Perspectives from the Past

PRIMARY SOURCES IN WESTERN

CIVILIZATIONS

Fifth Edition

Perspectives from the Past

PRIMARY SOURCES IN WESTERN CIVILIZATIONS

Fifth Edition

VOLUME 1

From the Ancient Near East through
the Age of Absolutism

JAMES M. BROPHY • JOSHUA COLE • JOHN ROBERTSON

THOMAS MAX SAFLEY • CAROL SYMES

W • W • NORTON & COMPANY   NEW YORK • LONDON

W. W. Norton & Company has been independent since its founding in 1923, when William Warder Norton and Mary D. Herter Norton first published lectures delivered at the People's Institute, the adult education division of New York City's Cooper Union. The firm soon expanded its program beyond the Institute, publishing books by celebrated academics from America and abroad. By mid-century, the two major pillars of Norton's publishing program—trade books and college texts—were firmly established. In the 1950s, the Norton family transferred control of the company to its employees, and today—with a staff of four hundred and a comparable number of trade, college, and professional titles published each year—W. W. Norton & Company stands as the largest and oldest publishing house owned wholly by its employees.

Editor: Jon Durbin
Editorial Assistant: Justin Cahill
Project Editor: Kate Feighery
Composition: DBS, Inc.
Manufacturing: Maple-Vail
Book design: Jack Meserole
Production manager: Eric Pier-Hocking

Acknowledgments and copyrights continue on page 539, which serves
as a continuation of the copyright page.

Library of Congress Cataloging-in-Publication Data

Perspectives from the past : primary sources in Western civilizations /
James M. Brophy . . . [et al.]. —5th ed.
  v. cm.
Includes bibliographical references.
Contents: v. 1. From the ancient Near East through the age of absolutism —v. 2.
From the age of exploration through contemporary times.
ISBN 978-0-393-91294-4 (v. 1 : pbk.)—**ISBN 978-0-393-91295-1** (v. 2 : pbk.)
1. Civilization, Western--History--Sources.
I. Brophy, James M.
CB245.P45 2012
909'.09821--dc23

                              2011043354

W. W. Norton & Company, Inc., 500 Fifth Avenue, New York, N.Y. 10110
www.wwnorton.com

W. W. Norton & Company Ltd., Castle House,
75/76 Wells Street, London W1T 3QT

1 2 3 4 5 6 7 8 9 0

ABOUT THE AUTHORS

JAMES M. BROPHY is professor of modern European history at the University of Delaware, where he has taught since 1992. He received his B.A. from Vassar College and did his graduate training at Universität Tübingen and Indiana University, where he specialized in the social and political history of nineteenth-century Europe. He is the author of *Capitalism, Politics, and Railroads in Prussia, 1830–1870* (1998), *Popular Culture and the Public Sphere in the Rhineland, 1800–1850* (2007), and numerous articles on nineteenth-century German history. He further serves on the board of editors for the journal, *Central European History*. He regularly teaches the Western civilization survey as well as courses and seminars on historiography, nationalism, modern European history, modern German history, and the Holocaust.

JOSHUA COLE is associate professor of history at the University of Michigan. He received his B.A. from Brown University and his M.A. and Ph.D. from the University of California, Berkeley. The author of *The Power of Large Numbers: Population, Politics, and Gender in Nineteenth-Century France* (2000), he has also published articles on French and German social and cultural history in the modern period. His current research is on the legacy of colonial violence in France, Algeria, and Madagascar, with a focus on the problems created by this history of violence in the postcolonial world. He has enjoyed teaching European history in a global context since 1993.

JOHN ROBERTSON received both his M.A. (1976) and his Ph.D. (1981) in ancient history from the University of Pennsylvania. A specialist in the social and economic history of the ancient Near East, he has published several articles in major scholarly journals and contributed articles to such major reference works as the *Anchor Bible Dictionary, Civilizations of the Ancient Near East,* and the *Blackwell Companion to the Ancient Near East.* He has also participated in archaeological excavations in Syria and Greece as well as the American Southwest. Since 1982, he has been a member of the faculty of the department of history at Central Michigan University, where he has taught the history of Western civilization for both the department of history and the university honors program, as well as more specialized courses in the history of the ancient Near East and the Islamic and modern Middle East.

THOMAS MAX SAFLEY teaches the history of early modern Europe at the University of Pennsylvania. A specialist in economic and social history, he has particular research interests in the history of marriage and the family, of poverty and charity, and of labor and business. In addition to numerous articles and reviews, he is the author of *Let No Man Put Asunder: The Control of Marriage in the German Southwest, 1550–1620* (1984), *Charity and Economy in the Orphanages of Early Modern Augsburg* (1996), *Matheus Miller's Memoir: A Merchant's Life in the Seventeenth Century* (2000), and *The Children of the Laboring Poor: Expectation and Experience among the Orphans of Early Modern*

Augsburg (2004). He is co-editor of *The Workplace before the Factory: Artisans and Proletarians, 1500–1800* (1993) and *The Reformation of Charity: The Secular and the Sacred in Early Modern Poor Relief* (2003). He also serves on the editorial board of the *Sixteenth Century Journal*. At the University of Pennsylvania, he regularly teaches the introductory survey of European history and advanced lecture courses on the early modern period. He also offers a broad array of undergraduate and graduate seminars.

CAROL SYMES is Associate Professor of History and Director of Undergraduate Studies in the History Department at the University of Illinois, Urbana-Champaign, where she has won the top teaching award in the College of Liberal Arts and Sciences. Her main areas of study include medieval Europe, especially France and England; cultural history; history of information media and communication technologies; and history of theatre. She is the author of *A Common Stage: Theater and Public Life in Medieval Arras.*

CONTENTS

CHAPTER 3 ✑ THE CIVILIZATION OF GREECE, 1000–400 B.C.E.   77

CHAPTER 4 ✑ THE GREEK WORLD EXPANDS, 400–150 B.C.E.   128

CHAPTER 5 ᴄᴏ THE CIVILIZATION OF ANCIENT ROME   156

CHAPTER 6 ᴄᴏ THE TRANSFORMATION OF ROME   182

CHAPTER 7 ᴄᴏ ROME'S THREE HEIRS, 500–950   220

CHAPTER 14 ❧ RELIGION, WARFARE, AND SOVEREIGNTY: 1540–1660   455

CHAPTER 15 ❧ ABSOLUTISM AND EMPIRE, 1660–1789   486

PREFACE FOR INSTRUCTORS

The authors of this text are very pleased to have been afforded the opportunity to design and compile this reader, which is the outgrowth of approximately nine decades of combined experience teaching the history of Western civilization. In the course of acquiring that experience, the authors were frustrated by what we perceived as serious shortcomings in most of the available supplementary readers. Among the more notable deficiencies are a frequent overemphasis on political and intellectual history at the expense of social and economic history and on elite culture at the expense of sources relating to the experiences of people of lesser socioeconomic station and, especially, of women. There is also an underrepresentation of sources relating the experiences and perspectives of European societies east of what is today Germany and a focus on Western civilization that often has neglected to address the West's important interactions with, and development of attitudes toward, non-Western peoples and civilizations. Some texts, in a laudable attempt to be more inclusive, incorporate more selections to serve up a veritable smorgasbord of thematically unlinked snippets, many of them so abbreviated or cited so disjointedly that the student can hardly gain a proper appreciation of their context or of the nature and structure of the documents from which they are derived. For ancient and medieval sources, this problem is all too often compounded by the use of translations that are either obsolete (from the standpoint of recent advances in philology) or rendered in an antiquated idiom that is hardly conducive to engaging students' interest. Finally, many readers are compiled by only one editor, who, whatever his or her experience and scholarly credentials, may understandably be hard pressed to command adequately the range and variety of primary sources available for examining the diverse aspects of Western civilization.

We by no means have the hubris to believe that what we have assembled will satisfy all the desiderata of every instructor. Nonetheless, to address the

concerns noted above, and others, we have endeavored to produce a text that incorporates, as much as possible, the following features:

- Selections that consist of complete texts or lengthy excerpts of primary-source documents, ranging from one to eight pages in length and rendered in authoritative and eloquent, yet idiomatic, translations.

- Recognition that visual artifacts are also meaningful primary sources. Each chapter of this edition contains two visual features (photographs, paintings, posters, cartoons, sculptures, etc.) intended to help students learn how to analyze and interpret visual sources.

- An appropriate balance of primary sources from the Western canon, works that are illustrative of the origins and development of Western political institutions, intellectual life, and high culture or that illustrate aspects of social and economic history as well as more mundane aspects of life in Western societies. In other words, we have strived to provide selections pertinent to the lives, roles, achievements, and contributions of elite and commoner, ruler and ruled, master and servant, man and woman.

- Selections that reflect the experiences and perspectives of women and the dynamics of gender relations, including family and household structure.

- Selections that attempt to place a focus on the western European experience within a broader, even global perspective, by including selections relating to eastern Europe, the ancient and Islamic Middle East, Africa, Asia, and the Western Hemisphere. Thus, interspersed among the works of Western authors are excerpts from ancient Egyptian and Babylonian literature and private letters, the Qur'an, and works of such figures as Ali ibn al-Athir, Ibn Battuta, Edward Morel, Mohandas Gandhi, Frantz Fanon, Tadataka Kuribayshi, and Achille Mbembe. Readings such as these are intended to help students trace the evolution of the concept of the West and its relations with the non-West—matters of immense significance as an increasingly global society stands at the beginning of the twenty-first century.

- The incorporation of several unifying questions and issues to link documents both within and among chapters in a coherent, pedagogically useful internal framework. The documents in this reader have been chosen with an overarching purpose of interweaving a number of thematic threads that compose vital elements in the colorful fabrics of Western civilization: What are the status, responsibilities, and rights of the individual within the local community and broader society, and how have they changed over time? How have people defined their own communities, and how have they viewed outsiders? Who should have power within and over the community and society, and why? How have people responded to changes in the material world around them? Who or what controls the cosmos, and how have humankind's perceptions of its appropriate role and function within the cosmos changed?

The pedagogical and critical apparatus provided in this reader has been designed to guide the student to an appreciation of the sources but without imparting too much in the way of historical interpretation. For each chapter we have supplied an introduction that provides a historical context for the readings and alerts the student to the thematic threads that link them. Each reading in turn has an introduction that supplies an even more specific context and alerts the student to issues of interpretation or biased perspective. Finally, each selection is accompanied by several questions intended to stimulate analysis and discussion. The placement of these questions after each selection is quite intentional, as it is our hope that students will engage each document without a preconceived or predetermined sense of why it may be important and will instead learn to trust their own critical capacities and discern the significance of a reading on their own.

While the Fifth Edition remains a wonderful collection of primary sources organized around the aforementioned features, it has also been made more affordable and compact to meet the changing needs of instructors and students. Nearly 100 instructors participated in our online survey to identify the most essential and highly teachable primary sources to include in the new edition. As a result, the Fifth Edition is more streamlined and compact. At the table of contents level, we have also brought it in closer alignment with our best-selling survey texts, *Western Civilizations*, Seventeenth Edition and *Western Civilizations*, Brief Third Edition by Cole, Symes, Coffin, and Stacey. Finally, as a result of the streamlining efforts, we were able to drop the standalone price of the text by 40%, and we can package each volume for $10 net with Norton's fine survey texts. Undoubtedly, students will be more inclined to buy our reader, and, we hope, to spend time reading it as well.

Obviously, to organize a project as complex as a reader of this kind and to bring it to a successful and timely fruition require the skills, support, inspiration, and dedication of many people other than the authors. We wish to express our admiration and profound gratitude to the editorial and marketing staff of W. W. Norton, especially to Kate Feighery, Jason Spears, Justin Cahill, who did a fantastic job researching sources and pulling the manuscript together in good order, Bethany Salminen for her work in securing permissions, and, most especially, to Jon Durbin, who assembled the team, helped us to define and refine our work, organized the project, offered useful insight and judicious criticism, and kept all of us on task and on time. The credit for this reader is surely as much theirs as ours.

For this edition we have included the following new documents:

- A Letter from the Hittite Queen to Ramesses II
- *Martyrdom of Perpetua*
- St. Benedict, from *The Rule*

- Procopius, from *Secret History*
- Mas𝒸udi, from *The Meadows of Gold*
- Bede, from *A History of the English Church and People*
- from The Anglo-Saxon Translation of *The Book of Genesis*
- from the *Song of Roland*
- Ali ibn al-Athir, An Arabic Account of the First Crusade
- Heloise, Letter to Abelard
- The Magna Carta: The "Great Charter" of 1215
- Jan Hus, from *The Church*
- from The Religious Peace of Augsburg
- Catherine the Great, from *Proposals for a New Code of Law*
- Daniel Defoe, from *The Complete English Tradesman*
- from The Charter of the Dutch West India Company

In addition, we would like to thank the following faculty for their valuable input as we developed the fifth edition:

- David Aliano, College of Mount Saint Vincent
- James Allen, Ramapo College of New Jersey
- Ken Bartlett, University of Toronto
- Benita Blessing, University of Massachusetts, Amherst
- Richard Brabander, Bridgewater State University
- Kathren Brown, Utah Valley University
- Jodi Campbell, Texas Christian University
- Peter Catapano, New York City College of Technology
- Tamara Chaplin, University of Illinois at Urbana-Champaign
- Frederick Corney, The College of William & Mary
- Jason Coy, College of Charleston
- Sarah Davis-Secord, University of Texas at Arlington
- Rene M Descartes, SUNY Cobleskill
- John Eastby, Hampden-Sydney College
- Benjamin Ehlers, University of Georgia
- Kathleen Fichtel, West Virginia University
- Deanna Forsman, North Hennepin Community College
- David Gallo, College of Mount Saint Vincent
- Steven Garfinkle, Western Washington University

- Norman Goda, University of Florida
- Peter Goddard, University of Guelph
- Andrew Goldman, Gonzaga University
- Rita V. Gomez, Anne Arundel Community College
- Robert Grasso, Monmouth University
- Madonna Hettinger, The College of Wooster
- Warren Johnston, Algoma University
- Philip Kaplan, University of North Florida
- Michael Kinney, Calhoun Community College
- Christine Kooi, Louisiana State University
- Glenn Kranking, Gustavus Adolphus College
- Chris Laney, Berkshire Community College
- Elizabeth Lehfeldt, Cleveland State University
- Janice Liedl, Laurentian University
- Kate Martin, Cape Cod Community College
- Martin Menke, Rivier College
- Jeffrey Lee Meriwether, Roger Williams University
- Lynn Mollenauer, University of North Carolina at Wilmington
- Rachel Nunez, Hollins University
- Bill Olejniczak, College of Charleston
- Daniel Opler, College of Mount Saint Vincent
- Christopher Otter, Ohio State University
- Matthew Pehl, Augustana College
- Samuel Pierce, College of Charleston
- Robert Policelli, University of North Carolina at Chapel Hill
- Peter Pozefsky, College of Wooster
- Sandra Pryor, Old Dominion University
- Matthew Ruane, Florida Institute of Technology
- David A. Serafini, Western Kentucky University
- David Shearer, University of Delaware
- Robert Simmons, Calhoun Community College
- Philip H. Slaby, Guilford College
- Susan L. Smith, Orange Coast College
- David Snyder, University of South Carolina

- Peter Utgaard, Cuyamaca College
- James Vanstone, John Abbott College
- Rachelle Wadsworth, Florida State College at Jacksonville
- Philip Whalen, Coastal Carolina University
- Aaron Wilson, Creighton University
- Matthew D. Zarzeczny, Ashland University

PREFACE FOR STUDENTS

Good Tips for Learning How to Analyze Primary Sources

The purpose of this collection of illustrations and documents is to provide the student with the raw materials of history, the sources, in the form of the objects and written words that survive from the past. Your textbook relies on such documents, known as primary sources, as well as on the works of many past and present historians who have analyzed and interpreted these sources—the secondary literature. In some cases the historians were themselves sources, eyewitnesses to the events they recorded. Authors of textbooks select which facts and interpretations they think you should know, and so the textbook filters what you think about the human past by limiting the information available to you. Textbooks are useful because they provide a coherent historical narrative for students of history, but it is important to remember that they are only an introduction to the rich complexity of human experience over time.

A collection of historical documents and artifacts provides a vital supplement to the textbook, but it also has problems. First, the sources, mostly not intended for us to read and study, exist for the reasons that prompted some people to create them and others to preserve them. These reasons may include a measure of lies, self-deception, or ignorance about what was really happening and being recorded. So we must ask the following questions about any document or object—a treaty, contract, painting, photograph, poem, newspaper article, or sculpture: Why does it exist? What specific purpose did it serve when it was done? Who is its author? What motives prompted the creator to produce this material in this form?

The second major problem is that we, the editors of this collection, have selected, from millions of possible choices, these particular documents and objects, and not others. Even in this process, because of the limitations of space and our own personal experiences, we present a necessarily partial and highly selective view of Western civilization (also because of space limitations, it has

been necessary to delete portions from some of the longer sections).* Our purpose is not to repeat what you can find in the textbook but to give you the opportunity to see and discuss how historians, now including you, make history out of documents and objects, and their understanding of why people behave the way they do.

The illustrations in this collection provide a glimpse at the millions of material objects that survive from the past. These churches, buildings, paintings, mosaics, sculptures, photographs, and other items make up an important set of sources for the historian to consider about the past. It is certainly difficult to appreciate an immense building or a small manuscript painting from a photograph. Nevertheless, the editors of this collection include illustrations in the Fifth Edition to make clear the full range of sources that historians utilize. Also, the illustrations in many cases complement the written documents and in every case provide opportunities for a broader discussion of historical questions and the variety of sources that can help answer them.

Before exploring in more detail what documents are, we should be clear about what history is. Simply put, history is what we can say about the human past, in this case about the vast area of Western civilization from its remote origins to the most recent past. We can say, or write, things about the past because people left us their words, in the form of documents, and we can, like detectives, question these sources and then try to understand what happened. Before the written word, there is no history in the strictest sense; instead there are preliterate societies and the tens of thousands of years for which we know only what the anthropologists and archaeologists can tell us from the physical remains of bodies and objects made by human hands. And yet during this time profoundly important human institutions like language, the family, and religion first appeared. History begins with writing because that is when the documentation starts. These accomplishments of our remote ancestors occurred over tens of thousands of years, broken into ages of stone, copper, and bronze. Objects and images, but no words, reveal advances in weapons, art, farming, and other activities.

Although history cannot exist without written documents, we must remember that this evidence is complex and ambiguous. In the first place, it first appears in ancient languages, and the majority of documents in this book were not originally in English. The act of translating the documents into modern English raises another barrier or filter, and we must use our imaginations to

---

We indicate omissions, no matter how brief, with three spaced asterisks (* *), running them in when the opening, middle, or closing of a paragraph has been deleted and centering them between lines when a full paragraph is dropped. Why asterisks, when ellipsis dots are the standard? Because authors use ellipsis dots, and we want to distinguish our deletions from theirs.

recreate the past worlds in which modern words like *liberty, race,* or *sin* had different meanings. One job of the historian is to understand the language of the documents in their widest possible contexts. All the authors intended their documents to communicate something, but as time passes, languages and contexts change, and so it becomes more difficult for us to figure out what a document meant then and may mean now. Language is an imperfect way to communicate, but we must make the best of what we have. If we recollect how difficult it is sometimes to understand the events we see and experience, then we can perhaps understand how careful we must be when we interpret someone else's report about an event in the past, especially when that past is far removed in space and time from our experience.

The documents give us the language, or testimony, of witnesses, observers, or people with some point to make. Some documents claim to reveal religious truths and interpreting these claims requires historians to inquire respectfully and sincerely. Historical evidence, like any other, must be examined for flaws, contradictions, lies, and what it tells us that the writer did not necessarily intend to reveal. Like a patient detective, we must question our witnesses with a full awareness of their limited and often-biased perception, piecing together our knowledge of their history with the aid of multiple testimonies and a broad context. Consider the document, whatever it is, as testimony and a piece of a bigger puzzle, many of the remaining pieces of which are missing or broken. It is useful at the beginning to be clear about the simple issues—What type of document is this evidence? Who wrote it? Where and when was it written? Why does it exist? Try to understand the context of the document by relating it to the wider world—how do words by Plato or about the Nazi Party fit with what you already know about ancient Greece or twentieth-century Germany?

When the document, or witness, has been correctly identified and placed in some context, we may then interrogate it further by asking questions about the words before us. Not all documents suggest the same questions, but there are some general questions that apply to nearly every document. One place to begin is to ask, Who or what is left out? Once you see the main point, it is interesting to ask what the documents tell us about people and subjects often left out of the records—women, children, or religious or ethnic minorities, for example. Or, if the document is about a religious minority, we can ask what it tells us about the majority. Take the document and try to turn it inside out by determining the basic assumptions or biases of its author, and then explore what has been intentionally or unintentionally left out. Look for anomalies— pieces of evidence that appear out of place or simply weird; they are often clues to understanding the distances between us and the sources. Another way to ask a fresh question of an old witness is to look beneath the surface and see what else is there. For example, if the document in question seems mainly to offer evidence on religion, ask what it tells us about the economy or contemporary eating habits

or whatever else might occur to you. Documents frequently reveal excellent information on topics far from their ostensible subjects, if we remember to ask.

Every document in this collection is some kind of story, either long or short. The stories are almost all nonfiction, at least in theory, but they all have characters; a plot, or story line; and above all a point to the story, the meaning. We have suggested some possible meanings in the sample questions at the end of each document, but these questions are just there to help your thinking or get a discussion going, about the many possible meanings of the documents. You can ask what the meaning was in the document's own time, as well as what we might now see as a meaning that makes sense to us of some pieces of the past. The point of the story in a document may often concern a central issue in history, the process of change. If history is what we can say about the human past, then the most important words describe how change occurs, for example, rapidly, as in revolutions and wars, or more slowly, as in marriage customs or family life. Every document casts some light on human change, and the meaning of the story often relates to why something changed.

History is often at its dullest when a document simply describes a static situation, for example, a law or farming. However, even a good description reveals choices and emphasis. If you ask, Why this law now? Why farm in this way? How did these activities influence human behavior? you can see that the real subject of nearly all documents is human change, on some level. You will find that people can and will strongly disagree about the meaning of a story: they can and will use the same evidence from a document to draw radically different meanings. This is one of the challenges of history and what makes it fun, for some explanations and meanings make more sense than others in the broader context of what you know about an episode or period of history. Argue about meaning, and you will learn something about not only your own biases and values but also the process of sifting facts for good arguments and answers. These skills have a value well beyond the study of history.

The documents and objects in this collection, even the most general works of philosophy or social analysis, reveal the particular and contingent aspects of history. Even the most abstract of these documents and objects comes from a specific time, place, and person and sheds some light on a unique set of circumstances. When history is like the other social sciences (anthropology, economics, sociology, political science, and others), it tries to deal with typical or average people, societies, or behavior. When history is like the other humanities (literature, philosophy, religion, art, and others), it stresses individual people, their quirks and uniqueness. The documents and objects also illustrate the contingent aspect of history, which unlike the social or natural sciences but like the humanities, appears to lack rules or laws. History depends on what people did, subject to the restrictions of their natures, resources, climate, and other natural factors—people with histories of their own! Rerunning this history is not like a

movie, and it would never turn out the same way twice, for it is specific and contingent to the way it turned out this time. The documents and objects do not tell a story of an orderly progression from simple to complex societies or from bad to good ones. Instead, history continues, and people cope, or not, with the issues of religious faith, family life, making a living, and creating artifacts and documents. These documents and objects collectively provide perspectives on how experiments in living succeeded or failed. We invite you to use them to learn more about the people of the past than the textbooks can say and to use your imaginations to get these witnesses to answer your questions about the process and meaning of human change.

WHERE TO BEGIN?

A Primary Source Checklist

This checklist is a series of questions that can be used to analyze most of the documents and objects in this reader.

✔ What type of document or object is this evidence?

✔ Why does the document or object exist? What motives prompted the author to create the material in this form?

✔ Who created this work?

✔ Who or what is left out—women, children, minorities, members of the majority?

✔ In addition to the main subject, what other kinds of information can be obtained?

✔ How do the subjects of the document or object relate to what we know about broader society?

✔ What was the meaning of the document or object in its own time? What is its meaning for the audience?

✔ What does the document or object tell us about change or stability

---

1 ✦ EARLY CIVILIZATIONS

In the history of humankind's sojourn on this planet, no development has been more momentous, or more fraught with consequence, than the emergence of civilization. Exactly what constitutes "civilization" has been debated by scholars for years. But as evidenced by the appearance of states, cities, complex economies, and writing, among other characteristics, civilizations can be said to have arisen independently in several areas across the globe. By far the earliest of them, however, arose in that region of southwestern Asia and northern Africa that we today call the Middle East.

But during the many preceding millennia of the eras that we now refer to as the Paleolithic (literally, "Old Stone Age") and Neolithic ("New Stone Age"), humankind also attained perhaps equally monumental achievements, without which cities and civilizations could never have developed. Those achievements are too numerous to catalogue here, but among the more significant are certainly the harnessing of fire, the creation of technologies for hunting wild animals and foraging for wild plants, and the domestication of those same wild-food sources in the process that resulted in agriculture and herding. The developments made the Neolithic village life possible. With these very early achievements, there also emerged a belief in powers and forces beyond the realm of the purely "natural," powers that, though unseen, might bring abundance or disaster if not properly recognized and, if necessary, propitiated. Such powers might be inherent in the life force of the animals and plants on which early humans depended; they might also lie in some mysterious, unknowable realm inhabited by the dead, including one's ancestors. Until relatively recently, historians had often relegated these so-called prehistoric achievements and ideas to an era of dim savagery that many believed was better left to the scrutiny of anthropologists and archaeologists. Today, however, more and more scholars are embracing the concept of "deep" or "macro" history, in the belief that even though these earliest human societies

and achievements date to a preliterate (i.e., before writing) era, we have been mistaken to deny them a place in the unfolding of human "history." Indeed, by calling them "prehistoric," perhaps we have been segregating our "modern" consciousness in the shallow end of the almost immeasurably deeper pool of what constitutes humankind's shared experience on this planet. We surely can embrace such a longer view of "history" while still recognizing the stupendous and rapid amplification of that human experience by the quantum leap ahead by the peoples of what is now the Middle East.

By about 5000 B.C.E.,[1] in what is now eastern Iraq, a Neolithic people to whom archaeologists refer as the Samarrans began to settle in villages where rainfall alone could not support agriculture. Their pioneering efforts in the technology of canal irrigation paved the way for the emergence of cities and, with them, the civilization of ancient Sumer. The world's first cities arose in the floodplain of Lower Mesopotamia, the land between the Tigris and Euphrates rivers (modern-day southern Iraq), more than five thousand years ago, as large population centers governed by administrators powerful enough to organize and direct the construction of large architectural complexes, quite likely temples. These efforts were fueled by agricultural production on an unprecedented scale, entailing the cultivation of thousands of acres of wheat, barley, and other foodstuffs. The floodplain's wondrous fertility could be unleashed only by the profuse application of irrigation water brought from the Euphrates and (perhaps to a lesser extent) the Tigris. Organizing the digging and maintaining of irrigation canals; the plowing, sowing, and harvesting of the fields; and the maintaining of huge herds of livestock was a truly formidable task.

By about 3200 B.C.E., the huge size and increasingly complex administration of these great estates necessitated the creation of a new technology that itself shaped the future of civilization: writing. Primitive pictographs incised on clay tablets evolved into a system that we today refer to as cuneiform (literally, "wedge-shaped") that spread throughout the ancient Near East, where it remained in use for almost three thousand years. The scribes of ancient Mesopotamia (and Anatolia, Syria, Iran, and even Egypt) bequeathed to us a remarkably durable legacy of tens of thousands of records—mostly clay tablets, but also inscriptions on stone monuments and objects. Most of the tablets are detailed accounts of the administration of temples, palaces, and public institutions, tediously dry in themselves but, when reconstructed into coherent archives, crucial evidence of social and economic organization. The remaining records—among them, royal inscriptions, letters, poems, hymns, prayers, law "codes," contracts, and a variety of literary works—provide, at best, tantalizing samples from what was once a vast corpus. Enough has survived, nonetheless, to enable us to reconstruct a complex sequence of dynasties and political configurations in the history of Mesopotamia and the Near East. But perhaps more appealing to our common humanity, these records allow us at least limited insight into the enduring structures

---

[1] B.C.E. means "before the common era."

of life and the everyday concerns of people who seem to have felt very strongly that their fortune and existence depended utterly on ensuring the continued good favor of their gods. Those gods might bestow on them benevolence and plenty or, just as likely, abandon them to destitution and catastrophe, the latter all too often brought by the rampages of "barbarian" invaders or the no less destructive rampages of the normally life-sustaining rivers.

By 2000 B.C.E., the solid foundations of Mesopotamian civilization had been shaken by some major tremors. Imperial dynasties established by the great conqueror Sargon of Akkad and then by the kings of the Third Dynasty of Ur had flourished then ebbed, although the idealized memory of Sargon's rule would inspire future Mesopotamian kings for the next fifteen hundred years. The next four hundred years ushered in chieftains of recently arrived tribal groups known as Amorites, who established themselves in small kingdoms in the urbanized regions of Sumer and Akkad. In time, one of those minor Amorite kingdoms, Babylon, was to establish itself, and its god Marduk, as supreme. With the ascent of its great king Hammurabi shortly after 1800 B.C.E., Babylon took center stage in Lower Mesopotamia (henceforth Babylonia), not to relinquish its leading role there until the era of Alexander the Great's successors. Babylon's rise was possible, though, only because Hammurabi proved himself a master player in an era when (as thousands of cuneiform tablets from the palace of Mari on the Euphrates testify for us) power politics, trade and diplomacy, and competition for prized resources encompassed an arena extending from Anatolia to the Persian Gulf and from Iran to the Mediterranean as far as Crete. His dynasty's fall, around one hundred fifty years later, would come at the hands of a relatively new player, the Hittite rulers of the Anatolian kingdom of Hatti. The Hittites' rise ushered onto the ancient Near Eastern stage speakers and writers of a language that we can identify as Indo-European and as thereby related to the later languages of western Europe (and India). When the curtain eventually lifted again in Babylonia, another new, nonindigenous ruling group, the Kassites, had taken charge. Yet, like the Amorites before them—and the Akkadian kings before them, the Kassites were captured—or, perhaps, captivated—by the enduring traditions and structures of an already ancient Sumerian civilization.

Civilization arose along the Nile River somewhat later than it had in the Tigris-Euphrates floodplain, but Egyptian civilization soon assumed its own distinct form and identity. According to their later traditions, the Egyptians believed that a king named Menes had been the first to unite the two rival kingdoms of Upper Egypt (the long Nile valley) and Lower Egypt (the Nile delta). From a modern vantage point, we detect scant traces of a ruler named Menes in the earliest Egyptian records, and most scholars are convinced that the unification of Egypt was much more complicated than the pulling together of two kingdoms. Nonetheless, by around 3100 B.C.E., what some have identified as the world's first unified nation-state had been created. For the next three thousand years, the people of Egypt regarded the absolute

rule of a semidivine king (who by the mid-second millennium B.C.E. came to be known as pharaoh) as the only desirable state of affairs. On his shoulders fell the responsibility of preserving the stability of the cosmos (what the Egyptians called ma'at), an essential ingredient of which was securing the unity of the "Two Lands" of Upper and Lower Egypt. Only the king's vigorous stewardship might avert chaos and calamity. Over time, there developed around the king's person a royal court and hierarchical administration that was served by a class of professional (and mostly male) bureaucrats ("scribes") highly trained in the hieroglyphic script and its hieratic derivative. Through their efforts, the manpower and resources of the kingdom could be marshaled to ensure the king's success, both in this world and the next. It is from the records they have left us—inscribed and painted on temple and tomb walls, or written on papyrus or even flakes of stone—that we glean our hard-won knowledge of ancient Egyptian history and culture.

Neither the grandeur of Egyptian kingship nor the king's preservation of cosmic harmony would have been possible, of course, without the Nile River. As the Greek "father of history" Herodotus so succinctly put it, Egypt is "the river's gift." Until the completion of the Aswan High Dam in the early 1970s, every year, between July and October, the Nile overflowed its banks, bringing life-sustaining water and rich silt that, together with the generative power of the sun, literally resurrected the black land of the Nile Valley. It may well be that in this annual resurrection of the land was born the Egyptian concept of a resurrection and continued existence after death (though only if proper preparations were made and precautions taken). Often, modern observers tend to focus on the Egyptians' supposed morbid preoccupation with death and the hereafter. In part, that perception stems from the accidents of archaeological preservation. Millennia of floods and silt deposits, combined with continued human occupation of town and village sites, have largely obliterated the towns and villages of the ancient Egyptians. Most of what has been left to us are the remains of temples and tombs, built in the low desert where the Nile's floods did not reach; that the remaining records say so much about kings, gods, and death should hardly surprise us. As some of the documents in this chapter make clear, however, the ancient Egyptians did not while away their lives dreamily pining for death.

By 2000 B.C.E., Egypt, like Mesopotamia, had been rocked by adversity, as the disintegration of the Old Kingdom brought, for the first time, the disruption of the divinely ordained, cosmic stability of ma'at that underpinned Egypt's civilization. The reunification forged by the rulers of Thebes (whose god Amun, like Babylon's Marduk, would soon emerge supreme) with the advent of the Middle Kingdom brought renewed strength and cultural vitality, as well as the assertion of Egyptian interests and power as far away as Nubia to the south, Crete to the north, and Palestine to the east. The Middle Kingdom also saw a reassertion of royal traditions and absolutism, though punctuated by the lingering memory of the chaos that had once plagued Egypt. In time, that threat of chaos would again

become real: "vile Asiatic" newcomers recently arrived from Palestine into the Nile Delta would assert political control as the Hyksos dynasties of Lower Egypt. Egypt would once again be divided, but now, for the first time, by the abomination of "barbarian" invasion.

FROM *Atrahasis:* An Account of the Great Flood

The theme of a great flood appears in several works of ancient Mesopotamian literature, including the Sumerian King List, The Epic of Gilgamesh, *and the following work, the earliest known example of flood literature which dates to about 1700 B.C.E. Its hero, Atrahasis (literally, "exceedingly wise"), is a figure of great antiquity who reappears under different names in later flood stories (including Ut-napishtim in* The Epic of Gilgamesh); *some scholars have traced versions of his name into later Greek, Roman, and Arabic tales. As will become apparent, however, this is much more than a flood story, for it also gives us one version of why and how, according to ancient Mesopotamian belief, humans came into being.*

From *Before the Muses: An Anthology of Akkadian Literature,* translated by Benjamin R. Foster 2nd ed. (Bethesda, Md.: CDL Press, 1993), pp. 159–183.

When gods were man,
They did forced labor, they bore drudgery.
Great indeed was the drudgery of the gods,
The forced labor was heavy, the misery too much:
The great Anunna-gods, the seven, were burdening
The Igigi-gods with forced labor.
Anu their father was king,
Their counsellor was the warrior Enlil,
Their prefect was Ninurta, . . .
Anu went up to heaven,
Enlil took the earth for his subjects,

      *   *   *

They burdened the Igigi-gods with forced labor.
The gods were digging watercourses,
The waterways of the gods, the life of the land,
The Igigi-gods were digging watercourses,
The waterways of the gods, the life of the land.
The Igigi-gods dug the Tigris river,
And the Euphrates thereafter.

Springs they opened up from the depths,
Wells . . . they established. . . .
They heaped up all the mountains. . . .
They counted years of drudgery, . . .
forced labor they bore night and day.
They were complaining, denouncing,
Muttering down in the ditch,
"Let us face up to our foreman the prefect,
"He must take off this our heavy burden upon us!
"The god, counsellor of the gods, the warrior,
"Come, let us remove him from his dwelling,
"Enlil, counsellor of the gods, the warrior,
"Come, let us remove him from his dwelling!" . . .

      *   *   *

"Now then, call for battle!
"Battle let us stir up, warfare!"
The gods heard his words,
They set fire to their tools,
They put fire to their spades,

And flame to their workbaskets.
Off they went, one and all,
To the gate of the warrior Enlil's abode.
It was night, half-way through the watch,
The house was surrounded, but the god did not
    know.
It was night, half-way through the watch,
Ekur was surrounded, but Enlil did not know!
Kalkal noticed it and looked out,
He touched the bolt and looked out.
Kalkal woke Nusku,
And they listened to the clamor of the Igigi-gods.
Nusku woke his lord,
He got him out of bed,
"My lord, your house is surrounded,
"Battle has run right up to your gate.
"Enlil, your house is surrounded,
"Battle has run right up to your gate!"
Enlil had provided weapons for his dwelling.
Enlil made ready to speak,
And said to the courier Nusku,
"Nusku, bar your gate,
Get your weapons and stand before me."
Nusku barred his gate,
Got his weapons and stood before Enlil.
Nusku made ready to speak,
And said to the warrior Enlil,
"My lord, your face is gone pale as tamarisk,
"Your own offspring! Why did you fear?
"My lord, your face is gone pale as tamarisk,
"Your own offspring! Why do you fear?
"Send that they bring Anu down here,
"And that they bring Enki before you."
He sent and they brought Anu down to him,
They brought Enki before him.
Anu, king of heaven, was present,
The king of the depths, Enki, was
With the great Anunna-gods present,
Enlil arose, the debate was underway.
Enlil made ready to speak,
And said to the great gods,
"Against me would they be trying this?
"Shall I make battle against my own offspring?
"What did I see with my very own eyes?
"Battle ran right up to my gate!"
Anu made ready to speak,

And said to the warrior Enlil,
"The reason why the Igigi-gods
"Surrounded your gate,
"Let Nusku go out, let him learn their cause,
"Let him take to your sons
"Your great command."
Enlil made ready to speak,
And said to the courier Nusku,
"Nusku, open your gate,
"Take your weapons, go out to the group.
"In the group of all the gods
"Bow down, stand up, and repeat to them our
    command:
    'Anu, your father,
    'Your counsellor, the warrior Enlil,
    'Your prefect, Ninurta,
    'And your bailiff Ennugi have sent me to say,
        "Who is the god who was instigator of
            battle?
        "Who is the god who was instigator of
            hostilities?
        "Who is it that stirred up war,
        "That battle has run up to the gate of
            Enlil?"'"

Nusku took the command, opened his gate,
Took his weapons and went with the command
    of Enlil.
In the group of all the gods,
He bowed down, stood up, set forth the command,
"Anu, your father,
"Your counsellor, the warrior Enlil,
"Your prefect, Ninurta,
"And your bailiff Ennugi have sent me to say:

    'Who is the god who was instigator of battle?
    'Who is the god who was instigator of
        hostilities?
    'Who is it that stirred up war, . . .

Ea made ready to speak,
And said to the gods his brethren,
"What do we denounce them for?
"Their forced labor was heavy, their misery too
    much.
"Every day the earth was . . .
"The outcry was loud, we could hear their clamor.

"There is a task to be done,
"Mami, the birth-goddess, is present,
"Let the mother-goddess create a human being,
"Let man assume the drudgery of god."
They summoned and asked the birth-goddess,
The midwife of the gods, wise Mami,
"Will you be the birth-goddess, creatress of
     humankind?
"Create a human being, let him bear the yoke,
"The yoke let him bear, the task of Enlil,
"Let man assume the drudgery of god."
Nintu made ready to speak,
And said to the great gods,
"It is not for me to do it,
"This task is Enki's.
"He is the one who purifies everything,
"Let him give me the clay so I can do the
     making."
Enki made ready to speak,
And said to the great gods,
"On the first, seventh, and fifteenth days of the
     month,
"I will establish a purification, a bath.
"Let one god be slaughtered,
"Then let the gods be purified in it.
"Let Nintu mix clay with his flesh and blood,
"Let that same god and man be thoroughly mixed
     in the clay.
"Let us hear the drumbeat for the rest of time,
"From the flesh of the god let a spirit remain,
"Let it make the living know its sign,
"Lest he be forgotten, let the spirit remain."
The great Anunna-gods, who administer destinies,
Answered "Yes!" in the assembly.
On the first, seventh, and fifteenth days of the
     month,
He established a purification, a bath.
They slaughtered Aw-ila, who had the inspiration,
     in their assembly.
Nintu mixed the clay with his flesh and blood.
That same god and man were thoroughly mixed
     in the clay.
For the rest of time they would hear the drumbeat,
From the flesh of the god a spirit remained.
It would make the living know its sign,
Lest he be forgotten, the spirit remained.

After she had mixed that clay,
He summoned the Anunna, the great gods.
The Igigi, the great gods, spat upon the clay.
Mami made ready to speak,
And said to the great gods,
"You ordered me the task and I have completed it!
"You have slaughtered the god, along with his
     inspiration.
"I have done away with your heavy forced labor,
"I have imposed your drudgery on man.
"You have bestowed clamor upon humankind.
     'That battle has run up to the gate of Enlil?'"
The Igigi answered him in the group,
They were defiant, the labor gang
"Every one of us gods has declared war,
"We formed our group in the ditch.
"Excessive drudgery has killed us,
"Our forced labor was heavy, our misery too
     much!
"And so every one of us gods
"Has resolved on a battle with Enlil."
Nusku took the command,
He went, he brought back . . . .
"My lord, you sent me to the group of the gods,
"I went, I bowed down, I stood up,
"I set forth your great command,
"All the Igigi-gods, the labor gangs, were defiant
     against it,

     'Every one of us gods has declared war,
     'We have formed our group in the ditch.
     'Excessive drudgery has killed us,
     'Our forced labor was heavy, the misery too
          much!
     'Now, every one of us gods
     'Has resolved on a battle with Enlil.'"

When he heard that speech,
Enlil's tears flowed down,
Enlil became disturbed at what he said.
He said to the warrior Anu,
"Noble one, you should take authority off with
     you to heaven.
"Take the power you still have.
"With the great gods in session before you,
"Summon one god, let them make a new
     authority."

"I have released the yoke, I have made restoration."
They heard this speech of hers,
They ran, restored, and kissed her feet, saying,
"Formerly we used to call you 'Mami',
"Now let your name be 'Mistress-of-All-the Gods'
    (Belet-kala-ili)."

*   *   *

Twelve hundred years had not gone by,
The land had grown numerous, the peoples had
    increased,
The land was bellowing like a bull.
The god was disturbed with their uproar,
Enlil heard their clamor.
He said to the great gods,
"The clamor of humankind has become
    burdensome to me,
"I am losing sleep to their uproar . . . .
"Let there be ague . . .
But he, Atrahasis, his god was Enki,
He was exceedingly wise.
He would speak with his god,
And his god would speak with him!
Atrahasis made ready to speak,
And said to his lord, . . .
"Will they impose the disease on us forever?"
Enki made ready to speak,
And said to his servant,
"Summon the elders
"At the usual time in your house.
"Command:

    'Let heralds proclaim,
    'Let them raise a loud clamor in the land:
        "Do not reverence your own gods,
        "Do not pray to your own goddesses,
        "Seek the door of Namtar,
        "Bring a baked loaf before it."'

"May the flour offering please him,
"May he be shamed by the gift and withdraw his
    hand."
Atrahasis received the command,
And assembled the elders to his gate.
Atrahasis made ready to speak,
And said to the elders,
"Elders . . .

"Command:

    'Let heralds proclaim,
    'Let them raise a loud clamor in the land:
        "Do not reverence your own gods,
        "Do not pray to your own goddesses,
        "Seek the door of Namtar,
        "Bring a baked loaf before it."'

"May the flour offering please him,
"May he be shamed by the gift and withdraw his
    hand."
Atrahasis received the command,
And assembled the elders to his gate.
Atrahasis made ready to speak,
And said to the elders,
"Elders . . .
"Command:

    'Let heralds proclaim,
    'Let them raise a loud clamor in the land:
        "Do not reverence your own gods,
        "Do not pray to your own goddesses,
        "Seek the door of Namtar,
        "Bring a baked loaf before it."'

"May the flour offering please him,
"May he be shamed by the gift and withdraw his
    hand."
The elders heeded his words,
They built a temple for Namtar in the city.
They commanded and the heralds proclaimed,
They raised a loud clamor in the land,
They did not reverence their own gods,
They did not pray to their own goddesses,
They sought the door of Namtar,
They brought a baked loaf before it.
The flour offering pleased him,
He was shamed by the gift and withdrew his hand.
The ague left them,
They resumed their clamor,

*   *   *

Twelve hundred years had not gone by,
The land had grown numerous, the peoples had
    increased,
The land was bellowing like a bull.

The god became disturbed by their uproar,
Enlil heard their clamor.
He said to the great gods,
"The clamor of humankind has become
     burdensome to me,
"I am losing sleep to their uproar.
"Cut off provisions for the peoples,
"Let plant life be too scanty for their hunger.
"Let Adad withdraw his rain,
"Below, let the flood not come up from the depths.
"Let the wind come to parch the ground,
"Let the clouds billow but discharge not a drop.
"Let the field reduce its yields,
"Let the grain-goddess close her bosom.
"Let there be no rejoicing for them, . . .

*   *   *

Enki made ready to speak,
Saying to his servant,
"Summon the elders
"At the usual time in your house.
"Command:

   'Let heralds proclaim,
   'Let them raise a loud clamor in the land:
       "Do not reverence your own gods,
       "Do not pray to your own goddesses,
       "Seek the door of Adad
       "Bring a baked loaf before it."'

"May the flour offering please him,
"May he be shamed by the gift and withdraw his
     hand.
"May he rain down mist in the morning,
"May he stealthily rain down dew in the night,
"That the fields just as stealthily bear ninefold."
They built a temple for Adad in the city.
They commanded and the heralds proclaimed,
They raised a loud clamor in the land,
They did not reverence their own gods,
They did not pray to their own goddesses,
They sought the door of Adad,
They brought a baked loaf before it.
The flour offering pleased him,
He was shamed by the gift and withdrew his hand.
He rained down mist in the morning,
And stealthily rained down dew in the night,

The fields just as stealthily bore ninefold.
Their handsome features returned,
Their former clamor resumed.

*   *   *

*[Enlil sends a famine. Atrahasis wants to communi-
cate with Enki, but apparently knows that the god
is now under oath not to speak directly with him.
He sleeps by the water for an indirect communication in dreams.]*

Out of the city he [Atrahasis] set his foot,
Every day he would weep,
Bringing dream offerings in the morning.
"My god would speak to me, but he is under oath,
"He will inform me in dreams.
"Enki would speak to me, but he is under oath,
"He will inform me in dreams." . . .
He cast the dream offering into the water,
He would sit facing the river, weeping constantly.
When the waterway was silent,
He made libation at night,
Sleep would come double fast.
He said to the waterway of the river,
"May the waterway take this, may the river bear it
     away,
"May my gift be set before Enki, my lord.
"May Enki see it and think of me,
"May he [   ],
"This night may I have a dream."
After he had sent the message by the waterway,
He sat down to weep facing the river,
From the bank [   ]
To the depths his present went down.
Enki heard his clamor,
He summoned his hairy hero-men and said,
"The man who [   ],
"Let this same one [   ],
"Go, take him my command,
"Ask him, tell me the news of his land."

*   *   *

The flood did not rise from the depths.
The womb of earth did not bear,
Plant life did not come forth.
People were not seen about,

The black fields whitened,
The broad plain was filled up with salts.
The first year they ate old grain,
The second year they exhausted their stores.
When the third year came,
Their features were gray from hunger,
Their faces were crusted, like crusted malt,
Life was ebbing, little by little.
Tall people shriveled in body,
They walked hunched in the street.
Broad-shouldered people turned slender,
Their long stance grew short.
Messengers took the command,
They went before the sea,
They stood and told him,
Their orders to Enki the leader

*   *   *

[Humanity has been saved from famine, apparently
by a flood of fish.]

Enlil was filled with anger at Enki,
"All we great Anunna-gods
"Resolved together on a rule.
"Anu and Adad watched over the upper regions,
"I watched over the lower earth.
"Where Enki went,
"He released the yoke, he made restoration.
"He let loose produce for the peoples,
"He put shade in the glare of the sun."
Enlil made ready to speak,
He said to the vizier Nusku,
"Let them bring to me the two comrades,
"Let them send them into my presence."
They brought to him the two comrades.
The warrior Enlil said to them,
"All we great Anunna-gods
"Resolved together on a rule.
"Anu and Adad watched over the upper regions,
"I watched over the lower earth.
"Where you (Enki) went
"You released the yoke, you made restoration.
"You let loose produce for the peoples,
"You put shade in the glare of the sun."

*   *   *

"Let us be sure to bind the leader Enki,
    who manages all, by oath."
Enki made ready to speak,
And said to the gods his brethren,
"Why would you bind me by oath [   ]?
"Am I to bring my hands against my own peoples?
"The flood that you are speaking of to me,
"Who is to do it? I do not know.
"Am I to produce a flood?
"The task of that is Enlil's.
"Let him choose,
"Let Shullat and Hanish go in front,
"Let Errakal tear out the mooring poles,
"Let Ninurta go make the dikes overflow.

*   *   *

The gods commanded annihilation,
Enlil committed the evil deed against the
    peoples.

[Atrahasis has had a dream from Enki, and wishes
to know its meaning.]

Atrahasis made ready to speak,
And said to his lord,
"Make me know the meaning of the dream,
"[   ] let me know, that I may look out for its
    consequence."
Enki made ready to speak,
And said to his servant,
"You might say, 'Am I to be looking out while in
    the bedroom?'
"Do you pay attention to the message that I speak
    for you:

    'Wall, listen to me!
    'Reed wall, pay attention to all my words!
    'Flee house, build boat,
    'Forsake possessions, and save life.
    'The boat that you build, . . .
    'Cover her with tarpaulins,
    'Roof her over like the depths,
    'So that the sun will not see inside her,
    'Let her be roofed over fore and aft.
    'The gear should be very firm,
    'The pitch should be firm, make her strong.

'I shall shower down upon you later
'A windfall of birds, a spate of fishes.'"

He opened the water clock and filled it,
He told it (the wall?) of the coming of the
    seven-day deluge.
Atrahasis received the command,
He assembled the elders at his gate.
Atrahasis made ready to speak,
And said to the elders,
"My god does not agree with your god,
"Enki and Enlil are constantly angry with each
    other.
"They have expelled me from the land.
"Since I have always reverenced Enki,
"He told me this. * * *
The carpenter carried his ax,
The reed-worker carried his stone.
The rich man carried the pitch,
The poor man brought the materials needed.

                    *   *   *

Pure animals he slaughtered, cattle . . .
Fat animals he killed, sheep . . .
He chose . . . and brought on board.
The birds flying in the heavens,
The cattle and of the cattle-god,
The creatures of the steppe,
[ ] he brought on board . . .
[ ] he invited his people . . .
[ ] to a feast.
[ ] his family he brought on board.
While one was eating and another was drinking,
He went in and out; he could not sit,
    he could not take his place,
For his heart was broken, he was retching gall.
The outlook of the weather changed,
Adad began to roar in the clouds.
The god they heard, his clamor.
He brought pitch to seal his door.
By the time he had bolted his door,
Adad was roaring in the clouds.
The winds were furious as he set forth,
He cut the mooring rope, he released the boat.

                    *   *   *

Anzu rent the sky with his talons, * * *
the flood came forth,
Its destructive power came upon the peoples like
    a battle.
One person did not see another,
They could not recognize each other in the catas-
    trophe.
The deluge bellowed like a bull,
The wind resounded like a screaming eagle.
The darkness was dense, the sun was gone,
The offspring became like flies.
The gods became afraid of the clamor of the
    deluge,
They took refuge in heaven,
They crouched outside.
Anu became afraid of the clamor of the deluge,
It was terrifying the gods.
Enki was beside himself,
That his sons were carried off before him.
Nintu, the great lady,
Gnawed her lips in agony.
The Anunna, the great gods,
Were sitting in thirst and hunger.
The goddess saw it, weeping,
The midwife of the gods, the wise Mami,
"Let the day grow dark,
"Let it turn back to gloom!
"In the assembly of the gods,
"How did I agree with them on annihilation?
"Was Enlil so strong that he forced me to speak?
"Like that Tiruru, did he make my speech confused?
"Of my own accord, from myself alone,
"To my own charge have I heard my people's
    clamor!
"My offspring—with no help from me—have be-
    come like flies.
"And as for me, how to dwell in this abode of
    grief, my clamor fallen silent?
"Shall I go up to heaven,
"I would take up my dwelling in a well-lardered
    house!
"Where has Anu gone to, the chief decision-maker,
"Whose sons, the gods, heeded his command?
"He who irrationally brought about the flood,
"And relegated the peoples to catastrophe?"

*   *   *

Nintu was wailing . . .
"As dragonflies a watercourse, they have filled the
   sea.
"Like rafts they lie against the river meadow,
"Like rafts capsized they lie against the bank.
"I saw and wept over them,
"I have exhausted my lamentation for them."
She wept, giving vent to her feelings,
While Nintu wailed, her emotion was spent.
The gods wept with her for the land.
She had her fill of woe, she was thirsty for beer.
Where she sat weeping, they too sat,
Like sheep, they filled a streambed.
Their lips were agonized with thirst,
They were suffering pangs of hunger.
Seven days and seven nights
There came the deluge, the storm, the flood.

[Atrahasis offers sacrifice to the gods.]

*   *   *

The gods sniffed the savor,
They were gathered like flies around the offering.
After they had eaten the offering,
Nintu arose to rail against all of them,
"Where has Anu come to, the chief decision-maker?
"Has Enlil drawn nigh the incense?
"They who irrationally brought about the flood,
"And relegated the peoples to catastrophe?
"You resolved upon annihilation,
"So now the people's bright countenances are
   turned gray."
Then she drew nigh the big fly ornaments . . .
"Mine is their woe! Proclaim my destiny!
"Let him get me out of my misery, let him show
   me the way.

*   *   *

"Let these flies be jewelry around my neck,
"That I may remember it every day and forever."
The warrior Enlil saw the vessel,
And was filled with anger at the Igigi-gods.
"All we great Anunna-gods
"Resolved together on an oath.
"Where did life escape?

"How did a man survive the catastrophe?"
Anu made ready to speak,
And said to the warrior Enlil,
"Who could do this but Enki?
"He revealed the command."
Enki made ready to speak,
And said to the great gods,
"I did it indeed for your sakes!
"I am responsible for safeguarding life.

*   *   *

Enlil made ready to speak,
And said to Ea the leader,
"Come, summon Nintu the birth-goddess,
"Do you and she take counsel together in the
   assembly."
Enki made ready to speak,
And said to Nintu the birth-goddess,
"You, birth-goddess, creatress of destinies,
"Establish death for all peoples! * * *
"Now then, let there be a third woman among the
   people,
"Among the people are the woman who has
   borne and the woman who has not borne.
"Let there be also among the people the she-
   demon,
"Let her snatch the baby from the lap of her who
   bore it,
"Establish high priestesses and priestesses,
"Let them be taboo, and so cut down childbirth.

*   *   *

REVIEW QUESTIONS

1. According to this account of the great flood,
   why were humans created?
2. Why did the gods decide to send a flood on
   humankind?
3. What does this myth suggest about the proper
   relationship between gods and humankind and,
   by extension, about the place of humans in the
   cosmos?
4. Does Atrahasis's role parallel that of a well-
   known figure from the Hebrew Bible's Book of
   Genesis?

FROM *The Epic of Gilgamesh*

With the exception of the Hebrew Bible, The Epic of Gilgamesh *is the most celebrated literary work of the ancient Near East. Although Gilgamesh almost certainly was an actual ruler of the Sumerian city of Uruk in the early third millennium* B.C.E., *the Akkadian epic that developed around him (elements of which can be found in even earlier Sumerian stories about him) is most prized today not as a historical source for his era but as one of world literature's earliest and most profound statements on the human condition, and especially on the inescapability of human mortality. And, although it is not included in the excerpt that follows, the epic also contains by far the most detailed account of the Flood that is to be found in Mesopotamian literature. (In fact, the discovery of a cuneiform tablet containing this story, with its obvious parallels to the story of Noah and the Flood in the biblical Book of Genesis, helped to foster continued archaeological expeditions to Iraq in the late nineteenth and early twentieth centuries.)*

From *The Epic of Gilgamesh: A New Translation, Analogues, Criticism,* translated by Benjamin R. Foster (New York: Norton, 2001), pp. 3–12, 60–62, 66, 80–82.

FROM **Tablet I**

He who saw the wellspring, the foundations of
    the land,
Who knew [. . .], was wise in all things,
Gilgamesh, who saw the wellspring, the foundations of the land,
Who knew [. . .], was wise in all things,
[He . . .] throughout,
Full understanding of it all he gained,
He saw what was secret and revealed what was
    hidden,
He brought back tidings from before the flood,
From a distant journey came home, weary, at
    peace,
Engraved all his hardships on a monument of
    stone,
He built the walls of ramparted Uruk,
The lustrous treasury of hallowed Eanna!
See its upper wall, whose facing gleams like copper,
Gaze at the lower course, which nothing will equal,
Mount the stone stairway, there from days of old,
Approach Eanna, the dwelling of Ishtar,
Which no future king, no human being will equal.

Go up, pace out the walls of Uruk,
Study the foundation terrace and examine the
    brickwork.
Is not its masonry of kiln-fired brick?
And did not seven masters lay its foundations?
One square mile of city, one square mile of
    gardens.
One square mile of clay pits, a half square mile of
    Ishtar's dwelling,
Three and a half square miles is the measure of
    Uruk!
[Search out] the foundation box of copper,
[Release] its lock of bronze,
Raise the lid upon its hidden contents,
Take up and read from the lapis tablet
Of him, Gilgamesh, who underwent many
    hardships.

[The narrator tells of the extraordinary characteristics of Gilgamesh. An old version of the epic began here.]

Surpassing all kings, for his stature renowned,
Heroic offspring of Uruk, a charging wild bull,
He leads the way in the vanguard,
He marches at the rear, defender of his comrades.

Mighty floodwall, protector of his troops,
Furious flood-wave smashing walls of stone,
Wild calf of Lugalbanda, Gilgamesh is perfect in
   strength,
Suckling of the subline wild cow, the woman
   Ninsun,
Towering Gilgamesh is uncannily perfect.
Opening passes in the mountains,
Digging wells at the highlands' verge,
Traversing the ocean, the vast sea, to the sun's
   rising,
Exploring the furthest reaches of the earth,
Seeking everywhere for eternal life,
Reaching in his might Utanapishtim the Distant
   One,
Restorer of holy places that the deluge had
   destroyed,
Founder of rites for the teeming peoples,
Who could be his like for kingly virtue?[1]
And who, like Gilgamesh, can proclaim, "I am
   king!"
Gilgamesh was singled out from the day of his
   birth,
Two-thirds of him was divine, one-third of him
   was human!
The Lady of Birth drew his body's image,
The God of Wisdom brought his stature to
   perfection.[2]

---

[1] Mesopotamian rulers sometimes boasted of restoring ancient temples that had been destroyed and forgotten long ago. Two lines up, the poet suggests that Gilgamesh became a dutiful king of this kind. Mesopotamian rulers also sometimes boasted of endowing temples with new offerings. This pair of lines (Restorer . . ., Founder . . .) sums up religious duties expected of a good king by citing two extremes of benefactions: those from the remote past and those beginning in his own reign.

[2] According to one Mesopotamian tradition, the first human being was created by Mami, goddess of birth, whom the gods thereupon rewarded with the title "Mistress of All the Gods," and Enki, god of wisdom, working together. This passage means that Gilgamesh was physically a perfect human being, so much so that he resembled the first human created by the gods more than the product of a normal birth.

   *   *   *

In the enclosure of Uruk he strode back and
   forth,
Lording it like a wild bull, his head thrust high.
The onslaught of his weapons had no equal.
His teammates stood forth by his game stick,
He was harrying the young men of Uruk beyond
   reason.
Gilgamesh would leave no son to his father,
Day and night he would rampage fiercely.

   *   *   *

Bold, superb, accomplished, and mature!
Gilgamesh would leave no girl to her [mother]!
The warrior's daughter, the young man's spouse,
Goddesses kept hearing their plaints.[3]

   *   *   *

They summoned the birth goddess, Aruru:

   You, Aruru, created [the boundless human
      race],
   Now, create what Anu commanded,
   To his stormy heart, let that one be equal,
   Let them contend with each other, that Uruk
      may have peace.

When Aruru heard this,
She conceived within her what Anu commanded.
Aruru wet her hands,
She pinched off clay, she tossed it upon the
   steppe,
She created valiant Enkidu in the steppe,
Offspring of potter's clay(?), with the force of the
   hero Ninurta.
Shaggy with hair was his whole body,
He was made lush with head hair, like a woman,
The locks of his hair grew thick as a grainfield.
He knew neither people nor inhabited land,
He dressed as animals do.

---

[3] Certain goddesses were believed to pay particular attention to prayers of women. In this case, they are moved by the constant complaints of the women of Uruk that Gilgamesh was mistreating the women and men of the city.

He fed on grass with gazelles,
With beasts he jostled at the water hole,
With wildlife he drank his fill of water.

*[A distraught hunter seeks his father's advice as to
how to stop Enkidu's interference with his trapping.
The father counsels him to go to Gilgamesh, who
will give him a woman to seduce Enkidu from his
untamed way of life.]*

A hunter, a trapping-man,
Encountered him at the edge of the water hole.
One day, a second, and a third he encountered
    him at the edge of the water hole.
When he saw him, the hunter stood stock-still
    with terror,
As for Enkidu, he went home with his beasts.
Aghast, struck dumb,
His heart in a turmoil, his face drawn,
With woe in his vitals,
His face like a traveler's from afar,

                    *   *   *

[Giving heed] to the advice of his father,
The hunter went forth [. . .].
He took the road, set off towards Uruk,
To [the king], Gilgamesh, [he said these words]:

    There is a certain fellow [who has come from
        the uplands],
    He is mightiest in the land, strength is his,
    Like the force of heaven, so mighty is his
        strength.
    He constantly ranges over the uplands,
    Constantly feeding on grass with his beasts,
    Constantly making his way to the edge of the
        water hole.
    I am too frightened to approach him.
    He has filled in the pits I dug,
    He has torn out my traps I set,
    He has helped the beasts, wildlife of the steppe,
        slip from my hands,
    He will not allow me to work the steppe.

Gilgamesh said to him, to the hunter:

    Go, hunter, take with you Shamhat the
        harlot,

    When the wild beasts draw near the water
        hole,
    Let her strip off her clothing, laying bare her
        charms.
    When he sees her, he will approach her,
    His beasts that grew up with him on the
        steppe will deny him.

Forth went the hunter, taking with him Shamhat
    the harlot,
They took the road, going straight on their way.
On the third day they arrived at the appointed
    place.
Hunter and harlot sat down to wait.
One day, a second day, they sat by the edge of the
    water hole,
The beasts came to the water hole to drink,
The wildlife came to drink their fill of water.
But as for him, Enkidu, born in the uplands,
Who feeds on grass with gazelles,
Who drinks at the water hole with beasts,
Who, with wildlife, drinks his fill of water,
Shamhat looked upon him, a human-man,
A barbarous fellow from the midst of the steppe:

    There he is, Shamhat, open your embrace,
    Open your embrace, let him take your charms!
    Be not bashful, take his vitality!
    When he sees you, he will approach you,
    Toss aside your clothing, let him lie upon
        you,
    Treat him, a human, to woman's work!
    His wild beasts that grew up with him will
        deny him,
    As in his ardor he caresses you!

Shamhat loosened her garments.
She exposed her loins, he took her charms.
She was not bashful, she took his vitality.
She tossed aside her clothing and he lay upon
    her,
She treated him, a human, to woman's work,
As in his ardor he caressed her.
Six days, seven nights was Enkidu aroused,
    flowing into Shamhat.
After he had his fill of her delights,
He set off towards his beasts.

When they saw him, Enkidu, the gazelles shied off,
The wild beasts of the steppe shunned his person.
Enkidu had spent himself, his body was limp,
His knees stood still, while his beasts went away.
Enkidu was too slow, he could not run as before,
But he had gained [reason] and expanded his
    understanding.

*[Shamhat urges Enkidu to return with her to Uruk,
artfully piquing his interest with tales of the pleasures awaiting him there, then feigning second
thoughts as she describes Gilgamesh.]*

He returned, he sat at the harlot's feet,
The harlot gazed upon his face,
While he listened to what the harlot was saying.
The harlot said to him, to Enkidu:

> You are handsome, Enkidu, you are become
>   like a god,
> Why roam the steppe with wild beasts?
> Come, let me lead you to ramparted Uruk,
> To the holy temple, abode of Anu and Ishtar,
> The place of Gilgamesh, who is perfect in
>   strength,
> And so, like a wild bull, he lords it over the
>   young men.

As she was speaking to him, her words found
    favor,
He was yearning for one to know his heart, a
    friend.
Enkidu said to her, to the harlot:

> Come, Shamhat, escort me
> To the lustrous hallowed temple, abode of Anu
>   and Ishtar,
> The place of Gilgamesh, who is perfect in
>   strength,
> And so, like a wild bull, he lords it over the
>   young men.
> I myself will challenge him, [I will speak out]
>   boldly,
> [I will] raise a cry in Uruk: I am the mighty
>   one!
> [I am come forward] to alter destinies!
> He who was born in the steppe [is mighty],
>   strength is his!

[Shamhat speaks.]

> [Come then], let him see your face,
> [I will show you Gilgamesh], where he is I
>   know full well.
> Come then, Enkidu, to ramparted Uruk,
> Where fellows are resplendent in holiday
>   clothing,
> Where every day is set for celebration,
> Where harps and drums are [played].
> And the harlots too, they are fairest of form,
> Rich in beauty, full of delights,
> Even the great (gods) are kept from sleeping at
>   night![4]
> Enkidu, you who [have not] learned to live,
> Oh, let me show you Gilgamesh, the joy-woe
>   man.
> Look at him, gaze upon his face,
> He is radiant with virility, manly vigor is his,
> The whole of his body is seductively gorgeous.
> Mightier strength has he than you,
> Never resting by day or night.
> O Enkidu, renounce your audacity!
> Gilgamesh is beloved of Shamash,
> Anu, Enlil, and Ea broadened his wisdom.
> Ere you come down from the uplands,
> Gilgamesh will dream of you in Uruk.

*[The scene shifts to Uruk, where Gilgamesh is
telling his mother, Ninsun, his dreams. She explains
them to him.]*

Gilgamesh went to relate the dreams, saying to
    his mother:

> Mother, I had a dream last night:
> There were stars of heaven around me,
> Like the force of heaven, something kept falling
>   upon me!
> I tried to carry it but it was too strong for me,
> I tried to move it but I could not budge it.
> The whole of Uruk was standing by it,
> The people formed a crowd around it,
> A throng was jostling towards it,

---

[4] The Mesopotamians considered a small group of the
gods "great" or "superior," above all the others.

Young men were mobbed around it,
Infantile, they were groveling before it!
[I fell in love with it], like a woman I caressed it,
I carried it off and laid it down before you,
Then you were making it my partner.

The mother of Gilgamesh, knowing and wise,
Who understands everything, said to her son,
Ninsun [the wild cow], knowing and wise,
Who understands everything, said to Gilgamesh:

> The stars of heaven around you,
> Like the force of heaven, what kept falling
>   upon you,
> Your trying to move it but not being able to
>   budge it,
> Your laying it down before me,
> Then my making it your partner,
> Your falling in love with it, your caressing it
>   like a woman,
> Means there will come to you a strong one,
> A companion who rescues a friend.
> He will be mighty in the land, strength will be
>   his,
> Like the force of heaven, so mighty will be his
>   strength.

                    *   *   *

Gilgamesh said to her, to his mother:

> Let this befall according to the command of
>   the great counselor Enlil,
> I want a friend for my own counselor,
> For my own counselor do I want a friend!

Even while he was having his dreams,
Shamhat was telling the dreams of Gilgamesh to
    Enkidu,
Each was drawn by love to the other.

[Eventually, Enkidu confronts Gilgamesh in Uruk; they fight; and they become fast friends and companions in fantastic adventures. They journey to the Pine Mountain to fell the trees there, but must first slay Humbaba, the terrifying monster who guards the forest. Afterwards, Ishtar, the goddess of love and sex, is smitten with Gilgamesh and offers to marry him, but, knowing the fate of her previous lovers, Gilgamesh spurns her. Grievously insulted, Ishtar approaches her father, Anu, the chief of the gods, to ask for the Bull of Heaven to send against Gilgamesh and Enkidu. At first reluctant, Anu evenually agrees, but the two heroes kill the Bull of Heaven as well and insult Ishtar with part of its carcass. The gods then decide that one of them must die: Enkidu. As Enkidu grows progressively more ill, Gilgamesh begins to mourn.]

FROM Tablet VIII

At the first glimmer of dawn,
Gilgamesh [lamented] his friend:

> Enkidu, my friend, your mother the gazelle,
> Your father the wild ass brought you into the
>   world,
> Onagers raised you on their milk,
> And the wild beasts taught you all the grazing
>   places.
> The pathways, O Enkidu, to the forest of
>   cedars,
> May they weep for you, without falling silent,
>   night and day.
> May the elders of the teeming city, ramparted
>   Uruk, weep for you,
> May the crowd who blessed our departure
>   weep for you.
> May the heights of highland and mountain
>   [weep for you],
> [. . .]
> May the lowlands wail like your mother.
> May [the forest] of balsam and cedar weep for
>   you,
> Which we slashed in our fury.
> May bear, hyena, panther, leopard, deer,
>   jackal,
> Lion, wild bull, gazelle, ibex, the beasts and
>   creatures of the steppe, weep for you.
> May the sacred Ulaya River weep for you, along
>   whose banks we once strode erect,
> May the holy Euphrates weep for you,
> Whose waters we libated from waterskins.

May the young men of ramparted Uruk weep
for you,
Who watched us slay the Bull of Heaven in
combat.
May the plowman weep for you [at his plow],
Who extolled your name in the sweet song of
harvest home.[5]
May they weep for you, [. . .] of the teeming
city of Uruk,
Who exalted your name at the first [. . .].
May the shepherd and herdsman weep for you,
Who held the milk and buttermilk to your
mouth,
May the [nurse] weep for you,
Who treated your rashes(?) with butter.
May the [. . .] weep for you,
Who held the ale to your mouth.
May the harlot weep for you,
Who massaged you with sweet-smelling oil.
May the wedding guests weep for you,
Who [. . .]
Like brothers may they weep for you,
Like sisters may they tear out their hair for
your sake.
[. . .] Enkidu, as your father, your mother,
I weep for you bitterly, [. . .]

Hear me, O young men, listen to me,
Hear me, O elders of [Uruk], listen to me!
I mourn my friend Enkidu,
I howl as bitterly as a professional keener.
Oh for the axe at my side, oh for the safeguard
by my hand,
Oh for the sword at my belt, oh for the shield
before me,
Oh for my best garment, oh for the raiment
that pleased me most!
An ill wind rose against me and snatched it away!
O my friend, swift wild donkey, mountain
onager, panther of the steppe!
O Enkidu my friend, swift wild donkey, moun-
tain onager, panther of the steppe!

You who stood by me when we climbed the
mountain,
Seized and slew the Bull of Heaven,
Felled Humbaba who [dwelt] in the forest of
cedar,
What now is this sleep that has seized you?
Come back to me! You hear me not.

But, as for him, he did not raise his head.
He touched his heart but it was not beating.
Then he covered his friend's face, like a bride's.
He hovered round him like an eagle,
Like a lioness whose cubs are in a pitfall,
He paced to and fro, back and forth,
Tearing out and hurling away the locks of his
hair,
Ripping off and throwing away his fine clothes
like something foul.

*[Gilgamesh commissions a memorial statue of
Enkidu.]*

At the first glimmer of dawn,
Gilgamesh sent out a proclamation to the land:

Hear ye, blacksmith, lapidary, metalworker,
goldsmith, jeweler!
Make [an image] of my friend,
[Such as no one ever] made of his friend!
The limbs of my friend [. . .]
[Your beard] of lapis, your chest of gold,
Your skin of [. . .]

I will lay you down in the ultimate resting
place,
In a perfect resting place I will surely lay you
down.
I will settle you in peaceful rest in the dwelling
sinister,
Rulers of the netherworld will do you homage.
I will have the people of Uruk shed bitter tears
for you,
I will make the pleasure-loving people
burdened down for you,
And, as for me, now that you are dead, I will
let my hair grow matted,
I will put on a lion skin and roam the steppe!

*   *   *

---

[5] Mesopotamian literature referred to work songs sung
when the crops were brought in from the harvest as
symbols of happiness and prosperity.

FROM **Tablet IX**

Gilgamesh was weeping bitterly for Enkidu, his
　friend,
As he roamed the steppe:

　Shall I not die too? Am I not like Enkidu?
　Oh woe has entered my vitals!
　I have grown afraid of death, so I roam the
　　steppe.
　Having come this far, I will go on swiftly
　Towards Utanapishtim, son of Ubar-Tutu.

*[To reach Utanapishtim, who corresponds to Atra-
hasis in the first reading in this chapter, Gilgamesh
must undertake a dangerous journey that culmi-
nates in a voyage by boat across a sea of lethal water. Finally, he reaches the far shore, where an
amazed Utanapishtim has watched him coming.]*

　　　　*　　　*　　　*

FROM **Tablet X**

Utanapishtim said to him, to Gilgamesh:

　Why are your cheeks emaciated, your face cast
　　down,
　Your heart wretched, your features wasted,
　Woe in your vitals,
　Your face like a traveler's from afar,
　Your features weathered by cold and sun,
　　Why are you clad in a lion skin, roaming the
　　　steppe?

*[Gilgamesh tells Utanapishtim his mission, wallow-
ing in the luxury of self-pity on the difficulties of
his quest.]*

Gilgamesh said to him, to Utanapishtim:

　My cheeks would not be emaciated, nor my
　　face cast down,
　Nor my heart wretched, nor my features
　　wasted,
　Nor would there be woe in my vitals,
　Nor would my face be like a traveler's from afar,
　Nor would my features be weathered by cold
　　and sun,

Nor would I be clad in a lion skin, roaming the
　steppe,
But for my friend, swift wild donkey, mountain
　onager, panther of the steppe,
But for Enkidu, my friend, swift wild donkey,
　mountain onager, panther of the steppe,
He who stood by me as we ascended the
　mountain,
Seized and killed the bull that came down from
　heaven,
Felled Humbaba who dwelt in the forest of
　cedars,
Killed lions at the mountain passes,
My friend whom I so loved, who went with me
　through every hardship,
Enkidu, whom I so loved, who went with me
　through every hardship,
The fate of mankind has overtaken him.
Six days and seven nights I wept for him,
I would not give him up for burial,
Until a worm fell out of his nose.
I was frightened [. . .]
I have grown afraid of death, so I roam the
　steppe,
My friend's case weighs heavy upon me.
A distant road I roam over the steppe,
My friend Enkidu's case weighs heavy upon
　me!
A distant path I roam over the steppe,
How can I be silent? How can I hold my
　peace?
My friend whom I loved is turned into clay,
Enkidu, my friend whom I loved, is turned into
　clay!
Shall I too not lie down like him,
And never get up, forever and ever?

Gilgamesh said to him, to Utanapishtim:

So it is to go find Utanapishtim, whom they
　call the "Distant One,"
I traversed all lands,
I came over, one after another, wearisome
　mountains,
Then I crossed, one after another, all the seas.
Too little sweet sleep has smoothed my
　countenance,

I have worn myself out in sleeplessness,
My muscles ache for misery,
What have I gained my trials?
I had not reached the tavern keeper when my
    clothes were worn out,
I killed bear, hyena, lion, panther, leopard, deer,
    ibex, wild beasts of the steppe,
I ate their meat, I [. . .] their skins.
Let them close behind me the doors of woe,
[Let them seal them] with pitch and tar,
For my part, I [. . .] no amusement,
For me, [. . .]

[*Gilgamesh asks Utanapishtim how he "came to stand in the gods' assembly and sought eternal life." Utanapishtim tells him the story of how, long ago, the gods had decided to send a great flood to destroy humankind, but how, at the instruction of Ea (Enki), he had built a great boat and had brought aboard it all manner of living things to survive the flood. After the flood subsided, Utanapishtim and his wife were granted immortality. He chides Gilgamesh for his self-pity and ostentatious mourning, all the more unseemly because the gods had favored him. The village idiot, he points out, wears rags and eats bad food, but no one accords him merit for that. After a gap in the text, Utanapishtim is found discoursing on the nature of death.*]

Utanapishtim said to him, to Gilgamesh:

Why, O Gilgamesh, did you prolong woe,
You who are [formed] of the flesh of gods and
    mankind,
You for whom [the gods] acted like fathers and
    mothers?

*   *   *

FROM Tablet XI

Now then, who will convene the gods for your
    sake,
That you may find the eternal life you seek?
Come, come, try not to sleep for six days and
    seven nights.

[*Utanapishtim has challenged Gilgamesh to go without sleep for a week; if he fails this test, how could he expect to live forever? Even as he speaks, Gilgamesh drifts off to sleep. Thus passes from the scene the all-night rowdy of Tablet I.*]

As he sat there on his haunches,
Sleep was swirling over him like a mist.
Utanapishtim said to her, to his wife:

Behold this fellow who seeks eternal life!
Sleep swirls over him like a mist.

[*Utanapishtim's wife, taking pity on Gilgamesh, urges her husband to awaken him and let him go home. Utanapishtim insists on a proof of how long he slept, lest Gilgamesh claim that he had only dozed. She is to bake him fresh bread every day and set it beside him, marking the wall for the day. The bread spoils progressively as Gilgamesh sleeps for seven days.*]

His wife said to him, to Utanapishtim the Distant
    One:

Do touch him that the man may wake up,
That he may return safe on the way whence he
    came,
That through the gate he came forth he may
    return to his land.

Utanapishtim said to her, to his wife:

Since the human race is duplicitous, he'll en-
    deavor to dupe you.
Come, come, bake his daily loaves, put them
    one after another by his head,
Then mark the wall for each day he has
    slept.

She baked his daily loaves for him, put them one
    after another by his head,
Then dated the wall for each day he slept.
The first loaf was dried hard,
The second was leathery, the third soggy,
The crust of the fourth turned white,
The fifth was gray with mold, the sixth was
    fresh,
The seventh was still on the coals when he
    touched him, the man woke up.

[Gilgamesh wakes at last. Claiming at first that he has scarcely dozed a moment, he sees the bread and realizes that he has slept for the entire time he was supposed to remain awake for the test. He gives up in despair. What course is left for him? Utanapishtim does not answer directly but orders the boatman to take him home. Further, the boatman himself is never to return. Thus access to Utanapishtim is denied the human race forever. Gilgamesh is bathed and given clothing that will stay magically fresh until his return to Uruk.]

Gilgamesh said to him, to Utanapishtim the
  Distant One:

  Scarcely had sleep stolen over me,
  When straightaway you touched me and roused
    me.

Utanapishtim said to him, to Gilgamesh:

  [Up with you], Gilgamesh, count your daily
    loaves,
  [That the days you have slept] may be known
    to you.
  The first loaf is dried hard,
  The second is leathery, the third soggy,
  The crust of the fourth has turned white,
  The fifth is gray with mold,
  The sixth is fresh,
  The seventh was still in the coals when I
    touched you and you woke up.

Gilgamesh said to him, to Utanapishtim the
  Distant One:

  What then should I do, Utanapishtim, whither
    should I go,
  Now that the Bereaver has seized my [flesh]?[6]
  Death lurks in my bedchamber,
  And wherever I turn, there is death!

Utanapishtim said to him, to Ur-Shanabi the
  boatman:

  Ur-Shanabi, may the harbor [offer] you no
    [haven],

---

6 "The Bereaver" is an epithet of death. It could also mean something like "kidnapper."

  May the crossing point reject you,
  Be banished from the shore you shuttled to.
  The man you brought here,
  His body is matted with filthy hair,
  Hides have marred the beauty of his flesh.
  Take him away, Ur-Shanabi, bring him to the
    washing place.
  Have him wash out his filthy hair with water,
    clean as snow,
  Have him throw away his hides, let the sea
    carry them off,
  Let his body be rinsed clean.
  Let his headband be new,
  Have him put on raiment worthy of him.
  Until he reaches his city,
  Until he completes his journey,
  Let his garments stay spotless, fresh and new.

Ur-Shanabi took him away and brought him to
  the washing place.
He washed out his filthy hair with water, clean as
  snow,
He threw away his hides, the sea carried them
  off,
His body was rinsed clean.
He renewed his headband,
He put on raiment worthy of him.
Until he reached his city,
Until he completed his journey,
His garments would stay spotless, fresh and new.

[Gilgamesh and Ur-Shanabi embark on their journey to Uruk. As they push off from the shore, Utanapishtim's wife intervenes, asking her husband to give the hero something to show for his quest. Gilgamesh brings the boat back to shore and waits expectantly. Utanapishtim tells him of a plant of rejuvenation. Gilgamesh dives for the plant by opening a shaft through the earth's surface to the water below. He ties stones to his feet, a technique used in traditional pearl diving in the Gulf. When he comes up from securing the plant, he is on the opposite side of the ocean, where he started from.]

Gilgamesh and Ur-Shanabi embarked on the
  boat,
They launched the boat, they embarked upon it.

His wife said to him, to Utanapishtim the Distant
  One:

Gilgamesh has come here, spent with exertion,
What will you give him for his homeward
  journey?

At that he, Gilgamesh, lifted the pole,
Bringing the boat back by the shore.
Utanapishtim said to him, to Gilgamesh:

Gilgamesh, you have come here, spent with
  exertion,
What shall I give you for your homeward
  journey?
I will reveal to you, O Gilgamesh, a secret
  matter,
And a mystery of the gods I will tell you.
There is a certain plant, its stem is like a
  thornbush,
Its thorns, like the wild rose, will prick [your
  hand].
If you can secure this plant, [. . .]
[. . .]

No sooner had Gilgamesh heard this,
He opened a shaft, [flung away his tools].
He tied heavy stones [to his feet],
They pulled him down into the watery depths
  [. . .].
He took the plant though it pricked [his hand].
He cut the heavy stones [from his feet],
The sea cast him up on his home shore.

*[Gilgamesh resolves to take the plant to Uruk to
experiment on an old man. While Gilgamesh is
bathing on the homeward journey, a snake eats the
plant and rejuvenates itself by shedding its skin.
Gilgamesh gives up. Immense quantities of water
have flooded up through the shaft he dug and
covered the place. He has left behind his tools so
cannot dig another shaft. He has also lost the boat,
so there is no going back.]*

Gilgamesh said to him, to Ur-Shanabi the
  boatman:

Ur-Shanabi, this plant is cure for heartache,
Whereby a man will regain his stamina.

I will take it to ramparted Uruk,
I will have an old man eat some and so test the
  plant.
His name shall be "Old Man Has Become
  Young-Again-Man."
I myself will eat it and so return to my carefree
  youth.

At twenty double leagues they took a bite to eat,
At thirty double leagues they made their camp.

Gilgamesh saw a pond whose water was cool,
He went down into it to bathe in the water.
A snake caught the scent of the plant,
[Stealthily] it came up and carried the plant away,
On its way back it shed its skin.

Thereupon Gilgamesh sat down weeping,
His tears flowed down his face,
He said to Ur-Shanabi the boatman:

For whom, Ur-Shanabi, have my hands been
  toiling?
For whom has my heart's blood been poured
  out?
For myself I have obtained no benefit,
I have done a good deed for a reptile!
Now, floodwaters rise against me for twenty
  double leagues,
When I opened the shaft, I flung away the
  tools.
How shall I find my bearings?
I have come much too far to go back, and I
  abandoned the boat on the shore.

*[Upon completing his journey, Gilgamesh invites
Ur-Shanabi to inspect the walls of Uruk, using the
same words used by the narrator in Tablet I.]*

At twenty double leagues they took a bite to eat,
At thirty double leagues they made their camp.
When they arrived in ramparted Uruk,
Gilgamesh said to him, to Ur-Shanabi the
  boatman:

Go up, Ur-Shanabi, pace out the walls of Uruk.
Study the foundation terrace and examine the
  brickwork.
Is not its masonry of kiln-fired brick?

TWO IMAGES OF SUMERIAN RULERSHIP (C. 2480 B.C.E.)

The first image (top) is a plaque of Ur-Nanshe, who ruled the Sumerian city-state of Lagash around 2480 B.C.E. He is shown both as a builder carrying a basket of bricks, with his family facing him (above), and enthroned (below). The second image (bottom), from a limestone monument known as the Vulture Stela, depicts Ur-Nanshe's successor Eannatum leading the troops of Lagash to victory against the rival city-state of Umma. The inscriptions on the stela record Lagash's victory and the terms it imposed on Umma. What do these images suggest about the status and responsibilities of Sumerian rulers? What do they suggest about the uses of cuneiform writing during the mid-third millennium B.C.E.?

And did not seven masters lay its foundations?
One square mile of city, one square mile of
    gardens,
One square mile of clay pits, a half square mile
    of Ishtar's dwelling,
Three and a half square miles is the measure of
    Uruk!

*   *   *

1. What kind of figure is Gilgamesh?
2. What becomes of his quest in this epic, and why?
3. What roles do the gods play in the story?
4. When his quest is completed, what is Gilgamesh's view of his fate?

FROM The Code of Hammurabi

Dating to the reign of Hammurabi of Babylon (the conventional dates for which are 1795–1750 B.C.E.), the Laws of Hammurabi are not the earliest Mesopotamian compilation of legal rulings known to us. They are, however, the longest and most diverse collection and undoubtedly constitute the single most informative document yet discovered regarding concepts of justice and social regulation in Mesopotamian society. Hammurabi's laws also provide extremely important evidence about the status and rights of women of various social classes in Babylonian society in the early second millennium B.C.E.

From *Law Collections from Mesopotamia and Asia Minor,* edited by Martha T. Roth, SBL Writings from the Ancient World Series, vol. 6 (Atlanta, Ga.: Scholars Press, 1995), pp. 76–135.

When the august god Anu, king of the Anunnaku deities, and the god Enlil, lord of heaven and earth, who determines the destinies of the land, allotted supreme power over all peoples to the god Marduk, the firstborn son of the god Ea, exalted him among the Igigu deities, named the city of Babylon with its august name and made it supreme within the regions of the world, and established for him within it eternal kingship whose foundations are as fixed as heaven and earth, at that time, the gods Anu and Enlil, for the enhancement of the well-being of the people, named me by my name: Hammurabi, the pious prince, who venerates the gods, to make justice prevail in the land, to abolish the wicked and the evil, to prevent the strong from oppressing the weak, to rise like the sun-god Shamash over all humankind, to illuminate the land.

I am Hammurabi, the shepherd, selected by the god Enlil, he who heaps high abundance and plenty, who perfects every possible thing for the city Nippur, the city known as band-of-heaven-and-earth, the pious provider of the Ekur temple;

the capable king, the restorer of the city Eridu, the purifier of the rites of the Eabzu temple;

the onslaught of the four regions of the world, who magnifies the reputation of the city Babylon, who gladdens the heart of his divine lord Marduk, whose days are devoted to the Esagil temple;

*   *   *

When the god Marduk commanded me to provide just ways for the people of the land in order

to attain appropriate behavior, I established truth and justice as the declaration of the land, I enhanced the well-being of the people.

*   *   *

1. If a man accuses another man and charges him with homicide but cannot bring proof against him, his accuser shall be killed.

*   *   *

2. If a man charges another man with practicing witchcraft but cannot bring proof against him, he who is charged with witchcraft shall go to the divine River Ordeal,[1] he shall indeed submit to the divine River Ordeal; if the divine River Ordeal should overwhelm him, his accuser shall take full legal possession of his estate; if the divine River Ordeal should clear that man and should he survive, he who made the charge of witchcraft against him shall be killed; he who submitted to the divine River Ordeal shall take full legal possession of his accuser's estate.

3. If a man comes forward to give false testimony in a case but cannot bring evidence for his accusation, if that case involves a capital offense, that man shall be killed.

*   *   *

6. If a man steals valuables belonging to the god or to the palace, that man shall be killed, and also he who received the stolen goods from him shall be killed.

7. If a man should purchase silver, gold, a slave, a slave woman, an ox, a sheep, a donkey, or anything else whatsoever, from a son of a man or from a slave of a man without witnesses or a contract—or if he accepts the goods for safekeeping—that man is a thief, he shall be killed.

8. If a man steals an ox, a sheep, a donkey, a pig, or a boat—if it belongs either to the god or to the palace, he shall give thirtyfold; if it belongs to a commoner, he shall replace it tenfold; if the thief does not have anything to give, he shall be killed.

*   *   *

15. If a man should enable a palace slave, a palace slave woman, a commoner's slave, or a commoner's slave woman to leave through the main city-gate, he shall be killed.

16. If a man should harbor a fugitive slave or slave woman of either the palace or of a commoner in his house and not bring him out at the herald's public proclamation, that householder shall be killed.

17. If a man seizes a fugitive slave or slave woman in the open country and leads him back to his owner, the slave owner shall give him 2 shekels of silver.

18. If that slave should refuse to identify his owner, he shall lead him off to the palace, his circumstances shall be investigated, and they shall return him to his owner.

19. If he should detain that slave in his own house and afterward the slave is discovered in his possession, that man shall be killed.

20. If the slave should escape the custody of the one who seized him, that man shall swear an oath by the god to the owner of the slave, and he shall be released.

21. If a man breaks into a house, they shall kill him and hang him in front of that very breach.

22. If a man commits a robbery and is then seized, that man shall be killed.

*   *   *

53. If a man neglects to reinforce the embankment of the irrigation canal of his field and does not reinforce its embankment, and then a breach opens in its embankment and allows the water to carry away the common irrigated area, the man in whose embankment the breach opened shall replace the grain whose loss he caused.

---

[1] The man would take an oath swearing to his innocence before the river god. He then would be required to plunge into the river. If he survived, he was deemed innocent; if he drowned, it was deemed the punishment of the river god, in whose name he had falsely sworn. [Editor.]

54. If he cannot replace the grain they shall sell him and his property, and the residents of the common irrigated area whose grain crops the water carried away shall divide (the proceeds).

55. If a man opens his branch of the canal for irrigation and negligently allows the water to carry away his neighbor's field, he shall measure and deliver grain in accordance with his neighbor's yield.

*   *   *

102. If a merchant should give silver to a trading agent for an investment venture, and he incurs a loss on his journeys, he shall return silver to the merchant in the amount of the capital sum.

103. If enemy forces should make him abandon whatever goods he is transporting while on his business trip, the trading agent shall swear an oath by the god and shall be released.

104. If a merchant gives a trading agent grain, wool, oil, or any other commodity for local transactions, the trading agent shall return to the merchant the silver for each transaction; the trading agent shall collect a sealed receipt for each payment in silver that he gives to the merchant.

105. If the trading agent should be negligent and not take a sealed receipt for each payment in silver that he gives to the merchant, any silver that is not documented in a sealed receipt will not be included in the final accounting.

*   *   *

108. If a woman innkeeper should refuse to accept grain for the price of beer but accepts only silver measured by the large weight, thereby reducing the value of beer in relation to the value of grain, they shall charge and convict that woman innkeeper and they shall cast her into the water.

109. If there should be a woman innkeeper in whose house criminals congregate, and she does not seize those criminals and lead them off to the palace authorities, that woman innkeeper shall be killed.

*   *   *

117. If an obligation is outstanding against a man and he sells or gives into debt service his wife, his son, or his daughter, they shall perform service in the house of their buyer or of the one who holds them in debt service for three years; their release shall be secured in the fourth year.

118. If he should give a male or female slave into debt service, the merchant may extend the term beyond the three years, he may sell him; there are no grounds for a claim.

119. If an obligation is outstanding against a man and he therefore sells his slave woman who has borne him children, the owner of the slave woman shall weigh and deliver the silver which the merchant weighed and delivered as the loan and he shall thereby redeem his slave woman.

*   *   *

128. If a man marries a wife but does not draw up a formal contract for her, she is not a wife.

129. If a man's wife should be seized lying with another male, they shall bind them and throw them into the water; if the wife's master allows his wife to live, then the king shall allow his subject (i.e., the other male) to live.

130. If a man pins down another man's virgin wife who is still residing in her father's house, and they seize him lying with her, that man shall be killed; that woman shall be released.

131. If her husband accuses his own wife of adultery, although she has not been seized lying with another male, she shall swear to her innocence by an oath by the god, and return to her house.

132. If a man's wife should have a finger pointed against her in accusation involving another male, although she has not been seized lying with another male, she shall submit to the divine River Ordeal for her husband.

*   *   *

134. If a man should be captured and there are not sufficient provisions in his house, his wife may enter another's house; that woman will not be subject to any penalty.

135. If a man should be captured and there are not sufficient provisions in his house, before his return his wife enters another's house and bears children, and afterwards her husband returns and

gets back to his city, that woman shall return to her first husband; the children shall inherit from their father.

136. If a man deserts his city and flees, and after his departure his wife enters another's house—if that man then should return and seize his wife, because he repudiated his city and fled, the wife of the deserter will not return to her husband.

*   *   *

138. If a man intends to divorce his first-ranking wife who did not bear him children, he shall give her silver as much as was her bridewealth and restore to her the dowry that she brought from her father's house, and he shall divorce her.

139. If there is no bridewealth, he shall give her 60 shekels of silver as a divorce settlement.

140. If he is a commoner, he shall give her 20 shekels of silver.

141. If the wife of a man who is residing in the man's house should decide to leave, and she appropriates goods, squanders her household possessions, or disparages her husband, they shall charge and convict her; and if her husband should declare his intention to divorce her, then he shall divorce her; neither her travel expenses, nor her divorce settlement, nor anything else shall be given to her. If her husband should not declare his intention to divorce her, then her husband may marry another woman and that first woman shall reside in her husband's house as a slave woman.

142. If a woman repudiates her husband, and declares, "You will not have marital relations with me"—her circumstances shall be investigated by the authorities of her city quarter, and if she is circumspect and without fault, but her husband is wayward and disparages her greatly, that woman will not be subject to any penalty; she shall take her dowry and she shall depart for her father's house.

143. If she is not circumspect but is wayward, squanders her household possessions, and disparages her husband, they shall cast that woman into the water.

*   *   *

150. If a man awards to his wife a field, orchard, house, or movable property, and makes out a sealed document for her, after her husband's death her children will not bring a claim against her; the mother shall give her estate to whichever of her children she loves, but she will not give it to an outsider.

151. If a woman who is residing in a man's house should have her husband agree by binding contract that no creditor of her husband shall seize her for his debts—if that man has a debt incurred before marrying that woman, his creditors will not seize his wife; and if that woman has a debt incurred before entering the man's house, her creditors will not seize her husband.

*   *   *

153. If a man's wife has her husband killed on account of (her relationship with) another male, they shall impale that woman.

154. If a man should carnally know his daughter, they shall banish that man from the city.

155. If a man selects a bride for his son and his son carnally knows her, after which he himself then lies with her and they seize him in the act, they shall bind that man and cast him into the water.

156. If a man selects a bride for his son and his son does not yet carnally know her, and he himself then lies with her, he shall weigh and deliver to her 30 shekels of silver; moreover, he shall restore to her whatever she brought from her father's house, and a husband of her choice shall marry her.

157. If a man, after his father's death, should lie with his mother, they shall burn them both.

158. If a man, after his father's death, should be discovered in the lap of the father's principal wife who had borne children, that man shall be disinherited from the paternal estate.

*   *   *

162. If a man marries a wife, she bears him children, and that woman then goes to her fate, her father shall have no claim to her dowry; her dowry belongs only to her children.

163. If a man marries a wife but she does not provide him with children, and that woman goes

to her fate—if his father-in-law then returns to him the bridewealth that that man brought to his father-in-law's house, her husband shall have no claim to that woman's dowry; her dowry belongs only to her father's house.

*   *   *

169. If he should be guilty of a grave offense deserving the penalty of disinheritance by his father, they shall pardon him for his first one; if he should commit a grave offense a second time, the father may disinherit his son.

*   *   *

188. If a craftsman takes a young child to rear and then teaches him his craft, he will not be reclaimed.

189. If he should not teach him his craft, that rearling shall return to his father's house.

190. If a man should not reckon the young child whom he took and raised in adoption as equal with his children, that rearling shall return to his father's house.

191. If a man establishes his household by reckoning as equal with any future children the young child whom he took and raised in adoption, but afterwards he has children of his own and then decides to disinherit the rearling, that young child will not depart empty-handed; the father who raised him shall give him a one-third share of his property as his inheritance and he shall depart; he will not give him any property from field, orchard, or house.

*   *   *

195. If a child should strike his father, they shall cut off his hand.

196. If an *awīlu* should blind the eye of another *awīlu*, they shall blind his eye.[2]

---

[2] The most basic meaning of *awīlu* is "man." In this context it seems to represent a free man, probably an owner of private land and with a status higher than that of a "commoner." [Editor.]

197. If he should break the bone of another *awīlu*, they shall break his bone.

198. If he should blind the eye of a commoner or break the bone of a commoner, he shall weigh and deliver 60 shekels of silver.

199. If he should blind the eye of an *awīlu's* slave or break the bone of an *awīlu's* slave, he shall weigh and deliver one-half of his value in silver.

200. If an *awīlu* should knock out the tooth of another *awīlu* of his own rank, they shall knock out his tooth.

201. If he should knock out the tooth of a commoner, he shall weigh and deliver 20 shekels of silver.

202. If an *awīlu* should strike the cheek of an *awīlu* who is of status higher than his own, he shall be flogged in the public assembly with 60 stripes of an ox whip.

203. If a member of the *awīlu*-class should strike the cheek of another member of the *awīlu*-class who is his equal, he shall weigh and deliver 60 shekels of silver.

204. If a commoner should strike the cheek of another commoner, he shall weigh and deliver 10 shekels of silver.

*   *   *

209. If an *awīlu* strikes a woman of the *awīlu*-class and thereby causes her to miscarry her fetus, he shall weigh and deliver 10 shekels of silver for her fetus.

210. If that woman should die, they shall kill his daughter.

211. If he should cause a woman of the commoner-class to miscarry her fetus by the beating, he shall weigh and deliver 5 shekels of silver.

212. If that woman should die, he shall weigh and deliver 30 shekels of silver.

*   *   *

218. If a physician performs major surgery with a bronze lancet upon an *awīlu* and thus causes the *awīlu's* death, or opens an *awīlu's* temple with a

bronze lancet and thus blinds the *awīlu*'s eye, they shall cut off his hand.

219. If a physician performs major surgery with a bronze lancet upon a slave of a commoner and thus causes the slave's death, he shall replace the slave with a slave of comparable value.

220. If he opens his (the commoner's slave's) temple with a bronze lancet and thus blinds his eye, he shall weigh and deliver silver equal to half his value.

*   *   *

226. If a barber shaves off the slave-hairlock of a slave not belonging to him without the consent of the slave's owner, they shall cut off that barber's hand.

227. If a man misinforms a barber so that he then shaves off the slave-hairlock of a slave not belonging to him, they shall kill that man and hang him in his own doorway; the barber shall swear, "I did not knowingly shave it off," and he shall be released.

*   *   *

These are the just decisions which Hammurabi, the able king, has established and thereby has directed the land along the course of truth and the correct way of life.

I am Hammurabi, noble king. I have not been careless or negligent toward humankind, granted to my care by the god Enlil, and with whose shepherding the god Marduk charged me. I have sought for them peaceful places, I removed serious difficulties, I spread light over them. With the mighty weapon which the gods Zababa and Ishtar bestowed upon me, with the wisdom which the god Ea allotted to me, with the ability which the god Marduk gave me, I annihilated enemies everywhere, I put an end to wars, I enhanced the well-being of the land, I made the people of all settlements lie in safe pastures, I did not tolerate anyone intimidating them. The great gods having chosen me, I am indeed the shepherd who brings peace, whose scepter is just. My benevolent shade is spread over my city, I held the people of the lands of Sumer and Akkad safely on my lap. They prospered under my protective spirit, I maintained them in peace, with my skillful wisdom I sheltered them.

In order that the mighty not wrong the weak, to provide just ways for the waif and the widow, I have inscribed my precious pronouncements upon my stela and set it up before the statue of me, the king of justice, in the city of Babylon, the city which the gods Anu and Enlil have elevated, within the Esagil, the temple whose foundations are fixed as are heaven and earth, in order to render the judgments of the land, to give the verdicts of the land, and to provide just ways for the wronged.

REVIEW QUESTIONS

1. Of the hundreds of records of litigation that exist from the era of Hammurabi and his successors, not one specifically states that a dispute was resolved in accordance with Hammurabi's laws; some, in fact, record rulings that directly contradict those laws. This has caused some scholars to question why Hammurabi had these laws compiled in the first place. Why do you think Hammurabi had his laws compiled? (Do the prologue and epilogue to the laws provide any clues?)

2. What principles of justice and compensation are evident in these laws, and what kinds of recourse did society have against wrongdoers?

3. What evidence of social classes in Babylonian society do they provide?

4. How did women's rights compare with those of men?

5. What do these laws tell us about Mesopotamian views on sexual activity?

6. What do they tell us about power and authority within Mesopotamian families?

Letters of Royal Women
of the Old Babylonian Period

Women's voices are all too infrequently heard in the documents of ancient Mesopotamia. But archeological excavations have recovered major portions of the palace archives (dating to the early second millennium B.C.E.) of the northern Mesopotamian cities of Mari and Karana, including cuneiform tablets containing letters to and from women of the royal houses of both places.

From *Mari and Karana: Two Old Babylonian Cities,* by Stephanie Dalley (Glenview, Ill.: Addison-Wesley Longman, 1984), pp. 104–9.

*   *   *

Speak to Iltani, thus Yasitna-abum your son. May Shamash and Marduk grant that my mother live forever for my sake. My mother called my name, and my heart came alive. Now, do send me a letter saying how you are, and give me new life. Whenever I reread your letter, the dust-storms of Adad are forgotten; my heart is replenished with life. The servant boy whom my mother sent to me is far too young. For that servant boy does not keep *me* regularly supplied; it is I who have to keep *him* regularly supplied! Whenever I go on a journey, not even so much as 2 litres of bread for my ration is carried behind me. May my mother send me another servant boy who will be able to carry 10 litres of bread for my ration behind me, and who will be able really to help.

*   *   *

Speak to my lady; thus Belassunu. Ever since the harvest I have written frequently to you, but you have never sent me a reply of any kind. The king had spoken to me saying, "Stay in Zarbat. As soon as I come, Usi-nawir will come with me, and he will let you plead your innocence." Now, why are you silent? He neither lets me plead my innocence nor lets me go. You are near the ruler where you are: write, that they may take me back to the ruler. What have I done wrong? Why have

you frowned upon me, and not pleaded my cause? Who will deal with the matter, and who has turned to help me?

*   *   *

Speak to my lord; thus Iltani thy servant. My lord wrote to me about letting go the oxen, sheep and donkeys belonging to Tazabru, saying: "If you do not let them go, I shall cut you into twelve pieces." That is what my lord wrote to me. Why has my lord written my death sentence to me? Only yesterday I spoke to my lord saying it was his own shepherd who had in the past kept his oxen and his sheep; he was pasturing them in Yashibatum. That is what I told my lord. Now, let my lord simply write that they are to take his oxen and sheep away from Yashibatum. If I have taken any of his oxen or sheep, may my lord inflict the punishment on me. Would I, without my lord's permission, would I have laid hands on and taken anything? Why then has my lord written my death sentence?

*   *   *

Speak to Iltani, my sister; thus Lamassani. I am well. The caravan comes regularly. You have never written to me to say how you are. I am still looking for a necklace of lapis lazuli, for which you wrote to me, and I shall send you a serving woman with it, but until now I have not found what you

wrote for, and so I have not yet sent a slavegirl. Are you not aware that I am receiving short rations of barley? For in the city of Ashur, barley is expensive and linseed oil is expensive. Your son Sin-rimeni often comes and goes, but you have never mentioned me to him; you have not heaped honour on my head in the household where I am staying. As you must be aware, I am receiving short rations: please provide me with barley and linseed oil.

*   *   *

Speak to Iltani my sister, thus Amat-Shamash your sister. May my divine lord and lady grant that you live forever for my sake. Previously when Aqba-hammu came to Sippar I gave him cause to honour my priestesshood, and he honoured me greatly, for he said to me: "When I go back to Karana, write to me and I shall send you a boat full of whatever you need. Offer a prayer for me to your divine lord." Now, I have written, and he has provided me with two servants. But you have not recalled my name; you never even sent me so much as a single jar of perfume; you never said: "Approach and offer a prayer for me to your divine lady." Instead you say: "What do you think I am for?" Apart from you, does a girl who has washed her husband's feet for one day not send her own sister provisions from then onwards? And the slaves whom my father gave me have grown old. Now, I have sent half a mina of silver to the king. Allow me my claim, and let him send to me slaves that have been captured recently, and who are trustworthy. Now, in recollection of you, I have sent to you five minas of first-rate wool and a basket of "shrimps."

*   *   *

Speak to the lady my mother, thus Erishti-Aya your daughter. May my divine lord and lady grant you long life for my sake. Why didn't you ever wear my dress, but sent it back to me, and made me dishonoured and accursed? I am your daughter, and you are the wife of a king. . . . Your husband and you put me into the cloister; but the soldiers who were taken captive pay me more respect than you! You should pay me respect, and then my divine lord and lady will honour you with the good opin-ion of the city and its inhabitants. I am sending you a nanny. Do send me something to make me happy, and then I will be happy. Don't neglect me.

*   *   *

Speak to my star, my father and my lord, thus your daughter Kiru. It really was a sign when I spoke to you in the courtyard saying: "You are going away, and so you will not be able to direct the country; the country will become hostile behind you." That is what I said to my father and lord, but he didn't listen to me. . . . Now, if I am truly a woman, may my lord and father pay heed to my words—I am always writing the words of the gods to my father!

*   *   *

About my worries I have written twice to my lord, and my lord has written to me saying: "Go into Ashlakka and don't cry." My lord wrote that to me, and now I have entered Ashlakka and my worries have been fully justified! The wife of Ibal-Addu is queen all right; that woman takes it upon herself to receive personally every delivery for Ash-lakka city and its towns. She made me sit in a corner holding my head in my hands like any idiot woman. Food and drink were regularly put in front of her, while my eyes envied and my mouth watered. She put a strong guard on me, and took no notice at all of appeals in my lord's name. So my fears have been fulfilled here . . . May my lord send someone to fetch me back to my lord, that I may look upon my lord's face.

*   *   *

REVIEW QUESTIONS

1. What kinds of roles and responsibilities did these women have? What needs and concerns do they seem most eager to communicate?
2. What were their relationships with the other members of their families and households?
3. What do these sources reveal about daily life in ancient Mesopotamia?

FROM The Instruction of Ptah-Hotep

In contrast to ancient Mesopotamian laws, no ancient Egyptian law code has survived, although various texts suggest that laws did indeed exist. This document, however, provides an excellent description of proper behavior in personal relations and, implicitly, a sense of Egyptian social values, at least among the elite. Dating perhaps as early as the late Old Kingdom, this text is presented as the instructions of the vizier (the most important royal official under the king himself), Ptah-hotep, to his son.

From *Ancient Egyptian Literature,* vol. 1, *The Old and Middle Kingdoms,* by Miriam Lichtheim (Berkeley: University of California Press, 1973), pp. 205–9.

Instruction of the Mayor of the city, the Vizier Ptahhotep, under the Majesty of King Isesi, who lives for all eternity. The mayor of the city, the vizier Ptahhotep, said:

O king, my lord!
Age is here, old age arrived,
Feebleness came, weakness grows,
Childlike one sleeps all day.
Eyes are dim, ears deaf,
Strength is waning through weariness,
The mouth, silenced, speaks not,
The heart, void, recalls not the past,
The bones ache throughout.
Good has become evil, all taste is gone,
What age does to people is evil in everything.
The nose, clogged, breathes not,
Painful are standing and sitting.

May this servant be ordered to make a staff of old
    age,
So as to tell him the words of those who heard,
The ways of the ancestors,
Who have listened to the gods.
May such be done for you,
So that strife may be banned from the people,
And the Two Shores may serve you!
Said the majesty of this god:
Instruct him then in the sayings of the past,
May he become a model for the children of the
    great,

May obedience enter him,
And the devotion of him who speaks to him,
No one is born wise.

Beginning of the formulations of excellent discourse spoken by the Prince, Count, God's Father, God's beloved, Eldest Son of the King, of his body, Mayor of the city and Vizier, Ptahhotep, in instructing the ignorant in knowledge and in the standard of excellent discourse, as profit for him who will hear, as woe to him who would neglect them. He spoke to his son:

1. Don't be proud of your knowledge,
   Consult the ignorant and the wise;
   The limits of art are not reached,
   No artist's skills are perfect;
   Good speech is more hidden than greenstone,
   Yet may be found among maids at the
       grindstones.

2. If you meet a disputant in action,
   A powerful man, superior to you,
   Fold your arms, bend your back,
   To flout him will not make him agree with
       you.
   Make little of the evil speech
   By not opposing him while he's in action;
   He will be called an ignoramus,
   Your self-control will match his pile of
       words.

3. If you meet a disputant in action
    Who is your equal, on your level,
    You will make your worth exceed his by
        silence,
    While he is speaking evilly,
    There will be much talk by the hearers,
    Your name will be good in the mind of the
        magistrates.

4. If you meet a disputant in action,
    A poor man, not your equal,
    Do not attack him because he is weak,
    Let him alone, he will confute himself.
    Do not answer him to relieve your heart,
    Do not vent yourself against your opponent,
    Wretched is he who injures a poor man,
    One will wish to do what you desire,
    You will beat him through the magistrates'
        reproof.

5. If you are a man who leads,
    Who controls the affairs of the many,
    Seek out every beneficent deed,
    That your conduct may be blameless.
    Great is justice, lasting in effect,
    Unchallenged since the time of Osiris.
    One punishes the transgressor of laws,
    Though the greedy overlooks this;
    Baseness may seize riches,
    Yet crime never lands its wares;
    In the end it is justice that lasts,
    Man says: "It is my father's ground."

6. Do not scheme against people,
    God punishes accordingly:
    If a man says: "I shall live by it,"
    He will lack bread for his mouth.
    If a man says: "I shall be rich,"
    He will have to say: "My cleverness has
        snared me."
    If he says: "I will snare for myself,"
    He will be unable to say: "I snared for my
        profit."
    If a man says: "I will rob someone,"
    He will end being given to a stranger.
    People's schemes do not prevail,

God's command is what prevails;
Live then in the midst of peace,
What they give comes by itself.

7. If you are one among guests
    At the table of one greater than you,
    Take what he gives as it is set before you;
    Look at what is before you,
    Don't shoot many glances at him,
    Molesting him offends the *ka*.[1]
    Don't speak to him until he summons,
    One does not know what may displease;
    Speak when he has addressed you,
    Then your words will please the heart.
    The nobleman, when he is behind food,
    Behaves as his *ka* commands him;
    He will give to him whom he favors,
    It is the custom when night has come.
    It is the *ka* that makes his hands reach out,
    The great man gives to the chosen man;
    Thus eating is under the counsel of god,
    A fool is who complains of it.

8. If you are a man of trust,
    Sent by one great man to another,
    Adhere to the nature of him who sent you,
    Give his message as he said it.
    Guard against reviling speech,
    Which embroils one great with another;
    Keep to the truth, don't exceed it,
    But an outburst should not be repeated.
    Do not malign anyone,
    Great or small, the *ka* abhors it.

9. If you plow and there's growth in the field,
    And god lets it prosper in your hand,
    Do not boast at your neighbors' side,
    One has great respect for the silent man:
    Man of character is man of wealth.
    If he robs he is like a crocodile in court.
    Don't impose on one who is childless,
    Neither decry nor boast of it;
    There is many a father who has grief,

---

[1] The term *ka* represents a complex concept linked to an individual's life force.

And a mother of children less content than
  another;
It is the lonely whom god fosters,
While the family man prays for a follower.

10.   If you are poor, serve a man of worth,
  That all your conduct may be well with the
    god.
  Do not recall if he once was poor,
  Don't be arrogant toward him
  For knowing his former state;
  Respect him for what has accrued to him,
  For wealth does not come by itself.
  It is their law for him whom they love,
  His gain, he gathered it himself;
  It is the god who makes him worthy
  And protects him while he sleeps.

11.   Follow your heart as long as you live,
  Do no more than is required,
  Do not shorten the time of "follow-the-heart,"
  Trimming its moment offends the *ka*.
  Don't waste time on daily cares
  Beyond providing for your household;
  When wealth has come, follow your heart,
  Wealth does no good if one is glum!

12.   If you are a man of worth
  And produce a son by the grace of god,
  If he is straight, takes after you,
  Takes good care of your possessions,
  Do for him all that is good,
  He is your son, your *ka* begot him,
  Don't withdraw your heart from him.
  But an offspring can make trouble:
  If he strays, neglects your counsel,
  Disobeys all that is said,
  His mouth spouting evil speech,
  Punish him for all his talk!
  They hate him who crosses you,
  His guilt was fated in the womb;
  He whom they guide can not go wrong,
  Whom they make boatless can not cross.

13.   If you are in the antechamber,
  Stand and sit as fits your rank,

Which was assigned you the first day.
Do not trespass—you will be turned back,
Keen is the face to him who enters announced,
Spacious the seat of him who has been called.
The antechamber has a rule,
All behavior is by measure;
It is the god who gives advancement,
He who uses elbows is not helped.

14.   If you are among the people,
  Gain supporters through being trusted;
  The trusted man who does not vent his
    belly's speech,
  He will himself become a leader.
  A man of means—what is he like?
  Your name is good, you are not maligned,
  Your body is sleek, your face benign,
  One praises you without your knowing.
  He whose heart obeys his belly
  Puts contempt of himself in place of love,
  His heart is bald, his body unanointed;
  The great-hearted is god-given,
  He who obeys his belly belongs to the enemy.

15.   Report your commission without faltering,
  Give your advice in your master's council.
  If he is fluent in his speech,
  It will not be hard for the envoy to report,
  Nor will he be answered, "Who is he to
    know it?"
  As to the master, his affairs will fail
  If he plans to punish him for it,
  He should be silent upon hearing: "I have
    told."

16.   If you are a man who leads,
  Whose authority reaches wide,
  You should do outstanding things,
  Remember the day that comes after.
  No strife will occur in the midst of honors,
  But where the crocodile enters hatred arises.

17.   If you are a man who leads,
  Listen calmly to the speech of one who
    pleads;
  Don't stop him from purging his body
  Of that which he planned to tell.

A man in distress wants to pour out his heart
More than that his case be won.
About him who stops a plea
One says: "Why does he reject it?"
Not all one pleads for can be granted,
But a good hearing soothes the heart.

18. If you want friendship to endure
In the house you enter
As master, brother, or friend,
In whatever place you enter,
Beware of approaching the women!
Unhappy is the place where it is done,
Unwelcome is he who intrudes on them.
A thousand men are turned away from their
    good:
A short moment like a dream,
Then death comes for having known them.
Poor advice is "shoot the opponent,"
When one goes to do it the heart rejects it.
He who fails through lust of them,
No affair of his can prosper.

19. If you want a perfect conduct,
To be free from every evil,
Guard against the vice of greed:
A grievous sickness without cure,
There is no treatment for it.
It embroils fathers, mothers,
And the brothers of the mother,
It parts wife from husband;
It is a compound of all evils,
A bundle of all hateful things.
That man endures whose rule is rightness,
Who walks a straight line;
He will make a will by it,
The greedy has no tomb.

20. Do not be greedy in the division,
Do not covet more than your share;
Do not be greedy toward your kin,
The mild has a greater claim than the harsh.
Poor is he who shuns his kin,
He is deprived of interchange.
Even a little of what is craved
Turns a quarreler into an amiable man.

21. When you prosper and found your house,
And love your wife with ardor,
Fill her belly, clothe her back,
Ointment soothes her body.
Gladden her heart as long as you live,
She is a fertile field for her lord.
Do not contend with her in court,
Keep her from power, restrain her—
Her eye is her storm when she gazes—
Thus will you make her stay in your
    house.

22. Sustain your friends with what you have,
You have it by the grace of god;
Of him who fails to sustain his friends
One says, "a selfish *ka*."
One plans the morrow but knows not what
    will be,
The right *ka* is the *ka* by which one is
    sustained.
If praiseworthy deeds are done,
Friends will say, "welcome!"
One does not bring supplies to town,
One brings friends when there is need.

23. Do not repeat calumny,
Nor should you listen to it,
It is the spouting of the hot-bellied.
Report a thing observed, not heard,
If it is negligible, don't say anything,
He who is before you recognizes worth.
If a seizure is ordered and carried out,
Hatred will arise against him who seizes;
Calumny is like a dream against which one
    covers the face.

24. If you are a man of worth
Who sits in his master's council,
Concentrate on excellence,
Your silence is better than chatter.
Speak when you know you have a
    solution,
It is the skilled who should speak in
    council;
Speaking is harder than all other work,
He who understands it makes it serve.

25. If you are mighty, gain respect through
        knowledge
     And through gentleness of speech.
     Don't command except as is fitting,
     He who provokes gets into trouble.
     Don't be haughty, lest you be humbled,
     Don't be mute, lest you be chided.
     When you answer one who is fuming,
     Avert your face, control yourself.
     The flame of the hot-heart sweeps across,
     He who steps gently, his path is paved.
     He who frets all day has no happy moment,
     He who's gay all day can't keep house.

26. Don't oppose a great man's action,
     Don't vex the heart of one who is burdened;
     If he gets angry at him who foils him,
     The *ka* will part from him who loves him.
     Yet he is the provider along with the god,
     What he wishes should be done for him.
     When he turns his face back to you after
        raging,
     There will be peace from his *ka;*
     As ill will comes from opposition,
     So goodwill increases love.

27. Teach the great what is useful to him,
     Be his aid before the people;
     If you let his knowledge impress his lord,
     Your sustenance will come from his *ka.*
     As the favorite's belly is filled,
     So your back will be clothed by it,
     And his help will be there to sustain you.
     For your superior whom you love
     And who lives by it,
     He in turn will give you good support.
     Thus will love of you endure
     In the belly of those who love you,
     He is a *ka* who loves to listen.

28. If you are a magistrate of standing,
     Commissioned to satisfy the many,
     Hew a straight line.
     When you speak don't lean to one side,
     Beware lest one complain:
     "Judges, he distorts the matter!"
     And your deed turns into a judgment of you.

29. If you are angered by a misdeed,
     Lean toward a man on account of his
        rightness;
     Pass it over, don't recall it,
     Since he was silent to you the first day.

30. If you are great after having been humble,
     Have gained wealth after having been poor
     In the past, in a town which you know,
     Knowing your former condition,
     Do not put trust in your wealth,
     Which came to you as gift of god;
     So that you will not fall behind one like
        you,
     To whom the same has happened.

31. Bend your back to your superior,
     Your overseer from the palace;
     Then your house will endure in its
        wealth,
     Your rewards in their right place.
     Wretched is he who opposes a superior,
     One lives as long as he is mild,
     Baring the arm does not hurt it.
     Do not plunder a neighbor's house,
     Do not steal the goods of one near you,
     Lest he denounce you before you are heard.
     A quarreler is a mindless person,
     If he is known as an aggressor
     The hostile man will have trouble in the
        neighborhood.

                    *   *   *

33. If you probe the character of a friend,
     Don't inquire, but approach him,
     Deal with him alone,
     So as not to suffer from his manner.
     Dispute with him after a time,
     Test his heart in conversation;
     If what he has seen escapes him,
     If he does a thing that annoys you,
     Be yet friendly with him, don't attack,
     Be restrained, don't let fly,
     Don't answer with hostility,
     Neither part from him nor attack him;
     His time does not fail to come,
     One does not escape what is fated.

34. Be generous as long as you live,
     What leaves the storehouse does not return;
     It is the food to be shared which is coveted,
     One whose belly is empty is an accuser;
     One deprived becomes an opponent,
     Don't have him for a neighbor.
     Kindness is a man's memorial
     For the years after the function.

35. Know your helpers, then you prosper,
     Don't be mean toward your friends,
     They are one's watered field,
     And greater then one's riches,
     For what belongs to one belongs to another.
     The character of a son-of-man is profit to
        him;
     Good nature is a memorial.

36. Punish firmly, chastise soundly,
     Then repression of crime becomes an
        example;
     Punishment except for crime
     Turns the complainer into an enemy.

37. If you take to wife a *špnt*[2]
     Who is joyful and known by her town,
     If she is fickle and likes the moment,
     Do not reject her, let her eat,
     The joyful brings happiness.

Epilogue

If you listen to my sayings,
All your affairs will go forward;
In their truth resides their value,
Their memory goes on in the speech of men,
Because of the worth of their precepts;
If every word is carried on,
They will not perish in this land.
If advice is given for the good,
The great will speak accordingly;
It is teaching a man to speak to posterity,
He who hears it becomes a master-hearer;
It is good to speak to posterity,
It will listen to it.

If a good example is set by him who leads,
He will be beneficent for ever,
His wisdom being for all time.
The wise feeds his *ba*[3] with what endures,
So that it is happy with him on earth.
The wise is known by his wisdom,
The great by his good actions;
His heart matches his tongue,
His lips are straight when he speaks;
He has eyes that see,
His ears are made to hear what will profit his son,
Acting with truth he is free of falsehood.
Useful is hearing to a son who hears;
If hearing enters the hearer,
The hearer becomes a listener,
Hearing well is speaking well.
Useful is hearing to one who hears,
Hearing is better than all else,
It creates good will.
How good for a son to grasp his father's words,
He will reach old age through them.

He who hears is beloved of god,
He whom god hates does not hear.
The heart makes of its owner a hearer or non-
    hearer,
Man's heart is his life-prosperity-health!
The hearer is one who hears what is said,
He who loves to hear is one who does what is said.
How good for a son to listen to his father,
How happy is he to whom it is said:
"The son, he pleases as a master of hearing."
The hearer of whom this is said,
He is well-endowed
And honored by his father;
His remembrance is in the mouth of the living,
Those on earth and those who will be.

If a man's son accepts his father's words,
No plan of his will go wrong.
Teach your son to be a hearer,
One who will be valued by the nobles;
One who guides his speech by what he was told,

---

[2] No single translation of *špnt* has been agreed upon.

[3] Like *ka*, the term *ba* is a complex concept intimately related to one's individuality. It is somewhat analogous to
our concept of "soul."

One regarded as a hearer.
This son excels, his deeds stand out,
While failure follows him who hears not.
The wise wakes early to his lasting gain,
While the fool is hard pressed.

The fool who does not hear,
He can do nothing at all;
He sees knowledge in ignorance,
Usefulness in harmfulness.
He does all that one detests
And is blamed for it each day;
He lives on that by which one dies,
His food is distortion of speech.
His sort is known to the officials,
Who say: "A living death each day."
One passes over his doings,
Because of his many daily troubles.

A son who hears is a follower of Horus,
It goes well with him when he has heard.
When he is old, has reached veneration,
He will speak likewise to his children,
Renewing the teaching of his father.
Every man teaches as he acts,
He will speak to the children,
So that they will speak to their children:
Set an example, don't give offense,
If justice stands firm your children will live.

*   *   *

Conceal your heart, control your mouth,
Then you will be known among the officials;
Be quite exact before your lord,
Act so that one will say to him: "He's the son of
    that one."

And those who hear it will say:
"Blessed is he to whom he was born!"
Be deliberate when you speak,
So as to say things that count;
Then the officials who listen will say:
"How good is what comes from his mouth!"
Act so that your lord will say of you:
"How good is he whom his father taught;
When he came forth from his body,
He told him all that was in his mind,
And he does even more than he was told."

Lo, the good son, the gift of god,
Exceeds what is told him by his lord,
He will do right when his heart is straight.
As you succeed me, sound in your body,
The king content with all that was done,
May you obtain many years of life!
Not small is what I did on earth,
I had one hundred and ten years of life
As gift of the king,
Honors exceeding those of the ancestors,
By doing justice for the king,
Until the state of veneration!

*   *   *

Review Questions

1. According to Ptah-hotep, what are the most
   important virtues in proper human relations?
2. Are those virtues to be applied differently to
   people of different rank and social class?
3. How much importance is ascribed to the ability to fight physically?

from The Book of the Dead

*Beginning in the late Old Kingdom, there were inscribed on the walls of the interior
chambers of pyramids magical texts that were intended to ensure that the deceased
king passed successfully into the next life. In the following centuries, these so-called
Pyramid Texts were developed further, and the possibility of proceeding into the*

next world became less exclusively focused on the king and his immediate family and more inclusive of Egyptians of lesser rank (what some scholars have referred to as the "democratization of death"). From this process emerged the collection of texts that has come to be known (erroneously) as The Book of the Dead. *The following selection has been referred to as the "Protestation of Guiltlessness" or the "Negative Confession." It was to be recited by the deceased as he or she appeared for judgment before the god Osiris and his entourage.*

From *Ancient Near Eastern Texts Relating to the Old Testament,* edited by James B. Pritchard, translated by H. L. Ginsberg (3d ed.; Princeton, N.J.: Princeton University Press, 1983).

*   *   *

What is said on reaching the Broad-Hall of the Two Justices, absolving X [the deceased] of every sin which he has committed, and seeing the faces of the gods:

Hail to thee, O great god, lord of the Two Justices! I have come to thee, my lord, I have been brought that I might see thy beauty. I know thee; I know thy name and the names of the forty-two gods who are with thee in the Broad-Hall of the Two Justices, who live on them who *preserve* evil and who drink their blood on that day of reckoning up character in the presence of Wennofer. Behold, "*Sati-mertifi,* Lord of Justice," is thy name. I have come to thee; I have brought thee justice; I have expelled deceit for thee.

I have not committed evil against men.

I have not mistreated cattle.

I have not committed sin in the place of truth.

I have not known that which is not.

I have not seen evil. . . .

My name has not reached the Master of the Barque.

I have not blasphemed a god.

I have not *done violence to* a poor man.

I have not done that which the gods abominate.

I have not defamed a slave to his superior.

I have not made anyone sick.

I have not made anyone weep.

I have not killed.

I have given no order to a killer.

I have not caused anyone suffering.

I have not cut down on the food-income in the temples.

I have not damaged the bread of the gods.

I have not taken the loaves of the blessed dead.

I have not had sexual relations with a boy.

I have not defiled myself.

I have neither increased or diminished the grain-measure.

I have not diminished the *aroura.*

I have not falsified a half-*aroura* of land.

I have not added to the weight of the balance.

I have not *weakened* the plummet of the scales.

I have not taken milk from the mouths of children.

I have not driven cattle away from their pasturage.

I have not snared the birds *of* the gods.

I have not caught fish in their marshes.

I have not held up the water in its season.

I have not built a dam against running water.

I have not quenched a fire at its proper time.

I have not neglected the appointed times and their meat-offerings.

I have not driven away the cattle of the god's property.

I have not stopped a god on his procession.

I am pure!—four times. My purity is the purity of that great *benu*-bird which is in Herakleopolis, because I am really that nose of the Lord of Breath, who makes all men to live, on that day of filling out the Eye of Horus in Heliopolis, in the second month of the second season, the last day, in the presence of the lord

of this land. I am the one who has seen the filling out of the Eye in Heliopolis. Evil will never happen to me in this land or in this Broad-Hall of the Two Justices, because I know the names of these gods who are in it, the followers of the great god.

O Wide-of-Stride, who comes forth from Heliopolis, I have not committed evil.

O Embracer-of-Fire, who comes forth from Babylon, I have not stolen.

O Nosey, who comes forth from Hermopolis, I have not been covetous.

O Swallower-of-Shadows, who comes forth from the pit, I have not robbed.

O Dangerous-of-Face, who came forth from *Rostau*, I have not killed men.

O *Ruti*, who comes forth from heaven, I have not damaged the grain-measure.

O His-Eyes-are-of-Flint, who comes forth from the shrine, I have not caused *crookedness*.

O Flamer, who comes forth *backward*, I have not stolen the property of a god.

O Breaker-of-Bones, who comes forth from Herakleopolis, I have not told lies.

O *Commander-of-Fire,* who comes forth from Memphis, I have not taken away food.

O Dweller-in-the-Pit, who comes forth from the west, I have not been contentious.

O White-of-Teeth, who comes forth from the Faiyum, I have not trespassed.

O Eater-of-Blood, who comes forth from the execution-block, I have not slain the cattle of the god.

O Eater-of-Entrails, who comes forth from the Thirty, I have not *practised usury*.

O Lord-of-Justice, who comes forth from *Ma'ati*, I have not stolen the *bread-ration*.

O Wanderer, who comes forth from Bubastis, I have not *gossiped*.

O *Aadi*, who comes forth from Heliopolis, my mouth has not gone on unchecked.

O *Djudju*-serpent, who comes forth from Busiris, I have not argued with *some one summoned because of* his property.

O *Wamemti*-serpent, who comes forth from the place of judgment, I have not committed adultery.

O *Maa-Intef,* who comes forth from the Temple of Min, I have not defiled myself.

O Superior-of-the-Nobles, who comes forth from *Imau*, I have not caused terror.

O Wrecker, who comes forth from *the Saite Nome*, I have not trespassed.

O Mischief-Maker, who comes forth from the sanctuary, I have not been overheated.

O Child, who comes forth from the Heliopolitan Nome, I have not been unresponsive to a matter of justice.

O *Ser-kheru*, who comes forth from *Wensi*, I have not been quarrelsome.

O Bastet, who comes forth from the sanctum, I have not winked.

O His-Face-Behind-Him, who comes forth from *Tep-het-djat*, I have not *been perverted*; I have not had sexual relations with a boy.

O Hot-of-Leg, who comes forth from the twilight, I have not swallowed my heart.

O Dark-One, who comes forth from the darkness, I have not been abusive.

O Bringer-of-His-Peace, who comes forth from Sais, I have not been overenergetic.

O Lord-of-Faces, who comes forth from the Heroonpolite Nome, my heart has not been hasty.

O Plan-Maker, who comes forth from *Utenet*, I have not transgressed my color; I have not washed the god.

O Lord-of-Horns, who comes forth from Siut, my voice is not too much about matters.

O *Nefer-tem*, who comes forth from Memphis, I have not committed sins; I have not done evil.

O *Tem-sep*, who comes forth from Busiris, I have not been abusive against a king.

O Acting-with-His-Heart, who comes forth from *Tjebu*, I have not waded in water.

O Flowing-One, who comes forth from Nun, my voice has not been loud.

O Commander-of-the-People, who comes forth from *his shrine*, I have not been abusive against a god.

O *Neheb-nefert*, who comes forth from *the Saite Nome*, I have never made puffings-up.

O *Neheb-kau*, who comes forth from the town, I have not made *discriminations for* myself.

O High-of-Head serpent, who comes forth from the cavern, my portion has not been too large, *not even* in my own property.

O *In-af* serpent, who comes forth from the cemetery, I have not blasphemed against my local god.

Words to be spoken by X [the deceased]:

Hail to you, ye gods who are in this Broad-Hall of the Two Justices! I know you; I know your names. I shall not fall for dread of you. Ye have not reported guilt of mine up to this god in whose retinue ye are; no deed of mine has come *from* you. Ye have spoken truth about me in the presence of the All-Lord, because I acted justly in Egypt. I have not been abusive to a god. No deed of mine has come *from* a king who is in his day.

Hail to you who are in the Broad-Hall of the Two Justices, who have no deceit in your bodies, who live on truth and who eat of truth in the presence of Horus, who is in his sun disc. May ye rescue me from Babi, who lives on the entrails *of elders* on that day of the great reckoning. Behold me—I have come to you without sin, without guilt, without evil, without a witness against me, without one against whom I have taken action. I live on truth, and I eat of truth. I have done that which men said and that with which gods are content. I have satisfied a god with that which he desires. I have given bread to the hungry, water to the thirsty, clothing to the naked, and a ferry-boat to him who was marooned. I have provided divine offerings for the gods and mortuary offerings for the dead. So rescue me, you; protect me, you. Ye will not make report against me in the presence of the great god. I am one pure of mouth and pure of hands, one to whom "Welcome, welcome, in peace!" is said by those who see him, because I have heard those great words which the ass discussed with the cat in the house of *the hippopotamus,* when the witness was His-Face-Behind-Him and he gave out a cry. I have seen the splitting of the *ished*-tree in *Rostau.* I am one who has a concern for the gods, who knows the *nature* of their bodies. I have come here to testify to justice and to bring the scales to their proper position in the cemetery.

O thou who art high upon his standard, Lord of the *Atef*-Crown, whose name has been made "Lord of Breath," mayest thou rescue me from thy messengers who give forth uncleanliness and create *destruction,* who have no covering up of their faces, because I have effected justice for the Lord of Justice, being pure—my front is pure, my rear is clean, my middle is in the flowing water of justice; there is no part of me free of justice. . . .

. . . "I will not announce thee," says the doorkeeper of the Broad-Hall of the Two Justices, "unless thou tellest my name." "Understander of Hearts, Searcher of Bodies is thy name." "Then to whom should I announce thee?" "To the god who is in his hour of service." "Thou shouldst tell it to the interpreter of the Two Lands." "Well, who is the interpreter of the Two Lands?" "It is Thoth."

"Come," says Thoth, "why hast thou come?" "I have come here to be announced." "What is thy condition?" "I am pure of sin. I have protected myself from the strife of those who are in their days. I am not among them." "Then to whom shall I announce thee? I shall announce thee to him whose ceiling is of fire, whose walls are living serpents, and whose pavement is water. Who is he?" "He is Osiris." "Then go thou. Behold, thou art announced. Thy bread is the Restored Eye; thy beer is the Restored Eye. Thou hast invocation-offerings upon earth in the Restored Eye." So spoke Osiris to X, the deceased.

Instructions for the Use of the Spell

To be done in conformance with what takes place in this Broad-Hall of the Two Justices. This spell is to be recited when one is clean and pure, clothed in fresh garments, shod with white sandals, painted with stibium, and anointed with myrrh, to whom cattle, fowl, incense, bread, beer, and vegetables have been offered. Then make thou this text in writing on a clean pavement with ochre smeared with earth upon which pigs and other small cattle have not trodden. As for him on whose behalf this book

IS MADE, HE SHALL BE PROSPEROUS AND HIS CHILDREN SHALL BE PROSPEROUS, WITHOUT *GREED*, BECAUSE HE SHALL BE A TRUSTED MAN OF the king AND HIS COURTIERS. LOAVES, JARS, BREAD, AND JOINTS OF MEAT SHALL BE GIVEN TO HIM FROM THE ALTAR OF the great god. HE CANNOT BE HELD BACK AT ANY DOOR OF THE WEST, BUT HE SHALL BE USHERED IN WITH the Kings of Upper and Lower Egypt, and he shall be in the retinue of Osiris.

Right and true a million times.

REVIEW QUESTIONS

1. What does this text reveal about the Egyptians' concept of the next life and in particular, about the individual's eligibility for it? Can you detect any parallels in the beliefs of later religious systems?
2. How, ideally, was one to conduct oneself in order to appear blameless before the gods?
3. What does this text have to say about Egyptian social values?

2 ✦ PEOPLES, GODS, AND EMPIRES, 1700–500 B.C.E.

Under the firm hand of the rulers of the Twelfth Dynasty, Egypt had reemerged as a unified, highly centralized monarchy served by an efficient corps of royal bureaucrats. By the seventeenth century B.C.E., however, that stability was shaken as "vile Asiatics" migrated from Palestine into the Nile Delta and asserted their own political authority as the Hyksos dynasties of Lower Egypt. With the onset of its Second Intermediate Period, then, Egypt was once again divided, but for the first time under the abominable yoke of "barbarian" conquerors. Once again, the unity of the "Two Lands" of Upper and Lower Egypt would be restored by the prowess of the rulers of Amun's city of Thebes, who expelled the foreigners, chased them back into Palestine, and subsequently, perhaps as insurance against a repetition of such an abomination, conquered and ruled most of the eastern Mediterranean seaboard from the Sinai to Syria as well as the region of Nubia, ranging into the interior of Africa.

The zenith of Egypt's New Kingdom Empire coincides with the era of the Late Bronze Age, a cosmopolitan age of unprecedented internationalism. As reflected vividly in the diplomatic correspondence found at the short-lived capital at Amarna as well as in the preserved cargo of a shipwreck discovered off the coast of Turkey at Ulu Burun, kings from Babylonia to Cyprus negotiated favors and offered their daughters in marriage. Maritime traders plied the sea routes of the Aegean and the eastern Mediterranean, carrying ingots of bronze, tusks of ivory, disks of blue glass, and pottery containers filled with valuable oils and resins. Envoys and ambassadors trudged well-worn caravan tracks, bearing messages from kings offering alliances to other kings or from local princes supplicating the pharaoh or informing him of depredations by outlaws. At the top of royal wish lists was the gold of Nubia, which the pharaoh had the power to dispense to royal "brothers" in Babylonia, Assyria, Hatti, Mittani, Alashiya (Cyprus), or Ahhiyawa (perhaps Mycenaean Greece). Many pounds of that same gold were expended on the burial of a short-lived pharaoh named Tutankhamun, whose abandoned birth name of Tutankhaten testifies to the genius (or psychosis) of his predecessor,

regarded by some experts as the first ruler to espouse monotheism, a religious system based on a single god (in this instance, the sun as personified in its disk, or aten). Later Egyptians would condemn Akhenaten's "revolution" as heresy and attempt to eradicate his memory. Only well after the internationalism of the Late Bronze Age had been disrupted and Egypt itself had become a "broken reed" would the Hebrews (perhaps not totally unrelated to those outlaws mentioned above) develop the concept of monotheism, a concept that eventually was to become one of the most central and enduring structures of civilization throughout the West, and the world.

The period 1200–1100 B.C.E. is a watershed in the history of the ancient Near East. Before 1200, the region enjoyed a vibrant internationalism set against the backdrop of competing great kingdoms, some of them with substantial empires. By 1100, most of those great kingdoms had disappeared—in some instances suddenly, perhaps even catastrophically; among them were the Hittite kingdom of Anatolia, the Kassite kingdom of Babylonia, the kingdom of Alashiya on Cyprus, and Mycenaean Greece. Others were in decline—most notably New Kingdom Egypt, whose empire in Syria and Palestine had waned and whose dynastic unity was dissolving. Scholars today still debate the impact of the invasion of the "Sea Peoples" on these events. In one prominent view, their invasions were the most catastrophic event to befall the ancient Near East prior to the arrival of Alexander's armies. Others see their arrival, though certainly shattering, as but one event in a concatenation of causes, both external and internal, that brought down the great Late Bronze Age kingdoms, ushered in a new configuration of states and peoples, and contributed to the ascendancy of iron over bronze as the preferred metal of technology.

Within the new configuration emerged peoples whose contributions to later Western and world civilizations were both profound and enduring. Among the Sea Peoples, memory of the Philistines has endured the longest, perhaps because the region in which they settled took on their name as Palestine. The Hebrew Bible depicts them as a potent and incorrigible threat to the early Israelites, and the ensuing animosity undoubtedly contributed to the modern (and surely unjustified) connotation of "philistine" as crude and unsophisticated. To their north, the long-established Canaanite craftsmen and traders of Tyre, Sidon, and Beirut whom the Greeks came to identify as Phoenicians established far-flung colonies and commercial routes along which their goods and reputation were carried to the Straits of Gibraltar and beyond. As part of their enterprise, they refined and disseminated a new technology (likely inspired by Egyptian hieroglyphs) that eventually would revolutionize both literacy and society—alphabetic writing. Meanwhile, emerging to the west of the Phoenicians were several tribal kingdoms of the Aramaeans, perhaps the most powerful of which was centered on the ancient city of Damascus. In time, Aramaean peoples spread across the Middle Eastern landscape as far away as Babylonia, bringing with them their language, Aramaic, and an alphabetic writing system that would eventually supplant the ancient cuneiform system. Aramaic became the official language of the Persian

Empire; it was the language spoken by Jesus Christ, and it remained the dominant spoken language throughout the Middle East until supplanted by Arabic in the wake of the Arab/Islamic conquests many centuries later.

The ancient Hebrews, or Israelites, had an impact on the shaping of Western civilization that dwarfs their impact on the history and culture of their own time. They emerged from almost total obscurity late during the second millennium B.C.E., in circumstances about which historians and archaeologists have yet to reach consensus and continually struggle to understand. According to the (hardly objective or verifiable) accounts in the Hebrew Bible, they came to dominate the area of modern Israel/Palestine under two kings, David and Solomon, whose reigns together encompassed less than a century (approximately 1000–920 B.C.E.). The civil war that erupted on Solomon's death left the previously united Hebrew monarchy irreparably divided into its two constituent parts: Israel in the north and Judah in the south.

Within a few centuries, however, both of these kingdoms, and most of the rest of the Middle East as well, were overcome by the reasserted might of Mesopotamian and then Persian Empires. The Assyrians destroyed Israel in 722 B.C.E. and by 650 had conquered virtually all of the Middle East, their kings celebrating their brutal conquests in vivid accounts that can shock even twenty-first-century sensibilities. One of their successors to imperial dominion, the Chaldaean king Nebuchadnezzar of Babylonia, captured Judah's capital, Jerusalem, in 587 and deported much of its population to Babylon—an event that began the Diaspora, the "dispersion" that has so dominated the experience of the Jewish people since that time. With Cyrus and his successors came the greatest of all ancient Near Eastern empires, that of the Achaemenid Persians, who developed a system and mentality of universal dominion that later empires emulated for centuries to come.

It was probably during the Captivity in Babylon that the displaced people of Judah (in Hebrew, yehudim—the word came to be "Jews") undertook in earnest the process of compiling and editing their ancient laws and traditions. The body of writings that was developed over the next several centuries—the Hebrew Bible, known in Christian tradition as the Old Testament—is, along with the New Testament, arguably the most influential corpus of literature in human history. Without a doubt, it is the ancient Near East's most significant contribution to the shaping of Western civilization. Its impact on the formation of later Islamic civilization worldwide, through its contribution to the teachings of the prophet Muhammad as reflected in the Qu'ran, is likewise beyond measuring. Furthermore, for the nearly two millennia before the archaeological rediscovery of ancient Mesopotamian civilization in the mid-nineteenth century and the decipherment of the cuneiform and hieroglyphic scripts, the Bible was the chief fount of knowledge of human history from the creation of the world (which some scholars, using Biblical evidence, dated to exactly 4004 B.C.E.) to the rise of the Greeks.

The theory of evolution and the modern discoveries of historians and archaeologists have undermined the historical value of much of the Bible's narrative.

*Obviously, then, it is not in the accuracy of their historical accounts that the He-
brews have had their greatest influence on later civilization. Rather, their singular
contribution lies in the unique perspective that dominated their sense of their
own history: their special relationship with a divine being who chose them as his
own people and established with them a covenant that promised them his support and protection. In return, they pledged to accept only him as their exclusive
deity and to govern their behavior, both cultic and social, in accordance with a
body of explicitly defined regulations handed down by him and him alone. The
working out of this covenant in the historical experience of the Hebrew people
provided the developmental context for concepts that became central to the tradition of Western civilization: divinely revealed law as the basis of the relationship
between God and humankind; and a monotheism founded on humankind's exclusive acceptance of a single, universal Supreme Being and Creator who demands justice and righteousness but is also capable of mercy and compassion.
These concepts today remain at the heart of the faiths of the "children of Abraham," the shared monotheistic tradition of Judaism, Christianity, and Islam.*

Akhenaton's *Hymn to the Aton*

*The nature of the relationship between the king and the gods and the religious focus
of the Egyptian royal court took on a significant (though short-lived) new direction
during the reign of the New Kingdom pharaoh Amunhotep IV, better known to history by the name he assumed, Akhenaton ("Beloved of the Aton"). Referred to by
some today as the heretic pharaoh, Akhenaton tried to redirect worship in the Egyptian royal court to an almost exclusive focus on the Aton, the personification of the
sun's power as manifested in the sun disk. Many scholars have seen in this an important precursor of the Hebrews' monotheism centered on their god, Yahweh; some, in
fact, have claimed that the Hebrews derived their monotheism from learning of
Akhenaton's reform during their captivity in Egypt (as described in the Hebrew
Bible's book of Exodus). The following hymn is generally ascribed to Akhenaton himself and shows some interesting parallels to Psalm 104 in the Hebrew Bible.*

From *Hymns, Prayers, and Songs: An Anthology of Ancient Egyptian Lyric Poetry,* translated by
John L. Foster, SBL Writings from the Ancient World Series, vol. 8 (Atlanta, Ga.: Scholars
Press, 1995), pp. 154–58.

In Praise of the living Horakhty who rejoices in
the Horizon in his Name of the divine Light
which is in the Sundisk, living eternally and forever, the living Aton, Great One who is in the
Festival, Lord of all the sundisk circles, Lord of
Heaven, Lord of Earth, Living on Maat, Lord of
the Two Lands, Nefer-kheper-rê Wa-en-rê, Son
of the Sun, Who lives on Maat, Lord of Appear-

ances, Akhenaton, One Great in his Time; and
the Great Royal Wife, whom he loves, Mistress of
the Two Lands, Nefer-neferu-aten Nefertiti, living,
healthy, flourishing forever and eternity. He says:

i

May you always appear thus gloriously in the
      horizon of the sky,
   O living Aton, origin of life!
Arisen from the eastern horizon,
   you have filled all earth with your splendor;
You are beautiful, great, dazzling, exalted above
      each land,
      yet your rays encompass the lands
      to the limits of all which you have created;
There in the Sun, you reach to their boundaries,
   making them bow to your Son, whom you
      love;
And though you are far, your rays are over the
      earth,
   and you are in the faces of those who watch
   your journeying.

ii

You go to rest in the western horizon,
   and earth is in a darkness like death,
With the sleepers in bedchambers, heads
      covered—
   the eye cannot discern its companion;
All their goods might be carried off—
   though they are near—without their knowing.
Every lion comes forth from his doorway,
   insects and snakes bite and sting;
Darkness shrouds, earth is silent—
   he who created them is at rest in his tomb.

iii

Dawn rises shining on the horizon,
   gleams from the sundisk as day.
You scatter the darkness, bestow your sunbeams,
   and the Two Lands offer thanksgiving.
The Sunfolk awaken and stand on their feet,
   for you have raised them up;

Their bodies are bathed, they put on their
      clothing,
   their arms raised in praise at your appearing.
Throughout the land
   they take up their work.

iv

The herds are at peace in their meadows,
   trees and the vegetation grow green,
Birds fly from their nests,
   their wings spread wide in praise of your
      Person;
All the small beasts leap about on their feet,
   and all who fly up or settle to rest
      live because you have shone upon them.
Ships go downstream or upstream as well,
   each path lies open because of your
      presence;
The fish in the River dart about in your sight,
   and your beams are deep in the Great Green
      Sea.

v

It is you who create the seed in women,
   shape the fluids into human beings,
Make the son alive in the womb of his mother,
   soothe him, ending his tears,
Nurturer from the womb to those given breath
   to bring into life all that he has created.
He descends from the womb to breathe
   on the day of his birth,
And you open his mouth, determine his nature,
   and minister to his needs.

vi

The fledgling in the egg speaks in the shell,
   so you give him breath within it to succor
      him;
And you have given to him his allotted time
   so that he might break out from the egg
To come forth peeping at that time
   and move about upon his own two feet
      when he emerges from it.

vii

How various are the things you have created,
    and they are all mysterious to the sight!
O sole God, without another of your kind,
    you created the world according to your desire,
        while you were alone,
With mankind and cattle and every sort of small
    beast,
    all those upon land, those who go upon feet,
Those who are on high soaring upon their wings,
    the foreign lands of Khor and Kush,
        and all that belongs to Egypt.

viii

You give each person his place in life,
    and you provide for his needs;
Each one has his sustenance,
    and his lifetime is reckoned for him.
Tongues are separated by words,
    the natures of persons as well;
And their skins are made different
    so you can distinguish the peoples.

ix

You create Hapy, the Nile, in the Underworld
    to bring him, at your desire, to nourish the
        people,
Just as you create them for yourself,
    Lord of them all, who is weary for them,
O Lord of all earth, who shines for them,
    O Aton of day, awesome in majesty.
All the foreign lands are far away,
    yet you make their lives possible,
For you have placed a Hapy in the sky
    that he might come down upon them—
Making waves upon the mountains like those of
    the Great Green Sea
    to water the fields in their villages.

x

How well ordered it is, your governing,
    O Lord of Eternity, Hapy in heaven!

You belong to the foreign peoples,
    to the small beasts of each land who go upon
        feet.
And Hapy comes from Below to beloved Egypt as
    well,
    while your rays are nursing each meadow.
You shine, and they live,
    they grow strong for you;
You fashion the seasons to make all your creation
    flourish—
    the winter for cooling
    and the heat which ripens;
And you have made the sky far off
    in order to shine down from it,
        to watch over all you have created.

xi

You are one alone,
    shining forth in your visible Form as the living
        Aton,
Glorious, giving light,
    far-off yet approaching nearby.
You create the numberless visible forms from
        yourself—
    you who are one alone—
Cities, towns, fields, the road, the River;
    and each eye looks to you as its shining
        example:
You are in the sun-disk of day,
    overseer of wherever you go and whatever
        shall be;
For you fashion their sight so that you may be
    complete—
    as they celebrate with one voice your
        creation.

xii

And you are in my heart;
    there is no other who knows you
Except for your son, Akhenaton,
    Nefer-kheper-rê Wa-en-rê.
Let him be wise with your counsel, your strength,
    that the world may approach your condition
        just as when you created it.

You have risen, and they are alive;
  you go to rest, and they die.
For you are the measure of Time itself,
  one lives by means of you.
Eyes shall be filled with beauty until your
    setting;
  all labor is set aside when you go to rest in the
    West.
Then rise! Let the creatures of earth thrive for the
    king!
And let me hasten on with every footstep
  as I have since you founded the world.
And raise them up for your son
  who came forth from your very body.

The King of Upper and Lower Egypt, who lives on Truth, Lord of the Two Lands, Nefer-Kheper-Rê Wa-en-rê, son of the Sun, who lives on Truth, Lord of Appearances, Akhenaton, one exalted in his own lifetime; and the Great Royal Wife, whom he loves, Nefer-neferu-aton Nefertiti, who lives and flourishes for eternity and everlasting.

REVIEW QUESTIONS

1. What kinds of powers does this hymn ascribe to the Aton?
2. What is the king's relationship to his newly elevated god?

A Letter from the Hittite Queen to Ramesses II

Our sources for the transnationalism of the Late Bronze Age Near East include not only more than 380 cuneiform tablets of diplomatic correspondence from Akhenaten's new (and short-lived) capital at Akhetaten (modern el-Amarna), but also cuneiform letters from the royal archives of the Hittite kings, who ruled their kingdom of Hatti from their capital at Hattusha (in modern Turkey). When the celebrated (and long-lived) pharaoh Ramesses II ascended the throne, Hatti was one of the Near East's great imperial powers and Egypt's most formidable rival for control of Syria and its lucrative ports. But later in his reign, Ramesses developed a peaceful relationship with his Hittite counterpart, Hattusili III. The following selection is one of the most remarkable documents from the Hittite royal archives: a copy of a cuneiform letter (written in Hittite, but undoubtedly subsequently transcribed into Akkadian, the Late Bronze Age language of international diplomacy) to Ramesses from Puduhepa, Hattusili's queen.

From *Hittite Diplomatic Texts*, edited by Gary Beckman, SBL Writings from the Ancient World Series, vol. 7 (2nd ed.; Atlanta, Ga.: Scholars Press, 1999), pp. 132–35.

Concerning the fact that you, my brother, wrote to me as follows: "At the time when your messengers came to me, they brought me back gifts, and I rejoiced." When I heard that, I rejoiced likewise. The wife of your brother (Puduhepa) enjoys full life. May the person of my brother (Ramses) likewise enjoy full life! Send me . . . , and may they be set with lapis luzuli! Furthermore, my lands enjoy full life. May your lands likewise enjoy full life! I have sent my greetings and my ornaments to my brother. May my brother likewise enjoy full life!

Concerning the fact that you, my brother, wrote to me as follows: "My sister wrote to me: 'I will give a daughter to you.' But you have withheld her. And now you are angry with me. Why have you not now given her to me?" I have indeed withheld my daughter. You will not disapprove of it; you will approve of it. At the moment I am not able to give her to you. . . . With whom should I compare the daughter of heaven and earth whom I will give to my brother? Should I compare her with the daughter of Babylonia, of Zulabi, or of Assyria? . . .

Does my brother not possess anything at all? Only if the Son of the Sun-god, the Son of the Storm-god, and the Sea have nothing, do you have nothing! But, my brother, you would enrich yourself somewhat at my expense! That is worthy neither of renown nor of lordliness.

Concerning the fact that I wrote to my brother as follows: "What civilian captives, cattle, and sheep will I give (as a dowry) to my daughter? In my lands I do not even have barley. The moment that the messengers reach you, let my brother send a rider to me. Let documents be brought to the lords of my land so that the civilian captives, cattle, and sheep which are in their charge may be taken away and accommodated." I myself have sent messengers and tablets to them (my local subordinates). Later they arrived at the palace(?) of His Majesty(?), together with the messengers. But your rider did not come back promptly, and my messenger did not come either. Thereupon I sent Zuzu, charioteer and intimate of the king, but he was delayed. At the moment that Pihasdu did arrive, it was already winter, and I did not transfer the civilian captives again. My brother, ask your messengers if this is so, or not so. . . .

Concerning the fact that you, my brother, wrote to me as follows: "Do not withhold the daughter from me any longer!" [. . .] Was she not approved by me? Do I hold back the daughter for myself? Rather, I wish that she had already arrived. . . . If I had not at any time (sincerely) given my own daughter to you, I would not have promised you the civilian captives, cattle, and sheep(?). . . .

. . . Concerning the fact that you, my brother, wrote to me as follows: "I write to my sister that withholding the daughter [is not right . . .]" . . . . But my brother has not accepted in his own mind my status as a sister and my dignity. . . .

Concerning the fact that you, my brother, wrote to me as follows: "Your messengers shall speak freely to the daughter." I have thereupon written this word to my brother: "When in the future, conditions are favorable, they will come(?)." That is why I have written to my brother.

If I had sent(?) the daughter to my brother precipitously(?), or if I had not given you the gifts appropriate for my brother or for his sister, what would my brother even then have said? Perhaps: "May the woman whom they gave to me have some support, and may it be generous for her! That would be lordly behavior."

The daughter of Babylonia and the daughter of Amurru whom I, the Queen, took for myself—were they not indeed a source of praise for me before the people of Hatti? It was I who did it. I took each daughter of a Great King, though a foreigner, as daughter-in-law. And if at some time his (the royal father's) messengers come in splendor to the daughter-in-law, or one of her brothers or sisters comes to her, is this not also a source of praise for me? Was there no woman available to me in Hatti? Did I not do this out of consideration for renown?

Did my brother have no wife at all? Did not my brother make them (marriage arrangements) out of consideration for his(!) brotherhood, my sisterhood, and our dignity? And when he did make them, they were indeed settled in conformity with (the arrangements of) the King of Babylonia. Did he not also take the daughter of the Great King, the King of Hatti, the mighty King, for marriage? If you should say: "The King of Babylonia is not a Great King," then my brother does not know the rank of Babylonia.

My personal deity who was responsible for this—when the Sun-goddess of Arinna, the Storm-god, Hebat, and Shaushga made me Queen—she joined me with your brother, and I produced sons and daughters, so that the people of Hatti often speak of my experience(?) and capacity for nur-

ture(?). My brother knows this. Furthermore, when I entered the royal household, the princesses I found in the household also gave birth under my care. I raised them (their children), and I also raised those whom I found already born. I made them military officers. . . . And may the gods likewise endow the daughter whom I will give to my brother with the Queen's experience(?) and capacity for nurture(?)! And I, the Queen, spoke thereby: "Her brothers will be concerned for her." If this is not acceptable to my brother, will I do anything displeasing to my brother?

Concerning the fact that you, my brother, wrote to me as follows: "When you turn over the daughter to me, then write to me about the matters which might be on your mind and which you might wish to write to me about." This message is just what one would expect from my brother! Since the Queen is coming to Amurru, I will be in your vicinity, and from there I will write to my brother whatever matters are on the Queen's mind. You, my brother, will not disapprove of them; you will approve of them. When the daughter arrives at my brother's bed, these matters of the Queen will be settled.

Concerning the fact that you, my brother, wrote to me as follows: "My sister wrote to me: 'When messengers traveled to visit the daughter of Babylonia who had been given to Egypt, they were left standing outside!'" Ellil-bel-nishe, messenger of the King of Babylonia, told me this information. Because I heard this information—should I not have written of it to my brother? I will not again do anything about which my brother has now expressed his disapproval to me. I will not again do to my brother anything which displeases my brother. If I do not know something, then I might do such a displeasing thing to my brother. But because I already know, I certainly will not do anything displeasing to my brother. Now I know that Egypt and Hatti will become a single country. Even if there is not now a treaty with Egypt, the Queen knows thereby how you will conclude it out of consideration for my dignity. The deity who installed me in this place has not denied me anything. She has not denied me happiness. You, as son-in-law, will take my daughter in marriage.

REVIEW QUESTIONS

1. Can you understand from this reading why experts often refer to the "Brotherhood of the Great Powers" when they speak of the transnational system of the Late Bronze Age?
2. How were relations solidified between the great powers of this era?
3. What does this letter reveal about the possible roles and status of royal women in the diplomacy of the era?

FROM The Book of I Kings: Solomon's Construction of Yahweh's Temple in Jerusalem

As recounted in the following selection from the First Book of Kings, 5–8, in the Hebrew Bible, the crowning achievement of the reign of the Israelite king Solomon was the building of the great temple of Yahweh in Jerusalem, perhaps sometime during the later tenth century B.C.E. That temple was part of a larger palace complex, no archaeological evidence of which has yet been recovered. This helps explain

why modern historians have been compelled to reassess the biblical accounts of the great power and extent of David's and Solomon's kingdom. Nonetheless, Solomon's First Temple, later destroyed by the Babylonians under Nebuchadnezzar in the sixth century B.C.E. (the Second Temple, rebuilt by Herod the Great in the first century B.C.E., was destroyed by the Romans in the first century C.E.),[1] became the central locus of ritual and worship in early Judaism and is an overriding reason for modern Israel's adamant refusal to share sovereignty over Jerusalem today.

From *Contemporary English Version* by American Bible Society (New York: American Bible Society, 1995).

King Hiram of Tyre had always been friends with Solomon's father David. When Hiram learned that Solomon was king, he sent some of his officials to meet with Solomon. Solomon sent a message back to Hiram: "Remember how my father David wanted to build a temple where the LORD his God could be worshiped? But enemies kept attacking my father's kingdom, and he never had the chance. Now, thanks to the LORD God, there is peace in my kingdom and no trouble or threat of war anywhere. The LORD God promised my father that when his son became king, he would build a temple for worshiping the LORD. So I've decided to do that. I'd like you to have your workers cut down cedar trees in Lebanon for me. I will pay them whatever you say and will even have my workers help them. We both know that your workers are more experienced than anyone else at cutting lumber."

Hiram was so happy when he heard Solomon's request that he said, "I am grateful that the LORD gave David such a wise son to be king of that great nation!" Then he sent back his answer: "I received your message and will give you all the cedar and pine logs you need. My workers will carry them down from Lebanon to the Mediterranean Sea. They will tie the logs together and float them along the coast to wherever you want them. Then they will untie the logs, and your workers can take them from there. To pay for the logs, you can provide the grain I need for my household." Hiram gave Solomon all the cedar and pine logs he needed. In return, Solomon gave Hiram about one hundred twenty-five thousand bushels of wheat and about one thousand one hundred gallons of pure olive oil each year. The LORD kept his promise and made Solomon wise. Hiram and Solomon signed a treaty and never went to war against each other.

Solomon ordered thirty thousand people from all over Israel to cut logs for the temple, and he put Adoniram in charge of these workers. Solomon divided them into three groups of ten thousand. Each group worked one month in Lebanon and had two months off at home. He also had eighty thousand workers to cut stone in the hill country of Israel, seventy thousand workers to carry the stones, and over three thousand assistants to keep track of the work and to supervise the workers. He ordered the workers to cut and shape large blocks of good stone for the foundation of the temple. Solomon's and Hiram's men worked with men from the city of Gebal, and together they got the stones and logs ready for the temple.

Solomon's workers started building the temple during Ziv, the second month of the year. It had been four years since Solomon became king of Israel, and four hundred eighty years since the people of Israel left Egypt. The inside of the LORD's temple was ninety feet long, thirty feet wide, and forty-five feet high. A fifteen-foot porch went all the way across the front of the temple. The windows were narrow on the outside but wide on the inside. Along the sides and back of the temple, there were three levels of storage rooms. The rooms on the bottom level were seven and a half feet wide, the rooms on the middle level were nine feet wide, and those on the top level were ten and

---

[1]C.E. means "common era."

a half feet wide. There were ledges on the outside of the temple that supported the beams of the storage rooms, so that nothing was built into the temple walls. Solomon did not want the noise of hammers and axes to be heard at the place where the temple was being built. So he had the workers shape the blocks of stone at the quarry.

The entrance to the bottom storage rooms was on the south side of the building, and stairs to the other rooms were also there. The roof of the temple was made out of beams and cedar boards. The workers finished building the outside of the temple. Storage rooms seven and a half feet high were all around the temple, and they were attached to the temple by cedar beams.

The LORD told Solomon: "If you obey my commands and do what I say, I will keep the promise I made to your father David. I will live among my people Israel in this temple you are building, and I will not desert them."

So Solomon's workers finished building the temple. The floor of the temple was made out of pine, and the walls were lined with cedar from floor to ceiling. The most holy place was in the back of the temple, and it was thirty feet square. Cedar boards standing from floor to ceiling separated it from the rest of the temple. The temple's main room was sixty feet long, and it was in front of the most holy place. The inside walls were lined with cedar to hide the stones, and the cedar was decorated with carvings of gourds and flowers.

The sacred chest was kept in the most holy place. This room was thirty feet long, thirty feet wide, and thirty feet high, and it was lined with pure gold. There were also gold chains across the front of the most holy place. The inside of the temple, as well as the cedar altar in the most holy place, was covered with gold. Solomon had two statues of winged creatures made from olive wood to put in the most holy place. Each creature was fifteen feet tall and fifteen feet across. They had two wings, and the wings were seven and a half feet long. Solomon put them next to each other in the most holy place. Their wings were spread out and reached across the room. The creatures were also covered with gold. The walls of the two rooms were decorated

with carvings of palm trees, flowers, and winged creatures. Even the floor was covered with gold. The two doors to the most holy place were made out of olive wood and were decorated with carvings of palm trees, flowers, and winged creatures. The doors and the carvings were covered with gold. The door frame came to a point at the top. The two doors to the main room of the temple were made out of pine, and each one had two sections so they could fold open. The door frame was shaped like a rectangle and was made out of olive wood. The doors were covered with gold and were decorated with carvings of palm trees, flowers, and winged creatures. The inner courtyard of the temple had walls made out of three layers of cut stones with one layer of cedar beams.

Work began on the temple during Ziv, the second month of the year, four years after Solomon became king of Israel. Seven years later the workers finished building it during Bul, the eighth month of the year. It was built exactly as it had been planned. Solomon's palace took thirteen years to build.

Forest Hall was the largest room in the palace. It was one hundred fifty feet long, seventy-five feet wide, and forty-five feet high, and was lined with cedar from Lebanon. It had four rows of cedar pillars, fifteen in a row, and they held up forty-five cedar beams. The ceiling was covered with cedar. Three rows of windows on each side faced each other, and there were three doors on each side near the front of the hall. Pillar Hall was seventy-five feet long and forty-five feet wide. A covered porch supported by pillars went all the way across the front of the hall. Solomon's throne was in Justice Hall, where he judged cases. This hall was completely lined with cedar. The section of the palace where Solomon lived was behind Justice Hall and looked exactly like it. He had a similar place built for his wife, the daughter of the king of Egypt.

From the foundation all the way to the top, these buildings and the courtyard were made out of the best stones carefully cut to size, then smoothed on every side with saws. The foundation stones were huge, good stones—some of them fifteen feet long

and others twelve feet long. The cedar beams and other stones that had been cut to size were on top of these foundation stones. The walls around the palace courtyard were made out of three layers of cut stones with one layer of cedar beams, just like the front porch and the inner courtyard of the temple.

Hiram was a skilled bronze worker from the city of Tyre. His father was now dead, but he also had been a bronze worker from Tyre, and his mother was from the tribe of Naphtali. King Solomon asked Hiram to come to Jerusalem and make the bronze furnishings to use for worship in the LORD's temple, and he agreed to do it. Hiram made two bronze columns twenty-seven feet tall and about six feet across. For the top of each column, he also made a bronze cap seven and a half feet high. The caps were decorated with seven rows of designs that looked like chains, with two rows of designs that looked like pomegranates. The caps for the columns of the porch were six feet high and were shaped like lilies. The chain designs on the caps were right above the rounded tops of the two columns, and there were two hundred pomegranates in rows around each cap. Hiram placed the two columns on each side of the main door of the temple. The column on the south side was called Jachin, and the one on the north was called Boaz. The lily-shaped caps were on top of the columns. This completed the work on the columns.

Hiram also made a large bowl called the Sea. It was seven and a half feet deep, about fifteen feet across, and forty-five feet around. Two rows of bronze gourds were around the outer edge of the bowl, ten gourds to every eighteen inches. The bowl itself sat on top of twelve bronze bulls with three bulls facing outward in each of four directions. The sides of the bowl were four inches thick, and its rim was like a cup that curved outward like flower petals. The bowl held about eleven thousand gallons.

Hiram made ten movable bronze stands, each one four and a half feet high, six feet long, and six feet wide. The sides were made with panels attached to frames decorated with flower designs. The panels themselves were decorated with figures of lions, bulls, and winged creatures. Each stand had four bronze wheels and axles and a round

frame twenty-seven inches across, held up by four supports eighteen inches high. A small bowl rested in the frame. The supports were decorated with flower designs, and the frame with carvings.

The side panels of the stands were square, and the wheels and axles were underneath them. The wheels were about twenty-seven inches high and looked like chariot wheels. The axles, rims, spokes, and hubs were made out of bronze. Around the top of each stand was a nine-inch strip, and there were four braces attached to the corners of each stand. The panels and the supports were attached to the stands, and the stands were decorated with flower designs and figures of lions, palm trees, and winged creatures. Hiram made the ten bronze stands from the same mold, so they were exactly the same size and shape. Hiram also made ten small bronze bowls, one for each stand. The bowls were six feet across and could hold about two hundred thirty gallons. He put five stands on the south side of the temple, five stands on the north side, and the large bowl at the southeast corner of the temple. Hiram made pans for hot ashes, and also shovels and sprinkling bowls.

This is a list of the bronze items that Hiram made for the LORD's temple: two columns; two bowl-shaped caps for the tops of the columns; two chain designs on the caps; four hundred pomegranates for the chain designs; ten movable stands; ten small bowls for the stands; a large bowl; twelve bulls that held up the bowl; pans for hot ashes, and also shovels and sprinkling bowls. Hiram made these bronze things for Solomon near the Jordan River between Succoth and Zarethan by pouring melted bronze into clay molds. There were so many bronze things that Solomon never bothered to weigh them, and no one ever knew how much bronze was used.

Solomon gave orders to make the following temple furnishings out of gold: the altar; the table that held the sacred loaves of bread; ten lampstands that went in front of the most holy place; flower designs; lamps and tongs; cups, lamp snuffers, and small sprinkling bowls; dishes for incense; fire pans; and the hinges for the doors to the most holy place and the main room of the temple. After the

LORD's temple was finished, Solomon put into its storage rooms everything that his father David had dedicated to the LORD, including the gold and the silver.

The sacred chest had been kept on Mount Zion, also known as the city of David. But Solomon decided to have the chest moved to the temple while everyone was in Jerusalem, celebrating the Festival of Shelters during Ethanim, the seventh month of the year. Solomon called together the important leaders of Israel. Then the priests and the Levites carried to the temple the sacred chest, the sacred tent, and the objects used for worship. Solomon and a crowd of people walked in front of the chest, and along the way they sacrificed more sheep and cattle than could be counted.

The priests carried the chest into the most holy place and put it under the winged creatures, whose wings covered the chest and the poles used for carrying it. The poles were so long that they could be seen from right outside the most holy place, but not from anywhere else. And they stayed there from then on. The only things kept in the chest were the two flat stones Moses had put there when the LORD made his agreement with the people of Israel at Mount Sinai, after bringing them out of Egypt. Suddenly a cloud filled the temple as the priests were leaving the most holy place. The LORD's glory was in the cloud, and the light from it was so bright that the priests could not stay inside to do their work. Then Solomon prayed:

"Our LORD, you said that you
would live in a dark cloud.
Now I have built a glorious temple
where you can live forever."

Solomon turned toward the people standing there. Then he blessed them and said: "Praise the LORD God of Israel! Long ago he brought his people out of Egypt. He later kept his promise to make my father David the king of Israel. The LORD also said that he had not chosen the city where his temple would be built. So when David wanted to build a temple for the LORD God of Israel, the LORD said, 'It's good that you want to build a temple where I can be worshiped. But you're not the one to do it. Your son will build a temple to honor me.' The LORD has done what he promised. I am the king of Israel like my father, and I've built a temple for the LORD our God. I've also made a place in the temple for the sacred chest. And in that chest are the two flat stones on which is written the solemn agreement the LORD made with our ancestors when he led them out of Egypt."

Solomon stood facing the altar with everyone standing behind him. Then he lifted his arms toward heaven and prayed: "LORD God of Israel, no other god in heaven or on earth is like you! You never forget the agreement you made with your people, and you are loyal to anyone who faithfully obeys your teachings. My father David was your servant, and today you have kept every promise you made to him. LORD God of Israel, you promised my father that someone from his family would always be king of Israel, if they do their best to obey you, just as he did. Please keep this promise you made to your servant David.

"There's not enough room in all of heaven for you, LORD God. How could you possibly live on earth in this temple I have built? But I ask you to answer my prayer. This is the temple where you have chosen to be worshiped. Please watch over it day and night and listen when I turn toward it and pray. I am your servant, and the people of Israel belong to you. So whenever any of us look toward this temple and pray, answer from your home in heaven and forgive our sins.

"Suppose someone accuses a person of a crime, and the accused has to stand in front of the altar in your temple and say, 'I swear I am innocent!' Listen from heaven and decide who is right. Then punish the guilty person and let the innocent one go free.

"Suppose your people Israel sin against you, and then an enemy defeats them. If they come to this temple and beg for forgiveness, listen from your home in heaven. Forgive them and bring them back to the land you gave their ancestors.

"Suppose your people sin against you, and you punish them by holding back the rain. If they turn toward this temple and pray in your name and stop

sinning, listen from your home in heaven and for-give them. The people of Israel are your servants, so teach them to live right. And please send rain on the land you promised them forever.

"Sometimes the crops may dry up or rot or be eaten by locusts or grasshoppers, and your people will be starving. Sometimes enemies may surround their towns, or your people will become sick with deadly diseases. Listen when anyone in Israel truly feels sorry and sincerely prays with arms lifted to-ward your temple. You know what is in everyone's heart. So from your home in heaven answer their prayers, according to the way they live and what is in their hearts. Then your people will worship and obey you for as long as they live in the land you gave their ancestors. Foreigners will hear about you and your mighty power, and some of them will come to live among your people Israel. If any of them pray toward this temple, listen from your home in heaven and answer their prayers. Then everyone on earth will worship you, just like your people Israel, and they will know that I have built this temple to honor you.

"Our LORD, sometimes you will order your people to attack their enemies. Then your people will turn toward this temple I have built for you in your chosen city, and they will pray to you. Answer their prayers from heaven and give them victory.

"Everyone sins. But when your people sin against you, suppose you get angry enough to let their enemies drag them away to foreign countries. Later, they may feel sorry for what they did and ask your forgiveness. Answer them when they pray to-ward this temple I have built for you in your cho-sen city, here in this land you gave their ancestors. From your home in heaven, listen to their sincere prayers and do what they ask. Forgive your people no matter how much they have sinned against you. Make the enemies who defeated them be kind to them. Remember, they are the people you chose and rescued from Egypt that was like a blazing fire to them.

"I am your servant, and the people of Israel be-long to you. So listen when any of us pray and cry out for your help. When you brought our ancestors out of Egypt, you told your servant Moses to say to them, 'From all people on earth, the LORD God has chosen you to be his very own.'"

When Solomon finished his prayer at the altar, he was kneeling with his arms lifted toward heaven. He stood up, turned toward the people, blessed them, and said loudly: "Praise the LORD! He has kept his promise and given us peace. Every good thing he promised to his servant Moses has hap-pened. The LORD our God was with our ancestors to help them, and I pray that he will be with us and never abandon us. May the LORD help us obey him and follow all the laws and teachings he gave our ancestors. I pray that the LORD our God will remember my prayer day and night. May he help everyone in Israel each day, in whatever way we need it. Then every nation will know that the LORD is the only true God. Obey the LORD our God and follow his commands with all your heart, just as you are doing today."

Solomon and the people dedicated the temple to the LORD by offering twenty-two thousand cattle and one hundred twenty thousand sheep as sacri-fices to ask the LORD's blessing. On that day, Solomon dedicated the courtyard in front of the temple and made it acceptable for worship. He of-fered the sacrifices there because the bronze altar in front of the temple was too small. Solomon and the huge crowd celebrated the Festival of Shelters at the temple for seven days. There were people from as far away as the Egyptian Gorge in the south and Lebo-Hamath in the north. Then on the eighth day, he sent everyone home. They said good-by and left, very happy, because of all the good things the LORD had done for his servant David and his people Israel.

*   *   *

REVIEW QUESTIONS

1. How are the wealth, skills, and products of the cities of Phoenicia represented in this selection?
2. Why did Solomon cause the temple to be built?
3. How is the temple intended to be a link between Yahweh and his people?

FROM The Annals of Ashurnasirpal II of Assyria

The ninth century B.C.E. witnessed the reemergence of Assyria under two powerful kings, Ashurnasirpal II and Shalmaneser III. Both kings waged far-flung military campaigns, the efficiency and brutality of which set the tone for the next two hundred fifty years of Assyrian conquest and empire. Ashurnasirpal's new capital city at Kalhu (Nimrud) on the Tigris River included a magnificent palace, the construction of which incorporated long cuneiform inscriptions celebrating his conquests and proclaiming his majesty and that of the chief Assyrian god, Ashur. The following selection includes the prologue to Ashurnasirpal's annals, followed by an account of his first year's campaign. As you read, you may find reason to agree with the assessment of the historian A. T. Olmstead, who characterized Ashurnasirpal's career as one of "calculated frightfulness."

From *Ancient Records of Assyria and Babylonia*, vol. I, by D. D. Luckenbill (Chicago: University of Chicago Press, 1926), pp. 138–45.

*   *   *

Unto Ninurta, the powerful, the almighty, the exalted, the chief of the gods, the valiant, the gigantic, the perfect, whose onslaught in battle cannot be equaled, the first(born) son, the destroyer of opposition, the first-born of Nudimmud, the hero of the Igigi, the powerful, the prince of the gods, the offspring of E-kur, who holds the bolt of heaven and earth, who opens the depths, who treads the broad earth, the god without whom the decisions of heaven and earth are not decided, the destroyer, the mighty one, the command of whose mouth is not void, pre-eminent in the (four) quarters (of the world), who gives scepter and law unto all cities, the impetuous ruler, the word of whose lips is not altered, (of) boundless strength, the master of the gods, the exalted, Utgallu, the lord of lords, whose hand controls the ends of heaven and earth, the king of battle, the strong one who conquers opposition, the triumphant, the perfect, the lord of the nether waters and of the oceans, the terrible, the merciless one whose onslaught is a storm (deluge), who overwhelms the land of enemies, who strikes down the wicked, the powerful god whose counsel is not void, the light of heaven and earth, who gives light unto the midst of the deep, who destroys the wicked, who brings to subjection the disobedient, who overthrows foes, whose name in the assembly of the gods no god can humble, the giver of life, the god Ab-u, to whom it is good to pray (?), who dwells in the city of Calah, the great lord, my lord, (I) Assur-nâsir-pal (do pray); the mighty king, king of the universe, the king without a rival, the king of the whole of the four quarters (of the world), the Sun of all peoples, favorite of Enlil and Ninurta, the beloved of Anu and Dagan, the worshiper of the great gods, the submissive one who is dear unto thy heart, the prince, the favorite of Enlil, whose priesthood is pleasing unto thy great godhead so that thou hast established his reign, the valiant hero who goes hither and yon trusting in Assur, his lord, and who is without a rival among the princes of the four quarters (of the world), the wonderful shepherd, who fears not opposition, the mighty flood who has no conqueror, the king who has brought into subjection those that were not submissive to him, who has brought under his sway the totality of all peoples, the mighty hero who treads on the neck of his foe, who tramples all enemies under foot, who shatters the might of the haughty, who goes about trusting in the great gods, his lords,

whose hand has conquered all the countries, who has brought under his sway all the mountain (regions) and has received their tribute, who has taken hostages, and who has established might over all lands.

When Assur, the lord, who called me by my name and has made great my kingdom, intrusted his merciless weapon unto my lordly hand, (I) Assur-nâsir-pal, the exalted prince, who fears the great gods, the powerful despot, conqueror of cities and mountains to their farthest borders, the king of rulers, who consumes the wicked, who is crowned with glory, who fears not opposition, the strong, the exalted, the unsparing, who destroys opposition, the king of all princes, the lord of lords, the shepherd(?), the king of kings, the exalted priest, the chosen of the hero Ninurta, the worshiper of the great gods, the avenger (of his fathers), the king who trusting in Assur and Shamash, the gods, his helpers, walks righteously and has cut down haughty mountain(eers) and princes who were his enemies, like reeds of the marsh, bringing all lands into subjection under his feet, who provides the offerings for the great gods, the rightful prince who has been permanently intrusted (with the task) of maintaining the cults(?) of the temples of his land, the work of whose hands and the offering of whose sacrifices the great gods of heaven and earth love, and whose priesthood in the temples they have established for all time,—their weapons they presented as my (v., his) royal gift,—the radiance of whose arms and the awe-inspiring splendor of whose rule have made him supreme over the kings of the four quarters (of the world), who has battled with all the enemies of Assur north and south and has laid tribute and tax upon them, conqueror of the foes of Assur; son of Tukulti-Ninurta, priest of Assur, who overcame all his enemies and fixed the bodies of his foes upon stakes; grandson of Adad-Nirâri, the priest, the viceroy of the great gods, who brought about the overthrow of those that did not obey him and established his sway over all; the descendant of Assur-daân, who freed(?) cities and founded temples. And now at the command of the great gods my sovereignty, my dominion, and my power are manifesting themselves; I am regal, I am lordly, I am exalted, I am mighty, I am honored, I am glorified, I am pre-eminent, I am powerful, I am valiant, I am lion-brave, and I am heroic! (I), Assur-nâsir-pal, the mighty king, the king of Assyria, chosen of Sin, favorite of Anu, beloved of Adad, mighty one among the gods, I am the merciless weapon that strikes down the land of his enemies; I am a king, mighty in battle, destroying cities and highlands, first in war, king of the four quarters (of the world), who has conquered his foes, destroyed all his enemies, king of all the regions (of earth), of all princes, every one of them, the king who has trampled down all who were not submissive to him, and who has brought under his sway the totality of all peoples. These decrees of destiny came forth at the word of the great gods, and for my destiny they duly ordained them. In (every) desire of my heart and undertaking of my hand, Ishtar, the lady, who loves my priesthood, was gracious unto me and her heart prompted to the waging of war and battle.

At that time Assur-nâsir-pal, the exalted prince, who fears the great gods, the desire of whose heart Enlil has caused him to attain, and whose mighty hand has conquered all princes who were disobedient unto him, conqueror of his foes, who shattered the power of the mighty in difficult regions,—when Assur, my great lord, who called me by name and made great my kingship over the kings of the four quarters (of the world), had made my name exceeding great, and had intrusted his merciless weapon unto my lordly power, and in his wrath had commanded me to conquer, to subdue and to rule; trusting in Assur, my lord, I marched by difficult roads over steep mountains with the hosts of my army, and there was none who opposed me.

In the beginning of my kingship, in the first year of my reign, when Shamash the judge of the (four) regions (of the world) had spread his kindly shadow over me, and I had seated myself upon the royal throne in might, and (when) he had placed in my hand the scepter, which rules the peoples, I mobilized my chariots and armies,

crossed over steep mountains by difficult roads which had not been prepared for the passage of chariots and troops, and marched to the land of Tumme. Libê, their fortified city, and the cities of Surra, Abuku, Arura, and Arubê, which lie among the mountains of Urini, Aruni and Etini, fortified cities, I captured. I slew great numbers of them; their spoil, their possessions and their cattle I carried off. The men escaped, and occupied a steep mountain; the mountain was exceeding steep and I did not go after them. The peak of the mountain rose like the point of an iron dagger, and no bird of heaven that flies comes to it. Like the nest of the eagle (vulture) their stronghold was situated within the mountain, whereinto none of the kings, my fathers, had penetrated. For three days the warrior searched out the mountain, his stout heart urging to battle; he climbed up on foot, he cast down the mountain, he destroyed their nest, he shattered their host. Two hundred of their fighting men I cut down with the sword; their heavy booty I carried off like a flock of sheep; with their blood I dyed the mountain red like wool; with the rest of them I darkened(?) the gullies and precipices of the mountain; their cities I destroyed, I devastated, I burned with fire. From the land of Tumme I departed, to the land of Kirruri I went down. Tribute from the lands of Kirruri, Simesi, Simera, Ulmania, Adaush, (from) the Hargeans and Harmaseans, —horses, mules, cattle, sheep, wine, vessels of copper, I received as their tribute and I imposed the carrying of the headpad(?) upon them.

While I was staying in the land of Kirruri, the awe-inspiring splendor of Assur, my lord, overwhelmed the men of the lands of Gilzani and Hubushkia; horses, silver, gold, lead, copper and vessels of copper they brought to me as their tribute. From the land of Kirruri I departed, and I entered by the pass of Hulun into the land of Kirhi, which lies inside. The cities of Hatu, Hataru, Nishtun, Irbidi, Mitkia, Arsania, Téla, and Halua, cities of the land of Kirhi which lie among the mighty mountains of Usu, Arua, and Arardi, I captured. Great numbers of them I slew, their spoil and their possessions I carried away. The men escaped and occupied a lofty mountain peak which was over against the city of Nishtun and which was suspended like a cloud from heaven. Against these men, unto whom none among the kings my fathers had come near, my warriors flew like birds; 260 of their fighting men I cut down with the sword, I cut off their heads, and I formed them into pillars. The rest of them built a nest on the rocks of the mountain like a bird. Their spoil and their possessions I brought down from the mountain, and the cities which were in the midst of the mighty ranges, I destroyed, I devastated, I burned with fire. All the men who had fled from before my arms came down and embraced my feet. Tribute and tax, and the carrying of the headpad(?) I imposed upon them. Bûbu, son of Bubâ, the governor of the city of Nishtun, I flayed in the city of Arbela and I spread his skin upon the city wall. At that time I fashioned an image of my own likeness, the glory of my power I inscribed thereon, and in the mountain of Eki, in the city of Assur-nâsir-pal, at the (river) source, I set it up.

In this (same) eponymy, on the twenty-fourth day of the month *Abu*, at the word of Assur and Ishtar, the great gods, my lords, I departed from Nineveh, against the cities which lie at the foot of the mighty mountains of Nipur and Pasate I marched. I captured the cities of Arkun, Ushhu and Pilazi and twenty cities of their neighborhood. Great numbers (of the inhabitants) I slew, their spoil and their possessions I carried off, their cities I burned with fire. All the men who had fled from before my arms, came down and embraced my feet, and I imposed forced labor upon them. From the cities at the foot of the mountains of Nipur and Pasate I departed, the Tigris I crossed, and I drew near to the land of Kutmuhi, I received tribute from the lands of Kutmuhi and Mushki—vessels of copper, cattle, sheep, and wine.

While I was staying in the land of Kutmuhi, they brought me the word: "The city of Sûru of Bît-Halupê has revolted, they have slain Hamatai, their governor, and Ahia-baba, the son of a nobody, whom they brought from Bît-Adini, they have set up as king over them." With the help of Adad and the great gods who have made great my

kingdom, I mobilized (my) chariots and armies and marched along the bank of the Habur. During my advance I received much tribute from Shulmanu-haman-ilâni of the city of Gardiganni, from Ilu-Adad of the city of Katna—silver, gold, lead, vessels of copper, and garments of brightly colored wool, and garments of linen. To the city of Sûru of Bît-Halupê I drew near, and the terror of the splendor of Assur, my lord, overwhelmed them. The chief men and the elders of the city, to save their lives, came forth into my presence and embraced my feet, saying: "If it is thy pleasure, slay! If it is thy pleasure, let live! That which thy heart desireth, do!" Ahiababa, the son of nobody, whom they had brought from Bît-Adini, I took captive. In the valor of my heart and with the fury of my weapons I stormed the city. All the rebels they seized and delivered them up. My officers I caused to enter into his palace and his temples. His silver, his gold, his goods and his possessions, copper, iron, lead, vessels of copper, cups of copper, dishes of copper, a great hoard of copper, alabaster, tables with inlay, the women of his palaces, his daughters, the captive rebels together with their possessions, the gods together with their possessions, precious stone from the mountains, his chariot with equipment, his horses, broken to the yoke, trappings of men and trappings of horses, garments of brightly colored wool and garments of linen, goodly oil, cedar, and fine sweet-scented herbs, panels(?) of cedar, purple and crimson wool, his wagons, his cattle, his sheep, his heavy spoil, which like the stars of heaven could not be counted, I carried off. Azi-ilu I set over them as my own governor. I built a pillar over against his city gate, and I flayed all the chief men who had revolted, and I covered the pillar with their skins; some I walled up within the pillar, some I impaled upon the pillar on stakes, and others I bound to stakes round about the pillar; many within the border of my own land I flayed, and I spread their skins upon the walls; and I cut off the limbs of the officers, of the royal officers who had rebelled. Ahiababa I took to Nineveh, I flayed him, I spread his skin upon the wall of Nineveh. My power and might I established over the land of Laké. While I was staying in the city of Sûru, (I received) tribute from all the kings of the land of Laké,—silver, gold, lead, copper, vessels of copper, cattle, sheep, garments of brightly colored wool, and garments of linen, and I increased the tribute and taxes and imposed them upon them. At that time, the tribute of Haiâani of the city of Hindani,—silver, gold, lead, copper, *umu*-stone, alabaster, purple wool, and (Bactrian) camels I received from him as tribute. At that time I fashioned a heroic image of my royal self, my power and my glory I inscribed thereon, in the midst of his palace I set it up. I fashioned memorial steles and inscribed thereon my glory and my prowess, and I set them up by his city gate.

*   *   *

REVIEW QUESTIONS

1. What is the relationship between the king and the gods? Do the king's conquests appear to be divinely sanctioned?
2. Would you characterize the Assyrians' attitude toward conquered peoples as benevolent?
3. To what kinds of techniques did the Assyrians resort in order to ensure their control?
4. What were the motives that underlay Ashurnasirpal's conquests?

THE ASSYRIAN ATTACK ON LACHISH (701 B.C.E.)

The Assyrian onslaught at the Israelite city of Lachish is depicted on a portion of a wall relief in the palace of the Assyrian king Sennacherib at Nineveh. What kinds of military technology did the Assyrian army employ? Can you see evidence of one fate of the vanquished? What might be the practical uses of images such as these?

HERODOTUS

FROM *The Histories:* Customs of the Persians

The Greek historian Herodotus, who wrote during the fifth century B.C.E., has long been lauded as the father of history (although some would call him the grandfather and accord Thucydides the appellation father*). Although modern historians are quite aware of Herodotus's own prejudices and gullibility, his* Histories *nonetheless remains our most important source for the history of the Persian invasions of Greece in 490 and 480-479 B.C.E. As background for that story, Herodotus also furnished a virtual travelogue of the peoples, places, and customs of the fifth century B.C.E. world. (In fact, his description of Egyptian customs remains an often-cited source on techniques of mummification.) In the following selection, Herodotus reports his knowledge of the customs of the Persians.*

From *Herodotus: The Histories,* edited by Walter Blanco and Jennifer Tolbert Roberts, translated by Walter Blanco (New York: Norton, 1992), pp. 48–50.

*   *   *

These are the customs I know the Persians to observe. They are not allowed to build statues, temples, and altars, and in fact they accuse those who do of silliness, in my opinion because unlike the Greeks, they don't think of the gods as having human form. It is their custom to climb to the mountaintops and sacrifice to Zeus, which is the name they give to the full circle of the sky. They sacrifice to the sun and the moon and the earth, as well as to fire, water, and air. At first, they sacrificed only to these, but they later learned to sacrifice to the Heavenly Aphrodite—they learned this from the Assyrians and the Arabians. The Assyrians call Aphrodite Mylitta, the Arabians call her Alilat, and the Persians call her Mitra.

This is the way the Persians sacrifice to the above-mentioned gods: they make no altars and light no fires when they are about to sacrifice. They don't pour libations or play the flute or wear garlands or sprinkle barley on their victims. Whenever someone wants to sacrifice to one of the gods, he leads the victim to a ritually pure place and invokes the god while wearing his turban wreathed, preferably, with myrtle. It is not allowed for the sacrificer to pray, in private, for good things for himself. Instead, he prays for the well-being of all the Persians and of the king, for the sacrificer, after all, is included among all the Persians. When he has cut up the sacrificial victim into pieces and then boiled the meat, he spreads out the tenderest grass—preferably clover—and then places all of the meat on top of it. When he has arranged the meat piece by piece, a Magus stands near and chants a hymn on the origin of the gods—anyway, that's the kind of hymn they say it is. It is not their custom to perform a sacrifice without a Magus. The sacrificer waits a little while, then carries away the meat and does whatever he wants with it.

The day of all days they celebrate the most is their own birthday. On that day, the right thing to do is to serve a bigger meal than on any other day. On that day, their rich people serve up oxen, horses, camels, and donkeys that have been roasted whole in ovens, while their poor people serve smaller cattle, like sheep and goats. They eat few main dishes, but lots of appetizers, one after another, and for this reason the Persians say that the Greeks eat a main course and then stop when

they are still hungry since after dinner nothing worth mentioning is brought out, though they wouldn't stop eating if it was. They love wine, but they are not allowed to vomit or to urinate in front of someone else. But though they have to be careful about that, they are accustomed to deliberate about their most important affairs when they are drunk, and then, on the next day, when they are sober, the master of the house they have been deliberating in proposes the decision that pleased them most. If they like it even when they are sober, they adopt it, but if not, they let it go. If they ever come to a provisional decision while sober, though, they then get drunk and reconsider it.

This is how you can tell if people who happen to meet each other on the street are social equals: instead of a verbal greeting, they kiss each other on the lips. If one is of slightly lower rank, they kiss each other's cheeks. If one is of a much lower rank, though, he prostrates himself and pays homage to the other. After themselves, Persians have the highest respect for the people who live closest to them, and next highest for those next closest, and so on. In accordance with this principle, they have the least respect for those who live farthest away. They consider themselves to be the best of people by far and others to share worth proportionally, so the people who live the farthest away are the worst. Subject nations ruled each other even under Median rule. That is, the Medes ruled over everything, but especially over those nearest to them, while those, in turn, ruled their neighbors, and so on. The Persians rank nations according to the same principle, by which each nation has a surrogate rule over the next one.

Nevertheless, the Persians are more inclined than other people to adopt foreign customs. For example, they wear Median clothes in the belief that they are more attractive than their own, and they wear Egyptian breastplates into war. They seek out and learn about all kinds of delights, and they even learned from the Greeks to have sex with boys. Each Persian man has many lawfully wedded wives, but many more mistresses.

Second only to being brave in battle, a man is considered manly if he has many sons to show for

himself, and every year the king sends gifts to the man who shows off the most sons. They believe that there is strength in numbers. They educate their sons from the age of five to the age of twenty in only three things: horseback riding, archery, and telling the truth. The boy does not come into the presence of his father until he is five years old—until then he lives with the women. This is done so that if he should die while he is growing up he won't cause any grief to his father.

I approve of that custom, and I also approve of the one that forbids even the king to put someone to death on the basis of only one charge, and that forbids any Persian to do any of his household slaves any irreparable harm on the basis of one charge either. If, however, he finds on review that there are more and greater offenses than services, then he may give way to anger.

They say that no one has yet killed his own father or mother. It is inevitable, they say, that any such child who has ever been born will be found on investigation to have been either a changeling or a bastard. They say that it just isn't likely that a true parent will be killed by his own child.

Whatever they are not allowed to do, they are also not allowed to talk about. They consider lying to be the most disgraceful of all things. After that, it is owing money—for many reasons, but mostly, they say, because it is necessary for somebody who owes money to tell lies.

No citizen who is an albino or who has leprosy is allowed into the city or to mingle with other Persians. They say that he has committed some offense against the sun. Foreigners who catch these diseases are driven out of the country by posses. Even white doves are driven out, charged with the same offense.

They don't spit, urinate, or wash their hands in rivers, or allow anyone else to, for they especially revere rivers.

The Persians don't notice it, though we do, but this also happens to be true of them: their names, which refer to their physical characteristics or to their social importance, all end in the same letter, which the Dorians call san and which the Ionians call sigma. If you look into it, you will find that

Persian names end in this letter—not some here and some there, but *all* of them.

I am able to say these things with certainty because I know them for a fact. There are things about the dead, though, which are concealed or referred to obliquely—for example that the corpse of a Persian man is not buried until it has been torn at by a bird or a dog. I know for sure, though, that the Magi practice this—because they do it openly—and that the Persians cover a corpse with wax before putting it in the ground. The Magi are very different from other people, including the Egyptian priests. The Egyptian priests refrain from killing any living thing, except what they ritually sacrifice. The Magi, however, will kill everything but dogs and people with their own hands. In fact,

they make a point of killing things, and go around killing ants and snakes and anything else that creeps, crawls, and flies. Well, that's how they've been practicing this custom since the beginning, so let it stay that way.

*   *   *

REVIEW QUESTIONS

1. How would you judge Herodotus's general opinion of Persian customs and values? Does he find things to admire about them?
2. Do any of his observations suggest to you that he might have been taken in by someone else's stories?

FROM The Torah: Laws

Modern scholars question the historicity of the Bible's account of the Hebrew Exodus, when thousands supposedly migrated from Egypt under the leadership of a man named Moses. The Egyptian records make no mention of such an event, nor is there any other evidence of it outside the biblical account. The impact of the Exodus story on the self-concept of the early Jewish people as having been chosen by God (who has identified himself by then as Yahweh) and whose fate is bound to their acceptance of him, is, however, immeasurable. As they made their way through the barren wilderness of the Sinai Desert, the Hebrews received from Yahweh a set of laws—the Decalogue, or Ten Commandments. These laws were to govern both their relationship with him and their behavior among themselves. In subsequent books of the Pentateuch (the first five books of the Hebrew Bible, the authorship of which was traditionally ascribed to Moses), these laws were expanded and elaborated on to form the basis of the Torah, the corpus of biblical law. The Torah remains today the very core of Judaism and of Jewish self-identity as a people chosen by God.

From *Contemporary English Version* by American Bible Society (New York: American Bible Society, 1995).

FROM The Book of Exodus

Moses led the people out of the camp to meet God, and they stood at the foot of the mountain. Mount Sinai was covered with smoke because the

LORD had come down in a flaming fire. Smoke poured out of the mountain just like a furnace, and the whole mountain shook. The trumpet blew louder and louder. Moses spoke, and God answered him with thunder. The LORD came down

to the top of Mount Sinai and told Moses to meet him there. Then he said, "Moses, go and warn the people not to cross the boundary that you set at the foot of the mountain. They must not cross it to come and look at me, because if they do, many of them will die. Only the priests may come near me, and they must obey strict rules before I let them. If they don't, they will be punished." Moses replied, "The people cannot come up the mountain. You warned us to stay away because it is holy." Then the LORD told Moses, "Go down and bring Aaron back here with you. But the priests and people must not try to push their way through, or I will rush at them like a flood!" After Moses had gone back down, he told the people what the LORD had said.

God said to the people of Israel:

I am the LORD your God, the one who brought you out of Egypt where you were slaves.

Do not worship any god except me.

Do not make idols that look like anything in the sky or on earth or in the ocean under the earth. Don't bow down and worship idols. I am the LORD your God, and I demand all your love. If you reject me, I will punish your families for three or four generations. But if you love me and obey my laws, I will be kind to your families for thousands of generations.

Do not misuse my name. I am the LORD your God, and I will punish anyone who misuses my name. Remember that the Sabbath Day belongs to me. You have six days when you can do your work, but the seventh day of each week belongs to me, your God. No one is to work on that day—not you, your children, your slaves, your animals, or the foreigners who live in your towns. In six days I made the sky, the earth, the oceans, and everything in them, but on the seventh day I rested. That's why I made the Sabbath a special day that belongs to me.

Respect your father and your mother, and you will live a long time in the land I am giving you.

Do not murder.

Be faithful in marriage.

Do not steal.

Do not tell lies about others.

Do not want anything that belongs to someone else. Don't want anyone's house, wife or husband, slaves, oxen, donkeys or anything else.

*   *   *

The LORD told Moses to say to the people of Israel: "With your own eyes, you saw me speak to you from heaven. So you must never make idols of silver or gold to worship in place of me. Build an altar out of earth, and offer on it your sacrifices of sheep, goats, and cattle. Wherever I choose to be worshiped, I will come down to bless you. If you ever build an altar for me out of stones, do not use any tools to chisel the stones, because that would make the altar unfit. And don't build an altar that requires steps; you might expose yourself when you climb up."

The LORD gave Moses the following laws for his people:

If you buy a Hebrew slave, he must remain your slave for six years. But in the seventh year you must set him free, without cost to him. If he was single at the time you bought him, he alone must be set free. But if he was married at the time, both he and his wife must be given their freedom. If you give him a wife, and they have children, only the man himself must be set free; his wife and children remain the property of his owner.

But suppose the slave loves his wife and children so much that he won't leave without them. Then he must stand beside either the door or the doorpost at the place of worship, while his owner punches a small hole through one of his ears with a sharp metal rod. This makes him a slave for life. A young woman who was sold by her father doesn't gain her freedom in the same way that a man does. If she doesn't please the man who bought her to be his wife, he must let her be bought back. He cannot sell her to foreigners; this would break the contract he made with her. If he selects her as a wife for his son, he must treat her as his own daughter. If the man later marries another woman, he must continue to provide food and clothing for the one he bought and to treat her as a wife. If he fails to do any of these things, she must be given her freedom without cost.

Death is the punishment for murder. But if you did not intend to kill someone, and I, the LORD, let it happen anyway, you may run for safety to a place that I have set aside. If you plan in advance to murder someone, there's no escape, not even by holding on to my altar. You will be dragged off and killed. Death is the punishment for attacking your father or mother.

Death is the punishment for kidnapping. If you sell the person you kidnapped, or if you are caught with that person, the penalty is death.

Death is the punishment for cursing your father or mother.

Suppose two of you are arguing, and you hit the other with either a rock or your fist, without causing a fatal injury. If the victim has to stay in bed, and later has to use a stick when walking outside, you must pay for the loss of time and do what you can to help until the injury is completely healed. That's your only responsibility.

Death is the punishment for beating to death any of your slaves. However, if the slave lives a few days after the beating, you are not to be punished. After all, you have already lost the services of that slave who was your property.

Suppose a pregnant woman suffers a miscarriage as the result of an injury caused by someone who is fighting. If she isn't badly hurt, the one who injured her must pay whatever fine her husband demands and the judges approve. But if she is seriously injured, the payment will be life for life, eye for eye, tooth for tooth, hand for hand, foot for foot, burn for burn, cut for cut, and bruise for bruise. If you hit one of your slaves and cause the loss of an eye, the slave must be set free. The same law applies if you knock out a slave's tooth—the slave goes free.

A bull that kills someone with its horns must be killed and its meat destroyed, but the owner of the bull isn't responsible for the death.

Suppose you own a bull that has been in the habit of attacking people, but you have refused to keep it fenced in. If that bull kills someone, both you and the bull must be put to death by stoning. However, you may save your own life by paying whatever fine is demanded. This same law applies if the bull gores someone's son or daughter. If the

bull kills a slave, you must pay the slave owner thirty pieces of silver for the loss of the slave, and the bull must be killed by stoning.

Suppose someone's ox or donkey is killed by falling into an open pit that you dug or left uncovered on your property. You must pay for the dead animal, and it becomes yours.

If your bull kills someone else's, yours must be sold. Then the money from your bull and the meat from the dead bull must be divided equally between you and the other owner.

If you refuse to fence in a bull that is known to attack others, you must pay for any animal it kills, but the dead animal will belong to you.

*   *   *

Suppose you borrow an animal from a neighbor, and it gets injured or dies while the neighbor isn't around. Then you must replace it. But if something happens to the animal while the owner is present, you do not have to replace it. If you had leased the animal, the money you paid the owner will cover any harm done to it.

Suppose a young woman has never been married and isn't engaged. If a man talks her into having sex, he must pay the bride price and marry her. But if her father refuses to let her marry the man, the bride price must still be paid. Death is the punishment for witchcraft.

Death is the punishment for having sex with an animal.

Death is the punishment for offering sacrifices to any god except me.

Do not mistreat or abuse foreigners who live among you. Remember, you were foreigners in Egypt.

Do not mistreat widows or orphans. If you do, they will beg for my help, and I will come to their rescue. In fact, I will get so angry that I will kill your men and make widows of their wives and orphans of their children.

Don't charge interest when you lend money to any of my people who are in need. Before sunset you must return any coat taken as security for a loan, because that is the only cover the poor have when they sleep at night. I am a merciful God,

and when they call out to me, I will come to help them.

Don't speak evil of me or of the ruler of your people. Don't fail to give me the offerings of grain and wine that belong to me. Dedicate to me your first-born sons and the first-born of your cattle and sheep. Let the animals stay with their mothers for seven days, then on the eighth day give them to me, your God.

You are my chosen people, so don't eat the meat of any of your livestock that was killed by a wild animal. Instead, feed the meat to dogs.

Don't spread harmful rumors or help a criminal by giving false evidence.

Always tell the truth in court, even if everyone else is dishonest and stands in the way of justice. And don't favor the poor, simply because they are poor. If you find an ox or a donkey that has wandered off, take it back where it belongs, even if the owner is your enemy.

If a donkey is overloaded and falls down, you must do what you can to help, even if it belongs to someone who doesn't like you. Make sure that the poor are given equal justice in court. Don't bring false charges against anyone or sentence an innocent person to death. I won't forgive you if you do.

Don't accept bribes. Judges are blinded and justice is twisted by bribes.

Don't mistreat foreigners. You were foreigners in Egypt, and you know what it is like.

Plant and harvest your crops for six years, but let the land rest during the seventh year. The poor are to eat what they want from your fields, vineyards, and olive trees during that year, and when they have all they want from your fields, leave the rest for wild animals.

Work the first six days of the week, but rest and relax on the seventh day. This law is not only for you, but for your oxen, donkeys, and slaves, as well as for any foreigners among you.

*   *   *

FROM **The Book of Leviticus**

If you curse your father or mother, you will be put to death, and it will be your own fault.

If any of you men have sex with another man's wife, both you and the woman will be put to death.

Having sex with one of your father's wives disgraces him. So both you and the woman will be put to death, just as you deserve. It isn't natural to have sex with your daughter-in-law, and both of you will be put to death, just as you deserve. It's disgusting for men to have sex with one another, and those who do will be put to death, just as they deserve. It isn't natural for a man to marry both a mother and her daughter, and so all three of them will be burned to death. If any of you have sex with an animal, both you and the animal will be put to death, just as you deserve.

If you marry one of your sisters, you will be punished, and the two of you will be disgraced by being openly forced out of the community. If you have sex with a woman during her monthly period, both you and the woman will be cut off from the people of Israel. The sisters of your father and mother are your own relatives, and you will be punished for having sex with any of them. If you have sex with your uncle's wife, neither you nor she will ever have any children. And if you marry your sister-in-law, neither of you will ever have any children. Obey my laws and teachings. Or else the land I am giving you will become sick of you and throw you out. The nations I am chasing out did these disgusting things, and I hated them for it, so don't follow their example. I am the LORD your God, and I have promised you their land that is rich with milk and honey. I have chosen you to be different from other people. That's why you must make a difference between animals and birds that I have said are clean and unclean—this will keep you from becoming disgusting to me. I am the LORD, the holy God. You have been chosen to be my people, and so you must be holy too. If you claim to receive messages from the dead, you will be put to death by stoning, just as you deserve.

*   *   *

Suppose some of your people become so poor that they have to sell themselves and become your slaves. Then you must treat them as servants,

rather than as slaves. And in the Year of Celebration they are to be set free, so they and their children may return home to their families and property. I brought them out of Egypt to be my servants, not to be sold as slaves. So obey me, and don't be cruel to the poor.

If you want slaves, buy them from other nations or from the foreigners who live in your own country, and make them your property. You can own them, and even leave them to your children when you die, but do not make slaves of your own people or be cruel to them.

*   *   *

Faithfully obey my laws, and I will send rain to make your crops grow and your trees produce fruit. Your harvest of grain and grapes will be so abundant, that you won't know what to do with it all. You will eat and be satisfied, and you will live in safety. I will bless your country with peace, and you will rest without fear. I will wipe out the dangerous animals and protect you from enemy attacks. You will chase and destroy your enemies, even if there are only five of you and a hundred of them, or only a hundred of you and ten thousand of them. I will treat you with such kindness that your nation will grow strong, and I will also keep my promises to you. Your barns will overflow with grain each year. I will live among you and never again look on you with disgust. I will walk with you—I will be your God, and you will be my people. I am the LORD your God, and I rescued you from Egypt, so that you would never again be slaves. I have set you free; now walk with your heads held high.

If you disobey me and my laws, and if you break our agreement, I will punish you terribly, and you will be ruined. You will be struck with incurable diseases and with fever that leads to blindness and depression. Your enemies will eat the crops you plant, and I will turn from you and let you be destroyed by your attackers. You will even run at the very rumor of attack. Then, if you still refuse to obey me, I will punish you seven times for each of your sins, until your pride is completely crushed. I will hold back the rain, so the sky above

you will be like iron, and the ground beneath your feet will be like copper. All of your hard work will be for nothing—and there will be no harvest of grain or fruit.

If you keep rebelling against me, I'll punish you seven times worse, just as your sins deserve! I'll send wild animals to attack you, and they will gobble down your children and livestock. So few of you will be left that your roads will be deserted.

If you remain my enemies after this, I'll remain your enemy and punish you even worse. War will break out because you broke our agreement, and if you escape to your walled cities, I'll punish you with horrible diseases, and you will be captured by your enemies. You will have such a shortage of bread, that ten women will be able to bake their bread in the same oven. Each of you will get only a few crumbs, and you will go hungry.

Then if you don't stop rebelling, I'll really get furious and punish you terribly for your sins! In fact, you will be so desperate for food that you will eat your own children. I'll destroy your shrines and tear down your incense altars, leaving your dead bodies piled on top of your idols. And you will be disgusting to me. I'll wipe out your towns and your places of worship and will no longer be pleased with the smell of your sacrifices. Your land will become so desolate that even your enemies who settle there will be shocked when they see it. After I destroy your towns and ruin your land with war, I'll scatter you among the nations.

While you are prisoners in foreign lands, your own land will enjoy years of rest and refreshment, as it should have done each seventh year when you lived there. In the land of your enemies, you will tremble at the rustle of a leaf, as though it were a sword. And you will become so weak that you will stumble and fall over each other, even when no one is chasing you. Many of you will die in foreign lands, and others of you will waste away in sorrow as the result of your sins and the sins of your ancestors.

Then suppose you realize that I turned against you and brought you to the land of your enemies because both you and your ancestors had stubbornly sinned against me. If you humbly confess what you have done and start living right, I'll keep

the promise I made to your ancestors Abraham, Isaac, and Jacob. I will bless your land and let it rest during the time that you are in a foreign country, paying for your rebellion against me and my laws.

No matter what you have done, I am still the LORD your God, and I will never completely reject you or become absolutely disgusted with you there in the land of your enemies. While nations watched, I rescued your ancestors from Egypt so that I would be their God. Yes, I am your LORD, and I will never forget our agreement.

*　*　*

FROM **The Book of Deuteronomy**

Suppose a man starts hating his wife soon after they are married. He might tell ugly lies about her, and say, "I married this woman, but when we slept together, I found out she wasn't a virgin."

If this happens, the bride's father and mother must go to the town gate to show the town leaders the proof that the woman was a virgin. Her father will say, "I let my daughter marry this man, but he started hating her and accusing her of not being a virgin. But he is wrong, because here is proof that she was a virgin!" Then the bride's parents will show them the bed sheet from the woman's wedding night.

The town leaders will beat the man with a whip because he accused his bride of not being a virgin. He will have to pay her father one hundred pieces of silver and will never be allowed to divorce her.

But if the man was right and there is no proof that his bride was a virgin, the men of the town will take the woman to the door of her father's house and stone her to death.

This woman brought evil into your community by sleeping with someone before she got married, and you must get rid of that evil by killing her.

People of Israel, if a man is caught having sex with someone else's wife, you must put them both to death. That way, you will get rid of the evil they have done in Israel.

If a man is caught in town having sex with an engaged woman who isn't screaming for help, they both must be put to death. The man is guilty of having sex with a married woman. And the woman is guilty because she didn't call for help, even though she was inside a town and people were nearby. Take them both to the town gate and stone them to death. You must get rid of the evil they brought into your community. If an engaged woman is raped out in the country, only the man will be put to death. Do not punish the woman at all; she has done nothing wrong, and certainly nothing deserving death. This crime is like murder, because the woman was alone out in the country when the man attacked her. She screamed, but there was no one to help her.

Suppose a woman isn't engaged to be married, and a man talks her into sleeping with him. If they are caught, they will be forced to get married. He must give her father fifty pieces of silver as a bride-price and can never divorce her. A man must not marry a woman who was married to his father. This would be a disgrace to his father.

REVIEW QUESTIONS

1. According to the Torah, what is Yahweh's relationship to his chosen people?
2. How are these chosen people to set themselves apart from other peoples? How are they to relate to them?
3. As reflected in these laws, what are the principal values and modes of acceptable behavior in Hebrew society?
4. What kinds of principles of compensation do these laws reflect, and how do they compare with the principles of compensation reflected in the laws of Hammurabi (see Chapter 1)?
5. What kinds of attitudes toward sexual behavior do these laws reflect? How is that behavior regulated?
6. What status and rights do women possess in the context of these laws?
7. What does Yahweh promise in return for obedience to his laws? For disobedience to them?

FROM The Book of Isaiah: Prophecies

The Book of Isaiah contains the writings of at least two different authors, separated in time by about one hundred fifty years: a prophet named Isaiah, from Jerusalem, whose career spanned the latter half of the eighth century B.C.E., and an unknown prophet, referred to now as the Second Isaiah, whose writings are included here. The Second Isaiah's career was in Babylon and encompassed the later part of the exile there (587–539 B.C.E.) as well as the conquest of Babylon by the Persian King Cyrus the Great. In the Second Isaiah's writings, Yahweh has assumed a role much larger than that of the exclusive God of a chosen people.

From *Contemporary English Version* by American Bible Society (New York: American Bible Society, 1995).

*   *   *

People of Israel,
I have chosen you
as my servant.
I am your Creator.
You were in my care
even before you were born.
Israel, don't be terrified!
You are my chosen servant,
my very favorite. I will bless the thirsty land
by sending streams of water;
I will bless your descendants
by giving them my Spirit.
They will spring up like grass or like willow
   trees
near flowing streams.
They will worship me
and become my people.
They will write my name
on the back of their hands. I am the LORD
   All-Powerful,
the first and the last,
the one and only God.
Israel, I have rescued you!
I am your King.
Can anyone compare with me?
If so, let them speak up
and tell me now.
Let them say what has happened

since I made my nation
long ago,
and let them tell
what is going to happen. Don't tremble with fear!
Didn't I tell you long ago?
Didn't you hear me?
I alone am God—
no one else is a mighty rock.
Those people who make idols
are nothing themselves,
and the idols they treasure
are just as worthless.
Worshipers of idols are blind,
stupid, and foolish.
Why make an idol or an image
that can't do a thing?
Everyone who makes idols
and all who worship them
are mere humans,
who will end up
sadly disappointed.
Let them face me in court
and be terrified.

*   *   *

People of Israel,
you are my servant,
so remember all of this.
Israel, I created you,

and you are my servant.
I won't forget you. Turn back to me!
I have rescued you
and swept away your sins
as though they were clouds.

Tell the heavens and the earth
to start singing!
Tell the mountains
and every tree in the forest
to join in the song!
The LORD has rescued his people;
now they will worship him.

Israel, I am your LORD.
I am your source of life,
and I have rescued you.
I created everything
from the sky above
to the earth below.
I make liars of false prophets
and fools of fortunetellers.
I take human wisdom
and turn it into nonsense.
I will make the message
of my prophets come true.
They are saying, "Jerusalem
will be filled with people,
and the LORD will rebuild
the towns of Judah."
I am the one who commands
the sea and its streams
to run dry.
I am also the one who says,
"Cyrus will lead my people
and obey my orders.
Jerusalem and the temple
will be rebuilt."

The LORD said to Cyrus, his chosen one:
I have taken hold
of your right hand
to help you capture nations
and remove kings from power.
City gates will open for you;
not one will stay closed.
As I lead you,

I will level mountains and break the iron bars
on bronze gates of cities.
I will give you treasures
hidden in dark
and secret places.
Then you will know that I,
the LORD God of Israel,
have called you by name.
Cyrus, you don't even know me!
But I have called you by name
and highly honored you because of Israel,
my chosen servant.
Only I am the LORD!
There are no other gods.
I have made you strong,
though you don't know me.
Now everyone from east to west
will learn that I am the LORD.
No other gods are real.
I create light and darkness,
happiness and sorrow.
I, the LORD, do all of this.

*   *   *

The clay doesn't ask,
"Why did you make me this way?
Where are the handles?"
Children don't have the right
to demand of their parents,
"What have you done
to make us what we are?"
I am the LORD, the Creator,
the holy God of Israel.
Do you dare question me
about my own nation
or about what I have done?
I created the world
and covered it with people;
I stretched out the sky
and filled it with stars.
I have done the right thing
by placing Cyrus in power,
and I will make the roads easy
for him to follow.
I am the LORD All-Powerful!
Cyrus will rebuild my city

and set my people free
without being paid a thing.
I, the LORD, have spoken.

*   *   *

Anyone who makes idols
will be confused
and terribly disgraced.
But Israel, I, the LORD,
will always keep you safe
and free from shame.

The LORD alone is God!
He created the heavens
and made a world
where people can live,
instead of creating
an empty desert.
The LORD alone is God;
there are no others.
The LORD did not speak
in a dark secret place
or command Jacob's descendants
to search for him in vain.
The LORD speaks the truth,
and this is what he says
to every survivor
from every nation:
"Gather around me!
Learn how senseless it is
to worship wooden idols
or pray to helpless gods.
"Why don't you get together
and meet me in court?
Didn't I tell you long ago
what would happen?
I am the only God!
There are no others.
I bring about justice,
and have the power to save.
"I invite the whole world
to turn to me and be saved.
I alone am God!
No others are real.
I have made a solemn promise,
one that won't be broken:

Everyone will bow down
and worship me.
They will admit that I alone
can bring about justice.
Everyone who is angry with me
will be terribly ashamed
and will turn to me.
I, the LORD, will give
victory and great honor
to the people of Israel."

City of Babylon,
You are delicate
and untouched,
but that will change.
Surrender your royal power
and sit in the dirt.
Start grinding grain!
Take off your veil.
Strip off your fancy clothes
and cross over rivers. You will suffer the shame
of going naked,
because I will take revenge,
and no one can escape. I am the LORD
    All-Powerful,
the holy God of Israel.
I am their Savior.
Babylon, be silent!
Sit in the dark.
No longer will nations
accept you as their queen.
I was angry with my people.
So I let you take their land
and bring disgrace on them.
You showed them no mercy,
but were especially cruel
to those who were old.
You thought that you
would be queen forever.
You didn't care what you did;
it never entered your mind
that you might get caught.
You think that you alone
are all-powerful,
that you won't be a widow
or lose your children.

All you care about is pleasure,
but listen to what I say.
Your magic powers and charms
will suddenly fail,
then you will be a widow
and lose your children.
You hid behind evil
like a shield and said,
"No one can see me!"
You were fooled by your wisdom
and your knowledge;
you felt sure that you alone
were in full control.
But without warning,
disaster will strike—
and your magic charms
won't help at all.
Keep using your magic powers
and your charms
as you have always done.
Maybe—just maybe—
you will frighten somebody!
You have worn yourself out,
asking for advice
from those who study the stars
and tell the future
month after month.
Go ask them how to be saved
from what will happen.
People who trust the stars
are as helpless
as straw
in a flaming fire.
No one can even keep warm, sitting by a fire
that feeds only on straw.
These are the fortunetellers
you have done business with
all of your life.
But they don't know
where they are going,
and they can't save you.

People of Israel,
you come from Jacob's family
and the tribe of Judah. You claim to worship me,
the LORD God of Israel,

but you are lying.
You call Jerusalem your home
and say you depend on me,
the LORD All-Powerful,
the God of Israel.
Long ago I announced
what was going to be,
then without warning,
I made it happen.
I knew you were stubborn
and hardheaded.
And I told you these things,
so that when they happened
you would not say,
"The idols we worship did this."
You heard what I said,
and you have seen it happen.
Now admit that it's true!
I will show you secrets
you have never known.

*   *   *

By the power of his Spirit
the LORD God has sent me
with this message:
People of Israel,
I am the holy LORD God,
the one who rescues you.
For your own good,
I teach you,
and I lead you
along the right path.
How I wish that you
had obeyed my commands!
Your success and good fortune
would then have overflowed
like a flooding river.
Your nation would be blessed
with more people
than there are grains of sand
along the seashore.
And I would never have let
your country be destroyed.
Now leave Babylon!
Celebrate as you go.
Be happy and shout

for everyone to hear,
"The LORD has rescued
his servant Israel!
He led us through the desert
and made water flow from a rock
to satisfy our thirst.
But the LORD has promised
that none who are evil
will live in peace."
Everyone, listen,
even you foreign nations
across the sea.
The LORD chose me
and gave me a name
before I was born.
He made my words pierce
like a sharp sword
or a pointed arrow;
he kept me safely hidden
in the palm of his hand.
The LORD said to me,
"Israel, you are my servant;
and because of you
I will be highly honored."
I said to myself,
"I'm completely worn out;
my time has been wasted.
But I did it for the LORD God,
and he will reward me."
Even before I was born,
the LORD God chose me
to serve him and to lead back
the people of Israel.
So the LORD has honored me
and made me strong.
Now the LORD says to me,
"It isn't enough for you
to be merely my servant.
You must do more than lead back
survivors
from the tribes
of Israel.
I have placed you here as a light
for other nations;
you must take my saving power
to everyone on earth."

Israel, I am the holy LORD God,
the one who rescues you.
You are slaves of rulers
and of a nation
who despises you. Now this is what I
     promise:
Kings and rulers will honor you
by kneeling at your feet.
You can trust me! I am your LORD,
the holy God of Israel,
and you are my chosen ones.

This is what the LORD says:
I will answer your prayers
because I have set a time
when I will help
by coming to save you.
I have chosen you
to take my promise of hope
to other nations. You will rebuild the country
from its ruins,
then people will come
and settle there.
You will set prisoners free
from dark dungeons
to see the light of day.
On their way home,
they will find plenty to eat,
even on barren hills.
They won't go hungry
or get thirsty;
they won't be bothered
by the scorching sun
or hot desert winds.
I will be merciful
while leading them along
to streams of water.
I will level the mountains
and make roads.
Then my people will return
from distant lands
in the north and the west
and from the city of Syene.

Tell the heavens and the earth
to celebrate and sing;

command every mountain
to join in the song.
The LORD's people have suffered,
but he has shown mercy
and given them comfort.
The people of Zion said,
"The LORD has turned away
and forgotten us."
The LORD answered,
"Could a mother forget a child
who nurses at her breast?
Could she fail to love an infant
who came from her own body?
Even if a mother could forget,
I will never forget you.
A picture of your city
is drawn on my hand.
You are always in my thoughts!
Your city will be built faster
than it was destroyed—those who attacked it
will retreat and leave.
Look around! You will see
your people coming home.
As surely as I live,
I, the LORD, promise
that your city with its people
will be as lovely as a bride
wearing her jewelry."

Jerusalem is now in ruins!
Nothing is left of the city.
But it will be rebuilt
and soon overcrowded;
its cruel enemies
will be gone far away.
Jerusalem is a woman
whose children were born
while she was in deep sorrow over the loss of her
    husband.
Now those children
will come and seek room
in the crowded city,
and Jerusalem will ask,
"Am I really their mother?
How could I have given birth
when I was still mourning

in a foreign land?
Who raised these children?
Where have they come from?"
The LORD God says:
"I will soon give a signal
for the nations
to return your sons
and your daughters
to the arms of Jerusalem.
The kings and queens
of those nations
where they were raised
will come and bow down.
They will take care of you
just like a slave
taking care of a child.
Then you will know
that I am the LORD.
You won't be disappointed
if you trust me."

Has anyone believed us
or seen the mighty power
of the LORD in action?
Like a young plant or a root
that sprouts in dry ground,
the servant grew up
obeying the LORD.
He wasn't some handsome king.
Nothing about the way he looked
made him attractive to us.
He was hated and rejected;
his life was filled with sorrow
and terrible suffering.
No one wanted to look at him.
We despised him and said,
"He is a nobody!"
He suffered and endured
great pain for us,
but we thought his suffering
was punishment from God.
He was wounded and crushed
because of our sins;
by taking our punishment,
he made us completely well.
All of us were like sheep

that had wandered off.
We had each gone our own way,
but the LORD gave him
the punishment we deserved.
He was painfully abused,
but he did not complain.
He was silent like a lamb
being led to the butcher,
as quiet as a sheep
having its wool cut off.
He was condemned to death
without a fair trial.
Who could have imagined
what would happen to him?
His life was taken away
because of the sinful things
my people had done. He wasn't dishonest
   or violent,
but he was buried in a tomb
of cruel and rich people. The LORD decided
   his servant
would suffer as a sacrifice
to take away the sin
and guilt of others.
Now the servant will live
to see his own descendants. He did everything

the LORD had planned.
By suffering, the servant
will learn the true meaning
of obeying the LORD.
Although he is innocent,
he will take the punishment
for the sins of others,
so that many of them
will no longer be guilty.
The LORD will reward him
with honor and power
for sacrificing his life.
Others thought he was a sinner,
but he suffered for our sins
and asked God to forgive us.

REVIEW QUESTIONS

1. According to the Second Isaiah, what now is the dominion of the Hebrews' God?
2. What role has Israel now assumed in relation to the other nations of the earth?
3. Does a messiah figure emerge in this document?
4. What is God's judgment of Babylon?

3 ❧ THE CIVILIZATION OF GREECE, 1000–400 B.C.E.

By the time that the uncharacteristically allied city-states of Hellas (Greece) had to face invasion by the massive forces of the Achaemenid Persian emperor Darius in 490 B.C.E., the much more ancient civilizations of Mesopotamia and Egypt (not to mention India and China) had been thriving for thousands of years. By 500 B.C.E., both Babylon and Egypt—in fact, the entire Near East— had fallen under the sway of the Persian Empire, which could boast of one of the more sophisticated imperial systems of antiquity and resources vastly superior to those of the upstarts from the Aegean, located on the empire's far western periphery. The Greeks themselves, from the Persian perspective, undoubtedly seemed to be a disorganized, belligerent, even barbarian people who were no real threat to continued Persian dominion.

Nonetheless, only eleven years after the Persians' first invasion, the Greeks had vanquished and expelled not only the invasion of Darius but also a second, even more massive invasion under the son and successor of Darius, Xerxes. The Greeks' improbable success came to be seen as one of the first events in the process by which the West, over many centuries, defined itself as an entity distinct from and, in its own eyes, generally superior to the East.

Scholars today recognize (as did ancient Greek writers) the tremendous debt the early Greeks owed to the older civilizations of the ancient Near East and Egypt. Indeed, to be aware of that debt, we need look no further than early Greek statuary and temple architecture, with their obviously Egyptian inspiration, or the Greek alphabet, borrowed from the Phoenicians, with whom the Greeks traded. However, within the unique context of early Greek society, political development, and culture, a number of concepts and issues emerged that have remained at the heart of the ongoing development of Western civilization and have had significant impact on the non-Western civilizations that, in the past two centuries, have increasingly been confronted with the ideas and values of the West. What are the appropriate roles and rights of the individual in society? To what

does the individual owe primary allegiance, the dictates of conscience or the laws of the state? How should a state be properly organized and governed, and by whom? What ought to be the respective roles of men and women in society? Do divine forces govern natural phenomena and human history? Indeed, do gods or a god even exist? Some have claimed that much of the history of Western culture subsequent to the era of the Greek city-states has centered on the continuing endeavor to answer these and other questions that the Greeks raised.

The Greeks took some giant steps in addressing these questions. In fact, they made perhaps their most significant contributions to that endeavor during the relatively brief "golden age" that accompanied Athens' rise to preeminence among the city-states after the defeat of the Persians. Classical Greek civilization achieved its loftiest heights in Athens during the decades prior to Athens' disastrous defeat by Sparta and its allies at the end of the Peloponnesian War. Less than seventy years later, Athens, Sparta, and the other previously independent city-states were compelled to cede their autonomy to the hegemony of the Macedonian king Philip II, whose son Alexander would inaugurate a new era during which the affairs of those city-states would take a backseat to the Hellenistic kingdoms. Nonetheless, the relatively brief zenith of the classical Greek city-states would, in time, be recognized as vastly out of proportion to their influence on the later course of Western civilization.

HOMER

FROM *The Odyssey*

The actual existence of the poet named Homer, and of the Trojan War about which he wrote, is still debated among scholars. The influence of the epic poems, the Iliad *and the* Odyssey, *that the later Greeks attributed to him is not. For the warrior aristocracy whose interests and tastes these poems reflected and for whom they were recited as entertainment, Homer's tales of the Greeks' siege of Troy and of the exploits of Odysseus and his men on their way home after that siege provided a vivid model of heroic values and behavior in a world where the gods intruded their designs regularly into human affairs. In the following selection from the* Odyssey, *the main hero, Odysseus, on his long and dangerous journey back to Ithaca on the Greek mainland after the Greeks have sacked Troy, has reached the land of Phaeacia. Its king, Alcinous, is determined to act as his worthy host.*

From *The Odyssey of Homer,* translated by Samuel Butler (London: Longmans, Green, & Co., 1900).

Now when the child of morning, rosy-fingered Dawn, appeared, Alcinous and Odysseus both rose, and Alcinous led the way to the Phaeacian place of assembly, which was near the ships. When they got there they sat down side by side on a seat of polished stone, while Athene took the form of one of Alcinous' servants, and went round the town in order to help Odysseus to get home. She went up to the citizens, man by man, and said: "Aldermen and town councilors of the Phaeacians, come to the assembly all of you and listen to the stranger who has just come off a long voyage to the house of King Alcinous. He looks like an immortal god."

With these words she made them all want to come, and they flocked to the assembly till seats and standing room were alike crowded. Everyone was struck with the appearance of Odysseus, for Athene had beautified him about the head and shoulders, making him look taller and stouter than he really was, that he might impress the Phaeacians favorably as being a very remarkable man, and might come off well in the many trials of skill to which they would challenge him. Then, when they were got together, Alcinous spoke:

"Hear me," said he, "aldermen and town councilors of the Phaeacians, that I may speak even as I am minded. This stranger, whoever he may be, has found his way to my house from somewhere or other either east or west. He wants an escort and wishes to have the matter settled. Let us then get one ready for him, as we have done for others before him. Indeed, no one who ever yet came to my house has been able to complain of me for not speeding him on his way soon enough. Let us draw a ship into the sea—one that has never yet made a voyage—and man her with two and fifty of our smartest young sailors. Then when you have made fast your oars each by his own seat, leave the ship and come to my house to prepare a feast. I will supply you with everything. I am giving these instructions to the young men who will form the crew. As regards you aldermen and town councilors, you will join me in entertaining our guest in the cloisters. I can take no excuses, and we will have Demodocus to sing to us; for there is no bard like him, whatever he may choose to sing about."

Alcinous then led the way, and the others followed after, while a servant went to fetch Demodocus. The fifty-two picked oarsmen went to the seashore as they had been told, and when they got there they drew the ship into the water, got her mast and sails inside her, bound the oars to the thole-pins with twisted thongs of leather, all in due course, and spread the white sails aloft. They moored the vessel a little way out from land, and then came on shore and went to the house of King Alcinous. The outhouses, yards, and all the precincts were filled with crowds of men in great multitudes both old and young; and Alcinous killed them a dozen sheep, eight full-grown pigs, and two oxen. These they skinned and dressed so as to provide a magnificent banquet.

A servant presently led in the famous bard Demodocus, whom the muse had dearly loved, but to whom she had given both good and evil, for though she had endowed him with a divine gift of song, she had robbed him of his eyesight. Pontonous set a seat for him among the guests, leaning it up against a bearing-post. He hung the lyre for him on a peg over his head, and showed him where he was to feel for it with his hands. He also set a fair table with a basket of victuals by his side, and a cup of wine from which he might drink whenever he was so disposed.

The company then laid their hands upon the good things that were before them, but as soon as they had had enough to eat and drink, the muse inspired Demodocus to sing the feats of heroes, and more especially a matter that was then in the mouths of all men, to wit, the quarrel between Odysseus and Achilles, and the fierce words that they heaped on one another as they sat together at a banquet. But Agamemnon was glad when he heard his chieftains quarreling with one another, for Apollo had foretold him this at Pytho when he crossed the stone floor to consult the oracle. Here was the beginning of the evil that by the will of Zeus fell both upon Danaans and Trojans.

Thus sang the bard, but Odysseus drew his purple mantle over his head and covered his face, for he was ashamed to let the Phaeacians see that he was weeping. When the bard left off singing, he wiped the tears from his eyes, uncovered his face,

and, taking his cup, made a drink offering to the gods; but when the Phaeacians pressed Demodocus to sing further, for they delighted in his lays, then Odysseus again drew his mantle over his head and wept bitterly. No one noticed his distress except Alcinous, who was sitting near him, and heard the heavy sighs that he was heaving. So he at once said, "Aldermen and town councilors of the Phaeacians, we have had enough now, both of the feast and of the minstrelsy that is its due accompaniment. Let us proceed therefore to the athletic sports so that our guest on his return home may be able to tell his friends how much we surpass all other nations as boxers, wrestlers, jumpers, and runners."

With these words he led the way, and the others followed after. A servant hung Demodocus' lyre on its peg for him, led him out of the cloister, and set him on the same way as that along which all the chief men of the Phaeacians were going to see the sports; a crowd of several thousands of people followed them, and there were many excellent competitors for all the prizes. Acroneos, Ocyalus, Elatreus, Nauteus, Prymneus, Anchialus, Eretmeus, Ponteus, Proreus, Thoon, Anabesineus, and Amphialus son of Polyneus son of Tecton. There was also Euryalus son of Naubolus, who was like Ares himself, and was the best looking man among the Phaeacians except Laodamas. Three sons of Alcinous—Laodamas, Halios, and Clytoneus—competed also.

The foot races came first. The course was set out for them from the starting post, and they raised a dust upon the plain as they all flew forward at the same moment. Clytoneus came in first by a long way; he left everyone else behind him by the length of the furrow that a couple of mules can plow in a fallow field. They then turned to the painful art of wrestling, and here Euryalus proved to be the best man. Amphialus excelled all the others in jumping, while at throwing the disc there was no one who could approach Elatreus. Alcinous' son Laodamas was the best boxer, and he it was who presently said, when they had all been diverted with the games, "Let us ask the stranger whether he excels in any of these sports. He seems very powerfully built; his thighs, calves, hands, and neck are of prodigious strength, nor is he at all old,

but he has suffered much lately, and there is nothing like the sea for making havoc with a man, no matter how strong he is."

"You are quite right, Laodamas," replied Euryalus, "go up to your guest and speak to him about it yourself."

When Laodamas heard this he made his way into the middle of the crowd and said to Odysseus, "I hope, sir, that you will enter yourself for some one or other of our competitions if you are skilled in any of them—and you must have gone in for many a one before now. There is nothing that does anyone so much credit all his life long as the showing himself a proper man with his hands and feet. Have a try therefore at something, and banish all sorrow from your mind. Your return home will not be long delayed, for the ship is already drawn into the water, and the crew is found."

Odysseus answered, "Laodamas, why do you taunt me in this way? My mind is set rather on cares than contests; I have been through infinite trouble, and am come among you now as a suppliant, praying your king and people to further me on my return home."

Then Euryalus reviled him outright and said: "I gather, then, that you are unskilled in any of the many sports that men generally delight in. I suppose you are one of those grasping traders that go about in ships as captains or merchants, and who think of nothing but of their outward freights and homeward cargoes. There does not seem to be much of the athlete about you."

"For shame, sir!" answered Odysseus, fiercely. "You are an insolent fellow—so true is it that the gods do not grace all men alike in speech, person, and understanding. One man may be of weak presence, but heaven has adorned him with such a good conversation that he charms everyone who sees him; his honeyed moderation carries his hearers with him so that he is leader in all assemblies of his fellows, and wherever he goes he is looked up to. Another may be as handsome as a god, but his good looks are not crowned with discretion. This is your case. No god could make a finer looking fellow than you are, but you are a fool. Your ill-judged remarks have made me exceedingly angry, and you are quite mistaken, for I excel in a

great many athletic exercises. Indeed, so long as I had youth and strength, I was among the first athletes of the age. Now, however, I am worn out by labor and sorrow, for I have gone through much both on the field of battle and by the waves of the weary sea. Still, in spite of all this I will compete, for your taunts have stung me to the quick."

So he hurried up without even taking his cloak off, and seized a disc, larger, more massive and much heavier than those used by the Phaeacians when disc-throwing among themselves. Then, swinging it back, he threw it from his brawny hand, and it made a humming sound in the air as he did so. The Phaeacians quailed beneath the rushing of its flight as it sped gracefully from his hand, and flew beyond any mark that had been made yet. Athene, in the form of a man, came and marked the place where it had fallen. "A blind man, sir," said she, "could easily tell your mark by groping for it—it is so far ahead of any other. You may make your mind easy about this contest, for no Phaeacian can come near to such a throw as yours."

Odysseus was glad when he found he had a friend among the lookers-on, so he began to speak more pleasantly. "Young men," said he, "come up to that throw if you can, and I will throw another disc as heavy or even heavier. If anyone wants to have a bout with me let him come on, for I am exceedingly angry. I will box, wrestle, or run, I do not care what it is, with any man of you all except Laodamas, but not with him because I am his guest, and one cannot compete with one's own personal friend. At least I do not think it a prudent or a sensible thing for a guest to challenge his host's family at any game, especially when he is in a foreign country. He will cut the ground from under his own feet if he does. But I make no exception as regards anyone else, for I want to have the matter out and know which is the best man.

"I am a good hand at every kind of athletic sport known among mankind. I am an excellent archer. In battle I am always the first to bring a man down with my arrow, no matter how many more are taking aim at him alongside of me. Philoctetes was the only man who could shoot better than I could when we Achaeans were before Troy and in practice. I far excel everyone else in the whole world, of those who still eat bread upon the face of the earth, but I should not like to shoot against the mighty dead, such as Heracles, or Eurytus the Oechalian—men who could shoot against the gods themselves. This in fact was how Eurytus came prematurely by his end, for Apollo was angry with him and killed him because he challenged him as an archer. I can throw a dart farther than anyone else can shoot an arrow. Running is the only point in respect of which I am afraid some of the Phaeacians might beat me, for I have been brought down very low at sea; my provisions ran short, and therefore I am still weak."

They all held their peace except King Alcinous, who began: "Sir, we have had much pleasure in hearing all that you have told us, from which I understand that you are willing to show your prowess, as having been displeased with some insolent remarks that have been made to you by one of our athletes, and which could never have been uttered by anyone who knows how to talk with propriety. I hope you will apprehend my meaning, and will explain to anyone of your chief men who may be dining with yourself and your family when you get home, that we have an hereditary aptitude for accomplishments of all kinds. We are not particularly remarkable for our boxing, nor yet as wrestlers, but we are singularly fleet of foot and are excellent sailors. We are extremely fond of good dinners, music, and dancing; we also like frequent changes of linen, warm baths, and good beds. So now, please, some of you who are the best dancers set about dancing, that our guest on his return home may be able to tell his friends how much we surpass all other nations as sailors, runners, dancers, and minstrels. Demodocus has left his lyre at my house, so run some one or other of you and fetch it for him."

*   *   *

REVIEW QUESTIONS

1. What does this selection reveal about the Greek ideal of masculine behavior?
2. What does it reveal about attitudes concerning hospitality?

HESIOD

FROM *Works and Days*

The partly autobiographical Works and Days *of Hesiod (c. 700 B.C.E.) reflects a world quite different from that of Homer's heroes. Indeed, in one part of this work Hesiod describes five ages of mankind that begin with a golden age of men who "lived like gods" but that decline thereafter, culminating in an age of bronze that coincides with the Homeric heroes ("a god-like race of hero-men") and then his own age, that of a race of iron, oppressed by hard labor and sorrow. As the following readings suggest, humankind's lot and the values of the time are in many ways quite different from those of Homer's world.*

*   *   *

FROM "On Work and Wealth"*

To you, foolish Perses, I will speak good sense. Badness can be got easily and in shoals: the road to her is smooth, and she lives very near us. But between us and Goodness the gods have placed the sweat of our brows: long and steep is the path that leads to her, and it is rough at the first; but when a man has reached the top, then indeed she is easy, though before that she was hard.

That man is altogether best who considers all things himself and marks what will be better afterwards and at the end; and he, again, is good who listens to a good adviser; but whoever neither thinks for himself nor keeps in mind what another man tells him, he is an unprofitable man. But do you at any rate, always remembering my charge, work, well-born Perses, that Hunger may hate you, and venerable Demeter richly crowned may love you and fill your barn with food; for Hunger is altogether a meet comrade for the sluggard. Both gods and men are angry with a man who lives idle,

for in nature he is like the stingless drones who waste the labor of the bees, eating without working; but let it be your care to order your work properly, that in the right season your barns may be full of victual. Through work men grow rich in flocks and substance, and working they are much better loved by the immortals. Work is no disgrace: it is idleness which is a disgrace. But if you work, the idle will soon envy you as you grow rich, for fame and renown attend on wealth. And whatever be your lot, work is best for you, if you turn your misguided mind away from other men's property to your work and attend to your livelihood as I bid you. An evil shame is the needy man's companion, shame which both greatly harms and prospers men: shame is with poverty, but confidence with wealth.

Wealth should not be seized: god-given wealth is much better; for if a man take great wealth violently and perforce, or if he steal it through his tongue, as often happens when gain deceives men's sense and dishonor tramples down honor, the gods soon blot him out and make that man's house low, and wealth attends him only for a little time. Alike with him who does wrong to a suppliant or a guest, or who goes up to his brother's bed and commits unnatural sin in lying with his wife, or who infatuately offends against fatherless children, or who abuses his old father at the cheerless threshold of

---

*From *Works and Days*, translated by Hugh G. Evelyn-White in *Homeric Hymns and Homerica* (Cambridge, Mass.: Harvard University Press, 1936), pp. 361–62.

old age and attacks him with harsh words, truly Zeus himself is angry, and at the last lays on him a heavy requital for his evil-doing. But do you turn your foolish heart altogether away from these things, and, as far as you are able, sacrifice to the deathless gods purely and cleanly, and burn rich meats also, and at other times propitiate them with libations and incense, both when you go to bed and when the holy light has come back, that they may be gracious to you in heart and spirit, and so you may buy another's holding and not another yours.

. . . He who adds to what he has, will keep off bright-eyed hunger; for if you add only a little to a little and do this often, soon that little will become great. What a man has by him at home does not trouble him: it is better to have your stuff at home, for whatever is abroad may mean loss. It is a good thing to draw on what you have; but it grieves your heart to need something and not to have it, and I bid you mark this. Take your fill when the cask is first opened and when it is nearly spent, but midways be sparing: it is poor saving when you come to the lees.

Let the wage promised to a friend be fixed; even with your brother smile—and get a witness; for trust and mistrust, alike ruin men.

Do not let a flaunting woman coax and cozen and deceive you: she is after your barn. The man who trusts womankind trusts deceivers.

There should be an only son, to feed his father's house, for so wealth will increase in the home; but if you leave a second son you should die old. Yet Zeus can easily give great wealth to a greater number. More hands mean more work and more increase.

If your heart within you desires wealth, do these things and work with work upon work.

*　　*　　*

"Pandora"*

For the gods have hidden and keep hidden what
   could be men's livelihood.
It could have been that easily in one day you
   could work out

enough to keep you for a year, with no more
   working.
Soon you could have hung up your steering oar
   in the smoke of the fireplace,
and the work the oxen and patient mules do
   would be abolished,
but Zeus in the anger of his heart hid it away
because the devious-minded Prometheus had
   cheated him;
and therefore Zeus thought up dismal sorrows
   for mankind.
He hid fire; but Prometheus, the powerful son of
   Iapetos,
stole it again from Zeus of the counsels, to give
   to mortals.
He hid it out of the sight of Zeus who delights
   in thunder
in the hollow fennel stalk. In anger the cloud-
   gatherer spoke to him:
"Son of Iapetos, deviser of crafts beyond all others,
you are happy that you stole the fire, and
   outwitted my thinking;
but it will be a great sorrow to you, and to men
   who come after.
As the price of fire I will give them an evil, and
   all men shall fondle
this, their evil, close to their hearts, and take
   delight in it."
  So spoke the father of gods and mortals; and
   laughed out loud.
He told glorious Hephaistos to make haste, and
   plaster
earth with water, and to infuse it with a human voice
and vigor, and make the face like the immortal
   goddesses,
the bewitching features of a young girl;
   meanwhile Athene
was to teach her her skills, and how to do the
   intricate weaving,
while Aphrodite was to mist her head in golden
   endearment
and the cruelty of desire and longings that wear
   out the body,

---

*From *Works and Days,* translated by Richard Lattimore (Ann Arbor: University of Michigan Press, 1959).

but to Hermes, the guide, the slayer of Argos, he
gave instructions
to put in her the mind of a hussy, and a
treacherous nature.
　　So Zeus spoke. And all obeyed Lord Zeus, the
son of Kronos.
The renowned strong smith modeled her figure
of earth, in the likeness
of a decorous young girl, as the son of Kronos
had wished it.
The goddess gray-eyed Athene dressed and
arrayed her; the Graces,
who are goddesses, and hallowed Persuasion put
necklaces
of gold upon her body, while the Seasons, with
glorious tresses,
put upon her head a coronal of spring flowers,
and Pallas Athene put all decor upon her body.
But into her heart Hermes, the guide, the slayer
of Argos,
put lies, and wheedling words of falsehood, and
a treacherous nature,
made her as Zeus of the deep thunder wished,
and he, the gods' herald,
put a voice inside her, and gave her the name of
woman,
Pandora, because all the gods who have their
homes on Olympos
had given her each a gift, to be a sorrow to men
who eat bread. Now when he had done with this
sheer, impossible
deception, the Father sent the gods' fleet
messenger, Hermes,
to Epimetheus, bringing her, a gift, nor did
Epimetheus
remember to think how Prometheus had told
him never
to accept a gift from Olympian Zeus, but always
to send it
back, for fear it might prove to be an evil for mankind.
He took the evil, and only perceived it when he
possessed her.
Since before this time the races of men had been
living on earth

free from all evils, free from laborious work, and
free from
all wearing sicknesses that bring their fates down
on men
(for men grow old suddenly in the midst of
misfortune;)
but the woman, with her hands lifting away the
lid from the great jar,
scattered its contents, and her design was sad
troubles for mankind.
Hope was the only spirit that stayed there in the
unbreakable
closure of the jar, under its rim, and could not
fly forth
abroad, for the lid of the great jar closed down
first and contained her;
this was by the will of cloud-gathering Zeus of
the aegis;
but there are other troubles by thousands that
hover about men,
for the earth is full of evil things, and the sea is
full of them;
there are sicknesses that come to men by day,
while in the night
moving of themselves they haunt us, bringing
sorrow to mortals,
and silently, for Zeus of the counsels took the
voice out of them.

So there is no way to avoid what Zeus has
intended.

REVIEW QUESTIONS

1. What kind of society does Hesiod's writing reflect?
2. How might one succeed in it?
3. According to Hesiod, what is the underlying
cause of man's misery, and what is the relationship of women to it?

Spartan Society and Values

Among all the Greek city-states, Sparta (also referred to by some authors as Lacedae-mon) was distinguished by the military ethic that governed virtually every aspect of its society. The life of the Spartan citizen was geared toward maintaining a constant state of military preparedness. For this achievement, no sacrifice was too great, as was heroically demonstrated by the Spartans who defended the pass at Thermopylae against the Persians in 480 B.C.E. The following selections shed light on the values and organization of Spartan society. The first, "The Spartan Creed," is the work of the Spartan poet Tyrtaeus, whose poetry continued to inspire Spartan warriors long after his death. The second selection is a description of Spartan laws and customs by Xenophon, an Athenian follower of the philosopher Socrates. Xenophon is known best for his work the Anabasis, *which describes the retreat, which he led, of a mercenary army stranded in Persian territory circa 400 B.C.E.*

Tyrtaeus: "The Spartan Creed"*

I would not say anything for a man nor take
    account of him
for any speed of his feet or wrestling skill he
    might have,
not if he had the size of a Cyclops and strength
    to go with it,
not if he could outrun Bóreas, the North Wind
    of Thrace,
not if he were more handsome and gracefully
    formed than Tithónos,
or had more riches than Midas had, or Kínyras
    too,
not if he were more of a king than Tantalid
    Pelops,
or had the power of speech and persuasion
    Adrastos had,
not if he had all splendors except for a fighting
    spirit.
For no man ever proves himself a good man in
    war
unless he can endure to face the blood and the
    slaughter,

go close against the enemy and fight with his
    hands.
Here is courage, mankind's finest possession,
    here is
the noblest prize that a young man can endeavor
    to win,
and it is a good thing his city and all the people
    share with him
when a man plants his feet and stands in the
    foremost spears
relentlessly, all thought of foul flight completely
    forgotten,
and has well trained his heart to be steadfast and
    to endure,
and with words encourages the man who is
    stationed beside him.
Here is a man who proves himself to be valiant
    in war.
With a sudden rush he turns to flight the rugged
    battalions
of the enemy, and sustains the beating waves of
    assault.
And he who so falls among the champions and
    loses his sweet life,
so blessing with honor his city, his father, and
    all his people,
with wounds in his chest, where the spear that
    he was facing has transfixed

---

*From *Greek Lyrics*, translated by Richmond Lattimore (Chicago: University of Chicago Press, 1960).

that massive guard of his shield, and gone
    through his breastplate as well,
why, such a man is lamented alike by the young
    and the elders,
and all his city goes into mourning and grieves
    for his loss.

His tomb is pointed to with pride, and so are
    his children,
and his children's children, and afterward all the
    race that is his.
His shining glory is never forgotten, his name is
    remembered,
and he becomes an immortal, though he lies
    under the ground,
when one who was a brave man has been killed
    by the furious War God
standing his ground and fighting hard for his
    children and land.
But if he escapes the doom of death, the
    destroyer of bodies,
and wins his battle, and bright renown for the
    work of his spear,
all men give place to him alike, the youth and
    the elders,
and much joy comes his way before he goes
    down to the dead.
Aging, he has reputation among his citizens. No
    one
tries to interfere with his honors or all he deserves;
all men withdraw before his presence, and yield
    their seats to him,
the youth, and the men his age, and even those
    older than he.
Thus a man should endeavor to reach this high
    place of courage
with all his heart, and, so trying, never be
    backward in war.

Xenophon: FROM "The Laws and Customs of the Spartans"*

*   *   *

But reflecting once how Sparta, one of the least populous of states, had proved the most powerful and celebrated city in Greece, I wondered by what means this result had been produced. When I proceeded, however, to contemplate the institutions of the Spartans, I wondered no longer.

Lycurgus, who made the laws for them, by obedience to which they have flourished, I not only admire, but consider to have been in the fullest sense a wise man; for he rendered his country preëminent in prosperity, not by imitating other states, but by making ordinances contrary to those of most governments.

With regard, for example, to the procreation of children, that I may begin from the beginning, other people feed their young women, who are about to produce offspring, and who are of the class regarded as well brought up, on the most moderate quantity of vegetable food possible, and on the least possible quantity of meat, while they either keep them from wine altogether, or allow them to use it only when mixed with water; and as the greater number of the men engaged in trades are sedentary, so the rest of the Greeks think it proper that their young women should sit quiet and spin wool. But how can we expect that women thus treated should produce a vigorous progeny? Lycurgus, on the contrary, thought that female slaves were competent to furnish clothes; and, considering that the production of children was the noblest duty of the free, he enacted, in the first place, that the female should practice bodily exercises no less than the male sex; and he thus appointed for the women contests with one another, just as for the men, expecting that when both parents were rendered strong a stronger offspring would be born from them.

---

*From *Xenophon's Minor Works,* translated by J. S. Watson (Bell: Bohn Classical Library, 1878).

Observing, too, that the men of other nations, when women were united to husbands, associated with their wives during the early part of their intercourse without restraint, he made enactments quite at variance with this practice; for he ordained that a man should think it shame to be seen going in to his wife, or coming out from her. When married people meet in this way, they must feel stronger desire for the company of one another, and whatever offspring is produced must thus be rendered far more robust than if the parents were satiated with each other's society.

In addition to these regulations, he also took from the men the liberty of marrying when each of them pleased, and appointed that they should contract marriages only when they were in full bodily vigour, deeming this injunction also conducive to the production of an excellent offspring. Seeing also that if old men chanced to have young wives, they watched their wives with the utmost strictness, he made a law quite opposed to this feeling; for he appointed that an old man should introduce to his wife whatever man in the prime of life he admired for his corporeal and mental qualities, in order that she might have children by him. If, again, a man was unwilling to associate with his wife, and yet was desirous of having proper children, he made a provision also with respect to him, that whatever women he saw likely to have offspring, and of good disposition, he might, on obtaining the consent of her husband, have children by her. Many similar permissions he gave; for the women are willing to have two families, and the men to receive brothers to their children, who are equal to them in birth and standing, but have no claim to share in their property.

Let him who wishes, then, consider whether Lycurgus, in thus making enactments different from those of other legislators, in regard to the procreation of children, secured for Sparta a race of men eminent for size and strength.

Having given this account of the procreation of children, I wish also to detail the education of those of both sexes. Of the other Greeks, those who say that they bring up their sons best set slaves over them to take charge of them, as soon as the children can understand what is said to them, and send them, at the same time, to schoolmasters, to learn letters, and music, and the exercises of the palaestra. They also render their children's feet delicate by the use of sandals, and weaken their bodies by changes of clothes; and as to food, they regard their appetite as the measure of what they are to take. But Lycurgus, instead of allowing each citizen to set slaves as guardians over his children, appointed a man to have the care of them all, one of those from whom the chief magistrates are chosen; and he is called the paedonomus. He invested this man with full authority to assemble the boys, and, if he found that any one was negligent of his duties, to punish him severely. He assigned him also some of the grown-up boys as whip-carriers, that they might inflict whatever chastisement was necessary; so that great dread of disgrace, and great willingness to obey, prevailed among them.

Instead, also, of making their feet soft with sandals, he enacted that they should harden them by going without sandals; thinking that, if they exercised themselves in this state, they would go up steep places with far greater ease, and descend declivities with greater safety; and that they would also leap, and skip, and run faster unshod, if they had their feet inured to doing so, than shod. Instead of being rendered effeminate, too, by a variety of dresses, he made it a practice that they should accustom themselves to one dress throughout the year; thinking that they would thus be better prepared to endure cold and heat.

As to food, he ordained that they should exhort the boys to take only such a quantity as never to be oppressed with overeating, and not to be strangers to living somewhat frugally; supposing that, being thus brought up, they would be the better able, if they should be required, to support toil under a scarcity of supplies, would be the more likely to persevere in exertion, should it be imposed on them, on the same quantity of provisions, and would be less desirous of sauces, more easily satisfied with any kind of food, and pass

their lives in greater health. He also considered that the fare which rendered the body slender would be more conducive to increasing its stature than that which expanded it with nutriment. Yet that the boys might not suffer too much from hunger, Lycurgus, though he did not allow them to take what they wanted without trouble, gave them liberty to steal certain things to relieve the cravings of nature; and he made it honourable to steal as many cheeses as possible. That he did not give them leave to form schemes for getting food because he was at a loss what to allot them, I suppose no one is ignorant; as it is evident that he who designs to steal must be wakeful during the night, and use deceit, and lay plots; and, if he would gain anything of consequence, must employ spies. All these things, therefore, it is plain that he taught the children from a desire to render them more dexterous in securing provisions, and better qualified for warfare.

Some one may say, "Why, then, if he thought it honourable to steal, did he inflict a great number of whiplashes on him who was caught in the act?" I answer, that in other things which men teach, they punish him who does not follow his instructions properly; and that the Spartans accordingly punished those who were detected as having attempted to steal in an improper manner. These boys he gave in charge to others to whip them at the altar of Diana Orthia; designing to show by this enactment that it is possible for a person, after enduring pain for a short time, to enjoy pleasure with credit for a long time. It is also shown by this punishment that, where there is need of activity, the inert person benefits himself the least, and occasions himself most trouble.

In order, too, that the boys, in case of the paedonomus being absent, may never be in want of a president, he appointed that whoever of the citizens may happen at any time to be present is to assume the direction of them, and to enjoin whatever he may think advantageous for them, and punish them if they do anything wrong. By doing this, Lycurgus has also succeeded in rendering the boys much more modest; for neither boys nor men respect any one so much as their rulers. And

that if, on any occasion, no full-grown man happen to be present, the boys may not even in that case be without a leader, he ordained that the most active of the grown-up youths take the command of each band; so that the boys there are never without a superintendent.

It appears to me that I must say something also of the boys as objects of affection; for this has likewise some reference to education. Among the other Greeks, a man and boy either form a union, as among the Boeotians, and associate together, or, as among the Eleians, the men gain the favour of the youths by means of attentions bestowed upon them; but there are some of the Greeks who prohibit the suitors for the boys' favours from having the least conversation with them. But Lycurgus, acting contrary to all these people also, thought proper, if any man, being himself such as he ought to be, admired the disposition of a youth, and made it his object to render him a faultless friend, and to enjoy his society, to bestow praise upon him, and regarded this as the most excellent kind of education; but if any man showed that his affections were fixed only on the bodily attractions of a youth, Lycurgus, considering this as most unbecoming, appointed that at Lacedaemon suitors for the favours of boys should abstain from intimate connexion with them, not less strictly than parents abstain from such intercourse with their children, or children of the same family from that with one another. That such a state of things is disbelieved by some, I am not surprised; for in most states the laws are not at all adverse to the love of youths; but Lycurgus, for his part, took such precautions with reference to it.

*   *   *

Lycurgus, then, having found the Spartans, like the other Greeks, taking their meals at home, and knowing that most were guilty of excess at them, caused their meals to be taken in public, thinking that his regulations would thus be less likely to be transgressed. He appointed them such a quantity of food, that they should neither be overfed nor feel stinted. Many extraordinary supplies are also furnished from what is caught in hunting, and for

these the rich sometimes contribute bread; so that the table is never without provisions, as long as they design the meal to last, and yet is never expensive.

Having put a stop likewise to all unnecessary drinking, which weakens alike the body and the mind, he gave permission that every one should drink when he was thirsty, thinking that the drink would then be most innoxious and most pleasant. When they take their meals together in this manner, how can any one ruin either himself or his family by gluttony or drunkenness? In other states, equals in age generally associate together, and with them modesty has but very little influence; but Lycurgus, at Sparta, mixed citizens of different ages, so that the younger are for the most part instructed by the experience of the older. It is a custom at these public meals, that whatever any one has done to his honour in the community is related; so that insolence, or disorder from intoxication, or any indecency in conduct or language, has there no opportunity of showing itself. The practice of taking meals away from home is also attended with these advantages, that the people are obliged to walk in taking their departure homewards, and to be careful that they may not stagger from the effects of wine, knowing that they will not remain where they dined, and that they must conduct themselves in the night just as in the day; for it is not allowable for any one who is still liable to military duty to walk with a torch.

As Lycurgus observed, too, that those who, after taking food, exercise themselves, become well-complexioned, plump, and robust, while those who are inactive are puffy, unhealthy-looking, and feeble, he did not neglect to give attention to that point; and as he perceived that when any one engages in labour from his own inclination, he proves himself to have his body in efficient condition, he ordered that the oldest in each place of exercise should take care that those belonging to it should never be overcome by taking too much food. With regard to this matter, he appears to me to have been by no means mistaken; for no one would easily find men more healthy, or more able-bodied, than the Spartans; for they exercise themselves alike in their legs, in their hands, and in their shoulders.

*   *   *

From acquiring money by unjust means, he prohibited them by such methods as the following. He instituted, in the first place, such a kind of money, that, even if but ten minae came into a house, it could never escape the notice either of masters or of servants; for it would require much room, and a carriage to convey it. In the next place, gold and silver are searched after, and, if they are discovered anywhere, the possessor of them is punished. How, then, could gain by traffic be an object of pursuit, in a state where the possession of money occasions more pain than the use of it affords pleasure?

That at Sparta the citizens pay the strictest obedience to the magistrates and laws, we all know. I suppose, however, that Lycurgus did not attempt to establish such an excellent order of things, until he had brought the most powerful men in the state to be of the same mind with regard to it. I form my opinion on this consideration, that, in other states, the more influential men are not willing even to appear to fear the magistrates, but think that such fear is unbecoming free men but in Sparta, the most powerful men not only put themselves under the magistrates, but even count it an honour to humble themselves before them, and to obey, when they are called upon, not walking, but running; supposing that if they themselves are the first to pay exact obedience, others will follow their example; and such has been the case. It is probable, also, that the chief men established the offices of the Ephors[1] in conjunction with Lycurgus, as they must have been certain that obedience is of the greatest benefit, alike in a state, and in an army, and in a family; and they doubtless considered that the greater power magistrates have, the greater effect will they produce on the citizens in enforcing obedience. The Ephors, accordingly, have full power to impose a fine on whomsoever they please, and to exact the fine without delay; they have power also to

---

[1] The five magistrates elected annually to govern the Spartan state [Editor].

degrade magistrates even while they are in office, and to put them in prison, and to bring them to trial for their life. Being possessed of such authority, they do not, like the magistrates in other states, always permit those who are elected to offices to rule during the whole year as they choose, but, like despots and presidents in gymnastic contests, punish on the instant whomsoever they find acting at all contrary to the laws.

Though there were many other excellent contrivances adopted by Lycurgus, to induce the citizens to obey the laws, the most excellent of all appears to me to be, that he did not deliver his laws to the people until he had gone, in company with the most eminent of his fellow-citizens, to Delphi, and consulted the god whether it would be more beneficial and advantageous for Sparta to obey the laws which he had made. As the god replied that it would be more beneficial in every way, he at once delivered them, deciding that it would be not only illegal, but impious, to disobey laws sanctioned by the oracle.

It is deserving of admiration, too, in Lycurgus, that he made it a settled principle in the community, that an honourable death is preferable to a dishonourable life; for whoever pays attention to the subject will find that fewer of those who hold this opinion die than of those who attempt to escape danger by flight. Hence we may say with truth, that safety attends for a much longer period on valour than on cowardice; for valour is not only attended with less anxiety and greater pleasure, but is also more capable of assisting and supporting us. It is evident, too, that good report accompanies valour; for almost everybody is willing to be in alliance with the brave.

How he contrived that such sentiments should be entertained, it is proper not to omit to mention. He evidently, then, intended a happy life for the brave, and a miserable one for the cowardly. In other communities, when a man acts as a coward, he merely brings on himself the name of coward, but the coward goes to the same market, and sits or takes exercise, if he pleases, in the same place with the brave men; at Sparta, however, every one

would be ashamed to admit a coward into the same tent with him, or to allow him to be his opponent in a match at wrestling. Frequently, too, a person of such character, when they choose opposite parties to play at ball, is left without any place, and in forming a chorus he is thrust into the least honourable position. On the road he must yield the way to others, and at public meetings he must rise up, even before his juniors. His female relatives he must maintain at home, and they too must pay the penalty of his cowardice, since no man will marry them. He is also not allowed to take a wife, and must at the same time pay the customary fine for being a bachelor. He must not walk about with a cheerful expression, or imitate the manners of persons of blameless character; else he will have to receive whipping from his betters. Since, then, such disgrace is inflicted on cowards, I do not at all wonder that death is preferred at Sparta to a life so dishonourable and infamous.

Lycurgus seems to me to have provided also, with great judgment, how virtue might be practised even to old age; for by adding to his other enactments the choice of senators at an advanced stage of life, he caused honour and virtue not to be disregarded even in old age.

It is worthy of admiration in him, too, that he attached consideration to the old age of the well-deserving; for by making the old men arbiters in the contest for superiority in mental qualifications, he rendered their old age more honourable than the vigour of those in the meridian of life. This contest is deservedly held in the greatest esteem among the people, for gymnastic contests are attended with honour, but they concern only bodily accomplishments; the contest for distinction in old age involves a decision respecting merits of the mind. In proportion, therefore, as the mind is superior to the body, so much are contests for mental eminence more worthy of regard than those concerning bodily superiority.

Is it not highly worthy of admiration, also, in Lycurgus, that when he saw that those who are disinclined to practice virtue are not qualified to increase the power of their country, he obliged all the

citizens of Sparta to cultivate every kind of virtue publicly. As private individuals, accordingly, who practise virtue, are superior in it to those who neglect it, so Sparta is naturally superior in virtue to all other states, as it is the only one that engages in a public cultivation of honour and virtue. Is it not also deserving of commendation, that, when other states punish any person that injures another, Lycurgus inflicted no less punishment on any one that openly showed himself unconcerned with becoming as good a man as possible? He thought, as it appears, that by those who make others slaves, or rob them, or steal anything, the individual sufferers only are injured, but that by the unprincipled and cowardly whole communities are betrayed; so that he appears to me to have justly imposed the heaviest penalties on such characters.

He also imposed on his countrymen an obligation, from which there is no exception, of practising every kind of political virtue; for he made the privileges of citizenship equally available to all those who observed what was enjoined by the laws, without taking any account either of weakness of body or scantiness of means; but if any one was too indolent to perform what the laws prescribed, Lycurgus appointed that he should be no longer counted in the number of equally privileged citizens.

That these laws are extremely ancient is certain; for Lycurgus is said to have lived in the time of the Heracleidae; but, ancient as they are, they are still very new to other communities; for, what is the most wonderful of all things, all men extol such institutions, but no state thinks proper to imitate them.

The regulations which I have mentioned are beneficial alike in peace and in war; but if any one wishes to learn what he contrived better than other legislators with reference to military proceedings, he may attend to the following particulars.

In the first place, then, the Ephors proclaim the age limits for the citizen draft to the army; artisans (non-citizens) are also called by the same order to serve supplying the troops. For the Spartans provide themselves in the field with an abundance of all those things which people use in a city; and of whatever instruments an army may require in common, orders are given to bring some on waggons, and others on beasts of burden, as by this arrangement anything left behind is least likely to escape notice.

For engagements in the field he made the following arrangements. He ordered that each soldier should have a purple robe and a brass shield; for he thought that such a dress had least resemblance to that of women, and was excellently adapted for the field of battle, as it is soonest made splendid, and is longest in growing soiled. He permitted also those above the age of puberty to let their hair grow, as he thought that they thus appeared taller, more manly, and more terrifying in the eyes of the enemy. . . .

*   *   *

REVIEW QUESTIONS

1. According to these readings, what was the preeminent role of the individual citizen within Spartan society?
2. What was the purpose of education among the Spartans?
3. What was the proper role of women in Spartan society? Why?
4. What values governed Spartan life?

HIPPOCRATES

FROM "On Airs, Waters, and Places"

One of the classical Greek philosopher-scientists whose names have become almost household words today is Hippocrates of Cos, the "father of medicine," in whose name modern physicians are obligated (in the "Hippocratic oath") to apply rational, humane treatment to the care and healing of their patients. Hippocrates himself was born around 460 B.C.E. on the Aegean island of Cos. During his career, he established a school of medical thought that focused on natural medicine, attention to personal hygiene, and simple common sense in emphasizing a rational (rather than magical, superstition-bound) approach to the study and care of the human body. By the second century C.E., Greek and Latin writers ascribed to Hippocrates a substantial body of written works dealing with human physiology; the diagnosis of illness; and the influence of lifestyle, diet, and environment on health. Scholars today continue to debate their authorship, but their contribution to later Western (and Islamic) civilizations is incalculable, not only in the realm of medicine, but also—as the selection below reflects—in shaping later, often destructive assumptions that linked supposedly innate superiorities and inferiorities of other human societies to their environment, climate, and lifestyle. In some instances, the judgments that the "Hippocratic" authors reached parallel more modern notions of ethnocentrism and racism—other elements of later Western thought that, like rationalism and democracy, can be traced to Classical roots.

In the following selection, Hippocrates first defines the criteria for assessing the impact of environment on human health—among them, winds, water quality, terrain, and personal habits and lifestyle of the inhabitants. Then, the author uses these criteria to assess and contrast the qualities of peoples inhabiting different regions of the world known to him.

From The Internet Classics Archive, translated by Francis Adams, http://classics.mit.edu//Hippocrates/airwatpl.html.

Part 1

Whoever wishes to investigate medicine properly, should proceed thus: in the first place to consider the seasons of the year, and what effects each of them produces for they are not at all alike, but differ much from themselves in regard to their changes. Then the winds, the hot and the cold, especially such as are common to all countries, and then such as are peculiar to each locality. We must also consider the qualities of the waters, for as they differ from one another in taste and weight, so also do they differ much in their qualities. In the same manner, when one comes into a city to which he is a stranger, he ought to consider its situation, how it lies as to the winds and the rising of the sun; for its influence is not the same whether it lies to the north or the south, to the rising or to the setting sun. These things one ought to consider most attentively, and concerning the waters which the

inhabitants use, whether they be marshy and soft, or hard, and running from elevated and rocky situations, and then if saltish and unfit for cooking; and the ground, whether it be naked and deficient in water, or wooded and well watered, and whether it lies in a hollow, confined situation, or is elevated and cold; and the mode in which the inhabitants live, and what are their pursuits, whether they are fond of drinking and eating to excess, and given to indolence, or are fond of exercise and labor, and not given to excess in eating and drinking.

Part 2

From these things he must proceed to investigate everything else. For if one knows all these things well, or at least the greater part of them, he cannot miss knowing, when he comes into a strange city, either the diseases peculiar to the place, or the particular nature of common diseases, so that he will not be in doubt as to the treatment of the diseases, or commit mistakes, as is likely to be the case provided one had not previously considered these matters. And in particular, as the season and the year advances, he can tell what epidemic diseases will attack the city, either in summer or in winter, and what each individual will be in danger of experiencing from the change of regimen. For knowing the changes of the seasons, the risings and settings of the stars, how each of them takes place, he will be able to know beforehand what sort of a year is going to ensue. Having made these investigations, and knowing beforehand the seasons, such a one must be acquainted with each particular, and must succeed in the preservation of health, and be by no means unsuccessful in the practice of his art. And if it shall be thought that these things belong rather to meteorology, it will be admitted, on second thoughts, that astronomy contributes not a little, but a very great deal, indeed, to medicine. For with the seasons the digestive organs of men undergo a change.

*   *   *

Part 12

I wish to show, respecting Asia and Europe, how, in all respects, they differ from one another, and concerning the figure of the inhabitants, for they are different, and do not at all resemble one another. To treat of all would be a long story, but I will tell you how I think it is with regard to the greatest and most marked differences. I say, then, that Asia differs very much from Europe as to the nature of all things, both with regard to the productions of the earth and the inhabitants, for everything is produced much more beautiful and large in Asia; the country is milder, and the dispositions of the inhabitants also are more gentle and affectionate. The cause of this is the temperature of the seasons, because it lies in the middle of the risings of the sun towards the east, and removed from the cold (and heat), for nothing tends to growth and mildness so much as when the climate has no predominant quality, but a general equality of temperature prevails. It is not everywhere the same with regard to Asia, but such parts of the country as lie intermediate between the heat and the cold, are the best supplied with fruits and trees, and have the most genial climate, and enjoy the purest waters, both celestial and terrestrial. For neither are they much burnt up by the heat, nor dried up by the drought and want of rain, nor do they suffer from the cold; since they are well watered from abundant showers and snow, and the fruits of the season, as might be supposed, grow in abundance, both such as are raised from seed that has been sown, and such plants as the earth produces of its own accord, the fruits of which the inhabitants make use of, training them from their wild state and transplanting them to a suitable soil; the cattle also which are reared there are vigorous, particularly prolific, and bring up young of the fairest description; the inhabitants too, are well fed, most beautiful in shape, of large stature, and differ little from one another either as to figure or size; and the country itself, both as regards its constitution and mildness of the seasons, may be said to bear a close resemblance to the spring. Manly courage, endurance of suffering, laborious enterprise, and high spirit, could not be

produced in such a state of things either among the native inhabitants or those of a different country, for there pleasure necessarily reigns. For this reason, also, the forms of wild beasts there are much varied. Thus it is, as I think, with the Egyptians and Libyans.

Part 13

But concerning those on the right hand of the summer risings of the sun as far as the Palus Maeotis (for this is the boundary of Europe and Asia), it is with them as follows: the inhabitants there differ far more from one another than those I have treated of above, owing to the differences of the seasons and the nature of the soil. But with regard to the country itself, matters are the same there as among all other men; for where the seasons undergo the greatest and most rapid changes, there the country is the wildest and most unequal; and you will find the greatest variety of mountains, forests, plains, and meadows; but where the seasons do not change much there the country is the most even; and, if one will consider it, so is it also with regard to the inhabitants; for the nature of some is like to a country covered with trees and well watered; of some, to a thin soil deficient in water; of others, to fenny and marshy places; and of some again, to a plain of bare and parched land. For the seasons which modify their natural frame of body are varied, and the greater the varieties of them the greater also will be the differences of their shapes.

Part 14

I will pass over the smaller differences among the nations, but will now treat of such as are great either from nature, or custom; and, first, concerning the Macrocephali. There is no other race of men which have heads in the least resembling theirs. At first, usage was the principal cause of the length of their head, but now nature cooperates with usage. They think those the most noble who have the longest heads. It is thus with regard to the usage: immediately after the child is born, and while its

head is still tender, they fashion it with their hands, and constrain it to assume a lengthened shape by applying bandages and other suitable contrivances whereby the spherical form of the head is destroyed, and it is made to increase in length. Thus, at first, usage operated, so that this constitution was the result of force: but, in the course of time, it was formed naturally; so that usage had nothing to do with it; for the semen comes from all parts of the body, sound from the sound parts, and unhealthy from the unhealthy parts. If, then, children with bald heads are born to parents with bald heads; and children with blue eyes to parents who have blue eyes; and if the children of parents having distorted eyes squint also for the most part; and if the same may be said of other forms of the body, what is to prevent it from happening that a child with a long head should be produced by a parent having a long head? But now these things do not happen as they did formerly, for the custom no longer prevails owing to their intercourse with other men. Thus it appears to me to be with regard to them.

Part 15

As to the inhabitants of Phasis [along the eastern shore at the Black Sea], their country is fenny, warm, humid, and wooded; copious and severe rains occur there at all seasons; and the life of the inhabitants is spent among the fens; for their dwellings are constructed of wood and reeds, and are erected amidst the waters; they seldom practice walking either to the city or the market, but sail about, up and down, in canoes constructed out of single trees, for there are many canals there. They drink the hot and stagnant waters, both when rendered putrid by the sun, and when swollen with rains. The Phasis itself is the most stagnant of all rivers, and runs the smoothest; all the fruits which spring there are unwholesome, feeble and imperfect growth, owing to the redundance of water, and on this account they do not ripen, for much vapor from the waters overspreads the country. For these reasons the Phasians have shapes different from those of all other men; for they are large in stature,

and of a very gross habit of body, so that not a joint nor vein is visible; in color they are sallow, as if affected with jaundice. Of all men they have the roughest voices, from their breathing an atmosphere which is not clear, but misty and humid; they are naturally rather languid in supporting bodily fatigue. The seasons undergo but little change either as to heat or cold; their winds for the most part are southerly, with the exception of one peculiar to the country, which sometimes blows strong, is violent and hot, and is called by them the wind cenchron. The north wind scarcely reaches them, and when it does blow it is weak and gentle. Thus it is with regard to the different nature and shape of the inhabitants of Asia and Europe.

Part 16

And with regard to the pusillanimity and cowardice of the inhabitants, the principal reason the Asiatics are more unwarlike and of gentler disposition than the Europeans is, the nature of the seasons, which do not undergo any great changes either to heat or cold, or the like; for there is neither excitement of the understanding nor any strong change of the body whereby the temper might be ruffled and they be roused to inconsiderate emotion and passion, rather than living as they do always in the state. It is changes of all kinds which arouse understanding of mankind, and do not allow them to get into a torpid condition. For these reasons, it appears to me, the Asiatic race is feeble, and further, owing to their laws; for monarchy prevails in the greater part of Asia, and where men are not their own masters nor independent, but are the slaves of others, it is not a matter of consideration with them how they may acquire military discipline, but how they may seem not to be warlike, for the dangers are not equally shared, since they must serve as soldiers, perhaps endure fatigue, and die for their masters, far from their children, their wives, and other friends; and whatever noble and manly actions they may perform lead only to the aggrandizement of their masters, whilst the fruits which they reap are dangers and death; and, in addition to all this, the lands of such persons must be laid waste by the enemy and want of cul-

ture. Thus, then, if any one be naturally warlike and courageous, his disposition will be changed by the institutions. As a strong proof of all this, such Greeks or barbarians in Asia as are not under a despotic form of government, but are independent, and enjoy the fruits of their own labors, are of all others the most warlike; for these encounter dangers on their own account, bear the prizes of their own valor, and in like manner endure the punishment of their own cowardice. And you will find the Asiatics differing from one another, for some are better and others more dastardly; of these differences, as I stated before, the changes of the seasons are the cause. Thus it is with Asia.

Part 17

In Europe there is a Scythian race, called Sauromatae, which inhabits the confines of the Palus Maeotis, and is different from all other races. Their women mount on horseback, use the bow, and throw the javelin from their horses, and fight with their enemies as long as they are virgins; and they do not lay aside their virginity until they kill three of their enemies, nor have any connection with men until they perform the sacrifices according to law. Whoever takes to herself a husband, gives up riding on horseback unless the necessity of a general expedition obliges her. They have no right breast; for while still of a tender age their mothers heat strongly a copper instrument constructed for this very purpose, and apply it to the right breast, which is burnt up, and its development being arrested, all the strength and fullness are determined to the right shoulder and arm.

Part 18

As the other Scythians have a peculiarity of shape, and do not resemble any other, the same observation applies to the Egyptians, only that the latter are oppressed by heat and the former by cold. What is called the Scythian desert is a prairie, rich in meadows, high-lying, and well watered; for the rivers which carry off the water from the plains are large. There live those Scythians which are called

Nomades, because they have no houses, but live in wagons. The smallest of these wagons have four wheels, but some have six; they are covered in with felt, and they are constructed in the manner of houses, some having but a single apartment, and some three; they are proof against rain, snow, and winds. The wagons are drawn by yokes of oxen, some of two and others of three, and all without horns, for they have no horns, owing to the cold. In these wagons the women live, but the men are carried about on horses, and the sheep, oxen, and horses accompany them; and they remain on any spot as long as there is provender for their cattle, and when that fails they migrate to some other place. They eat boiled meat, and drink the milk of mares, and also eat hippace, which is cheese prepared from the milk of the mare. Such is their mode of life and their customs.

Part 19

In respect of the seasons and figure of body, the Scythian race, like the Egyptian, have a uniformity of resemblance, different from all other nations; they are by no means prolific, and the wild beasts which are indigenous there are small in size and few in number, for the country lies under the Northern Bears, and the Rhiphaean mountains, whence the north wind blows; the sun comes very near to them only when in the summer solstice, and warms them but for a short period, and not strongly; and the winds blowing from the hot regions of the earth do not reach them, or but seldom, and with little force; but the winds from the north always blow, congealed, as they are, by the snow, ice, and much water, for these never leave the mountains, which are thereby rendered uninhabitable. A thick fog covers the plains during the day, and amidst it they live, so that winter may be said to be always present with them; or, if they have summer, it is only for a few days, and the heat is not very strong. Their plains are high-lying and naked, not crowned with mountains, but extending upwards under the Northern Bears. The wild beasts there are not large, but such as can be sheltered underground; for the cold of winter and the

barrenness of the country prevent their growth, and because they have no covert nor shelter. The changes of the seasons, too, are not great nor violent, for, in fact, they change gradually; and therefore their figures resemble one another, as they all equally use the same food, and the same clothing summer and winter, respiring a humid and dense atmosphere, and drinking water from snow and ice; neither do they make any laborious exertions, for neither body nor mind is capable of enduring fatigue when the changes of the seasons are not great. For these reasons their shapes are gross and fleshy, with ill-marked joints, of a humid temperament, and deficient in tone: the internal cavities, and especially those of the intestines, are full of humors; for the belly cannot possibly be dry in such a country, with such a constitution and in such a climate; but owing to their fat, and the absence of hairs from their bodies, their shapes resemble one another, the males being all alike, and so also with the women; for the seasons being of a uniform temperature, no corruption or deterioration takes place in the concretion of the semen, unless from some violent cause, or from disease.

Part 20

I will give you a strong proof of the humidity (laxity?) of their constitutions. You will find the greater part of the Scythians, and all the Nomades, with marks of the cautery on their shoulders, arms, wrists, breasts, hip-joints, and loins, and that for no other reason but the humidity and flabbiness of their constitution, for they can neither strain with their bows, nor launch the javelin from their shoulder owing to their humidity and atony: but when they are burnt, much of the humidity in their joints is dried up, and they become better braced, better fed, and their joints get into a more suitable condition. They are flabby and squat at first, because, as in Egypt, they are not swathed (?); and then they pay no attention to horsemanship, so that they may be adepts at it; and because of their sedentary mode of life; for the males, when they cannot be carried about on horseback, sit the most of their time in the wagon, and rarely practise

walking, because of their frequent migrations and shiftings of situation; and as to the women, it is amazing how flabby and sluggish they are. The Scythian race are tawny from the cold, and not from the intense heat of the sun, for the whiteness of the skin is parched by the cold, and becomes tawny.

Part 21

It is impossible that persons of such a constitution could be prolific, for, with the man, the sexual desires are not strong, owing to the laxity of his constitution, the softness and coldness of his belly, from all which causes it is little likely that a man should be given to venery; and besides, from being jaded by exercise on horseback, the men become weak in their desires. On the part of the men these are the causes; but on that of the women, they are embonpoint and humidity; for the womb cannot take in the semen, nor is the menstrual discharge such as it should be, but scanty and at too long intervals; and the mouth of the womb is shut up by fat and does not admit the semen; and, moreover, they themselves are indolent and fat, and their bellies cold and soft. From these causes the Scythian race is not prolific. Their female servants furnish a strong proof of this; for they no sooner have connection with a man than they prove with child, owing to their active course of life and the slenderness of body.

Part 22

And, in addition to these, there are many eunuchs among the Scythians, who perform female work, and speak like women. Such persons are called effeminates. The inhabitants of the country attribute the cause of their impotence to a god, and venerate and worship such persons, every one dreading that the like might befall himself; but to me it appears that such affections are just as much divine as all others are, and that no one disease is either more divine or more human than another, but that all are alike divine, for that each has its own nature, and that no one arises without a natural cause. But

I will explain how I think that the affection takes its rise. From continued exercise on horseback they are seized with chronic defluxions in their joints owing to their legs always hanging down below their horses; they afterwards become lame and stiff at the hip-joint, such of them, at least, as are severely attacked with it. They treat themselves in this way: when the disease is commencing, they open the vein behind either ear, and when the blood flows, sleep, from feebleness, seizes them, and afterwards they awaken, some in good health and others not. To me it appears that the semen is altered by this treatment, for there are veins behind the ears which, if cut, induce impotence; now, these veins would appear to me to be cut. Such persons afterwards, when they go in to women and cannot have connection with them, at first do not think much about it, but remain quiet; but when, after making the attempt two, three, or more times, they succeed no better, fancying they have committed some offence against the god whom they blame for the affection, they put on female attire, reproach themselves for effeminacy, play the part of women, and perform the same work as women do. This the rich among the Scythians endure, not the basest, but the most noble and powerful, owing to their riding on horseback; for the poor are less affected, as they do not ride on horses. And yet, if this disease had been more divine than the others, it ought not to have befallen the most noble and the richest of the Scythians alone, but all alike, or rather those who have little, as not being able to pay honors to the gods, if, indeed, they delight in being thus rewarded by men, and grant favors in return; for it is likely that the rich sacrifice more to the gods, and dedicate more votive offerings, inasmuch as they have wealth, and worship the gods; whereas the poor, from want, do less in this way, and, moreover, upbraid the gods for not giving them wealth, so that those who have few possessions were more likely to bear the punishments of these offences than the rich. But, as I formerly said, these affections are divine just as much as others, for each springs from a natural cause, and this disease arises among the Scythians from such a cause as I have stated. But it attacks other men in like manner, for

whenever men ride much and very frequently on horseback, then many are affected with rheums in the joints, sciatica, and gout, and they are inept at venery. But these complaints befall the Scythians, and they are the most impotent of men for the aforesaid causes, and because they always wear breeches, and spend the most of their time on horseback, so as not to touch their privy parts with the hands, and from the cold and fatigue they forget the sexual desire, and do not make the attempt until after they have lost their virility. Thus it is with the race of the Scythians.

Part 23

The other races in Europe differ from one another, both as to stature and shape, owing to the changes of the seasons, which are very great and frequent, and because the heat is strong, the winters severe, and there are frequent rains, and again protracted droughts, and winds, from which many and diversified changes are induced. These changes are likely to have an effect upon generation in the coagulation of the semen, as this process cannot be the same in summer as in winter, nor in rainy as in dry weather; wherefore, I think, that the figures of Europeans differ more than those of Asiatics; and they differ very much from one another as to stature in the same city; for vitiations of the semen occur in its coagulation more frequently during frequent changes of the seasons, than where they are alike and equable. And the same may be said of their dispositions, for the wild, and unsociable, and the passionate occur in such a constitution; for frequent excitement of the mind induces wildness, and extinguishes sociableness and mildness of disposition, and therefore I think the inhabitants of Europe more courageous than those of Asia; for a climate which is always the same induces indolence, but a changeable climate, laborious exertions both of body and mind; and from rest and indolence cowardice is engendered, and from laborious exertions and pains, courage. On this account the inhabitants of Europe are more warlike than the Asiatics, and also owing to their institutions, because they are not governed by kings like the latter,

for where men are governed by kings there they must be very cowardly, as I have stated before; for their souls are enslaved, and they will not willingly, or readily undergo dangers in order to promote the power of another; but those that are free undertake dangers on their own account, and not for the sake of others; they court hazard and go out to meet it, for they themselves bear off the rewards of victory, and thus their institutions contribute not a little to their courage.

Such is the general character of Europe and Asia.

Part 24

And there are in Europe other tribes, differing from one another in stature, shape, and courage: the differences are those I formerly mentioned, and will now explain more clearly. Such as inhabit a country which is mountainous, rugged, elevated, and well watered, and where the changes of the seasons are very great, are likely to have great variety of shapes among them, and to be naturally of an enterprising and warlike disposition; and such persons are apt to have no little of the savage and ferocious in their nature; but such as dwell in places which are low-lying, abounding in meadows and ill ventilated, and who have a larger proportion of hot than of cold winds, and who make use of warm waters—these are not likely to be of large stature nor well proportioned, but are of a broad make, fleshy, and have black hair; and they are rather of a dark than of a light complexion, and are less likely to be phlegmatic than bilious; courage and laborious enterprise are not naturally in them, but may be engendered in them by means of their institutions. And if there be rivers in the country which carry off the stagnant and rain water from it, these may be wholesome and clear; but if there be no rivers, but the inhabitants drink the waters of fountains, and such as are stagnant and marshy, they must necessarily have prominent bellies and enlarged spleens. But such as inhabit a high country, and one that is level, windy, and well-watered, will be large of stature, and like to one another; but their minds will be rather unmanly and gentle.

Those who live on thin, ill-watered, and bare soils, and not well attempered in the changes of the seasons, in such a country they are likely to be in their persons rather hard and well braced, rather of a blond than a dark complexion, and in disposition and passions haughty and self-willed. For, where the changes of the seasons are most frequent, and where they differ most from one another, there you will find their forms, dispositions, and nature the most varied. These are the strongest of the natural causes of difference, and next the country in which one lives, and the waters; for, in general, you will find the forms and dispositions of mankind to correspond with the nature of the country; for where the land is fertile, soft, and well-watered, and supplied with waters from very elevated situations, so as to be hot in summer and cold in winter, and where the seasons are fine, there the men are fleshy, have ill-formed joints, and are of a humid temperament; they are not disposed to endure labor, and, for the most part, are base in spirit; indolence and sluggishness are visible in them, and to the arts they are dull, and not clever nor acute. When the country is bare, not fenced, and rugged, blasted by the winter and scorched by the sun, there you may see the hardy, slender, with well-shaped joints, well-braced, and shaggy; sharp industry and vigilance accompany such a constitution; in morals and passions they are haughty and opinionative, inclining rather to the fierce than to the mild; and you will find them acute and ingenious as regards the arts, and excelling in military affairs; and likewise all the other productions of the earth corresponding to the earth itself. Thus it is with regard to the most opposite natures and shapes; drawing conclusions from them, you may judge of the rest without any risk of error.

REVIEW QUESTIONS

1. Which human groups does Hippocrates consider to be superior? On what basis?
2. Can you discern any parallels between what Hippocrates writes and more recent concepts of "race" and racial inferiority?

HERODOTUS

FROM *The Histories:*

The Second Persian Invasion of Greece

The Greeks' repelling of the Persian invasions of 490 and 480 to 479 B.C.E. can be regarded as one of the earliest events through which the West began to define itself as distinct from the East. Our knowledge of the invasions is derived almost entirely from the account by Herodotus, who wrote only a few decades after the actual events. His description of the war against the Persians is preceded by long discourses (often of questionable reliability) on the history and customs of other peoples who were involved in the war. The following excerpts, however, focus on the fierce resistance of the Spartans during the second invasion, led by the Persian king Xerxes. In the first selection, Xerxes asks the expatriate Spartan Demaratus how the Greeks can possibly stand up to Persia's might. (This is after Herodotus has given an accounting

of the composition of the Persian army. According to his figures, it numbered a fantastic—and impossible—2,641,610 warriors.) The following selection is Herodotus's account of the heroic stand of the Spartans under their king, Leonidas, at the mountain pass at Thermopylae.

From *Herodotus: The Histories,* edited by Walter Blanco and Jennifer Tobert Roberts, translated by Walter Blanco (New York: Norton, 1992), pp. 157–77, 191–97.

*   *   *

After the army had been counted and put in battle order, Xerxes wanted to ride past his troops and review them, which he did. He rode past the forces of each nation in his chariot, asking questions while his scribes wrote down the answers until he had gone from one end of the army to the other and reviewed both infantry and cavalry. After he had done this, the ships were dragged down into the sea and Xerxes transferred from his chariot to a Sidonian ship. He sat under a golden awning and sailed along the prows of the ships, asking questions and having answers written down just as he had done with the army. The captains had taken their ships back about four hundred feet from shore, lined them up with their prows facing land, and dropped anchor after posting the marines at their battle stations in full gear. Xerxes conducted his naval review while sailing between the ships' prows and the shore.

When he had sailed past his fleet and disembarked from his ship, Xerxes summoned Demaratus, son of Ariston, who was accompanying him on the campaign against Greece. As Demaratus approached, Xerxes called out to him and said, "Demaratus, there's something it would give me great pleasure to ask you about right now. You are a Greek, and as far as I can tell from you and the other Greeks who have had conversations with me, your city is by no means the smallest or the weakest. Tell me this, now, are the Greeks going to take up arms and resist? Because I believe that neither all the Greeks nor all the other people who live to the west put together are going to be able to resist my assault—unless they are united, that is. Still, I want to hear from you what you have to say about it."

When Xerxes had finished, Demaratus answered, "Should I tell you the truth, Your Majesty, or just something pleasing?" And Xerxes commanded him to tell the truth—he wouldn't like him any less than before.

When he heard this, Demaratus said, "Since you demand that I tell the truth by all means, Your Majesty, and not something you will later find to be a lie, why then, poverty is congenital to Greece, but bravery is an import, bought with skill and strict rules, and Greece uses bravery to fend off both poverty and despotism. Now, while I praise all Greeks who live in Dorian lands, I'm not really talking about all of them, but solely about the Lacedaemonians. First: there is no way they will ever accept any terms of slavery you bring to Greece. Second: they will oppose you in battle even if all the other Greeks come around to your way of thinking. Don't bother finding out whether there will be enough of them to do it. If there are a thousand, they will fight you, and they will fight you if there are fewer and fight you if there are more."

After Xerxes heard this, he said through his laughter, "What nonsense you talk, Demaratus! A thousand men fighting with an army like this! But come, now, tell me. You say that you yourself used to be king over these people. How would you like to fight with ten men right now? But really, if your citizens are all such as you describe them, then under your laws it would be fitting for you, as their king, to fight with twice that number. If each of them is worth ten men from my army, then I look for you to be worth twenty. That way you can make good on what you've said. Because if they are all like you and the other Greeks who come to talk to me—like you, that is, in size and shape—and you all brag in this way, then see to

it that your boast isn't made in vain. Come now, look at it reasonably. How could a thousand, or ten thousand, or fifty thousand men who are all equally free and not ruled by one man stand up to an army this size? Because if there are five thousand of them we will outnumber them by more than a thousand to one! If, like us, they were ruled by one man, they would either surpass themselves through fear of him or they would, under the lash, go up against forces that outnumbered them. But if they are left to their own devices, they won't do either. Anyway, I think that even if the numbers were the same, it would be hard for the Greeks to fight with just the Persians. We, too, have this quality you speak of. There isn't much of it—it's rare, but there are some of my Persian bodyguard who want to take on three Greeks at a time. You've never come up against them, and that's why you can talk so much drivel."

Demaratus answered, "I knew from the beginning, Your Majesty, that if I told you the truth, you wouldn't like what I had to say. But since you forced me to tell you the whole truth, I told you what the Spartans are like. You, though, more than anyone, know how much I love them now —they who stripped me of my rank and my privileges, who drove me from the city of my fathers and made me an exile while your father welcomed me and gave me an income and a home. A rational man is much more likely to appreciate goodwill than to reject it. As for me, I don't claim to be able to fight with ten men or with two. I wouldn't even willingly fight with one. But if I had to, or if a great cause spurred me on, then I would gladly fight—especially with one of those men who say they're a match for three Greeks. In the same way, when the Lacedaemonians fight one at a time, they are no worse than any other men, but when they fight together, they are the best in the world. Because though they're free, they aren't totally free. Custom is the despot who stands over them, and they secretly fear it more than your people fear you. They do whatever it commands, and its command is always the same: not to run away from any force, however large, but to stay in formation and either prevail or die. If I seem to

be talking drivel to you, then I'll keep quiet from now on. I spoke just now only because you made me, but let it be as you think best, Your Majesty."

Although Demaratus answered him in this way, Xerxes didn't get at all angry. Instead, he turned it into a joke and genially sent Demaratus away.

*   *   *

The Spartans sent Leonidas with an advance guard so that the other allies would go to war after seeing them do so and not use any delay on Sparta's part as an excuse for also collaborating with the Persians. Later, after celebrating the Carneian festival, which prevented them from going to battle immediately, they would station a guard in Sparta and march out on the double in full strength. Their allies had the same idea. The Olympic Games were taking place at the same time as these events, so the allies, too, sent their advance guards, never thinking that the battle of Thermopylae would be decided so quickly.

These, then, were their intentions. Meanwhile, when the Greeks at Thermopylae saw the Persians approaching the pass, they panicked and talked about retreat. In general, the Peloponnesians thought they should return to the Peloponnese and guard the Isthmus, but when the Phocians and Locrians became extremely agitated over this idea, Leonidas voted to stay where they were and to dispatch messengers calling on the allies to come to the rescue since they were too few to hold off the Persian army.

While the Greek commanders were discussing their plans, Xerxes sent out a mounted spy to see how many Greeks there were and what they were doing. He had already heard while still in Thessaly that a small army had gathered at Thermopylae, and that it was led by Lacedaemonians under the command of Leonidas, a descendant of Heracles. The horseman could not observe or even see the whole camp as he rode toward it, because some of the men were posted out of sight inside the wall, which they had rebuilt and were guarding. He did see the men outside the wall, though, and their weapons lying nearby. During that watch, the

Spartans happened to be stationed outside. He saw some of the men exercising, others combing their long hair. He was amazed at what he saw. He noted their numbers and, after carefully observing everything he could, trotted back unmolested. Nobody pursued him; nobody paid any attention to him at all. When he returned, he told Xerxes everything he had seen.

Xerxes heard it, but he couldn't understand that what they were doing was getting ready to kill or be killed. They seemed to him to be acting so absurdly that he sent for Demaratus, son of Ariston, who was in the camp. When he arrived, Xerxes asked him about everything in detail; he was eager to find out just what the Lacedaemonians were doing. Demaratus said, "I already told you about these men as we were setting out against Greece. You laughed at me for seeing that things would turn out just as they have. I keep trying to tell you the truth, Your Majesty, but it's a struggle. Listen to me now. Those men came here to fight with us for this pass, and that's what they are getting ready to do. It's their way. They comb their hair whenever they are about to risk their lives. But know this: if you defeat these men and the force that remains in Sparta, there are no other people on earth who will take up arms against you, because you are about to face the noblest king and the bravest men in all of Greece."

What he said seemed to Xerxes to be absolutely incredible, and Xerxes asked him for the second time how so few men could do battle with his army. Demaratus said, "Consider me a liar, Your Majesty, if things don't turn out as I say."

That's what he said, but Xerxes didn't believe him.

He let four days go by, expecting the Greeks to run away at any moment. When they had not only not left on the fifth day but seemed to be staying out of sheer reckless effrontery; Xerxes became furious and sent the Medes and Cissians out to attack them, with orders to bring them back into his presence alive. Waves of Medians rushed the Greeks. Many men fell, and others followed in their wake, but none retreated from the overwhelming disaster. The Medes made it clear to everyone and not least to the king himself that he

had many troops but few real men. Nevertheless, the battle lasted all day long.

The Medes finally retreated after being thoroughly manhandled. The Persians were the next to attack—the men Xerxes called his Immortals. They were under the command of Hydarnes, and indeed they thought that they would easily prevail, but it was no different for them when they mixed it up with the Greeks from what it had been for the Medes. It was just the same because they were fighting at very close quarters, using spears shorter than the Greeks', and were unable to take advantage of their numerical superiority. The Lacedaemonians fought a battle to remember! Among these men who knew nothing of warfare, they showed in all sorts of ways that they really knew how to fight—like when they turned their backs and pretended to run away, the barbarians would see them running and would chase after them shouting and making noise, and then the Greeks would wheel around and face the barbarians just as they were about to be overtaken and slaughter countless numbers of them.

A few of the Spartans fell there, too.

The Persians couldn't take the pass after attacking it company by company and in every other way, and they finally retreated.

They say that the king, who was observing these assaults, jumped up from his throne three times in fear for his army. That, then, is how the battle went on that day; and the barbarians fought with no more success the next day, either. They attacked in the belief that the small number of Greeks must have suffered so many casualties that they wouldn't even be able to raise their arms to resist. The Greeks, however, stood in formations of tribes and regiments and took turns in the fighting—all except the Phocians, who had been posted on the mountain to guard the trail. The Persians retreated when they didn't see anything different from what they had found the day before.

Xerxes was at a loss as to how to deal with this situation when a Malian, Ephialtes, son of Eurydemus, came to talk to the king in the hope of receiving a large gift. He told Xerxes about the trail leading through the mountains to Thermopylae and thereby doomed the Greek defenders at the pass. Ephialtes later fled to Thessaly in fear of

the Lacedaemonians, but at a meeting at Pylae, the Amphyctionic delegates—the Pylagorac—offered a reward for the fugitive. When he returned to Anticyra some time later, he was killed by Athenades, a man from Trachis. Now, Athenades killed Ephialtes for a different reason (which I will talk about in a later narrative), but the Lacedaemonians honored him for it nonetheless.

*   *   *

Xerxes was delighted with what Ephialtes had offered to do, and soon became positively overjoyed. He immediately dispatched Hydarnes and his Immortals, who left camp at dusk, at around the time the lamps are lit.

Malian locals discovered this trail and then guided the Thessalians over it to attack the Phocians after the Phocians had walled up the pass to hold off an invasion. That's how long the Malians have known about this deadly trail! The trail begins where the Asopus issues through the gorge, and its name is the same as the mountain's—the Anopaea. The Anopaea trail runs along the mountain ridge and leaves off at Alpeni, the first town on the Malian side of Locris, at a place called Black Ass Rock and the Cercopian Butts. This is the narrowest part of the pass.

The Persians crossed the Asopus and made their way over the trail through the night, keeping the Oeta Mountains on the right and the mountains of Trachis on the left. They reached the top of the mountain with the glimmering of dawn. As I have already said, a thousand heavily armed Phocians were stationed there to guard the trail and defend their own homeland. The Phocians had voluntarily given their oath to Leonidas to guard that mountain trail, and we know very well who was guarding the pass below.

The Persians could go up the mountain unnoticed because it was covered with oak trees, so the Phocians only found out that the Persians had already gotten up there when, on that perfectly still day, they heard the loud noise of fallen leaves crackling under the tramp of feet. The Phocians sprang up and were putting on their battle gear as the barbarians came in sight. The Persians were astonished to see men putting on their armor.

They had thought they would meet with no opposition, and yet here was an army! Hydarnes dreaded that the Phocians might be Spartans, so he asked Ephialtes where they were from. When he was sure of their nationality, he arrayed his Persians for battle. After being showered with arrows thick and fast, the Phocians thought the attack was aimed at them, and they ran up to the very top of the mountain ready to fight to the death; but they were mistaken, because the Persians under Ephialtes and Hydarnes paid no further attention to them and hurried down the mountain.

Meanwhile, Megistias the seer had examined the sacrificial animals and told the Greeks at Thermopylae that they would die at dawn. Also, deserters had told them during the night that the Persians were circling around behind them. Finally, their lookouts ran down from the mountaintops with the news at the dawn's early light. The Greeks then held a meeting, and their opinions were divided between those who would not leave their positions and those who took the opposite view. The two sides parted company: some retreated and scattered into their respective cities; others prepared to take their stand there with Leonidas.

It is said that Leonidas himself sent the others away, concerned lest they be destroyed—while as for him and the Spartans who were with him, they couldn't rightly abandon the post they had come to guard in the first place. I myself am inclined to the view that when Leonidas saw that his allies were balking, unwilling to stay with him and risk their lives, he must have ordered them to retreat, though he himself couldn't go home honorably. He would stay to leave eternal fame behind him, and see to it that Sparta's prosperity was not snuffed out. You see, the Spartans had consulted the Delphic oracle as soon as the war broke out, and the Pythian priestess had prophesied that either the Lacedaemonian people would be uprooted by the barbarians or their king would die. She uttered the prophecy in the following hexameter verses:

But for you, O dwellers in Sparta's wide land,
Either your glorious city shall be sacked by the
    men of Persia

Or, if not, she will mourn the action of Heracles,
The dead ruler over all the land of Lacedaemon.
The strength of bulls and lions cannot resist the
  foe,
For he has the strength of Zeus. No, he will not
  leave off,
I say, until he tears city or king limb from limb.

Leonidas dismissed the allies with this prophecy in mind, and because he wanted to be the only Spartan to win such fame; they did not go home in disarray over a difference of opinion.

For me, not the least evidence for this view is the well-known fact that Leonidas also tried to dismiss the army seer I mentioned—Megistias the Acarnanian, who they say descended from Melampus, and who foretold the future from his sacrificial animals. But although he had been dismissed to keep him from being killed with everyone else, he didn't leave; instead, he sent home his only son, who had gone to war with him.

The allies who had been dismissed obeyed Leonidas and left. Only the Thespians and the Thebans stayed with the Lacedaemonians. The Thebans remained without wanting to because Leonidas, regarding them as hostages, held them against their will. The Thespians, on the other hand, were very willing to stay. Refusing to abandon Leonidas or desert his men, they stayed behind and died along with them. The Thespian commander was Demophilus, son of Diadromes.

Xerxes poured out drink offerings at sunrise. He waited until about midmorning and then began the attack. This plan had been arranged in advance with Ephialtes, because the descent from the mountain would be much quicker, with much less ground to cover, than the march around and the climb up had been. The barbarians under Xerxes moved forward while the Greeks under Leonidas advanced like men who are going out to their deaths; and this time they went much farther out into the wider part of the pass than they had at first. In the first days of battle, concerned with protecting the defending wall, they would only make forays into the narrowest part and fight there. This time, as the two sides grappled with each other beyond the narrow neck of the pass, very many barbarians fell while their company commanders whipped each and every man, driving them constantly forward. Many of them fell into the sea and drowned; many others trampled each other alive; no one cared about the dying. And because they knew that death was coming from the troops who had circled the mountain, the Greeks fought the barbarians with all the strength they had, fought recklessly out of their minds.

Most of their spears were broken by now, so they slaughtered Persians with their swords. That brave man Leonidas fell in the struggle, and other renowned Spartans along with him. I have learned the names of these noble men, as I have learned the names of all the three hundred Spartans who perished. And, indeed, many brave Persians died there, too, two sons of Darius among them—Abrocomes and Hyperanthes, Darius' children by Phratagune, daughter of Artanes. This Artanes was the brother of King Darius, and the son of Hystaspes, son of Arsames. When he married his daughter to Darius, Artanes gave up his whole estate along with her since she was his only child.

Thus two brothers of Xerxes died in the battle.

There was a tremendous crush of Persians and Lacedaemonians around the body of Leonidas, until by sheer courage the Greeks dragged him away after beating back the enemy four times. The fight continued until Ephialtes arrived. The nature of the battle changed as soon as the Greeks realized that he was there. They fell back to the narrow part of the pass and, after ducking behind the wall, massed together on the hillock behind it and dug in—all except the Thebans. This mound is in the pass where the stone lion now stands in honor of Leonidas. The men defended themselves on this hillock with daggers, if they still had them, or with their hands and teeth, while some of the Persians came at them head-on after pulling down and demolishing the wall and others surrounded them and stood there burying them under arrows, spears, and stones.

They say that Dieneces the Spartan stood out even in this company of Lacedaemonians and Thespians. Just before the battle with the Persians,

he heard some Trachinian say that when the bar-barians shot their arrows the sky was so full of them that the sun was blotted out—that's how many Persians there were. Dieneces wasn't fazed at all. He pooh-poohed the Persian numbers, and is reported to have said that his Trachinian friend had brought good news, because if the Persians blotted out the sun they could have their battle in the shade rather than in the sunlight. They say Dieneces the Spartan left this and other witticisms to be remembered by. After him, they say, two Lacedaemonian brothers, Alpheus and Maron, sons of Orsiphantus, distinguished themselves. The most outstanding Thespian was named Dithyrambus, son of Harmatides.

The men were buried where they fell, along with those who had died before the departure of the men Leonidas had dismissed. There is an epitaph over the mass grave which says:

IN THIS PLACE FOUR THOUSAND
    PELOPONNESIANS FOUGHT
    FOUR MILLION MEN

That epitaph was for all the men. These words commemorate the Spartans alone:

STRANGER GO TELL THE
    LACEDAEMONIANS THAT WE WHO LIE
    HERE OBEYED THEIR ORDERS

*   *   *

REVIEW QUESTIONS

1. According to Herodotus, why does Xerxes decide to invade Greece? Do he or his generals fear the Greeks at all?
2. What special attributes of the Greeks make it possible for them to resist and eventually defeat the Persian forces?
3. Do the Persians, and Xerxes specifically, possess any flaws that ensure their eventual defeat?
4. How does Herodotus' account of the Spartans at Thermopylae compare with the readings preceding this one?

THUCYDIDES

FROM *The Peloponnesian Wars*

The costly Peloponnesian War of 431–404 B.C.E. was the culmination of years of growing tension between Sparta and its league of allies, on the one hand, and the Athenian Empire on the other. Our principal source for that war is the history written by the Athenian Thucydides, who tended to be much more rigorous than Herodotus in his assessment and use of historical evidence. In the first selection that follows, Thucydides recreates the speech given by the Athenian leader Pericles to honor those Athenians who fell in battle during the war's first year. It has come to be regarded as one of the classic statements of the values of a democracy. The second selection is Thucydides' account of the negotiations several years later between the envoys of the invading Athenian forces and the local authorities of Melos, an Aegean island that Athens was seeking to add to its empire.

From *The Peloponnesian Wars: A New Translation,* translated by Walter Blanco, edited by Walter Blanco and Jennifer Tolbert Roberts (New York: Norton, 1998), pp. 71–76, 227–231.

Pericles' Funeral Speech

That same winter, the Athenians observed an ancestral custom and arranged for the funeral, at the public expense, of the first men to die in the war. They always did it in the following way. Two days beforehand, they would build a tent and lay out the bones and ashes of the dead, and everyone would make whatever offerings he wished to his kin. On the day of the funeral procession, wagons brought in cypress coffins, one for each tribe, with every man's bones to be in the coffin of his tribe. There was one empty bier spread with a coverlet for the missing, the men who could not be found and carried away. Any man, citizen or stranger, could attend the funeral; women who were related to the dead were also present, mourning the dead right up to the grave. The soldiers were buried in the national cemetery, which is in the most beautiful suburb of the city. Those who die in war are always buried there, except for those who died at Marathon, for the Athenians decided that they had shown surpassing courage and buried them right on the battlefield in Marathon. When the coffins are covered with earth, a man who has been chosen by the city for his outstanding reputation and exceptional wisdom delivers a fitting eulogy over the dead. After this, they all depart. Thus are the dead buried, and the custom was observed throughout the whole war whenever it was necessary to do so. Now Pericles, son of Xanthippus, had been chosen to speak over these very first dead, and at the appropriate time, he stepped forward from the gravesite and up onto a podium built high enough so that the largest number of the audience could hear, and spoke as follows:

Most of those who have spoken in this place have praised the man who added this speech to our funeral customs. It was good, they said, for there to be an oration over the fallen men we honor with these rites. As for me, it would have seemed enough to show our respect for brave men who fell in action *with* action—like the one you see us publicly performing here, now, at this national gravesite—and not to risk letting the reputation for courage of so many depend on whether one man speaks

well or poorly. For it is hard to say the right thing when people barely agree as to the truth of it. The sympathetic, knowledgeable listener might, perhaps, think that what is said falls short of what he knows and wants to hear. Those who do not know the facts might, from envy, think some things exaggerated if they sound like more than they themselves can do, for praise of others is bearable only insofar as each man thinks he is capable of doing what he hears praised. They therefore begrudge and disbelieve in men who surpass their own abilities.

Nevertheless, since our forefathers thought fit that this should be so, I must observe our customs and try as best I can to satisfy your wishes and your expectations.

I will begin with our ancestors. It is both fitting and right on such an occasion as this to pay them the due regard of memory, because through their courage, they bequeathed this land they always occupied as a free state from one generation to the next down to the present day. They deserve our praise, but our fathers deserve even more because they, with great effort, added the empire we now possess to their inheritance and left it as a legacy for us, the living. We, who are still more or less in the prime of our lives, have enlarged most of that empire and have made our city self-sufficient both for war and peace. I will not go on at length about the things we did in our wars, through which each gain was made; or how our fathers or we ourselves readily defended ourselves against the attacks of hostile Greeks and barbarians alike. You know all that; let it go. But the way of life that brought us to our present state—the constitution, the customs, through which it has become great—these things I will first set forth before going on to the eulogy of these men, because I think it fitting that they be said on this occasion, and right for all this throng of citizens and noncitizens to give them heed.

We practice a politics that does not emulate the customs of our neighbors. On the contrary, we are the models, not the imitators, of others. Because we are governed for the many and not for the few, we go by the name of a democracy. As far as private interests are concerned, everyone has equal ac-

cess to the law; but you are distinguished in society and chosen for public service not so much by lot as because of your individual merit. Furthermore, your poverty will not keep you in obscurity if you can do something worthwhile for the city. We are generous towards one another in our public affairs; and though we keep a watchful eye on each other as we go about our daily business, we don't get angry at our neighbor if he does as he pleases, and we don't give him dirty looks, which are painful though they do not kill. Painless as our private lives may be, we are terrified of breaking the laws. We obey them as they are administered by whoever is in power, especially the laws meant to relieve victims of oppression, whether they have been enacted by statute or whether they are the unwritten laws that carry the undisputed penalty of shame.

In addition, we give our minds many a respite from their toils with games and festivals all year long and with the handsome private furnishings whose daily enjoyment dispels the cares of life. Because of its size, all sorts of merchandise comes pouring into our city from all over the world, and foreign goods are no less ours to enjoy than those that are produced right here.

Our approach to military training differs from that of our Spartan opponents in the following ways. We have an open city and do not, by periodically expelling foreigners, keep them from seeing and learning things lest some enemy benefit from what is open to his view. We trust less to our equipment and our guile than to our personal courage in action. When it comes to education, Spartans no sooner reach boyhood than they painfully train to become men, whereas we, who live a more relaxed life, will nevertheless advance to meet the same dangers as they. The proof is that while the Spartans will not march into our land on their own but only with all their allies, we, by ourselves, attacking on foreign soil, usually gain easy victories over men defending their homes. Because we send our own citizens on numerous expeditions by land while simultaneously conducting naval operations, not a single enemy has ever engaged with our whole combined force. Nevertheless, if they should meet with a contingent of our armed forces and defeat some of them somewhere, they boast that they have repelled us all; but if they lose, it is by all of us that they have been vanquished. And since we prefer to run risks with ease of mind rather than with harmful exercise, and with an ingrained rather than an enforced manliness, we do not worry about hardships to come and go to meet them no less boldly than do those who drill incessantly.

This city of ours is amazing for these reasons, but for others as well.

In the first place, we love nobility without ostentation and we have a virile love of knowledge. Furthermore, wealth is for us something to use, not something to brag about. And as to poverty, there is no shame in admitting to it—the real shame is in not taking action to escape from it. Finally, while there are those who manage both the city and their own private business, there are others who, though wrapped up in their work, nevertheless have a thorough knowledge of public affairs. For we are the only people who regard a man who takes no interest in politics to be leading not a quiet life, but a useless one. We are also the only ones who either make governmental decisions or at least frame the issues correctly, because we do not think that action is hampered by public discourse, but by failure to learn enough in advance, through discourse, about what action we need to take. We are especially daring in our analysis and performance of whatever we undertake, whereas for others, ignorance is confidence and reason a drag on action. The bravest men are rightly regarded as those who have the clearest knowledge of pleasure and pain but who do not shrink from danger because of it.

We are also markedly different from most others when it comes to doing good, because we make friends not by receiving favors, but by doing them. The one who does the favor is the firmer friend because his kindness towards the recipient keeps the debt of gratitude unpaid; but the friendship of the debtor has a duller edge because he knows that he reciprocates friendship not by doing favors, but by owing gratitude. And so we alone will also fearlessly help others, not from a calculation of

advantage but from the confidence that comes from our freedom.

To sum up, I tell you that this city, taken all in all, is the school of Greece, and as far as I am concerned, any man among us will exhibit a more fully developed personality than men elsewhere and will be able to take care of himself more gracefully and with the quickest of wit. The very strength our city has acquired through our way of life shows that this is not just a speechifying boast for this occasion, but the truth in action. Alone among today's cities, Athens proves stronger than its reputation, and no attacking enemy need be chagrined that he dies at the hands of an inferior, just as no subject state need censure our unworthiness to rule over it. Our power has not gone unnoticed, as you know only too well, and we have given great proofs to those who are living and yet to come as to why we should be the objects of their admiration. We need no more, not a Homer to sing our praises nor any other poet to please us with verses whose plots and fictions are hobbled by the truth. We have forced the earth and all its seas to make way before our daring, establishing an eternal memory everywhere of the vengeance we have taken and the good that we have done, and it was because they could not bear to think of losing such a city as this that these noble men fought and died, and it is fitting that each and every one of us who remain continue the struggle on her behalf.

This is why I have gone on for so long about our city—to teach the lesson that this struggle means more for us than for those who do not have our advantages, and to establish a foundation in fact for the eulogy I will now deliver. . . . But most of it has already been spoken, for the qualities I have extolled in the city were adorned by the valor of these men and of men like them, and it would be true of very few Greeks that words and deeds are so perfectly balanced as it is for these. For me, the end that came to these men makes plain a man's true worth, whether it came as the first sign or as the final confirmation of that worth. These men had human frailties, but it is only right that we emphasize their courage against the enemy in the defense of their fatherland. Their valor for the

common good erased any harm done by their private faults. None of these men put off the day of reckoning because, like a coward, he preferred to enjoy the pleasures of his wealth or because he hoped, being poor, that he might yet escape poverty and become rich. They yearned more to take vengeance on their enemies than they did for these things, whatever the danger, and believing that of all the dangers this was the noblest, they chose to punish their foes and relinquish the world, committing their hopes to an uncertain success and relying on themselves alone to enter the action they saw before them. They chose to save themselves by suffering and struggle but never by surrender, to flee disgrace and to withstand the battle with their bodies, and in that brief crisis of chance, at the height not of fear but of glory, they took their leave of us.

These were men worthy of their city! The rest of us must pray that our resolve against the enemy is safer, but we must be determined to be just as courageous. No one needs to harangue you, who know it so well, about how valor consists in driving off our enemies, but you must remember that the greatest gift to the city is not in public speeches but in daily beholding her power in action, in being like lovers to her. Thus when she is great in her glory, you will take it to heart that men knowingly, daringly, reverently built her power by doing what needed to be done, and that even when they perished in one of her enterprises, they did not think that the city was being deprived of their valor, but that they had freely made the handsomest possible investment in her. They offered up their bodies for the common good and took for themselves that undying praise and that most distinctive tomb—not the one in which they lie, but the one in which their fame remains to be eternally remembered in word and deed on every fitting occasion. The whole world is the tomb of famous men. Not just an inscribed tablet in their homeland commemorates them, but an unwritten memorial that lives on not in a monument, but in the minds even of strangers. You must now imitate these men. Think of happiness as freedom and freedom as courage, and do not worry over the dangers of war. It is not

the wretched of the earth, for whom there is no hope of improvement, who have reason to be reckless with their lives, but those for whom a change for the worse is a risk they must run for as long as they live and for whom the contrast would be the greatest if they faltered. To a thoughtful man, the knowledge that he is miserable after having proved himself a coward is more painful than a death he hardly feels in strength and comradeship.

Thus, you parents who are here now, I will not weep for you, only console you. You know that you have lived in troubled times. Lucky men, like these here, who have won the handsomest of deaths—for you, a proud grief—have lived for as long as they have been happy. I know it is hard to persuade you of this when you will often be reminded of your sons by the good fortune of others—good fortune in which you yourselves used to exult. And we feel grief not for the deprivation of the good things we have never known, but for what we had grown used to before it was snatched away.

Those who are still of child-bearing age must endure their sorrow in the hope of other children. For them, personally, a new generation will be a way to forget those who are gone; and it will carry the two benefits for the city of preventing underpopulation and of providing security. Those who do not expose their children to the risk of danger along with everyone else are not able to make decisions about equality and justice. To those of you who are past your prime, think of that larger part of your lives in which you were happy as profit. What follows will be short and eased by the good repute of these men. Only the love of honor never grows old, and it is not making money, as some people say, that pleases us most in our useless old age, but the esteem of others.

As to you, the sons and brothers of these men, I foresee that you will have a formidable task before you, because everyone praises those who have passed away, and it will be hard enough for you to be thought of as having fallen just short of their high valor, much less as having equaled it. You see, envy for the living derives from competition, but those who are no longer with us are honored with an unchallengeable good will.

And since I must also make some mention of womanly virtue to those who will now be widows, I will define it in this brief admonition: your greatest fame consists in being no worse than your natures, and in having the least possible reputation among males for good or ill.

I have spoken, in my turn, and according to our custom, what words I could for this occasion, and those who are interred have here been honored, for now, with our deeds. From this day on, the city will rear their children at public expense until they come of age, thus offering a tangible prize to these men and their survivors for their struggle. After all, the people who institute the greatest rewards for excellence will have the best citizens. And now that each of you has mourned your kin to the full, go on your way.

These funeral rites were celebrated that winter, after which the first year of the war came to an end. . . .

The Melian Dialogue

The following summer, Alcibiades sailed to Argos with twenty ships, seized three hundred Argives still suspected of having Spartan sympathies, and then imprisoned them on nearby islands under Athenian control. The Athenians also sent a fleet against the island of Melos. Thirty of the ships were their own, six were from Chios, and two were from Lesbos. Their own troops numbered twelve hundred hoplites, three hundred archers, and twenty mounted archers. There were also about fifteen hundred hoplites from their allies on the islands. The Melians are colonists from Sparta and would not submit to Athenian control like the other islanders. At first, they were neutral and lived peaceably, but they became openly hostile after Athens once tried to compel their obedience by ravaging their land. The generals Cleomedes, son of Lycomedes, and Tisias, son of Tisimachus, bivouacked on Melian territory with their troops, but before doing any injury to the land, they sent ambassadors to hold talks with the Melians. The Melian leadership, however, did not bring these men before the popular assembly. Instead, they

asked them to discuss their mission with the council and the privileged voters. The Athenian ambassadors spoke as follows.

"We know that what you are thinking in bringing us before a few voters, and not before the popular assembly, is that now the people won't be deceived after listening to a single long, seductive, and unrefuted speech from us. Well, those of you who are sitting here can make things even safer for yourselves. When we say something that seems wrong, interrupt immediately, and answer, not in a set speech, but one point at a time.—But say first whether this proposal is to your liking."

The Melian councillors said, "There can be no objection to the reasonableness of quiet, instructive talks among ourselves. But this military force, which is here, now, and not off in the future, looks different from instruction. We see that you have come as judges in a debate, and the likely prize will be war if we win the debate with arguments based on right and refuse to capitulate, or servitude if we concede to you."

ATHENIANS: Excuse us, but if you're having this meeting to make guesses about the future or to do anything but look at your situation and see how to save your city, we'll leave. But if that's the topic, we'll keep talking.

MELIANS: It's natural and understandable that in a situation like this, people would want to express their thoughts at length. But so be it. This meeting is about saving our city, and the format of the discussion will be as you have said.

ATHENIANS: Very well.

We Athenians are not going to use false pretenses and go on at length about how we have a right to rule because we destroyed the Persian empire, or about how we are seeking retribution because you did us wrong. You would not believe us anyway. And please do not suppose that you will persuade *us* when you say that you did not campaign with the Spartans although you were their colonists, or that you never did us wrong. No, each of us must exercise what power he really thinks he can, and we know and you know that in the human realm, justice is enforced only among those who can be equally constrained by it, and that those who have power use it, while the weak make compromises.

MELIANS: Since you have ruled out a discussion of justice and forced us to speak of expediency, it would be inexpedient, at least as we see it, for you to eradicate common decency. There has always been a fair and right way to treat people who are in danger, if only to give them some benefit for making persuasive arguments by holding off from the full exercise of power. This applies to you above all, since you would set an example for others of how to take the greatest vengeance if you fall.

ATHENIANS: We're not worried about the end of our empire, if it ever does end. People who rule over others, like the Spartans, are not so bad to their defeated enemies. Anyway, we're not fighting the Spartans just now. What is really horrendous is when subjects are able to attack and defeat their masters.—But you let us worry about all that. We are here to talk about benefiting our empire and saving your city, and we will tell you how we are going to do that, because we want to take control here without any trouble and we want you to be spared for both our sakes.

MELIANS: And just how would it be as much to our advantage to be enslaved, as for you to rule over us?

ATHENIANS You would benefit by surrendering before you experience the worst of consequences, and we would benefit by not having you dead.

MELIANS: So you would not accept our living in peace, being friends instead of enemies, and allies of neither side?

ATHENIANS: Your hatred doesn't hurt us as much as your friendship. That would show us as weak to our other subjects, whereas your hatred would be a proof of our power.

MELIANS: Would your subjects consider you reasonable if you lumped together colonists who had no connection to you, colonists from Athens, and rebellious colonists who had been subdued?

ATHENIANS: They think there's justice all around. They also think the independent islands are strong, and that we are afraid to attack them. So aside from adding to our empire, your subjugation will also enhance our safety, especially since you are islanders and we are a naval power. Besides, you're weaker than the others—unless, that is, you show that you too can be independent.

MELIANS: Don't you think there's safety in our neutrality? You turned us away from a discussion of justice and persuaded us to attend to what was in your interest. Now it's up to us to tell you about what is to our advantage and to try to persuade you that it is also to yours. How will you avoid making enemies of states that are now neutral, but that look at what you do here and decide that you will go after them one day? How will you achieve anything but to make your present enemies seem more attractive, and to force those who had no intention of opposing you into unwilling hostility?

ATHENIANS: We do not think the threat to us is so much from mainlanders who, in their freedom from fear, will be continually putting off their preparations against us, as from independent islanders, like you, and from those who are already chafing under the restraints of rule. These are the ones who are most likely to commit themselves to ill-considered action and create foreseeable dangers for themselves and for us.

MELIANS: Well then, in the face of this desperate effort you and your slaves are making, you to keep your empire and they to get rid of it, wouldn't we, who are still free, be the lowest of cowards if we didn't try everything before submitting to slavery?

ATHENIANS: No, not if you think about it prudently. This isn't a contest about manly virtue between equals, or about bringing disgrace on yourself. You are deliberating about your very existence, about standing up against a power far greater than yours.

MELIANS: But we know that there are times when the odds in warfare don't depend on the numbers. If we give up, our situation becomes hopeless right away, but if we fight, we can still hope to stand tall.

ATHENIANS: In times of danger, hope is a comfort that can hurt you, but it won't destroy you if you back it up with plenty of other resources. People who gamble everything on it (hope is extravagant by nature, you see) know it for what it really is only after they have lost everything. Then, of course, when you can recognize it and take precautions, it's left you flat. You don't want to experience that. You Melians are weak, and you only have one chance. So don't be like all those people who could have saved themselves by their own efforts, but who abandoned their realistic hopes and turned in their hour of need to invisible powers—to prophecies and oracles and all the other nonsense that conspires with hope to ruin you.

MELIANS: As you well know, we too think it will be hard to fight both your power and the fortunes of war, especially with uneven odds. Still, we believe that our fortune comes from god, and that we will not be defeated because we take our stand as righteous men against men who are in the wrong. And what we lack in power will be made up for by the Spartan League. They will have to help us, if only because of our kinship with them and the disgrace they would feel if they didn't. So it's not totally irrational for us to feel hopeful.

ATHENIANS: Well, when it comes to divine good will, we don't think we'll be left out. We're not claiming anything or doing anything outside man's thinking about the gods or about the way the gods themselves behave. Given what we believe about the gods and know about men, we think that both are always forced by the law of nature to dominate everyone they can. We didn't lay down this law, it was there—and we weren't the first to make use of it. We took it as it was and acted on it, and we will bequeath it as a living thing to future generations, knowing full well that if you or anyone else had the same power as we, you would do the same thing. So

we probably don't have to fear any disadvantage when it comes to the gods. And as to this opinion of yours about the Spartans, that you can trust them to help you because of their fear of disgrace—well, our blessings on your innocence, but we don't envy your foolishness. The Spartans do the right thing among themselves, according to their local customs. One could say a great deal about their treatment of others, but to put it briefly, they are more conspicuous than anyone else we know in thinking that pleasure is good and expediency is just. Their mindset really bears no relation to your irrational belief that there is any safety for you now.

MELIANS: But it's exactly because of this expediency that we trust them. They won't want to betray the Melians, their colonists, and prove themselves helpful to their enemies and unreliable to their well-wishers in Greece.

ATHENIANS: But don't you see that expediency is safe, and that doing the right and honorable thing is dangerous? On the whole, the Spartans are the last people to take big risks.

MELIANS: We think they'll take on dangers for us that they wouldn't for others and regard those dangers as less risky, because we are close to the Peloponnese from an operational point of view. Also, they can trust our loyalty because we are kin and we think alike.

ATHENIANS: Men who ask others to come to fight on their side don't offer security in good will but in real fighting power. The Spartans take this kind of thing more into consideration than others, because they have so little faith in their own resources that they even attack their neighbors with plenty of allies. So it's not likely that they'll try to make their way over to an island when we control the sea.

MELIANS: Then maybe they'll send their allies. The sea of Crete is large, and it is harder for those who control the sea to catch a ship than it is for the ship to get through to safety without being noticed. And if that doesn't work, they might turn against your territory or attack the rest of your allies, the ones Brasidas didn't get to. And then the fight would shift from a place where you have no interest to your own land and that of your allies.

ATHENIANS: It's been tried and might even be tried for you—though surely you are aware that we Athenians have never abandoned a siege out of fear of anyone.

But it occurs to us that after saying you were going to talk about saving yourselves, you haven't in any of this lengthy discussion mentioned anything that most people would rely on for their salvation. Your strongest arguments are in the future and depend on hope. What you've actually got is too meager to give you a chance of surviving the forces lined up against you now. You've shown a very irrational attitude—unless, of course, you intend to reach some more prudent conclusion than this after you send us away and begin your deliberations. For surely you don't mean to commit yourselves to that "honor" which has been so destructive to men in clear and present dangers involving "dishonor." Many men who could still see where it was leading them have been drawn on by the allure of this so-called "honor," this word with its seductive power, and fallen with open eyes into irremediable catastrophe, vanquished in their struggle with a fine word, only to achieve a kind of dishonorable honor because they weren't just unlucky, they were fools. You can avoid this, if you think things over carefully, and decide that there is nothing so disgraceful in being defeated by the greatest city in the world, which invites you to become its ally on fair terms—paying us tribute, to be sure, but keeping your land for yourselves. You have been given the choice between war and security. Don't be stubborn and make the wrong choice. The people who are most likely to succeed stand up to their equals, have the right attitude towards their superiors, and are fair to those beneath them.

We will leave now. Think it over, and always remember that you are making a decision about your country. You only have one, and its existence depends on this one chance to make a decision, right or wrong.

Then the Athenians withdrew from the discussion. The Melians, left to themselves, came to the

conclusion that had been implied by their responses in the talks. They answered the Athenians as follows: "Men of Athens, our decision is no different from what it was at first. We will not in this brief moment strip the city we have lived in for seven hundred years of its freedom. We will try to save it, trusting in the divine good fortune that has preserved us so far and in the help we expect from the Spartans and from others. We invite you to be our friends, to let us remain neutral, and to leave our territory after making a treaty agreeable to us both."

That was the Melian response. The talks were already breaking up when the Athenians said, "Well, judging from this decision, you seem to us to be the only men who can make out the future more clearly than what you can see, and who gaze upon the invisible with your mind's eye as if it were an accomplished fact. You have cast yourselves on luck, hope, and the Spartans, and the more you trust in them, the harder will be your fall."

REVIEW QUESTIONS

1. What, in Pericles' estimation, are the benefits of democracy?
2. What are the reasons for Athens' greatness?
3. How do the values of Athenian democracy compare with those of Spartan society?
4. How evident are Athens' democratic values in the Athenians' negotiations with the citizens of Melos?

SOPHOCLES

FROM *Antigone*

One of the foremost features of the culture of classical Athens was its focus on the rights, responsibilities, and potential of the individual and its celebration of human intellect and personality. Nowhere is this more evident than in the surviving works of the greatest of the Athenian tragedians, Aeschylus, Sophocles, and Euripides. Sophocles wrote his play Antigone, *from which the following excerpts are taken, shortly before 441 B.C.E. Like so many of the plays of this era,* Antigone *focuses on the nobility of spirit of the human being when faced with terrible conflict. Indeed, one well-known analysis of its impact characterizes it as the only work of literature that expresses "all the principal constants of conflict in the condition of man . . . : the confrontation of men and women; of age and of youth; of society and of the individual; of the living and the dead; of men and of god(s)."*

From *The Antigone of Sophocles,* translated by George Herbert Palmer (Boston: Houghton Mifflin, 1927).

THE PERSONS

CREON, King of Thebes

EURYDICE, his wife

HAEMON, his son, betrothed to Antigone

ANTIGONE, ⎫ his nieces, daughters of Oedipus and
ISMENE, ⎬ Jocasta, former King and Queen of
⎭ Thebes

WATCHMAN

MESSENGER

SECOND MESSENGER

BOY AND GUARDS, silent persons

CHORUS OF THEBAN ELDERS

The Scene throughout is at Thebes, in front of the palace. The Play begins at daybreak.

————

ANTIGONE: Ismene, my own sister, of all the woes begun in Oedipus can you imagine any that Zeus will not complete within our lives? There is no grief or crime, no degradation or dishonor, not to be found among the woes of you and me. And what is this new edict issued lately by our captain, people say, to the whole city? Do you know, and did you hear? Or have you failed to learn how on our friends fall evils from our foes?

ISMENE: To me, Antigone, have come no tidings of our friends, for good or ill, since we two lost two brothers, slain in mutual strife the self-same day. I know the Argive host retreated this last night, but I know nothing further—whether we gain or lose.

ANTIGONE: I guessed as much, and therefore brought you here alone outside the gate to learn the truth.

ISMENE: What is it, then? You seem to hint at some dark tale.

ANTIGONE: Yes. In his order for the burial of our brothers has not Creon honored the one, outraged the other? To Eteocles, they say, he paid each proper rite and custom and laid him in the ground, to be in honor with the dead below. But as for poor dead Polynices' body, they say he has proclaimed among our people that none shall hide it in a grave and mourn, but let it lie unwept, unburied, welcome provision for the birds who watch for such-like prey. These are, they say, the orders our good Creon has proclaimed for you and me—yes, even for me!—and now comes hither to make plain his will to such as do not know. Nor does he treat the matter lightly. But let one do what he forbids, and death by public stoning shall await him in the city. So it stands now, and you must quickly show if you are rightly born or the base child of noble parents.

ISMENE: But, my poor sister, if it has come to this, what further can I do to help or hinder?

ANTIGONE: Think, will you share my toil and strife?

ISMENE: In what bold deed? What is your plan?

ANTIGONE: To try if you with this hand's help will raise that body.

ISMENE: What! Bury him? In opposition to the State?

ANTIGONE: My brother, though, and yours. If you refuse, I will be found no traitor.

ISMENE: Reckless! When Creon too forbids?

ANTIGONE: 'T is not for him to keep me from my own.

ISMENE: Alas! consider, sister, how our father died, hated and scorned, because of self-exposed offences doing his eyes a violence with his own hand. And then his mother and his wife—ah, double title!—with twisted cord ended her life in shame. A third disaster came. Our pair of brothers in a single day, like wretched suicides, wrought out one common ruin by each other's hand. And now once more, when we are the only ones still left, think what a far worse fate we two shall meet if we, defying law, transgress our rulers' will and power. Nay, rather let us bear in mind that we are women, so not fit to strive with men. Moreover, since we are the subjects of those stronger than ourselves, we must obey these orders and orders harsher still. I, then, beseeching those beneath the earth to grant me pardon, seeing I am compelled, will bow to those in power. To act beyond one's sphere shows little wisdom.

ANTIGONE: I will not urge you. No! Nor if hereafter you desire, shall you with my consent give any aid. Be what you will, and I will bury

him. Good it would be to die in doing so. Dearly shall I lie with him, with my dear, after my pious sin. And longer must I satisfy those there below than people here, for there I shall lie ever. But you, if you think well, keep disregarding what the gods regard!

ISMENE: I mean no disregard. But to defy the State—it is not in me.

ANTIGONE: Make that, then, your excuse! I will go raise a grave over my dearest brother.

ISMENE: O my poor sister, how I fear for you!

ANTIGONE: Be not disturbed for me. Let your own course be true.

ISMENE: At least do not reveal what you have done. Keep it a secret. I will hide it too.

ANTIGONE: Ha? Speak it out! Far more my enemy if silent than if telling it to all!

ISMENE: Hot heart and chilling deeds!

ANTIGONE: I know I please those I most ought to please.

ISMENE: If you succeed. But you desire what cannot be.

ANTIGONE: Why, then, when strength shall fail me, I will cease.

ISMENE: Best not pursue at all what cannot be.

ANTIGONE: Speak thus, and I shall hate you. And he who died will hate you,—rightly too. Nay, leave me and my rash design to meet our doom, for I shall meet none equal to not dying nobly.

ISMENE: Go, then, if go you must. And yet of this be sure, that mad as is your going, dearly are you loved by those you love.

* * *

[*Enter* CREON.]

CREON: Sirs, our city's welfare, though shaken in a heavy surge, the gods have safely righted. Therefore by mandate I have brought you hither, parted from all the rest, because I know full well how in the time of Laïus you steadily respected the power of the throne. So also in the days when Oedipus upheld the State. And even when he fell, you stood around the children of his house with faithful hearts. Since, then, these two have fallen in one day by double doom, smiting and smitten in their own hand's guilt, I take possession of all power and of the throne through being next of kin to the two dead.

It is impossible fully to learn what a man is in heart and mind and judgment until he proves himself by test of office and of laws. For to my thinking he who ordering a great state catches at plans not through their being best, and then through fear holds his lips locked, appears and ever has appeared most base. Him who regards his friend more than his land I count no man at all. I therefore,—all-seeing Zeus bear witness!—never shall keep silence when I see woe coming on my citizens instead of weal. Nor would I ever make that man my friend who is my country's foe; because I know how it is she who saves us, and when we sail with her secure we find true friends.

Such are the principles by which I make this city prosper. And in accord herewith I now have issued public edict touching the sons of Oedipus: ordering that Eteocles, who fell fighting for this city after winning all distinction with his spear, be laid within a grave and given whatever honors meet the brave dead below. But for his brother Polynices, who coming back from exile tried by fire utterly to destroy his native land and his ancestral gods, tried even to taste the blood of his own kin or force them into bondage—this man we have proclaimed throughout the city none shall honor with a grave and none lament, but that his corpse be left unburied, for the birds and dogs to eat, disgraced for all to see. Such is my will. Never by act of mine shall bad men have more honor than the just. But he who is well minded toward this state alike in life or death by me is honored.

* * *

CREON: You there, now turning to the ground your face, do you acknowledge or deny you did this thing?

ANTIGONE: I say I did it. I deny not that I did.

CREON: (*To Watchman.*) Then go your way, clear of a heavy charge. [*Exit.*] (*To Antigone.*) Tell me, not at full length but briefly, did you know my edict against doing this?

ANTIGONE: I did. How could I help it? It was plain.

CREON: Yet you presumed to transgress laws?

ANTIGONE: Yes, for it was not Zeus who gave this edict; nor yet did Justice, dwelling with the gods below, make for men laws like these. I did not think such force was in your edicts that the unwritten and unchanging laws of God you, a mere man, could traverse. These are not matters of to-day or yesterday, but are from everlasting. No man can tell at what time they appeared. In view of them I would not, through fear of human will, meet judgment from the gods. That I shall die, I knew,—how fail to know it?—though you had never made an edict. And if before my time I die, I count it gain. For he who lives like me in many woes, how can he fail to find in death a gain? So then for me to meet this doom is not a grief at all. But when my mother's child had died if I had kept his corpse unburied, then I should have grieved. For this I do not grieve. And if I seem to you to have been working folly, it may be he who charges folly is the fool.

CHORUS: Plain is the headstrong temper of this child of headstrong father. She knows not how to bend in times of ill.

CREON: Yet know that spirits very stiff may soonest fail. The strongest iron, baked in the fire over-hard, you may see oftenest snap and break. By a little bit, I find, high-mettled steeds are managed. There is no place for pride in one who is dependent. She first set out in crime when she transgressed the established laws; and after that comes further crime in boasting here, laughing at having done so. I am no longer man, she is the man, if such power rests in her unchallenged. Be she my sister's child, or closer to my blood than all who bow before our household Zeus, she and her kin shall not escape the direst doom.

Yes, for I count her sister an equal plotter of this burial. Summon her hither! Even now I saw her in the house raving and uncontrolled. It often happens that the stealthy heart is caught before the act, when in the dark men fashion crooked deeds. But it is hateful, too, when one found out in wrong will give his guilt fine names.

ANTIGONE: Do you desire more than having caught to kill me?

CREON: No, nothing. Having that, I have the whole.

ANTIGONE: Then why delay? For nothing in your words can give me pleasure—and may they never please! So also you mine naturally displease. Yet how could I have gained glory more glorious than by now laying my own brother in the grave? All here would speak approval, did not terror seal their lips. Rulers, so fortunate in much besides, have this advantage too—that they can do and say whatever they may please.

CREON: Of all the race of Cadmus you alone see it so.

ANTIGONE: These also do, but curb their tongues through fear of you.

CREON: And are you not ashamed to act so unlike them?

ANTIGONE: 'T is no disgrace to honor one's own kin.

CREON: Was not he also of your blood who fell, his rival?

ANTIGONE: Mine, by one mother and one father too.

CREON: Why then pay honors which dishonor him?

ANTIGONE: He who is dead would not describe it so.

CREON: Yes, if you give like honor to his impious foe.

ANTIGONE: It was no slave who died. It was his brother.

CREON: Wasting the land. And he defending it.

ANTIGONE: But these are rites called for by Death itself.

CREON: The good and bad should not be like in lot.

ANTIGONE: Who knows if that is pity below?

CREON: A hated man is not beloved, though dead.

ANTIGONE: I take no part in hate. 'T is mine to love.

CREON: Down to the grave, then, if you needs must love, and love those there! But while I live, no woman masters me.

*   *   *

CHORUS: But here is Haemon, the youngest of your sons. Does he come grieving for the fate of his intended bride Antigone, vexed at his vanished nuptials?

[*Enter* HAEMON.]

*   *   *

CREON: Soon we shall know, better than seers could say. My son, because you heard the immutable decree passed on your promised bride, you are not here incensed against your father? Are we not dear to you, do what we may?

HAEMON: My father, I am yours; and with just judgment you may direct, and I shall follow. No marriage shall be counted greater gain than your wise guidance.

CREON: Yes, so it should be settled in your heart, my son, always to take your stand behind your father's judgment. Therefore men pray to rear obedient children and to have them in their homes, to recompense the foe with ill and honor as their father does the friend. If one begets unprofitable children, what shall we say but that he breeds pains for himself, loud laughter for his foes? Do not, my son, at pleasure's bidding, give up your wits for any woman. But know embraces soon grow cold when she who shares the home is false. What ulcer can be worse than the false friend? Then spurn the girl as if she were your foe, and let her seek a husband in the house of Hades. For having found her only, out of all the State, openly disobedient, recreant to that State I will not be, but I will have her life.

Let her appeal to Zeus, the god of kindred; but if I train my kin to be disorderly, I surely shall all those outside my kin. He who in private matters is a faithful man will prove himself upright in public too. But one who wantonly forces the law, and thinks to dictate to the rulers, wins no praise from me. No, whosoever is established by the State should be obeyed, in matters trivial and just or in their opposites. And the obedient man, I should be confident, would govern well and easily be governed, and posted in the storm of spears would hold his ground, a true and loyal comrade. Than lawlessness there is no greater ill. It ruins states, overturns homes, and joining with the spear-thrust breaks the ranks in rout. But in the steady lines what saves most lives is discipline. Therefore we must defend the public order and not at all subject it to a woman. Better be pushed aside, if need be, by a man than to be known as women's subjects.

CHORUS: Unless through age we are at fault, you seem to say with reason what you say.

HAEMON: Father, the gods plant wisdom in mankind, which is of all possessions highest. In what respects you have not spoken rightly I cannot say, and may I never learn; and still it may be possible for some one else to be right too. I naturally watch in your behalf all that men do or say or find to blame. For your eye terrifies the common man and checks the words you might not wish to hear; but it is mine to hear things uttered in the dark. I know how the whole city mourns this maid, as one who of all women least deservedly for noblest deeds meets basest death. "She who, when her brother had fallen in the fight and lay unburied, did not leave him to be torn by savage dogs and birds, is she not worthy to receive some golden honor?" Such guarded talk runs covertly about.

For me, my father, nothing I possess is dearer than your welfare. For what can bring to children greater glory than a successful father's noble name, or to a father than his son's renown? Do not then carry in your heart one fixed belief that what you say and nothing else is right. For he who thinks that he alone is wise, or that he has a tongue and mind no other has, will when laid open be found empty. However wise a man may be, it is no shame to learn, learn much, and not to be too firm. You see along the streams in winter how many trees bend down and save their branches; while those that stand up stiff go trunk and all to ruin. So he who tightly draws his vessel's sheet and will not slack, upsets the boat and ends his course with benches upside down. Be yielding, then, and admit change. For if from me, though younger, an opinion be allowed, I count it best that man should be by nature wise. But if that cannot be,—and usually the scale does not incline so— then it is well to learn from good advisers.

CHORUS: My lord, you ought, when Haemon speaks aright, to learn of him; and Haemon, you of him. For both have spoken well.

CREON: At our age shall we learn from one so young?

HAEMON: Only the truth. Young though I am, do not regard my years more than the facts.

CREON: The fact, you mean, of being gentle to the unruly.

HAEMON: I would not ask for gentleness to wicked persons.

CREON: But is not she tainted with some such ill?

HAEMON: With one accord the men of Thebes say no.

CREON: And shall the city tell me how to rule?

HAEMON: Surely you see how childish are such words!

CREON: Govern this land for others than myself?

HAEMON: No city is the property of one alone.

CREON: Is not the city reckoned his who rules?

HAEMON: Excellent ruling,—you alone, the land deserted!

CREON: He fights, it seems, the woman's battle.

HAEMON: If you are she. Indeed my care is all for you.

CREON: Perverted boy, pressing a cause against your father!

HAEMON: Because I see you causelessly do wrong.

CREON: Do I do wrong in reverencing my office?

HAEMON: It is not reverence to trample on the rights of gods.

CREON: A hateful heart that bends before a woman!

HAEMON: But never will you find me subservient to the base.

CREON: Why, all your argument is urged for her.

HAEMON: Yes, and for you and me, and for the gods below.

CREON: You shall not marry her this side the grave.

HAEMON: So then she dies; but if she dies, destroys another.

CREON: Will you assail me with your threats, audacious boy?

HAEMON: Is it a threat to combat silly schemes?

CREON: To your sorrow you shall teach, while yourself in need of teaching.

HAEMON: But that you are my father, I had counted you ill-taught.

CREON: Be a plaything for your mistress, but trifle not with me!

HAEMON: Will you then speak, and when you speak not listen?

CREON: And has it come to this? But, by Olympus, you shall not lightly heap reproach on insult. Bring me that piece of malice, straight-way to die before my eyes in presence of her bridegroom!

HAEMON: Not in my presence. Do not think it! She shall not die while I am near. And you youself shall see my face no more. Rave on then here with those who will submit!

[*Exit.*]

*   *   *

CHORUS: So you will put them both to death?

CREON: Not her who had no finger in the business. You say well.

CHORUS: And by what doom do you intend to slay the other?

CREON: Leading her where the ways are clear of humankind, I will shut her up alive in a stone cell, allowing only so much food for expiation that the whole city may escape the stain. And if she calls upon the Grave,—the only god she honors—she may obtain deliverance from death; or else will learn, though late, that honor done the Grave is labor lost.

[*Exit.*]

*   *   *

ANTIGONE: Men of my land, you see me taking my last walk here, looking my last upon the sunshine—never more. No, Hades, who brings all to bed, leads me alive along the strand of Acheron, missing my part in wedding song. Never did bridal hymn hymn me. But I shall be the bride of Acheron.

CHORUS: And yet you will in glory and with praise pass to the secret places of the dead. Not smitten with slow disease, nor meeting the sword's portion, but self-possessed, alone among mankind you go to the Grave alive.

ANTIGONE: I have heard of the pitiful end of the stranger from Phrygia, the daughter of Tantalus, on Mount Sipylus; o'er whom like cling-

ing ivy a rocky growth would creep, and from her wasting form the showers and snow, 't is said, are never absent, but drop upon her neck down from her weeping brows. Most like to her, God brings me to my rest.

CHORUS: Nay, nay! She was a god and sprung from gods. But we are mortals and of human birth. Yet for a mortal maid to win a godlike lot is high renown, whether one live or die.

ANTIGONE: Ah, I am mocked! Why, by our country's gods, taunt me when not yet gone but here before you? O thou my city, and ye great ones of my city, thou spring of Dircé, and thou grove of charioted Thebes, I call on you to witness how all unwept of friends and by what cruel laws I go to that sepulchral mound for an unheard-of burial. Ah, poor me! Having no home with mankind or with corpses, with living or with dead!

CHORUS: Onward pressing to the utmost verge of daring, on the deep foundation stone of Right you fell, my child,—a grievous fall. A father's penalty you pay.

ANTIGONE: Ah, there you touched my bitterest pang, my father's thrice-told woe, and all the doom of the great line of Labdacus. Alas, the horrors of my mother's bed! And the embraces—his very self begetting—of that father and that hapless mother from whom I here, distracted, once was born! To them I go, accursed, unwedded, now to dwell. Alas for you, my brother, who made an ill-starred marriage and in your death stripped me, alive, of all.

CHORUS: In pious actions there is piety. Yet power, when his whose right it is, may nowise be transgressed. Your self-willed temper slew you.

ANTIGONE: Unwept, unfriended, with no bridal song, poor I am led along the appointed way. Never again that sacred ball of fire may I, alas! behold. Yet for my tearless lot not a friend grieves.

CREON: Do you not know that groans and dirges before death would never cease, were it allowed to voice them? Away with her forthwith! And when, as I commanded, you have shut her in the vaulted tomb, leave her alone in solitude, to die if so she must, or let her live her life prisoned in such a home. Thus we are clear of what befalls the maid. Only from dwelling in the light above shall she be hindered.

ANTIGONE: O grave! O bridal chamber! Hollow home, forever holding me! whither I go to join my own; for far the greater number Persephassa has received among the dead, all gone! Last of them I, and most unhappy far, now go below before I reach the limit of my life; yet going, dearly cherish it among my hopes to have my coming welcome to my father, welcome to you, my mother, welcome too to you, my brother. When you all died, with my own hand I washed you, did you service, and poured libations at your graves. But, Polynices, for ministering to your corpse this is my recompense.

Rightly I honored you, the wise will think. Yet had I children, or were my husband mouldering in death, I might not in defiance of my townsmen have taken up the task. And wherefore so? I might have had another husband, had mine died, a child too by another man when I had lost my own; but mother and father hidden in the grave, there is no brother ever to be born. Yet when upon such grounds I held you first in honor, to Creon's eye I seemed to sin and to be over-bold, my brother dear. And now he leads me forth, a captive, deprived of bridal bed and song,—without experience of marriage or the rearing of a child,—that so poor I, cut off from friends but still alive, enter the caverned chambers of the dead.

What ordinance of heaven have I transgressed? Yet why in misery still look to gods or call on them for aid, when even this name of impious I got by piety! No, if such acts are pleasing to the gods, I may by suffering come to know my sin. But if these others rather sin, may they not suffer greater ill than they now wrongly wreak on me.

CHORUS: Still the same winds' same blasts of passion sway her.

CREON: Therefore her guards shall smart for their delay.

ANTIGONE: Ah me! The signal comes that death is nigh!

CHORUS: I cannot bid you hope it will not follow.

ANTIGONE: O city in the land of Thebes! Home of my fathers! And ye, ancestral gods! Men seize me and I cannot stay. Behold, O lords of Thebes, how I, last remnant of the royal line, now suffer, and from whom—I who revered the right.

[ANTIGONE *is led away.*]

*　　*　　*

[*Enter a messenger.*]

MESSENGER: Ye dwellers at the palace of Cadmus and Amphion, there is no human life, however placed, that I can praise or blame. For fortune raises, fortune overthrows, him who is now in good or evil fortune. No seer can tell the destinies of man. Creon was enviable once, I thought, through having saved this land of Cadmus from its foes. Winning full sovereignty he ruled the land, blest too in noble issue. Now all is gone. For when man parts with happiness, I count him not alive, but a mere breathing corpse. Let him have riches in his house, great riches if you will, and live in royal state; if happiness be absent, I would not pay a puff of smoke for all the rest, when weighed with joy.

CHORUS: What new disaster to our kings come you to tell?

MESSENGER: Dead! And the living caused the death.

CHORUS: Who is the slayer? Who has fallen? Speak!

MESSENGER: Haemon is gone. With violence his blood is shed.

CHORUS: What? By his father's hand, or by his own?

MESSENGER: His own, incensed against his father for the murder.

*　　*　　*

CHORUS: But lo! Our lord himself draws near, bringing in his arms clear proof—if we may say so—of wrong not wrought by others but by his erring self.

[*Enter* CREON, *bearing the body of* HAEMON.]

*　　*　　*

CREON: Alas, the sins of a presumptuous soul, stubborn and deadly! Ah, ye who see slayers and slain of kindred blood! Woe for my ill-starred plans! Alas, my boy, so young in life and young in sorrow! Woe! Woe! Thou, dead and gone? And by my folly, not thy own!

CHORUS: Ah me! It seems you see the right too late!

CREON: Unhappy I have learned it now. But then some god possessed me, smote on my head a heavy blow, drove me along a brutish path, and so—alas!—o'erthrew my joy and trampled it. Woe, woe, for the wearisome works of man!

[*Enter a second messenger.*]

SECOND MESSENGER: My lord, 't is having and still getting. You bear one sorrow in your arms; enter the house, and there you soon should see another.

CREON: What is there yet more sorrowful than this?

SECOND MESSENGER: The queen is dead, true mother of the dead here. Poor lady, she has fallen by wounds dealt even now.

CREON: Alas, alas! Insatiate gulf of death! Why, why thus cause my ruin? And cruel messenger, speeding my pain, what is the tale you tell? Why, one already dead you slay anew! What say you, boy? What tidings do you bring? Ah, must the slaughterous ending of my wife follow the death of him?

[*The Scene opens, and the body of* EURYDICE *is disclosed.*]

CHORUS: Here you may see! It shall be hid no longer.

CREON: Ah me! A fresh, a second grief poor I behold. What more has fate in waiting? Just now I took my child in my arms—alas!—and face to face behold another corse. Woe! Woe! unhappy mother! Woe, my child!

SECOND MESSENGER: Crazed, clinging to the altar, and closing her dark eyes, she first bemoaned the glorious grave of Megareus who died before, then this one's end; and with her last breath called down ill on you, the murderer of your children.

CREON: Alas! Alas! Fear thrills me. Will none strike home with two-edged sword? Poor I am steeped in sore distress.

SECOND MESSENGER: You were accused by her who died of causing both the deaths.

CREON: And by what sort of violence did she depart?

SECOND MESSENGER: Her own hand smote herself below the heart, soon as she learned the lamentable ending of her son.

CREON: Ah me! To no one else can this be shifted from my guilty self. 'T was I indeed that killed thee, wretched I! I say the truth, 't was I. Take me, my servants, take me straightway hence, to be no more than nothing.

CHORUS: Wise wishes these, if any way is wise in evil. Briefest is best, when evil clogs our feet.

CREON: Come, then, appear, fairest of fates that brings my final day! O come, best boon, and let me never see another day!

CHORUS: Time will determine that. The present needs our care. Let them whose right it is direct the rest!

CREON: All I desire is summed up in that prayer.

CHORUS: Pray no more now. From his appointed woe man cannot fly.

CREON: Then take away the useless man who by no will of his killed thee, my child, and thee too lying here. Alas poor me, who know not which to look on, where to turn! All in my hands was at cross purposes, and on my head fell fate I could not guide.

CHORUS: Wisdom is far the greater part of peace. The gods will have their dues. Large language, bringing to the proud large chastisement, at last brings wisdom.

*   *   *

REVIEW QUESTIONS

1. What is the dilemma with which Antigone is confronted?
2. Where, in her eyes, must her principal allegiance lie?
3. How does the fact that Antigone is a woman affect her treatment by Creon?
4. How do you think this play would have been received by a Spartan audience?

VASE DEPICTING A SLAVE, PERHAPS IN A SCENE FROM A GREEK PLAY (C. 450 B.C.E.)

Slaves at Athens included a variety of nationalities and were at the bottom of the socio-economic hierarchy. What does the depiction in this vase painting suggest about attitudes toward slaves? How do the physical features and clothing of this slave differ from what you have observed in other works of classical Greek art?

PLATO

FROM "Apology"

*Our knowledge of the life, personality, and teachings of the late-fifth-century B.C.E.
Athenian philosopher and social critic Socrates is derived almost entirely from the
dialogues composed by his most famous student, Plato. In them, Plato recreates Socrates' method of using questions and answers (what today we still refer to as the
"Socratic method") to examine and test commonly held opinions. In the following
excerpt from the "Apology" (a word that in ancient Greek referred to a defense of
one's actions or beliefs, not an expression of contrition or regret), Socrates, on trial
before an Athenian jury for allegedly subverting the youth of Athens by converting
them to gods of his own invention, defends his career as a teacher. (His eloquence
and intellect, in the end, did not save him from condemnation and subsequent execution in 399 B.C.E.)*

From *The Last Days of Socrates*, translated by Hugh Tredennick (New York: Penguin, 1969),
pp. 48–52, 72–76.

*   *   *

Here perhaps one of you might interrupt me
and say "But what is it that you do,
Socrates? How is it that you have been
misrepresented like this? Surely all this talk and
gossip about you would never have arisen if you
had confined yourself to ordinary activities, but
only if your behaviour was abnormal. Tell us the
explanation, if you do not want us to invent it for
ourselves." This seems to me to be a reasonable request, and I will try to explain to you what it is that
has given me this false notoriety; so please give me
your attention. Perhaps some of you will think that
I am not being serious; but I assure you that I am
going to tell you the whole truth.

I have gained this reputation, gentlemen, from
nothing more or less than a kind of wisdom. What
kind of wisdom do I mean? Human wisdom, I
suppose. It seems that I really am wise in this limited sense. Presumably the geniuses whom I mentioned just now are wise in a wisdom that is more
than human; I do not know how else to account
for it. I certainly have no knowledge of such wisdom, and anyone who says that I have is a liar

and wilful slanderer. Now, gentlemen, please do
not interrupt me if I seem to make an extravagant
claim; for what I am going to tell you is not my
own opinion; I am going to refer you to an unimpeachable authority. I shall call as witness to my
wisdom (such as it is) the god at Delphi.

You know Chaerephon, of course. He was a
friend of mine from boyhood, and a good dem-
ocrat who played his part with the rest of you in
the recent expulsion and restoration. And you
know what he was like; how enthusiastic he was
over anything that he had once undertaken. Well,
one day he actually went to Delphi and asked this
question of the god—as I said before, gentlemen,
please do not interrupt—he asked whether there
was anyone wiser than myself. The priestess replied that there was no one. As Chaerephon is
dead, the evidence for my statement will be supplied by his brother, who is here in court.

Please consider my object in telling you this. I
want to explain to you how the attack upon my
reputation first started. When I heard about the
oracle's answer, I said to myself "What does the
god mean? Why does he not use plain language?
I am only too conscious that I have no claim to

wisdom, great or small; so what can he mean by asserting that I am the wisest man in the world? He cannot be telling a lie; that would not be right for him."

After puzzling about it for some time, I set myself at last with considerable reluctance to check the truth of it in the following way. I went to interview a man with a high reputation for wisdom, because I felt that here if anywhere I should succeed in disproving the oracle and pointing out to my divine authority "You said that I was the wisest of men, but here is a man who is wiser than I am."

Well, I gave a thorough examination to this person—I need not mention his name, but it was one of our politicians that I was studying when I had this experience—and in conversation with him I formed the impression that although in many people's opinion, and especially in his own, he appeared to be wise, in fact he was not. Then when I began to try to show him that he only thought he was wise and was not really so, my efforts were resented both by him and by many of the other people present. However, I reflected as I walked away: "Well, I am certainly wiser than this man. It is only too likely that neither of us has any knowledge to boast of; but he thinks that he knows something which he does not know, whereas I am quite conscious of my ignorance. At any rate it seems that I am wiser than he is to this small extent, that I do not think that I know what I do not know."

After this I went on to interview a man with an even greater reputation for wisdom, and I formed the same impression again; and here too I incurred the resentment of the man himself and a number of others.

From that time on I interviewed one person after another. I realized with distress and alarm that I was making myself unpopular, but I felt compelled to put my religious duty first; since I was trying to find out the meaning of the oracle, I was bound to interview everyone who had a reputation for knowledge. And by Dog, gentlemen! (for I must be frank with you) my honest impression was this: it seemed to me, as I pursued

my investigation at the god's command, that the people with the greatest reputations were almost entirely deficient, while others who were supposed to be their inferiors were much better qualified in practical intelligence.

I want you to think of my adventures as a sort of pilgrimage undertaken to establish the truth of the oracle once for all. After I had finished with the politicians I turned to the poets, dramatic, lyric, and all the rest, in the belief that here I should expose myself as a comparative ignoramus. I used to pick up what I thought were some of their most perfect works and question them closely about the meaning of what they had written, in the hope of incidentally enlarging my own knowledge. Well, gentlemen, I hesitate to tell you the truth, but it must be told. It is hardly an exaggeration to say that any of the bystanders could have explained those poems better than their actual authors. So I soon made up my mind about the poets too: I decided that it was not wisdom that enabled them to write their poetry, but a kind of instinct or inspiration, such as you find in seers and prophets who deliver all their sublime messages without knowing in the least what they mean. It seemed clear to me that the poets were in much the same case; and I also observed that the very fact that they were poets made them think that they had a perfect understanding of all other subjects, of which they were totally ignorant. So I left that line of inquiry too with the same sense of advantage that I had felt in the case of the politicians.

Last of all I turned to the skilled craftsmen. I knew quite well that I had practically no technical qualifications myself, and I was sure that I should find them full of impressive knowledge. In this I was not disappointed; they understood things which I did not, and to that extent they were wiser than I was. But, gentlemen, these professional experts seemed to share the same failing which I had noticed in the poets; I mean that on the strength of their technical proficiency they claimed a perfect understanding of every other subject, however important; and I felt that this error more than outweighed their positive wisdom. So I made my-

self spokesman for the oracle, and asked myself whether I would rather be as I was—neither wise with their wisdom nor stupid with their stupidity —or possess both qualities as they did. I replied through myself to the oracle that it was best for me to be as I was.

The effect of these investigations of mine, gentlemen, has been to arouse against me a great deal of hostility, and hostility of a particularly bitter and persistent kind, which has resulted in various malicious suggestions, including the description of me as a professor of wisdom. This is due to the fact that whenever I succeed in disproving another person's claim to wisdom in a given subject, the bystanders assume that I know everything about that subject myself. But the truth of the matter, gentlemen, is pretty certainly this: that real wisdom is the property of God, and this oracle is his way of telling us that human wisdom has little or no value. It seems to me that he is not referring literally to Socrates, but has merely taken my name as an example, as if he would say to us "The wisest of you men is he who has realized, like Socrates, that in respect of wisdom he is really worthless."

That is why I still go about seeking and searching in obedience to the divine command, if I think that anyone is wise, whether citizen or stranger; and when I think that any person is not wise, I try to help the cause of God by proving that he is not. This occupation has kept me too busy to do much either in politics or in my own affairs; in fact, my service to God has reduced me to extreme poverty.

*   *   *

Well, gentlemen, for the sake of a very small gain in time you are going to earn the reputation—and the blame from those who wish to disparage our city—of having put Socrates to death, "that wise man"—because they will say I am wise even if I am not, these people who want to find fault with you. If you had waited just a little while, you would have had your way in the course of nature. You can see that I am well on in life and near to death. I am saying this not to

all of you but to those who voted for my execution, and I have something else to say to them as well.

No doubt you think, gentlemen, that I have been condemned for lack of the arguments which I could have used if I had thought it right to leave nothing unsaid or undone to secure my acquittal. But that is very far from the truth. It is not a lack of arguments that has caused my condemnation, but a lack of effrontery and impudence, and the fact that I have refused to address you in the way which would give you most pleasure. You would have liked to hear me weep and wail, doing and saying all sorts of things which I regard as unworthy of myself, but which you are used to hearing from other people. But I did not think then that I ought to stoop to servility because I was in danger, and I do not regret now the way in which I pleaded my case; I would much rather die as the result of this defence than live as the result of the other sort. In a court of law, just as in warfare, neither I nor any other ought to use his wits to escape death by any means. In battle it is often obvious that you could escape being killed by giving up your arms and throwing yourself upon the mercy of your pursuers; and in every kind of danger there are plenty of devices for avoiding death if you are unscrupulous enough to stick at nothing. But I suggest, gentlemen, that the difficulty is not so much to escape death; the real difficulty is to escape from doing wrong, which is far more fleet of foot. In this present instance, I, the slow old man, have been overtaken by the slower of the two, but my accusers, who are clever and quick, have been overtaken by the faster: by iniquity. When I leave this court I shall go away condemned by you to death, but they will go away convicted by Truth herself of depravity and wickedness. And they accept their sentence even as I accept mine. No doubt it was bound to be so, and I think that the result is fair enough.

Having said so much, I feel moved to prophesy to you who have given your vote against me; for I am now at that point where the gift of prophecy comes most readily to men: at the point of death. I tell you, my executioners, that as soon as I am

dead, vengeance shall fall upon you with a punishment far more painful than your killing of me. You have brought about my death in the belief that through it you will be delivered from submitting your conduct to criticism; but I say that the result will be just the opposite. You will have more critics, whom up till now I have restrained without your knowing it; and being younger they will be harsher to you and will cause you more annoyance. If you expect to stop denunciation of your wrong way of life by putting people to death, there is something amiss with your reasoning. This way of escape is neither possible nor creditable; the best and easiest way is not to stop the mouths of others, but to make yourselves as good men as you can. This is my last message to you who voted for my condemnation.

As for you who voted for my acquittal, I should very much like to say a few words to reconcile you to the result, while the officials are busy and I am not yet on my way to the place where I must die. I ask you, gentlemen, to spare me these few moments; there is no reason why we should not exchange fancies while the law permits. I look upon you as my friends, and I want you to understand the right way of regarding my present position.

Gentlemen of the jury—for *you* deserve to be so called—I have had a remarkable experience. In the past the prophetic voice to which I have become accustomed has always been my constant companion, opposing me even in quite trivial things if I was going to take the wrong course. Now something has happened to me, as you can see, which might be thought and is commonly considered to be a supreme calamity; yet neither when I left home this morning, nor when I was taking my place here in the court, nor at any point in any part of my speech did the divine sign oppose me. In other discussions it has often checked me in the middle of a sentence; but this time it has never opposed me in any part of this business in anything that I have said or done. What do I suppose to be the explanation? I will tell you. I suspect that this thing that has happened to me is a blessing, and we are quite mistaken in supposing death to be an evil. I have good grounds for thinking this, because my accustomed sign could not have failed to oppose me if what I was doing had not been sure to bring some good result.

We should reflect that there is much reason to hope for a good result on other grounds as well. Death is one of two things. Either it is annihilation, and the dead have no consciousness of anything; or, as we are told, it is really a change: a migration of the soul from this place to another. Now if there is no consciousness but only a dreamless sleep, death must be a marvellous gain. I suppose that if anyone were told to pick out the night on which he slept so soundly as not even to dream, and then to compare it with all the other nights and days of his life, and then were told to say, after due consideration, how many better and happier days and nights than this he had spent in the course of his life—well, I think that the Great King himself, to say nothing of any private person, would find these days and nights easy to count in comparison with the rest. If death is like this, then, I call it gain; because the whole of time, if you look at it in this way, can be regarded as no more than one single night. If on the other hand death is a removal from here to some other place, and if what we are told is true, that all the dead are there, what greater blessing could there be than this, gentlemen? If on arrival in the other world, beyond the reach of our so-called justice, one will find there the true judges who are said to preside in those courts, Minos and Rhadamanthys and Aeacus and Triptolemus and all those other half-divinities who were upright in their earthly life, would that be an unrewarding journey? Put it in this way: how much would one of you give to meet Orpheus and Musaeus, Hesiod and Homer? I am willing to die ten times over if this account is true. It would be a specially interesting experience for me to join them there, to meet Palamedes and Ajax the son of Telamon and any other heroes of the old days who met their death through an unfair trial, and to compare my fortunes with theirs—it would be rather amusing, I think—; and above all I should like to spend my time there, as here, in examining and searching people's

minds, to find out who is really wise among them, and who only thinks that he is. What would one not give, gentlemen, to be able to question the leader of that great host against Troy, or Odysseus, or Sisyphus, or the thousands of other men and women whom one could mention, to talk and mix and argue with whom would be unimaginable happiness? At any rate I presume that they do not put one to death there for such conduct; because apart from the other happiness in which their world surpasses ours, they are now immortal for the rest of time, if what we are told is true.

You too, gentlemen of the jury, must look forward to death with confidence, and fix your minds on this one belief, which is certain: that nothing can harm a good man either in life or after death, and his fortunes are not a matter of indifference to the gods. This present experience of mine has not come about mechanically; I am quite clear that the time had come when it was better for me to die and be released from my distractions. That is why my sign never turned me back. For my own part I bear no grudge at all against those who condemned me and accused me, although it was not with this kind intention that they did so, but be-cause they thought that they were hurting me; and that is culpable of them. However, I ask them to grant me one favour. When my sons grow up, gentlemen, if you think that they are putting money or anything else before goodness, take your revenge by plaguing them as I plagued you; and if they fancy themselves for no reason, you must scold them just as I scolded you, for neglecting the important things and thinking that they are good for something when they are good for nothing. If you do this, I shall have had justice at your hands, both I myself and my children.

Now it is time that we were going, I to die and you to live; but which of us has the happier prospect is unknown to anyone but God.

REVIEW QUESTIONS

1. What does Socrates identify as his mission?
2. Why might Socrates' activities have seemed subversive to some of the citizens of Athens?
3. What is his attitude toward his own death, and why?

4 ∾ THE GREEK WORLD EXPANDS, 400–150 B.C.E.

While Aristotle was composing his works Ethics *and* Politics, *his former pupil Alexander, the young king of Macedonia, was in the process of rendering his former tutor's discourse on the proper structure of the polis (the traditional Greek city-state) somewhat obsolete. Between 336 and his death in 322 B.C.E., Alexander achieved success almost beyond imagining: the subjugation of the vast Persian Empire, followed by further conquests that took his armies as far east as India. Yet, almost immediately on Alexander's death, his empire began to fragment, and in less than 300 years the Ptolemid, Seleucid, and Antigonid kingdoms all had succumbed to the ascending empires of the Romans from the west and the Parthians from the east. Political and military dominion, then, proved to be ephemeral. Not so fleeting, however, were the influence of Greek culture and urban institutions on the Near East (and the reciprocal influence of Near Eastern and Egyptian cultures on the Greeks) and the devastating impact of the invaders from the west on the previously established state structures of the areas they conquered.*

Historians, and the times during which they write, create history as much as do the great figures and civilizations about which they write. Nowhere is this more evident than in the history of Western perceptions of both Alexander and the new world order that he is claimed to have inaugurated. Until relatively recently, the West has made itself quite comfortable with an idealized image of Alexander the Great as a heroic figure whose conquests were aimed at harmoniously fusing Greek culture with the cultures of the Persian Empire. Likewise, Hellenistic civilization was regarded as mixed, essentially Greek in its inspiration but enriched by its contact with the older Near Eastern cultures. The rise of this point of view, understandably enough, coincided largely with the European colonial ascendancy over the Near and Far East and Africa that began during the nineteenth century C.E. With the disappearance of that colonialism over the past few decades, however, and as previously subject peoples have raised their own voices, there has come a dramatic reevaluation of Hellenistic civilization. The

idealized image of a cultural fusion has been replaced with an image of that civilization as more emphatically Greek and of the Greek ruling class of the Hellenistic kingdoms as a colonial presence that was quite determined to maintain its superiority and preserve a large degree of separation from the indigenous peoples. Meanwhile, the political traditions of the regions over which the Greeks ruled continued largely as they had for centuries.

As the Hellenistic world order of large kingdoms took shape, it is not surprising that the traditional institutions and parochial perspectives of the polis were found wanting. This is nowhere more evident than in the development of religion and philosophy in the Hellenistic era. Much of Greek religion had been bound directly to formal cult and ritual within the polis. As the expansion of Greek colonization into the Near Eastern world began to sever the links to the traditional religion of the polis, another kind of religious experience, the mystery religions, became increasingly popular because of their more universal appeal and their promise of salvation and mystical union with a divine presence. In many ways, the spread of these mystery religions established a milieu that later promoted the spread of Christianity in the eastern Mediterranean.

Much of the philosophical thought of Plato and Aristotle had resonated greatest within the political context of the traditional city-state. Although much of the thought of the great Hellenistic philosophers derived from their classical predecessors, it also liberated itself from the confines of the city-state, developing an increasingly universal appeal. Long after the absorption of the Hellenistic kingdoms into the Roman and Parthian empires, the Hellenistic schools of philosophy, and in particular, the Stoic teachings of a divine, universal natural law and the basic brotherhood of human beings, provided rich intellectual capital for the continued development of the legal, political, and spiritual traditions of the West.

In both the broad sweep of its cultural expansion and the increasingly universal appeal of the philosophical doctrines and systems of religious belief of the time, the new world order of the Hellenistic period can justifiably be regarded as the first truly cosmopolitan age. The widespread Greek cultural legacy endowed to the Near East set the stage for the eventual success, during the subsequent era of the Roman Empire, of what became the most successful of the cosmopolitan religions: Christianity.

PLATO

FROM *The Republic*

After the death of his teacher, Socrates, Plato established the Academy, a school of philosophical instruction in an olive grove on the outskirts of Athens. (The fame of this school is apparent in the modern application of the terms academy *and* academic *to institutions of higher learning.) Among the works that Plato produced there was* The Republic, *commonly regarded as one of the most influential statements of political philosophy ever written. Perhaps the central problem that Plato addresses is how to achieve a just society within the framework of the city-state. The following selection, which includes his famous Allegory of the Cave, offers some of his ideas on how to achieve that end.*

From *The Republic*, by Plato, translated by Richard W. Sterling and William C. Scott (New York: Norton, 1985), pp. 146–151, 209–215.

*   *   *

Book V

*   *   *

Now, then, can you think of any of the human arts in which men do not generally excel women? Let's not make a long story out of it by bringing up weaving and baking cakes and boiling vegetables, matters in which women take pride and would be mortified should a man best them in these skills.

You are surely correct in saying that the one sex excels the other in every respect. But it is also true that individually many women are more skilled than many men, even if your general proposition is true.

Then we must conclude that sex cannot be the criterion in appointments to government positions. No office should be reserved for a man just because he is a man or for a woman just because she is a woman. All the capabilities with which nature endows us are distributed among men and women alike. Hence women will have the rightful opportunity to share in every task, and so will men, even though women are the weaker of the two sexes.

Agreed.

Could we then assign all the tasks to the men and none to the women?

How could we propose such thing as that?

Well, then, we shall want to say instead that one woman has the capacity to be a doctor and another not, that one woman is naturally musical and another is unmusical.

Certainly.

Could we deny that there are some women who are warlike and natural athletes while others love neither war nor gymnastic?

I don't think we can.

Again, are there not women who love wisdom and those who do not? Are not some women high-spirited and some not?

There are all these kinds of women, too.

Hence it must also be true that one woman is fit to be a guardian and another unfit. For these are the same criteria we used when we were selecting men as guardians, are they not?

Yes.

As guardians of the state, then, women and men are naturally the same, except that one is weaker and the other stronger.

Apparently.

It follows that women with the requisite qualities must be chosen to live and guard together with men of like qualities since they have the necessary competence and are naturally kin.

By all means.

And the same natures ought to perform the same functions?

Yes.

So we have closed the circle. We agree that we do nothing against nature by educating the guardians' wives in music and gymnastic.

We are agreed.

Since we have legislated in harmony with nature, we have not proposed anything impractical or unattainable. On the contrary, we may say that if anything contradicts nature, it is the way things are done today.

So it appears.

Now we designed our inquiry to test whether our proposals would turn out to be both possible and desirable?

Yes.

Well, I take it we have just established that they are possible.

Yes.

Then we must see if we can agree that they are also desirable.

Clearly.

In preparing a woman to be a guardian, then, we won't prescribe one kind of education for women guardians and another for the men because their natures are the same.

No. There should be no differentiation.

Let me ask you a question.

About what?

About men. Do you think some are better and some worse, or are all alike?

They are certainly not all alike.

Then which do you think will become the better men in the city we are building: the guardians who are being educated in the manner we have prescribed or the cobblers who received instruction in the cobbler's art?

An absurd question.

I understand your answer. You mean that the guardians are the best of our citizens.

By far.

And will not the women guardians be the best of the women?

Yes.

And can we wish for the state anything better than that it should nurture the best possible men and women?

Nothing.

And the education we have prescribed in music and gymnastic will produce this outcome?

Without fail.

Therefore the institutions we have proposed for the state are not only possible, they are the best possible.

Quite so.

Then wearing virtue as a garment, the guardians' wives must go naked and take part alongside their men in war and the other functions of government, and no other duties will be required of them. Owing to the weakness of their gender, however, they shall perform the less burdensome tasks. When they are at their exercises for the body's benefit, any man who laughs at their nakedness will be "gathering unripe fruit," for he does not know what he ridicules nor where his laughter leads. He is ignorant of the fairest words ever spoken: what is beneficial must be beautiful; only the harmful is ugly.

You are right.

Having successfully reached this point in our legislation for women, we could compare ourselves with a swimmer who has surmounted a wave without being drowned by it. Our argument that men and women guardians should pursue all things in common turns out to be consistent in itself, since we have found our proposals to be both possible and beneficial.

That was no small wave, either.

You won't think it was so big when you see what the next one looks like.

Go ahead, then, and let me see.

Here it is. I think that everything we have said so far leads up to the following law.

What law?

That all the women shall belong to all the men and that none shall cohabit privately; that the children should also be raised in common and no child should know its parent nor the parent its child.

A far greater wave, indeed. Your proposal raises questions about both practicability and utility that will provoke the greatest misgivings.

I shouldn't think anyone would want to debate its utility. The desirability of having wives and children in common, were it possible, ought to be self-evident. But I suppose the main subject of dispute would be whether or not it would be possible to establish such a community.

I expect both aspects of the proposal will produce plenty of debate.

I see that you want to entangle me in both questions at once. I hoped for your consent in the matter of utility, so that I could escape from having to discuss it. Then I would only have to consider the question of feasibility.

Your escape efforts have been detected. You won't be allowed to run away, and you will be obliged to defend your case on both counts.

I will pay your penalty. But first, relent a little. Let me go on holiday, like men with lazy minds are wont to do, so that they may entertain themselves with their own thoughts as they walk alone. These men pursue their desires without pausing to inquire how they might be achieved. All such considerations they dismiss in order to spare themselves the trouble of weighing the possible against the impossible. They assume that what they wish is already at hand, giving their imaginations free rein in concocting the details and relishing in advance what they will do when everything is in place. So do idle minds become more idle still. I now yield to this same weakness. I would like to postpone the feasibility issue for later consideration. With your permission, I shall assume the feasibility of my proposal and proceed

to inquire how the rulers will arrange the particulars in practice. At the same time, I shall seek to demonstrate that nothing could be more beneficial to our city and its guardians than a successful implementation of our proposal. Let us consider this first, and then we can address the other issue.

Permission granted. Proceed as you suggest.

I suppose that worthy rulers will be prepared to command and worthy helpers ready to obey. In some of their commands the rulers will obey the laws. In those matters of detail that we have left to their discretion their commands will imitate the spirit of the laws.

Presumably they will.

As their lawgiver, you will have selected these men. You will apply the same criteria to select women whose natures are as similar as possible to those of the men. They will live in common houses and eat at common meals. There will be no private property. They will live together, learn together, and exercise together. The necessities of nature, I presume, would see to it that they will also mate with one another. Or is necessity too strong a word?

Not if you mean the necessities of love. They attract and compel most people with far greater force than all geometric necessities posited by the mathematicians.

You are right, Glaucon. But irregularity in sexual relations or in any other matters has no place in a happy city; the rules will not tolerate it.

They would be right.

Then it is evident that we must make marriage a sacred relationship, so far as may be. And those marriages that attain the highest degree of sanctity will produce the best results.

Agreed.

What will produce the best results? You can help me, Glaucon, for I have seen hunting dogs and a number of pedigreed cocks at your house. Have you noticed something about how they mate and breed?

What?

Well, first of all, even though all of them are thoroughbreds, some prove out better than others?

True.

So are you indiscriminate in how you breed them, or do you breed from the best?

From the best.

And which age do you select for the breeding? The young or the old or, so far as possible, those in their prime?

Those in their prime.

And if you failed to supervise the breeding in this way, you would have to expect that the quality of your stock of birds and hounds would deteriorate?

Certainly.

Would it be the same with horses and other animals?

Without doubt.

Well, then, old friend, if the same holds true for human beings, we can see how urgent is our need for rulers with the highest skills.

It does hold true, but what of it?

I say this because the rulers will have to employ many of the kinds of drugs we spoke of earlier. Remember we said that those who can be healed by submitting their bodies to diet and regimen do not need drugs and can be attended by an ordinary doctor. But we know that where it is necessary to prescribe drugs, a physician with greater imagination and audacity will be indispensable.

True, but what is your point?

I mean that the rulers will probably have to resort to frequent doses of lies and mystifications for the benefit of their subjects. You will recall that we said these kinds of lies could be advantageous if used after the manner of medical remedies.

And we were right.

And the right use of this sort of medicine will very often be imperative in matters of marriage and the begetting of children.

How so?

It follows necessarily from the conclusion we reached a moment ago. The best of the men must mate with the best of the women as often as possible. Inferior should mate with inferior as seldom as possible. In order to safeguard the quality of the stock the children of the best unions must be retained for nurture by the rulers, but the others not. And how all this will be managed must be known to none but the rulers, so that the guardian flock will not be divided by dissension.

*   *   *

Book VII

Here allegory may show us best how education—or the lack of it—affects our nature. Imagine men living in a cave with a long passageway stretching between them and the cave's mouth, where it opens wide to the light. Imagine further that since childhood the cave dwellers have had their legs and necks shackled so as to be confined to the same spot. They are further constrained by blinders that prevent them from turning their heads; they can see only directly in front of them. Next, imagine a light from a fire some distance behind them and burning at a higher elevation. Between the prisoners and the fire is a raised path along whose edge there is a low wall like the partition at the front of a puppet stage. The wall conceals the puppeteers while they manipulate their puppets above it.

So far I can visualize it.

Imagine, further, men behind the wall carrying all sorts of objects along its length and holding them above it. The objects include human and animal images made of stone and wood and all other material. Presumably, those who carry them sometimes speak and are sometimes silent.

You describe a strange prison and strange prisoners.

Like ourselves. Tell me, do you not think those men would see only the shadows cast by the fire on the wall of the cave? Would they have seen anything of themselves or of one another?

How could they if they couldn't move their heads their whole life long?

Could they see the objects held above the wall behind them or only the shadows cast in front?

Only the shadows.

If, then, they could talk with one another, don't you think they would impute reality to the passing shadows?

Necessarily.

Imagine an echo in their prison, bouncing off the wall toward which the prisoners were turned. Should one of those behind the wall speak, would the prisoners not think that the sound came from the shadows in front of them?

No doubt of it.

By every measure, then, reality for the prisoners would be nothing but shadows cast by artifacts.

It could be nothing else.

Imagine now how their liberation from bondage and error would come about if something like the following happened. One prisoner is freed from his shackles. He is suddenly compelled to stand up, turn around, walk, and look toward the light. He suffers pain and distress from the glare of the light. So dazzled is he that he cannot even discern the very objects whose shadows he used to be able to see. Now what do you suppose he would answer if he were told that all he had seen before was illusion but that now he was nearer reality, observing real things and therefore seeing more truly? What if someone pointed to the objects being carried above the wall, questioning him as to what each one is? Would he not be at a loss? Would he not regard those things he saw formerly as more real than the things now being shown him?

He would.

Again, let him be compelled to look directly at the light. Would his eyes not feel pain? Would he not flee, turning back to those things he was able to discern before, convinced that they are in every truth clearer and more exact than anything he has seen since?

He would.

Then let him be dragged away by force up the rough and steep incline of the cave's passageway, held fast until he is hauled out into the light of the sun. Would not such a rough passage be painful? Would he not resent the experience? And when he came out into the sunlight, would he not be dazzled once again and unable to see what he calls realities?

He could not see even one of them, at least not immediately.

Habituation, then, is evidently required in order to see things higher up. In the beginning he would most easily see shadows; next, reflections in the water of men and other objects. Then he would see the objects themselves. From there he would go on to behold the heavens and the heavenly phenomena—more easily the moon and stars by night than the sun by day.

Yes.

Finally, I suppose, he would be able to look on the sun itself, not in reflections in the water or in fleeting images in some alien setting. He would look at the sun as it is, in its own domain, and so be able to see what it is really like.

Yes.

It is at this stage that he would be able to conclude that the sun is the cause of the seasons and of the year's turning, that it governs all the visible world and is in some sense also the cause of all visible things.

This is surely the next step he would take.

Now, supposing he recalled where he came from. Supposing he thought of his fellow prisoners and of what passed for wisdom in the place they were inhabiting. Don't you think he would feel pity for all that and rejoice in his own change of circumstance?

He surely would.

Suppose there had been honors and citations those below bestowed upon one another. Suppose prizes were offered for the one quickest to identify the shadows as they go by and best able to remember the sequence and configurations in which they appear. All these skills, in turn, would enhance the ability to guess what would come next. Do you think he would covet such rewards? More, would he envy and want to emulate those who hold power over the prisoners and are in turn reverenced by them? Or would he not rather hold fast to Homer's words that it is "better to be the poor servant of a poor master," better to endure anything, than to believe those things and live that way?

I think he would prefer anything to such a life.

Consider, further, if he should go back down again into the cave and return to the place he was before, would not his eyes now go dark after so abruptly leaving the sunlight behind?

They would.

Suppose he should then have to compete once more in shadow watching with those who never left the cave. And this before his eyes had become accustomed to the dark and his dimmed vision still required a long period of habituation. Would he not be laughed at? Would it not be said that he had made the journey above only to come back with his eyes ruined and that it is futile even to attempt the ascent? Further, if anyone tried to release the prisoners and lead them up and they could get their hands on him and kill him, would they not kill him?

Of course.

Now, my dear Glaucon, we must apply the allegory as a whole to all that has been said so far. The prisoners' cave is the counterpart of our own visible order, and the light of the fire betokens the power of the sun. If you liken the ascent and exploration of things above to the soul's journey through the intelligible order, you will have understood my thinking, since that is what you wanted to hear. God only knows whether it is true. But, in any case, this is the way things appear to me: in the intelligible world the last thing to be seen—and then only dimly—is the idea of the good. Once seen, however, the conclusion becomes irresistible that it is the cause of all things right and good, that in the visible world it gives birth to light and its sovereign source, that in the intelligible world it is itself sovereign and the author of truth and reason, and that the man who will act wisely in private and public life must have seen it.

I agree, insofar as I can follow your thinking.

Come join me, then, in this further thought. Don't be surprised if those who have attained this high vision are unwilling to be involved in the affairs of men. Their souls will ever feel the pull from above and yearn to sojourn there. Such a preference is likely enough if the assumptions of our allegory continue to be valid.

Yes, it is likely.

By the same token, would you think it strange if someone returning from divine contemplation to the miseries of men should appear ridiculous? What if he were still blinking his eyes and not yet readjusted to the surrounding darkness before being compelled to testify in court about the shadows of justice or about the images casting the shadows? What if he had to enter into debate about the notions of such matters held fast by people who had never seen justice itself?

It would not be strange.

Nonetheless, a man with common sense would know that eyesight can be impaired in two different ways by dint of two different causes, namely, transitions from light into darkness and from darkness into light. Believing that the soul also meets with the same experience, he would not thoughtlessly laugh when he saw a soul perturbed and having difficulty in comprehending something. Instead he would try to ascertain whether the cause of its faded vision was the passage from a brighter life to unaccustomed darkness or from the deeper darkness of ignorance toward the world of light, whose brightness then dazzled the soul's eye. He will count the first happy, and the second he will pity. Should he be minded to laugh, he who comes from below will merit it more than the one who descends from the light above.

A fair statement.

If this is true, it follows that education is not what some professors say it is. They claim they can transplant the power of knowledge into a soul that has none, as if they were engrafting vision into blind eyes.

They do claim that.

But our reasoning goes quite to the contrary. We assert that this power is already in the soul of everyone. The way each of us learns compares with what happens to the eye: it cannot be turned away from darkness to face the light without turning the whole body. So it is with our capacity to know; together with the entire soul one must turn away from the world of transient things toward the world of perpetual being, until finally one learns to endure the sight of its most radiant

manifestation. This is what we call goodness, is it not?

Yes.

Then there must be some art that would most easily and effectively turn and convert the soul in the way we have described. It would lay no claim to produce sight in the soul's eye. Instead it would assume that sight is already there but wrongly directed; wrongly the soul is not looking where it should. This condition it would be the purpose of the art to remedy.

Such an art might be possible.

Wisdom, then, seems to be of a different order than those other things that are also called virtues of the soul. They seem more akin to the attributes of the body, for when they are not there at the outset, they can be cultivated by exercise and habit. But the ability to think is more divine. Its power is constant and never lost. It can be useful and benign or malevolent and useless, according to the purposes toward which it is directed. Or have you never observed in men who are called vicious but wise how sharp-sighted the petty soul is and how quickly it can pick out those things toward which it has turned its attention? All this shows that we have to do not with poor eyesight but with a soul under compulsion of evil, so that the keener his vision, the more harm he inflicts.

I have seen these things.

Consider then what would happen if such a soul had been differently trained from childhood or had been liberated early from the love of food and similar pleasures that are attached to us at birth like leaden weights. Supposing, I say, he were freed from all these kinds of things that draw the soul's vision downward. If he were then turned and converted to the contemplation of real things, he would be using the very same faculties of vision and be seeing them just as keenly as he now sees their opposites.

That is likely.

And must we not draw other likely and necessary conclusions from all that has been said so far? On the one hand, men lacking education and experience in truth cannot adequately preside over a city. Without a sense of purpose or duty in life they will also be without a sense of direction to govern their public and private acts. On the other hand, those who prolong their education endlessly are also unfit to rule because they become incapable of action. Instead, they suffer themselves to believe that while still living they have already been transported to the Islands of the Blessed.

So our duty as founders is to compel the best natures to achieve that sovereign knowledge we described awhile ago, to scale the heights in order to reach the vision of the good. But after they have reached the summit and have seen the view, we must not permit what they are now allowed to do.

What is that?

Remain above, refusing to go down again among those prisoners to share their labors and their rewards, whatever their worth may be.

Must we wrong them in this way, making them live a worse life when a better is possible?

My friend, you have forgotten again that the law is concerned not with the happiness of any particular class in the city but with the happiness of the city as a whole. Its method is to create harmony among the citizens by persuasion and compulsion, making them share the benefits that each is able to bestow on the community. The law itself produces such men in the city, not in order to let them do as they please but with the intention of using them to bind the city together.

True, I did forget.

Consider further, Glaucon, that in fact we won't be wronging the philosophers who come among us. When we require them to govern the city and be its guardians, we shall vindicate our actions. For we shall say to them that it is quite understandable that men of their quality do not participate in the public life of other cities. After all, there they develop autonomously without favor from the government. It is only just that self-educated men, owing nothing to others for their enlightenment, are not eager to pay anyone for it. But you have been begotten by us to be like kings and leaders in a hive of bees, governing the city for its good and yours. Your education is better and more complete, and you are better equipped

to participate in the two ways of life. So down you must go, each in turn, to where the others live and habituate yourselves to see in the dark. Once you have adjusted, you will see ten thousand times better than those who regularly dwell there. Because you have seen the reality of beauty, justice, and goodness, you will be able to know idols and shadows for what they are. Together and wide awake, you and we will govern our city, far differently from most cities today whose inhabitants are ruled darkly as in a dream by men who will fight with each other over shadows and use faction in order to rule, as if that were some great good. The truth is that the city where those who rule are least eager to do so will be the best governed and the least plagued by dissension. The city with the contrary kind of rulers will be burdened with the contrary characteristics.

I agree.

When we tell them this, will our students disobey us? Will they refuse to play their role in the affairs of state even when they know that most of the time they will be able to dwell with one another in a better world?

Certainly not. These are just requirements, and they are just men. Yet they will surely approach holding office as an imposed necessity, quite in the opposite frame of mind from those who now rule our cities.

Indeed, old friend. A well-governed city becomes a possibility only if you can discover a better way of life for your future rulers than holding office. Only in such a state will those who rule be really rich, not in gold but with the wealth that yields happiness: a life of goodness and wisdom. But such a government is impossible if men behave like beggars, turning to politics because of what is lacking in their private lives and hoping to find their good in the public business. When office and the power of governing are treated like prizes to be won in battle the result must be a civil war that will destroy the city along with the office seekers.

True.

Is there any life other than that of true philosophers that looks with scorn on political office?

None, by Zeus.

That is why we require that those in office should not be lovers of power. Otherwise there will be a fight among rival lovers.

Right.

Who else would you compel to guard the city? Who else than those who have the clearest understanding of the principles of good government and who have won distinction in another kind of life preferable to the life of politics?

No one else.

*　　*　　*

REVIEW QUESTIONS

1. In Plato's view, to whom ought the governing of the state be entrusted?
2. How were these individuals to be educated for such responsibility?
3. Were women to have any possible role in directing the state?
4. How do Plato's ideas compare with the values underlying the democratic system of Athens?
5. Do you see any influence of the Spartan system in Plato's ideas?
6. Does Plato draw any contrasts between the material and immaterial realms?

ARISTOTLE

FROM *Politics*

After twenty years as a student of Plato at the Academy and a subsequent three-year stint as a tutor for Alexander, the young son of King Philip II of Macedonia, Aristotle established his own school, the Lyceum, at Athens and taught there until almost the end of his life. Much of his work is a continuation of Plato's, although, in contrast to Plato's emphasis on the primacy of a world of universal forms or ideas, Aristotle asserted that those ideal forms could not exist independently of the world of matter, which could be directly experienced and observed by human senses. His two most important surviving works are the Ethics *and the* Politics. *The* Ethics *is his investigation of human character in order to determine what produces a good character and, therefore, happiness. Aristotle also believed, however, that the greatest degree of human happiness could be achieved only in the context of a properly ordered and governed city-state, the formation and characteristics of which are the focus of the* Politics.

From *The Politics of Aristotle*, edited by H. W. C. Davis, translated by Benjamin Jowett (Oxford: Oxford University Press, 1905), pp. 258–61, 264–68.

*   *   *

He who thus considers things in their first growth and origin, whether a state or anything else, will obtain the clearest view of them. In the first place (1) there must be a union of those who cannot exist without each other; for example, of male and female, that the race may continue; and this is a union which is formed, not of deliberate purpose, but because, in common with other animals and with plants, mankind have a natural desire to leave behind them an image of themselves. And (2) there must be a union of natural ruler and subject, that both may be preserved. For he who can foresee with his mind is by nature intended to be lord and master, and he who can work with his body is a subject, and by nature a slave; hence master and slave have the same interest. . . .

Of household management we have seen that there are three parts—one is the rule of a master over slaves, which has been discussed already, another of a father, and the third of a husband. A husband and father rules over wife and children, both free, but the rule differs, the rule over his children being a royal, over his wife a constitutional rule. For although there may be exceptions to the order of nature, the male is by nature fitter for command than the female, just as the elder and full-grown is superior to the younger and more immature. . . .

Now it is obvious that the same principle applies generally, and therefore almost all things rule and are ruled according to nature. But the kind of rule differs; the freeman rules over the slave after another manner from that in which the male rules over the female, or the man over the child; although the parts of the soul are present in all of them, they are present in different degrees. For the slave has no deliberative faculty at all; the woman has, but it is without authority, and the child has, but it is immature. So it must necessarily be with

the moral virtues also; all may be supposed to partake of them, but only in such manner and degree as is required by each for the fulfillment of his duty. . . . The courage of a man is shown in commanding, of a woman in obeying. . . . All classes must be deemed to have their special attributes; as the poet says of women, "Silence is a woman's glory," but this is not equally the glory of man. . . .

*   *   *

Next let us consider what should be our arrangements about property; should the citizens of the perfect state have possessions in common or not? . . .

There is always a difficulty in men living together and having things in common, but especially in their having common property. . . . The present arrangement, if improved as it might be by good customs and laws, would be far better, and would have the advantages of both systems. Property should be in a certain sense common, but, as a general rule, private. For when everyone has his separate interest, men will not complain of one another, and they will make more progress, because everyone will be attending to his own business. Yet among good men, and as regards use, "friends," as the proverb says, "will have all things common." . . . For although every human has his own property, some things he will place at the disposal of his friends, while of others he shares the use of them. . . .

Again, how immeasurably greater is the pleasure, when a man feels a thing to be his own! For love of self is a feeling implanted by nature and not given in vain, although selfishness is rightly condemned. This, however is not mere love of self, but love of self in excess, like the miser's love of money; for all, or almost all, men love money, and other such objects in a measure. Furthermore, there is the greatest pleasure in doing a kindness or service to friends or guests or companions, which can only be done when a man has private property. These advantages are lost by the excessive unification of the state. . . . No one, when men have all things in common, will any longer

set an example of liberality or do any liberal action; for liberality consists in the use a man makes of his own property.

Such legislation may have a specious appearance of benevolence. Men readily listen to it, and are easily induced to believe that in some wonderful manner everybody will become everybody's friend, especially when someone is heard denouncing the evils now existing in states, suits about contracts, convictions for perjury, flatteries of rich men, and the like, which are said to arise out of the possession of private property. These evils, however, are due to a very different cause— the wickedness of human nature. Indeed, we see that there is much more quarreling among those who have all things in common, though there are not many of them when compared with the vast numbers who have private property.

Again, we ought to reckon, not only the evils from which the citizens will be saved, but also the advantages which they will lose. The life which they are to lead appears to be quite impracticable. The error of Socrates must be attributed to the false notion of unity from which he starts. Unity there should be, both of the family and of the state, but in some respects only. For there is a point at which a state may attain such a degree of unity as to be no longer a state, or at which, without actually ceasing to exist, it will become an inferior state, like harmony passing into unison, or rhythm which has been reduced to a single foot. The state, as I was saying, is a plurality, which should be united and made into a community by education. . . . Let us remember that we should not disregard the experience of ages. . . .

*   *   *

. . . We have next to consider whether there is only one form of government or many; and if many, what they are, and how many; and what are the differences between them.

A constitution is the arrangement of powers in a state, especially of the supreme power, and the constitution is the government. For example, in democracies the people are supreme, but in oligarchies, the few; therefore, we say that the two

constitutions are different; and so in other cases. First let us consider what is the purpose of a state and how many forms of government there are by which human society is regulated. We have already said, earlier in this treatise, when drawing a distinction between household management and the rule of a governor, that man is by nature a political animal. And therefore men, even when they do not require one another's help, desire to live together all the same, and are in fact brought together by their common interests in proportion as they severally attain to any measure of well-being. Well-being is certainly the chief end of individuals and of states. . . .

The conclusion is evident: governments which have a regard to the common interest are constituted in accordance with strict principles of justice, and are therefore true forms; but those which regard only the interest of the rulers are all defective and perverted forms. For they are despotic, whereas a state is a community of free men.

Having determined these points, we have next to consider how many forms of constitution there are, and what they are; and in the first place what are the true forms, for when they are determined the perversions of them will at once be apparent. The words constitution and government have the same meaning; and the government, which is the supreme authority in states, is necessarily in the hands either of one, or of a few, or of many. The true forms of government, therefore, are those in which the one, or the few, or the many, govern with a view to the common interest; but governments which rule with a view to the private interest, whether of the one, or of the few, or of the many, are perversions. For citizens, if they are truly citizens, ought all to participate in the advantages of a state. We call that form of government in which one rules, and which regards the common interest, kingship or royalty; that in which more than one, but not many, rule, aristocracy. It is so called, either because the rulers are the best men, or because they have at heart the best interest of the state and of the citizens. But when the citizens at large administer the state for the common interest, the government is called

by the generic name—constitutional government. And there is a reason for this use of language. One man or a few may excel in virtue; but of virtue there are many kinds. As the number of rulers increases it becomes more difficult for them to attain perfection in every kind, though they may in military virtue, for this is found in the masses. Hence, in a constitutional government the fighting men have the supreme power, and those who possess arms are citizens.

Of the above-mentioned forms, the perversions are as follows: of royalty, tyranny; of aristocracy, oligarchy; of constitutional government, democracy. For tyranny is a kind of monarchy which has in view the interest of the monarch only; oligarchy has in view the interest of the wealthy; democracy, of the needy; none of them the common good of all.

*   *   *

. . . But a state exists for the sake of a good life, and not for the sake of life only. If life only were the object, slaves and brute animals might form a state, but they cannot, for they have no share in happiness or in a life of free choice. Nor does a state exist merely for the sake of alliance and security from injustice, nor yet for the sake of trade and mutual intercourse; for then the Tyrrhenians and the Carthaginians, and all who have commercial treaties with one another, would be citizens of one state. . . . Those who care for good government take into consideration the larger questions of virtue and vice in states. Whence it may be further inferred that virtue must be the serious care of a state which truly deserves the name. Otherwise the community becomes a mere alliance, which differs only in place from alliances of which the members live apart. And law is only a convention, "a surety to one another of justice," as the sophist Lycophron says, and has no real power to make the citizens good and just. . . .

Clearly then a state is not a mere society, having a common place, established for the prevention of crime and for the sake of trade. These are conditions without which a state cannot exist; but all of them together do not constitute a state,

which is a community of families and aggregations of families in well-being for the sake of a perfect and self-sufficing life. Such a community can only be established among those who live in the same place and intermarry. Hence arise in states family connections, brotherhoods, common sacrifices, amusements which draw men together. They are created by friendship, for friendship is the motive of society. The end is the good life, and these are the means towards it. And the state is the union of families and villages having for an end a perfect and self-sufficing life, by which we mean a happy and honorable life.

Our conclusion, then, is that political society exists for the sake of noble actions, and not of mere companionship. And they who contribute most to such a society have a greater share in it than those who have the same or a greater freedom or nobility of birth but are inferior to them in political virtue; or than those who exceed them in wealth but are surpassed by them in virtue. . . .

We maintain that the true forms of government are three, and that the best must be that which is administered by the best, and in which there is one man, or a whole family, or many persons, excelling in virtue, and both rulers and subjects are fitted, the one to rule, the others to be ruled, in such a manner as to attain the most eligible life. We showed at the commencement of our inquiry that the virtue of the good man is necessarily the same as the virtue of the citizen of the perfect state. Clearly then in the same manner, and by the same means through which a man becomes truly good, he will frame a state which will be truly good whether aristocratical, or under kingly rule, and the same education and the same habits will be found to make a good man a good statesman and king. . . .

*   *   *

We have now to inquire what is the best constitution for most states, and the best life for most men, neither assuming a standard of virtue which is above ordinary persons, nor an education which is exceptionally favored by nature and circumstances, nor yet an ideal state which is an inspiration only, but having regard to the life in which the majority are able to share, and to the form of government which states in general can attain. . . . If it was truly said in the *Ethics* that the happy life is the life according to unimpeded virtue and that virtue is a mean, then the life which is a mean and a mean attainable by everyone must be best. And the same criteria of virtue and vice are characteristic of cities and of constitutions; for the constitution is in pattern the life of the city.

Now in all states there are three elements; one class is very rich, another very poor, and a third in the mean. It is admitted that moderation and the mean are best, and therefore it will clearly be best to possess the gifts of fortune in moderation; for in that condition of life men are most ready to listen to reason. . . . Those who have too much of the goods of fortune, strength, wealth, friends, and the like, are neither willing nor able to submit to authority. The evil begins at home; for when they are boys, by reason of the luxury in which they are brought up, they never learn, even at school, the habit of obedience. On the other hand, the very poor, who are in the opposite extreme, are too degraded. So that the one class cannot obey, and can only rule despotically; the other knows not how to command and must be ruled like slaves. Thus arises a city, not of freemen, but of masters and slaves, the one despising, the other envying. Nothing can be more fatal to friendship and good fellowship in states than this; for good fellowship starts from friendship. When men are at enmity with one another, they would rather not even share the same path.

But a city ought to be composed, as far as possible, of equals and similars; and these are generally the middle classes. Wherefore a city which is composed of middle-class citizens is necessarily best constituted with respect to what we call the natural elements of a state. And this class of citizens is most secure in a state, for they do not, like the poor, covet their neighbors' goods; nor do others covet theirs, as the poor covet the goods of the rich. And as they neither plot against others nor are themselves plotted against, they pass through life safely. . . .

Thus it is manifest that the best political community is formed by citizens of the middle class, and that those states are likely to be well administered in which the middle class is large, and if possible larger than both the other classes, or at any rate than either singly, for the addition of the middle class turns the scale and prevents either of the extremes from being dominant. Great then is the good fortune of a state in which the citizens have a moderate and sufficient property. For where some possess much and the rest nothing, there may arise an extreme democracy, or a pure oligarchy; or a tyranny may grow out of either extreme—out of either the most rampant democracy or out of an oligarchy. But it is not so likely to arise out of a middle and nearly equal condition.

Democracies are safer and more permanent than oligarchies, because they have a middle class which is more numerous and has a greater share in the government. For when there is no middle class and the poor greatly exceed in number, troubles arise and the state soon comes to an end. A proof of the superiority of the middle class is that the best legislators have been of a middle rank; for example, Solon, as his own verses testify, and Lycurgus, for he was not a king. . . .

What then is the best form of government, and what makes it the best is evident. Of other states, since we say there are many kinds of democracy and oligarchy, it is not difficult to see which has the first and which the second or any other place in the order of excellence, now that we have determined which is best. For that which is nearest to the best must of necessity be the better, and that which is furthest from it the worse, if we are judging absolutely and not with reference to given conditions. I say "with reference to given conditions," since a particular government may be preferable for some, but another form may be better for others.

*   *   *

REVIEW QUESTIONS

1. In Aristotle's view, what constitutes a state?
2. What is the purpose of the state?
3. Ought women to have any role in the governing of the state?
4. What is Aristotle's view of democracy?
5. Do you find any of Aristotle's views pertinent to government and society of the late twentieth and early twenty-first centuries C.E.?

PLUTARCH

FROM "Life of Alexander"

The biographies produced by Plutarch are an important (though by no means entirely objective or accurate) source of knowledge of the lives of many great figures of the Greek and Roman past. The following selections reveal something of ancient opinion concerning Alexander's character and intentions. To a great extent, they also communicate a view of him that dominated much thinking until relatively recent times.

*   *   *

*Philonicus the Thessalian brought the horse Bucephalus to Philip, offering to sell him for thirteen talents; but when they went into the field to try him, they found him so very vicious and unmanageable, that he reared up when they endeavored to mount him, and would not so much as endure the voice of any of Philip's attendants. Upon which, as they were leading him away as wholly useless and untractable, Alexander, who stood by, said, "What an excellent horse do they lose, for want of skill and boldness to manage him!" Philip at first took no notice of what he said; but when he heard him repeat the same thing several times, and saw he was very frustrated to see the horse sent away, "Do you criticize," said Philip, "those who are older than yourself, as if you knew more, and were better able to manage him then they?" "I could manage this horse," replied Alexander, "better than others do." "And if you do not," said Philip, "what will you forfeit for your rashness?" "I will pay," answered Alexander, "the whole price of the horse." At this the whole company fell laughing; and as soon as the wager was settled among them, he immediately ran to the horse, and, taking hold of the bridle, turned him directly towards the sun, having, it seems, observed that he was disturbed at and afraid of the motion of his own shadow; then letting him go forward a little, still keeping the reins in his hand, and stroking him gently when he began to grow eager and fiery, . . . with one nimble leap, Alexander securely mounted him, and when he was seated, by little and little drew in the bridle, and curbed him without either striking or spurring him. Presently, when he found him free from all rebelliousness, and only impatient for the course, he let him go at full speed, inciting him now with a commanding voice, and urging him also with his heel. Philip and his friends looked on at first in silence and anxiety for the result, but when he came back rejoicing and triumphing for what he had performed, they all burst out into acclamations of applause; and his father, shedding tears, it is said, for joy, kissed him as he came down from his horse, and in his transport said, "O my son, carve out a kingdom equal to and worthy of yourself, for Macedonia is too small for you."

*   *   *

*After the company had drunk a good deal somebody began to sing the verses of a man named Pranichus . . . which had been written to humiliate and make fun of some Macedonian commanders who had recently been defeated by the barbarians. The older members of the party took offense at this and showed their resentment of both the poet and the singer, but Alexander and those sitting near him listened with obvious pleasure and told the man to continue. Thereupon Cleitus, who had already drunk too much and was rough and hot-tempered by nature, became angrier than ever and shouted that it was not right for Macedonians to be insulted in the presence of barbarians and enemies, even if they had met with misfortune, for they were better men than those who were laughing at them. Alexander retorted that if Cleitus was trying to disguise cowardice as misfortune, he must be pleading his own case. At this Cleitus sprang to his feet and shouted back, "Yes, it was my cowardice that saved your life, you who call yourself the son of the gods, when you were turning your back to Spithridates' sword. And it is the blood of these Macedonians and their wounds which have made you so great that you disown your father Philip and claim to be the son of Ammon!"

These words made Alexander furious. "You scum," he cried out, "do you think that you can keep on speaking of me like this, and stir up trouble among the Macedonians and not pay for it?" "Oh, but we Macedonians do pay for it," Cleitus retorted. "Just think of the rewards we get for all our efforts. It's the dead ones who are happy,

---

*From *Readings in Ancient History,* vol. 1, edited by William S. Davis (Boston: Allyn and Bacon, 1912).

*From *The Age of Alexander,* translated by Ian Scott-Kilvert (New York: Penguin, 1973), pp. 257–58, 307–9.

because they never lived to see Macedonians being beaten with Median rods, or begging the Persians for an audience with our own king." Cleitus blurted out all this impulsively, whereupon Alexander's friends jumped up and began to abuse him, while the older men tried to calm down both sides. . . . But Cleitus refused to take back anything and he challenged Alexander to speak out whatever he wished to say in front of the company, or else not invite to his table freeborn men who spoke their minds: it would be better for him to spend his time among barbarians and slaves, who would prostrate themselves before his white tunic and his Persian girdle. At this Alexander could no longer control his rage: he hurled one of the apples that lay on the table at Cleitus, hit him, and then looked around for his dagger. One of his bodyguards, Aristophanes, had already moved it out of harm's way, and the others crowded around him and begged him to be quiet. But Alexander leaped to his feet and shouted out in the Macedonian tongue for his bodyguard to turn out, a signal that this was an extreme emergency. . . . As Cleitus still refused to give way, . . . Alexander seized a spear from one of his guards, faced Cleitus as he was drawing aside the curtain of the doorway, and ran him through. With a roar of pain and a groan, Cleitus fell, and immediately the king's anger left him. When he came to himself and saw his friends standing around him speechless, he snatched the weapon out of the dead body and would have plunged it into his own throat if the guards had not forestalled him by seizing his hands and carrying him by force to his chamber.

There he spent the rest of the night and the whole of the following day sobbing in an agony of remorse. At last he lay exhausted by his grief, uttering deep groans but unable to speak a word, until his friends, alarmed at his silence, forced their way into his room. He paid no attention to what any of them said, except that when Aristander the diviner reminded him . . . that these events had long ago been ordained by fate, he seemed to accept this assurance.

REVIEW QUESTIONS

1. How would you characterize Plutarch's view of Alexander?
2. Is it completely unbiased?
3. What kind of leader does Alexander appear to be?
4. Does he have any apparent flaws?
5. What, according to Plutarch, were the motives underlying Alexander's conquests?

HELLENISTIC ARCHITECTURE IN THE NEAR EAST (C. 175 C.E.)

In the wake of Alexander's conquests, Greek culture and tastes were adopted by many of the native elites in the Near East. This "treasury" (perhaps a royal mausoleum in actuality) was carved into the sandstone of the city of Petra, now in modern Jordan. In the third and second centuries B.C.E., Petra was the capital of the Nabataean kings, much of whose wealth and power derived from Petra's importance as a major hub for long-distance caravan trade. How does the style of the architecture compare with that of Greek public buildings? What would have inspired non-Greeks to adopt Greek styles?

Epicurus

Principal Doctrines

With the exception of Stoicism, no Hellenistic philosophy has had more influence on the intellectual history of Western civilization than Epicureanism. Although later thinkers mistakenly perceived Epicureanism as a philosophy that espoused hedonistic pleasure seeking, in fact its founder, the Athenian philosopher Epicurus (341–270 B.C.E.), advocated a prudent pursuit of pleasure in the quest for peace of mind. Attaining that state entailed, among other things, an avoidance of excessive involvement in public affairs—very much in keeping with the escapism that in so many ways characterized the Hellenistic approach to life. The following selection provides the principal doctrines of his teaching.

From *Greek and Roman Philosophy after Aristotle,* by Jason L. Saunders (New York: Free Press, 1994).

1. A blessed and eternal being has no trouble himself and brings no trouble upon any other being; hence he is exempt from movements of anger and partiality, for every such movement implies weakness.

2. Death is nothing to us; for the body, when it has been resolved into its elements, has no feeling, and that which has no feeling is nothing to us.

3. The magnitude of pleasure reaches its limit in the removal of all pain. When pleasure is present, so long as it is uninterrupted, there is no pain either of body or of mind or of both together.

4. Continuous pain does not last long in the flesh; on the contrary, pain, if extreme, is present a very short time, and even that degree of pain which barely outweighs pleasure in the flesh does not last for many days together. Illnesses of long duration even permit of an excess of pleasure over pain in the flesh.

5. It is impossible to live a pleasant life without living wisely and well and justly, and it is impossible to live wisely and well and justly without living pleasantly. Whenever any one of these is lacking, when, for instance, the man is not able to live wisely, though he lives well and justly, it is impossible for him to live a pleasant life.

6. In order to obtain security from other men any means whatsoever of procuring this was a natural good.

7. Some men have sought to become famous and renowned, thinking that thus they would make themselves secure against their fellow-men. If, then, the life of such persons really was secure, they attained natural good; if, however, it was insecure, they have not attained the end which by nature's own prompting they originally sought.

8. No pleasure is in itself evil, but the things which produce certain pleasures entail annoyances many times greater than the pleasures themselves.

9. If all pleasure had been capable of accumulation, if this had gone on not only by recurrence in time, but all over the frame or, at any rate, over the principal parts of man's nature, there would never have been any difference between one pleasure and another, as in fact there is.

10. If the objects which are productive of pleasures to profligate persons really freed them from fears of the mind,—the fears, I mean, inspired by celestial and atmospheric phenomena, the fear of death, the fear of pain; if, further, they taught them to limit their desires, we should never have any fault to find with such persons, for they would then be

filled with pleasures to overflowing on all sides and would be exempt from all pain, whether of body or mind, that is, from all evil.

11. If we had never been molested by alarms at celestial and atmospheric phenomena, nor by the misgiving that death somehow affects us, nor by neglect of the proper limits of pains and desires, we should have had no need to study natural science.

12. It would be impossible to banish fear on matters of the highest importance, if a man did not know the nature of the whole universe, but lived in dread of what the legend tells us. Hence without the study of nature there was no enjoyment of unmixed pleasures.

13. There would be no advantage in providing security against our fellow-men, so long as we were alarmed by occurrences over our heads or beneath the earth or in general by whatever happens in the boundless universe.

14. When tolerable security against our fellow-men is attained, then on a basis of power sufficient to afford support and of material prosperity arises in most genuine form the security of a quiet private life withdrawn from the multitude.

15. Nature's wealth at once has its bounds and is easy to procure; but the wealth of vain fancies recedes to an infinite distance.

16. Fortune but seldom interferes with the wise man; his greatest and highest interests have been, are, and will be, directed by reason throughout the course of his life.

17. The just man enjoys the greatest peace of mind, while the unjust is full of the utmost disquietude.

18. Pleasure in the flesh admits no increase when once the pain of want has been removed; after that it only admits of variation. The limit of pleasure in the mind, however, is reached when we reflect on the things themselves and their congeners which cause the mind the greatest alarms.

19. Unlimited time and limited time afford an equal amount of pleasure, if we measure the limits of that pleasure by reason.

20. The flesh receives as unlimited the limits of pleasure; and to provide it requires unlimited time.

But the mind, grasping in thought what the end and limit of the flesh is, and banishing the terrors of futurity, procures a complete and perfect life, and has no longer any need of unlimited time. Nevertheless it does not shun pleasure, and even in the hour of death, when ushered out of existence by circumstances, the mind does not lack enjoyment of the best life.

21. He who understands the limits of life knows how easy it is to procure enough to remove the pain of want and make the whole of life complete and perfect. Hence he has no longer any need of things which are not to be won save by labor and conflict.

22. We must take into account as the end all that really exists and all clear evidence of sense to which we refer our opinions; for otherwise everything will be full of uncertainty and confusion.

23. If you fight against all your sensations, you will have no standard to which to refer, and thus no means of judging even those judgments which you pronounce false.

24. If you reject absolutely any single sensation without stopping to discriminate with respect to that which awaits confirmation between matter of opinion and that which is already present, whether in sensation or in feelings or in any presentative perception of the mind, you will throw into confusion even the rest of your sensations by your groundless belief and so you will be rejecting the standard of truth altogether. If in your ideas based upon opinion you hastily affirm as true all that awaits confirmation as well as that which does not, you will not escape error, as you will be maintaining complete ambiguity whenever it is a case of judging between right and wrong opinion.

25. If you do not on every separate occasion refer each of your actions to the end prescribed by nature, but instead of this in the act of choice or avoidance swerve aside to some other end, your acts will not be consistent with your theories.

26. All such desires as lead to no pain when they remain ungratified are unnecessary, and the longing is easily got rid of, when the thing desired is difficult to procure or when the desires seem likely to produce harm.

27. Of all the means which are procured by wisdom to ensure happiness throughout the whole of life, by far the most important is the acquisition of friends.

28. The same conviction which inspires confidence that nothing we have to fear is eternal or even of long duration, also enables us to see that even in our limited conditions of life nothing enhances our security so much as friendship.

29. Of our desires some are natural and necessary; others are natural, but not necessary; others, again, are neither natural nor necessary, but are due to illusory opinion.

30. Those natural desires which entail no pain when not gratified, though their objects are vehemently pursued, are also due to illusory opinion; and when they are not got rid of, it is not because of their own nature, but because of the man's illusory opinion.

31. Natural justice is a symbol or expression of expediency, to prevent one man from harming or being harmed by another.

32. Those animals which are incapable of making covenants with one another, to the end that they may neither inflict nor suffer harm, are without either justice or injustice. And those tribes which either could not or would not form mutual covenants to the same end are in like case.

33. There never was an absolute justice, but only an agreement made in reciprocal intercourse in whatever localities now and again from time to time, providing against the infliction or suffering of harm.

34. Injustice is not in itself an evil, but only in its consequence, viz. the terror which is excited by apprehension that those appointed to punish such offences will discover the injustice.

35. It is impossible for the man who secretly violates any article of the social compact to feel confident that he will remain undiscovered, even if he has already escaped ten thousand times; for right on to the end of his life he is never sure he will not be detected.

36. Taken generally, justice is the same for all, to wit, something found expedient in mutual intercourse; but in its application to particular cases of locality or conditions of whatever kind, it varies under different circumstances.

37. Among the things accounted just by conventional law, whatever in the needs of mutual intercourse is attested to be expedient, is thereby stamped as just, whether or not it be the same for all; and in case any law is made and does not prove suitable to the expediencies of mutual intercourse, then this is no longer just. And should the expediency which is expressed by the law vary and only for a time correspond with the prior conception, nevertheless for the time being it was just, so long as we do not trouble ourselves about empty words, but look simply at the facts.

38. Where without any change in circumstances the conventional laws, when judged by their consequences, were seen not to correspond with the notion of justice, such laws were not really just; but wherever the laws have ceased to be expedient in consequence of a change in circumstances, in that case the laws were for the time being just when they were expedient for the mutual intercourse of the citizens, and subsequently ceased to be just when they ceased to be expedient.

39. He who best knew how to meet fear of external foes made into one family all the creatures he could; and those he could not, he at any rate did not treat as aliens; and where he found even this impossible, he avoided all intercourse, and, so far as was expedient, kept them at a distance.

40. Those who were best able to provide themselves with the means of security against their neighbors, being thus in possession of the surest guarantee, passed the most agreeable life in each other's society; and their enjoyment of the fullest intimacy was such that, if one of them died before his time, the survivors did not lament his death as if it called for commiseration.

REVIEW QUESTIONS

1. What is Epicurus' view of the gods' role in the cosmos?
2. What is the role of human senses?
3. Does his view conflict with that of Plato?

EPICTETUS

FROM *The Manual:* Stoicism

The school of philosophy known as Stoicism, founded by Zeno of Citium, undoubtedly has had a more profound impact on the Western intellectual tradition than any other of the Hellenistic schools. In particular, its emphasis on a universal natural order governed by a divine plan greatly influenced the later development of both Roman imperial law and Christian thought. The literary remains of the early development of Stoic philosophy are quite fragmentary. Much better preserved is the systematic presentation of Stoic principles in The Manual of Epictetus *(60 c.e.–?), as set down probably by his student Arrian.*

From *The Manual of Epictetus*, translated by P. E. Matheson (Oxford: Clarendon Press, 1916).

1. Of all existing things some are in our power, and others are not in our power. In our power are thought, impulse, will to get and will to avoid, and, in a word, everything which is our own doing. Things not in our power include the body, property, reputation, office, and, in a word, everything which is not our own doing. Things in our power are by nature free, unhindered, untrammelled; things not in our power are weak, servile, subject to hindrance, dependent on others. Remember then that if you imagine that what is naturally slavish is free, and what is naturally another's is your own, you will be hampered, you will mourn, you will be put to confusion, you will blame gods and men; but if you think that only your own belongs to you, and that what is another's is indeed another's, no one will ever put compulsion or hindrance on you, you will blame none, you will accuse none, you will do nothing against your will, no one will harm you, you will have no enemy, for no harm can touch you.

Aiming then at these high matters, you must remember that to attain them requires more than ordinary effort; you will have to give up some things entirely, and put off others for the moment. And if you would have these also—office and wealth—it may be that you will fail to get them, just because your desire is set on the former, and you will certainly fail to attain those things which alone bring freedom and happiness.

Make it your study then to confront every harsh impression with the words, "You are but an impression, and not at all what you seem to be." Then test it by those rules that you possess; and first by this—the chief test of all—"Is it concerned with what is in our power or with what is not in our power?" And if it is concerned with what is not in our power, be ready with the answer that it is nothing to you.

2. Remember that the will to get promises attainment of what you will, and the will to avoid promises escape from what you avoid; and he who fails to get what he wills is unfortunate, and he who does not escape what he wills to avoid is miserable. If then you try to avoid only what is unnatural in the region within your control, you will escape from all that you avoid; but if you try to avoid disease or death or poverty you will be miserable.

Therefore let your will to avoid have no concern with what is not in man's power; direct it only to things in man's power that are contrary to nature. But for the moment you must utterly remove the will to get; for if you will to get something not in man's power you are bound to be unfortunate; while none of the things in man's power that you could honourably will to get is yet

within your reach. Impulse to act and not to act, these are your concern; yet exercise them gently and without strain, and provisionally.

3. When anything, from the meanest thing upwards, is attractive or serviceable or an object of affection, remember always to say to yourself, "What is its nature?" If you are fond of a jug, say you are fond of a jug; then you will not be disturbed if it be broken. If you kiss your child or your wife, say to yourself that you are kissing a human being, for then if death strikes it you will not be disturbed.

4. When you are about to take something in hand, remind yourself what manner of thing it is. If you are going to bathe put before your mind what happens in the bath—water pouring over some, others being jostled, some reviling, others stealing; and you will set to work more securely if you say to yourself at once: "I want to bathe, and I want to keep my will in harmony with nature," and so in each thing you do; for in this way, if anything turns up to hinder you in your bathing, you will be ready to say, "I did not want only to bathe, but to keep my will in harmony with nature, and I shall not so keep it, if I lose my temper at what happens."

5. What disturbs men's minds is not events but their judgements on events. For instance, death is nothing dreadful, or else Socrates would have thought it so. No, the only dreadful thing about it is men's judgement that it is dreadful. And so when we are hindered, or disturbed, or distressed, let us never lay the blame on others, but on ourselves, that is, on our own judgements. To accuse others for one's own misfortunes is a sign of want of education; to accuse oneself shows that one's education has begun; to accuse neither oneself nor others shows that one's education is complete.

6. Be not elated at an excellence which is not your own. If the horse in his pride were to say, "I am handsome," we could bear with it. But when you say with pride, "I have a handsome horse," know that the good horse is the ground of your pride. You ask then what you can call your own. The answer is—the way you deal with your impressions. Therefore when you deal with your impressions in accord with nature, then you may be proud indeed, for your pride will be in a good which is your own.

7. When you are on a voyage, and your ship is at anchorage, and you disembark to get fresh water, you may pick up a small shellfish or a truffle by the way, but you must keep your attention fixed on the ship, and keep looking towards it constantly, to see if the Helmsman calls you; and if he does, you have to leave everything, or be bundled on board with your legs tied like a sheep. So it is in life. If you have a dear wife or child given you, they are like the shellfish or the truffle, they are very well in their way. Only, if the Helmsman call, run back to your ship, leave all else, and do not look behind you. And if you are old, never go far from the ship, so that when you are called you may not fail to appear.

8. Ask not that events should happen as you will, but let your will be that events should happen as they do, and you shall have peace.

9. Sickness is a hindrance to the body, but not to the will, unless the will consent. Lameness is a hindrance to the leg, but not to the will. Say this to yourself at each event that happens, for you shall find that though it hinders something else it will not hinder you.

10. When anything happens to you, always remember to turn to yourself and ask what faculty you have to deal with it. If you see a beautiful boy or a beautiful woman, you will find continence the faculty to exercise there; if trouble is laid on you, you will find endurance; if ribaldry, you will find patience. And if you train yourself in this habit your impressions will not carry you away.

11. Never say of anything, "I lost it," but say, "I gave it back." Has your child died? It was given back. Has your wife died? She was given back. Has your estate been taken from you? Was not this also given back? But you say, "He who took it from me is wicked." What does it matter to you through whom the Giver asked it back? As long as He gives it you, take care of it, but not as your own; treat it as passers-by treat an inn.

12. If you wish to make progress, abandon reasonings of this sort: "If I neglect my affairs I shall have nothing to live on;" "If I do not punish my son, he will be wicked." For it is better to die of hunger, so that you be free from pain and free from fear, than to live in plenty and be troubled in mind. It is better for your son to be wicked than for you to be miserable. Wherefore begin with little things. Is your drop of oil spilt? Is your sup of wine stolen? Say to yourself, "This is the price paid for freedom from passion, this is the price of a quiet mind." Nothing can be had without a price. When you call your slave-boy, reflect that he may not be able to hear you, and if he hears you, he may not be able to do anything you want. But he is not so well off that it rests with him to give you peace of mind.

*   *   *

14. It is silly to want your children and your wife and your friends to live for ever, for that means that you want what is not in your control to be in your control, and what is not your own to be yours. In the same way if you want your servant to make no mistakes, you are a fool, for you want vice not to be vice but something different. But if you want not to be disappointed in your will to get, you can attain to that.

Exercise yourself then in what lies in your power. Each man's master is the man who has authority over what he wishes or does not wish, to secure the one or to take away the other. Let him then who wishes to be free not wish for anything or avoid anything that depends on others; or else he is bound to be a slave.

*   *   *

16. When you see a man shedding tears in sorrow for a child abroad or dead, or for loss of property, beware that you are not carried away by the impression that it is outward ills that make him miserable. Keep this thought by you: "What distresses him is not the event, for that does not distress another, but his judgement on the event." Therefore do not hesitate to sympathize with him so far as words go, and if it so chance, even to groan with him; but take heed that you do not also groan in your inner being.

17. Remember that you are an actor in a play, and the Playwright chooses the manner of it: if he wants it short, it is short; if long, it is long. If he wants you to act a poor man you must act the part with all your powers; and so if your part be a cripple or a magistrate or a plain man. For your business is to act the character that is given you and act it well; the choice of the cast is Another's.

18. When a raven croaks with evil omen, let not the impression carry you away, but straightway distinguish in your own mind and say, "These portents mean nothing to me; but only to my bit of a body or my bit of property or name, or my children or my wife. But for me all omens are favourable if I will, for, whatever the issue may be, it is in my power to get benefit therefrom."

19. You can be invincible, if you never enter on a contest where victory is not in your power. Beware then that when you see a man raised to honour or great power or high repute you do not let your impression carry you away. For if the reality of good lies in what is in our power, there is no room for envy or jealousy. And you will not wish to be praetor, or prefect or consul, but to be free; and there is but one way to freedom—to despise what is not in our power.

20. Remember that foul words or blows in themselves are no outrage, but your judgement that they are so. So when any one makes you angry, know that it is your own thought that has angered you. Wherefore make it your first endeavour not to let your impressions carry you away. For if once you gain time and delay, you will find it easier to control yourself.

21. Keep before your eyes from day to day death and exile and all things that seem terrible, but death most of all, and then you will never set your thoughts on what is low and will never desire anything beyond measure.

*   *   *

26. It is in our power to discover the will of Nature from those matters on which we have no

difference of opinion. For instance, when another man's slave has broken the wine-cup we are very ready to say at once, "Such things must happen." Know then that when your own cup is broken, you ought to behave in the same way as when your neighbour's was broken. Apply the same principle to higher matters. Is another's child or wife dead? Not one of us but would say, "Such is the lot of man;" but when one's own dies, straightway one cries, "Alas! miserable am I." But we ought to remember what our feelings are when we hear it of another.

27. As a mark is not set up for men to miss it, so there is nothing intrinsically evil in the world.

*   *   *

29. . . . Man, consider first what it is you are undertaking; then look at your own powers and see if you can bear it. Do you want to compete in the pentathlon or in wrestling? Look to your arms, your thighs, see what your loins are like. For different men are born for different tasks. Do you suppose that if you do this you can live as you do now—eat and drink as you do now, indulge desire and discontent just as before? Nay, you must sit up late, work hard, abandon your own people, be looked down on by a mere slave, be ridiculed by those who meet you, get the worst of it in everything—in honour, in office, in justice, in every possible thing. This is what you have to consider: whether you are willing to pay this price for peace of mind, freedom, tranquillity. If not, do not come near; do not be, like the children, first a philosopher, then a tax-collector, then an orator, then one of Caesar's procurators. These callings do not agree. You must be one man, good or bad; you must develop either your Governing Principle, or your outward endowments; you must study either your inner man, or outward things—in a word, you must choose between the position of a philosopher and that of a mere outsider.

*   *   *

31. For piety towards the gods know that the most important thing is this: to have right opinions about them—that they exist, and that they govern the universe well and justly—and to have set yourself to obey them, and to give way to all that happens, following events with a free will, in the belief that they are fulfilled by the highest mind. For thus you will never blame the gods, nor accuse them of neglecting you. But this you cannot achieve, unless you apply your conception of good and evil to those things only which are in our power, and not to those which are out of our power. For if you apply your notion of good or evil to the latter, then, as soon as you fail to get what you will to get or fail to avoid what you will to avoid, you will be bound to blame and hate those you hold responsible. For every living creature has a natural tendency to avoid and shun what seems harmful and all that causes it, and to pursue and admire what is helpful and all that causes it. It is not possible then for one who thinks he is harmed to take pleasure in what he thinks is the author of the harm, any more than to take pleasure in the harm itself. That is why a father is reviled by his son, when he does not give his son a share of what the son regards as good things; thus Polynices and Eteocles were set at enmity with one another by thinking that a king's throne was a good thing. That is why the farmer, and the sailor, and the merchant, and those who lose wife or children revile the gods. For men's religion is bound up with their interest. Therefore he who makes it his concern rightly to direct his will to get and his will to avoid, is thereby making piety his concern. But it is proper on each occasion to make libation and sacrifice and to offer first-fruits according to the custom of our fathers, with purity and not in slovenly or careless fashion, without meanness and without extravagance.

*   *   *

32. * * * Lay down for yourself from the first a definite stamp and style of conduct, which you will maintain when you are alone and also in the society of men. Be silent for the most part, or, if you speak, say only what is necessary and in a few words. Talk, but rarely, if occasion calls you, but

do not talk of ordinary things—of gladiators, or horse-races, or athletes, or of meats or drinks—these are topics that arise everywhere—but above all do not talk about men in blame or compliment or comparison. If you can, turn the conversation of your company by your talk to some fitting subject; but if you should chance to be isolated among strangers, be silent. Do not laugh much, nor at many things, nor without restraint.

Refuse to take oaths, altogether if that be possible, but if not, as far as circumstances allow.

Refuse the entertainments of strangers and the vulgar. But if occasions arise to accept them, then strain every nerve to avoid lapsing into the state of the vulgar. For know that, if your comrade has a stain on him, he that associates with him must needs share the stain, even though he be clean in himself.

For your body take just so much as your bare need requires, such as food, drink, clothing, house, servants, but cut down all that tends to luxury and outward show.

Avoid impurity to the utmost of your power before marriage, and if you indulge your passion, let it be done lawfully. But do not be offensive or censorious to those who indulge it, and do not be always bringing up your own chastity. If some one tells you that so and so speaks ill of you, do not defend yourself against what he says, but answer, "He did not know my other faults, or he would not have mentioned these alone."

It is not necessary for the most part to go to the games; but if you should have occasion to go, show that your first concern is for yourself; that is, wish that only to happen which does happen, and him only to win who does win, for so you will suffer no hindrance. But refrain entirely from applause, or ridicule, or prolonged excitement. And when you go away do not talk much of what happened there, except so far as it tends to your improvement. For to talk about it implies that the spectacle excited your wonder.

Do not go lightly or casually to hear lectures; but if you do go, maintain your gravity and dignity and do not make yourself offensive. When you are going to meet any one, and particularly some man of reputed eminence, set before your mind the thought, "What would Socrates or Zeno have done?" and you will not fail to make proper use of the occasion.

When you go to visit some great man, prepare your mind by thinking that you will not find him in, that you will be shut out, that the doors will be slammed in your face, that he will pay no heed to you. And if in spite of all this you find it fitting for you to go, go and bear what happens and never say to yourself, "It was not worth all this"; for that shows a vulgar mind and one at odds with outward things.

In your conversation avoid frequent and disproportionate mention of your own doings or adventures; for other people do not take the same pleasure in hearing what has happened to you as you take in recounting your adventures.

Avoid raising men's laughter; for it is a habit that easily slips into vulgarity, and it may well suffice to lessen your neighbour's respect.

It is dangerous too to lapse into foul language; when anything of the kind occurs, rebuke the offender, if the occasion allow, and if not, make it plain to him by your silence, or a blush or a frown, that you are angry at his words.

34. When you imagine some pleasure, beware that it does not carry you away, like other imaginations. Wait a while, and give yourself pause. Next remember two things: how long you will enjoy the pleasure, and also how long you will afterwards repent and revile yourself. And set on the other side the joy and self-satisfaction you will feel if you refrain. And if the moment seems come to realize it, take heed that you be not overcome by the winning sweetness and attraction of it; set in the other scale the thought how much better is the consciousness of having vanquished it.

35. When you do a thing because you have determined that it ought to be done, never avoid being seen doing it, even if the opinion of the multitude is going to condemn you. For if your action is wrong, then avoid doing it altogether, but if it is right, why do you fear those who will rebuke you wrongly?

*   *   *

37. If you try to act a part beyond your powers, you not only disgrace yourself in it, but you neglect the part which you could have filled with success.

38. As in walking you take care not to tread on a nail or to twist your foot, so take care that you do not harm your Governing Principle. And if we guard this in everything we do, we shall set to work more securely.

39. Every man's body is a measure for his property, as the foot is the measure for his shoe. If you stick to this limit, you will keep the right measure; if you go beyond it, you are bound to be carried away down a precipice in the end; just as with the shoe, if you once go beyond the foot, your shoe puts on gilding, and soon purple and embroidery. For when once you go beyond the measure there is no limit.

40. Women from fourteen years upwards are called "madam" by men. Wherefore, when they see that the only advantage they have got is to be marriageable, they begin to make themselves smart and to set all their hopes on this. We must take pains then to make them understand that they are really honoured for nothing but a modest and decorous life.

41. It is a sign of a dull mind to dwell upon the cares of the body, to prolong exercise, eating, drinking, and other bodily functions. These things are to be done by the way; all your attention must be given to the mind.

42. When a man speaks evil or does evil to you, remember that he does or says it because he thinks it is fitting for him. It is not possible for him to follow what seems good to you, but only what seems good to him, so that, if his opinion is wrong, he suffers, in that he is the victim of deception. In the same way, if a composite judgement which is true is thought to be false, it is not the judgement that suffers, but the man who is deluded about it. If you act on this principle you will be gentle to him who reviles you, saying to yourself on each occasion, "He thought it right."

*   *   *

44. It is illogical to reason thus, "I am richer than you, therefore I am superior to you," "I am more eloquent than you, therefore I am superior to you." It is more logical to reason, "I am richer than you, therefore my property is superior to yours," "I am more eloquent than you, therefore my speech is superior to yours." You are something more than property or speech.

*   *   *

46. On no occasion call yourself a philosopher, nor talk at large of your principles among the multitude, but act on your principles. For instance, at a banquet do not say how one ought to eat, but eat as you ought. Remember that Socrates had so completely got rid of the thought of display that when men came and wanted an introduction to philosophers he took them to be introduced; so patient of neglect was he. And if a discussion arise among the multitude on some principle, keep silent for the most part; for you are in great danger of blurting out some undigested thought. And when someone says to you, 'You know nothing,' and you do not let it provoke you, then know that you are really on the right road. For sheep do not bring grass to their shepherds and show them how much they have eaten, but they digest their fodder and then produce it in the form of wool and milk. Do the same yourself; instead of displaying your principles to the multitude, show them the results of the principles you have digested.

*   *   *

The signs of one who is making progress are: he blames none, praises none, complains of none, accuses none, never speaks of himself as if he were somebody, or as if he knew anything. And if any one compliments him he laughs in himself at his compliment; and if one blames him, he makes no defence. He goes about like a convalescent, careful not to disturb his constitution on its road to recovery, until it has got firm hold. He has got rid of the will to get, and his will to avoid is directed no longer to what is beyond our power but only to what is in our power and contrary to nature. In all things he exercises his will without strain. If men regard him as foolish or ignorant he pays no

heed. In one word, he keeps watch and guard on himself as his own enemy, lying in wait for him.

*   *   *

REVIEW QUESTIONS

1. As presented in this work, according to what principles is the practitioner of Stoicism to live his life?

2. Why do things happen as they do, and what should the proper Stoic's attitude be?

3. How do the principles of Stoicism contrast with those of Epicureanism?

5   THE CIVILIZATION OF ANCIENT ROME

During the same period that the Greeks and Persians were doing battle at Marathon and Thermopylae and Alexander was launching his invasion of the Near East, a new power that in time would supersede them both had begun gradually to emerge in the west. The rise of Rome is one of the most compelling stories of Western civilization: an insignificant settlement, confronted by dangerous enemies and often wracked by internal turmoil, succeeds not only in surviving but also in becoming first the master of Italy, then of the Mediterranean. In only a few centuries, Rome fashioned an empire that extended from Spain to Mesopotamia.

During the march to empire, of course, the Romans sustained casualties. Among them were their early system of government, a republic, and a society that was regulated by a strict code of law and by a tradition that emphasized respect for paternal authority and duty to family, state, and gods. In time, however, the republican system that had brought Rome to greatness was ripped apart by the demands of overseas dominion, to be replaced by rival, power-hungry generals and, eventually, by an emperor whose status eventually went from that of princeps ("first citizen") to dominus et deus ("lord and god"). As Roman government inexorably changed, so Roman society and values were transformed by the massive infusion of luxury brought by imperial possessions and the influence of Greek culture and philosophical ideas on venerable Roman traditions and behavior. Indeed, of the many parallels that have been drawn between the rise of Rome and the rise of the United States to global domination two millennia later, none has been more jarring, and perhaps more potentially instructive, than the perception of decline brought by the transformation of traditional values in the wake of involvement with the outside world. In both Rome and the United States, we can discern changes brought by the influence of foreign cultures and ideas as their respective dominions expanded; in both cases, the challenge of such changes brought a response, in the form of attempts to reassert the primacy of traditional values and attitudes. This process is nowhere more evident in the Roman world than in

the introduction and rapid spread of Christianity and the official Roman response to it. For both Roman and U.S. societies, the balance sheet of benefits and liabilities will surely be discussed for years to come.

Whatever the conclusions historians and others may reach in such matters, it remains indisputable that the Pax Romana *("Roman peace") over which the Roman emperors presided gave Western civilization the longest period of continuous peace and stability that it had ever seen or has seen since. In the names of our months and the nine planets of our solar system, in the names of some of our important governmental institutions (senate, consulate, diocese), in the architectural style and grandeur of some of our most important public buildings, we find constant reminders that, even with its slavery, gladiatorial games, and vomitoria, the age of imperial Rome remains the great golden age of Western civilization.*

FROM **The Twelve Tables**

Issued by a commission of Roman magistrates in 449 B.C.E., this codification of early Roman law was originally inscribed on twelve bronze plaques that were set up in the Forum in Rome. Our single most important source on the society and economy of early Rome, the Twelve Tables reflect, in relatively unvarnished fashion, the values that dominated life during the early years of the Roman Republic. (To borrow a modern expression, there was not much "kidding around.")

From *Roman Civilization: Selected Readings*, vol. 2, edited by Naphtali Lewis and Meyer Reinhold (New York: Columbia University Press, 1953), pp. 54–67.

Table I
Preliminaries to and Rules for a Trial

If plaintiff summons defendant to court, he shall go. If he does not go, plaintiff shall call witness thereto. Then only shall he take defendant by force.

If defendant shirks or takes to his heels, plaintiff shall lay hands on him.

If disease or age is an impediment, he [who summons defendant to court] shall grant him a team; he shall not spread with cushions the covered carriage if he does not so desire.

For a landowner, a landowner shall be surety; but for a proletarian person, let any one who is willing be his protector. . . .

When parties make a settlement of the case, the judge shall announce it. If they do not reach a settlement, they shall state the outline of their case in the meeting place or Forum before noon.

They shall plead it out together in person. After noon, the judge shall adjudge the case to the party present. If both be present, sunset shall be the time limit [of proceedings].

Table II
Further Enactments on Trials

Action under solemn deposit: 500 *as* pieces is the sum when the object of dispute under solemn deposit is valued at 1,000 in bronze or more, fifty pieces when less. Where the controversy concerns the liberty of a human being, fifty pieces shall be the solemn deposit under which the dispute should be undertaken.

If any of these be impediment for judge, referee, or party, on that account the day of trial shall be broken off.

Whoever is in need of evidence, he shall go on every third day to call out loudly before witness' doorway.

Table III
Execution; Law of Debt

When a debt has been acknowledged, or judgment about the matter has been pronounced in court, thirty days must be the legitimate time of grace. After that, the debtor may be arrested by laying on of hands. Bring him into court. If he does not satisfy the judgment, or no one in court offers himself as surety in his behalf, the creditor may take the defaulter with him. He may bind him either in stocks or in fetters; he may bind him with a weight no more than fifteen pounds, or with less if he shall so desire. The debtor, if he wishes, may live on his own. If he does not live on his own, the person who shall hold him in bonds shall give him one pound of grits for each day. He may give more if he so desires.

Unless they make a settlement, debtors shall be held in bonds for sixty days. During that time they shall be brought before the praetor's court in the meeting place on three successive market days, and the amount for which they are judged liable shall be announced; on the third market day they shall suffer capital punishment or be delivered up for sale abroad, across the Tiber.

On the third market day creditors shall cut pieces. Should they have cut more or less than their due, it shall be with impunity.

Against a stranger, title of ownership shall hold good forever.

Table IV
Patria Potestas: Rights of Head of Family

Quickly kill . . . a dreadfully deformed child.

If a father thrice surrender a son for sale, the son shall be free from the father.

A child born ten months after the father's death will not be admitted into a legal inheritance.

Table V
Guardianship; Succession

Females shall remain in guardianship even when they have attained their majority . . . except Vestal Virgins.

Conveyable possessions of a woman under guardianship of agnates[1] cannot be rightfully acquired by *usucapio*,[2] save such possessions as have been delivered up by her with a guardian's sanction.

According as a person shall will regarding his [household], chattels, or guardianship of his estate, this shall be binding.

If a person dies intestate, and has no self-successor, the nearest agnate kinsman shall have possession of deceased's household.

If there is no agnate kinsman, deceased's clansmen shall have possession of his household.

To persons for whom a guardian has not been appointed by will, to them agnates are guardians.

If a man is raving mad, rightful authority over his person and chattels shall belong to his agnates or to his clansmen.

A spendthrift is forbidden to exercise administration over his own goods. . . . A person who, being insane or a spendthrift, is prohibited from administering his own goods shall be under trusteeship of agnates.

---

[1] Male relatives on the father's side [Editor].

[2] Length of possession [Editor].

The inheritance of a Roman citizen-freedman shall be made over to his patron if the freedman has died intestate and without self-successor.

Items which are in the category of debts are not included in the division when they have with automatic right been divided into portions of an inheritance.

Debt bequeathed by inheritance is divided proportionally amongst each heir with automatic liability when the details have been investigated.

Table VI
Acquisition and Possession

When a party shall make bond or conveyance, the terms of the verbal declaration are to be held binding. * * *

A person who has been ordained a free man [in a will, on condition] that he bestow a sum of 10,000 pieces on the heir, though he has been sold by the heir, shall win his freedom by giving the money to the purchaser.

It is sufficient to make good such faults as have been named by word of mouth, and that for any flaws which the vendor had expressly denied, he shall undergo penalty of double damage.] * * *

Any woman who does not wish to be subjected in this manner to the hand of her husband should be absent three nights in succession every year, * * *

A person shall not dislodge from a framework a [stolen] beam which has been fixed in buildings or a vineyard. . . . Action [is granted] for double damages against a person found guilty of fixing such [stolen] beam.

Table VII
Rights Concerning Land

Ownership within a five-foot strip [between two pieces of land] shall not be acquired by long usage.

The width of a road [extends] to eight feet where it runs straight ahead, sixteen round a bend. . . .

Persons shall mend roadways. If they do not keep them laid with stone, a person may drive his beasts where he wishes.

If rainwater does damage . . . this must be restrained according to an arbitrator's order.

If a water course directed through a public place shall do damage to a private person, he shall have right of suit to the effect that damage shall be repaired for the owner.

Branches of a tree may be lopped off all round to a height of more than 15 feet. . . . Should a tree on a neighbor's farm be bent crooked by a wind and lean over your farm, action may be taken for removal of that tree.

It is permitted to gather up fruit falling down on another man's farm.

Table VIII
Torts or Delicts

If any person has sung or composed against another person a song such as was causing slander or insult to another, he shall be clubbed to death.

If a person has maimed another's limb, let there be retaliation in kind unless he makes agreement for settlement with him.

If he has broken or bruised a freeman's bone with his hand or a club, he shall undergo penalty of 300 *as* pieces; if a slave's, 150.

If he has done simple harm [to another], penalties shall be 25 *as* pieces.

If a four-footed animal shall be said to have caused loss, legal action . . . shall be either the surrender of the thing which damaged, or else the offer of assessment for the damage.

For pasturing on, or cutting secretly by night, another's crops acquired by tillage, there shall be capital punishment in the case of an adult malefactor . . . he shall be hanged and put to death as a sacrifice to Ceres. In the case of a person under the age of puberty, at the discretion of the praetor either he shall be scourged or settlement shall be made for the harm done by paying double damages.

Any person who destroys by burning any building or heap of corn [grain] deposited alongside a house shall be bound, scourged, and put to death by burning at the stake, provided that he has committed the said misdeed with malice aforethought; but if he shall have committed it by acci-

dent, that is, by negligence, it is ordained that he repair the damage, or, if he be too poor to be competent for such punishment, he shall receive a lighter chastisement.

Any person who has cut down another person's trees with harmful intent shall pay 25 *as* pieces for every tree.

If theft has been done by night, if the owner kill the thief, the thief shall be held lawfully killed.

It is forbidden that a thief be killed by day . . . unless he defend himself with a weapon; even though he has come with a weapon, unless he use his weapon and fight back, you shall not kill him. And even if he resists, first call out.

In the case of all other thieves caught in the act, if they are freemen, they should be flogged and adjudged to the person against whom the theft has been committed, provided that the malefactors have committed it by day and have not defended themselves with a weapon; slaves caught in the act of theft should be flogged and thrown from the Rock; boys under the age of puberty should, at the praetor's discretion, be flogged, and the damage done by them should be repaired.

If a person pleads on a case in theft in which the thief has not been caught in the act, the thief must compound for the loss by paying double damages. * * *

No person shall practice usury at a rate more than one twelfth . . . A usurer is condemned for quadruple amount. * * *

If a patron shall have defrauded his client, he must be solemnly forfeited.

Whosoever shall have allowed himself to be called as witness—or shall have been scales-balancer, if he does not as witness pronounce his testimony, he must be deemed dishonored and incapable of acting as witness.

Penalty . . . for false witness . . . a person who has been found guilty of giving false witness shall be hurled down from the Tarpeian Rock. . . .

No person shall hold meetings by night in the city.

Members [of associations] . . . are granted . . . the right to pass any binding rule they like for themselves provided that they cause no violation of public law.

Table IX
Public Law

*   *   *

The penalty shall be capital punishment for a judge or arbiter legally appointed who has been found guilty of receiving a bribe for giving a decision.

He who shall have roused up a public enemy, or handed over a citizen to a public enemy, must suffer capital punishment.

Putting to death . . . of any man who has not been convicted, whosoever he might be, is forbidden.

Table X
Sacred Law

A dead man shall not be buried or burned within the city.

One must not do more than this [at funerals]; one must not smooth the pyre with an axe. * * *

Women must not tear cheeks or hold chorus of "Alas!" on account of funeral.

When a man is dead one must not gather his bones in order to make a second funeral. An exception [in the case of] death in war or in a foreign land. . . .

Anointing by slaves is abolished, and every kind of drinking bout.

Let there be no costly sprinkling . . . no long garlands . . . no incense boxes. . . .

When a man wins a crown himself or through a chattel or by dint of valor, the crown bestowed on him . . . [may be laid in the grave] with impunity [on the man who won it] or on his father.

To make more than one funeral for one man and to make and spread more than one bier for him . . . this should not occur . . . and a person must not add gold. . . .

But him whose teeth shall have been fastened together with gold, if a person shall bury or burn him along with that gold, it shall be with impunity.

No new pyre or personal burning-mound must be erected nearer than sixty feet to another person's buildings without consent of the owner.

*   *   *

Table XI
Supplementary Laws

Intermarriage shall not take place between plebeians and patricians.

*   *   *

REVIEW QUESTIONS

1. What can you deduce from this selection about early Roman justice?
2. What are the roles and the rights of the family in early Roman law?
3. How important was corporal punishment in Roman law?

PLUTARCH

FROM *Lives*

By the early second century B.C.E., *Rome's conquests outside Italy, along with its increased exposure to Greek culture, began to have a significant impact on Rome's traditional values. In particular, leaders began to emerge whose individualistic behavior challenged ancient traditions that subjugated the interests of the individual to those of family and state. Plutarch's biography of Cato the Elder (234–149* B.C.E.*), however, presents the life of a Roman leader steeped in traditional values and opposed to the inroads that Greek culture was making into Roman society.*

From *Lives*, by Plutarch, translated by Bernadotte Perrin, vol. 2 (Cambridge, Mass.: Harvard University Press, 1914).

*   *   *

FROM Marcus Cato the Elder

The family of Marcus Cato, it is said, was of Tusculan origin, though he lived, previous to his career as soldier and statesman, on an inherited estate in the country of the Sabines. His ancestors commonly passed for men of no note whatever, but Cato himself extols his father, Marcus, as a brave man and good soldier. He also says that his grandfather, Cato, often won prizes for soldierly valour, and received from the state treasury, because of his bravery, the price of five horses which had been killed under him in battle. The Romans used to call men who had no family distinction, but were coming into public notice through their own achievements, "new men," and such they called Cato. But he himself used to say that as far as office and distinction went, he was indeed new, but having regard to ancestral deeds of valour, he was oldest of the old. His third name was not Cato at first, but Priscus. Afterwards he got the surname of Cato for his great abilities. The Romans call a man who is wise and prudent, *catus*.

*   *   *

His physical body—since he laboured from the very first with his own hands, held to a temperate way of life, and performed military duties—was very serviceable, vigorous, and healthy. His eloquence—a second body, as it were, and an instrument with which to perform not only necessary, but also high and noble services—he developed

and perfected in the villages and towns about Rome. There he served as advocate for all who needed him, and got the reputation of being, first a zealous pleader, and then a capable orator. Thenceforth the weight and dignity of his character revealed themselves more and more to those who had dealings with him; they saw that he was bound to be a man of great affairs, and have a leading place in the state. For he not only gave his services in legal contests without fee of any sort, but did not appear to cherish even the reputation won in such contests. For he was more desirous of high reputation in battles and campaigns against the enemy, and while he was yet a mere youth had his breast covered with honourable wounds. He says himself that he made his first campaign when he was seventeen years old, at the time when Hannibal was consuming Italy with the flames of his successes.

In battle, he showed himself effective in hand combat, sure and steadfast of foot, and with a fierce expression. With threatening speech and harsh cries he would advance upon the foe, for he rightly thought, and tried to show others, that often-times such action terrifies the enemy more than does the sword. On the march, he carried his own armour on foot, while a single servant followed in charge of his camp provisions. With this man, it is said, he was never angry, and never scolded him when he served up a meal; he actually assisted in most of such preparations, provided he was free from his military duties. Water was what he drank on his campaigns, except that once in a while, in a raging thirst, he would call for vinegar, or, when his strength was failing, would add a little wine.

Near his fields was the cottage which had once belonged to Manius Curius, a hero of three triumphs. To this he would often go, and the sight of the small farm and the simple dwelling led him to think of their former owner, who, though he had become the greatest of the Romans, had subdued the most warlike nations, and driven Pyrrhus out of Italy. Nevertheless, he tilled this little patch of ground with his own hands and occupied this cottage, after three triumphs. Here it was that the ambassadors of the Samnites once found him seated at his hearth cooking turnips, and offered him much gold; but he dismissed them, saying that a man whom such a meal satisfied had no need of gold, and for his part he thought that a more honourable thing than the possession of gold was the conquest of its possessors. Cato would go away with his mind full of these things, and on viewing again his own house and lands and servants and way of life, would increase the labours of his hands and reduce his extravagances.

*   *   *

The influence which Cato's oratory won for him increased, and men called him a Roman Demosthenes; but his manner of life was even more talked about and carried abroad. For his oratorical ability set before young men not only a goal which many already were striving eagerly to attain, but a man who worked with his own hands, as his fathers did, and was contented with a cold breakfast, a frugal dinner, simple clothing, and a humble dwelling—one who thought more of rejecting the extras of life than of possessing them. The Roman commonwealth had now grown too large to keep its earlier integrity. The conquest of many kingdoms and peoples had brought a large mixture of customs, and the adoption of ways of life of every sort. It was natural, therefore, that men should admire Cato, when they saw that, whereas other men were broken down by labors and weakened by pleasures, he was victor over both. And this too, not only while he was still young and ambitious, but even in his old age, after consulship and triumph. Then, like some victorious athlete, he persisted in the regimen of his training, and kept his mind unaltered to the last.

He tells us that he never wore expensive clothing; that he drank the same wine as his slaves; that as for fish and meats, he would buy enough for his dinner from the public stalls—and even this for Rome's sake, that he might strengthen his body for military service. He once inherited an embroidered Babylonian robe, but sold it at once; not a single one of his farm-houses had plastered walls; he never paid much for a slave, since he

did not want them to be delicately beautiful, but sturdy workers, such as grooms and herdsmen. And these he thought it his duty to sell when they got old, instead of feeding them when they were useless; and that in general, he thought nothing cheap that one could do without. He said also that he bought lands where crops were raised and cattle herded, not those where lawns were sprinkled and paths swept for pleasure.

These things were thought by some to be the result of the man's stinginess; but others excused them in the belief that he lived in this way only to correct and moderate the extravagance of others. However, for my part, I regard his treatment of his slaves like beasts of burden, using them to the utmost, and then, when they were old, driving them off and selling them, as the mark of a very mean nature, which recognizes no tie between man and man but that of profit. . . . A kindly man will take good care even of his horses when they are worn out with age, and of his dogs, too, not only in their puppyhood, but when their old age needs nursing. . . .

We should not treat living creatures like shoes or pots and pans, casting them aside when they are bruised and worn out with service; but, if for no other reason, than for the sake of practice in kindness to our fellow men, we should accustom ourselves to mildness and gentleness in our dealings with other creatures. I certainly would not sell even an ox that had worked for me, just because he was old, much less an elderly man, removing him from his habitual place and customary life, as it were from his native land, for a paltry price, useless as he is to those who sell him and as he will be to those who buy him. But Cato, boasting of such things, says that he left in Spain even the horse which had carried him through his military campaign, that he might not tax the city with the cost of its transportation home. Whether these things should be set down to greatness of spirit or littleness of mind, is an open question.

But in other matters, his self-restraint was beyond measure admirable. For instance, when he was in command of an army, he took for himself and his staff not more than three bushels of wheat

a month, and for his beasts of burden, less than a bushel and a half of barley a day. He received Sardinia to govern as his province; and whereas his predecessors used to charge the public treasury for their tents, couches, and clothing, . . . his simple economy stood out in an incredible contrast. He made no demands whatever upon the public treasury, and made his circuit of the cities on foot, followed by a single public officer, who carried his robe and cup for libations to the gods. And yet, though in such matters he showed himself mild and lenient to those under his authority, in other ways he displayed a dignity and severity proper to the administration of justice. He carried out the edicts of the government in a direct and masterful way so that the Roman power never inspired its subjects with greater fear or affection.

*　　*　　*

He dealt with the Athenians through an interpreter. He could have spoken to them directly, but he always clung to his native ways, and mocked at those who were lost in admiration of anything that was Greek.

*　　*　　*

Ten years after his consulship, Cato was a candidate for the censorship. This office towered, as it were, above every other civic honour, and was, in a way, the high point of a political career. The variety of its powers was great, including that of examining into the lives and manners of the citizens. Its creators thought that no one should be left to his own ways and desires, without inspection and review, either in his marrying, having children, ordering his daily life, or in the entertainment of his friends. Thinking that these things revealed a man's real character more than did his public and political career, they set men in office to watch, warn, and chastise, that no one should turn to vices and give up his native and customary way of life. They chose to this office one of the so-called patricians, and one of the plebeians. These officers were called censors, and they had authority to degrade a knight, or to expel a senator

who led a wild and disorderly life. They also revised the assessments of property, and arranged the citizens in lists [for military service] according to their social and political classes. There were other great powers also connected with the office.

Therefore, when Cato became a candidate, nearly all the best known and most influential men of the senatorial party united to oppose him. The men of noble parentage among them were moved by jealousy, thinking that nobility of birth would be trampled if men of lowly origin forced their way up to the summits of honour and power; while those who were conscious of base practices and of a departure from ancestral customs, feared the severity of the man, which was sure to be harsh and unyielding in the exercise of power. Therefore, after due consultation and preparation, they put up in opposition to Cato seven candidates for the office, who sought the favour of the people with promises of mild conduct in office, supposing that they wanted to be ruled with a lax and indulgent hand. Cato, on the contrary, showed no inclination to be agreeable whatever, but plainly threatened wrong-doers in his speeches, and loudly cried that the city had need of a great purification. He urged the people, if they were wise, not to choose the most agreeable physician, but the one who was most in earnest. He himself, he said, was such a physician, and so was Valerius Flaccus, of the patricians. With him as colleague, and him alone, he thought he could cut the excessive luxury and effeminacy of the time. As for the rest of the candidates, he saw that they were all trying to force their way into the office in order to administer it badly, since they feared those who would administer it well. And so truly great were the Roman voters, and so worthy of great leaders, that they did not fear Cato's rigour and haughty independence, but rejected those candidates who, it was believed, would do everything to please them, and elected Flaccus to the office along with Cato.

*   *   *

As censor, Cato paid not the slightest heed to his accusers, but grew still more strict. He cut off the pipes by which people conveyed part of the public water supply into their private houses and gardens; he upset and demolished all buildings that encroached on public land; he reduced the cost of public works to the lowest, and forced the rent of public lands to the highest possible figure. All these things brought much hatred upon him.

*   *   *

Still, it appears that the people approved of his censorship to an amazing extent. At any rate, after erecting a statue to his honour in the temple of Health, they commemorated in the inscription upon it, not the military commands nor the triumph of Cato, but, as the inscription may be translated, the fact "that when the Roman state was tottering to its fall, he was made censor, and by helpful guidance, wise restraints, and sound teachings, restored it again." . . .

*   *   *

He was also a good father, a considerate husband, and a household manager of no little talent; nor did he give only a fitful attention to this, as a matter of little or no importance. Therefore, I think I ought to give suitable instances of his conduct in these relations. He married a wife who was of higher birth than she was rich, thinking that, although the rich and the high-born may be alike given to pride, still, women of high birth have such a horror of what is disgraceful that they are more obedient to their husbands in all that is honourable. He used to say that the man who struck his wife or child, laid violent hands on the holiest of holy things. Also that he thought it more praiseworthy to be a good husband than a great senator, and there was nothing more to admire in Socrates of old than that he was always kind and gentle with his shrewish wife and stupid sons. After the birth of his own son, no business could be so urgent, unless it had a public character, as to prevent him from being present when his wife bathed and wrapped the babe. For the mother nursed it herself, and often gave her breast also to the infants of her slaves, that so they might come to cherish a brotherly affection for her son. As soon as the boy showed signs of understanding, his father

took him under his own charge and taught him to read, although he had an accomplished slave, Chilo by name, who was a school-teacher, and taught many boys. Still, Cato thought it not right, as he tells us himself, that his son should be scolded by a slave, or have his ears tweaked when he was slow to learn, still less that he should be indebted to his slave for such a priceless thing as education. He was therefore himself not only the boy's reading-teacher, but his tutor in law, and his athletic trainer, and he taught his son not merely to hurl the javelin and fight in armour and ride the horse, but also to box, to endure heat and cold, and to swim strongly through the eddies and billows of the Tiber. His "History of Rome," as he tells us himself, he wrote out with his own hand and in large characters, that his son might have in his own home an aid to acquaintance with his country's ancient traditions. He declares that his son's presence put him on guard against making indecencies of speech as if in the presence of the Vestal Virgins, and that he never bathed with him. This, indeed, would seem to have been a general taboo with the Romans, for even fathers-in-law avoided bathing with their sons-in-law, because they were ashamed to uncover their nakedness. Afterwards, however, when they had learned from the Greeks their freedom in going naked before men, they in their turn infected the Greeks with the practice of doing so even before women.

*   *   *

He owned many slaves, and usually bought those prisoners of war who were young and still capable of being reared and trained. Not one of his slaves ever entered another man's house unless sent there by Cato or his wife, and when any of them was asked what Cato was doing, he always answered that he did not know. A slave of his was expected either to be busy about the house, or to be asleep, and he preferred the sleepy ones. He thought these gentler than the wakeful ones, and that those who had enjoyed the gift of sleep were better for any kind of service than those who lacked it. In the belief that his slaves were led into most mischief by their sexual passions, he required that the males should have sex with the female

slaves of the house at a fixed price, but should never approach any other woman.

At the outset, when Cato was still poor and in military service, he found no fault at all with what was served up to him, declaring that it was shameful for a man to quarrel with a servant over food and drink. But afterwards, when his circumstances were improved and he used to entertain his friends and colleagues at table, no sooner was the dinner over than he would flog those slaves who had been unsatisfactory in preparing or serving it. He was always arranging that his slaves should have feuds and disagreements among themselves; harmony among them made him suspicious and fearful of them. He had those who were suspected of some capital offence brought to trial before all their fellow servants, and, if convicted, put to death.

*   *   *

He used to lend money also to those of his slaves who wished it, and they would buy boys with it, and after training and teaching them for a year, at Cato's expense, would sell them again. Many of these boys Cato would retain for himself, counting to the credit of the slave the highest price bid for his boy by outsiders. He tried to persuade his son also to such investments, by saying that it was not the part of a man, but of a widow woman, to lessen his property. But surely Cato was going too far when he said that a man should be admired and glorified like a god if the final inventory of his property showed that he had added to it more than he had inherited.

When he was now well on in years, there came as delegates from Athens to Rome, Carneades the Academic, and Diogenes the Stoic philosopher, to beg the reversal of a certain decision against the Athenian people, which imposed upon them a heavy fine. Upon the arrival of these philosophers, the most studious of the city's youth hastened to wait upon them, and became their devoted and admiring listeners. The charm of Carneades especially, which had boundless power, and a fame not inferior to its power, won large and sympathetic audiences, and filled the city, like a rushing mighty wind, with the noise of his praises. Report spread

far and wide that a Greek of amazing talent, who disarmed all opposition by the magic of his eloquence, had infused a tremendous passion into the youth of the city—in consequence of which they gave up their other pleasures and pursuits and were "possessed" about philosophy. The other Romans were pleased at this, and glad to see their young men lay hold of Greek culture and associate with such admirable men. But Cato, at the very outset, when this zeal for discussion came into the city, was distressed—fearing that the young men, by giving this direction to their ambition, should come to love a reputation based on mere words more than one achieved by military deeds. And when the fame of the visiting philosophers rose yet higher in the city, and their first speeches before the Senate were interpreted, at his own instance and request, by so conspicuous a man as Gaius Acilius, Cato determined, on some excuse or other, to rid the city of them all. So he rose in the Senate and condemned the city officials for keeping for so long a time a delegation composed of men who could easily secure anything they wished, so persuasive were they. "We ought," he said, "to make up our minds one way or another, and vote on what the delegation proposes, in order that these men may return to their schools and lecture to the sons of Greece, while the youth of Rome give ear to their laws and officials, as before."

This he did, not, as some think, out of personal hostility to Carneades, but because he was wholly opposed to philosophy, and made mock of all Greek culture and training, out of patriotic Roman zeal. He says, for instance, that Socrates was a mighty talker, who attempted, as best he could, to be his country's tyrant, by abolishing its customs, and by enticing his fellow citizens into opinions contrary to the laws. * * * And seeking to prejudice his son against Greek culture, he declared, in the tone of a prophet or a seer, that Rome would lose her empire when she had become infected with Greek literature. But time has certainly shown the emptiness of this pessimistic declaration, for while the city was at the height of its empire, she made every form of Greek learning and culture her own.

*   *   *

REVIEW QUESTIONS

1. What were the virtues that Cato prized most highly?
2. What were his reasons for opposing the spread of Greek culture?
3. How did he treat his slaves?
4. What were his attitudes toward women?

DIODORUS SICULUS

FROM *On Slavery in the Later Republic*

Rome's imperial conquests, besides exposing Roman values to alien influences, also produced a huge supply of captives who generally were reduced to slavery. The following selection describes the conditions of slaves set to work in the silver and gold mines of Spain, and then describes an especially destructive slave revolt on Sicily between 135 and 132 B.C.E.

From *On Slavery in the Later Republic, The Library of History,* vol. 3, by Diodorus Siculus, translated by C. H. Oldfather (Cambridge, Mass.: Harvard University Press, 1939), pp. 114–16.

*   *   *

. . . After the Romans had made themselves masters of Iberia, a multitude of Italians have swarmed to the mines and taken great wealth away with them, such was their greed. For they purchase a multitude of slaves whom they turn over to the overseers of the working of the mines; and these men, opening shafts in a number of places and digging deep into the ground, seek out the seams of earth which are rich in silver and gold; and not only do they go into the ground a great distance, but they also push their diggings many stades in depth and run galleries off at every angle, turning this way and that, in this manner bringing up from the depths the ore which gives them the profit they are seeking. . . .

But to continue with the mines, the slaves who are engaged in the working of them produce for their masters revenues in sums defying belief, but they themselves wear out their bodies both by day and by night in the diggings under the earth, dying in large numbers because of the exceptional hardships they endure. For no respite or pause is granted them in their labours, but compelled beneath blows of the overseers to endure the severity of their plight, they throw away their lives in this wretched manner, although certain of them who can endure it, by virtue of their bodily strength and their persevering souls, suffer such hardships over a long period; indeed death in their eyes is more to be desired than life, because of the magnitude of the hardships they must bear.

There was never a sedition of slaves so great as that which occurred in Sicily, whereby many cities met with grave calamities, innumerable men and women, together with their children, experienced the greatest misfortunes, and all the island was in danger of falling into the power of fugitive slaves. . . .

. . . The Servile War broke out for the following reason. The Sicilians, having shot up in prosperity and acquired great wealth, began to purchase a vast number of slaves, to whose bodies, as they were brought in droves from the slave markets, they at once applied marks and brands. The young men they used as cowherds, the others in such ways as they happened to be useful. But they treated them with a heavy hand in their service, and granted them the most meagre care, the bare minimum for food and clothing. . . .

The slaves, distressed by their hardships, and frequently outraged and beaten beyond all reason, could not endure their treatment. Getting together as opportunity offered, they discussed the possibility of revolt, until at last they put their plans into action. . . . The beginning of the whole revolt took place as follows.

There was a certain Damophilus of Enna, a man of great wealth but insolent of manner; he had abused his slaves to excess, and his wife Megallis vied even with her husband in punishing the slaves and in her general inhumanity towards them. The slaves, reduced by this degrading treatment to the level of brutes, conspired to revolt and to murder their masters. Going to Eunus they asked him whether their resolve had the favour of the gods. He, resorting to his usual mummery, promised them the favour of the gods, and soon persuaded them to act at once. Immediately, therefore, they brought together four hundred of their fellow slaves and, having armed themselves in such ways as opportunity permitted, they fell upon the city of Enna, with Eunus at their head and working his miracle of the flames of fire for their benefit. When they found their way into the houses they shed much blood, sparing not even suckling babes. Rather they tore them from the breast and dashed them to the ground, while as for the women—and under their husbands' very eyes— but words cannot tell the extent of their outrages and acts of lewdness! By now a great multitude of slaves from the city had joined them, who, after first demonstrating against their own masters their utter ruthlessness, then turned to the slaughter of others. When Eunus and his men learned that Damophilus and his wife were in the garden that lay near the city, they sent some of their band and dragged them off, both the man and his wife, fettered and with hands bound behind their backs, subjecting them to many outrages along the way. Only in the case of the couple's daughter were the slaves seen to show consideration throughout, and this was because of her kindly nature, in that to the extent of her power she was always compassionate and ready to succour the slaves. Thereby it was demonstrated that the others

were treated as they were, not because of some "natural savagery of slaves," but rather in revenge for wrongs previously received. The men appointed to the task, having dragged Damophilus and Megallis into the city, as we said, brought them to the theatre, where the crowd of rebels had assembled. But when Damophilus attempted to devise a plea to get them off safe and was winning over many of the crowd with his words, Hermeias and Zeuxis, men bitterly disposed towards him, denounced him as a cheat, and without waiting for a formal trial by the assembly the one ran him through the chest with a sword, the other chopped off his head with an axe. Thereupon Eunus was chosen king, not for his manly courage or his ability as a military leader, but solely for his marvels and his setting of the revolt in motion. . . .

Established as the rebels' supreme commander, he called an assembly and put to death all the citizenry of Enna except for those who were skilled in the manufacture of arms: these he put in chains and assigned them to this task. He gave Megallis to the maidservants to deal with as they might wish; they subjected her to torture and threw her over a precipice. He himself murdered his own masters, Antigenes and Pytho. Having set a diadem upon his head, and arrayed himself in full royal style, he proclaimed his wife queen (she was a fellow Syrian and of the same city) and appointed to the royal council such men as seemed to be gifted with superior intelligence. . . .

. . . In three days Eunus had armed, as best he could, more than six thousand men, besides others in his train who had only axes and hatchets, or slings, or sickles, or fire-hardened stakes, or even kitchen spits; and he went about ravaging the countryside. Then, since he kept recruiting untold numbers of slaves, he ventured even to do battle with Roman generals, and on joining combat repeatedly overcame them with his superior numbers, for he now had more than ten thousand soldiers.

Soon after, engaging in battle with a general arrived from Rome, Lucius Hypsaeus, who had eight thousand Sicilian troops, the rebels were victorious, since they now numbered twenty thousand. Before long their band reached a total of two hundred thousand, and in numerous battles with the Romans

they acquitted themselves well, and failed but seldom. As word of this was bruited about, a revolt of one hundred and fifty slaves, banded together, flared up in Rome, of more than a thousand in Attica, and of yet others in Delos and many other places. But thanks to the speed with which forces were brought up and to the severity of their punitive measures, the magistrates of these communities at once disposed of the rebels and brought to their senses any who were wavering on the verge of revolt. In Sicily, however, the trouble grew. Cities were captured with all their inhabitants, and many armies were cut to pieces by the rebels, until Rupilius, the Roman commander, recovered Tauromenium for the Romans by placing it under strict siege and confining the rebels under conditions of unspeakable duress and famine: conditions such that, beginning by eating the children, they progressed to the women, and did not altogether abstain even from eating one another. . . .

Finally, after Sarapion, a Syrian, had betrayed the citadel, the general laid hands on all the runaway slaves in the city, whom, after torture, he threw over a cliff. From there he advanced to Enna, which he put under siege in much the same manner, bringing the rebels into extreme straits and frustrating their hopes. . . . Rupilius captured this city also by betrayal, since its strength was impregnable to force of arms. Eunus, taking with him his bodyguards, a thousand strong, fled in unmanly fashion. . . .

. . . He met such an end as befitted his knavery, and died at Morgantina. Thereupon Rupilius, traversing the whole of Sicily with a few picked troops, sooner than had been expected rid it of every nest of robbers.

*   *   *

REVIEW QUESTIONS

1. According to Diodorus, to what kinds of treatment were slaves subjected in the second century B.C.E.?
2. How does Cato the Elder's treatment of his slaves compare with the conditions of slaves in the mines?

CICERO

FROM *On the Laws*

Whereas Cato the Elder epitomizes the traditionalists' resistance to the advances of Greek culture in the late Roman Republic, Cicero (106–43 B.C.E.) is that era's leading representative of Greek ideals. A foremost legal expert and compelling orator, he was a major political figure during the era of the rise of Julius Caesar. He was eventually executed after Caesar's assassination for advocating the restoration of the power of the Roman Senate. His most significant influence on the later Western intellectual tradition, however, lies in his prolific production as a writer. It was largely through his works that Greco-Roman thought was transmitted to later eras. The following selection is from Cicero's On the Laws, *in which, through the mechanism of dialogue that was used so well by earlier Greek philosophers, he propounds his concept of the ideal state.*

From *De Legibus* (*On the Laws*), by Cicero, translated by Clinton W. Keyes (Cambridge, Mass.: Harvard University Press, 1928), pp. 311–91.

*   *   *

ATTICUS: Yet if you ask what I expect of you, I consider it a logical thing that, since you have already written a treatise on the constitution of the ideal State, you should also write one on its laws. For I note that this was done by your beloved Plato, whom you admire, revere above all others, and love above all others.

MARCUS: Is it your wish, then, that, as he discussed the institutions of States and the ideal laws, . . . sometimes walking about, sometimes resting —you recall his description—we, in like manner, strolling or taking our ease among these stately poplars on the green and shady river bank, shall discuss the same subjects along somewhat broader lines than the practice of the courts calls for? * * *

MARCUS: And you are wise, for you must understand that in no other kind of discussion can one bring out so clearly what Nature's gifts to man are, what a wealth of most excellent possessions the human mind enjoys, what the purpose is, to strive after and accomplish which we have been born and placed in this world, what it is that unites men, and what natural fellowship there is among them. For it is only after all these things have been made clear that the origin of Law and Justice can be discovered.

ATTICUS: Then you do not think that the science of law is to be derived from the praetor's edict, as the majority do now, or from the Twelve Tables, as people used to think, but from the deepest mysteries of philosophy?

MARCUS: Quite right; for in our present conversation, Pomponius, we are not trying to learn how to protect ourselves legally, or how to answer clients' questions. Such problems may be important, and in fact they are; for in former times many eminent men made a specialty of their solution, and at present one person performs this duty with the greatest authority and skill. But in our present investigation we intend to cover the whole range of universal Justice and Law in such a way that our own civil law, as it is called, will be confined to a small and narrow corner. For we must explain the nature of Justice, and this must be sought for in the nature of man; we must also consider the laws by which States

ought to be governed; then we must deal with the enactments and decrees of nations which are already formulated and put in writing; and among these the civil law, as it is called, of the Roman people will not fail to find a place. ＊ ＊ ＊

MARCUS: . . . now let us investigate the origins of Justice.

Well then, the most learned men have determined to begin with Law, and it would seem that they are right, if, according to their definition, Law is the highest reason, implanted in Nature, which commands what ought to be done and forbids the opposite. This reason, when firmly fixed and fully developed in the human mind, is Law. And so they believe that Law is intelligence, whose natural function it is to command right conduct and forbid wrongdoing. . . . Now if this is correct, as I think it to be in general, then the origin of Justice is to be found in Law, for Law is a natural force; it is the mind and reason of the intelligent man, the standard by which Justice and Injustice are measured. But since our whole discussion has to do with the reasoning of the populace, it will sometimes be necessary to speak in the popular manner, and give the name of law to that which in written form decrees whatever it wishes, either by command or prohibition. For such is the crowd's definition of law. But in determining what Justice is, let us begin with that supreme Law which had its origin ages before any written law existed or any State had been established. ＊ ＊ ＊

＊   ＊   ＊

MARCUS: I will not make the argument long. Your admission leads us to this: that animal which we call man, endowed with foresight and quick intelligence, complex, keen, possessing memory, full of reason and prudence, has been given a certain distinguished status by the supreme God who created him; for he is the only one among so many different kinds and varieties of living beings who has a share in reason and thought, while all the rest are deprived of it. But what is more divine, I will not say in man only, but in all heaven and earth, than reason? And reason, when it is full grown and perfected, is rightly called wisdom. Therefore, since there is nothing better than reason, and since it exists both in man and God, the first common possession of man and God is reason. But those who have reason in common must also have right reason in common. And since right reason is Law, we must believe that men have Law also in common with the gods. Further, those who share Law must also share Justice; and those who share these are to be regarded as members of the same commonwealth. If indeed they obey the same authorities and powers, this is true in a far greater degree; but as a matter of fact they do obey this celestial system, the divine mind, and the God of transcendent power. Hence we must now conceive of this whole universe as one commonwealth of which both gods and men are members.

＊   ＊   ＊

MARCUS: The points which are now being briefly touched upon are certainly important; but out of all the material of the philosophers' discussions, surely there comes nothing more valuable than the full realization that we are born for Justice, and that right is based, not upon men's opinions, but upon Nature. This fact will immediately be plain if you once get a clear conception of man's fellowship and union with his fellow-men. For no single thing is so like another, so exactly its counterpart, as all of us are to one another. Nay, if bad habits and false beliefs did not twist the weaker minds and turn them in whatever direction they are inclined, no one would be so like his own self as all men would be like all others. And so, however we may define man, a single definition will apply to all. This is a sufficient proof that there is no difference in kind between man and man; for if there were, one definition could not be applicable to all men; and indeed reason, which alone raises us above the level of the beasts and enables us to draw inferences, to prove and disprove, to discuss and solve problems, and to

come to conclusions, is certainly common to us all, and, though varying in what it learns, at least in the capacity to learn it is invariable. For the same things are invariably perceived by the senses, and those things which stimulate the senses, stimulate them in the same way in all men; and those rudimentary beginnings of intelligence to which I have referred, which are imprinted on our minds, are imprinted on all minds alike; and speech, the mind's interpreter, though differing in the choice of words, agrees in the sentiments expressed. In fact, there is no human being of any race who, if he finds a guide, cannot attain to virtue.

*   *   *

MARCUS: The next point, then, is that we are so constituted by Nature as to share the sense of Justice with one another and to pass it on to all men. And in this whole discussion I want it understood that what I shall call Nature is that which is implanted in us by Nature; that, however, the corruption caused by bad habits is so great that the sparks of fire, so to speak, which Nature has kindled in us are extinguished by this corruption, and the vices which are their opposites spring up and are established. But if the judgments of men were in agreement with Nature, so that . . . they considered "nothing alien to them which concerns mankind," then Justice would be equally observed by all. For those creatures who have received the gift of reason from Nature have also received right reason, and therefore they have also received the gift of Law, which is right reason applied to command and prohibition. And if they have received Law, they have received Justice also. Now all men have received reason; therefore all men have received Justice. . . .

Now all this is really a preface to what remains to be said in our discussion, and its purpose is to make it more easily understood that Justice is inherent in Nature. After I have said a few words more on this topic, I shall go on to the civil law, the subject which gives rise to all this discourse. . . .

But you see the direction this conversation is to take; our whole discourse is intended to promote the firm foundation of States, the strengthening of cities, and the curing of the ills of peoples. For that reason I want to be especially careful not to lay down first principles that have not been wisely considered and thoroughly investigated. Of course I cannot expect that they will be universally accepted, for that is impossible; but I do look for the approval of all who believe that everything which is right and honourable is to be desired for its own sake, and that nothing whatever is to be accounted a good unless it is praiseworthy in itself, or at least that nothing should be considered a great good unless it can rightly be praised for its own sake.

*   *   *

MARCUS: Once more, then, before we come to the individual laws, let us look at the character and nature of Law, for fear that, though it must be the standard to which we refer everything, we may now and then be led astray by an incorrect use of terms, and forget the rational principles on which our laws must be based.

QUINTUS: Quite so, that is the correct method of exposition.

MARCUS: Well, then, I find that it has been the opinion of the wisest men that Law is not a product of human thought, nor is it any enactment of peoples, but something eternal which rules the whole universe by its wisdom in command and prohibition. Thus they have been accustomed to say that Law is the primal and ultimate mind of God, whose reason directs all things either by compulsion or restraint. Wherefore that Law which the gods have given to the human race has been justly praised; for it is the reason and mind of a wise lawgiver applied to command and prohibition.

*   *   *

MARCUS: So in the very beginning we must persuade our citizens that the gods are the lords and rulers of all things, and that what is done, is done by their will and authority; that they are

likewise great benefactors of man, observing the character of every individual, what he does, of what wrong he is guilty, and with what intentions and with what piety he fulfils his religious duties; and that they take note of the pious and the impious. For surely minds which are imbued with such ideas will not fail to form true and useful opinions. Indeed, what is more true than that no one ought to be so foolishly proud as to think that, though reason and intellect exist in himself, they do not exist in the heavens and the universe, or that those things which can hardly be understood by the highest reasoning powers of the human intellect are guided by no reason at all? In truth, the man that is not driven to gratitude by the orderly courses of the stars, the regular alternation of day and night, the gentle progress of the seasons, and the produce of the earth brought forth for our sustenance—how can such an one be accounted a man at all? And since all things that possess reason stand above those things which are without reason, and since

it would be sacrilege to say that anything stands above universal Nature, we must admit that reason is inherent in Nature. Who will deny that such beliefs are useful when he remembers how often oaths are used to confirm agreements, how important to our well-being is the sanctity of treaties, how many persons are deterred from crime by the fear of divine punishment, and how sacred an association of citizens becomes when the immortal gods are made members of it, either as judges or as witnesses?

REVIEW QUESTIONS

1. According to Cicero, what is the source of all law?
2. What is the relationship of civil law to law as Cicero defines it?
3. Do you find in this selection any evidence of a Stoic concept of universal human brotherhood and equality?

OVID

FROM *The Loves*

Ovid's works about love (or lust) reflect what some might regard as a certain shallowness in Roman social relations. Eventually, Emperor Augustus found his work so morally repugnant that he banished Ovid from Rome.

From *Amores*, by Ovid, translated by Guy Lee (London: John Murray, 1968), pp. 728–31.

*   *   *

Your husband? Going to the same dinner as us?
I hope it chokes him.

So I'm only to gaze at you, darling? Play gooseberry
while another man enjoys your touch?

You'll lie there snuggling up to him? He'll put his arm
round your neck whenever he wants?

No wonder Centaurs fought over Hippodamia
when the wedding wine began to flow.

I don't live in the forest nor am I part horse
but I find it hard to keep my hands off you.

However here's my plan. Listen carefully.
Don't throw my words of wisdom to the winds.

Arrive before him—not that I see what good
arriving first will do but arrive first all the
    same.

When he takes his place on the couch and you
    go to join him
looking angelic, secretly touch my foot.

Watch me for nods and looks that talk
and unobserved return my signals

in the language of eyebrows and fingers
with annotations in wine.

Whenever you think of our love-making
stroke that rosy cheek with your thumb.

If you're cross with me, darling,
press the lobe of your ear

but turn your ring round if you're pleased
with anything I say or do.

When you feel like cursing your fool of a
    husband
touch the table as if you were praying.

If he mixes you a drink, beware—tell him to
    drink it himself,
then quietly ask the waiter for what you want.

I'll intercept the glass as you hand it back
and drink from the side you drank from.

Refuse all food he has tasted first—
it has touched his lips.

Don't lean your gentle head against his shoulder
and don't let him embrace you

or slide a hand inside your dress
or touch your breasts. Above all don't kiss him.

If you do I'll cause a public scandal,
grab you and claim possession.

I'm bound to see all this. It's what I shan't see
that worries me—the goings on under your
    cloak.

Don't press your thigh or your leg against his
or touch his coarse feet with your toes.

I know all the tricks. That's why I'm worried.
I hate to think of him doing what I've done.

We've often made love under your cloak,
    sweetheart,
in a glorious race against time.

You won't do that, I know. Still,
to avoid all doubt don't wear one.

Encourage him to drink but mind—no kisses.
Keep filling his glass when he's not looking.

If the wine's too much for him and he drops
    off
we can take our cue from what's going on
    around us.

When you get up to leave and we all follow
move to the middle of the crowd.

You'll find me there—or I'll find you
so touch me anywhere you can.

But what's the good? I'm only temporizing.
Tonight decrees our separation.

Tonight he'll lock you in and leave me
desolated at your door.

Then he'll kiss you, then go further,
forcing his right to our secret joy.

But you *can* show him you're acting under duress.
Be mean with your love—give grudgingly—in
  silence.

He won't enjoy it if my prayers are answered.
And if they're not, at least assure me you won't.

But whatever happens tonight tell me tomorrow
you didn't sleep with him—and stick to that
  story.

*   *   *

REVIEW QUESTIONS

1. Does Ovid seem to have any moral scruples
   about adultery?
2. Would Cato the Elder have approved?

TACITUS

FROM *Germania*

*As the Romans' empire expanded, they came into contact with various peoples.
None of them was to have a more significant or enduring influence on the shaping
of Western civilization than the Germans, whose chieftains eventually would supplant Roman authority in western Europe. That at least some Romans had an ink-
ling of the Germans' later importance is evident in the* Germania *of the Roman
historian Tacitus, who wrote this work at the end of the first century* C.E.

From *The Agricola and Germany of Tacitus,* translated by A. J. Church and W. J. Brodribb
(Basingstoke, Eng.: Macmillan, 1877).

*   *   *

For my own part, I agree with those who think
that the tribes of Germany are free from all
taint of intermarriages with foreign nations,
and that they appear as a distinct, unmixed race,
like none but themselves. Hence, too, the same
physical peculiarities throughout so vast a population. All have fierce blue eyes, red hair, huge
frames, fit only for a sudden exertion. They are less
able to bear laborious work. Heat and thirst they
cannot in the least endure; to cold and hunger their
climate and their soil inure them.

   Their country, though somewhat various in
appearance, yet generally either bristles with forests or reeks with swamps; it is more rainy on
the side of Gaul, bleaker on that of Noricum and
Pannonia. It is productive of grain, but unfavourable to fruit-bearing trees; it is rich in flocks
and herds, but these are for the most part under-
sized, and even the cattle have not their usual
beauty or noble head. It is number that is chiefly
valued; they are in fact the most highly prized, indeed the only riches of the people. Silver and gold
the gods have refused to them, whether in kindness or in anger I cannot say. I would not, however, affirm that no vein of German soil produces
gold or silver, for who has ever made a search?
They care but little to possess or use them. You
may see among them vessels of silver, which have
been presented to their envoys and chieftains, held
as cheap as those of clay. The border population,
however, value gold and silver for their commer-

cial utility, and are familiar with, and show preference for, some of our coins. The tribes of the interior use the simpler and more ancient practice of the barter of commodities. They like the old and well-known money, coins milled, or showing a two-horse chariot. They likewise prefer silver to gold, not from any special liking, but because a large number of silver pieces is more convenient for use among dealers in cheap and common articles.

Even iron is not plentiful with them, as we infer from the character of their weapons. But few use swords or long lances. They carry a spear with a narrow and short head, but so sharp and easy to wield that the same weapon serves, according to circumstances, for close or distant conflict. As for the horse-soldier, he is satisfied with a shield and spear; the foot-soldiers also scatter showers of missiles, each man having several and hurling them to an immense distance, and being naked or lightly clad with a little cloak. There is no display about their equipment: their shields alone are marked with very choice colours. A few only have corslets, and just one or two here and there a metal or leathern helmet. Their horses are remarkable neither for beauty nor for fleetness. Nor are they taught various evolutions after our fashion, but are driven straight forward, or so as to make one wheel to the right in such a compact body that none is left behind another. On the whole, one would say that their chief strength is in their infantry, which fights along with the cavalry; admirably adapted to the action of the latter is the swiftness of certain foot-soldiers, who are picked from the entire youth of their country, and stationed in front of the line. Their number is fixed,—a hundred from each canton; and from this they take their name among their countrymen, so that what was originally a mere number has now become a title of distinction. Their line of battle is drawn up in a wedge-like formation. To give ground, provided you return to the attack, is considered prudence rather than cowardice. The bodies of their slain they carry off even in indecisive engagements. To abandon your shield is the basest of crimes; nor may a man thus disgraced be present at the sacred rites, or enter their council;

many, indeed, after escaping from battle, have ended their infamy with the halter.

They choose their kings by birth, their generals for merit. These kings have not unlimited or arbitrary power, and the generals do more by example than by authority. If they are energetic, if they are conspicuous, if they fight in the front, they lead because they are admired. But to reprimand, to imprison, even to flog, is permitted to the priests alone, and that not as a punishment, or at the general's bidding, but, as it were, by the mandate of the god whom they believe to inspire the warrior. They also carry with them into battle certain figures and images taken from their sacred groves. And what most stimulates their courage is, that their squadrons or battalions, instead of being formed by chance or by a fortuitous gathering, are composed of families and clans. Close by them, too, are those dearest to them, so that they hear the shrieks of women, the cries of infants. *They* are to every man the most sacred witnesses of his bravery—*they* are his most generous applauders. The soldier brings his wounds to mother and wife, who shrink not from counting or even demanding them and who administer both food and encouragement to the combatants.

Tradition says that armies already wavering and giving way have been rallied by women who, with earnest entreaties and bosoms laid bare, have vividly represented the horrors of captivity, which the Germans fear with such extreme dread on behalf of their women, that the strongest tie by which a state can be bound is the being required to give, among the number of hostages, maidens of noble birth. They even believe that the sex has a certain sanctity and prescience, and they do not despise their counsels, or make light of their answers. In Vespasian's days we saw Veleda, long regarded by many as a divinity. In former times, too, they venerated Aurinia, and many other women, but not with servile flatteries, or with sham deification.

*   *   *

Augury and divination by lot no people practise more diligently. The use of the lots is simple. A little bough is lopped off a fruit-bearing tree,

A MUMMY FROM THE TIME OF THE ROMAN EMPIRE (100 C.E.)

This painted and gilded case contains the mummy of a man with the very un-Egyptian name Artemidorus, who died evidently in his early twenties, shortly after 100 C.E. To what extent are classical and Egyptian artistic elements and symbolism mixed in the decoration of this case? Do you see evidence for the survival of ancient Egyptian religious beliefs and traditions under Roman rule? What is your assessment of the skill of the artist who painted Artemidorus' portrait?

and cut into small pieces; these are distinguished by certain marks, and thrown carelessly and at random over a white garment. In public questions the priest of the particular state, in private the father of the family, invokes the gods, and, with his eyes towards heaven, takes up each piece three times, and finds in them a meaning according to the mark previously impressed on them. If they prove unfavourable, there is no further consultation that day about the matter; if they sanction it, the confirmation of augury is still required. For they are also familiar with the practice of consulting the notes and the flight of birds. It is peculiar to this people to seek omens from horses. Kept at the public expense, in these same woods and groves, are white horses, pure from the taint of earthly labour; these are yoked to a sacred car, and accompanied by the priest and the king, or chief of the tribe, who note their neighings and snortings. No species of augury is more trusted, not only by the people and by the nobility, but also by the priests, who regard themselves as the ministers of the gods, and the horses as acquainted with their will. They have also another method of observing auspices, by which they seek to learn the result of an important war. Having taken, by whatever means, a prisoner from the tribe with whom they are at war, they pit him against a picked man of their own tribe, each combatant using the weapons of their country. The victory of the one or the other is accepted as an indication of the issue.

About minor matters the chiefs deliberate, about the more important the whole tribe. Yet even when the final decision rests with the people, the affair is always thoroughly discussed by the chiefs. They assemble, except in the case of a sudden emergency, on certain fixed days, either at new or at full moon; for this they consider the most auspicious season for the transaction of business. Instead of reckoning by days as we do, they reckon by nights, and in this manner fix both their ordinary and their legal appointments. Night they regard as bringing on day. Their freedom has this disadvantage, that they do not meet simultaneously or as they are bidden, but two or three days are wasted in the delays of assembling. When the multitude think proper, they sit down armed. Silence is proclaimed by the priests, who have on these occasions the right of keeping order. Then the king or the chief, according to age, birth, distinction in war, or eloquence, is heard, more because he has influence to persuade than because he has power to command. If his sentiments displease them, they reject them with murmurs; if they are satisfied, they brandish their spears. The most complimentary form of assent is to express approbation with their weapons.

In their councils an accusation may be preferred or a capital crime prosecuted. Penalties are distinguished according to the offence. Traitors and deserters are hanged on trees; the coward, the unwarlike, the man stained with abominable vices, is plunged into the mire of the morass, with a hurdle put over him. This distinction in punishment means that crime, they think, ought, in being punished, to be exposed, while infamy ought to be buried out of sight. Lighter offences, too, have penalties proportioned to them; he who is convicted, is fined in a certain number of horses or of cattle. Half of the fine is paid to the king or to the state, half to the person whose wrongs are avenged and to his relatives. In these same councils they also elect the chief magistrates, who administer law in the cantons and the towns. Each of these has a hundred associates chosen from the people, who support him with their advice and influence.

They transact no public or private business without being armed. It is not, however, usual for anyone to wear arms till the state has recognised his power to use them. Then in the presence of the council one of the chiefs, or the young man's father, or some kinsman, equips him with a shield and a spear. These arms are what the "toga" is with us, the first honour with which youth is invested. Up to this time he is regarded as a member of a household, afterwards as a member of the commonwealth. Very noble birth or great services rendered by the father secure for lads the rank of a chief; such lads attach themselves to men of mature strength and of long approved valour. It is

no shame to be seen among a chief's followers. Even in his escort there are gradations of rank, dependent on the choice of the man to whom they are attached. These followers vie keenly with each other as to who shall rank first with his chief, the chiefs as to who shall have the most numerous and the bravest followers. It is an honour as well as a source of strength to be thus always surrounded by a large body of picked youths; it is an ornament in peace and a defence in war. And not only in his own tribe but also in the neighbouring states it is the renown and glory of a chief to be distinguished for the number and valour of his followers, for such a man is courted by embassies, is honoured with presents, and the very prestige of his name often settles a war.

When they go into battle, it is a disgrace for the chief to be surpassed in valour, a disgrace for his followers not to equal the valour of the chief. And it is an infamy and a reproach for life to have survived the chief, and returned from the field. To defend, to protect him, to ascribe one's own brave deeds to his renown, is the height of loyalty. The chief fights for victory; his vassals fight for their chief. If their native state sinks into the sloth of prolonged peace and repose, many of its noble youths voluntarily seek those tribes which are waging some war, both because inaction is odious to their race, and because they win renown more readily in the midst of peril, and cannot maintain a numerous following except by violence and war. Indeed, men look to the liberality of their chief for their war-horse and their blood-stained and victorious lance. Feasts and entertainments, which, though inelegant, are plentifully furnished, are their only pay. The means of this bounty come from war and rapine. Nor are they as easily persuaded to plough the earth and to wait for the year's produce as to challenge an enemy and earn the honour of wounds. Nay, they actually think it tame and stupid to acquire by the sweat of toil what they might win by their blood.

Whenever they are not fighting, they pass much of their time in the chase, and still more in idleness, giving themselves up to sleep and to feasting, the bravest and the most warlike doing nothing, and surrendering the management of the household, of the home, and of the land, to the women, the old men, and all the weakest members of the family. They themselves lie buried in sloth, a strange combination in their nature that the same men should be so fond of idleness, so averse to peace. It is the custom of the states to bestow by voluntary and individual contribution on the chiefs a present of cattle or of grain, which, while accepted as a compliment, supplies their wants. They are particularly delighted by gifts from neighbouring tribes, which are sent not only by individuals but also by the state, such as choice steeds, heavy armour, trappings, and neckchains. We have now taught them to accept money also.

It is well known that the nations of Germany have no cities, and that they do not even tolerate closely contiguous dwellings. They live scattered and apart, just as a spring, a meadow, or a wood has attracted them. Their villages they do not arrange in our fashion, with the buildings connected and joined together, but every person surrounds his dwelling with an open space, either as a precaution against the disasters of fire, or because they do not know how to build. No use is made by them of stone or tile; they employ timber for all purposes, rude masses without ornament or attractiveness. Some parts of their buildings they stain more carefully with a clay so clear and bright that it resembles painting, or a coloured design. They are wont also to dig out subterranean caves, and pile on them great heaps of dung, as a shelter from winter and as a receptacle for the year's produce, for by such places they mitigate the rigour of the cold. And should an enemy approach, he lays waste the open country, while what is hidden and buried is either not known to exist, or else escapes him from the very fact that it has to be searched for.

They all wrap themselves in a cloak which is fastened with a clasp, or, if this is not forthcoming, with a thorn, leaving the rest of their persons bare. They pass whole days on the hearth by the fire. The wealthiest are distinguished by a dress which is not flowing, like that of the Sarmatae and Parthi, but is tight, and exhibits each limb. They also

wear the skins of wild beasts; the tribes on the Rhine and Danube in a careless fashion, those of the interior with more elegance, as not obtaining other clothing by commerce. These select certain animals, the hides of which they strip off and vary them with the spotted skins of beasts, the produce of the outer ocean, and of seas unknown to us. The women have the same dress as the men, except that they generally wrap themselves in linen garments, which they embroider with purple, and do not lengthen out the upper part of their clothing into sleeves. The upper and lower arm is thus bare, and the nearest part of the bosom is also exposed.

Their marriage code, however, is strict, and indeed no part of their manners is more praiseworthy. Almost alone among barbarians they are content with one wife, except a very few among them, and then not from sensuality, but because their noble birth procures for them many offers of alliance. The wife does not bring a dower to the husband, but the husband to the wife. The parents and relatives are present, and pass judgment on the marriage-gifts, gifts not meant to suit a woman's taste, nor such as a bride would deck herself with, but oxen, a caparisoned steed, a shield, a lance, and a sword. With these presents the wife is espoused, and she herself in her turn brings her husband a gift of arms. This they count their strongest bond of union, these their sacred mysteries, these their gods of marriage. Lest the woman should think herself to stand apart from aspirations after noble deeds and from the perils of war, she is reminded by the ceremony which inaugurates marriage that she is her husband's partner in toil and danger, destined to suffer and to dare with him alike both in peace and in war. The yoked oxen, the harnessed steed, the gift of arms, proclaim this fact. She must live and die with the feeling that she is receiving what she must hand down to her children neither tarnished nor depreciated, what future daughters-in-law may receive, and may be so passed on to her grandchildren.

Thus with their virtue protected they live uncorrupted by the allurements of public shows or the stimulant of feastings. Clandestine correspondence is equally unknown to men and women. Very rare for so numerous a population is adultery, the punishment for which is prompt, and in the husband's power. Having cut off the hair of the adulteress and stripped her naked, he expels her from the house in the presence of her kinsfolk, and then flogs her through the whole village. The loss of chastity meets with no indulgence; neither beauty, youth, nor wealth will procure the culprit a husband. No one in Germany laughs at vice, nor do they call it the fashion to corrupt and to be corrupted. Still better is the condition of those states in which only maidens are given in marriage, and where the hopes and expectations of a bride are then finally terminated. They receive one husband, as having one body and one life, that they may have no thoughts beyond, no further-reaching desires, that they may love not so much the husband as the married state. To limit the number of their children or to destroy any of their subsequent offspring is accounted infamous, and good habits are here more effectual than good laws elsewhere.

In every household the children, naked and filthy, grow up with those stout frames and limbs which we so much admire. Every mother suckles her own offspring, and never entrusts it to servants and nurses. The master is not distinguished from the slave by being brought up with greater delicacy. Both live amid the same flocks and lie on the same ground till the freeborn are distinguished by age and recognised by merit. The young men marry late, and their vigour is thus unimpaired. Nor are the maidens hurried into marriage; the same age and a similar stature is required; well-matched and vigorous they wed, and the offspring reproduce the strength of the parents. Sisters' sons are held in as much esteem by their uncles as by their fathers; indeed, some regard the relation as even more sacred and binding, and prefer it in receiving hostages, thinking thus to secure a stronger hold on the affections and a wider bond for the family. But every man's own children are his heirs and successors, and there are no wills. Should there be no issue, the next in succession to the property are his brothers

and his uncles on either side. The more relatives he has, the more numerous his connections, the more honoured is his old age; nor are there any advantages in childlessness.

It is a duty among them to adopt the feuds as well as the friendships of a father or a kinsman. These feuds are not implacable; even homicide is expiated by the payment of a certain number of cattle and of sheep, and the satisfaction is accepted by the entire family, greatly to the advantage of the state, since feuds are dangerous in proportion to a people's freedom.

No nation indulges more profusely in entertainments and hospitality. To exclude any human being from their roof is thought impious; every German, according to his means, receives his guest with a well-furnished table. When his supplies are exhausted, he who was but now the host becomes the guide and companion to further hospitality, and without invitation they go to the next house. It matters not; they are entertained with like cordiality. No one distinguishes between an acquaintance and a stranger, as regards the rights of hospitality. It is usual to give the departing guest whatever he may ask for, and a present in return is asked with as little hesitation. They are greatly charmed with gifts, but they expect no return for what they give, nor feel any obligation for what they receive.

On waking from sleep, which they generally prolong to a late hour of the day, they take a bath, oftenest of warm water, which suits a country where winter is the longest of the seasons. After their bath they take their meal, each having a separate seat and table of his own. Then they go armed to business, or no less often to their festal meetings. To pass an entire day and night in drinking disgraces no one. Their quarrels, as might be expected with intoxicated people, are seldom fought out with mere abuse, but commonly with wounds and bloodshed. Yet it is at their feasts that they generally consult on the reconciliation of enemies, on the forming of matrimonial alliances, on the choice of chiefs, finally even on peace and war, for they think that at no time is the mind more open to simplicity of purpose or more

warmed to noble aspirations. A race without either natural or acquired cunning, they disclose their hidden thoughts in the freedom of the festivity. Thus the sentiments of all having been discovered and laid bare, the discussion is renewed on the following day, and from each occasion its own peculiar advantage is derived. They deliberate when they have no power to dissemble; they resolve when error is impossible.

A liquor for drinking is made out of barley or other grain, and fermented into a certain resemblance to wine. The dwellers on the river-bank also buy wine. Their food is of a simple kind, consisting of wild-fruit, fresh game, and curdled milk. They satisfy their hunger without elaborate preparation and without delicacies. In quenching their thirst they are not equally moderate. If you indulge their love of drinking by supplying them with as much as they desire, they will be overcome by their own vices as easily as by the arms of an enemy.

One and the same kind of spectacle is always exhibited at every gathering. Naked youths who practise the sport bound in the dance amid swords and lances that threaten their lives. Experience gives them skill, and skill again gives grace; profit or pay are out of the question; however reckless their pastime, its reward is the pleasure of the spectators. Strangely enough they make games of hazard a serious occupation even when sober, and so venturesome are they about gaining or losing, that, when every other resource has failed, on the last and final throw they stake the freedom of their own persons. The loser goes into voluntary slavery; though the younger and stronger, he suffers himself to be bound and sold. Such is their stubborn persistency in a bad practice; they themselves call it honour. Slaves of this kind the owners part with in the way of commerce, and also to relieve themselves from the scandal of such a victory.

The other slaves are not employed after our manner with distinct domestic duties assigned to them, but each one has the management of a house and home of his own. The master requires from the slave a certain quantity of grain, of cattle, and of clothing, as he would from a tenant, and

this is the limit of subjection. All other household functions are discharged by the wife and children. To strike a slave or to punish him with bonds or with hard labour is a rare occurrence. They often kill them, not in enforcing strict discipline, but on the impulse of passion, as they would an enemy, only it is done with impunity. The freedmen do not rank much above slaves, and are seldom of any weight in the family, never in the state, with the exception of those tribes which are ruled by kings. There indeed they rise above the freedborn and the noble; elsewhere the inferiority of the freedman marks the freedom of the state.

Of lending money on interest and increasing it by compound interest they know nothing—a more effectual safeguard than if it were prohibited.

Land proportioned to the number of inhabitants is occupied by the whole community in turn, and afterwards divided among them according to rank. A wide expanse of plains makes the partition easy. They till fresh fields every year, and they have still more land than enough; with the richness and extent of their soil, they do not laboriously exert themselves in planting orchards, inclosing meadows, and watering gardens. Corn is the only produce required from the earth; hence even the year itself is not divided by them into as many seasons as with us. Winter, spring, and summer have both a meaning and a name; the name and blessings of autumn are alike unknown.

In their funerals there is no pomp; they simply observe the custom of burning the bodies of illustrious men with certain kinds of wood. They do not heap garments or spices on the funeral pile. The weapons of the dead man and in some cases his horse are consigned to the fire. A turf mound forms the tomb. Monuments with their lofty elaborate splendour they reject as oppressive to the dead. Tears and lamentations they soon dismiss; grief and sorrow but slowly. It is thought becoming for women to bewail, for men to remember, the dead.

Such on the whole is the account which I have received of the origin and manners of the entire German people.

*   *   *

REVIEW QUESTIONS

1. As described by Tacitus, what were some of the principal values that governed German society?
2. How did those values compare with values of imperial Roman society as evidenced in some of the preceding readings?
3. Can you discern parallels or contrasts between Tacitus' views on Germans and the earlier views (see Chapter 3) of Hippocrates on the people of Europe?

6 ✣ THE TRANSFORMATION OF ROME

By 300 C.E., the emperor Diocletian and his colleagues had reorganized the Roman Empire, which now appeared more prosperous and stable than it had been for decades. Paganism, a convenient but misleading name for the broad spectrum of ancient beliefs and religions, remained dominant; indeed, Diocletian soon began a vigorous persecution of the Christian sect. But this world was on the verge of a profound change. Starting with the conversion of the emperor Constantine in 312 C.E., Christianity gradually triumphed, becoming the official religion of Rome. Missionary work among the barbarian tribes succeeded in bringing new peoples such as the Franks into the Christian fold. The barbarian kingdoms and the Christian Church, through its bishops and monasteries, transformed the legacies of the ancient world and created the new society of early medieval Europe.

In the centuries before Christianity emerged from persecution, the new faith found adherents because of its promise of salvation, the supportive and caring nature of early Christian communities, and the witness of generations of martyrs. In addition to the texts collected into the New Testament and approved by Church leaders, many other documents reveal both the spirit of the early martyrs and the effects of martyrdom on the people who witnessed it. The account of Perpetua's imprisonment and death in 205 C.E. is a powerful example.

After Christianity became the empire's official religion, Augustine of Hippo (in North Africa) was perhaps the most significant voice of this late Roman world. His many books continued to influence theologians in the medieval and early modern periods and beyond. Augustine tried to account for the sack of Rome in 410 C.E. in terms that strengthened Christian beliefs and denied pagans the chance to blame the new religion for the empire's defeats. Augustine, laying the foundations for doctrines on original sin and predestination of the saved and damned, also took on one of the empire's most important social and economic institutions, slavery, and fitted it into Christian belief. Augustine also wrote a spiritual autobiography, The Confessions, *that was a model of self-reflection for many centuries.*

As emperor and high priest of the Roman state cult, Constantine and his successors retained the same legal rights over Christianity that earlier rulers had exercised over pagan cults. This is reflected in the Roman legal system, which was based on imperial decrees and legal commentaries. The fifth-century C.E. Theodosian Code and the great compilations made under Emperor Justinian in the next century thus show the Christian Roman emperors trying to incorporate the newly official religion into a legal system originally attuned to more ancient values.

One of Christianity's distinctive institutions, originating in Egypt, was the monastery, and the Rule *of Saint Benedict (d. 547) demonstrates how a community dedicated to poverty, chastity, and obedience organized a common life for people wanting to escape the secular world and its temptations. Not everyone was called to be a nun or a monk, but this style of life defined perfection for Christians after the opportunities for martyrdom waned. The late empire's internal decay encouraged people to abandon the world, but it also attracted its most serious external threat. Tribes such as the Vandals and Visigoths, seeking protection on the frontiers from less Romanized peoples like the Huns, may have weakened an empire they probably wanted to preserve, even as they sought to assimilate and emulate Roman values.*

The Teaching of Jesus According to the Gospel of Matthew

Among the eastern religions that gained popularity in the Roman Empire was Judaism, especially that version of it espoused by the Christians: followers of an itinerant Jewish preacher named Yeshua (in Latin, Jesus), whose career in Judaea ended with his death by crucifixion sometime around 30 C.E. The chief records of his life and teachings are contained in the gospels ("good news"), a number of which were composed in the decades after his death. Only four—those of Mark, Matthew, Luke, and John—were later accepted as authoritative. All were originally written in Greek. Jesus himself would have spoken Aramaic and Hebrew.

From *The Contemporary English Version*, by American Bible Society (New York: American Bible Society, 1995).

*   *   *

Years later, John the Baptist started preaching in the desert of Judea. He said, "Turn back to God! The kingdom of heaven will soon be here." John was the one the prophet Isaiah was talking about, when he said,

"In the desert someone
is shouting,
'Get the road ready
for the Lord!
Make a straight path
for him.'"

John wore clothes made of camel's hair. He had a leather strap around his waist and ate grasshoppers and wild honey.

From Jerusalem and all Judea and from the Jordan River Valley crowds of people went to John. They told how sorry they were for their sins, and he baptized them in the river.

Many Pharisees and Sadducees also came to be baptized. But John said to them:

"You bunch of snakes! Who warned you to run from the coming judgment? Do something to show that you have really given up your sins. And don't start telling yourselves that you belong to Abraham's family. I tell you that God can turn these stones into children for Abraham. An ax is ready to cut the trees down at their roots. Any tree that doesn't produce good fruit will be chopped down and thrown into a fire.

"I baptize you with water so that you will give up your sins. But someone more powerful is going to come, and I am not good enough even to carry his sandals. He will baptize you with the Holy Spirit and with fire. His threshing fork is in his hand, and he is ready to separate the wheat from the husks. He will store the wheat in a barn and burn the husks in a fire that never goes out."

Jesus left Galilee and went to the Jordan River to be baptized by John. But John kept objecting and said, "I ought to be baptized by you. Why have you come to me?"

Jesus answered, "For now this is how it should be, because we must do all that God wants us to do." Then John agreed.

So Jesus was baptized. And as soon as he came out of the water, the sky opened, and he saw the Spirit of God coming down on him like a dove. Then a voice from heaven said, "This is my own dear Son, and I am pleased with him."

When Jesus saw the crowds, he went up on the side of a mountain and sat down. Jesus' disciples gathered around him, and he taught them:

"God blesses those people
who depend only on him.
They belong to the kingdom
of heaven! God blesses those people
who grieve.
They will find comfort!
God blesses those people
who are humble.
The earth will belong
to them!
God blesses those people
who want to obey him more than to eat or drink.
They will be given
what they want!
God blesses those people
who are merciful.
They will be treated
with mercy!
God blesses those people
whose hearts are pure.
They will see him!
God blesses those people
who make peace.
They will be called
his children!
God blesses those people
who are treated badly
for doing right.
They belong to the kingdom
of heaven.

"God will bless you when people insult you, mistreat you, and tell all kinds of evil lies about you

because of me. Be happy and excited! You will have a great reward in heaven. People did these same things to the prophets who lived long ago.

"You are like salt for everyone on earth. But if salt no longer tastes like salt, how can it make food salty? All it is good for is to be thrown out and walked on.

"You are like light for the whole world. A city built on top of a hill cannot be hidden, and no one would light a lamp and put it under a clay pot. A lamp is placed on a lampstand, where it can give light to everyone in the house. Make your light shine, so that others will see the good that you do and will praise your Father in heaven.

"Don't suppose that I came to do away with the Law and the Prophets. I did not come to do away with them, but to give them their full meaning. Heaven and earth may disappear. But I promise you that not even a period or comma will ever disappear from the Law. Everything written in it must happen. If you reject even the least important command in the Law and teach others to do the same, you will be the least important person in the kingdom of heaven. But if you obey and teach others its commands, you will have an important place in the kingdom. You must obey God's commands better than the Pharisees and the teachers of the Law obey them. If you don't, I promise you that you will never get into the kingdom of heaven.

"You know that our ancestors were told, 'Do not murder' and 'A murderer must be brought to trial.' But I promise you that if you are angry with someone, you will have to stand trial. If you call someone a fool, you will be taken to court. And if you say that someone is worthless, you will be in danger of the fires of hell. So if you are about to place your gift on the altar and remember that someone is angry with you, leave your gift there in front of the altar. Make peace with that person, then come back and offer your gift to God.

"Before you are dragged into court, make friends with the person who has accused you of doing wrong. If you don't, you will be handed over to the judge and then to the officer who will put you in jail. I promise you that you will not get out until you have paid the last cent you owe.

"You know the commandment which says, 'Be faithful in marriage.' But I tell you that if you look at another woman and want her, you are already unfaithful in your thoughts. If your right eye causes you to sin, poke it out and throw it away. It is better to lose one part of your body, than for your whole body to end up in hell. If your right hand causes you to sin, chop it off and throw it away! It is better to lose one part of your body, than for your whole body to be thrown into hell.

"You have been taught that a man who divorces his wife must write out divorce papers for her. But I tell you not to divorce your wife unless she has committed some terrible sexual sin. If you divorce her, you will cause her to be unfaithful, just as any man who marries her is guilty of taking another man's wife.

"You know that our ancestors were told, 'Don't use the Lord's name to make a promise unless you are going to keep it.' But I tell you not to swear by anything when you make a promise! Heaven is God's throne, so don't swear by heaven. The earth is God's footstool, so don't swear by the earth. Jerusalem is the city of the great king, so don't swear by it. Don't swear by your own head. You cannot make one hair white or black. When you make a promise, say only 'Yes' or 'No.' Anything else comes from the devil.

"You know that you have been taught, 'An eye for an eye and a tooth for a tooth.' But I tell you not to try to get even with a person who has done something to you. When someone slaps your right cheek, turn and let that person slap your other cheek. If someone sues you for your shirt, give up your coat as well. If a soldier forces you to carry his pack one mile, carry it two miles. When people ask you for something, give it to them. When they want to borrow money, lend it to them.

"You have heard people say, 'Love your neighbors and hate your enemies.' But I tell you to love your enemies and pray for anyone who mistreats you. Then you will be acting like your Father in heaven. He makes the sun rise on both good and

bad people. And he sends rain for the ones who do right and for the ones who do wrong. If you love only those people who love you, will God reward you for that? Even tax collectors love their friends. If you greet only your friends, what's so great about that? Don't even unbelievers do that? But you must always act like your Father in heaven."

*   *   *

"When you pray, don't be like those show-offs who love to stand up and pray in the meeting places and on the street corners. They do this just to look good. I can assure you that they already have their reward.

"When you pray, go into a room alone and close the door. Pray to your Father in private. He knows what is done in private, and he will reward you.

"When you pray, don't talk on and on as people do who don't know God. They think God likes to hear long prayers. Don't be like them. Your Father knows what you need before you ask.

"You should pray like this:

Our Father in heaven,
help us to honor
your name.
Come and set up
your kingdom,
so that everyone on earth
will obey you,
as you are obeyed
in heaven.
Give us our food for today. Forgive us for
  doing wrong,
as we forgive others.
Keep us from being tempted
and protect us from evil.

"If you forgive others for the wrongs they do to you, your Father in heaven will forgive you. But if you don't forgive others, your Father will not forgive your sins.

"When you go without eating, don't try to look gloomy as those show-offs do when they go without eating. I can assure you that they already have their reward. Instead, comb your hair and wash your face. Then others won't know that you are going without eating. But your Father sees what is done in private, and he will reward you.

"Don't store up treasures on earth! Moths and rust can destroy them, and thieves can break in and steal them. Instead, store up your treasures in heaven, where moths and rust cannot destroy them, and thieves cannot break in and steal them. Your heart will always be where your treasure is.

"Your eyes are like a window for your body. When they are good, you have all the light you need. But when your eyes are bad, everything is dark. If the light inside you is dark, you surely are in the dark.

"You cannot be the slave of two masters! You will like one more than the other or be more loyal to one than the other. You cannot serve both God and money.

"I tell you not to worry about your life. Don't worry about having something to eat, drink, or wear. Isn't life more than food or clothing? Look at the birds in the sky! They don't plant or harvest. They don't even store grain in barns. Yet your Father in heaven takes care of them. Aren't you worth more than birds?

"Can worry make you live longer? Why worry about clothes? Look how the wild flowers grow. They don't work hard to make their clothes. But I tell you that Solomon with all his wealth wasn't as well clothed as one of them. God gives such beauty to everything that grows in the fields, even though it is here today and thrown into a fire tomorrow. He will surely do even more for you! Why do you have such little faith? Don't worry and ask yourselves, 'Will we have anything to eat? Will we have anything to drink? Will we have any clothes to wear?' Only people who don't know God are always worrying about such things. Your Father in heaven knows that you need all of these. But more than anything else, put God's work first and do what he wants. Then the other things will be yours as well.

"Don't worry about tomorrow. It will take care of itself. You have enough to worry about today.

"Don't condemn others, and God won't condemn you. God will be as hard on you as you are

on others! He will treat you exactly as you treat them.

"You can see the speck in your friend's eye, but you don't notice the log in your own eye. How can you say, 'My friend, let me take the speck out of your eye,' when you don't see the log in your own eye? You're nothing but show-offs! First, take the log out of your own eye. Then you can see how to take the speck out of your friend's eye.

"Don't give to dogs what belongs to God. They will only turn and attack you. Don't throw pearls down in front of pigs. They will trample all over them.

"Ask, and you will receive. Search, and you will find. Knock, and the door will be opened for you. Everyone who asks will receive. Everyone who searches will find. And the door will be opened for everyone who knocks. Would any of you give your hungry child a stone, if the child asked for some bread? Would you give your child a snake if the child asked for a fish? As bad as you are, you still know how to give good gifts to your children. But your heavenly Father is even more ready to give good things to people who ask.

"Treat others as you want them to treat you. This is what the Law and the Prophets are all about.

"Go in through the narrow gate. The gate to destruction is wide, and the road that leads there is easy to follow. A lot of people go through that gate. But the gate to life is very narrow. The road that leads there is so hard to follow that only a few people find it.

"Watch out for false prophets! They dress up like sheep, but inside they are wolves who have come to attack you. You can tell what they are by what they do. No one picks grapes or figs from thornbushes. A good tree produces good fruit, and a bad tree produces bad fruit. A good tree cannot produce bad fruit, and a bad tree cannot produce good fruit. Every tree that produces bad fruit will be chopped down and burned. You can tell who the false prophets are by their deeds.

"Not everyone who calls me their Lord will get into the kingdom of heaven. Only the ones who obey my Father in heaven will get in. On the day of judgment many will call me their Lord. They will say, 'We preached in your name, and in your name we forced out demons and worked many miracles.' But I will tell them, 'I will have nothing to do with you! Get out of my sight, you evil people!'

"Anyone who hears and obeys these teachings of mine is like a wise person who built a house on solid rock. Rain poured down, rivers flooded, and winds beat against that house. But it did not fall, because it was built on solid rock.

"Anyone who hears my teachings and doesn't obey them is like a foolish person who built a house on sand. The rain poured down, the rivers flooded, and the winds blew and beat against that house. Finally, it fell with a crash."

When Jesus finished speaking, the crowds were surprised at his teaching. He taught them like someone with authority, and not like their teachers of the Law of Moses.

*   *   *

REVIEW QUESTIONS

1. What were the chief features of Jesus's teaching, according to these excerpts?
2. How do these teachings challenge the norms of the society in which Jesus lived? How does he represent himself as breaking with tradition?
3. Jesus speaks often of the "kingdom of heaven." What does he seem to mean by this? How might this "kingdom" stand in contrast to the kingdoms and empires that dominated the world in Jesus's own time? How might his teachings have been perceived by those in power?

The Martyrdom of Perpetua

In 203 C.E., a number of Christians were arrested, tried, and convicted by the Roman governor of Carthage (in North Africa). Among them was a young, well-born woman named Vivia (or Vibia) Perpetua, who was accompanied by her slave, Felicitas. Perpetua was nursing a young child at the time, and Felicitas was in the late stages of pregnancy. The following text features a first-hand account of these events in Perpetua's own words, the oldest surviving autobiographical writing associated with a Christian woman. The text has come down to us in both Latin and Greek editions.

From *A Lost Tradition: Women Writers of the Early Church*, by Patricia Wilson-Kastner, G. Ronald Kastner, Ann Millin, Rosemary Rader, and Jeremiah Reedy (Lanham, Md.: United Press of America, 1981), pp. 19–32.

1. If instances of ancient faith which both testified to the grace of God and edified persons were written expressly for God's honor and humans' encouragement, why shouldn't recent events be similarly recorded for those same purposes? For these events will likewise become part of the past and vital to posterity, in spite of the fact that contemporary esteem for antiquity tends to minimize their value. And those who maintain that there is a single manifestation of the one Holy Spirit throughout the ages ought to consider that since a fullness of grace has been decreed for the last days of the world these recent events should be considered of greater value because of their proximity to those days. For "In the last days," says the Lord, "I shall diffuse my spirit over all humanity and their sons and daughters shall prophesy; the young shall see visions, and the old shall dream dreams."[1]

Just as we valued those prophecies so we acknowledge and reverence the new visions which were promised. And we consider the other powers of the Holy Spirit to be instruments of the Church to which that same Spirit was sent to administer all gifts to all people, just as the Lord allotted. For this reason we deem it necessary to disseminate the written accounts for the glory of God, lest anyone with a weak or despairing faith might think that supernatural grace prevailed solely among the ancients who were honored either by their experience of martyrdom or visions. For God always fulfills what he promises, either as proof to non-believers or as an added grace to believers.

And so, brothers and dear ones, we share with you those things which we have heard and touched with our hands,[2] so that those of you who were eye-witnesses of these deeds may be reminded of the glory of the Lord, and those of you now learning of it through this narration may associate yourselves with the holy martyrs and, through them, with the Lord Jesus Christ to whom there is glory and honor forever.[3] Amen.

2. Arrested were some young catechumens; Revocatus and Felicitas (both servants), Saturninus, Secundulus, and Vibia Perpetua, a young married woman about twenty years old, of good family and upbringing.[4] She had a father, mother, two brothers (one was a catechumen like herself), and an infant son at the breast. The following account of her martyrdom is her own, a record in her own words of her perceptions of the event.

---

[1] Acts 2:17–18. Cf. Joel 2:28.

[2] I John 1:3. Cf. 1 Cor. 7:17; Rom. 12:3.

[3] I John 1:3.

[4] A catechumen was one receiving instruction in the basic beliefs and teachings of the Christian faith prior to baptism.

3. While I was still with the police authorities (she said) my father out of love for me tried to dissuade me from my resolution. "Father," I said, "do you see here, for example, this vase, or pitcher, or whatever it is?" "I see it," he said. "Can it be named anything else than what it really is?", I asked, and he said, "No." "So I also cannot be called anything else than what I am, a Christian." Enraged by my words my father came at me as though to tear out my eyes. He only annoyed me, but he left, overpowered by his diabolical arguments.

For a few days my father stayed away. I thanked the Lord and felt relieved because of my father's absence. At this time we were baptized and the Spirit instructed me not to request anything from the baptismal waters except endurance of physical suffering.[5]

A few days later we were imprisoned. I was terrified because never before had I experienced such darkness. What a terrible day! Because of crowded conditions and rough treatment by the soldiers the heat was unbearable. My condition was aggravated by my anxiety for my baby. Then Tertius and Pomponius, those kind deacons who were taking care of our needs, paid for us to be moved for a few hours to a better part of the prison where we might refresh ourselves. Leaving the dungeon we all went about our own business. I nursed my child, who was already weak from hunger. In my anxiety for the infant I spoke to my mother about him, tried to console my brother, and asked that they care for my son.[6] I suffered intensely because I sensed their agony on my account. These were the trials I had to endure for many days. Then I was granted the privilege of having my son remain with me in prison. Being relieved of my anxiety and concern for the infant, I immediately regained my strength. Suddenly the prison became my palace, and I loved being there rather than any other place.

4. Then my brother said to me, "Dear sister, you already have such a great reputation that you could ask for a vision indicating whether you will be condemned or freed." Since I knew that I could speak with the Lord, whose great favors I had already experienced, I confidently promised to do so. I said I would tell my brother about it the next day. Then I made my request and this is what I saw.

There was a bronze ladder of extraordinary height reaching up to heaven, but it was so narrow that only one person could ascend at a time.[7] Every conceivable kind of iron weapon was attached to the sides of the ladder: swords, lances, hooks, and daggers. If anyone climbed up carelessly or without looking upwards, he/she would be mangled as the flesh adhered to the weapons. Crouching directly beneath the ladder was a monstrous dragon who threatened those climbing up and tried to frighten them from ascent.

Saturus went up first. Because of his concern for us he had given himself up voluntarily after we had been arrested. He had been our source of strength but was not with us at the time of the arrest).[8] When he reached the top of the ladder he turned to me and said, "Perpetua, I'm waiting for you, but be careful not to be bitten by the dragon." I told him that in the name of Jesus Christ the dragon could not harm me. At this the dragon slowly lowered its head as though afraid of me. Using its head as the first step, I began my ascent.

At the summit I saw an immense garden, in the center of which sat a tall, grey-haired man dressed like a shepherd, milking sheep. Standing around him were several thousand white-robed people. As he raised his head he noticed me and said, "Welcome, my child." Then he beckoned me to approach and gave me a small morsel of the cheese he was making. I accepted it with cupped hands and ate it. When all those surrounding us said "Amen," I awoke, still tasting the sweet cheese. I immediately told my brother about the vision, and we

---

[5] Apparently after baptism the newly baptized could pray for a special grace or gift. Cf. Tertullian, *De Bapt.* 20.

[6] From the rest of the account it appears that Perpetua's mother was bringing the child to and from prison.

[7] Cf. Jacob's ladder in Gen. 28:12.

[8] Since Saturus was not listed as a catechumen he was probably the instructor of the others prior to their arrest.

both realized that we were to experience the sufferings of martyrdom. From then on we gave up having any hope in this world.

5. A few days later there was a rumor that our case was to be heard. My father, completely exhausted from his anxiety, came from the city to see me, with the intention of weakening my faith. "Daughter", he said, "have pity on my grey head. Have pity on your father if I have the honor to be called father by you, if with these hands I have brought you to the prime of your life, and if I have always favored you above your brothers, do not abandon me to the reproach of men. Consider your brothers; consider your mother and your aunt; consider your son who cannot live without you. Give up your stubbornness before you destroy all of us. None of us will be able to speak freely if anything happens to you."

These were the things my father said out of love, kissing my hands and throwing himself at my feet. With tears he called me not daughter, but woman. I was very upset because of my father's condition. He was the only member of my family who would find no reason for joy in my suffering. I tried to comfort him saying, "Whatever God wants at this tribunal will happen, for remember that our power comes not from ourselves but from God." But utterly dejected, my father left me.

6. One day as we were eating we were suddenly rushed off for a hearing. We arrived at the forum and the news spread quickly throughout the area near the forum, and a huge crowd gathered. We went up to the prisoners' platform. All the others confessed when they were questioned. When my turn came my father appeared with my son. Dragging me from the step, he begged: "Have pity on your son!"

Hilarion, the governor, who assumed power after the death of the proconsul Minucius Timinianus,[9] said, "Have pity on your father's grey head; have pity on your infant son; offer sacrifice for the emperors' welfare". But I answered, "I will not." Hi-

larion asked, "Are you a Christian?" And I answered, "I am a Christian." And when my father persisted in his attempts to dissuade me, Hilarion ordered him thrown out, and he was beaten with a rod. My father's injury hurt me as much as if I myself had been beaten, and I grieved because of his pathetic old age. Then the sentence was passed; all of us were condemned to the beasts. We were overjoyed as we went back to the prison cell. Since I was still nursing my child who was ordinarily in the cell with me, I quickly sent the deacon Pomponius to my father's house to ask for the baby, but my father refused to give him up. Then God saw to it that my child no longer needed my nursing, nor were my breasts inflamed. After that I was no longer tortured by anxiety about my child or by pain in my breasts.

7. A few days later while all of us were praying, in the middle of a prayer I suddenly called out the name "Dinocrates." I was astonished since I hadn't thought about him till then. When I recalled what had happened to him I was very disturbed and decided right then that I had not only the right, but the obligation, to pray for him. So I began to pray repeatedly and to make moaning sounds to the Lord in his behalf. During that same night I had this vision: I saw Dinocrates walking away from one of many very dark places. He seemed very hot and thirsty, his face grimy and colorless. The wound on his face was just as it had been when he died. This Dinocrates was my blood-brother who at the age of seven died very tragically from a cancerous disease which so disfigured his face that his death was repulsive to everyone. It was for him that I now prayed. But neither of us could reach the other because of the great distance between. In the place where Dinocrates stood was a pool filled with water, and the rim of the pool was so high that it extended far above the boy's height. Dinocrates stood on his toes as if to drink the water but in spite of the fact that the pool was full, he could not drink because the rim was so high![10]

---

[9] There is no real information about Minucius Timinianus, but Hilarion is mentioned as an African proconsul by Tertullian, *Ad Scapulam* 3.1. Hilarion was evidently temporarily serving as governor until a new one would be appointed.

[10] The reason Dinocrates was unable to drink the water may have been due to his dying before being baptized. Augustine (*De Anima* 1.12) maintained that the boy had committed sins after baptism and had not been cleansed of those sins prior to death.

I realized that my brother was in trouble, but I was confident that I could help him with his problem. I prayed for him every day until we were transferred to the arena prison where we were to fight wild animals on the birthday of Geta Caesar.[11] And I prayed day and night for him, moaning and weeping so that my petition would be granted.

8. On the day that we were kept in chains, I had the following vision: I saw the same place as before, but Dinocrates was clean, well-dressed, looking refreshed. In place of the wound there was a scar, and the fountain which I had seen previously now had its rim lowered to the boy's waist. On the rim, over which water was flowing constantly, there was a golden bowl filled with water. Dinocrates walked up to it and began to drink; the bowl never emptied. And when he was no longer thirsty, he gladly went to play as children do. Then I awoke, knowing that he had been relieved of his suffering.

9. A few days passed. Pudens, the official in charge of the prison (the official who had gradually come to admire us for our persistence), admitted many prisoners to our cell so that we might mutually encourage each other. As the day of the games drew near, my father, overwhelmed with grief, came again to see me. He began to pluck out his beard and throw it on the ground. Falling on his face before me, he cursed his old age, repeating such things as would move all creation. And I grieved because of his old age.

10. The day before the battle in the arena, in a vision I saw Pomponius the deacon coming to the prison door and knocking very loudly. I went to open the gate for him. He was dressed in a loosely fitting white robe, wearing richly decorated sandals. He said to me, "Perpetua, come. We're waiting for you!" He took my hand and we began to walk over extremely rocky and winding paths. When we finally arrived short of breath, at the arena, he led me to the center saying, "Don't be frightened! I'll be here to help you." He left me and I stared out over a huge crowd which watched me with apprehension. Because I knew that I had to fight with the beasts, I wondered why they hadn't yet been turned loose in the arena. Coming towards me was some type of Egyptian, horrible to look at, accompanied by fighters who were to help defeat me. Some handsome young men came forward to help and encourage me. I was stripped of my clothing, and suddenly I was a man. My assistants began to rub me with oil as was the custom before a contest, while the Egyptian was on the opposite side rolling in the sand. Then a certain man appeared, so tall that he towered above the amphitheatre. He wore a loose purple robe with two parallel stripes across the chest; his sandals were richly decorated with gold and silver. He carried a rod like that of an athletic trainer, and a green branch on which were golden apples. He motioned for silence and said, "If this Egyptian wins, he will kill her with the sword; but if she wins, she will receive this branch." Then he withdrew.

We both stepped forward and began to fight with our fists. My opponent kept trying to grab my feet but I repeatedly kicked his face with my heels. I felt myself being lifted up into the air and began to strike at him as one who was no longer earthbound. But when I saw that we were wasting time, I put my two hands together, linked my fingers, and put his head between them. As he fell on his face I stepped on his head. Then the people began to shout and my assistants started singing victory songs. I walked up to the trainer and accepted the branch.[12] He kissed me and said, "Peace be with you, my daughter." And I triumphantly headed towards the Sanavivarian Gate.[13] Then I woke up realizing that I would be contending not with wild animals but with the devil himself. I knew, however, that I would win. I have recorded the events which occurred up to the day before the final contest. Let anyone who wishes to record the events of the contest itself, do so.

---

[11] This incidental reference to the celebration of games on Geta's birthday helps establish the date of the martyrdom somewhere between 200 [and] 205.

[12] The branch was the reward presented to the victor in any kind of official combat or contest.

[13] The Porta Sanavivaria (Gate of Life) was the gate by which the victors would exit. Those who were defeated were carried out through the Porta Libitinensis, which derived its name from the goddess presiding over funeral rites.

11. The saintly Saturus also related a vision which he had and it is recorded here in his own hand. Our suffering had ended (he said), and we were being carried towards the east by four angels whose hands never touched us. And we floated upward, not in a supine position, but as though we were climbing a gentle slope. As we left the earth's atmosphere we saw a brilliant light, and I said to Perpetua who was at my side, "This is what the Lord promised us. We have received his promise."

And while we were being carried along by those four angels we saw a large open space like a splendid garden landscaped with rose trees and every variety of flower. The trees were as tall as cypresses whose leaves rustled gently and incessantly. And there in that garden-sanctuary were four other angels, more dazzling than the rest. And when they saw us they showed us honor, saying to the other angels in admiration, "Here they are! They have arrived."

And those four angels who were carrying us began trembling in awe and set us down. And we walked through a violet-strewn field where we met Jocundus, Saturninus, and Artaxius who were burned alive in that same persecution, and Quintus, also a martyr, who had died in prison. We were asking them where they had been, when the other angels said to us, "First, come this way. Go in and greet the Lord."

12. We went up to a place where the walls seemed constructed of light. At the entrance of the place stood four angels who put white robes on those who entered. We went in and heard a unified voice chanting endlessly, "Holy, holy, holy." We saw a white haired man sitting there who, in spite of his snowy white hair, had the features of a young man. His feet were not visible. On his right and left were four elderly gentlemen and behind them stood many more. As we entered we stood in amazement before the throne. Four angels supported us as we went up to kiss the aged man, and he gently stroked our faces with his hands. The other elderly men said to us, "Stand up." We rose and gave the kiss of peace. Then they told us to enjoy ourselves. I said to Perpetua, "You have your wish." She answered, "I thank God, for although I was happy on earth, I am much happier here right now."

13. Then we went out, and before the gates we saw Optatus the bishop on the right and Aspasius the priest and teacher on the left, both looking sad as they stood there separated from each other. They knelt before us saying, "Make peace between us, for you've gone away and left us this way." But we said to them "Aren't you our spiritual father, and our teacher? Why are you kneeling before us?" We were deeply touched and we embraced them. And Perpetua began to speak to them in Greek and we invited them into the garden beneath a rose tree. While we were talking with them, the angels said to them, "Let them refresh themselves, and if you have any dissensions among you, forgive one another." This disturbed both of them and the angels said to Optatus, "Correct your people who flock to you as though returning from the games, fighting about the different teams." It seemed to us that they wanted to close the gates, and there we began to recognize many of our friends, among whom were martyrs. We were all sustained by an indescribable fragrance which completely satisfied us. Then in my joy, I awoke.

14. The remarkable visions narrated above were those of the blessed martyrs Saturus and Perpetua, just as they put them in writing. As for Secundulus, while he was still in prison God gave him the grace of an earlier exit from this world, so that he could escape combat with the wild beasts. But his body, though not his soul, certainly felt the sword.

15. As for Felicitas, she too was touched by God's grace in the following manner. She was pregnant when arrested, and was now in her eighth month. As the day of the contest approached she became very distressed that her martyrdom might be delayed, since the law forbade the execution of a pregnant woman. Then she would later have to shed her holy and innocent blood among common criminals. Her friends in martyrdom were equally sad at the thought of abandoning such a good friend to travel alone on the same road to hope.

And so, two days before the contest, united in grief they prayed to the Lord. Immediately after the prayers her labor pains began. Because of the additional pain natural for an eighth-month delivery,

she suffered greatly during the birth, and one of the prison guards taunted her; "If you're complaining now, what will you do when you'll be thrown to the wild beasts? You didn't think of them when you refused to sacrifice." She answered, "Now it is I who suffer, but then another shall be in me to bear the pain for me, since I am now suffering for him." And she gave birth to a girl whom one of her sisters reared as her own daughter.

16. Since the Holy Spirit has permitted, and by permitting has willed, that the events of the contest be recorded, we have no choice but to carry out the injunction (rather, the sacred trust) of Perpetua, in spite of the fact that it will be an inferior addition to the magnificent events already described. We are adding an instance of Perpetua's perseverance and lively spirit. At one time the prisoners were being treated with unusual severity by the commanding officer because certain deceitful men had intimated to him that the prisoners might escape by some magic spells. Perpetua openly challenged him; "Why don't you at least allow us to freshen up, the most noble of the condemned, since we belong to Caesar and are about to fight on his birthday? Or isn't it to your credit that we should appear in good condition on that day?" The officer grimaced and blushed, then ordered that they be treated more humanely and that her brothers and others be allowed to visit and dine with them. By this time the prison warden was himself a believer.

17. On the day before the public games, as they were eating the last meal commonly called the free meal, they tried as much as possible to make it instead an *agape*.[14] In the same spirit they were exhorting the people, warning them to remember the judgment of God, asking them to be witnesses to the prisoners' joy in suffering, and ridiculing the curiosity of the crowd. Saturus told them, "Won't tomorrow's view be enough for you? Why are you so eager to see something you hate? Friends today, enemies tomorrow! Take a good look so you'll rec-

ognize us on that day." Then they all left the prison amazed, and many of them began to believe.

18. The day of their victory dawned, and with joyful countenances they marched from the prison to the arena as though on their way to heaven. If there was any trembling it was from joy, not fear. Perpetua followed with quick step as a true spouse of Christ, the darling of God, her brightly flashing eyes quelling the gaze of the crowd. Felicitas too, joyful because she had safely survived childbirth and was now able to participate in the contest with the wild animals, passed from one shedding of blood to another: from midwife to gladiator, about to be purified after child-birth by a second baptism. As they were led through the gate they were ordered to put on different clothes; the men, those priests of Saturn, the women, those of the priestesses of Ceres. But that noble woman stubbornly resisted even to the end. She said, "We've come this far voluntarily in order to protect our rights, and we've pledged our lives not to recapitulate [sic] on any such matter as this. We made this agreement with you." Injustice bowed to justice and the guard conceded that they could enter the arena in their ordinary dress. Perpetua was singing victory psalms as if already crushing the head of the Egyptian. Revocatus, Saturninus and Saturus were warning the spectators, and as they came within sight of Hilarion they informed him by nods and gestures: "You condemn us; God condemns you." This so infuriated the crowds that they demanded the scourging of these men in front of the line of gladiators. But the ones so punished rejoiced in that they had obtained yet another share in the Lord's suffering.

19. Whoever said, "Ask and you shall receive," granted to these petitioners the particular death that each one chose. For whenever the martyrs were discussing among themselves their choice of death, Saturus used to say that he wished to be thrown in with all the animals so that he might wear a more glorious crown. Accordingly, at the outset of the show he was matched against a leopard but then called back; then he was mauled by a bear on the exhibition platform. Now Saturus detested nothing as much as a bear and he had

---

[14] The *agape* or "love feast" was the common meal shared by the early Christian communities. It was the visible expression of the love Christians felt for each other as co-sharers of the love of Christ.

already decided to die by one bite from the leopard. Consequently, when he was tied to a wild boar the professional gladiator who had tied the two together was pierced instead and died shortly after the games ended, while Saturus was merely dragged about. And when he was tied up on the bridge in front of the bear, the bear refused to come out of his den; and so a second time Saturus was called back unharmed.

20. For the young women the devil had readied a mad cow, an animal not usually used at these games, but selected so that the women's sex would be matched with that of the animal. After being stripped and enmeshed in nets, the women were led into the arena. How horrified the people were as they saw that one was a young girl and the other, her breasts dripping with milk, had just recently given birth to a child. Consequently both were recalled and dressed in loosely fitting gowns.

Perpetua was tossed first and fell on her back. She sat up, and being more concerned with her sense of modesty than with her pain, covered her thighs with her gown which had been torn down one side. Then finding her hair-clip which had fallen out, she pinned back her loose hair thinking it not proper for a martyr to suffer with dishevelled hair; it might seem that she was mourning in her hour of triumph. Then she stood up. Noticing that Felicitas was badly bruised, she went to her, reached out her hands and helped her to her feet. As they stood there the cruelty of the crowds seemed to be appeased and they were sent to the Sanavivarian Gate. There Perpetua was taken care of by a certain catechumen, Rusticus, who stayed near her. She seemed to be waking from a deep sleep (so completely had she been entranced and imbued with the Spirit). She began to look around her and to everyone's astonishment asked, "When are we going to be led out to that cow, or whatever it is." She would not believe that it had already happened until she saw the various markings of the tossing on her body and clothing. Then calling for her brother she said to him and to the catechumen, "Remain strong in your faith and love one another. Do not let our excruciating sufferings become a stumbling block for you."

21. Meanwhile, at another gate Saturus was similarly encouraging the soldier, Pudens. "Up to the present," he said, "I've not been harmed by any of the animals, just as I've foretold and predicted. So that you will now believe completely, watch as I go back to die from a single leopard bite." And so at the end of that contest, Saturus was bitten once by the leopard that had been set loose, and bled so profusely from that one wound that as he was coming back the crowd shouted in witness to his second baptism: "Salvation by being cleansed; Salvation by being cleansed;"[15] And that man was truly saved who was cleansed in this way.

Then Saturus said to Pudens the soldier, "Goodbye, and remember my faith. Let these happenings be a source of strength for you, rather than a cause for anxiety." Then asking Pudens for a ring from his finger, he dipped it into the wound and returned it to Pudens as a legacy, a pledge and remembrance of his death. And as he collapsed he was thrown with the rest to that place reserved for the usual throat-slitting. And when the crowd demanded that the prisoners be brought out into the open so that they might feast their eyes on death by the sword, they voluntarily arose and moved where the crowd wanted them. Before doing so they kissed each other so that their martyrdom would be completely perfected by the rite of the kiss of peace.

The others, without making any movement or sound, were killed by the sword. Saturus in particular, since he had been the first to climb the ladder and was to be Perpetua's encouragement, was the first to die. But Perpetua, in order to feel some of the pain, groaning as she was struck between the ribs, took the gladiator's trembling hand [and] guided it to her throat. Perhaps it was that so great a woman, feared as she was by the unclean spirit, could not have been slain had she not herself willed it.

O brave and fortunate martyrs, truly called and chosen to give honor to our Lord Jesus Christ! And anyone who is elaborating upon, or who reverences

---

[15] One of the customary greetings of good omen before and after the public baths was "Salvum lotum," here used ironically by the crowd in the amphitheater.

STILICHO AND HIS FAMILY (395 C.E.)

The two panels of this ivory diptych (DIP-tick) date to around the year 395 C.E. and they would originally have been joined by hinges, making a portable object that could open and close—or be displayed on a flat surface. On the right is the Roman general Stilicho (c. 359–408), dressed as a conventional Roman soldier; on the left are his wife, Serena (holding a flower), and his young son, Eucherius (holding a book). Stilicho was the son of a Vandal chieftain and an unknown (Roman) woman. Serena came from an aristocratic Roman family and was the adopted niece of the Emperor Theodosius I (r. 379–95). At the time of their marriage, Stilicho was the effective ruler of the Western Roman Empire. What do these images reveal about Roman identity and values during a time of intense political and cultural change? What do they suggest about the status and chosen identity of Stilicho himself? How might this object have been used?

or worships that honor, should read these more recent examples, along with the ancient, as sources of encouragement for the Christian community. In this way, there will be new examples of courage witnessing to the fact that even in our day the same Holy Spirit is still efficaciously present, along with the all powerful God the Father and Jesus Christ our Lord, to whom there will always be glory and endless power. Amen.

*   *   *

REVIEW QUESTIONS

1. First-hand accounts of this kind are rare, and it is especially unusual to have a text that preserves the words of a young woman from one of Rome's provinces. How might this document have survived and circulated? What clues to its preservation and audience are given in the text?

2. Perpetua's father is an important figure in this account. What do his interactions with his daughter and with Roman authorities tell us about traditional Roman values, and about the ways that Christianity opposed these values?

3. What can we learn by analyzing Perpetua's visions? In particular, what do you make of the fact that she "became a man" when she was stripped and entered the arena? More generally, what do Perpetua's words and actions reveal about gender roles in Roman provincial society?

ST. AUGUSTINE

FROM *City of God* AND *Confessions*

Augustine (354–430 C.E.) is considered the greatest "father" and theologian of the early Church, second only to Saint Paul in his influence. The son of a pagan father and a Christian mother, he was born in North Africa and educated at Carthage, but his ambitions took him to Italy as a young man. While working as a teacher in Milan, he came under the influence of the city's charismatic bishop, Ambrose, another important Church Father. In 386, after years of deliberation and doubt, he converted to Christianity and was soon appointed bishop of Hippo Regius in his native North Africa. His best-known works are his autobiographical Confessions *and* The City of God, *a monumental defense of Christianity published in response to the sack of Rome by the Visigoths in 410 C.E. The following excerpts from the latter book come from the introduction, where Augustine lays out his thesis and begins his analysis of the nature of freedom, sin, and slavery. The short excerpt from the* Confessions *describes a youthful crime that appears to have haunted Augustine throughout his life.*

FROM *City of God*, Book I*

Here, my dear Marcellinus, is the fulfilment of my promise, a book in which I have taken upon myself the task of defending the glorious City of God against those who prefer their own gods to the Founder of that City. I treat of it both as it exists in this world of time, a stranger among the ungodly, living by faith, and as it stands in the security of its everlasting seat. This security it now awaits in steadfast patience, until 'justice returns to judgement'; but it is to attain it hereafter in virtue of its ascendancy over its enemies, when the final victory is won and peace established. The task is long and arduous; but God is our helper.

I know how great is the effort needed to convince the proud of the power and excellence of humility, an excellence which makes it soar above all the summits of this world, which sway in their temporal instability, overtopping them all with an eminence not arrogated by human pride, but granted by divine grace. For the King and Founder of this City which is our subject has revealed in the Scripture of his people this statement of the divine Law, 'God resists the proud, but he gives grace to the humble.' This is God's prerogative; but man's arrogant spirit in its swelling pride has claimed it as its own, and delights to hear this verse quoted in its own praise: 'To spare the conquered, and beat down the proud.'[1]

Therefore I cannot refrain from speaking about the city of this world,[2] a city which aims at dominion, which holds nations in enslavement, but is itself dominated by that very lust of domination. I must consider this city as far as the scheme of this work demands and as occasion serves.

1. THE ENEMIES OF CHRISTIANITY WERE SPARED BY THE BARBARIANS AT THE SACK OF ROME, OUT OF RESPECT FOR CHRIST.

From this world's city there arise enemies against whom the City of God has to be defended, though many of these correct their godless errors and become useful citizens of that City. But many are inflamed with hate against it and feel no gratitude for the benefits offered by its Redeemer. The benefits are unmistakable; those enemies would not today be able to utter a word against the City if, when fleeing from the sword of their enemy, they had not found, in the City's holy places, the safety on which they now congratulate themselves. The barbarians spared them for Christ's sake; and now these Romans assail Christ's name. The sacred places of the martyrs and the basilicas of the apostles bear witness to this, for in the sack of Rome they afforded shelter to fugitives, both Christian and pagan. The bloodthirsty enemy raged thus far, but here the frenzy of butchery was checked; to these refuges the merciful among the enemy conveyed those whom they had spared outside, to save them from encountering foes who had no such pity. Even men who elsewhere raged with all the savagery an enemy can show, arrived at places where practices generally allowed by laws of war were forbidden and their monstrous passion for violence was brought to a sudden halt; their lust for taking captives was subdued.

In this way many escaped who now complain of this Christian era, and hold Christ responsible for the disasters which their city endured. But they do not make Christ responsible for the benefits they received out of respect for Christ, to which they owed their lives. They attribute their deliverance to their own destiny; whereas if they had any right judgement they ought rather to attribute the harsh cruelty they suffered at the hands of their enemies to the providence of God. For God's providence constantly uses war to correct and chasten the corrupt morals of mankind, as it also uses such afflictions to train men in a righteous and laudable way of life, removing to a better state those whose life is approved, or else keeping them in this world for further service.

Moreover, they should give credit to this Christian era for the fact that these savage barbarians showed mercy beyond the custom of war—whether they so acted in general in honour of the

---

*From *City of God*, by St. Augustine, translated by Henry Bettenson (New York: Penguin, 1972), pp. 5–9, 874–76.
[1] Virgil, *Æneid* VI: 853.
[2] I.e., Rome.

name of Christ, or in places specially dedicated to Christ's name, buildings of such size and capacity as to give mercy a wider range. For this clemency our detractors ought rather to give thanks to God; they should have recourse to his name in all sincerity, so as to escape the penalty of everlasting fire, seeing that so many of them assumed his name dishonestly, to escape the penalty of immediate destruction. Among those whom you see insulting Christ's servants with such wanton insolence there are very many who came unscathed through that terrible time of massacre only by passing themselves off as Christ's servants. And now with ungrateful pride and impious madness they oppose his name in the perversity of their hearts, so that they may incur the punishment of eternal darkness; but then they took refuge in that name, though with deceitful lips, so that they might continue to enjoy this transitory light.

2. THAT VICTORS SHOULD SPARE THE VANQUISHED OUT OF RESPECT FOR THEIR GODS IS SOMETHING UNEXAMPLED IN HISTORY.

We have the records of many wars, both before the foundation of Rome and after its rise to power. Let our enemies read their history, and then produce instances of the capture of any city by foreign enemies when those enemies spared any whom they found taking refuge in the temples of their gods. Let them quote any barbarian general who gave instructions, at the storming of a town, that no one should be treated with violence who was discovered in this temple or that. Aeneas saw Priam at the altar,

> polluting with his blood
> The fire which he had consecrated.

And Diomedes and Ulysses

> Slew all the warders of the citadel
> And snatched with bloody hands the sacred
>   image;
> Nor shrank to touch the chaplets virginal
> Of the dread goddess.

And there is no truth in the statement that comes after,

> The Grecian hopes then failed, and ebbed
>   away.[3]

For what in fact followed was the Greek victory, the destruction of Troy by fire and sword, the slaughter of Priam at the altar.

And it was not because Troy lost Minerva that Troy perished. What loss did Minerva herself first incur, that led to her own disappearance? Was it, perhaps, the loss of her guards? There can be no doubt that their death made her removal possible—the image did not preserve the men; the men were preserving the image. Why then did they worship her, to secure her protection for their country and its citizens? She could not guard her own keepers.

3. THE FOLLY OF THE ROMANS IN CONFIDING THEIR SAFETY TO THE HOUSEHOLD GODS WHO HAD FAILED TO PROTECT TROY.

There you see the sorts of gods to whom the Romans gladly entrusted the preservation of their city. Pitiable folly! Yet the Romans are enraged by such criticisms from us, while they are not incensed at the authors of such quotations; in fact they pay money to become acquainted with their works, and they consider that those who merely instruct them in these works merit an official salary and an honoured position in the community. Virgil certainly is held to be a great poet; in fact he is regarded as the best and the most renowned of all poets, and for that reason he is read by children at an early age—they take great draughts of his poetry into their unformed minds, so that they may not easily forget him, for, as Horace[4] remarks,

> New vessels will for long retain the taste
> Of what is first poured into them.

---

[3] These are quotations from the *Æneid* of Virgil (70–19 B.C.E.), Augustine's favorite poet.
[4] Quintus Horatius Flaccus (65–8 B.C.E.).

Now in Virgil, Juno is introduced as hostile to the Trojans, and when she urges Aeolus, king of the winds, against them, she says,

> A race I hate sails the Etruscan sea
> Bringing to Italy Troy's vanquished gods,
> And Troy itself.

Ought the Romans, as prudent men, to have entrusted the defence of Rome to gods unable to defend themselves? Juno no doubt spoke like a woman in anger, heedless of what she was saying. But consider what is said by Aeneas himself, who is so often called "the pious."

> Panthus, the priest of Phoebus and the citadel,
> Snatching his conquered gods and his young
>   grandson
> Rushes in frenzy to the door.

He does not shrink from calling the gods "conquered," and he speaks of them as being entrusted to him, rather than the other way round, when he is told, "To thee, Troy now entrusts her native gods."

If Virgil speaks of such gods as "vanquished," and tells how, after their overthrow, they only succeeded in escaping because they were committed to the care of a man, what folly it is to see any wisdom in committing Rome to such guardians, and in supposing that it could not be sacked while it retained possession of them. To worship "vanquished" gods as protectors and defenders is to rely not on divinities but on defaulters. It is not sensible to assume that Rome would have escaped this disaster had these gods not first perished; the sensible belief is that those gods would have perished long before, had not Rome made every effort to preserve them. Anyone who gives his mind to it can see that it is utter folly to count on invincibility by virtue of the possession of defenders who have been conquered and to attribute destruction to the loss of such guardian deities as these. In fact, the only possible cause of destruction was the choice of such perishable defenders. When the poets wrote and sang of "vanquished gods," it was not because it suited their whim to lie—they were men of sense, and truth compelled them to admit the facts.

But I must deal with this subject in fuller detail in a more convenient place. For the present I will return to the ingratitude of those who blasphemously blame Christ for the disasters which their moral perversity deservedly brought upon them, and I will deal with the subject as briefly as I can. They were spared for Christ's sake, pagans though they were; yet they scorn to acknowledge this. With the madness of sacrilegious perversity they use their tongues against the name of Christ; yet with those same tongues they dishonestly claimed that name in order to save their lives, or else, in places sacred to him, they held their tongues through fear. They were kept safe and protected there where his name stood between them and the enemy's violence. And so they issue from that shelter to assail him with curses of hate.

*   *   *

15. MAN'S NATURAL FREEDOM; AND THE SLAVERY CAUSED BY SIN.

This relationship is prescribed by the order of nature, and it is in this situation that God created man. For he says, "Let him have lordship over the fish of the sea, the birds of the sky . . . and all the reptiles that crawl on the earth."[5] He did not wish the rational being, made in his own image, to have dominion over any but irrational creatures, not man over man, but man over the beasts. Hence the first just men were set up as shepherds of flocks, rather than as kings of men, so that in this way also God might convey the message of what was required by the order of nature, and what was demanded by the deserts of sinners—for it is understood, of course, that the condition of slavery is justly imposed on the sinner. That is why we do not hear of a slave anywhere in the Scriptures until Noah, the just man, punished his son's sin with this word; and so that son deserved this name because of his misdeed, not because of his nature. The origin of the Latin word for slave, *servus,* is believed to be derived from the

---

[5] Genesis 1:26.

fact that those who by the laws of war could rightly be put to death by the conquerors, became *servi,* slaves, when they were preserved, receiving this name from their preservation. But even this enslavement could not have happened, if it were not for the deserts of sin. For even when a just war is fought it is in defence of his sin that the other side is contending; and victory, even when the victory falls to the wicked, is a humiliation visited on the conquered by divine judgement, either to correct or to punish their sins. We have a witness to this in Daniel, a man of God, who in captivity confesses to God his own sins and the sins of his people, and in devout grief testifies that they are the cause of that captivity. The first cause of slavery, then, is sin, whereby man was subjected to man in the condition of bondage; and this can only happen by the judgement of God, with whom there is no injustice, and who knows how to allot different punishments according to the deserts of the offenders.

Now, as our Lord above says, "Everyone who commits sin is sin's slave,"[6] and that is why, though many devout men are slaves to unrighteous masters, yet the masters they serve are not themselves free men; 'for when a man is conquered by another he is also bound as a slave to his conqueror.' And obviously it is a happier lot to be slave to a human being than to a lust; and, in fact, the most pitiless domination that devastates the hearts of men, is that exercised by this very lust for domination, to mention no others. However, in that order of peace in which men are subordinate to other men, humility is as salutary for the servants as pride is harmful to the masters. And yet by nature, in the condition in which God created man, no man is the slave either of man or of sin. But it remains true that slavery as a punishment is also ordained by that law which enjoins the preservation of the order of nature, and forbids its disturbance; in fact, if nothing had been done to contravene that law, there would have been nothing to require the discipline of slavery as a punishment. That explains also the Apostle's admonition

to slaves, that they should be subject to their masters, and serve them loyally and willingly.[7] What he means is that if they cannot be set free by their masters, they themselves may thus make their slavery, in a sense, free, by serving not with the slyness of fear, but with the fidelity of affection, until all injustice disappears and all human lordship and power is annihilated, and God is all in all.

16. EQUITY IN THE RELATION OF MASTER AND SLAVE.

This being so, even though our righteous fathers had slaves, they so managed the peace of their households as to make a distinction between the situation of children and the condition of slaves in respect of the temporal goods of this life; and yet in the matter of the worship of God—in whom we must place our hope of everlasting goods—they were concerned, with equal affection, for all the members of their household. This is what the order of nature prescribes, so that this is the source of the name *paterfamilias,* a name that has become so generally used that even those who exercise unjust rule rejoice to be called by this title. On the other hand, those who are genuine "fathers of their household" are concerned for the welfare of all in their households in respect of the worship and service of God, as if they were all their children, longing and praying that they may come to the heavenly home, where it will not be a necessary duty to give orders to men, because it will no longer be a necessary duty to be concerned for the welfare of those who are already in the felicity of that immortal state. But until that home is reached, the fathers have an obligation to exercise the authority of masters greater than the duty of slaves to put up with their condition as servants.

However, if anyone in the household is, through his disobedience, an enemy to the domestic peace, he is reproved by a word, or by a blow, or any other kind of punishment that is just and legitimate, to the extent allowed by human society; but this is for the benefit of the offender, intended to readjust him

---

[6] John 8:54.

[7] Ephesians 6:5.

to the domestic peace from which he had broken away. For just as it is not an act of kindness to help a man, when the effect of the help is to make him lose a greater good, so it is not a blameless act to spare a man, when by so doing you let him fall into a greater sin. Hence the duty of anyone who would be blameless includes not only doing no harm to anyone but also restraining a man from sin or punishing his sin, so that either the man who is chastised may be corrected by his experience, or others may be deterred by his example. Now a man's house ought to be the beginning, or rather a small component part of the city, and every beginning is directed to some end of its own kind, and every component part contributes to the completeness of the whole of which it forms a part. The implication is quite apparent, that domestic peace contributes to the peace of the city—that is, the ordered harmony of those who live together in a house in the matter of giving and obeying orders, contributes to the ordered harmony concerning authority and obedience obtaining among the citizens. Consequently it is fitting that the father of a household should take his rules from the law of the city, and govern his household in such a way that it fits in with the peace of the city.

FROM *Confessions**

4

It is certain, O Lord, that theft is punished by your law, the law that is written in men's hearts and cannot be erased however sinful they are. For no thief can bear that another thief should steal from him, even if he is rich and the other is driven to it by want. Yet I was willing to steal, and steal I did, although I was not compelled by any lack, unless it were the lack of a sense of justice or a distaste for what was right and a greedy love of doing wrong. For of what I stole I already had plenty, and much

---

*From *Confessions*, by St. Augustine, translated by R. S. Pine-Coffin (New York: Penguin, 1961), pp. 47–49.

better at that, and I had no wish to enjoy the things I coveted by stealing, but only to enjoy the theft itself and the sin. There was a pear-tree near our vineyard, loaded with fruit that was attractive neither to look at nor to taste. Late one night a band of ruffians, myself included, went off to shake down the fruit and carry it away, for we had continued our games out of doors until well after dark, as was our pernicious habit. We took away an enormous quantity of pears, not to eat them ourselves, but simply to throw them to the pigs. Perhaps we ate some of them, but our real pleasure consisted in doing something that was forbidden.

Look into my heart, O God, the same heart on which you took pity when it was in the depths of the abyss. Let my heart now tell you what prompted me to do wrong for no purpose, and why it was only my own love of mischief that made me do it. The evil in me was foul, but I loved it. I loved my own perdition and my own faults, not the things for which I committed wrong, but the wrong itself. My soul was vicious and broke away from your safe keeping to seek its own destruction looking for no profit in disgrace but only for disgrace itself.

5

The eye is attracted by beautiful objects, by gold and silver and all such things. There is great pleasure, too, in feeling something agreeable to the touch, and material things have various qualities to please each of the other senses. Again, it is gratifying to be held in esteem by other men and to have the power of giving them orders and gaining the mastery over them. This is also the reason why revenge is sweet. But our ambition to obtain all these things must not lead us astray from you, O Lord, nor must we depart from what your law allows. The life we live on earth has its own attractions as well, because it has a certain beauty of its own in harmony with all the rest of this world's beauty. Friendship among men, too, is a delightful bond, uniting many souls in one. All these things and their like can be occasions of sin because, good though they are, they are of the lowest order of good, and if we are too much tempted by them we abandon those higher and better things,

your truth, your law, and you yourself, O Lord our God. For these earthly things, too, can give joy, though not such joy as my God, who made them all, can give, because *honest men will rejoice in the Lord; upright hearts will not boast in vain.*

When there is an inquiry to discover why a crime has been committed, normally no one is satisfied until it has been shown that the motive might have been either the desire of gaining, or the fear of losing, one of those good things which I said were of the lowest order. For such things are attractive and have beauty, although they are paltry trifles in comparison with the worth of God's blessed treasures. A man commits murder and we ask the reason. He did it because he wanted his victim's wife or estates for himself, or so that he might live on the proceeds of robbery, or because he was afraid that the other might defraud him of something, or because he had been wronged and was burning for revenge. Surely no one would believe that he would commit murder for no reason but the sheer delight of killing? Sallust tells us that Catiline was a man of insane ferocity, "who chose to be cruel and vicious without apparent reason"; but we are also told that his purpose was "not to allow his men to lose heart or waste their skill through lack of practice." If we ask the reason for this, it is obvious that he meant that once he had made himself master of the government by means of this continual violence, he would obtain honour, power, and wealth and would no longer go in fear of the law because of his crimes or have to face difficulties through lack of funds. So even Catiline did not love crime for crime's sake. He loved something quite different, for the sake of which he committed his crimes.

6

If the crime of theft which I committed that night as a boy of sixteen were a living thing, I could speak to it and ask what it was that, to my shame, I loved in it. I had no beauty because it was a robbery. It is true that the pears which we stole had beauty, because they were created by you, the good God, who are the most beautiful of all beings and the Creator of all things, the supreme Good and my own true Good. But it was not the pears that my unhappy soul desired. I had plenty of my own, better than those, and I only picked them so that I might steal. For no sooner had I picked them than I threw them away, and tasted nothing in them but my own sin, which I relished and enjoyed. If any part of one of those pears passed my lips, it was the sin that gave it flavour.

*   *   *

Review Questions

1. How does Augustine interpret the meaning of the sack of Rome? How does he use classical authors to defend his position?
2. How does he justify slavery?
3. What light does he shed on the daily life of Roman slaves?
4. What troubled Augustine about the memory of stealing the pears?

FROM The Theodosian Code: Christian Revisions of the Roman Legal Tradition

This compilation of Roman law was made in Constantinople during the reign of Emperor Theodosius II (r. 408–50), in an attempt to codify and arrange the many disparate senatorial statutes and imperial decisions that made up the Roman legal system. Theodosius also wanted to ensure that these legal traditions were updated to account for the powerful roles played by Christian bishops in Roman governance. The resulting laws also reflect the ways in which the adoption of Christianity had resulted in the creation of new types of criminal law and the enacting of legislation designed to silence or punish "heretics."

From *The Theodosian Code and Novels and the Sirmondian Constitutions*, translated by Clyde Pharr (Princeton, N.J.: Princeton University Press, 1980), pp. 440–51.

Book 16

TITLE 1
THE CATHOLIC FAITH

1. Emperors Valentinian and Valens, Augustuses, to Symmachus, Prefect of the City

If any judge or apparitor [sponsor] should appoint men of the Christian religion as custodians of temples, he shall know that neither his life nor his fortunes will be spared.

Given on the fifteenth day before the kalends of December at Milan in the year of the consulship of Valentinian and Valens Augustuses.—November 17, 365; 364.

2. Emperors Gratian, Valentinian, and Theodosius, Augustuses: An Edict to the People of the City of Constantinople

It is Our will that all the peoples who are ruled by the administration of Our Clemency shall practice that religion which the divine Peter the Apostle transmitted to the Romans, as the religion which he introduced makes clear even unto this day. It is evident that this is the religion that is followed by the Pontiff Damascus and by Peter, Bishop of Alexandria, a man of apostolic sanctity; that is, according to the apostolic discipline and the evangelic doctrine, we shall believe in the single Deity of the Father, the Son, and the Holy Spirit, under the concept of equal majesty and of the Holy Trinity.

We command that those persons who follow this rule shall embrace the name of Catholic Christians. The rest, however, whom We adjudge demented and insane, shall sustain the infamy of heretical dogmas, their meeting places shall not receive the name of churches, and they shall be smitten first by divine vengeance and secondly by the retribution of Our own initiative, which We shall assume in accordance with the divine judgment.

Given on the third day before the kalends of March at Thessalonica in the year of the fifth consulship of Gratian Augustus and the first consulship of Theodosius Augustus.—February 28, 380.

3. The same Augustuses to Auxonius, Proconsul of Asia

We command that all churches shall immediately be surrendered to those bishops who confess that the Father, the Son, and the Holy Spirit are of one majesty and virtue, of the same glory, and of one splendor; to those bishops who produce no dissonance by unholy distinction, but who affirm the concept of the Trinity by the assertion of three Persons and the unity of the Divinity;

to those bishops who appear to have been associated in the communion of Nectarius, Bishop of the Church of Constantinople, and of Timotheus, Bishop of the City of Alexandria in Egypt; to those bishops also who, in the regions of the Orient, appear to be communicants with Pelagius, Bishop of Laodicea, and with Diodorus, Bishop of Tarsus; also, in the Proconsular Province of Asia and in the Diocese of Asia, with Amphilochius, Bishop of Iconium, and with Optimus, Bishop of Antioch; in the Diocese of Pontus, with Helladius, Bishop of Caesarea, and with Otreius of Melitene, and with Gregorius, Bishop of Nyssa; with Terennius, Bishop of Scythia, and with Marmarius, Bishop of Martianopolis. Those bishops who are of the communion and fellowship of such acceptable priests must be permitted to obtain the Catholic churches. All, however, who dissent from the communion of the faith of those who have been expressly mentioned in this special enumeration shall be expelled from their churches as manifest heretics and hereafter shall be altogether denied the right and power to obtain churches, in order that the priesthood of the true Nicene faith may remain pure, and after the clear regulations of Our law, there shall be no opportunity for malicious subtlety.

Given on the third day before the kalends of August at Heraclea in the year of the consulship of Eucherius and Syagrius.—July 30, 381.

4. Emperors Valentinian, Theodosius, and Arcadius, Augustuses, to Eusignius, Praetorian Prefect

We bestow the right of assembly upon those persons who believe according to the doctrines which in the times of Constantius of sainted memory were decreed as those that would endure forever, when the priests had been called together from all the Roman world and the faith was set forth at the Council of Ariminum by these very persons who are now known to dissent, a faith which was also confirmed by the Council of Constantinople. The right of voluntary assembly shall also be open to those persons for whom We have so ordered. If those persons who suppose that the right of assembly has been granted to them alone should attempt to provoke any agitation against the regulation of Our Tranquillity, they shall know that, as authors of sedition and as disturbers of the peace of the Church, they shall also pay the penalty of high treason with their life and blood. Punishment shall no less await those persons who may attempt to supplicate Us surreptitiously and secretly, contrary to this Our regulation.

Given on the tenth day before the kalends of February at Milan in the year of the consulship of Emperor Designate Honorius and of Evodius.—January 23, 386.

TITLE 2
BISHOPS, CHURCHES, AND CLERICS

1. Emperor Constantine Augustus

We have learned that clerics of the Catholic Church are being so harassed by a faction of heretics that they are being burdened by nominations and by service as tax receivers, as public custom demands, contrary to the privileges granted them. It is Our pleasure, therefore, that if Your Gravity should find any person thus harassed, another person shall be chosen as a substitute for him and that henceforward men of the aforesaid religion shall be protected from such outrages.

Given on the day before the kalends of November in the year of the third consulship of Constantine Augustus and of Licinius Caesar.—October 31, 313(?).

2. The same Augustus to Octavianus, Governor of Lucania [Basilicata] and of Bruttium [Calabra]

Those persons who devote the services of religion to divine worship, that is, those who are called clerics, shall be exempt from all compulsory public services whatever, lest, through the sacrilegious malice of certain persons, they should be called away from divine services.

Given on the twelfth day before the kalends of November in the year of the fifth consulship of Constantine Augustus and the consulship of Licinius Caesar.—October 21, 319; 313.

INTERPRETATION: This law by special ordinance directs that no person whatsoever by sacrilegious ordinance shall presume to make tax collectors or tax gatherers of clerics. The law commands that such clerics shall be free from every compulsory public service, that is, from every duty and servitude, and shall zealously serve the Church.

3. The same Augustus to Bassus, Praetorian Prefect

A constitution was issued which directs that thenceforth no decurion [government official] or descendant of a decurion or even any person provided with adequate resources and suitable to undertake compulsory public services shall take refuge in the name and the service of the clergy, but that in the place of deceased clerics thereafter only those persons shall be chosen as substitutes who have slender fortunes and who are not held bound to such compulsory municipal services. But We have learned that those persons also are being disturbed who became associated with the clergy before the promulgation of the aforesaid law. We command, therefore, that the latter shall be freed from all annoyance, and that the former, who in evasion of public duties have taken refuge in the number of the clergy after the issuance of the law, shall be completely separated from that body, shall be restored to their orders and to the municipal councils, and shall perform their municipal duties.

Posted on the fifteenth day before the kalends of August in the year of the sixth consulship of Constantine Augustus and the consulship of Constantius Caesar.—July 18, 320; 329.

4. The same Augustus to the People

Every person shall have the liberty to leave at his death any property that he wishes to the most holy and venerable council of the Catholic Church. Wills shall not become void. There is nothing which is more due to men than that the expression of their last will, after which they can no longer will anything, shall be free and the power of choice, which does not return again, shall be unhampered.

Posted on the fifth day before the nones of July at Rome in the year of the second consulship of Crispus and Constantine Caesars.—July 3, 321.

5. The same Augustus to Helpidius

Whereas We have learned that certain ecclesiastics and others devoting their services to the Catholic sect have been compelled by men of different religions to the performance of lustral [purifying] sacrifices, We decree by this sanction that, if any person should suppose that those who devote their services to the most sacred law may be forced to the ritual of an alien superstition, he shall be beaten publicly with clubs, provided that his legal status so permits. If, however, the consideration of his honorable rank protects him from such an outrage, he shall sustain the penalty of a very heavy fine, which shall be vindicated to the municipalities.

Given on the eighth day before the kalends of June at Sirmium in the year of the consulship of Severus and Rufinus.—May (December) 25, 323.

6. The same Augustus to Ablavius, Praetorian Prefect

Exemption from compulsory public services shall not be granted by popular consent, nor shall it be granted indiscriminately to all who petition under the pretext of being clerics, nor shall great numbers be added to the clergy rashly and beyond measure, but rather, when a cleric dies, another shall be selected to replace the deceased, one who has no kinship with a decurion family and who has not the wealth of resources whereby he may very easily support the compulsory public services. Thus, if there should be a dispute about the name of any person between a municipality and the clergy, if equity claims him for public service and if he is adjudged suitable for membership in the municipal council through either lineage or wealth, he shall be removed from the clergy and shall be delivered to the municipality. For the wealthy must assume secular obligations, and the poor must be supported by the wealth of the churches.

Posted on the kalends of June in the year of the seventh consulship of Constantine Augustus and the consulship of Constantius Caesar.—June 1, 326; 329.

7. The same Augustus to Valentinus, Governor of Numidia

Lectors [liturgical readers] of the divine scriptures, subdeacons, and the other clerics who through the injustice of heretics have been summoned to the municipal councils shall be absolved, and in the future, according to the practice of the Orient,[1] they shall by no means be summoned to the municipal councils, but they shall possess fullest exemption.

Given on the nones of February at Sofia (Serdica) in the year of the consulship of Gallicanus and Symmachus.—February 5, 330.

8. Emperor Constantius Augustus to the Clergy, Greetings

According to the sanction which you are said to have obtained previously, no person shall obligate you and your slaves to new tax payments, but you shall enjoy exemption. Furthermore, you shall not be required to receive quartered persons, and if any of you, for the sake of a livelihood, should wish to conduct a business, they shall possess tax exemption.

Given on the sixth day before the kalends of September in the year of the consulship of Placidus and Romulus.—August 27, 343.

9. The same Augustus to Severianus, Proconsul of Achaea [western Greece]

All clerics must be exempt from compulsory services as decurions and from every annoyance of municipal duties. Their sons, moreover, must continue in the Church, if they are not held obligated to the municipal councils.

Given on the third day before the ides of April in the year of the consulship of Limenius and Catullinus.—April 11, 349.

10. Emperors Constantius and Constans Augustuses to all the Bishops throughout the various provinces.

In order that organizations in the service of the churches may be filled with a great multitude of people, tax exemption shall be granted to clerics and their acolytes, and they shall be protected from the exaction of compulsory public services of a menial nature. They shall by no means be subject to the tax payments of tradesmen, since it is manifest that the profits which they collect from stalls and workshops will benefit the poor. We decree also that their men who engage in trade shall be exempt from all tax payments. Likewise, the exaction of services for the maintenance of the supplementary postwagons shall cease. This indulgence We grant to their wives, children, and servants, to males and females equally, for We command that they also shall continue exempt from tax assessments.

Given on the seventh day before the kalends of June at Constantinople in the year of the sixth consulship of Constantius and the consulship of Constans.—May 26, 353; 320; 346.

11. The same Augustuses to Longinianus, Prefect of Egypt

We formerly sanctioned that bishops and clerics of the Catholic faith who possess nothing at all and are useless with respect to patrimony shall not be summoned to compulsory public services as decurions. But We learn that they are being disturbed in their life of perfection, to no public advantage. Therefore, We direct that their sons also who are not financially responsible and who are found to be below the legal age shall sustain no molestation.

Given on the fourth day before the kalends of March in the year of the seventh consulship of Constantius Augustus and the consulship of Constans Augustus.—February 26, 354; 342.

12. The same Augustuses to their dear friend Severus, Greetings

By a law of Our Clemency We prohibit bishops to be accused in the courts, lest there should

---

[1] Rome's eastern provinces.

be an unrestrained opportunity for fanatical spirits to accuse them, while the accusers assume that they will obtain impunity by the kindness of the bishops. Therefore, if any person should lodge any complaint, such complaint must unquestionably be examined before other bishops, in order that an opportune and suitable hearing may be arranged for the investigation of all concerned.

Given as a letter on the ninth day before the kalends of October.—September 23. Received on the nones of October in the year of the consulship of Arbitio and Lollianus.—October 7, 355.

INTERPRETATION: It is specifically prohibited that any person should dare to accuse a bishop before secular judges, but he shall not delay to submit to the hearing of bishops whatever he supposes may be due him according to the nature of the case, so that the assertions which he makes against the bishop may be decided in a court of other bishops.

13. The same Augustus and Julian Caesar to Leontius

We command that the privileges granted to the Church of the City of Rome and to its clerics shall be firmly guarded.

Given on the fourth day before the ides of November at Milan in the year of the ninth consulship of Constantius Augustus and the second consulship of Julian Caesar.—November 10, 357; 356.

14. The same Augustus and Julian Caesar to Bishop Felix

Clerics shall be protected from every injustice of an undue suit and from every wrong of an unjust exaction, and they shall not be summoned to compulsory public services of a menial nature. Moreover, when tradesmen are summoned to some legally prescribed tax payment, all clerics shall cease to be affected by such a disturbance; for if they have accumulated anything by thrift, foresight, or trading, but still in accordance with honesty, this must be administered for the use of the poor and needy, and whatever they have been

able to acquire and collect from their workshops and stalls they shall regard as having been collected for the profit of religion.

(1) Moreover, with respect to their men who are employed in trade, the statutes of the sainted Emperor, that is, of Our father,[2] provided with manifold regulations that the aforesaid clerics should abound in numerous privileges. (2) Therefore, with respect to the aforesaid clerics, the requirement of extraordinary services and all molestation shall cease. (3) Moreover, they and their resources and substance shall not be summoned to furnish supplementary postwagons.

(4) All clerics shall be assisted by the prerogative of this nature, namely, that wives of clerics and also their children and attendants, males and females equally, and their children, shall continue to be exempt forever from tax payments and free from such compulsory public services.

Given on the eighth day before the ides of December at Milan—December 6. Read into the records on the fifth day before the kalends of January in the year of the ninth consulship of Constantius Augustus and the second consulship of Julian Caesar.—December 28, 357; 356. Or: Read in court proceedings, acta, 2, 8, 1, n. 4.

*   *   *

29. Emperors Arcadius and Honorius, Augustuses, to Hierius, Vicar of Africa

We direct that whatever statutes were enacted by Our fathers at different times with respect to the sacrosanct churches shall remain inviolate and unimpaired. None of their privileges, therefore, shall be altered, and protection shall be granted to all those persons who serve the churches, for We desire that reverence shall be increased in Our time rather than that any of the privileges which were formerly granted should be altered.

Given on the tenth day before the kalends of April at Milan in the year of the consulship of Olybrius and Probinus.—March 23, 395.

---

[2] I.e., Constantine.

30. The same Augustuses to Theodorus, Praetorian Prefect

We decree nothing new by the present sanction; rather, We confirm those privileges that appear to have been granted formerly. We prohibit, therefore, under threat of punishment, that privileges which were formerly obtained through reverence for religion shall be curtailed, so that those who serve the Church may also enjoy fully those special benefits which the Church enjoys.

Given on the day before the kalends of February at Milan in the year of the consulship of Caesarius and Atticus.—January 31, 397.

31. The same Augustuses to Theodorus, Praetorian Prefect

If any person should break forth into such sacrilege that he should invade Catholic churches and should inflict any outrage on the priests and ministers, or on the worship itself and on the place of worship, whatever occurs shall be brought to the notice of the authorities by letters of the municipal senates, magistrates, and curators, and by official reports of the apparitors who are called rural police, so that the names of those who could be recognized may be revealed. Moreover, if the offense is said to have been perpetrated by a multitude, some, if not all, can nevertheless be recognized, and by their confession the names of their accomplices may be disclosed. Thus the governor of the province shall know that the outrage to the priests and ministers of the Catholic Church, to the divine worship, and to the place of worship itself must be punished with a capital sentence against the aforesaid convicted or confessed criminals. The governor shall not wait until the bishop shall demand the avenging of his own injury, since the bishop's sanctity leaves nothing to him except the glory of forgiving. It shall be not only permissible but even laudable for all persons to prosecute as a public crime the atrocious outrages committed against priests and ministers and to exact punishment from such criminals. But if it should be impossible to bring to court a violent multitude by the operation of civil apparitors and by the help of the municipal senates and landholders, in case the multitude pro-

tects itself by arms or by the difficulty of the places, the African judges shall prefix the contents of this law to letters which they shall send to the Respectable Count of Africa, and they shall demand the aid of the armed apparitors, in order that the perpetrators of such crimes may not escape.

Given on the seventh day before the kalends of May at Milan in the year of the fourth consulship of Honorius Augustus and the consulship of Eutychianus.—April 25, 398; January 15, 409.

32. The same Augustuses to Caesarius, Praetorian Prefect

If perchance the bishops should suppose that they are in need of clerics, they will more properly ordain them from the number of monks. They shall not incur disfavor by holding those persons who are bound by public and private accounts but shall have those already approved.

Given on the seventh day before the kalends of August in the year of the fourth consulship of Honorius Augustus and the consulship of Eutychianus.—July 26, 398(?).

*   *   *

TITLE 3
MONKS

1. Emperors Valentinian, Theodosius, and Arcadius Augustuses to Tatianus, Praetorian Prefect

If any persons should be found in the profession of monks, they shall be ordered to seek out and to inhabit desert places and desolate solitudes.

Given on the fourth day before the nones of September at Verona in the year of the fourth consulship of Valentinian Augustus and the consulship of Neoterius.—September 2, 390.

2. The same Augustuses to Tatianus, Praetorian Prefect

We direct that the monks to whom the municipalities had been forbidden, since they are strengthened by judicial injustices, shall be restored to their original status, and the aforesaid law shall be repealed. Thus indeed, We revoke such a decree of Our Clemency, and We grant them free ingress into the towns.

Given on the fifteenth day before the kalends of May at Constantinople in the year of the second consulship of Arcadius Augustus and the consulship of Rufinus.—April 17, 392.

*   *   *

REVIEW QUESTIONS

1. Judging from these laws, what can you conclude about the relationship between the Roman government and the Christian religion after the conversion of Constantine?

2. What groups and individuals emerge as having special legal privileges within the Christian Roman Empire? Which groups and individuals have their rights curtailed?

3. Although the Code was compiled in the Greek-speaking Eastern Roman Empire, it was written in the traditional Latin language of Roman law and bureaucracy. How would you summarize the main assumptions and precepts of Roman legal thought, based on these excerpts from the Code? How do these compare with the older principles of Roman law summarized in the Twelve Tables (p. 157)?

SAINT BENEDICT

FROM *The Rule*

Benedict of Nursia (c. 480–547 C.E.) was a well-born Roman and the founder of an important monastery at Monte Cassino, in south-central Italy. Dissatisfied with other varieties of monasticism, which he critiques in the following excerpt, he drew on Egyptian and Syriac models to formulate a new and very practical set of rules that would structure the daily life, work, and prayer of all the monks within the walls of his monastery, which he conceived as a self-sustaining community that could protect itself from the violence and temptations of the outside world. This Rule *continues to form the basis of religious life in Benedictine monasteries around the globe.*

From *The Rule of Saint Benedict*, translated by Abbot Gasquet (London: Chatto & Windus, 1909).

Chapter I
Of the Several Kinds of Monks and Their Lives

It is recognized that there are four kinds of monks. The first are the Cenobites: that is, those who live in a monastery under a Rule or an abbot. The second kind is that of Anchorites, or Hermits, who not in the first fervour of conversion, but after long trial in the monastery, and already taught by the example of many others, have learnt to fight against the devil, are well prepared to go forth from the ranks of the brotherhood to the single combat of the desert. They can now, by God's help, safely fight against the vices of their flesh and against evil thoughts singly, with their own hand and arm and without the encouragement of a companion.

The third and worst kind of monks is that of the Sarabites, who have not been tried under any Rule nor schooled by an experienced master, as gold is

proved in the furnace, but soft as is lead and still in their works cleaving to the world, are known to lie to God by their tonsure. These in twos or threes, or more frequently singly, are shut up, without a shepherd; not in our Lord's fold, but in their own. The pleasure of carrying out their particular desires is their law, and whatever they dream of or choose this they call holy; but what they like not, that they account unlawful.

The fourth class of monks is called Gyrovagi (or Wanderers). These move about all their lives through various countries, staying as guests for three or four days at different monasteries. They are always on the move and never settle down, and are slaves to their own wills and to the enticements of gluttony. In every way they are worse than the Sarabites, and of their wretched way of life it is better to be silent than to speak.

Leaving these therefore aside, let us by God's help set down a Rule for Cenobites, who are the best kind of monks.

Chapter II
What the Abbot Should Be

An abbot to be fit to rule a monastery should ever remember what he is called, and in his acts illustrate his high calling. For in a monastery he is considered to take the place of Christ, since he is called by His name as the apostle saith, *Ye have received the spirit of the adoption of sons, whereby we cry, Abba, Father.*[1] Therefore the abbot should neither teach, ordain, nor require anything against the command of our Lord (God forbid!), but in the minds of his disciples let his orders and teaching be mingled with the leaven of divine justice.

The abbot should ever be mindful that at the dread judgment of God there will be inquiry both as to his teaching and as to the obedience of his disciples. Let the abbot know that any lack of goodness, which the master of the family shall find in his flock, will be accounted the shepherd's fault. On the other hand, he shall be acquitted in so far as he shall have shown all the watchfulness of a shepherd over a restless and disobedient flock: and if as their pastor he shall have employed every care to cure their corrupt manners, he shall be declared guiltless in the Lord's judgment, and he may say with the prophet, *I have not hidden Thy justice in my heart; I have told Thy truth and Thy salvation;*[2] but *they contemned and despised me.*[3] And then in the end shall death be inflicted as a meet punishment upon the sheep which have not responded to his care. . . .

Let him make no distinction of persons in the monastery. Let not one be loved more than another, save such as be found to excel in obedience or good works. Let not the free-born be put before the serf-born in religion, unless there be other reasonable cause for it. If upon due consideration the abbot shall see such cause he may place him where he pleases; otherwise let all keep their own places, because *whether bond or free we are all one in Christ,*[4] and bear an equal burden of service under one Lord: *for with God there is no accepting of persons.*[5] For one thing only are we preferred by Him, if we are found better than others in good works and more humble. Let the abbot therefore have equal love for all, and let all, according to their deserts, be under the same discipline.

The abbot in his teaching should always observe that apostolic rule which saith, *Reprove, entreat, rebuke.*[6] That is to say, as occasions require he ought to mingle encouragement with reproofs. Let him manifest the sternness of a master and the loving affection of a father. He must reprove the undisciplined and restless severely, but he should exhort such as are obedient, quiet and patient, for their better profit. We charge him, however, to reprove and punish the stubborn and negligent. Let him not shut his eyes to the sins of offenders; but, directly they begin to show themselves and to grow, he must use every means to root them up utterly, remembering the fate of Heli, the priest of

---

[1] Romans 8:15.

[2] Psalms 39:11.
[3] Isaiah 1:2.
[4] 1 Corinthians 9:27.
[5] Ephesians 6:9.
[6] 2 Timothy 4:2.

Silo. To the more virtuous and apprehensive, indeed, he may for the first or second time use words of warning; but in dealing with the stubborn, the hard-hearted, the proud and the disobedient, even at the very beginning of their sin, let him chastise them with stripes and with bodily punishment, knowing that it is written, *The fool is not corrected with words.*[7] And again, *Strike thy son with a rod and thou shalt deliver his soul from death.*[8]

The abbot ought ever to bear in mind what he is and what he is called; he ought to know that to whom more is entrusted, from him more is exacted. Let him recognize how difficult and how hard a task he has undertaken, to rule souls and to make himself a servant to the humours of many. . . .

Chapter III
On Taking Counsel of the Brethren

Whenever any weighty matters have to be transacted in the monastery let the abbot call together all the community and himself propose the matter for discussion. After hearing the advice of the brethren let him consider it in his own mind, and then do what he shall judge most expedient. We ordain that all must be called to council, because the Lord often reveals to a younger member what is best. And let the brethren give their advice with all humble subiection, and presume not stiffly to defend their own opinion. Let them rather leave the matter to the abbot's discretion, so that all submit to what he shall deem best. As it becometh disciples to obey their master, so doth it behove the master to dispose of all things with forethought and justice.

In all things, therefore, every one shall follow the Rule as their master, and let no one rashly depart from it. In the monastery no one is to be led by the desires of his own heart, neither shall any one within or without the monastery presume to argue wantonly with his abbot. If he presume to do so let him be subjected to punishment according to the Rule.

The abbot, however, must himself do all things in the fear of God and according to the Rule, knowing that he shall undoubtedly have to give an account of his whole government to God, the most just Judge.

If anything of less moment has to be done in the monastery let the abbot take advice of the seniors only, as it is written, *Do all things with counsel, and thou shalt not afterwards repent of it.*[9] . . .

Chapter V
On Obedience

The first degree of humility is prompt obedience. This is required of all who, whether by reason of the holy servitude to which they are pledged, or through fear of hell, or to attain to the glory of eternal life, hold nothing more dear than Christ. Such disciples delay not in doing what is ordered by their superior, just as if the command had come from God. Of such our Lord says, *At the hearing of the ear he hath obeyed me.*[10] And to the teachers He likewise says, *He that heareth you, heareth me.*[11]

For this reason such disciples, surrendering forthwith all they possess, and giving up their own will, leave unfinished what they were working at, and with the ready foot of obedience in their acts follow the word of command. Thus, as it were, at the same moment comes the order of the master and the finished work of the disciple: with the speed of the fear of God both go jointly forward and are quickly effected by such as ardently desire to walk in the way of eternal life. These take the narrow way, of which the Lord saith, *Narrow is the way which leads to life.*[12] That is, they live not as they themselves will, neither do they obey their own desires and pleasures; but following the command and direction of another and abiding in their monasteries, their desire is to be ruled by an abbot. Without doubt such as these carry out that

---

[7] Proverbs 23:13.
[8] Proverbs 23:14.
[9] Ecclesiasticus 32:24.
[10] Psalms 17:45.
[11] Luke 10:16.
[12] Matthew 7:14.

saying of our Lord, *I came not to do my own will, but the will of Him Who sent me.*[13]

This kind of obedience will be both acceptable to God and pleasing to men, when what is ordered is not done out of fear, or slowly and coldly, grudgingly, or with reluctant protest. Obedience shown to superiors is indeed given to God, Who Himself hath said, *He that heareth you, heareth Me.*[14] What is commanded should be done by those under obedience, with a good will, since *God loveth a cheerful giver.*[15] If the disciple obey unwillingly and murmur in word as well as in heart, it will not be accepted by God, Who considereth the heart of a murmurer, even if he do what was ordered. For a work done in this spirit shall have no reward; rather shall the doer incur the penalty appointed for murmurers if he amend not and make not satisfaction.

Chapter VI
On Silence

Let us do as the prophet says, *I have said, I will keep my ways, that I offend not with my tongue. I have been watchful over my mouth: I held my peace and humbled myself and was silent from speaking even good things.*[16] Here the prophet shows that, for the sake of silence, we are at times to abstain even from good talk. If this be so, how much more needful is it that we refrain from evil words, on account of the penalty of the sin! Because of the importance of silence, therefore, let leave to speak be seldom given, even to perfect disciples, although their talk be of good and holy matters and tending to edification, since it is written, *In much speaking, thou shalt not escape sin.*[17] The master, indeed, should speak and teach: the disciple should hold his peace and listen.

Whatever, therefore, has to be asked of the prior, let it be done with all humility and with reverent submission. But as to coarse, idle words, or such as move to laughter, we utterly condemn and ban them in all places. We do not allow any disciple to give mouth to them. . . .

Chapter XIX
Of the Manner of Singing the Office

We believe that the Divine Presence is everywhere, and that the eyes of the Lord behold both the good and the bad in all places. Especially do we believe without any doubt that this is so when we assist at the Divine Office. Let us therefore always be mindful of what the prophet says, *Serve ye the Lord in fear;*[18] and again, *Sing ye His praises with understanding;*[19] and, *In the sight of angels I will sing praise to Thee.*[20] Wherefore let us consider how it behoveth us to be in the sight of God and the angels, and so let us take our part in the psalmody that mind and voice accord together.

Chapter XX
On Reverence at Prayer

If, when we wish to obtain some favour from those who have the power to help us, we dare not ask except with humility and reverence, how much more reason is there that we should present our petitions to the Lord God of the universe in all lowliness of heart and purity of devotion. We may know for certain that we shall be heard, not because we use many words, but on account of the purity of our hearts and our tears of sorrow. Our prayer, therefore, should be short and pure, unless by some inspiration of divine grace it be prolonged. All prayer made by the community in common, however, should be short; and when the prior (that is, the superior) has given the sign, let all rise together. . . .

Chapter XXII
How the Monks Are to Sleep

All shall sleep in separate beds and each shall receive, according to the appointment of his abbot,

---

[13] John 5:30.
[14] Luke 10:16.
[15] 2 Corinthians 9:7.
[16] Psalms 38:2, 3.
[17] Proverbs 18:21.

[18] Psalms 2:11.
[19] Psalms 46:8.
[20] Psalms 137:1.

bedclothes, fitted to the condition of his life. If it be possible let them all sleep in a common dormitory, but if their great number will not allow this they may sleep in tens or twenties, with seniors to have charge of them. Let a candle be constantly burning in the room until morning, and let the monks sleep clothed and girt with girdles or cords; but they are not to have knives by their sides in their beds, lest perchance they be injured whilst sleeping. In this way the monks shall always be ready to rise quickly when the signal is given and hasten each one to come before his brother to the Divine Office, and yet with all gravity and modesty.

The younger brethren are not to have their beds next to each other, but amongst those of the elders. When they rise for the Divine Office let them gently encourage one another, because of the excuses made by those that are drowsy. . . .

Chapter XXXII
Concerning the Iron Tools or Other Goods of the Monastery

Let the abbot appoint brethren, of whose life and moral conduct he is sure, to keep the iron tools, the clothes, or other property of the monastery. To these he shall allot the various things to be kept and collected, as he shall deem expedient. The abbot shall hold a list of these things that, as the brethren succeed each other in their appointed work, he may know what he gives and what he receives back. If any one shall treat the property of the monastery in a slovenly or careless way let him be corrected; if he does not amend let him be subjected to regular discipline.

Chapter XXXIII
Ought Monks to Have Anything of Their Own?

Above all others, let this vice be extirpated in the monastery. No one, without leave of the abbot, shall presume to give, or receive, or keep as his own, anything whatever: neither book, nor tablets, nor pen: nothing at all. For monks are men who can claim no dominion even over their own bodies or wills. All that is necessary, however, they may hope from the Father of the monastery; but they shall keep nothing which the abbot has not given or allowed. All things are to be common to all, as it is written, *Neither did any one say or think that aught was his own.*[21] Hence if any one shall be found given to this most wicked vice let him be admonished once or twice, and if he do not amend let him be subjected to correction. . . .

Chapter XLVIII
Of Daily Manual Labour

Idleness is an enemy of the soul. Because this is so the brethren ought to be occupied at specified times in manual labour, and at other fixed hours in holy reading. We therefore think that both these may be arranged for as follows: from Easter to the first of October, on coming out from Prime, let the brethren labour till about the fourth hour.[22] From the fourth till close upon the sixth hour[23] let them employ themselves in reading. On rising from table after the sixth hour let them rest on their beds in strict silence; but if any one shall wish to read, let him do so in such a way as not to disturb any one else.

Let None be said somewhat before the time, about the middle of the eighth hour,[24] and after this all shall work at what they have to do till evening. If, however, the nature of the place or poverty require them to labour at gathering in the harvest, let them not grieve at that, for then are they truly monks when they live by the labour of their hands, as our Fathers and the Apostles did. Let everything, however, be done with moderation for the sake of the faint-hearted.

From the first of October till the beginning of Lent let the brethren be occupied in reading till the end of the second hour.[25] At that time Tierce shall be said, after which they shall labour at the work

---

[21] Acts 4:32.
[22] In summer, about 9:00 A.M.
[23] About noon.
[24] About 3:20 P.M.
[25] In winter, about 9 A.M.

enjoined them till None.[26] At the first signal for the Hour of None all shall cease to work, so as to be ready when the second signal is given. After their meal they shall be employed in reading or on the psalms.

On the days of Lent, from the morning till the end of the third[27] hour, the brethren are to have time for reading, after which let them work at what is set them to do till the close of the tenth hour.[28] During these Lenten days let each one have some book from the library which he shall read through carefully. These books are to be given out at the beginning of Lent.

It is of much import that one or two seniors be appointed to go about the monastery at such times as the brethren are free to read, in order to see that no one is slothful, given to idleness or foolish talking instead of reading, and so not only makes no profit himself but also distracts others. If any such be found (which God forbid) let him be corrected once or twice, and if he amend not let him be subjected to regular discipline of such a character that the rest may take warning. Moreover one brother shall not associate with another at unsuitable hours.

On Sunday also, all, save those who are assigned to various offices, shall have time for reading. If, however, any one be so negligent and slothful as to be unwilling or unable to read or meditate, he must have some work given him, so as not to be idle. For weak brethren, or those of delicate constitutions, some work or craft shall be found to keep them from idleness, and yet not such as to crush them by the heavy labour or to drive them away. The weakness of such brethren must be taken into consideration by the abbot. . . .

---

[26] About 1:20 P.M.
[27] About 10:00 A.M.
[28] About 2:40 P.M.

REVIEW QUESTIONS

1. How does Benedict justify the need for a new rule to organize religious life? What is wrong with the other varieties of monasticism that he identifies?

2. Although many portions of the *Rule* regulate worship in the monastery, Benedict pays close attention to practical matters: governance, decision making, eating, sleeping, work, relationships. Why would he consider these things so fundamental to monastic spirituality? What do we learn about daily life at Monte Cassino?

3. What can you infer from this source about the world outside the monastery? How might the events of Benedict's lifetime have shaped his *Rule*?

GREGORY OF TOURS

FROM *History of the Franks*

Gregory, bishop of Tours (538–94 C.E.), was descended from a long line of provincial nobles and bishops in Gaul. His History of the Franks *relates how the Franks and other tribes conquered and settled a key area of the Roman Empire, as seen through the eyes of a Gallo-Roman aristocrat. These selections discuss how and why the Frankish chieftain Clovis converted to Roman Christianity in 496 C.E., and his role in solidifying a new dynasty. Barbarian tribes had not yet produced historians or documents, so we must depend on the views of relative outsiders such as Gregory for details on their earliest history.*

From *History of the Franks by Gregory of Tours*, edited by Ernest Brehaut (New York: Columbia University Press, 1944), pp. 36–45.

*   *   *

After these events Childeric died [c. 482 C.E.] and Clovis his son reigned in his stead. In the fifth year of his reign Siagrius, king of the Romans, son of Egidius, had his seat in the city of Soissons which Egidius, who has been mentioned before, once held. And Clovis came against him with Ragnachar, his kinsman, because he used to possess the kingdom, and demanded that they make ready a battle-field. And Siagrius did not delay nor was he afraid to resist. And so they fought against each other and Siagrius, seeing his army crushed, turned his back and fled swiftly to king Alaric at Toulouse. And Clovis sent to Alaric to send him back, otherwise he was to know that Clovis would make war on him for his refusal. And Alaric was afraid that he would incur the anger of the Franks on account of Siagrius, seeing it is the fashion of the Goths to be terrified, and he surrendered him in chains to Clovis' envoys. And Clovis took him and gave orders to put him under guard, and when he had got his kingdom he directed that he be executed secretly.

At that time many churches were despoiled by Clovis' army, since he was as yet involved in heathen error. Now the army had taken from a certain church a vase of wonderful size and beauty, along with the remainder of the utensils for the service of the church. And the bishop of the church sent messengers to the king asking that the vase at least be returned, if he could not get back any more of the sacred dishes. On hearing this the king said to the messenger: "Follow us as far as Soissons, because all that has been taken is to be divided there and when the lot assigns me that dish I will do what the father asks."

Then when he came to Soissons and all the booty was set in their midst, the king said: "I ask of you, brave warriors, not to refuse to grant me in addition to my share, yonder dish," that is, he was speaking of the vase just mentioned. In answer to the speech of the king those of more sense replied: "Glorious king, all that we see is yours, and we ourselves are subject to your rule. Now do what seems well-pleasing to you; for no one is able to resist your power." When they said this a foolish, envious and excitable fellow lifted his battle-ax and struck the vase, and cried in a loud voice: "You shall get nothing here except what the lot fairly bestows on you." At this all were stupefied, but the king endured the insult with the gentleness of patience, and taking the vase he handed it over to the messenger of the church, nursing the wound deep in his heart.

And at the end of the year he ordered the whole army to come with their equipment of armor, to show the brightness of their arms on the field of March. And when he was reviewing them all carefully, he came to the man who struck the vase, and said to him: "No one has brought armor so carelessly kept as you; for neither your spear nor sword nor ax is in serviceable condition." And seizing his ax he cast it to the earth, and when the other had bent over somewhat to pick it up, the king raised his hands and drove his own ax into the man's head. "This," said he, "is what you did at Soissons to the vase."

Upon the death of this man, he ordered the rest to depart, raising great dread of himself by this action. He made many wars and gained many victories. In the tenth year of his reign he made war on the Thuringi and brought them under his dominion.

Now the king of the Burgundians was Gundevech, of the family of king Athanaric the persecutor, whom we have mentioned before. He had four sons; Gundobad, Godegisel, Chilperic and Godomar. Gundobad killed his brother Chilperic with the sword, and sank his wife in water with a stone tied to her neck. His two daughters he condemned to exile; the older of these, who became a nun, was called Chrona, and the younger Clotilda. And as Clovis often sent embassies to Burgundy, the maiden Clotilda was found by his envoys. And when they saw that she was of good bearing and wise, and learned that she was of the family of the king, they reported this to King Clovis, and he sent an embassy to Gundobad without delay asking her in marriage. And Gundobad was afraid to refuse, and surrendered her to the men, and they took the girl and brought her swiftly to the king. The king was very glad when he saw her, and married her, having already by a concubine a son named Theodoric.

He had a first-born son by queen Clotilda, and as his wife wished to consecrate him in baptism, she tried unceasingly to persuade her husband, saying: "The gods you worship are nothing, and they will be unable to help themselves or any one else. For they are graven out of stone or wood or some metal. And the names you have given them are names of men and not of gods, as Saturn, who is declared to have fled in fear of being banished from his kingdom by his son; as Jove himself, the foul perpetrator of all shameful crimes, committing incest with men, mocking at his kinswomen, not able to refrain from intercourse with his own sister as she herself says: *Jovisque et soror et conjunx.*[1] What could Mars or Mercury do? They are endowed rather with the magic arts than with the power of the divine name. But he ought rather to be worshipped who created by his word heaven and earth, the sea and all that in them is out of a state of nothingness, who made the sun shine, and adorned the heavens with stars, who filled the waters with creeping things, the earth with living things and the air with creatures that fly, at whose nod the earth is decked with growing crops, the trees with fruit, the vines with grapes, by whose hand mankind was created, by whose generosity all that creation serves and helps man whom he created as his own."

But though the queen said this the spirit of the king was by no means moved to belief, and he said: "It was at the command of our gods that all things were created and came forth, and it is plain that your God has no power and, what is more, he is proven not to belong to the family of the gods." Meantime the faithful queen made her son ready for baptism; she gave command to adorn the church with hangings and curtains, in order that he who could not be moved by persuasion might be urged to belief by this mystery. The boy, whom they named Ingomer, died after being baptized, still wearing the white garments in which he became regenerate.

At this the king was violently angry, and reproached the queen harshly, saying: "If the boy had been dedicated in the name of my gods he would certainly have lived; but as it is, since he was baptized in the name of your God, he could not live at all." To this the queen said: "I give thanks to the omnipotent God, creator of all, who has judged me

---

[1] "And of Jove both sister and wife." Virgil, *Æneid* I: 46–47.

not wholly unworthy, that he should deign to take to his kingdom one born from my womb. My soul is not stricken with grief for his sake, because I know that, summoned from this world as he was in his baptismal garments, he will be fed by the vision of God."

After this she bore another son, whom she named Chlodomer at baptism; and when he fell sick, the king said: "It is impossible that anything else should happen to him than happened to his brother, namely, that being baptized in the name of your Christ, he should die at once." But through the prayers of his mother, and the Lord's command, he became well.

The queen did not cease to urge him to recognize the true God and cease worshiping idols. But he could not be influenced in any way to this belief, until at last a war arose with the Alamanni, in which he was driven by necessity to confess what before he had of his free will denied. It came about that as the two armies were fighting fiercely, there was much slaughter, and Clovis's army began to be in danger of destruction. He saw it and raised his eyes to heaven, and with remorse in his heart he burst into tears and cried: "Jesus Christ, whom Clotilda asserts to be the son of the living God, who art said to give aid to those in distress, and to bestow victory on those who hope in thee, I beseech the glory of thy aid, with the vow that if thou wilt grant me victory over these enemies, and I shall know that power which she says that people dedicated in thy name have had from thee, I will believe in thee and be baptized in thy name. For I have invoked my own gods, but, as I find, they have withdrawn from aiding me; and therefore I believe that they possess no power, since they do not help those who obey them. I now call upon thee, I desire to believe thee, only let me be rescued from my adversaries." And when he said this, the Alamanni turned their backs, and began to disperse in flight. And when they saw that their king was killed, they submitted to the dominion of Clovis, saying: "Let not the people perish further, we pray; we are yours now." And he stopped the fighting, and after encouraging his men, retired in peace and told the queen how he had had merit to win the victory by

calling on the name of Christ. This happened in the fifteenth year of his reign.

Then the queen asked saint Remi, bishop of Rheims, to summon Clovis secretly, urging him to introduce the king to the word of salvation. And the bishop sent for him secretly and began to urge him to believe in the true God, maker of heaven and earth, and to cease worshiping idols, which could help neither themselves nor any one else. But the king said: "I gladly hear you, most holy father; but there remains one thing: the people who follow me cannot endure to abandon their gods; but I shall go and speak to them according to your words." He met with his followers, but before he could speak the power of God anticipated him, and all the people cried out together: "O pious king, we reject our mortal gods, and we are ready to follow the immortal God whom Remi preaches." This was reported to the bishop, who was greatly rejoiced, and bade them get ready the baptismal font.

The squares were shaded with tapestried canopies, the churches adorned with white curtains, the baptistery set in order, the aroma of incense spread, candles of fragrant odor burned brightly, and the whole shrine of the baptistery was filled with a divine fragrance: and the Lord gave such grace to those who stood by that they thought they were placed amid the odors of paradise. And the king was the first to ask to be baptized by the bishop. Another Constantine advanced to the baptismal font, to terminate the disease of ancient leprosy and wash away with fresh water the foul spots that had long been borne. And when he entered to be baptized, the saint of God began with ready speech: "Gently bend your neck, Sigamber; worship what you burned; burn what you worshipped."

The holy bishop Remi was a man of excellent wisdom and especially trained in rhetorical studies, and of such surpassing holiness that he equalled the miracles of Silvester. For there is extant a book of his life which tells that he raised a dead man. And so the king confessed all-powerful God in the Trinity, and was baptized in the name of the Father, Son and holy Spirit, and was anointed with the

holy ointment with the sign of the cross of Christ. And of his army more than 3000 were baptized. His sister also, Albofled, was baptized, who not long after passed to the Lord. And when the king was in mourning for her, the holy Remi sent a letter of consolation which began in this way: "The reason of your mourning pains me, and pains me greatly, that Albofled your sister, of good memory, has passed away. But I can give you this comfort, that her departure from the world was such that she ought to be envied rather than mourned." Another sister also was converted, Lanthechild by name, who had fallen into the heresy of the Arians, and she confessed that the Son and the holy Spirit were equal to the Father, and was anointed.

At that time the brothers Gundobad and Godegisel were kings of the country about the Rhone and the Saône together with the province of Marseilles. And they, as well as their people, belonged to the Arian sect.[2] And since they were fighting with each other, Godegisel, hearing of the victories of King Clovis, sent an embassy to him secretly, saying: "If you will give me aid in attacking my brother, so that I may be able to kill him in battle or drive him from the country, I will pay you every year whatever tribute you yourself wish to impose." Clovis accepted this offer gladly, and promised aid whenever need should ask. And at a time agreed upon he marched his army against Gundobad. On hearing of this, Gundobad, who did not know of his brother's treachery, sent to him, saying: "Come to my assistance, since the Franks are in motion against us and are coming to our country to take it. Therefore let us be united against a nation hostile to us, lest because of division we suffer in turn what other peoples have suffered." And the other said: "I will come with my army, and will give you aid."

And these three, namely, Clovis against Gundobad and Godegisel, were marching their armies to the same point, and they came with all their warlike equipment to the stronghold named Dijon. And they fought on the river Ouche, and Godegisel joined Clovis, and both armies crushed the people of Gundobad. And he perceived the treachery of his brother, whom he had not suspected, and turned his back and began to flee, hastening along the banks of the Rhone, and he came to the city of Avignon. And Godegisel having won the victory, promised to Clovis a part of his kingdom, and departed quietly and entered Vienne in triumph, as if he now held the whole kingdom.

King Clovis increased his army further, and set off after Gundobad to drag him from his city and slay him. He heard it, and was terrified, and feared that sudden death would come to him. However he had with him Aridius, a man famed for energy and wisdom, and he sent for him and said: "Difficulties wall me in on every side, and I do not know what to do, because these barbarians have come upon us to slay us and destroy the whole country." To this Aridius answered: "You must soften the fierceness of this man in order not to perish. Now if it is pleasing in your eyes, I will pretend to flee from you and to pass over to his side, and when I come to him, I shall prevent his harming either you or this country. Only be willing to do what he demands of you by my advice, until the Lord in his goodness deigns to make your cause successful." And Gundobad said: "I will do whatever you direct."

When he said this, Aridius bade him good-by and departed, and going to King Clovis he said: "Behold I am your humble servant, most pious king, I come to your protection, leaving the wretched Gundobad. And if your goodness condescends to receive me, both you and your children shall have in me a true and faithful servant." Clovis received him very readily, and kept him by him, for he was entertaining in story-telling, ready in counsel, just in judgment, and faithful in what was put in his charge. Then when Clovis with all his army sat around the walls of the city, Aridius said: "O King, if the glory of your loftiness should kindly consent to hear the few words of my lowliness, though you do not need counsel, yet I would utter them with entire faithfulness, and they will be

---

[2] Followers of the bishop Arius (c. 250–336 C.E.) who taught that Jesus was not equal to God the Father in divinity. His teachings were deemed heretical at the First Council of Nicea in 325.

advantageous to you and to the cities through which you purpose to go. Why," said he, "do you keep your army here, when your enemy sits in a very strong place? If you ravage the fields, lay waste the meadows, cut down the vineyards, lay low the olive-yards, and destroy all the produce of the country, you do not, however, succeed in doing him any harm. Send an embassy rather and impose tribute to be paid you every year, so that the country may be safe and you may rule forever over a tributary. And if he refuses, then do whatever pleases you." The king took this advice, and commanded his army to return home. Then he sent an embassy to Gundobad, and ordered him to pay him every year a tribute. And he paid it at once and promised that he would pay it for the future.

Later he regained his power, and now contemptuously refused to pay the promised tribute to King Clovis, and set his army in motion against his brother Godegisel, and shut him up in the city of Vienne and besieged him. And when food began to be lacking for the common people, Godegisel was afraid that the famine would extend to himself, and gave orders that the common people be expelled from the city.

When this was done, there was driven out, among the rest, the artisan who had charge of the aqueduct. And he was indignant that he had been cast out from the city with the rest, and went to Gundobad in a rage to inform him how to burst into the city and take vengeance on his brother. Under his guidance an army was led through the aqueduct, and many with iron crowbars went in front, for there was a vent in the aqueduct closed with a great stone, and when this had been pushed away with crowbars, by direction of the artisan, they entered the city, and surprised from the rear the defenders who were shooting arrows from the wall.

The trumpet was sounded in the midst of the city, and the besiegers seized the gates, and opened them and entered at the same time, and when the people between these two battle lines were being slain by each army, Godegisel sought refuge in the church of the heretics, and was slain there along with the Arian bishop. Finally the Franks who were with Godegisel gathered in a tower. But Gundobad ordered that no harm should be done to a single one of them, but seized them and sent them in exile to king Alaric at Toulouse, and he slew the Burgundian senators who had conspired with Godegisel. He restored to his own dominion all the region which is now called Burgundy. He established milder laws for the Burgundians lest they should oppress the Romans.

*   *   *

REVIEW QUESTIONS

1. According to Gregory, what qualities does a barbarian chieftain need to display in order to succeed? What does this excerpt reveal about the nature of kingship among the Franks?
2. Why does Clovis agree to accept Christianity? What is the role of his wife, Clotilda? What can we infer about the status of women in Frankish society, based on this passage?
3. What is the significance—for Clovis, for his people, and for Gregory—of his conversion? Does it seem to change his nature as a man and a king?
4. What vestiges of the Roman Empire remain in the world of Clovis and his people? What does this source reveal about change and continuity in the former provinces of Rome?

7 ❧ ROME'S THREE HEIRS, 500–950

Roman control over most of the western Mediterranean weakened in the fifth century, and soon Rome itself became the capital of an Ostrogothic kingdom in Italy. A world formerly centered on the "Middle Sea" began to take a different shape. In the eastern Mediterranean, the Roman Empire endured. This state, smaller after the rise of Islam and the loss of North Africa, Egypt, Syria, and Palestine, is now known as the Byzantine Empire. Ancient culture continued to evolve here in the setting of Eastern Orthodox Christianity and a nearly incessant struggle for survival against Slavic, Muslim, and eventually western Christian neighbors.

The Arabian Peninsula, largely neglected by the neighboring Roman and Persian Empires, unified in the seventh century under the influence of Muhammad of Mecca. The new religion of Islam, partially drawing on and extending Jewish and Christian traditions but containing a specific revelation and message for the Arabian peoples, unified Arabia with a mission. Armies spread the new faith as they quickly extended Muslim conquests across Africa to the west and crossed to the Iberian Peninsula, and the religion spread through Mesopotamia, Persia, and northern India to the east. The collected revelations of Muhammad, in the form of the Qu'ran, brought a knowledge of the religion as well as the Arabic language to all the new peoples converted into the world of Islam. Islamic scholars and schools preserved much of ancient Greek, Syrian, and Persian culture and soon contributed new insights in the sciences and history. Much of the West's knowledge of ancient Greek thought came through translations of Arabic sources.

In northwestern Europe, the barbarian kingdoms were gradually being converted to Christianity and were becoming the center of a third culture, shaped by the combined influences of Roman civilization and Germanic heritage. European monasteries preserved and copied classical Latin and early Christian texts that became the core of early medieval culture. The religious frontiers between the Eastern Orthodox, Roman Catholic, and Muslim worlds in Europe masked deep ethnic divisions and eventual splits in the apparent unity of the faiths. All three

cultures preserved parts of the classical legacy while despising paganism and some ancient values not suited to the newer religions.

For a time in the sixth century, the emperor Justinian seemed poised to restore imperial authority in large parts of the West, but his failures and the rise of Islam resulted in a more compact Byzantine state. For nearly a thousand years, Byzantine culture produced distinctive artistic works and writers. In the West there was no Roman emperor until the coronation of Charlemagne in 800. The resurgent Frankish state in the West helped to halt the advance of Islam in Europe and extended the frontiers of Christendom into the pagan Germanic and Slavic lands to the east. Government depended on the personalities of individual rulers, and in Charlemagne the Franks benefited from the rule of a king who was also interested in sponsoring the revival of learning and the arts. Anglo-Saxon England, remaining outside the Carolingian Empire, also contributed monks and missionaries, as well as a distinctive literature, to this early medieval culture. In the Muslim world, the caliphate of Baghdad presided over a golden age of Arabic culture under Harun al Rashid (786–809). This ruler established contacts with the Christian West and sent Charlemagne an elephant (an animal not seen in Europe since the Romans and a marvel of the age) and a clock, which did not last as long as the elephant.

By about the year 1000, three centers of power had replaced the Roman Empire of late antiquity. Islamic rulers held sway over the southern and eastern shores of the Mediterranean, and in the East a Greek state calling itself a Roman Empire still endured. In the West a distinctly Latin Christendom emerged from the end of Rome and the subsequent barbarian kingdoms, but this world was insecure and beset by powerful enemies on all sides.

MOSAICS OF JUSTINIAN AND THEODORA, CHURCH OF SAN VITALE, RAVENNA (C. 500 C.E.)

Justinian (top) holds a communion dish, Theodora (bottom) a chalice. The emperor commissioned these mosaics for an important church in Ravenna, the capital of a part of Byzantine Italy. What does this mosaic suggest about the position of the imperial family in the Church? What does it suggest about the relationships among different powerful groups: the imperial family, the aristocracy, the army, and the clergy?

222

PROCOPIUS

FROM *Secret History*

Procopius (c. 500–565), bishop of Caesaria, was a scholar active in the service of Justinian (r. 527–65) and the emperor's exact contemporary. He became an official court historian and biographer, and most of his surviving writings present a flattering picture of Justinian's reign and accomplishments. But in the text known as the Secret History—*in the original Greek, the "unpublished writings"—Procopius tells a very different story. The following excerpts explain his rationale for producing (and hiding) this work and present alternative portraits of the "real" Justinian and his wife, the empress Theodora.*

From *Procopius: Secret History*, translated by Richard Atwater (Ann Arbor: University of Michigan Press, 1963), pp. 35–36, 39–49.

*   *   *

In what I have written on the Roman wars up to the present point, the story was arranged in chronological order and as completely as the times then permitted. What I shall write now follows a different plan, supplementing the previous formal chronicle with a disclosure of what really happened throughout the Roman Empire. You see, it was not possible, during the life of certain persons, to write the truth of what they did, as a historian should. If I had, their hordes of spies would have found out about it, and they would have put me to a most horrible death. I could not even trust my nearest relatives. That is why I was compelled to hide the real explanation of many matters glossed over in my previous books.

These secrets it is now my duty to tell and reveal the remaining hidden matters and motives. Yet when I approach this different task, I find it hard indeed to have to stammer and retract what I have written before about the lives of Justinian and Theodora. Worse yet, it occurs to me that what I am now about to tell will seem neither probable nor plausible to future generations, especially as time flows on and my story becomes ancient history. I fear they may think me a writer of fiction, and even put me among the poets.

However, I have this much to cheer me, that my account will not be unendorsed by other testimony: so I shall not shrink from the duty of completing this work.

*   *   *

VII. Outrages of the Blues

The people had since long previous time been divided, as I have explained elsewhere, into two factions, the Blues and the Greens. Justinian, by joining the former party, which had already shown favor to him, was able to bring everything into confusion and turmoil, and by its power to sink the Roman state to its knees before him. Not all the Blues were willing to follow his leadership, but there were plenty who were eager for civil war. Yet even these, as the trouble spread, seemed the most prudent of men, for their crimes were less awful than was in their power to commit. Nor did the Green partisans remain quiet, but showed their resentment as violently as they could, though one by one they were continually punished; which, indeed,

urged them each time to further recklessness. For men who are wronged are likely to become desperate.

Then it was that Justinian, fanning the flame and openly inciting the Blues to fight, made the whole Roman Empire shake on its foundation, as if an earthquake or a cataclysm had stricken it, or every city within its confines had been taken by the foe. Everything everywhere was uprooted: nothing was left undisturbed by him. Law and order, throughout the State, overwhelmed by distraction, were turned upside down.

First the rebels revolutionized the style of wearing their hair. For they had it cut differently from the rest of the Romans: not molesting the mustache or beard, which they allowed to keep on growing as long as it would, as the Persians do, but clipping the hair short on the front of the head down to the temples, and letting it hang down in great length and disorder in the back, as the Massageti do. This weird combination they called the Hun haircut.

Next they decided to wear the purple stripe on their togas, and swaggered about in a dress indicating a rank above their station: for it was only by ill-gotten money they were able to buy this finery. And the sleeves of their tunics were cut tight about the wrists, while from there to the shoulders they were of an ineffable fullness; thus, whenever they moved their hands, as when applauding at the theater or encouraging a driver in the hippodrome, these immense sleeves fluttered conspicuously, displaying to the simple public what beautiful and well-developed physiques were these that required such large garments to cover them. They did not consider that by the exaggeration of this dress the meagerness of their stunted bodies appeared all the more noticeable. Their cloaks, trousers, and boots were also different: and these too were called the Hun style, which they imitated.

Almost all of them carried steel openly from the first, while by day they concealed their two-edged daggers along the thigh under their cloaks. Collecting in gangs as soon as dusk fell, they robbed their betters in the open Forum and in the narrow alleys, snatching from passersby their mantles, belts, gold brooches, and whatever they had in their hands. Some they killed after robbing them, so they could not inform anyone of the assault. . . .

Yet all of this disturbed people less than Justinian's offenses against the State. For those who suffer the most grievously from evildoers are relieved of the greater part of their anguish by the expectation they will sometime be avenged by law and authority. Men who are confident of the future can bear more easily and less painfully their present troubles; but when they are outraged even by the government what befalls them is naturally all the more grievous, and by the failing of all hope of redress they are turned to utter despair. And Justinian's crime was that he was not only unwilling to protect the injured, but saw no reason why he should not be the open head of the guilty faction; he gave great sums of money to these young men, and surrounded himself with them: and some he even went so far as to appoint to high office and other posts of honor.

VIII. Character and Appearance of Justinian

Now this went on not only in Constantinople, but in every city: for like any other disease, the evil, starting there, spread throughout the entire Roman Empire. But the Emperor was undisturbed by the trouble, even when it went on continually under his own eyes at the hippodrome. For he was very complacent and resembled most the silly ass, which follows, only shaking its ears, when one drags it by the bridle. As such Justinian acted, and threw everything into confusion.

As soon as he took over the rule from his uncle, his first measure was to spend the public money without restraint, now that he had control of it. He gave much of it to the Huns who, from time to time, entered the state; and in consequence the Roman provinces were subject to constant incursions, for these barbarians, having once tasted Roman wealth, never forgot the road that led to it. And he threw much money into the sea in the form of moles, as if to master the eternal roaring of the breakers. For he jealously hurled stone breakwaters

far out from the mainland against the onset of the sea, as if by the power of wealth he could outmatch the might of ocean.

He gathered to himself the private estates of Roman citizens from all over the Empire: some by accusing their possessors of crimes of which they were innocent, others by juggling their owners' words into the semblance of a gift to him of their property. And many, caught in the act of murder and other crimes, turned their possessions over to him and thus escaped the penalty for their sins.

Others, fraudulently disputing title to lands happening to adjoin their own, when they saw they had no chance of getting the best of the argument, with the law against them, gave him their equity in the claim so as to be released from court. Thus, by a gesture that cost him nothing, they gained his favor and were able illegally to get the better of their opponents.

I think this is as good a time as any to describe the personal appearance of the man. Now in physique he was neither tall nor short, but of average height; not thin, but moderately plump; his face was round, and not bad looking, for he had good color, even when he fasted for two days. To make a long description short, he much resembled Domitian, Vespasian's son. He was the one whom the Romans so hated that even tearing him into pieces did not satisfy their wrath against him, but a decree was passed by the Senate that the name of this Emperor should never be written, and that no statue of him should be preserved. And so this name was erased in all the inscriptions at Rome and wherever else it had been written, except only where it occurs in the list of emperors; and nowhere may be seen any statue of him in all the Roman Empire, save one in brass, which was made for the following reason.

Domitian's wife was of free birth and otherwise noble; and neither had she herself ever done wrong to anybody, nor had she assented in her husband's acts. Wherefore she was dearly loved; and the Senate sent for her, when Domitian died, and commanded her to ask whatever boon she wished. But she asked only this: to set up in his memory one brass image, wherever she might desire. To this the

Senate agreed. Now the lady, wishing to leave a memorial to future time of the savagery of those who had butchered her husband, conceived this plan: collecting the pieces of Domitian's body, she joined them accurately together and sewed the body up again into its original semblance. Taking this to the statue makers, she ordered them to produce the miserable form in brass. So the artisans forthwith made the image, and the wife took it, and set it up in the street which leads to the Capitol, on the right hand side as one goes there from the Forum: a monument to Domitian and a revelation of the manner of his death until this day.

Justinian's entire person, his manner of expression and all of his features might be clearly pointed out in this statue.

Now such was Justinian in appearance; but his character was something I could not fully describe. For he was at once villainous and amenable; as people say colloquially, a moron. He was never truthful with anyone, but always guileful in what he said and did, yet easily hoodwinked by any who wanted to deceive him. His nature was an unnatural mixture of folly and wickedness. What in olden times a peripatetic philosopher said was also true of him, that opposite qualities combine in a man as in the mixing of colors. I will try to portray him, however, insofar as I can fathom his complexity.

This Emperor, then, was deceitful, devious, false, hypocritical, two-faced, cruel, skilled in dissembling his thought, never moved to tears by either joy or pain, though he could summon them artfully at will when the occasion demanded, a liar always, not only offhand, but in writing, and when he swore sacred oaths to his subjects in their very hearing. Then he would immediately break his agreements and pledges, like the vilest of slaves, whom indeed only the fear of torture drives to confess their perjury. A faithless friend, he was a treacherous enemy, insane for murder and plunder, quarrelsome and revolutionary, easily led to anything evil, but never willing to listen to good counsel, quick to plan mischief and carry it out, but finding even the hearing of anything good distasteful to his ears.

How could anyone put Justinian's ways into words? These and many even worse vices were disclosed in him as in no other mortal: nature seemed to have taken the wickedness of all other men combined and planted it in this man's soul. And besides this, he was too prone to listen to accusations; and too quick to punish. For he decided such cases without full examination, naming the punishment when he had heard only the accuser's side of the matter. Without hesitation he wrote decrees for the plundering of countries, sacking of cities, and slavery of whole nations, for no cause whatever. So that if one wished to take all the calamities which had befallen the Romans before this time and weigh them against his crimes, I think it would be found that more men had been murdered by this single man than in all previous history.

He had no scruples about appropriating other people's property, and did not even think any excuse necessary, legal or illegal, for confiscating what did not belong to him. And when it was his, he was more than ready to squander it in insane display, or give it as an unnecessary bribe to the barbarians. In short, he neither held on to any money himself nor let anyone else keep any: as if his reason were not avarice, but jealousy of those who had riches. Driving all wealth from the country of the Romans in this manner, he became the cause of universal poverty.

Now this was the character of Justinian, so far as I can portray it.

IX. How Theodora Most Depraved of All Courtesans, Won His Love

He took a wife: and in what manner she was born and bred, and, wedded to this man, tore up the Roman Empire by the very roots, I shall now relate.

Acacius was the keeper of wild beasts used in the amphitheater in Constantinople; he belonged to the Green faction and was nicknamed the Bearkeeper. This man, during the rule of Anastasius, fell sick and died, leaving three daughters named Comito, Theodora and Anastasia: of whom the eldest was not yet seven years old. His widow took a second husband, who with her undertook to keep up Acacius's family and profession. But Asterius, the dancing master of the Greens, on being bribed by another, removed this office from them and assigned it to the man who gave him the money. For the dancing masters had the power of distributing such positions as they wished.

When this woman saw the populace assembled in the amphitheater, she placed laurel wreaths on her daughters' heads and in their hands, and sent them out to sit on the ground in the attitude of suppliants. The Greens eyed this mute appeal with indifference; but the Blues were moved to bestow on the children an equal office, since their own animal-keeper had just died.

When these children reached the age of girlhood, their mother put them on the local stage, for they were fair to look upon; she sent them forth, however, not all at the same time, but as each one seemed to her to have reached a suitable age. Comito, indeed, had already become one of the leading hetaerae of the day.

Theodora, the second sister, dressed in a little tunic with sleeves, like a slave girl, waited on Comito and used to follow her about carrying on her shoulders the bench on which her favored sister was wont to sit at public gatherings. Now Theodora was still too young to know the normal relation of man with maid, but consented to the unnatural violence of villainous slaves who, following their masters to the theater, employed their leisure in this infamous manner. And for some time in a brothel she suffered such misuse.

But as soon as she arrived at the age of youth, and was now ready for the world, her mother put her on the stage. Forthwith, she became a courtesan, and such as the ancient Greeks used to call a common one, at that: for she was not a flute or harp player, nor was she even trained to dance, but only gave her youth to anyone she met, in utter abandonment. Her general favors included, of course, the actors in the theater; and in their productions she took part in the low comedy scenes. For she was very funny and a good mimic, and immediately became popular in this art. There was no shame in the girl, and no one ever saw her dis-

mayed: no role was too scandalous for her to accept without a blush.

She was the kind of comedienne who delights the audience by letting herself be cuffed and slapped on the cheeks, and makes them guffaw by raising her skirts to reveal to the spectators those feminine secrets here and there which custom veils from the eyes of the opposite sex. With pretended laziness she mocked her lovers, and coquettishly adopting ever new ways of embracing, was able to keep in a constant turmoil the hearts of the sophisticated. And she did not wait to be asked by anyone she met, but on the contrary, with inviting jests and a comic flaunting of her skirts herself tempted all men who passed by, especially those who were adolescent.

On the field of pleasure she was never defeated. Often she would go picnicking with ten young men or more, in the flower of their strength and virility, and dallied with them all, the whole night through. When they wearied of the sport, she would approach their servants, perhaps thirty in number, and fight a duel with each of these; and even thus found no allayment of her craving. Once, visiting the house of an illustrious gentleman, they say she mounted the projecting corner of her dining couch, pulled up the front of her dress, without a blush, and thus carelessly showed her wantonness. And though she flung wide three gates to the ambassadors of Cupid, she lamented that nature had not similarly unlocked the straits of her bosom, that she might there have contrived a further welcome to his emissaries.

Frequently, she conceived, but as she employed every artifice immediately, a miscarriage was straightway effected. Often, even in the theater, in the sight of all the people, she removed her costume and stood nude in their midst, except for a girdle about the groin: not that she was abashed at revealing that, too, to the audience, but because there was a law against appearing altogether naked on the stage, without at least this much of a fig-leaf. Covered thus with a ribbon, she would sink down to the stage floor and recline on her back. Slaves to whom the duty was entrusted would then scatter grains of barley from above into the calyx of this passion flower, whence geese, trained for the purpose, would next pick the grains one by one with their bills and eat. When she rose, it was not with a blush, but she seemed rather to glory in the performance. For she was not only impudent herself, but endeavored to make everybody else as audacious. Often when she was alone with other actors, she would undress in their midst and arch her back provocatively, advertising like a peacock both to those who had experience of her and to those who had not yet had that privilege her trained suppleness.

So perverse was her wantonness that she should have hid not only the customary part of her person, as other women do, but her face as well. Thus those who were intimate with her were straightway recognized from that very fact to be perverts, and any more respectable man who chanced upon her in the Forum avoided her and withdrew in haste, lest the hem of his mantle, touching such a creature, might be thought to share in her pollution. For to those who saw her, especially at dawn, she was a bird of ill omen. And toward her fellow-actresses she was as savage as a scorpion: for she was very malicious.

Later, she followed Hecebolus, a Tyrian who had been made governor of Pentapolis, serving him in the basest of ways; but finally she quarreled with him and was sent summarily away. Consequently, she found herself destitute of the means of life, which she proceeded to earn by prostitution, as she had done before this adventure. She came thus to Alexandria, and then traversing all the East, worked her way to Constantinople; in every city plying a trade (which it is safer, I fancy, in the sight of God not to name too clearly) as if the Devil were determined there be no land on earth that should not know the sins of Theodora.

Thus was this woman born and bred, and her name was a byword beyond that of other common wenches on the tongues of all men.

But when she came back to Constantinople, Justinian fell violently in love with her. At first he kept her only as a mistress, though he raised her to patrician rank. Through him Theodora was able immediately to acquire an unholy power and

exceedingly great riches. For she seemed to him the sweetest thing in the world, and like all lovers, he desired to please his charmer with every possible favor and requite her with all his wealth. The extravagance added fuel to the flames of passion. With her now to help spend his money he plundered the people more than ever, not only in the capital, but throughout the Roman Empire. As both of them had for a long time been of the Blue party, they gave this faction almost complete control of the affairs of state.

REVIEW QUESTIONS

1. What reasons does Procopius give for distinguishing between official and secret history? Are these distinctions valid?
2. How might you account for Procopius's extremely negative view of Empress Theodora?
3. After reading these excerpts, do you think that Procopius is a reliable source of information? Why or why not? Even if this is not an accurate portrayal of Justinian and Theodora, what does it reveal about Procopius himself and the world in which he lived?

MUHAMMAD

FROM The Qu'ran

The prophet Muhammad (c. 570–632) brought the message of Islam first to the Arab peoples of his home city, Mecca. Muslims, those who submit to the will of the one God (Allah), follow the revelations committed to Muhammad and the Prophet's teachings, which were collected shortly after his death and compose the Qu'ran. Following are two suras (chapters) from the Qu'ran, an excerpt from number 2, the Cow, and number 47, Muhammad; they are typical of the style and content of the Qu'ran.

From *Al-Quran: A Contemporary Translation*, by Ahmed Ali (Princeton, N.J.: Princeton University Press, 2001), pp. 31–39.

Cow

O men, eat only the things of the earth
that are lawful and good.
Do not walk in the footsteps of Satan,
your acknowledged enemy.
He will ask you to indulge in evil, indecency,
and to speak lies of God you cannot even conceive.
When it is said to them:
"Follow what God has revealed,"
they reply: "No, we shall follow only what
our fathers had practiced,"—
even though their fathers had no wisdom
    or guidance!

The semblance of the infidels
is that of a man
who shouts to one that cannot hear
more than a call and a cry.
They are deaf, dumb and blind,
and they fail to understand.
O believers, eat what is good of the food
We have given you, and be grateful to God,
if indeed you are obedient to Him.
Forbidden to you are carrion and blood,
and the flesh of the swine,
and that which has been
consecrated (or killed)
in the name of any other than God.

If one is obliged by necessity
to eat it without intending to transgress,
or reverting to it, he is not guilty of sin;
for God is forgiving and kind.
Those who conceal any part of the Scriptures
that God has revealed, and thus make
a little profit thereby,
take nothing but fire as food;
and God will not turn to them on the Day
   of Resurrection,
nor nourish them for growth;
and their doom will be painful.
They are those who bartered away
good guidance for error, and pardon for
   punishment:
How great is their striving for the Fire!
That is because God has revealed
the Book containing the truth;
but those who are at variance about it
have gone astray in their contrariness.

Piety does not lie in turning your face
to East or West:
Piety lies in believing in God,
the Last Day and the angels,
the Scriptures and the prophets,
and disbursing your wealth out of love for God
among your kin and the orphans,
the wayfarers and mendicants,
freeing the slaves, observing your devotional
   obligations,
and in paying the *zakat*[1] and fulfilling a pledge
   you have given,
and being patient in hardship, adversity,
and times of peril.
These are the men who affirm the truth,
and they are those who follow the straight
   path.
O believers, ordained for you is retribution
for the murdered,
(whether) a free man (is guilty)
of (the murder of) a free man, or a slave of
   a slave,

---

[1] The practice of giving a portion of one's wealth to the poor—one of the Five Pillars of Islam.

or a woman of a woman.
But he who is pardoned some of it by his brother
should be dealt with equity,
and recompense (for blood) paid with a grace.
This is a concession from your Lord and
   a kindness.
He who transgresses in spite of it
shall suffer painful punishment.
In retribution there is life (and preservation).
O men of sense, you may haply take heed for
   yourselves.
It is ordained that when any one of you
nears death, and he owns goods and chattels,
he should bequeath them equitably
to his parents and next of kin.
This is binding on those who are upright and
   fear God.
And any one who changes the will, having heard
   it,
shall be guilty and accountable;
for God hears all and knows every thing.
He who suspects wrong or partiality
on the part of the testator
and brings about a settlement,
does not incur any guilt,
for God is verily forgiving and merciful.

O believers, fasting is enjoined on you
as it was on those before you,
so that you might become righteous.
Fast a (fixed) number of days,
but if someone is ill or is travelling
(he should complete) the number of days (he
   had missed);
and those who find it hard to fast
should expiate by feeding a poor person.
For the good they do with a little hardship is
   better for men.
And if you fast it is good for you,
if you knew.
Ramadan is the month in which the Qu'ran
   was revealed
as guidance to man and clear proof of the
   guidance,
and criterion (of falsehood and truth).
So when you see the new moon you should fast
   the whole month;

but a person who is ill or travelling
(and fails to do so) should fast on other days,
as God wishes ease and not hardship for you,
so that you complete the (fixed) number (of
    fasts),
and give glory to God
for the guidance, and be grateful.
When My devotees enquire of you about Me,
I am near, and answer the call
of every supplicant when he calls.
It behoves them to hearken to Me
and believe in Me
that they may follow the right path.
You are allowed to sleep with your wives
on the nights of the fast:
They are your dress as you are theirs.
God is aware you were cheating yourselves,
so He turned to you and pardoned you.
So now you may have intercourse with them,
and seek what God has ordained for you.
Eat and drink until the white thread
of dawn appears clear from the dark line,
then fast until the night falls;
and abstain from your wives (when you have
    decided)
to stay in the mosques for assiduous devotion.
These are the bounds fixed by God,
so keep well within them.
So does God make His signs clear to men
that they may take heed for themselves.
And do not consume each other's wealth in vain,
nor offer it to men in authority with intent
of usurping unlawfully and knowingly
a part of the wealth of others.

They ask you of the new moons.
Say: "These are periods set for men (to reckon)
    time,
and for pilgrimage."
Piety does not lie in entering the house through
    the back door,[2]

for the pious man is he who follows the straight
    path.
Enter the house through the main gate,[3]
and obey God. You may haply find success.
Fight those in the way of God who fight you,
but do not be aggressive:
God does not like aggressors.
And fight those (who fight you) wheresoever you
    find them,
and expel them from the place
they had turned you out from.
Oppression is worse than killing.
Do not fight them by the Holy Mosque
unless they fight you there.
If they do, then slay them:
Such is the requital for unbelievers.
But if they desist, God is forgiving and kind.
Fight them till sedition comes to end,
and the law of God (prevails).
If they desist, then cease to be hostile,
except against those who oppress.
(Fighting during) the holy month
(if the sanctity) of the holy month (is violated)
is (just) retribution.
So if you are oppressed,
oppress those who oppress you to the same
    degree,
and fear God, and know that God
is with those who are pious
and follow the right path.
Spend in the way of God,
and do not seek destruction at your own hands.
So do good;
for God loves those who do good.
Perform the pilgrimage and holy visit ('Umra,
    to Mecca)
in the service of God.
But if you are prevented, send an offering
which you can afford as sacrifice,
and do not shave your heads until
the offering has reached the place of sacrifice.
But if you are sick or have ailment of the scalp
(preventing the shaving of hair),
then offer expiation by fasting

---

[2] It means the same thing as is meant by the English expression 'through the back door,' i.e., clandestinely. Here it has more than one implication, as the verse deals with the new moon and reckoning "periods," e.g., the period of fasting, a woman's monthly courses, etc.

[3] That is, seek attainment through the right way.

or else giving alms or a sacrificial offering.
When you have security, then those of you who
   wish
to perform the holy visit along with the pilgrimage,
should make a sacrifice according to their means.
But he who has nothing,
should fast for three days during the pilgrimage
and seven on return, completing ten.
This applies to him whose family does not live
near the Holy Mosque.
Have fear of God, and remember that God
is severe in punishment.

Known are the months of pilgrimage.
If one resolves to perform the pilgrimage in
   these months,
let him not indulge in concupiscence, sin or
   quarrel.
And the good you do shall be known to God.
Provide for the journey,
and the best of provisions is piety.
O men of understanding, obey Me.
It is no sin to seek the favours of your Lord
   (by trading).
When you start from 'Arafat in a concourse,
remember God at the monument that is sacred
(al-Mash'ar al-haram),
and remember Him as He has shown you the way,
for in the olden days you were a people astray.
Then move with the crowd impetuously,
and pray God to forgive you your sins.
God is surely forgiving and kind.
When you have finished the rites and ceremonies,
remember God as you do your fathers,
in fact with a greater devotion.
There are some who say:
"Give us, O Lord, in the world";
but they will forego their share in the life
   to come.
But some there are who pray:
"Give us of good in the world, O Lord,
and give us of good in the life to come,
and suffer us not to suffer the torment of Hell."
They are those who will surely have their share
of whatsoever they have earned;
for God is swift at the reckoning.

Remember God during the stated days;
but if a person comes away after two days,
it will not be a sin; and if one tarries,
he will not transgress, if he keep away from evil.
Follow the law of God, and remember
that you will have to gather before Him in
   the end.
There is a man who talks well
of the world to your pleasing,
and makes God witness to what is in his heart,
yet he is the most contentious;
For when his back is turned
he goes about spreading disorder in the land,
destroying fields and flocks;
but God does not love disorder.
Whenever he is told: "Obey God,"
his arrogance leads him to more sin;
and sufficient for him shall be Hell:
How evil a place of wide expanse!
And there is a man who is willing to sell
even his soul to win the favour of God;
and God is compassionate to His creatures.
O believers, come to full submission to God.
Do not follow in the footsteps of Satan
your acknowledged foe.
If you falter even after Our signs
have reached you, then do not forget
that God is all-powerful and all-wise.
Are they waiting for God to appear
in the balconies of clouds
with a host of angels,
and the matter to be settled?
But all things rest
with God in the end.

Ask the children of Israel
how many a clear sign We had given them.
But if one changes the favour of God
after having received it, then remember,
God is severe in revenge.
Enamoured are the unbelievers
of the life of this world,
and scoff at the faithful.
But those who keep from evil and follow the
   straight path
will have a higher place than they
on the Day of Reckoning;

for God gives in measure without number
whomsoever He will.
Men belonged to a single community,
and God sent them messengers
to give them happy tidings and warnings,
and sent the Book with them containing the truth
to judge between them in matters of dispute;
but only those who received it differed
after receiving clear proofs,
on account of waywardness
(and jealousies) among them.
Then God by His dispensation showed those
    who believed
the way to the truth about which they were
    differing;
for God shows whom He please
the path that is straight.
Do you think you will find your way to Paradise
even though you have not known
what the others before you have gone through?
They had suffered affliction and loss,
and were shaken and tossed about
so that even the Apostle
had to cry out with his followers:
"When will the help of God arrive?"
Remember, the help of God is ever at hand.
They ask you of what they should give in charity.
Tell them: "What you can spare of your wealth
as should benefit the parents, the relatives,
the orphans, the needy, the wayfarers,
for God is not unaware of the good deeds that
    you do."
Enjoined on you is fighting,
and this you abhor.
You may dislike a thing
yet it may be good for you;
or a thing may haply please you
but may be bad for you.
Only God has knowledge, and you do not know.

They ask you of war in the holy month.
Tell them: "To fight in that month is a great sin.
But a greater sin in the eyes of God
is to hinder people from the way of God,
and not to believe in Him,
and to bar access to the Holy Mosque
and turn people out of its precincts;

and oppression is worse than killing.
They will always seek war against you
till they turn you away from your faith, if
    they can.
But those of you who turn back on their faith
and die disbelieving
will have wasted their deeds
in this world and the next.
They are inmates of Hell,
and shall there abide for ever.
Surely those who believe,
and those who leave their homes
and fight in the way of God,
may hope for His benevolence,
for God is forgiving and kind.
They ask you of (intoxicants,) wine and gambling.
Tell them: "There is great enervation though
    profit in them[4]
for men; but their enervation is greater than
    benefit.
And they ask you what they should give.
Tell them: "The utmost you can spare."
So does God reveal His signs: You may haply reflect
On this world and the next.
And they ask you about the orphans.
Tell them: "Improving their lot is much better;
    and if
you take interest in their affairs, they are your
    brethren;
and God is aware who are corrupt and who
    are honest;
and if He had pleased
He could surely have imposed on you hardship,
for God is all-powerful and all-wise.
Do not marry idolatrous women
unless they join the faith.
A maid servant who is a believer
is better than an idolatress
even though you may like her.
And do not marry your daughters to idolaters
until they accept the faith.
A servant who is a believer is better than
    an idolater

---

[4] The basic meaning of *ithm* is drunkenness or enervation (*Taj* and Ibn Faris) of which the wine of Paradise
is free.

even though you may like him.
They invite you to Hell, but God
calls you to Paradise and pardon by His grace.
And He makes His signs manifest that men
may haply take heed.

*   *   *

Muhammad

In the name of Allah, most benevolent, ever-
   merciful.

THOSE WHO DISBELIEVE
and obstruct (others) from the way of God
will have wasted their deeds.
But those who believe and do the right,
and believe what has been revealed to
   Muhammad,
which is the truth from their Lord,
will have their faults condoned by Him
and their state improved.
That is because those who refuse to believe
only follow what is false; but those who believe
follow the truth from their Lord.
That is how God gives men precepts of wisdom.
So, when you clash with the unbelievers,
smite their necks until you overpower them,
then hold them in bondage.
Then either free them graciously
or after taking a ransom,
until war shall have come to end.
If God had pleased
He could have punished them (Himself),
but He wills to test some of you through some
   others.
He will not allow the deeds
of those who are killed in the cause of God
to go waste.
He will show them the way,
and better their state,
And will admit them into gardens
with which he has acquainted them.
O you who believe, if you help (in the cause of)
   God
He will surely come to your aid,
and firmly plant your feet.

As for the unbelievers, they will suffer misfortunes,
and their deeds will be rendered ineffective.
That is so as they were averse
to what has been revealed by God,
and their actions will be nullified.
Have they not journeyed in the land
and seen the fate of those before them?
Destroyed they were utterly by God;
and a similar (fate) awaits the unbelievers.
This is so for God is the friend of those who
   believe
while the unbelievers have no friend.

Verily God will admit those who believe and do
   the right
into gardens with streams of water running by.
But the unbelievers revel and carouse
and subsist like beasts, and Hell will be their
   residence.
How many were the habitations,
mightier than your city which has turned you out,
which We destroyed;
and they did not have a helper.
Can one who stands on a clear proof from his
   Lord,
be like one enamoured of his evil deeds
and follows his inane desires?
The semblance of Paradise promised the pious
   and devout
(is that of a garden) with streams of water that
   will not go rank,
and rivers of milk whose taste will not undergo a
   change,
and rivers of wine delectable to drinkers,
and streams of purified honey,
and fruits of every kind in them, and forgiveness
   of their Lord.
Are these like those who will live for ever in the
   Fire
and be given boiling water to drink
which will cut their intestines to shreds?
There are some who listen to you; but as soon
   as they go
from you they say to those who were given
   knowledge:
"What is this he is saying now?"
They are those whose hearts

have been sealed by God, and they follow their
   own lusts.
But those who are rightly guided will be given
greater guidance by Him, and they will have
   their intrinsic piety.
Do they wait for any thing but the Hour (of
   change),
that it may come upon them suddenly?
Its signs have already appeared.
How then will they be warned when it has come
   upon them?
Know then, therefore, there is no god but He,
and ask forgiveness for your sins
and those of believing men and women.
God knows your wanderings
and your destination.

Those who believe say: "How is it no *Surah*[5] was
   revealed?"
But when a categorical Surah is revealed
that mentions war, you should see those
who are sceptical
staring at you like a man in the swoon of death.
Alas the woe for them!
Obedience and modest speech (would have been
   more becoming).
And when the matter has been determined
it is best for them to be true to God.
Is it possible that if placed in authority
you will create disorder in the land
and sever your bonds of relationship?
They are those who were condemned by God,
whose ears were blocked by Him and their eyes
   blinded.
Do they not ponder
on what the Qu'ran says?
Or have their hearts been sealed with locks?
Those who turn their backs
after the way of guidance has been opened to them,
have been surely tempted by Satan
and beguiled by illusory hopes.
This was so because they said to those
who disdain what God has revealed:

"We shall obey you in some things."
But God knows their secret intentions well.
How will it be when the angels draw out their
   souls
striking their faces and their backs?
Because they followed what displeases God,
and they were averse to pleasing Him.
So We nullified their deeds.

Do they whose minds are filled with doubt, think
that God will not expose their malice?
Had We pleased We could have shown them to you
that you could know them by their marks,
and recognise them from the way
they twist their words.
Yet God knows all your deeds.
We shall try you in order to know
who are the fighters among you,
and who are men of fortitude,
and verify your histories.
Surely those who do not believe, and obstruct
   others
from the path of God, and oppose the Prophet
after the way of guidance has been opened
   to them,
will not hurt God in the least,
and He will nullify all that they have done.
O you who believe, obey God and the Prophet,
and do not waste your deeds.
Those who do not believe and obstruct others
from the way of God, and die disbelieving,
will not be pardoned by God.
So do not become weak-kneed and sue for peace,
for you will have the upper hand
as God is with you and will not overlook your deeds.
Verily the life of this world
is no more than a sport and frivolity.
If you believe and fear God,
He will give you your reward,
and will not ask for your possessions.
If He asks for all you possess and insist upon it,
you will become niggardly,
and it will bring out your malevolence.
Beware! You are called to spend in the way of God,
yet some among you close their fists.
But he who is niggardly is so for his own self:

---

[5] A word meaning both "revelation" and a chapter (*sura*)
   of the Qu'ran.

God is above need, and it is you who are needy.
If you turn away then God
will bring other people in your place
who, moreover, will not be like you.

*   *   *

REVIEW QUESTIONS

1. What aspects of Muslim belief are revealed in these suras? What are the obligations of those who submit to Islam? What are their rewards?

2. How do Muhammad's teachings compare with those of Jesus (see pp. 183–187). What do their similarities and differences reveal about the relationships among Judaism, Christianity, and Islam?

3. What do these suras suggest about the historical conditions in which Muhammad and his followers lived?

MAS^CUDI

FROM *The Meadows of Gold*

*The Muslim polymath Abu al-Hasan Ali ibn al-Husayn ibn Ali al-Mas^cudi
(c. 896–956) was born in Baghdad and traveled widely throughout the Middle East
and Asia. Over the course of his extraordinary life, he authored more than thirty
books on such varied subjects as philosophy, political science, medicine, astronomy,
and law. Only two have survived, and the work originally entitled* Meadows of Gold
and Mines of Gems *is one of these. Written in classical Arabic, it traces the history of
the world from the creation of Adam and Eve to Mas^cudi's own day. The only portion
currently translated into English deals with the Abbasid caliphate. The excerpts below
focus on the reign of Harun al-Rashid (r. 786–809), a contemporary of Charlemagne,
who also figured prominently in the compilation of stories known as* The 1001 Nights.

From *The Meadows of Gold: The Abbasids,* translated and edited by Paul Lunde and Caroline Stone (New York: Kegan Paul International, 1989), pp. 62–67, 71.

Harun al-Rashid and the Death of Hadi

Hadi[1] wished to strip his brother of the title of heir apparent, in order to give it to his own son, Ja'far. He had imprisoned Yahya ibn Khalid, the Barmakid, and wanted to kill him; but Yahya, who was responsible for Harun al-Rashid's interests, said to him one day:

'O Commander of the Faithful, if that thing which I ask heaven to spare us and keep far from us, by granting your majesty long life, should come to pass, do you think, I repeat, do you think that the people would recognize the authority of your son Ja'far, who has not yet reached the age of reason, to lead the prayers, the pilgrimage and the holy wars?'

'No, I don't think so,' he replied.

---

[1] Abu Abdullah Musa ibn Mahdi al-Hadi, who ruled as caliph from 785–786.

'Are you not afraid,' continued Yahya, 'that they will raise one of the leading men of your family to the throne, and that the power will pass from your issue to others? You yourself will have stirred up your subjects to break their oath and hold their faith cheap. If, on the other hand, you were to respect the oath of allegiance made to your brother, and if you were to have your son accepted as his heir, it would be the strongest possible position. Then, when Ja'far comes of age, you can ask your brother to yield the supreme power to him.'

'By God,' replied the Caliph, 'you are suggesting a plan that had never occurred to me.'

But later, he determined at all costs to force Harun to give up his rights, with or without his consent, and he severely restrained his movements. Yahya advised his master Harun to ask permission to go out hunting and urged him to spend as much time as possible doing so, since the horoscope cast at the moment of Hadi's birth predicted that his time would be short.

Harun asked and obtained leave to go. He followed the banks of the Euphrates into the region of Hit and Anbar, and then struck inland in the direction of Samawa. Hadi wrote to recall him and, when Harun delayed even more, cursed him roundly. It even occurred to Hadi to go in the direction of al-Haditha, but he fell ill there and turned back. His illness took so serious a turn that no one dared go into him, except the youngest eunuchs. He signed to them to bring him his mother Khaizuran and, when she was at his bedside, he said:

'I am going to die tonight, and my brother Harun will immediately succeed me, for you know the sentence pronounced against me by fate at the very moment of my birth at Rayy. I have had to refuse you what you asked and have had to impose my orders upon you, in accordance with the dictates of policy, but to do so always went against the affection which religion demands of a son. Far, however, from having been an ungrateful child, I have never ceased to protect you, nor to be dutiful and loyal.'

Then he took his mother's hand in farewell, laid it on his heart and breathed his last. Hadi, like his brother Harun, was born at Rayy. His death, the accession of Harun al-Rashid and the birth of Ma'mun, all took place on the same night.

The Dream of Mahdi

It is said that one day one of the great men of the dynasty, who was guilty of many crimes, was brought before Hadi. The Caliph reminded him of them, one after another.

'O Commander of the Faithful,' the man replied, 'to make excuses for the things which you accuse me of having done, would mean contradicting you; to accept your charges would be an admission of my guilt. I prefer to say, with the poet:

> If what you hope for from punishment is
>   satisfaction,
> Why deprive yourself of the satisfaction of
>   forgiveness?'

Hadi set him free and gave him a present.

A number of chroniclers, learned in the history of this dynasty, relate that Hadi said to his brother Harun al-Rashid:

'It seems to me that you are ceaselessly talking to yourself about the fulfilment of the dream and that you hope for that which is still far from you—but first "you must pluck the thorns from the tragacanth".[2]

'O Commander of the Faithful,' replied Harun, 'those you have raised shall be laid low and those you have humbled shall be exalted, and the unjust man shall feel his shame. If power comes into my hands, I shall heal him whom you have broken and I shall give to him whom you have refused. Your children shall be set above my children and your sons shall marry my daughters, and thus will I pay my debt to the Imam Mahdi.'

These words melted Hadi's anger and his face shone with joy. He said:

'Harun, that is just what I would have expected of you. Come here.'

Harun rose, kissed his brother's hand and was going back to his place when Hadi said to him:

---

[2] A natural gum derived from legumes. The Greek words *tarjos* and *akantha* mean "goat thorn"; thus, to remove the "thorn" from this compound would be impossible.

'No, by the most illustrious shaikh and glorious king, you shall sit nowhere but by me, in the place of honour.' Then he said:

'O treasurer, bring a million dinars to my brother immediately and as soon as the taxes are collected, you are to give him half.'

When Harun wished to withdraw, they led his mount right up to the edge of the carpet.

Amr al-Rumi said:

'I asked Harun al-Rashid about the dream, and he quoted Mahdi's own words:

"I dreamed that I gave a branch of a tree to Hadi and another to Harun. Hadi's branch bore only a few leaves towards the top, while that of Harun, on the other hand, was covered with foliage along all its length."'

Mahdi related his dream to the physician Ibn Ishaq al-Saimari, who interpreted it, saying:

'They will both reign, but the reign of Hadi will be short, while that of Harun will endure longer than that of any other Caliph. His days will be the best of days and his age the best of ages.'

Amr al-Rumi adds that when Harun al-Rashid came to the throne, he married his daughter Hamduna to Ja'far, and his other daughter, Fatima, to Ismail—both sons of Hadi—and that he kept all the promises which he had made to his predecessor.

The Sword Samsama

Abd Allah ibn al-Dahhak relates the following tradition, according to al-Haitham ibn Adi:

'Mahdi had given his son Hadi a famous sword named Samsama, which had belonged to Amr ibn Ma'dikarib. One day, after he had become Caliph, Hadi had this sword brought in and a great basket filled with dinars. Then he ordered his chamberlain:

"Let the poets enter!"

When they had come in, he asked them to choose the sword as subject for their verse. Ibn Yamin of Basra spoke first, and said:

Hadi, the trustworthy, alone among men
Possesses the Samsama of Amr al-Zubaidi;
We have heard that the sword of Amr

Was the best blade ever closed in a sheath.
The lightning flash lit it with fire
And death tempered it with poison, sudden
  and terrible.
When you unsheath it, it shines like the sun
So that a man can scarcely look upon it.
The temper of its steel flashes on the blade
Like the ripples of clear water.
At the moment of striking, what does it matter
Whether it cuts with the left edge or the right?

"Take the sword and the basket of dinars," said the Caliph. "I give you them both."

Ibn Yamin distributed the contents of the basket to the other poets, saying:

"You came here with me and it is because of me that you have not been rewarded; this sword will take the place of any other fee."

Hadi sent to him later and bought the sword back from him for 50,000 dinars.'

The story of this reign, so interesting in spite of its being cut short, is told at length in the *Historical Annals* and the *Intermediate History*.

All help comes from God!

The Accession of Harun al-Rashid

Allegiance was sworn to Harun, son of Mahdi, at Baghdad, the City of Peace, on a Friday, on the morning after the night that Hadi died. It was the twelfth day before the end of Rabi' 170 AH/786 AD. Harun died in a village called Sanabadh near Tus on a Saturday, the 4th of Jumada II, 193 AH/809 AD. His reign had lasted twenty-three years and six months, or, according to another tradition, twenty-three years, two months and eighteen days. He was twenty-one years and two months old when he became caliph. He died at the age of forty-four years and four months.

As soon as the caliphate came to Harun al-Rashid, he summoned Yahya ibn Khalid, the Barmakid, and said to him:

'My dear little father, it was you who placed me on this throne, it was by your aid and the blessing of heaven—yes, by your happy influence and wise advice! And now I invest you with absolute power.'

And he gave him his seal. This occasion is commemorated in the following lines by Ibrahim al-Mawsili:

Did you not see how the sun was pale and wan
But when Harun took power it blazed with
    light?
This was because of the good fortune of
    Harun,
The generous, the faithful agent of God.
He is the sun's elect, Yahya the sun's vizier.

Raita, the daughter of Abu al-Abbas al-Saffah, died a few months after the accession of Harun al-Rashid or, according to another version, at the end of the reign of Hadi. The mother of both that caliph and Rashid, Khaizuran, died in 173 AH/789 AD and Rashid walked on foot at the head of the funeral procession. The revenues of this princess amounted to 160 million dirhams.

The Last Pilgrimage of Harun al-Rashid

In the year 188 AH/804 AD, Harun al-Rashid went on his last pilgrimage to Mecca. They say that Abu Bakr ibn Ayyash, one of the most highly learned men of the age, said, as Harun al-Rashid was going through Kufa on his return from this pilgrimage:

'Harun al-Rashid will never travel this road again, nor will it be taken by any of the Abbasid Caliphs who come after him.'

'Does this prophecy come from your knowledge of the invisible world?' he was asked.

'Yes,' replied Abu Bakr.

'Is it a revelation from Heaven?'

'Yes.'

'Addressed directly to you?'

'No,' he replied, 'but to Muhammad—may the prayers and peace of God be upon him—and transmitted by him who was murdered in this place.' And with his hand he indicated the place in Kufa where Ali—may God be content with him—was killed.

REVIEW QUESTIONS

1. What are the attributes of a good Caliph? How do Hadi and Harun al-Rashid exemplify these characteristics?

2. What role do dreams and visions play in these historical vignettes? Why might they have been considered important?

3. What do these excerpts tell us about Muslim society under the Abbasid caliphate? What classes of people are represented? What do we learn about them?

BEDE

FROM *A History of the English Church and People*

Bede (d. 735), often known as the Venerable Bede, was an Anglo-Saxon monk from Northumbria (northen England). Known in his own day as "Bede the Computer," he wrote Latin treatises on the accurate calculation of historical time as well as commentaries on the Bible, saints' lives, and histories. His most famous work, excerpted here, tells the story of England's conversion to Christianity and the establishment of what Bede liked to call the "English Church," which he saw as uniting the disparate peoples

of Britain, Celtic and Anglo-Saxon, in their allegiance to the Roman pope. The following passages illustrate two of the ways in which English tribal leaders were influenced by Roman missionaries, and eventually persuaded to adopt the Christian religion.

From *Bede: A History of the English Church and People*, translated by Leo Serley-Price and revised by R. E. Latham (New York: Barnes & Noble, 1993), pp. 66–71, 126–29.

The Conversion of Ethelbert, King of Kent

CHAPTER 23: THE HOLY POPE GREGORY SENDS AUGUSTINE AND OTHER MONKS TO PREACH TO THE ENGLISH NATION, AND ENCOURAGES THEM IN A LETTER TO PERSEVERE IN THEIR MISSION [A.D. 596]

In the year of our Lord 582, Maurice, fifty-fourth in succession from Augustus, became Emperor, and ruled for twenty-one years. In the tenth year of his reign, Gregory, an eminent scholar and administrator, was elected Pontiff of the apostolic Roman see, and ruled it for thirteen years, six months, and ten days. In the fourteenth year of this Emperor, and about the one hundred and fiftieth year after the coming of the English to Britain, Gregory was inspired by God to send his servant Augustine with several other God-fearing monks to preach the word of God to the English nation. Having undertaken this task in obedience to the Pope's command and progressed a short distance on their journey, they became afraid, and began to consider returning home. For they were appalled at the idea of going to a barbarous, fierce, and pagan nation, of whose very language they were ignorant. They unanimously agreed that this was the safest course, and sent back Augustine—who was to be consecrated bishop in the event of their being received by the English—so that he might humbly request the holy Gregory to recall them from so dangerous, arduous, and uncertain a journey. In reply, the Pope wrote them a letter of encouragement, urging them to proceed on their mission to preach God's word, and to trust themselves to his aid. This letter ran as follows:

'GREGORY, Servant of the servants of God, to the servants of our Lord. My very dear sons, it is better never to undertake any high enterprise than to abandon it when once begun. So with the help of God you must carry out this holy task which you have begun. Do not be deterred by the troubles of the journey or by what men say. Be constant and zealous in carrying out this enterprise which, under God's guidance, you have undertaken: and be assured that the greater the labour, the greater will be the glory of your eternal reward. When Augustine your leader returns, whom We have appointed your abbot, obey him humbly in all things, remembering that whatever he directs you to do will always be to the good of your souls. May Almighty God protect you with His grace, and grant me to see the result of your labours in our heavenly home. And although my office prevents me from working at your side, yet because I long to do so, I hope to share in your joyful reward. God keep you safe, my dearest sons.

'Dated the twenty-third of July, in the fourteenth year of the reign of the most pious Emperor Maurice Tiberius Augustus, and the thirteenth year after his Consulship: the fourteenth indiction.'

CHAPTER 25: AUGUSTINE REACHES BRITAIN, AND FIRST PREACHES IN THE ISLE OF THANET BEFORE KING ETHELBERT, WHO GRANTS PERMISSION TO PREACH IN KENT [A.D. 597]

Reassured by the encouragement of the blessed father Gregory, Augustine and his fellow-servants of Christ resumed their work in the word of God, and arrived in Britain. At this time the most powerful king there was Ethelbert, who reigned in Kent and whose domains extended northwards to the river Humber, which forms the boundary between the

north and south Angles. To the east of Kent lies the large island of Thanet, which by English reckoning is six hundred hides[1] in extent; it is separated from the mainland by a waterway about three furlongs broad called the Wantsum, which joins the sea at either end and is fordable only in two places. It was here that God's servant Augustine landed with companions, who are said to have been forty in number. At the direction of blessed Pope Gregory, they had brought interpreters from among the Franks, and they sent these to Ethelbert, saying that they came from Rome bearing very glad news, which infallibly assured all who would receive it of eternal joy in heaven and an everlasting kingdom with the living and true God. On receiving this message, the king ordered them to remain in the island where they had landed, and gave directions that they were to be provided with all necessaries until he should decide what action to take. For he had already heard of the Christian religion, having a Christian wife of the Frankish royal house named Bertha, whom he had received from her parents on condition that she should have freedom to hold and practise her faith unhindered with Bishop Liudhard, whom they had sent as her helper in the faith.

After some days, the king came to the island and, sitting down in the open air, summoned Augustine and his companions to an audience. But he took precautions that they should not approach him in a house; for he held an ancient superstition that, if they were practisers of magical arts, they might have opportunity to deceive and master him. But the monks were endowed with power from God, not from the Devil, and approached the king carrying a silver cross as their standard and the likeness of our Lord and Saviour painted on a board. First of all they offered prayer to God, singing a litany for the eternal salvation both of themselves and of those to whom and for whose sake they had come. And when, at the king's command, they had sat down and preached the word of life to the king and his court, the king said: 'Your words and promises are fair indeed; but they are

new and uncertain, and I cannot accept them and abandon the age-old beliefs that I have held together with the whole English nation. But since you have travelled far, and I can see that you are sincere in your desire to impart to us what you believe to be true and excellent, we will not harm you. We will receive you hospitably and take care to supply you with all that you need; nor will we forbid you to preach and win any people you can to your religion.' The king then granted them a dwelling in the city of Canterbury, which was the chief city of all his realm, and in accordance with his promise he allowed them provisions and did not withdraw their freedom to preach. Tradition says that as they approached the city, bearing the holy cross and the likeness of our great King and Lord Jesus Christ as was their custom, they sang in unison this litany: 'We pray Thee, O Lord, in all Thy mercy, that Thy wrath and anger may be turned away from this city and from Thy holy house, for we are sinners. Alleluia.'

CHAPTER 26: THE LIFE AND DOCTRINE OF THE PRIMITIVE CHURCH ARE FOLLOWED IN KENT: AUGUSTINE ESTABLISHES HIS EPISCOPAL SEE IN THE KING'S CITY

As soon as they had occupied the house given to them they began to emulate the life of the apostles and the primitive Church. They were constantly at prayer; they fasted and kept vigils; they preached the word of life to whomsoever they could. They regarded worldly things as of little importance, and accepted only the necessities of life from those they taught. They practised what they preached, and were willing to endure any hardship, and even to die for the truth which they proclaimed. Before long a number of heathen, admiring the simplicity of their holy lives and the comfort of their heavenly message, believed and were baptized. On the east side of the city stood an old church, built in honour of Saint Martin during the Roman occupation of Britain, where the Christian queen of whom I have spoken went to pray. Here they first assembled to sing the psalms, to pray, to say Mass, to preach, and to baptize, until the king's own con-

---

[1] *hide*: measurement of land, usually equivalent to about 120 acres.

version to the Faith gave them greater freedom to preach and to build and restore churches everywhere.

At length the king himself, among others, edified by the pure lives of these holy men and their gladdening promises, the truth of which they confirmed by many miracles, believed and was baptized. Thenceforward great numbers gathered each day to hear the word of God, forsaking their heathen rites and entering the unity of Christ's holy Church as believers. While the king was pleased at their faith and conversion, it is said that he would not compel anyone to accept Christianity; for he had learned from his instructors and guides to salvation that the service of Christ must be accepted freely and not under compulsion. Nevertheless, he showed greater favour to believers, because they were fellow-citizens of the kingdom of heaven. And it was not long before he granted his teachers in his capital of Canterbury a place of residence appropriate to their station, and gave them possessions of various kinds to supply their wants.

The Conversion of Edwin, King of Northumbrians

CHAPTER 13: EDWIN HOLDS A COUNCIL WITH HIS CHIEF MEN ABOUT ACCEPTING THE FAITH OF CHRIST. THE HIGH PRIEST DESTROYS HIS OWN ALTARS [A.D. 627]

When he heard this,[2] the king [Edwin] answered that is was his will as well as his duty to accept the Faith that Paulinus taught, but said that he must still discuss the matter with his principal advisers and friends so that, if they were in agreement with him, they might all be cleansed together in Christ the Fount of Life. Paulinus agreed, and the king kept his promise. He summoned a council of the wise men, and asked each in turn his opinion of this strange doctrine and this new way of worshipping the godhead that was being proclaimed to them.

---

[2] That is, the assurances of the Roman missionary Paulinus.

Coifi, the Chief Priest, replied without hesitation: 'Your Majesty, let us give careful consideration to this new teaching; for I frankly admit that, in my experience, the religion that we have hitherto professed seems valueless and powerless. None of your subjects has been more devoted to the service of our gods than myself; yet there are many to whom you show greater favour, who receive greater honours, and who are more successful in all their undertakings. Now, if the gods had any power, they would surely have favoured myself, who have been more zealous in their service. Therefore, if on examination you perceive that these new teachings are better and more effectual, let us not hesitate to accept them.'

Another of the king's chief men signified his agreement with this prudent argument, and went on to say: 'Your Majesty, when we compare the present life of man on earth with that time of which we have no knowledge, it seems to me like the swift flight of a single sparrow through the banqueting-hall where you are sitting at dinner on a winter's day with your thanes and counsellors. In the midst there is a comforting fire to warm the hall; outside, the storms of winter rain or snow are raging. This sparrow flies swiftly in through one door of the hall, and out through another. While he is inside, he is safe from the winter storms; but after a few moments of comfort, he vanishes from sight into the wintry world from which he came. Even so, man appears on earth for a little while; but of what went before this life or of what follows, we know nothing. Therefore, if this new teaching has brought any more certain knowledge, it seems only right that we should follow it.' The other elders and counsellors of the king, under God's guidance, gave similar advice.

Coifi then added that he wished to hear Paulinus' teaching about God in greater detail; and when, at the king's bidding, this had been given, he exclaimed: 'I have long realized that there is nothing in our way of worship; for the more diligently I sought after truth in our religion, the less I found. I now publicly confess that this teaching clearly reveals truths that will afford us the blessings of life, salvation, and eternal happiness. Therefore, Your

Majesty, I submit that the temples and altars that we have dedicated to no advantage be immediately desecrated and burned.' In short, the king granted blessed Paulinus full permission to preach, renounced idolatry, and professed his acceptance of the Faith of Christ. And when he asked the Chief Priest who should be the first to profane the altars and shrines of the idols, together with the enclosures that surrounded them, Coifi replied: 'I will do this myself; for now that the true God has granted me knowledge, who more suitably than I can set a public example and destroy the idols that I worshipped in ignorance?' So he formally renounced his empty superstitions and asked the king to give him arms and a stallion—for hitherto it had not been lawful for the Chief Priest to carry arms or to ride anything but a mare—and, thus equipped, he set out to destroy the idols. Girded with a sword and with a spear in his hand, he mounted the king's stallion and rode up to the idols. When the crowd saw him, they thought he had gone mad; but without hesitation, as soon as he reached the temple, he cast into it the spear he carried and thus profaned it. Then, full of joy at his knowledge of the worship of the true God, he told his companions to set fire to the temple and its enclosures and destroy them. The site where these idols once stood is still shown, not far east of York, beyond the river Derwent, and is known today as Goodmanham. Here it was that the Chief Priest, inspired by the true God, desecrated and destroyed the altars that he had himself dedicated.

CHAPTER 14: EDWIN AND HIS PEOPLE ACCEPT THE FAITH, AND ARE BAPTIZED BY PAULINUS [A.D. 627]

So King Edwin, with all the nobility of his kingdom and a large number of humbler folk, accepted the Faith and were washed in the cleansing waters of Baptism in the eleventh year of his reign, which was the year of our Lord 627, and about one hundred and eighty years after the first arrival of the English in Britain. The king's Baptism took place at York on Easter Day, the 12th of April, in the church of Saint Peter the Apostle, which the king had hastily built of timber during the time of his instruction and preparation for Baptism; and in this city he established the see of his teacher and bishop Paulinus. Soon after his Baptism, at Paulinus' suggestion, he gave orders to build on the same site a larger and more noble basilica of stone, which was to enclose the little oratory he had built before. The foundations were laid, and the walls of a square church began to rise around this little oratory; but before they reached their appointed height, the cruel death of the king left the work to be completed by Oswald his successor. Thenceforward for six years, until the close of Edwin's reign, Paulinus preached the word in that province with the king's full consent and approval, and as many as were predestined to eternal life believed and were baptized. . . .

REVIEW QUESTIONS

1. Analyze the two conversion processes that Bede describes. What do they reveal about Anglo-Saxon culture, the role of the king, and the king's relationship with his people?

2. Why, ultimately, did both Ethelbert and Edwin decide to become Christian, according to Bede? What did they—and their peoples—stand to gain?

3. Compare these conversion experiences with that of Clovis (pp. 215–219). What do the differences and similarities suggest about the cultural ties between the Anglo-Saxons and the Franks?

FROM The Anglo-Saxon Translation of *The Book of Genesis*

Following the initial missionary efforts of Latin-speaking emissaries from Rome, the bishops and monastic communities of Anglo-Saxon England became active in developing new ways to spread knowledge of the Christian faith to lay audiences. One powerful mechanism for doing this was to translate portions of the Gospels (the New Testament) or the Hebrew Bible (the Old Testament) into the Anglo-Saxon vernacular. But as this excerpt from an Anglo-Saxon version of Genesis reveals, translation often involves much more than translating words: concepts, customs, social structures, assumptions, and values must also be translated in order to make them comprehensible to a new audience. Comparing the resulting version of the story with that written in the Hebrew Bible reveals a great deal about the Anglo-Saxon worldview and the profound ways in which it differed from that of the ancient Hebrews. As you read, bear in mind that this text was actually written down in verse at about the same time as the epic poem Beowulf.

Genesis 3:1–7 (Revised Standard Version of the Hebrew Bible)*

Now the serpent was more subtle than any other wild creature that the Lord God had made. He said to the woman, "Did God say, 'You shall not eat of any tree of the garden'?" And the woman said to the serpent, "We may eat of the fruit of the trees of the garden; but God said, 'You shall not eat of the fruit of the tree which is in the midst of the garden, neither shall you touch it, lest you die.'" But the serpent said to the woman, "You will not die. For God knows that when you eat of it your eyes will be opened, and you will be like God, knowing good and evil." So when the woman saw that the tree was good for food, and that it was a delight to the eyes, and that the tree was to be desired to make one wise, she took of its fruit and ate; and she also gave some to her husband, and he ate. Then the eyes of both were opened, and they knew that they were naked; and they sewed fig leaves together and made themselves aprons.

The Anglo-Saxon Translation*

442   Then an adversary of God eager in his accoutrements got himself ready: he had an evil sense of purpose. He set on his head a concealing helm and fastened it very tightly and secured it with clasps. He had in him knowledge of plenty of speeches of perverse words. From there he wound his way upwards and passed through the gates

---

*From the *Revised Standard Version of the Bible*, National Council of Churches of Christ in America, http://quod.lib.umich.edu/r/rsv/.

*From *Anglo-Saxon Poetry: An Anthology of Old English Poems in Prose Translations with Introduction and Headnotes*, by S. A. J. Bradley (New York: Everyman's Library, 1982), pp. 25–32.

of hell—he had a strong sense of purpose—and hovered aloft, malevolent-minded. He beat down the fire on both sides with his fiend's strength: he meant surreptitiously to seduce, to lead astray and to pervert with wicked deeds the followers of the Lord, men, so that they would become repugnant to God.

453 He journeyed on then with his fiend's strength until in the kingdom of earth he came upon the perfected Adam, God's wisely created handiwork, and his wife also, a most beautiful woman, so that they could accomplish much good whom mankind's ordaining Lord himself had appointed as his subordinates.

460 And near them stood two trees which were laden with a crop and covered with fruit according as God the Ruler, the high King of heaven, had planted them with his hands in order that thereby the children of men, each person, might choose between good and evil, well-being and woe. Their fruit was not alike. The one was so pleasant, beautiful and radiant, graceful and admirable—that was the tree of life. He would be allowed thereafter to live on and to exist in the world in eternity who ate of that fruit, so that age did not harm him after that nor severe sickness, but he would be allowed from then on always to live among pleasures and to have his existence and the heaven-King's favour here in the world and to have as his pledge assured honours in that high heaven when he should journey there. Then there was the other, entirely black, obscure and dark—that was the tree of death which brought forth much bitterness. Each man soever that tasted of what grew on that tree must needs become aware of the two things, the divergent ways of good and of evil in this world, and thereafter he would have to live by his sweat and in sorrows, forever under punishment. Old age must needs rob him of valorous deeds, of

pleasures and of authority, and death be decreed him. For a little while he would enjoy his life and then go to the darkest of realms, into the fire, and would have to minister to fiends there where there will exist for an infinite duration the greatest of all perils for men. That the malignant creature, the devil's secret messenger who was contending against God, well knew.

491 He turned himself then into the form of a snake and then wound himself about the tree of death with the cunning of a devil; there he plucked a fruit and went thence back again to where he perceived the heaven-King's handiwork. Then in his first utterance the malignant creature began to question him with lies:

496 'Do you long for anything, Adam, from God above? I have journeyed here from far away on his business; it was not long since that I sat by his very self. He then commanded me to go on this mission. He commanded that you should eat of this fruit and he declared that your strength and skill and your mind would grow greater, and your body much more beautiful, your limbs more handsome, and he declared that to you there would prove no want of any wealth in the world. You have now done the will of the heaven-King and your loyal duty to him and served your Master to his satisfaction and you have made yourself precious to the Lord. I heard him in his splendour praise your deeds and your words and speak about your way of life. Accordingly, you are to carry out what his messengers bring word of here into this country. Broad are the green regions in the world and God, the Ruler of all, sits above in the most exalted realm of the heavens. The Lord of men is unwilling himself to have the hardships of travelling on this mission; rather he sends his subordinate to speak with you. Now he has commanded me to teach you by messages cunning skills. Carry out his bid-

ding confidently. Take this fruit into your hand, bite it and taste it. Within your breast you will become untrammelled and your outward form will become the more beautiful. God the Ruler, your Lord, has sent you this help from the heaven-kingdom.'

522 Adam, the self-determined man, standing there on the earth, spoke out:

523 'When I heard the triumphant Lord, mighty God, speak with stern voice, and when he commanded me to establish myself here and to keep his behests and gave me this wife, this lovely woman, and commanded me take heed that I should not be brought to ruin or utterly betrayed over that tree of death, he declared that he would have to inhabit black hell who of his own volition did anything evil. I do not know whether you come with lies from a hidden motive or whether you are the messenger of the Lord from heaven. You see, I cannot make any sense of your suggestions, of your words and reasons, your mission and declarations. I do know what he, our Saviour, himself enjoined upon me when I saw him last: he commanded me to honour and keep well his word and carry out his precepts. You are not like any of his angels whom I saw before, nor have you shown me any token that my Master has sent to me out of his favour and out of his grace. Therefore I cannot obey you, and you may go your way. I have a firm trust above in the almighty God who fashioned me here with his arms and with his hands. He is capable of endowing me with every advantage from his high kingdom, even if he did not send his subordinate.'

547 He turned himself, the malevolent creature, to where in earth's domain he saw the woman Eve standing, beautifully formed; and he declared to her that it would prove the greatest harm in the world to all their children thereafter:

551 'I am certain that the Lord God will be incensed against the two of you when I return from this journey along the lengthy road if I personally tell him this message, that you two do not properly act upon whatever message he sends here from the east on this occasion. Now he himself will have to make the journey, according to your answer. His spokesman is not allowed to speak his business, therefore I am certain that in his heart he, the mighty God, is going to be incensed against you. But if you, a compliant woman, will listen to my words then you will be able to think circumspectly about a remedy for it. Consider in your heart that you can fend off punishment from the pair of you, as I shall show you.

564 'Eat of this fruit. Then your eyes will become so clear that you will afterwards be able to see as widely as beyond the whole world and the throne of your Master himself, and henceforth to enjoy his favour. You will be able moreover to manipulate Adam if you command his desire and he trusts in your words. If you tell him truly what an exemplary precept you yourself hold in your bosom, because you have carried out God's bidding and counsel, he will abandon in his heart this distasteful antagonism and his ill response, if we two both talk to him with effect. Coax him carefully so that he carries out your counsel, lest you should both be forced to prove abhorrent to God your Ruler.

578 'If you achieve that design, most excellent lady, I will conceal from your Master that Adam spoke so much insult and so many contemptible words to me. He accuses me of lies and says that I am a messenger intent upon malicious and hostile things, and not an angel of God. But I know the whole race of angels and the lofty roofs of the heavens so well, so long has been the time I have eagerly served God, my Master, the Lord

himself, with loyal resolution. I am not like a devil.'

588   So he led her on with lies and by cunning coaxed on the woman in that mischief until the snake's thinking began to seethe up inside her—the ordaining Lord had defined for her a frailer resolution—so that she began to let her mind go along with those counsels. Therefore she received from the abhorrent foe, against the word of the Lord, the tree of death's injurious fruit. A deed more evil was not defined for men. It is a great wonder that eternal God, the Prince, would ever tolerate it that so many a servant should be led astray by lies as happened because of those counsels.

599   She ate of the fruit then and violated the word and the will of the Ruler of all. Then through the gift of the abhorrent foe who betrayed her with lies and subtly defrauded her, which came to her because of his doings, she was enabled to see far afield so that heaven and earth seemed brighter to her and all this world more beautiful and God's work great and mighty—although she did not view it by means of a human perception, but the destroyer who had lent her the vision assiduously deluded her in her spirit so that she could gaze so widely over the heavenly domain.

609   Then the apostate spoke out of his malevolence; he did not teach her anything at all of profit:

611   'Now you can see for yourself, so I do not need to tell you it, virtuous Eve, that appearances and forms are different since you trusted in my words and carried out my counsels. Now light shines out before you and gracious radiance towards you which I have brought from God, gleaming from out of the heavens. Now you can lay hold on it.

Tell Adam what powers of vision you possess through my coming. If even now he carries out my counsels in modest manner, then I shall give him abundance of this light with which, so virtuous, I have adorned you. I shall not reproach him for those blasphemies, even though he is not worthy of being excused for he expressed much that was abhorrent to me.'

623   So must her children live in their turn: when they do something abhorrent they must achieve an amicable settlement, make good the blaspheming of their Master and enjoy his favour from then on.

626   To Adam then she went, the most lovely of women, the most beautiful of wives that might come into the world, because she was the work of the hand of the heaven-King, even though she had then been subtly corrupted and led astray by lies so that they were to prove abhorrent to God through the enemy's scheming and were to lose the esteem and favour of their Master through the devil's devices and to forfeit the kingdom of heaven for many a season. Misery replete will befall the man who does not keep on his guard while he enjoys self-determination.

636   One unblessed apple she carried in her hand, one lay at her heart, the fruit of the tree of death which the Lord of lords had previously forbidden her; and the Prince of glory had uttered this pronouncement, that men, his servants, lay under no necessity of suffering that great death, but he, the holy Lord, granted to each one of his people the kingdom of heaven and copious wealth if they would let be that one fruit which the abhorrent tree bore on its boughs, filled with bitterness: it was death's tree which the Lord forbade them. Her, then, and the mentality of Eve, the frail mind of woman, he seduced who was hostile to God and in hatred

of the heaven-King, so that she believed in his words, carried out his counsels, and accepted in trust that he had brought those precepts from God which he so carefully communicated to her in his words and showed her a sign and gave assurance of his good faith and honest intent. Then she spoke to her master:

655 'Adam, my lord, this fruit is so sweet and delectable in my breast, and this handsome messenger is God's good angel: I see by his apparel that he is the envoy of our Master, the King of heaven. His favour is better for us to win than his enmity. If you spoke anything hurtful to him today he will nevertheless forgive it, if we two are willing to pay him deference. What will it avail you, such detestable quarrelling with your Master's messenger? We need his favour. He can intercede for us with the Ruler of all, the King of heaven. I can see from here where he himself is sitting—it is to the south-east—surrounded with wealth, who shaped the world. I see his angels moving about him on their wings, the hugest of all throngs, of multitudes the most joyous. Who could give me such discernment if God, the Ruler of heaven, had not sent it directly to me? I can hear amply and see so widely into all the world and beyond this spacious creation, I can hear the ethereal merriment in the heavens. My mind has become enlightened within and without since I ate the fruit. I have some of it here in my hands now, virtuous master. I give it to you gladly. I believe that it has come from God, brought by his command— so this messenger has told me with truthful words. It is like nothing else on earth except that, as this envoy says, it has come directly from God.'

684 She talked to him repeatedly and coaxed him the whole day towards the dismal act, that they should violate their Lord's will. The malignant messenger stayed; he foisted desires upon them, enticed them with cunning and audaciously dogged them. The fiend remained very close, who had travelled on the audacious journey along the lengthy road: he meant to make man fall into that great and mortal sin, to misguide people and lead them astray so that they should forgo God's benefaction, the Almighty's gift, possession of the kingdom of heaven. Indeed, the hellish mischief-maker well knew that they must be subject to God's wrath and imprisonment in hell and of necessity undergo that forcible oppression once they had broken God's command, when with lying words he misguided the lovely woman, the most beautiful of wives, into that indiscretion, so that she spoke under his will and became as an instrument to him in misguiding God's handiwork.

704 She talked quite often to Adam, then, this most lovely of women, until the man's mind was changed, so that he put his trust in the promise which the woman expressed to him in her words. Yet she did it out of loyal intent. She did not know that there were to follow so many hurts and terrible torments for humankind because she took to heart what she heard in the counsellings of that abhorrent messenger; but rather she thought that she was gaining the favour of the heavenly King with those words which she presented to the man as a sign, and gave assurance of her good faith until within his breast Adam's determination wavered and his heart began to incline towards her desire. From the woman he accepted hell and departure hence, though it was not so called, but had the name of fruit. Yet it was the sleep of death and the yoke of the devil, hell and death, and the perdition of men, the murder of mankind, that unholy fruit which they took as their food.

REVIEW QUESTIONS

1. Carefully compare this excerpt from the Anglo-Saxon Genesis with the parallel portion of the Hebrew Genesis to which it corresponds. What are the major differences—in length, style, structure, and content?

2. How do these differences constitute historical evidence that can assist in constructing a picture of Anglo-Saxon society in the centuries following the arrival of Roman missionaries?

3. The Anglo-Saxon depiction of Eve, in particular, departs from that of the Hebrew Bible. What does this reveal about the status of women in Anglo-Saxon society?

EINHARD

FROM *The Life of Charlemagne*

The author of this official biography of Charlemagne (r. 768–814) was his close friend and younger contemporary, Einhard (c. 775–840). One of the many able scholars who were attracted to the Carolingian court, Einhard appears to have been an intimate member of Charlemagne's household circle and, after Charlemagne's death, a close associate and supporter of his son, Louis the Pious (r. 814–40). In his efforts to glorify Charlemagne's memory and legacy, he modeled this biography on an earlier life of the first Roman emperor, Augustus Caesar.

From *Two Lives of Charlemagne*, edited by Lewis Thorpe (New York: Penguin, 1969), pp. 73–82.

*   *   *

The Emperor's Private Life

What has gone before is a fair picture of Charlemagne and all that he did to protect and enlarge his kingdom, and indeed to embellish it. I shall now speak of his intellectual qualities, his extraordinary strength of character, whether in prosperity or adversity, and all the other details of his personal and domestic life.

After the death of his father, at the time when he was sharing the kingship with Carloman, Charlemagne bore with such patience this latter's hatred and jealousy that everyone was surprised that he never lost his temper with his brother.

Then, at the bidding of his mother, he married the daughter of Desiderius, the King of the Longobards [Lombards, of northern Italy]. Nobody knows why, but he dismissed this wife after one year. Next he married Hildigard, a woman of most noble family, from the Swabian race. By her he had three sons, Charles, Pepin and Lewis, and the same number of daughters, Rotrude, Bertha and Gisela. He had three more daughters, Theoderada, Hiltrude and Rothaide, two of these by his third wife, Fastrada, who was from the race of Eastern Franks or Germans, and the last by a concubine whose name I cannot remember. Fastrada died and he married Luitgard, from the Alamanni, but she bore him no children. After Luitgard's death, he took four concubines: Madelgard, who bore him a daughter Ruothilde; Gersvinda, of the Saxon race, by whom he had a daughter Adaltrude; Regina,

who bore him Drogo and Hugo; and Adallinda, who became the mother of Theodoric.

Charlemagne's own mother, Bertrada, lived with him in high honour to a very great age. He treated her with every respect and never had a cross word with her, except over the divorce of King Desiderius' daughter, whom he had married on her advice. Bertrada died soon after Hildigard, living long enough to see three grandsons and as many granddaughters in her son's house. Charlemagne buried her with great honour in the church of Saint Denis, where his father lay.

He had a single sister, Gisela by name, who from her childhood onwards had been dedicated to the religious life. He treated her with the same respect which he showed his mother. She died a few years before Charlemagne himself, in the nunnery where she had spent her life.

Charlemagne was determined to give his children, his daughters just as much as his sons, a proper training in the liberal arts which had formed the subject of his own studies. As soon as they were old enough he had his sons taught to ride in the Frankish fashion, to use arms and to hunt. He made his daughters learn to spin and weave wool, use the distaff and spindle, and acquire every womanly accomplishment, rather than fritter away their time in sheer idleness.

Of all his children he lost only two sons and one daughter prior to his own death. These were his eldest son Charles, Pepin whom he had made King of Italy, and Rotrude, the eldest of his daughters, who had been engaged to Constantine, the Emperor of the Greeks.[1] Pepin left one son, called Bernard, and five daughters, Adelhaid, Atula, Gundrada, Berthaid and Theoderada. Charlemagne gave clear proof of the affection which he bore them all, for after the death of Pepin he ordered his grandson Bernard to succeed and he had his granddaughters brought up with his own girls. He bore the death of his two sons and his daughter with less fortitude than one would have expected, considering the strength of his

character; for his emotions as a father, which were very deeply rooted, made him burst into tears.

When the death of Hadrian, the Pope of Rome [r. 772–795] and his close friend, was announced to him, he wept as if he had lost a brother or a dearly loved son. He was firm and steady in his human relationships, developing friendship easily, keeping it up with care and doing everything he possibly could for anyone whom he had admitted to this degree of intimacy.

He paid such attention to the upbringing of his sons and daughters that he never sat down to table without them when he was at home, and never set out on a journey without taking them with him. His sons rode at his side and his daughters followed along behind. Hand-picked guards watched over them as they closed the line of march. These girls were extraordinarily beautiful and greatly loved by their father. It is a remarkable fact that, as a result of this, he kept them with him in his household until the very day of his death, instead of giving them in marriage to his own men or to foreigners, maintaining that he could not live without them. The consequence was that he had a number of unfortunate experiences, he who had been so lucky in all else that he undertook. However, he shut his eyes to all that happened, as if no suspicion of any immoral conduct had ever reached him, or as if the rumour was without foundation.

I did not mention with the others a son called Pepin who was born to Charlemagne by a concubine. He was handsome enough, but a hunchback. At a moment when his father was wintering in Bavaria, soon after the beginning of his campaign against the Huns, this Pepin pretended to be ill and conspired with certain of the Frankish leaders who had won him over to their cause by pretending to offer him the kingship. The plot was discovered and the conspirators were duly punished. Pepin was tonsured and permitted to take up, in the monastery of Prūm, the life of a religious for which he had already expressed a vocation.

Earlier on there had been another dangerous conspiracy against Charlemagne in Germany. All

---

[1] Constantine II (780–797).

the plotters were exiled, some having their eyes put out first, but the others were not maltreated physically. Only three of them were killed. These resisted arrest, drew their swords and started to defend themselves. They slaughtered a few men in the process and had to be destroyed themselves, as there was no other way of dealing with them.

The cruelty of Queen Fastrada is thought to have been the cause of both these conspiracies, since it was under her influence that Charlemagne seemed to have taken actions which were fundamentally opposed to his normal kindliness and good nature. Throughout the remainder of his life he so won the love and favour of all his fellow human beings, both at home and abroad, that no one ever levelled against him the slightest charge of cruelty or injustice.

He loved foreigners and took great pains to make them welcome. So many visited him as a result that they were rightly held to be a burden not only to the palace, but to the entire realm. In his magnanimity he took no notice at all of this criticism, for he considered that his reputation for hospitality and the advantage of the good name which he acquired more than compensated for the great nuisance of their being there.

The Emperor was strong and well built. He was tall in stature, but not excessively so, for his height was just seven times the length of his own feet. The top of his head was round, and his eyes were piercing and unusually large. His nose was slightly longer than normal, he had a fine head of white hair and his expression was gay and good-humoured. As a result, whether he was seated or standing, he always appeared masterful and dignified. His neck was short and rather thick, and his stomach a trifle too heavy, but the proportions of the rest of his body prevented one from noticing these blemishes. His step was firm and he was manly in all his movements. He spoke distinctly, but his voice was thin for a man of his physique. His health was good, except that he suffered from frequent attacks of fever during the last four years of his life, and towards the end he was lame in one foot. Even then he continued to do exactly as he wished, instead of following the advice of his doctors, whom he came positively to dislike after

they advised him to stop eating the roast meat to which he was accustomed and to live on stewed dishes.

He spent much of his time on horseback and out hunting, which came naturally to him, for it would be difficult to find another race on earth who could equal the Franks in this activity. He took delight in steam-baths at the thermal springs, and loved to exercise himself in the water whenever he could. He was an extremely strong swimmer and in this sport no one could surpass him. It was for this reason that he built his palace at Aachen and remained continuously in residence there during the last years of his life and indeed until the moment of his death. He would invite not only his sons to bathe with him, but his nobles and friends as well, and occasionally even a crowd of his attendants and bodyguards, so that sometimes a hundred men or more would be in the water together.

He wore the national dress of the Franks. Next to his skin he had a linen shirt and linen drawers; and then long hose and a tunic edged with silk. He wore shoes on his feet and bands of cloth wound round his legs. In winter he protected his chest and shoulders with a jerkin made of otter skins or ermine. He wrapped himself in a blue cloak and always had a sword strapped to his side, with a hilt and belt of gold or silver. Sometimes he would use a jewelled sword, but this was only on great feast days or when ambassadors came from foreign peoples. He hated the clothes of other countries, no matter how becoming they might be, and he would never consent to wear them. The only exception to this was one day in Rome when Pope Hadrian entreated him to put on a long tunic and a Greek mantle, and to wear shoes made in the Roman fashion; and then a second time, when Leo, Hadrian's successor, persuaded him to do the same thing. On feast days he walked in procession in a suit of cloth of gold, with jewelled shoes, his cloak fastened with a golden brooch and with a crown of gold and precious stones on his head. On ordinary days his dress differed hardly at all from that of the common people.

He was moderate in his eating and drinking, and especially so in drinking; for he hated to see

drunkenness in any man, and even more so in himself and his friends. All the same, he could not go long without food, and he often used to complain that fasting made him feel ill. He rarely gave banquets and these only on high feast days, but then he would invite a great number of guests. His main meal of the day was served in four courses, in addition to the roast meat which his hunters used to bring in on spits and which he enjoyed more than any other food. During his meal he would listen to a public reading or some other entertainment. Stories would be recited for him, or the doings of the ancients told again. He took great pleasure in the books of Saint Augustine and especially in those which are called *The City of God*.

He was so sparing in his use of wine and every other beverage that he rarely drank more than three times in the course of his dinner. In summer, after his midday meal, he would eat some fruit and take another drink; then he would remove his shoes and undress completely, just as he did at night, and rest for two or three hours. During the night he slept so lightly that he would wake four or five times and rise from his bed. When he was dressing and putting on his shoes he would invite his friends to come in. Moreover, if the Count of the Palace told him that there was some dispute which could not be settled without the Emperor's personal decision, he would order the disputants to be brought in there and then, hear the case as if he were sitting in tribunal and pronounce a judgement. If there was any official business to be transacted on that day, or any order to be given to one of his ministers, he would settle it at the same time.

He spoke easily and fluently, and could express with great clarity whatever he had to say. He was not content with his own mother tongue, but took the trouble to learn foreign languages. He learnt Latin so well that he spoke it as fluently as his own tongue; but he understood Greek better than he could speak it. He was eloquent to the point of sometimes seeming almost garrulous.

He paid the greatest attention to the liberal arts; and he had great respect for men who taught them, bestowing high honours upon them. When he was learning the rules of grammar he received tuition from Peter the Deacon of Pisa, who by then was an old man, but for all other subjects he was taught by Alcuin, surnamed Albinus, another Deacon, a man of the Saxon race who came from Britain and was the most learned man anywhere to be found. Under him the Emperor spent much time and effort in studying rhetoric, dialectic and especially astrology. He applied himself to mathematics and traced the course of the stars with great attention and care. He also tried to learn to write. With this object in view he used to keep writing-tablets and notebooks under the pillows on his bed, so that he could try his hand at forming letters during his leisure moments; but, although he tried very hard, he had begun too late in life and he made little progress.

Charlemagne practised the Christian religion with great devotion and piety, for he had been brought up in this faith since earliest childhood. This explains why he built a cathedral of such great beauty at Aachen, decorating it with gold and silver, with lamps, and with lattices and doors of solid bronze. He was unable to find marble columns for his construction anywhere else, and so he had them brought from Rome and Ravenna.

As long as his health lasted, he went to church morning and evening with great regularity, and also for early-morning Mass, and the late-night hours. He took the greatest pains to ensure that all church ceremonies were performed with the utmost dignity, and he was always warning the sacristans to see that nothing sordid or dirty was brought into the building or left there. He donated so many sacred vessels made of gold and silver, and so many priestly vestments, that when service time came even those who opened and closed the doors, surely the humblest of all church dignitaries, had no need to perform their duties in their everyday clothes.

He made careful reforms in the way in which the psalms were chanted and the lessons read. He was himself quite an expert at both of these exercises, but he never read the lesson in public and he would sing only with the rest of the congregation and then in a low voice.

He was most active in relieving the poor and in that form of really disinterested charity which the Greeks call *eleemosyna*. He gave alms not only in his own country and in the kingdom over which he reigned, but also across the sea in Syria, Egypt, Africa, Jerusalem, Alexandria and Carthage. Wherever he heard that Christians were living in want, he took pity on their poverty and sent them money regularly. It was, indeed, precisely for this reason that he sought the friendship of kings beyond the sea, for he hoped that some relief and alleviation might result for the Christians living under their domination.

Charlemagne cared more for the church of the holy Apostle Peter in Rome than for any other sacred and venerable place. He poured into its treasury a vast fortune in gold and silver coinage and in precious stones. He sent so many gifts to the Pope that it was impossible to keep count of them. Throughout the whole period of his reign nothing was ever nearer to his heart than that, by his own efforts and exertion, the city of Rome should regain its former proud position. His ambition was not merely that the church of Saint Peter should remain safe and protected thanks to him, but that by means of his wealth it should be more richly adorned and endowed than any other church. However much he thought of Rome, it still remains true that throughout his whole reign of forty-seven years he went there only four times to fulfil his vows and to offer up his prayers.

These were not the sole reasons for Charlemagne's last visit to Rome. The truth is that the inhabitants of Rome had violently attacked Pope Leo [r. 795–816], putting out his eyes and cutting off his tongue, and had forced him to flee to the King for help. Charlemagne really came to Rome to restore the Church, which was in a very bad state indeed, but in the end he spent the whole winter there. It was on this occasion that he received the title of Emperor and Augustus. At first he was far from wanting this. He made it clear that he would not have entered the cathedral that day at all, although it was the greatest of all the festivals of the Church, if he had known in advance what the Pope was planning to do. Once he

had accepted the title, he endured with great patience the jealousy of the so-called Roman Emperors, who were most indignant at what had happened. He overcame their hostility only by the sheer strength of his personality, which was much more powerful than theirs. He was for ever sending messengers to them, and in his dispatches he called them his brothers.

Now that he was Emperor, he discovered that there were many defects in the legal system of his own people, for the Franks have two separate codes of law which differ from each other in many points. He gave much thought to how he could best fill the gaps, reconcile the discrepancies, correct the errors and rewrite the laws which were ill-expressed. None of this was ever finished; he added a few sections, but even these remained incomplete. What he did do was to have collected together and committed to writing the laws of all the nations under his jurisdiction which still remained unrecorded.

At the same time he directed that the age-old narrative poems, barbarous enough, it is true, in which were celebrated the warlike deeds of the kings of ancient times, should be written out and so preserved. He also began a grammar of his native tongue.

*   *   *

REVIEW QUESTIONS

1. According to Einhard, what aspects of Charlemagne's policies and personality made him an effective ruler? Does Einhard seem to be masking any of the emperor's weaknesses? Why?

2. What can we learn from this source about the role and status of women in the Carolingian court?

3. How does this portrait of Charlemagne by an intimate member of his court compare with that of Justinian by Procopius (pp. 224–226)? How would you account for the differences in tone, style, and content?

8 ✠ THE EXPANSION OF EUROPE, 950–1100

The central Middle Ages witnessed tremendous economic growth, which began in agriculture, the basis of the medieval economy. All societies in Europe, North Africa, and the Middle East remained overwhelmingly rural and depended on villages of peasants to produce the food and supplies needed to sustain urban life and emerging state bureaucracies. Better technology for vital tools such as plows and harnesses, accurate record keeping, and more benign weather all contributed to the improved yields in crops and flocks.

About the year 1000, Christian Europe had only a few small cities, whereas the Muslim world contained many large ones in Spain, Sicily, and the Middle East. Most European cities rapidly increased in population in the following centuries, a growth that depended on adequate food supplies, either produced locally or acquired through trade. People living in towns also needed certain rights and liberties to transact business, and urban people wanted secure land ownership; personal liberty, including freedom of travel; and a sound coinage. Merchants did not want to resort to feuds and vendettas to settle their disputes. Kings and lords were prepared to grant some liberties to towns in exchange for money. Urban wealth largely resulted from trade and a modest level of artisan manufactures, especially cloth.

Fending off invaders (like the Vikings) and dispensing justice remained the main tasks of medieval rulers in this era. But secular rulers also had a new rival: the papacy. Beginning in the eleventh century, powerful voices within the Church called for a series of reforms that would not only eradicate perceived abuses of clerical authority but would also strengthen the power of the clergy and aggrandize the role of the Roman pope. Eventually, this reformed Church had the authority to define more closely all liberties and duties, but this was not usually good news for women or for religious or ethnic minorities. Persecution and subjugation were also the result of a new Christian ideology: crusading. In an effort to quell violence within Europe, the papacy took advantage of a call for assistance from the Byzantine emperor Alexius Commenus, urging fractious nobles and landless knights to seek salvation, glory, and treasure overseas. But

many Crusaders chose to use this mandate closer to home, assaulting and even massacring communities of Jesus. Meanwhile, the rhetoric of crusading entered into popular storytelling traditions and inflamed a parallel discourse of religious warfare within certain Muslim communities.

POPE GREGORY VII

Letter to Bishop Hermann of Metz

Pope Gregory VII (r. 1073–85) wrote this letter to Bishop Hermann of Metz to justify his decision to excommunicate Emperor Henry IV of Germany and to explain his views on the role of the Church in the world. The pope's dispute with Henry IV concerned the emperor's claim to appoint bishops and abbots. The pope considered these appointments to be in the Church's jurisdiction, and other reformers were also troubled by churchmen who became vassals of a secular lord. Homage and fealty for fiefs gave the appearance that secular power was superior to spiritual power. This letter is a concise statement of the reform movement's position.

From *The Correspondence of Pope Gregory VII*, edited by Ephriam Emerton (New York: Columbia University Press, 1969), pp. 166–75.

Gregory to his beloved brother in Christ, Hermann, bishop of Metz, greeting . . .

We know you to be ever ready to bear labor and peril in defense of the truth, and doubt not that this is a gift from God. It is a part of his unspeakable grace and his marvelous mercy that he never permits his chosen ones to wander far or to be completely cast down; but rather, after a time of persecution and wholesome probation, makes them stronger than they were before. On the other hand, just as among cowards one who is worse than the rest is broken down by fear, so among the brave one who acts more bravely than the rest is stirred thereby to new activity. We remind you of this by way of exhortation that you may stand more joyfully in the front ranks of the Christian host, the more confident you are that they are the nearest to God the conqueror.

You ask us to fortify you against the madness of those who babble with accursed tongues about the authority of the Holy Apostolic See not being able to excommunicate King Henry as one who despises the law of Christ, a destroyer of churches and of the empire, a promoter and partner of heresies, nor to release anyone from his oath of fidelity to him; but it has not seemed necessary to reply to this request, seeing that so many and such convincing proofs are to be found in Holy Scripture. Nor do we believe that those who abuse and contradict the truth to their utter damnation do this as much from ignorance as from wretched and desperate folly. And no wonder! It is ever the way of the wicked to protect their own iniquities by calling upon others like themselves; for they think it of no account to incur the penalty of falsehood.

To cite but a few out of the multitude of proofs: Who does not remember the words of our

Lord and Savior Jesus Christ: "Thou art Peter and on this rock I will build my Church, and the gates of hell shall not prevail against it. And I will give thee the keys of the kingdom of heaven and whatsoever thou shalt bind on earth shall be bound in heaven and whatsoever thou shalt loose on earth shall be loosed in heaven." Are kings excepted here? Or are they not of the sheep which the Son of God committed to St. Peter? Who, I ask, thinks himself excluded from this universal grant of the power of binding and loosing to St. Peter unless, perchance, that unhappy man who, being unwilling to bear the yoke of the Lord, subjects himself to the burden of the Devil and refuses to be numbered in the flock of Christ? His wretched liberty shall profit him nothing; for if he shakes off from his proud neck the power divinely granted to Peter, so much the heavier shall it be for him in the day of judgment.

This institution of the divine will, this foundation of the rule of the Church, this privilege granted and sealed especially by a heavenly decree to St. Peter, chief of the Apostles, has been accepted and maintained with great reverence by the holy fathers, and they have given to the Holy Roman Church, as well in general councils as in their other acts and writings, the name of "universal mother." They have not only accepted her expositions of doctrine and her instructions in our holy religion, but they have also recognized her judicial decisions. They have agreed as with one spirit and one voice that all major cases, all especially important affairs and the judgments of all churches ought to be referred to her as to their head and mother, that from her there shall be no appeal, that her judgments may not and cannot be reviewed or reversed by anyone.

Thus Pope Gelasius, writing to the emperor Anastasius, gave him these instructions as to the right theory of the principate of the Holy and Apostolic See, based upon divine authority:

Although it is fitting that all the faithful should submit themselves to all priests who perform their sacred functions properly, how much the more should they accept the judgment of that prelate who has been appointed by the supreme divine ruler to be superior to all priests and whom the loyalty of the whole later Church has recognized as such. Your Wisdom sees plainly that no human capacity whatsoever can equal that of him whom the word of Christ raised above all others and whom the reverend Church has always confessed and still devotedly holds as its Head.

So also Pope Julius, writing to the eastern bishops in regard to the powers of the same Holy and Apostolic See, says:

You ought, my brethren, to have spoken carefully and not ironically of the Holy Roman and Apostolic Church, seeing that our Lord Jesus Christ addressed her respectfully, saying, "Thou art Peter and upon this rock I will build my church, and the gates of hell shall not prevail against it; and I will give thee the keys of the kingdom of heaven." For it has the power, granted by a unique privilege, of opening and shutting the gates of the celestial kingdom to whom it will.

To whom, then, the power of opening and closing Heaven is given, shall he not be able to judge the earth? God forbid! Do you remember what the most blessed Apostle Paul says: "Know ye not that we shall judge angels? How much more things that pertain to this life?"

So Pope Gregory declared that kings who dared to disobey the orders of the Apostolic See should forfeit their office. He wrote to a certain senator and abbot in these words:

If any king, priest, judge or secular person shall disregard this decree of ours and act contrary to it, he shall be deprived of his power and his office and shall learn that he stands condemned at the bar of God for the wrong that he has done. And unless he shall restore what he has wrongfully taken and shall have done fitting penance for his unlawful acts he shall be excluded from the sacred body and blood of our Lord and Savior Jesus Christ and at the last judgment shall receive condign punishment.

RUNESTONE AT APSA, SWEDEN (SIDE B)

This stone bears inscriptions in two different runic alphabets. Side B (pictured here) records that the stone was erected at the place where an annual assembly (in Norse, the Thing*) was traditionally held, and that its sponsor was a woman called Þóra (Thora), who was commemorating her husband, Œpir, "who armed his men in the west." It also indicates that their son witnessed the placing of the stone. Side A says simply, "Þóra raised this stone in memory of Œpir, her husband."*

Stones such as these can be found throughout Scandinavia. They commemorate the extraordinary adventures and travels of Norsemen who went on "viking" (raiding) expeditions as far west as North America and as far to the east as the lands of the Muslim caliphate. Most date from the most intense period of Viking activity, the late ninth to eleventh centuries, and all carry inscriptions in a variety of ancient alphabets whose letters are known as runes. *Some of the stones originally were painted in bright colors, and many of the inscriptions are in verse.*

256

RUNESTONE AT KJULA, SWEDEN.

The inscription on this stone records that it was raised by Alríkr (Alaric), son of Sigriðr (Sigrid), in memory of his father, a man known as Spjót ("Spear"), famous for attacking and raiding towns in the west—probably En-gland.

Think about the many ways that these runestones function as historical sources. How would you use such information—the practice of erecting these stones, their placement in the landscape, their inscriptions—to reconstruct Norse culture? For example, what do they tell us about the role of women in these societies? What do they indicate about the interactions among far-flung peoples? What do they suggest about the men they commemorate and the families these men left behind?

257

Now then, if the blessed Gregory, most gentle of doctors, decreed that kings who should disobey his orders about a hospital for strangers should be not only deposed but excommunicated and condemned in the last judgment, how can anyone blame us for deposing and excommunicating Henry, who not only disregards apostolic judgments, but so far as in him lies tramples upon his mother the Church, basely plunders the whole kingdom and destroys its churches—unless indeed it were one who is a man of his own kind?

As we know also through the teaching of St. Peter in his letter touching the ordination of Clement, where he says: "If any one were friend to those with whom he is not on speaking terms, that man is among those who would like to destroy the Church of God and, while he seems to be with us in the body, he is against us in mind and heart, and he is a far worse enemy than those who are without and are openly hostile. For he, under the forms of friendship, acts as an enemy and scatters and lays waste the Church." Consider then, my best beloved, if he passes so severe a judgment upon him who associates himself with those whom the pope opposes on account of their actions, with what severity he condemns the man himself to whom the pope is thus opposed.

But now, to return to our point: Is not a sovereignty invented by men of this world who were ignorant of God subject to that which the providence of Almighty God established for his own glory and graciously bestowed upon the world? The Son of God we believe to be God and man, sitting at the right hand of the Father as High Priest, head of all priests and ever making intercession for us. He despised the kingdom of this world wherein the sons of this world puff themselves up and offered himself as a sacrifice upon the cross.

Who does not know that kings and princes derive their origin from men ignorant of God who raised themselves above their fellows by pride, plunder, treachery, murder—in short, by every kind of crime—at the instigation of the Devil, the prince of this world, men blind with greed and intolerable in their audacity? If, then, they strive to bend the priests of God to their will, to whom

may they more properly be compared than to him who is chief over all the sons of pride? For he, tempting our High Priest, head of all priests, son of the Most High, offering him all the kingdoms of this world, said: "All these will I give thee if thou wilt fall down and worship me."

Does anyone doubt that the priests of Christ are to be considered as fathers and masters of kings and princes and of all believers? Would it not be regarded as pitiable madness if a son should try to rule his father or a pupil his master and to bind with unjust obligations the one through whom he expects to be bound or loosed, not only on earth but also in heaven? Evidently recognizing this the emperor Constantine the Great, lord over all kings and princes throughout almost the entire earth, as St. Gregory relates in his letter to the emperor Mauritius, at the holy synod of Nicaea took his place below all the bishops and did not venture to pass any judgment upon them but, even addressing them as gods, felt that they ought not to be subject to his judgment but that he ought to be bound by their decisions.

Pope Gelasius, urging upon the emperor Anastasius not to feel himself wronged by the truth that was called to his attention said: "There are two powers, O august Emperor, by which the world is governed, the sacred authority of the priesthood and the power of kings. Of these the priestly is by so much the greater as they will have to answer for kings themselves in the day of divine judgment;" and a little further: "Know that you are subject to their judgment, not that they are to be subjected to your will."

In reliance upon such declarations and such authorities, many prelates have excommunicated kings or emperors. If you ask for illustrations: Pope Innocent excommunicated the emperor Arcadius because he consented to the expulsion of St. John Chrysostom from his office. Another Roman pontiff deposed a king of the Franks, not so much on account of his evil deeds as because he was not equal to so great an office, and set in his place Pippin, father of the emperor Charles the Great, releasing all the Franks from the oath of fealty which they had sworn to him. And this is

often done by Holy Church when it absolves fighting men from their oaths to bishops who have been deposed by apostolic authority. So St. Ambrose, a holy man but not bishop of the whole Church, excommunicated the emperor Theodosius the Great for a fault which did not seem to other prelates so very grave and excluded him from the Church. He also shows in his writings that the priestly office is as much superior to royal power as gold is more precious than lead. He says: "The honor and dignity of bishops admit of no comparison. If you liken them to the splendor of kings and the diadem of princes, these are as lead compared to the glitter of gold. You see the necks of kings and princes bowed to the knees of priests, and by the kissing of hands they believe that they share the benefit of their prayers." And again: "Know that we have said all this in order to show that there is nothing in this world more excellent than a priest or more lofty than a bishop."

Your Fraternity should remember also that greater power is granted to an exorcist when he is made a spiritual emperor for the casting out of devils, than can be conferred upon any layman for the purpose of earthly dominion. All kings and princes of this earth who live not piously and in their deeds show not a becoming fear of God are ruled by demons and are sunk in miserable slavery. Such men desire to rule, not guided by the love of God, as priests are, for the glory of God and the profit of human souls, but to display their intolerable pride and to satisfy the lusts of their mind. Of these St. Augustine says in the first book of his Christian doctrine: "He who tries to rule over men—who are by nature equal to him—acts with intolerable pride." Now if exorcists have power over demons, as we have said, how much more over those who are subject to demons and are limbs of demons! And if exorcists are superior to these, how much more are priests superior to them!

Furthermore, every Christian king when he approaches his end asks the aid of a priest as a miserable suppliant that he may escape the prison of hell, may pass from darkness into light and may appear at the judgment seat of God freed from the bonds of sin. But who, layman or priest, in his last moments has ever asked the help of any earthly king for the safety of his soul? And what king or emperor has power through his office to snatch any Christian from the might of the Devil by the sacred rite of baptism, to confirm him among the sons of God and to fortify him by the holy chrism? Or—and this is the greatest thing in the Christian religion—who among them is able by his own word to create the body and blood of the Lord? or to whom among them is given the power to bind and loose in Heaven and upon earth? From this it is apparent how greatly superior in power is the priestly dignity.

Or who of them is able to ordain any clergyman in the Holy Church—much less to depose him for any fault? For bishops, while they may ordain other bishops, may in no wise depose them except by authority of the Apostolic See. How, then, can even the most slightly informed person doubt that priests are higher than kings? But if kings are to be judged by priests for their sins, by whom can they more properly be judged than by the Roman pontiff?

In short, all good Christians, whosoever they may be, are more properly to be called kings than are evil princes; for the former, seeking the glory of God, rule themselves rigorously; but the latter, seeking their own rather than the things that are of God, being enemies to themselves, oppress others tyrannically. The former are the body of the true Christ; the latter, the body of the Devil. The former rule themselves that they may reign forever with the supreme ruler. The power of the latter brings it to pass that they perish in eternal damnation with the prince of darkness who is king over all the sons of pride.

It is no great wonder that evil priests take the part of a king whom they love and fear on account of honors received from him. By ordaining any person whomsoever, they are selling their God at a bargain price. For as the elect are inseparably united to their Head, so the wicked are firmly bound to him who is head of all evil—especially against the good. But against these it is of no use to argue, but rather to pray God with tears and

groans that he may deliver them from the snares of Satan, in which they are caught, and after trial may lead them at last into knowledge of the truth.

So much for kings and emperors who, swollen with the pride of this world, rule not for God but for themselves. But since it is our duty to exhort everyone according to his station, it is our care with God's help to furnish emperors, kings and other princes with the weapons of humility that thus they may be strong to keep down the floods and waves of pride. We know that earthly glory and the cares of this world are wont especially to cause rulers to be exalted, to forget humility and, seeking their own glory, strive to excel their fellows. It seems therefore especially useful for emperors and kings, while their hearts are lifted up in the strife for glory, to learn how to humble themselves and to know fear rather than joy. Let them therefore consider carefully how dangerous, even awesome is the office of emperor or king, how very few find salvation therein, and how those who are saved through God's mercy have become far less famous in the Church by divine judgment than many humble persons. From the beginning of the world to the present day we do not find in all authentic records emperors or kings whose lives were as distinguished for virtue and piety as were those of a countless multitude of men who despised the world—although we believe that many of them were saved by the mercy of God. Not to speak of Apostles and Martyrs, who among emperors and kings was famed for his miracles as were St. Martin, St. Antony and St. Benedict? What emperor or king ever raised the dead, cleansed lepers or opened the eyes of the blind? True, Holy Church praises and honors the emperor Constantine, of pious memory, Theodosius and Honorius, Charles and Louis, as lovers of justice, champions of the Christian faith and protectors of churches, but she does not claim that they were illustrious for the splendor of their wonderful works. Or to how many names of kings or emperors has Holy Church ordered churches or altars to be dedicated or masses to be celebrated?

Let kings and princes fear lest the higher they are raised above their fellows in this life, the deeper they may be plunged in everlasting fire. Wherefore it is written: "The mighty shall suffer mighty torments." They shall render unto God an account for all men subject to their rule. But if it is no small labor for the pious individual to guard his own soul, what a task is laid upon princes in the care of so many thousands of souls! And if Holy Church imposes a heavy penalty upon him who takes a single human life, what shall be done to those who send many thousands to death for the glory of this world? These, although they say with their lips, *mea culpa,* for the slaughter of many, yet in their hearts they rejoice at the increase of their glory and neither repent of what they have done nor regret that they have sent their brothers into the world below. So that, since they do not repent with all their hearts and will not restore what they have gained by human bloodshed, their penitence before God remains without the fruits of a true repentance.

Wherefore they ought greatly to fear, and they should frequently be reminded that, as we have said, since the beginning of the world and throughout the kingdoms of the earth very few kings of saintly life can be found out of an innumerable multitude, whereas in one single chair of successive bishops—the Roman—from the time of the blessed Apostle Peter nearly a hundred are counted among the holiest of men. How can this be, except because the kings and princes of the earth, seduced by empty glory, prefer their own interests to the things of the Spirit, whereas pious pontiffs, despising vainglory, set the things of God above the things of the flesh. The former readily punish offenses against themselves but are not troubled by offenses against God; the latter quickly forgive those who sin against them but do not easily pardon offenders against God. The former, far too much given to worldly affairs, think little of spiritual things; the latter, dwelling eagerly upon heavenly subjects, despise the things of this world.

All Christians, therefore, who desire to reign with Christ are to be warned not to reign through

ambition for wordly power. They are to keep in mind the admonition of that most holy pope Gregory in his book on the pastoral office: "Of all these things what is to be followed, what held fast, except that the man strong in virtue shall come to his office under compulsion? Let him who is without virtue not come to it even though he be urged thereto." If, then, men who fear God come under compulsion with fear and trembling to the Apostolic See where those who are properly ordained become stronger through the merits of the blessed Apostle Peter, with what awe and hesitation should men ascend the throne of a king where even good and humble men like Saul and David become worse! What we have said above is thus stated in the decrees of the blessed pope Symmachus—though we have learned it by experience: "He, that is St. Peter, transmitted to his successors an unfailing endowment of merit together with an inheritance of innocence;" and again: "For who can doubt that he is holy who is raised to the height of such an office, in which if he is lacking in virtue acquired by his own merits, that which is handed down from his predecessor is sufficient. For either he raises men of distinction to bear this burden or he glorifies them after they are raised up."

Wherefore let those whom Holy Church, of its own will and with deliberate judgment, not for fleeting glory but for the welfare of multitudes, has called to royal or imperial rule—let them be obedient and ever mindful of the blessed Gregory's declaration in that same pastoral treatise: "When a man disdains to be the equal of his fellow men, he becomes like an apostate angel. Thus Saul, after his period of humility, swollen with pride, ran into excess of power. He was raised in humility, but rejected in his pride, as God bore witness, saying: 'Though thou wast little in thine own sight, wast thou not made the head of the tribes of Israel?' " and again: "I marvel how, when he was little to himself he was great before God, but when he seemed great to himself he was little before God." Let them watch and remember what God says in the Gospel: "I seek not my own glory," and, "He who would be first among you, let him be the ser-

vant of all." Let them ever place the honor of God above their own; let them embrace justice and maintain it by preserving to everyone his right; let them not enter into the counsels of the ungodly, but cling to those of religion with all their hearts. Let them not seek to make Holy Church their maid-servant or their subject, but recognizing priests, the eyes of God, as their masters and fathers, strive to do them becoming honor.

If we are commanded to honor our fathers and mothers in the flesh, how much more our spiritual parents! If he that curseth his father or his mother shall be put to death, what does he deserve who curses his spiritual father or mother? Let not princes, led astray by carnal affection, set their own sons over that flock for whom Christ shed his blood if a better and more suitable man can be found. By thus loving their own son more than God they bring the greatest evils upon the Church. For it is evident that he who fails to provide to the best of his ability so great and necessary an advantage for our holy mother, the Church, does not love God and his neighbor as befits a Christian man. If this one virtue of charity be wanting, then whatever of good the man may do will lack all saving grace.

But if they do these things in humility, keeping their love for God and their neighbor as they ought, they may count upon the mercy of him who said: "Learn of me, for I am meek and lowly of heart." If they humbly imitate him, they shall pass from their servile and transient reign into the kingdom of eternal liberty.

*   *   *

REVIEW QUESTIONS

1. What does Pope Gregory VII think is the right relationship between the Church and secular authority?
2. How effectively does he use evidence to support his case?
3. How might a supporter of Henry IV answer the pope's arguments?

ANNA COMNENA

FROM *The Alexiad*

Anna Comnena (1083–after 1148), an imperial princess, wrote The Alexiad, *an admiring biography of her father. In this selection, she is describing how Emperor Alexius engaged his mother, Anna Dalassena, in the governance of the Byzantine Empire, with a digression on Anna Dalassena's own qualities. Byzantine royal families allowed women a wide scope for participating in government. Alexius spent much of his reign defending the empire from Turkish advances in Asia Minor, and his request for help from the West was one of the motivations for the First Crusade, the centerpiece of Anna's history.*

From *The Alexiad of Anna Comnena*, edited by E. R. A. Sewter (New York: Penguin, 1969), pp. 116–23.

*   *   *

Gradually and surreptitiously he involved her more and more in state affairs; on occasions he even declared openly that without her brains and good judgement the Empire would not survive. By these means he bound her more closely to himself, but prevented her from attaining her own goal and frustrated it. She had in mind the last stage of life and dreamed of monasteries in which she would drag out her remaining years in the contemplation of wisdom. Such was her intention, the constant aim of her prayers. Despite this longing in her heart, despite the total preoccupation with a higher life, she also loved her son to a quite exceptional degree and wished somehow to bear with him the storms that buffeted the Empire (if I may apply seafaring metaphor to the manifold troubles and tumults to which it was exposed). She desired to guide the ship of state on the best possible course, in fair weather or in tempest (when waves crashed on to it from all sides), especially since the young man had only just taken his seat in the stern and put his hand to the tiller, with no previous experience of storms, winds and waves of such violence. She was constrained, therefore, by

a mother's affection for her son, and governed with him, sometimes even grasping the reins (to change the metaphor) and alone driving the chariot of power—and without accident or error. The truth is that Anna Dalassena was in any case endowed with a fine intellect and possessed besides a really first-class aptitude for governing. On the other hand, she was distracted from it by her love for God. When in the month of August (in the same indiction) Robert's crossing to Epirus compelled Alexius to leave the capital, he brought to light and put into operation his cherished plan: the whole executive power was entrusted to his mother alone and the decision was confirmed publicly in a chrysobull.[1] As it is the historian's duty not merely to summarize the deeds and decrees of good men, but as far as he can to give some details of the former and transmit the latter in full, I myself will set out the terms of this document, omitting only the subtle refinements of the scribe. It ran thus: "When danger is foreseen or some other dreadful occurrence is expected, there is no safeguard stronger than a mother who is understanding and loves her son,

---

[1] An imperial decree sealed with gold.

for if she gives counsel, her advice will be reliable; if she offers prayers, they will confer strength and certain protection. Such at any rate has been the experience of myself, your emperor, in the case of my own revered mother, who has taught and guided and sustained me throughout, from my earliest years. She had a place in aristocratic society, but her first concern was for her son and his faith in her was preserved intact. It was well known that one soul animated us, physically separated though we were, and by the grace of Christ that happy state has persisted to this day. Never were those cold words, 'mine' and 'yours,' uttered between us, and what was even more important, the prayers she poured out during all that time reached the ears of the Lord and have raised me now to the imperial throne. After I took in my hand the imperial sceptre, she found it intolerable that she was not bearing an equal share in my labours, to the interests both of your emperor and of the whole people. But now I am preparing with God's help to do battle with Rome's enemies; with much forethought an army is being recruited and thoroughly equipped; not the least of my cares, however, has been the provision of an efficient organization in financial and civil affairs. Fortunately, an impregnable bulwark for good government has been found—in the appointment of my revered mother, of all women most honoured, as controller of the entire administration. I, your emperor, therefore decree explicitly in this present chrysobull the following: because of her vast experience of secular affairs (despite the very low value she sets upon such matters), whatever she decrees in writing (whether the case be referred to her by the logothete, or by his subordinate officers, or by any other person who prepares memoranda or requests or judgements concerning remissions of public debts) shall have permanent validity as if I myself, your Serene Emperor, had issued them or after dictating them had had them committed to writing. Whatever decisions or orders are made by her, written or unwritten, reasonable or unreasonable, provided that they bear her seal (the Transfiguration and the Assumption), shall be regarded as coming from myself, by the fact that they carry the

'In the month . . .' of the current logothete.[2] Moreover, with regard to promotions and successions to the tribunals and fiscs, and in the matter of honours, offices and donations of immovable property, my saintly mother shall have full power to take whatever action shall seem good to her. Further, if any persons are promoted to the tribunals or succeed to the fiscs and are honoured with the highest or medium or lowest dignities, they shall thereafter retain these positions on a permanent basis. Again, increases of salary, additional gifts, reductions of tax, economies and diminution of payments shall be settled by her without question. In brief, nothing shall be reckoned invalid which she commands either in writing or by word of mouth, for her words and her decisions shall be reckoned as my own and none of them shall be annulled. In years to come they shall have the force of law permanently. Neither now nor in the future shall my mother be subjected to inquiry or undergo any examination whatsoever at the hands of anybody, whoever he may be. The same provision shall also hold good for her ministers and the chancellor of the time, whether their actions seem to be reasonable or ridiculous. It shall be absolutely impossible in the future to demand account of any action taken by them under the terms of this present chrysobull."

The reader may be surprised by the honour conferred on his mother by the emperor in this matter, since he yielded her precedence in everything, relinquishing the reins of government, as it were, and running alongside as she drove the imperial chariot; only in the title of emperor did he share with her the privileges of his rank. And this despite the fact that he had already passed his boyhood years and was of an age which in the case of men like him is particularly susceptible to the lust for power. Wars against the barbarians, with all their attendant trials and tribulations he was prepared to face himself, but the entire administration of affairs, the choice of civil magistrates, the accounts of the imperial revenues and expen-

---

[1] Auditor of accounts.

diture he left to his mother. At this point the reader may well censure him for transferring the government of the Empire to the gynaeconitis,[3] but had he known this woman's spirit, her surpassing virtue, intelligence and energy, his reproaches would soon have turned to admiration. For my grandmother had an exceptional grasp of public affairs, with a genius for organization and government; she was capable, in fact, of managing not only the Roman Empire, but every other empire under the sun as well. She had vast experience and a wide understanding of the motives, ultimate consequences, interrelations good and bad of various courses of action, penetrating quickly to the right solution, adroitly and safely carrying it out. Her intellectual powers, moreover, were paralleled by her command of language. She was indeed a most persuasive orator, without being verbose or long-winded. Nor did the inspiration of the argument readily desert her, for if she began on a felicitous note, she was also most successful in ending her speeches with just the right words. She was already a woman of mature years when she was called upon to exercise imperial authority, at a time of life when one's mental powers are at their best, when one's judgement is fully developed and knowledge of affairs is widest—all qualities that lend force to good administration and government. It is natural that persons of this age should not merely speak with greater wisdom than the young (as the tragic playwright says), but also act in a more expedient way. In the past, when Anna Dalassena was still looked upon as a younger woman, she had impressed everyone as "having an old head on young shoulders"; to the observant her face alone revealed Anna's inherent virtue and gravity. But, as I was saying, once he had seized power my father reserved for himself the struggles and hard labour of war, while she became so to speak an onlooker, but he made her sovereign and like a slave said and did whatever she commanded. He loved her exceedingly and depended on her for advice (such was his affection for her). His right hand he devoted to her

service; his ears listened for her bidding. In all things he was entirely subservient, in fact, to her wishes. I can sum up the whole situation thus: he was in theory the emperor, but she had real power. She was the legislator, the complete organizer and governor, while he confirmed her arrangements, written and unwritten, the former by his signature, the latter by his spoken approval. One might say that he was indeed the instrument of her power— he was not emperor, for all the decisions and ordinances of his mother satisfied him, not merely as an obedient son, but as an attentive listener to her instruction in the art of ruling. He was convinced that she had attained perfection in everything and easily excelled all men of that generation in prudence and understanding of affairs.

Such were the events that marked the beginning of the reign. One could hardly at that stage call Alexius emperor once he had entrusted to her the supreme authority. Another person might yield here to the claims of panegyric and extol the native land of this remarkable woman; he might trace her descent from the Adriani Dalasseni and Charon, while he embarked on the ocean of their achievements. But I am writing history and my fitting task is not to describe her through the family and kinsmen, but by reference to her character, her virtue, and the events which form the proper subject of history. To return once more to my grandmother, I must add this: not only was she a very great credit to her own sex, but to men as well; indeed, she contributed to the glory of the whole human race. The women's quarters in the palace had been the scene of utter depravity ever since the infamous Constantine Monomachos had ascended the throne and right up to the time when my father became emperor had been noted for foolish love intrigues, but Anna effected a reformation; a commendable decorum was restored and the palace now enjoyed a discipline that merited praise. She instituted set times for the singing of sacred hymns, stated hours for breakfast; there was now a special period in which magistrates were chosen. She herself set a firm example to everybody else, with the result that the palace assumed the appearance rather of a monastery

---

[3] I. e. the women's quarters within the palace.

under the influence of this really extraordinary woman and her truly saintly character; for in self-control she surpassed the famous women of old, heroines of many a legend, as the sun outshines all stars. As for her compassion for the poor and her generosity to the needy, no words could do justice to them. Her house was a refuge for penniless relatives, but no less for strangers. Priests and monks she honoured in particular: they shared her meals and no one ever saw her at table without some of them as guests. Her outward serenity, true reflection of character, was respected by angels but terrorized even the demons, and pleasure-loving fools, victims of their own passions, found a single glance from her more than they could bear; yet to the chaste she seemed gentle and gay. She knew exactly how to temper reserve and dignity; her own reserve never gave the impression of harshness or cruelty, nor did her tenderness seem too soft or unrestrained—and this, I fancy, is the true definition of propriety: the due proportion of warm humanity and strict moral principle. She was by nature thoughtful and was always evolving new ideas, not, as some folk whispered, to the detriment of the state; on the contrary, they were wholesome schemes which restored to full vigour the already corrupted empire and revived, as far as one could, the ruined fortunes of the people. In spite of her preoccupation with matters of government, she by no means neglected the duties incumbent on a religious woman, for the greater part of the night was spent by her in the chanting of sacred hymns and she wore herself out with continual prayers and vigils. Nevertheless, at dawn or even at second cock-crow, she was applying herself anew to state business, attending to the choice of magistrates and answering the petitions of suppliants with the help of her secretary Gregory Genesius. Now if some orator had decided to make this the subject of a panegyric, he would no doubt have exalted her and praised her to the skies (as is the way of encomiasts) for her deeds and thoughts and superiority to all others; the famous ones of old, both men and women, who were renowned for their virtue would certainly have been thrown into the shade. But such licence is not for the writer of history. Those who know her virtue, therefore, her dignified character, her never-failing sagacity and the loftiness and sublimity of her spirit, must not blame my history, if I have done less than justice to her great qualities.

*   *   *

REVIEW QUESTIONS

1. What does Anna's account reveal about the role of women within the Byzantine court? What does it reveal about the values and culture of the Eastern Roman Empire?
2. How does this picture of women's activities compare with that in Einhard's *Life of Charlemagne* (pp. 248–252)? How does it compare with Procopius's portrait of an earlier Byzantine empress, Theodora (pp. 226–228). How might you explain these differences?
3. What does Anna have to say about the proper way to write history, and about herself as an historian?

FROM *The Song of Roland*

This chanson de geste *("song about great deeds") tells the story of Charlemagne's heroic vassal Roland; his betrayal by his stepfather, Ganelon; and the avenging of his ignominious death at the hands of a Muslim army. Some of the elements that make up this epic may have begun to circulate in Charlemagne's own time, around the year 800, but when the poem was eventually committed to writing, around 1100, it more closely reflected the very recent events of the First Crusade, as well as the culture and values of the warriors from many parts of Europe who spoke the language we call French. (Indeed, the oldest surviving manuscript of the poem was produced in England.) In the following excerpt, news of Roland's death has reached Charlemagne, and now the Frankish and Muslim armies prepare for battle. The Muslim emir (commander) is Baligant.*

From *The Song of Roland*, translated by Robert Harrison (New York: Mentor, 1970), pp. 146–56.

226

Dismounting from his horse, the emperor
  [Charlemagne]
has stretched out prone upon the lush green
  grass
and turned his face to meet the rising sun.
With all his heart he prays aloud to God:
3100 "True Father, keep me safe from harm today,
as Thou most certainly protected Jonah
when he was in the body of the whale,
as Thou hath saved the king of Nineveh,
and Daniel from excruciating pain
when he was down within the lions' den,
and all three children in a burning fire!
Allow Thy love to be with me today!
And grant me, in Thy mercy, if it please Thee,
the power to avenge my nephew Roland!"
3110 Now having prayed, he rises to his feet
and on his forehead makes the mighty sign.°
The king climbs on his prancing destrier,
his stirrup held by Naimes and Jozeran,
and takes in hand his shield and sharpened
  lance.

His build is rugged, trim, and well-
  proportioned,
his features clean, his bearing confident.
He rides out, seated firmly in the saddle;
from front and rear alike the trumpets
  sound;
the oliphant booms out above the rest.
3120 The Frenchmen weep with tenderness for
  Roland.

227

With easy grace the emperor rides on,
his flowing beard fanned out upon his
  byrnie.
For love of him, the others do the same:
a hundred thousand Franks are known by
  this.
They pass those hills and soaring rocky
  bluffs,
those sunken glades, those harrowing
  ravines,
then leave behind the passes and the waste-
  lands:
they've made their way into the Spanish
  march
and set up camp upon a broad plateau.

3111. *mighty sign:* the sign of the Cross.

3130 The envoys hurry back to Baligant.
A Syrian delivers his report:
"We've had a look at arrogant King
  Charles.
His men are bold, they have no heart to fail
  him,
so arm yourself—you'll have a battle soon!"
"That's gallantry I hear!" says Baligant.
"To let my pagans know this, sound your
  trumpets."

228

Throughout the host they beat upon the
  drums
and sound those horns and brilliant clarions:
the pagans all dismount to arm themselves.
3140 The emir does not intend to lag behind:
he dons a saffron-yellow skirted byrnie
and laces up his jeweled golden casque
and then upon his left side straps his
  sword.
Through vanity he's given it a name;
because he's heard them speak of Charles's
  sword,
[he lets his own be known as "Précieuse."]°
This then will be his war cry in the field;
he orders all his knights to sing it out.
He hangs about his neck a great, broad
  shield:
3150 its boss is made of gold with crystal border,
its shoulder strap of roundel-patterned silk.
He grasps his spear, the one he calls Maltet:
its handle was as heavy as a beam,
and its tip alone would overload a mule.
Now Baligant gets on his destrier;
at his stirrup is Marcule of Outremer.
This noble lord° is lengthy in the stride
and narrow-hipped and broad across the
  back;
his chest is deep and beautifully molded,

3160 his shoulders wide, his features very clean,
his look ferocious, and his curly head
as white as flowers in the summertime.
His valor has been proven many times.
God, what a lord, if he were but a Christian!
He spurs his horse until the bright blood
  flows
and brings him to a gallop, leaps a ditch
some fifty feet in width, could it be measured.
The pagans shout: "This man should hold
  the marches!
No Frenchman who may come to fight with
  him
3170 will fail, to die, whatever he may wish.
King Charles is crazy not to have withdrawn." AOI

229

The picture of a baron, the emir
displays a beard as white as any flower;
a man supremely learned in his law,
as well as bold and arrogant in battle.
His son Malprimes is very chivalrous,
robust and tall, the image of his forebears.
He tells his father: "Let us ride, my lord;
if we see Charles at all, I'll be surprised."
3180 Says Baligant: "Oh yes, for he is very brave—
great praise for him is found in many
  gestes—
but since his nephew Roland is no more,
he won't possess the strength to hold us off."
  AOI

230

"Malprimes, fair son," continues Baligant,
"just yesterday brave Roland was brought
  down,
along with valiant, bold Olivier,
the dozen peers, whom Charles once held so
  dear,
and twenty thousand fighting men from
  France.
I wouldn't give a glove for all the rest.

3146. A line missing from the Oxford ms. and supplied
from V⁴.
3157. *This noble lord:* Baligant.

3190   Undoubtedly the emperor's returning:
the Syrian, my messenger, reported
that he has made up ten immense battalions.
The man who sounds the oliphant is
    brave—
his comrade's clear-voiced trumpet rackets
    back—
and thus they ride as leaders, up ahead,
in company with fifteen thousand Franks,
the bachelors, whom Charles has called his
    children.
Behind them are at least that many more.
These men will fight with lordly arrogance."
3200   Malprimes says: "I request of you the
    stroke."° AOI

231

"Malprimes," says Baligant to him, "my son,
I grant you what you've asked of me just
    now.
Go out at once and strike against the French.
I'll send along the Persian king Torleu
and Dapamort, another Lycian° king.
If you can blunt that overbearing pride
I'll let you have that section of my country
that lies between Cheirant° and Val Marchis."°
The other answers him: "I thank you, sire!"
3210   and stepping forward, he accepts the gift
(a land which once belonged to King Flurit)
at such a time that he will never see it;
nor was he ever seised° of it, nor vested.

232

The emir goes riding through that mighty
    host,
the massive figure of his son behind him.

King Dapamort and King Torleu together
establish quickly thirty battle corps
of chevaliers in numbers past belief;
the smallest one contains some fifty thou-
    sand.
3220   The first is formed of men from Butentrot,°
the second of big-headed men from
    Misnes—°
along the vertebrae all down their backs
these men have tufted bristles, just like hogs.
    AOI
The third is formed of Nubles and of Blos;
the fourth contains Slavonians and Bruns;°
the fifth is formed of Sorz and of Sorabi;°
the sixth contains Armenians and Moors;
in the seventh are the men from Jericho;
the eighth is formed of blacks; the ninth of
    Gros;
3230   and the tenth is formed of troops from
    strong Balide,
a race of men who never seek the Good. AOI
With all his heart, the emir now swears an
    oath
upon the flesh and wonders of Mohammed:
"Like a madman, Charles of France keeps
    riding on;
unless he turns aside, there'll be a battle,
and he shall have his golden crown no
    more."

233

They make up ten battalions after that.
The first is formed of ugly Canaanites
who made their way cross-country from Val
    Fuit;

3200. *the stroke:* the first blow of the battle—see v. 866, n.
3205. *Lycian:* pertaining to Lycia, a province in southwestern Asia Minor.
3208. *Cheirant* is probably Kairouan in Tunisia, a city sacred to the Moslem world. *Val Marchis* may be the city of Marrakech in Morocco.
3213. *seised:* a legal term meaning possessed.

3220. *Butentrot:* a valley in the Taurus Mountains, of southern Asia Minor; its inhabitants at the time of the First Crusade were a tribe of recreant Slavs who had renounced Christianity and had become Moslems.
3221. *Misnes:* the Milceni from Lusatia, a realm lying in the area of eastern Germany and Poland.
3225: *Bruns:* probably the inhabitants of Braunschweig, a province of central Germany.
3226. *Sorabi:* a Slavonic tribe dwelling along the Elbe River in northern Germany.

3240 the next is formed of Turks; the third of
          Persians;
       and the fourth is formed of Petchenegs . . .°
       and the fifth is formed of Solteras and
          Avars°;
       and the sixth of Ormaleus and of Eugiez;
       and the seventh of the race of Samuel°;
       the eighth of men from Bruise°; the ninth,
          Clavers°;
       and the tenth of those from Occian Deserta°:
       a race that does not serve Almighty God,
       you'll never hear of men more infamous;
       their skins are every bit as hard as iron,
3250 and thus they have no need for casques or
          hauberks.
       In combat they are treacherous and brutal.
          AOI

234

       The emir has drawn up ten battalions more.
       The first one is of giants from Malprose;
       the next of Huns; the third Hungarians;
       and the fourth is formed of men from long
          Baldise;
       and the fifth is formed of those from Val
          Peneuse;
       and the sixth is formed of . . . Marose°;
       and the seventh of the Leus and Astrimoines;

the eighth, Argoilles men; and the ninth,
   Clarbone;
3260 and the tenth is formed of bearded troops
   from Fronde:
a race that has no love for God at all.
The Frankish *geste* counts thirty battle corps,
a mighty force amassed where trumpets
   sound.
The pagans make a brave show as they ride.
   AOI

235

The emir, a man of vast authority,
commands that they precede him with his
   dragon,
the flags of Termagant and of Mohammed,
and an effigy of villainous Apollo.
Ten Canaanites go riding all around,
3270 in high-pitched voices screaming
   exhortation:
"Whoever wants to have our gods' protection
should pray and offer penitential psalms!"
The pagans let their heads and chins sink
   down
and tilt their shining helmets toward the
   earth.
The French say: "Gluttons, you are soon to
   die!
May utter wrack and ruin be yours today!
Oh Lord of all of us, look after Charles,
and [let us fight]° this battle in his name!"
   AOI

236

The emir, a man of great sagacity,
3280 now calls upon his son and both the kings:
"My lords and barons, you shall ride ahead
of my battalions; you shall lead them all,
except the finest three. These I'll hold back:
the first, the Turks; the second, Ormaleus;

3241. *Petchenegs:* a barbarian tribe from central Asia which terrorized the civilized world in the eleventh century. The remainder of this line is unknown; the scribe made a blunder and recopied here the end of the preceding line.
3242. *Avars:* a Caucasian tribe which ranged from the Black Sea to the Adriatic and raided northern Italy and southern Germany.
3244. *the race of Samuel:* the Bulgarians who, led by their czar Samuel, invaded the Roman Empire repeatedly in the tenth and eleventh centuries.
3245. *Bruise:* probably the city of Broussa in Asia Minor, a pilgrimage site. *Clavers:* Slavs.
3246. *Occian Deserta:* probably the Theme of Opsicianum, a political and military subdivision of the Byzantine Empire located in northwestern Asia Minor.
3257. Here there is a blank space in the Oxford text, and the other mss. have variant readings.

3278. *let us fight:* a reconstruction of an unintelligible place in the Oxford ms.

and the third, the one of giants from Mal-
  prose.
The men from Occian will stay with me,
so they may go against the French and
  Charles.
If he will fight with me, the emperor
is sure to lose the head from off his torso,
3290 and that's the only 'justice' he shall have."

237

The hosts are large, the battle corps are
  handsome.
Between them there's no hill nor rise nor
  valley
nor woods nor brake—no place where one
  could hide.
They see each other clearly on the plain.
Says Baligant: "My pagan fighting men,
ride forward, seek them out, and give them
  battle!"
Amborre of Oluferne holds up the ensign.
The pagans bellow out its name—"Précieuse!"
"Today will be your downfall," say the
  French,
3300 then loudly they renew the cry "Monjoy!"
The emperor gives word to sound his trumpets
and the oliphant, which heartens all the rest.
The pagans say: "This host of Charles looks
  good;
we'll have a brutal, unrelenting fight." AOI

238

The plain is broad, the country flat and
  open.
Light flashes off those jeweled golden
  casques
and off those shields and saffron-yellow
  byrnies
and lances with their rolled-up battle flags.
The trumpets sound, their tones are very
  clear;

3310 the oliphant's high note sings out the charge.
The emir just now has called upon his
  brother,
Canabeus, the king of Floredée,
who rules that country clear to Val Sevrée,
and shown him the battalions of King
  Charles:
"Look: there's the pride of celebrated France!
The emperor is riding very fiercely;
he's with those bearded soldiers in the rear.
Across their byrnies they've thrown out their
  beards,
which are as white as snow on top of frost.
3320 These men will fight with lances and with
  swords;
our battle will be vicious and unyielding,
a trial of arms like no one's ever seen."
Then, farther than a peeled switch can be
  thrown,
the emir rides out ahead of his companions
and setting an example tells them this:
"Come, pagans; I'm already on my way!"
He menacingly shook his lance's shaft
and swung its head around to point toward
  Charles. AOI

239

Now Charlemagne, on seeing the emir
3330 and the dragon and the ensign and the
  flag—
the Arab forces there are so immense,
they've spread out over every bit of land
except for that the emperor is holding—
in ringing tones the king of France calls out:
"French barons, you are splendid fighting
  men;
you've waged so many battles in the field—
you see how vile and base these pagans are,
and all their laws aren't worth a denier.
Their army's huge, my lords, but what's the
  difference?
3340 Whoever will not come with me, get out!"
At this he digs his spurs into his horse
and causes Tencendur to make four leaps.

The Frenchmen say: "This king's a fighting
 man!
Ride on, lord—not a one of us will fail you."

240

The day was clear, the sunlight radiant,
the hosts superb, the companies immense;
the lead battalions stand there, face to face.
Count Guinemant, along with Count Rabel,
both let their prancing horses' reins fall slack
3350 and spur them on. At this, the Frenchmen
 charge
and go to the attack with sharpened spears.
 AOI

241

The count Rabel is a rugged chevalier:
he rakes his horse with spurs of finest gold
and goes to strike Torleu, the Persian king.
No shield nor byrnie can withstand his blow;
he drives his gilded lance into the body
and throws him dead upon a little bush.
The French say: "Help us now, Almighty God!
King Charles is in the right—we mustn't fail
 him." AOI

242

3360 And Guinemant accosts a Lycian king.
He shatters his fleuron-emblazoned shield,
and afterward he rips apart his byrnie;
he shoves his pennant deep into the body
and, laugh or cry who will, he drops him
 dead.
And at this stroke, the men from France call
 out:
"Attack them, barons, don't let up at all!
King Charles is in the right against these
 [pagans,]°
and God has left His verdict up to us." AOI

243

Malprimes, who sits upon a pure white
 horse,
3370 now hurls himself into the crowd of Franks,
repeatedly goes striking mighty blows
and piling corpses one upon the other.
Before the others Baligant calls out:
"My barons, for a long time I have fed°
 you;
now look: my son goes seeking after
 Charles,
defying many knights by force of arms—
I'll never ask for any better vassal—
so take your sharpened spears and give him
 help!"
The pagans, moving forward at this word,
3380 strike brutal blows; the carnage is immense.
The fighting is incredible and heavy:
none harsher has occurred before or since.
 AOI

244

The hosts are large, the companies
 aggressive,
and all of the battalions have engaged.
The pagans fight astonishingly well.
God!—so many shafts are snapped in two
and shields destroyed and byrnies stripped of
 mail!
Just look at how the ground about is littered!
Upon the battlefield, the soft green grass
3390 [is all vermillioned by the running blood.]°
The emir encourages his retinue:
"Lay on, my lords, against this Christian
 race!"
The battle is extremely fierce and stubborn;
there's been none harder fought before or
 since.

3374. *fed:* OF *nurrit,* literally to nourish. See Introduction.
3390. This line, missing from the Oxford ms., is supplied
from V⁴.

3367. *pagans:* this word is supplied from V⁴.

No truce will be announced until night falls.
    AOI

245

The emir exhorts the members of his race:
"Strike, pagans—that's what you've come
    here for!
I'll make you gifts of pretty, high-born
    women,
and also give you honors, lands, and fiefs."
3400   The pagans say: "For that we'll have to
    fight."
Attacking with full force, they lose their
    spears;
a hundred thousand swords and more are
    drawn.
Just look at all this grim, relentless
    slaughter:
whoever stands with them will see a battle.
    AOI

246

The emperor now calls upon his French:
"I hold you dear and trust you, lords and
    barons;
so many battles you have fought for me
and kingdoms overwhelmed and kings
    deposed!
I'm well aware I owe you recompense
3410   in personal assistance, lands, and wealth.
Avenge your sons, your brothers, and your
    heirs

who died at Roncesvals the other evening!
I know you're in the right against the
    pagans."
The Franks reply: "Sire, what you say is
    true."
Some twenty thousand men who stand
    nearby
swear loyalty to him in unison—
on pain of death or torture they won't fail
    him.
Not one of them neglects to use his lance;
before long they'll be fighting with their
    swords.
3420   The battle is astonishingly brutal. AOI

REVIEW QUESTIONS

1. Compare and contrast the poem's descriptions of the Christian Franks and the "pagan" Saracens. What do you make of the fact that they are similar in so many respects? Why does the poet admire Baligant in particular (ci. 3156–67)?

2. Scholars are still mystified by the meaning of the letters AOI, which appear after many of the stanzas in the poem's original manuscript, but they almost certainly indicate places where a performer might add a musical interlude or embellishment. What is historically significant about the fact that this poem (or portions of it) functioned as a dramatic entertainment?

3. What can you conclude about the values of this poem's intended audience? How might it have resonated with the first generation of crusaders?

The Charter of Liberties for St. Omer

William of Normandy, count of Flanders, issued this famous charter of liberties to the citizens of St. Omer in 1127. Such charters were the foundations of urban freedom, and they reveal what city people needed to conduct their businesses. William also benefited from this arrangement, and the charter embodies the results of some hard bargaining between the merchants and their lord.

From *The Saxons in England*, by J. M. Kemble (London: Quaritch, 1876).

I, William, by the grace of God, Count of Flanders, not wishing to reject the petition of the citizens of St. Omer—especially as they have willingly received my petition about the consulate of Flanders, and because they have always been honest and faithful to me—grant them the laws written below, and command that those laws remain inviolate.

1. First that to every man I will show peace, and I will protect and defend them with good will just as I do my other men. And I grant that justice be done to all of them by my bailiffs, and I wish that they do justice to me also. I grant liberty to my bailiffs such as my other bailiffs have.

2. If any citizen of St. Omer lend money to any one, and the borrower freely acknowledge this in the presence of lawful men of that town and of his heirs, if the debt be unpaid on the agreed date, he or his goods may be detained until all be paid. If he be unwilling to pay, or deny the agreement, he shall be detained until he pay the debt if he be convicted on the testimony of two bailiffs or two sworn men. * * *

5. All those who have their gild and belong to it, and who reside within the limits of the town, I make free of toll at the port of Dixmude and at the port of Gravelines; and throughout all the land of Flanders I make them free of *sewerp*. I grant them the toll which the people of Arras pay at Bapaume.

6. If any of them go to the land of the Emperor for trade, he shall not be forced to lose his gild by any of my people.

7. If it should happen that at any time I should acquire land outside of Flanders, or if a treaty of peace be made between me and my uncle, Henry, King of the English, I will cause them to be made free of all toll in the land acquired, or in the whole land of England, or I will make them free of all customs by the terms of such treaty. * * *

9. All who dwell within the walls of St. Omer, or who dwell there in the future, I make free from *cavagium, i.e.,* from head-tax, and from suit of court. * * *

11. Moreover they have asked the king of France and Ralph of Peronne that wherever they go in their lands they may be free of toll, transit dues, and passage; I wish this to be granted to them. * * *

13. As I wish the citizens of Flanders to be free henceforward from all customs, I shall require from them no *scot*, or *taille*, or forced loan.

14. The thirty pounds a year I had from St. Omer and whatever I ought to have from there, I grant for the restoration of their damaged property, and for the maintenance of their gild. The burgesses shall see to it that there is good and stable coinage during my life whereby the town may be improved.

15. Since the guards who nightly watch the castle of St. Omer have had a fee decreed from of old to be in oats, cheeses, and goatskins, and since they have been accustomed to take bread and one or two denarii from every house unjustly on the feasts of St. Omer and St. Bertin and at the Nativity, or to take guarantees from the poor for these things, we decree that they shall not dare in the future to take anything above their stipend.

16. Whoever comes to Nieuport from any place shall have permission to come to St. Omer with his goods in whatever ship he pleases.

17. If I make peace with Stephen, Count of Boulogne, I shall make them free of toll and sewerp throughout all his lands and at Wissant.

18. I grant for their use the pasture in the wood near St. Omer, which is called Lo, and the marshes, meadows, whins and fallow lands, except the land of the lepers, just as it was in the time of Count Robert the Bearded.

19. I make free from all toll the houses which are in the care of the advocate of the Abbey of St. Bertin, namely, those which are inhabited. Each gives twelve denarii at the feast of St. Michael, twelve denarii as *brotban*, and twelve denarii as *byrban*. Those which are empty pay nothing. ✳ ✳ ✳

25. The following have promised that this agreement shall be observed by all, and they have sealed

their promise with an oath: Louis, King of the French; William, Count of Flanders; Ralph of Peronne, etc.

REVIEW QUESTIONS

1. According to this document, what freedoms are crucial to the well-being and commercial endeavors of an urban community?

2. What did Count William stand to gain from protecting these freedoms? Why would some great lords and kings have resisted townspeople's efforts to win such liberties?

3. What can you gather about town governance in St. Omer? How much agency did townspeople have when it came to shaping social, political, and economic institutions?

FROM The Anonymous of Mainz: A Hebrew Account of the First Crusade

The summoning of the First Crusade, by Pope Urban II at Clermont in 1095, resulted in widespread enthusiasm in western Europe for an armed expedition to the Muslim east to recover Jerusalem. But on the way, some crusaders passing through the Rhineland engaged in massacres of Jewish populations, most notably in the city of Mainz. This Jewish record of the massacre, though anonymous, is close to the original events and bears all the marks of being derived from an eyewitness account of what occurred. The author quotes and paraphrases extensively from Hebrew Scripture, and these passages remain in quotation marks.

From *European Jewry and the First Crusade*, by Robert Chazan (Berkeley: University of California Press, 1987), pp. 225–27, 232–42. Bracketed insertions are Chazan's; insertions in braces are editorial.

Spring, 1096

I shall begin the account of the former persecution. May the Lord protect us and all Israel from persecution.

It came to pass in the year one thousand twenty-eight after the destruction of the Temple that this evil befell Israel. There first arose the princes and nobles and common folk in France, who took counsel and set plans to ascend and "to rise up like

eagles" and to do battle and "to clear a way" for journeying to Jerusalem, the Holy City, and for reaching the sepulcher of the Crucified, "a trampled corpse" "who cannot profit and cannot save for he is worthless." They said to one another: "Behold we travel to a distant land to do battle with the kings of that land. 'We take our souls in our hands' in order to kill and to subjugate all those kingdoms that do not believe in the Crucified. How much more so [should we kill and subjugate] the Jews, who killed and crucified him." They taunted us from every direction. They took counsel, ordering that either we turn to their abominable faith or they would destroy us "from infant to suckling." They—both princes and common folk—placed an evil sign upon their garments, a cross, and helmets upon their heads.

When the [Jewish] communities in France heard, they were seized by consternation, fear, and trembling. . . . They wrote letters and sent emissaries to all the [Jewish] communities along the Rhine River, [asking that they] fast and deprive themselves and seek mercy from [God "who] dwells on high," so that he deliver them [the Jews] from their [the crusaders'] hands. When the letters reached the saintly ones who were in that land, they—those men of God, "the pillars of the universe," who were in Mainz—wrote in reply to France. Thus was it written in them [their letters]: "All the [Jewish] communities have decreed a fast. We have done our part. May God save us and save you from 'all distress and hardship.' We are greatly fearful for you. We, however, have less reason to fear [for ourselves], for we have heard not even a rumor [of such developments]." Indeed we did not hear that a decree had been issued and that "a sword was to afflict us mortally."

When the crusaders began to reach this land, they sought funds with which to purchase bread. We gave them, considering ourselves to be fulfilling the verse: "Serve the king of Babylon, and live." All this, however, was of no avail, for our sins brought it about that the burghers in every city to which the crusaders came were hostile to us, for their [the burghers'] hands were also with them [the crusaders] to destroy vine and stock all along the way to Jerusalem.

It came to pass that, when the crusaders came, battalion after battalion, like the army of Sennacherib, some of the princes in the empire said: "Why do we sit thus? Let us also go with them. For every man who sets forth on this journey and undertakes to ascend to the impure sepulcher dedicated to the Crucified will be assured paradise." Then the crusaders along with them [the princes] gathered from all the provinces until they became as numerous "as the sands of the sea," including both princes and common folk. They circulated a report. . . . "Anyone who kills a single Jew will have all his sins absolved." Indeed there was a certain nobleman, Ditmar by name, who announced that he would not depart from this empire until he would kill one Jew—then he would depart. Now when the holy community in Mainz heard this, they decreed a fast. "They cried out mightily to the Lord" and they passed night and day in fasting. Likewise they recited dirges both morning and evening, both small and great. Nonetheless our God "did not turn away from his awesome wrath" against us. For the crusaders with their insignia came, with their standards before our houses. When they saw one of us, they ran after him and pierced him with a spear, to the point that we were afraid even to cross our thresholds.

It came to pass on the eighth of the month of Iyyar {May 3, 1096}, on the Sabbath, the measure of justice began to manifest itself against us. The crusaders and burghers arose first against the saintly ones, the pious of the Almighty in Speyer. They took counsel against them, [planning] to seize them together in the synagogue. But it was revealed to them and they arose [early] on the Sabbath morning and prayed rapidly and left the synagogue. When they [the crusaders and burghers] saw that their plan for seizing them together was foiled, they rose against them [the Jews] and killed eleven of them. From there the decree began to fulfill that which is said: "Begin at my sanctuary." When Bishop John heard, he came with a large force and helped the [Jewish] community wholeheartedly and brought them indoors and saved them from their [the crusaders' and burghers'] hands. He seized some of the burghers

and "cut off their hands." He was a pious one among the nations. Indeed God brought about well-being and salvation through him. R. Moses ben Yekutiel the *parnas*, {a leader}, "stood on the breach" and extended himself on their behalf. Through him all those forcibly converted who remained "here and there" in the empire of Henry returned [to Judaism]. Through the emperor, Bishop John removed the remnant of the community of Speyer to his fortified towns, and the Lord turned to them, for the sake of his great Name. The bishop hid them until the enemies of the Lord passed. They [the Jews] remained there, fasting and weeping and mourning. "They despaired deeply," for every day the crusaders and the gentiles and Emicho—may his bones be ground up—and the common folk gathered against them, to seize them and to destroy them. Through R. Moses the *parnas*, Bishop John saved them, for the Lord inclined his heart to save them without bribery. This was from the Lord, in order to give us there "a remnant and a residue" through him.

*   *   *

It came to pass that, when the saintly ones, the pious of the Almighty, the holy community in Mainz, heard that some of the community of Speyer had been killed and the community of Worms [had been attacked] twice, then their spirit collapsed and "their hearts melted and turned to water." They cried out to the Lord and said: " 'Ah Lord God of Israel! Are you wiping out the remnant of Israel?' 'Where are all your wondrous deeds about which our ancestors told us, saying: "Truly the Lord brought you up from Egypt." But now you have abandoned us, delivering us into the hands of the gentiles for destruction.' " Then all the leaders of Israel gathered from the community and came to the archbishop and his ministers and servants and said to them: "What are we to do with regard to the report which we have heard concerning our brethren in Speyer and Worms who have been killed?" They said to them: "Heed our advice and bring all your moneys into our treasury and into the treasury of the archbishop. Then you and your wives and your children and all your retinue bring

into the courtyard of the archbishop. Thus will you be able to be saved from the crusaders." They contrived and gave this counsel in order to surrender us and to gather us up and to seize us "like fish enmeshed in a fatal net." In addition, the archbishop gathered his ministers and servants—exalted ministers, nobles and grandees—in order to assist us and to save us from the crusaders. For at the outset it was his desire to save us, but ultimately he failed.

It came to pass on a certain day that a gentile woman came and brought with her a goose that she had raised since it was a gosling. This goose went everywhere that the gentile woman went. She said to all passersby: "Behold this goose understands that I intend to go on the crusade and wishes to go with me." Then the crusaders and burghers gathered against us, saying to us: "Where is your source of trust? How will you be saved? Behold the wonders that the Crucified does for us!" Then all of them came with swords and spears to destroy us. Some of the burghers came and would not allow them [to do so]. At that time they stood . . . and killed along the Rhine River, until they killed one of the crusaders. Then they said: "All these things the Jews have caused." Then they almost gathered [against us]. When the saintly ones saw all these things, their hearts melted. They [the Christians] spoke harshly with them, [threatening] to assault and attack us. When they [the Jews] heard their words, they said—from great to small: "If only we might die by the hand of the Lord, rather than die at the hands of the enemies of the Lord. For he is a merciful God, the only king in his universe."

They left their houses empty and came to the synagogue only on the sabbath, that last sabbath prior to our disaster, when "a few" entered to pray. R. Judah ben R. Isaac entered there to pray on that Sabbath. They wept copiously, to the point of exhaustion, for they saw that this was the decree of the King of kings. There was a venerable scholar, R. Baruch ben R. Isaac, and he said to us: "Know that a decree has truly and surely been enacted against us, and we will not be able to be saved. For tonight we—I and my son-in-law Judah—heard the souls praying here loudly, [with a sound] like

weeping. When we heard the sound, we thought that perhaps they [those praying] came from the courtyard of the archbishop and that some of the community had returned to pray in the synagogue at midnight out of pain and anguish. We ran to the door of the synagogue, but it was closed. We heard the sound, but we comprehended nothing. We returned home shaken, for our house was close to the synagogue." When we heard these words, we fell on our faces and said: " 'Ah Lord God! Are you wiping out the remnant of Israel?' " They went and recounted these incidents to their brethren in the courtyard of the burgrave and in the courtyard of the archbishop. They likewise wept copiously.

It came to pass on the new moon of Sivan that the wicked Emicho—may his bones be ground up on iron millstones—came with a large army outside the city, with crusaders and common folk. For he also said: "It is my desire to go on the crusade." He was our chief persecutor. He had no mercy on the elderly, on young men and young women, on infants and sucklings, nor on the ill. He made the people of the Lord "like dust to be trampled." "Their young men he put to the sword and their pregnant women he ripped open." They camped outside the city for two days. Then the heads of the [Jewish] community said: "Let us send him money, along with our letters, so that the [Jewish] communities along the way will honor him. Perhaps the Lord will treat us with his great lovingkindness." For previously they had liberally spent their moneys, giving the archbishop and the burgrave and their ministers and their servants and the burghers approximately four hundred marks, so that they might aid them. It availed them nothing. We were unlike Sodom and Gomorrah, for in their case ten [righteous] were sought in order to save them. For us neither twenty nor ten were sought.

*   *   *

It came to pass at midday that the wicked Emicho—may his bones be ground up—he and all his army—came, and the burghers opened up to him the gates. Then the enemies of the Lord said one to another: "Behold the gates have been opened by themselves. All this the Crucified has done for us, so that we might avenge his blood on the Jews." They came with their standards to the archbishop's gate, where the children of the sacred covenant were—an army as numerous "as the sands on the seashore." When the saintly and God-fearing saw the huge multitude, they trusted in and cleaved to their Creator. They donned armor and strapped on weapons—great and small—with R. Kalonymous ben Meshullam at their head.

There was a pious one, one of the great men of the generation, Rabbi Menahem ben Rabbi David the *levi*. He said: "All the congregation, sanctify the revered and awesome Name unreservedly." They all replied: . . . [He said]: "All of you must do as did the sons of our ancestor Jacob when he sought to reveal to them the time of redemption, at which point the Divine Presence left him. [Jacob said]: 'Perhaps I too am sullied as was my grandfather Abraham [from whom proceeded Ishmael] or like my father Isaac [from whom proceeded Esau.'] [His sons said to him: 'Hear O Israel! The Lord is our God; the Lord is one.'] [Do] as did our ancestors when they answered and said, as they received the Torah at this very time on Mount Sinai: 'We shall do and hear.' " They then called out loudly: "Hear O Israel! The Lord is our God, the Lord is one." They all then drew near to the gate to do battle with the crusaders and with the burghers. They did battle one with another around the gate. Our sins brought it about that the enemy overcame them and captured the gate. The men of the archbishop, who had promised to assist, fled immediately, in order to turn them over to the enemy, for they are "splintered reeds." Then the enemy came into the courtyard and found R. Isaac ben R. Moses [and others and struck them] a mortal sword blow. Not so for the fifty-three souls who fled with R. Kalonymous through the chambers of the archbishop, exiting into a long room called . . . and remaining there.

*   *   *

When the children of the sacred covenant saw that the decree had been issued and that the enemy had overcome them, they all cried out—young

men and old men, young women and children, menservants and maidservants—and wept for themselves and their lives. They said: "We shall suffer the yoke of awe of the sacred. For the moment the enemy will kill us with the easiest of the four deaths—by the sword. But we shall remain alive; our souls [will repose] in paradise, in the radiance of the great light, forever." They all said acceptingly and willingly: "Ultimately one must not question the ways of the Holy One blessed be he and blessed be his Name, who gave us his Torah and commanded us to put to death and to kill ourselves for the unity of his holy Name. Blessed are we if we do his will and blessed are all those who are killed and slaughtered and who die for the unity of his Name. Not only are they privileged to enter the world to come and sit in the circle of the saintly, 'the pillars of the universe.' What is more, they exchange a world of darkness for a world of light, a world of pain for a world of happiness, a transitory world for a world that is eternal and everlasting."

*   *   *

It came to pass that, when the enemy came to the chambers and broke down the doors and found them convulsing, still writhing in their blood, they took their money and stripped them naked. They struck those remaining and left not "a remnant or a residue." Thus they did in all the chambers where there were children of Israel, [children of] the sacred covenant, with the exception of one chamber which was too strong. The enemy did battle against it till evening. When the saintly ones [in that chamber] saw that the enemy was mightier than they were, the men and the women rose up and slaughtered the children. Subsequently, they slaughtered one another. Some fell on their swords or knives. The saintly women threw rocks through the windows. The enemy in turn struck them with rocks. They [the Jewish women] endured all these rocks, until their flesh and faces became shredded. They cursed and blasphemed the crusaders in the name of the Crucified, the profane and despised, the son of lust: "Upon whom do you rely? 'Upon a trampled corpse!'" Then the crusaders advanced to break down the door.

There was a notable lady, Rachel the daughter of R. Isaac ben R. Asher. She said to her companions: "I have four children. On them as well have no mercy, lest these uncircumcised come and seize them and they remain in their pseudo-faith. With them as well you must sanctify the holy Name." One of her companions came and took the knife. When she saw the knife, she cried loudly and bitterly. She beat her face, crying and saying: " 'Where is your steadfast love, O Lord?' " She took Isaac her small son—indeed he was very lovely—and slaughtered him. She . . . said to her companions: "Wait! Do not slaughter Isaac before Aaron." But the lad Aaron, when he saw that his brother had been slaughtered, cried out: "Mother, Mother, do not slaughter me!" He then went and hid himself under a bureau. She took her two daughters, Bella and Matrona, and sacrificed them to the Lord God of Hosts, who commanded us not to abandon pure awe of him and to remain loyal to him. When the saintly one finished sacrificing her three children before our Creator, she then lifted her voice and called out to her son: "Aaron, Aaron, where are you? I shall not have pity or mercy on you either." She pulled him by the leg from under the bureau, where he had hidden, and sacrificed him before the sublime and exalted God. She then put them under her two sleeves, two on one side and two on the other, near her heart. They convulsed near her, until the crusaders seized the chamber. They found her sitting and mourning them. They said to her: "Show us the money which you have under your sleeves." When they saw the slaughtered children, they smote her and killed her. With regard to them and to her it is said: "Mother and babes were dashed to death together." She died with them, as did the [earlier] saintly one with her seven sons. With regard to her it is said: "The mother of the child is happy." The crusaders killed all those in the chamber and stripped them naked. They were still writhing and convulsing in their blood, as they stripped them. "See, O Lord, and behold, how abject I have become."

Subsequently they threw them from the chambers through the windows naked, heap upon heap and mound upon mound, until they formed a high

heap. Many of the children of the sacred covenant, as they were thrown, still had life and would signal with their fingers: "Give us water that we might drink." When the crusaders saw this, they would ask them: "Do you wish to sully yourselves [with the waters of the baptism]?" They would shake their heads and would look at their Father in heaven as a means of saying no and would point with their fingers to the Holy One blessed be he. The crusaders then killed them.

All these things were done by those whom we have designated by name. The rest of the community all the more proclaimed the unity of the sacred Name, and all fell in the hands of the Lord.

Then the crusaders began to exult in the name of the Crucified. They lifted their standards and came to the remnant of the community, to the courtyard of the burgrave. They besieged them as well and did battle against them and seized the entranceway to the courtyard and smote them also.

There was a certain man, named Moses ben Helbo. He called to his sons and said to them: "My sons Simon and Helbo. At this moment hell and paradise are open [before you]. Into which do you wish to enter?" They answered him and said: "Bring us into paradise." They stretched forth their necks. The enemy smote them, the father along with the sons.

There was a Torah scroll there in the chamber. The crusaders came into the chamber, found it, and tore it to shreds. When the saintly and pure daughters of royalty [the Jewish women] saw that the Torah had been torn, they called out loudly to their husbands: "Behold, behold the holy Torah. The enemy is tearing it." Then they all, the men and the women, said together: "Woe for the holy Torah, 'perfect in beauty,' 'the delight of our eyes.' We used to bow before it in the synagogue; we used to kiss it; we used to honor it. How has it now fallen into the hands of the unclean and uncircumcised." When the men heard the words of the saintly women, "they became exceedingly zealous" for the Lord our God and for the holy and beloved Torah. There was there a young man named R. David ben Rabbi Menahem. He said to them: "My brethren, rend your garments over the honor of the Torah." They rent their garments as our teacher commanded. They then found a crusader in a chamber and they all—both men and women—rose up and stoned him. He fell and died. Now when the burghers and crusaders saw that he had died, they did battle against them. They went up on the roof over the place where the children of the covenant were, broke the roof, shot at them with arrows, and pierced them with spears.

*   *   *

I know not how much is missing here. May God save us from this exile. The end of the former persecutions.

REVIEW QUESTIONS

1. According to this account, what factors and motives led to the slaughter of Jews in certain communities? What can you conclude about the conditions in which Jews lived prior to the First Crusade?

2. The anonymous author of this account quotes extensively from the Hebrew Bible. Why? What rhetorical and historical functions might such scriptural passages serve?

3. What does the story about the goose reveal about the crusaders' mind-set? Does this story seem credible? Why or not? Why did the author include it here?

ALI IBN AL-ATHIR

An Arabic Account of the First Crusade

Ali ibn al-Athir (1160–1233) was a historian who may at one time have been in contact with the great leader Salah ad-Din (Saladin, c. 1138–1193), who successfully marshalled Muslim forces against the Christian crusaders. Ibn al-Athir's major work, The Complete History of the World, *includes a description of the events leading up to the First Crusade and provides another valuable perspective on the causes of the crusading movement and the motivations of the crusaders.*

From *Arab Historians of the Crusades*, Arabic sources translated by Francesco Gabrielli, translated from the Italian by E. J. Costello (Berkeley: University of California Press, 1969), pp. 3–12.

The Franks Seize Antioch

The power of the Franks first became apparent when in the year 478/1085–86 they invaded the territories of Islām and took Toledo and other parts of Andalusia, as was mentioned earlier. Then in 484/1091 they attacked and conquered the island of Sicily[1] and turned their attention to the African coast. Certain of their conquests there were won back again but they had other successes, as you will see.

In 490/1097 the Franks attacked Syria. This is how it all began: Baldwin, their King,[2] a kinsman of Roger the Frank who had conquered Sicily, assembled a great army and sent word to Roger saying: 'I have assembled a great army and now I am on my way to you, to use your bases for my conquest of the African coast. Thus you and I shall become neighbours.'

Roger called together his companions and consulted them about these proposals. 'This will be a fine thing both for them and for us!' they declared, 'for by this means these lands will be converted to the Faith!' At this Roger raised one leg and farted loudly, and swore that it was of more use than their advice.[3] 'Why?' 'Because if this army comes here it will need quantities of provisions and fleets of ships to transport it to Africa, as well as reinforcements from my own troops. Then, if the Franks succeed in conquering this territory they will take it over and will need provisioning from Sicily. This will cost me my annual profit from the harvest. If they fail they will return here and be an embarrassment to me here in my own domain. As well as all this Tamīm[4] will say that I have broken faith with him and violated our treaty, and friendly relations and communications between us will be disrupted. As far as we are concerned, Africa is always there. When we are strong enough we will take it.'

He summoned Baldwin's messenger and said to him: 'If you have decided to make war on the Muslims your best course will be to free Jerusalem from

---

[1] This date clearly refers to the end of the Norman conquest.

[2] This Baldwin (*Bardawil*) is a mythical character, compounded of the various Baldwins of Flanders and Jerusalem; or else the first Baldwin is mistakenly thought to have been already a king in the West.

[3] This passage is characteristic of the contempt with which the Muslims usually spoke of their enemies, as well as giving a fairly accurate picture of Roger's political acumen.

[4] The Zirid amīr of Tunisia Tamīm ibn Mu'ízz.

their rule and thereby win great honour. I am bound by certain promises and treaties of allegiance with the rulers of Africa.' So the Franks made ready and set out to attack Syria.

Another story is that the Fatimids of Egypt were afraid when they saw the Seljuqids extending their empire through Syria as far as Gaza, until they reached the Egyptian border and Atsiz[5] invaded Egypt itself. They therefore sent to invite the Franks to invade Syria and so protect Egypt from the Muslims.[6] But God knows best.

When the Franks decided to attack Syria they marched east to Constantinople, so that they could cross the straits and advance into Muslim territory by the easier, land route. When they reached Constantinople, the Emperor of the East refused them permission to pass through his domains. He said: 'Unless you first promise me Antioch, I shall not allow you to cross into the Muslim empire.' His real intention was to incite them to attack the Muslims, for he was convinced that the Turks, whose invincible control over Asia Minor he had observed, would exterminate every one of them. They accepted his conditions and in 490/1097 they crossed the Bosphorus at Constantinople. Iconium and the rest of the area into which they now advanced belonged to Qilij Arslān ibn Sulaimān ibn Qutlumísh, who barred their way with his troops. They broke through[7] in rajab 490/July 1097, crossed Cilicia,[8] and finally reached Antioch, which they besieged.

When Yaghi Siyān, the ruler of Antioch, heard of their approach, he was not sure how the Christian people of the city would react, so he made the Muslims go outside the city on their own to dig trenches, and the next day sent the Christians out alone to continue the task. When they were ready to return home at the end of the day he refused to allow them. 'Antioch is yours,' he said, 'but you will have to leave it to me until I see what happens between us and the Franks.' 'Who will protect our children and our wives?' they said. 'I shall look after them for you.' So they resigned themselves to their fate, and lived in the Frankish camp for nine months, while the city was under siege.

Yaghi Siyān showed unparalleled courage and wisdom, strength and judgment. If all the Franks who died had survived they would have overrun all the lands of Islām. He protected the families of the Christians in Antioch and would not allow a hair of their heads to be touched.

After the siege had been going on for a long time the Franks made a deal with one of the men who were responsible for the towers. He was a cuirass-maker called Ruzbih[9] whom they bribed with a fortune in money and lands. He worked in the tower that stood over the river-bed, where the river flowed out of the city into the valley. The Franks sealed their pact with the cuirass-maker, God damn him! and made their way to the water-gate. They opened it and entered the city. Another gang of them climbed the tower with ropes. At dawn, when more than 500 of them were in the city and the defenders were worn out after the night watch, they sounded their trumpets. Yaghi Siyān woke up and asked what the noise meant. He was told that trumpets had sounded from the citadel and that it must have been taken. In fact the sound came not from the citadel but from the tower. Panic seized Yaghi Siyān and he opened the city gates and fled in terror, with an escort of thirty pages. His army commander arrived, but when he discovered on enquiry that Yaghi Siyān had fled, he made his escape by another gate. This was of great help to the Franks, for if he had stood firm for an hour, they would have been wiped out. They entered the city by the gates and sacked it, slaughtering all the Muslims they found there. This happened in jumada I (491/April/May 1098).[10] As

---

[5] A general of the Seljuqid Sultan Malikshāh, who in 1076 attacked Egypt from Palestine.

[6] Of course the Fatimids were also Muslims, but they were heretics and so opposed to the rest of *sunni* [sic] Islām.

[7] At Dorylaeum.

[8] Literally 'the land of the son of Armenus' as the Arab writers call the Lesser Armenia of the Cilician Roupenians.

---

[9] *Firūz* is an alternative reading.

[10] June 3 according to European sources.

for Yaghi Siyān, when the sun rose he recovered his self control and realized that his flight had taken him several *farsakh*[11] from the city. He asked his companions where he was, and on hearing that he was four *farsakh* from Antioch he repented of having rushed to safety instead of staying to fight to the death. He began to groan and weep for his desertion of his household and children. Overcome by the violence of his grief he fell fainting from his horse. His companions tried to lift him back into the saddle, but they could not get him to sit up, and so left him for dead while they escaped. He was at his last gasp when an Armenian shepherd came past, killed him, cut off his head and took it to the Franks at Antioch.

The Franks had written to the rulers of Aleppo and Damascus to say that they had no interest in any cities but those that had once belonged to Byzantium. This was a piece of deceit calculated to dissuade these rulers from going to the help of Antioch.

The Muslim Attack on the Franks, and Its Results

When Qawām ad-Daula Kerbuqā[12] heard that the Franks had taken Antioch he mustered his army and advanced into Syria, where he camped at Marj Dabiq. All the Turkish and Arab forces in Syria rallied to him except for the army from Aleppo. Among his supporters were Duqāq ibn Tutūsh,[13] the Ata-beg Tughtikīn, Janāh ad-Daula of Hims, Arslān Tash of Sanjār, Sulaimān ibn Artūq and other less important amīrs. When the Franks heard of this they were alarmed and afraid, for their troops were weak and short of food. The Muslims advanced and came face to face with the Franks in front of Antioch. Kerbuqā, thinking that the present crisis would force the Muslims to remain loyal to him, alienated them by his pride and ill-treatment of them. They plotted in secret anger to betray him and desert him in the heat of battle.

After taking Antioch the Franks camped there for twelve days without food. The wealthy ate their horses and the poor ate carrion and leaves from the trees. Their leaders, faced with this situation, wrote to Kerbuqā to ask for safe-conduct through his territory but he refused, saying 'You will have to fight your way out.' Among the Frankish leaders were Baldwin,[14] Saint-Gilles, Godfrey of Bouillon, the future Count of Edessa, and their leader Bohemond of Antioch. There was also a holy man who had great influence over them, a man of low cunning, who proclaimed that the Messiah had a lance buried in the Qusyān, a great building in Antioch:[15] 'And if you find it you will be victorious and if you fail you will surely die.' Before saying this he had buried a lance in a certain spot and concealed all trace of it. He exhorted them to fast and repent for three days, and on the fourth day he led them all to the spot with their soldiers and workmen, who dug everywhere and found the lance as he had told them.[16] Whereupon he cried 'Rejoice! For victory is secure.' So on the fifth day they left the city in groups of five or six. The Muslims said to Kerbuqā: 'You should go up to the city and kill them one by one as they come out; it is easy to pick them off now that they have split up.' He replied: 'No, wait until they have all come out and then we will kill them.' He would not allow them to attack the enemy and when some Muslims killed a group of Franks, he went himself to forbid such behaviour and prevent its recurrence. When all the Franks had come out and not one was left in Antioch, they began to attack strongly, and the Muslims turned and fled. This was Kerbuqā's fault, first because he

---

[11] One *farsakh* (parasang) is about four miles.
[12] The Turkish amir of Mosul.
[13] The Seljuqid Lord of Damascus, soon to be succeeded by his general, the Ata-beg Tughtikin, whose name comes next on the list and who was to be one of the most active and tenacious opponents of the Crusades during this first phase of conquest.

[14] Baldwin of Le Bourg, later Baldwin II.
[15] The Church of St. Peter in Antioch, called in Byzantine sources Κασσιανός and in Arabic sources *Qusyān*, from the name of the man whose son was raised from the dead by St. Peter.
[16] The Finding of the Sacred Lance, at the instigation of Peter Bartholomew, seen through rationalistic Muslim eyes.

had treated the Muslims with such contempt and scorn, and second because he had prevented their killing the Franks. The Muslims were completely routed without striking a single blow or firing a single arrow. The last to flee were Suqmān ibn Artūq and Janāh ad-Daula, who had been sent to set an ambush. Kerbuqā escaped with them. When the Franks saw this they were afraid that a trap was being set for them, for there had not even been any fighting to flee from, so they dared not follow them. The only Muslims to stand firm were a detachment of warriors from the Holy Land, who fought to acquire merit in God's eyes and to seek martyrdom. The Franks killed them by the thousand and stripped their camp of food and possessions, equipment, horses and arms, with which they re-equipped themselves.

The Franks Take Ma'arrat an-Nu'mān

After dealing this blow to the Muslims the Franks marched on Ma'arrat an-Nu'mān and besieged it. The inhabitants valiantly defended their city. When the Franks realized the fierce determination and devotion of the defenders they built a wooden tower as high as the city wall and fought from the top of it, but failed to do the Muslims any serious harm. One night a few Muslims were seized with panic and in their demoralized state thought that if they barricaded themselves into one of the town's largest buildings they would be in a better position to defend themselves, so they climbed down from the wall and abandoned the position they were defending. Others saw them and followed their example, leaving another stretch of wall undefended, and gradually, as one group followed another, the whole wall was left unprotected and the Franks scaled it with ladders. Their appearance in the city terrified the Muslims, who shut themselves up in their houses. For three days the slaughter never stopped; the Franks killed more than 100,000 men and took innumerable prisoners. After taking the town the Franks spent six weeks shut up there, then sent an expedition to 'Arqa, which they besieged for four months. Although they breached the wall in many places they

failed to storm it. Munqidh, the ruler of Shaizar, made a treaty with them about 'Arqa and they left it to pass on to Hims. Here too the ruler Janāh ad-Daula made a treaty with them, and they advanced to Acre by way of an-Nawaqir. However they did not succeed in taking Acre.

The Franks Conquer Jerusalem

Taj ad-Daula Tutūsh[17] was the Lord of Jerusalem but had given it as a feoff to the amīr Suqmān ibn Artūq the Turcoman. When the Franks defeated the Turks at Antioch the massacre demoralized them, and the Egyptians, who saw that the Turkish armies were being weakened by desertion, besieged Jerusalem under the command of al-Afdal ibn Badr al-Jamali.[18] Inside the city were Artūq's sons, Suqmān and Ilghazi, their cousin Sunij and their nephew Yaquti. The Egyptians brought more than forty siege engines to attack Jerusalem and broke down the walls at several points. The inhabitants put up a defence, and the siege and fighting went on for more than six weeks. In the end the Egyptians forced the city to capitulate, in sha'bān 489/August 1096.[19] Suqmān, Ilghazi and their friends were well treated by al-Afdal, who gave them large gifts of money and let them go free. They made for Damascus and then crossed the Euphrates. Suqmān settled in Edessa and Ilghazi went on into Iraq. The Egyptian governor of Jerusalem was a certain Iftikhār ad-Daula, who was still there at the time of which we are speaking.

After their vain attempt to take Acre by siege, the Franks moved on to Jerusalem and besieged it for more than six weeks. They built two towers, one of which, near Sion, the Muslims burnt down, killing everyone inside it. It had scarcely ceased to burn before a messenger arrived to ask for help and to bring the news that the other side of the city had fallen. In fact Jerusalem was taken from the north on the

---

17 A Syrian Seljuqid, Malikshāh's brother.
18 The Fatimid vizier.
19 If this date were correct the connection with the fall of Antioch would no longer exist. In fact the date given here is wrong: the Egyptians took Jerusalem in August 1098.

morning of Friday 22 sha'bān 492/15 July 1099. The population was put to the sword by the Franks, who pillaged the area for a week. A band of Muslims barricaded themselves into the Oratory of David[20] and fought on for several days. They were granted their lives in return for surrendering. The Franks honoured their word, and the group left by night for Ascalon. In the Masjid al-Aqsa the Franks slaughtered more than 70,000 people, among them a large number of Imams and Muslim scholars, devout and ascetic men who had left their homelands to live lives of pious seclusion in the Holy Place. The Franks stripped the Dome of the Rock[21] of more than forty silver candelabra, each of them weighing 3,600 drams, and a great silver lamp weighing forty-four Syrian pounds, as well as a hundred and fifty smaller silver candelabra and more than twenty gold ones, and a great deal more booty. Refugees from Syria reached Baghdād in ramadan, among them the qadi Abu Sa'd al-Hárawi. They told the Caliph's ministers a story that wrung their hearts and brought tears to their eyes. On Friday they went to the Cathedral Mosque and begged for help, weeping so that their hearers wept with them as they described the sufferings of the Muslims in that Holy City: the men killed, the women and children taken prisoner, the homes pillaged. Because of the terrible hardships they had suffered, they were allowed to break the fast.

*   *   *

It was the discord between the Muslim princes, as we shall describe, that enabled the Franks to overrun the country. Abu l-Muzaffar al-Abiwardi[22]

composed several poems on this subject, in one of which he says:

> We have mingled blood with flowing tears, and there is no room left in us for pity(?)
> To shed tears is a man's worst weapon when the swords stir up the embers of war.
> Sons of Islām, behind you are battles in which heads rolled at your feet.
> Dare you slumber in the blessed shade of safety, where life is as soft as an orchard flower?
> How can the eye sleep between the lids at a time of disaster that would waken any sleeper?
> While your Syrian brothers can only sleep on the backs of their chargers, or in vultures' bellies!
> Must the foreigners feed on our ignominy, while you trail behind you the train of a pleasant life, like men whose world is at peace?
> When blood has been spilt, when sweet girls must for shame hide their lovely faces in their hands!
> When the white swords' points are red with blood, and the iron of the brown lances is stained with gore!
> At the sound of sword hammering on lance young children's hair turns white.
> This is war, and the man who shuns the whirlpool to save his life shall grind his teeth in penitence.
> This is war, and the infidel's sword is naked in his hand, ready to be sheathed again in men's necks and skulls.
> This is war, and he who lies in the tomb at Medina seems to raise his voice and cry: 'O sons of Hashim![23]
> I see my people slow to raise the lance against the enemy: I see the Faith resting on feeble pillars.

---

[20] The *Mihrāb Dawūd*, called the Tower of David in the European sources, in the citadel at Jerusalem. Not to be confused with a small sanctuary of the same name in the Temple precinct.

[21] The rock from which, the Muslims believe, Muhammad ascended into heaven. Over it was built the so-called 'Mosque of Umar', the chief Islamic monument in Jerusalem. It was from this Mosque that the conquerors took their booty. Nearby, but separate from it, is the 'Farthest Mosque' (al-Masjid al-Aqsa), where according to Ibn al-Athir the armies of the Cross showed even greater barbarity. The two sanctuaries are often confused in both Arabic and European sources.

[22] An Iraqi poet of the eleventh and twelfth centuries.

---

[23] The Prophet, who from the tomb raises his voice to rebuke his descendants (the sons of Hashim), that is, the unworthy Caliphs whose opposition to the Crusades is only half-hearted.

For fear of death the Muslims are evading the fire of battle, refusing to believe that death will surely strike them.'

Must the Arab champions then suffer with resignation, while the gallant Persians shut their eyes to their dishonour?

REVIEW QUESTIONS

1. How does Ibn al-Athir describe the behavior and motivations of Roger and his fellow crusaders? How does this depiction compare with that of the Anonymous of Mainz (pp. 274–279)?

2. What does Ibn al-Athir reveal about Muslim leaders' immediate responses to the Crusade? What do we learn about divisions within and among various Islamic peoples?

3. This description was written at least a century after the events it describes, at a time when the many of the crusaders' conquests had been reversed. Why do we need to take that into account as we read and extract information from it?

9 ✌ THE CONSOLIDATION OF EUROPE, 1100–1300

In the wake of the First Crusade, the most lucrative trade with the Muslim world required reliable contracts to encourage merchants to invest or risk their lives in overseas trade. These contracts rested on a legal framework partly inherited from the Romans but also borrowed from the Byzantines and Muslims and reinvented in the new trading centers. As certain families amassed fortunes in trade and the rest of the population benefited from a general increase in prosperity, the use of written documents in business and family life became more common throughout urban society. Literacy, once useful mainly to the Church, became a valuable money-making skill and generated jobs for copyists and notaries. An ability to manipulate numbers was also valuable.

As the economic and social vitality of the High Middle Ages strengthened the institutions of Church, monarchy, and city governments, people faced the problem of determining the relationships among these different centers of power. The processes of crusade and colonization expanded the frontiers of Western Christendom and brought Europeans into conflicts with their neighbors. By 1300, the papacy in Rome had become the center of a huge ecclesiastical bureaucracy, and new religious orders such as the Cistercians, Franciscans, and Dominicans and an intricate system of canon law buttressed the Church's authority. The university, perhaps the most distinctive legacy of the Middle Ages, supplied the Church with an educated clergy trained in the new disciplines of theology and canon law.

The movement for reforming the church in the eleventh century had raised the issues of clerical celibacy and the proper relations between the Church and the secular world. A series of powerful popes increased the Church's authority by successfully claiming that the Church should not be subordinate to any earthly power. One of the papacy's tools for uniting Western Christendom behind its teachings was the escalating rhetoric of crusading. Eventually, the Church used the Crusades as a way to fight heretics and even political opponents.

Meanwhile, creative minds were finding new answers to old questions about faith. What was happening at the universities often seemed remote from the daily lives of most people, but Saint Thomas Aquinas applied the recently revived tools of Aristotelian logic to the basic concerns, in order to harmonize faith and reason. Many artistic developments accompanied all this religious and intellectual fervor,

and the great cathedrals and churches rising across Europe are testimony to that society's prosperity and values. However, the increased control exercised by the Church and secular states led to increased restriction of woman's roles and the silencing of their voices. Still, many strong witnesses to female authority survive, and are represented here by Heloise, abbess of the Paraclete, and the polymath Hildegard of Bingen.

HELOISE

Letter to Abelard

Most of what we know about Heloise (c. 1101?–1164) comes from the letters that she exchanged with her former teacher and husband, Peter Abelard. She was the niece of Fulbert, a priest and canon of Notre Dame cathedral in Paris, and had received an excellent education at the royal abbey of Argenteuil. With the exception of Abelard, she was the most famous scholar of her day, and Fulbert had entrusted her to Abelard for further education when she came to live in Paris. But the pair eventually became lovers and were secretly married when Heloise became pregnant. Fulbert, enraged at this betrayal of his trust, had Abelard castrated. Thereafter, Heloise and Abelard separated.

The following is the first of her letters to survive, and it would have been written sometime after the year 1125, when Heloise had become head of a new community of religious women. Abelard, for his part, had failed to make the transition to monastic life and was still making many enemies.

From *Abelard and Heloise: The Letters and Other Writings*, translated by William Levitan, selected songs and poems translated by Stanley Lombardo and Barbara Thorburn (Indianapolis: Hackett Publishing), pp. 49–62.

First Letter
Heloise to Abelard

To her lord, no, her father
To her husband, no, her brother
From his handmaid, no, his daughter
His wife, no, his sister—

To Abelard from Heloise.

The other day, my most beloved,
one of your men brought me a copy
of the letter you wrote as consolation
for your friend.
From what was written at its head I knew at once
that it was yours, and I began to read it
with a warmth as great as the love
with which I hold its writer in my heart.
I hoped that at least by its words
I could be restored to life,
as if by some image
of the one whose real substance I have lost.
Almost every line, I noticed,
was filled with vinegar and gall,

as it told the sad story
of our entrance into monastic life
and the unending crosses which you,
my only one,
have always had to bear.

The letter well fulfilled the promise you made
your friend at its beginning, that he would think
his own troubles small or nothing next to yours.
You wrote of your persecution
at the hands of your teachers,
the supreme betrayal
of the mutilation of your body,
and the enmity and hateful malice
of Alberic and Lotulf, who were once
your fellow students.
You wrote of what happened, through their in-
     trigue,
to the glorious book of your *Theology*
and to you yourself
when you were condemned as if to prison.
You wrote of the plots of your abbot and false
     brothers,
the attacks of those spurious apostles
which the same enemies instigated against you,
and the scandal which arose when you gave
the Paraclete[1] its uncustomary name.
And then, when you came to those unbearable
     assaults
which still are launched against you by that tyrant
and by the worst of all monks you call your sons,
you brought the sad story to an end.

No one, I am sure, could read or hear it without
     tears,
and my own grief became fresh with every detail,
and it grows greater still as the danger to you
even now is increasing.
We are all driven to despair of your life,
and every day our hearts beat in fear
of some final word of your death.
So, by that Christ who keeps you for his own
     even now,

we beg of you,
as we are his handmaids and yours,
write to us,
tell us of those storms
in which you find yourself tossed.
We are all you have left: let us share
your grief or your joy.

A community of grief can bring some comfort
to one in need of it, since many shoulders
lighten any burden or even make it
seem to disappear.
If, on the other hand, this storm abates
even just a little, you must write to us quickly
when your letters will bring us more joy.
But whatever it is you write to us about,
it will be no small relief, for in this way
at least you will show you are thinking of us.
Seneca teaches us by his own example
how much joy there is in letters from absent
     friends,
as he writes to his friend Lucilius:

"I am grateful that you write to me often,
for you show yourself to me in the one way you
     can.
When I receive a letter from you, we are suddenly
     together.
If images of absent friends bring joy,
if they refresh our memory and soothe the ache
of absence even with their false and empty solace,
how much more joy is there in a letter,
which carries the true signature of an absent
     friend?"[2]

And I am grateful to God that here at least
is a way you can grant us your presence,
one which no malice will hinder,
no obstacle impede,
and no negligence—I beg of you—delay.

You have written your friend a long letter of con-
     solation,
addressing his adversities but recounting
your own.

---

[1] The monastery for women founded by Heloise and
Abelard. Its name reflects its dedication to the Holy
Spirit (in Greek, Paraclete).

[2] *Epistulae ad Lucilium* 40.1.

But as you told of them in such detail,
while your mind was on his consolation,
you have worsened our own desolation;
while you were treating his wounds,
you have inflicted new wounds upon us
and have made our old wounds bleed.
I beg of you,
heal these wounds you have made, who are so
    careful
to tend the wounds made by others.
You have done what you ought
for a friend and comrade
and have paid your debt to friendship and com-
    radeship.
But you are bound to us by a greater debt,
for we are not your friends but your most loving
    friends,
not your comrades but your daughters—yes,
it is right to call us that, or even use
a name more sacred and more sweet
if one can be imagined.

We need no arguments or testimony
to prove the obligation you have toward us:
if men will keep their silence, the facts will
    speak
for themselves.
You alone, after God, are the founder of this place,
you alone the builder of this oratory,
you alone the architect of this congregation.
Nothing you have built
is on the foundation of another:[3]
it is all your creation, everything here.
Before you, this was a wilderness,
an empty range for wild beasts and outlaws;
it knew no human settlement and not a house
    stood.
Among these lairs of beasts, these dens of outlaws,
where the name of God was never pronounced,
you raised a tabernacle of the Lord
and dedicated a temple of the Holy Spirit
for him to call his own.
Nothing you brought to the task
was from the wealth of kings and princes,

though you could have had so much at your dis-
    posal:
it was all to be yours, whatever was done here,
yours alone.
The clerics and students who came flooding here
to learn from you provided all that was needed;
and suddenly, those who were used to living
on the benefices of the Church,
who had learned how to receive offerings
but not how to make them,
who had opened their hands to take
but not to give,
now became prodigal in their gifts
and even pressed them upon you.

Yes, it is yours,
truly yours, this newly planted garden,
whose living shoots are young, still delicate,
and need watering to thrive.[4]
From the nature of women alone the garden is
    tender
and would not be hardy even if it were not new.
Its cultivation, then, must be more careful,
in the way Saint Paul intended when he wrote:

"I have planted, Apollos has watered,
and God has given the increase."[5]

He had planted the Corinthians in the faith
by the doctrine he had preached, and his student
    Apollos
had watered them with his encouragement,
and the grace of God bestowed on them
the increase of their virtues.
But you are tending another's vine
in a vineyard you have not planted,
and it has turned to bitterness for you,
all your words wasted and vain.[6]
While you lavish your care on another's vine,
remember what you owe your own.

[4] Abelard uses similar terms to speak of the Paraclete in his Sermon 30, which seeks to raise funds for the new convent.

[5] 1 Cor. 3:6.

[6] Cf. Jer. 2:21.

[3] Cf. Rom. 15:20.

You try to teach rebels and do not succeed;
you are casting pearls of God's word before
    swine.[7]
While you lavish so much on those who defy you,
consider what you owe those who obey.
While you squander so much on your enemies,
think what you owe your daughters.
But leave aside these others for a moment—
remember what you owe *me*,
and all you owe
this whole community of devoted women
you may repay at once to her who is,
with more devotion, your only one.

The wealth of your learning
knows better than the poverty of my own
how many treatises the Fathers have composed—
long, weighty, careful treatises—to teach,
encourage, and, yes, console women in religious
    orders.
That is why, in the tender early time
of my convent life long ago,
your oblivion came as no small surprise to me
when, unpersuaded by any reverence for God,
or any love for me, or any example
set by these same Fathers,
you did not try to console me as I foundered,
overwhelmed in sorrow day after day—
never once, neither by a word when we were
    together
nor a letter when we were apart—
and yet you would know
that you are bound to me by a greater debt,
obliged to me by the sacrament of marriage,
and beholden to me further by what is plain
to everyone:
that I have always held you in my heart
with a love that has no measure.

You know, my dearest,
all the world knows, how much I have lost in
    you,
how that supreme, that notorious betrayal

robbed me of my very self
when it robbed me of you,
and how incomparably worse than the loss itself
is the pain from the way it happened.
This greater pain must have a greater solace,
and it can come only from you, not from another.
As you alone are the source of my grief,
you alone can grant the grace of consolation.
You alone have the power to make me sad,
to make me happy or to console me,
and you alone owe me this debt,
now above all,
when I have so completely fulfilled your com-
    mands
in every particular
that, rather than commit a single offense
against you,
I threw myself away at your command.
And the greater irony is that my love
then turned to such insanity
that the one thing it desired above all else
was the one thing it put irrevocably beyond its
    reach
in that one instant when, at your command,
I changed my habit along with my heart
to show that my body along with my heart
belonged only to you.

I never wanted anything in you
but you alone,
nothing of what you have
but you yourself,
never a marriage, never a dowry,
never any pleasure, any purpose of my own—
as you well know—
but only yours.[8]
The name of wife may have the advantages
of sanctity and safety, but to me
the sweeter name will always be *lover*
or, if your dignity can bear it,
concubine or *whore*.

---

[7] Cf. Matt. 7:6.

[8] In the margin of his own manuscript copy of the letter, the poet Petrarch wrote at this point, "You are acting throughout with gentleness and perfect sweetness, Heloise."

Do you imagine
I debased myself to earn your gratitude
and preserve your glorious distinction in the
    world?
You were not so entirely oblivious
when it suited your own purposes in that letter
to your friend,
and did not think it beneath your dignity
to set out at least some of the arguments
I used when I tried to dissuade you
from this marriage of ours and its disastrous bed.
You kept your silence, though, about most of the
    reasons
why I preferred love over marriage,
freedom over a chain.
So I call my God to witness now:
If great Augustus, ruler of the world,
ever thought to honor me by making me his wife
and granted me dominion over the earth,
it would be dearer to me
and more honorable to be called
not his royal consort but your whore.

No man's real worth is measured by his property
    or power:
fortune belongs to one category of things
and virtue to another.[9]
And no woman should think herself any the less
    for sale
if she prefers a rich man to a poor one
in marriage and wants what she would get
in a husband more than the husband himself.
Reward such greed with cash and not devotion,
for she is after property alone
and is prepared to prostitute herself

to an even richer man given the chance.
This is the argument the philosopher
Aspasia used with Xenophon and his wife
in the dialogue of Aeschines the Socratic.
After she set out her argument
aimed at reconciling the pair,
the philosopher capped her proof with this con-
    clusion:
"Therefore, if you two are not convinced
that no worthier man exists and no finer woman
    exists
anywhere on earth, then above all else
you will always be seeking that one thing
you think is best—
to have the best of all possible husbands
or the best of all possible wives."[10]

This notion goes beyond philosophy
and should not be called the pursuit of wisdom
but wisdom itself.
There is a blessed delusion among the married,
a happy fantasy that perfect love
keeps their marital ties intact less through the
    restraint
of their bodies than through the chastity
of their hearts.
But what is a delusion for other women,
for me is the manifest truth.
What other women only think about their hus-
    bands,
I—and the entire world—not only believe
but *know* to be true about you,
and in this way my love is far from any delusion.

Has there been a philosopher or even a king
whose renown could equal yours?[11]

---

[9] This argument will find its way into Abelard's *Ethics* (Luscombe 1971, 48): "If this were true [that merit depends on external circumstances], then great wealth could make someone better or more worthy (that is, if wealth in itself could bring about merit or the increase of merit), and the richer men are, the better they could become because out of their abundance of riches they could add more in deeds to their devotion. But to think that wealth can add to real happiness or the worthiness of the soul, or to think that its lack can detract from the merits of the poor is utterly insane."

---

[10] Cicero, *De Inventione* 1.31.52. Aspasia was the companion (the "concubine or whore," as it were) of the Athenian leader Pericles, widely respected for her character and intellect. In Cicero, Aspasia's words are reported by Socrates, but Heloise has bypassed the middleman and gone straight to the source, the original philosopher herself.

[11] Petrarch wrote in the margin of his manuscript copy at this point, "About Peter's fame—if love doesn't make her testimony suspect."

Has there been any region of the country,
any city, any town that did not boil
with excitement just to see you?
Has there been a single person
who did not come running
to catch a glimpse as you came into sight,
who did not stretch his neck and strain his
    eyes
to follow you as you left?
Has there been a woman, married or unmarried,
who did not long for you when you were gone
or lust for you when you were present?
Has there been a great lady or even a queen
who did not envy me the pleasures of my bed?

And two things that belonged to you alone
would win the heart of any woman—
your beautiful voice and your gift for writing
    songs.
These are not common among philosophers, I
    know,
but for you they were amusements, a diversion
from your philosophical work.
You left countless songs,
both in the classical meter of love
and in the rhythms of love as well,
that kept your name on everyone's lips;
and they were of such surpassing sweetness
that their melodies alone would not allow
even the unlettered to forget you.[12]
For this above all, women sighed with love for
    you.
And since most of the songs told of your love and
    mine,

in what then seemed an instant my name was
    sung
in every corner of the country,
and the envy of women was kindled against me.[13]
Has there been a grace of mind or body
that you did not possess when you were young?
And is there now, of all the women then
who envied me,
a single one who does not feel compassion
when my own calamity has cut me
from those joys?
Is there any man or woman, even among
our ancient enemies, who is not softened now
by the pity owed to me?

I am entirely guilty; as you know,
I am entirely innocent.
For blame does not reside in the action itself
but in the disposition of the agent,
and justice does not weigh what is done
but what is in the heart.[14]
And what my heart has always been toward you,
you alone can judge, who have put me to the test.
I submit it all for your examination,
and rest my case on your testimony alone.

Now answer me one question if you can:
why, after our entrance into religious life—
which you alone decided, you alone—
why I have fallen into such neglect

---

[12] The indications here are that these songs were in Latin. The distinction between "meter" and "rhythm" is between verse forms based on syllable quantity (as in classical Latin) and syllable quality or stress accent (as in the accented verse of much medieval Latin poetry). The "classical meter of love," then, is the elegiac couplet, the standard form of classical Latin love poetry. The "unlettered" are those who did not know Latin but who nonetheless found it easy to memorize Abelard's songs because of the qualities Heloise notes. Outside what may be preserved in *The Letters of Two Lovers* . . . , little of Abelard's elegiac poetry addressed to Heloise survives; . . .

[13] Petrarch commented in the margin at this point, "*Muliebriter*—Just like a woman." Far from descending into vanity, however, Heloise is adapting Abelard's own remarks about the role of fame and envy in his life to help confirm a parallel between their experiences. In the next sections, she proceeds to apply to herself the specific language Abelard used about his castration, the examination of his book at the Council of Soissons, and his isolation at St. Gildas of Rhuys, and refers to her own "*calamitas*—calamity."

[14] What evidently has been an issue of mutual concern between them will become central to the doctrine of Abelard's *Ethics*, that intentions alone, not actions in themselves, are subject to moral judgment; see, e.g., *Ethics* (Luscombe 1971, 52): "Indeed, we call an intention good, that is, right in itself; we do not say of an action, however, that it takes on any good in itself but rather that it proceeds from a good intention."

and oblivion with you that I am neither
restored to life with a word when we are together
nor comforted with a letter when we are apart.
Yes, tell me if you can,
and I will tell you
what I, no, what everyone suspects—
that it was appetite and not affection
that connected you to me, your lust and not your
    love;
and that when what you desired suddenly became
impossible,
everything you put on for its sake
also disappeared.
My most beloved,
this is not my inference alone but everyone's,
not private and particular to me
but public and universal.
I wish it were just mine alone,
for then your love could find
someone to defend it, someone I could turn to
to relieve the pain I am suffering now.
I wish there were
some plausible excuse I could invent,
for then I could find, in defending you,
some way of covering my own cheapness.

Remember what I ask, I beg of you—
you will find it is small and easy to do:
so long as I am cheated of your presence,
present me with an image of yourself
at least in words,
of which you have an exceptional supply.
I cannot expect your generosity in substance
if I find you miserly in words.
Up to now
I had thought I deserved so much from you
since everything I have done was for your sake
and even now I continue in your service.
It was not any commitment to the religious life
that forced me to the rigors of the convent
when I was the young woman I once was:
it was your command alone.
If even in this
I deserve nothing from you, then you may judge
how all my work here has been wasted.
I can expect no reward from God since it is
    clear

I have yet done nothing out of love for him.
I followed *you* as you went striding off
to God and to his monastery—
No,
I did not follow: I went first.
Were you haunted by the image of Lot's wife
turning back[15]
when you delivered me up to these vows and holy
    vestments
even before you delivered yourself to God?
That you doubted me in this one thing, my
    love,
overwhelmed me with grief and shame.
But, as God knows,
I would have followed you
to Vulcan's flames if you commanded it,
and without a moment's hesitation
I would have gone first.

My heart was never my own but was always
with you,
and now even more, if it is not with you
it is nowhere:
without you it cannot exist at all.[16]
Let it be at peace with you, I beg of you.
And it will be at peace with you if you are kind,
if you return grace for grace,[17] small things for
    large,
words for real substance.
My love, I wish your love
had less confidence in me,
so that it would be more careful and concerned.
But now it seems the more secure of me
I have made you feel, the more negligent
you have become.

Recall what I have done, I beg of you.
Remember what you owe me.
In the days
when we shared the pleasures of the flesh,
no one was sure if I acted out of love or lust.
Now the end confirms the beginning.

---

[15] See Gen. 19:26.
[16] Petrarch's marginal comment is "*Amicissime et elegan-
    ter*—Written with elegance and the greatest love."
[17] Cf. John 1:16.

I have denied myself all pleasure to follow your
    will:
I kept nothing for myself but to become yours.
If you now give me less when I deserve
so much more,
if you now give me nothing at all,
think what your injustice will be then.
And it is so small a thing I ask and so easy
for you to do.
So, by that God who claims your dedication,
I beg of you,
grant me your presence in the one way you can—
by writing me some word of comfort,
so that at least in this one way
I may be restored to life,
readier and fit for my own service to God.
In the days
when you sought me out for pleasures long ago,
you showered me with letter after letter,
and with your songs you set your Heloise
on the lips of everyone, and every home
and every street re-echoed
Heloise.
Is it not better now to summon me to God
than it once was to call me to your bed?

Think what you owe me, remember what I ask,
I beg of you,
and I will end my long letter
with these brief words—

Farewell, my only one.

REVIEW QUESTIONS

1. What does this letter reveal about gender roles
   in twelfth-century Europe? How does Heloise
   herself understand her own role in society?
2. Heloise was known for her beautiful and ornate
   Latin prose style, and in this letter she quotes
   from both classical sources and from the Bible.
   How does she make use of these two cultural
   legacies?
3. Many (male) scholars of the nineteenth and
   twentieth centuries alleged that this letter could
   not have been written by Heloise, or by any
   woman with a sincere religious vocation. Why
   would they make such allegations? Do you
   think they are plausible?

HILDEGARD OF BINGEN

Letter to the Clergy of Mainz

*Hildegard of Bingen (1098–1179) was a German abbess whose creative genius ex-
tended to preaching, founding convents, and above all writing down her visionary
prophesies. She was also a prolific composer of sacred songs and plays. Hildegard's
remarkable career as an abbess demonstrates one of the few opportunities women
had to be in charge of an institution in the medieval world. In this letter to the
male clergy of Mainz, Hildegard is objecting to the interdict her convent is experiencing because of a dispute over a burial.*

From *The Letters of Hildegard of Bingen*, edited by Joseph L. Baird (Oxford: Oxford
University Press, 1994), pp. 76–79.

By a vision, which was implanted in my soul by God the Great Artisan before I was born, I have been compelled to write these things because of the interdict by which our superiors have bound us, on account of a certain dead man buried at our monastery, a man buried without any objection, with his own priest officiating. Yet only a few days after his burial, these men ordered us to remove him from our cemetery. Seized by no small terror, as a result, I looked as usual to the True Light, and, with wakeful eyes, I saw in my spirit that if this man were disinterred in accordance with their commands, a terrible and lamentable danger would come upon us like a dark cloud before a threatening thunderstorm.

Therefore, we have not presumed to remove the body of the deceased inasmuch as he had confessed his sins, had received extreme unction and communion, and had been buried without objection. Furthermore, we have not yielded to those who advised or even commanded this course of action. Not, certainly, that we take the counsel of upright men or the orders of our superiors lightly, but we would not have it appear that, out of feminine harshness we did injustice to the sacraments of Christ, with which this man had been fortified while he was still alive. But so that we may not be totally disobedient we have, in accordance with their injunction, ceased from singing the divine praises and from participation in Mass, as had been our regular monthly custom.

As a result, my sisters and I have been greatly distressed and saddened. Weighed down by this burden, therefore, I heard these words in a vision: It is improper for you to obey human words ordering you to abandon the sacraments of the Garment of the Word of God, Who, born virginally of the Virgin Mary, is your salvation. Still, it is incumbent upon you to seek permission to participate in the sacraments from those prelates who laid the obligation of obedience upon you. For ever since Adam was driven from the bright region of paradise into the exile of this world on account of his disobedience, the conception of all people is justly tainted by that first transgression. There-

fore, in accordance with God's inscrutable plan, it was necessary for a man free from all pollution to be born in human flesh, through whom all who are predestined to life might be cleansed from corruption and might be sanctified by the communion of his body so that he might remain in them and they in him for their fortification. That person, however, who is disobedient to the commands of God, as Adam was, and is completely forgetful of Him must be completely cut off from participation in the sacrament of His body, just as he himself has turned away from Him in disobedience. And he must remain so until, purged through penitence, he is permitted by the authorities to receive the communion of the Lord's body again. In contrast, however, a person who is aware that he has incurred such a restriction not as a result of anything that he has done, either consciously or deliberately, may be present at the service of the life-giving sacrament, to be cleansed by the Lamb without sin, Who, in obedience to the Father, allowed Himself to be sacrificed on the altar of the cross that he might restore salvation to all.

In that same vision I also heard that I had erred in not going humbly and devoutly to my superiors for permission to participate in the communion, especially since we were not at fault in receiving that dead man into our cemetery. For, after all, he had been fortified by his own priest with proper Christian procedure, and, without objection from anyone, was buried in our cemetery, with all Bingen joining in the funeral procession. And so God has commanded me to report these things to you, our lords and prelates. Further, I saw in my vision also that by obeying you we have been celebrating the divine office incorrectly, for from the time of your restriction up to the present, we have ceased to sing the divine office, merely reading it instead. And I heard a voice coming from the Living Light concerning the various kinds of praises, about which David speaks in the psalm: "Praise Him with sound of trumpet: praise Him with psaltery and harp," and so forth up to this point: "Let every spirit praise the Lord." These words use outward, visible things to teach

us about inward things. Thus the material composition and the quality of these instruments instruct us how we ought to give form to the praise of the Creator and turn all the convictions of our inner being to the same. When we consider these things carefully, we recall that man needed the voice of the living Spirit, but Adam lost this divine voice through disobedience. For while he was still innocent, before his transgression, his voice blended fully with the voices of the angels in their praise of God. Angels are called spirits from that Spirit which is God, and thus they have such voices by virtue of their spiritual nature. But Adam lost that angelic voice which he had in paradise, for he fell asleep to that knowledge which he possessed before his sin, just as a person on waking up only dimly remembers what he had seen in his dreams. And so when he was deceived by the trick of the devil and rejected the will of his Creator, he became wrapped up in the darkness of inward ignorance as the just result of his iniquity.

God, however, restores the souls of the elect to that pristine blessedness by infusing them with the light of truth. And in accordance with His eternal plan, He so devised it that whenever He renews the hearts of many with the pouring out of the prophetic spirit, they might, by means of His interior illumination, regain some of the knowledge which Adam had before he was punished for his sin.

And so the holy prophets, inspired by the Spirit which they had received, were called for this purpose: not only to compose psalms and canticles (by which the hearts of listeners would be inflamed) but also to construct various kinds of musical instruments to enhance these songs of praise with melodic strains. Thereby, both through the form and quality of the instruments, as well as through the meaning of the words which accompany them, those who hear might be taught, as we said above, about inward things, since they have been admonished and aroused by outward things. In such a way, these holy prophets get beyond the music of this exile and recall to mind that divine melody of praise which Adam, in company with the angels, enjoyed in God before his fall.

Men of zeal and wisdom have imitated the holy prophets and have themselves, with human skill, invented several kinds of musical instruments, so that they might be able to sing for the delight of their souls, and they accompanied their singing with instruments played with the flexing of the fingers, recalling, in this way, Adam, who was formed by God's finger, which is the Holy Spirit. For, before he sinned, his voice had the sweetness of all musical harmony. Indeed, if he had remained in his original state, the weakness of mortal man would not have been able to endure the power and the resonance of his voice.

But when the devil, man's great deceiver, learned that man had begun to sing through God's inspiration and, therefore, was being transformed to bring back the sweetness of the songs of heaven, mankind's homeland, he was so terrified at seeing his clever machinations go to ruin that he was greatly tormented. Therefore, he devotes himself continually to thinking up and working out all kinds of wicked contrivances. Thus he never ceases from confounding confession and the sweet beauty of both divine praise and spiritual hymns, eradicating them through wicked suggestions, impure thoughts, or various distractions from the heart of man and even from the mouth of the Church itself, wherever he can, through dissension, scandal, or unjust oppression.

Therefore, you and all prelates must exercise the greatest vigilance to clear the air by full and thorough discussion of the justification for such actions before your verdict closes the mouth of any church singing praises to God or suspends it from handling or receiving the divine sacraments. And you must be especially certain that you are drawn to this action out of zeal for God's justice, rather than out of indignation, unjust emotions, or a desire for revenge, and you must always be on your guard not to be circumvented in your decisions by Satan, who drove man from celestial harmony and the delights of paradise.

Consider, too, that just as the body of Jesus Christ was born of the purity of the Virgin Mary through the operation of the Holy Spirit so, too, the canticle of praise, reflecting celestial harmony,

is rooted in the Church through the Holy Spirit. The body is the vestment of the spirit, which has a living voice, and so it is proper for the body, in harmony with the soul, to use its voice to sing praises to God. Whence, in metaphor, the prophetic spirit commands us to praise God with clashing cymbals and cymbals of jubilation, as well as other musical instruments which men of wisdom and zeal have invented, because all arts pertaining to things useful and necessary for mankind have been created by the breath that God sent into man's body. For this reason it is proper that God be praised in all things.

And because sometimes a person sighs and groans at the sound of singing, remembering, as it were, the nature of celestial harmony, the prophet, aware that the soul is symphonic and thoughtfully reflecting on the profound nature of the spirit, urges us in the psalm to confess to the Lord with the harp and to sing a psalm to Him with the ten-stringed psaltery. His meaning is that the harp, which is plucked from below, relates to the discipline of the body; the psaltery, which is plucked from above, pertains to the exertion of the spirit; the ten chords, to the fulfillment of the law.

Therefore, those who, without just cause, impose silence on a church and prohibit the singing of God's praises and those who have on earth unjustly despoiled God of His honor and glory will lose their place among the chorus of angels, unless they have amended their lives through true penitence and humble restitution. Moreover, let those who hold the keys of heaven beware not to open those things which are to be kept closed nor to close those things which are to be kept open, for harsh judgment will fall upon those who rule, unless, as the apostle says, they rule with good judgment.

And I heard a voice saying thus: Who created heaven? God. Who opens heaven to the faithful? God. Who is like Him? No one. And so, O men of faith, let none of you resist Him or oppose Him, lest He fall on you in His might and you have no helper to protect you from His judgment. This time is a womanish time, because the dispensation of God's justice is weak. But the strength of God's justice[1] is exerting itself, a female warrior battling against injustice, so that it might fall defeated.

REVIEW QUESTIONS

1. Why does Hildegard need to defend the importance of music? Why would the bishop of Mainz have curtailed the use of music in religious worship at the convent as part of the interdict?

2. What are the sources of Hildegard's authority, according to her letter? How does she use her authority to challenge the decisions of the bishop and clergy of Mainz?

3. Compare this letter with that of Heloise (pp. 287–294). How does it complicate our understanding of gender roles in the twelfth century?

---

[1] In Latin, *justicia* (justice) is a feminine noun.

ECCLESIA AND *SYNAGOGA* FROM THE CATHEDRAL OF STRASBOURG

These two magnificent statues were sculpted for the cathedral at Strasbourg around the year 1230. Each is larger than life size (about six and a half feet tall), and they would have flanked the entrance to the south transept. Allegorical representations of the Church and the Synagogue were common during the Middle Ages. They were invariably depicted as women (the Latin nouns ecclesia *and* synagoga *are feminine) adorned with certain attributes and posed in distinctive ways. Both of these female figures are beautiful and youthful, but Ecclesia (left) stands proudly erect, wearing a crown, and carrying a victorious banner in the form of cross; her left hand cradles a Eucharistic chalice. Synagoga, in contrast, stands dejectedly, her head bowed and her eyes blindfolded; she holds a broken spear, and an open scroll dangles from her left hand.*

The sculptures, wall paintings, and stained glass of medieval churches helped to communicate complex concepts and stories. What messages do these statues convey? What importance should we attach to the gender of these statues? What did medieval authorities gain by depicting these allegorical figures as women? How might someone such as Hildegard of Bingen (see pp. 295–297) have responded to these figures?

The Magna Carta:
The "Great Charter" of 1215

Magna Carta, issued in June of 1215, was a response to both long-term trends and recent disasters. The barons of England were, most of them, descendants of Norman warriors who had helped their lord, William the Conqueror, subdue and colonize the Anglo-Saxon kingdom after 1066. For nearly a century and a half thereafter, England's strong position vis-à-vis the French king had allowed these men to control lands on both sides of the English Channel. But when John inherited the English throne in 1199, he was forced to contend with the fact that the power of the new French king, Philip Augustus, was growing. Although he had considerable talents as an administrator, he was no warrior; his chief subjects resented both his inability to hold onto Normandy and his tendency to interfere in their affairs. When many of England's bishops, barons, and other lords subsequently rebelled against him, they forced him to put his seal on this contract, which is a curious mixture of lofty ideals and practical details about how John should govern his realm and not infringe on the liberties of his most powerful subjects.

From *Select Documents of English Constitutional History*, edited by George Burton Adams and H. Morse Stephens (Basingstoke: Macmillan, 1901); translation modified and annotated by Carol Symes, with reference to the Latin original.

John, by the grace of God, king of England, lord of Ireland, duke of Normandy and Aquitaine, count of Anjou, to the archbishops, bishops, abbots, earls,[1] barons, justiciars,[2] foresters, sheriffs, reeves,[3] servants, and all bailiffs and his faithful people, greeting. Know that out of respect for God and for the good of our soul and those of all our predecessors and of our heirs; to the honor of God and the exaltation of Holy Church; and the improvement of our kingdom; by the advice of our venerable fathers Stephen, archbishop of Canterbury, primate of all England and Cardinal of the Holy Roman Church, Henry, archbishop of Dublin, William of London, Peter of Winchester, Joscelyn of Bath and Glastonbury, Hugh of Lincoln, Walter of Worcester, William of Coventry, and Benedict of Rochester, bishops; of Master Pandulf, subdeacon and member of the household of the lord Pope, of Brother Aymeric, master of the Knights of the Temple in England; and of the noblemen William Marshall, earl of Pembroke, William, earl of Salisbury, William, earl Warren, William, earl of Arundel, Alan of Galloway, constable of Scotland, Warren Fitz-Gerald, Peter Fitz-Herbert, Hubert de Burgh, seneschal of Poitou, Hugh de Nevil, Matthew Fitz-Herbert, Thomas Bassett, Alan Bassett, Philip d'Albini, Robert de Ropesle, John Marshall, John Fitz-Hugh, and others of our faithful:[4]

1. We have in the first place granted to God, and by this our present charter confirmed, for us and our

---

[1] An Anglo-Saxon word for a nobleman or great lord—as opposed to *baron*, a Norman French word meaning something similar.

[2] A Latin term for judges and court officials.

[3] An Anglo-Saxon term for an elected official; sheriffs are "shire-reeves," reeves with oversight of a shire (an Anglo-Saxon administrative unit).

[4] It is worth noting that nearly all of the noblemen mentioned by name are of Norman descent.

heirs forever, that the English Church shall be free, and shall hold its rights entire and its liberties uninjured; and we will that it thus be observed: which is shown by this, that the freedom of elections, which is considered to be most important and especially necessary to the English Church, we, of our pure and spontaneous will, granted, and by our charter confirmed, before the contest between us and our barons had arisen, and obtained a confirmation of it by the Lord Pope Innocent III; which we will observe and which we will shall be observed in good faith by our heirs forever.

We have granted moreover to all free men of our kingdom, for us and our heirs forever, all the liberties written below, to be had and held by themselves and by their heirs from us and from our heirs.

2. If any of our earls or barons, or others holding from us in chief by military service, shall die, and when he has died his heir shall be of full age and owe relief,[5] he shall have his inheritance by the ancient [law of] relief: that is to say, the heir or heirs of an earl [in exchange] for the whole barony of an earl a hundred pounds; the heir or heirs of a baron [in exchange] for a whole barony a hundred pounds; the heir or heirs of a knight, [in exchange] for a whole knight's fee, a hundred shillings at most; and who owes less let him give less according to the ancient custom of fiefs.

3. If moreover the heir of any one of such shall be underage, and shall be in wardship,[6] when he comes of age he shall have his inheritance without relief and without a fine.

4. The custodian of the land of such a minor heir shall not take from the land of the heir any except reasonable products, reasonable customary payments, and reasonable services, and this without destruction or waste of men or of property; and if we shall have committed the custody of the land of any such a one to the sheriff or to any other who is to be responsible to us for its proceeds, and that man shall have caused destruction or waste during his custody, we will recover damages from him, and the land shall be committed to two legal and discreet men of that fief, who shall be responsible for its proceeds to us or to him to whom we have assigned them; and if we shall have given or sold to anyone the custody of any such land, and he has caused destruction or waste there, he shall lose that custody, and it shall be handed over to two legal and discreet men of that fief who shall be in like manner responsible to us, as is said above.

5. The custodian, moreover, so long as he shall have the custody of the land, must keep up the houses, parks, warrens, fish ponds, mills, and other things pertaining to the land, from the proceeds of the land itself; and he must return to the heir, when he has come to full age, all his land, furnished with ploughs and implements of husbandry according as the time of wainage[7] requires and as the proceeds of the land are able reasonably to sustain.

6. Heirs shall be married without disparity: that is, before the marriage is contracted it shall be announced to the relatives by blood of the heir himself.

7. A widow, after the death of her husband, shall have her marriage portion and her inheritance immediately and without obstruction, nor shall she give anything [in exchange] for her dowry or for her marriage portion, or [in exchange] for her inheritance, which inheritance her husband and she held on the day of the death of her husband; and she may remain in the house of her husband for forty days after his death, within which time her dowry shall be assigned to her.

8. No widow shall be compelled to marry so long as she prefers to live without a husband, provided she gives security that she will not marry without our consent, if she holds [property] from us, or without the consent of her lord from whom she holds [property], if she holds from another.

9. Neither we nor our bailiffs will seize any land or rent for any debt, so long as the chattels of the

---

[5] An inheritance tax.

[6] That is, a ward of the crown and under the personal protection of the king.

[7] An Anglo-Saxon term: "carting," or the means of transporting the fruits of the harvest.

debtor are sufficient for the payment of the debt; nor shall the pledges of a debtor be distrained[8] so long as the principal debtor himself has enough for the payment of the debt; and if the principal debtor fails in the payment of the debt, not having the wherewithal to pay it, the pledges shall be responsible for the debt; and if they wish, they shall have the lands and the rents of the debtor until they shall have been satisfied for the debt which they have before paid for him, unless the principal debtor shall have shown himself to be quit in that respect towards those pledges.

10. If any one has taken anything from the Jews, by way of a loan, [whether] more or less, and dies before that debt is paid, the debt shall not draw interest so long as the heir is under age, from whomsoever he holds; and if that debt falls into our hands, we will take nothing except the chattel contained in the agreement.

11. And if any one dies leaving a debt owing to the Jews, his wife shall have her dowry, and shall pay nothing of that debt; and if there remain minor children of the dead man, necessaries shall be provided for them corresponding to the holding of the dead man; and from the remainder shall the debt be paid, saving the service [owed] to the [debtor's] lords. In the same way debts are to be treated which are owed to others than the Jews.

12. No scutage[9] or aid[10] shall be imposed in our kingdom except by the common council of our kingdom, except for the ransoming of our body, for making our oldest son a knight, and for once marrying our oldest daughter, and for these purposes it shall be only a reasonable aid; in the same way it shall be done concerning the aids [usually paid by merchants] of the city of London.

13. And the city of London shall have all its ancient liberties and free customs, as well by land as by water. Moreover, we will and grant that all other cities and boroughs and villages and ports shall have all their liberties and free customs.

14. And for holding a common council of the kingdom concerning the assessment of an aid otherwise than in the three cases mentioned above, or concerning the assessment of a scutage, we shall cause to be summoned the archbishops, bishops, abbots, earls, and greater barons by our letters, individually; and besides we shall cause to be summoned generally, by our sheriffs and bailiffs all those who hold from us in chief, for [meeting on] a certain day, that is at the end of forty days at least, and for a certain place; and in all the letters of that summons, we will express the cause of the summons; and when the summons has thus been given, the business shall proceed on the appointed day, on the advice of those who shall be present, even if not all of those who were summoned have come.

15. We will not grant to any one, moreover, that he shall take an aid from his free men, except for ransoming his body, for making his oldest son a knight, and for once marrying his oldest daughter; and for these purposes only a reasonable aid shall be taken.

16. No one shall be compelled to perform any greater service for a knight's fief, or for any other free tenement,[11] than is [usually] owed for it.

17. The common pleas shall not follow our court, but shall be held in some certain place.[12]

18. The recognition of *novel disseisin, mort d'ancestor,* and *darrein presentment* shall be held only in their own counties and in this manner:[13] we, or (if we are outside of the kingdom) our principal justiciar, will send two justiciars through each county four times a year, who with four

---

8 Imprisoned or forced to pay: "pledges" in this context means those who have promised to pay the debt in the event that the debtor himself is unable to do so.

9 A kind of tax.

10 A loan to the crown, usually a forced loan.

---

11 Holding, usually of land.

12 That is, the king's court should no longer be itinerant, sitting in judgment whenever the king is traveling around the realm, but should instead be convened in a fixed location at certain times.

13 These Norman French terms are legal neologisms inserted into the Latin text of the charter. *Novel disseisin* refers to the recovery of recently seized land; *mort d'ancestor* ("death of the ancestor") is an inheritance claim; and *darrein presentment* refers to cases concerning nomination to ecclesiastical office.

knights of each county, elected by the county, shall hold in the county, and on the day and in the place of the county court, the aforesaid assizes[14] of the county.

19. And if the aforesaid assizes cannot be held within the day of the county court, a sufficient number of knights and free-holders shall remain from those who were present at the county court on that day to give the judgments, according as the business is more or less.

20. A free man shall not be fined for a small offence, except in proportion to the measure of the offence; and for a great offence he shall be fined in proportion to the magnitude of the offence, saving his freehold;[15] and a merchant in the same way, saving his merchandise; and the villain[16] shall be fined in the same way, saving his wainage, if he shall be at our mercy; and none of the above fines shall be imposed except by the oaths of honest men of the neighborhood.

21. Earls and barons shall only be fined by their peers, and only in proportion to their offence.

22. A cleric shall be fined, like those before mentioned, only in proportion to his lay holding, and not according to the extent of his ecclesiastical benefice.

23. No vill[17] or man shall be compelled to make bridges over the rivers except those which ought to do it of old and rightfully.

24. No sheriff, constable, coroners, or other bailiffs of ours shall hold pleas of our crown.

25. All counties, hundreds, wapentakes, and trithings[18] shall be [valued] at the ancient rents and without any increase, excepting our demesne[19] manors.

26. If any person holding a lay fief from us shall die, and our sheriff or bailiff shall show our letters-patent[20] of our summons concerning a debt which the deceased owed to us, it shall be lawful for our sheriff or bailiff to attach and levy on the chattels of the deceased found on his lay fief, to the value of that debt, in the view of legal men, so nevertheless that nothing be removed thence until the clear debt to us shall be paid; and the remainder shall be left to the executors for the fulfillment of the will of the deceased; and if nothing is owed to us by him, all the chattels shall go to the deceased, saving to his wife and children their reasonable shares.

27. If any free man dies intestate, his chattels shall be distributed by the hands of his near relatives and friends, under the oversight of the Church, saving to each one the debts which the deceased owed to him.

28. No constable or other bailiff of ours shall take anyone's grain or other chattels, without immediately paying for them in money, unless he is able to obtain a postponement at the goodwill of the seller.

29. No constable shall require any knight to give money in place of his ward[21] of a castle if he is willing to furnish that ward in his own person or through another honest man, if he himself is not able to do it for a reasonable cause; and if we shall lead or send him into the army he shall be free from ward in proportion to the amount of time during which he has been in the army through us.

30. No sheriff or bailiff of ours, or anyone else, shall take horses or wagons from any free man for carrying purposes, except by the permission of that free man.

31. Neither we nor our bailiffs will take the wood of another man for castles, or for anything else which we are doing, except by the permission of him to whom the wood belongs.

32. We will not hold the lands of those convicted of a felony for more than a year and a day, after which the lands shall be returned to the lords of the fiefs.

---

[14] A Norman French term meaning "sitting" that is, local hearings on minor civil cases.

[15] In other words, his fine cannot be so great as to result in liquidation of his real property.

[16] From the Latin *villanus*, meaning "villager" or even "farmhand."

[17] Community or village.

[18] These are all Anglo-Saxon terms designating successively smaller divisions of land.

[19] A Norman French term referring to lands—domains—from which the king derives revenue directly.

---

[20] Literally, "open letters," sealed documents whose contents were plainly visible (not secret).

[21] The responsibility for guarding or keeping watch.

33. All the fish-weirs on the Thames and the Medway [rivers], and throughout all England, shall be done away with, except those on the coast.

34. The writ which is called *præcipe*[22] shall not be given in the future to any one concerning any tenement by which a free man can lose his court.

35. There shall be one measure of wine throughout our whole kingdom, and one measure of ale, and one measure of grain, that is the London quarter, and one width of dyed cloth and of russets and of halbergets,[23] that is two ells within the selvages; of weights, moreover it shall be as of measures.

36. Nothing shall henceforth be given or taken [in exchange] for a writ of inquisition concerning life or limbs, but it shall be given freely and not denied.

37. If any one holds from us by fee farm or by socage or by burgage,[24] and from another he holds land by military service, we will not have the guardianship of the heir or of his land which is of the fief of another, on account of that fee farm, or socage, or burgage; nor will we have the custody of that fee farm, or socage, or burgage, unless that fee farm itself owes military service. We will not have the guardianship of the heir or of the land of anyone who holds land from another by military service on account of any petty serjeanty[25] which he holds from us by the service of paying to us knives or arrows, or things of that kind.

38. No bailiff in the future shall put any one to his law on his simple affirmation, without credible witnesses brought for this purpose.[26]

39. No free man shall be taken or imprisoned or dispossessed, or outlawed, or banished, or in any way destroyed, nor will we act against him, nor send [anyone] against him, except by the legal judgment of his peers or by the law of the land.

40. To no one will we sell, to no one will we deny or delay right or justice.

41. All merchants shall be safe and secure in going out from England and coming into England and in remaining and going through England, as well by land as by water, for buying and selling, free from all evil tolls, by the ancient and rightful customs, except in time of war, and if they are of a land at war with us; and if such are found in our land at the beginning of war, they shall be attached[27] without injury to their bodies or goods, until it shall be known from us or from our principal justiciar in what way the merchants of our land are treated who shall be then found in the country which is at war with us; and if ours are safe there, the others shall be safe in our land.

42. It is allowed henceforth to any one to go out from our kingdom, and to return, safely and securely, by land and by water, for the sake of their fidelity to us, except in time of war for some short time, for the common good of the kingdom; excepting persons imprisoned and outlawed according to the law of the realm, and people of a land at war with us, and merchants of whom it shall be done as is before said.

43. If any one holds from any escheat,[28] as from the honor of Wallingford, or Nottingham, or Boulogne, or Lancaster, or from other escheats which are in our hands and are baronies, and he dies, his heir shall not give any other relief, nor do to us any other service than he would do to the baron, if that barony was in the hands of the baron; and we will hold it in the same way as the baron held it.

44. Men who dwell outside the forest shall not henceforth come before our justiciars of the forest, on common summons, unless they are in a plea of, or pledges for, any person or persons who are arrested on account of the forest.

45. We will not make [any men] justiciars, constables, sheriffs or bailiffs unless they be such men as know the law of the realm and are well inclined to observe it.

---

[22] From the Latin command "seize."

[23] Types of cloth: one dyed a dark reddish brown, the other of uncertain texture and hue.

[24] Anglo-Saxon terms, referring to ancient rights and customs of land holding.

[25] A Norman French term meaning "minor military service."

---

[26] That is, no one should be questioned in a legal matter unless he has been sworn in before legal witnesses.

[27] Arrested or arraigned.

[28] A situation in which the holder of a fief has died without an heir or has been convicted of a crime.

46. All barons who have founded abbeys for which they have charters from kings of England, or ancient tenure, shall have their custody when they have become vacant, as they ought to have.[29]

47. All forests which have been afforested in our time shall be disafforested immediately; and so it shall be concerning river banks which in our time have been fenced in.[30]

48. All the bad customs concerning forests and warrens and concerning foresters and warreners, sheriffs and their servants, river banks and their guardians shall be inquired into immediately in each county by twelve sworn knights of the same county, who shall be elected by the honest men of the same county, and within forty days after the inquisition has been made, they shall be entirely destroyed by them, never to be restored, provided that we be first informed of it, or our justiciar, if we are not in England.

49. We will give back immediately all hostages and charters which have been delivered to us by Englishmen as security for peace or for faithful service.

50. We will remove absolutely from their bailiwicks the relatives of Gerard de Athyes, so that for the future they shall have no bailiwick in England: Engelard de Cygony, Andrew, Peter and Gyon de Chancelles, Gyon de Cygony, Geoffrey de Martin and his brothers, Philip Mark and his brothers, and Geoffrey his nephew and their whole retinue.

51. And immediately after the reëstablishment of peace we will remove from the kingdom all foreign-born soldiers, cross-bow men, sergeants, and mercenaries who have come with horses and arms for the injury of the realm.

52. If any one shall have been dispossessed or removed by us without legal judgment of his peers, from his lands, castles, franchises, or his right, we will restore them to him immediately; and if contention arises about this, then it shall be done according to the judgment of the twenty-five barons, of whom mention is made below concerning the security of the peace. Concerning all those things, however, from which any one has been removed or of which he has been deprived without legal judgment of his peers by King Henry [II] our father, or by King Richard our brother, which we have in our hand, or which others hold, and which it is our duty to guarantee, we shall have respite according to the usual dispensation of crusaders: excepting those things about which the suit has been begun or the inquisition made by our writ before our assumption of the cross; when, however, we shall return from our journey, or if by chance we desist from the journey, we will immediately show full justice in regard to them.[31]

53. We shall, moreover, have the same respite, and in the same manner, about showing justice in regard to the forests which are to be disafforested or to remain forests, which Henry our father or Richard our brother made into forests; and concerning the custody of lands which are in the fief of another, custody of which we have until now had on account of a fief which any one has held from us by military service; and concerning the abbeys which have been founded in fiefs of others than ourselves, in which the lord of the fief has asserted for himself a right; and when we return, or if we should desist from our journey, we will immediately show full justice to those complaining in regard to them.

54. No one shall be seized nor imprisoned on the appeal of a woman concerning the death of any one except her husband.

---

[29] That is, lords who have been granted a controlling interest in abbeys located in their domains are allowed to collect taxes and tithes when the office of the abbot is vacant. Such lords often had a strong say in the selection of abbots.

[30] Those areas that have been recently declared to be royal forests, and thus the property of the king, should revert to being common land.

[31] This clause and the next, as well as clause 57 below, have to do with seizure of property or other exactions made by John and his immediate predecessors on the grounds that revenue or goods were needed to finance or equip a crusade. Henry II (r. 1154–89) may have taken an oath to go on crusade in order to do just this (he never went). Richard (r. 1189–99) participated in the Third Crusade (1189–92). John himself never went on crusade or seems to have had any intention of doing so.

55. All fines which have been imposed unjustly and against the law of the land, and all penalties imposed unjustly and against the law of the land are altogether excused, or will be on the judgment of the twenty-five barons of whom mention is made below in connection with the security of the peace, or on the judgment of the majority of them, along with the aforesaid Stephen, archbishop of Canterbury, if he is able to be present, and others whom he may wish to call for this purpose along with him. And if he should not be able to be present, nevertheless the business shall go on without him, provided that if any one or more of the aforesaid twenty-five barons are in a similar suit they should be removed as far as this particular judgment goes, and others who shall be chosen and put upon oath, by the remainder of the twenty-five, shall be substituted for them for this purpose.

56. If we have dispossessed or removed any Welshmen from their lands, or franchises, or other things, without legal judgment of their peers, in England, or in Wales, they shall be immediately returned to them; and if a dispute shall have arisen over this, then it shall be settled in the borderland by judgment of their peers, concerning holdings of England according to the law of England, concerning holdings of Wales according to the law of Wales, and concerning holdings of the borderland according to the law of the borderland. The Welsh shall do the same to us and ours.

57. Concerning all those things, however, from which any one of the Welsh shall have been removed or dispossessed without legal judgment of his peers, by King Henry our father, or King Richard our brother, which we hold in our hands, or which others hold, and we are bound to guarantee to them, we shall have respite till the usual period of crusaders, those being excepted about which suit was begun or inquisition made by our command before our assumption of the cross. When, however, we shall return, or if by chance we shall desist from our journey, we will show full justice to them immediately, according to the laws of the Welsh and the aforesaid parts.

58. We will give back the son of Llewellyn[32] immediately, and all the hostages from Wales and the charters which had been liberated to us as a security for peace.

59. We will act toward Alexander, king of the Scots,[33] concerning the return of his sisters and his hostages, and concerning his franchises and his right, according to the manner in which we shall act toward our other barons of England, unless it ought to be otherwise by the charters which we hold from William his father, formerly king of the Scots, and this shall be by the judgment of his peers in our court.

60. Moreover, all those customs and franchises mentioned above which we have conceded in our kingdom—and which are to be fulfilled, as far as pertains to us, in respect to our men—all men of our kingdom, as well clergy as laymen, shall observe as far as pertains to them, in respect to their men.

61. Since, moreover, for the sake of God, and for the improvement of our kingdom, and for the better quieting of the hostility sprung up lately between us and our barons, we have made all these concessions; wishing them to enjoy these in a complete and firm stability forever, we make and concede to them the security described below; that is to say, that they shall elect twenty-five barons of the kingdom, whom they will, who ought with all their power to observe, hold, and cause to be observed, the peace and liberties which we have conceded to them, and by this our present charter confirmed to them; in this manner, that if we or our justiciar, or our bailiffs, or any one of our servants shall have

---

[32] Llywelyn ab Iorwerth, often known as Llewellyn the Great (c. 1172–1240). He was the ruler of Gwynedd (northern Wales) and the *de facto* leader of the Welsh. He had aligned himself with the Norman barons against John, who was holding his son hostage, and used this position to demand certain concessions. The situation was further complicated by the fact that John's illegitimate daughter, Joan, was married to the Welsh prince.

[33] Alexander II (r. 1214–49): he, too, took advantage of the situation.

done wrong in any way toward any one, or shall have transgressed any of the articles of peace or security; and the wrong shall have been shown to four barons of the aforesaid twenty-five barons, let those four barons come to us or to our justiciar, if we are out of the kingdom, laying before us the transgression, and let them ask that we cause that transgression to be corrected without delay. And if we shall not have corrected the transgression or, if we shall be out of the kingdom, if our justiciar shall not have corrected it within a period of forty days, counting from the time in which it has been shown to us or to our justiciar, if we are out of the kingdom; the aforesaid four barons shall refer the matter to the remainder of the twenty-five barons, and let these twenty-five barons with the whole community of the country distress and injure us in every way they can; that is to say by the seizure of our castles, lands, possessions, and in such other ways as they can until it shall have been corrected according to their judgment, saving our person and that of our queen, and those of our children; and when the correction has been made, let them devote themselves to us as they did before. And let whoever in the country wishes take an oath that in all the above-mentioned measures he will obey the orders of the aforesaid twenty-five barons, and that he will injure us as far as he is able with them, and we give permission to swear publicly and freely to each one who wishes to swear, and no one will we ever forbid to swear. All those, moreover, in the country who of themselves and their own will are unwilling to take an oath to the twenty-five barons as to distressing and injuring us along with them, we will compel to take the oath by our mandate, as before said. And if any one of the twenty-five barons shall have died or departed from the land or shall in any other way be prevented from taking the above-mentioned action, let the remainder of the aforesaid twenty-five barons choose another in his place, according to their judgment, who shall take an oath in the same way as the others. In all those things, moreover, which are committed to those five and twenty barons to carry out, if perhaps the twenty-

five are present, and some disagreement arises among them about something, or if any of them when they have been summoned are not willing or are not able to be present, let that be considered valid and firm which the greater part of those who are present arrange or command, just as if the whole twenty-five had agreed in this; and let the aforesaid twenty-five swear that they will observe faithfully all the things which are said above, and with all their ability cause them to be observed. And we will obtain nothing from any one, either by ourselves or by another by which any of these concessions and liberties shall be revoked or diminished; and if any such thing shall have been obtained, let it be invalid and void, and we will never use it by ourselves or by another.

62. And all ill-will, grudges, and anger sprung up between us and our men, clergy and laymen, from the time of the dispute, we have fully renounced and pardoned to all. Moreover, all transgressions committed on account of this dispute, from Easter in the sixteenth year of our reign [1215] till the restoration of peace, we have fully remitted to all, clergy and laymen, and as far as pertains to us, fully pardoned. And moreover we have caused to be made for them testimonial letters-patent of lord Stephen, archbishop of Canterbury, lord Henry, archbishop of Dublin, and of the aforesaid bishops and of Master Pandulf, in respect to that security and the concessions named above.

63. Wherefore we will and firmly command that the Church of England shall be free, and that the men in our kingdom shall have and hold all the aforesaid liberties, rights and concessions, well and peacefully, freely and quietly, fully and completely, for themselves and their heirs, from us and our heirs, in all things and places, forever, as before said. It has been sworn, moreover, as well on our part as on the part of the barons, that all these things spoken of above shall be observed in good faith and without any evil intent. Witness the above named and many others. Given by our hand in the meadow which is called Runnymede, between Windsor and Staines, on the fifteenth day of June, in the seventeenth year of our reign.

REVIEW QUESTIONS

1. Study the organization of this charter carefully. What does the order of the various clauses reveal about the issues that were most important to the English barons?
2. How would you summarize the barons' main grievances? What would you identify as the most important concessions being granted by the king?
3. What does a close reading of this document reveal about political, social, economic, and ethnic tensions within John's realm—and beyond its borders? What can you conclude about the legal status of "ordinary" men and women in England?

THOMAS AQUINAS

FROM *Summa Theologica*

Thomas Aquinas (c. 1225–1274) was a Dominican theologian, university professor, and author of the Summa Theologica, *the most influential theological work of the Middle Ages.* Theology *was a new term devised to define the recent academic subject of applying the tools of reason to religious truths. This confidence in human ability to understand a reasonable universe working according to God's logical plans and laws is central to the values of medieval humanism. In these sections of the* Summa Theologica, *Thomas analyzes proofs of God's existence and the meaning of humanity's creation. This translation, faithful to the content of the original, rearranges for a modern audience a very formal style of scholastic argument.*

From *St. Thomas Aquinas: Summa Theologica*, edited by Timothy S. McDermott (Westminster, Md.: Christian Classics, 1989), pp. 12–13, 144–49.

*　　*　　*

There Is a God. There are Five Ways of Proving There is a God:

The first and most obvious way is based on change. We see things changing. Now anything changing is being changed by something else. (For things changing are on the way to realization, whereas things causing change are already realized: they are realizing something else's potential, and for that they must themselves be real. The actual heat of a fire causes wood, already able to be hot, to become actually hot, and so causes change in the wood. Now the actually hot cannot at the same time be potentially hot, but only potentially cold. So what changes cannot as such be causing the change, but must be being changed by something else.) This something else, if itself changing, is being changed by yet another thing; and this last by another. Now we must stop somewhere, otherwise there will be no first cause of the change, and, as a result, no subsequent causes. (Only when acted upon by a first cause do intermediate causes produce a change; if a hand does not move the stick, the stick will not move anything else.) We arrive

then at some first cause of change not itself being changed by anything, and this is what everybody understands by *God*.

The second way is based on the very notion of cause. In the observable world causes derive their causality from other causes; we never observe, nor ever could, something causing itself, for this would mean it preceded itself, and this is not possible. But the deriving of causality must stop somewhere; for in the series of causes an earlier member causes an intermediate and the intermediate a last (whether the intermediate be one or many). Now eliminate a cause and you also eliminate its effects: you cannot have a last cause, nor an intermediate one, unless you have a first. Given no stop in the series of causes, no first cause, there will be no intermediate causes and no last effect; which contradicts observation. So one is forced to suppose some first cause, to which everyone gives the name *God*.

The third way is based on what need not be and on what must be, and runs as follows. Some of the things we come across can be but need not be, for we find them springing up and dying away, thus sometimes in being and sometimes not. Now everything cannot be like this, for a thing that need not be, once was not; and if everything need not be, once upon a time there was nothing. But if that were true there would be nothing even now, because something that does not exist can only be brought into being by something already existing. If nothing was in being nothing could be brought into being, and nothing would be in being now, which contradicts observation. Not everything therefore is the sort of thing that need not be; some things must be, and these may or may not owe this necessity to something else. But just as a series of causes must have a stop, so also a series of things which must be and owe this to other things. One is forced to suppose something which must be, and owes this to nothing outside itself; indeed it itself is the cause that other things must be.

The fourth way is based on the gradation observed in things. Some things are better, truer, more ex-

cellent than others. Such comparative terms describe varying degrees of approximation to a superlative; for example, things are hotter and hotter the nearer they approach what is hottest. Something therefore is the truest and best and most excellent of things, and hence the most fully in being; for Aristotle says that the truest things are the things most fully in being. Now *when many things possess some property in common, the one most fully possessing it causes it in the others: fire*, as Aristotle says, *the hottest of all things, causes all other things to be hot*. Something therefore causes in all other things their being, their goodness, and whatever other perfection they have. And this is what we call *God*.

The fifth way is based on the guidedness of nature. Goal-directed behaviour is observed in all bodies obeying natural laws, even when they lack awareness. Their behaviour hardly ever varies and practically always turns out well, showing that they truly tend to goals and do not merely hit them by accident. But nothing lacking awareness can tend to a goal except it be directed by someone with awareness and understanding; the arrow, for example, requires an archer. Everything in nature, therefore, is directed to its goal by someone with understanding, and this we call *God*.

*   *   *

The Genesis of Man

God formed man from the slime of the earth and breathed into his face the breath of life, and man became a living soul. Only what possesses existence and is subject of its own existence—substance— properly exists; all supervening properties exist not as themselves possessing existence but as forms under which a substance exists. Whiteness's existence is really the existence of something as white. This is true of all non-subsistent forms; so, properly speaking, it is not such forms but the things of which they are forms that come into existence. The soul however is a subsistent form and can properly be said both to exist and to come into existence. But since it does not come from pre-existent matter

(only bodies do that) it must come by a new creation. Only God can create. All secondary agents presuppose material provided by a primary agent, which they then transform. Since the human soul does not come into existence by transformation of pre-existent matter, it must be produced by God's immediate creation. The soul however is only part of man, and naturally perfect only when united to its body, so it was fittingly created in its body, not before it. If it was a natural species of thing the soul would be a sort of angel; but by nature it is the form of a body, the formal element in an animal. Forms in matter are caused by forms in matter, when composite material things generate one another. The only immaterial thing that can produce something material without needing previous material is God; he alone can create new matter. So Adam's body was formed by God immediately, there being no preceding human body that could generate a body of like species to itself. Because the senses are mainly concentrated in the face, other animals have faces close to the ground to look for food and provender; but men have raised faces so that their senses, especially the finest and most discriminating sense of sight, may experience sense-objects in every direction of heaven and earth. Man's upright carriage also releases his hands for various useful purposes. And since he does not have to use his mouth for gathering food, it is not oblong and hard as in other animals but adapted for speech, the special work of reason. So man's upright carriage is not like that of the plants, for they have their roots (which are their mouths) in the earth.

It is not good for man to be alone; let us make him a help that is like himself. The help God makes for man is not for any sort of work (for there other men would be more help than a woman) but for producing children. In plants, which have no nobler function in life than propagation, the active and passive abilities to propagate are joined at all times. In the higher animals however there is more to life than that, so the active male and passive female partners mate only at certain times, constituting the sort of unity a plant is always. Aristotle called the female *a male manqué.* The particular nature of the active male seed intends to produce a perfect likeness of itself, and when females are conceived this is due to weak seed, or unsuitable material, or external influences like the dampness of the south wind. But this is because nature as a whole intends women; and in this sense they are not manqué but intended by God, the author of nature as a whole. The type of subordination in which servants are managed in their master's interests came in after sin; but the subordination seen in households or cities, where management is for the benefit of the subordinates themselves, would have obtained even without sin. And such is the natural inequality and subordination of women to men, who are by nature more reasonable and discerning. [Some say God should not have produced Eve to be an occasion of sin for Adam, but] if God removed from the world everything which man has made an excuse for sin, the world would be a poor place. What is a general good must not be sacrificed because of some particular abuse, especially since God is powerful enough to turn any evil to good account. Forming Eve from Adam's rib signified companionship, not domination (so not from his head) nor yet subjection (so not from his feet); and it also symbolized the establishment of the church by the sacraments of blood and water flowing from the side of Christ sleeping on the cross.

Let us make man after our own image and likeness. An image not only resembles, it expresses: however like each other two eggs may be, one does not express the other and is not its image. But the resemblance man bears God derives from God as from an original, so scripture describes man as made to God's image; where the preposition *to* signifies approach to something at a distance, the original in this case being infinitely distant from the image. An image must also resemble its original in species, or in some attribute like shape peculiar to that species, where likeness in species means likeness down to the last thing differentiating the species. Things in general resemble God in existing, some things also in being alive, and some finally in intellectual discernment: the closest likeness to God in creation. Properly speaking then, only creatures with intellect are made to God's image. And the point at which

such creatures most closely resemble God is when they imitate his self-understanding and love. So there are three levels to the imaging of God by man: the very nature of mind gives to all men a natural aptitude for understanding and loving God; grace adds to some men an actual if imperfect understanding and love of God; and the glory of heaven brings this to perfection. The principal constituent of God's image in man, mind, is found in both male and female human beings; which is why Genesis says *To God's image he created him (namely, mankind); male and female he created them.* A secondary image of God as beginning and end of creation is however to be found only in male man, the beginning and end of woman: and this is what made St Paul say that *the man is the image and glory of God, and the woman the glory of man, for Adam was not from Eve but Eve from Adam, and Adam was not for Eve, but Eve for Adam.*

That man is made in the image of God's nature implies that all three persons of God are represented in him. In other creatures, and in other parts of man than his mind, there is not the same image or likeness in species to God, but only the sort of trace that all causes leave even in effects unlike in species. Thus we talk of tracks left by animals as traces, fires leave traces of themselves in ashes, and armies traces in the ravaged countryside. An image of the uncreated Trinity can be found in creatures with reason, who utter a word in their minds, and in whose wills a love issues, so representing God in species. In other creatures there is no such word-source or word or love; but a trace of the fact that source, word and love exist in its maker. For a creature's shaping and conditioning indicate that it *comes from* somewhere; its specific form indicates its maker's *word* as a house's shape indicates its architect's idea; and its functional order indicates its maker's *love* as a house's uses indicate what its architect willed. A first image of the Trinity in our minds is found in our activities of thinking out and formulating an inner word from the information we have, and then bursting out from this in a love. But since such activities exist implicitly in their sources [memory, understanding and will], a secondary

image of the Trinity exists in our powers and dispositions to act. The kind of word and love we have in our heart varies according to what it is we are conceiving and loving: stone or horse. So God's image is to be found in the conceiving of a word that expresses what we know of God and a love flowing from that; in other words, in the soul attending directly to God. Though the mind can also attend indirectly to God (as to an object seen in a mirror) when, as Augustine says, it remembers and understands and loves itself, and perceives there a trinity: not God indeed, but an image of God; and then moves through that to God.

God made man right. No one can wilfully turn away from happiness, for man wants happiness by nature. So no one seeing God for what he is can wilfully turn his back on God. Plainly then, since Adam sinned, he had not seen God for what he is. The disembodied state of the soul after death differs from its present embodied state in being unnatural; but Adam's state of innocence and man's state after sin differ as integrated and disintegrated states of a soul which has preserved its natural way of existence unimpaired. In the state of innocence, just as now, man's soul was adapted to controlling and perfecting and giving life to his body, but in so fully integrated a way that his body was completely at the service of his soul without hindrance. And since the way of understanding appropriate to a soul that must control and perfect the body's animal life is by recourse to sense-experience, this was also Adam's way of understanding. The things that were made in the beginning were made not only to be themselves but to start other things existing, and that is why they were produced in a state of perfection. Adam was created mature in body, capable of immediate procreation, and mature in soul, capable of immediate education and instruction of others. So he knew all that men normally have to learn, everything implicit in the first self-evident premises, all natural knowledge: *he gave all animals their names.* And since controlling his own and other people's lives also involved knowing life as destined to a goal beyond nature, Adam needed to

know the supernatural things required to direct life in that state of innocence, just as nowadays we need the faith. But Adam did not know other things not naturally knowable but not required for directing life: such as men's thoughts, or the indeterminate future, or details like the number of pebbles in some river.

The integrated state of Adam in which his reason was submissive to God, his lower powers to his reason, and his body to his soul, seems to imply that he possessed God's grace from the start; for this is an integration not written into man's nature, otherwise it would have remained after sin. The primary submissiveness of Adam's reason to God must have been more than natural, and therefore due to a gift of grace; for effects cannot be more potent than their cause. In us feeling is partly but not wholly subject to reason: sometimes our feelings pre-empt and hamper reasoned assessment, whilst at other times they presuppose it. In the state of innocence the lower appetites were completely subject to reason, and all feelings presupposed reasoned assessment. Virtues are what dispose our reason towards God and our lower powers towards the standards set by reason; so the very rightness of man's first state required him to possess all virtue. Some virtues, like charity and justice, contain no implication of imperfection, and others, like faith and hope, imply imperfections which were compatible with Adam's state (not yet seeing God and not in full enjoyment of him); so these existed in Adam without qualification, both the dispositions and the acts that proceed from them. But virtues like repentance and compassion that imply imperfections incompatible with Adam's state could only exist inactively, as dispositions to act when required, in the way Aristotle says shame exists in an earnest man.

Let him rule the fishes of the sea and the birds of the sky and the beasts of the earth. In nature the less perfect serve the more perfect: plants feed on the earth, animals on plants, and men on both plants and animals. Moreover, the instincts of animals to behave in certain particular ways is a sort of sharing in man's universal practical sense which can reason out all behaviour. So the subordination of animals to man is natural. To think wild and aggressive animals were originally peaceable, not only to men but also to other animals, is quite irrational. How could man by sinning change the nature of animals from vegetarian to carnivorous? Hostility between animals is natural, but it no more made them insubordinate to man then than it makes them insubordinate to God and his providence now. Man would have been an instrument of that providence then, just as he is now with domesticated animals, giving his tame hawks hens to eat. Instinctively geese follow a leader and bees obey a queen: all animals share by nature in the practical sense we have by reason. And at that time all animals would have obeyed man of their own accord, as the ones he has domesticated do today. Man was master of other things to the measure that he was master of himself. He shares reason with the angels, sense-powers with other animals, natural vital powers with plants, and the body itself with all non-living things. Reason is master, not subject (so man never had mastery over angels); feelings of aggression and desire man masters to some extent by reason's command (and so in the state of innocence he could command animals); but his own body and vital forces man masters not by command but by use (and so in the state of innocence he could not command plants and non-living things to change their behaviour, but would have had no trouble using their behaviour for his purposes). Of course, disparities existed in that first state: disparities first of all in sex and age, but also in moral and intellectual proficiency (men being free to work to different extents at doing and willing and knowing things), and again in physical strength (since this is influenced by food and climate and the stars one is born under). But none of this would have implied natural defect or sin. Free men exist for their own ends, as Aristotle says; whereas slaves serve others. Such slavery can't exist without suffering: everyone values his own good, and does not willingly cede it exclusively to another. But men can be subordinate to one another and yet remain free, if the good being served is their own

or a common good. Such subordination would have existed in the state of innocence, since man is by nature a social animal, and people living a social life need some single authority to look to their common good. If some men are more knowledgeable and just than others the right thing is to use that to the others' benefit.

Death entered the world through sin. Before sin then, man must have been immortal. Not because he was immaterial like angels, or made of a kind of matter that cannot lose its form like the stars of heaven, nor because of some inherent disposition preserving him from his natural mortality like the glorified in heaven, but because God gave his soul supernatural ability to preserve his body from decay as long as it itself remained submissive to God. In the state of innocence man preserved his body from external injury by his own wits, helped by God's providence which so cared for him that nothing dangerous took him by surprise. As Augustine says *Adam was provided with food against hunger, with drink against thirst, and with the tree of life against the ravages of old age.* But the tree of life couldn't be the sole source of immortality. For one thing the tree of life couldn't give the soul its ability to preserve the body from injury; and for another, the potency of any material thing is finite and the effects of the tree of life would wear off in time, after which man would either move on to a life in the spirit or need another dose.

Increase and multiply and fill the earth. Unless there had been reproduction in the state of innocence to propagate the human race, man would have urgently needed to sin, seeing it would have brought such good. For among corruptible things, in which only the species lasts for ever, nature's main aim is the good of the species and its reproduction. Only among incorruptible substances is nature interested in individuals. So man needed to reproduce for the sake of his perishable body; though as regards his imperishable soul man needed nature (or better the author of nature, who alone creates human souls) to be interested in a multitude of individuals for their own sakes. So in the state of innocence reproduction was needed not for conservation of the species but for multiplication of individuals. In the present state of things, when owners multiply, property must be divided up, since, as Aristotle says, common property breeds discord. But in the state of innocence men's wills would have been well enough disposed for them to use their common property in a manner suited to each without danger of discord; as we indeed often see good men doing nowadays.

Some early theologians seeing intercourse besmirched by lust in our present state, thought reproduction would have happened without intercourse in the state of innocence. But this is unreasonable. It is in man's nature, like that of other animals, both before and after sin, to reproduce by intercourse, and nature has provided him with the organs needed for the purpose. In our present state the natural mating of male and female is somewhat disfigured by unbalanced desire, but this would not have happened in the state of innocence where the lower powers obeyed reason. Because animals lack reason, people sometimes say that men become like animals during intercourse, when reason is unable to balance the pleasure and heat of desire. But in the state of innocence nothing would have escaped reason in that way. Yet the pleasure would not have been any less; in fact it would have been greater given the greater purity of nature and sensitivity of body men then had. Rule by reason requires not that the pleasure should be less, but that the desire for it should be within reasonable bounds. Men who eat moderately can take as much pleasure in their food as gluttons do, but their desire doesn't wallow in the pleasure. In the state of innocence there would have been no great esteem for sexual abstinence, which we esteem nowadays not because it reduces fruitfulness but because it tempers lust.

Things beyond nature only faith can teach, and for faith we need authority. So, without God's authority, we can only assert what is in the nature of things. Now scripture tells us God created man right, so that his limbs, for example, would obey his properly ordered will. But a properly ordered will tends only to the behaviour appropriate to one's age. So newly-born infants would only have had power to move their limbs appropriately to

their age, sucking the breast and so on. Weakness of seed or unsuitable material are not the only causes of females being conceived, but also external circumstances such as the direction of the wind or an idea in the mind. And this would have been particularly likely in the state of innocence, when the body was more subordinate to the mind, so that the sex of the child could have been decided by the parent. The integrated state in which man was created was a state of our nature, not deriving from the natural constitution of man, but from a gift of God given to human nature as a whole. We know this because its opposite, inherited sin, attaches to nature as a whole and passes from parent to child. When authority is silent we can only believe what accords with nature. Now men naturally learn by sense-experience, so those born in a state of innocence would also have acquired their knowledge over a period of time by discovery and instruction, though without the difficulties we have. And, as infants, they would no more have had mature use of their reason than they had of their bodily limbs.

People who locate Paradise at the equator do so because they think the evenness of day and night produces a temperate climate there, never too cold and never too hot. Aristotle however expressly says that the region is so hot that it is uninhabitable; and this seems more likely, seeing that even countries where the sun never passes directly overhead have excessively hot climates from mere proximity to the sun. In any case we believe Paradise to be situated in the most temperate locality, whether that be on the equator or elsewhere.

*   *   *

REVIEW QUESTIONS

1. What ideas tie together Thomas's five ways of proving there is a God?
2. How does Thomas see the natural relationship between men and women?
3. For Thomas, what is humanity's proper place in nature? Why?

DANTE ALIGHIERI

FROM *The Divine Comedy*

Dante Alighieri (1265–1321), a Florentine poet and part-time politician who was exiled from his native city for his views on the political role of the papacy, completed his masterpiece, The Divine Comedy, *toward the end of his life. Dante's earlier poetry centered on Beatrice, the great love of his life, and her early death changed the direction of his artistic development. Praised as divine after his death, the* Comedy, *beginning sadly in Hell and ending happily in Heaven, consists of one hundred cantos in a then-new poetic style. This complex poem is a window on the values of its age, because Dante allows himself to comment on many aspects of history as he tours Hell, Purgatory, and Paradise, seeing many famous people of the past and of his own present. Canto V describes the fate of the carnal in Hell, as seen by Dante and his guide and master, the Roman poet Virgil.*

From *The Divine Comedy*, by Dante Alighieri, translated by John Ciardi (New York: Norton, 1954), pp. 25–29.

*　　*　　*

Canto V

CIRCLE TWO

THE CARNAL

*The Poets leave Limbo and enter the Second Circle.
Here begin the torments of Hell proper, and here,
blocking the way, sits Minos, the dread and semi-
bestial judge of the damned who assigns to each soul
its eternal torment. He orders the Poets back; but Virgil silences him as he earlier silenced Charon, and the
Poets move on.*

*They find themselves on a dark ledge swept by a
great whirlwind, which spins within it the souls of
the Carnal, those who betrayed reason to their appetites. Their sin was to abandon themselves to the
tempest of their passions: so they are swept forever in
the tempest of Hell, forever denied the light of reason
and of God. Virgil identifies many among them.
Semiramis is there, and Dido, Cleopatra, Helen,
Achilles, Paris, and Tristan. Dante sees Paolo and
Francesca swept together, and in the name of love he
calls to them to tell their sad story. They pause from
their eternal flight to come to him, and Francesca
tells their history while Paolo weeps at her side.
Dante is so stricken by compassion at their tragic tale
that he swoons once again.*

So we went down to the second ledge alone;
a smaller circle[1] of so much greater pain
the voice of the damned rose in a bestial moan.

There Minos[2] sits, grinning, grotesque, and hale.
He examines each lost soul as it arrives
and delivers his verdict with his coiling tail.

That is to say, when the ill-fated soul
appears before him it confesses all,[3]
and that grim sorter of the dark and foul

decides which place in Hell shall be its
　　end,
then wraps his twitching tail about himself
one coil for each degree it must descend.

The soul descends and others take its
　　place:
each crowds in its turn to judgment, each
　　confesses,
each hears its doom and falls away through
　　space.

"O you who come into this camp of woe,"
cried Minos when he saw me turn away
without awaiting his judgment, "watch where
　　you go

once you have entered here, and to whom you
　　turn!
Do not be misled by that wide and easy
　　passage!"
And my Guide to him: "That is not your
　　concern;

it is his fate to enter every door.
This has been willed where what is willed
　　must be,
and is not yours to question. Say no
　　more."

---

[1] The pit of Hell tapers like a funnel. The circles of ledges
accordingly grow smaller as they descend.

[2] Like all the monsters Dante assigns to the various offices of Hell, Minos is drawn from classical mythology.
He was the son of Europa and of Zeus, who descended
to her in the form of a bull. Minos became a mytho-
logical king of Crete, so famous for his wisdom and
justice that after death his soul was made judge of the
dead. Virgil presents him fulfilling the same office at

Aeneas' descent to the underworld. Dante, however,
transforms him into an irate and hideous monster with
a tail. The transformation may have been suggested by
the form Zeus assumed for the rape of Europa—the
monster is certainly bullish enough here—but the obvious purpose of the brutalization is to present a figure
symbolic of the guilty conscience of the wretches who
come before it to make their confessions. Dante freely
reshapes his materials to his own purposes.

[3] Just as the souls appeared eager to cross Acheron, so
they are eager to confess even while they dread. Dante
is once again making the point that sinners elect their
Hell by an act of their own will.

Now the choir of anguish, like a wound,
strikes through the tortured air. Now I have
    come
to Hell's full lamentation,[4] sound beyond sound.

I came to a place stripped bare of every
    light
and roaring on the naked dark like seas
wracked by a war of winds. Their hellish
    flight

of storm and counterstorm through time
    foregone,
sweeps the souls of the damned before its charge.
Whirling and battering it drives them on,

and when they pass the ruined gap of Hell[5]
through which we had come, their shrieks begin
    anew.
There they blaspheme the power of God eternal.

And this, I learned, was the never ending flight
of those who sinned in the flesh, the carnal and
    lusty
who betrayed reason to their appetite.

As the wings of wintering starlings bear them on
in their great wheeling flights, just so the blast
wherries these evil souls through time foregone.

Here, there, up, down, they whirl and, whirling,
    strain
with never a hope of hope to comfort them,
not of release, but even of less pain.

As cranes go over sounding their harsh
    cry,
leaving the long streak of their flight in
    air,
so come these spirits, wailing as they fly.

And watching their shadows lashed by wind, I
    cried:
"Master, what souls are these the very air
lashes with its black whips from side to
    side?"

"The first of these whose history you would
    know,"
he answered me, "was Empress of many
    tongues.[6]
Mad sensuality corrupted her so

that to hide the guilt of her debauchery
she licensed all depravity alike,
and lust and law were one in her decree.

She is Semiramis of whom the tale is told
how she married Ninus and succeeded him
to the throne of that wide land the Sultans
    hold.

The other is Dido;[7] faithless to the ashes
of Sichaeus, she killed herself for love.
The next whom the eternal tempest lashes

---

[4] It is with the second circle that the real tortures of Hell
begin.

[5] At the time of the Harrowing of Hell a great earthquake
shook the underworld shattering rocks and cliffs.
Ruins resulting from the same shock are noted in
Canto XII, 34, and Canto XXI, 112 ff. At the beginning
of Canto XXIV, the Poets leave the *bolgia* of the Hyp-
ocrites by climbing the ruined slabs of a bridge that was
shattered by this earthquake.

   Here begin the punishments for the various sins of
incontinence (the sins of the She-Wolf). Those are
punished who sinned by excess of sexual passion. Since
this is the most natural sin and the sin most nearly associated with love, its punishment is the lightest of all
to be found in Hell proper. The Carnal are whirled and
buffeted endlessly through the murky air (symbolic of
the beclouding of their reason by passion) by a great
gale (symbolic of their lust).

[6] Semiramis, a legendary queen of Assyria who assumed
full power at the death of her husband, Ninus.

[7] Queen and founder of Carthage. She had vowed to remain faithful to her husband, Sichaeus, but she fell in
love with Aeneas. When Aeneas abandoned her she
stabbed herself on a funeral pyre she had had prepared.
According to Dante's own system of punishments, she
should be in the Seventh Circle with the suicides. The
only clue Dante gives to the tempering of her punishment is his statement that "she killed herself for love."
Dante always seems readiest to forgive in that name.

is sense-drugged Cleopatra. See Helen there,
from whom such ill arose. And great Achilles,[8]
who fought at last with love in the house of
        prayer.

And Paris. And Tristan." As they whirled above
he pointed out more than a thousand shades
of those torn from the mortal life by love.

I stood there while my Teacher one by one
named the great knights and ladies of dim time;
and I was swept by pity and confusion.

At last I spoke: "Poet, I should be glad
to speak a word with those two swept together[9]
so lightly on the wind and still so sad."

And he to me: "Watch them. When next they pass,
call to them in the name of love that drives
and damns them here. In that name they will
        pause."

Thus, as soon as the wind in its wild course
brought them around, I called: "O wearied souls!
if none forbid it, pause and speak to us."

As mating doves that love calls to their nest
glide through the air with motionless raised
        wings,
borne by the sweet desire that fills each breast—

Just so those spirits turned on the torn sky
from the band where Dido whirls across the air;
such was the power of pity in my cry.

"O living creature, gracious, kind, and good,
going this pilgrimage through the sick night,
visiting us who stained the earth with blood,

were the King of Time our friend, we would
        pray His peace
on you who have pitied us. As long as the wind
will let us pause, ask of us what you please.

The town where I was born lies by the shore
where the Po descends into its ocean rest
with its attendant streams in one long murmur.

Love, which in gentlest hearts will soonest
        bloom
seized my lover with passion for that sweet body
from which I was torn unshriven to my
        doom.

Love, which permits no loved one not to
        love,
took me so strongly with delight in him
that we are one in Hell, as we were above.[10]

---

[8] Achilles is placed among this company because of his passion for Polyxena, the daughter of Priam. For love of her, he agreed to desert the Greeks and to join the Trojans, but when he went to the temple for the wedding (according to the legend Dante has followed), he was killed by Paris.

[9] Paolo and Francesca (PAH-oe-loe: Frahn-CHAY-ska). Dante's treatment of these two lovers is certainly the tenderest and most sympathetic accorded any of the sinners in Hell, and legends immediately began to grow about this pair.

   The facts are these. In 1275 Giovanni Malatesta (Djoe-VAH-nee Mahl-ah-TEH-stah) of Rimini, called Giovanni the Lame, a somewhat deformed but brave and powerful warrior, made a political marriage with Francesca, daughter of Guido da Polenta of Ravenna. Francesca came to Rimini and there an amour grew between her and Giovanni's younger brother Paolo. Despite the fact that Paolo had married in 1269 and had become the father of two daughters by 1275, his affair with Francesca continued for many years. It was sometime between 1283 and 1286 that Giovanni surprised them in Francesca's bedroom and killed both of them.

   Around these facts the legend has grown that Paolo was sent by Giovanni as his proxy to the marriage, that Francesca thought he was her real bridegroom and accordingly gave him her heart irrevocably at first sight. The legend obviously increases the pathos, but nothing in Dante gives it support.

[10] At many points of *The Inferno* Dante makes clear the principle that the souls of the damned are locked so blindly into their own guilt that none can feel sympathy for another, or find any pleasure in the presence of another. The temptation of many readers is to interpret this line romantically: i.e., that the love of Paolo and Francesca survives Hell itself. The more Dantean interpretation, however, is that they add to one another's anguish (a) as mutual reminders of their sin, and (b) as insubstantial shades of the bodies for which they once felt such great passion.

Love led us to one death. In the depths of Hell
Caïna waits for him[11] who took our lives."
This was the piteous tale they stopped to tell.

And when I had heard those world-offended lovers
I bowed my head. At last the Poet spoke:
"What painful thoughts are these your lowered
      brow covers?"

When at length I answered, I began: "Alas!
What sweetest thoughts, what green and young
      desire
led these two lovers to this sorry pass."

Then turning to those spirits once again,
I said: "Francesca, what you suffer here
melts me to tears of pity and of pain.

But tell me: in the time of your sweet sighs
by what appearances found love the way
to lure you to his perilous paradise?"

And she: "The double grief of a lost bliss
is to recall its happy hour in pain.
Your Guide and Teacher knows the truth of this.

But if there is indeed a soul in Hell
to ask of the beginning of our love
out of his pity, I will weep and tell:

On a day for dalliance we read the rhyme
of Lancelot,[12] how love had mastered him.
We were alone with innocence and dim time.[13]

Pause after pause that high old story drew
our eyes together while we blushed and paled;
but it was one soft passage overthrew

our caution and our hearts. For when we read
how her fond smile was kissed by such a lover,
he who is one with me alive and dead

breathed on my lips the tremor of his kiss.
That book, and he who wrote it, was a pander.[14]
That day we read no further." As she said this,

the other spirit, who stood by her, wept
so piteously, I felt my senses reel
and faint away with anguish. I was swept

by such a swoon as death is, and I fell,
as a corpse might fall, to the dead floor of Hell.

*   *   *

REVIEW QUESTIONS

1. How does Dante use this poetic format to critique the culture and values of his own time?
2. Why does the poet describe himself as being so affected by the story of Paolo and Francesca? Why would he describe the reading of literature as a dangerous thing—especially in a work such as this?
3. In most of the other rings of Hell, Dante encounters few women; but in this circle, there are many. What does this suggest about Dante's own attitude toward women, or that of his contemporaries?

---

[11] Giovanni Malatesta was still alive at the writing. His fate is already decided, however, and upon his death, his soul will fall to Caïna, the first ring of the last circle, where lie those who performed acts of treachery against their kin.

[12] The story exists in many forms. The details Dante makes use of are from an Old French version.

[13] The original simply reads "We were alone, suspecting nothing." "Dim time" is rhyme-forced, but not wholly outside the legitimate implications of the original, I hope. The old courtly romance may well be thought of as happening in the dim ancient days. The apology, of course, comes after the fact: one does the possible, then argues for justification, and there probably is none.

---

[14] *Galeotto*, the Italian word for "pander," is also the Italian rendering of the name of Gallehault, who in the French Romance Dante refers to here, urged Lancelot and Guinevere on to love.

POPE BONIFACE VIII

Papal Bull *Unam Sanctam*

This official statement of papal policy, known as a "bull" from the lead seal (bulla) that carried the pope's insignia, was issued by Boniface VIII (r. 1294–1303) in 1302. Its short title comes from the opening Latin words, "one holy," which capture Boniface's central argument, made in response to a challenge by the French king Philip IV (r. 1285–1314). Philip disputed the papacy's claim to authority over the churches in his realm, and eventually went so far as to claim that the pope should be subordinate to his own superior, secular power.

From *Corpus Iuris Canonici*, vol. 2, edited by E. Friedberg (Leipzig, 1881).

That there is one holy, Catholic and apostolic church we are bound to believe and to hold, our faith urging us, and this we do firmly believe and simply confess; and that outside this church there is no salvation or remission of sins, as her spouse proclaims in the Canticles, "One is my dove, my perfect one. She is the only one of her mother, the chosen of her that bore her"; which represents one mystical body whose head is Christ, while the head of Christ is God. In this church there is one Lord, one faith, one baptism. At the time of the Flood there was one ark, symbolizing the one church. It was finished in one cubit and had one helmsman and captain, namely Noah, and we read that all things on earth outside of it were destroyed. This church we venerate and this alone, the Lord saying through his prophet, "Deliver, O God, my soul from the sword, my only one from the power of the dog." He prayed for the soul, that is himself, the head, and at the same time for the body, which he called the one church on account of the promised unity of faith, sacraments and charity of the church. This is that seamless garment of the Lord which was not cut but fell by lot. Therefore there is one body and one head of this one and only church, not two heads as though it were a monster, namely Christ and Christ's vicar,

Peter and Peter's successor, for the Lord said to this Peter, "Feed my sheep." He said "My sheep" in general, not these or those, whence he is understood to have committed them all to Peter. Hence, if the Greeks or any others say that they were not committed to Peter and his successors, they necessarily admit that they are not of Christ's flock, for the Lord says in John that there is one sheepfold and one shepherd.

We are taught by the words of the Gospel that in this church and in her power there are two swords, a spiritual one and a temporal one. For when the apostles said "Here are two swords," meaning in the church since it was the apostles who spoke, the Lord did not reply that it was too many but enough. Certainly anyone who denies that the temporal sword is in the power of Peter has not paid heed to the words of the Lord when he said, "Put up thy sword into its sheath." Both then are in the power of the church, the material sword and the spiritual. But the one is exercised for the church, the other by the church, the one by the hand of the priest, the other by the hand of kings and soldiers, though at the will and suffrance of the priest. One sword ought to be under the other and the temporal authority subject to the spiritual power. For, while the apostle says,

"There is no power but from God and those that are ordained of God," they would not be ordained unless one sword was under the other and, being inferior, was led by the other to the highest things. For, according to the blessed Dionysius,[1] it is the law of divinity for the lowest to be led to the highest through intermediaries. In the order of the universe all things are not kept in order in the same fashion and immediately but the lowest are ordered by the intermediate and inferiors by superiors. But that the spiritual power excels any earthly one in dignity and nobility we ought the more openly to confess in proportion as spiritual things excel temporal ones. Moreover we clearly perceive this from the giving of tithes, from benediction and sanctification, from the acceptance of this power and from the very government of things. For, the truth bearing witness, the spiritual power has to institute the earthly power and to judge it if it has not been good. So is verified the prophecy of Jeremias concerning the church and the power of the church, "Lo, I have set thee this day over the nations and over kingdoms" etc.

Therefore, if the earthly power errs, it shall be judged by the spiritual power, if a lesser spiritual power errs it shall be judged by its superior, but if the supreme spiritual power errs it can be judged only by God not by man, as the apostle witnesses, "The spiritual man judgeth all things and he himself is judged of no man." Although this authority was given to a man and is exercised by a man it is not human but rather divine, being given to Peter at God's mouth, and confirmed to him and to his successors in him, the rock whom the Lord acknowledged when he said to Peter himself "Whatsoever thou shalt bind" etc. Whoever therefore resists this power so ordained by God resists the ordinance of God unless, like the Manicheans,[2] he imagines that there are two beginnings, which we judge to be false and heretical, as Moses witnesses, for not "in the beginnings" but "in the beginning" God created heaven and earth. Therefore we declare, state, define and pronounce that it is altogether necessary to salvation for every human creature to be subject to the Roman Pontiff.

REVIEW QUESTIONS

1. What does Pope Boniface VIII see as the right relation between the Church and secular power?
2. How do his arguments and evidence differ from those of his predecessor Gregory VII (pp. 254–261)?
3. What, in practice, did the last sentence of this bull mean? What are its implications?

---

[1] According to the Acts of the Apostles (17:34), a certain Athenian citizen called Dionysius the Areopagite was converted by the apostle Paul. Centuries later, a body of mystical writings was attributed to him, and he was also misidentified as St. Denis, the first bishop of Paris (d. c. 251 C.E.).

[2] Followers of the third-century visionary Mani, Manicheans were condemned as heretics by the Church. They espoused a dualistic view of the world, in which the good power of God is opposed by the equally powerful forces of evil.

10 ✎ CRISIS, UNREST, AND OPPORTUNITY, 1300–1500

By about 1300, Europe's economic and demographic growth seemed to stall. Medieval society reached limits on its geographic frontiers, could not count on increased agricultural yields from depleted soils, and no longer experienced big productivity gains from improved technologies in artisan manufacturing. Signs of trouble, famines and increased mortality, appeared long before the devastating plague of 1348, which killed at least one-third of the population in Europe and the Middle East and was especially lethal in the great cities such as Cairo and Florence. The long fourteenth century, calamitous for its repeated epidemics and wars such as the century-long episodic conflict between France and England, is a bridge between the confident thirteenth century and notable recoveries of the fifteenth century.

Much of Europe exhibited similar religious, economic, social, and psychological responses to repeated outbreaks of plague. The basic institutions of late medieval life—the family, papacy, monarchies, and universities—endured the high levels of mortality, proving the strength of late medieval people and their culture. However, these same institutions offered few practical explanations for the new killer, leading to a crisis in belief and a search for scapegoats that focused on traditional targets: the Jews, "heretic," and other outsiders.

Giovanni Boccaccio, an eyewitness to the plague's course through Florence where it killed more than half the population, recorded in his introduction to the Decameron *the impressions of a survivor and described a culture preoccupied with piety, melancholy, and death. Meanwhile, The Church, with the papacy in Avignon and on the verge of schism, faced new challenges to its authority. Theologians such as John Wyclif and Jan Hus raised fundamental questions about the sacraments and how the Church functioned in the world.*

In the eastern Mediterranean, the Ottoman state advanced into the Balkans and finally destroyed the last remnant of the Byzantine Empire by taking Constantinople in 1453. Another distinctive feature of this period was the triumph of

vernacular culture, as authors such as Dante (in Italian), Chaucer (in English), and Christine de Pisan (in French) captured the spirit of their times and addressed the growing number of readers who wanted literature and art that responded to the crises and questions of real life.

GIOVANNI BOCCACCIO

FROM *The Decameron*

Giovanni Boccaccio (1313–1374), was a native of the city of Florence and a survivor of the Black Death. Around 1351, in the immediate aftermath of the plague, he put together a compilation of one hundred comic tales told in the Florentine dialect and framed them as the amusements devised by a party of ten young people—seven men and three woman—who have escaped from the plague-ridden city for a period of ten days. (Hence the title of the collection, which means "ten days.") The following is an excerpt from the preface to this book, in which Boccaccio describes the effects of the plague on the people of Florence.

From *The Decameron: A New Translation*, selected, translated, and edited by Mark Musa and Peter Bondanella (New York: Norton, 1977), pp. 3–10.

FROM Introduction

Whenever, gracious ladies, I consider how compassionate you are by nature, I realize that in your judgment the present work will seem to have had a serious and painful beginning, for it recalls in its opening the unhappy memory of the deadly plague just passed, dreadful and pitiful to all those who saw or heard about it. But I do not wish this to frighten you away from reading any further, as if you were going to pass all of your time sighing and weeping as you read. This horrible beginning will be like the ascent of a steep and rough mountainside, beyond which there lies a most beautiful and delightful plain, which seems more pleasurable to the climbers in proportion to the difficulty of their climb and their descent. And just as pain is the extreme limit of pleasure, so misery ends by unanticipated happiness. This brief pain (I say brief since it contains few words) will be quickly followed by the sweetness and the delight, which I promised you before, and which, had I not promised, might not be expected from such a beginning. To tell the truth, if I could have conveniently led you by any other way than this, which I know is a bitter one, I would have gladly done so; but since it is otherwise impossible to demonstrate how the stories you are

THE TRIUMPH OF DEATH (C. 1340)   FRANCESCO TRAINI (?)

This painting is part of a series of frescos decorating the Camposanto, the famous cemetery of Pisa. The frescos are by local tradition attributed to the Pisan painter Francesco Traini. This fresco was probably painted just before the arrival of the bubonic plague in Pisa in 1348, and it incorporates images of death formed in the years of famine and during the epidemics of the early fourteenth century. What overall impression of death does this fresco convey? In particular, find the image of Death and consider her role in the fresco. One of the many striking parts of this fresco is the detail in which the three living riders confront the three corpses. What can we learn about the mentality of a people who commissioned this fresco to decorate a cemetery?

322

about to read came to be told, I am almost obliged by necessity to write about it this way.

Let me say, then, that thirteen hundred and forty-eight years had already passed after the fruitful Incarnation of the Son of God when into the distinguished city of Florence, more noble than any other Italian city, there came the deadly pestilence. It started in the East, either because of the influence of heavenly bodies or because of God's just wrath as a punishment to mortals for our wicked deeds, and it killed an infinite number of people. Without pause it spread from one place and it stretched its miserable length over the West. And against this pestilence no human wisdom or foresight was of any avail; quantities of filth were removed from the city by officials charged with this task; the entry of any sick person into the city was prohibited; and many directives were issued concerning the maintenance of good health. Nor were the humble supplications, rendered not once but many times to God by pious people, through public processions or by other means, efficacious; for almost at the beginning of springtime of the year in question the plague began to show its sorrowful effects in an extraordinary manner. It did not act as it had done in the East, where bleeding from the nose was a manifest sign of inevitable death, but it began in both men and women with certain swellings either in the groin or under the armpits, some of which grew to the size of a normal apple and others to the size of an egg (more or less), and the people called them *gavoccioli*. And from the two parts of the body already mentioned, within a brief space of time, the said deadly *gavoccioli* began to spread indiscriminately over every part of the body; and after this, the symptoms of the illness changed to black or livid spots appearing on the arms and thighs, and on every part of the body, some large ones and sometimes many little ones scattered all around. And just as the *gavoccioli* were originally, and still are, a very certain indication of impending death, in like manner these spots came to mean the same thing for whoever had them. Neither a doctor's advice nor the strength of medicine could do anything to cure this illness; on the contrary, either the nature of the illness was such

that it afforded no cure, or else the doctors were so ignorant that they did not recognize its cause and, as a result, could not prescribe the proper remedy (in fact, the number of doctors, other than the well-trained, was increased by a large number of men and women who had never had any medical training); at any rate, few of the sick were ever cured, and almost all died after the third day of the appearance of the previously described symptoms (some sooner, others later), and most of them died without fever or any other side effects.

This pestilence was so powerful that it was communicated to the healthy by contact with the sick, the way a fire close to dry or oily things will set them aflame. And the evil of the plague went even further: not only did talking to or being around the sick bring infection and a common death, but also touching the clothes of the sick or anything touched or used by them seemed to communicate this very disease to the person involved. What I am about to say is incredible to hear, and if I and others had not witnessed it with our own eyes, I should not dare believe it (let alone write about it), no matter how trustworthy a person I might have heard it from. Let me say, then, that the power of the plague described here was of such virulence in spreading from one person to another that not only did it pass from one man to the next, but, what's more, it was often transmitted from the garments of a sick or dead man to animals that not only became contaminated by the disease, but also died within a brief period of time. My own eyes, as I said earlier, witnessed such a thing one day: when the rags of a poor man who died of this disease were thrown into the public street, two pigs came upon them, as they are wont to do, and first with their snouts and then with their teeth they took the rags and shook them around; and within a short time, after a number of convulsions, both pigs fell dead upon the ill-fated rags, as if they had been poisoned. From these and many similar or worse occurrences there came about such fear and such fantastic notions among those who remained alive that almost all of them took a very cruel attitude in the matter; that is, they completely avoided the sick and their possessions; and in so doing, each

one believed that he was protecting his good health.

There were some people who thought that living moderately and avoiding all superfluity might help a great deal in resisting this disease, and so, they gathered in small groups and lived entirely apart from everyone else. They shut themselves up in those houses where there were no sick people and where one could live well by eating the most delicate of foods and drinking the finest of wines (doing so always in moderation), allowing no one to speak about or listen to anything said about the sick and the dead outside; these people lived, spending their time with music and other pleasures that they could arrange. Others thought the opposite: they believed that drinking too much, enjoying life, going about singing and celebrating, satisfying in every way the appetites as best one could, laughing, and making light of everything that happened was the best medicine for such a disease; so they practiced to the fullest what they believed by going from one tavern to another all day and night, drinking to excess; and often they would make merry in private homes, doing everything that pleased or amused them the most. This they were able to do easily, for everyone felt he was doomed to die and, as a result, abandoned his property, so that most of the houses had become common property, and any stranger who came upon them used them as if he were their rightful owner. In addition to this bestial behavior, they always managed to avoid the sick as best they could. And in this great affliction and misery of our city the revered authority of the laws, both divine and human, had fallen and almost completely disappeared, for, like other men, the ministers and executors of the laws were either dead or sick or so short of help that it was impossible for them to fulfill their duties; as a result, everybody was free to do as he pleased.

Many others adopted a middle course between the two attitudes just described: neither did they restrict their food or drink so much as the first group nor did they fall into such dissoluteness and drunkenness as the second; rather, they satisfied their appetites to a moderate degree. They did not

shut themselves up, but went around carrying in their hands flowers, or sweet-smelling herbs, or various kinds of spices; and often they would put these things to their noses, believing that such smells were a wonderful means of purifying the brain, for all the air seemed infected with the stench of dead bodies, sickness, and medicines.

Others were of a crueler opinion (though it was, perhaps, a safer one): they maintained that there was no better medicine against the plague than to flee from it; and convinced of this reasoning, not caring about anything but themselves, men and women in great numbers abandoned their city, their houses, their farms, their relatives, and their possessions and sought other places, and they went at least as far away as the Florentine countryside— as if the wrath of God could not pursue them with this pestilence wherever they went but would only strike those it found within the walls of the city! Or perhaps they thought that Florence's last hour had come and that no one in the city would remain alive.

And not all those who adopted these diverse opinions died, nor did they all escape with their lives; on the contrary, many of those who thought this way were falling sick everywhere, and since they had given, when they were healthy, the bad example of avoiding the sick, they, in turn, were abandoned and left to languish away without care. The fact was that one citizen avoided another, that almost no one cared for his neighbor, and that relatives rarely or hardly ever visited each other—they stayed far apart. This disaster had struck such fear into the hearts of men and women that brother abandoned brother, uncle abandoned nephew, sister left brother, and very often wife abandoned husband, and—even worse, almost unbelievable— fathers and mothers neglected to tend and care for their children, as if they were not their own.

Thus, for the countless multitude of men and women who fell sick, there remained no support except the charity of their friends (and these were few) or the avarice of servants, who worked for inflated salaries and indecent periods of time and who, in spite of this, were few and far between; and those few were men or women of little wit (most

of them not trained for such service) who did little else but hand different things to the sick when requested to do so or watch over them while they died, and in this service, they very often lost their own lives and their profits. And since the sick were abandoned by their neighbors, their parents, and their friends and there was a scarcity of servants, a practice that was almost unheard of before spread through the city: when a woman fell sick, no matter how attractive or beautiful or noble she might be, she did not mind having a manservant (whoever he might be, no matter how young or old he was), and she had no shame whatsoever in revealing any part of her body to him—the way she would have done to a woman—when the necessity of her sickness required her to do so. This practice was, perhaps, in the days that followed the pestilence, the cause of looser morals in the women who survived the plague. And so, many people died who, by chance, might have survived if they had been attended to. Between the lack of competent attendants, which the sick were unable to obtain, and the violence of the pestilence, there were so many, many people who died in the city both day and night that it was incredible just to hear this described, not to mention seeing it! Therefore, out of sheer necessity, there arose among those who remained alive customs which were contrary to the established practices of the time.

It was the custom, as it is again today, for the women, relatives, and neighbors to gather together in the house of a dead person and there to mourn with the women who had been dearest to him; on the other hand, in front of the deceased's home, his male relatives would gather together with his male neighbors and other citizens, and the clergy also came (many of them, or sometimes just a few) depending upon the social class of the dead man. Then, upon the shoulders of his equals, he was carried to the church chosen by him before death with the funeral pomp of candles and chants. With the fury of the pestilence increasing, this custom, for the most part, died out and other practices took its place. And so, not only did people die without having a number of women around them, but there were many who passed away without even

having a single witness present, and very few were granted the piteous laments and bitter tears of their relatives; on the contrary, most relatives were somewhere else, laughing, joking, and amusing themselves; even the women learned this practice too well, having put aside, for the most part, their womanly compassion for their own safety. Very few were the dead whose bodies were accompanied to the church by more than ten or twelve of their neighbors, and these dead bodies were not even carried on the shoulders of honored and reputable citizens but rather by gravediggers from the lower classes that were called *becchini*. Working for pay, they would pick up the bier and hurry it off, not to the church the dead man had chosen before his death but, in most cases, to the church closest by, accompanied by four or six churchmen with just a few candles, and often none at all. With the help of these *becchini*, the churchmen would place the body as fast as they could in whatever unoccupied grave they could find, without going to the trouble of saying long or solemn burial services.

The plight of the lower class and, perhaps, a large part of the middle class, was even more pathetic: most of them stayed in their homes or neighborhoods either because of their poverty or their hopes for remaining safe, and every day they fell sick by the thousands; and not having servants or attendants of any kind, they almost always died. Many ended their lives in the public streets, during the day or at night, while many others who died in their homes were discovered dead by their neighbors only by the smell of their decomposing bodies. The city was full of corpses. The dead were usually given the same treatment by their neighbors, who were moved more by the fear that the decomposing corpses would contaminate them than by any charity they might have felt towards the deceased: either by themselves or with the assistance of porters (when they were available), they would drag the corpse out of the home and place it in front of the doorstep where, usually in the morning, quantities of dead bodies could be seen by any passerby; then, they were laid out on biers, or for lack of biers, on a plank. Nor did a bier carry only one corpse; sometimes it was used for two or

three at a time. More than once, a single bier would serve for a wife and husband, two or three brothers, a father or son, or other relatives, all at the same time. And countless times it happened that two priests, each with a cross, would be on their way to bury someone, when porters carrying three or four biers would just follow along behind them; and where these priests thought they had just one dead man to bury, they had, in fact, six or eight and sometimes more. Moreover, the dead were honored with no tears or candles or funeral mourners but worse: things had reached such a point that the people who died were cared for as we care for goats today. Thus, it became quite obvious that what the wise had not been able to endure with patience through the few calamities of everyday life now became a matter of indifference to even the most simple-minded people as a result of this colossal misfortune.

So many corpses would arrive in front of a church every day and at every hour that the amount of holy ground for burials was certainly insufficient for the ancient custom of giving each body its individual place; when all the graves were full, huge trenches were dug in all of the cemeteries of the churches and into them the new arrivals were dumped by the hundreds; and they were packed in there with dirt, one on top of another, like a ship's cargo, until the trench was filled.

But instead of going over every detail of the past miseries which befell our city, let me say that the same unfriendly weather there did not, because of this, spare the surrounding countryside any evil; there, not to speak of the towns which, on a smaller scale, were like the city, in the scattered villages and in the fields the poor, miserable peasants and their families, without any medical assistance or aid of servants, died on the roads and in their fields and in their homes, as many by day as by night, and they died not like men but more like wild animals. Because of this they, like the city dwellers, became careless in their ways and did not look after their possessions or their businesses; furthermore, when they saw that death was upon them, completely neglecting the future fruits of their past labors, their

livestock, their property, they did their best to consume what they already had at hand. So, it came about that oxen, donkeys, sheep, pigs, chickens and even dogs, man's most faithful companion, were driven from their homes into the fields, where the wheat was left not only unharvested but also unreaped, and they were allowed to roam where they wished; and many of these animals, almost as if they were rational beings, returned at night to their homes without any guidance from a shepherd, satiated after a good day's meal.

Leaving the countryside and returning to the city, what more can one say, except that so great was the cruelty of Heaven, and, perhaps, also that of man, that from March to July of the same year, between the fury of the pestiferous sickness and the fact that many of the sick were badly treated or abandoned in need because of the fear that the healthy had, more than one hundred thousand human beings are believed to have lost their lives for certain inside the walls of the city of Florence whereas, before the deadly plague, one would not have estimated that there were actually that many people dwelling in that city.

Oh, how many great palaces, beautiful homes, and noble dwellings, once filled with families, gentlemen, and ladies, were now emptied, down to the last servant! How many notable families, vast domains, and famous fortunes remained without legitimate heir! How many valiant men, beautiful women, and charming young men, who might have been pronounced very healthy by Galen, Hippocrates, and Aesculapius (not to mention lesser physicians), dined in the morning with their relatives, companions, and friends and then in the evening took supper with their ancestors in the other world!

Reflecting upon so many miseries makes me very sad; therefore, since I wish to pass over as many as I can, let me say that as our city was in this condition, almost emptied of inhabitants, it happened (as I heard it later from a person worthy of trust) that one Tuesday morning in the venerable church of Santa Maria Novella there was hardly any congregation there to hear the holy services ∗ ∗ ∗

*   *   *

Review Questions

1. According to Boccaccio, how did his neighbors explain and respond to the devastations of the Black Death?

2. What does Boccaccio say about the social effects of the plague? How does he describe its effects on the behavior of women, specifically?

3. Given that this account is the preface to a book of mostly bawdy or comic tales, can we take this testimony at face value? Do you think that Boccaccio is a reliable historical source? Why or why not?

GEOFFREY CHAUCER

FROM *The Canterbury Tales: The "Pardoner's Tale"*

Geoffrey Chaucer (c. 1340–1400) was an English civil servant and poet who, like Boccaccio, had survived the Black Death. He never finished his most famous work, The Canterbury Tales, *framed (like Boccaccio's* Decameron*) as series of stories, in this case told by a diverse group of pilgrims making their way to the shrine of Saint Thomas Becket at Canterbury. One of these pilgrims is a "pardoner," a contemporary slang term for a priest or cleric who makes his living selling indulgences ("pardons") for sins. Here, the Pardoner introduces himself and his cynical attitude toward the people he dupes, then launches into a story that reveals even more about his character. Although Chaucer's language (known as Middle English) may seem difficult at first, you will find that it is quite easy to understand if you read it aloud.*

From *The Canterbury Tales: Nine Tales and the General Prologue: A Norton Critical Edition* by Geoffrey Chaucer, edited by V. A. Kolve and Glending Olson, (New York: Norton, 1989), pp. 192–207.

The Prologue

"Lordinges," quod he, "in chirches whan I preche,
I peyne me° to han an hauteyn° speche,   *take pains / elevated*
And ringe it out as round as gooth° a belle,   *sounds*
For I can al by rote° that I telle.   *know all by memory*
My theme° is alwey oon,° and evere was—   *text / always the same*
Radix malorum est Cupiditas.[1]

---

[1] "Avarice (the love of money) is the root of all evil."

First I pronounce° whennes° that I come,   *proclaim / whence, from where*
And thanne my bulles[2] shewe I, alle and somme.°   *one and all*
Oure lige lordes seel[3] on my patente,°   *license*
That shewe I first, my body° to warente,°   *person / authorize*
That no man be so bold, ne preest ne clerk,°   *neither priest nor scholar*
Me to destourbe of Cristes holy werk;
And after that thanne telle I forth my tales.
Bulles of popes and of cardinales,
Of patriarkes,° and bishoppes I shewe,   *heads of churches*
And in Latyn I speke a wordes fewe
To saffron with my predicacioun,[4]
And for to stire° hem to devocioun.   *stir*
Thanne shewe I forth my longe cristal stones,°   *glass cases*
Y-crammed ful of cloutes° and of bones—   *rags*
Reliks been they, as wenen they echoon.[5]
Thanne have I in latoun[6] a sholder-boon
Which that was of an holy Jewes shepe.
'Goode men,' seye I, 'tak of my wordes kepe:°   *heed*
If that this boon be wasshe° in any welle,   *washed, dunked*
If cow, or calf, or sheep, or oxe swelle,°   *swell (up)*
That any worm hath ete, or worm y-stonge,[7]
Tak water of that welle, and wash his tonge,
And it is hool° anon;° and forthermore,   *healed / at once*
Of pokkes° and of scabbe and every sore   *pox*
Shal every sheep be hool,° that of this welle   *healed*
Drinketh a draughte. Tak kepe° eek° what I telle: *heed / also*
If that the good-man that the bestes° oweth°   *animals / owns*
Wol every wike,° er° that the cok him croweth,   *week / before*
Fastinge,° drinken of this welle a draughte—   *(While) fasting*
As thilke° holy Jewe[8] bure eldres taughte—   *that same*
His bestes and his stoor° shal multiplye.   *stock*
    And, sires, also it heleth° jalousye: *heals*
For though a man be falle in jalous rage,
Let maken with this water his potage,[9]
And nevere shal he more his wyf mistriste,°   *mistrust*

---

[2] Bulls, writs of indulgence for sin, purchasable in lieu
   of other forms of penance.
[3] Bishop's seal.
[4] "With which to season my preaching." (Saffron is a
   yellow spice.)
[5] "They are (saints') relics, or so they all suppose."
[6] Latten, a metal like brass.
[7] "Who has eaten any (poisonous) worm, or whom a
   snake has stung (bitten)."
[8] Jacob.
[9] "Have his soup made with this water."

Though he the sooth° of hir defaute° wiste°—   *truth / erring / should know*
Al° had she taken° preestes two or three.   *Even if / taken (as lovers)*
   Heer is a miteyn° eek, that ye may see: *mitten*
He that his hond wol putte in this miteyn,
He shal have multiplying of his greyn°   *grain*
Whan he hath sowen, be it whete° or otes,°   *wheat / oats*
So that he offre pens, or elles grotes.[10]
   Good men and wommen, o° thing warne° I yow: *one / tell*
If any wight° be in this chirche now,   *person*
That hath doon sinne horrible, that he
Dar° nat for shame of it y-shriven[11] be,   *Dare*
Or any womman, be she yong or old,
That hath y-maked hir housbonde cokewold,°   *a cuckold*
Swich° folk shul have no power ne no grace   *Such*
To offren° to my reliks in this place.   *To offer (money)*
And whoso findeth him out of swich blame,°   *not deserving such blame*
He wol com up and offre a° Goddes name,   *make an offering in*
And I assoille° him by the auctoritee°   *(will) absolve / authority*
Which that by bulle y-graunted was to me.'
   By this gaude° have I wonne,° yeer° by yeer,   *trick / earned / year*
An hundred mark sith I was pardoner.[12]
I stonde lyk a clerk° in my pulpet,   *scholar*
And whan the lewed° peple is doun y-set,   *ignorant, unlearned*
I preche, so as ye han herd bifore,
And telle an hundred false japes° more.   *tricks, stories*
Thanne peyne I me° to strecche forth the nekke,   *I take pains*
And est and west upon the peple I bekke°   *nod*
As doth a dowve,° sittinge on a berne.°   *dove / in a barn*
Myn hondes and my tonge goon so yerne°   *rapidly*
That it is joye to see my bisinesse.
Of avaryce and of swich° cursednesse   *such*
Is al my preching, for° to make hem free°   *in order / generous*
To yeven hir pens, and namely unto me.[13]
For myn entente° is nat but for to winne,°   *intention / profit*
And nothing° for correccioun of sinne: *not at all*
I rekke° nevere, whan that they ben beried,°   *care / buried*
Though that hir soules goon a-blakeberied![14]
For certes,° many a predicacioun°   *certainly / sermon*
Comth ofte tyme of yvel° entencioun: *evil*

---

[10] "Provided that he offers (to me) pennies or else groats (coins worth fourpence)."

[11] Confessed and absolved.

[12] "A hundred marks (coins worth thirteen shillings fourpence) since I became a pardoner."

[13] "In giving their pence, and particularly to me."

[14] Blackberrying, i.e., wandering.

Som for plesaunce° of folk and flaterye,   *the entertainment*
To been avaunced by ypocrisye,[15]
And som for veyne glorie,° and som for hate.   *vainglory*
For whan I dar non other weyes debate,[16]
Than wol I stinge him[17] with my tonge smerte°   *sharp*
In preching, so that he shal nat asterte°   *leap up (to protest)*
To been° defamed falsly, if that he   *At being*
Hath trespased to° my brethren[18] or to me.   *wronged*
For, though I telle noght his propre° name,   *own*
Men shal wel knowe that it is the same
By signes and by othere circumstances.
Thus quyte° I folk that doon us displesances;°   *requite / offenses*
Thus spitte I out my venim under hewe°   *hue, coloring*
Of holynesse, to semen° holy and trewe.   *seem*
    But shortly° myn entente I wol devyse:°   *briefly / describe*
I preche of no thing but for coveityse.°   *out of covetousness*
Therfore my theme is yet, and evere was,
Radix malorum est cupiditas.
Thus can I preche agayn° that same vyce   *against*
Which that I use,° and that is avaryce.   *practice*
But though myself be gilty in that sinne,
Yet can I maken other folk to twinne°   *part*
From avaryce, and sore° to repente.   *ardently*
But that is nat my principal entente:
I preche nothing but for coveityse.
Of this matere° it oughte y-nogh suffyse.   *subject*
    Than telle I hem ensamples many oon°   *examples many a one*
Of olde stories longe tyme agoon,°   *past*
For lewed° peple loven tales olde;   *unlearned*
Swich° thinges can they wel reporte° and holde.°   *Such / repeat / remember*
What, trowe ye, the whyles I may preche[19]
And winne° gold and silver for° I teche,   *obtain / because*
That I wol live in povert° wilfully?°   *poverty / willingly*
Nay, nay, I thoghte° it nevere, trewely!   *considered*
For I wol preche and begge in sondry° londes;   *various*
I wol nat do no labour with myn hondes,
Ne make baskettes,[20] and live therby,
By cause I wol nat beggen ydelly.°   *without profit*

---

[15] To seek advancement through hypocrisy.

[16] "For when I dare enter into contest (argument) no other way."

[17] Some enemy.

[18] Fellow pardoners.

[19] "What? do you believe (that) as long as I can preach."

[20] St. Paul was said to have been a basket maker.

I wol non of the Apostles counterfete:°   *imitate*
I wol have money, wolle,° chese, and whete,   *wool*
Al° were it yeven of° the povereste page,°   *Even if / given by / servant*
Or of° the povereste widwe° in a village,   *by / poorest widow*
Al sholde hir children sterve for famyne.[21]
Nay! I wol drinke licour° of the vyne,   *liquor, wine*
And have a joly wenche in every toun.
But herkneth,° lordinges, in conclusioun: *listen*
Youre lyking is that I shall telle a tale.
Now have I dronke a draughte of corny° ale,   *malty*
By God, I hope I shal yow telle a thing
That shal by resoun° been at° youre lyking.   *with reason / to*
For though myself be a ful vicious° man,   *evil, vice-ridden*
A moral tale yet I yow telle can,

Which I am wont to preche for to winne.[22]
Now holde youre pees,° my tale I wol beginne."   *peace*

The Tale

In Flaundres whylom was° a compaignye   *once (there) was*
Of yonge folk, that haunteden folye—
As ryot, hasard, stewes, and tavernes,[23]
Where as° with harpes, lutes, and giternes,°   *There where / guitars*
They daunce and pleyen at dees° bothe day and night,   *dice*
And eten also and drinken over hir might,°   *beyond their capacity*
Thurgh which they doon the devel sacrifyse°   *make sacrifice to the devil*
Withinne that develes temple,[24] in cursed wyse,°   *way*
By superfluitee° abhominable.   *excess*
Hir othes° been so grete and so dampnable,°   *oaths, curses / condemnable*
That it is grisly for to here hem swere.
Our blissed Lordes body they totere°—   *tear apart*
Hem thoughte° Jewes rente° him noght y-nough— *It seemed to them / tore*
And ech° of hem at otheres sinne lough.°   *each / laughed*
And right anon thanne comen tombesteres°   *female tumblers, dancers*
Fetys and smale, and yonge fruytesteres,[25]
Singeres with harpes, baudes,° wafereres,°   *bawds / girls selling cakes*

---

[21] "Even though her children should die of hunger."
[22] "Which I am in the habit of preaching, in order to make some money."
[23] "Of young folk who gave themselves up to folly—(such) as excessive revelry, gambling with dice, (visiting) brothels and taverns."
[24] The tavern.
[25] "Shapely and slender, and young girls selling fruit."

Whiche been the verray° develes officeres   *the very*
To kindle and blowe the fyr of lecherye
That is annexed° unto glotonye: *joined (as a sin)*
The Holy Writ take I to my witnesse
That luxurie° is in wyn and dronkenesse.   *lechery*
   Lo, how that dronken Loth° unkindely°   *Lot / unnaturally*
Lay by his doghtres two, unwitingly;°   *unknowingly*
So dronke he was, he niste° what he wroghte.°   *knew not / did*
   Herodes,° whoso wel the stories soghte,°   *Herod / should seek out*
Whan he of wyn was repleet° at his feste,   *replete, full*
Right at his owene table he yaf° his heste°   *gave / command*
To sleen the Baptist John ful giltelees.°   *guiltless (innocent)*
   Senek° seith a good word doutelees: *Seneca*
He seith, he can no difference finde
Bitwix a man that is out of his minde
And a man which that is dronkelewe,°   *drunken*
But that woodnesse, y-fallen in a shrewe,[26]
Persevereth lenger° than doth dronkenesse.   *Continues longer*
O glotonye,° ful of cursednesse!   *gluttony*
O cause first° of oure confusioun!°   *first cause / ruin*
O original° of oure dampnacioun,   *origin*
Til Crist had boght us with his blood agayn!

Lo, how dere,° shortly for to sayn,°   *costly / to speak briefly*
Aboght was thilke cursed vileinye;[27]
Corrupt° was al this world for glotonye!   *Corrupted*
Adam oure fader and his wyf also
Fro Paradys to labour and to wo
Were driven for that vyce, it is no drede.°   *doubt*
For whyl that Adam fasted, as I rede,°   *read*
He was in Paradys; and whan that he
Eet of the fruyt defended° on the tree,   *forbidden*
Anon° he was outcast to wo and peyne.°   *Immediately / pain*
O glotonye, on thee wel oghte us pleyne![28]
   O, wiste a man° how manye maladyes   *(if) a man knew*
Folwen of° excesse and of glotonyes,   *Follow on*
He wolde been the more mesurable°   *measured, temperate*
Of his diete, sittinge at his table.
Allas! the shorte throte, the tendre mouth,[29]

---

[26] "Except that madness, having afflicted a miserable man."

[27] "Bought was that same cursed, evil deed."

[28] "Oh, gluttony, we certainly ought to complain against you."

[29] "The brief pleasure of swallowing, the mouth accustomed to delicacies."

Maketh that,° est and west, and north and south,   *Causes*
In erthe, in eir,° in water, men to swinke°   *air / labor*
To gete a glotoun deyntee° mete and drinke!   *dainty*
Of this matere,° O Paul, wel canstow trete:°   *subject / canst thou treat*
"Mete° unto wombe,° and wombe eek unto mete,   *Meat / belly*
Shal God destroyen bothe," as Paulus seith.[30]
Allas! a foul thing is it, by my feith,
To seye this word, and fouler is the dede,
Whan man so drinketh of the whyte and rede[31]
That of his throte he maketh his privee,°   *privy (toilet)*
Thurgh thilke° cursed superfluitee.°   *that same / excess*
    The apostel,[32] weping, seith ful pitously,
"Ther walken manye of whiche yow told have I"—
I seye it now weping with pitous voys—
"They been enemys of Cristes croys,°   *cross*
Of which the ende is deeth: wombe° is her° god!"   *belly / their*
O wombe! O bely! O stinking cod,[33]
Fulfild of donge and of corrupcioun![34]
At either ende of thee foul is the soun.°   *sound*
How° greet labour and cost is thee to finde!°   *What / to provide for*
Thise cookes, how they stampe,° and streyne,° and
    grinde,   *pound / strain*
And turnen substaunce into accident,[35]
To fulfille al thy likerous talent!°   *lecherous (here, gluttonous) appetite*
Out of the harde bones knokke they
The mary,° for they caste noght° awey   *marrow / nothing*
That may go thurgh the golet° softe and swote;°   *gullet / sweet*
Of spicerye° of leef, and bark, and rote°   *spices / root(s)*
Shal been his sauce y-maked by delyt,°   *to give pleasure*
To make him yet a newer° appetyt.   *renewed*
But certes, he that haunteth swich delyces[36]
Is deed, whyl that° he liveth in tho° vyces.   *while / those*
    A lecherous thing is wyn, and dronkenesse
Is ful of stryving° and of wrecchednesse.   *quarreling*
O dronke man, disfigured is thy face,
Sour is thy breeth, foul artow° to embrace,   *art thou*

---

[30] 1 Corinthians 6:13.

[31] Wines.

[32] St. Paul. See Philippians 3:18–19.

[33] "Bag," i.e., the stomach.

[34] "Filled up with dung and with decaying matter."

[35] "And turn substance into accident" (a scholastic joke: *sub-staunce* means "essence, essential qualities"; *accident*, "external appearances").

[36] "But truly, he that gives himself up to such pleasures."

And thurgh thy dronke nose semeth the soun°   *sound*
As though thou seydest ay° "Sampsoun, Sampsoun";[37]   *ever*
And yet, God wot,° Sampsoun drank nevere no wyn.   *knows*
Thou fallest,[38] as it were a stiked swyn;°   *stuck pig*
Thy tonge is lost, and al thyn honest cure,°   *care for decency*
For dronkenesse is verray sepulture°   *the true tomb*
Of mannes wit° and his discrecioun.°   *understanding / discretion*
In whom that° drinke hath dominacioun,   *In him whom*
He can no conseil° kepe, it is no drede.°   *secrets / doubt*
Now kepe yow fro the whyte and fro the rede—
And namely° fro the whyte wyn of Lepe[39]   *especially*
That is to selle° in Fishstrete° or in Chepe.°   *for sale / Fish Street / Cheapside*
This wyn of Spaigne crepeth subtilly
In othere wynes growinge faste by,[40]
Of° which ther ryseth swich fumositee,°   *From / vapor*
That whan a man hath dronken draughtes three
And weneth° that he be at hoom in Chepe,   *thinks*
He is in Spaigne, right at the toune of Lepe,
Nat at The Rochel,° ne at Burdeux toun;°   *La Rochelle / Bordeaux*
And thanne wol he seye, "Sampsoun, Sampsoun."
    But herkneth,° lordinges, o° word I yow preye,   *listen / one*
That alle the sovereyn actes,° dar I seye,   *supreme deeds*
Of victories in the Olde Testament,
Thurgh verray° God, that is omnipotent,   *true*
Were doon in abstinence and in preyere:
Loketh the Bible, and ther ye may it lere.°   *learn*
    Loke Attila,[41] the grete conquerour,
Deyde° in his sleep, with shame and dishonour,   *Died*
Bledinge ay° at his nose in dronkenesse: *continually*
A capitayn shoulde live in sobrenesse.
And over al this, avyseth yow right wel°   *be well advised*
What was comaunded unto Lamuel°—   *Lemuel*
Nat Samuel, but Lamuel, seye I—
Redeth the Bible, and finde it expresly
Of wyn-yeving to hem that han justyse.[42]
Namore of this, for it may wel suffyse.

---

[37] A witty kind of onomatopoeia—the snoring sound
seems to say "Samson," who was betrayed.

[38] Down.

[39] Near Cadiz.

[40] The wines sold as French are often mixed with the
cheaper wines of Spain.

[41] The Hun.

[42] Concerning the giving of wine to those responsible for
the law (see Proverbs 31.4–5).

And now that I have spoke of glotonye,
Now wol I yow defenden° hasardrye.°   *forbid / gambling at dice*
Hasard is verray moder° of lesinges,°   *the true mother / lies*
And of deceite and cursed forsweringes,°   *perjuries*
Blaspheme of Crist, manslaughtre, and wast° also   *waste*
Of catel° and of tyme; and forthermo,   *goods*
It is repreve° and contrarie of honour   *a reproach*
For to ben holde a commune hasardour.°   *gambler*
And ever the hyer° he is of estaat°   *higher / in social rank*
The more is he y-holden desolaat:°   *considered debased*
If that a prince useth° hasardrye,   *practices*
In alle governaunce and policye
He is, as by commune opinioun,
Y-holde the lasse in reputacioun.

Stilbon, that was a wys° embassadour,   *wise*
Was sent to Corinthe in ful greet honour,
For Lacidomie° to make hire alliaunce.°   *Lacedaemon (Sparta) / their alliance*
And whan he cam, him happede par chaunce°   *it happened by chance*
That alle the grettest° that were of that lond,   *greatest (men)*
Pleyinge atte° hasard he hem fond.   *at (the)*
For which, as sone as it mighte be,°   *could be*
He stal him° hoom agayn to his contree,   *stole away*
And seyde, "Ther wol I nat lese° my name,°   *lose / (good) name*
Ne I wol nat take on me so greet defame,°   *dishonor*
Yow for to allye° unto none hasardours.°   *to ally / gamblers*
Sendeth othere wyse embassadours—
For by my trouthe, me were levere dye°   *I would rather die*
Than I yow sholde to hasardours allye.
For ye that been so glorious in honours
Shul nat allyen yow with hasardours
As by my wil, ne as by my tretee."°   *negotiations*
This wyse philosophre, thus seyde he.

Loke eek° that to the king Demetrius   *also*
The king of Parthes,° as the book seith us,[43]   *Parthia*
Sente him a paire of dees° of gold in scorn,   *dice*
For he hadde used hasard ther-biforn;
For which he heeld his glorie or his renoun°   *renown*
At no value or reputacioun.
Lordes may finden other maner pley
Honeste° y-nough to dryve the day awey.   *Honorable*

Now wol I speke of othes° false and grete   *oaths, curses*
A word or two, as olde bokes trete.
Gret swering° is a thing abhominable,   *cursing*

---

[43] The *Policraticus* of John of Salisbury, which also contains
the preceding story.

And false swering[44] is yet more reprevable.°   *reproachable*
The heighe° God forbad swering at al—   *high*
Witnesse on Mathew—but in special
Of swering seith the holy Jeremye,°   *Jeremiah*
"Thou shalt swere sooth° thyn othes° and nat lye,   *truly / oaths*
And swere in dome,° and eek in rightwisnesse;"°   *(good) judgment / righteousness*
But ydel° swering is a cursednesse.°   *vain / wickedness*
Bihold and see, that in the first table°   *tablet (of Moses)*
Of heighe Goddes hestes° honurable,   *commandments*
How that the seconde heste of him is this:
"Tak nat my name in ydel° or amis."°   *in vain / amiss (wrongly)*
Lo, rather° he forbedeth swich° swering   *earlier (in the list) / such*
Than homicyde or many a cursed thing—
I seye that, as by ordre,° thus it stondeth—   *in terms of the order*
This knoweth, that his hestes understondeth,[45]
How that the second heste of God is that.
And forther over,° I wol thee telle al plat°   *moreover / flatly*
That vengeance shal nat parten° from his hous   *depart*
That° of his othes is to° outrageous.   *Who / too*
"By Goddes precious herte," and "By his nayles,"
And "By the blode of Crist that is in Hayles,[46]
Seven is my chaunce,[47] and thyn is cink° and treye;"°   *five / three*
"By Goddes armes, if thou falsly pleye,
This dagger shal thurghout thyn herte go!"
This fruyt cometh of the bicched bones two—[48]
Forswering,° ire,° falsnesse, homicyde.   *Perjury / anger*
Now for the love of Crist that for us dyde,
Lete° youre othes, bothe grete and smale.   *Cease*
But, sires, now wol I telle forth my tale.
    Thise ryotoures° three of which I telle,   *rioters, revelers*
Longe erst er° pryme° rong of any belle,   *before / 9 A.M.*
Were set hem° in a taverne for to drinke;   *Had set themselves down*
And as they sat, they herde a belle clinke
Biforn a cors° was° caried to his grave.   *corpse / (which) was (being)*
That oon of hem gan callen to his knave,
"Go bet," quod he, "and axe redily,[49]

---

[44] I.e., Of oaths.

[45] "[He] knows this, who understands His commandments."

[46] An abbey in Gloucestershire supposed to possess (as a high relic) some of Christ's blood.

[47] Throw.

[48] This fruit, i.e., result, comes from the two cursed dice. (Dice were made of bone; hence "bones" here.)

[49] The one of them proceeded to call to his servant-boy, "Go quickly," he said, "and ask straightway."

What cors is this that passeth heer forby;°   *by here*
And looke that thou reporte his name wel."[50]
     "Sire," quod this boy, "it nedeth never-a-del.°   *it isn't at all necessary*
It was me told, er° ye cam heer two houres.   *before*
He was, pardee,[51] an old felawe° of youres;   *companion*
And sodeynly he was y-slayn to-night,
For-dronke,° as he sat on his bench upright.   *Dead drunk*
Ther cam a privee° theef men clepeth° Deeth,   *secret / call*
That in this contree° al the peple sleeth,°   *region / kills*
And with his spere he smoot his herte atwo,[52]
And wente his wey withouten wordes mo.°   *more*
He hath a thousand slayn this pestilence.°   *(during) this plague*
And maister, er° ye come in his presence,   *before*
Me thinketh° that it were necessarie   *It seems to me*
For to be war° of swich an adversarie: *aware, careful*
Beth redy for to mete him everemore.°   *always*
Thus taughte me my dame,° I sey namore."   *mother*
"By Seinte Marie," seyde this taverner,°   *tavernkeeper*
"The child seith sooth, for he hath slayn this yeer,
Henne° over a myle, withinne a greet village,   *Hence, from here*
Bothe man and womman, child, and hyne,° and page;°   *laborer / servant*
I trowe° his habitacioun be there.   *believe*
To been avysed° greet wisdom it were,   *forewarned*
Er that° he dide a man a dishonour."   *Before*
     "Ye,° Goddes armes," quod° this ryotour,°   *Aye, yes / said / reveler*
"Is it swich peril with him for to mete?
I shal him seke by wey° and eek° by strete,   *road / also*
I make avow to° Goddes digne° bones!   *avow (it) by / worthy*
Herkneth, felawes, we three been al ones:°   *all of one mind*
Lat ech° of us holde up his hond til other,°   *each / to the other*
And ech of us bicomen otheres° brother,   *the others'*
And we wol sleen° this false traytour Deeth.   *slay*
He shal be slayn, he that so manye sleeth,
By Goddes dignitee,° er it be night."   *worthiness*
     Togidres° han thise three hir trouthes plight°   *Together / plighted their troth*
To live and dyen ech of hem for other,°   *one another*
As though he were his owene y-boren° brother.   *born*
And up they sterte,° al dronken in this rage,°   *leaped / passion*
And forth they goon towardes that village

---

[50] Correctly.

[51] A weak form of the oath "by God," based on the French *par dieu.*

[52] "And with his spear he struck his heart in two." (Death was often shown in the visual arts as a hideous skeleton menacing men with a spear or arrow.)

Of which the taverner hadde spoke biforn,
And many a grisly ooth thanne han they sworn,
And Cristes blessed body they to-rente°—   *tore apart*
Deeth shal be deed, if that they may him hente.°   *seize*
   Whan they han goon nat fully half a myle,
Right° as they wolde han troden° over a style,°   *Just / stepped / stile*
An old man and a povre° with hem mette.   *poor (one)*
This olde man ful mekely° hem grette,°   *meekly / greeted them*
And seyde thus, "Now, lordes, God yow see!"°   *may God protect you*
   The proudest of thise ryotoures three
Answerde agayn, "What, carl,° with sory grace!°   *Hey, fellow / confound you*
Why artow al forwrapped save thy face?[53]
Why livestow° so longe in so greet age?"   *livest thou*
This olde man gan loke in° his visage,   *scrutinized*
   And seyde thus, "For° I ne can nat finde   *Because*
A man, though that I walked into Inde,°   *India*
Neither in citee nor in no village,
That wolde chaunge his youthe for myn age;
And therfore moot° I han myn age stille,   *must*
As longe time as it is Goddes wille.
Ne Deeth, allas! ne wol nat han my lyf.
Thus walke I, lyk° a resteleees caityf,°   *like / captive*
And on the ground, which is my modres° gate,   *mother's*
I knokke with my staf bothe erly and late,
And seye, 'Leve° moder, leet me in!   *Dear*
Lo, how I vanish,° flesh, and blood, and skin!   *waste away*
Allas! whan shul my bones been at reste?
Moder, with yow wolde I chaunge° my cheste°   *exchange / chest (of clothes)*
That in my chambre longe tyme hath be,°   *been*
Ye, for an heyre clout° to wrappe me!'   *haircloth (for burial)*
But yet to me she wol nat do that grace,
For which ful pale and welked° is my face.   *withered*
   But sires, to yow it is no curteisye[54]
To speken to an old man vileinye,°   *rudeness*
But° he trespasse° in worde or elles° in dede.   *Unless / offend / else*
In Holy Writ ye may yourself wel rede,°   *read*
'Agayns° an old man, hoor° upon his heed,   *Before / hoary, white*
Ye sholde aryse.' Wherfor I yeve yow reed:[55]
Ne dooth unto an old man noon harm now,
Namore than that ye wolde men did to yow
In age, if that ye so longe abyde.°   *remain (alive)*

---

[53] "Why art thou all wrapped up, except for thy face?"
[54] "But, sirs, it is not courteous of you."
[55] "'You should stand up (in respect).' Therefore I give you (this) advice."

And God be with yow, wher ye go° or ryde;   *walk*
I moot° go thider as° I have to go."   *must / thither where*

    "Nay, olde cherl, by God, thou shalt nat so,"
Seyde this other hasardour° anon;°   *gambler / at once*
"Thou partest° nat so lightly, by Seint John!   *departest*
Thou spak right now of thilke° traitour Deeth   *that same*
That in this contree alle oure frendes sleeth.
Have heer my trouthe,° as° thou art his espye,°   *pledge / since / spy*
Telle wher he is, or thou shalt it abye,°   *pay for*
By God, and by the holy sacrament!
For soothly thou art oon of his assent°   *in league with him*
To sleen us yonge folk, thou false theef!"

    "Now, sires," quod he, "if that yow be so leef°   *desirous*
To finde Deeth, turne up this croked° wey,   *crooked*
For in that grove I lafte° him, by my fey,°   *left / faith*
Under a tree, and there he wol abyde:°   *stay*
Nat for youre boost he wole him nothing hyde.[56]
See ye that ook?° right ther ye shul him finde.   *oak*
God save yow, that boghte agayn° mankinde,   *redeemed*

    And yow amende!"° Thus seyde this olde man.   *make you better*
And everich° of thise ryotoures° ran,   *each / revelers*
Til he cam to that tree, and ther they founde
Of florins° fyne of golde y-coyned° rounde   *florins, coins / coined*
Wel ny an° eighte busshels, as hem thoughte.°   *nearly / it seemed to them*
No lenger thanne° after Deeth they soughte,   *No longer then*
But ech° of hem so glad was of that sighte—   *each*
For that the florins been so faire and brighte—
That doun they sette hem by this precious hord.
The worste of hem he spake the firste word.

    "Brethren," quod he, "take kepe° what that I seye: *heed*
My wit° is greet, though that I bourde° and pleye.   *understanding / jest*
This tresor° hath Fortune unto us yiven°   *treasure / given*
In mirthe and jolitee° our lyf to liven,   *merriment*
And lightly as it comth, so wol we spende.
Ey! Goddes precious dignitee!° who wende°   *worthiness / would have supposed*
To-day that we sholde han so fair a grace?°   *favor*
But° mighte this gold be caried fro this place   *If only*
Hoom to myn hous—or elles unto youres—
For wel ye woot° that al this gold is oures—   *know*
Thanne were we in heigh felicitee.°   *supreme happiness*
But trewely, by daye it may nat be:°   *be (done)*
Men wolde seyn that we were theves stronge,°   *flagrant*
And for oure owene tresor doon us honge.°   *have us hanged*

---

[56] "He won't conceal himself at all because of your boasting."

This tresor moste y-caried be by nighte,
As wysly° and as slyly° as it mighte.°   *prudently / craftily / can (be)*
Wherfore I rede° that cut° among us alle   *advise / lots, straws*
Be drawe,° and lat se wher the cut wol falle;   *drawn, pulled*
And he that hath the cut with herte blythe
Shal renne° to the toune, and that ful swythe,°   *run / quickly*
And bringe us breed and wyn ful prively.°   *secretly*
And two of us shul kepen° subtilly°   *guard / carefully*
This tresor wel; and if he wol nat tarie,°   *tarry*
Whan it is night we wol this tresor carie,
By oon assent, where as us thinketh best."[57]
That oon of hem the cut broughte in his fest,°   *fist*
And bad hem drawe, and loke wher it wol falle;
And it fil on the yongeste of hem alle,
And forth toward the toun he wente anon.
And also sone as° that he was agon,   *as soon as*
That oon of hem° spak thus unto that other: *The one of them*
"Thou knowest wel thou art my sworne brother;
Thy profit° wol I telle thee anon.   *Something to thy advantage*
Thou woost° wel that oure felawe is agon,°   *knowest / gone*
And heer is gold, and that° ful greet plentee,   *that (in)*
That shal departed° been among us three.   *divided*
But natheles,° if I can shape° it so   *nonetheless / arrange*
That it departed were among us two,
Hadde I nat doon a freendes torn° to thee?"   *turn*
    That other answerde, "I noot° how that may be: *know not*
He woot how that the gold is with us tweye.
What shal we doon? what shal we to him seye?"
    "Shal it be conseil?"° seyde the firste shrewe;° *a secret / wretch*
"And I shal tellen in a wordes fewe
What we shal doon, and bringe it wel aboute."
"I graunte,"° quod that other, "out of doute,[58]   *grant (it)*
That, by my trouthe, I wol thee nat biwreye."°   *betray*
    "Now," quod the firste, "thou woost° wel
      we be tweye,°   *knowest / two*
And two of us shul strenger° be than oon.   *stronger*
Looke whan that he is set,° that right anoon°   *has sat down / right away*
Arys° as though thou woldest with him pleye;   *Arise (get up)*
And I shal ryve° him thurgh the sydes tweye°   *stab / through his two sides*
Whyl that thou strogelest° with him as in game,°   *strugglest / as if in play*
And with thy dagger looke° thou do the same;   *take heed*
And thanne shall al this gold departed° be,   *divided*
My dere freend, bitwixen me and thee.

---

[57] "By common assent, wherever seems to us best."
[58] You can be sure.

Thanne may we bothe oure lustes° al fulfille,   *desires*
And pleye at dees° right at oure owene wille."   *dice*
And thus acorded° been thise shrewes° tweye   *agreed / cursed fellows*
To sleen the thridde, as ye han herd me seye.

   This yongest, which that wente unto the toun,
Ful ofte in herte he rolleth up and doun[59]
The beautee of thise florins newe and brighte.
"O Lord!" quod he, "if so were that I mighte
Have al this tresor to myself allone,
Ther is no man that liveth under the trone°   *throne*
Of God that sholde live so mery as I!"
And atte laste° the feend,° our enemy,   *at (the) last / devil*
Putte in his thought that he shold poyson beye,°   *buy poison*
With which he mighte sleen his felawes tweye°—   *two companions*
For-why the feend fond him in swich lyvinge[60]
That he had leve° him to sorwe bringe: *permission (from God)*
For this was outrely° his fulle entente,°   *completely / purpose*
To sleen hem bothe, and nevere to repente.
And forth he gooth—no lenger wolde he tarie—
Into the toun, unto a pothecarie,°   *apothecary, pharmacist*
And preyed° him that he him wolde selle   *asked*
Som poyson, that° he mighte his rattes quelle,°   *so that / kill his rats*
And eek° ther was a polcat° in his hawe,°   *also / weasel / yard*
That, as he seyde, his capouns° hadde y-slawe,°   *capons / killed*
And fayn° he wolde wreke him,° if he mighte,   *gladly / avenge himself*
On vermin, that destroyed° him by nighte.   *were ruining*
   The pothecarie answerde, "And thou shalt have
A thing that, also° God my soule save,   *so (may)*
In al this world ther nis no° creature,   *is not any*
That ete or dronke hath of this confiture°   *mixture*
Noght but the mountance of a corn of whete,[61]
That he ne shal his lyf anon° forlete.°   *at once / lose*
Ye,° sterve° he shal, and that in lasse whyle°   *Yes / die / shorter time*
Than thou wolt goon a paas° nat but° a myle,   *walk at normal pace / only*
This poyson is so strong and violent."
   This cursed man hath in his hond y-hent°   *grasped*
This poyson in a box, and sith° he ran   *afterward*
Into the nexte strete unto a man
And borwed [of] him large botels° three,   *bottles (probably of leather)*
And in the two his poyson poured he—
The thridde he kepte clene for his° drinke—   *his (own)*
For al the night he shoop him° for to swinke°   *was preparing himself / work*

---

[59] Thinks on.

[60] "Because the fiend [the devil] found him living in such a way."

[61] "No more than the quantity of a grain of wheat."

In caryinge of the gold out of that place.
And whan this ryotour, with sory grace,[62]
Hadde filled with wyn his grete botels three,
To his felawes agayn repaireth° he.   *returns*
    What nedeth it to sermone° of it more?   *speak*
For right as they hadde cast° his deeth bifore,   *planned*
Right so they han him slayn, and that anon.°   *immediately*
And whan that this was doon, thus spak that oon:
"Now lat us sitte and drinke, and make us merie,
And afterward we wol his body berie."°   *bury*
And with that word it happed° him, par cas,°   *befell / by chance*
To take the botel ther° the poyson was,   *where*
And drank, and yaf° his felawe drink also,   *gave*
For which anon they storven° bothe two.   *died*
    But certes, I suppose that Avicen
Wroot nevere in no canon, ne in no fen,

Mo wonder signes of empoisoning[63]
Than hadde thise wrecches two, er° hir° ending.   *before / their*
Thus ended been thise homicydes two,
And eek° the false empoysoner° also.°   *also / poisoner / as well*
    O cursed sinne of alle cursednesse!
O traytours° homicyde, O wikkednesse!   *traitorous*
O glotonye, luxurie,° and hasardrye!   *lechery*
Thou blasphemour of Crist with vileinye°   *vile speech*
And othes grete, of usage° and of pryde!   *out of habit*
Allas! mankinde, how may it bityde°   *happen*
That to thy Creatour which that thee wroghte,
And with his precious herte-blood thee boghte,°   *redeemed*
Thou art so fals and so unkinde,° allas!   *unnatural*
    Now, goode men, God forgeve° yow youre trespas,   *may God forgive*
And ware yow fro° the sinne of avaryce.   *make you beware of*
Myn holy pardoun may yow alle waryce°—   *cure*
So that ye offre nobles or sterlinges,[64]
Or elles silver broches, spones,° ringes.   *spoons*
Boweth youre heed° under this holy bulle!   *head*
Cometh up, ye wyves, offreth of youre wolle!°   *wool*
Youre names I entre heer in my rolle° anon:°   *roll, list / at once*
Into the blisse of hevene shul ye gon.
I yow assoile,° by myn heigh power—   *absolve*
Yow that wol offre°—as clene and eek as cleer°   *make an offering / pure*

---

[62] Blessed by evil.

[63] "But truly, I would guess that Avicenna—an Arab physician and author—never described, in any treatise or chapter, more terrible symptoms of poisoning."

[64] "As long as you offer nobles [gold coins] or silver pennies."

As ye were born.—And, lo, sires, thus I preche.
And Jesu Crist, that is our soules leche,°   *healer, doctor*
So graunte° yow his pardon to receyve,   *May He grant*
For that is best; I wol yow nat deceyve.
    But sires, o° word forgat I in my tale: *a, one*
I have relikes and pardon in my male°   *pouch*
As faire as any man in Engelond,
Whiche were me yeven° by the Popes hond.   *given*
If any of yow wol of devocioun°   *out of devotion*
Offren and han myn absolucioun,
Cometh forth anon, and kneleth heer adoun,
And mekely receyveth my pardoun;
Or elles, taketh pardon as ye wende,°   *travel*
Al newe and fresh, at every myles ende—
So that ye offren alwey newe and newe[65]
Nobles or pens,° which that be gode and trewe.   *pence*
It is an honour to everich° that is heer   *every one*
That ye mowe° have a suffisant° pardoneer   *may / capable*
T'assoille° yow, in contree as ye ryde,   *To absolve*

For aventures whiche that may bityde.[66]
Peraventure° ther may falle oon or two   *By chance*
Doun of his hors, and breke his nekke atwo.°   *in two*
Look which a seuretee° is it to you alle   *what a security*
That I am in youre felaweship y-falle,
That may assoille yow, bothe more and lasse,°   *great and small*
Whan that the soule shal fro the body passe.
I rede° that oure Host heer shal biginne,   *advise*
For he is most envoluped° in sinne.   *enveloped, wrapped up*
Com forth, sire Hoste, and offre first anon,°   *first now*
And thou shalt kisse the reliks everichon,°   *every one*
Ye, for a grote:° unbokel° anon thy purs."   *groat (four pence) / unbuckle*
    "Nay, nay," quod° he, "thanne have I Cristes curs!   *said*
Lat be," quod he, "it shal nat be, so theech!°   *as I hope to prosper*
Thou woldest make me kisse thyn olde breech°   *breeches*
And swere it were a relik of a seint,
Thogh it were with thy fundement° depeint!°   *fundament (rectum) / stained*
But by the croys° which that Seint Eleyne° fond,   *(true) Cross / St. Helena*
I wolde I hadde thy coillons° in myn hond   *testicles*
In stede of relikes or of seintuarie.[67]
Lat cutte hem of! I wol thee helpe hem carie.[68]

---

[65] "As long as you make offering anew each time (of)."
[66] "In respect to things which may befall."
[67] Holy things.
[68] "Have them cut off! I'll help thee carry them."

Thay shul be shryned° in an hogges tord!"°   *enshrined / turd*
  This Pardoner answerde nat a word;
So wrooth° he was, no word ne wolde he seye.   *wroth, angered*
  "Now," quod our Host, "I wol no lenger pleye
With thee, ne with noon other angry man."
But right anon the worthy Knight bigan,
"Whan that he saugh that al the peple lough,°   *laughed*
"Namore of this, for it is right y-nough!°   *quite enough*
Sire Pardoner, be glad and mery of chere;°   *mood*
And ye, sire Host, that been to me so dere,
I prey yow that ye kisse the Pardoner.
And Pardoner, I prey thee, drawe thee neer,
And, as we diden, lat us laughe and pleye."
Anon° they kiste, and riden forth hir weye.°   *At once / (on) their way*

*   *   *

REVIEW QUESTIONS

1. How do the character of the Pardoner and the tale he tells reflect contemporary trends and problems within the late medieval Church and society? What can you discern about Chaucer's attitude toward the sale of indulgences or false relics?

2. How does the Pardoner's Tale reflect the realities of life in the world after the Black Death?

3. Did you find that the reading of Middle English became easier as you became more accustomed to it? How different is this language from our own? What words and phrases are still in use today? What might that reveal about continuities over time?

CHRISTINE DE PISAN

FROM *The Book of the City of Ladies*

Christine de Pisan (1365–after 1429) was the highly educated daughter of a Venetian physician at the court of Charles VI of France. Widowed at an early age, Christine became a writer to support her family, becoming the first professional woman of letters. Her most famous work, The Book of the City of Ladies, *is both a historical treatise on women and a defense of them. In this selection, the allegorical figure of Lady Rectitude introduces the subject of virtuous women.*

From *The Book of the City of Ladies*, by Christine de Pisan, translated by Earl Jeffrey Richards (New York: Persea Books, 1982), pp. 206–15.

*   *   *

Rectitude Says That Many Women Are Loved for Their Virtues More Than Other Women for Their Prettiness

"If we assumed that women who wished to be loved tried, for this reason, to be pretty, conceited, cute, and vain, then I can show you that such action will not make wise and worthwhile men love them more quickly or better and that, in fact, honest, virtuous, and simple women will more readily and more deeply be loved by men who love honor than pretty women, even if we suppose that these honest women are less beautiful. One could answer that, since women attract men with virtue and integrity and since it is bad that men be attracted, it would be better if women were less good. But of course this argument has no validity at all, for one should not neglect the cultivation and advancement of the good in spite of however much fools abuse it, and everyone must do his duty by acting well regardless of what might happen. I will give you an example to prove that women are loved for their virtue and integrity. First I could tell you about the many women who are saints in Paradise who were desired by men because of their honesty.

"Consider Lucretia, whom I spoke to you about before and who was raped: her great integrity was the reason why Tarquin became enamored, much more so than because of her beauty. For once, when her husband was dining with this Tarquin (who afterward raped her) and with many other knights, the subject of their conversation turned to their wives, and each one claimed that his own was the best. In order to discover the truth and to prove which one of their wives was worthy of the highest praise, they got up and rode home, and those women found occupied in the most honest occupation and activity were to be the most celebrated and honored. Lucretia, of all these wives, turned out to be the most honestly occupied, for her husband found her, such a wise and upright woman, clothed in a simple gown, sitting at home among her women servants, working in wool, and discoursing on various subjects. This same Tarquin, the king's son, arrived there with her husband and saw her outstanding honesty, her smile and fair conduct, and her serene manner. He was so captivated by her that he began to plan the folly which he committed later."

Here She Speaks of Queen Blanche, the Mother of Saint Louis, and of Other Good and Wise Ladies Loved for Their Virtue

"The most noble Queen Blanche, mother of Saint Louis, was similarly loved for great learning, prudence, virtue, and goodness by Thibault, the count of Champagne. Even though she had already passed the flower of her youth, this noble count—hearing the wise and good queen speak to him so judiciously after he had gone to war against Saint Louis, sensibly reproving him, telling him he ought not to have acted this way, considering the good deeds her son had done for him—looked at her intently, amazed by her enormous goodness and virtue, and was so overwhelmed by love that he did not know what to do. He did not dare confess his love for fear of death, for he realized that she was so good that she would never consent to his proposition. From that time onward he suffered much grief because of the mad desire which oppressed him. Nevertheless, he told her then not to fear his continuing to wage war against the king and that he wished to be her subject totally, that she should be certain that everything he possessed, body and soul, was entirely subject to her command. So he loved her all his life, from that hour on, and he never stopped loving her in spite of the slight chance he had of ever winning her love. He made his laments to Love in his poems, where he praised his lady most graciously. These beautiful poems of his were put to music in a charming way. He had them inscribed in his bedroom in Provins and also in Troyes, and they appear there

to this day. And so I could tell you about many others."

And I, Christine, replied, "Indeed, my lady, I have seen in my own experience several cases similar to the one you mention, for I know of virtuous and wise women who, from what they have confessed to me in lamenting their distress, have been propositioned more frequently after their peak of beauty and youthfulness than when they were in their greatest flower. Concerning this, they have told me, 'Gods! What can this possibly mean? Do these men see in me some foolish behavior which would give them the slightest glimmer of hope that I would agree to commit such foolishness?' But I realize now, from what you say, that their outstanding goodness caused them to be loved. And this is very much against the opinion of many people who claim that an honest woman who intends to be chaste will never be desired or propositioned unless she herself so wishes."

Christine Speaks, and Rectitude Responds in Her Reply to Those Men Who Claim That Women Are Naturally Greedy

"I do not know what more to tell you, my dear lady, for all my questions are answered. It seems to me that you have disproven the slanders put forth by so many men against women. Likewise, what they so often claim is not true, that greed is, among feminine vices, a very natural thing."

She answered, "My dear friend, let me assure you that greed is no more natural in women than it is in men, and God only knows whether men are less greedy! You can see that the latter is in fact the case because considerably more evil occurs and recurs in the world because of the rapacity of different men than because of the greed of women. But, just as I told you before, the fool sees his neighbor's peccadillo and fails to see his own enormous crime. Since one commonly sees women taking delight in collecting cloth and thread and such trifles which go into a household,

women are thought to be greedy. I can, however, assure you that there are many women who, were they to possess anything, would not be greedy or stingy in bestowing honors and giving generously where what they have could be used well, just as one poor person would do for an even poorer person in need. Women are usually kept in such financial straits that they guard the little that they can have, knowing they can recover this only with the greatest pain. So some people consider women greedy because some women have foolish husbands, great wastrels of property and gluttons, and the poor women, who know well that their households need what their husbands spend foolishly and that in the end their poor children will have to pay for it, are unable to refrain from speaking to their husbands and from urging them to spend less. Thus, such behavior is not at all avarice or greed, but is a sign of great prudence. Of course I am referring to those women who act with discretion. One sees so much quarreling in these marriages because the husbands do not like such urging and so blame their wives for something which they should praise them for. It is clear from the alms which these women so freely give that the vice of avarice is not to be found in them. God knows how many prisoners, even in the lands of the Saracens, how many destitute and needy noblemen and others have been and are every day, in this world here below, comforted and helped by women and their property."

And I, Christine, then said, "Indeed, my lady, your remarks remind me that I have seen women show themselves honorable in prudent generosity, and today I am acquainted with women who rejoice when they can say, 'See, the money is put to good use there, and no greedy man can hoard it away in some coffer.' For although Alexander the Great was said to be generous, I can tell you that I never saw any examples of it."

Rectitude then began to laugh and said, "Indeed, my friend, the ladies of Rome were not greedy when their city was gravely afflicted with war, when the public treasury was completely spent on warriors. The Romans had terrible trouble finding money to finance a large army which

they had to raise. But the ladies, with their liberality—even the widows—collected all their jewels and property together, sparing nothing, and freely gave them to the princes of Rome. The ladies received great praise for this deed, and afterward their jewels were given back to them, and quite rightly so, for they had saved Rome."

Here She Speaks of the Rich and Generous Lady Named Busa

"In the *Faits des Romains* the generosity of a rich and upright woman named Busa, or Paulina, is described. She lived in Apuleia during the time when Hannibal was ravaging the Romans with fire and arms, despoiling almost all of Italy of men and goods. Many Romans retreated after the great defeat at the battle of Cannae, where Hannibal won such a noble victory, and they fled the battlefield wounded or injured. But this valiant Lady Busa received as many as she could take in, until she sheltered some ten thousand in her household, for she was extremely wealthy and had them cared for at her expense. All of them, having been helped by her wealth as much as by the aid and comfort she afforded them, were able to return to Rome and put the army back on its feet, for which she was highly praised. So do not doubt, dear friend, that I could tell you more about the endless generosity, bounty, and liberality of women.

"And even without going back to look for historical examples, how many other examples of the generosity of ladies from your own time could be mentioned! Was not the generosity great which was shown by the Dame de la Rivière, named Marguerite, who is still alive and was formerly the wife of Monsieur Burel de la Rivière, first chamberlain of the wise King Charles? On one occasion among others it happened that this lady, as she was always wise, valiant, and well-bred, was attending a very fine celebration which the duke of Anjou, later king of Sicily, was holding in Paris. At this celebration there were a large number of noble ladies and knights and gentlemen in fine array. This lady, who was young and beautiful, realized while she watched the noble knights assembled there, that a most noteworthy knight of great fame among those then living, named Emerion de Poumiers, was missing from the company of knights. She, of course, allowed that this Sir Emerion was too old to remember her, but his goodness and valiance made the lady remember him, and she felt there could be no more beautiful an ornament for such an assembly than so noteworthy and famous a man, even if he were old, so she inquired where the missing knight was. She was told that he was in prison in the Châtelet in Paris because of a debt of five hundred francs that he had incurred during his frequent travels in arms. 'Ah!' said the noble lady, 'what a shame for this kingdom to suffer a single hour of such a man imprisoned for debt!' Whereupon she removed the gold chaplet which she was wearing on her rich and fair head and replaced it with a chaplet of periwinkle on her blond hair. She gave the gold chaplet to a certain messenger and said, 'Go and give this chaplet as a pledge for what he owes, and let him be freed immediately and come here.' This was done and she was highly praised for it."

She Speaks Here of the Princesses and Ladies of France

Then I, Christine, spoke again. "My lady, since you have recalled a lady from my own time and since you have come to the history of the ladies of France and of those ladies still living, let me ask you whether you think it is a good idea to lodge some of them in our City. For why should they be forgotten, and foreign women as well?"

She replied, "I can answer you, Christine, that there are certainly a great many virtuous ladies of France, and I would be more than pleased if they were among our citizens. First of all, the noble queen of France, Isabella of Bavaria, will not be refused, reigning now by the grace of God, and in whom there is not a trace of cruelty, extortion, or any other evil vice, but only great love and good will toward her subjects.

"We can equally praise the fair, young, good, and wise duchess of Berry, wife of Duke John, son of the late King John of France and brother of wise King Charles. In the flower of her youth this noble duchess conducted herself so chastely, so sensibly, and so wisely that all the world praised and reputed her for her excellent virtue.

"What could I say about Valentina Visconti, the duchess of Orléans, wife of Duke Louis, son of Charles, the wise king of France, and daughter of the duke of Milan? What more could be said about such a prudent lady? A lady who is strong and constant in heart, filled with devotion to her lord and good teaching for her children, well-informed in government, just toward all, sensible in her conduct, and virtuous in all things—and all this is well known.

"What more could be said concerning the duchess of Burgundy, wife of Duke John, son of Philip, the son of the late King John of France? Is she not extraordinarily virtuous, loyal to her lord, kind in heart and manners, excellent in her morals and lacking a single vice?

"Is not the countess of Clermont, daughter of the duke of Berry mentioned above from his first marriage, and wife of Count John of Clermont, son of the duke of Bourbon and heir to the duchy, is she not everything which every lofty princess must be, devoted to her love, well-bred in everything, beautiful, wise, and good? In short, her virtues shine forth in her good conduct and honorable bearing.

"And what about that one woman among others whom you love singularly as much for the goodness of her virtues as for the favors she has extended to you and to whom you are much beholden, the noble duchess of Holland and countess of Hainault, daughter of the late Duke Philip of Burgundy mentioned above, and sister of the present duke? This lady should be ranked among the most perfect ladies, loyal-hearted, most prudent, wise in government, charitable, supremely devoted to God, and, in short, wholly good.

"Should not the duchess of Bourbon also be recalled among princesses known for their honor and laudability in all things?

"What more shall I tell you? I would need much time to recount all their great virtues.

"The good and beautiful countess of Saint-Pol, noble and upright, daughter of the duke of Bar, second cousin of the king of France, should also be ranked among the good women.

"Similarly the woman whom you love, Anne, daughter of the late count of La Marche and sister of the present duke, married to Ludwig of Bavaria, brother of the queen of France, does not discredit the company of women endowed with grace and praise, for her excellent virtues are well-known to God and the world.

"In spite of the slanderers, there are so many good and beautiful women among the ranks of countesses, baronesses, ladies, maidens, bourgeois women, and all classes that God should be praised who upholds them all. May He correct those women with shortcomings! Do not think otherwise, for I assure you of its truth, even if many jealous and slanderous people say the opposite."

And I, Christine, replied, "My lady, hearing this from you is a supreme joy for me."

She answered, "My dear friend, it seems to me I have now more than adequately executed my office in the City of Ladies. I have built it up with beautiful palaces and many fair inns and mansions. I have populated it for your sake with noble ladies and with such great numbers of women from all classes that it is already completely filled. Now let my sister Justice come to complete the rest, and this should satisfy you."

Christine Addresses Herself to All Princesses and to All Women

"Most excellent, revered, and honored princesses of France and of all lands, and all ladies and maidens, and, indeed, all women who have loved and do love and will love virtue and morality, as well as all who have died or who are now living or who are to come, rejoice and exult in our new City which, thanks to God, is already formed and almost finished and populated. Give thanks to God who has

led me to undertake this great labor and the desirable task of establishing for you honorable lodging within city walls as a perpetual residence for as long as the world endures. I have come this far hoping to reach the conclusion of my work with the aid and comfort of Lady Justice, who, in accordance with her promise, will unfailingly help me until the City is finished and wholly completed. Now, my most honored ladies, pray for me."

*   *   *

REVIEW QUESTIONS

1. Christine was outspokenly critical of the ways that women were represented by the male authors of her own day, notably Boccaccio. How might she have responded to the depictions of women in the *Decameron* (pp. 321–326) or even in Dante's *Inferno* (pp. 314–317)?
2. How does Christine use history to make her case for women?
3. What does Christine see as the correct way for men and women to relate in society?

FROM *The Trial of Jeanne d'Arc*

Jeanne d'Arc appeared on the scene in 1429 as French fortunes in the Hundred Years' War were at their lowest. Taking command of the Dauphin's army, and then lifting the siege of Orleans, she had him crowned as Charles VII at Rheims and revived the French cause. Captured by the Burgundians and then sold to their English allies, Jeanne was tried as a heretic and eventually burned at the stake in Rouen in May of 1431. Although she was dead before the age of twenty, Jeanne's career is a remarkable episode in the history of France and of late medieval women. The following excerpts from her trial include some of Jeanne's own words and reveal the concerns of the prosecutors.

From *The Trial of Jeanne d'Arc*, edited by W. P. Barrett (London: Routledge and Paul, 1931), pp. 50–51, 68–70, 73–74, 125–26, 318–19.

*   *   *

First Inquiry after the Oath

When she had thus taken the oath the said Jeanne was questioned by us about her name and her surname. To which she replied that in her own country she was called Jeannette, and after she came to France, she was called Jeanne. Of her surname she said she knew nothing. Consequently she was questioned about the district from which she came. She replied she was born in the village of Domrémy, which is one with the village of Greux; and in Greux is the principal church.

Asked about the name of her father and mother, she replied that her father's name was Jacques d'Arc, and her mother's Isabelle.

Asked where she was baptized, she replied it was in the church of Domrémy.

Asked who were her godfathers and godmothers, she said one of her godmothers was named Agnes, another Jeanne, another Sibylle; of her godfathers, one was named Jean Lingué, another

Jean Barrey: she had several other godmothers, she had heard her mother say.

Asked what priest had baptized her, she replied that it was master Jean Minet, as far as she knew.

Asked if he was still living, she said she believed he was.

Asked how old she was, she replied she thought nineteen. She said moreover that her mother taught her the Paternoster, Ave Maria, and Credo; and that no one but her mother had taught her her Credo.

* * *

Asked whether the voice which spoke to her was that of an angel, or of a saint, male or female, or straight from God, she answered that the voice was the voice of St. Catherine and of St. Margaret. And their heads were crowned in a rich and precious fashion with beautiful crowns. "And to tell this," she said, "I have God's permission. If you doubt it, send to Poitiers where I was examined before."

Asked how she knew they were these two saints, and how she knew one from the other, she answered she knew well who they were, and easily distinguished one from the other.

Asked how she knew one from the other, she answered she knew them by the greeting they gave her. She said further that a good seven years have passed since they undertook to guide her. She said also she knows the saints because they tell her their names.

Asked if the said saints are dressed in the same cloth, she answered: "I will tell you no more now; I have not leave to reveal it. If you do not believe me, send to Poitiers!" She said also that there were some revelations made directly to the king of France, and not to those who question her.

Asked if the saints are the same age, she answered that she had not leave to say.

Asked if the saints spoke at the same time, or one after another, she answered: "I have not leave to tell you; nevertheless I have always had counsel from both."

Asked which one appeared first, she answered: "I did not recognize them immediately; I knew

well enough once, but I have forgotten; if I had leave I would gladly tell you. It is written down in the register at Poitiers." She added that she had received comfort from St. Michael.

Asked which of the apparitions came to her first, she answered that St. Michael came first.

Asked whether it was a long time ago that she first heard the voice of St. Michael, she answered: "I do not speak of St. Michael's voice, but of his great comfort."

Asked which was the first voice which came to her when she was about thirteen, she answered that it was St. Michael whom she saw before her eyes; and he was not alone, but accompanied by many angels from heaven. She said also that she came into France only by the instruction of God.

Asked if she saw St. Michael and these angels corporeally and in reality, she answered: "I saw them with my bodily eyes as well as I see you; and when they left me, I wept; and I fain would have had them take me with them too."

Asked in what form St. Michael appeared, she answered: "There is as yet no reply to that, for I have not had leave to answer."

Asked what St. Michael said to her the first time, she answered: "You will get no further reply to-day." She said the voices told her to answer boldly. She said she had indeed once told her king everything that had been revealed to her, since it concerned him. She said, however, that she had not yet leave to reveal what St. Michael said. She added that she wished her examiner had a copy of the book at Poitiers, provided that God desired it.

Asked if the voices told her not to tell her revelations without their permission, she answered: "I will not answer you further about that; and what I have permission to, that I will gladly answer. If the voices forbade me, I did not understand."

Asked what sign she gives that this revelation comes from God, and that it is St. Catherine and St. Margaret who speak to her, she answered: "I have told you often enough that it is St. Catherine and St. Margaret; believe me if you will."

Asked if it is forbidden for her to tell, she answered: "I have not quite understood whether that is permitted or not."

Asked how she can distinguish such points as she will answer, and such as she will not, she answered that on some points she had asked permission, and on some points she had received it. Furthermore she said she would rather be torn asunder by horses than have come to France without God's leave.

Asked if God ordered her to wear a man's dress, she answered that the dress is a small, nay, the least thing. Nor did she put on man's dress by the advice of any man whatsoever; she did not put it on, nor did she do aught, but by the command of God and the angels.

Asked whether it seemed to her that this command to assume male attire was lawful, she answered: "Everything I have done is at God's command; and if He had ordered me to assume a different habit, I should have done it, because it would have been His command."

Asked if she did it at the order of Robert de Baudricourt she said no.

Asked if she thought she had done well to take man's dress, she answered that everything she did at God's command she thought well done, and hoped for good warrant and succour in it.

Asked if, in this particular case, by taking man's dress, she thought she had done well, she answered that she had done nothing in the world but by God's commands.

Asked whether, when she saw the voice coming to her, there was a light, she answered that there was a great deal of light on all sides, as was most fitting. She added to the examiner that not all the light came to him alone!

*   *   *

Asked whether, when she went to Orleans, she had a standard or banner, in French *estandart ou banière,* and what colour it was, she answered she had a banner, with a field sown with lilies; the world was depicted on it, and two angels, one at each side; it was white, of white linen or boucassin, and on it were written, she thought, these names, JHESUS MARIA; and it was fringed with silk.

Asked if these names JHESUS MARIA were written above, or below, or at the side, she answered, at the side, she believed.

Asked which she preferred, her standard or her sword, she answered she much preferred her standard to her sword.

Asked who persuaded her to have this painting on her standard, she answered: "I have told you often enough that I have done nothing but by God's command." She said also that she herself bore the standard, when attacking the enemy, so as not to kill anyone; she never has killed anyone, she said.

Asked what force her king gave her when he set her to work, she answered that he gave her 10 or 12,000 men; and she went first to Orleans, to the fortress of Saint-Loup, and then to the fortress of the Bridge.

Asked to which fortress she ordered her men to retire, she says she does not remember. She added that she was confident of raising the siege of Orleans, for it had been revealed to her, and she had told the king so before going there.

Asked whether, when the assault was to be made, she did not tell her men that she would receive arrows, crossbolts and stones hurled by catapults or cannons, she answered no; there were a hundred wounded, or more. But she had indeed told her men not to fear and they would raise the siege. She said also that at the assault upon the fortress of the Bridge she was wounded in the neck by an arrow or crossbolt; but she received great comfort from St. Margaret, and was better in a fortnight. But she did not on account of that give up her riding or work.

Asked if she knew beforehand that she would be wounded, she answered that she did indeed, and she had told her king so; but that notwithstanding she would not give up her work. And it was revealed to her by the voices of the two saints, namely the blessed Catherine and Margaret. She added that she herself was the first to plant the ladder against the said fortress of the Bridge; and as she was raising the ladder she was wounded in the neck with the crossbolt, as she had said.

*   *   *

Asked on the subject of the woman's dress offered her so that she might hear Mass, she answered that she would not put it on till it should please Our

Lord. And if it be that she must be brought to judgment she requests the Lords of the Church to grant her the mercy of a woman's dress and a hood for her head; she would die rather than turn back from what Our Lord commanded her; she firmly believed God would not let her be brought so low, or be presently without His help or miracle.

Asked why, if she wore man's dress at God's bidding, she asked for a woman's robe in the event of her death, she answered: "It is enough for me that it be long."

Asked if her godmother, who saw the fairies, was held to be a wise woman, she answered that she was held and reputed to be an honest woman, and not a witch or sorceress.

Asked whether her saying she would take a woman's dress if they would let her go would please God, she answered that if she were given permission to go in woman's dress she would immediately put on man's dress and do what Our Lord bade her. So she had formerly answered: and nothing would induce her to swear not to take up arms or to wear man's dress, to accomplish our Lord's will.

Asked about the age of the garments worn by St. Catherine and St. Margaret, she answered: "You already have my reply on this matter, and you will get none other from me. I have answered you as best I can."

Asked if she did not believe heretofore that the fairies were evil spirits, she answered she knew nothing of that.

Asked how she knew that St. Catherine and St. Margaret hated the English, she answered: "They love those whom God loves, and hate whom He hates."

Asked if God hated the English, she answered that of God's love or His hatred for the English, or of what He would do to their souls, she knew nothing, but she was certain that, excepting those who died there, they would be driven out of France, and God would send victory to the French and against the English.

Asked if God was for the English when they were prospering in France, she answered that she knew not whether God hated the French, but she believed it was His will to suffer them to be beaten for their sins, if they were in a state of sin.

*   *   *

The Trial for Relapse

On Monday following, the day after Holy Trinity Sunday, we the said judges repaired to Jeanne's prison to observe her state and disposition. * * *

Now because the said Jeanne was wearing a man's dress, a short mantle, a hood, a doublet and other garments used by men (which at our order she had recently put off in favour of woman's dress), we questioned her to find out when and for what reason she had resumed man's dress and rejected woman's clothes. Jeanne said she had but recently resumed man's dress and rejected woman's clothes.

Asked why she had resumed it, and who had compelled her to wear it, she answered that she had taken it of her own will, under no compulsion, as she preferred man's to woman's dress.

She was told that she had promised and sworn not to wear man's dress again, and answered that she never meant to take such an oath.

Asked for what reason she had assumed male costume, she answered that it was more lawful and convenient for her to wear it, since she was among men, than to wear woman's dress. She said she had resumed it because the promises made to her had not been kept, which were to permit her to go to Mass and receive her Saviour, and to take off her chains.

Asked whether she had not abjured and sworn in particular not to resume this male costume, she answered that she would rather die than be in chains, but if she were allowed to go to Mass, if her chains were taken off and she were put in a gracious prison and were given a woman as companion, she would be good and obey the Church.

As we her judges had heard from certain people that she had not yet cut herself off from her illusions and pretended revelations, which she had previously renounced, we asked her

whether she had not since Thursday heard the voices of St. Catherine and St. Margaret. She answered yes.

Asked what they told her, she answered that they told her God had sent her word through St. Catherine and St. Margaret of the great pity of this treason by which she consented to abjure and recant in order to save her life; that she had damned herself to save her life. She said that before Thursday they told her what to do and say then, which she did. Further her voices told her, when she was on the scaffold or platform before the people, to answer the preacher boldly. The said Jeanne declared that he was a false preacher, and had accused her of many things she had not done. She said that if she declared God had not sent her she would damn herself, for in truth she was sent from God. She said that her voices had since told her that she had done a great evil in declaring that what she had done was wrong. She said that what she had declared and recanted on Thursday was done only for fear of the fire.

Asked if she believed her voices to be St. Catherine and St. Margaret, she answered yes, and they came from God.

Asked to speak truthfully of the crown which is mentioned above, she replied: "In everything, I told you the truth about it in my trial, as well as I could."

*　　*　　*

REVIEW QUESTIONS

1. Why do the prosecutors seem preoccupied with the issues of Jeanne's dress and appearance?
2. On what grounds is Jeanne being tried for heresy? What are her crimes, according to the tribunal?
3. In what other ways can legal testimony such as this be used as a historical evidence source? What are the potential pitfalls and limitations of such sources?

JAN HUS

FROM *The Church*

Jan Hus (c. 1373–1415) was a Czech preacher and writer active in Prague. Influenced by the writings of the English theologian John Wyclif (c. 1330–1384), called for radical reforms in the Church. Summoned under safe conduct to the Council of Constance, he was nevertheless accused of heresy, convicted, and burned at the stake. Hus thus became a national martyr in his native Bohemia, which remained for centuries in rebellion against the Catholic Church. This chapter from his book The Church *expresses his opinions on the papacy.*

From *The Church by John Hus*, edited by David S. Schaff (New York: Scribner's, 1915).

Chapter XII
Christ the True Roman Pontiff upon Salvation Depends

To the honor of our Lord Jesus Christ, which honor and also Christ the aforesaid doctors nowhere mention in their writing, this conclusion is proved, namely, "to be subject to the Roman pontiff is necessary for salvation for every human being."[1] From this it is clear, that no one can be saved unless he is meritoriously subject to Jesus Christ. But Christ is the Roman pontiff, just as he is the head of the universal church and every particular church. Therefore the conclusion is a true one. The consequence is clear from the major premise. And the minor premise is clear from the things said above and from what is said in I Peter 2:25, "For ye were sometime going astray like sheep but are now returned unto the shepherd and bishop of your souls," and also from Heb. 7:22: "By so much also hath Jesus become the surety of a better covenant and they indeed have been made free, many in number, according to the law because that by death they are hindered from continuing. But this man, because he continueth forever, hath his priesthood unchangeable, wherefore also he is able to save to the uttermost, drawing near through himself to the Lord and always living to intercede for us. For such a high priest became us holy, guileless, undefiled, separated from sinners and made higher than the heavens, who needeth not daily like those priests, to offer up sacrifices first for his own sins and then for the sins of the people, for this he did once for all when he offered himself."

Truly this is the most holy and chief Roman pontiff, sitting at God's right hand and dwelling with us, for he said: "And lo, I am with you all the days, even unto the consummation of the age," Matt. 28:20. For that person, Christ, is everywhere present, since he is very God whose right it is to be everywhere without limitation. He is the bishop, who baptizes and takes away the sins of the world, John 1:29. He is the one who joins in marriage so that no man may put asunder: "What God hath joined together let not man put asunder," Matt. 19:6. He is the one who makes us priests: "He made us a kingdom and priests," Rev. 1:6. He performs the sacrament of the eucharist, saying: "This is my body," Luke 22:19. This is he who confirms his faithful ones: "I will give you a mouth of wisdom which all your adversaries will not be able to withstand or gainsay," Luke 21:15. He it is who feeds his sheep by his word and example and by the food of his body. All these things, however, he does on his part indefectibly, because he is a holy priest, guileless, undefiled, separated from sinners and made higher than the heavens. He is the bishop holding supreme guardianship over his flock, because he sleeps not nor is he, that watches over Israel, weary. He is the pontiff who in advance makes the way easy for us to the heavenly country. He is the pope—*papa*—because he is the wonderful Prince of Peace, the Father of the future age. For, indeed, such a pontiff became us who, since he was in the form of God, did not think it robbery to be equal with God but emptied himself, taking upon him the form of a servant, because he humbled himself by being made obedient unto death, even the death of the cross. Wherefore God hath highly exalted and given him a name which is above every name, that at the name of Jesus every knee should bow, of things in heaven, of things on the earth, and things in hell [Phil. 2:6 *sqq.*].

To this the conclusion follows, namely: "To be subject to the Roman pontiff is necessary for salvation for every human being." But there is no other such pontiff except the Lord Jesus Christ himself, our pontiff. . . .

Chapter XIII
The Pope Not the Head of the Church but Christ's Vicar

Further, the aforesaid doctors lay down in their writing that "the pope is head of the Roman church and the college of cardinals the body, and

---

[1] From Boniface VIII's bull *Unam sanctam*. The expression in the next sentence, "meritoriously," refers to the mediæval doctrine of merit in proportion to our good works.

that they are very successors and princes of the apostle Peter and the college of Christ's other apostles in ecclesiastical office for the purpose of discerning and defining all catholic and church matters, correcting and purging all errors in respect to them and, in all these matters, to have the care of all the churches and of all the faithful of Christ. For in order to govern the church throughout the whole world it is fitting there should always continue to be such manifest and true successors in the office of Peter, the prince of the apostles, and of the college of the other apostles of Christ. And such successors cannot be found or procured on the earth other than the pope, the existing head, and the college of cardinals, the existing body, of the aforesaid Roman church." . . .

I assume that the pope stands for that spiritual bishop who, in the highest way and in the most similar way, occupies the place of Christ, just as Peter did after the ascension. But if any person whatsoever is to be called pope—whom the Western church accepts as Roman bishop—appointed to decide as the final court ecclesiastical cases and to teach the faithful whatever he wishes, then there is an abuse of the term, because according to this view, it would be necessary in cases to concede that the most unlettered layman or a female, or a heretic and antichrist, may be pope. This is plain, for Constantine II, an unlettered layman, was suddenly ordained a priest and through ambition made pope and then was deposed and all the things which he ordained were declared invalid, about A.D. 707. And the same is plain from the case of Gregory, who was unlettered and consecrated another in addition to himself. And as the people were displeased with the act, a third pope was superinduced. Then these quarrelling among themselves, the emperor came to Rome and elected another as sole pope. As for a female, it is plain in the case of Agnes, who was called John Anglicus,[2] and of her Castrensis, 5:3, writes: "A certain woman sat in the papal chair two years and five months,

following Leo. She is said to have been a girl, called Agnes, of the nation of Mainz, was led about by her paramour in a man's dress in Athens and named John Anglicus. She made such progress in different studies that, coming to Rome, she read the trivium to an audience of great teachers. Finally, elected pope, she was with child by her paramour, and, as she was proceeding from St. Peter's to the Lateran, she had the pains of labor in a narrow street between the Colosseum and St. Clement's and gave birth to a child. Shortly afterward she died there and was buried. For this reason it is said that all the popes avoid this street. Therefore, she is not put down in the catalogue of popes."

As for a heretic occupying the papal chair we have an instance in Liberius, of whom Castrensis writes, . . . that at Constantius's command he was exiled for three years because he wished to favor the Arians. At the counsel of the same Constantius, the Roman clergy ordained Felix pope who, during the sessions of a synod condemned and cast out two Arian presbyters, Ursacius and Valens, and when this became known, Liberius was recalled from exile, and being wearied by his long exile and exhilarated by the reoccupation of the papal chair, he yielded to heretical depravity; and when Felix was cast down, Liberius with violence held the church of Peter and Paul and St. Lawrence so that the clergy and priests who favored Felix were murdered in the church, and Felix was martyred, Liberius not preventing.

As for antichrist occupying the papal chair, it is evident that a pope living contrary to Christ, like any other perverted person, is called by common consent antichrist. In accordance with John 2:22, many are become antichrists. And the faithful will not dare to deny persistently that it is possible for the man of sin to sit in the holy place. Of him the Saviour prophesied when he said: "When ye see the abomination of desolation, which is spoken of by Daniel, standing in the holy place." Matt. 24:15. The apostle also says: "Let no man beguile you in any wise, for it will not be except the falling away come first and the man of sin be revealed, the son of perdition; he that opposeth and exalteth himself against all that is called God or is worshipped; so

---

[2] The alleged female Pope Agnes (John VIII, about 855), whom Hus refers again and again in his writings. . . .

that he sitteth in the temple of God setting himself forth as God," II Thess. 2:3–4. And it is apparent from the *Chronicles* how the papal dignity has sunk. . . .

. . . No pope is the most exalted person of the catholic church but Christ himself; therefore no pope is the head of the catholic church besides Christ. The conclusion is valid reasoning from description to the thing described. Inasmuch as the head of the church is the capital or chief person of the church, yea, inasmuch as the head is a name of dignity and of office—dignity in view of predestination, and office in view of the administration of the whole church—it follows that no one may reasonably assert of himself or of another without revelation that he is the head of a particular holy church, although if he live well he ought to hope that he is a member of the holy catholic church, the bride of Christ. Therefore, we should not contend in regard to the reality of the incumbency whether any one, whoever he may be, living with us is the head of a particular holy church but, on the ground of his works, we ought assume that, if he is a superior, ruling over a particular holy church, then he is the superior in that particular church, and this ought to be assumed of the Roman pontiff, unless his works gainsay it, for the Saviour said: "Beware of false prophets which come unto you in sheep's clothing but inwardly they are ravening wolves. By their fruits ye shall know them." Matt. 7:15. Also John 10:38: "Believe the works." . . .

In the same way, it is not of necessity to salvation for all Christians, living together, that they should believe expressly that any one is head of any church whatsoever unless his evangelical life and works plainly moved them to believe this. For it would be all too much presumption to affirm that we are heads of any particular church which perhaps might be a part of holy mother church. How, therefore, may any one of us without revelation presume to assert of himself or of another that he is the head, since it is said truly, Ecclesiasticus 9, that "no one knows, so far as predestination goes, whether one is worthy of love or hatred."

Likewise, if we examine in the light of the feeling and influence with which we influence infe-

riors and, on the other hand, examine by the mirror of Scripture, according to which we should regulate our whole life, then we would choose rather to be called servants and ministers of the church than its heads. For it is certain that if we do not fulfil the office of a head, we are not heads, as Augustine, *de decem chordis* says: that a perverse husband is not the head of his wife, much less is a prelate of the church, who alone from God could have a dignity of this kind, the head of a particular church in case he fall away from Christ.[3]

Therefore, after Augustine has shown that a truly Christian wife ought to mourn over the fornication of her husband, not for carnal reasons, but out of love and for the chastity due to the man Christ—he says consequentially that Christ speaks in the hearts of good women, where the husband does not hear, and he goes on to say: "Mourn over the injuries done by thy husband, but do not imitate them that he may rather imitate you in that which is good. For in that wherein he does wrong, do not regard him as thy head but me, thy Lord." And he proves that this ought to be the case and says: "If he is the head in that wherein he does wrong and the body follow its head, they both go over the precipice. But that the Christian may not follow this bad head, let him keep himself to the head of the church, Christ, to whom he owes his chastity, to whom he yields his honor, no longer a single man but now a man wedded to his mother, the church." Blessed, therefore, be the head of the church, Christ, who cannot be separated from his bride which is his mystical body, as the popes have often been separated from the church by heresy.

But some of the aforesaid doctors say that the pope is the bodily head of the church militant and this head ought always to be here with the church, but in this sense Christ is not the bodily head. Here is meant that the same difficulty remains, namely, that they prove the first part of the statement. For

---

[3] Not an exact quotation. The inference is drawn by Hus. The Sermon on the Ten Strings, Psalms 144:9, has much to say on the relation of husband and wife on the basis of "Thou shalt not commit adultery."

it remains for them to prove that the pope is the head of holy church, a thing they have not proved. And, before that, it remains for them to prove that Christ is not the bodily head of the church militant, inasmuch as Christ is a bodily person, because the man who is the head of the church militant, who is Christ, is present through all time with his church unto the consummation of the age, in virtue of his divine personality. Similarly, he is present by grace, giving his body to the church to be eaten in a sacramental and spiritual way. Wherefore, is not that bridegroom, who is the head of the church, much more present with us than the pope, who is removed from us two thousand miles and incapable of influencing of himself our feeling or movements? Let it suffice, therefore, to say, that the pope may be the vicar of Christ and may be so to his profit, if he is a faithful minister predestinated unto the glory of the head, Jesus Christ.[4]

*   *   *

REVIEW QUESTIONS

1. What sources of authority in the Church does Hus accept? Which does he deny?
2. How do Hus's arguments compare with those that Gregory VII and Boniface VIII raised in defense of papal authority (see pp. 254–261 and 318–319)?
3. In what ways was Hus a threat to the organized Church? In what ways was he an asset?

---

[4] The same thought is expressed in Reply to Palecz, *Mon.*, 1:321: "God gave Christ to be the head over the militant church, that he might preside over it most excellently without any hindrance of local distance . . . and pour into it, as the head pours into the body, movement, feeling and a gracious life whether there be no pope or a woman be pope."

11 CONQUEST, COMMERCE, AND COLONIZATION, 1300–1600

The commercial revolution of the Middle Ages fostered a desire by Europeans to extend trading networks. Trade was not the only motive for travel. Religious pilgrimages and missions, the Crusades, and greed also motivated some people to venture beyond the frontiers of Europe. Successful trade depended on reliable knowledge about the world. Better maps and accounts of travels made it possible for people to find their way over the vast stretches of Asia to China or across the Atlantic. The most adventurous travel was by sea, and better ships, sails, ropes, compasses, and astrolabes made it easier to sail long distances out of sight of land. The great inland sea, the Mediterranean, whose waters touched Africa, Asia, and Europe, witnessed the first advances in sailing techniques, and also the first experiments in European colonization on islands like Crete and Cyprus. Muslim merchants continued to dominate the trading networks in the Indian Ocean.

Beginning in the mid-thirteenth century, missionaries such as William of Rubruck and intrepid merchants such as the Polos of Venice followed the Silk Road across central Asia to China, "the east beyond the east." A small trade continued along this route to Europe until the mid-fourteenth century, when plague and changes in the Mongol Empire made travel across Asia more difficult. Accounts of the East and its immense riches in spices, precious gems and gold, and silk continued to intrigue Europeans. Muslim travelers such as Ibn Battuta displayed a similar curiosity about Muslim states across Asia. In the fifteenth century, Chinese explorers made it all the way to Madagascar off the coast of southern Africa. The impulse to explore so far from home waned when the emperors stopped supporting these trading voyages. If Europeans wanted regular trade with China, they needed to find new, safe routes not controlled by the emerging Islamic Ottoman and Mamluk Empires in the East.

The Portuguese, facing the Atlantic, the Ocean Sea, began to explore the west coast of Africa in search of gold. In the fourteenth century, Portuguese and Italian sailors found the islands—the Azores and Madeira, both uninhabited, and

the Canaries, peopled by the Canarians. Spanish and French traders and explorers also took an interest in the opportunities for trade and settlement, but only the Portuguese sailed farther south beyond the Saharan coast. Merchants and sailors from Lisbon hoped to confirm ancient speculations that it was possible to circumnavigate Africa and find a way to the Indian Ocean. Explorations of the West African coast opened up a lucrative trade in gold and slaves that made tiny Portugal a world power. The patronage of Prince Henry the Navigator (1394–1460) established a seafaring tradition that enabled Bartolomeu Dias to round the Cape of Good Hope in 1488. Vasco de Gama sailed for India in 1497 and eventually rewarded his investors with fabulous profits in spices.

Only after reaching the "new worlds" of Asia and Africa did Europeans "discover" the Americas. The Italian-born Christopher Columbus (c. 1450–1506) convinced Isabella of Castile and Ferdinand of Aragon to gamble on a sea route across the perilous Atlantic to the East. Until his dying day, Columbus remained convinced that the people he called Indians lived off the coast of Asia. His search for wealth was frustrated, moreover, but he laid the foundations for trading in slaves and the exploitation of indigenous peoples that reached its bloody culmination with Hernando Cortéz, in Mexico in 1519, and the Pizarros in Peru, in 1533.

At the same time, a demographic catastrophe occurred in the Americas, as European diseases, such as smallpox, wiped out a high percentage (in some places perhaps as much as 90 percent) of the population. Colonists planning to make money in the mines or the newly established sugar plantations thus relied increasingly on African slaves for labor. Supplying slaves to the new world thus became an increasingly lucrative trade and the first global economy.

WILLIAM OF RUBRUCK

FROM *On the Mongols*

William of Rubruck, a Franciscan monk from Flanders, was sent in 1253 to the Mongols by Louis IX of France, then on crusade in the East. The Mongol Empire, established by Chingis, or Genghis, Khan (1167–1227) and extended by successors such as Mangu (1251–1259), had sent scouting parties as far west as Poland and Hungary. In the first section of this account, William describes Mongol culture to the French king. In the second section, he is at the Mongol capital of Caracorum in Mongolia, seeking another audience with Mangu.

From *The Journey of William of Rubruck to the Eastern Parts of the World, 1253–55: As Narrated by Himself,* translated and edited by William Woodville Rockhill (London: Hakluyt Society, 1900), pp. 56–66, 68–83, 235–239.

Commerce and Conquest

The matrons make for themselves most beautiful (luggage) carts, which I would not know how to describe to you unless by a drawing, and I would depict them all to you if I knew how to paint. A single rich Moal or Tartar has quite c or cc such carts with coffers. Baatu has xxvi wives, each of whom has a large dwelling, exclusive of the other little ones which they set up after the big one, and which are like closets, in which the sewing girls live, and to each of these (large) dwellings are attached quite cc carts. And when they set up their houses, the first wife places her dwelling on the extreme west side, and after her the others according to their rank, so that the last wife will be in the extreme east; and there will be the distance of a stone's throw between the *iurt* of one wife and that of another. The *ordu* of a rich Moal seems like a large town, though there will be very few men in it. One girl will lead xx or xxx carts, for the country is flat, and they tie the ox or camel carts the one after the other, and a girl will sit on the front one driving the ox, and all the others follow after with the same gait. Should it happen that they come to some bad piece of road, they untie them, and take them across one by one. So they go along slowly, as a sheep or an ox might walk.

When they have fixed their dwelling, the door turned to the south, they set up the couch of the master on the north side. The side for the women is always the east side, that is to say, on the left of the house of the master, he sitting on his couch with his face turned to the south. The side for the men is the west side, that is, on the right. Men coming into the house would never hang up their bows on the side of the women

And over the head of the master is always an image of felt, like a doll or statuette, which they call the brother of the master; another similar one is above the head of the mistress, which they call the brother of the mistress, and they are attached to the wall; and higher up between the two of them is a little lank one (*macilenta*), who is, as it were, the guardian of the whole dwelling. The mistress places in her house on her right side, in a conspicuous place at the foot of her couch, a goat-skin full of wool or other stuff, and beside it a very little statuette looking in the direction of the attendants and women. Beside the entry on the women's side is yet another image, with a cow's tit for the women, who milk the cows; for it is part of the duty of the women to milk the cows. On the other side of the entry, toward the men, is another statue with a mare's tit for the men who milk the mares.

And when they have come together to drink, they first sprinkle with liquor this image which is over the master's head, then the other images in order. Then an attendant goes out of the dwelling with a cup and liquor, and sprinkles three times to the south, each time bending the knee, and that to do reverence to the fire; then to the east, and that to do reverence to the air; then to the west to do reverence to the water; to the north they sprinkle for the dead. When the master takes the cup in hand and is about to drink, he first pours a portion on the ground. If he were to drink seated on a horse, he first before he drinks pours a little on the neck or the mane of the horse. Then when the attendant has sprinkled toward the four quarters of the world he goes back into the house, where two attendants are ready with two cups and platters to carry drink to the master and the wife seated near him upon the couch. And when he hath several wives, she with whom he hath slept that night sits beside him in the day, and it becometh all the others to come to her dwelling that day to drink, and court is held there that day, and the gifts which are brought that day are placed in the treasury of that lady. A bench with a skin of milk, or some other drink, and with cups, stands in the entry.

In winter they make a capital drink of rice, of millet, and of honey; it is clear as wine: and wine is carried to them from remote parts. In summer they care only for *cosmos*. There is always *cosmos* near the house, before the entry door, and beside it stands a guitar-player with his guitar. Lutes and vielles such as we have I did not see there, but many other instruments which are unknown among us. And when the master begins to drink, then one of the attendants cries with a loud voice, "Ha!" and the guitarist strikes his guitar, and when they have a great feast they all clap their hands, and also dance about to the sound of the guitar, the

men before the master, the women before the mistress. And when the master has drunken, then the attendant cries as before, and the guitarist stops. Then they drink all around, and sometimes they do drink right shamefully and gluttonly. And when they want to challenge anyone to drink, they take hold of him by the ears, and pull so as to distend his throat, and they clap and dance before him. Likewise, when they want to make a great feasting and jollity with someone, one takes a full cup, and two others are on his right and left, and thus these three come singing and dancing towards him who is to take the cup, and they sing and dance before him; and when he holds out his hand to take the cup, they quickly draw it back, and then again they come back as before, and so they elude him three or four times by drawing away the cup, till he hath become well excited and is in good appetite, and then they give him the cup, and while he drinks they sing and clap their hands and strike with their feet.

The Food of the Tartars

Of their food and victuals you must know that they eat all their dead animals without distinction, and with such flocks and herds it cannot be but that many animals die. Nevertheless, in summer, so long as lasts their *cosmos,* that is to say mare's milk, they care not for any other food. So then if it happens that an ox or a horse dies, they dry its flesh by cutting it into narrow strips and hanging it in the sun and the wind, where at once and without salt it becomes dry without any evil smell. With the intestines of horses they make sausages better than pork ones, and they eat them fresh. The rest of the flesh they keep for winter. With the hides of oxen they make big jars, which they dry in admirable fashion in the smoke. With the hind part of the hide of horses they make most beautiful shoes. With the flesh of a single sheep they give to eat to L men or C; for they cut it up very fine in a platter with salt and water, for they make no other sauce; and then with the point of a knife or a fork which they make for the purpose, like that which we use to eat coddled pears or apples, they give to each of the bystanders a mouthful or two according to the number of the guests. Prior to this, before the flesh of the sheep is served, the master takes what pleases him; and furthermore if he gives to anyone a special piece, it is the custom that he who receives it shall eat it himself, and he may not give it to another; but if he cannot eat it all he carries it off with him, or gives it to his servant if he be present, who keeps it; otherwise he puts it away in his *captargac,* which is a square bag which they carry to put such things in, in which they store away bones when they have not time to gnaw them well, so that they can gnaw them later and that nothing of the food be lost. ✶ ✶ ✶

The Animals They Eat, Their Clothes, and Their Hunting

The great lords have villages in the south, from which millet and flour are brought to them for the winter. The poor procure (these things) by trading sheep and pelts. The slaves fill their bellies with dirty water, and with this they are content. They catch also rats, of which many kinds abound here. Rats with long tails they eat not, but give them to their birds. They eat mice and all kinds of rats which have short tails. There are also many marmots, which are called *sogur,* and which congregate in one hole in winter, xx or xxx together, and sleep for six months; these they catch in great numbers. There are also conies, with a long tail like a cat's, and on the end of the tail they have black and white hairs. They have also many other kinds of small animals good to eat, which they know very well how to distinguish. I saw no deer there. I saw few hares, many gazelles. Wild asses I saw in great numbers, and these are like mules. I saw also another kind of animal which is called *arcali,* which has quite the body of a sheep, and horns bent like a ram's, but of such size that I could hardly lift the two horns with one hand, and they make of these horns big cups. They have hawks and peregrine falcons in great numbers, which they all carry on their right hand. And they always put a little thong around the hawk's neck, which hangs down to the middle of its breast, by which, when they cast it at its prey, they pull down with the left hand the head and breast of the hawk, so that it be not struck by

the wind and carried upward. So it is that they procure a large part of their food by the chase.

Of their clothing and customs you must know, that from Cataia, and other regions of the east, and also from Persia and other regions of the south, are brought to them silken and golden stuffs and cloth of cotton, which they wear in summer. From Ruscia, Moxel, and from greater Bulgaria and Pascatir, which is greater Hungary, and Kerkis, all of which are countries to the north and full of forests, and which obey them, are brought to them costly furs of many kinds, which I never saw in our parts, and which they wear in winter. And they always make in winter at least two fur gowns, one with the fur against the body, the other with the fur outside exposed to the wind and snow; these latter are usually of the skins of wolves or foxes or papions; and while they sit in the dwelling they have another lighter one. The poor make their outside (gowns) of dog and kid (skins).

When they want to chase wild animals, they gather together in a great multitude and surround the district in which they know the game to be, and gradually they come closer to each other till they have shut up the game in among them as in an enclosure, and then they shoot them with their arrows. They make also breeches with furs. The rich furthermore wad their clothing with silk stuffing, which is extraordinarily soft, light and warm. The poor line their clothes with cotton cloth, or with the fine wool which they are able to pick out of the coarser. With this coarser they make felt to cover their houses and coffers, and also for bedding. With wool and a third of horse hair mixed with it they make their ropes. They also make with felt covers, saddle-cloths and rain cloaks; so they use a great deal of wool. You have seen the costume of the men.

How the Men Shave and the Women Adorn Themselves

The men shave a square on the tops of their heads, and from the front corners (of this square) they continue the shaving to the temples, passing along both sides of the head. They shave also the temples and the back of the neck to the top of the cervical cavity, and the forehead as far as the crown of the head, on which they leave a tuft of hair which falls down to the eyebrows. They leave the hair on the sides of the head, and with it they make tresses which they plait together to the ears.

And the dress of the girls differs not from the costume of the men, except that it is somewhat longer. But on the day following her marriage, (a woman) shaves the front half of her head, and puts on a tunic as wide as a nun's gown, but everyway larger and longer, open before, and tied on the right side. For in this the Tartars differ from the Turks; the Turks tie their gowns on the left, the Tartars always on the right. Furthermore they have a head-dress, which they call *bocca*, made of bark, or such other light material as they can find, and it is big and as much as two hands can span around, and is a cubit and more high, and square like the capital of a column. This *bocca* they cover with costly silk stuff, and it is hollow inside, and on top of the capital, or the square on it, they put a tuft of quills or light canes also a cubit or more in length. And this tuft they ornament at the top with peacock feathers, and round the edge (of the top) with feathers from the mallard's tail, and also with precious stones. The wealthy ladies wear such an ornament on their heads, and fasten it down tightly with an amess, for which there is an opening in the top for that purpose, and inside they stuff their hair, gathering it together on the back of the tops of their heads in a kind of knot, and putting it in the *bocca*, which they afterwards tie down tightly under the chin. So it is that when several ladies are riding together, and one sees them from afar, they look like soldiers, helmets on head and lances erect. For this *bocca* looks like a helmet, and the tuft above it is like a lance. And all the women sit their horses astraddle like men. And they tie their gowns with a piece of blue silk stuff at the waist and they wrap another band at the breasts, and tie a piece of white stuff below the eyes which hangs down to the breast. And the women there are wonderfully fat,

and she who has the least nose is held the most beautiful. They disfigure themselves horribly by painting their faces. They never lie down in bed when having their children.

The Duties of the Women and Their Work

It is the duty of the women to drive the carts, get the dwellings on and off them, milk the cows, make butter and *gruit*, and to dress and sew skins, which they do with a thread made of tendons. They divide the tendons into fine shreds, and then twist them into one long thread. They also sew the boots, the socks and the clothing. They never wash clothes, for they say that God would be angered thereat, and that it would thunder if they hung them up to dry. They will even beat those they find washing them. Thunder they fear extraordinarily; and when it thunders they will turn out of their dwellings all strangers, wrap themselves in black felt, and thus hide themselves till it has passed away. Furthermore, they never wash their bowls, but when the meat is cooked they rinse out the dish in which they are about to put it with some of the boiling broth from the kettle, which they pour back into it. They also make the felt and cover the houses.

The men make bows and arrows, manufacture stirrups and bits, make saddles, do the carpentering on (the framework of) their dwellings and the carts; they take care of the horses, milk the mares, churn the *cosmos* or mare's milk, make the skins in which it is put; they also look after the camels and load them. Both sexes look after the sheep and goats, sometimes the men, othertimes the women, milking them.

They dress skins with a thick mixture of sour ewe's milk and salt. When they want to wash their hands or head, they fill their mouths with water, which they let trickle on to their hands, and in this way they also wet their hair and wash their heads.

As to their marriages, you must know that no one among them has a wife unless he buys her; so it sometimes happens that girls are well past marriageable age before they marry, for their parents always keep them until they sell them. They observe the first and second degrees of consanguinity, but no degree of affinity; thus (one person) will have at the same time or successively two sisters. Among them no widow marries, for the following reason: they believe that all who serve them in this life shall serve them in the next, so as regards a widow they believe that she will always return to her first husband after death. Hence this shameful custom prevails among them, that sometimes a son takes to wife all his father's wives, except his own mother; for the *orda* of the father and mother always belongs to the youngest son, so it is he who must provide for all his father's wives who come to him with the paternal household, and if he wishes it he uses them as wives, for he esteems not himself injured if they return to his father after death. When then anyone has made a bargain with another to take his daughter, the father of the girl gives a feast, and the girl flees to her relatives and hides there. Then the father says: "Here, my daughter is yours; take her wheresoever you find her." Then he searches for her with his friends till he finds her, and he must take her by force and carry her off with a semblance of violence to his house.

Of Their Justice and Judgments, Death and Burial

As to their justice you must know that when two men fight together no one dares interfere, even a father dare not aid a son; but he who has the worse of it may appeal to the court of the lord, and if anyone touches him after the appeal, he is put to death. But action must be taken at once without any delay, and the injured one must lead him (who has offended) as a captive. They inflict capital punishment on no one unless he be taken in the act or confesses. When one is accused by a number of persons, they torture him so that he confesses. They punish homicide with capital punishment, and also cohabiting with a woman not one's own. By not one's own, I mean not his wife or bond-woman, for with one's slaves one may do as one

pleases. They also punish with death grand larceny, but as for petty thefts, such as that of a sheep, so long as one has not repeatedly been taken in the act, they beat him cruelly, and if they administer an hundred blows they must use an hundred sticks: I speak of the case of those beaten under order of authority. In like manner false envoys, that is to say persons who pass themselves off as ambassadors but who are not, are put to death. Likewise sorcerers, of whom I shall however tell you more, for such they consider to be witches.

When anyone dies, they lament with loud wailing, then they are free, for they pay no taxes for the year. And if anyone is present at the death of an adult, he may not enter the dwelling even of Mangu Chan for the year. If it be a child who dies, he may not enter it for a month. Beside the tomb of the dead they always leave a tent if he be one of the nobles, that is of the family of Chingis, who was their first father and lord. Of him who is dead the burying place is not known. And always around these places where they bury their nobles there is a camp with men watching the tombs. I did not understand that they bury treasure with their dead. The Comans raise a great tumulus over the dead, and set up a statue to him, its face to the east, and holding a cup in its hand at the height of the navel. They make also pyramids to the rich, that is to say, little pointed structures, and in some places I saw great tiled covered towers, and in others stone houses, though there were no stones thereabout. Over a person recently dead I saw hung on long poles the skins of xvi horses, four facing each quarter of the world; and they had placed also *cosmos* for him to drink, and meat for him to eat, and for all that they said of him that he had been baptised. Farther east I saw other tombs in shape like great yards covered with big flat stones, some round, some square, and four high vertical stones at the corners facing the four quarters of the world. When anyone sickens he lies on his couch, and places a sign over his dwelling that there is a sick person therein, and that no one shall enter. So no one visits a sick person, save him who serves him. And when anyone from the great *ordu* is ill, they place guards all round the *ordu*, who permit no one

to pass those bounds. For they fear lest an evil spirit or some wind should come with those who enter. They call, however, their priests, who are these same soothsayers.

*   *   *

Friar William's Last Audience with Mangu

On Pentecost day (31st May) Mangu Chan called me before him, and also the Tuin with whom I had discussed; but before I went in, the interpreter, master William's son, said to me that we should have to go back to our country, and that I must not raise any objection, for he understood that it was a settled matter. When I came before the Chan, I had to bend the knees, and so did the Tuin beside me, with his interpreter. Then (the Chan) said to me: "Tell me the truth, whether you said the other day, when I sent my secretaries to you, that I was a Tuin." I replied: "My lord, I did not say that; I will tell you what I said, if it pleases you." Then I repeated to him what I had said, and he replied: "I thought full well that you did not say it, for you should not have said it; but your interpreter translated badly." And he held out toward me the staff on which he leaned, saying: "Fear not." And I, smiling, said in an undertone: "If I had been afraid, I should not have come here." He asked the interpreter what I had said, and he repeated it to him. After that he began confiding to me his creed: "We Moal," he said, "believe that there is only one God, by whom we live and by whom we die, and for whom we have an upright heart." Then I said: "May it be so, for without His grace this cannot be." He asked what I had said; the interpreter told him. Then he added: "But as God gives us the different fingers of the hand, so he gives to men divers ways. God gives you the Scriptures, and you Christians keep them not. You do not find (in them, for example) that one should find fault with another, do you?" "No, my lord," I said; "but I told you from the first that I did not want to wrangle with anyone." "I do not intend to say it," he said, "for you. Likewise you do not find that a man should depart

from justice for money." "No, my lord," I said. "And truly I came not to these parts to obtain money; on the contrary I have refused what has been offered me." And there was a secretary present, who bore witness that I had refused an *iascot* and silken cloths. "I do not say it," he said, "for you. God gave you therefore the Scriptures, and you do not keep them; He gave us diviners, we do what they tell us, and we live in peace."

He drank four times, I believe, before he finished saying all this. And I was listening attentively for him to say something else of his creed, when he began talking of my return journey, saying: "You have stayed here a long while; I wish you to go back. You have said that you would not dare take my ambassadors with you; will you take my words, or my letters?" And from that time I never found the opportunity nor the time when I could show him the Catholic Faith. For no one can speak in his presence but so much as he wishes, unless he be an ambassador; for an ambassador can say whatever he chooses, and they always ask if he wishes to say something more. As for me, it was not allowed me to speak more; I had only to listen to him, and reply to his questions. So I answered him that he should make me understand his words, and have them put down in writing, for I would willingly take them as best I could. Then he asked me if I wanted gold or silver or costly clothing. I said: "We take no such things; but we have no travelling money, and without your assistance we cannot get out of your country." He said: "I will have you given all you require while in my possessions; do you want anything more?" I replied: "That suffices us." Then he asked: "How far do you wish to be taken?" I said: "Our power extends to the country of the king of Hermenia; if we were (escorted) that far, it would suffice me." He answered: "I will have you taken that far; after that look out for yourself." And he added: "There are two eyes in the head; but though they be two, they have but one sight, and when one turns its glance there goes the other. You came from Baatu, and so you must go back by way of him." When he had said this, I asked permission of him to speak. "Speak," he said. Then I said: "My lord, we are not men of war. We wish that

those should have dominion over the world who rule it most justly, in accordance with the will of God. Our office is to teach men to live after the will of God. For that we have come here, and willingly would we remain here if it pleased you. Since it pleases you that we go back, that must then be. I will go back, and I will carry your letters as well as I can, as you have ordered. I would ask of your majesty that since I shall carry your letters, I may also come back to you with your consent; principally because you have poor slaves at Bolat, who are of our tongue, and who have no priest to teach them and their sons their religion, and willingly would I remain with them." Then he replied: "If your masters should send you back to me (you will be welcome)." I said: "My lord, I know not the will of my masters; but I have their permission to go wherever I wish, where it is needful to preach the word of God; and it seems to me that it is very needful in these parts; so whether he sends back envoys by us or not, if it pleases you I will come back."

Then he remained silent and sat for a long time as if thinking, and the interpreter told me to speak no more. So I waited anxiously for what he would reply. Finally he said: "You have a long way to go, comfort yourself with food, so that you may reach your country in good health." And he had me given to drink, and then I went out from before him, and after that I went not back again. If I had had the power to work by signs and wonders like Moses, perhaps he would have humbled himself.

*   *   *

REVIEW QUESTIONS

1. What valuable insights does William offer about Mongol culture?
2. According to William, how does the role of women in Mongol society compare with that of European women?
3. What ideas about religion determine the outlooks of Mangu and William?

IBN BATTUTA

FROM *The Travels*

Ibn Battuta (1304–c. 1377), from Tangier in Morocco, was an extraordinary traveler whose journeys took him as far as China and India. He wrote extensive accounts of his travels; here he describes Muslim Cairo at its zenith, before the Black Death.

From *The Travels of Ibn Battuta*, A.D. *1325–1354*, edited by H. A. R. Gibb (London: Hakluyt Society, 1958), pp. 41–53.

*   *   *

Commerce

I arrived at length at the city of Miṣr, mother of cities and seat of Pharaoh the tyrant, mistress of broad provinces and fruitful lands, boundless in multitude of buildings, peerless in beauty and splendour, the meeting-place of comer and goer, the stopping-place of feeble and strong. Therein is what you will of learned and simple, grave and gay, prudent and foolish, base and noble, of high estate and low estate, unknown and famous; she surges as the waves of the sea with her throngs of folk and can scarce contain them for all the capacity of her situation and sustaining power. Her youth is ever new in spite of length of days, and the star of her horoscope does not move from the mansion of fortune; her conquering capital (*al-Qāhira*) has subdued the nations, and her kings have grasped the forelocks of both Arab and non-Arab. She has as her peculiar possession the majestic Nile, which dispenses her district from the need of entreating the distillation [of the rain]; her territory is a month's journey for a hastening traveller, of generous soil, and extending a friendly welcome to strangers.

Ibn Juzayy remarks: Of Cairo the poet says—

No common town is Cairo, by thy life! Nay, she
Is heaven on earth for those with eyes to see;

Her youth those boys and maids with lustrous eyes,
Kawthar her Nile, her Rawḍa Paradise.

*   *   *

It is said that in Cairo there are twelve thousand water-carriers who transport water on camels, and thirty thousand hirers of mules and donkeys, and that on its Nile there are thirty-six thousand vessels belonging to the Sultan and his subjects, which sail upstream to Upper Egypt and downstream to Alexandria and Damietta, laden with goods and commodities of all kinds. On the bank of the Nile opposite Cairo is the place known as al-Rawḍa ['the Garden'], which is a pleasure park and promenade, containing many beautiful gardens. The people of Cairo are fond of pleasure and amusement. I once witnessed a fête there which was held for al-Malik al-Nāṣir's recovery from a fracture which he had suffered in his hand. All the merchants decorated their bazaars and had rich stuffs, ornaments, and silken fabrics hung up in their shops for several days.

The Mosque of 'Amr b. al-'Āṣ, and the Colleges, Hospital, and Convents

The Mosque of 'Amr b. al-'Āṣ is a noble mosque, highly venerated and widely celebrated. The Friday service is held in it, and the road runs right

through it from east to west. To the west of it is the cell where the Imām Abū 'Abdallāh al-Shāfi'ī used to teach. As for the madrasas in Cairo, they are too many for anyone to count; and as for the Māristān, which is "between the two castles" near the mausoleum of al-Malik al-Manṣūr Qalā'ūn, no description is adequate to its beauties. It is equipped with innumerable conveniences and medicaments, and its revenue is reported to be a thousand dinars a day. The convents too are numerous. The people there call them *khawāniq,* the singular being *khānqa,* and the amīrs in Cairo vie with one another in building them.

Each convent in Cairo is affected to the use of a separate congregation of poor brethren, most of whom are Persians, men of good education and adepts in the "way" of Sufism. Each has a shaikh and a warden, and the organization of their affairs is admirable. It is one of their customs in the matter of their food that the steward of the house comes in the morning to the faqīrs, each of whom then specifies what food he desires. When they assemble for meals, each person is given his bread and soup in a separate dish, none sharing with another. They eat twice a day. They receive winter clothing and summer clothing and a monthly allowance varying from twenty to thirty dirhams each. Every Thursday night they are given sugar cakes, soap to wash their clothes, the price of admission to the bath-house, and oil to feed their lamps. These men are celibate; the married men have separate convents. Amongst the stipulations required of them are attendance at the five daily prayers, spending the night in the convent, and assembly in mass in a chapel within the convent. Another of their customs is that each one of them sits upon a prayer-carpet reserved for his exclusive use. When they pray the dawn prayer they recite the chapters of *Victory,* of *the Kingdom,* and of *'Amma.* After this copies of the Holy Qur'ān are brought, divided into sections, and each faqīr takes a section. After 'sealing' the Qur'ān and reciting a *dhikr,* the Qur'ān-readers give a recital according to the custom of the Easterners. They hold a similar service following the mid-afternoon prayer.

They have a regular ritual for the admission of newcomers. The applicant comes to the gate of the convent and takes up his stand there, with his waist girt, a prayer mat on his shoulder, the staff in his right hand and the jug in his left. The gate-keeper informs the steward of the convent that he is there. The steward then comes out to him and asks him from what country he has come, what convents he has stayed in on his way, and who was his spiritual director (*shaikh*). When he has ascertained the truth of his answers, he admits him into the convent, spreads his prayer-mat for him in a place befitting his station, and shows him the lavatory. The newcomer renews his ablutions and, returning to his mat, ungirds his waist, and prays two prostrations, then he clasps the hand of the shaikh and those of the others present, and takes his seat amongst them. Another custom of theirs is that on Fridays the servant collects all their prayer-mats and takes them to the mosque, where he spreads them in readiness for their coming. The faqīrs come out in a body, accompanied by their shaikh, proceed to the mosque, and pray each on his own mat. When they have finished the prayer they recite the Qur'ān according to their custom, and thereafter return in a body to the convent, accompanied by their shaikh.

The Qarāfa of Cairo and Its Sanctuaries

At [Old] Cairo too is [the cemetery called] al-Qarāfa, a place of vast repute for blessed power, whose special virtue is affirmed in a tradition related by al-Qurṭubī amongst others, for it is a part of the amount al-Muqaṭṭam, of which God has promised that it shall be one of the gardens of Paradise. These people build in the Qarāfa beautiful domed chapels and surround them by walls, so that they look like houses, and they construct chambers in them and hire the services of Qur'ān-readers, who recite night and day in beautiful voices. There are some of them who build a religious house or a madrasa by the side of the mausoleum. They go out every Thursday evening to

spend the night there with their children and womenfolk and make a circuit of the famous sanctuaries. They go out also to spend the night there on the night of mid-Sha'bān, and the market-people take out all kinds of eatables.

Among the celebrated sanctuaries is the imposing holy shrine where rests the head of al-Ḥusain b. 'Alī * * *. Beside it is a vast convent, of wonderful workmanship, on the doors of which there are silver rings, and plates also on them of the same metal. This shrine is paid its full meed of respect and veneration.

Amongst the monuments is the tomb of the Lady (*Sayyida*) Nafīsa, daughter of Zaid b. 'Alī b. al-Ḥusain b. 'Alī (upon them be peace). She was a woman answered in prayer and zealous in her devotions. This mausoleum is of elegant construction and resplendent brightness, and beside it is a convent which is visited by a great concourse during the days of the feast dedicated to her. Another is the tomb of the Imām Abū 'Abdallāh Muḥammad b. Idrīs al-Shāfi'ī, close by which is a large convent. The mausoleum enjoys an immense revenue and is surmounted by the famous dome, of admirable workmanship and marvellous construction, an exceedingly fine piece of architecture and exceptionally lofty, the diameter of which exceeds thirty cubits. The Qarāfa of Cairo contains also an incalculable number of graves of men eminent for learning and religion, and in it lie a goodly number of the Companions and of the leading figures of both earlier and later generations (God be pleased with them). * * *

*   *   *

The Egyptian Nile

The Egyptian Nile surpasses all rivers of the earth in sweetness of taste, breadth of channel and magnitude of utility. Cities and villages succeed one another along its banks without interruption and have no equal in the inhabited world, nor is any river known whose basin is so intensively cultivated as that of the Nile. There is no river on earth but it which is called a sea; God Most High has

said "If thou fearest for him, cast him into the *yamm*," thus calling it *yamm*, which means "sea" (*bahr*). It is related in an unimpeachable Tradition that the Prophet of God (God's blessing and peace upon him) reached on the night of his Ascension the Lote-Tree of the Extremity, and lo, at its base were four streams, two outer streams and two inner streams. He asked Gabriel (peace be upon him) what streams these were, and he replied 'The two inner streams flow through Paradise, and as for the two outer streams they are the Nile and Euphrates'. It is also related in the Traditions of the Prophet that the Nile, Euphrates, Saiḥān and Jaiḥān are, each one, rivers of Paradise. The course of the Nile is from south to north, contrary to all the great rivers. One extraordinary thing about it is that it begins to rise in the extreme hot weather, at the time when rivers generally diminish and dry up, and begins to subside at the time when rivers increase in volume and overflow. The river of Sind [Indus] resembles it in this respect, and will be mentioned later. The first beginning of the Nile flood is in Ḥazīrān, that is June; and when its rise amounts to sixteen cubits, the land-tax due to the Sultan is payable in full. If it rises another cubit, there is plenty in that year, and complete well-being. But if it reaches eighteen cubits it does damage to the cultivated lands and causes an outbreak of plague. If it falls short of sixteen by a cubit, the Sultan's land-tax is diminished, and if it is two cubits short the people make solemn prayers for rain and there is the greatest misery.

The Nile is one of the five great rivers of the world, which are the Nile, Euphrates, Tigris, Saiḥūn [Syr Darya] and Jaiḥūn [Amu Darya]; five other rivers rival these, the river of Sind, which is called Panj Āb [i.e. Five Rivers], the river of Hindustān which is called the Kank [or Gang, i.e. Ganges]—to it the Hindus go on pilgrimage, and when they burn their dead they throw the ashes of them into it, and they say that it comes from Paradise—the river Jūn, also in Hindustān, the river Itil [Volga] in the Qifjaq [Kipchak] steppe, on the shore of which is the city of al-Sarā, and the river Sarū in the land of al-Khiṭā [Cathay], on the banks of which is the city of Khān-Bāliq [Pe-

king], whence it descends to the city of al-Khansā [Hang-chow] and from there to the city of al-Zaitūn [Zayton] in the land of China. We shall speak of all these in their proper places, if God will. Some distance below Cairo the Nile divides into three sections, and none of these streams can be crossed except by boat, winter or summer. The inhabitants of every township have canals led off the Nile; when it is in flood it fills these and they inundate the cultivated fields.

The Pyramids and Berbās

These are among the marvels which have been celebrated through the course of ages, and there is much talk and theorizing amongst men about them, their significance and the origin of their construction. They aver that all branches of knowledge which came into existence before the Deluge were derived from Hermes the Ancient, who lived in the remotest part of the Saʿīd [Upper Egypt]; he is also called by the name of Khanūkh [Enoch] that is Idrīs (on him be peace). It is said that he was the first to speculate on the movements of the spheres and the celestial bodies, and the first to construct temples and glorify God in them; and that he warned men of the coming of the Deluge, and fearing for the disappearance of knowledge and destruction of the practical arts built the pyramids and berbas, in which he depicted all the practical arts and their tools, and made diagrams of the sciences, in order that they might remain immortalized. It is said also that the seat of learning and kingship in Egypt was the city of Manūf [Memphis], which is one *barīd* from al-Fusṭāṭ. When Alexandria was built, the people removed to it, and it became the seat of learning and kingship until the coming of Islām, when ʿAmr b. al-ʿĀṣ (God be pleased with him) laid out the city of al-Fusṭāṭ, which remains the capital of Egypt to this day.

The pyramids is an edifice of solid hewn stone, of immense height and circular plan, broad at the base and narrow at the top, like the figure of a cone. They have no doorways and the manner of their erection is unknown. One of the tales related about them is that a certain king of Egypt before the Flood dreamed a dream which filled him with terror and determined him to build these pyramids on the western side of the Nile, as a depository for the sciences and for the bodies of the kings. He asked the astrologers whether they would be opened in the future at any spot, and they told him that an opening would be made on the north side, and informed him of the exact spot where the opening would begin, and of the sum of money which would be expended in making the opening. He then ordered to be deposited in that place the sum of money which they had told him would be spent in breaching it. By pressing forward its construction, he completed it in sixty years, and wrote this inscription upon them: "We erected these pyramids in the space of sixty years; let him who will, pull them down in the space of six hundred years; yet to pull down is easier than to build." Now when the Caliphate devolved upon the Commander of the Faithful al-Maʾmūn, he proposed to pull them down, and although one of the Egyptian shaikhs advised him not to do so he persisted in his design and ordered that they should be breached from the north side. So they set about lighting fires up against them and then sprinkling them with vinegar and battering them with a mangonel, until the breach which is still to be seen in them was opened up. There they found, facing the hole, a sum of money which the Commander of the Faithful ordered to be weighted. He then calculated what had been spent on making the breach, and finding the two sums equal, was greatly astonished. At the same time they found the breadth of the wall to be twenty cubits.

The Sultan of Egypt

The Sultan of Egypt at the time of my entry was al-Malik al-Nāṣir Abuʾl-Fatḥ Muḥammad, son of al-Malik al-Manṣūr Saif al-Dīn Qalāʾūn al-Ṣāliḥī. Qalāʾūn was known as al-Alfī ['the Thousand-man'] because al-Malik al-Ṣāliḥ bought him for a thousand dinars of gold. He came originally from Qifjaq [Kipchak]. Al-Malik al-Nāṣir (God's mercy upon him) was a man of generous character and

great virtues, and sufficient proof of his nobility is furnished by his devotion to the service of the two holy sanctuaries of Mecca and Madīna and the works of beneficence which he does every year to assist the pilgrims, in furnishing camels loaded with provisions and water for those without means and the helpless, and for carrying those who cannot keep up with the caravan or are too weak to walk on foot, both on the Egyptian pilgrim-road and on that from Damascus. He also built a great convent at Siryāqus, in the outskirts of Cairo. But the convent built by our lord the Commander of the Faithful and Defender of the Faith, the refuge of the poor and needy, Caliph of God upon earth, whose zeal in the Holy War transcends its obligations, Abū ʿInān (God be his strength and aid, and grant him the signal victory, and prosper him), in the outskirts of his sublime residence, the luminous city (God guard it), has no equal to it in the inhabited world for perfection of architecture, beauty of construction, and plaster carving such as none of the Easterners can accomplish. We shall speak in due course of the schools, hospitals, and convents which he (God be his strength) has founded in his land (God guard it and preserve it by the prolongation of his reign).

*   *   *

REVIEW QUESTIONS

1. Based on this description, how does old Cairo compare with a contemporary European city?
2. According to Ibn Battuta, what are the most important features of a city?
3. How much does the author seem to know about the pyramids and the Nile?

DOUKAS

FROM *Decline and Fall of Byzantium to the Ottoman Turks*

Doukas (or Ducas), a fifteenth-century Byzantine historian, was descended from a noble Greek family. For a time he worked for the Genoese colonial administration at New Phocaea in Asia Minor. Doukas wrote his history to illustrate what he hoped were temporary Ottoman triumphs over the Greek world. The historian was present at the Ottoman siege of Lesbos in 1462, after which he disappears from the historical record, probably through death or enslavement. This section of Doukas's history concerns the conquest of Constantinople in 1453.

From *Decline and Fall of Byzantium to the Ottoman Turks*, by Doukas, translated by Harry J. Magoulias (Detroit: Wayne State University Press, 1975), pp. 220–27, 240–41.

*   *   *

When all preparations had been completed according to plan, Mehmed sent an envoy to the emperor inside the City with the following message, "The preparations for the assault have been concluded. It is now time to consummate what we planned long ago. Let us leave the outcome of this undertaking to God. What say you? Do you wish to quit the City and go wherever you like together with your officials and their possessions, leaving behind the populace un-

harmed by us and by you? Or do you choose to resist and to lose your life and belongings, and to have the Turks take the populace captive and scatter them throughout the earth?" The emperor and the senate answered, "If you so wish, as your fathers did before you, you too, by the grace of God, can live peacefully with us. They regarded my parents as their fathers, and as such honored them, and they looked upon this City as their fatherland. In time of difficulty, they entered within her walls and were saved. No one who resisted her lived long. Keep the fortresses and the lands which have been unjustly seized from us as justly yours. Extract as much tribute annually as we are able to pay you, and depart in peace. Can you be certain that victory instead of defeat awaits you? The right to surrender the City to you belongs neither to me nor to anyone who dwells therein. Rather than to have our lives spared, it is our common resolve willingly to die."

When the tyrant heard this reply, he despaired of a peaceful surrender of the City. He therefore instructed the heralds to announce to the entire army the day on which the assault would be launched. He also affirmed on oath that he desired for himself no gain other than the buildings and walls of the City. As for the treasures and captives to be taken, he declared, "Let those be your reward." The troops shouted their approval.

As night fell, he sent heralds around the camp with instructions that large torches and fires should be lighted at every tent. And once the torches were burning, they were all to chant and shout in their foul and impious tongue. This strange spectacle was indeed incredible. As the torches poured their light over land and sea, brighter than the sun, they illuminated the entire City, Galata, all the islands, ships and boats as far as Skutari. The entire surface of the water flashed so brightly that it was like lightning. Would that it had been lightning, the lightning which not only produces light but also burns and utterly consumes everything! The Romans thought that fire had fallen on the camp and ran up to the breach in the wall. When they saw the Turks dancing and heard their joyous shouts, they foresaw the future. With a contrite heart they prayed to God, "Spare us, O Lord, from Thy just wrath and deliver us from the hands of the enemy." The spectacle and din affected the citizens so much that they appeared to be half-dead, unable to breathe either in or out.

Giovanni labored throughout the night. He ordered all the brushwood in the City gathered and placed at the breach. He also constructed a second fosse within for protection where the walls had been destroyed. The Romans realized that their movements were conspicuous and that they could not pass through the gate to oppose the Turks at the outer fortifications because the fallen walls exposed them. There were, however, some old men who knew of an underground sallyport located at the lower end of the palace that, many years before, had been sealed shut. When the emperor was informed of its existence, he commanded that it be opened. The soldiers could now sally through because it was screened by solid walls, and they gave battle to the Turks in the enclosure. The name of this hidden door was Kerkoporta.

On Sunday, the tyrant began to engage in full scale warfare. Right into the evening and through the night he gave no rest to the Romans. That Sunday was the Feast of All Saints, the twenty-seventh day of May.

From daybreak he engaged in light skirmishes until the ninth hour [3 p.m.], and after the ninth hour he arrayed the army from the palace to the Golden Gate. He also deployed the eighty ships from the Xyloporta Gate to the Plataea Gate. The remaining ships, which were stationed at the Double Columns, began an encircling maneuver, starting from the Horaia Gate and continuing past the Acropolis of Demetrios the Great and the small postern located at the Hodegetria monastery. Sailing past the Great Palace and crossing the harbor, they completed the encirclement as far as Vlangas. In addition to all kinds of equipment, each vessel carried a scaling ladder equal to the height of the walls.

Just as the sun set, the call to battle rang out. The battle array was most formidable indeed! The tyrant himself was on horseback on Monday evening. Exactly opposite the fallen walls he gave battle with his faithful slaves, young and all-powerful, fighting like lions, more than ten thousand of them. To the rear and on both flanks there were more than one hundred thousand fighting

cavalrymen. To the south of these and as far as the harbor of the Golden Gate there were another hundred thousand troops and more. From the spot where the ruler was standing to the extremities of the palace there were another fifty thousand soldiers. The troops on the ships and at the bridge were beyond number.

The City's defenders were deployed in the following manner: The emperor and Giovanni Giustiniani were stationed at the fallen walls, outside the stockade in the enclosure, with about three thousand Latins and Romans. The grand duke was posted at the Imperial Gate with about five hundred troops. At the sea walls and along the battlements from the Xyloporta Gate to the Horaia Gate, more than five hundred crossbowmen and archers were arrayed. Making the complete circuit from the Horaia Gate to the Golden Gate there was stationed in each bastion a single archer, crossbowman, or gunner. They spent the entire night on watch with no sleep at all.

The Turks with Mehmed rushed to the walls, carrying a great number of scaling ladders which had been constructed beforehand. Behind the lines, the tyrant, brandishing an iron mace, forced his archers to the walls by using both flattery and threats. The City's defenders fought back bravely with all the strength they could muster. Giovanni and his men, supported by the emperor in arms, together with all his troops, fought back courageously.

But just as Fortune's feats of arms were about to snatch victory from Turkish hands, from the very middle of the embattled Roman troops, God removed their general, a mighty warrior of gigantic stature. He was wounded just before dawn by lead shot which went through the back of his arm, penetrating his iron breastplate which had been forged in the manner of Achilles' weapons. Unable to relieve the pain of the wound, he cried out to the emperor, "Stand your ground bravely, and I will retire to the ship to attend to my wound. Then I will quickly return." It was in that hour that the words spoken by Jeremias to the Jews were fulfilled, "Thus shall ye say to Sedekias: Thus saith the Lord God of Israel. Behold, I will turn back the weapons of war *which are in your hands,*

wherewith ye fight against the king of Babylon and the Chaldeans that have besieged you from outside the wall; and I will gather them into the midst of this city. And I will fight against you with an outstretched hand *or with an* uplifted *arm with wrath and anger and* great irritation. *And I will smite the dwellers in this city, both men and cattle with grievous death, and they shall die. I will not spare them, and I will not have compassion upon them!"[1]* When the emperor beheld Giovanni in retreat, he lost heart and so did his companions. Yet they continued the fight with all their strength.

The Turks gradually made their way to the walls, and, using their shields for cover, threw up their scaling ladders. Thwarted, however, by stone-throwers from above, they achieved nothing. Their assault, therefore, was repulsed. All the Romans with the emperor held their ground against the enemy, and all their strength and purpose were exerted to prevent the Turks from entering through the fallen walls. Unbeknown to them, however, God willed that the Turks would be brought in by another way. When they saw the sallyport, to which we referred above, open, some fifty of the tyrant's renowned slaves leaped inside. They climbed to the top of the walls and zealously slew anyone they met and struck down the sentinels who discharged missiles from above. It was a sight filled with horror! Some of the Romans and Latins who were preventing the Turks from attaching scaling ladders to the walls were cut to pieces, while others, closing their eyes, jumped from the wall and ended their lives horribly by smashing their bodies. Unimpeded, the Turks threw up the scaling ladders and ascended like soaring eagles.

The Romans and the emperor did not know what had happened because the entry of the Turks took place at a distance; indeed, their paramount concern was the enemy before them. The fierce Turkish warriors outnumbered the Romans twenty to one. The Romans, moreover, were not as experienced in warfare as the ordinary Turks. Their attention and concern, therefore, were focused on the Turkish ground attack. Then sud-

---

[1] Jeremiah 21: 3–6. Doukas's additions are in italics.

denly arrows fell from above, slaughtering many Romans. When they looked up and saw the Turks, they fled behind the walls. Unable to enter through the Gate of Charisios because of the press of the multitude, only those got through who were stronger and able to trample down the weaker. When the tyrant's troops witnessed the rout of the Romans, they shouted with one voice and pursued them inside, trampling upon the wretches and slaughtering them. When they reached the gate, they were unable to get through because it was blocked by the bodies of the dead and the dying. The majority entered through the breaches in the walls and they cut down all those they met.

The emperor, despairing and hopeless, stood with sword and shield in hand and poignantly cried out, "Is there no one among the Christians who will take my head from me?" He was abandoned and alone. Then one of the Turks wounded him by striking him flush, and he, in turn, gave the Turk a blow. A second Turk delivered a mortal blow from behind and the emperor fell to the earth. They slew him as a common soldier and left him, because they did not know he was the emperor.

Only three Turks perished and all the rest made their way inside. It was the first hour of the day [6 a.m.], and the sun had not yet risen. As they entered the City and spread out from the Gate of Charisios to the palace, they slew those who resisted and those who fled. Some two thousand fighting men were slaughtered. The Turks were apprehensive because they had estimated that within the City there must be at least fifty thousand soldiers. Consequently, they slew the two thousand. Had they known that the total number of armed troops did not exceed eight thousand men, they would not have killed any of them. This nation is a lover of money and if a patricide fell into their hands, they would release him for gold. How much truer this would be for him who had done no wrong but had instead been wronged by them. After the conflict I met many Turks who related the following to me, "Fearful of those ahead of us, we slew as many as we met. Had we known that there was such a dearth of men in the City, we would have sold them all like sheep."

Some of the Azabs, that is, the tyrant's retinue who are also called Janissaries, overran the palace. Others swarmed over the Monastery of the Great Forerunner called Petra and the Monastery of Chora in which was found the icon of my Immaculate Mother of God. O tongue and lips, how can I relate what happened there to the icon because of your sins? While the apostates were anxious to go elsewhere for more plunder, one of the infidels, extending his befouled hands, hacked the icon into four pieces with an axe. Casting lots, each received his equal share and its accompanying ornament. After they seized the monastery's precious vessels, they rode off.

Breaking into the protostrator's home, they broke open the coffers full of treasures amassed long ago. In so doing, they aroused the noblewomen from their sleep. It was the twenty-ninth day of May, and the morning sleep of the youths and maidens was sweet indeed; they slept unafraid and carefree as they had done yesterday and the day before.

Then a great horde of mounted infidels charged down the street leading to the Great Church. The actions of both Turks and Romans made quite a spectacle! In the early dawn, as the Turks poured into the City and the citizens took flight, some of the fleeing Romans managed to reach their homes and rescue their children and wives. As they moved, bloodstained, across the Forum of the Bull and passed the Column of the Cross [Forum of Constantine], their wives asked, "What is to become of us?" When they heard the fearful cry, "The Turks are slaughtering Romans within the City's walls," they did not believe it at first. They cursed and reviled the ill-omened messenger instead. But behind him came a second, and then a third, and all were covered with blood, and they knew that the cup of the Lord's wrath had touched their lips. Monks and nuns, therefore, and men and women, carrying their infants in their arms and abandoning their homes to anyone who wished to break in, ran to the Great Church. The thoroughfare, overflowing with people, was a sight to behold!

Why were they all seeking refuge in the Great Church? Many years before they had heard from some false prophets that the City was fated to be surrendered to the Turks who would enter with

great force, and that the Romans would be cut down by them as far as the Column of Constantine the Great. Afterwards, however, an angel, descending and holding a sword, would deliver the empire and the sword to an unknown man, extremely plain and poor, standing at the Column. "Take this sword," the angel would say, "and avenge the people of the Lord." Then the Turks would take flight and the Romans would follow hard upon them, cutting them down. They would drive them from the City and from the West, and from the East as far as the borders of Persia, to a place called Monodendrion. Because they fully expected these prophecies to be realized, some ran and advised others to run also. This was the conviction of the Romans who long ago had contemplated what their present action would be, contending, "If we leave the Column of the Cross behind us, we will avoid future wrath." This was the cause then of the flight into the Great Church. In one hour's time that enormous temple was filled with men and women. There was a throng too many to count, above and below, in the courtyards and everywhere. They bolted the doors and waited, hoping to be rescued by the anonymous savior.

O miserable Romans! O wretches! The temple which only yesterday you called a cave and altar of heretics, and not one of you would enter so as not to be defiled because the liturgy was offered by clerics who had embraced Church Union, and now, because of the impending wrath you push your way inside, seeking to be saved. But not even the impending just wrath could move your hearts to peace. And even if, in such a calamity, an angel were to descend from heaven and say to you, "If you will accept the Union and a state of peace in the Church, I will expel the enemy from the City," even then you would not assent. And if you did assent, it would only be a lie! They who but a few days before had said, "It would be better to fall into the hands of the Turks than into the clutches of the Franks," knew this was true.

Pillaging, slaughtering, and taking captives on the way, the Turks reached the temple before the termination of the first hour. The gates were barred, but they broke them with axes. They en-

tered with swords flashing and, beholding the myriad populace, each Turk caught and bound his own captive. There was no one who resisted or who did not surrender himself like a sheep. Who can recount the calamity of that time and place? Who can describe the wailing and the cries of the babes, the mothers' tearful screams and the fathers' lamentations? The commonest Turk sought the most tender maiden. The lovely nun, who heretofore belonged only to the one God, was now seized and bound by another master. The rapine caused the tugging and pulling of braids of hair, the exposure of bosoms and breasts, and outstretched arms. The female slave was bound with her mistress, the master with his slave, the archimandrite with the doorkeeper, tender youths with virgins, who had never been exposed to the sun and hardly ever seen by their own fathers, were dragged about, forcibly pushed together and flogged. The despoiler led them to a certain spot, and placing them in safekeeping, returned to take a second and even a third prize. The abductors, the avengers of God, were in a great hurry. Within one hour they had bound everyone, the male captives with cords and the women with their own veils. The infinite chains of captives who like herds of kine and flocks of sheep poured out of the temple and the temple sanctuary made an extraordinary spectacle! They wept and wailed and there was none to show them mercy.

What became of the temple treasures? What shall I say and how shall I say it? My tongue is stuck fast in my larynx. I am unable to draw breath through my sealed mouth. In that same hour the dogs hacked the holy icons to pieces, removing the ornaments. As for the chains, candelabra, holy altar coverings, and lamps, some they destroyed and the rest they seized. All the precious and sacred vessels of the holy sacristy, fashioned from gold and silver and other valuable materials, they collected in an instant, leaving the temple desolate and naked; absolutely nothing was left behind.

*   *   *

Three days after the Fall, Mehmed released the ships so that they might sail to their own province

and city. They carried so much cargo that they almost sank from the weight. What cargo did they carry? Costly apparel, silver, gold, copper and tin vessels, and books beyond number. They were filled to capacity with captives—priests and laymen, nuns and monks. The tents at the fosse were also teeming with captives and with the multifarious articles enumerated above. It was indeed spectacular to see a barbarian wearing an episcopal *sakkos*,[2] and another girded about with a golden stole and leading around dogs that were arrayed in fabrics embroidered with golden lambs instead of in coarse blankets. Others were sitting and feasting, eating a variety of fruits from the sacred patens in front of them, and drinking unwatered wine from the sacred chalices. Innumerable books were loaded onto the wagons and hauled in all directions; they were dispersed throughout East and West. For a single gold coin, ten books were sold—the works of Aristotle and Plato, books of theological content and on every subject. Gold and silver were pulled from the Evangelistaries which were adorned with many different jewels; some were sold and the rest were thrown away. All the icons were thrown to the flames and the meats they ate were roasted by the fire that was kindled.

On the fifth day Mehmed visited Galata. Ordering a census taken of all the inhabitants, he found that many of the homes had been bolted because the Latins had fled in the ships. He ordered the homes opened and an inventory taken of their belongings. He stipulated that should the owners return within a period of three months, they would be allowed to repossess their possessions, but if they failed to return, all would then be confiscated by the ruler. Afterwards, he commanded the entire army with the assistance of the outlying villages to demolish and raze the walls of Galata. Once this was accomplished they would be dismissed. His orders were executed. The land walls were overthrown but the walls along the harbor were allowed to stand.

In order to prepare enough lime to rebuild the fallen walls of the City, Mehmed ordered the lime-slakers to work the whole month of August. After five thousand families were registered from both the eastern and western provinces, Mehmed instructed them and their entire households to take up residence in the City by September on penalty of death. He next appointed his slave Sulayman *eparch*. He converted the Great Church into an altar for his God and Muhammad, but left the other churches desolate. He returned triumphant to Adrianople with innumerable captives and booty.

He departed from the City on the eighteenth day of June, taking with him in wagons and on horseback all the noblewomen and their daughters. The wife of the grand duke died en route near the village of Mesene and she was buried there. She was renowned for her charity and compassion for the indigent and for being a prudent woman who exercised restraint over the many passions of the spirit.

Mehmed's majestic triumphal entry into Adrianople was followed—and what a spectacle it was—by all the noblewomen and Christian governors and rulers streaming in and greeting him with "Hail!" With what heart and intent did their lips and mouths say this? Afraid that they might suffer the same fate as the City, they involuntarily made their submission with gifts. The tyrant was sitting on his throne, haughty and proud, boasting about the fall of the City. The Christian rulers stood there trembling and wondering what the future held in store for them.

First, he demanded of the Serb ambassador the annual payment of twelve thousand gold coins to the Turkish throne. The despots of the Peloponnesos were instructed to appear in person annually with gifts to make their obeisance and to submit the payment of ten thousand gold coins. The lord of Chios was to make an annual payment of six thousand gold coins and the lord of Mitylene three thousand gold coins annually. The emperor of Trebizond and all those who resided along the Black Sea were to come annually with gifts to make obeisance and to pay the tribute.

*   *   *

---

[2] An episcopal garment.

REVIEW QUESTIONS

1. How does Doukas explain the reason for the fall of Constantinople?
2. What signs of bias appear in Doukas's account of the Turks and Sultan Mehmed?
3. What difference did the end of the Byzantine state make to the history of the eastern Mediterranean? How does Doukas describe the immediate aftermath of Turkish occupation?

ALVISE DA MOSTO

Voyage to Africa

Alvise da Mosto (died 1483), also known as Cadamosto, was a member of a prominent family in the Venetian nobility. Alvise passed his early years as a merchant, visiting Flanders and Portugal. In 1454, he accompanied a Portuguese expedition engaged in trade and exploration south of the Sahara. The account of this voyage and another one the following year constitutes one of the earliest European descriptions of central Africa. This excerpt contains Alvise's first impressions of the empire of Mali (here called Melli), inhabited by the people he called the Azanegi (Tuaregs) and the Wolof people, a large tribe south of the Senegal River.

From *The Voyages of Cadamosto*, translated and edited by G. R. Crone (London: Hakluyt Society, 1937), pp. 20–33.

*   *   *

You should know that these people have no knowledge of any Christians except the Portuguese, against whom they have waged war for [thirteen or] fourteen years, many of them having been taken prisoners, as I have already said, and sold into slavery. It is asserted that when for the first time they saw sails, that is, ships, on the sea (which neither they nor their forefathers had ever seen before), they believed that they were great sea-birds with white wings, which were flying, and had come from some strange place: when the sails were lowered for the landing, some of them, watching from far off, thought that the ships were fishes. Others again said that they were phantoms that went by night, at which they were greatly terrified. The reason for this belief was because these caravels within a short space of time appeared at many places, where attacks were delivered, especially at night, by their crews. Thus one such assault might be separated from the next by a hundred or more miles, according to the plans of the sailors, or as the winds, blowing hither and thither, served them. Perceiving this, they said amongst themselves, "If these be human creatures, how can they travel so great a distance in one night, a distance which we could not go in three days?" Thus, as they did not understand the art of navigation, they all thought that the ships were phantoms. This I know is testified to by many Portuguese who at that time were trading in caravels on this coast, and also by those who were captured on these raids. And from this it may be judged how strange many of our ways appeared to them, if such an opinion could prevail.

Beyond the said mart of Edon [Oden], six days journey further inland, there is a place called

Tagaza, that is to say in our tongue "cargador," where a very great quantity of rock-salt is mined. Every year large caravans of camels belonging to the above mentioned Arabs and Azanaghi, leaving in many parties, carry it to Tanbutu [Timbuktu]; thence they go to Melli, the empire of the Blacks, where, so rapidly is it sold, within eight days of its arrival all is disposed of at a price of two to three hundred *mitigalli* a load, according to the quantity [a *mitigallo* is worth about a ducat]: then with the gold they return to their homes.

In this empire of Melli it is very hot, and the pasturage is very unsuitable for fourfooted animals: so that of the majority which come with the caravans no more than twenty-five out of a hundred return. There are no quadrupeds in this country, because they all die, and many also of the Arabs and Azanaghi sicken in this place and die, on account of the great heat. It is said that on horseback it is about forty days from Tagaza to Tanbutu, and thirty from Tanbutu to Melli.

I enquired of them what the merchants of Melli did with this salt, and was told that a small quantity is consumed in their country. Since it is below the meridional and on the equinoctial, where the day is constantly about as long as the night, it is extremely hot at certain seasons of the year: this causes the blood to putrefy, so that were it not for this salt, they would die. The remedy they employ is as follows: they take a small piece of the salt, mix it in a jar with a little water, and drink it every day. They say that this saves them. The remainder of this salt they carry away on a long journey in pieces as large as a man can, with a certain knack, bear on his head.

You must know that when this salt is carried to Melli by camel it goes in large pieces [as it is dug out from the mines], of a size most easily carried on camels, two pieces on each animal. Then at Melli, these Blacks break it in smaller pieces, in order to carry it on their heads, so that each man carries one piece, and thus they form a great army of men on foot, who transport it a great distance. Those who carry it have two forked sticks, one in each hand: when they are tired, they plant them in the ground, and rest their load upon them. In this way they carry it until they reach certain waters: I could not learn from them whether it is fresh or sea water, so that I do not know if it is a river or the sea, though they consider it to be the sea. [I think however it must be a river, for if it were the sea, in such a hot country there would be no lack of salt.] These Blacks are obliged to carry it in this way, because they have no camels or other beasts of burden, as these cannot live in the great heat. It may be imagined how many men are required to carry it on foot, and how many are those who consume it every year. Having reached these waters with the salt, they proceed in this fashion: all those who have the salt pile it in rows, each marking his own. Having made these piles, the whole caravan retires half a day's journey. Then there come another race of Blacks who do not wish to be seen or to speak. They arrive in large boats, from which it appears that they come from islands, and disembark. Seeing the salt, they place a quantity of gold opposite each pile, and then turn back, leaving salt and gold. When they have gone, the negroes who own the salt return: if they are satisfied with the quantity of gold, they leave the salt and retire with the gold. Then the Blacks of the gold return, and remove those piles which are without gold. By the other piles of salt they place more gold, if it pleases them, or else they leave the salt. In this way, by long and ancient custom, they carry on their trade without seeing or speaking to each other. Although it is difficult to believe this, I can testify that I have had this information from many merchants, Arab as well as Azanaghi, and also from persons in whom faith can be placed.

How the Emperor Sought to Take One of These Traders Prisoner

Reflecting upon this, I asked the merchants how it came to be that the Emperor of Melli, who, they said, was so great a lord, had not wished so to proceed as to find out by love or by other means what people these were who did not wish to speak or to be seen. They replied that, not many years previously, an Emperor of Melli determined at all costs to get one of them in his power, and having taken counsel about it, ordered some of his men to leave a few days before the salt caravan, and

proceed to the place where it was customary to pile the salt, to dig trenches near by, in which to conceal themselves. When the Blacks returned to set the gold by the salt, they were to attack them and to take two or three, whom they were to convey under close guard to Melli. To be brief, this was done. They seized four, the others taking to flight: of the four they released three, surmising that one would satisfy the desires of the lord, and not wishing to anger these Blacks more. They spoke to this man in several Negro languages, but he would not reply, or speak at all, neither would he eat. He lived four days and then died. For this reason these Blacks of Melli are of the opinion, after the experience they had with him who would not speak, that they are dumb. Others think that they behave thus from disdain [of doing what their ancestors had never done]. This death vexed all the Blacks of Melli, for on account of it their lord could not achieve his intention. On returning to him they related the incident in due order.

Then the lord was very displeased with them, and asked what the Blacks looked like. They replied they were very black in colour, with well-formed bodies, a span higher than they themselves. The lower lip, more than a span in width, hung down, huge and red, over the breast, displaying the inner part glistening like blood.[1] The upper lip was as small as their own. This form of the lips displayed the gums and teeth, the latter, they said, being bigger than their own: they had two large teeth on each side, and large black eyes. Their appearance is terrifying, and the gums exude blood, as do the lips.

Because of this incident, none of the emperor's men have since been willing to embroil themselves in similar affairs, since, as a result of the capture and death of this one Negro, it was three years before the others would resume the customary exchange of gold for salt. It was thought that their lips became putrid, being in a warmer country than ours: so that these Blacks, having borne much sickness and death [for this space of time], and having no other way of obtaining the salt to cure themselves, resumed the accustomed trade. On

this account, it is our opinion, being unable to live without salt, they set off their plight against our action, just as the Emperor did not care whether these Blacks spoke or not, so long as he had the profit of the gold. This is what I understood from this incident, and since it is related by so many we can accept it. Because I have seen and understood such things in the world, I am one of those who are willing to believe this and other matters to be possible.

The gold thus brought to Melli is divided in three parts: one portion goes with the caravan which takes the road from Melli to a place that is called Cochia. This is the route which runs towards Soria [and il Cairo]: the second and third portions go with a caravan from Melli to Tanbutu. There they are separated: one portion goes to Atoet, whence it is carried to Tunis in Barbary through all the coast beyond: the other part goes to the above mentioned Hoden, whence it spreads towards Orā and Hona, towns in Barbary within the Strecto de Zibelterra, Afezes, Amarochos, Arzib, Azafi, and Amessa, towns in Barbary beyond the Straits. In these places it is bought by us Italians and other Christians from the Moors with the various merchandize we give them.

To return to my first subject, this is the best thing that is brought from the said land and country of the Azanaghi, that is, the brown men. Of that portion of the gold which is brought every year to Hoden, as described already, some quantity is carried to the sea coast, and sold to the Spaniards who are continuously stationed on the said island of Argin for the trade of merchandize, in exchange for other things.

In this land of the brown men, no money is coined, and they have never used it. Nor, formerly, was money to be found in any of their towns. Their sole method is to barter article for article, or two articles for one, and by such means they live. It is true that I understand that inland these Azanaghi, and also the Arabs in some of their districts, are wont to employ white cowries, of those small kinds which are brought to Venice from the Levant. They give certain numbers of these according to the things they have to buy. I should explain that the gold they sell they give by the

---

[1] This suggests the use of the labret, which is still worn by the Lobi women.

weight of a *mitigallo;* according to the practice in Barbary, this *mitigallo* is of the value of a ducat, more or less.

*   *   *

The Rio de Senega, Which Divides the Desert from the Fertile Land

When we had passed in sight of this Cauo Bianco, we sailed on our journey to the river called the Rio de Senega, the first river of the Land of the Blacks, which debouches on this coast. This river separates the Blacks from the brown people called Azanaghi, and also the dry and arid land, that is, the above mentioned desert, from the fertile country of the Blacks. The river is large; its mouth being over a mile wide, and quite deep. There is another mouth a little distance beyond, with an island between. Thus it enters the sea by two mouths, and before each of them about a mile out to sea are shoals and broad sand-banks. In this place the water increases and decreases every six hours, that is, with the rise and fall of the tide. The tide ascends the river more than sixty miles, according to the information I have had from Portuguese who have been [many miles] up it [in caravels]. He who wishes to enter this river must go in with the tide, on account of the shoals and banks at the mouth. From Cauo Bianco it is 380 miles to the river: all the coast is sandy to within about twenty miles of the mouth. It is called Costa de Antte rotte, and is of the Azanaghi, or brown men.

It appears to me a very marvellous thing that beyond the river all men are very black, tall and big, their bodies well formed; and the whole country green, full of trees, and fertile: while on this side, the men are brownish, small, lean, ill-nourished, and small in stature: the country sterile and arid. This river is said to be a branch of the river Nile, of the four royal rivers: it flows through all Ethiopia, watering the country as in Egypt: passing through "lo caiero," it waters all the land of Egypt. This river has many other very large branches, in addition to that of Senega, and they are great rivers on this coast of Ethiopia, of which more will be related later.

The Lords Who Rule on the Coast of Capo Verde

The country of these first Blacks of the Kingdom of Senega is at the beginning of the first Kingdom of Ethiopia. It is all low-lying country, and many people live on the banks of this river. They are called Zilofi. For a great distance beyond, it is low country, and beyond the river likewise, except for Cauo Verde, which is the highest land on all this coast, for 400 miles beyond this Cauo Verde, and for 900 miles on this side of the said cape, the whole coast is flat. [And the people who dwell along its banks are called Gilofi. And all this coast and the known country behind is all lowland as far as the river, and also beyond this river to Capo Verde. This Cape is the highest land on the whole coast, that is for four hundred miles beyond the said Cape.]

The King of Senega in my time was called Zuchalin [Zucolin—a youth of twenty-two years. This Kingdom does not descend by inheritance] but in this land there are divers lesser lords, who [three or four of whom] through jealousy, at times agree among themselves, and set up a King of their own, if he is in truth of noble parentage. This King rules as long as is pleasing to the said lords [that is, according to the treatment they receive from him]. Frequently [they banish him by force: and as frequently] the King makes himself so powerful that he can defend himself against them. Thus his position is not stable and firm, as is that of the Soldan of Babilonia: but he is always in dread of deposition [death or exile].

You must know that this King is lord of a very poor people, and has no city in his country, but villages with huts of straw only. [They do not know how to build houses with walls:] they have no lime with which to build walls, and there is great lack of stones. This Kingdom, also, is very small; it extends no more than two hundred miles along the coast, and, from the information I had, about the same distance inland or a little more. The king lives thus: he has no fixed income [from taxes]: save that each year the lords of the country, in order to stand well with him, present him with horses, which are much esteemed owing to their

scarcity, forage, beasts such as cows and goats, vegetables, millet, and the like. The King supports himself by raids, which result in many slaves from his own as well as neighbouring countries. He employs these slaves [in many ways, mainly] in cultivating the land allotted to him: but he also sells many to the Azanaghi [and Arab] merchants in return for horses and other goods, and also to Christians, since they have begun to trade with these Blacks.

The King is permitted to have as many wives as he wishes, as also are all the chiefs and men of this country, that is, as many as they can support. Thus this King has always thirty of them, though he favours one more than another, according to those from whom they are descended. This is his manner of living with his wives: he has certain villages and places, in some of which he keeps eight or ten of them. Each has a house of her own, with young servants to attend her, and slaves to cultivate the possessions and lands assigned by the lord, [with the fruits of which they are able to support themselves]. They have also a certain number of beasts, such as cows and goats, for their use; in this way his wives have the land sown and the beasts tended, and so gain a living. When the King arrives at one of these villages, he goes to the house of one of his wives, for they are obliged to provide, out of this produce, for him and those accompanying him. Every morning, at sunrise, each prepares three or four dishes of various foods, either meat, fish, or other Moorish foods according to their practice. These are sent by their slaves to be put at the disposal of their lord, so that within an hour forty or fifty dishes are assembled; when the time at which the lord wishes to eat has arrived, he picks out whatever tempts him, and gives the remainder to those in his train. But he never gives his people abundance to eat, so that they are always hungry. In this fashion he journeys from place to place without giving any thought to his victuals, and lodges sometimes with one wife, sometimes with another, so that he begets numerous sons, for when one is pregnant he leaves her alone. All the other chiefs of this country live in this same fashion.

The Customs of the Blacks, and Their Beliefs

The faith of these first Blacks is Muhammadanism: they are not however, as are the white Moors, very resolute in this faith, especially the common people. The chiefs adhere to the tenets of the Muhammadans because they have around them priests of the Azanaghi or Arabs, [who have reached this country]. These give them some instruction in the laws of Muhammad, enlarging upon the great disgrace of being rulers and yet living without any divine law, and behaving as do their people and lowly men, who live without laws; and since they have converse with none but these Azanaghi and Arab priests, they are converted to the law of Muhammad. But since they have had converse with Christians, they believe less in it, for our customs please them, and they also realise our wealth and ingenuity in everything as compared with theirs. They say that the God, who has bestowed so many benefits, has shown his great love for us, which could only be if his law were good—but that, none the less, theirs is still the law of God, through which they will find salvation, as we through ours.

These people dress thus: almost all constantly go naked, except for a goatskin fashioned in the form of drawers, with which they hide their shame. But the chiefs and those of standing wear a cotton garment—for cotton grows in these lands. Their women spin it into cloth of a span in width. They are unable to make wider cloth because they do not understand how to card it for weaving. When they wish to make a larger piece, they sew four or five of these strips together. These garments are made to reach half way down the thigh, with wide sleeves to the elbow. They also wear breeches of this cotton, which are tied across, and reach to the ankles, and are otherwise so large as to be from thirty to thirty-five, or even forty *palmi* round the top; when they are girded round the waist, they are much crumpled and form a sack in front, and the hinder part reaches to the ground, and waggles like a tail—the most comical thing to be seen in the world. They would come in these wide petticoats with these tails and ask us

if we had ever seen a more beautiful dress or fashion: for they hold it for certain that they are the most beautiful garments in the world. Their women, both married and single, all go covered with girdles, below which they wear a sheet of these cotton strips bound across, half way down their legs. Men and women always go barefoot. They wear nothing on their heads: the hair of both sexes is fashioned into neat tresses arranged in various styles, though their hair by nature is no longer than a span. You must know also that the men of these lands perform many women's tasks, such as spinning, washing clothes and such things. It is always very hot there, and the further one goes inland, the greater the heat: by comparison, it is no colder in these parts in January than it is in April in our country of Italy.

Men Clean in Their Persons and Filthy in Eating

The men and women are clean in their persons, since they wash themselves all over four or five times a day: but in eating they are filthy, and ill-mannered. In matters of which they have no experience they are credulous and awkward, but in those to which they are accustomed they are the equal of our skilled men. They are talkative, and never at a loss for something to say: in general they are great liars and cheats: but on the other hand, charitable, receiving strangers willingly, and providing a night's lodging and one or two meals without any charge.

*   *   *

REVIEW QUESTIONS

1. What does da Mosto's account reveal about the earliest phases of the African slave trade?
2. His description of the silent trade is the first extended account we have of this remarkable type of barter. How plausible is this account, and what might it teach the economic historian about markets?
3. Alvise da Mosto was the first European ethnographer of the Wolof. What perspective frames his view of the Wolof? What contrasts are there in the way he described them, compared to the way William of Rubruck described the Mongols (pp. 359–365)? How do you account for these differences?

CHRISTOPHER COLUMBUS

Letter on His First Voyage

Christopher Columbus (c. 1450–1506) was born somewhere around Genoa and made his living as a sailor from an early age. Columbus saw much of the Mediterranean and Atlantic world and acquired real skill as a mapmaker and navigator. Self-taught in geography, Columbus developed an erroneous theory of the globe's size that made sailing across the Atlantic to China and Japan a daring but plausible adventure. After he had spent years looking for a patron among the rulers of Europe, Isabella of Castile took the lead (along with her husband Ferdinand of Aragon) in sponsoring Columbus's first voyage. This letter is one of his earliest accounts of this trip in 1492.

From *Selected Documents Illustrating the Four Voyages of Christopher Columbus,* translated and edited by Cecil Jane (London: Hakluyt Society, 1930), pp. 3–18.

Sir, As I know that you will be pleased at the great victory with which Our Lord has crowned my voyage, I write this to you, from which you will learn how in thirty-three days, I passed from the Canary Islands to the Indies with the fleet which the most illustrious king and queen, our sovereigns, gave to me. And there I found very many islands filled with people innumerable, and of them all I have taken possession for their highnesses, by proclamation made and with the royal standard unfurled, and no opposition was offered to me. To the first island which I found, I gave the name *San Salvador,* in emembrance of the Divine Majesty, Who has marvellously bestowed all this; the Indians call it "Guanahani." To the second, I gave the name *Isla de Santa María de Concepción;* to the third, *Fernandina;* to the fourth, *Isabella;* to the fifth, *Isla Juana,* and so to each one I gave a new name.

When I reached Juana, I followed its coast to the westward, and I found it to be so extensive that I thought that it must be the mainland, the province of Catayo. And since there were neither towns nor villages on the seashore, but only small hamlets, with the people of which I could not have speech, because they all fled immediately, I went forward on the same course, thinking that I should not fail to find great cities and towns. And, at the end of many leagues, seeing that there was no change and that the coast was bearing me northwards, which I wished to avoid, since winter was already beginning and I proposed to make from it to the south, and as moreover the wind was carrying me forward, I determined not to wait for a change in the weather and retraced my path as far as a certain harbour known to me. And from that point, I sent two men inland to learn if there were a king or great cities. They travelled three days' journey and found an infinity of small hamlets and people without number, but nothing of importance. For this reason, they returned.

I understood sufficiently from other Indians, whom I had already taken, that this land was nothing but an island. And therefore I followed its coast eastwards for one hundred and seven leagues to the point where it ended. And from that cape, I saw another island, distant eighteen leagues from the former, to the east, to which I at once gave the name "Española." And I went there and followed its northern coast, as I had in the case of Juana, to the eastward for one hundred and eighty-eight great leagues in a straight line. This island and all the others are very fertile to a limitless degree, and this island is extremely so. In it there are many harbours on the coast of the sea, beyond comparison with others which I know in Christendom, and many rivers, good and large, which is marvellous. Its lands are high, and there are in it very many sierras and very lofty mountains, beyond comparison with the island of Teneriffe. All are most beautiful, of a thousand shapes, and all are accessible and filled with trees of a thousand kinds and tall, and they seem to touch the sky. And I am told that they never lose their foliage, as I can understand, for I saw them as green and as lovely as they are in Spain in May, and some of them were flowering, some bearing fruit, and some in another stage, according to their nature. And the nightingale was singing and other birds of a thousand kinds in the month of November there where I went. There are six or eight kinds of palm, which are a wonder to behold on account of their beautiful variety, but so are the other trees and fruits and plants. In it are marvellous pine groves, and there are very large tracts of cultivatable lands, and there is honey, and there are birds of many kinds and fruits in great diversity. In the interior are mines of metals, and the population is without number. Española is a marvel.

The sierras and mountains, the plains and arable lands and pastures, are so lovely and rich for planting and sowing, for breeding cattle of every kind, for building towns and villages. The harbours of the sea here are such as cannot be believed to exist unless they have been seen, and so with the rivers, many and great, and good waters, the majority of which contain gold. In the trees and fruits and plants, there is a great difference from those of Juana. In this island, there are many spices and great mines of gold and of other metals.

The people of this island, and of all the other islands which I have found and of which I have information, all go naked, men and women, as their mothers bore them, although some women

cover a single place with the leaf of a plant or with a net of cotton which they make for the purpose. They have no iron or steel or weapons, nor are they fitted to use them, not because they are not well built men and of handsome stature, but because they are very marvellously timorous. They have no other arms than weapons made of canes, cut in seeding time, to the ends of which they fix a small sharpened stick. And they do not dare to make use of these, for many times it has happened that I have sent ashore two or three men to some town to have speech, and countless people have come out to them, and as soon as they have seen my men approaching they have fled, even a father not waiting for his son. And this, not because ill has been done to anyone; on the contrary, at every point where I have been and have been able to have speech, I have given to them of all that I had, such as cloth and many other things, without receiving anything for it; but so they are, incurably timid. It is true that, after they have been reassured and have lost their fear, they are so guileless and so generous with all they possess, that no one would believe it who has not seen it. They never refuse anything which they possess, if it be asked of them; on the contrary, they invite anyone to share it, and display as much love as if they would give their hearts, and whether the thing be of value or whether it be of small price, at once with whatever trifle of whatever kind it may be that is given to them, with that they are content. I forbade that they should be given things so worthless as fragments of broken crockery and scraps of broken glass, and ends of straps, although when they were able to get them, they fancied that they possessed the best jewel in the world. So it was found that a sailor for a strap received gold to the weight of two and a half *castellanos*, and others much more for other things which were worth much less. As for new *blancas*, for them they would give everything which they had, although it might be two or three *castellanos'* weight of gold or an *arroba* or two of spun cotton. . . . They took even the pieces of the broken hoops of the wine barrels and, like savages, gave what they had, so that it seemed to me to be wrong and I forbade it. And I gave a thousand handsome good things, which I had brought, in order that they might conceive affection, and more than that, might become Christians and be inclined to the love and service of their highnesses and of the whole Castilian nation, and strive to aid us and to give us of the things which they have in abundance and which are necessary to us. And they do not know any creed and are not idolaters; only they all believe that power and good are in the heavens, and they are very firmly convinced that I, with these ships and men, came from the heavens, and in this belief they everywhere received me, after they had overcome their fear. And this does not come because they are ignorant; on the contrary, they are of a very acute intelligence and are men who navigate all those seas, so that it is amazing how good an account they give of everything, but it is because they have never seen people clothed or ships of such a kind.

And as soon as I arrived in the Indies, in the first island which I found, I took by force some of them, in order that they might learn and give me information of that which there is in those parts, and so it was that they soon understood us, and we them, either by speech or signs, and they have been very serviceable. I still take them with me, and they are always assured that I come from Heaven, for all the intercourse which they have had with me; and they were the first to announce this wherever I went, and the others went running from house to house and to the neighbouring towns, with loud cries of, 'Come! Come to see the people from Heaven!' So all, men and women alike, when their minds were set at rest concerning us, came, so that not one, great or small, remained behind, and all brought something to eat and drink, which they gave with extraordinary affection. In all the island, they have very many canoes, like rowing *fustas*, some larger, some smaller, and some are larger than a *fusta* of eighteen benches. They are not so broad, because they are made of a single log of wood, but a *fusta* would not keep up with them in rowing, since their speed is a thing incredible. And in these they navigate among all those islands, which are innumerable, and carry their goods. One of these canoes I have seen with seventy and eighty men in her, and each one with his oar.

In all these islands, I saw no great diversity in the appearance of the people or in their manners and language. On the contrary, they all understand one another, which is a very curious thing, on account of which I hope that their highnesses will determine upon their conversion to our holy faith, towards which they are very inclined.

I have already said how I have gone one hundred and seven leagues in a straight line from west to east along the seashore of the island Juana, and as a result of that voyage, I can say that this island is larger than England and Scotland together, for, beyond these one hundred and seven leagues, there remain to the westward two provinces to which I have not gone. One of these provinces they call "Avan," and there the people are born with tails; and these provinces cannot have a length of less than fifty or sixty leagues, as I could understand from those Indians whom I have and who know all the islands.

The other, Española, has a circumference greater than all Spain, from Colibre, by the seacoast, to Fuenterabia in Vizcaya, since I voyaged along one side one hundred and eighty-eight great leagues in a straight line from west to east. It is a land to be desired and, seen, it is never to be left. And in it, although of all I have taken possession for their highnesses and all are more richly endowed than I know how, or am able, to say, and I hold them all for their highnesses, so that they may dispose of them as, and as absolutely as, of the kingdoms of Castile, in this Española, in the situation most convenient and in the best position for the mines of gold and for all intercourse as well with the mainland here as with that there, belonging to the Grand Khan, where will be great trade and gain, I have taken possession of a large town, to which I gave the name *Villa de Navidad,* and in it I have made fortifications and a fort, which now will by this time be entirely finished, and I have left in it sufficient men for such a purpose with arms and artillery and provisions for more than a year, and a *fusta,* and one, a master of all sea-craft, to build others, and great friendship with the king of that land, so much so, that he was proud to call me, and to treat me as, a

brother. And even if he were to change his attitude to one of hostility towards these men, he and his do not know what arms are and they go naked, as I have already said, and are the most timorous people that there are in the world, so that the men whom I have left there alone would suffice to destroy all that land, and the island is without danger for their persons, if they know how to govern themselves.

In all these islands, it seems to me that all men are content with one woman, and to their chief or king they give as many as twenty. It appears to me that the women work more than the men. And I have not been able to learn if they hold private property; what seemed to me to appear was that, in that which one had, all took a share, especially of eatable things.

In these islands I have so far found no human monstrosities, as many expected, but on the contrary the whole population is very well-formed, nor are they Negroes as in Guinea, but their hair is flowing, and they are not born where there is intense force in the rays of the sun; it is true that the sun has there great power, although it is distant from the equinoctial line twenty-six degrees. In these islands, where there are high mountains, the cold was severe this winter, but they endure it, being used to it and with the help of meats which they eat with many and extremely hot spices. As I have found no monsters, so I have had no report of any, except in an island "Quaris," the second at the coming into the Indies, which is inhabited by a people who are regarded in all the islands as very fierce and who eat human flesh. They have many canoes with which they range through all the islands of India and pillage and take as much as they can. They are no more malformed than the others, except that they have the custom of wearing their hair long like women, and they use bows and arrows of the same cane stems, with a small piece of wood at the end, owing to lack of iron which they do not possess. They are ferocious among these other people who are cowardly to an excessive degree, but I make no more account of them than of the rest. These are those who have intercourse with the women of "Matinino," which is the first island

met on the way from Spain to the Indies, in which there is not a man. These women engage in no feminine occupation, but use bows and arrows of cane, like those already mentioned, and they arm and protect themselves with plates of copper, of which they have much.

In another island, which they assure me is larger than Española, the people have no hair. In it, there is gold incalculable, and from it and from the other islands, I bring with me Indians as evidence.

In conclusion, to speak only of that which has been accomplished on this voyage, which was so hasty, their highnesses can see that I will give them as much gold as they may need, if their highnesses will render me very slight assistance; moreover, spice and cotton, as much as their highnesses shall command; and mastic, as much as they shall order to be shipped and which, up to now, has been found only in Greece, in the island of Chios, and the Seignory sells it for what it pleases; and aloe wood, as much as they shall order to be shipped, and slaves, as many as they shall order to be shipped and who will be from the idolaters. And I believe that I have found rhubarb and cinamon, and I shall find a thousand other things of value, which the people whom I have left there will have discovered, for I have not delayed at any point, so far as the wind allowed me to sail, except in the town of Navidad, in order to leave it secured and well established, and in truth, I should have done much more, if the ships had served me, as reason demanded.

This is enough . . . and the eternal God, our Lord, Who gives to all those who walk in His way triumph over things which appear to be impossible, and this was notably one; for, although men have talked or have written of these lands, all was conjectural, without suggestion of ocular evidence, but amounted only to this, that those who heard for the most part listened and judged it to be rather a fable than as having any vestige of truth. So that, since Our Redeemer has given this victory to our most illustrious king and queen, and to

their renowned kingdoms, in so great a matter, for this all Christendom ought to feel delight and make great feasts and give solemn thanks to the Holy Trinity with many solemn prayers for the great exaltation which they shall have, in the turning of so many peoples to our holy faith, and afterwards for temporal benefits, for not only Spain but all Christians will have hence refreshment and gain.

This, in accordance with that which has been accomplished, thus briefly.

Done in the caravel, off the Canary Islands, on the fifteenth of February, in the year one thousand four hundred and ninety-three.

At your orders.   El Almirante.

After having written this, and being in the sea of Castile, there came on me so great a south-south-west wind, that I was obliged to lighten ship. But I ran here to-day into this port of Lisbon, which was the greatest marvel in the world, whence I decided to write to their highnesses. In all the Indies, I have always found weather like May; where I went in thirty-three days and I had returned in twenty-eight, save for these storms which have detained me for fourteen days, beating about in this sea. Here all the sailors say that never has there been so bad a winter nor so many ships lost.

Done on the fourth day of March.

REVIEW QUESTIONS

1. What can we learn about Columbus's personality and motives from this letter?
2. Columbus provides here the first Western account of the people he called Indians. What do we learn about his interests and abilities as an ethnographer?
3. Compare this account to those of William of Rubruck (pp. 359–365) and Alvise da Mosto (pp. 376–381). What can you conclude from their similiarities and differences?

CONQUEST OF MEXICO, FLORENTINE CODEX (C. 1555)

The Franciscan friar Bernardino de Sahagún (d. 1590) directed the team of Nahua artists who produced the Florentine Codex. This book is an account of Cortéz's expedition of 1519, which resulted in the destruction of the Aztec Empire. The story is told in Nahuatl, and is accompanied by over 100 illustrations. Scholars have debated the extent to which the text and pictures allowed the Nahua to express their own views of these events. Sahagún began collecting information in the 1540s, and this chapter may have been composed around 1555. These six pictures show characteristic battle scenes; in the last one, the native Mexicans have captured a Spanish cannon. Guns and steel certainly played a role in the Spanish conquest of Mexico. What evidence do these pictures provide of this? Perhaps even more striking were the roles of horses. What advantages did these animals provide the Spaniards? Why would indigenous artists have been involved in a project like this? What are the advantages and short-comings of this historical source?

12 ❧ RENAISSANCE IDEALS AND REALITIES, c. 1350–1550

The Renaissance began as an Italian phenomenon, occurring between c. 1350 and 1520, that spread to the rest of Europe over the course of the 1500s and early 1600s. Its principal manifestations were the revival of classicism and naturalism in arts and literature, the rise of the modern dynastic state as the dominant political structure, and an economic crisis fueled by industrial change and economic contraction.

Until recently, scholars have traditionally viewed the Renaissance as a period of great change. Contemporaries used the term rinascita *to express their sense of a rebirth, a perfection in the arts. Some modern scholars view the period as one of fundamental change, an abrupt departure from the past, and have identified the following several characteristics that set the Renaissance apart as a discrete period of history. Scholars and artists revived classical antiquity as a subject of study and emulation. The state emerged as a work of art, that is, as a calculated design by persons in pursuit of power. The universal man, well rounded in physical and intellectual endeavors, became the political and pedagogical ideal of the age. The social mobility born of a rapidly changing economy led to an aristocracy of merit, a fusion of nobility and bourgeoisie in which achievement mattered more than lineage.*

All of these characteristics have been criticized and reviewed by latter-day historians of the Renaissance, most of whom would emphasize its continuity with the Middle Ages. Few, however, would disagree that the age was unusually self-conscious—aware of its achievements, intrigued by its potential, and impatient of its limits. The following selections capture something of this mentality.

LEON BATTISTA ALBERTI

FROM *I Libri della Famiglia*

Leon Battista Alberti (1404–1474) embodied the Renaissance universal man. Born the illegitimate son of a Florentine merchant, he was an athlete, polymath, and artist. He earned a degree in canon law at the University of Bologna in 1428 and migrated to Rome, where he entered papal service. It was there, in 1438, that he began to write On the Family. *Written in the form of a dialogue among the members of the Alberti family, gathered at the deathbed of Leon Battista's father in 1421, it examines the ideal family as a unit for the begetting and rearing of children, for the amassing and maintaining of fortunes, and for the accumulation and exercise of power. It was also a sly exercise in satire, insofar as it indirectly criticizes his brothers and uncles for violating his father's dying wish that Leon Battista be treated as a legitimate member of the family.*

From *I Libri della Famiglia*, translated by Renee New Watkins (Columbia: University of South Carolina Press, 1969).

*   *   *

XIII

Lionardo: If I had children, you may be sure I should think about them, but my thoughts would be untroubled. My first consideration would only be to make my children grow up with good character and virtue. Whatever activities suited their taste would suit me. Any activity which is not dishonest is not displeasing to an honorable mind. The activities which lead to honor and praise belong to honorable and wellborn men. Certainly I will admit that every son cannot achieve all that his father might wish. If he does something he is able to do, however, I like that better than to have him strike out in a direction where he cannot follow through. I also think it is more praiseworthy for a man, even if he does not altogether succeed, to do his best in some field rather than sit inactive, inert, and idle. There is an old saying which our ancestors often repeated: "Idleness is the mother of vice." It is an ugly and hateful thing to see a man keep himself forever useless, like that idle fellow who when they asked him why he spent all day as if condemned to sit or lie on public benches, answered "I am waiting to get fat." The man who heard him was disgusted, and asked him rather to try to fatten up a pig, since at least something useful might come of it. Thus quite correctly he showed him what an idle fellow amounts to, which is less than a pig.

I'll go further, Adovardo. However rich and noble a father may be, he should try to have his son learn, besides the noble skills, some occupation which is not degrading. By means of this occupation in case of misfortune he can live honestly by his own labor and the work of his hands. Are the vicissitudes of this world so little or so infrequent that we can ignore the possibility of adverse circumstances? Was not the son of Perseus, king of Macedonia, seen sweating and soiled in a Roman factory, employed in making his living with heavy and painful labor? If the instability of things could thus transport the son of a famous and powerful king to such depths of poverty and need,

it is right for us private citizens as well as for men of higher station to provide against every misfortune. If none in our house ever had to devote himself to such laboring occupations, thank fortune for it, and let us make sure that none will have to in the future. A wise and foresightful pilot, to be able to survive in adverse storms, carries more rope, anchors, and sheets than he needs for good weather. So let the father see that his sons enjoy some praiseworthy and useful activity. In this matter let him consider first of all the honesty of the work, and then adapt his course to what he knows his son can actually accomplish, and finally try to choose a field in which, by applying himself, the young man can hope to earn a reputation.

*   *   *

Battista: Whatever you think. The only question we have is what are the things that make a family fortunate. Go on with what you have to say and we shall listen.

*   *   *

Lionardo: In our discussion we may establish four general precepts as sound and firm foundation for all the other points to be developed or added. I shall name them. In the family the number of men must not diminish but augment; possessions must not grow less, but more; all forms of disgrace are to be shunned—a good name and fine reputation is precious and worth pursuing; hatreds, enmities, rancor must be carefully avoided, while good will, numerous acquaintances, and friendships are something to look for, augment, and cultivate.

*   *   *

If a family is not to fall for these reasons into what we have described as the most unfortunate condition of decline, but is to grow, instead, in fame and in the prosperous multitude of its youth, we must persuade our young men to take wives. We must use every argument for this purpose, offer incentive, promise reward, employ all our wit, persistence, and cunning. A most appropriate reason for taking a wife may be found in what we

were saying before, about the evil of sensual indulgence, for the condemnation of such things may lead young men to desire honorable satisfactions. As other incentives, we may also speak to them of the delights of this primary and natural companionship of marriage. Children act as pledges and securities of marital love and kindness. At the same time they offer a focus for all a man's hopes and desires. Sad, indeed, is the man who has labored to get wealth and power and lands, and then has no true heir and perpetuator of his memory. No one can be more suited than a man's true and legitimate sons to gain advantages by virtue of his character, position, and authority, and to enjoy the fruits and rewards of his labor. If a man leaves such heirs, furthermore, he need not consider himself wholly dead and gone. His children keep his own position and his true image in the family. Dido, the Phoenician, when Aeneas left her, his mistress, cried out with tears, among her great sorrows no desire above this one: "Ah, had I but a small Aeneas now, to play beside me." As you were first poisoned, wretched and abandoned woman, by that man whose fatal and consuming love you did embrace, so another little Aeneas might by his similar face and gestures have offered you some consolation in your grief and anguish.

*   *   *

When, by the urging and counsel of their elders and of the whole family, young men have arrived at the point of marriage, their mothers and other female relatives and friends, who have known the virgins of the neighborhood from earliest childhood and know the way their upbringing has formed them, should select all the well-born and well-brought-up girls and present that list to the new groom-to-be. He can then choose the one who suits him best. The elders of the house and all of the family shall reject no daughter-in-law unless she is tainted with the breath of scandal or bad reputation. Aside from that, let the man who will have to satisfy her satisfy himself. He should act as do wise heads of families before they acquire some property—they like to look it over several

times before they actually sign a contract. It is good in the case of any purchase and contract to inform oneself fully and to take counsel. One should consult a good number of persons and be very careful in order to avoid belated regrets. The man who has decided to marry must be still more cautious. I recommend that he examine and anticipate in every way, and consider for many days, what sort of person it is he is to live with for all his years as husband and companion. Let him be minded to marry for two purposes: first to perpetuate himself in his children, and second to have a steady and constant companion all his life. A woman is needed, therefore, who is likely to bear children and who is desirable as a perpetual mate.

*   *   *

To sum up this whole subject in a few words, for I want above all to be brief on this point, let a man get himself new kinsmen of better than plebeian blood, of a fortune more than diminutive, of a decent occupation, and of modest and respectable habits. Let them not be too far above himself, lest their greatness overshadow his own honor and position. Too high a family may disturb his own and his family's peace and tranquillity, and also, if one of them falls, you cannot help to support him without collapsing or wearing yourself out as you stagger under a weight too great for your arms and your strength. I also do not want the new relatives to rank too low, for while the first error puts you in a position of servitude, the second causes expense. Let them be equals, then, and, to repeat, modest and respectable people.

*   *   *

We have, as I said, made the house numerous and full of young people. It is essential to give them something to do now, and not let them grow lazy. Idleness is not only useless and generally despised in young men, but a positive burden and danger to the family. I do not need to teach you to shun idleness, when I know you are hard workers and active. I do encourage you to continue as

you are doing in every sort of activity and hard discipline that you may attain excellence and deserve fame. Only think this matter over and consider whether any man, even if he is not necessarily ambitious of gaining glory but merely a little shy of falling into disgrace, can ever be, in actuality or even if we merely try to imagine him, a man not heartily opposed to idleness and to mere sitting. Who has ever dreamed he might reach any grace or dignity without hard work in the noblest arts, without assiduous efforts, without plenty of sweat poured out in manly and strenuous exertions? Certainly a man who would wish for the favor of praise and fame must avoid and resist idleness and inertia just as he would do major and hateful enemies. There is nothing that leads more quickly to dishonor and disgrace than idleness. The lap of the idler has always been the nest and lair of vice. Nothing is so harmful and pestilent in public and private life as the lazy and passive citizen. From idleness springs lasciviousness; from lasciviousness comes a contempt for the law; from disobedience to law comes ruin and the destruction of the country itself. To the extent that men tolerate the first resistance of men's will to the customs and ways of the country, their spirits soon turn to arrogance, pride, and the harmful power of avarice and greed. Thieves, murderers, adulterers, and all sorts of criminals and evil men run wild.

*   *   *

To this I might add that man ought to give some reward to God, to satisfy him with good works in return for the wonderful gifts which He gave to the spirit of man exalting and magnifying it beyond that of all other earthly beings. Nature, that is, God, made man a composite of two parts, one celestial and divine, the other most beautiful and noble among mortal things. He provided him with a form and a body suited to every sort of movement, so as to enable him to perceive and to flee from that which threatened to harm and oppose him. He gave him speech and judgment so that he would be able to seek after and to find what he needed and could use. He gave him

movement and sentiment, desire and the power of excitement, so that he might clearly appreciate and pursue useful things and shun those harmful and dangerous to him. He gave him intelligence, teachability, memory and reason, qualities divine in themselves and which enable man to investigate, to distinguish, to know what to avoid and what to desire in order best to preserve himself. To these great gifts, admirable beyond measure, God added still another power of the spirit and mind of man, namely moderation. As a curb on greed and on excessive lusts, he gave him modesty and the desire for honor. Further, God established in the human mind a strong tie to bind together human beings in society, namely justice, equity, liberality, and love. These are the means by which a man can gain the favor and praise of other men, as well as the mercy and grace of the creator. Beyond this, God filled the manly breast with powers that make man able to bear fatigue, adversity, and the hard blows of fortune. He is able to undertake what is difficult, to overcome sorrow, not even to fear death—such are his qualities of strength, of endurance and fortitude, such can be his contempt for transitory things. These are qualities which enable us to honor and serve God as fully as we should, with piety, with moderation, and with every other perfect and honorable deed. Let us agree, then, that man was not born to languish in idleness but to labor and create magnificent and great works, first for the pleasure and glory of God, and second for his own enjoyment of that life of perfect virtue and its fruit, which is happiness.

*   *   *

Let men seek their own happiness first, and they will obtain the happiness of their family also. As I have said, happiness cannot be gained without good works and just and righteous deeds. Works are just and good which not only do no harm to anyone, but which benefit many. Works are righteous if they are without a trace of the dishonorable or any element of dishonesty. The best works are those which benefit many people. Those are most virtuous, perhaps, which cannot

be pursued without strength and nobility. We must give ourselves to manly effort, then, and follow the noblest pursuits.

It seems to me, before we dedicate ourselves to any particular activity, it would be wise to think over and examine the question of what is our easiest way to reach or come near to happiness. Not every man easily attains happiness. Nature did not make all men of the same humor, or of the same intelligence or will, or equally endowed with skill and power. Rather nature planned that where I might be weak, you would make good the deficiency, and in some other way you would lack the virtue found in another. Why this? So that I should have need of you, and you of him, he of another, and some other of me. In this way one man's need for another serves as the cause and means to keep us all united in general friendship and alliance. This may, indeed, have been the source and beginning of republics. Laws may have begun thus rather than as I was saying before; fire and water alone may not have been the cause of so great a union among men as society gives them. Society is a union sustained by laws, by reason, and by custom.

Let us not digress. To decide which is the most suitable career for himself, a man must take two things into account: the first is his own intelligence, his mind and his body, everything about himself; and the second, the question requiring close consideration, is that of outside supports, the help and resources which are necessary or useful and to which he must have early access, welcome, and free right of use if he is to enter the field for which he seems more suited than for any other. Take an example: if a man wished to perform great feats of arms while he knew he was himself but a weak fellow, not very robust, incapable of bearing up through dust and storm and sun, this would not be the right profession for him to pursue. If I, being poor, longed to devote my life to letters, though I had not the money to pay the considerable expenses attached to such a career, again this would be a poor choice of career. If you are equipped with numerous relatives, plenty of friends, abundant wealth, and if you possess

within yourself intelligence, eloquence, and such tact as to keep you out of any rough or awkward situations, and you decide to dedicate yourself to civic affairs, you might do extremely well.

*   *   *

We should also consider at this point how much reward and profit, how much honor and fame, you can gain from any work or achievement you undertake to perform. The only condition is that you surpass everyone else in the field. In every craft the most skilled master, as you know, gains most riches and has the best position and the greatest stature among his companions. Think how even in so humble a profession as shoemaking men search out the best among the cobblers. If it is true of the humblest occupations that the most skilled practitioners are ever most in demand and so become most famous, consider whether in the highest professions the opposite suddenly holds true. In fact you will find it still more to the point to be the best in these, or at least one of the best. If you succeed in these fields, you know that you have been given a greater portion of happiness than other men. If you are learned, you realize the misfortune of the ignorant. You know, in addition, that the unhappiest lot falls to those who, being ignorant, desire still to appear learned.

*   *   *

Consider in your own mind what a boon to know more than others and to put the knowledge to good use at the right time and place. If you think it over, I am sure you will realize that in every field a man who would appear to be valuable must be valuable in fact. Now we have stated this much: that youth should not be wasted but should be directed to some honorable kind of work, that a man should do his utmost in that work, and that he should choose the field which will be most helpful to his family and bring him most fame. A career should suit our own nature and the state of our fortunes, and should be pursued in such a way that we may never, by our own fault at least, fall short of the first rank.

Riches, however, are for nearly everyone the primary reason for working at all. They are also most useful in making it possible to persevere in our undertakings until we win approval and attain public favor, position, and fame. This is the time, therefore, to explain how wealth is acquired and how it is kept. It was also one of the four things which we said were necessary to bring about and to preserve contentment in a family. Now, then, let us begin to accumulate wealth. Perhaps the present moment, as the evening grows dark, is just right for this subject, for no occupation seems less attractive to a man of large and liberal spirit than the kind of labor by which wealth is in fact gathered. If you will count over in your imagination the actual careers that bring great profits, you will see that all basically concern themselves with buying and selling or with lending and collecting the returns. Having neither petty nor vulgar minds, I imagine you probably find these activities, which are solely directed to making a profit, somewhat below you. They seem entirely to lack honor and distinction.

*   *   *

Those who thus dismiss all mercenary activities are wrong, I believe. If the pursuit of wealth is not as glorious as are other great pursuits, yet a man is not contemptible if, being unsuited by nature to achieve anything much in other finer fields of work, he devotes himself to this kind of activity. Here, it may be, he knows he is not inadequately equipped to do well. Here everyone admits he is very useful to the republic and still more to his own family. Wealth, if it is used to help the needy, can gain a man esteem and praise. With wealth, if it is used to do great and noble things and to show a fine magnanimity and splendor, fame and dignity can be attained. In emergencies and times of need we see every day how useful is the wealth of private citizens to the country itself. From public funds alone it is not always possible to pay the wages of those whose arms and blood defend the country's liberty and dignity. Nor can republics increase their glory and their might without enormous expenditure.

*   *   *

Why have I gone on at length on these topics? Only to show you that, among occupations, there are quite a few, both honorable and highly esteemed, by means of which wealth in no small measure may be gained. One of these occupations, as you know, is that of merchant. You can easily call to mind other similar careers which are both honorable and highly profitable. You want to know, then, what they are. Let us run through them. We shall spread out all the occupations before us and choose the best among them, then we shall try to define how they make us wealthy and prosperous. Occupations that do not bring profit and gain will never make you rich. Those that bring frequent and large profits are the ones that make you rich. The only system for becoming rich, by our own industry and by the means that luck, friends, or anyone's favor can give us, is to make profits. And how do men grow poor? Ill fortune certainly plays a part, this I admit, but excluding fortune, let us speak here of industry. If riches come through profits, and these through labor, diligence, and hard work, then poverty, which is the reverse of profit, will follow from the reverse of these virtues, namely from neglect, laziness, and sloth. These are the fault neither of fortune nor of others, but of oneself. One grows poor, also, by spending too much. Prodigality dissipates wealth and throws it away. The opposite of prodigality, the opposite of neglect, are carefulness and conscientiousness, in short, good management. Good management is the means to preserve wealth. Thus we have found out that to become rich one must make profits, keep what one has gained, and exercise rational good management.

*   *   *

REVIEW QUESTIONS

1. What, according to Alberti, is the role and nature of a father?
2. How is a father's authority different from other kinds of authority?
3. What is the role of education in the formation of human nature?
4. How does this view differ from that of other authors?
5. What is Alberti's definition of honor?
6. What is its relationship to the family? Why is it so important to Alberti?
7. How might Alberti define the family?

LEONARDO DA VINCI

FROM *The Notebooks*

Leonardo da Vinci (1452–1519) was born in the countryside of Florence, the illegitimate son of a notary in the town of Vinci. He was self-taught and could read Latin only poorly. He was left-handed, a condition viewed by contemporaries as a deformity. Sometime around 1481, he moved to Milan, where his patrons were the dukes Gian Galeazzo (1476–94) and Ludovico Sforza (1494–1500). During the French invasion of 1499, Leonardo fled Milan and led a peripatetic existence until 1508, when

he returned to the city. In 1513, he was taken to France, where he lived the remainder of his days. He is widely acclaimed as a genius, the designer of futuristic machines of many sorts. Among these was a device for grinding concave mirrors and lenses that made possible the invention of the telescope in 1509. He was a great artist in many media as well as a keen observer of nature. His interests ranged from aerodynamics to physics to biology to anatomy to optics. His writings on perspective are drawn from his notebooks, which he wrote backward, in a mirror hand, and in no particular order, and which were never published in his lifetime.

From *Leonardo da Vinci's Notebooks*, translated by Edward MacCurdy (London: Duckworth & Co., 1906).

*   *   *

Principle of Perspective

All things transmit their image to the eye by means of pyramids; the nearer to the eye these are intersected the smaller the image of their cause will appear.

If you should ask how you can demonstrate these points to me from experience, I should tell you, as regards the vanishing point which moves with you, to notice as you go along by lands ploughed in straight furrows, the ends of which start from the path where you are walking, you will see that continually each pair of furrows seem to approach each other and to join at their ends.

As regards the point that comes to the eye, it may be comprehended with greater ease; for if you look in the eye of anyone you will see your own image there; consequently if you suppose two lines to start from your ears and proceed to the ears of the image which you see of yourself in the eye of the other person, you will clearly recognise that these lines contract so much that when they have continued only a little way beyond your image as mirrored in the said eye they will touch one another in a point.

The thing that is nearer to the eye always appears larger than another of the same size which is more remote.

Perspective is of such a nature that it makes what is flat appear in relief, and what is in relief appear flat.

The perspective by means of which a thing is represented will be better understood when it is seen from the view-point at which it was drawn.

If you wish to represent a thing near, which should produce the effect of natural things, it is impossible for your perspective not to appear false, by reason of all the illusory appearances and errors in proportion of which the existence may be assumed in a mediocre work, unless whoever is looking at this perspective finds himself surveying it from the exact distance, elevation, angle of vision or point at which you were situated to make this perspective. Therefore it would be necessary to make a window of the size of your face or in truth a hole through which you would look at the said work. And if you should do this, then without any doubt your work will produce the effect of nature if the light and shade are correctly rendered, and you will hardly be able to convince yourself that these things are painted. Otherwise do not trouble yourself about representing anything, unless you take your view-point at a distance of at least twenty times the maximum width and height of the thing that you represent; and this will satisfy every beholder who places himself in front of the work at any angle whatever.

If you wish to see a proof of this quickly, take a piece of a staff like a small column eight times

as high as its width without plinth or capital, then measure off on a flat wall forty equal spaces which are in conformity with the spaces; they will make between them forty columns similar to your small column. Then let there be set up in front of the middle of these spaces, at a distance of four braccia from the wall, a thin band of iron, in the centre of which there is a small round hole of the size of a large pearl; place a light beside this hole so as to touch it, then go and place your column above each mark of the wall and draw the outline of the shadow, then shade it and observe it through the hole in the iron.

In Vitolone there are eight hundred and five conclusions about perspective.

Perspective

No visible body can be comprehended and well judged by human eyes, except by the difference of the background where the extremities of this body terminate and are bounded, and so far as its contour lines are concerned no object will seem to be separated from this background. The moon, although far distant from the body of the sun, when by reason of eclipses it finds itself between our eyes and the sun, having the sun for its background will seem to human eyes to be joined and attached to it.

Perspective comes to aid us where judgment fails in things that diminish.

It is possible to bring about that the eye does not see distant objects as much diminished as they are in natural perspective, where they are diminished by reason of the convexity of the eye, which is obliged to intersect upon its surface the pyramids of every kind of image that approach the eye at a right angle. But the method that I show here in the margin cuts these pyramids at right angles near the surface of the pupil. But whereas the convex pupil of the eye can take in the whole of our hemisphere, this will show only a single star; but

where many small stars transmit their images to the surface of the pupil these stars are very small; here only one will be visible but it will be large; and so the moon will be greater in size and its spots more distinct. You should place close to the eye a glass filled with the water mentioned in chapter four of book 113 'Concerning Natural Things', water which causes things congealed in balls of crystalline glass to appear as though they were without glass.

Of the eye. Of bodies less than the pupil of the eye that which is nearest to it will be least discerned by this pupil—and from this experience it follows that the power of sight is not reduced to a point.

But the images of objects which meet in the pupil of the eye are spread over this pupil in the same way as they are spread about in the air; and the proof of this is pointed out to us when we look at the starry heavens without fixing our gaze more upon one star than upon another, for then the sky shows itself to us strewn with stars, and they bear to the eye the same proportions as in the sky, and the spaces between them also are the same.

Natural perspective acts in the opposite way, for the greater the distance the smaller does the thing seen appear, and the less the distance the larger it appears. But this invention constrains the beholder to stand with his eye at a small hole, and then with this small hole it will be seen well. But since many eyes come together to see at the same time one and the same work produced by this art, only one of them will have a good view of the function of this perspective and all the others will only see it confusedly. It is well therefore to shun this compound perspective, and to keep to the simple which does not purport to view planes foreshortened but as far as possible in exact form.

And of this simple perspective in which the plane intersects the pyramid that conveys the images to the eye that are at an equal distance from the visual faculty, an example is afforded us by the curve of the pupil of the eye upon which these pyramids intersect at an equal distance from the visual faculty.

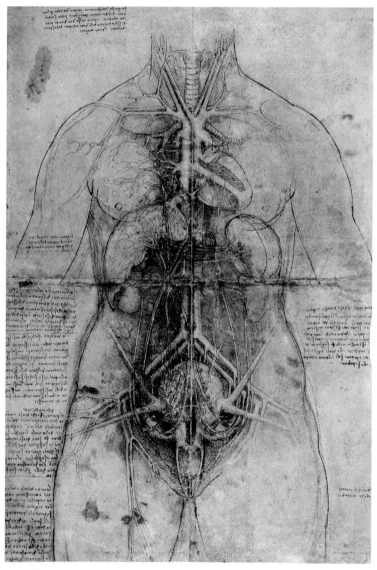

DRAWING OF A WOMAN'S TORSO   LEONARDO DA VINCI

During his period of service to the Duke of Milan, 1482–1499, Leonardo da Vinci began a wide range of scientific studies, in addition to his artistic creativity. These included reflections on geometry, mechanics and architecture, sketches for public works, advanced weapons, and fanciful inventions. He also undertook a series of anatomical studies based on the dissection of human cadavers, an illegal and immoral activity in his day. The "Drawing of a Woman's Torso" is one of the results. What does this sketch reveal about the importance of naturalism in Renaissance art? How might such studies have influenced later developments in the science of human anatomy? What new perspectives does this image cast on the so-called glorification of man during the Renaissance?

Of Equal Things the More Remote Appears Smaller

The practice of perspective is divided into two parts, of which the first treats of all the things seen by the eye at whatsoever distance, and this in itself shows all these things diminished as the eye beholds them, without the man being obliged to stand in one place rather than in another, provided that the wall does not foreshorten it a second time.

But the second practice is a combination of perspective made partly by art and partly by nature, and the work done according to its rules has no part that is not influenced by natural and accidental perspective. Natural perspective I understand has to do with the flat surface on which this perspective is represented; which surface, although it is parallel to it in length and height, is constrained to diminish the distant parts more than its near ones. And this is proved by the first of what has been said above, and its diminution is natural.

Accidental perspective, that is that which is created by art, acts in the contrary way; because it causes bodies equal in themselves to increase on the foreshortened plane, in proportion as the eye is more natural and nearer to the plane, and as the part of this plane where it is represented is more remote from the eye.

*   *   *

REVIEW QUESTIONS

1. According to Leonardo, what is the relationship between perspective in nature and perspective in the human eye?
2. What is the relationship between perspective and mathematical principles?
3. Is perspective a constant or contingent?
4. What implications does this have for painting?
5. How might it shape the enterprise of reading?

BALDESAR CASTIGLIONE

FROM *The Book of the Courtier*

Baldesar Castiglione (1478–1529) was born near Mantua and educated in Milan. He entered the service of the duke of Milan in 1496. After the duke was carried to France as a prisoner, Castiglione returned to Mantua. In 1504, he entered the court of Guidobaldo of Montefeltro, duke of Urbino, where he remained until 1524; this is the setting of The Book of the Courtier. *Although he wrote elegant verse in Latin and Italian, this reflection on courtly life was Castiglione's claim to fame. Fashioned as a discourse among courtiers and ladies of the court, it described the ideal courtier and presented the Renaissance man.*

From *The Book of the Courtier*, by Count Baldesar Castiglione, translated by Leonard Eckstein Opdycke (New York: Charles Scribner's Sons, 1903), pp. 22–23, 25–26, 59, 175–77, 247.

*   *   *

"I wish, then, that this Courtier of ours should be nobly born and of gentle race; because it is far less unseemly for one of ignoble birth to fail in worthy deeds, than for one of noble birth, who, if he strays from the path of his predecessors, stains his family name, and not only fails to achieve but loses what has been achieved already; for noble birth is like a bright lamp that manifests and makes visible good and evil deeds, and kindles and stimulates to virtue both by fear of shame and by hope of praise. And since this splendour of nobility does not illumine the deeds of the humbly born, they lack that stimulus and fear of shame, nor do they feel any obligation to advance beyond what their predecessors have done; while to the nobly born it seems a reproach not to reach at least the goal set them by their ancestors. And thus it nearly always happens that both in the profession of arms and in other worthy pursuits the most famous men have been of noble birth, because nature has implanted in everything that hidden seed which gives a certain force and quality of its own essence to all things that are derived from it, and makes them like itself: as we see not only in the breeds of horses and of other animals, but also in trees, the shoots of which nearly always resemble the trunk; and if they sometimes degenerate, it arises from poor cultivation. And so it is with men, who if rightly trained are nearly always like those from whom they spring, and often better; but if there be no one to give them proper care, they become like savages and never reach perfection.

*   *   *

"But to return to our subject: I say that there is a middle state between perfect grace on the one hand and senseless folly on the other; and those who are not thus perfectly endowed by nature, with study and toil can in great part polish and amend their natural defects. Besides his noble birth, then, I would have the Courtier favoured in this regard also, and endowed by nature not only with talent and beauty of person and feature, but with a certain grace and (as we say) air that shall make him

at first sight pleasing and agreeable to all who see him; and I would have this an ornament that should dispose and unite all his actions, and in his outward aspect give promise of whatever is worthy the society and favour of every great lord." * * *

—"But to come to some details, I am of opinion that the principal and true profession of the Courtier ought to be that of arms; which I would have him follow actively above all else, and be known among others as bold and strong, and loyal to whomsoever he serves. And he will win a reputation for these good qualities by exercising them at all times and in all places, since one may never fail in this without severest censure. And just as among women, their fair fame once sullied never recovers its first lustre, so the reputation of a gentleman who bears arms, if once it be in the least tarnished with cowardice or other disgrace, remains forever infamous before the world and full of ignominy. Therefore the more our Courtier excels in this art, the more he will be worthy of praise; and yet I do not deem essential in him that perfect knowledge of things and those other qualities that befit a commander; since this would be too wide a sea, let us be content, as we have said, with perfect loyalty and unconquered courage, and that he be always seen to possess them. For the courageous are often recognized even more in small things than in great; and frequently in perils of importance and where there are many spectators, some men are to be found, who, although their hearts be dead within them, yet, moved by shame or by the presence of others, press forward almost with their eyes shut, and do their duty God knows how. While on occasions of little moment, when they think they can avoid putting themselves in danger without being detected, they are glad to keep safe. But those who, even when they do not expect to be observed or seen or recognized by anyone, show their ardour and neglect nothing, however paltry, that may be laid to their charge,— they have that strength of mind which we seek in our Courtier.

"Not that we would have him look so fierce, or go about blustering, or say that he has taken his cuirass to wife, or threaten with those grim scowls

that we have often seen in Berto; because to such men as this, one might justly say that which a brave lady jestingly said in gentle company to one whom I will not name at present; who, being invited by her out of compliment to dance, refused not only that, but to listen to the music, and many other entertainments proposed to him,—saying always that such silly trifles were not his business; so that at last the lady said, 'What is your business, then?' He replied with a sour look, 'To fight.' Then the lady at once said, 'Now that you are in no war and out of fighting trim, I should think it were a good thing to have yourself well oiled, and to stow yourself with all your battle harness in a closet until you be needed, lest you grow more rusty than you are;' and so, amid much laughter from the bystanders, she left the discomfited fellow to his silly presumption.

"Therefore let the man we are seeking, be very bold, stern, and always among the first, where the enemy are to be seen; and in every other place, gentle, modest, reserved, above all things avoiding ostentation and that impudent self-praise by which men ever excite hatred and disgust in all who hear them."

*   *   *

"I would have him more than passably accomplished in letters, at least in those studies that are called the humanities, and conversant not only with the Latin language but with the Greek, for the sake of the many different things that have been admirably written therein. Let him be well versed in the poets, and not less in the orators and historians, and also proficient in writing verse and prose, especially in this vulgar tongue of ours; for besides the enjoyment he will find in it, he will by this means never lack agreeable entertainment with ladies, who are usually fond of such things. And if other occupations or want of study prevent his reaching such perfection as to render his writings worthy of great praise, let him be careful to suppress them so that others may not laugh at him, and let him show them only to a friend whom he can trust: because they will at least be of this service to him, that the exercise will enable him to judge the work of others. For it very rarely happens that a man who is not accustomed to write, however learned he may be, can ever quite appreciate the toil and industry of writers, or taste the sweetness and excellence of style, and those latent niceties that are often found in the ancients.

"Moreover these studies will also make him fluent, and as Aristippus said to the tyrant, confident and assured in speaking with everyone. Hence I would have our Courtier keep one precept fixed in mind; which is that in this and everything else he should be always on his guard, and diffident rather than forward, and that he should keep from falsely persuading himself that he knows that which he does not know. * * *

Then my lady Duchess said:

"Do not wander from your subject, my lord Magnifico, but hold to the order given you and describe the Court Lady, to the end that so noble a Lady as this may have someone competent to serve her worthily."

The Magnifico continued:

"Then, my Lady, to show that your commands have power to induce me to essay even that which I know not how to do, I will speak of this excellent Lady as I would have her; and when I have fashioned her to my liking, not being able then to have another such, like Pygmalion I will take her for my own.

"And although my lord Gaspar has said that the same rules which are set the Courtier, serve also for the Lady, I am of another mind; for while some qualities are common to both and as necessary to man as to woman, there are nevertheless some others that befit woman more than man, and some are befitting man to which she ought to be wholly a stranger. The same I say of bodily exercises; but above all, methinks that in her ways, manners, words, gestures and bearing, a woman ought to be very unlike a man; for just as it befits him to show a certain stout and sturdy manliness, so it is becoming in a woman to have a soft and dainty tenderness with an air of womanly sweetness in her every movement, which, in her going or staying or saying what you will, shall always make her seem the woman, without any likeness of a man.

"Now, if this precept be added to the rules that these gentlemen have taught the Courtier, I certainly think she ought to be able to profit by many of them, and to adorn herself with admirable accomplishments, as my lord Gaspar says. For I believe that many faculties of the mind are as necessary to woman as to man; likewise gentle birth, to avoid affectation, to be naturally graceful in all her doings, to be mannerly, clever, prudent, not arrogant, not envious, not slanderous, not vain, not quarrelsome, not silly, to know how to win and keep the favour of her mistress and of all others, to practise well and gracefully the exercises that befit women. I am quite of the opinion, too, that beauty is more necessary to her than to the Courtier, for in truth that woman lacks much who lacks beauty. Then, too, she ought to be more circumspect and take greater care not to give occasion for evil being said of her, and so to act that she may not only escape a stain of guilt but even of suspicion, for a woman has not so many ways of defending herself against false imputations as has a man.

"But as Count Ludovico has explained very minutely the chief profession of the Courtier, and has insisted it be that of arms, methinks it is also fitting to tell what in my judgment is that of the Court Lady: and when I have done this, I shall think myself quit of the greater part of my duty.

"Laying aside, then, those faculties of the mind that she ought to have in common with the Courtier (such as prudence, magnanimity, continence, and many others), and likewise those qualities that befit all women (such as kindness, discretion, ability to manage her husband's property and her house and children if she be married, and all those capacities that are requisite in a good housewife), I say that in a lady who lives at court methinks above all else a certain pleasant affability is befitting, whereby she may be able to entertain politely every sort of man with agreeable and seemly converse, suited to the time and place, and to the rank of the person with whom she may speak, uniting with calm and modest manners, and with that seemliness which should ever dispose all her actions, a quick vivacity of spirit whereby she

may show herself alien to all indelicacy; but with such a kindly manner as shall make us think her no less chaste, prudent and benign, than agreeable, witty and discreet; and so she must preserve a certain mean (difficult and composed almost of contraries), and must barely touch certain limits but not pass them.

"Thus, in her wish to be thought good and pure, the Lady ought not to be so coy and seem so to abhor company and talk that are a little free, as to take her leave as soon as she finds herself therein; for it might easily be thought that she was pretending to be thus austere in order to hide something about herself which she feared others might come to know; and such prudish manners are always odious. Nor ought she, on the other hand, for the sake of showing herself free and agreeable, to utter unseemly words or practise a certain wild and unbridled familiarity and ways likely to make that believed of her which perhaps is not true; but when she is present at such talk, she ought to listen with a little blush and shame.

"Likewise she ought to avoid an errour into which I have seen many women fall, which is that of saying and of willingly listening to evil about other women. For those women who, on hearing the unseemly ways of other women described, grow angry thereat and seem to disbelieve it and to regard it almost monstrous that a woman should be immodest,—they, by accounting the offence so heinous, give reason to think that they do not commit it. But those who go about continually prying into other women's intrigues, and narrate them so minutely and with such zest, seem to be envious of them and to wish that everyone may know it, to the end that like matters may not be reckoned as a fault in their own case; and thus they fall into certain laughs and ways that show they then feel greatest pleasure. And hence it comes that men, while seeming to listen gladly, usually hold such women in small respect and have very little regard for them, and think these ways of theirs are an invitation to advance farther, and thus often go such lengths with them as bring them deserved reproach, and finally esteem them so lightly as to despise their company and even find them tedious.

"And on the other hand, there is no man so shameless and insolent as not to have reverence for those women who are esteemed good and virtuous; because this gravity (tempered with wisdom and goodness) is as it were a shield against the insolence and coarseness of the presumptuous. Thus we see that a word or laugh or act of kindness (however small it be) from a virtuous woman is more prized by everyone, than all the endearments and caresses of those who show their lack of shame so openly; and if they are not immodest, by their unseemly laughter, their loquacity, insolence and like scurrile manners, they give sign of being so. * * *

"I think then that the aim of the perfect Courtier, which has not been spoken of till now, is so to win for himself, by means of the accomplishments ascribed to him by these gentlemen, the favour and mind of the prince whom he serves, that he may be able to say, and always shall say, the truth about everything which it is fitting for the prince to know, without fear or risk of giving offence thereby; and that when he sees his prince's mind inclined to do something wrong, he may be quick to oppose, and gently to make use of the favour acquired by his good accomplishments, so as to banish every bad intent and lead his prince into the path of virtue. And thus, possessing the goodness which these gentlemen have described, together with readiness of wit and pleasantness, and shrewdness and knowledge of letters and many other things,—the Courtier will in every case be able deftly to show the prince how much honour and profit accrue to him and his from justice, liberality, magnanimity, gentleness, and the other virtues that become a good prince; and on the other hand how much infamy and loss proceed from the vices opposed to them. Therefore I think that just as music, festivals, games, and the other pleasant accomplishments are as it were the flower, in like manner to lead or help one's prince towards right, and to frighten him from wrong, are the true fruit of Courtiership.

"And since the merit of well-doing lies chiefly in two things, one of which is the choice of an end for our intentions that shall be truly good, and the other ability to find means suitable and fitting to conduce to that good end marked out,—certain it is that that man's mind tends to the best end, who purposes to see to it that his prince shall be deceived by no one, shall hearken not to flatterers or to slanderers and liars, and shall distinguish good and evil, and love the one and hate the other.

*　　*　　*

REVIEW QUESTIONS

1. What does Castiglione mean by "grace"? How is it created?
2. To what extent is grace the product of birth or nature?
3. How is grace gendered?
4. What does a courtier's conduct tell others about his status?
5. If status was once thought to reside in one's birth and lineage, how does the courtier alter that notion?
6. How does Castiglione's courtier differ from a medieval monk or knight?
7. Is the courtier's virtue the expression of his nature, cultivation, or education?

PORTRAIT OF POPE LEO X AND TWO CARDINALS (1518)   RAPHAEL

This intriguing portrait of Pope Leo X and two of his cardinals, relatives elevated through acts of nepotism, reveals the full sophistication of Raphael's artistry. He created an attractive painting of his patron in full papal regalia. At the same time, he subtly included less attractive hints about the subject's office and character. What might this portrait tell us of Leo's character? What does the portrait tell us about Renaissance values? Is Raphael exercising a subtle criticism of the church through his portrait of its head? If so, what elements of his criticism are explicit in the painting?

GIOVANNI PICO DELLA MIRANDOLA

FROM "Oration on the Dignity of Man"

Giovanni Pico della Mirandola (1463–1494) is a singular figure in the history of Renaissance humanism. Although the corpus of his published works remained small as a result of his early death, the breadth of his learning won him the admiration of scholars past and present. He received a thorough classical education in Greek and Latin, and studied the scholastic tradition of the Middle Ages as well as Jewish and Arabic philosophy. His conception of the dignity of man and harmony among philosophers found expression in his "Oration on the Dignity of Man." In 1486, Pico published his 900 theses, inviting all scholars to a public debate in January 1487. Before it could take place, however, Pope Innocent VIII appointed a commission to examine the theses, some of which were found to be heretical. An attempt to defend the incriminated points plunged Pico into a conflict with ecclesiastical authorities that lasted several years. The oration, never published in its author's lifetime, was written as an introductory speech for the disputation.

From *Reflections on the Philosophy of the History of Mankind,* by J. G. Herder and F. E. Manuel (Chicago: University of Chicago Press, 1968).

I have read in the records of the Arabians, reverend Fathers, that Abdala the Saracen, when questioned as to what on this stage of the world, as it were, could be seen most worthy of wonder, replied: "There is nothing to be seen more wonderful than man." In agreement with this opinion is the saying of Hermes Trismegistus: "A great miracle, Asclepius, is man." But when I weighed the reason for these maxims, the many grounds for the excellence of human nature reported by many men failed to satisfy me—that man is the intermediary between creatures, the intimate of the gods, the king of the lower beings, by the acuteness of his senses, by the discernment of his reason, and by the light of his intelligence the interpreter of nature, the interval between fixed eternity and fleeting time, and (as the Persians say) the bond, nay, rather, the marriage song of the world, on David's testimony but little lower than the angels. Admittedly great though these reasons be, they are not the principal grounds, that is, those which may rightfully claim for themselves the privilege of the highest admiration. For why should we not admire more the angels themselves and the blessed choirs of heaven? At last it seems to me I have come to understand why man is the most fortunate of creatures and consequently worthy of all admiration and what precisely is that rank which is his lot in the universal chain of Being—a rank to be envied not only by brutes but even by the stars and by minds beyond this world. It is a matter past faith and a wondrous one. Why should it not be? For it is on this very account that man is rightly called and judged a great miracle and a wonderful creature indeed.

But hear, Fathers, exactly what this rank is and, as friendly auditors, conformably to your kindness, do me this favor. God the Father, the supreme Architect, had already built this cosmic home we behold, the most sacred temple of His godhead, by the laws of His mysterious wisdom. The region above the heavens He had adorned with

Intelligences, the heavenly spheres He had quick-ened with eternal souls, and the excrementary and filthy parts of the lower world He had filled with a multitude of animals of every kind. But, when the work was finished, the Craftsman kept wishing that there were someone to ponder the plan of so great a work, to love its beauty, and to wonder at its vast-ness. Therefore, when everything was done (as Moses and Timaeus bear witness), He finally took thought concerning the creation of man. But there was not among His archetypes that from which He could fashion a new offspring, nor was there in His treasure-houses anything which He might bestow on His new son as an inheritance, nor was there in the seats of all the world a place where the latter might sit to contemplate the universe. All was now complete; all things had been assigned to the highest, the middle, and the lowest orders. But in its final creation it was not the part of the Father's power to fail as though exhausted. It was not the part of His wisdom to waver in a needful matter through poverty of counsel. It was not the part of His kindly love that he who was to praise God's divine generosity in regard to others should be compelled to condemn it in regard to himself.

At last the best of artisans ordained that that creature to whom He had been able to give noth-ing proper to himself should have joint possession of whatever had been peculiar to each of the dif-ferent kinds of being. He therefore took man as a creature of indeterminate nature and, assigning him a place in the middle of the world, addressed him thus: "Neither a fixed abode nor a form that is thine alone nor any function peculiar to thyself have we given thee, Adam, to the end that accord-ing to thy longing and according to thy judgment thou mayest have and possess what abode, what form, and what functions thou thyself shalt desire. The nature of all other beings is limited and con-strained within the bounds of laws prescribed by Us. Thou, constrained by no limits, in accordance with thine own free will, in whose hand We have placed thee, shalt ordain for thyself the limits of thy nature. We have set thee at the world's center that thou mayest from thence more easily observe whatever is in the world. We have made thee nei-ther of heaven nor of earth, neither mortal nor im-mortal, so that with freedom of choice and with honor, as though the maker and molder of thyself, thou mayest fashion thyself in whatever shape thou shalt prefer. Thou shalt have the power to degener-ate into the lower forms of life, which are brutish. Thou shalt have the power, out of thy soul's judg-ment, to be reborn into the higher forms, which are divine."

O supreme generosity of God the Father, O highest and most marvelous felicity of man! To him it is granted to have whatever he chooses, to be whatever he wills. Beasts as soon as they are born (so says Lucilius) bring with them from their mother's womb all they will ever possess. Spiritual beings, either from the beginning or soon there-after, become what they are to be for ever and ever. On man when he came into life the Father conferred the seeds of all kinds and the germs of every way of life. Whatever seeds each man cul-tivates will grow to maturity and bear in him their own fruit. If they be vegetative, he will be like a plant. If sensitive, he will become brutish. If ra-tional, he will grow into a heavenly being. If in-tellectual, he will be an angel and the son of God. And if, happy in the lot of no created thing, he withdraws into the center of his own unity, his spirit, made one with God, in the solitary darkness of God, who is set above all things, shall surpass them all. Who would not admire this our cha-meleon? Or who could more greatly admire aught else whatever? It is man who Asclepius of Athens, arguing from his mutability of character and from his self-transforming nature, on just grounds says was symbolized by Proteus in the mysteries. Hence those metamorphoses renowned among the He-brews and the Pythagoreans.

*   *   *

REVIEW QUESTIONS

1. How does Pico reorder the hierarchy of cre-ation?

2. What does he claim for human nature that sets it apart?
3. How does Pico conceive of human will?
4. What implications does that conception have?

5. What is Pico's understanding of the relationship of humankind to God?
6. What are its implications?

NICCOLÒ MACHIAVELLI

FROM *The Prince*

Niccolò Machiavelli (1469–1527) was the son of a Florentine lawyer. Little is known of him until 1498, when he entered the service of the Florentine Republic of Pier Soderini as secretary to the second chancery, a minor bureaucratic post he held for fourteen years. From this position, Machiavelli observed the political process of his day. A staunch republican, he lost his position in government in 1512, when Soderini's republic was toppled and the Medici of Florence were restored to power by a papal army. He spent the rest of his days in retirement, possibly trying to restore himself to the graces of the Medici and the pope, but certainly engaged in the scholarly and literary pursuits that would establish his reputation as a political analyst. Among the fruits of these labors was The Prince, *written in 1513. Of the many observations and ideas expressed in this short work, two at least became fundamental truths of modern politics. One was the necessity of national unity based on a common language, culture, and economy. The other was the preservation of national unity through the concentration and exercise of power by the state. As controversial as they were prescient in Machiavelli's day, these ideas encouraged later scholars to number him among the first modern students of politics.*

From *The Prince*, by Niccolò Machiavelli, translated by Robert M. Adams, A Norton Critical Edition, 2d ed. (New York: Norton, 1977), pp. 31–32, 44–50.

How to Measure the Strength of Any Prince's State

There is one other consideration to bear in mind regarding these civil principates; that is, whether a prince is strong enough to stand on his own feet in case of need, or whether he is in constant need of help from others. And to make the matter clearer, let me say that in my opinion princes control their own destiny when they command enough money or men to assemble an adequate army and make a stand against anyone who attacks them. I think princes who need outside protection are those who can't take the field against their foes, but have to hide behind their walls and defend themselves there. I've already mentioned

the first class, and will save whatever else I have to say about them till later. As for the others, all I can say is that they should keep their cities well fortified and well supplied, and pay no heed to the surrounding countryside. Whenever a man has fortified his city strongly, and has dealt with his subjects as I described above and will describe further below, people will be slow to attack him; men are always wary of tasks that seem hard, and it can't seem easy to attack a prince whose city is in fine fettle, and whose people do not hate him.

*   *   *

Thus a prince who has a strong city and does not earn his people's hatred cannot be attacked, or if he were, that attacker would be driven off to his own disgrace; because the way things keep changing in this world, it's almost impossible for a prince with his armies to devote an entire year to a siege while doing nothing else. Maybe someone will object: when the people see their possessions outside the walls being burnt up, they will get impatient; a long siege and their own self-interest will make them forget the prince. But to this I answer that a brave, strong prince will overcome all these problems, giving his subjects hope at one minute that the storm will soon pass, stirring them up at another moment to fear the enemy's cruelty, and on still other occasions restraining those who seem too rash. Besides, the enemy will generally do his burning and ravishing of the countryside as soon as he begins the siege, when men's minds are still passionate and earnest for the defense; thus the prince has less reason to worry, because, after a few days, when tempers have cooled, the harm will already have been done, the losses inflicted, and there will clearly be no cure. At that point, the people will rally even more strongly behind their prince, because they will feel he owes them something, since their houses were burnt and their fields ravaged in defense of his cause. Indeed, men are so constructed that they feel themselves committed as much by the benefits they grant as by those they receive. Hence, all things considered, it should not be hard for a prudent prince to keep his subjects in good

spirits throughout a siege, as long as he does not run short of food or weapons.

*   *   *

On the Reasons Why Men Are Praised or Blamed—Especially Princes

It remains now to be seen what style and principles a prince ought to adopt in dealing with his subjects and friends. I know the subject has been treated frequently before, and I'm afraid people will think me rash for trying to do so again, especially since I intend to differ in this discussion from what others have said. But since I intend to write something useful to an understanding reader, it seemed better to go after the real truth of the matter than to repeat what people have imagined. A great many men have imagined states and princedoms such as nobody ever saw or knew in the real world, for there's such a difference between the way we really live and the way we ought to live that the man who neglects the real to study the ideal will learn how to accomplish his ruin, not his salvation. Any man who tries to be good all the time is bound to come to ruin among the great number who are not good. Hence a prince who wants to keep his post must learn how not to be good, and use that knowledge, or refrain from using it, as necessity requires.

Putting aside, then, all the imaginary things that are said about princes, and getting down to the truth, let me say that whenever men are discussed (and especially princes because they are prominent), there are certain qualities that bring them either praise or blame. Thus some are considered generous, others stingy (I use a Tuscan term, since "greedy" in our speech means a man who wants to take other people's goods; we call a man "stingy" who clings to his own); some are givers, others grabbers; some cruel, others merciful; one man is treacherous, another faithful; one is feeble and effeminate, another fierce and spirited; one humane, another proud; one lustful, another chaste; one straightforward, another sly; one

harsh, another gentle; one serious, another playful; one religious, another skeptical, and so on. I know everyone will agree that among these many qualities a prince certainly ought to have all those that are considered good. But since it is impossible to have and exercise them all, because the conditions of human life simply do not allow it, a prince must be shrewd enough to avoid the public disgrace of those vices that would lose him his state. If he possibly can, he should also guard against vices that will not lose him his state; but if he cannot prevent them, he should not be too worried about indulging them. And furthermore, he should not be too worried about incurring blame for any vice without which he would find it hard to save his state. For if you look at matters carefully, you will see that something resembling virtue, if you follow it, may be your ruin, while something else resembling vice will lead, if you follow it, to your security and well-being.

On Liberality and Stinginess

Let me begin, then, with the first of the qualities mentioned above, by saying that a reputation for liberality is doubtless very fine; but the generosity that earns you that reputation can do you great harm. For if you exercise your generosity in a really virtuous way, as you should, nobody will know of it, and you cannot escape the odium of the opposite vice. Hence if you wish to be widely known as a generous man, you must seize every opportunity to make a big display of your giving. A prince of this character is bound to use up his entire revenue in works of ostentation. Thus, in the end, if he wants to keep a name for generosity, he will have to load his people with exorbitant taxes and squeeze money out of them in every way he can. This is the first step in making him odious to his subjects; for when he is poor, nobody will respect him. Then, when his generosity has angered many and brought rewards to a few, the slightest difficulty will trouble him, and at the first approach of danger, down he goes. If by chance he foresees this, and tries to change his ways, he will immediately be labelled a miser.

Since a prince cannot use this virtue [*virtù*] of liberality in such a way as to become known for it unless he harms his own security, he won't mind, if he judges prudently of things, being known as a miser. In due course he will be thought the more liberal man, when people see that his parsimony enables him to live on his income, to defend himself against his enemies, and to undertake major projects without burdening his people with taxes. Thus he will be acting liberally toward all those people from whom he takes nothing (and there are an immense number of them), and in a stingy way toward those people on whom he bestows nothing (and they are very few). In our times, we have seen great things being accomplished only by men who have had the name of misers; all the others have gone under. Pope Julius II, though he used his reputation as a generous man to gain the papacy, sacrificed it in order to be able to make war; the present king of France has waged many wars without levying a single extra tax on his people, simply because he could take care of the extra expenses out of the savings from his long parsimony. If the present king of Spain had a reputation for generosity, he would never have been able to undertake so many campaigns, or win so many of them.

*   *   *

On Cruelty and Clemency: Whether It Is Better to Be Loved or Feared

Continuing now with our list of qualities, let me say that every prince should prefer to be considered merciful rather than cruel, yet he should be careful not to mismanage this clemency of his. People thought Cesare Borgia was cruel, but that cruelty of his reorganized the Romagna, united it, and established it in peace and loyalty. Anyone who views the matter realistically will see that this prince was much more merciful than the people of Florence, who, to avoid the reputation of cruelty, allowed Pistoia to be destroyed. Thus, no prince should mind being called cruel for what he

does to keep his subjects united and loyal; he may make examples of a very few, but he will be more merciful in reality than those who, in their tenderheartedness, allow disorders to occur, with their attendant murders and lootings. Such turbulence brings harm to an entire community, while the executions ordered by a prince affect only one individual at a time. A new prince, above all others, cannot possibly avoid a name for cruelty, since new states are always in danger. And Virgil, speaking through the mouth of Dido, says:

Res dura et regni novitas me talia cogunt
Moliri, et late fines custode tueri.[1]

Yet a prince should be slow to believe rumors and to commit himself to action on the basis of them. He should not be afraid of his own thoughts; he ought to proceed cautiously, moderating his conduct with prudence and humanity, allowing neither overconfidence to make him careless, nor overtimidity to make him intolerable.

Here the question arises: is it better to be loved than feared, or vice versa? I don't doubt that every prince would like to be both; but since it is hard to accommodate these qualities, if you have to make a choice, to be feared is much safer than to be loved. For it is a good general rule about men, that they are ungrateful, fickle, liars and deceivers, fearful of danger and greedy for gain. While you serve their welfare, they are all yours, offering their blood, their belongings, their lives, and their children's lives, as we noted above—so long as the danger is remote. But when the danger is close at hand, they turn against you. Then, any prince who has relied on their words and has made no other preparations will come to grief; because friendships that are bought at a price, and not with greatness and nobility of soul, may be paid for but they are not acquired, and they cannot be used in time of need. People are less concerned with offending a man who makes himself loved than one

who makes himself feared: the reason is that love is a link of obligation which men, because they are rotten, will break any time they think doing so serves their advantage; but fear involves dread of punishment, from which they can never escape.

Still, a prince should make himself feared in such a way that, even if he gets no love, he gets no hate either; because it is perfectly possible to be feared and not hated, and this will be the result if only the prince will keep his hands off the property of his subjects or citizens, and off their women. When he does have to shed blood, he should be sure to have a strong justification and manifest cause; but above all, he should not confiscate people's property, because men are quicker to forget the death of a father than the loss of a patrimony. Besides, pretexts for confiscation are always plentiful; it never fails that a prince who starts living by plunder can find reasons to rob someone else. Excuses for proceeding against someone's life are much rarer and more quickly exhausted.

*   *   *

Returning to the question of being feared or loved, I conclude that since men love at their own inclination but can be made to fear at the inclination of the prince, a shrewd prince will lay his foundations on what is under his own control, not on what is controlled by others. He should simply take pains not to be hated, as I said.

The Way Princes Should Keep Their Word

How praiseworthy it is for a prince to keep his word and live with integrity rather than by craftiness, everyone understands; yet we see from recent experience that those princes have accomplished most who paid little heed to keeping their promises, but who knew how craftily to manipulate the minds of men. In the end, they won out over those who tried to act honestly.

You should consider then, that there are two

---

[1] "Severe pressures and the newness of the regime compel me to these measures. I must maintain the borders against foreign enemies."

ways of fighting, one with laws and the other with force. The first is properly a human method, the second belongs to beasts. But as the first method does not always suffice, you sometimes have to turn to the second. Thus a prince must know how to make good use of both the beast and the man. Ancient writers made subtle note of this fact when they wrote that Achilles and many other princes of antiquity were sent to be reared by Chiron the centaur, who trained them in his discipline. Having a teacher who is half man and half beast can only mean that a prince must know how to use both these two natures, and that one without the other has no lasting effect.

Since a prince must know how to use the character of beasts, he should pick for imitation the fox and the lion. As the lion cannot protect himself from traps, and the fox cannot defend himself from wolves, you have to be a fox in order to be wary of traps, and a lion to overawe the wolves. Those who try to live by the lion alone are badly mistaken. Thus a prudent prince cannot and should not keep his word when to do so would

go against his interest, or when the reasons that made him pledge it no longer apply. Doubtless if all men were good, this rule would be bad; but since they are a sad lot, and keep no faith with you, you in your turn are under no obligation to keep it with them.

*   *   *

REVIEW QUESTIONS

1. What, according to Machiavelli, is the basis of political authority?
2. How does his theory differ from others of his day?
3. When he claims that a prince must assume many guises, what is Machiavelli saying about his understanding of human nature?
4. What is the role of artifice in political authority?
5. What might Machiavelli's prince have in common with Castiglione's courtier?

DESIDERIUS ERASMUS OF ROTTERDAM

FROM *Ten Colloquies*

Desiderius Erasmus of Rotterdam (1476–1536) was one of the greatest scholars of his day, measured in terms of his writings and their influence. Educated at Deventer in the Netherlands and in Paris, he began his career as an editor, translator, and popularizer of classical texts. In the humanistic tradition, he used classical tropes as models for his own society, a practice that made him not only a great scholar but also a great satirist. His chief intellectual commitment, however, was the renewal of Christian piety through the study of Christian literature, the Bible and church fathers above all. In this context he is often viewed as the great exponent of Christian humanism, the northern European variant of classical Italian humanism. His translation of the Bible inspired the biblical scholarship of sixteenth-century reformers. His editions of patristic sources remain authoritative to this day. His Ten

Colloquies *were written as popular texts to inculcate elegant Latin and to inspire Christian conduct.*

From *Ten Colloquies*, by Desiderius Erasmus, translated by Craig R. Thompson (Upper Saddle River, N.J.: Prentice Hall, 1986).

"Cyclops, or the Gospel Bearer"

CANNIUS: What's Polyphemus hunting here?

POLYPHEMUS: What could I be hunting without dogs or spear? Is that your question?

CANNIUS: Some wood nymph, perhaps.

POLYPHEMUS: A good guess. Look, here's my hunting net.

CANNIUS: What a sight! Bacchus in a lion's skin —Polyphemus with a book—a cat in a saffron gown!

POLYPHEMUS: I've painted this little book not only in saffron but bright red and blue, too.

CANNIUS: I'm not talking about saffron; I said something in Greek. Seems to be a soldierly book, for it's protected by bosses, plates, and brass clasps.

POLYPHEMUS: Take a good look at it.

CANNIUS: I'm looking. Very fine, but you haven't yet decorated it enough.

POLYPHEMUS: What's lacking?

CANNIUS: You should have added your coat of arms.

POLYPHEMUS: What coat of arms?

CANNIUS: The head of Silenus peering out of a wine jug. But what's the book about? The art of drinking?

POLYPHEMUS: Be careful you don't blurt out blasphemy.

CANNIUS: What, you don't mean it's something sacred?

POLYPHEMUS: The most sacred of all, the Gospels.

CANNIUS: By Hercules! What has Polyphemus to do with the Gospels?

POLYPHEMUS: You might as well ask what a Christian has to do with Christ.

CANNIUS: I'm not sure a halberd isn't more fitting for the likes of you. If I were at sea and met a stranger who looked like this, I'd take him for a pirate; if I met him in a wood, for a bandit.

POLYPHEMUS: Yet this very Gospel teaches us not to judge a man by appearances. Just as a haughty spirit often lurks under an ash-colored cowl, so a cropped head, curled beard, stern brow, wild eyes, plumed cap, military cloak, and slashed breeches sometimes cover a true Christian heart.

CANNIUS: Of course. Sometimes a sheep lurks in wolf's clothing, too. And if you trust fables, an ass in a lion's skin.

POLYPHEMUS: What's more, I know a man who has a sheep's head and a fox's heart. I could wish him friends as fair as his eyes are dark, and a character as shining as his complexion.

CANNIUS: If a man with a sheepskin cap has a sheep's head, what a load *you* carry, with both a sheep and an ostrich on your head. And isn't it rather ridiculous to have a bird on your head and an ass in your heart?

POLYPHEMUS: That hurt!

CANNIUS: But it would be well if, as you've decorated the Gospels with various ornaments, the Gospels in turn adorned you. You've decorated them with colors; I wish they might embellish you with good morals.

POLYPHEMUS: I'll take care of that.

CANNIUS: After your fashion, yes.

POLYPHEMUS: But insults aside, you don't condemn those who carry a volume of the Gospels about, do you?

CANNIUS: I'd be the last person in the world to do that.

POLYPHEMUS: What? I seem to you the least person in the world, when I'm taller than you by an ass's head?

CANNIUS: I don't believe you'd be that much taller even if the ass pricked up its ears.

POLYPHEMUS: Certainly by a buffalo's.

CANNIUS: I like the comparison. But I said "last"; I wasn't calling you "least."

POLYPHEMUS: What's the difference between an egg and an egg?

CANNIUS: What's the difference between middle finger and little finger?

POLYPHEMUS: The middle one's longer.

CANNIUS: Very good! What's the difference between ass ears and wolf ears?

POLYPHEMUS: Wolf ears are shorter.

CANNIUS: That's right.

POLYPHEMUS: But I'm in the habit of measuring long and short by span and ell, not by ears.

CANNIUS: Well, the man who carried Christ was called Christopher. You, who carry the Gospels, ought to be called Gospel-bearer instead of Polyphemus.

POLYPHEMUS: Don't you think it's holy to carry the Gospels?

CANNIUS: No—unless you'd agree that asses are mighty holy.

POLYPHEMUS: How so?

CANNIUS: Because one of them can carry three thousand books of this kind. I should think you'd be equal to that load if fitted with the right packsaddle.

POLYPHEMUS: There's nothing farfetched in thus crediting an ass with holiness because he carried Christ.

CANNIUS: I don't envy you that holiness. And if you like, I'll give you relics of the ass that carried Christ, so you can kiss them.

POLYPHEMUS: A gift I'll be glad to get. For by touching the body of Christ that ass was consecrated.

CANNIUS: Obviously those who smote Christ touched him too.

POLYPHEMUS: But tell me seriously, isn't carrying the Gospel about a reverent thing to do?

CANNIUS: Reverent if done sincerely, without hypocrisy.

POLYPHEMUS: Let monks have hypocrisy! What has a soldier to do with hypocrisy?

CANNIUS: But first tell me what hypocrisy is.

POLYPHEMUS: Professing something other than what you really mean.

CANNIUS: But what does carrying a copy of the Gospels profess? A gospel life, doesn't it?

POLYPHEMUS: I suppose so.

CANNIUS: Therefore, when the life doesn't correspond to the book, isn't that hypocrisy?

POLYPHEMUS: Apparently. But what is it truly to bear the Gospel?

CANNIUS: Some bear it in their hands, as the Franciscans do their Rule. Parisian porters, and asses and geldings, can do the same. There are those who bear it in their mouths, harping on nothing but Christ and the Gospel. That's pharisaical. Some bear it in their hearts. The true Gospel bearer, then, is one who carries it in hands and mouth *and* heart.

POLYPHEMUS: Where are these?

CANNIUS: In churches—the deacons, who bear the book, read it to the congregation, and have it by heart.

POLYPHEMUS: Though not all who bear the Gospel in their hearts are devout.

CANNIUS: Don't quibble. A man doesn't bear it in his heart unless he loves it through and through. Nobody loves it wholeheartedly unless he emulates the Gospel in his manner of living.

POLYPHEMUS: I don't follow these subtleties.

CANNIUS: But I'll tell you more bluntly. If you carry a jar of Beaune wine on your shoulder, it's just a burden, isn't it?

POLYPHEMUS: That's all.

CANNIUS: But if you hold the wine in your throat, and presently spit it out?

POLYPHEMUS: Useless—though, really, I'm not accustomed to doing that!

CANNIUS: But if—as you *are* accustomed—you take a long drink?

POLYPHEMUS: Nothing more heavenly.

CANNIUS: Your whole body glows; your face turns rosy; your expression grows merry.

POLYPHEMUS: Exactly.

CANNIUS: The Gospel has the same effect when it penetrates the heart. It makes a new man of you.

POLYPHEMUS: So I don't seem to you to live according to the Gospel?

CANNIUS: You can best decide that question yourself.

POLYPHEMUS: If it could be decided with a battle-ax—

CANNIUS: If someone called you a liar or a rake to your face, what would you do?

POLYPHEMUS: What would I do? He'd feel my fists.

CANNIUS: What if someone hit you hard?

POLYPHEMUS: I'd break his neck for that.

CANNIUS: But your book teaches you to repay insults with a soft answer; and "Whosoever shall smite thee on thy right cheek, turn to him the other also."

POLYPHEMUS: I've read that, but it slipped my mind.

CANNIUS: You pray frequently, I dare say.

POLYPHEMUS: That's pharisaical.

CANNIUS: Long-winded but ostentatious praying is pharisaical. But your book teaches us to pray without ceasing, yet sincerely.

POLYPHEMUS: Still, I do pray sometimes.

CANNIUS: When?

POLYPHEMUS: Whenever I think of it—once or twice a week.

CANNIUS: What do you pray?

POLYPHEMUS: The Lord's Prayer.

CANNIUS: How often?

POLYPHEMUS: Once. For the Gospel forbids vain repetitions as "much speaking."

CANNIUS: Can you concentrate on the Lord's Prayer while repeating it?

POLYPHEMUS: Never tried. Isn't it enough to say the words?

CANNIUS: I don't know, except that God hears only the utterance of the heart. Do you fast often?

POLYPHEMUS: Never.

CANNIUS: But your book recommends prayer and fasting.

POLYPHEMUS: I'd recommend them too, if my belly did not demand something else.

CANNIUS: But Paul says that those who serve their bellies aren't serving Jesus Christ. Do you eat meat on any day whatever?

POLYPHEMUS: Any day it's offered.

CANNIUS: Yet a man as tough as you are could live on hay or the bark of trees.

POLYPHEMUS: But Christ said that a man is not defiled by what he eats.

CANNIUS: True, if it's eaten in moderation, without giving offense. But Paul, the disciple of Christ, prefers starvation to offending a weak brother by his food; and he calls upon us to follow his example, in order that we may please all men in all things.

POLYPHEMUS: Paul's Paul, and I'm me.

CANNIUS: But Egon's job is to feed she-goats.

POLYPHEMUS: I'd rather eat one.

CANNIUS: A fine wish! You'll be a billygoat rather than a she-goat.

POLYPHEMUS: I said *eat* one, not *be* one.

CANNIUS: Very prettily said. Are you generous to the poor?

POLYPHEMUS: I've nothing to give.

CANNIUS: But you would have, if you lived soberly and worked hard.

POLYPHEMUS: I'm fond of loafing.

CANNIUS: Do you keep God's commandments?

POLYPHEMUS: That's tiresome.

CANNIUS: Do you do penance for your sins?

POLYPHEMUS: Christ has paid for us.

CANNIUS: Then why do you insist you love the Gospel?

POLYPHEMUS: I'll tell you. A certain Franciscan in our neighborhood kept babbling from the pulpit against Erasmus' New Testament. I met the man privately, grabbed him by the hair with my left hand, and punched him with my right. I gave him a hell of a beating; made his whole face swell. What do you say to that? Isn't that promoting the Gospel? Next I gave him absolution by banging him on the head three times with this very same book, raising three lumps, in the name of Father, Son, and Holy Ghost.

CANNIUS: The evangelical spirit, all right! This is certainly defending the Gospel with the Gospel.

POLYPHEMUS: I ran across another member of the same order who never stopped raving against Erasmus. Fired with evangelical zeal, I threatened the fellow so much he begged pardon on both knees and admitted the devil had put him up to saying what he said. If he hadn't done this, my halberd would have bounced against his head. I looked as fierce as Mars in battle. This took place before witnesses.

CANNIUS: I'm surprised the man didn't drop dead on the spot. But let's go on. Do you live chastely?

POLYPHEMUS: I may when I'm old. But shall I confess the truth to you, Cannius?

CANNIUS: I'm no priest. If you want to confess, find somebody else.

POLYPHEMUS: Usually I confess to God, but to you I admit I'm not yet a perfect follower of the Gospel; just an ordinary fellow. My kind have four Gospels. Four things above all we Gospelers seek: full bellies; plenty of work for the organs below the belly; a livelihood from somewhere or other; finally, freedom to do as we please. If we get these, we shout in our cups, "Io, triumph; Io, Paean! The Gospel flourishes! Christ reigns!"

CANNIUS: That's an Epicurean life, surely, not an evangelical one.

POLYPHEMUS: I don't deny it, but you know Christ is omnipotent and can turn us into other men in the twinkling of an eye.

CANNIUS: Into swine, too, which I think is more likely than into good men.

POLYPHEMUS: I wish there were no worse creatures in the world than swine, oxen, asses, and camels! You can meet many men who are fiercer than lions, greedier than wolves, more lecherous than sparrows, more snappish than dogs, more venomous than vipers.

CANNIUS: But now it's time for you to begin changing from brute to man.

POLYPHEMUS: You do well to warn me, for prophets these days declare the end of the world is at hand.

CANNIUS: All the more reason to hurry.

POLYPHEMUS: I await the hand of Christ.

CANNIUS: See that you are pliant material for his hand! But where do they get the notion that the end of the world is near?

POLYPHEMUS: They say it's because men are behaving now just as they did before the Flood overwhelmed them. They feast, drink, stuff themselves, marry and are given in marriage, whore, buy, sell, pay and charge interest, build buildings. Kings make war, priests are zealous to increase their wealth, theologians invent syllogisms, monks roam through the world, the commons riot, Erasmus writes colloquies. In short, no calamity is lacking: hunger, thirst, robbery, war, plague, sedition, poverty. Doesn't this prove human affairs are at an end?

CANNIUS: In this mass of woes, what worries you most?

POLYPHEMUS: Guess.

CANNIUS: That your purse is full of cobwebs.

POLYPHEMUS: Damned if you haven't hit it!— Just now I'm on my way back from a drinking party. Some other time, when I'm more sober, I'll argue with you about the Gospel, if you like.

CANNIUS: When shall I see you sober?

POLYPHEMUS: When I'm sober.

CANNIUS: When will you be so?

POLYPHEMUS: When you see me so. Meantime, my dear Cannius, good luck.

CANNIUS: I hope you, in turn, become what you're called.

POLYPHEMUS: To prevent you from outdoing me in courtesy, I pray that Cannius, as the name implies, may never be lacking a can!

REVIEW QUESTIONS

1. Why does Erasmus use the dialogue form?
2. What might he be saying, not only about his readers but also about voice and perspective?
3. What is the older mode of Christianity that Erasmus parodies?
4. What is wrong with it?
5. What ideal of Christian behavior emerges in the colloquy?
6. How might it differ from the older form?
7. How might it be better suited to the instabilities of life in Renaissance Europe?

SIR THOMAS MORE

FROM *Utopia*

Sir Thomas More (1478–1535) was born on Milk Street, in London, the "brightest star that ever shined in the via lactea," *according to Thomas Fuller. His father, John More, was a butler at Lincoln's Inn, later raised to the knighthood and made a judge first in the court of common pleas and later on the king's bench. The son was educated in the household of John Morton, archbishop of Canterbury, and at Christ Church, Oxford. Compelled by his father to study law, More entered New Inn in 1494 and Lincoln's Inn in 1496. He lived with the monks at the London Charterhouse and developed there the discipline and devotion that would serve him well in later troubles. Yet he decided on married rather than monastic life. He wed Jane Colet in 1505 and they had four children. More was an early advocate of education for women; he insisted that his son and daughters be taught by the best tutors available. Despite his many interests—intellectual, religious, and domestic—the law remained his career. City, monarchy, and church called on his services.*

He was part of a London trade delegation to the cities of the Hanse in 1515. During this service, he wrote Book II of Utopia, *describing a pagan, communist city-state in which all policies and institutions were governed by reason. Such a state contrasted notably with the polity of Christian Europe with its greed, self-interest, and violence, as More described it in Book I. The complete work, which drew heavily on descriptions of the new world as well as passages from classical literature, was published in 1516 in Louvain. It established More's international reputation as a man of letters. But public affairs constantly drew him out of his study. In 1523, he served as speaker of the House of Commons, and in 1529, he succeeded Cardinal Wolsey as lord chancellor under Henry VIII. The king favored More, keeping him in attendance, visiting him at home, and enjoying his learned conversation. They fell out over Henry's growing dispute with the Catholic Church. More resigned his office in 1532, the day after the clergy were deprived of the power to enact constitutions without royal consent. Refusal to swear the Oath of Supremacy in 1534, by which he would have recognized Henry as the supreme head of the church in England, made More guilty of treason. He was martyred in 1535, in his own words "the king's good servant but God's first."*

From *Utopia*, by Sir Thomas More, translated by Robert M. Adams, A Norton Critical Edition, 2d ed. (New York: Norton, 1975), pp. 30–33, 40–42, 50–51, 64.

*   *   *

"But as a matter of fact, my dear More, to tell you what I really think, as long as you have private property, and as long as cash money is the measure of all things, it is really not possible for a nation to be governed justly or happily. For justice cannot exist where all the best things in life are held by the worst citizens; nor can anyone be happy where property is limited

to a few, since those few are always uneasy and the many are utterly wretched.

"So I reflect on the wonderfully wise and sacred institutions of the Utopians who are so well governed with so few laws. Among them virtue has its reward, yet everything is shared equally, and all men live in plenty. I contrast them with the many other nations which are constantly passing new ordinances and yet can never order their affairs satisfactorily. In these other nations, whatever a man can get he calls his own private property; but all the mass of laws old and new don't enable him to secure his own, or defend it, or even distinguish it from someone else's property. Different men lay claim, successively or all at once, to the same property; and thus arise innumerable and interminable lawsuits—fresh ones every day. When I consider all these things, I become more sympathetic to Plato and do not wonder that he declined to make laws for any people who refused to share their goods equally. Wisest of men, he easily perceived that the one and only road to the welfare of all lies through the absolute equality of goods. I doubt whether such equality can ever be achieved where property belongs to individual men. However abundant goods may be, when every man tries to get as much as he can for his own exclusive use, a handful of men end up sharing the whole thing, and the rest are left in poverty. The result generally is two sorts of people whose fortunes ought to be interchanged: the rich are rapacious, wicked, and useless, while the poor are unassuming, modest men who work hard, more for the benefit of the public than of themselves.

"Thus I am wholly convinced that unless private property is entirely done away with, there can be no fair or just distribution of goods, nor can mankind be happily governed. As long as private property remains, by far the largest and the best part of mankind will be oppressed by a heavy and inescapable burden of cares and anxieties. This load, I admit, may be lightened a little bit under the present system, but I maintain it cannot be entirely removed. Laws might be made that no one should own more than a certain amount of land or receive more than a certain income. Or laws might be passed to prevent the prince from becoming too powerful and the populace too unruly. It might be made unlawful for public offices to be solicited, or put up for sale, or made burdensome for the officeholder by great expense. Otherwise, officeholders are tempted to get their money back by fraud or extortion, and only rich men can afford to seek positions which ought to be held by wise men. Laws of this sort, I agree, may have as much effect as good and careful nursing has on men who are chronically or even terminally sick. The social evils I mentioned may be alleviated and their effects mitigated for a while, but so long as private property remains, there is no hope at all of effecting a cure and restoring society to good health. While you try to cure one part, you aggravate the disease in other parts. Suppressing one symptom causes another to break out, since you cannot give something to one man without taking it away from someone else."

"But I don't see it that way," I replied. "It seems to me that men cannot possibly live well where all things are in common. How can there be plenty of commodities where every man stops working? The hope of gain will not spur him on; he will rely on others, and become lazy. If a man is driven by want of something to produce it, and yet cannot legally protect what he has gained, what can follow but continual bloodshed and turmoil, especially when respect for magistrates and their authority has been lost? I for one cannot conceive of authority existing among men who are equal to one another in every respect."

*   *   *

"As for the relative ages of the governments," Raphael replied, "you might judge more accurately if you had read their histories. If we believe these records, they had cities before there were even human inhabitants here. What ingenuity has discovered or chance hit upon could have turned up just as well in one place as the other. As a matter of fact, I believe we surpass them in natural intelligence, but they leave us far behind in their diligence and zeal to learn.

"According to their chronicles, they had heard nothing of men-from-beyond-the-equator (that's their name for us) until we arrived, except that once, some twelve hundred years ago, a ship which a storm had blown toward Utopia was wrecked on their island. Some Romans and Egyptians were cast ashore, and never departed. Now note how the Utopians profited, through their diligence, from this one chance event. They learned every single useful art of the Roman civilization either directly from their guests, or indirectly from hints and surmises on which they based their own investigations. What benefits from the mere fact that on a single occasion some Europeans landed there! If a similar accident has hitherto brought any men here from their land, the incident has been completely forgotten, as it will be forgotten in time to come that I was ever in their country. From one such accident they made themselves masters of all our useful inventions, but I suspect it will be a long time before we accept any of their institutions which are better than ours. This willingness to learn, I think, is the really important reason for their being better governed and living more happily than we do, though we are not inferior to them in brains or resources."

*   *   *

Their Occupations

Agriculture is the one occupation at which everyone works, men and women alike, with no exceptions. They are trained in it from childhood, partly in the schools where they learn theory, and partly through field trips to nearby farms, which make something like a game of practical instruction. On these trips they not only watch the work being done, but frequently pitch in and get a workout by doing the jobs themselves.

Besides farm work (which, as I said, everybody performs), each person is taught a particular trade of his own, such as wool-working, linen-making, masonry, metal-work, or carpentry. There is no other craft that is practiced by any considerable number of them. Throughout the island people wear, and down through the centuries they have always worn, the same style of clothing, except for the distinction between the sexes, and between married and unmarried persons. Their clothing is attractive, does not hamper bodily movement, and serves for warm as well as cold weather; what is more, each household can make its own.

Every person (and this includes women as well as men) learns a second trade, besides agriculture. As the weaker sex, women practice the lighter crafts, such as working in wool or linen; the heavier crafts are assigned to the men. As a rule, the son is trained to his father's craft, for which most feel a natural inclination. But if anyone is attracted to another occupation, he is transferred by adoption into a family practicing the trade he prefers. When anyone makes such a change, both his father and the authorities make sure that he is assigned to a grave and responsible householder. After a man has learned one trade, if he wants to learn another, he gets the same permission. When he has learned both, he pursues whichever he likes better, unless the city needs one more than the other.

The chief and almost the only business of the syphogrants is to manage matters so that no one sits around in idleness, and assure that everyone works hard at his trade. But no one has to exhaust himself with endless toil from early morning to late at night, as if he were a beast of burden. Such wretchedness, really worse than slavery, is the common lot of workmen in all countries, except Utopia. Of the day's twenty-four hours, the Utopians devote only six to work. They work three hours before noon, when they go to dinner. After dinner they rest for a couple of hours, then go to work for another three hours. Then they have supper, and at eight o'clock (counting the first hour after noon as one), they go to bed and sleep eight hours.

The other hours of the day, when they are not working, eating, or sleeping, are left to each man's individual discretion, provided he does not waste them in roistering or sloth, but uses them busily in some occupation that pleases him. Generally these periods are devoted to intellectual activity.

For they have an established custom of giving public lectures before daybreak; attendance at these lectures is required only of those who have been specially chosen to devote themselves to learning, but a great many other people, both men and women, choose voluntarily to attend. Depending on their interests, some go to one lecture, some to another. But if anyone would rather devote his spare time to his trade, as many do who don't care for the intellectual life, this is not discouraged; in fact, such persons are commended as especially useful to the commonwealth.

*   *   *

But in all this, you may get a wrong impression, if we don't go back and consider one point more carefully. Because they allot only six hours to work, you might think the necessities of life would be in scant supply. This is far from the case. Their working hours are ample to provide not only enough but more than enough of the necessities and even the conveniences of life. You will easily appreciate this if you consider how large a part of the population in other countries exists without doing any work at all. In the first place, hardly any of the women, who are a full half of the population, work; or, if they do, then as a rule their husbands lie snoring in the bed. Then there is a great lazy gang of priests and so-called religious men. Add to them all the rich, especially the landlords, who are commonly called gentlemen and nobility. Include with them their retainers, that mob of swaggering bullies. Finally, reckon in with these the sturdy and lusty beggars, who go about feigning some disease as an excuse for their idleness. You will certainly find that the things which satisfy our needs are produced by far fewer hands than you had supposed.

And now consider how few of those who do work are doing really essential things. For where money is the standard of everything, many superfluous trades are bound to be carried on simply to satisfy luxury and licentiousness. Suppose the multitude of those who now work were limited to a few trades, and set to producing more and more

of those conveniences and commodities that nature really requires. They would be bound to produce so much that the prices would drop, and the workmen would be unable to gain a living. But suppose again that all the workers in useless trades were put to useful ones, and that all the idlers (who now guzzle twice as much as the workingmen who make what they consume) were assigned to productive tasks—well, you can easily see how little time each man would have to spend working, in order to produce all the goods that human needs and conveniences require—yes, and human pleasure too, as long as it's true and natural pleasure.

*   *   *

Their Gold and Silver

For these reasons, therefore, they have accumulated a vast treasure, but they do not keep it like a treasure. I'm really quite ashamed to tell you how they do keep it, because you probably won't believe me. I would not have believed it myself if someone had just told me about it; but I was there, and saw it with my own eyes. It is a general rule that the more different anything is from what people are used to, the harder it is to accept. But, considering that all their other customs are so unlike ours, a sensible man will not be surprised that they use gold and silver quite differently than we do. After all, they never do use money among themselves, but keep it only for a contingency which may or may not actually arise. So in the meanwhile they take care that no one shall overvalue gold and silver, of which money is made, beyond what the metals themselves deserve. Anyone can see, for example, that iron is far superior to either; men could not live without iron, by heaven, any more than without fire or water. But gold and silver have, by nature, no function that we cannot easily dispense with. Human folly has made them precious because they are rare. Like a most wise and generous mother, nature has placed the best things everywhere and in the open, like

air, water, and the earth itself; but she has hidden away in remote places all vain and unprofitable things.

If in Utopia gold and silver were kept locked up in some tower, foolish heads among the common people might well concoct a story that the prince and the senate were out to cheat ordinary folk and get some advantage for themselves. They might indeed put the gold and silver into beautiful plate-ware and rich handiwork, but then in case of necessity the people would not want to give up such articles, on which they had begun to fix their hearts, only to melt them down for soldiers' pay. To avoid all these inconveniences, they thought of a plan which conforms with their institutions as clearly as it contrasts with our own. Unless we've actually seen it working, their plan may seem ridiculous to us, because we prize gold so highly and are so careful about protecting it. With them it's just the other way. While they eat from pottery dishes and drink from glass cups, well made but inexpensive, their chamber pots and stools—all their humblest vessels, for use in the common halls and private homes—are made of gold and silver. The chains and heavy fetters of slaves are also made of these metals. Finally, criminals who are to bear through life the mark of some disgraceful act are forced to wear golden rings on their ears, golden bands on their fingers, golden chains around their necks, and even golden crowns on their heads. Thus they hold gold and silver up to scorn in every conceivable way. As a result, when they have to part with these metals, which other nations give up with as much agony as if they were being disemboweled, the Utopians feel it no more than the loss of a penny.

*   *   *

Slaves

The Utopians enslave prisoners of war only if they are captured in wars fought by the Utopians themselves. The children of slaves are not automatically enslaved, nor are any men who were enslaved in a foreign country. Most of their slaves are either their own former citizens, enslaved for some heinous offense, or else men of other nations who were condemned to death in their own land. Most are of the latter sort. Sometimes the Utopians buy them at a very modest rate, more often they ask for them, get them for nothing, and bring them home in considerable numbers. These kinds of slaves are kept constantly at work, and are always fettered. The Utopians deal with their own people more harshly than with others, feeling that their crimes are worse and deserve stricter punishment because, as it is argued, they had an excellent education and the best of moral training, yet still couldn't be restrained from wrongdoing. A third class of slaves consists of hardworking penniless drudges from other nations who voluntarily choose to become slaves in Utopia. Such people are treated well, almost as well as citizens, except that they are given a little extra work, on the score that they're used to it. If one of them wants to leave, which seldom happens, no obstacles are put in his way, nor is he sent off empty-handed.

*   *   *

REVIEW QUESTIONS

1. Why did More choose to call the place *Utopia*, literally "Nowhere"?
2. What possibilities created by the discovery of a new world does More explore in *Utopia*?
3. How are More's Utopians different from what medieval Europeans would have considered Christian?
4. How does More's attitude toward the people of Utopia reflect attitudes of the Renaissance?
5. How might *Utopia* be critical of Renaissance society?
6. What do More's Utopians have in common with the kind of Christian Erasmus described in his colloquy "Cyclops, or the Gospel-Bearer"?

13 ⤫ THE AGE OF DISSENT AND DIVISION, 1500–1600

The year 1492 marked both the end of the expansion of Christianity in Europe, with the final expulsion of the Jews and Muslims from the Iberian Peninsula, and the beginning of the expansion of European Christianity across the globe. So, too, it marked the nadir of papal ambition, venality, and corruption, and thereby the medieval Christian hierarchy. In that year, the Borgia pope, Alexander VI, whom contemporaries such as Machiavelli knew to be rapacious, murderous, treacherous, and ambitious, was elected.

Within a generation of the Reconquista of Spain, the German lands of the grandson of Ferdinando and Isabella of Spain would be split between two very different understandings of Christianity: what it meant to be a Christian, what the Church was and how it was to be constituted, and what the nature of worship was. In part, the Reformation arose in response to perceptions of papal bellicosity and immorality; it belonged to an older tradition of reformatio. Equally, however, the Reformation was heir to the Renaissance: the philological skills and discoveries of fifteenth-century humanists enabled new approaches to the study of the Bible, and the humanist emphasis on historical accuracy led to a call for a return to apostolic Christianity. That return to the text of Scripture, along with a new sensitivity to historical periods, brought theologians such as Martin Luther to reconsider not only devotional practices but the very structure of authority of medieval Christendom—the papal hierarchy—and others, such as John Calvin, to return to the Acts of the Apostles for a vision of the true church.

Even as Christendom divided against itself in Europe, it expanded through the persons of conquistadores to create worlds unimagined in the European tradition. Reformation and expansion both came through bloodshed. In Germany, peasants and artisans fought lords and emperor to institute the godly law they found in the Bible, only to be massacred. In France, the Low Countries, and England, as well as the Holy Roman Empire, Christians executed Christians

over questions of the Eucharist, the place of images in worship, and the cult of the saints. Churches divided from one another, each defining itself against the others, even as all confronted worlds for which neither the Bible nor the classical tradition had prepared them.

MARTIN LUTHER

FROM *The Large Catechism,* 1530

Martin Luther (1483–1546), one of the founders of Protestantism, was born of peasant stock. His father had left his fields for the copper mines of Mansfeld in Saxon, where he flourished economically and rose to the status of town councilor. His son, Martin, received a primary education from the Brethren of the Common Life and enrolled at the University of Erfurt in 1501, where he earned his bachelor of arts in 1502 and his master of arts in 1505. His father hoped that his son would continue the family's rise to prominence by pursuing a legal career. These aspirations were shattered when Luther unexpectedly entered a monastery in 1505. As a member of the order of Augustinian Hermits, he began formal training in theology. Selected for advanced training in theology, he made his way to the University of Wittenberg, where he received his doctorate in 1512 and occupied the chair of biblical theology. Even as his academic career prospered, his inner life suffered. Luther was beset by doubts about his own salvation, the result of a consciousness both of his own weakness and of divine righteousness. Long study and meditation led him to a resolution that became the basis for his theology of justification. Salvation was the result of divine grace, freely given; the forgiven conscience could be at peace; the soul could serve God joyfully. Luther having experienced this new conviction, it is not surprising that the extravagant claims surrounding the sale of indulgences in 1517 provoked him to public protest. The form and text of that protest became known as the "95 Theses." His objection to the claim that the pope could remit the temporal punishment of sins led him deeper and deeper into controversy and ultimately to schism. By 1520, the rift between Luther and the Catholic Church had become irreparable and extended to far more issues than papal power. His The Large Catechism, whose Preface follows, reveals another dimension of Luther's reform: his engagement in the care of souls. Through catechism, a process of recitation and repetition, young people were to be brought to a proper understanding of God's Will and Word. It reveals Luther's familiarity with the Christian Church's past and his hope for its future.

From *The Large Catechism of Martin Luther,* translated by Robert H. Fischer (Philadelphia: Augsburg Fortress Press, 1959).

Martin Luther's Preface[1]

It is not for trivial reasons that we constantly treat the Catechism and strongly urge others to do the same. For we see to our sorrow that many pastors and preachers[2] are very negligent in this respect and despise both their office and this teaching itself. Some because of their great and lofty learning, others because of sheer laziness and gluttony, behave in this matter as if they were pastors or preachers for their bellies' sake and had nothing to do but live off the fat of the land all their days, as they used to do under the papacy.

Everything that they are to teach and preach is now available to them in clear and simple form in the many excellent books which are in reality what the old manuals claimed in their titles to be: "Sermons That Preach Themselves," "Sleep Soundly," "Prepared!" and "Treasury."[3] However, they are not so upright and honest as to buy these books, or if they have them, to examine and read them. Such shameful gluttons and servants of their bellies would make better swineherds or dogkeepers than spiritual guides and pastors.

Now that they are free from the useless, bothersome babbling of the Seven Hours,[4] it would be fine if every morning, noon, and evening they would read, instead, at least a page or two from the Catechism, the Prayer Book,[5] the New Testament, or something else from the Bible and would pray the Lord's Prayer for themselves and their parishioners. In this way they might show honor and gratitude to the Gospel, through which they have been delivered from so many burdens and troubles, and they might feel a little shame because, like pigs and dogs, they remember no more of the Gospel than this rotten, pernicious, shameful, carnal liberty. As it is, the common people take the Gospel altogether too lightly, and even our utmost exertions accomplish but little. What, then, can we expect if we are sluggish and lazy, as we used to be under the papacy?

Besides, a shameful and insidious plague of security and boredom has overtaken us. Many regard the Catechism as a simple, silly teaching which they can absorb and master at one reading. After reading it once they toss the book into a corner as if they are ashamed to read it again. Indeed, even among the nobility there are some louts and skinflints who declare that we can do without pastors and preachers from now on because we have everything in books and can learn it all by ourselves. So they blithely let parishes fall into decay, and brazenly allow both pastors and preachers to suffer distress and hunger. This is what one can expect of crazy Germans. We Germans have such disgraceful people among us and must put up with them.

As for myself, let me say that I, too, am a doctor and a preacher—yes, and as learned and experienced as any of those who act so high and mighty. Yet I do as a child who is being taught the Catechism. Every morning, and whenever else I have time, I read and recite word for word the Lord's Prayer, the Ten Commandments, the Creed, the Psalms, etc. I must still read and study the Catechism daily, yet I cannot master it as I wish, but must remain a child and pupil of the Catechism, and I do it gladly. These dainty, fastidious fellows would like quickly, with one reading, to become doctors above all doctors, to know all there is to be known. Well, this, too, is a sure sign that they despise both their office and the people's souls, yes, even God and his Word. They need not fear a fall, for they have already fallen all too horribly. What they need is to become children and begin learning their ABC's, which they think they have outgrown long ago.

---

[1] In the German edition of the Book of Concord, 1580, this Longer Preface (which dates from 1530) appeared after the Shorter Preface in accordance with the order observed in the fourth German volume of the Jena edition of Luther's Works (1556).

[2] Preachers (*Prediger*) were limited to preaching; pastors (*Pfarrherren*) exercised the full ministerial office.

[3] Titles of medieval sermon books.

[4] The seven canonical hours, daily prayers prescribed by the medieval Breviary.

[5] Luther published the "Little Prayer Book" (*Betbüchlein*) in 1522 to replace Roman Catholic devotional books.

Therefore, I beg these lazy-bellies and pre-sumptuous saints, for God's sake, to get it into their heads that they are not really and truly such learned and great doctors as they think. I implore them not to imagine that they have learned these parts of the Catechism perfectly, or at least suffi-ciently, even though they think they know them ever so well. Even if their knowledge of the Cate-chism were perfect (though that is impossible in this life), yet it is highly profitable and fruitful daily to read it and make it the subject of meditation and conversation. In such reading, conversation, and meditation the Holy Spirit is present and bestows ever new and greater light and fervor, so that day by day we relish and appreciate the Catechism more greatly. This is according to Christ's promise in Matt. 18:20, "Where two or three are gathered in my name, there am I in the midst of them."

Nothing is so effectual against the devil, the world, the flesh, and all evil thoughts as to occupy oneself with the Word of God, talk about it, and meditate on it. Psalm 1 calls those blessed who "meditate on God's law day and night."[6] You will never offer up any incense or other savor more po-tent against the devil than to occupy yourself with God's commandments and words and to speak, sing, and meditate on them. This, indeed, is the true holy water, the sign which routs the devil and puts him to flight.[7]

For this reason alone you should eagerly read, recite, ponder, and practice the Catechism, even if the only blessing and benefit you obtain from it is to rout the devil and evil thoughts. For he cannot bear to hear God's Word. God's Word is not like some empty tale, such as the one about Dietrich of Bern,[8] but as St. Paul says in Rom. 1:16, it is "the power of God," indeed, the power of God which burns the devil and gives us immeasurable strength, comfort, and help.

Why should I waste words? Time and paper would fail me if I were to recount all the blessings that flow from God's Word. The devil is called the master of a thousand arts. What, then, shall we call God's Word, which routs and destroys this master of a thousand arts with all his wiles and might? It must, indeed, be master of more than a hundred thousand arts. Shall we frivolously despise this might, blessing, power, and fruit—especially we who would be pastors and preachers? If so, we de-serve not only to be refused food but also to be chased out by dogs and pelted with dung. Not only do we need God's Word daily as we need our daily bread; we also must use it daily against the daily, incessant attacks and ambushes of the devil with his thousand arts.

If this were not enough to admonish us to read the Catechism daily, there is God's command. That alone should be incentive enough. Deut. 6:7, 8 solemnly enjoins that we should always meditate upon his precepts whether sitting, walking, stand-ing, lying down, or rising, and keep them before our eyes and in our hands as a constant token and sign. Certainly God did not require and command this so solemnly without good reason. He knows our dan-ger and need. He knows the constant and furious at-tacks and assaults of the devil. So he wishes to warn, equip, and protect us against them with good "ar-mor" against their "flaming darts,"[9] and with a good antidote against their evil infection and poison. O what mad, senseless fools we are! We must ever live and dwell in the midst of such mighty enemies as the devils, and yet we despise our weapons and ar-mor, too lazy to give them a thought!

Look at these bored, presumptuous saints who will not or cannot read and study the Catechism daily. They evidently consider themselves much wiser than God himself, and wiser than all his holy angels, prophets, apostles, and all Christians! God himself is not ashamed to teach it daily, for he knows of nothing better to teach, and he always keeps on teaching this one thing without varying it with anything new or different. All the saints know

---

[6] Ps. 1:2.

[7] I.e., the Word of God really does what holy water was formerly believed to accomplish.

[8] Luther frequently cited the legend of Dietrich of Bern as an example of lies and fables.

[9] Eph. 6:11, 16.

of nothing better or different to learn, though they cannot learn it to perfection. Are we not most marvelous fellows, therefore, if we imagine, after reading or hearing it once, that we know it all and need not read or study it any more? Most marvelous fellows, to think we can finish learning in one hour what God himself cannot finish teaching! Actually, he is busy teaching it from the beginning of the world to the end, and all prophets and saints have been busy learning it and have always remained pupils, and must continue to do so.

This much is certain: anyone who knows the Ten Commandments perfectly knows the entire Scriptures. In all affairs and circumstances he can counsel, help, comfort, judge, and make decisions in both spiritual and temporal matters. He is qualified to sit in judgment upon all doctrines, estates, persons, laws, and everything else in the world.

What is the whole Psalter but meditations and exercises based on the First Commandment? Now, I know beyond a doubt that such lazy-bellies and presumptuous fellows do not understand a single Psalm, much less the entire Scriptures, yet they pretend to know and despise the Catechism, which is a brief compend and summary of all the Holy Scriptures.

Therefore, I once again implore all Christians, especially pastors and preachers, not to try to be doctors prematurely and to imagine that they know everything. Vain imaginations, like new cloth, suffer shrinkage! Let all Christians exercise themselves in the Catechism daily, and constantly put it into practice, guarding themselves with the greatest care and diligence against the poisonous infection of such security or vanity. Let them continue to read and teach, to learn and meditate and ponder. Let them never stop until they have proved by experience that they have taught the devil to death and have become wiser than God himself and all his saints.

If they show such diligence, then I promise them—and their experience will bear me out—that they will gain much fruit and God will make excellent men of them. Then in due time they themselves will make the noble confession that the longer they work with the Catechism, the less they know of it and the more they have to learn. Only then, hungry and thirsty, will they truly relish what now they cannot bear to smell because they are so bloated and surfeited. To this end may God grant his grace! Amen.

Preface[10]

This sermon has been undertaken for the instruction of children and uneducated people. Hence from ancient times it has been called, in Greek, a "catechism"—that is, instruction for children. Its contents represent the minimum of knowledge required of a Christian. Whoever does not possess it should not be reckoned among Christians nor admitted to a sacrament,[11] just as a craftsman who does not know the rules and practices of his craft is rejected and considered incompetent. For this reason young people should be thoroughly instructed in the various parts of the Catechism or children's sermons and diligently drilled in their practice.

Therefore, it is the duty of every head of a household to examine his children and servants at least once a week and ascertain what they have learned of it, and if they do not know it, to keep them faithfully at it. I well remember the time when there were old people who were so ignorant that they knew nothing of these things—indeed, even now we find them daily—yet they come to Baptism and the Sacrament of the Altar and exercise all the rights of Christians, although those who come to the sacrament ought to know more and have a fuller understanding of all Christian doctrine than children and beginners at school. As for the common people, however, we should be satisfied if they learned the three parts[12] which

---

[10] The Shorter Preface is based on a sermon of May 18, 1528 (*WA*, 301:2).

[11] This was not only a proposal of Luther, but also a medieval prescription; cf. John Surgant, *Manuale Curatorum* (1502), etc.

[12] Ten Commandments, Creed, Lord's Prayer. From 1525 on catechetical instruction in Wittenberg was expanded to include material on Baptism and the Lord's Supper.

have been the heritage of Christendom from ancient times, though they were rarely taught and treated correctly, so that all who wish to be Christians in fact as well as in name, both young and old, may be well-trained in them and familiar with them.

I. THE TEN COMMANDMENTS OF GOD

1. You shall have no other gods before me.
2. You shall not take the name of God in vain.
3. You shall keep the Sabbath day holy.
4. You shall honor father and mother.
5. You shall not kill.
6. You shall not commit adultery.
7. You shall not steal.
8. You shall not bear false witness against your neighbor.
9. You shall not covet your neighbor's house.
10. You shall not covet his wife, man-servant, maid-servant, cattle, or anything that is his.[13]

II. THE CHIEF ARTICLES OF OUR FAITH

I believe in God, the Father almighty, maker of heaven and earth:

And in Jesus Christ, his only Son, our Lord: who was conceived by the Holy Spirit, born of the virgin Mary, suffered under Pontius Pilate, was crucified, dead, and buried: he descended into hell, the third day he rose from the dead, he ascended into heaven, and sits on the right hand of God, the Father almighty, whence he shall come to judge the living and the dead.

I believe in the Holy Spirit, the holy Christian church,[14] the communion of saints, the forgiveness of sins, the resurrection of the body, and the life everlasting. Amen.

III. THE PRAYER, OR OUR FATHER, WHICH CHRIST TAUGHT

Our Father who art in heaven, hallowed be thy name. Thy kingdom come, thy will be done, on earth as it is in heaven. Give us this day our daily bread; and forgive us our debts, as we also have forgiven our debtors; and lead us not into temptation, but deliver us from evil. For thine is the kingdom and the power and the glory, forever. Amen.[15]

These are the most necessary parts of Christian instruction. We should learn to repeat them word for word. Our children should be taught the habit of reciting them daily when they rise in the morning, when they go to their meals, and when they go to bed at night; until they repeat them they should not be given anything to eat or drink. Every father has the same duty to his household; he should dismiss man-servants and maid-servants if they do not know these things and are unwilling to learn them. Under no circumstances should a person be tolerated if he is so rude and unruly that he refuses to learn these three parts in which everything contained in Scripture is comprehended in short, plain, and simple terms, for the dear fathers or apostles, whoever they were,[16] have thus summed up the doctrine, life, wisdom, and learning which constitute the Christian's conversation, conduct, and concern.

When these three parts are understood, we ought also to know what to say about the sacraments which Christ himself instituted, Baptism and the holy Body and Blood of Christ, according to the texts of Matthew and Mark at the end of their Gospels where they describe how Christ said farewell to his disciples and sent them forth.

BAPTISM

"Go and teach all nations, and baptize them in the name of the Father and of the Son and of the Holy

---

[13] Ex. 20:2–17; cf. Deut. 5:6–21.

[14] The translation of *ecclesiam catholicam* by *eine christliche Kirche* was common in fifteenth-century Germany.

[15] Matt. 6:9–13; cf. Luke 11:2–4.

[16] Luther was not interested in defending the apostolic authorship of the Creed.

Spirit" (Matt. 28:19). "He who believes and is baptized will be saved; but he who does not believe will be condemned" (Mark 16:16).

It is enough for an ordinary person to know this much about Baptism from the Scriptures. The other sacrament may be dealt with similarly, in short, simple words according to the text of St. Paul.

THE SACRAMENT [OF THE ALTAR]

"Our Lord Jesus Christ on the night when he was betrayed took bread, gave thanks, and broke it and gave it to his disciples, saying, 'Take and eat, this is my body, which is given for you. Do this in remembrance of me.'

"In the same way also the cup, after supper, saying, 'This cup is the new testament in my blood, which is shed for you for the forgiveness of sins. Do this, as often as you drink it, in remembrance of me' " (I Cor. 11:23–25).

Thus we have, in all, five parts covering the whole of Christian doctrine, which we should constantly teach and require young people to recite word for word. Do not assume that they will learn and retain this teaching from sermons alone. When these parts have been well learned, you may assign them also some Psalms or some hymns,[17] based on these subjects, to supplement and confirm their knowledge. Thus our youth will be led into the Scriptures so that they make progress daily.

However, it is not enough for them simply to learn and repeat these parts verbatim. The young people should also attend preaching, especially at the time designated for the Catechism,[18] so that they may hear it explained and may learn the meaning of every part. Then they will also be able to repeat what they have heard and give a good, correct answer when they are questioned, and thus the preaching will not be without benefit and fruit. The reason we take such care to preach on the Catechism frequently is to impress it upon our youth, not in a lofty and learned manner but briefly and very simply, so that it may penetrate deeply into their minds and remain fixed in their memories.

Now we shall take up the above-mentioned parts one by one and in the plainest possible manner say about them as much as is necessary.

REVIEW QUESTIONS

1. Why is the catechism so important to Martin Luther?
2. To whom is the catechism to be taught, and by whom is it to be taught?
3. What matters, issues, or ideas does the catechism teach?
4. What purposes does the catechism serve in the reformation of Luther?
5. What concerns on the part of Luther do these purposes reflect?

---

[17] Luther himself wrote six hymns based on the parts of the Catechism.

[18] Preaching and instruction on the Catechism especially during Lent.

SEBASTIAN LOTZER

The Twelve Articles of the Peasants of Swabia

The Twelve Articles of the Peasants of Swabia, adopted at the free imperial city of Memmingen in 1525, is one of the signal documents of the great agrarian revolt known as the Peasants' War of 1525. More than any other such document, it specifically linked the

THE HOLY COMMUNION BY THE PROTESTANTS AND
RIDE TO HELL OF THE CATHOLICS (date unknown)

LUCAS CRANACH THE YOUNGER

Lucas Cranach the Younger (1515–1586) developed his art while apprenticed to his father, Lucas Cranach the Elder. So well did he learn that his paintings and woodcuts, usually individual portraits or allegorical scenes, are difficult to distinguish from those of his father. This particular woodcut, whose date is unknown, captures the potential of this print medium to communicate through images meaning beyond words. Cranach the Younger was an early master. What activities occur on each side of the image? What does Cranach want his viewers to know? How does the Renaissance aesthetic of balance and symmetry reinforce the central message of the image? What central themes of the Reformation appear before your eyes?

*social and political grievances of the peasants with the evangelical principles of the Re-
formation. Ironically, this document was not composed by a peasant but by a townsman,
the journeyman furrier and lay preacher Sebastian Lotzer. To do so, he summarized and
condensed the long (several hundred articles) list of demands put forward by the peasants of Baltringen. The Memmingen preacher Christoph Schappeler added a preamble
and supplied biblical references in the margins. This document acquired its importance
because it was quickly printed and widely disseminated. In many areas of the revolt, it
was adopted as the basis for lists of grievances and proposals for settlement.*

From *The Revolution of 1525: The German Peasants' War from a New Perspective*, translated by
Thomas A. Brady Jr. (Baltimore: Johns Hopkins University Press, 1981), pp. 195–201.

The Just and Fundamental Articles of All the Peasantry and Tenants of Spiritual and Temporal Powers by Whom They Think Themselves Oppressed

To the Christian reader, the peace and grace of God through Jesus Christ.

There are many antichrists who, now that the peasants are assembled together, seize the chance to mock the gospel, saying, "Is this the fruit of the new gospel: to band together in great numbers and plot conspiracies to reform and even topple the spiritual and temporal powers—yes, even to murder them?" The following articles answer all these godless, blasphemous critics. We want two things: first, to make them stop mocking the word of God; and second, to establish the Christian justice of the current disobedience and rebellion of all the peasants.

First of all, the gospel does not cause rebellions and uproars, because it tells of Christ, the promised Messiah, whose words and life teach nothing but love, peace, patience, and unity. And all who believe in this Christ become loving, peaceful, patient, and one in spirit. This is the basis of all the articles of the peasants (as we will clearly show): to hear the gospel and to live accordingly. How then can the antichrists call the gospel a cause of rebellion and of disobedience? It is not the gospel that drives some antichrists and foes of the gospel to resist and reject these demands and require-

ments, but the devil, the deadliest foe of the gospel, who arouses through unbelief such opposition in his own followers. His aim is to suppress and abolish the word of God, which teaches love, peace, and unity.

Second, it surely follows that the peasants, whose articles demand this gospel as their doctrine and rule of life, cannot be called "disobedient" or "rebellious." For if God deigns to hear the peasants' earnest plea that they may be permitted to live according to his word, who will dare deny his will? Who indeed will dare question his judgment? Who will dare oppose his majesty? Did he not hear the children of Israel crying to him and deliver them out of Pharaoh's hand? And can he not save his own today as well? Yes, he will save them, and soon! Therefore, Christian reader, read these articles diligently, and then judge for yourself.

These are the Articles.

THE FIRST ARTICLE

First of all, we humbly ask and beg—and we all agree on this—that henceforth we ought to have the authority and power for the whole community to elect and appoint its own pastor. We also want authority to depose a pastor who behaves improperly. This elected pastor should preach to us the holy gospel purely and clearly, without human additions or human doctrines or precepts. For constant preaching of the true faith impels us to

beg God for his grace, that he may instill in us and confirm in us that same true faith. Unless we have his grace in us, we remain mere, useless flesh and blood. For the Scripture clearly teaches that we may come to God only through true faith and can be saved only through His mercy. This is why we need such a guide and pastor; and thus our demand is grounded in Scripture.

THE SECOND ARTICLE

Second, although the obligation to pay a just tithe prescribed in the Old Testament is fulfilled in the New, yet we will gladly pay the large tithe on grain—but only in just measure. Since the tithe should be given to God and distributed among his servants, so the pastor who clearly preaches the word of God deserves to receive it. From now on we want to have our church wardens, appointed by the community, collect and receive this tithe and have our elected pastor draw from it, with the whole community's consent, a decent and adequate living for himself and his. The remainder should be distributed to the village's own poor, again with the community's consent and according to need. What then remains should be kept in case some need to be called up to defend the country; and then the costs can be met from this reserve, so that no general territorial tax will be laid upon the poor folk.

Wherever one or more villages have sold off the tithe to meet some emergency, those purchasers who can show that they bought the tithe with the consent of the whole village shall not be simply expropriated. Indeed we hope to reach fair compromises with such persons, according to the facts of the case, and to redeem the tithe in installments. But wherever the tithe holder—be he clergyman or layman—did not buy the tithe from the whole village but has it from ancestors who simply seized it from the village, we will not, ought not, and do not intend to pay it any longer, except (as we said above) to support our elected pastor. And we will reserve the rest or distribute it to the poor, as the Bible commands. As for the small tithe, we will not pay it at all, for the Lord God created cattle for man's free use; and it is an unjust tithe invented by men alone. Therefore, we won't pay it anymore.

THE THIRD ARTICLE

Third, it has until now been the custom for the lords to own us as their property. This is deplorable, for Christ redeemed and bought us all with his precious blood, the lowliest shepherd as well as the greatest lord, with no exceptions. Thus the Bible proves that we are free and want to be free. Not that we want to be utterly free and subject to no authority at all; God does not teach us that. We ought to live according to the commandments, not according to the lusts of the flesh. But we should love God, recognize him as our Lord in our neighbor, and willingly do all things God commanded us at his Last Supper. This means we should live according to his commandment, which does not teach us to obey only the rulers, but to humble ourselves before everyone. Thus we should willingly obey our elected and rightful ruler, set over us by God, in all proper and Christian matters. Nor do we doubt that you, as true and just Christians, will gladly release us from bondage or prove to us from the gospel that we must be your property.

THE FOURTH ARTICLE

Fourth, until now it has been the custom that no commoner might catch wild game, wildfowl, or fish in the running waters, which seems to us altogether improper, unbrotherly, selfish, and contrary to God's Word. In some places the rulers protect the game to our distress and great loss, for we must suffer silently while the dumb beasts gobble up the crops God gave for man's use, although this offends both God and neighbor. When the Lord God created man, he gave him dominion over all animals, over the birds of the air, and the fish in the waters. Thus we demand that if someone owns a stream, lake, or pond, he should have to produce documentary proof of ownership and

show that it was sold to him with the consent of the whole village. In that case we do not want to seize it from him with force but only to review the matter in a Christian way for the sake of brotherly love. But whoever cannot produce adequate proof of ownership and sale should surrender the waters to the community, as is just.

THE FIFTH ARTICLE

Fifth, we have another grievance about woodcutting, for our lords have seized the woods for themselves alone; and when the poor commoner needs some wood, he has to pay twice the price for it. We think that those woods whose lords, be they clergymen or laymen, cannot prove ownership by purchase should revert to the whole community. And the community should be able to allow in an orderly way each man to gather firewood for his home and building timber free, though only with permission of the community's elected officials. If all the woods have been fairly purchased, then a neighborly and Christian agreement should be reached with their owners about their use. Where the woods were simply seized and then sold to a third party, however, a compromise should be reached according to the facts of the case and the norms of brotherly love and Holy Writ.

THE SIXTH ARTICLE

Sixth, there is our grievous burden of labor services, which the lords daily increase in number and kind. We demand that these obligations be properly investigated and lessened. And we should be allowed, graciously, to serve as our forefathers did, according to God's word alone.

THE SEVENTH ARTICLE

Seventh, in the future we will not allow the lords to oppress us any more. Rather, a man shall have his holding on the proper terms on which it has been leased, that is, by the agreement between lord and peasant. The lord should not force or press the tenant to perform labor or any other service without

pay, so that the peasant may use and enjoy his land unburdened and in peace. When the lord needs labor services, however, the peasant should willingly serve his own lord before others; yet a peasant should serve only at a time when his own affairs do not suffer and only for a just wage.

THE EIGHTH ARTICLE

Eighth, we have a grievance that many of us hold lands that are overburdened with rents higher than the land's yield. Thus the peasants lose their property and are ruined. The lords should have honorable men inspect these farms and adjust the rents fairly, so that the peasant does not work for nothing. For every laborer is worthy of his hire.

THE NINTH ARTICLE

Ninth, we have a grievance against the way serious crimes are punished, for they are constantly making new laws. We are not punished according to the severity of the case but sometimes out of great ill will and sometimes out of favoritism. We think that punishments should be dealt out among us according to the ancient written law and the circumstances of the case, and not according to the judge's bias.

THE TENTH ARTICLE

Tenth, we have a grievance that some people have seized meadows and fields belonging to the community. We shall restore these to the community, unless a proper sale can be proved. If they were improperly bought, however, then a friendly and brotherly compromise should be reached, based on the facts.

THE ELEVENTH ARTICLE

Eleventh, we want the custom called death taxes totally abolished. We will not tolerate it or allow widows and orphans to be so shamefully robbed of their goods, as so often happens in various ways, against God and all that is honorable. The very ones

who should be guarding and protecting our goods have skinned and trimmed us of them instead. Had they the slightest legal pretext, they would have grabbed everything. God will suffer this no longer but will wipe it all out. Henceforth no one shall have to pay death taxes, whether small or large.

CONCLUSION

Twelfth, we believe and have decided that if any one or more of these articles is not in agreement with God's Word (which we doubt), then this should be proved to us from Holy Writ. We will abandon it, when this is proved by the Bible. If some of our articles should be approved and later found to be unjust, they shall be dead, null, and void from that moment on. Likewise, if Scripture truly reveals further grievances as offensive to God and a burden to our neighbor, we will reserve a place for them and declare them included in our list. We, for our part, will live and exercise our-

selves in all Christian teachings, for which we will pray to the Lord God. For he alone, and no other, can give us the truth. The peace of Christ be with us all.

REVIEW QUESTIONS

1. What do the Twelve Articles tell you about relations between the common man and his lords?
2. What are the priorities of the Twelve Articles?
3. What is most important to the petitioners?
4. Why is it so important?
5. What is second in importance?
6. What changes are the petitioners asking for the tithe?
7. What is Godly Law?
8. What might be its applications?
9. What are the implications of Godly Law for the lords?

JOHN CALVIN

FROM Draft of Ecclesiastical Ordinances, September and October 1541

John (Jean) Calvin (1509–1564) was born of bourgeois parents in the city of Noyon in Picardy. Destined by his father for an ecclesiastical career, he received several benefices to finance his education as early as 1521. In 1523, he transferred to the University of Paris, where he imbibed the spirit of humanism from such teachers as Mathurin Cordier and Guillaume Bude. Calvin earned a master of arts degree at Paris and, without abandoning his study of classical languages and literature, turned to law at Orléans in 1528. By 1532, he had earned a doctorate of law. Sometime during his legal training or shortly thereafter, Calvin converted to Protestantism. The year 1534 was decisive for Calvin. Forced to flee Paris because of the proscription of Protestantism, he made his way to Basel, where he began work on his great systematic theology, Institutes of the Christian Religion *(1536). It was immediately recognized as a superb normative statement of reformed theology and established Calvin's stature as a leader among Protestants despite his youth. As the first edition went to press, Calvin made his way to Geneva, where Guillaume Farel enlisted his aid in the*

THE CRUCIFIXION (c. 1596–1600)   EL GRECO

Domenikos Theotokopoulos, better known as El Greco, "the Greek" (1541–1614), is one of the most recognizable and puzzling masters of the Late Renaissance. His dramatic, expressionistic style combined elements of the mannerist and Venetian schools in ways utterly unique. He settled in Toledo, the religious capital of Spain in 1577, after spending his early career in Italy, and received a number of large commissions to decorate some of the churches of the city, as well as the monumental palace of El Escorial. A private commission, executed as part of a retable for the Lady María of Aragon, The Crucifixion is one of his most famous and powerful works. As you view the painting, what do you think are its most striking elements? Can you identify the figures grouped around the cross? What do their postures, gestures and expressions seem to indicate? How does this painting capture the central themes of the Counter-Reformation?

reform of the city. The early years of the Reformation in Geneva were stormy, and the doctrines advocated by Calvin met with considerable opposition. In a dispute over church discipline, the city council banished the Protestant pastors. Calvin made his way to Strasbourg, where he remained as a colleague of Martin Bucer and minister to the French refugee church until 1541. Meanwhile, political and religious chaos in Geneva eventually forced the government to seek the return of Calvin. He reluctantly consented, but only with the assurance that his entire original scheme of church polity would be instituted. The ecclesiastical ordinance adopted in 1541 encapsulated that polity and became influential for reformed churches throughout Europe. Written four years later, his Catechism of the Church of Geneva *offers a different vision of the reformer's range of activity. He was no less deeply committed to the inner life of the faithful than he was to the explication of doctrine or the organization of the church. The dedication summarizes the role of education in preserving an embattled and isolated religious community. Calvin remained in Geneva from 1541 until his death in 1564, by which time the city that had accepted reform so reluctantly had been transformed into the center of an international Reformation.*

From *John Calvin*, by G. R. Potter and M. Greengrass (London: Edward Arnold, 1983), pp. 71–76.

First there are four orders of offices instituted by our Saviour for the government of his Church: namely, the pastors, then the doctors, next the elders [*nominated and appointed by the government*,] and fourthly the deacons. If we wish to see the Church well-ordered and maintained we ought to observe this form of government.

The Duty of Pastors

Pastors are sometimes named in the Bible as overseers, elders and ministers. Their work is to proclaim the Word of God, to teach, admonish, exhort and reprove publicly and privately, to administer the sacraments and, with the elders or their deputies, to issue fraternal warnings.

The Examination of Pastors

This consists of two parts. The first concerns doctrine—to find out if the candidate has a good and sound knowledge of the Bible; and, secondly, comes his suitability for expounding this to the people for their edification.

Further, to avoid any danger of his having any wrong ideas, it is fitting that he should profess to accept and uphold the teaching approved by the Church.

Questions must be asked to find out if he is a good teacher and he must privately set forth the teaching of our Lord.

Next, it must be ascertained that he is a man of good principles without any known faults.

The Selection of Pastors

First the ministers should choose someone suitable for the position [*and notify the government*]. Then he is to be presented to the council. If he is approved, he will be accepted and received by the council [*as it thinks fit*]. He is then given a certificate to be produced when he preaches to the people, so that he can be received by the common consent of the faithful. If he is found to be unsuitable and this is demonstrated by evidence, there must be a new selection to find another.

As to the manner of introducing him, because the ceremonies previously used led to a great deal

of superstition, all that is needed is that a minister should explain the nature of the position to which he has been appointed and then prayers and pleas should be made that our Lord will give him grace to do what is needed.

After election he must take an oath of allegiance to the government following a written form as required of a minister.

Weekly Meetings to be Arranged

In the first place it is desirable that all ministers should meet together once a week. This is to maintain purity and agreement in their teaching and to hold Bible discussions. Attendance shall be compulsory unless there is good reason for absence. . . . As for the preachers in the villages under the control of the government, it is for the city ministers to urge them to attend whenever possible. . . .

What Should be Done in Cases of Difference About Doctrine

If any differences of opinion concerning doctrine should arise, the ministers should gather together and discuss the matter. If necessary, they should call in the elders and commissioners [appointed by the government] to assist in the settlement of any difficulties.

There must be some means available to discipline ministers . . . to prevent scandalous living. In this way, respect for the ministry can be maintained and the Word of God not debased by any minister bringing it into scorn and derision. Those who deserve it must be corrected, but at the same time care must be taken to deal with gossip and malicious rumours which can bring harm to innocent parties.

But it is of first importance to notice that certain crimes are quite incompatible with the ministry and cannot be dealt with by fraternal rebuke. Namely heresy, schism, rebellion against Church discipline, open blasphemy deserving civil punishment, simony and corrupt inducement, intriguing to take over one another's position, leaving the Church without special permission, forgery.

There Follows the Second Order Which We Have Called the Doctors

The special duty of the doctors is to instruct the faithful in sound doctrine so that the purity of the gospel is not corrupted by ignorance or wrong opinion.

As thing stand at present, every agent assisting in the upholding of God's teaching is included so that the Church is not in difficulties from a lack of pastors and ministers. This is in common parlance the order of school teachers. The degree nearest the minister and closely joined to the government of the Church is the lecturer in theology.

Establishment of a College

Because it is only possible to profit from such teaching if one is first instructed in languages and humanities, and also because it is necessary to lay the foundations for the future . . . a college should be instituted for instructing children to prepare them for the ministry as well as for civil government.

In the first place suitable accommodation needs to be provided for the teaching of children and others who want to take advantage of it. We also need a literate, scholarly and trained teacher who can take care of the establishment and their education. He should be chosen and paid on the understanding that he should have under his charge teachers in languages and logic, if they can be found. He should also have some student teachers (bacheliers) to teach the little ones. . . .

All who are engaged must be subject to the same ecclesiastical ordinances as apply to the ministers.

There is to be no other school in the city for small children, although the girls are to have a separate school of their own as has been the case up to now.

No one is to be appointed without the approval of the ministers—essential to avoid trouble. [The candidate must first have been notified to the government and then presented to the council. Two members of the 'council of 24' should be present at all interviews.]

Here Follows the Third Order, or Elders

Their duty is to supervise every person's conduct. In friendly fashion they should warn backsliders and those of disorderly life. After that, where necessary, they should report to the Company [of pastors] who will arrange for fraternal correction. . . .

As our Church is now arranged, it would be most suitable to have two elected from the 'council of 24', four from the 'council of 60' and six from the 'council of 200'. They should be men of good repute and conduct. . . . They should be chosen from each quarter of the city so that they can keep an eye on the whole of it.

Method of Choosing the Elders

Further we have decided upon the machinery for choosing them. The 'council of 24' will be asked to nominate the most suitable and adequate men they can discover. In order to do this, they should discuss the matter with the ministers and then present their suggestions to the 'council of 200' for approval. If they are found worthy [and approved], they must take an oath in the same form as it is presented to the ministers. At the end of the year and after the elections to the council, they should present themselves to the government so that a decision can be made as to whether they shall be reappointed or not, but they should not be changed frequently and without good cause provided that they are doing their work faithfully.

The Fourth Order of Ecclesiastical Government, Namely, the Deacons

There have always been two kinds of these in the early Church. One has to receive, distribute and care for the goods of the poor (i.e. daily alms as well as possessions, rents and pensions); the other has to tend and look after the sick and administer the allowances to the poor as is customary. [*In order to avoid confusion*], since we have officials and hospital staff, [*one of the four officials of the said hospital should be responsible for the whole of its*

property and revenues and he should have an adequate salary in order to do his work properly].

Concerning the Hospital[1]

Care should be taken to see that the general hospital is properly maintained. This applies to the sick, to old people no longer able to work, to widows, orphans, children and other poor people. These are to be kept apart and separate from others and to form their own community.

Care for the poor who are scattered throughout the city shall be the responsibility of the officials. In addition to the hospital for those visiting the city, which is to be kept up, separate arrangements are to be made for those who need special treatment. To this end a room must be set apart to act as a reception room for those that are sent there by the officials. . . .

Further, both for the poor people in the hospital and for those in the city who have no means, there must be a good physician and surgeon provided at the city's expense. . . .

As for the plague hospital, it must be kept entirely separate.

Begging

In order to stop begging, which is contrary to good order, the government should use some of its officers to remove any beggars who are obstinately present when people come out of Church.

And this especially if it should happen that the city is visited by this sourge of God.

Of the Sacraments

Baptism is to take place only at sermon time and is to be administered only by ministers or their assistants. A register is to be kept of the names of the

---

[1] The Geneva general hospital had been established in 1535 in one of the series of measures by which the city had broken all connections with the Roman Catholic Church, and which consolidated the various confraternities and eight charitable foundations of the city.

children and of their parents: the justice department is to be informed of any bastard.

Since the Supper was instituted by our Lord to be more often observed by us and also since this was the case in the early Church until such time as the devil upset everything by setting up the mass in its place, the defect ought to be remedied by celebrating it a little more frequently. All the same, for the time being we have agreed and ordained that it should be administered four times a year, i.e. at Christmas, Easter, Pentecost and the first Sunday in September in the autumn.

The ministers shall distribute the bread in orderly and reverent fashion and no other person shall offer the chalice except those appointed (or the deacons) along with the ministers and for this reason there is no need for many plates and cups.

The tables should be set up close to the pulpit so that the mystery can be more suitably set forth near by.

Celebration should take place only in church and at the most suitable time.

Of the Order Which Must be Observed in Obedience to Those in Authority, for the Maintenance of Supervision in the Church

A day should be fixed for the consistory. The elders should meet once a week with the ministers, on a Thursday, to ensure that there is no disorder in the Church and to discuss together any necessary remedial action.

Since they have neither the power nor the authority to use force, we have agreed to assign one of our officials to them to summon those whom they wish to admonish.

If any one should deliberately refuse to appear, the council is to be informed so as to take action.

If any one teaches things contrary to the received doctrine he shall be summoned to a conference. If he listens to reason, let him be sent back without any scandal or disgrace. If he is obstinate,

he should be admonished several times until it is apparent that greater severity is needed: then he shall be forbidden to attend the communion of the Supper and he shall be reported to the magistrates.

If any one fails to come to church to such a degree that there is real dislike for the community of believers manifested, or if any one shows that he cares nothing for ecclesiastical order, let him be admonished, and if he is tractable let him be amicably sent back. If however he goes from bad to worse, after having been warned three times, let him be cut off from the Church and be denounced to the magistrate. . . .

[*All this must be done in such a way that the ministers have no civil jurisdiction nor use anything but the spiritual sword of the word of God as St Paul commands them; nor is the authority of the consistory to diminish in any way that of the magistrate or ordinary justice. The civil power must remain unimpaired. In cases where, in future, there may be a need to impose punishments or constrain individuals, then the ministers and the consistory, having heard the case and used such admonitions and exhortations as are appropriate, should report the whole matter to the council which, in turn, will judge and sentence according to the needs of the case.*]

*   *   *

REVIEW QUESTIONS

1. What is the church according to Calvin?
2. What is its structure?
3. What do the four offices tell us about the function of the church?
4. What is the purpose of the church?
5. What are its goals?
6. What are the practices of the church and the relation of those practices to the process of becoming a Christian?
7. What is the relation between the church and salvation?

JOHN CALVIN

FROM Catechism of the Church of Geneva, Being a Form of Instruction for Children in the Doctrine of Christ, 1545

From *Tracts Relating to the Reformation*, vol. 2, by John Calvin, translated by Henry Beveridge (Edinburgh: The Calvin Translation Society, 1844–1851), pp. 34–37.

Dedication.

JOHN CALVIN TO THE FAITHFUL MINISTERS OF CHRIST THROUGHOUT EAST FRIESLAND, WHO PREACH THE PURE DOCTRINE OF THE GOSPEL.

Seeing it becomes us to endeavour by all means that unity of faith, which is so highly commended by Paul, shine forth among us, to this end chiefly ought the formal profession of faith which accompanies our common baptism to have reference. Hence it were to be wished, not only that a perpetual consent in the doctrine of piety should appear among all, but also that one CATECHISM were common to all the Churches. But as, from many causes, it will scarcely ever obtain otherwise than that each Church shall have its own Catechism, we should not strive too keenly to prevent this; provided, however, that the variety in the mode of teaching is such, that we are all directed to one Christ, in whose truth being united together, we may grow up into one body and one spirit, and with the same mouth also proclaim whatever belongs to the sum of faith. Catechists not intent on this end, besides fatally injuring the Church, by sowing the materials of dissension in religion, also introduce an impious profanation of baptism. For where can any longer be the utility of baptism unless this remain as its foundation—that we all agree in one faith?

Wherefore, those who publish Catechisms ought to be the more carefully on their guard, lest, by producing anything rashly, they may not for the present only, but in regard to posterity also, do grievous harm to piety, and inflict a deadly wound on the Church.

This much I wished to premise, as a declaration to my readers, that I myself too, as became me, have made it my anxious care not to deliver any thing in this Catechism of mine that is not agreeable to the doctrine received among all the pious. This declaration will not be found vain by those who will read with candour and sound judgment. I trust I have succeeded at least so far that my labour, though it should not satisfy, will be acceptable to all good men, as being in their opinion useful.

In writing it in Latin, though some perhaps will not approve of the design, I have been influenced by many reasons, all of which it is of no use to detail at present. I shall only select such as seem to me sufficient to obviate censure.

First, In this confused and divided state of Christendom, I judge it useful that there should be public testimonies, whereby churches which, though widely separated by space, agree in the doctrine of Christ, may mutually recognise each other. For besides that this tends not a little to mutual confirmation, what is more to be desired than that mutual congratulations should pass between them, and that they should devoutly commend each other to the Lord? With this view, bishops were wont in old time, when as yet consent in faith existed and flourished among all, to send Synodal Epistles beyond sea, by which, as a kind of badges,

they might maintain sacred communion among the churches. How much more necessary is it now, in this fearful devastation of the Christian world, that the few churches which duly worship God, and they too scattered and hedged round on all sides by the profane synagogues of Antichrist, should mutually give and receive this token of holy union, that they may thereby be incited to that fraternal embrace of which I have spoken?

But if this is so necessary in the present day, what shall our feelings be concerning posterity, about which I am so anxious, that I scarcely dare to think? Unless God miraculously send help from heaven, I cannot avoid seeing that the world is threatened with the extremity of barbarism. I wish our children may not shortly feel, that this has been rather a true prophecy than a conjecture. The more, therefore, must we labour to gather together, by our writings, whatever remains of the Church shall continue, or even emerge, after our death. Writings of a different class will show what were our views on all subjects in religion, but the agreement which our churches had in doctrine cannot be seen with clearer evidence than from catechisms. For therein will appear, not only what one man or other once taught, but with what rudiments learned and unlearned alike amongst us, were constantly imbued from childhood, all the faithful holding them as their formal symbol of Christian communion. This was indeed my principal reason for publishing this Catechism.

A second reason, which had no little weight with me, was, because I heard that it was desired by very many who hoped it would not be unworthy of perusal. Whether they are right or wrong in so judging is not mine to decide, but it became me to yield to their wish. Nay, necessity was almost laid upon me, and I could not with impunity decline it. For having seven years before published a brief summary of religion, under the name of a Catechism, I feared that if I did not bring forward this one, I should cause (a thing I wished not) that the former should on the other hand be excluded. Therefore if I wished to consult the public good, it behoved me to take care that this one which I preferred should occupy the ground.

Besides, I deem it of good example to testify to the world, that we who aim at the restitution of the Church, are everywhere faithfully exerting ourselves, in order that, at least, the use of the Catechism which was abolished some centuries ago under the Papacy, may now resume its lost rights. For neither can this holy custom be sufficiently commended for its utility, nor can the Papists be sufficiently condemned for the flagrant corruption, by which they not only set it aside, by converting it into puerile trifles, but also basely abuse it to purposes of impure and impious superstition. That spurious Confirmation, which they have substituted in its stead, they deck out like a harlot, with great splendour of ceremonies, and gorgeous shows without number; nay, in their wish to adorn it, they speak of it in terms of execrable blasphemy, when they give out that it is a sacrament of greater dignity than baptism, and call those only half Christians who have not been besmeared with their oil. Meanwhile, the whole proceeding consists of nothing but theatrical gesticulations, or rather the wanton sporting of apes, without any skill in imitation.

To you, my very dear brethren in the Lord, I have chosen to inscribe this work, because some of your body, besides informing me that you love me, and that the most of you take delight in my writings, also expressly requested me by letter to undertake this labour for their sake. Independently of this, it would have been reason sufficient, that what I learned of you long ago, from the statement of grave and pious men, had bound me to you with my whole soul. I now ask what I am confident you will of your own accord do—have the goodness to consult for the utility of this token of my goodwill towards you! Farewell. May the Lord increase you more and more in the spirit of wisdom, prudence, zeal, and fortitude, to the edification of his Church.

GENEVA, *2d December*, 1545.

TO THE READER.

It has ever been the practice of the Church, and one carefully attended to, to see that children should be duly instructed in the Christian religion.

That this might be done more conveniently, not only were schools opened in old time, and individuals enjoined properly to teach their families, but it was a received public custom and practice, to question children in the churches on each of the heads, which should be common and well known to all Christians. To secure this being done in order, there was written out a formula, which was called a Catechism or Institute. Thereafter the devil miserably rending the Church of God, and bringing upon it fearful ruin, (of which the marks are still too visible in the greater part of the world,) overthrew this sacred policy, and left nothing behind but certain trifles, which only beget superstition, without any fruit of edification. Of this description is that confirmation, as they call it, full of gesticulations which, worse than ridiculous, are fitted only for apes, and have no foundation to rest upon. What we now bring forward, therefore, is nothing else than the use of things which from ancient times were observed by Christians, and the true worshippers of God, and which never were laid aside until the Church was wholly corrupted.

REVIEW QUESTIONS

1. What is the purpose of catechism for John Calvin, and how does his purpose differ from that of Martin Luther?
2. Who, according to Calvin, should be taught catechism, and who should do the teaching?
3. How did Calvin reconcile the unity of faith, which he hoped his catechism would serve, and the diversity of local circumstances and observances, which he expected would be the case?
4. What do this hope for unity and this admission of diversity tell us about the Reformation as Calvin understood it?
5. Use the catechism as a measure of the reformers' concerns and goals to explain how had these changed between 1530, when Luther published his *Large Catechism*, and 1545, when Calvin dedicated the *Catechism of the Church of Geneva*. Do the titles reveal anything?
6. Why did Calvin compose his catechism in Latin rather than a vernacular language, as did Martin Luther?

SAINT IGNATIUS OF LOYOLA

FROM *The Spiritual Exercises*

Saint Ignatius of Loyola (1491–1556), the great mystic and founder of the Society of Jesus, was born into a hidalgo family and spent his early manhood in military service to the king of Spain. Wounded in battle, he spent his convalescence reading the lives of saints, which awoke in him a sense of spiritual inadequacy not unlike those which fired the religious engagements of Martin Luther and John Calvin. His early attempts at reconciliation, in the form of physical austerities practiced on pilgrimage to Montserrat and in the hermitage at Manresa, failed to reassure him of his soul's salvation, just as they failed to ease the spiritual torments of the young Luther. The scholastically trained Luther sought solace in the systematic study of the Bible; the uneducated Loyola found it in visions of God. Loyola spent the next decade educating himself and seeking his mission. After a pilgrimage to the Holy Land in 1523, Loyola began his formal education by studying elementary Latin with schoolboys in Barcelona. He attended the universities in Alcalá and Salamanca, preached in the

streets, and was arrested by the Inquisition on suspicion of heresy. He attended the University of Paris from 1528 to 1535 and began to gather around him the companions who would form the initial core of the Society of Jesus. In 1534, he and nine companions swore an oath of poverty and chastity and promised either to undertake a crusade to the Holy Land or, failing that, to offer absolute obedience to the pope. At the center of this group was not only the man Loyola but his series of devotions and meditations that would later be published as The Spiritual Exercises *(1548). These exercises offered a practical and ascetic meditation on the life and death of Christ that drew much from the systematic meditations of the* devotio moderna *("modern devotions"). This system instructed those who made or directed a religious retreat in order to stimulate an imitation of Christ that would be expressed in apostolic action as well as religious devotion. In 1535, Loyola and his company left for Italy. He was ordained in Venice in 1537. Finding no passage to the Holy Land, they continued to Rome, where they preached in the streets and ministered to the poor. Introduced to Pope Paul III by Gasparo Contarini, a great advocate of monastic reform, the company received a charter of foundation as the Society of Jesus in 1540. Constituted an order of clerks regular, devoted to educating the young and propagating the faith, sworn to poverty and obedience, the Jesuits grew quickly to become one of the most influential Catholic orders of the early modern period, a model of piety, discipline, education, and service.*

From *The Spiritual Exercises of St. Ignatius of Loyola,* translated from the *Autograph* by Father Elder Mullen, S. J. (New York: P. J. Kennedy and Sons, 1914).

To Have the True Sentiment Which We Ought to Have in the Church Militant

Let the following Rules be observed.

First Rule. All judgment laid aside, we ought to have our mind ready and prompt to obey, in all, the true Spouse of Christ our Lord, which is our holy Mother the Church Hierarchical.

Second Rule. To praise confession to a Priest, and the reception of the most Holy Sacrament of the Altar once in the year, and much more each month, and much better from week to week, with the conditions required and due.

Third Rule. To praise the hearing of Mass often, likewise hymns, psalms, and long prayers, in the church and out of it; likewise the hours set at the time fixed for each Divine Office and for all prayer and all Canonical Hours.

Fourth Rule. To praise much Religious Orders, virginity and continence, and not so much marriage as any of these.

Fifth Rule. To praise vows of Religion, of obedience, of poverty, of chastity and of other perfections of supererogation. And it is to be noted that as the vow is about the things which approach to Evangelical perfection, a vow ought not to be made in the things which withdraw from it, such as to be a merchant, or to be married, etc.

Sixth Rule. To praise relics of the Saints, giving veneration to them and praying to the Saints; and to praise Stations, pilgrimages, Indulgences, pardons, Cruzadas, and candles lighted in the churches.

Seventh Rule. To praise Constitutions about fasts and abstinence, as of Lent, Ember Days, Vigils, Friday and Saturday; likewise penances, not only interior, but also exterior.

Eighth Rule. To praise the ornaments and the buildings of churches; likewise images, and to venerate them according to what they represent.

Ninth Rule. Finally, to praise all precepts of the Church, keeping the mind prompt to find reasons in their defence and in no manner against them.

Tenth Rule. We ought to be more prompt to find good and praise as well the Constitutions and recommendations as the ways of our Superiors. Because, although some are not or have not been such, to speak against them, whether preaching in public or discoursing before the common people, would rather give rise to fault-finding and scandal than profit; and so the people would be incensed against their Superiors, whether temporal or spiritual. So that, as it does harm to speak evil to the common people of Superiors in their absence, so it can make profit to speak of the evil ways to the persons themselves who can remedy them.

Eleventh Rule. To praise positive and scholastic learning. Because, as it is more proper to the Positive Doctors, as St. Jerome, St. Augustine and St. Gregory, etc., to move the heart to love and serve God our Lord in everything; so it is more proper to the Scholastics, as St. Thomas, St. Bonaventure, and to the Master of the Sentences, etc., to define or explain for our times the things necessary for eternal salvation; and to combat and explain better all errors and all fallacies. For the Scholastic Doctors, as they are more modern, not only help themselves with the true understanding of the Sacred Scripture and of the Positive and holy Doctors, but also, they being enlightened and clarified by the Divine virtue, help themselves by the Councils, Canons and Constitutions of our holy Mother the Church.

Twelfth Rule. We ought to be on our guard in making comparison of those of us who are alive to the blessed passed away, because error is committed not a little in this; that is to say, in saying, this one knows more than St. Augustine; he is another, or greater than, St. Francis; he is another St. Paul in goodness, holiness, etc.

Thirteenth Rule. To be right in everything, we ought always to hold that the white which I see, is black, if the Hierarchical Church so decides it, believing that between Christ our Lord, the Bridegroom, and the Church, His Bride, there is the same Spirit which governs and directs us for the salvation of our souls. Because by the same Spirit and our

Lord Who gave the ten Commandments, our holy Mother the Church is directed and governed.

Fourteenth Rule. Although there is much truth in the assertion that no one can save himself without being predestined and without having faith and grace; we must be very cautious in the manner of speaking and communicating with others about all these things.

Fifteenth Rule. We ought not, by way of custom, to speak much of predestination; but if in some way and at some times one speaks, let him so speak that the common people may not come into any error, as sometimes happens, saying: Whether I have to be saved or condemned is already determined, and no other thing can now be, through my doing well or ill; and with this, growing lazy, they become negligent in the works which lead to the salvation and the spiritual profit of their souls.

Sixteenth Rule. In the same way, we must be on our guard that by talking much and with much insistence of faith, without any distinction and explanation, occasion be not given to the people to be lazy and slothful in works, whether before faith is formed in charity or after.

Seventeenth Rule. Likewise, we ought not to speak so much with insistence on grace that the poison of discarding liberty be engendered. So that of faith and grace one can speak as much as is possible with the Divine help for the greater praise of His Divine Majesty, but not in such way, nor in such manners, especially in our so dangerous times, that works and free will receive any harm, or be held for nothing.

Eighteenth Rule. Although serving God our Lord much out of pure love is to be esteemed above all; we ought to praise much the fear of His Divine Majesty, because not only filial fear is a thing pious and most holy, but even servile fear—when the man reaches nothing else better or more useful—helps much to get out of mortal sin. And when he is out, he easily comes to filial fear, which is all acceptable and grateful to God our Lord: as being at one with the Divine Love.

*   *   *

REVIEW QUESTIONS

1. What do you suppose Loyola means by the *Church Militant?*
2. How might the Jesuits have been soldiers of Christ?

3. Loyola asks the members of his order to "praise" in order to be "thinking with the Church." How does this serve the Church?
4. What specifically does Loyola ask the Jesuits to praise?
5. What do the "Rules for Thinking with the Church" tell us about the Church?

SAINT FRANCIS XAVIER

FROM "Letter from India"

Saint Francis Xavier (l506–1552) was one of the original companions of Saint Ignatius of Loyola and one of the original members of the Society of Jesus. The two became friends during their student years at the University of Paris. Shortly after the founding of the Society, Loyola sent Xavier on a mission to Portugal's mercantile empire in South Asia. After a voyage that lasted more than a year, he arrived in Goa on the Coromandel coast of India, accompanied by the Portuguese governor, Don Martin Alfonso de Sousa, and two fellow missionaries, Father Paul and Francis Mancias, not yet in holy orders. It was at Sousa's behest that Xavier turn his attention to the pearl-fishing villages of Cape Comorin, in an effort to spread Christianity among those peoples and, so, bring them more fully into the Portuguese sphere of influence. It was from Comorin that Xavier wrote the following letter. He would remain there two years before spreading his mission to the East Indies and Japan. He died in 1552, waiting to extend his work to China. His was a life of extraordinary hardship and danger as well as extraordinary activity and achievement. To him belongs credit for extending Roman Christianity and Western ideas to Asian peoples.

From *The Life and Letters of St Francis Xavier*, vol. 1, edited by Henry James Coleridge, 2d ed. (London: Burns and Oates, 1890), pp. 151–63.

To the Society at Rome

May the grace and charity of Christ our Lord always help and favour us! Amen.

It is now the third year since I left Portugal. I am writing to you for the third time, having as yet received only one letter from you, dated February 1542. God is my witness what joy it caused me. I only received it two months ago—later than is usual for letters to reach India, because the vessel which brought it had passed the winter at Mozambique.

I and Francis Mancias are now living amongst the Christians of Comorin. They are very numerous, and increase largely every day. When I first

came I asked them, if they knew anything about our Lord Jesus Christ? but when I came to the points of faith in detail and asked them what they thought of them, and what more they believed now than when they were Infidels, they only replied that they were Christians, but that as they are ignorant of Portuguese, they know nothing of the precepts and mysteries of our holy religion. We could not understand one another, as I spoke Castilian and they Malabar; so I picked out the most intelligent and well read of them, and then sought out with the greatest diligence men who knew both languages. We held meetings for several days, and by our joint efforts and with infinite difficulty we translated the Catechism into the Malabar tongue. This I learnt by heart, and then I began to go through all the villages of the coast, calling around me by the sound of a bell as many as I could, children and men. I asembled them twice a day and taught them the Christian doctrine: and thus, in the space of a month, the children had it well by heart. And all the time I kept telling them to go on teaching in their turn whatever they had learnt to their parents, family, and neighbours.

Every Sunday I collected them all, men and women, boys and girls, in the church. They came with great readiness and with a great desire for instruction. Then, in the hearing of all, I began by calling on the name of the most holy Trinity, Father, Son, and Holy Ghost, and I recited aloud the Lord's Prayer, the *Hail Mary*, and the Creed in the language of the country: they all followed me in the same words, and delighted in it wonderfully. Then I repeated the Creed by myself, dwelling upon each article singly. Then I asked them as to each article, whether they believed it unhesitatingly; and all, with a loud voice and their hands crossed over their breasts, professed aloud that they truly believed it. I take care to make them repeat the Creed oftener than the other prayers; and I tell them that those who believe all that is contained therein are called Christians. After explaining the Creed I go on to the Commandments, teaching them that the Christian law is contained in those ten precepts, and that every one who observes them all faithfully is a good and true Christian and is certain of eternal salvation, and that, on the other hand, whoever neglects

a single one of them is a bad Christian, and will be cast into hell unless he is truly penitent for his sin. Converts and heathen alike are astonished at all this, which shows them the holiness of the Christian law, its perfect consistency with itself, and its agreement with reason. . . .

*   *   *

The fruit that is reaped by the baptism of infants, as well as by the instruction of children and others, is quite incredible. These children, I trust heartily, by the grace of God, will be much better than their fathers. They show an ardent love for the Divine law, and an extraordinary zeal for learning our holy religion and imparting it to others. Their hatred for idolatry is marvellous. They get into feuds with the heathen about it, and whenever their own parents practise it, they reproach them and come off to tell me at once. Whenever I hear of any act of idolatrous worship, I go to the place with a large band of these children, who very soon load the devil with a greater amount of insult and abuse than he has lately received of honour and worship from their parents, relations, and acquaintances. The children run at the idols, upset them, dash them down, break them to pieces, spit on them, trample on them, kick them about, and in short heap on them every possible outrage.

I had been living for nearly four months in a Christian village, occupied in translating the Catechism. A great number of natives came from all parts to entreat me to take the trouble to go to their houses and call on God by the bedsides of their sick relatives. Such numbers also of sick made their own way to us, that I had enough to do to read a Gospel over each of them. At the same time we kept on with our daily work, instructing the children, baptizing converts, translating the Catechism, answering difficulties, and burying the dead. For my part I desired to satisfy all, both the sick who came to me themselves, and those who came to beg on the part of others, lest if I did not, their confidence in, and zeal for, our holy religion should relax, and I thought it wrong not to do what I could in answer to their prayers. But the thing grew to such a pitch that it was impossible for me myself to satisfy all,

and at the same time to avoid their quarrelling among themselves, every one striving to be the first to get me to his own house; so I hit on a way of serving all at once. As I could not go myself, I sent round children whom I could trust in my place. They went to the sick persons, assembled their families and neighbours, recited the Creed with them, and encouraged the sufferers to conceive a certain and wellfounded confidence of their restoration. Then after all this, they recited the prayers of the Church. To make my tale short, God was moved by the faith and piety of these children and of the others, and restored to a great number of sick persons health both of body and soul. How good He was to them! He made the very disease of their bodies the occasion of calling them to salvation, and drew them to the Christian faith almost by force!

I have also charged these children to teach the rudiments of Christian doctrine to the ignorant in private houses, in the streets, and the crossways. As soon as I see that this has been well started in one village, I go on to another and give the same instructions and the same commission to the children, and so I go through in order the whole number of their villages. When I have done this and am going away, I leave in each place a copy of the Christian doctrine, and tell all those who know how to write to copy it out, and all the others are to learn it by heart and to recite it from memory every day. Every feast day I bid them meet in one place and sing all together the elements of the faith. For this purpose I have appointed in each of the thirty Christian villages men of intelligence and character who are to preside over these meetings, and the Governor, Don Martin Alfonso, who is so full of love for our Society and of zeal for religion, has been good enough at our request to allot a yearly revenue of 4000 gold *fanams* for the salary of these catechists. He has an immense friendship for ours, and desires with all his heart that some of them should be sent hither, for which he is always asking in his letters to the King.

*   *   *

We have in these parts a class of men among the pagans who are called Brahmins. They keep up the worship of the gods, the superstitious rites of religion, frequenting the temples and taking care of the idols. They are as perverse and wicked a set as can anywhere be found, and I always apply to them the words of holy David, "from an unholy race and a wicked and crafty man deliver me, O Lord." They are liars and cheats to the very backbone. Their whole study is, how to deceive most cunningly the simplicity and ignorance of the people. They give out publicly that the gods command certain offerings to be made to their temples, which offerings are simply the things that the Brahmins themselves wish for, for their own maintenance and that of their wives, children, and servants. Thus they make the poor folk believe that the images of their gods eat and drink, dine and sup like men, and some devout persons are found who really offer to the idol twice a day, before dinner and supper, a certain sum of money. The Brahmins eat sumptuous meals to the sound of drums, and make the ignorant believe that the gods are banqueting. When they are in need of any supplies, and even before, they give out to the people that the gods are angry because the things they have asked for have not been sent, and that if the people do not take care, the gods will punish them by slaughter, disease, and the assaults of the devils. And the poor ignorant creatures, with the fear of the gods before them, obey them implicitly. ✱ ✱ ✱

The heathen inhabitants of the country are commonly ignorant of letters, but by no means ignorant of wickedness. All the time I have been here in this country I have only converted one Brahmin, a virtuous young man, who has now undertaken to teach the Catechism to children. As I go through the Christian villages, I often pass by the temples of the Brahmins, which they call pagodas. One day lately, I happened to enter a pagoda where there were about two hundred of them, and most of them came to meet me. We had a long conversation, after which I asked them what their gods enjoined them in order to obtain the life of the blessed. There was a long discussion amongst them as to who should answer me. At last, by common consent, the commission was given to one of them, of greater age and experience than the rest, an old man, of more than eighty years. He asked me in return, what commands the God of the Christians

laid on them. I saw the old man's perversity, and I refused to speak a word till he had first answered my question. So he was obliged to expose his ignorance, and replied that their gods required two duties of those who desired to go to them hereafter, one of which was to abstain from killing cows, because under that form the gods were adored; the other was to show kindness to the Brahmins, who were the worshippers of the gods. This answer moved my indignation, for I could not but grieve intensely at the thought of the devils being worshipped instead of God by these blind heathen, and I asked them to listen to me in turn. Then I, in a loud voice, repeated the Apostles' Creed and the Ten Commandments. After this I gave in their own language a short explanation, and told them what Paradise is, and what Hell is, and also who they are who go to Heaven to join the company of the blessed, and who are to be sent to the eternal punishments of hell. Upon hearing these things they all rose up and vied with one another in embracing me, and in confessing that the God of the Christians is the true God, as His laws are so agreeable to reason. Then they asked me if the souls of men like those of other animals perished together with the body. God put into my mouth arguments of such a sort, and so suited to their ways of thinking, that to their great joy I was able to prove to them the immortality of the soul. I find, by the way, that the arguments which are to convince these ignorant people must by no means be subtle, such as those which are found in the books of learned schoolmen, but must be such as their minds can understand. They asked me again how the soul of a dying person goes out of the body, how it was, whether it was as happens to us in dreams, when we seem to be conversing with our friends and acquaintance? (Ah, how often this happens to me, dearest brothers, when I am dreaming of you!) Was this because the soul then leaves the body? And again, whether God was black or white? For as there is so great a variety of colour among men, and the Indians being black themselves, consider their own colour the best, they believe that their gods are black. On this account the great majority of their idols are as black

as black can be, and moreover are generally so rubbed over with oil as to smell detestably, and seem to be as dirty as they are ugly and horrible to look at. To all these questions I was able to reply so as to satisfy them entirely. But when I came to the point at last, and urged them to embrace the religion which they felt to be true, they made that same objection which we hear from many Christians when urged to change their life,—that they would set men talking about them if they altered their ways and their religion, and besides, they said that they should be afraid that, if they did so, they would have nothing to live on and support themselves by.

I have found just one Brahmin and no more in all this coast who is a man of learning: he is said to have studied in a very famous Academy. Knowing this, I took measures to converse with him alone. He then told me at last, as a great secret, that the students of this Academy are at the outset made by their masters to take an oath not to reveal their mysteries, but that, out of friendship for me, he would disclose them to me. One of these mysteries was that there only exists one God, the Creator and Lord of heaven and earth, whom men are bound to worship, for the idols are simply images of devils, The Brahmins have certain books of sacred literature which contain, as they say, the laws of God. The masters teach in a learned tongue, as we do in Latin. He also explained to me these divine precepts one by one; but it would be a long business to write out his commentary, and indeed not worth the trouble. Their sages keep as a feast our Sunday. On this day they repeat at different hours this one player: "I adore Thee, O God; and I implore Thy help for ever." They are bound by oath to repeat this prayer frequently, and in a low voice. My friend added, that the law of nature permitted them to have more wives than one, and their sacred books predicted that the time would come when all men should embrace the same religion. After all this he asked me in my turn to explain the principal mysteries of the Christian religion, promising to keep them secret. I replied, that I would not tell him a word about them unless he promised beforehand to publish abroad what I should tell him of the reli-

gion of Jesus Christ. He made the promise, and then I carefully explained to him those words of Jesus Christ in which our religion is summed up: "He who believes and is baptized shall be saved." This text, with my commentary on it, which embraced the whole of the Apostles' Creed, he wrote down carefully, as well as the Commandments, on account of their close connection with the Creed. He told me also that one night he had dreamt that he had been made a Christian to his immense delight, and that he had become my brother and companion. He ended by begging me to make him a Christian secretly. But as he made certain conditions opposed to right and justice, I put off his baptism. I don't doubt but that by God's mercy he will one day be a Christian. I charged him to teach the ignorant and unlearned that there is only one God, Creator of heaven and earth; but he pleaded the obligation of his oath, and said he could not do so, es-

pecially as he was much afraid that if he did it he should become possessed by an evil spirit. ✶ ✶ ✶

REVIEW QUESTIONS

1. What was involved in the conversion of Asian peoples to Christianity?
2. What were the greatest challenges that Xavier and his fellows confronted?
3. How did Xavier's values shape his perception of Asian peoples?
4. How would you describe the reception of Christian missionaries and Christianity among the people of Cape Comorin?
5. How might Xavier and his mission have shaped the interaction and understanding of East and West?

SAINT TERESA OF ÁVILA

FROM *The Life of Teresa of Jesus*

Saint Teresa of Ávila (1515–1582) was a Spanish mystic, spiritual author, and monastic reformer. Her worldly achievements were great, to which the Discalced Carmelites still bear witness; in addition, the beauty of her inner life, as revealed in her writings, earned her recognition as one of the world's great female religious authors. Teresa was born in central Spain, the daughter of a wealthy hidalgo. At age fourteen, she was sent to a boarding school, where she became ill and began to consider her life's vocation. Despite paternal opposition, Teresa became a novice in a Carmelite convent around 1535. Her health collapsed again, leaving her an invalid for three years. During her convalescence, she began the series of meditations that would establish her reputation as a mystic. It took her fifteen years to perfect the prayers and meditations that would lead to her ecstatic visions and conversations with God. Her most celebrated work, The Life, *written in obedience to her confessors and directors, captured this process as the history of a soul, much like Augustine's* Confessions. *They*

combine religious ardor with human candor, an insistence that her experiences were a gift of God with an unwillingness to claim any spiritual distinction.

In 1558, Teresa began to consider the restoration of Carmelite life to its original observance of austerity. It required complete separation from the world to promote prayerful meditation, such as was enjoined in the Primitive Carmelite Rule of 1247. In 1562, with the authorization of Pope Pius IV, Teresa and four companions opened the first convent of the Carmelite reform. Despite intense opposition from secular and ecclesiastical officials, her efforts eventually won the approval of the Carmelite general as well as his mandate to extend her reform to men. In 1567, she met a young Carmelite priest, Juan de Yepes, later canonized as Saint John of the Cross, a brilliant friar who helped her initiate the Carmelite reform for men. In her lifetime, she saw sixteen convents and twelve monasteries established. The last decades of her life were given to this work. Forty years after her death, she was canonized; in 1970, she was made a doctor of the Church.

From *The Life of Theresa of Jesus: The Autobiography of Teresa of Avila,* translated by E. Allison Peters (New York: Bantam Doubleday Dell, 1991), pp. 68–71.

*   *   *

I have strayed far from any intention, for I was trying to give the reasons why this kind of vision cannot be the work of the imagination. How could we picture Christ's Humanity by merely studying the subject or form any impression of His great beauty by means of the imagination? No little time would be necessary if such a reproduction was to be in the least like the original. One can indeed make such a picture with one's imagination, and spend time in regarding it, and considering the form and the brilliance of it; little by little one may even learn to perfect such an image and store it up in the memory. Who can prevent this? Such a picture can undoubtedly be fashioned with the understanding. But with regard to the vision which we are discussing there is no way of doing this: we have to look at it when the Lord is pleased to reveal it to us—to look as He wills and at whatever He wills. And there is no possibility of our subtracting from it or adding to it, or any way in which we can obtain it, whatever we may do, or look at it when we like or refrain from looking at it. If we try to look at any particular part of it, we at once lose Christ.

For two years and a half things went on like this and it was quite usual for God to grant me this favour. It must now be more than three years since He took it from me as a continually recurring favour, by giving me something else of a higher kind, which I shall describe later. Though I saw that He was speaking to me, and though I was looking upon that great beauty of His, and experiencing the sweetness with which He uttered those words—sometimes stern words—with that most lovely and Divine mouth, and though, too, I was extremely desirous of observing the colour of His eyes, or His height, so that I should be able to describe it, I have never been sufficiently worthy to see this, nor has it been of any use for me to attempt to do so; if I tried, I lost the vision altogether. Though I sometimes see Him looking at me compassionately, His gaze has such power that my soul cannot endure it and remains in so sublime a rapture that it loses this beauteous vision in order to have the greater fruition of it all. So there is no question here of our wanting or not wanting to see the vision. It is clear that the Lord wants of us only humility and shame, our acceptance of what is given us and our praise of its Giver.

This refers to all visions, none excepted. There is nothing that we can do about them; we cannot see more or less of them at will; and we can neither call them up nor banish them by our own efforts. The Lord's will is that we shall see quite

clearly that they are produced, not by us but by His Majesty. Still less can we be proud of them: on the contrary, they make us humble and fearful, when we find that, just as the Lord takes from us the power of seeing what we desire, so He can also take from us these favours and His grace, with the result that we are completely lost. So while we live in this exile let us always walk with fear.

Almost invariably the Lord showed Himself to me in His resurrection body, and it was thus, too, that I saw Him in the Host. Only occasionally, to strengthen me when I was in tribulation, did He show me His wounds, and then He would appear sometimes as He was on the Cross and sometimes as in the Garden. On a few occasions I saw Him wearing the crown of thorns and sometimes He would also be carrying the Cross—because of my necessities, as I say, and those of others—but always in His glorified flesh. Many are the affronts and trials that I have suffered through telling this and many are the fears and persecutions that it has brought me. So sure were those whom I told of it that I had a devil that some of them wanted to exorcize me. This troubled me very little, but I was sorry when I found that my confessors were afraid to hear my confessions or when I heard that people were saying things to them against me. None the less, I could never regret having seen these heavenly visions and I would not exchange them for all the good things and delights of this world. I always considered them a great favour from the Lord, and I think they were the greatest of treasures; often the Lord Himself would reassure me about them. I found my love for Him growing exceedingly: I used to go to Him and tell Him about all these trials and I always came away from prayer comforted and with new strength. I did not dare to argue with my critics, because I saw that that made things worse, as they thought me lacking in humility. With my confessor, however, I did discuss these matters; and whenever he saw that I was troubled he would comfort me greatly.

As the visions became more numerous, one of those who had previously been in the habit of helping me and who used sometimes to hear my confessions when the minister was unable to do so, began to say that it was clear I was being deceived by the devil. So, as I was quite unable to resist it, they commanded me to make the sign of the Cross whenever I had a vision, and to snap my fingers at it so as to convince myself that it came from the devil, whereupon it would not come again: I was not to be afraid, they said, and God would protect me and take the vision away. This caused me great distress: as I could not help believing that my visions came from God, it was a terrible thing to have to do; and, as I have said, I could not possibly wish them to be taken from me. However, I did as they commanded me. I besought God often to set me free from deception; indeed, I was continually doing so and with many tears. I would also invoke Saint Peter and Saint Paul, for the Lord had told me (it was on their festival that He had first appeared to me) that they would prevent me from being deluded; and I used often to see them very clearly on my left hand, though not in an imaginary vision. These glorious Saints were in a very real sense my lords.

To be obliged to snap my fingers at a vision in which I saw the Lord caused me the sorest distress. For, when I saw Him before me, I could not have believed that the vision had come from the devil even if the alternative were my being cut to pieces. So this was a kind of penance to me, and a heavy one. In order not to have to be so continually crossing myself, I would carry a cross in my hand. This I did almost invariably; but I was not so particular about snapping my fingers at the vision, for it hurt me too much to do that. It reminded me of the way the Jews had insulted Him, and I would beseech Him to forgive me, since I did it out of obedience to him who was in His own place, and not to blame me, since he was one of the ministers whom He had placed in His Church. He told me not to worry about it and said I was quite right to obey, but He would see that my confessor learned the truth. When they made me stop my prayer He seemed to me to have become angry, and He told me to tell them that this was tyranny. He used to show me ways of knowing that the visions were not of the devil; some of these I shall describe later.

⁕   ⁕   ⁕

REVIEW QUESTIONS

1. What distinguishes Teresa's spirituality from that of Ignatius of Loyola?

2. Might we call her spirituality feminine?
3. Is Teresa's piety private or public? In what ways?
4. Are visions portable?
5. Are they entirely private?
6. How does language fail Teresa?

FROM *Canons and Decrees of the Council of Trent*

The great centerpiece of Catholic reform and reaction was the ecumenical Council of Trent, held in several sessions between 1545 and 1563. From the beginning of the sixteenth century, Catholic clergy, secular leaders, and Protestant reformers had called for an ecumenical council to address the inadequacies of the Catholic Church. Popes had resisted the tactic just as insistently for fear that such a council might be used to limit papal authority, as, indeed, had been the case in the fifteenth century. Pope Paul III, however, realized that a council might serve the cause of papal authority as well as that of church reform and accordingly called a council to meet in the city of Trent, located in imperial territory but still close to Rome. Agreements on procedures and the leadership of papal legates assured that the council remained firmly under papal direction and set a tone of doctrinal and disciplinary conservatism. Its deliberations and decisions divide themselves into three great periods. The first period, 1545–47, was devoted to dogma. The council rejected the Protestant teaching on Scripture as the sole source of religious truth and insisted that Scripture and tradition were equally authoritative. It retained the traditional seven sacraments. Most important, it rejected the Protestant doctrine of justification. During the second period, 1551–52, the council reasserted the traditional Catholic teaching on the Eucharist, rejecting the interpretations of Luther, Zwingli, and Calvin. Long delayed by political events and papal indifference, the council reconvened for the third and last time in 1562. In its final year, the council defined the Mass, addressed various liturgical issues, and resolved disciplinary issues such as clerical residency and training. Viewed in its entirety, the Council of Trent strengthened the authority of the papacy in the Catholic Church. If its decrees and canons were largely conservative, they were also unmistakable in their clarity and uniformity. In its pronouncements on discipline, it laid the foundations for a better-educated, more conscientious clergy. The Council of Trent clearly defined Catholic Christianity in opposition to Protestantism.

From *Canons and Decrees of the Council of Trent*, translated by H. J. Schroeder (London: Herder, 1941).

*   *   *

Fourth Session
Celebrated on the Eighth Day
of April 1546

DECREE CONCERNING THE CANONICAL SCRIPTURES

The holy, ecumenical and general Council of Trent, lawfully assembled in the Holy Ghost, the same three legates of the Apostolic See presiding, keeps this constantly in view, namely, that the purity of the Gospel may be preserved in the Church after the errors have been removed. This, of old promised through the Prophets in the Holy Scriptures, our Lord Jesus Christ, the Son of God, promulgated first with His own mouth, and then commanded it to be preached by His Apostles to every creature as the source at once of all saving truth and rules of conduct. It also clearly perceives that these truths and rules are contained in the written books and in the unwritten traditions, which, received by the Apostles from the mouth of Christ Himself, or from the Apostles themselves, the Holy Ghost dictating, have come down to us, transmitted as it were from hand to hand. Following, then, the examples of the orthodox Fathers, it receives and venerates with a feeling of piety and reverence all the books both of the Old and New Testaments, since one God is the author of both; also the traditions, whether they relate to faith or to morals, as having been dictated either orally by Christ or by the Holy Ghost, and preserved in the Catholic Church in unbroken succession. It has thought it proper, moreover, to insert in this decree a list of the sacred books, lest a doubt might arise in the mind of someone as to which are the books received by this council. They are the following: of the Old Testament, the five books of Moses, namely, Genesis, Exodus, Leviticus, Numbers, Deuteronomy; Josue, Judges, Ruth, the four books of Kings, two of Paralipomenon, the first and second of Esdras, the latter of which is called Nehemias, Tobias, Judith, Esther, Job, the Davidic Psalter of 150 Psalms, Proverbs, Ecclesiastes, the Canticle of Canticles, Wisdom, Ecclesiasticus, Isaias, Jeremias, with Baruch, Ezechiel, Daniel, the twelve minor Prophets, namely, Osee, Joel, Amos, Abdias, Jonas, Micheas, Nahum, Habacuc, Sophonias, Aggeus, Zacharias, Malachias; two books of Machabees, the first and second. Of the New Testament, the four Gospels, according to Matthew, Mark, Luke and John; the Acts of the Apostles written by Luke the Evangelist; fourteen Epistles of Paul the Apostle, to the Romans, two to the Corinthians, to the Galatians, to the Ephesians, to the Philippians, to the Colossians, two to the Thessalonians, two to Timothy, to Titus, to Philemon, to the Hebrews; two of Peter the Apostle, three of John the Apostle, one of James the Apostle, one of Jude the Apostle, and the Apocalypse of John the Apostle. If anyone does not accept as sacred and canonical the aforesaid books in their entirety and with all their parts, as they have been accustomed to be read in the Catholic Church and as they are contained in the old Latin Vulgate Edition, and knowingly and deliberately rejects the aforesaid traditions, let him be anathema. Let all understand, therefore, in what order and manner the council, after having laid the foundation of the confession of faith, will proceed, and who are the chief witnesses and supports to whom it will appeal in confirming dogmas and in restoring morals in the Church.

DECREE CONCERNING THE EDITION AND USE
OF THE SACRED BOOKS

Moreover, the same holy council considering that not a little advantage will accrue to the Church of God if it be made known which of all the Latin editions of the sacred books now in circulation is to be regarded as authentic, ordains and declares that the old Latin Vulgate Edition, which, in use for so many hundred years, has been approved by the Church, be in public lectures, disputations, sermons and expositions held as authentic, and that no one dare or presume under any pretext whatsoever to reject it.

Furthermore, to check unbridled spirits, it decrees that no one relying on his own judgment shall, in matters of faith and morals pertaining to the edification of Christian doctrine, distorting the

Holy Scriptures in accordance with his own conceptions, presume to interpret them contrary to that sense which holy mother Church, to whom it belongs to judge of their true sense and interpretation, has held and holds, or even contrary to the unanimous teaching of the Fathers, even though such interpretations should never at any time be published. Those who act contrary to this shall be made known by the ordinaries and punished in accordance with the penalties prescribed by the law.

And wishing, as is proper, to impose a restraint in this matter on printers also, who, now without restraint, thinking what pleases them is permitted them, print without the permission of ecclesiastical superiors the books of the Holy Scriptures and the notes and commentaries thereon of all persons indiscriminately, often with the name of the press omitted, often also under a fictitious press-name, and what is worse, without the name of the author, and also indiscreetly have for sale such books printed elsewhere, this council decrees and ordains that in the future the Holy Scriptures, especially the old Vulgate Edition, be printed in the most correct manner possible, and that it shall not be lawful for anyone to print or to have printed any books whatsoever dealing with sacred doctrinal matters without the name of the author, or in the future to sell them, or even to have them in possession, unless they have first been examined and approved by the ordinary, under penalty of anathema and fine prescribed by the last Council of the Lateran. If they be regulars they must in addition to this examination and approval obtain permission also from their own superiors after these have examined the books in accordance with their own statutes. Those who lend or circulate them in manuscript before they have been examined and approved, shall be subject to the same penalties as the printers, and those who have them in their possession or read them, shall, unless they make known the authors, be themselves regarded as the authors. The approbation of such books, however, shall be given in writing and shall appear authentically at the beginning of the book, whether it be written or printed, and all this, that is, both the examination

and approbation, shall be done gratuitously, so that what ought to be approved may be approved and what ought to be condemned may be condemned.

Furthermore, wishing to repress that boldness whereby the words and sentences of the Holy Scriptures are turned and twisted to all kinds of profane usages, namely, to things scurrilous, fabulous, vain, to flatteries, detractions, superstitions, godless and diabolical incantations, divinations, the casting of lots and defamatory libels, to put an end to such irreverence and contempt, and that no one may in the future dare use in any manner the words of Holy Scripture for these and similar purposes, it is commanded and enjoined that all people of this kind be restrained by the bishops as violators and profaners of the word of God, with the penalties of the law and other penalties that they may deem fit to impose.

*   *   *

Twenty-third Session
Which Is the Seventh under the Supreme Pontiff, Pius IV, Celebrated on the Fifteenth Day of July 1563 The True and Catholic Doctrine Concerning the Sacrament of Order, Defined and Published by the Holy Council of Trent in the Seventh Session in Condemnation of Current Errors

FROM CHAPTER I
THE INSTITUTION OF THE PRIESTHOOD
OF THE NEW LAW

Sacrifice and priesthood are by the ordinance of God so united that both have existed in every law. Since therefore in the New Testament the Catholic Church has received from the institution of Christ the holy, visible sacrifice of the Eucharist, it must also be confessed that there is in that Church a new, visible and external priesthood, into which

the old has been translated. That this was instituted by the same Lord our Savior, and that to the Apostles and their successors in the priesthood was given the power of consecrating, offering and administering His body and blood, as also of forgiving and retaining sins, is shown by the Sacred Scriptures and has always been taught by the tradition of the Catholic Church.

CHAPTER II
THE SEVEN ORDERS

But since the ministry of so holy a priesthood is something divine, that it might be exercised in a more worthy manner and with greater veneration, it was consistent that in the most well-ordered arrangement of the Church there should be several distinct orders of ministers, who by virtue of their office should minister to the priesthood, so distributed that those already having the clerical tonsure should ascend through the minor to the major orders. For the Sacred Scriptures mention unmistakably not only the priests but also the deacons, and teach in the most definite words what is especially to be observed in their ordination; and from the very beginning of the Church the names of the following orders and the duties proper to each one are known to have been in use, namely, those of the subdeacon, acolyte, exorcist, lector and porter, though these were not of equal rank; for the subdiaconate is classed among the major orders by the Fathers and holy councils, in which we also read very often of other inferior orders.

CHAPTER III
THE ORDER OF THE PRIESTHOOD IS TRULY A SACRAMENT

Since from the testimony of Scripture, Apostolic tradition and the unanimous agreement of the Fathers it is clear that grace is conferred by sacred ordination, which is performed by words and outward signs, no one ought to doubt that order is truly and properly one of the seven sacraments of holy Church. For the Apostle says: *I admonish thee*

that thou stir up the grace of God which is in thee by the imposition of my hands. For God has not given us the spirit of fear, but of power and of love and of sobriety.

CHAPTER IV
THE ECCLESIASTICAL HIERARCHY AND ORDINATION

But since in the sacrament of order, as also in baptism and confirmation, a character is imprinted which can neither be effaced nor taken away, the holy council justly condemns the opinion of those who say that the priests of the New Testament have only a temporary power, and that those who have once been rightly ordained can again become laymen if they do not exercise the ministry of the word of God. And if anyone should assert that all Christians without distinction are priests of the New Testament, or that they are all *inter se* endowed with an equal spiritual power, he seems to do nothing else than derange the ecclesiastical hierarchy, which is *an army set in array*; as if, contrary to the teaching of St. Paul, all are apostles, all prophets, all evangelists, all pastors, all doctors. Wherefore, the holy council declares that, besides the other ecclesiastical grades, the bishops, who have succeeded the Apostles, principally belong to this hierarchical order, and have been placed, as the same Apostle says, by the Holy Ghost to rule the Church of God; that they are superior to priests, administer the sacrament of confirmation, ordain ministers of the Church, and can perform many other functions over which those of an inferior order have no power. The council teaches furthermore, that in the ordination of bishops, priests and the other orders, the consent, call or authority, whether of the people or of any civil power or magistrate is not required in such wise that without this the ordination is invalid; rather does it decree that all those who, called and instituted only by the people or by the civil power or magistrate, ascend to the exercise of these offices, and those who by their rashness assume them, are not ministers of the Church, but are to be regarded as thieves and robbers, who

have not entered by the door. These are the things which in general it has seemed good to the holy council to teach to the faithful of Christ regarding the sacrament of order. The contrary, however, it has resolved to condemn in definite and appropriate canons in the following manner, in order that all, making use with the help of Christ of the rule of faith, may in the midst of the darkness of so many errors recognize more easily the Catholic truth and adhere to it.

CANONS ON THE SACRAMENT OF ORDER

Canon 1. If anyone says that there is not in the New Testament a visible and external priesthood, or that there is no power of consecrating and offering the true body and blood of the Lord and of forgiving and retaining sins, but only the office and bare ministry of preaching the Gospel; or that those who do not preach are not priests at all, let him be anathema.

Canon 2. If anyone says that besides the priesthood there are not in the Catholic Church other orders, both major and minor, by which, as by certain steps, advance is made to the priesthood, let him be anathema.

Canon 3. If anyone says that order or sacred ordination is not truly and properly a sacrament instituted by Christ the Lord, or that it is some human contrivance devised by men unskilled in ecclesiastical matters, or that it is only a certain rite for choosing ministers of the word of God and of the sacraments, let him be anathema.

Canon 4. If anyone says that by sacred ordination the Holy Ghost is not imparted and that therefore the bishops say in vain: *Receive ye the Holy Ghost,* or that by it a character is not imprinted, or that he who has once been a priest can again become a layman, let him be anathema.

Canon 5. If anyone says that the holy unction which the Church uses in ordination is not only not required but is detestable and pernicious, as also are the other ceremonies of order, let him be anathema.

Canon 6. If anyone says that in the Catholic Church there is not instituted a hierarchy by di-vine ordinance, which consists of bishops, priests and ministers, let him be anathema.

Canon 7. If anyone says that bishops are not superior to priests, or that they have not the power to confirm and ordain, or that the power which they have is common to them and to priests, or that orders conferred by them without the consent or call of the people or of the secular power are invalid, or that those who have been neither rightly ordained nor sent by ecclesiastical and canonical authority, but come from elsewhere, are lawful ministers of the word and of the sacraments, let him be anathema.

Canon 8. If anyone says that the bishops who are chosen by the authority of the Roman pontiff are not true and legitimate bishops, but merely human deception, let him be anathema.

*   *   *

Twenty-fifth Session Which Is the Ninth and Last under the Supreme Pontiff, Pius IV, Begun on the Third and Closed on the Fourth Day of December 1563

DECREE CONCERNING PURGATORY

Since the Catholic Church, instructed by the Holy Ghost, has, following the sacred writings and the ancient tradition of the Fathers, taught in sacred councils and very recently in this ecumenical council that there is a purgatory, and that the souls there detained are aided by the suffrages of the faithful and chiefly by the acceptable sacrifice of the altar, the holy council commands the bishops that they strive diligently to the end that the sound doctrine of purgatory, transmitted by the Fathers and sacred councils, be believed and maintained by the faithful of Christ, and be everywhere taught and preached. The more difficult and subtle questions, however, and those that do not make for edification and from which there is for the most part no increase in piety, are to be excluded from popular instructions to uneducated

people. Likewise, things that are uncertain or that have the appearance of falsehood they shall not permit to be made known publicly and discussed. But those things that tend to a certain kind of curiosity or superstition, or that savor of filthy lucre, they shall prohibit as scandals and stumbling blocks to the faithful. The bishops shall see to it that the suffrages of the living, that is, the sacrifice of the mass, prayers, alms and other works of piety which they have been accustomed to perform for the faithful departed, be piously and devoutly discharged in accordance with the laws of the Church, and that whatever is due on their behalf from testamentary bequests or other ways, be discharged by the priests and ministers of the Church and others who are bound to render this service not in a perfunctory manner, but diligently and accurately.

ON THE INVOCATION, VENERATION, AND RELICS OF SAINTS, AND ON SACRED IMAGES

The holy council commands all bishops and others who hold the office of teaching and have charge of the *cura animarum,* that in accordance with the usage of the Catholic and Apostolic Church, received from the primitive times of the Christian religion, and with the unanimous teaching of the holy Fathers and the decrees of sacred councils, they above all instruct the faithful diligently in matters relating to intercession and invocation of the saints, the veneration of relics, and the legitimate use of images, teaching them that the saints who reign together with Christ offer up their prayers to God for men, that it is good and beneficial suppliantly to invoke them and to have recourse to their prayers, assistance and support in order to obtain favors from God through His Son, Jesus Christ our Lord, who alone is our redeemer and savior; and that they think impiously who deny that the saints who enjoy eternal happiness in heaven are to be invoked, or who assert that they do not pray for men, or that our invocation of them to pray for each of us individually is idolatry, or that it is opposed to the word of God and inconsistent with the honor of the *one*

mediator of God and men, Jesus Christ, or that it is foolish to pray vocally or mentally to those who reign in heaven. Also, that the holy bodies of the holy martyrs and of others living with Christ, which were the living members of Christ and the temple of the Holy Ghost, to be awakened by Him to eternal life and to be glorified, are to be venerated by the faithful, through which many benefits are bestowed by God on men, so that those who maintain that veneration and honor are not due to the relics of the saints, or that these and other memorials are honored by the faithful without profit, and that the places dedicated to the memory of the saints for the purpose of obtaining their aid are visited in vain, are to be utterly condemned, as the Church has already long since condemned and now again condemns them. Moreover, that the images of Christ, of the Virgin Mother of God, and of the other saints are to be placed and retained especially in the churches, and that due honor and veneration is to be given them; not, however, that any divinity or virtue is believed to be in them by reason of which they are to be venerated, or that something is to be asked of them, or that trust is to be placed in images, as was done of old by the Gentiles who placed their hope in idols; but because the honor which is shown them is referred to the prototypes which they represent, so that by means of the images which we kiss and before which we uncover the head and prostrate ourselves, we adore Christ and venerate the saints whose likeness they bear. That is what was defined by the decrees of the councils, especially of the Second Council of Nicaea, against the opponents of images.

Moreover, let the bishops diligently teach that by means of the stories of the mysteries of our redemption portrayed in paintings and other representations the people are instructed and confirmed in the articles of faith, which ought to be borne in mind and constantly reflected upon; also that great profit is derived from all holy images, not only because the people are thereby reminded of the benefits and gifts bestowed on them by Christ, but also because through the saints the miracles of God and salutary examples are set

before the eyes of the faithful, so that they may give God thanks for those things, may fashion their own life and conduct in imitation of the saints and be moved to adore and love God and cultivate piety. But if anyone should teach or maintain any thing contrary to these decrees, let him be anathema. If any abuses shall have found their way into these holy and salutary observances, the holy council desires earnestly that they be completely removed, so that no representation of false doctrines and such as might be the occasion of grave error to the uneducated be exhibited. And if at times it happens, when this is beneficial to the illiterate, that the stories and narratives of the Holy Scriptures are portrayed and exhibited, the people should be instructed that not for that reason is the divinity represented in picture as if it can be seen with bodily eyes or expressed in colors or figures. Furthermore, in the invocation of the saints, the veneration of relics, and the sacred use of images, all superstition shall be removed, all filthy quest for gain eliminated, and all lasciviousness avoided, so that images shall not be painted and adorned with a seductive charm, or the celebration of saints and the visitation of relics be perverted by the people into boisterous festivities and drunkenness, as if the festivals in honor of the saints are to be celebrated with revelry and with no sense of decency. Finally, such zeal and care should be exhibited by the bishops with regard to these things that nothing may appear that is disorderly or unbecoming and confusedly arranged, nothing that is profane, nothing disrespectful, since holiness becometh the house of God. That these things may be the more faithfully observed, the holy council decrees that no one is permitted to erect or cause to be erected in any place or church, howsoever exempt, any unusual image unless it has been approved by the bishop; also that no new miracles be accepted and no relics recognized unless they have been investigated and approved by the same bishop, who, as soon as he has obtained any knowledge of such matters, shall, after consulting theologians and other pious men, act thereon as he shall judge consonant with truth and piety. But if any doubtful or grave abuse is to be eradicated, or if indeed any graver question concerning these matters should arise, the bishop, before he settles the controversy, shall await the decision of the metropolitan and of the bishops of the province in a provincial synod; so, however, that nothing new or anything that has not hitherto been in use in the Church, shall be decided upon without having first consulted the most holy Roman pontiff.

*   *   *

REVIEW QUESTIONS

1. How does the Council of Trent approach the question of the authority of Scripture?
2. Why did it set that discussion in terms of a list of books the council recognized as sacred?
3. On what basis might the council claim the authority to name the books of the Bible and determine the correct translation?
4. What are the seven orders? What is their place in Christianity and their function? What is the nature of their authority?
5. What do these decrees suggest about the practice of Catholicism in the years following the Reformation?

14 ❧ RELIGION, WARFARE, AND SOVEREIGNTY, 1540–1660

The challenge to the authority of classical culture that the new worlds posed, combined with the fragmentation of the medieval Christian Church—the "body of all believers"—laid the foundation in the second half of the sixteenth century for profound crises of political and social order and of epistemology, the very foundation of human knowledge. In their efforts to describe what they saw in the Americas, European conquistadores and clergy were forced to adopt analogies: hundreds of species of plants and animals were not to be found in the writings of Pliny, the great and trusted botanist and zoologist of the ancient world, or in the Bible. The cultures of the Americas posed new models of social and political relations, opening new possibilities for the ordering of political relations and calling into question the very nature of political authority.

Within Europe, civil wars arose in the wake of the fragmentation of the Christian Church. The wars of religion in France, 1562–98, led astute observers such as Montaigne to question the claim of each side to know the truth, and to question whether human reason was sufficient to discern the truth. In all the religious wars, beginning with the German Peasants' War of 1525 and culminating in the Thirty Years' War, 1618–48, the social order was overthrown, as peasant killed lord, brother killed brother, son killed father, and neighbor killed neighbor. What was it to be human? To be savage? And where was God while Christian slaughtered Christian?

The crisis of the seventeenth century was not simply intellectual and spiritual but also had real material aspects. The expansion of Europe into new worlds changed patterns of consumption and production, thus contributing to the overthrow of traditional work processes and lifestyles. It created a tremendous influx of wealth that aided the rise of new economic and political powers, both social groups and nation-states, and that contributed to chronic inflation. Changes in society, economy, and politics created tensions that found expression in the violence of the period. Religious wars were seldom entirely religious in cause or in

consequence. The almost constant march and countermarch of armies not only destroyed life and property but also disrupted agriculture and spread disease. The struggle for existence, difficult under the best of circumstances in the early modern period, became much more difficult in the age of crisis.

By 1660, peasants had risen in unprecedented numbers against their lords; common Englishmen had executed their king; Europeans had witnessed multiple incidents of cannibalism in their own villages; and the medieval epistemology, that very base by which Europeans could be certain of the veracity of what they knew, had collapsed. New formulations were being tentatively put forward, but they did not yet replace the old certainties that had been irrecoverably lost.

GIOVANNI MICHIEL

FROM A Venetian Ambassador's Report on the St. Bartholomew's Day Massacre

The struggle for supremacy in northern Italy, which marked the last half of the fifteenth century, gave rise to a new form of diplomacy, including structures and procedures that would be fundamental to relations among all modern states. Requiring continuous contact and communication, Renaissance states turned to permanent diplomacy, distinguished by the use of accredited resident ambassadors rather than ad hoc missions of medieval legates. The tasks of a permanent ambassador were to represent his government at state ceremonies, to gather information, and, occasionally, to enter into negotiations. Nowhere was this system more fully and expertly articulated than by the Republic of Venice in the late fifteenth and sixteenth centuries. Its ambassadors were chosen with unusual care from the most prominent families of the city. They were highly educated, and their duties were carefully defined. Among the latter were weekly dispatches reporting all matters of any interest to Venice. These reports were regularly read and debated in the senate, which replied with questions, instructions, and information of its own. As a result, Venetian ambassadors were among the most skilled and respected in early modern Europe. In this report, Giovanni Michiel interprets the events of St. Bartholomew's Day in 1572. The massacre of Huguenots, instigated by the Queen Mother, Catherine de Medici, outraged Protestant Europe and dashed all hopes for peace in France. Of particular interest is the ambassador's harshly realistic account of the political motives for so violent an act of statecraft.

From *Pursuit of Power: Venetian Ambassadors' Reports on Spain, Turkey and France in the Age of Phillip II, 1560–1600*, by James C. Davis (New York: HarperCollins, 1970), pp. 72–76, 78–79.

*   *   *

Turning to the queen, Admiral de Coligny said, "Madame, the king refuses to involve himself in one war. God grant that he may not be caught up in another which he cannot avoid."

By these words he meant, some say, that if they abandoned the prince of Orange things might go badly for him, and there would be a danger that if the prince failed to win or was actually driven out by the Spanish or for some other reason, then he might enter France with his French and German followers and it might be necessary to drive him out by force. However, everyone understood his words in a very different sense, namely that he was giving notice that he planned to stir up new storms and renew the rioting and civil war. When the queen carefully pondered this it became the chief reason, taken together with the other considerations, why she hurried to prepare that fate for him which he eventually met.

*   *   *

Then, at the dinner hour on Friday, while the admiral was returning on foot from the court to his lodgings and reading a letter, someone fired an arquebus at him. The shot came from a window which faced a bit obliquely on the street, near the royal palace called the Louvre. But it did not strike him in the chest as intended because it so happened that the admiral was wearing a pair of slippers which made walking difficult and, wanting to take them off and hand them to a page, he had just started to turn around. So the arquebus shot tore off a finger on his left hand and then hit his right arm near the wrist and passed through it to the other side near the elbow. If he had simply walked straight ahead it would have hit him in the chest and killed him.

As you can imagine, news of the event caused great excitement, especially at court. Everyone supposed it had been done by order of the duke of Guise to avenge his family, because the window from which the shot was fired belonged to his mother's house, which had purposely been left empty after she had gone to stay in another. When the news was reported to the king, who happened to be playing tennis with the duke of Guise, they say he turned white and looked thunderstruck. Without saying a word he withdrew into his chambers and made it obvious that he was extremely angry.

*   *   *

On Saturday the admiral's dressings were changed and the word was given out—which may or may not have been true—that the wound was not a mortal one and that there was no danger even that he would lose the arm. The Huguenots only blustered all the more, and everyone waited to see what would happen next. The duke of Guise knew he might be attacked, so he armed himself and stuck close to his uncle, the duke of Aumale, and as many relatives, friends and servants as possible.

But before long the situation changed. Late Saturday night, just before the dawn of Saint Bartholomew's Day, the massacre or slaughter was carried out. The French say the king ordered it. How wild and terrifying it was in Paris (which has a larger population than any other city in Europe), no one can imagine. Nor can one imagine the rage and frenzy of those who slaughtered and sacked, as the king ordered the people to do. Nor what a marvel, not to say a miracle, it was that the common people did not take advantage of this freedom to loot and plunder from Catholics as well as Huguenots, and ravenously take whatever they could get their hands on, especially since the city is incredibly wealthy. No one would ever imagine that a people could be armed and egged on by their ruler, yet not get out of control once they were worked up. But it was not God's will that things should reach such a pass.

The slaughter went on past Sunday for two or three more days, despite the fact that edicts were issued against it and the duke of Nevers was sent riding through the city along with the king's natural brother to order them to stop the killing. The massacre showed how powerfully religion can

affect men's minds. On every street one could see the barbarous sight of men cold-bloodedly outraging others of their own people, and not just men who had never done them any harm but in most cases people they knew to be their neighbors and even their relatives. They had no feeling, no mercy on anyone, even those who kneeled before them and humbly begged for their lives. If one man hated another because of some argument or lawsuit all he had to say was "This man is a Huguenot" and he was immediately killed. (That happened to many Catholics.) If their victims threw themselves in the river as a last resort and tried to swim to safety, as many did, they chased them in boats and then drowned them. There was a great deal of looting and pillaging and they say the goods taken amounted to two million because many Huguenots, including some of the richest of them, had come to live in Paris after the most recent edict of pacification. Some estimate the number who were killed as high as four thousand, while others put it as low as two thousand.

The killing spread to all the provinces and most of the major cities and was just as frenzied there, if not more so. They attacked anyone, even the gentry, and as a result all the leaders who did not escape have been killed or thrown in prison. It is true that Montgomery and some others who were pursued by the duke of Guise escaped to England, but they are not major figures. And the king has terrified them enough so they won't make any trouble.

*   *   *

REVIEW QUESTIONS

1. According to the report, at what level of society did the St. Bartholomew's Day Massacre originate?
2. How was a person identified as Huguenot or Catholic?
3. What does that say about religious identity in early modern France?
4. Do we know from this report who ordered the assassination of Admiral de Coligny?
5. Who caused the massacre?
6. What do we learn about the relation of religion to politics and political action?

REGINALD SCOT

FROM *Discoverie of Witchcraft*

Reginald Scot (1538–1599) was a Kentish squire who witnessed a number of fraudulent accusations of witchcraft in the villages of his shire during the reign of Elizabeth I. In 1584, he wrote his Discoverie of Witchcraft, *which contains a remarkable exposition of magical elements in medieval Catholicism and a protest against the persecution of harmless old women. Scot doubted that God could ever have allowed witches to exercise supernatural powers, much less demand that they be persecuted for it. In this regard, he deserves to be ranked among the skeptics on the question of witchcraft, although he never denied the existence of witches. According to Scot, all "witches" fell into one of four categories. First were the innocent, those falsely accused. Second were the deluded, those convinced through their own misery that they*

were witches. Third were the malefactors, those who harmed people and damaged property, though not by supernatural means. Fourth were imposters, those who posed as witches and conjurers. Scot denied that any of these "witches" had access to supernatural powers. Malefactors and imposters were, in fact, the witches named in the Bible as not being suffered to live. They were the only witches Scot admitted. His work is said to have made a great impression in the magistracy and clergy of his day. Nonetheless, his remained a minority opinion. Most contemporaries understood as tantamount to atheism any denial of the reality of spirits or the possibility of the supernatural. The persecution of witches continued unabated into the eighteenth century; many thousands, mostly harmless old women, fell victim to the rage.

From *Discoverie of Witchcraft*, by Reginald Scot, 1584, edited by Brinsley Nicholson (London: E. Stock, 1886).

*   *   *

The inconvenience growing by mens credulitie herein, with a reproofe of some churchmen, which are inclined to the common conceived opinion of witches omnipotencie, and a familiar example thereof. But the world is now so bewitched and over-run with this fond error, that even where a man shuld seeke comfort and counsell, there shall hee be sent (in case of necessitie) from God to the divell; and from the Physician, to the coosening witch, who will not sticke to take upon hir, by wordes to heale the lame (which was proper onelie to Christ: and to them whom he assisted with his divine power) yea, with hir familiar & charmes she will take upon hir to cure the blind: though in the tenth of S. *Johns* Gospell it be written, that the divell cannot open the eies of the blind. And they attaine such credit as I have heard (to my greefe) some of the ministerie affirme, that they have had in their parish at one instant, xvii. or xviii. witches: meaning such as could worke miracles supernaturallie. Whereby they manifested as well their infidelitie and ignorance, in conceiving Gods word; as their negligence and error in instructing their flocks. For they themselves might understand, and also teach their parishoners, that God onelie worketh great woonders; and that it is he which sendeth such punishments to the wicked,

and such trials to the elect: according to the saieng of the Prophet *Haggai,* I smote you with blasting and mildeaw, and with haile, in all the labours of your hands; and yet you turned not unto me, saith the Lord. And therefore saith the same Prophet in another place; You have sowen much, and bring in little. And both in *Joel* and *Leviticus,* the like phrases and proofes are used and made. But more shalbe said of this hereafter.

*   *   *

At the assises holden at *Rochester,* Anno 1581, one *Margaret Simons,* the wife of *John Simons,* of *Brenchlie* in *Kent,* was araigned for witchcraft, at the instigation and complaint of divers fond and malicious persons; and speciallie by the meanes of one *John Ferrall* vicar of that parish: with whom I talked about that matter, and found him both fondlie assotted in the cause, and enviouslie bent towards hir: and (which is worse) as unable to make a good account of his faith, as shee whom he accused. That which he, for his part, laid to the poore womans charge, was this.

His sonne (being an ungratious boie, and prentise to one *Robert Scotchford* clothier, dwelling in that parish of *Brenchlie*) passed on a daie by hir house; at whome by chance hir little dog barked. Which thing the boie taking in evill part, drewe his knife, & pursued him therewith even to hir

doore: whom she rebuked with some such words as the boie disdained, & yet neverthelesse would not be persuaded to depart in a long time. At the last he returned to his maisters house, and within five or sixe daies fell sicke. Then was called to mind the fraie betwixt the dog and the boie: insomuch as the vicar (who thought himselfe so privileged, as he little mistrusted that God would visit his children with sicknes) did so calculate; as he found, partlie through his owne judgement, and partlie (as he himselfe told me) by the relation of other witches, that his said sonne was by hir bewitched. Yea, he also told me, that this his sonne (being as it were past all cure) received perfect health at the hands of another witch.

He proceeded yet further against hir, affirming, that alwaies in his parish church, when he desired to read most plainelie, his voice so failed him, as he could scant be heard at all. Which hee could impute, he said, to nothing else, but to hir inchantment. When I advertised the poore woman hereof, as being desirous to heare what she could saie for hir selfe; she told me, that in verie deed his voice did much faile him, speciallie when he strained himselfe to speake lowdest. How beit, she said that at all times his voice was hoarse and lowe: which thing I perceived to be true. But sir, said she, you shall understand, that this our vicar is diseased with such a kind of hoarsenesse, as divers of our neighbors in this parish, not long since, doubted that he had the French pox; & in that respect utterly refused to communicate with him: untill such time as (being therunto injoined by M. D. *Lewen* the Ordinarie) he had brought frō *London* a certificat, under the hands of two physicians, that his hoarsenes proceeded from a disease in the lungs. Which certificat he published in the church, in the presence of the whole congregation: and by this meanes hee was cured, or rather excused of the shame of his disease. And this I knowe to be true by the relation of divers honest men of that parish. And truelie, if one of the Jurie had not beene wiser than the other, she had beene condemned thereupon, and upon other as ridiculous matters as this. For the name of a witch is so odious, and hir power so feared among the common people, that if the honestest bodie living chance to be arraigned thereupon, she shall hardlie escape condemnation.

A Confutation of the Common Conceived Opinion of Witches and Witchcraft, and How Detestable a Sinne It Is to Repaire to Them for Counsell or Helpe in Time of Affliction

But whatsoever is reported or conceived of such manner of witchcrafts, I dare avow to be false and fabulous (coosinage, dotage, and poisoning excepted:) neither is there any mention made of these kind of witches in the Bible. If Christ had knowne them, he would not have pretermitted to invaie against their presumption, in taking upon them his office: as, to heale and cure diseases; and to worke such miraculous and supernaturall things, as whereby he himselfe was speciallie knowne, beleeved, and published to be God; his actions and cures consisting (in order and effect) according to the power of our witchmoongers imputed to witches. Howbeit, if there be any in these daies afflicted in such strange sort, as Christs cures and patients are described in the new testament to have beene: we flie from trusting in God to trusting in witches, who doo not onelie in their coosening art take on them the office of Christ in this behalfe; but use his verie phrase of speech to such idolators, as com to seeke divine assistance at their hands, saieng; Go thy waies, thy sonne or thy daughter, &c. shall doo well, and be whole.

*   *   *

In like manner I say, he that attributeth to a witch, such divine power, as dulie and onelie apperteineth unto GOD (which all witchmongers doo) is in hart a blasphemer, an idolater, and full of grosse impietie, although he neither go nor send to hir for assistance.

A Further Confutation of Witches Miraculous and Omnipotent Power, by Invincible Reasons and Authorities, with Dissuasions from Such Fond Credulitie

If witches could doo anie such miraculous things, as these and other which are imputed to them, they might doo them againe and againe, at anie time or place, or at anie mans desire: for the divell is as strong at one time as at another, as busie by daie as by night, and readie enough to doo all mischeefe, and careth not whom he abuseth. And in so much as it is confessed, by the most part of witchmoongers themselves, that he knoweth not the cogitation of mans heart, he should (me thinks) sometimes appeere unto honest and credible persons, in such grosse and corporall forme, as it is said he dooth unto witches: which you shall never heare to be justified by one sufficient witnesse. For the divell indeed entreth into the mind, and that waie seeketh mans confusion.

The art alwaies presupposeth the power; so as, if they saie they can doo this or that, they must shew how and by what meanes they doo it; as neither the witches, nor the witchmoongers are able to doo. For to everie action is required the facultie and abilitie of the agent or dooer; the aptnes of the patient or subject; and a convenient and possible application. Now the witches are mortall, and their power dependeth upon the analogie and consonancie of their minds and bodies; but with their minds they can but will and understand; and with their bodies they can doo no more, but as the bounds and ends of terrene sense will suffer: and therefore their power extendeth not to doo such miracles, as surmounteth their owne sense, and the understanding of others which are wiser than they; so as here wanteth the vertue and power of the efficient. And in reason, there can be no more vertue in the thing caused, than in the cause, or that which proceedeth of or from the benefit of the cause. And we see, that ignorant and impotent women, or witches, are the causes of incantations and charmes; wherein we shall perceive there is none effect, if we will credit our owne experience and sense unabused, the rules of philosophie, or the word of God. For alas! What an unapt instrument is a toothles, old, impotent, and unweldie woman to flie in the aier? Truelie, the divell little needs such instruments to bring his purposes to passe.

It is strange, that we should suppose, that such persons can worke such feates: and it is more strange, that we will imagine that to be possible to be doone by a witch, which to nature and sense is impossible; speciallie when our neighbours life dependeth upon our credulitie therein; and when we may see the defect of abilitie, which alwaies is an impediment both to the act, and also to the presumption thereof. And bicause there is nothing possible in lawe, that in nature is impossible; therefore the judge dooth not attend or regard what the accused man saith; or yet would doo: but what is prooved to have beene committed, and naturallie falleth in mans power and will to doo. For the lawe saith, that To will a thing unpossible, is a signe of a mad man, or of a foole, upon whom no sentence or judgement taketh hold. Furthermore, what Jurie will condemne, or what Judge will give sentence or judgement against one for killing a man at *Berwicke;* when they themselves, and manie other sawe that man at *London,* that verie daie, wherein the murther was committed; yea though the partie confesse himself guiltie therein, and twentie witnesses depose the same? But in this case also I saie the judge is not to weigh their testimonie, which is weakened by lawe; and the judges authoritie is to supplie the imperfection of the case, and to mainteine the right and equitie of the same.

Seeing therefore that some other things might naturallie be the occasion and cause of such calamities as witches are supposed to bring; let not us that professe the Gospell and knowledge of Christ, be bewitched to beleeve that they doo such things, as are in nature impossible, and in sense and reason incredible. If they saie it is doone through the divels helpe, who can work miracles; whie doo not theeves

bring their busines to passe miraculouslie, with whom the divell is as conversant as with the other? Such mischeefes as are imputed to witches, happen where no witches are; yea and continue when witches are hanged and burnt: whie then should we attribute such effect to that cause, which being taken awaie, happeneth neverthelesse?

＊   ＊   ＊

What Testimonies and Witnesses Are Allowed to Give Evidence against Reputed Witches, by the Report and Allowance of the Inquisitors Themselves, and Such as Are Speciall Writers Heerein

Excommunicat persons, partakers of the falt, infants, wicked servants, and runnawaies are to be admitted to beare witnesse against their dames in this mater of witchcraft: bicause (saith *Bodin* the champion of witchmoongers) none that be honest are able to detect them. Heretikes also and witches shall be received to accuse, but not to excuse a witch. And finallie, the testimonie of all infamous persons in this case is good and allowed. Yea, one lewd person (saith *Bodin*) may be received to accuse and condemne a thousand suspected witches. And although by lawe, a capitall enimie may be challenged; yet *James Sprenger,* and *Henrie Institor,* (from whom *Bodin,* and all the writers that ever I have read, doo receive their light, authorities and arguments) saie (upon this point of lawe) that The poore frendlesse old woman must proove, that hir capitall enimie would have killed hir, and that hee hath both assalted & wounded hir; otherwise she pleadeth all in vaine. If the judge aske hir, whether she have anie capitall enimies; and she rehearse other, and forget hir accuser; or else answer that he was hir capital enimie, but now she hopeth he is not so: such a one is nevertheles admitted for a witnes. And though by lawe, single witnesses are not admittable; yet if one depose she hath bewitched hir cow; another, hir sow; and the third, hir butter:

these saith (saith *M. Mal.* and *Bodin*) are no single witnesses: bicause they agree that she is a witch.

The Fifteene Crimes Laid to the Charge of Witches, by Witchmongers, Speciallie by Bodin, in Dæmonomania

They denie God, and all religion.

Answere. Then let them die therefore, or at the least be used like infidels, or apostataes.

They cursse, blaspheme, and provoke God with all despite.

Answere. Then let them have the law expressed in *Levit.* 24. and *Deut.* 13 & 17.

They give their faith to the divell, and they worship and offer sacrifice unto him.

Ans. Let such also be judged by the same lawe.

They doo solemnelie vow and promise all their progenie unto the divell.

Ans. This promise proceedeth from an unsound mind, and is not to be regarded; bicause they cannot performe it, neither will it be prooved true. Howbeit, if it be done by anie that is sound of mind, let the cursse of *Jeremie,* 32.36. light upon them, to wit, the sword, famine and pestilence.

They sacrifice their owne children to the divell before baptisme, holding them up in the aire unto him, and then thrust a needle into their braines.

Ans. If this be true, I maintaine them not herein: but there is a lawe to judge them by. Howbeit, it is so contrarie to sense and nature, that it were follie to beleeve it; either upon *Bodins* bare word, or else upon his presumptions; speciallie when so small commoditie and so great danger and inconvenience insueth to the witches thereby.

They burne their children when they have sacrificed them.

Ans. Then let them have such punishment, as they that offered their children unto *Moloch: Levit.* 20. But these be meere devises of witchmoongers and inquisitors, that with extreame tortures have wroong such confessions from them; or else with false reports have beelied them; or by flatterie & faire words and promises have woon it at their hands, at the length.

They sweare to the divell to bring as manie into that societie as they can.

Ans. This is false, and so prooved elsewhere.

They sweare by the name of the divell.

Ans. I never heard anie such oth, neither have we warrant to kill them that so doo sweare; though indeed it be verie lewd and impious.

They use incestuous adulterie with spirits.

Ans. This is a stale ridiculous lie, as is prooved apparentlie hereafter.

They boile infants (after they have murthered them unbaptised) untill their flesh be made potable.

Ans. This is untrue, incredible, and impossible.

They eate the flesh and drinke the bloud of men and children openlie.

Ans. Then are they kin to the *Anthropophagi* and *Canibals.* But I beleeve never an honest man in *England* nor in *France,* will affirme that he hath seene any of these persons, that are said to be witches, do so; if they shuld, I beleeve it would poison them.

They kill men with poison.

Ans. Let them be hanged for their labour.

They kill mens cattell.

Ans. Then let an action of trespasse be brought against them for so dooing.

They bewitch mens corne, and bring hunger and barrennes into the countrie; they ride and flie in the aire, bring stormes, make tempests, &c.

Ans. Then will I worship them as gods; for those be not the works of man nor yet of witch: as I have elsewhere prooved at large.

They use venerie with a divell called *Incubus,* even when they lie in bed with their husbands, and have children by them, which become the best witches.

Ans. This is the last lie, verie ridiculous, and confuted by me elsewhere.

Of Foure Capitall Crimes Objected against Witches, All Fullie Answered and Confuted as Frivolous

First therefore they laie to their charge idolatrie. But alas without all reason: for such are properlie knowne to us to be idolaters, as doo externall worship to idols or strange gods. The furthest point that idolatrie can be stretched unto, is, that they, which are culpable therein, are such as hope for and seeke salvation at the hands of idols, or of anie other than God; or fixe their whole mind and love upon anie creature, so as the power of God be neglected and contemned thereby. But witches neither seeke nor beleeve to have salvation at the hands of divels, but by them they are onlie deceived; the instruments of their phantasie being corrupted, and so infatuated, that they suppose, confesse, and saie they can doo that, which is as farre beyond their power and nature to doo, as to kill a man at *Yorke* before noone, when they have beene seene at *London* in that morning, &c. But if these latter idolaters, whose idolatrie is spirituall, and committed onelie in mind, should be punished by death; then should everie covetous man, or other, that setteth his affection anie waie too much upon an earthlie creature, be executed, and yet perchance the witch might escape scotfree.

Secondlie, apostasie is laid to their charge, whereby it is inferred, that they are worthie to die. But apostasie is, where anie of sound judgement forsake the gospell, learned and well knowne unto them; and doo not onelie embrace impietie and infidelitie; but oppugne and resist the truth erstwhile by them professed. But alas these poore women go not about to defend anie impietie, but after good admonition repent.

Thirdlie, they would have them executed for seducing the people. But God knoweth they have small store of Rhetorike or art to seduce; except to tell a tale of Robin good-fellow be to deceive and seduce. Neither may their age or sex admit that opinion or accusation to be just: for they themselves are poore seduced soules. I for my part (as else-where I have said) have prooved this point to be false in most apparent sort.

Fourthlie, as touching the accusation, which all the writers use herein against them for their carnall copulation with *Incubus:* the follie of mens credulitie is as much to be woondered at and derided, as the others vaine and impossible confessions. For the divell is a spirit, and hath neither

flesh nor bones, which were to be used in the performance of this action. And since he also lacketh all instruments, substance, and seed ingendred of bloud; it were follie to staie overlong in the confutation of that, which is not in the nature of things. And yet must I saie somewhat heerein, bicause the opinion hereof is so stronglie and universallie received, and the fables thereupon so innumerable; wherby *M. Mal. Bodin, Hemingius, Hyperius, Danaeus, Erastus,* and others that take upon them to write heerein, are so abused, or rather seeke to abuse others; as I woonder at their fond credulitie in this behalfe. For they affirme undoubtedlie, that the divell plaieth *Succubus* to the man, and carrieth from him the seed of generation, which he delivereth as *Incubus* to the woman, who manie times that waie is gotten with child; which will verie naturallie (they saie) become a witch, and such one they affirme *Merline* was.

＊   ＊   ＊

By What Meanes the Common People Have Beene Made Beleeve in the Miraculous Works of Witches, a Definition of Witchcraft, and a Description Thereof

The common people have beene so assotted and bewitched, with whatsoever poets have feigned of witchcraft, either in earnest, in jest, or else in derision; and with whatsoever lowd liers and couseners for their pleasures heerein have invented, and with whatsoever tales they have heard from old doting women, or from their mothers maids, and with whatsoever the grandfoole their ghostlie father, or anie other morrow masse preest had informed them; and finallie with whatsoever they have swallowed up through tract of time, or through their owne timerous nature or ignorant conceipt, concerning these matters of hagges and witches: as they have so settled their opinion and credit thereupon, that they thinke it heresie to doubt in anie part of the matter; speciallie because they find this word

witchcraft expressed in the scriptures; which is as to defend praieng to saincts, bicause *Sanctus, Sanctus, Sanctus* is written in *Te Deum.*

And now to come to the definition of witchcraft, which hitherto I did deferre and put off purposelie: that you might perceive the true nature thereof, by the circumstances, and therefore the rather to allow of the same, seeing the varietie of other writers. Witchcraft is in truth a cousening art, wherin the name of God is abused, prophaned and blasphemed, and his power attributed to a vile creature. In estimation of the vulgar people, it is a supernaturall worke, contrived betweene a corporall old woman, and a spirituall divell. The maner thereof is so secret, mysticall, and strange, that to this daie there hath never beene any credible witnes thereof. It is incomprehensible to the wise, learned or faithfull; a probable matter to children, fooles, melancholike persons and papists. The trade is thought to be impious. The effect and end thereof to be sometimes evill, as when thereby man or beast, grasse, trees, or corne, &c; is hurt: sometimes good, as whereby sicke folkes are healed, theeves bewraied, and true men come to their goods, &c. The matter and instruments, wherewith it is accomplished, are words, charmes, signes, images, characters, &c; the which words although any other creature do pronounce, in manner and forme as they doo, leaving out no circumstance requisite or usually for that action: yet none is said to have the grace or gift to perform the matter, except she be a witch, and so taken either by hir owne consent, or by others imputation.

Reasons to Proove That Words and Characters Are But Bables, and That Witches Cannot Doo Such Things as the Multitude Supposeth They Can, Their Greatest Woonders Prooved Trifles, of a Yoong Gentleman Cousened

That words, characters, images, and such other trinkets, which are thought so necessarie instru-

ments for witchcraft (as without the which no such thing can be accomplished) are but bables, devised by couseners, to abuse the people withall; I trust I have sufficientlie prooved. And the same maie be further and more plainelie perceived by these short and compendious reasons following.

First, in that *Turkes* and infidels, in their witchcraft, use both other words, and other characters than our witches doo and also such as are most contrarie. In so much as, if ours be bad, in reason theirs should be good. If their witches can doo anie thing, ours can doo nothing. For as our witches are said to renounce Christ, and despise his sacraments: so doo the other forsake *Mahomet*, and his lawes, which is one large step to christianitie.

It is also to be thought, that all witches are couseners; when mother *Bungie*, a principall witch, so reputed, tried, and condemned of all men, and continuing in that exercise and estimation manie yeares (having cousened & abused the whole realme, in so much as there came to hir, witchmongers from all the furthest parts of the land, she being in diverse bookes set out with authoritie, registred and chronicled by the name of the great witch of *Rochester,* and reputed among all men for the cheefe ringleader of all other witches) by good proofe is found to be a meere cousener; confessing in hir death bed freelie, without compulsion or inforcement, that hir cunning consisted onlie in deluding and deceiving the people: saying that she had (towards the maintenance of hir credit in that cousening trade) some sight in physicke and surgerie, and the assistance of a freend of hirs, called *Heron,* a professor thereof. And this I know, partlie of mine owne knowledge, and partlie by the testimonie of hir husband, and others of credit, to whome (I saie) in hir death bed, and at sundrie other times she protested these things; and also that she never had indeed anie materiall spirit or divell (as the voice went) nor yet knew how to worke anie supernaturall matter, as she in hir life time made men beleeve she had and could doo.

*   *   *

Againe, who will mainteine, that common witchcrafts are not cousenages, when the great and famous witchcrafts, which had stolne credit not onlie from all the common people, but from men of great wisdome and authoritie, are discovered to be beggerlie slights of cousening varlots? Which otherwise might and would have remained a perpetuall objection against me. Were there not three images of late yeeres found in a doonghill, to the terror & astonishment of manie thousands? In so much as great matters were thought to have beene pretended to be doone by witchcraft. But if the Lord preserve those persons (whose destruction was doubted to have beene intended thereby) from all other the lewd practises and attempts of their enimies; I feare not, but they shall easilie withstand these and such like devises, although they should indeed be practised against them. But no doubt, if such bables could have brought those matters of mischeefe to passe, by the hands of traitors, witches, or papists; we should long since have beene deprived of the most excellent jewell and comfort that we enjoy in this world. Howbeit, I confesse, that the feare, conceipt, and doubt of such mischeefous pretenses may breed inconvenience to them that stand in awe of the same. And I wish, that even for such practises, though they never can or doo take effect, the practisers be punished with all extremitie: bicause therein is manifested a traiterous heart to the Queene, and a presumption against God.

*   *   *

REVIEW QUESTIONS

1. What is witchcraft?
2. How does Scot depict it?
3. According to Scot, what characterizes witches and witchcraft?
4. How does Scot confound the very notion of witchcraft?
5. Where does he locate the source of all power to override the laws of nature?
6. What sort of power is left to witches?
7. What, according to Scot, is the relation of witches to the natural world?

THE PLUNDERING AND BURNING OF A VILLAGE, A HANGING, AND
PEASANTS AVENGE THEMSELVES (1633)

JACQUES CALLOT

These three prints, often referred to as *The Horrors of War, powerfully reveal commonplace events of the early seventeenth century: the ravages of war on a small village, the punishment of unruly troops, and the violence of the violated. How does Callot portray rural life? What general aspects of the Iron Century does Callot capture in his images? Why do you think Callot decided to reveal the underbelly of 17th-century warfare rather than portraying it in more heroic terms?*

HANS JAKOB CHRISTOPH VON GRIMMELSHAUSEN

FROM *Simplicissimus*

Hans Jakob Christoph von Grimmelshausen (1621–1676), author of Simplicissimus, *the greatest German novel of the seventeenth century and one of the great works of all German literature, was born at Gelnhausen, near Hanau in Hesse Kassel. The troubled times of the Thirty Years' War (1618–1648), which found eloquent consideration in his writing, are reflected in his life. He lost his parents early, probably in the 1634 sack of Gelnhausen by troops under Ferdinand, cardinal-infante of Spain, and was himself kidnapped by marauding Hessian troops the following year. His experiences became the stuff of his novel. In 1636, he joined the imperial army. In 1639, he became secretary to Reinhard von Schauenburg, the commandant at Offenburg, on whose staff he served until 1647. At the end of the war, he was commandant on the Inn. Soon after the war he became the steward of the Schauenburg estates, married, and converted to Catholicism. In 1667, Grimmelshausen was appointed magistrate and tax collector at Renchen, a town belonging to the bishopric of Strasbourg. His duties evidently left him free to write; he published his masterpiece,* Simplicissimus, *in 1669. Modeled on the Spanish picaresque romance,* Simplicissimus *sketched the development of a human soul measured against the background of a land riven by warfare. It gave free rein to its author's narrative gifts: his realist detail, coarse humor, and social criticism.* Simplicissimus *is widely considered a historical document for its vivid picture of seventeenth-century Germany. Grimmelshausen's life ended as it began, in the shadow of war. In 1674, Renchen was occupied by French troops, and his household was broken up. He died in 1676, once more in military service.*

From *Simplicissimus*, by Hans Jakob Christoph von Grimmelshausen, translated by A. T. S. Goodrich (London: Heinemann, 1912).

Book I

CHAPTER I
TREATS OF SIMPLICISSIMUS'S RUSTIC DESCENT AND OF HIS UPBRINGING ANSWERING THERETO

There appeareth in these days of ours (of which many do believe that they be the last days) among the common folk, a certain disease which causeth those who do suffer from it (so soon as they have either scraped and higgled together so much that they can, besides a few pence in their pocket, wear a fool's coat of the new fashion with a thousand bits of silk ribbon upon it, or by some trick of fortune have become known as men of parts) forthwith to give themselves out gentlemen and nobles of ancient descent. Whereas it doth often happen that their ancestors were day-labourers, carters, and porters, their cousins donkey-drivers, their brothers turnkeys and catchpolls, their sisters harlots, their mothers bawds—yea, witches even: and in a word, their whole pedigree of thirty-two quarterings as full of dirt and stain as ever was the sugarbakers' guild of Prague. Yea, these new sprigs of nobility be often themselves as black as if they had been born and bred in Guinea.

With such foolish folk I desire not to even myself, though 'tis not untrue that I have often

fancied I must have drawn my birth from some great lord or knight at least, as being by nature disposed to follow the nobleman's trade had I but the means and the tools for it. 'Tis true, moreover, without jesting, that my birth and upbringing can be well compared to that of a prince if we overlook the one great difference in degree. How! did not my dad (for so they call fathers in the Spessart) have his own palace like any other, so fine as no king could build with his own hands, but must let that alone for ever. 'Twas painted with lime, and in place of unfruitful tiles, cold lead and red copper, was roofed with that straw whereupon the noble corn doth grow, and that he, my dad, might make a proper show of nobility and riches, he had his wall round his castle built, not of stone, which men do find upon the road or dig out of the earth in barren places, much less of miserable baked bricks that in a brief space can be made and burned (as other great lords be wont to do), but he did use oak, which noble and profitable tree, being such that smoked sausage and fat ham doth grow upon it, taketh for its full growth no less than a hundred years; and where is the monarch that can imitate him therein? His halls, his rooms, and his chambers did he have thoroughly blackened with smoke, and for this reason only, that 'tis the most lasting colour in the world, and doth take longer to reach to real perfection than an artist will spend on his most excellent paintings. The tapestries were of the most delicate web in the world, wove for us by her that of old did challenge Minerva to a spinning match. His windows were dedicated to St. Papyrius for no other reason than that that same paper doth take longer to come to perfection, reckoning from the sowing of the hemp or flax whereof 'tis made, than doth the finest and clearest glass of Murano: for his trade made him apt to believe that whatever was produced with much paint was also more valuable and more costly; and what was moss costly was best suited to nobility. Instead of pages, lackeys, and grooms, he had sheep, goats, and swine, which often waited upon me in the pastures till I drove them home. His armoury was well furnished with ploughs, mattocks, axes, hoes, shovels, pitch-

forks, and hayforks, with which weapons he daily exercised himself; for hoeing and digging he made his military discipline, as did the old Romans in time of peace. The yoking of oxen was his generalship, the piling of dung his fortification, tilling of the land his campaigning, and the cleaning out of stables his princely pastime and exercise. By this means did he conquer the whole round world so far as he could reach, and at every harvest did draw from it rich spoils. But all this I account nothing of, and am not puffed up thereby, lest any should have cause to jibe at me as at other newfangled nobility, for I esteem myself no higher than was my dad, which had his abode in a right merry land, to wit, in the Spessart, where the wolves do howl good-night to each other. But that I have as yet told you nought of my dad's family, race and name is for the sake of precious brevity, especially since there is here no question of a foundation for gentlefolks for me to swear myself into; 'tis enough if it be known that I was born in the Spessart.

Now as my dad's manner of living will be perceived to be truly noble, so any man of sense will easily understand that my upbringing was like and suitable thereto: and whoso thinks that is not deceived, for in my tenth year had I already learned the rudiments of my dad's princely exercises: yet as touching studies I might compare with the famous Amphistides, of whom Suidas reports that he could not count higher than five: for my dad had perchance too high a spirit, and therefore followed the use of these days, wherein many persons of quality trouble themselves not, as they say with bookworms' follies, but have their hirelings to do their inkslinging for them. Yet was I a fine performer on the bagpipe, whereon I could produce most dolorous strains. But as to knowledge of things divine, none shall ever persuade me that any lad of my age in all Christendom could there beat me, for I knew nought of God or man, of Heaven or hell, of angel or devil, nor could discern between good and evil. So may it be easily understood that I, with such knowledge of theology, lived like our first parents in Paradise, which in their innocence knew nought of sickness or death

or dying, and still less of the Resurrection. O noble life! (or, as one might better say, O noodle's life!) in which none troubles himself about medicine. And by this measure ye can estimate my proficiency in the study of jurisprudence and all other arts and sciences. Yea, I was so perfected in ignorance that I knew not that I knew nothing. So say I again, O noble life that once I led! But my dad would not suffer me long to enjoy such bliss, but deemed it right that as being nobly born, I should nobly act and nobly live: and therefore began to train me up for higher things and gave me harder lessons.

*　　*　　*

CHAPTER IV

HOW SIMPLICISSIMUS'S PALACE WAS STORMED, PLUNDERED, AND RUINATED, AND IN WHAT SORRY FASHION THE SOLDIERS KEPT HOUSE THERE

Although it was not my intention to take the peaceloving reader with these troopers to my dad's house and farm, seeing that matters will go ill therein, yet the course of my history demands that I should leave to kind posterity an account of what manner of cruelties were now and again practised in this our German war: yea, and moreover testify by my own example that such evils must often have been sent to us by the goodness of Almighty God for our profit. For, gentle reader, who would ever have taught me that there was a God in Heaven if these soldiers had not destroyed my dad's house, and by such a deed driven me out among folk who gave me all fitting instruction thereupon? Only a little while before, I neither knew nor could fancy to myself that there were any people on earth save only my dad, my mother and me, and the rest of our household, nor did I know of any human habitation but that where I daily went out and in. But soon thereafter I understood the way of men's coming into this world, and how they must leave it again. I was only in shape a man and in name a Christian: for the rest I was but a beast. Yet the Almighty looked upon my innocence with a pitiful eye, and would bring me to a knowledge both of Himself and of myself. And although He had a thousand ways to lead me thereto, yet would He doubtless use that one only by which my dad and my mother should be punished: and that for an example to all others by reason of their heathenish upbringing of me.

The first thing these troopers did was, that they stabled their horses: thereafter each fell to his appointed task: which task was neither more nor less than ruin and destruction. For though some began to slaughter and to boil and to roast so that it looked as if there should be a merry banquet forward, yet others there were who did but storm through the house above and below stairs. Others stowed together great parcels of cloth and apparel and all manner of household stuff, as if they would set up a frippery market. All that they had no mind to take with them they cut in pieces. Some thrust their swords through the hay and straw as if they had not enough sheep and swine to slaughter: and some shook the feathers out of the beds and in their stead stuffed in bacon and other dried meat and provisions as if such were better and softer to sleep upon. Others broke the stove and the windows as if they had a never-ending summer to promise. Houseware of copper and tin they beat flat, and packed such vessels, all bent and spoiled, in with the rest. Bedsteads, tables, chairs, and benches they burned, though there lay many cords of dry wood in the yard. Pots and pipkins must all go to pieces, either because they would eat none but roast flesh, or because their purpose was to make there but a single meal.

Our maid was so handled in the stable that she could not come out; which is a shame to tell of. Our man they laid bound upon the ground, thrust a gag into his mouth, and poured a pailful of filthy water into his body: and by this, which they called a Swedish draught, they forced him to lead a party of them to another place where they captured men and beasts, and brought them back to our farm, in which company were my dad, my mother, and our Ursula.

And now they began: first to take the flints out of their pistols and in place of them to jam the peasants' thumbs in and so to torture the poor

rogues as if they had been about the burning of witches: for one of them they had taken they thrust into the baking oven and there lit a fire under him, although he had as yet confessed no crime: as for another, they put a cord round his head and so twisted it tight with a piece of wood that the blood gushed from his mouth and nose and ears. In a word each had his own device to torture the peasants, and each peasant his several torture. But as it seemed to me then, my dad was the luckiest, for he with a laughing face confessed what others must out with in the midst of pains and miserable lamentations: and such honour without doubt fell to him because he was the householder. For they set him before a fire and bound him fast so that he could neither stir hand nor foot, and smeared the soles of his feet with wet salt, and this they made our old goat lick off, and so tickle him that he well nigh burst his sides with laughing. And this seemed to me so merry a thing that I must needs laugh with him for the sake of fellowship, or because I knew no better. In the midst of such laughter he must needs confess all that they would have of him, and indeed revealed to them a secret treasure, which proved far richer in pearls, gold, and trinkets than any would have looked for among peasants. Of the women, girls, and maidservants whom they took, I have not much to say in particular, for the soldiers would not have me see how they dealt with them. Yet this I know, that one heard some of them scream most piteously in divers corners of the house; and well I can judge it fared no better with my mother and our Ursel than with the rest. Yet in the midst of all this miserable ruin I helped to turn the spit, and in the afternoon to give the horses drink, in which employ I encountered our maid in the stable, who seemed to me wondrously tumbled, so that I knew her not, but with a weak voice she called to me, "O lad, run away, or the troopers will have thee away with them. Look to it well that thou get hence: thou seest in what plight . . ." And more she could not say.

*   *   *

CHAPTER XV

HOW SIMPLICISSIMUS WAS PLUNDERED, AND HOW HE DREAMED OF THE PEASANTS AND HOW THEY FARED IN TIMES OF WAR

Now when I came home I found that my fireplace and all my poor furniture, together with my store of provisions, which I had grown during the summer in my garden and had kept for the coming winter, were all gone. "And whither now?" thought I. And then first did need teach me heartily to pray: and I must summon all my small wits together, to devise what I should do. But as my knowledge of the world was both small and evil, I could come to no proper conclusion, only that 'twas best to commend myself to God and to put my whole confidence in Him: for otherwise I must perish. And besides all this those things which I had heard and seen that day lay heavy on my mind: and I pondered not so much upon my food and my sustenance as upon the enmity which there is ever between soldiers and peasants. Yet could my foolish mind come to no other conclusion than this—that there must of a surety be two races of men in the world, and not one only, descended from Adam, but two, wild and tame, like other unreasoning beasts, and therefore pursuing one another so cruelly.

With such thoughts I fell asleep, for mere misery and cold, with a hungry stomach. Then it seemed to me, as if in a dream, that all the trees which stood round my dwelling suddenly changed and took on another appearance: for on every treetop sat a trooper, and the trunks were garnished, in place of leaves, with all manner of folk. Of these, some had long lances, others musquets, hangers, halberts, flags, and some drums and fifes. Now this was merry to see, for all was neatly distributed and each according to his rank. The roots, moreover, were made up of folk of little worth, as mechanics and labourers, mostly, however, peasants and the like; and these nevertheless gave its strength to the tree and renewed the same when it was lost: yea more, they repaired the loss of any fallen leaves from among themselves to their own great damage: and all the time they lamented over

them that sat on the tree, and that with good reason, for the whole weight of the tree lay upon them and pressed them so that all the money was squeezed out of their pockets, yea, though it was behind seven locks and keys: but if the money would not out, then did the commissaries so handle them with rods (which thing they call military execution) that sighs came from their heart, tears from their eyes, blood from their nails, and the marrow from their bones. Yet among these were some whom men call light o' heart; and these made but little ado, took all with a shrug, and in the midst of their torment had, in place of comfort, mockery for every turn.

CHAPTER XVI
OF THE WAYS AND WORKS OF SOLDIERS NOWADAYS, AND HOW HARDLY A COMMON SOLDIER CAN GET PROMOTION

So must the roots of these trees suffer and endure toil and misery in the midst of trouble and complaint, and those upon the lower boughs in yet greater hardship: yet were these last mostly merrier than the first named, yea and moreover, insolent and swaggering, and for the most part godless folk, and for the roots a heavy unbearable burden at all times. And this was the rhyme upon them:

Hunger and thirst, and cold and heat, and work
   and woe, and all we meet;
And deeds of blood and deeds of shame, all may
   ye put to the landsknecht's name.

Which rhymes were the less like to be lyingly invented in that they answered to the facts. For gluttony and drunkenness, hunger and thirst, wenching and dicing and playing, riot and roaring, murdering and being murdered, slaying and being slain, torturing and being tortured, hunting and being hunted, harrying and being harried, robbing and being robbed, frighting and being frighted, causing trouble and suffering trouble, beating and being beaten: in a word, hurting and harming, and in turn being hurt and harmed—this was their whole life. And in this career they let nothing hinder them: neither winter nor summer, snow nor ice, heat nor cold, rain nor wind, hill nor dale, wet nor dry; ditches, mountain-passes, ramparts and walls, fire and water, were all the same to them. Father nor mother, sister nor brother, no, nor the danger to their own bodies, souls, and consciences, nor even loss of life and of heaven itself, or aught else that can be named, will ever stand in their way, for ever they toil and moil at their own strange work, till at last, little by little, in battles, sieges, attacks, campaigns, yea, and in their winter quarters too (which are the soldiers' earthly paradise, if they can but happen upon fat peasants) they perish, they die, they rot and consume away, save but a few, who in their old age, unless they have been right thrifty rievers and robbers, do furnish us with the best of all beggars and vagabonds.

Next above these hard-worked folk sat old henroost-robbers, who, after some years and much peril of their lives, had climbed up the lowest branches and clung to them, and so far had had the luck to escape death. Now these looked more serious, and somewhat more dignified than the lowest, in that they were a degree higher ascended: yet above them were some yet higher, who had yet loftier imaginings because they had to command the very lowest. And these people did call coat-beaters, because they were wont to dust the jackets of the poor pikemen, and to give the musqueteers oil enough to grease their barrels with.

Just above these the trunk of the tree had an interval or stop, which was a smooth place without branches, greased with all manner of ointments and curious soap of disfavour, so that no man save of noble birth could scale it, in spite of courage and skill and knowledge, God knows how clever he might be. For 'twas polished as smooth as a marble pillar or a steel mirror. Just over that smooth spot sat they with the flags: and of these some were young, some pretty well in years: the young folk their kinsmen had raised so far: the older people had either mounted on a silver ladder which is called the Bribery Backstairs or else on a step which Fortune, for want of a better client, had left for them. A little further up sat higher folk,

and these had also their toil and care and annoyance: yet had they this advantage, that they could fill their pokes with the fattest slices which they could cut out of the roots, and that with a knife which they called "War-contribution." And these were at their best and happiest when there came a commissary-bird flying overhead, and shook out a whole panfull of gold over the tree to cheer them: for of that they caught as much as they could, and let but little or nothing at all fall to the lowest branches: and so of these last more died of hunger than of the enemy's attacks, from which danger those placed above seemed to be free. Therefore was there a perpetual climbing and swarming going on on those trees; for each would needs sit in those highest and happiest places: yet were there some idle, worthless rascals, not worth their commissariat-bread, who troubled themselves little about higher places, and only did their duty. So the lowest, being ambitious, hoped for the fall of the highest, that they might sit in their place, and if it happened to one among ten thousand of them that he got so far, yet would such good luck come to him only in his miserable old age when he was more fit to sit in the chimney-corner and roast apples than to meet the foe in the field. And if any man dealt honestly and carried himself well, yet was he ever envied by others,

and perchance by reason of some unlucky chance of war deprived both of office and of life. And nowhere was this more grievous than at the before-mentioned smooth place on the tree: for there an officer who had had a good sergeant or corporal under him must lose him, however unwillingly, because he was now made an ensign. And for that reason they would take, in place of old soldiers, ink-slingers, footmen, overgrown pages, poor noblemen, and at times poor relations, tramps and vagabonds. And these took the very bread out of the mouths of those that had deserved it, and forthwith were made Ensigns.

*   *   *

REVIEW QUESTIONS

1. Who is Simplicissimus?
2. What is his relation to nature?
3. What does he consider noble and base?
4. What does Grimmelshausen tell us about the conduct of the Thirty Years' War?
5. What happens to the character of Simplicissimus when he witnesses the violence of war?
6. What did the Thirty Years' War do to the land and its occupants?

MICHEL EYQUEM DE MONTAIGNE

FROM "Of Cannibals"

Michel Eyquem de Montaigne (1533–1592) originated the essay as a literary form. Born of a wealthy family at the Château de Montaigne, near Libourne, he was first educated by a tutor who spoke to him in Latin but no French. Until he was six years old, Montaigne learned the classical language as his native tongue. He was further educated at the Collège du Guyenne, where his fluency intimidated some of the finest Latinists in France, and studied law at Toulouse. In 1554, his father purchased an office in the Cour des Aides of Périgeaux, a fiscal court later incorporated into the Parlement of Bordeaux, a position he soon resigned to his son. Montaigne spent

thirteen years in office at work he found neither pleasant nor useful. In 1571, he retired to the family estate. Apart from brief visits to Paris and Rouen, periods of travel, and two terms as mayor of Bordeaux (1581–85), Montaigne spent the rest of his life as a country gentleman. His life was not all leisure. He became gentleman-in-ordinary to the king's chamber and spent the period 1572–76 trying to broker a peace between Catholics and Huguenots. His first two books of the Essais *appeared in 1580; the third and last volume appeared in 1588. These essays are known for their discursive, conversational style, in which Montaigne undertook explorations of custom, opinion, and institutions. They gave voice to his opposition to all forms of dogmatism that were without rational basis. He observed life with a degree of skepticism, emphasizing the limits of human knowledge and the contradictions in human behavior. Indeed, Montaigne's essays are often cited as examples of an epistemological crisis borne of the new discoveries, theological debates, and social tensions that marked the early modern period.*

From *The Complete Essays of Montaigne*, translated by Donald M. Frame (Stanford: Stanford University Press, 1958).

When King Pyrrhus passed over into Italy, after he had reconnoitered the formation of the army that the Romans were sending to meet him, he said: "I do not know what barbarians these are" (for so the Greeks called all foreign nations), "but the formation of this army that I see is not at all barbarous." The Greeks said as much of the army that Flamininus brought into their country, and so did Philip, seeing from a knoll the order and distribution of the Roman camp, in his kingdom, under Publius Sulpicius Galba. Thus we should beware of clinging to vulgar opinions, and judge things by reason's way, not by popular say.

I had with me for a long time a man who had lived for ten or twelve years in that other world which has been discovered in our century, in the place where Villegaignon landed, and which he called Antarctic France. This discovery of a boundless country seems worthy of consideration. I don't know if I can guarantee that some other such discovery will not be made in the future, so many personages greater than ourselves having been mistaken about this one. I am afraid we have eyes bigger than our stomachs, and more curiosity than capacity. We embrace everything, but we clasp only wind.

*   *   *

This man I had was a simple, crude fellow—a character fit to bear true witness; for clever people observe more things and more curiously, but they interpret them; and to lend weight and conviction to their interpretation, they cannot help altering history a little. They never show you things as they are, but bend and disguise them according to the way they have seen them; and to give credence to their judgment and attract you to it, they are prone to add something to their matter, to stretch it out and amplify it. We need a man either very honest, or so simple that he has not the stuff to build up false inventions and give them plausibility; and wedded to no theory. Such was my man; and besides this, he at various times brought sailors and merchants, whom he had known on that trip, to see me. So I content myself with his information, without inquiring what the cosmographers say about it.

*   *   *

Now, to return to my subject, I think there is nothing barbarous and savage in that nation, from what I have been told, except that each man calls barbarism whatever is not his own practice; for

indeed it seems we have no other test of truth and reason than the example and pattern of the opinions and customs of the country we live in. *There is always the perfect religion, the perfect government, the perfect and accomplished manners in all things.* Those people are wild, just as we call wild the fruits that Nature has produced by herself and in her normal course; whereas really it is those that we have changed artificially and led astray from the common order, that we should rather call wild. The former retain alive and vigorous their genuine, their most useful and natural, virtues and properties, which we have debased in the latter in adapting them to gratify our corrupted taste. And yet for all that, the savor and delicacy of some uncultivated fruits of those countries is quite as excellent, even to our taste, as that of our own. It is not reasonable that art should win the place of honor over our great and powerful mother Nature. We have so overloaded the beauty and richness of her works by our inventions that we have quite smothered her. Yet wherever her purity shines forth, she wonderfully puts to shame our vain and frivolous attempts:

> Ivy comes readier without our care;
> In lonely caves the arbutus grows more fair;
> No art with artless bird song can compare.
>
>   Propertius

All our efforts cannot even succeed in reproducing the nest of the tiniest little bird, its contexture, its beauty and convenience; or even the web of the puny spider. All things, says Plato, are produced by nature, by fortune, or by art; the greatest and most beautiful by one or the other of the first two, the least and most imperfect by the last.

These nations, then, seem to me barbarous in this sense, that they have been fashioned very little by the human mind, and are still very close to their original naturalness. The laws of nature still rule them, very little corrupted by ours; and they are in such a state of purity that I am sometimes vexed that they were unknown earlier, in the days when there were men able to judge them better than we. I am sorry that Lycurgus and Plato did not know of them; for it seems to me that what we actually see in these nations surpasses not only all the pictures in which poets have idealized the golden age and all their inventions in imagining a happy state of man, but also the conceptions and the very desire of philosophy. They could not imagine a naturalness so pure and simple as we see by experience; nor could they believe that our society could be maintained with so little artifice and human solder. This is a nation, I should say to Plato, in which there is no sort of traffic, no knowledge of letters, no science of numbers, no name for a magistrate or for political superiority, no custom of servitude, no riches or poverty, no contracts, no successions, no partitions, no occupations but leisure ones, no care for any but common kinship, no clothes, no agriculture, no metal, no use of wine or wheat. The very words that signify lying, treachery, dissimulation, avarice, envy, belittling, pardon—unheard of. How far from this perfection would he find the republic that he imagined: *Men fresh sprung from the gods.*

These manners nature first ordained.

                                                      Virgil

For the rest, they live in a country with a very pleasant and temperate climate, so that according to my witnesses it is rare to see a sick man there; and they have assured me that they never saw one palsied, bleary-eyed, toothless, or bent with age. They are settled along the sea and shut in on the land side by great high mountains, with a stretch about a hundred leagues wide in between. They have a great abundance of fish and flesh which bear no resemblance to ours, and they eat them with no other artifice than cooking. The first man who rode a horse there, though he had had dealings with them on several other trips, so horrified them in this posture that they shot him dead with arrows before they could recognize him.

Their buildings are very long, with a capacity of two or three hundred souls; they are covered with the bark of great trees, the strips reaching to the ground at one end and supporting and leaning on one another at the top, in the manner of some of our barns, whose covering hangs down to the ground and acts as a side. They have wood so hard

that they cut with it and make of it their swords and grills to cook their food. Their beds are of a cotton weave, hung from the roof like those in our ships, each man having his own; for the wives sleep apart from their husbands.

They get up with the sun, and eat immediately upon rising, to last them through the day; for they take no other meal than that one. Like some other Eastern peoples, of whom Suidas tells us, who drank apart from meals, they do not drink then; but they drink several times a day, and to capacity. Their drink is made of some root, and is of the color of our claret wines. They drink it only lukewarm. This beverage keeps only two or three days; it has a slightly sharp taste, is not at all heady, is good for the stomach, and has a laxative effect upon those who are not used to it; it is a very pleasant drink for anyone who is accustomed to it. In place of bread they use a certain white substance like preserved coriander. I have tried it; it tastes sweet and a little flat.

The whole day is spent in dancing. The younger men go to hunt animals with bows. Some of the women busy themselves meanwhile with warming their drink, which is their chief duty. Some one of the old men, in the morning before they begin to eat, preaches to the whole barnful in common, walking from one end to the other, and repeating one single sentence several times until he has completed the circuit (for the buildings are fully a hundred paces long). He recommends to them only two things: valor against the enemy and love for their wives. And they never fail to point out this obligation, as their refrain, that it is their wives who keep their drink warm and seasoned.

There may be seen in several places, including my own house, specimens of their beds, of their ropes, of their wooden swords and the bracelets with which they cover their wrists in combats, and of the big canes, open at one end, by whose sound they keep time in their dances. They are close shaven all over, and shave themselves much more cleanly than we, with nothing but a wooden or stone razor. They believe that souls are immortal, and that those who have deserved well of the gods are lodged in that part of heaven where the sun rises, and the damned in the west.

They have some sort of priests and prophets, but they rarely appear before the people, having their home in the mountains. On their arrival there is a great feast and solemn assembly of several villages—each barn, as I have described it, makes up a village, and they are about one French league from each other. The prophet speaks to them in public, exhorting them to virtue and their duty; but their whole ethical science contains only these two articles: resoluteness in war and affection for their wives. He prophesies to them things to come and the results they are to expect from their undertakings, and urges them to war or holds them back from it; but this is on the condition that when he fails to prophesy correctly, and if things turn out otherwise than he has predicted, he is cut into a thousand pieces if they catch him, and condemned as a false prophet. For this reason, the prophet who has once been mistaken is never seen again.

*   *   *

They have their wars with the nations beyond the mountains, further inland, to which they go quite naked, with no other arms than bows or wooden swords ending in a sharp point, in the manner of the tongues of our boar spears. It is astonishing what firmness they show in their combats, which never end but in slaughter and bloodshed; for as to routs and terror, they know nothing of either.

Each man brings back as his trophy the head of the enemy he has killed, and sets it up at the entrance to his dwelling. After they have treated their prisoners well for a long time with all the hospitality they can think of, each man who has a prisoner calls a great assembly of his acquaintances. He ties a rope to one of the prisoner's arms, by the end of which he holds him, a few steps away, for fear of being hurt, and gives his dearest friend the other arm to hold in the same way; and these two, in the presence of the whole assembly, kill him with their swords. This done, they roast him and eat him in common and send

some pieces to their absent friends. This is not, as people think, for nourishment, as of old the Scythians used to do; it is to betoken an extreme revenge. And the proof of this came when they saw the Portuguese, who had joined forces with their adversaries, inflict a different kind of death on them when they took them prisoner, which was to bury them up to the waist, shoot the rest of their body full of arrows, and afterward hang them. They thought that these people from the other world, being men who had sown the knowledge of many vices among their neighbors and were much greater masters than themselves in every sort of wickedness, did not adopt this sort of vengeance without some reason, and that it must be more painful than their own; so they began to give up their old method and to follow this one.

I am not sorry that we notice the barbarous horror of such acts, but I am heartily sorry that, judging their faults rightly, we should be so blind to our own. I think there is more barbarity in eating a man alive than in eating him dead; and in tearing by tortures and the rack a body still full of feeling, in roasting a man bit by bit, in having him bitten and mangled by dogs and swine (as we have not only read but seen within fresh memory, not among ancient enemies, but among neighbors and fellow citizens, and what is worse, on the pretext of piety and religion), than in roasting and eating him after he is dead.

*   *   *

So we may well call these people barbarians, in respect to the rules of reason, but not in respect to ourselves, who surpass them in every kind of barbarity.

Their warfare is wholly noble and generous, and as excusable and beautiful as this human disease can be; its only basis among them is their rivalry in valor. They are not fighting for the conquest of new lands, for they still enjoy that natural abundance that provides them without toil and trouble with all necessary things in such profusion that they have no wish to enlarge their boundaries. They are still in that happy state of desiring only as much as their natural needs demand; anything beyond that is superfluous to them.

They generally call those of the same age, brothers; those who are younger, children; and the old men are fathers to all the others. These leave to their heirs in common the full possession of their property, without division or any other title at all than just the one that Nature gives to her creatures in bringing them into the world.

If their neighbors cross the mountains to attack them and win a victory, the gain of the victor is glory, and the advantage of having proved the master in valor and virtue; for apart from this they have no use for the goods of the vanquished, and they return to their own country, where they lack neither anything necessary nor that great thing, the knowledge of how to enjoy their condition happily and be content with it. These men of ours do the same in their turn. They demand of their prisoners no other ransom than that they confess and acknowledge their defeat. But there is not one in a whole century who does not choose to die rather than to relax a single bit, by word or look, from the grandeur of an invincible courage; not one who would not rather be killed and eaten than so much as ask not to be. They treat them very freely, so that life may be all the dearer to them, and usually entertain them with threats of their coming death, of the torments they will have to suffer, the preparations that are being made for that purpose, the cutting up of their limbs, and the feast that will be made at their expense. All this is done for the sole purpose of extorting from their lips some weak or base word, or making them want to flee, so as to gain the advantage of having terrified them and broken down their firmness. For indeed, if you take it the right way, it is in this point alone that true victory lies:

It is no victory
Unless the vanquished foe admits your mastery.
Claudian

The Hungarians, very bellicose fighters, did not in olden times pursue their advantage beyond putting the enemy at their mercy. For having

wrung a confession from him to this effect, they let him go unharmed and unransomed, except, at most, for exacting his promise never again to take up arms against them.

We win enough advantages over our enemies that are borrowed advantages, not really our own. It is the quality of a porter, not of valor, to have sturdier arms and legs; agility is a dead and corporeal quality; it is a stroke of luck to make our enemy stumble, or dazzle his eyes by the sunlight; it is a trick of art and technique, which may be found in a worthless coward, to be an able fencer. The worth and value of a man is in his heart and his will; there lies his real honor. Valor is the strength, not of legs and arms, but of heart and soul; it consists not in the worth of our horse or our weapons, but in our own. He who falls obstinate in his courage, *if he has fallen, he fights on his knees.* He who relaxes none of his assurance, no matter how great the danger of imminent death; who, giving up his soul, still looks firmly and scornfully at his enemy—he is beaten not by us, but by fortune; he is killed, not conquered.

*   *   *

To return to our story. These prisoners are so far from giving in, in spite of all that is done to them, that on the contrary, during the two or three months that they are kept, they wear a gay expression; they urge their captors to hurry and put them to the test; they defy them, insult them, reproach them with their cowardice and the number of battles they have lost to the prisoners' own people.

I have a song composed by a prisoner which contains this challenge, that they should all come boldly and gather to dine off him, for they will be eating at the same time their own fathers and grandfathers, who have served to feed and nourish his body. "These muscles," he says, "this flesh and these veins are your own, poor fools that you are. You do not recognize that the substance of your ancestors' limbs is still contained in them. Savor them well; you will find in them the taste of your own flesh." An idea that certainly does not smack of barbarity. Those that paint these people dying, and who show the execution, portray the prisoner spitting in the face of his slayers and scowling at them. Indeed, to the last gasp they never stop braving and defying their enemies by word and look. Truly here are real savages by our standards; for either they must be thoroughly so, or we must be; there is an amazing distance between their character and ours.

The men there have several wives, and the higher their reputation for valor the more wives they have. It is a remarkably beautiful thing about their marriages that the same jealousy our wives have to keep us from the affection and kindness of other women, theirs have to win this for them. Being more concerned for their husbands' honor than for anything else, they strive and scheme to have as many companions as they can, since that is a sign of their husbands' valor.

*   *   *

Three of these men, ignorant of the price they will pay some day, in loss of repose and happiness, for gaining knowledge of the corruptions of this side of the ocean; ignorant also of the fact that of this intercourse will come their ruin (which I suppose is already well advanced: poor wretches, to let themselves be tricked by the desire for new things, and to have left the serenity of their own sky to come and see ours!)—three of these men were at Rouen, at the time the late King Charles IX was there. The king talked to them for a long time; they were shown our ways, our splendor, the aspect of a fine city. After that, someone asked their opinion, and wanted to know what they had found most amazing. They mentioned three things, of which I have forgotten the third, and I am very sorry for it; but I still remember two of them. They said that in the first place they thought it very strange that so many grown men, bearded, strong, and armed, who were around the king (it is likely that they were talking about the Swiss of his guard) should submit to obey a child, and that one of them was not chosen to command instead. Second (they have a way in their language of speaking of men as halves of one another), they had noticed that there were among us men full

THE "ARMADA PORTRAIT" OF QUEEN ELIZABETH (c. 1588)

GEORGE GOWER

The English portraitist George Gower (1540–1596) became Sergeant Painter to Queen Elizabeth I of England in 1581. This, his most famous painting notwithstanding, we know little of the artist or his career. A number of portraits survive from the period before his court appointment. Thereafter, he created portraits of many English aristocrats and supervised the decoration of the royal palace at Hampton Court. The "Armada Portrait" commemorates the defeat of the Spanish Armada in 1588. What elements of the painting indicate the importance of the sea and of naval power for England? Given that warfare was commonly understood to be "man's work," how does Gower handle the apparent contradiction of a warrior queen? How does he signal his patroness's firmness of command without making her masculine? How does he glorify Glorianna?

478

and gorged with all sorts of good things, and that their other halves were beggars at their doors, emaciated with hunger and poverty; and they thought it strange that these needy halves could endure such an injustice, and did not take the others by the throat, or set fire to their houses.

I had a very long talk with one of them; but I had an interpreter who followed my meaning so badly, and who was so hindered by his stupidity in taking in my ideas, that I could get hardly any satisfaction from the man. When I asked him what profit he gained from his superior position among his people (for he was a captain, and our sailors called him king), he told me that it was to march foremost in war. How many men followed him? He pointed to a piece of ground, to signify as many as such a space could hold; it might have been four or five thousand men. Did all his authority expire with the war? He said that this much remained, that when he visited the villages dependent on him, they made paths for him through the underbrush by which he might pass quite comfortably.

All this is not too bad—but what's the use? They don't wear breeches.

*   *   *

REVIEW QUESTIONS

1. What lessons does Montaigne draw from accounts of the New World?
2. Why do you suppose Montaigne chose cannibalism, of all possible topics, to compare European and American cultures?
3. How do Montaigne's ideas reflect the crisis of the iron century?
4. Are there any human constants for Montaigne?
5. Does he believe in a single human nature, a single ideal of virtue?

HUGO GROTIUS

FROM *On the Law of War and Peace*

Hugo Grotius (1583–1645) was a Dutch statesman, jurist, theologian, poet, philologist, and historian, a man of all-embracing knowledge whose writings were of fundamental importance in the formulation of international law. He was born in Delft, the son of the burgomaster and curator at the University of Leiden. Grotius was precocious; he matriculated at the University of Leiden at age eleven. By age fifteen, he had edited the encyclopedia of Martianus Capella and accompanied a diplomatic mission to the king of France, who described Grotius as the "miracle of Holland." He earned his doctorate in law at the University of Orléans and became a distinguished jurist at The Hague. In 1601, he was appointed historiographer of the States of Holland.

He wrote a number of minor but memorable legal treatises before publishing his great work, On the Law of War and Peace, *in 1625. Grotius argued that the entire law of humankind was based on four fundamental precepts: neither a state nor an individual may attack another state or individual, neither a state nor an individual may appropriate what belongs to another state or individual, neither a state nor*

an individual may disregard treaties or contracts, and neither a state nor an individual may commit a crime. In the case of a violation of one of these precepts, compensation might be sought either by war or by individual action. These principles and the arguments that surrounded them significantly aided the development of a theory of state sovereignty and international relations in the early modern period. During the remainder of his life, Grotius remained involved in the political as well as the intellectual affairs of his day. Besides creating a vast corpus of written works, he participated in the government of the United Provinces of the Netherlands. He was eventually imprisoned for his support of Arminianism and managed to escape hidden in a trunk. He spent the rest of his life in exile, honored as one of the great intellectuals of the seventeenth century but unacknowledged by his own country.

From *The Rights of War and Peace*, by Hugo Grotius (Washington and London: M. Walter Dunne, 1901).

*   *   *

VIII

And here is the proper place for refuting the opinion of those, who maintain that, every where and without exception, the sovereign power is vested in the people, so that they have a right to restrain and punish kings for an abuse of their power. However there is no man of sober wisdom, who does not see the incalculable mischiefs, which such opinions have occasioned, and may still occasion; and upon the following grounds they may be refuted.

From the Jewish, as well as the Roman Law, it appears that any one might engage himself in private servitude to whom he pleased. Now if an individual may do so, why may not a whole people, for the benefit of better government and more certain protection, completely transfer their sovereign rights to one or more persons, without reserving any portion to themselves? Neither can it be alledged that such a thing is not to be presumed, for the question is not, what is to be presumed in a doubtful case, but what may lawfully be done. Nor is it any more to the purpose to object to the inconveniences, which may, and actually do arise from a people's thus surrendering their rights. For it is not in the power of man to devise any form of government free from imperfections and dangers. As a dramatic writer says, "you must either

take these advantages with those imperfections, or resign your pretensions to both."

Now as there are different ways of living, some of a worse, and some of a better kind, left to the choice of every individual; so a nation, "under certain circumstances, WHEN for instance, the succession to the throne is extinct, or the throne has by any other means become vacant," may choose what form of government she pleases. Nor is this right to be measured by the excellence of this or that form of government, on which there may be varieties of opinion, but by the will of the people.

There may be many reasons indeed why a people may entirely relinquish their rights, and surrender them to another: for instance, they may have no other means of securing themselves from the danger of immediate destruction, or under the pressure of famine it may be the only way, through which they can procure support. For if the Campanians, formerly, when reduced by necessity surrendered themselves to the Roman people in the following terms:—"Senators of Rome, we consign to your dominion the people of Campania, and the city of Capua, our lands, our temples, and all things both divine and human," and if another people as Appian relates, offered to submit to the Romans, and were refused, what is there to prevent any nation from submitting in the same manner to one powerful sovereign? It may also

happen that a master of a family, having large possessions, will suffer no one to reside upon them on any other terms, or an owner, having many slaves, may give them their liberty upon condition of their doing certain services, and paying certain rents; of which examples may be produced. Thus Tacitus, speaking of the German slaves, says, "Each has his own separate habitation, and his own household to govern. The master considers him as a tenant, bound to pay a certain rent in corn, cattle, and wearing apparel. And this is the utmost extent of his servitude."

Aristotle, in describing the requisites, which fit men for servitude, says, that "those men, whose powers are chiefly confined to the body, and whose principal excellence consists in affording bodily service, are naturally slaves, because it is their interest to be so." In the same manner some nations are of such a disposition that they are more calculated to obey than to govern, which seems to have been the opinion which the Cappadocians held of themselves, who when the Romans offered them a popular government, refused to accept it, because the nation they said could not exist in safety without a king. Thus Philostratus in the life of Apollonius, says, that it was foolish to offer liberty to the Thracians, the Mysians, and the Getae, which they were not capable of enjoying. The example of nations, who have for many ages lived happily under a kingly government, has induced many to give the preference to that form. Livy says, that the cities under Eumenes would not have changed their condition for that of any free state whatsoever. And sometimes a state is so situated, that it seems impossible it can preserve its peace and existence, without submitting to the absolute government of a single person, which many wise men thought to be the case with the Roman Republic in the time of Augustus Cæsar. From these, and causes like these it not only may, but generally does happen, that men, as Cicero observes in the second book of his offices, willingly submit to the supreme authority of another.

Now as property may be acquired by what has been already styled just war, by the same means the rights of sovereignty may be acquired. Nor is the term sovereignty here meant to be applied to monarchy alone, but to government by nobles, from any share in which the people are excluded. For there never was any government so purely popular, as not to require the exclusion of the poor, of strangers, women, and minors from the public councils. Some states have other nations under them, no less dependent upon their will, than subjects upon that of their sovereign princes. From whence arose that question, Are the Collatine people in their own power? And the Campanians, when they submitted to the Romans, are said to have passed under a foreign dominion. In the same manner Acarnania and Amphilochia are said to have been under the dominion of the Aetolians; Peraea and Caunus under that of the Rhodians; and Pydna was ceded by Philip to the Olynthians. And those towns, that had been under the Spartans, when they were delivered from their dominion, received the name of the free Laconians. The city of Cotyora is said by Xenophon to have belonged to the people of Sinope. Nice in Italy, according to Strabo, was adjudged to the people of Marseilles; and the island of Pithecusa to the Neapolitans. We find in Frontinus, that the towns of Calati and Caudium with their territories were adjudged, the one to the colony of Capua, and the other to that of Beneventum. Otho, as Tacitus relates, gave the cities of the Moors to the Province of Baetia. None of these instances, any more than the cessions of other conquered countries could be admitted, if it were a received rule that the rights of sovereigns are under the controul and direction of subjects.

Now it is plain both from sacred and profane history, that there are kings, who are not subject to the controul of the people in their collective body; God addressing the people of Israel, says, if thou shalt say, "I will place a king over me"; and to Samuel "Shew them the manner of the king, who shall reign over them." Hence the King is said to be anointed over the people, over the inheritance of the Lord, over Israel. Solomon is styled King over all Israel. Thus David gives thanks to God, for subduing the people under him. And Christ says, "the Kings of the nations bear rule

over them." There is a well known passage in Horace, "Powerful sovereigns reign over their own subjects, and the supreme being over sovereigns themselves." Seneca thus describes the three forms of government, "Sometimes the supreme power is lodged in the people, sometimes in a senate composed of the leading men of the state, sometimes this power of the people, and dominion over the people themselves is vested in a single person." Of the last description are those, who, as Plutarch says, exercise authority not according to the laws, but over the laws. And in Herodutus, Otanes describes a monarch as one whose acts are not subject to controul. Dion Prusaeensis also and Pausanias define a monarchy in the same terms.

Aristotle says there are some kings, who have the same right, which the nation elsewhere possesses over persons and property. Thus when the Roman Princes began to exercise regal power, the people it was said had transferred all their own personal sovereignty to them, which gave rise to the saying of Marcus Antoninus the Philosopher, that no one but God alone can be judge of the Prince. Dion. L. liii. speaking of such a prince, says, "he is perfectly master of his own actions, to do whatever he pleases, and cannot be obliged to do any thing against his will." Such anciently was the power of the Inachidae established at Argos in Greece. For in the Greek Tragedy of the Suppliants, Aeschylus has introduced the people thus addressing the King: "You are the state, you the people; you the court from which there is no appeal, you preside over the altars, and regulate all affairs by your supreme will." King Theseus himself in Euripides speaks in very different terms of the Athenian Republic; "The city is not governed by one man, but in a popular form, by an annual succession of magistrates." For according to Plutarch's explanation, Theseus was the general in war, and the guardian of the laws; but in other respects nothing more than a citizen. So that they who are limited by popular controul are improperly called kings. Thus after the time of Lycurgus, and more particularly after the institution of the

Ephori, the Kings of the Lacedaemonians are said by Polybius, Plutarch, and Cornelius Nepos, to have been Kings more in name than in reality. An example which was followed by the rest of Greece. Thus Pausanias says of the Argives to the Corinthians, "The Argives from their love of equality have reduced their kingly power very low; so that they have left the posterity of Cisus nothing more than the shadow of Kings." Aristotle denies such to be proper forms of government, because they constitute only a part of an Aristocracy or Democracy.

Examples also may be found of nations, who have not been under a perpetual regal form, but only for a time under a government exempt from popular controul. Such was the power of the Amimonians among the Cnidians, and of the Dictators in the early periods of the Roman history, when there was no appeal to the people, from whence Livy says, the will of the Dictator was observed as a law. Indeed they found this submission the only remedy against imminent danger, and in the words of Cicero, the Dictatorship possessed all the strength of royal power.

It will not be difficult to refute the arguments brought in favour of the contrary opinion. For in the first place the assertion that the constituent always retains a controul over the sovereign power, which he has contributed to establish, is only true in those cases where the continuance and existence of that power depends upon the will and pleasure of the constituent: but not in cases where the power, though it might derive its origin from that constituent, becomes a necessary and fundamental part of the established law. Of this nature is that authority to which a woman submits when she gives herself to a husband. Valentinian the Emperor, when the soldiers who had raised him to the throne, made a demand of which he did not approve, replied; "Soldiers, your election of me for your emperor was your own voluntary choice; but since you have elected me, it depends upon my pleasure to grant your request. It becomes you to obey as subjects, and me to consider what is proper to be done."

Nor is the assumption true, that all kings are made by the people, as may be plainly seen from the instances adduced above, of an owner admitting strangers to reside upon his demesnes on condition of their obedience, and of nations submitting by right of conquest. Another argument is derived from a saying of the Philosophers, that all power is conferred for the benefit of the governed and not of the governing party. Hence from the nobleness of the end, it is supposed to follow, that subjects have a superiority over the sovereign. But it is not universally true, that all power is conferred for the benefit of the party governed. For some powers are conferred for the sake of the governor, as the right of a master over a slave, in which the advantage of the latter is only a contingent and adventitious circumstance. In the same manner the gain of a Physician is to reward him for his labour; and not merely to promote the good of his art. There are other kinds of authority established for the benefit of both parties, as for instance, the authority of a husband over his wife. Certain governments also, as those which are gained by right of conquest, may be established for the benefit of the sovereign; and yet convey no idea of tyranny, a word which in its original signification, implied nothing of arbitrary power or injustice, but only the government or authority of a Prince. Again, some governments may be formed for the advantage both of subjects and sovereign, as when a people, unable to defend themselves, put themselves under the protection and dominion of any powerful king. Yet it is not to be denied, but that in most governments the good of the subject is the chief object which is regarded: and that what Cicero has said after Herodotus, and Herodotus after Hesiod, is true, that Kings were appointed in order that men might enjoy complete justice.

Now this admission by no means goes to establish the inference that kings are amenable to the people. For though guardianships were invented for the benefit of wards, yet the guardian has a right to authority over the ward. Nor, though a guardian may for mismanagement be removed from his trust, does it follow that a king may for the same reason be deposed. The cases are quite different, the guardian has a superior to judge him; but in governments, as there must be some dernier resort, it must be vested either in an individual, or in some public body, whose misconduct, as there is no superior tribunal before which they can be called, God declares that he himself will judge. He either punishes their offences, should he deem it necessary; or permits them for the chastisement of his people.

This is well expressed by Tacitus: he says, "you should bear with the rapacity or luxury of rulers, as you would bear with drought, or excessive rains, or any other calamities of nature. For as long as men exist there will be faults and imperfections; but these are not of uninterrupted continuance, and they are often repaired by the succession of better times." And Marcus Aurelius speaking of subordinate magistrates, said, that they were under the controul of the sovereign: but that the sovereign was amenable to God. There is a remarkable passage in Gregory of Tours, where that Bishop thus addresses the King of France, "If any of us, Sir, should transgress the bounds of justice, he may be punished by you. But if you exceed them, who can call you to account? For when we address you, you may hear us if you please; but if you will not, who can judge you, except him, who has declared himself to be righteousness?" Among the maxims of the Essenes, Porphyry cites a passage, that "no one can reign without the special appointment of divine providence." Irenaeus has expressed this well, "Kings are appointed by him at whose command men are created; and their appointment is suited to the condition of those, whom they are called to govern." There is the same thought in the Constitutions of Clement, "You shall fear the King, for he is of the Lord's appointment."

Nor is it an objection to what has been said, that some nations have been punished for the offences of their kings, for this does not happen, because they forbear to restrain their kings, but because they seem to give, at least a tacit consent to their vices, or perhaps, without respect to this, God may use that sovereign power which he has over the life

and death of every man to inflict a punishment upon the king by depriving him of his subjects.

*   *   *

REVIEW QUESTIONS

1. What is the relation between political power and will according to Grotius?

2. How does Grotius define the state? The sovereign state?
3. Where does Grotius locate sovereignty?
4. Does sovereignty have a moral component?
5. What is sovereignty's relation to property? To the good of the people?

FROM The Religious Peace of Augsburg

On September 25, 1555, the Religious Peace of Augsburg officially ended the religious struggle between the Catholic authorities, led by the Holy Roman emperor Charles V, and the forces of the Schmalkaldic League, an alliance of Lutheran princes. It made permanent the division of Christian church within the Holy Roman Empire by establishing the principle that each ruling authority could determine the official religion of its realm, either Lutheranism in accordance with the Augsburg Confession or Catholicism. This principle was later referred to as cuius regio, eius religio. *Subjects had to submit or migrate.*

From *Select Documents*, edited by E. Reich (London: P. S. King: 1905), pp. 230–32.

*   *   *

15. In order to bring peace to the Holy Roman Empire of the Germanic Nation between the Roman Imperial Majesty and the Electors, Princes and Estates, let neither his Imperial Majesty nor the Electors, Princes, etc., do any violence or harm to any estate of the empire on the account of the Augsburg Confession, but let them enjoy their religious belief, liturgy and ceremonies as well as their estates and other rights and privileges in peace; and complete religious peace shall be obtained only by Christian means of amity, or under threat of punishment of the Imperial ban.

16. Likewise the Estates espousing the Augsburg Confession shall let all the Estates and Princes who cling to the old religion live in absolute peace and in the enjoyment of all their estates, rights, and privileges.

17. However, all such as do not belong to the two above named religions shall not be included in the present peace but be totally excluded from it.

18. And since it has proved to be a matter of great dispute what was to happen with the bishoprics, priories and other ecclesiastical benefices of such Catholic priests who would in course of time abandon the old religion, we have in virtue of the powers of Roman Emperors ordained as follows: where an archbishop, bishop or prelate or any other priest of our old religion shall abandon the same, his archbishopric, bishopric, prelacy and other benefices together with all their income and rev-

enues which he has so far possessed, shall be abandoned by him without any further objection or delay. The chapter and such [as] are entitled to it by common law or the custom of the place shall elect a person espousing the old religion who may enter on the possession and enjoyment of all the rights and incomes of the place without any further hindrance and without prejudging any ultimate amicable transaction of religion.

19. Some of the abbeys, monasteries and other ecclesiastical estates having been confiscated and turned into churches, schools, and charitable institutions, it is herewith ordained that such estates which their original owners had not possessed at the time of the Treaty of Passau [1552] shall be comprised in the present treaty of peace.

20. The ecclesiastical jurisdiction over the Augsburg Confession, dogma, appointment of ministers, church ordinances, and ministries hitherto practiced (but apart from all the rights of Electors, Princes and Estates colleges and monasteries to taxes in money or tithes) shall from now cease and the Augsburg Confession shall be left to the free and untrammeled enjoyment of their religion, ceremonies, appointment of ministers, as is stated in a subsequent separate article, until the final transaction of religion will take place.

*   *   *

23. No Estate shall try to persuade the subjects of other Estates to abandon their religion or protect them against their own magistrates. Such as had from olden times the rights of patronage are not included in the present article.

24. In case our subjects whether belonging to the old religion or the Augsburg confession should intend leaving their homes with their wives and children in order to settle in another, they shall be hindered neither in the sale of their estates after due payment of the local taxes nor injured in their honor.

REVIEW QUESTIONS

1. Why do we call this document a "religious peace"?
2. What does the Religious Peace specifically allow?
3. What does the Religious Peace specifically disallow?
4. Does the Religious Peace constitute an act of toleration?
5. What is the particular significance of Article 18, the so-called ecclesiastical reservation?
6. What grounds for future conflicts does this "religious peace" contain?

15 ❧ ABSOLUTISM AND EMPIRE, 1660–1789

The word transition *best characterizes the economy and society of early modern Europe. Although the forms of production and exchange remained corporatist and traditional, elements of individualism and capitalism exerted increasingly strong influence. Accordingly, European society, which remained in large part hierarchical and patriarchal, showed signs of an emergent class structure. Evidence of these changes remained regional, being more marked in certain places and times than in others. Nonetheless, the evidence of such a transition can be seen nearly everywhere in Europe, driven by forces that gripped the entire continent.*

For much of this period, the population remained locked in a struggle to survive. Beset by periodic famine and disease, life seemed tenuous and expectancies were short. Given high and early mortality, marriages occurred relatively late in life, and truncated families were commonplace. Beginning in the late seventeenth century, however, mortality began to decline. By the eighteenth century, populations were expanding across Europe.

The principal cause of the change in demographic dynamics was an increase in food supply that can be attributed in turn to a gradual change in agricultural techniques. Throughout the early modern period, traditional agricultural practices gradually yielded to techniques known generally as scientific farming. Landowners who sought gain in the marketplaces of Europe needed more direct control over land use and the ability to respond flexibly to market conditions. As a result, they enclosed communal lands and turned to the kinds of husbandry that would increase harvests and profits. The result was an increased food supply that eventually freed Europe from its age-old cycle of feast and famine.

An increasing population put new pressures on industry by raising the demand for manufactured goods and supplying a ready labor force to produce them. Rural manufacturing in the form of extensive production networks, known as the putting-out system, increased industrial productivity and captured surplus

population in industrial work processes. Those who could not find such employment fled to the cities, which also grew rapidly. It is interesting that urban manufacturing remained largely traditional, that is, highly regulated and guild based, throughout the early modern period.

The greatest single force for change between 1500 and 1800 was the expansion of long-distance commerce based on the development of overseas empires and the consolidation of central states. Capitalist practices had existed since the late fourteenth century at least, but the possibility of large profits from direct trade with Asia and the Americas offered new scope for their application. The development of mercantilist theories, which advocated the expansion of trade as a source of political power, combined with capitalist ambitions to facilitate global commerce. As a result, enterprises such as charter companies emerged on a larger scale. The supplies of goods traded and their profitability promoted the refinement of commercial facilities such as commodity exchanges, stock markets, and banking techniques. Moreover, the activities of these enterprises introduced new commodities in such volumes that new tastes emerged and old patterns of consumption were transformed.

Growing populations and expanding economies notwithstanding, the society of early modern Europe remained traditional. It was hierarchical in structure; each individual's place was fixed by birthright. Authority was patriarchal in nature, modeled on the supposedly absolute authority of the father within his family. Yet transition was also evident here. Economic change created mobility. New wealth encouraged social and political aspirations as bourgeois everywhere chafed under the exclusivity of the aristocracy and sought admission to their ranks. New poverty created a class of have-nots that challenged the established order and threatened its security.

Observers and theorists viewed the transformation of Europe's economy and society with some trepidation. In most instances, their responses were reactionary. They returned to notions of fatherhood for a model of authority that could withstand the changing times. As the period progressed, however, more and more theorists turned to philosophical reason to find general laws of human interaction that might be applied to govern economic and social behavior.

Absolutism refers to a particular conception of political authority that emerged in the wake of this transition and its attendant disorders in the later sixteenth century. It asserted order, where Europeans felt order had been undermined in political and social relations, by positing a vision of a society that had its apex in the person of a single ruler. At the center of all conceptions of absolutism was the will of the ruler: For all theorists, that will was absolute, not merely sovereign but determinative of all political relations. Such an understanding of the nature and operation of political power required a number of developments, not the least of which were a military and a bureaucracy to carry out the king's will.

By the end of the period, there would be calls for enlightened absolutism, whereby reason guided the will of the sovereign, but the will of the monarch was still the agent of political life. Among theorists, several emerged who countered the notion of absolute monarchy with that of sovereignty placed in the hands of property owners. Moreover, they argued persuasively that the exercise of sovereignty was limited in accordance with the principles of natural law.

No monarch in this period was truly absolute—such an effective expression of the will of the ruler requires greater technological and military support than any ruler prior to the nineteenth century could have. Many, however, were largely successful in representing themselves as the center of all political life in their states, nurturing courts and bureaucracies that reflected images of omniscient and powerful rulers. These same courts provided both a milieu and the financial support for philosophes such as Voltaire and scientists such as Galileo, even as those intellectuals were calling into question the ethics of and the social bases for absolutism.

JEAN BODIN

FROM *On Sovereignty*

Jean Bodin (1529–1596) was born a bourgeois in Angers. He entered a Carmelite monastery in 1545, apparently set on an ecclesiastical career, but obtained release from his vows around 1549. He pursued a course of study at the royal Collège de Quatre Langues in Paris. By 1550, he was well trained in humanist studies and went on to become one of the greatest scholars of his day. His continual search for religious truth placed him repeatedly under suspicion of heresy, but no clear evidence exists to support a conversion to Calvinism. Bodin continued his studies and attended the University of Toulouse, where he studied law during the 1550s. In 1561, he launched his public career by serving as an advocate before the parliament in Paris. Bodin soon came to the attention of high officials and dignitaries and received special commissions from the king as early as 1570. In 1571, he entered the service of Francis, duke of Alençon, a prince of the blood. During his service to Alençon, and in the aftermath of the St. Bartholomew's Day massacre, Bodin published his great work, Six livres de la république (1576), a systematic exposition of public law. It included an absolutist theory of royal government, from which the following selection is drawn. Bodin's theory was based on the controversial notion, which proved highly influential in the development of royal absolutism, that sovereignty was indivisible and that high powers of government could not be shared by

separate agents or agencies. His notion that all governmental powers were concentrated in the king of France can be seen as a direct response to the anarchy of civil war that gripped the kingdom during the second half of the sixteenth century. In 1576, Bodin was chosen as a deputy for the Third Estate of the Estates-General of Blois. Though a royalist, Bodin opposed the civil wars that raged in France and became a leading spokesperson against royal requests for increased taxation and religious uniformity. It cost him royal favor and high office. With the death in 1584 of his patron, the duke of Alençon, Bodin's career in high politics ended. He retired to Laon, where he died.

From *On Sovereignty*, by Jean Bodin, edited by Julian H. Franklin (Cambridge: Cambridge University Press, 1992), pp. 46–50.

Book I

* * *

CHAPTER 8
ON SOVEREIGNTY

Sovereignty is the absolute and perpetual power of a commonwealth, which the Latins call *maiestas;* the Greeks *akra exousia, kurion arche,* and *kurion politeuma;* and the Italians *segnioria,* a word they use for private persons as well as for those who have full control of the state, while the Hebrews call it *tomech shévet*—that is, the highest power of command. We must now formulate a definition of sovereignty because no jurist or political philosopher has defined it, even though it is the chief point, and the one that needs most to be explained, in a treatise on the commonwealth. Inasmuch as we have said that a commonwealth is a just government, with sovereign power, of several households and of that which they have in common, we need to clarify the meaning of sovereign power.

* * *

We shall conclude, then, that the sovereignty of the monarch is in no way altered by the presence of the Estates. On the contrary, his majesty is all the greater and more illustrious when all his people publicly acknowledge him as sovereign, even though, in an assembly like this, princes, not wishing to rebuff their subjects, grant and pass many things that they would not consent to had they not been overcome by the requests, petitions, and just complaints of a harassed and afflicted people which has most often been wronged without the knowledge of the prince, who sees and hears only through the eyes, ears, and reports of others.

We thus see that the main point of sovereign majesty and absolute power consists of giving the law to subjects in general without their consent. Not to go to other countries, we in this kingdom have often seen certain general customs repealed by edicts of our kings without hearing from the Estates when the injustice of the rules was obvious. Thus the custom concerning the inheritance by mothers of their children's goods, which was observed in this kingdom throughout the entire region governed by customary law, was changed without assembling either the general or local estates. Nor is this something new. In the time of King Philip the Fair, the general custom of the entire kingdom, by which the losing party in a case could not be required to pay expenses, was suppressed by an edict without assembling the Estates.

* * *

CHAPTER 10
ON THE TRUE MARKS OF SOVEREIGNTY

Since there is nothing greater on earth, after God, than sovereign princes, and since they have been

established by Him as His lieutenants for commanding other men, we need to be precise about their status so that we may respect and revere their majesty in complete obedience, and do them honor in our thoughts and in our speech. Contempt for one's sovereign prince is contempt toward God, of whom he is the earthly image. That is why God, speaking to Samuel, from whom the people had demanded a different prince, said "It is me that they have wronged."

To be able to recognize such a person—that is, a sovereign—we have to know his attributes, which are properties not shared by subjects. For if they were shared, there would be no sovereign prince. Yet the best writers on this subject have not treated this point with the clarity it deserves, whether from flattery, fear, hatred, or forgetfulness.

We read that Samuel, after consecrating the king that God had designated, wrote a book about the rights of majesty. But the Hebrews have written that the kings suppressed his book so that they could tyrannize their subjects. Melanchthon thus went astray in thinking that the rights of majesty were the abuses and tyrannical practices that Samuel pointed out to the people in a speech. "Do you wish to know," said Samuel, "the ways of tyrants? It is to seize the goods of subjects to dispose of at his pleasure, and to seize their women and their children in order to abuse them and to make them slaves." The word *mishpotim* as it is used in this passage does not mean rights, but rather practices and ways of doing things. Otherwise this good prince, Samuel, would have contradicted himself. For when accounting to the people for the stewardship that God had given him, he said, "Is there anyone among you who can say that I ever took gold or silver from him, or any present whatsoever?" And thereupon the whole people loudly praised him for never having done a wrong or taken anything from anyone no matter who.

*   *   *

We may thus conclude that the first prerogative of a sovereign prince is to give law to all in general and each in particular. But this is not sufficient. We have to add "without the consent of any other, whether greater, equal, or below him." For if the prince is obligated to make no law without the consent of a superior, he is clearly a subject; if of an equal, he has an associate; if of subjects, such as the senate or the people, he is not sovereign. The names of grandees that one finds affixed to edicts are not put there to give the law its force, but to witness it and to add weight to it so that the enactment will be more acceptable. For there are very ancient edicts, extant at Saint Denys in France, issued by Philip I and Louis the Fat in 1060 and 1129 respectively, to which the seals of their queens Anne and Alix, and of Robert and Hugh, were affixed. For Louis the Fat, it was year twelve of his reign; for Adelaide, year six.

When I say that the first prerogative of sovereignty is to give law to all in general and to each in particular, the latter part refers to privileges, which are in the jurisdiction of sovereign princes to the exclusion of all others. I call it a privilege when a law is made for one or a few private individuals, no matter whether it is for the profit or the loss of the person with respect to whom it is decreed. Thus Cicero said, *Privilegium de meo capite latum est.* "They have passed," he said, "a capital privilege against me." He is referring to the authorization to put him on trial decreed against him by the commoners at the request of the tribune Clodius. He calls this the *lex Clodia* in many places, and he bitterly protests that privileges could be decreed only by the great Estates of the people as it was laid down by the laws of the Twelve Tables in the words: *Privilegia, nisi comitiis centuriatis irroganto, qui secus faxit capital esto.*[1] And all those who have written of regalian rights agree that only the sovereign can grant privileges, exemptions, and immunities, and grant dispensations from edicts and ordinances. In monarchies, however, privileges last only for the lifetime of the monarchs, as the emperor Tiberius, Suetonius re-

---

[1] "Let no privileges be imposed except in the *comita centuriata;* let him who has done otherwise be put to death."

ports, informed all those who had received privileges from Augustus.

*   *   *

Book II

Ignorance of the exact meaning of the term "tyrant" has led many people astray, and has been the cause of many inconveniences. We have said that a tyrant is someone who makes himself into a sovereign prince by his own authority—without election, or right of succession, or lot, or a just war, or a special calling from God. This is what is understood by tyrant in the writings of the ancients and in the laws that would have him put to death. Indeed, the ancients established great prizes and rewards for those who killed tyrants, offering titles of nobility, prowess, and chivalry to them along with statues and honorific titles, and even all the tyrant's goods, because they were taken as true liberators of the fatherland, or of the motherland, as the Cretans say. In this they did not distinguish, between a good and virtuous prince and a bad and wicked one, for no one has the right to seize the sovereignty and make himself the master of those who had been his companions, no matter what pretenses of justice and virtue he may offer. In strictest law, furthermore, use of the prerogatives reserved to sovereignty is punishable by death. Hence if a subject seeks, by whatever means, to invade the state and steal it from his king or, in a democracy or aristocracy, to turn himself from a fellow-citizen into lord and master, he deserves to be put to death. In this respect our question does not pose any difficulty.

*   *   *

At this point there are many questions one may ask, such as whether a tyrant, who I said may be justly killed without form or shape of trial, be-

comes legitimate if, after having encroached upon sovereignty by force or fraud, he has himself elected by the Estates. For it seems that the solemn act of election is an authentic ratification of the tyranny, an indication that the people have found it to their liking. But I say that it is nevertheless permissible to kill him, and to do so by force unless the tyrant, stripping off his authority, has given up his arms and put power back into the hands of the people in order to have its judgment. What tyrants force upon a people stripped of power cannot be called consent. Sulla, for example, had himself made dictator for eighty years by the Valerian law, which he got published with a powerful army camped inside the city of Rome. But Cicero said that this was not a law. Another example is Caesar, who had himself made permanent dictator by the Servian law; and yet another is Cosimo de Medici who, having an army inside Florence, had himself elected duke. When objections were raised, he set off a volley of gunfire in front of the palace, which induced the lords and magistrates to get on with it more quickly.

*   *   *

So much then for the tyrant, whether virtuous or wicked, who makes himself a sovereign lord on his own authority. But the chief difficulty arising from our question is whether a sovereign prince who has come into possession of the state by way of election, or lot, or right of succession, or just war, or by a special calling from God, can be killed if he is cruel, oppressive, or excessively wicked. For that is the meaning given to the word tyrant. Many doctors and theologians, who have touched upon this question, have resolved that it is permissible to kill a tyrant without distinction, and some, putting two words together that are incompatible, have spoken of a king-tyrant (*roi tyran*), which has caused the ruin of some very fine and flourishing monarchies.

But to decide this question properly we need to distinguish between a prince who is absolutely sovereign and one who is not, and between subjects and foreigners. It makes a great difference whether we say that a tyrant can be lawfully killed by a

foreign prince or by a subject. For just as it is glorious and becoming, when the gates of justice have been shut, for someone, whoever he may be, to use force in defense of the goods, honor, and life of those who have been unjustly oppressed—as Moses did when he saw his brother being beaten and mistreated and had no way of getting justice—so is it a most beautiful and magnificent thing for a prince to take up arms in order to avenge an entire people unjustly oppressed by a tyrant's cruelty, as did Hercules, who traveled all over the world exterminating tyrant-monsters and was deified for his great feats. The same was done by Dion, Timoleon, Aratus, and other generous princes, who obtained the title of chastisers and correctors of tyrants. This, furthermore, was the sole cause for which Tamerlane, prince of the Tartars, declared war on Bajazet, who was then besieging Constantinople, Tamerlane saying that he had come to punish him for tyranny and to deliver the afflicted peoples. He defeated Bajazet in a battle fought on the plateau of Mount Stella, and after he had killed and routed three hundred thousand Turks, he had the tyrant chained inside a cage until he died. In this case it makes no difference whether this virtuous prince proceeds against a tyrant by force, deception, or judicial means. It is however true that if a virtuous prince has seized a tyrant, he will obtain more honor by putting him on trial and punishing him as a murderer, parricide, and thief, rather than acting against him by the common law of peoples (*droit des gens*).

But as for subjects, and what they may do, one has to know whether the prince is absolutely sovereign, or is properly speaking not a sovereign. For if he is not absolutely sovereign, it follows necessarily that sovereignty is in the people or the aristocracy. In this latter case there is no doubt that it is permissible to proceed against the tyrant either by way of law if one can prevail against him, or else by way of fact and open force, if one cannot otherwise have justice. Thus the Senate took the first way against Nero, the second against Maximinus inasmuch as the Roman emperors were no more than princes of the republic, in the sense of first persons and chief citizens, with

sovereignty remaining in the people and the Senate.

* * *

But if the prince is sovereign absolutely, as are the genuine monarchs of France, Spain, England, Scotland, Ethiopia, Turkey, Persia, and Moscovy—whose power has never been called into question and whose sovereignty has never been shared with subjects—then it is not the part of any subject individually, or all of them in general, to make an attempt on the honor or the life of the monarch, either by way of force or by way of law, even if he has committed all the misdeeds, impieties, and cruelties that one could mention. As to the way of law, the subject has no right of jurisdiction over his prince, on whom all power and authority to command depends; he not only can revoke all the power of his magistrates, but in his presence, all the power and jurisdiction of all magistrates, guilds and corporations, Estates and communities, cease, as we have said and will say again even more elaborately in the proper place. And if it is not permissible for a subject to pass judgment on his prince, or a vassal on his lord, or a servant on his master—in short, if it is not permissible to proceed against one's king by way of law—how could it be licit to do so by way of force? For the question here is not to discover who is the strongest, but only whether it is permissible in law, and whether a subject has the power to condemn his sovereign prince.

A subject is guilty of treason in the first degree not only for having killed a sovereign prince, but also for attempting it, advising it, wishing it, or even thinking it. And the law finds this so monstrous [as to subject it to a special rule of sentencing]. Ordinarily, if someone who is accused, seized, and convicted dies before he has been sentenced, his personal status is not diminished, no matter what his crime, even if it was treason. But treason in the highest degree can never be purged by the death of the person accused of it, and even someone who was never accused is considered in law as having been already sentenced. And although evil thoughts are not subject to punish-

ment, anyone who has thought of making an attempt on the life of his sovereign prince is held to be guilty of a capital crime, no matter whether he repented of it. In fact there was a gentleman from Normandy who confessed to a Franciscan friar that he had wanted to kill King Francis I but had repented of this evil wish. The Franciscan gave him absolution, but still told the king about it; he had the gentleman sent before the Parlement of Paris to stand trial, where he was condemned to death by its verdict and thereupon executed. And one cannot say that the court acted from fear, in view of the fact that it often refused to verify edicts and letters patent even when the king commanded it. And in Paris a man, named Caboche, who was completely mad and out of his senses, drew a sword against King Henry II without any effect or even attempt. He too was condemned to die without consideration of his insanity, which the law ordinarily excuses no matter what murder or crime the madman may have committed.

*   *   *

As for Calvin's remark that if there existed in these times magistrates especially constituted for the defense of the people and to restrain the licentiousness of kings, like the ephors in Sparta, the tribunes in Rome, and the demarchs in Athens, then those magistrates should resist, oppose, and prevent their licentiousness and cruelty—it clearly shows that it is never licit, in a proper monarchy, to attack a sovereign king, or defend one's self against him, or to make an attempt upon his life or honor, for he spoke only of democratic and aristocratic states. I have shown above that the kings of Sparta were but simple senators and captains. And when he speaks of the Estates, he says "possible," not daring to be definite. In any event there is an important difference between attacking the honor of one's prince and resisting his tyranny, between killing one's king and opposing his cruelty.

We thus read that the Protestant princes of Germany, before taking up arms against the emperor, asked Martin Luther if it were permissible. He frankly replied that it was not permissible no mat-

ter how great the charge of impiety or tyranny. But he was not heeded; and the outcome of the affair was miserable, bringing with it the ruin of some great and illustrious houses of Germany. *Quia nulla iusta causa videri potest,* said Cicero, *adversus patriam arma capiendi.*[2] Admittedly, it is quite certain that the sovereignty of the German Empire does not lie in the person of the emperor, as we shall explain in due course. But since he is the chief, they could have taken up arms against him only with the consent of the Estates or its majority, which was not obtained. It would have been even less permissible against a sovereign prince.

I can give no better parallel than that of a son with respect to his father. The law of God says that he who speaks evil of his father or his mother shall be put to death. If the father be a murderer, a thief, a traitor to his country, a person who has committed incest or parricide, a blasphemer, an atheist, and anything else one wants to add, I confess that the entire gamut of penalties will not suffice for his punishment; but I say that it is not for his son to lay hands on him, *quia nulla tanta impietas, nullum tantum factum est quod sit parricidio vindicandum,*[3] as it was put by an orator of ancient times. And yet Cicero, taking up this question, says that love of country is even greater. Hence the prince of our country, being ordained and sent by God, is always more sacred and ought to be more inviolable than a father.

I conclude then that it is never permissible for a subject to attempt anything against a sovereign prince, no matter how wicked and cruel a tyrant he may be. It is certainly permissible not to obey him in anything that is against the law of God or nature—to flee, to hide, to evade his blows, to suffer death rather than make any attempt upon his life or honor. For oh, how many tyrants there would be if it were lawful to kill them! He who taxes too heavily would be a tyrant, as the vulgar understand it; he who gives commands that the

---

[2] "Because there can never be a just cause to take up arms against one's country."

[3] "Because there is no impiety so great, and no crime so great that it ought to be avenged by patricide."

people do not like would be a tyrant, as Aristotle defined a tyrant in the *Politics;* he who maintains guards for his security would be a tyrant; he who punishes conspirators against his rule would be a tyrant. How then should good princes be secure in their lives? I would not say that it is illicit for other princes to proceed against tyrants by force of arms, as I have stated, but it is not for subjects.

*   *   *

REVIEW QUESTIONS

1. What, according to Bodin, is the definition of *sovereignty?*
2. In describing its prerogatives, would Bodin have agreed with Machiavelli?
3. Can sovereignty be mixed? Why?
4. Is it permissible to resist a tyrant?
5. Can a sovereign ruler be a tyrant?
6. May one resist a sovereign?

THOMAS HOBBES

FROM *Leviathan*

Thomas Hobbes (1588–1679) was an English philosopher whose mechanistic and deterministic theories of political life were highly controversial in his own time. Born in Malmesbury, Hobbes attended Magdalen Hall, Oxford, and became tutor to William Cavendish, later the Earl of Devonshire, in 1608. With his student, he undertook several tours of the Continent, where he met and spoke with leading intellectual lights of the day, including Galileo and Descartes. Around 1637, he became interested in the constitutional struggle between Parliament and Charles I and set to work writing a "little treatise in English" in defense of the royal prerogative. Before its publication in 1650, the book circulated privately in 1640 under the title Elements of Law, Natural and Politic. *Fearing arrest by Parliament, Hobbes fled to Paris, where he remained for the next eleven years. While in exile, he served as math tutor to the Prince of Wales, later Charles II, from 1646 to 1648. His great work,* Leviathan *(1651), was a forceful argument for political absolutism. Its title, taken from the horrifying sea monster of the Old Testament, suggested the power and authority Hobbes thought necessary to compel obedience and order in human society. Strongly influenced by mechanical philosophy, he treated human beings as matter in motion, subject to certain physical, rational laws. According to Hobbes, people feared one another and lived in a state of constant competition and conflict. For this reason, they must submit to the absolute, supreme authority of the state, a social contract among selfish individuals moved by fear and necessity. Once delegated, that authority was irrevocable and indivisible. Ironically, these theories found favor neither with royalists nor with antiroyalists. Charles II believed that it was written in justification of the Commonwealth. The French feared its attacks on the papacy. After the Restoration, Parliament added* Leviathan *to a list of books to be investigated for atheistic tendencies.*

Despite frustrations over the reception of his political theories, Hobbes retained his intellectual vigor. At age eighty-four, he wrote an autobiography in Latin and translated the works of Homer into English. He died at age ninety-one.

From *Leviathan*, by Thomas Hobbes, edited by E. Hershey Sneath (Needham, Eng.: Ginn Press, 1898).

*   *   *

Of the Causes, Generation, and Definition of a Commonwealth

The final cause, end, or design of men, who naturally love liberty and dominion over others, in the introduction of that restraint upon themselves in which we see them live in commonwealths is the foresight of their own preservation, and of a more contented life thereby; that is to say, of getting themselves out from that miserable condition of war which is necessarily consequent . . . to the natural passions of men when there is no visible power to keep them in awe and tie them by fear of punishment to the performance of their covenants, and observation of the laws of nature. . . .

For the laws of nature, as "justice," "equity," "modesty," "mercy," and, in sum, "doing to others as we would be done to," of themselves, without the terror of some power to cause them to be observed, are contrary to our natural passions, that carry us to partiality, pride, revenge, and the like. And covenants without the sword are but words, and of no strength to secure a man at all. Therefore, notwithstanding the laws of nature, which every one has then kept when he has the will to keep them, when he can do it safely, if there be no power erected, or not great enough for our security; every man will, and may lawfully rely on his own strength and art, for protection against all other men. And in all places where men have lived by small families, to rob and spoil one another has been a trade, and so far from being reputed against the law of nature that the greater spoils they gained, the greater was their honor; and men observed no other laws therein but the laws of honor; that is, to abstain from cruelty, leaving to men their lives and instruments of livelihood. And as small families did then, so now do cities and kingdoms, which are but greater families, for their own security enlarge their dominions upon all pretenses of danger and fear of invasion or assistance that may be given to invaders, and endeavor as much as they can to subdue or weaken their neighbors by open force and secret arts, for lack of other protection, justly; and are remembered for it in later ages with honor.

Nor is it the joining together of a small number of men that gives them this security, because in small numbers small additions on the one side or the other make the advantage of strength so great as is sufficient to carry the victory; and therefore gives encouragement to an invasion. The multitude sufficient to confide in for our security is not determined by any certain number but by comparison with the enemy we fear; and is then sufficient when the advantage of the enemy is not so visible and conspicuous to determine the event of war as to move him to attempt it.

And should there not be so great a multitude, even if their actions be directed according to their particular judgments and particular appetites, they can expect thereby no defense nor protection, neither against a common enemy nor against the injuries of one another. For being distracted in opinions concerning the best use and application of their strength, they do not help but hinder one another, and reduce their strength by mutual opposition to nothing; whereby they are easily not only subdued by a very few that agree together, but also, when there is no common enemy, they make war upon each other for their particular interests. For if we could suppose a great multitude of men to consent in the observation of justice and

other laws of nature without a common power to keep them all in awe, we might as well suppose all mankind to do the same; and then there neither would be, nor need to be, any civil government or commonwealth at all, because there would be peace without subjection.

Nor is it enough for the security which men desire should last all the time of their life that they be governed and directed by one judgment for a limited time, as in one battle or one war. For though they obtain a victory by their unanimous endeavor against a foreign enemy, yet afterwards, when either they have no common enemy or he that by one group is held for an enemy is by another group held for a friend, they must needs, by the difference of their interests, dissolve, and fall again into a war among themselves.

It is true that certain living creatures, as bees and ants, live sociably one with another, which are therefore by Aristotle numbered among political creatures, and yet have no other direction, than their particular judgments and appetites; nor speech whereby one of them can signify to another what he thinks expedient for the common benefit; and therefore some man may perhaps desire to know why mankind cannot do the same. To which I answer:

First, that men are continually in competition for honor and dignity, which these creatures are not; and consequently among men there arises on the ground envy and hatred and finally war, but among these not so.

Secondly, that among these creatures the common good differ not from the private; and being by nature inclined to their private, they procure thereby the common benefit. But man, whose joy consists in comparing himself with other men, can relish nothing but what is eminent.

Thirdly, that these creatures, having not, as man, the use of reason, do not see nor think they see any fault, in the administration of their common business; whereas among men, there are very many that think themselves wiser and abler to govern the public better than the rest; and these strive to reform and innovate, one this way, another that way, and thereby bring it into distraction and civil war.

Fourthly, that these creatures, though they have some use of voice in making known to one another their desires and other affections, yet lack that art of words by which some men can represent to others that which is good in the likeness of evil; and evil in the likeness of good; and augment or diminish the apparent greatness of good and evil, making men discontented and troubling their peace at their pleasure.

Fifthly, irrational creatures cannot distinguish between "injury" and "damage"; and, therefore, as long as they be at ease they are not offended with their fellows; whereas man is then most troublesome when he is most at ease; for then it is that he loves to show his wisdom and control the actions of them that govern the commonwealth.

Lastly, the agreement of these creatures is natural, that of men is by covenant only, which is artificial; and therefore, it is no wonder if there be somewhat else required besides covenant to make their agreement constant and lasting, which is a common power to keep them in awe and to direct their actions to the common benefit.

The only way to erect such a common power which may be able to defend them from the invasion of foreigners and the injuries of one another, and thereby to secure them in such sort so that by their own industry and by the fruits of the earth they may nourish themselves and live contentedly, is to confer all their power and strength upon one man, or upon one assembly of men that may reduce all their wills, by plurality of voices, unto one will; which is as much as to say, to appoint one man or assembly of men to bear their person; and every one to accept and acknowledge himself to be author of whatsoever he that so bears their person shall act or cause to be acted in those things which concern the common peace and safety, and therein to submit their wills every one to his will, and their judgments to his judgment. This is more than consent or concord; it is a real unity of them all in one and the same person, made by covenant of every man with every man, in such manner as if every man should say to every man, "I authorize and give up my right of governing myself to this man, or to this assembly

of men, on this condition, that you give up your right to him and authorize all his actions in like manner." This done, the multitude so united in one person is called a "commonwealth," in Latin *civitas*. This is the generation of that great "leviathan," or rather, to speak more reverently, of that "mortal god," to which we owe, under the "immortal God," our peace and defense. For by this authority, given him by every particular man in the commonwealth, he has the use of so much power and strength conferred on him that, by terror thereof, he is enabled to form the wills of them all to peace at home and mutual aid against their enemies abroad. And in him consists the essence of the commonwealth, which, to define it, is "one person, of whose acts a great multitude, by mutual covenants one with another, have made themselves the author, to the end he may use the strength and means of them all as he shall think expedient for their peace and common defense."

And he that carries this person is called "sovereign" and said to have "sovereign power"; and every one besides, his "subject."

The attaining to this sovereign power is by two ways. One, by natural force, as when a man makes his children to submit themselves and their children to his government, as being able to destroy them if they refuse; or by war subdues his enemies to his will, giving them their lives on that condition. The other is when men agree among themselves to submit to some man or assembly of men voluntarily, on confidence that they will be protected by him against all others. This latter, may be called a political commonwealth, or commonwealth by "institution," and the former, a commonwealth by "acquisition." ✳ ✳ ✳

Of the Office of the Sovereign Representative

The office of the sovereign, be it a monarch or an assembly, consists in the end for which he was trusted with the sovereign power, namely, the securing of "the safety of the people"; to which he is obliged by the law of nature, and to render an account thereof to God, the author of that law, and to none but him. But by safety here is not meant a bare preservation but also all other contentments of life which every man by lawful industry, without danger or hurt to the commonwealth, shall acquire to himself.

And this is to be done, not by care applied to individuals further than their protection from injuries when they shall complain, but by a general provision contained in public instruction, both of doctrine and example, and in the making and executing of good laws to which individual persons may apply their own cases.

And because, if the essential rights of sovereignty . . . be taken away, the commonwealth is thereby dissolved and every man returns into the condition and calamity of a war with every other man, which is the greatest evil that can happen in this life; it is the office of the sovereign, to maintain those rights entire, and consequently against his duty, first, to transfer to another or to lay from himself any of them. For he that deserts the means deserts the ends; and he deserts the means when, being the sovereign, he acknowledges himself subject to the civil laws and renounces the power of supreme judicature, or of making war or peace by his own authority; or of judging of the necessities of the commonwealth; or of levying money and soldiers when and as much as in his own conscience he shall judge necessary; or of making officers and ministers both of war and peace; or of appointing teachers and examining what doctrines are conformable or contrary to the defense, peace, and good of the people. Secondly, it is against his duty to let the people be ignorant or misinformed of the grounds and reasons of those his essential rights, because thereby men are easy to be seduced and drawn to resist him when the commonwealth shall require their use and exercise.

And the grounds of these rights have the need to be diligently and truly taught, because they cannot be maintained by any civil law or terror of legal punishment. For a civil law that shall forbid rebellion (and such is all resistance to the essential rights of the sovereignty), is not, as a civil law, any

obligation, but by virtue only of the law of nature that forbids the violation of faith; which natural obligation if men know not, they cannot know the right of any law the sovereign makes. And for the punishment, they take it but for an act of hostility which when they think they have strength enough, they will endeavor by acts of hostility, to avoid. * * *

To the care of the sovereign belongs the making of good laws. But what is a good law? By a good law I mean not a just law; for no law can be unjust. The law is made by the sovereign power, and all that is done by such power is warranted and owned by every one of the people; and that which every man will have so, no man can say is unjust. It is in the laws of a commonwealth as in the laws of gaming; whatsoever the gamesters all agree on is injustice to none of them. A good law is that which is "needed" for the "good of the people" and "perspicuous."

For the use of laws, which are but rules authorized, is not to bind the people from all voluntary actions but to direct and keep them in such a motion as not to hurt themselves by their own impetuous desires, rashness, or indiscretion; as hedges are set not to stop travellers, but to keep them in their way. And, therefore, a law that is not needed, having not the true end of a law, is not good. A law may be conceived to be good when it is for the benefit of the sovereign, though it be not necessary for the people, but it is not so. For the good of the sovereign and people cannot be separated. It is a weak sovereign, that has weak subjects, and a weak people, whose sovereign lacks power to rule them at his will. Unnecessary laws are not good laws but traps for money; which, where the right of sovereign power is acknowledged, are superfluous, and where it is not acknowledged, insufficient to defend the people. * * *

It belongs also to the office of the sovereign to make a right application of punishments and rewards. And seeing the end of punishing is not revenge and discharge of anger, but correction, either of the offender, or of others by his example; the severest punishments are to be inflicted for those crimes that are of most danger to the public; such as are those which proceed from malice to the government established; those that spring from contempt of justice; those that provoke indignation in the multitude; and those which, unpunished, seem authorized, as when they are committed by sons, servants, or favorites of men in authority. For indignation carries men not only against the actors and authors of injustice, but against all power that is likely to protect them; as in the case of Tarquin, when for the insolent act of one of his sons he was driven out of Rome and the monarchy itself dissolved. But crimes of infirmity, such as are those which proceed from great provocation, from great fear, great need, or from ignorance, whether the fact be a great crime or not, there is place many times for leniency without prejudice to the commonwealth; and leniency, when there is such place for it, is required by the law of nature. The punishment of the leaders and teachers in a commotion, not the poor seduced people, when they are punished, can profit the commonwealth by their example. To be severe to the people is to punish that ignorance which may in great part be imputed to the sovereign, whose fault it was that they were no better instructed.

In like manner it belongs to the office and duty of the sovereign, to apply his rewards so that there may arise from them benefit to the commonwealth, wherein consists their use, and end; and is then done when they that have well served the commonwealth are, with as little expense of the common treasure as is possible, so well recompensed as others thereby may be encouraged both to serve the same as faithfully as they can and to study the arts by which they may be enabled to do it better. To buy with money or preferment from a popular ambitious subject to be quiet and desist from making ill impressions in the minds of the people has nothing of the nature of reward (which is ordained not for disservice, but for service past), nor a sign of gratitude, but of fear; nor does it tend to the benefit but to the damage of the public. It is a contention with ambition like that of Hercules with the monster Hydra which,

having many heads, for every one that was vanquished there grew up three. For in like manner, when the stubbornness of one popular man is overcome with reward there arise many more, by the example, that do the same mischief in hope of like benefit; and as all sorts of manufacture, so also malice increases by being salable. And though sometimes a civil war may be deferred by such ways as that, yet the danger grows still the greater and the public ruin more assured. It is therefore against the duty of the sovereign, to whom the public safety is committed, to reward those that aspire to greatness by disturbing the peace of their country, and not rather to oppose the beginnings of such men with a little danger than after a longer time with greater. ✴ ✴ ✴

When the sovereign himself is popular, that is, revered and beloved of his people, there is no danger at all from the popularity of a subject. For soldiers are never so generally unjust as to side with their captain though they love him, against their sovereign, when they love not only his person but also his cause. And therefore those who by violence have at any time suppressed the power of their lawful sovereign, before they could settle themselves in his place have been always put to the trouble of contriving their titles to save the people from the shame of receiving them. To have a known right to sovereign power is so popular a quality as he that has it needs no more, for his own part, to turn the hearts of his subjects to him but that they see him able absolutely to govern his own family; nor, on the part of his enemies, but a disbanding of their armies. For the greatest and most active part of mankind has never hitherto been well contented with the present.

Concerning the offices of one sovereign to another, which are comprehended in that law which is commonly called the "law of nations," I need not say anything in this place because the law of nations and the law of nature is the same thing. And every sovereign has the same right, in securing the safety of his people that any particular man can have in securing the safety of his own body. And the same law that dictates to men that have no civil government what they ought to do and what to avoid in regard of one another dictates the same to commonwealths, that is, to the consciences of sovereign princes and sovereign assemblies, there being no court of natural justice but in the conscience only; where not man but God reigns whose laws, such of them as oblige all mankind, in respect of God as he is the author of nature are "natural," and in respect of the same God as he is King of kings are "laws."

✴   ✴   ✴

REVIEW QUESTIONS

1. What is Hobbes's view of human nature?
2. What, according to Hobbes, motivates human beings?
3. What, according to Hobbes, is the purpose of the state?
4. Why do human beings come together to form a political society?
5. What are the responsibilities of the sovereign?
6. What is the sovereign's highest obligation?
7. Does Hobbes hold out any hope that the state can improve human nature?

SIAMESE EMBASSY TO LOUIS XIV, IN 1686 (1686)   NICOLAS III DE LARMESSIN

Nicolas III Larmessin (c. 1640–1725) was a member of the de Larmessin (also: de L'Armessin) family, a famous French dynasty of engravers, printers and booksellers, who were active during the seventeenth and eighteenth centuries. Art historians attribute a number of important portraits to him as well as the many engravings for books, calendars, almanacs and decorative purposes, for which he is best known. Here he commemorates the Siamese embassy to the court of Louis XIV in 1686. What might have made this event a fit subject for an engraving? How does the artist glorify the French king? What elements of court ritual in an age of absolutism are readily visible? In a period of burgeoning imperialism, what propaganda purposes might this image have served?

Coffee House Society

Coffee is an example of the impact of overseas trade and colonial empire on the consumption and lifestyle of ordinary Europeans. The bean's historical origins are shrouded in legend. What seems clear is that they were taken to Arabia from Africa during the fifteenth century and placed under cultivation. Introduced into Europe during the sixteenth and seventeenth centuries, they gained almost immediate popularity. Served at coffeehouses, the first of which was established in London around 1650, coffee's consumption became an occasion for transacting political, social, commercial, or literary business. So great was the demand for coffee that European merchants took it from the Arabian Peninsula to Java, Indonesia, and the Americas. The following descriptions by two anonymous authors give some sense of the ways in which colonial products shaped European culture in the seventeenth century.

From *Selections from the Sources of English History*, edited by Charles W. Colby (New York: Longmans, Green, 1899), pp. 208–12.

*   *   *

1673

A coffee-house is a lay conventicle, good-fellowship turned puritan, ill-husbandry in masquerade, whither people come, after toping all day, to purchase, at the expense of their last penny, the repute of sober companions: A Rota [club] room, that, like Noah's ark, receives animals of every sort, from the precise diminutive band, to the hectoring cravat and cuffs in folio: a nursery for training up the smaller fry of virtuosi in confident tattling, or a cabal of kittling [carping] critics that have only learned to spit and mew; a mint of intelligence, that, to make each man his pennyworth, draws out into petty parcels, what the merchant receives in bullion: he, that comes often, saves twopence a week in Gazettes, and has his news and his coffee for the same charge, as at a threepenny ordinary they give in broth to your chop of mutton; it is an exchange, where haberdashers of political small-wares meet, and mutually abuse each other, and the public, with bottomless stories, and headless notions; the rendezvous of idle pamphlets, and persons more idly employed to read them; a high court of justice, where every little fellow in a camlet cloak takes upon him to transpose affairs both in church and state, to show reasons against acts of parliament, and condemn the decrees of general councils.

*   *   *

As you have a hodge-podge of drinks, such too is your company, for each man seems a leveller, and ranks and files himself as he lists, without regard to degrees or order; so that often you may see a silly fop and a worshipful justice, a griping rook and a grave citizen, a worthy lawyer and an errant pickpocket, a reverend nonconformist and a canting mountebank, all blended together to compose an oglio [medley] of impertinence.

If any pragmatic, to show himself witty or eloquent, begin to talk high, presently the further tables are abandoned, and all the rest flock round (like smaller birds, to admire the gravity of the madge-howlet [barn-owl]). They listen to him awhile with their mouths, and let their pipes go out, and coffee grow cold, for pure zeal of attention, but on the sudden fall all a yelping at once

with more noise, but not half so much harmony, as a pack of beagles on the full cry. To still this bawling, up starts Capt. All-man-sir, the man of mouth, with a face as blustering as that of Æolus and his four sons, in painting, and a voice louder than the speaking trumpet, he begins you the story of a sea-fight; and though he never were further, by water, than the Bear-garden, . . . yet, having pirated the names of ships and captains, he persuades you himself was present, and performed miracles; that he waded knee-deep in blood on the upper-deck, and never thought to serenade his mistress so pleasant as the bullets whistling; how he stopped a vice-admiral of the enemy's under full sail; till she was boarded, with his single arm, instead of grappling-irons, and puffed out with his breath a fire-ship that fell foul on them. All this he relates, sitting in a cloud of smoke, and belching so many common oaths to vouch it, you can scarce guess whether the real engagement, or his romancing account of it, be the more dreadful: however, he concludes with railing at the conduct of some eminent officers (that, perhaps, he never saw), and protests, had they taken his advice at the council of war, not a sail had escaped us.

He is no sooner out of breath, but another begins a lecture on the Gazette, where, finding several prizes taken, he gravely observes, if this trade hold, we shall quickly rout the Dutch, horse and foot, by sea: he nicknames the Polish gentlemen wherever he meets them, and enquires whether Gayland and Taffaletta be Lutherans or Calvinists? *stilo novo* he interprets a vast new stile, or turnpike, erected by his electoral highness on the borders of Westphalia, to keep Monsieur Turenne's cavalry from falling on his retreating troops: he takes words by the sound, without examining their sense: Morea he believes to be the country of the Moors, and Hungary a place where famine always keeps her court, nor is there anything more certain, than that he made a whole room full of fops, as wise as himself, spend above two hours in searching the map for Aristocracy and Democracy, not doubting but to have found them there, as well as Dalmatia and Croatia.

1675

Though the happy Arabia, nature's spicery, prodigally furnishes the voluptuous world with all kinds of aromatics, and divers other rarities; yet I scarce know whether mankind be not still as much obliged to it for the excellent fruit of the humble coffee-shrub, as for any other of its more specious productions: for, since there is nothing we here enjoy, next to life, valuable beyond health, certainly those things that contribute to preserve us in good plight and eucrasy, and fortify our weak bodies against the continual assaults and batteries of disease, deserve our regards much more than those which only gratify a liquorish palate, or otherwise prove subservient to our delights. As for this salutiferous berry, of so general a use through all the regions of the east, it is sufficiently known, when prepared, to be moderately hot, and of a very drying attenuating and cleansing quality; whence reason infers, that its decoction must contain many good physical properties, and cannot but be an incomparable remedy to dissolve crudities, comfort the brain, and dry up ill humours in the stomach. In brief, to prevent or redress, in those that frequently drink it, all cold drowsy rheumatic distempers whatsoever, that proceed from excess of moisture, which are so numerous, that but to name them would tire the tongue of a mountebank.

*   *   *

Lastly, for diversion. It is older than Aristotle, and will be true, when Hobbes is forgot, that man is a sociable creature, and delights in company. Now, whither shall a person, wearied with hard study, or the laborious turmoils of a tedious day, repair to refresh himself? Or where can young gentlemen, or shop-keepers, more innocently and advantageously spend an hour or two in the evening, than at a coffee-house? Where they shall be sure to meet company, and, by the custom of the house, not such as at other places, stingy and reserved to themselves, but free and communicative; where every man may modestly begin his story,

and propose to, or answer another, as he thinks fit. Discourse is *pabulum animi, cos ingenii;* the mind's best diet, and the great whetstone and incentive of ingenuity; by that we come to know men better than by their physiognomy. *Loquere, ut te videam,* speak, that I may see thee, was the philosopher's adage. To read men is acknowledged more useful than books; but where is there a better library for that study, generally, than here, amongst such a variety of humours, all expressing themselves on divers subjects, according to their respective abilities?

*   *   *

In brief, it is undeniable, that, as you have here the most civil, so it is, generally, the most intelligent society; the frequenting whose converse, and observing their discourses and department, cannot but civilise our manners, enlarge our understandings, refine our language, teach us a generous confidence and handsome mode of address, and brush off that *pudor rubrusticus* (as, I remember, Tully somewhere calls it), that clownish kind of modesty frequently incident to the best natures, which renders them sheepish and ridiculous in company.

So that, upon the whole matter, spite of the idle sarcasms and paltry reproaches thrown upon it, we may, with no less truth than plainness, give this brief character of a well-regulated coffee-house (for our pen disdains to be an advocate for any sordid holes, that assume that name to cloak the practice of debauchery), that it is the sanctuary of health, the nursery of temperance, the delight of frugality, an academy of civility, and free-school of ingenuity.

*   *   *

REVIEW QUESTIONS

1. How would you describe coffeehouse society in the late seventeenth century?
2. What is the attitude of each of our two anonymous authors? How and why do they differ?
3. What is the significance of reading the gazette?
4. What are the virtues of coffee?
5. How could coffee drinking be considered a vice in early modern Europe?

JOHN LOCKE

FROM *Two Treatises on Government*

John Locke (1632–1704) was an English philosopher whose thought contributed to the Enlightenment. He grew up in a liberal Puritan family, the son of an attorney who fought in the civil war against Charles I, and attended Christ Church College, Oxford. He received his bachelor of arts in 1656, lectured in classical languages while earning his master of arts, and entered Oxford's medical school to avoid being forced to join the clergy. In 1666, Locke attached himself to the household of the Earl of Shaftesbury and his fortunes to the liberal Whig Party. Between 1675 and 1679, he lived in France, where he made contact with leading intellectuals of the late seventeenth century. On his return to England, he plunged into the controversy

*surrounding the succession of James II, an avowed Catholic with absolutist preten-
sions, to the throne of his brother, Charles II. Locke's patron, Shaftesbury, was imprisoned for his opposition, and Locke went into exile in 1683. Though he was
involved to some extent in the Glorious Revolution of 1688, he returned to England
in 1689, in the entourage of Mary, Princess of Orange, who would assume the
throne with her husband, William. The* Two Treatises on Government *(1690) were
published anonymously, although readers commonly assumed Locke's authorship.
More interesting is the time at which they were written. Most scholars assume that
they were written immediately before publication, as a justification of the revolution
just completed. Other scholars believe, however, that the treatises were written from
exile as a call to revolution, a riskier, much more inflammatory project. The first
treatise comprises a long attack on Robert Filmer's* Patriarcha, *a denial of the patriarchal justification of the absolute monarch. The second treatise constructs in the
place of patriarchy a theory of politics based on natural law, which provides the foundation of human freedom. The social contract creates a political structure by consent
of the governed and designed to preserve those freedoms established in natural law.
Locke's treatises inspired the political theories of the Enlightenment.*

From *First Treatise* in *Two Treatises on Government*, edited by Ernst Rhys (New York: Dutton, 1993).

*   *   *

Chapter VI
Of Paternal Power

It may perhaps be censured an impertinent criticism in a discourse of this nature to find fault with words and names that have obtained in the world. And yet possibly it may not be amiss to offer new ones when the old are apt to lead men into mistakes, as this of paternal power probably has done, which seems so to place the power of parents over their children wholly in the father, as if the mother had no share in it; whereas if we consult reason or revelation, we shall find she has an equal title, which may give one reason to ask whether this might not be more properly called parental power? For whatever obligation Nature and the right of generation lays on children, it must certainly bind them equal to both the concurrent causes of it. And accordingly we see the positive law of God everywhere joins them together without distinction, when it commands the obedience of children: "Honour thy father and thy mother"; "Whosoever curseth his father or his mother"; "Ye shall fear every man his mother and his father"; "Children, obey your parents" etc., is the style of the Old and New Testament.

*   *   *

Though I have said above "That all men by nature are equal," I cannot be supposed to understand all sorts of "equality." Age or virtue may give men a just precedency. Excellency of parts and merit may place others above the common level. Birth may subject some, and alliance or benefits others, to pay an observance to those to whom Nature, gratitude, or other respects, may have made it due; and yet all this consists with the equality which all men are in in respect of jurisdiction or dominion one over another, which was the equality I there spoke of as proper to the business in hand, being that equal right that every man hath to his natural freedom, without being subjected to the will or authority of any other man.

Children, I confess, are not born in this full state of equality, though they are born to it. Their

PALACE AND GARDENS OF VERSAILLES (1668)   PIERRE PATEL

Patel's famous print of the palace at Versailles captures the grand scale of monarchy in the seventeenth century. Note not only the size of the palace but also its location in the center of carefully planned gardens, boulevards, and buildings. Versailles was truly a theater for the display of political power. Why was such a theater of power necessary? What can be learned from the iconography of power that was built into Versailles, such as the function of gardens or the location of boulevards or alleys or broad open spaces? How might Versailles have functioned not only as a theater of power but also as a prison for the powerful?

parents have a sort of rule and jurisdiction over them when they come into the world, and for some time after, but it is but a temporary one. The bonds of this subjection are like the swaddling clothes they are wrapt up in and supported by in the weakness of their infancy. Age and reason as they grow up loosen them, till at length they drop quite off, and leave a man at his own free disposal.

Adam was created a perfect man, his body and mind in full possession of their strength and reason, and so was capable from the first instance of his being to provide for his own support and preservation, and govern his actions according to the dictates of the law of reason God had implanted in him. From him the world is peopled with his descendants, who are all born infants, weak and helpless, without knowledge or understanding. But to supply the defects of this imperfect state till the improvement of growth and age had removed them, Adam and Eve, and after them all parents were, by the law of Nature, under an obligation to preserve, nourish and educate the children they had begotten, not as their own workmanship, but the workmanship of their own Maker, the Almighty, to whom they were to be accountable for them.

The law that was to govern Adam was the same that was to govern all his posterity, the law of reason. But his offspring having another way of entrance into the world, different from him, by a natural birth, that produced them ignorant, and without the use of reason, they were not presently under that law. For nobody can be under a law that is not promulgated to him; and this law being promulgated or made known by reason only, he that is not come to the use of his reason cannot be said to be under this law; and Adam's children being not presently as soon as born under this law of reason, were not presently free. For law, in its true notion, is not so much the limitation as the direction of a free and intelligent agent to his proper interest, and prescribes no farther than is for the general good of those under that law. Could they be happier without it, the law, as a useless thing, would of itself vanish; and that ill deserves the name of confinement which hedges us in only from bogs and precipices. So that however it may be mistaken, the end of law is not to abolish or restrain, but to preserve and enlarge freedom. For in all the states of created beings, capable of laws, where there is no law there is no freedom. For liberty is to be free from restraint and violence from others, which cannot be where there is no law; and is not, as we are told, "a liberty for every man to do what he lists." For who could be free, when every other man's humour might domineer over him? But a liberty to dispose and order freely as he lists his person, actions, possessions, and his whole property within the allowance of those laws under which he is, and therein not to be subject to the arbitrary will of another, but freely follow his own.

The power, then, that parents have over their children arises from that duty which is incumbent on them, to take care of their offspring during the imperfect state of childhood. To inform the mind, and govern the actions of their yet ignorant nonage, till reason shall take its place and ease them of that trouble, is what the children want, and the parents are bound to. For God having given man an understanding to direct his actions, has allowed him a freedom of will and liberty of acting, as properly belonging thereunto within the bounds of that law he is under. But whilst he is in an estate wherein he has no understanding of his own to direct his will, he is not to have any will of his own to follow. He that understands for him must will for him too; he must prescribe to his will, and regulate his actions, but when he comes to the estate that made his father a free man, the son is a free man too.

This holds in all the laws a man is under, whether natural or civil. Is a man under the law of Nature? What made him free of that law? what gave him a free disposing of his property, according to his own will, within the compass of that law? I answer, an estate wherein he might be supposed capable to know that law, that so he might keep his actions within the bounds of it. When he has acquired that state, he is presumed to know how far that law is to be his guide, and how far he may make use of his freedom, and so comes to have it; till then, somebody else must guide

him, who is presumed to know how far the law allows a liberty. If such a state of reason, such an age of discretion made him free, the same shall make his son free too. Is a man under the law of England? what made him free of that law—that is, to have the liberty to dispose of his actions and possessions, according to his own will, within the permission of that law? a capacity of knowing that law. Which is supposed, by that law, at the age of twenty-one, and in some cases sooner. If this made the father free, it shall make the son free too. Till then, we see the law allows the son to have no will, but he is to be guided by the will of his father or guardian, who is to understand for him. And if the father die and fail to substitute a deputy in this trust, if he hath not provided a tutor to govern his son during his minority, during his want of understanding, the law takes care to do it: some other must govern him and be a will to him till he hath attained to a state of freedom, and his understanding be fit to take the government of his will. But after that the father and son are equally free, as much as tutor and pupil, after nonage, equally subjects of the same law together, without any dominion left in the father over the life, liberty, or estate of his son, whether they be only in the state and under the law of Nature, or under the positive laws of an established government.

*　　*　　*

The freedom then of man, and liberty of acting according to his own will, is grounded on his having reason, which is able to instruct him in that law he is to govern himself by, and make him know how far he is left to the freedom of his own will. To turn him loose to an unrestrained liberty, before he has reason to guide him, is not the allowing him the privilege of his nature to be free, but to thrust him out amongst brutes, and abandon him to a state as wretched and as much beneath that of a man as theirs. This is that which puts the authority into the parents' hands to govern the minority of their children. God hath made it their business to employ this care on their offspring, and hath placed in them suitable inclinations of tenderness

and concern to temper this power, to apply it as His wisdom designed it, to the children's good as long as they should need to be under it.

But what reason can hence advance this care of the parents due to their offspring into an absolute, arbitrary dominion of the father, whose power reaches no farther than by such a discipline as he finds most effectual to give such strength and health to their bodies, such vigour and rectitude to their minds, as may best fit his children to be most useful to themselves and others, and, if it be necessary to his condition, to make them work when they are able for their own subsistence; but in this power the mother, too, has her share with the father.

Nay, this power so little belongs to the father by any peculiar right of Nature, but only as he is guardian of his children, that when he quits his care of them he loses his power over them, which goes along with their nourishment and education, to which it is inseparably annexed, and belongs as much to the foster-father of an exposed child as to the natural father of another. So little power does the bare act of begetting give a man over his issue, if all his care ends there, and this be all the title he hath to the name and authority of a father. And what will become of this paternal power in that part of the world where one woman hath more than one husband at a time? or in those parts of America where, when the husband and wife part, which happens frequently, the children are all left to the mother, follow her, and are wholly under her care and provision? And if the father die whilst the children are young, do they not naturally everywhere owe the same obedience to their mother, during their minority, as to their father, were he alive? And will any one say that the mother hath a legislative power over her children that she can make standing rules which shall be of perpetual obligation, by which they ought to regulate all the concerns of their property, and bound their liberty all the course of their lives, and enforce the observation of them with capital punishments? For this is the proper power of the magistrate, of which the father hath not so much as the shadow. His command over his children is but

temporary, and reaches not their life or property. It is but a help to the weakness and imperfection of their nonage, a discipline necessary to their education. And though a father may dispose of his own possessions as he pleases when his children are out of danger of perishing for want, yet his power extends not to the lives or goods which either their own industry, or another's bounty, has made theirs, nor to their liberty neither, when they are once arrived to the enfranchisement of the years of discretion. The father's empire then ceases, and he can from thenceforward no more dispose of the liberty of his son than that of any other man. And it must be far from an absolute or perpetual jurisdiction from which a man may withdraw himself, having licence from Divine authority to "leave father and mother and cleave to his wife."

*   *   *

Chapter VII
Of Political or Civil Society

God, having made man such a creature that, in His own judgment, it was not good for him to be alone, put him under strong obligations of necessity, convenience, and inclination, to drive him into society, as well as fitted him with understanding and language to continue and enjoy it. The first society was between man and wife, which gave beginning to that between parents and children, to which, in time, that between master and servant came to be added. And though all these might, and commonly did, meet together, and make up but one family, wherein the master or mistress of it had some sort of rule proper to a family, each of these, or all together, came short of "political society," as we shall see if we consider the different ends, ties, and bounds of each of these.

Conjugal society is made by a voluntary compact between man and woman, and though it consist chiefly in such a communion and right in one another's bodies as is necessary to its chief end, procreation, yet it draws with it mutual support

and assistance, and a communion of interests too, as necessary not only to unite their care and affection, but also necessary to their common offspring, who have a right to be nourished and maintained by them till they are able to provide for themselves.

For the end of conjunction between male and female being not barely procreation, but the continuation of the species, this conjunction betwixt male and female ought to last, even after procreation, so long as is necessary to the nourishment and support of the young ones, who are to be sustained by those that got them till they are able to shift and provide for themselves. This rule, which the infinite wise Maker hath set to the works of His hands, we find the inferior creatures steadily obey. In those vivaporous animals which feed on grass the conjunction between male and female lasts no longer than the very act of copulation, because the teat of the dam being sufficient to nourish the young till it be able to feed on grass, the male only begets, but concerns not himself for the female or young, to whose sustenance he can contribute nothing. But in beasts of prey the conjunction lasts longer, because the dam, not being able well to subsist herself and nourish her numerous offspring by her own prey alone (a more laborious as well as more dangerous way of living than by feeding on grass), the assistance of the male is necessary to the maintenance of their common family, which cannot subsist till they are able to prey for themselves, but by the joint care of male and female. The same is observed in all birds (except some domestic ones, where plenty of food excuses the cock from feeding and taking care of the young brood), whose young, needing food in the nest, the cock and hen continue mates till the young are able to use their wings and provide for themselves.

And herein, I think, lies the chief, if not the only reason, why the male and female in mankind are tied to a longer conjunction than other creatures—viz., because the female is capable of conceiving, and, *de facto*, is commonly with child again, and brings forth too a new birth, long before the former is out of a dependency for support

on his parents' help and able to shift for himself, and has all the assistance due to him from his parents, whereby the father, who is bound to take care for those he hath begot, is under an obligation to continue in conjugal society with the same woman longer than other creatures, whose young, being able to subsist of themselves before the time of procreation returns again, the conjugal bond dissolves of itself, and they are at liberty till Hymen, at his usual anniversary season, summons them again to choose new mates. Wherein one cannot but admire the wisdom of the great Creator, who, having given to man an ability to lay up for the future as well as supply the present necessity, hath made it necessary that society of man and wife should be more lasting than of male and female amongst other creatures, that so their industry might be encouraged, and their interest better united, to make provision and lay up goods for their common issue, which uncertain mixture, or easy and frequent solutions of conjugal society, would mightily disturb.

But though these are ties upon mankind which make the conjugal bonds more firm and lasting in a man than the other species of animals, yet it would give one reason to inquire why this compact, where procreation and education are secured and inheritance taken care for, may not be made determinable, either by consent, or at a certain time, or upon certain conditions, as well as any other voluntary compacts, there being no necessity, in the nature of the thing, nor to the ends of it, that it should always be for life—I mean, to such as are under no restraint of any positive law which ordains all such contracts to be perpetual.

But the husband and wife, though they have but one common concern, yet having different understandings, will unavoidably sometimes have different wills too. It therefore being necessary that the last determination (i.e., the rule) should be placed somewhere, it naturally falls to the man's share as the abler and the stronger. But this, reaching but to the things of their common interest and property, leaves the wife in the full and true possession of what by contract is her peculiar right, and at least gives the husband no more power over

her than she has over his life; the power of the husband being so far from that of an absolute monarch that the wife has, in many cases, a liberty to separate from him where natural right or their contract allows it, whether that contract be made by themselves in the state of Nature or by the customs or laws of the country they live in, and the children, upon such separation, fall to the father or mother's lot as such contract does determine.

For all the ends of marriage being to be obtained under politic government, as well as in the state of Nature, the civil magistrate doth not abridge the right or power of either, naturally necessary to those ends—viz., procreation and mutual support and assistance whilst they are together, but only decides any controversy that may arise between man and wife about them. If it were otherwise, and that absolute sovereignty and power of life and death naturally belonged to the husband, and were necessary to the society between man and wife, there could be no matrimony in any of these countries where the husband is allowed no such absolute authority. But the ends of matrimony requiring no such power in the husband, it was not at all necessary to it. The condition of conjugal society put it not in him; but whatsoever might consist with procreation and support of the children till they could shift for themselves—mutual assistance, comfort, and maintenance—might be varied and regulated by that contract which first united them in that society, nothing being necessary to any society that is not necessary to the ends for which it is made.

*   *   *

Let us therefore consider a master of a family with all these subordinate relations of wife, children, servants and slaves, united under the domestic rule of a family, with what resemblance soever it may have in its order, offices, and number too, with a little commonwealth, yet is very far from it both in its constitution, power, and end; or if it must be thought a monarchy, and the paterfamilias the absolute monarch in it, absolute monarchy will have but a very shattered and short power, when it is plain by what has been said before, that

the master of the family has a very distinct and differently limited power both as to time and extent over those several persons that are in it; for excepting the slave (and the family is as much a family, and his power as paterfamilias as great, whether there be any slaves in his family or no) he has no legislative power of life and death over any of them, and none too but what a mistress of a family may have as well as he. And he certainly can have no absolute power over the whole family who has but a very limited one over every individual in it. But how a family, or any other society of men, differ from that which is properly political society, we shall best see by considering wherein political society itself consists.

Man being born, as has been proved, with a title to perfect freedom and an uncontrolled enjoyment of all the rights and privileges of the law of Nature, equally with any other man, or number of men in the world, hath by nature a power not only to preserve his property—that is, his life, liberty, and estate, against the injuries and attempts of other men, but to judge of and punish the breaches of that law in others, as he is persuaded the offence deserves, even with death itself, in crimes where the heinousness of the fact, in his opinion, requires it. But because no political society can be, nor subsist, without having in itself the power to preserve the property, and in order thereunto punish the offences of all those of that society, there, and there only, is political society where every one of the members hath quitted this natural power, resigned it up into the hands of the community in all cases that exclude him not from appealing for protection to the law established by it. And thus all private judgment of every particular member being excluded, the community comes to be umpire, and by understanding indifferent rules and men authorised by the community for their execution, decides all the differences that may happen between any members of that society concerning any matter of right, and punishes those offences which any member hath committed against the society with such penalties as the law has established; whereby it is easy to discern who are, and are not, in political society together. Those who are united into

one body, and have a common established law and judicature to appeal to, with authority to decide controversies between them and punish offenders, are in civil society one with another; but those who have no such common appeal, I mean on earth, are still in the state of Nature, each being where there is no other, judge for himself and executioner; which is, as I have before showed it, the perfect state of Nature.

And thus the commonwealth comes by a power to set down what punishment shall belong to the several transgressions they think worthy of it, committed amongst the members of that society (which is the power of making laws), as well as it has the power to punish any injury done unto any of its members by any one that is not of it (which is the power of war and peace); and all this for the preservation of the property of all the members of that society, as far as is possible. But though every man entered into society has quitted his power to punish offences against the law of Nature in prosecution of his own private judgment, yet with the judgment of offences which he has given up to the legislative, in all cases where he can appeal to the magistrate, he has given up a right to the commonwealth to employ his force for the execution of the judgments of the commonwealth whenever he shall be called to it, which, indeed, are his own judgments, they being made by himself or his representative. And herein we have the original of the legislative and executive power of civil society, which is to judge by standing laws how far offences are to be punished when committed within the commonwealth; and also by occasional judgments founded on the present circumstances of the fact, how far injuries from without are to be vindicated, and in both these to employ all the force of all the members when there shall be need.

Wherever, therefore, any number of men so unite into one society as to quit every one his executive power of the law of Nature, and to resign it to the public, there and there only is a political or civil society. And this is done wherever any number of men, in the state of Nature, enter into society to make one people one body politic under

one supreme government: or else when any one joins himself to, and incorporates with any government already made. For hereby he authorises the society, or which is all one, the legislative thereof, to make laws for him as the public good of the society shall require, to the execution whereof his own assistance (as to his own decrees) is due. And this puts men out of a state of Nature into that of a commonwealth, by setting up a judge on earth with authority to determine all the controversies and redress the injuries that may happen to any member of the commonwealth, which judge is the legislative or magistrates appointed by it. And wherever there are any number of men, however associated, that have no such decisive power to appeal to, there they are still in the state of Nature.

And hence it is evident that absolute monarchy, which by some men is counted for the only government in the world, is indeed inconsistent with civil society, and so can be no form of civil government at all. For the end of civil society being to avoid and remedy those inconveniencies of the state of Nature which necessarily follow from every man's being judge in his own case, by setting up a known authority to which every one of that society may appeal upon any injury received, or controversy that may arise, and which every one of the society ought to obey. Wherever any persons are who have not such an authority to appeal to, and decide any difference between them there, those persons are still in the state of Nature. And so is every absolute prince in respect of those who are under his dominion.

For he being supposed to have all, both legislative and executive, power in himself alone, there is no judge to be found, no appeal lies open to any one, who may fairly and indifferently, and with authority decide, and from whence relief and redress may be expected of any injury or inconveniency that may be suffered from him, or by his order. So that such a man, however entitled, Czar, or Grand Signior, or how you please, is as much in the state of Nature, with all under his dominion, as he is with the rest of mankind. For wherever any two men are, who have no standing rule and common judge to appeal to on earth, for the determination of controversies of right betwixt them, there they are still in the state of Nature, and under all the inconveniencies of it, with only this woeful difference to the subject, or rather slave of an absolute prince. That whereas, in the ordinary state of Nature, he has a liberty to judge of his right, according to the best of his power to maintain it; but whenever his property is invaded by the will and order of his monarch, he has not only no appeal, as those in society ought to have, but, as if he were degraded from the common state of rational creatures, is denied a liberty to judge of, or defend his right, and so is exposed to all the misery and inconveniencies that a man can fear from one, who being in the unrestrained state of Nature, is yet corrupted with flattery and armed with power.

*   *   *

Chapter VIII
Of the Beginning of Political Societies

Men being, as has been said, by nature all free, equal, and independent, no one can be put out of this estate and subjected to the political power of another without his own consent, which is done by agreeing with other men, to join and unite into a community for their comfortable, safe, and peaceable living, one amongst another, in a secure enjoyment of their properties, and a greater security against any that are not of it. This any number of men may do, because it injures not the freedom of the rest; they are left, as they were, in the liberty of the state of Nature. When any number of men have so consented to make one community or government, they are thereby presently incorporated, and make one body politic, wherein the majority have a right to act and conclude the rest.

For, when any number of men have, by the consent of every individual, made a community, they have thereby made that community one body, with a power to act as one body, which is only by the will and determination of the majority.

For that which acts any community, being only the consent of the individuals of it, and it being one body, must move one way, it is necessary the body should move that way whither the greater force carries it, which is the consent of the majority, or else it is impossible it should act or continue one body, one community, which the consent of every individual that united into it agreed that it should; and so every one is bound by that consent to be concluded by the majority. And therefore we see that in assemblies empowered to act by positive laws where no number is set by that positive law which empowers them, the act of the majority passes for the act of the whole, and of course determines as having, by the law of Nature and reason, the power of the whole.

And thus every man, by consenting with others to make one body politic under one government, puts himself under an obligation to every one of that society to submit to the determination of the majority, and to be concluded by it; or else this original compact, whereby he with others incorporates into one society, would signify nothing, and be no compact if he be left free and under no other ties than he was in before in the state of Nature. For what appearance would there be of any compact? What new engagement if he were no farther tied by any decrees of the society than he himself thought fit and did actually consent to? This would be still as great a liberty as he himself had before his compact, or any one else in the state of Nature, who may submit himself and consent to any acts of it if he thinks fit.

*   *   *

Whosoever, therefore, out of a state of Nature unite into a community, must be understood to give up all the power necessary to the ends for which they unite into society to the majority of the community, unless they expressly agreed in any number greater than the majority. And this is done by barely agreeing to unite into one political society, which is all the compact that is, or needs be, between the individuals that enter into or make up a commonwealth. And thus, that which begins and actually constitutes any political so-

ciety is nothing but the consent of any number of freemen capable of majority, to unite and incorporate into such a society. And this is that, and that only, which did or could give beginning to any lawful government in the world.

*   *   *

Every man being, as has been showed, naturally free, and nothing being able to put him into subjection to any earthly power, but only his own consent, it is to be considered what shall be understood to be a sufficient declaration of a man's consent to make him subject to the laws of any government. There is a common distinction of an express and a tacit consent, which will concern our present case. Nobody doubts but an express consent of any man, entering into any society, makes him a perfect member of that society, a subject of that government. The difficulty is, what ought to be looked upon as a tacit consent, and how far it binds—*i.e.,* how far any one shall be looked on to have consented, and thereby submitted to any government, where he has made no expressions of it at all. And to this I say, that every man that hath any possession or enjoyment of any part of the dominions of any government doth hereby give his tacit consent, and is as far forth obliged to obedience to the laws of that government, during such enjoyment, as any one under it, whether this his possession be of land to him and his heirs for ever, or a lodging only for a week; or whether it be barely travelling freely on the highway; and, in effect, it reaches as far as the very being of any one within the territories of that government.

To understand this the better, it is fit to consider that every man when he at first incorporates himself into any commonwealth, he, by his uniting himself thereunto, annexes also, and submits to the community those possessions which he has, or shall acquire, that do not already belong to any other government. For it would be a direct contradiction for any one to enter into society with others for the securing and regulating of property, and yet to suppose his land, whose property is to be regulated by the laws of the society, should be exempt from the jurisdiction of that government to

which he himself, and the property of the land, is a subject. By the same act, therefore, whereby any one unites his person, which was before free, to any commonwealth, by the same he unites his possessions, which were before free, to it also; and they become, both of them, person and possession, subject to the government and dominion of that commonwealth as long as it hath a being. Whoever therefore, from thenceforth, by inheritance, purchases permission, or otherwise enjoys any part of the land so annexed to, and under the government of that commonweal, must take it with the condition it is under—that is, of submitting to the government of the commonwealth, under whose jurisdiction it is, as far forth as any subject of it.

But since the government has a direct jurisdiction only over the land and reaches the possessor of it (before he has actually incorporated himself in the society) only as he dwells upon and enjoys that, the obligation any one is under by virtue of such enjoyment to submit to the government begins and ends with the enjoyment; so that whenever the owner, who has given nothing but such a tacit consent to the government will, by donation, sale or otherwise, quit the said possession, he is at liberty to go and incorporate himself into any other commonwealth, or agree with others to begin a new one *in vacuis locis,* in any part of the world they can find free and unpossessed; whereas he that has once, by actual agreement and any express declaration, given his consent to be of any commonweal, is perpetually and indispensably obliged to be, and remain unalterably a subject to it, and can never be again in the liberty of the state of Nature, unless by any calamity the government he was under comes to be dissolved.

But submitting to the laws of any country, living quietly and enjoying privileges and protection under them, makes not a man a member of that society; it is only a local protection and homage due to and from all those who, not being in a state of war, come within the territories belonging to any government, to all parts whereof the force of its law extends. But this no more makes a man a member of that society, a perpetual subject of that commonwealth, than it would make a man a sub-

ject to another in whose family he found it convenient to abide for some time, though, whilst he continued in it, he were obliged to comply with the laws and submit to the government he found there. And thus we see that foreigners, by living all their lives under another government, and enjoying the privileges and protection of it, though they are bound, even in conscience, to submit to its administration as far forth as any denizen, yet do not thereby come to be subjects or members of that commonwealth. Nothing can make any man so but his actually entering into it by positive engagement and express promise and compact. This is that which, I think, concerning the beginning of political societies, and that consent which makes any one a member of any commonwealth.

Chapter IX
Of the Ends of Political Society and Government

If man in the state of Nature be so free as has been said, if he be absolute lord of his own person and possessions, equal to the greatest and subject to nobody, why will he part with his freedom, this empire, and subject himself to the dominion and control of any other power? To which it is obvious to answer, that though in the state of Nature he hath such a right, yet the enjoyment of it is very uncertain and constantly exposed to the invasion of others; for all being kings as much as he, every man his equal, and the greater part no strict observers of equity and justice, the enjoyment of the property he has in this state is very unsafe, very insecure. This makes him willing to quit this condition which, however free, is full of fears and continual dangers; and it is not without reason that he seeks out and is willing to join in society with others who are already united, or have a mind to unite for the mutual preservation of their lives, liberties and estates, which I call by the general name—property.

The great and chief end, therefore, of men uniting into commonwealths, and putting themselves under government, is the preservation of

their property; to which in the state of Nature there are many things wanting.

Firstly, there wants an established, settled, known law, received and allowed by common consent to be the standard of right and wrong, and the common measure to decide all controversies between them. For though the law of Nature be plain and intelligible to all rational creatures, yet men, being biased by their interest, as well as ignorant for want of study of it, are not apt to allow of it as a law binding to them in the application of it to their particular cases.

Secondly, in the state of Nature there wants a known and indifferent judge, with authority to determine all differences according to the established law. For every one in that state being both judge and executioner of the law of Nature, men being partial to themselves, passion and revenge is very apt to carry them too far, and with too much heat in their own cases, as well as negligence and unconcernedness, make them too remiss in other men's.

Thirdly, in the state of Nature there often wants power to back and support the sentence when right, and to give it due execution. They who by any injustice offended will seldom fail where they are able by force to make good their injustice. Such resistance many times makes the punishment dangerous, and frequently destructive to those who attempt it.

*   *   *

REVIEW QUESTIONS

1. According to Locke, what is the nature of political society?
2. How does political society come into being?
3. How does Locke's notion of a social contract compare with that of Hobbes?
4. What are the ends of political society?
5. What are the implications of Locke's reasoning for early modern economic thinking?

ADAM SMITH

FROM *The Wealth of Nations*

Though best remembered for his towering system of political economy, An Inquiry into the Nature and Causes of the Wealth of Nations *(1776), Adam Smith (1723–1790) was one of the most important social philosophers of the eighteenth century. His economic writings constitute only a part of his larger view of social and political development. Born the son of a minor government official, he entered the University of Glasgow in 1737, already a center of what became known as the Scottish Enlightenment, where he was deeply influenced by another great moral and economic philosopher, Francis Hutcheson. After completing his education at Oxford, he returned to Scotland, where he embarked on a series of public lectures in Edinburgh. In 1752, he was appointed professor of logic at Glasgow, and in 1754, he assumed the chair in moral philosophy. He would look on his tenure as the happiest and most honorable of his life. It was certainly the most productive. There he made the acquaintance of some of the leading intellectual lights of his day: James Watt, of steam-engine fame; David Hume, the great philosopher; and Andrew Cochrane. The last was the founder of the Political Economy Club and the likely source of much of*

Smith's information on business and commerce. In 1759, Smith published his first important work, The Theory of Moral Sentiments, *in which he attempted to describe universal principles of human nature. His answer to the question of moral judgment was the thesis of the "inner man," or "impartial spectator," which is the conscience in each human being and whose pronouncements cannot be ignored. Thus, human beings can be driven by passions and self-interests and simultaneously capable of ethics and generosity. This principle foreshadowed the "invisible hand" that would guide economic behavior in* The Wealth of Nations. *He began work on this classic text after resigning his post at Glasgow to serve as tutor to the young Duke of Buccleuch. When it finally appeared, it continued the themes first addressed in* The Theory of Moral Sentiments, *the resolution of passion and reason in human behavior, and now, human history. According to Smith, society evolves through four broad stages, each with appropriate institutions: simple hunters, nomadic herders, feudal farmers, and commercial workers. The guiding force in this development is human nature, motivated by self-interest but guided by disinterested reason. Most of the book is given over to a discussion of the function of the invisible hand in the final, current stage. Whereas conscience provided the necessary guidance in* The Theory of Moral Sentiments, *competition assumes that function in* The Wealth of Nations. *Competition rendered markets self-regulating and ensured that prices and wages never stray far from their "natural" levels. Much of the book, especially Book IV, where he places his discussion of colonies, is given over to a polemic against restriction, through both regulation and monopoly, in economic life.* The Wealth of Nations *appeared to great acclaim and earned its author fame and fortune. He published nothing more.*

From *An Inquiry into the Nature and Causes of the Wealth of Nations*, by Adam Smith (Edinburgh: Thomas Nelson, 1838).

*   *   *

Of the Motives for Establishing New Colonies

The interest which occasioned the first settlement of the different European colonies in America and the West Indies, was not altogether so plain and distinct as that which directed the establishment of those of ancient Greece and Rome.

GREEK COLONIES WERE SENT OUT WHEN THE POPULATION GREW TOO GREAT AT HOME.

All the different states of ancient Greece possessed, each of them, but a very small territory, and when the people in any one of them multiplied beyond what that territory could easily maintain, a part of them were sent in quest of a new habitation in some remote and distant part of the world; the warlike neighbours who surrounded them on all sides, rendering it difficult for any of them to enlarge very much its territory at home. * * *

THE MOTHER CITY CLAIMED NO AUTHORITY.

The mother city, though she considered the colony as a child, at all times entitled to great favour and assistance, and owing in return much gratitude and respect, yet considered it as an emancipated child, over whom she pretended to claim no direct authority or jurisdiction.

The colony settled its own form of government, enacted its own laws, elected its own magistrates, and made peace or war with its neighbours as an

independent state, which had no occasion to wait for the approbation or consent of the mother city. Nothing can be more plain and distinct than the interest which directed every such establishment.

ROMAN COLONIES WERE SENT OUT TO SATISFY THE DEMAND FOR LANDS AND TO ESTABLISH GARRISONS IN CONQUERED TERRITORIES.

Rome, like most of the other ancient republics, was originally founded upon an Agrarian law, which divided the public territory in a certain proportion among the different citizens who composed the state. The course of human affairs, by marriage, by succession, and by alienation, necessarily deranged this original division, and frequently threw the lands, which had been allotted for the maintenance of many different families into the possession of a single person. To remedy this disorder, for such it was supposed to be, a law was made, restricting the quantity of land which any citizen could possess to five hundred jugera, about three hundred and fifty English acres. This law, however, though we read of its having been executed upon one or two occasions, was either neglected or evaded, and the inequality of fortunes went on continually increasing. The greater part of the citizens had no land, and without it the manners and customs of those times rendered it difficult for a freeman to maintain his independency. * * * The people became clamorous to get land, and the rich and the great, we may believe, were perfectly determined not to give them any part of theirs. To satisfy them in some measure, therefore, they frequently proposed to send out a new colony.

THEY WERE ENTIRELY SUBJECT TO THE MOTHER CITY.

But conquering Rome was, even upon such occasions, under no necessity of turning out her citizens to seek their fortune, if one may say so, through the wide world, without knowing where they were to settle. She assigned them lands generally in the conquered provinces of Italy, where,

being within the dominions of the republic, they could never form any independent state; but were at best but a sort of corporation, which, though it had the power of enacting bye-laws for its own government, was at all times subject to the correction, jurisdiction, and legislative authority of the mother city. The sending out a colony of this kind, not only gave some satisfaction to the people, but often established a sort of garrison too in a newly conquered province, of which the obedience might otherwise have been doubtful. A Roman colony, therefore, whether we consider the nature of the establishment itself, or the motives for making it, was altogether different from a Greek one. The words accordingly, which in the original languages denote those different establishments, have very different meanings. The Latin word (*Colonia*) signifies simply a plantation. The Greek word (απoιηια), on the contrary, signifies a separation of dwelling, a departure from home, a going out of the house. But, though the Roman colonies were in many respects different from the Greek ones, the interest which prompted to establish them was equally plain and distinct. Both institutions derived their origin either from irresistible necessity, or from clear and evident utility.

THE UTILITY OF THE AMERICAN COLONIES IS NOT SO EVIDENT.

The establishment of the European colonies in America and the West Indies arose from no necessity: and though the utility which has resulted from them has been very great, it is not altogether so clear and evident. It was not understood at their first establishment, and was not the motive either of that establishment or of the discoveries which gave occasion to it; and the nature, extent, and limits of that utility are not, perhaps, well understood at this day.

THE VENETIANS HAD A PROFITABLE TRADE IN EAST INDIA GOODS.

The Venetians, during the fourteenth and fifteenth centuries, carried on a very advantageous commerce

in spiceries, and other East India goods, which they distributed among the other nations of Europe. They purchased them chiefly in Egypt, at that time under the dominion of the Mammeluks, the enemies of the Turks, of whom the Venetians were the enemies; and this union of interest, assisted by the money of Venice, formed such a connection as gave the Venetians almost a monopoly of the trade.

THIS WAS ENVIED BY THE PORTUGUESE AND LED THEM TO DISCOVER THE CAPE OF GOOD HOPE PASSAGE.

The great profits of the Venetians tempted the avidity of the Portuguese. They had been endeavouring, during the course of the fifteenth century, to find out by sea a way to the countries from which the Moors brought them ivory and gold dust across the Desart. They discovered the Madeiras, the Canaries, the Azores, the Cape de Verd islands, the coast of Guinea, that of Loango, Congo, Angola, and Benguela, and finally, the Cape of Good Hope. They had long wished to share in the profitable traffic of the Venetians, and this last discovery opened to them a probable prospect of doing so. In 1497, Vasco de Gama sailed from the port of Lisbon with a fleet of four ships, and, after a navigation of eleven months, arrived upon the coast of Indostan, and thus completed a course of discoveries which had been pursued with great steadiness, and with very little interruption, for near a century together.

COLUMBUS ENDEAVOURED TO REACH THE EAST INDIES BY SAILING WESTWARDS.

Some years before this, while the expectations of Europe were in suspense about the projects of the Portuguese, of which the success appeared yet to be doubtful, a Genoese pilot formed the yet more daring project of sailing to the East Indies by the West. The situation of those countries was at that time very imperfectly known in Europe. The few European travellers who had been there had magnified the distance; perhaps through simplicity and ignorance, what was really very great, appearing almost infinite to those who could not measure it;

or, perhaps, in order to increase somewhat more the marvellous of their own adventures in visiting regions so immensely remote from Europe. The longer the way was by the East, Columbus very justly concluded, the shorter it would be by the West. He proposed, therefore, to take that way, as both the shortest and the surest, and he had the good fortune to convince Isabella of Castile of the probability of his project. He sailed from the port of Palos in August 1492, near five years before the expedition of Vasco de Gama set out from Portugal, and, after a voyage of between two and three months, discovered first some of the small Bahama or Lucayan islands, and afterwards the great island of St. Domingo.

COLUMBUS MISTOOK THE COUNTRIES HE FOUND FOR THE INDIES.

But the countries which Columbus discovered, either in this or in any of his subsequent voyages, had no resemblance to those which he had gone in quest of. Instead of the wealth, cultivation and populousness of China and Indostan, he found, in St. Domingo, and in all the other parts of the new world which he ever visited, nothing but a country quite covered with wood, uncultivated, and inhabited only by some tribes of naked and miserable savages. He was not very willing, however, to believe that they were not the same with some of the countries described by Marco Polo, the first European who had visited, or at least had left behind him any description of China or the East Indies; and a very slight resemblance, such as that which he found between the name of Cibao, a mountain in St. Domingo, and that of Cipango, mentioned by Marco Polo, was frequently sufficient to make him return to this favourite prepossession, though contrary to the clearest evidence. In his letters to Ferdinand and Isabella he called the countries which he had discovered, the Indies. He entertained no doubt but that they were the extremity of those which had been described by Marco Polo, and that they were not very distant from the Ganges, or from the countries which had been conquered by Alexander. Even when at last convinced

that they were different, he still flattered himself that those rich countries were at no great distance, and in a subsequent voyage, accordingly, went in quest of them along the coast of Terra Firma, and towards the isthmus of Darien.

HENCE THE NAMES EAST AND WEST INDIES.

In consequence of this mistake of Columbus, the name of the Indies has stuck to those unfortunate countries ever since; and when it was at last clearly discovered that the new were altogether different from the old Indies, the former were called the West, in contradistinction to the latter, which were called the East Indies.

THE COUNTRIES DISCOVERED WERE NOT RICH.

It was of importance to Columbus, however, that the countries which he had discovered, whatever they were, should be represented to the court of Spain as of very great consequence; and, in what constitutes the real riches of every country, the animal and vegetable productions of the soil, there was at that time nothing which could well justify such a representation of them.

*   *   *

SO COLUMBUS RELIED ON THE MINERALS.

Finding nothing either in the animals or vegetables of the newly discovered countries, which could justify a very advantageous representation of them, Columbus turned his view towards their minerals; and in the richness of the productions of this third kingdom, he flattered himself, he had found a full compensation for the insignificancy of those of the other two. The little bits of gold with which the inhabitants ornamented their dress, and which, he was informed, they frequently found in the rivulets and torrents that fell from the mountains, were sufficient to satisfy him that those mountains abounded with the richest gold mines. St. Domingo, therefore, was represented as a country abounding with gold, and upon that account (according to the prejudices not only of the present times, but of those times), an inexhausti-

ble source of real wealth to the crown and kingdom of Spain.

THE COUNCIL OF CASTILE WAS ATTRACTED BY THE GOLD, COLUMBUS PROPOSING THAT THE GOVERNMENT SHOULD HAVE HALF THE GOLD AND SILVER DISCOVERED.

In consequence of the representations of Columbus, the council of Castile determined to take possession of countries of which the inhabitants were plainly incapable of defending themselves. The pious purpose of converting them to Christianity sanctified the injustice of the project. But the hope of finding treasures of gold there, was the sole motive which prompted to undertake it; and to give this motive the greater weight, it was proposed by Columbus that the half of all the gold and silver that should be found there should belong to the crown. This proposal was approved of by the council.

*   *   *

THE SUBSEQUENT SPANISH ENTERPRISES WERE ALL PROMPTED BY THE SAME MOTIVE.

All the other enterprises of the Spaniards in the new world, subsequent to those of Columbus, seem to have been prompted by the same motive. It was the sacred thirst of gold that carried Oieda, Nicuessa, and Vasco Nugnes de Balboa, to the isthmus of Darien, that carried Cortez to Mexico, and Almagro and Pizzarro to Chile and Peru. When those adventurers arrived upon any unknown coast, their first enquiry was always if there was any gold to be found there; and according to the information which they received concerning this particular, they determined either to quit the country or to settle in it.

*   *   *

IN THIS CASE EXPECTATIONS WERE TO SOME EXTENT REALISED, SO FAR AS THE SPANIARDS WERE CONCERNED.

In the countries first discovered by the Spaniards, no gold or silver mines are at present known which

are supposed to be worth the working. The quantities of those metals which the first adventurers are said to have found there, had probably been very much magnified, as well as the fertility of the mines which were wrought immediately after the first discovery. What those adventurers were reported to have found, however, was sufficient to inflame the avidity of all their countrymen. Every Spaniard who sailed to America expected to find an Eldorado. Fortune too did upon this what she has done upon very few other occasions. She realized in some measure the extravagant hopes of her votaries, and in the discovery and conquest of Mexico and Peru (of which the one happened about thirty, the other about forty years after the first expedition of Columbus), she presented them with something not very unlike that profusion of the precious metals which they sought for.

A project of commerce to the East Indies, therefore, gave occasion to the first discovery of the West. A project of conquest gave occasion to all the establishments of the Spaniards in those newly discovered countries. The motive which excited them to this conquest was a project of gold and silver mines; and a course of accidents, which no human wisdom could foresee, rendered this project much more successful than the undertakers had any reasonable grounds for expecting.

BUT THE OTHER NATIONS WERE NOT SO SUCCESSFUL.

The first adventures of all the other nations of Europe, who attempted to make settlements in America, were animated by the like chimerical views; but they were not equally successful. It was more than a hundred years after the first settlement of the Brazils, before any silver, gold, or diamond mines were discovered there. In the English, French, Dutch, and Danish colonies, none have ever yet been discovered; at least none that are at present supposed to be worth the working. The first English settlers in North America, however, offered a fifth of all the gold and silver which should be found there to the king, as a motive for granting them their patents. In the patents to Sir Walter Raleigh, to the London and Plymouth companies, to the council of Plymouth, &c. this fifth was accordingly reserved to the crown. To the expectation of finding gold and silver mines, those first settlers too joined that of discovering a north-west passage to the East Indies. They have hitherto been disappointed in both.

Causes of the Prosperity of New Colonies

The colony of a civilized nation which takes possession either of a waste country, or of one so thinly inhabited, that the natives easily give place to the new settlers, advances more rapidly to wealth and greatness than any other human society.

COLONISTS TAKE OUT KNOWLEDGE AND REGULAR GOVERNMENT.

The colonists carry out with them a knowledge of agriculture and of other useful arts, superior to what can grow up of its own accord in the course of many centuries among savage and barbarous nations. They carry out with them too the habit of subordination, some notion of the regular government which takes place in their own country, of the system of laws which supports it, and of a regular administration of justice; and they naturally establish something of the same kind in the new settlement. But among savage and barbarous nations, the natural progress of law and government is still slower than the natural progress of arts, after law and government have been so far established, as is necessary for their protection.

LAND IS PLENTIFUL AND CHEAP.

Every colonist gets more land than he can possibly cultivate. He has no rent, and scarce any taxes to pay. No landlord shares with him in its produce, and the share of the sovereign is commonly but a trifle. He has every motive to render as great as possible a produce, which is thus to be almost entirely his own. But his land is commonly so extensive, that with all his own industry, and with all the industry of other people whom he can get

to employ, he can seldom make it produce the tenth part of what it is capable of producing.

WAGES ARE HIGH.

He is eager, therefore, to collect labourers from all quarters, and to reward them with the most liberal wages. But those liberal wages, joined to the plenty and cheapness of land, soon make those labourers leave him, in order to become landlords themselves, and to reward, with equal liberality, other labourers, who soon leave them for the same reason that they left their first master.

*   *   *

Of the Advantages Which Europe Has Derived from the Discovery of America, and from That of a Passage to the East Indies by the Cape of Good Hope

THE ADVANTAGES DERIVED BY EUROPE FROM AMERICA ARE (1) THE ADVANTAGES OF EUROPE IN GENERAL, AND (2) THE ADVANTAGES OF THE PARTICULAR COUNTRIES WHICH HAVE COLONIES.

Such are the advantages which the colonies of America have derived from the policy of Europe.

What are those which Europe has derived from the discovery and colonization of America?

Those advantages may be divided, first, into the general advantages which Europe, considered as one great country, has derived from those great events; and, secondly, into the particular advantages which each colonizing country has derived from the colonies which particularly belong to it, in consequence of the authority or dominion which it exercises over them.

(1) THE GENERAL ADVANTAGES TO EUROPE ARE (A) AN INCREASE OF ENJOYMENTS.

The general advantages which Europe, considered as one great country, has derived from the discovery and colonization of America, consist, first, in the increase of its enjoyments; and secondly, in the augmentation of its industry.

The surplus produce of America, imported into Europe, furnishes the inhabitants of this great continent with a variety of commodities which they could not otherwise have possessed, some for conveniency and use, some for pleasure, and some for ornament, and thereby contributes to increase their enjoyments.

(B) AN AUGMENTATION OF INDUSTRY NOT ONLY IN THE COUNTRIES WHICH TRADE WITH AMERICA DIRECTLY, BUT ALSO IN OTHER COUNTRIES WHICH DO NOT SEND THEIR PRODUCE TO AMERICA OR EVEN RECEIVE ANY PRODUCE FROM AMERICA.

The discovery and colonization of America, it will readily be allowed, have contributed to augment the industry, first, of all the countries which trade to it directly; such as Spain, Portugal, France, and England; and, secondly, of all those which, without trading to it directly, send, through the medium of other countries, goods to it of their own produce; such as Austrian Flanders, and some provinces of Germany, which, through the medium of the countries before mentioned, send to it a considerable quantity of linen and other goods. All such countries have evidently gained a more extensive market for their surplus produce, and must consequently have been encouraged to increase its quantity.

*   *   *

Those great events may even have contributed to increase the enjoyments, and to augment the industry of countries which, not only never sent any commodities to America, but never received any from it. Even such countries may have received a greater abundance of other commodities from countries of which the surplus produce had been augmented by means of the American trade. This greater abundance, as it must necessarily have increased their enjoyments, so it must likewise have augmented their industry. A greater number of new equivalents of some kind or other must have been presented to them to be exchanged for the

surplus produce of that industry. A more extensive market must have been created for that surplus produce, so as to raise its value, and thereby encourage its increase. The mass of commodities annually thrown into the great circle of European commerce, and by its various revolutions annually distributed among all the different nations comprehended within it, must have been augmented by the whole surplus produce of America. A greater share of this greater mass, therefore, is likely to have fallen to each of those nations, to have increased their enjoyments, and augmented their industry.

*   *   *

(2) THE PARTICULAR ADVANTAGES OF THE COLONISING COUNTRIES ARE (A) THE COMMON ADVANTAGES DERIVED FROM PROVINCES, (B) THE PECULIAR ADVANTAGES DERIVED FROM PROVINCES IN AMERICA.

The particular advantages which each colonizing country derives from the colonies which particularly belong to it, are of two different kinds; first, those common advantages which every empire derives from the provinces subject to its dominion; and, secondly, those peculiar advantages which are supposed to result from provinces of so very peculiar a nature as the European colonies of America.

The common advantages which every empire derives from the provinces subject to its dominion, consist, first, in the military force which they furnish for its defence; and, secondly, in the revenue which they furnish for the support of its civil government. * * *

(A) THE COMMON ADVANTAGES ARE CONTRIBUTIONS OF MILITARY FORCES AND REVENUE, BUT NONE OF THE COLONIES HAVE EVER FURNISHED MILITARY FORCE.

The European colonies of America have never yet furnished any military force for the defence of the mother country. Their military force has never yet been sufficient for their own defence; and in the different wars in which the mother countries have been engaged, the defence of their colonies has generally occasioned a very considerable distraction of the military force of those countries. In this respect, therefore, all the European colonies have, without exception, been a cause rather of weakness than of strength to their respective mother countries.

AND THE COLONIES OF SPAIN AND PORTUGAL ALONE HAVE CONTRIBUTED REVENUE.

The colonies of Spain and Portugal only have contributed any revenue towards the defence of the mother country, or the support of her civil government. The taxes which have been levied upon those of other European nations, upon those of England in particular, have seldom been equal to the expence laid out upon them in time of peace, and never sufficient to defray that which they occasioned in time of war. Such colonies, therefore, have been a source of expence and not of revenue to their respective mother countries.

(B) THE EXCLUSIVE TRADE IS THE SOLE PECULIAR ADVANTAGE.

The advantages of such colonies to their respective mother countries, consist altogether in those peculiar advantages which are supposed to result from provinces of so very peculiar a nature as the European colonies of America; and the exclusive trade, it is acknowledged, is the sole source of all those peculiar advantages.

THE EXCLUSIVE TRADE OF EACH COUNTRY IS A DISADVANTAGE TO THE OTHER COUNTRIES.

In consequence of this exclusive trade, all that part of the surplus produce of the English colonies, for example, which consists in what are called enumerated commodities, can be sent to no other country but England. Other countries must afterwards buy it of her. It must be cheaper therefore in England than it can be in any other country, and must contribute more to increase the enjoyments of England than those of any other country. It must likewise contribute more to encourage her industry. For all those parts of her own surplus

produce which England exchanges for those enumerated commodities, she must get a better price than any other countries can get for the like parts of theirs, when they exchange them for the same commodities. The manufactures of England, for example, will purchase a greater quantity of the sugar and tobacco of her own colonies, than the like manufactures of other countries can purchase of that sugar and tobacco. So far, therefore, as the manufactures of England and those of other countries are both to be exchanged for the sugar and tobacco of the English colonies, this superiority of price gives an encouragement to the former, beyond what the latter can in these circumstances enjoy. The exclusive trade of the colonies, therefore, as it diminishes, or, at least, keeps down below what they would otherwise rise to, both the enjoyments and the industry of the countries which do not possess it; so it gives an evident advantage to the countries which do possess it over those other countries.

*   *   *

REVIEW QUESTIONS

1. How, according to Smith, did the colonial empires of early modern Europe differ from those of the ancient world?
2. What was the motive force of empire?
3. How does Smith explain the eventual success of the colonies in America?
4. What benefits does he think derive from empire? What costs?
5. How do we explain Smith's apparent indifference to the exploitation of native or slave populations?

CATHERINE THE GREAT

FROM Proposals for a New Code of Law

Catherine II (1729–1796), a German princess who became Tsarina of Russia after disposing of her ineffectual husband, was one of the most successful European monarchs of the eighteenth century and one of the most remarkable female rulers of all time. She followed Peter the Great in regarding Russia as a European power. Among her many achievements was the addition of some 200,000 square miles to the territory of the Russian Empire. Nor were her interests limited to expansion. She also took effective measures to modernize the empire's administration and improve its society. In 1767 Catherine summoned an assembly to draft a new code of laws for Russia and gave detailed instructions to the members about the principles they should apply. The proposed code never went into effect, but the proposal breathes the spirit of the Enlightenment.

From *Documents of Catherine the Great: The Correspondence with Voltaire and the Instruction of 1767 in the English Text of 1768*, translated by W. F. Reddaway (Cambridge: Cambridge University Press, 1931), pp. 216–17, 219, 231, 241, 244, 256, 258.

*   *   *

6. Russia is a European State.

7. This is clearly demonstrated by the following Observations: The Alterations which *Peter the Great* undertook in Russia succeeded with the greater Ease, because the Manners, which prevailed at that Time, and had been introduced amongst us by a Mixture of different Nations, and the Conquest of foreign Territories, were quite unsuitable to the Climate. *Peter the First*, by introducing the Manners and Customs of Europe among the European People in his Dominions, found at that Time such Means as even he himself was not sanguine enough to expect. . . .

8. The Possessions of the Russian Empire extend upon the terrestrial Globe to 32 Degrees of Latitude, and to 165 of Longitude.

9. The Sovereign is absolute; for there is no other Authority but that which centers in his single Person, that can act with a Vigor proportionate to the Extent of such a vast Dominion.

10. The Extent of the Dominion requires an absolute Power to be vested in that Person who rules over it. It is expedient so to be, that the quick Dispatch of Affairs, sent from distant Parts, might make ample Amends for the Delay occasioned by the great Distance of the Places.

11. Every other Form of Government whatsoever would not only have been prejudicial to Russia, but would even have proved its entire Ruin.

12. Another Reason is: That it is better to be subject to the Laws under one Master, than to be subservient to many.

13. What is the true End of Monarchy? Not to deprive People of their natural Liberty; but to correct their Actions, in order to attain the *supreme Good*.

14. The Form of Government, therefore, which best attains this End, and at the same Time sets less Bounds than others to natural Liberty, is that which coincides with the Views and Purposes of rational Creatures, and answers the End, upon which we ought to fix a steadfast Eye in the Regulations of civil Polity.

15. The Intention and the End of Monarchy, is the Glory of the Citizens, of the State, and of the Sovereign.

16. But, from this Glory, a Sense of Liberty arises in a People governed by a Monarch; which may produce in these States as much Energy in transacting the most important Affairs, and may contribute as much to the Happiness of the Subjects, as even Liberty itself. . . .

33. The Laws ought to be so framed, as to secure the Safety of every Citizen as much as possible.

34. The Equality of the Citizens consists in this; that they should all be subject to the same Laws.

35. This Equality requires Institutions so well adapted, as to prevent the Rich from oppressing those who are not so wealthy as themselves, and converting all the Charges and Employments entrusted to them as Magistrates only, to their own private Emolument. . . .

37. In a State or Assemblage of People that live together in a Community, where there are Laws, Liberty can only consist *in doing that which every One ought to do*, and *not to be constrained to do that which One ought not to do*.

38. A Man ought to form in his own Mind an exact and clear Idea of what Liberty is. *Liberty is the Right of doing whatsoever the Laws allow:* And if any one Citizen could do what the Laws forbid, there would be no more Liberty; because others would have an equal Power of doing the same.

39. The political Liberty of a Citizen is the Peace of Mind arising from the Consciousness, that every Individual enjoys his peculiar Safety; and in order that the People might attain this Liberty, the Laws ought to be so framed, that no one Citizen should stand in Fear of another; but that all of them should stand in Fear of the same Laws. . . .

123. The Usage of Torture is contrary to all the Dictates of Nature and Reason; even Mankind itself cries out against it, and demands loudly the total Abolition of it. . . .

180. That Law, therefore, is highly beneficial to the Community where it is established, which ordains that every Man shall be judged by his Peers and Equals. For when the Fate of a Citizen is in Question, all Prejudices arising from the Difference of Rank or Fortune should be stifled; because they ought to have no Influence between the Judges and the Parties accused. . . .

194. (1.) No Man ought to be looked upon as *guilty*, before he has received his judicial Sentence; nor can the Laws deprive him of *their* Protection, before it is proved that he *has forfeited all Right* to it. What Right therefore can Power give to any to inflict Punishment upon a Citizen at a Time, when it is yet dubious, whether he is *Innocent* or *guilty*? ...

250. A Society of Citizens, as well as every Thing else, requires a certain fixed Order: There ought to be *some to govern*, and *others to obey*.

251. And this is the Origin of every Kind of Subjection; which feels itself more or less alleviated, in Proportion to the Situation of the Subjects. ...

252. And, consequently, as the Law of Nature commands Us to take as much Care, as lies in *Our* Power, of the Prosperity of all the People; we are obliged to alleviate the Situation of the Subjects, as much as sound Reason will permit.

253. And therefore, to shun all Occasions of reducing People to a State of Slavery, except the *utmost* Necessity should *inevitably* oblige us to do it; in that Case, it ought not to be done for our own Benefit; but for the Interest of the State: Yet even that Case is extremely uncommon.

254. Of whatever Kind Subjection may be, the civil Laws ought to guard, on the one Hand, against the *Abuse* of Slavery, and, on the other, against the *Dangers* which may arise from it. ...

269. It seems too, that the Method of exacting their Revenues, *newly* invented by the Lords, diminishes both the *Inhabitants*, and the *Spirit of Agriculture* in Russia. Almost all the Villages are *heavily* taxed. The Lords, who seldom or never *reside* in their Villages, lay an Impost on every Head of one, two, and even five Rubles, without the least Regard to the *Means* by which their Peasants may be able to *raise* this Money.

270. It is highly necessary that the Law should prescribe a Rule to the Lords, for a more judicious Method of raising their Revenues; and oblige them to levy *such* a Tax, as *tends least* to separate the Peasant from his House and Family; this would be the Means by which Agriculture would become more extensive, and Population be more increased in the Empire.

REVIEW QUESTIONS

1. Which articles and which instructions, coincide with the liberal or enlightened principles that were spreading across Europe in the late seventeenth and eighteenth centuries?

2. These liberal sentiments notwithstanding, what makes this document a classic exercise in absolute monarchy?

3. Why does Catherine include the curious instruction in Article 6?

4. How does Catherine understand such concepts as "society" and the "laws of nature"?

5. How does Catherine understand monarchy? How do her ideas differ from those of other absolute monarchs you may have studied?

DANIEL DEFOE

FROM *The Complete English Tradesman*

Daniel Defoe (c. 1659–1731) was an English writer who gained fame as an early proponent of the novel, helping to popularize its form through the success of Robinson Crusoe. *He was a prolific writer on an extraordinary range of subjects, publishing more than five hundred novels, pamphlets, essays and journals in his lifetime. He is*

also considered a pioneer of economic journalism, of which the following excerpt from his book The Complete English Tradesman *might be considered a prime example. It reflects an unusually exact, practical knowledge of trade, its potentials and pitfalls. Defoe's knowledge reflects the fact that he actively engaged in many enterprises. In it he attempts to defend trade as practiced by the English, which he clearly sees as the cornerstone of national prosperity, power, and glory.*

From *The Complete English Tradesman*, by Daniel Defoe (London, 1724), chap. XXV as reprinted in *The Western Tradition: From the Ancient World to Louis XIV*, edited by Eugen Weber (Lexington, Mass.: D. C. Heath, 1995), pp. 476–81.

The instances which we have given in the last chapter abundantly make for the honor of the British traders; and we may venture to say, at the same time, are very far from doing dishonor to the nobility who have from time to time entered into alliance with them; for it is very well known that, besides the benefit which we reap by being a trading nation, which is our principal glory, trade is a very different thing in England than it is in many other countries and is carried on by persons who, both in their education and descent, are far from being the dregs of the people.

King Charles II, who was perhaps the prince of all the kings that ever reigned in England, who best understood the country and the people he governed, used to say, that the tradesmen were the only gentry in England. His majesty spoke it merrily, but it had a happy signification in it, such as was peculiar to the bright genius of that prince, who, though he was not the best governor, was the best acquainted with the world of all the princes of his age, if not of all the men in it; and I make no scruple to advance these three points in honor of our country; viz.

1. That we are the greatest trading country in the world because we have the greatest exportation of the growth and product of our land and of the manufacture and labor of our people; and the greatest importation and consumption of the growth, product, and manufactures of other countries from abroad, of any nation in the world.

2. That our climate is the best and most agreeable to live in because a man can be more out of doors in England than in other countries.

3. That our men are the stoutest and best because, strip them naked from the waist upwards, and give them no weapons at all but their hands and heels, and turn them into a room or stage, and lock them in with the like number of other men of any nation, man for man, and they shall beat the best men you shall find in the world.

As so many of our noble and wealthy families, as we have shown, are raised by and derived from trade, so it is true, and indeed it cannot well be otherwise, that many of the younger branches of our gentry, and even of the nobility itself, have descended again into the spring from whence they flowed and have become tradesmen; and thence it is that, as I said above, our tradesmen in England are not, as it generally is in other countries, always of the meanest of our people. Nor is trade itself in England, as it generally is in other countries, the meanest thing the men can turn their hand to; but, on the contrary, trade is the readiest way for men to raise their fortunes and families; and therefore it is a field for men of figure and of good families to enter upon.

Having thus done a particular piece of justice to ourselves, in the value we put upon trade and tradesmen in England, it reflects very much upon the understandings of those refined heads who pretend to depreciate that part of the nation which is so infinitely superior in wealth to the families who call themselves gentry, and so infinitely more numerous.

As to the wealth of the nation, that undoubtedly lies chiefly among the trading part of the people; and though there are a great many families

raised within few years, in the late war, by great employments and by great actions abroad, to the honor of the English gentry, yet how many more families among the tradesmen have been raised to immense estates, even during the same time, by the attending circumstances of the war; such as the clothing, the paying, the victualling and furnishing, etc., both army and navy? And by whom have the prodigious taxes been paid, the loans supplied, and money advanced upon all occasions? By whom are the banks and companies carried on, and on whom are the customs and excises levied? Have not the trade and tradesmen borne the burden of the war? And do they not still pay four millions a year interest for the public debts? On whom are the funds levied, and by whom the public credit supported? Is not trade the unexhausted fund of all funds, and upon which all the rest depend?

As is the trade, so in proportion are the tradesmen; and how wealthy are tradesmen in almost all the several parts of England, as well as in London? How common is it to see a tradesman go off the stage, even but from mere shop-keeping, with from ten to forty thousand pounds' estate to divide among his family! When, on the contrary, take the gentry in England, from one end to the other, except a few here and there, what with excessive high living, which is of late grown so much into a disease, and the other ordinary circumstances of families, we find few families of the lower gentry, that is to say from six or seven hundred a year downwards, but they are in debt, and in necessitous circumstances, and a great many of greater estates also.

On the other hand, let any one who is acquainted with England, look but abroad into the several counties, especially near London, or within fifty miles of it; how are the ancient families worn out by time and family misfortunes, and the estates possessed by a new race of tradesmen, grown up into families of gentry, and established by the immense wealth gained, as I may say, behind the counter; that is, in the shop, the warehouse, and the counting-house.

How many noble seats, superior to the palaces of sovereign princes, in some countries, do we see erected within few miles of this city by tradesmen, or the sons of tradesmen, while the seats and castles of the ancient gentry, like their families, look worn out and fallen into decay!

Again, in how superior a port do our tradesmen live, to what the middling gentry either do or can support! An ordinary tradesman now, not in the city only, but in the country, shall spend more money by the year, than a gentleman of four or five hundred pounds a year too; whereas the gentleman shall, at the best, stand stock still just where he began, nay, perhaps, decline: and as for the lower gentry, from a hundred pounds a year to three hundred, or thereabouts, though they are often as proud and high in their appearance as the other; as to them, I say, a shoemaker in London shall keep a better house, spend more money, clothe his family better, and yet grow rich too. It is evident where the difference lies; an estate's a pond, but trade's a spring: the first, if it keeps full, and the water wholesome, by the ordinary supplies and drains from the neighboring grounds, it is well, and it is all that is expected; but the other is an unexhausted current, which not only fills the pond and keeps it full, but is continually running over, and fills all the lower ponds and places about it.

This being the case in England, and our trade being so vastly great, it is no wonder that the tradesmen in England fill the lists of our nobility and gentry; no wonder that the gentlemen of the best families marry tradesmen's daughters, and put their younger sons apprentices to tradesmen; and how often do these younger sons come to buy the elder sons' estates, and restore the family, when the elder and head of the house, proving rakish and extravagant, has wasted his patrimony, and is obliged to make out the blessing of Israel's family, where the younger son bought the birthright, and the elder was doomed to serve him!

Trade is so far here from being inconsistent with a gentleman, that, in short, trade in England makes gentlemen, and has peopled this nation with gentlemen; for, after a generation or two, the tradesman's children, or at least their grandchildren, come to be as good gentlemen, statesmen, parliament-men, privy-counselors, judges, bishops,

and noblemen, as those of the highest birth and the most ancient families; as we have shown. Nor do we find any defect either in the genius or capacities of the posterity of tradesmen, arising from any remains of mechanic blood, which, it is pretended, should influence them; but all the gallantry of spirit, greatness of soul, and all the generous principles that can be found in any of the ancient families, whose blood is the most untainted, as they call it, with the low mixtures of a mechanic race, are found in these; and, as is said before, they generally go beyond them in knowledge of the world, which is the best education.

We see the tradesmen of England, as they grow wealthy, coming every day to the herald's office to search for the coats of arms of their ancestors, in order to paint them upon their coaches, and grave them upon their plate, embroider them upon their furniture, or carve them upon the pediments of their new houses; and how often do we see them trace the registers of their families up to the prime nobility, or the most ancient gentry of the kingdom!

In this search we find them often qualified to raise new families, if they do not descend from old; as was said of a certain tradesman of London, that if he could not find the ancient race of gentlemen, from which he came, he would begin a new race, who should be as good gentlemen as any that went before him.

Thus, in the late wars between England and France, how was our army full of excellent officers, who went from the shop, and behind the counter, into the camp, and who distinguished themselves there by their merits and gallant behavior! And several such came to command regiments, and even to be general officers, and to gain as much reputation in the service as any, as Colonel Pierce, Wood, Richards, and several others that may be named.

All this confirms what I have said before, viz., that trade in England neither is or ought to be compared with what it is in other countries; or the tradesmen depreciated as they are abroad, and as some of our gentry would pretend to do in England; but that as many of our best families rose from trade, so many branches of the best families in England, under the nobility, have stooped so low as to put apprentices to tradesmen in London, and to set up and follow those trades when they have come out of their times, and have thought it no dishonor to their blood.

To bring this once more home to the ladies, who are scandalized at that mean step, which they call it, of marrying a tradesman, it may be told them, for their humiliation, that, however they think fit to act, sometimes those tradesmen come of better families than their own; and oftentimes, when they have refused them to their loss, those very tradesmen have married ladies of superior fortune to them, and have raised families of their own, who, in one generation, have been superior to those nice ladies both in dignity and estate; and have, to their great mortification, been ranked above them upon all public occasions.

The word "tradesman," in England, does not sound so harsh as it does in other countries; and to say a gentleman-tradesman, is not so much nonsense as some people would persuade us to reckon it; and, indeed, the very name of an English tradesman, will and does already obtain in the world; and as our soldiers, by the late war, gained the reputation of being some of the best troops in the world; and our seamen are at this day, and very justly too, esteemed the best sailors in the world; so the English tradesman may be allowed to rank with the best gentlemen in Europe.

And hence it is natural to ask, whence comes all this to be so? How is it produced? War has not done it; no, nor so much as helped or assisted to it; it is not by any martial exploits; we have made no conquests abroad, added no new kingdoms to the British Empire, reduced no neighboring nations, or extended the possession of our monarchs into the properties of others; we have gained nothing by war and encroachment; nay, we have lost all the dominions which our ancient kings for some hundreds of years held in France; and, instead of being enriched by war and victory, on the contrary, we have been torn in pieces by civil wars and rebellions, and that several times, to the ruin of our richest families, and the slaughter of our nobility and gentry.

These things prove abundantly that the greatness of the British nation is not owing to war and conquests, to enlarging its dominions by the sword, or subjecting the people of other countries to our power; but it is allowing to trade, to the increase of our commerce at home, and the extending it abroad.

It is owing to trade that new discoveries have been made in lands unknown, and new settlements and plantations made, new colonies planted, and new governments formed in the uninhabited islands and the uncultivated continent of America; and those plantings and settlements have again enlarged and increased the trade, and thereby the wealth and power of the nation by whom they were discovered and planted. We have not increased our power, or the number of our subjects, by subduing the nations which possess those countries, and incorporating them into our own, but have entirely planted our colonies, and peopled the countries with our own subjects. Excepting the Negroes, which we transport from Africa to America as slaves to work in the sugar and tobacco plantations, all our colonies, as well in the islands as on the continent of America, are entirely peopled from Great Britain and Ireland, and chiefly the former; the natives having either removed further up into the country, or, by their own folly and treachery raising war against us, been destroyed and cut off.

As trade has thus extended our colonies abroad, so it has (except those colonies) kept our people at home, where they are multiplied to that prodigious degree, and do still continue to multiply in such a manner that, if it goes on so, time may come that all the lands in England will do little more than serve for gardens for them and to feed their cows, and their corn and cattle be supplied from Scotland and Ireland.

What is the reason that we see numbers of French, and of Scots, and Germans, in all the foreign nations in Europe, and especially filling up their armies and courts, and that you see few or no English there?

What is the reason that, when we want to raise armies, or to man navies, in England, we are obliged to press the seamen, and to make laws, and empower the justices of peace and magistrates of towns, to force men to go for soldiers, and enter into the service, or allure them by giving bounty-money as an encouragement to men to list themselves; whereas the people of other nations, and even the Scots and Irish, travel abroad and run into all the neighbor-nations, to seek service and to be admitted into their pay?

What is it but trade, the increase of business at home, and the employment of the poor in the business and manufactures of this kingdom, by which the poor get so good wages, and live so well, that they will not list for soldiers; and have so good pay in the merchants' service, that they will not serve on board the ships of war, unless they are forced to do it?

What is the reason that, in order to supply our colonies and plantations with people, besides the encouragement given in those colonies to all people that will come hither to plant and to settle, we are obliged to send away thither all our petty offenders, and all the criminals that we think fit to spare from the gallows, besides what we formerly called the kidnapping trade, that is to say, the arts made use of to wheedle and draw away young, vagrant, and indigent people, and people of desperate fortunes, to sell themselves, that is, bind themselves for servants, the number of which are very great?

Poverty fills armies, mans navies, and peoples colonies. In vain the drums beat for soldiers to serve in the armies for five pence a day, and the king's captains invite seamen to serve in the royal navy for twenty-three shillings per month, in a country where the ordinary laborer can have nine shillings a week for his labor, and the manufacturers earn from twelve to sixteen shillings a week for their work, and while trade gives thirty shillings per month wages to the seamen on board merchant ships, men will always stay or go, as the pay gives them encouragement; and this is the reason why it has been so much more difficult to raise and recruit armies in England, than it has been in Scotland and Ireland, France and Germany.

The same trade that keeps our people at home, is the cause of the well-living of the people here;

for as frugality is not the national virtue of England, so the people that get much, spend much; and as they work hard, so they live well, eat and drink well, clothe warm, and lodge soft. In a word, the working, manufacturing people of England eat the fat, drink the sweet, live better, and fare better, than the working poor of any other nation in Europe; they make better wages of their work; and spend more of the money upon their backs and bellies than in any other country. This expense of the poor, as it causes a prodigious consumption both of the provisions and of the manufactures of our country at home, so two things are undeniably the consequence of that part.

1. The consumption of provisions increases the rent and value of the lands; and this raises the gentlemen's estates, and that again increases the employment of people, and consequently the numbers of them, as well those that are employed in the husbandry of land, breeding and feeding of cattle, etc., as of servants to the gentlemen's families, who as their estates increase in value, so they increase their families and equipages.

2. As the people get greater wages, so they, I mean the same poorer part of the people, clothe better, and furnish better; and this increases the consumption of the very manufactures they make; then that consumption increases the quantity made; and this creates what we call inland trade, by which innumerable families are employed, and the increase of the people maintained; and by which increase of trade and people the present growing prosperity of this nation is produced.

The whole glory and greatness of England then, being thus raised by trade, it must be unaccountable folly and ignorance in us to lessen that one article in our own esteem, which is the only fountain from whence we all, take us as a nation, are raised, and by which we are enriched and maintained. The Scripture says, speaking of the riches and glory of the city of Tyre, which was indeed at that time the great port or emporium of the world for foreign commerce, from whence all the silks and fine manufactures of Persia and India were exported all over the western world, "that her merchants were princes," and in another place, "by thy traffic thou hast increased thy riches." Certain it is, that our traffic has increased our riches; and it is also certain, that the flourishing of our manufacture is the foundation of all our traffic, as well our merchandise as our inland trade.

REVIEW QUESTIONS

1. Why, according to Defoe, is English trade so prosperous?
2. How does trade contribute to the wealth of England?
3. How does trade contribute to the well-being of Englishmen?
4. Why is trade the best means to combat poverty?
5. How does empire contribute to English trade and prosperity?
6. How does Defoe's understanding of trade differ from that of Adam Smith, who believed that the unrestrained pursuit of profit by individuals actually created prosperity for all?

FROM The Charter of the Dutch West India Company

A chartered company of Dutch merchants, the Dutch West India Company received its charter from the Dutch Republic for a trade monopoly in the West Indies on June 2, 1621. The monopoly included all trade to and from the Caribbean,

especially the slave trade between Africa and the Americas. The company intended to displace all competition, of which the Spanish and Portuguese were the greatest, from its monopoly region. Although it enjoyed only mixed success in this regard, the company and its charter became the vehicles for Dutch colonization in the New World.

From *Van Rensselaer Bowier Manuscripts*, translated by A. J. F. van Laer (Albany, NY: University of the State of New York, 1908), pp. 87–115.

Charter granted by the High and Mighty Lords the States General to the West India Company, dated the 3d of June 1621.

The States General of the United Netherlands to all who shall see these presents or hear them read, greeting, Be it known, that we, noticing that the prosperity of this country and the welfare of its inhabitants consist principally in navigation and trade, which from time immemorial has been carried on by this country with good fortune and great blessing with all countries and kingdoms; and desiring that the aforesaid inhabitants not only be maintained in their former navigation, commerce and trade, but also that their commerce may be increased as much as possible, especially in conformity with the treaties, alliances, conventions and covenants concerning commerce and navigation formerly made with other princes, republics and nations, which we intend shall be punctually kept and observed in all their parts; and finding by experience that without the common help, aid and means of a general company, no profitable business can be carried on, protected and maintained in the parts hereafter designated on account of the great risk from pirates, extortions and the like, which are incurred on such long and distant voyages; we, therefore, many other and different pregnant reasons and considerations also us thereunto moving, after mature deliberation of Council, and for very pressing causes, have resolved that the navigation, trade and commerce in the West Indies, Africa and other countries hereafter designated, shall henceforth not be carried on otherwise than with the common united strength of the merchants and inhabitants of this country and that to this end there shall be established a general company, which, on account of our great love for the common weal and in order to conserve the trade and welfare of the inhabitants of this country, we will maintain and strengthen with our help, favor and assistance, so far as the present state and condition of this country will in any way admit, and for that purpose furnish with a proper charter and endow with the privileges and exemptions hereafter enumerated, to wit:

I. That for the period of twenty-four years no native or inhabitant of this country shall be permitted, except in the name of this United Company, from these United Netherlands nor even from any place outside of them, to sail to or trade with the coasts and countries of Africa, from the Tropic of Cancer to the Cape of Good Hope; nor to or with the countries of America, or the West Indies, beginning at the south end of *Terra Nova*, through the Straits of Magellan, *le Maire*, and other straits and passages situated thereabouts, to the Strait of *Anjan*, neither on the North Sea nor on the South Sea, nor to or with any islands situated on the one side or the other, or between both; nor to or with the Australian or South Lands, extending and lying between the two meridians of the Cape of Good Hope in the east, and of the east end of New Guinea in the west, inclusive. And whoever shall venture, without the consent of this Company, to sail to or to traffic with any places within the aforesaid limits granted to this Company, shall forfeit the ships and goods which shall be found trading upon the aforesaid coasts and lands, the which in the name of the aforesaid Company may immediately and everywhere be attached, seized and held as confiscated property for the behoof of the same. And in case such ship or goods shall have

been sold or taken to other countries or ports, the owners and partners may be levied on for the value of those ships and goods; except only, that they, who before the date of this charter shall have sailed from these or other countries to any of the aforesaid coasts, shall be permitted to continue their trade till they have sold their goods and come back to this country, or otherwise until the expiration of their charter if they have been granted any before this date, and no longer. Provided, that after the first of July, sixteen hundred and twenty-one, the day and time of the commencement of this charter, no one shall be permitted to send any ships or goods to the places comprehended in this charter even if this Company should not be fully organized before that date; but proper provision shall be made against those who knowingly and fraudulently seek to frustrate our good intentions for the common weal; it being understood that the salt trade at *Ponte del Ré* may be continued according to the conditions and instructions already given, or to be given by us respecting it, without being in any way restricted by this charter.

II. That further the aforesaid Company, in our name and by our authority, within the limits hereinbefore set forth, shall have power to make contracts, leagues and alliances with the princes and natives of the countries therein comprised also to build any fortresses and strongholds there; to appoint, transfer, discharge and replace governors, troops and officers of justice and for other necessary services, for the preservation of the places, the maintenance of good order, police and justice, in general for the furtherance of trade, as according to circumstances they shall see fit; moreover, they may promote the settlement of fertile and uninhabited districts, and do all that the service of this country and the profit and increase of trade shall require. And the [directors] of the Company shall regularly communicate to us and transmit such contracts and alliances as they shall have made with the aforesaid princes and nations, likewise [report] the situation of the fortresses, strongholds and settlements by them begun.

III. Provided that when they have chosen a governor general and prepared instructions for him, the same must be approved, and the commission given by us; and further, that such governor general, as also other vice governors, commanders and officers, shall be obliged to take the oath of allegiance to us and also to the Company.

IV. And if the aforesaid Company in any of the aforesaid places be cheated under the pretense of friendship or badly treated, or if any money or goods entrusted by them be kept without their receiving restitution or payment, they may according to circumstances and the best of their ability cause the loss to be made good by all such means as can properly be employed.

V. And as it will also be necessary for the establishment, security and defense of this trade to take some troops along, we will, according to the condition of the country and the situation of affairs, furnish the said Company with such troops for field and garrison duty as shall be necessary, provided they be paid and supported by the Company.

VI. Which troops, besides the oath already taken to us and to his Excellency, shall swear to obey the commands of the said Company and to help promote their interests to the utmost of their ability.

VII. That the provosts of the Company on shore shall have power to apprehend any soldiers or other of the military that have enlisted in the service of the aforesaid Company and to confine them on board ship in whatever city, place or jurisdiction of this country they may be found; provided the provosts first inform the officers and magistrates of the cities and places where this occurs.

VIII. That we will not take any ships, ordnance or ammunition belonging to the Company, for the use of this country, except with the consent of the said Company.

IX. We have further granted, privileged and conceded this Company, and do hereby grant and concede, that they may pass freely with all their ships and goods without paying toll to any of the United Provinces and that they may use this freedom in the same manner as the free inhabitants of the cities of this country enjoy their freedom,

notwithstanding some persons who are not free should be members of this Company.

X. That all the goods which this Company during the eight next ensuing years shall carry out of this country to the West Indies and Africa, and other places comprised within the aforesaid limits, and those which they shall bring thence into this country shall be exempt from outgoing and ingoing convoy charges; provided, that if at the expiration of the aforesaid eight years, the state and condition of this country will not admit of this eight years' freedom's continuing for another term of years, then outgoing convoy charges and license fees on the said goods and merchandise coming from the places mentioned in this charter and again exported from this country, during the whole term of this charter shall not be rated higher by us than they are rated at present; unless we should be again engaged in war, in which case all the aforesaid goods and merchandises shall not be rated higher by us than they were in the last list in time of war.

XI. And in order that this Company may have a good government, to the greatest profit and satisfaction of all the participants, we have ordained that the said government shall be vested in five Chambers of directors—one at Amsterdam which shall have the management of four ninths; one Chamber in Zealand, of two ninths; one Chamber on the *Maze*, of one ninth; one Chamber in the *Noorder-quartier*; of one ninth; and the fifth Chamber in Friesland together with *Stadt ende Landen*, also of one ninth—upon the conditions set forth in the register of our resolutions and the agreement drawn up respecting it. And the provinces in which there are no Chambers shall be accommodated with as many directors, divided among the respective Chambers, as the number of hundred thousand guilders which they shall furnish to the Company.

XII. That the Chamber of Amsterdam shall consist of twenty directors; the Chamber of Zealand of twelve; the Chambers of the *Maze* and of the *Noorder-quartier* each of fourteen; and the Chamber of Friesland together with *Stadt ende Landen* also of fourteen directors. If it shall hereafter appear that this work can not be carried on

without a greater number of persons, then more may be added after notice to the Nineteen and our approbation, but not otherwise.

XIII. And the States of the respective united provinces are authorized to make such regulations, either for their Noble Mightinesses' ordinary deputies or for the magistrates of the cities of their province, concerning the registration of the participants and the election of directors, as they think proper, according to the constitution of their province; provided that no person in the Chamber of Amsterdam shall be chosen a director who shall not in his own name participate in the Company for the sum of six thousand guilders; in the Chamber of Zealand for four thousand guilders; and in the Chambers of the *Maze*, of the *Noorder-quartier*, and of Friesland, with *Stadt ende Landen*, for the like sum of four thousand guilders.

XIV. That the first directors shall serve for the term of six years and that at the expiration of the said term, first one third part of the number of directors, selected by lot, shall be changed; and two years after a like third part; and again after two years, the last third part; and thenceforth successively, the oldest in the service shall be retired; and in the place of [each] retiring director or of such as shall at any time die, or for other reason leave a vacancy, three others shall be nominated by the directors, both remaining and retiring, together with those chief participants who in person and at their own expense shall care to join them, from which number the aforesaid respective provinces, deputies or magistrates, shall elect new directors and successively supply the vacancies; and they shall be considered chief participants who in their own name participate for the same amount as the respective directors.

XV. That the accounts of the equipment and fitting out of the ships, with their appurtenances, shall be rendered three months after the departure of the ships and that one month thereafter copies shall be sent to us and to the respective Chambers; and the Chambers shall (as often as we see fit or they are requested by the [other] Chambers) send to us and to each other an account of the returns and also of the sales of the same.

XVI. That every six years a general accounting shall be made of all outfits and returns, as also of all gains and losses of the Company, to wit, one relating to trade and one relating to war, each separate; which accounts shall be rendered publicly, notices being previously posted, to the end that every one who is interested may attend the hearing of the said accounts; and if before the expiration of the seventh year the accounts are not rendered in the manner aforesaid, the directors shall forfeit their commissions, which shall be appropriated to the use of the poor, and they shall nevertheless be held to render their accounts as aforesaid within such time and under such penalty as shall be fixed by us respecting the delinquents. And none the less a dividend shall meantime be declared from the profits of the trade as often as it shall be found that ten per cent has been gained.

XVII. No one shall be permitted during the continuance of this charter to withdraw his capital or sums advanced from this Company; nor shall any new participants be admitted. If at the expiration of twenty-four years it shall be judged well to continue this Company or to erect a new one, a final accounting and estimate shall be made by the Nineteen, with our approval, of all that belongs to the Company, and also of their necessary expenses, and after the aforesaid settlement and estimate any one may withdraw his money or, in proportion thereof, in whole or in part, continue and share in the succeeding Company; and the succeeding Company shall in such case take the remainder, which shall be found according to the accounting and estimate, and pay the participants who do not think fit to continue in the Company their share at such times at the Nineteen, with our knowledge and approbation, shall think proper.

XVIII. That so often as it shall be necessary to have a general Assembly of the aforesaid Chambers, it shall be by Nineteen persons, of whom eight shall come from the Chamber of Amsterdam, four from Zealand, two from the *Maze*, two from the *Noorder-quartier*, two from Friesland and *Stadt ende Landen*; provided, that the nineteenth person, or so many more as we shall at any time think fit, shall be deputed by us for the purpose of helping to direct the affairs of the Company in the aforesaid Assembly.

XIX. By which general Assembly of the aforesaid Chambers, all matters relating to this Company shall be considered and decided; provided, that in matters of war, our approbation of their resolution shall be asked.

XX. The aforesaid general Assembly being summoned, it shall meet, whenever they are about to fit out, to resolve how many ships they shall send to each place for the account of the Company in general, and no individual Chamber shall be permitted to undertake anything not included in the aforesaid common resolution but [all] shall be bound to carry it into effect and to execute it. And if any Chamber should fail to comply with the common resolution, or be found to act in violation thereof, we have authorized, and by these presents do authorize, the said Assembly immediately to cause reparation to be made for such failure or violation, wherein, on request, we will assist them.

XXI. The said general Assembly shall be held the first six years in the city of Amsterdam, and the following two years in Zealand; and so on alternately in the aforesaid two places.

XXII. The directors who by commission of the Company shall go from home to attend the aforesaid Assembly or otherwise, shall have for their expenses and daily allowance four guilders a day, besides boat and stage fare; it being understood that those who go from one city to another to attend the meetings of the Chambers as directors and managers shall receive no allowance or traveling expenses at the charge of the Company.

XXIII. And if it should happen that in the aforesaid general Assembly any weighty matter came before them, wherein they could not agree, or even in which one side should scruple to impose its decision on the other, the same shall be left to our decision; and whatever shall be determined upon shall be followed and carried into execution.

XXIV. And all the inhabitants of this country, and also of other countries, shall be notified by public posting of notices within the month after the date hereof that they may be admitted into this Company during five months from the first of July,

this year, sixteen hundred and twenty-one, and that they may pay the money they wish to invest in three payments; to wit, one third at the expiration of the aforesaid five months and the other two thirds within the three next succeeding years, unless the aforesaid general Assembly shall find it necessary to extend the time, whereof the participants shall be notified by posting of notices.

XXV. The ships returning from a voyage shall come to the place they sailed from; and if, by stress of wind and weather, the vessels which sailed out from one district shall arrive in another—as those from Amsterdam or the *Noorder-quartier* in Zealand or the *Maze*; or from Zealand in Holland; or those from Friesland, with *Stadt ende Landen*, in another district—each Chamber shall nevertheless retain the direction and management of the ships and goods it sent out and be allowed to send and transport the goods to the places whence the vessels sailed, either in the same or other vessels; provided that the directors of that Chamber shall be required to be present in person at the place where the vessels and goods shall have arrived and not to appoint factors to superintend the business; but in case it shall not be convenient for them to travel, they shall commit this business to the Chamber in whose district the vessels arrived.

XXVI. If any Chamber shall have obtained any goods or returns from the places included within the limits of this charter with which another is not provided, it shall be required to send such goods on request to the Chamber which is unprovided, according to the situation of the case; and when they have sold out to send more. And in like manner, if the managers of the respective Chambers have need of any persons for crews or other purposes, from the cities where there are Chambers or directors, they shall request and employ [the aid of] the directors of this Company therefore and not make use of any factors.

XXVII. And if any of the provinces think fit to appoint an agent to collect the money from their inhabitants, deposit the amount in bulk in any Chamber, and receive the payment of dividends, the Chamber shall be required to give such agent access, that he may obtain information of the state of the disbursements and receipts, and of the debts and assets; provided that the money brought in by such agent shall amount to fifty thousand guilders or upwards.

XXVIII. The directors shall have for commissions one per cent on the outfits and returns, and also on the prizes, and a half per cent on gold and silver; which commissions shall be divided—to the Chamber of Amsterdam, four ninths; the Chamber of Zealand, two ninths; the *Maze*, one ninth; the *Noorder-quartier*, one ninth; and Friesland with *Stadt ende Landen*, a like ninth.

XXIX. Provided that they shall not receive commissions on the ordnance and value of the ships more than once. They shall, moreover, have no commission on the ships, ordnance and other things with which we shall strengthen the Company, nor on the money which they shall collect for the Company, nor on the profits they receive from the goods; nor shall they charge the Company with any salaries, expenses of traveling or board of those to whom they shall commit the fitting out and purchasing of goods necessary therefore.

XXX. The bookkeepers and cashiers shall have a salary paid them by the directors out of their commissions.

XXXI. The directors shall not deliver or sell to the Company any ships, merchandise, or goods belonging to themselves in whole or in part, nor buy or cause to be bought of the said Company, directly or indirectly, any goods or merchandise, nor have any portion or part therein, on forfeiture by those who shall be found to have acted to the contrary of one year's commissions for the use of the poor and on pain of being deposed from their directorship.

XXXII. The directors shall be obliged to give notice, by posting of bills, as often as they have a fresh importation of goods and merchandise, to the end that every one may have seasonable knowledge of it before they proceed to a final sale.

XXXIII. And if it should happen that in one Chamber or another any of the directors should get into such a situation that he could not make good what was entrusted to him for his administration and in consequence thereof any loss should occur, said loss shall be charged against the money which such directors have in the Company, which [investment] is also especially pledged for their ad-

ministration; the same shall also be the case as to all the participants who, on account of goods purchased or otherwise, shall become debtors to the Company, and to all intents it shall be reckoned as if the money which they put in had from the beginning been counterbalanced and wiped out by what they owe the Company.

XXXIV. The directors of the respective Chambers shall be responsible for their cashiers and bookkeepers.

XXXV. That all the goods of this Company which shall be disposed of by weight shall be sold by one standard of weight, to wit, that of the weight of Amsterdam; and that all such goods may be sold on board ship, or in store, without paying any excise, impost or weigh money; provided that, once being sold, they shall not be delivered in any other way than at the Weigh-house and that the impost and weigh money shall be paid as often as they are alienated in the same manner as other goods subject to weigh money.

XXXVI. That the persons or goods of the directors shall not be arrested, attached or encumbered in order to obtain from them an account of the administration of the Company nor for the payment of the salaries or wages of those whom they have employed in the service of the Company; but those who wish to make any such demands upon them must bring the matter before the ordinary judges.

XXXVII. Whenever any ship shall return from a voyage, the admirals or commanders of the fleets, ship or ships shall be obliged to come and report to us the success of the voyage within ten days after their arrival and shall make out and deliver a report in writing, if the case requires it.

XXXVIII. And if it should happen (which we by no means expect) that any one ventured to injure or hinder in any way the navigation, commerce, trade or traffic of this Company, contrary to the common law or to the contents of the aforesaid treaties, leagues and covenants, they shall have the right to protect themselves against such actions and shall govern themselves according to the instructions to be issued by us concerning them.

XXXIX. We have, moreover, promised, and do promise, that we will maintain and defend this Company against every person in [their rights of] free navigation and trade, and to that end will assist them with a sum of ten hundred thousand guilders, to be paid in five years, whereof the first two hundred thousand guilders shall be paid them when the first payment shall be made by the participants; provided, that we, with half the aforesaid ten hundred thousand guilders, shall receive and bear profit and risk in the same manner as the other participants of this Company.

XL. And if by a powerful and continued obstruction of the aforesaid navigation and trade, the affairs within the limits of this Company should be brought to a state of open war, we will, if the situation of this country will in any wise admit of it, give them for their assistance sixteen ships of war, the smallest one of one hundred and fifty lasts burden, with four good, well-sailing yachts, the smallest of forty lasts burden, which shall be properly mounted and provided in all respects, both with brass and other cannon, and a proper quantity of ammunition, together with double suits of running and standing rigging, sails, cables, anchors and other things thereto belonging, such as are proper to be provided and used in all great expeditions; upon condition that they shall be manned, victualed and supported at the expense of the Company and that the Company shall be obliged to add thereto sixteen like ships of war and four yachts, mounted and provided as above, to be used in like manner for the defense of trade and all exploits of war; provided that all the ships of war and merchantmen (which likewise shall be provided and manned as is fitting) shall be under an admiral appointed by us after previous advice of the aforesaid general Assembly and shall obey our commands, together with the resolutions of the Company, and if need be, shall be used together for purposes of war, in such manner, however, that the merchantmen shall not unnecessarily hazard their lading.

XLI. And if it should happen that the country should be greatly eased of its burdens and that this Company should be put to the heavy charges of war, we have further promised, and do promise, to increase the aforesaid subsidy in such manner as the situation of this country will permit and the affairs of the Company shall require.

XLII. We have moreover ordained that in case of war all the prizes which may be taken from enemies and pirates within the aforesaid limits by the Company or those who have been sent to its assistance; also the goods which shall be seized by virtue of our proclamations—after deducting all necessary expenses and the damage which the Company may have suffered in taking each prize, together with the dues of His Excellency as admiral in chief agreeable to our resolution to that effect adopted on the first of April, sixteen hundred and two, and the tenth part for the officers, sailors and soldiers who have taken the prize—shall remain at the disposal of the directors of the aforesaid Company; provided that the account of them shall be kept separate and distinct from the account of trade and commerce, that the net proceeds of the said prizes shall be employed in fitting out ships, paying the troops, fortifications, garrisons and like matters of war and defense, by sea and land, and that there shall be no distribution unless the said proceeds shall amount to so much that a notable share may be distributed without weakening the said defense and after paying the expenses of the war, which distribution shall be made separately and apart from that on account of trade; and the distribution shall be made, one tenth part for the use of the United Netherlands and the remainder for the participants of this Company, in exact proportion to their invested capital.

XLIII. Provided, however, that all the prizes and goods taken by virtue of our proclamations shall be brought and tried before the council of the admiralty of the district to which they are brought, that it may take cognizance of them and determine the legality or illegality of the said prizes, the administration of the goods brought in remaining, nevertheless, with the Company, pending the process, and that under a proper inventory, and saving to those who might be injured by the sentence of the admiralty the right of appeal, agreeable to the instructions given the admiralty; provided that the vendue masters and other officers of the admiralty shall neither receive nor claim any fees from prizes which shall be sold for the benefit of this Company and in [connection with] which they are not employed.

XLIV. The directors of this Company shall solemnly promise and swear that they will act well and faithfully in their administration and render good and just accounts of their transactions; that they will in all things consult the greatest profit of the Company and, as much as possible, prevent its meeting with losses; that they will not give the greatest participant any greater advantage in the payments or distribution of money than the least; that, in collecting and receiving outstanding debts, they will not excuse one more than another; that they, for their own account, will invest, and during the continuance of their administration will continue the investment of all such sums of money as by this charter are stipulated; and moreover, that they will, as far as concerns them, to the utmost of their power, observe and keep all and every the particulars and articles herein contained.

XLV. All of which privileges, freedoms and exemptions, together with the assistance above mentioned, in all their points and articles, we have granted, allowed, promised and pledged to the aforesaid Company, and do hereby grant, allow and pledge with full knowledge of the matter, promising to allow them to enjoy the same quietly and peaceably. We likewise order that the same shall be kept and observed by all magistrates, officers and subjects of these United Netherlands and that they shall not do anything contrary to the same directly or indirectly, either within or without the said United Netherlands, upon pain of being punished therefore both in person and property as disturbers of the common welfare of this country and transgressors of our ordinance. We further promise that we will maintain and uphold the Company in the contents of this our charter, by all treaties of peace, alliances and covenants with the neighboring princes, kingdoms and countries, without suffering anything to be done or transacted that might tend to diminish its value. Wherefore we expressly charge and command all governors, justiciaries, officers, magistrates and inhabitants of these United Netherlands to permit and suffer the Company and its directors to enjoy quietly and peaceably all the benefits of this charter, license and privilege, ceasing all opposition and obstruction to it. And in

order that none may pretend ignorance of this, we have ordered a summary of the contents of this charter to be publicly proclaimed and placarded wherever necessary, for we have found this to be for the best interests of the country. Given under our great seal, paraph and the signature of our secretary, at the Hague, on the third day of the month of June, in the year sixteen hundred and twenty-one.

Was paraphed, *I. Magnus*

By order of the aforesaid Honorable Lords the States General.

C. Aersscn

[Having a seal pendent of red wax, on a cord of white silk.]

REVIEW QUESTIONS

1. Why did the West India Company receive a charter from the Dutch Republic?
2. How is the company structured? What does that structure tell you about its decision making?
3. Why does the company wish to exercise a monopoly?
4. What unusual powers are granted to the company to protect its monopoly?
5. Does the company suffer from any obvious weaknesses in its organization?
6. Given the content of this charter, how would you describe the relationship between trade and politics?

Credits

Photo Credits

Chapter 1: p. 23 (top) Erich Lessing/Art Resource; (bottom) Giraudon/Art Resource; Chapter 2: p. 61 Erich Lessing/Art Resource; Chapter 3: p. 122 University of Pennsylvannia Museum neg. #S8-120800; Chapter 4: p. 145 Art Resource; Chapter 5: p. 176 The British Museum; Chapter 6: p. 195 The Bridgeman Art Library International; Chapter 7: p. 222 (top) Archivo Iconografico, S.A./Corbis; (bottom) Archivo Iconografico, S.A./Corbis; Chapter 8: p. 256 Berig/Wikimedia Commons; p. 257 Berig/Wikimedia Commons; Chapter 9: p. 298 (left) Foto Marburg/Art Resource, NY; (right) Foto Marburg/Art Resource, NY; Chapter 10: p. 322 (top & bottom) Alinari/Art Resource; Chapter 11: p. 386 University of Utah Press; Chapter 12: p. 396 Milan, Ambrosiana—Anatomical Notebooks; p. 402 Scala/Art Resource; Chapter 13: p. 426 BPK BERLIN/Kupferstichkabinett, SMB/J´rg P. Anders/Art Resource, NY; p. 431 AISA/Everett Collection; Chapter 14: p. 466 (top) Josie Piller and Debra Doty, University Art Gallery, University of Pittsburgh, (middle) Bettmann/Corbis, (bottom) Josie Piller and Debra Doty, University Art Gallery, University of Pittsburgh; p. 478 The Gallery Collection/Corbis; Chapter 15: p. 500 PHGCOM/WIKIMEDIA COMMONS; p. 505 Giraudon/Art Resource

Text Credits

Ibn al-Athir: "Arab Account of the Crusade" From *Arab Historians of the Crusades*, Arabic sources translated by Francesco Gabrielli, translated from the Italian by E. J. Costello. Copyright © 1969 by Routledge & Kegan Paul Ltd. Published by the University of California Press. Reprinted by permission of the University of California Press.

Leon B. Alberti: Reprinted by permission of Waveland Press, Inc. from Alberti, *The Family in Renaissance Florence, Book Three: I Libri Della Famiglia*, translated by Renee Neu Watkins. (Long Grove, IL: Waveland Press, Inc., 1994). All rights reserved.

Ahmed Ali: From *Al-Quran: A Contemporary Translation*, by Ahmed Ali (Karashi, Pakistan: Akrash Publishing). Copyright © 1995, Akrash Publishing. We have made diligent efforts to contact the copyright holder to obtain permission to reprint this selection. If you have information that would help us, please write to Permissions Department, W. W. Norton & Company, Inc., 500 Fifth Avenue, New York, NY 10110.

Dante Alighieri: "Canto V, Circle Two: The Carnal," pp. 25–28. From *The Divine Comedy* by Dante Alighieri, translated by John Ciardi. Copyright 1954, 1957, 1959, 1960, 1961, 1965, 1967, 1970 by the Ciardi Family Publishing Trust. Used by permission of W.W. Norton & Company, Inc.

American Bible Society: Scripture taken from the Contemporary English Version © 1991, 1992, 1995 by American Bible Society, Used by Permission.

W.P. Barrett: From *The Trial of Jeanne d'Arc*, edited and translated by W.P. Barrett, Copyright © 1931 by Routledge. Reproduced by permission of Taylor & Francis Books UK.

Gary Beckman (trans.): "Letters from the Hittite Queen to Ramesses II." From *Hittite Diplomatic Texts, 2nd Edition*, SBL Writings from The Ancient World Series. Pp. 132–135. Reprinted by permission of the Society for Biblical Literature.

Ibn Battuta: From *The Travels of Ibn Battuta, A.D. 1325–1354*, edited and translated by H.A.R. Gibb (London: Hakluyt Society, 1958), pp. 41–53. Reprinted by permission.

Jean Bodin: From *On Sovereignty*, pp. 46-50. Copyright © Cambridge University Press 1992. Reprinted with the permission of Cambridge University Press.

S.A.J. Bradley (ed.): "Anglo-Saxon translation of Genesis" *From Anglo-Saxon Poetry: An Anthology of Old English Poems in Prose Translations* with Introduction and Headnotes, by S. A. J. Bradley, pp. 25–32. Copyright © 1982 New York: Everyman's Library.

Catherine the Great: "Proposals for a New Code of Law" From *Documents of Catherine the Great: The Correspondence with Voltaire and the Instruction of 1767 in the English Text of 1768*, translated by W. F. Reddaway. Copyright © 1931 Cambridge University Press. Reprinted with permission from Cambridge University Press.

Geoffrey Chaucer: From *The Canterbury Tales: Nine Tales and the General Prologue: A Norton Critical Edition* by Geoffrey Chaucer, edited by V.A. Kolve and Glending Olson, pp. 192–207. Copyright © 1989 by W.W. Norton & Company. Used by permission of W.W. Norton & Company, Inc.

Robert Chazan: "Anonymous Mainz Account," *European Jewry and the First Crusade* by Robert Chazan, pp. 225–242. © 1987 Regents of the University of California. Published by the University of California Press. Reprinted by permission of the publisher.

Cicero: Reprinted by permission of the publishers and the Trustees of the Loeb Classical Library from *Cicero: Volume XVI – De Republica/De Legibus*, Loeb Classical Library Vol. 213, translated by Clinton W. Keyes, pp. 311–323, 329–339, 381–391 (odd), Cambridge, Mass.: Harvard University Press, Copyright © 1928, by the President and Fellows of Harvard College, The Loeb Classical Library ® is a registered trademark of the President and Fellows of Harvard College.

Christopher Columbus: "The First Voyage of Christopher Columbus," *Selected Documents Illustrating the Four Voyages of Columbus, Vol. 1*, edited and translated by Cecil Jane, The Hakluyt Society, 1930. Reprinted by permission of David Higham Associates, Ltd.

Columella: From "The Twelve Tables" and "Management of a Large Estate," *Roman Civilization, Selected Readings, Vol. 2*, ed. Lewis & Reinhold, pp. 54–67. Reprinted by permission of Columbia University Press.

Praise for On The Shoulders of Giant,
selected as an Amazon Top 10 Science Book

"World-renowned physicist and best-selling author Stephen Hawking presents a revolutionary look at the momentous discoveries that changed our
perception of the world with this first-ever compilation of seven classic
works on physics and astronomy. His choice of landmark writings by some
of the world's great thinkers traces the brilliant evolution of modern science
and shows how each figure built upon the genius of his predecessors."
— Review in the Amazon Top 10 Science Announcement

"Acclaimed physicist Hawking has collected in this single illuminating
volume the classic works of physics and astronomy that in their day
revolutionized humankind's perceptions of the world . . . Taken together,
these writings document the evolution of our conception of the universe
from a pre-Copernican cosmos with a stationary earth at its center to one
in which the very wave of time and space are relative . . . In an essay introducing each work, he gives a short and sweet biography of its author and
an explanation of its significance, as well as the occasional gem, like
Galileo's handwritten renunciation of his beliefs before the Inquisition. To
read the works themselves is to feel the thrill and mystery of intimacy with
oft-cited documents. Despite the volume's heftiness, Hawking has given
these works a setting that is elegantly simple, effectively broadening."
—*Publishers Weekly*

"The [essays] provide useful historical and personal context for rediscover-
ing path-working, and affirm that modern scientific achievement is the
result of our ability to perceive the universe from our perspective—
standing on the shoulders of giants-atop-giants."
—Fred Bortz, *Dallas Morning News* special correspondent

"At 1,264 pages, this book is heavy in a lot of ways—but it's also an
eminently authoritative and readable text for anyone with an
interest in the universe around us."
—Hilary Davidson, in the *Sunday Boulder Camera*

"This single volume allows readers to see thoughts and ideas on the structure of the universe flowed from one scientific era to another . . . Summing Up: Highly recommended."
—J. R. Kraus, University of Denver, in *Choice*

"Wow! That's the only word I can think of to describe this book. That rating means that in my opinion there is no way it could be improved upon. It is a work of art."
—Barry Newbold, who rated it a 10 on a scale of 10 in his review for the *Northern Advocate*

"[On the Shoulders of Giants] is a massive, well-bound tome. If you could take only one book to a desert island, this would be enough to keep you thinking for the rest of your life."
—Hugh McCarroll in the *Sunday Star Times*

ON THE
SHOULDERS
of
GIANTS

THE GREAT WORKS OF PHYSICS AND ASTRONOMY

EDITED, WITH COMMENTARY, BY

STEPHEN
HAWKING

RUNNING PRESS
PHILADELPHIA • LONDON

Library of Congress Cataloging-in-Publication Number 2002100441
ISBN-13: 978-0-7624-1698-1
ISBN-10: 0-7624-1698-X

Author photo courtesy of Book Laboratory
Cover and Interior design: Bill Jones
Editor: Deborah Grandinetti
Typography: Scribe

Text of *On the Revolutions of Heavenly Spheres* courtesy
of Annapolis: St. John's Bookstore, ©1939.
Text of *Harmonies of the World* courtesy of Annapolis:
St. John's Bookstore, ©1939.
Text of *Dialogues Concerning Two New Sciences* courtesy of Dover Publications.
Text of *Principia* and *System of the World* courtesy of
New York: Daniel Adee, ©1848.
Selections from *The Principle of Relativity: A Collection
of Papers on the Special and General Theory of Relativity*,
courtesy of Dover Publications.

This book may be ordered by mail from the publisher.
Please include $2.50 for postage and handling.
But try your bookstore first!

Running Press Book Publishers
2300 Chestnut Street Suite 200
Philadelphia, PA 19103-4371

Visit us on the web!
www.runningpress.com

Contents

G

A NOTE ON THE TEXTS

The texts in this book are based on translations of the original, printed editions. We have made no attempt to modernize the authors' own distinct usage, spelling or punctuation, or to make the texts consistent with each other in this regard. Here are other relevant details:

On the Revolutions of Heavenly Spheres, by Nicolaus Copernicus, was first published in 1543 under the title *De revolutionibus orbium colestium*. This translation is by Charles Glen Wallis.

Dialogues Concerning Two New Sciences, by Galileo Galilei, was originally published in 1638 under the title *Discorsi e Dimostrazioni Matematiche, intorno à due nuoue scienze*, by the Dutch publish Louis Elzevir. Our text is based on the translation by Henry Crew and Alfonso deSalvio.

We have selected Book Five of the five-book *Harmonies of the World* by Johannes Kepler. Kepler completed the work in the spring of 1618, publishing it under the title, *Harmonices Mundi*. This translation is by Charles Glen Wallis.

The Principia, by Isaac Newton, was originally published in 1687 under the title of *Philosophiae naturalis principia mathematica* (*The Mathematical Principles of Natural Philosophy*). This translation is by Andrew Motte.

We haven chosen seven works by Albert Einstein from *The Principles of Relativity: A Collection of Original Papers on the Special Theory of Relativity*, by H.A. Lorentz, A. Einstein, H. Minkowski and H. Weyl. The entire collection was originally published in German, under the title "Des Relativitatsprinzip" in 1922. Our text comes from the translation by W. Perrett and G.B. Jeffery.

The Editors

INTRODUCTION

IF I HAVE SEEN FARTHER, IT IS BY STANDING ON THE SHOULDERS OF GIANTS, WROTE ISAAC NEWTON IN A LETTER TO ROBERT HOOKE IN 1676. ALTHOUGH NEWTON WAS REFERRING TO HIS DISCOVERIES IN OPTICS RATHER THAN HIS MORE IMPORTANT WORK ON GRAVITY AND THE LAWS OF MOTION, IT IS AN APT COMMENT ON HOW SCIENCE, AND INDEED THE WHOLE OF CIVILIZATION, IS A SERIES OF INCREMENTAL ADVANCES, EACH BUILDING ON WHAT WENT BEFORE. THIS IS THE THEME OF THIS FASCINATING VOLUME, WHICH USES THE ORIGINAL TEXTS TO TRACE THE EVOLUTION OF OUR PICTURE OF THE HEAVENS FROM THE REVOLUTIONARY CLAIM OF NICOLAUS COPERNICUS THAT THE EARTH ORBITS THE SUN TO THE EQUALLY REVOLUTIONARY PROPOSAL OF ALBERT EINSTEIN THAT SPACE AND TIME ARE CURVED AND WARPED BY MASS AND ENERGY. IT IS A COMPELLING STORY BECAUSE BOTH COPERNICUS AND EINSTEIN HAVE BROUGHT ABOUT PROFOUND CHANGES IN WHAT WE SEE AS OUR POSITION IN THE ORDER OF THINGS. GONE IS OUR PRIVILEGED PLACE AT THE CENTER OF THE UNIVERSE, GONE ARE ETERNITY AND CERTAINTY, AND GONE ARE ABSOLUTE SPACE AND TIME TO BE REPLACED BY RUBBER SHEETS.

IT IS NO WONDER BOTH THEORIES ENCOUNTERED VIOLENT OPPOSITION: THE INQUISITION IN THE CASE OF THE COPERNICAN THEORY AND THE NAZIS IN THE CASE OF RELATIVITY. WE NOW HAVE A TENDENCY

TO DISMISS AS PRIMITIVE THE EARLIER WORLD PICTURE OF ARISTOTLE AND PTOLEMY IN WHICH THE EARTH WAS AT THE CENTER AND THE SUN WENT ROUND IT. HOWEVER WE SHOULD NOT BE TOO SCORNFUL OF THEIR MODEL, WHICH WAS ANYTHING BUT SIMPLE-MINDED. IT INCORPORATED ARISTOTLE'S DEDUCTION THAT THE EARTH IS A ROUND BALL RATHER THAN A FLAT PLATE AND IT WAS REASONABLY ACCURATE IN ITS MAIN FUNCTION, THAT OF PREDICTING THE APPARENT POSITIONS OF THE HEAVENLY BODIES IN THE SKY FOR ASTROLOGICAL PURPOSES. IN FACT, IT WAS ABOUT AS ACCURATE AS THE HERETICAL SUGGESTION PUT FOR-WARD IN 1543 BY COPERNICUS THAT THE EARTH AND THE PLANETS MOVED IN CIRCULAR ORBITS AROUND THE SUN.

GALILEO FOUND COPERNICUS' PROPOSAL CON-VINCING NOT BECAUSE IT BETTER FIT THE OBSERVA-TIONS OF PLANETARY POSITIONS BUT BECAUSE OF ITS SIMPLICITY AND ELEGANCE, IN CONTRAST TO THE COMPLICATED EPICYCLES OF THE PTOLEMAIC MODEL. IN *DIALOGUES CONCERNING TWO SCIENCES*, GALILEO'S CHARACTERS, SALVIATI AND SAGREDO, PUT FORWARD PERSUASIVE ARGUMENTS IN SUPPORT OF COPERNICUS. YET, IT WAS STILL POSSIBLE FOR HIS THIRD CHARACTER, SIMPLICIO, TO DEFEND ARISTOTLE AND PTOLEMY AND TO MAINTAIN THAT IN REALITY THE EARTH WAS AT REST AND THE SUN WENT ROUND THE EARTH.

IT WAS NOT UNTIL KEPLER'S WORK MADE THE SUN-CENTERED MODEL MORE ACCURATE AND NEWTON GAVE IT LAWS OF MOTION THAT THE EARTH-

CENTERED PICTURE FINALLY LOST ALL CREDIBILITY. IT WAS QUITE A SHIFT IN OUR VIEW OF THE UNIVERSE: IF WE ARE NOT AT THE CENTER, IS OUR EXISTENCE OF ANY IMPORTANCE? WHY SHOULD GOD OR THE LAWS OF NATURE CARE ABOUT WHAT HAPPENS ON THE THIRD ROCK FROM THE SUN, WHICH IS WHERE COPERNICUS HAS LEFT US? MODERN SCIENTISTS HAVE OUT-COPERNICUSED COPERNICUS BY SEEKING AN ACCOUNT OF THE UNIVERSE IN WHICH MAN (IN THE OLD PRE-POLITICALLY CORRECT SENSE) PLAYED NO ROLE. ALTHOUGH THIS APPROACH HAS SUCCEEDED IN FINDING OBJECTIVE IMPERSONAL LAWS THAT GOVERN THE UNIVERSE, IT HAS NOT (SO FAR AT LEAST) EXPLAINED WHY THE UNIVERSE IS THE WAY IT IS RATHER THAN BEING ONE OF THE MANY OTHER POSSIBLE UNIVERSES THAT WOULD ALSO BE CONSISTENT WITH THE LAWS.

SOME SCIENTISTS WOULD CLAIM THAT THIS FAILURE IS ONLY PROVISIONAL, THAT WHEN WE FIND THE ULTIMATE UNIFIED THEORY, IT WILL UNIQUELY PRESCRIBE THE STATE OF THE UNIVERSE, THE STRENGTH OF GRAVITY, THE MASS AND CHARGE OF THE ELECTRON AND SO ON. HOWEVER, MANY FEATURES OF THE UNIVERSE (LIKE THE FACT THAT WE ARE ON THE THIRD ROCK, RATHER THAN THE SECOND OR FOURTH) SEEM ARBITRARY AND ACCIDENTAL AND NOT THE PREDICTIONS OF A MASTER EQUATION. MANY PEOPLE (MYSELF INCLUDED) FEEL THAT THE APPEARANCE OF SUCH A COMPLEX AND STRUCTURED UNIVERSE FROM SIMPLE LAWS REQUIRES THE INVOCATION OF SOMETHING CALLED THE ANTHROPIC PRINCIPLE, WHICH RESTORES

US TO THE CENTRAL POSITION WE HAVE BEEN TOO MODEST TO CLAIM SINCE THE TIME OF COPERNICUS. THE ANTHROPIC PRINCIPLE IS BASED ON THE SELF-EVIDENT FACT THAT WE WOULDN'T BE ASKING QUESTIONS ABOUT THE NATURE OF THE UNIVERSE IF THE UNIVERSE HADN'T CONTAINED STARS, PLANETS AND STABLE CHEMICAL COMPOUNDS, AMONG OTHER PREREQUISITES OF (INTELLIGENT?) LIFE AS WE KNOW IT. IF THE ULTIMATE THEORY MADE A UNIQUE PREDICTION FOR THE STATE OF THE UNIVERSE AND ITS CONTENTS, IT WOULD BE A REMARKABLE COINCIDENCE THAT THIS STATE WAS IN THE SMALL SUBSET THAT ALLOWS LIFE.

HOWEVER THE WORK OF THE LAST THINKER IN THIS VOLUME, ALBERT EINSTEIN, RAISES A NEW POSSIBILITY. EINSTEIN PLAYED AN IMPORTANT ROLE IN THE DEVELOPMENT OF QUANTUM THEORY WHICH SAYS THAT A SYSTEM DOESN'T JUST HAVE A SINGLE HISTORY AS ONE MIGHT HAVE THOUGHT. RATHER IT HAS EVERY POSSIBLE HISTORY WITH SOME PROBABILITY. EINSTEIN WAS ALSO ALMOST SOLELY RESPONSIBLE FOR THE GENERAL THEORY OF RELATIVITY IN WHICH SPACE AND TIME ARE CURVED AND BECOME DYNAMIC. THIS MEANS THAT THEY ARE SUBJECT TO QUANTUM THEORY AND THAT THE UNIVERSE ITSELF HAS EVERY POSSIBLE SHAPE AND HISTORY. MOST OF THESE HISTORIES WILL BE QUITE UNSUITABLE FOR THE DEVELOPMENT OF LIFE BUT A VERY FEW HAVE ALL THE CONDITIONS NEEDED. IT DOESN'T MATTER IF THESE FEW HAVE A VERY LOW PROBABILITY RELATIVE TO THE OTHERS: THE LIFELESS UNIVERSES WILL HAVE NO ONE TO OBSERVE THEM. IT IS

SUFFICIENT THAT THERE IS AT LEAST ONE HISTORY IN WHICH LIFE DEVELOPS, AND WE OURSELVES ARE EVIDENCE FOR THAT, THOUGH MAYBE NOT FOR INTELLIGENCE. NEWTON SAID HE WAS "*STANDING ON THE SHOULDERS OF GIANTS.*" BUT AS THIS VOLUME ILLUSTRATES SO WELL, OUR UNDERSTANDING DOESN'T ADVANCE JUST BY SLOW AND STEADY BUILDING ON PREVIOUS WORK. SOMETIMES AS WITH COPERNICUS AND EINSTEIN, WE HAVE TO MAKE THE INTELLECTUAL LEAP TO A NEW WORLD PICTURE. MAYBE NEWTON SHOULD HAVE SAID, "*I USED THE SHOULDERS OF GIANTS AS A SPRINGBOARD.*"

Nicolaus Copernicus

(1473-1543)

HIS LIFE AND WORK

Nicolaus Copernicus, a sixteenth-century Polish priest and mathematician, is often referred to as the founder of modern astronomy. That credit goes to him because he was the first to conclude that the planets and Sun did not revolve around the earth. Certainly there was speculation that a heliocentric—or sun-centered—universe had existed as far back as Aristarchus (d. 230 B.C.), but the idea was not seriously considered before Copernicus. Yet to understand the contributions of Copernicus, it is important to consider the religious and cultural implications of scientific discovery in his time.

As far back as the fourth century B.C., the Greek thinker and philosopherAristotle (384-322 B.C.) devised a planetary system in his book, *On the Heavens, (De Caelo)* and concluded that because the Earth's shadow on the Moon during eclipses was always round, the world was spherical in shape rather than flat. He also surmised the Earth was round because when one watched a ship sail out to sea one noticed that the hull disappeared over the horizon before the sails did.

In Aristotle's geocentric vision, the earth was stationary and the planets Mercury, Venus, Mars, Jupiter, and Saturn, as well as the sun and the moon performed circular orbits around the earth. Aristotle also believed the stars were fixed to the celestial sphere, and his scale of the universe purported these fixed stars to be not much further beyond the orbit of Saturn. He believed in perfect circular motions and had good evidence to

1

believe the earth to be at rest. A stone dropped from a tower fell straight down. It did not fall to the west, as we would expect it to do if the earth rotated from west to east. (Aristotle did not consider that the stone might partake in the Earth's rotation). In an attempt to combine physics with the metaphysical, Aristotle devised his theory of a "prime mover," which held that a mystical force behind the fixed stars caused the circular motions he observed. This model of the universe was accepted and embraced by theologians, who often interpreted prime movers as angels, and Aristotle's vision endured for centuries. Many modern scholars believe universal acceptance of this theory by religious authorities hindered the progress of science, as to challenge Aristotle's theories was to call into question the authority of the church itself.

Five centuries after Aristotlels death, an Egyptian named Claudius Ptolemaeus (Ptolemy, 87-150 A.D.), created a model for the universe that more accurately predicted the movements and actions of spheres in the heavens. Like Aristotle, Ptolemy believed the earth was stationary. Objects fell to the center of the earth, he reasoned, because the earth must be fixed at the center of the universe. Ptolemy ultimately elaborated a system in which the celestial bodies moved around the circumference of their own epicycles (a circle in which a planet moves and which has a center that is itself carried around at the same time on the circumference of a larger circle. To accomplish this, he put the Earth slightly off center of the universe and called this new center the "equant"—an imaginary point that helped him account for observable planetary movements. By custom designing the sizes of circles, Ptolemy was better able to predict the motions of celestial bodies. Western Christendom had little quarrel with Ptolemy's geocentric system, which left room in the universe behind the fixed stars to accommodate a heaven and a hell, and so the church adopted the Ptolemaic model of the universe as truth.

Aristotle and Ptolemy's picture of the cosmos reigned, with few significant modifications, for well over a thousand years. It wasn't until 1514 that the Polish priest Nicolaus Copernicus revived the heliocentric model of the universe. Copernicus proposed it merely as a model for calculating planetary positions because he was concerned that the church might label him a heretic if he proposed it as a description of reality. Copernicus became convinced, through his own study of planetary motions, that the earth was merely another planet and the sun was the center of the universe. This hypothesis became known as a heliocentric model. Copernicus' breakthrough marked one of the greatest paradigm shifts in world history, opening the way to modern astronomy and broadly affecting science, philosophy and religion. The elderly priest was hesitant to divulge his theory, lest it provoke church authorities to any angry response, and so he withheld his work from all but a few astronomers. Copernicus' landmark *De Revolutionibus* was published while he was on his deathbed, in 1543. He

did not live long enough to witness the chaos his heliocentric theory would cause.

Copernicus was born on February 19, 1473 in Torun, Poland, into a family of merchants and municipal officials who placed a high priority on education. His uncle, Lukasz Watzenrode, prince-bishop of Ermland, ensured that his nephew received the best academic training available in Poland. In 1491, Copernicus enrolled at Cracow University, where he pursued a course of general studies for four years before traveling to Italy to study law and medicine, as was common practice among Polish elites at the time. While studying at the University of Bologna (where he would eventually become a professor of astronomy), Copernicus boarded at the home of Domenico Maria de Novara, the renowned mathematician of whom Copernicus would ultimately become a disciple. Novara was a critic of Ptolemy, whose second-century astronomy he regarded with skepticism. In November 1500, Copernicus observed a lunar eclipse in Rome. Although he spent the next few years in Italy studying medicine, he never lost his passion for astronomy.

After receiving the degree of Doctor of Canon Law, Copernicus practiced medicine at the episcopal court of Heilsberg, where his uncle lived. Royalty and high clergy requested his medical services, but Copernicus spent most of his time in service of the poor. In 1503, he returned to Poland and moved into his uncle's bishopric palace in Lidzbark Warminski. There he tended to the administrative matters of the diocese, as well as serving as an advisor to his uncle. After his uncle's death in 1512, Copernicus moved permanently to Frauenburg and would spend the rest of his life in priestly service. But the man who was a scholar in mathematics, medicine and theology was only beginning the work for which he would become best known.

In March of 1513, Copernicus purchased 800 building stones, and a barrel of lime from his chapter so that he could build an observation tower. There, he made use of astronomical instruments such as quadrants, parallactics and astrolabes to observe the sun, moon and stars. The following year, he wrote a brief *Commentary on the Theories of the Motions of Heavenly Objects from Their Arrangements* (*De hypothesibus motuum coelestium a se constitutis commentariolus*), but he refused to publish the manuscript and only discreetly circulated it among his most trusted friends. The *Commentary* was a first attempt to propound an astronomical theory that the earth moves and the sun remains at rest. Copernicus had become dissatisfied with the Aristotelian-Ptolemaic astronomical system that had dominated Western thought for centuries. The center of the earth, he thought, was not the center of the universe, but merely the center of the Moon's orbit. Copernicus had come to believe that apparent perturbations in the observable motion of the planets was a result of the earth's own rotation around its axis and of its travel in orbit. "We revolve around the Sun," he concluded in *Commentary*, "like any other planet.

Despite speculation about a sun-centered universe as far back as the third century B.C. by Aristarchus, theologians and intellectuals felt more comfortable with a geocentric theory, and the premise was barely challenged in earnest. Copernicus prudently abstained from disclosing any of his views in public, preferring to develop his ideas quietly by exploring mathematical calculations and drawing elaborate diagrams, and to keep his theories from circulating outside of a select group of friends. When, in 1514, Pope Leo X summoned Bishop Paul of Fossombrone to recruit Copernicus to offer an opinion on reforming the ecclesiastical calendar, the Polish astronomer replied that knowledge of the motions of the sun and moon in relation to the length of the year was insufficient to have any bearing on reform. The challenge must have preoccupied Copernicus, however, for he later wrote to Pope Paul III, the same Pope who commissioned Michaelangelo to paint the Sistine Chapel, with some relevant observations, which later served to form the foundation of the Gregorian calendar seventy years later.

Still, Copernicus feared exposing himself to the contempt of the populace and the church, and he spent years working privately to amend and expand the *Commentary*. The result was *On the Revolutions of Heavenly Spheres (De Revolutionibus Orbium Coelestium)* which he completed in 1530, but withheld from publication for thirteen years. The risk of the church's condemnation was not, however, the only reason for Copernicus' hesitancy to publish. Copernicus was a perfectionist and considered his observations in constant need of verification and revision. He continued to lecture on these principles of his planetary theory, even appearing before Pope Clement VII, who approved of his work. In 1536, Clement formally requested that Copernicus publish his theories. But it took a former pupil, 25-year-old Georg Joachim Rheticus of Germany, who relinquished his chair in mathematics in Wittenberg so that he could study under Copernicus, to persuade his master to publish *On the Revolutions*. In 1540, Rheticus assisted in the editing of the work and presented the manuscript to a Lutheran printer in Nuremberg, ultimately giving birth to the Copernican Revolution.

When *On the Revolutuons* appeared in 1543, it was attacked by Protestant theologians who held the premise of a heliocentric universe to be unbiblical. Copernicus' theories, they reasoned, might lead people to believe that they are simply part of a natural order, and not the masters of nature, the center around which nature was ordered. Because of this clerical opposition, and perhaps also general incredulity at the prospect of a non-geocentric universe, between 1543 and 1600, fewer than a dozen scientists embraced Copernican theory. Still, Copernicus had done nothing to resolve the major problem facing any system in which the earth rotated on its axis (and revolved around the sun), namely, how it is that terrestrial bodies stay with the rotating Earth. The answer was proposed by Giordano Bruno, an Italian scientist and avowed Copernican, who suggested that space might have no boundaries and that the solar system might be

one of many such systems in the universe. Bruno also expanded on some purely speculative areas of astronomy that Copernicus did not explore in *On the Revolutions*. In his writings and lectures, the Italian scientist held that there were infinite worlds in the universe with intelligent life, some perhaps with beings superior to humans. Such audacity brought Bruno to the attention of the Inquisition, which tried and condemned him for his heretical beliefs. He was burned at the stake in 1600.

On the whole, however, the book did not have an immediate impact on modern astronomic study. In *On the Revolutions*, Copernicus did not actually put forth a heliocentric system, but rather a heliostatic one. He considered the Sun to be not precisely at the center of the universe, but only close to it, so as to account for variations in observable retrogression and brightness. The earth, he asserted, made one full rotation on its axis daily, and orbited around the sun once yearly. In the first section of the book's six sections, he took issue with the Ptolemaic system, which placed all heavenly bodies in orbit around the earth, and established the correct heliocentric order: Mercury, Venus, Mars, Jupiter and Saturn (the six planets known at the time). In the second section, Copernicus used mathematics (namely epicycles and equants) to explain the motions of the stars and planets, and reasoned that the sun's motion coincided with that of the earth. The third section gives a mathematical explanation of the precession of the equinoxes, which Copernicus attributes to the Earth's gyration around its axis. The remaining sections of *On the Revolutions* focus on the motions of the planets and the moon.

Copernicus was the first to position Venus and Mercury correctly, establishing with remarkable accuracy the order and distance of the known planets. He saw these two planets (Venus and Mercury) as being closer to the sun, and noticed that they revolved at a faster rate inside the Earth's orbit.

Before Copernicus, the sun was thought to be another planet. Placing the sun at the virtual center of the planetary system was the beginning of the Copernican revolution. By moving the Earth away from the center of the universe, where it was presumed to anchor all heavenly bodies, Copernicus was forced to address theories of gravity. Pre-Copernican gravitational explanations had posited a single center of gravity (the earth,) but Copernicus theorized that each heavenly body might have its own gravitational qualities and asserted that heavy objects everywhere tended toward their own center. This insight would eventually lead to the theory of universal gravitation, but its impact was not immediate.

By 1543, Copernicus had become paralyzed on his right side and weakened both physically and mentally. The man who was clearly a perfectionist had no choice but to surrender control of his manuscript, *On the Revolutions* , in the last stages of printing. He entrusted his student, George Rheticus with the manuscript, but when Rheticus

was forced to leave Nuremberg, the manuscript fell into the hands of Lutheran theologian Andreas Osiander. Osiander, hoping to appease advocates of the geocentric theory, made several alterations without Copernicus's knowledge and consent. Osiander placed the word "hypothesis" on the title page, deleted important passages, and added his own sentences which diluted the impact and certainty of the work. Copernicus was said to have received a copy of the printed book in Frauenburg on his deathbed, unaware of Osiander's revisions. His ideas lingered in relative obscurity for nearly one hundred years, but the seventeenth century would see men like Galileo Galilei, Johannes Kepler and Isaac Newton build on his theories of a heliocentric universe, effectively obliterating Aristotelian ideas. Many have written about the unassuming Polish priest who would change the way people saw the universe, but the German writer and scientist Johann Wolfgang von Goethe may have been the most eloquent when he wrote of the contributions of Copernicus:

> *Of all discoveries and opinions, none may have exerted a greater effect on the human spirit than the doctrine of Copernicus. The world had scarcely become known as round and complete in itself when it was asked to waive the tremendous privilege of being the center of the universe. Never, perhaps, was a greater demand made on mankind — for by this admission so many things vanished in mist and smoke! What became of Eden, our world of innocence, piety and poetry; the testimony of the senses; the conviction of a poetic-religious faith? No wonder his contemporaries did not wish to let all this go and offered every possible resistance to a doctrine which in its converts authorized and demanded a freedom of view and greatness of thought so far unknown, indeed not even dreamed of.*

> — *Johann Wolfgang von Goethe*

INTRODUCTION

To the Reader Concerning the Hypotheses of this Work[1]

[*b*][2] Since the newness of the hypotheses of this work—which sets the earth in motion and puts an immovable sun at the centre of the universe—has already received a great deal of publicity, I have no doubt that certain of the savants have taken grave offense and think it wrong to raise any disturbance among liberal disciplines which have had the right set-up for a long time now. If, however, they are willing to weigh the matter scrupulously, they will find that the author of this work has done nothing which merits blame. For it is the job of the astronomer to use painstaking and skilled observation in gathering together the history of the celestial movements, and then since he cannot by any line of reasoning reach the true causes of these movements—to think up or construct whatever causes or hypotheses he pleases such that, by the assumption of these causes, those same movements can be calculated from the principles of geometry for the past and for the future too. This artist is markedly outstanding in both of these respects: for it is not necessary that these hypotheses should be true, or even probably; but it is enough if they provide a calculus which fits the observations—unless by some chance there is anyone so ignorant of geometry and optics as to hold the epicycle of Venus as probable and to believe this to be a cause why Venus alternately precedes and follows the sun at an angular distance of up to 40° or more. For who does not see that it necessarily follows from this assumption that the diameter of the planet in its perigee should appear more than four times greater, and the body of the planet more than sixteen times greater, than in its apogee? Nevertheless the experience of all the ages is opposed to that.[3] There are also other things in this discipline which are just as absurd, but it is not necessary to examine them right now. For it is sufficiently clear that this art is absolutely and profoundly ignorant of the causes of the apparent irregular movements. And if it constructs and thinks up causes—and it has certainly thought up a good many—nevertheless it does not think them up in order to persuade anyone of their truth but only in order that they may provide a correct basis for calculation. But since for one and the same movement varying hypotheses are proposed

---

[1]This foreword, at first ascribed to Copernicus, is held to have been written by Andrew Osiander, a Lutheran theologian and friend of Copernicus, who saw the *De Revolutionibus* through the press.

[2]The numbers within the brackets refer to the pages of the first edition, published in 1543 at Nuremberg.

[3]Ptolemy makes Venus move on an epicycle the ratio of whose radius to the radius of the eccentric circle carrying the epicycle itself is nearly three to four. Hence the apparent magnitude of the planet would be expected to vary with the varying distance of the planet from the Earth, in the ratios stated by Osiander.

Moreover, it was found that, whenever the planet happened to be on the epicycle, the mean position of the sun appeared in line with *EPA*. And so, granted the ratios of epicycle and eccentric, Venus would never appear from the Earth to be at an angular distance of much more than 40° from the centre of her epicycle, that is to say, from the mean position of the sun, as it turned out by observation.

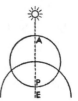

from time to time, as eccentricity or epicycle for the movement of the sun, the astronomer much prefers to take the one which is easiest to [i𝑖ᵃ] grasp. Maybe the philosopher demands probability instead; but neither of them will grasp anything certain or hand it on, unless it has been divinely revealed to him. Therefore let us permit these new hypotheses to make a public appearance among old ones which are themselves no more probable, especially since they are wonderful and easy and bring with them a vast storehouse of learned observations. And as far as hypotheses go, let no one expect anything in the way of certainty from astronomy, since astronomy can offer us nothing certain, lest, if anyone take as true that which has been constructed for another use, he go away from this discipline a bigger fool than when he came to it. Farewell.

PREFACE AND DEDICATION TO POPE PAUL III

[i𝑏] I can reckon easily enough, Most Holy Father, that as soon as certain people learn that in these books of mine which I have written about the revolutions of the spheres of the world I attribute certain motions to the terrestrial globe, they will immediately shout to have me and my opinion hooted off the stage. For my own works do not please me so much that I do not weigh what judgments others will pronounce concerning them. And although I realize that the conceptions of a philosopher are placed beyond the judgment of the crowd, because it is his loving duty to seek the truth in all things, in so far as God has granted that to human reason; nevertheless I think we should avoid opinions utterly foreign to rightness. And when I considered how absurd this "lecture" would be held by those who know that the opinion that the Earth rests immovable in the middle of the heavens as if their centre had been confirmed by the judgments of many ages—if I were to assert to the contrary that the Earth moves; for a long time I was in great difficulty as to whether I should bring to light my commentaries written to demonstrate the Earth's movement, or whether it would not be better to follow the example of the Pythagoreans and certain others who used to hand down the mysteries of their philosophy not in writing but by word of mouth and only to their relatives and friends—witness the letter of Lysis to Hipparchus. They however seem to me to have done that not, as some judge, out of a jealous unwillingness to communicate their doctrines but in order that things of very great beauty which have been investigated by the loving care of great men should not be scorned by those who find it a bother to expend any great energy on letters—except on the money-making variety—or who are provoked by the exhortations and examples of others to the liberal study of philosophy but on account of their natural [ii𝑎] stupidity hold the position among philosophers that drones hold among bees. Therefore, when I weighed these things in my mind, the scorn which I had to fear on account of the newness and absurdity of my opinion almost drove me to abandon a work already undertaken.

But my friends made me change my course in spite of my long-continued hesitation and even resistance. First among them was Nicholas Schonberg, Cardinal of Capua, a man distinguished in all branches of learning; next to him was my devoted friend Tiedeman Giese, Bishop of Culm, a man filled with the greatest zeal for the divine and liberal arts: for he in particular urged me frequently and even spurred me on by added reproaches into publishing this book and letting come to light a work which I had kept hidden among my things for not merely nine years, but for almost four times nine years. Not a few other learned and distinguished men demanded the same thing of me, urging me to refuse no longer—on account of the fear which I felt— to contribute my work to the common utility of those who are really interested in mathematics: they said that the absurder my teaching about the movement of the Earth now seems to very many persons, the more wonder and thanksgiving will it be the object of, when after the publication of my commentaries those same persons see the fog of absurdity dissipated by my luminous demonstrations. Accordingly I was led by such persuasion and by that hope finally to permit my friends to undertake the publication of a work which they had long sought from me.

But perhaps Your Holiness will not be so much surprised at my giving the results of my nocturnal study to the light—after having taken such care in working them out that I did not hesitate to put in writing my conceptions as to the movement of the Earth—as you will be eager to hear from me what came into my mind that in opposition to the general opinion of mathematicians and almost in opposition to common sense I should dare to imagine some movement of the Earth. And so I am unwilling to hide from Your Holiness that nothing except my knowledge that mathematicians have not agreed with one another in their researches moved me to think out a different scheme of drawing up the movements of the spheres of the world. For in the first place mathematicians are so uncertain about the movements of the sun and moon that they can neither demonstrate nor observe the unchanging magnitude of the [ii^b] revolving year. Then in setting up the solar and lunar movements and those of the other five wandering stars, they do not employ the same principles, assumptions, or demonstrations for the revolutions and apparent movements. For some make use of homocentric circles only, others of eccentric circles and epicycles, by means of which however they do not fully attain what they seek. For although those who have put their trust in homocentric circles have shown that various different movements can be composed of such circles, nevertheless they have not been able to establish anything for certain that would fully correspond to the phenomena. But even if those who have thought up eccentric circles seem to have been able for the most part to compute the apparent movements numerically by those means, they have in the meanwhile admitted a great deal which seems to contradict the first principles of regularity of movement. Moreover, they have

9

not been able to discover or to infer the chief point of all, *i.e.*, the form of the world and the certain commensurability of its parts. But they are in exactly the same fix as someone taking from different places hands, feet, head, and the other limbs—shaped very beautifully but not with reference to one body and without correspondence to one another—so that such parts made up a monster rather than a man. And so, in the process of demonstration which they call "method," they are found either to have omitted something necessary or to have admitted something foreign which by no means pertains to the matter; and they would by no means have been in this fix, if they had followed sure principles. For if the hypotheses they assumed were not false, everything which followed from the hypotheses would have been verified without fail; and though what I am saying may be obscure right now, nevertheless it will become clearer in the proper place.

Accordingly, when I had meditated upon this lack of certitude in the traditional mathematics concerning the composition of movements of the spheres of the world, I began to be annoyed that the philosophers, who in other respects had made a very careful scrutiny of the least details of the world, had discovered no sure scheme for the movements of the machinery of the world, which has been built for us by the Best and Most Orderly Workman of all. Wherefore I took the trouble to reread all the books by philosophers which I could get hold of, to see if any of them even supposed that the movements of the spheres of the world [*iv*ᵃ] were different from those laid down by those who taught mathematics in the schools. And as a matter of fact, I found first in Cicero that Nicetas thought that the Earth moved. And afterwards I found in Plutarch that there were some others of the same opinion: I shall copy out his words here, so that they may be known to all:

> *Some think that the Earth is at rest; but Philolaus the Pythagorean says that it moves around the fire with an obliquely circular motion, like the sun and moon. Herakleides of Pontus and Ekphantus the Pythagorean do not give the Earth any movement of locomotion, but rather a limited movement of rising and setting around its centre, like a wheel.*[1]

Therefore I also, having found occasion, began to meditate upon the mobility of the Earth. And although the opinion seemed absurd, nevertheless because I knew that others before me had been granted the liberty of constructing whatever circles they pleased in order to demonstrate astral phenomena, I thought that I too would be readily permitted to test whether or not, by the laying down that the Earth had some movement, demonstrations less shaky than those of my predecessors could be found for the revolutions of the celestial spheres.

[1] *De placitis philosophorum*, III, 13.

And so, having laid down the movements which I attribute to the Earth farther on in the work, I finally discovered by the help of long and numerous observations that if the movements of the other wandering stars are correlated with the circular movement of the Earth, and if the movements are computed in accordance with the revolution of each planet, not only do all their phenomena follow from that but also this correlation binds together so closely the order and magnitudes of all the planets and of their spheres or orbital circles and the heavens themselves that nothing can be shifted around in any part of them without disrupting the remaining parts and the universe as a whole.

Accordingly, in composing my work I adopted the following order: in the first book I describe all the locations of the spheres or orbital circles together with the movements which I attribute to the earth, so that this book contains as it were the general set-up of the universe. But afterwards in the remaining books I correlate all the movements of the other planets and their spheres or orbital circles with the mobility of the Earth, so that it can be gathered from that how far the apparent movements of the remaining planets and their orbital circles can be saved by being correlated with the movements of the Earth. And I have no doubt that talented and learned mathematicians will agree with me, if—as philosophy [iv^b] demands in the first place—they are willing to give not superficial but profound thought and effort to what I bring forward in this work in demonstrating these things. And in order that the unlearned as well as the learned might see that I was not seeking to flee from the judgment of any man, I preferred to dedicate these results of my nocturnal study to Your Holiness rather than to anyone else; because, even in this remote corner of the earth where I live, you are held to be most eminent both in the dignity of your order and in your love of letters and even of mathematics; hence, by the authority of your judgment you can easily provide a guard against the bites of slanderers, despite the proverb that there is no medicine for the bite of a sycophant.

But if perchance there are certain "idle talkers" who take it upon themselves to pronounce judgment, although wholly ignorant of mathematics, and if by shamelessly distorting the sense of some passage in Holy Writ to suit their purpose, they dare to reprehend and to attack my work; they worry me so little that I shall even scorn their judgments as foolhardy. For it is not unknown that Lactantius, otherwise a distinguished writer but hardly a mathematician, speaks in an utterly childish fashion concerning the shape of the Earth, when he laughs at those who have affirmed that the Earth has the form of a globe. And so the studious need not be surprised if people like that laugh at us. Mathematics is written for mathematicians; and among them, if I am not mistaken, my labours will be seen to contribute something to the ecclesiastical commonwealth, the principate of which Your Holiness now holds. For not many years ago under Leo X when the Lateran Council was considering the question of reforming

the Ecclesiastical Calendar, no decision was reached, for the sole reason that the magnitude of the year and the months and the movements of the sun and moon had not yet been measured with sufficient accuracy. From that time on I gave attention to making more exact observations of these things and was encouraged to do so by that most distinguished man, Paul, Bishop of Fossombrone, who had been present at those deliberations. But what have I accomplished in this matter I leave to the judgment of Your Holiness in particular and to that of all other learned mathematicians. And so as not to appear to Your Holiness to make more promises concerning the utility of this book than I can fulfill, I now pass on to the body of the work.

BOOK ONE[1]

Among the many and varied literary and artistic studies upon which the natural talents of man are nourished, I think that those above all should be embraced and pursued with the most loving care which have to do with things that are very beautiful and very worthy of knowledge. Such studies are those which deal with the godlike circular movements of the world and the course of the stars, their magnitudes, distances, risings and settings, and the causes of the other appearances in the heavens; and which finally explicate the whole form. For what could be more beautiful than the heavens which contain all beautiful things? Their very names make this clear: *Caelum* (heavens) by naming that which is beautifully carved; and *Mundus* (world), purity and elegance. Many philosophers have called the world a visible god on account of its extraordinary excellence. So if the worth of the arts were measured by the matter with which they deal, this art—which some call astronomy, others astrology, and many of the ancients the consummation of mathematics—would be by far the most outstanding. This art which is as it were the head of all the liberal arts and the one most worthy of a free man leans upon nearly all the other branches of mathematics. Arithmetic, geometry, optics, geodesy, mechanics, and whatever others, all offer themselves in its service. And since a property of all good arts is to draw the mind of man away from the vices and direct it to better things, these arts can do that more plentifully, over and above the unbelievable pleasure of mind (which they furnish). For who, after applying himself to things which he sees established in the best order and directed by divine ruling, would not through diligent contemplation of them and through a certain habituation be awakened to that which is best and would not wonder at the Artificer of all things, in Whom is all happiness and every good? For the divine Psalmist surely did not say gratuitously that he took pleasure in the workings of God and rejoiced in the works of His hands, unless by means of these things as by some sort of vehicle we are transported to the contemplation of the highest Good.

Now as regards the utility and ornament which they confer upon a commonwealth—to pass over the innumerable advantages they give to private citizens—Plato makes an extremely good point, for in the seventh book of the *Laws* he says that this study should be pursued in especial, that through it the orderly arrangement of days into months and years and the determination of the times for solemnities and sacrifices should keep the state alive and watchful; and he says that if anyone denies that this study is necessary for a man who is going to take up any of the highest branches of learning, then such a person is thinking foolishly; and he thinks that it is impossible for anyone to become godlike or be called so who has no necessary knowledge of the sun, moon, and the other stars.

[1] The three introductory paragraphs are found in the Thorn centenary and Warsaw editions

However, this more divine than human science, which inquires into the highest things, is not lacking in difficulties. And in particular we see that as regards its principles and assumptions, which the Greeks call "hypotheses," many of those who undertook to deal with them were not in accord and hence did not employ the same methods of calculation. In addition, the courses of the planets and the revolution of the stars cannot be determined by exact calculations and reduced to perfect knowledge unless, through the passage of time and with the help of many prior observations, they can, so to speak, be handed down to posterity. For even if Claud Ptolemy of Alexandria, who stands far in front of all the others on account of his wonderful care and industry, with the help of more than forty years of observations brought this art to such a high point that there seemed to be nothing left which he had not touched upon; nevertheless we see that very many things are not in accord with the movements which should follow from his doctrine but rather with movements which were discovered later and were unknown to him. Whence even Plutarch in speaking of the revolving solar year says, "So far the movement of the stars has overcome the ingenuity of the mathematicians." Now to take the year itself as my example, I believe it is well known how many different opinions there are about it, so that many people have given up hope of risking an exact determination of it. Similarly, in the case of the other planets I shall try—with the help of God, without Whom we can do nothing—to make a more detailed inquiry concerning them, since the greater the interval of time between us and the founders of this art—whose discoveries we can compare with the new ones made by us—the more means we have of supporting our own theory. Furthermore, I confess that I shall expound many things differently from my predecessors—although with their aid, for it was they who first opened the road of inquiry into these things.

1. THE WORLD IS SPHERICAL

[1ª] In the beginning we should remark that the world is globe-shaped; whether because this figure is the most perfect of all, as it is an integral whole and needs no joints; or because this figure is the one having the greatest volume and thus is especially suitable for that which is going to comprehend and conserve all things; or even because the separate parts of the world i.e., the sun, moon, and stars are viewed under such a form; or because everything in the world tends to be delimited by this form, as is apparent in the case of drops of water and other liquid bodies, when they become delimited of themselves. And so no one would hesitate to say that this form belongs to the heavenly bodies.

2. THE EARTH IS SPHERICAL TOO

The Earth is globe-shaped too, since on every side it rests upon its centre. But it is not perceived straightway to be a perfect sphere, on account of the great height of its mountains and the lowness of its valleys, though they modify its universal roundness to only a very small extent.

That is made clear in this way. For when people journey northward from anywhere, the northern vertex of the axis of daily revolution gradually moves overhead, and the other moves downward to the same extent; and many stars situated to the north are seen not to set, and many to the south are seen not to rise any more. So Italy does not see Canopus, which is visible to Egypt. And Italy sees the last star of Fluvius, which is not visible to this region situated in a more frigid zone. Conversely, for people who travel southward, the second group of stars becomes higher in the sky; while those become lower which for us are high up.

Moreover, the inclinations of the poles have everywhere the same ratio with places at equal distances from the poles of the Earth and that [1b] happens in no other figure except the spherical. Whence it is manifest that the Earth itself is contained between the vertices and is therefore a globe.

Add to this the fact that the inhabitants of the East do not perceive the evening eclipses of the sun and moon; nor the inhabitants of the West, the morning eclipses; while of those who live in the middle region—some see them earlier and some later.

Furthermore, voyagers perceive that the waters too are fixed within this figure; for example, when land is not visible from the deck of a ship, it may be seen from the top of the mast, and conversely, if something shining is attached to the top of the mast, it appears to those remaining on the shore to come down gradually, as the ship moves from the land, until finally it becomes hidden, as if setting.

Moreover, it is admitted that water, which by its nature flows, always seeks lower places—the same way as earth—and does not climb up the shore any farther than the convexity of the shore allows. That is why the land is so much higher where it rises up from the ocean.

3. How Land and Water Make Up a Single Globe

And so the ocean encircling the land pours forth its waters everywhere and fills up the deeper hollows with them. Accordingly it was necessary for there to be less water than land, so as not to have the whole earth soaked with water—since both of them tend toward the same centre on account of their weight—and so as to leave some portions of land—such as the islands discernible here and there—for the preservation of living creatures. For what is the continent itself and the *orbis terrarum* except an island which is larger than the rest? We should not listen to certain Peripatetics who maintain that there is ten times more water than land and who arrive at that conclusion because in the transmutation of the elements the liquefaction of one part of earth results in ten

parts of water. And they say that land has emerged for a certain distance because, having hollow spaces inside, it does not balance everywhere with respect to weight and so the centre of gravity is different from the centre of magnitude. But they fall into error through ignorance of geometry; for they do not know that there cannot be seven times more water than land and some part of the land still remain dry, unless the land abandon its centre of gravity and give place to the waters as being heavier. For spheres are to one another as the cubes of their diameters. If therefore there were seven parts of water and one part of land, [2ᵃ] the diameter of the land could not be greater than the radius of the globe of the waters. So it is even less possible that the water should be ten times greater. It can be gathered that there is no difference between the centres of magnitude and of gravity of the Earth from the fact that the convexity of the land spreading out from the ocean does not swell continuously, for in that case it would repulse the sea-waters as much as possible and would not in any way allow interior seas and huge gulfs to break through. Moreover, from the seashore outward the depth of the abyss would not stop increasing, and so no island or reef or any spot of land would be met with by people voyaging out very far. Now it is well known that there is not quite the distance of two miles—at practically the centre of the *orbis terrarum*—between the Egyptian and the Red Sea. And on the contrary, Ptolemy in his *Cosmography* extends inhabitable lands as far as the median circle, and he leaves that part of the Earth as unknown, where the moderns have added Cathay and other vast regions as far as 60° longitude, so that inhabited land extends in longitude farther than the rest of the ocean does. And if you add to these the islands discovered in our time under the princes of Spain and Portugal and especially America—named after the ship's captain who discovered her—which they consider a second *orbis terrarum* on account of her so far unmeasured magnitude—besides many other islands heretofore unknown, we would not be greatly surprised if there were antiphodes or antichthones. For reasons of geometry compel us to believe that America is situated diametrically opposite to the India of the Ganges.

And from all that I think it is manifest that the land and the water rest upon one centre of gravity; that this is the same as the centre of magnitude of the land, since land is the heavier; that parts of land which are as it were yawning are filled with water; and that accordingly there is little water in comparison with the land, even if more of the surface appears to be covered by water.

Now it is necessary that the land and the surrounding waters have the figure which the shadow of the Earth casts, for it eclipses the moon by projecting a perfect circle upon it. Therefore the Earth is not a plane, as Empedocles and Anaximenes opined; or a tympanoid, as Leucippus; or a scaphoid, as Heracleitus; or hollowed out in any other way, as Democritus; or again a cylinder, as Anaximander; and it is not infinite in its

lower part, with the density increasing rootwards, as Xenophanes thought; but it is perfectly round, as the philosophers perceived.

4. The Movement of the Celestial Bodies is Regular, Circular, and Everlasting—Or Else Compounded of Circular Movements

[2ᵇ] After this we will recall that the movement of the celestial bodies is circular. For the motion of a sphere is to turn in a circle; by this very act expressing its form, in the most simple body, where beginning and end cannot be discovered or distinguished from one another, while it moves through the same parts in itself.

But there are many movements on account of the multitude of spheres or orbital circles.[1] The most obvious of all is the daily revolution—which the Greeks call νυχ-θήμερν; i.e., having the temporal span of a day and a night. By means of this movement the whole world—with the exception of the Earth—is supposed to be borne from east to west. This movement is taken as the common measure of all movements, since we measure even time itself principally by the number of days.

Next, we see other as it were antagonistic revolutions; i.e., from west to east, on the part of the sun, moon, and the wandering stars. In this way the sun gives us the year, the moon the months—the most common periods of time; and each of the other five planets follows its own cycle. Nevertheless these movements are manifoldly different from the first movement. First, in that they do not revolve around the same poles as the first movement but follow the oblique ecliptic; next, in that they do not seem to move in their circuit regularly. For the sun and moon are caught moving at times more slowly and at times more quickly. And we perceive the five wandering stars sometimes even to retrograde and to come to a stop between these two movements. And though the sun always proceeds straight ahead along its route, they wander in various ways, straying sometimes towards the south, and at other times towards the north—whence they are called "planets." Add to this the fact that sometimes they are nearer the Earth—and are then said to be at their perigee—and at other times are farther away—and are said to be at their apogee.

We must however confess that these movements are circular or are composed of many circular movements, in that they maintain these irregularities in accordance with a constant law and with fixed periodic returns: and that could not take place, if they were not circular. For it is only the circle which can bring back what is past and over with; and in this way, for example, the sun by a movement composed of circular movements brings back to us the inequality of days and nights and the four seasons of the

[1]The "orbital circle" (orbis) is the great circle whereon the planet moves in its sphere (sphaera). Copernicus; uses the word orbis which designates a circle primarily rather than a sphere because, while the sphere may be necessary for the mechanical explanation of the movement, only the circle is necessary for the mathematical.

year. [3ª] Many movements are recognized in that movement, since it is impossible that a simple heavenly body should be moved irregularly by a single sphere. For that would have to take place either on account of the inconstancy of the motor virtue—whether by reason of an extrinsic cause or its intrinsic nature—or on account of the inequality between it and the moved body. But since the mind shudders at either of these suppositions, and since it is quite unfitting to suppose that such a state of affairs exists among things which are established in the best system, it is agreed that their regular movements appear to us as irregular, whether on account of their circles having different poles or even because the earth is not at the centre of the circles in which they revolve. And so for us watching from the Earth, it happens that the transits of the planets, on account of being at unequal distances from the Earth, appear greater when they are nearer than when they are farther away, as has been shown in optics: thus in the case of equal arcs of an orbital circle which are seen at different distances there will appear to be unequal movements in equal times. For this reason I think it necessary above all that we should note carefully what the relation of the Earth to the heavens is, so as not—when we wish to scrutinize the highest things—to be ignorant of those which are nearest to us, and so as not—by the same error—to attribute to the celestial bodies what belongs to the Earth.

5. Does the Earth Have a Circular Movement? And of Its Place

Now that it has been shown that the Earth too has the form of a globe, I think we must see whether or not a movement follows upon its form and what the place of the Earth is in the universe. For without doing that it will not be possible to find a sure reason for the movements appearing in the heavens. Although there are so many authorities for saying that the Earth rests in the centre of the world that people think the contrary supposition inopinable and even ridiculous; if however we consider the thing attentively, we will see that the question has not yet been decided and accordingly is by no means to be scorned. For every apparent change in place occurs on account of the movement either of the thing seen or of the spectator, or on account of the necessarily unequal movement of both. For no movement is perceptible relatively to things moved equally in the same directions—I mean relatively to the thing seen and the spectator. Now it is from the Earth that the celestial circuit is beheld and presented to our sight. Therefore, if some movement should belong to the Earth [3ᵇ] it will appear, in the parts of the universe which are outside, as the same movement but in the opposite direction, as though the things outside were passing over. And the daily revolution in especial is such a movement. For the daily revolution appears to carry the whole universe along, with the exception of the Earth and the things around it. And if

you admit that the heavens possess none of this movement but that the Earth turns from west to east, you will find—if you make a serious examination—that as regards the apparent rising and setting of the sun, moon, and stars the case is so. And since it is the heavens which contain and embrace all things as the place common to the universe, it will not be clear at once why movement should not be assigned to the contained rather than to the container, to the thing placed rather than to the thing providing the place.

As a matter of fact, the Pythagoreans Herakleides and Ekphantus were of this opinion and so was Hicetas the Syracusan in Cicero; they made the Earth to revolve at the centre of the world. For they believed that the stars set by reason of the interposition of the Earth and that with cessation of that they rose again. Now upon this assumption there follow other things, and a no smaller problem concerning the place of the Earth, though it is taken for granted and believed by nearly all that the Earth is the centre of the world. For if anyone denies that the Earth occupies the midpoint or centre of the world yet does not admit that the distance (between the two) is great enough to be compared with (the distance to) the sphere of the fixed stars but is considerable and quite apparent in relation to the orbital circles of the sun and the planets; and if for that reason he thought that their movements appeared irregular because they are organized around a different centre from the centre of the Earth, he might perhaps be able to bring forward a perfectly sound reason for movement which appears irregular. For the fact that the wandering stars are seen to be sometimes nearer the Earth and at other times farther away necessarily argues that the centre of the Earth is not the centre of their circles. It is not yet clear whether the Earth draws near to them and moves away or they draw near to the Earth and move away.

And so it would not be very surprising if someone attributed some other movement to the earth in addition to the daily revolution. As a matter of fact, Philolaus the Pythagorean—no ordinary mathematician, whom Plato's biographers say Plato went to Italy for the sake of seeing—is supposed to have held that the Earth moved in a circle and wandered in some other movements and was one of the planets.

Many however have believed that they could show by geometrical reasoning that the Earth is in the middle of the world; that it has the proportionality of a point in relation to the immensity of the heavens, occupies the central position, and for this reason is immovable, because, when the universe moves, the centre [4ª] remains unmoved and the things which are closest to the centre are moved the most slowly.

6. On the Immensity of the Heavens in Relation to the Magnitude of the Earth

It can be understood that this great mass which is the Earth is not comparable with

the magnitude of the heavens, from the fact that the boundary circles—for that is the translation of the Greek ὁρίζοντες—cut the whole celestial sphere into two halves; for that could not take place if the magnitude of the Earth in comparison with the heavens, or its distance from the centre of the world, were considerable. For the circle bisecting a sphere goes through the centre of the sphere, and is the greatest circle which it is possible to circumscribe.

Now let the horizon be the circle *ABCD*, and let the Earth, where our point of view is, be *E*, the centre of the horizon by which the visible stars are separated from those which are not visible. Now with a dioptra or horoscope or level placed at *E*, the beginning of Cancer is seen to rise at point *C*; and at the same moment the beginning of Capricorn appears to set at *A*. Therefore, since *AEC* is in a straight line with the dioptra, it is clear that this line is a diameter of the ecliptic, because the six signs bound a semicircle, whose centre *E* is the same as that of the horizon. But when a revolution has taken place and the beginning of Capricorn arises at *B*, then the setting of Cancer will be visible at *D*, and *BED* will be a straight line and a diameter of the ecliptic. But

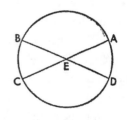

it has already been seen that the line *AEC* is a diameter of the same circle; therefore, at their common section, point *E* will be their centre. So in this way the horizon always bisects the ecliptic, which is a great circle of the sphere. But on a sphere, if a circle bisects one of the great circles, then the circle bisecting is a great circle. Therefore the horizon is a great circle; and its centre is the same as that of the ecliptic, as far as appearance goes; although nevertheless the line passing through the centre of the Earth and the line touching to the surface are necessarily different; but on account of their immensity in comparison with the Earth they are like parallel lines, which on account of the great distance between the termini appear to be one line, when the space contained between them [4ᵇ] is in no perceptible ratio to their length, as has been shown in optics.

From this argument it is certainly clear enough that the heavens are immense in comparison with the Earth and present the aspect of an infinite magnitude, and that in the judgment of sense-perception the Earth is to the heavens as a point to a body and as a finite to an infinite magnitude. But we see that nothing more than that has been shown, and it does not follow that the Earth must rest at the centre of the world. And we should be even more surprised if such a vast world should wheel completely around during the space of twenty-four hours rather than that its least part, the Earth, should. For saying that the centre is immovable and that those things which are closest to the centre are moved least does not argue that the Earth rests at the centre of the

world. That is no different from saying that the heavens revolve but the poles are at rest and those things which are closest to the poles are moved least. In this way Cynosura (the pole star) is seen to move much more slowly than Aquila or Canicula because, being very near to the pole, it describes a smaller circle, since they are all on a single sphere, the movement of which stops at its axis and which does not allow any of its parts to have movements which are equal to one another. And nevertheless the revolution of the whole brings them round in equal times but not over equal spaces.

The argument which maintains that the Earth, as a part of the celestial sphere and as sharing in the same form and movement, moves very little because very near to its centre advances to the following position: therefore the Earth will move, as being a body and not a centre, and will describe in the same time arcs similar to, but smaller than, the arcs of the celestical circle. It is clearer than daylight how false that is; for there would necessarily always be noon at one place and midnight at another, and so the daily risings and settings could not take place, since the movement of the whole and the part would be one and inseparable.

But the ratio between things separated by diversity of nature is so entirely different that those which describe a smaller circle turn more quickly than those which describe a greater circle. In this way Saturn, the highest of the wandering stars, completes its revolution in thirty years, and the moon which is without doubt the closest to the Earth completes its circuit in a month, and finally the Earth itself will be considered to complete a circular movement in the space of a day and a night. So this same problem concerning the daily revolution comes up again. And also the question about the place of the Earth becomes even less certain on account of what was just said. For that demonstration proves nothing except that the heavens are of an indefinite magnitude with respect to the Earth. But it is not at all clear how far this immensity stretches out. On the contrary, since the minimal and indivisible corpuscles, which are called atoms, are not perceptible to sense, they do not, when taken in twos or in some small number, constitute a visible body; but they can be taken in such a large quantity that there will at last be enough to form a visible magnitude. So it is as regards the place of the earth; for although it is not at the centre of the world, nevertheless the distance is as nothing, particularly in comparison with the sphere of the fixed stars.

7. WHY THE ANCIENTS THOUGHT THE EARTH WAS AT REST AT THE MIDDLE OF THE WORLD AS ITS CENTRE

[5ª] Wherefore for other reasons the ancient philosophers have tried to affirm that the Earth is at rest at the middle of the world, and as principal cause they put forward heaviness and lightness. For Earth is the heaviest element; and all things of any weight are borne towards it and strive to move towards the very centre of it.

since the Earth is a globe towards which from every direction heavy things by

own nature are borne at right angles to its surface, the heavy things would fall on one another at the centre if they were not held back at the surface; since a straight line making right angles with a plane surface where it touches a sphere leads to the centre. And those things which are borne toward the centre seem to follow along in order to be at rest at the centre. All the more then will the Earth be at rest at the centre; and, as being the receptacle for falling bodies, it will remain immovable because of its weight.

They strive similarly to prove this by reason of movement and its nature. For Aristotle says that the movement of a body which is one and simple is simple, and the simple movements are the rectilinear and the circular. And of rectilinear movements, one is upward, and the other is downward. As a consequence, every simple movement is either toward the centre, *i.e.*, downward, or away from the centre, *i.e.*, upward, or around the centre, *i.e.*, circular. Now it belongs to earth and water, which are considered heavy, to be borne downward, *i.e.*, to seek the centre: for air and fire, which are endowed with lightness, move upward, *i.e.*, away from the centre. It seems fitting to grant rectilinear movement to these four elements and to give the heavenly bodies a circular movement around the centre. So Aristotle. Therefore, said Ptolemy of Alexandria, if the Earth moved, even if only by its daily rotation, the contrary of what was said above would necessarily take place. For this movement which would traverse the total circuit of the Earth in twenty-four hours would necessarily be very headlong and of an unsurpassable velocity. Now things which are suddenly and violently whirled around are seen to be utterly unfitted for reuniting, and the more unified are seen to become dispersed, unless some constant force constrains them to stick together. And a long time ago, he says, the scattered Earth would have passed beyond the heavens, as is certainly ridiculous; [5b] and *a fortiori* so would all the living creatures and all the other separate masses which could by no means remain unshaken. Moreover, freely falling bodies would not arrive at the places appointed them, and certainly not along the perpendicular line which they assume so quickly. And we would see clouds and other things floating in the air always borne toward the west.

8. Answer to the Aforesaid Reasons and Their Inadequacy

For these and similar reasons they say that the Earth remains at rest at the middle of the world and that there is no doubt about this. But if someone opines that the Earth revolves, he will also say that the movement is natural and not violent. Now things which are according to nature produce effects contrary to those which are violent. For things to which force or violence is applied get broken up and are unable to subsist for a long time. But things which are caused by nature are in a right condition and are kept in their best organization. Therefore Ptolemy had no reason to fear that

the Earth and all things on the Earth would be scattered in a revolution caused by the efficacy of nature, which is greatly different from that of art or from that which can result from the genius of man. But why didn't he feel anxiety about the world instead, whose movement must necessarily be of greater velocity, the greater the heavens are than the Earth? Or have the heavens become so immense, because an unspeakably vehement motion has pulled them away from the centre, and because the heavens would fall if they came to rest anywhere else?

Surely if this reasoning were tenable, the magnitude of the heavens would extend infinitely. For the farther the movement is borne upward by the vehement force, the faster will the movement be, on account of the ever-increasing circumference which must be traversed every twenty-four hours: and conversely, the immensity of the sky would increase with the increase in movement. In this way, the velocity would make the magnitude increase infinitely, and the magnitude the velocity. And in accordance with the axiom of physics that *that which is infinite cannot be traversed or moved in any way*, then the heavens will necessarily come to rest.

But they say that beyond the heavens there isn't any body or place or void or anything at all; and accordingly it is not possible for the heavens to move outward; in that case it is rather surprising that something can be held together by nothing. But if the heavens were infinite and were finite only with respect to a hollow space inside, then it will be said with more truth that there is nothing outside the heavens, since anything [6ª] which occupied any space would be in them; but the heavens will remain immobile. For movement is the most powerful reason wherewith they try to conclude that the universe is finite.

But let us leave to the philosophers of nature the dispute as to whether the world is finite or infinite, and let us hold as certain that the Earth is held together between its two poles and terminates in a spherical surface. Why therefore should we hesitate any longer to grant to it the movement which accords naturally with its form, rather than put the whole world in a commotion—the world whose limits we do not and cannot know? And why not admit that the appearance of daily revolution belongs to the heavens but the reality belongs to the Earth? And things are as when Aeneas said in Virgil: "We sail out of the harbor, and the land and the cities move away." As a matter of fact, when a ship floats on over a tranquil sea, all the things outside seem to the voyagers to be moving in a movement which is the image of their own, and they think on the contrary that they themselves and all the things with them are at rest. So it can easily happen in the case of the movement of the Earth that the whole world should be believed to be moving in a circle. Then what would we say about the clouds and the other things floating in the air or falling or rising up, except that not only the Earth and the watery element with which it is conjoined are moved in this way but also no

23

small part of the air and whatever other things have a similar kinship with the Earth? whether because the neighbouring air, which is mixed with earthly and watery matter, obeys the same nature as the Earth or because the movement of the air is an acquired one, in which it participates without resistance on account of the contiguity and perpetual rotation of the Earth. Conversely, it is no less astonishing for them to say that the highest region of the air follows the celestial movement, as is shown by those stars which appear suddenly—I mean those called "comets" or "bearded stars" by the Greeks. For that place is assigned for their generation; and like all the other stars they rise and set. We can say that that part of the air is deprived of terrestrial motion on account of its great distance from the Earth. Hence the air which is nearest to the Earth and the things floating in it will appear tranquil, unless they are driven to and fro by the wind or some other force, as happens. For how is the wind in the air different from a current in the sea?

But we must confess that in comparison with the world the movement of falling and of rising bodies is twofold and is in general compounded of the rectilinear and the circular. As regards things which move downward on account of their weight [6ᵇ] because they have very much earth in them, doubtless their parts possess the same nature as the whole, and it is for the same reason that fiery bodies are drawn upward with force. For even this earthly fire feeds principally on earthly matter; and they define flame as glowing smoke. Now it is a property of fire to make that which it invades to expand; and it does this with such force that it can be stopped by no means or contrivance from breaking prison and completing its job. Now expanding movement moves away from the centre to the circumference; and so if some part of the Earth caught on fire, it would be borne away from the centre and upward. Accordingly, as they say, a simple body possesses a simple movement—this is first verified in the case of circular movement—as long as the simple body remain in its unity in its natural place. In this place, in fact, its movement is none other than the circular, which remains entirely in itself, as though at rest. Rectilinear movement, however, is added to those bodies which journey away from their natural place or are shoved out of it or are outside it somehow. But nothing is more repugnant to the order of the whole and to the form of the world than for anything to be outside of its place. Therefore rectilinear movement belongs only to bodies which are not in the right condition and are not perfectly conformed to their nature—when they are separated from their whole and abandon its unity. Furthermore, bodies which are moved upward or downward do not possess a simple, uniform, and regular movement—even without taking into account circular movement. For they cannot be in equilibrium with their lightness or their force of weight. And those which fall downward possess a slow movement at the beginning but increase their velocity as they fall. And conversely we note that this earthly fire—

and we have experience of no other—when carried high up immediately dies down, as if through the acknowledged agency of the violence of earthly matter.

Now circular movement always goes on regularly, for it has an unfailing cause; but (in rectilinear movement) the acceleration stops, because, when the bodies have reached their own place, they are no longer heavy or light, and so the movement ends. Therefore, since circular movement belongs to wholes and rectilinear to parts, we can say that the circular movement stands with the rectilinear, as does animal with sick. And the fact that Aristotle divided simple movement into three genera: away from the centre, toward the centre, and around the centre, will be considered merely as an act of reason, just as we distinguish between line, point, and surface, though none of them can subsist without the others or [7ª] without body.

In addition, there is the fact that the state of immobility is regarded as more noble and godlike than that of change and instability, which for that reason should belong to the Earth rather than to the world. I add that it seems rather absurd to ascribe movement to the container or to that which provides the place and not rather to that which is contained and has a place, *i.e.*, the Earth. And lastly, since it is clear that the wandering stars are sometimes nearer and sometimes farther away from the Earth, then the movement of one and the same body around the centre—and they mean the centre of the Earth—will be both away from the centre and toward the centre. Therefore it is necessary that movement around the centre should be taken more generally; and it should be enough if each movement is in accord with its own centre. You see therefore that for all these reasons it is more probably that the Earth moves than that it is at rest—especially in the case of the daily revolution, as it is the Earth's very own. And I think that is enough as regards the first part of the question.

9. Whether Many Movements Can Be Attributed to the Earth, and Concerning the Centre of the World

Therefore, since nothing hinders the mobility of the Earth, I think we should now see whether more than one movement belongs to it, so that it can be regarded as one of the wandering stars. For the apparent irregular movement of the planets and their variable distances from the Earth—which cannot be understood as occurring in circles homocentric with the Earth—make it clear that the Earth is not the centre of their circular movements. Therefore, since there are many centres, it is not foolhardy to doubt whether the centre of gravity of the Earth rather than some other is the centre of the world. I myself think that gravity or heaviness is nothing except a certain natural appetency implanted in the parts by the divine providence of the universal Artisan, in order that they should unite with one another in their oneness and wholeness and come

together in the form of a globe. It is believable that this affect is present in the sun, moon, and the other bright planets and that through its efficacy they remain in the spherical figure in which they are visible, though they nevertheless accomplish their circular movements in many different ways. Therefore if the Earth too possesses movements different from the one around its centre, then they will necessarily be movements which similarly appear on the outside in the many bodies; and we find the yearly revolution among these movements. For if the annual revolution were changed from being solar to being terrestrial, and immobility were granted to the sun, [7ᵇ] the risings and settings of the signs and of the fixed stars—whereby they become morning or evening stars—will appear in the same way; and it will be seen that the stoppings, retrogressions, and progressions of the wandering stars are not their own, but are a movement of the Earth and that they borrow the appearances of this movement. Lastly, the sun will be regarded as occupying the centre of the world. And the ratio of order in which these bodies succeed one another and the harmony of the whole world teaches us their truth, if only—as they say—we would look at the thing with both eyes.

10. ON THE ORDER OF THE CELESTIAL ORBITAL CIRCLES

I know of no one who doubts that the heavens of the fixed stars is the highest up of all visible things. We see that the ancient philosophers wished to take the order of the planets according to the magnitude of their revolutions, for the reason that among things which are moved with equal speed those which are the more distant seem to be borne along more slowly, as Euclid proves in his *Optics*. And so they think that the moon traverses its circle in the shortest period of time, because being next to the Earth, it revolves in the smallest circle. But they think that Saturn, which completes the longest circuit in the longest period of time, is the highest. Beneath Saturn, Jupiter. After Jupiter, Mars.

There are different opinions about Venus and Mercury, in that they do not have the full range of angular elongations from the sun that the others do.[1] Wherefore some place them above the sun, as Timaeus does in Plato; some, beneath the sun, as Ptolemy and a good many moderns. Alpetragius makes Venus higher than the sun and Mercury lower. Accordingly, as the followers of Plato suppose that all the planets—which are otherwise dark bodies—shine with light received from the sun, they think that if the planets were below the sun, they would on account of their slight distance from the sun be viewed as only half—or at any rate as only partly—spherical. For the light which they receive is reflected by them upward for the most part, *i.e.*, towards the sun, as we see in the case of the new moon or the old. Moreover, they say that necessarily the sun would sometimes be obscured through their interposition and that its light would be

[1]The greatest angular elongation of Venus from the sun is approximately 45°; that of Mercury, approximately 24°; while Saturn, Jupiter, and Mars have the full range of possible angular elongation, *i.e.*, up to 180°.

eclipsed in proportion to their magnitude; and as that has never appeared to take place, they think that these planets cannot by any means be below the sun.[1]

On the contrary, those who place Venus and Mercury below the sun claim as a reason the amplitude of the space which they find between the sun and the moon. [8a] For they find that the greatest distance between the Earth and the moon, *i.e.,* $64^1/_6$ units, whereof the radius of the Earth is one, is contained almost 18 times in the least distance between the sun and the Earth. This distance is 1160 such units, and therefore the distance between the sun and the moon is 1096 such units. And then, in order for such a vast space not to remain empty, they find that the intervals between the perigees and apogees—according to which they reason out the thickness of the spheres[2]—add up to approximately the same sum: in such fashion that the apogee of the moon may be succeeded by the perigee of Mercury, that the apogee of Mercury may be followed by the perigee of Venus, and that finally the apogee of Venus may nearly touch the perigee of the sun. In fact they calculate that the interval between the perigee and the apogee of Mercury contains approximately $177^1/_2$ of the aforesaid units and that the remaining space is nearly filled by the 910 units of the interval between the perigee and apogee of Venus.[3] Therefore they do not admit that these planets have a certain opacity, like that of the moon; but that they shine either by their own proper light or because their entire bodies are impregnated with sunlight, and that accordingly they do not obscure the sun, because it is an extremely rare occurrence for them to be interposed between our sight and the sun, as they usually withdraw (from the sun) latitudinally. In addition, there is the fact that they are small bodies in comparison with the sun, since Venus even though larger than Mercury can cover scarcely one one-hundredth part of the sun, as al-Battani the Harranite maintains, who holds that the diameter of the sun is ten times greater, and therefore it would not be easy to see such a little speck in the midst of such beaming light. Averroes, however, in his paraphrase of Ptolemy records having seen something blackish, when he observed the

[1]The transit of Venus across the face of the sun was first observed—by means of a telescope—in 1639.

[2]That is to say, the thickness of the sphere would measured by the ratio of the diameter of the epicycle to the diameter of the sphere, or, in the accompanying diagram, by the distance between the inmost and the outmost of the three homocentric circles.

[3]The succession of the orbital circles according to their perigees and apogees may be represented in the following diagram, which has been drawn to scale.

conjunction of the sun and Mercury which he had computed. And so they judge that these two planets move below the solar circle.

But how uncertain and shaky this reasoning is, is clear from the fact that though the shortest distance of the moon is 38 units whereof the radius of the Earth is one unit—according to Ptolemy, but more than 49 such units by a truer evaluation, as will be shown below—nevertheless we do not know that this great space contains anything except air, or if you prefer, what they call the fiery element.

Moreover, there is the fact that the diameter of the epicycle of Venus—by reason of which Venus has an angular digression of approximately 45° on either side of the sun—would have to be six times greater than the distance from the centre of the Earth to its perigee, as will be shown in the proper place.[1] Then what will they say is contained in all this space, which [8ᵇ] is so great as to take in the Earth, air, ether, moon and Mercury, and which moreover the vast epicycle of Venus would occupy if it revolved around an immobile Earth?

Furthermore, how unconvincing is Ptolemy's argument that the sun must occupy the middle position between those planets which have the full range of angular elongation from the sun and those which do not is clear from the fact that the moon's full range of angular elongation proves its falsity.

But what cause will those who place Venus below the sun, and Mercury next, or separate them in some other order—what cause will they allege why these planets do not also make longitudinal circuits separate and independent of the sun, like the other planets[2]—if indeed the ratio of speed or slowness does not falsify their order? Therefore it will be necessary either for the Earth not to be the centre to which the order of the planets and their orbital circles is referred, or for there to be no sure reason for their order and for it not to be apparent why the highest place is due to Saturn rather than to Jupiter or some other planet. Wherefore I judge that what Martianus Capella—who wrote the *Encyclopedia*—and some other Latins took to be the case is by no means to be despised. For they hold that Venus and Mercury circle around the sun as a centre; and they hold that for this reason Venus and Mercury do not have any farther elongation from the sun than the convexity of their orbital circles permits; for they do not make a circle around the earth as do the others, but have perigee and apogee interchangeable (in the sphere of the fixed stars). Now what do they mean except that the centre of their spheres is around the sun? Thus the orbital circle of Mercury will be

---

[1]According to Ptolemy, the ratio of the radius of Venus' epicycle to the radius of its eccentric is between 2 to 3 and 3 to 4, or approximately $43\frac{1}{6}$ to 60. Now since at perigee the epicycle subtracts from the mean distance, or radius of the eccentric circle, that which at apogee it adds to the mean distance, the ratio of Venus' distance at perigee to its distance at apogee is approximately 1 to 6. That is to say, in the passage from apogee to perigee, the ratio of increase, in the apparent magnitude of the planet should be approximately 36 to 1, as the apparent magnitude varies inversely in the ratio of the square of the distance. But no such increase in the magnitude of the planet is apparent. This opposition between an appearance and the consequences of an hypothesis made to save another appearance is still present within Copernicus' own scheme.

[2]Ptolemy makes the centres of the epicycles of Venus and Mercury travel around the Earth longitudinally at the same rate as the mean sun, and in such fashion that the mean sun is always on the straight line extending from the centre of the Earth through the centres of their epicycles, while the centres of the epicycles of the upper planets may be at any angular distance from the mean sun.

enclosed within the orbital circle of Venus—which would have to be more than twice as large—and will find adequate room for itself within that amplitude.[1] Therefore if anyone should take this as an occasion to refer Saturn, Jupiter, and Mars also to this same centre, provided he understands the magnitude of those orbital circles to be such as to comprehend and encircle the Earth remaining within them, he would not be in error, as the table of ratios of their movements makes clear.[2] For it is manifest that the planets are always nearer the Earth at the time of their evening rising, *i.e.*, when they are opposite to the sun and the Earth is in the middle between them and the sun. But they are farthest away from the Earth at the time of their evening setting, *i.e.*, when they are occulted in the neighbourhood of the sun, namely, when we have the sun between them and the Earth. All that shows clearly enough that their centre is more directly related to the sun and is the same as that to which Venus and Mercury refer

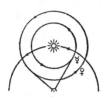

[1] As in the following diagram which has been drawn to scale.

[2] Take the case of Mars. In Ptolemy, the ratio of its epicycle to its eccentric is 39$\frac{1}{2}$ to 60, or approximately 2 to 3. Mars has 37 cycles of anomaly, or movement on the epicycle, and 42 cycles of longitude, or movement of the epicycle on the eccentric, in 79 solar years; or for the sake of easiness let us say that the ratio of the sun's movement to either of the planets' two movements is 2 to 1. Copernicus is here suggesting that if the centre of the planet's movement is placed around the moving sun, then the Ptolemaic cycles of anomaly will represent the number of times the sun has overtaken the planet in longitude: thus the 37 cycles of anomaly plus the 42 cycles of longitude add up to the 79 solar revolutions. That is to say, the sun will now be traveling around the Earth on a circle which has the same relative magnitude as the Martian epicycle in Ptolemy and bears an epicycle having the same relative magnitude as Ptolemy's Martian eccentric circle, on which epicycle Mars travels in the opposite direction at half the speed of the sun. Under both hypotheses the appearances from the Earth will be the same, as can be seen in the following diagrams.

For according to the Ptolemaic hypothesis, let the Earth be at the center of the approximately homocentric circles of the sun, Mars, and the ecliptic. Let the radius of the planet's epicycle be to the radius of the planet's eccentric as 2 to 3. Now, first, let the sun be viewed at the beginning of Leo, and let the planet at the perigee of its epicycle be viewed at the beginning of Aquarius, in opposition to the sun. Next, let the sun move 240° eastwards, to the beginning of Aries; and during the same interval let the epicycle move 120° eastwards, to the beginning of Gemini, and the planet 120° eastwards on the epicycle. Now the planet will be found to appear in Taurus, about 36° west of the sun.

But if according to the semi-Copernican hypothesis, the sun is made to revolve around the Earth on a circle having the same relative magnitude as Mars' Ptolemaic epicycle, while Mars is placed on an epicycle which has the same relative magnitude as its Ptolemaic eccentric and has its centre at the sun; and if the apparent positions of Mars and the sun are first the same as before, and the sun moves 240° eastwards, bearing along the deferent of Mars, while Mars moves 120° westwards on its epicycle; then Mars will once more be found to appear in Taurus, approximately 36° west of the sun.

PTOLEMAIC HYPOTHESIS

SEMI-COPERNICAN HYPOTHESIS

Movement of Sun=240°
Movement of Eccentric=120°
Movement of Epicycle=120°

Movement of Sun=240°
Movement of Mars=120°

their revolutions.[1] But as they all have one common centre, it is necessary that the space left between the convex orbital circle of Venus and the concave orbital circle of Mars should be viewed as an orbital circle [9a] or sphere homocentric with them in respect to both surfaces, and that it should receive the Earth and its satellite the moon and whatever is contained beneath the lunar globe. For we can by no means separate the moon from the Earth, as the moon is incontestably very near to the Earth—especially since we find in this expanse a place for the moon which is proper enough and sufficiently large. Therefore we are not ashamed to maintain that this totality—which the moon embraces—and the centre of the Earth too traverse that great orbital circle among the other wandering stars in an annual revolution around the sun; and that the centre of the world is around the sun. I also say that the sun remains forever immobile and that whatever apparent movement belongs to it can be verified of the mobility of the Earth; that the magnitude of the world is such that, although the distance from the sun to the Earth in relation to whatsoever planetary sphere you please possesses magnitude which is sufficiently manifest in proportion to these dimensions, this distance, as compared with the sphere of the fixed stars, is imperceptible. I find it much more easy to grant that than to unhinge the understanding by an almost infinite multitude of spheres—as those who keep the earth at the centre of the world are forced to do. But we should rather follow the wisdom of nature, which, as it takes very great care not to have produced anything superfluous or useless, often prefers to endow one thing with many effects. And though all these things are difficult, almost inconceivable, and quite contrary to the opinion of the multitude, nevertheless in what follows we will with God's help make them clearer than day—at least for those who are not ignorant of the art of mathematics.

Therefore if the first law is still safe—for no one will bring forward a better one than that the magnitude of the orbital circles should be measured by the magnitude of time—then the order of the spheres will follow in this way—beginning with the highest: the first and highest of all is the sphere of the fixed stars, which comprehends itself and all things, and is accordingly immovable. In fact it is the place of the universe, *i.e.*, it is that to which the movement and position of all the other stars are referred. For in the deduction of terrestrial movement, we will however give the cause why there are appearances such as to make people believe that even the sphere of the fixed stars somehow moves. Saturn, the first of the wandering stars follows; it completes its circuit in

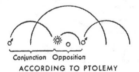

Conjunction Opposition
ACCORDING TO PTOLEMY

[1]Copernicus is asking what reason there is why the planets are always found to be at their apogees at the time of conjunction with the sun, and at their perigees at the time of opposition, since according to the Ptolemaic scheme the reverse is also possible—as is evident from the accompanying diagram.

But if the sun and not the Earth is the centre of the planet's movements, the reason is obvious.

Conjunction Opposition
ACCORDING TO COPERNICUS

30 years. After it comes Jupiter moving in a 12-year period of revolution. Then Mars, which completes a revolution every 2 years. The place fourth in order is occupied by the annual revolution [9ᵇ] in which we said the Earth together with the orbital circle of the moon as an epicycle is comprehended. In the fifth place, Venus, which completes its revolution in 7$\frac{1}{2}$ months. The sixth and final place is occupied by Mercury, which completes its revolution in a period of 88 days.[1] In the center of all rests the sun. For who would place this lamp of a very beautiful temple in another or better place than this wherefrom it can illuminate everything at the same time? As a matter of fact, not unhappily do some call it the lantern; others, the mind and still others, the pilot of the world. Trismegistus calls

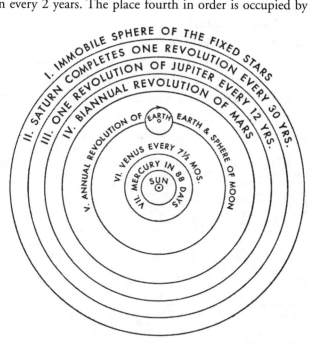

[1]In order to see how Copernicus, derived the length of his periods of revolution, consider the following Ptolemaic ratios for the lower planets:

	Cycles of anomaly	Cycles of longitude	Solar years
Mercury	145	46 +	46 +
Venus	5	8 —	8 —

It is noteworthy that the number of cycles of longitude in one year is equal to the number of solar cycles. Moreover, the two planets have a limited angular elongation from the sun. In order to explain these two peculiar appearances Copernicus sets the Earth in motion on the circumference of a circle which encloses the orbits of Venus and Mercury, with the sun at the centre of all three orbits. Thus the planet's cycles of anomaly in so many years become the number of times the planet has overtaken the Earth, as they revolve around the sun. That is to say, in so many solar years the planet will have traveled around the sun a number of times which is equal to the sum of its cycles of anomaly and its cycles in longitude. Thus, for example, Venus travels around the sun approximately 13 times in 8 solar years; hence its period of revolution is approximately 7$\frac{1}{2}$ months; and similarly, that of Mercury is approximately 88 days—although for some obscure reason Copernicus actually writes down 9 months for Venus (*nono mense reducitur*) and 80 days for Mercury (*octaginta dierum spatio circumcurrens*).

The reader may intuit from the following diagrams the equipollence, with respect to the appearances, of the Ptolemaic and the Copernican explanations of the movement of Venus.

Now, on Ptolemy's hypothesis, let the Earth be placed at the centre of the ecliptic, the solar circle, and the orbital circle of Venus, which carries the planetary epicycle. The radius of the epicycle is to that of the orbital circle approximately as 3 is to 4. First let the sun be situated at the middle of Scorpio, and let Venus be in conjunction with the sun and at the perigee of its epicycle. Next let the sun move 180° eastwards to the middle of Taurus, and similarly the centre of the epicycle; during this same interval the planet will move 112$\frac{1}{2}$° eastwards on its epicycle and will be found to appear in the middle of Aries approximately, or 30° west of the sun.

But according to the Copernican hypothesis, let us place the sun at the centre of the orbital circles of Venus and the Earth, which preserve the relative magnitudes of the Ptolemaic epicycle and orbital circle of Venus, but let us keep the Earth at the centre of the ecliptic, as far as appearances go, since the distance between the Earth and the sun is imperceptible in comparison with the magnitude of the sphere of the fixed stars. Now if the Earth is placed in the middle of Taurus, as viewed from the sun, and the planet at its perigee between the Earth and the sun, in such fashion that Venus and the sun would appear in the middle of Scorpio, while Venus moves eastwards 292$\frac{1}{2}$°, then the sun will be found to appear in the middle of Taurus, and the planet itself in middle of Aries or 30° west of the sun.

But let us turn to the three upper planets.

	Cycles of anomaly	Cycles of longitude	Solar years
Mars	37	42 +	79
Jupiter	65	6 —	71 —
Saturn	57	2 +	59 —

It is here noteworthy that according to the Ptolemaic hypothesis the sum of the revolutions of the eccentric circle and the revolutions in anomaly is equal to the number of solar cycles; and also that, the conjunctions with the sun take place at the planet's apogee, and the oppositions at its perigee.

(continued p. 26)

it a "visible god"; Sophocles' Electra, "that which gazes upon all things." And so the sun, as if resting on a kingly throne, governs the family of stars which wheel around. Moreover, the Earth is by no means cheated of the services of the moon; but, as Aristotle says in the *De Animalibus*, the earth has the closest kinship with the moon. The Earth moreover is fertilized by the sun and conceives offspring every year.

Therefore in this ordering we find [10a] that the world has a wonderful commensurability and that there is a sure bond of harmony for the movement and magnitude of the orbital circles such as cannot be found in any other way.[1] For now the careful observer can note why progression and retrogradation appear greater in Jupiter than in

But according to Copernicus the Ptolemaic cycles of anomaly will now represent the number of times the Earth has overtaken the planet; and the period of revolution in longitude will stay the alone. Thus, for example, Saturn will have two revolutions in longitude in 59 years, or one revolution around the sun in about 30 years. The planet will be revolving directly on its eccentric circle instead of on its Ptolemaic epicycle, and the Earth will now be revolving on an inner circle which has the same relative magnitude as the former epicycle. The two hypotheses, of course, are equipollent here too, with respect to appearances.

In other words, in constructing a theory to account for four coincidences which were left unexplained by Ptolemy, namely, (1) the equality between the number of cycles in longitude and the solar cycles, in the two lower planets; (2) the equality between the solar cycles and the sum of the cycles of anomaly and longitude, in the upper planets; (3) the limited angular digressions of Mercury and Venus away from the sun; and (4) the apogeal conjunctions and perigeal oppositions of Saturn, Jupiter, and Mars, Copernicus has telescoped the eccentric circle of Venus and that of Mercury into one circle carrying the Earth; and he has furthermore collapsed the three epicycles of Saturn, Jupiter, and Mars into this same one circle. That is to say, one circle is now doing the work of five.

COPERNICAN HYPOTHESIS

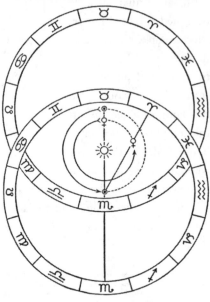

Movement of Earth=180°
Movement of Venus=292½°

---

[1] Let us recall the Ptolemaic ratios between the radius of the epicycle and that of the eccentric circle, and also the eccentricity.

	Epicycle	Eccentric	Eccentricity
Mercury	22½	60	3
Venus	43⅙	60	1¼
Mars	39½	60	6
Jupiter	11½	60	2⅖
Saturn	6½	60	3¼

By the Ptolemaic scheme it is impossible to compute the magnitudes of the eccentric circles themselves relative to one another, as there is no common measure. But now that the eccentric circles of Mercury and Venus and the epicycles of Mars, Jupiter, and Saturn have all been reduced to the orbital circle of the Earth, it is easy to calculate the relative magnitudes of the orbital circles—heretofore the epicycles of the lower planets and the eccentric circles of the upper—since, by reason of the necessary commensurability between epicycle and eccentric, they are all commensurable with the orbital circle of the Earth. Thus, for example, if we take the distance from the Earth to the sun as 1, the planets will observe the following approximate distances from the sun.

Mercury	⅓	Earth	1	Jupiter	5
Venus	¾	Mars	1½	Saturn	9

Saturn and smaller than in Mars; and in turn greater in Venus than in Mercury.[1] And why these reciprocal events appear more often in Saturn than in Jupiter, and even less often in Mars and Venus than in Mercury.[2] In addition, why when Saturn, Jupiter, and Mars are in opposition (to the mean position of the sun) they are nearer to the Earth than at the time of their occultation and their reappearance. And especially why at the times when Mars is in opposition to the sun, it seems to equal Jupiter in magnitude and to be distinguished from Jupiter only by a reddish color, but when discovered through careful observation by means of a sextant is found with difficulty among the stars of second magnitude?[3] All these things proceed from the same cause, which resides in the movement of the Earth.

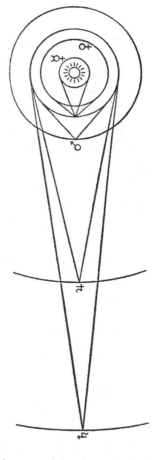

But that there are no such appearances among the fixed stars argues that they are at an immense height away, which makes the circle of annual movement or its image disappear from before our eyes since every visible thing has a certain distance beyond which it is no longer seen, as is shown in optics. For the brilliance of their lights shows that there is a very great distance between Saturn the highest of the planets and the sphere of the fixed stars. It is by this mark in particular that they are distinguished from the planets, as it is proper to have the greatest difference between the moved and the unmoved. How exceedingly fine is the godlike work of the Best and Greatest Artist!

11. A DEMONSTRATION OF THE THREEFOLD MOVEMENT OF THE EARTH

Therefore since so much and such great testimony on the part of the planets is consonant with the mobility of the Earth, we shall now give a summary of its movement,

---

[1] In the three upper planets, the angles which measure the apparent progression and retrogradation have as their vertex the centre of the planet and as their sides the tangents drawn to the orbital circle of the Earth. In the two lower planets, however, the vertex of the angle is at the centre of the Earth and the sides are the tangents drawn to the orbital circle of the planet. It is easy to see that, on account of the relative magnitudes of the orbital circles, the arcs of progression and retrogradation will appear smaller in Saturn than in Jupiter, and smaller in Jupiter than in Mars, and greater in Venus than in Mercury.

[2] The interchanges of progression and retrogradation are proportional to the number of times the Earth overtakes the outer planets and the inner planets overtake the Earth. Now the Earth overtakes Saturn more often than Jupiter, Jupiter more often than Mars, Mars more often than overtaken by Venus, and overtaken less often by Venus than by Mercury. Hence the frequency of progression and retrogradation is in that order.

[3] According to the Ptolemaic scheme, it can be inferred only from the changes in magnitude of the planet Mars what its relative distances from the Earth are at perigee and apogee. But according to the Copernican scheme, it follows from the relative distances of the planet at perigee and at apogee—which are as 1 to 5—that the apparent diameter of the planet should vary inversely in that ratio—assuming that the planet could be seen when in conjunction with the sun.

insofar as the appearances can be shown forth by its movement as by an hypothesis. We must allow a threefold movement altogether.

The first—which we said the Greeks called νυχθημἐρινος—is the proper circuit of day and night, which goes around the axis of the earth from west to east—as the world is held to move in the opposite direction—and describes the equator or the equinoctial circle—which some, imitating the Greek expression [10ᵇ] ἰσηἐρινος call the equidial.

The second is the annual movement of the centre, which describes the circle of the (zodiacal) signs around the sun similarly from west to east, *i.e.*, towards the signs which follow (from Aries to Taurus) and moves along between Venus and Mars, as we said, together with the bodies accompanying it. So it happens that the sun itself seems to traverse the ecliptic with a similar movement. In this way, for example, when the centre of the Earth is traversing Capricorn, the sun seems to be crossing Cancer; and when Aquarius, Leo, and so on, as we were saying.

It has to be understood that the equator and the axis of the Earth have a variable inclination with the circle and the plane of the ecliptic. For if they remained fixed and only followed the movement of the centre simply, no inequality of days and nights would be apparent, but it would always be the summer solstice or the winter solstice or the equinox, or summer or winter, or some other season of the year always remaining the same. There follows then the third movement, which is the declination: it is also an annual revolution but one towards the signs which precede (from Aries to Pisces), or westwards, *i.e.*, turning back counter to the movement of the centre; and as a consequence of these two movements which are nearly equal to one another but in opposite directions, it follows that the axis of the Earth and the greatest of the parallel circles on it, the equator, always look towards approximately the same quarter of the world, just as if they remained immobile. The sun in the meanwhile is seen to move along the oblique ecliptic with that movement with which the centre of the earth moves, just as if the centre of the earth were the centre of the world—provided you

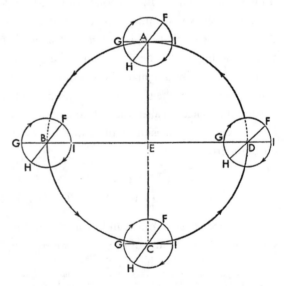

remember that the distance between the sun and the earth in comparison with the sphere of the fixed stars is imperceptible to us.

Since these things are such that they need to be presented to sight rather than merely to be talked about, let us draw the circle *ABCD*, which will represent the annual circuit of the centre of the earth in the plane of the ecliptic, and let *E* be the sun around its centre. I will cut this circle into four equal parts by means of the diameters *AEC* and *BED*. Let the point *A* be the beginning of Cancer; *B* of Libra; *E* of Capricorn; and *D* of Aries. Now let us put the centre of the earth first at *A*, around which we shall describe the terrestrial equator *FGHI*, but not in the same plane (as the ecliptic) except that the diameter *GAI* is the common section of the circles, *i.e.*, of the equator and the ecliptic. Also let the diameter *FAH* be drawn at right angles to *GAI*; and let *F* be the limit of the greatest southward declination (of the equator), and *H* of the northward declination. With this set-up, the Earth-dweller will see the sun—which is at the centre *E*—at the point of the winter solstice in Capricorn—[11ᵃ] which is caused by the greatest northward declination at *H* being turned toward the sun; since the inclination of the equator with respect to line *AE* describes by means of the daily revolution the winter tropic, which is parallel to the equator at the distance comprehended by the angle of inclination *EAH*. Now let the centre of the Earth proceed from west to east; and let *F*, the limit of greatest declination, have just as great a movement from east to west, until at *B* both of them have traversed quadrants of circles. Meanwhile, on account of the equality of the revolutions, angle *EAI* will always remain equal to angle *AEB*; the diameters will always stay parallel to one another—*FAH* to *FBH* and *GAI* to *GBI*; and the equator will remain parallel to the equator. And by reason of the cause spoken of many times already, these lines will appear in the immensity of the sky as the same. Therefore from the point *B* the beginning of Libra, *E* will appear to be in Aries, and the common section of the two circles (of the ecliptic and the equator) will fall upon line *GBIE*, in respect to which the daily revolution has no declination; but every declination will be on one side or the other of this line. And so the sun will be soon in the spring equinox. Let the centre of the Earth advance under the same conditions; and when it has completed [11ᵇ] a semicircle at *C*, the sun will appear to be entering Cancer. But since *F* the southward declination of the equator is now turned toward the sun, the result is that the sun is seen in the north, traversing the summer tropic in accordance with angle of inclination *ECF*. Again, when *F* moves on through the third quadrant of the circle, the common section *GI* will fall on line *ED*, whence the sun, seen in Libra, will appear to have reached the autumn equinox. But then as, in the same progressive movement, *HF* gradually turns in the direction of the sun, it will make the situation at the beginning return, which was our point of departure.

In another way: Again in the underlying plane let *AEC* be both the diameter (of the ecliptic) and its common section with the circle perpendicular to its plane. In this circle let *DGFI*, the meridian passing through the poles of the Earth be described around *A* and *C*, in turn, *i.e.*, in Cancer and in Capricorn. And let the axis of the Earth be *DF*, the north pole *D*, the south pole *F*, and *GI* the diameter of the equator. Therefore when *F* is turned in the direction of the sun, which is at E, and the inclination of the equator is northward in proportion to angle *IAE*, then the movement around the axis will describe—with the diameter *KL* and at the distance *LI*—parallel to the equator the southern circle, which appears with respect to the sun as the tropic of Capricorn. Or—to speak more correctly—this movement around the axis describes, in the direction of *AE*, a conic surface, which has the centre of the earth as its vertex and a circle parallel to the equator as its base.[1] Moreover in the opposite sign, *C*, the same things take place but conversely. Therefore it is clear how the two mutually opposing movements, *i.e.*, that of the centre and that of the inclination, force the axis of the Earth to remain balanced in the same way and to keep a similar position, and how they make all things appear as if they were movements of the sun.

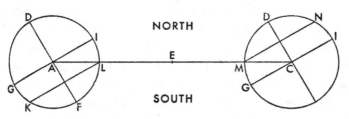

Now we said that the yearly revolutions of the centre and of the declination were approximately equal, because if they were exactly so, then the points of equinox and solstice and the obliquity of the ecliptic in relation to the sphere of the fixed stars could not change at all. But as the difference is very slight, [12ᵃ] it is not revealed except as it increases with time: as a matter of fact, from the time of Ptolemy to ours there has been a precession of the equinoxes and solstices of about 21°. For that reason some have believed that the sphere of the fixed stars was moving, and so they choose a ninth higher sphere. And when that was not enough, the moderns added a tenth, but without attaining the end which we hope we shall attain by means of the movement of the Earth. We shall use this movement as a principle and a hypothesis in demonstrating other things.

12. ON THE STRAIGHT LINES IN A CIRCLE

Because the proofs which we shall use in almost the entire work deal with straight lines and arcs, with plane and spherical triangles, and because Euclid's *Elements*, although they clear up much of this, do not have what is here most required, namely, how to find the sides from the angles and the angles from the sides, since the angle

---

[1]Or, in other words, the axis of the terrestrial equator describes around the axis of the terrestrial ecliptic a double conic surface having its vertices at the centre of the Earth, in a period of revolution equal approximately to that of the Earth's centre.

does not measure the subtending straight line—just as the line does not measure the angle—but the arc does, there has accordingly been found a method whereby the lines subtending any arc may become known. By means of these lines, or chords, it is possible to determine the arc corresponding to the angle: and conversely by means of the arc to determine the straight line, or chord, which subtends the angle. So it does not seem irrelevant, if we treat of these lines, and also of the sides and angles of plane and spherical triangles—which Ptolemy discussed a few at a time here and there—in order that these questions may be answered here once and for all and that what we are going to teach may become clearer. Now, by the common agreement of mathematicians, we divide the circle into 360 degrees. Now the ancients employed a diameter of 120 parts. But in order to avoid the complication of minutes and seconds in the multiplication and division of the numbers attached to the lines, as the lines are usually incommensurable in length, and often in square too; some of their successors established a rational diameter of 1,200,000 parts or of 2,000,000 parts, or of some other rational quantity—from the time when Arabic numerals came into general use. This mathematical notation surpasses any other—Greek or Latin—[12ᵇ] in a certain singular ease of employment and readily accommodates itself to every class of computation. For that reason we too have taken a division of the diameter into 200,000 parts as sufficient to exclude any very noticeable error. For as regards things which are not related as number to number, it is enough to attain a close approximation. But we will unfold this in six theorems and a problem—following Ptolemy fairly closely.

FIRST THEOREM

The diameter of a circle being given, the sides of the triangle, tetragon, hexagon, and decagon, which the same circle circumscribes, are also given.

Half the diameter, or the radius, is equal to the side of the hexagon, (Euclid, IV, 15); the square on the side of the triangle is three times the square on the side of the hexagon, (Euclid, XIII, 12); and the square on the side of the tetragon is twice the square on the side of the hexagon, Euclid as is shown in Euclid's *Elements* (IV, 9 and I, 47). Therefore the side of a hexagon is given in length as 100,000 parts, that of the tetragon as 141,422 parts, and that of the triangle as 173,205 parts.

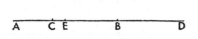

Now, let *AB* be the side of the hexagon; and by Euclid, II, 11, or VI, 30, let it be cut in mean and extreme ratio at point *C*; and let *CB* be the greater segment to which its equal *BD* is added. Therefore the whole *ABD* will have been cut in extreme and mean ratio, and the lesser segment *BD* will be the side of the decagon inscribed in the

circle, and *AB* will be the side of the inscribed hexagon, as is made clear by Euclid, XIII, 5 and 9.

But *BD* will be given in this way: let *AB* be bisected at *E*, and it will be clear from Euclid, XIII, 3 that

$$\text{sq. } EBD = 5 \text{ sq. } EB.$$

But

$$EB = 50{,}000.$$

Whence

$$5 \text{ sq. } EB \text{ is given.}$$

Hence

$$EBD = 111{,}803.$$

And

$$BD = EBD - EB = 111{,}803 - 50{,}000 = 61{,}803,$$

which is the side of the decagon sought.

Moreover the side of the pentagon, the square on which is equal to the sum of the squares on the side of the hexagon and on the side of the decagon (*Elements*, XIII, 10), is given as 117,557 parts.

Therefore the diameter of the circle being given, the sides of the triangle, tetragon, pentagon, hexagon and decagon, which may be inscribed in the same circle, have been given—as was to be shown.

PORISM

Furthermore, it is clear that when the chord subtending an arc has been given, that chord too can be found which subtends the rest [13ᵃ] of the semicircle..

Since the angle in a semicircle is right, and in right triangles the square on the chord subtending the right angle, *i.e.*, the square on the diameter, is equal to the sum of the squares on the sides comprehending the right angle; therefore—since the side of the decagon, which subtends 36° of the circumference, has been shown to have 61,803 parts whereof the diameter has 200,000 parts—the chord which subtends the remaining 144° of the semicircle has 190,211 parts.

And in the case of the side of the pentagon, which is equal to 117,557 parts of the diameter and subtends an arc of 72°, a straight line of 161,803 parts is given, and it subtends remaining 108° of the circle.

SECOND THEOREM

If a quadrilateral is inscribed in a circle, the rectangle comprehended by the diagonals is equal to the two rectangles which are comprehended by the two pairs of opposite sides.

For let the quadrilateral *ABCD* be inscribed in a circle; I say that the rectangle

comprehended by the diagonals *AC* and *DB* is equal to those comprehended by *AB*, *CD* and by *AD*, *BC*.

For let us make

angle *ABE* = angle *CBD*.

Therefore by addition

angle *ABD* = angle *EBC*,

taking angle *EBD* as common to both. Moreover

angle *ACB* = angle *BDA*

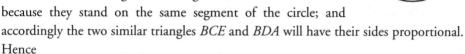

because they stand on the same segment of the circle; and accordingly the two similar triangles *BCE* and *BDA* will have their sides proportional. Hence

BC : *BD* = *EC* : *AD*.

And

rect. *EC*, *BD* = rect. *BC*, *AD*.

But also the triangles *ABE* and *CBD* are similar, because

angle *ABE* = angle *CBD*.

And

angle *BAC* = angle *BDC*,

because they intercept the same arc of the circle.
So again,

AB : *BD* = *AE* : *CD*

And

rect. *AB*, *DC* = rect. *AE*, *BD*.

But it has already been made clear that

rect. *AD*, *BC* = rect. *BD*, *EC*.

Accordingly, taken as a whole,

rect. *BD*, *AC* = rect. *AD*, *BC* + rect. *AB*, *CD*,

as it was opportune to have shown.

THIRD THEOREM

Hence if straight lines subtending unequal arcs in a semicircle are given, the chord subtending the arc whereby the greater arc exceeds the smaller is also given.

[13ᵇ] In the semicircle *ABCD* with diameter *AD*, let the straight lines *AB* and *AC*

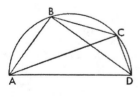

subtending unequal arcs be given. To us, who wish to discover the chord subtending *BC*, there are given by means of the aforesaid the chords *BD* and *CD* subtending the remaining arcs of the semicircle, and these chords bound the quadrilateral *ABCD* in the semicircle. The diagonals *AC*

and *BD* have been given together with the three sides *AB*, *AD*, and *CD*. And, as has already been shown,

rect. *AC*, *BD* = rect. *AB*, *CD* + rect. *AD*, *BC*.

Therefore,

rect. *AD*, *BC* = rect. *AC*, *BD* – rect. *AB*, *CD*.

Accordingly, in so far as the division may be carried out,

(*AC-BD* – *AB-CD*) ÷ *AD* = *BC*,

which was sought.

Further when, for example, the sides of the pentagon and hexagon are given from the above, by this computation a line is given subtending 12°—which is the difference between the arcs—and it is equal to 20,905 parts of the diameter.

FOURTH THEOREM

Given a chord subtending any arc, the chord subtending half of the arc is also given.

Let us describe the circle *ABC*, whose diameter is *AC*, and let the arc *BC* be given together with the chord subtending it, and let the line *EF* from the centre *E* cut *BC* at right angles. Accordingly by Euclid, III, 3, it will bisect chord *BC* at *F*, and the arc at *D*. Let the chords subtending arcs *AB* and *BD* be drawn. Since the triangles *ABC* and *EFC* are right and also similar—for they have angle *ECF* in common; therefore, as

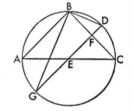

CF = ¹/₂ *BFC*,

so

EF = ¹/₂ *AB*.

But chord *AB* is given, for it subtends the remaining arc of the semicircle. Therefore *EF* is given; and so is line *DF* the remainder of the radius. Let the diameter *DEG* be completed, and let *BG* be joined. Therefore in triangle *BDG* line *BF* falls from the right angle at *B* perpendicular to the base. Accordingly,

rect. *GD*, *DF* = sq. *BD*.

Therefore *BD* is given in length, and it subtends half of the arc *BDC*.

And since a chord subtending 12° has already been given, the chord subtending 6° is given as 10,467 parts; that subtending 3°, as 5235 parts; that subtending 1¹/₂°, as 2618 parts; and that subtending 45', as 1309 parts.

[14ª] FIFTH THEOREM

Again, when chords are given subtending two arcs, the chord subtending the whole arc made up of them is also given.

Let there be given in the circle the two chords subtending the arcs *AB* and *BC*; I say that the chord subtending the whole arc *ABC* is also given.

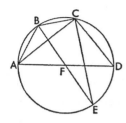

For let the diameters *AFD* and *BFE* be drawn, and also the chords *BD* and *CE*, which are given by means of the foregoing, on account of chords *AB* and *BC* being given; and

chord *DE* = chord *AB*.

The joining of *CD* completes the quadrilateral *BCDE*, whose diagonals *BD* and *CE* are given together with the three sides *BC*, *DE*, and *BE*; and the remaining side *CD* will be given by the second theorem; accordingly chord *CA* which subtends the remaining part of the semicircle will be given, and it subtends the whole arc *ABC* and is what was sought.

Furthermore, since so far there have been discovered chords which subtend 3°, $1^1/_2$°, and $^3/_4$°; by means of these intervals a table can be constructed with the most exact ratios. Nevertheless if we ascend through the degrees and add one arc to another arc either by halves or by some other mode, there is not unjustified doubt concerning the chords subtending those arcs, as the graphical ratios by which they can be shown are lacking to us. Nothing, however, prevents us from going on with that by some mode which is this side of error perceptible to sense and which is least unconsonant with the assumed number. This was what Ptolemy too sought as regards the chords subtending arcs of 1° or of $^1/_2$°; and he admonished us in the first place.

SIXTH THEOREM

The ratio of the arcs is greater than the ratio of the greater to the smaller of the chords.

Let there be in a circle two unequal successive arcs *AB* and *BC*, and let *BC* be the greater. I say that

arc *BC* : arc *AB* > chord *BC* : chord *AB*.

These chords comprehend angle *B*, and let that be bisected by line *BD*. And let *AC* be joined, which cuts *BD* at point *E*. Similarly let *AD* and *CD* be joined; then

AD = CD,

because they subtend equal arcs.

Accordingly, since in triangle *ABC*, the line which bisects the angle also cuts *AC* [14^b] at *E*, then

EC, segment of base : *AE* = *BC* : *AB* (Euclid, VI, 3)

and since

BC > AB,

then

EC > EA.

Let *DF* be erected perpendicular to *AC*; it will bisect *AC* at point *F*. And *F* must necessarily be found in the greater segment *EC*. And since in every triangle the greater angle is subtended by the greater side, in the triangle *DEF*

$$\text{side } DE > \text{side } DF,$$

and further,

$$AD > DE,$$

wheretofore the circumference described with *D* as center and *DE* as radius will cut *AD* and pass beyond *DF*. Therefore let it cut *AD* at *H*, and let it be extended in the straight line *DFI*. Since

$$\text{sect. } EDI > \text{trgl. } EDF,$$

while

$$\text{trgl. } DEA > \text{sect. } DEH,$$

therefore

$$\text{trgl. } DEF : \text{trgl. } DEA < \text{sect. } DEI : \text{sect. } DEH.$$

But sectors are proportional to their arcs or to the angles at the centre; while triangles under the same vertex are proportional to their bases. Accordingly

$$\text{angle } EDF : \text{angle } ADE > \text{base } EF : \text{base } AE.$$

Therefore, *componendo*,

$$\text{angle } FDA : \text{angle } ADE > \text{base } AF : \text{base } AE.$$

And, in the same way,

$$\text{angle } CDA : \text{angle } ADE > \text{base } AC : \text{base } AE.$$

But, *separando*,

$$\text{angle } CDE : \text{angle } EDA > \text{base } CE : \text{base } EA.$$

But

$$\text{angle } CDE : \text{angle } EDA = \text{arc } CB : \text{arc } AB.$$

And

$$\text{base } CE : \text{base } AE = \text{chord } CB : \text{chord } AB.$$

Therefore

$$\text{arc } CB : \text{arc } AB > \text{chord } BC : \text{chord } AB,$$

as was to be shown.

PROBLEM

But since the arc is always greater than the straight line subtending it—as the straight line is the shortest of those lines which have the same termini—nevertheless in going from greater to lesser sections of the circle, the inequality approaches equality, so that finally the circular line and the straight line go out of existence simultaneously at the point of tangency on the circle. Therefore it is necessary that just before that moment they differ from one another by no discernible difference.

42

For example, let arc AB be 3° and arc AC $1^1/_2$°. It has been shown that

$$\text{ch. } AB = 5235,$$

where diameter = 200,000,

and that

$$\text{ch. } AC = 2618.$$

And though

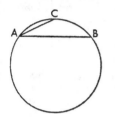

$$\text{arc } AB = 2 \text{ [15ª] arc } AC,$$

yet

$$\text{ch. } AB < 2 \text{ ch. } AC$$

and

$$\text{ch. } AC - 2617 = 1.$$

But if we make

$$\text{arc } AB = 1^1/_2°$$

and

$$\text{arc } AC = {}^3/_4°,$$

then

$$\text{ch. } AB = 2618$$

and

$$\text{ch. } AC = 1309,$$

and even though chord AC ought to be greater than half of chord AD, it is seen to be no different from the half. And the ratios of the arcs and the straight lines are now apparently the same. Therefore, since we see that we have come so far that the difference between the straight and the circular line evades sense-perception as completely as if there were only one line, we do not hesitate to take 1309 as subtending ${}^3/_4$° and in the same ratio to fit the chord to the degree and to the remaining parts (of the degree); and so with the addition of ${}^1/_4$° to the ${}^3/_4$° we establish 1° as subtended by 1745, ${}^1/_2$° by $872^1/_2$, and ${}^1/_3$° by approximately 582.

Nevertheless I think it will be enough if in the table we give only the halves of the chords subtending twice the arc, whereby we may concisely comprehend in the quadrant what it used to be necessary to spread out over the semicircle; and especially because the halves come more frequently into use in demonstration and calculation than the whole chords do. Now we have set forth a table increasing by ${}^1/_6$°'s and having three columns. In the first column are the degrees and sixth parts of a degree. The second contains the numerical length of half the chord subtending twice the arc. The third contains the difference between the numerical lengths of each half chord, and by means of these differences we can make proportional additions in taking half-chords of a particular number of minutes. The table follows:

TABLE OF THE CHORDS IN A CIRCLE

Arcs		Halves of the chords subtending twice the arcs	Differences between each half-chord	Arcs		Halves of the chords subtending twice the arcs	Differences between each half-chord	Arcs		Halves of the chords subtending twice the arcs	Differences between each half-chord
Deg.	Min.			Deg.	Min.			Deg.	Min.		
0	10	291	291	7	40	13341	288	15	10	26163	280
0	20	582	291	7	50	13629	288	15	20	26443	281
0	30	873	290	8	0	13917	288	15	30	26724	280
0	40	1163	291	8	10	14205	288	15	40	27004	280
0	50	1454	291	8	20	14493	288	15	50	27284	280
1	0	1745	291	8	30	14781	288	16	0	27564	279
1	10	2036	291	8	40	15069	287	16	10	27843	279
1	20	2327	290	8	50	15356	287	16	20	28122	279
1	30	2617	291	9	0	15643	288	16	30	28401	279
1	40	2908	291	9	10	15931	287	16	40	28680	279
1	50	3199	291	9	20	16218	287	16	50	28959	278
2	0	3490	291	9	30	16505	287	17	0	29237	278
2	10	3781	290	9	40	16792	286	17	10	29515	278
2	20	4071	291	9	50	17078	287	17	20	29793	278
2	30	4362	291	10	0	17365	286	17	30	30071	277
2	40	4653	290	10	10	17651	286	17	40	30348	277
2	50	4943	291	10	20	17937	286	17	50	30625	277
3	0	5234	290	10	30	18223	286	18	0	30902	276
3	10	5524	290	10	40	18509	286	18	10	31178	276
3	20	5814	291	10	50	18795	286	18	20	31454	276
3	30	6105	290	11	0	19081	285	18	30	31730	276
3	40	6395	290	11	10	19366	286	18	40	32006	276
3	50	6685	290	11	20	19652	285	18	50	32282	275
4	0	6975	290	11	30	19937	285	19	0	32557	275
4	10	7265	290	11	40	20222	285	19	10	32832	274
4	20	7555	290	11	50	20507	284	19	20	33106	275
4	30	7845	290	12	0	20791	285	19	30	33381	274
4	40	8135	290	12	10	21076	284	19	40	33655	274
4	50	8425	290	12	20	21360	284	19	50	33929	273
5	0	8715	290	12	30	21644	284	20	0	34202	273
5	10	9005	290	12	40	21928	284	20	10	34475	273
5	20	9295	290	12	50	22212	283	20	20	34748	273
5	30	9585	289	13	0	22495	283	20	30	35021	272
5	40	9874	290	13	10	22778	284	20	40	35293	272
5	50	10164	289	13	20	23062	282	20	50	35565	272
6	0	10453	289	13	30	23344	283	21	0	35837	271
6	10	10742	289	13	40	23627	283	21	10	36108	271
6	20	11031	289	13	50	23910	282	21	20	36379	271
6	30	11320	289	14	0	24192	282	21	30	36650	270
6	40	11609	289	14	10	24474	282	21	40	36920	270
6	50	11898	289	14	20	24756	282	21	50	37190	270
7	0	12187	289	14	30	25038	281	22	0	37460	270
7	10	12476	288	14	40	25319	282	22	10	37730	269
7	20	12764	289	14	50	25601	281	22	20	37999	269
7	30	13053	288	15	0	25882	281	22	30	38268	269

TABLE OF THE CHORDS IN A CIRCLE

Arcs		Halves of the chords subtending twice the arcs	Differences between each half-chord	Arcs		Halves of the chords subtending twice the arcs	Differences between each half-chord	Arcs		Halves of the chords subtending twice the arcs	Differences between each half-chord
Deg.	Min.			Deg.	Min.			Deg.	Min.		
22	40	38587	268	30	10	50252	251	37	40	61107	230
22	50	38805	268	30	20	50503	251	37	50	61337	229
23	0	39073	268	30	30	50754	250	38	0	61566	229
23	10	39341	267	30	40	51004	250	38	10	61795	229
23	20	39608	267	30	50	51254	250	38	20	62024	227
23	30	39875	266	31	0	51504	249	38	30	62251	228
23	40	40141	267	31	10	51753	249	38	40	62479	227
23	50	40408	266	31	20	52002	248	38	50	62706	226
24	0	40674	265	31	30	52250	248	39	0	62932	226
24	10	40939	265	31	40	52498	247	39	10	63158	225
24	20	41204	265	31	50	52745	247	39	20	63383	225
24	30	41469	265	32	0	52992	246	39	30	63608	224
24	40	41734	264	32	10	53238	246	39	40	63832	224
24	50	41998	264	32	20	53484	246	39	50	64056	223
25	0	42262	263	32	30	53730	245	40	0	64279	222
25	10	42525	263	32	40	53975	245	40	10	64501	222
25	20	42788	263	32	50	54220	244	40	20	64723	222
25	30	43051	262	33	0	54464	244	40	30	64945	221
25	40	43313	262	33	10	54708	243	40	40	65166	220
25	50	43575	262	33	20	54951	243	40	50	65386	220
26	0	43837	261	33	30	55194	242	41	0	65606	219
26	10	44098	261	33	40	55436	242	41	10	65825	219
26	20	44359	261	33	50	55678	241	41	20	66044	218
26	30	44620	260	34	0	55919	241	41	30	66262	218
26	40	44880	260	34	10	56160	240	41	40	66480	217
26	50	45140	259	34	20	56400	241	41	50	66697	216
27	0	45399	259	34	30	56641	239	42	0	66913	216
27	10	45658	259	34	40	56880	239	42	10	67129	215
27	20	45917	258	34	50	57119	239	42	20	67344	215
27	30	46175	258	35	0	57358	238	42	30	67559	214
27	40	46433	257	35	10	57596	237	42	40	67773	214
27	50	46690	257	35	20	57833	237	42	50	67987	213
28	0	46947	257	35	30	58070	237	43	0	68200	212
28	10	47204	256	35	40	58307	236	43	10	68412	212
28	20	47460	256	35	50	58543	236	43	20	68624	211
28	30	47716	255	36	0	58779	235	43	30	68835	211
28	40	47971	255	36	10	59014	234	43	40	69046	210
28	50	48226	255	36	20	59248	234	43	50	69256	210
29	0	48481	254	36	30	59482	234	44	0	69466	209
29	10	48735	254	36	40	59716	233	44	10	69675	208
29	20	48989	253	36	50	59949	232	44	20	69883	208
29	30	49242	253	37	0	60181	232	44	30	70091	207
29	40	49495	253	37	10	60413	232	44	40	70298	207
29	50	49748	252	37	20	60645	231	44	50	70505	206
30	0	50000	252	37	30	60876	231	45	0	70711	205

Arcs		Halves of the chords subtending twice the arcs	Differences between each half-chord	Arcs		Halves of the chords subtending twice the arcs	Differences between each half-chord	Arcs		Halves of the chords subtending twice the arcs	Differences between each half-chord
Deg.	Min.			Deg.	Min.			Deg.	Min.		
45	10	70916	205	52	40	79512	176	60	10	86747	145
45	20	71121	204	52	50	79688	176	60	20	86892	144
45	30	71325	204	53	0	79864	174	60	30	87036	142
45	40	71529	203	53	10	80038	174	60	40	87178	142
45	50	71732	202	53	20	80212	174	60	50	87320	142
46	0	71934	202	53	30	80386	172	61	0	87462	141
46	10	72136	201	53	40	80558	172	61	10	87603	140
46	20	72337	200	53	50	80730	172	61	20	87743	139
46	30	72537	200	54	0	80902	170	61	30	87882	138
46	40	72737	199	54	10	81072	170	61	40	88020	138
46	50	72936	199	54	20	81242	169	61	50	88158	137
47	0	73135	198	54	30	81411	169	62	0	88295	136
47	10	73333	198	54	40	81580	168	62	10	88431	135
47	20	73531	197	54	50	81748	167	62	20	88566	135
47	30	73728	196	55	0	81915	167	62	30	88701	134
47	40	73924	195	55	10	82082	166	62	40	88835	133
47	50	74119	195	55	20	82248	165	62	50	88968	133
48	0	74314	194	55	30	82413	164	63	0	89101	131
48	10	74508	194	55	40	82577	164	63	10	89232	131
48	20	74702	194	55	50	82741	163	63	20	89363	130
48	30	74896	194	56	0	82904	162	63	30	89493	129
48	40	75088	192	56	10	83066	162	63	40	89622	129
48	50	75280	191	56	20	83228	161	63	50	89751	128
49	0	75471	190	56	30	83389	160	64	0	89879	127
49	10	75661	190	56	40	83549	159	64	10	90006	127
49	20	75851	189	56	50	83708	159	64	20	90133	125
49	30	76040	189	57	0	83867	158	64	30	90258	125
49	40	76299	188	57	10	84025	157	64	40	90383	124
49	50	76417	187	57	20	84182	157	64	50	90507	124
50	0	76604	187	57	30	84339	156	65	0	90631	122
50	10	76791	186	57	40	84495	155	65	10	90753	122
50	20	76977	185	57	50	84650	155	65	20	90875	121
50	30	77162	185	58	0	84805	154	65	30	90996	120
50	40	77347	184	58	10	84959	153	65	40	91116	119
50	50	77531	184	58	20	85112	152	65	50	91235	119
51	0	77715	182	58	30	85264	151	66	0	91354	118
51	10	77897	182	58	40	85415	151	66	10	91472	118
51	20	78079	182	58	50	85566	151	66	20	91590	116
51	30	78261	181	59	0	85717	149	66	30	91706	116
51	40	78442	180	59	10	85866	149	66	40	91822	114
51	50	78622	179	59	20	86015	148	66	50	91936	114
52	0	78801	179	59	30	86163	147	67	0	92050	114
52	10	78980	178	59	40	86310	147	67	10	92164	112
52	20	79158	177	59	50	86457	145	67	20	92276	112
52	30	79335	177	60	0	86602	145	67	30	92388	111

TABLE OF THE CHORDS IN A CIRCLE

Arcs		Halves of the chords subtending twice the arcs	Differences between each half-chord	Arcs		Halves of the chords subtending twice the arcs	Differences between each half-chord	Arcs		Halves of the chords subtending twice the arcs	Differences between each half-chord
Deg.	Min.			Deg.	Min.			Deg.	Min.		
67	40	92499	110	75	10	96667	75	82	40	99182	37
67	50	92609	109	75	20	96742	73	82	50	99219	36
68	0	92718	109	75	30	96815	72	83	0	99255	35
68	10	92827	108	75	40	96887	72	83	10	99290	34
68	20	92935	107	75	50	96959	71	83	20	99324	33
68	30	93042	106	76	0	97030	69	83	30	99357	32
68	40	93148	105	76	10	97099	70	83	40	99389	32
68	50	93253	105	76	20	97169	68	83	50	99421	31
69	0	93358	104	76	30	97237	67	84	0	99452	30
69	10	93462	103	76	40	97304	67	84	10	99482	29
69	20	93565	102	76	50	97371	66	84	20	99511	28
69	30	93667	102	77	0	97437	65	84	30	99539	28
69	40	93769	101	77	10	97502	64	84	40	99567	27
69	50	93870	99	77	20	97566	64	84	50	99594	26
70	0	93969	99	77	30	97630	62	85	0	99620	24
70	10	94068	99	77	40	97692	62	85	10	99644	24
70	20	94167	97	77	50	97754	61	85	20	99668	24
70	30	94264	97	78	0	97815	60	85	30	99692	22
70	40	94361	96	78	10	97875	59	85	40	99714	22
70	50	94457	95	78	20	97934	58	85	50	99736	20
71	0	94552	94	78	30	97992	58	86	0	99756	20
71	10	94646	93	78	40	98050	57	86	10	99776	19
71	20	94739	93	78	50	98107	56	86	20	99795	18
71	30	94832	92	79	0	98163	55	86	30	99813	17
71	40	94924	91	79	10	98218	54	86	40	99830	17
71	50	95015	90	79	20	98272	53	86	50	99847	16
72	0	95105	90	79	30	98325	53	87	0	99863	15
72	10	95195	89	79	40	98378	52	87	10	99878	14
72	20	95284	88	79	50	98430	51	87	20	99892	13
72	30	95372	87	80	0	98481	50	87	30	99905	12
72	40	95459	86	80	10	98531	49	87	40	99917	11
72	50	95545	85	80	20	98580	49	87	50	99928	11
73	0	95630	85	80	30	98629	47	88	0	99939	10
73	10	95715	84	80	40	98676	47	88	10	99949	9
73	20	95799	83	80	50	98723	46	88	20	99958	8
73	30	95882	82	81	0	98769	45	88	30	99966	7
73	40	95964	81	81	10	98814	44	88	40	99973	6
73	50	96045	81	81	20	98858	44	88	50	99979	6
74	0	96126	80	81	30	98902	42	89	0	99985	4
74	10	96206	79	81	40	98944	42	89	10	99989	4
74	20	96285	78	81	50	98986	41	89	20	99993	3
74	30	96363	77	82	0	99027	40	89	30	99996	2
74	40	96440	77	82	10	99067	39	89	40	99998	1
74	50	96517	75	82	20	99106	38	89	50	99999	1
75	0	96592	75	82	30	99144	38	90	0	100000	0

13. ON THE SIDES AND ANGLES OF PLANE RECTILINEAR TRIANGLES

I

[19ᵇ] The sides of a triangle whose angles are given are given.

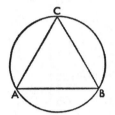

I say let there be the triangle *ABC*, around which a circle is circumscribed, by Euclid, IV, 5. Therefore arcs *AB*, *BC*, and *CA* will be given in degrees whereof 360° are equal to two right angles. Now given the arcs, the subtending sides of the triangle inscribed in the circle are also given by the table drawn up, where the diameter is assumed to have 200,000 parts.

II

But if two sides of the triangle are given together with one of the angles, the remaining side and the remaining angles may become known.

For the given sides are either equal or unequal. But the given angle is either right or acute or obtuse. Again, the given sides either comprehend the angle or they do not comprehend it.

Therefore in triangle *ABC* first let the two given sides *AB* and *AC* be equal, and let them comprehend the given angle *A*.

Therefore the remaining angles at base *BC* are also given—since they are equal—as half of the remainder, when *A* is subtracted from two right angles. And if the angle given first was at the base, then its equal is soon given, and from the two of them the remaining angle that goes to make up two right angles. But given the angles of a triangle, the sides are given; and moreover the base *BC* is given from the table in the parts whereof *AB* or *AC* as radius has 100,000 parts or whereof the diameter has 200,000 parts.

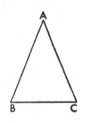

III

But if the angle BAC comprehended by the given sides is right, the same thing will result.

Since it is obvious that

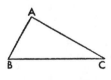

[20ᵃ] sq. *AB* + sq. *AC* = sq. *BC*;

therefore *BC* is given in length and the sides in their ratio to one another. But the segment of a circle which comprehends a right triangle is a semicircle, and base *BC* is the diameter. Therefore *AB* and *AC* as subtending the remaining angles *C* and *B* will be

given in the parts whereof *BC* has 200,000 parts. And the ratio of the table will reveal the angles in the degrees whereof 180° are equal to two right angles.

The same thing will result if *BC* is given together with one of the sides comprehending the right angle, as I judge has been clearly established.

IV

But now let the given angle ABC be acute, and also let it be comprehended by the given sides AB and BC.

And from point *A* drop a perpendicular to *BC* extended, if necessary, according as it falls inside or outside the triangle, and let it be *AD*. By this perpendicular the two right triangles *ABD* and *ADC* are distinguished, and since the angles in *ABD* are given—for *D* is a right angle, and *B* is given by hypothesis; therefore *AD* and *BD* are given by the table as subtending angles *A* and *B* in the parts whereof *AB*, the diameter of the circle, has 200,000 parts. And in the same ratio wherein *AB* was given in length, *AD* and *BD* are given similarly; and *CD*, which is the difference between *BC* and *BD*, is given also.

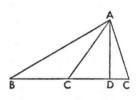

Therefore in the right triangle *ADC*, the sides *AD* and *CD* being given, *AC* the side sought and angle *ACD* are given according to what has been shown above.

V

And it will not turn out differently, if angle *B* is obtuse.

For the perpendicular *AD* dropped from point *A* to straight line *BC* extended makes the triangle *ABD* have its angles given. For angle *ABD*, which is exterior to angle *ABC*, is given; and

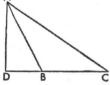

angle *D* = 90°.

Therefore sides *BD* and *AD* are given in the parts whereof *AB* has 200,000. And since *BA* and *BC* have a given ratio to one another, therefore *AB* too is given in the same parts, wherein *BD* and the whole *CBD* are given.

Accordingly in the right triangle *ADC*, since the two sides *AD* and *CD* are given, side *AC* and angles *BAC* and *ACB*, which were sought for, are also given.

VI

But let either of the given sides, *AC* or *AB*, be the one subtending the given angle *B*. [20b] Therefore *AC* is given by the table in parts whereof the diameter of the circle circumscribing the triangle *ABC* has 200,000 and according to the given ratio of *AC*

to *AB*. *AB* is given in similar parts, and by the table the angle *ACB* is given together with the remaining angle *BAC*, by which chord *CB* is also given. And by this ratio they are given in any magnitude.

VII

Given all the sides of the triangle, the angles are given.

It is too well known to be worth mentioning that each angle of an equilateral triangle is one third of two right angles.

It is also clear in the case of an isosceles triangle. For each of the equal sides is to the third side as half of the diameter is to the side subtending the arc by which the angle comprehended by the equal sides is given according to the table, wherein the 360° around the centre are equal to four right angles.[1] Then the two angles at the base are given as half of the supplementary angle.

Therefore it now remains to show this in the case of scalene triangles, which we divide in the same way into right triangles. Therefore let there be the scalene triangle *ABC* of which the sides are given, and upon the side which is the longest, namely *BC*, drop the perpendicular *AD*. Now Euclid, II, 13 tells us that if *AB* subtends the acute angle, then

$$(\text{sq. } AC + \text{sq. } BC) - \text{sq. } AB = 2 \text{ rect. } BC, CD.$$

Now it is necessary for angle *C* to be acute; for otherwise *AB* would be the longest side contrary to the hypotheses, according to Euclid, I, 17 - 19. Therefore *BD* and *DC* are given, and there will be the right triangles *ABC* and *ADC* with their sides and angles given—as has so often happened before—and so the angles of triangle *ABC* which were sought become established.

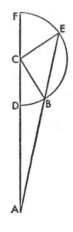

Another way. Similarly Euclid, III, 36 will perhaps give us an easy method, if with *BC* the shorter side as radius and with point *C* as centre, we describe a circle which will cut either one or both of the remaining sides.

First, let it cut both: *AB* at point *E* and *AC* at *D*; and let line *ADC* extended to point *F* in order to complete the diameter *DCF*. And with this construction it is clear from that proposition of Euclid that

[21ᵃ] rect. *FA, AD* = rect. *BA, AE*,

since each is equal to the square on the tangent to the circle from *A*. But the whole *AF* is given, as all its segments are given, since

[1] As in the subjoined figure:

radius *CF* = radius *CD* = *BC*,

and

$$AD = CA - CD.$$

Wherefore, as the rectangle *BA*, *AE* is given, *AE* also is given in length; and so is the remainder *BE* subtending arc *BE*. By joining *EC* we shall have the isosceles triangle *BCE* with all its sides given. Therefore the angle *EBC* is given. Hence in the triangle *ABC* the remaining angles at *C* and at *A* may become known by means of what has been shown above.

However, let the circle not cut *AB* as in the other figure, where *AB* falls upon the concave circumference; nevertheless *BE* will be given, and in the isosceles triangle *BCE* angle *CBE* will be given and also the exterior angle *ABC*. And by the same method as before the remaining angles are given.

And we have said enough concerning rectilinear triangles, in which a great part of geodesy consists. Now let us turn to spherical triangles.

14. ON SPHERICAL TRIANGLES

In this place we take that triangle as spherical which is comprehended by three arcs of great circles on a spherical surface. But we take the difference and magnitude of the angles from the arc of a great circle, *i.e.*, a great circle described with the point of section as a pole; and this arc is the arc intercepted by the quadrants of the circles comprehending the angle. For as the arc thus intercepted is to the whole circumference, so is the angle of section to four right angles—which we have said contain 360 equal degrees.

I

*[21*b*] If there are three arcs of the great circles of a sphere, and if any two of them joined together are longer than the third; it is clear that a spherical triangle can be constructed from them.*

For Euclid, XI, 23 shows in the case of angles what is here proposed in the case of arcs. Since there is the same ratio between angles as between arcs, and since the great circles are those circles which pass through the centre of the sphere; it is manifest that those three sectors of circles, *i.e.*, the sectors to which the three arcs belong, form a solid angle at the centre of the sphere. Therefore what was proposed has been established.

II

Any arc of a (spherical) triangle must be less than a semicircle.

For the semicircle makes no angle at the centre but falls upon it in a straight line.

But the remaining two angles which intercept the arcs cannot complete a solid angle at the centre, and so they cannot complete a spherical triangle.

And I think this is the reason why Ptolemy in his exposition of triangles of this genus, especially as regards the figure of the spherical sector, argues that none of the arcs taken together must be greater than a semicircle.

III

In spherical triangles having a right angle, the chord subtending twice the side opposite the right angle is to a chord subtending twice one of the sides comprehending the right angle as the diameter of the sphere is to the chord which subtends the angle comprehended in the great circle of the sphere by the first side and by the remaining side.

For let there be the spherical triangle *ABC*, of which the angle at *C* is right. I say that

ch. 2 *AB* : ch. 2 *BC* = dmt. sph. : ch. 2 *BAC* gr. circ. sph.

With *A* as a pole draw *DE* the arc of a great circle, and let *ABD* and *ACE* the quadrants of the circles be completed. And from the centre *F* of the sphere draw the common sections of the circles: *FA* the common section of circles *ABD* and *ACE*, [22ª] *FE* of circles *ACE* and *DE*, and *FD* of circles *ABD* and *DE*; and moreover, *FC* of the circles *AC* and *BC*. Then draw *BG* at right angles to *FA*, *BI* at right angles to *FC*, and *DK* at right angles to *FE*; and let *GI* be joined.

Since if a circle cuts a circle described through its poles, it cuts it at right angles; therefore the angle *AED* will be right; and angle *ACB* is right by hypothesis; and each of the planes *EDF* and *BCF* is perpendicular to plane *AEF*. Wherefore if a line be erected in the underlying plane of *AFE* at right angles 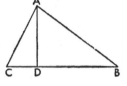 to point *K* in the common section, this line and *KD* will comprehend a right angle, by the definition of planes which are perpendicular to one another. Wherefore, by Euclid, XI, 4, line *KD* is perpendicular to circle *AEF*. But *BI* was erected in the same relation to the same plane; and so by Euclid, XI, 6, *DK* is parallel to *BI* and *FD* is parallel to *GB*, because

angle *FGB* = angle *GFD* = 90°.

And by Euclid, XI, 10,

angle *FDK* = angle *GBI*.

But

angle *FKD* = 90°,

and by definition

GI is perpendicular to *IB*.

Accordingly the sides of similar triangles are proportional; and

$$DF : BG = DK : BI.$$

But

$$BI = \frac{1}{2} \text{ ch. } 2 \, CB,$$

since it is at right angles to the radius from center F; and for the same reason,

$$BG = \frac{1}{2} \text{ ch. } 2 \, BA,$$

$$DK = \frac{1}{2} \text{ ch. } 2 \, DE, \text{ or } \frac{1}{2} \text{ ch. } 2 \, DAE,$$

and

$$DF = \frac{1}{2} \text{ dmt. sph.,}$$

Therefore it is clear that

$$\text{ch. } 2 \, AB : \text{ch. } 2 \, BC = \text{dmt.} : \text{ch. } 2 \, DAE \text{ (or ch. } 2 \, DE),$$

as it was time to show.

IV

In any triangle having a right angle, if another angle and any side are given, the remaining angle and the remaining sides will be given.

For let there be the triangle ABC having the angle A right and having one of the other two angles, namely B, given.

Let us take three cases of the given side. For it is either adjacent to both the given angles, as AB, or only to the right angle, as AC, or is opposite the right angle, as BC.

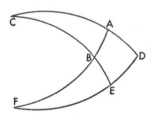

Therefore let AB be the side given first; and with C as a pole let arc [22b] DE of the great circle be described. Let the quadrants CAD and CBE be completed; and let AB and DE be extended, until they cut one another at point F. Therefore conversely the pole of CAD will be at F, because

$$\text{angle } A = \text{angle } D = 90°.$$

And since, if in a sphere the great circles cut one another at right angles, they will bisect one another and pass through the poles of one another; therefore ABF and DEF are quadrants of circles. And since AB is given, BF the remainder of the quadrant is also given; and the vertical angle EBF is equal to the given angle ABC. But by what has been shown above

$$\text{ch. } 2 \, BF : \text{ch. } 2 \, EF = \text{dmt. sph.} : \text{ch. } 2 \, EBF.$$

But three of the chords have been given:

dmt. sph.,

ch. 2 BF,

ch. 2 EBF,

or the half-chords; and therefore by Euclid, VI, 15, there is also given

$^1/_2$ ch. 2 *EF*;

and by the table the arc *EF* itself and *DE* the remainder of the quadrant, or the angle at *C*, which was sought. Similarly and alternately,

ch. 2 *DE* : ch. 2 *AB* = ch. 2 *EBC* : ch. 2 *CB*.

But *DE*, *AB*, and *CE* on the quadrants of the circle have already been given; and therefore the fourth chord, subtending twice arc *CB*, will be given, and also the side *CB*, which was sought.

And since

ch. 2 *CB* : ch. 2 *CA* = ch. 2 *BF* : ch. 2 *EF*,

because they both have the ratio of

dmt. sph. : ch. 2 *CBA*,

and because things which have the same ratio to one and the same thing have the same ratio to one another; therefore with the three chords *BF*, *EF*, and *CB* given, the fourth chord *CA* is also given; and arc *CA* is the third side of the triangle *ABC*.

But now let *AC* be the side assumed as given, and let our problem be to find the sides *AB* and *BC* together with the remaining angle *C*. Again similarly and by inversion,

ch. 2 *CA* : ch. 2 *CB* = ch. 2 *ABC* : dmt.

Hence the side *CB* is given, and also *AD* and *BE* the remainders of the quadrants of the circles. And so again,

ch. 2 *AD* : ch. 2 *BE* = ch. 2 *ABF*, *i.e.*, dmt., : ch. 2 *BF*.

Therefore arc *BF* is given, and the side *AB*, which is the remainder.

And similarly,

ch. 2 *BC* : ch. 2 *AB* = 2 ch. *CBE* : ch. 2 *DE*.

Hence arc *DE*, or twice the remaining angle at *C*, will be given.

Furthermore, if it was *BC* which was assumed, again as before, *AC* and the remainders *AD* and *BE* will be given. Hence arc *BF* and the remaining side *AB* are given by means of the diameter and the chords [23a] subtending them, as has often been said. And as in the preceding theorem, by means of arcs *BC*, *AB*, and *CBE* being given, the arc *ED*, *i.e.*, the remaining angle at *C*, which we were seeking, is discovered.

And so again in the triangle *ABC* with two angles *A* and *B* given, of which *A* is right, and with one of the three sides given, the third angle and the remaining sides are given, as was to be shown.

V

The sides of a right triangle, of which the angles are given, are also given.

Let the preceding diagram be kept. On account of the angle *C* being given, the arc *DE* and *EF* the remainder of the quadrant are given. And since *BEF* is a right angle, because *BE* was let fall from the pole of arc *DEF*; and since angle *EBF* is equal to its vertical angle, which was given; therefore the triangle *BEF*, having the right angle *E* and the angle at *B* given together with the side *EF*, has its sides and angles given by the preceding theorem. Therefore *BF* is given, and so is *AB* the remainder of the quadrant. And similarly in the triangle *ABC* the remaining sides *AC* and *BC* are shown as above.

VI

If in the same sphere two triangles have right angles and another angle equal to another angle and one side equal to one side—whether the sides be adjacent to the equal angles or lie opposite one of the equal angles—they will have the remaining sides equal to the remaining sides and the remaining angle equal to the remaining angle.

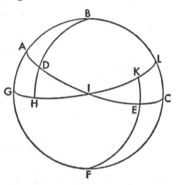

Let there be the hemisphere *ABC*, in which the two triangles *ABD* and *CEF* are taken. Let the angles at *A* and *C* be right; and furthermore let the angle *ADB* be equal to *CEF*, and one side to one side. And first let the equal sides be adjacent to the equal angles, *i.e.*, let *AD* be equal to *CE*. I say moreover that side *AB* is equal to side *CF*, side *BD* to *EF*, and the remaining angle *ABD* to the remaining angle *CFE*.

For with *B* and *F* as poles, draw *GHI* and *IKL* the quadrants of the great circles. And let quadrants *ADI* and *CEI* be completed. They necessarily cut one another at the pole of the hemisphere, point *I*, [23b] because

angle *A* = angle *C* = 90°

and quadrants *GHI* and *CEI* have been drawn through the poles of the circle *ABC*.

Therefore, since it has been assumed that

side *AD* = side *CE*

then by subtraction

arc *DI* = arc *EI*.

And

angle *IDH* = angle *IEK*;

for they are placed at the vertices of the angles assumed as equal; and

angle *H* = angle *K* = 90°.

As things which have the same ratio to the same are in the same ratio; and since by Theorem III in this chapter,

$$\text{ch. 2 } ID : \text{ch. 2 } HI = \text{dmt. sph.} : \text{ch. 2 } IDH,$$

and

$$\text{ch. } EI : \text{ch. 2 } KI = \text{dmt. sph.} : \text{ch. 2 } IEK;$$

therefore

$$\text{ch. 2 } ID : \text{ch. 2 } HI = \text{ch. 2 } EI : \text{ch. 2 } IK.$$

And by Euclid's *Elements*, V, 14, since

$$\text{ch. 2 } DI = \text{ch. 2 } IE$$

therefore

$$\text{ch. 2 } HI = \text{ch. 2 } IK.$$

And as in equal circles equal chords cut off equal arcs, and as the parts of multiples are in the same ratio (as the multiples); therefore the plain arcs IH and IK will be equal; and so will GH and KL the remainders of the quadrants. Whence it is clear that

$$\text{angle } B = \text{angle } F,$$

and since, by the inverse of the third theorem,

$$\text{ch. 2 } AD : \text{ch. 2 } BD = \text{ch. 2 } HG : \text{ch 2 } BDH, \text{ or dmt.,}$$

and

$$\text{ch. 2 } EC : \text{ch. 2 } EF = \text{ch. 2 } KL : \text{ch. 2 } FEK, \text{ or dmt.,}$$

wherefore

$$\text{ch. 2 } AD : \text{ch. 2 } BD = \text{ch. 2 } EC : \text{ch. 2 } EF$$

and

$$AD = CE.$$

Therefore, by Euclid's *Elements*, V, 14,

$$\text{arc } BD = \text{arc } EF,$$

on account of the chords subtending twice the area being equal.

In the same way with BD and EF equal, we will show that the remaining sides and angles are equal.

And in turn, if sides AB and CF are assumed to be equal, the results will follow the same identity of ratio.

VII

Now also even if there is no right angle, but provided that the sides which are adjacent to the equal angles are equal to one another, the same thing will be shown.

In this way if in the two triangles ABD and CEF

$$\text{angle } B = \text{angle } F$$

and

$$\text{angle } D = \text{angle } E,$$

and if side *BD* is adjacent to the equal [24ᵃ], angles and

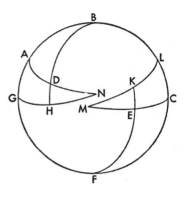

$$\text{side } BD = \text{side } EF,$$

I say that again the triangles are equilateral and equiangular.

For once more with *B* and *F* as poles, describe *GH* and *KL*, the arcs of the great circles. And let *AD* and *GH* extended intersect at *N*; and let *EC* and *LK* similarly extended intersect at *M*.

Therefore since in the two triangles *HDN* and *EKM*

$$\text{angle } HDN = \text{angle } KEM,$$

because they are placed at the vertex of the angles assumed equal; and since

$$\text{angle } H = \text{angle } K = 90°$$

on account of the intersection of circles described through the poles of one another; and

$$\text{side } DH = \text{side } EK;$$

therefore the triangles are equiangular and equilateral by the preceding proof. And again because

$$\text{arc } GH = \text{arc } KL$$

on account of its being assumed that

$$\text{angle } B = \text{angle } F;$$

therefore by addition

$$\text{arc } GHN = \text{arc } MKL,$$

by the axiom concerning the addition of equals. And therefore there are these two triangles *AGN* and *MCL* where

$$\text{side } GN = \text{side } ML,$$
$$\text{angle } ANG = \text{angle } CML,$$

and

$$\text{angle } G = \text{angle } L = 90°.$$

So the triangles will have their sides and angles equal. Therefore when equals have been subtracted from equals, the remainders will be equal:

$$\text{arc } AD = \text{arc } CE,$$
$$\text{arc } AB = \text{arc } CF,$$

and

$$\text{angle } BAD = \text{angle } ECF,$$

as was to be shown.

VIII

Now further, if two triangles have two sides equal to two sides and an angle equal to an angle, whether the angle which the equal sides comprehend, or an angle at the base, they will also have base equal to base and the remaining angles equal to the remaining angles.

As in the preceding diagram, let

$$\text{side } AB = \text{side } CF$$

and

$$\text{side } AD = \text{side } CE.$$

And first let

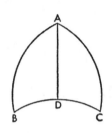

$$\text{angle } A = \text{angle } C,$$

which is comprehended by the equal sides. I say also that

$$\text{base } BD = \text{base } EF,$$
$$\text{angle } B = \text{angle } F,$$

and

$$\text{angle } BDA = \text{angle } CEF.$$

For we shall have the two triangles AGN and CLM, where

$$\text{angle } G = \text{angle } L = 90°.$$

And since

$$\text{angle } GAN = 180°—\text{angle } BAD,$$

and

$$\text{angle } MCL = 180°—\text{angle } ECF,$$

then

$$\text{angle } GAN = \text{angle } MCL.$$

Therefore the triangles are equiangular and equilateral.

Wherefore since

$$\text{arc } AN = \text{arc } CM$$

and

$$\text{arc } AD = \text{arc } CE,$$

then by subtraction

$$\text{arc } DN = \text{arc } ME.$$

But it has already been made clear that

$$\text{angle } DNH = \text{angle } EMK,$$

and

$$\text{angle } H = \text{angle } K = 90°.$$

Therefore the two triangles DHN and EMK will also be equiangular and equilateral. [24b] Hence (by the subtraction of equals)

$$\text{arc } BD = \text{arc } EF$$

and

$$\text{arc } GH = \text{arc } KL.$$

Hence

$$\text{angle } B = \text{angle } F,$$

and

$$\text{angle } ADB = \text{angle } FEC.$$

But if instead of sides AD and CE it be assumed that

$$\text{base } BD = \text{base } EF,$$

which are opposite the equal angles; and if the rest stays the same; then the proof will be similar. For since

$$\text{exterior angle } GAN = \text{exterior angle } MCL,$$

$$\text{angle } G = \text{angle } L = 90°,$$

and

$$\text{side } AG = \text{side } CL;$$

in the same way as before we shall have the two triangles AGN and MCL as equiangular and equilateral. And moreover, as parts of them,

$$\text{trgl. } DNH = \text{trgl. } MEK,$$

because

$$\text{angle } H = \text{angle } K = 90°,$$

$$\text{angle } DNH = \text{angle } KME,$$

and by subtraction from the quadrant

$$\text{side } DH = \text{side } EK.$$

Whence the same things follow as before.

IX

Moreover, in isosceles spherical triangles the angles at the base are equal to one another.

Let there be triangle ABC, where

$$\text{side } AB = \text{side } AC.$$

I say that on the base angle ABC = angle ACB.

From the vertex A drop a great circle which will cut the base at right angles, *i.e.*, a circle through the poles of the base; and let this circle be AD. Therefore, since in the two triangles ABD and ADC

$$\text{side } BA = \text{side } AC,$$

and

$$\text{side } AD = \text{side } AD,$$

and

$$\text{angle } BDA = \text{angle } CDA = 90°,$$

it is clear from what was shown above that

$$\text{angle } ABC = \text{angle } ACB,$$

as was to be shown.

PORISM

Hence it follows that the arc from the vertex of an isosceles triangle which falls at right angles upon the base will at the same time bisect the base and the angle comprehended by the equal sides, and vice versa. And that is clear from what has been shown above.

X

If two triangles in the same sphere have the sides of the one severally equal to the sides of the other, they will have the angles of the one severally equal to the angles of the other.

For in each triangle the three segments of great circles form pyramids which have as their apexes the centre of the sphere and as their bases the plane triangles which are comprehended by the straight lines subtending the arcs of the convex triangles. And those pyramids are similar and [25ª] equal by the definition of similar and equal solid figures (Euclid, XI, Def. 10); now the ratio of similarity is that the angles taken in any order will be severally equal to one another. Therefore the triangles will have their angles equal to one another.

In particular, those who define similarity of figures more generally say that similar figures are those which have similar declinations, and have corresponding angles equal to one another. Whence I think it is manifest that in a sphere the triangles which are equilateral are similar, just as in the case of plane triangles.

XI

Every triangle which has two sides and an angle given will have the remaining sides and angles given.

For if the two sides are given as equal, the angles at the base will be equal, and by drawing an arc from the vertex at right angles to the base, what is sought will easily be found by means of the Porism to the ninth theorem.

But if however the sides given are unequal, as in triangle *ABC*, where angle *A* is

given together with two sides, the sides either comprehend the given angle or do not comprehend it: First, let the given sides *AB* and *AC* comprehend it. And with *C* as a pole draw arc *DEF* of a great circle; and let the quadrants *CAD* and *CBE* be completed; and let *AB* extended cut *DE* at point *F*. So also in the triangle *ADF*,

$$\text{side } AD = 90° - \text{arc } AC;$$

and

$$\text{angle } BAD = 180° - \text{angle } CAB.$$

For the ratios and dimensions of these angles are the same as those of angles occurring at the intersection of straight lines and planes. And

$$\text{angle } D = 90°.$$

Therefore by the fourth theorem of this chapter, triangle *ADF* will have its sides and angles given. And again in triangle *BEF* angle *F* has been found, and

$$\text{angle } E = 90°$$

on account of the intersection of circles through the poles of one another; and

$$\text{side } BF = \text{arc } ABF - \text{arc } AB.$$

Therefore by the same theorem triangle *BEF* also will have its angles and sides given. Whence *BC* the side sought is given, as

$$BC = 90° - BE,$$

and *BC* is the side sought. And

$$\text{arc } DE = \text{arc } DEF - \text{arc } EF.$$

And so angle *C* is given. Any by means of angle *EBF*, the vertical angle *ABC*, which was sought, is given.

But if in place of side *AB*, side *CB* which is opposite to the given angle is assumed, the same thing will result. For *AD* and *BE* the remainders of quadrants are given; and by the same argument the two triangles *ADF* and *BEF* will have their sides and angles given, as before.

Whence, as was intended, *ABC* the triangle set before us will have its sides and angles given.

[25ᵇ] XII

Furthermore, if any two angles are given together with one side, there will be the same result.

For let the construction in the previous figure stay; and in triangle *ABC* let the two angles *ACB* and *BAC* be given together with side *AC*, which is adjacent to both angles. Now if one of the angles given were right, then everything else would follow from the ratios by the preceding fourth theorem. But we wish to keep the theorems different and to have neither of the angles right. Therefore

$$AD = 90° - AC.$$

And

$$\text{angle } BAD = 180° - \text{angle } BAC.$$

And

$$\text{angle } D = 90°.$$

Therefore by the fourth theorem in this chapter, triangle *AFD* will have its angles and sides given. But through angle *C* being given, the arc *DE* is given, and so is the remainder

$$\text{arc } EF = 90° - \text{arc } DE.$$

And

angle $BEF = 90°$;

and

angle F = angle F.

In the same way by the fourth theorem BE and BF are given; and through them we can discover sides AB and BC, which were sought.

Moreover, if one of the given angles is opposite the given side, namely if angle ABC is given in place of angle ACB, and if the rest stayed the same, then it can be shown in similar fashion that the whole triangle ADF will be established as having its sides and angles given; and similarly the part of it which is triangle BEF; since on account of angle F being common to both, angle EBF being at the vertex of the given angle, and angle E being right, it is shown as above that all the sides are given. And from that there follows what I said. For all these things are always tied together by a mutual and perpetual bond, as befits the form of a globe.

XIII

Finally, all the sides of a triangle being given, the angles are given.

Let all the sides of triangle ABC be given: I say that all the angles too are found.

For the triangle either will have equal sides or it will not. First therefore let AB and AC be equal. It is clear that the halves of chords subtending twice those sides will be equal. And let these halves be BE and CE, which on account of being at an equal distance from the centre of the sphere will cut one another at point E in DE the common section of the circles, as is clear from Euclid, III, Def. 4, [26ª] and its converse.

But by Euclid, III, 3, in plane ABD

angle $DEB = 90°$;

and in plane ACD similarly

angle $DEC = 90°$.

Therefore by Euclid, XI, Def. 3, BEC is the angle of inclination of the planes; and we shall find it as follows; for since there is a straight line subtending BC, we shall have a rectilinear triangle BEC with its sides given on account of their arcs being given; and then since the angles may be found, we shall have the angle BEC, which was sought, *i.e.*, we shall have the spherical angle BAC; and we shall have the others as above.

But if the triangle is scalene, as in the second figure, it is clear that the halves of the chords subtending twice the sides will by no means touch one another. For if

arc AC > arc AB,

then, as

$$CF = {}^1/_2 \text{ ch. } 2\ AC,$$

CF will fall lower down. But if

$$\text{arc } AC < \text{arc } AB,$$

then *CF* will fall higher up, according as such lines become nearer and farther away from the centre, by Euclid, III, 15. Now however let *FG* be drawn parallel to *BE*; and at point *G* let it cut *BD* the common section of the two circles (*AB* and *BC*). And let *GC* be joined. Therefore it is clear that

$$\text{angle } EFG = \text{angle } AEB = 90°$$

And too

$$\text{angle } EFC = 90°;$$

for

$$CF = {}^1/_2 \text{ ch. } 2\ AC.$$

Therefore angle *CFG* will be the angle of section of circles *AB* and *AC*; and we shall find this angle too. For

$$DF : FG = DE : EB,$$

since triangles *DFG* and *DEB* are similar. Therefore *FG* is given in the parts wherein *FC* is also given; and

$$DG : DB = DE : EB.$$

Hence *DG* will be given in the same parts whereof *DC* has 100,000. But as the angle *GDC* is given through the arc *BC*, therefore by the second theorem on plane triangles the side *GC* is given in the same parts wherein the remaining sides of the plane triangle *GFC* are given. Therefore by the last theorem on plane triangles we shall have the angle *GFC*, *i.e.*, the spherical angle *BAC*, which was sought; and then we shall find the remaining angles by the eleventh theorem on spherical triangles.

XIV

If a given arc of a circle is cut anywhere so that both of the segments together are less than a semicircle, and if the ratio of half of the chord subtending twice one segment to the half

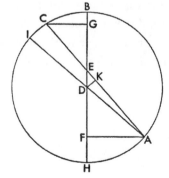

of the chord subtending twice the other segment is given, [26ᵇ] *the arcs of those segments will also be given.*

For let arc *ABC* be given, around centre *D*; and let *ABC* be cut at point *B* anywhere, but in such a way that the segments are less than a semicircle; and let

$${}^1/_2 \text{ ch. } 2\ AB : {}^1/_2 \text{ ch. } 2\ BC$$

be somehow given in length: I say that the axes *AB* and *BC* are also given.

For let the straight line *AC* be drawn, which the diameter cuts at point *E*; and from the termini *A* and *C* let the perpendiculars *AF* and *CG* fall upon the diameter. And of necessity

$$AF = {}^1\!/_2 \text{ ch. } 2\,AB$$

and

$$CG = {}^1\!/_2 \text{ ch. } 2\,BC.$$

Therefore in the right triangles *AEF* and *CEG*

$$\text{angle } AEF = \text{angle } CEG,$$

because they are vertical angles. And the triangles which are therefore equiangular and similar have the sides opposite the equal angles proportional:

$$AF : CG = AE : EC.$$

Therefore we shall have *AE* and *EC* in the parts wherein *AF* or *GC* has been given. But the chord subtending arc *ABC* is given in the parts wherein the radius *DEB*, *AK* the half of chord *AC*, and the remainder *EK* are given. Let *DA* and *DK* be joined, and they will be given in the parts wherein *BD* is given: *DK* will be given as half of the chord subtending the remaining segment which is supplementary to arc *ABC* and is comprehended by angle *DAK*. And therefore angle *ADK* is given, which comprehends half of arc *ABC*. But in the triangle *EDK* having two sides given and angle *EKD* right, angle *EDK* will also be given. Hence the whole angle *EDA* comprehending the arc *AB* will be given. Thereby also the remainder *CB* will be manifest. And it was this that we were trying to show.

XV

If all the angles of a triangle are given, even though now is a right angle, all the sides are given.

Let there be the triangle *ABC*, all the angles of which are given but none of which is right. I say that all the sides are given too.

For from some one of the angles, say *A*, drop the arc *AD* through the poles of *CB*. *AD* will cut *BC* at right angles, and it will fall within the triangle, unless one of the angles at the base—angle *B* or angle *C*—is obtuse and the other acute. If that were the case, the arc would have to be drawn from the obtuse angle to the base. So with the quadrants *BAF*, *CAG*, and *DAE* completed and with *B* and *C* as poles, let the arcs *EF* and *EG* [27a] be drawn.

Therefore

$$\text{angle } F = \text{angle } G = 90°.$$

Therefore in the right triangle *EAF*

$${}^1\!/_2 \text{ ch. } 2\,AE : {}^1\!/_2 \text{ ch. } 2\,EF = {}^1\!/_2 \text{ dmt. sph. } : {}^1\!/_2 \text{ ch. } 2\,EAF$$

Similarly in right triangle *AEG*

$^1/_2$ ch. 2 *AE* : $^1/_2$ ch. 2 *EG* = $^1/_2$ dmt. sph. : $^1/_2$ ch. 2 *EAG*.
Therefore, *ex aequali*,

$^1/_2$ ch. 2 *EF* : $^1/_2$ ch. 2 *EG* = $^1/_2$ ch. 2 *EAF* : $^1/_2$ ch. 2 *EAG*.

And because arcs *FE* and *EG* arc given, since

arc *FE* = 90° – angle *B*

and

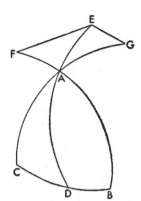

arc *EG* = 90° – angle *C*;

thence we shall have the ratio between angles *EAF* and *EAG* given, *i.e.*, the ratio between *BAD* and *CAD*, which are their vertical angles. Now the whole angle *BAC* has been given; therefore by the foregoing theorem, angles *BAD* and *CAD* will also be given. Then by the fifth theorem we shall determine sides *AB*, *BD*, *AC*, *CD*, and the whole of arc *BC*.

This much said enroute concerning triangles, according as they are necessary for our undertaking, will be sufficient. For if they had to be treated in greater detail, the work would be of unusual size.

[27ᵇ] BOOK TWO

Since we have expounded briefly the three terrestrial movements, by means of which we promised to demonstrate all the planetary appearances, now we shall fulfill our promise by proceeding from the whole to the parts and examining and investigating particular questions to the extent of our powers. Now we shall begin with the best-known movement of all, the revolution of day and night—which we said the Greeks called νυχθήμερος and which we have taken as belonging wholly and immediately to the terrestrial globe, since from this movement arise the months, years, and other variously named periods of time, as number from unity. Therefore we shall say only a few words about the inequality of days and nights, the rising and setting of the sun and of the parts of the ecliptic and the signs, and the consequences of this type of revolution; for many people have written about these subjects copiously enough and what they say is in harmony and agreement with our conceptions. It is of no importance if we take up in an opposite fashion what others have demonstrated by means of a motionless earth and a giddy world and race with them toward the same goal, since things related reciprocally happen to be inversely in harmony with one another. Nevertheless we shall omit nothing necessary. But no one should be surprised if we still speak of the rising and setting of the sun and stars, *et cetera*; but he should realize that we are speaking in the usual manner of speech which can be recognized by all and that we are nevertheless always keeping in mind that: "To us who are being carried by the Earth, the sun and the moon seem to pass over; and the stars return to their former positions and again move away."

1. On the Circles and Their Names

We have said that the equator is the greatest of the parallel circles on the terrestrial globe described around the axis of its daily revolution and that the ecliptic is the circle through the middle [28ª] of the signs under which the centre of the Earth moves in a circle in its annual revolution.

But since the ecliptic crosses the equator obliquely; in proportion to the inclination of the axis of the Earth to it, it describes in the course of the daily revolution two circles which touch it on either side of the equator, as if the farthest limits to its obliquity. These circles are called the tropics. For on them the sun appears to make its "tropes," *i.e.*, its winter and summer changes of direction. Whence the northern circle used to be called the tropic of the summer solstice and the other the tropic of the shortest day, as was set forth in our summary exposition of the circular movements of the Earth.

66

Next follows the so-called horizon, which the Latins call the boundary circle; for it is the boundary between that part of the world which is visible to us and that part which lies hidden. All stars which set are seen to have their rising on it; and it has its centre on the surface of the Earth and its pole at the point directly overhead. But since it is impossible to compare the Earth with the immensity of the heavens—for according to our hypothesis even the total distance between the sun and the moon is indiscernible beside the magnitude of the heavens—the circle of the horizon appears to bisect the heavens, as if it went through the centre of the world, as we demonstrated in the beginning.

But when the horizon is oblique to the equator, it too touches on either side of the equator twin parallel circles, *i.e.*, the northern circle of the always visible stars and the southern circle of the always hidden stars. The first circle was called the arctic, and the second the antarctic by Proclus and the Greeks; and they become greater or smaller in proportion to the obliquity of the horizon or the elevation of the pole of the equator.[1]

There remains the meridian circle which passes through the poles of the horizon and through the poles of the equator too and hence is perpendicular to both circles. The sun's reaching it gives us midday and midnight.

But these two circles which have their centres on the surface of the Earth, *i.e.*, the horizon and the meridian, are wholly consequent upon the movement of the Earth and upon our sight at some particular place. For the eye everywhere becomes as it were the centre of the sphere of all things which are visible to it on all sides.

Furthermore all the circles assumed on the Earth produce circles in the heavens as their likenesses and images, as will be shown more clearly in cosmography and in connection with the dimensions of the Earth. And these circles at any rate are the ones having proper names, though there are infinite ways of designating and naming others.

2. ON THE OBLIQUITY OF THE ECLIPTIC AND THE DISTANCE OF THE TROPICS AND HOW THEY ARE DETERMINED

[28b] Since the ecliptic lies between the tropics and crosses the equator obliquely, I therefore think that we should now try to observe what the distance between the tropics is and hence what the angle of section between the equator and the ecliptic is. For in order to perceive this by sense with the help of artificial instruments, by means of which the job can be done best, it is necessary to have a wooden square prepared, or preferably a square made from some other more solid material, from stone or metal; for the wood might not stay in the same condition on account of some alteration in the atmosphere and might mislead the observer. Now one surface of it should be very

---

[1]That is to say, the magnitude of the circle of the always visible stars varies inversely with the obliquity of the horizon and directly with the elevation of the poles of the equator.

carefully planed, and it should be of sufficient area to admit being divided into sections, that is, a side should be about 5 or 6 feet long. Now with one of the corners (of the square) as centre and with a side as radius, let a quadrant of a circle be drawn and divided into 90 equal degrees; and let each of the degrees be subdivided into 60 minutes, or whatever number can be taken. Next let a cylindrical pointer which has been well turned on a lathe be set up at the centre (of the quadrant) and fixed in such a way as to be perpendicular to the surface and to extend out from it a little, say perhaps a finger's width or less.

When the instrument has been prepared in this way, the next thing to do is to exhibit the line of the meridian on a piece of flooring which lies in the plane of the horizon and which has been made even as carefully as is possible by means of a hydroscope or ground-level, so as not to have a slope in any part of it. The piece of flooring should have a circle drawn on it and a cylinder erected at the center of the circle: we shall take observations and mark the point where at some time before midday the extremity of the shadow of the cylinder touches the circumference of the circle, We shall do the same thing in the afternoon, and then shall bisect the arc of the circle lying between the two points we have already marked. In this way a straight line drawn from the centre through the point of section will indicate infallibly for us the south and the north.

Accordingly the plane surface of the instrument should be set up on this piece of flooring as a base and fixed perpendicular to it with the centre (of the quadrant) to the south, so that a plumb-line from the centre would fall exactly at right angles to the meridian line. For it comes about in this way that the surface of the instrument exhibits the meridian circle. Hence on the days of summer and winter solstice the shadows of the sun at noon [29a] are to be observed according as they are cast by the pointer, or cylinder, from the centre (of the quadrant); and some mark is to be made on the arc of the quadrant, so that the place of the shadow may be kept more surely. And we shall note down the centre of the shadow in degrees and minutes as accurately as is possible. For if we do this, the arc between the marked shadows—the summer—and winter—solstitial shadows—will be found and will show us the distance between the tropics and also the total obliquity of the ecliptic.[1] By taking half of the arc, we shall have the distance of the tropics from the equator, and it will be clear what the angle of inclination is between the equator and the ecliptic.

Now Ptolemy took the interval between the aforesaid limits—the northern and the southern—as 47°42'40", whereof the circle has 360°, as he found had been observed by Hipparchus and Eratosthenes before his time; and there are 11ᴾ whereof the whole circle has 83ᴾ. Hence half the arc—and half the arc has 23°51'20", whereof

---

[1]Since the distance between the sun and the Earth is imperceptible in relation to the radius of the sphere of the fixed stars, the centre of the quadrant may be taken as the centre of the sphere of the fixed stars.

the circle has 360°—showed the distance of the tropics from the equator and what the angle of section with the ecliptic was. Accordingly Ptolemy believed that these things were invariably such and would always remain so. But these distances have been found to have decreased continually from that time down to ours. For it has already been discovered by us and some of our contemporaries that the distance between the tropics is not more than 46°58' approximately and that the angle of section is 23°29'. Hence it is clear enough that the obliquity of the ecliptic is not fixed. More on this below, where we shall show by a probable enough conclusion that it was never greater than 23°52' and will not ever be less than 23°28'.

3. On the Arcs and Angles of the Intersections of the Equator, Ecliptic, and Meridian, by Means of Which Declinations and Right Ascensions are Determined, and on the Computation of These Arcs and Angles

Accordingly as we were saying in the case of the horizon that the parts of the world have their risings and settings on it, we say that the meridian circle [29ᵇ] halves the heavens. During the space of twenty-four hours this circle is crossed by both the ecliptic and the equator and divides both of their circumferences by cutting them at the spring and at the autumnal intersection and in turn has its circumference divided by the arc intercepted by those two circles. Since they are all great circles, they form a spherical right triangle; for the angle is right where the meridian circle by definition cuts the equator described through its poles. Now the arc of the meridian circle, or any arc of a circle passing through the poles (of the equator) and intercepted in this way is called the declination of a segment of the ecliptic; and the corresponding arc on the equator is called the right ascension occurring at the same time as the similar arc on the ecliptic.

All this is easily demonstrated in a convex triangle. For let the circle *ABCD* be a circle passing simultaneously through the poles of the ecliptic and of the equator—most people call this circle the "colure"—let the semi-circle of the ecliptic be *AEC*, the semicircle of the equator *BED*; let the spring equinox be at point *E*, the summer solstice at *A*, and the winter solstice at *C*. Now let *F* be taken as the pole of daily revolution, and on the ecliptic let

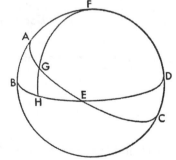

arc *EG* = 30°,

for example, and let it be cut off by *FGH* the quadrant of a circle.

Then it is clear that in triangle EGH
$$\text{side } EG = 30°,$$
$$\text{angle } GEH \text{ is given,}$$
since at its least, in conformity with the greatest declination AB,
$$\text{angle } GFH = 23°28'$$
$$\text{where 4 rt. angles} = 360°;$$
and
$$\text{angle } GHE = 90°.$$
Therefore by the fourth theorem on sphericals, triangle EHG will have its sides and angles given. For it was shown that
$$\text{ch. 2 } EG : \text{ch. 2 } GH = \text{ch. 2 } AGE, \text{ or dmt. sph. : ch. 2 } AB$$
and their halves are in the same ratio. And since
$$^1/_2 \text{ ch. 2 } AGE = \text{radius} = 100,000,$$
$$^1/_2 \text{ ch. 2 } AB = 39,822,$$
and
$$^1/_2 \text{ ch. 2 } EG = 50,000;$$
and since, if four numbers are proportional, the product of the means is equal to the product of the extremes; therefore
$$^1/_2 \text{ ch. 2 } GH = 19,911,$$
and hence, by the table,
$$\text{arc } GH = 11°29',$$
which is the declination of segment EG,
$$\text{side } FG = 78°31',$$
$$\text{side } AG = 60°,$$
since they are the remainders of the quadrants, and
$$\text{angle } FAG = 90°.$$
In the same way
$$[30^a] \ ^1/_2 \text{ ch. 2 } FG : {}^1/_2 \text{ ch. 2 } AG = {}^1/_2 \text{ ch. 2 } FGH : {}^1/_2 \text{ ch. 2 } BH.$$
Now since three of these chords are given, the fourth will also be given, that is to say,
$$\text{arc } BH = 62°6',$$
which is the right ascension from the summer solstice, and
$$HE = 27°54'$$
from the spring equinox. Similarly, since
$$\text{side } FG = 78°31',$$
$$\text{side } AF = 64°30',$$
and
$$AGE = 90°;$$
then, since angles AGF and HGE are vertical angles,

angle *AGF* = angle *HGE* = 63°29$^1/_2$'.

In the rest we shall do as in this example. But we should not be ignorant of the fact that the meridian circle cuts the ecliptic at right angles in the signs where the ecliptic touches the tropics, for then the meridian circle cuts it through its poles, as we said. But at the equinoctial points the meridian makes an angle less than a right angle by the angle of inclination of the ecliptic, so that in conformity with the least inclination of the ecliptic it makes an angle of 66°32'.

Moreover we should note that equal sides and equal angles of the triangles follow upon equal arcs of the ecliptic being taken from the points of solstice or equinox. In this way if we

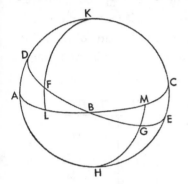

draw the equatorial arc *ABC* and the ecliptic *BDE* as intersecting at point *B*, where the equinox is, and if we take as equal the arcs *FB* and *BG* and also arcs *KFL* and *HGM* two quadrants of circle described through the poles of daily revolution; there will be the two triangles *FLB* and *BMG*, wherein

side *BF* = side *BG*

angle *FLB* = angle *GBM*

and

angle *FLB* = angle *GMB* = 90°.

Therefore by the sixth theorem on spherical triangles the sides and angles are equal. Hence

declination *FL* = declination *GM*

rt. ascension *LB* = rt. ascension *BM*

and

angle *LFB* = angle *MGB*.

This same fact will be manifest upon the assumption of equal arcs described from a point of solstice, for example, when *AB* and *BC* on different sides of their point of contact *B*, the solstice, are equally distant from it. For when the arcs *DA* and *DB* (and *DC*) have been drawn from the pole of the equator, there will similarly be the two triangles *ABD* and *DBC*.

Then

base *AB* = base *BC*

side *BD* is common

and

angle *ABD* = angle *CBD* = 90°.

Accordingly by the eighth theorem on sphericals the triangles will be shown to have equal sides and angles. It is clear from this that such angles and arcs laid out in one quadrant of the ecliptic [30^b] are in accord with the remaining quadrants of the full circle.

We shall subjoin an example of these things in the tables. In the first column are placed the degrees of the ecliptic; in the following column, the declinations answering to those degrees; and in the third column the minutes, which are the differences between the particular declinations and the declinations which occur at the time of greatest obliquity of the ecliptic: the greatest of these differences is 24'.

We shall do the same thing in the table of ascensions and the table of meridian angles. For it is necessary for all things which are consequences of the obliquity of the ecliptic to be changed with a change in it. Furthermore, in the right ascensions an extremely slight difference is found, one which does not exceed $1/10$ "time" and which in the space of an hour makes only $1/150$ "time."—The ancients give the name of "time" to the parts of the equator which arise together with the parts of the ecliptic. Each of these circles, as we have often said, has 360 parts; but in order to distinguish between them, most of the ancients called the parts of ecliptic "degrees" and those of

TABLE OF DECLINATIONS OF THE DEGREES OF THE ECLIPTIC

Ecliptic Deg.	Declination Deg.	Min.	Difference Min.	Ecliptic Deg.	Declination Deg.	Min.	Difference Min.	Ecliptic Deg.	Declination Deg.	Min.	Difference Min.
1	0	24	0	31	11	50	11	61	20	23	20
2	0	48	1	32	12	11	12	62	20	35	21
3	1	12	1	33	12	32	12	63	20	47	21
4	1	36	2	34	12	52	13	64	20	58	21
5	2	0	2	35	13	12	13	65	21	9	21
6	2	23	2	36	13	32	14	66	21	20	22
7	2	47	3	37	13	52	14	67	21	30	22
8	3	11	3	38	14	12	14	68	21	40	22
9	3	35	4	39	14	31	14	69	21	49	22
10	3	58	4	40	14	50	14	70	21	58	22
11	4	22	4	41	15	9	15	71	22	7	22
12	4	45	4	42	15	27	15	72	22	15	23
13	5	9	5	43	15	46	16	73	22	23	23
14	5	32	5	44	16	4	16	74	22	30	23
15	5	55	5	45	16	22	16	75	22	37	23
16	6	19	6	46	16	39	17	76	22	44	23
17	6	41	6	47	16	56	17	77	22	50	23
18	7	4	7	48	17	13	17	78	22	55	23
19	7	27	7	49	17	30	18	79	23	1	24
20	7	49	8	50	17	46	18	80	23	5	24
21	8	12	8	51	18	1	18	81	23	10	24
22	8	34	8	52	18	17	18	82	23	13	24
23	8	57	9	53	18	32	19	83	23	17	24
24	9	19	9	54	18	47	19	84	23	20	24
25	9	41	9	55	19	2	19	85	23	22	24
26	10	3	10	56	19	16	19	86	23	24	24
27	10	25	10	57	19	30	20	87	23	26	24
28	10	46	10	58	19	44	20	88	23	27	24
29	11	8	10	59	19	57	20	89	23	28	24
30	11	29	11	60	20	10	20	90	23	28	24

the equator "times"; and we will copy them for the remainder of the work.—Therefore since the difference is so small that it can be properly neglected, we are not peeved at having to place it in a separate column.

Hence these tables can be made to apply to any other obliquity of the ecliptic, if in conformity with the ratio of difference between the least and greatest obliquity of the ecliptic we make the proper corrections. For example, if with an obliquity of 23°34' we wish to know how great a declination follows from taking it distance of 30° from the equator along the ecliptic, we find that in the table there are 11°29' in the column of declinations and 11' in the column of differences. These 11' would be all added in the case of the greatest obliquity of the ecliptic, which is, as we said, an obliquity of 23°52'. But it has already been laid down that the obliquity is 23°34' and is accordingly greater than the least obliquity by 6', which are one quarter of 24', which is the excess of the greatest obliquity over the least. Now

TABLE OF RIGHT ASCENSIONS

Ecliptic	Equator		Difference	Ecliptic	Equator		Difference	Ecliptic	Equator		Difference
Deg.	Deg.	Min.	Min.	Deg.	Deg.	Min.	Min.	Deg.	Deg.	Min.	Min.
1	0	55	0	31	28	54	4	61	58	51	4
2	1	50	0	32	29	51	4	62	59	54	4
3	2	45	0	33	30	50	4	63	60	57	4
4	3	40	0	34	31	46	4	64	62	0	4
5	4	35	0	35	32	45	4	65	63	3	4
6	5	30	0	36	33	43	5	66	64	6	3
7	6	25	1	37	34	41	5	67	65	9	3
8	7	20	1	38	35	40	5	68	66	13	3
9	8	15	1	39	36	38	5	69	67	17	3
10	9	11	1	40	37	37	5	70	68	21	3
11	10	6	1	41	38	36	5	71	69	25	3
12	11	0	2	42	39	35	5	72	70	29	3
13	11	57	2	43	40	34	5	73	71	33	3
14	12	52	2	44	41	33	6	74	72	38	2
15	13	48	2	45	42	32	6	75	73	43	2
16	14	43	2	46	43	31	6	76	74	47	2
17	15	39	2	47	44	32	5	77	75	52	2
18	16	34	3	48	45	32	5	78	76	57	2
19	17	31	3	49	46	32	5	79	78	2	2
20	18	27	3	50	47	33	5	80	79	7	2
21	19	23	3	51	48	34	5	81	80	12	1
22	20	19	3	52	49	35	5	82	81	17	1
23	21	15	3	53	50	36	5	83	82	22	1
24	22	10	4	54	51	37	5	84	83	27	1
25	23	9	4	55	52	38	4	85	84	33	1
26	24	6	4	56	53	41	4	86	85	38	0
27	25	3	4	57	54	43	4	87	86	43	0
28	26	0	4	58	55	45	4	88	87	48	0
29	26	57	4	59	56	46	4	89	88	54	0
30	27	54	4	60	57	48	4	90	90	0	0

$$3' : 11 \fallingdotseq 6' : 24'.$$

When I add 3' to the 11°29', I shall have 11°32', which will then measure the declination of the arc of the ecliptic 30° from the equator.

The same thing can be done in the table of meridian angles and right ascensions, except that we must always add the differences in the case of right ascensions but subtract them in the case of the meridian angles, so that everything may proceed correctly in conformity with the time.

TABLE OF THE MERIDIAN ANGLES

Eclip-tic	Angle		Differ-ence	Eclip-tic	Angle		Differ-ence	Eclip-tic	Angle		Differ-ence
Deg.	Deg.	Min.	Min.	Deg.	Deg.	Min.	Min.	Deg.	Deg.	Min.	Min.
1	66	32	24	31	69	35	21	61	78	7	12
2	66	33	24	32	69	48	21	62	78	29	12
3	66	34	24	33	70	0	20	63	78	51	11
4	66	35	24	34	70	13	20	64	79	14	11
5	66	37	24	35	70	26	20	65	79	36	11
6	66	39	24	36	70	39	20	66	79	59	10
7	66	42	24	37	70	53	20	67	80	22	10
8	66	44	24	38	71	7	19	68	80	45	10
9	66	47	24	39	71	22	19	69	81	9	9
10	66	51	24	40	71	36	19	70	81	33	9
11	66	55	24	41	71	52	19	71	81	58	8
12	66	59	24	42	72	8	18	72	82	22	8
13	67	4	23	43	72	24	18	73	82	46	7
14	67	10	23	44	72	39	18	74	83	11	7
15	67	15	23	45	72	55	17	75	83	35	6
16	67	21	23	46	73	11	17	76	84	0	6
17	67	27	23	47	73	28	17	77	84	25	6
18	67	34	23	48	73	47	17	78	84	50	5
19	67	41	23	49	74	6	16	79	85	15	5
20	67	49	23	50	74	24	16	80	85	40	4
21	67	56	23	51	74	42	16	81	86	5	4
22	68	4	22	52	75	1	15	82	86	30	3
23	68	13	22	53	75	21	15	83	86	55	3
24	68	22	22	54	75	40	15	84	87	19	3
25	68	32	22	55	76	1	14	85	87	53	2
26	68	41	22	56	76	21	14	86	88	17	2
27	68	51	22	57	76	42	14	87	88	41	1
28	69	2	21	58	77	3	13	88	89	6	1
29	69	13	21	59	77	24	13	89	89	33	0
30	69	24	21	60	77	45	13	90	90	0	0

4. How to Determine the Declination and Right Ascension of any Star Which Is Placed Outside the Ecliptic But Whose Longitude and Latitude Have Been Established; and with What Degree of the Ecliptic It Halves the Heavens

[32ᵇ] These things have been set down concerning the ecliptic and the equator and their intersections. But as regards the daily revolution, it is of interest not only to know what parts of the ecliptic appear, by means of which the causes of the sun's appearing where it does are discovered, but also to know that there is a similar demonstration of the declination from the equator and of the right ascension in the case of those fixed or wandering stars which are outside the ecliptic but whose longitude and latitude have been given.

Therefore let the circle *ABCD* be described through the poles of the equator and of the ecliptic; let *AEC* be the semicircle of the equa-
tor above pole *F*; let *BED* be the semicircle of the ecliptic about pole *G*; and let its intersection with the equator be at point *E*. Now from the pole *G* let the arc *GHKL* be drawn through a star, and let the position of the star be given as point *H*, and let *FHMN* a quadrant of a circle fall through *H* from the pole of daily movement.

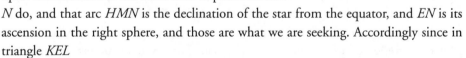

Then it is clear that the star which is at *H* falls upon the meridian at the same time as points *M* and *N* do, and that arc *HMN* is the declination of the star from the equator, and *EN* is its ascension in the right sphere, and those are what we are seeking. Accordingly since in triangle *KEL*

side *KE* is given,

angle *KEL* is given,

and

angle *EKL* = 90°,

therefore by the fourth theorem on spherical triangles,

side *KL* is given,

side *EL* is given,

and

angle *KLE* is given.

Therefore by addition

arc *HKL* is given.

And on that account, in triangle *HLN*,

angle *HLN* is given,

angle *LNH* = 90°,

and

side *HL* is given.

Therefore by the same fourth theorem on sphericals there are also given the remaining sides: *HN* the declination of the star, and *LN*, and the remaining distance *NE*, the right ascension, which measures the distance the sphere turns from the equinox to the star.

—Or in another way. If in the foregoing you take *KE* the arc of the ecliptic as the right ascension of *LE*, conversely *LE* will be given by the table of right ascensions; and so will *LK*, as the declination corresponding to *LE*; [33ª] and the angle *KLE* will be given by the table of meridian angles; and hence the remaining sides and angles, as we have showed, may be learned.—

Then by means of the right ascension *EN*, the number of degrees of *EM* the arc of the ecliptic are given. And in conformity with these things the star together with point *M* halves the heavens.

5. On the Sections of the Horizon

Now the horizon of a right sphere is different from the horizon of an oblique sphere. For the horizon to which the equator is perpendicular, or which passes through the poles of the equator, is called a right horizon.

We call the horizon which has some inclination with the equator the horizon of an oblique sphere.

Therefore on a right horizon all the stars rise and set, and the days are always equal to the nights. For this horizon bisects all the parallel circles described by the diurnal movement, and passes through their poles; and there occurs there what we have already explained in the case of the meridian circle. Here, however, we are taking the day as extending from sunrise to sunset, and not from light to darkness, as the crowds understand it, *i.e.*, from early morning twilight to the first street lights; but we shall say more on this subject in connection with the rising and setting of the signs.

On the contrary, where the axis of the Earth is perpendicular to the horizon there are no risings or settings, but all the stars turn in a gyre and are always visible or hidden, unless they are affected by some other motion, such as the annual movement around the sun. Consequently, there day lasts perpetually for the space of half a year and night for the rest of the time; and there is nothing else to differentiate summer and winter, since there the horizon coincides with the equator.

Furthermore, in an oblique sphere certain stars rise and set; and certain others are always visible or always hidden; and meanwhile the days and nights are unequal there

where an oblique horizon touches two parallel circles in proportion to its inclination. And of these circles, the one nearer the visible pole is the boundary of the always visible stars, and conversely the circle nearer the hidden pole is the boundary for the always hidden stars. Therefore the horizon, as falling completely between these boundaries, cuts all the parallel circles in the middle into unequal arcs, except the equator, which is the greatest of the parallels; and great circles bisect one another. Therefore an oblique horizon in the upper hemisphere cuts off axes of parallels in the direction of the visible pole which are greater than the arcs which are toward the southern and hidden [33b] pole; and the converse is the case in the hidden hemisphere. The sun becomes visible in these horizons by reason of the diurnal movement and causes the inequality of days and nights.

6. WHAT THE DIFFERENCES BETWEEN THE MIDDAY SHADOWS ARE

There are differences between the midday shadows on account of which some people are called periscian, others amphiscian, and still others heteroscian. The periscian are those whom we might call "circumumbratile," that is to say, "throwing the shadow of the sun on every side." And they live where the distance between the vertex, or pole, of the horizon and the pole of the Earth is less or no greater than that between the tropic and the equator. For there the parallels which the horizon touches as the boundaries of the always apparent or always hidden stars are greater than, or equal to, the tropics. And so the summer sun high up among the always apparent stars at that time throws the shadow of a pointer in every direction. But where the horizon touches the tropics, the tropics become the boundaries of the always apparent and the always hidden stars. Wherefore instead of there being midnight the sun at its (winter) solstice seems to graze the Earth, at which time the whole circle of the ecliptic coincides with the horizon; and straightway six signs rise at the same time, and on the opposite side six signs set at the same time, and the pole of the ecliptic coincides with the pole of the horizon.

The amphiscian, who cast midday shadows on both sides, are those who live between the tropics. This is the space which the ancients called the middle zone. And since throughout that whole tract the circle of the ecliptic passes directly over head twice, as is shown in the second theorem of the *Phaenomena* of Euclid, the shadows of pointers are cast in two directions there: for as the sun moves back and forth, the pointers throw their shadows sometimes to the south and sometimes to the north.

The rest of us who inhabit the region between the two others are heteroscian, because we cast our midday shadows in only one direction, *i.e.*, towards the north.

Now the ancient mathematicians were accustomed to divide the world into seven climates, through Meröe, Siona, Alexandria, Rhodes, the Hellespont, the middle of the Pontus, Boristhenes, Byzantium, and so on with the single parallel circles taken according to the differences between the longest days and according to the lengths of the shadows, which they observed by means of pointers at noon on the days of equinoxes and solstices, and [34ᵃ] according to the elevation of the pole or the latitude of some segment. Since these things have partly changed through time, they are not exactly the same as they once were, on account of the variable obliquity of the ecliptic, as we said, of which the ancients were ignorant; or, to speak more correctly, on account of the variable inclination of the equator to the plane of the ecliptic, upon which these things depend. But the elevations of the pole or the latitudes of the places and the equinoctial shadows agree with those which antiquity discovered and made note of. That would necessarily take place, since the equator depends upon the pole of the terrestrial globe. Wherefore those segments are not accurately enough designated and defined by shadows falling on special days, but more correctly by their distances from the equator, which remain perpetually. But although this variability of the tropics, because very slight, admits but slight diversity of days and of shadows in southern places, it becomes more apparent to those who are moving northward. Therefore as regards the shadows of pointers, it is clear that for any given altitude of the sun the length of the shadow is derivable and vice versa.

In this way if there is the pointer *AB* which casts a shadow *BC*; since the pointer is perpendicular to the plane of the horizon, angle *ABC* must always be right, by the definition of lines perpendicular to a plane. Wherefore if *AC* be joined, we shall have a right triangle *ABC*; and for a given altitude of the sun we shall have angle *ACB* given. And by the first theorem on plane triangles the ratio of the pointer *AB* to its shadow *BC* will be given, and *BC* will be given in length. Conversely, moreover, when *AB* and *BC* are given, it will be clear from the third theorem on plane triangles what angle *ACB* is and what the elevation of the sun making that shadow at that time is. In this way the

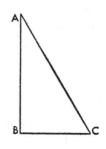

ancients in describing the regions of the terrestrial globe gave the lengths of the midday shadows sometimes at the equinoxes and sometimes at the solstices.

7. How the Longest Day, the Distance of Rising, and the Inclination of the Sphere are Derived from One Another, and on the Differences Between Days

[34ᵇ] In this way too for any obliquity of the sphere or inclination of the horizon we will demonstrate simultaneously the longest and the shortest day together with the

distance of rising (of the sun) and the difference of the remaining days. Now the distance of rising is the arc of the horizon intercepted between the summer solstitial and the winter solstitial sunrises, or the sum of the distances of the solstitial from the equinoctial sunrise.

Therefore let *ABCD* be the meridian circle, and let *BED* be the semicircle of the horizon in the eastern hemisphere, and let *AEC* be the similar semicircle of the equa-

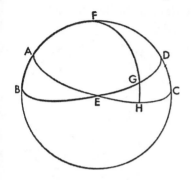

tor with *F* as its northern pole. Let point *G* be taken as the rising of the sun at the summer solstice, and let *FGH* the arc of a great circle be drawn. Therefore since the motion of the terrestrial sphere takes place around pole *F* of the equator, then necessarily points *G* an *H* will fit onto the meridian *ABCD* at the same time, since parallel circles are around the same poles through which pass the great circles which intercept similar arcs on the parallel circles. Wherefore the selfsame time from the rising at *G* to midday measures also the arc *AEH*; and the time from midnight to sunrise measures *CH* the remaining and subterranean arc of the semicircle. Now *AEC* is a semicircle; and *AE* and *EC* are quadrants of circles, since they are drawn through the pole of *ABCD*. On that account, *EH* will be half the difference between the longest day and the equinox; and *EG* will be the distance between the equinoctial and the solstitial sunrise. Therefore since in triangle *EHG* angle *GEH*, the obliquity of the sphere, is established by means of arc *AB*, and angle *GHE* is right, and side *GH* is given as the distance from the summer tropic to the equator; the remaining sides are also given by the fourth theorem on sphericals: side *EH* as half the difference between the longest day and the equinox, and side *GE* as the distance of sunrise. Moreover, if together with side *GH* side *EH*, (half) the difference between the longest day and the equinox, or else *EG*, is given; angle *E* of the inclination of the sphere is given, and hence *FD* the elevation of the pole above the horizon.

But even if it is not the tropic but some other point *G* in the ecliptic which is taken, nevertheless arcs *EG* and *EH* will become manifest: since by the table of declinations set out above *GH* the arc of declination for that degree of the ecliptic becomes known, and the rest can be demonstrated in the same way.

Hence it also follows that the degrees of the ecliptic which are equally distant from the tropic cut off equal arcs of the horizon [35a] between the equinoctial sunrise and the same degrees and make the lengths of days and nights inversely equal. And that is so because the parallels which pass through each of those degrees of the ecliptic are equal, since each of the degrees has the same declination.

But when equal arcs are taken between the equinoctial intersection and the two degrees (on the ecliptic), again the distances of rising are equal but in different directions; and the duration of days and nights are inversely equal, because on each side of the equinox the durations describe equal arcs of parallels, according as the signs themselves which are equally distant from the equinox have equal declinations from the equator.

For in the same figure let *GM* and *KN* the arcs of parallels be described cutting the horizon *BED* at points *G* and *K*, and let *LKO* a quadrant of a great circle be drawn from the south pole *L*. Therefore since

declination HG = declination KO,

there will be two triangles *DFG* and *BLK*, wherein two sides of the one are equal to two sides of the other:

FG = LK

and the elevations of the poles are equal,

FD = LB,

and

angle D = angle B = 90°.

Therefore

base DG = base BK;

and hence, as the distances of sunrise are the remainders of the quadrants

GE = EK.

Wherefore since here too,

side EG = side EK,
side GH = side KO,

and

vertical angle KEO = vertical angle GEH;
side EH = side EO.

And

EH + 90° = OE + 90°.

Hence

arc AEH = arc OEC.

But since great circles described through the poles of parallel circles cut off similar arcs, *GM* and *KN* will be similar and equal, as was to be shown.

But all this can be shown differently. In the same way let the meridian circle *ABCD* be described with centre *E*. Let the diameter of the equator and the common section of the two circles be *AEC*; let *BED* be the diameter of the horizon and the meridian line, let *LEM* be the axis of the sphere; and let *L* be the apparent pole and *M* the hidden. Let *AF* be taken as the distance of the summer solstice or as some other declination; and to *AF* let *GF* be drawn as the diameter of a parallel and its common section with the meridian; *FG* will cut the axis at *K* and the meridian line at *N*.

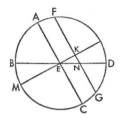

Therefore, [35ᵇ] since by the definition of Posidonius those lines are parallel which neither move toward nor move away from one another but which everywhere make the perpendicular lines between them equal,

$$KE = \tfrac{1}{2} \text{ ch. } 2\, AF.$$

Similarly *KN* will be half of the chord subtending twice the arc of the parallel circle whose radius is *FK*. And twice this arc is the difference between the equinoctial day and the other day. And this is true because all the semicircles of which these lines are the common sections and diameters—namely, *BED* of the oblique horizon, *LEM* of the right horizon, *AEC* of the equator, and *FKG* of the parallel—are perpendicular to the plane of circle *ABCD*. And by Euclid's *Elements*, XI, 19, the common sections which they make with one another are perpendicular to the same plane at points *E, K,* and *N*: and by XI, 6, these common sections are parallel to one another.

And *K* is the centre of the parallel circle; and *E* is the centre of the sphere. Wherefore *EN* is half the chord subtending twice the arc of the horizon which is the difference between sunrise on the parallel and the equinoctial sunrise. Therefore, since the declination *AF* was given together with *FL* the remainder of the quadrant, *KE* half of the chord subtending twice arc *AF* and *FK* half the chord subtending twice arc *FL* will be established in terms of the parts whereof *AE* has 100,000. But in the right triangle *EKN* angle *KEN* is given by *DL* the elevation of the pole, and the remaining angle *KNE* is equal to *AEB*, because in the oblique sphere the parallels are equally inclined to the horizon; and the sides are given in the same parts whereof the radius has 100,000. Therefore *KN* will be given in the parts whereof *FK* the radius of the parallel has 100,000; for *KN* is equal to half the chord subtending the arc which measures the distance between the equinoctial day and a day on the parallel; and this arc is similarly given in the degrees whereof the parallel circle has 360°.

From this it is clear that

$$FK : KN = \tfrac{1}{2} \text{ ch. } 2\, FL : \tfrac{1}{2} \text{ ch. } 2\, AF \text{ comp. } \tfrac{1}{2} \text{ ch. } 2\, AB : \tfrac{1}{2} \text{ ch. } 2\, DL$$

and

$$\tfrac{1}{2} \text{ ch. } 2\, FL : \tfrac{1}{2} \text{ ch. } 2\, AF \text{ comp. } \tfrac{1}{2} \text{ ch. } 2\, AB : \tfrac{1}{2} \text{ ch. } 2\, DL = FK : KE \text{ comp. } EK : KN.$$

That is to say, *EK* is taken as a mean between *FK* and *KN*. Similarly too

$$BE : EN = BE : EK \text{ comp. } KE : EN,$$

as Ptolemy shows in greater detail by means of spherical segments. So I think that not only the inequality of days and nights can be determined; but also that in the case of the moon and the stars whose declination on the parallels described through them by the daily movement has been given, the segments (of the parallels) which are above the horizon can be distinguished from those which are below; and hence the risings and settings (of the moon or stars) can be easily understood.

TABLE OF DIFFERENCE OF THE ASCENSIONS IN AN OBLIQUE SPHERE

Declin ation	Elevation of the Pole											
	31°		32°		33°		34°		35°		36°	
	Times	Min.	Times	Min.	Times	Min.	Times	Min.	Times	Min.	Times	Min.
1	0	36	0	37	0	39	0	40	0	42	0	44
2	1	12	1	15	1	18	1	21	1	24	1	27
3	1	48	1	53	1	57	2	2	2	6	2	11
4	2	24	2	30	2	36	2	42	2	48	2	55
5	3	1	3	8	3	15	3	23	3	31	3	39
6	3	37	3	46	3	55	4	4	4	13	4	23
7	4	14	4	24	4	34	4	45	4	56	5	7
8	4	51	5	2	5	14	5	26	5	39	5	52
9	5	28	5	41	5	54	6	8	6	22	6	36
10	6	5	6	20	6	35	6	50	7	6	7	22
11	6	42	6	59	7	15	7	32	7	49	8	7
12	7	20	7	38	7	56	8	15	8	34	8	53
13	7	58	8	18	8	37	8	58	9	18	9	39
14	8	37	8	58	9	19	9	41	10	3	10	26
15	9	16	9	38	10	1	10	25	10	49	11	14
16	9	55	10	19	10	44	11	9	11	25	12	2
17	10	35	11	1	11	27	11	54	12	22	12	50
18	11	16	11	43	12	11	12	40	13	9	13	39
19	11	56	12	25	12	55	13	26	13	57	14	29
20	12	38	13	9	13	40	14	13	14	46	15	20
21	13	20	13	53	14	26	15	0	15	36	16	12
22	14	3	14	37	15	13	15	49	16	27	17	5
23	14	47	15	23	16	0	16	38	17	17	17	58
24	15	31	16	9	16	48	17	29	18	10	18	52
25	16	16	16	56	17	38	18	20	19	3	19	48
26	17	2	17	45	18	28	19	12	19	58	20	45
27	17	50	18	34	19	19	20	6	20	54	21	44
28	18	38	19	24	20	12	21	1	21	51	22	43
29	19	27	20	16	21	6	21	57	22	50	23	45
30	20	18	21	9	22	1	22	55	23	51	24	48
31	21	10	22	3	22	58	23	55	24	53	25	53
32	22	3	22	59	23	56	24	56	25	57	27	0
33	22	57	23	54	24	19	25	59	27	3	28	9
34	23	55	24	56	25	59	27	4	28	10	29	21
35	24	53	25	57	27	3	28	10	29	21	30	35
36	25	53	27	0	28	9	29	21	30	35	31	52

TABLE OF DIFFERENCE OF THE ASCENSIONS IN AN OBLIQUE SPHERE

Declination	Elevation of the Pole										
	37°		38°		39°		40°		41°		42°
	Times	Min.	Times	Min.	Times	Min.	Times	Min.	Times	Min.	Times	Min.
1	0	45	0	47	0	49	0	50	0	52	0	54
2	1	31	1	34	1	37	1	41	1	44	1	48
3	2	16	2	21	2	26	2	31	2	37	2	42
4	3	1	3	8	3	15	3	22	3	29	3	37
5	3	47	3	55	4	4	4	13	4	22	4	31
6	4	33	4	43	4	53	5	4	5	15	5	26
7	5	19	5	30	5	42	5	55	6	8	6	21
8	6	5	6	18	6	32	6	46	7	1	7	16
9	6	51	7	6	7	22	7	38	7	55	8	12
10	7	38	7	55	8	13	8	30	8	49	9	8
11	8	25	8	44	9	3	9	23	9	44	10	5
12	9	13	9	34	9	55	10	16	10	39	11	2
13	10	1	10	24	10	46	11	10	11	35	12	0
14	10	50	11	14	11	39	12	5	12	31	12	58
15	11	39	12	5	12	32	13	0	13	28	13	58
16	12	29	12	57	13	26	13	55	14	26	14	58
17	13	19	13	49	14	20	14	52	15	25	15	59
18	14	10	14	42	15	15	15	49	16	24	17	1
19	15	2	15	36	16	11	16	48	17	25	18	4
20	15	55	16	31	17	8	17	47	18	27	19	8
21	16	49	17	27	18	7	18	47	19	30	20	13
22	17	44	18	24	19	6	19	49	20	34	21	20
23	18	39	19	22	20	6	20	52	21	39	22	28
24	19	36	20	21	21	8	21	56	22	46	23	38
25	20	34	21	21	22	11	23	2	23	55	24	50
26	21	34	22	24	23	16	24	10	25	5	26	3
27	22	35	23	28	24	22	25	19	26	17	27	18
28	23	37	24	33	25	30	26	30	27	31	28	36
29	24	41	25	40	26	40	27	43	28	48	29	57
30	25	47	26	49	27	52	28	59	30	7	31	19
31	26	55	28	0	29	7	30	17	31	29	32	45
32	28	5	29	13	30	54	31	31	32	54	34	14
33	29	18	30	29	31	44	33	1	34	22	35	47
34	30	32	31	48	33	6	34	27	35	54	37	24
35	31	51	33	10	34	33	35	59	37	30	39	5
36	33	12	34	35	36	2	37	34	39	10	40	51

TABLE OF DIFFERENCE OF THE ASCENSIONS IN AN OBLIQUE SPHERE

Declin ation	Elevation of the Pole											
	43°		44°		45°		46°		47°		48°	
	Times	Min.	Times	Min.	Times	Min.	Times	Min.	Times	Min.	Times	Min.
1	0	56	0	58	1	0	1	2	1	4	1	7
2	1	52	1	56	2	0	2	4	2	9	2	13
3	2	48	2	54	3	0	3	7	3	13	3	20
4	3	44	3	52	4	1	4	9	4	18	4	27
5	4	41	4	51	5	1	5	12	5	23	5	35
6	5	37	5	50	6	2	6	15	6	28	6	42
7	6	34	6	49	7	3	7	18	7	34	7	50
8	7	32	7	48	8	5	8	22	8	40	8	59
9	8	30	8	48	9	7	9	26	9	47	10	8
10	9	28	9	48	10	9	10	31	10	54	11	18
11	10	27	10	49	11	13	11	37	12	2	12	28
12	11	26	11	51	12	16	12	43	13	11	13	39
13	12	26	12	53	13	21	13	50	14	20	14	51
14	13	27	13	56	14	26	14	58	15	30	16	5
15	14	28	15	0	15	32	16	7	16	42	17	19
16	15	31	16	5	16	40	17	16	17	54	18	34
17	16	34	17	10	17	48	18	27	19	8	19	51
18	17	38	18	17	18	58	19	40	20	23	21	9
19	18	44	19	25	20	9	20	53	21	40	22	29
20	19	50	20	35	21	21	22	8	22	58	23	51
21	20	59	21	46	22	34	23	25	24	18	25	14
22	22	8	22	58	23	50	24	44	25	40	26	40
23	23	19	24	12	25	7	26	5	27	5	28	8
24	24	32	25	28	26	26	27	27	28	31	29	38
25	25	47	26	46	27	48	28	52	30	0	31	12
26	27	3	28	6	29	11	30	20	31	32	32	48
27	28	22	29	29	30	38	31	51	33	7	34	28
28	29	44	30	54	32	7	33	25	34	46	36	12
29	31	8	32	22	33	40	35	2	36	28	38	0
30	32	35	33	53	35	16	36	43	38	15	39	53
31	34	5	35	28	36	56	38	29	40	7	41	52
32	35	38	37	7	38	40	40	19	42	4	43	57
33	37	16	38	50	40	30	42	15	44	8	46	9
34	38	58	40	39	42	25	44	18	46	20	48	31
35	40	46	42	33	44	27	46	23	48	36	51	3
36	42	39	44	33	46	36	48	47	51	11	53	47

Table of Difference of the Ascensions in an Oblique Sphere

Declin ation	Elevation of the Pole										
	49°		50°		51°		52°		53°		54°	
	Times	Min.	Times	Min.	Times	Min.	Times	Min.	Times	Min.	Times	Min.
1	1	9	1	12	1	14	1	17	1	20	1	23
2	2	18	2	23	2	28	2	34	2	39	2	45
3	3	27	3	35	3	43	3	51	3	59	4	8
4	4	37	4	47	4	57	5	8	5	19	5	31
5	5	47	5	50	6	12	6	26	6	40	6	55
6	6	57	7	12	7	27	7	44	8	1	8	19
7	8	7	8	25	8	43	9	2	9	23	9	44
8	9	18	9	38	10	0	10	22	10	45	11	9
9	10	30	10	53	11	17	11	42	12	8	12	35
10	11	42	12	8	12	35	13	3	13	32	14	3
11	12	55	13	24	13	53	14	24	14	57	15	31
12	14	9	14	40	15	13	15	47	16	23	17	0
13	15	24	15	58	16	34	17	11	17	50	18	32
14	16	40	17	17	17	56	18	37	19	19	20	4
15	17	57	18	39	19	19	20	4	20	50	21	38
16	19	16	19	59	20	44	21	32	22	22	23	15
17	20	36	21	22	22	11	23	2	23	56	24	53
18	21	57	22	47	23	39	24	34	25	33	26	34
19	23	20	24	14	25	10	26	9	27	11	28	17
20	24	45	25	42	26	43	27	46	28	53	30	4
21	26	12	27	14	28	18	29	26	30	37	31	54
22	27	42	28	47	29	56	31	8	32	25	33	47
23	29	14	30	23	31	37	32	54	34	17	35	45
24	31	4	32	3	33	21	34	44	36	13	37	48
25	32	26	33	46	35	10	36	39	38	14	39	59
26	34	8	35	32	37	2	38	38	40	20	42	10
27	35	53	37	23	39	0	40	42	42	33	44	32
28	37	43	39	19	41	2	42	53	44	53	47	2
29	39	37	41	21	43	12	45	12	47	21	49	44
30	41	37	43	29	45	29	47	39	50	1	52	37
31	43	44	45	44	47	54	50	16	52	53	55	48
32	45	57	48	8	50	30	53	7	56	1	59	19
33	48	19	50	44	53	20	56	13	59	28	63	21
34	50	54	53	30	56	20	59	42	63	31	68	11
35	53	40	56	34	59	58	63	40	68	18	74	32
36	56	42	59	59	63	47	68	26	74	36	90	0

TABLE OF DIFFERENCE OF THE ASCENSIONS IN AN OBLIQUE SPHERE

Declin ation	Elevation of the Pole											
	55°		56°		57°		58°		59°		60°	
	Times	Min.	Times	Min.	Times	Min.	Times	Min.	Times	Min.	Times	Min.
1	1	26	1	29	1	32	1	36	1	40	1	44
2	2	52	2	58	3	5	3	12	3	20	3	28
3	4	17	4	27	4	38	4	49	5	0	5	12
4	5	44	5	57	6	11	6	25	6	41	6	57
5	7	11	7	27	7	44	8	3	8	22	8	43
6	8	38	8	58	9	19	9	41	10	4	10	29
7	10	6	10	29	10	54	11	20	11	47	12	17
8	11	35	12	1	12	30	13	0	13	32	14	5
9	13	4	13	35	14	7	14	41	15	17	15	55
10	14	35	15	9	15	45	16	23	17	4	17	47
11	16	7	16	45	17	25	18	8	18	53	19	41
12	17	40	18	22	19	6	19	53	20	43	21	36
13	19	15	20	1	20	50	21	41	22	36	23	34
14	20	52	21	42	22	35	23	31	24	31	25	35
15	22	30	23	24	24	22	25	23	26	29	27	39
16	24	10	25	9	26	12	27	19	28	30	29	47
17	25	53	26	57	28	5	29	18	30	35	31	59
18	27	39	28	48	30	1	31	20	32	44	34	19
19	29	27	30	41	32	1	33	26	34	58	36	37
20	31	19	32	39	34	5	35	37	37	17	39	5
21	33	15	34	41	36	14	37	54	39	42	41	40
22	35	14	36	48	38	28	40	17	42	15	44	25
23	37	19	39	0	40	49	42	47	44	57	47	20
24	39	29	41	18	43	17	45	26	47	49	50	27
25	41	45	43	44	45	54	48	16	50	54	53	52
26	44	9	46	18	48	41	51	19	54	16	57	39
27	46	41	49	4	51	41	54	38	58	0	61	57
28	49	24	52	1	54	58	58	19	62	14	67	4
29	52	20	55	16	58	36	62	31	67	18	73	46
30	55	32	58	52	62	45	67	31	73	55	90	0
31	59	6	62	58	67	42	74	4	90	0		
32	63	10	67	53	74	12	90	0				
33	68	1	74	19	90	0			*The vacant spaces go to*			
34	74	33	90	0					*stars which neither rise*			
35	90	0							*nor set*			
36												

8. ON THE HOURS AND PARTS OF THE DAY AND NIGHT

[38ᵇ] Accordingly it is clear from this that if from the table we take the difference of days which correspond to the declination of the sun and is found under the given elevation of the pole and add it to a quadrant of a circle in the case of a northern declination and subtract it in the case of a southern declination, and then double the result, we shall have the length of that day and the span of night, which is the remainder of the circle.

Any of these segments divided by 15 "times" will show how many equal hours there are (in that day). But by taking a twelfth part of the segment we shall have the duration of one seasonal hour. Now the hours get their name from their day, whereof each hour is always the twelfth part. Hence the hours are found to have been called summer-solstitial, equinoctial, and winter-solstitial by the ancients.

But there were not any others in use at first except the twelve hours from sunrise to sunset; and they divided the night into four vigils or watches. This set-up of the hours lasted a long time by the tacit consent of mankind. And for its sake were water-clocks invented: by the addition and subtraction of dripping water people adjusted the hours to the different lengths of days, so as not to have distinctions in time obscured by a cloud. But afterwards when equal hours common to day and night came into general use, as making it easier to tell the time, then the seasonal hours became obsolete, so that if you asked any ordinary person whether it was the first, third or sixth, ninth, or eleventh hour of the day, he would not have any answer to make or would make one which had nothing to do with the matter. Furthermore, at present some measure the number of equal hours from noon, some from sunset, some from midnight, and others from sunrise, according as it is instituted by the state.

9. ON THE OBLIQUE ASCENSION OF THE PARTS OF THE ECLIPTIC AND HOW THE DEGREE WHICH IS IN THE MIDDLE OF THE HEAVENS IS DETERMINED WITH RESPECT TO THE DEGREE WHICH IS RISING

[39ᵃ] Now that the lengths and differences of days and nights have been expounded, there follows in proper order an exposition of oblique ascensions, that is to say, together with what "times" (of the equator) the dodekatemoria, i.e., the twelve parts of the ecliptic, or some other arcs of it, cross the horizon. For the differences between right and oblique ascensions are the same as the differences between the equinox and a different day, as we set forth. Furthermore, the ancients borrowed the names of animals for twelve constellations of unmoving stars, and, beginning at the spring equinox, called them Aries, Taurus, Gemini, Cancer, and so on in order.

Therefore for the sake of greater clearness let the meridian circle *ABCD* be repeated; and the equatorial semicircle *AEC* and the horizon *BED*, which cut one another at point *E*. Now let point *H* be taken as the equinox. Let the ecliptic *FHI* pass through this point and cut the horizon at *L*; and through this intersection let *KLM* the quadrant of a great circle fall from *K* the pole of the equator. Thus it is perfectly clear that arc *HL* of the ecliptic and arc *HE* of the equator cross the horizon together, but that in the right sphere (arc *HL*) was rising together with arc *HEM*. Arc *EM* is the difference between these ascensions; and we have already shown that it is half the difference between the equinox and the different day. But in a

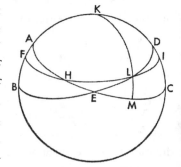

northern declination what was there added (to the quadrant of a circle) is here subtracted (from the right ascension); but in a southern declination it is added to the right ascension, so that the ascension may become oblique. And hence the extent that the whole sign or some other arc of the ecliptic has emerged may become manifest by means of the numbered ascensions from beginning to end.

From this it follows that when some degree of the ecliptic is given, the rising of which has been measured from the equinox, the degree which is in the middle of the heavens is also given. For when the declination of a degree rising at L has been given as corresponding to arc *HL* the distance from the equinox, and arc *HEM* is the right ascension, and the whole *AHEM* is the arc of half a day: then the remainder *AH* is given. And *AH* is the right ascension of arc *FH*, which is also given by the table, or because angle *AHF* the angle of section is given together with side *AH*, and angle *FAH* is right. And so *FHL* the whole arc between the degree rising and the degree in the middle of the heavens is given.

Conversely, if the degree which is in the middle of the heavens, namely arc *FH*, is given first, we shall also know the sign which [39ᵇ] is rising. For arc *AF* the declination will be known; and by means of the angle of obliquity of the sphere, arc *AFB* and arc *FB* the remainder will become known. Now in triangle *BFL* angle *BFL* and side *FB* are given by the above, and angle *FBL* is right. Therefore side *FHL*, which was sought, is given; or by a different method, as below.

10. On the Angle of Section of the Ecliptic with the Horizon

Moreover, as the ecliptic is oblique to the axis of the sphere, it makes various angles with the horizon. For we have already said in the case of the differences of the shadows that two opposite degrees of the ecliptic pass through the axis of the horizon of those

who live between the tropics. But I think it will be sufficient for our purpose if we demonstrate the angles which we the heteroscian inhabitants find. By means of these angles the universal ratio of them may easily be understood. Accordingly I think it is clear enough that in the oblique sphere when the equinox or the beginning of Aries is rising, the more the greatest southward declination increases—and this declination is measured from the beginning of Capricorn which is in the middle of the heavens at this time—the more the ecliptic is inclined and verges towards the horizon; and conversely, when the ecliptic has a greater elevation (above the horizon), it makes a greater eastern angle, when the beginning of Libra is emerging and the beginning of Cancer is in the middle of the heavens; since these three circles, the equator, the ecliptic, and the horizon, coincide in one common section at the poles of the meridian circle, and the arcs of the meridian circle intercepted by them show how great the angle of rising should be judged to be.

But in order that the way of taking the measurements of the other parts of the ecliptic may be clear, again let *ABC* be the meridian circle, let *BED* be the semicircle of the horizon, let *AEC* be the semi-circle of the ecliptic, and let any degree of the ecliptic be rising at *E*.

Our problem is to find how great angle *AEB* is, according as four right angles are equal to 360°. Therefore since *E* is given as the rising degree, there are given by the foregoing the degree which is in the middle of the heavens and the arc *AE*.
And since

angle *ABE* = 90°;

ch. 2 *AE* : ch. 2 *AB* = dmt. sph. : ch. 2 *AEB*.

[40ª] Therefore too

angle *AEB* is given.

But if the degree given is not rising but the degree in the middle of the heavens—and let it be *A*—nevertheless angle *AEB* will be the measure of the eastern angle or angle of rising. For with *E* as pole, let *FGH* the quadrant of a great circle be described, and let the quadrants *EAG* and *EBH* be completed.
Therefore since

meridian altitude *AB* is given,

and

$$AF = 90°—AB,$$

and by the foregoing

angle *FAG* is given,

and

angle $FGA = 90°$;

therefore

arc FG is given,

and

$$90° — FG = GH,$$

which measures the sought angle of rising. Similarly, it is also made evident here how for the degree which is in the middle of the heavens the degree which is rising is given, because

$$\text{ch. } 2\ GH : 2\ AB = \text{dmt. sph. : ch. } 2\ AE,$$

as in spherical triangles.

We are subjoining three sets of tables of these things. The first will be the table of ascensions in the right sphere, beginning with Aries and increasing by sixtieth parts of the ecliptic. The second will be that of ascensions in the oblique sphere, proceeding by steps of 6° in the ecliptic, from the parallel for which there is a polar elevation of 39° to the parallel which has a polar elevation of 57°—increasing the elevation by 3°'s each time. The remaining table contains the angles made with the horizon and proceeds through the ecliptic by steps of 6° beneath the same seven segments. These tables have been set up in accordance with the least obliquity of the ecliptic, namely 23°28', which is approximately right for our age.

TABLE OF THE ASCENSIONS OF THE SIGNS IN THE REVOLUTION
OF THE RIGHT SPHERE

Ecliptic Signs	Deg.	Ascensions Times	Min.	One Degree Times	Min.	Ecliptic Signs	Deg.	Ascensions Times	Min.	One Degree Times	Min.
Aries ♈	6	5	30	0	55	Libra ♎	6	185	30	0	55
	12	11	0	0	55		12	191	0	0	55
	18	16	34	0	56		18	196	34	0	56
	24	22	10	0	56		24	202	10	0	56
	30	27	54	0	57		30	207	54	0	57
Taurus ♉	6	33	43	0	58	Scorpio ♏	6	213	43	0	58
	12	39	35	0	59		12	219	35	0	59
	18	45	32	1	0		18	225	32	1	0
	24	51	37	1	1		24	231	37	1	1
	30	57	48	1	2		30	237	48	1	2
Gemini ♊	6	64	6	1	3	Sagittarius ♐	6	244	6	1	3
	12	70	29	1	4		12	250	29	1	4
	18	76	57	1	5		18	256	57	1	5
	24	83	27	1	5		24	263	27	1	5
	30	90	0	1	5		30	270	0	1	5
Cancer ♋	6	96	33	1	5	Capricornus ♑	6	276	33	1	5
	12	103	3	1	5		12	283	3	1	5
	18	109	31	1	5		18	289	31	1	5
	24	115	54	1	4		24	295	54	1	4
	30	122	12	1	3		30	302	12	1	3
Leo ♌	6	128	23	1	2	Aquarius ♒	6	308	23	1	2
	12	134	28	1	1		12	314	28	1	1
	18	140	25	1	0		18	320	25	1	0
	24	146	17	0	59		24	326	17	0	59
	30	152	6	0	58		30	332	6	0	58
Virgo ♍	6	157	50	0	57	Pisces ♓	6	337	50	0	57
	12	163	26	0	56		12	343	26	0	56
	18	169	0	0	56		18	349	0	0	56
	24	174	30	0	55		24	354	30	0	55
	30	180	0	0	55		30	360	0	0	55

TABLE OF THE ASCENSIONS IN THE OBLIQUE SPHERE

Ecliptic Signs	Elevation of the Pole of the Equator												
	39°		42°		45°		48°		51°		54°		57°	
	Ascension		Ascension		Ascension		Ascension		Ascension		Ascension		Ascension	
	Times	Min.	Times	Min.	Times	Min.	Times	Min.	Times	Min.	Times	Min.	Times	Min.
♈ 6	3	34	3	20	3	6	2	50	2	32	2	12	1	49
12	7	10	6	44	6	15	5	44	5	8	4	27	3	40
18	10	50	10	10	9	27	8	39	7	47	6	44	5	34
24	14	32	13	39	12	43	11	40	10	28	9	7	7	32
30	18	26	17	21	16	11	14	51	13	26	11	40	9	40
♉ 6	22	30	21	12	19	46	18	14	16	25	14	22	11	57
12	26	39	25	10	23	32	21	42	19	38	17	13	14	23
18	31	0	29	20	27	29	25	24	23	2	20	17	17	2
24	35	38	33	47	31	43	29	25	26	47	23	42	20	2
30	40	30	38	30	36	15	33	41	30	49	27	26	23	22
♊ 6	45	39	43	31	41	7	38	23	35	15	31	34	27	7
12	51	8	48	52	46	20	43	27	40	8	36	13	31	26
18	56	56	54	35	51	56	48	56	45	28	41	22	36	20
24	63	0	60	36	57	54	54	49	51	15	47	1	41	49
30	69	25	66	59	64	16	61	10	57	34	53	28	48	2
♋ 6	76	6	73	42	71	0	67	55	64	21	60	7	54	55
12	83	2	80	41	78	2	75	2	71	34	67	28	62	26
18	90	10	87	54	85	22	82	29	79	10	75	15	70	28
24	97	27	95	19	92	55	90	11	87	3	83	22	78	55
30	104	54	102	54	100	39	98	5	95	13	91	50	87	46
♌ 6	112	24	110	33	108	30	106	11	103	33	100	28	96	48
12	119	56	118	16	116	25	114	20	111	58	109	13	105	58
18	127	29	126	0	124	23	122	32	120	28	118	3	115	13
24	135	4	133	46	132	21	130	48	128	59	126	56	124	31
30	142	38	141	33	140	23	139	3	137	38	135	52	133	52
♍ 6	150	11	149	19	148	23	147	20	146	8	144	47	143	12
12	157	41	157	1	156	19	155	29	154	38	153	36	153	24
18	165	7	164	40	164	12	163	41	163	5	162	24	162	47
24	172	34	172	21	172	6	171	51	171	33	171	12	170	49
30	180	0	180	0	180	0	180	0	180	0	180	0	180	0

TABLE OF THE ASCENSIONS IN THE OBLIQUE SPHERE, II

Ecliptic		Elevation of the Pole of the Equator												
		39°		42°		45°		48°		51°		54°		57°
		Ascension		Ascension		Ascension		Ascension		Ascension		Ascension		Ascension
Signs		Times Min.		Times Min.		Times Min.		Times Min.		Times Min.		Times Min.		Times Min.
♎	6	187	26	187	39	187	54	188	9	188	27	188	48	189	11
	12	194	53	195	19	195	48	196	19	196	55	197	36	198	23
	18	202	21	203	0	203	41	204	30	205	24	206	25	207	36
	24	209	49	210	41	211	37	212	40	213	52	215	13	216	48
	30	217	22	218	27	219	37	220	57	222	22	224	8	226	8
♏	6	224	56	226	14	227	38	229	12	231	1	233	4	235	29
	12	232	56	234	0	235	37	237	28	239	32	241	57	244	47
	18	240	31	241	44	243	35	245	40	248	2	250	47	254	2
	24	247	36	249	27	251	30	253	49	256	27	259	32	263	12
	30	255	36	257	6	259	21	261	52	264	47	268	10	272	14
♐	6	262	8	264	41	267	5	269	49	272	57	276	38	281	5
	12	269	50	272	6	274	38	277	31	280	50	284	45	289	32
	18	276	58	279	19	281	58	248	58	288	26	292	32	297	34
	24	283	54	286	18	289	0	292	5	295	39	299	53	305	5
	30	290	75	293	1	295	45	298	50	302	26	306	42	311	58
♑	6	297	0	299	24	302	6	305	11	308	45	312	59	318	11
	12	303	4	305	25	308	4	311	4	314	32	318	38	323	40
	18	308	52	311	8	313	40	316	33	319	52	323	47	328	34
	24	314	21	316	29	318	53	321	37	324	45	328	26	332	53
	30	319	30	321	30	323	45	326	19	329	11	332	34	336	38
♒	6	324	21	326	13	328	16	330	35	333	13	336	18	339	58
	12	330	0	330	40	332	31	334	36	336	58	339	43	342	58
	18	333	21	334	50	336	27	338	18	340	22	342	47	345	37
	24	337	30	338	48	340	3	341	46	343	35	345	38	348	3
	30	341	34	342	39	343	49	345	9	346	34	348	20	350	20
♓	6	345	29	346	21	347	17	348	20	349	32	350	53	352	28
	12	349	11	349	51	350	33	351	21	352	14	353	16	354	26
	18	352	50	353	16	353	45	354	16	354	52	355	33	356	20
	24	356	26	356	40	356	23	357	10	357	53	357	48	358	11
	30	360	0	360	0	360	0	360	0	360	0	360	0	360	0

TABLE OF THE ANGLES MADE BY THE ECLIPTIC WITH THE HORIZON

Ecliptic Sign		39° Angles Deg. Min.		42° Angles Deg. Min.		45° Angles Deg. Min.		48° Angles Deg. Min.		51° Angles Deg. Min.		54° Angles Deg. Min.		57° Angles Deg. Min.		Ecliptic Sign	
♈	0	27	32	24	32	21	32	18	32	15	32	12	32	9	32	30	
	6	27	37	24	36	21	36	18	36	15	35	12	35	9	35	24	
	12	27	49	24	39	21	48	18	47	15	45	12	43	9	41	18	
	18	28	13	25	9	22	6	19	3	15	59	12	56	9	53	12	
	24	28	45	25	40	22	34	19	29	16	23	13	18	10	13	6	♓
	30	29	27	26	15	23	11	20	5	16	56	13	45	10	31	30	
♉	6	30	19	27	9	23	59	20	48	17	34	14	20	11	2	24	
	12	31	21	28	9	24	56	20	41	18	23	15	3	11	40	18	
	18	32	35	29	20	26	3	22	43	19	21	15	56	12	26	12	
	24	34	5	30	43	27	23	24	2	20	41	16	59	13	20	6	♒
	30	35	40	32	17	28	52	25	26	21	52	18	14	14	26	30	
♊	6	37	29	34	1	30	37	27	5	23	11	19	42	15	48	24	
	12	39	32	36	4	32	32	28	56	25	15	21	25	17	23	18	
	18	41	44	38	14	34	41	31	3	27	18	23	25	19	16	12	
	24	44	8	40	32	37	2	33	22	29	35	25	37	21	26	6	♑
	30	46	41	43	11	39	33	35	53	32	5	28	6	23	52	30	
♋	6	49	18	45	51	42	15	38	35	34	44	30	50	26	36	24	
	12	52	3	48	34	45	0	41	8	37	55	33	43	29	34	18	
	18	54	44	51	20	47	48	44	13	40	31	36	40	32	39	12	
	24	57	30	54	5	50	38	47	6	43	33	39	43	35	50	6	♐
	30	60	4	56	42	53	22	49	54	46	21	42	43	38	56	30	
♌	6	62	40	59	27	56	0	52	34	49	9	45	37	41	57	24	
	12	64	59	61	44	58	26	55	7	51	46	48	19	44	48	18	
	18	67	7	63	56	60	20	57	26	54	6	50	47	47	24	12	
	24	68	59	65	52	62	42	59	30	56	17	53	7	49	47	6	♏
	30	70	38	67	27	64	18	61	17	58	9	54	50	52	38	30	
♍	6	72	0	68	53	65	51	62	46	59	37	56	27	53	16	24	
	12	73	4	70	2	66	59	63	56	60	53	57	50	54	46	18	
	18	73	51	70	50	67	49	64	48	61	46	58	45	55	44	12	
	24	74	19	71	20	68	20	65	19	62	18	59	17	56	16	6	♎
	30	74	28	71	28	68	28	65	28	62	28	59	28	56	28	0	

11. ON THE USE OF THESE TABLES

[42b] Now the use of these tables is clear from the demonstrations, since if we take the right ascension corresponding to the known degree of the sun and if for every equal hour measured from noon we add 15 "times" to it—not counting the 360° of the whole circle, if there is more than that—the sum of the right ascensions will show the degree of the ecliptic in the middle of the heavens at the proposed hour.

Similarly if you do the same thing in the case of the oblique ascension of your region, you will have the rising degree of the ecliptic for the hour measured from sunrise.

Moreover, in the case of certain stars which are outside the ecliptic but of which the right ascension has been established—as we taught above—by their right ascension from the beginning of Aries the degrees of the ecliptic which are in the middle of the heavens together with them are given according to the table; and by their oblique ascension the degree of the ecliptic which arises with them, according as the ascensions and parts of the ecliptic are placed in corresponding regions of the tables. It is possible to operate with the setting similarly but by means of the position opposite.

Moreover, if to the right ascension in the middle of the heavens a quadrant of a circle is added, the sum is the oblique ascension of the rising degree. Wherefore the rising degree is given by means of the degree in the middle of the heavens, and vice versa.

There follows the table of the angles of the ecliptic and the horizon, which are measured at the rising degree of the ecliptic. Hence it is understood how great the elevation of the 90th degree of the ecliptic is above the horizon; and it is particularly necessary to know that in the case of solar eclipses.

12. ON THE ANGLES AND ARCS OF THE CIRCLES WHICH PASS THROUGH THE POLES OF THE HORIZON AND INTERSECT THE SAME CIRCLE OF THE ECLIPTIC

In what follows we shall expound the ratio of the angles and arcs made by the intersection of the ecliptic with the circles through the vertex of the horizon, in the cases wherein the intersections have some altitude above the horizon. But we spoke above concerning the meridian altitude of the sun or of any degree of the ecliptic which is in the middle of the heavens, and concerning the angle of section with the meridian, since [43a] the meridian circle is also one of those circles which pass through the vertex of the horizon. Moreover we have already talked about the angle of the rising sign, the complementary angle to which is the angle which is comprehended by a great circle passing through the vertex of the horizon and by the rising ecliptic. Therefore there remain to be considered the mean sections, that is, the mean sections of the meridian circle with the semicircles of the ecliptic and the horizon.

Let the above figure be repeated. Let *G* be taken as any point on the ecliptic between midday and the point of rising or setting. Through *G* from *F* the pole of the horizon let fall *FGH* a quadrant of a circle.

"Hour" *AGE* is given

as the whole arc of the ecliptic between the meridian and the horizon, and by hypothesis

AG is given.

Similarly, because

meridian altitude *AB* is given,

and

meridian angle *FAG* is given;

therefore

AF is given.

And by what has been shown concerning spherical triangles,

arc *FG* is given.

And hence

altitude of *G* is given,

because

$$90° - FG = GH.$$

And

meridian angle *FAG* is given.

And those are what we were looking for.

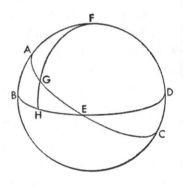

En route, we have taken from Ptolemy these truths about the angles and intersections of the ecliptic, and have referred ourselves to the geometry of spherical triangles. If anyone wishes to pursue this study at length, he can find by himself more utilities than we have given examples of.

13. On the Rising and Setting of the Stars

The rising and setting of the stars also seems to depend upon the daily revolution, not only the simple risings and settings of which we have just spoken but also those which occur in the morning or evening; because although their occurrence is affected by the course of the annual revolution, it will be better to speak of them here.

The ancient mathematicians distinguish the true risings and settings from the apparent. The morning rising of the star is true when the star rises at the same time as the sun; and the morning setting is true, when the star sets at sunrise; for morning is said to occur at the midpoint of this time. But the evening rising is true when the star rises at sunset; and the evening setting is true when the star sets at the same time as the

sun; for evening is said to occur at the midpoint of this time, namely the time [43ᵇ] between the time which is beginning and the time which ceases with night.

But the morning rising of a star is apparent when it rises first in the twilight before sunrise and begins to be apparent; and the morning setting is apparent when the star is seen to set very early before the sun rises. The evening rising is apparent when the star is seen to rise first in the evening; and the evening setting is apparent, when the star ceases to be apparent some time after sunset, and the star is occulted by the approach of the sun, until they come forth in their previous order at the morning rising.

This is true of the fixed stars and of the planets Saturn, Jupiter, and Mars. But Venus and Mercury rise and set in a different fashion. For they are not occulted by the approach of the sun, as the higher planets are; and they are not uncovered again by its departure. But, coming in front, they mingle with the radiance of the sun and free themselves. But when the higher planets have an evening rising and a morning setting, they are not obscured at any time, so as not to traverse the night with their illumination. But the lower planets remain hidden indifferently from sunset to sunrise, and cannot be seen anywhere. There is still another difference, namely that in higher planets the true morning risings and settings are prior to the apparent ones; and the evening risings and settings are posterior to the apparent, according as in the morning they precede the rising of the sun and in the evening follow its setting. But in the lower planets the apparent morning and evening risings are posterior to the true, while the apparent settings are prior to the true.

Now it can be understood from the above, where we expounded the oblique ascension of any star having a known position, how (the risings and settings) may be discerned, and together with what degree of the ecliptic the star rises or sets and at what position, or degree opposite—if the sun has become apparent by that time—the star has its true morning or evening rising or setting. The apparent risings and settings differ from the true according to the clarity and magnitude of the star, so that the stars which give a more powerful light are less dimmed by the rays of the sun than those which are less luminous. And the boundaries of occultation and apparition are determined in the lower hemisphere, between the horizon and the sun, on the arcs of circles which pass through the poles of the horizon. And the limits are 12° for the primary stars, 11° for Saturn, 10° for Jupiter, 11¹/₂° for Mars, 5° for Venus, and 10° for Mercury. But in this whole period during which what is left of daylight yields to night—this period embraces twilight, or dusk—there are 18° of the aforesaid circle. When the sun has traversed these degrees, the smaller stars too begin to be apparent. By this distance the mathematicians determine [44ᵃ] a parallel below the horizon in the lower hemisphere, and they say that when the sun has reached this parallel, day has ended and night has begun. Therefore when we have learned with what degree of the

ecliptic the star rises or sets and what the angle of section of the ecliptic with the horizon at that point is, and if then too we find as many degrees of the ecliptic between the rising degree and the sun as are sufficient to give the sun an altitude below the horizon in accord with the prescribed limits of the star in question; we shall pronounce that the first emergence or occultation of the star has taken place.

But what we have expounded, in the foregoing explanation, in the case of the altitude of the sun above the Earth agrees in all respects with its descent below the Earth. For there is no difference in the corresponding positions; and consequently those stars which are setting in the visible hemisphere are rising in the hidden hemisphere; and everything is the converse, and is easy to understand. What has been said concerning the rising and setting of the stars and the daily revolution of the terrestrial globe shall be sufficient.

14. On Investigating the Positions of the Stars and the Catalogue of the Fixed Stars

After the daily revolution of the terrestrial globe and its consequences have been expounded by us, the demonstrations relating to the annual circuit ought to follow now. But since some of the ancient mathematicians thought the phenomena of the fixed stars ought to come first as being the first beginnings of this art, accordingly we decided to act in accordance with this opinion, as among our principles and hypotheses we had assumed that the sphere of the fixed stars, to which the wanderings of all the planets are equally referred, is wholly immobile. But no one should be surprised at our following this order, although Ptolemy in his *Almagest* held that an explanation of the fixed stars could not be given, unless knowledge of the positions of the sun and moon had preceded it, and accordingly he judged that whatever had to do with the fixed stars should be put off till then. We think that this opinion must be opposed. But if you understand it of the numbers with which the apparent motion of the sun and moon is computed perhaps the opinion will stand. For Menelaus the geometer discovered the positions of many stars by means of the numbers relating to their conjunctions with the moon. [44b] But we shall do a much better job if we determine a star by the aid of instruments after examining carefully the positions of the sun and moon, as we will show how in a little while. We are even admonished by the wasted attempt of those who thought that the magnitude of the solar year could be defined simply by the equinoxes or solstices without the fixed stars. We shall never agree with them on that, so much so that there will nowhere be greater discord. Ptolemy called our attention to this: when he had evaluated the solar year in his time not without suspicion of an error which might emerge with the passage of time, he admonished posterity to examine the further certainty of the thing later on. Therefore it seemed to us to be

worth the trouble to show how by means of artificial instruments the positions of the sun and moon may be determined, that is, how far distant they are from the spring equinox or some other cardinal points of the world. The knowledge of these positions will afford us some facilities for investigating the other stars, and thus we shall be able to set forth before your eyes the sphere of the fixed stars and an image of it embroidered with constellations.

Now we have set forth above with what instruments the distance of the tropics, the obliquity of the ecliptic, and the inclination of the sphere, or the altitude of the pole of the equator, may be determined. In the same way we can determine any other altitude of the sun at midday. This altitude will exhibit to us through its difference from the inclination of the sphere how great the declination of the sun from the equator is. Then by means of this declination the position of the sun at midday will become clear as measured from the solstice or the equinox. Now the sun seems to traverse approximately 1° during the space of 24 hours; 2$^1/_2$' come as the hourly allotment. Hence its position at any other definite hour will easily be determined.

But for observing the positions of the moon and stars another instrument is constructed, which Ptolemy calls the astrolabe. For let two circles, or rather four-sided rims of circles, be constructed in such a way that they may have their concave and convex surfaces at right angles to the plane sides. These rims are to be equal and similar in every respect and of a suitable size, in order not to become hard to handle through being too large, though they must be of sufficient amplitude to be divided into degrees and minutes. Their width and thickness [45ª] should be at least one thirtieth of the diameter. Therefore they are to be fitted together and joined at right angles to one another, having their convex sides as it were on the surface of the same sphere, and their concave sides on the surface of another single sphere. Now one of the circles should have the relative position of the ecliptic; and the other, that of the circle which passes through both poles, *i.e.*, the poles of the equator and of the ecliptic. Therefore the circle of the ecliptic is to be divided along its sides into the conventional number of 360°, which are again to be subdivided according to the capacity of the instrument. Moreover, when quadrants on the other circle have been measured from the ecliptic, the poles of the ecliptic should be marked on it; and when a distance proportionate to the obliquity has been measured from those points, the poles of the equator are also to be marked down. When these circles are finished, two other circles should be prepared and constructed around the same poles of the ecliptic: they will move about these poles, one circle inside and one circle outside. They should be of equal thicknesses between their plane surfaces, and the width of their plane surfaces should be equal to that of the others; and they should be so constructed that at all points the concave surface of the larger will touch the convex surface of the ecliptic; and the convex surface

of the smaller, the concave surface of the ecliptic. Nevertheless do not let their revolutions be impeded, but have them able to traverse freely and easily both the ecliptic together with its meridian circle and one another. Therefore we shall make holes in these circles diametrically opposite the poles of the ecliptic, and pass axles through these holes, so that by means of these axles the circles will be bound together and carried along. Moreover, the inside circle should be divided into 360° in such fashion that the single quadrant of 90° will be at the poles. Furthermore, within the concavity of the inside circle a fifth circle should be placed which can be turned in the same plane and which has an apparatus fixed to its plane surfaces which has openings diametrically opposite and reflectors or eyepieces, through which the light of the sun, as in a dioptra, can break through and go out along the diameter of the circle. And certain appliances or pointers for numbers are fitted on to this fifth circle at opposite points for the sake of observing the latitudes on the container circle. Finally, a sixth circle is to be applied which will embrace and support the whole astrolabe, which is hung on to it by means of fastenings at the poles of the equator; this last circle is to be placed upon some sort of column, or stand, and made to rest upon it perpendicular to the plane of the horizon. Moreover, the poles (of the equator) should be adjusted to the inclination of the sphere, so that the outmost circle will have a position similar to that of a natural meridian and will by no means waver from it.

Therefore after the instrument has been prepared in this way, when we wish to determine the position of some star, then in the evening or at the approach of sunset and at a time when the moon too is visible, we shall adjust the outer circle to the degree of the ecliptic, in which [45ᵇ] we have determined—by the methods spoken of—that the sun is at that time. And we shall turn the intersection of the (ecliptic and the outer) circle towards the sun itself, until both of them—I mean the ecliptic and the outer circle which passes through its poles—cast shadows on themselves evenly.[1] Then we shall turn the inner circle towards the moon; and with the eye placed in its plane we shall mark its position on the ecliptic part of the instrument there where we shall view the moon as opposite, or as it were bisected by the same plane. That will be the position of the moon as seen in longitude. For without the moon there is no way of discovering the positions of the stars, as the moon alone among all is a partaker of both day and night. Then after nightfall, when the star whose position we are seeking is visible, we shall adjust the outer circle to the position of the moon; and thus, as we did in the case of the sun, we shall bring the position of the astrolabe into relation with the moon. Then also we shall turn the inner circle towards the star, until the star seems to be in contact with the plane surfaces of the circle and is viewed through the eyepieces which are on the little circle contained (by the inner circle). For in this way we shall

[1] *i.e.*, until the shadows intersect as two straight lines at right angles to one another.

have discovered the longitude and latitude of the star. When this is being done, the degree of the ecliptic which is in the middle of the heavens will be before the eyes; and accordingly it will be obvious at what hour the thing itself was done.[1]

For example, in the 2nd year of the Emperor Antoninus Pius, on the 9th day of Pharmuthi, the 8th month by the Egyptian calendar, Ptolemy, who was then at Alexandria and wished to observe at the time of sunset the position of the star which is in the breast of Leo and is called Basiliscus or Regulus, adjusted his astrolabe to the setting sun at 5 equatorial hours after midday. At this time the sun was at $3^1/_{24}°$ of Pisces, and by moving the inner circle he found that the moon was $92^1/_8°$ east of the sun: hence it was seen that the position of the moon was then at $5^1/_6°$ of Gemini. After half an hour—which made six hours since noon—when the star had already begun to be apparent and 4° of Gemini was in the middle of the heavens, he turned the outer circle of the instrument to the already determined position of the moon. Proceeding with the inner circle, he took the distance of the star from the moon as $57^1/_{10}°$ to the east. Accordingly the moon had been found at $92^1/_8°$ from the setting sun, as was said—which placed the moon at $5^1/_6°$ of Gemini; but it was correct for the moon to have moved $^1/_4°$ in the space of half an hour; since the hourly allotment in the movement of the moon is more or less $^1/_2°$; but on account of the then subtractive parallax of the moon it must have been slightly less than $^1/_4°$, [46a] that is to say, about $^1/_6°$: hence the moon was at $5^1/_3°$ of Gemini. But when we have discussed the parallaxes of

[1]Legend:
1. Circle through poles of ecliptic
2. Ecliptic
3. Outer circle
4. Inner circle
5. Little circle
6. Meridian circle
A and A₁. Poles of equator
BCC₁B₁. Axis of ecliptic
D. Zenith, or pole of horizon

The astrolabe is constructed as an image of the Ptolemaic heavens, or as a "smaller world." Accordingly the astrolabe in operation is an imitation of the revolving heavens on a reduced scale.

The astrolabe is set up with the meridian circle (6) fixed in the meridian line and with the northern and southern poles of the equator (A and A₁) pointing towards the celestial poles above and below the horizon, as the meridian does not change during the course of the daily revolution. The degrees of the celestial ecliptic are marked off on the ecliptic circle (2), with the solstices or equinoxes at the intersections of the ecliptic (2) and the circle through the poles of the ecliptic (1). The outer circle (3) is turned to that point on the ecliptic where the position of the sun is computed to be, and then this intersection of the outer circle and the ecliptic is turned towards the sun itself, until each circle casts its shadow in the form of a straight line intersecting the other shadow at right angles. Now as the revolution of the outer circle around the axis of the equator makes the axis of the ecliptic, the circle through the poles of the ecliptic, the inner circle, and the little circle swing round the axis of the equator, and as the pole of the ecliptic revolves around the pole of the equator during the daily revolution; the turning towards the sun of the intersection of the two circles serves to bring the yearly and daily movement of the sun into proper ratio with one

COPERNICUS' ASTROLABE

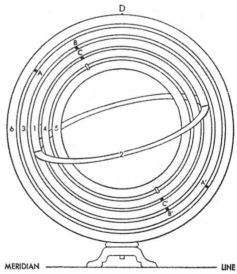

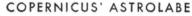

MERIDIAN ——————————————— LINE

another; and the cruciform shadow is a sign that the wooden astrolabe occupies the relative position in the astrolabe that the celestial ecliptic occupies at this moment of the daily revolution. The inner circle (4) can now be turned towards the moon in order to mark on the ecliptic the lunar longitude, and the little circle (5) can be wheeled around in the plane of the inner circle, in order to mark the lunar latitude on the graduated inner circle.

the moon, the difference will not appear to have been so great; and hence it will be evident enough that the position of the moon viewed was more than $5^1/_3$° but a little less than $5^2/_5$°. The addition of $57^1/_{10}$° to this locates the position of the star at 2°30' of Leo at a distance of about $32^1/_2$° from the summer solstice of the sun and with a northern latitude of $^1/_6$°. This was the position of Basiliscus; and consequently the way was laid open to the other fixed stars. This observation of Ptolemy's was made in the year of Our Lord 139 by the Roman calendar, on the 24th day of February, in the 1st year of the 229th Olympiad.

That most outstanding of mathematicians took note of what position at that time each of the stars had in relation to the spring equinox, and catalogued the constellations of the celestial animals. Thus he helps us not a little in this our enterprise and relieves us of some difficult enough labour, so that we, who think that the positions of the stars should not be referred to the equinoxes which change with time but that the equinoxes should be referred to the sphere of the fixed stars, can easily draw up a description of the stars from any other unchanging starting-point. We decided to begin this description with the Ram as being the first sign, and with its first star, which is in its head—so that in this way a configuration which is absolute and always the same will be possessed by those stars which shine together as if fixed and clinging perpetually and at the same time to the throne which they have seized. But by the marvellous care and industry of the ancients the stars were distributed into forty-eight constellations with the exception of those which the circle of the always hidden stars removed from the fourth climate, which passes approximately through Rhodes; and in this way the unconstellated stars remained unknown to them. According to the opinion of Theo the Younger in the *Aratean Treatise* the stars were not arranged in the form of images for any other reason except that their great multitude might be divided into parts and that they might be designated separately by certain names in accordance with an ancient enough custom, since even in Hesiod and Homer we read the names of the Pleiades, Hyas, Arcturus, and Orion. Accordingly in the description of the stars according to longitude we shall not employ the "twelve divisions," or dodekatemoria, which are measured from the equinoxes or solstices, but the simple and conventional number of degrees. We shall follow Ptolemy as to the rest with the exception of a few cases, where we have either found some corruption or a different state of affairs. We shall however teach you in the following book how to find out what their distances are from those cardinal points (*i.e.*, the equinoxes).

CATALOGUE OF THE SIGNS AND OF THE STARS
AND FIRST THOSE OF THE NORTHERN REGION

Constellations	Longitude			Latitude		Magnitude
	Deg.	Min.		Deg.	Min.	
URSA MINOR, OR THE LITTLE BEAR,						
OR CYNOSURA						
The (star) at the tip of the tail	53	30	N	66	0	3
The (star) to the east in the tail	55	50	N	70	0	4
The (star) at the base of the tail	69	20	N	74	0	4
The more southern (star) on the western						
side of the quadrilateral	83	0	N	75	20	4
The northern (star) on the same side	87	0	N	77	40	4
The more southern of the stars on the						
eastern side	100	30	N	72	40	2
The more northern on the same side	109	30	N	74	50	2
7 stars: 2 of second magnitude, 1 of third,						
4 of fourth						
The most southern unconstellated star near						
the Cynosure, in a straight line with the						
eastern side	103	20	N	71	10	4
URSA MAJOR, OR THE GREAT BEAR						
The star in the muzzle	78	40	N	39	50	4
The western star in the two eyes	79	10	N	43	0	5
The star to the east of that	79	40	N	43	0	5
The more western star of the two in the						
forehead	79	30	N	47	10	5
The star to the east in the forehead	81	0	N	47	0	5
The western star in the right ear	81	30	N	50	30	5
The more western of the two in the neck	85	50	N	43	50	4
The eastern	92	50	N	44	20	4

NORTHERN SIGNS						
The more northern of the two in the breast	94	20	N	44	0	4
The more southern	93	20	N	42	0	4
The star at the knee of the left foreleg	89	0	N	35	0	3
The more northern of the two in the left						
forefoot	89	50	N	29	0	3
The more southern	88	40	N	28	30	3
At the knee of the right foreleg	89	0	N	36	0	4
The star below the knee	101	10	N	33	30	4
The star on the shoulder	104	0	N	49	0	2
The star on the flanks	105	30	N	44	30	2
The star at the base of the tail	116	30	N	51	0	3
The star in the left hind leg	117	20	N	46	30	2
The more western of the two in the left hind foot	106	0	N	29	38	3
The star to the east of that	107	30	N	28	15	3
[47ª] The star in the hollow of the left leg	115	0	N	35	15	4
The more northern of the two which are in						
the right hind foot	123	10	N	25	50	3

NORTHERN SIGNS

Constellations	Longitude			Latitude		Magnitude
	Deg.	Min.		Deg.	Min.	
The more southern	123	40	N	25	0	3
The first of the three in the tail after the base	125	30	N	53	30	2
The middle star	131	20	N	55	40	2
The star which is last and at the tip of the tail	143	10	N	54	0	2
27 stars: 6 of second magnitude, 8 of third,						
8 of fourth, and 5 of fifth						
UNCONSTELLATED STARS NEAR THE GREAT BEAR						
The star to the south of the tail	141	10	N	39	45	3
The more obscure star to the west	133	30	N	41	20	5
The star between the forefeet of the Bear						
and the head of the Lion	98	20	N	17	15	4
The star more to the north than that one	96	40	N	19	10	4
The last of the three obscure stars	99	30	N	20	0	0 obscure
The one to the west of that	95	30	N	22	4	5 obscure
The one more to the west	94	30	N	23	1	5 obscure
The star between the forefeet and the Twins	100	20	N	22	1	5 obscure
8 unconstellated stars: 1 of third magnitude,						
2 of fourth, 1 of fifth, 4 obscure						
DRACO, OR THE DRAGON						
The star in the tongue	200	0	N	76	30	4
On the jaws	215	10	N	78	30	4 greater
Above the eye	216	30	N	75	40	3
In the cheek	229	40	N	75	20	4
Above the head	233	30	N	75	30	3
The most northern star in the first curve of						
the neck	258	40	N	82	20	4
The most southern	295	50	N	78	15	4
The star in between	262	10	N	80	20	4
The star to the east of them at the second curve	282	50	N	81	10	4
The more southern star on the western side						
of the quadrilateral	331	20	N	81	40	4
The more northern star on the same side	343	50	N	83	0	4
The more northern star on the eastern side	1	0	N	78	50	4
The more southern on the same side	346	10	N	77	50	4
The more southern star in the triangle at the						
third curve	4	0	N	80	30	4
The more western of the other two in the triangle	15	0	N	81	40	5
The star to the east	19	30	N	80	15	5
<The star to the east> in the triangle to the west	66	20	N	83	30	4
The more southern of the remaining two in the						
same triangle	43	40	N	83	30	4

NORTHERN SIGNS

Constellations	Longitude			Latitude		Magnitude
	Deg.	Min.		Deg.	Min.	
[47ᵇ] The star which is more northern than the two above	35	10	N	84	50	4
Of the small stars west of the triangle, the more eastern	200	0	N	87	30	6
The more western	195	0	N	86	50	6
The most southern of the three which are in a straight line towards the east	152	30	N	81	15	5
The one in the middle	152	50	N	83	0	5
The most northern	151	0	N	84	50	3
The more northern of the two which follow towards the west	153	20	N	78	0	3
The more southern	156	30	N	74	40	4 greater
The star to the west of them, in the coil of the tail	156	0	N	70	0	3
The more western of the two rather distant from that one	120	40	N	64	40	4
The star to the east of it	124	30	N	65	30	3
The star to the east in the tail	192	30	N	61	15	3
At the tip of the tail	186	30	N	56	15	3
Therefore 31 stars: 8 of third magnitude, 16 of fourth, 5 of fifth, 2 of sixth						
CEPHEUS						
In the right foot	28	40	N	75	40	4
In the left foot	26	20	N	64	15	4
On the right side beneath the belt	0	40	N	71	10	4
The star which touches the top of the right shoulder	340	0	N	69	0	3
The star which touches the right joint of the elbow	332	40	N	72	0	4
The star to the east which touches the same elbow	333	20	N	74	0	4
The star on the chest	352	0	N	65	30	5
On the right arm	1	0	N	62	30	4 greater
The most southern of the three on the tiara	339	40	N	60	15	5
The one in the middle	340	40	N	61	15	4
The most northern	342	20	N	61	30	5
11 stars: 1 of third magnitude, 7 of fourth, 3 of fifth						
Of the two unconstellated stars, the one to the west of the tiara	337	0	N	64	0	5
The one to the east of the tiara	344	40	N	59	30	4
BOÖTES, OR ARCTURUS						
The more western of the three in the left hand	145	40	N	58	40	5
The middle one of the three, the more southern	147	30	N	58	20	5
The more eastern of the three	149	0	N	60	10	5
The star in the left joint of the elbow	143	0	N	54	40	5

NORTHERN SIGNS

Constellations	Longitude			Latitude		Magnitude
	Deg.	Min.		Deg.	Min.	
On the left shoulder	163	0	N	49	0	3
On the head	170	0	N	53	50	4 greater
On the right shoulder	179	0	N	48	40	4
[48ª] The more southern of the two on the crook	179	0	N	53	15	4
The star more to the north, at the tip of the crook	178	20	N	57	30	4
The more northern of the two under the shoulder and on the spear	181	0	N	46	10	4 greater
The more southern	181	50	N	45	30	5
At the extremity of the right hand	181	35	N	41	20	5
The more western of the two in the palm	180	0	N	41	40	5
The one to the east	180	20	N	42	30	5
At the extremity of the handle of the crook	181	0	N	40	20	5
On the right leg	183	20	N	40	15	3
The more eastern of the two in the belt	169	0	N	41	40	4
The more western	168	20	N	42	10	4 greater
At the right heel	178	40	N	28	0	3
The more northern of the three on the left ham	164	40	N	28	0	3
The middle one of the three	163	50	N	26	30	4
The more southern of them	164	50	N	25	0	4
22 stars: 4 of third magnitude, 9 of fourth, 9 of fifth						
The unconstellated star between the thighs, which they call Arcturus	170	20	N	31	30	1
CORONA BOREALIS, OR THE NORTHERN CROWN						
The brilliant star in the crown	188	0	N	44	30	2 greater
The most western of all	185	0	N	46	10	4 greater
The eastern star towards the north	185	10	N	48	0	5
The eastern star more to the north	193	0	N	50	30	6
The star to the south-east of the brilliant one	191	30	N	44	45	4
The next star to the east	190	30	N	44	50	4
The star farther to the east	194	40	N	46	10	4
The most eastern of all in the crown	195	0	N	49	20	4
8 stars: 1 of second magnitude, 5 of fourth, 1 of fifth, 1 of sixth						
ENGONASI, OR THE KNEELING MAN						
On the head	221	0	N	37	30	3
At the right arm-pit	207	0	N	43	0	3
On the right arm	205	0	N	40	10	3
In the right flank	201	20	N	37	10	4
On the left shoulder	220	20	N	49	30	4 greater
[48ᵇ] In the left flank	231	0	N	42	0	4

NORTHERN SIGNS

Constellations	Longitude			Latitude		Magnitude
	Deg.	Min.		Deg.	Min.	
\<The more eastern\> of the three in the left palm	238	50	N	52	50	4 greater
The more northern of the remaining two	235	0	N	54	0	4 greater
The more southern	234	50	N	53	0	4
On the right side	207	10	N	56	10	3
On the left side	213	30	N	53	30	4
On the \<lower part of the\> left buttock	213	20	N	56	10	5
At the beginning of the left leg	214	30	N	58	30	5
The most western of the three in the left ham	217	20	N	59	50	3
The more eastern	218	40	N	60	20	4
The most eastern	219	40	N	61	15	4
At the left knee	237	10	N	61	0	4
On the \<upper part of the\> left buttock	225	30	N	69	20	4
The most western of the three in the left foot	188	40	N	70	15	6
The middle star	220	10	N	71	15	6
The most eastern of the three	223	0	N	72	0	6
At the beginning of the right leg	207	0	N	60	15	4 greater
The more northern on the right ham	198	50	N	63	0	4
At the right knee	189	0	N	65	30	4 greater
The more southern of the two under the right knee	186	40	N	63	40	4
The more northern	183	30	N	64	15	4
On the right shin	184	30	N	60	0	4
At the extremity of the right foot, the same as the tip of Boötes' crook	178	20	N	57	30	4

Besides that last one, 28 stars: 6 of third magnitude, 17 of fourth, 2 of fifth, 3 of sixth

The unconstellated star to the south of the right arm	26	0	N	38	10	5

LYRA, OR THE LYRE

The brilliant star which is called Lyra or Fidicula	250	40	N	62	0	1
The more northern of the two adjacent stars	253	40	N	62	40	4 greater
The more southern	253	40	N	61	0	4 greater
The star which is at the centre of the beginning of the horns	262	0	N	60	0	4
The more northern of the two which are next and to the east	265	20	N	61	20	4
The more southern	265	0	N	60	20	4
The more northern of the two westerly stars on the cross-piece	254	20	N	56	10	3
The more southern	254	10	N	55	0	4 smaller
The more northern of the two easterly stars on the cross-piece	257	30	N	55	20	3
The more southern	258	20	N	54	45	4 smaller

NORTHERN SIGNS

Constellations	Longitude			Latitude		Magnitude
	Deg.	Min.		Deg.	Min.	
10 stars: 1 of first magnitude, 2 of third magnitude, 7 of fourth						
[49ª] CYGNUS, OR THE SWAN						
At the mouth	267	50	N	49	20	3
On the head	272	20	N	50	30	5
In the middle of the neck	279	20	N	54	30	4 greater
In the breast	291	50	N	56	20	3
The brilliant star in the tail	302	30	N	60	0	2
In the elbow of the right wing	282	40	N	64	40	3
The most southern of the three in the flat of the wing	285	50	N	69	40	4
The middle star	284	30	N	71	30	4 greater
The last of the three, and at the tip of the wing	310	0	N	74	0	4 greater
At the elbow of the left wing	294	10	N	49	30	3
In the middle of the left wing	298	10	N	52	10	4 greater
At the tip of the same	300	0	N	74	0	3
In the left foot	303	20	N	55	10	4 greater
At the left knee	307	50	N	57	0	4
The more western of the two in the right foot	294	30	N	64	0	4
The more eastern	296	0	N	64	30	4
The nebulous star at the right knee	305	30	N	63	45	5
17 stars: 1 of second magnitude, 5 of third, 9 of fourth, 2 of fifth						
AND TWO UNCONSTELLATED STARS NEAR THE SWAN						
The more southern of the two under the left wing	306	0	N	49	40	4
The more northern	307	10	N	51	40	4
CASSIOPEIA						
On the head	1	10	N	45	20	4
On the breast	4	10	N	46	45	3 greater
On the girdle	6	20	N	47	50	4
Above the seat, at the hips	10	0	N	49	0	3 greater
At the knees	13	40	N	45	30	3
On the leg	20	20	N	47	45	4
At the extremity of the foot	355	0	N	48	20	4
On the left arm	8	0	N	44	20	4
On the left forearm	7	40	N	45	0	5
On the right forearm	357	40	N	50	0	6
At the foot of the chair	8	20	N	52	40	4
At the middle of the settle	1	10	N	51	40	3 smaller
At the extremity	27	10	N	51	40	6
13 stars: 4 of third magnitude, 6 of fourth, 1 of fifth, 2 of sixth						

NORTHERN SIGNS

Constellations	Longitude			Latitude		Magnitude
	Deg.	Min.		Deg.	Min.	
[49ᵇ] PERSEUS						
The nebulous star at the extremity of the right hand	21	0	N	40	30	nebulous
On the right forearm	24	30	N	37	30	4
On the right shoulder	26	0	N	34	30	4 smaller
On the left shoulder	20	50	N	32	20	4
On the head, or a nebula	24	0	N	34	30	4
On the shoulder-blades	24	50	N	31	10	4
The brilliant star on the right side	28	10	N	30	0	2
The most western of the three on the same side	28	40	N	27	30	4
The middle one	30	20	N	27	40	4
The remaining one of the three	31	0	N	27	30	3
On the left forearm	24	0	N	27	0	4
The brilliant star in the left hand and in the head of Medusa	23	0	N	23	0	2
The easterly star on the head of the same	22	30	N	21	0	4
The more western on the head of the same	21	0	N	21	0	4
The most western	20	10	N	22	15	4
On the right knee	38	10	N	28	15	4
The one to the west of this one at the knee	37	10	N	28	10	4
The more western of the two on the belly	35	40	N	25	10	4
The more eastern	37	20	N	26	15	4
On the right hip	37	30	N	24	30	5
On the right calf	39	40	N	28	45	5
On the left hip	30	10	N	21	40	4 greater
On the left knee	32	0	N	19	50	3
On the left calf	31	40	N	14	45	3 greater
On the left heel	24	30	N	12	0	3 smaller
On the top part of the left foot	29	40	N	11	0	3 greater
26 stars: 2 of second magnitude, 5 of third, 16 of fourth, 2 of fifth, 1 nebulous						
UNCONSTELLATED STARS AROUND PERSEUS						
To the east of the left hand	34	10	N	31	0	5
To the north of the right hand	38	20	N	31	0	5
To the west of Medusa's head	18	0	N	20	40	obscure
3 stars: 2 of fifth magnitude, 1 obscure						
[50ᵃ] AURIGA, OR THE CHARIOTEER						
The more southern of the two on the head	55	50	N	30	0	4
The more northern	55	40	N	30	50	4
The brilliant star on the left shoulder, which is called Capella	48	20	N	22	30	1
On the right shoulder	56	10	N	20	0	2
On the right forearm	54	30	N	15	15	4
On the palm of the right hand	56	10	N	13	30	4 greater
On the left forearm	45	20	N	20	40	4 greater
The star to the west of the Haedi	45	30	N	18	0	4 smaller

NORTHERN SIGNS

Constellations	Longitude			Latitude		Magnitude
	Deg.	Min.		Deg.	Min.	
The star on the palm of the left hand which is to the east of the Haedi	46	0	N	18	0	4 greater
On the left calf	53	10	N	10	10	3 small
On the right calf and at the tip of the northern horn of Taurus	49	0	N	5	0	3 greater
At the ankle	49	20	N	8	30	5
On the buttocks	49	40	N	12	20	5
The small star on the left foot	24	0	N	10	20	6
14 stars: 1 of first magnitude, 1 of second, 2 of third, 7 of fourth, 2 of fifth, 1 of sixth						
OPHIUCHUS, OR THE SERPENT-HOLDER						
On the head	228	10	N	36	0	3
The more western of the two on the right shoulder	231	20	N	27	15	4 greater
The more eastern	232	20	N	26	45	4
The more western of the two on the left shoulder	216	40	N	33	0	4
The more eastern	218	0	N	31	50	4
At the left elbow	211	40	N	34	30	4
The more western of the two in the left hand	208	20	N	17	0	4
The more eastern	209	20	N	12	30	3
At the right elbow	220	0	N	15	0	4
The more western in the right hand	205	40	N	18	40	4 smaller
The more eastern	207	40	N	14	20	4
At the right knee	224	30	N	4	30	3
On the right shin	227	0	N	2	15	3 greater
The most western of the four on the right foot	226	20	S	2	15	4 greater
The more easterly	227	40	S	1	30	4 greater
The next to the east	228	20	S	0	20	4 greater
The most easterly	229	10	S	1	45	5 greater
The star which touches the heel	229	30	S	1	0	5
[50b] At the left knee	215	30	N	11	50	3
The most northern of the three in a straight line on the lower part of the left leg	215	0	N	5	20	5 greater
The middle one	214	0	N	3	10	5
The most southern of the three	213	10	N	1	40	5 greater
The star on the left heel	215	40	N	0	40	5
The star touching the hollow of the left foot	214	0	S	0	45	4
24 stars: 5 of third magnitude, 13 of fourth, 6 of fifth						
UNCONSTELLATED STARS AROUND OPHIUCHUS						
The most northern of the three to the east of the right shoulder	235	20	N	28	10	4
The middle one	236	0	N	26	20	4
The most southern of the three	233	40	N	25	0	4
Another one, farther to the east of the three	237	0	N	27	0	4

NORTHERN SIGNS

Constellations	Longitude			Latitude		Magnitude
	Deg.	Min.		Deg.	Min.	
A star separate from the four, to the north	238	0	N	33	0	4
Therefore 5 unconstellated stars: all of						
fourth magnitude						
SERPENS OPHIUCHI, OR THE SERPENT						
On the quadrilateral, the star in the cheeks	192	10	N	38	0	4
The star touching the nostrils	201	0	N	40	0	4
On the temples	197	40	N	35	0	3
At the beginning of the neck	195	20	N	34	15	3
At the middle of the quadrilateral, and on						
the jaws	194	40	N	37	15	4
To the north of the head	201	30	N	42	30	4
At the first curve of the neck	195	0	N	29	15	3
The most northern of the three to the east	198	10	N	26	30	4
The middle one	197	40	N	25	20	3
The most southern of the three	199	40	N	24	0	3
The star to the west of the left hand of						
Ophiuchus	202	0	N	16	30	4
The star to the east of the same hand	211	30	N	16	15	5
The star to the east of the right hip	227	0	N	10	30	4
The more southern of the two to the east of						
that	230	20	N	8	30	4 greater
The more northern	231	10	N	10	30	4
To the east of the right hand, in the coil of						
the tail	237	0	N	20	0	4
Farther east in the tail	242	0	N	21	10	4
At the tip of the tail	251	40	N	27	0	4 greater
18 stars: 5 of third magnitude, 12 of fourth,						
1 of fifth						
[51ᵃ] SAGITTA, OR THE ARROW						
At the head	273	30	N	39	20	4
The most eastern of the three on the shaft	270	0	N	39	10	6
The middle one	269	10	N	39	50	5
The most western of the three	268	0	N	39	0	5
At the notch	266	40	N	38	45	5
5 stars: 1 of fourth magnitude, 3 of fifth,						
1 of sixth						
AQUILA, OR THE EAGLE						
In the middle of the head	270	30	N	26	50	4
On the neck	268	10	N	27	10	3
The brilliant star on the shoulder-blades,						
which is called Aquila	267	10	N	29	10	2 greater
The star to the north which is very near	268	0	N	30	0	3 smaller
The more western on the left shoulder	266	30	N	31	30	3
The more eastern	269	20	N	31	30	5
The star to the west in the right shoulder	263	0	N	28	40	5
The star to the east	264	30	N	26	40	5 greater

NORTHERN SIGNS

Constellations	Longitude			Latitude		Magnitude
	Deg.	Min.		Deg.	Min.	
The star in the tail, which touches the milky circle	265	30	N	26	30	3
9 stars: 1 of second magnitude, 4 of third, 1 of fourth, 3 of fifth						
UNCONSTELLATED STARS AROUND AQUILA						
The more western star south of the head	272	0	N	21	40	3
The more eastern	272	20	N	29	10	3
Away from the right shoulder and to the south-west	259	20	N	25	0	4 greater
To the south	261	30	N	20	0	3
Farther south	263	0	N	15	30	5
West of all	254	30	N	18	10	3
6 unconstellated stars: 4 of third magnitude, 1 of fourth, and 1 of fifth						
DELPHINUS, OR THE DOLPHIN						
The most western of the three in the tail	281	0	N	29	10	3 smaller
The more northern of the two remaining	282	0	N	29	0	4 smaller
The more southern	282	0	N	26	40	4
The more southern on the western side of the rhomboid	281	50	N	32	0	3 smaller
The more northern on the same side	283	30	N	33	50	3 smaller
The more southern on the eastern side	284	40	N	32	0	3 smaller
The more northern on the same side	286	50	N	33	10	3 smaller
The most southern of the three between the tail and the rhombus	280	50	N	34	15	6
The more western of the other two to the north	280	50	N	31	50	6
The more eastern	282	20	N	31	30	6
10 stars: 5 of third magnitude, 2 of fourth, 3 of sixth						
[51b] EQUI SECTIO, OR THE SECTION OF THE HORSE						
The more western of the two on the head	289	40	N	20	30	obscure
The more eastern	292	20	N	20	40	obscure
The more western of the two at the mouth	289	40	N	25	30	obscure
The more eastern	291	21	N	25	0	obscure
4 stars: all obscure						
PEGASUS, OR THE WINGED HORSE						
Within the open mouth	298	40	N	21	30	3 greater
The more northern of the two close together on the head	302	40	N	16	50	3
The more southern	301	20	N	16	0	4
The more southern of the two on the mane	314	40	N	15	0	5
The more northern	313	50	N	16	0	5
The more western of the two on the neck	312	10	N	18	0	3
The more eastern	313	50	N	19	0	4

NORTHERN SIGNS

Constellations	Longitude			Latitude		Magnitude
	Deg.	Min.		Deg.	Min.	
On the left pastern	305	40	N	36	30	4 greater
On the left knee	311	0	N	34	15	4 greater
On the right pastern	317	0	N	41	10	4 greater
The more western of the two close together on the breast	319	30	N	29	0	4
The more eastern	320	20	N	29	30	4
The more northern of the two on the right knee	322	20	N	35	0	3
The more southern	321	50	N	24	30	5
The more northern of the two beneath the wing, on the body	327	50	N	25	40	4
The more southern	328	20	N	25	0	4
At the shoulder-blades and juncture of the wing	350	0	N	19	40	2 smaller
On the right shoulder and at the beginning of the leg	325	30	N	31	0	2 smaller
At the tip of the wing	335	30	N	12	30	2 smaller
At the navel, and on the head of Andromeda too	341	10	N	26	0	2 smaller
20 stars: 4 of second magnitude, 4 of third, 9 of fourth, 3 of fifth						
ANDROMEDA						
On the shoulder-blades	348	40	N	24	30	3
On the right shoulder	349	40	N	27	0	4
On the left shoulder	347	40	N	23	0	4
The most southern of the three on the right arm	347	0	N	32	0	4
The most northern	348	0	N	33	30	4
The middle one of the three	348	20	N	32	20	5
The most southern of the three on the top of the right hand	343	0	N	41	0	4
The middle star	344	0	N	42	0	4
[52ª] The most northern of the three	345	30	N	44	0	4
On the left arm	347	30	N	17	30	4
At the left elbow	349	0	N	15	50	3
The most southern of the three on the girdle	357	10	N	25	20	3
The middle one	355	10	N	30	0	3
The most northern	355	20	N	32	30	3
On the left foot	10	10	N	23	0	3
On the right foot	10	30	N	37	10	4 greater
To the south of those two	8	30	N	35	20	4 greater
The more northern of the two under the hamstrings	5	40	N	29	0	4
The more southern	5	20	N	28	0	4
At the right knee	5	30	N	35	30	5
The more northern of the two on the flowing robe	6	0	N	34	30	5
The more southern	7	30	N	32	30	5

NORTHERN SIGNS

Constellations	Longitude			Latitude		Magnitude
	Deg.	Min.		Deg.	Min.	
The unconstellated star west of the right hand	5	0	N	44	0	3
23 stars: 7 of third magnitude, 12 of fourth,						
4 of fifth						
TRIANGULUM, OR THE TRIANGLE						
At the vertex of the triangle	4	20	N	16	30	3
The most western of the three on the base	9	20	N	20	40	3
The middle one	9	30	N	20	20	4
The most eastern of the three	10	10	N	19	0	3
4 stars: 3 of third magnitude, 1 of fourth						

Therefore in the northern region there are 360 stars, all in all: 3 of first magnitude, 18 of second, 81 of third, 177 of fourth, 58 of fifth, 13 of sixth, 1 nebulous, and 9 obscure.

THE SIGNS AND STARS WHICH ARE IN THE MIDDLE AND AROUND THE ECLIPTIC

Constellations	Longitude			Latitude		Magnitude
	Deg.	Min.		Deg.	Min.	
AIRES, OR THE RAM						
The star which is first of all and the more						
western of the two on the horn	0	0	N	7	20	3 smaller
The more eastern on the horn	1	0	N	8	20	3
The more northern of the two in the opening						
of the jaws	4	20	N	7	40	5
The more southern	4	50	N	6	0	5
On the neck	9	50	N	5	30	5
On the kidneys	10	50	N	6	0	6
At the beginning of the tail	14	40	N	4	50	5
The most western of the three on the tail	17	10	N	1	40	4
The middle one	18	40	N	2	30	4
[52b] The most eastern	20	20	N	1	50	4
On the hips	13	0	N	1	10	5
On the ham	11	20	S	1	30	5
At the tip of the hind foot	8	10	S	5	15	4 greater
13 stars: 2 of third magnitude, 4 of fourth,						
6 of fifth, 1 of sixth						
UNCONSTELLATED STARS AROUND ARIES						
The brilliant star over the head	3	50	N	10	0	3 greater
The very northerly star above the back	15	0	N	10	10	4
The most northern of the remaining three						
small stars	14	40	N	12	40	5
The middle one	13	0	N	10	40	5
The most southern	12	30	N	10	40	5
5 stars: 1 of third magnitude, 1 of fourth,						
3 of fifth						
TAURUS, OR THE BULL						
The most northern of the four in the section	19	40	S	6	0	4
The next after that	19	20	S	7	15	4
The third	18	0	S	8	30	4

IN THE MIDDLE, AND AROUND THE ECLIPTIC

Constellations	Longitude			Latitude		Magnitude
	Deg.	Min.		Deg.	Min.	
The fourth and most southern	17	50	S	9	15	4
On the right shoulder	23	0	S	9	30	5
In the breast	27	0	S	8	0	3
At the right knee	30	0	S	12	40	4
On the right pastern	26	20	S	14	50	4
At the left knee	35	30	S	10	0	4
On the left pastern	36	20	S	13	30	4
Of the five called Hyades and on the face, the one at the nostrils	32	0	S	5	45	3 smaller
Between that star and the northern eye	33	40	S	4	15	3 smaller
Between that same star and the southern eye	34	10	S	8	50	3 smaller
The brilliant star, in the very eye, called Palilicius by the Romans	36	0	S	5	10	1
On the northern eye	35	10	S	3	0	3 smaller
The star south of the horn between the base and the ear	40	30	S	4	0	4
The more southern of the two on the same horn	43	40	S	5	0	4
The more northern	43	20	S	3	30	5
At the extremity of the same	50	30	S	2	30	3
To the north of the base of the horn	49	0	S	4	0	4
At the extremity of the horn and on the right foot of Auriga	49	0	N	5	0	3
The more northern of the two in the north ear	35	20	N	4	30	5
The more southern	35	0	N	4	30	5 Apogee of Venus: 48°20'
[53ª] The more western of the two small stars on the neck	30	20	N	0	40	5
The more eastern	32	20	N	1	0	6
The more southern on the western side of the quadrilateral on the neck	31	20	N	5	0	5
The more northern on the same	32	10	N	7	10	5
The more southern on the eastern side	35	20	N	3	0	5
The more northern on the same side	35	0	N	5	0	5
The northern limit of the western side of the Pleiades	25	30	N	4	30	5
The southern limit of the same side	25	50	N	4	40	5
The very narrow limit of the eastern side of the Pleiades	27	0	N	5	20	5
A small star of the Pleiades, separated from the limits	26	0	N	3	0	5

32 stars, apart from that which is at the tip of the northern horn: 1 of first magnitude, 6 of third, 11 of fourth, 13 of fifth, 1 of sixth

UNCONSTELLATED STARS AROUND TAURUS

| Between the foot and below the shoulder | 18 | 20 | S | 17 | 30 | 4 |

In the Middle, and Around the Ecliptic

Constellations	Longitude			Latitude		Magnitude
	Deg.	Min.		Deg.	Min.	
The most western of the three to the south of the horn	43	20	S	2	0	5
The middle one	47	20	S	1	45	5
The most eastern of the three	49	20	S	2	0	5
The more northern of the two under the tip of the same horn	52	20	S	6	20	5
The more southern	52	20	S	7	40	5
The most western of the five under the northern horn	50	20	N	2	40	5
The next to the east	52	20	N	1	0	5
The third and to the east	54	20	N	1	20	5
The more northern of the remaining two	55	40	N	3	20	5
The more southern	56	40	N	1	15	5
11 unconstellated stars: 1 of fourth magnitude, 10 of fifth						
GEMINI, OR THE TWINS						
On the head of the western Twin, Castor	76	40	N	9	30	2
The reddish star on the head of the eastern Twin, Pollux	79	50	N	6	15	2
At the left elbow of the western Twin	70	0	N	10	0	4
On the left arm	72	0	N	7	20	4
At the shoulder-blades of the same Twin	75	20	N	5	30	4
On the right shoulder of the same	77	20	N	4	50	4
On the left shoulder of the eastern Twin	80	0	N	2	40	4
On the right side of the western Twin	75	0	N	2	40	5
On the left side of the eastern Twin	76	30	N	3	0	5
[53b] At the left knee of the western Twin	66	30	N	1	30	3
At the left knee of the eastern	71	35	S	2	30	3
On the left groin of the same	75	0	S	0	30	3
At the hollow of the right knee of the same	74	40	S	0	40	3
The more western star in the foot of the western Twin	60	0	S	1	30	4 greater
The more eastern star in the same foot	61	30	S	1	15	4
At the extremity of the foot of the western Twin	63	30	S	3	30	4
On the top of the foot of the eastern Twin	65	20	S	7	30	3
On the bottom of the foot of the same	68	0	S	10	30	4
18 stars: 2 of second magnitude, 5 of third, 9 of fourth, 2 of fifth						
UNCONSTELLATED STARS AROUND GEMINI						
The star west of the top of the foot of the western Twin	57	30	8	0	40	4
The brilliant star to the west of the knee of the same	59	50	N	5	50	4 greater
To the west of the left knee of the eastern Twin	68	30	S	2	15	5
The most northern of the three east of the right hand of the eastern Twin	81	40	S	1	20	5

IN THE MIDDLE, AND AROUND THE ECLIPTIC

Constellations	Longitude Deg.	Min.		Latitude Deg.	Min.	Magnitude
The middle one	79	40	S	3	20	5
The most southern of the three, and in the neighbourhood of the right arm	79	20	S	4	30	5
The brilliant star to the east of the three	84	0	S	2	40	4
7 unconstellated stars; 3 of fourth magnitude, 4 of fifth						
CANCER, OR THE CRAB						
The nebulous star in the breast, which is called Praeses	93	40	N	0	40	nebulous
The more northern of the two west of the quadrilateral	91	0	N	1	15	4 smaller
The more southern	91	20	S	1	10	4 smaller
The more northern of the two to the east, which are called the Asses	93	40	N	2	40	4 greater
The southern Ass	94	40	S	0	10	4 greater
On the claws or the southern arm	99	50	S	5	30	4
On the northern arm	91	40	N	11	50	4
At the extremity of the northern foot	86	0	N	1	0	5
At the extremity of the southern foot	90	30	S	7	30	4 greater
9 stars: 7 of fourth magnitude, 1 of fifth, 1 nebulous						
UNCONSTELLATED STARS AROUND CANCER						
Above the elbow of the southern claw	103	0	S	2	40	4 smaller
East of the extremity of the same claw	105	0	S	5	40	4 smaller
[54ᵃ] The more western of the two above the little cloud	97	20	N	4	50	5
The more eastern	100	20	N	7	15	5
4 unconstellated stars: 2 of fourth magnitude, 2 of fifth						
LEO, OR THE LION						
At the nostrils	101	40	N	10	0	4
At the opening of the jaws	104	30	N	7	30	4
The more northern of the two on the head	107	40	N	12	0	3
The more southern	107	30	N	9	30	3 greater
The most northern of the three on the neck	113	30	N	11	0	3 Apogee of Mars: 109°50'
The middle one	115	30	N	8	30	2
The most southern of the three	114	0	N	4	30	3
At the heart, the star called Basiliscus or Regulus	115	50	N	0	10	1
The more southern of the two on the breast	116	50	S	1	50	4
A little to the west of the star at the heart	113	20	S	0	15	5
At the knee of the right foreleg	110	40		0	0	5
On the right pad	117	30	S	3	40	6
At the knee of the left foreleg	122	30	S	4	10	4
On the left pad	115	50	S	4	15	4

IN THE MIDDLE, AND AROUND THE ECLIPTIC

Constellations	Longitude			Latitude		Magnitude
	Deg.	Min.		Deg.	Min.	
At the left arm-pit	122	30	S	0	10	4
The most western of the three on the belly	120	20	N	4	0	6
The more northern of the two to the east	126	20	N	5	20	6
The more southern	125	40	N	2	20	6
The more western of the two on the loins	124	40	N	12	15	5
The more eastern	127	30	N	13	40	2
The more northern of the two on the rump	127	40	N	11	30	5
The more southern	129	40	N	9	40	3
At the hips	133	40	N	5	50	3
At the hollow of the knee	135	0	N	1	15	4
On the lower part of the leg	135	0	S	0	50	4
On the hind foot	134	0	S	3	0	5
At the tip of the tail	137	50	N	11	50	1 smaller
27 stars: 2 of first magnitude, 2 of second, 6 of third, 8 of fourth, 5 of fifth, 4 of sixth						
UNCONSTELLATED STARS AROUND LEO						
The more western of the two above the back	119	20	N	13	20	5
The more eastern	121	30	N	15	30	5
The most northern of the three below the belly	129	50	N	1	10	4 smaller
[54b] The middle one	130	30	S	0	30	5
The most southern of the three	132	20	S	2	40	5
The star farthest north between the extremities of Leo and the nebulous complex called Coma Berenices	138	10	N	30	0	luminous
The more western of the two to the south	133	50	N	25	0	obscure
The star to the east, in the shape of an ivy leaf	141	50	N	25	30	obscure
8 unconstellated stars: 1 of fourth magnitude, 4 of fifth, 1 luminous, 2 obscure						
VIRGO, OR THE VIRGIN						
The more southwestern of the two on the top of the head	139	40	N	4	15	5
The more northeastern	140	20	N	5	40	5
The more northern of the two on the face	144	0	N	8	0	5
The more southern	143	30	N	5	30	5
At the tip of the left and southern wing	142	20	N	6	0	3
The most western of the four on the left wing	151	35	N	1	10	3
The next to the east	156	30	N	2	50	3
The third	160	30	N	2	50	5
The last and most eastward of the four	164	20	N	1	40	4
On the right side beneath the girdle	157	40	N	8	30	3
The most western of the three on the right and northern wing	151	30	N	13	50	5
The more southern of the two remaining	153	30	N	11	40	6 Apogee of Jupiter: 154°20'

IN THE MIDDLE, AND AROUND THE ECLIPTIC

Constellations	Longitude			Latitude		Magnitude
	Deg.	Min.		Deg.	Min.	
The more northern of them, called Vindemiator	155	30	N	15	10	3 greater
On the left hand, called Spica	170	0	S	2	0	1
Beneath the girdle and on the right buttock	168	10	N	8	40	3
The more northern of the two on the western side of the quadrilateral on the left hip	169	40	N	2	20	5
The more southern	170	20	N	0	10	6
The more northern of the two on the eastern side	173	20	N	1	30	4
The more southern	171	20	N	0	20	5
At the left knee	175	0	N	1	30	5
On the posterior side of the right hip	171	20	N	8	30	5
On the flowing robe, in the middle	180	0	N	7	30	4
More to the south	180	40	N	2	40	4
More to the north	181	40	N	11	40	4 Apogee of Mercury: 183°20'
On the left and southern foot	183	20	N	0	30	4
On the right and southern foot	186	0	N	9	50	3
26 Stars: 1 of first magnitude, 7 of third, 6 of fourth, 10 of fifth, 2 of sixth						
UNCONSTELLATED STARS AROUND VIRGO						
[55ᵃ] The most western of the three in a straight line under the left arm	158	0	S	3	30	5
The middle one	162	20	S	3	30	5
The most eastern	165	35	S	3	20	5
The most western of the three in a straight line under Spica	170	30	S	7	20	6
The middle one, which is also a double star	171	30	S	8	20	5
The most eastern of the three	173	20	S	7	50	6
6 unconstellated stars: 4 of fifth magnitude, 2 of sixth						
CHELAE, OR THE CLAWS						
The bright one of the two at the extremity of the southern claw	191	20	N	0	40	2 greater
The more obscure star to the north	190	20	N	2	30	5
The bright one of the two at the extremity of the northern claw	195	30	N	8	30	2
The more obscure star to the west of that	191	0	N	8	30	5
In the middle of the southern claw	197	20	N	1	40	4
In the same claw, but to the west	194	40	N	1	15	4
At the middle of the northern claw	200	50	N	3	45	4
In the same claw, but to the east	206	20	N	4	30	4
8 stars: 2 of second magnitude, 4 of fourth, 2 of fifth						

IN THE MIDDLE, AND AROUND THE ECLIPTIC

Constellations	Longitude			Latitude		Magnitude
	Deg.	Min.		Deg.	Min.	
UNCONSTELLATED STARS AROUND THE CHELAE						
The most western of the three north of the northern claw	199	30	N	9	0	5
The more southern of the two to the east	207	0	N	6	40	4
The more northern	207	40	N	9	15	4
The most eastern of the three between the claws	205	50	N	5	30	6
The more northern of the remaining two to the west	203	40	N	2	0	4
The more southern	204	30	N	1	30	5
The most western of the three beneath the southern claw	196	20	S	7	30	3
The more northern of the remaining two to the east	204	30	S	8	10	4
The more southern	205	20	S	9	40	4
9 unconstellated stars: 1 of third magnitude, 5 of fourth, 2 of fifth, 1 of sixth						
SCORPIO, OR THE SCORPION						
The most northern of the three bright stars on the forehead	209	40	N	1	20	3 greater
The middle one	209	0	S	1	40	3
The most southern of the three	209	0	S	5	0	3
More to the south and in the foot	209	20	S	7	50	3
The more northern of the two adjacent bright stars	210	20	N	1	40	4
The more southern	210	40	N	0	30	4
The most western of the three bright stars on the body	214	0	S	3	45	3
The reddish star in the middle, called Antares	216	0	S	4	0	2 greater
The most eastern of the three	217	50	S	5	30	3
[55^b] The more western of the two at the extremity of the foot	212	40	S	6	10	5
The more eastern	213	50	S	6	40	5
At the first vertebra of the body	221	50	S	11	0	3
At the second vertebra	222	10	S	15	0	4
The more northern of the double at the third	223	20	8	18	40	4
The more southern of the double	223	30	S	18	0	3
At the fourth vertebra	226	30	8	19	30	3 Apogee of Saturn: 226°30'
At the fifth	231	30	S	18	50	3
At the sixth vertebra	233	50	S	16	40	3
At the seventh, and next to the sting	232	20	S	15	10	3
The more eastern of the two on the sting	230	50	S	13	20	3
The more western	230	20	S	13	30	4
21 stars: 1 of second magnitude, 13 of third, 5 of fourth, 2 of fifth						

IN THE MIDDLE, AND AROUND THE ECLIPTIC

Constellations	Longitude			Latitude		Magnitude
	Deg.	Min.		Deg.	Min.	
UNCONSTELLATED STARS AROUND SCORPIO						
The nebulous star to the east of the sting	234	30	S	12	15	nebulous
The more western of the two north of the sting	228	50	S	6	10	5
The more eastern	232	50	S	4	10	5
3 unconstellated stars: 2 of fifth magnitude, 1 nebulous						
SAGITTARIUS, OR THE ARCHER						
At the head of the arrow	237	50	S	6	30	3
In the palm of the left hand	241	0	S	6	30	3
On the southern part of the bow	241	20	S	10	50	3
The more southern of the two to the north	242	20	S	1	30	3
More northward, at the extremity of the bow	240	0	N	2	50	4
On the left shoulder	248	40	S	3	10	3
To the west and on the dart	246	20	S	3	50	4
The nebulous double star in the eye	248	30	N	0	45	nebulous
The most western of the three on the head	249	0	N	2	10	4
The middle one	251	0	N	1	30	4 greater
The most eastward	252	30	N	2	0	4
The most southern of the three on the northern garment	254	40	N	2	50	4
The middle one	255	40	N	4	30	4
The most northern	256	10	N	6	30	4
The obscure star east of the three	259	0	N	5	30	6
The most northern of the two on the southern. garment	262	50	N	5	0	5
The more southern	261	0	N	2	0	6
On the right shoulder	255	40	S	1	50	5
[56a] At the right elbow	258	10	S	2	50	5
At the shoulder-blades	253	20	S	2	30	5
At the foreshoulder	251	0	S	4	30	4 greater
Beneath the arm-pit	249	40	S	6	45	3
On the pastern of the left foreleg	251	0	S	23	0	2
At the knee of the same leg	250	20	S	18	0	2
On the pastern of the right foreleg	240	0	S	13	0	3
At the left shoulder blade	260	40	S	13	30	3
At the knee of the right foreleg	260	0	S	20	10	3
The more western on the northern side of the quadrilateral at the beginning of the tail	261	0	S	4	50	5
The more eastern on the same side	261	10	S	4	50	5
The more western on the southern side	261	50	S	5	50	5
The more eastern on the same side	263	0	S	6	50	5
31 stars: 2 of second magnitude, 9 of third, 9 of fourth, 8 of fifth, 2 of sixth, 1 nebulous.						

IN THE MIDDLE, AND AROUND THE ECLIPTIC

Constellations	Longitude			Latitude		Magnitude
	Deg.	Min.		Deg.	Min.	
CAPRICORNUS, OR THE GOAT						
The most northern of the three on the western horn	270	40	N	7	30	3
The middle one	271	0	N	6	40	6
The most southern of the three	270	40	N	5	0	3
At the extremity of the eastern horn	272	20	N	8	0	6
The most southern of the three at the opening of the jaws	272	20	N	0	45	6
The more western of the two remaining	272	0	N	1	45	6
The more eastern	272	10	N	1	30	6
Under the right eye	270	30	N	0	40	5
The more northern of the two on the neck	275	0	N	4	50	6
The more southern	275	10	S	0	50	5
At the right knee	274	10	S	6	30	4
At the left knee, which is bent	275	0	S	8	40	4
On the left shoulder	280	0	S	7	40	4
The more western of the two contiguous stars below the belly	283	30	S	6	50	4
The more eastern	283	40	S	6	0	5
The most eastern of the three in the middle of the body	282	0	S	4	15	5
The more southern of the two remaining to the west	280	0	S	7	0	5
The more northern	280	0	S	2	50	5
The more western of the two on the back	280	0		0	0	4
The more eastern	284	20	S	0	50	4
The more western of the two on the southern part of the spine	286	40	S	4	45	4
[56ᵇ] The more eastern	288	20	S	4	30	4
The more western of the two at the base of the tail	288	40	S	2	10	3
The more eastern	289	40	S	2	0	3
The more western of the four in the northern part of the tail	290	10	S	2	20	4
The most northern of the remaining three	292	0	S	5	0	5
The middle one	291	0	S	2	50	5
The most northern, at the extremity of the tail	292	0	N	4	20	5
28 stars: 4 of third magnitude, 9 of fourth, 9 of fifth, 6 of sixth						
AQUARIUS, OR THE WATER-BOY						
On the head	293	40	N	15	45	5
The brighter of the two on the right shoulder	299	40	N	11	0	3
The more obscure	298	30	N	9	40	5
On the left shoulder	290	0	N	8	50	3
Under the arm-pit	290	40	N	6	15	5
The most eastern of the three under the left hand and on the coat	280	0	N	5	30	3
The middle one	279	30	N	8	0	4

IN THE MIDDLE, AND AROUND THE ECLIPTIC

Constellations	Longitude			Latitude		Magnitude
	Deg.	Min.		Deg.	Min.	
The most western of the three	278	0	N	8	30	3
At the right elbow	302	50	N	8	45	3
The farthest north on the right hand	303	0	N	10	45	3
The more western of the two remaining to the south	305	20	N	9	0	3
The more eastern	306	40	N	8	30	3
The more western of the two adjacent stars on the right hip	299	30	N	3	0	4
The more eastern	300	20	N	2	10	5
On the right buttock	302	0	S	0	50	4
The more southern of the two on the left buttock	295	0	S	1	40	4
The more northern	295	30	N	4	0	6
The more southern of the two on the right shin	305	0	S	6	30	3
The more northern	304	40	S	5	0	4
On the left hip	301	0	S	5	40	5
The more southern of the two on the left shin	300	40	S	10	0	5
The northern star beneath the knee	302	10	S	9	0	5
The first star in the fall of water from the hand	303	20	N	2	0	4
More to the south-east	308	10	N	0	10	4
To the east at the first bend in the water	311	0	S	1	10	4
To the east of that	313	20	S	0	30	4
In the second and southern bend	313	50	S	1	40	4
The more northern of the two to the east	312	30	S	3	30	4
The more southern	312	50	S	4	10	4
Farther off to the south	314	10	S	8	15	5
[57a] Eastward, the more western of the two adjacent	316	0	S	11	0	5
The more eastern	316	30	S	10	50	5
The most northern of the three at the third bend in the water	315	0	S	14	0	5
The middle one	316	0	S	14	45	5
The most eastern of the three	316	30	S	15	40	5
The most northern of three in a similar figure to the east	310	20	S	14	10	4
The middle one	310	50	S	15	0	4
The most southern of the three	311	40	S	15	45	4
The most western of the three at the last bend in the water	305	10	S	14	50	4
The more southern of the two to the east	306	0	S	15	20	4
The more northern	306	30	S	14	0	4
The last in the water, and in the mouth of the southern Fish	300	20	S	23	0	1

42 stars: 1 of first magnitude, 9 of third,
18 of fourth, 13 of fifth, 1 of sixth

IN THE MIDDLE, AND AROUND THE ECLIPTIC

| Constellations | Longitude | | | Latitude | | Magnitude |
	Deg.	Min.		Deg.	Min.	
UNCONSTELLATED STARS AROUND AQUARIUS						
The most western of the three east of the						
bend in the water	320	0	S	15	30	4
The more northern of the two remaining	323	0	S	14	20	4
The more southern	322	20	S	18	15	4
3 stars: greater than fourth magnitude						
PISCES, OR THE FISH						
In the mouth of the western Fish	315	0	N	9	15	4
The more southern of the two on the occiput	317	30	N	7	30	4 greater
The more northern	321	30	N	9	30	4
The more western of the two on the back	319	20	N	9	20	4
The more eastern	324	0	N	7	30	4
The more western one on the belly	319	20	N	4	30	4
The more eastern	323	0	N	2	30	4
On the tail of the same Fish	329	20	N	6	20	4
On the fishing-line, the first star from the tail	334	20	N	5	45	6
To the east of that	336	20	N	2	45	6
The most western of the three bright stars to						
the east	340	30	N	2	15	4
The middle one	343	50	N	1	10	4
The most eastern	346	20	S	1	20	4
The more northern of the two small stars on						
the curvature	345	40	S	2	0	6
The more southern	346	20	S	5	0	6
The most western of the three after the curvature	350	20	S	2	20	4
The middle one	352	0	S	4	40	4
The most eastern one	354	0	S	7	45	4
[57^b] At the knot of the two fishing-lines	356	0	S	8	30	3
In the northern line, west of the knot	354	0	S	4	20	4
The most southern of the three to the east	353	30	N	1	30	5
The middle one	353	40	N	5	20	3
The most northern of the three and the last in						
the line	353	50	N	9	0	4
THE EASTERN FISH						
The more northern of the two in the mouth	355	20	N	21	45	5
The more southern	355	0	N	21	30	5
The most eastern of the three small stars on						
the head	352	0	N	20	0	6
The middle one	351	0	N	19	50	6
The most western of the three	350	20	N	23	0	6
The most western of the three on the southern						
fin, near the left elbow of Andromeda	349	0	N	14	20	4
The middle one	349	40	N	13	0	4
The most eastern of the three	351	0	N	12	0	4
The more northern of the two on the belly	355	30	N	17	0	4
The more southern	352	40	N	15	20	4

IN THE MIDDLE, AND AROUND THE ECLIPTIC

Constellations	Longitude			Latitude		Magnitude
	Deg.	Min.		Deg.	Min.	
On the eastern fin, near the tail	353	20	N	11	45	4
34 stars: 2 of third magnitude, 22 of fourth, 3 of fifth, 7 of sixth						
UNCONSTELLATED STARS AROUND PISCES						
The more western on the northern side of the quadrilateral under the western Fish	324	30	S	2	40	4
The more eastern	325	35	S	2	30	4
The more western on the southern side	324	0	S	5	50	4
The more eastern	325	40	S	5	30	4
4 unconstellated stars: of fourth magnitude						

Therefore, all in all, there are 348 stars in the zodiac: 5 of first magnitude, 9 of second, 65 of third, 132 of fourth, 105 of fifth, 27 of sixth, 3 nebulous, 2 obscure; and, over and above the count, the Coma, which we said above was called Coma Berenices by Conon the mathematician.

THE STARS OF THE SOUTHERN REGION

Constellations	Longitude			Latitude		Magnitude
	Deg.	Min.		Deg.	Min.	
CETUS, OR THE WHALE						
At the extremity of the nose	11	0	S	7	45	4
The most eastern of the three in the jaws	11	0	S	11	20	3
The middle one, in the middle of the mouth	6	0	S	11	30	3
The most western of the three, on the cheek	3	50	S	14	0	3
In the eye	4	0	S	8	10	4
Northward, in the hair	5	30	S	6	20	4
[58ª] Westward, in the mane	1	0	S	4	10	4
The more northern on the western side of the quadrilateral in the breast	355	20	S	24	30	4
The more southern	356	40	S	28	0	4
The more northern of the two to the east	0	0	S	25	10	4
The more southern	0	0	S	27	30	3
The middle one of the three on the body	345	20	S	25	20	3
The most southern	346	20	S	30	30	4
The most northern of the three	348	20	S	20	0	3
The more eastern of the two at the tail	343	0	S	15	20	3
The more western	338	20	S	15	40	3
The more northern on the eastern side of the quadrilateral in the tail	335	0	S	11	40	5
The more southern	334	0	S	13	40	5
The more northern of the two remaining to the west	332	40	S	13	0	5
The more southern	332	20	S	14	0	5
At the northern extremity of the tail	327	40	8	9	30	3
At the southern extremity of the tail	329	0	S	20	20	3
22 stars: 10 of third magnitude, 8 of fourth, 4 of fifth						

SOUTHERN SIGNS

Constellations	Longitude			Latitude		Magnitude
	Deg.	Min.		Deg.	Min.	
ORION						
The nebulous star on the head	50	20	S	16	30	nebulous
The bright, reddish star on the right shoulder	55	20	S	17	0	1
On the left shoulder	43	40	S	17	30	2 greater
East of that star	48	20	S	18	0	4 smaller
At the right elbow	57	40	S	14	30	4
On the right forearm	59	40	S	11	50	6
The more eastern on the southern side of the quadrilateral in the right hand	59	50	S	10	40	4
The more western	59	20	S	9	45	4
The more eastern on the northern side	60	40	S	8	15	6
The more western on the same side	59	0	S	8	15	6
The more western of the two on the club	55	0	S	3	45	5
The more eastern	57	40	S	3	15	5
The most eastern of the four in a straight line on the back	50	50	S	19	40	4
More western	49	40	S	20	0	6
Still more western	48	40	S	20	20	6
Most western	47	30	S	20	30	5
The most northern of the nine on the shield	43	50	S	8	0	4
The second	42	40	S	8	10	4
The third	41	20	S	10	15	4
The fourth	39	40	S	12	50	4
The fifth	38	30	S	14	15	4
The sixth	37	50	S	15	50	3
[58b] The seventh	38	10	S	17	10	3
The eighth	38	40	S	20	20	3
The last and most southern	39	40	S	21	30	3
The most western of the three bright stars on the sword-belt	48	40	S	24	10	2
The middle one	50	40	S	24	50	2
The most eastern of the three in a straight line	52	40	S	25	30	2
On the hilt of the sword	47	10	S	25	50	3
The most northern of the three on the sword	50	10	S	28	40	4
The middle one	50	0	S	29	30	3
The most southern one	50	20	S	29	50	3 smaller
The more eastern of the two at the tip of the sword	51	0	S	30	30	4
The more western	49	30	S	30	50	4
On the left foot, the bright star which belongs to Fluvius too	42	30	S	31	30	1
On the left shin	44	20	S	30	15	4 greater
At the right heel	46	40	S	31	10	4
At the right knee	53	30	S	33	30	3

38 stars: 2 of first magnitude, 4 of second,
8 of third, 15 of fourth, 3 of fifth, 5 of sixth,
and 1 nebulous

Southern Signs

Constellations	Longitude			Latitude		Magnitude
	Deg.	Min.		Deg.	Min.	
FLUVIUS, OR THE RIVER						
After the left foot of Orion, and at the beginning of Fluvius	41	40	S	31	50	4
The most northern star within the bend of Orion's leg	42	10	S	28	15	4
The more eastern of the two after that	41	20	S	29	50	4
The more western	38	0	S	28	15	4
The more eastern of the next two	36	30	S	25	15	4
The more western	33	30	S	25	20	4
The most eastern of the three after them	29	40	S	26	0	4
The middle one	29	0	S	27	0	4
The most western of the three	26	18	S	27	50	4
The most eastern of the four after the interval	20	20	S	82	50	3
More western	18	0	S	31	0	4
Still more western	17	30	S	28	50	3
The most western of all four	15	30	S	28	0	3
Again similarly, the most eastward of the four	10	30	S	25	30	3
More westward	8	10	S	23	50	4
Still more westward	5	30	S	23	10	3
The most westward of the four	3	50	S	23	15	4
The star in the bend of Fluvius which touches the breast of Cetus	358	30	S	32	10	4
East of that	359	10	S	34	50	4
The most westward of the three to the seat	2	10	S	38	30	4
[59a] The middle one	7	10	S	38	10	4
The most eastward of the three	10	50	S	39	0	5
The more northern of the two on the western side of the quadrilateral	14	40	S	41	30	4
The more southern	14	50	S	42	30	4
The more western on the eastern side	15	30	S	43	20	4
The most eastward of those four	18	0	S	43	20	4
The more northern of the two contiguous stars towards the east	27	30	S	50	20	4
The more southern	28	20	S	51	45	4
The more eastern of the two at the bend	21	30	S	53	50	4
The more western	19	10	S	53	10	4
The most eastern of the three in the remaining space	11	10	S	53	0	4
The middle one	8	10	S	53	30	4
The most western of the three	5	10	S	52	0	4
The bright star at the extremity of the river	353	30	S	53	30	1
34 stars; 1 of first magnitude, 5 of third, 27 of fourth, 1 of fifth						
LEPUS, OR THE RABBIT						
The more northern one on the western side of the quadrilateral at the ears	43	0	S	35	0	5
The more southern	43	10	S	36	30	5
The more northern one on the eastern side	44	40	S	35	30	5

SOUTHERN SIGNS

Constellations	Longitude			Latitude		Magnitude
	Deg.	Min.		Deg.	Min.	
The more southern	44	40	S	36	40	5
At the chin	42	30	S	39	40	4 greater
At the extremity of the left forefoot	39	30	S	45	15	4 greater
In the middle of the body	48	50	S	41	30	3
Beneath the belly	48	10	S	44	20	3
The more northern of the two on the hind feet	54	20	S	44	0	4
The more southern	52	20	S	45	50	4
On the loins	53	20	S	38	20	4
At the tip of the tail	56	0	S	38	10	4
12 stars: 2 of third magnitude, 6 of fourth, 4 of fifth						
CANIS, OR THE DOG						
The very bright star called Canis, in the mouth	71	0	S	39	10	1 very great
On the ears	73	0	S	35	0	4
On the head	74	40	S	36	30	5
The more northern of the two on the neck	76	40	S	37	45	4
The more southern	78	40	S	40	0	4
On the breast	73	50	S	42	30	5
The more northern of the two at the right knee	69	30	S	41	15	5
The more southern	69	20	S	42	30	5
At the extremity of the forefoot	64	20	S	41	20	3
[59b] The more western of the two on the left knee	68	0	S	46	30	5
The more eastern	69	30	S	45	50	5
The more eastern of the two on the left shoulder	78	0	S	46	0	4
The more western	75	0	S	47	0	5
On the left hip	80	0	S	48	45	3 smaller
Beneath the belly between the thighs	77	0	S	51	30	3
In the hollow of the right foot	76	20	S	55	10	4
At the extremity of the same foot	77	0	S	55	40	3
At the tip of the tail	85	30	S	50	30	3 smaller
18 stars: 1 of first magnitude, 5 of third, 5 of fourth, 7 of fifth						
UNCONSTELLATED STARS AROUND CANIS						
North of the head of the Dog	72	50	S	25	15	4
The most southern in a straight line under the hind feet	63	20	S	60	30	4
The more northern	64	40	S	58	45	4
Still more northern	66	20	S	57	0	4
The last and farthest north of the four	67	30	S	56	0	4
The most western of the three westward as it were in a straight line	50	20	S	55	30	4
The middle one	53	40	S	57	40	4
The most eastern of the three	55	40	S	59	30	4

SOUTHERN SIGNS

Constellations	Longitude			Latitude		Magnitude
	Deg.	Min.		Deg.	Min.	
The more western of the two bright stars beneath them	52	20	S	59	40	2
The more western	49	20	S	57	40	2
The remaining star, more southern	45	30	S	59	30	4
11 stars: 2 of second magnitude, 9 of fourth						
CANICULA, OR PROCYON, OR THE LITTLE BITCH						
On the neck	78	20	S	14	0	4
The bright star on the thigh, that is,						
Προκύων or Canicula, the Dog-star	82	30	S	16	10	1
2 stars: 1 of first magnitude, 1 of fourth						
ARGO, OR THE SHIP						
The more western of the two at the extremity of the Ship	93	40	S	42	40	5
The more eastern	97	40	S	43	20	3
The more northern of the two on the stern	92	10	S	45	0	4
The more southern	92	10	S	46	0	4
West of the two	88	40	S	45	30	4
The bright star in the middle of the shield	89	40	S	47	15	4
The most western of the three beneath the shield	88	40	S	49	45	4
The most eastern	92	40	S	49	50	4
The middle one of the three	91	40	S	49	15	4
At the extremity of the rudder	97	20	S	49	50	4
The more northern of the two on the stern keel	87	20	S	53	0	4
The more southern	87	20	S	58	30	3
[60ª] The most northern on the cross-bank of the stem	93	30	S	55	30	5
The most western of the three on the same cross-bank	95	30	S	58	30	5
The middle one	96	40	S	57	15	4
The most eastern	99	50	S	57	45	4
The bright star to the east on the cross bank	104	30	S	58	20	2
The more western of the two obscure stars beneath that	101	30	S	60	0	5
The more eastern	104	20	S	59	20	5
The more western of the two east of the aforesaid bright star	106	30	S	56	40	5
The more eastern	107	40	S	57	0	5
The most northern of the three on the small shields and at the foot of the mast	119	0	S	51	30	4 greater
The middle one	119	30	S	55	30	4 greater
The most southern of the three	117	20	S	57	10	4
The more northern of the two contiguous stars beneath them	122	30	S	60	0	4
The more southern	122	20	S	61	15	4

Southern Signs

Constellations	Longitude			Latitude		Magnitude
	Deg.	Min.		Deg.	Min.	
The more southern of the two in the middle of the mast	113	30	S	51	30	4
The more northern	112	40	S	49	0	4
The more western of the two at the top part of the sail	111	40	S	43	20	4
The more eastern	112	20	S	43	30	4
Below the third star east of the shield	98	30	S	54	30	2 smaller
In the section of the bridge	100	50	S	51	15	2
Between the oars in the keel	95	0	S	63	0	4
The obscure star east of that	102	20	S	64	30	6
The bright star, east of that and below the cross-bank	113	20	S	63	50	2
The bright star to the south, more within the keel	121	50	S	69	40	2
The most western of the three to the east of that	128	30	S	65	40	3
The middle one	134	40	S	65	50	3
The most eastern	139	20	S	65	50	2
The more western of the two in the section	144	20	S	62	50	3
The more eastern	151	20	S	62	15	3
The more western in the northwestern oar	57	20	S	65	50	4 greater
The more eastern	73	30	S	65	40	3 greater
The more western one in the remaining oar; Canopus	70	30	S	75	0	1
The remaining star east of that	82	20	S	71	50	3 greater

45 stars: 1 of first magnitude, 6 of second, 8 of third, 22 of fourth, 7 of fifth, 1 of sixth

Hydra						
Of the two more western of the five on the head, the more southern, at the nostrils	97	20	S	15	0	4
The more northern of the two, and in the eye	98	40	S	13	40	4
On the occiput, the more northern of the two to the east	99	0	S	11	30	4
[60b] The more southern, and at the jaws	98	50	S	14	45	4
East of all those and on the cheeks	100	50	S	12	15	4
The more western of the two at the beginning of the neck	103	40	S	11	50	5
The more eastern	106	40	S	13	30	4
The middle one of the three at the curve of the neck	111	40	S	15	20	4
East of that	114	0	S	14	50	4
The most southern	111	40	S	17	10	4
The obscure and northern star of the two contiguous to the south	112	30	S	19	45	6
The bright one and to the south-east	113	20	S	20	30	2
The most western of the three after the curve in the neck	119	20	S	26	30	4

SOUTHERN SIGNS

Constellations	Longitude Deg.	Min.		Latitude Deg.	Min.	Magnitude
The most eastern	124					
	30	S	23	15	4	
The middle one	122	0	S	24	0	4
The most western of the three in a straight line	131	20	S	24	30	3
The middle one	133	20	S	23	0	4
The most eastern one	136	20	S	23	10	3
The more northern of the two beneath the base of the Cup	144	50	S	25	45	4
The more southern	145	40	S	30	10	4
East of them, the most western of the three on the triangle	155	30	S	31	20	4
The most southern	157	50	S	34	10	4
The most eastern of the same three	159	30	S	31	40	3
East of the Crow, near the tail	173	20	S	13	30	4
At the extremity of the tail	186	50	S	17	30	4

25 stars: 1 of second magnitude, 3 of third,
19 of fourth, 1 of fifth, 1 of sixth

UNCONSTELLATED STARS AROUND HYDRA

Constellations	Longitude Deg.	Min.		Latitude Deg.	Min.	Magnitude
South of the head	96	0	S	23	15	3
East of those on the neck	124	20	S	26	0	3

2 unconstellated stars: of third magnitude

CRATER, OR THE CUP

Constellations	Longitude Deg.	Min.		Latitude Deg.	Min.	Magnitude
On the base of the Cup and in Hydra too	139	40	S	23	0	4
The more southern of the two in the middle of the Cup	146	0	S	19	30	4
The more northern of them	143	30	S	18	0	4
On the southern rim of the Cup	150	20	S	18	30	4 greater
On the northern part of the rim	142	40	S	13	40	4
On the southern part of the stem	152	30	S	16	30	4 smaller
On the northern part	145	0	S	11	50	4

7 stars: of fourth magnitude

[61a] CORVUS, OR THE CROW

Constellations	Longitude Deg.	Min.		Latitude Deg.	Min.	Magnitude
On the beak, and in Hydra too	158	40	S	21	30	5
On the neck	157	40	S	19	40	5
In the breast	160	0	S	18	10	5
On the right wing, the western wing	160	50	S	14	50	3
The more western of the two on the eastern wing	160	0	S	12	30	3
The more eastern	161	20	S	11	45	4
At the extremity of the foot, and in Hydra too	163	50	S	18	10	3

7 Stars: 5 of third magnitude, 1 of fourth,
1 of fifth

CENTAURUS, OR THE CENTAUR

Constellations	Longitude Deg.	Min.		Latitude Deg.	Min.	Magnitude
The most southern of the four on the head	183	50	S	21	20	5
The more northern	183	20	S	13	50	5

SOUTHERN SIGNS

Constellations	Longitude			Latitude		Magnitude
	Deg.	Min.		Deg.	Min.	
The more western of the two in the middle	182	30	S	20	30	5
The more eastern and last of the four	182	20	S	20	0	5
On the left and western shoulder	179	30	S	25	30	3
On the right shoulder	189	0	S	22	30	3
On the left forearm	182	30	S	17	30	4
The more northern of the two on the western side of the quadrilateral on the shield	191	30	S	22	30	4
The more southern	192	30	S	23	45	4
Of the remaining two, the one at the top of the shield	195	20	S	18	15	4
The more southern	196	50	S	20	50	4
The most western of the three on the right side	186	40	S	28	20	4
The middle one	187	20	S	29	20	4
The most eastern	188	30	S	28	0	4
On the right arm	189	40	S	26	30	4
On the right elbow	196	10	S	25	15	3
At the extremity of the right hand	200	50	S	24	0	4
The bright star at the junction of the human body	191	20	S	33	30	3
The more eastern of the two obscure stars	191	0	S	31	0	5
The more western	189	50	S	30	20	5
At the beginning of the back	185	30	S	33	50	5
West of that, on the horse's back	182	20	S	37	30	5
The most eastern of the three on the loins	179	10	S	40	0	3
The middle one	178	20	S	40	20	4
The most western of the three	176	0	S	41	0	5
The more western of the two contiguous stars on the right hip.	176	0	S	46	10	2
The more eastern	176	40	S	46	45	4
On the breast, beneath the horse's wing	191	40	S	40	45	4
[61b] The more western of the two under the belly	179	50	S	43	0	2
The more eastern	181	0	S	43	45	3
In the hollow of the right hind foot	183	20	S	51	10	2
On the pastern of the same	188	40	S	51	40	2
In the hollow of the left <hind> foot	188	40	S	55	10	4
Under the muscle of the same foot	184	30	S	55	40	4
On top of the right forefoot	181	40	S	41	10	1
At the left knee	197	30	S	45	20	2
The unconstellated star below the right thigh	188	0	S	49	10	3

37 stars: 1 of first magnitude, 5 of second, 7 of third, 15 of fourth, 9 of fifth

BESTIA QUAM TENET CENTAURUS, OR THE BEAST HELD BY THE CENTAUR—THE WOLF

Constellations	Longitude			Latitude		Magnitude
At the top of the hind foot and in the hand of the Centaur	201	20	S	24	50	3

SOUTHERN SIGNS

Constellations	Longitude			Latitude		Magnitude
	Deg.	Min.		Deg.	Min.	
On the hollow of the same foot	199	10	S	20	10	3
The more western of the two on the foreshoulder	204	20	S	21	15	4
The more eastern	207	30	S	21	0	4
In the middle of the body	206	20	S	25	10	4
On the belly	203	30	S	27	0	5
On the hip	204	10	S	29	0	5
The more northern of the two at the beginning of the hip	208	0	S	28	30	5
The more southern	207	0	S	30	0	5
The upmost part of the loins	208	40	S	33	10	5
The most southern of the three at the extremity of the tail	195	20	S	31	20	5
The middle one	195	10	S	30	0	4
The most northern of the three	196	20	S	29	20	4
The more southern of the two at the throat	212	10	S	17	0	4
The more northern	212	40	S	15	20	4
The more western of the two at the opening of the jaws	209	0	S	13	30	4
The more eastern	210	0	S	12	50	4
The more southern of the two on the forefoot	240	40	S	11	80	4
The more northern	239	50	S	10	0	4
19 stars: 2 of third magnitude, 11 of fourth, 6 of fifth						
ARA OR THURIBULUM, THE ALTAR OR THE CENSER						
The more northern of the two at the base	231	0	S	22	40	5
The more southern	233	40	S	25	45	4
At the center of the altar	229	30	S	26	30	4
[62ª] The most northern of the three on the hearth	224	0	S	30	20	5
The more southern of the remaining two contiguous stars	228	30	S	34	10	4
The more northern	228	20	S	33	20	4
In the midst of the flames	224	10	S	34	10	4
7 Stars: 5 of fourth magnitude, 2 of fifth						
CORONA AUSTRINA, OR SOUTHERN CROWN						
The more western star on the outer periphery	242	30	S	21	30	4
East of that on the crown	245	0	S	21	0	5
East of that too	246	30	S	20	20	5
Farther east of that also	248	10	S	20	0	4
East of that and west of the knee of Sagittarius	249	30	S	18	30	5
The bright star to the north on the knee	250	40	S	17	10	4
The more northern	250	10	S	16	0	4
Still more northern	249	50	S	15	20	4

Southern Signs

Constellations	Longitude			Latitude		Magnitude
	Deg.	Min.		Deg.	Min.	
The more eastern of the two on the northern part of the periphery	248	30	S	15	50	6
The more western	248	0	S	14	50	6
Some distance west of those	245	10	S	14	40	5
Still west of that	243	0	S	15	50	5
The last star, more towards the south	242	30	S	18	30	5
13 stars: 5 of fourth magnitude, 6 of fifth, 2 of sixth						
PISCIS AUSTRINUS, OR THE SOUTHERN FISH						
In the mouth, and the same as at the extremity of Aqua	300	20	S	23	0	1
The most western of the three on the head	294	0	S	21	20	4
The middle one	297	30	S	22	15	4
The most eastern	299	0	S	22	30	4
At the gills	297	40	S	16	15	4
On the southern and dorsal fin	288	30	S	19	30	5
The more eastern of the two in the belly	294	30	S	15	10	5
The more western	292	10	S	14	30	4
The most eastern of the three on the northern fin	288	30	S	15	15	4
The middle one	285	10	S	16	30	4
The most western of the three	284	20	S	18	10	4
At the extremity of the tail	289	20	S	22	15	4
11 stars beside the first: 9 of fourth magnitude, 2 of fifth						
[62ᵇ] UNCONSTELLATED STARS AROUND PISCIS AUSTRINUS						
The most western of the bright stars west of Piscis	271	20	S	22	20	3
The middle one	274	30	S	22	10	3
The most eastern of the three	277	20	S	21	0	3
The obscure star west of that	275	20	S	20	50	5
The more southern of the two remaining to the north	277	10	S	16	0	4
The more northern	277	10	S	14	50	4
6 stars: 3 of third magnitude, 2 of fourth, 1 of fifth						

In the southern region 316 stars: 7 of first magnitude, 18 of second, 60 of third, 167 of fourth, 54 of fifth, 9 of sixth, and 1 nebulous. And so there are altogether 1024 stars: 15 of first magnitude, 45 of second, 206 of third, 476 of fourth, 217 of fifth, 49 of sixth, 11 obscure, and 5 nebulous.

BOOK THREE

1. On the Precessions of the Solstices and Equinoxes

[63ª] Having depicted the appearance of the fixed stars in relation to the annual revolution, we must pass on; and we shall treat first of the change of the equinoxes, by reason of which even the fixed stars are believed to move. Now we find that the ancient mathematicians made no distinction between the "turning" or natural year, which begins at an equinox or solstice, and the year which is determined by means of some one of the fixed stars. That is why they thought the Olympic years, which they measured from the rising of Canicula, were the same as the years measured from the summer solstice, since they did not yet know the distinction between the two.

But Hipparchus of Rhodes, a man of wonderful acumen, was the first to call attention to the fact that there was a difference in the length of these two kinds of year. While making careful observations of the magnitude of the year, he found that it was longer as measured from the fixed stars than as measured from the equinoxes or solstices. Hence he believed that the fixed stars too possessed a movement eastward, but one so slow as not to be immediately perceptible. But now through the passage of time, the movement has become very evident. By it we discern a rising and setting of the signs and stars which are already far different from those risings and settings described by the ancients; and we see that the twelve parts of the ecliptic have receded from the signs of the fixed stars by a rather great interval, although in the beginning they agreed in name and in position.

Moreover, an irregular movement has been found; and wishing to assign the cause for its irregularity, astronomers have brought forward different theories. Some maintained that there was a sort of swinging movement of the suspended world—like the movement in latitude which we find in the case of the planets—and that back and forth within fixed limits as far out as the world has gone forward in one direction it will come back again in the other at some time,[1] and that the extent of its digression from the middle on either side was not more than 8°. But this already outdated theory can no longer hold, especially because [63ᵇ] it is already clear enough that the head of the constellation of Aries has become more than three times 8° distant from the spring equinox—and similarly for other stars—and no trace of a regression has been perceived during so many ages. Others indeed have opined that the sphere of the fixed stars moves forward but does so by irregular steps; and nevertheless they have failed to define any fixed mode of movement.

[1] *i.e.,* the sphere of the world has rotated westward and will at some time rotate eastward the same distance.

Moreover, there is an additional surprise of nature, in that the obliquity of the ecliptic does not appear so great to us as before Ptolemy—as we said above.

For the sake of a cause for these facts some have thought up a ninth sphere and others a tenth: they thought these facts could be explained through those spheres; but they were unable to produce what they had promised. Already an eleventh sphere has begun to see the light of day; and in talking of the movement of the Earth we shall easily prove that this number of circles is superfluous.

For, as we have already set out separately in Book I, the two revolutions, that is, of the annual declination and of the centre of the Earth, are not altogether equal, namely because the restoration of the declination slightly anticipates the period of the centre, whence it necessarily follows that the equinoxes seem to arrive before their time—not that the sphere of the fixed stars is moved eastward, but rather that the equator is moved westward, as it is inclined obliquely to the plane of the ecliptic in proportion to the amount of deflexion of the axis of the terrestrial globe. For it seems more accurate to say that the equator is inclined obliquely to the ecliptic than that the ecliptic, a greater circle, is inclined to the equator, a smaller. For the ecliptic, which is described by the distance between the sun and the Earth during the annual circuit, is much greater than the equator, which is described by the daily movement of the Earth around its axis. And in this way the common sections of the equator and the oblique ecliptic are perceived, with the passage of time, to get ahead, while the stars are perceived to lag behind. But the measure of this movement and the ratio of its irregularity were hidden from our predecessors, because the period of revolution was not yet known on account of its surprising slowness—I mean that during the many ages after it was first noticed by men, it has advanced through hardly a fifteenth part of a circle, or 24°. Nevertheless, we shall state things with as much certitude as possible, with the aid of what we have learned concerning these facts from the history of observations down to our own time.

2. HISTORY OF THE OBSERVATIONS CONFIRMING THE IRREGULAR PRECESSION OF THE EQUINOXES AND SOLSTICES

[64a] Accordingly in the 36th year of the first of the seventy-six-year periods of Callippus, which was the 30th year after the death of Alexander the Great, Timochares the Alexandrian, who was the first to investigate the positions of the fixed stars, recorded that Spica, which is in the constellation of Virgo, had an angular elongation of $82\frac{1}{3}°$ from the point of summer solstice with a southern latitude of 2°; and that the star in the forehead of Scorpio which is the most northward of the three and is first in the order of formation of the sign had a latitude of $1\frac{1}{3}°$ and a longitude of 32° from the autumn equinox.

And again in the 48th year of the same period he found that Spica in Virgo had a longitude of $82^1/_2°$ from the summer solstice but had kept the same latitude.

Now Hipparchus in the 50th year of the third period of Callippus, in the 196th year since the death of Alexander, found that the star called Regulus, which is in the breast of Leo, was $29^5/_6°$ to the east of the summer solstice.

Next Menelaus, the Roman geometer, in the first year of Trajan's reign, $i.e.$, in the 99th year since the birth of Christ, and in the 422nd year since the death of Alexander, recorded that Spica in Virgo had a longitude of $86^1/_4°$ from the (summer) solstice and that the star in the forehead of Scorpio had a longitude of $35^{11}/_{12}°$ from the autumn equinox.

Following them, Ptolemy, in the second year of the reign of Antoninus Pius, in the 462nd year since the death of Alexander, discovered that Regulus in Leo had a longitude of $32^1/_2°$ from the (summer) solstice; Spica, $86^1/_2°$; and that the star in the forehead of Scorpio had a longitude of $36^1/_3°$ from the autumn equinox, with no change in latitude—as was set forth above in drawing up the tables. And we have passed these things in review, just as they were recorded by our predecessors.

After a great lapse of time, however, in the 1202nd year after the death of Alexander, came the observations of al-Battani the Harranite; and we may place the utmost confidence in them. In that year Regulus, or Basiliscus, was seen to have attained a longitude of 44°5' from the (summer) solstice; and the star in the forehead of Scorpio, one of 47°50' [64^b] from the autumn equinox. The latitude of these stars stayed completely the same, so that there is no longer any doubt on that score.

Wherefore in the year of Our Lord 1525, in the year after leap-year by the Roman calendar and 1849 Egyptian years after the death of Alexander, we were taking observations of the often mentioned Spica, at Frauenburg, in Prussia. And the greatest altitude of the star on the meridian circle was seen to be approximately 27°. We found that the latitude of Frauenburg was $54°19^1/_2°$. Wherefore its declination from the equator stood to be 8°40'. Hence its position became known as follows:

For we have described the meridian circle $ABCD$ through the poles of the ecliptic and the equator. Let AEC be the diameter and common section with the equator; and BED is the diameter and common section with the ecliptic. Let F be the north pole of the ecliptic and FEG its axis; and let B be the beginning of Capricorn and D of Cancer. Now let

arc $BH = 2°$,

which is the southern latitude of the star. And from point H let HL be drawn parallel to BD; and let HL cut the axis of the ecliptic at I and the equator at K. Moreover, let

arc $MA = 8°40'$,

in proportion to the southern declination of the star; and from point M let MN be drawn parallel to AC.

MN will cut HIL the parallel to the ecliptic; therefore let MN cut HIL at point O; and if the straight line OP is drawn at right angles to MN and AC, then

$$OP = \tfrac{1}{2} \text{ ch. } 2 \, AM.$$

But the circles having the diameters FG, HL, and MN are perpendicular to plane $ABCD$; and by Euclid's *Elements*, XI, 19, their common sections are at right angles to the same plane in points O and I. Hence by XI, 6, they (the common sections) are parallel to one another. And since I is the centre of the circle whose diameter is HL, therefore line OI will be equal to half the chord subtending twice an arc in a circle of diameter HL— an arc similar to the arc which measures the longitude of the star from the beginning of Libra, and this arc is what we are looking for. It is found in this way:

Since the exterior angle is equal to its interior and opposite,

$$\text{angle } AEB = \text{angle } OKP$$

and

$$\text{angle } OPK = 90°.$$

Accordingly

[65a] $OP : OK = \tfrac{1}{2} \text{ ch. } 2 \, AB : BE = \tfrac{1}{2} \text{ ch. } 2 \, AH : HIK.$

For the lines comprehend triangles similar to OPK.

But

$$\text{arc } AB = 23°28\tfrac{1}{2}',$$

and

$$\tfrac{1}{2} \text{ ch. } 2 \, AB = 39,832,$$
$$\text{where } BE = 100,000.$$

And

$$\text{arc } ABH = 25°28\tfrac{1}{2}',$$
$$\tfrac{1}{2} \text{ ch. } 2 \, ABH = 43,010,$$
$$\text{arc } MA = 8°40',$$

which is the declination,

and

$$\tfrac{1}{2} \text{ ch. } 2 \, MA = 15,069.$$

It follows from this that

$$HIK = 107,978,$$
$$OK = 37,831,$$

and by subtraction

$$HO = 70,147.$$

But

$$HOI = \frac{1}{2} \text{ ch. } HGL$$

and

$$\text{arc } HGL = 176°.$$

Then

$$HOI = 99,939,$$
$$\text{where } BE = 100,000.$$

And therefore by subtraction,

$$OI = HOI - HO = 29,792.$$

But in so far as HOI = radius = 100,000,

$$OI = 29,810$$
$$\frac{1}{2} \text{ ch. 2 arc } 17°21'.$$

This was the distance of Spica in (the constellation) Virgo from the beginning of Libra; and the position of the star was here. Moreover, ten years before, in 1515, we found that it had a declination of 8°36'; and its position was 17°14' distant from the beginning of the Balances.

Now Ptolemy recorded that it had a declination of only $\frac{1}{2}°$. Therefore its position was at 26°40' of the (zodiacal sign) Virgo, which seems to be more or less true in comparison with the previous observations.

Hence it appears clearly enough that during nearly the whole period of 432 years from Timochares to Ptolemy the equinoxes and solstices were moved according to a precession of 1° per 100 years—if a constant ratio is set up between the time and the amount of precession, which added up to $4\frac{1}{3}°$. For in the 266 years between Hipparchus and Ptolemy the longitude of Basiliscus in Leo from the summer solstice moved $2\frac{2}{3}°$, so that here too, by taking the time into comparison, there is found a precession of 1° per 100 years.

Moreover, because during the 782 mean years between the observation of Menelaus and that of al-Battani the first star in the forehead of Scorpio had a change in longitude of 11°55', it will certainly seem that 1° should be assigned not to 100 years but rather to 66 years; but for the 741 years after Ptolemy, 1° to only 65 years.

If finally the remaining space of 645 years is compared with the difference of 9°11' given by our observation, there will be 71 years allotted to 1°.

From this it is clear that the precession of the equinoxes was slower [65^b] during the 400 years before Ptolemy than during the time between Ptolemy and al-Battani, and that the precession in this middle period was speedier than in the time from al-Battani to us.

Moreover, there is found a difference in the movement of obliquity, since Aristarchus of Samos found that the obliquity of the ecliptic and the equator was 23°51'20", just as Ptolemy did; al-Battani, 23°35'; 190 years later Arzachel the

Spaniard, 23°34'. And similarly after 230 years Prophatius the Jew found that the obliquity was approximately 2' smaller. And in our time it has not been found greater than 23°28$^1/_2$'. Hence it is also clear that the movement was least from the time of Aristarchus to that of Ptolemy and greatest from that of Ptolemy to that of al-Battani.

3. The Hypotheses by Means of Which the Mutation of the Equinoxes and of the Obliquity of the Ecliptic and the Equator are Shown

Accordingly it seems clear from this that the solstices and equinoxes change around in an irregular movement. No one perhaps will bring forward a better reason for this than that there is a certain deflexion of the axis of the Earth and the poles of the equator. For that seems to follow upon the hypothesis of the movement of the Earth, since it is clear that the ecliptic remains perpetually unchangeable—the constant latitudes of the fixed stars bear witness to that—while the equator moves. For if the movement of the axis of the Earth were simply and exactly in proportion to the movement of the centre, there would not appear at all any precession of the equinoxes and solstices, as we said; but as these movements differ from one another by a variable difference, it was necessary for the solstices and equinoxes to precede the positions of the stars in an irregular movement.

The same thing happens in the case of the movement of declination, which changes the obliquity of the ecliptic irregularly—although this obliquity should be assigned more rightly to the equator.

For this reason you should understand two reciprocal movements belonging wholly to the poles, like hanging balances, since the poles and circles in a sphere imply one another mutually and are in agreement. Therefore there will be one movement which changes the inclination of those circles [66^a] by moving the poles up and down in proportion to the angle of section. There is another which alternately increases and decreases the solstitial and equinoctial precessions by a movement taking place crosswise. Now we call these movements "librations," or "swinging movements," because like hanging bodies swinging over the same course between two limits, they become faster in the middle and very slow at the extremes. And such movements occur very often in connection with the latitudes of the planets, as we shall see in the proper place.

They differ moreover in their periods, because the irregular movement of the equinoxes is restored twice during one restoration of obliquity. But as in every apparent irregular movement, it is necessary to understand a certain mean, through which the ratio of irregularity can be determined; so in this case too it was quite necessary to consider the mean poles and the mean equator and also the mean equinoxes and points of solstice. The poles and the terrestrial equator, by being deflected in opposite directions

away from these mean poles, though within fixed limits, make those regular movements appear to be irregular. And so these two librations competing with one another make the poles of the earth in the passage of time describe certain lines similar to a twisted garland.

But since it is not easy to explain these things adequately with words, and still

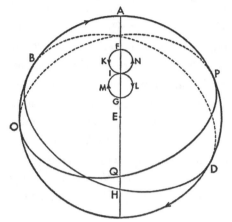

less—I fear—to have them grasped by the hearing, unless they are also viewed by the eyes, therefore let us describe on a sphere circle *ABCD* which is the ecliptic. Let the north pole (of the ecliptic) be *E*, the beginning of Capricornus *A*, that of Cancer *C*, that of Aries *B*, and that of Libra *D*. And through points *A* and *C* and pole *E* let circle *AEC* be drawn. And let the greatest distance between the north poles of the ecliptic and of the equator be *EF*, and the least *EG*. Similarly let *I* be the pole in the middle position, and around *I* let the equator *BHD* be described, and let that be called the mean equator; and let *B* and *D* be called the mean equinoxes.

Let the poles of the equator, the equinoxes, and the equator be all carried around *E* by an always regular movement westward, *i.e.*, counter to the order of the signs in the sphere of the fixed stars, and with a slow movement, as I said. Now let there be understood two reciprocal movements of the terrestrial poles like hanging bodies—one of them between the limits *F* and *G*, which will be called the movement of anomaly,[1]— *i.e.*, irregularity—of declination; the other from westward to eastward, and from eastward to westward. This second movement, which has twice the velocity of the first, we shall call the anomaly of the equinoxes. As both of these movements belong to the poles of the earth, they deflect the poles in a surprising way.

For first with *F* as the north pole of the earth, [66ᵇ] the equator described around the pole will pass through the same sections *B* and *D*, *i.e.*, through the poles of circle *AFEC*. But it will make greater angles of obliquity in proportion to arc *FI*. Now the second movement supervening does not allow the terrestrial pole, which was about to cross from the assumed starting point *F* to the mean obliquity at *I*, to proceed in a straight line along *FI*, but draws it aside in a circular movement towards its farthest eastward latitude, which is at *K*. The intersection of the apparent equator *OQP* described around this position will not be in *B* but to the east of it in *O*, and the precession of the equinoxes will be decreased in proportion to arc *BO*. Changing its direction and

[1]The term *anomaly* will be used to designate a regular movement the compounding of which with the principal regular movement being considered makes that principal movement appear irregular.

moving westwards, the pole is carried by the two simultaneously competing movements to the mean position *I*. And the apparent equator is in all respects identical with the regular or mean equator. Crossing there, the pole of the earth moves westward and separates the apparent equator from the mean equator and increases the precession of the equinoxes up to the other limit *L*. There changing its direction again, it subtracts what it had just added to the precession of the equinoxes, until, when situated at point *G*, it causes the least obliquity at the same common section *B*, where once more the movement of the equinoxes and solstices will appear very slow, in approximately the same way as at *F*. At this time the irregularity of the equinoxes stands to have completed its revolution, since it has passed from the mean through both extremes and back to the mean; while the movement of obliquity in going from greatest declination to least has completed only half its circuit. Moving on from there, the pole advances eastward to the farthest limit *M*; and, after reversing its direction there becomes one with the mean pole *I*; and once more it proceeds westward and after reaching the limit *N* finally [67ª] completes what we called the twisted line *FKILGMINF*. And so it is clear that in one cycle of obliquity the pole of the Earth reaches the westward limit twice and the eastward limit twice.

4. HOW THE RECIPROCAL MOVEMENT OR MOVEMENT OF LIBRATION IS COMPOSED OF CIRCULAR MOVEMENTS

Accordingly we shall make clear exactly how this movement agrees with the appearances. In the meantime someone will ask how the regularity of these librations is to be understood, since it was said in the beginning that the celestial movement was regular, or composed of regular and circular movements. But here in either case of libration two movements are apparent as one movement between two limits, and the two limits necessarily make a cessation of movement intervene. For we acknowledge that there are twin movements, which are demonstrated from regular movements in this way.

Let there be the straight line *AB*, and let it be cut into four equal parts at points *C*, *D*, and *E*. Let the homocentric circles *ADB* and *CDE* be described around *D* in the same plane. And in the selfsame plane *ADB* and *CDE*, let any point *F* be taken on the circumference of the inner circle; and with *F* as centre and radius equal to *FD* let circle *GHD* be described. And let it cut the straight line *AB* at point *H*; and let the diameter *DFG* be drawn. We have to show that when the twin movements of circles *GHD* and *CFE* compete

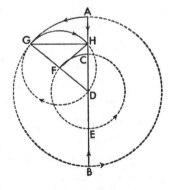

with one another, the movable point *H* proceeds back and forth along the same straight line *AB* by a reciprocal motion.

This will take place if we understand that *H* is moved in a different direction from *F* and through twice the distance, since the angle same *CDF* which is situated at the centre of circle *CFE* and on the circumference of circle *GHD* comprehends both arcs of the equal circles: arc *FC* and arc *GH* which is twice arc *FC*.

It is laid down that at some time upon the coincidence of the straight lines *ACD* and *DFG* the moving point *H* will be at *G*, which will then coincide with *A*; and *F* will be at *C*. Now, however, the centre *F* has moved towards the right along *CF*, and *H* has moved along the circumference to the left twice the distance *CF* [67ᵇ] or vice versa; accordingly *H* will be deflected along line *AB*; otherwise the part would be greater than the whole, as it is easy to see. But *H* has moved away from its first position along the length *AH* made by the bent line *DFH*, which is equal to *AD*; and *H* has moved for a distance by which the diameter *DFG* exceeds chord *DH*. And in this way *H* will be made to arrive at centre *D*, which will be the point of tangency of circle *DHG* with straight line *AB*, namely when *GD* is at right angles to *AB*; and then *H* will reach the other limit at *B*, and from that position it will move back again according to the same ratio.

Therefore it is clear that movement along a straight line is compounded of two circular movements which compete with one another in this way; and that a reciprocal and irregular movement is composed of regular movements; as was to be shown. Moreover it follows from this that the straight line *GH* will always be at right angles to *AB*; for lines *DH* and *HG*, being in a semicircle, will always comprehend a right angle. And accordingly

$$GH = {}^1/_2 \text{ ch. } 2 \, AG;$$

and

$$DH = {}^1/_2 \text{ ch. } 2 \, (90° - AG),$$

because circle *AGB* has twice the diameter of circle *HGD*.

5. A DEMONSTRATION OF THE IRREGULARITY OF THE EQUINOCTIAL PRECESSION AND THE OBLIQUITY

For this reason some call this movement of the circle a movement in width, *i.e.*, along the diameter. But they determine its periodicity and its regularity by means of the circumference, and its magnitude by means of the chords subtending. On that account it is easily shown that the movement appears irregular and faster at the centre and slower [68ᵃ] at the circumference.

For let there be the semicircle *ABC* with centre *D* and diameter *ADC*, and let it be bisected at point *B*. Now let equal arcs *AE* and *BF* be taken, and from points *F* and *E*

let *EG* and *FK* be drawn perpendicular to *ADC*. Therefore, since

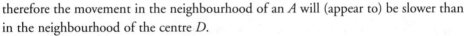

$$2 DK = 2 \text{ ch. } BF,$$

and

$$2 EG = 2 \text{ ch. } AE,$$

then

$$DK = EG.$$

But by Euclid's *Elements*, III, 7,

$$AG < GE;$$

hence

$$AG < DK.$$

But *GA* and *KD* will take up equal time because

$$\text{arc } AE = \text{arc } BF;$$

therefore the movement in the neighbourhood of an *A* will (appear to) be slower than in the neighbourhood of the centre *D*.

Having shown this, let us take *L* as the centre of the Earth, so that the straight line *DL* is perpendicular to plane *ABC* of the semicircle; and with *L* as centre and through points *A* and *C* let arc *AMC* of a circle be described; and let *LDM* be drawn in a straight line. Accordingly the pole of the semicircle *ABC* will be at *M*, and *ADC* will be the common section of the circles. Let *LA* and *LC* be joined; and similarly *LK* and *LG* too. And let *LK* and *LG* extended in straight lines cut arc *AMC* at *N* and *O*. Therefore, since angle *LDK* is right, angle *LKD* is acute. Wherefore too the line *LK* is longer than *LD*, and all the more is side *LG* greater than side *LK*, and *LA* than *LG* in the obtuse triangles. Therefore the circle described with *L* as centre and *LK* as radius will fall beyond *LD*, but will cut *LG* and *LA*; let it be described, and let it be *PKRS*. And since

$$\text{trgl. } LDK < \text{sect. } LPK,$$

while

$$\text{trgl. } LGA > \text{sect. } LRS,$$

on that account

$$\text{trgl. } LDK : \text{sect. } LPK < \text{trgl. } LGA : \text{sect. } LRS.$$

Hence, alternately also,

$$\text{trgl. } LDK : \text{trgl. } LGA < \text{sect. } LPK : \text{sect. } LRS.$$

And by Euclid's *Elements*, VI, 1,

$$\text{trgl. } LDK : \text{trgl. } LGA = \text{base } DK : \text{base } AG.$$

But

$$\text{sect. } LPK : \text{sect. } LRS = \text{angle } DLK : \text{angle } RLS = \text{arc } MN : \text{arc } OA.$$

Therefore

$$\text{base } DK : \text{base } GA < \text{arc } MN : \text{arc } OA.$$

But we have already shown that

$$DK > GA.$$

All the more then

[68ᵇ] $MN > OA.$

And arcs MN and OA are understood as having been described during equal intervals of time by the poles of the earth in accordance with the equal arcs of anomaly AE and BF—as was to be shown. But since the difference between greatest and least obliquity is so slight as not to exceed $2/5°$, there will be no sensible difference between the curved line AMC and the straight line ADC; and so no error will arise if we work simply with line ADC and semicircle ABC.

Practically the same thing happens in the case of the other movement of the poles, which has to do with the equinoxes, since this movement does not ascend to the mean degree, as will be apparent below. Once more let there be the circle $ABCD$ through the poles of the ecliptic and the mean equator. We may call it the mean colure of Cancer. Let the semicircle of the ecliptic be DEB and the mean equator AEC; and let them cut one another at point E, where the mean equinox will be. Now let the pole of the equator be F, and let the great circle FEI be described through it. On that account it will be the colure of the mean or regular equinoxes.

Therefore for the sake of an easier demonstration let us separate the libration of the equinoxes from the obliquity of the ecliptic. On the colure EF let arc FG be taken,

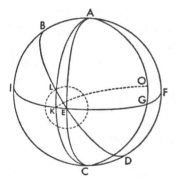

and through that distance let G the apparent pole of the equator be understood as removed from F the mean pole. And with G as a pole let $ALKC$ the semicircle of the apparent equator be described. It will cut the ecliptic at L. Therefore point L will be the apparent equinox; and its distance from the mean equinox will be measured by arc LE, which is produced by arc EK the equal of FG.

But with K as a pole we shall describe circle AGC; and let it be understood that the equatorial pole during the time in which the libration FG takes place does not remain the "true" pole at point G, but, driven by another libration or swinging movement, moves away in the direction of the oblique ecliptic through arc GO. Therefore while ecliptic BED abides, the "true" equator will be changed to the "apparent" in accordance with the transposition of the pole to O. And similarly the movement of intersection L the apparent equinox will be faster in the neighbourhood of the mean (equinox) E and very slow in the neighbourhood of the extreme equinoxes, more or less in proportion to the swinging movement of the poles which we have already demonstrated—as was worth the trouble of our attention.

6. On the Regular Movements of the Precession of the Equinoxes and of the Inclination of the Ecliptic

[69ª] Now every apparent irregular circular movement passes through four termini: there is the terminus where it appears slow and the terminus where it appears fast, as if at the extremes, and the terminus where it appears to have a mean velocity, as if at the means, since from the point which is the end of decrease in velocity and the beginning of increase it passes on to a mean velocity; and from the mean velocity it increases till it becomes fast; again after being fast it approaches a mean velocity, whence for the remainder of the cycle it changes to its former slowness.

By means of that it is possible to know in what part of the circle the position of the non-uniform movement, or irregularity, is at a given time; and too by means of these indications the restitution of the irregularity is perceptible.[1] Accordingly in a quadrisected circle let A be the position of greatest slowness, B the mean of increasing velocity, C the end of the increase and the beginning of the decrease, and D the mean of decreasing velocity. Therefore, since, as was reported above, the apparent movement of the precession of the equinoxes was found to be rather slow in the time between Timochares and Ptolemy in comparison with the other times, and because for a while it appeared regular and uniform, as is shown by the observations of Aristyllus, Hipparchus, Agrippa, and Menelaus which were made at the middle of that time; it argues that the apparent movement of the equinoxes had been simply at its slowest and at the middle of this time was at the beginning of increase in velocity, when the cessation of the decrease conjoined to the beginning of the increase by reason of mutual compensation made the movement seem uniform for the time being. Accordingly Timochares' observation must be placed in the fourth quadrant of the circle along DA; but Ptolemy's falls in the first quadrant along AB. Again, because in the second interval, the one between Ptolemy and al-Battani the Harranite the movement is found to have been faster than in the third, it is clear that the point of highest velocity was passed during the second interval of time, and the irregularity had already reached the third quadrant of the circle along CD, and that from the third interval down to us the restoration of the irregularity was nearly completed and has nearly returned to its starting-point with Timochares. For if we divide the cycle of 1819 years between Timochares and us into the customary 360 parts, we shall have proportionally an arc of $85\frac{1}{2}°$ for 432 years; $146°51'$ for 742 years; and the remaining arc of $127°39'$ for the remaining 645 years.

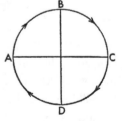

[1]This circle is not the circle of libration, of course, but a circle which typifies the cycle in velocity which results from compounding the libration with the regular movement of precession of the equinoxes.

We have made these determinations by an obvious and simple inference; [69ᵇ] but upon working them over with stricter calculations, to see how exactly they agree with observations, we find that the movement of irregularity during the 1819 Egyptian years has already exceeded its complete revolution by 21°24', and that the time of the period comprehends only 1717 Egyptian years. In accordance with this ratio it is discovered that the first segment of the circle has 90°35'; the second, 155°34'; while the third period of 543 years will comprehend the remaining 113°51' of the circle. Now that these things have been set up in this way, the mean movement of the precession of the equinoxes is also disclosed; and it is 23°57' for these same 1717 years, at the end of which the whole movement of irregularity was restored to its pristine status, since for the 1819 years we have an apparent movement of approximately 25°1'.

But in 102 years after Timochares—the difference between the 1717 years and the 1819 years—the apparent movement must have been about 1°4', because it is probable that the apparent movement was then a little greater than to need only 1° per 100 years, since it was decreasing without yet having reached the end of the decrease. Hence, if we subtract 1°4' from 25°1' there will remain, as we said, for the 1717 Egyptian years a mean and regular movement of 23°57', now corrected according to the apparent and irregular movement: hence the complete and regular revolution of the precession of the equinoxes arises in 25,816 years, during which time 15 cycles of irregularity are traversed and approximately $1/28$ cycle over and above.

Moreover, the movement of obliquity, whose restoration we said was twice as slow as the irregular precession of the equinoxes, accords with this ratio. For the fact that Ptolemy reports that during the 400 years between the time of Aristarchus of Samos and his own the obliquity of 23°51'20" had hardly changed at all indicates that the obliquity was then close to the limit of greatest obliquity, namely when the precession of the equinoxes was in its slowest motion. But now also when the same restoration of slowness is approaching, the inclination of the axis is not at its greatest but is near its least. In the middle of the time in between, al-Battani the Harranite, as was said, found that the inclination was 23°35'; 190 years after him Arzachel the Spaniard, 23°34'; and similarly 230 years later Prophatius the Jew found it approximately 2' less. Finally as regards our own times, we in 30 years of frequent observation found it approximately 23°28²/₅'—from which George Peurbach and John of Monteregium, [70ᵃ] our nearest predecessors, differ slightly. Here again it is perfectly obvious that for the 900 years after Ptolemy the change in obliquity was greater than for any other interval of time.

Therefore since we already have the cycle of irregularity of precession in 1717 years, we shall also have half the period of obliquity in that time, and in 3434 years its complete restoration. Wherefore if we divide the 360° by the number of the 3434 years or 180° by 1717, the quotient will be the annual movement of simple anomaly of

6'17"24'"9"". These in turn distributed through the 365 days give a daily movement of 1"2'"2"".

Similarly, when the mean precession of equinoxes has been distributed through the 1717 years—and there was 23°57'—an annual movement of 50"12'"5"" will be the result; and this distributed through the 365 days will give a daily movement of 8'"15"".

But in order that the movements may be more in the open and may be found right at hand when there is need of them, we shall draw up their tables or canons by the continuous and equal addition of annual movement—60 parts always being carried over into the minutes or degrees, if the sum exceeds that—and for the sake of convenience we shall keep on adding until we reach the 60th year, since the same configuration of numbers returns every sixty years, only with the denominations of degrees and minutes moved up, so that what were formerly seconds become minutes and so on.[1] By this abridgement in the form of brief tables, it will be possible merely by a double entry to determine and infer the regular movements for the years in question among the 3600 years. This is also the case with the number of days.

Moreover, in our computations of the celestial movements we shall employ the Egyptian years, which alone among the legal years are found equal. For it is necessary for the measure to agree with the measured; but that is not the case with the years of the Romans, Greeks, and Persians, for intercalations are made not in any single way, but according to the will of the people. But the Egyptian year contains no ambiguity as regards the fixed number of 365 days, in which throughout twelve equal months— which they name in order by these names: Thoth, Phaophi, Athyr, Chiach, Tybi, Mechyr, Phamenoth, Pharmuthi, Pachon, Pauni, Epiphi, and Mesori—in which, I say, six periods of 60 days are comprehended evenly together with the five remaining days, which they call the intercalary days. For that reason Egyptian years are most convenient for calculating regular movements. Any other years are easily reducible to them by resolving the days.

---

[1] That is to say, the same configurations of numbers return in multiples of sixty years, because the cycle of movement is divided according to the sexagesimal system—jut as it would return in multiples of ten years if the circle were divided according to the decimal system.

REGULAR MOVEMENT OF THE PRECESSION OF THE EQUINOXES IN YEARS AND PERIODS OF SIXTY YEARS

Egyptian Years	Longitude					*Position of the Birth of Christ—5°32'*	Egyptian Years	Longitude				
	60°	°	'	"	'''			60°	°	'	"	'''
1	0	0	0	50	12		31	0	0	25	56	14
2	0	0	1	40	24		32	0	0	26	46	26
3	0	0	2	30	36		33	0	0	27	36	38
4	0	0	3	20	48		34	0	0	28	26	50
5	0	0	4	11	0		35	0	0	29	17	2
6	0	0	5	1	12		36	0	0	30	7	15
7	0	0	5	51	24		37	0	0	30	57	27
8	0	0	6	41	36		38	0	0	31	47	38
9	0	0	7	31	48		39	0	0	32	37	51
10	0	0	8	22	0		40	0	0	33	28	3
11	0	0	9	12	12		41	0	0	34	18	15
12	0	0	10	2	25		42	0	0	35	8	27
13	0	0	10	52	37		43	0	0	35	58	39
14	0	0	11	42	49		44	0	0	36	48	51
15	0	0	12	33	1		45	0	0	37	39	3
16	0	0	13	23	13		46	0	0	38	29	15
17	0	0	14	13	25		47	0	0	39	19	27
18	0	0	15	3	37		48	0	0	40	9	40
19	0	0	15	53	49		49	0	0	40	59	52
20	0	0	16	44	1		50	0	0	41	50	4
21	0	0	17	34	13		51	0	0	42	40	16
22	0	0	18	24	25		52	0	0	43	30	28
23	0	0	19	14	37		53	0	0	44	20	40
24	0	0	20	4	50		54	0	0	45	10	52
25	0	0	20	55	2		55	0	0	46	1	4
26	0	0	21	45	14		56	0	0	46	51	16
27	0	0	22	35	26		57	0	0	47	41	28
28	0	0	23	25	38		58	0	0	48	31	40
29	0	0	24	15	50		59	0	0	49	21	52
30	0	0	25	6	2		60	0	0	50	12	5

REGULAR MOVEMENT OF THE PRECESSION OF THE EQUINOXES IN YEARS AND PERIODS OF SIXTY YEARS

Days	Longitude					*Position of the Birth of Christ—5°32'*	Days	Longitude				
	60°	°	'	"	'''			60°	°	'	"	'''
1	0	0	0	0	8		31	0	0	0	4	15
2	0	0	0	0	16		32	0	0	0	4	24
3	0	0	0	0	24		33	0	0	0	4	32
4	0	0	0	0	33		34	0	0	0	4	40
5	0	0	0	0	41		35	0	0	0	4	48
6	0	0	0	0	49		36	0	0	0	4	57
7	0	0	0	0	57		37	0	0	0	5	5
8	0	0	0	1	6		38	0	0	0	5	13
9	0	0	0	1	14		39	0	0	0	5	21
10	0	0	0	1	22		40	0	0	0	5	30
11	0	0	0	1	30		41	0	0	0	5	38
12	0	0	0	1	39		42	0	0	0	5	46
13	0	0	0	1	47		43	0	0	0	5	54
14	0	0	0	1	55		44	0	0	0	6	3
15	0	0	0	2	3		45	0	0	0	6	11
16	0	0	0	2	12		46	0	0	0	6	19
17	0	0	0	2	20		47	0	0	0	6	27
18	0	0	0	2	28		48	0	0	0	6	36
19	0	0	0	2	36		49	0	0	0	6	44
20	0	0	0	2	45		50	0	0	0	6	52
21	0	0	0	2	53		51	0	0	0	7	0
22	0	0	0	3	1		52	0	0	0	7	9
23	0	0	0	3	9		53	0	0	0	7	17
24	0	0	0	3	18		54	0	0	0	7	25
25	0	0	0	3	26		55	0	0	0	7	33
26	0	0	0	3	34		56	0	0	0	7	42
27	0	0	0	3	42		57	0	0	0	7	50
28	0	0	0	3	51		58	0	0	0	7	58
29	0	0	0	3	59		59	0	0	0	8	6
30	0	0	0	4	7		60	0	0	0	8	15

MOVEMENT OF THE SIMPLE ANOMALY OF EQUINOXES IN YEARS AND PERIODS OF SIXTY YEARS

Egyptian Years	Longitude					Egyptian Years	Longitude			
	60° °	′	″	‴			60° °	′	″	‴
1	0 0	6	17	24		31	0 3	14	59	28
2	0 0	12	34	48		32	0 3	21	16	52
3	0 0	18	52	12		33	0 3	27	34	16
4	0 0	25	9	36		34	0 3	33	51	41
5	0 0	31	27	0		35	0 3	40	9	5
6	0 0	37	44	24		36	0 3	46	26	29
7	0 0	44	1	49		37	0 3	52	43	53
8	0 0	50	19	13		38	0 3	59	1	17
9	0 0	56	36	36		39	0 4	5	18	42
10	0 1	2	54	1		40	0 4	11	36	6
11	0 1	9	11	25		41	0 4	17	53	30
12	0 1	15	28	49		42	0 4	24	10	54
13	0 1	21	46	13		43	0 4	30	28	18
14	0 1	28	3	38		44	0 4	36	45	42
15	0 1	34	21	2		45	0 4	43	3	0
16	0 1	40	38	26		46	0 4	49	20	31
17	0 1	46	55	50		47	0 4	55	37	55
18	0 1	53	13	14		48	0 5	1	55	19
19	0 1	59	30	38		49	0 5	8	12	43
20	0 2	5	48	3		50	0 5	14	30	7
21	0 2	12	5	27		51	0 5	20	47	31
22	0 2	18	22	51		52	0 5	27	4	55
23	0 2	24	40	15		53	0 5	33	22	20
24	0 2	30	57	39		54	0 5	39	39	44
25	0 2	37	15	3		55	0 5	45	57	8
26	0 2	43	32	27		56	0 5	52	14	32
27	0 2	49	49	52		57	0 5	58	31	56
28	0 2	56	7	16		58	0 6	4	49	20
29	0 3	2	24	40		59	0 6	11	6	45
30	0 3	8	42	4		60	0 6	17	24	9

Position of the Birth of Christ–6°45′

MOVEMENT OF THE SIMPLE ANOMALY OF EQUINOXES IN YEARS AND PERIODS OF SIXTY YEARS

Days	Longitude					Days	Longitude			
	60°	°	′	″	‴		60°	°	′	″ ‴
1	0	0	0	1	2	31	0	0	0	32 3
2	0	0	0	2	4	32	0	0	0	33 5
3	0	0	0	3	6	33	0	0	0	34 7
4	0	0	0	4	8	34	0	0	0	35 9
5	0	0	0	5	10	35	0	0	0	36 11
6	0	0	0	6	12	36	0	0	0	37 13
7	0	0	0	7	14	37	0	0	0	38 15
8	0	0	0	8	16	38	0	0	0	39 17
9	0	0	0	9	18	39	0	0	0	40 19
10	0	0	0	10	20	40	0	0	0	41 21
11	0	0	0	11	22	41	0	0	0	42 23
12	0	0	0	12	24	42	0	0	0	43 25
13	0	0	0	13	26	43	0	0	0	44 27
14	0	0	0	14	28	44	0	0	0	45 29
15	0	0	0	15	30	45	0	0	0	46 31
16	0	0	0	16	32	46	0	0	0	47 33
17	0	0	0	17	34	47	0	0	0	48 35
18	0	0	0	18	36	48	0	0	0	49 37
19	0	0	0	19	38	49	0	0	0	50 39
20	0	0	0	20	40	50	0	0	0	51 41
21	0	0	0	21	42	51	0	0	0	52 43
22	0	0	0	22	44	52	0	0	0	53 45
23	0	0	0	23	46	53	0	0	0	54 47
24	0	0	0	24	48	54	0	0	0	55 49
25	0	0	0	25	50	55	0	0	0	56 51
26	0	0	0	26	52	56	0	0	0	57 53
27	0	0	0	27	54	57	0	0	0	58 55
28	0	0	0	28	56	58	0	0	0	59 57
29	0	0	0	29	58	59	0	0	1	0 59
30	0	0	0	31	1	60	0	0	1	2 2

Position of the Birth of Christ–6°45′

7. WHAT THE GREATEST DIFFERENCE IS BETWEEN THE REGULAR AND THE APPARENT PRECESSION OF THE EQUINOXES

[72ᵇ] Now that the mean movements have been set out in this way, we must inquire what the greatest difference is between the regular and the apparent movement of the equinoxes, or what the diameter of the small circle is, through which the movement of anomaly turns.[1] For when this is known, it will be easy to discern various other differences in the movements. As was written above, between the observation of Timochares, which came first, and that of Ptolemy in the second year of the reign of Antoninus Pius, there were 432 years; and during that time the mean movement was 6° and the apparent 4°20'. So the difference between them is 1°40'. And the movement of double[2] anomaly was 90°35'. Moreover, it seems that at the middle of this period of time or around there the apparent movement reached its peak of greatest slowness. At that time the (position of the) apparent movement necessarily agreed with the mean movement, and the true equinox and the mean equinox occurred at the same section of the circles.[3] Wherefore if we make a distribution of the movement and the time into two equal parts, there will be in each part as differences between the irregular and the regular movement $^{10}/_{12}°$, which the circle of anomaly comprehends on either side beneath an arc of $45°17^{1}/_{2}'$. But since all these differences are very small and do not amount to $1^{1}/_{2}°$ on the ecliptic, and the straight lines are almost equal to the arcs subtended by them, and there is scarcely any diversity found in the third-minutes: we who are staying within the minutes will make no error if we employ straight lines instead of arcs.

[73ᵃ] Let *ABC* be a part of the ecliptic and on it let the mean equinox be *B*. And with *B* as pole let there be described the semicircle *ADC*, and let it cut the ecliptic at points *A* and *C*. Moreover let *DB* be drawn from the pole of the ecliptic, it will bisect the semicircle at *D*; and let *D* be understood to be limit of greatest slowness and beginning of the increase.[4] In the quadrant *AD* let

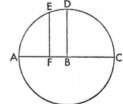

$$\text{arc } DE = 45°17^{1}/_{2}';$$

and through point *E* from the pole of the ecliptic, let fall *EF*; and let

$$BF = 50'.$$

Our problem is to find out from this what the whole *BFA* is.

---

[1] *i.e.*, what the diameter of the small circle is, along which the libration takes place back and forth.

[2] The anomaly of precession is called the "double" anomaly because it completes two cycles for one cycle of the anomaly of obliquity.

[3] As Copernicus showed in Chapter 4, the movement of the libration, considered above, appears fastest around the centre of the circle. Hence the apparent movement itself will appear slowest when the fastest movement of libration is in opposition to the mean movement with which it is compounded. And the fastest libration is in opposition to the mean movement when the apparent equinox is swinging eastward and is in the neighbourhood of the centre of the circle or the mean equinox.

[4] Thus, circle *ADC* is the circle of libration transferred from the pole of the ecliptic to around the equinox—as in the last diagram in Chapter 5.

Accordingly it is clear that

$$2\ BF = \text{ch. } 2\ DE.$$

But

$$FB : AFB = 7107 : 10,000 = 50' : 70'.$$

Hence

$$AB = 1°10',$$

and that is the greatest difference between the mean and the apparent movement of the equinoxes, which we were seeking; and the greatest polar deflexion of 28' follows upon it.

[72^b] For with this set-up let ABC be the arc of the ecliptic, BDE the mean equatorial arc, and B the mean section of the apparent equinoxes, either Aries or Libra, and through the poles of DBE let fall BF. Now along arc ABC on both sides let

$$\text{arc } BI = \text{arc } BK = 1°10';$$

hence, by addition,

$$\text{arc } IBK = 2°20'.$$

Moreover, let there be drawn at right angles to FB extended to FBH the two arcs IG and HK of the apparent equators. Now I say "at right angles," [73^a] though the poles of IG and IK are usually outside of circle BF, since the movement of obliquity gets mixed in, as was seen in the hypothesis, but on account of the distance being very slight—for at its greatest it does not exceed 90°/350—we employ these angles as angles which are right to sense-perception. For no great error will appear on that account. Therefore in triangle IBG

$$\text{angle } IBG = 66°20',$$

since its complement, as being the angle of mean obliquity of the ecliptic,

$$\text{angle } DBA = 23°40'.$$

And

$$\text{angle } BGI = 90°.$$

Moreover,

$$\text{angle BIG} \doteq \text{angle IBD},$$

because they are alternate angles. And

$$\text{side } IB = 70'.$$

Therefore too

$$\text{arc } BG = 28',$$

and that is the distance between the poles of the mean and the apparent equator.

Similarly in triangle BHK,

$$\text{angle } BHK = \text{angle } IGB$$

and

angle *HBK* = angle *IBG*,

and

side *BK* = side *BI*.

Moreover,

BH = *BG* = 28'.

For

GB : *IB* = *BH* : *BK*;

and the movements will be of the same ratio in the poles as in the intersections.

8. ON THE PARTICULAR DIFFERENCES IN THE MOVEMENTS AND THE TABLE OF THEM

[73^b] Therefore since

arc *AB* = 70',

and since arc *AB* does not appear to differ from the chord subtending it lengthwise, it will not be difficult to exhibit certain other differences between the mean and the apparent movements. The Greeks call the differences προσθαφαιρέις, or "additosubtractions," and later writers "aequationes," by the subtraction or addition of which the apparent movements are made to harmonize (with the mean movements). We shall employ the Greek word as being more fitting. Therefore if

arc *ED* = 3°,

then in accordance with the ratio of *AB* to the chord *BF*,

arc *BF* = 4',

which is the additosubtraction. And if

ED = 6°,

then

arc *BF* = 7';

and if

ED = 9°,

then

BF = 11',

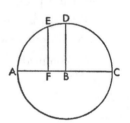

and so on.

We think we should use a similar ratio in the case of the change of obliquity also, where, as we said, a difference of 24' has been found between the greatest and the least obliquity. These 24' subtend a semicircle of simple anomaly every 1717 years, and the mean differences subtending a quadrant of a circle will be 12', where the pole of the small circle of this anomaly will be at an obliquity of 23°40'.

And in this way, as we said, we shall extract the remaining parts of difference approximately in proportion to the aforesaid as in the subjoined table. And if through

these demonstrations the apparent movements can be compounded by various modes, nevertheless that mode is better whereby all the particular additosubtractions may be taken separately, that the calculus of their movements may be easier to understand and may agree better with the explanations of what has been demonstrated.

Accordingly we have drawn up a table of sixty rows, increasing by 3°'s. For in this way it will not be spread over too much space, and it will not seem to be compressed into too little—as we shall do in the case of the similar remaining tables. The table will have only four main columns, the first two of which will contain the degrees of both semicircles; and we call them the common numbers, because the obliquity of the circle of signs is taken from the simple number, and twice the number applies to the additosubtractions of the movement of the equinoxes; and the numbers have their commencement at the beginning of the increase [74ª] (in velocity).[1] In the third column will be placed the additosubtractions of the equinoxes corresponding to the single 3°'s; and they are to be added to, or subtracted from, the mean movement— which we measure from the head of Aries at the spring equinox. The subtractive additosubtractions correspond to the numbers in the first semicircle of the anomaly or the first column; and the additive, to those in the second column and the second semicircle. Finally, in the last column are the minutes, which are called the differences in the proportions of obliquity and which go up to 60', since in place of the difference of 24' between greatest and least obliquity we are putting 60', and we adjust the proportional minutes to them in the same ratio in proportion to the other differences of obliquity. On that account we place 60' as corresponding to the beginning and end of the anomaly; but where the difference of obliquity is 22', as in the anomaly of 33°, we put 55' instead. In this way we put 50' in place of 20', as in the anomaly of 48°; and so on for the rest, as in the subjoined table.[2]

---

[1] *i.e.*, in the foregoing diagram, the first quadrant comprises the arc *DA*; and the fourth quadrant the arc *CD*.

[2] Thus, let line *FIG*, as in Chapter 3, represent the colors of the solstices. Point *F* is the limit of greatest obliquity of the ecliptic, point *G* that of the least; and thus the distance *FG* is 28'. The distance *KN* of the libration of the equinoxes is 2°20'. In the foregoing table the anomalies of precession and of obliquity we taken as starting at point *I* and proceeding along the route *INFKILGM*.

ADDITIONS-AND-SUBTRACTIONS OF EQUINOXES, OBLIQUITY OF THE ECLIPTIC

Common Numbers		Additions-and-Subtractions of Movement of Equinoxes		Proportional Minutes of Obliquity	Common Numbers		Additions-and-Subtractions of Movement of Equinoxes		Proportional Minutes of Obliquity
Deg.	Deg.	Deg.	Min.		Deg.	Deg.	Deg.	Min.	
3	357	0	4	60	93	267	1	10	28
6	354	0	7	60	96	264	1	10	27
9	351	0	11	60	99	261	1	9	25
12	348	0	14	59	102	258	1	9	24
15	345	0	18	59	105	255	1	8	22
18	342	0	21	59	108	252	1	7	21
21	339	0	25	58	111	249	1	5	19
24	336	0	28	57	114	246	1	4	18
27	333	0	32	56	117	243	1	2	16
30	330	0	35	56	120	240	1	1	15
33	327	0	38	55	123	237	0	59	14
36	324	0	41	54	126	234	0	56	12
39	321	0	44	53	129	231	0	54	11
42	318	0	47	52	132	228	0	52	10
45	315	0	49	51	135	225	0	49	9
48	312	0	52	50	138	222	0	47	8
51	309	0	54	49	141	219	0	44	7
54	306	0	56	48	144	216	0	41	6
57	303	0	9	46	147	213	0	38	5
60	300	1	1	45	150	210	0	35	4
63	297	1	2	44	153	207	0	32	3
66	294	1	4	42	156	204	0	28	3
69	291	1	5	41	159	201	0	25	2
72	288	1	7	39	162	198	0	21	1
75	285	1	8	38	165	195	0	18	1
78	282	1	9	36	168	192	0	14	1
81	279	1	9	35	171	189	0	11	0
84	276	1	10	33	174	186	0	7	0
87	273	1	10	32	177	183	0	4	0
90	270	1	10	30	180	180	0	0	0

9. On the Examination and Correction of That Which Was Set Forth Concerning the Precession of the Equinoxes

[75ª] But since by an inference we took the beginning of increase in the movement of anomaly as occurring in the middle of the time from the 36th year of the first period of Callippus to the 2nd year of Antoninus, and we take the order of the movement of anomaly from that beginning; it is still necessary for us to test whether we did that correctly and whether it agrees with the observations.

Let us consider again the three observations of the stars made by Timochares, Ptolemy, and al-Battani the Harranite: And it is clear that there were 432 Egyptian years in the first interval and 742 years in the second. The regular movement in the first span of time was 6°; the irregular movement 4°20'; and the movement of double anomaly 90°35', subtracting 1°40' from the regular movement. During the second interval the regular movement was 10°21', the irregular 11¹/₂°; and the movement of double anomaly was 155°34', adding 1°9' to the regular movement.

Now as before let the arc of the ecliptic be *ABC*, and let *B*—which is to be the mean spring equinox—be taken as a pole; let

arc *AB* = 1°10',

and let the small circle *ADCE* be described. But let the regular movement of *B* be understood as in the direction of *A*, *i.e.*, westward; and let *A* be the westward limit, where the irregular equinox is westernmost; and *C* the eastern limit, where the irregular equinox is easternmost. Furthermore, from the pole of the ecliptic drop *DBE* through point *B*. *DBE* together with the ecliptic will cut the small circle *ADCE* into four equal parts, since circles described through the poles of one another cut one another at right angles. However since the movement in the semicircle *ADC* is eastward, and the move-

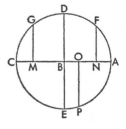

ment remaining in *CEA* is westward, the extreme slowness of the apparent equinox will be at *D* on account of its resistance to the forward movement of *B*; but there will be at *E* the greatest velocity for the movements moving forwards in the same direction.

Moreover on either side of *D* let

arc *FD* = arc *DG* = 45°17¹/₂'

Let *F* be the first terminus of the anomaly—the one observed by Timochares; *G* the second—the one observed by Ptolemy; and *P* the third—the one observed by al-Battani. And through these points let fall great circles *FN*, *GM*, and *OP* through the poles of the ecliptic; and they all [75ᵇ] appear in this very small circle rather much like straight lines. Therefore

arc *FDG* = 99°35',

where circle $ADCE = 360°$,

wherefrom

$$-add.\ MN = 1°40',$$
$$where\ ABC = 2°20'.$$

And

$$arc\ GCEP = 155°34',$$

wherefrom

$$+ add.\ MBO = 109'.$$

Accordingly, by subtraction,

$$arc\ PAF = 113°51'$$

wherefrom

$$+ add.\ ON = 31'$$
$$where\ AB = 70'.$$

But since by addition

$$arc\ DGCEP = 200°51'$$

and

$$EP = DGCEP - 180° = 200°51';$$

therefore by the table of chords in a circle, as if a straight line,

$$BO = 356,$$
$$where\ AB = 1,000.$$

But

$$BO \doteq 24',$$
$$where\ AB = 70';$$

and

$$MB = 50'.$$

Hence, by addition,

$$MBO = 74',$$

and,

$$NO = MN - MBO = 26'.$$

But, in the foregoing

$$MBO = 69',$$

and

$$NO = 31'.$$

Hence NO has a deficiency of 5'; and MO has an excess of 5'. Accordingly the circle $ADCE$ must be revolved, until there is compensation on both sides.

But this will take place if

$$arc\ DG = 42^1/_2°,$$

so that by subtraction,

arc $DF = 48°5'$.

For by this both errors will seem to be corrected and everything else will be all right, since—with the beginning at D the limit of greatest slowness—

arc $DGCEPAF = 311°55'$,

which is the movement of anomaly at the first terminus; at the second terminus

arc $DG = 42^1/_2°$;

and at the third terminus

arc $DGCEP = 198°4'$.

Now since

$AB = 70'$;

at the first terminus

+ add. $BN = 52'$,

by what has been shown; at the second terminus

−add. $MB = 47^1/_2'$;

and at the third terminus again

+ add. $BO\ 21'$.

Therefore during the first interval

arc $MN = 1°40'$,

and during the second interval

arc $MBO = 1°9'$;

and they agree exactly with the observations. Moreover, by those means a simple anomaly of $155°57^1/_2°$ is made evident at the first terminus; at the second terminus, one of $21°15'$; and at the third terminus, a simple anomaly of $99°2'$—as was to be shown.

10. What the Greatest Difference Is Between the Intersections of the Equator and the Ecliptic

[76a] In the same way we shall confirm what we expounded concerning the change in obliquity of the ecliptic and the equator and shall find it to be correct. For we have in Ptolemy for the second year of Antoninus Pius a corrected simple anomaly of $21^1/_4°$; and a greatest obliquity of $23°51'20''$ was found to go with it. From this position down to the observation made by us there have been 1387 years, during which the movement of simple anomaly is reckoned to be $144°04'$; and at this time an obliquity of approximately $23°28^2/_5'$ is found.

In connection with this let there be drawn again arc ABC of the ecliptic, or instead of it a straight line on account of the shortness of the arc; and above it the semicircle of simple anomaly around pole B, as before. And let A be the limit of greatest declination and C the limit of least declination; and it is the difference between them which we are examining. Therefore in the small circle let

$$\text{arc } AE = 21°15',$$

and,

$$\text{arc } ED = AD - AE = 68°45';$$

while, by calculation,

$$\text{arc } EDF = 144°4'$$

and,

$$\text{arc } DF = EDF - ED = 75°19'.$$

Drop perpendiculars *EG* and *EK* upon the diameter *ABC*.

Now on the great circle

$$\text{arc } GK = 22'56'',$$

on account of the difference in obliquities from Ptolemy to us. But on account of being like a straight line,

$$GB = \frac{1}{2} \text{ ch. 2 } ED = 932,$$

where *AC* the diameter's image = 2,000.

And also

$$KB = \frac{1}{2} \text{ ch. 2 } DF = 967.$$

And

$$GK = 1899,$$

where *AC* = 2,000.

But according as

$$GK = 22'56'',$$
$$AC \; 24',$$

the difference between greatest and least obliquity which we have been examining. So it is established that the greatest obliquity which occurred during the time between Timochares and Ptolemy was 23°52' and a least obliquity of 23°28' is now approaching. [76ᵇ] Hence also whatever mean inclinations of these circles there happen to be are discovered by the same mathematical reasoning we expounded in connection with the precession.

11. ON DETERMINING THE POSITIONS OF THE REGULAR MOVEMENTS OF THE EQUINOXES AND OF THE ANOMALY

With all that unfolded, it remains for us to determine the positions of the movements of the spring equinox. Some people call these positions "roots," because computations may be drawn from them for any given time. Ptolemy considered that the farthest point in history to which our knowledge of this question extends was the beginning of the reign of Nabonassar of the Chaldees, whom many people—taken in by the similarity of the names—have thought to be Nabuchodonoso, and whom the ratio of time and the computation of Ptolemy—which according to the historians falls in the

reign of Shalmaneser of the Chaldees—declare to have been much later. But we, seeking better known times, have judged it sufficient if we start with the first Olympiad, which—measured from the summer solstice—is found to have preceded Nabonassar by 28 years. At this time Canicula was beginning to rise for the Greeks, and the Olympic games' were being held, as Censorinus and other trustworthy authors report. Whence, according to the more exact reckoning of the times which is necessary in calculating the heavenly movements, there are 27 years and 247 days from the first Olympiad at noon on the first day of the month Hekatombaion by the Greek calendar to Nabonassar and noon of the first day of the month of Thoth by the Egyptian calendar.

From this to the death of Alexander there are 424 Egyptian years.

But from the decease of Alexander to the beginning of the years of Julius Caesar, there are 278 Egyptian years $118^1/_2$ days up to the midnight before the Kalends of January, which Julius Caesar took as the beginning of the year instituted by him; it was in his third year as Pontifex Maximus and during the consulship of Marcus Aemilius Lepidus that he instituted this year. And so the later years have been called Julian from the year as established by Julius Caesar.

And from the fourth consulship of Caesar to Octavius Augustus there are by the Roman calendar 18 years up to the Kalends of January, although it was on the 16th day before the Kalends of February that Augustus was proclaimed Emperor and son of the deified Julius Caesar by the Senate and the other citizens according to the decree of Numatius Plancus, in the seventh year of the consulship of Marcus Vipsanus and himself. But inasmuch as two years before this the Egyptians came into the power of the Romans after the fall of Antony [77ᵃ] and Cleopatra, the Egyptians reckon 15 years $246^1/_2$ days up to noon of the first day of the month Thoth, which by the Roman calendar was the 3rd day before the Kalends of September.

Accordingly from Augustus to the years of Christ, which begin similarly in January, there are 27 years by the Roman calendar but 29 years $130^1/_2$ days by the Egyptian.

From this to the 2nd year of Antoninus, when, as Claud Ptolemy says, the positions of the stars were observed by him, there are 138 Roman years 55 days. And these years add 34 days to the Egyptian reckoning.

Between the first Olympiad and that moment of time there have been altogether 913 years 101 days, for which time the regular precession of the equinoxes was 12°44', and the simple anomaly was 95°44'.

But in the second year of Antoninus, as has been narrated, the spring equinox was 6°40' to the west of the first of the stars which are in the head of Aries; and since there was a double anomaly of $42^1/_2$°, there was a subtractive difference of 48' between the regular and the apparent movement. And when this difference was restored to the 6°40' of the apparent movement, it made the mean position of the spring equinox to

be at 7°28'. If to this we add the 360° of a circle, and from the sum subtract 12°44', we shall have the mean position of the spring equinox at 354°44'—that is to say, the one which was then 5°16' east of the first star of Aries—for the first Olympiad which began on noon of the first day of the month Hekatombaion among the Athenians.

In the same way if from the 21°15' of simple anomaly 95°45' are subtracted, there will remain a position of simple anomaly of 285°30' for the same beginning of the Olympiads.

And again by a series of additions of movement made in accordance with the lengths of time—the 360° are not counted where there is an excess above that—we shall have the position or root of the regular movement at the death of Alexander as 1°2', and the position of the movement of simple anomaly as 332°52'; at the beginning of the years of Caesar a mean movement of 4°55' and an anomaly of 2°2'; and at the beginning of the years of Christ a position of the mean movement at 5°32' and an anomaly of 6°45'; and in this way we shall determine the roots of movements for whatever beginnings of time are chosen.

12. ON THE COMPUTATION OF THE PRECESSION OF THE SPRING EQUINOX AND THE OBLIQUITY

[77[b]] Therefore, whenever we wish to determine the position of the spring equinox, if the years from the assumed beginning to the given time are unequal, such as those of the Roman calendar, which we use commonly, we shall reduce them to equal or Egyptian years. For we do not use any other years than the Egyptian in calculating the regular movements, on account of the reason which we mentioned. In so far as the number of years is greater than a period of 60 years, we shall divide it into periods of 60 years; and when we enter the tables of movement through these 60-year periods, we shall pass over as supernumerary the first column appearing in the movements; and beginning with the second column, we shall determine the 60°'s, if there are any, together with the other degrees and minutes, which follow.[1] Next as the second entry and from the first column, as they are found, we shall take the 60°'s, degrees and minutes corresponding to the remaining years. We shall do the same thing in the case of days and the periods of 60 days, since we wish to connect the days with their regular movements according to the table of days and minutes, although in this case the minutes of days or even the days themselves are not wrongly neglected on account of the slowness of their movements, as within the daily movement there is a question only of seconds or third minutes. Therefore when we have made a sum of all these together with their root, by adding single numbers to single numbers within the same species—not counting six 60°'s, if they occur—we shall have the mean position of the spring equinox, its distance to the west of the first star of the Ram, or the distance of that star east of the equinox.

---

[1] That is to say, reading the column of degrees as 60°'s, the minutes as degrees, and so on.

In the same way we shall determine the anomaly too.

But we shall find placed in the last column of the table of additosubtractions and corresponding to the simple anomaly the proportional minutes: we shall set them aside and save them. Then, in the third column of the same table and corresponding to the double anomaly we shall find the additosubtraction, *i.e.*, the degrees and minutes by which the true movement differs from the mean. And if the double anomaly is less than a semicircle, we shall subtract the additosubtraction from the mean movement. But if, by having more than 180°, the double anomaly exceeds a semicircle, we shall add [78ª] the additosubtraction to the mean movement. And that which is thus the sum or remainder will comprehend the true and apparent precession of the spring equinox, or in turn the then angular elongation of the first star of Aries from the spring equinox. But if you seek the position of any other star, add its number as assigned in the catalogue of the stars.

But since things which have to do with the laboratory usually become clearer by means of some examples, let our problem be to find the true position of the spring equinox together with the obliquity of the ecliptic for the 16th day before the Kalends of May in the year of Our Lord 1525, and how great the angular distance of Spica in Virgo from the same equinox is. Therefore, it is clear that in the 1524 Roman years 106 days from the beginning of the years of Our Lord up to this time, there has been an intercalation of 381 days, *i.e.*, 1 year 16 days, which in terms of equal years make 1525 years 122 days: there are twenty-five periods of 60 years and 25 years over, and two periods of 60 days and 2 days over. But to the twenty-five periods of 60 years there correspond in the table of mean movement 20°55'2"; to the 25 years, 20'55"; to the two periods of 60 days, 16"; the remaining 2 days are in third minutes. All these together with their root—which was 5°32'—add up to 26°48', the mean precession of the spring equinox. Similarly, the movement of simple anomaly in the twenty-five periods of 60 years has been two 60°'s and 37°15'3"; in the 25 years, 2°37'15"; in the two periods of 60 days, 2'4"; and in the 2 days, 2". There also, together with the root—which is 6°45'—add up to 166°40', the simple anomaly. I shall save as corresponding to this anomaly the proportional minutes found in the last column of the table of the additosubtractions; for they will come into use in investigating the obliquity; and only 1' is found in this case. Next, as corresponding to the double anomaly of 333°20', I find 32' as the additosubtraction, which is additive because the double anomaly is greater than a semicircle. And when it is added to the mean movement, there comes about a true and apparent precession of the spring equinox of 27°21'. And lastly if to that we add the 170° which is the angular distance of Spica in Virgo from the first star in Aries, I shall have its position [78ᵇ] to the east of the spring equinox at 17°21' of Libra, it was found at approximately the time of our observation.

Now the obliquity of the ecliptic and its declination have the ratio that when there are 60 proportional minutes, the differences located in the table of declinations—I mean the differences at greatest and least obliquity—are added in their entirety to the degrees of the declinations. But in this case, 1' adds only 24" to the obliquity. Wherefore the declinations of the degrees of the ecliptic placed in the table remain as they are throughout this time on account of the least obliquity already approaching as, though at some other time they would be more obviously changeable. In this way, for example, if the simple anomaly were 99°, as it was in the 1380th Egyptian year of Our Lord, there are given by it 25 proportional minutes. But 24' is the difference between greatest and least obliquity and

$$60' : 24' = 25' : 10'.$$

And the addition of 10' to 28' gives an obliquity of 23°38' for that time. If then I should wish to know the declination of any degree on the ecliptic, for example, 3° of Taurus, which is 33° distant from the equinox, I find in the table 12°32', with a difference of 12'. But

$$60' : 25' = 12' : 5';$$

and the addition of 5' to 32' gives 12°37' for 33° of the ecliptic. We can do the same thing in the case of the angles of section of the ecliptic and the equator and the right ascensions—if it is not better to make use of the ratios of spherical triangles—except that it is always necessary to add in the case of the angles of section and to subtract in the case of the right ascensions, so that all things may be corrected to accord with their time.

13. ON THE MAGNITUDE AND DIFFERENCE OF THE SOLAR YEAR

But that this is the way it is with the precession of the equinoxes and solstices—the precession being due to the inclination of the Earth's axis, as we said—will also be confirmed by the annual movement of the centre of the Earth, as it affects the appearance of the sun, which we must now discuss. It follows of absolute necessity that the magnitude of the year, when referred to one of the equinoxes or solstices, is found unequal on account of the irregular change of the termini. For these things imply one another mutually.

Wherefore we must separate and distinguish [79ª] the seasonal year from the sidereal year. For we call that the natural year which times the four seasonal changes of the year for us; and that the sidereal, the revolutions of which are referred to some one of the fixed stars. Now the observations of the ancients make clear in many ways that the natural year, which is also called the revolving year, is unequal. For Callippus, Aristarchus of Samos, and Archimedes of Syracuse determined the year as containing a quarter of a day in addition to the 365 whole days—taking the beginning of the year at the summer solstice, after the Athenian manner.

But Claud Ptolemy, realizing that the apprehension of the solstices was detailed and difficult, did not rely upon their observations very much and went over rather to Hipparchus, who left after him records not so much of the solar solstices as of the equinoxes in Rhodes and reported that there was some small deficiency in the quarter-day; and afterwards Ptolemy decided that the deficiency was $1/300$th part of a day—as follows. For he took the autumn equinox observed as accurately as possible by Hipparchus at Alexandria in the 177th year after the death of Alexander the Great, at midnight of the third intercalary day by the Egyptian calendar—which the fourth intercalary day follows. Then Ptolemy compared it with the equinox as observed by himself at Alexandria in the third year of Antoninus, which was the 463rd year since the death of Alexander, on the 9th day of Athyr, the third month of the Egyptians, at approximately one hour after the rising of the sun. Accordingly between this observation and that of Hipparchus there were 285 Egyptian years 70 days $7^1/_5$ hours, though there should have been 71 days 6 hours, if the revolving year had a full quarter-day in addition to the whole days. Accordingly the 285 years were deficient by $19/_{20}$th of a day, whence it follows that a whole day fell out in 300 years. Moreover, he made a similar inference from the spring equinox. For what he recorded as reported by Hipparchus in the 178th year of Alexander on the 27th day of Mechir, the 6th month by the Egyptian calendar, at sunrise, he himself found in the 463rd year of Alexander on the 7th day of Pachon the 9th month by the Egyptian calendar at a little more than one hour after midday; and in the same way the 285 years were deficient by $19/_{20}$th of a day. By the aid of these indications Ptolemy determined the revolving year as having 365 days 14 min. (of a day) 48 sec. (or 5 hours 55 min. 12 sec.).[1]

Afterwards al-Battani in Arata, Syria, [79b] in the 1206th year after the death of Alexander observed the autumn equinox with no less diligence and found that it occurred after the 7th day of the month Pachon, approximately $7^2/_5$ hours later in the night, *i.e.*, $4^3/_5$ hours before the light of the 8th day. Accordingly, comparing his own observation with that of Ptolemy made in the third year of Antoninus one hour after sunrise at Alexandria—which is 10° to the west of Arata—he corrected Ptolemy's observation for the meridian at Arata and found the equinox must have occurred at $1^2/_3$ hours after sunrise. Accordingly in the period of 743 equal years the sum of the quarter-days amounted to 178 extra days and $17^3/_5$ hours instead of $185^1/_4$ days. Accordingly since there was deficiency of 7 days $2/_5$ hours, it was seen that the quarter-day was deficient by $1/_{106}$th of a day. Therefore in accordance with the number of years he subtracted one 743rd part of the 7 days $2/_5$ hours (which is 13 min. of an hour 36 sec.) from the quarter-day and recorded the natural year as containing 365 days 5 hours 46 min. 24 sec.

---

[1] *i.e.*, Ptolemy found $1/300$th part of a day lacking to a full quarter-day.

We too made observations of the autumn equinox at Frauenburg in the year of Our Lord 1515 on the 18th day before the Kalends of October: but according to the Egyptian calendar it was the 1840th year after the death of Alexander on the 6th day of the month Phaophi, half an hour after sunrise. But since Arata is about 25° to the east of this spot—which makes $1^2/_3$ hours—therefore during the time between our equinox and that of al-Battani there were 633 Egyptian years and 153 days $6^3/_4$ hours in place of 158 days 6 hours. But between the observation made by Ptolemy at Alexandria and the place and date of our observation, there were 1376 Egyptian years 332 days $^1/_2$ hour. For there is about an hour's difference between us and Alexandria. Therefore during the 633 years between al-Battani and us there have fallen out 4 days $23^3/_4$ hours, or 1 day per 128 years; but during the 1376 years after Ptolemy approximately 12 days, $i.e.$, 1 day per 115 years, and again the year has become unequal on both sides.

[80ª] Moreover, we determined the spring equinox, which occurred in the year of Our Lord 1516, $4^1/_3$ hours after midnight on the 5th day before the Ides of March; and since the spring equinox of Ptolemy—the meridian of Alexandria being corrected for ours—there have been 1376 Egyptian years 332 days $16^1/_3$ hours, in which it is apparent that the distances between the spring and autumn equinoxes are unequal. And so it is of much importance that the solar year as determined in this way should be equal. For the fact that at the autumnal equinoxes between Ptolemy and us, as was shown, in accordance with the equal distribution of years, the quarter-day should be deficient in the 115th part of a day makes the equinox come half a day later than al-Battani's. And the period from al-Battani to us, where the quarter-day must have been deficient in the 128th part of a day, is not consonant with Ptolemy, but the date precedes by a full day the equinox observed by him, and the equinox of Hipparchus by two days. Similarly the time of al-Battani's equinox as measured from Ptolemy's precedes the equinox of Hipparchus by 2 days.

Therefore the equality of the solar year is more correctly measured from the sphere of the fixed stars, as Thebites ben Chora was the first to find; and its magnitude is 365 days 15 minutes (of a day) 23 seconds (which are approximately 6 hours 9 min. 12 sec.) according to a probable argument taken from the fact that the year appears longer in the slower passage of the equinoxes and solstices than in the faster and in accordance with a fixed proportion; and that could not be the case, if there were no equality with reference to the sphere of the fixed stars. Wherefore Ptolemy is not to be listened to in that part where he thinks that it is absurd and irrelevant to measure the annual regularity of the sun through its restitutions with reference to some one of the fixed stars and that this is no more fitting than if someone were to take Jupiter or Saturn as the measure of that regularity. And so there is a ready reason why the seasonal year was longer before Ptolemy and after him became shorter, by a variable difference.

But also in the case of the astral or sidereal year an error can come about, but nevertheless a very slight one and far less than the one which we have already described; and it occurs because this same movement of the centre of the Earth around the sun appears irregular by reason of a twofold irregularity. [80b] The first and simple irregularity relates to the annual restoration; the other, which varies the first by changing it around, is perceptible not immediately but after a long stretch of time; and accordingly it is not simple or easy to know the ratio of the equality of the year. For if anyone wishes to determine it simply in relation to the fixed distance of some star having a known position—which can be done by using an astrolabe and with the help of the moon, in the way we described in the case of Basiliscus in Leo—he will not avoid error completely, unless at that time the sun on account of the movement of the Earth either has no additosubtraction or else obtains similar and equal additosubtractions at both termini. But unless this happens and unless there is some difference made manifest in accordance with the irregularity, an equal circuit will certainly not seem to have taken place in equal times. But if in both termini the total difference is subtracted or added proportionally, the job will be perfect. Furthermore, the apprehension of the difference requires a prior knowledge of the mean movement, which we are seeking for that reason; and we are versed in this business as in the Archimedean quadrature of the circle.

Nevertheless in order to arrive at the resolution of this knotty problem some time—we find four causes altogether for the appearance of irregularity. The *first* is the irregular precession of the equinoxes, which we have expounded; the *second* is that whereby the sun seems to traverse unequal arcs on the ecliptic, which occurs approximately annually; the *third* is the one which varies this irregularity which we call the second. There remains the *fourth*, which changes the highest and lowest apsides[1] of the centre of the Earth, as will appear below. Of all these only the second was marked by Ptolemy; and it by itself could not produce the inequality of the year but contributes to it through being involved in the others.

But for demonstrating the difference between the regular and the apparent movement of the sun the most accurate ratio of the year does not seem necessary; and it seems to be enough if in the demonstration we take as the magnitude of the year the $365^1/_4$ days, in which the movement of the first irregularity is completed, since that which stands out so little, when taken on the total circle, vanishes utterly when taken on a lesser magnitude. But on account of the excellence of the order and the facility in teaching we are here expounding first the regular movements of the annual revolution of the centre of the Earth by means of necessary demonstrations. And then we shall build up the regular movements together with the difference between the regular and the apparent movement.

---

[1] The apsides are the positions of greatest and least altitudinal distance of a planet from the sun.

14. On the Regular and Mean Movements of the Revolutions of the Centre of the Earth

[81ª] We find that the magnitude of the year and its equality is only 1 second 10 thirds greater than Thebith ben Chora recorded it to be, so that it contains 365 days 15 minutes 24 seconds 10 third-minutes—which amounts to 6 hours 9 minutes 40 seconds, and its fixed equality with reference to the sphere of the fixed stars is disclosed.

Therefore, when we have multiplied the 360° of a circle by 365 days and have divided the sum by 365 days 15 minutes 24 seconds 10 third-minutes, we shall have the movement of an Egyptian year as 359°44'49"7'"4"" and the movement during 60 similar years—not counting the total circles—will be 344°49'7"4'". Again, if we divide the annual movement by 365 days, we shall have a daily movement of 59'8"11'"22"".

But if we add to these the mean and regular precession of the equinoxes, we shall compose another regular annual movement in seasonal years of 359°45'39"19'"9"" and a daily movement 59'8"19'"37"". And for this reason we can call the former movement of the sun—to use the common expression—the regular and simple movement; and the latter, the regular and composite movement. And we shall set them out in tables, as we did with the precession of the equinoxes. The regular movement of the anomaly of the sun is added to them; but we shall speak of that later.

TABLE OF THE MEAN AND SIMPLE MOVEMENT OF THE SUN IN YEARS AND PERIODS OF SIXTY YEARS

Egyptian Years	Movement 60°	°	'	"	'''		Egyptian Years	Movement 60°	°	'	"	'''
1	5	59	44	49	7		31	5	52	9	22	39
2	5	59	29	38	14		32	5	51	54	11	46
3	5	59	14	27	21		33	5	51	39	0	53
4	5	58	59	16	28		34	5	51	23	50	0
5	5	58	44	5	35		35	5	51	8	39	7
6	5	58	28	54	42		36	5	50	53	28	14
7	5	58	13	43	49		37	5	50	38	17	21
8	5	57	58	32	56		38	5	50	23	6	28
9	5	57	43	22	3		39	5	50	7	55	35
10	5	57	28	11	10		40	5	49	52	44	42
11	5	57	13	0	17		41	5	49	37	33	49
12	5	56	57	49	24		42	5	49	22	22	56
13	5	56	42	38	31		43	5	49	7	12	3
14	5	56	27	27	38		44	5	48	52	1	10
15	5	56	12	16	46		45	5	48	36	50	18
16	5	55	57	5	53		46	5	48	21	39	25
17	5	55	41	55	0		47	5	48	6	28	32
18	5	55	26	44	7		48	5	47	51	17	39
19	5	55	11	33	14		49	5	47	36	6	46
20	5	54	56	22	21		50	5	47	20	55	53
21	5	54	41	11	28		51	5	47	5	45	0
22	5	54	26	0	35		52	5	46	50	34	7
23	5	54	10	49	42		53	5	46	35	23	14
24	5	53	55	38	49		54	5	46	20	12	21
25	5	53	40	27	56		55	5	46	5	1	28
26	5	53	25	17	3		56	5	45	49	50	35
27	5	53	10	6	10		57	5	45	34	39	42
28	5	52	54	55	17		58	5	45	19	28	49
29	5	52	39	44	24		59	5	45	4	17	56
30	5	52	24	33	32		60	5	44	49	7	4

Position of the Birth of Christ–27°31'

TABLE OF THE REGULAR AND SIMPLE MOVEMENT OF THE SUN IN DAYS AND PERIODS OF SIXTY DAYS

Days	Movement 60°	°	'	"	'''		Days	Movement 60°	°	'	"	'''
1	0	0	59	8	11		31	0	30	33	13	52
2	0	1	58	16	22		32	0	31	32	22	3
3	0	2	57	24	34		33	0	32	31	30	15
4	0	3	56	32	45		34	0	33	30	38	26
5	0	4	55	40	56		35	0	34	29	46	37
6	0	5	54	49	8		36	0	35	28	54	49
7	0	6	53	57	19		37	0	36	28	3	0
8	0	7	53	5	30		38	0	37	27	11	11
9	0	8	52	13	42		39	0	38	26	19	23
10	0	9	51	21	53		40	0	39	25	27	34
11	0	10	50	30	5		41	0	40	24	35	45
12	0	11	49	38	16		42	0	41	23	43	57
13	0	12	48	46	27		43	0	42	22	52	8
14	0	13	47	54	39		44	0	43	22	0	20
15	0	14	47	2	50		45	0	44	21	8	31
16	0	15	46	11	1		46	0	45	20	16	42
17	0	16	45	19	13		47	0	46	19	24	54
18	0	17	44	27	24		48	0	47	18	33	5
19	0	18	43	35	35		49	0	48	17	41	16
20	0	19	42	43	47		50	0	49	16	49	28
21	0	20	41	51	58		51	0	50	15	57	39
22	0	21	41	0	9		52	0	51	15	5	50
23	0	22	40	8	21		53	0	52	14	14	2
24	0	23	39	16	32		54	0	53	13	22	13
25	0	24	38	24	44		55	0	54	12	30	25
26	0	25	37	32	55		56	0	55	11	38	36
27	0	26	36	41	6		57	0	56	10	46	47
28	0	27	35	49	18		58	0	57	9	54	59
29	0	28	34	57	29		59	0	58	9	3	10
30	0	29	34	5	41		60	0	59	8	11	22

Position of the Birth of Christ–27°31'

TABLE OF THE REGULAR COMPOSITE MOVEMENT OF THE SUN IN YEARS AND PERIODS OF SIXTY YEARS

Egyptian Years	Movement					Egyptian Years	Movement				
	60°	°	'	"	'''		60°	°	'	"	'''
1	5	59	45	39	19	31	5	52	35	18	53
2	5	59	31	18	38	32	5	52	21	58	12
3	5	59	16	57	57	33	5	52	6	37	31
4	5	59	2	37	16	34	5	51	52	16	51
5	5	58	48	16	35	35	5	51	38	56	10
6	5	58	33	55	54	36	5	51	23	35	29
7	5	58	19	35	14	37	5	51	9	14	48
8	5	58	5	14	33	38	5	50	55	54	7
9	5	57	50	53	52	39	5	50	40	33	26
10	5	57	36	33	11	40	5	50	26	12	46
11	5	57	22	12	30	41	5	50	11	52	5
12	5	57	7	51	49	42	5	49	57	31	24
13	5	56	53	31	8	43	5	49	43	10	43
14	5	56	39	10	28	44	5	49	28	50	2
15	5	56	24	49	47	45	5	49	14	29	21
16	5	56	10	29	6	46	5	49	0	8	40
17	5	55	56	8	25	47	5	48	45	48	0
18	5	55	41	47	44	48	5	48	31	27	19
19	5	55	27	27	3	49	5	48	17	6	38
20	5	55	13	6	23	50	5	48	2	45	57
21	5	54	58	45	42	51	5	47	48	25	16
22	5	54	44	25	1	52	5	47	34	4	35
23	5	54	30	4	20	53	5	47	19	43	54
24	5	54	15	43	39	54	5	47	5	23	14
25	5	54	1	22	58	55	5	46	51	2	33
26	5	53	47	2	17	56	5	46	36	41	52
27	5	53	32	41	37	57	5	46	22	21	11
28	5	53	18	20	56	58	5	46	8	0	30
29	5	53	4	0	15	59	5	45	53	39	49
30	5	52	48	39	34	60	5	45	39	19	9

Position of the Birth of Christ—278°2'

TABLE OF THE REGULAR COMPOSITE MOVEMENT OF THE SUN

Egyptian Years	Movement					Egyptian Years	Movement				
	60°	°	'	"	'''		60°	°	'	"	'''
1	0	0	59	8	19	31	0	30	33	18	8
2	0	1	58	16	39	32	0	31	32	26	27
3	0	2	57	24	58	33	0	32	31	34	47
4	0	3	56	33	18	34	0	33	30	43	6
5	0	4	55	41	38	35	0	34	29	51	26
6	0	5	54	49	57	36	0	35	28	59	46
7	0	6	53	58	17	37	0	36	28	8	5
8	0	7	53	6	36	38	0	37	27	16	25
9	0	8	52	14	56	39	0	38	26	24	45
10	0	9	51	23	16	40	0	39	25	33	4
11	0	10	50	31	35	41	0	40	24	41	24
12	0	11	49	39	55	42	0	41	23	49	43
13	0	12	48	48	15	43	0	42	22	58	3
14	0	13	47	56	34	44	0	43	22	6	23
15	0	14	47	4	54	45	0	44	21	14	42
16	0	15	46	13	13	46	0	45	20	23	2
17	0	16	45	21	33	47	0	46	19	31	21
18	0	17	44	29	53	48	0	47	18	39	41
19	0	18	43	38	12	49	0	48	17	48	1
20	0	19	42	46	32	50	0	49	16	56	20
21	0	20	41	54	51	51	0	50	16	4	40
22	0	21	41	3	11	52	0	51	15	13	0
23	0	22	40	11	31	53	0	52	14	21	19
24	0	23	39	19	50	54	0	53	13	29	39
25	0	24	38	28	10	55	0	54	12	37	58
26	0	25	37	36	30	56	0	55	11	46	18
27	0	26	36	44	49	57	0	56	10	54	38
28	0	27	35	53	9	58	0	57	10	2	57
29	0	28	35	1	28	59	0	58	9	11	17
30	0	29	34	9	48	60	0	59	8	19	37

Position of the Birth of Christ—278°2'

169

Table of the Regular Movement of Anomaly[1] of the Sun in Years and Periods of Sixty Years

Egyptian Years	*Movement* 60°	°	′	″	‴		*Egyptian Years*	*Movement* 60°	°	′	″	‴
1	5	59	44	24	46	Position of the Birth of Christ–211°19′	31	5	51	56	48	11
2	5	59	28	49	33		32	5	51	41	12	58
3	5	59	13	14	20		33	5	51	25	37	45
4	5	58	57	39	7		34	5	51	10	2	32
5	5	58	42	3	54		35	5	50	54	27	19
6	5	58	26	28	41		36	5	50	38	52	6
7	5	58	10	53	27		37	5	50	23	16	52
8	5	57	55	18	14		38	5	50	7	41	39
9	5	57	39	43	1		39	5	49	52	6	26
10	5	57	24	7	48		40	5	49	36	31	13
11	5	57	8	32	35		41	5	49	20	56	0
12	5	56	52	57	22		42	5	49	5	20	47
13	5	56	37	22	8		43	5	48	49	45	33
14	5	56	21	46	55		44	5	48	34	10	20
15	5	56	6	11	42		45	5	48	18	35	7
16	5	55	50	36	29		46	5	48	2	59	54
17	5	55	35	1	16		47	5	47	47	24	41
18	5	55	19	26	3		48	5	47	31	49	28
19	5	55	3	50	49		49	5	47	16	14	14
20	5	54	48	15	36		50	5	47	0	39	1
21	5	54	32	40	23		51	5	46	45	3	48
22	5	54	17	5	10		52	5	46	29	28	35
23	5	54	1	29	57		53	5	46	13	53	22
24	5	53	45	54	44		54	5	45	58	18	9
25	5	53	30	19	30		55	5	45	42	42	55
26	5	53	14	44	17		56	5	45	26	7	42
27	5	52	59	9	4		57	5	45	11	32	29
28	5	52	43	33	51		58	5	44	55	57	16
29	5	52	27	58	38		59	5	44	40	22	3
30	5	52	12	23	25		60	5	44	24	46	50

Movement of Anomaly of the Sun in Days and Periods of Sixty Days

Egyptian Years	*Movement* 60°	°	′	″	‴		*Egyptian Years*	*Movement* 60°	°	′	″	‴
1	0	0	59	8	7	Position of the Birth of Christ–211°19′	31	0	30	33	11	48
2	0	1	58	16	14		32	0	31	32	19	55
3	0	2	57	24	22		33	0	32	31	28	3
4	0	3	56	32	29		34	0	33	30	36	10
5	0	4	55	40	36		35	0	34	29	44	17
6	0	5	54	48	44		36	0	35	28	52	25
7	0	6	53	56	51		37	0	36	28	0	32
8	0	7	53	4	58		38	0	37	27	8	39
9	0	8	52	13	6		39	0	38	26	16	47
10	0	9	51	21	13		40	0	39	25	24	54
11	0	10	50	29	21		41	0	40	24	33	2
12	0	11	49	37	28		42	0	41	23	41	8
13	0	12	48	45	35		43	0	42	22	49	16
14	0	13	47	53	43		44	0	43	21	57	24
15	0	14	47	1	50		45	0	44	21	5	31
16	0	15	46	9	57		46	0	45	20	13	38
17	0	16	45	18	5		47	0	46	19	21	46
18	0	17	44	26	12		48	0	47	18	29	53
19	0	18	43	34	19		49	0	48	17	38	0
20	0	19	42	42	27		50	0	49	16	46	8
21	0	20	41	50	34		51	0	50	15	54	15
22	0	21	40	58	42		52	0	51	15	2	23
23	0	22	40	6	49		53	0	52	14	10	30
24	0	23	39	14	56		54	0	53	13	18	37
25	0	24	38	23	4		55	0	54	12	26	45
26	0	25	37	31	11		56	0	55	11	34	52
27	0	26	36	39	18		57	0	56	10	42	59
28	0	27	35	47	26		58	0	57	9	51	7
29	0	28	34	55	33		59	0	58	8	59	14
30	0	29	34	3	41		60	0	59	8	7	22

[1]Any regular movement which, when compounded with a mean movement, causes an appearance of irregularity is called a movement of anomaly. In this case, the regular movement of anomaly is the movement of the eccentric circle, or the first epicycle.

15. THEOREMS PREREQUISITE FOR DEMONSTRATING THE APPARENT IRREGULARITY OF THE MOVEMENT OF THE SUN

[84ᵇ] But for the sake of making a better determination of the apparent irregular movement of the sun we shall now demonstrate more clearly that—with the sun occupying the central position in the world and with the Earth revolving around it as around a centre—if, as we said, there is a distance between the Earth and the sun which cannot be perceived in relation to the immensity of the sphere of the fixed stars; then the sun will be seen to have a regular motion with reference to any point or star in the same sphere (of the fixed stars).

For let *AB* be the greatest circle in the world in the plane of the ecliptic. Let *C* be

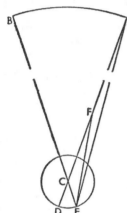

its centre, and let the sun be situated there. And in accordance with the distance *CD* between the sun and the Earth—in comparison with which the depth of the world is immense—let the circle *CDE*, in which the annual revolution of the centre of the Earth is located, be described in the same plane of the ecliptic: I say that the sun will seem to have a regular motion with reference to any point or star taken on circle *AB*.

Let some point be taken; and let it be *A*. And to *A* let the view of the sun from the Earth—which is at *D*—be extended as *DCA*. Now let the Earth be moved anywhere through arc *DE*; and let *AE* and *DE* be drawn from *E* the position of the Earth. Therefore the sun will now be seen from *E* at point *B*. And since *AC* is immense in comparison with *CD* or *CE* its equal, *AE* too will be immense in comparison with *CE*. For let any point *F* be taken on *AC*, and let *EF* be joined. Therefore since two straight lines from the termini *C* and *E* of the base fall outside triangle *EFC* on point *A*; by the converse of Euclid's *Elements*, I, 21,

angle *FAE* < angle *EFC*.

Wherefore the straight lines extended to immensity comprehend at last an angle *CAE* so acute that it is no longer perceptible; and

angle *CAE* = angle *BCA* − angle *AEC*.

Moreover, on account of the slightness of the difference between them angles *BCA* and *AEC* seem to be equal; and lines *AC* and *AE* seem to be parallel; and the sun seems to have [85ᵃ] a regular motion with reference to any point on the sphere of the fixed stars, just as if it were revolving around the centre *E*, as was to be shown.

But its irregular movement is demonstrated, because the movement of the centre of the Earth in its annual revolution is not absolutely around the centre of the sun.

That can be understood in two ways, either through an eccentric circle, *i.e.*, one whose centre is not the centre of the sun, or through an epicycle on a homocentric circle.

Now it is made clear through an eccentric in this way. For let *ABCD* be an eccentric circle in the plane of the ecliptic; and let its centre *E* be no very slight distance away from the centre of the sun or world. Let the centre of the world be *F*; and let *AEFD* be the diameter (of circle *ABCD*) passing through both centres. And let its apogee be at *A*—which is called the highest apsis by the Romans—the place farthest removed from the centre of the world, and *D* the perigee, which is nearest (to the centre of the world) and is the lowest apsis.

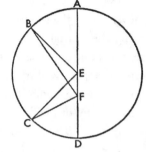

Therefore while the Earth is moved regularly in its orbital circle *ABCD* around its centre *E*, as has been already said, there will appear to be an irregular movement around *F*.

For let

arc *AB* = arc *CD*;

and let the straight lines *BE*, *CB*, *BF*, and *CF* be drawn.

Angle *AEB* = angle *CED*,

because angles *AEB* and *CED* are intercepting equal arcs around the centre *E*. But angle *CFD* is the angle of sight, and

ext. angle *CFD* > int. angle *CED*.

But

angle *AEB* = angle *CED*.

Hence

angle *CFD* > angle *AEB*.

But also

ext. angle *AEB* > int. angle *AFB*;

and hence by so much more

angle *CFD* > angle *AFB*.

But an equal time produces both angle *CFD* and angle *AFB* because

arc *AB* = arc *CD*.

Therefore the movement will appear regular from around *E* and irregular from around *F*.

Moreover, it is possible to see the same thing more simply, because arc *AB* is farther away from *F* than arc *CD* is. For by Euclid, III, 7, lines *AF* and *BF* by which arc *AB* is intercepted are longer than *CF* and *DF* by which arc *CD* is intercepted, and, as is shown in optics, equal magnitudes which are nearer appear greater than the ones farther away. And so what was proposed in the case of the eccentric circle is manifest.

The same thing will also be made clear by means of an epicycle on a homocentric circle. For let the centre of the homocentric circle *ABCD* and the centre of the world where the sun is be at *E*; and in the same plane let *A* be the centre of epicycle *FG*. And through both centres let the straight line *CEAF* be drawn. Let *F* be the apogee of the epicycle; and *I*, the perigee. Therefore it is clear that there is regularity [85ᵇ] in *A*, but apparent irregularity in epicycle *FG*. For if the movement of *A* takes place in the direction of *B*, *i.e.*, eastward, while the movement of the centre of the Earth is from its apogee *F* westward; then in the perigee—which is *I*—*E* will appear to be moving faster, because the two movements of *A* and *I* are in the same direction. But in the apogee, which is *F*, point *E* will seem to be moved more slowly, namely because it is moved only by the excelling movement out of two contraries; and the Earth situated at *G* is to the west of the regular movement but at *K* is to the east of it, and the distance of the Earth from the regular movement is measured by arcs *AK* and *AG*, in accordance with which the sun will seem to move irregularly.

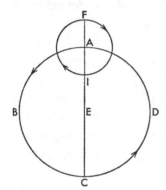

But whatever things take place by means of the epicycle can happen in the same way by means of the eccentric circle, which the transit of the planet in the epicycle describes equal to the homocentric circle and in the same plane; and the centre of the eccentric circle is at a distance from the centre of the homocentric circle equal to the radius of the epicycle. And all this occurs in three ways, since, if the epicycle on the homocentric circle and the planet on the epicycle made similar revolutions but with movements opposite to one another, the movement of the planet will trace a fixed eccentric circle, *i.e.*, one whose apogee and perigee possess unchanging locations.

In this way let *ABC* be the homocentric circle, and the centre of the world *D*, the diameter *ADC*. And let us put down that, when the epicycle is at *A*, the planet is in the apogee of the epicycle, which is at *G*, and its radius is in the straight line *DAG*. Now let arc *AB* of the homocentric circle be taken; and with centre *B* and radius equal to *AG*, let the epicycle *EF* be described, and let *BD* and *BE* be extended in a straight line; and let the arc *EF* be similar to arc *AB*, but let arc *EF* be taken in the opposite direction. And let the planet or Earth be in *F*. Let *BF* be joined. And on line *AD* let

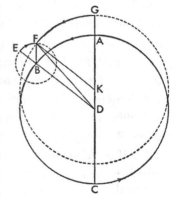

$$DK = BF.$$

Therefore, since

$$\text{angle } EBF = \text{angle } BDA,$$

and for those reasons

$$BF = DK$$

and BF is parallel to DK; and since, if straight lines are joined to equal and parallel straight lines, they are also equal and parallel by Euclid, I, 33; and since

$$DK = AG$$

[86ª] and AK is their common annex;

$$GAK = AKD$$

and therefore

$$GAK = KF.$$

Therefore the circle described with centre K and radius KAG will pass through F. By means of a movement compounded of AB and EF point F describes this circle as eccentric and equal to the homocentric and accordingly fixed too. For when the epicycle makes proportionally equal revolutions with the homocentric circle, the apsides of the eccentric circle so described necessarily remain in the same place.

But if the centre and the circumference of the epicycle make proportionately unequal revolutions, then the movement of the planet will not designate a fixed eccentric circle but one whose centre and apsides are carried westward or eastward, according as the movement of the planet is faster or slower than the centre of its epicycle. In this way if

$$\text{angle } EBF > \text{angle } BDA,$$

let

$$\text{angle } BDM = \text{angle } EBF.$$

It will similarly be shown that if on line DM there be taken DL equal to BF, the circle described with L as centre and with radius LMN equal to AD will pass through planet F. Hence it is clear that by the composite movement of the planet there is described arc NF of the eccentric circle, whose apogee meanwhile travels from point G westward along arc GN.

On the contrary, if the movement of the planet in the epicycle were slower, then the centre of the eccentric circle should follow it eastward, whither the centre of the epicycle is carried; that is if

$$\text{angle } EBF = \text{angle } BDM > \text{angle } BDA,$$

it is clear that what we have spoken of will take place.

From all that it is clear that the same irregularity of appearance is always produced

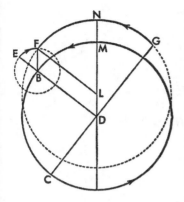

whether by means of an epicycle on a homocentric circle or by means of an eccentric circle equal to the homocentric; and they by no means differ from one another, provided the distance between the centres (of the homocentric and the eccentric) is equal to the radius of the epicycle. Accordingly it is not easy to determine which of them exists in the heavens. Indeed Ptolemy, where he understood simple irregularity and certain and immutable locations for the apsides—as he thought was the case in the sun—judged that the scheme of eccentricity was sufficient. But to the moon and to the five planets which wander in two or more different ways [86^b] he applied eccentric circles carrying epicycles.

From this moreover it is easily demonstrated that the greatest difference between regularity and appearance is seen at the time when the planet appears in the mean position between the highest and the lowest apsis in the case of the eccentric circle, but in the case of the epicycle at its point of contact (with the circle carrying the epicycle), as in Ptolemy.

In the case of the eccentric circle thus: For let there be the circle *ABCD* around the centre *E*; and *AEC* the diameter through *F* the sun, which is off centre. Now let line *BFD* be drawn through *F* at right angles to the diameter; and let *BE* and *ED* be joined. Let *A* be the apogee and *C* the perigee; and let *B* and *D* be the means appearing between them.

I say that no angle greater than angle *B* or *D* can be constructed with its vertex on the circumference and line *EF* as its base.

For let points *G* and *H* be taken on either side of *B*; and let *GD*, *GE*, and *GF* be joined, and also *HE*, *HF*, and *HD*. Since line *FG* is nearer the centre than line *DF*,

line *FG* > line *DF*.

And therefore

angle *GDF* > angle *DGF*.

But

angle *EDG* = angle *EGD*,

because sides *EG* and *ED* falling upon the base are equal.
And therefore

angle *EDF* > angle *EGF*.

But
$$\text{angle } EDF = \text{angle } EBF.$$
Similarly too
$$\text{line } DF > \text{line } FH;$$
and
$$\text{angle } FHD > \text{angle } FDH.$$
But
$$\text{angle } EHD = \text{angle } EDH,$$
because
$$\text{line } EH = \text{line } ED.$$
Therefore, by subtraction,
$$\text{angle } EDF > \text{angle } EHF.$$
But
$$\text{angle } EDF = \text{angle } EBF.$$
Therefore no angle greater than the angles at points B and D will ever be constructed with line EF as base. And so the greatest difference between regularity and appearance is found in the mean position between apogee and perigee.

16. ON THE APPARENT IRREGULARITY OF THE SUN

These things have been demonstrated generally; and they are applicable not only to the apparent movements of the sun but also to the irregularity of the other planets. Now we shall investigate what relates to the sun and the Earth, first in respect to what has been handed down to us by Ptolemy and the other ancients, and then in respect to what modern times and experience have taught us. Ptolemy found [87a] that $94^1/_2$ days were comprehended between the spring equinox and the summer solstice, and $92^1/_2$ between the solstice and the autumn equinox. Therefore in accordance with the ratio of time during the first interval there was a mean and regular movement of 93°9'; during the second interval, one of 91°11'.

Let $ABCD$ be the circle of the year as divided in this way; and let E be the centre. Let
$$\text{arc } AB = 93°9'$$
for the first period of time; and let
$$\text{arc } BC = 91°11'$$
for the second. Let the spring equinox be viewed from A; the summer solstice from B; the autumn equinox from C; and the remaining winter solstice from D. Let AC and BD be joined.

AC and BD cut one another at right angles at F, where we set up the sun.

Therefore since

$$\text{arc } ABC > 180°$$

and too

$$\text{arc } AB > \text{arc } BC;$$

Ptolemy understood from this that the centre of the circle was located between lines *BF* and *FA*, and the apogee between the spring equinox and the summer tropic of the sun. Now let *IEG*, which will cut *BFD* in *L*, be drawn through centre *E* parallel to *AFC*, and let *HEK*, which will cut *AF* in *M*, be drawn parallel to *BFD*. In this way there will be constructed the right parallelogram whose diameter *FE* extended in the straight line *FEN* will indicate the Earth's greatest distance in length from the sun and the position of the apogee in *N*.

Therefore since

$$\text{arc } ABC = 184°19',$$

and

$$\text{arc } AH = {}^1\!/_2 \text{ arc } ABC = 92°9{}^1\!/_2';$$
$$\text{arc } HB = \text{arc } AGB - \text{arc } AH = 59°.$$

Again

$$\text{arc } AG = \text{arc } AH - 90° = 2°10'.$$

Now

$$LF = {}^1\!/_2 \text{ ch. } 2 AG = 377,$$
$$\text{where radius} = 10{,}000.$$

But

$$EL = {}^1\!/_2 \text{ ch. } 2 BH = 172.$$

And, as two sides of triangle *ELF* are given,

$$\text{side } EF = 414 \ {}^1\!/_{24} \text{ radius } NE$$
$$\text{where radius } NE = 10{,}000.$$

But

$$EF : EL = NE : {}^1\!/_2 \text{ ch. } 2 NH.$$

Therefore

$$\text{arc } NH = 24{}^1\!/_2°.$$

And thus

$$\text{angle } NEH \text{ is given,}$$

and

$$\text{angle } NEH = \text{angle } LFE,$$

which is the angle of apparent movement. By such an interval therefore did the highest apsis before Ptolemy precede the summer solstice of the sun. But

$$\text{arc } IK - 90°,$$

and

[87^b] arc IC = arc AG

and

arc DK = arc HB.

Hence

arc CD = arc IK − (arcs IC + DK) = 86°51'

and

arc DA = arc CDA − arc CD = 88°49'.

But to the 86°51' there correspond 88$^1/_8$ days; and to the 88°49', 90 days and 3 hours—the eighth part of a day. During these periods the sun on account of the regular movement of the Earth seemed to cross from the autumn equinox to the winter solstice and for the remainder of the year to return from the winter solstice to the spring equinox. Indeed Ptolemy testifies that he found these things no different from what were reported by Hipparchus before him. Wherefore he judged that for the remainder of time the highest apsis would be 24$^1/_2$° before the summer tropic and that the eccentricity of—as I said—a 24th part of the radius would remain perpetually.

But now it is found that both of them have changed by a manifest difference. Al-Battani noted it as being 93 days 35 minutes (of a day) from the spring equinox to the summer solstice, and 186 days 37 minutes to the autumn, from which by Ptolemy's rule he elicited an eccentricity of not more than 346 parts whereof the radius has 10,000. Arzachel the Spaniard agrees with him in the ratio of eccentricity but reported an apogee 12°10' west of the solstice, and al-Battani viewed it as 7°43' west of the same solstice. By these tokens it has been grasped that there still remains another irregularity in the movement of the centre of the Earth, as has been attested by the observations of our time also. For during the ten and more years in which we applied our intelligence to investigating these things and especially in the year of Our Lord 1515, we found that there were 186 days 5$^1/_2$ minutes from the spring equinox to the autumnal. And so as not to deceive ourselves in determining the solstices—which some suspected had happened in the case of our predecessors—we took certain other positions of the sun into consideration in this business which were not difficult to observe even in comparison with the equinoxes, such as the mean positions in the signs of Taurus, Leo, Scorpio, and Aquarius. Therefore we found that there were 45 days 16 minutes from the autumn equinox to the middle point of Scorpio, and 178 days 53$^1/_2$ minutes to the spring equinox. Now the regular movement during the first interval was 44°37'; and during the second interval 176°19'.

[88^a] Now that these preparations have been made, let circle $ABCD$ be repeated; and let A be the point from which the sun was seen at the spring equinox; B the point at which the autumn equinox was viewed; and C the midpoint of Scorpio. Let AB and CD, which cut one another at F the centre of the sun, be joined; and let arc AC be subtended.

Therefore, since

$$\text{arc } CB = 44°37',$$
$$\text{angle } BAC = 44°37',$$
where 2 rt. angles = 360°.

And

$$\text{angle } BFC = 45°,$$
where 4 rt. angles = 360°;

and is the angle of apparent movement; but

$$\text{angle } BFC = 90°,$$
where 2 rt. angles = 60°.

Hence,

$$\text{angle } ACD = 45°23',$$

because

$$\text{arc } AD = 45°23'.$$

But

$$\text{arc } ACB = 176°19',$$

and

$$\text{arc } AC = \text{arc } ACB - \text{arc } BC = 131°42',$$

and

$$\text{arc } CAD = \text{arc } AC + \text{arc } AD = 177°5'.$$

Therefore, since

$$\text{arc } ACB < 180°,$$

and

$$\text{arc } CAD < 180°,$$

it is clear that the centre of the circle is located in the remainder BD. And let the centre be E. And through E let the diameter LEFG be drawn. Let L be the apogee and G the perigee. Let EK be erected perpendicular to CFD. But the chords subtending the given arcs are also given by the table:

$$AC = 182,494$$

and

$$CFD = 199,934,$$
where diameter = 200,000.

Accordingly, as triangle ACF has its angles given, the ratio of the sides will be given by the first rule for plane triangles.

$$CF = 97,697,$$

according as

$$AC = 182,494;$$

and for that reason

$$FK = \frac{1}{2} CD - CF = 2,000.$$

And since

$$180° - \text{arc } CAD = 2°55';$$

and since

$$EK = \frac{1}{2} \text{ ch. } 2°55' = 2,534;$$

then, in triangle EFK, as the two sides FK and KE comprehending the right angle have been given, the triangle will have its sides and angles given:

$$EF = 323,$$
$$\text{where } EL = 10,000;$$

and

$$\text{angle } EFK = 51\frac{2}{3}°$$
$$\text{where 4 rt. angles} = 360°.$$

Therefore, by addition,

$$\text{angle } AFL = 96\frac{2}{3}°$$

and, by subtraction,

$$\text{angle } BFL = 83\frac{1}{3}°.$$

But

$$EF1^{\text{P}}56',$$
$$\text{where } EL = 60^{\text{P}}.$$

This is the distance of the sun from the centre of the orbital circle: and it has now become approximately $\frac{1}{31}$st (of the radius of the orbital circle), [88^{b}] though to Ptolemy it seemed to he $\frac{1}{24}$th. And the apogee, which was at that time $24\frac{1}{2}°$ to the west of the summer solstice, is now $6\frac{2}{3}°$ to the east of it.

17. DEMONSTRATION OF THE FIRST AND ANNUAL IRREGULARITY OF THE SUN TOGETHER WITH ITS PARTICULAR DIFFERENCES

Therefore since many differences of the irregular movement of the sun are found, we judge that the difference which occurs annually and is more known than the rest should be deduced first.

Accordingly let circle ABC be constructed again, around centre E with diameter

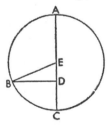

AEC; apogee at A, perigee at C; and the sun at D. Now it has been shown that the greatest difference between regular and apparent movement occurs at the position which with respect to the apparent movement is midway between the apsides. For that reason let BD be erected perpendicular to AEC, and let it cut the circumference in point B, and let BE be joined. Therefore, since

in right triangle *BDE* two sides have been given, namely *BE* which is the radius of the circle and *DE* the distance of the sun from the centre; the triangle will have its angles given. And angle *DBE* will be given, which is the difference between the angle *BEA* of regular movement and right angle *EDB* the angle of apparent movement.

But as *DE* is made greater or less, the whole species of the triangle changes. Thus, before Ptolemy

angle *B* = 2°23';

in the time of al-Battani and Arzachel

angle *B* = 1°59';

but at present

angle *B* = 1°51'.

And for Ptolemy

arc *AB* = 92°23',

which is intercepted by angle *AEB*, and

arc *BC* = 87°37'.

For al-Battani

arc *AB* = 91°59'

and

arc *BC* = 88°1'.

And at present

arc *AB* = 91°51'

and

arc *BC* = 88°9'.

Whence too the remaining differences are manifest. For let any other arc *AB* be taken, as in the following figure: and let angle *AEB* be given, and the interior angle *BED*, and the two sides *BE* and *ED*. By the calculus of plane triangles there will be given [89ª] angle *EBD*, the additosubtraction, the difference between the regular and the apparent movement. And it is necessary for these differences to change on account of the change of side *ED*, as has already been said.

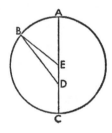

18. ON THE EXAMINATION OF THE REGULAR MOVEMENT IN LONGITUDE

These things have been set forth concerning the annual irregularity of the sun, but not by means of the simple difference so appearing but by means of the difference still mingled with that which the length of time has disclosed.

We shall distinguish them from one another later on. Meanwhile, the mean and regular movement of the centre of the Earth will be given in numbers which will be the more certain the more that movement is separated from any differences of irregularity and the more it extends in time. Now that will be established in this way.

We have taken that autumn equinox which was observed by Hipparchus at Alexandria in the 32nd year of the third period of Callippus—which, as was said above, was the 177th year after the death of Alexander—at midnight after the third intercalary day, which the fourth day followed. But according as Alexandria is approximately 1 hour to the east of Cracow in longitude, it was approximately 1 hour before midnight. Therefore according to the calculation handed on above the position of the autumn equinox in the sphere of the fixed stars was 176°10' from the head of Aries and that was the apparent position of the sun. It was $114^1/_2°$ distant from the highest apsis.

In accordance with this model let there be traced around centre D the circle ABC which the centre of the Earth describes. Let ADC be the diameter; and let the sun be situated on the diameter at point E; the apogee in A; and the perigee in C. But let B be the point where the sun appears in the autumn equinox, and let the straight lines BD and BE be joined.

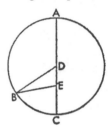

Since

$$\text{angle } DEB = 114^1/_2°,$$

and is seen to measure the distance of the sun from the apogee; and

$$\text{side } DE = 414,$$

$$\text{where } BD = 10,000;$$

therefore, by the fourth theorem on plane triangles, triangle BDE has its sides and angles given. And

$$\text{angle } BDE = \text{angle } BDA = \text{angle } BED = 2°10'.$$

[89b] But

$$\text{angle } BED = 114°30'.$$

Hence

$$\text{angle } BDA = 116°40';$$

and the mean or regular position of the sun is 178°20' from the head of the Ram in the sphere of the fixed stars.

With this we have compared the autumn equinox observed by us in Frauenburg under the same meridian of Cracow in the year of Our Lord 1515, on the 18th day before the Kalends of October, in the 1840th year since the death of Alexander, on the 6th day of Phaophi the second month by the Egyptian calendar, half an hour after sunrise. At this time the position of the autumn equinox by calculation and observation was 152°45' in the sphere of the fixed stars and was 83°29' distant from the highest apsis in accordance with the preceding demonstration.

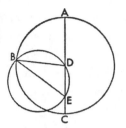

Now let

angle *BEA* = 83°20',

where 2 rt. angles = 180°;

and two sides of the triangle are given:

BD = 10,000

and

DE = 323.

By the fourth theorem on plane triangles

angle *DBE* 1°50'.

For, if a circle circumscribes triangle *BDE*, then, as on the circumference,

angle *BED* = 166°40',

where 2 rt. angles = 360°.

And

ch. *BD* = 19,864

where dmt. = 20,000.

And as

BD : *DE* is given,

ch. *DE* 640,

and

DE = ch. *DBE*

and, as on circumference,

angle *DBE* = 1°50';

but, as at centre,

angle *DBE* = 3°40'.

And this was the additosubtraction and difference between the regular and the apparent movement. And

angle *BDA* = angle *DBE* + angle *BED* = 1°50' + 83°20' = 85°10',

the distance of the regular movement from the apogee, and hence the mean position of the sun is 154°35' in the sphere of the fixed stars.

Therefore in the time between both observations there are 1662 Egyptian years 37 days 18 minutes (of a day) 45 seconds. And the mean and regular movement over and above the whole revolutions—of which there were 1660—is approximately 336°15', which is consonant with the number which we set out in the table of regular movements.

19. ON DETERMINING THE POSITIONS OF THE REGULAR MOVEMENT OF THE SUN AT THE BEGINNINGS (OF YEARS)

[90ª] Accordingly in the flow of time between the death of Alexander the Great and the observation made by Hipparchus there were 176 years 362 days $27^1/_2$ minutes,

in which the mean movement was 312°43', according to calculation. When these degrees are subtracted from the sum of the 178°20' of Hipparchus' observation and from the 360° of the circle, there will remain, for noon of the first day of Thoth the first month of the Egyptians at the beginning of the years named after the death of Alexander, a position of 225°37' beneath the meridian of Cracow and of Frauenburg, the place of our observation.

From this to the beginning of the Roman years of Julius Caesar in 278 years $118^1/_2$ days the mean movement is 46°27' over and above the complete revolutions. The addition of these degrees to the degrees of the position of Alexander gives 272°4' as Caesar's position at midnight before the Kalends of January, from which the Romans are accustomed to take the beginning of their years and days.

Then in 45 years 12 days, or in 323 years $130^1/_2$ days from the death of Alexander the Great, there arises the position of Christ at 272°31'.

And since Christ was born in the third year of the 194th Olympiad, the calculations which give 775 years and $12^1/_2$ days from the beginning of the year of the first Olympiad to midnight before the Kalends of January similarly give 96°16' as the position of the first Olympiad at noon of the first day of the month Hekatombaion, the anniversary of which day is now the Kalends of July according to the Roman calendar.

In this way the beginnings of the simple movement of the sun are determined with respect to the sphere of the fixed stars. Moreover, the positions of the composite movement are given by the addition of the precession of the equinoxes and similarly to the others: the Olympic position at 90°59'; the position of Alexander at 226°38'; that of Caesar at 276°59'; and that of Christ at 278°2'. All these things, as we said, are taken with respect to the Cracow meridian.

20. On the Second and Twofold Irregularity Which Occurs in the Case of the Sun on Account of the Change of the Apsides

[90^b] But there is now a greater difficulty in connexion with the inconstancy of the apsis of the sun, since, although Ptolemy thought it to be fixed, others have thought it to follow the movement of the starry sphere, according as they judged that the fixed stars moved too. Arzachel opined that this movement also was irregular, that is to say, as happening to retrograde—from the token that, although, as was said, al-Battani had found the apogee 7°44' to the west of the solstice (for previously during the 740 years after Ptolemy it had progressed approximately 17°), it seemed to Arzachel 193 years later to have retrograded approximately $4^1/_2$°. And accordingly he thought there was some other movement made by the centre of the annual orbital circle in a small circle, in accordance with which (movement) the apogee was deflected back and

forth and the centre of the circle (of the year) was at unequal distances from the centre of the world. That was a good enough device, but it was not accordingly accepted, because upon a universal comparison it is not consonant with the rest; that is to say, if the succession in the order of movement is considered: namely, that at some time before Ptolemy the movement came to a standstill, that during 740 years or thereabouts it traversed 17°, that in the 200 years thereafter it retrograded 4° or 5°, that in the time remaining down to us it progressed, and that no other retrogradation was perceived during the total time, and no more standstills, though they necessarily intervene in the case of contrary movements back and forth. And this can by no means be understood as occurring in uniform and circular movement. Wherefore it is believed by many that some error had crept into their observations. But each mathematician is alike in his care and industry, so that it is doubtful which one we should follow in preference to the other. At all events, I confess that nowhere is there greater difficulty than in determining the apogee of the sun, where we ratiocinate with very small and hardly perceptible magnitudes, since in the neighbourhood of the perigee and apogee (a movement of) 1° effects only a variation of approximately 2' in the additosubtraction, but in the neighbourhood of the mean apsides (a movement of) 1' effects 5° or 6° (in the additosubtraction); and so a slight [91ᵃ] error can propagate itself greatly. Hence in placing the apogee at $6^2/_3$° of Cancer, we were not content to rely upon the instruments of the horoscope, unless the eclipses of the sun and moon gave us more certainty, since if any error lay concealed in our observations, the eclipses would uncover it without fail. Therefore, in accordance with most likelihood, we can apply our intelligence to conceiving the movement as a whole: it is eastward, but irregular, since after that standstill between Hipparchus and Ptolemy the apogee has appeared to be in continuous, orderly, and increased progression down to our time, with the exception of the movement which occurred erroneously—it is believed—between al-Battani and Arzachel, as all the rest seems to be in harmony. For it seems to follow from the same ratio of circular movement that the additosubtraction (of the movement) of the sun similarly does not stop decreasing and that corrections are made for these two irregularities in conjunction with the first and simple anomaly of the obliquity of the ecliptic or something similar.

But in order for this to become more clear, let the circle AB around centre C be in the plane of the ecliptic. And let the diameter be ACB, and on ACB let D be the globe of the sun as it were at the centre of the world; and let another quite small circle EF be described around centre C in such a way as not to comprehend the sun. And let it be understood that the centre of the annual revolution of the Earth moves around this small circle with a rather slow progress. And since the small circle EF together with line AD has a rather slow movement eastward and the centre of the annual revolution has

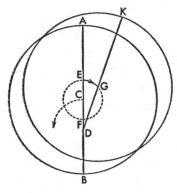

a rather slow movement westward along circle *EF*, sometimes the centre of the annual orbital circle will be found at its greatest distance which is *DE*, and sometimes at its least which is *DF*, and with a slower movement at the greatest distance and a faster movement at the least. And along the middle curves the small circle makes the distance between the centres increase and decrease with time, and it makes the highest apsis alternately precede and follow the apsis or apogee which is on line *ACD* as if in the middle position. In this way, if arc *EG* is taken and with *G* as centre a circle equal to *AB* is described, the then highest apsis will be on line *DGK* and *DG* will be a shorter distance than *DE*, by Euclid, III, 8.

And these things are demonstrated by means of a circle eccentric to an eccentric circle as above; and by means of the epicycle [91ᵇ] on the epicycle as follows: Let circle *AB* be homocentric with the world and with the sun, and let *ABC* be the diameter, whereon the highest apsis is. And with *A* as centre let the epicycle *DE* be described; and again with *D* as centre, the epicycle *FG*, whereon the Earth revolves. And all in the same plane of the ecliptic. Let the movement of the first epicycle be eastward and approximately annual; and that of the second too, *i.e.*, *D*, be similar but westward. And let both have proportionately equal revolutions with respect to line *AC*. Moreover, let the centre of the Earth moving westward from *F* add a little movement to *D*.

From this it is clear that when the Earth is at *F*, it will make the apogee of the sun to be farthest away; and when at *G* it will make the apogee to be nearest; but in the mean arcs of epicycle *FG*, it will make the apogee precede or follow, increased or decreased, greater or less; and hence it will make the movement appear irregular, as has been demonstrated before of the epicycle and the eccentric circle.

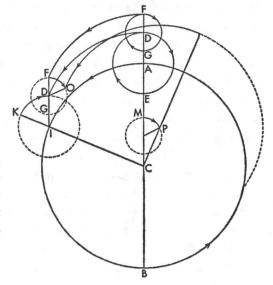

Now let arc *AI* be taken. And with point *I* as centre let the epicyclical epicycle be taken again. And let *CI* be joined and extended in the straight line *CIK*.

angle *KID* = angle *ACI*

on account of the revolutions being proportionately equal. Therefore, as we demonstrated above, point D will describe around centre L an eccentric circle equal to homocentric circle AB, and with an eccentricity CL equal to DI; and F will describe an eccentric circle having an eccentricity CLM equal to IDF; and G similarly an eccentric circle having an eccentricity CN equal to IG. Meanwhile, if the centre of the Earth has by now measured [92ª] any arc FO on its second epicycle, point O will not describe an eccentric circle whose centre is on line AC but one whose centre is on a line parallel (to DO), such as LP. But if OI and CP are joined,

$$OI = CP,$$

but

$$OI < IF$$

and

$$CP < CM.$$

And

$$\text{angle } DIO = \text{angle } LCP,$$

by Euclid, I, 8. And that is the interval whereby the apogee of the sun on line CP will be seen to precede A.

From this moreover it is clear that the same thing occurs through the eccentric circle having an epicycle, since with the eccentric circle alone pre-existing which epicycle D describes around centre L, the centre of the Earth revolves through arc FO in accordance with the aforesaid conditions, *i.e.,* (in a movement) less than the annual revolution. For it will describe, as before, another circle eccentric to the first, around centre P; and the same things will occur again. And since so many ways lead to the same number, I could not really say which one is right, except that the perpetual harmony of numbers and appearances compels us to believe that it is some one of them.

21. HOW GREAT THE SECOND DIFFERENCE IN THE IRREGULARITY OF THE SUN IS

Therefore, since it has already been seen that the second irregularity follows after that first and simple anomaly of the obliquity of the ecliptic or its similitude, we shall have its fixed differences, if some error on the part of past observers does not stand in the way. For according to calculation we have a simple anomaly of approximately 165°39' for the year of Our Lord 1515, and also its beginning by a calculation backwards to approximately 64 years before the birth of Christ, from which time to us there has been a passage of 1580 years. Now the greatest eccentricity of that beginning has been found by us to be 414, whereof the radius is 10,000. But the eccentricity of our time, as was shown, is 323.

Now let *AB* be a straight line, and on it let *B* be the sun and centre of the world. Let *AB* be the greatest eccentricity and *BD* the least. Let a small circle be described whose diameter is *AD*, and let

$$\text{arc } AC - 165°39',$$

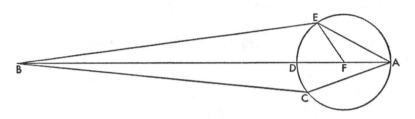

in proportion to the first simple anomaly. Since line *AB* has [92b] been found at the beginning of the simple anomaly, *i.e.*, at *A*, and

$$AB = 414,$$

and now

$$\text{line } BC = 323,$$

therefore we shall now have triangle *ABC* with sides *AB* and *BC* given; and also one angle *CAD* given, because *CD* the remaining arc of the semicircle is given, *i.e.*,

$$\text{arc } CD = 14°21'.$$

Therefore, by what we have shown concerning plane triangles, there are given the remaining side *AC* and angle *ABC*, the difference between the mean and the irregular movement of the apogee; and inasmuch as line *AC* subtends the given arc, diameter *AD* of circle *ACD* will also be given. For since

$$\text{angle } CAD = 14°21',$$
$$CB = 2496$$

where diameter of circle circumscribing triangle = 20,000,

and since

$$BC : AB \text{ is given,}$$
$$AB = 3225 = \text{ch. } ACB = \text{ch. } 341°26'.$$

Hence by subtraction

$$\text{angle } CBD = 4°13',$$
$$\text{where 2 rt. angles} = 360°.$$

And

ch. *CBD* = *AC* = 735.

Therefore

$$AC \ 95,$$
$$\text{where } AB = 414.$$

And according as *AC* subtends the given arc, it will have a ratio to *AD* as to a diameter. Therefore

$$AD = 96,$$

where *ADB* = 414;

and, by subtraction,

$$DB = 321,$$

and that is the distance of the least eccentricity. But, as on the circumference

angle *CBD* = 4°13',

and as at the centre

angle *CBD* = 2°6$^1/_2$',

which is the additosubtraction to be subtracted from the regular movement of *AB* around centre *B*. Now let there be drawn the straight line *BE* touching the circle at point *E*; and with centre *F* taken, let *EF* be joined. Therefore, since in right triangle *BEF*,

side *EF* = 48,

and

side *BDF* = 369,

EF = 1300,

where radius *FB* = 10,000.

And

$$EF = {}^1/_2 \text{ ch. } 2 \ EBF;$$

and

angle *EBF* = 7°28',

where 4 rt. angles = 360°;

and that is the greatest additosubtraction between the regular movement at *F* and the apparent at *E*.

Hence the remaining and particular differences can be discovered: for instance, if

angle *AFE* = 6°.

For we shall have the triangle with sides *EF* and *FB* and angle *EFB* given. Hence

angle *EBF* = 41',

which is the additosubtraction. [93ª] But if

angle *AFE* = 12°,

add. = 1°23'.

And if

angle *AFE* = 18°,

add. = 2°3';

and so for the rest in this way, as was said above in the case of the additosubtractions for the annual revolution.

22. How the Regular Movement of the Apogee of the Sun and the Irregular Movement Are Unfolded

Therefore, since the time in which the greatest eccentricity coincided with the beginning of the first and simple anomaly was the third year of the 178th Olympiad but the 259th year of Alexander the Great by the Egyptian calendar, and on that account the simultaneously true and mean position of the apogee was at $5\frac{1}{2}°$ of Gemini, *i.e.*, $65\frac{1}{2}°$ from the spring equinox; and since the precession of the equinoxes—the true at that time coinciding with the mean—was 4°38': the subtraction of 4°38' from $65\frac{1}{2}°$ leaves 60°52' from the head of Aries in the sphere of the fixed stars as the position of the apogee.

Again in the second year of the 573rd Olympiad and in the 1515th year of Our Lord, the position of the apogee was found at $6\frac{2}{3}°$ of Cancer. But by calculation the precession of the spring equinox was $27\frac{1}{4}°$; and the subtraction of $27\frac{1}{4}°$ from 96°40' leaves 69°25'. Now it was shown that with a first anomaly of 165°39' existing at that time there was an additosubtraction of 2°7', by which the true locus preceded the mean. Wherefore it was clear that the mean locus of the apogee of the sun was 71°32'.

Therefore during the middle 1580 Egyptian years the mean and regular movement of the apogee was 10°41'. And when we have divided that by the number of the years, we shall have an annual rate of 24"20"'14"".

23. On the Correction of the Anomaly of the Sun and the Determination of Its Prior Positions

[93^b] If we subtract these 24"20"'14"" from the simple annual movement, which was 359°44'49"7"'4"" there will remain an annual regular movement of anomaly of 359°44'24"46"'50"". Again, the distribution of 359°44'24"46"'50"" through the 365 days will give a daily rate of 59'8"7"'22"" in accord with what was set out above in the tables. Hence we shall have the positions at the established beginnings of years—starting at the 1st Olympiad. For it was shown that on the 18th day before the Kalends of October in the second year of the 573rd Olympiad at half an hour after sunrise the mean apogee of the sun was at 71°32', from which the sun had a distance of 82°58'. And from the first Olympiad there have been 2290 Egyptian years 281 days 46 minutes, during which the movement of anomaly—the whole cycles not being counted—was 42°33'. The subtraction of 42°33' from 82°58' leaves 40°25' as the position of anomaly for the first Olympiad.

And similarly, as above, the position for the Alexander years is 166°38'; for the Caesar years, 211°11'; and for the years of Our Lord, 211°19'.

24. Table of the Differences Between Regular and Apparent Movement

But in order that those things which we have shown concerning the (additive and subtractive) differences between the regular and apparent movements of the sun may be better fitted up for use, we shall also set out a table of them, having sixty rows and six orders of columns.

For the two first columns of both semicircles—that is to say, of the ascending and the descending semicircles—will contain numbers increasing by 3°'s, as above in the case of the movements of the equinoxes.

In the third column will be inscribed the degrees of additosubtraction arising from the movement [94a] or anomaly of the solar apogee; and this additosubtraction ascends to the height of approximately $7^1/_2°$, according as it fits each row of degrees.

The fourth place is given over to the proportional minutes, which go up to 60'; and they are reckoned according to the differences between the greater and the lesser additosubtractions arising from the simple anomaly. For since the greatest of these differences is 32', the sixtieth part will be 32". Therefore in accordance with the magnitude of the difference, which we derive from the eccentricity by the mode described above, we put down a number up to 60 to correspond to the single items in the column of the 3°'s.

In the fifth column the single additosubtractions arising from the annual and first anomaly are set up in accordance with the least distance of the sun from the centre.

In the sixth and final column, the differences between these additosubtractions and the additosubtractions which occur at greatest eccentricity.[1] The table is as follows:

---

[1]The movements on the homocentric circle, on the first epicycle, and on the second epicycle we proportionately equal. Hence, from the first two columns of the table are to be taken the movement on the second epicycle, or arc KJ; and from the third column, the additosubtraction to be applied to the annual anomaly or movement of the first epicycle; this additosubtraction, angle KFJ, corrects the mean anomaly from H to I. (Proportional minutes corresponding to arc KJ are to be saved.) Then from the fifth column is to be taken the additosubtraction GEI, corresponding to angle GFI. But since the true position of the sun, is not at I but at J, the additosubtraction most be corrected for the difference between angle FEI and angle FIJ. The proportional minutes which have been saved enable one to adjust the final difference, angle IEJ, according as chord FJ varies in length between FL and FK: that is to say, the change in eccentricity according to the movement around circle CO may be considered as it were a variation in the length of the radius of the corrected epicycle HK.

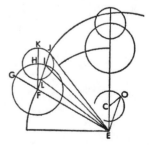

TABLE OF THE ADDITIONS-AND-SUBTRACTIONS OF THE MOVEMENT OF THE SUN

Common Numbers		Additions-and-subtractions arising from movement of the centre		Proportional minutes	Additions-and-subtractions arising from eccentric orbital circle or first epicycle		Differences	Common Numbers		Additions-and-subtractions arising from movement of the centre		Proportional minutes	Additions-and-subtractions arising from eccentric orbital circle or first epicycle		Differences
Deg.	Deg.	Deg.	Min.		Deg.	Min.	Min.	Deg.	Deg.	Deg.	Min.		Deg.	Min.	Min.
3	357	0	21	60	0	6	1	93	267	7	24	30	1	50	32
6	354	0	41	60	0	11	3	96	264	7	24	29	1	50	33
9	351	1	2	60	0	17	4	99	261	7	24	27	1	50	32
12	348	1	23	60	0	22	6	102	258	7	23	26	1	49	32
15	345	1	44	60	0	27	7	105	255	7	21	24	1	48	31
18	342	2	3	59	0	33	9	108	252	7	18	23	1	47	31
21	339	2	24	59	0	38	11	111	249	7	13	21	1	45	31
24	336	2	44	59	0	43	13	114	246	7	6	20	1	43	30
27	333	3	4	58	0	48	14	117	243	6	58	18	1	40	30
30	330	3	23	57	0	53	16	120	240	6	49	16	1	38	29
33	327	3	41	57	0	58	17	123	237	6	37	15	1	35	28
36	324	4	0	56	1	3	18	126	234	6	25	14	1	32	27
39	321	4	18	55	1	7	20	129	231	6	14	12	1	29	25
42	318	4	35	54	1	12	21	132	228	6	50	11	1	25	24
45	315	4	51	53	1	16	22	135	225	5	44	10	1	21	23
48	312	5	6	51	1	20	23	138	222	5	28	9	1	17	22
51	309	5	20	50	1	24	24	141	219	5	19	7	1	12	21
54	306	5	34	49	1	28	25	144	216	4	51	6	1	7	20
57	303	5	47	47	1	31	27	147	213	4	30	5	1	3	18
60	300	6	3	46	1	34	28	150	210	4	9	4	0	58	17
63	297	6	12	44	1	37	29	153	207	3	46	3	0	53	14
66	294	6	27	42	1	39	29	156	204	3	23	3	0	47	13
69	291	6	33	41	1	42	30	159	201	3	1	2	0	42	12
72	288	6	42	40	1	44	30	162	198	2	37	1	0	36	10
75	285	6	51	39	1	46	30	165	195	2	12	1	0	30	9
78	282	6	58	38	1	48	31	168	192	1	47	1	0	24	7
81	279	7	5	36	1	49	31	171	189	1	21	0	0	18	5
84	276	7	11	35	1	49	31	174	186	0	54	0	0	12	4
87	273	7	16	33	1	50	31	177	183	0	27	0	0	6	2
90	270	7	21	32	1	51	32	180	180	0	0	0	0	0	0

25. ON THE CALCULATION OF THE APPARENT MOVEMENT OF THE SUN

[95ᵇ] From that, I think, it is now sufficiently clear how the apparent position of the sun is calculated for any given time. For we must seek the true position of the spring equinox for that time or its precession together with its first and simple anomaly, as we have set forth above, and then the mean simple movement of the centre of the Earth—or you may call it the movement of the sun—and the annual anomaly, by means of the tables of regular movements; and they are added to their established beginnings. Accordingly you will take the number of the first simple anomaly found in the first or second column of the preceding table; and in the third column[1] you will find the corresponding additosubtraction for correcting the annual anomaly, and in the following column the proportional minutes; save the proportional minutes. Now add the additosubtraction to the annual anomaly, if the first (and simple anomaly) or its number contained in the first column—is less than a semicircle; otherwise subtract. For the remainder or aggregate will be the corrected anomaly of the sun; now by means of this take the additosubtraction arising from the annual (eccentric) orbital circle (or first epicycle)—which is found in the fifth column—and the difference in the following column. If this difference, when adjusted to the proportional minutes you have saved, amounts to something, it is always added to this additosubtraction, and the additosubtraction thus becomes corrected and is subtracted from the mean position of the sun, if the number of the annual anomaly is found in the first column or is less than a semicircle, but it is added, if the annual anomaly is greater or is found in one of the other columns of numbers. For that which in this way becomes the remainder or aggregate will determine the true position of the sun as measured from the head of the constellation of Aries, and if finally the true precession of the spring equinox is added to this (position of the sun), it will straightway show the distance of the sun from the equinox in degrees of the ecliptic among the twelve signs.

But if you wish to do that in another way, take the regular composite movement instead of the simple, and do the other things we spoke of, except that instead of the precession of the equinox, you add or subtract merely its additosubtraction, as the case demands. And so the rational explanation of the appearance of the sun by means of the mobility of the Earth is consonant with ancient and modern findings; and it is all the more [96ᵃ] presumed to hold for the future.

But furthermore, we are not ignorant of the fact that, if anyone thought that the centre of the annual revolutions were fixed as the centre of the world but that the sun moved in accordance with two movements similar and equal to those which we

---

[1] *i.e.*, since the movements on the first epicycle and on the second epicycle are proportionately equal to one another.

demonstrated in the case of the centre of the eccentric circle, everything will be manifest which was manifest before—the same numbers and the same demonstrations—since nothing else is changed in them except their situation, especially those which have to do with the sun. For then the movement of the centre of the Earth round the centre of the world would be absolute and simple, as the other two movements would be attributed to the sun itself. And on that account there will still remain some doubt as to which of these centres is the centre of the world, as we said ambiguously in the beginning that the centre of the world was at the sun or around the sun. But we shall say more about this question in our explanation of the five wandering stars; and we shall decide the issue to the extent that we are able, holding it enough, if we apply to the apparent movement of the sun calculations which have certitude and are not misleading.

26. ON THE NYXΘHMEPON, *i.e.*, THE DIFFERENCE OF THE NATURAL DAY

In connection with the sun there still remains something to be said about the inequality of the natural day. This time is comprehended by the space of twenty-four hours, which up to now we have used as the common and certain measure of the celestial movements. But some, like the Chaldees and the ancient Jews, define such a day as the time between two sunrises; others, like the Athenians, as that between two sunsets; or like the Romans, from midnight to midnight; or like the Egyptians, from noon to noon. Now it is clear that during this time the revolution proper to the terrestrial globe is completed together with that which is added by the annual revolution in accordance with the apparent movement of the sun.[1] The apparent irregular course of the sun in especial shows that this addition is unequal, as does the fact that the natural day takes place with respect to the poles of the equator, but the year with respect to the ecliptic. Wherefore that apparent time cannot be the common and certain measure of movement, since day does not accord with day in every respect; and so it was necessary to choose among them some mean and equal day, by which it would be possible [96ᵇ]

[1]In Ptolemy the daily revolution and the annual movement were in opposite directions, and thus the solar day was slightly longer than the sidereal day. Here the daily revolution of the Earth and its annual movement are both of them in the same direction, *i.e.*, eastward, and the solar day remains longer than the sidereal day on account of the third movement of the Earth, *i.e.*, the declination of the pole of the Earth, which is approximately equal to the annual revolution but in the opposite direction.

Let *A* be the sun, *CF* and *DEF* the Earth with centre *B* and *G*. And let *FBC* and *FGD* be the same meridian line. Let the centre of the Earth move from *B* to *G* during the space of 24 equatorial hours. As the movement of declination keeps the axis of the Earth parallel to itself, so too the meridian line *FBC* or *FGD* will be parallel to itself at the end of one daily revolution, but it will not be one with *GEA*, the line from the centre of the Earth to the centre of the sun, until the Earth has further revolved through arc *DE*. That is to say, the solar day is equal to the 360° of sidereal day *DEFD* plus arc *DE*.

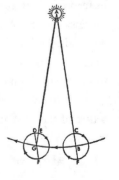

to measure regularity of movement without trouble. Therefore since in the circle of the total year there are 365 revolutions around the poles of the Earth, to which there accretes approximately one whole supernumerary revolution on account of the daily addition made by the apparent progress of the sun: consequently one 365th part of that would fill out the natural day upon an equal basis.

Wherefore we must define and separate the equal day from the apparent and irregular. Accordingly we call that the equal day which comprehends the whole revolution of the equator and over and above that the portion which the sun is seen to traverse with regular movement during that time; but the unequal and apparent day that which comprehends the 360 "times"[1] of one revolution of the equator and in addition that which ascends in the horizon or meridian together with the apparent progress of the sun. Although the difference between these days is very slight and not immediately perceptible, nevertheless it becomes evident after the passage of a certain number of days.

There are two causes for this: the irregularity of the apparent movement of the sun and the unequal ascension of the oblique ecliptic. The first cause, which exists by reason of the irregular apparent movement of the sun, has already been explained, since in the case of the semicircle in which the highest apsis holds the midpoint there is a deficiency of $4^3/_4$ "times" with respect to the ecliptic, according to Ptolemy, and in the case of the other semicircle, in which the lowest apsis is, there is a similar excess of the same amount. Accordingly the total excess of one semicircle over the other was $9^1/_2$ "times."

But in the case of the other cause—which has to do with the rising and setting—the greatest difference occurs between the semicircles comprehending each solstice. This is the difference which exists between the shortest and the longest day and which is most variable, as being particular to each region. The difference which is measured from noon or midnight is comprehended by four termini everywhere, since from 16° of Taurus to 14° of Leo, 88° (of the ecliptic) cross the meridian together with approximately 93 "times"; and from 14° of Leo to 16° of Scorpio, 92° (of the ecliptic) and 87 "times" pass over the meridian, so that in the latter case there is a deficiency of 5 "times" and in the former case an excess of 5 "times." And so the sum of the days in the first segment exceeds those in the second by ten "times"—which make two thirds of one hour; and the same thing takes place conversely in the other semicircle within the remaining termini set diametrically opposite to these. Now the mathematicians chose [97ª] to take the natural day from noon or midnight rather than from sunrise or sunset. For the difference which is taken from the horizon is more manifold; for it extends to a certain number of hours, and moreover it is not everywhere the same but varies manifoldly according to the obliquity of the sphere. But the one which pertains to the meridian is everywhere the same and is more simple. Therefore the total difference, which is constituted by the aforesaid causes: the apparent

---

[1] The unit parts of the equator we called "times" instead of degrees.

irregular progress of the sun and the irregular passage over the meridian, in the time before Ptolemy, took its beginning of decrease at the midpoint of Aquarius and, increasing from the beginning of Scorpio, added up to $8^1/_3$ "times"; and now decreasing from 20° of Aquarius or thereabouts to 10° of Scorpio and increasing from 10° of Scorpio to 20° of Aquarius, it has contracted to 7 "times" 48'. For these things too are changed on account of the inconstancy of the perigee and the eccentricity with the passage of time. Finally, moreover, if the greatest difference in the precession of the equinoxes is taken into account, the total difference of the natural days can extend itself to above 10 "times" for a period of years. In this the third cause of the inequality of days was hidden up to now, because the revolution of the equator was found regular in respect to the mean and regular equinox but not in respect to the apparent equinoxes, which—as is clear enough—are not wholly regular. Therefore the doubling of the 10 "times" makes $1^1/_3$ hours, by which sometimes the longer days can exceed the shorter.

These things can perhaps be neglected this side of manifest error in connexion with the annual progress of the sun and rather slow movement of the fixed stars; but on account of the speed of the moon—by reason of which an inexactitude of $5/_6$° in the movement of the sun can cause error—they are by no means to be neglected. Accordingly, the method of reducing the irregular and apparent time—wherein all differences agree—to the equal time, is as follows.

For any period of time proposed there must be sought in each limit of the time—I mean in the beginning and the end—the mean position of the sun with respect to the mean equinox according to its regular movement which we called composite, and also the true apparent position with respect to the true equinox; and we must consider how many "times" the right ascensions [97b] at midday or midnight have amounted to, or how many "times" intervened between the first true position and the second true position. For if they are equal to the degrees between the two mean positions, then the apparent time assumed will be equal to the mean time. But if the "times" exceed, the excess should be added to the given time; and if they are deficient, the deficiency should be subtracted from the apparent time. For if we take the sums and remainders, we shall have the time reduced to equality by taking for one "time" four minutes of an hour or ten seconds of a minute of a day. But if the equal time is given, and you want to know how much apparent time corresponds to it, you will do the contrary.

Now for the first Olympiad we have the mean position of the sun at 90°59' in relation to the mean spring equinox, on noon of the first day of Hekatombaion, the first month by the Athenian calendar, and at 0°36' of Cancer in relation to the apparent equinox. But for the years of Our Lord we have the mean movement of the sun at 8°2' of Capricorn and the true movement at 8°48' of the same. Therefore 178 "times" 54' ascend in the right sphere from 0°36' of Cancer to 8°48' of Capricorn, and they exceed the distance of the mean positions by 1 "times" 51', which make 7 minutes of an hour. And so for the rest, by means of which the course of the moon can be examined most accurately: we shall speak of that in the following book.

BOOK FOUR

[98ª] Since in the preceding book, to the extent that our mediocrity was able, we explained the appearances due to the movement of the Earth around the sun, and we proposed by that same means to determine the movements of all the planets; the circular movement of the moon interrupts us now and does so of necessity because through her in particular, who shares in both night and day, the positions of the stars are apprehended and examined; then, because she alone of all the planets refers her revolutions however irregular directly to the centre of the earth and is most closely akin to the earth. And on that account, in so far as she is considered in herself, she does not indicate anything about the mobility of the Earth—except perhaps in the case of the daily movement; and for that reason the ancients believed that the Earth was the centre of the world and the centre common to all revolutions. In our explanation of the circular movement of the moon we do not differ from the ancients as regards the opinion that it takes place around the Earth. But we shall bring forward certain things which are different from what we received from our elders and are more consonant; by means of them we shall try to set up the movement of the moon with more certitude, in so far as that is possible.

1. The Hypotheses of the Circles of the Moon According to the Opinion of the Ancients

Accordingly the movement of the moon has the following property: it does not follow the ecliptic but follows an incline proper to itself, which bisects the ecliptic and is in turn bisected by it, and from this line of intersection the moon crosses over into both latitudes. These facts are as firmly established as the solstices in the annual movement of the sun. As the year belongs to the sun, so the month belongs to the moon. Now the middle positions at the sections are called (by some) ecliptic; by others, nodes—and the conjunctions and oppositions of the sun and moon occurring at those positions are called ecliptic. [98ᵇ] For there are not any other points common to both circles except these in which the eclipses of the sun and moon can take place. For in other places the divagation of the moon keeps the sun and moon from opposing one another with their lights; but, as they pass by, they do not block one another. Moreover, the orbital circle of the moon with its four "hinges" or cardinal points revolves obliquely around the centre of the Earth in a regular movement of approximately 3' per day, and it completes its revolution in 19 years. Accordingly the moon is perceived always to move eastward in this orbital circle and in its plane, but sometimes with least velocity and at other times with greatest velocity. For it is slower, the higher up it is; and faster, the nearer to Earth; and this fact can be apprehended more easily in the case of the moon than in that of any other planet on account of the nearness of the moon.

Accordingly the ancients understood that change in velocity to occur on account of an epicycle; in running around this epicycle the moon, when in the upper semicircle, subtracts from the regular movement, but when in the lower semicircle, it adds the same amount to it. Besides, it has been demonstrated that those things which take place through an epicycle can take place through an eccentric circle. But the ancients chose the epicycle because the moon seemed to admit to a twofold irregularity. For when it was at the highest or the lowest apsis of the epicycle, there was no apparent difference from regular movement. But around the point of contact of the epicycle and the greater circle there was a variable difference, for the difference was far greater when the half moon was waxing or waning than when there was a full moon; and this in a fixed and orderly succession. Wherefore they thought that the circle in which the epicycle moved was not homocentric with the Earth; but that there was an eccentric circle carrying an epicycle in which the moon was moved in accordance with the law that in all mean oppositions and conjunctions of the sun and moon the epicycle should be at the apogee of the eccentric circle but in the mean quadrants of the (synodic) circle[1] at the perigee of the eccentric circle. Therefore they imagined two equal and mutually opposing movements around the centre of the Earth—namely, that of the epicycle eastward and that of the centre of the eccentric circle and its apsides westward, with the line of the mean position of the sun always half-way between them. And in this way the epicycle traverses the eccentric circle twice a month.

And in order that these things may be brought before our eyes, let *ABCD* be the oblique lunar circle homocentric with the Earth. Let it be quadrisected by the diameters *AEC* and *BED*; and let *E* be the centre of the Earth. Now on line *AC* there will be the mean conjunction of the sun and moon and at the same position and time the apogee of the eccentric circle—whose centre is *F*—and the centre [99a] of the epicycle *MN*. Now let the apogee of the eccentric circle be moved as far westward as the epicycle eastward, and let them both move regularly around *E* in regular and monthly revolutions as measured by the mean conjunctions or oppositions of the sun. And let line *AEC* of the mean position of the sun be always half way between them; and furthermore let the moon move westward from the apogee of the

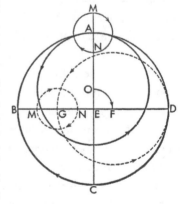

epicycle. For astronomers think that the appearances agree with this set-up. For since the epicycle in the time of half a month moves the distance of a semicircle away from the sun but completes a full revolution from the apogee of the eccentric circle; as a consequence,

at the midpoint of this time—when the moon is half full—the moon and the apogee are in opposition to one another along diameter *BD*; and the epicycle is at the perigee of the eccentric circle, as at point *G* where—having become nearer to the Earth—it makes greater differences of irregularity. For when equal magnitudes are set out at unequal intervals, the one which is nearer to the eye appears the greater. Accordingly the differences will be least when the epicycle is at *A*, but greatest when it is at *G*, since the diameter *MN* of the epicycle will be to line *AE* in its least ratio but will be to *GE* in a greater ratio than to all the other lines which are found in the rest of the positions, since *GE* is the shortest line and *AE* or its equal *DE* the longest of all those lines which can be extended from the centre of the Earth to the eccentric circle.

2. ON THE INADEQUACY OF THOSE ASSUMPTIONS

Our predecessors assumed that such a composition of circles was consonant with lunar appearances. But if we consider the thing itself rather carefully, we shall not find this hypothesis very fitting or adequate, as we can prove by reason and sense. For while they admit that the movement of the centre of the epicycle is regular around the centre of the Earth, they must also admit that the movement is irregular on its own eccentric circle which it describes. If—for example—it is assumed that

angle *AEB* = angle *AED* = 45°,

so that by addition

angle *BED* = 90°;

and if the centre of the epicycle is taken in *G* [99b] and *GF* is joined; it is clear that

angle *GFD* > angle *GEF*,

the exterior than the interior and opposite angle. Wherefore the dissimilar arcs *DAB* and *DG* are both described during one period of time, so that when

arc *DAB* = 90°;

arc *DG* > 9W,

and arc *DG* has been described by the centre of the epicycle during this same time. But it is clear at half moon

arc *DAB* = arc *DG* = 180° :

therefore the movement of the epicycle on the eccentric circle which it describes is not regular.

But if this is so, what shall we reply to the axiom: *The movement of the heavenly bodies is regular except for seeming irregular with respect to appearances;* if the apparent regular movement of the epicycle is really irregular and takes place utterly contrary to the principle set up and assumed? But if you say that the epicycle moves regularly

around the centre of the Earth and that that takes care sufficiently of the regularity, then what sort of regularity will that be which occurs in a circle foreign to the epicycle, in which its movement does not exist, and not in its own eccentric circle?

We also are amazed at the fact that they mean the regularity of the moon in its epicycle to be understood not in relation to the centre of the Earth, namely, in respect to line *EGM*, to which the regularity having to do with the centre of the epicycle should rightly be referred, but in relation to some other different point, which has the Earth midway between it and the centre of the eccentric circle, and that line *IGH* is, as it were, the index of the regularity of the moon in the epicycle. And that shows well enough that this movement is really irregular. For the appearances which in part follow upon this hypothesis force this admission. And now that the moon traverses its own epicycle irregularly, we may mark what the line of reasoning would be like if we should try to confirm the irregularity of apparent movement by means of real irregularities. For what else shall we be doing except giving a hold to those who detract from this art?

Furthermore, experience and sense-perception teach us that the parallaxes of the moon are not consonant with those which the ratio of the circles promises. For the parallaxes, which are called commutations, take place on account of the magnitude of the Earth being evident in the neighbourhood of the moon. For since the straight lines which are extended from the centre of the Earth and its surface do not appear parallel but [100ª] in accord with a manifest inclination cut one another in the body of the moon, they are necessarily able to make for irregularity in the apparent movement of the moon, so that the moon is seen in a different position by those viewing it obliquely along the convexity of the Earth and by those who behold the moon from the centre or vertex (of the Earth). Accordingly such parallaxes vary in proportion to the distance of the moon from the Earth. For by the consensus of all the mathematicians the greatest distance is $64^{1}/_{6}$ units whereof the radius of the Earth is one unit; but in accordance with the commensurability of these things the least distance should be 33ᴾ33', so that the moon would move towards us through approximately half the total distance— and by the ensuing proportion it was necessary for the parallaxes at greatest and least distance to differ from one another in the ratio of the squares.[1] But we see that those parallaxes, which occur at the time of the half moon waxing or waning, even in the perigee of the epicycle differ slightly or not at all from those which occur at the eclipses of the sun and moon, as we shall show satisfactorily in the proper place.

---

[1] Literally, in duplicate ratio.

But the body itself of the moon makes perfectly clear that error, because for the same reason it would appear twice as large and twice as small in its diameter. But just as circles are in the ratio of the squares[1] of their diameters, the moon should seem almost four times greater in its quadratures when nearest the earth than when opposite the sun, if it were a full moon shining; but since a half moon is shining, nevertheless it should shine with twice the area of light as a full moon there—although the contrary of this is self-evident. If someone who is not content with simple sight wishes to make an experiment with the dioptra of Hipparchus or some other instruments by which the diameter of the moon may be determined, he will find that the diameter does not vary except in so far as the epicycle without the eccentric circle demands. For that reason Menelaus and Timochares in investigating the fixed stars by means of the positions of the moon did not hesitate to use the same lunar diameter always as $1/_2°$, which the moon was seen to occupy most of the time.

3. ANOTHER THEORY OF THE MOVEMENT OF THE MOON

In this way it is perfectly clear that it is not an eccentricity which makes the epicycle appear greater and smaller, but some other relation of circles. [100b] For let AB be the epicycle which

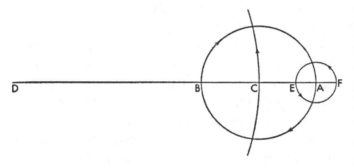

we shall call first and greater; and let C be its centre. Let D be the centre of the Earth, and from D let the straight line DC be extended to the highest apsis of the epicycle; and with A as centre let another small epicycle EF also be described—and all this in the same plane of the oblique circle of the moon. Now let C be moved eastward but A westward; and again let the moon be moved eastward from F the upper part of EF. And let such an order be kept that when line DE is one with line of the mean position of the sun, the moon is always nearest to centre C, i.e., is in point E, but in the quadratures is farthest away at F. I say that the lunar appearances agree with this set-up.

For it follows that twice a month the moon runs around epicycle EF, during which time C makes one revolution with respect to the mean position of the sun. And the new and the full moon will be seen to cause the least circle, namely, that whereof the radius is CE; but the moon in its quadratures will cause the greatest circle with radius CF; and thus again in the conjunctions and oppositions it will make lesser differences between the regular and the apparent movement, but in the quadratures greater differences by

---

[1] Literally, in duplicate ratio.

means of similar but unequal arcs around centre *E*. And since the centre of the epicycle is always in a circle homocentric with the Earth, it will not exhibit such diverse parallaxes but parallaxes in conformity with the epicycle. And the reason will be evident why the body of the moon is seen somehow similar to itself; and all the other things which are perceived in the movement of the moon will come about in this way.

We shall demonstrate them successively by means of our hypothesis, although the same things can take place through eccentric circles, as in the case of the sun—the due proportion being kept. Now we shall take our start from the regular movements, as we did above, without which the irregular movement cannot be separated out. But here there is no small difficulty on account of the parallaxes, which we mentioned; and for that reason the position (of the moon) is not observable by means of astrolabes and other such instruments. But the kindness of nature makes provision for human longing even in this respect, so that the position (of the moon) is more surely determinable through its eclipses than by means of instruments and without any suspicion of error. [101ª] For since the other parts of the world are pure and are filled with the light of day, it stands to reason that night is nothing except the shadow of the Earth, which has the figure of a cone and ends in a point. Falling upon this cone, the moon is dimmed; and, when placed at the midpoint of its darkness, is understood to have arrived without any doubt at the position opposite the sun. But the eclipses of the sun, which take place when the moon moves in front of it, do not offer such a certain determination of the position of the moon. For it happens that the conjunction of the sun and moon is seen by us at some given time, although in relation to the centre of the Earth the conjunction has passed or has not yet taken place, because of the aforesaid parrallax. And accordingly in different parts of the Earth we view the same eclipse of the sun as unequal in magnitude and duration and not similar in all respects. But in the case of the eclipses of the moon no such hindrance occurs, since the Earth transmits the axis of that blotting shadow through its centre from the sun; and for that reason the eclipses of the moon are best fitted for determining the course of the moon with the utmost certainty.

4. On the Revolutions of the Moon and Its Particular Movements

Among the ancients who cared to hand these things down to posterity by means of numbers was found Meton the Anthenian, who flourished around the 37th Olympiad. He reported that in 19 solar years there were 235 full months, whence that great ἐννεαδεκὰτερις year, *i.e.*, year of nineteen years, was called the Metontic year. That number was so suitable that it was set up publicly in the market place at Athens

and other famous cities, and even down to the present it has remained in common use, because they think that through it the beginnings and ends of the months are established in a sure order and that through it also the solar year of 365^1/$_4$ days is commensurable with the months. Hence the Callippic period of 76 years, in which there is an intercalation of 19 days and which they call the Callippic year.

But Hipparchus discovered through careful study that in 304 years there was an excess of a total day, and that (the Callippic year) was verifiable only when the solar year was ^{1}/$_{300}$ of a day smaller. And so by some men that year was called the great year of Hipparchus, [101^b] in which there were 3760 full months. These years are called more simply and crassly, so to speak, Minerva's, when the recurrences of anomaly and of latitude are also sought, for the sake of which that same Hipparchus was making further investigations. For by comparing the readings which he took in making careful observation of the lunar eclipses with those which he had got from the Chaldees, he determined the time in which the revolutions of the months and of the anomaly recurred simultaneously to be 345 Egyptian years 82 days and 1 hour; and during that time there were 4267 full months and 4573 cycles of anomaly. Therefore when the number of months has been reduced to days and there are 126,007 days 1 hour, one month is found equal to 29 days 31 minutes 50 seconds 8 thirds 9 fourths 20 fifths. According to that ratio the movement during any time is manifest. For the division of the 360° of revolution of one month by the number of days in a month produces a daily movement of the moon in relation to the sum of 12°11'26"41'"20""18"'''. The multiplication of that by 365 makes—in addition to the 12 revolutions—an annual movement of 129°37'21"28'"29"".

Furthermore, since the 4267 months and 4573 cycles of anomaly are given in numbers which are composite with respect to one another, that is, as being numbered by the common measure of 17, the ratio of 4267 months to 4573 cycles of anomaly will in least terms be the ratio of 251 to 269; and by Euclid, X, 15, we shall have the proportion of the revolution of the moon to the movement of anomaly in that ratio. Accordingly, when we have multiplied the (annual) movement of the moon by 269 and divided the product by 251, the quotient will be annual movement of anomaly of 13 full revolutions and 88°43'8"40'"20"" and hence a daily movement of 13°3'53"56'"29"".

But the revolution in latitude has another ratio. For it does not agree with the prescribed time in which the anomaly has recurred; but we understand that the latitude of the moon has returned only at that time when a later eclipse of the moon is in every respect similar and equal to an earlier, so that both obscurations are in the same part of the moon and are equal, i.e., in magnitude and duration. And this happens when the distances of the moon from the highest or the lowest apsis are

equal. For then the moon is understood to have traversed equal shadows in equal time. [102ª] Now according to Hipparchus such a returning occurs once in 5458 months, to which there correspond 5923 revolutions of latitude. And by that ratio the particular movements of latitude in years and days will be established, as in the case of the others. For when we have multiplied the movement of the moon away from the sun by 5923 months and divided the product by 5458, we shall have an annual movement of the moon in latitude of 13 revolutions 148°42'46"49'"3"" and a daily movement of 13°13'45"39'"40"".

Hipparchus gave this as the rate of the regular movements of the moon, and no one before him had made a closer approximation. Nevertheless the succeeding ages did not show these movements absolved by all the same numbers. For Ptolemy found the same mean movement away from the sun as did Hipparchus, but an annual movement of anomaly deficient with respect to the former in 1"11'"39"" and an annual movement of latitude with an excess of 53'"41"". But now after the passage of many ages since Hipparchus we also found a mean annual movement deficient in 1" 2'"49"" and a movement of anomaly deficient in only 24'"49"". Moreover, there is an excess of 1"1'"44"" in the movement in latitude. And so the regular movement of the moon, whereby it differs from the terrestrial movement, will be an annual movement of 129°37'22"32'"40"", a movement of anomaly of 88°43'9"5'"9"" and a movement in latitude of 148°42'45"17'"21"".

MOVEMENT OF THE MOON IN YEARS AND PERIODS OF SIXTY YEARS

Egyptian Years	60°	°	'	"	'''		Egyptian Years	60°	°	'	"	'''
1	2	9	37	22	36		31	0	58	18	40	48
2	4	19	14	45	12		32	3	7	56	3	25
3	0	28	52	7	49		33	5	17	33	26	1
4	2	38	29	30	25		34	1	27	10	48	38
5	4	48	6	53	2		35	3	36	48	11	14
6	0	57	44	15	38		36	5	46	25	33	51
7	3	7	21	38	14		37	1	56	2	56	27
8	5	16	59	0	51		38	4	5	40	19	3
9	0	26	36	23	27		39	0	15	17	41	40
10	3	36	13	46	4		40	2	24	55	4	16
11	5	45	31	8	40		41	4	34	32	26	53
12	1	55	28	31	17		42	0	44	9	49	29
13	4	5	5	53	53		43	2	53	47	12	5
14	0	14	43	16	29		44	5	3	24	34	42
15	2	24	20	39	6		45	1	13	1	57	18
16	4	33	58	1	42		46	3	22	39	19	55
17	0	43	35	24	19		47	5	32	16	42	31
18	2	53	12	46	55		48	1	41	54	5	8
19	5	2	50	9	31		49	3	51	31	27	44
20	1	12	27	32	8		50	0	1	8	50	20
21	3	22	4	54	44		51	2	10	46	12	57
22	5	31	42	17	21		52	4	20	23	35	33
23	1	41	19	39	57		53	0	30	0	58	10
24	3	50	57	2	34		54	2	39	38	20	46
25	0	0	34	25	10		55	4	49	15	43	22
26	2	10	11	47	46		56	0	58	53	5	59
27	4	19	49	10	23		57	3	8	30	28	35
28	0	29	26	32	59		58	5	18	7	51	12
29	2	39	3	55	36		59	1	27	45	13	48
30	4	49	41	18	12		60	3	37	22	36	25

Position of the Birth of Christ—209°58'

MOVEMENT OF THE MOON IN DAYS AND PERIODS OF SIXTY DAYS

Days	60°	°	'	"	'''		Days	60°	°	'	"	'''
1	0	12	11	26	41		31	6	17	54	47	26
2	0	24	22	53	23		32	6	30	6	14	8
3	0	36	34	20	4		33	6	42	17	40	49
4	0	48	45	46	46		34	6	54	29	7	31
5	1	0	57	13	27		35	7	6	40	34	12
6	1	13	8	40	9		36	7	18	52	0	54
7	1	25	20	6	50		37	7	31	3	27	35
8	1	37	31	33	32		38	7	43	14	54	17
9	1	49	43	0	13		39	7	55	26	20	58
10	2	1	54	26	55		40	8	7	37	47	40
11	2	14	5	53	36		41	8	19	49	14	21
12	2	26	17	20	18		42	8	32	0	41	3
13	2	38	28	47	0		43	8	44	12	7	44
14	2	50	40	13	41		44	8	56	23	34	26
15	3	2	51	40	22		45	9	8	35	1	7
16	3	15	3	7	4		46	9	20	46	27	49
17	3	27	14	33	45		47	9	32	57	54	30
18	3	39	26	0	27		48	9	45	9	21	12
19	3	51	37	27	8		49	9	57	20	47	53
20	4	3	48	53	50		50	10	9	32	14	35
21	4	16	0	20	31		51	10	21	43	41	16
22	4	28	11	47	13		52	10	33	55	7	58
23	4	40	23	13	54		53	10	46	6	34	40
24	4	52	34	40	36		54	10	58	18	1	21
25	5	4	46	7	17		55	11	10	29	28	2
26	5	16	57	33	59		56	11	22	40	54	43
27	5	29	9	0	40		57	11	34	52	21	25
28	5	41	20	27	22		58	11	47	3	48	7
29	5	53	31	54	3		59	11	59	15	14	48
30	6	5	43	20	45		60	12	11	26	41	31

Position of the Birth of Christ—209°58'

MOVEMENT OF ANOMALY OF THE MOON IN YEARS AND PERIODS OF SIXTY YEARS

Egyptian Years	Movement				
	60°	°	'	"	'''
1	1	28	43	9	7
2	2	57	26	18	14
3	4	26	9	27	21
4	5	54	52	36	29
5	1	23	35	45	36
6	2	52	18	54	43
7	4	21	2	3	59
8	5	49	45	12	58
9	1	18	28	22	5
10	2	47	11	31	12
11	4	15	54	40	19
12	5	44	37	49	27
13	1	13	20	58	34
14	2	42	4	7	41
15	4	10	47	16	48
16	5	39	30	25	56
17	1	8	13	35	3
18	2	36	56	44	10
19	4	5	39	53	17
20	5	34	23	2	25
21	1	3	6	11	32
22	2	31	49	20	39
23	4	0	32	29	46
24	5	29	15	38	54
25	0	57	58	48	1
26	2	26	41	57	8
27	3	55	25	6	15
28	5	24	8	15	23
29	0	52	51	24	30
30	2	21	34	33	37
31	3	50	17	42	44
32	0	19	0	51	52
33	3	47	43	0	59
34	0	16	27	10	6
35	3	45	10	19	13
36	0	13	53	28	21
37	3	42	36	37	28
38	0	11	19	46	35
39	3	40	2	55	42
40	0	8	46	4	50
41	3	37	29	13	57
42	0	6	12	23	4
43	3	34	55	32	11
44	0	3	38	41	19
45	3	32	21	50	26
46	0	1	4	59	33
47	3	29	48	8	40
48	0	58	31	17	48
49	3	27	14	26	55
50	0	55	57	36	2
51	3	24	40	45	9
52	0	53	23	54	17
53	3	22	7	3	24
54	0	50	50	12	31
55	3	19	33	21	38
56	0	48	16	30	46
57	3	16	59	39	53
58	0	45	42	49	0
59	3	14	25	58	7
60	4	43	9	7	15

Position of the Birth of Christ–207°7'

MOVEMENT OF LUNAR ANOMALY IN PERIODS OF SIXTY DAYS

Days	Movement				
	60°	°	'	"	'''
1	0	13	3	53	56
2	0	26	7	47	53
3	0	39	11	41	49
4	0	52	15	35	46
5	1	5	19	29	42
6	1	18	23	23	39
7	1	31	27	17	35
8	1	44	31	11	32
9	1	57	35	5	28
10	2	10	38	59	25
11	2	23	42	53	21
12	2	36	46	47	18
13	2	49	50	41	14
14	3	2	54	35	11
15	3	15	58	29	7
16	3	29	2	23	4
17	3	42	6	17	0
18	3	55	10	10	57
19	4	8	14	4	53
20	4	21	17	58	50
21	4	34	21	52	46
22	4	47	25	46	43
23	5	0	29	40	39
24	5	13	33	34	36
25	5	26	37	28	32
26	5	39	41	22	29
27	5	52	45	16	25
28	6	5	49	10	22
29	6	18	53	4	18
30	6	31	56	58	15
31	6	45	0	52	11
32	6	58	4	46	8
33	7	11	8	40	4
34	7	24	12	34	1
35	7	37	16	27	57
36	7	50	20	21	54
37	8	3	24	15	50
38	8	16	28	9	47
39	8	29	32	3	43
40	8	42	35	57	40
41	8	55	39	51	36
42	9	8	43	45	33
43	9	21	47	39	29
44	9	34	51	33	26
45	9	47	55	27	22
46	10	0	59	21	19
47	10	14	3	15	15
48	10	27	7	9	12
49	10	40	11	3	8
50	10	53	14	57	5
51	11	6	18	51	1
52	11	19	22	44	58
53	11	32	26	38	54
54	11	45	30	32	51
55	11	58	34	26	47
56	12	11	38	20	44
57	12	24	42	14	40
58	12	37	46	8	37
59	12	50	50	2	33
60	13	3	53	56	30

Position of the Birth of Christ–207°7'

LUNAR MOVEMENT IN LATITUDE IN YEARS AND PERIODS OF SIXTY YEARS

Egyptian Years	Movement					Egyptian Years	Movement				
	60°	°	′	″	‴		60°	°	′	″	‴
1	2	28	42	45	17	31	4	50	5	23	57
2	4	57	25	30	34	32	1	18	48	9	14
3	1	26	8	15	52	33	3	47	30	54	32
4	3	54	51	1	9	34	0	16	13	39	48
5	0	23	33	46	26	35	2	44	56	25	6
6	2	52	16	31	44	36	5	13	39	10	24
7	5	20	59	17	1	37	1	42	21	55	41
8	1	49	42	2	18	38	4	11	4	40	58
9	4	18	24	47	36	39	0	39	47	26	16
10	0	47	7	32	53	40	3	8	30	11	33
11	3	15	50	18	10	41	5	37	12	56	50
12	5	44	33	3	28	42	2	5	55	42	8
13	2	13	15	48	45	43	4	34	38	27	25
14	4	41	58	34	2	44	1	3	21	12	42
15	1	10	41	19	20	45	3	32	3	58	0
16	3	39	24	4	37	46	0	0	46	43	17
17	0	8	6	49	54	47	2	29	29	28	34
18	2	36	49	35	12	48	4	58	12	13	52
19	5	5	32	20	29	49	1	26	54	59	8
20	1	34	15	5	46	50	3	55	37	44	26
21	4	2	57	51	4	51	0	24	29	29	44
22	0	31	40	36	21	52	2	53	3	15	1
23	3	0	23	21	38	53	5	21	46	0	18
24	5	29	6	6	56	54	1	50	28	45	36
25	1	57	48	52	13	55	4	19	11	30	53
26	4	26	31	37	30	56	0	47	54	16	10
27	0	55	14	22	48	57	3	16	37	1	28
28	3	23	57	8	5	58	5	45	19	46	45
29	5	52	39	53	22	59	2	14	2	32	2
30	2	21	21	12	38 40	60	4	42	45	17	21

Position of the Birth of Christ—129°45′

MOVEMENT IN LATITUDE OF THE MOON IN DAYS AND PERIODS OF SIXTY DAYS

Days	Movement					Days	Movement				
	60°	°	′	″	‴		60°	°	′	″	‴
1	0	13	13	45	39	31	6	50	6	35	20
2	0	26	27	31	18	32	7	3	20	20	59
3	0	39	41	16	58	33	7	16	34	6	39
4	0	52	55	2	37	34	7	29	47	52	18
5	1	6	8	48	16	35	7	43	1	37	58
6	1	19	22	33	56	36	7	56	15	23	37
7	1	32	36	19	35	37	8	9	29	9	16
8	1	45	50	5	14	38	8	22	42	54	56
9	1	59	3	50	54	39	8	35	56	40	35
10	2	12	17	36	33	40	8	49	10	26	14
11	2	25	31	22	13	41	9	2	24	11	54
12	2	38	45	7	52	42	9	15	37	57	33
13	2	51	58	53	31	43	9	28	51	43	13
14	3	5	12	39	11	44	9	42	5	28	52
15	3	18	26	24	50	45	9	55	19	14	31
16	3	31	40	10	29	46	10	8	33	0	11
17	3	44	53	56	9	47	10	21	46	45	50
18	3	58	7	41	48	48	10	35	0	31	29
19	4	11	21	27	28	49	10	48	14	17	9
20	4	24	35	13	7	50	11	1	28	2	48
21	4	37	48	58	46	51	11	14	41	48	28
22	4	51	2	44	26	52	11	27	55	34	7
23	5	4	16	30	5	53	11	41	9	19	46
24	5	17	30	15	44	54	11	54	23	5	26
25	5	30	44	1	24	55	12	7	36	51	5
26	5	43	57	47	3	56	12	20	50	36	44
27	5	57	11	32	43	57	12	34	4	22	24
28	6	10	25	18	22	58	12	47	18	8	3
29	6	23	39	4	1	59	13	0	31	53	43
30	6	36	25	49	41	60	13	13	45	39	22

Position of the Birth of Christ—129°45′

5. DEMONSTRATION OF THE FIRST IRREGULARITY OF THE MOON WHICH OCCURS AT THE NEW AND AT THE FULL MOON

[105^b] We have set out the regular movements of the moon, according as they can be known by us at present. Now we must approach the ratio of irregularity which we shall demonstrate by way of the epicycle, and first the irregularity which occurs in the conjunction and oppositions with the sun, in connexion with which the ancient mathematicians exercised their amazing genius in triads of lunar eclipses. We shall also follow the road thus prepared for us by them, and we shall take three eclipses carefully observed by Ptolemy and compare them with three others noted with no less care, in order to examine the regular movements already set out, to see if they have been set out correctly. In explaining them we shall in imitation of the ancients employ as regular the mean movement of the sun and moon away from the position of the spring equinox, since the variation which occurs on account of the irregular precession of equinoxes is not perceptible in such a short time or even in ten years.

Accordingly, Ptolemy took as first the eclipse occurring in the 17th year of Hadrian's reign, after the close of the 20th day of the month Pauni by the Egyptian calendar; and it was the year of Our Lord 133 on the 6th day of May or the day before the Nones. There was a total eclipse, the midtime of which was a quarter of an equal hour before midnight at Alexandria; but at Frauenburg or Cracow it was an hour and a quarter before the midnight which the seventh day followed; and the sun was at $12^1/_4°$ of Taurus, but according to the mean movement at 12°21' of Taurus.

He says that the second occurred in the 19th year of Hadrian, when two days of Chiach—the fourth Egyptian month had passed: that was in the year of Our Lord 134, 13 days before the Kalends of November. There was an eclipse from the north covering ten twelfths of its diameter. The midtime was one equatorial hour before midnight at Alexandria, but two hours before midnight at Cracow; and the sun was at $25^1/_6°$ of Libra but by its mean movement at 26°43' of the same.

The third eclipse occurred in the 20th year of Hadrian, when 19 days of Pharmuthi—the eighth Egyptian month—had passed; in the year of Our Lord [106^a] 135, when the 6th day of March had passed. The moon was again eclipsed in the north to the extent of half its diameter. The midtime was four equatorial hours past midnight at Alexandria, but at Cracow it was three hours after midnight, that morning being the Nones of March. At that time the sun was at $14^1/_2°$ of Pisces, but by its mean movement at 11°44' of Pisces.

Now it is clear that in the middle space of time between the first and the second eclipse the moon traversed as much space as the sun in its apparent movement—not

counting the full circles—*i.e.*, 161°55'; and between the second and the third eclipse, 138°55'. Now in the first interval there were 1 year 166 days 23³/₄ equal hours according to apparent time, but by corrected time 23⁵/₈ hours; but in the second interval 1 year 137 days 5 hours simply, but 5¹/₂ hours correctly.

And during the first interval the regular movement of the sun and the moon measured as one—not counting the circles—was 169°37', and there was a movement of anomaly of 110°21'; in the second interval the similarly regular movement of the sun and the moon was 137°34' and there was a movement of anomaly of 81°36'. Therefore it is clear that during the first interval the 110°21' of the epicycle subtract 7°42' from the mean movement of the moon; and during the second interval the 81°36' of the epicycle add 1°21'.

With these things thus before us, let there be described the lunar epicycle *ABC*, in which the first eclipse of the moon is at *A*, the second at *B*, and the remaining one at

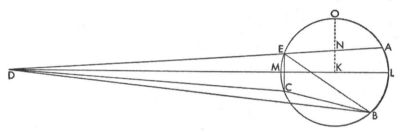

C, and in the order as above let the transit of the moon be understood as occurring westward. And let

$$\text{arc } AB = 110°21',$$

hence

$$-\text{ add. } AB = 7°42',$$

as we said; and let

$$\text{arc } BC = 81°36',$$

hence

$$+\text{ add. } BDC = 1°21'.$$

And, as the remainder of the circle,

$$\text{arc } CA = 168°3'$$

and it adds the remainder of the additosubtraction, *i.e.*,

$$+\text{ add. } CDA = 6°21'.$$

Since on the ecliptic

$$\text{arc } AB = 7°42',$$

therefore

$$\text{angle } ADB = 7°42',$$

where 2 rt. angles = 180°.

But

angle ADB = 15°24',

[106[b]] where 2 rt. angles = 360°.

And, as on the circumference and as an exterior angle of triangle BDE,

angle AEB = 110°21' :

therefore

angle EBD = 94°57'.

But the sides of triangles whose angles are given are themselves given:

DE = 147,396

and

BE = 26,798,

where diameter of circle circumscribing triangle = 200,000.

Again, since on the ecliptic

arc AEC = 6°21',

angle EDC = 6°21',

where 2 rt. angles = 180°.

But

angle EDC = 12°42',

where 2 rt. angles = 360°.

And

angle AEC = 191°57'.

And

angle ECD = angle AEC – angle CDE = 179°15'.

Therefore the sides are given:

DE = 199,996

and

CE = 22,120,

where the diameter of the circle circumscribing triangle = 200,000.

But

CE = 16,302

and

BE = 26,798,

where DE = 147,396.

Again, since in triangle BEC

side BE is given,

side EC is given,

and

angle CEB = 81°36'

and hence

arc BC = 81°36' :

therefore, by the proofs concerning plane triangles,

side BC = 17,960.

But since the diameter of the epicycle = 200,000, and

arc BC = 81°36',

chord BC = 130,694.

And in accordance with the ratio given

ED = 1,072,684

and

CE = 118,637,

and

arc CB = 72°46'10".

But, by construction,

arc CEA = 168°3'.

Therefore, by subtraction,

arc EA = 95°16'50"

and

chord EA = 147,786.

Hence by addition

line AED = 1,220,470.

But since segment EA is less than a semicircle, the centre of the epicycle will not be in [107ª] it but in the remainder $ABCE$. Therefore let K be the centre, and let $DMKL$ be drawn through both apsides, and let L be the highest apsis and M the lowest, Now, by Euclid, III, 36, it is clear that

rect. AD, DE = rect. LD, DM.

Now since LM, the diameter of the circle—to which DM is added in a straight line—is bisected at K, then

rect. LD, DM + sq. KM = sq. DK.

Therefore

DK = 1,148,556

where KL = 100,000;

and on that account,

LK = 8,706

where DKL = 100,000

211

and *LK* is the radius of the epicycle. Having done that, draw *KNO* perpendicular to *AD*. Since *KD*, *DE*, and *EA* have their ratios to one another given in the parts whereof *LK* = 100,000, and since

$$NE = \frac{1}{2} AE = 73{,}893 :$$

therefore, by addition,

$$DEN = 1{,}146{,}577.$$

But in triangle *DKN*

side *DK* is given,

side *ND* is given,

and

angle $N = 90°$;

on that account, at the centre,

angle $NKD = 86°38\frac{1}{2}'$

and

arc $MEO = 86°38\frac{1}{2}'.$

Hence,

arc $LAO = 180° -$ arc $NEO = 93°21\frac{1}{2}'.$

Now

arc $OA = \frac{1}{2}$ arc $AOE = 47°38\frac{1}{2}'$;

and

arc $LA =$ arc $LAO -$ arc $OA = 45°43'$,

which is the distance—or position of anomaly—of the moon from the highest apsis of the epicycle at the first eclipse. But

arc $AB = 110°21'.$

Accordingly, by subtraction,

arc $LB = 64°38'$,

which is the anomaly at the second eclipse. And by addition

arc $LBC = 146°14'$,

where the third eclipse falls. Now it will also be clear that since

angle $DKN = 86°38\frac{1}{2}'$,

where 4 rt. angles = 360°,

angle $KDN = 90° -$ angle $DKN = 3°21\frac{1}{2}'$;

and that is the additosubtraction which the anomaly adds at the first eclipse. Now

angle $ADB = 7°42'$;

therefore, by subtraction,

angle $LDB = 4°20\frac{1}{2}'$,

which arc *LB* subtracts from the regular movement of the moon at the second eclipse. And since

[107^b] angle *BDC* = 1°21',

and therefore, by subtraction,

angle *CDM* = 2°49',

the subtractive additosubtraction caused by arc *LBC* at the third eclipse; therefore the mean position of the moon, *i.e.*, of centre *K*, at the first eclipse was 9°53' of Scorpio, because its apparent position was at 13°15' of Scorpio; and that was the number of degrees of the sun diametrically opposite in Taurus. And thus the mean movement of the moon at the second eclipse was at 29^1/$_2$° of Aries; and in the third eclipse, at 17°4' of Virgo. Moreover, the regular distances of the moon from the sun were 177°33' for the first eclipse, 182°47' for the second, 185°20' for the last. So Ptolemy.

Following his example, let us now proceed to a third trinity of eclipses of the moon, which were painstakingly observed by us. The first was in the year of Our Lord 1511, after October 6th had passed. The moon began to be eclipsed 1^1/$_8$ equal hours before midnight, and was completely restored 2^1/$_3$ hours after midnight, and in this way the middle of the eclipse was at ^{7}/$_{12}$ hours after midnight—the morning following being the Nones of October, the 7th. There was a total eclipse, while the sun was in 22°25' of Libra but by regular movement at 24°13' of Libra.

We observed the second eclipse in the year of Our Lord 1522, in the month of September, after the lapse of five days. The eclipse was total, and began at ^{2}/$_5$ equal hours before midnight, but its midpoint occurred 1^1/$_3$ hours after midnight, which the 6th day followed—the 8th day before the Ides of September. The sun was in 22^1/$_5$° of Virgo but, according to its regular movement, in 23°59' of Virgo.

We observed the third in the year of Our Lord 1523, at the close of August 25th. It began 2^4/$_5$ hours after midnight, was a total eclipse, and the midtime was 4^5/$_{12}$ hours after the midnight prior to the 7th day before the Kalends of September. The sun was in 11°21' of Virgo but according to its mean movement at 13°2' of Virgo.

And here it is also manifest that the distance between the true positions of the sun and the moon from the first eclipse to the second was 329°47', [108^a] but from the second to the third it was 349°9'. Now the time from the first eclipse to the second was 10 equal years 337 days ^{3}/$_4$ hours according to apparent time, but by corrected equal time ^{4}/$_5$ hours. From the second to the third there were 354 days 3 hours 5 minutes; but according to equal time 3 hours 9 minutes.

During the first interval the mean movement of the sun and the moon measured as one—not counting the complete circles—amounted to 334°47', and the movement of anomaly to 250°36', subtracting approximately 5° from the regular movement; in the second interval the mean movement of the sun and moon was 346°10'; and the movement of anomaly was 306°43', adding 2°59' to the mean movement.

Now let *ABC* be the epicycle, and let 21 be the position of the moon at the middle of the first eclipse, *B* at the second, *C* at the third. And let the movement of the

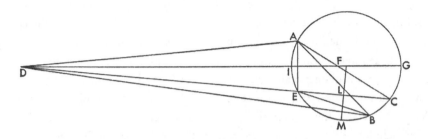

epicycle be understood as proceeding from *C* to *B* and from *B* to *A*, *i.e.*, from above, westward, and from below, eastward. And

$$\text{arc } ACB = 250°36',$$

and, as we said, it subtracts 5° from the mean movement during the first interval of time. But

$$\text{arc } BAC = 306°43',$$

which adds 2°59' to the mean movement of the moon; and accordingly by subtraction the remainder

$$\text{arc } AC = 197°19',$$

which subtracts the remaining 2°1'. But since arc *AC* is greater than a semicircle and is subtractive, then it must contain the highest apsis. For the highest apsis cannot be in area *BA* or *CBA*, which are additive and each less than a semicircle; but the lesser movement is placed by the apogee. Therefore let *D* be taken opposite as the centre of the Earth; and let *AD*, *DB*, *DEC*, *AB*, *AE*, and *EB* be joined.

Now since in triangle *DBE*

$$\text{exterior angle } CEB = 53°17',$$

because angle *CEB* intercepts arc *CB*, and

$$\text{arc } CB = 360° - \text{arc } BAC;$$

and since, as at the centre,

$$\text{angle } BDE = 2°59',$$

but, as at the circumference,

$$\text{angle } BDE = 5°58';$$

and since, therefore, by subtraction,

$$\text{angle } EBD = 47°19';$$

wherefore

$$\text{side } BE = 1042$$

and

$$\text{side } DE = 8024$$

= [108^b] where radius of circle circumscribing the triangle = 10,000.
Similarly, as standing on arc *AC* of the circumference,

angle *AEC* = 197°19',

and, as at the centre,

angle *ADC* = 2°1',

but, as on the circumference,

angle *ADC* = 4°2';

therefore, by subtraction,

angle *DAE* = 193°17',

where 2 rt. angles = 360°.

Therefore the sides are also given in the parts whereof the radius of the circle circumscribing triangle *ADE* = 10,000:

AE = 702

and

DE = 19,865 :

but whereas

DE = 8,024,
AE = 283

and

BE = 1042.

Therefore once more we shall have triangle *ABE*, wherein

side *AE* is given,
side *EB* is given,

and

angle *AEB* = 250°36',

where 2 rt. angles = 360°.

Accordingly by what we have shown concerning plane triangles

AB = 1,227

where *EB* = 1,042.

Accordingly in this way we have got hold of the ratios of the three lines *AB*, *EB*, and *ED*; and hence they will become manifest in terms of the parts whereof the radius of the epicycle = 10,000:

ch. *AB* = 16,323,
ED = 106,751,

and

ch. *EB* = 13,853.

Whence also

arc *EB* = 87°41';

and
$$\text{arc } EBC = \text{arc } EB + \text{arc } BC = 140°58';$$
and
$$\text{ch. } CE = 18{,}851,$$
and, by addition,
$$CED = 125{,}602.$$

Now let the centre of the epicycle be set forth: it necessarily falls in segment *EAC* as being greater than a semicircle. And let *F* be the centre; and let *DIFG* be extended in a straight line through both apsides, *I* the lowest and *G* the highest. Again it is clear that
$$\text{rect. } CD, DE = \text{rect. } GD, DI.$$
But
$$\text{rect. } GD, DI + \text{sq. } FI = \text{sq. } DF.$$
Therefore
$$DIF = 116{,}226,$$
$$\text{where } FG = 10{,}000.$$

Accordingly
$$FG = 8{,}604,$$
$$\text{where } DF = 100{,}000,$$
—which agrees with what we find reported by most of our predecessors after Ptolemy's time.

[109ᵃ] Now from centre *F* let *FL* be drawn at right angles to *EC* and extended in the straight line *FLM*. It will bisect *CE* at point *I*. Now since
$$\text{line } ED = 106{,}751$$
and
$${}^{1}/_{2}CE = LF = 9{,}426;$$
therefore, by addition,
$$DEL = 116{,}177$$
$$\text{where } FG = 10{,}000$$
$$\text{and where } DF = 116{,}226.$$

Therefore, in triangle *DFL*
$$\text{side } DF \text{ is given,}$$
$$\text{side } DL \text{ is given,}$$
$$\text{angle } DFL = 88°21',$$
and, by subtraction,
$$\text{angle } FDL = 1°39';$$
and similarly
$$\text{arc } IEM = 88°21'$$

and
$$\text{arc } MC = {}^1/_2 \text{ arc } EBC = 70°29';$$
hence, by addition,
$$\text{arc } IMC = 158°50',$$
and
$$\text{arc } GC = 180° - \text{arc } IMC = 21°10'.$$
And this was the distance of the moon from the apogee of the epicycle, or the position of anomaly at the third eclipse. And at the second eclipse
$$\text{arc } GCB = 74°27';$$
and at the first eclipse
$$\text{arc } GBA = 183°51'.$$
Again at the third eclipse, and as at the centre,
$$\text{angle } IDE = 1°39',$$
which is the subtractive additosubtraction. And at the second eclipse
$$\text{angle } IDB = 4°38',$$
which is still a subtractive addition-and-subtraction, because
$$\text{angle } IDB = \text{angle } GDC + \text{angle } CDB = 1°39' + 2°59'.$$
And accordingly
$$\text{angle } ADI = \text{angle } ADB - \text{angle } IDB = 5° - 4°38' = 22'$$
which are added to the regular movement at the first eclipse.

For that reason the position of regular movement of the moon in the first eclipse was 22°3' of Aries, but the position of the apparent movement was at 22°25'; and the sun was opposite, at the same number of degrees of Libra. In this way too the mean position of the moon in the second eclipse was at 26°50' of Pisces, but in the third eclipse, at 13° of Pisces, and the mean lunar movement by which it is separated from the annual movement of the Earth, was 177°50' at the first eclipse; at the second eclipse, 182°51'; and at the third eclipse, 179°58'.

6. CONFIRMATION OF WHAT HAS BEEN SET OUT CONCERNING THE MOON'S MOVEMENTS OF ANOMALY IN LONGITUDE

Moreover, by means of these things which are set out concerning the eclipses of the moon, it will be possible to test whether we have set out the regular movements of the moon correctly. For it was shown that in the second of the two eclipses the distance of the moon from the sun was 182°47', and (the movement) of anomaly was 64°38'; [109b] but in the second of those eclipses occurring in our time the movement of the moon away from the sun was 182°51' but (the movement) of anomaly was 74°27'. It is clear that in the intervening time there were 17,166 full months and as it were a

movement of 4' and a movement of anomaly—not counting the whole cycles—of 9°49'. Now the time which intervenes between the 19th year of Hadrian on the 2nd day of the Egyptian month Chiach 2 hours before midnight, followed by the 3rd day of the month, and the 1522nd year of Our Lord on September 5th, $1^1/_3$ hours after midnight amounts to 1388 Egyptian years 302 days $3^1/_3$ hours by apparent time; and when corrected, 3 hours 34 minutes after midnight.

And in that time after the 17,165 complete revolutions of equal months there was according to Ptolemy and Hipparchus a movement away from the sun of 359°38'. And according to Hipparchus the movement of anomaly was 9°39', but according to Ptolemy 9°11'. Accordingly the lunar movement away from the sun calculated by Hipparchus and Ptolemy is deficient in 26', and the movement of anomaly of Ptolemy and of Hipparchus is deficient in 38'. These minutes swell our movements, and are consonant with the numbers which we have set out.

7. On the Positions of the Moon in Longitude and Anomaly

Now we shall speak of these things, as above; and here we are to determine positions for the established beginnings of calendar years of the Olympiads, of the years of Alexander, Caesar, and Our Lord, and any additional one desired. Therefore if we consider the second of the three ancient eclipses—the one which occurred in the 19th year of Hadrian, on the 2nd day of the Egyptian month Chiach, one equatorial hour before midnight at Alexandria but for us under the Cracow meridian at 2 hours before midnight—we shall find from the beginning of the years of Our Lord to this movement 133 Egyptian years 325 days 22 hours simply, but 21 hours 37 minutes correctly. During this time the movement of the moon according to our calculation was 332°49' and (the movement) of anomaly was 217°32'. [110ᵃ] And when they have been subtracted from the findings for the eclipse, each from its own kind, there remain 209°58' as the mean position of the moon away from the sun, and a position of anomaly of 207°7' at the beginning of the years of Our Lord at midnight before the Kalends of January.

Again (from the 1st Olympiad) to the beginning of the years of Our Lord, there are 193 Olympiads 2 years $194^1/_2$ days, which make 775 Egyptian years $12^1/_2$ days, but by corrected time 12 hours 11 minutes. Similarly from the death of Alexander to the birth of Christ, they compute 323 Egyptian years $130^1/_2$ days by apparent time, but by corrected time 12 hours 16 minutes. And from Caesar to Christ there are 45 Egyptian years 12 days, in which the ratios of equal and apparent time agree.

Accordingly when we have deducted the movements corresponding to the intervals of time from the positions at the birth of Christ, by subtracting single items from single items, we shall have for noon of the 1st day of the month Hekatombaion of the

1st Olympiad a regular lunar distance from the sun of 39°43' and a distance of anomaly of 46°20'.

At the beginning of the years of Alexander at noon on the first day of the month Thoth the moon was 310°44' distant from the sun, and the movement of anomaly was 85°41'.

And at the beginning of the years of Julius Caesar at midnight before the Kalends of January the moon was 350°39' distant from the sun, and the movement of anomaly was 17°58'. All this with reference to the Cracow meridian, since Gynopolis—commonly called Frauenburg—where we took our observations at the mouth of the Vistula, lies under this meridian, as the eclipses of the sun and moon observed in both places at the same time teach us; and Dyrrhachium in Macedonia—which was called Epidamnum in antiquity—is also under this meridian.

8. ON THE SECOND IRREGULARITY OF THE MOON AND WHAT RATIO THE FIRST EPICYCLE HAS TO THE SECOND

Accordingly, in this way the regular movement of the moon together with its first irregularity has been demonstrated. Now we must inquire into what ratio the first epicycle has to the second and both of them to the distance of the centre of the Earth. But, as we said, the greatest difference (between regular and apparent movement) is found in the mean quadratures when the half moon is waxing or waning, and that difference is $7^2/_3°$, [110^b] as even the observations of the ancients record. For they were making observations of the time in which the half moon had nearly reached the mean distance of the epicycle and was in the neighbourhood of the tangent from the centre of the Earth—and that is easily perceptible by means of the calculus set forth above. And as the moon was then at about 90° of the ecliptic measured from its rising or setting, they were aware of the error which the parallax could bring into the movement of longitude. For at that time the circle through the vertex of the horizon divides the ecliptic at right angles and does not admit any parallax in longitude but the parallax falls wholly in latitude. Then by means of the astrolabe they determined the position of the moon in relation to the sun. When they made their comparison, the moon was found to differ from its regular movement by $7^2/_3°$, as we said, instead of by 5°.

Now let epicycle AB be described; and let its centre be C. Let the centre of the Earth be D, and from D let the straight line $DBCA$ be extended. Let A be the apogee of the epicycle, B the perigee; and let DE be drawn tangent to the epicycle, and let CE be joined. Accordingly since the greatest additosubtraction is at the tangent and in this case is 7°40', and hence

$$\text{angle } BDE = 7°40',$$

and

$$\text{angle } CED = 90°,$$

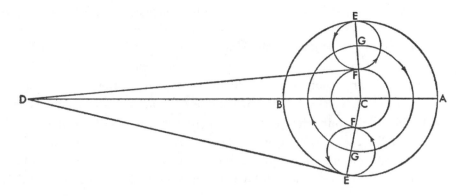

as being at the point of tangency of circle *AB*:
wherefore

$$CE = 1334,$$

where radius $CD = 10,000.$

But at the full moon it was much shorter, that is,

$$CE \doteqdot 860.$$

Let *CE* be such again, and let

$$CF = 860.$$

Point *F*, which the new moon and the full moon occupy, will be circumcurrent around the same centre; and accordingly, by subtraction,

$$FE = 474$$

and is the diameter of the second epicycle. Let *FE* be bisected at centre *G*, and by addition

$$CFG = 1097$$

and will be the radius of the circle which the centre of the second epicycle describes. And so it is established that

$$CG : GE = 1097 : 237,$$

where $CD = 10,000.$

9. On the Remaining Difference, by Reason of Which the Moon Seems to Move Irregularly Away from the Highest Apsis of Its Epicycle

[111ª] By this induction it is given to understand how the moon is moved irregularly in its first epicycle, and that its greatest difference occurs when the half moon is horn-shaped or gibbous. Once more, let *AB* be that first epicycle, which the centre of the second epicycle describes through its mean movement; let *C* be the centre, *A* the highest apsis, and *B* the lowest. Let point *E* be taken anywhere in the circumference, and let *CE* be joined. Now let

$$CE : EF = 1097 : 237.$$

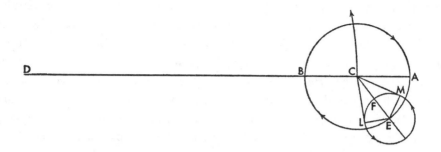

And with radius *EF* let the second epicycle be described around centre *E*. And let the straight lines *CL* and *CM* be drawn tangent to it on both sides. Let the movement of the small epicycle be from *A* to *E*, *i.e.*, from above, westward; and let the movement of the moon be from *F* to *L*, still westward. Accordingly it is clear that, since movement *AE* is regular, the second epicycle by virtue of its motion *FL* adds arc *EL* to the regular movement and by virtue of *MF* subtracts from the regular movement. But since in triangle *CEL*

$$\text{angle } L = 90°,$$

and

$$EL = 237,$$
$$\text{where } CE = 1,097.$$

Therefore

$$EL = 2,160,$$
$$\text{where } CE = 10,000.$$

And by the table

$$EL = \tfrac{1}{2} \text{ ch. } 2 \ ECL.$$

And

$$\text{angle } ECL = \text{angle } MCF,$$

since the triangles are similar and equal. And that is the greatest difference by which the moon varies in its movement from the highest apsis of the first epicycle. It occurs when the moon by its mean movement is 38°46' distant on either side of the line of mean movement of the Earth. And so it is perfectly clear that these greatest additosubtractions occur at a mean distance of 38°46' between the sun and moon, and at the same distance on either side of the mean opposition.

10. How the Apparent Movement of the Moon Is Demonstrated from the Regular Movements

[111ᵇ] Having seen all that first, we now wish to show by means of diagrams how the regular and apparent movements of the moon are separated out from those regular

lunar movements which were set before us, taking our example from among the observations of Hipparchus, so that in this way our teaching may at the same time be confirmed experimentally. Accordingly in the 197th year from the death of Alexander, on the 17th day of Pauni, which is the 10th month in the Egyptian calendar, when $9^1/_3$ hours of the day had passed at Rhodes, Hipparchus by an observation of the sun and moon through an astrolabe found that they were 48°6' distant from one another, and that the moon was to the east of the sun. And since he judged that the position of the sun was in $10^9/_{10}$° of Cancer, as a consequence the moon was at 29° of Leo. At that time 29° of Scorpio was rising, and 10° of Virgo was in the middle of the heavens over Rhodes, which has an elevation of the north pole of 36°. By this argument it is clear that the moon, which was situated at 90° of the ecliptic from the meridian had at that time admitted no parallax in vision or else one imperceptible in longitude. But since this observation was made $3^1/_3$ hours after midday of the 17th—which corresponds at Rhodes to four equatorial hours—at Cracow it was $3^1/_6$ equatorial hours after midday in accordance with the distance which makes Rhodes a sixth of an hour nearer to us than Alexandria. Accordingly from the death of Alexander there were 196 years, 286 days, $3^1/_6$ hours simply, but $3^1/_3$ hours by equal time. At that time the sun by its mean movement had arrived at 12°3' of Cancer, but by its apparent movement at 10°40' of Cancer, whence the moon appeared in truth to be at 28°37' of Leo. But the regular movement of the moon according to the monthly revolution was at 45°9', and the movement of anomaly was 333° away from the highest apsis by our calculations.

With this example before us let us describe the first epicycle *AB*. Let *C* be its centre. [112ª] Let *ACB* be its diameter, and let *ACB* be extended as *ABD* in a straight line to the centre of the Earth. And in the epicycle, let

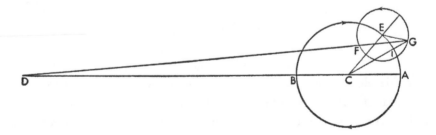

arc *ABE* = 333°.

Let *CE* be joined and again cut in *F*, so that

$$EF = 237,$$

where *EC* = 1,097.

And with *E* as centre and *EF* as radius, let *FG* the epicycle of the epicycle be described. Let the moon be at point *G*; and let

$$\text{arc } FG = 90°18',$$

in the ratio of double to the regular movement away from the sun, which was 45°9'. And let *CG*, *EG*, and *DG* be joined. Accordingly, since in triangle *CEG* two sides are given:

$$CE = 1,097$$

and

$$EG = EF = 237;$$

and

$$\text{angle } GEC = 90°18';$$

therefore, by what we have shown concerning plane triangles

$$\text{side } CG = 1,123$$

and

$$\text{angle } ECG = 12°11'.$$

By this means there are determined arc *EI* and the additive additosubtraction caused by the anomaly; and, by addition,

$$\text{arc } ABEI = 345°11'.$$

And, by subtraction,

$$\text{angle } GCA = 14°49',$$

and is the true distance of the moon from the highest apsis of epicycle *AB*; and

$$\text{angle } BCG = 165°11'.$$

Wherefore in triangle *GDC* two sides are given also.

$$GC = 1,123,$$

$$\text{where } CD = 10,000;$$

and

$$\text{angle } GCD = 165°11'.$$

Hence

$$\text{angle } CDG = 1°29',$$

the additosubtraction which was added to the mean movement of the moon. Hence the true distance of the moon from the mean movement of the sun is 46°34', and its apparent position is at 28°37' of Leo, and is 47°57' distant from the true position of the sun. And there is a deficiency of 9' according to Hipparchus' observation.

But in order that no one on that account should suspect that either his investigation or ours is wrong—though the deficiency is very slight—nevertheless I shall show that neither he nor we committed any error but that this is the way things rightly are. For if we recollect that the lunar circle which the moon itself follows is oblique, we will admit that it produces some sort of longitudinal irregularity in the ecliptic, especially around the mean positions, which lie between the northern and the southern limits of latitude and the ecliptic sections, in approximately the same way as between the oblique [112ᵇ] ecliptic and the equator, as we expounded in connection with the

inequality of the natural day. And so if we transfer the ratios to the orbital circle of the moon, which Ptolemy recorded as being inclined to the ecliptic, we find that at those positions the ratios cause a 7' difference in longitude in relation to the ecliptic—and twice that difference is 14'; and the difference increases and decreases proportionally, since when the sun and moon are a quadrant of a circle distant from one another, and if the limit of northern or southern latitude is at the midpoint between them, then the arc intercepted on the ecliptic will be 14' greater than a quadrant of the lunar circle; and conversely in the other quadrants, which the ecliptic sections halve, the circles through the poles of the ecliptic intercept an arc that much less than a quadrant. So in the present case. Since the moon was in the neighbourhood of the mean position between the southern limit of latitude and the ascending ecliptic section—which the moderns call the head of the Dragon—and the sun had already passed by the other descending section—which they call the tail; it is not surprising if when the moon's distance of 47°57' in its own orbital circle was referred to the ecliptic, it increased by at least 7', without the fact of the sun declining in the west causing any subtractive parallax of vision. We shall speak more clearly of all that in our explanation of the parallaxes.

And so the distance of the luminaries, which Hipparchus determined by his instrument as being 48°6', agrees with our calculation perfectly and as it were unanimously.

11. On the Table of the Lunar Additions-and-Subtractions Or *Aequationes*

Accordingly, I judge that the mode of determining the motions of the moon is understood generally from this example, since in triangle *CEG*, the two sides *GE* and *CE* always remain the same. But we determine the remaining side *GC* together with angle *ECG*—which is the additosubtraction to be used in correcting the anomaly—according to angle *GEC* which changes continually but which is given. Then in triangle *CDG*, since the two sides *DC* and *GC* together with angle *DCG* have been computed, in the same way angle *D* at the centre of the Earth, the angular difference between the true and the regular movement, becomes established.

So that these things may be at hand, [113ᵃ] we shall set out a table of the additosubtractions, which will contain six columns. For after the two columns of common numbers of the circle, in the third column will come the additosubtractions which are caused by the small epicycle and vary the regular movement of the first epicycle in accordance with the bi-monthly revolution. Then, we shall leave the fourth column vacant for the time being, and fill up the fifth column first, in which we shall inscribe the additosubtractions caused by the first and greater epicycle which occur at the mean conjunctions and oppositions of the sun and moon, and the greatest is 4°56'. In the next to the last column will be placed the numbers whereby the additosubtractions

which occur at half moon exceed the former additosubtractions, and the greatest of these excesses is 2°44'. But in order that the other excesses may be evaluated, the proportional minutes have been worked out, and this is the ratio of them. For we have taken 2°44' as 60 minutes in relation to any other excesses occurring at the point of tangency of the (small) epicycle (with the line from the centre of the Earth).

In this way, in the same example,

$$CG = 1123,$$

where $CD = 10,000.$

And that makes the greatest additosubtraction at the point of tangency of the (small) epicycle (with the line from the centre of the Earth) to be 6°29', which exceeds the first additosubtraction by 1°33'. But

$$2°44' : 1°33' = 60° : 34°;$$

and so we have the ratio of the excess which occurs at the semicircle of the small epicycle to the excess corresponding to the given arc of 90°18'. Therefore we shall write down 34 minutes in that part of the table corresponding to 90°. In this way we shall find the minutes which are proportional to the arcs inscribed in the table; and we shall set them out in the fourth column.

Finally we have added the degrees of northern and southern latitude in the last column, and we shall speak of them below. For convenience and ease of operation advise us to put them in this order.

Table of Additions-and-Subtractions of the Moon

Common Numbers		Additions-and-subtractions caused by small epicycle		Proportional Minutes	Additions-and-subtractions caused by great epicycle		Excesses		Degrees of Northern Latitudude	
Deg.	Deg.	Deg.	Min.		Deg.	Min.	Deg.	Min.	Deg.	Min.
3	357	0	51	0	0	14	0	7	4	59
6	354	1	40	0	0	28	0	14	4	58
9	351	2	28	1	0	43	0	21	4	56
12	348	3	15	1	0	57	0	28	4	53
15	345	4	1	2	1	11	0	35	4	50
18	342	4	47	3	1	24	0	43	4	45
21	339	5	31	3	1	38	0	50	4	40
24	336	6	13	4	1	51	0	56	4	34
27	333	6	54	5	2	5	1	4	4	27
30	330	7	34	5	2	17	1	12	4	20
33	327	8	10	6	2	30	1	18	4	12
36	324	8	44	7	2	42	1	25	4	3
39	321	9	16	8	2	54	1	30	3	53
42	318	9	47	10	3	6	1	37	3	43
45	315	10	14	11	3	17	1	42	3	32
48	312	10	30	12	3	27	1	48	3	20
51	309	11	0	13	3	38	1	52	3	8
54	306	11	21	15	3	47	1	57	2	56
57	303	11	38	16	3	56	2	2	2	44
60	300	11	50	18	4	5	2	6	2	30
63	297	12	2	19	4	13	2	10	2	16
66	294	12	12	21	4	20	2	15	2	2
69	291	12	18	22	4	27	2	18	1	47
72	288	12	23	24	4	33	2	21	1	33
75	285	12	27	25	4	39	2	25	1	18
78	282	12	28	27	4	43	2	28	1	2
81	279	12	26	28	4	47	2	30	0	47
84	276	12	23	30	4	51	2	34	0	31
87	273	12	17	32	4	53	2	37	0	16
90	270	12	12	34	4	55	2	40	0	0
93	267	12	3	35	4	56	2	42	0	16
96	264	11	53	37	4	56	2	42	0	31
99	261	11	41	38	4	55	2	43	0	47
102	258	11	27	39	4	54	2	43	1	2
105	255	11	10	41	4	51	2	44	1	18
108	252	10	52	42	4	48	2	44	1	33
111	249	10	35	43	4	44	2	43	1	47
114	246	10	17	45	4	39	2	41	2	2
117	243	9	57	46	4	34	2	38	2	16
120	240	9	35	47	4	27	2	35	2	30
123	237	9	13	48	4	20	2	31	2	44
126	234	8	50	49	4	11	2	27	2	56
129	231	8	25	50	4	2	2	22	3	9
132	228	7	59	51	3	53	2	18	3	21
135	225	7	33	52	3	42	2	13	3	32
138	222	7	7	53	3	31	2	8	3	43
141	219	6	38	54	3	19	2	1	3	53
144	216	6	9	55	3	7	1	53	4	3
147	213	5	40	56	2	53	1	46	4	12
150	210	5	11	57	2	40	1	37	4	20
153	207	4	42	57	2	25	1	28	4	27
156	204	4	11	58	2	10	1	20	4	34
159	201	3	41	58	1	55	1	12	4	40
162	198	3	10	59	1	39	1	4	4	45
165	195	2	39	59	1	23	0	53	4	50
168	192	2	7	59	1	7	0	43	4	53
171	189	1	36	60	0	51	0	33	4	56
174	186	1	4	60	0	34	0	22	4	58
177	183	0	32	60	0	17	0	11	4	59
180	180	0	0	60	0	0	0	0	5	0

12. ON THE COMPUTATION OF THE COURSE OF THE MOON

[114ᵇ] Accordingly the method of computing the apparent movement of the moon is clear from what has been shown and is as follows. We shall reduce to equal time the time for which we are seeking the position of the moon proposed to us. By means of the time we shall deduce the mean movements of longitude, anomaly, and latitude—which last we shall also define soon—as we did in the case of the sun, from the given beginning of the years of Our Lord, or from some other beginning, and we shall declare the positions of the single movements at the time set before us. Then we shall seek in the table twice the regular longitude of the moon or twice its angular distance from the sun and[1] the corresponding additosubtraction found in the third column; and we shall note the proportional minutes which are in the next column. Accordingly if the number with which we entered upon the table was found in the first column or is less than 180°, we shall add the additosubtraction to the lunar anomaly; but if it is greater than 180° or is in the second column, the additosubtraction will be subtracted from the anomaly; and we shall have the corrected anomaly of the moon and its true angular distance from the highest apsis.

And entering the table again with this (distance) we shall determine the corresponding additosubtraction in the fifth column and the excess which follows in the sixth column, which the second (the small) epicycle adds (to the additosubtraction), over and above the first epicycle. The proportional part of this excess taken in accordance with the ratio of the 60 minutes is always added to this additosubtraction. The sum is subtracted from the mean movement of longitude or latitude, if the corrected anomaly is less than 180° or a semicircle; and it is added, if the anomaly is greater. And in this way we shall have the true distance of the moon from the mean position of the sun and the corrected movement of latitude. Wherefore the true position of the moon will not be unknown, either its distance from the first star of Aries in the case of the simple movement of the sun or its distance from the spring equinox in the case of the composite movement or the addition of the precession. Finally by means of the corrected movement in latitude we shall have in the seventh and last place of the table the degrees of latitude which measure the distance of the moon from the ecliptic. That latitude will be northern at the time when the movement of latitude is found in the first part of the table, [115ᵃ] i.e., if it is less than 90° or greater than 270°; otherwise it will be following a southern latitude. And so the moon will be coming down from the north to 180°, and afterwards it will be going up from the southern limit, until it has completed the remaining parts of the circle. Thus the apparent course of the moon has somehow as many affairs around the centre of the Earth as the Earth has around the sun.

[1] Because the moon traverses the small epicycle twice during one synodic month, the time of one revolution with respect to the sun.

13. HOW THE MOVEMENT OF LUNAR LATITUDE IS EXAMINED AND DEMONSTRATED

Now too we must give the ratio of the lunar movement in latitude, and it seems more difficult to discover, as it is complicated by more attendant circumstances. For, as we said before, if two eclipses of the moon were similar and equal in all respects, *i.e.*, with the parts eclipsed having the same position to the north or to the south and at the same ascending or descending ecliptic section: its distance from the Earth or from the highest apsis would be equal, since in this harmony the moon is understood to have completed its whole circles of latitude by true movement. For since the shadow of the Earth is conoid, and if a right cone is cut in a plane parallel with the base, the section is a circle which is smaller the greater the distance from the base and greater the shorter the distance from the base, and similarly equal at an equal distance. And so the moon at equal distances from the Earth traverses equal circles of shadow and presents to our vision equal disks of itself. Hence the moon, standing out with equal parts in the same direction according to an equal distance from the centre of the shadow makes us certain of equal latitudes, from which it necessarily follows that the moon has returned to its former position in latitude and is now distant from the same ecliptic node by an equal interval. But that is especially true if the position fulfils two of those conditions. For its approach to the Earth or withdrawal from it changes the total magnitude of the shadow, [115^b] but so slightly that it can hardly be grasped. Accordingly the greater the interval of time between both eclipses, the more definite can we have the movement in latitude of the moon, as was said in the case of the sun.

But since you rarely find two eclipses agreeing in these conditions—and up to now none have come our way—nevertheless we note there is another method which will give us the same result, since—the other conditions remaining—if the moon is eclipsed in different directions and at opposite sections, then it will signify that at the second eclipse the moon has arrived at a position diametrically opposite to the former and in addition to the whole circles has described a semicircle; and that will seem to be satisfactory for investigating the thing.

Accordingly we have found two eclipses fairly close in these respects: the first in the 7th year of Ptolemy Philometor, which was the 150th year of Alexander when—as Claud says—27 days of Phamenoth the 7th month of the Egyptians had passed, in the night which the 28th day followed. And the moon was eclipsed from the beginning of the 8th hour till the end of the 10th hour in Alexandrian nocturnal seasonal hours, to the extent of seven-twelfths of the lunar diameter, and it was eclipsed from the north around a descending section. Therefore the midtime of the eclipse was, he says, 2 seasonal hours after midnight, which make $2^1/_3$ equatorial hours, since the sun was at 6° of Taurus, but $1^1/_3$ hours after midnight at Cracow.

We have taken the second eclipse beneath the same Cracow meridian in the year of Our Lord 1519, after the 4th day before the Nones of June, when the sun was at 21° of Gemini. The midtime of the eclipse was $11^3/_5$ equatorial hours after midday; and the moon was eclipsed for approximately eight-twelfths of its diameter, from the south, at an ascending section.

Accordingly, from the beginning of the years of Alexander (to the first eclipse) there are 149 Egyptian years 206 days $14^1/_3$ hours at Alexandria, but at Cracow $13^1/_3$ hours according to apparent time, but $13^1/_2$ upon correction. At that time the position of anomaly by our calculation, which agreed approximately with Ptolemy's, was at 163°33' of regular movement; and there was a subtractive additosubtraction of 1°23', by which the true position of the moon was exceeded by the regular. But from the established beginning of the years of Alexander to the second eclipse [116ᵃ] there are 1832 Egyptian years 295 days 11 hours 45 minutes by apparent time, but by equal time 11 hours 55 minutes: whence the regular movement of the moon was 182°18'. The position of anomaly was 159°55', but as corrected it was 161°13'; and the additive additosubtraction, by which the regular movement was exceeded by the apparent, was 1°44'.

Accordingly it is clear that in both eclipses the distance of the moon from the Earth was equal, and the sun was approximately at the apogee in both cases, but there was a difference of one-twelfth in the eclipses. But since the diameter of the moon usually occupies approximately $1/_2$°, as we will show afterwards, its twelfth part will be $2^1/_2$', which corresponds to approximately $1/_2$° in the oblique circle of the moon at the ecliptic sections. And so the moon was $1/_2$° farther away from the ascending section at the second eclipse than from the descending section at the first eclipse. Hence it is clear that the true movement in latitude of the moon was $179^1/_2$° after the complete revolutions. But the lunar anomaly between the first and second eclipse adds 21'—which is the difference between the additosubtractions—to the regular (movement). Accordingly we shall have a regular lunar movement in latitude of 179°51' after the full circles. Now the time between the two eclipses was 1683 years 88 days 22 hours 35 minutes by apparent time, which agreed with the equal (time). During that time there were 40,577 complete equal revolutions and 179°51', which agree with the numbers which we have already set down.

14. ON THE POSITIONS OF LUNAR ANOMALY IN LATITUDE

However, in order to determine the positions of the moon's movement in relation to the established beginnings of calendar years, we have here also assumed two lunar eclipses, not at the same section and not at diametrically opposite parts, as in the foregoing, but at equal distances north or south, and fulfilling all the other requirements,

[116^b] as we said, in accordance with Ptolemy's rule, and in this way we shall solve our problem without any error.

Accordingly, the first eclipse, which we have already used in investigating other movements of the moon, is the one which we said was observed by Claud Ptolemy in the 19th year of Hadrian when two days of the month Chiach had passed, one equatorial hour before midnight at Alexandria, but at Cracow two hours before midnight, which the third day followed. The moon was eclipsed at the midpoint of the eclipse to the extent of ten-twelfths of the diameter, *i.e.*, ten-twelfths from the north, while the sun was at 25°10' of Libra, and the position of lunar anomaly was 64°38' and its subtractive additosubtraction was 4°20' around the descending section.

We made careful observations of the other eclipse at Rome, in the year of Our Lord 1500, after the Nones of November, 2 hours after midnight, and it was the 8th daybreak before the Ides of November. But at Cracow which is 5° to the east, it was 2²/₅ hours after midnight, while the sun was at 23°16' of Scorpio; and once more there was a ten-twelfths eclipse from the north.

Therefore, since the death of Alexander there have passed 1824 Egyptian years 84 days 14 hours 20 minutes by apparent time, but by equal time 14 hours 16 minutes. Accordingly the mean movement of the moon was 174°14', and the lunar anomaly was 294°44', but as corrected it was 291°35'; and there was an additive additosubtraction of 4°27'.

Accordingly it is clear that at both these eclipses the distances of the moon from the highest apsis was approximately equal, and at both times the sun was at its mean apsis, and the magnitude of the shadows was equal. All that makes clear that the latitude of the moon was southern and equal; and hence that the moon was at an equal distance from the sections but was ascending at the second eclipse and descending at the first. Accordingly between both eclipses there are 1366 Egyptian years 358 days 4 hours 20 minutes by apparent time, but by equal time 4 hours 24 minutes, wherein the movement in latitude was 159°55'.

Now let *ABCD* be the oblique circle of the moon; and let *AB* be its diameter and common section with the ecliptic. Let *C* be the northern limit, and *D* the southern; [117^a] *A* the ecliptic section descending, and *B* the ecliptic section ascending. Now let there be taken *AF* and *BE* two equal arcs in the south, according as the first eclipse was at point *F* and the second at *E*. And again let *FK* be the subtractive additosubtraction at the first eclipse, and *EL* the additive additosubtraction at the second.

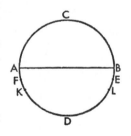

Accordingly, since

$$\text{arc } KL = 159°55'$$

and

$$\text{arc } FK = 4°20'$$

and

$$\text{arc } EL = 4°27';$$
$$\text{arc } FKLE = \text{arcs } FK + KL + LE = 168°42'.$$

And

$$180° - 168°42' = 11°18°.$$

Now

$$\text{arc } AF = \text{arc } BE = \frac{1}{2}(11°18') = 5°39',$$

which is the true distance of the moon from section AB, and on that account

$$\text{arc } AFK = 9°59'.$$

Hence it is clear that K the mean position in latitude is 99°59' away from the northern limit.

From the death of Alexander to this position and time of Ptolemy's observation there are 457 Egyptian years 91 days 10 hours by apparent time, but by equal time 9 hours 54 minutes, during which the mean movement in latitude is 50°59'. And when 50°59' is subtracted from 99°59', there remain 49° for noon on the first day of Thoth the first month by the Egyptian calendar at the beginning of the years of Alexander but on the Cracow meridian. Hence for each of the other beginnings there are given in accordance with the differences of time the positions of the course of the moon in latitude as taken in relation to the northern limit, from which we measure the movement.

Now from the first Olympiad to the death of Alexander there are 451 Egyptian years 247 days—from which in accordance with equality of time 7 minutes of an hour are subtracted—and during that time the progress in latitude was 136°57'. Again from the first Olympiad to Caesar there are 780 Egyptian years 12 hours, but 10 minutes of an hour are added to the equal time; and during that time the movement is 206°53'. Then come 45 years 12 days up to Christ. Accordingly if 136°57' are subtracted from 49° plus the 360° of the circle, there remain 272°3' for noon of the first day of the month Hekatombaion of the first Olympiad.

Now if 206°53' are added to 272°3', the sum will be 118°56' for midnight before the Kalends of January [117b] at the beginning of the Julian years.

Finally, with the addition of 10°49' the sum becomes 129°45' as the position (at the beginning of the years) of Our Lord similarly at midnight before the Kalends of January.

15. CONSTRUCTION OF THE INSTRUMENT FOR
OBSERVING PARALLAXES

But chance and the hindrance of the lunar parallaxes did not grant to us, as it had to Ptolemy, the occasion of discovering experimentally that the greatest latitude of the moon—in accordance with the angle of section of its orbital circle and the ecliptic—is 5°, whereof the circle is 360°. For he was watching at Alexandria—which has 30°58' as the elevation of the north pole—until the moon should come most near to the vertex of the horizon, namely when it was at the beginning of Cancer and at the northern limit, which can be foreknown by means of calculations. Therefore at that time by means of an instrument which he called the parallacticon and which was constructed for measuring the parallaxes of the moon, he found that the least distance was only $2^1/_8$° from the vertex, and if any parallax had occurred at this distance it would necessarily have been very slight in such a small spatial interval. Accordingly by the subtraction of $2^1/_8$° from 30°58'[1] the remainder is 28°50$^1/_2$', which exceeds the greatest obliquity of the ecliptic—which at that time was 23°51'20"—by approximately 5°; and this latitude for the moon is found to agree in every respect with the other particulars.

But the instrument for observing parallaxes consists of three straight-edges. Two of them are of equal length and are at least eight or nine feet long; the third is somewhat longer. The latter and one of the former two are joined to both extremities of the remaining straight-edge, by carefully making holes and fitting cylinders or pivots into them in such a way that while the straight-edges are movable in a plane surface they do not wobble at all at the joints. Now in the longer straight-edge a straight line should be drawn from the centre of its place of joining through its total length, and the line is made equal to the distance between the places of joining (on the other straight-edge) measured as accurately as possible. This line is divided into 1,000 equal parts—or into more, if that can be done; and the division of the remainder should be carried on [118ᵃ] in the same unit parts, until it reaches 1414 parts, which subtend the side of a square that may be inscribed in a circle whose radius has 1,000 parts. It will be all right to cut off as superfluous the remainder of the straight-edge over and above this. In the other ruler too, there should be drawn from the centre of the joining-place a line equal to those 1,000 parts or to the distance between the centres of the two joining-places; the ruler should have eyepieces fastened to it on one side, as in a dioptra, which sight may have passage through. The eyepieces should be so adjusted that the sight-passages do not at all swerve away from the line already drawn the length of the straight-edge, but keep at an equal distance; and provided also that the line as extended from its terminus to the longer ruler can touch the divided line. And in this way by means of the rulers an isosceles triangle is made, the base of which will be along the parts of the divided line.

[1]The elevation of the north pole above the horizon is equal to the declination of the vertex of the horizon from the equator.

Then a pole, which has been divided crosswise in the best manner and well smoothed, should be erected on a firm base. The ruler which has the two joining-places should be affixed to this pole by means of pivots, around which the instrument may swing, like a swinging door, but in such a way that the straight line through the centres of the joining-places will always correspond to the plumbline of the ruler and point towards the vertex of the horizon, as if its axis. Accordingly when a person who wishes to find the distance of some star from the vertex of the horizon has the star itself in full view along a straight line through the eyepieces, then by the application underneath of the ruler with the divided line, he should learn how many unit parts—whereof the diameter of the circle has 20,000—subtend the angle between the line of vision and the axis of the horizon; and by means of the table he will get the sought arc of the great circle passing through the star and the vertex of the horizon.

16. HOW THE PARALLAXES OF THE MOON ARE DETERMINED

By means of this instrument, as we said, Ptolemy found the greatest latitude of the moon to be 5°. Next he turned to observing the parallax and said he discovered that at Alexandria it was 1°7', while the sun was at 5°28' of Libra and the mean movement of the moon away from the sun was 78°13', the regular anomaly was 262°20'; the movement in latitude was 354°40'; the additive additosubtraction was 7°26'; [118^b] and accordingly the position of the moon was at 3°9' of Capricorn. The corrected movement in latitude was 2°6'; the northern latitude of the moon was 4°59'; its declination from the equator was 23°49'; and the latitude of Alexandria was 30°58'. The moon, he says, as seen through the instrument, was approximately in the meridian circle at 50°45' from the vertex of the horizon, i.e., 1°7' more than the computation demanded. Hence by the rule of the ancients concerning the eccentric circle and the epicycle, he shows that the distance of the moon from the centre of the Earth was then 39^{P}45' whereof the radius of the Earth is 1^P; and what next follows from the ratio of the circles, namely that the greatest distance of the moon from the Earth—which they say occurs at a new and at a full moon in the apogee of the epicycle—is 64^{P}10', but the least distance—at the quadratures and at the half moon in the perigee of the epicycle—is only 33^{P}33'. Hence he even evaluated the parallaxes, which occur at about 90° from the vertex (of the horizon): the least at 53'34", and the greatest at 1°43'—as it is possible to see in a broad outline what he built up concerning them. But now it is perfectly obvious to those wishing to consider the question that these things are far otherwise, as we have found out experimentally very often.

However, we shall review two observations, by which it is again made clear that our hypotheses as to the moon have more certitude than his, because they are found to

agree better with the appearances and to leave nothing in doubt. In the 1522nd year since the birth of Christ, on the 5th day before the Kalends of October, after the passage of $5^2/_3$ equal hours since midday, at about sunset at Frauenburg we found by means of the parallactic instrument that the centre of the moon, which was in the meridian circle, was 82°50' distant from the vertex of the horizon. Accordingly from the beginning of the years of Our Lord to this hour there were 1522 Egyptian years 284 days $17^2/_3$ hours by apparent time but by equal time 17 hours 24 minutes. Wherefore the apparent position of the sun was by calculation at 13°29' of Libra and the regular movement of the moon away from the sun [119ª] was 87°6'; the regular anomaly was 357°39'; but the true (the corrected) anomaly was 358°40', and it added 7'; and thus the true position of the moon was at 12°32' of Aries. The mean movement in latitude was 197°1' from the northern limit, the true was 197°8'; the southern latitude of the moon was 4°47'; the moon had a declination of 27°41' from the equator; the latitude of the place of our observation was 54°19', and the addition of 54°19' to the lunar declination makes the true distance of the moon from the pole of the horizon to be 82°. Accordingly the 50' not accounted for belong to the parallax, which by Ptolemy's teaching should be 1°17'.

Once more we made another observation at the same place in the 1524th year of Our Lord on the 7th day before the Ides of August 6 hours after midday; and we saw through the same instrument the moon at 82° from the vertex of the horizon. Accordingly from the beginning of the years of Our Lord to this hour there were 1524 Egyptian years 234 days 18 hours (by apparent time) and also 18 hours by exact time. The position of the sun was by calculation at 24°14' of Leo; the mean movement of the moon away from the sun was 97°6'; the regular anomaly was 242°10'; the corrected anomaly was 239°43', adding approximately 7° to the mean movement; wherefore the true position of the moon was at 9°39' of Sagittarius; the mean movement of latitude was 193°19'; the true, 200°17'; the southern latitude of the moon was 4°41'; the southern declination was 26°36', and the addition of 26°36' to 54°19' of the latitude of the place of observation makes the distance of the moon from the pole of the horizon to be 80°55'. But there appeared to be 82°. Accordingly the difference of 1°5' came from the lunar parallax, which according to Ptolemy should have been 1°38' and also according to the theory of the ancients, as the harmonic ratio, which follows from their hypotheses, forces you to admit.

17. Distance of the Moon from the Earth and Demonstration of Their Ratio in Parts Whereof the Radius of the Earth Is the Unit

[119ᵇ] From this it will now be made apparent how great the distance of the moon from the earth is. And without this distance a sure ratio cannot be given for the parallaxes, for they are mutually related. And it will be established in this way. Let *AB* be a

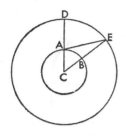

great circle of the Earth, and let C be its centre. Around C let another circle be described in comparison with which the Earth has considerable magnitude, and let this circle be DE. Let D be the pole of the horizon, and let the centre of the moon be at E, so that DE its distance from the vertex is known. Accordingly, since at the first observation,

$$\text{angle } DAE = 82°50'$$

and by calculation

$$\text{angle } ACE = 82°$$

and hence

$$\text{angle } DAE - \text{angle } ACE = 50',$$

which belonged to the parallax; we have triangle ACE with its angles given and therefore with its sides given. For since

$$\text{angle } CAE \text{ is given,}$$
$$\text{side } CE = 99,219$$

where diameter of circle circumscribing triangle $AEC = 100,000$ and

$$AC = 1,454;$$

and

$$CE68^{\text{P}},$$
$$\text{where } AC, \text{ radius of Earth, } = 1^{\text{P}}.$$

And this was the distance of the moon from the centre of the Earth at the first observation.

But at the second observation

$$\text{angle } DAE = 82°,$$

as the apparent movement; and, by calculation,

$$\text{angle } ACE = 80°55;$$

and, by subtraction,

$$\text{angle } AEC = 1°5'.$$

Accordingly,

$$\text{side } EC = 99,027$$

and

$$\text{side } AC = 1894$$

where diameter of circle circumscribing triangle $= 100,000$.

And so

$$CB = 56^{\text{P}}42',$$
$$\text{where the radius of Earth } = 1^{\text{P}}.$$

And that was the distance of the moon.

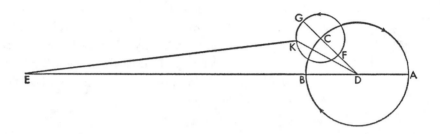

But now let *ABC* be the greater epicycle of the moon; and let its centre be *D*. Let *E* be taken as the centre of the Earth, and from *E* let the straight line *EBDA* be drawn, so that *A* is the apogee and *B* the perigee. Now let

arc *ABC* = 242°10',

in accordance with the computed regularity of the lunar anomaly.
And with *C* as centre let epicycle *FGK* be described, whereon

arc *FGK* = 194°10',

twice the distance of the moon from the sun. And let *DK* be joined.

Thus,

angle *GDK* = − add. [120ª] 2°27';

and, by subtraction,

corr. anomaly = 59°43',

since

arc *CDB* = arc *ABC* − 180° = 62°10',

and

angle *BEK* = 7°,

Therefore, in triangle *KDE* the angles are given in the degrees whereof 2 rt. angles = 180°; and the ratio of the sides is also given:

DE = 91,856

and

EK = 86,354,

where diameter of circle circumscribing triangle *KDE* = 100,000.

But

KE = 94,010

where *DE* = 100,000.

Now it was shown above that

DF = 8,600

and

DFG = 13,340.

236

Accordingly it follows from the given ratio that when, as was shown,

$$EK = 56P42',$$

where radius of the Earth = 1P;

then

$$DE = 60P18',$$
$$DF = 5P11',$$
$$DFG = 8P2';$$

and hence, as extended in a straight line.

$$EDG = 68^1/_3P;$$

and that is the greatest altitude of the half moon. Furthermore,

$$ED - DG = 52°17',$$

which is its least distance. And thus, at its greatest,

$$EDF = 65^1/_2P,$$

which is the altitude occurring at the bright, full moon; and at its least,

$$EDF - DF = 55P8'.$$

And we should not be moved by the fact that others—and especially those to whom the parallaxes of the moon could not become known except partially, on account of the location of their places—estimate the greatest distance of the new moon and the full moon to be 64P10'. But the greater nearness of the moon to the horizon—for it is clear that the parallaxes are filled out in relation to the horizon—has allowed us to perceive them more perfectly, and we have not found the parallaxes to differ by more than 1' on account of the difference caused by the nearness of the moon to the horizon.

18. ON THE DIAMETER OF THE MOON AND ON THE DIAMETER OF THE TERRESTRIAL SHADOW IN THE PLACE OF PASSAGE OF THE MOON

[120b] Moreover, the apparent diameters of the moon and the shadow vary with the distance of the moon from the Earth. Wherefore it is pertinent to speak of them. And although the diameters of the sun and the moon are rightly determined through the dioptra of Hipparchus, nevertheless in the case of the moon astronomers judge that this is done with more certainty through some particular eclipses of the moon, in which the moon is at an equal distance from its highest or lowest apsis, especially if at that time the sun too is in the same relative situation, so that the circle of shadow which the moon passes through is found equal—unless the eclipses themselves are unequal in extent. For it is clear that the comparison of the difference in extent of the eclipses with the latitude of the moon shows how much of the circle around the centre of the Earth the diameter of the moon subtends. When that has been perceived, the semidiameter of the shadow is also known.

All this will be made clearer by an example. In this way at the midpoint of the first eclipse $^3/_{12}$ of the diameter of the moon was eclipsed; and the moon had a latitude of 47'54"; but at the other eclipse $^{10}/_{12}$ of the diameter was eclipsed, and the latitude was 29'37". The difference between the extent of the eclipses is $^7/_{12}$ of the diameter; the difference in latitude is 18'17"; and the $^{12}/_{12}$ are proportional to the 31'20" which the diameter of the moon subtends. Accordingly it is clear that the centre of the moon at the midpoint of the first eclipse was about a quarter of the moon's diameter—or 7'50" of latitude—beyond the shadow if these 7'50" are subtracted from the 47'54" of the total latitude, 40'4" remain as the semidiameter of the shadow; just as at the other eclipse the shadow occupied—in proportion to $^1/_3$ of the lunar diameter—10'27" more than the latitude of the centre of the moon. The addition of 29'37" to 10'27" similarly makes the semidiameter of the shadow to be 40'4". And so in accordance with Ptolemy's conclusion, when the sun and moon are in conjunction or opposition at their greatest distance from the Earth, the diameter of the moon is 31'20"—[121ª] as he admits he found the sun's diameter to be through the dioptra of Hipparchus—but the diameter of the shadow is 1°21'20"; and he believed that the diameters were in the ratio of 13 to 5, *i.e.*, the ratio of double plus three-fifths.

19. How the Distances of the Sun and Moon from the Earth, Their Diameters and That of the Shadow at the Place of Crossing of the Moon, and the Axis of the Shadow Are Demonstrated Simultaneously

But even the sun has some parallax; and since it is very slight, it is not perceived so easily, except that the following things are related reciprocally: namely the distance of the sun and moon from the Earth, their diameters and that of the shadow at the crossing of the moon, and the axis of the shadow; and for that reason they are mutually productive of one another in analytical demonstrations. First we shall review Ptolemy's conclusions on these things, and how he demonstrated them, and we shall draw out from them what seems the most true. He assumed $31^1/_3$' as the apparent diameter of the sun, which he employed without any qualification. He assumed as equal to that the diameter of the full and new moon when at its apogee, which he says was at a distance of 64ᴾ10', whereof the radius of the Earth is 1ᴾ.

From that he demonstrated the rest in this way: Let *ABC* be the circle of the solar globe around centre *D*; and let *EFG* be the circle of the terrestrial globe around its centre *K* at its greatest distance from the sun. Let *AG* and *CE* be straight lines touching both circles, and let them as extended meet at the apex of the shadow, as at point *S*. And let *DKS* be a line through the centres of the sun and the Earth. Moreover, let *AK* and *KC* be drawn, and let *AC* and *GE* be joined, which should hardly differ at all from

the diameters on account of the great distance between them. Now on *DKS* let equal segments *LK* and *KM* be taken in proportion to the distance of the moon in the apogee when new and when full: in his opinion 64P10', where *EK* is 1P. Let *QMR* be the diameter of the shadow at this crossing of the moon; and let *NLO* be the diameter of the moon at right angles to *DK*, and let it be extended as *LOP*.

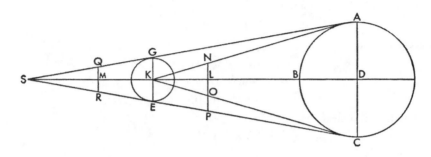

The first problem is to find

$$DK : KE.$$

Accordingly, since

$$\text{angle } NKD = 31\tfrac{1}{3}',$$
$$\text{where 4 rt. angles} = 360°$$

and [121b]

$$\text{angle } LKO = \tfrac{1}{2} \text{ angle } NKO,$$
$$\text{angle } LKO = 15\tfrac{2}{3}'.$$

And

$$\text{angle } L = 90°.$$

Accordingly, in triangle *LKO*, which has its angles given,

$$KL : LO \text{ is given,}$$

and

$$LO = 17\text{P}33',$$

and

$$LK = 64\text{P}10',$$
$$\text{where } KE = 1\text{P}$$

And because

$$LO : MR = 5 : 13,$$
$$MR = 45'38''.$$

But since *LOP* and *MR* are parallel to *KE* at equal intervals, on that account

$$LOP + MR = 2 \ KE.$$

And

$$OP = LOP - (MR + LO) - 56'49''.$$

Now by Euclid, VI, 2,

$$EC : PC = KC : OC = KD : LD = KE : OP = 60' : 56'49".$$

Hence

$$LD = 56'49",$$

where $DLK = 1$P.

And accordingly, by subtraction,

$$KL = 3'11".$$

But according as

$$KL = 64\text{P}10',$$

where $FK = 1$P,

$$KD = 1210\text{P}.$$

Now it is also clear that

$$MR = 45'38".$$

Hence

$$KE : MR \text{ is given}$$

and

$$KMS : MS \text{ is given}.$$

And of the whole KMS

$$KM = 14'22".$$

And, *separando*,

$$KMS = 268\text{P}$$

where $KM = 64\text{P}10'.$

So in truth Ptolemy.

But others after Ptolemy, since they found that these things did not agree sufficiently with the appearances, published other things concerning all this. None the less
they admit that the greatest distance of the full moon and the new moon from the
Earth is 64P10'; and that the apparent diameter of the sun at its apogee is $31^1/_3'$. They
even grant that the diameter of the shadow at the place of crossing of the moon is as
13 to 5, even as Ptolemy himself. Nevertheless they deny that the apparent diameter of
the moon at that time is greater than $29^1/_2'$; and for that reason they put the diameter
of the shadow at approximately $1°16^3/_4'$. They hold that it follows from this that at its
apogee the distance of the sun from the Earth is 1146P and that the axis of the shadow
is 254P, whereof the radius of the Earth is 1P. [122ª] And astronomers attribute these
things to the Harranite philosopher (al-Battani) as the discoverer, although they cannot
be joined together at all reasonably. We considered that these things must be adjusted
and corrected as follows, since we put the apparent diameter of the sun in its apogee at
31'40"—for it should be somewhat greater now than before Ptolemy—and that of the
full or the new moon in its highest apsis at 30' and the diameter of the shadow in its

crossing at $80^3/_5$'. For astronomers should have a slightly greater ratio than that of 5 to 13, that is to say 150 to 403. And the whole sun is not covered by the moon, unless the moon is at a lesser distance from the Earth than 62ᴾ, whereof the radius of the Earth is 1ᴾ. For when these things are put down in this way they seem to be connected with one another and the rest in a sure fashion and to be consonant with the apparent eclipses of the sun and moon. And in accordance with the foregoing demonstration:

$$LO = 17'85''$$

where KE radius of Earth = 1ᴾ.

And for that reason

$$MR = 46'1'',$$

and

$$OP = 56'51''.$$

And

$$DLK = 1179 \text{ P},$$

the distance from the Earth of the sun at its apogee; and

$$KMS = 265,$$

which is the axis of the shadow.

20. On the Magnitude of These Three Celestial Bodies: the Sun, Moon, and Earth, and Their Comparison with One Another

Hence it is also manifest that

$$LK : KD = 1 : 18$$

and

$$LO : DC = 1 : 18.$$

Now

$$1 : 18 = 17'8'' : 5ᴾ27'$$

where KE = 1ᴾ.

And

$$SK : KE = 265ᴾ : 1ᴾ = SKD : DC = 1444ᴾ : 5ᴾ27'.$$

For they are all proportional; and that will be the ratio of the diameters of the sun and Earth. But, as globes are in the ratio of the cubes[1] of their diameters, accordingly

$$(5ᴾ27')^3 - 161^7/_8ᴾ;$$

and the sun is $161^7/_8$ greater than the terrestrial globe.

Again, since

$$\text{moon's radius} = 17'9''$$

[1] *literally*, in the triplicate ratio.

where KE = 1P,

[122[b]] Earth's diameter: moon's diameter = 7 : 2, *i.e.*, in the triple sesquialter ratio. When the cube[1] of that ratio is taken, it shows that the Earth is $42^7/_8$ greater than the moon. And hence the sun will be $6,999^{62}/_{63}$ greater than the moon.

21. ON THE APPARENT DIAMETER OF THE SUN AND ITS PARALLAXES

But since the same magnitude when farther away appears smaller than when nearer; for that reason it happens that the sun, moon, and the shadow of the Earth vary with their unequal distances from the Earth no less than do their parallaxes. By means of the aforesaid, all these things are easily determinable for any elongation whatsoever. That is first made manifest in the case of the sun. For since we have shown that the Earth at its farthest is 10,323 parts distant from the sun, whereof the radius of the orbital circle of annual revolution = 10,000; and at its nearest the Earth has a distance of 9,678 parts of the remainder of the diameter: accordingly the highest apsis is 1179P whereof the radius of the Earth is 1P, the lowest apsis will be 1105P, and so the mean apsis will be 1142P. Accordingly in the right triangle[2]

$$1,000,000 \div 1179 = 848^3 = \frac{1}{2} \text{ ch. 2 } (2'55''),$$

which is the small angle of greatest parallax, and that is found around the horizon. Similarly, as the least distance is 1105P,

$$1,000,000 - 1105 = 905^4 = \frac{1}{2} \text{ ch. 2 } (3'7'');$$

and 3'7" measures the angle of greatest parallax of the lowest apsis. Now it was shown that the diameter of the sun is 5P27', whereof the diameter of the Earth is 1P, and that it appears at the highest apsis as 31'48". For

$$1179P : 5P27' = 2,000,000 : 9,245;$$

$$\text{where diameter of circle} = 2,000,000,$$

and

$$\frac{1}{2} \text{ ch. } 2(31'48'') = 9245.$$

It follows that at the least distance of 1105P there is an apparent diameter of 33'54". Therefore the difference between them is 2'6"; but there is a difference of only 12" [123[a]] between the parallaxes. Ptolemy considered that both of these differences should be ignored on account of their smallness; for 1' or 2' is not easily perceptible to the senses, much less than are a few seconds perceptible. Wherefore if we keep the greatest parallax of the sun at 3' everywhere, we shall be seen to have made no error.

[1] *literally,* the triplicate.
[2] *i.e.,* the right triangle formed by the line joining the centres of the sun and the Earth, the tangent from the centre of the sun to the Earth's surface, and the radius of the Earth to that point of tangency.
[3] *i.e.,* when the highest apsis = 1179P, 1P = 848 whereof radius of circle = 1,000,000.
[4] Similarily, where the lowest apsis = 1105P, 1P = 905 whereof radius of circle = 1,000,000.

Now we shall determine the mean apparent diameters of the sun through its mean distances; or, as do others, through the apparent hourly movement of the sun, which they believe to be to its diameter as 5 to 66 or as 1 to $14^1/_5$. For its hourly movement is approximately proportional to its distance.

22. On the Unequal Apparent Diameter of the Moon and Its Parallaxes

A greater diversity in the apparent diameter and parallaxes appears in the case of the moon as being the nearest planet. For since its greatest distance from the Earth is $65^1/_2$P at new moon and full moon, its least distance—will by the above demonstrations be 55P8'; and the greatest (altitudinal) elongation of the half moon will be 68P21', and the least 52P17'. Accordingly we shall have the parallaxes of the setting or rising moon at these four termini, when we have divided the radius of the circle by the distances of the moon from the Earth: the parallax of the farthest half moon will be 50'18" and that of the farthest new or full moon will be 52'24"; the parallax of the nearest full or new moon will be 62'21" and that of the nearest half moon 65'45".

Furthermore by this the apparent diameters of the moon are established. For it was shown that the diameter of the Earth is to the diameter of the moon as 7 to 2, and the radius of the Earth will be to the diameter of the moon as 7 to 4. Moreover, the parallaxes are in that ratio to the apparent diameters of the moon, since the straight lines, which comprehend the angles of the greater parallaxes, do not differ at all from the apparent diameters at the same crossing of the moon; and the angles, (or arcs of parallax) are approximately proportional to the chords subtending them; and their difference is not perceptible to sense. By this summary it is clear that at the first limit of the parallaxes which have been already set forth the apparent [123b] diameter of the moon will be $28^3/_4$'; at the second, approximately 30'; at the third, 35'38"; and at the last limit, 37'34". By the hypothesis of Ptolemy and others the diameter would have been approximately 1°, and so it ought to have been, as the half moon at that time was shedding as much light on the Earth as the full moon would.

23. What the Ratio of Difference Between the Shadows of the Earth Is

We have already made clear that

shadow's diameter; moon's diameter = 403 : 150.

For that reason at a full or a new moon, when the sun is at its apogee, the shadow's is found to be 80'36" at its least and 95'44" at its greatest; and the greatest difference is 15'8". Moreover, the shadow of the Earth varies, even in the same place of crossing of the moon, on account of the unequal distance of the Earth from the sun, as follows:

For, as in the foregoing diagram, let *DKS* the straight line through the centres of the sun and the Earth be drawn again, and also *CES* the line of tangency. As was shown, when

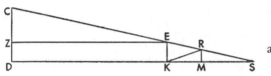

distance *DK* = 1179P,

where *KE* = 1P

and

KM = 62P

then the semidiameter of the shadow

$$MR = 46'1''$$

where *KE* = 1P;

and (*KR* being joined)

$$\text{angle } MKR = 42'32'',$$

which is the angle of sight, and the axis of the shadow

$$KMS = 265\text{P}.$$

Now when the Earth is nearest to the sun, so that

$$DK = 1105\text{P},$$

we shall evaluate the shadow of the Earth at the same crossing of the moon, as follows: For let *EZ* be drawn parallel to *DK*. Then

$$CZ : ZE = EK : KS.$$

But

$$CZ = 4\text{P}27'$$

and

$$ZE = 1105\text{P}.$$

For

$$ZE = DK$$

and

$$DZ = KE,$$

as *KZ* is a parallelogram. Accordingly

$$KS = 248\text{P}19'$$

where *KE* = 1P.

Now

$$KM = 62;$$

and accordingly, by subtraction,

$$MS = 186\text{P}19'.$$

But since

$$SM : MR = SK : KE,$$

therefore

$$MR = 45'1'',$$
where [124a] $KE = 1\text{P}.$

And hence

$$\text{angle } MKR = 41'35'',$$

which is the angle of sight. Whence it happens that on account of the approach and withdrawal of the sun and the Earth, the greatest difference in the diameters of the shadow at the same place of crossing of the moon is 1', whereof $EK = 1\text{P}$, in proportion to an angle of sight of 57", whereof 4 rt. angles = 360°.

Furthermore, in the first case

$$\text{shadow's diameter : moon's diameter} > 13 : 5;$$

but here

$$\text{shadow's diameter : moon's diameter} < 13 : 5,$$

as 13 : 5 is a sort of mean ratio. Wherefore we shall make but slight error if we employ it as everywhere the same, thus saving labour and following the judgment of the ancients.

24. ON THE TABLE OF THE PARTICULAR PARALLAXES IN THE CIRCLE PASSING THROUGH THE POLES OF THE HORIZON

Moreover, it will not be difficult now to determine all the single parallaxes of the sun and the moon. For let there be drawn again *AB* the terrestrial circle through the vertex of the horizon, with *C* as its centre. And in the same plane let *DE* be the orbital circle of the moon, *FG* that of the sun, *CDF* the line through the vertex of the horizon; and let line *CEG* be drawn, in which the true positions of the sun and the moon are understood to be, and let the lines of sight *AG* and *AE* be joined to those points. Therefore the parallaxes of the sun are measured by angle *AGC*, those of the moon 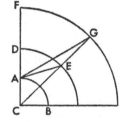 by angle *AEC*. Moreover, there is a parallax between the sun and moon which is measured by angle *GAE*, which is determined according to the difference between angles *AGC* and *AEC*. Now let us take angle *ACG*, with which we wish to compare those angles; and, for example, let

$$\text{angle } ACG = 30°.$$

Now it is clear from what we have shown concerning plane triangles that when

$$\text{line } CG = 1142\text{P},$$
$$\text{where } AC = 1\text{P},$$
$$\text{angle } AGC = 1\tfrac{1}{2}',$$

which is the difference between the true and the seeming altitude of the sun. But when

$$\text{angle } ACG = 60°,$$
$$\text{angle } AGC = 2'36''.$$

Everything will be similarly clear as regards the remaining angles.

But in the case of the moon at its four limits: If at the greatest lunar distance from the Earth, wherein, as we said,

$$CE = 68\text{P}21',$$
[124b] where $CA = 1\text{P}$,
$$\text{angle } DCE = 30°,$$
where 4 rt. angles = 360°,

we shall have triangle ACE in which the two sides AC and CE together with angle ACE have been given. From that we find that

$$\text{parallax } AEC = 25'28''.$$

And when

$$CE = 65^1/_2\text{P}$$
$$\text{angle } AEC = 26'36''.$$

Similarly in the third case when

$$CE = 55\text{P}8',$$
$$\text{parallax } AEC = 31'42''.$$

Finally, at the least distance when

$$CE = 52\text{P}17',$$
$$\text{angle } AEC = 33'27''.$$

Again, when

$$\text{arc } DE = 60°,$$

the parallaxes in the same order will be as follows:

$$\text{First parallax} = 43'55'',$$
$$\text{second parallax} = 45'51'',$$
$$\text{third parallax} = 54^1/_2',$$

and

$$\text{fourth parallax} = 57^1/_2'.$$

We shall inscribe all these things after the order of the subjoined table, which for the sake of convenience we shall extend like all the other tables into a series of thirty rows but proceeding by 6°'s by which twice the arcs from the vertex of the horizon—of which the greatest is 90°—are given to be understood. But we have divided the table into nine columns. For in the first and second will be found the common numbers of the circle. We shall put the parallaxes of the sun in the third, and in the next the lunar parallaxes, and in the fifth column the differences, by which the least parallaxes, which occur at the half moon and at the apogee, are deficient as measured by the parallaxes occurring at the apogee of the full moon or the new moon. The sixth column will

contain the parallaxes which the full or bright moon produces at its perigee; and in the next column are the minutes of difference, by which the parallaxes which occur at half

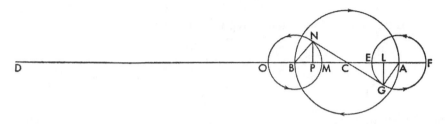

moon when the moon is nearest to us exceed those occurring at half moon in the apogee. Then, the two spaces which are left are reserved for the proportional minutes, by which the parallaxes between these four limits can be computed. We shall set forth these parallaxes, and first in connection with the apogee and the parallaxes which are between the first two limits—as follows.

Let circle [125ª] *AB* be the first epicycle of the moon, and let *C* be its centre. With *D* taken as the centre of the Earth, let the straight line *DBCA* be drawn; and with apogee *A* as centre let the second epicycle *EFG* be described. Now let

arc *EG* = 60°,

and let *AG* and *CG* be joined. Accordingly, since in the foregoing it was shown that

straight line *CE* = 5ᴾ11',

where radius of Earth = 1ᴾ,

straight line *DC* = 60ᴾ 18',

and

straight line *EF* = 2ᴾ51',

then in triangle *ACG*

side *GA* = 1ᴾ25'

and

side *AC* = 6ᴾ36';

and

angle *CAG* is given,

which is the angle comprehended by *GA* and *AC*. Accordingly, by what has been shown concerning plane triangles,

side *CG* = 6ᴾ7'.

Accordingly, as extended in a straight line,

DCG = *DCL* = 66ᴾ25'.

But

$$DCE = 65^1/_2\text{P}.$$

Therefore, by subtraction,

$$EL55^1/_2{}',$$

and that is the excess. Moreover, by this given ratio, when

$$DCE = 60\text{P};$$
$$EF = 2\text{P}37',$$

and

$$EL = 46'.$$

Therefore, according as,

$$EF = 60',$$
$$\text{excess } EL \doteqdot 18'.$$

We shall mark these down in the eighth column of the table as corresponding to 60° (in the first column).

We shall show something similar in the case of perigee B. Let the second epicycle MNO be drawn again around centre B, and let

$$\text{angle } MBN = 60°.$$

For, as before, triangle BCN will have its sides and angles given, and similarly

$$\text{excess } MP = 55^1/_2{}'$$
$$\text{where Earth's radius} = 1\text{P}.$$

But that is because

$$DBM = 55\text{P}8'.$$

If

$$DBM = 60\text{P};$$
$$MBO = 3\text{P}7',$$

and

$$\text{excess } MP = 55'.$$

Now

$$3\text{P}7' : 55' = 60' : 18';$$

and so on, the same as before. Nevertheless there is a difference of a few seconds. We shall do this for the rest; and thus we shall fill out the eighth column of the table. But if we were to employ instead of them, those (proportional minutes) which were set

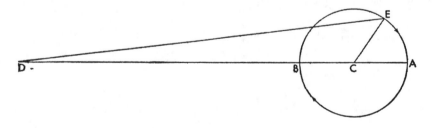

out in the table of additosubtractions, we shall make no error. For they are approximately the same—and it is a question of very small numbers. [125^b] There remain the proportional minutes which occur at the mean termini, namely between the second and the third termini.

Now let circle AB be the first epicycle at the new or full moon. Let C be its centre; and let D be taken as the centre of the Earth. And let the straight line $DBCA$ be extended. Now from apogee A let some arc be taken: for instance, let

$$\text{arc } AE = 60°;$$

and let DE and CE be joined. For we shall have the triangle DCE, in which two sides are given:

$$CD = 60\text{P}19'$$

and

$$CE = 5\text{P}11'.$$

Now angle DCE is an interior angle, and

$$\text{angle } DCE = 180° - \text{angle } ACE.$$

Accordingly, by what we have shown concerning triangles,

$$DE = 63\text{P}4'.$$

But

$$DBA = 65^1/_2\text{P},$$

and

$$DBA - ED = 2\text{P}26'.$$

Now

$$AB = 10\text{P}22';$$

and

$$10\text{P}22' : 2\text{P}26' = 60' : 14'.$$

And they are inscribed in the table in the ninth column opposite 60°. Following this example, we have completed the rest and filled out the table, which follows. And we have added another table of the semidiameters of the sun and the moon, and the shadow of the Earth, so that as far as possible they may be at hand.

TABLE OF THE PARALLAXES OF THE SUN AND MOON

Common Numbers	Parallaxes of the sun	Parallax of the moon at the second limit		Differences between the first and second limit of the moon: to be subtracted		Parallax of the moon at the third limit		Differences between the third and forth lunar limit: to be added		Proportional minutes of the smaller epicycle	Proportional minutes of the greater epicycle
Deg.	Deg.	Min.	Sec.	Min.	Sec.	Min.	Sec.	Min.	Sec.		
6	354	0	10	2	46	0	7	3	18	0 12	0	0
12	348	0	19	5	33	0	14	6	36	0 23	1	0
18	342	0	29	8	19	0	21	9	53	0 34	3	1
24	336	0	38	11	4	0	28	13	10	0 45	4	2
30	330	0	47	13	49	0	35	16	26	0 56	5	3
36	324	0	56	16	32	0	42	19	40	1 6	7	5
42	318	1	5	19	5	0	48	22	47	1 16	10	7
48	312	1	13	21	39	0	55	25	47	1 26	12	9
54	306	1	22	24	9	1	1	28	49	1 35	15	12
60	300	1	31	26	36	1	8	31	42	1 45	18	14
66	294	1	39	28	57	1	14	34	31	1 54	21	17
72	288	1	46	31	14	1	19	37	14	2 3	24	20
78	282	1	53	33	25	1	24	39	50	2 11	27	23
84	276	2	0	35	31	1	29	42	19	2 19	30	26
90	270	2	7	37	31	1	34	44	40	2 26	34	29
96	264	2	13	39	24	1	39	46	54	2 33	37	32
102	258	2	20	41	10	1	44	49	0	2 40	39	35
108	252	2	26	42	50	1	48	50	59	2 46	42	38
114	246	2	31	44	24	1	52	52	49	2 53	45	41
120	240	2	36	45	51	1	56	54	30	3 0	47	44
126	234	2	40	47	8	2	0	56	2	3 6	49	47
132	228	2	44	48	15	2	2	57	23	3 11	51	49
138	222	2	49	49	15	2	3	58	36	3 14	53	52
134	216	2	52	50	10	2	4	59	39	3 17	55	54
150	210	2	54	50	55	2	4	60	31	3 20	57	56
156	204	2	56	51	29	2	5	61	12	3 22	58	57
162	198	2	58	51	56	2	5	61	47	3 23	59	58
168	192	2	59	52	13	2	6	62	9	3 23	59	59
174	186	3	0	52	22	2	6	62	19	3 24	60	60
180	180	3	0	52	24	2	6	62	21	3 24	60	60

TABLE OF THE SEMIDIAMETERS OF THE SUN, MOON, AND SHADOW

Common Numbers		Semidiameter of the Sun		Semidiameter of the Moon		Semidiameter of the Shadow		Variation of the Shadow
Deg.	Deg.	Min.	Sec.	Min.	Sec.	Min.	Sec.	Min.
6	354	15	50	15	0	40	18	0
12	358	15	50	15	1	40	21	0
18	342	15	51	15	3	40	26	1
24	336	15	52	15	6	40	34	2
30	330	15	53	15	9	40	42	3
36	324	15	55	15	14	40	56	4
42	318	15	57	15	19	41	10	6
48	312	16	0	15	25	41	26	9
54	306	16	3	15	32	41	44	11
60	300	16	6	15	39	42	2	14
66	294	16	9	15	47	42	24	16
72	288	16	12	15	56	42	40	19
78	282	16	15	16	5	43	13	22
84	276	16	19	16	13	43	34	25
90	270	16	22	16	22	43	58	27
96	264	16	26	16	30	44	20	31
102	258	16	29	16	39	44	44	33
108	252	16	32	16	47	45	6	36
114	246	16	36	16	55	45	20	39
120	240	16	39	17	4	45	52	42
126	234	16	42	17	12	46	13	45
132	228	16	45	17	19	46	32	47
138	222	16	48	17	26	46	51	49
144	216	16	50	17	32	47	7	51
150	210	16	53	17	38	47	23	53
156	204	16	54	17	41	47	31	54
162	198	16	55	17	44	47	39	55
168	192	16	56	17	46	47	44	56
174	186	16	57	17	48	47	49	56
180	180	16	57	17	49	47	52	57

25. ON COMPUTING THE PARALLAX OF THE SUN
AND MOON

[127ª] We shall also set out briefly the mode of computing the parallaxes of the sun and moon by the table. If for the distance of the sun or twice the distance of the moon from the vertex of the horizon we take the corresponding parallaxes in the table—the solar parallaxes simply but the lunar parallaxes at the four limits—and if we take the first proportional minutes corresponding to twice the movement of the moon or twice its distance from the sun; by means of these minutes we shall determine the parts of the difference between the first and the last terminus which are proportional to sixty minutes; we shall always subtract these parts from the parallaxes following next, and we shall always add the later parts to the parallax at the next to the last limit. And we shall have two corrected parallaxes of the moon at the apogee and perigee; the lesser epicycle increases or decreases these parallaxes. Then we shall take the last proportional minutes corresponding to the lunar anomaly; and by means of them we shall determine the proportional part of the difference between the two parallaxes found nearest; we shall always add this proportional part to the first corrected parallax, the parallax at the apogee; and the result will be the parallax of the moon sought for that place and time, as in the following example.

Let the distance of the moon from the vertex (of the horizon) be 54°, the mean movement of the moon 15°, and the corrected anomaly 100°: I wish to find from them by means of the table the lunar parallax. I double the degrees of distance, and the result is 108°, to which in the table there correspond a difference of 1'48" between the first and second limit, a parallax of 42'50" at the second limit, a parallax of 50'69" at the third limit, and a difference of 2'46" between the third and the fourth limit—which I shall mark down separately. Doubling the movement of the moon makes 30°; I find five of the first proportional minutes corresponding to it, and with them I determine 9" to be the part of the first difference which is proportional to sixty minutes: I subtract these 9" from the 42'50" of the parallax, and the remainder is 42'41". Similarly the proportional part of the second difference—which was 2'46"—is 14"; and I add it to the 50'59" of the parallax at the third limit; the sum is 51'13". The difference between these parallaxes is 8'32". After this I take the last proportional minutes corresponding to the corrected anomaly, and there are 39'. By means of them I take 4'50" as the proportional part of the difference of 8'32"; [127ᵇ] I add this 4'50" to the first corrected parallax, and the sum is 47'31", which will be the sought parallax of the moon in the circle of altitude.

But since any other parallaxes of the moon differ very little from the parallaxes at full moon and new moon, it would seem to be sufficient if we kept within the mean

limits everywhere, for we have great need of them for the sake of predicting eclipses. The rest do not require such great examination, which will be held to offer perhaps less in the way of utility than in the satisfaction of curiosity.

26. How the Parallaxes of Longitude and Latitude Are Distinguished

Now the parallax is divided simply into the parallax of longitude and that of latitude, or the parallax between the sun and moon is distinguished according to the arcs and angles of the intersection of the ecliptic and the circle through the poles of the horizon; since it is clear that when this circle falls at right angles upon the ecliptic, it makes no parallax in longitude, but the parallax is transferred wholly to latitude, as the circle is wholly a circle of latitude and altitude. But where conversely the ecliptic falls at right angles upon the horizon and becomes wholly the same as the circle of altitude; then, if the moon has no latitude, it does not admit anything except a parallax in longitude, but if it has a digression in latitude, it does not escape some parallax in latitude.

In this way let circle ABC be the ecliptic, and let it be at right angles to the horizon, and let A be the pole of the horizon. Accordingly circle ABC will be the same as the circle of altitude of a moon without latitude. Let B be the position of the moon, and BC its total parallax in longitude.

But when it also has latitude, let DBE be the circle described through the poles of the ecliptic and with DB or BE as the latitude of the moon, it is clear that side AD or AE will not be equal to AB; and the angle at D or E will not be right, since DA and EA are not circles through the poles of DBE; and the parallax will participate in latitude, and it will do so all the more the nearer the moon is to the vertex. For let triangle ADE keep the same base, but let sides AD and AE be shorter and comprehend acuter angles at the base; the greater the distance of the moon from the vertex is, the more like right angles will the angles be.

Now let ABC be the ecliptic, and DBE the oblique circle of altitude of a moon not having latitude, as being at an ecliptic section. [128ª] Let B be the ecliptic section, and BE the parallax in the circle of altitude. Let there be drawn EF the arc of a circle through the poles of ABC. Accordingly since in triangle BEF angle EBF is given, as was shown above, and

$$\text{angle } F = 90°,$$

and side BE is also given: by what has been shown concerning spherical triangles, the remaining sides are given: BF the parallax in longitude and FE the parallax in latitude,

which agree with parallax *BE*. But since *BE*, *EF*, and *FB* on account of their shortness differ but slightly and imperceptibly from straight lines, we shall not make an error if we use the right triangle as rectilinear; and on that account the ratio will become easy.

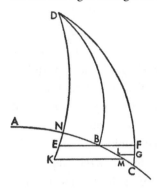

For let circle *ABC* be drawn as the ecliptic, and let *DB* the oblique circle through the poles of the horizon fall upon it. Let *B* be the position in longitude of the moon and *FB* the northern latitude or *BE* the southern. Let the vertex of the horizon be *D*, and from *D* let fall on the moon the circles of altitude *DEK* or *DFC*, whereon are the parallaxes *EK* and *FG*. For the true positions of the moon in longitude and latitude will be at points *E* or *F*, but the seeming positions will be at *K* or *G*. And from *K* and *G* let arcs *KM* and *LG* be drawn at right angles to the ecliptic *ABC*. Accordingly, since the longitude and latitude of the moon have been established together with the latitude of the region; in triangle *DEB* two sides *DB* and *BE* will be known and also *ABD* the angle of section and

angle *DBE* = angle *ABD* + 90°.

Accordingly the remaining side *DE* will be given together with angle *DEB*.

Similarly in triangle *DBF* since two sides *DB* and *BF* are given together with angle *DBF*, which with angle *ABD* makes up a right angle, *DF* will also be given together with angle *DFB*. Accordingly parallaxes *EK* and *FG* on arcs *DE* and *DF* are given by the table, and so is *DE* or *DF*, the true distance of the moon from the vertex, and similarly the seeming distance *DEK* or *DFG*. But in triangle *EBN*, which has the intersection of *DE* with the ecliptic at point *N*, angle *NEB* is given, and base *BE* is given, and angle *NBE* is right: the remaining angle *BNE* will become known too together with the remaining sides *BN* and *NE*. And similarly in the whole triangle *NKM*, as angles *M* and *N* and the whole side *KEN* are given, the base *KM* will be established. *KM* is the seeming southern latitude of the moon, and its excess over *EB* is the parallax of latitude: and the remaining side *NBM* is given: by the subtraction of *NB* from *NBM* the remainder *BM* will be the parallax in longitude.

Moreover, thus in the northern triangle *BFC*, since side *BF* is given together with angle *BFC* [128b] and angle *B* is right, the remaining sides *BLC* and *FGC* together with the remaining angle *C* are given; and after the subtraction of *FG* from *FGC* there remains *GC*, which is a side given in triangle *GLC* together with the angle *LCG* and angle *CLG*, which is right. Accordingly the remaining sides are given: *GL* and *LC*, and hence *BL* which is the remainder of *BC* and is the parallax in longitude; and *GL* is the seeming latitude, and its parallax is the excess of *BF* the true latitude over *GL*.

As you see however, this computation, which deals with very small magnitudes, contains more labour than fruitfulness. For it will be sufficient if we use angle *ABD* instead of *DCB* and angle *DBF* instead of *DEB*, and as before, simply the mean *DB* instead of arcs *DE* and *DF*—neglecting the latitude of the moon. For no error will appear because of that, especially in regions of the northern part of the Earth; but in very southern regions, where *B* touches the vertex of the horizon at the greatest latitude of 5° and when the moon is at its perigee, there is a difference of approximately 6'. But in the ecliptic conjunctions with the sun, where the latitude of the moon cannot exceed $1/_2$°, there can be a difference of merely $1^3/_4$'. Accordingly it is clear from this that the parallax is always added to the true position of the moon in the eastern quadrant of the ecliptic and is always subtracted in the other quadrant, so that we may have the seeming longitude of the moon; and may have the seeming latitude through the parallax in latitude, since if the true latitude and the parallax are in the same direction, they are added together; if in different directions, the lesser is subtracted from the greater, and the remainder is the seeming latitude of that same part, to which the greater falls away.

27. CONFIRMATION OF WHAT HAS BEEN EXPOUNDED CONCERNING THE PARALLAXES OF THE MOON

Accordingly we can confirm by many other observations (such as the following one) that the parallaxes of the moon as set forth above are in conformity with the appearances. We made this observation at Bologna, after sunset on the seventh day before the Ides of March, in the year of Christ 1497. For we observed how long [129ª] the moon would occult the bright star of the Hyades (which the Romans call Paliticium), and with this in mind, we saw the star brought into contact with the shadowy part of the lunar body and already lying hidden between the horns of the moon at the end of the fifth hour of the night, though the star was nearer the southern horn by three quarters as it were of the width or diameter of the moon. And since according to the tables the star was at 2°52' of Gemini with a southerly latitude of $5^1/_6$°, it was clear that to eyesight the centre of the moon was half a diameter to the west of the star, and accordingly its seen position was 2°36' in longitude and approximately 5°6' in latitude.

Accordingly from the beginning of the years of Christ there have been 1497 Egyptian years 76 days 23 hours at Bologna; but at Cracow, which is approximately 8° farther east, 23 hours 36 minutes, to which equal time adds 4 minutes. For the sun was at $28^1/_2$° of Pisces and therefore the regular movement of the moon away from the sun was 74°, the regular anomaly was 111°10', the true position of the moon was at 3°24' of Gemini, the southerly latitude 4°35', for the true movement of latitude was 203°41'. Moreover, at that time at Bologna, 26° of Scorpio was rising, with an angle of $57^1/_2$°;

and the moon was 83° from the vertex of the horizon, and the angle of section between the circle of altitude and the ecliptic was approximately 29°, the parallax of the moon was 1°51' in longitude and 30' in latitude. Those things agree perfectly with the observations; and all the less will anyone doubt that our hypotheses and what results from them are correct.

28. ON THE MEAN OPPOSITIONS AND CONJUNCTIONS OF THE SUN AND MOON

The method of investigating the conjunctions and oppositions of the sun and the moon is clear from what has been said so far concerning their movement. For in relation to that approaching time at which we think this or that conjunction or opposition will take place, we shall seek the regular movement of the moon; and if we find that the regular movement has already completed a circle, we understand a full conjunction at the semicircle. [129b] But since that rarely presents itself, we shall have to observe the distance between the sun and the moon; and when we have divided it by the daily movement of the moon, we shall know by how much time the one of them is in advance of the other, or how far off in the future the conjunction or the opposition is. Therefore we shall seek out the movements and positions for this time, and with them we shall set up ratios for the true new moons and full moons; and we shall distinguish the ecliptic conjunctions from the others, as we shall indicate below. When we have got these things set up, it will be possible to go on into any number of months and continue through some number of years by means of the table of twelve months, which contains the time and the regular movements of the anomaly of the sun and the moon and the regular movement of the moon in latitude—joining single movements to the single movements already found. But, we shall put down the anomaly of the sun as true, so as to have it as corrected immediately. For its difference is not perceptible to sense in one or more years on account of its slowness at its beginning, *i.e.*, at its highest apsis.

TABLE OF THE CONJUNCTION AND OPPOSITION OF SUN AND MOON

Months	Divisions of Time				Movements of Lunar Anomaly				Movement in Latitude of the Moon			
	Days	Min. of Day	Sec.	Thirds	60°	Deg.	Min.	Sec.	60°	Deg.	Min.	Sec.
1	29	31	50	8	0	25	49	0	0	30	40	13
2	59	3	40	16	0	51	38	0	1	1	20	27
3	88	35	30	24	1	17	27	0	1	32	0	41
4	118	7	20	32	1	43	16	0	2	2	40	55
5	147	39	10	40	2	9	5	0	2	33	21	9
6	177	11	0	48	2	34	34	0	3	4	1	23
7	206	42	50	57	3	0	43	0	3	34	41	36
8	236	14	41	25	3	26	32	0	4	5	21	50
9	265	46	31	13	3	52	21	0	4	36	2	4
10	295	18	21	21	4	18	10	0	5	6	42	18
11	324	50	11	29	4	4	59	0	5	37	22	32
12	354	22	1	37	5	9	48	0	0	8	2	46

THE HALF MONTH BETWEEN THE FULL AND NEW MOON

1/2	14	45	55	4	3	12	54	30	3	15	20	6

MOVEMENT OF SOLAR ANOMALY

Months	60°	°	′	″	Months	60°	°	′	″
1	0	29	6	18	7	3	23	44	6
2	0	58	12	36	8	3	52	50	24
3	1	27	18	54	9	4	21	56	42
4	1	56	25	12	10	4	51	3	0
5	2	25	31	30	11	5	20	9	19
6	2	54	57	48	12	5	49	15	37

THE HALF MONTH

	1/2	0	14	33	9

29. ON THE CLOSE EXAMINATION OF THE TRUE CONJUNCTIONS AND OPPOSITIONS OF THE SUN AND MOON

[130^b] Since we possess, as was said, the time of mean conjunction or opposition of these heavenly bodies together with their movements, then the true distance between them, whereby they precede or follow one another, will be necessary in order to find their true (conjunctions and oppositions). For if the (true) moon is prior to the sun in (mean) conjunction or opposition, it is clear that the true one will be in the future; but if the sun, then it is already past the true one which we are seeking. This is made clear by the additosubtractions in the case of both of them, since if there were no additosubtractions, or if they were equal and of the same quality, *viz.*, both additive or both subtractive, it is clear that at the same moment the true conjunctions or oppositions and the mean ones coincide. But if they are unequal, the difference indicates what their distance is and that the star to which the additive or subtractive difference belongs precedes or follows. But when they are in different parts (of their circles) that star all the more precedes whose additosubtraction is subtractive; and the adding together of the additosubtractions shows what the distance between them is. In connection with this we shall decide how many whole hours can be is traversed by the moon—taking two hours for every degree of distance.

In this way, if there were about 6° of distance, we should take 12 hours as corresponding to them. Therefore we shall seek the true movement of the moon away from the sun for the interval of time thus set up; and we shall do that easily, when we know that the mean movement of the moon is 1°1' per 2 hours, but that the true hourly movement of anomaly around the full moon or the new moon is approximately 50'. In 6 hours that makes the regular movement to be 3°3', and the true movement of anomaly 5°; and in the table of lunar additosubtractions we shall note the difference between the additosubtractions and add it to the mean movement—if the anomaly is in the lower part of the circle—and subtract it if the anomaly is in the upper. For the sum or the remainder is the true movement of the moon for the hours taken. Therefore that movement, if equal to the distance first existing, is sufficient. Otherwise the distance multiplied by the number of estimated hours should be divided by this movement; or else we shall divide the true simple distance by the hourly movement taken. [131^a] For the quotient will be the true difference in time in hours and minutes between the mean and the true conjunction or opposition. We shall add this difference to the mean time of conjunction or opposition, if the moon is west of the sun, or to the position of the sun diametrically opposite: or we shall subtract, if the moon is eastward; and we shall have the time of true conjunction or opposition, although we must

confess that the anomaly of the sun too adds or subtracts something, but it is rightly neglected, as in the whole tract and at greatest elongation—which extends beyond 7°—the anomaly cannot fill 1'; and the method of evaluating the lunar movements is more certain.

For those who rely only upon the hourly movement of the moon, which they call the hourly excelling movement, make mistakes sometimes and are forced rather often to repeat their calculations. For the moon is changeable even from hour to hour and does not stay like itself. Accordingly, for the time of true conjunction or opposition, we shall work out the true movement in latitude, so as to learn the latitude of the moon and work out the true position of the sun in relation to the spring equinox, i.e., in the signs, whereby the true position of the moon is known to lie the same or opposite to it. And since time is here understood as mean and equal with respect to the Cracow meridian, we shall reduce it to apparent time by the method described above. But if we should wish to set this up for any other place than Cracow, we shall note its longitude and take four minutes of an hour for each degree of longitude and four seconds of an hour for each minute of longitude; and we shall add them to the Cracow time, if the other place is to the east, and subtract them, if it is to the west. And the sum or the remainder will be the time of conjunction or opposition of the sun and moon.

30. HOW THE ECLIPTIC CONJUNCTIONS AND OPPOSITIONS OF THE SUN AND MOON ARE DISTINGUISHED FROM THE OTHERS

In the case of the moon it is easily discernible whether or not they are ecliptic; since, if the latitude of the moon is less than half the diameters of the moon and the shadow, it will undergo an eclipse, but if greater, it will not. But there is more than enough bother in the case of the sun, as the parallax of each of them, by which for the most part the visible conjunction differs from the true, is mixed up in it. Accordingly when we have examined [131^b] what the parallax in longitude between the sun and moon is at the time of true conjunction, similarly we shall look for the apparent (angular) elongation of the moon from the sun at the interval of an hour before the true conjunction in the eastern quarter of the ecliptic or after the true conjunction in the western quarter, in order to understand how far the moon seems to move away from the sun in one hour. Therefore when we have divided the parallax by this hourly movement, we shall have the difference in time between the true and the seen conjunction, When that is subtracted from the time of the true conjunction in the eastern part of the ecliptic or added in the western—for in the eastern part the seen conjunction precedes the true, and in the western it follows it—the result will be the time of seen conjunction which we were looking for. Therefore we shall reckon the seen latitude of the

moon in relation to the sun for this time, or the distance between the centres of the sun and the moon at the seen conjunction, after deducting the parallax of the sun. If this latitude is greater than half the diameters of the sun and moon, the sun will not undergo an eclipse; but if smaller, it will. From this it is clear that if the moon at the time of true conjunction does not have any parallax in longitude, the seen and the true conjunction will be the same, and the conjunction will take place at 90° of the ecliptic as measured from the east or the west.

31. How Great an Eclipse of the Sun or Moon Will Be

Therefore, after we have learned that the sun or moon will undergo an eclipse, we shall easily come to know how great the eclipse will be—in the case of the sun by means of the seen latitude between the sun and moon at the time of seen conjunction. For if we subtract the latitude from half the diameters of the sun and the moon, the remainder is the eclipse of the sun as measured along its diameter; and when we have multiplied that by twelve and divided the product by the diameter of the sun, we shall have the number of twelfths of the eclipse of the sun. But if there is no latitude between the sun and the moon, there will be a total eclipse of the sun or as much of it as the moon can cover.

Approximately the same method (is used) in the case of a lunar eclipse, except that instead of the seen latitude we employ the simple latitude. When the latitude is subtracted from half the diameters of the moon and shadow, the remainder is the part of [132a] the moon eclipsed, provided the latitude of the moon is not less than half the diameters of the moon and shadow, as taken along the diameter of the moon. For then there will be a total eclipse. And furthermore the lesser latitude even adds some delay in the darkness; and the delay will be greatest when there is no latitude—as I think is perfectly clear to those who consider it. Accordingly, in the case of a particular eclipse of the moon, when we have multiplied the eclipsed part by twelve and divided the product by the diameter of the moon, we shall have the number of twelfths of the eclipse—just as in the case of the sun.

32. How to Know Beforehand How Long an Eclipse Will Last

It remains to see how long an eclipse will last. It should be noted that we use the arcs which occur in the case of the sun, moon, and shadow as straight lines; for they are so small that they do not seem to be different from straight lines.

Accordingly let us take point A as the centre of the sun or of the shadow, and line BC as the passage of the orb of the moon. And let B be the centre of the moon touching

the sun or shadow at the beginning of incidence and *C* at the end of its transit. Let *AB* and *BC* be joined, and let fall *AD* perpendicular to *BC*.

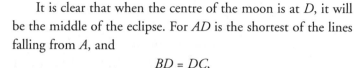

It is clear that when the centre of the moon is at *D*, it will be the middle of the eclipse. For *AD* is the shortest of the lines falling from *A*, and

$$BD = DC,$$

since

$$AB = AC,$$

and *AB* or *AC* is equal to half the sum of the diameters of the sun and the moon in a solar eclipse and to that of the diameters of the moon and shadow in a lunar eclipse; and *AD* is the true latitude of the moon or the seen latitude at the middle of the eclipse. Accordingly, when we have subtracted the square on *AD* from the square on *AB*, the remainder is the square on *BD*. Therefore *BD* will be given in length. When we have divided it by the true hourly movement of the moon during the eclipse of the moon, or by the visible movement in the case of a solar eclipse, we shall have the time of half the duration. But the moon very often delays in the middle of the darkness—that happens when half the sum of the diameters of the moon and the shadow exceeds the latitude of the moon by more than the moon's diameter, as we said. Accordingly when we have placed *E* the centre of the moon at the starting-point of the total [132ᵇ] obscuration, when the moon touches the concave circumference of the shadow, and *F* at the other point of contact, when the moon first emerges, and have joined *AE* and *AF*, it will be made clear in the same way as before that *ED* and *DF* are the halves of the delay in darkness, because *AD* is the known latitude of the moon, and *AE* or *AF* is that whereby the half of the diameter of the shadow is greater than half the diameter of the moon. Therefore *DE* or *DF* will be established; and once more when we have divided it by the true hourly movement of the moon, we shall have the time of half the delay, which we were looking for.

Nevertheless we must notice here that since the moon moves in its own orbital circle, it does not, by the mediation of the circles passing through the poles of the ecliptic, cut arcs of longitude on the ecliptic wholly equal to the arcs in its own orbital circle. But the difference is very slight, so that at the total distance of 12° from the ecliptic section, which is approximately the farthest limit of the eclipses of the sun and moon, the arcs of the circles do not differ from one another by 2', which makes $1/15$ hour; on that account we often use one instead of the other as if they were the same. So too we use the same latitude of the moon at the limits of the eclipses as at the middle of the eclipse, although the latitude of the moon is always increasing or decreasing, and on that account the intervals of incidence and withdrawal are not wholly equal, but the difference is so slight that it seems a waste of time to examine them more closely.

In this way the times, durations, and magnitudes of eclipses have been unfolded with respect to the diameters.

But since it is the opinion of many persons that the parts eclipsed should be distinguished not with respect to the diameters but with respect to the surfaces, for it is not lines but surfaces which are eclipsed: 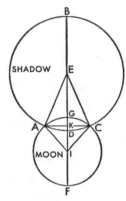 accordingly let *ABCD* be the circle of the sun or of the shadow, and let *E* be its centre. Let *AFCG* be the lunar circle, and let *I* be its centre. Let the circles cut one another 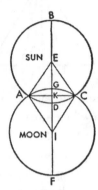 in points *A* and *C*, let the straight line *BEIF* be drawn through the centres of both, and let *AE, EC, IA, IC* be joined and line *AKC* at right angles to *BF*. By means of this we wish to examine how great *ADCG* the surface obscured is, or how many twelfths of the whole surface of the orb of the moon or sun belong to the part eclipsed. Accordingly since the semidiameters *AE* and *AI* of each circle are given by the above, and also *EI* the distance between their centres or the lunar latitude, we shall have [133ª] triangle *AEI* with its sides given; and for that reason with its angles given by the demonstrations above; and angle *AEI* is similar and equal to angle *EIC*. Accordingly

arcs *ADC* and *AGC* will be given,

where the circumference = 360°.

Furthermore, in the measurement of the circle Archimedes of Syracuse records that

circumference : diameter < $3^1/_7$: 1

but

circumference : diameter > $3^{10}/_{71}$: 1.

Ptolemy assumed as a mean between these

3P8'30" : 1P.

By means of this ratio

arcs *AGC* and *ADG* will be given,

in terms of the same parts as the semidiameters *AE* and *AI*.
And

quad. *EA, AD* = sector *AEC,*

and

quad. *IA, AG* = sector *AIC.*

But in the isosceles triangles *AEC* and *AIC* the common base *AKC* and the perpendiculars *EK* and *KI* are given. And accordingly the quadrilateral *AK, KE* is given, which is the area of triangle *AEC*—and similarly the quadrilateral *AK, KI* is the area of triangle *ACI*. Accordingly

sect. *AFCK* – trgl. *AIC* = seg. circ. *AFC*

and

sect. *ABCK* – trgl. *AEC* = seg. circ. *ABC*

and hence,

figure *ADCG* is given,

which was sought.

And moreover, the total area of the circle—which is comprehended by *BE* and *BAD* in a solar eclipse or by *FI* and *FAG* in a lunar eclipse—was given. Accordingly it will be manifest how many twelfths of the total circle of the sun or moon was eclipsed in *ADCG*. Let all this—which has been treated in more detail by others—be enough now concerning the moon: for we are in a hurry to get to the revolutions of the remaining five planets, which will be spoken of in the books following.

BOOK FIVE

[133^b] Up to now we have been explaining to the best of our ability the revolutions of the Earth around the sun and of the moon around the Earth. Now we are turning to the movements of the five wandering stars: the mobility of the Earth binds together the order and magnitude of their orbital circles in a wonderful harmony and sure commensurability, as we said in our brief survey in the first book, when we showed that the orbital circles do not have their centres around the Earth but rather around the sun. Accordingly it remains for us to demonstrate all these things singly and with greater clarity; and let us fulfil our promises adequately, in so far as we can, particularly by measuring the appearances by the experiments which we have got from the ancients or from our own times, in order that the ratio of the movements may be held with greater certainty. Now in Plato's *Timaeus* each of these five stars is named in accordance with its visible aspect: Saturn, Phaenon—as if to say "shining" or "appearing," for Saturn is hidden less than the others, and emerges more quickly after undergoing occultation by the sun; Jupiter, Phaeton from his radiance; Mars, Pyrois from his fiery glow; Venus sometimes φωσφόρος and sometimes ἕοπερος, *i.e.*, Lucifer and Vesperugo, according as she shines at morning or evening; and finally Mercury, Stilbon from his sparkling and twinkling light. Moreover the planets have greater irregularities in longitude and in latitude than the moon.

1. ON THEIR REVOLUTIONS AND MEAN MOVEMENTS

Two longitudinal movements which are quite different appear in the planets. One of them is on account of the movement of the Earth, as we said; and the other is proper to each planet. We may rightly call the first the movement of parallax, since it is the one which makes the planets appear to have stoppings, progressions, and retrogradations— [134^a] not that the planet which always progresses by its own movement, is pulled in different directions, but that it appears to do so by reason of the parallax caused by the movement of the Earth taken in relation to the differing magnitudes of their orbital circles.

Accordingly it is clear that the true position of Saturn, Jupiter, and Mars become visible to us only at the time when they are in opposition to the sun; and that occurs approximately in the middle of their retrogradations. For at that time they fall on a straight line with the mean position of the sun, and lay aside their parallax.

Furthermore there is a different ratio in the case of Venus and Mercury: for they are hidden at the time they are in conjunction with the sun, and they show only the digressions which they make on either side away from the sun: hence they are never found without parallax.

Therefore the revolution of parallax—I mean the movement of the Earth with respect to the planet—is private to each planet; and the planet and the Earth are mutually explanatory of it. For we say that the movement of parallax is nothing except that wherein the regular movement of the Earth exceeds their movement, as in the case of Saturn, Jupiter, and Mars, or is exceeded by it, as in the case of Venus and Mercury. But since such periods of parallax are found unequal by a manifest difference, the ancients recognized that the movements of these planets too were irregular and had apsides; of circles to which their irregularity returned, and the ancients supposed that these apsides had perpetual seats in the sphere of the fixed stars. By that argument the road is opened for learning their mean movements and equal periods. For when the ancients had recorded in memory the position of some planet with respect to its exact distance from the sun and a fixed star, and after an interval of time found that it had arrived at the same position with an equal distance from the sun; the planet was seen to have completed its whole movement of irregularity and to have returned through all to its former relationship with the Earth. And so by means of the time which intervened they calculated the number of whole and equal revolutions and from them the particular movements of the planet. Ptolemy surveyed the circuits through a number of years, according as, he acknowledged, he got them from Hipparchus. Now he means solar years to be understood as the years measured from an equinox or solstice. But it has already been made clear that such years are not quite equal; on that account we shall use years measured from the fixed stars, and by means of them the movements of these five planets have been reconstituted more correctly by us, according as in our time [134^b] we found there was some deficiency in them or excess, as follows.

For the Earth has 57 revolutions in respect to Saturn—we call this the movement of parallax—in 59 of our solar years 1 day 6 minutes of a day 48 seconds approximately: during this time the planet has by its own movement completed two circuits plus 1°6'6".

Jupiter is outrun by the Earth 65 times in 71 solar years minus 5 days 45 minutes 27 seconds: during this time the planet by its own movement has 6 revolutions minus 5°41'2$^1/_2$".

Mars has 37 revolutions of parallax in 79 solar years 2 days 27 minutes 3 seconds: during this time the planet by its own movement completes 42 periods plus 2°24'56".

Venus outruns the movement of the Earth 5 times in 8 solar years minus 2 days 26 minutes 46 seconds. And during this time it has 13 revolutions minus 2°24'40" around the sun.

Finally, Mercury completes 145 periods of parallax, by which it outruns the movement of the Earth, in 46 solar years plus 34 minutes of a day 23 seconds. And it has 191 revolutions around the sun in that time plus 34 minutes of a day 23 seconds approximately.

Accordingly the single circuits of parallax are as follows: for the single planets;

Saturn:	378 days	5 min.	32 sec.	11 thirds
Jupiter:	398 days	23 min.	25 sec.	56 thirds
Mars:	779 days	56 min.	19 sec.	7 thirds
Venus:	583 days	45 min.	17 sec.	24 thirds
Mercury:	115 days	52 min.	42 sec.	12 thirds

When we have reduced these circuits to the degrees of a circle and multiplied by the ratio of 365 to the number of days and minutes, we shall have as the annual movements (of parallax):

Saturn:	347°32'2"54'''12''''
Jupiter:	329°25'8"15'''6''''
Mars:	168°28'29"13'''12''''
Venus:	225°1'48"54'''30''''
Mercury:	3 (360°) + 53°56'46"54'''40''''

[135ᵃ] The three-hundred-sixty-fifth part of these is the daily movement:

Saturn:	57'7"44'''
Jupiter:	54'9"3'''49''''
Mars:	27'41"40'''8''''
Venus:	36'49"28'''35''''
Mercury:	3°6'24"7'''43''''

according as they are set out in the following tables, like the mean movement of the sun and moon.

But we thought it unnecessary to set down their proper movements in this way. For the proper movements are determined by the subtraction of the movements of parallax from the mean movement of the sun, as the proper movement of the planet and the mean movement of parallax compose the mean movement of the sun. For the proper annual movements in relation to the sphere of the fixed stars are as follows for the upper planets:

Saturn:	12°12'46"12'''52''''
Jupiter:	30°19'40"51'''58''''
Mars:	191°16'19"53'''52''''

But in the case of Venus and Mercury, since their proper movements are not apparent to us,[1] the movement of the sun itself is used by us instead; and it furnishes a way of investigating and demonstrating their apparent movements, in the following tables.

[1] The proper movements of Venus and Mercury are not apparent to us in that their positions are never viewed without parallax.

SATURN'S MOVEMENT OF PARALLAX IN YEARS AND PERIODS OF SIXTY YEARS

Egyptian Years	Movement 60°	°	′	″	‴	Egyptian Years	Movement 60°	°	′	″	‴
1	5	47	32	3	9	31	5	33	33	37	59
2	5	35	4	6	19	32	5	11	5	41	9
3	5	22	36	9	29	33	5	8	37	44	19
4	5	10	8	12	38	34	4	56	9	47	28
5	4	57	40	15	48	35	4	43	41	50	38
6	4	45	12	18	58	36	4	31	13	53	48
7	4	32	44	22	7	37	4	18	45	56	57
8	4	20	16	25	17	38	4	6	18	0	7
9	4	7	48	28	27	39	3	53	50	3	17
10	3	55	20	31	36	40	3	41	22	6	26
11	3	42	52	34	46	41	3	18	54	9	36
12	3	30	24	37	56	42	3	16	26	12	46
13	3	17	56	41	5	43	3	3	58	15	55
14	3	5	28	44	15	44	2	51	30	19	5
15	2	53	0	47	25	45	2	39	2	22	15
16	2	40	32	50	34	46	2	26	34	25	24
17	2	28	4	53	44	47	2	14	6	28	34
18	2	15	36	56	54	48	2	1	38	31	44
19	2	3	9	0	3	49	1	49	10	34	53
20	1	50	41	3	13	50	1	36	42	38	3
21	1	38	13	6	23	51	1	24	14	41	13
22	1	25	45	9	32	52	1	11	46	44	22
23	1	13	17	12	42	53	1	59	18	47	32
24	1	0	49	15	52	54	0	46	50	50	42
25	0	48	21	19	1	55	0	34	22	43	51
26	0	35	53	22	11	56	0	21	54	57	1
27	0	23	25	25	21	57	0	9	27	0	11
28	0	10	57	28	30	58	0	56	59	3	20
29	5	58	29	31	40	59	5	44	31	6	30
30	5	46	1	34	50	60	5	32	3	9	40

SATURN'S MOVEMENT OF PARALLAX IN PERIODS OF SIXTY DAYS

Days	Movement 60°	°	′	″	‴	Days	Movement 60°	°	′	″	‴
1	0	0	57	7	44	31	0	29	30	59	46
2	0	1	54	15	28	32	0	30	28	7	30
3	0	2	51	23	12	33	0	31	25	15	14
4	0	3	48	30	56	34	0	32	22	22	58
5	0	4	45	38	40	35	0	33	19	30	42
6	0	5	42	46	24	36	0	34	16	38	26
7	0	6	39	54	8	37	0	35	13	46	1
8	0	7	37	1	52	38	0	36	10	53	55
9	0	8	34	9	36	39	0	37	8	1	39
10	0	9	31	17	20	40	0	38	5	9	23
11	0	10	28	25	4	41	0	39	2	17	7
12	0	11	25	32	49	42	0	39	59	24	51
13	0	12	22	40	33	43	0	40	56	32	35
14	0	13	13	48	17	44	0	41	53	40	19
15	0	14	16	56	1	45	0	42	50	48	3
16	0	15	14	3	45	46	0	43	47	55	47
17	0	11	11	11	29	47	0	44	45	3	31
18	0	17	8	19	13	48	0	45	42	11	16
19	0	18	5	26	57	49	0	46	39	19	0
20	0	19	2	34	41	50	0	47	36	26	44
21	0	19	59	42	25	51	0	48	33	34	28
22	0	20	56	50	9	52	0	49	30	42	12
23	0	21	53	57	53	53	0	50	27	49	56
24	0	22	51	5	38	54	0	51	24	57	40
25	0	23	48	13	22	55	0	52	22	5	24
26	0	24	45	21	6	56	0	53	19	13	8
27	0	25	42	28	50	57	0	54	16	20	52
28	0	26	39	36	34	58	0	55	13	28	36
29	0	27	36	44	18	59	0	56	10	36	20
30	0	28	33	52	2	60	0	57	7	44	5

Jupiter's Movement of Parallax in Years and Periods of Sixty Years

Egyptian Years	Movement					Egyptian Years	Movement				
	60°	°	′	″	‴		60°	°	′	″	‴
1	5	29	25	8	15	31	2	11	59	15	48
2	4	58	50	16	30	32	1	41	24	24	3
3	4	28	15	24	45	33	1	10	49	32	18
4	3	57	40	33	0	34	0	40	14	40	33
5	3	27	5	41	15	35	0	9	39	48	48
6	2	56	30	49	30	36	5	39	4	57	8
7	2	25	55	57	45	37	5	8	30	5	18
8	1	55	21	6	0	38	4	37	55	13	33
9	1	24	46	14	15	39	4	7	20	21	48
10	0	54	11	22	31	40	3	36	45	30	4
11	0	23	36	30	46	41	3	6	10	38	19
12	5	53	1	39	1	42	2	35	35	46	34
13	5	22	25	47	16	43	2	5	0	54	49
14	4	51	51	55	31	44	1	34	26	3	4
15	4	21	17	3	46	45	1	3	51	11	19
16	3	50	42	12	1	46	0	33	16	19	34
17	3	20	7	20	16	47	0	2	41	27	49
18	2	49	32	28	31	48	5	32	6	36	4
19	2	18	57	35	46	49	5	1	31	44	19
20	1	48	22	45	2	50	4	30	56	52	34
21	1	17	47	58	17	51	4	0	22	0	50
22	0	47	13	1	32	52	3	29	47	9	5
23	0	16	38	9	47	53	2	59	12	17	20
24	5	45	3	18	2	54	2	28	37	25	33
25	5	15	28	26	17	55	1	58	2	33	50
26	4	44	53	34	32	56	1	27	27	42	5
27	4	14	18	42	47	57	0	56	52	50	20
28	3	43	43	51	2	58	0	26	17	58	35
29	3	13	8	59	17	59	5	55	43	6	50
30	2	42	34	7	33	60	5	25	8	15	6

Jupiter's Movement of Parallax in Periods or Sixty Days

Days	Movement					Days	Movement				
	60°	°	′	″	‴		60°	°	′	″	‴
1	0	0	54	9	3	31	0	27	58	40	58
2	0	1	49	18	7	32	0	28	52	50	2
3	0	2	42	27	11	33	0	29	46	59	5
4	0	3	36	36	15	34	0	30	41	8	9
5	0	4	30	45	19	35	0	31	35	17	13
6	0	5	24	54	22	36	0	32	29	26	17
7	0	6	19	3	26	37	0	33	23	35	21
8	0	7	13	12	30	38	0	34	17	44	25
9	0	8	7	21	34	39	0	35	11	53	29
10	0	9	1	30	38	40	0	36	6	2	32
11	0	9	55	39	41	41	0	37	0	11	36
12	0	10	49	48	45	42	0	37	54	20	40
13	0	11	43	57	49	43	0	38	48	29	44
14	0	12	38	6	53	44	0	39	42	38	47
15	0	13	32	15	57	45	0	40	36	47	51
16	0	14	26	25	1	46	0	41	30	56	55
17	0	15	20	34	4	47	0	42	25	5	59
18	0	16	14	43	8	48	0	43	19	15	3
19	0	17	8	52	12	49	0	44	13	24	6
20	0	18	3	1	16	60	0	45	7	33	10
21	0	18	57	10	20	51	0	46	1	42	14
22	0	19	51	19	23	52	0	46	55	51	18
23	0	20	45	28	27	53	0	47	50	0	22
24	0	21	39	37	31	64	0	48	44	9	26
25	0	22	33	46	35	55	0	49	38	18	29
26	0	23	27	55	39	56	0	50	32	27	33
27	0	24	22	4	43	57	0	51	26	36	37
28	0	25	16	13	46	58	0	52	20	45	41
29	0	26	10	22	50	59	0	53	14	54	45
30	0	27	4	31	54	60	0	54	9	3	49

MARS' MOVEMENT OF PARALLAX IN YEARS AND PERIODS OF SIXTY YEARS

Egyptian Years	Movement					Egyptian Years	Movement				
	60°	°	′	″	‴		60°	°	′	″	‴
1	2	48	28	30	36	31	3	2	43	48	38
2	5	36	57	1	12	32	5	51	12	19	14
3	2	25	25	31	48	33	2	39	40	49	50
4	5	13	54	2	24	34	5	28	9	20	26
5	2	2	22	33	0	35	2	16	37	51	2
6	4	50	51	3	36	36	5	5	6	21	38
7	1	39	19	34	12	37	1	53	34	52	14
8	4	27	48	4	48	38	4	42	3	22	50
9	1	16	16	35	24	39	1	30	31	53	26
10	4	4	45	6	0	40	4	19	0	24	2
11	0	53	13	36	36	41	1	7	28	54	38
12	3	41	42	7	12	42	3	55	57	25	14
13	0	30	10	37	46	43	0	44	25	55	50
14	3	18	39	8	24	44	3	32	54	26	26
15	0	7	7	39	1	45	0	21	22	57	3
16	2	55	36	9	37	46	3	9	51	27	39
17	5	44	4	40	13	47	5	58	19	58	15
18	2	32	33	10	49	48	2	46	48	28	51
19	5	21	1	41	25	49	5	35	16	59	27
20	2	9	30	12	1	50	2	23	45	30	3
21	4	57	58	42	37	51	5	12	14	0	39
22	1	46	27	13	13	52	2	0	42	31	15
23	4	34	55	43	49	53	4	49	11	1	51
24	1	23	24	14	25	54	1	37	39	32	27
25	4	11	52	45	1	55	4	26	8	3	3
26	1	0	21	15	37	56	1	14	36	33	39
27	3	48	49	46	13	57	4	3	5	4	15
28	0	37	18	16	49	58	0	51	33	34	51
29	3	25	46	47	25	59	3	40	2	5	27
30	0	14	15	18	2	60	0	28	30	36	4

MARS' MOVEMENT OF PARALLAX IN PERIODS OF SIXTY DAYS

Days	Movement					Days	Movement				
	60°	°	′	″	‴		60°	°	′	″	‴
1	0	0	27	41	40	31	0	14	18	31	51
2	0	0	55	23	20	32	0	14	46	13	31
3	0	1	23	5	1	33	0	15	14	55	12
4	0	1	50	46	41	34	0	15	41	36	52
5	0	2	18	28	21	35	0	16	9	18	32
6	0	2	46	10	2	36	0	16	37	0	13
7	0	3	13	51	42	37	0	17	4	41	53
8	0	3	41	33	22	38	0	17	32	23	33
9	0	4	9	15	3	39	0	18	0	5	14
10	0	4	36	35	43	40	0	18	27	46	54
11	0	5	4	38	24	41	0	18	55	28	35
12	0	5	32	20	4	42	0	19	23	10	15
13	0	6	0	1	44	43	0	19	50	51	55
14	0	6	27	43	25	44	0	20	18	33	36
15	0	6	55	25	5	45	0	20	46	15	16
16	0	7	23	6	45	46	0	21	13	56	56
17	0	7	50	48	26	47	0	21	41	38	37
18	0	8	18	30	6	48	0	22	9	20	17
19	0	8	46	11	47	49	0	22	37	1	57
20	0	9	13	53	27	50	0	23	4	43	38
21	0	9	41	35	7	51	0	23	32	25	18
22	0	10	9	16	48	52	0	24	0	6	59
23	0	10	36	58	28	53	0	24	27	48	39
24	0	11	4	40	8	54	0	24	55	30	19
25	0	11	32	21	48	55	0	25	23	12	0
26	0	12	0	3	29	56	0	25	50	53	40
27	0	12	27	45	9	57	0	26	18	35	20
28	0	12	59	25	50	58	0	26	46	17	1
29	0	13	23	8	30	59	0	27	13	58	41
30	0	13	50	50	11	60	0	27	41	40	22

VENUS' MOVEMENT OF PARALLAX IN YEARS AND PERIODS OF SIXTY YEARS

Egyptian Years	Movement 60°	°	'	"	'''	Egyptian Years	Movement 60°	°	'	"	'''
1	3	45	1	45	3	31	2	15	54	16	53
2	1	30	3	30	7	32	0	0	56	1	57
3	5	15	5	15	11	33	3	45	57	47	1
4	3	0	7	0	14	34	1	30	59	32	4
5	0	45	8	45	18	35	5	16	1	17	8
6	4	30	10	30	22	36	3	1	3	2	12
7	2	15	12	15	25	37	0	46	4	47	15
8	0	0	14	0	29	38	4	31	6	32	19
9	3	45	15	45	33	39	2	16	8	17	23
10	1	30	17	30	36	40	0	1	10	2	26
11	5	15	19	15	40	41	3	46	11	47	30
12	3	0	21	0	44	42	1	31	13	32	34
13	0	45	22	45	47	43	5	16	15	17	37
14	4	30	24	30	51	44	3	1	17	2	41
15	2	15	26	15	55	45	0	46	18	47	45
16	0	0	28	0	58	46	4	31	20	32	48
17	3	45	29	46	2	47	2	16	22	17	52
18	1	30	31	31	6	48	0	1	24	2	56
19	5	15	33	16	9	49	3	46	25	47	59
20	3	0	35	1	13	50	1	31	27	33	3
21	0	45	36	46	17	51	5	16	29	18	7
22	4	30	38	31	20	52	3	1	31	3	10
23	2	15	40	16	24	53	0	46	32	48	14
24	0	0	42	1	28	54	4	31	34	33	18
25	3	45	43	46	31	55	2	16	36	18	21
26	1	30	45	31	35	56	0	1	38	3	25
27	5	15	47	16	39	57	3	46	39	48	29
28	3	0	49	1	42	58	1	31	41	33	32
29	0	45	50	46	46	59	5	16	43	18	36
30	4	20	52	31	50	60	3	1	45	3	40

VENUS' MOVEMENT OF PARALLAX IN PERIODS OF SIXTY DAYS

Days	Movement 60°	°	'	"	'''	Days	Movement 60°	°	'	"	'''
1	0	0	36	59	28	31	0	19	6	43	46
2	0	1	13	58	57	32	0	19	43	43	14
3	0	1	50	58	25	33	0	20	20	42	43
4	0	2	27	57	54	34	0	20	57	42	11
5	0	3	4	57	22	35	0	21	34	41	40
6	0	3	41	56	51	36	0	22	11	41	9
7	0	4	18	56	20	37	0	22	48	40	37
8	0	4	55	55	48	38	0	23	25	40	6
9	0	5	32	55	17	39	0	24	2	39	34
10	0	6	9	54	45	40	0	24	39	39	3
11	0	6	46	54	14	41	0	25	16	38	31
12	0	7	23	53	43	42	0	25	53	38	0
13	0	8	0	53	11	43	0	26	30	37	29
14	0	8	37	52	40	44	0	27	7	36	57
15	0	9	14	52	8	45	0	27	44	36	26
16	0	9	51	51	37	46	0	28	21	35	54
17	0	10	28	51	5	47	0	28	58	35	23
18	0	11	5	50	34	48	0	29	35	34	52
19	0	11	42	50	2	49	0	30	12	34	20
20	0	12	19	49	31	50	0	30	49	33	49
21	0	12	56	48	59	51	0	31	26	33	17
22	0	13	33	48	28	52	0	32	3	32	46
23	0	14	0	47	57	53	0	32	40	32	14
24	0	14	47	47	26	54	0	33	17	31	43
25	0	15	24	46	54	55	0	33	54	31	12
26	0	16	1	46	23	56	0	34	31	30	40
27	0	16	38	45	51	57	0	35	8	30	9
28	0	17	15	45	20	58	0	35	45	29	37
29	0	17	52	44	48	59	0	36	22	29	6
30	0	18	29	44	17	60	0	36	59	28	35

MERCURY'S MOVEMENT OF PARALLAX IN YEARS AND PERIODS OF SIXTY YEARS

Egyptian Years	60°	°	'	"	'''	Egyptian Years	60°	°	'	"	'''
1	0	53	57	23	6	31	3	52	38	56	21
2	1	47	54	46	13	32	4	46	36	19	28
3	2	41	52	9	19	33	5	40	33	42	34
4	3	35	49	32	26	34	0	34	31	5	41
5	4	29	46	55	32	35	1	28	28	28	47
6	5	23	44	18	39	36	2	22	25	51	54
7	0	17	41	41	45	37	3	16	23	15	0
8	1	11	39	4	52	38	4	10	20	38	7
9	2	5	36	27	58	39	5	4	18	1	13
10	3	59	33	51	5	40	5	58	15	24	20
11	4	53	31	14	11	41	0	52	12	47	26
12	5	47	28	37	18	42	1	46	10	10	33
13	0	41	26	0	24	43	2	40	7	33	39
14	1	35	23	23	31	44	3	34	4	56	46
15	2	29	20	46	37	45	4	28	2	19	52
16	3	23	18	9	44	46	5	21	59	42	59
17	4	17	15	32	50	47	0	15	57	6	5
18	5	11	12	55	57	48	1	9	54	29	12
19	0	5	10	19	3	49	2	57	51	52	18
20	5	59	7	42	10	50	2	57	49	15	25
21	0	53	5	5	16	51	3	51	46	38	31
22	1	47	2	28	23	52	4	45	44	1	38
23	2	40	59	51	29	53	5	39	41	24	44
24	3	34	57	14	36	54	0	33	38	47	51
25	4	28	54	37	42	55	1	27	36	10	57
26	5	22	52	0	49	56	2	21	33	34	4
27	0	16	49	23	55	57	3	15	30	57	10
28	1	10	46	47	2	58	4	9	28	20	17
29	2	4	44	10	8	59	5	3	25	43	23
30	2	58	41	33	15	60	5	57	23	6	30

MERCURY'S MOVEMENT OF PARALLAX IN PERIODS OF SIXTY DAYS

Days	60°	°	'	"	'''	Days	60°	°	'	"	'''
1	0	3	6	24	13	31	1	36	18	31	3
2	0	6	12	48	27	32	1	39	24	55	17
3	0	9	19	12	41	33	1	42	31	19	31
4	0	12	25	36	54	34	1	45	37	43	44
5	0	15	32	1	8	35	1	48	44	7	58
6	0	18	38	25	22	36	1	51	50	32	12
7	0	21	44	49	35	37	1	54	56	56	25
8	0	24	51	13	49	38	1	58	3	20	39
9	0	27	57	38	3	39	2	1	9	44	53
10	0	31	4	2	16	40	2	4	16	9	6
11	0	34	10	26	30	41	2	7	22	33	20
12	0	37	16	50	44	42	2	10	28	57	34
13	0	40	23	14	57	43	2	13	35	21	47
14	0	43	29	39	11	44	2	16	41	46	1
15	0	46	36	3	25	45	2	19	48	10	15
16	0	49	42	27	38	46	2	22	54	34	28
17	0	52	48	51	52	47	2	26	0	58	42
18	0	55	55	16	6	48	2	29	7	22	56
19	0	59	1	40	19	49	2	32	13	47	9
20	1	2	8	4	33	50	2	35	20	11	23
21	1	5	14	28	47	51	2	38	26	35	37
22	1	8	20	53	0	52	2	41	32	59	50
23	1	11	27	17	14	53	2	44	39	24	4
24	1	14	33	41	28	54	2	47	45	48	18
25	1	17	40	5	41	55	2	50	52	12	31
26	1	20	46	29	55	56	2	53	58	36	45
27	1	23	52	54	9	57	2	57	5	0	59
28	1	26	59	18	22	58	3	0	11	25	12
29	1	30	5	42	36	59	3	3	17	49	26
30	1	33	12	6	50	60	3	6	24	13	40

2. DEMONSTRATION OF THE REGULAR AND APPARENT MOVEMENTS OF THESE PLANETS ACCORDING TO THE THEORY OF THE ANCIENTS

[140^b] Accordingly this is the way the mean movements are. Now let us turn to the apparent irregularity. The ancient mathematicians who kept the earth immobile imagined in the case of Saturn, Jupiter, Mars, and Venus eccentric circles bearing epicycles, and another further eccentric circle, with respect to which the epicycle and the planet in the epicycle should move regularly.

In this way let *AB* be an eccentric circle, and let its centre be at *C*. Let *ABC* be its diameter, whereon *D* is the centre of the Earth, so that *A* is the apogee and *B* the perigee. Let *DC* be bisected at *E*, and with *E* as centre let *FG* another eccentric circle to the first be described. Let *H* be anywhere on this eccentric circle, and with *H* as centre let the epicycle *IK* be described. Through its centre let there be drawn the straight line *IHKC* and similarly *LHME*. Now let it be understood that on account of the latitudes of the planet the eccentric circles are inclined to the plane of the ecliptic and similarly the epicycle to the plane of the eccentric circle; but here they are represented as if in one plane for the sake of ease of demonstration. Accordingly the ancients say that this whole plane together with points *E* and *C* moves around *D*—the centre of the ecliptic—in the movement of the sphere of the fixed stars: by this they mean that these

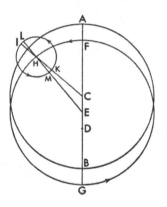

points have unchanging positions in the sphere of the fixed stars. And they say that the epicycle moves eastward in circle *FHG* but in accordance with line *IHC*, and in relation to this line the planet revolves regularly in epicycle *IK*. But it is clear that the regularity of the epicycle should occur in relation to *E* the centre of its deferent,[1] and the revolution of the planet in relation to line *LME*. Accordingly they concede that in this case the regularity of the circular movement can occur with respect to a foreign and not the proper centre; similarly and more so in the case of Mercury. But I think I have already made a sufficient refutation of that in the case of the moon. These and similar things furnished us with an occasion for working out the mobility of the Earth and some other ways by which regularity and the principles of this art might be preserved, and the ratio of apparent irregularity rendered more constant.

3. GENERAL DEMONSTRATION OF APPARENT IRREGULARITY ON ACCOUNT OF THE MOVEMENT OF THE EARTH

[141^a] Accordingly there are two reasons why the regular movement of a planet should appear irregular: on account of the movement of the Earth and on account of

---

[1]The deferent of an epicycle is the circle on the circumference of which the centre of the epicycle moves.

its proper movement. We shall make both of them clear generally and separately by ocular demonstration, whereby they can be better distinguished from one another; and we shall begin with the movement which mixes itself with all of them on account of the movement of the Earth: and first in the case of Venus and Mercury, which are comprehended by the (orbital) circle of the Earth.

Therefore let AB be the circle eccentric to the sun, which the centre of the Earth describes during its annual circuit in the way we explained above; and let C be its centre. But now let us put down that the planet has no other irregularity except this one;

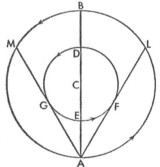

and that will be the case if we make DE, the orbital circle of Venus or Mercury, homocentric with AB; and DE should be inclined to AB on account of its latitude. But for the sake of ease of demonstration they can be thought of as if in the same plane. Let the Earth be assumed at point A; and from A let there be drawn the lines of sight AFL and AGM touching the circle of the planet at points F and G; and let ACB the diameter common to both circles be drawn.

Now let the movement of both the Earth and the planet be in the same direction, *i.e.*, eastward, but with greater velocity in the case of the planet than in that of the Earth. Therefore C and line ACB will appear to the eye borne along at A to move in accordance with the mean movement of the sun; but the planet in circle DFG as in an epicycle will traverse arc FDG eastward in greater time than it will the remaining arc GEF westward; and in the upper arc it will add the total angle FAG to the mean movement of the sun, and in the lower arc will subtract the same. Accordingly where the subtractive movement of the planet, especially around E the perigee, is greater than the additive (movement) of C, it will seem to A to retrograde in proportion to the excelling (movement)—as happens in these planets, when line CE has a greater ratio to line AE than the movement at A has to the movement of the planet, according to the demonstrations of Apollonius of Perga, as will be said later. But where the additive movement is equal to the subtractive, [141^b] the planet will seem to come to a stop on account of the mutual equilibrium; all this agrees with the appearances.

Accordingly if there were no other irregularity in the movement of the planet, as Apollonius opined, this would be sufficient. But the greatest angular elongations from the mean movement of the sun, which these planets have in the morning and evening and which are understood by angles FAE and GAE, are not everywhere equal, neither the one to the other, nor are the sums of the two equal; for the apparent reason that the route of these planets is not along circles homocentric with the terrestrial circle but along certain others, by which they effect the second irregularity.

The same thing is also demonstrated in the case of the three upper planets, Saturn, Jupiter, and Mars, which circle around the Earth. For let the former circle of the Earth be drawn again, and let *DE* be as an exterior homocentric circle in the same plane: let the position of the planet be taken anywhere, at point *D*; and from *D* let there be drawn *DACBE* the common diameter and *DF* and *DG* straight lines touching the orbital circle of the Earth at points *F* and *G*. It is manifest that from point *A* only will the true position of the planet in *DE*

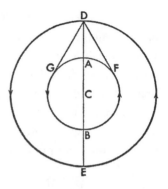

the line of mean movement of the sun be apparent, when the planet is opposite the sun and is nearest to the Earth. For when the Earth is in the opposite position at *B*, the opposition (of the planet and the sun), although in the same straight line, will not be at all apparent on account of the closeness of the sun to *C*. But as the movement of the Earth is speedier, so that it outruns the movement of the planet, it will seem along *FBG* the arc of apogee to add the total angle *GDF* to the movement of the planet and along the remaining arc *GAF* to subtract the same, according as arc *GAF* is smaller. But where the subtractive movement of the Earth excels the additive movement of the planet, especially in the neighbourhood of *A*, the planet will seem to be left behind by the Earth, to move westward and to come to a stop at the place where there is least difference between the movements which are contrary according to sight.

And so it is once more manifest that all these apparent movements—which the ancients were looking into by means of the epicycles of the individual planets—occur on account of the movement of the Earth. But since in spite of the opinion of Apollonius and the ancients the movement of the planet is not found regular, as the irregular revolution of the Earth with respect to the planet produces that; accordingly the planets are not carried in a homocentric circle but in some other which we shall demonstrate straightway.

4. WHY THE PROPER MOVEMENTS OF THE PLANETS APPEAR IRREGULAR

[142ᵃ] But since their proper movements in longitude follow approximately the same mode except for Mercury, which is seen to differ from them, we shall treat of those four planets together, but another place has been given over to Mercury. Accordingly as the ancients placed one movement in two eccentric circles, as was shown, we have decreed two regular movements out of which the apparent irregularity is compounded either by a circle eccentric to an eccentric circle, or by the epicycle of an epicycle or by a combination of an eccentric circle carrying an epicycle. For they can

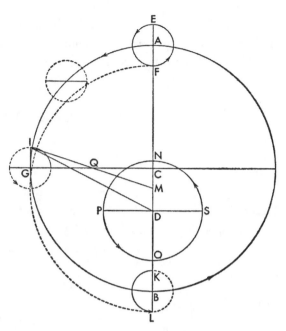

all effect the same irregularity, as we demonstrated above in the case of the sun and the moon.

Accordingly let *AB* be an eccentric circle around centre *C*. Let *ACB* be the diameter drawn through the highest and lowest apsis of the planet and containing the mean position of the sun. On *ACB* let *D* be the centre of the orbital circle of the Earth; and with the highest apsis *A* as centre and the third part of *CD* as radius, let epicycle *EF* be described. Let *F* be its perigee, and let the planet be placed there. Now let the movement of the epicycle along eccentric circle *AB* take place eastward; and let the movement of the planet in the upper arc (of the epicycle) take place similarly eastward [142b] but in the remaining arc westward; and let the revolutions of the epicycle and the planet be proportionately equal to one another.

On that account when the epicycle is at the highest apsis of the eccentric circle and the planet on the contrary is at the perigee of the epicycle, the relation between their movements is reversed[1] with respect to one another, since both the planet and the epicycle have traversed their semicircle. But in both mean quadrants each will have its mean apsis, and then only will the diameter[2] of the epicycle be parallel to line *AB*; and at the midpoints (between the mean quadrants and the perigee or apogee) the diameter will be perpendicular to *AB*: the rest of the time always moving towards *AB* or moving away. All that is easily understood as following from the movements.

Hence it will also be demonstrated that by this composite movement the planet does not describe a perfect circle in accordance with the theory of the ancient mathematicians but a curve differing imperceptibly from one.

For let the same epicycle *KL* be drawn again, and let *B* be its centre. Let *AG* the quadrant of a circle be assumed, and let *HI* be an epicycle around *G*. Let *CD* be cut into three equal parts, and let

---

[1]That is to say, during the hemicycle of movement wherein the epicycle is passing from the lowest to the highest apsis of the eccentric circle and the planet is passing from the apogee to the perigee of the epicycle, the movement on the epicycle adds to the movement on the eccentric circle; but during the hemicycle wherein the epicycle is passing from the highest to the lowest apsis, the movement on the epicycle subtracts from the movement on the eccentric circle.

[2]In this passage Copernicus is speaking as if the planet were borne around the epicycle by the revolving diameter, although he usually speaks as if the diameter of the epicycle pointed perpetually at the centre of the homocentric circle.

$$CM = {}^1/_3 CD = GI.$$

And let GC and IM, which cut one another at Q, be joined.

Accordingly since, by hypothesis

$$\text{arc } AG = \text{arc } HI$$

and

$$\text{angle } ACG = 90°;$$

then

$$\text{angle } HGI = 90°.$$

And

$$\text{angle } IQG = \text{angle } MQC,$$

because they are vertical angles. Therefore triangles GIQ and QCM are equiangular; and they have correspondingly equal sides, since by hypothesis

$$\text{base } GI = \text{base } CM.$$

And

$$QI > QC = QI > QG;$$

therefore

$$IQM > GQC,$$

but

$$FM = ML = AC = CG.$$

Therefore the circle which is described around centre M through points F and L and is hence equal to circle AB will cut line IM. The same demonstration will hold in the opposite quadrant. Accordingly by the regular movements of the epicycle in the eccentric circle the planet in the epicycle will not describe a perfect circle but a quasi-circle—as was to be demonstrated.[1]

Now around centre D let NO the annual orbital circle of the Earth be described; let IDR be extended; and let PDS be drawn parallel to CG. Accordingly IDR will be the straight line of the true movement of the planet; GC, the straight line of the mean and regular movement. And R will be the true apogee of the Earth with respect to the planet; and S, the mean apogee. Accordingly angle RDS or IDP is the difference between the regular and the apparent movement of both, namely between angle ACG and angle CDI.

But in place of eccentric circle AB we may take an equal homocentric circle around D as the deferent of the epicycle, whose radius is equal to DC and which is the deferent of the other epicycle, whose semi-diameter is half MD.[2] New let the first epicycle be moved [143ª] eastward, but the second in the opposite direction; and lastly let the planet on it (*i.e.*,

---

[1]As has been pointed out, if in the foregoing diagram we consider a point X so situated on semi-diameter CA that CX is equal to GI (and consequently DM is equal to MX), then since the planet on reaching point I has expended one quarter of its periodic time and has traversed one quarter of a full revolution about point X, evidently point X is analogous to the centre of a Ptolemaic equant, point M (the centre of the quasi-circle) to the centre of the Ptolemaic deferent, and point D (the centre of the sun for Copernicus) to the centre of the Earth.

[2]As in the accompanying diagram:

on the second epicycle) be deflected by the twofold movement. The same things will happen as before and no differently from in the moon, or by some other of the aforesaid modes.

But here we have chosen the eccentric circle bearing the epicycle, because by remaining always between the sun and C centre D is meantime found to have changed, as was shown in the case of solar appearances. But as the remaining appearances do not accord proportionately with this change there must be some other irregularity in those planetary movements: this irregularity, although very slight, is perceptible in the case of Mars and Venus, as will be seen in the right place.

Accordingly we shall soon demonstrate from observations that these hypotheses are sufficient for the appearances; and we shall do that first in the case of Saturn, Jupiter, and Mars: in them the position of the apogee and the distance CD are very difficult to find and of the greatest importance, since the rest is easily demonstrable by means of the apogee and the distance CD. Now in this case we shall use the method we used concerning the moon, namely a comparison of three ancient solar oppositions with the same number of modern ones, which the Greeks call their "acronychial gleams" and we the "deeps of the night," namely when the planet opposite the sun falls upon the straight line of the mean movement of the sun, where it throws off all that irregularity which the movement of the Earth brings to it. Such positions are determined by observations with an astrolabe and by computation of the oppositions of the sun, until it is clear that the planet has arrived at a point opposite the Sun.

5. DEMONSTRATIONS OF THE MOVEMENT OF SATURN

Accordingly we shall begin with Saturn by taking three oppositions once observed by Ptolemy. The first of them occurred in the 11th year of Hadrian on the 7th day of the month Pachom at the first hour of night; in the year of Our Lord 127 on the 7th day before the Kalends of April, 17 equal hours after midnight in relation to the Cracow meridian, which we find an hour distant from Alexandria. Now the position of the planet in relation to the sphere of the fixed stars, to which as to the starting-point of the regular movement we are referring all these things, was found to be at approximately 174°40', since [143b] the sun by its simple movement was then opposite at 354°40' from the horn of Aries, the starting-point assumed.

The second opposition was in the 17th year of Hadrian on the 18th day of the month Epiphi by the Egyptian calendar; but by the Roman, in the year of Our Lord 133 on the 3rd day before the Nones of June, 11 equatorial hours after midnight: he found the planet at 243°3', while by its mean movement the sun was at 63°3', 15 hours after midnight.

He recorded the third as occurring in the 20th year of Hadrian on the 24th day of the month Mesori by the Egyptian calendar; which was in the year of Our Lord 136 on the 8th day before the Ides of July, 11 hours after midnight (similarly according to the Cracow meridian) at 277°37', while by its mean movement the sun was at 97°37'.

Accordingly in the first interval there are 6 years 70 days 55 minutes (of a day), during which the planet is moved 62°23' in relation to sight, and the mean movement of the Earth with respect to the planet, *i.e.*, the movement of parallax, is 352°44'. Accordingly the 7°16' in which the circle is deficient belong to the mean movement of the planet, so that it is 75°39'.

In the second interval there are 3 Egyptian years 35 days 50 minutes; the apparent movement of the planet is 34°34', (the movement) of parallax 356°43'; and the remaining 3°17' of a circle are added to the apparent movement of the planet, so that the mean movement is 37°51'.

After this survey let *ABC* the eccentric circle of the planet be described. Let *D* be its centre, and *FDG* its diameter, whereon *E* is the centre of the great orbital circle of the Earth. Now let *A* be the centre of the epicycle at the first opposition to the sun; *B*, at the second; and *C*, at the third; and around them let the same epicycle be described with a radius equal to one-third of *DE*. Let the centres *A*, *B*, and *C* be joined to *D* and *E* by straight lines, which will cut the

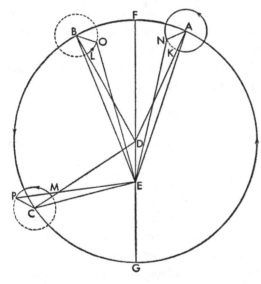

circumference of the epicycle at points *K*, *L*, and *M*. And let there be taken arc *KN* similar to *AF*, arc *LO* similar to *BF*, and *MP* similar to *FBC*; and let *EN*, *EO*, and *EP* be joined. Therefore by computation

arc *AB* = 75°39'

and

arc *BC* = 37°51';

and of the angles of apparent movement,

angle *NEO* = 68°23'

and

angle *OEP* = 34°34'.

Our problem is to examine the positions of highest and lowest apsis, *i.e.*, of *F* and *G*, together with the distance *DE* between the centres, without which there is no way of discerning the regular and the apparent [144ᵃ] movement.

But here too we run into as great a difficulty as in this part of Ptolemy, since, if the given angle *NEO* comprehended the given arc *AB*, and (angle) *OEP* (arc) *BC*, the entrance to demonstrating what we are looking for would be already opened. But the known arc *AB* subtends the unknown angle *AEB*, and similarly the unknown angle

BEC is subtended by the known arc *BC*; for it was necessary for both of them to be known. But *AEN*, *BEO*, and *CEP*, the differences between the angles, cannot be perceived, unless arcs *AF*, *FB*, and *FBC* are first set up as similar to those on the epicycle; accordingly these things are mutually dependent so as to be simultaneously known or unknown. Therefore those who were destitute of the means of demonstration relied upon detours and the *a posteriori* method, as the straightforward and *a priori* approach was not open. So Ptolemy in this investigation expended his energies in a prolix argument and a great multitude of calculations, which I judge boring and supererogatory to review, especially as in our calculations, which follow, we shall copy the same method approximately.

Finally in going over his calculations again he found that
$$\text{arc } AF = 57°1',$$
$$\text{arc } BF = 18°37',$$

and
$$\text{arc } FBC = 56\tfrac{1}{2}°.$$

But
$$\text{ecc.} = 6^{\text{P}}50',$$
$$\text{where } DF = 60^{\text{P}}.$$

But
$$\text{ecc.} = 1139,$$
$$\text{where } DF = 10{,}000.$$

Now
$$\tfrac{3}{4}(1139) \fallingdotseq 854,$$

and
$$\tfrac{1}{4}(1139) \fallingdotseq 1285.$$

Hence
$$DE = 854$$

and
$$\text{rad. ep.} = 285.$$

Making these assumptions and borrowings for our hypothesis, [144^{b}] we shall show that these things agree with the appearances observed.

Now at the first solar opposition, in triangle *ADE*,
$$\text{side } AD = 10{,}000,$$

and
$$\text{side } DE = 854;$$

and
$$\text{angle } ADE = 180° - \text{angle } ADF.$$

Hence, by means of what we have shown concerning plane triangles,

side AE = 10,489,

and

angle DEA = 53°6',

and

angle DAE = 3°55',
where 4 rt. angles = 360°.

But

angle KAN = angle ADF = 57°1'.

Therefore by addition

angle NAE = 60°56'.

Accordingly in triangle NAE two sides are given:
side AE = 10,489,
side NA = 285
where AD = 10,000,

and

angle NAE is given.

Hence

angle AEN = 1°22';

and, by subtraction,

angle NED = 51°44',
where 4 rt. angles = 360°.

Similarly at the second solar opposition. For in triangle BDE
side DE = 854,
where BD = 10,000;

and

angle BDE = 180° − BDF = 161°22'.

So triangle BDE too has its sides and angles given:
side BE = 10,812,
where BD = 10,000,

and

angle DBE = 1°27',

and

angle BED = 17°11'.

But

angle OBL = angle BDF = 18°36'.

Therefore, by addition

angle EBO = 20°3'.

Accordingly in triangle EBO two sides are given together with angle EBO:

$$BE = 10,812$$

and

$$BO = 285.$$

By what we have shown concerning plane triangles

$$\text{angle } BEO = 32'.$$

Hence

$$\text{angle } BED = 16°39'.$$

Moreover, in the third solar opposition, in triangle CDE, as before,

side CD is given

and

side DE is given;

and

$$\text{angle } CDE = 180° - 56°29'.$$

By the fourth rule for plane triangles

$$\text{base } CE = 10,512,$$

$$\text{where } CD = 10,000;$$

and

$$\text{angle } DCE = 3°53'$$

and, by subtraction,

$$\text{angle } CED = 52°36'.$$

Therefore, by addition,

$$\text{angle } ECP = 60°22',$$

$$\text{where 4 rt. angles} = 360°.$$

So also in triangle ECP two sides are given together with angle ECP; furthermore,

$$\text{angle } CEP = 1°22',$$

whence, by subtraction,

$$\text{angle } PED = 51°14'.$$

Hence, of the total angles of apparent movement,

$$\text{angle } OEN = 68°23',$$

and

$$\text{angle } OEP = 34°35',$$

which agree with the observations. And the position of the highest apsis of the eccentric circle

$$F = 226°20'$$

from the head of Aries. And as the then existing precession of [145a] the spring equinox was 6°40',

$$226°20' + 6°40' = 23° \text{ of Scorpio,}$$

in accordance with Ptolemy's conclusion. For the apparent position of the planet at this third solar opposition, as was reported above, was 227°37'. And as the angle of apparent movement,

$$\text{angle } PED = 51°14'.$$

Hence

$$227°37' - 51°14' = 226°23',$$

which is the position of the highest apsis of the eccentric circle.

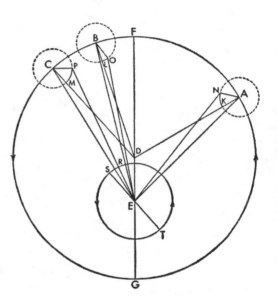

Now let there be described *RST* the annual orbital circle of the Earth, which will cut line *PE* at point *R*; and let the diameter *SET* be drawn parallel to the line of mean movement of the planet. Accordingly, as

$$\text{angle } SED = \text{angle } CDF,$$

angle *SER* will be the difference and the additosubtraction between the apparent and mean movement, *i.e.*, between angles *CDF* and *PED*, and

$$\text{angle } SER = 5°16'.$$

And there is the same difference between the mean and the true movements of parallax. Now

$$\text{arc } RT = 180° - \text{arc } SER = 174°44',$$

which is the regular movement of parallax from starting-point *T*, *i.e.*, from the mean conjunction of the sun and the planet, to this third solar opposition or true opposition of the Earth and the planet.

Accordingly at the time of this observation, namely in the 20th year of the reign of Hadrian, but in the 136th year of Our Lord on the 8th day before the Ides of July, 11 hours after midnight, we have the movement of anomaly of Saturn from the highest apsis of its eccentric circle as $56^1/_2°$, and the mean movement of parallax as 174°44', as was timely to demonstrate on account of what follows.

6. ON THREE OTHER SOLAR OPPOSITIONS OF SATURN RECENTLY OBSERVED

[145^b] Now since the computation of the movement of Saturn handed down by Ptolemy has no small discrepancy with our times, and since it cannot be understood right away in what quarter the error lies, we are forced to make new observations, out of which we have again taken three solar oppositions. The first opposition was in the

year of Our Lord 1514, on the 3rd day before the Nones of May $1^1/_5$ hours before midnight, at which time Saturn was discovered at 205°24'.

The second was in the year of Our Lord 1520 on the third day before the Ides of July at midday, and the planet was at 273°25'.

The third was in the year of Our Lord 1527 on the 6th day before the Ides of October $6^2/_5$ hours after midnight; and Saturn appeared at 7' from the horn of Aries.

Accordingly between the first and second solar oppositions there are 6 Egyptian years 70 days 33 minutes (of a day), during which time the apparent movement of Saturn is 68°1'.

From the second to the third there are 7 Egyptian years 89 days 46 minutes, and the apparent movement of the planet is 86°42'; and the mean movement during the first interval is 75°39'; and during the second, 88°29'. Accordingly in investigating the highest apsis and the eccentricity, we must at first abide by the rule of Ptolemy, just as if the planet moved in a simple eccentric circle; and although that is not sufficient, nevertheless we shall be led fairly near and shall arrive at the truth more easily.

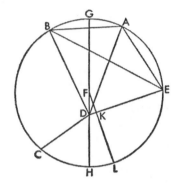

Accordingly, let *ABC* be the circle in which the planet is moved regularly: and let the first opposition be at *A*, the second at *B*, and the third at *C*. Let the centre of the orbital circle of the Earth be taken within it as *D*. Let *AD*, *BD*, and *CD* be joined, and let any one of them be extended in a straight line to the opposite part of the circumference—say *CDE*—and let *AE* and *BE* be joined.

Accordingly, since

angle *BDC* = 86°42',

where 2 rt. angles = 180°;

angle *BDE* = [146ᵃ] 93°18';

but

angle *BDE* = 186°36',

where 2 rt. angles = 360°.

And, as intercepting arc *BC*,

angle *BED* = 88°29',

and

angle *DBE* = 84°55'.

Accordingly, as the angles of triangle *BDE* are given, the sides are given by the table:

BE = 19,953

and

$$DE = 13,501$$

where diameter of circle circumscribing triangle = 20,000.

Similarly in triangle *ADE*, since

$$\text{angle } ADC = 154°43',$$

where 2 rt. angles = 180°;

$$\text{angle } ADE = 180° - \text{angle } ADC = 25°17';$$

but

$$\text{angle } ADE = 50°34',$$

where 2 rt. angles = 360°.

And, as intercepting arc *ABC*,

$$\text{angle } AED = 164°8',$$

and

$$\text{angle } DAE = 145°18' :$$

hence the sides are established:

$$DE = 19,090$$

and

$$AE = 8,542,$$

where diameter of circle circumscribing triangle *ADE* = 20,000.

But

$$AE = 6,043$$

where *DE* = 13,501 and

$$BE = 19,953.$$

Hence too, in triangle *ABE*, these two sides *BE* and *EA* have been given; and, as intercepting arc *AB*,

$$\text{angle } AEB = 75°39'.$$

Accordingly by what we have shown concerning plane triangles,

$$AB = 15,647$$

where *BE* = 19,968.

But according as

$$\text{ch. } AB = 12,266,$$

where diameter of eccentric circle = 20,000;

$$EB = 15,664$$

and

$$DE = 10,599.$$

Accordingly, in proportion to chord *BE*,

$$\text{arc } BAE = 103°7'.$$

Hence, by addition,

$$\text{arc } EABC = 191°36';$$

and
$$\text{arc } CE = 360° - \text{arc } EABC = 168°24';$$
and hence
$$\text{ch. } CDE = 19{,}898.$$
And
$$CD = CDE - DE = 9{,}299.$$

And now it is manifest that, if *CDE* were the diameter of the eccentric circle, the positions of highest and lowest apsis would fall upon it, and the distance between the centres would be evident; but because segment *EABC* is greater, the centre will be in it. Let *F* be the centre, and let the diameter *GFDG* be extended through *F* and *D*, and let *FKL* be drawn at right angles to *CDE*.

Now it is manifest that
$$\text{rect. } CD, DE = \text{rect. } GD, DH.$$
But
$$\text{rect. } GD, DH + \text{sq. } FD = \text{sq. } (^1/_2 GDH) = \text{sq. } FDH.$$
Accordingly
$$\text{sq. } FDH - \text{rect. } CD, DE = \text{sq. } FD.$$
Therefore
$$FD = 1{,}200$$
$$\text{where radius } GF = 10{,}000;$$
but
$$FD = 7^P12'$$
$$\text{where radius} = 60^P,$$
[146^b] which differs little from Ptolemy.

But since
$$CDK = {}^1/_2 CDE = 9{,}949$$
and
$$CD = 9{,}299,$$
therefore
$$DK = CDK - CD = 650,$$
$$\text{where } GF = 10{,}000$$
$$\text{and } FD = 1{,}200.$$
But
$$DK = 5{,}411$$
$$\text{where } FD = 10{,}000.$$
And since
$$DK = {}^1/_2 \text{ ch. } 2 \ DFK,$$
$$\text{angle } DFK = 32°45',$$

where 4 rt. angles = 360°;
and as standing at the centre of the circle it intercepts a similar chord and arc *HL* on the circumference.

But

$$\text{arc } CHL = \tfrac{1}{2}CLE = 84°13';$$

therefore

$$\text{arc } CH = CHL - HL = 51°28',$$

which is the distance from the third opposition to the perigee.
Now

$$180° - 51°28' = CBG = 128°32'$$

from the highest apsis to the third opposition. And since

$$\text{arc } CB = 88°29',$$

$$\text{arc } BG = CBG - CB = 40°3',$$

from the highest apsis to the second solar opposition. Then, as

$$\text{arc } BGA = 75°39',$$

$$\text{arc } GA = BGA - BG = 35°36'$$

from the first opposition to the apogee *G*.

Now let *ABC* be a circle with diameter *FDEG*, centre *D*, apogee *F*, perigee *G*. Let

arc *AF* = 35°36',

arc *FB* = 40°3',

and

arc *FBC* = 128°32'.

Now let *DE* be taken as three quarters of what has already been shown to be the distance between the centres, *i.e.*, let

DE = 900;

and

quarter distance = 300

where radius = 10,000.

And with that quarter distance as radius, let the epicycle be described around centres *A*, *B*, and *C*—and let

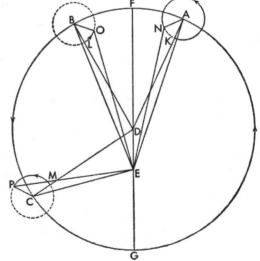

the figure be completed according to the hypothesis set before us. But if with this layout we wish to elicit the observed positions of Saturn [147ª] by the method handed down above and soon to be repeated, we shall find some discrepancy.

And—to speak briefly, so as not to burden the reader with many words or seem to have laboured more in indicating by-ways than in pointing out the high road—these

things will, by means of what we have shown concerning triangles, necessarily lead us to the conclusion that

$$\text{angle } NEO = 67°35'$$

and

$$\text{angle } OEP = 87°12'.$$

But angle OEP is $1/_2$° greater than the apparent angle, and the angle NEO is 26' smaller. And we find that they square with one another only if we move the apogee forward a little, and set up

$$\text{arc } AF = 38°50',$$
$$\text{arc } FB = 36°49',$$
$$\text{arc } FBC = 125°18',$$
$$DE = 854,$$

which is the distance between the centres, and

$$\text{rad. ep.} = 285,$$

where $FD = 10,000$;

and that agrees approximately with Ptolemy, as set out above. For it is clear from this that these magnitudes agree with the three apparent solar oppositions observed.

Since at the first opposition, in triangle ADE,

$$\text{side } DE = 854,$$

where $AD = 10,000$,

and

$$\text{angle } ADE = 141°10',$$

where angle ADE + angle ADF = 2 rt. angles;

hence it is shown that

$$\text{side } AE = 10,679,$$

where radius $FD = 10,000$,

$$\text{angle } DAE = 2°52',$$

and

$$\text{angle } DEA = 35°58'.$$

Similarly in triangle AEN, since

$$\text{angle } KAN = \text{angle } ADF;$$
$$\text{angle } EAN = 41°42',$$

and

$$\text{side } AN = 285,$$

where $AE = 10,679$.

Hence

$$\text{angle } AEN = 1°3'.$$

But

angle DEA = 35°58';

accordingly, by subtraction,

angle DEN = 34°55'.

In the second solar opposition triangle DEB has two sides given:

DE = 854,

where DB = 10,000

and

angle BDE = 153°11'.

Accordingly

BE = 10,697,

angle DBE = 2°45',

and

angle BED = 34°4'.

But

angle LBO = angle BDF;

therefore, as at the centre,

angle EBO = 39°34'.

Now this angle is comprehended by the given sides

BO = 285

and

BE = 10,697;

hence

angle BEO = 59'.

And

angle OED = angle BED – angle BEO 33°5'.

But in the first solar opposition it has already been shown that

angle DEN = 34°55'.

Therefore by addition

angle OEN = 68°

by which the distance of the first solar opposition from the second becomes apparent; and it harmonizes with the observations.

The same thing will be shown at the third opposition.

In triangle CDE

angle CDE = 54°42',

side CD = 10,000,

and

side DE = 854;

[147^b] hence

side EC = 9,532,

angle CED = 121°5',

and

angle DCE = 4°13';

therefore by addition

angle PCE = 129°31'.

So again in triangle EPC

side CE = 9,532

and

side PC = 285,

and

angle PCE = 129°31' :

hence

angle PEC = 1°18'.

And

angle PED = angle CED - angle PEO = 119°47'

from the highest apsis of the eccentric circle to the position of the planet at the third opposition.

Now it was shown that there were 33°5' to the second solar opposition: accordingly between the second and third solar oppositions of Saturn there remain 86°42', which agree with the observations. Now the position of Saturn was found by observation at that time to be at 7' from the assumed starting-point of the first star of Aries, and it was shown that there were 60°13' from it to the lowest apsis of the eccentric circle: accordingly the lowest apsis is approximately $60^1/_3$°, and the position of the highest apsis is diametrically opposite at $240^1/_3$°.

Now let RST the great orbital circle of the Earth be set around its centre E, and let its diameter SET be parallel to CD the line of mean movement; and let

angle FDC = angle DES.

Therefore the Earth and our point of sight will be on line PE, namely at point R. Now

angle PES = 5°31',

and angle PES or arc RS is the difference between FDC the angle of regular movement and DEP the angle of apparent movement.

Now

arc RT = 180° − 5°31' = 174°29'

which is the distance of the planet from the apogee of the orbital circle, i.e., from T, as if from the mean position of the sun.

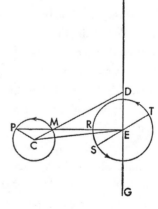

And so we have demonstrated that in the year of Our Lord 1527 on the sixth day before the Ides of October at $6^2/_5$ hours after midnight, the movement of anomaly of Saturn from the highest apsis of the eccentric circle was 125°18', the movement of parallax was 174°29', and the position of the highest apsis was at 240°21' from the first star of Aries in the sphere of the fixed stars.

7. ON THE EXAMINATION OF THE MOVEMENT OF SATURN

[148ª] Now it was shown that Saturn at the time of the last of the three observations of Ptolemy was by its movement of parallax at 174°44', and the position of the highest apsis of the eccentric circle was at 226°23', from the head of the constellation of Aries. Accordingly it is clear that in the midtime between the two observations Saturn has completed 1344 revolutions minus $^1/_4$° of regular parallaxes.

Now from the 20th year of Hadrian on the 24th day of the Egyptian month Mesori one hour before midday to the year of Our Lord 1527 on the 6th day before the Ides of October at 6 hours (after midnight, the time) of this observation, there are 1392 Egyptian years 75 days 48 minutes (of a day).

Hence if we wish to get the movement itself from the table, we shall similarly find 359°45', the movement beyond the 1343 revolutions of parallax. Accordingly what was set down concerning the mean movements of Saturn is correct. Moreover during that time the simple movement of the sun is 82°30'. If 359°45' are subtracted from 82°30', the remainder is the 82°45' of the mean movement of Saturn, which are already being added up in its 47th revolution, in harmony with the computation. Meanwhile too the position of the highest apsis of the eccentric circle has been moved forward to 13°58' in the sphere of the fixed stars. Ptolemy believed it to be fixed in the same way, but now it appears to move approximately 1° per 100 years.

8. ON DETERMINING THE POSITIONS OF SATURN

Now from the beginning of the years of Our Lord to the 20th of Hadrian on the 24th day of the month Mesori at 1 hour before midday, the time of Ptolemy's observation, there are 135 Egyptian years 222 days 27 minutes (of a day), during which time Saturn's movement of parallax was 328°55'. The subtraction of 328°55' from 174°44' leaves 205°49' [148ᵇ] as the locus of distance of the mean position of the sun from the mean (position) of Saturn, and as its movement of parallax at midnight before the Kalends of January.

From the first Olympiad to this locus 775 Egyptian years $12^1/_2$ days comprehend a movement of 70°55' besides the whole revolutions. The subtraction of 70°55' from 205°49' leaves 134°54' for the beginning of the Olympiads at noon on the 1st day of the month Hekatombaion.

Then after 451 years 247 days there are 13°7' besides the whole revolutions: the addition of 13°7' to 134°54' puts the locus (of the years) of Alexander the Great at 148°1' on noon of the 1st day of the month Thoth by the Egyptian calendar; and there are 278 years 118$^1/_2$ days to (years of) Caesar; the movement is 247°20', and it sets up the locus at 35°21' on midnight before the Kalends of January.

9. ON THE PARALLAXES OF SATURN, WHICH ARISE FROM THE ANNUAL ORBITAL CIRCLE OF THE EARTH, AND HOW GREAT THE DISTANCE OF SATURN IS (FROM THE EARTH)

In this way it has been demonstrated that the regular movements of Saturn in longitude are at one with the apparent. For the other apparent movements which occur in the case of Saturn are, as we said, parallaxes arising from the annual orbital circle of the Earth, since, as the magnitude of the Earth in relation to the distance of the moon causes parallaxes, so too its orbital circle, in which it revolves annually, should in the case of the five wandering stars cause (parallaxes) which are far more evident in proportion to the magnitude of the orbital circle. Now such parallaxes cannot be determined, unless the altitude of the planet—which, however, it is possible to apprehend through any one observation of a parallax—becomes known first.

We have such (an observation) in the case of Saturn in the year of Our Lord 1514 on the sixth day before the Kalends of May 5 equatorial hours after the preceding midnight. For Saturn was seen to be in a straight line with the stars in the forehead of Scorpio, namely with the second and third stars, which have the same longitude and are at 209° of the sphere of the fixed stars. Accordingly the position of Saturn is made evident through them. Now there are 1514 Egyptian years 61 days 13 minutes (of a day) from the beginning of the years of Our Lord to this time; and according to [149ª] calculation the mean position of the sun was at 315°41', the anomaly of parallax of

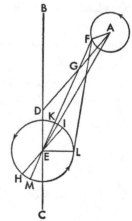

Saturn was at 116°31', and for that reason the mean position of Saturn was 199°10' and that of the highest apsis of the eccentric circle was at approximately 240$^1/_3$°.

Now in accordance with our problem, let *ABC* be the eccentric circle: let *D* be its centre, and on the diameter *BDC* let *B* be the apogee, *C* the perigee, and *E* the centre of the orbital circle of the Earth. Let *AD* and *AE* be joined, and with *A* as centre and $^1/_3$ *DE* as radius let the epicycle be drawn. On the epicycle let *F* be the position of the planet; and let

angle *DAF* = angle *ADB*.

And through *E* the centre of the orbital circle of the Earth let *HI* be drawn, as if in the same plane with circle *ABC*, and as

a diameter, parallel to *AD*, so as to have it understood that with respect to the planet the apogee of the orbital circle is at *H* and the perigee at *I*.

Now on the orbital circle let

$$\text{arc } HL = 116°31'$$

in accordance with the computation of the anomaly of parallax; let *FL* and *EL* be joined, and let *FKEM* produced cut both arcs of the orbital circle.

Accordingly since by hypothesis

$$\text{angle } ADB = \text{angle } DAF = 41°10',$$

and

$$\text{angle } ADE = 180° - ADB = 138°50';$$

and

$$DE = 854$$
$$\text{where } AD = 10,000:$$

whence in triangle *ADE*

$$\text{side } AE = 10,667,$$
$$\text{angle } DEA = 38°9',$$

and

$$\text{angle } EAD = 3°1':$$

therefore by addition

$$\text{angle } EAF = 44°12'.$$

So again in triangle *FAE*

$$\text{side } FA = 285$$
$$\text{where } AE = 10,667,$$
$$\text{side } FKE = 10,465,$$

and

$$\text{angle } AEF = 1°5':$$

accordingly it is manifest that

$$\text{angle } AEF + \text{angle } DAE = 4°6',$$

which is the total difference or additosubtraction between the mean and the true position of the planet. Wherefore if the position of the Earth had been at *K* or *M*, the position of Saturn would have been apparent as if from centre *E* and would have been seen to be at 203°16' from the constellation of Aries. But with the Earth at *L*, Saturn is seen to be at 209°. The difference [149b] of 5°44' goes to the parallax in accord with angle *KFL*. But by calculation of the regular movement

$$\text{arc } HL = 116°31',$$

and

$$\text{arc } ML = \text{arc } HL - \text{add. } HM = 112°25'.$$

And by subtraction[1]

---

[1] Arc *MLIK* = 180°.

$$\text{arc } LIK = 67°35' :$$

hence

$$\text{angle } KEL = 67°35'.$$

Wherefore in triangle *FEL* the angles are given, and the ratio of the sides is given too:
Hence

$$EL = 1,090$$
$$\text{where } EF = 10,465,$$
$$\text{and } AD = BD = 10,000;$$

but

$$EL = 6\text{P}32',$$
$$\text{where } BD = 60\text{P},$$

by usage of the ancients;

and there is very little difference between that and what Ptolemy gave.

Accordingly

$$BDE = 10,854,$$

and, as the remainder of the diameter

$$CE = 9,146.$$

But since the epicycle when at *B* always subtracts 285 from the altitude of the planet, but adds the same amount, *i.e.*, its radius, when at *C*; on that account the greatest distance of Saturn from centre *E* will be 10,569, and the least 9,431, where *BD* = 10,000. By this ratio the altitude of the apogee of Saturn is 9P42', where the radius of the orbital circle of the Earth = 1P; and the altitude of the perigee is 8P39': hence it is quite evident by the mode set forth above in the case of the small parallaxes of the moon that the parallaxes of Saturn can be greater. And when Saturn is at the apogee,

$$\text{greatest parallax} = 5°45';$$

and when at the perigee,

$$\text{greatest parallax} = 6°39';$$

and they differ from one another by 44'—measuring the angles by the lines coming from the planet and tangent to the orbital circle of the Earth. In this way the particular differences in the movement of Saturn have been found, and we shall afterwards set them out simultaneously and in conjunction with those of the five planets.

10. DEMONSTRATIONS OF THE MOVEMENT OF JUPITER

Having solved the problems concerning Saturn, we shall use the same method and order of demonstration in the case of the movement of Jupiter too, and first we shall repeat three positions reported and demonstrated by Ptolemy, and by the foreshown transformation of circles we shall reconstitute them as the same or as very little different.

The first of the solar oppositions was in the 17th year of Hadrian on the 1st day of the month Epiphi by the Egyptian calendar 1 hour before the following midnight [150ᵃ] at 23°11' of Scorpio, as he says, but after deducting the precession of the equinoxes, at 226°33'.

He recorded the second as occurring on the 21st year of Hadrian on the 13th day of the month Phaophi by the Egyptian calendar 2 hours before the following midnight, at 7°54' of Pisces; but with respect to the sphere of the fixed stars it was 331°16'.

The third was during the 1st year of Antoninus in the month Athyr during the night following the 20th day of the month 5 hours after midnight, at 7°45' in the sphere of the fixed stars.

Accordingly from the first opposition to the second there were 3 Egyptian years 106 days 23 hours, and the apparent movement of the planet was 104°43'. From the second to the third opposition there was 1 year 37 days 7 hours, and the apparent movement of the planet was 36°29'. During the first interval of time the mean movement was 99°55'; during the second it was 33°26'.

Now he found that the arc of the eccentric circle from the highest apsis to the first opposition was 77°15'; and next, 2°50' from the second opposition to the lowest apsis; and from that to the third opposition, 30°36'. Now the eccentricity of the whole circle was 5¹/₂ᵖ whereof the radius is 60ᵖ; but it is 917, whereof the radius would be 10,000; and all that corresponds approximately to the observations.

Now let *ABC* be the circle; and from the first opposition to the second let

arc *AB* = 99°55';

and let

arc *BC* = 33°26'.

Through the centre *D* let diameter *FDG* be drawn, so that from the highest apsis *F*

FA = *77°15'*,

FAB = *177°10'*,

and

GC = 30°36'.

Now let *E* be taken as the centre of the orbital circle of the Earth. Let the distance between the centres be equal to three-quarters 917, *i.e.*, let

DE = 687;

let

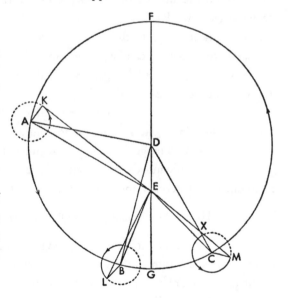

rad. ep. = 229,

which is one-quarter distance, and let the epicycle be described at points *A*, *B*, and *C*. Let *AD*, *BD*, *CD*, *AE*, *BE*, and *CE* be joined; and in the epicycles let *AK*, *BL*, and *BM* be joined in such a way that

angle *DAK* = angle *ADF*,

angle *DBL* = angle *FDB*,

and

angle *DCM* = angle *FDC*.

Finally let *K*, *L*, and *M* be joined to *E* by straight lines.

Accordingly, since in triangle *ADE*

angle *ADE* = 102°45',

because angle *ADF* is given; and

side *DE* = 687,

where *AD* = 10,000;

side *AE* = 10,174,

angle *EAD* = 3°48',

and

angle *DEA* = 73°27';

and by addition

angle *EAK* = 81°3'.

Accordingly in [150ᵇ] triangle *AEK* two sides have been given:

EA = 10,174

and

AK = 229,

and

angle *EAK* = 81°3';

it will be clear that

angle *AEK* = 1°17'.

Hence, by subtraction,

angle *KEO* = 72°10'.

Something similar will be shown in triangle *BED*. For the sides *BD* and *DE* always remain equal to the corresponding sides in the first triangle; but

angle *BDE* = 2°50'.

For that reason

base *BE* = 9,314,

where *DB* = 10,000;

and

angle *DBE* = 12'.

So once more, in triangle *ELB* two sides are given; and

$$\text{angle } EBL = 177°22';$$

moreover

$$\text{angle } LEB = 4'.$$

But

$$\text{angle } FEL = \text{angle } FDB - 16' = 176°54'.$$

And as

$$\text{angle } KED = 72°10';$$

$$\text{angle } KEL = \text{angle } FEL - \text{angle } KED = 104°44',$$

which is the angle of apparent movement between the first and the second termini observed; and there is approximate agreement.

Similarly at the third opposition, in triangle *CDE* two sides *CD* and *DE* have been given, and

$$\text{angle } CDE = 30°36';$$

$$\text{base } EC = 9,410$$

and

$$\text{angle } DCE = 2°8'.$$

Whence in triangle *ECM*

$$\text{angle } ECM = 147°49';$$

hence

$$\text{angle } CEM = 39';$$

and because the exterior angle is equal to the sum of the interior and opposite angles

$$\text{angle } DXE = \text{angle } ECX + \text{angle } CEX = 2°47'$$

and

$$\text{angle } FDC - \text{angle } DEM = 2°47'.$$

Hence

$$\text{angle } GEM = 180° - \text{angle } DEM = 33°23';$$

and, by addition,

$$\text{angle } LEM = [151^a] \; 36°29',$$

which is the distance from the second opposition to the third; and that agrees with the observations. But since this third solar opposition was found to be at 7°45' (in the sphere of the fixed stars) and 33°23' to the east of the lowest apsis; the remainder of the semicircle gives us the position of the highest apsis as 154°22' in the sphere of the fixed stars.

Now around *E* let there be drawn *RST* the annual orbital circle of the Earth with diameter *SET* parallel to line *DC*. Now it has been made clear that

$$\text{angle } GDC = \text{angle } GER = 30°36';$$

and

angle DXE = angle RES = arc RS = 2°47',
the distance of the planet from the mean perigee of the
orbital circle. Hence by addition

arc TSR = 182°47',

which is the distance from the highest apsis of the orbital circle.

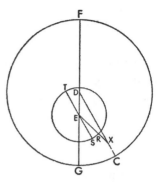

And by this we have confirmation of the fact that at
the time of the third opposition of Jupiter during the first
year of Antoninus on the 20th day of the month Athyr
by the Egyptian calendar 5 hours after the following midnight the planet Jupiter by its anomaly of parallax was at
182°47'. Its regular position in longitude was at 4°58', and the position of the highest
apsis of the eccentric circle was at 154°22'. All these things are in perfect agreement
with our hypothesis of the mobility of the Earth and absolute regularity (of movement).

11. ON THREE OTHER OPPOSITIONS OF JUPITER RECENTLY OBSERVED

Having recorded three positions of the planet Jupiter and evaluated them in this
way, we shall set up three others in their place, which we observed with greatest care at
the solar oppositions of Jupiter.

The first was in the year of Our Lord 1520 on the day before the Kalends of May
11 hours after the preceding midnight, at 220°18' of the sphere of the fixed stars.

The second was in the year of Our Lord 1526 on the fourth day before the
Kalends of December 3 hours after midnight, at 48°34'.

But the third opposition was in the year of Our Lord 1529 on the Kalends of
February 18 hours after midnight, at 113°44'.

From the first [151^b] to the second there are 6 years 212 days 40 minutes (of a
day), during which time the apparent movement of Jupiter was 208°6'. From the second to the third opposition there are 2 Egyptian years 66 days 39 minutes (of a day),
and the apparent movement of the planet is 65°10'. But the regular movement of the
planet during the first interval is 199°40', and during
the second 66°10'.

With this as a paradigm let eccentric circle ABC be
described, in which the planet is assumed to move simply and regularly. And let the three positions observed
be designated in the order of the letters A, B, and C in
such a way that

arc AB = 199°40'

and

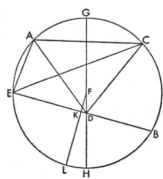

$$\text{arc } BC = 66°10',$$

on that account

$$\text{arc } AC = 360° - (AB + BC) = 94°10'.$$

Moreover let D be taken as the centre of the annual orbit of the Earth. Let AD, BD and CD be joined; and let any of them, say DB, be extended in a straight line BDE to both arcs of the circle; and let AC, AE and CE be joined.

Accordingly, since

$$\text{angle } BDC = 65°10',$$

where 4 rt. angles at centre = 360°;

and that is the angle of apparent movement, and since

$$\text{angle } CDE = 180° - 65°10' = 114°50',$$

but

$$\text{angle } CDE = 229°40',$$

where 2 rt. angles at circumference 360°;

and since, as standing on arc BC of circumference,

$$\text{angle } CED = 66°10',$$

and accordingly

$$\text{angle } DCE = 64°10';$$

therefore, as triangle CDE has its angles given, it has its sides given too:

$$CE = 18,150$$

and

$$ED = 10,918$$

where diameter of circle circumscribing triangle = 20,000.

Similarly, in triangle ADE, since

$$\text{angle } ADB = 151°54',$$

which is the remainder of the circle after the subtraction of the given distance between the first opposition and the second; accordingly

$$\text{angle } ADE = 180° - 151°54' = 28°6',$$

as at the centre, but as on the circumference

$$\text{angle } ADE = 56°12';$$

and, as on arc BCA of the circumference

$$\text{angle } AED = 160°20';$$

and

$$\text{angle } EAD = 143°28'.$$

Hence

$$\text{side } AE = 9,420$$

and

$$\text{side } ED = 18,992$$

where diameter of circle circumscribing triangle ADE = 20,000.
But

$$AE = 5,415$$
where ED = 10,918
and CE = 18,150

Again therefore we shall have triangle EAC, of which the two sides EA and EC are given; and, as standing on arc AC of the circumference

angle AEC = 94°10'.

[152ᵃ] Hence it will be shown that, as standing on arc AE,

angle ACE = 30°40',
angle ACE + arc AC = 124°50',

and

$$CE = \text{ch. } EAC = 17,727$$
where diameter of eccentric circle = 20,000.

And by the ratio given before,

$$DE = 10,665,$$

and

arc $BCAE$ = 191°.

It follows that

arc EB = 360° − 191° = 169°

and

$$BDE = \text{ch. } EB = 19,908$$

and by subtraction

$$BD = 9,243.$$

Accordingly, since $BCAE$ is the greater segment, it will contain F the centre of the circle. Now let the diameter $GFDH$ be drawn. It is manifest that

rect. ED, DB = rect. GD, DH,

which is therefore also given. But

rect. GD, DH + sq. FD = sq. FDH.

Now

sq. FDH − rect. GD, DH = sq. FD.

Therefore

$$FD = 1,193,$$
where FG = 10,000,

but

$$FD = 7^{\text{P}}9',$$
where FG = 60ᴾ.

Now let *BE* be bisected at *K*, and let *FKL* be extended; accordingly *FKL* will be at rt. angles to *BE*. And since

$$BDK = {}^1/_2 \, BE = 9,954$$

and

$$DB = 9,243,$$

then, by subtraction,

$$DK = 711.$$

Accordingly in triangle *DFK*, which has its sides given,

$$\text{angle } DFK = 36°35',$$

and similarly

$$\text{arc } HL = 36°35'.$$

But

$$\text{arc } LHB = 84{}^1/_2°;$$

and, by subtraction,

$$\text{arc } BH = 47°55',$$

which is the distance of the second position from the perigee. And

$$\text{arc } BCG = 180° - 47°55' = 132°5',$$

which is the distance of the apogee from the second position. And

$$\text{arc } BCG - \text{arc } BC = 132°5' - 66°10' = 65°55',$$

which is the distance from the third position to the apogee *G*. Now

$$99°10' - 65°55' = 28°15',$$

which is the distance from the apogee to the first position of the epicycle. That harmonizes too little with the appearances, as the planet does not run through the proposed eccentric circle: hence this method of demonstration which is based upon an uncertain principle cannot give us any certainty. One sign of this among others is that Ptolemy in the case of Saturn recorded a too great distance between the centres and in the case of Jupiter a too small distance; but the same thing seemed a great enough distance to us, so that evidently upon the assumption of different arcs of circles for the same planet [152^b] that which is sought does not come about in the same way. Not otherwise was it possible to compound the apparent and the regular movements at the three proposed termini and then at all the termini, unless we kept the total egression of eccentricity of the centres which was recorded by Ptolemy as 5^{P}30', whereof the radius of the eccentric circle is 60^P, but which is 917 parts, whereof the radius is 10,000. And let the arc from the highest apsis to the first opposition be 45°2'; from the lowest apsis to the second opposition 64°42'; and from the third opposition to the highest apsis 49°8'.

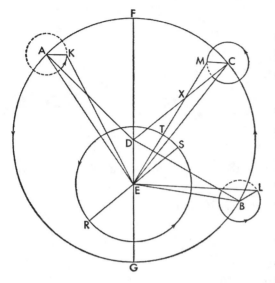

For let the above figure of the eccentric circle carrying an epicycle be repeated, inasmuch as it fits this example. So by our hypothesis

$$DE = 687,$$

which is three-quarters of the total distance between the centres. And

radius of epicycle = 229,

where $FD = 10,000$,

which is the remaining quarter of the distance. Accordingly, since

angle $ADF = 45°2'$,

triangle ADE will have the two sides AD and DE given, together with angle ADE; hence it is shown that

side $AE = 10,496$,

where $AD = 10,000$;

and

angle $DAE = 2°39'$.

And since

angle DAK = angle ADF,

by addition

angle $EAK = 47°41'$.

Also in triangle AEK the two sides AK and AE are given. Hence

angle $AEK = 57'$.

Now

angle KED = angle ADF − (angle AEK + angle DAE) = $41°26'$,

as the angle of apparent movement at the first solar opposition.

[153ª] In triangle BDE a similar thing will be shown. Since the two sides BD and DE are given, and

angle $BDE = 64°42'$;

side $BE = 9,725$

where $BD = 10,000$

and

angle $BDE = 3°40'$.

Furthermore, in triangle BEL the two sides BE and BL are also given, and

angle $EBL = 118°58'$:

angle $BEL = 1°10'$;

and hence

$$\text{angle } DEL = 110°28'.$$

But it has already been made clear that

$$\text{angle } AED = 41°26',$$

therefore, by addition,

$$\text{angle } KEL = 151°54'.$$

Hence

$$360° - 151°54' = 208°6',$$

the angle of apparent movement between the first and the second solar oppositions; and that agrees with the observations.

Finally, at the third opposition, in triangle CDE, sides DC and DE are given in the same way; and

$$\text{angle } CDE = 130°52'.$$

On account of angle FDC being given,

$$\text{side } CE = 10,463,$$
$$\text{where } CD = 10,000,$$

and

$$\text{angle } DCE = 2°51'.$$

Therefore, by addition,

$$\text{angle } ECM = 51°59'.$$

Now in triangle ECM the two sides CM and CE are given together with angle MCE:

$$\text{angle } MEC = 1°,$$

and

$$\text{angle } MEC + \text{angle } DCE = \text{angle } FDC - \text{angle } DEM,$$

and angles FDC and DEM are the angles of regular and apparent movement. And hence, at the third solar opposition,

$$\text{angle } DEM = 45°17'.$$

But it has already been shown that

$$\text{angle } DEL = 90°28';$$

accordingly

$$\text{angle } LEM = 65°10',$$

which is the distance between the second and the third solar oppositions observed; and that agrees with the observations. But since the third position of Jupiter was viewed at 113°44' of the sphere of the fixed stars, it shows that the position of the highest Jovial apsis is at approximately 159°.

But if around centre E we now describe RST the orbital circle of the Earth, of which the diameter RES is parallel to DC, then it will be manifest that at the third opposition of Jupiter

angle *FDX* = angle *DES* = 49°8',

and that the apogee of the regular movement in parallax is at R.

But now that the Earth has passed through 180° plus arc *ST*, it is in conjunction with Jupiter at its solar opposition; and

arc *ST* = 3°51',

according as angle *SET* has been shown to be of the same magnitude.

And so it is clear from this that in the year of Our Lord, 1529, on the Kalends of February 19 hours after midnight, [153b] the regular movement of anomaly of parallax of Jupiter was at 183°51', but by its proper movement Jupiter was at 109°52'; and the apogee of the eccentric circle is approximately 159° from the horn of the constellation of the Ram, as was to be investigated.

12. CONFIRMATION OF THE REGULAR MOVEMENT OF JUPITER

But it has already been seen above that at the last of the three solar oppositions observed by Ptolemy the planet Jupiter by its proper movement was at 4°58' with an anomaly of parallax of 182°47'. Hence it is clear that during the time between the two observations the movement of parallax of Jupiter was 1°5' besides the full revolutions and its proper movement was approximately 104°54'. The time, however, which flowed between the 1st year of Antoninus on the 20th day of the month Athyr by the Egyptian calendar at 5 hours after the following midnight and the year of Our Lord 1529 on the Kalends of February 18 hours after the preceding midnight was 1392 Egyptian years 99 days 37 minutes of a day, to which time there similarly corresponds according to the above calculation 1°5' besides the whole revolutions, by which the regular revolutions of the Earth has anticipated Jupiter 1267 times; and so the number is seen to harmonize with the observations and is held as certain and exact.

And it is also manifest that during this time the highest and lowest apsides of the eccentric circle moved $4^1/_2$° to the east. The equal distribution (of the movement) yields approximately 1° per 300 years.

13. POSITIONS TO BE ASSIGNED TO THE MOVEMENT OF JUPITER

But the time from the last of the three observations, in the 1st year of Antoninus on the 20th day of the month Athyr at 4 hours after the following midnight, going back to the beginning of the years of Our Lord, amounts to 136 Egyptian years 314 days 10 minutes (of a day), during which time the mean movement of [154a] parallax was 84°31'. The subtraction of 84°31' from 182°47' leaves 98°16' for the movement up to midnight on the Kalends of January at the beginning of the years of Our Lord.

Backward to the first Olympiad there were 775 Egyptian years $12\frac{1}{2}$ days, during which time a movement of 70°58' was reckoned besides the whole revolutions. The subtraction of 70°58' from 98°16' leaves 27°18' as the position for the Olympiad.

Coming down from there for 451 years 247 days, there are 110°52', which together with the movement for the first Olympiad amount to 138°10' for the position of the years of Alexander at noon of the 1st day of the month Thoth by the Egyptian calendar. And so for any others.

14. ON INVESTIGATING THE PARALLAXES OF JUPITER AND ITS ALTITUDE IN RELATION TO THE ORBITAL CIRCLE OF TERRESTRIAL REVOLUTION

In order to investigate the remaining apparent movements of parallax in the case of Jupiter, we carefully observed its position in the year of Our Lord 1520 on the 12th day before the Kalends of March 6 hours before noon, and we perceived through the instrument that Jupiter was 4°31' to the west of the first bright star in the forehead of Scorpio; and since the position of the fixed star was at 209°40', it is clear that the position of Jupiter was at 205°9' in the sphere of the fixed stars.

Accordingly from the beginning of the years of Christ to the time of this observation there were 1520 equal years 62 days 15 minutes (of a day), during which time the mean movement of the sun is calculated to have been 309°16', and the anomaly of parallax 111°15', whereby the mean position of the planet Jupiter is put at 198°1'. And since at this our time the position of the highest apsis of the eccentric circle was found to be at 159°, the anomaly of the eccentric circle of Jupiter was 39°1'.

Following this example, let eccentric circle *ABC* be described with centre *D* and diameter *ADC*. Let *A* be the apogee, and *C* the perigee; and for that reason let *E* the centre of the annual orbital circle of the Earth be on *DC*. Now let

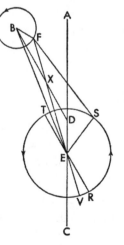

arc *AB* = 39°1';

and with *B* as centre let the epicycle be described with *BF* as radius equal to one third of distance *DE*. Let

angle *DBF* = angle [154ᵇ] *ADB*;

and let the straight lines *BD*, *BE*, and *FE* be joined. Accordingly since in triangle *BDE* two sides are given:

DE = 687,

where *BD* = 10,000;

and since these two sides comprehend the given angle *BDE*, and

angle *BDE* = 140°59' :

it will be shown that

$$\text{base } BE = 10,543$$

and

$$\text{angle } DBE = \text{angle } ADB - \text{angle } BED = 2°21',$$

which is the difference between angle *BED* and angle *ADB*. Therefore, by addition,

$$\text{angle } EBF = 41°22'.$$

Accordingly in triangle *EBF* angle *EBF* is given together with the two sides comprehending it:

$$EB = 10,543$$

and

$$BF = {}^1/_3 \, DE = 229,$$
$$\text{where } BD = 10,000.$$

It follows from this that

$$\text{side } FE = 10,373$$

and

$$\text{angle } BEF = 50'.$$

Now as lines *BD* and *FE* out one another in point *X*,

$$\text{angle } DXE = \text{angle } BDA - \text{angle } FED$$

and angles *FED* and *BDA* are the angles of mean and true movement; and

$$\text{angle } DXE = \text{angle } DBE + \text{angle } BEF = 3°11'.$$

Now

$$\text{angle } FED = 39°1' - 3°11' = 35°50'$$

from the highest apsis of the eccentric circle to the planet.
But the position of the highest apsis was at 159°; and

$$159° + 35°50' = 194°50',$$

which was the true position of Jupiter with respect to centre *E*, but the apparent position was at 205°9'. Accordingly, the difference of 10°19' is due to the parallax.

Now let *RST* the orbital circle of the Earth be described around centre *E*; and let its diameter *RET* be parallel to *DB*, so that *R* is the apogee of parallax. Moreover, in accordance with the measure of the mean anomaly of parallax, let

$$\text{arc } RS = 111°15';$$

and let *FEV* be extended in a straight line to both arcs of the orbital circle of the Earth. The true apogee of the planet will be at *V*; angle *REV* is equal to the difference between regular and apparent movement; and

$$\text{angle } REV = \text{angle } DXE.$$

Hence, by addition,

$$\text{arc } VRS = 114°26',$$

and by subtraction

305

angle *FES* = 65°34'.

[155ª] But since

angle *EFS* = 10°19';

angle *FSE* = 104°7'.

Hence, as in triangle *EFS* the angles are given, the ratio of the sides will be given too:

FE : *ES* = 9,698 : 1,791.

Accordingly

FE = 10,373

and

ES = 1,916,

where *BD* = 10,000.

For Ptolemy however

ES = 11P30',

where radius of eccentric circle = 60P;

and that is approximately the same ratio as

1,916 : 10,000;

and therein we do not seem to differ from Ptolemy at all.

Accordingly

dmtr. *ADC* : dmtr. *RET* = 5P13' : 1P.

Similarly

AD : *ES* = *AD* : *RE* = 5P13'9" : 1P

thus

DE = 21'9"

and

BF = 7'10".

Accordingly, when Jupiter is at apogee,

(*ADF* − *BF*) : radius of orbital circle of Earth = 5P27'29" : 1P.

And when Jupiter is at perigee;

(*EC* + *BF*) : radius of orbital circle of Earth = 4P58'49" : 1P;

and when in the mean positions, as is proportional. Hence it is gathered that Jupiter at apogee has a greatest parallax of 10°35', and at perigee 11°35': there is a difference of 1° between them. So the regular movements of Jupiter have been demonstrated to be at one with the apparent.

15. On the Planet Mars

We must now inspect the revolutions of Mars by taking three ancient solar oppositions, with which we shall connect the mobility of the Earth in antiquity. Accordingly of those oppositions which Ptolemy recorded, the first was in the 15th year of Hadrian

on the 26th day of Tybi the 5th month by the Egyptian calendar 1 equatorial hour after the midnight following. And he says that it was at 21° of Gemini, but in relation to the sphere of the fixed stars was at 84°20'.

He noted the second opposition [155ᵇ] as occurring in the 19th year of Hadrian on the 6th day of Pharmuthi the 8th month by the Egyptian calendar 3 hours before the following midnight at 28°50' of Leo but at 142°10' in the sphere of the fixed stars.

The third was in the 2nd year of Antoninus on the 12th day of Epiphi the 11th month by the Egyptian calendar 2 equatorial hours before the following midnight at 2°34' of Sagittarius but at 235°54' of the sphere of the fixed stars.

Accordingly, between the first and second oppositions there are 4 Egyptian years 69 days 20 hours or 50 minutes of a day, and the apparent movement of the planet was 67°50' besides the whole revolutions. From the second opposition to the third there were 4 years 96 days and 1 hour, and the apparent movement of the star was 93°44'. Now during the first interval the mean movement was 81°44' besides the complete revolutions; during the second interval it was 95°28'. Then he found that the total distance between the centres was 12ᴾ, whereof the radius of the eccentric circle was 60ᴾ; but it was 2,000 whereof the radius was 10,000. And the mean movement from the first opposition to the highest apsis was 41°33'; and then it was 40°11' from the highest apsis to the second opposition; and from the third opposition to the lowest apsis it was 44°21': But by our hypothesis of regular movements there will be three-quarters of that distance, i.e., 1,500 between the centres of the eccentric circle and the orbital circle of the Earth, and the remaining quarter of 500 will be the radius of the epicycle.

Now thus let eccentric circle ABC be described with centre D, and with FDG as the diameter through both apsides; and let E the centre of the orbital circle of annual

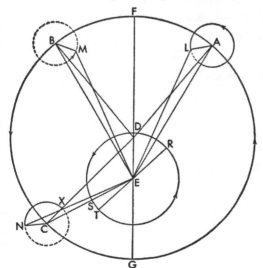

revolution be on the diameter. Let A, B, and C be the points of solar opposition, in that order; and let

arc AF = 41°34',
arc FB = 40°11',

and

arc CG = 44°21'.

At the separate points A, B, and C let the epicycle be described with one-third of distance DE as radius. And let AD, BD, CD, AE, BE, and CE be joined. On the epicycle let AL, BM, and CN be joined, but in such a way that

$$\text{angle } DAL = \text{angle } ADF,$$
$$\text{angle } DBM = \text{angle } BDF,$$

and

$$\text{angle } DCN = \text{angle } CDF.$$

Accordingly, since in triangle ADE

$$\text{angle } ADE = 138°26',$$

because angle FDA was given and also the two sides, *viz.*,

$$DE = 1,500$$
$$\text{where } AD = 10,000;$$

it follows from this that

$$\text{side } AE = 11,172,$$

and

$$\text{angle } DAE = 5°7'.$$

[156ª] Hence, by addition,

$$\text{angle } EAL = 46°41'.$$

So also in triangle EAL angle EAL is given, together with the two sides:

$$AE = 11,172$$

and

$$AL = 500,$$
$$\text{where } AD = 10,000.$$

Moreover,

$$\text{angle } AEL = 1°56';$$

and

$$\text{angle } AEL + \text{angle } DAE = 7°3',$$

which is the total difference between angles ADF and LED; and hence

$$\text{angle } DEL = 34\frac{1}{2}°.$$

Similarly at the second opposition: in triangle BDE

$$\text{angle } BDE = 139°49'$$

and

$$\text{side } DE = 1,500$$
$$\text{where } BD = 10,000.$$

Hence

$$\text{side } BE = 11,188,$$
$$\text{angle } BED = 35°13',$$

and

$$\text{angle } DBE = 4°58'.$$

Therefore

$$\text{angle } EBM = 45°13'$$

308

and is comprehended by the given sides *BE* and *BM*, from which it follows that

$$\text{angle } BEM = 1°53',$$

and by subtraction

$$\text{angle } DEM = 33°20'.$$

Accordingly

$$\text{angle } LEM = 47°50',$$

whereby the movement of the planet from the first solar opposition to the second is apparent; and the number is consonant with experience.

Again at the third solar opposition: triangle *CDE* has the two sides *CD* and *DE* given, which comprehend angle *CDE*. And

$$\text{angle } CDE = 44°21';$$

hence

$$\text{base } CE = 8,988,$$
$$\text{where } CD = 10,000$$
$$\text{and } DE = 1,500;$$

and

$$\text{angle } CED = 135°39',$$

and

$$\text{angle } DCE = 6°42'.$$

This again in triangle *CEN*

$$\text{angle } ECN = 142°21'$$

and is comprehended by the known sides *EC* and *CN* : hence too

$$\text{angle } CEN = 1°52'.$$

[156^b] Therefore by subtraction

$$\text{angle } NED = 127°5'$$

at the third solar opposition. But it has already been shown that

$$\text{angle } DEM = 33°20'.$$

Hence by subtraction

$$\text{angle } MEN = 93°45',$$

and is the angle of apparent movement between the second and the third solar oppositions, wherein the calculation agrees sufficiently with the observations. But at this last observed opposition of Mars the planet was seen at 235°54', being 127°5' distant from the apogee of the eccentric circle, as was shown: therefore the position of the apogee of the eccentric circle of Mars was at 108°50' in the sphere of the fixed stars.

Now let *RST* the annual orbital circle of the Earth be described around centre *E* with diameter *RET* parallel to *DC*, so that *R* is the apogee of parallax and *T* the perigee. Accordingly the planet was seen on *EX* at 235°54', in longitude, and it was shown that

$$\text{angle } DXE = 8°34',$$

the difference between the regular and the apparent movement; and on that account

$$\text{mean movement} = 244\frac{1}{2}°;$$

but, at the centre,

$$\text{angle } SET = \text{angle } DXE = 8°34'.$$

Accordingly

$$\text{arc } RS = \text{arc } RT - \text{arc } ST = 180° - 8°34' = 171°26',$$

the mean movement of parallax of the planet. Furthermore among other things we have demonstrated by this hypothesis of the mobility of the Earth that in the 2nd year of Antoninus on the 12th day of the month Epiphi by the Egyptian calendar 10 equal hours after midday the planet Mars by its mean movement in longitude was at $244\frac{1}{2}°$, and the anomaly of parallax was at 171°26'.

16. ON THREE OTHER SOLAR OPPOSITIONS OF MARS WHICH HAVE BEEN OBSERVED RECENTLY

We have compared these three of Ptolemy's observations of Mars with three other observations, which we did not take carelessly. The first was in the year of Our Lord 1512 on the Nones of June, 1 hour after midnight, and the position of Mars was found to be at 235°33', according as the sun was opposite [157ª] at 55°33' from the first star of Aries in the sphere of the fixed stars as a starting point.

The second was in the year of Our Lord 1518 on the day before the Ides of December 8 hours after midday; and the planet was apparent at 63°2'.

The third was in the year of Our Lord 1523 on the 8th day before the Kalends of March 8 hours before Boon, at 183°20'.

Accordingly from the first to the second opposition there were 6 Egyptian years 191 days 45 minutes (of a day); from the second to the third 4 years 72 days 23 minutes.

During the first interval of time the apparent movement was 187°29', and the regular movement was 168°7'. During the second interval of time the apparent movement was 80°18', and the regular was 83°.

Now let the eccentric circle of Mars be repeated again, except that here

$$\text{arc } AB = 168°7'$$

and

$$\text{arc } BC = 83°.$$

Accordingly, by the same method which we employed in the case of Saturn and Jupiter—let us pass over in silence the multitude, complication, and boredom of the calculations—we finally find that the apogee of Mars is on arc BC. For it is manifest that the apogee cannot be in arc AB because there the apparent movement is 19°22' greater than the mean. Again the apogee cannot be in arc CA, because even if BC the arc preceding CA is the lesser, nevertheless arc BC exceeds the apparent movement by

a greater difference than arc *CA* does. But it was shown above that in the eccentric circle the lesser and decreased movement takes place around the apogee. Accordingly the apogee will be held correctly to be in arc *BC*.

Let the apogee be *F*; and let *FDG* be the diameter of the circle. And let the centre of the orbital circle of the Earth be on the diameter. Accordingly, we find that

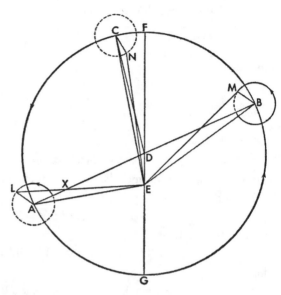

arc *FCA* = 125°29',

arc *BF* = 66°18',

and

arc *FC* = 16°36';

but

DE = 1,460,

where radius *DE* = 10,000 which is the distance between the centres; and semi-diameter of epicycle = 500 : whence the apparent and regular movements are shown to be consonant with one another and to agree with experiments.

Therefore let the figure be filled out, as before. For it will be shown that, since in triangle *ADE* two sides *AD* and *DE* are known and

angle *ADE* = 54°31'

from the first opposition of Mars to the perigee;

angle *DAE* = 7°24',

and by subtraction

angle *AED* = 118°5';

and

side *AE* = 9,229.

Now by hypothesis

angle *DAL* = angle *FDA*.

Accordingly by addition

angle *EAL* = 132°53'.

So too in triangle *EAL* the two sides *EA* and *AL* comprehending the given angle at *A* are themselves given; [157b] accordingly

angle *AEL* = 2°12',

and

angle *LED* = 115°53'.

Similarly it will be shown in the case of the second opposition that, since in triangle *BDE* the two given sides *DB* and *BE* comprehend angle *BDE*, and

angle *BDE* = 113°35',

then by what we have shown concerning plane triangles

angle *DBE* = 7°11',

angle *DEB* = 59°13',

and

base *BE* = 10,668,

where *DB* = 10,000

and *BM* = 500.

And by addition

angle *EBM* = 73°36'.

So too in triangle *EBM*, since the sides comprehending the given angle are given, it will be shown that

angle *BEM* = 2°36';

and by subtraction

angle *DEM* = 56°38'.

Then

angle *MEG* = 180° − angle *DEM* = 123°22'.

But it has already been shown that

angle *LED* = 115°53';

hence

angle *LEG* = 64°7';

and

angle *LEG* + angle *GEM* = 187°29',

where 4 rt. angles = 360°.

And that agrees with the apparent distance from the first opposition to the second.

A similar thing can be seen at the third opposition. For it has been shown that

angle *DCE* = 2°6',

and

side *EC* = 11,407,

where *CD* = 10,000.

Accordingly, as

angle *ECN* = 18°42',

and as sides *CE* and *CN* of triangle *ECN* have already been given, it will be clear [158ª] that

angle *CEN* = 50'.

And

angle *CEN* + angle *DCE* = 2°56',

which is the difference by which angle *DEN* of apparent movement is exceeded by angle *FDC* of regular movement. Therefore

angle *DEN* = 13°40',

which agrees approximately with the apparent movement observed between the second and the third oppositions.

Accordingly, since the planet Mars, as we told you, was apparent in this position at 133°20' from the head of the constellation of Aries; and it has been shown that

angle *FEN* ≒ 13°40';

it is manifest upon calculation backward that the position of the apogee of the eccentric circle at this last observation was at 119°40' in the sphere of the fixed stars.

At the time of Antoninus, Ptolemy found it at 108°50', and so during the time between then and now it has moved $10^{10}/_{12}$° eastward. Moreover we have found a lesser distance between the centres, *i.e.*, 40, whereof the radius of the eccentric circle is given as 10,000—not because either Ptolemy or ourselves made a slip, but manifestly because the centre of this orbital circle of the Earth has approached the centre of the orbital circle of Mars, while the sun has remained immobile. For these things correspond approximately to one another, as will be shown below clearer than day.

Now let the annual orbital circle of the Earth be described around the centre *E*; and let its diameter *SER* be parallel to *CD* on account of the equality of revolutions. Let *R* be the regular apogee with respect to the planet, *S* the perigee, and *T* the Earth. Now let *ET* be extended; the line of sight of the planet will thus cut *CD* at point *X*. Now the line of sight along *ETX*, as was said at the last opposition, is at 133°20' of longitude.

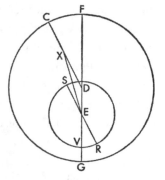

Moreover, it has been shown that

angle *DXE* = 2°56',

for angle *DXE* is the difference by which angle *XDF* of mean movement exceeds angle *XED* of apparent movement. But angle *SET* is equal to its alternate angle *DXE*, and is the additosubtraction arising from the parallax. Now

180° – 2°56' = 177°4',

which is the regular movement of the anomaly of parallax from *R* the apogee of the regular movement—and hence we have shown here that in the year of Our Lord 1523 on the 8th day before the Kalends of March, 7 equatorial hours before noon, the planet Mars by its mean movement in longitude was at 136°16'; and its regular anomaly of parallax was at 177°4', and the highest apsis of the eccentric circle was at 119°40', as was to be shown.

17. Confirmation of the Movement of Mars

[158^b] Now it was made clear above that in the last of Ptolemy's three observations Mars by its mean movement was at $244^1/_2$°, and its anomaly of parallax was at 171°26'. Accordingly during the year between there was a movement of 5°38' besides the complete revolutions. Now for the 2nd year of Antoninus on the 12th day of Epiphi the 11 month by the Egyptian calendar 9 hours after midday, i.e., 3 equatorial hours before the following midnight, with respect to the Cracow meridian, to the year of Our Lord 1523 on the 8th day before the Kalends of March 7 hours before noon, there were 1384 Egyptian years 251 days 19 minutes (of a day). During that time there were by the above calculation 5°38' and 648 complete revolutions of anomaly of parallax. Now the regular movement of the sun was held to be $257^1/_2$°. The subtraction from $257^1/_2$° of the 5°38' of the movement of parallax leaves 251°52' as the mean movement of Mars in longitude. And all that agrees approximately with what was set down just now.

18. Determination of the Position of Mars

Now from the beginning of the years of Our Lord to the 2nd year of Antoninus on the 12th day of the month Epiphi by the Egyptian calendar at 3 hours before midnight there were 138 Egyptian years 180 days 52 minutes (of a day), and during that time the movement of parallax was 293°4'. And when 293°4' is subtracted from the 171°26' of Ptolemy's last observation—a complete revolution being borrowed—there remain 238°22' at the (beginning of) the first year of Our Lord on midnight of the Kalends of January.

From the first Olympiad to this time there were 775 Egyptian years $12^1/_2$ days, during which the movement of parallax was 254°1'. When 254°1' has similarly been subtracted from 238°22' and a revolution borrowed, its [159^a] position at the first Olympiad remains as 344°21'.

Similarly by calculating the movements according to the other intervals of time we shall have its position at the beginning of the years of Alexander as 120°39' and at the beginning of the years of Caesar as 211°25'.

19. How Great the Orbital Circle of Mars Is in Terms of the Parts of Which the Annual Orbital Circle of the Earth Is the Unit

Moreover we took observations of the conjunction of Mars with the first bright star of the Chelae—called the southern Claw—which occurred in 1512 on the Kalends of January, For on the morning of that day 6 equatorial hours before noon we saw Mars

$1/4°$ distant from the fixed star but deflected towards the solstitial rising, by which it was signified that Mars was already in longitude $1/8°$ to the east of the star but $1/5°$ distant in northern latitude. Now it was established that the position of the star was 191°20' with a northern latitude of 40'. So it was clear that the position of Mars was at 191°28' with a northern latitude of 51'. But at this time the anomaly of parallax by calculation was 98°28'; the mean position of the sun was at 262°, and the mean position of Mars at 163°32', and the anomaly of the eccentric circle was 43°52'.

With that before us let the eccentric circle *ABC* be described. Let *D* be its centre, *ADC* its diameter, *A* the apogee, *C* the perigee, and let

ecc. *DE* = 1,460,

where *AD* = 10,000.

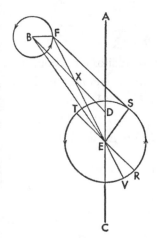

Now let

arc *AB* = 43°52'.

Now with *B* as centre and radius *BF* of 500, whereof *AD* is 10,000, let the epicycle be described. Let

angle *DBF* = angle *ADB*;

and let *BD*, *BE*, *BF*, and *FE* be joined. Moreover, let *RST* the great orbital circle of the Earth be described around centre *E* with its diameter *RET* parallel to *BD*; and on the diameter let *R* be the apogee of the planet's regular movement of parallax, and *T* the perigee. Now let the Earth be at *S*; and in accordance with the regular anomaly of parallax as computed, let

arc *RS* = 98°28'.

Let *FE* be extended in the straight line *FEV*, which will cut *BD* at point *X* and the convex arc of the orbital circle of the Earth at *V*, where the true apogee of parallax is.

Accordingly, in triangle *BDE* [159b] two sides are given:

DE = 1,460,

where, *BD* = 10,000;

and they comprehend angle *BDE*. And

angle *ADB* = 43°52';

now

angle *BDE* = 180° − 43°52' = 136°8'.

Hence it will be shown that

base *BE* = 11,097

and

angle *DBE* = 5°13'.

But by hypothesis

angle *DBF* = angle *ABD*;

by addition

angle *EBF* = 49°5',

and is comprehended by the given sides *EB* and *BF*. On that account

angle *BEF* = 2°

and

side *FE* = 10,776,

where *DB* = 10,000.

Accordingly

angle *DXE* = 7°13',

because

angle *DXE* = angle *XBE* + angle *XEB*,

the interior and opposite angles. Angle *DXE* is the subtractive additosubtraction, the difference by which angle *ADB* exceeds angle *XED*, and by which the mean position of Mars exceeds the true. Now the mean position is reckoned as 163°32'; therefore the true position is to the west at 156°19'. But its position appears to be at 191°28' to those viewing it from *S*. Therefore its parallax, or commutation, is 35°9' eastward. Therefore it is clear that

angle *EFS* = 35°9'.

Now as *RT* is parallel to *BD*,

angle *DXE* = angle *REV*,

and similarly

arc *RV* = 7°13'.

Thus, by addition,

arc *VRS* = 105°41',

which is the corrected anomaly of parallax, and hence angle *VES* exterior to triangle *FES* is given. Hence, as being interior and opposite

angle *FSE* = 70°32',

where 2 rt. angles = 180°.

But as the angles of the triangle are given, the ratio of the sides is given too: therefore

FE = 9,428

and

ES = 5,727

where diameter of circle circumscribing triangle = 10,000.

Accordingly

[160ª] *ES* ≐ 6,580,

where *EF* = 10,776

and *BD* = 10,000;

and that is approximately the same as Ptolemy's findings. But by addition

$$ADE = 11,460,$$

and by subtraction

$$EC = 8,540.$$

And at the lowest apsis of the eccentric circle the epicycle adds the 500 which it subtracts at A the highest apsis, so that the remainder at the highest apsis is 10,960, and the sum at the lowest apsis is 9,040. Accordingly, in so far as the radius of the orbital circle of the Earth is 1P, Mars will have a greatest distance of 1P39'57" at its apogee, a least distance of 1P22'26", and a mean distance of 1P39'11". So too in the case of Mars the movements, magnitudes, and distances have been explicated in a fixed ratio by means of the movement of the Earth.

20. ON THE PLANET VENUS

Now that we have set out the movements of the three higher planets Saturn, Jupiter, and Mars which circle around the Earth, it is time to speak of the planets which the Earth circles around. And first of Venus, which admits an easier and clearer demonstration of its movement than does Mercury, if only the necessary observations of some positions are not wanting; since if its greatest distances, *i.e.*, at morning and at evening, in either direction from the mean position of the sun are found equal to one another, then we have as certain that the highest or lowest apsis of the eccentric circle of Venus is at the midpoint between these two positions of the sun. The apsides are distinguished from one another by the fact that such equal (angular) elongations are smaller when they take place around the apogee and greater when they take place around the perigee. Finally at its other positions we perceive through the differences by which the angular elongations exceed one another how far distant the orb of Venus is from the highest or lowest apsis and also what its eccentricity is, according as these things have been passed on to us by Ptolemy with great clarity, so that there is no need to repeat them separately, except in so far as things from Ptolemy's observations are applicable to our hypothesis of terrestrial mobility.

He took as his first observation one made by the mathematician Theo of Alexandria in the 16th year of Hadrian, he tells us, on the 21st day of the month Pharmuthi, at the first hour of the following night; and that was in the year of Our Lord 132 on the evening of the 8th day before the Ides of March. And Venus was seen at its greatest evening distance of $47^{1}/_{4}°$ from the mean position of the sun, [160b] while the mean position of the sun was by calculation at 337°41' in the sphere of the fixed stars. With this observation he compared one of his own which he said he made in the 4th year of Antoninus on the 12th day of the month Thoth at daybreak, *i.e.*, in the year of Our Lord 142 on the early morning of the third day before the Kalends of August.

He says that at this time the greatest morning elongation of Venus was equal to the previous elongation and was 47°15' from the mean position of the sun, which was at 119° in the sphere of the fixed stars and which on the previous date had been at 337°41'. Now it is manifest that midway between these mean positions are the apsides diametrically opposite one another at $48^1/_3$° and $228^1/_3$°. When the $6^2/_3$° of the precession of the equinoxes has been added to both of them, they will fall upon 25° of Taurus and of Scorpio according to Ptolemy, and the diametrically opposite highest and lowest apsides of Venus must be at those positions.

Once more for the further confirmation of the thing, he assumed another observation made by Theo in the 4th year of Hadrian at morning twilight on the 20th day of the month Athyr, which was in the year of Our Lord 119 on the morning of the fourth day before the Ides of October, at which time Venus was again found at a great distance of 47°32' from the mean position of the sun at 181°13'. With that he connected his own observation made in the 21st year of Hadrian, which was the year of Our Lord 136, on the 9th day of the month Mechyr by the Egyptian calendar but by the Roman calendar the 8th day before the Kalends of January, at the first hour of the following night, and the evening distance was found to be 47°32' from the mean position of the sun at 265°25'. But in the preceding observation made by Theo the mean position of the sun was at 191°13'. Again the apsides fall midway between these positions, at 48°20' and at 228°20' approximately, where the apogee and the perigee must be. And they are distant from the equinoxes at 25° of Taurus and at 25° of Scorpio, and Ptolemy separated them by two other observations as follows.

The first observation was made by Theo in the 13th year of Hadrian on the 3rd day of the month Epiphi, but in the year of Our Lord 129 at early morning on the 12th day before the Kalends of January, and he found the farthest morning elongation of Venus to be 44°48', while the sun by its mean movement was at $48^{10}/_{12}$°, and Venus was apparent at 4° of the sphere of the fixed stars. Ptolemy himself made the other observation in the 21st year of Hadrian on the 2nd day of the month [161ª] Tybi by the Egyptian calendar, which was by the Roman calendar the year of Our Lord 136 on the 5th day before the Kalends of January at the 1st hour of the following night, while the sun by its mean movement was at 228°54', from which Venus had a greatest evening elongation of 47°16' and was itself apparent at $276^1/_6$°. Hence the apsides are distinguished from one another, that is to say, the highest is put at $48^1/_3$°, where the shorter wanderings of Venus are, and the lowest at $228^1/_3$°, where the greater wanderings are—as was to be demonstrated.

21. WHAT THE RATIO OF THE DIAMETERS OF THE ORBITAL CIRCLE OF THE EARTH AND OF VENUS IS

Furthermore from these last two observations the ratio of the diameters of the orbital circles of the Earth and Venus will be apparent. For let *AB* the orbital circle of the Earth be described around centre *C*. Let *ACB* be its diameter through both apsides; and on *ACB* let *D* be taken as the centre of the orbital circle of Venus which is eccentric to circle *AB*. Now let *A* be the position of the apogee; and when the Earth is there, the centre of the orbital circle of Venus is at its greatest distance, while *AB* is the line of mean movement of the sun—$48^1/_3°$ at *A*

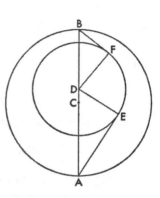

and $228^1/_3°$ at *B*. Now let the straight lines *AE* and *BF* be drawn touching the orbital circle of Venus at points *E* and *F*, and let *DE* and *DF* be joined. Accordingly, since as at the centre

$$\text{angle } DAE = 44^4/_5°,$$

and

$$\text{angle } AED = 90°,$$

then triangle *DAE* will have its angles given and hence its sides:

$$DE = {}^1/_2 \text{ ch. } 2\, DAE = 7{,}046,$$
$$\text{where } AD = 10{,}000.$$

In the same way in the right triangle *BDF*

$$\text{angle } DBF = 47^1/_3°,$$

and

$$\text{ch. } DF = 7{,}346,$$
$$\text{where } BD = 10{,}000.$$

Accordingly

$$BD = 9{,}582,$$
$$\text{where } DF = DE = 7{,}046.$$

Hence by addition

$$ACB = 19{,}582$$

and

$$AC = {}^1/_2 ACB = 9{,}791;$$

and by subtraction

$$CD = 209.$$

Accordingly, in so far as

$$[161^\text{b}]\ AC = 1^\text{P},$$

$$DE = 43^1/_6',$$

and

$$CD \doteq 1^1/_4';$$

and

$$DE = DF \doteq 7,193$$

and

$$CD \doteq 213,$$
where $AC = 10,000$.

And that was to be demonstrated.

22. ON THE TWOFOLD MOVEMENT OF VENUS

But by the argument from two of Ptolemy's observations, Venus does not have a simple regular movement around D. He made the first observation in the 18th year of Hadrian on the 2nd day of the month Pharmuthi by the Egyptian calendar, but by the Roman calendar it was the year of Our Lord 134 at early morning on the 12th day before the Kalends of March. For at that time the sun by its mean movement was at $318^{10}/_{12}°$; and Venus, which was apparent in the morning at $275^1/_4°$ of the ecliptic, had reached a farthest limit of elongation of $43°35'$.

He made the second in the 3rd year of Antoninus on the 4th day of the month Pharmuthi by the Egyptian calendar, which by the Roman calendar was in the year of Our Lord 140 on the evening of the 12th day before the Kalends of March. And at that time the mean position of the sun was at $318^{10}/_{12}°$; and Venus was at a greatest evening elongation of $48^1/_3°$ and was visible at $7^{10}/_{12}°$ in longitude.

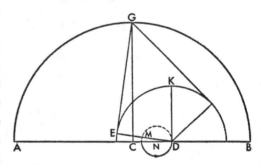

With that set out, let point G be taken as the position of the Earth in the same terrestrial orbital circle, so that arc AG is a quadrant of a circle—the quadrant which measures how far the sun diametrically opposite at both observations according to its mean movement was seen to be west of the apogee of the eccentric circle of Venus. Let GC be joined, and let DK be drawn parallel to GC. Let GE and GF be drawn touching the orbital circle of Venus; and let DE, DF, and DG be joined. Accordingly, since,

angle $EGC = 43°35'$,

which was the morning elongation at the time of the first observation, and since

angle $CGF = 48^1/_3°$,

which was the evening elongation at the time of the second observation;

$$\text{angle } EGF = \text{angle } EGC + \text{angle } CGF = 91^{11}/_{12}°;$$

and accordingly

$$\text{angle } DGF = {}^1/_2 EGF = 45°47^1/_2';$$

and by subtraction

$$\text{angle } CGD = 2°23'.$$

But

$$\text{angle } DCG = 90°.$$

Accordingly, as the angles of triangle CGD are given, the ratios of the sides are given too; and

$$CD = 416,$$

where $CG = 10,000$.

Now it has already been shown that the distance between the centres was 208; and now the distance has become approximately twice as great. Accordingly, if CD is bisected at point M, similarly

$$[162^a] \; DM = 208,$$

the total variation in this approach and withdrawal. Again if DM is bisected at N, it will be seen to be the mean and regular point in this movement.

Hence, as in the case of the three higher planets, the movement of Venus happens to be compounded of two regular movements, either by reason of the epicycle of an eccentric circle, as above, or by any other of the aforesaid modes. This planet however is somewhat different from the others in the order and commensurability of its movements; and, as I opine, there will be an easier and more convenient demonstration by means of the eccentric circle of an eccentric circle. In this way let us take N as centre and DN as radius and describe a small circle, on which (the centre of) the orbital circle of Venus is borne and moved around according to the law that whenever the Earth falls upon diameter ACB, on which the highest and lowest apsides of the eccentric circle are, the centre of orbital circle of the planet will always be at least distance, *i.e.*, at point M; and when the Earth is at its mean apsis, *i.e.*, at G, the centre of the orbital circle of the planet will reach point D and the greatest distance CD. Hence you are given to understand that at the time when the Earth has made one orbital circuit, the centre of the orbital circle of the planet has made two revolutions around centre N in the same direction as the Earth, *i.e.*, eastward. For according to such an hypothesis in the case of Venus, all the regular and apparent movements agree with the observations, as will be shown later. Now all this which has so far been demonstrated concerning Venus is found to be consonant with our times, except that the eccentricity has decreased approximately one sixth, so that what before was 416 is now 350, as many observations teach us.

23. ON THE EXAMINATION OF THE MOVEMENT OF VENUS

In this connection I have taken two positions observed very accurately, the first by Timochares in the 13th year of Ptolemy Philadelphus the 52nd year after the death of Alexander in the early morning [162^b] of the 18th day of Mesori the eight month by the Egyptian calendar; and it was recorded that Venus was seen to have occupied the position of the fixed star which is westernmost of the four stars in the left wing of Virgo and is sixth in the description of the sign; its longitude $151^1/_2°$, its northern latitude $1^1/_6°$; and it is of third magnitude. Accordingly the position of Venus was made manifest in this way; and the mean position of the sun was by calculation at 194°23'.

With this as an example, let the figure be drawn with point A still at 48°20':

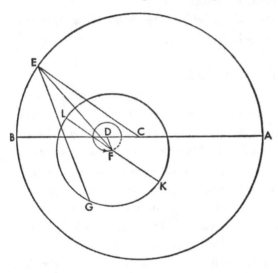

arc AE = 146°3',

and by subtraction

arc BE = 33°57'.

Angle CEG = 42°53',

which is the angular distance of the planet from the mean position of the sun. Accordingly, since

line CD = 312,

where CE = 10,000,

and

angle BCE = 33°57';

in triangle CDE

angle CED = 1°1',

and

base DE = 9,743.

But

angle CDF = $2BCE$ = 67°54';

and

angle BDF = 180° − 67°54' = 112°6'.

And, as the exterior angle of triangle CDE,

angle BDE = 33°57'.

Hence it is clear that

angle EDF = 144°4',

DF = 104,

where DE = 9,743.

So in triangle DEF

angle DEF = 20',

and by addition
$$\text{angle } CEF = 1°21',$$
and
$$\text{side } EF = 9,831.$$
But it has already been shown that
$$\text{angle } CEG = 42°53';$$
accordingly, by subtraction,
$$\text{angle } FEG = 41°32';$$
and, as radius of the orbital circle,
$$FG = 7,193,$$
$$\text{where } EF = 9,831$$
Accordingly, since in triangle EFG angle FEG and the ratios of the sides are given, the remaining angles are given too. And
$$[163^a] \text{ angle } EFG = 72°5'.$$
$$\text{Arc } KLG = 180° + \text{angle } EFG = 252°5',$$
measured from the highest apsis of the orbital circle. And so we have shown that in the 13th year of Ptolemy Philadelphus on the 18th day of the month Mesori the anomaly of parallax of Venus was 252°5'.

We ourselves made observations of a second position of Venus in the year of Our Lord 1529 on the 4th day before the Ides of March, 1 hour after sunset and at the beginning of the 8th hour after midday. We saw the moon begin to occult Venus at the midpoint of the dark part between the horns, and the occultation lasted till the end of the hour or a little later, until the planet was seen to emerge towards the west on the other side at the midpoint of the gibbosity of the horns. Accordingly it is clear that at the middle of the hour or thereabouts, the centres of the moon and Venus were in conjunction, and we had a full view at Frauenburg. Venus was still in her evening increase (of elongation) and this side of the point of tangency of the orbital circle with a line from the Earth. Accordingly from the birth of Christ there have been 1529 Egyptian years 87 days $7^1/_2$ hours by apparent time but by equal time 7 hours 34 minutes, and the mean position of the sun considered simply had reached 332°11'; and the precession of the equinoxes was 27°24'. The regular movement of the moon was 33°57' away from the sun, the regular movement of anomaly was 205°1', and the movement in latitude was 71°59'. Hence it is reckoned that the true position of the moon was at 10°, but measured from the equinox it was at 7°24' of Taurus with a northern latitude of 1°13'. But since the 15° of Libra were rising, on that account the lunar parallax in longitude was 48°32', and so the apparent position (of the moon) was at 6°26' of Taurus; but its longitude in the sphere of the fixed stars was 9°11' with a northern latitude of 41'; and the apparent position of Venus was at an evening distance of 37°1' from the

mean position of the sun, and the distance of the Earth from the highest apsis of Venus was 76°9' to the west.

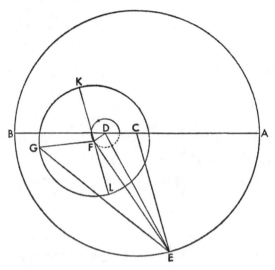

Now let the figure be drawn again according to the previous mode of construction, except that

> angle *ECA* = 76°9',

and

> angle *CDF* = 2*ECA* = 152°18';

and

> ecc. *CD* = 246,

as it is found today; and

> *DF* = 104,

where *CE* = 10,000. Therefore in triangle *CDE*, by subtraction

> angle *DCE* = 103°51'

and is comprehended by the given sides. From that it will be shown that

> angle *CED* = 1°15',

and

> base *DE* = 10,056,

and

> angle [163b] *CDE* = 74°54'.

But

> angle *CDF* = 2*ACE* = 152°18'.

And

> angle *EDF* = angle *CDF* - angle *CDE* = 77°24'.

So again in triangle *DEF* two sides are given;

> *DF* = 104,

where *DE* = 10,056;

and they comprehend the given angle *EDF*. Moreover,

> angle *DEF* = 35',

and

> base *EF* = 10,034.

Hence by addition

> angle *CEF* = 1°50'.

Furthermore,

> angle *CEG* = 37°1',

which measures the apparent distance of the planet from the mean position of the sun.

Now

$$\text{angle } FEG = \text{angle } CEG - \text{angle } CEF = 35°11'.$$

Similarly in triangle EFG two sides are given:

$$EF = 10,034,$$

$$\text{where } FG = 7,193$$

and the angle at E is given: hence too the remaining angles are calculable;

$$\text{angle } EGF = 53^1/_2°$$

and

$$\text{angle } EFG = 91°19',$$

which is the distance of the planet from the true perigee of its orbital circle.

But since diameter KFL has been drawn parallel to CE, so that K is the apogee of the regular movement and L is the perigee, and since

$$\text{angle } EFL = \text{angle } CEF;$$

then

$$\text{angle } LFG = \text{angle } EFG - \text{angle } EFL = 89°29';$$

and

$$\text{arc } KG = 180° - 89°29' = 90°31',$$

which is the planet's anomaly of parallax as measured from the highest apsis of regular movement of the orbital circle—and that is what we were investigating at the time of this observation of ours.

But at the time of the observation made by Timochares the anomaly was 252°5'; accordingly during the years between there was a movement of 198°26' besides the 1115 complete revolutions. Now the time from the 13th year of Ptolemy [164a] Philadelphus at early morning on the 18th day of the month Mesori to the year of Our Lord 1529 on the 4th day before the Ides of March $7^1/_2$ hours after midday was 1800 Egyptian years 236 days 40 minutes (of a day) approximately.

Accordingly when we have multiplied the movement of 1115 revolutions and 198°26' by 365 days, and divided the product by 1800 years 226 days 40 minutes, we shall have an annual movement of 225°1'45"3'''40''''.

Once more the distribution of this through 365 days leaves a daily movement of 36'59"28''', which were added to the table which we set out above.

24. ON THE POSITIONS OF THE ANOMALY OF VENUS

Now from the first Olympiad to the 13th year of Ptolemy Philadelphus at early morning of the 18th day of the month Mesori there are 503 Egyptian years 228 days 40 minutes (of a day), during which time the movement was reckoned to be 290°39'. But if 290°39' is subtracted from 252°5' and 360° is borrowed, the remainder will be 321°26', the position of the movement at the beginning of the first Olympiad.

The remaining positions are in proportion to the movement and time so often spoken of: 81°52' at the beginning of the years of Alexander; 70°26' at the beginning of the years of Caesar; and 126°45' at the beginning of the years of Our Lord.

25. ON MERCURY

It has been shown how Venus is bound up with the movement of the Earth and in what ratio of circles the regularity of its movement is concealed. Mercury remains, and without fail will also submit to the principle assumed, although it has more complicated wanderings than Venus or any of the aforesaid planets. It has been established experimentally by ancient observations that in the sign of Libra, Mercury has its least angular elongations from the sun and has *greater* elongations in the opposite sign, as is right. But Mercury does not have its *greatest* elongations in this position but in some other positions higher and beyond, as in Gemini and Aquarius, particularly at the time of Antoninus according to Ptolemy; and that occurs in the case of no other planet. When the ancient mathematicians, who supposed the reason for this [164b] to be the immobility of the Earth and the movement of Mercury in its great epicycle along an eccentric circle, had noticed that one simple eccentric circle could not account satisfactorily for these appearances, not only did they grant that the movement on the eccentric circle was not around its own centre but around a foreign centre, but they were also compelled to admit that this same eccentric circle carrying the epicycle moved along another small circle, as they admitted the moon's eccentric circle did. And so there were three centres, namely that of the eccentric circle carrying the epicycle, that of the small circle, and that of the circle which the moderns call the equant. They passed over the first two circles and acknowledged that the epicycle did not move regularly except around the centre of the equant, which was the most foreign to the true centre, to its ratio, and to both the centres already extant. But they judged that the appearances of this planet could be saved by no other scheme, as Ptolemy declares at great length in his *Composition*.

But in order that this last planet may be freed from the liability to injury and disparagement and that the regularity of its movement in relation to the mobility of the Earth may be no less clear than in the case of the other preceding planets; we shall assign to it too a circle eccentric to an eccentric circle instead of the epicycle which the ancients assumed, but in a way different from that of Venus. And nevertheless an epicycle does move on the eccentric circle, but the planet is not borne on its circumference but up and down along its diameter: that can take place through regular circular movements, as was set forth above in connection with the precession of the equinoxes. And it is not surprising, since Proclus in his commentary on the *Elements* of Euclid admits that a straight line can be described by many movements, by all of which movements its appearance will be demonstrable.

But in order that the hypothesis may be grasped more perfectly, let *AB* be the great orbital circle of the Earth with centre *C* and diameter *ACB*. And on *ACB* between points *B* and *C* let *D* be taken as a centre and with one-third *CD* as radius let the small circle *EF* be described, so that *F* is its greatest distance from *C*, and *E* its least. Let *HI*

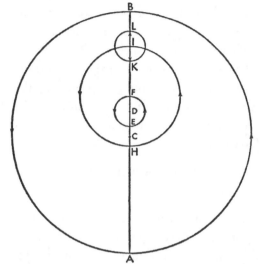

the orbital circle of Mercury be described around centre *F*; and then with *I* the highest apsis as centre let the epicycle which the planet traverses be added. Let *HI* be the orbital circle which is eccentric to an eccentric circle and carries the epicycle. When the figure has been drawn in this way, all those things will fall in order on the straight line *AHCEDFKILB*.

Meanwhile let the planet be set up at *K*, *i.e.*, at the least distance *KF* from centre *F*. [165ª] Now with that point established as the starting-point of the revolutions of Mercury, let it be understood that the centre *F* makes two revolutions for every one of the Earth, and in the same direction too, *i.e.*, eastward; similarly too the planet on *LK*, but along the diameter, up and down with respect to the centre of circle *HI*.

For it follows from this that whenever the Earth is at *A* or *B*, the centre of the orbital circle of Mercury is at *F*, which is the position farthest away from *C*; but whenever the Earth is at the middle quadrants, the centre is at *E* which is the position nearest (to *C*), and this in a manner contrary to that of Venus. Moreover, according to this law Mercury traversing the diameter of epicycle *KL* is nearest to the centre of the orbital circle carrying the epicycle, *i.e.*, is at *K*, when the Earth falls upon the diameter *AB*; and when the Earth is at its mean positions, the planet will be at *L* the most distant position. In this way there take place the two twin revolutions of the centre of the orbital circle on the circumference of the small circle *EF* and of the planet along the diameter *LK* which are equal to one another and commensurable with the annual movement of the Earth.

But meanwhile let the epicycle or line *FI* be moved by its own proper movement along orbital circle *HI*, and let its centre move regularly, completing one revolution simply and with respect to the sphere of the fixed stars in approximately 88 days. But by that movement, whereby it outruns the movement of the Earth and which we call the movement of parallax, it has with respect to the Earth one revolution in 116 days,

as can be derived more exactly [165[b]] from the table of mean movements. Hence it follows that Mercury by its own proper movement does not always describe the same circumference of a circle, but in proportion to its distance from the centre of its orbital circle it describes a circumference of greatly varying magnitude, least at point *K*, greatest at *L*, and middling around *I*, in practically the same way as was viewed in the case of the lunar epicycle on an epicycle. But what the moon did on the circumference, Mercury does on the diameter by means of a reciprocal movement which is nevertheless compounded of regular movements. We showed above in connection with the precession of the equinoxes how that takes place. But we shall bring to bear some other things concerning this, farther down in connection with latitudes. And this hypothesis is sufficient for all the appearances which are seen to be Mercury's, as is manifest from the history of the observations of Ptolemy and others.

26. ON THE POSITIONS OF THE HIGHEST AND LOWEST APSIDES OF MERCURY

For Ptolemy observed Mercury in the 1st year of Antoninus after sunset on the 20th day of the month Epiphi, while the planet in the evening was at its greatest angular distance from the mean position of the sun. Now at this time there had been 137 Christian years 188 days $42^1/_2$ minutes (of a day) at Cracow, and accordingly the mean position of the sun according to our calculation was at 63°50', and the planet observed through the instrument was at 7° of Cancer, he says. But after the subtraction of the precession of the equinoxes, which at that time was 6°40', it was shown that the position of Mercury was at 90°20' from the beginning of Aries in the sphere of the fixed stars, and its greatest angular elongation from the mean position of the sun was $26^1/_2$°.

He made a second observation in the 4th year of Antoninus on the early morning of the 19th day of the month Phamenoth when 140 years 67 days 12 minutes (of a day) approximately had passed since the beginning of the years of Christ, and the mean position of the sun was at 303°19'. Now Mercury was apparent through the instrument at $13^1/_2$° of Capricorn, but it was at approximately 276°49' from the fixed beginning of Aries, and accordingly the greatest morning distance was similarly $26^1/_2$°. Accordingly since the limits of elongation on either side of the mean position of the sun are equal, it is necessary that the apsides of Mercury be either way at the midpoint between these positions, *i.e.*, between 226°49' and 90°20'. And they are 3°34' and 183°34' diametrically opposite, where the highest and the lowest apsides [166[a]] of Mercury must be.

As in the case of Venus, the apsides are distinguished through two observations. He made the first in the 19th year of Hadrian on the early morning of the 15th day of the month Athyr, while the mean position of the sun was at 182°38'. The greatest

morning distance of Mercury from the sun was 19°3', since the apparent position of Mercury was at 163°35'. And in the same 19th year of Hadrian, which was the year of Our Lord 135, at dusk of the 19th day of the month Pachon by the Egyptian calendar, Mercury was found by the aid of the instrument at 27°43' in the sphere of the fixed stars, while the sun by its mean movement was at 4°28'. Again it was shown that the greatest evening distance of the planet was 23°15'—which is greater than the previous distance—whence it was clear enough that the apogee of Mercury at that time could be only at approximately 183$^1/_2$°—as was to be taken note of.

27. How Great the Eccentricity of Mercury Is and What the Commensurability of Its Circles Is

Moreover through this the distance between the centres and the magnitudes of the orbital circles are demonstrated simultaneously, For let *AB* be the straight line passing through *A* the highest and *B* the lowest apsis of Mercury, and also the diameter of the great circle, whose centre is *D*. And with *D* taken as centre let the orbital circle of the planet be described. Therefore let lines *AE* and *BF* be drawn touching the orbital circle, and let *DE* and *DF* be joined.

Accordingly, since at the first of the two preceding observations the greatest morning distance of the planet was seen to be 19°3',

angle *CAE* = 19°3'.

But at the second observation the greatest evening distance was seen to be 23$^1/_4$°. Accordingly, as both of the right triangles *AED* and *BFD* have their angles given, [166^b] the ratios of their sides will be given too, so that, as radius of the orbital circle,

ED = 32,639,

where *AD* = 100,000.

But

FD = 39,474,

where *BD* = 100,000.

But according as

FD = *ED*

as radius of the orbital circle,

FD = 32,639,

where *AD* = 100,000;

and by subtraction

DB = 82,685

Hence

$$AC = \frac{1}{2}AB = 91{,}342;$$

and by subtraction

$$CD = 8{,}658,$$

which is the distance between the centres. And the radius of the orbital circle of Mercury will be 21'26", where $AC = 1^P = 60'$;

and

$$CD = 5'4";$$

and

$$DF = 35{,}733$$

and

$$CD = 9{,}479,$$

where $AC = 100{,}000$

as was to be demonstrated.

But these magnitudes also do not stay everywhere the same; but are quite different from those found in connection with the mean apsides, as the apparent morning and evening longitudes observed at those positions and recorded by Theo and Ptolemy teach us. For Theo observed the evening limit of Mercury in the 14th year of Hadrian on the 18th day of the month Mesori after sunset; and at 129 years 216 days 45 minutes (of a day) after the birth of Christ, while the mean position of the sun was $93\frac{1}{2}°$, *i.e.*, approximately at the mean apsis of Mercury. Now the planet was seen through the instrument to be $3\frac{10}{12}°$ to the west of Basiliscus in Leo; and on that account its position was $119\frac{3}{4}°$ and its greatest evening distance was $26\frac{3}{4}°$.

Ptolemy reported that the second limit was observed by him in the 2nd year of Antoninus on the 21st day of the month Mesori at early morning, at which time there had been 138 Christian years 219 days 12 minutes, and the mean position of the sun was similarly 93°39'; [167ª] and the greatest morning distance of Mercury from that was found to be $20\frac{1}{4}°$. For Mercury was visible at $73\frac{2}{5}°$ in the sphere of the fixed stars.

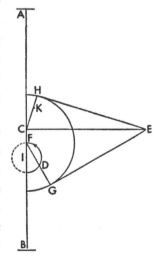

Therefore let *ACDB* which is the diameter of the great orbital circle (of the Earth) and which passes through the apsides of Mercury, be again drawn, as before; and at point *C* let *CE* the line of mean movement of the sun be erected at right angles. Let point *F* be taken between *C* and *D*; and let the orbital circle of Mercury be described around *F*. Let the straight lines *EH* and *EG* touch this small circle; and let *FG*, *FH*, and *EF* be joined.

Now once more our problem is to find point F, and what ratio radius FG has to AC. For since

$$\text{angle } CEG = 26^1/_4°,$$

and

$$\text{angle } CEH = 20^1/_4°;$$

accordingly by addition

$$\text{angle } HEG = 46^1/_2°.$$

And

$$\text{angle } HEF = {}^1/_2 HEG = 23^1/_4°.$$

And so by subtraction

$$\text{angle } CEF = 3°.$$

For that reason the sides of the right triangle CEF are given:

$$CF = 524$$

and

$$FE = 10,014,$$
$$\text{where } CE = AC = 10,000.$$

But it has been shown already that

$$CD = 948,$$

while the Earth is at the highest or lowest apsis of the planet. Hence DF will be the excess (of CD over CF) and the diameter of the small circle which the centre of the orbital circle of Mercury describes.

$$DF = 424,$$

and

$$\text{radius } IF = 212.$$

Hence by addition

$$CFI = 736.$$

Similarly, as in triangle HEF

$$\text{angle } H = 90°,$$

and

$$\text{angle } HEF = 23^1/_4° :$$

hence

$$FH = 3,947,$$
$$\text{where } EF = 10,000.$$

But

$$FH = 3,953,$$
$$\text{where } EF = 10,014$$
$$\text{and } CE = 10,000.$$

Now it has been shown above that

$$FK = 3,573.$$

Therefore by subtraction

$$HK = 380,$$

which is the greatest difference in the planet's distance from F the centre of its orbital circle; and this greatest difference is found when the planet is between its highest or lowest apsis and its mean apsis. On account of this varying distance from F the centre of its orbital circle, the planet describes unequal circles in proportion to the varying distances—the least distance being 3,573, the greatest 3,953, and the mean 3,763—as was to be demonstrated.

28. Why the Angular Digressions of Mercury at Around 60° From the Perigee Appear Greater Than Those at the Perigee

Hence too it will seem less surprising that Mercury has greater angular digressions at a distance of 60° from the perigee than when at the perigee, since they are also greater than the ones which we have already demonstrated; consequently it was held by the ancients that in one revolution [167$^\text{b}$] of the Earth, Mercury's orb was twice very near to the Earth.

For let the construction be made such that

$$\text{angle } BCE = 60°.$$

On that account

$$\text{angle } BIF = 120°$$

For F is put down as making two revolutions for one of E the Earth. Therefore let EF and EI be joined. Accordingly, since it has been shown that

$$CI = 736,$$

where $EC = 10,000,$

and

$$\text{angle } ECI = 60°;$$

hence in triangle ECI

$$\text{base } EI = 9,655;$$

and

$$\text{angle } CEI 3°47',$$

which is the difference between angle ACE and angle CIE. But

$$\text{angle } ACE = 120°.$$

Accordingly

$$\text{angle } CIE = 116°13'.$$

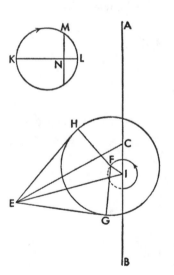

But also
$$\text{angle } FIB = 120°,$$
since by construction
$$\text{angle } FIB = 2 \ ECI;$$
and
$$\text{angle } CIF = 180° - 120° = 60°;$$
[and
$$\text{angle } BIE = 63°47']$$
hence by subtraction
$$\text{angle } EIF = 56°13'.$$
But it was shown that
$$IF = 212,$$
where $EI = 9,655$;
and EI and IF comprehend the given angle EIF. Hence it is inferred that
$$\text{angle } FEI = 1°4';$$
and by subtraction
$$\text{angle } CEF = 2°44',$$
which is the difference between the centre of the orbital circle of the planet and the mean position of the sun; and
$$\text{side } EF = 9,540.$$

Now let GH the orbital circle of Mercury be described around centre F; and from E let EG be drawn touching the orbital circle, and let FG and FH be joined.

We must first examine how great the radius FG or FH is under these circumstances; and we shall do that as follows:

For let a small circle be taken, whose
$$\text{diameter} = 380,$$
where $AC = 10,000$.

And let it be understood that the planet on straight line FG or FH approaches and recedes from centre F along that diameter or along a line equal to it, as we set forth above in connection with the precession of the equinoxes. And in accordance with our hypothesis, wherein angle BCE intercepts 60° of the circumference, let
$$\text{arc } KM = 120°;$$
and let MN be drawn at right angles to KL. And since
$$MN = {}^1/_2 \text{ ch. } 2ML = {}^1/_2 \text{ ch. } 2 \ KM,$$
then
$$LN = 95,$$
which is one quarter of the diameter—as is shown by [168ª] Euclid's *Elements*, XIII, 12 and V, 15. Accordingly,

$$KN = {}^3/_4 \, KL = 285.$$

Line *KN* and the least distance of the planet added together make the distance sought for this position, *i.e.*,

$$FG = FH = 3,858,$$
$$\text{where } AC = 10,000$$
$$\text{and } EF = 9,540.$$

Wherefore two sides of right triangle *FEG* or *FEH* have been given: so angle *FEG* or *FEH* will also be given. For

$$FG = FH = 4,044,$$
$$\text{where } EF = 10,000;$$

and

$$FG = FH = \text{ch. } 23°52',$$

so that by addition

$$\text{angle } GEH = 47°44'.$$

But at the lowest apsis only $46^1/_2°$ is seen, and at the mean apsis similarly $46^1/_2°$. Accordingly the elongation here becomes $1°14'$ greater, not because the orbital circle of the planet is nearer to the Earth than it was at the perigee, but because the planet is here describing a greater circle than there. All these things are consonant with both present and past observations, and follow from the regular movements.

29. Examination of the Mean Movements of Mercury

For it is found by the ancient observations that in the 21st year of Ptolemy Philadelphus in the morning twilight of the 19th day of the month Thoth by the Egyptian calendar, Mercury was apparent on the straight line passing through the first and second of the stars in the forehead of Scorpio and was two lunar diameters distant to the east but was separated from the first star by one lunar diameter to the north. Now it is known that the position of the first star is $209^2/_3°$ in longitude and $1^1/_3°$ in northern latitude; and the position of the second is $209°$ in longitude and $1^5/_6°$ in southern latitude. From that it was concluded that the position of Mercury was $110^2/_3°$ in longitude and approximately $1^5/_6°$ in northern latitude. Now there were 59 years 17 days 45 minutes (of a day) since the death of Alexander; and the mean position of the sun according to our calculation was $228°8'$; and the morning distance of the star was $17°28'$ and was still increasing, as was noted during the four following days. Hence it was certain that the planet had not yet arrived at the farthest morning limit or at the point of tangency of its orbital circle, but was still moving in the lower part of the circumference nearer to the Earth. But since the highest apsis was at $183°20'$, there were $44°48'$ to the mean position of the sun.

[168^b] Therefore again let *ACB* be the diameter of the great orbital circle, as above; and from centre *C* let *CE* the line of mean movement of the sun be drawn, in such fashion that

angle *ACE* = 44°48'.

And let there be described around centre *I* the small circle on which the centre *F* of the eccentric circle is home. And since by hypothesis

angle *BIF* = 2 angle *ACE*,

let

angle *BIF* = 89°36'.

And let *EF* and *EI* be joined.

Accordingly, in triangle *ECI* two sides have been given:

CI = 736$^1/_2$,

where *CE* = 10,000.

And sides *CI* and *CE* comprehend the given angle *ECI*. And

angle *ECI* = 180° − angle *ACE* = 135°12'; side

EI = 10,534;

and

angle *CEI* = 2°49',

which is the excess of angle *ACE* over angle *EIC*. Therefore too

angle *CIE* = 41°59'.

But

angle *CIF* = 180° − angle *BIF* = 90°24'.

Therefore by addition

angle *EIF* = 132°23';

and angle *EIF* is comprehended by the given sides *EI* and *IF* of triangle *EFI*, and

side *EI* = 10,534

and

side *IF* = 211$^1/_2$,

where *AC* = 10,000,

Hence

angle *FEI* = 50';

and

side *EF* = 10,678

And by subtraction

angle $CEF = 1°59'$.

Now let the small circle LM be taken; and let

diameter $LM = 380$,

where $AC = 10,000$.

And in accordance with the hypothesis let

arc $LN = 89°36'$.

Let chord LN also be drawn; and let NR be drawn perpendicular to LM. Accordingly, since

sq. LN = rect. LM, LR;

that ratio being given,

side $LR \doteqdot 189$,

where diameter $LM = 380$.

That straight line, *i.e.*, LR, measures the distance of the planet from F the centre of its orbital circle at the time when line EC has completed angle ACE. Accordingly, by the addition of this [169^a] line to the least distance

$$189 + 3,573 = 3,672,$$

which is the distance at this position.

Accordingly, with the centre F and radius 3,762, let a circle be described; and let EG be drawn cutting the convex circumference at point G, in such a way that

angle $CEG = 17°28'$,

which is the apparent angular elongation of the planet from the mean position of the sun. Let FG be joined; and let FK be drawn parallel to CE. Now

angle FEG = angle CEG – angle CEF = $15°29'$.

Hence in triangle EFG two sides have been given;

$$EF = 10,678,$$

and

$$FG = 3,762,$$

and

angle $FEG = 15°29'$:

whence it will be clear that

angle $EFG = 3346$.

Now, since

angle EFK = angle CEF,

angle KFG = angle EFG – angle RFK = $31°48'$;

and

arc $KG = 31°48'$,

which is the distance of the planet from K the mean perigee of its orbital circle.

arc $KG + 180° = 211°48'$,

which was the mean movement of the anomaly of parallax at the time of this observation—as was to be shown.

30. ON THREE MODERN OBSERVATIONS OF THE MOVEMENTS OF MERCURY

The ancients have directed us to this method of examining the movement of this planet, but they were favoured by a clearer atmosphere at a place, where the Nile—so they say—does not give out vapours as the Vistula does among us. For nature has denied that convenience to us who inhabit a colder region, where fair weather is rarer; and furthermore on account of the great obliquity of the sphere it is less frequently possible to see Mercury, as its rising does not fall within our vision at its greatest distance from the sun when it is in Aries or Pisces, and its setting in Virgo and Libra is not visible; and it is not apparent in Cancer or Gemini at evening or early morning, and never at night, except when the sun has receded through the greater part of Leo. On this account the planet has made us take many detours and undergo much labour in order to examine its wanderings. On this account we have borrowed three positions from those which have been carefully observed at Nuremburg.

The first observation was taken by Bernhard Walther, a pupil of Regiomontanus, in the year of Our Lord 1491 on the 9th of September, the fifth day before the Ides, 5 equal hours after midnight, by means of an astrolabe brought into relation with the Hyades. And he saw Mercury at $13^1/_2°$ [169^b] of Virgo with a northern latitude of $1^5/_6°$; and at that time the planet was at the beginning of its morning occultation, while during the preceding days its morning (elongation) had decreased continuously. Accordingly there were 1491 Egyptian years 258 days $12^1/_2$ minutes (of a day) since the beginning of the years of Our Lord; the simple mean position of the sun was at from the spring equinox but in 26°47' of Virgo, wherein the position of Mercury was approximately $13^1/_2°$.

The second was taken by Johann Schöner in the year of Our Lord 1504 on the 5th day before the Ides of January $6^1/_2$ hours after midnight, when 10° of Scorpio was in the middle of the heavens over Nuremburg; and the planet was apparent at $3^1/_3°$ of Capricorn with a northern latitude of 45'. Now by our calculation the mean position of the sun away from the spring equinox was at 27°7' of Capricorn and a morning Mercury was 23°42' to the west of that.

The third observation was taken by this same Johann Schöner in the same year 1504 on the 15th day before the Kalends of April, at which time he found Mercury at $26^1/_{10}°$ of Aries with a northern latitude of approximately 3°, while 25° of Cancer was in the middle of the heavens over Nuremburg—as seen through an astrolabe brought into relation with the Hyades, at $12^1/_2$ hours after midday, at which time the mean

position of the sun away from the spring equinox was at 5°39' of Aries, and an evening Mercury was 21°17' away from the sun.

Accordingly from the first position to the second, there are 12 Egyptian years 125 days 3 minutes (of a day) 45 seconds, during which time the simple movement of the sun was 120°14', and Mercury's movement of anomaly of parallax was 316°1'. During the second interval there were 69 days 31 minutes 45 seconds the simple mean position of the sun was 68°32', and Mercury's mean anomaly of parallax was 216°.

Accordingly we wish to examine the movements of Mercury during our time by means of these three observations, and I think we must grant that the commensurability of the circles has remained from Ptolemy's time to now, since in the case of the other planets the good authorities who preceded us are not found to have been mistaken here. If we have the position of the apsis of the eccentric circle together with these observations, nothing further should be desired in the case of the apparent movement of this planet. Now we have taken the position of the highest apsis as $211\frac{1}{2}°$, *i.e.*, at $28\frac{1}{2}°$ of Scorpio; for it was not possible to take it as less without prejudice to the observations. And so we shall have the anomaly of the eccentric circle—I mean [170ª] the distance of the mean movement of the sun from the apogee—as 298°15' at the first terminus, as 58°29' at the second, and as 127°1' at the third.

Therefore let the figure be constructed as before, except that

angle ACE = 61°45',

which measures the westward distance of the line of mean movement of the sun from the apogee at the time of the first observation; and then the rest according to the hypothesis. And since

$$IC = 736\frac{1}{2},$$

where AC = 10,000;

and angle ECI in triangle ECI is also given; then

angle CEI = 3°35',

and

side IE = 10,369,

where EC = 10,000;

and

$$IF = 211\frac{1}{2}.$$

So in triangle EFI also there are two sides having a given ratio; and since by construction

angle BIF = 2 angle ACE;

angle BIF = $123\frac{1}{2}°$,

and

$$\text{angle } CIF = 180° - 123^1/_2° = 56^1/_2°.$$

Therefore by addition

$$\text{angle } EIF = 114°40'.$$

Accordingly

$$\text{angle } IEF = 1°5',$$

and

$$\text{side } EF = 10,371.$$

Hence

$$\text{angle } CEF = 2^1/_2°.$$

But in order that we may know how greatly the orbital circle, whose centre is F, is increased by the movement of approach and withdrawal from the apogee or perigee, let a small circle be drawn and quadrisected by the diameters LM, NR at centre O. And let

$$\text{angle } POM = 2 \text{ angle } ACE = 123^1/_2°;$$

and from point P let PS be drawn perpendicular to LM. Accordingly by the ratio given,

$$OP : OS = LO : OS = 10,000 : 8,349 = 190 : 105.$$

Whence

$$LS = 295,$$
$$\text{where } [170^b] \ AC = 10,000;$$

and LS measures the farther removal of the planet from centre F. As the least distance is 3,573,

$$LS + 3,573 = 3,868,$$

which is the present distance.

And with 3,868 as radius and F as centre, let circle HG be drawn. Let EG be joined; and let EF be extended in the straight line EFH. Accordingly, it has been shown that

$$\text{angle } CEF = 2^1/_2°,$$

and by observation

$$\text{angle } GEC = 13^1/_4°,$$

which is the morning distance of the planet from the mean sun. Therefore by addition

$$\text{angle } FEG = 15^3/_4°.$$

But in triangle EFG

$$EF : EG = 10,371 : 3,868;$$

and angle EFG is also given; that shows us that

$$\text{angle } EGF = 49°8'.$$

Hence

$$\text{angle } GFH = 64°53',$$

as it is the exterior angle; and

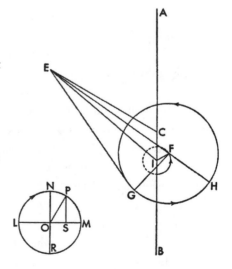

339

$$360° - \text{angle } GFH = 295°7',$$

which is the true anomaly of parallax. And

$$295°7' + \text{angle } CEF = 297°37',$$

the mean and regular anomaly of parallax—which is what we were looking for. And

$$297°37' + 316°1' = 253°38',$$

which is the regular anomaly of parallax at the second observation—and we shall show that this number is certain and is consonant with the observations.

For let us make

$$\text{angle } ACE = 58°29'$$

in accordance with the second movement of anomaly of the eccentric circle. Then also in triangle CEI two sides are given:

$$IC = 736,$$

where $EC = 10,000$;

and IC and EC comprehend angle ECI, and

$$\text{angle } ECI = 121°31';$$

accordingly

$$\text{side } EI = 10,404$$

and

$$\text{angle } CEI = 3°28'.$$

Similarly, since in triangle EIF
angle $EIF = 118°3'$,
and

$$\text{side } IF = 211^1/_2°,$$

where $IE = 10,404$:

$$\text{side } EF = 10,505,$$

and

$$\text{angle } IEF = 61'.$$

And so by subtraction

$$\text{angle } FEC = 2°27',$$

which is the additive additosubtraction of the eccentric circle; and the addition of angle FEC to the mean movement of parallax makes the true movement to be 256°5'.

Now also in the epicycle of approach [171ª] and withdrawal let us take

$$\text{angle } LOP = 2 \text{ angle } ACE = 116°58'.$$

Then too, as in right triangle OPS

$$OP : OS = 1,000 : 455;$$
$$OS = 85,$$

where $OP = OL = 190$.

And by addition

$$LOS = 276.$$

The addition of *LOS* to the least distance of 3,573 makes 3,849.

With 3,849 as radius let circle *HG* be described around centre *F*, so that the apogee of parallax is at point *H* from which the planet has the westward distance of 103°55' of arc *HG*, which measures the difference between a full revolution and the 256°5' of the movement of corrected parallax. And on that account

$$\text{angle } EFG = 180° - 103°55' = 76°5'.$$

So again in triangle *EFG* two sides are given:

$$FG = 3,849,$$

$$\text{where } EF = 10,505.$$

On that account

$$\text{angle } FEG = 21°19';$$

and

$$\text{angle } CEG = \text{angle } FEG + \text{angle } CEF = 23°46'.$$

That is the apparent distance between *C* the centre of the great orbital circle and *G* the planet; and it differs very little from the observation.

All this will be further confirmed by the third example, wherein we have set down that

$$\text{angle } ACE = 127°1',$$

or

$$\text{angle } BCE = 180° - 127°1' = 52°59'.$$

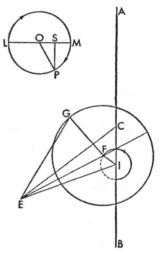

Hence it is shown that

$$\text{angle } CEI = 3°31',$$

and

$$\text{side } IE = 9,575,$$

$$\text{where } EC = 10,000.$$

And since by construction

$$\text{angle } EIF = 49°28',$$

and the sides comprehending angle *EIF* are given:

$$FI = 211^{1}/_{2},$$

$$\text{where } EI = 9,575;$$

$$\text{side } EF = 9,440,$$

and

$$\text{angle } IEF - 59'.$$

$$\text{Angle } FEC = \text{angle } IEC - 59' = 2°32',$$

which is the subtractive additosubtraction of the anomaly of the eccentric circle. When the 2°32' has been added to the mean anomaly of parallax, which we reckoned as 109°38' after adding the 216° of the second (movement of anomaly), the sum will be the 112°10' of the true anomaly of parallax.

Now in the epicycle let

$$\text{angle } LOP = 2 \text{ angle } ECI = 105°58';$$

here too by the ratio $PO : OS$,

$$OS = 52,$$

so that by addition

$$LOS = 242.$$

Now the least distance is 3,573; and

$$3,573 + 242 = 3,815,$$

which is the corrected distance.

With 3,815 as radius and F as centre, let the circle be described, in which the highest apsis of parallax is H, which is on the straight line made by extending line EFH. And in proportion to the true anomaly of parallax [171^b] let

$$\text{arc } HG = 112°10';$$

and let GF be joined. Therefore

$$\text{angle } GFE = 180° - 112°10' = 67°50',$$

which is comprehended by the given sides:

$$GF = 3,815$$

and

$$EF = 9,440.$$

Hence

$$\text{angle } FEG = 23°50'.$$

Now angle CEF is the additosubtraction; and

$$\text{angle } CEG = \text{angle } FEG - \text{angle } CEF = 21°18',$$

which is the apparent angular distance between the evening planet and the centre of the great orbital circle. And that is approximately the distance found by observation.

Therefore these three positions which are in agreement with observations testify indubitably that the position of the highest apsis, of the eccentric circle is the one which we assumed at $211\frac{1}{2}°$ in the sphere of the fixed stars for our time; and that what follows is also certain, namely, that the regular anomaly of parallax was 297°37' at the first position, 253°38' at the second, and 109°38' at the third position; and that is what we were looking for.

But at the ancient observation made in the 21st year of Ptolemy Philadelphus in the early morning of the 19th day of Thoth, the 1st month of the Egyptian calendar the position of the highest apsis of the eccentric circle was 182°20' according to Ptolemy, and the position of regular anomaly of parallax was 211°47'. Now the time between this latest and that ancient observation amounts to 1768 Egyptian years 200 days 33 minutes (of a day), during which time the highest apsis of the eccentric circle moved 28°10' in the sphere of the fixed stars, and the movement of parallax was

257°51' besides the 5,570 complete [172ª] revolutions—as approximately 63 periods are completed in 20 years and that amounts to 5,544 periods in 1,760 years and 26 revolutions in the remaining 8 years 200 days. Similarly in the 1,768 years 200 days 33 minutes there are in addition to the 5,570 revolutions 257°51', which is the distance between the position observed in ancient times and the one observed by us. That agrees with the numbers which we set out in the tables. Now when we have compared the 28°10' with the time during which the apogee of the eccentric circle has moved, it will be seen to have moved 1° per 63 years, if only the movement were regular.

31. ON DETERMINING THE FORMER POSITIONS OF MERCURY

Accordingly there have been 1504 Egyptian years 87 days 48 minutes (of a day) from the beginning of the years of Our Lord to the hour of the last observation, during which time Mercury's movement of anomaly of parallax was 63°14'—not counting the complete revolutions. When 63°14' has been subtracted from 109°38', it will leave 46°24' as the position of the movement of anomaly at the beginning of the years of Our Lord.

Again between that time and the beginning of the first Olympiad there are 775 Egyptian years 12¹/₂ days, during which the movement was calculated to be 95°3' besides the whole revolutions.

If 95°3' is subtracted from the position at the beginning of the years of our Lord and one revolution is borrowed, 311°21' will be left as the position at the time of the first Olympiad.

Moreover between this and the death of Alexander there are 451 years 247 days, and by computation the position is 213°3'.

32. ON ANOTHER EXPLANATION OF APPROACH AND WITHDRAWAL

But before we leave Mercury, let us survey another method no less credible than the former, by which that approach and withdrawal can take place and can be understood.

For let *GHKP* be a circle quadrisected at centre *F*, and around centre *F* let *LM* a small homocentric circle be inscribed. And again, with *L* as centre and radius *LFO* equal to *FG* or *FH*, let another circle *OR* be described.

Now let it be postulated that this whole configuration of circles [172ᵇ] together with its sections *GFR*

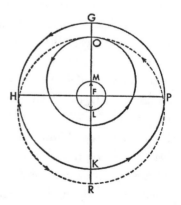

and *HFP* moves eastward around centre *F* in a daily movement of approximately 2°7'—namely, a movement as great as that whereby the movement of parallax of the planet exceeds the movement of the Earth in the ecliptic—away from the apogee of the eccentric circle of the planet; and the planet meanwhile furnishes the remaining movement away from *G* along *OR* the proper circle of parallax; and this movement is approximately equal to the terrestrial movement. Let it also be assumed that in this same annual revolution the centre of *OR*, the orbital circle which carries the planet, is borne by a movement of libration along a diameter *LFM* which is twice as great as the one which we laid down at first; and let it move back and forth, as was said above.

With this as the set-up, we have placed the Earth by its mean movement in a position corresponding to the apogee of the eccentric circle of the planet; and at that time the centre of the orbital circle carrying the planet, at *L*; and the planet itself, at point *O*. The planet then being at its least distance from *F* will describe by its whole movement its least circle, whose radius is *FO*. Consequently, when the Earth is in the neighbourhood of the mean apsis, the planet falling upon point *H* at its greatest distance from *F* will describe its greatest arcs, namely in proportion to the circle having *F* as centre. For at that time *OR* the deferent coincides with circle *GH* on account of the unity of centre at *F*. Hence as the Earth advances in the direction of the perigee and the centre of the orbital circle *OR* towards *M* the other extreme, the orbital circle itself is placed beyond *GK*, and the planet at *R* again is at its least distance from *F*, and the same things occur as in the beginning. For here the three revolutions—namely, that of the Earth through the apogee of the eccentric orbital circle of Mercury, the libration of the centre along diameter *LM*, and the movement of the planet in the same direction away from line *FG*—are equal to one another, and only the movement of the sections *GH* and *KP* away from the apsis of the eccentric circle is different from those revolutions, as we said.

And so in the case of this planet nature has sported a wonderful variety, but one which she has confirmed by a perpetual, certain, and unchanging order. And we should note here that the planet does not traverse the middle spaces of quadrants *GH* and *KP* without any irregularity in longitude, provided that the diversity of the centres, which comes into play, necessarily makes some additosubtraction; but the instability of that centre prevents that. For if, for example, the centre abided at *L* and the planet proceeded from *O*, then it would admit greatest irregularity at *H* in proportion [173ª] to the eccentricity *FL*. But it follows from the assumptions that the planet proceeding from *O* begins and promises to cause the irregularity which is due to *FL* the distance between the centres; but as the mobile centre approaches the midpoint *F*, more and more is taken away from the promised irregularity, and it is made void to such an extent that it wholly vanishes at the mean sections *H* and *P*, where you would expect

it to be greatest. And nevertheless, as we acknowledge, when the planet is made small beneath the rays of the sun,[1] it undergoes occultation; and when the planet is rising or setting in the morning or evening, it is not discernible on the curves of the circle. And we are unwilling to pass over this method which is no less rationable than the former, and which will come into open use in connection with the movements in latitude.

33. On the Tables of the Additosubtractions of the Five Wandering Stars

These things have been demonstrated concerning the regular and apparent movements of Mercury and the other planets and set out in numbers. And by their example the way to calculating differences of movement for certain other positions will be clear. And for this use we have made ready separate tables for each planet: six column, thirty rows, ascending by triads of 3°, as is usual. The first two columns will contain the common numbers—both of the anomaly of the eccentric circle and of the parallax. The third, the sums of the additosubtractions of the eccentric circle—I mean the total differences occurring between the regular and irregular movements of the orbital circles. The fourth, the proportional minutes—and they go up to 60'—by which the parallaxes are increased or diminished on account of the greater or lesser distance of the Earth. The fifth, the additosubtractions which are the parallaxes occurring at the highest apsis of the eccentric circle and which arise from the great orbital circle. The sixth and last, their excesses over the parallaxes which take place at the lowest apsis of the eccentric circle. And the tables are as follows:

[1] *i.e.*, when the planet is in conjunction with the sm.

ADDITIONS-AND-SUBTRACTIONS OF SATURN

Common Numbers		Additosubtractions of the eccentric circle		Proportional Minutes	Parallaxes of the orbital circle of the Earth		Excesses over the parallax of the lowest apsis	
Deg.	Deg.	Deg.	Min.	Min.	Deg.	Min.	Deg.	Min.
3	357	0	20	0	0	17	0	2
6	354	0	40	0	0	34	0	4
9	351	0	58	0	0	51	0	6
12	348	1	17	0	1	3	0	8
15	345	1	36	1	1	23	0	10
18	342	1	55	1	1	40	0	12
21	339	2	13	1	1	56	0	14
24	336	2	31	2	2	11	0	16
27	333	2	49	2	2	26	0	18
30	330	3	6	3	2	42	0	19
33	327	3	33	3	2	56	0	21
36	324	3	39	4	3	10	0	23
39	321	3	55	4	3	25	0	24
42	318	4	10	5	3	38	0	26
45	315	4	25	6	3	52	0	27
48	312	4	39	7	4	5	0	29
51	309	4	52	8	4	17	0	31
54	306	5	5	9	4	28	0	33
57	303	5	17	10	4	38	0	34
60	300	5	29	11	4	49	0	35
63	297	5	41	12	4	59	0	36
66	294	5	50	13	5	8	0	37
69	291	5	59	14	5	17	0	38
72	288	6	7	16	5	24	0	38
75	285	6	14	17	5	31	0	39
78	282	6	19	18	5	37	0	39
81	279	6	23	19	5	42	0	40
84	276	6	27	21	5	46	0	41
87	273	6	29	22	5	50	0	42
90	270	6	31	23	5	52	0	42
93	267	6	31	25	5	52	0	43
96	264	6	30	27	5	53	0	44
99	261	6	28	29	5	53	0	45
102	258	6	26	31	5	51	0	46
105	255	6	22	32	5	48	0	46
108	252	6	17	34	5	45	0	45
111	249	6	12	35	5	40	0	45
114	246	6	6	36	5	36	0	44
117	243	5	58	38	5	29	0	43
120	240	5	49	39	5	22	0	42
123	237	5	40	41	5	13	0	41
126	234	5	28	42	5	3	0	40
129	231	5	16	44	4	52	0	39
132	228	5	3	46	4	41	0	37
135	225	4	48	47	4	29	0	35
138	222	4	33	48	4	15	0	34
141	219	4	17	50	4	1	0	32
144	216	4	0	51	3	46	0	30
147	213	3	42	52	3	30	0	28
150	210	3	24	53	3	13	0	26
153	207	3	6	54	2	56	0	24
156	204	2	46	55	2	38	0	22
159	201	2	27	56	2	21	0	19
162	198	2	7	57	2	2	0	17
165	195	1	46	58	1	42	0	14
168	192	1	25	59	1	22	0	12
171	189	1	4	59	1	2	0	9
174	186	0	43	60	0	42	0	7
177	183	0	22	60	0	21	0	4
180	180	0	0	60	0	0	0	0

ADDITIONS-AND-SUBTRACTIONS OF JUPITER

Common Numbers		Additosubtractions of the eccentric circle		Proportional Minutes		Parallaxes of the orbital circle of the Earth		Excesses over the parallax of the lowest apsis	
Deg.	Deg.	Deg.	Min.	Min.	Sec.	Deg.	Min.	Deg.	Min.
3	357	0	16	0	3	0	28	0	2
6	354	0	31	0	12	0	56	0	4
9	351	0	47	0	18	1	25	0	6
12	348	1	2	0	30	1	53	0	8
15	345	1	18	0	45	2	19	0	10
18	342	1	33	1	3	2	46	0	13
21	339	1	48	1	23	3	13	0	15
24	336	2	2	1	48	3	40	0	17
27	333	2	17	2	18	4	6	0	19
30	330	2	31	2	50	4	32	0	21
33	327	2	44	3	26	4	57	0	23
36	324	2	58	4	10	5	22	0	25
39	321	3	11	5	40	5	47	0	27
42	318	3	23	6	43	6	11	0	29
45	315	3	35	7	48	6	34	0	31
48	312	3	47	8	50	6	56	0	34
51	309	3	58	9	53	7	18	0	36
54	306	4	8	10	57	7	39	0	38
57	303	4	17	12	0	7	58	0	40
60	300	4	26	13	10	8	17	0	42
63	297	4	35	14	20	8	35	0	44
66	294	4	42	15	30	8	52	0	46
69	291	4	50	16	50	9	8	0	48
72	288	4	56	18	10	9	22	0	50
75	285	5	1	19	17	9	35	0	52
78	282	5	5	20	40	9	47	0	54
81	279	5	9	22	20	9	59	0	55
84	276	5	12	23	50	10	8	0	56
87	273	5	14	25	23	10	17	0	57
90	270	5	15	26	57	10	24	0	58
93	267	5	15	28	33	10	25	0	59
96	264	5	15	30	12	10	33	1	0
99	261	5	14	31	43	10	34	1	1
102	258	5	12	33	17	10	34	1	2
105	255	5	10	34	50	10	33	1	3
108	252	5	6	36	21	10	29	1	3
111	249	5	1	37	47	10	23	1	3
114	246	4	55	39	0	10	15	1	3
117	243	4	49	40	25	10	5	1	2
120	240	4	41	41	50	9	54	1	1
123	237	4	32	43	18	9	41	1	0
126	234	4	23	44	46	9	25	1	0
129	231	4	13	46	11	9	8	0	59
132	228	4	2	47	37	8	56	0	58
135	225	3	50	49	2	8	27	0	57
138	222	3	38	50	22	8	5	0	55
141	219	3	25	51	46	7	39	0	53
144	216	3	13	53	6	7	12	0	50
147	213	2	59	54	10	6	43	0	47
150	210	2	45	55	15	6	13	0	43
153	207	2	30	56	12	5	41	0	39
156	204	2	15	57	0	5	7	0	35
159	201	1	59	57	37	4	32	0	31
162	198	1	43	58	6	3	56	0	27
165	195	1	27	58	34	3	18	0	23
168	192	1	11	59	3	2	40	0	19
171	189	0	53	59	36	2	0	0	15
174	186	0	35	59	58	1	20	0	11
177	183	0	17	60	0	0	40	0	6
180	180	0	0	60	0	0	0	0	0

ADDITIONS-AND-SUBTRACTIONS OF MARS

Common Numbers		Addito-subtractions of the eccentric circle		Proportional Minutes		Parallaxes of the orbital circle of the Earth		Excesses over the parallax of the lowest apsis	
Deg.	Deg.	Deg.	Min.	Min.	Sec.	Deg.	Min.	Deg.	Min.
3	357	0	32	0	0	1	8	0	8
6	354	1	5	0	2	2	16	0	17
9	351	1	37	0	7	3	24	0	25
12	348	2	8	0	15	4	31	0	33
15	345	2	39	0	28	5	38	0	41
18	342	3	10	0	42	6	45	0	50
21	339	3	41	0	57	7	52	0	59
24	336	4	11	1	13	8	58	1	8
27	333	4	41	1	34	10	5	1	16
30	330	5	10	2	1	11	11	1	25
33	327	5	38	2	31	12	16	1	34
36	324	6	6	3	2	13	22	1	43
39	321	6	32	3	32	14	26	1	52
42	318	6	58	4	3	15	31	2	2
45	315	7	23	4	37	16	35	2	11
48	312	7	47	5	16	17	39	2	20
51	309	8	10	6	2	18	42	2	30
54	306	8	32	6	50	19	45	2	40
57	303	8	53	7	39	20	47	2	50
60	300	9	12	8	30	21	49	3	0
63	297	9	30	9	27	22	50	3	11
66	294	9	47	10	25	23	48	3	22
69	291	10	3	11	28	24	47	3	34
72	288	10	19	12	33	25	44	3	46
75	285	10	32	13	38	26	40	3	59
78	282	10	42	14	46	27	35	4	11
81	279	10	50	16	4	28	29	4	24
84	276	10	56	17	24	29	21	4	36
87	273	11	1	18	45	30	12	4	50
90	270	11	5	20	8	31	0	5	8
93	267	11	7	21	32	31	45	5	20
96	264	11	8	22	58	32	30	5	35
99	261	11	7	24	32	33	13	5	51
102	258	11	5	26	7	33	53	6	7
105	255	11	1	27	43	34	30	6	25
108	252	10	56	29	21	35	3	6	45
111	249	10	45	31	2	35	34	7	4
114	246	10	33	32	46	35	59	7	25
117	243	10	11	34	41	36	21	7	46
120	240	10	7	36	16	36	37	8	11
123	237	9	51	38	1	36	49	8	34
126	234	9	33	39	46	36	54	8	59
129	231	9	13	41	30	36	53	9	24
132	228	8	50	43	12	36	45	9	49
135	225	8	27	44	50	36	25	10	17
138	222	8	2	46	26	35	59	10	47
141	219	7	36	48	1	35	25	11	15
144	216	7	7	49	35	34	30	11	45
147	213	6	37	51	2	33	24	12	12
150	210	6	34	52	22	32	3	12	35
153	207	6	0	53	38	30	26	13	24
156	204	5	25	54	50	28	5	13	28
159	201	4	49	56	0	26	5	13	7
162	198	4	12	57	6	23	28	12	47
165	195	3	35	57	54	20	21	12	12
168	192	2	57	58	22	16	51	10	59
171	189	1	18	58	50	13	1	9	1
174	186	1	39	59	11	8	51	6	40
177	183	0	57	59	44	4	32	3	28
180	180	0	0	60	0	0	0	0	0

ADDITIONS-AND-SUBTRACTIONS OF VENUS

Common Numbers		Addito-subtractions of the eccentric circle		Proportional Minutes		Parallaxes of the orbital circle of the Earth		Excesses over the parallax of the lowest apsis	
Deg.	Deg.	Deg.	Min.	Min.	Sec.	Deg.	Min.	Deg.	Min.
3	357	0	6	0	0	1	15	0	1
6	354	0	13	0	0	2	30	0	2
9	351	0	19	0	10	3	45	0	3
12	348	0	25	0	39	4	59	0	5
15	345	0	31	0	58	6	13	0	6
18	342	0	36	1	20	7	28	0	7
21	339	0	42	1	39	8	42	0	9
24	336	0	48	2	23	9	56	0	11
27	333	0	53	2	59	11	10	0	12
30	330	0	59	3	38	12	24	0	13
33	327	1	4	4	18	13	37	0	14
36	324	1	10	5	3	14	50	0	16
39	321	1	15	5	45	16	3	0	17
42	318	1	20	6	32	17	16	0	18
45	315	1	25	7	22	18	28	0	20
48	312	1	29	8	18	19	40	0	21
51	309	1	33	9	31	20	52	0	22
54	306	1	36	10	48	22	3	0	24
57	303	1	40	12	8	23	14	0	26
60	300	1	43	13	32	24	24	0	27
63	297	1	46	15	8	25	34	0	28
66	294	1	49	16	35	26	43	0	30
69	291	1	52	18	0	27	52	0	32
72	288	1	54	19	33	28	57	0	34
75	285	1	56	21	8	30	4	0	36
78	282	1	58	22	32	31	9	0	38
81	279	1	59	24	7	32	13	0	41
84	276	2	0	25	30	33	17	0	43
87	273	2	0	27	5	34	20	0	45
90	270	2	0	28	28	35	21	0	47
93	267	2	0	29	58	36	20	0	50
96	264	2	0	31	28	37	17	0	53
99	261	1	59	32	57	38	13	0	55
102	258	1	58	34	26	39	7	0	58
105	255	1	57	35	55	40	0	1	0
108	252	1	55	37	23	40	49	1	4
111	249	1	53	38	52	41	36	1	8
114	246	1	51	40	19	42	18	1	11
117	243	1	48	41	45	42	59	1	14
120	240	1	45	43	10	43	35	1	18
123	237	1	42	44	37	44	7	1	22
126	234	1	39	46	6	44	32	1	26
129	231	1	35	47	36	44	49	1	50
132	228	1	31	49	6	45	4	1	36
135	225	1	27	50	12	45	10	1	41
138	222	1	22	51	17	45	5	1	47
141	219	1	17	52	33	44	51	1	53
144	216	1	12	53	48	44	22	2	0
147	213	1	7	54	28	43	36	2	6
150	210	1	1	55	0	42	34	2	13
153	207	0	55	55	57	41	12	2	19
156	204	0	49	56	47	39	20	2	34
159	201	0	43	57	33	36	58	2	27
162	198	0	37	58	16	33	58	2	27
165	195	0	31	58	59	30	14	2	27
168	192	0	25	59	39	25	42	2	16
171	189	0	19	59	48	20	20	1	56
174	186	0	13	59	54	14	7	1	26
177	183	0	7	59	58	7	16	0	46
180	180	0	0	60	0	0	16	0	0

ADDITIONS-AND-SUBTRACTIONS OF MERCURY

Common Numbers		Addito-subtractions of the eccentric circle		Proportional Minutes		Parallaxes of the orbital circle of the Earth		Excesses over the parallax of the lowest apsis	
Deg.	Deg.	Deg.	Min.	Min.	Sec.	Deg.	Min.	Deg.	Min.
3	357	0	8	0	3	0	44	0	8
6	354	0	17	0	12	1	28	0	15
9	351	0	26	0	24	2	12	0	23
12	348	0	34	0	50	2	56	0	31
15	345	0	43	1	43	3	41	0	38
18	342	0	51	2	42	4	25	0	45
21	339	0	59	3	51	5	8	0	53
24	336	1	8	5	10	5	51	1	1
27	333	1	16	6	41	6	34	1	8
30	330	1	24	8	29	7	15	1	16
33	327	1	32	10	35	7	57	1	24
36	324	1	39	12	50	8	38	1	32
39	321	1	46	15	7	9	18	1	40
42	318	1	53	17	26	9	59	1	47
45	315	2	0	19	47	10	38	1	55
48	312	2	6	22	8	11	17	2	2
51	309	2	12	24	31	11	54	2	10
54	306	2	18	26	17	12	31	2	18
57	303	2	24	29	17	13	7	2	26
60	300	2	29	31	39	13	41	2	34
63	297	2	34	33	59	14	14	2	42
66	294	2	38	36	12	14	46	2	51
69	291	2	43	38	29	15	17	2	59
72	288	2	47	40	45	15	46	3	8
75	285	2	50	42	58	16	14	3	16
78	282	2	53	45	6	16	40	3	24
81	279	2	56	46	59	17	4	3	32
84	276	2	58	48	50	17	27	3	40
87	273	2	59	50	36	17	48	3	48
90	270	3	0	52	2	18	6	3	56
93	267	3	0	53	43	18	23	4	3
96	264	3	1	55	4	18	37	4	11
99	261	3	0	56	14	18	48	4	19
102	258	2	59	57	14	18	56	4	27
105	255	2	58	58	1	19	2	4	34
108	252	2	56	58	40	19	3	4	42
111	249	2	55	59	14	19	3	4	49
114	246	2	53	59	40	18	59	4	54
117	243	2	49	59	57	18	53	4	58
120	240	2	44	60	0	18	42	5	2
123	237	2	39	59	49	18	27	5	4
126	234	2	34	59	35	18	8	5	6
129	231	2	28	59	19	17	44	5	9
132	228	2	22	58	59	17	17	5	9
135	225	2	16	58	32	16	44	5	6
138	222	2	10	57	56	16	7	5	3
141	219	2	3	56	41	15	25	4	59
144	216	1	55	55	27	14	38	4	52
147	213	1	47	54	55	13	47	4	41
150	210	1	38	54	25	12	52	4	26
153	207	1	29	53	54	11	51	4	10
156	204	1	19	53	23	10	44	3	53
159	201	1	10	52	54	9	34	3	33
162	198	1	0	52	33	8	20	3	10
165	195	0	51	52	18	7	4	2	43
168	192	0	41	52	8	5	43	2	14
171	189	0	31	52	3	4	19	1	43
174	186	0	21	52	2	2	54	1	9
177	183	0	10	52	2	1	27	0	35
180	180	0	0	52	2	0	0	0	0

34. HOW THE POSITIONS IN LONGITUDE OF THE FIVE PLANETS ARE CALCULATED

[178b] Therefore by means of the tables drawn up in this way by us we shall calculate without any difficulty the positions in longitude of the five wandering stars. There is approximately the same method of computation in all of them, though the three outer planets differ slightly from Venus and Mercury in this respect.

Therefore let us speak of Saturn, Jupiter, and Mars first. In their case the calculation is such that the mean movements—that is, the simple movement of the sun and the movement of parallax of the planet—are sought for any given time by the method described above. Next, the position of the highest apsis of the eccentric circle is subtracted from the simple position of the sun, and the movement of parallax is subtracted from the remainder; the first remainder is the anomaly of the eccentric circle of the planet. We shall look it up among the common numbers in one of the first two columns of the table, and correspondingly in the third column we shall take the additosubtraction of the eccentric circle, and the proportional minutes in the following column. We shall add this additosubtraction to the movement of anomaly of parallax and subtract it from the anomaly of the eccentric circle, if the number whereby we entered (the table) was found in the first column; and conversely we shall subtract it from the anomaly of the eccentric circle—if the number was found in the second column. The sum or remainder will be the corrected anomaly of parallax or the corrected anomaly of the eccentric circle—the proportional minutes being reserved for a use we shall speak of soon. Then we shall look up this corrected anomaly (of parallax) in the first two columns of common numbers; and from the corresponding place in the fifth column we shall take the additosubtraction arising from the movement of parallax, together with its excess found in the last column; and of that excess we shall take the proportional part in accordance with the number of proportional minutes; and we shall always add this proportional part to the additosubtraction. The sum will be the true parallax of the planet; and is to be subtracted from the corrected anomaly of parallax, if the (corrected anomaly) is less than a semicircle, or added, if greater than a semicircle. For in this way we shall have the true and apparent distance of the planet westward from the mean position of the sun; and when we have subtracted that distance from the mean position of the sun, the remainder will be the sought position of the planet [179a] in the sphere of the fixed stars, and the addition of the precession of the equinoxes will determine the position of the planet in relation to the spring equinox.

In the case of Venus and Mercury we shall use the distance from the highest apsis to the mean position of the sun as the anomaly of the eccentric circle; and by means of this anomaly we shall correct the movement of parallax and the anomaly of the

eccentric circle, as was said already. But if the additosubtraction of the eccentric circle and the corrected parallax are of the same quality or species (*i.e.*, are both additive or both subtractive), they are simultaneously added to or subtracted from the mean position of the sun. But if they are of different species, the lesser is subtracted from the greater; and by means of the remainder there will take place that which we have just mentioned, according to the additive or subtractive property of the greater number; and the final result will be the position which we are looking for.

35. On the Stations and Retrogradations of the Five Wandering Stars

Moreover, the knowledge of where and when the stations, retrogradations, and returns take place and how great they are seems also to pertain to the account of movement in longitude. The mathematicians, especially Apollonius of Perga, have dealt a good deal with them; but they have done so under the assumption of only one irregular movement, namely, that whereby the planets are moved with respect to the sun and which we have called the parallax due to the great orbital circle of the Earth.

For if the circles of the planets—whereon all the planets are borne with unequal periods of revolution but in the same direction, *i.e.*, towards the east—are homocentric with the great orbital circle of the Earth, and some planet on its own orbital circle and within the great orbital circle, such as Venus or Mercury, has greater velocity than the movement of the Earth has; *and if a straight line drawn from the Earth cuts the orbital circle of the planet in each a way that half the segment comprised within the orbital circle has the same ratio to the line which extends from our point of vision the Earth to the lower and convex are of the intersected orbital circle, as does the movement of the Earth to the velocity of the planet then, if a point is made at the extremity of this line drawn to the arc which is at the perigee of the circle of the planet, the point will separate the retrogradation from the progression, so that when the planet is at that position, it will have the appearance of stopping.*

Similarly in the case of the three outer planets which have a movement slower than the velocity [179b] of the Earth, *if a straight line drawn through our point of vision cuts the great orbital circle, in such a way that half the segment comprised within the orbital circle has the same ratio to the line which extends from the planet to our point of vision located on the nearer and convex surface of the orbital circle, as does the movement of the planet to the velocity of the Earth; then the planet when in that position will present to our vision the appearance of stopping.*

But if half the segment comprised within the circle, as was said, *has a greater ratio to the remaining external segment than the velocity of the Earth has to the velocity of Venus or Mercury, or than the movement of any of the three upper planets has to the velocity of the*

Earth; then the planet will progress eastward; but if the ratio is less, then it will retrograde westward.

In order to demonstrate all this, Apollonius took a certain lemma, which was in accord with the hypothesis of the immobility of the Earth but which none the less squares with our principle of terrestrial mobility and which for that reason we too shall employ. And we can enunciate it in this form: *if the greater side of a triangle is so cut that one of the segments is not less than the adjoining side, then this segment will have a greater ratio to the remaining segment than the angles on the side cut, taken in reverse order will have to one another.*

For let BC be the greater side of triangle ABC; and if on side BC

$$CD < AC,$$

then I say that

$$CD : BD > \text{angle } ABC : \text{angle } BCA.$$

Now it is demonstrated as follows. Let the parallelogram $ADCE$ be completed; and BA and CE extended will meet at point E. Accordingly since

$$AE < AC,$$

the circle described with centre A and radius AE will pass through C or beyond it. Now let GEC be the circle, and let it pass through C. Since

$$\text{trgl. } AEF > \text{sect. } AEG,$$

while

$$\text{trgl. } AEC < \text{sect. } AEC;$$

then

$$\text{trgl. } AEF : \text{trgl. } AEC > \text{sect. } AEG : \text{sect. } AEC.$$

But

$$\text{trgl. } AEF : \text{trgl. } AEC = \text{base } FE : \text{base } EC.$$

Therefore

$$FE : EC > \text{angle } FAE : \text{angle } EAG.$$

But

$$FE : EC = CD : DB.$$

And

$$\text{angle } FAE = \text{angle } ABC;$$

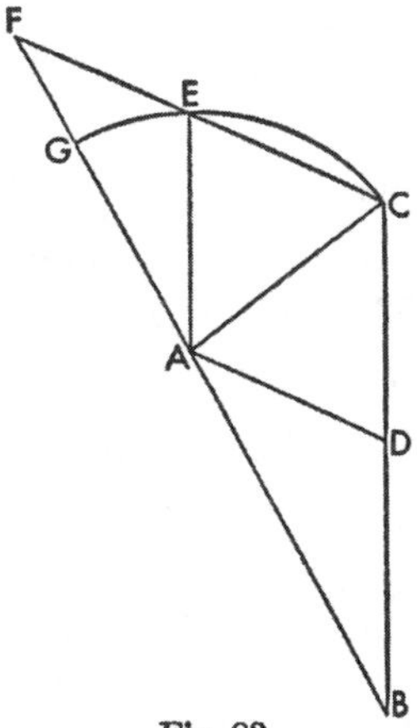

and

$$\text{angle } EAC = \text{angle } BCA.$$

Accordingly

[180a] $CD : DB > \text{angle } ABC : \text{angle } ACB.$

Now it is manifest that the ratio will be much greater if it is not assumed that

$$CD = AC = AE$$

but that

$$CD > AE.$$

Fig. 83

Now let *ABC* be the circle of Venus or Mercury around centre *D*; and let the Earth *E* outside the circle be movable around the same centre *D*. From *E* our point of vision let the straight line *ECDA* be drawn through the centre of the circle; and let *A* be the position farthest from the Earth, and *C* the nearest. And let *DC* be put down as having a greater ratio to *CE* than the movement of the point of vision has to the velocity of the planet. Accordingly it is possible to find a line *EFB* such that half *BF* has the same ratio to *FE* that the movement of the point of vision has to the movement of the planet. For let line *EFB* be moved away from centre *D* and be decreased along *FB* and increased along *EF*, until we meet with what is demanded.

I say that *when the planet is set up at point F, it will present to us the appearance of stopping; and that whatever size of the arc we take on either side of F, we shall find the planet progressing, if the arc is taken in the direction of the apogee, and retrograding, if in as direction of the perigee.*

For first let the arc *FG* be taken in the direction of the apogee: let *EGK* be extended, and let *BG*, *DG*, and *DF* be joined. Accordingly since in triangle *BGE* segment *BF* of the greater side *BE* is greater than *BG*, then

$$BF : EF > \text{angle } FEG : \text{angle } GBF.$$

Furthermore,

$${}^1/_2 BF : FE > \text{angle } FEG : 2 \text{ angle } GBF,$$

i.e.,

$${}^1/_2 BF : FE > \text{angle } FEG : \text{angle } GDF.$$

But

$${}^1/_2 BF : FE = \text{movement of Earth} : \text{movement of planet.}$$

Therefore

$$\text{angle } FEG : \text{angle } GDF < \text{velocity of Earth} : \text{velocity of planet.}$$

Now let

$$\text{angle } FEL : \text{angle } FDG = \text{movement of Earth} : \text{movement of planet.}$$

Therefore

$$\text{angle } FEL > \text{angle } FEG.$$

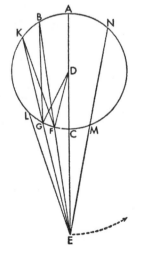

Accordingly, during the time in which the planet traverses arc *GF* of the orbital circle, our line of sight [180b] will be thought to have traversed during that time the contrary space between line *EF* and line *EL*. It is manifest that in the same time in which to our sight arc *GF* transports the planet westward in accordance with the smaller angle *FEG*, the passage of the Earth drags it back eastward in accordance with the greater angle *FEL*, so that the planet will go on increasing its angular distance eastward by angle *GEL* and will not seem to have come to a stop yet.

Now it is manifest that the opposite of this can be shown by the same means. If in the same diagram we put down that

$$^1/_2 GK : GE = \text{movement of Earth : velocity of planet;}$$

and if we take arc GF in the direction of the perigee and away from straight line EK, and join KF and make triangle KEF, where

$$GE > EF;$$

then

$$KG : GE < \text{angle } FEG : \text{angle } FKG.$$

Thus too

$$^1/_2 KG : GE < \text{angle } FEG : 2 \text{ angle } FKG,$$

i.e.,

$$^1/_2 KG : GE < \text{angle } FEG : \text{angle } GDF,$$

conversely to what was shown before. And it is inferred by the same means that

$$\text{angle } GDF : \text{angle } FEG < \text{velocity of planet : velocity of line of sight.}$$

Accordingly, when angle GDF has been made greater, so that the angles have the same ratio, then the planet will complete a greater movement westwards than progression demands.

Hence it is also manifest that if we make

$$\text{arc } FC = \text{arc } CM$$

the second station will be at point M; and if line EMN is drawn,

$$^1/_2 MN : ME = {}^1/_2 BF : FE = \text{velocity of Earth : velocity of planet;}$$

and accordingly points M and F will designate the two stations and will determine the whole arc FCM as retrogressive and the remainder of the circle as progressive.

Moreover, it follows that at certain distances

$$DC : CE > \text{velocity of Earth : velocity of planet;}$$

and it will not be possible to draw another straight line in the ratio (which the velocity of the Earth has to the velocity of the planet); and the planet will not seem to stop or to retrograde. For since it was assumed that in triangle DEG

$$DC < EG;$$

$$\text{angle } CEG : \text{angle } CDG < DC : CE$$

but

$$DC : CE > \text{velocity of Earth : velocity of planet.}$$

Therefore also

$$\text{angle } CEG : \text{angle } CDG < \text{velocity of Earth : velocity of planet.}$$

Where that occurs, the planet will progress; [181ª] and we shall not find anywhere in the orbital circle of the planet an arc through which it seems to retrograde. All this concerning Venus and Mercury, which are inside the great orbital circle (of the Earth).

We can demonstrate this concerning the three outer planets by the same method and with the same diagrams—merely by reversing the names, so that we put down

ABC as the great orbital circle of the Earth and as the circuit of our point of vision and the planet at *E*, whose movement in its own orbital circle is less than the speed of our point of vision in the great orbital circle. The rest of the demonstration will proceed as before.

36. HOW THE TIMES, POSITIONS, AND ARCS OF THE RETROGRADATIONS ARE DETERMINED

Now if the orbital circles which bear the wandering stars were homocentric with the great orbital circle, it would be easy to establish that which the demonstrations promise, as the ratio of the velocity of the planet to the velocity of the point of vision would always be the same. But the orbital circles are eccentric, and hence their movements appear as irregular. For that reason it will be necessary for us to assume irregular and corrected movements everywhere as the differences of velocity and to employ them in the demonstrations, and not the simple and regular movements, except when the planet happens to be at its mean longitudes, the only place where it seems to be carried in its orbital circle with a mean movement.

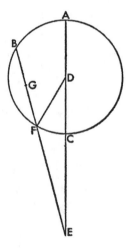

Now we shall show this in the case of Mars, so that the retrogradations of the other planets may become clearer by means of this example. For let *ABC* be the great orbital circle, on which our point of vision revolves; and let the planet be at point *E*. From the planet let the straight line *ECDA* be drawn through the centre of the orbital circle; and let *EFB* also be drawn. Half of chord *BF*—i.e., chord *GF*—will have the ratio to line *EF* which the varying velocity of the planet has to the velocity of the line of sight, whereby it exceeds the planet. Our problem is to find arc *FC* of half the retrogradation, or *ABF*, so as to know at what distance from its farthest position from *A* the planet becomes stationary and what the angle comprehended by *FEC* is. For by means of this we shall foretell the time and position of such an affection of the planet.

Now let the planet be placed at the mean apsis of the eccentric circle, where the movements of longitude and of anomaly differ very little from the regular movements. Therefore in the case of the planet Mars, since its mean movement (that is half of the line *BF*) [181^b] is 1ᴾ8°7", the motion of parallax, which is the relation of our vision to the mean movement of the star, consists of one part and is the straight line *EF*. Hence

$$EB = 3ᴾ16'14"$$

and likewise

$$\text{rect. } BE, EF = 3ᴾ16'14".$$

Now we have shown that

$$DA = 6,580,$$

where $DE = 10,000$,

and DA is the radius of the orbital circle.

But

$$DA = 39\text{P}29',$$
$$= \text{where } DE = 60\text{P};$$

and

$$AE : EC = 99\text{P}29' : 20\text{P}31'.$$

And

$$\text{rect. } AE, EC = \text{rect. } BE, EF = 2{,}041\text{P}4'.$$

Accordingly by reduction

$$2{,}041\text{P}4' \div 3\text{P}16'14'' = 624\text{P}4',$$

and similarly

$$\text{side } EF = 24\text{P}58'52'',$$

where $DE = 60\text{P}$.

But

$$EF = 4{,}163$$

where $DE = 10{,}000$

and $DF = 6{,}580$.

Accordingly, as the sides of triangle DEF are given,

$$\text{angle } DEF = 27°15',$$

which is the angular retrogradation of the planet, and

$$\text{angle } CDF = 16°50',$$

which is the angular anomaly of parallax. Accordingly, since the planet, when first stationary, appeared on line EF; and the planet, when opposite the sun, on line EC; if the planet is not moved eastward, the 16°15' of arc CF will comprehend the 27°25' of angle AEF found to be the retrogradation; but according to the ratio set forth of the velocity of the planet to the velocity of our line of sight, 16°5' corresponds to the section of the anomaly of parallax and approximately 19°6'39" corresponds (to the section of the anomaly) of longitude of the planet. Now

$$27°15' - 19°6'39'' = 8°8',$$

which is the distance from the other station to the solar opposition—and there are approximately $36^1/_2$ days during which the anomaly in longitude is 19°6'39"—and hence the total retrogradation is 16°16' in 73 days. These things which have been demonstrated for the mean longitudes of the eccentric circle can be similarly demonstrated for other positions—the planet being credited with an always varying velocity, according as its position demands, as we said.

Hence in Saturn, Jupiter, and Mars the same way of demonstration is open, provided we take the point of sight instead of the planet and the planet instead of the point of sight. Now the reverse of what occurs in the orbital circles which the Earth encloses occurs in the orbital circles which enclose the Earth; and let that be enough, so that we won't have to repeat the same old song. Nevertheless, since the variable movement of the planet with respect to the point of sight and to the ambiguity of the stationary points—of which the theorem of Apollonius does not relieve us—give no little difficulty; I do not know whether it would not be better to investigate the stations simply and in connection with the nearest position, by the method whereby we investigate by means of the known numbers of their movements the conjunction of the planet, when opposite the sun, with the line of mean movement of the sun, or the conjunction of any of the planets. And we shall leave that to your pleasure.

BOOK SIX

[182ª] We have indicated to the best of our ability what power and effect the assumption of the revolution of the Earth has in the case of the apparent movement in longitude of the wandering stars and in what a sure and necessary order it places all the appearances. It remains for us to occupy ourselves with the movements of the planets by which they digress in latitude and to show how in this case too the selfsame mobility of the Earth exercises its command and prescribes laws for them here also. Moreover this is a necessary part of the science, as the digressions of these planets cause no little variation in the rising and setting, apparitions and occultations, and the other appearances of which there has been a general exposition above. And their true positions are said to be known only when their longitude together with their latitude in relation to the ecliptic has been established. Accordingly by means of the assumption of the mobility of the Earth we shall do with perhaps greater compactness and more becomingly what the ancient mathematicians thought to have demonstrated by means of the immobility of the Earth.

1. General Exposition of the Digression in Latitude of the Five Wandering Stars

The ancients found in all the planets two digressions in latitude answering to their twofold irregularity in longitude—one digression taking place by reason of the eccentricity of the orbital circles, and the other in accordance with the epicycles. In place of the epicycles, as has been often repeated, we have taken the single great orbital circle of the Earth—not that the orbital circle has some inclination with respect to the plane of the ecliptic fixed once and forever, since they are the same, but that the orbital circles of the planets are inclined to this plane [182ᵇ] with a variable obliquity, and this variability is regulated according to the movement and revolutions of the great orbital circle of the Earth.

But since the three higher planets, Saturn, Jupiter, and Mars, move longitudinally under different laws from those under which the remaining two do, so also they differ not a little in their latitudinal movement. Accordingly, the ancients first examined where and how great their farthest northern limits in latitude were. Ptolemy found the limits in the case of Saturn and Jupiter around the beginning of Libra, but in the case of Mars around the end of Cancer near the apogee of the eccentric circle. But in our time we found this northern limit in the case of Saturn at 7° of Scorpio, in the case of Jupiter at 27° of Libra, in the case of Mars at 27° of Leo, according as the apogees have been changing around down to our time; for the inclinations and the cardinal points of latitude follow upon the movement of those orbital circles. At corrected or apparent

distances of 90° between these limits, they seem to be making no digression in latitude, wherever the Earth happens to be at that time. Therefore, when they are at these mean longitudes, they are understood to be at the common section of their orbital circles with the ecliptic, just as the moon was at the ecliptic sections. Ptolemy calls these points the nodes: the ascending node, after which the planet enters upon northern latitudes; and the descending node, after which the planet crosses over into southern latitudes— not that the great orbital circle of the Earth, which always remains the same in the plane of the ecliptic, gives them any latitude; but every digression in latitude is measured from the nodes and varies greatly in positions different from the nodes. And according as the Earth approaches other positions, where the planets are seen to be opposite the sun and *acronycti*, the planets always move with a greater digression than in any other position of the Earth: in the northern semicircle to the north, and in the southern to the south, and with greater variation than the approach or withdrawal of the Earth demands. By that happening, it is known that the inclination of their orbital circles is not fixed, but that it changes in a certain movement of libration commensurable with the revolutions of the great circle of the Earth, as will be said a little farther on.

Now Venus and Mercury seem to digress somewhat differently but under a fixed law which has been observed to hold at the mean, highest, and lowest apsides. For at the mean longitudes, namely when the line of the mean movement of the sun is at a quadrant's distance from their highest or lowest apsis, and the planets as evening or morning stars are themselves at a distance of a quadrant of their orbital circle from the same line of mean movement of the sun; [183a] the ancients found that the planets had not digressed from the ecliptic, and hence the ancients understood them to be at that time the common section of their separate orbital circles and the ecliptic. This section passes through their apogees and perigees; and accordingly when they are higher or lower than the Earth, they then make manifest digressions—the greatest digressions at their greatest distances from the Earth, *i.e.*, at the evening apparition or at the morning occultation, when Venus is farthest north, and Mercury farthest south. And conversely at a position nearer to the Earth, when they undergo occultation in the evening or emerge in the morning, Venus is to the south, and Mercury to the north. Vice versa, when the Earth is at the position opposite to this and at the other mean apsis namely, when the anomaly of the eccentric circle is 270°—Venus is apparent at its greater southern distance from the Earth, and Mercury is to the north, and at a nearer position of the Earth Venus is to the north, and Mercury to the south. At the solstice of the Earth at the apogee of these planets, Ptolemy found that the latitude of Venus the morning star was northern, and of Venus the evening star, southern; and inversely in the case of Mercury: southern when the morning star, and northern when the evening star. These relations are similarly reversed at the opposite position of the perigee, so that

Venus Lucifer is seen in the south, and Venus Vesperugo in the north; but Mercury as morning star in the north, and Mercury as evening star in the south. And the ancients found that at both these positions the northern digression of Venus was always greater than the southern, and that the southern digression of Mercury was greater than the northern.

Taking this as an occasion, the ancients reasoned out a twofold latitude for this position, and a threefold latitude universally. They called the first latitude, which occurs at the mean longitudes, the inclination; the second, which occurs at the highest and lowest apsides, the obliquation; and the third one, which occurs in conjunction with the second, the deviation: it is always northern in the case of Venus and southern in the case of Mercury. Between these four limits the latitudes are mixed with one another, and alternately increase and decrease and yield mutually; and we shall give the right causes for all that.

2. HYPOTHESES OF THE CIRCLES ON WHICH THE PLANETS ARE MOVED IN LATITUDE

Accordingly in the case of these five planets we must assume that their orbital circles are inclined to the plane of the ecliptic—the common section being through the diameter of the ecliptic—by a variable but regular inclination, [183^b] since in Saturn, Jupiter, and Mars the angle of section receives a certain libration around that section as around an axis, like the libration which we demonstrated in the case of the precession of the equinoxes, but simple and commensurable with the movement of parallax. The angle of section is increased and decreased by this libration within a fixed period, so that, whenever the Earth is nearest to the planet, i.e., to the planet in opposition to the sun, the greatest inclination of the orbital circle of the planet occurs; at the contrary position the least inclination; at the mean position, the mean inclination: consequently, when the planet is at its farthest limit of northern or southern latitude, its latitude appears much greater at the nearness of the Earth than at its greatest distance from the Earth. And although this irregularity can be caused only by the unequal distances of the Earth, in accordance with which things nearer seem greater than things farther away; nevertheless there is a rather great difference between the excess and the deficiency of these planetary latitudes: and that cannot take place unless the orbital circles too have a movement of libration with respect to their obliquity. But, as we said before, in the case of things which are undergoing a libration, we must take a certain mean between the extremes.

In order that this may be clearer, let *ABCD* be the Earth's great orbital circle in the plane of the ecliptic with centre *E*; and let *FGKL* the orbital circle of the planet be inclined to *ABCD* in a mean and permanent declination whereof *F* is the northern limit in latitude, *K* the southern, *G* the descending node of section, and *BED* the

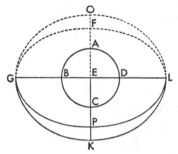

common section, which is extended in the straight lines *GB* and *DL*. And those four termini do not change, except along with the movement of the apsides. Let it be understood however that the movement of the planet in longitude takes place not on the plane of circle *FG* but on *OP*, another circle which is inclined to and homocentric with *FG*. These two circles cut one another in that same [184ª] straight line *GBDL*. Therefore, while the planet is being borne on orbital circle *OP*, it meanwhile falls upon plane *FK* by the movement of libration, goes beyond plane *FK* in either direction, and on that account makes the latitude appear variable.

For first let the planet be at point *O* at its greatest northern latitude and at its position nearest to the Earth in *A*; then the latitude of the planet will increase in proportion to *OGF* the angle of greatest inclination of orbital circle *OGP*. This movement (of libration) is a movement of approach and withdrawal, because by hypothesis it is commensurable with the movement of parallax: if then the Earth is at *B*, point *O* will coincide with *F*, and the latitude of the planet will appear less in the same position than before; and it will be much less if the Earth is at point *C*. For *O* will cross over to the farthest and most diverse part of its libration, and will leave only as much latitude as is in excess over the subtractive libration of the northern latitude, namely over the angle equal to *OGF*. Hence the latitude of the planet around *F* in the north will increase throughout the remaining semicircle *CDA*, until the Earth returns to the first point *A*, from which it set out. There will be the same way of progress for the meridian planet set up around point *K*—the movement of the Earth starting from *C*. But if the planet, in opposition to the sun or hidden by it, is at one of the nodes *G* or *L*, even though at that time the orbital circles *FK* and *OP* have their greatest inclination to one another, on that account no planetary latitude is perceptible, namely because the planet is at the common section of the orbital circles. From that, I judge, it is easily understood how the northern latitude of the planet decreases from *F* to *G*; and the southern latitude increases from *G* to *K*, but vanishes totally at *L* and becomes northern. And this is the way with those three higher planets.

Venus and Mercury differ from them no little in their latitudes, as in longitude, because they have the common sections of the orbital circles located through the apogee and perigee. Now their greatest inclinations at the mean apsides become changeable by a movement of libration, as in the case of the higher planets; but they undergo furthermore a libration dissimilar to the first. Nevertheless both librations are commensurable with the revolutions of the Earth, but not in the same way. For the first libration has the following property; when there has been one revolution of the Earth

with respect to the apsides of the planets, there have been two revolutions of the movement of libration having as an immobile axis the section through the apogee and the
perigee, which we spoke of; so that whenever the line of mean movement of the sun is
at the perigee or apogee of the planets, the greatest angle of section occurs; while the
least angle occurs at the mean longitudes. [184b] But the second libration supervening
upon this one differs from it in that, by possessing a movable axis, it has the following
effect: namely, that when the Earth is located at a mean longitude, the planet of Venus
or Mercury is always on the axis, *i.e.*, at the common section of this libration, but
shows its greatest deviation when the Earth is in line with its apogee or perigee—Venus
always being to the north, as was said, and Mercury to the south; although on account
of the former simple inclination they should at this time be lacking latitude.

For example, when the mean movement of the sun is at the apogee of Venus and
Venus is in the same position, it is manifest that, in accordance with the simple inclination and the first libration, Venus, being at the common section of its orbital circle
with the plane of the ecliptic, would at that time have had no latitude; but the second
libration, which has its section or axis along the transverse diameter of the eccentric
orbital circle and cuts at right angles the diameter passing through the highest and lowest apsis, adds its greatest deviation to the planet. But if at this time Venus is in one of
the other quadrants and around the mean apsides of its orbital circle, then the axis of
this libration will coincide with the line of mean movement of the sun, and Venus itself
will add to the northern obliquity the greatest deviation, which it subtracts from the
southern obliquity and leaves smaller. In this way the libration of deviation is made
commensurate with the movement of the Earth.

In order that these things may be grasped more easily, let *ABCD* be drawn again
as the great orbital circle. Let *FGK* be the orbital circle of Venus or Mercury: it is eccentric to circle *ABC* and inclined to it in accordance with the equal inclination *FGK*. Let

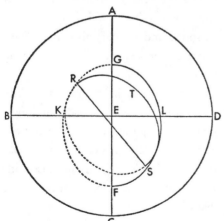

FG be the common section of these two
circles through *F* the apogee of the orbital
circle and *G* the perigee. First for the sake
of an easier demonstration let us put down
GKF the inclination of the eccentric orbital
circle as simple and fixed, or, if you prefer,
as midway between the greatest and the
least inclination, except that the common
section *FG* [185a] changes according to the
movement of the perigee and apogee.
When the Earth is on this common sec-
tion, *i.e.*, at *A* or *C*, and the planet is on the

same line, it is manifest that at that time the planet would have no latitude, since all latitude is sideways in the semicircles *GKF* and *FLG*, whereon the planet effects its northern or southern approaches, as has been said, in proportion to the inclination of circle *FKG* to the plane of the ecliptic. Now some call this digression of the planet the obliquation; others, the reflexion. But when the Earth is at *B* or *D*, *i.e.*, at the mean apsides of the planet, there will be the same latitudes *FKG* and *GFL* above and below; and they call them the declinations. And so these latitudes differ nominally rather than really from the former latitudes, and even the names are interchanged at the middle positions. But since the angle of inclination of these circles is found to be greater in the obliquation than in the declination, the ancients understood this as taking place through a certain libration, curving itself around section *FG* as an axis, as was said above. Accordingly since the angle of section is known in both cases, it will be easy to understand from the difference between them how great the libration from least to greatest inclination is.

Now let there be understood another circle, the circle of deviation, which is inclined to circle *GKFL* and homocentric in the case of Venus but eccentric to the eccentric circle in the case of Mercury, as will be said later: And let *RS* be their common section as axis of libration, an axis movable in a circle, in such fashion that when the Earth is at *A* or *B*, the planet is at the farthest limit of deviation, wherever that is, as at point *T*; and as far as the Earth has advanced from *A*, so far away from *T* let the planet be understood to have moved, while the inclination of the circle of deviation decreases, so that when the Earth bas measured the quadrant *AB*, the planet should be understood as having arrived at the node of this latitude, *i.e.*, at *R*. But as at this time the planes coincide at the mean movement of libration and are tending in different directions, the remaining semicircle of the deviation, which before was southerly, becomes northern; and as Venus passes into this semicircle, Venus avoids the south and seeks the north again, never to seek the south by this libration, just as Mercury, by crossing in the opposite direction, stays in the south; and Mercury also differs from Venus in that its libration takes place not in a circle homocentric with an eccentric circle but in a circle eccentric to an eccentric circle.

We employed an epicycle instead of this eccentric circle in demonstrating the irregularity in the movement in longitude. But since there we were considering longitude without latitude, and here latitude [185^b] without longitude, and as one and the same revolution comprehends and brings them to pass equally; it is clear enough that it is one and the same movement and one and the same libration which can cause both irregularities and be eccentric and have an inclination at the same time; and that there is no other hypothesis besides this which we have just spoken of and will say more about below.

3. HOW GREAT THE INCLINATIONS OF THE ORBITAL
CIRCLES OF SATURN, JUPITER, AND MARS ARE

After setting out our hypothesis for the digressions of the five planets, we must descend to the things themselves and discern singulars; and first how great the inclinations of the single circles are. We measure these inclinations against the great circle which passes through the poles of the circle having the inclination and is at right angles to the ecliptic; the transits in latitude are observed in relation to this great circle. For when we have apprehended these (inclinations), the way of learning the latitudes of each planet will be disclosed. Beginning once more with the three higher planets, we find that according to Ptolemy the digression of Saturn in opposition to the sun at the farthest limits of southern latitude was 3°5', the digression of Jupiter 2°7', that of Mars 7°; but in opposite positions, namely when they were in conjunction with the sun, the digression of Saturn was 2°2', that of Jupiter 1°5', and that of Mars only 5', so that it almost touched the ecliptic—according as it is possible to mark the latitudes from the observations which he took in the neighbourhood of their occultations and apparitions.

Let that be kept before us; and in the plane which is at right angles to the ecliptic and through its centre, let *AB* be the common section (of the plane) with the ecliptic, and *CD* the common section (of the plane) with any of the three eccentric circles

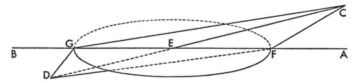

through the greatest northern and southern limits. Moreover, let *E* be the centre of the ecliptic, and *FEG* the diameter of the great orbital circle of the Earth. Now let *D* be the southern latitude and *C* the northern; and let *CF*, *CG*, *DF*, and *DG* be joined.

But the ratios of *EG* the great orbital circle of the Earth to *ED* the eccentric circle of the planet at any of their given positions have already been demonstrated above in the cases of the single (planets). But the positions of greatest latitudes have been given by the observations. Therefore, since angle *BGD*, the angle of greatest southern latitude and an exterior angle of triangle *EGD*, has been given, the interior and opposite angle *GED*, the angle of greatest southern inclination of the eccentric circle to the plane of the ecliptic, will also be given by what has been shown concerning plane triangles.

Similarly we shall demonstrate the least inclination by mean of the least southern latitude, namely by means of angle [186ᵃ] *EFD*. Since in triangle *EFD* the ratio of side *EF* to side *ED* is given together with angle *EFD*, we shall have *GED* given, the exterior angle and angle of least southern inclination: hence from the difference between

both declinations we shall have the total libration of the eccentric circle in relation to the ecliptic. Moreover against these angles of inclination we shall measure the opposite northern latitudes, that is to say, angles *AFC* and *EGC*; and if they agree with the observations, it will be a sign that we have not erred at all.

Now as our example we shall take Mars, which has a greater digression in latitude than any of the others. Ptolemy marked the greatest southern latitude as being approximately 7° in the case of the perigee of Mars, and the greatest northern latitude as 4°20' at the apogee. But as we have assumed that

$$\text{angle } BGD = 6°50',$$

we shall find that correspondingly

$$\text{angle } AFC \doteq 4°30'.$$

For since

$$EG : ED = 1^P : 1^P22'26''$$

and since

$$\text{angle } BCD = 6°50';$$
$$\text{angle } DEG \doteq 1°51',$$

which is the angle of greatest southern inclination.
And since

$$EF : CE = 1^P : 1^P39'57'',$$

and

$$\text{angle } CEF = \text{angle } DEG = 1°51',$$

it follows that, as angle *CFA* is the exterior angle which we spoke of,

$$\text{angle } CFA = 4^1/_2°,$$

when the planet is in opposition to the sun.

Similarly, in the opposite position where it is in conjunction with the sun, if we assume that

$$\text{angle } DFE = 5',$$

then, since sides *DE* and *EF* and angle *EFD* are given,

$$\text{angle } EDF = 4',$$

and, as exterior angle,

$$\text{angle } DEG \doteq 9',$$

which is the angle of least inclination. And that will show us that

$$\text{angle } CGE = 6',$$

which is the angle of northern latitude. Therefore, by the subtraction of the least inclination from the greatest,

$$1°5' - 9' = 1°42'$$

which is the libration of this inclination, and

$$^1/_2(1°42') \doteq 50^1/_2'.$$

In the case of the other two, Jupiter and Saturn, there is a similar method for discovering the angles of the inclinations together with the latitudes; for the greatest inclination of Jupiter is 1°42', and the least 1°18'; [186ᵇ] so that its total libration does not comprehend more than 24'. Now the greatest inclination of Saturn is 2°44', and the least 2°16'; and the libration between them is 19'. Hence by means of the least angles of inclination, which occur at the opposite position, when the planets are hidden beneath the sun, their digressions in latitude away from the ecliptic will be exhibited: that of Saturn as 2°3' and that of Jupiter as 1°6'—as were to be shown and reserved for the tables to be drawn up below.[1]

4. On the Exposition of the Other Latitudes in Particular and in General

Now that these things have been shown, the latitudes of these three planets will be made clear in general and in particular. For as before, let *AB* the line through the farthest limits of digression be the common section of the plane perpendicular to the ecliptic. And let the northern limit be at *A*; and let *CD*, which cuts *AB* in point *D*, be

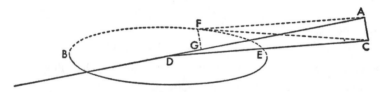

the perpendicular common section of the orbital circle of the planet. And with *D* as centre let *EF* the great orbital circle of the Earth be described. From the opposition, which is at *E*, let any known arc, such as *EF*, be measured, and from *F* and from *C*, the position of the planet, let the perpendiculars *CA* and *FG* be drawn to *AB*; and let *FA* and *FC* be joined.

We are first looking to see how great *ADC* the angle of inclination of the eccentric circle is, with this set-up. Now it has been shown that the inclination was greatest when the Earth was at point *E*. Moreover it has been made clear that the total libration is commensurate with the revolution of the Earth on circle *EF* in relation to the diameter *BE*, as the nature of libration demands. Therefore on account of arc *EF* being given, the ratio of *ED* to *EG* will be given; and that is the ratio of the total libration to which angle *ADC* has just now decreased. For that reason angle *ADC* is given in this case. Accordingly triangle *ADC* has all its angles given together with its sides. But since by the foregoing, *CD* has a given ratio to *ED*, the ratio of *CD* to the remainder *DG* is given. Accordingly the ratios of *CD* and *AD* to *GD* are given. And hence the remainder *AG* is given. Hence too *FG* is given; for

$$FG = \frac{1}{2} \text{ ch. } 2 \, EF.$$

Therefore as two sides of the right triangle AGF have been given, side AF is given, and the ratio of AF to AC. Finally as two sides of right triangle ACF [187ª] have been given, angle AFC will be given; and that is the angle of apparent latitude, which we were looking for.

Once more we shall take Mars as our example of this. Let its limit of greatest southern latitude be around A, which is approximately at its lowest apsis. Now let the position of the planet be at C, where—as has been demonstrated—the angle of inclination was greatest, i.e., 1°50', when the Earth was at point E. Now let us put the Earth at point F and the movement of parallax at 45° in accordance with arc EF: therefore

$$\text{line } FG = 7{,}071,$$

where $ED = 10{,}000$,

and

$$GE = 10{,}000 - 7{,}071 = 2{,}929,$$

which is the remainder of the radius. Now it has been shown that

$$\frac{1}{2} \text{ libration of angle } ADC = 50\frac{1}{2}°;$$

and half of the libration has the following ratio of increase and decrease in this case,

$$DE : GE = 50\frac{1}{2}' : 15'.$$

Now at present

$$\text{angle } ADC = 1°50' - 15' = 1°35',$$

which is the angle of inclination. On that account triangle ADC will have its sides and angles given; and since it has been shown above that

$$CD = 9{,}040,$$

where $ED = 6{,}580$;

$$FG = 4{,}653,$$
$$AD = 9{,}036,$$

and by subtraction

$$AEG = 4{,}383,$$

and

$$AC = 249\frac{1}{2}.$$

Accordingly, in right triangle AFG, since

$$\text{perpendicular } AG = 4{,}383$$

and

$$\text{base } FG = 4{,}653$$
$$\text{side } AF = 6{,}392.$$

Thus finally in triangle ACF, whereof

$$\text{angle } CAF = 90°$$

and sides AC and AF are given,

$$\text{angle } ACF = 2°15',$$

which is the angle of apparent latitude in relation to the Earth placed at *F*. We shall apply similar reasoning in the case of Saturn and Jupiter.

5. ON THE LATITUDES OF VENUS AND MERCURY

Venus and Mercury remain, and their transits in latitude will be demonstrated, as I said, by means of three simultaneous and complicated latitudinal divagations. [187^b] In order that they may be discerned separately, we shall begin with the one which the ancients call declination, as if from a simpler handling of it. And it happens to the declination alone to be sometimes separate from the others; and that occurs around the mean longitudes and around the nodes in accordance with the exact movements in longitude when the Earth has moved through a quadrant of a circle from the apogee or perigee of the planet. For when the Earth is very near, a northern or southern latitude of 6°22' is found in the case of Venus, and 4°5' in the case of Mercury; but at the greatest distance from the Earth, 1°2' in the case of Venus; and in the case of Mercury, 1°45'. Thereby the angles of inclination at this position are made manifest by means of the tables of additosubtractions which have been drawn up; and for Venus in that position at its greatest distance from the Earth the latitude is 1°2', and at its least distance 6°22', and on either side (of the mean latitude) the arc of the circle (through the poles of the orbital circle and perpendicular to the plane of the ecliptic) is approximately 2$^1/_2$°; but in the case of Mercury the 1°45' at its greatest distance and the 4°5' at its least demand 6$^1/_4$° as the (total) arc of its circle: consequently the angle of inclination of the circles of Venus is 2°30', and that of Mercury is 6$^1/_4$°, whereof four right angles are equal to 360°. By means of these (angles) the particular latitudes of declination can be unfolded, as we shall demonstrate, and first in the case of Venus.

For in the plane of the ecliptic and through the centre of the perpendicular plane, let *ABC* be the common section (of the two planes) and *DBE* the common section (of the perpendicular plane) with the plane of the orbital circle of Venus. And let *A* be the

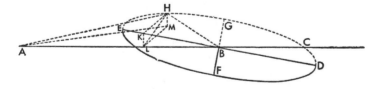

centre of the Earth, *B* the centre of the orbital circle of the planet, and *ABE* the angle of inclination of the orbital circle to the ecliptic. Let circle *DFEG* be described around *B*, and let diameter *FBG* be drawn perpendicular to diameter *DE*. Now let it be understood that the plane of the circle is so related to the assumed perpendicular plane that lines in the plane of the circle which are drawn at right angles to *DE* are parallel to one

another and to the plane of the ecliptic; and in the plane of the circle line *FBG* alone has been drawn.

Now our problem is to find out, by means of the given straight lines *AB* and *BC* together with angle *ABE* the given angle of inclinations, how far distant in latitude the planet is, when, for example, [188ª] it is 45° distant from *E* the point nearest to the Earth; and, following Ptolemy, we have chosen this position so that it may become apparent whether the inclination of the orbital circle adds any difference in longitude to Venus or Mercury. For such differences should be most visible around the positions midway between the limits *D*, *F*, *E*, and *G*, because the planet when situated at these four limits has the same longitude as it would have without declination, as is manifest of itself.

Therefore, as was said, let us assume that
$$\text{arc } EH = 45°;$$
and let *HK* be drawn perpendicular to *BE*, and *KL* and *HM* perpendicular to the plane of the ecliptic; and let *HB*, *LM*, *AM*, and *AH* be joined. We shall have the right parallelogram *LKHM*, as *HK* is parallel to the plane of the ecliptic. For angle *LAM* comprehends the additosubtraction in longitude; and angle *HAM* comprehends the transit in latitude, since *HM* also falls perpendicular upon the same plane of the ecliptic. Accordingly, since
$$\text{angle } HBE = 45°;$$
$$HK = {}^1/_2 \text{ ch. } 2 \, HE = 7{,}071,$$
$$\text{where } EB = 10{,}000.$$

Similarly in triangle *KBL*
$$\text{angle } BKL = 2{}^1/_2°$$
and
$$\text{angle } BLK = 90°,$$
and
$$\text{side } BK = 7{,}071,$$
$$\text{where } BE = 10{,}000;$$
hence
$$\text{side } KL = 308$$
and
$$\text{side } BL = 7{,}064.$$
But since, by what was shown above,
$$AB : BE \fallingdotseq 10{,}000 : 7{,}193;$$
then
$$HK = 5{,}086,$$
and

$$HM = KL = 221,$$

and

$$BL = 5,081;$$

hence, by subtraction,

$$LA = 4,919.$$

Moreover, as in triangle ALM side AL is given,

$$LM = HK,$$

and

$$\text{angle } ALM = 90°;$$

then

$$\text{side } AM = 7,075$$

and

$$\text{angle } MAL = 45°57',$$

which is the additosubtraction or great parallax of Venus according to calculation. Similarly, as in triangle MAH

$$\text{side } AM = 7,075$$

and

$$\text{side } MH = KL;$$
$$\text{angle } MAH = 1°47',$$

which is the angular declination in latitude.

And if it is not boring to examine what difference in the longitude of Venus is caused by this inclination, let us take triangle ALH, as we understand side LH to be the diagonal of parallelogram $LKHM$. For

$$LH = 5,091,$$
$$\text{where } AL = 4,919$$

and

$$\text{angle } ALK = 90° :$$

hence

$$\text{side } AH = 7,079.$$

Accordingly, as the ratio of the sides is given,

$$\text{angle } HAL = 45°59'.$$

But it has been shown that

$$\text{angle } MAL = 45°57';$$

therefore there is a difference of only 2', as was to be shown.

Again, in the case of Mercury, [188ᵇ] with a similar scheme of declination we shall demonstrate the latitudes with the help of a diagram similar to the foregoing: wherein

$$\text{arc } EH = 45°,$$

so that again

$$HK = KB = 7,071,$$

where side $AB = 10,000$.

Accordingly, as can be gathered from the differences in longitude which have already been demonstrated, in this case

$$BK = KH = 2,975,$$

where radius $BH = 3,953$

and $AB = 9,964$.

And since it has been shown that

angle of inclination $ABE = 6°15'$,

where 4 rt. angles = 360°;

accordingly, as the angles of right triangle BKL are given,

base $KL = 304$

and

perpendicular $BL = 2,778$.

And so by subtraction

$$AL = 7,186.$$

But also

$$LM = HK = 2,795;$$

accordingly, as in triangle ALM

angle $L = 90°$

and sides AL and LM have been given;

side $AM = 7,710$

and

angle $LAM = 21°16'$,

which is the additosubtraction calculated.

Similarly, since in triangle AMH side AM has been given,

side $MH = KL$

and

angle $M = 90°$,

which is comprehended by sides AM and MH;

angle $MAH = 2°16'$,

which is the latitude sought for. But if we wish to inquire how much is due to the true and the apparent additosubtraction, let us take LH the diagonal of the parallelogram: we deduce from the sides (of the parallelogram) that

$$LH = 2,811.$$

And

$$AL = 7,186.$$

Hence

angle *LAH* = 21°23',

which is the additosubtraction of apparent movement and has an excess of approximately 7' over the previously reckoned difference, (angle *LAM*), as was to be shown.

6. ON THE SECOND TRANSIT IN LATITUDE OF VENUS AND MERCURY ACCORDING TO THE OBLIQUATION OF THEIR ORBITAL CIRCLES IN THE APOGEE AND THE PERIGEE

That is enough on the transit in latitude of these planets, which occurs around the mean longitudes of their orbital circles: we have said that these latitudes are called the declinations. Now we must speak of those latitudes which occur at the perigee and apogee and to which the third digression, the deviation, is conjoined—not as the latitudes occur in the three higher planets, but as follows, in order that the third digression may be more easily separated and discerned by reason. For Ptolemy observed that these latitudes appeared greatest at the time when the planets were on the straight lines from the centre of the Earth which touch the orbital circles; and that occurs, [189ᵃ] as we said, at their greatest morning and evening distances from the sun. He found that the northern latitudes of Venus were $1/3$° greater than the southern, but that the southern latitudes of Mercury were approximately $1/2$° greater than the northern. But, wishing to reduce the difficulty and labour of calculations, he took in accordance with a certain mean ratio $2 1/2$° in different directions of latitude; the latitude themselves subtend these degrees in the circle perpendicular to the ecliptic and around the Earth, against which circle the latitudes are measured—especially as he did not think the error would on that account be very great, as we shall soon show. But if we take only $2 1/2$° as the equal digression on each side of the ecliptic and exclude the deviation for the time being, until we have determined the latitudes of the obliquations, our demonstrations will be simpler and easier. Accordingly we must first show that this latitudinal digression is greatest around the point of tangency of the eccentric circle, where the additosubtractions in longitude are also greatest.

For let there be drawn the common section of the plane of the ecliptic and the plane of the eccentric circle of Venus or Mercury—the common section through the apogee and the perigee; and on it let *A* be taken as the position of the Earth and *B* as

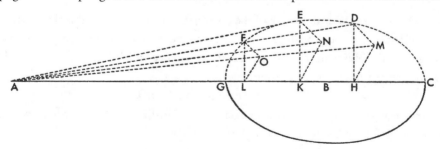

the centre of eccentric circle *CDEFG* which is inclined to the ecliptic, so that straight lines drawn anywhere at right angles to *CG* comprehend angles equal to the obliquation; and let *AE* be drawn tangent to the circle, and *AD* as cutting it somewhere. Moreover, from points *D*, *E*, and *F* let *DH*, *EK*, and *FL* be drawn perpendicular to line *CG*, and *DM*, *EN*, and *FO* perpendicular to the underlying plane of the ecliptic; and let *MH*, *NK*, and *OL* be joined, and also *AN* and *AOM*; for *AOM* is a straight line, since its three points are each in two planes—namely, in the plane of the ecliptic and in the plane *ADM* perpendicular to the plane of the ecliptic.

Accordingly since in the present obliquation the angles *HAM* and *KAN* comprehend the additosubtractions of these planets; and the angles *DAM* and *EAN* are the digressions in latitude: [189^b] I say, first, that angle *EAN*, the angle situated at the point of tangency, where the additosubtraction in longitude is also approximately greatest, is the greatest of all the angles of latitude.

For since angle *EAK* is greater than any of the others,

$$KE : EA > HD : DA$$

and

$$KE : EA > LF : FA.$$

But

$$EK : EN = HD : DM = LF : FO.$$

For, as we said,

$$\text{angle } EKN = \text{angle } HDM = \text{angle } LFO;$$

and

$$\text{angle } M = \text{angle } N = \text{angle } O = 90°.$$

Therefore

$$NE : EA > MD : DA$$

and

$$NE : EA > DF : FA;$$

and again

$$\text{angle } DMA = \text{angle } ENA = \text{angle } OFA = 90°.$$

Accordingly

$$\text{angle } EAN > \text{angle } DAM,$$

and angle *EAN* is greater than each of the other angles constructed in this way. Whence it is manifest that among the differences occurring between the additosubtractions and arising from the obliquation in longitude, the difference which is determined at point *E* in the greatest transit is the greatest. For

$$HD : HM = KE : KN = LF : FO,$$

on account of their subtending equal angles (in similar triangles). And since these lines are in the same ratio as the differences between them,

$$EK - KN : EA > HD - HM : AD$$

and

$$EK - KN : EA > LF - FO : AF.$$

Hence it is also clear that the additosubtractions in longitude of the segments of the eccentric circle will have the same ratio to the transits in latitude as the greatest additosubtraction in longitude has to the greatest transit in latitude, since

$$KE : EN = LF : FO = HD : DM,$$

—as was set before us to be demonstrated.

7. HOW GREAT THE ANGLES OF OBLIQUATION OF VENUS AND MERCURY ARE

Having first noted all that, let us see how great an angle is comprehended by the obliquation of the planes of either planet; and let us repeat what was said before: each planet has 5° between its greatest and least distance (in latitude), so that for the most part they become more northern or southern at contrary times and in accordance with their position on the orbital circle, for when the transit or manifest difference of Venus makes a digression greater or less than 5° through the apogee or perigee of the eccentric circle, the transit of Mercury however is more or less at $1/_2$°.

[190ª] Accordingly as before, let ABC be the common section of the ecliptic and the eccentric circle; and let the orbital circle of the planet be described around centre

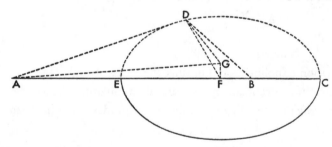

B oblique to the plane of the ecliptic in the way set forth. Now from the centre of the Earth let straight line AD be drawn touching the orbital circle at point D; and from D let DF be drawn perpendicular to CBE and DG perpendicular to the underlying plane of the ecliptic; and let BD, FG, and AG be joined. Moreover, let it be assumed that

angle $DAG = 2^1/_2$°,

where 4 rt. angles = 360°,

which is half the difference in latitude set forth for each planet.

Our problem is to find how great the angle of obliquation between the planes is, i.e., to find angle DFG.

Accordingly, since in the case of the planet Venus it has been shown that

the greater distance, at the apogee = 10,208,

where radius = 7,193,

and

the lesser, at the perigee = 9,792,

and

the mean distance = 10,000,

which Ptolemy decided to assume in this demonstration, as he wished to avoid labour and difficulty and to make an epitome; for where the extremes do not cause any great difference, it is better to use the mean. Accordingly,

$$AB : BD = 10,000 : 7,193,$$

and

angle $ADB = 90°$.

Therefore

side $AD = 6,947$.

Again, since

angle $DAG = 2^1/_2°$

and

angle $AGD = 90°$;

accordingly, the angles of triangle AGD are given, and

side $DG = 303$,

where $AD = 6,947$.

Thus also, two sides DF and DG have been given, and

angle $DGF = 90°$;

hence

angle $DFG = 3°29'$,

which is the angle of inclination or obliquation. But since the excess of angle DAF over angle FAG comprehends the difference made by the parallax in longitude, hence that difference is to be determined by the measurement of those magnitudes. For it has been shown that

$$AD = 6,947$$

and

$$DF = 4,997,$$

where $DG = 303$.

Now

sq. AD – sq. DG = sq. AG,

and

sq. FD – sq. DG = sq. GF;

therefore

$$AG = 6,940$$

and

$$FG = 4,988.$$

But

$$FG = 7,187,$$
$$\text{where } AG = 10,000,$$

and

$$\text{angle } FAG = 45°57';$$

and

$$DF = 7,193,$$
$$\text{where } AD = 10,000,$$

and

$$\text{angle } DA \fallingdotseq F46°.$$

Therefore at the greatest obliquation the additosubtraction of the parallax is deficient by approximately 3'. [190^b] Now it was made clear that at the mean apsis the angle of inclination of the orbital circles was $2^1/_2°$; but here it has increased by approximately 1°, which the first movement of libration—of which we have spoken—has added to it.

There is a similar demonstration in the case of Mercury. For the greatest distance of the orbital circle from the Earth is 10,948, where the radius of the orbital circle is 3,573; the least is 9,052; and the mean between these is 10,000. Moreover

$$AB : BD = 10,000 : 3,573.$$

Therefore

$$\text{side } AD = 9,340;$$

and since

$$BD : BF = AB : AD;$$

therefore

$$DF = 3,337.$$

And since

$$\text{angle } DAG = 2^1/_2°,$$

which is the angle of latitude;

$$DG = 407,$$
$$\text{where } DF = 3,337.$$

And so in triangle DFG the ratio of these two sides is given, and

$$\text{angle } G = 90°;$$

hence

$$\text{angle } DF \fallingdotseq G7°.$$

And that is the angle of inclination or obliquation between the orbital circle of Mercury and the plane of the ecliptic. But it has been shown that around the mean longitudes or quadrants the angle of inclination was 6°15'. Therefore 45' have now been added to it by the movement of libration.

There is a similar argument in picking out the additosubtractions and their differences, after it has been shown that

$$DG = 407,$$
$$\text{where } AD = 9,340$$
$$\text{and } DF = 3,337$$

Accordingly,

$$\text{sq. } AD - \text{sq. } DG = \text{sq. } AG,$$

and

$$\text{sq. } DF - \text{sq. } DG = \text{sq. } FG.$$

Therefore

$$AG = 9,331$$

and

$$FG = 3,314;$$

hence it is inferred that

$$\text{angle } GAF = 20°48',$$

which is the additosubtraction, and

$$\text{angle } DAF = 20°56',$$

which is approximately 8' greater than the angle proportionate to the obliquation. It still remains for us to see if such angles of obliquation and the latitudes in accordance with the greatest and least distance of the orbital circle are found to be in conformity with those gathered from observation.

Wherefore once more with the same diagram; and first at the greatest distance of the orbital circle of Venus, let

$$AB : BD = 10,208 : 7,193.$$

And since

$$\text{angle } ADB = 90°;$$
$$DF = 5,102.$$

[191ª] But it has been found that

$$\text{angle } DFG = 3°29',$$

which is the angle of obliquation; hence

$$\text{side } DG = 309,$$
$$\text{where } AD = 7,238.$$

Accordingly,

$$DG = 427,$$
$$\text{where } AD = 10,000;$$

whence it is concluded that at the greatest distance from the Earth

$$\text{angle } DAG = 2°27'.$$

But at the least distance

$$AB = 9,792,$$
where radius of orbital circle = 7,193.

And

$$AD = 6,644,$$
which is perpendicular to the radius; and similarly, since
$$BD : DF = AB : AD,$$
$$DF = 4,883.$$

But

$$\text{angle } DFG = 3°28';$$
therefore

$$DG = 297,$$
where $AD = 6,644$.
And as the sides of the triangle have been given,
$$\text{angle } DAG = 2°34'.$$
But neither 3' nor 4' is large enough to be measured by means of an astrolabe; therefore that which was considered to be the greatest latitude of obliquation of the planet Venus is correct.

Again, let the greatest distance of the orbital circle of Mercury be taken, *i.e.*, let
$$AB : AD = 10,948 : 3,573;$$
consequently, by demonstrations similar to the foregoing, we still infer that
$$AD = 9,452$$
and

$$DF = 3,085.$$
But here too we have it recorded that
$$\text{angle } DFG = 7°,$$
which is the angle of obliquation; hence
$$DG = 376,$$
where $DF = 3,085$
and $DA = 9,452$.
Accordingly, as the sides of right triangle DAG are given,
$$\text{angle } DAG \doteqdot 2°17',$$
which is the greatest digression in latitude. But at the least distance
$$AB : BD = 9,052 : 3,573;$$
therefore

$$AD = 8,317$$
and

$$DF = 3,283.$$
Now since by reason of this same (obliquation)

$$DF : DG = 3,283 : 400,$$
$$\text{where } AD = 8,317;$$

whence

$$\text{angle } DAG = 2°45'.$$

Accordingly there is a difference of at least 13' between the $2^1/_2°$ of the digression in latitude according to the mean ratio and the digression at the apogee; and at the most a difference of 15' between the mean digression and that at the perigee. And in making our calculations according to the mean ratio we shall use $^1/_4°$ as the difference; for it is not sensibly diverse from the observed differences.

Having demonstrated these things and also that the greatest additosubtractions in longitude have the same ratio to the greatest transit in latitude as the additosubtractions in the remaining sections of the orbital circle have to the particular transits in latitude, we shall have at hand the numbers of all the latitudes, which occur on account of the obliquation of the orbital circle of Venus and Mercury. But we have calculated only those latitudes which occur midway between the apogee and the perigee, as we said; and it was shown that the greatest of these latitudes is $2^1/_2°$, and the greatest [191^b] additosubtraction in the case of Venus is 46° and that in the case of Mercury about 22°. And in the tables of irregular movements we have already placed the additosubtractions opposite the particular sections of the orbital circles. Accordingly in the case of each of the two planets we shall take from the $2^1/_2°$ a part proportionate to the excess of the greatest additosubtraction over each of the lesser additosubtractions; we shall inscribe it in the table to be drawn up below with all its numbers; and in this way we shall have unfolded all the particular latitudes of the obliquations which occur when the Earth is at their highest apsis and at their lowest—just as we set forth the latitudes of the declinations in the case of the mean quadrants and mean longitudes. The latitudes which occur between these four limits can be unfolded by the subtle art of mathematics with the help of the proposed hypothesis of circles but not without labour. Now Ptolemy—who is compendious wherever he can be so—seeing that each of these aspects of latitude as a whole and in all its parts increased and decreased proportionally, like the latitude of the moon, accordingly took twelve parts of it, since their greatest latitude is 5° and that number is a twelfth part of 60, and made proportional minutes out of them, to be used not only in the case of these two planets but also in that of the three higher planets, as will be made clear below.

8. On the Third Aspect of the Latitude of Venus and Mercury, Which They Call the Deviation

Now that these things have been set forth, it still remains to say something about the third movement in latitude, which is the deviation. The ancients, who held the

Earth down at the centre of the world, believed that the deviation took place by reason of the inclination of an eccentric circle which has an epicycle and which revolves around the centre of the Earth—the deviation occurring most greatly when the epicycle is at the apogee or perigee and being always $1/_6°$ to the north in the case of Venus and $3/_4°$ to the south in the case of Mercury, as we said before. It is not however sufficiently clear whether they meant the inclination of the orbital circles to be equal and always the same: for their numbers indicate that, when they order a sixth part of the proportional minutes to be taken as the deviation of Venus, and three parts out of four as that of Mercury. That does not hold, unless the angle of inclination always remains [192ª] the same, as is demanded by the ratio of the minutes, which they take as their base. But if the angle remains the same, it is impossible to understand how the latitude of the planets suddenly springs back from the common section into the same latitude which it had just left, unless you say that takes place in the manner of refraction of light, as in optics. But here we are dealing with movement, which is not instantaneous but is by its own nature measured by time. Accordingly we must acknowledge that a libration such as we have expounded is present in those (circles) and makes the parts of the circle move over in different directions: And that necessarily follows, as the numbers differ $1/_5°$ in the case of Mercury. That should seem less surprising, if in accordance with our hypothesis this latitude is variable and not wholly simple but does not produce any apparent error, as is to be seen in the case of all differences, as follows:

For in the plane perpendicular to the ecliptic let (*ABC*) be the common section (of the two planes), and in the common section let *A* be the centre of the Earth and *B* the centre of the circle *CDF* at greatest or least distance from the Earth and as it were through the poles of the inclined orbital circle. And when the centre of the orbital circle is at the apogee or

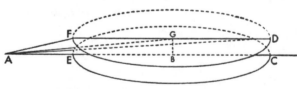

the perigee, *i.e.*, on line *AB*, the planet, wherever it is, is at its greatest deviation, in accordance with the circle parallel to the orbital circle; and *DF* is the diameter parallel to *CBE*, the diameter of the orbital circle. And *DF* and *CBE* are put down as the common sections of the planes perpendicular to plane *CDF*. Now let *DF* be bisected at *G*, which will be the centre of the parallel circle; and let *BG*, *AG*, *AD*, and *AF* be joined. Let us put down that

angle BAG = 10',

as in the greatest deviation of Venus. Accordingly, in triangle *ABG*

angle B = 90°;

and we have the following ratio for the sides:

$$AB : BG = 10,000 : 29.$$

But

$$\text{line } ABC = 17,193;$$

and by subtraction

$$AE = 2,807;$$

and

$$^1/_2 \text{ ch. 2 } CD = {}^1/_2 \text{ ch. 2 } EF = BG.$$

Accordingly

$$\text{angle } CAD = 6'$$

and

$$\text{angle } EAF \doteqdot 15'.$$

Now

$$\text{angle } BAG - \text{angle } CAD = 4',$$

while

$$\text{angle } EAF - \text{angle } BAG = 5';$$

and those differences can be neglected on account of their smallness. Accordingly, when the Earth is situated at its apogee or perigee, the apparent deviation of Venus will be slightly more or less than 10', [192^b] in whatever part of its orbital circle the planet is.

But in the case of Mercury when

$$\text{angle } BAG = 45',$$

and

$$AB : BG = 10,000 : 131,$$

and

$$ABC = 13,573,$$

and by subtraction

$$AE = 6,827;$$

then

$$\text{angle } CAD = 33°$$

and

$$\text{angle } EA \doteqdot F70'.$$

Accordingly, angle CAD has a deficiency of 12', and angle EAF has an excess of 25'. But these differences are practically obliterated beneath the rays of the sun before Mercury emerges into our sight, wherefore the ancients considered only its apparent and as it were simple deviation. But if anyone wishes to examine with least labour the precise ratio of their passages when hidden beneath the sun, we shall show how that takes place, as follows. We shall take Mercury as our example, because it makes a more considerable deviation than Venus.

For let *AB* be the straight line in the common section of the orbital circle of the planet and the ecliptic, while the Earth—which is at *A*—is at the apogee or the perigee

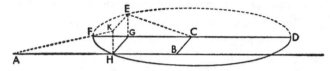

of the planet's orbital circle. Now let us put down that

$$AB = 10,000$$

indifferently, as if the mean between greatest and least distance, as we did in the case of the obliquation. Now around centre *C* let there be described circle *DEF*, which is parallel to the eccentric orbital circle at a distance *CB*; and the planet on this parallel circle be understood as being at this time at its greatest deviation. Let *DCF* be the diameter of this circle, which is also necessarily parallel to *AB*; and *DCF* and *AB* are in the same plane perpendicular to the orbital circle of the planet. Therefore, for example, let

arc *EF* = 45°,

in relation to which we shall examine the deviation of the planet. And let *EG* be drawn perpendicular to *CF*, and *EK* and *GH* perpendicular to the underlying plane of the orbital circle. Let the right parallelogram be completed by joining *HK*; and let *AE*, *AK*, and *EC* also be joined.

Now in the greatest deviation of Mercury

BC = 131,

where *AB* = 10,000.

And

CE = 3,573;

and the angles of the right triangle *EGC* are given; hence

side *EG* = *KH* = 2526.

And since

BH = *EG* = *CG*,

AH = *BA* – *BH* = 7,474.

Accordingly, since in triangle *AHK*

angle *H* = 90°

and the sides of comprehending angle *H* are given;

side *AK* = 7,889.

But

side *KE* = *CB* = *GH* = 131.

Accordingly, since in triangle [193ª] *AKE* the two sides *AK* and *KE* comprehending the right angle *K* have been given, angle *KAE* is given, which answers to the deviation we were seeking for the postulated arc *EF* and differs very little from the angle observed. We shall do similarly in the case of Venus and the other planets; and we shall inscribe our findings in the subjoined table.

Having made this exposition, we shall work out proportional minutes for the deviations between these limits. For let *ABC* be the eccentric orbital circle of Venus or Mercury; and let *A* and *C* be the nodes of this movement in latitude, and *B* the limit of greatest deviation. And with *B* as centre let there be described the small circle *DFG*, with the diameter *DBF* across it, along which diameter the libration of the movement of deviation takes place. And since it has been laid down that when the Earth is at the apogee or the perigee of the eccentric orbital circle of the planet, the planet itself is at its greatest deviation, namely in point *F*, where at this time the circle carrying the planet touches the small circle. Now let the Earth be

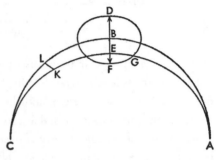

somewhere removed from the apogee or perigee of the eccentric circle of the planet; and in accordance with this movement let a similar arc *FG* be taken on the small circle. Let circle *AGC* be described, which bears the planet and will cut the small circle, and the diameter *DF* at point *E*; and let the planet be taken as being on this circle at point *K* in accordance with arc *EK* which is by hypothesis similar to arc *FG*; and let *KL* be drawn perpendicular to circle *ABC*.

Our problem is to find by means of *FG*, *EK*, and *BE* the magnitude of *KL*, *i.e.*, the distance of the planet from circle *ABC*. For since by means of arc *FG* arc *EG* will be given as a straight line hardly different from a circular or convex line, and *EF* will similarly be given in terms of the parts, whereof *BF* and the remainder *BE* will be given; for

$$BF : BE = \text{ch. } 2\ CE : \text{ch. } 2\ CK = BE : KL.$$

Accordingly if we put down *BF* and the radius of circle *CE* in terms of the same number, sixty, we shall have from them the number which picks out *BE*. When that number has been multiplied by itself and the product divided by sixty, we shall have *KL*, the minutes proportional to arc *EK*; and we shall inscribe them similarly in the fifth and last column of the table which follows:

LATITUDES OF SATURN, JUPITER, AND MARS

Common Numbers		SATURN				JUPITER				MARS				Proportional Minutes	
		Northern		Southern		Northern		Southern		Northern		Southern			
Deg.	Deg.	Deg.	Min.	Deg.	Min.	Deg.	Min.	Deg.	Min.	Deg.	Min.	Deg.	Min.	Deg.	Min.
3	357	2	3	2	2	1	6	1	5	0	6	0	5	59	48
6	354	2	4	2	2	1	7	1	5	0	7	0	5	59	36
9	351	2	4	2	3	1	7	1	5	0	9	0	6	59	6
12	348	2	5	2	3	1	8	1	6	0	9	0	6	58	36
15	345	2	5	2	3	1	8	1	6	0	10	0	8	57	48
18	342	2	6	2	3	1	8	1	6	0	11	0	8	57	0
21	339	2	6	2	4	1	9	1	7	0	12	0	9	56	48
24	336	2	7	2	4	1	9	1	7	0	13	0	9	54	36
27	333	2	8	2	5	1	10	1	8	0	14	0	10	53	18
30	330	2	8	2	5	1	10	1	8	0	14	0	11	52	0
33	327	2	9	2	6	1	11	1	9	0	15	0	11	50	12
36	324	2	10	2	7	1	11	1	9	0	16	0	12	48	24
39	321	2	10	2	7	1	12	1	10	0	17	0	12	46	24
42	318	2	11	2	8	1	12	1	10	0	18	0	13	44	24
45	315	2	11	2	9	1	13	1	11	0	19	0	15	42	12
48	312	2	12	2	10	1	13	1	11	0	20	0	16	40	0
51	309	2	13	2	11	1	14	1	12	0	22	0	18	37	36
54	306	2	14	2	12	1	14	1	13	0	23	0	20	35	12
57	303	2	15	2	13	1	15	1	14	0	25	0	22	32	36
60	300	2	16	2	15	1	16	1	15	0	27	0	24	30	0
63	297	2	17	2	16	1	17	1	17	0	29	0	25	27	12
66	294	2	18	2	18	1	18	1	18	0	31	0	27	24	24
69	291	2	20	2	19	1	19	1	19	0	33	0	29	21	24
72	288	2	21	2	21	1	21	1	21	0	35	0	31	18	24
75	285	2	22	2	22	1	22	1	22	0	37	0	34	15	24
78	282	2	24	2	24	1	24	1	24	0	40	0	37	12	24
81	279	2	25	2	26	1	25	1	25	0	42	0	39	9	24
84	276	2	27	2	27	1	27	1	27	0	45	0	42	6	24
87	273	2	28	2	28	1	28	1	28	0	48	0	45	3	12
90	270	2	30	2	30	1	30	1	30	0	51	0	49	0	0
93	267	2	31	2	31	1	31	1	31	0	55	0	52	3	12
96	264	2	33	2	33	1	33	1	33	0	59	0	56	6	24
99	261	2	34	2	34	1	34	1	34	1	2	1	0	9	9
102	258	2	36	2	36	1	36	1	36	1	6	1	4	12	12
105	255	2	37	2	37	1	37	1	37	1	11	1	8	15	15
108	252	2	39	2	39	1	39	1	39	1	15	1	12	18	18
111	249	2	40	2	40	1	40	1	40	1	19	1	17	21	21
114	246	2	42	2	42	1	42	1	42	1	25	1	22	24	24
117	243	2	43	2	43	1	43	1	43	1	31	1	28	27	12
120	240	2	45	2	45	1	44	1	44	1	36	1	34	30	0
123	237	2	46	2	46	1	46	1	46	1	41	1	40	32	37
126	234	2	47	2	48	1	47	1	47	1	47	1	47	35	12
129	231	2	49	2	49	1	49	1	49	1	54	1	55	37	36
132	228	2	50	2	51	1	50	1	51	2	2	2	5	40	6
135	225	2	52	2	53	1	53	1	53	2	10	2	15	42	12
138	222	2	53	2	54	1	52	1	54	2	19	2	26	44	24
141	219	2	54	2	55	1	53	1	55	2	29	2	38	47	24
144	216	2	55	2	56	1	55	1	57	2	37	2	48	48	24
147	213	2	56	2	57	1	56	1	58	2	47	3	4	50	12
150	210	2	57	2	58	1	58	1	59	2	51	3	20	52	0
153	207	2	58	2	59	1	59	2	1	3	12	3	32	53	18
156	204	2	59	3	0	2	0	2	2	3	23	3	52	54	36
159	201	2	59	3	1	2	1	2	3	3	34	4	13	55	48
162	198	3	0	3	2	2	2	2	4	3	46	4	36	57	0
165	195	3	0	3	2	2	2	2	5	3	57	5	0	57	48
168	192	3	1	3	3	2	3	2	5	4	9	5	23	58	36
171	189	3	1	3	3	2	3	2	6	4	17	5	48	59	6
174	186	3	2	3	4	2	4	2	6	4	23	6	15	59	36
177	183	3	2	3	4	2	4	2	7	4	27	6	35	59	48
180	180	3	2	3	5	2	4	2	7	4	30	6	50	60	0

LATITUDES OF VENUS AND MERCURY

Common Numbers		VENUS				MERCURY				Deviation of Venus		Deviation of Mercury		Proportional Minutes of the Deviation	
		Declination		Obliquation		Declination		Obliquation							
Deg.	Deg.	Deg.	Min.	Deg.	Min.	Deg.	Min.	Deg.	Min.	Deg.	Min.	Deg.	Min.	Deg.	Min.
3	357	1	2	0	4	0	7	1	45	0	5	0	33	59	36
6	354	1	2	0	8	0	7	1	45	0	11	0	33	59	12
9	351	1	1	0	12	0	7	1	45	0	16	0	33	58	25
12	348	1	1	0	16	0	7	1	44	0	22	0	33	57	14
15	345	1	0	0	21	0	7	1	44	0	27	0	33	55	41
18	342	1	0	0	25	0	7	1	43	0	33	0	33	54	9
21	339	0	59	0	29	0	7	1	42	0	38	0	33	52	12
24	336	0	59	0	33	0	7	1	40	0	44	0	34	49	43
27	333	0	58	0	37	0	7	1	38	0	49	0	34	47	21
30	330	0	57	0	41	0	8	1	36	0	55	0	34	45	4
33	327	0	56	0	45	0	8	1	34	1	0	0	34	42	0
36	324	0	55	0	49	0	8	1	30	1	6	0	34	39	15
39	321	0	53	0	53	0	8	1	27	1	11	0	35	35	53
42	318	0	51	0	57	0	8	1	23	1	16	0	35	32	51
45	315	0	49	1	1	0	8	1	19	1	21	0	35	29	41
48	312	0	46	1	5	0	8	1	15	1	26	0	36	23	40
51	309	0	44	1	9	0	8	1	11	1	31	0	36	26	34
54	306	0	41	1	13	0	8	1	8	1	35	0	36	30	39
57	303	0	38	1	17	0	8	1	4	1	40	0	37	17	40
60	300	0	35	1	20	0	8	0	59	1	44	0	38	15	0
63	297	0	32	1	24	0	8	0	54	1	48	0	38	12	20
66	294	0	29	1	28	0	9	0	49	1	52	0	39	9	55
69	291	0	26	1	32	0	9	0	44	1	56	0	39	7	38
72	288	0	23	1	35	0	9	0	38	2	0	0	40	5	39
75	285	0	20	1	38	0	9	0	32	2	3	0	41	3	57
78	282	0	16	1	42	0	9	0	26	2	7	0	42	2	34
81	279	0	12	1	46	0	9	0	21	2	10	0	42	1	28
84	276	0	8	1	50	0	10	0	16	2	14	0	43	0	40
87	273	0	4	1	54	0	10	0	8	2	17	0	44	0	10
90	270	0	0	1	57	0	10	0	0	2	20	0	45	0	0
93	267	0	5	2	0	0	10	0	8	2	23	0	45	0	10
96	264	0	10	2	3	0	10	0	15	2	25	0	46	0	40
99	261	0	15	2	6	0	10	0	23	2	27	0	47	1	28
102	258	0	20	2	9	0	11	0	31	2	28	0	48	2	34
105	255	0	26	2	12	0	11	0	40	2	29	0	48	3	57
108	252	0	32	2	15	0	11	0	48	2	29	0	49	5	39
111	249	0	38	2	17	0	11	0	57	2	30	0	50	7	38
114	246	0	44	2	20	0	11	1	6	2	30	0	51	9	55
117	243	0	50	2	22	0	11	1	16	2	30	0	51	12	20
120	240	0	59	2	24	0	12	1	25	2	29	0	52	15	0
123	237	1	8	2	26	0	12	1	35	2	28	0	53	17	40
126	234	1	18	2	27	0	12	1	45	2	26	0	54	20	39
129	231	1	28	2	29	0	12	1	55	2	23	0	55	23	34
132	228	1	38	2	30	0	12	2	6	2	20	0	56	26	40
135	225	1	48	2	30	0	13	2	16	2	16	0	57	29	41
138	222	1	59	2	30	0	13	2	27	2	11	0	57	32	51
141	219	2	11	2	29	0	13	2	37	2	6	0	58	35	53
144	216	2	25	2	28	0	13	2	47	2	0	0	59	39	25
147	213	2	43	2	26	0	13	2	57	1	53	1	0	42	0
150	210	3	3	2	22	0	13	3	7	1	46	1	1	45	4
153	207	3	23	2	18	0	13	3	17	1	38	1	2	47	21
156	204	3	44	2	12	0	14	3	26	1	29	1	3	49	43
159	201	4	5	2	4	0	14	3	34	1	20	1	4	52	12
162	198	4	26	1	55	0	14	3	42	1	10	1	5	54	9
165	195	4	49	1	42	0	14	3	48	0	59	1	6	55	41
168	192	5	13	1	27	0	14	3	54	0	48	1	7	57	14
171	189	5	36	1	9	0	14	3	58	0	36	1	7	58	25
174	186	5	52	0	48	0	14	4	2	0	24	1	8	59	12
177	183	6	7	0	25	0	14	4	4	0	12	1	9	59	36
180	180	6	22	0	0	0	14	4	5	0	0	1	10	60	0

9. ON THE CALCULATION OF THE LATITUDES OF THE FIVE WANDERING STARS

[195^b] Now this is the method of calculating the latitudes of the five wandering stars by means of these tables. For in the case of Saturn, Jupiter, and Mars we shall take the discrete, or corrected, anomaly of the eccentric circle among the common numbers: in the case of Mars, the anomaly as is; in that of Jupiter, after the subtraction of 20°; and in that of Saturn, after the addition of 50°. Accordingly we shall note the numbers which occur in the region of the 60's, in the proportional minutes placed in the last column. Similarly by means of the corrected anomaly of parallax we shall determine the proper number of each planet, corresponding to the latitude: the first and northern latitude, if the proportional minutes are in the first half of the column—which happens when the anomaly of the eccentric circle is less than 90° or more than 270°; the second and southern latitude, if the proportional minutes are in the second half of the column, *i.e.*, if the anomaly of the eccentric circle, whereby the table was entered upon, was more than 90° or less than 270°. Accordingly if we adjust one of these latitudes to its 60's, the result will be the distance north or south of the ecliptic in accordance with the denomination of the circles assumed.

But in the case of Venus and Mercury the three latitudes of declination, obliquation, and deviation, which are marked down separately, are to be taken first by means of the corrected anomaly of parallax, except that in the case of Mercury one tenth of the obliquation is to be subtracted, if the anomaly of the eccentric circle and its number are found in the first column of the table, or merely added, if in the second column of the table; and the remainder or sum is to be kept.

And we must discern whether their denominations are northern or southern, since if the corrected anomaly of parallax is in the apogeal semicircle, *i.e.*, is less than 90° or more than 270° and the anomaly of the eccentric circle is also less than a semicircle; or again, if the anomaly of parallax is in the perigeal arc, *i.e.*, is more than 90° and less than 270° and the anomaly of the eccentric circle is greater than a semicircle; the declination of Venus will be northern and that of Mercury southern. But if the anomaly of parallax is in the perigeal arc and the anomaly of the eccentric circle is less than a semicircle; [196^a] or if the anomaly of parallax is in the apogeal arc and the anomaly of the eccentric circle is more than a semicircle; conversely the declination of Venus will be southern and that of Mercury northern. But in the case of the obliquation, if the anomaly of parallax is less than a semicircle and the anomaly of the eccentric circle is apogeal; or if the anomaly of parallax is greater than a semicircle and the anomaly of the eccentric circle is perigeal; the obliquation of Venus will be to the north and that of Mercury to the south; and vice versa. But the deviations of Venus always remain northern and those of Mercury southern.

Then, corresponding to the corrected anomaly of the eccentric circle, the proportional minutes should be taken which are common to all the five planets, although they are ascribed to the three higher planets. These are assigned to the obliquation and lastly to the deviation. After this, when we have added 90° to the same anomaly of the eccentric circle, we shall once more take the sum and find the common proportional minutes which correspond to it and assign them to the latitude of declination. Having placed these things in this order, we shall adjust each of the three particular latitudes set forth to their proportional minutes; and the result will be the corrected latitude for the position and time, so that at last we may have the sum of the three latitudes of the two planets. If all the latitudes are of one denomination, they are added together; but if not, only the two are added which have the same denomination; and according as the sum is greater or less than the third latitude, which is different from there, there will be a subtraction; and the remainder will be the predominant latitude sought for.

Galileo Galilei

(1564-1642)

HIS LIFE AND WORK

In 1633, ninety years after the death of Copernicus, the Italian astronomer and mathematician Galileo Galilei was taken to Rome to stand trial before the Inquisition for heresy. The charge stemmed from the publication of Galileo's *Dialogue Concerning the Two Chief World Systems: Ptolemaic and Copernican* (*Dialogo sopra Ii due massimi sistemi del mondo: Ttolemaico, e Ccopernicono*). In this book, Galileo forcefully asserted, in defiance of a 1616 edict against the propagation of Copernican doctrine, that the heliocentric system was not just a hypothesis but was the truth. The outcome of the trial was never in doubt. Galileo admitted that he might have gone too far in his arguments for the Copernican system, despite previous warnings by the Roman Catholic church. A majority of the cardinals in the tribunal found him "vehemently suspected of heresy" for supporting and teaching the idea that the earth moves and is not the center of the universe, and they sentenced him to life imprisonment.

Galileo was also forced to sign a handwritten confession and to renounce his beliefs publicly. On his knees, and with his hands on the Bible, he pronounced this abjuration in Latin:

> *I, Galileo Galilei, son of the late Vincenzio Galilei of Florence, aged 70 years, tried personally by this court, and kneeling before You, the most Eminent and Reverend Lord Cardinals, Inquisitors-General*

throughout the Christian Republic against heretical depravity, having before my eyes the Most Holy Gospels, and laying on them my own hands; I swear that I have always believed, I believe now, and with God's help I will in future believe all which the Holy Catholic and Apostolic Church doth hold, preach, and teach.

But since I, after having been admonished by this Holy Office entirely to abandon the false opinion that the sun was the centre of the universe and immoveable, and that the earth was not the centre of the same and that it moved, and that I was neither to hold, defend, nor teach in any manner whatever, either orally or in writing, the said false doctrine; and after having received a notification that the said doctrine is contrary to Holy Writ, I did write and cause to be printed a book in which I treat of the said already condemned doctrine, and bring forward arguments of much efficacy in its favour, without arriving at any solution: I have been judged vehemently suspected of heresy, that is, of having held and believed that the sun is the centre of the universe and immoveable, and that the earth is not the centre of the same, and that it does move.

Nevertheless, wishing to remove from the minds of your Eminences and all faithful Christians this vehement suspicion reasonably conceived against me, I abjure with sincere heart and unfeigned faith, I curse and detest the said errors and heresies, and generally all and every error and sect contrary to the Holy Catholic Church. And I swear that for the future I will neither say nor assert in speaking or writing such things as may bring upon me similar suspicion; and if I know any heretic, or one suspected of heresy, I will denounce him to this Holy Office, or to the Inquisitor and Ordinary of the place in which I may be.

I also swear and promise to adopt and observe entirely all the penances which have been or may be by this Holy Office imposed on me. And if I contravene any of these said promises, protests, or oaths (which God forbid!) I submit myself to all the pains and penalties which by the Sacred Canons and other Decrees general and particular are against such offenders imposed and promulgated. So help me God and the

Holy Gospels, which I touch with my own hands.

I Galileo Galilei aforesaid have abjured, sworn, and promised, and hold myself bound as above; and in token of the truth, with my own hand have subscribed the present schedule of my abjuration, and have recited it word by word. In Rome, at the Convent della Minerva, this 22nd day of June, 1633. I, Galileo Galilei, have abjured as above, with my own hand.

Legend has it that as Galileo rose to his feet, he uttered under his breath, "Eppur si muove"—"And yet, it moves." The remark captivated scientists and scholars for centuries, as it represented defiance of obscurantism and nobility of purpose in the search for truth under the most adverse circumstances. Although an oil portrait of Galileo dating from 1640 has been discovered bearing the inscription "Eppur si muove," most historians regard the story as myth. Still, it is entirely within Galileo's character to have only paid lip service to the church's demands in his abjuration and then to have returned to his scientific studies, whether they adhered to non-Copernican principles or not. After all, what had brought Galileo before the Inquisition was his publication of *Two Chief World Systems*, a direct challenge to the church's 1616 edict forbidding him from teaching the Copernican theory of the earth in motion around the sun as anything but a hypothesis. "Eppur si mouve" may not have concluded his trial and abjuration, but the phrase certainly punctuated Galileo's life and accomplishments.

Born in Pisa on February 18, 1564, Galileo Galilei was the son of Vincenzo Galilei, a musician and mathematician. The family moved to Florence when Galileo was young, and there he began his education in a monastery. Although from an early age Galileo demonstrated a penchant for mathematics and mechanical pursuits, his father was adamant that he enter a more useful field, and so in 1581 Galileo enrolled in the University of Pisa to study medicine and the philosophy of Aristotle. It was in Pisa that Galileo's rebelliousness emerged. He had little or no interest in medicine and began to study mathematics with a passion. It is believed that while observing the oscillations of a hanging lamp in the cathedral of Pisa, Galileo discovered the isochronism of the pendulum—the period of swing is independent of its amplitude—which he would apply a half-century later in building an astronomical clock.

Galileo persuaded his father to allow him to leave the university without a degree, and he returned to Florence to study and teach mathematics. By 1586, he had begun to question the science and philosophy of Aristotle, preferring to reexamine the work of the great mathematician Archimedes, who was also known for discovering and perfecting methods of integration for calculating areas and volumes. Archimedes also gained a

reputation for his invention of many machines ultimately used as engines of war, such as giant catapults to hurl boulders at an advancing army and large cranes to topple ships. Galileo was inspired mainly by Archimedes' mathematical genius, but he too was swept up in the spirit of invention, designing a hydrostatic balance to determine an object's density when weighed in water.

In 1589, Galileo became a professor of mathematics at the University of Pisa, where he was required to teach Ptolemaic astronomy—the theory that the sun and the planets revolve around the earth. It was in Pisa, at the age of twenty-five, that Galileo obtained a deeper understanding of astronomy and began to break with Aristotle and Ptolemy. Lecture notes recovered from this period show that Galileo had adopted the Archimedean approach to motion; specifically, he was teaching that the density of a falling object, not its weight, as Aristotle had maintained, was proportional to the speed at which it fell. Galileo is said to have demonstrated his theory by dropping objects of the different weights but the same density from atop the leaning tower of Pisa. In Pisa, too, he wrote *On motion* (*De motu*), a book that contradicted the Aristotelian theories of motion and established Galileo as a leader in scientific reformation.

After his father's death in 1592, Galileo did not see much of a future for himself in Pisa. The pay was dismal, and with the help of a family friend, Guidobaldo del Monte, Galileo was appointed to the chair in mathematics at the University of Padua, in the Venetian Republic. There, Galileo's reputation blossomed. He remained at Padua for eighteen years, lecturing on geometry and astronomy as well as giving private lessons on cosmography, optics, arithmetic and the use of the sector in military engineering. In 1593, he assembled treatises on fortifications and mechanics for his private students and invented a pump that could raise water under power of a single horse.

In 1597, Galileo invented a calculating compass that proved useful to mechanical engineers and military men. He also began a correspondence with Johannes Kepler, whose book *Mystery of the Cosmos* (*Mysterium cosmographicum*) Galileo had read. Galileo sympathized with Kepler's Copernican views, and Kepler hoped that Galileo would openly support the theory of a heliocentric earth. But Galileo's scientific interests were still focused on mechanical theories, and he did not follow Kepler's wishes. Also at that time Galileo had developed a personal interest in Marina Gamba, a Venetian woman by whom he had a son and two daughters. The eldest daughter, Virginia, born in 1600, maintained a very close relationship with her father, mainly through an exchange of correspondence, for she spent most of her short adult life in a convent, taking the name Maria Celeste in tribute to her father's interest in celestial matters.

In the first years of the seventeenth century, Galileo experimented with the pendulum and explored its association with the phenomenon of natural acceleration. He

also began work on a mathematical model describing the motion of falling bodies, which he studied by measuring the time it took balls to roll various distances down inclined planes. In 1604, a supernova observed in the night sky above Padua renewed questions about Aristotle's model of the unchanging heavens. Galileo thrust himself into the forefront of the debate, delivering several provocative lectures, but he was hesitant to publish his theories. In October 1608, a Dutchman by the name of Hans Lipperhey applied for a patent on a spyglass that could make faraway objects appear closer. Upon hearing of the invention, Galileo set about attempting to improve it. Soon he had designed a nine-power telescope, three times more powerful than Lipperhey's device, and within a year, he had produced a thirty-power telescope. When he pointed the scope toward the skies in January 1610, the heavens literally opened up to humankind. The moon no longer appeared to be a perfectly smooth disc but was seen to be a mountainous and full of craters. Through his telescope, Galileo determined that the Milky Way was actually a vast gathering of separate stars. But most important, he sighted four moons around Jupiter, a discovery that had tremendous implications for many of the geocentrically inclined, who held that all heavenly bodies revolved exclusively around the earth. That same year, he published *The Starry Messenger* (*Sidereus Nuncius*), in which he announced his discoveries and which put him in the forefront of contemporary astronomy. He felt unable to continue teaching Aristotelian theories, and his renown enabled him to take a position in Florence as mathematician and philosopher to the grand duke of Tuscany.

Once free from the responsibilities of teaching, Galileo was able to devote himself to telescopy. He soon observed the phases of Venus, which confirmed Copernicus' theory that the planet revolved around the sun. He also noted Saturn 's oblong shape, which he attributed to numerous moons revolving around the planet, for his telescope was unable to detect Saturn's rings.

The Roman Catholic Church affirmed and praised Galileo's discoveries but did not agree with his interpretations of them. In 1613, Galileo published *Letters on Sunspots*, marking the first time in print that he had defended the Copernican system of a heliocentric universe. The work was immediately attacked and its author denounced, and the Holy Inquisition soon took notice. When in 1616 Galileo published a theory of tides, which he believed was proof that the earth moved, he was summoned to Rome to answer for his views. A council of theologians issued an edict that Galileo was practicing bad science when he taught the Copernican system as fact. But Galileo was never officially condemned. A meeting with Pope Paul V led him to believe that the pontiff held him in esteem and that he could continue to lecture under the pontiff's protection. He was, however, strongly warned that Copernican theories ran contrary to the Scriptures and that they may only be presented as hypotheses.

When upon Paul's death in 1623 one of Galileo's friends and supporters, Cardinal Barberini, was elected pope, taking the name Urban VIII, Galileo presumed that the 1616 edict would be reversed. Urban told Galileo that he himself was responsible for omitting the word "heresy" from the edict and that as long as Galileo treated Copernican doctrine as hypothesis and not truth, he would be free to publish. With this assurance, over the next six years Galileo worked on *Dialogue Concerning the Two Chief World Systems*, the book that would lead to his imprisonment.

Two Chief World Systems takes the form of a polemic between an advocate of Aristotle and Ptolemy and a supporter of Copernicus, who seek to win an educated everyman over to the respective philosophies. Galileo prefaced the book with a statement in support of the 1616 edict against him, and by presenting the theories through the book's characters, he is able to avoid openly declaring his allegiance to either side. The public clearly perceived, nonetheless, that in *Two Chief World Systems* Galileo was disparaging Aristotelianism. In the polemic, Aristotle's cosmology is only weakly defended by its simpleminded supporter and is viciously attacked by the forceful and persuasive Copernican. The book achieved a great success, despite being the subject of massive protest upon publication. By writing it in vernacular Italian rather than Latin, Galileo made it accessible to a broad range of literate Italians, not just to churchmen and scholars. Galileo's Ptolemaic rivals were furious at the dismissive treatment that their scientific views had been given. In Simplicio, the defender of the Ptolemaic system, many readers recognized a caricature of Simplicius, a sixth-century Aristotelian commentator. Pope Urban VIII, meanwhile, thought that Simplicio was meant as a caricature of himself. He felt misled by Galileo, who apparently had neglected to inform him of any injunction in the 1616 edict when he sought permission to write the book. Galileo, on the other hand, never received a written injunction, and seemed to be unaware of any violations on his part.

By March 1632, the church had ordered the book's printer to discontinue publication, and Galileo was summoned to Rome to defend himself. Pleading serious illness, Galileo refused to travel, but the pope insisted, threatening to have Galileo removed in chains. Eleven months later, Galileo appeared in Rome for trial. He was made to abjure the heresy of the Copernican theory and was sentenced to life imprisonment. Galileo's life sentence was soon commuted to gentle house arrest in Siena under the guard of Archbishop Ascanio Piccolomini, a former student of Galileo's. Piccolomini permitted and even encouraged Galileo to resume writing. There, Galileo began his final work, *Dialogues Concerning Two New Sciences*, an examination of his accomplishments in physics. But the following year, when Rome got word of the preferential treatment Galileo was receiving from Piccolomini, it had him removed to another home, in the

hills above Florence. Some historians believe that it was upon his transfer that Galileo actually said "Eppur si muove," rather than at his public abjuration following the trial.

The transfer brought Galileo closer to his daughter Virginia, but soon she died, after a brief illness, in 1634. The loss devastated Galileo, but he eventually he was able to resume working on *Two New Sciences*, and he finished the book within a year. However, the Congregation of the Index, the church censor, would not allow Galileo to publish it. The manuscript had to be smuggled out of Italy to Leiden, in Protestant northern Europe, by Louis Elsevier, a Dutch publisher, before it could appear in print in 1638. *Dialogues Concerning Two New Sciences*, which set out the laws of accelerated motion governing falling bodies, is widely held to be the cornerstone of modern physics. In this book, Galileo reviewed and refined his previous studies of motion, as well as the principles of mechanics. The two new sciences Galileo focuses on are the study of the strength of materials (a branch of engineering), and the study of motion (kinematics, a branch of mathematics). In the first half of the book, Galileo described his inclined-plane experiments in accelerated motion. In the second half, Galileo took on the intractable problem of calculating the path of a projectile fired from a cannon. At first it had been thought that, in keeping with Aristotelian principles, a projectile followed a straight line until it lost its "impetus" and fell straight to the ground. Later, observers noticed that it actually returned to earth on a curved path, but the reason this happened and an exact description of the curve no one could say—until Galileo. He concluded that the projectile's path is determined by two motions—one vertical, caused by gravity, which forces the projectile down, and one horizontal, governed by the principle of inertia.

Galileo demonstrated that the combination of these two independent motions determined the projectile's course along a mathematically describable curve. He showed this by rolling a bronze ball coated in ink down an inclined plane and onto a table, whence it fell freely off the edge and onto the floor. The inked ball left a mark on the floor where it hit, always some distance out from the table's edge. Thus Galileo proved that the ball continued to move horizontally, at a constant speed, while gravity pulled it down vertically. He found that the distance increased in proportion to the square of the time elapsed. The curve achieved a precise mathematical shape, which the ancient Greeks had termed a parabola.

So great a contribution to physics was *Two New Sciences* that scholars have long maintained that the book anticipated Isaac Newton's laws of motion. By the time of its publication, however, Galileo had gone blind. He lived out the remaining years of his life in Arcetri, where he died on January 8, 1642. Galileo's contributions to humanity were never understated. Albert Einstein recognized this when he wrote: "Propositions arrived at purely by logical means are completely empty as regards reality. Because

Galileo saw this, and particularly because he drummed it into the scientific world, he is the father of modern physics—indeed of modern science."

In 1979, Pope John Paul II stated that the Roman Catholic church may have mistakenly condemned Galileo, and he called for a commission specifically to reopen the case. Four years later, the commission reported that Galileo should not have been condemned, and the church published all the documents relevant to his trial. In 1992, the pope endorsed the commission's conclusion.

DIALOGUES CONCERNING TWO SCIENCES

FIRST DAY

Interlocutors: Salviati, Sagredo And Simplicio

Salv. The constant activity which you Venetians display in your famous arsenal suggests to the studious mind a large field for investigation, especially that part of the work which involves mechanics; for in this department all types of instruments and machines are constantly being constructed by many artisans, among whom there must be some who, partly by inherited experience and partly by their own observations, have become highly expert and clever in explanation.

Sagr. You are quite right. Indeed, I myself, being curious by nature, frequently visit this place for the mere pleasure of observing the work of those who, on account of their superiority over other artisans, we call "first rank men." Conference with them has often helped me in the investigation of certain effects including not only those which are striking, but also those which are recondite and almost incredible. At times also I have been put to confusion and driven to despair of ever explaining something for which I could not account, but which my senses told me to be true. And notwithstanding the fact that what the old man told us a little while ago is proverbial and commonly accepted, yet it seemed to me altogether false, like many another saying which is current among the ignorant; for I think they introduce these expressions in order to give the appearance of knowing something about matters which they do not understand.

Salv. You refer, perhaps, to that last remark of his when we asked the reason why they employed stocks, scaffolding and bracing of larger dimensions for launching a big

vessel than they do for a small one; and he answered that they did this in order to avoid the danger of the ship parting under its own heavy weight [*vasta mole*], a danger to which small boats are not subject?

Sagr. Yes, that is what I mean; and I refer especially to his last assertion which I have always regarded as a false, though current, opinion; namely, that in speaking of these and other similar machines one cannot argue from the small to the large, because many devices which succeed on a small scale do not work on a large scale. Now, since mechanics has its foundation in geometry, where mere size cuts no figure, I do not see that the properties of circles, triangles, cylinders, cones and other solid figures will change with their size. If, therefore, a large machine be constructed in such a way that its parts bear to one another the same ratio as in a smaller one, and if the smaller is sufficiently strong for the purpose for which it was designed, I do not see why the larger also should not be able to withstand any severe and destructive tests to which it may be subjected.

Salv. The common opinion is here absolutely wrong. Indeed, it is so far wrong that precisely the opposite is true, namely, that many machines can be constructed even more perfectly on a large scale than on a small; thus, for instance, a clock which indicates and strikes the hour can be made more accurate on a large scale than on a small. There are some intelligent people who maintain this same opinion, but on more reasonable grounds, when they cut loose from geometry and argue that the better performance of the large machine is owing to the imperfections and variations of the material. Here I trust you will not charge

[51]

me with arrogance if I say that imperfections in the material, even those which are great enough to invalidate the clearest mathematical proof, are not sufficient to explain the deviations observed between machines in the concrete and in the abstract. Yet I shall say it and will affirm that, even if the imperfections did not exist and matter were absolutely perfect, unalterable and free from all accidental variations, still the mere fact that it is matter makes the larger machine, built of the same material and in the same proportion as the smaller, correspond with exactness to the smaller in every respect except that it will not be so strong or so resistant against violent treatment; the larger the machine, the greater its weakness. Since I assume matter to be unchangeable and always the same, it is clear that we are no less able to treat this constant and invariable property in a rigid manner than if it belonged to simple and pure mathematics. Therefore, Sagredo, you would do well to change the opinion which you, and perhaps also many other students of mechanics, have entertained concerning the ability of machines and structures to resist external disturbances, thinking that when they are

built of the same material and maintain the same ratio between parts, they are able equally, or rather proportionally, to resist or yield to such external disturbances and blows. For we can demonstrate by geometry that the large machine is not proportionately stronger than the small. Finally, we may say that, for every machine and structure, whether artificial or natural, there is set a necessary limit beyond which neither art nor nature can pass; it is here understood, of course, that the material is the same and the proportion preserved.

Sagr. My brain already reels. My mind, like a cloud momentarily illuminated by a lightning-flash, is for an instant filled with an unusual light, which now beckons to me and which now suddenly mingles and obscures strange, crude ideas. From what you have said it appears to me impossible to build two similar structures of the same material, but of different sizes and have them proportionately strong; and if this were so, it would

[52]

not be possible to find two single poles made of the same wood which shall be alike in strength and resistance but unlike in size.

Salv. So it is, Sagredo. And to make sure that we understand each other, I say that if we take a wooden rod of a certain length and size, fitted, say, into a wall at right angles, i. e., parallel to the horizon, it may be reduced to such a length that it will just support itself; so that if a hair's breadth be added to its length it will break under its own weight and will be the only rod of the kind in the world.[1] Thus if, for instance, its length be a hundred times its breadth, you will not be able to find another rod whose length is also a hundred times its breadth and which, like the former, is just able to sustain its own weight and no more: all the larger ones will break while all the shorter ones will be strong enough to support something more than their own weight. And this which I have said about the ability to support itself must be understood to apply also to other tests; so that if a piece of scantling [*corrente*] will carry the weight of ten similar to itself, a beam [*trave*] having the same proportions will not be able to support ten similar beams.

Please observe, gentlemen, how facts which at first seem improbable will, even on scant explanation, drop the cloak which has hidden them and stand forth in naked and simple beauty. Who does not know that a horse falling from a height of three or four cubits will break his bones, while a dog falling from the same height or a cat from a height of eight or ten cubits will suffer no injury? Equally harmless would be the fall of a grasshopper from a tower or the fall of an ant from the distance of the moon. Do not children fall with impunity from heights which would cost their elders a broken

1. The author here apparently means that the solution is unique. *[Trans.]*

leg or perhaps a fractured skull? And just as smaller animals are proportionately stronger and more robust than the larger, so also smaller plants are able to stand up better than larger. I am certain you both know that an oak two hundred cubits [*braccia*] high would not be able to sustain its own branches if they were distributed as in a tree of ordinary size; and that nature cannot produce a horse as large as twenty ordinary horses or a giant ten times taller than an

[53]

ordinary man unless by miracle or by greatly altering the proportions of his limbs and especially of his bones, which would have to be considerably enlarged over the ordinary. Likewise the current belief that, in the case of artificial machines the very large and the small are equally feasible and lasting is a manifest error. Thus, for example, a small obelisk or column or other solid figure can certainly be laid down or set up without danger of breaking, while the very large ones will go to pieces under the slightest provocation, and that purely on account of their own weight. And here I must relate a circumstance which is worthy of your attention as indeed are all events which happen contrary to expectation, especially when a precautionary measure turns out to be a cause of disaster. A large marble column was laid out so that its two ends rested each upon a piece of beam; a little later it occurred to a mechanic that, in order to be doubly sure of its not breaking in the middle by its own weight, it would be wise to lay a third support midway; this seemed to all an excellent idea; but the sequel showed that it was quite the opposite, for not many months passed before the column was found cracked and broken exactly above the new middle support.

Simp. A very remarkable and thoroughly unexpected accident, especially if caused by placing that new support in the middle.

Salv. Surely this is the explanation, and the moment the cause is known our surprise vanishes; for when the two pieces of the column were placed on level ground it was observed that one of the end beams had, after a long while, become decayed and sunken, but that the middle one remained hard and strong, thus causing one half of the column to project in the air without any support. Under these circumstances the body therefore behaved differently from what it would have done if supported only upon the first beams; because no matter how much they might have sunken the column would have gone with them. This is an accident which could not possibly have happened to a small column, even though made of the same stone and having a length corresponding to its thickness, i. e., preserving the ratio between thickness and length found in the large pillar.

[54]

Sagr. I am quite convinced of the facts of the case, but I do not understand why

the strength and resistance are not multiplied in the same proportion as the material; and I am the more puzzled because, on the contrary, I have noticed in other cases that the strength and resistance against breaking increase in a larger ratio than the amount of material. Thus, for instance, if two nails be driven into a wall, the one which is twice as big as the other will support not only twice as much weight as the other, but three or four times as much.

Salv. Indeed you will not be far wrong if you say eight times as much; nor does this phenomenon contradict the other even though in appearance they seem so different.

Sagr. Will you not then, Salviati, remove these difficulties and clear away these obscurities if possible: for I imagine that this problem of resistance opens up a field of beautiful and useful ideas; and if you are pleased to make this the subject of to-day's discourse you will place Simplicio and me under many obligations.

Salv. I am at your service if only I can call to mind what I learned from our Academician[2] who had thought much upon this subject and according to his custom had demonstrated everything by geometrical methods so that one might fairly call this a new science. For, although some of his conclusions had been reached by others, first of all by Aristotle, these are not the most beautiful and, what is more important, they had not been proven in a rigid manner from fundamental principles. Now, since I wish to convince you by demonstrative reasoning rather than to persuade you by mere probabilities, I shall suppose that you are familiar with present-day mechanics so far as it is needed in our discussion. First of all it is necessary to consider what happens when a piece of wood or any other solid which coheres firmly is broken; for this is the fundamental fact, involving the first and simple principle which we must take for granted as well known.

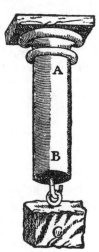

Fig. 1

To grasp this more clearly, imagine a cylinder or prism, AB, made of wood or other solid coherent material. Fasten the upper end, A, so that the cylinder hangs vertically. To the lower end, B, attach the weight C. It is clear that however great they may be, the tenacity and coherence [*tenacità e*

[55]

coerenza] between the parts of this solid, so long as they are not infinite, can be overcome by the pull of the weight C, a weight which can be increased indefinitely until finally the solid breaks like a rope. And as in the case of the rope whose strength we know to be derived from a multitude of hemp threads which compose it, so in the case

2. I. e. Galileo: The author frequently refers to himself under this name. [*Trans.*]

of the wood, we observe its fibres and filaments run lengthwise and render it much stronger than a hemp rope of the same thickness. But in the case of a stone or metallic cylinder where the coherence seems to be still greater the cement which holds the parts together must be something other than filaments and fibres; and yet even this can be broken by a strong pull.

Simp. If this matter be as you say I can well understand that the fibres of the wood, being as long as the piece of wood itself, render it strong and resistant against large forces tending to break it, But how can one make a rope one hundred cubits long out of hempen fibres which are not more than two or three cubits long, and still give it so much strength? Besides, I should be glad to hear your opinion as to the manner in which the parts of metal, stone, and other materials not showing a filamentous structure are put together; for, if I mistake not, they exhibit even greater tenacity.

Salv. To solve the problems which you raise it will be necessary to make a digression into subjects which have little bearing upon our present purpose.

Sagr. But if, by digressions, we can reach new truth, what harm is there in making one now, so that we may not lose this knowledge, remembering that such an opportunity, once omitted, may not return; remembering also that we are not tied down to a fixed and brief method but that we meet solely for our own entertainment? Indeed, who knows but that we may thus

[56]

frequently discover something more interesting and beautiful than the solution originally sought? I beg of you, therefore, to grant the request of Simplicio, which is also mine; for I am no less curious and desirous than he to learn what is the binding material which holds together the parts of solids so that they can scarcely be separated. This information is also needed to understand the coherence of the parts of fibres themselves of which some solids are built up.

Salv. I am at your service, since you desire it. The first question is, How are fibres, each not more than two or three cubits in length, so tightly bound together in the case of a rope one hundred cubits long that great force [violenza] is required to break it?

Now tell me, Simplicio, can you not hold a hempen fibre so tightly between your fingers that I, pulling by the other end, would break it before drawing it away from you? Certainly you can. And now when the fibres of hemp are held not only at the ends, but are grasped by tile surrounding medium throughout their entire length is it not manifestly more difficult to tear them loose from what holds them than to break them? But in the case of the rope the very act of twisting causes the threads to bind one another in such a way that when the rope is stretched with a great force the fibres break rather than separate from each other.

At the point where a rope parts the fibres are, as everyone knows, very short, nothing like a cubit long, as they would be if the parting of the rope occurred, not by the breaking of the filaments, but by their slipping one over the other.

Sagr. In confirmation of this it may be remarked that ropes sometimes break not by a lengthwise pull but by excessive twisting. This, it seems to me, is a conclusive argument because tile threads bind one another so tightly that the compressing fibres do not permit those which are compressed to lengthen the spirals even that little bit by which it is necessary for them to lengthen in order to surround the rope which, on twisting, grows shorter and thicker.

[57]

Salv. You are quite right. Now see how one fact suggests another. The thread held between the fingers does not yield to one who wishes to draw it away even when pulled with considerable force, but resists because it is held back by a double compression, seeing that the upper finger presses against the lower as hard as the lower against the upper. Now, if we could retain only one of these pressures there is no doubt that only half the original resistance would remain; but since we are not able, by lifting, say, the upper finger, to remove one of these pressures without also removing the other, it becomes necessary to preserve one of them by means of a new device which causes the thread to press itself against the finger or against some other solid body upon which it rests; and thus it is brought about that the very force which pulls it in order to snatch it away compresses it more and more as the pull increases. This is accomplished by wrapping the thread around the solid in the manner of a spiral; and will be better understood by means of a figure. Let AB and CD be two cylinders between which is stretched the thread EF: and for the sake of greater clearness we will imagine it to be a small cord. If these two cylinders be pressed strongly together, the cord EF, when drawn by the end F, will undoubt-

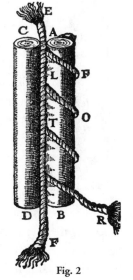

Fig. 2

edly stand a considerable pull before it slips between the two compressing solids. But if we remove one of these cylinders the cord, though remaining in contact with the other, will not thereby be prevented from slipping freely. On the other hand, if one holds the cord loosely against the top of the cylinder A, winds it in the spiral form AFLOTR, and then pulls it by the end R, it is evident that the cord will begin to bind the cylinder; the greater the number of spirals the more tightly will the cord be pressed against the cylinder by any given pull. Thus as the number of turns increases, the line

of contact becomes longer and in consequence more resistant; so that the cord slips and yields to the tractive force with increasing difficulty.

[58]

Is it not clear that this is precisely the kind of resistance which one meets in the case of a thick hemp rope where the fibres form thousands and thousands of similar spirals? And, indeed, the binding effect of these turns is so great that a few short rushes woven together into a few interlacing spirals form one of the strongest of ropes which I believe they call pack rope [*susta*].

Sagr. What you say has cleared up two points which I did not previously understand. One fact is how two, or at most three, turns of a rope around the axle of a windlass cannot only hold it fast, but can also prevent it from slipping when pulled by the immense force of the weight [*forza del peso*] which it sustains; and moreover how, by turning the windlass, this same axle, by mere friction of the rope around it, can wind up and lift huge stones while a mere boy is able to handle the slack of the rope. The other fact has to do with a simple but clever device, invented by a young kinsman of mine, for the purpose of descending from a window by means of a rope without lacerating the palms of his hands, as had happened to him shortly before and greatly to his discomfort. A small sketch will make this clear. He took a wooden cylinder, AB, about as thick as a walking stick and about one span long: on this he cut a spiral channel of about one turn and a half, and large enough to just receive the rope which he wished to use. Having introduced the rope at the end A and led it out again at the end B, he enclosed both the cylinder and the rope in a case of wood or tin, hinged along the side so that it could be easily opened and closed. After he had fastened the rope to a firm support above, he could, on grasping and squeezing the case with both hands, hang by his arms. The pressure on the rope, lying between the case and the cylinder, was such that he could, at will, either grasp the case more tightly and hold himself from slipping, or slacken his hold and descend as slowly as he wished.

Fig. 3

[59]

Salv. A truly ingenious device! I feel, however, that for a complete explanation other considerations might well enter; yet I must not now digress upon this particular topic since you are waiting to hear what I think about the breaking strength of other materials which, unlike ropes and most woods, do not show a filamentous structure.

The coherence of these bodies is, in my estimation, produced by other causes which may be grouped under two heads. One is that much-talked-of repugnance which nature exhibits towards a vacuum; but this horror of a vacuum not being sufficient, it is necessary to introduce another cause in the form of a gluey or viscous substance which binds firmly together the component parts of the body.

First I shall speak of the vacuum, demonstrating by definite experiment the quality and quantity of its force [*virtù*]. If you take two highly polished and smooth plates of marble, metal, or glass and place them face to face, one will slide over the other with the greatest ease, showing conclusively that there is nothing of a viscous nature between them. But when you attempt to separate them and keep them at a constant distance apart, you find the plates exhibit such a repugnance to separation that the upper one will carry the lower one with it and keep it lifted indefinitely, even when the latter is big and heavy.

This experiment shows the aversion of nature for empty space, even during the brief moment required for the outside air to rush in and fill up the region between the two plates. It is also observed that if two plates are not thoroughly polished, their contact is imperfect so that when you attempt to separate them slowly the only resistance offered is that of weight; if, however, the pull be sudden, then the lower plate rises, but quickly falls back, having followed the upper plate only for that very short interval of time required for the expansion of the small amount of air remaining between the plates, in consequence of their not fitting, and for the entrance of the surrounding air. This resistance which is exhibited between the two plates is doubtless likewise present between the parts of a solid, and enters, at least in part, as a concomitant cause of their coherence.

[60]

Sagr. Allow me to interrupt you for a moment, please; for I want to speak of something which just occurs to me, namely, when I see how the lower plate follows the upper one and how rapidly it is lifted, I feel sure that, contrary to the opinion of many philosophers, including perhaps even Aristotle himself, motion in a vacuum is not instantaneous. If this were so the two plates mentioned above would separate without any resistance whatever, seeing that the same instant of time would suffice for their separation and for the surrounding medium to rush in and fill the vacuum between them. The fact that the lower plate follows the upper one allows us to infer, not only that motion in a vacuum is not instantaneous, but also that, between the two plates, a vacuum really exists, at least for a very short time, sufficient to allow the surrounding medium to rush in and fill the vacuum; for if there were no vacuum there would be no need of any motion in the medium. One must admit then that a vacuum is sometimes

produced by violent motion [*violenza*] or contrary to the laws of nature, (although in my opinion nothing occurs contrary to nature except the impossible, and that never occurs).

But here another difficulty arises. While experiment convinces me of the correctness of this conclusion, my mind is not entirely satisfied as to the cause to which this effect is to be attributed. For the separation of the plates precedes the formation of the vacuum which is produced as a consequence of this separation; and since it appears to me that, in the order of nature, the cause must precede the effect, even though it appears to follow in point of time, and since every positive effect must have a positive cause, I do not see how the adhesion of two plates and their resistance to separation—actual facts—can be referred to a vacuum as cause when this vacuum is yet to follow. According to the infallible maxim of the Philosopher, the non-existent can produce no effect.

Simp. Seeing that you accept this axiom of Aristotle, I hardly think you will reject another excellent and reliable maxim of his, namely, Nature undertakes only that which happens without resistance; and in this saying, it appears to me, you will find the solution of your difficulty. Since nature abhors a vacuum, she prevents that from which a vacuum would follow as a necessary consequence. Thus it happens that nature prevents the separation of the two plates.

[61]

Sagr. Now admitting that what Simplicio says is an adequate solution of my difficulty, it seems to me, if I may be allowed to resume my former argument, that this very resistance to a vacuum ought to be sufficient to hold together the parts either of stone or of metal or the parts of any other solid which is knit together more strongly and which is more resistant to separation. If for one effect there be only one cause, or if, more being assigned, they can be reduced to one, then why is not this vacuum which really exists a sufficient cause for all kinds of resistance?

Salv. I do not wish just now to enter this discussion as to whether the vacuum alone is sufficient to hold together the separate parts of a solid body; but I assure you that the vacuum which acts as a sufficient cause in the case of the two plates is not alone sufficient to bind together the parts of a solid cylinder of marble or metal which, when pulled violently, separates and divides. And now if I find a method of distinguishing this well known resistance, depending upon the vacuum, from every other kind which might increase the coherence, and if I show you that the aforesaid resistance alone is not nearly sufficient for such an effect, will you not grant that we are bound to introduce another cause? Help him, Simplicio, since he does not know what reply to make.

Simp. Surely, Sagredo's hesitation must be owing to another reason, for there can be no doubt concerning a conclusion which is at once so clear and logical.

Sagr. You have guessed rightly, Simplicio. I was wondering whether, if a million of gold each year from Spain were not sufficient to pay the army, it might not be necessary to make provision other than small coin for the pay of the soldiers.[3]

But go ahead, Salviati; assume that I admit your conclusion and show us your method of separating the action of the vacuum from other causes; and by measuring it show us how it is not sufficient to produce the effect in question.

Salv. Your good angel assist you. I will tell you how to separate the force of the vacuum from the others, and afterwards how to measure it. For this purpose let us consider a continuous substance whose parts lack all resistance to separation except that derived from a vacuum, such as is the case with water, a fact fully demonstrated by our Academician in one of his treatises. Whenever a cylinder of water is subjected to a pull and

[62]

offers a resistance to the separation of its parts this can be attributed to no other cause than the resistance of the vacuum. In order to try such an experiment I have invented a device which I can better explain by means of a sketch than by mere words. Let CABD represent the cross section of a cylinder either of metal or, preferably, of glass, hollow inside and accurately turned. Into this is introduced a perfect fitting cylinder of wood, represented in cross section by EGHF, and capable of up-and-down motion. Through the middle of this cylinder is bored a hole to receive an iron wire, carrying a hook at the end K, while the upper end of the wire, I, is provided with a conical head. The wooden cylinder is countersunk at the top so as to receive, with a perfect fit, the conical head I of the wire, IK, when pulled down by the end K.

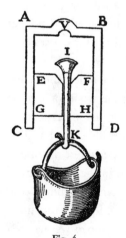

Fig. 4

Now insert the wooden cylinder EH in the hollow cylinder AD, so as not to touch the upper end of the latter but to leave free a space of two or three finger-breadths; this space is to be filled with water by holding the vessel with the mouth CD upwards, pushing down on the stopper EH, and at the same time keeping the conical head of the wire, I, away from the hollow portion of the wooden cylinder. The air is thus allowed to escape alongside the iron wire (which does not make a close fit) as soon as one presses down on the wooden stopper. The air having been allowed to escape and the iron wire having been drawn back so that it fits snugly against the conical depression in the wood,

3. The bearing of this remark becomes clear on reading what Salviati says below. [Trans.]

invert the vessel, bringing it mouth downwards, and hang on the hook K a vessel which can be filled with sand or any heavy material in quantity sufficient to finally separate the upper surface of the stopper, EF, from the lower surface of the water to which it was attached only by the resistance of the vacuum. Next weigh the stopper and wire together with the attached vessel and its contents; we shall then have the force of the vacuum [*forza del vacuo*].

[63]

If one attaches to a cylinder of marble or glass a weight which, together with the weight of the marble or glass itself, is just equal to the sum of the weights before mentioned, and if breaking occurs we shall then be justified in saying that the vacuum alone holds the parts of the marble and glass together; but if this weight does not suffice and if breaking occurs only after adding, say, four times this weight, we shall then be compelled to say that the vacuum furnishes only one fifth of the total resistance [*resistenza*].

Simp. No one can doubt the cleverness of the device; yet it presents many difficulties which make me doubt its reliability. For who will assure us that the air does not creep in between the glass and stopper even if it is well packed with tow or other yielding material? I question also whether oiling with wax or turpentine will suffice to make the cone, I, fit snugly on its seat. Besides, may not the parts of the water expand and dilate? Why may not the air or exhalations or some other more subtile substances penetrate the pores of the wood, or even of the glass itself?

Salv. With great skill indeed has Simplicio laid before us the difficulties; and he has even partly suggested how to prevent the air from penetrating the wood or passing between the wood and the glass. But now let me point out that, as our experience increases, we shall learn whether or not these alleged difficulties really exist. For if, as is the case with air, water is by nature expansible, although only under severe treatment, we shall see the stopper descend; and if we put a small excavation in the upper part of the glass vessel, such as indicated by V, then the air or any other tenuous and gaseous substance, which might penetrate the pores of glass or wood, would pass through the water and collect in this receptacle V. But if these things do not happen we may rest assured that our experiment has been performed with proper caution; and we shall discover that water does not dilate and that glass does not allow any material, however tenuous, to penetrate it.

Sagr. Thanks to this discussion, I have learned the cause of a certain effect which I have long wondered at and despaired of understanding. I once saw a cistern which had been provided with a pump under the mistaken impression that the water might thus be drawn with less effort or in greater quantity than by means of the ordinary bucket.

[64]

The stock of the pump carried its sucker and valve in the upper part so that the water was lifted by attraction and not by a push as is the case with pumps in which the sucker is placed lower down. This pump worked perfectly so long as the water in the cistern stood above a certain level; but below this level the pump failed to work. When I first noticed this phenomenon I thought the machine was out of order; but the workman whom I called in to repair it told me the defect was not in the pump but in the water which had fallen too low to be raised through such a height; and he added that it was not possible, either by a pump or by any other machine working on the principle of attraction, to lift water a hair's breadth above eighteen cubits; whether the pump be large or small this is the extreme limit of the lift. Up to this time I had been so thoughtless that, although I knew a rope, or rod of wood, or of iron, if sufficiently long, would break by its own weight when held by the upper end, it never occurred to me that the same thing would happen, only much more easily, to a column of water. And really is not that thing which is attracted in the pump a column of water attached at the upper end and stretched more and more until finally a point is reached where it breaks, like a rope, on account of its excessive weight?

Salv. That is precisely the way it works; this fixed elevation of eighteen cubits is true for any quantity of water whatever, be the pump large or small or even as fine as a straw. We may therefore say that, on weighing the water contained in a tube eighteen cubits long, no matter what the diameter, we shall obtain the value of the resistance of the vacuum in a cylinder of any solid material having a bore of this same diameter. And having gone so far, let us see how easy it is to find to what length cylinders of metal, stone, wood, glass, etc., of any diameter can be elongated without breaking by their own weight.

[65]

Take for instance a copper wire of any length and thickness; fix the upper end and to the other end attach a greater and greater load until finally the wire breaks; let the maximum load be, say, fifty pounds. Then it is clear that if fifty pounds of copper, in addition to the weight of the wire itself which maybe, say, 1/8 ounce, is drawn out into wire of this same size we shall have the greatest length of this kind of wire which can sustain its own weight. Suppose the wire which breaks to be one cubit in length and 1/8 ounce in weight; then since it supports 50 lbs. in addition to its own weight, i. e., 4800 eighths-of-an-ounce, it follows that all copper wires, independent of size, can sustain themselves up to a length of 4801 cubits and no more. Since then a copper rod can sustain its own weight up to a length of 4801 cubits it follows that that part of the

breaking strength [*resistenza*] which depends upon the vacuum, comparing it with the remaining factors of resistance, is equal to the weight of a rod of water, eighteen cubits long and as thick as the copper rod. If, for example, copper is nine times as heavy as water, the breaking strength [*resistenza allo strapparsi*] of any copper rod, in so far as it depends upon the vacuum, is equal to the weight of two cubits of this same rod. By a similar method one can find the maximum length of wire or rod of any material which will just sustain its own weight, and can at the same time discover the part which the vacuum plays in its breaking strength.

Sagr. It still remains for you to tell us upon what depends the resistance to breaking, other than that of the vacuum; what is the gluey or viscous substance which cements together the parts of the solid? For I cannot imagine a glue that will not burn up in a highly heated furnace in two or three months, or certainly within ten or a hundred. For if gold, silver and glass are kept for a long while in the molten state and are removed from the furnace, their parts, on cooling, immediately reunite and bind themselves together as before. Not only so, but whatever difficulty arises with respect to the cementation of the parts of the glass arises also with regard to the parts of the glue; in other words, what is that which holds these parts together so firmly?

[66]

Salv. A little while ago, I expressed the hope that your good angel might assist you. I now find myself in the same straits. Experiment leaves no doubt that the reason why two plates cannot be separated, except with violent effort, is that they are held together by the resistance of the vacuum; and the same can be said of two large pieces of a marble or bronze column. This being so, I do not see why this same cause may not explain the coherence of smaller parts and indeed of the very smallest particles of these materials. Now, since each effect must have one true and sufficient cause and since I find no other cement, am I not justified in trying to discover whether the vacuum is not a sufficient cause?

Simp. But seeing that you have already proved that the resistance which the large vacuum offers to the separation of two large parts of a solid is really very small in comparison with that cohesive force which binds together the most minute parts, why do you hesitate to regard this latter as something very different from the former?

Salv. Sagredo has already answered this question when he remarked that each individual soldier was being paid from coin collected by a general tax of pennies and farthings, while even a million of gold would not suffice to pay the entire army. And who knows but that there may be other extremely minute vacua which affect the smallest particles so that that which binds together the contiguous parts is throughout of the same mintage? Let me tell you something which has just occurred to me and which I do not

offer as an absolute fact, but rather as a passing thought, still immature and calling for more careful consideration. You may take of it what you like; and judge the rest as you see fit. Sometimes when I have observed how fire winds its way in between the most minute particles of this or that metal and, even though these are solidly cemented together, tears them apart and separates them, and when I have observed that, on removing the fire, these particles reunite with the same tenacity as at first, without any loss of quantity in the case of gold and with little loss in the case of other metals, even though these parts have been separated for a long while, I have thought that the explanation might lie in the fact that the extremely fine particles of fire, penetrating the slender pores of the metal (too small to admit even the finest particles of air or of many other fluids), would fill the small intervening vacua and would set free these small particles from the attraction which these same vacua exert upon them and which prevents their separation.

[67]

Thus the particles are able to move freely so that the mass [*massa*] becomes fluid and remains so as long as the particles of fire remain inside; but if they depart and leave the former vacua then the original attraction [*attrazzione*] returns and the parts are again cemented together.

In reply to the question raised by Simplicio, one may say that although each particular vacuum is exceedingly minute and therefore easily overcome, yet their number is so extraordinarily great that their combined resistance is, so to speak, multiplied almost without limit. The nature and the amount of force [*forza*] which results [*risulta*] from adding together an immense number of small forces [*debolissimi momenti*] is clearly illustrated by the fact that a weight of millions of pounds, suspended by great cables, is overcome and lifted, when the south wind carries innumerable atoms of water, suspended in thin mist, which moving through the air penetrate between the fibres of the tense ropes in spite of the tremendous force of the hanging weight. When these particles enter the narrow pores they swell the ropes, thereby shorten them, and perforce lift the heavy mass [*mole*].

Sagr. There can be no doubt that any resistance, so long as it is not infinite, may be overcome by a multitude of minute forces. Thus a vast number of ants might carry ashore a ship laden with grain. And since experience shows us daily that one ant can easily carry one grain, it is clear that the number of grains in the ship is not infinite, but falls below a certain limit. If you take another number four or six times as great, and if you set to work a corresponding number of ants they will carry the grain ashore and the boat also. It is true that this will call for a prodigious number of ants, but in my opinion this is precisely the case with the vacua which bind together the least particles of a metal.

Salv. But even if this demanded an infinite number would you still think it impossible?
Sagr. Not if the mass [*mole*] of metal were infinite; otherwise. . .

[68]

Salv. Otherwise what? Now since we have arrived at paradoxes let us see if we cannot prove that within a finite extent it is possible to discover an infinite number of vacua. At the same time we shall at least reach a solution of the most remarkable of all that list of problems which Aristotle himself calls wonderful; I refer to his *Questions in*

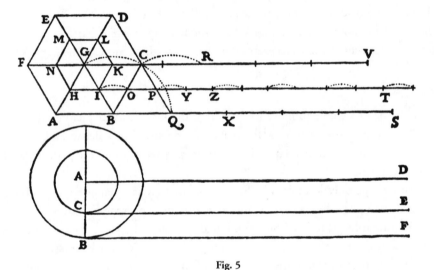

Fig. 5

Mechanics. This solution may be no less clear and conclusive than that which he himself gives and quite different also from that so cleverly expounded by the most learned Monsignor di Guevara.[4]

First it is necessary to consider a proposition, not treated by others, but upon which depends the solution of the problem and from which, if I mistake not, we shall derive other new and remarkable facts. For the sake of clearness let us draw an accurate figure. About G as a center describe an equiangular and equilateral polygon of any number of sides, say the hexagon ABCDEF. Similar to this and concentric with it, describe another smaller one which we shall call HIKLMN. Prolong the side AB, of the larger hexagon, indefinitely toward S; in like manner prolong the corresponding side HI of the smaller hexagon, in the same direction, so that the line HT is parallel to AS; and through the center draw the line GV parallel to the other two.

4. Bishop of Teano; b. 1561, d. 1641. *[Trans.]*

[69]

This done, imagine the larger polygon to roll upon the line AS, carrying with it the smaller polygon. It is evident that, if the point B, the end of the side AB remains fixed at the beginning of the rotation, the point A will rise and the point C will fall describing the arc CQ until the side BC coincides with the line BQ, equal to BC. But during this rotation the point I, on the smaller polygon, will rise above the line IT because IB is oblique to AS; and it will not again return to the line IT until the point C shall have reached the position Q. The point I, having described the arc IO above the line HT, will reach the position O at the same time the side IK assumes the position OP; but in the meantime the center G has traversed a path above GV and does not return to it until it has completed the arc GC. This step having been taken, the larger polygon has been brought to rest with its side BC coinciding with the line BQ while the side IK of the smaller polygon has been made to coincide with the line OP, having passed over the portion IO without touching it; also the center G will have reached the position C after having traversed all its course above the parallel line GV. And finally the entire figure will assume a position similar to the first, so that if we continue the rotation and come to the next step, the side DC of the larger polygon will coincide with the portion QX and the side KL of the smaller polygon, having first skipped the arc PY, will fall on YZ, while the center still keeping above the line GV will return to it at R after having jumped the interval CR. At the end of one complete rotation the larger polygon will have traced upon the line AS, without break, six lines together equal to its perimeter; the lesser polygon will likewise have imprinted six lines equal to its perimeter, but separated by the interposition of five arcs, whose chords represent the parts of HT not touched by the polygon: the center G never reaches the line GV except at six points. From this it is clear that the space traversed by the smaller polygon is almost equal to that traversed by the larger, that is, the line HT approximates the line AS, differing from it only by the length of one chord of one of these arcs, provided we understand the line HT to include the five skipped arcs.

[70]

Now this exposition which I have given in the case of these hexagons must be understood to be applicable to all other polygons, whatever the number of sides, provided only they are similar, concentric, and rigidly connected, so that when the greater one rotates the lesser will also turn however small it may be. You must also understand that the lines described by these two are nearly equal provided we include in the space traversed by the smaller one the intervals which are not touched by any part of the perimeter of this smaller polygon.

Let a large polygon of, say, one thousand sides make one complete rotation and thus lay off a line equal to its perimeter; at the same time the small one will pass over an approximately equal distance, made up of a thousand small portions each equal to one of its sides, but interrupted by a thousand spaces which, in contrast with the portions that coincide with the sides of the polygon, we may call empty. So far the matter is free from difficulty or doubt.

But now suppose that about any center, say A, we describe two concentric and rigidly connected circles; and suppose that from the points C and B, on their radii, there are drawn the tangents CE and BF and that through the center A the line AD is drawn parallel to them, then if the large circle makes one complete rotation along the line BF, equal not only to its circumference but also to the other two lines CE and AD, tell me what the smaller circle will do and also what the center will do. As to the center it will certainly traverse and touch the entire line AD while the circumference of the smaller circle will have measured off by its points of contact the entire line CE, just as was done by the above mentioned polygons. The only difference is that the line HT was not at every point in contact with the perimeter of the smaller polygon, but there were left untouched as many vacant spaces as there were spaces coinciding with the sides. But herein the case of the circles the circumference of the smaller one never leaves the line CE, so that no part of the latter is left untouched, nor is there ever a time when some point on the circle is not in contact with the straight line. How now can the smaller circle traverse a length greater than its circumference unless it go by jumps?

Sagr. It seems to me that one may say that just as the center of the circle, by itself, carried along the line AD is constantly in contact with it, although it is only a single point, so the points on the circumference of the smaller circle, carried along by the motion of the larger circle, would slide over some small parts of the line CE.

[71]

Salv. There are two reasons why this cannot happen. First because there is no ground for thinking that one point of contact, such as that at C, rather than another, should slip over certain portions of the line CE. But if such slidings along CE did occur they would be infinite in number since the points of contact (being mere points) are infinite in number: an infinite number of finite slips will however make an infinitely long line, while as a matter of fact the line CE is finite. The other reason is that as the greater circle, in its rotation, changes its point of contact continuously the lesser circle must do the same because B is the only point from which a straight line can be drawn to A and pass through C. Accordingly the small circle must change its point of contact whenever the large one changes: no point of the small circle touches the straight line CE in more than one point. Not only so, but even in the rotation of the polygons there

was no point on the perimeter of the smaller which coincided with more than one point on the line traversed by that perimeter; this is at once clear when you remember that the line IK is parallel to BC and that therefore IK will remain above IP until BC coincides with BQ, and that IK will not lie upon IP except at the very instant when BC occupies the position BQ; at this instant the entire line IK coincides with OP and immediately afterwards rises above it.

Sagr. This is a very intricate matter. I see no solution. Pray explain it to us.

Salv. Let us return to the consideration of the above mentioned polygons whose behavior we already understand. Now in the case of polygons with 100000 sides, the line traversed by the perimeter of the greater, i. e., the line laid down by its 100000 sides one after another, is equal to the line traced out by the 100000 sides of the smaller, provided we include the 100000 vacant spaces interspersed. So in the case of the circles, polygons having an infinitude of sides, the line traversed by the continuously distributed [*continuamente disposti*] infinitude of sides is in the greater circle equal to the line laid down by the infinitude of sides in the smaller circle but with the exception that these latter alternate with empty spaces; and since the sides are not finite in number, but infinite, so also are the intervening empty spaces not finite but infinite.

[72]

The line traversed by the larger circle consists then of an infinite number of points which completely fill it; while that which is traced by the smaller circle consists of an infinite number of points which leave empty spaces and only partly fill the line. And here I wish you to observe that after dividing and resolving a line into a finite number of parts, that is, into a number which can be counted, it is not possible to arrange them again into a greater length than that which they occupied when they formed a *continuum* [*continuate*] and were connected without the interposition of as many empty spaces. But if we consider the line resolved into an infinite number of infinitely small and indivisible parts, we shall be able to conceive the line extended indefinitely by the interposition, not of a finite, but of an infinite number of infinitely small indivisible empty spaces.

Now this which has been said concerning simple lines must be understood to hold also in the case of surfaces and solid bodies, it being assumed that they are made up of an infinite, not a finite, number of atoms. Such a body once divided into a finite number of parts cannot be reassembled so as to occupy more space than before unless we interpose a finite number of empty spaces, that is to say, spaces free from the substance of which the solid is made. But if we imagine the body, by some extreme and final analysis, resolved into its primary elements, infinite in number, then we shall be able to think of them as indefinitely extended in space, not by the interposition of a finite,

but of an infinite number of empty spaces. Thus one can easily imagine a small ball of gold expanded into a very large space without the introduction of a finite number of empty spaces, always provided the gold is made up of an infinite number of indivisible parts.

Simp. It seems to me that you are travelling along toward those vacua advocated by a certain ancient philosopher.

Salv. But you have failed to add, "who denied Divine Providence," an inapt remark made on a similar occasion by a certain antagonist of our Academician.

Simp. I noticed, and not without indignation, the rancor of this ill-natured opponent; further references to these affairs I omit, not only as a matter of good form, but also because I know how unpleasant they are to the good tempered and well ordered mind of one so religious and pious, so orthodox and God-fearing as you.

But to return to our subject, your previous discourse leaves with me many difficulties which I am unable to solve. First among these is that, if the circumferences of the two circles are equal to the two straight lines, CE and BF, the latter considered as a *continuum*, the former as interrupted with an infinity of empty points, I do not see how it is possible to say that the line AD described by the center, and made up of an infinity of points, is equal to this center which is a single point. Besides, this building up of lines out of points, divisibles out of indivisibles, and finites out of infinites, offers me an obstacle difficult to avoid; and the necessity of introducing a vacuum, so conclusively refuted by Aristotle, presents the same difficulty.

[73]

Salv. These difficulties are real; and they are not the only ones. But let us remember that we are dealing with infinities and indivisibles, both of which transcend our finite understanding, the former on account of their magnitude, the latter because of their smallness. In spite of this, men cannot refrain from discussing them, even though it must be done in a roundabout way.

Therefore I also should like to take the liberty to present some of my ideas which, though not necessarily convincing, would, on account of their novelty, at least, prove somewhat startling. But such a diversion might perhaps carry us too far away from the subject under discussion and might therefore appear to you inopportune and not very pleasing.

Sagr. Pray let us enjoy the advantages and privileges which come from conversation between friends, especially upon subjects freely chosen and not forced upon us, a matter vastly different from dealing with dead books which give rise to many doubts but remove none. Share with us, therefore, the thoughts which our discussion has suggested to you; for since we are free from urgent business there will be abundant time

to pursue the topics already mentioned; and in particular the objections raised by Simplicio ought not in anywise to be neglected.

Salv. Granted, since you so desire. The first question was, How can a single point be equal to a line? Since I cannot do more at present I shall attempt to remove, or at least diminish, one improbability by introducing a similar or a greater one, just as sometimes a wonder is diminished by a miracle.[5]

And this I shall do by showing you two equal surfaces, together with two equal solids located upon these same surfaces as bases, all four of which diminish continuously and uniformly in such a way that their remainders always preserve equality among themselves, and finally both the surfaces and the solids terminate their previous constant equality by degenerating, the one solid and the one surface into a very long line, the other solid and the other surface into a single point; that is, the latter to one point, the former to an infinite number of points.

[74]

Sagr. This proposition appears to me wonderful, indeed; but let us hear the explanation and demonstration.

Salv. Since the proof is purely geometrical we shall need a figure. Let AFB be a semicircle with center at C; about it describe the rectangle ADEB and from the center draw the straight lines CD and CE to the points D and E. Imagine the radius CF to be drawn perpendicular to either of the lines AB or DE, and the entire figure to rotate

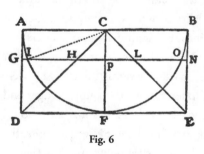

Fig. 6

about this radius as an axis. It is clear that the rectangle ADEB will thus describe a cylinder, the semicircle AFB a hemisphere, and the triangle CDE, a cone. Next let us remove the hemisphere but leave the cone and the rest of the cylinder, which, on account of its shape, we will call a "bowl." First we shall prove that the bowl and the cone are equal; then we shall show that a plane drawn parallel to the circle which forms

the base of the bowl and which has the line DE for diameter and F for a center—a plane whose trace is GN—cuts the bowl in the points G, I, O, N, and the cone in the points H, L, so that the part of the cone indicated by CHL is always equal to the part of the bowl whose profile is represented by the triangles GAI and BON. Besides this we shall prove that the base of the cone, i. e., the circle whose diameter is HL, is equal to the circular surface which forms the base of this portion of the bowl, or as one might say, equal to a ribbon whose width is GI. (Note by the way the nature of mathematical

definitions which consist merely in the imposition of names or, if you prefer, abbreviations of speech established and introduced in order to avoid the tedious drudgery which you and I now experience simply because we have not agreed to call this surface a "circular band" and that sharp solid portion of the bowl a "round razor.")

[75]

Now call them by what name you please, it suffices to understand that the plane, drawn at any height whatever, so long as it is parallel to the base, i. e., to the circle whose diameter is DE, always cuts the two solids so that the portion CHL of the cone is equal to the upper portion of the bowl; likewise the two areas which are the bases of these solids, namely the band and the circle HL, are also equal. Here we have the miracle mentioned above; as the cutting plane approaches the line AB the portions of the solids cut off are always equal, so also the areas of their bases. And as the cutting plane comes near the top, the two solids (always equal) as well as their bases (areas which are also equal) finally vanish, one pair of them degenerating into the circumference of a circle, the other into a single point, namely, the upper edge of the bowl and the apex of the cone. Now, since as these solids diminish equality is maintained between them up to the very last, we are justified in saying that, at the extreme and final end of this diminution, they are still equal and that one is not infinitely greater than the other. It appears therefore that we may equate the circumference of a large circle to a single point. And this which is true of the solids is true also of the surfaces which form their bases; for these also preserve equality between themselves throughout their diminution and in the end vanish, the one into the circumference of a circle, the other into a single point. Shall we not then call them equal seeing that they are the last traces and remnants of equal magnitudes? Note also that, even if these vessels were large enough to contain immense celestial hemispheres, both their upper edges and the apexes of the cones therein contained would always remain equal and would vanish, the former into circles having the dimensions of the largest celestial orbits, the latter into single points. Hence in conformity with the preceding we may say that all circumferences of circles, however different, are equal to each other, and are each equal to a single point.

Sagr. This presentation strikes me as so clever and novel that, even if I were able, I would not be willing to oppose it; for to deface so beautiful a structure by a blunt pedantic attack would be nothing short of sinful. But for our complete satisfaction pray give us this geometrical proof that there is always equality between these solids and between their bases; for it cannot, I think, fail to be very ingenious, seeing how subtle is the philosophical argument based upon this result.

[76]

Salv. The demonstration is both short and easy. Referring to the preceding figure, since IPC is a right angle the square of the radius IC is equal to the sum of the squares on the two sides IP, PC; but the radius IC is equal to AC and also to GP, while CP is equal to PH. Hence the square of the line GP is equal to the sum of the squares of IP and PH, or multiplying through by 4, we have the square of the diameter GN equal to the sum of the squares on IO and HL. And, since the areas of circles are to each other as the squares of their diameters, it follows that the area of the circle whose diameter is GN is equal to the sum of the areas of circles having diameters IO and HL, so that if we remove the common area of the circle having IO for diameter the remaining area of the circle GN will be equal to the area of the circle whose diameter is HL. So much for the first part. As for the other part, we leave its demonstration for the present, partly because those who wish to follow it will find it in the twelfth proposition of the second book of *De centro gravitatis solidorum* by the Archimedes of our age, Luca Valerio,[6] who made use of it for a different object, and partly because, for our purpose, it suffices to have seen that the above-mentioned surfaces are always equal and that, as they keep on diminishing uniformly, they degenerate, the one into a single point, the other into the circumference of a circle larger than any assignable; in this fact lies our miracle.[7]

Sagr. The demonstration is ingenious and the inferences drawn from it are remarkable. And now let us hear something concerning the other difficulty raised by Simplicio, if you have anything special to say, which, however, seems to me hardly possible, since the matter has already been so thoroughly discussed.

[77]

Salv. But I do have something special to say, and will first of all repeat what I said a little while ago, namely, that infinity and indivisibility are in their very nature incomprehensible to us; imagine then what they are when combined. Yet if we wish to build up a line out of indivisible points, we must take an infinite number of them, and are, therefore, bound to understand both the infinite and the indivisible at the same time. Many ideas have passed through my mind concerning this subject, some of which, possibly the more important, I may not be able to recall on the spur of the moment; but in the course of our discussion it may happen that I shall awaken in you, and especially in Simplicio, objections and difficulties which in turn will bring to memory that which, without such stimulus, would have lain dormant in my mind. Allow me therefore the customary liberty of introducing some of our human fancies, for indeed we

6. Distinguished Italian mathematician; born at Ferrara about 1552; admitted to the Accademia dei Lincei 1612; died 1618. *[Trans.]*
7. *Cf.* above. *[Trans.]*

may so call them in comparison with supernatural truth which furnishes the one true and safe recourse for decision in our discussions and which is an infallible guide in the dark and dubious paths of thought.

One of the main objections urged against this building up of continuous quantities out of indivisible quantities [*continuo d' indivisibili*] is that the addition of one indivisible to another cannot produce a divisible, for if this were so it would render the indivisible divisible. Thus if two indivisibles, say two points, can be united to form a quantity, say a divisible line, then an even more divisible line might be formed by the union of three, five, seven, or any other odd number of points. Since however these lines can be cut into two equal parts, it becomes possible to cut the indivisible which lies exactly in the middle of the line. In answer to this and other objections of the same type we reply that a divisible magnitude cannot be constructed out of two or ten or a hundred or a thousand indivisibles, but requires an infinite number of them.

Simp. Here a difficulty presents itself which appears to me insoluble. Since it is clear that we may have one line greater than another, each containing an infinite number of points, we are forced to admit that, within one and the same class, we may have something greater than infinity, because the infinity of points in the long line is greater than the infinity of points in the short line. This assigning to an infinite quantity a value greater than infinity is quite beyond my comprehension.

[78]

Salv. This is one of the difficulties which arise when we attempt, with our finite minds, to discuss the infinite, assigning to it those properties which we give to the finite and limited; but this I think is wrong, for we cannot speak of infinite quantities as being the one greater or less than or equal to another. To prove this I have in mind an argument which, for the sake of clearness, I shall put in the form of questions to Simplicio who raised this difficulty.

I take it for granted that you know which of the numbers are squares and which are not.

Simp. I am quite aware that a squared number is one which results from the multiplication of another number by itself; thus 4, 9, etc., are squared numbers which come from multiplying 2, 3, etc., by themselves.

Salv. Very well; and you also know that just as the products are called squares so the factors are called sides or roots; while on the other hand those numbers which do not consist of two equal factors are not squares. Therefore if I assert that all numbers, including both squares and non-squares, are more than the squares alone, I shall speak the truth, shall I not?

Simp. Most certainly.

Salv. If I should ask further how many squares there are one might reply truly that there are as many as the corresponding number of roots, since every square has its own root and every root its own square while no square has more than one root and no root more than one square.

Simp. Precisely so.

Salv. But if I inquire how many roots there are, it cannot be denied that there are as many as there are numbers because every number is a root of some square. This being granted we must say that there are as many squares as there are numbers because they are just as numerous as their roots, and all the numbers are roots. Yet at the outset we said there are many more numbers than squares, since the larger portion of them are not squares. Not only so, but the proportionate number of squares diminishes as we pass to larger numbers. Thus up to 100 we have 10 squares, that is, the squares constitute 1/10 part of all the numbers; up to 10000, we find only 1/100 part to be squares; and up to a million only 1/1000 part; on the other hand in an infinite number, if one could conceive of such a thing, he would be forced to admit that there are as many squares as there are numbers all taken together.

[79]

Sagr. What then must one conclude under these circumstances?

Salv. So far as I see we can only infer that the totality of all numbers is infinite, that the number of squares is infinite, and that the number of their roots is infinite; neither is the number of squares less than the totality of all numbers, nor the latter greater than the former; and finally the attributes "equal," "greater," and "less," are not applicable to infinite, but only to finite, quantities. When therefore Simplicio introduces several lines of different lengths and asks me how it is possible that the longer ones do not contain more points than the shorter, I answer him that one line does not contain more or less or just as many points as another, but that each line contains an infinite number. Or if I had replied to him that the points in one line were equal in number to the squares; in another, greater than the totality of numbers; and in the little one, as many as the number of cubes, might I not, indeed, have satisfied him by thus placing more points in one line than in another and yet maintaining an infinite number in each? So much for the first difficulty.

Sagr. Pray stop a moment and let me add to what has already been said an idea which just occurs to me. If the preceding be true, it seems to me impossible to say either that one infinite number is greater than another or even that it is greater than a finite number, because if the infinite number were greater than, say, a million it would follow that on passing from the million to higher and higher numbers we would be approaching the infinite; but this is not so; on the contrary, the larger the number to

which we pass, the more we recede from [this property of] infinity, because the greater the numbers the fewer [relatively] are the squares contained in them; but the squares in infinity cannot be less than the totality of all the numbers, as we have just agreed; hence the approach to greater and greater numbers means a departure from infinity.[8]

[80]

Salv. And thus from your ingenious argument we are led to conclude that the attributes "larger," "smaller," and "equal" have no place either in comparing infinite quantities with each other or in comparing infinite with finite quantities.

I pass now to another consideration. Since lines and all continuous quantities are divisible into parts which are themselves divisible without end, I do not see how it is possible to avoid the conclusion that these lines are built up of an infinite number of indivisible quantities because a division and a subdivision which can be carried on indefinitely presupposes that the parts are infinite in number, otherwise the subdivision would reach an end; and if the parts are infinite in number, we must conclude that they are not finite in size, because an infinite number of finite quantities would give an infinite magnitude. And thus we have a continuous quantity built up of an infinite number of indivisibles.

Simp. But if we ran carry on indefinitely the division into finite parts what necessity is there then for the introduction of non-finite parts?

Salv. The very fact that one is able to continue, without end, the division into finite parts [in parti quante] makes it necessary to regard the quantity as composed of an infinite number of immeasurably small elements [di infiniti non quanti]. Now in order to settle this matter I shall ask you to tell me whether, in your opinion, a continuum is made up of a finite or of an infinite number of finite parts [parti quante].

Simp. My answer is that their number is both infinite and finite; potentially infinite but actually finite [infinite, in potenza; e finite, in atto]; that is to say, potentially infinite before division and actually finite after division; because parts cannot be said to exist in a body which is not yet divided or at least marked out; if this is not done we say that they exist potentially.

Salv. So that a line which is, for instance, twenty spans long is not said to contain actually twenty lines each one span in length except after division into twenty equal parts; before division it is said to contain them only potentially. Suppose the facts are as you say; tell me then whether, when the division is once made, the size of the original quantity is thereby increased, diminished, or unaffected.

Simp. It neither increases nor diminishes.

---

8. A certain confusion of thought appears to be introduced here through a failure to distinguish between the *number n* and the *class* of the first *n* numbers; and likewise from a failure to distinguish infinity as a number from infinity as the class of all numbers. *[Trans.]*

Salv. That is my opinion also. Therefore the finite parts [*parti quante*] in a *continuum*, whether actually or potentially present, do not make the quantity either larger or smaller; but it is perfectly clear that, if the number of finite parts actually contained in the whole is infinite in number, they will make the magnitude infinite. Hence the number of finite parts, although existing only potentially, cannot be infinite unless the magnitude containing them be infinite; and conversely if the magnitude is finite it cannot contain an infinite number of finite parts either actually or potentially.

[81]

Sagr. How then is it possible to divide a *continuum* without limit into parts which are themselves always capable of subdivision?

Salv. This distinction of yours between actual and potential appears to render easy by one method what would be impossible by another. But I shall endeavor to reconcile these matters in another way; and as to the query whether the finite parts of a limited *continuum* [*continuo terminato*] are finite or infinite in number I will, contrary to the opinion of Simplicio, answer that they are neither finite nor infinite.

Simp. This answer would never have occurred to me since I did not think that there existed any intermediate step between the finite and the infinite, so that the classification or distinction which assumes that a thing must be either finite or infinite is faulty and defective.

Salv. So it seems to me. And if we consider discrete quantities I think there is, between finite and infinite quantities, a third intermediate term which corresponds to every assigned number; so that if asked, as in the present case, whether the finite parts of a *continuum* are finite or infinite in number the best reply is that they are neither finite nor infinite but correspond to every assigned number. In order that this may be possible, it is necessary that those parts should not be included within a limited number, for in that case they would not correspond to a number which is greater; nor can they be infinite in number since no assigned number is infinite; and thus at the pleasure of the questioner we may, to any given line, assign a hundred finite parts, a thousand, a hundred thousand, or indeed any number we may please so long as it be not infinite. I grant, therefore, to the philosophers, that the *continuum* contains as many finite parts as they please and I concede also that it contains them, either actually or potentially, as they may like; but I must add that just as a line ten fathoms [*canne*] in length contains ten lines each of one fathom and forty lines each of one cubit [*braccia*] and eighty lines each of half a cubit, etc., so it contains an infinite number of points; call them actual or potential, as you like, for as to this detail, Simplicio, I defer to your opinion and to your judgment.

[82]

Simp. I cannot help admiring your discussion; but I fear that this parallelism between the points and the finite parts contained in a line will not prove satisfactory, and that you will not find it so easy to divide a given line into an infinite number of points as the philosophers do to cut it into ten fathoms or forty cubits; not only so, but such a division is quite impossible to realize in practice, so that this will be one of those potentialities which cannot be reduced to actuality.

Salv. The fact that something can be done only with effort or diligence or with great expenditure of time does not render it impossible; for I think that you yourself could not easily divide a line into a thousand parts, and much less if the number of parts were 937 or any other large prime number. But if I were to accomplish this division which you deem impossible as readily as another person would divide the line into forty parts would you then be more willing, in our discussion, to concede the possibility of such a division?

Simp. In general I enjoy greatly your method; and replying to your query, I answer that it would be more than sufficient if it prove not more difficult to resolve a line into points than to divide it into a thousand parts.

Salv. I will now say something which may perhaps astonish you; it refers to the possibility of dividing a line into its infinitely small elements by following the same order which one employs in dividing the same line into forty, sixty, or a hundred parts, that is, by dividing it into two, four, etc. He who thinks that, by following this method, he can reach an infinite number of points is greatly mistaken; for if this process were followed to eternity there would still remain finite parts which were undivided.

Indeed by such a method one is very far from reaching the goal of indivisibility; on the contrary he recedes from it and while he thinks that, by continuing this division and by multiplying the multitude of parts, he will approach infinity, he is, in my opinion, getting farther and farther away from it. My reason is this. In the preceding discussion we concluded that, in an infinite number, it is necessary that the squares and cubes should be as numerous as the totality of the natural numbers [*tutti i numeri*], because both of these are as numerous as their roots which constitute the totality of the natural numbers. Next we saw that the larger the numbers taken the more sparsely distributed were the squares, and still more sparsely the cubes; therefore it is clear that the larger the numbers to which we pass the farther we recede from the infinite number; hence it follows that, since this process carries us farther and farther from the end sought, if on turning back we shall find that any number can be said to be infinite, it must be unity. Here indeed are satisfied all those conditions which are requisite for an infinite number; I mean that unity contains in itself as many squares as there are cubes and natural numbers [*tutti i numeri*].

[83]

Simp. I do not quite grasp the meaning of this.

Salv. There is no difficulty in the matter because unity is at once a square, a cube, a square of a square and all the other powers [*dignità*]; nor is there any essential peculiarity in squares or cubes which does not belong to unity; as, for example, the property of two square numbers that they have between them a mean proportional; take any square number you please as the first term and unity for the other, then you will always find a number which is a mean proportional. Consider the two square numbers, 9 and 4; then 3 is the mean proportional between 9 and 1; while 2 is a mean proportional between 4 and 1; between 9 and 4 we have 6 as a mean proportional. A property of cubes is that they must have between them two mean proportional numbers; take 8 and 27; between them lie 12 and 18; while between 1 and 8 we have 2 and 4 intervening; and

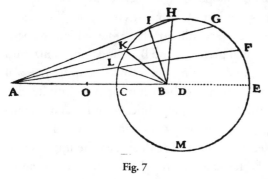

Fig. 7

between 1 and 27 there lie 3 and 9. Therefore we conclude that unity is the only infinite number. These are some of the marvels which our imagination cannot grasp and which should warn us against the serious error of those who attempt to discuss the infinite by assigning to it the same properties which we employ for the finite, the natures of the two having nothing in common.

With regard to this subject I must tell you of a remarkable property which just now occurs to me and which will explain the vast alteration and change of character which a finite quantity would undergo in passing to infinity. Let us draw the straight line AB of arbitrary length and let the point C divide it into two unequal parts; then I say that, if pairs of lines be drawn, one from each of the terminal points A and B, and if the ratio between the lengths of these lines is the same as that between AC and CB, their points of intersection will all lie upon the circumference of one and the same circle.

[84]

Thus, for example, AL and BL drawn from A and B, meeting at the point L, bearing to one another the same ratio as AC to BC, and the pair AK and BK meeting at K also bearing to one another the same ratio, and likewise the pairs AI, BI, AH, BH, AG, BG, AF, BF, AE, BE, have their points of intersection L, K, I, H, G, F, E, all lying upon the circumference of one and the same circle. Accordingly if we imagine the point C to

move continuously in such a manner that the lines drawn from it to the fixed terminal points, A and B, always maintain the same ratio between their lengths as exists between the original parts, AC and CB, then the point C will, as I shall presently prove, describe a circle. And the circle thus described will increase in size without limit as the point C approaches the middle point which we may call O; but it will diminish in size as C approaches the end B. So that the infinite number of points located in the line OB will, if the motion be as explained above, describe circles of every size, some smaller than the pupil of the eye of a flea, others larger than the celestial equator. Now if we move any of the points lying between the two ends O and B they will all describe circles, those nearest O, immense circles; but if we move the point O itself, and continue to move it according to the aforesaid law, namely, that the lines drawn from O to the terminal points, A and B, maintain the same ratio as the original lines AO and OB, what kind of a line will be produced? A circle will be drawn larger than the largest of the others, a circle which is therefore infinite, But from the point O a straight line will also be drawn perpendicular to BA and extending to infinity without ever turning, as did the others, to join its last end with its first; for the point C, with its limited motion, having described the upper semicircle, CHE, proceeds to describe the lower semicircle EMC, thus returning to the starting point.

[85]

But the point O having started to describe its circle, as did all the other points in the line AB, (for the points in the other portion OA describe their circles also, the largest being those nearest the point O) is unable to return to its starting point because the circle it describes, being the largest of all, is infinite; in fact, it describes an infinite straight line as circumference of its infinite circle. Think now what a difference there is between a finite and an infinite circle since the latter changes character in such a manner that it loses not only its existence but also its possibility of existence; indeed, we already clearly understand that there can be no such thing as an infinite circle; similarly there can be no infinite sphere, no infinite body, and no infinite surface of any shape. Now what shall we say concerning this metamorphosis in the transition from finite to infinite? And why should we feel greater repugnance, seeing that, in our search after the infinite among numbers we found it in unity? Having broken up a solid into many parts, having reduced it to the finest of powder and having resolved it into its infinitely small indivisible atoms why may we not say that this solid has been reduced to a single *continuum* [*un solo continuo*] perhaps a fluid like water or mercury or even a liquified metal? And do we not see stones melt into glass and the glass itself under strong heat become more fluid than water?

Sagr. Are we then to believe that substances become fluid in virtue of being resolved into their infinitely small indivisible components?

Salv. I am not able to find any better means of accounting for certain phenomena of which the following is one. When I take a hard substance such as stone or metal and when I reduce it by means of a hammer or fine file to the most minute and impalpable powder, it is clear that its finest particles, although when taken one by one are, on account of their smallness, imperceptible to our sight and touch, are nevertheless finite in size, possess shape, and capability of being counted. It is also true that when once heaped up they remain in a heap; and if an excavation be made within limits the cavity will remain and the surrounding particles will not rush in to fill it; if shaken the particles come to rest immediately after the external disturbing agent is removed; the same effects are observed in all piles of larger and larger particles, of any shape, even if spherical, as is the case with piles of millet, wheat, lead shot, and every other material.

[86]

But if we attempt to discover such properties in water we do not find them; for when once heaped up it immediately flattens out unless held up by some vessel or other external retaining body; when hollowed out it quickly rushes in to fill the cavity; and when disturbed it fluctuates for a long time and sends out its waves through great distances.

Seeing that water has less firmness [*consistenza*] than the finest of powder, in fact has no consistence whatever, we may, it seems to me, very reasonably conclude that the smallest particles into which it can be resolved are quite different from finite and divisible particles; indeed the only difference I am able to discover is that the former are indivisible. The exquisite transparency of water also favors this view; for the most transparent crystal when broken and ground and reduced to powder loses its transparency; the finer the grinding the greater the loss; but in the case of water where the attrition is of the highest degree we have extreme transparency. Gold and silver when pulverized with acids [*acque forti*] more finely than is possible with any file still remain powders,[9] and do not become fluids until the finest particles [*gl' indivisibili*] of fire or of the rays of the sun dissolve them, as I think, into their ultimate, indivisible, and infinitely small components.

Sagr. This phenomenon of light which you mention is one which I have many times remarked with astonishment. I have, for instance, seen lead melted instantly by means of a concave mirror only three hands [*palmi*] in diameter. Hence I think that if the mirror were very large, well-polished and of a parabolic figure, it would just as readily and quickly melt any other metal, seeing that the small mirror, which was not well

9. It is not clear what Galileo here means by saying that gold and silver when treated with acids still remain powders. [*Trans.*]

429

polished and had only a spherical shape, was able so energetically to melt lead and burn every combustible substance. Such effects as these render credible to me the marvels accomplished by the mirrors of Archimedes.

[87]

Salv. Speaking of the effects produced by the mirrors of Archimedes, it was his own books (which I had already read and studied with infinite astonishment) that rendered credible to me all the miracles described by various writers. And if any doubt had remained the book which Father Buonaventura Cavalieri[10] has recently published on the subject of the burning glass [*specchio ustorio*] and which I have read with admiration would have removed the last difficulty.

Sagr. I also have seen this treatise and have read it with pleasure and astonishment; and knowing the author I was confirmed in the opinion which I had already formed of him that he was destined to become one of the leading mathematicians of our age. But now, with regard to the surprising effect of solar rays in melting metals, must we believe that such a furious action is devoid of motion or that it is accompanied by the most rapid of motions?

Salv. We observe that other combustions and resolutions are accompanied by motion, and that, the most rapid; note the action of lightning and of powder as used in mines and petards; note also how the charcoal flame, mixed as it is with heavy and impure vapors, increases its power to liquify metals whenever quickened by a pair of bellows. Hence I do not understand how the action of light, although very pure, can be devoid of motion and that of the swiftest type.

Sagr. But of what kind and how great must we consider this speed of light to be? Is it instantaneous or momentary or does it like other motions require time? Can we not decide this by experiment.

Simp. Everyday experience shows that the propagation of light is instantaneous; for when we see a piece of artillery fired, at great distance, the flash reaches our eyes without lapse of time; but the sound reaches the ear only after a noticeable interval.

Sagr. Well, Simplicio, the only thing I am able to infer from this familiar bit of experience is that sound, in reaching our ear, travels more slowly than light; it does not inform me whether the coming of the light is instantaneous or whether, although extremely rapid, it still occupies time. An observation of this kind tells us nothing more than one in which it is claimed that "As soon as the sun reaches the horizon its light reaches our eyes"; but who will assure me that these rays had not reached this limit earlier than they reached our vision?

10. One of the most active investigators among Galileo's contemporaries; born at Milan 1598; died at Bologna 1647; a Jesuit father, first to introduce the use of logarithms into Italy and first to derive the expression for the focal length of a lens having unequal radii of curvature. His "method of indivisibles" is to be reckoned as a precursor of the infinitesimal calculus. [*Trans.*]

[88]

Salv. The small conclusiveness of these and other similar observations once led me to devise a method by which one might accurately ascertain whether illumination, i. e., the propagation of light, is really instantaneous. The fact that the speed of sound is as high as it is, assures us that the motion of light cannot fail to be extraordinarily swift. The experiment which I devised was as follows:

Let each of two persons take a light contained in a lantern, or other receptacle, such that by the interposition of the hand, the one can shut off or admit the light to the vision of the other. Next let them stand opposite each other at a distance of a few cubits and practice until they acquire such skill in uncovering and occulting their lights that the instant one sees the light of his companion he will uncover his own. After a few trials the response will be so prompt that without sensible error [*svario*] the uncovering of one light is immediately followed by the uncovering of the other, so that as soon as one exposes his light he will instantly see that of the other. Having acquired skill at this short distance let the two experimenters, equipped as before, take up positions separated by a distance of two or three miles and let them perform the same experiment at night, noting carefully whether the exposures and occultations occur in the same manner as at short distances; if they do, we may safely conclude that the propagation of light is instantaneous; but if time is required at a distance of three miles which, considering the going of one light and the coming of the other, really amounts to six, then the delay ought to be easily observable. If the experiment is to be made at still greater distances, say eight or ten miles, telescopes may be employed, each observer adjusting one for himself at the place where he is to make the experiment at night; then although the lights are not large and are therefore invisible to the naked eye at so great a distance, they can readily be covered and uncovered since by aid of the telescopes, once adjusted and fixed, they will become easily visible.

Sagr. This experiment strikes me as a clever and reliable invention. But tell us what you conclude from the results.

Salv. In fact I have tried the experiment only at a short distance, less than a mile, from which I have not been able to ascertain with certainty whether the appearance of the opposite light was instantaneous or not; but if not instantaneous it is extraordinarily rapid—I should call it momentary; and for the present I should compare it to motion which we see in the lightning flash between clouds eight or ten miles distant from us. We see the beginning of this light—I might say its head and source—located at a particular place among the clouds; but it immediately spreads to the surrounding ones, which seems to be an argument that at least some time is required for propagation; for if the illumination were instantaneous and not gradual, we should not be able to distinguish its origin—its center, so to speak—from its outlying portions. What a sea

we are gradually slipping into without knowing it! With vacua and infinities and indivisibles and instantaneous motions, shall we ever be able, even by means of a thousand discussions, to reach dry land?

[89]

Sagr. Really these matters lie far beyond our grasp. Just think; when we seek the infinite among numbers we find it in unity; that which is ever divisible is derived from indivisibles; the vacuum is found inseparably connected with the plenum; indeed the views commonly held concerning the nature of these matters are so reversed that even the circumference of a circle turns out to be an infinite straight line, a fact which, if my memory serves me correctly, you, Salviati, were intending to demonstrate geometrically. Please therefore proceed without further digression.

Salv. I am at your service; but for the sake of greater clearness let me first demonstrate the following problem:

> *Given a straight line divided into unequal parts which bear to each other any ratio whatever, to describe a circle such that two straight lines drawn from the ends of the given line to any point on the circumference will bear to each other the same ratio as the two parts of the given line, thus making those lines which are drawn from the same terminal points homologous.*

[90]

Let AB represent the given straight line divided into any two unequal parts by the point C; the problem is to describe a circle such that two straight lines drawn from the terminal points, A and B, to any point on the circumference will bear to each other the same ratio as the part AC bears to BC, so that lines drawn from the same terminal points are homologous. About C as center describe a circle having the shorter part CB of the given line, as radius. Through A draw a straight line AD which shall be tangent to the circle at D and indefinitely prolonged toward E. Draw the radius CD which will be perpendicular to AE. At B erect a perpendicular to AB; this perpendicular will intersect AE at some point since the angle at A is acute; call this point of intersection E, and from it draw a perpendicular to AE which will intersect AB prolonged in F. Now I say the two straight lines FE and FC are equal. For if we join E and C, we shall have two triangles, DEC and BEC, in which the two sides of the one, DE and EC, are equal to the two sides of the other, BE and EC, both DE and EB being tangents to the circle DB while the bases DC and CB are likewise equal; hence the two angles, DEC and

BEC, will be equal. Now since the angle BCE differs from a right angle by the angle CEB, and the angle CEF also differs from a right angle by the angle CED, and since

these differences are equal, it follows that the angle FCE is equal to CEF; consequently the sides FE and FC are equal. If we describe a circle with F as center and FE as radius it will pass through the point C; let CEG be such a circle. This is the circle sought, for if we draw lines from the terminal points A and B to any point on its circumference they will bear to each other the same ratio as the two portions AC and BC which meet at

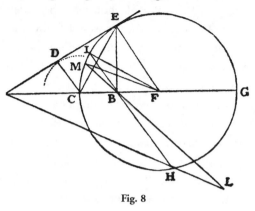

Fig. 8

the point C. This is manifest in the case of the two lines AE and BE, meeting at the point E, because the angle E of the triangle AEB is bisected by the line CE, and therefore AC:CB=AE:BE. The same may be proved of the two lines AG and BG terminating in the point G. For since the triangles AFE and EFB are similar, we have AF:FE=EF:FB, or AF:FC=CF:FB, and *dividendo* AC:CF=CB:BF, or AC:FG=CB:BF; also *componendo* we have both AB:BG=CB:BF and AG:GB=CF:FB=AE:EB=AC:BC.   Q. E. D.

[91]

Take now any other point in the circumference, say H, where the two lines AH and BH intersect; in like manner we shall have AC:CB=AH:HB. Prolong HB until it meets the circumference at I and join IF; and since we have already found that AB:BG=CB:BF it follows that the rectangle AB.BF is equal to the rectangle CB.BG or IB.BH. Hence AB:BH=IB:BF. But the angles at B are equal and therefore AH:HB=IF:FB=EF:FB=AE:EB.

Besides, I may add, that it is impossible for lines which maintain this same ratio and which are drawn from the terminal points, A and B, to meet at any point either inside or outside the circle, CEG. For suppose this were possible; let AL and BL be two such lines intersecting at the point L outside the circle: prolong LB till it meets the circumference at M and join MF. If AL:BL=AC:BC=MF:FB, then we shall have two triangles ALB and MFB which have the sides about the two angles proportional, the angles at the vertex, B, equal, and the two remaining angles, FMB and LAB, less than right angles (because the right angle at M has for its base the entire diameter CG and not merely a part BF: and the other angle at the point A is acute because the line AL

433

the homologue of AC, is greater than BL, the homologue of BC). From this it follows that the triangles ABL and MBF are similar and therefore AB:BL=MB:BF, making the rectangle AB.BF=MB.BL; but it has been demonstrated that the rectangle AB.BF is equal to CB.BG; whence it would follow that the rectangle MB.BL is equal to the rectangle CB.BG which is impossible; therefore the intersection cannot fall outside the circle. And in like manner we can show that it cannot fall inside; hence all these intersections fall on the circumference.

But now it is time for us to go back and grant the request of Simplicio by showing him that it is not only not impossible to resolve a line into an infinite number of points but that this is quite as easy as to divide it into its finite parts. This I will do under the following condition which I am sure, Simplicio, you will not deny me, namely, that you will not require me to separate the points, one from the other, and show them to you, one by one, on this paper; for I should be content that you, without separating the four or six parts of a line from one another, should show me the marked divisions or at most that you should fold them at angles forming a square or a hexagon: for, then, I am certain you would consider the division distinctly and actually accomplished.

[92]

Simp. I certainly should.

Salv. If now the change which takes place when you bend a line at angles so as to form now a square, now an octagon, now a polygon of forty, a hundred or a thousand angles, is sufficient to bring into actuality the four, eight, forty, hundred, and thousand parts which, according to you, existed at first only potentially in the straight line, may I not say, with equal right, that, when I have bent the straight line into a polygon having an infinite number of sides, i. e., into a circle, I have reduced to actuality that infinite number of parts which you claimed, while it was straight, were contained in it only potentially? Nor can one deny that the division into an infinite number of points is just as truly accomplished as the one into four parts when the square is formed or into a thousand parts when the millagon is formed; for in such a division the same conditions are satisfied as in the case of a polygon of a thousand or a hundred thousand sides. Such a polygon laid upon a straight line touches it with one of its sides, i. e., with one of its hundred thousand parts; while the circle which is a polygon of an infinite number of sides touches the same straight line with one of its sides which is a single point different from all its neighbors and therefore separate and distinct in no less degree than is one side of a polygon from the other sides. And just as a polygon, when rolled along a plane, marks out upon this plane, by the successive

contacts of its sides, a straight line equal to its perimeter, so the circle rolled upon such a plane also traces by its infinite succession of contacts a straight line equal in length to its own circumference. I am willing, Simplicio, at the outset, to grant to the Peripatetics the truth of their opinion that a continuous quantity [*il continuo*] is divisible only into parts which are still further divisible so that however far the division and subdivision be continued no end will be reached; but I am not so certain that they will concede to me that none of these divisions of theirs can be a final one, as is surely the fact, because there always remains "another"; the final and ultimate division is rather one which resolves a continuous quantity into an infinite number of indivisible quantities, a result which I grant can never be reached by successive division into an ever-increasing number of parts.

[93]

But if they employ the method which I propose for separating and resolving the whole of infinity [*tutta la infinità*], at a single stroke (an artifice which surely ought not to be denied me), I think that they would be contented to admit that a continuous quantity is built up out of absolutely indivisible atoms, especially since this method, perhaps better than any other, enables us to avoid many intricate labyrinths, such as cohesion in solids, already mentioned, and the question of expansion and contraction, without forcing upon us the objectionable admission of empty spaces [in solids] which carries with it the penetrability of bodies. Both of these objections, it appears to me, are avoided if we accept the above-mentioned view of indivisible constituents.

Simp. I hardly know what the Peripatetics would say since the views advanced by you would strike them as mostly new, and as such we must consider them. It is however not unlikely that they would find answers and solutions for these problems which I, for want of time and critical ability, am at present unable to solve. Leaving this to one side for the moment, I should like to hear how the introduction of these indivisible quantities helps us to understand contraction and expansion avoiding at the same time the vacuum and the penetrability of bodies.

Sagr. I also shall listen with keen interest to this same matter which is far from clear in my mind; provided I am allowed to hear what, a moment ago, Simplicio suggested we omit, namely, the reasons which Aristotle offers against the existence of the vacuum and the arguments which you must advance in rebuttal.

Salv. I will do both. And first, just as, for the production of expansion, we employ the line described by the small circle during one rotation of the large one—a line greater than the circumference of the small circle—so, in order to explain contraction, we point out that, during each rotation of the smaller circle, the larger one describes a straight line which is shorter than its circumference.

[94]

For the better understanding of this we proceed to the consideration of what happens in the case of polygons. Employing a figure similar to the earlier one, construct the two hexagons, ABC and HIK, about the common center L and let them roll along the parallel lines HOM and AB*c*. Now holding the vertex I fixed, allow the smaller

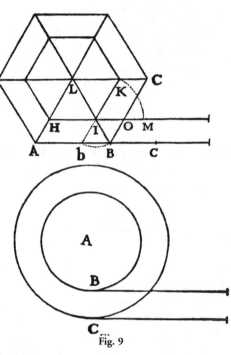

Fig. 9

polygon to rotate until the side IK lies upon the parallel, during which motion the point K will describe the arc KM, and the side KI will coincide with IM. Let us see what, in the meantime, the side CB of the larger polygon has been doing. Since the rotation is about the point I, the terminal point B, of the line IB, moving backwards, will describe the arc B*b* underneath the parallel *c*A so that when the side KI coincides with the line MI, the side BC will coincide with *bc*, having advanced only through the distance B*c*, but having retreated through a portion of the line BA which subtends the arc B*b*. If we allow the rotation of the smaller polygon to go on it will traverse and describe along its parallel a line equal to its perimeter; while the larger one will traverse and describe a line less than its perimeter by as many times the length *b*B as there are sides less one; this line is approximately equal to that described by the smaller polygon exceeding it only by the distance *b*B. Here now we see, without any difficulty, why the larger polygon, when carried by the smaller, does not measure off with its sides a line longer than that traversed by the smaller one; this is because a portion of each side is superposed upon its immediately preceding neighbor.

[95]

Let us next consider two circles, having a common center at A, and lying upon their respective parallels, the smaller being tangent to its parallel at the point B; the larger, at the point C. Here when the small circle commences to roll the point B does not remain at rest for a while so as to allow BC to move backward and carry with it the

point C, as happened in the case of the polygons, where the point I remained fixed until the side KI coincided with MI and the line IB carried the terminal point B backward as far as *b*, so that the side BC fell upon *bc*, thus superposing upon the line BA, the portion B*b*, and advancing by an amount B*c*, equal to MI, that is, to one side of the smaller polygon. On account of these superpositions, which are the excesses of the sides of the larger over the smaller polygon, each net advance is equal to one side of the smaller polygon and, during one complete rotation, these amount to a straight line equal in length to the perimeter of the smaller polygon.

But now reasoning in the same way concerning the circles, we must observe that whereas the number of sides in any polygon is comprised within a certain limit, the number of sides in a circle is infinite; the former are finite and divisible; the latter infinite and indivisible. In the case of the polygon, the vertices remain at rest during an interval of time which bears to the period of one complete rotation the same ratio which one side bears to the perimeter; likewise, in the case of the circles, the delay of each of the infinite number of vertices is merely instantaneous, because an instant is such a fraction of a finite interval as a point is of a line which contains an infinite number of points. The retrogression of the sides of the larger polygon is not equal to the length of one of its sides but merely to the excess of such a side over one side of the smaller polygon, the net advance being equal to this smaller side; but in the circle, the point or side C, during the instantaneous rest of B, recedes by an amount equal to its excess over the side B, making a net progress equal to B itself. In short the infinite number of indivisible sides of the greater circle with their infinite number of indivisible retrogressions, made during the infinite number of instantaneous delays of the infinite number of vertices of the smaller circle, together with the infinite number of progressions, equal to the infinite number of sides in the smaller circle—all these, I say, add up to a line equal to that described by the smaller circle, a line which contains an infinite number of infinitely small superpositions, thus bringing about a thickening or contraction without any overlapping or interpenetration of finite parts.

[96]

This result could not be obtained in the case of a line divided into finite parts such as is the perimeter of any polygon, which when laid out in a straight line cannot be shortened except by the overlapping and interpenetration of its sides. This contraction of an infinite number of infinitely small parts without the interpenetration or overlapping of finite parts and the previously mentioned [see above] expansion of an infinite number of indivisible parts by the interposition of indivisible vacua is, in my opinion, the most that can be said concerning the contraction and rarefaction of bodies, unless we give up the impenetrability of matter and introduce empty spaces of finite size.

If you find anything here that you consider worth while, pray use it; if not regard it, together with my remarks, as idle talk; but this remember, we are dealing with the infinite and the indivisible.

Sagr. I frankly confess that your idea is subtle and that it impresses me as new and strange; but whether, as a matter of fact, nature actually behaves according to such a law I am unable to determine; however, until I find a more satisfactory explanation I shall hold fast to this one. Perhaps Simplicio can tell us something which I have not yet heard, namely, how to explain the explanation which the philosophers have given of this abstruse matter; for, indeed, all that I have hitherto read concerning contraction is so dense and that concerning expansion so thin that my poor brain can neither penetrate the former nor grasp the latter.

Simp. I am all at sea and find difficulties in following either path, especially this new one; because according to this theory an ounce of gold might be rarefied and expanded until its size would exceed that of the earth, while the earth, in turn, might be condensed and reduced until it would become smaller than a walnut, something which I do not believe; nor do I believe that you believe it. The arguments and demonstrations which you have advanced are mathematical, abstract, and far removed from concrete matter; and I do not believe that when applied to the physical and natural world these laws will hold.

[97]

Salv. I am not able to render the invisible visible, nor do I think that you will ask this. But now that you mention gold, do not our senses tell us that that metal can be immensely expanded? I do not know whether you have observed the method employed by those who are skilled in drawing gold wire, of which really only the surface is gold, the inside material being silver. The way they draw it is as follows: they take a cylinder or, if you please, a rod of silver, about half a cubit long and three or four times as wide as one's thumb; this rod they cover with gold-leaf which is so thin that it almost floats in air, putting on not more than eight or ten thicknesses. Once gilded they begin to pull it, with great force, through the holes of a draw-plate; again and again it is made to pass through smaller and smaller holes, until, after very many passages, it is reduced to the fineness of a lady's hair, or perhaps even finer; yet the surface remains gilded. Imagine now how the substance of this gold has been expanded and to what fineness it has been reduced.

Simp. I do not see that this process would produce, as a consequence, that marvellous thinning of the substance of the gold which you suggest: first, because the original gilding consisting of ten layers of gold-leaf has a sensible thickness; secondly, because in drawing out the silver it grows in length but at the same time diminishes proportionally

in thickness; and, since one dimension thus compensates the other, the area will not be so increased as to make it necessary during the process of gilding to reduce the thinness of the gold beyond that of the original leaves.

Salv. You are greatly mistaken, Simplicio, because the surface increases directly as the square root of the length, a fact which I can demonstrate geometrically.

Sagr. Please give us the demonstration not only for my own sake but also for Simplicio, provided you think we can understand it.

[98]

Salv. I'll see if I can recall it on the spur of the moment. At the outset, it is clear that the original thick rod of silver and the wire drawn out to an enormous length are two cylinders of the same volume, since they are the same body of silver. So that, if I

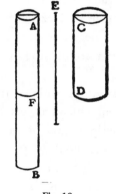

determine the ratio between the surfaces of cylinders of the same volume, the problem will be solved. I say then,

The areas of cylinders of equal volumes, neglecting the bases, bear to each other a ratio which is the square root of the ratio of their lengths.

Take two cylinders of equal volume having the altitudes AB and CD, between which the line E is a mean proportional. Then I claim that, omitting the bases of each cylinder, the surface of the cylinder AB is to that of the cylinder CD as the length AB is to the line E, that is, as the square root of AB is to the square root of CD. Now cut off the cylinder AB at F so that

Fig. 10

the altitude AF is equal to CD. Then since the bases of cylinders of equal volume bear to one another the inverse ratio of their heights, it follows that the area of the circular base of the cylinder CD will be to the area of the circular base of AB as the altitude BA is to DC: moreover, since circles are to one another as the squares of their diameters, the said squares will be to each other as BA is to CD. But BA is to CD as the square of BA is to the square of E: and, therefore, these four squares will form a proportion; and likewise their sides; so the line AB is to E as the diameter of circle C is to the diameter of the circle A. But the diameters are proportional to the circumferences and the circumferences are proportional to the areas of cylinders of equal height; hence the line AB is to E as the surface of the cylinder CD is to the surface of the cylinder AF. Now since the height AF is to AB as the surface of AF is to the surface of AB; and since the height AB is to the line E as the surface CD is to AF, it follows, *ex aequali in proportione perturbata*,[11] that the height AF is to E as the surface CD is to the surface AB, and *convertendo*, the surface of the cylinder AB is to the surface of the cylinder CD as the line E is to AF, i. e., to CD, or as AB is to E which is the square root of the ratio of AB to CD.   Q. E. D.

[99]

If now we apply these results to the case in hand, and assume that the silver cylinder at the time of gilding had a length of only half a cubit and a thickness three or four times that of one's thumb, we shall find that, when the wire has been reduced to the fineness of a hair and has been drawn out to a length of twenty thousand cubits (and perhaps more), the area of its surface will have been increased not less than two hundred times. Consequently the ten leaves of gold which were laid on have been extended over a surface two hundred times greater, assuring us that the thickness of the gold which now covers the surface of so many cubits of wire cannot be greater than one twentieth that of an ordinary leaf of beaten gold. Consider now what degree of fineness it must have and whether one could conceive it to happen in any other way than by enormous expansion of parts; consider also whether this experiment does not suggest that physical bodies [*materie fisiche*] are composed of infinitely small indivisible particles, a view which is supported by other more striking and conclusive examples.

Sagr. This demonstration is so beautiful that, even if it does not have the cogency originally intended;—although to my mind, it is very forceful—the short time devoted to it has nevertheless been most happily spent.

Salv. Since you are so fond of these geometrical demonstrations, which carry with them distinct gain, I will give you a companion theorem which answers an extremely interesting query. We have seen above what relations hold between equal cylinders of different height or length; let us now see what holds when the cylinders are equal in area but unequal in height, understanding area to include the curved surface, but not the upper and lower bases. The theorem is:

The volumes of right cylinders having equal curved surfaces are inversely proportional to their altitudes.

[100]

Let the surfaces of the two cylinders, AE and CF, be equal but let the height of the latter, CD, be greater than that of the former, AB: then I say that the volume of the cylinder AE is to that of the cylinder CF as the height CD is to AB. Now since the surface of CF is equal to the surface of AE, it follows that the volume of CF is less than that of AE; for, if they were equal the surface of CF would, by the preceding proposition, exceed that of AE, and the excess would be so much the greater if the volume of the cylinder CF were greater than that of AE. Let us now take a cylinder ID having a volume equal

11. See *Euclid*, Book V, Def. 20., Tadhunter's Ed., p. 137 (London, 1877.) *[Trans.]*

to that of AE; then, according to the preceding theorem, the surface of the cylinder ID is to the surface of AE as the altitude IF is to the mean proportional between IF and AB. But since one datum of the problem is that the surface of AE is equal to that of CF, and since the surface ID is to the surface CF as the altitude IF is to the altitude CD, it follows that CD is a mean proportional between IF and AB. Not only so, but since the volume of the cylinder ID is equal to that of AE, each will bear the same ratio to the volume of the cylinder CF; but the volume ID is to the volume CF as the altitude IF is to the altitude CD; hence the volume of AE is to the volume of CF as the length IF is to the length CD, that is, as the length CD is to the length AB.   Q. E. D.

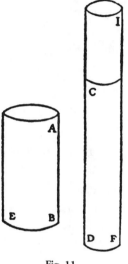

This explains a phenomenon upon which the common people always look with wonder, namely, if we have a piece of stuff which has one side longer than the other, we can make from it a cornsack, using the customary wooden base, which will hold more when the short side of the cloth is used for the height of the sack and the long side is wrapped around the wooden base, than with the alternative arrangement. So that, for instance, from a piece of cloth which is six cubits on one side and twelve on the other, a sack can be made which will hold more when the side of twelve cubits is wrapped around the wooden base,

Fig. 11

leaving the sack six cubits high than when the six cubit side is put around the base making the sack twelve cubits high. From what has been proven above we learn not only the general fact that one sack holds more than the other, but we also get specific and particular information as to how much more, namely, just in proportion as the altitude of the sack diminishes the contents increase and *vice versa.*

[101]

Thus if we use the figures given which make the cloth twice as long as wide and if we use the long side for the seam, the volume of the sack will be just one-half as great as with the opposite arrangement. Likewise if we have a piece of matting which measures 7 x 25 cubits and make from it a basket, the contents of the basket will, when the seam is lengthwise, be seven as compared with twenty-five when the seam runs endwise.

Sagr. It is with great pleasure that we continue thus to acquire new and useful information. But as regards the subject just discussed, I really believe that, among those who are not already familiar with geometry, you would scarcely find four persons in a hundred who would not, at first sight, make the mistake of believing that bodies

having equal surfaces would be equal in other respects. Speaking of areas, the same error is made when one attempts, as often happens, to determine the sizes of various cities by measuring their boundary lines, forgetting that the circuit of one may equal to the circuit of another while the area of the one is much greater than that of the other. And this is true not only in the case of irregular, but also of regular surfaces, where the polygon having the greater number of sides always contains a larger area than the one with the less number of sides, so that finally the circle which is a polygon of an infinite number of sides contains the largest area of all polygons of equal perimeter. I remember with particular pleasure having seen this demonstration when I was studying the sphere of Sacrobosco[12] with the aid of a learned commentary.

[102]

Salv. Very true! I too came across the same passage which suggested to me a method of showing how, by a single short demonstration, one can prove that the circle has the largest content of all regular isoperimetric figures; and that, of other figures, the one which has the larger number of sides contains a greater area than that which has the smaller number.

Sagr. Being exceedingly fond of choice and uncommon propositions, I beseech you to let us have your demonstration.

Salv. I can do this in a few words by proving the following theorem:

> *The area of a circle is a mean proportional between any two regular and similar polygons of which one circumscribes it and the other is isoperimetric with it. In addition, the area of the circle is less than that of any circumscribed polygon and greater than that of any isoperimetric polygon. And further, of these circumscribed polygons, the one which has the greater number of sides is smaller than the one which has a less number; but, on the other hand, that isoperimetric polygon which has the greater number of sides is the larger.*

Let A and B be two similar polygons of which A circumscribes the given circle and B is isoperimetric with it. The area of the circle will then be a mean proportional between the areas of the polygons. For if we indicate

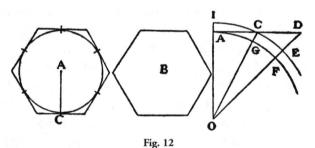

Fig. 12

12. See interesting biographical note on Sacrobosco [John Holywood] in *Ency. Brit.*, 11th Ed. *[Trans.]*

the radius of the circle by AC and if we remember that the area of the circle is equal to that of a right-angled triangle in which one of the sides about the right angle is equal to the radius, AC, and the other to the circumference; and if likewise we remember that the area of the polygon A is equal to the area of a right-angled triangle one of

[103]

whose sides about the right angle has the same length as AC and the other is equal to the perimeter of the polygon itself; it is then manifest that the circumscribed polygon bears to the circle the same ratio which its perimeter bears to the circumference of the circle, or to the perimeter of the polygon B which is, by hypothesis, equal to the circumference of the circle. But since the polygons A and B are similar their areas are to each other as the squares of their perimeters; hence the area of the circle A is a mean proportional between the areas of the two polygons A and B. And since the area of the polygon A is greater than that of the circle A, it is clear that the area of the circle A is greater than that of the isoperimetric polygon B, and is therefore the greatest of all regular polygons having the same perimeter as the circle.

We now demonstrate the remaining portion of the theorem, which is to prove that, in the case of polygons circumscribing a given circle, the one having the smaller number of sides has a larger area than one having a greater number of sides; but that on the other hand, in the case of isoperimetric polygons, the one having the more sides has a larger area than the one with less sides. To the circle which has O for center and OA for radius draw the tangent AD; and on this tangent lay off, say, AD which shall represent one-half of the side of a circumscribed pentagon and AC which shall represent one-half of the side of a heptagon; draw the straight lines OGC and OFD; then with O as a center and OC as radius draw the arc ECI. Now since the triangle DOC is greater than the sector EOC and since the sector COI is greater than the triangle COA, it follows that the triangle DOC bears to the triangle COA a greater ratio than the sector EOC bears to the sector COI, that is, than the sector FOG bears to the sector GOA. Hence, *componendo et permutando*, the triangle DOA bears to the sector FOA a greater ratio than that which the triangle COA bears to the sector GOA, and also 10 such triangles DOA bear to 10 such sectors FOA a greater ratio than 14 such triangles COA bear to 14 such sectors GOA, that is to say, the circumscribed pentagon bears to the circle a greater ratio than does the heptagon. Hence the pentagon exceeds the heptagon in area.

[104]

But now let us assume that both the heptagon and the pentagon have the same perimeter as that of a given circle. Then I say the heptagon will contain a larger area

than the pentagon. For since the area of the circle is a mean proportional between areas of the circumscribed and of the isoperimetric pentagons, and since likewise it is a mean proportional between the circumscribed and isoperimetric heptagons, and since also we have proved that the circumscribed pentagon is larger than the circumscribed hexagon, it follows that this circumscribed pentagon bears to the circle a larger ratio than does the heptagon, that is, the circle will bear to its isoperimetric pentagon a greater ratio than to its isoperimetric heptagon. Hence the pentagon is smaller than its isoperimetric heptagon. Q. E. D.

Sagr. A very clever and elegant demonstration! But how did we come to plunge into geometry while discussing the objections urged by Simplicio, objections of great moment, especially that one referring to density which strikes me as particularly difficult?

Salv. If contraction and expansion [*condensazione e rarefazzione*] consist in contrary motions, one ought to find for each great expansion a correspondingly large contraction. But our surprise is increased when, every day, we see enormous expansions taking place almost instantaneously. Think what a tremendous expansion occurs when a small quantity of gunpowder flares up into a vast volume of fire! Think too of the almost limitless expansion of the light which it produces! Imagine the contraction which would take place if this fire and this light were to reunite, which, indeed, is not impossible since only a little while ago they were located together in this small space. You will find, upon observation, a thousand such expansions for they are more obvious than contractions since dense matter is more palpable and accessible to our senses.

[105]

We can take wood and see it go up in fire and light, but we do not see them recombine to form wood; we see fruits and flowers and a thousand other solid bodies dissolve largely into odors, but we do not observe these fragrant atoms coming together to form fragrant solids. But where the senses fail us reason must step in; for it will enable us to understand the motion involved in the condensation of extremely rarefied and tenuous substances just as clearly as that involved in the expansion and dissolution of solids. Moreover we are trying to find out how it is possible to produce expansion and contraction in bodies which are capable of such changes without introducing vacua and without giving up the impenetrability of matter; but this does not exclude the possibility of there being materials which possess no such properties and do not, therefore, carry with them consequences which you call inconvenient and impossible. And finally, Simplicio, I have, for the sake of you philosophers, taken pains to find an explanation of how expansion and contraction can take place without our admitting the penetrability of matter and introducing vacua, properties which you deny and

dislike; if you were to admit them, I should not oppose you so vigorously. Now either admit these difficulties or accept my views or suggest something better.

Sagr. I quite agree with the peripatetic philosophers in denying the penetrability of matter. As to the vacua I should like to hear a thorough discussion of Aristotle's demonstration in which he opposes them, and what you, Salviati, have to say in reply. I beg of you, Simplicio, that you give us the precise proof of the Philosopher and that you, Salviati, give us the reply.

Simp. So far as I remember, Aristotle inveighs against the ancient view that a vacuum is a necessary prerequisite for motion and that the latter could not occur without the former. In opposition to this view Aristotle shows that it is precisely the phenomenon of motion, as we shall see, which renders untenable the idea of a vacuum. His method is to divide the argument into two parts. He first supposes bodies of different weights to move in the same medium; then supposes, one and the same body to move in different media.

[106]

In the first case, he supposes bodies of different weight to move in one and the same medium with different speeds which stand to one another in the same ratio as the weights; so that, for example, a body which is ten times as heavy as another will move ten times as rapidly as the other. In the second case he assumes that the speeds of one and the same body moving in different media are in inverse ratio to the densities of these media; thus, for instance, if the density of water were ten times that of air, the speed in air would be ten times greater than in water. From this second supposition, he shows that, since the tenuity of a vacuum differs infinitely from that of any medium filled with matter however rare, any body which moves in a plenum through a certain space in a certain time ought to move through a vacuum instantaneously; but instantaneous motion is an impossibility; it is therefore impossible that a vacuum should be produced by motion.

Salv. The argument is, as you see, *ad hominem*, that is, it is directed against those who thought the vacuum a prerequisite for motion. Now if I admit the argument to be conclusive and concede also that motion cannot take place in a vacuum, the assumption of a vacuum considered absolutely and not with reference to motion, is not thereby invalidated. But to tell you what the ancients might possibly have replied and in order to better understand just how conclusive Aristotle's demonstration is, we may, in my opinion, deny both of his assumptions. And as to the first, I greatly doubt that Aristotle ever tested by experiment whether it be true that two stones, one weighing ten times as much as the other, if allowed to fall, at the same instant, from a height of, say, 100 cubits, would so differ in speed that when the heavier had reached the ground, the other would not have fallen more than 10 cubits.

Simp. His language would seem to indicate that he had tried the experiment, because he says: *We see the heavier*, now the word *see* shows that he had made the experiment.

[107]

Sagr. But I, Simplicio, who have made the test can assure you that a cannon ball weighing one or two hundred pounds, or even more, will not reach the ground by as much as a span ahead of a musket ball weighing only half a pound, provided both are dropped from a height of 200 cubits.

Salv. But, even without further experiment, it is possible to prove clearly, by means of a short and conclusive argument, that a heavier body does not move more rapidly than a lighter one provided both bodies are of the same material and in short such as those mentioned by Aristotle. But tell me, Simplicio, whether you admit that each falling body acquires a definite speed fixed by nature, a velocity which cannot be increased or diminished except by the use of force [*violenza*] or resistance.

Simp. There can be no doubt but that one and the same body moving in a single medium has a fixed velocity which is determined by nature and which cannot be increased except by the addition of momentum [*impeto*] or diminished except by some resistance which retards it.

Salv. If then we take two bodies whose natural speeds are different, it is clear that on uniting the two, the more rapid one will be partly retarded by the slower, and the slower will be somewhat hastened by the swifter. Do you not agree with me in this opinion?

Simp. You are unquestionably right.

Salv. But if this is true, and if a large stone moves with a speed of, say, eight while a smaller moves with a speed of four, then when they are united, the system will move with a speed less than eight; but the two stones when tied together make a stone larger than that which before moved with a speed of eight. Hence the heavier body moves with less speed than the lighter; an effect which is contrary to your supposition. Thus you see how, from your assumption that the heavier body moves more rapidly than the lighter one, I infer that the heavier body moves more slowly.

[108]

Simp. I am all at sea because it appears to me that the smaller stone when added to the larger increases its weight and by adding weight I do not see how it can fail to increase its speed or, at least, not to diminish it.

Salv. Here again you are in error, Simplicio, because it is not true that the smaller stone adds weight to the larger.

Simp. This is, indeed, quite beyond my comprehension.

Salv. It will not be beyond you when I have once shown you the mistake under which you are laboring. Note that it is necessary to distinguish between heavy bodies in motion and the same bodies at rest. A large stone placed in a balance not only acquires additional weight by having another stone placed upon it, but even by the addition of a handful of hemp its weight is augmented six to ten ounces according to the quantity of hemp. But if you tie the hemp to the stone and allow them to fall freely from some height, do you believe that the hemp will press down upon the stone and thus accelerate its motion or do you think the motion will be retarded by a partial upward pressure? One always feels the pressure upon his shoulders when he prevents the motion of a load resting upon him; but if one descends just as rapidly as the load would fall how can it gravitate or press upon him? Do you not see that this would be the same as trying to strike a man with a lance when he is running away from you with a speed which is equal to, or even greater than, that with which you are following him? You must therefore conclude that, during free and natural fall, the small stone does not press upon the larger and consequently does not increase its weight as it does when at rest.

[109]

Simp. But what if we should place the larger stone upon the smaller?

Salv. Its weight would be increased if the larger stone moved more rapidly; but we have already concluded that when the small stone moves more slowly it retards to some extent the speed of the larger, so that the combination of the two, which is a heavier body than the larger of the two stones, would move less rapidly, a conclusion which is contrary to your hypothesis. We infer therefore that large and small bodies move with the same speed provided they are of the same specific gravity.

Simp. Your discussion is really admirable; yet I do not find it easy to believe that a bird-shot falls as swiftly as a cannon ball.

Salv. Why not say a grain of sand as rapidly as a grindstone? But, Simplicio, I trust you will not follow the example of many others who divert the discussion from its main intent and fasten upon some statement of mine which lacks a hair's-breadth of the truth and, under this hair, hide the fault of another which is as big as a ship's cable. Aristotle says that "an iron ball of one hundred pounds falling from a height of one hundred cubits reaches the ground before a one-pound ball has fallen a single cubit." I say that they arrive at the same time. You find, on making the experiment, that the larger outstrips the smaller by two finger-breadths, that is, when the larger has reached

the ground, the other is short of it by two finger-breadths; now you would not hide behind these two fingers the ninety-nine cubits of Aristotle, nor would you mention my small error and at the same time pass over in silence his very large one. Aristotle declares that bodies of different weights, in the same medium, travel (in so far as their motion depends upon gravity) with speeds which are proportional to their weights; this he illustrates by use of bodies in which it is possible to perceive the pure and unadulterated effect of gravity, eliminating other considerations, for example, figure as being of small importance [*minimi momenti*], influences which are greatly dependent upon the medium which modifies the single effect of gravity alone. Thus we observe that gold, the densest of all substances, when beaten out into a very thin leaf, goes floating through the air; the same thing happens with stone when ground into a very fine powder. But if you wish to maintain the general proposition you will have to show that the same ratio of speeds is preserved in the case of all heavy bodies, and that a stone of twenty pounds moves ten times as rapidly as one of two; but I claim that this is false and that, if they fall from a height of fifty or a hundred cubits, they will reach the earth at the same moment.

[110]

Simp. Perhaps the result would be different if the fall took place not from a few cubits but from some thousands of cubits.

Salv. If this were what Aristotle meant you would burden him with another error which would amount to a falsehood; because, since there is no such sheer height available on earth, it is clear that Aristotle could not have made the experiment; yet he wishes to give us the impression of his having performed it when he speaks of such an effect as one which we see.

Simp. In fact, Aristotle does not employ this principle, but uses the other one which is not, I believe, subject to these same difficulties.

Salv. But the one is as false as the other; and I am surprised that you yourself do not see the fallacy and that you do not perceive that if it were true that, in media of different densities and different resistances, such as water and air, one and the same body moved in air more rapidly than in water, in proportion as the density of water is greater than that of air, then it would follow that any body which falls through air ought also to fall through water. But this conclusion is false inasmuch as many bodies which descend in air not only do not descend in water, but actually rise.

Simp. I do not understand the necessity of your inference; and in addition I will say that Aristotle discusses only those bodies which fall in both media, not those which fall in air but rise in water.

[111]

Salv. The arguments which you advance for the Philosopher are such as he himself would have certainly avoided so as not to aggravate his first mistake. But tell me now whether the density [*corpulenza*] of the water, or whatever it may be that retards the motion, bears a definite ratio to the density of air which is less retardative; and if so fix a value for it at your pleasure.

Simp. Such a ratio does exist; let us assume it to be ten; then, for a body which falls in both these media, the speed in water will be ten times slower than in air.

Salv. I shall now take one of those bodies which fall in air but not in water, say a wooden ball, and I shall ask you to assign to it any speed you please for its descent through air.

Simp. Let us suppose it moves with a speed of twenty.

Salv. Very well. Then it is clear that this speed bears to some smaller speed the same ratio as the density of water bears to that of air; and the value of this smaller speed is two. So that really if we follow exactly the assumption of Aristotle we ought to infer that the wooden ball which falls in air, a substance ten times less-resisting than water, with a speed of twenty would fall in water with a speed of two, instead of coming to the surface from the bottom as it does; unless perhaps you wish to reply, which I do not believe you will, that the rising of the wood through the water is the same as its falling with a speed of two. But since the wooden ball does not go to the bottom, I think you will agree with me that we can find a ball of another material, not wood, which does fall in water with a speed of two.

Simp. Undoubtedly we can; but it must be of a substance considerably heavier than wood.

Salv. That is it exactly. But if this second ball falls in water with a speed of two, what will be its speed of descent in air? If you hold to the rule of Aristotle you must reply that it will move at the rate of twenty; but twenty is the speed which you your-self have already assigned to the wooden ball; hence this and the other heavier ball will each move through air with the same speed. But now how does the Philosopher har-monize this result with his other, namely, that bodies of different weight move through the same medium with different speeds—speeds which are proportional to their weights? But without going into the matter more deeply, how have these common and obvious properties escaped your notice?

[112]

Have you not observed that two bodies which fall in water, one with a speed a hun-dred times as great as that of the other, will fall in air with speeds so nearly equal that

one will not surpass the other by as much as one hundredth part? Thus, for example, an egg made of marble will descend in water one hundred times more rapidly than a hen's egg, while in air falling from a height of twenty cubits the one will fall short of the other by less than four finger breadths. In short, a heavy body which sinks through ten cubits of water in three hours will traverse ten cubits of air in one or two pulse-beats; and if the heavy body be a ball of lead it will easily traverse the ten cubits of water in less than double the time required for ten cubits of air. And here, I am sure, Simplicio, you find no ground for difference or objection. We conclude, therefore, that the argument does not bear against the existence of a vacuum; but if it did, it would only do away with vacua of considerable size which neither I nor, in my opinion, the ancients ever believed to exist in nature, although they might possibly be produced by force [*violenza*] as may be gathered from various experiments whose description would here occupy too much time.

Sagr. Seeing that Simplicio is silent, I will take the opportunity of saying something. Since you have clearly demonstrated that bodies of different weights do not move in one and the same medium with velocities proportional to their weights, but that they all move with the same speed, understanding of course that they are of the same substance or at least of the same specific gravity; certainly not of different specific gravities, for I hardly think you would have us believe a ball of cork moves with the same speed as one of lead; and again since you have clearly demonstrated that one and the same body moving through differently resisting media does not acquire speeds which are inversely proportional to the resistances, I am curious to learn what are the ratios actually observed in these cases.

[113]

Salv. These are interesting questions and I have thought much concerning them. I will give you the method of approach and the result which I finally reached. Having once established the falsity of the proposition that one and the same body moving through differently resisting media acquires speeds which are inversely proportional to the resistances of these media, and having also disproved the statement that in the same medium bodies of different weight acquire velocities proportional to their weights (understanding that this applies also to bodies which differ merely in specific gravity), I then began to combine these two facts and to consider what would happen if bodies of different weight were placed in media of different resistances; and I found that the differences in speed were greater in those media which were more resistant, that is, less yielding. This difference was such that two bodies which differed scarcely at all in their speed through air would, in water, fall the one with a speed ten times as great as that of the other. Further, there are bodies which will fall rapidly in air, whereas if placed in

water not only will not sink but will remain at rest or will even rise to the top: for it is possible to find some kinds of wood, such as knots and roots, which remain at rest in water but fall rapidly in air.

Sagr. I have often tried with the utmost patience to add grains of sand to a ball of wax until it should acquire the same specific gravity as water and would therefore remain at rest in this medium. But with all my care I was never able to accomplish this. Indeed, I do not know whether there is any solid substance whose specific gravity is, by nature, so nearly equal to that of water that if placed anywhere in water it will remain at rest.

[114]

Salv. In this, as in a thousand other operations, men are surpassed by animals. In this problem of yours one may learn much from the fish which are very skillful in maintaining their equilibrium nor only in one kind of water, but also in waters which are notably different either by their own nature or by some accidental muddiness or through salinity, each of which produces a marked change. So perfectly indeed can fish keep their equilibrium that they are able to remain motionless in any position. This they accomplish, I believe, by means of an apparatus especially provided by nature, namely, a bladder located in the body and communicating with the mouth by means of a narrow tube through which they are able, at will, to expel a portion of the air contained in the bladder: by rising to the surface they can take in more air; thus they make themselves heavier or lighter than water at will and maintain equilibrium.

Sagr. By means of another device I was able to deceive some friends to whom I had boasted that I could make up a ball of wax that would be in equilibrium in water. In the bottom of a vessel I placed some salt water and upon this some fresh water; then I showed them that the ball stopped in the middle of the water, and that, when pushed to the bottom or lifted to the top, would not remain in either of these places but would return to the middle.

Salv. This experiment is not without usefulness. For when physicians are testing the various qualities of waters, especially their specific gravities, they employ a ball of this kind so adjusted that, in certain water, it will neither rise nor fall. Then in testing another water, differing ever so slightly in specific gravity [peso], the ball will sink if this water be lighter and rise if it be heavier. And so exact is this experiment that the addition of two grains of salt to six pounds of water is sufficient to make the ball rise to the surface from the bottom to which it had fallen. To illustrate the precision of this experiment and also to clearly demonstrate the non-resistance of water to division, I wish to add that this notable difference in specific gravity can be produced not only by solution of some heavier substance, but also by merely heating or cooling; and so sensitive

is water to this process that by simply adding four drops of another water which is slightly warmer or cooler than the six pounds one can cause the ball to sink or rise; it will sink when the warm water is poured in and will rise upon the addition of cold water. Now you can see how mistaken are those philosophers who ascribe to water viscosity or some other coherence of parts which offers resistance to separation of parts and to penetration.

[115]

Sagr. With regard to this question I have found many convincing arguments in a treatise by our Academician; but there is one great difficulty of which I have not been able to rid myself, namely, if there be no tenacity or coherence between the particles of water how is it possible for those large drops of water to stand out in relief upon cabbage leaves without scattering or spreading out?

Salv. Although those who are in possession of the truth are able to solve all objections raised, I would not arrogate to myself such power; nevertheless my inability should not be allowed to becloud the truth. To begin with let me confess that I do not understand how these large globules of water stand out and hold themselves up, although I know for a certainty, that it is not owing to any internal tenacity acting between the particles of water; whence it must follow that the cause of this effect is external. Beside the experiments already shown to prove that the cause is not internal, I can offer another which is very convincing. If the particles of water which sustain themselves in a heap, while surrounded by air, did so in virtue of an internal cause then they would sustain themselves much more easily when surrounded by a medium in which they exhibit less tendency to fall than they do in air; such a medium would be any fluid heavier than air, as, for instance, wine: and therefore if some wine be poured about such a drop of water, the wine might rise until the drop was entirely covered, without the particles of water, held together by this internal coherence, ever parting company.

[116]

But this is not the fact; for as soon as the wine touches the water, the latter without waiting to be covered scatters and spreads out underneath the wine if it be red. The cause of this effect is therefore external and is possibly to be found in the surrounding air. Indeed there appears to be a considerable antagonism between air and water as I have observed in the following experiment. Having taken a glass globe which had a mouth of about the same diameter as a straw, I filled it with water and turned it mouth downwards; nevertheless, the water, although quite heavy and prone to descend, and the air, which is very light and disposed to rise through the water, refused, the one to

descend and the other to ascend through the opening, but both remained stubborn and defiant. On the other hand, as soon as I apply to this opening a glass of red wine, which is almost inappreciably lighter than water, red streaks are immediately observed to ascend slowly through the water while the water with equal slowness descends through the wine without mixing, until finally the globe is completely filled with wine and the water has all gone down into the vessel below. What then can we say except that there exists, between water and air, a certain incompatibility which I do not understand, but perhaps. . .

Simp. I feel almost like laughing at the great antipathy which Salviati exhibits against the use of the word antipathy; and yet it is excellently adapted to explain the difficulty.

Salv. Alright, if it please Simplicio, let this word antipathy be the solution of our difficulty. Returning from this digression, let us again take up our problem. We have already seen that the difference of speed between bodies of different specific gravities is most marked in those media which are the most resistant: thus, in a medium of quicksilver, gold not merely sinks to the bottom more rapidly than lead but it is the only substance that will descend at all; all other metals and stones rise to the surface and float. On the other hand the variation of speed in air between balls of gold, lead, copper, porphyry, and other heavy materials is so slight that in a fall of 100 cubits a ball of gold would surely not outstrip one of copper by as much as four fingers. Having observed this I came to the conclusion that in a medium totally devoid of resistance all bodies would fall with the same speed.

Simp. This is a remarkable statement, Salviati. But I shall never believe that even in a vacuum, if motion in such a place were possible, a lock of wool and a bit of lead can fall with the same velocity.

[117]

Salv. A little more slowly, Simplicio. Your difficulty is not so recondite nor am I so imprudent as to warrant you in believing that I have not already considered this matter and found the proper solution. Hence for my justification and for your enlightenment hear what I have to say. Our problem is to find out what happens to bodies of different weight moving in a medium devoid of resistance, so that the only difference in speed is that which arises from inequality of weight. Since no medium except one entirely free from air and other bodies, be it ever so tenuous and yielding, can furnish our senses with the evidence we are looking for, and since such a medium is not available, we shall observe what happens in the rarest and least resistant media as compared with what happens in denser and more resistant media. Because if we find as a fact that the variation of speed among bodies of different specific gravities is less and less according

as the medium becomes more and more yielding, and if finally in a medium of extreme tenuity, though not a perfect vacuum, we find that, in spite of great diversity of specific gravity [*peso*], the difference in speed is very small and almost inappreciable, then we are justified in believing it highly probable that in a vacuum all bodies would fall with the same speed. Let us, in view of this, consider what takes place in air, where for the sake of a definite figure and light material imagine an inflated bladder. The air in this bladder when surrounded by air will weigh little or nothing, since it can be only slightly compressed; its weight then is small being merely that of the skin which does not amount to the thousandth part of a mass of lead having the same size as the inflated bladder. Now, Simplicio, if we allow these two bodies to fall from a height of four or six cubits, by what distance do you imagine the lead will anticipate the bladder? You may be sure that the lead will not travel three times, or even twice, as swiftly as the bladder, although you would have made it move a thousand times as rapidly.

Simp. It may be as you say during the first four or six cubits of the fall; but after the motion has continued a long while, I believe that the lead will have left the bladder behind not only six out of twelve parts of the distance but even eight or ten.

[118]

Salv. I quite agree with you and doubt not that, in very long distances, the lead might cover one hundred miles while the bladder was traversing one; but, my dear Simplicio, this phenomenon which you adduce against my proposition is precisely the one which confirms it. Let me once more explain that the variation of speed observed in bodies of different specific gravities is not caused by the difference of specific gravity but depends upon external circumstances and, in particular, upon the resistance of the medium, so that if this is removed all bodies would fall with the same velocity; and this result I deduce mainly from the fact which you have just admitted and which is very true, namely, that, in the case of bodies which differ widely in weight, their velocities differ more and more as the spaces traversed increase, something which would not occur if the effect depended upon differences of specific gravity. For since these specific gravities remain constant, the ratio between the distances traversed ought to remain constant whereas the fact is that this ratio keeps on increasing as the motion continues. Thus a very heavy body in a fall of one cubit will not anticipate a very light one by so much as the tenth part of this space; but in a fall of twelve cubits the heavy body would outstrip the other by one-third, and in a fall of one hundred cubits by 90/100, etc.

Simp. Very well: but, following your own line of argument, if differences of weight in bodies of different specific gravities cannot produce a change in the ratio of their speeds, on the ground that their specific gravities do not change, how is it possible for the medium, which also we suppose to remain constant, to bring about any change in the ratio of these velocities?

Salv. This objection with which you oppose my statement is clever; and I must meet it. I begin by saying that a heavy body has an inherent tendency to move with a constantly and uniformly accelerated motion toward the common center of gravity, that is, toward the center of our earth, so that during equal intervals of time it receives equal increments of momentum and velocity. This, you must understand, holds whenever all external and accidental hindrances have been removed; but of these there is one which we can never remove, namely, the medium which must be penetrated and thrust aside by the falling body. This quiet, yielding, fluid medium opposes motion through it with a resistance which is proportional to the rapidity with which the medium must give way to the passage of the body; which body, as I have said, is by nature continuously accelerated so that it meets with more and more resistance in the medium and hence a diminution in its rate of gain of speed until finally the speed reaches such a point and the resistance of the medium becomes so great that, balancing each other, they prevent any further acceleration and reduce the motion of the body to one which is uniform and which will thereafter maintain a constant value. There is, therefore, an increase in the resistance of the medium, not on account of any change in its essential properties, but on account of the change in rapidity with which it must yield and give way laterally to the passage of the falling body which is being constantly accelerated.

[119]

Now seeing how great is the resistance which the air offers to the slight momentum [*momento*] of the bladder and how small that which it offers to the large weight [*peso*] of the lead, I am convinced that, if the medium were entirely removed, the advantage received by the bladder would be so great and that coming to the lead so small that their speeds would be equalized. Assuming this principle, that all falling bodies acquire equal speeds in a medium which, on account of a vacuum or something else, offers no resistance to the speed of the motion, we shall be able accordingly to determine the ratios of the speeds of both similar and dissimilar bodies moving either through one and the same medium or through different space-filling, and therefore resistant, media. This result we may obtain by observing how much the weight of the medium detracts from the weight of the moving body, which weight is the means employed by the falling body to open a path for itself and to push aside the parts of the medium, something which does not happen in a vacuum where, therefore, no difference [of speed] is to be expected from a difference of specific gravity. And since it is known that the effect of the medium is to diminish the weight of the body by the weight of the medium displaced, we may accomplish our purpose by diminishing in just this proportion the speeds of the falling bodies, which in a non-resisting medium we have assumed to be equal.

[120]

Thus, for example, imagine lead to be ten thousand times as heavy as air while ebony is only one thousand times as heavy. Here we have two substances whose speeds of fall in a medium devoid of resistance are equal: but, when air is the medium, it will subtract from the speed of the lead one part in ten thousand, and from the speed of the ebony one part in one thousand, i. e. ten parts in ten thousand. While therefore lead and ebony would fall from any given height in the same interval of time, provided the retarding effect of the air were removed, the lead will, in air, lose in speed one part in ten thousand; and the ebony, ten parts in ten thousand. In other words, if the elevation from which the bodies start be divided into ten thousand parts, the lead will reach the ground leaving the ebony behind by as much as ten, or at least nine, of these parts. Is it not clear then that a leaden ball allowed to fall from a tower two hundred cubits high will outstrip an ebony ball by less than four inches? Now ebony weighs a thousand times as much as air but this inflated bladder only four times as much; therefore air diminishes the inherent and natural speed of ebony by one part in a thousand; while that of the bladder which, if free from hindrance, would be the same, experiences a diminution in air amounting to one part in four. So that when the ebony ball, falling from the tower, has reached the earth, the bladder will have traversed only three-quarters of this distance. Lead is twelve times as heavy as water; but ivory is only twice as heavy. The speeds of these two substances which, when entirely unhindered, are equal will be diminished in water, that of lead by one part in twelve, that of ivory by half. Accordingly when the lead has fallen through eleven cubits of water the ivory will have fallen through only six. Employing this principle we shall, I believe, find a much closer agreement of experiment with our computation than with that of Aristotle.

In a similar manner we may find the ratio of the speeds of one and the same body in different fluid media, not by comparing the different resistances of the media, but by considering the excess of the specific gravity of the body above those of the media. Thus, for example, tin is one thousand times heavier than air and ten times heavier than water; hence, if we divide its unhindered speed into 1000 parts, air will rob it of one of these parts so that it will fall with a speed of 999, while in water its speed will be 900, seeing that water diminishes its weight by one part in ten while air by only one part in a thousand.

[121]

Again take a solid a little heavier than water, such as oak, a ball of which will weigh let us say 1000 drachms; suppose an equal volume of water to weigh 950, and an equal volume of air, 2; then it is clear that if the unhindered speed of the ball is 1000, its

speed in air will be 998, but in water only 50, seeing that the water removes 950 of the 1000 parts which the body weighs, leaving only 50.

Such a solid would therefore move almost twenty times as fast in air as in water, since its specific gravity exceeds that of water by one part in twenty. And here we must consider the fact that only those substances which have a specific gravity greater than water can fall through it—substances which must, therefore, be hundreds of times heavier than air; hence when we try to obtain the ratio of the speed in air to that in water, we may, without appreciable error, assume that air does not, to any considerable extent, diminish the free weight [*assoluta gravità*], and consequently the unhindered speed [*assoluta velocità*] of such substances. Having thus easily found the excess of the weight of these substances over that of water, we can say that their speed in air is to their speed in water as their free weight [*totale gravità*] is to the excess of this weight over that of water. For example, a ball of ivory weighs 20 ounces; an equal volume of water weighs 17 ounces; hence the speed of ivory in air bears to its speed in water the approximate ratio of 20:3.

Sagr. I have made a great step forward in this truly interesting subject upon which I have long labored in vain. In order to put these theories into practice we need only discover a method of determining the specific gravity of air with reference to water and hence with reference to other heavy substances.

Simp. But if we find that air has levity instead of gravity what then shall we say of the foregoing discussion which, in other respects, is very clever?

Salv. I should say that it was empty, vain, and trifling. But can you doubt that air has weight when you have the clear testimony of Aristotle affirming that all the elements have weight including air, and excepting only fire? As evidence of this he cites the fact that a leather bottle weighs more when inflated than when collapsed.

Simp. I am inclined to believe that the increase of weight observed in the inflated leather bottle or bladder arises, not from the gravity of the air, but from the many thick vapors mingled with it in these lower regions. To this I would attribute the. increase of weight in the leather bottle.

[122]

Salv. I would not have you say this, and much less attribute it to Aristotle; because, if speaking of the elements, he wished to persuade me by experiment that air has weight and were to say to me: "Take a leather bottle, fill it with heavy vapors and observe how its weight increases," I would reply that the bottle would weigh still more if filled with bran; and would then add that this merely proves that bran and thick vapors are heavy, but in regard to air I should still remain in the same doubt as before. However, the experiment of Aristotle is good and the proposition is true. But I cannot say as much

of a certain other consideration, taken at face value; this consideration was offered by a philosopher whose name slips me; but I know I have read his argument which is that air exhibits greater gravity than levity, because it carries heavy bodies downward more easily than it does light ones upward.

Sagr. Fine indeed! So according to this theory air is much heavier than water, since all heavy bodies are carried downward more easily through air than through water, and all light bodies buoyed up more easily through water than through air; further there is an infinite number of heavy bodies which fall through air but ascend in water and there is an infinite number of substances which rise in water and fall in air. But, Simplicio, the question as to whether the weight of the leather bottle is owing to thick vapors or to pure air does not affect our problem which is to discover how bodies move through this vapor-laden atmosphere of ours. Returning now to the question which interests me more, I should like, for the sake of more complete and thorough knowledge of this matter, not only to be strengthened in my belief that air has weight but also to learn, if possible, how great its specific gravity is. Therefore, Salviati, if you can satisfy my curiosity on this point pray do so.

[123]

Salv. The experiment with the inflated leather bottle of Aristotle proves conclusively that air possesses positive gravity and not, as some have believed, levity, a property possessed possibly by no substance whatever; for if air did possess this quality of absolute and positive levity, it should on compression exhibit greater levity and, hence, a greater tendency to rise; but experiment shows precisely the opposite.

As to the other question, namely, how to determine the specific gravity of air, I have employed the following method. I took a rather large glass bottle with a narrow neck and attached to it a leather cover, binding it tightly about the neck of the bottle: in the top of this cover I inserted and firmly fastened the valve of a leather bottle, through which I forced into the glass bottle, by means of a syringe, a large quantity of air. And since air is easily condensed one can pump into the bottle two or three times its own volume of air. After this I took an accurate balance and weighed this bottle of compressed air with the utmost precision, adjusting the weight with fine sand. I next opened the valve and allowed the compressed air to escape; then replaced the flask upon the balance and found it perceptibly lighter: from the sand which had been used as a counterweight I now removed and laid aside as much as was necessary to again secure balance. Under these conditions there can be no doubt but that the weight of the sand thus laid aside represents the weight of the air which had been forced into the flask and had afterwards escaped. But after all this experiment tells me merely that the weight of the compressed air is the same as that of the sand removed from the balance;

when however it comes to knowing certainly and definitely the weight of air as compared with that of water or any other heavy substance this I cannot hope to do without first measuring the volume [*quantità*] of compressed air; for this measurement I have devised the two following methods.

According to the first method one takes a bottle with a narrow neck similar to the previous one; over the mouth of this bottle is slipped a leather tube which is bound tightly about the neck of the flask; the other end of this tube embraces the valve attached to the first flask and is tightly bound about it. This second flask is provided with a hole in the bottom through which an iron rod can be placed so as to open, at will, the valve above mentioned and thus permit the surplus air of the first to escape after it has once been weighed: but his second bottle must be filled with water. Having prepared everything in the manner above described, open the valve with the rod; the air will rush into the flask containing the water and will drive it through the hole at the bottom, it being clear that the volume [*quantità*] of water thus displaced is equal to the volume [*mole e quantità*] of air escaped from the other vessel. Having set aside this displaced water, weigh the vessel from which the air has escaped (which is supposed to have been weighed previously while containing the compressed air), and remove the surplus of sand as described above; it is then manifest that the weight of this sand is precisely the weight of a volume [*mole*] of air equal to the volume of water displaced and set aside; this water we can weigh and find how many times its weight contains the weight of the removed sand, thus determining definitely how many times heavier water is than air; and we shall find, contrary to the opinion of Aristotle, that this is not 10 times, but, as our experiment shows, more nearly 400 times.

[124]

The second method is more expeditious and can be carried out with a single vessel fitted up as the first was. Here no air is added to that which the vessel naturally contains but water is forced into it without allowing any air to escape; the water thus introduced necessarily compresses the air. Having forced into the vessel as much water as possible, filling it, say, three-fourths full, which does not require any extraordinary effort, place it upon the balance and weigh it accurately; next hold the vessel mouth up, open the valve, and allow the air to escape; the volume of the air thus escaping is precisely equal to the volume of water contained in the flask. Again weigh the vessel which will have diminished in weight on account of the escaped air; this loss in weight represents the weight of a volume of air equal to the volume of water contained in the vessel.

Simp. No one can deny the cleverness and ingenuity of your devices; but while they appear to give complete intellectual satisfaction they confuse me in another direction. For since it is undoubtedly true that the elements when in their proper places

have neither weight nor levity, I cannot understand how it is possible for that portion of air, which appeared to weigh, say, 4 drachms of sand, should really have such a weight in air as the sand which counterbalances it. It seems to me, therefore, that the experiment should be carried out, not in air, but in a medium in which the air could exhibit its property of weight if such it really has.

[125]

Salv. The objection of Simplicio is certainly to the point and must therefore either be unanswerable or demand an equally clear solution. It is perfectly evident that that air which, under compression, weighed as much as the sand, loses this weight when once allowed to escape into its own element, while, indeed, the sand retains its weight. Hence for this experiment it becomes necessary to select a place where air as well as sand can gravitate; because, as has been often remarked, the medium diminishes the weight of any substance immersed in it by an amount equal to the weight of the displaced medium; so that air in air loses all its weight. If therefore this experiment is to be made with accuracy it should be performed in a vacuum where every heavy body exhibits its momentum without the slightest diminution. If then, Simplicio, we were to weigh a portion of air in a vacuum would you then be satisfied and assured of the fact?

Simp. Yes truly: but this is to wish or ask the impossible.

Salv. Your obligation will then be very great if, for your sake, I accomplish the impossible. But I do not want to sell you something which I have already given you; for in the previous experiment we weighed the air in vacuum and not in air or other medium. The fact that any fluid medium diminishes the weight of a mass immersed in it, is due, Simplicio, to the resistance which this medium offers to its being opened up, driven aside, and finally lifted up. The evidence for this is seen in the readiness with which the fluid rushes to fill up any space formerly occupied by the mass; if the medium were not affected by such an immersion then it would not react against the immersed body. Tell me now, when you have a flask, in air, filled with its natural amount of air and then proceed to pump into the vessel more air, does this extra charge in any way separate or divide or change the circumambient air? Does the vessel perhaps expand so that the surrounding medium is displaced in order to give more room? Certainly not.

[126]

Therefore one is able to say that this extra charge of air is not immersed in the surrounding medium for it occupies no space in it, but is, as it were, in a vacuum. Indeed, it is really in a vacuum; for it diffuses into the vacuities which are not completely filled

by the original and uncondensed air. In fact I do not see any difference between the enclosed and the surrounding media: for the surrounding medium does not press upon the enclosed medium and, *vice versa*, the enclosed medium exerts no pressure against the surrounding one; this same relationship exists in the case of any matter in a vacuum, as well as in the case of the extra charge of air compressed into the flask. The weight of this condensed air is therefore the same as that which it would have if set free in a vacuum. It is true of course that the weight of the sand used as a counterpoise would be a little greater *in vacuo* than in free air. We must, then, say that the air is slightly lighter than the sand required to counterbalance it, that is to say, by an amount equal to the weight *in vacuo* of a volume of air equal to the volume of the sand.*

[127]

Simp. The previous experiments, in my opinion, left something to be desired: but now I am fully satisfied.

Salv. The facts set forth by me up to this point and, in particular, the one which shows that difference of weight, even when very great, is without effect in changing the speed of falling bodies, so that as far as weight is concerned they all fall with equal speed: this idea is, I say, so new, and at first glance so remote from fact, that if we do not have the means of making it just as clear as sunlight, it had better not be mentioned; but having once allowed it to pass my lips I must neglect no experiment or argument to establish it.

Sagr. Not only this but also many other of your views are so far removed from the commonly accepted opinions and doctrines that if you were to publish them you would stir up a large number of antagonists; for human nature is such that men do not look with favor upon discoveries—either of truth or fallacy—in their own field, when made by others than themselves. They call him an innovator of doctrine, an unpleasant title, by which they hope to cut those knots which they cannot untie, and by subterranean mines they seek to destroy structures which patient artisans have built with customary tools. But as for ourselves who have no such thoughts, the experiments and

---

* At this point in an annotated copy of the original edition the following note by Galileo is found.

[Sagr. A very clever discussion, solving a wonderful problem, because it demonstrates briefly and concisely the manner in which one may find the weight of a body *in vacuo* by simply weighing it in air. The explanation is as follows: when a heavy body is immersed in air it loses in weight an amount equal to the weight of a volume [*mole*] of air equivalent to the volume [*mole*] of the body itself. Hence if one adds to a body, without expanding it, a quantity of air equal to that which it displaces and weighs it, he will obtain its absolute weight *in vacuo*, since, without increasing it in size, he has increased its weight by just the amount which it lost through immersion in air.

When therefore we force a quantity of water into a vessel which already contains its normal amount of air, without allowing any of this air to escape it is clear that this normal quantity of air will be compressed and condensed into a smaller space in order to make room for the water which is forced in; it is also clear that the volume of air thus compressed is equal to the volume of water added. If now the vessel be weighed in air in this condition, it is manifest that the weight of the water will be increased by that of an equal volume of air; the total weight of water and air thus obtained is equal to the weight of the water alone *in vacuo*.

Now record the weight of the entire vessel and then allow the compressed air to escape; weigh the remainder; the difference of these two weights will be the weight of the compressed air which, in volume, is equal to that of the water. Next find the weight of the water alone and add to it that of the compressed air; we shall then have the water alone *in vacuo*. To find the weight of the water we shall have to remove it from the vessel and weigh the vessel alone; subtract this weight from that of the vessel and water together. It is clear that the remainder will be the weight of the water alone in air.]

[128]

arguments which you have thus far adduced are fully satisfactory; however if you have any experiments which are more direct or any arguments which are more convincing we will hear them with pleasure.

Salv. The experiment made to ascertain whether two bodies, differing greatly in weight will fall from a given height with the same speed offers some difficulty; because, if the height is considerable, the retarding effect of the medium, which must be penetrated and thrust aside by the falling body, will be greater in the case of the small momentum of the very light body than in the case of the great force [*violenza*] of the heavy body; so that, in a long distance, the light body will be left behind; if the height be small, one may well doubt whether there is any difference; and if there be a difference it will be inappreciable.

It occurred to me therefore to repeat many times the fall through a small height in such a way that I might accumulate all those small intervals of time that elapse between the arrival of the heavy and light bodies respectively at their common terminus, so that this sum makes an interval of time which is not only observable, but easily observable. In order to employ the slowest speeds possible and thus reduce the change which the resisting medium produces upon the simple effect of gravity it occurred to me to allow the bodies to fall along a plane slightly inclined to the horizontal. For in such a plane, just as well as in a vertical plane, one may discover how bodies of different weight behave: and besides this, I also wished to rid myself of the resistance which might arise from contact of the moving body with the aforesaid inclined plane. Accordingly I took two balls, one of lead and one of cork, the former more than a hundred times heavier than the latter, and suspended them by means of two equal fine threads, each four or five cubits long.

[129]

Pulling each ball aside from the perpendicular, I let them go at the same instant, and they, falling along the circumferences of circles having these equal strings for semidiameters, passed beyond the perpendicular and returned along the same path. This free vibration [*per lor medesime le andate e le tornate*] repeated a hundred times showed clearly that the heavy body maintains so nearly the period of the light body that neither in a hundred swings nor even in a thousand will the former anticipate the latter by as much as a single moment [*minimo momento*], so perfectly do they keep step. We can also observe the effect of the medium which, by the resistance which it offers to motion, diminishes the vibration of the cork more than that of the lead, but without altering the frequency of either; even when the arc traversed by the cork did not exceed five or six degrees while that of the lead was fifty or sixty, the swings were performed in equal times.

Simp. If this be so, why is not the speed of the lead greater than that of the cork, seeing that the former traverses sixty degrees in the same interval in which the latter covers scarcely six?

Salv. But what would you say, Simplicio, if both covered their paths in the same time when the cork, drawn aside through thirty degrees, traverses an arc of sixty, while the lead pulled aside only two degrees traverses an arc of four? Would not then the cork be proportionately swifter? And yet such is the experimental fact. But observe this: having pulled aside the pendulum of lead, say through an arc of fifty degrees, and set it free, it swings beyond the perpendicular almost fifty degrees, thus describing an arc of nearly one hundred degrees; on the return swing it describes a little smaller arc; and after a large number of such vibrations it finally comes to rest. Each vibration, whether of ninety, fifty, twenty, ten, or four degrees occupies the same time: accordingly the speed of the moving body keeps on diminishing since in equal intervals of time, it traverses arcs which grow smaller and smaller.

Precisely the same things happen with the pendulum of cork, suspended by a string of equal length, except that a smaller number of vibrations is required to bring it to rest, since on account of its lightness it is less able to overcome the resistance of the air; nevertheless the vibrations, whether large or small, are all performed in time-intervals which are not only equal among themselves, but also equal to the period of the lead pendulum. Hence it is true that, if while the lead is traversing an arc of fifty degrees the cork covers one of only ten, the cork moves more slowly than the lead; but on the other hand it is also true that the cork may cover an arc of fifty while the lead passes over one of only ten or six; thus, at different times, we have now the cork, now the lead, moving more rapidly. But if these same bodies traverse equal arcs in equal times we may rest assured that their speeds are equal.

[130]

Simp. I hesitate to admit the conclusiveness of this argument because of the confusion which arises from your making both bodies move now rapidly, now slowly and now very slowly, which leaves me in doubt as to whether their velocities are always equal.

Sagr. Allow me, if you please, Salviati, to say just a few words. Now tell me, Simplicio, whether you admit that one can say with certainty that the speeds of the cork and the lead are equal whenever both, starting from rest at same moment and descending the same slopes, always traverse equal spaces in equal times?

Simp. This can neither be doubted nor gainsaid.

Sagr. Now it happens, in the case of the pendulums, that each of them traverses now an arc of sixty degrees, now one of fifty, or thirty or ten or eight or four or two, etc.; and when they both swing through an are of sixty degrees they do so in equal

intervals of time; the same thing happens when the are is fifty degrees or thirty or ten or any other number; and therefore we conclude that the speed of the lead in an arc of sixty degrees is equal to the speed of the cork when the latter also swings through an arc of sixty degrees; in the case of a fifty-degree arc these speeds are also equal to each other; so also in the case of other arcs. But this is not saying that the speed which occurs in an arc of sixty is the same as that which occurs in an arc of fifty; nor is the speed in an arc of fifty equal to that in one of thirty, etc.; but the smaller the arcs, the smaller the speeds; the fact observed is that one and the same moving body requires the same time for traversing a large arc of sixty degrees as for a small arc of fifty or even a very small arc of ten; all these arcs, indeed, are covered in the same interval of time. It is true therefore that the lead and the cork each diminish their speed [*moto*] in proportion as their arcs diminish; but this does not contradict the fact that they maintain equal speeds in equal arcs.

[131]

My reason for saying these things has been rather because I wanted to learn whether I had correctly understood Salviati, than because I thought Simplicio had any need of a clearer explanation than that given by Salviati which like everything else of his is extremely lucid, so lucid, indeed, that when he solves questions which are difficult not merely in appearance, but in reality and in fact, he does so with reasons, observations and experiments which are common and familiar to everyone.

In this manner he has, as I have learned from various sources, given occasion to a highly esteemed professor for undervaluing his discoveries on the ground that they are commonplace, and established upon a mean and vulgar basis; as if it were not a most admirable and praiseworthy feature of demonstrative science that it springs from and grows out of principles well-known, understood and conceded by all.

But let us continue with this light diet; and if Simplicio is satisfied to understand and admit that the gravity inherent [*interna gravità*] in various falling bodies has nothing to do with the difference of speed observed among them, and that all bodies, in so far as their speeds depend upon it, would move with the same velocity, pray tell us, Salviati, how you explain the appreciable and evident inequality of motion; please reply also to the objection urged by Simplicio—an objection in which I concur—namely, that a cannon ball falls more rapidly than a bird-shot. From my point of view, one might expect the difference of speed to be small in the case of bodies of the same substance moving through any single medium, whereas the larger ones will descend, during a single pulse-beat, a distance which the smaller ones will not traverse in an hour, or in four, or even in twenty hours; as for instance in the case of stones and fine sand and especially that very fine sand which produces muddy water and which in many hours will

not fall through as much as two cubits, a distance which stones not much larger will traverse in a single pulse-beat.

[132]

Salv. The action of the medium in producing a greater retardation upon those bodies which have a less specific gravity has already been explained by showing that they experience a diminution of weight. But to explain how one and the same medium produces such different retardations in bodies which are made of the same material and have the same shape, but differ only in size, requires a discussion more clever than that by which one explains how a more expanded shape or an opposing motion of the medium retards the speed of the moving body. The solution of the present problem lies, I think, in the roughness and porosity which are generally and almost necessarily found in the surfaces of solid bodies. When the body is in motion these rough places strike the air or other ambient medium. The evidence for this is found in the humming which accompanies the rapid motion of a body through air, even when that body is as round as possible. One hears not only humming, but also hissing and whistling, whenever there is any appreciable cavity or elevation upon the body. We observe also that a round solid body rotating in a lathe produces a current of air. But what more do we need? When a top spins on the ground at its greatest speed do we not hear a distinct buzzing of high pitch? This sibilant note diminishes in pitch as the speed of rotation slackens, which is evidence that these small rugosities on the surface meet resistance in the air. There can be no doubt, therefore, that in the motion of falling bodies these rugosities strike the surrounding fluid and retard the speed; and this they do so much the more in proportion as the surface is larger, which is the case of small bodies as compared with greater.

Simp. Stop a moment please, I am getting confused. For although I understand and admit that friction of the medium upon the surface of the body retards its motion and that, if other things are the same, the larger surface suffers greater retardation, I do not see on what ground you say that the surface of the smaller body is larger. Besides if, as you say, the larger surface suffers greater retardation the larger solid should move more slowly, which is not the fact. But this objection can be easily met by saying that, although the larger body has a larger surface, it has also a greater weight, in comparison with which the resistance of the larger surface is no more than the resistance of the small surface in comparison with its smaller weight; so that the speed of the larger solid does not become less. I therefore see no reason for expecting any difference of speed so long as the driving weight [*gravità movente*] diminishes in the same proportion as the retarding power [*facolta ritardante*] of the surface.

[133]

Salv. I shall answer all your objections at once. You will admit, of course, Simplicio, that if one takes two equal bodies, of the same material and same figure, bodies which would therefore fall with equal speeds, and if he diminishes the weight of one of them in the same proportion as its surface (maintaining the similarity of shape) he would not thereby diminish the speed of this body.

Simp. This inference seems to be in harmony with your theory which states that the weight of a body has no effect in either accelerating or retarding its motion.

Salv. I quite agree with you in this opinion from which it appears to follow that, if the weight of a body is diminished in greater proportion than its surface, the motion is retarded to a certain extent; and this retardation is greater and greater in proportion as the diminution of weight exceeds that of the surface.

Simp. This I admit without hesitation.

Salv. Now you must know, Simplicio, that it is not possible to diminish the surface of a solid body in the same ratio as the weight, and at the same time maintain similarity of figure. For since it is clear that in the case of a diminishing solid the weight grows less in proportion to the volume, and since the volume always diminishes more rapidly than the surface, when the same shape is maintained, the weight must therefore diminish more rapidly than the surface. But geometry teaches us that, in the case of similar solids, the ratio of two volumes is greater than the ratio of their surfaces; which, for the sake of better understanding, I shall illustrate by a particular case.

Take, for example, a cube two inches on a side so that each face has an area of four square inches and the total area, i. e., the sum of the six faces, amounts to twenty-four square inches; now imagine this cube to be sawed through three times so as to divide it into eight smaller cubes, each one inch on the side, each face one inch square, and the total surface of each cube six square inches instead of twenty-four as in the case of the larger cube. It is evident therefore that the surface of the little cube is only one-fourth that of the larger, namely, the ratio of six to twenty-four; but the volume of the solid cube itself is only one-eighth; the volume, and hence also the weight, diminishes therefore much more rapidly than the surface. If we again divide the little cube into eight others we shall have, for the total surface of one of these, one and one-half square inches, which is one-sixteenth of the surface of the original cube; but its volume is only one-sixty-fourth part.

[134]

Thus, by two divisions, you see that the volume is diminished four times as much as the surface. And, if the subdivision be continued until the original solid be reduced to

a fine powder, we shall find that the weight of one of these smallest particles has diminished hundreds and hundreds of times as much as its surface. And this which I have illustrated in the case of cubes holds also in the case of all similar solids, where the volumes stand in sesquialteral ratio to their surfaces. Observe then how much greater the resistance, arising from contact of the surface of the moving body with the medium, in the case of small bodies than in the case of large; and when one considers that the rugosities on the very small surfaces of fine dust particles are perhaps no smaller than those on the surfaces of larger solids which have been carefully polished, he will see how important it is that the medium should be very fluid and offer no resistance to being thrust aside, easily yielding to a small force. You see, therefore, Simplicio, that I was not mistaken when, not long ago, I said that the surface of a small solid is comparatively greater than that of a large one.

Simp. I am quite convinced; and, believe me, if I were again beginning my studies, I should follow the advice of Plato and start with mathematics, a science which proceeds very cautiously and admits nothing as established until it has been rigidly demonstrated.

Sagr. This discussion has afforded me great pleasure; but before proceeding further I should like to hear the explanation of a phrase of yours which is new to me, namely, that similar solids are to each other in the sesquialteral ratio of their surfaces; for although I have seen and understood the proposition in which it is demonstrated that the surfaces of similar solids are in the duplicate ratio of their sides and also the proposition which proves that the volumes are in the triplicate ratio of their sides, yet I have not so much as heard mentioned the ratio of the volume of a solid to its surface.

[135]

Salv. You yourself have suggested the answer to your question and have removed every doubt. For if one quantity is the cube of something of which another quantity is the square does it not follow that the cube is the sesquialteral of the square? Surely. Now if the surface varies as the square of its linear dimensions while the volume varies as the cube of these dimensions may we not say that the volume stands in sesquialteral ratio to the surface?

Sagr. Quite so. And now although there are still some details, in connection with the subject under discussion, concerning which I might ask questions yet, if we keep making one digression after another, it will be long before we reach the main topic which has to do with the variety of properties found in the resistance which solid bodies offer to fracture; and, therefore, if you please, let us return to the subject which we originally proposed to discuss.

Salv. Very well; but the questions which we have already considered are so numerous and so varied, and have taken up so much time that there is not much of this day left to spend upon our main topic which abounds in geometrical demonstrations calling for careful consideration. May I, therefore, suggest that we postpone the meeting until to-morrow, not only for the reason just mentioned but also in order that I may bring with me some papers in which I have set down in an orderly way the theorems and propositions dealing with the various phases of this subject, matters which, from memory alone, I could not present in the proper order.

Sagr. I fully concur in your opinion and all the more willingly because this will leave time to-day to take up some of my difficulties with the subject which we have just been discussing. One question is whether we are to consider the resistance of the medium as sufficient to destroy the acceleration of a body of very heavy material, very large volume, and spherical figure. I say *spherical* in order to select a volume which is contained within a minimum surface and therefore less subject to retardation.

[136]

Another question deals with the vibrations of pendulums which may be regarded from several viewpoints; the first is whether all vibrations, large, medium, and small, are performed in exactly and precisely equal times: another is to find the ratio of the times of vibration of pendulums supported by threads of unequal length.

Salv. These are interesting questions: but I fear that here, as in the case of all other facts, if we take up for discussion any one of them, it will carry in its wake so many other facts and curious consequences that time will not remain to-day for the discussion of all.

Sagr. If these are as full of interest as the foregoing, I would gladly spend as many days as there remain hours between now and nightfall; and I dare say that Simplicio would not be wearied by these discussions.

Simp. Certainly not; especially when the questions pertain to natural science and have not been treated by other philosophers.

Salv. Now taking up the first question, I can assert without hesitation that there is no sphere so large, or composed of material so dense but that the resistance of the medium, although very slight, would check its acceleration and would, in time reduce its motion to uniformity; a statement which is strongly supported by experiment. For if a falling body, as time goes on, were to acquire a speed as great as you please, no such speed, impressed by external forces [*motore esterno*], can be so great but that the body will first acquire it and then, owing to the resisting medium, lose it. Thus, for instance, if a cannon ball, having fallen a distance of four cubits through the air and having acquired a speed of, say, ten units [*gradi*] were to strike the surface of the water, and if

the resistance of the water were not able to chock the momentum [*impeto*] of the shot, it would either increase in speed or maintain a uniform motion until the bottom were reached: but such is not the observed fact; on the contrary, the water when only a few cubits deep hinders and diminishes the motion in such a way that the shot delivers to the bed of the river or lake a very slight impulse.

[137]

Clearly then if a short fall through the water is sufficient to deprive a cannon ball of its speed, this speed cannot be regained by a fall of even a thousand cubits. How could a body acquire, in a fall of a thousand cubits, that which it loses in a fall of four? But what more is needed? Do we not observe that the enormous momentum, delivered to a shot by a cannon, is so deadened by passing through a few cubits of water that the ball, so far from injuring the ship, barely strikes it? Even the air, although a very yielding medium, can also diminish the speed of a falling body, as may be easily understood from similar experiments. For if a gun be fired downwards from the top of a very high tower the shot will make a smaller impression upon the ground than if the gun had been fired from an elevation of only four or six cubits; this is clear evidence that the momentum of the ball, fired from the top of the tower, diminishes continually from the instant it leaves the barrel until it reaches the ground. Therefore a fall from ever so great an altitude will not suffice to give to a body that momentum which it has once lost through resistance of the air, no matter how it was originally acquired. In like manner, the destructive effect produced upon a wall by a shot fired from a gun at a distance of twenty cubits cannot be duplicated by the fall of the same shot from any altitude however great. My opinion is, therefore, that under the circumstances which occur in nature, the acceleration of any body falling from rest reaches an end and that the resistance of the medium finally reduces its speed to a constant value which is thereafter maintained.

Sagr. These experiments are in my opinion much to the purpose; the only question is whether an opponent might not make bold to deny the fact in the case of bodies [*moli*] which are very large and heavy or to assert that a cannon ball, falling from the distance of the moon or from the upper regions of the atmosphere, would deliver a heavier blow than if just leaving the muzzle of the gun.

[138]

Salv. No doubt many objections may be raised not all of which can be refuted by experiment: however in this particular case the following consideration must be taken into account, namely, that it is very likely that a heavy body falling from a height will,

on reaching the ground, have acquired just as much momentum as was necessary to carry it to that height; as may be clearly seen in the case of a rather heavy pendulum which, when pulled aside fifty or sixty degrees from the vertical, will acquire precisely that speed and force which are sufficient to carry it to an equal elevation save only that small portion which it loses through friction on the air. In order to place a cannon ball at such a height as might suffice to give it just that momentum which the powder imparted to it on leaving the gun we need only fire it vertically upwards from the same gun; and we can then observe whether on falling back it delivers a blow equal to that of the gun fired at close range; in my opinion it would be much weaker. The resistance of the air would, therefore, I think, prevent the muzzle velocity from being equalled by a natural fall from rest at any height whatsoever.

We come now to the other questions, relating to pendulums, a subject which may appear to many exceedingly arid, especially to those philosophers who are continually occupied with the more profound questions of nature. Nevertheless, the problem is one which I do not scorn. I am encouraged by the example of Aristotle whom I admire especially because he did not fail to discuss every subject which he thought in any degree worthy of consideration.

Impelled by your queries I may give you some of my ideas concerning certain problems in music, a splendid subject, upon which so many eminent men have written: among these is Aristotle himself who has discussed numerous interesting acoustical questions. Accordingly, if on the basis of some easy and tangible experiments, I shall explain some striking phenomena in the domain of sound, I trust my explanations will meet your approval.

[139]

Sagr. I shall receive them not only gratefully but eagerly. For, although I take pleasure in every kind of musical instrument and have paid considerable attention to harmony, I have never been able to fully understand why some combinations of tones are more pleasing than others, or why certain combinations not only fail to please but are even highly offensive. Then there is the old problem of two stretched strings in unison; when one of them is sounded, the other begins to vibrate and to emit its note; nor do I understand the different ratios of harmony [*forme delle consonanze*] and some other details.

Salv. Let us see whether we cannot derive from the pendulum a satisfactory solution of all these difficulties. And first, as to the question whether one and the same pendulum really performs its vibrations, large, medium, and small, all in exactly the same time, I shall rely upon what I have already heard from our Academician. He has clearly shown that the time of descent is the same along all chords, whatever the arcs which

subtend them, as well along an arc of 180° (i. e., the whole diameter) as along one of 100°, 60°, 10°, 2°, 1/2°, or 4'. It is understood, of course, that these arcs all terminate at the lowest point of the circle, where it touches the horizontal plane.

If now we consider descent along arcs instead of their chords then, provided these do. not exceed 90°, experiment shows that they are all traversed in equal times; but these times are greater for the chord than for the arc, an effect which is all the more remarkable because at first glance one would think just the opposite to be true. For since the terminal points of the two motions are the same and since the straight line included between these two points is the shortest distance between them, it would seem reasonable that motion along this line should be executed in the shortest time; but this is not the case, for the shortest time—and therefore the most rapid motion— is that employed along the arc of which this straight line is the chord.

As to the times of vibration of bodies suspended by threads of different lengths, they bear to each other the same proportion as the square roots of the lengths of the thread; or one might say the lengths are to each other as the squares of the times; so that if one wishes to make the vibration-time of one pendulum twice that of another, he must make its suspension four times as long. In like manner, if one pendulum has a suspension nine times as long as another, this second pendulum will execute three vibrations during each one of the first; from which it follows that the lengths of the suspending cords bear to each other the [inverse] ratio of the squares of the number of vibrations performed in the same time.

[140]

Sagr. Then, if I understand you correctly, I can easily measure the length of a string whose upper end is attached at any height whatever even if this end were invisible and I could see only the lower extremity. For if I attach to the lower end of this string a rather heavy weight and give it a to-and-fro motion, and if I ask a friend to count a number of its vibrations, while I, during the same time interval, count the number of vibrations of a pendulum which is exactly one cubit in length, then knowing the number of vibrations which each pendulum makes in the given interval of time one can determine the length of the string. Suppose, for example, that my friend counts 20 vibrations of the long cord during the same time in which I count 240 of my string which is one cubit in length; taking the squares of the two numbers, 20 and 240, namely 400 and 57600, then, I say, the long string contains 57600 units of such length that my pendulum will contain 400 of them; and since the length of my string is one cubit, I shall divide 57600 by 400 and thus obtain 144. Accordingly I shall call the length of the string 144 cubits.

Salv. Nor will you miss it by as much as a hand's breadth, especially if you observe a large number of vibrations.

Sagr. You give me frequent occasion to admire the wealth and profusion of nature when, from such common and even trivial phenomena, you derive facts which are not only striking and new but which are often far removed from what we would have imagined. Thousands of times I have observed vibrations especially in churches where lamps, suspended by long cords, had been inadvertently set into motion; but the most which I could infer from these observations was that the view of those who think that such vibrations are maintained by the medium is highly improbable: for, in that case, the air must needs have considerable judgment and little else to do but kill time by pushing to and fro a pendent weight with perfect regularity. But I never dreamed of learning that one and the same body, when suspended from a string a hundred cubits long and pulled aside through an arc of 90° or even 1° or 1/2°, would employ the same time in passing through the least as through the largest of these arcs; and, indeed, it still strikes me as somewhat unlikely. Now I am waiting to hear how these same simple phenomena can furnish solutions for those acoustical problems-solutions which will be at least partly satisfactory.

[141]

Salv. First of all one must observe that each pendulum has its own time of vibration so definite and determinate that it is not possible to make it move with any other period [altro periodo] than that which nature has given it. For let any one take in his hand the cord to which the weight is attached and try, as much as he pleases, to increase or diminish the frequency [frequenza] of its vibrations; it will be time wasted. On the other hand, one can confer motion upon even a heavy pendulum which is at rest by simply blowing against it; by repeating these blasts with a frequency which is the same as that of the pendulum one can impart considerable motion. Suppose that by the first puff we have displaced the pendulum from the vertical by, say, half an inch; then if, after the pendulum has returned and is about to begin the second vibration, we add a second puff, we shall impart additional motion; and so on with other blasts provided they are applied at the right instant, and not when the pendulum is coming toward us since in this case the blast would impede rather than aid the motion. Continuing thus with many impulses [impulsi] we impart to the pendulum such momentum [impeto] that a greater impulse [forza] than that of a single blast will be needed to stop it.

Sagr. Even as a boy, I observed that one man alone by giving these impulses at the right instant was able to ring a bell so large that when four, or even six, men seized the rope and tried to stop it they were lifted from the ground, all of them together being unable to counterbalance the momentum which a single man, by properly-timed pulls, had given it.

[142]

Salv. Your illustration makes my meaning clear and is quite as well fitted, as what I have just said, to explain the wonderful phenomenon of the strings of the cittern [*cetera*] or of the spinet [*cimbalo*], namely, the fact that a vibrating string will set another string in motion and cause it to sound not only when the latter is in unison but even when it differs from the former by an octave or a fifth. A string which has been struck begins to vibrate and continues the motion as long as one hears the sound [*risonanza*]; these vibrations cause the immediately surrounding air to vibrate and quiver; then these ripples in the air expand far into space and strike not only all the strings of the same instrument but even those of neighboring instruments. Since that string which is tuned to unison with the one plucked is capable of vibrating with the same frequency, it acquires, at the first impulse, a slight oscillation; after receiving two, three, twenty, or more impulses, delivered at proper intervals, it finally accumulates a vibratory motion equal to that of the plucked string, as is clearly shown by equality of amplitude in their vibrations. This undulation expands through the air and sets into vibration not only strings, but also any other body which happens to have the same period as that of the plucked string. Accordingly if we attach to the side of an instrument small pieces of bristle or other flexible bodies, we shall observe that, when a spinet is sounded, only those pieces respond that have the same period as the string which has been struck; the remaining pieces do not vibrate in response to this string, nor do the former pieces respond to any other tone.

If one bows the base string on a viola rather smartly and brings near it a goblet of fine, thin glass having the same tone [*tuono*] as that of the string, this goblet will vibrate and audibly resound. That the undulations of the medium are widely dispersed about the sounding body is evinced by the fact that a glass of water may be made to emit a tone merely by the friction of the finger-tip upon the rim of the glass; for in this water is produced a series of regular waves. The same phenomenon is observed to better advantage by fixing the base of the goblet upon the bottom of a rather large vessel of water filled nearly to the edge of the goblet; for if, as before, we sound the glass by friction of the finger, me shall see ripples spreading with the utmost regularity and with high speed to large distances about the glass. I have often remarked, in thus sounding a rather large glass nearly full of water, that at first the waves are spaced with great uniformity, and when, as sometimes happens, the tone of the glass jumps an octave higher I have noted that at this moment each of the aforesaid waves divides into two; a phenomenon which shows clearly that the ratio involved in the octave [*forma dell' ottava*] is two.

[143]

Sagr. More than once have I observed this same thing, much to my delight and also to my profit. For a long time I have been perplexed about these different harmonies since the explanations hitherto given by those learned in music impress me as not sufficiently conclusive. They tell us that the diapason, i. e. the octave, involves the ratio of two, that the diapente which we call the fifth involves a ratio of 3:2, etc.; because if the open string of a monochord be sounded and afterwards a bridge be placed in the middle and the half length be sounded one hears the octave; and if the bridge be placed at 1/3 the length of the string, then on plucking first the open string and afterwards 2/3 of its length the fifth is given; for this reason they say that the octave depends upon the ratio of two to one [*contenuta trà'l due e l'uno*] and the fifth upon the ratio of three to two. This explanation does not impress me as sufficient to establish 2 and 3/2 as the natural ratios of the octave and the fifth; and my reason for thinking so is as follows. There are three different ways in which the tone of a string may be sharpened, namely, by shortening it, by stretching it and by making it thinner. If the tension and size of the string remain constant one obtains the octave by shortening it to one-half, i. e., by sounding first the open string and then one-half of it; but if length and size remain constant and one attempts to produce the octave by stretching he will find that it does not suffice to double the stretching weight; it must be quadrupled; so that, if the fundamental note is produced by a weight of one pound, four will be required to bring out the octave.

And finally if the length and tension remain constant, while one changes the size[13] of the string he will find that in order to produce the octave the size must be reduced to 1/4 that which gave the fundamental. And what I have said concerning the octave, namely, that its ratio as derived from the tension and size of the string is the square of that derived from the length, applies equally well to all other musical intervals [*intervalli musici*].

[144]

Thus if one wishes to produce a fifth by changing the length he finds that the ratio of the lengths must be sesquialteral, in other words he sounds first the open string, then two-thirds of it; but if he wishes to produce this same result by stretching or thinning the string then it becomes necessary to square the ratio 3/2 that is by taking 9/4 [*dupla sesquiquarta*]; accordingly, if the fundamental requires a weight of 4 pounds, the higher note will be produced not by 6, but by 9 pounds; the same is true in regard to size, the string which gives the fundamental is larger than that which yields the fifth in the ratio of 9 to 4.

13. For the exact meaning of "size" see below. [*Trans.*]

In view of these facts, I see no reason why those wise philosophers should adopt 2 rather than 4 as the ratio of the octave, or why in the case of the fifth they should employ the sesquialteral ratio, 3/2, rather than that of 9/4 Since it is impossible to count the vibrations of a sounding string on account of its high frequency, I should still have been in doubt as to whether a string, emitting the upper octave, made twice as many vibrations in the same time as one giving the fundamental, had it not been for the following fact, namely, that at the instant when the tone jumps to the octave, the waves which constantly accompany the vibrating glass divide up into smaller ones which are precisely half as long as the former.

Salv. This is a beautiful experiment enabling us to distinguish individually the waves which are produced by the vibrations of a sonorous body, which spread through the air, bringing to the tympanum of the ear a stimulus which the mind translates into sound. But since these waves in the water last only so long as the friction of the finger continues and are, even then, not constant but are always forming and disappearing, would it not be a fine thing if one had the ability to produce waves which would persist for a long while, even months and years, so as to easily measure and count them?

Sagr. Such an invention would, I assure you, command my admiration.

[145]

Salv. The device is one which I hit upon by accident; my part consists merely in the observation of it and in the appreciation of its value as a confirmation of something to which I had given profound consideration; and yet the device is, in itself, rather common. As I was scraping a brass plate with a sharp iron chisel in order to remove some spots from it and was running the chisel rather rapidly over it, I once or twice, during many strokes, heard the plate emit a rather strong and clear whistling sound; on looking at the plate more carefully, I noticed a long row of fine streaks parallel and equidistant from one another. Scraping with the chisel over and over again, I noticed that it was only when the plate emitted this hissing noise that any marks were left upon it; when the scraping was not accompanied by this sibilant note there was not the least trace of such marks. Repeating the trick several times and making the stroke, now with greater now with less speed, the whistling followed with a pitch which was correspondingly higher and lower. I noted also that the marks made when the tones were higher were closer together; but when the tones were deeper, they were farther apart. I also observed that when, during a single stroke, the speed increased toward the end the sound became sharper and the streaks grew closer together, but always in such a way as to remain sharply defined and equidistant. Besides whenever the stroke was accompanied by hissing I felt the chisel tremble in my grasp and a sort of shiver run through my band. In short we see and hear in the case of the chisel precisely that which

is, seen and heard in the case of a whisper followed by a loud voice; for, when the breath is emitted without the production of a tone, one does not feel either in the throat or mouth any motion to speak of in comparison with that which is felt in the larynx and upper part of the throat when the voice is used, especially, when the tones employed are low and strong.

At times I have also observed among the strings of the spinet two which were in unison with two of the tones produced by the aforesaid scraping; and among those which differed most in pitch I found two which were separated by an interval of a perfect fifth. Upon measuring the distance between the markings produced by the two scrapings it was found that the space which contained 45 of one contained 30 of the other, which is precisely the ratio assigned to the fifth.

[146]

But now before proceeding any farther I want to call your attention to the fact that, of the three methods for sharpening a tone, the one which you refer to as the fineness of the string should be attributed to its weight. So long as the material of the string is unchanged, the size and weight vary in the same ratio. Thus in the case of gut-strings, we obtain the octave by making one string 4 times as large as the other; so also in the case of brass one wire must have 4 times the size of the other; but if now we wish to obtain the octave of a gut-string, by use of brass wire, we must make it, not four times as large, but four times as heavy as the gutstring: as regards size therefore the metal string is not four times as big but four times as heavy. The wire may therefore be even thinner than the gut notwithstanding the fact that the latter gives the higher note. Hence if two spinets are strung, one with gold wire the other with brass, and if the corresponding strings each have the same length, diameter, and tension it follows that the instrument strung with gold will have a pitch about one-fifth lower than the other because gold has a density almost twice that of brass. And here it is to be noted that it is the weight rather than the size of a moving body which offers resistance to change of motion [*velocità del moto*] contrary to what one might at first glance think. For it seems reasonable to believe that a body which is large and light should suffer greater retardation of motion in thrusting aside the medium than would one which is thin and heavy; yet here exactly the opposite is true.

Returning now to the original subject of discussion, I assert that the ratio of a musical interval is not immediately determined either by the length, size, or tension of the strings but rather by the ratio of their frequencies, that is, by the number of pulses of air waves which strike the tympanum of the ear, causing it also to vibrate with the same frequency. This fact established, we may possibly explain why certain pairs of notes, differing in pitch produce a pleasing sensation, others a less pleasant effect and

still others a disagreeable sensation. Such an explanation would be tantamount to an explanation of the more or less perfect consonances and of dissonances. The unpleasant sensation produced by the latter arises, I think, from the discordant vibrations of two different tones which strike the ear out of time [*sproporzionatamente*]. Especially harsh is the dissonance between notes whose frequencies are incommensurable; such a case occurs when one has two strings in unison and sounds one of them open, together with a part of the other which bears the same ratio to its whole length as the side of a square bears to the diagonal; this yields a dissonance similar to the augmented fourth or diminished fifth [*tritono o semidiapente*].

[147]

Agreeable consonances are pairs of tones which strike the ear with a certain regularity; this regularity consists in the fact that the pulses delivered by the two tones, in the same interval of time, shall be commensurable in number, so as not to keep the ear drum in perpetual torment, bending in two different directions in order to yield to the ever-discordant impulses.

The first and most pleasing consonance is, therefore, the octave since, for every pulse given to the tympanum by the lower string, the sharp string delivers two; accordingly at every other vibration of the upper string both pulses are delivered simultaneously so that one-half the entire number of pulses are delivered in unison. But when two strings are in unison their vibrations always coincide and the effect is that of a single string; hence we do not refer to it as consonance. The fifth is also a pleasing interval since for every two vibrations of the lower string the upper one gives three, so that considering the entire number of pulses from the upper string one-third of them will strike in unison, i. e., between each pair of concordant vibrations there intervene two single vibrations; and when the interval is a fourth, three single vibrations intervene. In case the interval is a second where the ratio is 9/8 it is only every ninth vibration of the upper string which reaches the ear simultaneously with one of the lower; all the others are discordant and produce a harsh effect upon the recipient ear which interprets them as dissonances.

Simp. Won't you be good enough to explain this argument a little more clearly?

[148]

Salv. Let AB denote the length of a wave [*lo spazio e la dilatazione d'una vibrazione*] emitted by the lower string and CD that of a higher string which is emitting the octave of AB; divide AB in the middle at E. If the two strings begin their motions at A and C, it is clear that when the sharp vibration has reached the end D,

the other vibration will have travelled only as far as E, which, not being a terminal point, will emit no pulse; but there is a blow delivered at D. Accordingly when the one wave comes back from D to C, the other passes on from E to B; hence the two pulses from B and C strike the drum of the ear simultaneously. Seeing that these vibrations are repeated again and again in the same manner, we conclude that each alternate pulse from CD falls in unison with one from AB. But each of the pulsations at the terminal points, A and B, is constantly accompanied by one which leaves always from C or always from D. This is clear because if we suppose the waves to reach A and

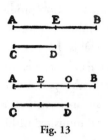

Fig. 13

C at the same instant, then, while one wave travels from A to B, the other will proceed from C to D and back to C, so that waves strike at C and B simultaneously; during the passage of the wave from B back to A the disturbance at C goes to D and again returns to C, so that once more the pulses at A and C are simultaneous.

Next let the vibrations AB and CD be separated by an interval of a fifth, that is, by a ratio of 3/2; choose the points E and O such that they will divide the wave length of the lower string into three equal parts and imagine the vibrations to start at the same instant from each of the terminals A and C. It is evident that when the pulse has been delivered at the terminal D, the wave in AB has travelled only as far as O; the drum of the ear receives, therefore, only the pulse from D. Then during the return of the one vibration from D to C, the other will pass from O to B and then back to O, producing an isolated pulse at B—a pulse which is out of time but one which must be taken into consideration.

Now since we have assumed that the first pulsations started from the terminals A and C at the same instant, it follows that the second pulsation, isolated at D, occurred after an interval of time equal to that required for passage from C to D or, what is the same thing, from A to O; but the next pulsation, the one at B, is separated from the preceding by only half this interval, namely, the time required for passage from O to B. Next while the one vibration travels from O to A, the other travels from C to D, the result of which is that two pulsations occur simultaneously at A and D. Cycles of this kind follow one after another, i. e., one solitary pulse of the lower string interposed between two solitary pulses of the upper string. Let us now imagine time to be divided into very small equal intervals; then if we assume that, during the first two of these intervals, the disturbances which occurred simultaneously at A and C have travelled as far as O and D and have produced a pulse at D; and if we assume that during the third and fourth intervals one disturbance returns from D to C, producing a pulse at C, while the other, passing on from O to B and back to O, produces a pulse at B; and if finally, during the fifth and sixth intervals, the disturbances travel from O and C to A

and D, producing a pulse at each of the latter two, then the sequence in which the pulses strike the ear will be such that, if we begin to count time from any instant where two pulses are simultaneous, the ear drum will, after the lapse of two of the said intervals, receive a solitary pulse; at the end of the third interval, another solitary pulse; so also at the end of the fourth interval; and two intervals later, i. e., at the end of the sixth interval, will be heard two pulses in unison. Here ends the cycle—the anomaly, so to speak—which repeats itself over and over again.

[149]

Sagr. I can no longer remain silent; for I must express to you the great pleasure I have in hearing such a complete explanation of phenomena with regard to which I have so long been in darkness. Now I understand why unison does not differ from a single tone; I understand why the octave is the principal harmony, but so like unison as often to be mistaken for it and also why it occurs with the other harmonies. It resembles unison because the pulsations of strings in unison always occur simultaneously, and those of the lower string of the octave are always accompanied by those of the upper string; and among the latter is interposed a solitary pulse at equal intervals and in such a manner as to produce no disturbance; the result is that such a harmony is rather too much softened and lacks fire. But the fifth is characterized by its displaced beats and by the interposition of two solitary beats of the upper string and one solitary beat of the lower string between each pair of simultaneous pulses; these three solitary pulses are separated by intervals of time equal to half the interval which separates each pair of simultaneous beats from the solitary beats of the upper string. Thus the effect of the fifth is to produce a tickling of the ear drum such that its softness is modified with sprightliness, giving at the same moment the impression of a gentle kiss and of a bite.

Salv. Seeing that you have derived so much pleasure from these novelties, I must show you a method by which the eye may, enjoy the same game as the ear. Suspend three balls of lead, or other heavy material, by means of strings of different length such that while the longest makes two vibrations the shortest will make four and the medium three; this will take place when the longest string measures 16, either in hand breadths or in any other unit, the medium 9 and the shortest 4, all measured in the same unit.

Now pull all these pendulums aside from the perpendicular and release them at the same instant; you will see a curious interplay of the threads passing each other in various manners but such that at the completion of every fourth vibration of the longest pendulum, all three will arrive simultaneously at the same terminus, whence they start over again to repeat the same cycle. This combination of vibrations, when produced on strings is precisely that which yields the interval of the octave and the intermediate fifth.

If we employ the same disposition of apparatus but change the lengths of the threads, always however in such a way that their vibrations correspond to those of agreeable musical intervals, we shall see a different crossing of these threads but always such that, after a definite interval of time and after a definite number of vibrations, all the threads, whether three or four, will reach the same terminus at the same instant, and then begin a repetition of the cycle.

[150]

If however the vibrations of two or more strings are incommensurable so that they never complete a definite number of vibrations at the same instant, or if commensurable they return only after a long interval of time and after a large number of vibrations, then the eye is confused by the disorderly succession of crossed threads. In like manner the ear is pained by an irregular sequence of air waves which strike the tympanum without any fixed order.

But, gentlemen, whither have we drifted during these many hours lured on by various problems and unexpected digressions? The day is already ended and we have scarcely touched the subject proposed for discussion. Indeed we have deviated so far that I remember only with difficulty our early introduction and the little progress made in the way of hypotheses and principles for use in later demonstrations.

Sagr. Let us then adjourn for to-day in order that our minds may find refreshment in sleep and that we may return to-morrow, if so please you, and resume the discussion of the main question.

Salv. I shall not fail to be here to-morrow at the same hour, hoping not only to reader you service but also to enjoy your company.

END OF THE FIRST DAY

[151]

SECOND DAY

Sagr. While Simplicio and I were awaiting your arrival we were trying to recall that last consideration which you advanced as a principle and basis for the results you intended to obtain; this consideration dealt with the resistance which all solids offer to fracture and depended upon a certain cement which held the parts glued together so that they would yield and separate only under considerable pull [*potente attrazzione*]. Later we tried to find the explanation of this coherence, seeking it mainly in the vacuum; this was the occasion of our many digressions which occupied the entire day and led us far afield from the original question which, as I have already stated, was the consideration of the resistance [*resistenza*] that solids offer to fracture.

Salv. I remember it all very well. Resuming the thread of our discourse, whatever the nature of this resistance which solids offer to large tractive forces [*violenta attrazione*] there can at least be no doubt of its existence; and though this resistance is very great in the case of a direct pull, it is found, as a rule, to be less in the case of bending forces [*nel violentargli per traverso*]. Thus, for example, a rod of steel or of glass will sustain a longitudinal pull of a thousand pounds while a weight of fifty pounds would be quite sufficient to break it if the rod were fastened at right angles into a vertical wall.

[152]

It is this second type of resistance which we must consider, seeking to discover in what proportion it is found in prisms and cylinders of the same material whether alike or unlike in shape, length, and thickness. In this discussion I shall take for granted the well-known mechanical principle which has been shown to govern the behavior of a bar, which we call a lever, namely, that the force bears to the resistance the inverse ratio of the distances which separate the fulcrum from the force and resistance respectively.

Simp. This was demonstrated first of all by Aristotle, in his *Mechanics*.

Salv. Yes, I am willing to concede him priority in point of time; but as regards rigor of demonstration the first place must be given to Archimedes, since upon a single proposition proved in his book on Equilibrium[14] depends not only the law of the lever but also those of most other mechanical devices.

Sagr. Since now this principle is fundamental to all the demonstrations which you propose to set forth would it not be advisable to give us a complete and thorough proof of this proposition unless possibly it would take too much time?

Salv. Yes, that would be quite proper, but it is better I think to approach our subject in a manner somewhat different from that employed by Archimedes, namely, by first assuming merely that equal weights placed in a balance of equal arms will produce equilibrium—a principle also assumed by Archimedes—and then proving that it is no less true that unequal weights produce equilibrium when the arms of the steelyard have lengths inversely proportional to the weights suspended from them; in other words, it amounts to the same thing whether one places equal weights at equal distances or unequal weights at distances which bear to each other the inverse ratio of the weights.

In order to make this matter clear imagine a prism or solid cylinder, AB, suspended at each end to the rod [*linea*] HI, and supported by two threads HA and IB; it is evident that if I attach a thread, C, at the middle point of the balance beam HI, the entire prism AB will, according to the principle assumed, hang in equilibrium since one-half its weight lies on one side, and the other half on the other side, of the point of suspension C. Now suppose the prism to be divided into unequal parts by a plane

14. *Works of Archimedes.* Trans. By T. L. Heath, pp. 189-220. [*Trans.*]

through the line D, and let the part DA be the larger and DB the smaller: this division having been made, imagine a thread ED, attached at the point E and supporting the parts AD and DB, in order that these parts may remain in the same position relative to line HI: and since the relative position of the prism and the beam HI remains unchanged, there can be no doubt but that the prism will maintain its former state of equilibrium.

But circumstances would remain the same if that part of the prism which is now held up, at the ends, by the threads AH and DE were supported at the middle by a single thread GL; and likewise the other part DB would not change position if held by a

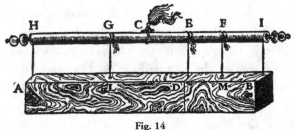

Fig. 14

thread FM placed at its middle point. Suppose now the threads HA, ED, and IB to be removed, leaving only the two GL and FM, then the same equilibrium will be maintained so long as the suspension is at C. Now let us consider that we have here two heavy bodies AD and DB hung at the ends G and F, of a balance beam GF in equilibrium about the point C, so that the line CG is the distance from C to the point of suspension of the heavy body AD, while CF is the distance at which the other heavy body DB is supported. It remains now only to show that these distances bear to each other the inverse ratio of the weights themselves, that is, the distance GC is to the distance CF as the prism DB is to the prism DA—a proposition which we shall prove as follows: Since the line GE is the half of EH, and since EF is the half of EI, the whole length GF will be half of the entire line HI, and therefore equal to CI: if now we subtract the common part CF the remainder GC will be equal to the remainder FI, that is, to FE, and if to each of these we add CE we shall have GE equal to CF: hence GE:EF=FC:CG. But GE and EF bear the same ratio to each other as do their doubles HE and EI, that is, the same ratio as the prism AD to DB. Therefore, by equating ratios we have, *convertendo*, the distance GC is to the distance CF as the weight BD is to the weight DA, which is what I desired to prove.

[154]

If what precedes is clear, you will not hesitate, I think, to admit that the two prisms AD and DB are in equilibrium about the point C since one-half of the whole body AB lies on the right of the suspension C and the other half on the left; in other words, this arrangement is equivalent to two equal weights disposed at equal distances. I do not see how any one can doubt, if the two prisms AD and DB were transformed into cubes, spheres, or into any other figure whatever and if G and F were retained as points of suspension, that they would remain in equilibrium about the point C, for it is only too evident that change of figure does not produce change of weight so long as the mass [*quantità di materià*] does not vary. From this we may derive the general conclusion that any two heavy bodies are in equilibrium at distances which are inversely proportional to their weights.

This principle established, I desire, before passing to any other subject, to call your attention to the fact that these forces, resistances, moments, figures, etc., may be considered either in the abstract, dissociated from matter, or in the concrete, associated with matter. Hence the properties which belong to figures that are merely geometrical and non-material must be modified when we fill these figures with matter and therefore give them weight. Take, for example, the lever BA which, resting upon the support E, is used to lift a heavy stone D. The principle just demonstrated makes it clear that a force applied at the extremity B will just suffice to equilibrate the resistance offered by the heavy body D provided this force [*momento*] bears to the force [*momento*] at D the same ratio as the distance AC bears to the distance CB; and this is true so long as we consider only the moments of the single force at B and of the resistance at D, treating the lever as an immaterial body devoid of weight. But if we take into account the weight of the lever itself—an instrument which may be made either of wood or of iron—it is manifest that, when this weight has been added to the

[155]

force at B, the ratio will be changed and must therefore be expressed in different terms. Hence before going further let us agree to distinguish between these two points of view; when we consider an instrument in the abstract, i. e., apart from the weight of its own material, we shall speak of "taking it in an absolute sense" [*prendere assolutamente*]; but if we fill one of these simple and absolute figures with matter and thus give it weight, we shall refer to such a material figure as a "moment" or "compound force" [*momento o forza composta*].

Sagr. I must break my resolution about not leading you off into a digression; for I cannot concentrate my attention upon what is to follow until a certain doubt is

removed from my mind, namely, you seem to compare the force at B with the total weight of the stone D, a part of which—possibly the greater part—rests upon the horizontal plane: so that . . .

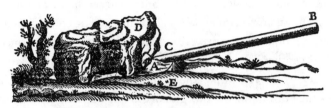

Fig. 15

Salv. I understand perfectly. you need go no further. However please observe that I have not mentioned the total weight of the stone; I spoke only of its force [*momento*] at the point A, the extremity of the lever BA, which force is always less than the total weight of the stone, and varies with its shape and elevation.

Sagr. Good: but there occurs to me another question about which I am curious. For a complete understanding of this matter, I should like you to show me, if possible, how one can determine what part of the total weight is supported by the underlying plane and what part by the end A of the lever.

Salv. The explanation will not delay us long and I shall therefore have pleasure in granting your request. In the accompanying figure, let us understand that the weight having its center of gravity at A rests with the end B upon the horizontal plane and with the other end upon the lever CG. Let N be the fulcrum of a lever to which the force [*potenza*] is applied at G. Let fall the perpendiculars, AO and CF, from the center A and the end C. Then I say, the magnitude [*momento*] of the entire weight bears to the magnitude of the force [*momento della potenza*] at G a ratio compounded of the ratio between the two distances GN and NC and the ratio between FB and BO. Lay off a distance X such that its ratio to NC is the same as that of BO to FB; then, since the total weight A is counterbalanced by the two forces at B and at C, it follows that the force at B is to that at C as the distance FO is to the distance OB.

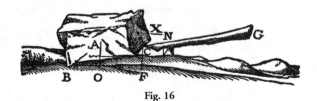

Fig. 16

[156]

Hence, *componendo*, the sum of the forces at B and C, that is, the total weight A [*momento di tutto 'l peso A*], is to the force at C as the line FB is to the line BO, that is, as NC is to X: but the force [*momento della potenza*] applied at C is to the force applied at G as the distance GN is to the distance NC; hence it follows, *ex æquali in proportione perturbata,*[15] that the entire weight A is to the force applied at G as the distance GN is to X. But the ratio of GN to X is compounded of the ratio of GN to NC and of NC to X, that is, of FB to BO; hence the weight A bears to the equilibrating force at G a ratio compounded of that of GN to NC and of FB to BO: which was to be proved.

Let us now return to our original subject; then, if what has hitherto been said is clear, it will be easily understood that,

PROPOSITION I

A prism or solid cylinder of glass, steel, wood or other breakable material which is capable of sustaining a very heavy weight when applied longitudinally is, as previously remarked, easily broken by the transverse application of a weight which may be much smaller in proportion as the length of the cylinder exceeds its thickness.

Let us imagine a solid prism ABCD fastened into a wall at the end AB, and supporting a weight E at the other end; understand also that the wall is vertical and that the prism or cylinder is fastened at right angles to the wall. It is clear that, if the cylinder breaks, fracture will occur at the point B where the edge of the mortise act as a fulcrum for the lever BC, to which the force is applied; the thickness of the solid BA is the other arm of the lever along which is located the resistance. This resistance opposes the separation of the part BD, lying outside the wall, from that portion lying inside. From the preceding, it follows that the magnitude [*momento*] of the force applied at C bears to the magnitude [*momento*] of the resistance, found in the thickness of the prism, i. e., in the attachment of the base BA to its contiguous parts, the same ratio which the length CB bears to half the length BA; if now we define absolute resistance to fracture as that offered to a longitudinal pull (in which case the stretching force acts in the same direction as that through which the body is moved), then it follows that the absolute resistance of the prism BD is to the breaking load placed at the end of the lever BC in the same ratio as the length BC is to the half of AB in the case of a prism, or the semidiameter in the case of a cylinder.

15. For definition of *perturbata* see Todhunter's *Euclid.* Book V, Def. 20. [*Trans.*]

[157]

This is our first proposition.[16] Observe that in what has here been said the weight of the solid BD itself has been left out of consideration, or rather, the prism has been assumed to

Fig. 17

be devoid of weight. But if the weight of the prism is to be taken account of in conjunction with the weight E, we must add to the weight E one half that of the prism BD: so that if, for example, the latter weighs two pounds and the weight E is ten pounds we must treat the weight E as if it were eleven pounds.

Simp. Why not twelve?

Salv. The weight E, my dear Simplicio, hanging at the extreme end C acts upon the lever BC with its full moment of ten pounds: so also would the solid BD if suspended at the same point exert its full moment of two pounds; but, as you know, this solid is uniformly distributed throughout its entire length, BC, so that the parts which lie near the end B are less effective than those more remote.

Accordingly if we strike a balance between the two, the weight of the entire prism may be considered as concentrated at its center of gravity which lies midway of the lever BC. But a weight hung at the extremity C exerts a moment twice as great as it would if suspended from the middle: therefore if we consider the moments of both as located at the end C we must add to the weight E one-half that of the prism.

[158]

Simp. I understand perfectly; and moreover, if I mistake not, the force of the two weights BD and E, thus disposed, would exert the same moment as would the entire weight BD together with twice the weight E suspended at the middle of the lever BC.

Salv. Precisely so, and a fact worth remembering. Now we can readily understand

16. The one fundamental error which is implicitly introduced into this proposition and which is carried through the entire discussion of the Second Day consists in a failure to see that, in such a beam, there must be equilibrium between the forces of tension and compression over any cross-section. The correct point of view seems first to have been found by E. Mariotte in 1680 and by A. Parent in 1713. Fortunately this error does not vitiate the conclusions of the subsequent propositions which deal only with proportions—not actual strength—of beams. Following K. Pearson (Todhunter's *History of Elasticity*) one might say that Galileo's mistake lay in supposing the fibres of the strained beam to be inextensible. Or, confessing the anachronism, one might say that the error consisted in taking the lowest fibre of the beam as the neutral axis. *[Trans.]*

PROPOSITION II

How and in what proportion a rod, or rather a prism, whose width is greater than its thickness offers more resistance to fracture when the force is applied in the direction of its breadth than in the direction of its thickness.

For the sake of clearness, take a ruler *ad* whose width is *ac* and whose thickness, *cb*, is much less than its width. The question now is why will the ruler, if stood on edge, as in the first figure, withstand a great weight T, while, when laid flat, as in the second figure, it will not support the weight X which is less than T. The answer is evident when we remember that in the one case the fulcrum is at the line *bc*, and in the other case at *ca*, while the distance at which the force is applied is the same in both cases, namely, the length *bd*: but in the first case the distance of the

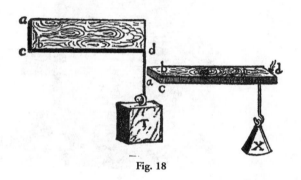

Fig. 18

resistance from the fulcrum-half the line *ca*-is greater than in the other case where it is only half of *bc*. Therefore the weight T is greater than X in the same ratio as half the width *ca* is greater than half the thickness *bc*, since the former acts as a lever arm for *ca*, and the latter for *cb*, against the same resistance, namely, the strength of all the fibres in the cross-section *ab*. We conclude, therefore, that any given ruler, or prism, whose width exceeds its thickness, will offer greater resistance to fracture when standing on edge than when lying flat, and this in the ratio of the width to the thickness.

PROPOSITION III

Considering now the case of a prism or cylinder growing longer in a horizontal direction, we must find out in what ratio the moment of its own weight increases in comparison with its resistance to fracture. This moment I find increases in proportion to the square of the length.

[159]

In order to prove this let AD be a prism or cylinder lying horizontal with its end A firmly fixed in a wall. Let the length of the prism be increased by the addition of the portion BE. It is clear that merely changing the length of the lever from AB to AC will, if we disregard its weight, increase the moment of the force [at the end] tending to pro-

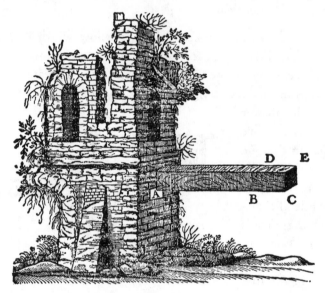

Fig. 19

duce fracture at A in the ratio of CA to BA. But, besides this, the weight of the solid portion BE, added to the weight of the solid AB increases the moment of the total weight in the ratio of the weight of the prism AE to that of the prism AB, which is the same as the ratio of the length AC to AB.

It follows, therefore, that, when the length and weight are simultaneously increased in any given proportion, the moment, which is the product of these two, is increased in a ratio which is the square of the preceding proportion. The conclusion is then that the bending moments due to the weight of prisms and cylinders which have the same thickness but different lengths, bear to each other a ratio which is the square of the ratio of their lengths, or, what is the same thing, the ratio of the squares of their lengths.

[160]

We shall next show in what ratio the resistance to fracture [bending strength], in prisms and cylinders, increases with increase of thickness while the length remains unchanged. Here I say that

PROPOSITION IV

In prisms and cylinders of equal length, but of unequal thicknesses,
the resistance to fracture increases in the same ratio as the cube of the
diameter of the thickness, i. e., of the base.

Let A and B be two cylinders of equal lengths DG, FH; let their bases be circular but unequal, having the diameters CD and EF. Then I say that the

resistance to fracture offered by the cylinder B is to that offered by A as the cube of the diameter FE is to the cube of the diameter DC. For, if we consider the resistance to fracture by longitudinal pull as dependent upon the bases, i. e., upon the circles EF and DC, no one can doubt that the strength [*resistenza*] of the cylinder B is greater than that of A in the same propor-

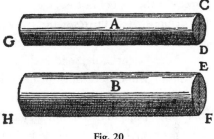

Fig. 20

tion in which the area of the circle EF exceeds that of CD; because it is precisely in this ratio that the number of fibres binding the parts of the solid together in the one cylinder exceeds that in the other cylinder.

But in the case of a force acting transversely it must be remembered that we are employing two levers in which the forces are applied at distances DG, FH, and the fulcrums are located at the points D and F; but the resistances are applied at distances which are equal to the radii of the circles DC and EF, since the fibres distributed over these entire cross-sections act as if concentrated at the centers. Remembering this and remembering also that the arms, DG and FH, through which the forces G and H act are, equal, we can understand that the resistance, located at the center of the base EF, acting against the force at H, is more effective [*maggiore*] than the resistance at the center of the base CD opposing the force G, in the ratio of the radius FE to the radius DC. Accordingly the resistance to fracture offered by the cylinder B is greater than that of the cylinder A in a ratio which is compounded of that of the area of the circles EF and DC and that of their radii, i. e., of their diameters; but the areas of circles are as the squares of their diameters. Therefore the ratio of the resistances, being the product of the two preceding ratios, is the same as that of the cubes of the diameters. This is what I set out to prove. Also since the volume of a cube varies as the third power of its edge we may say that the resistance [strength] of a cylinder whose length remains constant varies as the third power of its diameter.

[161]

From the preceding we are able to conclude that

COROLLARY

The resistance [strength] of a prism or cylinder of constant length varies in the sesquialteral ratio of its volume.

This is evident because the volume of a prism or cylinder of constant altitude varies directly as the area of its base, i. e., as the square of a side or diameter of this base; but, as just demonstrated, the resistance [strength] varies as the cube of this same side or diameter. Hence the resistance varies in the sesquialteral ratio of the volume—consequently also of the weight-of the solid itself.

Simp. Before proceeding further I should like to have one of my difficulties removed. Up to this point you have not taken into consideration a certain other kind of resistance which, it appears to me, diminishes as the solid grows longer, and this is quite as true in the case of bending as in pulling; it is precisely thus that in the case of a rope we observe that a very long one is less able to support a large weight than a short one. Whence, I believe, a short rod of wood or iron will support a greater weight than if it were long, provided the force be always applied longitudinally and not transversely, and provided also that we take into account the weight of the rope itself which increases with its length.

Salv. I fear, Simplicio, if I correctly catch your meaning, that in this particular you are making the same mistake as many others; that is if you mean to say that a long rope, one of perhaps 40 cubits, cannot bold up so great a weight as a shorter length, say one or two cubits, of the same rope.

Simp. That is what I meant, and as far as I see the proposition is highly probable.

Salv. On the contrary, I consider it not merely improbable but false; and I think I can easily convince you of your error. Let AB represent the rope, fastened at the upper end A: at the lower end attach a weight C whose force is just sufficient to break the rope. Now, Simplicio, point out the exact place where you think the break ought to occur.

[162]

Simp. Let us say D.

Salv. And why at D?

Simp. Because at this point the rope is not strong enough to support, say, 100 pounds, made up of the portion of the rope DB and the stone C.

Salv. Accordingly whenever the rope is stretched [*violentata*] with the weight of 100 pounds at D it will break there.

Simp. I think so.

Salv. But tell me, if instead of attaching the weight at the end of the rope, B, one fastens it at a point nearer D, say, at E: or if, instead of fixing the upper end of the rope at A, one fastens it at some point F, just above D, will not the rope, at the point D, be subject to the same pull of 100 pounds?

Simp. It would, provided you include with the stone C the portion of rope EB.

Salv. Let us therefore suppose that the rope is stretched at the point D with a weight of 100 pounds, then according to your own admission it will break; but FE is only a small portion of AB; how can you therefore maintain that the long rope is weaker than the short one? Give up then this erroneous view which you share with many very intelligent people, and let us proceed.

Now having demonstrated that, in the case of [uniformly loaded] prisms and cylinders of constant thickness, the moment of force tending to produce fracture [*momento sopra le proprie resistenze*] varies as the square of the length; and having likewise shown that, when the length is constant and the thickness varies, the resistance to fracture varies as the cube of the side, or diameter, of the base, let us pass to the investigation of the case of solids which simultaneously vary in both length and thickness. Here I observe that,

Fig. 21

PROPOSITION V

Prisms and cylinders which differ in both length and thickness offer resistances to fracture [i. e., can support at their ends loads] which are directly proportional to the cubes of the diameters of their bases and inversely proportional to their lengths.

[163]

Let ABC and DEF be two such cylinders; then the resistance [bending strength] of the cylinder AC bears to the resistance of the cylinder DF a ratio which is the product of the cube of the diameter AB divided by the cube of the diameter DE, and of the length EF divided by the length BC. Make EG equal to BC: let H be a third proportional to the lines AB and DE; let I be a fourth proportional, [AB/DE=H/I]: and let I:S=EF:BC.

Now since the resistance of the cylinder AC is to that of the cylinder DG as the cube of AB is to the cube of DE, that is, as the length AB is to the length I; and since the resistance of the cylinder DG is to that of the cylinder DF as the length FE is to EG, that is, as I is to S, it follows that the length AB is to S as the resistance of the

cylinder AC is to that of the cylinder DF. But the line AB bears to S a ratio which is the product of AB/I and I/S. Hence the resistance [bending strength] of the cylinder AC bears to the resistance of the cylinder DF a ratio which is the product of AB/I (that is, AB^3/DE^3) and of I/S (that is, EF/BC): which is what I meant to prove.

This proposition having been demonstrated, let us next consider the case of prisms and cylinders which are similar. Concerning these we shall show that,

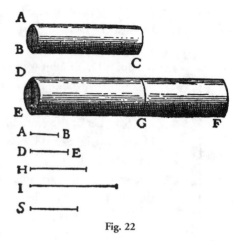

Fig. 22

PROPOSITION VI

In the case of similar cylinders and prisms, the moments [stretching forces] which result from multiplying together their weight and length [i. e., from the moments produced by their own weight and length], which latter acts as a lever-arm, bear to each other a ratio which is the sesquialteral of the ratio between the resistances of their bases.

In order to prove this let us indicate the two similar cylinders by AB and CD: then the magnitude of the force [*momento*] in the cylinder AB, opposing the resistance of its base B, bears to the magnitude [*momento*] of the force at CD, opposing the resistance of its base D, a ratio which is the sesquialteral of the ratio

[164]

between the resistance of the base B and the resistance of the base D. And since the solids AB and CD, are effective in opposing the resistances of their bases B and D, in proportion to their weights and to the mechanical advantages [*forze*] of their lever arms respectively, and since the advantage [*forza*] of the lever arm AB is equal to the advantage [*forza*] of the lever arm CD (this is true because in virtue of the similarity of the cylinders the length AB is to the radius of the base B as the length CD is

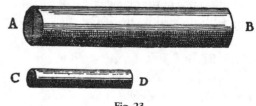

Fig. 23

to the radius of the base D), it follows that the total force [*momento*] of the cylinder AB is to the total force [*momento*] of the cylinder CD as the weight alone of the cylinder AB is to the weight alone of the cylinder CD, that is, as the volume of the cylinder AB [*l'istesso cilindro AB*] is to the volume CD [*all'istesso CD*]: but these are as the cubes of the diameters of their bases B and D; and the resistances of the bases, being to each other as their areas, are to each other consequently as the squares of their diameters. Therefore the forces [*momenti*] of the cylinders are to each other in the sesquialteral ratio of the resistance of their bases.[17]

Simp. This proposition strikes me as both new and surprising: at first glance it is very different from anything which I myself should have guessed: for since these figures are similar in all other respects, I should have certainly thought that the forces [*momenti*] and the resistances of these cylinders would have borne to each other the same ratio.

Sagr. This is the proof of the proposition to which I referred, at the very beginning of our discussion, as one imperfectly understood by me.

Salv. For a while, Simplicio, I used to think, as you do, that the resistances of similar solids were similar; but a certain casual observation showed me that similar solids do not exhibit a strength which is proportional to their size, the larger ones being less fitted to undergo rough usage just as tall men are more apt than small children to be injured by a fall. And, as we remarked at the outset, a large beam or column falling

[165]

from a given height will go to pieces when under the same circumstances a small scantling or small marble cylinder will not break. It was this observation which led me to the investigation of the fact which I am about to demonstrate to you: it is a very remarkable thing that, among the infinite variety of solids which are similar one to another, there are no two of which the forces [*momenti*], and the resistances of these solids are related in the same ratio.

Simp. You remind me now of a passage in Aristotle's *Questions in Mechanics* in which he tries to explain why it is that a wooden beam becomes weaker and can be more easily bent as it grows longer, notwithstanding the fact that the shorter beam is thinner and the longer one thicker: and, if I remember correctly, he explains it in terms of the simple lever.

17. The preceding paragraph beginning with Prop. VI is of more than usual interest as illustrating the confusion of terminology current in the time of Galileo. The translation given is literal except in the case of those words for which the Italian is supplied. The facts which Galileo has in mind are so evident that it is difficult to see how one can here interpret "*moment,*" to mean the force "*opposing the resistance of its base,*" unless "*the force of the lever arm .AB*" be taken to mean "*the mechanical advantage of the lever made up of AB and the radius of the base B*"; and similarly for "*the force of the lever arm CD.*" [*Trans.*]

Salv. Very true: but, since this solution seemed to leave room for doubt, Bishop di Guevara,[18] whose truly learned commentaries have greatly enriched and illuminated this work, indulges in additional clever speculations with the hope of thus overcoming all difficulties; nevertheless even he is confused as regards this particular point, namely, whether, when the length and thickness of these solid figures increase in the same ratio, their strength and resistance to fracture, as well as to bending, remain constant. After much thought upon this subject I have reached the following result. First I shall show that,

PROPOSITION VII

Among heavy prisms and cylinders of similar figure, there is one and only one which under the stress of its own weight lies just on the limit between breaking and not breaking: so that every larger one is unable to carry the bad of its own weight and breaks; while every smaller one is able to withstand some additional force tending to break it.

Let AB be a heavy prism, the longest possible that will just sustain its own weight, so that if it be lengthened the least bit it will break. Then, I say, this prism is unique among all similar prisms—infinite in number—in occupying that boundary line between breaking and not breaking; so that every larger one will break under its own weight,

[166]

and every smaller one win not break, but will be able to withstand some force in addition to its own weight.

Let the prism CE be similar to, but larger than, AB: then, I say, it will not remain intact but will break under its own weight. Lay off the portion CD, equal in length to AB. And, since, the resistance [bending strength] of CD is to that of AB as the cube of the thickness of CD is to the cube of the thickness of AB, that is, as the prism CE is to the similar prism AB, it follows that the weight of CE is the utmost load which a prism of the length CD can sustain; but the length of CE is greater; therefore the prism CE will break. Now take another prism FG which is smaller than AB. Let FH equal AB, then it can be shown in a similar manner that the resistance

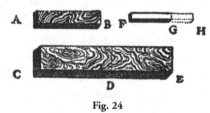

Fig. 24

[bending strength] of FG is to that of AB as the prism FG is to the prism AB provided the distance AB that is FH, is equal to the distance FG; but AB is greater than FG,

18. Bishop of Teano; b. 1561; d. 1641. *[Trans.]*

and therefore the moment of the prism FG applied at G is not sufficient to break the prism FG.

Sagr. The demonstration is short and clear; while the proposition which, at first glance, appeared improbable is now seen to be both true and inevitable. In order therefore to bring this prism into that limiting condition which separates breaking from not breaking, it would be necessary to change the ratio between thickness and length either by increasing the thickness or by diminishing the length. An investigation of this limiting state will, I believe, demand equal ingenuity.

Salv. Nay, even more; for the question is more difficult; this I know because I spent no small amount of time in its discovery which I now wish to share with you.

PROPOSITION VIII

Given a cylinder or prism of the greatest length consistent with its not breaking under its own weight; and having given a greater length, to find the diameter of another cylinder or prism of this greater length which shall be the only and largest one capable of withstanding its own weight.

Let BC be the largest cylinder capable of sustaining its own weight; and let DE be a length greater than AC: the problem is to find the diameter of the cylinder which, having the length DE, shall be the largest one just able to withstand its own weight.

[167]

Let I be a third proportional to the lengths DE and AC; let the diameter FD be to the diameter BA as DE is to I; draw the cylinder FE; then, among all cylinders having the same proportions, this is the largest and only one just capable of sustaining its own weight.

Let M a third proportional to DE and I: also let O be a fourth proportional to DE, I, and M; lay off FG equal to AC. Now since the diameter FD is to the diameter AB as the length DE is to I, and since O is a fourth proportional to DE, I and M, it follows that $FD^3:BA^3=DE:O$. But the resistance [bending strength] of the cylinder DG

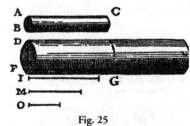

Fig. 25

is to the resistance of the cylinder BC as the cube of FD is to the cube of BA: hence the resistance of the cylinder DG is to that of cylinder BC as the length DE is to O. And since the moment of the cylinder BC is held in equilibrium by [*e equale alla*] its resistance., we shall accomplish our end (which is to prove that the moment of the

cylinder FE is equal to the resistance located at FD), if we show that the moment of the cylinder FE is to the moment of the cylinder BC as the resistance DF is to the resistance BA, that is, as the cube of FD is to the cube of BA, or as the length DE is to O. The moment of the cylinder FE is to the moment of the cylinder DG as the square of DE is to the square of AC, that is, as the length DE is to I; but the moment of the cylinder DG is to the moment of the cylinder BC, as the square of DF is to the square of BA, that is, as the square of DE is to the square of I, or as the square of I is to the square of M, or, as I is to O. Therefore by equating ratios, it results that the moment of the cylinder FE is to the moment of the cylinder BC as the length DE is to O, that is, as the cube of DF is to the cube of BA, or as the resistance of the base DF is to the resistance of the base BA; which was to be proven.

Sagr. This demonstration, Salviati, is rather long and difficult to keep in mind from a single hearing. Will you not, therefore, be good enough to repeat it?

Salv. As you like; but I would suggest instead a more direct and a shorter proof: this will, however, necessitate a different figure.

[168]

Sagr. The favor will be that much greater: nevertheless I hope you will oblige me by putting into written form the argument just given so that I may study it at my leisure.

Salv. I shall gladly do so. Let A denote a cylinder of diameter DC and the largest capable of sustaining its own weight: the problem is to determine a larger cylinder which shall be at once the maximum and the unique one capable of sustaining its own weight.

Let E be such a cylinder, similar to A, having the assigned length, and having a diameter KL. Let MN be a third proportional to the two lengths DC and KL: let MN also be the diameter of another cylinder,

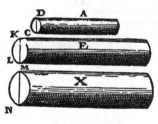

Fig. 26

X, having the same length as E: then, I say, X is the cylinder sought. Now since the resistance of the base DC is to the resistance of the base KL as the square of DC is to the square of KL, that is, as the square of KL is to the square of MN, or, as the cylinder E is to the cylinder X, that is, as the moment E is to the moment X; and since also the resistance [bending strength] of the base KL is to the resistance of the base MN as the cube of KL is to the cube of MN, that is, as the cube of DC is to the cube of KL, or, as the

cylinder A is to the cylinder E, that is, as the moment of A is to the moment of E; hence it follows, *ex æquali in proportione perturbata*,[19] that the moment of A is to the moment of X as the resistance of the base DC is to the resistance of the base MN; therefore moment and resistance; are related to each other in prism X precisely as they are in prism A.

Let us now generalize the problem; then it will read as follows:

> *Given a cylinder AC in which moment and resistance [bending strength] are related in any manner whatsoever, let DE be the length of another cylinder; then determine what its thickness must be in order that the relation between its moment and resistance shall be identical with that of the cylinder AC.*

Using Fig. 25 in the same manner as above, we may say that, since the moment of the cylinder FE is to the moment of the portion DG as the square of ED is to the square of FG, that is, as the length DE is to I; and since the moment of the cylinder FG is to the moment of the cylinder AC as the square of FD is to the square of AB, or, as the square of ED is to the square of I, or, as the square of I is to the square of M, that is, as the length I is to O; it follows, *ex æquali*, that the moment of the cylinder FE is to

[169]

the moment of the cylinder AC as the length DE is to O, that is, as the cube of DE is to the cube of I, or, as the cube of FD is to the cube of AB, that is, as the resistance of the base FD is to the resistance of the base AB; which was to be proven.

From what has already been demonstrated, you can plainly see the impossibility of increasing the size of structures to vast dimensions either in art or in nature; likewise the impossibility of building ships, palaces, or temples of enormous size in such a way that their oars, yards, beams, iron-bolts, and, in short, all their other parts will hold together; nor can nature produce trees of extraordinary size because the branches would break down under their own weight; so also it would be impossible to build up the bony structures of men, horses, or other animals so as to hold together and perform their normal functions if these animals were to be increased enormously in height; for this increase in height can be accomplished only by employing a material which is harder and stronger than usual, or by enlarging the size of the bones, thus changing their shape until

---

19. For definition of *perturbata* see Todhunter's *Euclid*, Book V, Def. 20. *[Trans.]*

the form and appearance of the animals suggest a monstrosity. This is perhaps what our wise Poet had in mind, when he says, in describing a huge giant:

"Impossible it is to reckon his height
"So beyond measure is his size." [20]

To illustrate briefly, I have sketched a bone whose natural length has been increased three times and whose thickness has been multiplied until, for a correspondingly large animal, it would perform the same function which the small bone performs for its small animal. From the figures here shown you can see how out of proportion the enlarged bone appears. Clearly then if one wishes to maintain in a great giant the same proportion of limb as that found in an ordinary man he must either find a harder and stronger material for making the bones, or he must admit a diminution of

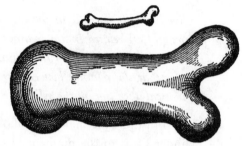

Fig. 27

[170]

strength in comparison with men of medium stature; for if his height be increased inordinately he will fall and be crushed under his own weight. Whereas, if the size of a body be diminished, the strength of that body is not diminished in the same proportion; indeed the smaller the body the greater its relative strength. Thus a small dog could probably carry on his back two or three dogs of his own size; but I believe that a horse could not carry even one of his own size.

Simp. This may be so; but I am led to doubt it on account of the enormous size reached by certain fish, such as the whale which, I understand, is ten times as large as an elephant; yet they all support themselves.

Salv. Your question, Simplicio, suggests another principle, one which had hitherto escaped my attention and which enables giants and other animals of vast size to support themselves and to move about as well as smaller animals do. This result may be secured either by increasing the strength of the bones and other parts intended to carry not only their weight but also the superincumbent load; or, keeping the proportions of the bony structure constant, the skeleton will hold together in the same manner or even more easily, provided one diminishes, in the proper proportion, the weight of the bony material, of the flesh, and of anything else which the skeleton has to carry. It is this

20. *Non si può compartir quanto sia lungo,*
Si smisuratamente è tutto grosso.
Ariosto's *Orlando Furioso*, XVII, 30 *[Trans.]*

second principle which is employed by nature in the structure of fish, making their bones and muscles not merely light but entirely devoid of weight.

Simp. The trend of your argument, Salviati, is evident. Since fish live in water which on account of its density [*corpulenza*] or, as others would say, heaviness [*gravità*] diminishes the weight [*peso*] of bodies immersed in it, you mean to say that, for this reason, the bodies of fish will be devoid of weight and will be supported without injury to their bones. But this is not all; for although the remainder of the body of the fish may be without weight, there can be no question but that their bones have weight. Take the case of a whale's rib, having the dimensions of a beam; who can deny its great weight or its tendency to go to the bottom when placed in water? One would, therefore, hardly expect these great masses to sustain themselves.

[171]

Salv. A very shrewd objection! And now, in reply, tell me whether you have ever seen fish stand motionless at will under water, neither descending to the bottom nor rising to the top, without the exertion of force by swimming?

Simp. This is a well-known phenomenon.

Salv. The fact then that fish are able to remain motionless under water is a conclusive reason for thinking that the material of their bodies has the same specific gravity as that of water; accordingly, if in their make-up there are certain parts which are heavier than water there must be others which are lighter, for otherwise they would not produce equilibrium.

Hence, if the bones are heavier, it is necessary that the muscles or other constituents of the body should be lighter in order that their buoyancy may counterbalance the weight of the bones. In aquatic animals therefore circumstances are just reversed from what they are with land animals inasmuch as, in the latter, the bones sustain not only their own weight but also that of the flesh, while in the former it is the flesh which supports not only its own weight but also that of the bones. We must therefore cease to wonder why these enormously large animals inhabit the water rather than the land, that is to say, the air.

Simp. I am convinced and I only wish to add that what we call land animals ought really to be called air animals, seeing that they live in the air, are surrounded by air, and breathe air.

Sagr. I have enjoyed Simplicio's discussion including both the question raised and its answer. Moreover I can easily understand that one of these giant fish, if pulled ashore, would not perhaps sustain itself for any great length of time, but would be crushed under its own mass as soon as the connections between the bones gave way.

Salv. I am inclined to your opinion; and, indeed, I almost think that the same thing would happen in the case of a very big ship which floats on the sea without going to pieces under its load of merchandise and armament, but which on dry land and in air would probably fall apart. But let us proceed and show how:

[172]

Given a prism or cylinder, also its own weight and the maximum load which it can carry, it is then possible to find a maximum length beyond which the cylinder cannot be prolonged without breaking under its own weight.

Let AC indicate both the prism and its own weight; also let D represent the maximum load which the prism can carry at the end C without fracture; it is required to find the maximum to which the length of the said prism can be increased without breaking. Draw AH of such a length that the weight of the prism AC is to the sum of AC and twice the weight D as the length CA is to AH; and let AG be a mean proportional between CA and AH; then, I say, AG is the length sought. Since the moment of

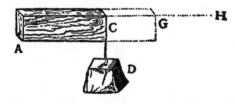

Fig. 28

the weight [*momento gravante*] D attached at the point C is equal to the moment of a weight twice as large as D placed at the middle point AC, through which the weight of the prism AC acts, it follows that the moment of the resistance of the prism AC located at A is equivalent to twice the weight D plus the weight of AC, both acting through the middle point of AC. And since we have agreed that the moment of the weights thus located, namely, twice D plus AC, bears to the moment of AC the same ratio which the length HA bears to CA and since AG is a mean proportional between these two lengths, it follows that the moment of twice D plus AC is to the moment of AC as the square of GA is to the square of CA. But the moment arising from the weight [*momento premente*] of the prism GA is to the moment of AC as the square of GA is to the square of CA; thence AG is the maximum length sought, that is, the length up to which the prism AC may be prolonged and still support itself, but beyond which it will break.

Hitherto we have considered the moments and resistances of prisms and solid cylinders fixed at one end with a weight applied at the other end; three cases were discussed, namely, that in which the applied force was the only one acting, that in which the weight of the prism itself is also taken into consideration, and that in which the weight of the prism alone is taken into consideration. Let us now consider these same

[173]

prisms and cylinders when supported at both ends or at a single point placed some-where between the ends.

In the first place, I remark that a cylinder carrying only its own weight and hav-ing the maximum length, beyond which it will break, will, when supported either in the middle or at both ends, have twice the length of one which is mortised into a wall and supported only at one end. This is very evident because, if we denote the cylinder by ABC and if we assume that one-half of it, AB, is the greatest possible length capable of supporting its own weight with one end fixed at B, then, for the same

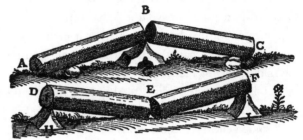

Fig. 29

reason, if the cylinder is carried on the point G, the first half will be counterbalanced by the other half BC. So also in the case of the cylinder DEF, if its length be such that it will support only one-half this length when the end D is held fixed, or the other half when the end F is fixed, then it is evident that when supports, such as H and I, are placed under the ends D and F respectively the moment of any additional force or weight placed at E will produce fracture at this point.

A more intricate and difficult problem is the following: neglect the weight of a solid such as the preceding and find whether the same force or weight which produces fracture when applied at the middle of a cylinder, supported at both ends, win also break the cylinder when applied at some other point nearer one end than the other.

Thus, for example, if one wished to break a stick by holding it with one hand at each end and applying his knee at the middle, would the same force be required to break it in the same manner if the knee were applied, not at the middle, but at some point nearer to one end?

Sagr. This problem, I believe, has been touched upon by Aristotle in his *Questions in Mechanics.*

[174]

Salv. His inquiry however is not quite the same; for he seeks merely to discover why it is that a stick may be more easily broken by taking hold, one hand at each end of the stick, that is, far removed from the knee, than if the hands were closer together. He gives a general explanation, referring it to the lengthened lever arms which are

secured by placing the hands at the ends of the stick. Our inquiry calls for something more: what we want to know is whether, when the hands are retained at the ends of the stick, the same force is required to break it wherever the knee be placed.

Sagr. At first glance this would appear to be so, because the two lever arms exert, in a certain way, the same moment, seeing that as one grows, shorter the other grows correspondingly longer.

Salv. Now you see how readily one falls into error and what caution and circumspection are required to avoid it. What you have just said appears at first glance highly probable, but on closer examination it proves to be quite far from true; as will be seen from the fact that whether the knee—the fulcrum of the two levers—be placed in the middle or not makes such a difference that, if fracture is to be produced at any other point than the middle, the breaking force at the middle, even when multiplied four, ten, a hundred, or a thousand times would not suffice. To begin with we shall offer some general considerations and then pass to the determination of the ratio in which the breaking force must change in order to produce fracture at one point rather than another.

Let AB denote a wooden cylinder which is to be broken in the middle, over the supporting point C, and let DE represent an identical cylinder which is to be broken

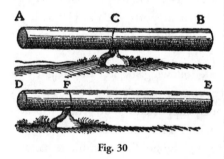

Fig. 30

just over the supporting point F which is not in the middle. First of all it is clear that, since the distances AC and CB are equal, the forces applied at the extremities B and A must also be equal. Secondly since the distance DF is less than the distance AC the moment of any force acting at D is less than the moment of the same force at A, that is, applied at the distance CA; and the moments are less in the ratio of the length DF to AC; consequently it is necessary to increase the force [*momento*] at D in order to overcome, or even to balance, the resistance at F; but in comparison with the length AC the distance DF can be diminished indefinitely: in order therefore to counterbalance the resistance at F it will be necessary to increase indefinitely the force [*forza*] applied at D.

[175]

On the other hand, in proportion as we increase the distance FE over that of CB, we must diminish the force at E in order to counterbalance the resistance at F; but the distance FE, measured in terms of CB, cannot be increased indefinitely by sliding the fulcrum F toward the end D; indeed, it cannot even be made double the length CB.

Therefore the force required at E to balance the resistance at F will always be more than half that required at B. It is clear then that, as the fulcrum F approaches the end D, we must of necessity indefinitely increase the sum of the forces applied at E and D in order to balance, or overcome, the resistance at F.

Sagr. What shall we say, Simplicio? Must we not confess that geometry is the most powerful of all instruments for sharpening the wit and training the mind to think correctly? Was not Plato perfectly right when he wished that his pupils should be first of all well grounded in mathematics? As for myself, I quite understood the property of the lever and how, by increasing or diminishing its length, one can increase or diminish the moment of force and of resistance; and yet, in the solution of the present problem I was not slightly but greatly, deceived.

Simp. Indeed I begin to understand that while logic is an excellent guide in discourse, it does not, as regards stimulation to discovery, compare with the power of sharp distinction which belongs to geometry.

Sagr. Logic, it appears to me, teaches us how to test the conclusiveness of any argument or demonstration already discovered and completed; but I do not believe that it teaches us to discover correct arguments and demonstrations. But it would be better if Salviati were to show us in just what proportion the forces must be increased in order to produce fracture as the fulcrum is moved from one point to another along one and the same wooden rod.

[176]

Salv. The ratio which you desire is determined as follows:

> *If upon a cylinder one marks two points at which fracture is to be produced, then the resistances at these two points will bear to each other the inverse ratio of the rectangles formed by the distances from the respective points to the ends of the cylinder.*

Let A and B denote the least forces which will bring about fracture of the cylinder at C; likewise E and F the smallest forces which will break it at D. Then, I say, that the sum of the forces A and B is to the sum of the forces E and F as the area of the rectangle AD.DB is to the area of the rectangle AC.CB. Because the sum of the forces A and B bears to the sum of the forces E and F a ratio which is the product of the three following ratios, namely, (A+B)/B, B/F, and F/(F+E); but the length BA is to the length CA as the sum of the forces A and B is to

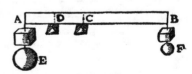

Fig. 31

the force B; and, as the length DB is to the length CB, so is the force B to the force F; also as the length AD is to AB, so is the force F to the sum of the forces F and E.

Hence it follows that the sum of the forces A and B bears to the sum of the forces E and F a ratio which is the product of the three following ratios, namely, BA/CA, BD/BC, and AD/AB. But DA/CA is the product of DA/BA and BA/CA. Therefore the sum of the forces A and B bears to the sum of the forces E and F a ratio which is the product of DA:CA and DB:CB. But the rectangle AD.DB bears to the rectangle AC.CB a ratio which is the product of DA/CA and DB/CB. Accordingly the sum of the forces A and B is to the sum of the forces E and F as the rectangle AD.DB is to the rectangle AC.CB, that is, the resistance to fracture at C is to the resistance to fracture at D as the rectangle AD.DB is to the rectangle AC.CB.   Q. E. D.

[177]

Another rather interesting problem may be solved as a consequence of this theorem, namely,

> *Given the maximum weight which a cylinder or prism can support*
> *at its middle-point where the resistance is a minimum, and given also*
> *a larger weight, find that point in the cylinder for which this Larger*
> *weight is the maximum load that can be supported.*

Let that one of the given weights which is larger than the maximum weight supported at the middle of the cylinder AB bear to this maximum weight the same ratio which the length E bears to the length F. The problem is to find that point in the cylinder at which this larger weight becomes the maximum that can be supported. Let G be

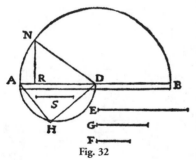

Fig. 32

a mean proportional between the lengths E and F. Draw AD and S so that they bear to each other the same ratio as E to G; accordingly S will be less than AD.

Let AD be the diameter of a semicircle AHD, in which take AH equal to S; join the points H and D and lay off DR equal to HD. Then, I say, R is the point sought, namely, the point at which the given weight, greater than the maximum supported at the middle of the cylinder D, would become the maximum load.

On AB as diameter draw the semicircle ANB: erect the perpendicular RN and join the points N and D. Now since the sum of the squares on NR and RD is equal to the

square of ND, that is, to the square of AD, or to the sum of the squares of AH and HD; and, since the square of HD is equal to the square of DR, it follows that the square of NR, that is, the rectangle AR.RB, is equal to the square of AH, also therefore to the square of S; but the square of S is to the square of AD as the length F is to the length E, that is, as the maximum weight supported at D is to the larger of the two given weights. Hence the latter will be the maximum load which can be carried at the point R; which is the solution sought.

Sagr. Now I understand thoroughly; and I am thinking that, since the prism AB grows constantly stronger and more resistant to the pressure of its load at points which are more and more removed from the middle, we could in the case of large heavy beams cut away a considerable portion near the ends which would notably lessen the weight, and which, in the beam work of large rooms, would prove to be of great utility and convenience.

[178]

It would be a fine thing if one could discover the proper shape to give a solid in order to make it equally resistant at every point, in which case a load placed at the middle would not produce fracture more easily than if placed at any other point.[21]

Salv. I was just on the point of mentioning an interesting and remarkable fact connected with this very question. My meaning will be clearer if I draw a figure. Let DB represent a prism; then, as we have already shown, its resistance to fracture [bending strength] at the end AD, owing to a load placed at the end B, will be less than the resistance at CI in the ratio of the length CB to AB. Now imagine this same prism to be cut through diagonally along the line FB so that the opposite faces will be triangular; the side facing us will be FAB. Such a solid will have properties different from those of the prism; for, if the load remain at B, the resistance against fracture [bending strength] at C will be less than that at A in the ratio of the length CB to the length AB. This is easily proved: for if CNO represents a cross-section parallel to AFD, then the length FA bears to the length CN, in the triangle FAB, the same ratio which the length AB bears to the length CB. Therefore, if we imagine A and C to be the points at which the fulcrum is placed, the lever arms in the two cases BA, AF and BC, CN will be proportional [simili]. Hence the moment of any force applied at B and

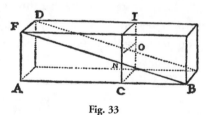

Fig. 33

21. The reader will notice that two different problems are here involved. That which is suggested in the last remark of Sagredo is the following: To find a beam whose maximum stress has the same value when a constant load moves from one end of the beam to the other.
The second problem—the one which Salviati proceeds to solve—is the following:
To find a beam in all cross-sections of which the maximum stress is the same for a constant load in a fixed position. [Trans.]

acting through the arm BA, against a resistance placed at a distance AF will be equal to that of the same force at B acting through the arm BC against the same resistance located at a distance CN. But now, if the force still be applied at B, the resistance to be overcome when the fulcrum is at C, acting through the arm CN, is less than the resistance with the fulcrum at A in the same proportion as the rectangular cross-section CO is less than the rectangular cross-section AD, that is, as the length CN is less than AF, or CB than BA.

Consequently the resistance to fracture at C, offered by the portion OBC, is less than the resistance to fracture at A, offered by the entire block DAB, in the same proportion as the length CB is smaller than the length AB.

By this diagonal saw-cut we have now removed from the beam, or prism DB, a portion, i. e., a half, and have left the wedge, or triangular prism, FBA. We thus have two solids possessing opposite properties; one body grows stronger as it is shortened

[179]

while the other grows weaker. This being so it would seem not merely reasonable, but inevitable, that there exists a line of section such that, when the superfluous material his been removed, there will remain a solid of such figure that it will offer the same resistance [strength] at all points.

Simp. Evidently one must, in passing from greater to less, encounter equality.

Sagr. But now the question is what path the saw should follow in making the cut.

Simp. It seems to me that this ought not to be a difficult task: for if by sawing the prism along the diagonal line and removing half of the material, the remainder acquires a property just the opposite to that of the entire prism, so that at every point where the latter gains strength the former becomes weaker, then it seems to me that by taking a middle path, i. e., by removing half the former half, or one-quarter of the whole, the strength of the remaining figure will be constant at a those points where, in the two previous figures, the gain in one was equal to the loss in the other.

Salv. You have missed the mark, Simplicio. For, as I shall presently show you, the amount which you can remove from the prism without weakening it is not a quarter but a third. It now remains, as suggested by Sagredo, to discover the path along which the saw must travel: this, as I shall prove, must be a parabola. But it is first necessary to demonstrate the following lemma:

> *If the fulcrums are so, placed under two levers or balances that the arms through which the forces act are to each other in the same ratio as the squares of the arms through which the resistances act, and if these resistances are to each other in the same ratio as the arms through which they act, then the forces will be equal.*

[180]

Let AB and CD represent two levers whose lengths are divided by their fulcrums in such a way as to make the distance EB bear to the distance FD a ratio which is equal to the square of the ratio between the distances EA and FC. Let the resistances located at A and C be to each other as EA is to FC. Then, I say, the forces which must be applied at B and D in order to hold in equilibrium the resistances at A and C are equal.

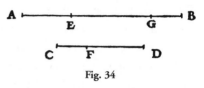

Fig. 34

Let EG be a mean proportional between EB and FD. Then we shall have BE:EG=EG:FD=AE:CF. But this last ratio is precisely that which we have assumed to exist between the resistances at A and C. And since EG:FD=AE:CF, it follows, *permutando*, that EG:AE=FD:CF. Seeing that the distances DC and GA are divided in the same ratio by the points F and E, it follows that the same force which, when applied at D, will equilibrate the resistance at C, would if applied at G equilibrate at A a resistance equal to that found at C.

But one datum of the problem is that the resistance at A is to the resistance at C as the distance AE is to the distance CF, or as BE is to EG. Therefore the force applied at G, or rather at D, will, when applied at B, just balance the resistance located at A.   Q. E. D.

This being clear draw the parabola FNB in the face FB of the prism DB. Let the prism be sawed along this parabola whose vertex is at B. The portion of the solid which

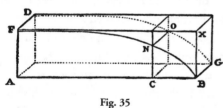

Fig. 35

remains will be included between the base AD, the rectangular plane AG, the straight line BG and the surface DGBF, whose curvature is identical with that of the parabola FNB. This solid will have, I say, the same strength at every point. Let the solid be cut by a plane CO parallel to the plane AD.

Imagine the points A and C to be the fulcrums of two levers of which one will have the arms BA and AF; the other BC and CN. Then since in the parabola FBA, we have BA:BC=AF^2:CN^2, it is clear that the arm BA of one lever is to the arm BC of the other lever as the square of the arm AF is to the square of the other arm CN. Since the resistance to be balanced by the lever BA is to the resistance to be balanced by the lever BC in the same ratio as the rectangle DA is to the rectangle OC, that is as the length AF is to the length CN, which two lengths are the other arms of the levers, it follows, by the lemma just demonstrated, that the same force which, when applied at BG will equilibrate the resistance at DA, will also balance the resistance at CO. The same is true for any other section. Therefore this parabolic solid is equally strong throughout.

[181]

It can now be shown that, if the prism be sawed along the line of the parabola FNB, one-third part of it will be removed; because the rectangle FB and the surface FNBA bounded by the parabola are the bases of two solids included between two parallel planes, i. e., between the rectangles FB and DG; consequently the volumes of these two solids bear to each other the same ratio as their bases. But the area of the rectangle is one and a half times as large as the area FNBA under the parabola; hence by cutting the prism along the parabola we remove one-third of the volume. It is thus seen how one can diminish the weight of a beam by as much as thirty-three per cent without diminishing its strength; a fact of no small utility in the construction of large vessels, and especially in supporting the decks, since in such structures lightness is of prime importance.

Sagr. The advantages derived from this fact are so numerous that it would be both wearisome and impossible to mention them all; but leaving this matter to one side, I should like to learn just how it happens that diminution of weight is possible in the ratio above stated. I can readily understand that, when a section is made along the diagonal, one-half the weight is removed; but, as for the parabolic section removing one-third of the prism, this I can only accept on the word of Salviati who is always reliable; however I prefer first-hand knowledge to the word of another.

Salv. You would like then a demonstration of the fact that the excess of the volume of a prism over the volume of what we have called the parabolic solid is one-third of the entire prism. This I have already given you on a previous occasion; however I shall now try to recall the demonstration in which I remember having used a certain lemma from Archimedes' book *On Spirals*,[22] namely, given any number of lines, differing in length one from another by a common difference which is equal to the shortest of these lines; and given also an equal number of lines each of which has the same length as the longest of the first mentioned series; then the sum of the squares of the lines of this second group will be less than three times the sum of the squares of the lines in the first group. But the sum of the squares of the second group will be greater than three times the sum of the squares of all excepting the longest of the first group.

[182]

Assuming this, inscribe in the rectangle ACBP the parabola AB. We have now to prove that the mixed triangle BAP whose sides are BP and PA, and whose base is the parabola BA, is a third part of the entire rectangle CP. If this is not true it will be either greater or less than a third. Suppose it to be less by an area which is represented by X.

22. For demonstration of the theorem here cited, see "*Works of Archimedes*" translated by T. L. Heath (Camb. Univ. Press 1897) p. 107 and p. 162. *[Trans.]*

By drawing lines parallel to the sides BP and CA, we can divide the rectangle CP into equal parts; and if the process be continued we shall finally reach a division into parts so small that each of them will be smaller than the area X; let the rectangle OB represent one of these parts and, through the points where the other parallels cut the parabola, draw lines parallel to AP. Let us now describe about our "mixed triangle" a figure made up of rectangles such as BO, IN, HM, FL, EK, and GA; this figure will also be less than a third part of the rectangle CP because the excess of this figure above the area of

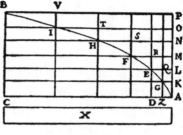

Fig. 36

the "mixed triangle" is much smaller than the rectangle BO which we have already made smaller than X.

Sagr. More slowly, please; for I do not see how the excess of this figure described about the "mixed triangle" is much smaller than the rectangle BO.

Salv. Does not the rectangle BO have an area which is equal to the sum of the areas of all the little rectangles through which the parabola passes? I mean the rectangles BI, IH, HF, FE, EG, and GA of which only a part lies outside the "mixed triangle." Have we not taken the rectangle BO smaller than the area X? Therefore if, as our opponent might say, the triangle plus X is equal to a third part of this rectangle CP, the circumscribed figure, which adds to the triangle an area less than X, will still remain smaller than a third part of the rectangle, CP. But this cannot be, because this circumscribed figure is larger than a third of the area. Hence it is not true that our "mixed triangle" is less than a third of the rectangle.

[183]

Sagr. You have cleared up my difficulty; but it still remains to be shown that the circumscribed figure is larger than a third part of the rectangle CP, a task which will not, I believe, prove so easy.

Salv. There is nothing very difficult about it. Since in the parabola $DE^2:ZG^2=DA:AZ=$ rectangle KE: rectangle AG, seeing that the altitudes of these two rectangles, AK and KL, are equal, it follows that $ED^2:ZG^2=LA^2:AK^2=$ rectangle KE: rectangle KZ. In precisely the same manner it may be shown that the other rectangles LF, MH, NI, OB, stand to one another in the same ratio as the squares of the lines MA, NA, OA, PA.

Let us now consider the circumscribed figure, composed of areas which bear to each other the same ratio as the squares of a series of lines whose common difference in length is equal to the shortest one in the series; note also that the rectangle CP is

made up of an equal number of areas each equal to the largest and each equal to the rectangle OB. Consequently, according to the lemma of Archimedes, the circumscribed figure is larger than a third part of the rectangle CP; but it was also smaller, which is impossible. Hence the "mixed triangle" is not less than a third part of the rectangle CP.

Likewise, I say, it cannot be greater. For, let us suppose that it is greater than a third part of the rectangle CP and let the area X represent the excess of the triangle over the third part of the rectangle CP; subdivide the rectangle into equal rectangles and continue the process until one of these subdivisions is smaller than the area X. Let BO represent such a rectangle smaller than X. Using the above figure, we have in the "mixed triangle" an inscribed figure, made up of the rectangles VO, TN, SM, RL, and QK, which will not be less than a third part of the large rectangle CP.

For the "mixed triangle" exceeds the inscribed figure by a quantity less than that by which it exceeds the third part of the rectangle CP; to see that this is true we have only to remember that the excess of the triangle over the third part of the rectangle CP is equal to the area X, which is less than the rectangle BO, which in turn is much less than the excess of the triangle over the inscribed figure. For the rectangle BO is made

[184]

up of the small rectangles AG, GF, EF, FH, HI, and IB; and the excess of the triangle over the inscribed figure is less than half the sum of these little rectangles. Thus since the triangle exceeds the third part of the rectangle CP by an amount X, which is more than that by which it exceeds the inscribed figure, the latter will also exceed the third part of the rectangle, CP. But, by the lemma which we have assumed, it is smaller. For the rectangle CP, being the sum of the largest rectangles, bears to the component rectangles of the inscribed figure the same ratio which the sum of all the squares of the lines equal to the longest bears to the squares of the lines which have a common difference, after the square of the longest has been subtracted.

Therefore, as in the case of squares, the sum total of the largest rectangles, i. e., the rectangle CP, is greater than three times the sum total of those having a common difference minus the largest; but these last make up the inscribed figure. Hence the "mixed triangle" is neither greater nor less than the third part of rectangle CP; it is therefore equal to it.

Sagr. A fine, clever demonstration; and all the more so because it gives us the quadrature of the parabola, proving it to be four-thirds of the inscribed[23] triangle, a fact which Archimedes demonstrates by means of two different, but admirable, series of many propositions. This same theorem has also been recently established

23. Distinguish carefully between this triangle and the "mixed triangle" above mentioned. [Trans.]

by Luca Valerio,[24] the Archimedes of our age; his demonstration is to be found in his book dealing with the centers of gravity of solids.

Salv. A book which, indeed, is not to be placed second to any produced by the most eminent geometers either of the present or of the past; a book which, as soon as it fell into the hands of our Academician, led him to abandon his own researches along these lines; for he saw how happily everything had been treated and demonstrated by Valerio.

[185]

Sagr. When I was informed of this event by the Academician himself, I begged of him to show the demonstrations which he had discovered before seeing Valerio's book; but in this I did not succeed.

Salv. I have a copy of them and will show them to you; for you will enjoy the diversity of method employed by these two authors in reaching and proving the same conclusions; you will also find that some of these conclusions are explained in different ways, although both are in fact equally correct.

Sagr. I shall be much pleased to see them and will consider it a great favor if you will bring them to our regular meeting. But in the meantime, considering the strength of a solid formed from a prism by means of a parabolic section, would it not, in view of the fact that this result promises to be both interesting and useful in many mechanical operations, be a fine thing if you were to give some quick and easy rule by which a mechanician might draw a parabola upon a plane surface?

Salv. There are many ways of tracing these curves; I will mention merely the two which are the quickest of all. One of these is really remarkable; because by it I can trace thirty or forty parabolic curves with no less neatness and precision, and in a shorter time than another man can, by the aid of a compass, neatly draw four or six circles of different sizes upon paper. I take a perfectly round brass ball about the size of a walnut and project it along the surface of a metallic mirror held in a nearly upright position, so that the ball in its motion will press slightly upon the mirror and trace out a fine sharp parabolic line; this parabola will grow longer and narrower as the angle of elevation increases. The above experiment furnishes clear and tangible evidence that the path of a projectile is a parabola; a fact first observed by our friend and demonstrated by him in his book on motion which we shall take up at our next meeting. In the execution of this method, it is advisable to slightly heat and moisten the ball by rolling in the hand in order that its trace upon the minor may be more distinct.

24. An eminent Italian mathematician, contemporary with Galileo. [Trans.]

[186]

The other method of drawing the desired curve upon the face of the prism is the following: Drive two nails into a wall at a convenient height and at the same level; make the distance between these nails twice the width of the rectangle upon which it is desired to trace the semiparabola. Over these two nails hang a light chain of such a length that the depth of its sag is equal to the length of the prism. This chain will assume the form of a parabola,[25] so that if this form be marked by points on the wall we shall have described a complete parabola which can be divided into two equal parts by drawing a vertical line through a point midway between the two nails. The transfer of this curve to the two opposing faces of the prism is a matter of no difficulty; any ordinary mechanic will know how to do it.

By use of the geometrical lines drawn upon our friend's compass,[26] one may easily lay off those points which will locate this same curve upon the same face of the prism.

Hitherto we have demonstrated numerous conclusions pertaining to the resistance which solids offer to fracture. As a starting point for this science, we assumed that the resistance offered by the solid to a straight-away pull was known; from this base one might proceed to the discovery of many other results and their demonstrations; of these results the number to be found in nature is infinite. But, in order to bring our daily conference to an end, I wish to discuss the strength of hollow solids, which are employed in art—and still oftener in nature—in a thousand operations for the purpose of greatly increasing strength without adding to weight; examples of these are seen in the bones of birds and in many kinds of reeds which are light and highly resistant both to bending and breaking. For if a stem of straw which carries a head of wheat heavier than the entire stalk were made up of the same amount of material in solid form, it would

[187]

offer less resistance to bending and breaking. This is an experience which has been verified and confirmed in practice where it is found that a hollow lance or a tube of wood or metal is much stronger than would be a solid one of the same length and weight, one which would necessarily be thinner; men have discovered, therefore, that in order to make lances strong as well as light they must make them hollow. We shall now show that:

In the case of two cylinders, one hollow the other solid but having equal volumes and equal lengths, their resistances [bending strengths] are to each other in the ratio of their diameters.

25. It is now well known that this curve is not a parabola but a catenary the equation of which was first given, 49 years after Galileo's death, by James Bernoulli. *[Trans.]*

26. The geometrical and military compass of Galileo, described in Nat. Ed. Vol. 2. *[Trans.]*

Let AE denote a hollow cylinder and IN a solid one of the same weight and length; then, I say, that the resistance against fracture exhibited by the tube AE bears to that of the solid cylinder IN the same ratio as the diameter AB to the diameter IL. This is very evident; for since the tube and the solid cylinder IN have the same volume and length, the area of the circular base IL will be equal to that of the annulus AB which is the base of the tube AE. (By annulus is here meant the area which lies between two concentric circles of different radii.) Hence their resistances to a straight-away pull are equal; but in producing fracture by a transverse pull we employ, in the case of the cylinder IN, the length LN as one lever arm, the point L as a fulcrum, and the diameter LI, or its half, as the opposing lever arm: while in the case of the tube, the length BE which plays the part of the first lever arm is equal to LN, the opposing lever arm beyond the fulcrum, B, is the diameter AB, or its half. Manifestly then the resistence [bending strength] of the tube exceeds that of the solid cylinder in the proportion in which the diameter AB exceeds the diameter IL which is the desired result.

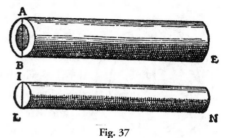

Fig. 37

[188]

Thus the strength of a hollow tube exceeds that of a solid cylinder in the ratio of their diameters whenever the two are made of the same material and have the same weight and length.

It may be well next to investiage the general case of tubes and solid cylinders of constant length, but with the weight and the hollow portion variable. First we shall show that:

Given a hollow tube, a solid cylinder may be determined which will be equal [eguale] to it.

The method is very simple. Let AB denote the external and CD the internal diameter of the tube. In the larger circle lay off the line AE equal in length to the diameter CD; join the points E and B. Now since the angle at E inscribed in a semicircle, AEB, is a right-angle, the area of the circle whose diameter is AB is equal to the sum of the areas of the two circles whose respective diameters are AE and EB. But AE is the diameter of the hollow portion of the tube. Therefore the area of the circle whose diameter is EB is the same as the area of the annulus ACBD. Hence a solid cylinder of circular base having a diamter EB will have the same volume as the walls of the tube of equal length.

By use of this theorem, it is easy:

To find the ratio between the resistance [bending strength] of any tube and that of any cylinder of equal length.

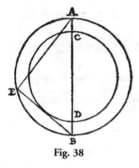

Fig. 38

Let ABE denote a tube and RSM a cylinder of equal length: it is required to find the ratio between their resistances. Using the preceding proposition, determine a cylinder ILN which shall have the same volume and length as the tube. Draw a line V of such a length that it will be related to IL and RS (diameters of the bases of the cylinders IN and RM), as follows: V:RS=RS:IL. Then, I say, the resistance of the tube AE is to that of the cylinder RM as the length of the line AB is to the length

[189]

V. For, since the tube AE is equal both in volume and length, to the cylinder IN, the resistance of the tube will bear to the resistance of the cylinder the same ratio as the line AB to IL; but the resistance of the cylinder IN is to that of the cylinder RM as the cube of IL is to the cube of RS, that is, as the length IL is to length V: therefore, *ex æquali*, the resistance [bending strength] of the tube AE bears to the resistance of the cylinder RM the same ratio as the length AB to V.   Q.E.D.

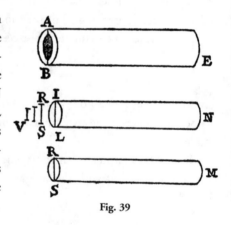

Fig. 39

END OF SECOND DAY.

[190]

THIRD DAY

CHANGE OF POSITION. [De Motu Locali]

My purpose is to set forth a very new science dealing with a very ancient subject. There is, in nature, perhaps nothing older than motion, concerning which the books

written by philosophers are neither few nor small; nevertheless I have discovered by experiment some properties of it which are worth knowing and which have not hitherto been either observed or demonstrated. Some superficial observations have been made, as, for instance, that the free motion [*naturalem motum*] of a heavy falling body is continuously accelerated;[27] but to just what extent this acceleration occurs has not yet been announced; for so far as I know, no one bas yet pointed out that the distances traversed, during equal intervals of time, by a body falling from rest, stand to one another in the same ratio as the odd numbers beginning with unity.[28]

It has been observed that missiles and projectiles describe a curved path of some sort; however no one has pointed out the fact that this path is a parabola. But this and other facts, not few in number or less worth knowing, I have succeeded in proving; and what I consider more important, there have been opened up to this vast and most excellent science, of which my work is merely the beginning, ways and means by which other minds more acute than mine will explore its remote corners.

This discussion is divided into three parts; the first part deals with motion which is steady or uniform; the second treats of motion as we find it accelerated in nature; the third deals with the so-called violent motions and with projectiles.

[191]

UNIFORM MOTION

In dealing with steady or uniform motion, we need a single definition which I give as follows:

DEFINITION

By steady or uniform motion, I mean one in which the distances traversed by the moving particle during any equal intervals of time, are themselves equal.

CAUTION

We must add to the old definition (which defined steady motion simply as one in which equal distances are traversed in equal times) the word "any," meaning by this, all equal intervals of time; for it may happen that the moving body will traverse equal distances during some equal intervals of time and yet the distances traversed during some small portion of these time-intervals may not be equal, even though the time-intervals be equal.

27. "Natural motion" of the author has here been translated into "free motion"-since this is the term used to-day to distinguish the "natural" from the "violent" motions of the Renaissance. *[Trans.]*
28. A theorem demonstrated below. *[Trans.]*

From the above definition, four axioms follow, namely:

AXIOM I

In the case of one and the same uniform motion, the distance traversed during a longer interval of time is greater than the distance traversed during a shorter interval of time.

AXIOM II

In the case of one and the same uniform motion, the time required to traverse a greater distance is longer than the time required for a less distance.

AXIOM III

In one and the same interval of time, the distance traversed at a greater speed is larger than the distance traversed at a less speed.

[192]

AXIOM IV

The speed required to traverse a longer distance is greater than that required to traverse a shorter distance during the same time-interval.

THEOREM I, PROPOSITION I

If a moving particle, carried uniformly at a constant speed, traverses two distances the time-intervals required are to each other in the ratio of these distances.

Let a particle move uniformly with constant speed through two distances AB, BC, and let the time required to traverse AB be represented by DE; the time required

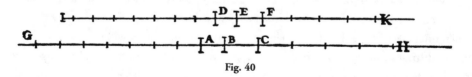

Fig. 40

to traverse BC, by EF; then I say that the distance AB is to the distance BC as the time DE is to the time EF.

Let the distances and times be extended on both sides towards G, H and I, K; let AG be divided into any number whatever of spaces each equal to AB, and in like manner lay off in DI exactly the same number of time-intervals each equal to DE. Again lay off in CH any number whatever of distances each equal to BC; and in FK exactly the same number of time-intervals each equal to EF; then will the distance BG and the time EI be equal and arbitrary multiples of the distance BA and the time ED; and likewise the distance HB and the time KE are equal and arbitrary multiples of the distance CB and the time FE.

And since DE is the time required to traverse AB, the whole time EI will be required for the whole distance BG, and when the motion is uniform there will be in EI as many time-intervals each equal to DE as there are distances in BG each equal to BA; and likewise it follows that KE represents the time required to traverse HB.

Since, however, the motion is uniform, it follows that if the distance GB is equal to the distance BH, then must also the time IE be equal to the time EK; and if GB is greater than BH, then also IE will be greater than EK; and if less, less.[29] There are then four quantities, the first AB, the second BC, the third DE, and the fourth EF; the time IE and the distance GB are arbitrary multiples of the first and the third, namely of the distance AB and the time DE.

[193]

But it has been proved that *both* of these latter quantities are either equal to, greater than, or less than the time EK and the space BH, which are arbitrary multiples of the second and the fourth. Therefore the first is to the second, namely the distance AB is to the distance BC, as the third is to the fourth, namely the time DE is to the time EF.   Q.E.D.

THEOREM II, PROPOSITION II

If a moving particle traverses two distances in equal intervals of time, these distances will bear to each other the same ratio as the speeds. And conversely if the distances are as the speeds then the times are equal.

Referring to Fig. 40, let AB and BC represent the two distances traversed in equal time-intervals, the distance AB for instance with the velocity DE, and the distance BC with the velocity EF. Then, I say, the distance AB is to the distance BC as the velocity DE is to the velocity EF. For if equal multiples of both distances and speeds be taken,

29. The method here employed by Galileo is that of Euclid as set forth in the famous 5th Definition of the Fifth Book of his *Elements*, for which see *art. Geometry* Ency. Brit. 11th Ed. p. 683. *[Trans.]*

as above, namely, GB and IE of AB and DE respectively, and in like manner HB and KE of BC and EF, then one may infer, in the same manner as above, that the multiples GB and IE are either less than, equal to, or greater than equal multiples of BH and EK. Hence the theorem is established.

Theorem III, Proposition III

In the case of unequal speeds, the time-intervals required to traverse a given space are to each other inversely as the speeds.

Let the larger of the two unequal speeds be indicated by A; the smaller, by B; and let the motion corresponding to both traverse the given space CD. Then I say the time required to traverse the distance CD at speed A is to the time required to traverse the same distance at speed B,

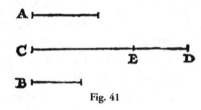

Fig. 41

as the speed B is to the speed A. For let CD be to CE as A is to B; then, from the preceding, it follows that the time required to complete the distance CD at speed A is the same as

[194]

the time necessary to complete CE at speed B; but the time needed to traverse the distance CE at speed B is to the time required to traverse the distance CD at the same speed as CE is to CD; therefore the time in which CD is covered at speed A is to the time in which CD is covered at speed B as CE is to CD, that is, as speed B is to speed A.
Q. E. D.

Theorem IV, Proposition IV

If two particles are carried with uniform motion, but each with a different speed, the distances covered by them during unequal intervals of time bear to each other the compound ratio of the speeds and time intervals.

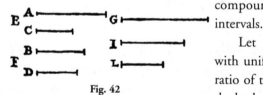

Fig. 42

Let the two particles which are carried with uniform motion be E and F and let the ratio of the speed of the body E be to that of the body F as A is to B; but let the ratio of the time consumed by the motion of E be to the time consumed by the motion of F as C is to D. Then, I say, that the distance covered by E, with speed A in time C, bears to

the space traversed by F with speed B in time D a ratio which is the product of the ratio of the speed A to the speed B by the ratio of the time C to the time D. For if G is the distance traversed by E at speed A during the time-interval C, and if G is to I as the speed A is to the speed B; and if also the time-interval C is to the time-interval D as I is to L, then it follows that I is the distance traversed by F in the same time that G is traversed by E since G is to I in the same ratio as the speed A to the speed B. And since I is to L in the same ratio as the time-intervals C and D, if I is the distance traversed by F during the interval C, then L will be the distance traversed by F during the interval D at the speed B.

But the ratio of G to L is the product of the ratios G to I and I to L, that is, of the ratios of the speed A to the speed B and of the time-interval C to the time-interval D. Q. E. D.

[195]

THEOREM V, PROPOSITION V

If two particles are moved at a uniform rate, but with unequal speeds, through unequal distances, then the ratio of the time-intervals occupied will be the product of the ratio of the distances by the inverse ratio of the speeds.

Let the two moving particles be denoted by A and B, and let the speed of A be to the speed of B in the ratio of V to T; in like manner let the distances traversed be in the ratio of S to R; then I say that the ratio of the time-interval during which the motion of A occurs to the time-interval occupied by the motion of B is the product of the ratio of the speed T to the speed V by the ratio of the distance S to the distance R.

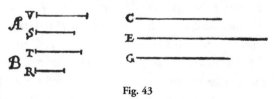

Fig. 43

Let C be the time-interval occupied by the motion of A, and let the time-interval C bear to a time-interval E the same ratio as the speed T to the speed V.

And since C is the time-interval during which A, with speed V, traverses the distance S and since T, the speed of B, is to the speed V, as the time-interval C is to the time-interval E, then E will be the time required by the particle B to traverse the distance S. If now we let the time-interval E be to the time-interval G as the distance S is to the distance R, then it follows that G is the time required by B to traverse the space R. Since the ratio of C to G is the product of the ratios C to E and E to G (while also

the ratio of C to E is the inverse ratio of the speeds of A and B respectively, i. e., the ratio of T to V); and since the ratio of E to G is the same as that of the distances S and R respectively, the proposition is proved.

[196]

THEOREM VI, PROPOSITION VI

If two particles are carried at a uniform rate, the ratio of their speeds will be the product of the ratio of the distances traversed by the inverse ratio of the time-intervals occupied.

Let A and B be the two particles which move at a uniform rate; and let the respective distances traversed by them have the ratio of V to T, but let the time-intervals be as S to R. Then I say the speed of A will bear to the speed of B a ratio which is the product

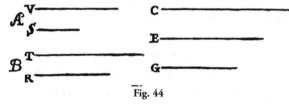

Fig. 44

of the ratio of the distance V to the distance T and the time-interval R to the time-interval S.

Let C be the speed at which A traverses the distance V during the time-interval S; and let the speed C bear the same ratio to another speed E as V bears to T; then E will be the speed at which B traverses the distance T during the time-interval S. If now the speed E is to another speed G as the time-interval R is to the time-interval S, then G will be the speed at which the particle B traverses the distance T during the time-interval R. Thus we have the speed C at which the particle A covers the distance V during the time S and also the speed G at which the particle B traverses the distance T during the time R. The ratio of C to G is the product of the ratio C to E and E to G; the ratio of C to E is by definition the same as the ratio of the distance V to distance T; and the ratio of E to G is the same as the ratio of R to S. Hence follows the proposition.

Salv. The preceding is what our Author has written concerning uniform motion. We pass now to a new and more discriminating consideration of naturally accelerated motion, such as that generally experienced by heavy falling bodies; following is the title and introduction.

[197]

NATURALLY ACCELERATED MOTION

The properties belonging to uniform motion have been discussed in the preceding section; but accelerated motion remains to be considered.

And first of all it seems desirable to find and explain a definition best fitting natural phenomena. For anyone may invent an arbitrary type of motion and discuss its properties; thus, for instance, some have imagined helices and conchoids as described by certain motions which are not met with in nature, and have very commendably established the properties which these curves possess in virtue of their definitions; but we have decided to consider the phenomena of bodies falling with an acceleration such as actually occurs in nature and to make this definition of accelerated motion exhibit the essential features of observed accelerated motions. And this, at last, after repeated efforts we trust we have succeeded in doing. In this belief we are confirmed mainly by the consideration that experimental results are seen to agree with and exactly correspond with those properties which have been, one after another, demonstrated by us. Finally, in the investigation of naturally accelerated motion we were led, by hand as it were, in following the habit and custom of nature herself, in all her various other processes, to employ only those means which are most common, simple and easy.

For I think no one believes that swimming or flying can be accomplished in a manner simpler or easier than that instinctively employed by fishes and birds.

When, therefore, I observe a stone initially at rest falling from an elevated position and continually acquiring new increments of speed, why should I not believe that such increases take place in a manner which is exceedingly simple and rather obvious to everybody? If now we examine the matter carefully we find no addition or increment more simple than that which repeats itself always in the same manner. This we readily understand when we consider the intimate relationship between time and motion; for just as uniformity of motion is defined by and conceived through equal times and equal spaces (thus we call a motion uniform when equal distances are traversed during equal time-intervals), so also we may, in a similar manner, through equal time-intervals, conceive additions of speed as taking place without complication; thus we may picture to our mind a motion as uniformly and continuously accelerated when, during any equal intervals of time whatever, equal increments of speed are given to it.

[198]

Thus if any equal intervals of time whatever have elapsed, counting from the time at which the moving body left its position of rest and began to descend, the amount of speed acquired during the first two time-intervals will be double that acquired during the first time-interval alone; so the amount added during three of these time-intervals will be treble; and that in four, quadruple that of the first time-interval. To put the matter more clearly, if a body were to continue its motion with the same speed which it had acquired during the first time-interval and were to retain this same uniform speed, then its motion would be twice as slow as that which it would have if its velocity had been acquired during *two* time-intervals.

And thus, it seems, we shall not be far wrong if we put the increment of speed as proportional to the increment of time; hence the definition of motion which we are about to discuss may be stated as follows: A motion is said to be uniformly accelerated, when starting from rest, it acquires, during equal time-intervals, equal increments of speed.

Sagr. Although I can offer no rational objection to this or indeed to any other definition, devised by any author whomsoever, since all definitions are arbitrary, I may nevertheless without offense be allowed to doubt whether such a definition as the above, established in an abstract manner, corresponds to and describes that kind of accelerated motion which we meet in nature in the case of freely falling bodies. And since the Author apparently maintains that the motion described in his definition is that of freely falling bodies, I would like to clear my mind of certain difficulties in order that I may later apply myself more earnestly to the propositions and their demonstrations.

Salv. It is well that you and Simplicio raise these difficulties. They are, I imagine, the same which occurred to me when I first saw this treatise, and which were removed either by discussion with the Author himself, or by turning the matter over in my own mind.

[199]

Sagr. When I think of a heavy body falling from rest, that is, starting with zero speed and gaining speed in proportion to the time from the beginning of the motion; such a motion as would, for instance, in eight beats of the pulse acquire eight degrees of speed; having at the end of the fourth beat acquired four degrees; at the end of the second, two; at the end of the first, one: and since time is divisible without limit, it follows from all these considerations that if the earlier speed of a body is less than its present speed in a constant ratio, then there is no degree of speed however small (or, one may say, no degree of slowness however great) with which we may not find this body travelling after starting from infinite slowness, i.e., from rest. So that if that speed which it had at the end of the fourth beat was such that, if kept uniform, the body would traverse two miles in an hour, and if keeping the speed which it had at the end of the second beat, it would traverse one mile an hour, we must infer that, as the instant of starting is more and more nearly approached, the body moves so slowly that, if it kept on moving at this rate, it would not traverse a mile in an hour, or in a day, or in a year or in a thousand years; indeed, it would not traverse a span in an even greater time; a phenomenon which baffles the imagination, while our senses show us that a heavy falling body suddenly acquires great speed.

Salv. This is one of the difficulties which I also at the beginning, experienced, but which I shortly afterwards removed; and the removal was effected by the very experiment which creates the difficulty for you. You say the experiment appears to show that immediately after a heavy body starts from rest it acquires a very considerable speed: and I say that the same experiment makes clear the fact that the initial motions of a falling body, no matter how heavy, are very slow and gentle. Place a heavy body upon a yielding material, and leave it there without any pressure except that owing to its own weight; it is clear that if one lifts this body a cubit or two and allows it to fall upon the same material, it will, with this impulse, exert a new and greater pressure than that caused by its mere weight; and this effect is brought about by the [weight of the] falling body together with the velocity acquired during the fall, an effect which will be greater and greater according to the height of the fall, that is according as the velocity of the falling body becomes greater. From the quality and intensity of the blow we are thus enabled to accurately estimate the speed of a falling body.

[200]

But tell me, gentlemen, is it not true that if a block be allowed to fall upon a stake from a height of four cubits and drives it into the earth, say, four finger-breadths, that coming from a height of two cubits it will drive the stake a much less distance, and from the height of one cubit a still less distance; and finally if the block be lifted only one finger-breadth how much more will it accomplish than if merely laid on top of the stake without percussion? Certainly very little. If it be lifted only the thickness of a leaf, the effect will be altogether imperceptible. And since the effect of the blow depends upon the velocity of this striking body, can any one doubt the motion is very slow and the speed more than small whenever the effect [of the blow] is imperceptible? See now the power of truth; the same experiment which at first glance seemed to show one thing, when more carefully examined, assures us of the contrary.

But without depending upon the above experiment, which is doubtless very conclusive, it seems to me that it ought not to be difficult to establish such a fact by reasoning alone. Imagine a heavy stone held in the air at rest; the support is removed and the stone set free; then since it is heavier than the air it begins to fall, and not with uniform motion but slowly at the beginning and with a continuously accelerated motion. Now since velocity can be increased and diminished without limit, what reason is there to believe that such a moving body starting with infinite slowness, that is, from rest, immediately acquires a speed of ten degrees rather than one of four, or of two, or of one, or of a half, or of a hundredth; or, indeed, of any of the infinite number of small values [of speed]? Pray listen. I hardly think you will refuse to grant that the gain of speed of the stone falling from rest follows the same sequence as the diminution and

loss of this same speed when, by some impelling force, the stone is thrown to its former elevation: but even if you do not grant this, I do not see how you can doubt that the ascending stone, diminishing in speed, must before coming to rest pass through every possible degree of slowness.

Simp. But if the number of degrees of greater and greater slowness is limitless, they will never be all exhausted, therefore such an ascending heavy body will never reach rest, but will continue to move without limit always at a slower rate; but this is not the observed fact.

[201]

Salv. This would happen, Simplicio, if the moving body were to maintain its speed for any length of time at each degree of velocity; but it merely passes each point without delaying more than an instant: and since each time-interval however small may be divided into an infinite number of instants, these will always be sufficient [in number] to correspond to the infinite degrees of diminished velocity.

That such a heavy rising body does not remain for any length of time at any given degree of velocity is evident from the following: because if, some time-interval having been assigned, the body moves with the same speed in the last as in the first instant of that time-interval, it could from this second degree of elevation be in like manner raised through an equal height, just as it was transferred from the first elevation to the second, and by the same reasoning would pass from the second to the third and would finally continue in uniform motion forever.

Sagr. From these considerations it appears to me that we may obtain a proper solution of the problem discussed by philosophers, namely, what causes the acceleration in the natural motion of heavy bodies? Since, as it seems to me, the force [*virtù*] impressed by the agent projecting the body upwards diminishes continuously, this force, so long as it was greater than the contrary force of gravitation, impelled the body upwards; when the two are in equilibrium the body ceases to rise and passes through the state of rest in which the impressed impetus [*impeto*] is not destroyed, but only its excess over the weight of the body has been consumed—the excess which caused the body to rise. Then as the diminution of the outside impetus [*impeto*] continues, and gravitation gains the upper hand, the fall begins, but slowly at first on account of the opposing impetus [*virtù impressa*], a large portion of which still remains in the body; but as this continues to diminish it also continues to be more and more overcome by gravity, hence the continuous acceleration of motion.

Simp. The idea is clever, yet more subtle than sound; for even if the argument were conclusive, it would explain only the case in which a natural motion is preceded by a violent motion, in which there still remains active a portion of the external force [*virtù*

esterna]; but where there is no such remaining portion and the body starts from an antecedent state of rest, the cogency of the whole argument fails.

Sagr. I believe that you are mistaken and that this distinction between cases which you make is superfluous or rather non-existent. But, tell me, cannot a projectile receive from the projector either a large or a small force [*virtù*] such as will throw it to a height of a hundred cubits, and even twenty or four or one?

[202]

Simp. Undoubtedly, yes.

Sagr. So therefore this impressed force [*virtù impressa*] may exceed the resistance of gravity so slightly as to raise it only a finger-breadth; and finally the force [*virtù*] of the projector may be just large enough to exactly balance the resistance of gravity so that the body is not lifted at all but merely sustained. When one holds a stone in his hand does he do anything but give it a force impelling [*virtù impellente*] it upwards equal to the power [*facoltà*] of gravity drawing it downwards? And do you not continuously impress this force [*virtù*] upon the stone as long as you hold it in the hand? Does it perhaps diminish with the time during which one holds the stone?

And what does it matter whether this support which prevents the stone from falling is furnished by one's hand or by a table or by a rope from which it hangs? Certainly nothing at all. You must conclude, therefore, Simplicio, that it makes no difference whatever whether the fall of the stone is preceded by a period of rest which is long, short, or instantaneous provided only the fall does not take place so long as the stone is acted upon by a force [*virtù*] opposed to its weight and sufficient to hold it at rest.

Salv. The present does not seem to be the proper time to investigate the cause of the acceleration of natural motion concerning which various opinions have been expressed by various philosophers, some explaining it by attraction to the center, others to repulsion between the very small parts of the body, while still others attribute it to a certain stress in the surrounding medium which closes in behind the falling body and drives it from one of its positions to another. Now, all these fantasies, and others too, ought to be examined; but it is not really worth while. At present it is the purpose of our Author merely to investigate and to demonstrate some of the properties of accelerated motion (whatever the cause of this acceleration may be)—meaning thereby a motion, such that the momentum of its velocity [*i momenti della sua velocità*] goes on increasing after departure from rest, in simple proportionality to the time, which is the same as saying that in equal time-intervals the body receives equal increments of velocity; and if we find the properties [of accelerated motion] which will be demonstrated later are realized in freely falling and accelerated bodies, we may conclude that the

assumed definition includes such a motion of falling bodies and that their speed [*accelerazione*] goes on increasing as the time and the duration of the motion.

[203]

Sagr. So far as I see at present, the definition might have been put a little more clearly perhaps without changing the fundamental idea, namely, uniformly accelerated motion is such that its speed increases in proportion to the space traversed; so that, for example, the speed acquired by a body in falling four cubits would be double that acquired in falling two cubits and this latter speed would be double that acquired in the first cubit. Because there is no doubt but that a heavy body falling from the height of six cubits has, and strikes with, a momentum [*impeto*] double that it had at the end of three cubits, triple that which it had at the end of one.

Salv. It is very comforting to me to have had such a companion in error; and moreover let me tell you that your proposition seems so highly probable that our Author himself admitted, when I advanced this opinion to him, that he had for some time shared the same fallacy. But what most surprised me was to see two propositions so inherently probable that they commanded the assent of everyone to whom they were presented, proven in a few simple words to be not only false, but impossible.

Simp. I am one of those who accept the proposition, and believe that a falling body acquires force [*vires*] in its descent, its velocity increasing in proportion to the space, and that the momentum [*momento*] of the falling body is doubled when it falls from a doubled height; these propositions, it appears to me, ought to be conceded without hesitation or controversy.

Salv. And yet they are as false and impossible as that motion should be completed instantaneously; and here is a very clear demonstration of it. If the velocities are in proportion to the spaces traversed, or to be traversed, then these spaces are traversed in equal intervals of time; if, therefore, the velocity with which the falling body traverses a space of eight feet were double that with which it covered the first four feet (just as the one distance is double the other) then the time-intervals required for these passages would be equal. But for one and the same body to fall eight feet and four feet in the same time is possible only in the case of instantaneous [discontinuous] motion; but observation shows us that the motion of a falling body occupies time, and less of it in covering a distance of four feet than of eight feet; therefore it is not true that its velocity increases in proportion to the space.

[204]

The falsity of the other proposition may be shown with equal clearness. For if we consider a single striking body the difference of momentum in its blows can depend

only upon difference of velocity; for if the striking body falling from a double height were to deliver a blow of double momentum, it would be necessary for this body to strike with a doubled velocity; but with this doubled speed it would traverse a doubled space in the same time-interval; observation however shows that the time required for fall from the greater height is longer.

Sagr. You present these recondite matters with too much evidence and ease; this great facility makes them less appreciated than they would be had they been presented in a more abstruse manner. For, in my opinion, people esteem more lightly that knowledge which they acquire with so little labor than that acquired through long and obscure discussion.

Salv. If those who demonstrate with brevity and clearness the fallacy of many popular beliefs were treated with contempt instead of gratitude the injury would be quite bearable; but on the other hand it is very unpleasant and annoying to see men, who claim to be peers of anyone in a certain field of study, take for granted certain conclusions which later are quickly and easily shown by another to be false. I do not describe such a feeling as one of envy, which usually degenerates into hatred and anger against those who discover such fallacies; I would call it a strong desire to maintain old errors, rather than accept newly discovered truths. This desire at times induces them to unite against these truths, although at heart believing in them, merely for the purpose of lowering the esteem in which certain others are held by the unthinking crowd. Indeed, I have heard from our Academician many such fallacies held as true but easily refutable; some of these I have in mind.

[205]

Sagr. You must not withhold them from us, but, at the proper time, tell us about them even though an extra session be necessary. But now, continuing the thread of our talk, it would seem that up to the present we have established the definition of uniformly accelerated motion which is expressed as follows:

A motion is said to be equally or uniformly accelerated when, starting from rest, its momentum (celeritatis momenta) receives equal increments in equal times.

Salv. This definition established, the Author makes a single assumption, namely,

The speeds acquired by one and the same body moving down planes of different inclinations are equal when the heights of these planes are equal.

By the height of an inclined plane we mean the perpendicular let fall from the upper end of the plane upon the horizontal line drawn through the lower end of the same plane. Thus, to illustrate, let the line AB be horizontal, and let the planes CA and CD be inclined to it; then the Author calls the perpendicular CB the "height" of the planes CA and CD; he supposes that the speeds acquired by one and the same body, descending along the planes CA and CD to the terminal points A and D are equal since the heights of these planes are the same, CB; and also it must be understood that this speed is that which would be acquired by the same body falling from C to B.

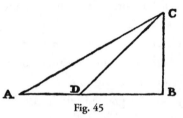

Fig. 45

Sagr. Your assumption appears to me so reasonable that it ought to be conceded without question, provided of course there are no chance or outside resistances, and that the planes are hard and smooth, and that the figure of the moving body is perfectly round, so that neither plane nor moving body is rough. All resistance and opposition having been removed, my reason tells me at once that a heavy and perfectly round ball descending along the lines CA, CD, CB would reach the terminal points A, D, B, with equal momenta [*impeti eguali*].

[206]

Salv. Your words are very plausible; but I hope by experiment to increase the probability to an extent which shall be little short of a rigid demonstration.

Imagine this page to represent a vertical wall, with a nail driven into it; and from the nail let there be suspended a lead bullet of one or two ounces by means of a fine vertical thread, AB, say from four to six feet long, on this wall draw a horizontal line DC, at right angles to the vertical thread AB, which hangs about two finger-breadths in front of the wall. Now bring the thread AB with the attached ball into the position AC and set it free; first it will be observed to descend along the arc CBD, to pass the point B, and to travel along the

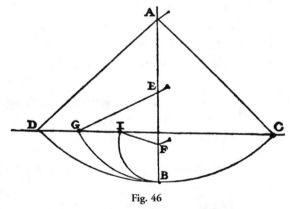

Fig. 46

arc BD, till it almost reaches the horizontal CD, a slight shortage being caused by the resistance of the air and the string; from this we may rightly infer that the ball in its

descent through the arc CB acquired a momentum [*impeto*] on reaching B, which was just sufficient to carry it through a similar arc BD to the same height. Having repeated this experiment many times, let us now drive a nail into the wall close to the perpendicular AB, say at E or F, so that it projects out some five or six finger-breadths in order that the thread, again carrying the bullet through the are CB, may strike upon the nail E when the bullet reaches B, and thus compel it to traverse the are BG, described about E as center. From this we can see what can be done by the same momentum [*impeto*] which previously starting at the same point B carried the same body through the arc BD to the horizontal CD. Now, gentlemen, you will observe with pleasure that the ball swings to the point G in the horizontal, and you would see the same thing happen if the obstacle were placed at some lower point, say at F, about which the ball would describe the arc BI, the rise of the ball always terminating exactly on the line CD. But when the nail is placed so low that the remainder of the thread below it will not reach to the height CD (which would happen if the nail were placed

[207]

nearer B than to the intersection of AB with the horizontal CD) then the thread leaps over the nail and twists itself about it.

This experiment leaves no room for doubt as to the truth of our supposition; for since the two arcs CB and DB are equal and similarly placed, the momentum [*momento*] acquired by the fall through the arc CB is the same as that gained by fall through the arc DB; but the momentum [*momento*] acquired at B, owing to fall through CB, is able to lift the same body [*mobile*] through the arc BD; therefore, the momentum acquired in the fall BD is equal to that which lifts the same body through the same arc from B to D; so, in general, every momentum acquired by fall through an arc is equal to that which can lift the same body through the same arc. But all these momenta [*momenti*] which cause a rise through the arcs BD, BG, and BI are equal, since they are produced by the same momentum, gained by fall through CB, as experiment shows. Therefore all the momenta gained by fall through the arcs DB, GB, IB are equal.

Sagr. The argument seems to me so conclusive and the experiment so well adapted to establish the hypothesis that we may, indeed, consider it as demonstrated.

Salv. I do not wish, Sagredo, that we trouble ourselves too much about this matter, since we are going to apply this principle mainly in motions which occur on plane surfaces, and not upon curved, along which acceleration varies in a manner greatly different from that which we have assumed for planes.

So that, although the above experiment shows us that the descent of the moving body through the arc CB confers upon it momentum [*momento*] just sufficient to

carry it to the same height through any of the arcs BD, BG, BI, we are not able, by similar means, to show that the event would be identical in the case of a perfectly round ball descending along planes whose inclinations are respectively the same as the chords of these arcs. It seems likely, on the other hand, that, since these planes form angles at the point B, they will present an obstacle to the ball which has descended along the chord CB, and starts to rise along the chord BD, BG, BI.

In striking these planes some of its momentum [*impeto*] will be lost and it will not be able to rise to the height of the line CD; but this obstacle, which interferes with the experiment, once removed, it is clear that the momentum [*impeto*] (which gains in

[208]

strength with descent) will be able to carry the body to the same height. Let us then, for the present, take this as a postulate, the absolute truth of which will be established when we find that the inferences from it correspond to and agree perfectly with experiment. The author having assumed this single principle passes next to the propositions which he clearly demonstrates; the first of these is as follows:

THEOREM I, PROPOSITION I

The time in which any space is traversed by a body starting from rest and uniformly accelerated is equal to the time in which that same space would be traversed by the same body moving at a uniform speed whose value is the mean of the highest speed and the speed just before acceleration began.

Let us represent by the line AB the time in which the space CD is traversed by a body which starts from rest at C and is uniformly accelerated; let the final and highest value of the speed gained during the interval AB be represented by the line EB drawn at right angles to AB; draw the line AE, then all lines drawn from equidistant points on AB and parallel to BE will represent the increasing values of the speed, beginning with the instant A. Let the point F bisect the line EB; draw FG parallel to BA, and GA parallel to FB, thus forming a parallelogram AGFB which will be equal in area to the triangle AEB, since the side GF bisects the side AE at the point I; for if the parallel lines in the triangle AEB are extended to GI, then the sum of all the parallels contained in the quadrilateral is equal to the sum of those

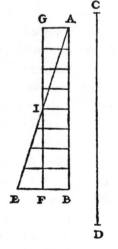

Fig. 47

contained in the triangle AEB; for those in the triangle IEF are equal to those contained in the triangle GIA, while those included in the trapezium AIFB are common. Since each and every instant of time in the time-interval AB has its corresponding point on the line AB, from which points parallels drawn in and limited by the triangle AEB represent the increasing values of the growing velocity, and since parallels contained within the rectangle represent the values of a speed which is not increasing, but constant, it appears, in like manner, that the momenta [*momenta*] assumed by the moving body may also be represented, in the case of the accelerated motion, by the increasing parallels of the triangle AEB, and, in the case of the uniform motion, by the

[209]

parallels of the rectangle GB. For, what the momenta may lack in the first part of the accelerated motion (the deficiency of the momenta being represented by the parallels of the triangle AGI) is made up by the momenta represented by the parallels of the triangle IEF.

Hence it is clear that equal spaces will be traversed in equal times by two bodies, one of which, starting from rest, moves with a uniform acceleration, while the momentum of the other, moving with uniform speed, is one-half its maximum momentum under accelerated motion.   Q.E.D.

THEOREM II, PROPOSITION II

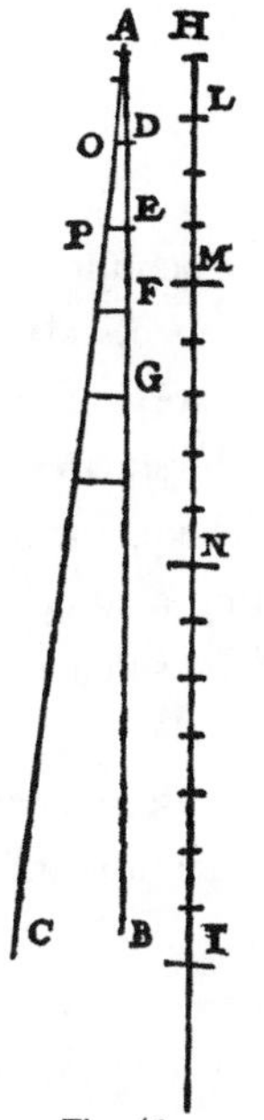

Fig. 48

The spaces described by a body falling from rest with a uniformly accelerated motion are to each other as the squares of the time-intervals employed in traversing these distances.

Let the time beginning with any instant A be represented by the straight line AB in which are taken any two time-intervals AD and AE. Let HI represent the distance through which the body, starting from rest at H, falls with uniform acceleration. If HL represents the space traversed during the time-interval AD, and HM that covered during the interval AE, then the space MH stands to the space LH in a ratio which is the square of the ratio of the time AE to the time AD; or we may say simply that the distances HM and HL are related as the squares of AE and AD.

Draw the line AC making any angle whatever with the line AB; and from the points D and E, draw the parallel lines DO and EP; of these two lines, DO represents the greatest velocity attained during the interval AD, while EP represents the maximum velocity acquired during the interval AE. But it has just been proved that so far as distances traversed are concerned it is precisely the same whether a body falls from rest with a uniform acceleration or whether it falls during an equal time-interval with a constant speed which is one-half the maximum speed attained during the accelerated motion. It follows therefore that the distances HM and HL are the same as would be traversed, during the time-intervals AE and AD, by uniform velocities equal to one-half those represented by DO and EP respectively. If, therefore, one can show that the distances HM and HL are in the same ratio as the squares of the time-intervals AE and AD, our proposition will be proven.

[210]

But in the fourth proposition of the first book [see above] it has been shown that the spaces traversed by two particles in uniform motion bear to one another a ratio which is equal to the product of the ratio of the velocities by the ratio of the times. But in this case the ratio of the velocities is the same as the ratio of the time-intervals (for the ratio of AE to AD is the same as that of 1/2 EP to 1/2 DO or of EP to DO). Hence the ratio of the spaces traversed is the same as the squared ratio of the time intervals.   Q.E.D.

Evidently then the ratio of the distances is the square of the ratio of the final velocities, that is, of the lines EP and DO, since these are to each other as AE to AD.

COROLLARY I

Hence it is clear that if we take any equal intervals of time whatever, counting from the beginning of the motion, such as AD, DE, EF, FG, in which the spaces HL, LM, MN, NI are traversed, these spaces will bear to one another the same ratio as the series of odd numbers, 1, 3, 5, 7; for this is the ratio of the differences of the squares of the lines [which represent time], differences which exceed one another by equal amounts, this excess being equal to the smallest line [viz. the one representing a single time-interval]: or we may say [that this is the ratio] of the differences of the squares of the natural numbers beginning with unity.

While, therefore, during equal intervals of time the velocities increase as the natural numbers, the increments in the distances traversed during these equal time-intervals are to one another as the odd numbers beginning with unity.

Sagr. Please suspend the discussion for a moment since there just occurs to me an idea which I want to illustrate by means of a diagram in order that it may be clearer both to you and to me.

Let the line AI represent the lapse of time measured from the initial instant A; through A draw the straight line AF making A any angle whatever; join the terminal points I and F; divide the time AI in half at C; draw CB parallel to IF. Let us consider CB as the maximum value of the velocity which increases from zero at the beginning, in simple proportionality to the intercepts on the triangle ABC of lines drawn parallel to BC; or what is the same thing, let us suppose the velocity to increase in proportion to the time; then I admit without question, in view of the preceding argument, that the space described by a body falling in the aforesaid manner will be equal to the space traversed by the same body during the same length of time travelling with a uniform speed equal, to EC, the

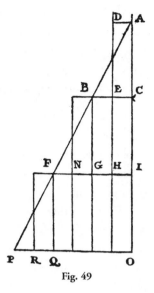

Fig. 49

[211]

half of BC. Further let us imagine that the body has fallen with accelerated motion so that, at the instant C, it has the velocity BC. It is clear that if the body continued to descend with the same speed BC, without acceleration, it would in the next time-interval CI traverse double the distance covered during the interval AC, with the uniform speed EC which is half of BC; but since the falling body acquires equal increments of speed during equal increments of time, it follows that the velocity BC, during the next time-interval CI will be increased by an amount represented by the parallels of the triangle BFG which is equal to the triangle ABC. If, then, one adds to the velocity GI half of the velocity FG, the highest speed acquired by the accelerated motion and determined by the parallels of the triangle BFG, he will have the uniform velocity with which the same space would have been described in the time CI; and since this speed IN is three times as great as EC it follows that the space described during the interval a is three times as great as that described during the interval AC. Let us imagine the motion extended over another equal time-interval IO, and the triangle extended to APO; it is then evident that if the motion continues during the interval IO, at the constant rate IF acquired by acceleration during the time AI, the space traversed during the interval IO will be four times that traversed during the first interval AC, because the speed IF is four times the speed EC. But if we enlarge our triangle so as to include FPQ which is equal to ABC, still assuming the acceleration to be constant, we shall add to the uniform speed an increment RQ, equal to EC; then the value of the equivalent uniform speed during the time-interval IO will be five times that during the first time-interval AC; therefore the space traversed will be quintuple that during the first interval

AC. It is thus evident by simple computation that a moving body starting from rest and acquiring velocity at a rate proportional to the time, will, during equal intervals of time, traverse distances which are related to each other as the odd numbers beginning with unity, 1, 3, 5;[30] or considering the total space traversed, that covered in double time will be quadruple that covered during unit time; in

[212]

triple time, the space is nine times as great as in unit time. And in general the spaces traversed are in the duplicate ratio of the times, i. e., in the ratio of the squares of the times.

Simp. In truth, I find more pleasure in this simple and clear argument of Sagredo than in the Author's demonstration which to me appears rather obscure; so that I am convinced that matters are as described, once having accepted the definition of uniformly accelerated motion. But as to whether this acceleration is that which one meets in nature in the case of falling bodies, I am still doubtful; and it seems to me, not only for my own sake but also for all those who think as I do, that this would be the proper moment to introduce one of those experiments-and there are many of them, I understand-which illustrate in several ways the conclusions reached.

Salv. The request which you, as a man of science, make, is a very reasonable one; for this is the custom-and properly so-in those sciences where mathematical demonstrations are applied to natural phenomena, as is seen in the case of perspective, astronomy, mechanics, music, and others where the principles, once established by well-chosen experiments, become the foundations of the entire superstructure. I hope therefore it will not appear to be a waste of time if we discuss at considerable length this first and most fundamental question upon which hinge numerous consequences of which we have in this book only a small number, placed there by the Author, who has done so much to open a pathway hitherto closed to minds of speculative turn. So far as experiments go they have not been neglected by the Author; and often, in his company, I have attempted in tile following manner to assure myself that the acceleration actually experienced by falling bodies is that above described.

[213]

A piece of wooden moulding or scantling, about 12 cubits long, half a cubit wide, and three finger-breadths thick, was taken; on its edge was cut a channel a little more

---

30. As illustrating the greater elegance and brevity of modern analytical methods, one may obtain the result of Prop. II directly from the fundamental equation

$s = 1/2g(t2^2 - t1^2) = g/2(t2 + t1)(t2 - t1)$

where g is the acceleration of gravity and s, the space traversed between the instants $t1$ and $t2 = 1$, say one second, then $s = g/2(t2 + t1)$ where $t2 + t1$, must always be an odd number, seeing that it is the sum of two consecutive terms in the series of natural numbers. *[Trans.]*

than one finger in breadth; having made this groove very straight, smooth, and polished, and having lined it with parchment, also as smooth and polished as possible, we rolled along it a hard, smooth, and very round bronze ball. Having placed this board in a sloping position, by lifting one end some one or two cubits above the other, we rolled the ball, as I was just saying, along the channel, noting, in a manner presently to be described, the time required to make the descent. We repeated this experiment more than once in order to measure the time with an accuracy such that the deviation between two observations never exceeded one-tenth of a pulse-beat. Having performed this operation and having assured ourselves of its reliability, we now rolled the ball only one-quarter the length of the channel; and having measured the time of its descent, we found it precisely one-half of the former. Next we tried other distances, comparing the time for the whole length with that for the half, or with that for two-thirds, or three-fourths, or indeed for any fraction; in such experiments, repeated a full hundred times, we always found that the spaces traversed were to each other as the squares of the times, and this was true for all inclinations of the plane, i. e., of the channel, along which we rolled the ball. We also observed that the times of descent, for various inclinations of the plane, bore to one another precisely that ratio which, as we shall see later, the Author had predicted and demonstrated for them.

For the measurement of time, we employed a large vessel of water placed in an elevated position; to the bottom of this vessel was soldered a pipe of small diameter giving a thin jet of water, which we collected in a small glass during the time of each descent, whether for the whole length of the channel or for a part of its length; the water thus collected was weighed, after each descent, on a very accurate balance; the differences and ratios of these weights gave us the differences and ratios of the times, and this with such accuracy that although the operation was repeated many, many times, there was no appreciable discrepancy in the results.

Simp. I would like to have been present at these experiments; but feeling confidence in the care with which you performed them, and in the fidelity with which you relate them, I am satisfied and accept them as true and valid.

Salv. Then we can proceed without discussion.

[214]

COROLLARY II

Secondly, it follows that, starting from any initial point, if we take any two distances, traversed in any time-intervals whatsoever, these time-intervals bear to one another the same ratio as one of the distances to the mean proportional of the two distances.

For if we take two distances ST and SY measured from the initial point S, the mean proportional of which is SX, the time of fall through ST is to the time of fall through SY as ST is to SX; or one may say the time of fall through SY is to the time of fall through ST as SY is to SX. Now since it has been shown that the spaces traversed are in the same ratio as the squares of the times; and since, moreover, the ratio of the space SY to the space ST is the square of the ratio SY to SX, it follows that the ratio of the times of fall through SY and ST is the ratio of the respective distances SY and SX.

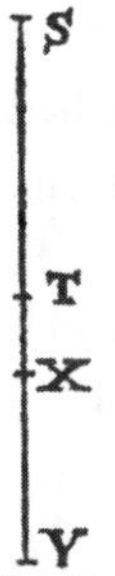

Fig. 50

SCHOLIUM

The above corollary has been proven for the case of vertical fall; but it holds also for planes inclined at any angle; for it is to be assumed that along these planes the velocity increases in the same ratio, that is, in proportion to the time, or, if you prefer, as the series of natural numbers.[31]

Salv. Here, Sagredo, I should like, if it be not too tedious to Simplicio, to interrupt for a moment the present discussion in order to make some additions on the basis of what has already been proved and of what mechanical principles we have already learned from our Academician. This addition I make for the better establishment on logical and experimental grounds, of the principle which we have above considered; and what is more important, for the purpose of deriving it geometrically, after first demonstrating a single lemma which is fundamental in the science of motion [*impeti*].

Sagr. If the advance which you propose to make is such as will confirm and fully establish these sciences of motion, I will gladly devote to it any length of time. Indeed,

[215]

I shall not only be glad to have you proceed, but I beg of you at once to satisfy the curiosity which you have awakened in me concerning your proposition; and I think that Simplicio is of the same mind.

Simp. Quite right.

Salv. Since then I have your permission, let us first of all consider this notable fact, that the momenta or speeds [*i momenti o le velocità*] of one and the same moving body vary with the inclination of the plane.

The speed reaches a maximum along a vertical direction, and for other directions diminishes as the plane diverges from the vertical. Therefore the impetus, ability, energy, [*l'impeto, il talento l'energia*] or, one might say, the momentum [*il momento*] of descent of the moving body is diminished by the plane upon which it is supported and along which it rolls.

---

31. The dialogue which intervenes between this Scholium and the following theorem was elaborated by Viviani, at the suggestion of Galileo. See *National Edition*, viii, 23. *[Trans.]*

For the sake of greater clearness erect the line AB perpendicular to the horizontal AC; next draw AD, AE, AF, etc., at different inclinations to the horizontal. Then I say that all the momentum of the falling body is along the vertical and is a maximum when it falls in that direction; the momentum is less along DA and still less along EA, and even less yet along the more inclined plane FA. Finally on the horizontal plane the momentum vanishes altogether; the body finds itself in a condition of indifference as to motion or rest; has no inherent tendency to move in any direction, and offers no resistance to being set in motion. For just as a heavy body or system of bodies cannot of itself move upwards, or recede from the common center [*comun centro*] toward which all heavy things tend, so it is impossible for any body of its own accord to assume any motion other than one which carries it nearer to the aforesaid common center. Hence, along the horizontal, by which we understand a surface, every point of which is equidistant from this same common center, the body will have no momentum whatever.

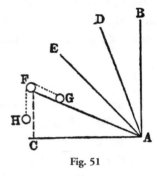

Fig. 51

[216]

This change of momentum being clear, it is here necessary for me to explain something which our Academician wrote when in Padua, embodying it in a treatise on mechanics prepared solely for the use of his students, and proving it at length and conclusively when considering the origin and nature of that marvellous machine, the screw. What he proved is the manner in which the momentum [*impeto*] varies with the inclination of the plane, as for instance that of the plane FA, one end of which is elevated through a vertical distance FC. This direction FC is that along which the momentum of a heavy body becomes a maximum; let us discover what ratio this momentum bears to that of the same body moving along the inclined plane FA. This ratio, I say, is the inverse of that of the aforesaid lengths. Such is the lemma preceding the theorem which I hope to demonstrate a little later.

It is clear that the impelling force [*impeto*] acting on a body in descent is equal to the resistance or least force [*resistenza o forza minima*] sufficient to bold it at rest. In order to measure this force and resistance [*forza e resistenza*] I propose to use the weight of another body. Let us place upon the plane FA a body G connected to the weight H by means of a cord passing over the point F; then the body H will ascend or descend, along the perpendicular, the same distance which the body G ascends or descends along the inclined plane FA; but this distance will not be equal to the rise or fall of G along the vertical in which direction alone G, as other bodies, exerts its force

[*resistenza*]. This is clear. For if we consider the motion of the body G, from A to F in the triangle AFC to be made up of a horizontal component AC and a vertical component CF, and remember that this body experiences no resistance to motion along the horizontal (because by such a motion the body neither gains nor loses distance from the common center of heavy things) it follows that resistance is met only in consequence of the body rising through the vertical distance CF.

[217]

Since then the body G in moving from A to F offers resistance only in so far as it rises through the vertical distance CF, while the other body H must fall vertically through the entire distance FA, and since this ratio is maintained whether the motion be large or small, the two bodies being inextensibly connected, we are able to assert positively that, in case of equilibrium (bodies at rest) the momenta, the velocities, or their tendency to motion [*propensioni al moto*], i. e., the spaces which would be traversed by them in equal times, must be in the inverse ratio to their weights. This is what has been demonstrated in every case of mechanical motion.[32] So that, in order to hold the weight G at rest, one must give H a weight smaller in the same ratio as the distance CF is smaller than FA. If we do this, FA:FC=weight G:weight H; then equilibrium will occur, that is, the weights H and G will have the some impelling forces [*momenti eguali*], and the two bodies will come to rest.

And since we are agreed that the impetus, energy, momentum or tendency to motion of a moving body is as great as the force or least resistance [*forza o resistenza minima*] sufficient to stop it, and since we have found that the weight H is capable of preventing motion in the weight G it follows that the less weight H whose entire force [*momento totale*] is along the perpendicular, FC, will be an exact measure of the component of force [*momento parziale*] which the larger weight G exerts along the plane FA. But the measure of the total force [*total momento*] on the body G is its own weight, since to prevent its fall it is only necessary to balance it with an equal weight, provided this second weight be free to move vertically; therefore the component of the force [*momento parziale*] on G along the inclined plane FA will bear to the maximum and total force on this same body G along the perpendicular FC the same ratio as the weight H to the weight G. This ratio is, by construction, the same which the height, FC, of the inclined plane bears to the length FA. We have here the lemma which I proposed to demonstrate and which, as you will see, has been assumed by our Author in the second part of the sixth proposition of the present treatise.

Sagr. From what you have shown thus far, it appears to me that one might infer, arguing *ex aequali con la proportione perturbata*, that the tendencies [*momenti*] of one

32. A near approach to the principle of virtual work enunciated by John Bernoulli in 1717. [*Trans.*]

and the same body to move along planes differently inclined, but having the same vertical height, as FA and FI, are to each other inversely as the lengths of the planes.

[218]

Salv. Perfectly right. This point established, I pass to the demonstration of the following theorem:

If a body falls freely along smooth planes inclined at any angle whatsoever, but of the same height, the speeds with which it reaches the bottom are the same.

First we must recall the fact that on a plane of any inclination whatever a body starting from rest gains speed or momentum [*la quantitá dell'impeto*] in direct proportion to the time, in agreement with the definition of naturally accelerated motion given by the Author. Hence, as he has shown in the preceding proposition, the distances traversed are proportional to the squares of the times and therefore to the squares of the speeds, the speed relations are here the same as in the motion first studied [i. e., *vertical motion*], since in each case the gain of speed is proportional to the time.

Let AB be an inclined plane whose height above the level BC is AC. As we have seen above the force impelling [*l'impeto*] a body to fall along the vertical AC is to the force which drives the same body along the inclined plane AB as AB is to AC. On the incline AB , lay off AD a third proportional to AB and AC; then the force producing motion along AC is to that along AB (i. e., along AD) as the length AC is to the length AD. And therefore the body will traverse the space AD, along the incline AB, in the same time which it would occupy in falling the vertical distance AC, (since the forces [*momenti*] are in the same ratio as these distances); also the speed at C is to the speed at D as the distance AC is to the distance AD. But, according to the definition of accelerated motion, the speed at B is to the speed of the same body at D as the time required to traverse AB is to the time required for AD; and, according to the last corollary of the second proposition, the time of passing through the distance AB bears to the time of passing through AD the same ratio as the distance AC (a mean proportional between AB and AD) to AD. Accordingly the two speeds at B and C each bear to the speed at D the same ratio, namely, that of the distances AC and AD; hence they are equal. This is the theorem which I set out to prove.

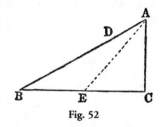

Fig. 52

From the above we are better able to demonstrate the following third preposition of the Author in which he employs the following principle, namely, the time required to traverse an inclined plane is to that required to fall through the vertical height of the plane in the same ratio as the length of the plane to its height.

[219]

For, according to the second corollary of the second reposition, if BA represents the time required to pass over the distance BA, the time required to pass the distance AD will be a mean proportional between these two distances and will be represented by the line AC; but if AC represents the time needed to traverse AD it will also represent the time required to fall through the distance AC, since the distances AC and AD are traversed in equal times; consequently if AB represents the time required for AB then AC will represent the time required for AC. Hence the times required to traverse AB and AC are to each other as the distances AB and AC.

In like manner it can be shown that the time required to fall through AC is to the time required for any other incline AE as the length AC is to the length AE; therefore, *ex aequali*, the time of fall along the incline AB is to that along AE as the distance AB is to the distance AE, etc.[33]

One might by application of this same theorem, as Sagredo will readily see, immediately demonstrate the sixth proposition of the Author; but let us here end this digression which Sagredo has perhaps found rather tedious, though I consider it quite important or the theory of motion.

Sagr. On the contrary it has given me great satisfaction, and indeed I find it necessary for a complete grasp of this principle.

Salv. I will now resume the reading of the text.

[220]

THEOREM III, PROPOSITION III

If one and the same body, starting from rest, falls along an inclined plane and also along a vertical, each having the same height, the times of descent will be to each other as the lengths of the inclined plane and the vertical.

Let AC be the inclined plane and AB the perpendicular, each having the same vertical height above the horizontal, namely, BA; then I say, the time of descent of one and

---

33 Putting this argument in a modern and evident notation, one has AC=1/2 gt2c and AD = 1/2 AC/AB gt2/d If now AC^2=AB.AD, it follows at once that t_d=t_c. [Trans.] Q.D.E.

the same body along the plane AC bears a ratio to the time of fall along the perpendicular AB, which is the same as the ratio of the length AC to the AB.

[221]

Let DG, EI and LF be any lines parallel to the horizontal CB; then it follows from what has preceded that a body starting from A will acquire the same speed at the point G as at D, since in each case the vertical fall is the same; in like manner the speeds at I and E will be the same; so also those at L and F. And in general the speeds at the two extremities of any parallel drawn from any point on AB to the corresponding point on AC will be equal.

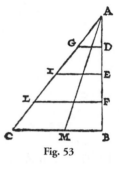

Fig. 53

[222]

Thus the two distances AC and AB are traversed at the same speed. But it has already been proved that if two distances are traversed by a body moving with equal speeds, then the ratio of the times of descent will be the ratio of the distances themselves; therefore, the time of descent along AC is to that along AB as the length of the plane AC is to the vertical distance AB.   Q.E.D.

[223]

Sagr. It seems to me that the above could have been proved clearly and briefly on the basis of a proposition already demonstrated, namely, that the distance traversed in the case of accelerated motion along AC or AB is the same as that covered by a uniform speed whose value is one-half the maximum speed, CB; the two distances AC and

[224]

AB having been traversed at the same uniform speed it is evident, from Proposition I, that the times of descent will be to each other as the distances.

COROLLARY

Hence we may infer that the times of descent along planes having different inclinations, but the same vertical height stand to one another in the same ratio as the lengths of the planes. For consider any plane AM extending from A to the horizontal CB; then it may be demonstrated in the same manner that the time of descent along AM is to the time along AB as the distance AM is to AB; but since the time along AB is to that along AC as the length AB is to the length AC, it follows, *ex æquali*, that as AM is to AC so is the time along AM to the time along AC.

Theorem IV, Proposition IV

The times of descent along planes of the same length but of different inclinations are to each other in the inverse ratio of the square roots of their heights.

From a single point B draw the planes BA and BC, having the same length but different inclinations; let AE and CD be horizontal lines drawn to meet the perpendicular BD; and let BE represent the height of the plane AB, and BD the height of BC; also

[225]

let BI be a mean proportional to BD and BE; then the ratio of BD to BI is equal to the square root of the ratio of BD to BE. Now, I say, the ratio of the times of descent along BA and BC is the ratio of BD to BI; so that the time of descent along BA is related to the height of the other plane BC, namely BD as the time along BC is related to the height BI. Now it must be proved that the time of descent along BA is to that along BC as the length BD is to the length BI.

Draw IS parallel to DC; and since it has been shown that the time of fall along BA is to that along the vertical BE as BA is to BE; and also that the time along BE is to that along BD as BE is to BI; and likewise that the time along BD is to that along BC as BD is to BC, or as BI to

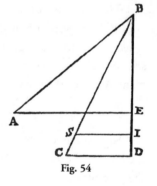

Fig. 54

BS; it follows, *ex æquali*, that the time along BA is to that along BC as BA to BS, or BC to BS. However, BC is to BS as BD is to BI; hence follows our proposition.

Theorem V, Proposition V

The times of descent along planes of different length, slope and height bear to one another a ratio which is equal to the product of the ratio of the lengths by the square root of the inverse ratio of their heights.

Draw the planes AB and AC, having different inclinations, lengths, and heights. My theorem then is that the ratio of the time of descent along AC to that along AB is equal to the product of the ratio of AC to AB by the square root of the inverse ratio of their heights.

For let AD be a perpendicular to which are drawn the horizontal lines BG and CD; also let AL be a mean proportional to the heights AG and AD; from the point L draw a horizontal line meeting AC in F; accordingly AF will be a mean proportional between AC and AE. Now since the time of descent along AC is to that along AE as the length AF is to AE; and since the time along AE is to that along AB as AE is to AB, it is clear that the time along AC is to that along AB as AF is to AB.

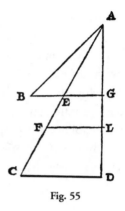

Fig. 55

[226]

Thus it remains to be shown that the ratio of AF to AB is equal to the product of the ratio of AC to AB by the ratio of AG to AL, which is the inverse ratio of the square roots of the heights DA and GA. Now it is evident that, if we consider the line AC in connection with AF and AB, the ratio of AF to AC is the same as that of AL to AD, or AG to AL which is the square root of the ratio of the heights AG and AD; but the ratio of AC to AB is the ratio of the lengths themselves. Hence follows the theorem.

THEOREM VI, PROPOSITION VI

If from the highest or lowest point in a vertical circle there be drawn any inclined planes meeting the circumference the times of descent along these chords are each equal to the other.

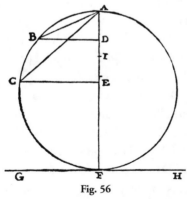

Fig. 56

On the horizontal line GH construct a vertical circle. From its lowest point—the point of tangency with the horizontal—draw the diameter FA and from the highest point, A, draw inclined planes to B and C, any points whatever on the circumference; then the times of descent along these are equal. Draw BD and CE perpendicular to the diameter; make AI a mean proportional between the heights of the planes, AE and AD; and since the, rectangles FA.AE and FA.AD are respectively equal to the squares of AC and AB, while the rectangle FA.AE is to the rectangle FA.AD as AE is to AD, it follows that the square of AC is to the square of AB as the length AE is to the length AD. But since the length AE is to AD as the square of AI is to the square of AD, it follows that the squares on the lines AC and AB

are to each other as the squares on the lines AI and AD, and hence also the length AC is to the length AB as AI is to AD. But it has previously been demonstrated that the ratio of the time of descent along AC to that along AB is equal to the product of the two ratios AC to AB and AD to AI; but this last ratio is the same as that of AB to AC. Therefore the ratio of the time of descent along AC to that along AB is the product of the two ratios, AC to AB and AB to AC. The ratio of these times is therefore unity. Hence follows our proposition.

By use of the principles of mechanics [*ex mechanicis*] one may obtain the same result, namely, that a falling body will require equal times to traverse the distances CA

[227]

and DA, indicated in the following figure. Lay off BA equal to DA, and let fall the perpendiculars BE and DF; it follows from the principles of mechanics that the component of the momentum [*momentum ponderis*] acting along the inclined plane ABC is

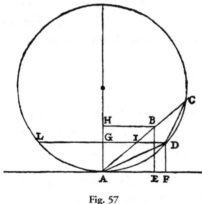

Fig. 57

to the total momentum [i. e., the momentum of the body falling freely] as BE is to BA; in like manner the momentum along the plane AD is to its total momentum [i. e., the momentum of the body falling freely] as DF is to DA, or to BA. Therefore the momentum of this same weight along the plane DA is to that along the plane ABC as the length DF is to the length BE; for this reason, this same weight will in equal times according to the second proposition of the first book, traverse spaces along the planes CA and DA which are to each other as the lengths BE and DF. But it can be shown that CA is to DA as BE is to DF. Hence the falling body will traverse the two paths CA and DA in equal times.

Moreover the fact that CA is to DA as BE is to DF may be demonstrated as follows: Join C and D; through D, draw the line DGL parallel to AF and cutting the line AC in I; through B draw the line BH, also parallel to AF. Then the angle ADI will be equal to the angle DCA, since they subtend equal arcs LA and DA, and since the angle DAC is common, the sides of the triangles, CAD and DAI, about the common angle will be proportional to each other; accordingly as CA is to DA so is DA to IA, that is as BA is to IA, or as HA is to GA, that is as BE is to DF.   Q.E.D.

The same proposition may be more easily demonstrated as follows: On the horizontal line AB draw a circle whose diameter DC is vertical. From the upper end of this diameter draw any inclined plane, DF, extending to meet the circumference; then,

I say, a body will occupy the same time in falling along the plane DF as along the diameter DC. For draw FG parallel to AB and perpendicular to DC; join FC; and since the time of fall along DC is to that along DG as the mean proportional between CD and

[228]

GD is to GD itself; and since also DF is a mean proportional between DC and DG, the angle DFC inscribed in a semicircle being a right-angle, and FG being perpendicular to DC, it follows that the time of fall along DC is to that along DG as the length FD is to GD. But it has already been demonstrated that the time of descent along DF is to that along DG as the length DF is to DG; hence the times of descent along DF and DC each bear to the time of fall along DG the same ratio; consequently they are equal.

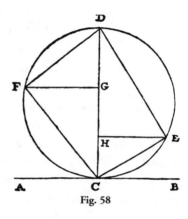

Fig. 58

In like manner it may be shown that if one draws the chord CE from the lower end of the diameter, also the line EH parallel to the horizon, and joins the points E and D, the time of descent along EC, will be the same as that along the diameter, DC.

COROLLARY I

From this it follows that the times of descent along all chords drawn through either C or D are equal one to another.

COROLLARY II

It also follows that, if from any one point there be drawn a vertical line and an inclined one along which the time of descent is the same, the inclined line will be a chord of a semicircle of which the vertical line is the diameter.

COROLLARY III

Moreover the times of descent along inclined planes will be equal when the vertical heights of equal lengths of these planes are to each other as the lengths of the planes themselves; thus it is clear that the times of descent along CA and DA, in the figure just before the last, are equal, provided the vertical height of AB (AB being equal to AD), namely, BE, is to the vertical height DF as CA is to DA.

Sagr. Please allow me to interrupt the lecture for a moment in order that I may clear up an idea which just occurs to me; one which, if it involve no fallacy, suggests at

[229]

least a freakish and interesting circumstance, such as often occurs in nature and in the realm of necessary consequences.

If, from any point fixed in a horizontal plane, straight lines be drawn extending indefinitely in all directions, and if we imagine a point to move along each of these lines with constant speed, all starting from the fixed point at the same instant and moving with equal speeds, then it is clear that all of these moving points will lie upon the circumference of a circle which grows larger and larger, always having the aforesaid fixed point as its center; this circle spreads out in precisely the same manner as the little waves do in the case of a pebble allowed to drop into quiet water, where the impact of the stone starts the motion in all directions, while the point of impact remains the center of these ever-expanding circular waves. But imagine a vertical plane from the highest point of which are drawn lines inclined at every angle and extending indefinitely; imagine also that heavy particles descend along these lines each with a naturally accelerated motion and each with a speed appropriate to the inclination of its line.

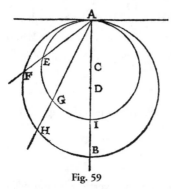

Fig. 59

If these moving particles are always visible, what will be the locus of their positions at any instant? Now the answer to this question surprises me, for I am led by the preceding theorems to believe that these particles will always lie upon the circumference of a single circle, ever increasing in size as the particles recede farther and farther from the point at which their motion began. To be more definite, let A be the fixed point from which are drawn the lines AF and AH inclined at any angle whatsoever. On the perpendicular AB take any two points C and D about which, as centers, circles are described passing through the point A, and cutting the inclined lines at the points F, H, B, E, G, I. From the preceding theorems it is clear that, if particles start, at the same instant, from A and descend along these lines, when one is at E another will be at G and another at I; at a later instant they will be found simultaneously at F, H and B; these, and indeed an infinite number of other particles travelling along an infinite

[230]

number of different slopes will at successive instants always lie upon a single ever-expanding circle. The two kinds of motion occurring in nature give rise therefore to two infinite series of circles, at once resembling and differing from each other; the one

takes its rise in the center of an infinite number of concentric circles; the other has its origin in the contact, at their highest points, of an infinite number of eccentric circles; the former are produced by motions which are equal and uniform; the latter by motions which are neither uniform nor equal among themselves, but which vary from one to another according to the slope.

Further, if from the two points chosen as origins of motion, we draw lines not only along horizontal and vertical planes but in all directions then just as in the former cases, beginning at a single point ever-expanding circles are produced, so in the latter case an infinite number of spheres are produced about a single point, or rather a single sphere which expands in size without limit; and this in two ways, one with the origin at the center, the other on the surface of the spheres.

Salv. The idea is really beautiful and worthy of the clever mind of Sagredo.

Simp. As for me, I understand in a general way how the two kinds of natural motions give rise to the circles and spheres; and yet as to the production of circles by accelerated motion and its proof, I am not entirely clear; but the fact that one can take the origin of motion either at the inmost center or at the very top of the sphere leads one to think that there may be some great mystery hidden in these true and wonderful results, a mystery related to the creation of the universe (which is said to be spherical in shape), and related also to the seat of the first cause [*prima causa*].

Salv. I have no hesitation in agreeing with you. But profound considerations of this kind belong to a higher science than ours [*a più alte dottrine che la nostre*]. We must be satisfied to belong to that class of less worthy workmen who procure from the quarry the marble out of which, later, the gifted sculptor produces those masterpieces which lay hidden in this rough and shapeless exterior. Now, if you please, let us proceed.

[231]

THEOREM VII, PROPOSITION VII

If the heights of two inclined planes are to each other in the same ratio as the squares of their lengths, bodies starting from rest will traverse these planes in equal times.

Take two planes of different lengths and different inclinations, AE and AB, whose heights are AF and AD: let AF be to AD as the square of AE is to the square of AB; then, I say, that a body, starting from rest at A, will traverse the planes AE and AB in equal times. From the vertical line, draw the horizontal parallel lines EF and DB, the latter cutting AE at G. Since $FA:DA=DV:EA^2:BA^2$, and since $FA:DA=EA:GA$, it follows that $EA:GA=EA^2:BA^2$. Hence BA is a mean proportional between FA and GA.

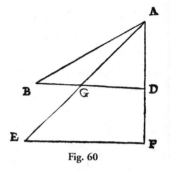

Now since the time of descent along AB bears to the time along AG the same ratio which AB bears to AG and since also the time of descent along AG is to the time along AE as AG is to a mean proportional between AG and AE, that is, to AB, it follows, *ex æquali*, that the time along AB is to the time along AE as AB is to itself. Therefore the times are equal.

Q.E.D.

Fig. 60

THEOREM VIII, PROPOSITION VIII

The times of descent along all inclined planes which intersect one and the same vertical circle, either at its highest or lowest point, are equal to the time of fall along the vertical diameter; for those planes which fall short of this diameter the times are shorter; for planes which cut this diameter, the times are longer.

Let AB be the vertical diameter of a circle which touches the horizontal plane. It has already been proven that the times of descent along planes drawn from either end, A or B, to the circumference are equal. In order to show that the time of descent along

[232]

the plane DF which falls short of the diameter is shorter we may draw the plane DB which is both longer and

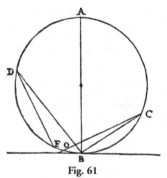

Fig. 61

less steeply inclined than DF; whence it follows that the time along DF is less than that along DB and consequently along AB. In like manner, it is shown that the time of descent along CO which cuts the diameter is greater: for it is both longer and less steeply inclined than CB. Hence follows the theorem.

THEOREM IX, PROPOSITION IX

If from any point on a horizontal line two planes, inclined at any angle, are drawn, and if they are cut by a line which makes with them angles alternately equal to the angles between these planes and the horizontal, then the times required to traverse those portions of the plane cut off by the aforesaid line are equal.

Through the point C on the horizontal line X, draw two planes CD and CE inclined at any angle whatever: at any point in the line CD lay off the angle CDF equal to the angle XCE; let the line DF cut CE at F so that the angles CDF and CFD are alternately equal to XCE and LCD; then, I say, the times of descent over CD and CF are equal. Now since the angle CDF is equal to the angle XCE by construction, it is evident that the angle CFD must be equal to the angle DCL. For if the common angle DCF be subtracted from the three angles of the triangle CDF, together equal to two right angles, (to which are also equal all the

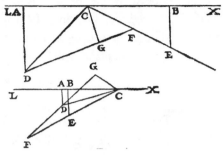

Fig. 62

angles which can be described about the point C on the lower side of the line LX) there remain in the triangle two angles, CDF and CFD, equal to the two angles XCE and LCD; but, by hypothesis, the angles CDF and XCE are equal; hence the remaining angle CFD is equal to the remainder DCL. Take CE equal to CD; from the points D and E draw DA and EB perpendicular to the horizontal line XL; and from the point C draw CG perpendicular to DF. Now since the angle CDG is equal to the angle ECB and since DGC and CBE are right angles, it follows that the triangles CDG and CBE are equiangular; consequently DC:CG=CE:EB. But DC is equal to CE, and therefore CG is equal to EB.

[233]

Since also the angles at C and at A, in the triangle DAC, are equal to the angles at F and G in the triangle CGF, we have CD:DA=FC:CG and, *permutando*, DC:CF=DA:CG=DA:BE. Thus the ratio of the heights of the equal planes CD and CE is the same as the ratio of the lengths DC and CF. Therefore, by Corollary I of Prop. VI, the times of descent along these planes will be equal.   Q.E.D.

An alternative proof is the following: Draw FS perpendicular to the horizontal line AS. Then, since the triangle CSF is similar to the triangle DGC, we have SF:FC=GC:CD; and since the triangle CFG is similar to the triangle DCA, we have FC:CG=CD:DA. Hence, *ex æquali*, SF:CG=CG:DA. Therefore CG is a mean proportional between SF and DA, while

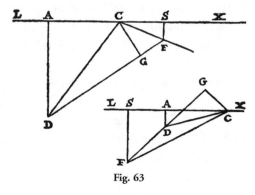

Fig. 63

549

DA:SF=DA^2:CG^2. Again since the triangle ACD is similar to the triangle CGF, we have DA:DC=GC:CF and, *permutando*, DA:CG=DC:CF: also DA^2:CG^2=DC^2:CF^2. But it has been shown that DA^2:CG^2=DA:FS. Therefore DC^2:CF^2=DA:FS. Hence from the above Prop. VII, since the heights DA and FS of the planes CD and CF are to each other as the squares of the lengths of the planes, it follows that the times of descent along these planes will be equal.

THEOREM X, PROPOSITION X

The times of descent along inclined planes of the same height, but of different slope, are to each other as the lengths of these planes; and this is true whether the motion starts from rest or whether it is preceded by a fall from a constant height.

Let the paths of descent be along ABC and ABD to the horizontal plane DC so that the falls along BD and BC are preceded by the fall along AB; then, I say, that the time of descent along BD is to the time of descent along BC as the length BD is to BC. Draw the horizontal line AF and extend DB until it cuts this line at F; let FE be a mean

[234]

proportional between DF and FB; draw EO parallel to DC; then AO will be a mean proportional between CA and AB. If now we represent the time of fall along AB by the length AB, then the time of descent along FB will be represented by the distance FB; so also the time of fall through the entire distance AC will be represented by the mean proportional AO: and for the entire distance FD by FE. Hence the time of fall along the remainder, BC, will be represented by BO, and that along the remainder, BD, by BE; but since BE:BO=BD:BC, it follows, if we allow the bodies to fall first along AB and FB, or, what is the same thing, along the common stretch AB, that the times of descent along BD and BC will be to each other as the lengths BD and BC.

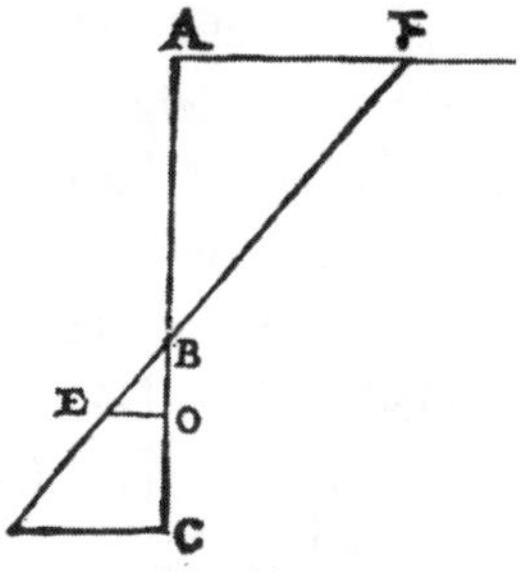

But we have previously proven that the time of descent, from rest at B, along BD is to the time along BC

Fig. 64

in the ratio which the length BD bears to BC. Hence the times of descent along different planes of constant height are to each other as the lengths of these planes, whether the motion starts from rest or is preceded by a fall from a constant height. Q.E.D.

THEOREM XI, PROPOSITION XI

If a plane be divided into any two parts and if motion along it starts from rest, then the time of descent along the first part is to the time of descent along the remainder as the length of this first part is to the excess of a mean proportional between this first part and the entire length over this first part.

Let the fall take place, from rest at A, through the entire distance AB which is divided at any point C; also let AF be a mean proportional between the entire length BA and the first part AC; then CF will denote the excess of the mean proportional FA over the first part AC. Now, I say, the time of descent along AC will be to the time of subsequent fall through CB as the length AC is to CF. This is evident, because the time along AC is to the time along the entire distance AB as AC is to the mean proportional AF. Therefore, *dividendo*, the time along AC will be to the time along the remainder CB as AC is to CF. If we agree to represent the time along AC by the length AC then the time along CB will be represented by CF.

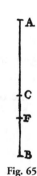

Fig. 65

Q.E.D.

[235]

In case the motion is not along the straight line ACB but along the broken line ACD to the horizontal line BD, and if from F we draw the horizontal line FE, it may in like manner be proved that the time along AC is to the time along the inclined line CD as AC is to CE. For the time along AC is to the time along CB as AC is to CF; but it has already been shown time along CB, after the fall through the distance AC, is to the time along CD, after descent through the same distance AC, as CB is to CD, or, as CF is to CE; therefore, *ex æquali*, the time along AC will be to the time along CD as the length AC is to the length CE.

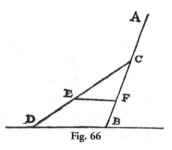

Fig. 66

THEOREM XII, PROPOSITION XII

If a vertical plane and any inclined plane are limited by two horizontals, and if we take mean proportionals between the lengths of these planes and those portions of them which lie between their point

of intersection and the upper horizontal, then the time of fall along the perpendicular bears to the time required to traverse the upper part of the perpendicular plus the time required to traverse the lower part of the intersecting plane the same ratio which the entire length of the vertical bears to a length which is the sum of the mean proportional on the vertical plus the excess of the entire length of the inclined plane over its mean proportional.

Let AF and CD be two horizontal planes limiting the vertical plane AC and the inclined plane DF; let the two last-mentioned planes intersect at B. Let AR be a mean proportional between the entire vertical AC and its upper part AB; and let FS be a mean proportional between FD and its upper part FB. Then, I say, the time of fall along the entire vertical path AC bears to the time of fall along its upper portion AB plus the time of fall along the lower part of the inclined plane, namely, BD, the same ratio which the length AC bears to the mean proportional on the vertical, namely, AR, plus the length SD which is the excess of the entire plane DF over its mean proportional FS.

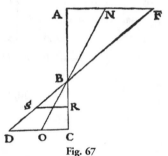

Fig. 67

Join the points R and S giving a horizontal line RS. Now since the time of fall through the entire distance AC is to the time along the portion AB as CA is to the mean proportional AR it follows that, if we agree to represent the time of fall through AC by the distance AC, the time of fall through the distance AB will be represented by AR; and the time of descent through the remainder, BC, will be represented by RC. But, if the time along AC is taken to be equal to the length AC, then the time along FD will be equal to the distance FD; and we may likewise infer that the time of descent

[236]

along BD, when preceded by a fall along FB or AB, is numerically equal to the distance DS. Therefore the time required to fall along the path AC is equal to AR plus RC; while the time of descent along the broken line ABD will be equal to AR plus SD.

Q.E.D.

The same thing is true if, in place of a vertical plane, one takes any other plane, as for instance NO; the method of proof is also the same.

PROBLEM I, PROPOSITION XIII

Given a perpendicular line of limited length, it is required to find a plane having a vertical height equal to the perpendicular and so inclined that a body, having fallen from rest along the perpendicular, will make its descent along the inclined plane in the same time which it occupied in falling through the given perpendicular.

Let AB denote the given perpendicular: prolong this line to C making BC equal to AB, and draw the horizontal lines CE and AG. It is required to draw a plane from B to the horizontal line CE such that after a body starting from rest at A has fallen through the distance AB, it will complete its path along this plane in an equal time. Lay off CD equal to BC, and draw the line BD. Construct the line BE equal to the sum of BD and DC; then, I say, BE is the required plane. Prolong EB till it intersects the horizontal AG at G. Let GF be a mean proportional between GE and GB; then EF:FB=EG:GF, and EF²:FB²=EG²:GF²=EG:GB. But EG is twice GB; hence the square of EF is twice the square of FB; so also is the square of DB twice the square of BC. Consequently EF:FB=DB:BC,

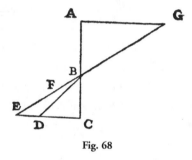

Fig. 68

and *componendo et permutando* EB:DB+BC=BF:BC. But EB=DB+BC; hence BF=BC=BA. If we agree that the length AB shall represent the time of fall along the line AB, then GB will represent the time of descent along GB, and GF the time along the entire distance GE; therefore BF will represent the time of descent along the difference of these paths, namely, BE, after fall from G or from A.   Q.E.F.

[237]

PROBLEM II, PROPOSITION XIV

Given an inclined plane and a perpendicular passing through it, to find a length on the upper part of the perpendicular through which a body will fall from rest in the same time which is required to traverse the inclined plane after fall through the vertical distance just determined.

Let AC be the inclined plane and DB the perpendicular. It is required to find on the vertical AD a length which will be traversed by a body, falling from rest, in the same time which is needed by the same body to traverse the plane AC after the aforesaid fall.

Draw the horizontal CB; lay off AE such that BA+2AC:AC=AC:AE, and lay off AR such that BA:AC=EA:AR. From R draw RX perpendicular to DB; then, I say, X is the

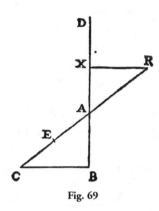

Fig. 69

point sought. For since BA+2AC:AC=AC:AE, it follows, *dividendo*, that BA+AC:AC=CE:AE. And since BA:AC=EA:AR, we have, *componendo*, BA+AC:AC=ER:RA. But BA+AC:AC=CE:AE, hence CE:EA=ER:RA= sum of the antecedents: sum of the consequents =CR:RE. Thus RE is seen to be a mean proportional between CR and RA. Moreover since it has been assumed that BA:AC=EA:AR, and since by similar triangles we have BA:AC=XA:AR, it follows that EA:AR=XA:AR. Hence EA and XA are equal. But if we agree that the time of fall through RA shall be represented by the length RA, then the time of fall along RC will be represented by the length RE which is a mean proportional between RA and RC; likewise AE will represent the time of descent along AC after descent along RA or along AX. But the time of fall through XA is represented by the length XA, while RA represents the time through RA. But it has been shown that XA and AE are equal.   Q.E.F.

[238]

PROBLEM III, PROPOSITION XV

*Given a vertical line and a plane inclined to it, it is required to find
a length on the vertical line below its point of intersection which will
be traversed in the same time as the inclined plane, each of these
motions having been preceded by a fall through the given vertical line.*

Let AB represent the vertical line and BC the inclined plane; it is required to find a length on the perpendicular below its point of intersection, which after a fall from A will be traversed in the same time which is needed for BC after an identical fall from A. Draw the horizontal AD, intersecting the prolongation of CB at D; let DE be a

[239]

mean proportional between CD and DB; lay off BF equal to BE; also let AG be a third proportional to BA and AF. Then, I say, BG is the distance which a body, after falling through AB, will traverse in the same time which is needed for the

plane BC after the same preliminary fall. For if we assume that the time of fall along AB is represented by AB, then the time for DB will be represented by DB. And since DE is a mean proportional between BD and DC, this same DE will represent the time of descent along the entire distance DC while BE will represent the time required for the difference of these paths, namely, BC, provided in each case the fall is from rest at D or at A. In like manner we may infer that BF represents the time of descent through the distance BG after the same preliminary fall; but BF is equal to BE. Hence the problem is solved.

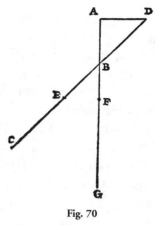

Fig. 70

THEOREM XIII, PROPOSITION XVI

If a limited inclined plane and a limited vertical line are drawn from the same point, and if the time required for a body, starting from rest, to traverse each of these is the same, then a body falling from any higher altitude will traverse the inclined plane in less time than is required for the vertical line.

Let EB be the vertical line and CE the inclined plane, both starting from the common point E, and both traversed in equal times by a body starting from rest at E; extend the vertical line upwards to any point A, from which falling bodies are allowed to start. Then, I say that, after the fall through AE, the inclined plane EC will be traversed in less time than the perpendicular EB. Join CB, draw the horizontal AD, and prolong CE backwards until it meets the latter in D; let DF be a mean proportional between CD and DE while AG is made a mean proportional between BA and AE. Draw FG and DG; then since the times of descent along EC and EB, starting from rest at E, are equal, it follows, according to Corollary II of Proposition VI that the angle at C is a right angle; but the angle at A is also a right angle

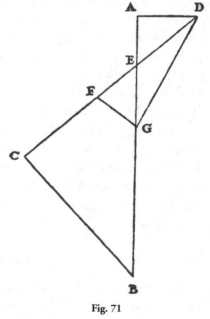

Fig. 71

555

and the angles at the vertex E are equal; hence the triangles AED and CEB are equiangular and the sides about the equal angles are proportional; hence BE:EC=DE:EA. Consequently the rectangle BE.EA is equal to the rectangle CE.ED; and since the rectangle CD.DE exceeds the rectangle CE.ED by the square of ED, and since the rectangle BA.AE exceeds the rectangle BE.EA by the square of EA, it follows that the excess of the rectangle CD.DE over the rectangle BA.AE, or what is the same thing, the excess of the square of FD over the square of AG, will be equal to the excess of the square of DE over the square of AE, which excess is equal to the square of AD. Therefore $FD^2=GA^2+AD^2=GD^2$. Hence DF is equal to DG, and the angle DGF is equal to the angle DFG while the angle EGF is less than the angle EFG, and the opposite side EF is less than the opposite side EG. If now we agree to represent the time of fall through AE by the length AE, then the time along DE will be represented by DE. And since AG is a mean proportional between BA and AE, it follows that AG will represent the time of fall through the total distance AB, and the difference EG will represent the time of fall, from rest at A, through the difference of path EB.

In like manner EF represents the time of descent along EC, starting from rest at D or falling from rest at A. But it has been shown that EF is less than EG; hence follows the theorem.

COROLLARY

From this and the preceding proposition, it is clear that the vertical distance covered by a freely falling body, after a preliminary fall, and during the time-interval required to traverse an inclined plane, is greater than the length of the inclined plane, but less than the distance traversed on the inclined plane during an equal time, without any preliminary fall. For since we have just shown that bodies falling from an elevated point A will traverse the plane EC in Fig. 71 in a shorter time than the vertical EB, it is evident that the distance along EB which will be traversed during a time equal to that of descent along EC will be less than the whole of EB. But now in order to show that this vertical distance is greater than the length of the inclined plane EC, we reproduce Fig. 70 of the preceding theorem in which the vertical length BG is traversed in

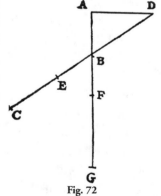

Fig. 72

[240]

the same time as BC after a preliminary fall through AB. That BG is greater than BC is shown as follows: since BE

and FB are equal while BA is less than BD, it follows that FB will bear to BA a greater ratio than EB bears to BD; and, *componendo*, FA will bear to BA a greater ratio than ED to DB; but FA:AB=GF:FB (since AF is a mean proportional between BA and AG) and in like manner ED:BD=CE:EB. Hence GB bears to BF a greater ratio than CB bears to BE; therefore GB is greater than BC.

PROBLEM IV, PROPOSITION XVII

Given a vertical line and an inclined plane, it is required to lay off a distance along the given plane which will be traversed by a body, after fall along the perpendicular, in the same time-interval which is needed for this body to fall from rest through the given perpendicular.

Let AB be the vertical line and BE the inclined plane. The problem is to determine on BE a distance such that a body, after falling through AB, will traverse it in a time equal to that required to traverse the perpendicular AB itself, starting from, rest.

Draw the horizontal AD and extend the plane until it meets this line in D. Lay off FB equal to BA; and choose the point E such that BD:FD=DF:DE. Then, I say, the time of descent along BE, after fall through AB, is equal to the time of fall, from rest at A, through AB. For, if we assume that the length AB represents the tune of fall through AB, then the time of fall through DB will be represented by the time DB; and since BD:FD=DF:DE, it follows that DF will represent the time of descent along the entire plane DE while BF represents the time through the portion BE starting from rest at D; but the time of descent along BE after the preliminary descent along DB is the same as that after a preliminary fall through AB. Hence the time of descent along BE after AB will be BF which of course is equal to the time of fall through AB from rest at A.

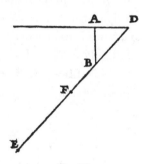

Fig. 73

Q.E.F.

[241]

PROBLEM V, PROPOSITION XVIII

Given the distance through which a body will fall vertically from rest during a given time-interval, and given also a smaller time-interval, it is required to locate another [equal] vertical distance which the body will traverse during this given smaller time-interval.

Let the vertical line be drawn through A, and on this line lay off the distance AB which is traversed by a body falling from rest at A, during a time which may also be represented by AB. Draw the horizontal line CBE, and on it lay off BC to represent the given interval of time which is shorter than AB. It is required to locate, in the perpendicular above mentioned, a distance which is equal to AB and which will be descended in a time equal to BC. Join the points A and C; then, since BC<BA, it follows that the angle BAC<angle BCA. Construct the angle CAE equal to BCA and let E be the point where AE intersects the horizontal line; draw ED at right angles to AE, cutting the vertical at D; lay off DF equal to BA. Then, I say, that FD is that portion of the vertical which a body starting from rest at A will traverse during the assigned time-interval BC. For, if in the right-angled triangle AED a perpendicular be drawn from the right-angle at E to the side AD, then AE will be a mean proportional between DA and AB while BE will be a mean proportional between BD and BA, or between FA and AB (seeing that FA is equal to DB); and since it has been agreed to represent the time of fall through AB by the distance AB, it follows that AE, or EC, will represent the time of fall through the entire distance AD, while EB will represent the time through AF. Consequently the remainder BC will represent the time of fall through the remaining distance FD.   Q.E.F.

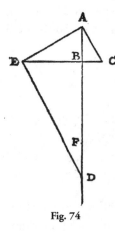

Fig. 74

[242]

PROBLEM VI, PROPOSITION XIX

Given the distance through which a body falls in a vertical line from rest and given also the time of fall, it is required to find the time in which the same body will, later, traverse an equal distance chosen anywhere in the same vertical line.

On the vertical line AB, lay off AC equal to the distance fallen from rest at A, also locate at random an equal distance DB. Let the time of fall through AC be represented by the length AC. It is required to find the time necessary to traverse DB after fall from rest at A. About the entire length AB describe the semicircle

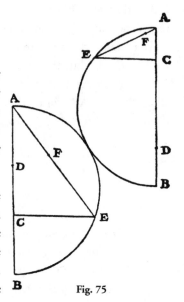

Fig. 75

AEB; from C draw CE perpendicular to AB; join the points A and E; the line AE will be longer than EC; lay off EF equal to EC. Then, I say, the difference FA will represent the time required for fall through DB. For since AE is a mean proportional between BA and AC and since AC represents the time of fall through AC, it follows that AE will represent the time through the entire distance AB. And since CE is a mean proportional between DA and AC (seeing that DA=BC) it follows that CE, that is, EF, will represent the time of fall through AD. Hence the difference AF will represent the time of fall through the difference DB.   Q.E.D.

COROLLARY

Hence it is inferred that if the time of fall from rest through any given distance is represented by that distance itself, then the time of fall, after the given distance has been increased by a certain amount, will be represented by the excess of the mean proportional between the increased distance and the original distance over the mean proportional between the original distance and the increment. Thus, for instance, if we agree that AB represents the time of fall, from rest at A, through the distance AB, and that AS is the increment, the time required to traverse AB, after fall through SA, will be the excess of the mean proportional between SB and BA over the mean proportional between BA and AS.

[243]

PROBLEM VII, PROPOSITION XX

Given any distance whatever and a portion of it laid off from the point at which motion begins, it is required to find another portion which lies at the other end of the distance and which is traversed in the same time as the first given portion.

Let the given distance be CB and let CD be that part of it which is laid off from the beginning of motion. It is required to find another part, at the end B, which is traversed in the same time as the assigned portion CD. Let BA be a mean proportional between BC and CD; also let CE be a third proportional to BC and CA. Then, I say, EB will be the distance which, after fall from C, will be traversed in the same time as CD itself. For if we agree that CB shall represent the time through the entire distance CB, then BA (which, of course, is a mean proportional between BC and CD) will represent the time along CD; and since CA is a mean proportional between BC and CE, it follows that CA will be the time through CE; but the total length

Fig. 76

CB represents the time through the total is distance CB. Therefore the difference BA will be the time along the difference of distances, EB, after falling from C; but this same BA was the time of fall through CD. Consequently the distances CD and EB are traversed, from rest at A, in equal times.   Q.E.F.

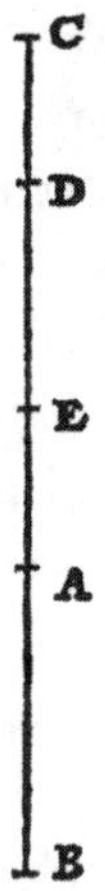

C
D
E
A
B

Fig. 77

[244.]

Theorem XIV, Proposition XXI

If, on the path of a body falling vertically from rest, one lays off a portion which is traversed in any time you please and whose upper terminus coincides with the point where the motion begins, and if this fall is followed by a motion deflected along any inclined plane, then the space traversed along the inclined plane, during a time-interval equal to that occupied in the previous vertical fall, will be greater than twice, and less than three times, the length of the vertical fall.

Let AB be a vertical line drawn downwards from the horizontal line AE, and let it represent the path of a body falling from rest at A; choose any portion AC of this path. Through C draw any inclined plane, CG, along which the motion is

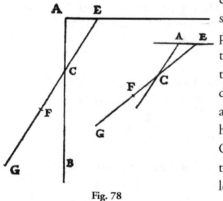

continued after fall through AC. Then, I say, that the distance traversed along this plane CG, during the time-interval equal to that of the fall through AC, is more than twice, but less than three times, this same distance AC. Let us lay off CF equal to AC, and extend the plane GC until it meets the horizontal in E; choose G such that CE:EF=EF:EG. If now we assume that the time of fall along AC is represented by the length AC, then CE will represent the time of descent along CE, while CF, or CA, will

Fig. 78

represent the time of descent along CG. It now remains to be shown that the distance CG is more than twice., and less than three times, the distance CA itself. Since CE:EF=EF:EG, it follows that CE:EF=CF:FG; but EC<EF; therefore CF will be less than FG and GC will be more than twice FC, or AC. Again since FE<2EC (for EC is greater than CA, or CF), we have GF less than twice FC, and also GC less than three times CF, or CA.   Q.E.D.

This proposition may be stated in a more general form; since what has been proven for the case of a vertical and inclined plane holds equally well in the case of motion along a plane of any inclination followed by motion along any plane of less steepness, as can be seen from the adjoining figure. The method of proof is the same.

[245]

PROBLEM VIII, PROPOSITION XXII

Given two unequal time-intervals, also the distance through which a body will fall along a vertical line, from rest, during the shorter of these intervals, it is required to pass through the highest point of this vertical line a plane so inclined that the time of descent along it will be equal to the longer of the given intervals.

Let A represent the longer and B the shorter of the two unequal time-intervals, also let CD represent the length of the vertical fall, from rest, during the time B.

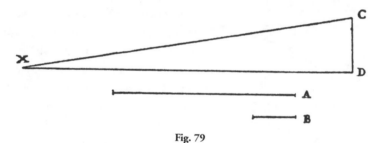

Fig. 79

It is required to pass through the point C a plane of such a slope that it will be traversed in the time A.

Draw from the point C to the horizontal a line CX of such a length that B:A=CD:CX. It is clear that CX is the plane along which a body will descend in the given time A. For it has been shown that the time of descent along an inclined plane bears to the time of fall through its vertical height the same ratio which the length of the plane bears to its vertical height. Therefore the time along CX is to the time along CD as the length CX is to the length CD, that is, as the time-interval A is to the time-interval B: but B is the time required to traverse the vertical distance, CD, starting from rest; therefore A is the time required for descent along the plane CX.

Problem IX, Proposition XXIII

Given the time employed by a body in falling through a certain distance along a vertical line, it is required to pass through the lower terminus of this vertical fall, a plane so inclined that this body will, after its vertical fall, traverse on this plane, during a time-interval equal to that of the vertical fall, a distance equal to any assigned

[246]

distance, provided this assigned distance is more than twice and less than three times, the vertical fall.

Let AS be any vertical line, and let AC denote both the length of the vertical fall, from rest at A, and also the time required for this fall. Let IR be a distance more than twice and less than three times, AC. It is required to pass a plane through the point C so inclined that a body, after fall through AC, will, during the time AC, traverse a

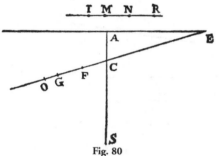

Fig. 80

distance equal to IR. Lay off RN and NM each equal to AC. Through the point C, draw a plane CE meeting the horizontal, AE, at such a point that IM:MN=AC:CE. Extend the plane to O, and lay off CF, FG and GO equal to RN, NM, and MI respectively. Then, I say, the time along the inclined plane CO, after fall through AC, is equal to the time of fall, from rest at A, through AC. For since OG:GF=FC:CE, it follows, *componendo*, that OF:FG=OF:FC=FE:EC, and since an antecedent is to its consequent as the sum of the antecedents is to the sum of the consequents, we have OE:EF=EF:EC. Thus EF is a mean proportional between OE and EC. Having agreed to represent the time of fall through AC by the length AC it follows that EC will represent the time along EC, and EF the time along the entire distance EO, while the difference CF will represent the time along the difference CO; but CF=CA; therefore the problem is solved. For the time CA is the time of fall, from rest at A, through CA while CF (which is equal to CA) is the time required to traverse CO after descent along EC or after fall through AC.   Q.E.F.

It is to be remarked also that the same solution holds if the antecedent motion takes place, not along a vertical, but along an inclined plane. This case is illustrated in

[247]

the following figure where the antecedent motion is along the inclined plane AS underneath the horizontal AE. The proof is identical with the preceding.

SCHOLIUM

On careful attention, it will be clear that, the nearer the given line IR approaches to
three times the length AC, the nearer the inclined plane, CO, along which the second

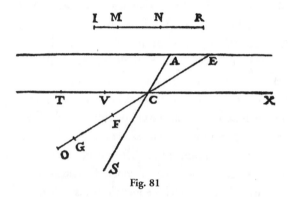

Fig. 81

motion takes place, approaches the perpendicular along which the space traverse
during the time AC, will be three times the distance AC. For if. IR be taken nearly
equal to three times AC, then IM will be almost equal to MN; and since, by construction, IM:MN=AC:CE, it follows that CE is but little greater than CA: consequently the point E will lie near the point A, and the lines CO and CS, forming a
very acute angle, will almost coincide. But, on the other band, if the given line, IR,
be only the least bit longer than twice AC, the line IM will be very short; from
which it follows that AC will be very small in comparison with CE which is now so
long that it almost coincides with the horizontal line drawn through C. Hence we
can infer that, if, after descent along the inclined plane AC of the adjoining figure,
the motion is continued along a horizontal line, such as CT, the distance traversed
by a body, during a time equal to the time of fall through AC, will be exactly twice
the distance AC. The argument here employed is the same as the preceding. For it
is clear, since OE:EF=EF:EC, that FC measures the time of descent along CO. But,
if the horizontal line TC which is twice as long as CA, be divided into two equal
parts at V then this line must be extended indefinitely in the direction of X before
it will intersect the line AE produced; and accordingly the ratio of the infinite
length TX to the infinite length VX is the same as the ratio of the infinite distance
VX to the infinite distance CX.

The same result may be obtained by another method of approach, namely, by returning to the same line of argument which was employed in the proof of the first proposition. Let us consider the triangle ABC, which, by lines drawn parallel to its

[248]

base, represents for us a velocity increasing in proportion to the time; if these lines are infinite in number, just as the points in the line AC are infinite or as the number of instants in any interval of time is infinite, they will form the area of the triangle. Let us now suppose that the maximum velocity attained-that represented by the line BC—to be continued, without acceleration and at constant value through another interval of time equal to the first. From these velocities will be built up, in a similar manner, the area of the

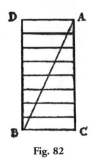

Fig. 82

parallelogram ADBC, which is twice that of the triangle ABC; accordingly the distance traversed with these velocities during any given interval of time will be twice that traversed with the velocities represented by the triangle during an equal interval of time. But along a horizontal plane the motion is uniform since here it experiences neither acceleration nor retardation; therefore we conclude that the distance CD traversed during a time-interval equal to AC is twice the distance AC; for the latter is covered by a motion, starting from rest and increasing in speed in proportion to the parallel lines in the triangle, while the former is traversed by a motion represented by the parallel lines of the parallelogram which, being also infinite in number, yield an area twice that of the triangle.

Furthermore we may remark that any velocity once imparted to a moving body will be rigidly maintained as long as the external causes of acceleration or retardation are removed, a condition which is found only on horizontal planes; for in the case of planes which slope downwards there is already present a cause of acceleration, while on planes sloping upward there is retardation; from this it follows that motion along a horizontal plane is perpetual; for, if the velocity be uniform, it cannot be diminished or slackened, much less destroyed. Further, although any velocity which a body may have acquired through natural fall is permanently maintained so far as its own nature [*suapte natura*] is concerned, yet it must be remembered that if, after descent along a plane inclined downwards, the body is deflected to a plane inclined upward, there is already existing in this latter plane a cause of retardation; for in any such plane this same body is subject to a natural acceleration downwards. Accordingly we have here the superposition of two different states, namely, the velocity acquired during the preceding fall which if acting alone would carry the body at a uniform rate to infinity, and the velocity which results from a natural acceleration downwards common to all bodies. It seems altogether reasonable, therefore, if we wish to trace the future history of a body which has descended along some inclined

plane and has been deflected along some plane inclined upwards, for us to assume that the maximum speed acquired during descent is permanently maintained during the ascent. In the ascent, however, there

[249]

supervenes a natural inclination downwards, namely, a motion which, starting from rest, is accelerated at the usual rate. If perhaps this discussion is a little obscure, the following figure will help to make it clearer.

Let us suppose that the descent has been made along the downward sloping plane AB, from which the body is deflected so as to continue its motion along the upward sloping plane BC; and first let these planes be of equal length and placed so as to make equal angles with the horizontal line GH. Now it is well known that a body, starting from rest at A, and descending along AB, acquires a speed which is proportional to the time, which is a maximum at B, and which is maintained by the body so long as all causes of fresh acceleration or retardation are removed; the acceleration to which I refer is that to which the body would be subject if its motion were continued along the plane AB extended, while the retardation is that which the body would encounter if its motion were deflected along the plane BC inclined upwards; but, upon the horizontal plane GH, the body would maintain a uniform velocity equal to that

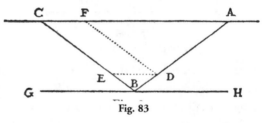

Fig. 83

which it had acquired at B after fall from A; moreover this velocity is such that, during an interval of time equal to the time of descent through AB, the body will traverse a horizontal distance equal to twice AB. Now let us imagine this same body to move with the same uniform speed along the plane BC so that here also during a time-interval equal to that of descent along AB, it will traverse along BC extended a distance twice AB; but let us suppose that, at the very instant the body begins its ascent it is subjected, by its very nature, to the same influences which surrounded it during its descent from A along AB, namely, it descends from rest under the same acceleration as that which was effective in AB, and it traverses, during an equal interval of time, the same distance along this second plane as it did along AB; it is clear that, by thus superposing upon the body a uniform motion of ascent and an accelerated motion of descent, it will be carried along the plane BC as far as the point C where these two velocities become equal.

If now we assume any two points D and E, equally distant from the vertex B, we may then infer that the descent along BD takes place in the same time as the ascent

along BE. Draw DF parallel to BC; we know that, after descent along AD, the body will ascend along DF; or, if, on reaching D, the body is carried along the horizontal DE, it will reach E with the same momentum [*impetus*] with which it left D; hence from E the body will ascend as far as C, proving that the velocity at E is the same as that at D.

From this we may logically infer that a body which descends along any inclined plane and continues its motion along a plane inclined upwards will, on account of the

[250]

momentum acquired, ascend to an equal height above the horizontal; so that if the descent is along AB the body will be carried up the plane BC as far as the horizontal line ACD: and this is true whether the inclinations of the planes are the same or different, as in the case of

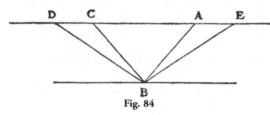

Fig. 84

the planes AB and BD. But by a previous postulate the speeds acquired by fall along variously inclined planes having the same vertical height are the same. If therefore the planes EB and BD have the same slope, the descent along EB will be able to drive the body along BD as far as D; and since this propulsion comes from the speed acquired on reaching the point B, it follows that this speed at B is the same whether the body has made its descent along AB or EB. Evidently then the body will be carried up BD whether the descent has been made along AB or along EB. The time of ascent along BD is however greater than that along BC, just as the descent along EB occupies more time than that along AB; moreover it has been demonstrated that the ratio between the lengths of these times is the same as that between the lengths of the planes. We must next discover what ratio exists between the distances traversed in equal times along planes of different slope, but of the same elevation, that is, along planes which are included between the same parallel horizontal lines. This is done as follows:

THEOREM XV, PROPOSITION XXIV

Given two parallel horizontal planes and a vertical line connecting them; given also an inclined plane passing through the lower extremity of this vertical line; then, if a body fall freely along the vertical line and have its motion reflected along the inclined plane, the distance which it will traverse along this plane, during a time equal to that of the vertical fall, is greater than once but less than twice the vertical line.

566

Let BC and HG be the two horizontal planes, connected by the perpendicular AE; also let EB represent the inclined plane along which the motion takes place after the

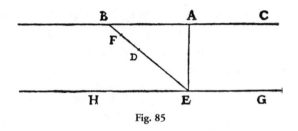

Fig. 85

body has fallen along AE and has been reflected from E towards B. Then, I say, that, during a time equal to that of fall along AE, the body will ascend the inclined plane through a distance which is greater than AE but less than twice AE. Lay off ED equal

[251]

to AE and choose F so that EB:BD=BD:BF. First we shall show that F is the point to which the moving body will be carried after reflection from E towards B during a time equal to that of fall along AE; and next we shall show that the distance EF is greater than EA but less than twice that quantity.

Let us agree to represent the time of fall along AE by the length AE, then the time of descent along BE, or what is the same thing, ascent along EB will be represented by the distance EB.

Now, since DB is a mean proportional between EB and BF, and since BE is the time of descent for the entire distance BE, it follows that BD will be the time of descent through BF, while the remainder DE will be the time of descent along the remainder FE. But the time of descent along the fall from rest at B is the same as the time of ascent from E to F after reflection from E with the speed acquired during fall either through AE or BE. Therefore DE represents the time occupied by the body in passing from E to F, after fall from A to E and after reflection along EB. But by construction ED is equal to AE. This concludes the first part of our demonstration.

Now since the whole of EB is to the whole of BD as the portion DB is to the portion BF, we have the whole of EB is to the whole of BD as the remainder ED is to the remainder DF; but EB>BD and hence ED>DF, and EF is less than twice DE or AE.   Q.E.D.

The same is true when the initial motion occurs, not along a perpendicular, but upon an inclined plane: the proof is also the same provided the upward sloping plane is less steep, i. e., longer, than the downward sloping plane.

THEOREM XVI, PROPOSITION XXV

If descent along any inclined plane is followed by motion along a horizontal plane, the time of descent along the inclined plane bears to the time required to traverse any assigned length of the horizontal plane the same ratio which twice the length of the inclined plane bears to the given horizontal length.

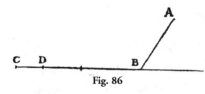

Fig. 86

Let CB be any horizontal line and AB an inclined plane; after descent along AB let the motion continue through the assigned horizontal distance BD. Then, I say, the time of descent along AB bears to the time spent in traversing BD the same ratio twice AB bears to BD. For, lay off BC equal to twice AB then it follows, from a previous proposition, that the time of descent along AB is equal to the time required to traverse BC; but the time along BC is to the time along DB as the length CB is to the length BD. Hence the time of

[252]

descent along AB is to the time along BD as twice the distance AB is to the distance BD.   Q.E.D.

PROBLEM X, PROPOSITION XXVI

Given a vertical height joining two horizontal parallel lines; given also a distance greater than once and less than twice this vertical height, it is required to pass through the foot of the given perpendicular an inclined plane such that, after fall through the given vertical height, a body whose motion is deflected along the plane will traverse the assigned distance in a time equal to the time of vertical fall.

Let AB be the vertical distance separating two parallel horizontal lines AO and BC; also let FE be greater than once and less than twice BA. The problem is to pass a plane through B, extending to the upper horizontal line, and such that a body, after having fallen from A to B, will, if its motion be deflected along the inclined plane, traverse a distance equal to EF in a time equal to that of fall along AB. Lay off ED equal to AB; then the remainder DF will be less than AB since the entire length EF is less than twice this quantity; also lay off DI equal to DF, and choose the point X such that EI:ID=DF:FX; from B, draw the plane BO equal in length to EX. Then, I say, that the

568

plane BO is the one along which, after fall through AB, a body will traverse the assigned distance FE in a time equal to the time of fall through AB. Lay off BR and RS equal to ED and DF respectively; then since EI:ID=DF:FX, we have, *componendo*, ED:DI=DX:XF=ED:DF=EX:XD=BO:OR=RO:OS. If we represent the time of fall

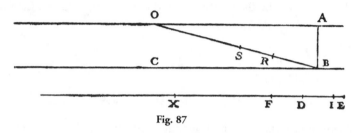

Fig. 87

along AB by the length AB, then OB will represent the time of descent along OB, and RO will stand for the time along OS, while the remainder BR will represent the time required for a body starting from rest at O to traverse the remaining distance SB. But the time of descent along SE starting from rest at O is equal to the time of ascent from B to S after fall through AB. Hence BO is that plane, passing through B, along which a body, after fall through AB, will traverse the distance BS, equal to the assigned distance EF, in the time-interval BR or BA. Q.E.F.

[253]

THEOREM XVII, PROPOSITION XXVII

If a body descends along two inclined planes of different lengths but of the same vertical height, the distance which it will traverse, in the lower part of the longer plane, during a time-interval equal to that of descent over the shorter plane, is equal to the length of the shorter plane plus a portion of it to which the shorter plane bears the same ratio which the longer plane bears to the excess of the longer over the shorter plane.

Let AC be the longer plane, AB, the shorter, and AD the common elevation; on the lower part of AC lay off CE equal to AB. Choose F such that CA:AE=CA:CA-AB=CE:EF. Then, I say, that FC is that distance which will, after fall from A, be traversed during a time-interval equal to that required

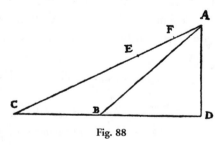

Fig. 88

569

for descent along AB. For since CA:AE=CE:EF, it follows that the remainder EA: the remainder AF=CA:AE. Therefore AE is a mean proportional between AC and AF. Accordingly if the length AB is employed to measure the time of fall along AB, then the distance AC will measure the time of descent through AC; but the time of descent through AF is measured by the length AE, and that through FC by EC. Now EC=AB; and hence follows the proposition.

[254]

Problem XI, Proposition XXVIII

Let AG be any horizontal line touching a circle; let AB be the diameter passing through the point of contact; and let AE and EB represent any two chords. The problem is to determine what ratio the time of fall through AB bears to the time of descent over both AE and EB. Extend BE till it meets the tangent at G, and draw AF so as to bisect the angle BAE. Then, I say, the time through AB is to the sum of the times along AE and EB as the length AE is to the sum of the lengths AE and EF. For since the angle FAB is equal to the angle FAE, while the angle EAG is equal to the angle ABF it fol-

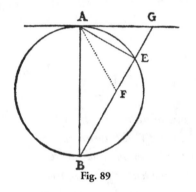

Fig. 89

lows that the entire angle GAF is equal to the sum of the angles FAB and ABF. But the angle GFA is also equal to the sum of these two angles. Hence the length GF is equal to the length GA; and since the rectangle BG.GE is equal to the square of GA, it will also be equal to the square of GF, or BG:GF=GF:GE. If now we agree to represent the time of descent along AE by the length AE, then the length GE will represent the time of descent along GE, while GF will stand for the time of descent through the entire distance GB; so also EF will denote the time through EB after fall from G or from A along AE. Consequently the time along AE, or AB, is to the time along AE and EB as the length AE is to AE+EF.   Q.E.D.

A shorter method is to lay off GF equal to GA, thus making GF a mean proportional between BG and GE. The rest of the proof is as above.

Theorem XVIII, Proposition XXIX

*Given a limited horizontal line, at one end of which is erected a limit-
ed vertical line whose length is equal to one-half the given horizontal*

line; then a body, falling through this given height and having its motion deflected into a horizontal direction, will traverse the given horizontal distance and vertical line in less time than it will any other vertical distance plus the given horizontal distance.

[255]

Let BC be the given distance in a horizontal plane; at the end B erect a perpendicular, on which lay off BA equal to half BC. Then, I say, that the time required for a body, starting from rest at A, to traverse the two distances, AB and BC, is the least of all possible times in which this same distance BC together with a vertical portion, whether greater or less than AB, can be traversed.

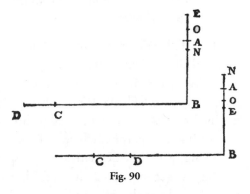

Fig. 90

Lay off EB greater than AB, as in the first figure, and less than AB, as in the second. It must be shown that the time required to traverse the distance EB plus BC is greater than that required for AB plus BC. Let us agree that the length AB shall represent the time along AB, then the time occupied in traversing the horizontal portion BC will also be AB, seeing that BC=2AB; consequently the time required for both AB and BC will be twice AB. Choose the point O such that EB:BO=BO:BA, then BO will represent the time of fall through EB. Again lay off the horizontal distance BD equal to twice BE; whence it is clear that BO represents the time along BD after fall through EB. Select a point N such that DB:BC=EB:BA=OB:BN. Now since the horizontal motion is uniform and since OB is the time occupied in traversing BD, after fall from E, it follows that NB will be the time along BC after fall through the same height EB. Hence it is clear that OB plus BN represents the time of traversing EB plus BC; and since twice BA is the time along AB plus BC. it remains to be shown that OB+BN>2BA.

But since EB:BO=BO:BA, it follows that $EB:BA=OB^2:BA^2$. Moreover since EB:BA=OB:BN it follows that $OB:BN=OB^2:BA^2$. But OB:BN=(OB:BA)(BA:BN), and therefore AB:BN=OB:BA, that is, BA is a mean proportional between BO and BN. Consequently OB+BN>2BA.   Q.E.D.

[256]

THEOREM XIX, PROPOSITION XXX

*A perpendicular is let fall from any point in a horizontal line; it is
required to pass through any other point in this same horizontal line
a plane which shall cut the perpendicular and along which a body
will descend to the perpendicular in the shortest possible time. Such
a plane will cut from the perpendicular a portion equal to the distance of the assumed point in the horizontal from the upper end of
the perpendicular.*

Let AC be any horizontal line and B any point in it from which is dropped
the vertical line BD. Choose any point C in the horizontal line and lay off, on
the vertical, the distance BE equal to BC;
join C and E. Then, I say, that of all
inclined planes that can be passed through
C, cutting the perpendicular, CE is that
one along which the descent to the perpendicular is accomplished in the shortest
time. For, draw the plane CF cutting the
vertical above E, and, the plane CG cutting
the vertical below E; and draw IK, a parallel vertical line, touching at C a circle
described with BC as radius. Let EK be
drawn parallel to CF, and extended to meet
the tangent, after cutting the circle at L.
Now it is clear that the time of fall along
LE is equal to the time along CE; but the
time along KE is greater than along LE;
therefore the time along KE is greater than
along CE. But the time along KE is equal
to the time along CF, since they have the

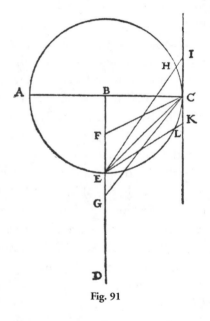

Fig. 91

same length and the same slope; and, in like manner, it follows that the planes
CG and IE, having the same length and the same slope, will be traversed in
equal times. Also, since HE<IE, the time along HE will be less than the time
along IE. Therefore also the time along CE (equal to the time along HE), will
be shorter than the time along IE.   Q.E.D.

572

THEOREM XX, PROPOSITION XXXI

If a straight line is inclined at any angle to the horizontal and if, from any assigned point in the horizontal, a plane of quickest descent is to be drawn to the inclined line, that plane will be the one which bisects the angle contained between two lines drawn from

[257]

the given point, one perpendicular to the horizontal line, the other perpendicular to the inclined line.

Let CD be a line inclined at any angle to the horizontal AB; and from any assigned point A in the horizontal draw AC perpendicular to AB, and AE perpendicular to CD; draw FA so as to bisect the angle CAE. Then, I say, that of all the planes which can be drawn through the point A, cutting the line CD at any points whatsoever AF is the one of quickest descent [*in quo tempore omnium brevissimo fiat descensus*]. Draw FG parallel to AE; the alternate angles GFA and FAE will be equal; also the angle EAF is equal to the angle FAG. Therefore the sides GF and GA of the triangle FGA are equal. Accordingly if we describe a circle about G as center, with GA as radius, this circle will

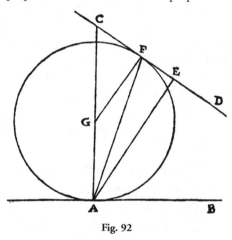

Fig. 92

pass through the point F, and will touch the horizontal at the point A and the inclined line at F; for GFC is a right angle, since GF and AE are parallel. It is clear therefore that all lines drawn from A to the inclined line, with the single exception of FA, will extend beyond the circumference of the circle, thus requiring more time to traverse any of them than is needed for FA.

Q.E.D.

LEMMA

If two circles one lying within the other are in contact, and if any straight line be drawn tangent to the inner circle, cutting the outer circle, and if three lines be drawn from the point at which the circles are in contact to three points on the tangential straight line, namely,

the point of tangency on the inner circle and the two points where the straight line extended cuts the outer circle, then these three lines will contain equal angles at the point of contact.

Let the two circles touch each other at the point A, the center of the smaller being at B, the center of the larger at C. Draw the straight line FG touching the inner

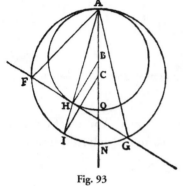

Fig. 93

circle at H, and cutting the outer at the points F and G; also draw the three lines AF, AH, and AG. Then, I say, the angles contained by these lines, FAH and GAH, are equal. Prolong AH to the circumference at I; from the centers of the circles, draw BH and CI; join the centers B and C and extend the line until it reaches the point of contact at A and cuts the circles at the points O and N. But now the lines BH and CI are parallel, because the angles ICN and HBO are equal, each being twice the angle IAN. And since BH, drawn from the center to the point of contact is perpendicular to FG, it follows that CI will also be perpendicular to FG and that the arc FI is equal to the arc IG; consequently the angle FAI is equal to the angle IAG.   Q.E.D.

THEOREM XXI, PROPOSITION XXXII

If in a horizontal line any two points are chosen and if through one of these points a line be drawn inclined towards the other, and if from this other point a straight line is drawn to the inclined line in such a direction that it cuts off from the inclined line a portion equal to the distance between the two chosen points on the horizontal line, then the time of descent along the line so drawn is less than along any other straight line drawn from the same point to the same inclined line. Along other lines which make equal angles on opposite side of this line, the times of descent are the same.

Let A and B be any two points on a horizontal line: through B draw an inclined straight line BC, and from B lay off a distance BD equal to BA; join the points A and D. Then, I say, the time of descent along AD is less than along any other line drawn from A to the inclined line BC. From the point A draw AE perpendicular to BA; and from the point D draw DE perpendicular to BD, intersecting AE at E. Since in the isosceles triangle ABD, we have the angles BAD and BDA equal, their complements

DAE and EDA are equal. Hence if, with E as center and EA as radius, we describe a circle it will pass through D and will touch the lines BA and BD at the points A and D. Now since A is the end of the vertical line AE, the descent along AD will occupy less time than along any other line drawn from the extremity A to the line BC and extending beyond the circumference of the circle; which concludes the first part of the proposition.

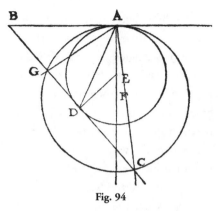

Fig. 94

[259]

If however, we prolong the perpendicular line AE, and choose any point F upon it, about which as center, we describe a circle of radius FA, this circle, AGC, will cut the tangent line in the points G and C. Draw the lines AG and AC which will according to the preceding lemma, deviate by equal angles from the median line AD. The time of descent along either of these lines is the same, since they start from the highest point A, and terminate on the circumference of the circle AGC.

PROBLEM XII, PROPOSITION XXXIII

Given a limited vertical line and an inclined plane of equal height, having a common upper terminal; it is required to find a point on the vertical line, extended upwards, from which a body will fall and, when deflected along the inclined plane, will traverse it in the same time-interval which is required for fall, from rest, through the given vertical height.

Let AB be the given limited vertical line and AC an inclined plane having the same altitude. It is required to find on the vertical BA, extended above A, a point from which a falling body will traverse the distance AC in the same time which is spent in falling, from rest at A, through the given vertical line AB. Draw the line DCE at right angles to AC, and lay off CD equal to AB; also join the points A and D; then the angle ADC will be greater than the angle CAD, since the side CA is greater than either AB or CD.

[260]

Make the angle DAE equal to the angle ADE, and draw EF perpendicular to AE; then EF will cut the inclined plane, extended both ways, at F. Lay off AI and AG each equal to CF; through G draw the horizontal line GH. Then, I say, H is the point sought.

For, if we agree to let the length AB represent the time of fall along the vertical AB, then AC will likewise represent the time of descent from rest at A, along AC; and since,

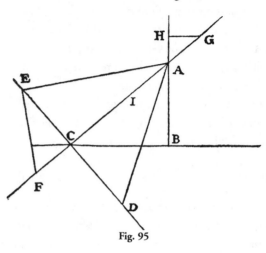

in the right-angled triangle AEF, the line EC has been drawn from the right angle at E perpendicular to the base AF, it follows that AE will be a mean proportional between FA and AC, while CE will be a mean proportional between AC and CF, that is between CA and AI. Now, since AC represents the time of descent from A along AC, it follows that AE will be the time along the entire distance AF, and EC the time along AI. But since in the isosceles triangle AED the side EA is equal to the side

Fig. 95

ED it follows that ED will represent the time of fall along AF, while EC is the time of fall along AI. Therefore CD, that is AB, will represent the time of fall, from rest at A, along IF; which is the same as saying that AB is the time of fall, from G or from H, along AC.   E.F.

PROBLEM XIII, PROPOSITION XXXIV

Given a limited inclined plane and a vertical line having their highest point in common, it is required to find a point in the vertical line extended such that a body will fall from it and then traverse the inclined plane in the same time which is required to traverse the inclined plane alone starting from rest at the top of said plane.

Let AC and AB be an inclined plane and a vertical line respectively, having a common highest point at A. It is required to find a point in the vertical line, above A, such that a body, falling from it and afterwards having its motion directed along AB, will traverse both the assigned part of the vertical line and the plane AB in the same time

[261]

which is required for the plane AB alone, starting from rest at A. Draw BC a horizontal line and lay off AN equal to AC; choose the point L so that AB:BN=AL:LC, and lay off AI equal to AL; choose the point E such that CE, laid off on the vertical AC

produced, will be a third proportional to AC and BI. Then, I say, CE is the distance sought; so that, if the vertical line is extended above A and if a portion AX is laid off equal to CE, then a body falling from X will traverse both the distances, XA and AB, in the same time as that required, when starting from A, to traverse AB alone.

Draw XR parallel to BC and intersecting BA produced in R; next draw ED parallel to BC and meeting BA produced in D; on AD as diameter describe a semicircle; from B draw BF perpendicular to AD, and prolong it till it meets the circumference of the circle; evidently FB is a mean proportional between AB and BD, while FA is a

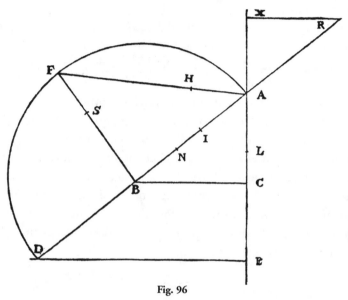

Fig. 96

mean proportional between DA and AB. Take BS equal to BI and FH equal to FB. Now since AB:BD=AC:CE and since BF is a mean proportional between AB and BD, while BI is a mean proportional between AC and CE, it follows that BA:AC=FB:BS, and since BA:AC=BA:BN=FB:BS we shall have, *convertendo*, BF:FS=AB:BN=AL:LC. Consequently the rectangle formed by FB and CL is equal to the rectangle whose sides are AL and SF; moreover, this rectangle AL.SF is the excess of the rectangle AL.FB, or

[262]

AI.BF, over the rectangle AI.BS, or AI.IB. But the rectangle FB.LC is the excess of the rectangle AC.BF over the rectangle AL.BF; and moreover the rectangle AC.BF is equal to the rectangle AB.BI since BA:AC=FB:BI; hence the excess of the rectangle AB.BI over the rectangle AI.BF, or AI.FH, is equal to the excess of the rectangle AI.FH over the rectangle AI.IB; therefore twice the rectangle AI.FH is equal to the sum of the

rectangles AB.BI and AI.IB, or $2AI.FH=2AI.IB+\overline{BI}^2$. Add $\overline{AI}^2$ to each side, then $2AI.IB+\overline{BI}^2+\overline{AI}^2=\overline{AB}^2=2AI.FH=AI^2$. Again add $\overline{BF}^2$ to each side, then $AB^2+BF^2=\overline{AF}^2$ $=2AI.FH+\overline{AI}^2+\overline{BF}^2=2AI.FH+\ \overline{AI}^2+\overline{FH}^2$. But $\overline{AF}^2=2AH.HF+\overline{AH}^2+\overline{HF}^2$; and hence $2AI.FH+\overline{AI}^2+\overline{FH}^2=2AH.HF+\overline{AH}^2+\overline{HF}^2$. Subtracting $\overline{HF}^2$ from each side we have $2AI.FH+\overline{AI}^2=2AH.HF+\overline{AH}^2$. Since now FH is a factor common to both rectangles, it follows that AH is equal to AI; for if AH were either greater or smaller than AI, then the two rectangles AH.HF plus the square of HA would be either larger or smaller than the two rectangles AI.FH plus the square of IA, a result which is contrary to what we have just demonstrated.

If now we agree to represent the time of descent along AB by the length AB, then the time through AC will likewise be measured by AC; and IB, which is a mean proportional between AC and CE, will represent the time through CE, or XA, from rest at X. Now, since AF is a mean proportional between DA and AB, or between RB and AB, and since BF, which is equal to FH, is a mean proportional between AB and BD, that is between AB and AR, it follows, from a preceding proposition [Proposition XIX, corollary], that the difference AH represents the time of descent along AB either from rest at R or after fall from X, while the time of descent along AB, from rest at A, is measured by the length AB. But as has just been shown, the time of fall through XA is measured by IB, while the time of descent along AB, after fall, through RA or through XA, is IA. Therefore the time of descent through XA plus AB is measured by the length AB, which, of course, also measures the time of descent, from rest at A, along AB alone.   Q.E.F.

[263]

PROBLEM XIV, PROPOSITION XXXV

Given an inclined plane and a limited vertical line, it is required to find a distance on the inclined plane which a body, starting from rest, will traverse in the same time as that needed to traverse both the vertical and the inclined plane.

Let AB be the vertical line and BC the inclined plane. It is required to lay off on BC a distance which a body, starting from rest, will traverse in a time equal to that which is occupied by fall through the vertical AB and by descent of the plane. Draw the horizontal line AD, which intersects at E the prolongation of the inclined plane CB; lay off BF equal to BA, and about E as center, with EF as radius describe the circle FIG. Prolong FE until it intersects the circumference at G. Choose a point H such that GB:BF=BH:HF. Draw the line HI tangent to the circle at I. At B draw the line

BK perpendicular to FC, cutting the line EIL at L; also draw LM perpendicular to EL and cutting BC at M. Then, I say, BM is the distance which a body, starting from rest at B, will traverse in the same time which is required to descend from rest at A through both distances, AB and BM. Lay off EN equal to EL; then since GB:BF=BH:HF, we

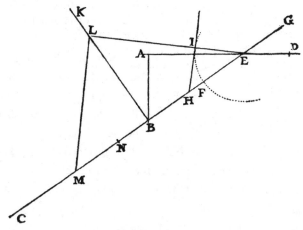

Fig. 97

shall have, *permutando*, GB:BH=BF:HF, and, *dividendo*, GH:BH=BH:HF,. Consequently the rectangle GH.HF is equal to the square on BH; but this same rectangle is also equal to the square on HI; therefore BH is equal to HI. Since, in the quadrilateral ILBH, the sides HB and HI are equal and since the angles at B and I are right angles, it follows that the sides BL and LI are also equal: but EI=EF; therefore the

[264]

total length LE, or NE, is equal to the sum of LB and EF. If we subtract the common part FF, the remainder FN will be equal to LB: but, by construction, FB=BA and, therefore, LB=AB+BN. If again we agree to represent the time of fall through AB by the length AB, then the time of descent along EB will be measured by EB; moreover since EN is a mean proportional between ME and EB it will represent the time of descent along the whole distance EM; therefore the difference of these distances, BM, will be traversed, after fall from EB, or AB, in a time which is represented by BN. But having already assumed the distance AB as a measure of the time of fall through AB, the time of descent along AB and BM is measured by AB+BN. Since EB measures the time of fall, from rest at E, along EB, the time from rest at B along BM will be the mean proportional between BE and BM, namely, BL. The time therefore for the path AB+BM, starting from rest at A is AB+BN; but the time for BM alone, starting from rest at B, is BL; and since it has already been shown that BL=AB+BN, the proposition follows.

Another and shorter proof is the following: Let BC be the inclined plane and BA the vertical; at B draw a perpendicular to EC, extending it both ways; lay off BH equal

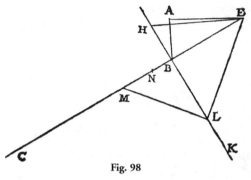

Fig. 98

to the excess of BE over BA; make the angle HEL equal to the angle BHE; prolong EL until it cuts BK in L; at L draw LM perpendicular to EL and extend it till it meets BC in M; then, I say, BM is the portion of BC sought. For, since the angle MLE is a right angle, BL will be a mean proportional between MB and BE, while LE is a mean proportional between ME and BE; lay off EN equal to LE; then NE=EL=LH, and HB=NE-BL. But also HB=NE-(NB+BA); therefore BN+BA=BL. If now we assume the length EB as a measure of the time of descent along EB, the time of descent, from rest at B, along BM will be represented by BL; but, if the descent along BM is from rest at E or at A, then the time of descent will be measured by BN; and AB will measure the time along AB. Therefore the time required to traverse AB and BM, namely, the sum of the distances AB and BN, is equal to the time of descent, from rest at B, along BM alone.   Q.E.F.

[265]

LEMMA

Let DC be drawn perpendicular to the diameter BA; from the extremity B draw the line BED at random; draw the line FB. Then, I say, FB is a mean proportional between DB and BE. Join the points E and F. Through B, draw the tangent BG which will be parallel to CD. Now, since the angle DBG is equal to the angle FDB, and since the alternate angle of GBD is equal to EFB, it follows that the triangles FDB and FEB are similar and hence BD:BF=FB:BE.

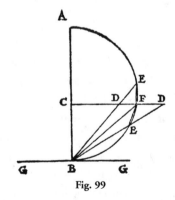

Fig. 99

LEMMA

Let AC be a line which is longer than DF, and let the ratio of AB to BC be greater than that of DE to EF. Then, I say, AB is greater than DE. For, if AB bears to BC a ratio greater than that of DE to EF, then DE will bear to some length shorter than EF,

the same ratio which AB bears to BC. Call this length EG; then since AB:BC=DE:EG, it follows, *componendo et convertendo*, that CA:AB=GD:DE. But since CA is greater than GD, it follows that BA is greater than DE.

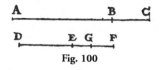

Fig. 100

LEMMA

Let ACIB be the quadrant of a circle; from B draw BE parallel to AC; about any point in the line BE describe a circle BOES, touching AB at B and intersecting the circumference of the quadrant at I. Join the points C and B; draw the line CI, prolonging it to S. Then, I say, the line is always less than CO. Draw the line AI touching the circle BOE. Then, if the line DI be drawn, it will be equal to DB; but, since DB touches the quadrant, DI will also be tangent to it and will be at right angles to AI; thus AI touches the circle BOE at I. And since the angle AIC is greater than the angle ABC, subtending as it does a larger arc, it follows that the angle SIN is also greater than the angle ABC. Wherefore the arc IES is greater than the arc BO, and the line CS, being nearer the center, is longer that CB. Consequently CO is greater than CI, since SC:CB=OC:CI.

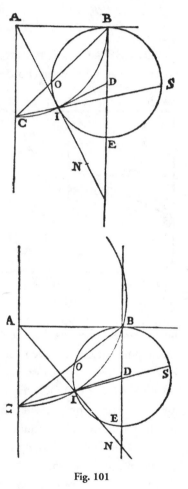

Fig. 101

[266]

This result would be all the more marked if, as in the second figure, the arc BIC were less than a quadrant. For the perpendicular DB would then cut the circle CIB; and so also would DI which is equal to BD; the angle DIA would be obtuse and therefore the line AIN would cut the circle BIE. Since the angle ABC is less than the angle AIC, which is equal to SIN, and still less than the angle which the tangent at I would make with the line SI, it follows that the arc SEI is far greater than the arc BO; whence, etc.

Q.E.D.

[267]

THEOREM XXII, PROPOSITION XXXVI

*If from the lowest point of a vertical circle, a chord is drawn sub-
tending an are not greater than a quadrant, and if from the two ends
of this chord two other chords be drawn to any point on the arc, the
time of descent along the two latter chords will be shorter than along
the first, and shorter also, by the same amount, than along the lower
of these two latter chords.*

Let CBD be an arc, not exceeding a quadrant, taken from a vertical circle whose
point is C; let CD be the chord [*planum elevatum*] subtending this arc, and let there

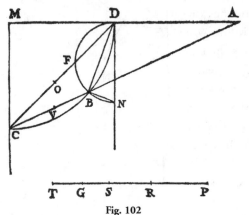

Fig. 102

be two other chords drawn from C and
D to any point B on the arc. Then, I
say, the time of descent along the two
chords [*plana*] DB and BC is shorter
than along DC alone, or along BC
alone, starting from rest at B. Through
the point D, draw the horizontal line
MDA cutting CB extended at A: draw
DN and MC at right angles to MD,
and BN at right angles to BD; about the
right-angled triangle DBN describe the
semicircle DFBN, cutting DC at F.
Choose the point O such that DO will
be a mean proportional between CD and DF; in like manner select V so that AV is a
mean proportional between CA and AB. Let the length PS represent the time of
descent along the whole distance DC or BC, both of which require the same time. Lay
off PR such that CD:DO=*time*PS.*time*PR. Then PR will represent the time in which
a body, starting from D, will traverse the distance DF, while RS will measure the time
in which the remaining distance, FC, will be traversed. But since PS is also the time of
descent, from rest at B, along BC, and if we choose T such that BC:CD=PS:PT then
PT will measure the time of descent from A to C, for we have already shown [Lemma]
that DC is a mean proportional between AC and CB. Finally choose the point G such
that CA:AV=PT:PG, then PG will be the time of descent from A to B, while GT will
be the residual time of descent along BC following descent from A to B. But, since the
diameter, DN, of the circle DFN is a vertical line, the chords DF and DB will be traversed in equal times; wherefore if one can prove that a body will traverse BC, after

582

descent along DB, in a shorter time than it will FC after descent along DF he will have proved the theorem. But a body descending from D along DB will traverse BC in the same time as if it had come from A along AB, seeing that the body acquires the same momentum in descending along DB as along AB.

[268]

Hence it remains only to show that descent along BC after AB is quicker than along FC after DF. But we have already shown that GT represents the time along BC after AB; also that RS measures the time along FC after DF. Accordingly it must be shown that RS is greater than GT, which may be done as follows: Since SP:PR=CD:DO, it follows, *invertendo et convertendo*, that RS:SP=OC:CD; also we have SP:PT=DC:CA. And since TP:PG=CA:AV, it follows, *invertendo*, that PT:TG=AC:CV, therefore, *ex æquali*, RS:GT=OC:CV. But, as we shall presently show, OC is greater than CV; hence the time RS is greater than the time GT, which was to be shown. Now, since [Lemma] CF is greater than CB and FD smaller than BA, it follows that CD:DF>CA:AB. But CD:DF=CO:OF, seeing that CD:DO=DO:DF; and CA:AB=CV²:VB². Therefore CO:OF>CV:VB, and, according to the preceding lemma, CO>CV. Besides this it is clear that the time of descent along DC is to the time along DBC as DOC is to the sum of DO and CV.

[269]

SCHOLIUM

From the preceding it is possible to infer that the path of quickest descent [*lationem omnium velocissimam*] from one point to another is not the shortest path, namely, a straight line, but the are of a circle.[34] In the quadrant BAEC, having the side BC vertical, divide the arc AC into any number of equal parts, AD, DE, EF, FG, GC, and from C draw straight lines to the points A, D, E, F, G; draw also the straight lines AD, DE, EF, FG, GC. Evidently descent along the path ADC is quicker than along AC alone or along DC from rest at D. But a body, starting from rest at A, will traverse C more quickly than the path ADC; while, if it starts from rest at A, it will traverse the path DEC in a shorter time

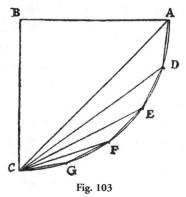

Fig. 103

34. It is well known that the first correct solution for the problem of quickest descent, under the condition of a constant force was given by John Bernoulli (1667-1748). *[Trans.]*

than DC alone. Hence descent along the three chords, ADEC, will take less time than along the two chords ADC. Similarly, following descent along ADE, the time required to traverse EFC is less than that needed for EC alone. Therefore descent is more rapid along the four chords ADEFC than along the three ADEC. And finally a body, after descent along ADEF, will traverse the two chords, FGC, more quickly than FC alone. Therefore, along the five chords, ADEFGC, descent will be more rapid than along the four, ADEFC. Consequently the nearer the inscribed polygon approaches a circle the shorter is the time required for descent from A to C.

What has been proven for the quadrant holds true also for smaller arcs; the reasoning is the same.

Problem XV, Proposition XXXVII

*Given a limited vertical line and an inclined plane of equal altitude;
it is required to find a distance on the inclined plane which is equal
to the vertical line and which is traversed in an interval equal to the
time of fall along the vertical line.*

Let AB be the vertical line and AC the inclined plane. We must locate, on the inclined plane, a distance equal to the vertical line AB and which will be traversed by a body starting from rest at A in the same time needed for fall along the vertical line. Lay off AD equal to AB, and bisect the remainder DC at I. Choose the point E such that AC:CI=CI:AE and lay off DG equal to AE. Clearly EG is equal to AD, and also to AB. And further, I say that EG is that distance which will be traversed by a body, starting from rest at A, in the same time which is required for that body to fall through the distance AB. For since

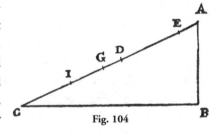

Fig. 104

AC:CI=CI:AE=ID:DG, we have, *convertendo*, CA:AI=DI:IG. And since the whole of CA is to the whole of AI as the portion CI is to the portion IG, it follows that the remainder IA is to the remainder AG as the whole of CA is to the whole of AI. Thus AI is seen to be a mean proportional between CA and AG, while CI is a mean proportional between CA and AE. If therefore the time of fall along AB is represented

[270]

by the length AB, the time along AC will be represented by AC, while CI, or ID, will measure the time along AE. Since AI is a mean proportional between CA and AG, and

since CA is a measure of the time along the entire distance AC, it follows that AI is the time along AG, and the difference IC is the time along the difference GC; but DI was the time along AE. Consequently the lengths DI and IC measure the times along AE and CG respectively. Therefore the remainder DA represents the time along EG, which of course is equal to the time along AB.   Q.E.F.

COROLLARY

From this it is clear that the distance sought is bounded at each end by portions of the inclined plane which are traversed in equal times.

PROBLEM XVI, PROPOSITION XXXVIII

Given two horizontal planes cut by a vertical line, it is required to find a point on the upper part of the vertical line from which bodies may fall to the horizontal planes and there, having their motion deflected into a horizontal direction, will, during an interval equal to the time of fall, traverse distances which bear to each other any assigned ratio of a smaller quantity to a larger.

Let CD and BE be the horizontal planes cut by the vertical ACB, and let the ratio of the smaller quantity to the larger be that of N to FG. It is required to find in the upper part of the vertical line, AB, a point from which a body falling to the plane CD and there having its motion deflected along this plane, will traverse, during an interval equal to its time of fall a distance such that if another body, falling from this same point to the plane BE, there have its motion deflected along this plane and continued during

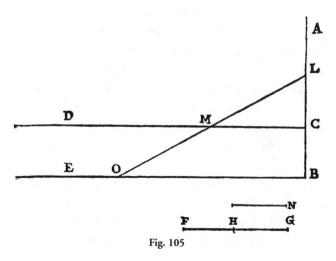

Fig. 105

an interval equal to its time of fall, will traverse a distance which bears to the former distance the ratio of FG to N. Lay off GH equal to N, and select the point L so that FH:HG=BC:CL. Then, I say, L is the point sought. For, if we lay off CM equal to twice CL, and draw the line LM cutting the plane BE at O, then BO will be equal to twice BL. And since FH:HG=BC:CL, we have, *componendo et convertendo*, HG:GF=N:GF=CL:LB=CM:BO. It is clear that, since CM is double the distance LC, the space CM is that which a body falling from L through LC will traverse in the plane CD; and, for the same reason, since BO is twice the distance BL, it is clear that BO is the distance which a body, after fall through LB, will traverse during an interval equal to the time of its fall through LB.   Q.E.F.

[271]

Sagr. Indeed, I think we may concede to our Academician, without flattery, his claim that in the principle [*principio*, i. e., accelerated motion] laid down in this treatise he has established a new science dealing with a very old subject. Observing with what ease and clearness he deduces from a single principle the proofs of so many theorems, I wonder not a little how such a question escaped the attention of Archimedes, Apollonius, Euclid and so many other mathematicians and illustrious philosophers, especially since so many ponderous tomes have been devoted to the subject of motion.

[272]

Salv. There is a fragment of Euclid which treats of motion, but in it there is no indication that he ever began to investigate the property of acceleration and the manner in which it varies with slope. So that we may say the door is now opened, for the first time, to a new method fraught with numerous and wonderful results which in future years will command the attention of other minds.

Sagr. I really believe that just as, for instance, the few properties of the circle proven by Euclid in the Third Book of his Elements lead to many others more recondite, so the principles which are set forth in this little treatise will, when taken up by speculative minds, lead to many another more remarkable result; and it is to be believed that it will be so on account of the nobility of the subject, which is superior to any other in nature.

During this long and laborious day, I have enjoyed these simple theorems more than their proofs, many of which, for their complete comprehension, would require more than an hour each; this study, if you will be good enough to leave the book in my hands, is one which I mean to take up at my leisure after we have read the remain-

ing portion which deals with the motion of projectiles; and this if agreeable to you we shall take up to-morrow.

Salv. I shall not fail to be with you.

END OF THE THIRD DAY.

[273]

FOURTH DAY

Salviati. Once more, Simplicio is here on time; so let us without delay take up the question of motion. The text of our Author is as follows:

THE MOTION OF PROJECTILES

In the preceding pages we have discussed the properties of uniform motion and of motion naturally accelerated along planes of all inclinations. I now propose to set forth those properties which belong to a body whose motion is compounded of two other motions, namely, one uniform and one naturally accelerated; these properties, well worth knowing, I propose to demonstrate in a rigid manner. This is the kind of motion seen in a moving projectile; its origin I conceive to be as follows:

Imagine any particle projected along a horizontal plane without friction; then we know, from what has been more fully explained in the preceding pages, that this particle will move along this same plane with a motion which is uniform and perpetual, provided the plane has no limits. But if the plane is limited and elevated, then the moving particle, which we imagine to be a heavy one, will on passing over the edge of the plane acquire, in addition to its previous uniform and perpetual motion, a downward propensity due to its own weight; so that the resulting motion which I call projection [*projectio*], is compounded of one which is uniform and horizontal and of another which is vertical and naturally accelerated. We now proceed to demonstrate some of its properties, the first of which is as follows:

[274]

THEOREM I, PROPOSITION I

A projectile which is carried by a uniform horizontal motion compounded with a naturally accelerated vertical motion describes a path which is a semi-parabola.

Sagr. Here, Salviati, it will be necessary to stop a little while for my sake and, I believe, also for the benefit of Simplicio; for it so happens that I have not gone very far in my study of Apollonius and am merely aware of the fact that he treats of the parabola and other conic sections, without an understanding of which I hardly think one will be able to follow the proof of other propositions depending upon them. Since even in this first beautiful theorem the author finds it necessary to prove that the path of a projectile is a parabola, and since, as I imagine, we shall have to deal with only this kind of curves, it will be absolutely necessary to have a thorough acquaintance, if not with all the properties which Apollonius has demonstrated for these figures, at least with those which are needed for the present treatment.

Salv. You are quite too modest, pretending ignorance of facts which not long ago you acknowledged as well known—I mean at the time when we were discussing the strength of materials and needed to use a certain theorem of Apollonius which gave you no trouble.

Sagr. I may have chanced to know it or may possibly have assumed it, so long as needed, for that discussion; but now when we have to follow all these demonstrations about such curves we ought not, as they say, to swallow it whole, and thus waste time and energy.

Simp. Now even though Sagredo is, as I believe, well equipped for all his needs, I do not understand even the elementary terms; for although our philosophers have treated the motion of projectiles, I do not recall their having described the path of a projectile except to state in a general way that it is always a curved line, unless the projection be vertically upwards. But if the little Euclid which I have learned since our previous discussion does not enable me to understand the demonstrations which are to follow, then I shall be obliged to accept the theorems on faith without fully comprehending them.

[275]

Salv. On the contrary, I desire that you should understand them from the Author himself, who, when he allowed me to see this work of his, was good enough to prove

for me two of the principal properties of the parabola because I did not happen to have at hand the books of Apollonius. These properties, which are the only ones we shall need in the present discussion, he proved in such a way that no prerequisite knowledge was required. These theorems are, indeed, given by Apollonius, but after many preceding ones, to follow which would take a long while. I wish to shorten our task by deriving the first property purely and simply from the mode of generation of the parabola and proving the second immediately from the first.

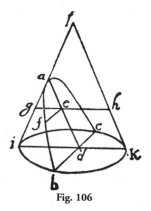

Fig. 106

Beginning now with the first, imagine a right cone, erected upon the base *ibkc* with apex at *l*. The section of this cone made by a plane drawn parallel to the side *lk* is the curve which is called a *parabola*. The base of this parabola *bc* cuts at right angles the diameter *ik* of the circle *ibkc*, and the axis *ad* is parallel to the side *lk*; now having taken any point in the curve *bfa* draw the straight line *fe* parallel to *bd*; then, I say, the square of *bd* is to the square of *fe* in the same ratio as the axis *ad* is to the portion *ae*. Through the point *e* pass a plane parallel to the circle *ibkc*, producing in the cone a circular section whose diameter is the line *geh*. Since *bd* is at right angles to *ik* in the circle *ibk*, the square of *bd* is equal to the rectangle formed by *id* and *dk*; so also in the upper circle which passes through the points *gfh* the square of *fe* is equal to the rectangle formed by *ge* and *eh*; hence the square of *bd* is to the square of *fe* as the rectangle *id.dk* is to the rectangle *ge.eh*. And since the line *ed* is parallel to *hk*, the line *eh*, being parallel to *dk*, is equal to it; therefore the rectangle *ge.eh* as *id* is to *id.dk* is to the rectangle *ge*, that is, as *da* is to *ae*; whence also the rectangle *id.dk* is to the rectangle *ge.eh*, that is, the square of *bd* is to the square of *fe*, as the axis *da* is to the portion *ae*. Q.E.D.

[276]

The other proposition necessary for this discussion we demonstrate as follows. Let us draw a parabola whose axis *ca* is prolonged upwards to a point *d*; from any point *b* draw the line *bc* parallel to the base of the parabola; if now the point *d* is chosen so that *da* = *ca*, then, I say, the straight line drawn through the points *b* and *d* will be tangent to the parabola at *b*. For imagine, if possible, that this line cuts the parabola above or that its prolongation cuts it below, and through any point *g* in it draw the straight line *fge*. And since the square of *fe* is greater than the square of *ge*, the square of *fe* will bear a greater ratio to the square of *bc* than the square of *ge* to that of *bc*; and since, by the preceding proposition, the square of *fe* is to that of *bc* as the line *ea* is to *ca*, it follows that the line *ea* will bear to the line *ca* a greater ratio than the square of *ge* to that of

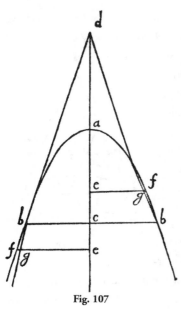

Fig. 107

bc, or, than the square of *ed* to that of *cd* (the sides of the triangles *deg* and *dcb* being proportional). But the line *ea* is to *ca*, or *da*, in the same ratio as four times the rectangle *ea.ad* is to four times the square of *ad*, or, what is the same, the square of *cd*, since this is four times the square of *ad*; hence four times the rectangle *ea.ad* bears to the square of *cd* a greater ratio than the square of *ed* to the square of *cd*; but that would make four times the rectangle *ea.ad* greater than the square of *ed*; which is false, the fact being just the opposite, because the two portions *ea* and *ad* of the line *ed* are not equal. Therefore the line *db* touches the parabola without cutting it.   Q.E.D.

Simp. Your demonstration proceeds too rapidly and, it seems to me, you keep on assuming that all of Euclid's theorems are as familiar and available to me

[277]

as his first axioms, which is far from true. And now this fact which you spring upon us, that four times the rectangle *ea.ad* is less than the square of *de* because the two portions *ea* and *ad* of the line *de* are not equal brings me little composure of mind, but rather leaves me in suspense.

Salv. Indeed, all real mathematicians assume on the part of the reader perfect familiarity with at least the elements of Euclid; and here it is necessary in your case only to recall a proposition of the Second Book in which he proves that when a line is cut into equal and also into two unequal parts, the rectangle formed on the unequal parts is less than that formed on the equal (i. e, less than the square on half the line), by an amount which is the square of the difference between the equal and unequal segments. From this it is clear that the square of the whole line which is equal to four times the square of the half is greater than four times the rectangle of the unequal parts. In order to understand the following portions of this treatise it will be necessary to keep in mind the two elemental theorems from conic sections which we have just demonstrated; and these two theorems are indeed the only ones which the Author uses. We can now resume the text and see how he demonstrates his first proposition in which he shows that a body falling with a motion compounded of a uniform horizontal and a naturally accelerated [*naturale descendente*] one describes a semi-parabola.

Let us imagine an elevated horizontal line or plane *ab* along which a body moves with uniform speed from *a* to *b*. Suppose this plane to end abruptly at *b*; then at this

point the body will, on account of its weight, acquire also a natural motion downwards along the perpendicular *bn*. Draw the line *be* along the plane *ba* to represent the flow, or measure, of time; divide this line into a number of segments, *bc*, *cd*, *de*, representing equal intervals of time; from the points *b*, *c*, *d*, *e*, let

[278]

fall lines which are parallel to the perpendicular *bn*. On the first of these lay off any distance *ci*, on the second a distance four times as long, *df*; on the third, one nine times as long, *eh*; and so on, in proportion to the squares of *cb*, *db*, *eb*, or, we may say, in the squared ratio of these same lines. Accordingly we see that while the body moves from *b* to *c* with uniform speed, it also falls perpendicularly through the distance *ci*, and at the end of the time-interval *bc* finds itself at the point *i*. In like manner at the end of the time-interval *bd*, which is the double of *bc*, the vertical fall will be four times the first distance *ci*; for it has been shown in a previous discussion that the distance traversed by a freely falling body varies as the square of the time; in like manner the space *eh* traversed during the time *be* will be nine times *ci*; thus it is evident that the distances *eh*, *df*, *ci* will be to one another as the squares of the lines *be*, *bd*, *bc*. Now from the points *i*, *f*, *h* draw the straight lines *io*, *fg*, *hl* parallel to *be*; these lines *hl*, *fg*, *io* are equal to *eb*, *db* and *cb*, respectively; so also are the lines *bo*, *bg*, *bl* respectively equal to *ci*, *df*, and *eh*. The square of *hl* is to that of *fg* as the line *lb* is to *bg*; and the square of *fg* is to that of *io* as *gb* is to *bo*; therefore the points *i*, *f*, *h*, lie on one and the same parabola. In like manner it may be shown that, if we take equal time-intervals of any size whatever, and if we imagine the particle to be carried by a similar compound motion, the positions of this particle, at the ends of these time-intervals, will lie on one and the same parabola. Q.E.D.

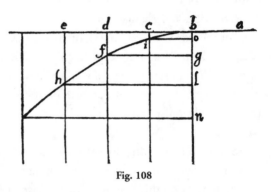

Fig. 108

Salv. This conclusion follows from the converse of the first of the two propositions given above. For, having drawn a parabola through the points *b* and *h*, any other two points, *f* and *i*, not falling on the parabola must lie either within or without; consequently the line *fg* is either longer or shorter than the line which terminates on the parabola. Therefore the square of *hl* will not bear to the square of *fg* the same ratio as the line *lb* to *bg*, but a greater or smaller; the fact is, however, that the square of *hl* *does*

bear this same ratio to the square of *fg*. Hence the point *f* does lie on the parabola and so do all the others.

[279]

Sagr. One cannot deny that the argument is new, subtle and conclusive, resting as it does upon this hypothesis, namely, that the horizontal motion remains uniform, that the vertical motion continues to be accelerated downwards in proportion to the square of the time, and that such motions and velocities as these combine without altering, disturbing, or hindering each other,[35] so that as the motion proceeds the path of the projectile does not change into a different curve: but this, in my opinion, is impossible. For the axis of the parabola along which we imagine the natural motion of a falling body to take place stands perpendicular to a horizontal surface and ends at the center of the earth; and since the parabola deviates more and more from its axis no projectile can ever reach the center of the earth or, if it does, as seems necessary, then the path of the projectile must transform itself into some other curve very different from the parabola.

Simp. To these difficulties, I may add others. One of these is that we suppose the horizontal plane, which slopes neither up nor down, to be represented by a straight line as if each point on this line were equally distant from the center, which is not the case; for as one starts from the middle [of the line] and goes toward either end, he departs farther and farther from the center (of the earth] and is therefore constantly going uphill. Whence it follows that the motion cannot remain uniform through any distance whatever, but must continually diminish. Besides, I do not see how it is possible to avoid the resistance of the medium which must destroy the uniformity of the horizontal motion and change the law of acceleration of falling bodies. These various difficulties render it highly improbable that a result derived from such unreliable hypotheses should hold true in practice.

Salv. All these difficulties and objections which you urge are so well founded that it is impossible to remove them; and, as for me, I am ready to admit them all, which indeed I think our Author would also do. I grant that these conclusions proved in the abstract will be different when applied in the concrete and will be fallacious to this extent, that neither will the horizontal motion be uniform nor the natural acceleration be in the ratio assumed, nor the path of the projectile a parabola, etc. But, on the other hand, I ask you not to begrudge our Author that which other eminent men have assumed even if not strictly true. The authority of Archimedes alone will satisfy everybody. In his Mechanics and in his first quadrature of the parabola he takes for granted

---

35. A very near approach to Newton's Second Law of Motion. *[Trans.]*

that the beam of a balance or steelyard is a straight line, every point of which is equidistant from the common center of all heavy bodies, and that the cords by which heavy bodies are suspended are parallel to each other.

Some consider this assumption permissible because, in practice, our instruments and the distances involved are so small in comparison with the enormous distance from the center of the earth that we may consider a minute of arc on a great circle as a straight line, and may regard the perpendiculars let fall from its two extremities as parallel. For if in actual practice one had to consider such small quantities, it would be

[280]

necessary first of all to criticise the architects who presume, by use of a plumbline, to erect high towers with parallel sides. I may add that, in all their discussions, Archimedes and the others considered themselves as located at an infinite distance from the center of the earth, in which case their assumptions were not false, and therefore their conclusions were absolutely correct. When we wish to apply our proven conclusions to distances which, though finite, are very large, it is necessary for us to infer, on the basis of demonstrated truth, what correction is to be made for the fact that our distance from the center of the earth is not really infinite, but merely very great in comparison with the small dimensions of our apparatus. The largest of these will be the range of our projectiles—and even here we need consider only the artillery—which, however great, will never exceed four of those miles of which as many thousand separate us from the center of the earth; and since these paths terminate upon the surface of the earth only very slight changes can take place in their parabolic figure which, it is conceded, would be greatly altered if they terminated at the center of the earth.

As to the perturbation arising from the resistance of the medium this is more considerable and does not, on account of its manifold forms, submit to fixed laws and exact description. Thus if we consider only the resistance which the air offers to the motions studied by us, we shall see that it disturbs them all and disturbs them in an infinite variety of ways corresponding to the infinite variety in the form, weight, and velocity of the projectiles. For as to velocity, the greater this is, the greater will be the resistance offered by the air; a resistance which will be greater as the moving bodies become less dense [*men gravi*]. So that although the falling body ought to be displaced [*andare accelerandosi*] in proportion to the square of the duration of its motion, yet no matter how heavy the body, if it falls from a very considerable height, the resistance of the air will be such as to prevent any increase in speed and will render the motion uniform; and in proportion as the moving body is less dense [*men grave*] this uniformity will be so much the more quickly attained and after a shorter fall. Even horizontal

motion which, if no impediment were offered, would be uniform and constant is altered by the resistance of the air and finally ceases; and here again the less dense [*piu leggiero*] the body the quicker the process.

[281]

Of these properties [*accidenti*] of weight, of velocity, and also of form [*figura*], infinite in number, it is not possible to give any exact description; hence, in order to handle this matter in a scientific way, it is necessary to cut loose from these difficulties; and having discovered and demonstrated the theorems, in the case of no resistance., to use them and apply them with such limitations as experience will teach. And the advantage of this method will not be small; for the material and shape of the projectile may be chosen, as dense and round as possible, so that it will encounter the least resistance in the medium. Nor will the spaces and velocities in general be so great but that we shall be easily able to correct them with precision.

In the case of those projectiles which we use, made of dense [*grave*] material and round in shape, or of lighter material and cylindrical in shape, such as arrows, thrown from a sling or crossbow, the deviation from an exact parabolic path is quite insensible. Indeed, if you will allow me a little greater liberty, I can show you, by two experiments, that the dimensions of our apparatus are so small that these external and incidental resistances, among which that of the medium is the most considerable, are scarcely observable.

I now proceed to the consideration of motions through the air, since it is with these that we are now especially concerned; the resistance of the air exhibits itself in two ways: first by offering greater impedance to less dense than to very dense bodies, and secondly by offering greater resistance to a body in rapid motion than to the same body in slow motion.

Regarding the first of these, consider the case of two balls having the same dimensions, but one weighing ten or twelve times as much as the other; one, say, of lead, the other of oak, both allowed to fall from an elevation of 150 or 200 cubits.

Experiment shows that they will reach the earth with slight difference in speed, showing us that in both cases the retardation caused by the air is small; for if both balls start at the same moment and at the same elevation, and if the leaden one be slightly retarded and the wooden one greatly retarded, then the former ought to reach the earth a considerable distance in advance of the latter, since it is ten times as heavy. But this does not happen; indeed, the gain in distance of one over the other does not amount to the hundredth part of the entire fall. And in the case of a ball of stone weighing only a third or half as much as one of lead, the difference in their times of reaching the earth will be scarcely noticeable. Now since the speed [*impeto*] acquired by a leaden ball in

falling from a height of 200 cubits is so great that if the motion remained uniform the ball would, in an interval of time equal to that of the fall, traverse 400 cubits, and since this speed is so considerable in comparison with those which, by use of bows or other machines except fire arms, we are able to give to our projectiles, it follows that we may, without sensible error, regard as absolutely true those propositions which we are about to prove without considering the resistance of the medium.

[282]

Passing now to the second case, where we have to show that the resistance of the air for a rapidly moving body is not very much greater than for one moving slowly, ample proof is given by the following experiment. Attach to two threads of equal length—say four or five yards—two equal leaden balls and suspend them from the ceiling; now pull them aside from the perpendicular, the one through 80 or more degrees, the other through not more than four or five degrees; so that, when set free, the one falls, passes through the perpendicular, and describes large but slowly decreasing arcs of 160, 150, 140 degrees, etc.; the other swinging through small and also slowly diminishing arcs of 10, 8, 6, degrees, etc.

In the first place it must be remarked that one pendulum passes through its arcs of 180°, 160°, etc., in the same time that the other swings through its 10°, 8°, etc., from which it follows that the speed of the first ball is 16 and 18 times greater than that of the second. Accordingly, if the air offers more resistance to the high speed than to the low, the frequency of vibration in the large arcs of 180° or 160°, etc., ought to be less than in the small arcs of 10°, 8°, 4°, etc., and even less than in arcs of 2°, or 1°; but this prediction is not verified by experiment; because if two persons start to count the vibrations, the one the large, the other the small, they will discover that after counting tens and even hundreds they will not differ by a single vibration, not even by a fraction of one.

[283]

This observation justifies the two following propositions, namely, that vibrations of very large and very small amplitude all occupy the same time and that the resistance of the air does not affect motions of high speed more than those of low speed, contrary to the opinion hitherto generally entertained.

Sagr. On the contrary, since we cannot deny that the air hinders both of these motions, both becoming slower and finally vanishing, we have to admit that the retardation occurs in the same proportion in each case. But how? How, indeed, could the resistance offered to the one body be greater than that offered to the other except by the impartation of more momentum and speed [*impeto e velocità*] to the fast body than

to the slow? And if this is so the speed with which a body moves is at once the cause and measure [*cagione e misura*] of the resistance which it meets. Therefore, all motions, fast or slow, are hindered and diminished in the same proportion; a result, it seems to me, of no small importance.

Salv. We are able, therefore, in this second case to say that the errors, neglecting those which are accidental, in the results which we are about to demonstrate are small in the case of our machines where the velocities employed are mostly very great and the distances negligible in comparison with the semi-diameter of the earth or one of its great circles.

Simp. I would like to hear your reason for putting the projectiles of fire arms, i. e., those using powder, in a different class from the projectiles employed in bows, slings, and crossbows, on the ground of their not being equally subject to change and resistance from the air.

Salv. I am led to this view by the excessive and, so to speak, supernatural violence with which such projectiles are launched; for, indeed, it appears to me that without exaggeration one might say that the speed of a ball fired either from a musket or from a piece of ordnance is supernatural. For if such a ball be allowed to fall from some great elevation its speed will, owing to the resistance of the air, not go on increasing indefinitely; that which happens to bodies of small density in falling through short distances—I mean the reduction of their motion to uniformity— will also happen to a ball of iron or lead after it has fallen a few thousand cubits; this terminal or final speed [*terminata velocità*] is the maximum which such a heavy body can naturally acquire in falling through the air. This speed I estimate to be much smaller than that impressed upon the ball by the burning powder.

An appropriate experiment will serve to demonstrate this fact. From a height of one hundred or more cubits fire a gun [*archibuso*] loaded with a lead bullet, vertically downwards upon a stone pavement; with the same gun shoot against a similar stone from a distance of one or two cubits, and observe which of the two balls is the more flattened. Now if the ball which has come from the greater elevation is found to be the less flattened of the two, this will show that the air has hindered and diminished the speed initially imparted to the bullet by the powder, and that the air will not permit a bullet to acquire so great a speed, no matter from what height it falls; for if the speed impressed upon the ball by the fire does not exceed that acquired by it in falling freely [*naturalmente*] then its downward blow ought to be greater rather than less.

[284]

This experiment I have not performed, but I am of the opinion that a musket-ball or cannon-shot, falling from a height as great as you please, will not deliver so strong a

blow as it would if fired into a wall only a few cubits distant, i. e., at such a short range that the splitting or rending of the air will not be sufficient to rob the shot of that excess of supernatural violence given it by the powder.

The enormous momentum [*impeto*] of these violent shots may cause some deformation of the trajectory, making the beginning of the parabola flatter and less curved than the end; but, so far as our Author is concerned, this is a matter of small consequence in practical operations, the main one of which is the preparation of a table of ranges for shots of high elevation, giving the distance attained by the ball as a function of the angle of elevation; and since shots of this kind are fired from mortars [*mortari*] using small charges and imparting no supernatural momentum [*impeto sopranaturale*] they follow their prescribed paths very exactly.

But now let us proceed with the discussion in which the Author invites us to the study and investigation of the motion of a body [*impeto del mobile*] when that motion is compounded of two others; and first the case in which the two are uniform, the one horizontal, the other vertical.

[285]

THEOREM II, PROPOSITION II

When the motion of a body is the resultant of two uniform motions, one horizontal, the other perpendicular, the square of the resultant momentum is equal to the sum of the squares of the two component momenta.[36]

Let us imagine any body urged by two uniform motions and let *ab* represent the vertical displacement, while *bc* represents the displacement which, in the same interval of time, takes place in a horizontal direction. If then the distances *ab* and *bc* are traversed, during the same time-interval, with uniform motions the corresponding momenta will be to each other as the distances *ab* and *bc* are to each other; but the body which is urged by these

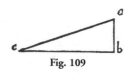

Fig. 109

two motions describes the diagonal *ac*; its momentum is proportional to *ac*. Also the square of *ac* is equal to the sum of the squares of *ab* and *bc*. Hence the square of the resultant momentum is equal to the sum of the squares of the two momenta *ab* and *bc*.   Q.E.D.

36. In the original this theorem reads as follows:
"*Si aliquod mobile duplici motu æquabili moveatur, nempe orizontali et perpendiculari, impetus seu momentum lationis ex utroque motu compositæ erit potentia æqualis ambobus momentis priorum motuum.*"
For the justification of this translation of the word "potentia" and of the use of the adjective "resultant" see below. [*Trans.*]
37. See above. [*Trans.*]

Simp. At this point there is just one slight difficulty which needs to be cleared up; for it seems to me that the conclusion just reached contradicts a previous proposition[37] in which it is claimed that the speed [*impeto*] of a body coming from *a* to *b* is equal to that in coming from *a* to *c*; while now you conclude that the speed [*impeto*] at *c* is greater than that at *b*.

Salv. Both propositions, Simplicio, are true., yet there is a great difference between them. Here we are speaking of a body urged by a single motion which is the resultant of two uniform motions, while there we were speaking of two bodies each urged with naturally accelerated motions, one along the vertical *ab* the other along the inclined plane *ac*. Besides the time-intervals were there not supposed to be equal, that along the incline *ac* being greater than that along the vertical *ab*; but the motions of which we now speak, those along *ab*, *bc*, *ac*, are uniform and simultaneous.

[286]

Simp. Pardon me; I am satisfied; pray go on.

Salv. Our Author next undertakes to explain what happens when a body is urged by a motion compounded of one which is horizontal and uniform and of another which is vertical but naturally accelerated; from these two components results the path of a projectile, which is a parabola. The problem is to determine the speed [*impeto*] of the projectile at each point. With this purpose in view our Author sets forth as follows the manner, or rather the method, of measuring such speed [*impeto*] along the path which is taken by a heavy body starting from rest and falling with a naturally acceler-ated motion.

THEOREM III, PROPOSITION III

Let the motion take place along the line *ab*, starting from rest at *a*, and in this line choose any point *c*. Let *ac* represent the time, or the measure of the time, required for

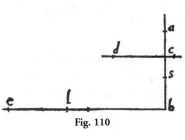

Fig. 110

the body to fall through the space *ac*; let *ac* also rep-resent the velocity [*impetus seu momentum*] at *c* acquired by a fall through the distance *ac*. In the line *ab* select any other point *b*. The problem now is to determine the velocity at b acquired by a body in falling through the distance *ab* and to express this in terms of the velocity at *c*, the measure of which is the length *ac*. Take *as* a mean proportion-al between *ac* and *ab*. We shall prove that the velocity at *b* is to that at *c* as the length *as* is to the length *ac*. Draw the horizontal line *cd*, having twice the length of *ac*, and

[287]

be, having twice the length of *ba*. It then follows, from the preceding theorems, that a body falling through the distance *ac*, and turned so as to move along the horizontal *cd* with a uniform speed equal to that acquired on reaching *c* will traverse the distance *cd* in the same interval of time as that required to fall with accelerated motion from *a* to *c*. Likewise *be* will be traversed in the same time as *ba*. But the time of descent through *ab* is *as*; hence the horizontal distance *be* is also traversed in the time *as*. Take a point *l* such that the time *as* is to the time *ac* as *be* is to *bl*; since the motion along *be* is uniform, the distance *bl*, if traversed with the speed [*momentum celeritatis*] acquired at *b*, will occupy the time *ac*; but in this same time-interval, *ac*, the distance *cd* is traversed with the speed acquired in *c*. Now two speeds are to each other as the distances traversed in equal intervals of time. Hence the speed at *c* is to the speed at *b* as *cd* is to *bl*. But since *dc* is to *be* as their halves, namely, as *ca* is to *ba*, and since *be* is to *bl* as *ba* is to *sa*; it follows that *dc* is to *bl* as *ca* is to *sa*. In other words, the speed at *c* is to that at *b* as *ca* is to *sa*, that is, as the time of fall through *ab*.

The method of measuring the speed of a body along the direction of its fall is thus clear; the speed is assumed to increase directly as the time.

But before we proceed further, since this discussion is to deal with the motion compounded of a uniform horizontal one and one accelerated vertically downwards—the path of a projectile, namely, a parabola-it is necessary that we define some common standard by which we may estimate the velocity, or momentum [*velocitatem, impetum seu momentum*] of both motions; and since from the innumerable uniform velocities one only, and that not selected at random, is to be compounded with a velocity acquired by naturally accelerated motion, I can think of no simpler way of selecting and measuring this than to assume another of the same kind.[38] For the sake of clearness, draw the vertical line *ac* to meet the horizontal line *bc*. *Ac* is the height and *bc* the amplitude of the semi-parabola *ab*, which is the resultant of the two motions, one that of a body falling from rest at *a*, through the distance *ac*, with naturally accelerated motion, the other a uniform motion along the horizontal *ad*.

[288]

The speed acquired at *c* by a fall through the distance *ac* is determined by the height *ac*; for the speed of a body falling from the same elevation is always one and the same; but along the horizontal one may give a body an infinite number of uniform speeds. However, in order that I may select one out of this multitude and separate it from the rest in a perfectly definite manner, I will extend the height *ca* upwards to *e* just as far

---

38. Galileo here proposes to employ as a standard of velocity the terminal speed of a body falling freely from a given height. *[Trans.]*

as is necessary and will call this distance *ae* the "sublimity." Imagine a body to fall from rest at *e*; it is clear that we may make its terminal speed at *a* the same as that with which

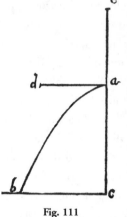

Fig. 111

the same body travels along the horizontal line *ad*; this speed will be such that, in the time of descent along *ea*, it will describe a horizontal distance twice the length of *ea*. This preliminary remark seems necessary.

The reader is reminded that above I have called the horizontal line *cb* the "amplitude" of the semi-parabola *ab*; the axis *ac* of this parabola, I have called its "altitude"; but the line *ea* the fall along which determines the horizontal speed I have called the "sublimity." These matters having been explained, I proceed with the demonstration.

Sagr. Allow me, please, to interrupt in order that I may point out the beautiful agreement between this thought of the Author and the views of Plato concerning the origin of the various uniform speeds with which the heavenly bodies revolve. The latter chanced upon the idea that a body could not pass from rest to any given speed and maintain it uniformly except by passing through all the degrees of speed intermediate between the given speed and rest. Plato thought that God, after having created the heavenly bodies, assigned them the proper and uniform speeds with which they were forever to revolve; and that He made them start from rest and move over definite distances under a natural and rectilinear acceleration such as governs the motion of terrestrial bodies. He added that once these bodies had gained their proper and permanent speed, their rectilinear motion was converted into a circular one, the only motion capable of maintaining uniformity, a motion in which the body revolves without either receding from or approaching its desired goal. This conception is truly worthy of Plato; and it is to be all the more highly prized since its underlying principles remained hidden until discovered by our Author who removed from them the mask and poetical dress and set forth the idea in correct historical perspective.

[289]

In view of the fact that astronomical science furnishes us such complete information concerning the size of the planetary orbits, the distances of these bodies from their centers of revolution, and their velocities, I cannot help thinking that our Author (to whom this idea of Plato was not unknown) bad some curiosity to discover whether or not a definite "sublimity" might be assigned to each planet, such that, if it were to start from rest at this particular height and to fall with naturally accelerated motion along a

straight line, and were later to change the speed thus acquired into uniform motion, the size of its orbit and its period of revolution would be those actually observed.

Salv. I think I remember his having told me that he once made the computation and found a satisfactory correspondence with observation. But he did not wish to speak of it, lest in view of the odium which his many new discoveries had already brought upon him, this might be adding fuel to the fire. But if any one desires such information he can obtain it for himself from the theory set forth in the present treatment.

We now proceed with the matter in hand, which is to prove:

PROBLEM I, PROPOSITION IV

To determine the momentum of a projectile at each particular point in its given parabolic path.

Let *bec* be the semi-parabola whose amplitude is *cd* and whose height is *db*, which latter extended upwards cuts the tangent of the parabola *ca* in *a*. Through the vertex draw the horizontal line *bi* parallel to *cd*. Now if the amplitude *cd* is equal to the entire height *da*, then *bi* will be equal to *ba* and also to *bd*; and if we take *ab* as the measure of the time required for fall through the distance *ab* and also of the momentum acquired at *b* in consequence of its fall from rest at *a*, then if we turn into a horizontal direction the momentum acquired by fall through *ab* [*impetum ab*] the space traversed in the same interval of time will be represented by *dc* which is twice *bi*. But a body which falls from rest at *b* along the line *bd* will during the same time-interval fall through the height of the parabola *bd*.

[290]

Hence a body falling from rest at *a*, turned into a horizontal direction with the speed *ab* will traverse a space equal to *dc*. Now if one superposes upon this motion a fall along *bd*, traversing the height *bd* while the parabola *bc* is described, then the momentum of the body at the terminal point *c* is the resultant of a uniform horizontal momentum, whose value is represented by *ab*, and of another momentum acquired by fall from *b* to the terminal point *d* or *c*; these two momenta are equal. If, therefore, we take *ab* to be the measure of one of these momenta, say, the uniform horizontal one, then *bi*, which is equal to *bd*, will represent the momentum acquired at *d* or *c*; and *ia* will represent the resultant of these two momenta, that is, the total momentum with which the projectile, travelling along the parabola, strikes at *c*.

With this in mind let us take any point on the parabola, say *e*, and determine the momentum with which the projectile passes that point. Draw the horizontal *ef* and take *bg* a mean proportional between *bd* and *bf*. Now since *ab*, or *bd*, is assumed to be

the measure of the time and of the momentum [*momentum velocitatis*] acquired by falling from rest at *b* through the distance *bd*, it follows that *bg* will measure the time

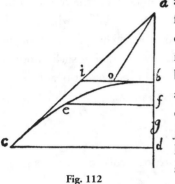

and also the momentum [*impetus*] acquired at *f* by fall from *b*. If therefore we lay off *bo*, equal to *bg*, the diagonal line joining *a* and *o* will represent the momentum at the point *e*; because the length *ab* has been assumed to represent the momentum at *b* which, after diversion into a horizontal direction, remains constant; and because *bo* measures the momentum at *f* or *e*, acquired by fall, from rest at *b*, through the height *bf*. But the square of *ao* equals the sum of the squares of *ab* and *bo*. Hence the theorem sought.

Fig. 112

Sagr. The manner in which you compound these different momenta to obtain their resultant strikes me as so novel that my mind is left in no small confusion. I do not refer to the composition of two uniform motions, even when unequal, and when one takes place along a horizontal, the other along a vertical direction; because in this case I am thoroughly convinced that the resultant is a motion whose square is equal to the sum of the squares of the two components. The confusion arises when one undertakes to compound a uniform horizontal motion with a vertical one which is naturally accelerated. I trust, therefore, we may pursue this discussion more at length.

[291]

Simp. And I need this even more than you since I am not yet as clear in my mind as I ought to be concerning those fundamental propositions upon which the others rest. Even in the case of the two uniform motions, one horizontal, the other perpendicular, I wish to understand better the manner in which you obtain the resultant from the components. Now, Salviati, you understand what we need and what we desire.

Salv. Your request is altogether reasonable and I will see whether my long consideration of these matters will enable me to make them clear to you. But you must excuse me if in the explanation I repeat many things already said by the Author.

Concerning motions and their velocities or momenta [*movimenti e lor velocità o impeti*] whether uniform or naturally accelerated, one cannot speak definitely until he has established a measure for such velocities and also for time. As for time we have the already widely adopted hours, first minutes and second minutes. So for velocities, just as for intervals of time, there is need of a common standard which shall be understood and accepted by everyone, and which shall be the same for all. As has already been stated, the Author considers the velocity of a freely falling body adapted to this purpose,

since this velocity increases according to the same law in all parts of the world; thus for instance the speed acquired by a leaden ball of a pound weight starting from rest and falling vertically through the height of, say, a spear's length is the same in all places; it is therefore excellently adapted for representing the momentum [*impeto*] acquired in the case of natural fall.

It still remains for us to discover a method of measuring momentum in the case of uniform motion in such a way that all who discuss the subject will form the same conception of its size and velocity [*grandezza e velocità*]. This will prevent one person from imagining it larger, another smaller, than it really is; so that in the composition of a given uniform motion with one which is accelerated different men may not obtain different values for the resultant. In order to determine and represent such a momentum

[292]

and particular speed [*impeto e velocità particolare*] our Author has found no better method than to use the momentum acquired by a body in naturally accelerated motion. The speed of a body which has in this manner acquired any momentum whatever will, when converted into uniform motion, retain precisely such a speed as, during a time-interval equal to that of the fall, will carry the body through a distance equal to twice that of the fall. But since this matter is one which is fundamental in our discussion it is well that we make it perfectly clear by means of some particular example.

Let us consider the speed and momentum acquired by a body falling through the height, say, of a spear [*picca*] as a standard which we may use in the measurement of other speeds and momenta as occasion demands; assume for instance that the time of such a fall is four seconds [*minuti secondi d'ora*]; now in order to measure the speed acquired from a fall through any other height, whether greater or less, one must not conclude that these speeds bear to one another the same ratio as the heights of fall; for instance, it is not true that a fall through four times a given height confers a speed four times as great as that acquired by descent through the given height; because the speed of a naturally accelerated motion does not vary in proportion to the time. As has been shown above, the ratio of the spaces is equal to the square of the ratio of the times.

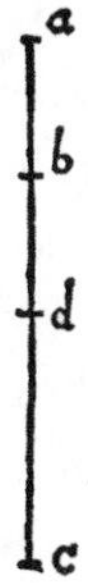

If, then, as is often done for the sake of brevity, we take the same limited straight line as the measure of speed, and of the time, and also of the space traversed during that time, it follows that the duration of fall and the speed acquired by the same body in passing over any other distance, is not represented by this second distance, but by a mean proportional between the two distances. This I can better illustrate by an example. In the vertical line *ac*, lay off the portion *ab* to represent the distance traversed by a body falling freely with

Fig. 113

603

accelerated motion: the time of fall may be represented by any limited straight line, but for the sake of brevity, we shall represent it by the same length *ab*; this length may also be employed as a measure of the momentum and speed acquired during the motion; in short, let *ab* be a measure of the various physical quantities which enter this discussion.

[293]

Having agreed arbitrarily upon *ab* as a measure of these three different quantities, namely, space, time, and momentum, our next task is to find the time required for fall through a given vertical distance *ac*, also the momentum acquired at the terminal point *c*, both of which are to be expressed in terms of the time and momentum represented by *ab*. These two required quantities are obtained by laying off *ad*, a mean proportional between *ab* and *ac*; in other words, the time of fall from *a* to *c* is represented by *ad* on the same scale on which we agreed that the time of fall from *a* to *b* should be represented by *ab*. In like manner we may say that the momentum [*impeto o grado di velocità*] acquired at *c* is related to that acquired at *b*, in the same manner that the line *ad* is related to *ab*, since the velocity varies direct as the time, a conclusion, which although employed as a postulate in Proposition III, is here amplified by the Author.

This point being clear and well-established we pass to the consideration of the momentum [*impeto*] in the case of two compound motions, one of which is compounded of a uniform horizontal and a uniform vertical motion, while the other is compounded of a uniform horizontal and a naturally accelerated vertical motion. If both components are uniform, and one at right angles to the other, we have already seen that the square of the resultant is obtained by adding the squares of the components as will be clear from the following illustration.

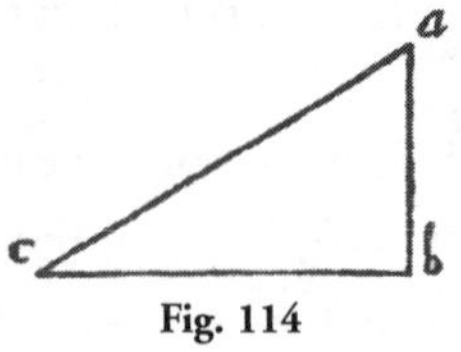

Fig. 114

Let us imagine a body to move along the vertical *ab* with a uniform momentum [*impeto*] of 3, and on reaching *b* to move toward *c* with a momentum [*velocità ed impeto*] of 4, so that during the same time-interval it will traverse 3 cubits along the vertical and 4 along the horizontal. But a particle which moves with the resultant velocity [*velocità*] will, in the same time, traverse the diagonal *ac*, whose length is not 7 cubits—the sum of *ab* (3) and *bc* (4)—but 5, which is *in potenza* equal to the sum of 3 and 4, that is, the squares of 3 and 4 when added make 25, which is the square of *ac*, and is equal to the sum of the squares of *ab* and *bc*. Hence *ac* is represented by the side—or we may say the root—of a square whose area is 25, namely 5.

As a fixed and certain rule for obtaining the momentum which results from two

[294]

uniform momenta, one vertical, the other horizontal, we have therefore the following: take the square of each, add these together, and extract the square root of the sum, which will be the momentum resulting from the two. Thus, in the above example, the body which in virtue of its vertical motion would strike the horizontal plane with a momentum [*forza*] of 3, would owing to its horizontal motion alone strike at c with a momentum of 4; but if the body strikes with a momentum which is the resultant of these two, its blow will be that of a body moving with a momentum [*velocità e forza*] of 5; and such a blow will be the same at all points of the diagonal *ac*, since its components are always the same and never increase or diminish.

Let us now pass to the consideration of a uniform horizontal motion compounded with the vertical motion of a freely falling body starting from rest. It is at once clear that the diagonal which represents the motion compounded of these two is not a straight line, but, as has been demonstrated, a semi-parabola, in which the momentum [*impeto*] is always increasing because the speed [*velocità*] of the vertical component is always increasing. Wherefore, to determine the momentum [*impeto*] at any given point in the parabolic diagonal, it is necessary first to fix upon the uniform horizontal momentum [*impeto*] and then, treating the body as one falling freely, to find the vertical momentum at the given point; this latter can be determined only by taking into account the duration of fall, a consideration which does not enter into the composition of two uniform motions where the velocities and momenta are always the same; but here where one of the component motions has an initial value of zero and increases its speed [*velocità*] in direct proportion to the time, it follows that the time must

determine the speed [*velocità*] at the assigned point. It only remains to obtain the momentum resulting from these two components (as in the case of uniform motions) by placing the square of the resultant equal to the sum of the squares of the two components. But here again it is better to illustrate by means of an example.

On the vertical *ac* lay off any portion *ab* which we shall employ as a measure of the space traversed by a body falling freely along the perpendicular, likewise as a measure of the time and also of the speed [*grado di velocità*]

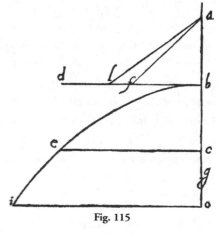

Fig. 115

or, we may say, of the momenta [*impeti*]. It is at once clear that if the momentum of a body at *b*, after having fallen

from rest at *a*, be diverted along the horizontal direction *bd*, with uniform motion, its speed will be such that, during the time-interval *ab*, it will traverse a distance which is represented by the line *bd* and which is twice as great as *ab*. Now choose a point *c*, such that *bc* shall be equal to *ab*, and through *c* draw the line *ce* equal and parallel to *bd*; through the points *b* and *e* draw the parabola *bei*. And since, during the time-interval *ab*, the horizontal distance *bd* or *ce*, double the length *ab*, is traversed with the momentum *ab*, and since during an equal time-interval the vertical distance *bc* is traversed, the body acquiring at *c* a momentum represented by the same horizontal, *bd*, it follows that during the time *ab* the body will pass from *b* to *e* along the parabola *be*, and will reach *e* with a momentum compounded of two momenta each equal to *ab*. And since one of these is horizontal and the other vertical, the square of the resultant momentum is equal to the sum of the squares of these two components, i. e., equal to twice either one of them.

Therefore, if we lay off the distance *bf*, equal to *ba*, and draw the diagonal *af*, it follows that the momentum [*impeto e percossa*] at *e* will exceed that of a body at *b* after having fallen from *a*, or what is the same thing, will exceed the horizontal momentum [*percossa dell'impeto*] along *bd*, in the ratio of *af* to *ab*.

Suppose now we choose for the height of fall a distance *bo* which is not equal to but greater than *ab*, and suppose that *bg* represents a mean proportional between *ba* and *bo*; then, still retaining *ba* as a measure of the distance fallen through, from rest at *a*, to *b*, also as a measure of the time and of the momentum which the falling body acquires at *b*, it follows that *bg* will be the measure of the time and also of the momentum which the body acquires in falling from *b* to *o*. Likewise just as the momentum *ab* during the time *ab* carried the body a distance along the horizontal equal to twice *ab*, so now, during the time-interval *bg*, the body will be carried in a horizontal direction through a distance which is greater in the ratio of *bg* to *ba*. Lay off *lb* equal to *bg* and draw the diagonal *al*, from which we have a quantity compounded of two velocities [*impeti*] one horizontal, the other vertical; these determine the parabola. The horizontal and uniform velocity is that acquired at *b* in falling from *a*; the other is that acquired at *o*, or, we may say, at *i*, by a body falling through the distance *bo*, during a time measured by the line *bg*, which line *bg* also represents the momentum of the body.

296

And in like manner we may, by taking a mean proportional between the two heights, determine the momentum [*impeto*] at the extreme end of the parabola where the height is less than the sublimity *ab*; this mean proportional is to be drawn along the

horizontal in place of *bf,* and also another diagonal in place of *af,* which diagonal will represent the momentum at the extreme end of the parabola.

To what has hitherto been said concerning the momenta, blows or shocks of projectiles, we must add another very important consideration; to determine the force and energy of the shock [*forza ed energia della percossa*] it is not sufficient to consider only the speed of the projectiles, but we must also take into account the nature and condition of the target which, in no small degree, determines the efficiency of the blow. First of all it is well known that the target suffers violence from the speed [*velocità*] of the projectile in proportion as it partly or entirely stops the motion; because if the blow falls upon an object which yields to the impulse [*velocità del percuziente*] without resistance such a blow will be of no effect; likewise when one attacks his enemy with a spear and overtakes him at an instant when he is fleeing with equal speed there will be no blow but merely a harmless touch. But if the shock falls upon an object which yields only in part then the blow will not have its full effect, but the damage will be in proportion to the excess of the speed of the projectile over that of the receding body; thus, for example, if the shot reaches the target with a speed of 10 while the latter recedes with a speed of 4, the momentum and shock [*impeto e percossa*] will be represented by 6. Finally the blow will be a maximum, in so far as the projectile is concerned, when the target does not recede at all but if possible completely resists and stops the motion of the projectile. I have said *in so far as the projectile is concerned* because if the target should approach the projectile the shock of collision [*colpo e l'incontro*] would be greater in proportion as the sum of the two speeds is greater than that of the projectile alone.

Moreover it is to be observed that the amount of yielding in the target depends not only upon the quality of the material, as regards hardness, whether it be of iron, lead, wool, etc., but also upon its position. If the position is such that the shot strikes

[297]

it at right angles, the momentum imparted by the blow [*impeto del colpo*] will be a maximum; but if the motion be oblique, that is to say slanting, the blow will be weaker; and more and more so in proportion to the obliquity; for, no matter how hard the material of the target thus situated, the entire momentum [*impeto e moto*] of the shot will not be spent and stopped; the projectile will slide by and will, to some extent, continue its motion along the surface of the opposing body.

All that has been said above concerning the amount of momentum in the projectile at the extremity of the parabola must be understood to refer to a blow received on a line at right angles to this parabola or along the tangent to the parabola at the given point; for, even though the motion has two components, one horizontal, the other

vertical, neither will the momentum along the horizontal nor that upon a plane perpendicular to the horizontal be a maximum, since each of these will be received obliquely.

Sagr. Your having mentioned these blows and shocks recalls to my mind a problem, or rather a question, in mechanics of which no author has given a solution or said anything which diminishes my astonishment or even partly relieves my mind.

My difficulty and surprise consist in not being able to see whence and upon what principle is derived the energy and immense force [*energia e forza immensa*] which makes its appearance in a blow; for instance we see the simple blow of a hammer, weighing not more than 8 or 10 lbs., overcoming resistances which, without a blow, would not yield to the weight of a body producing impetus by pressure alone, even though that body weighed many hundreds of pounds. I would. like to discover a method of measuring the force [*forza*] of such a percussion. I can hardly think it infinite, but incline rather to the view that it has its limit and can be counterbalanced and measured by other forces, such as weights, or by levers or screws or other mechanical instruments which are used to multiply forces in a manner which I satisfactorily understand.

Salv. You are not alone in your surprise at this effect or in obscurity as to the cause of this remarkable property. I studied this matter myself for a while in vain; but my confusion merely increased until finally meeting our Academician I received from him

[298]

great consolation. First he told me that he also had for a long time been groping in the dark; but later he said that, after having spent some thousands of hours in speculating and contemplating thereon, he had arrived at some notions which are far removed from our earlier ideas and which are remarkable for their novelty. And since now I know that you would gladly hear what these novel ideas are I shall not wait for you to ask but promise that, as soon as our discussion of projectiles is completed, I will explain all these fantasies, or if you please, vagaries, as far as I can recall them from the words of our Academician. In the meantime we proceed with the propositions of the author.

Proposition V, Problem

Having given a parabola, find the point, in its axis extended upwards, from which a particle must fall in order to describe this same parabola.

Let *ab* be the given parabola, *hb* its amplitude, and *he* its axis extended. The problem is to find the point *e* from which a body must fall in order that, after the momentum

which it acquires at *a* has been diverted into a horizontal direction, it will describe the parabola *ab*. Draw the horizontal *ag*, parallel to *bh*, and having laid off *af* equal to *ah*, draw the straight line *bf* which will be a tangent to the parabola at *b*, and will intersect the horizontal *ag* at *g*: choose *e* such that *ag* will be a mean proportional between *af* and *ae*. Now I say that *e* is the point above sought. That is, if a body falls from rest at this point *e*, and if the momentum acquired at the point *a* be diverted into a horizontal direction, and compounded with the momentum acquired at *h* in falling from rest at *a*, then the body will describe the parabola *ab*. For if we understand *ea* to be the

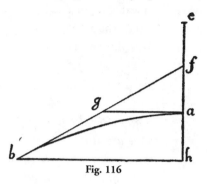

Fig. 116

measure of the time of fall from *e* to *a*, and also of the momentum acquired at *a*, then *ag* (which is a mean proportional between *ea* and *af*) will represent the time and momentum of fall from *f* to *a* or, what is the same thing, from *a* to *h*; and since a body falling from *e*, during the time *ea*, will, owing to the momentum acquired at *a*, traverse at uniform speed a horizontal distance which is twice *ea*, it follows that, the body will. if impelled by the same momentum, during the time-interval *ag* traverse a distance equal to twice *ag* which is the half of *bh*. This is true because, in the case of uniform motion, the spaces traversed vary directly as the times. And likewise if the

[299]

motion be vertical and start from rest, the body will describe the distance *ah* in the time *ag*. Hence the amplitude *bh* and the altitude *ah* are traversed by a body in the same time. Therefore the parabola *ab* will be described by a body falling from the sublimity of *e*.

Q.E.F.

COROLLARY

Hence it follows that half the base, or amplitude, of the semi-parabola (which is one-quarter of the entire amplitude) is a mean proportional between its altitude and the sublimity from which a falling body will describe this same parabola.

PROPOSITION VI, PROBLEM

Given the sublimity and the altitude of a parabola, to find its amplitude.

Let the line *ac*, in which lie the given altitude *cb* and sublimity *ab*, be perpendicular to the horizontal line *cd*. The problem is to find the amplitude, along the horizontal

cd, of the semi-parabola which is described with the sublimity *ba* and altitude *bc*. Lay off *cd* equal to twice the mean proportional between *cb* and *ba*. Then *cd* will be the amplitude sought, as is evident from the preceding proposition.

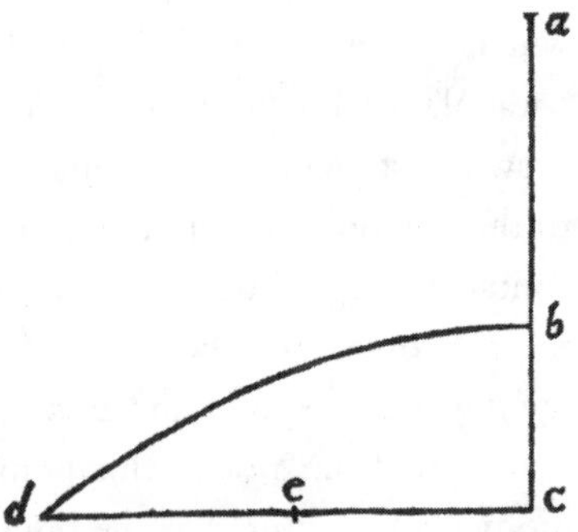

THEOREM. PROPOSITION VII

If projectiles describe semi-parabolas of the same amplitude, the momentum required to describe that one whose amplitude is double its attitude is less than that required for any other.

Fig. 117

Let *bd* be a semi-parabola whose amplitude *cd* is double its altitude *cb*; on its axis extended upwards lay off *ba* equal to its altitude *bc*. Draw the line *ad* which will be a tangent to the parabola at *d* and will cut the horizontal line *be* at the point *e*, making *be* equal to *bc* and also to *ba*. It is evident that this parabola will be described by a projectile whose uniform horizontal momentum is that which it would acquire at *b* in falling from rest at *a* and whose naturally accelerated vertical momentum is that of the body falling to *c*, from rest at *b*. From this it follows that the momentum at the terminal point *d*, compounded of these two, is represented by the diagonal *ae*, whose square is equal to the sum of the squares of the two components. Now let *gd* be any other parabola whatever having the same amplitude *cd*, but whose altitude *cg* is either greater or less than the altitude *bc*. Let *hd* be the tangent cutting the horizontal through

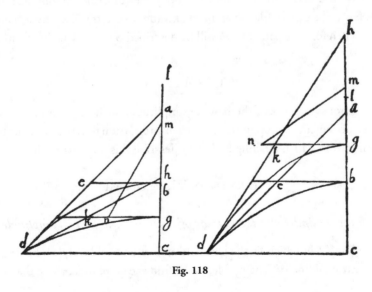

Fig. 118

[300]

g at *k*. Select a point *l* such that *hg:gk=gk:gl*. Then from a preceding proposition [V], it follows that *gl* will be the height from which a body must fall in order to describe the parabola *gd*.

Let *gm* be a mean proportional between *ab* and *gl*, then *gm* will [Prop. IV] represent the time and momentum acquired at *g* by a fall from *l*, for *ab* has been assumed as a measure of both time and momentum. Again let *gn* be a mean proportional between *bc* and *cg*; it will then represent the time and momentum which the body acquires at *c* in falling from *g*. If now we join *m* and *n*, this line *mn* will represent the momentum at *d* of the projectile traversing the parabola *dg*, which momentum is, I say, greater than that of the projectile travelling along the parabola *bd* whose measure was given by *ae*. For since *gn* has been taken as a mean proportional between *bc* and *gc*, and since *bc* is equal to *be* and also to *kg* (each of them being the half of *dc*) it follows that *cg:gn=gn:gk*, and as *cg* or (*hg*) is to *gk* so is ng^2 to gk^2: but by construction *hg:gk=gk:gl*. Hence $ng^2:gk^2=gk:gl$. But $gk:gl=gk^2:gm^2$, since *gm* is a mean proportional between *kg* and *gl*. Therefore the three squares *ng*, *kg*, *mg* form a continued proportion, $gn^2:gk^2=gk^2:gm^2$. And the sum of the two extremes which is equal to the square of *mn* is greater than twice the square of *gk*; but the square of *ae* is double the square of *gk*. Hence the square of *mn* is greater than the square of *ae* and the length *mn* is greater than the length *ae*.

Q.E.F.

[301]

COROLLARY

Conversely it is evident that less momentum will be required to send a projectile from the terminal point *d* along the parabola *bd* than along any other parabola having an elevation greater or less than that of the parabola *bd*, for which the tangent at *d* makes an angle of 45° with the horizontal. From which it follows that if projectiles are fired from the terminal point *d*, all having the same speed, but each having a different elevation, the maximum range, i. e., amplitude of the semi-parabola or of the entire parabola, will be obtained when the elevation is 45°: the other shots, fired at angles greater or less will have a shorter range.

Sagr. The force of rigid demonstrations such as occur only in mathematics fills me with wonder and delight. From accounts given by gunners, I was already aware of the fact that in the use of cannon and mortars, the maximum range, that is the one in which the shot goes farthest, is obtained when the elevation is 45° or, as they say, at the sixth point of the quadrant; but to understand why this happens far outweighs the mere information obtained by the testimony of others or even by repeated experiment.

Salv. What you say is very true. The knowledge of a single fact acquired through a discovery of its causes prepares the mind to understand and ascertain other facts without need of recourse to experiment, precisely as in the present case, where by argumentation alone the Author proves with certainty that the maximum range occurs when the elevation is 45°. He thus demonstrates what has perhaps never been observed in experience, namely, that of other shots those which exceed or fall short of 45° by equal amounts have equal ranges; so that if the balls have been fired one at an elevation of 7 points, the other at 5, they will strike the level at the same distance: the same is true if the shots are fired at 8 and at 4 points, at 9 and at 3, etc. Now let us hear the demonstration of this.

[302]

THEOREM. PROPOSITION VIII

The amplitudes of two parabolas described by projectiles fired with the same speed, but at angles of elevation which exceed and fall short of 45° by equal amounts, are equal to each other.

In the triangle *mcb* let the horizontal side *bc* and the vertical *cm*, which form a right angle at *c*, be equal to each other; then the angle *mbc* will be a semi-right angle; let the line *cm* be prolonged to *d*, such a point that the two angles at *b*, namely *mbe* and *mbd*, one above and the other below the diagonal *mb*, shall be equal. It is now to be proved that in the case of two parabolas described by two projectiles fired from *b* with the same speed, one at the angle of *ebc*, the other at the angle of *dbc*, their amplitudes will be equal. Now since the external angle *bmc* is equal to the sum of the internal angles *mbd* and *dbm* we may also equate to them the angle *mbc*, but if we replace the angle *dbm* by *mbe*, then this same angle *mbc* is equal to the two *mbe* and *bdc*: and if we subtract from each side of this equation the angle *mbe*, we have the remainder *bdc* equal to the remainder *ebc*. Hence the two triangles *dcb* and *bce* are similar. Bisect the straight lines *dc* and *ec* in the points *h* and *f*: and draw the lines *hi* and *fg* parallel to the horizontal *cb*, and choose *l* such that *dh:hi=ih:hl*. Then the triangle *ihl* will be similar to *ihd*, and also to the triangle *egf*; and since *ih* and *gf* are equal, each being half of *bc*, it follows that *hl* is equal to *fe* and also to *fc*; and if we add to each of these the common part *fh*, it will be seen that *ch* is equal to *fl*.

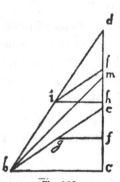

Fig. 119

Let us now imagine a parabola described through the points *h* and *b* whose altitude is *hc* and sublimity *hl*. Its amplitude will be *cb* which is double the length *hi* since

hi is a mean proportional between *dh* (or *ch*) and *hl.* The line *db* is tangent to the parabola at *b*, since *ch* is equal to *hd*. If again we imagine a parabola described through the points *f* and *b*, with a sublimity *fl* and altitude *fc*, of which the mean proportional is *fg*, or one-half of *cb*, then, as before, will *cb* be the amplitude and the line *eb* a tangent at *b*; for *ef* and *fc* are equal.

[303]

But the two angles *dbc* and *ebc*, the angles of elevation, differ by equal amounts from a 45° angle. Hence follows the proposition.

THEOREM. PROPOSITION IX

The amplitudes of two parabolas are equal when their altitudes and sublimities are inversely proportional.

Let the altitude *gf* of the parabola *fh* bear to the altitude *cb* of the parabola *bd* the same ratio which the sublimity *ba* bears to the sublimity *fe*; then I say the amplitude *hg* is equal to the amplitude *dc*. For since the first of these quantities, *gf*, bears to the second *cb* the same ratio which the third, *ba*, bears to the fourth *fe*, it follows that the area of the rectangle *gf.fe* is equal to that of the rectangle *cb.ba*; therefore squares which are equal to these rectangles are equal to each other. But [by Proposition VI] the square of half of *gh* is equal to the rectangle *gf.fe*; and the square of half of

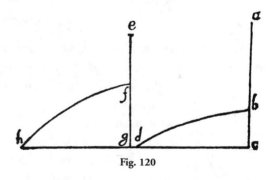

Fig. 120

cd is equal to the rectangle *cb.ba*. Therefore these squares and their sides and the doubles of their sides are equal. But these last are the amplitudes *gh* and *cd*. Hence follows the proposition.

LEMMA FOR THE FOLLOWING PROPOSITION

If a straight line be cut at any point whatever and mean proportionals between this line and each of its parts be taken, the sum of the

squares of these mean proportionals is equal to the square of the entire line.

Let the line *ab* be cut at *c*. Then I say that the square of the mean proportional between *ab* and *ac* plus the square of the mean proportional between *ab* and *cb* is equal to the square of the whole line *ab*. This is evident as soon as we describe a semicircle upon the entire line *ab*, erect a perpendicular *cd* at *c*, and draw *da* and *db*. For *da* is a mean proportional between *ab* and *ac* while *db* is a mean proportional between *ab* and *bc*: and since the angle *adb*, inscribed in a semicircle, is

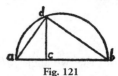

Fig. 121

a right angle the sum of the squares of the lines *da* and *db* is equal to the square of the entire line *ab*. Hence follows the proposition.

[304]

THEOREM. PROPOSITION X

The momentum [impetus seu momentum] acquired by a particle at the terminal point of any semi-parabola is equal to that which it would acquire in falling through a vertical distance equal to the sum of the sum of the sublimity and the altitude of the semi-parabola.[39]

Let *ab* be a semi-parabola having a sublimity *da* and an altitude *ac*, the sum of which is the perpendicular *dc*. Now I say the momentum of the particle at *b* is the same as that which it would acquire in falling freely from *d* to *c*. Let us take the length of *dc* itself as a measure of time and momentum, and lay off *cf* equal to the mean proportional between *cd* and *da*; also lay off *ce* a mean proportional between *cd* and *ca*. Now *cf* is the measure of the time and of the momentum acquired by fall, from rest at *d*, through the distance *da*; while *ce* is the time and momentum of fall, from rest at *a*, through the distance *ca*; also the diagonal *ef* will represent a momentum which is the resultant of these two, and is therefore the momentum at the terminal point of the parabola, *b*.

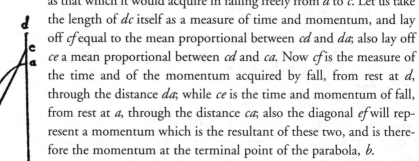

Fig. 122

And since *dc* has been cut at some point *a* and since *cf* and *ce* are mean proportionals between the whole of *cd* and its parts, *da* and *ac*, it follows, from the preceding lemma, that the sum of the squares of these mean proportionals is equal to the square of the whole: but the square of *ef* is also equal to the sum of these same squares; whence it follows that the line *ef* is equal to *dc*.

---

39. In modern mechanics this well-known theorem assumes the following form: *The speed of a projectile at any point is that produced by a fall from the directrix. [Trans.]*

Accordingly the momentum acquired at *c* by a particle in falling from *d* is the same as that acquired at *b* by a particle traversing the parabola *ab*.   Q.E.D.

COROLLARY

Hence it follows that, in the case of all parabolas where the sum of the sublimity and altitude is a constant, the momentum at the terminal point is a constant.

[305]

PROBLEM. PROPOSITION XI

Given the amplitude and the speed [impetus] at the terminal point of a semi-parabola, to find its altitude.

Let the given speed be represented by the vertical line *ab*, and the amplitude by the horizontal line *bc*; it is required to find the sublimity of the semi-parabola whose terminal speed is *ab* and amplitude *bc*. From what precedes [Cor. Prop. V] it is clear

[306]

that half the amplitude *bc* is a mean proportional between the altitude and sublimity of the parabola of which the terminal speed is equal, in accordance with the preceding proposition, to the speed acquired by a body in falling from rest at *a* through the distance *ab*. Therefore the line *ba* must be cut at a point such that the rectangle formed by its two parts will be equal to the square of half *bc*, namely *bd*. Necessarily, therefore, *bd* must not exceed the half of *ba*; for all the rectangles formed by parts of a straight line the one of greatest area is obtained when the line is divided into two equal parts. Let *e* be the middle point of the line *ab*; and now if *bd* be equal to *be* the problem is solved; for *be* will be the altitude and *ea* the sublimity of the parabola. (Incidentally we may observe a consequence already demonstrated, namely: of all parabolas described with any given terminal speed that for which the elevation is 45° will have the maximum amplitude.)

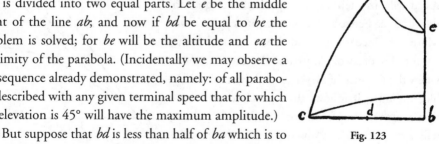

Fig. 123

But suppose that *bd* is less than half of *ba* which is to be divided in such a way that the rectangle upon its parts may be equal to the square of *bd*. Upon *ea* as diameter describe a semicircle *efa*, in which draw the chord *af*, equal to y: join *fe* and lay off the distance *eg* equal to *fe*.

Then the rectangle *bg.ga* plus the square of *eg* will be equal to the square of *ea*, and hence also to the sum of the squares of *af* and *fe*. If now we subtract the equal squares of *fe* and *ge* there remains the rectangle *bg.ga* equal to the square of *af*, that is, of *bd*, a line which is a mean proportional between *bg* and *ga*; from which it is evident that the semi-parabola whose amplitude is *bc* and whose terminal speed [*impetus*] is represented by *ba* has an altitude *bg* and a sublimity *ga*.

If however we lay off *bi* equal to *ga*, then *bi* will be the altitude of the semi-parabola *ic*, and *ia* will be its sublimity. From the preceding demonstration we are able to solve the following problem.

PROBLEM. PROPOSITION XII

To compute and tabulate the amplitudes of all semi-parabolas which are described by projectiles fired with the same initial speed [impetus].

From the foregoing it follows that, whenever the sum of the altitude and sublimity is a constant vertical height for any set of parabolas, these parabolas are described by projectiles having the same initial speed; all vertical heights thus obtained are therefore included between two parallel horizontal lines. Let *cb* represent a horizontal line and *ab* a vertical line of equal length; draw the diagonal *ac*; the angle *acb* will be one of 45°; let *d* be the middle point of the vertical line *ab*. Then the semi-parabola *dc* is the one which is determined by the sublimity *ad* and the altitude *db*, while its terminal speed at *c* is that which would be acquired at *b* by a particle falling from rest at *a*. If now *ag* be drawn parallel to *bc*, the sum of the altitude and sublimity for any other semi-parabola having the same terminal speed will, in the manner explained, be equal to the distance between the parallel lines *ag* and *bc*. Moreover, since it has already been shown that the amplitudes of two semi-parabolas are the same when their angles of elevation differ from 45° by like amounts, it follows that the same computation which is employed for the larger elevation will serve also for the smaller. Let us also assume 10000 as the greatest amplitude for a parabola

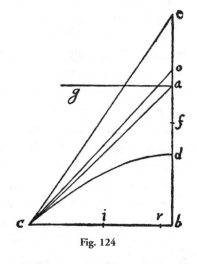

Fig. 124

whose angle of elevation is 45°; this then will be the length of the line *ba* and the amplitude of the semi-parabola *bc*. This number, 10000, is selected because in these

calculations we employ a table of tangents in which this is the value of the tangent of 45°. And now, coming down to business, draw the straight line *ce* making an acute angle *ecb* greater than *acb*: the problem now is to draw the semi-parabola to which the line *ec* is a tangent and for which the sum of the sublimity and the altitude is the distance *ba*. Take the length of the tangent[40] *be* from the table of tangents, using the angle *bce* as an argument: let *f* be the middle point of *be*; next find a third proportional to *bf* and *bi* (the half of *bc*), which is of necessity greater than *fa*.[41] Call this *fo*. We have now discovered that, for the parabola inscribed in the triangle *ecb* having the tangent *ce* and the amplitude *cb*, the altitude is *bf* and the sublimity *fo*. But the total length of *bo* exceeds the distance

[307]

between the parallels *ag* and *cb*, while our problem was to keep it equal to this distance: for both the parabola sought and the parabola *dc* are described by projectiles fired from *c* with the same speed. Now since an infinite number of greater and smaller parabolas, similar to each other, may be described within the angle *bce* we must find another parabola which like *cd* has for the sum of its altitude and sublimity the height *ba*, equal to *bc*.

Therefore lay off *cr* so that, *ob*:*ba*=*bc*:*cr*; then *cr* will be the amplitude of a semi-parabola for which *bce* is the angle of elevation and for which the sum of the altitude and sublimity is the distance between the parallels *ga* and *cb*, as desired. The process is therefore as follows: One draws the tangent of the given angle *bce*; takes half of this tangent, and adds to it the quantity, *fo*, which is a third proportional to the half of this tangent and the half of *bc*; the desired amplitude *cr* is then found from the following proportion *ob*:*ba*:*bc*:*cr*. For example let the angle *ech* be one of 50°; its tangent is 11918, half of which, namely *bf*, is 5959; half of *bc* is 5000; the third proportional of these halves is 4195, which added to *bf* gives the value 10154 for *bo*. Further, as *ob* is to *ab*, that is, as 10154 is to 10000, so is *bc*, or 10000 (each being the tangent of 45°) to *cr*, which is the amplitude sought and which has the value 9848, the maximum amplitude being *bc*, or 10000. The amplitudes of the entire parabolas are double these, namely, 19696 and 20000. This is also the amplitude of a parabola whose angle of elevation is 40°, since it deviates by an equal amount from one of 45°.

Sagr. In order to thoroughly understand this demonstration I need to be shown how the third proportional of *bf* and *bi* is, as the Author indicates, necessarily greater than *fa*.

40. The reader will observe that the word "tangent" is here used in a sense somewhat different from that of the preceding sentence. The "tangent *ec*" is a line which touches the parabola at *c*, but the "tangent *eb*" is the side of the right-angled triangle which lies opposite the angle *ecb*, a line whose length is proportional to the numerical value of the tangent of this angle. [*Trans.*]
41. This fact is demonstrated in the third paragraph below. [*Trans.*]

[308]

Salv. This result can, I think, be obtained as follows. The square of the mean proportional between two lines is equal to the rectangle formed by these two lines. Therefore the square of *bi* (or of *bd* which is equal to *bi*) must be equal to the rectangle formed by *fb* and the desired third proportional. This third proportional is necessarily greater than *fa* because the rectangle formed by *bf* and *fa* is less than the square of *bd* by an amount equal to the square of *df*, as shown in Euclid, II. 1. Besides it is to be observed that the point *f*, which is the middle point of the tangent *eb*, falls in general above *a* and only once at *a*; in which cases it is self-evident that the third proportional to the half of the tangent and to the sublimity *bi* lies wholly above *a*. But the Author has taken a case where it is not evident that the third proportional is always greater than *fa*, so that when laid off above the point *f* it extends beyond the parallel *ag*.

Now let us proceed. It will be worth while, by the use of this table, to compute another giving the altitudes of these semi-parabolas described by projectiles having the same initial speed. The construction is as follows:

[309]

AMPLITUDES OF SEMI-PARABOLAS DESCRIBED WITH THE SAME INITIAL SPEED.		AMPLITUDES OF SEMI-PARABOLAS DESCRIBED WITH THE SAME INITIAL SPEED.	
ANGLE OF ELEVATION	ANGLE OF ELEVATION	ANGLE OF ELEVATION	ANGLE OF ELEVATION
45° 10000		1° 3	46° 5173
46 9994	44°	2 13	47 5346
47 9976	43	3 28	48 5523
48 9945	42	4 50	49 5698
49 9902	41	5 76	50 5868
50 9848	40	6 108	51 6038
51 9782	39	7 150	52 6207
52 9704	38	8 194	53 6379
53 9612	37	9 245	54 6546
54 9511	36	10 302	55 6710
55 9396	35	11 365	56 6873
56 9272	34	12 432	57 7033
57 9136	33	13 506	58 7190
58 8989	32	14 585	59 7348
59 8829	31	15 670	60 7502
60 8659	30	16 760	61 7049
61 8481	29	17 855	62 7796
62 8290	28	18 955	63 7939
63 8090	27	19 1060	64 8078
64 7880	26	20 1170	65 8214

65	7660	25		21	1285	66	8346
66	7431	24		22	1402	67	8474
67	7191	23		23	1527	68	8597
68	6944	22		24	1685	69	8715
69	6692	21		25	1786	70	8830

AMPLITUDES OF SEMI-PARABOLAS DESCRIBED WITH THE SAME INITIAL SPEED.				ALTITUDES OF SEMI-PARABOLAS DESCRIBED WITH THE SAME INITIAL SPEED.			
ANGLE OF ELEVATION		ANGLE OF ELEVATION		ANGLE OF ELEVATION		ANGLE OF ELEVATION	
70°	6428	20		26°	1922	71°	8940
71	6157	19		27	2061	72	9045
72	5878	18		28	2204	73	9144
73	5592	17		29	2351	74	9240
74	5300	16		30	2499	75	9330
75	5000	15		31	2653	76	9415
76	4694	14		32	2810	77	9493
77	4383	13		33	2967	78	9567
78	4067	12		34	3128	79	9636
79	3746	11		35	3289	80	9698
80	3420	10		36	3456	81	9755
81	3090	9		37	3621	82	9806
82	2756	8		38	3793	83	9851
83	2419	7		39	3962	84	9890
84	2079	6		40	4132	85	9924
85	1736	5		41	4302	86	9951
86	1391	4		42	4477	87	9972
87	1044	3		43	4654	88	9987
88	698	2		44	4827	89	9998
89	349	1		45	5000	90	10000

[310]

PROBLEM. PROPOSITION XIII

From the amplitudes of semi-parabolas given in the preceding table to find the altitudes of each of the parabolas described with the same initial speed.

Let *bc* denote the given amplitude; and let *ob*, the sum of the altitude and sublimity, be the measure of the initial speed which is understood to remain constant. Next we must find and determine the altitude, which we shall accomplish by so dividing *ob* that the rectangle contained by its parts shall be equal to the square of half the amplitude, *bc*. Let *f* denote this point of division and *d* and *i* be the middle points of *ob* and *bc* respectively. The square of *ib* is equal to the rectangle *bf.fo*; but the square

of *do* is equal to the sum of the rectangle *bf.fo* and the square of *fd*. If, therefore, from the square of *do* we subtract the square of *bi* which is equal to the rectangle *bf.fo*, there will remain the square of *fd*. The altitude in question, *bf*, is now obtained by adding to this length, *fd*, the line *bd*. The process is then as follows: From the square of half of *bo* which is known, subtract the square of *bi* which as also known; take the square root of the remainder and add to it the known length *db*; then you have the required altitude, *bf.*

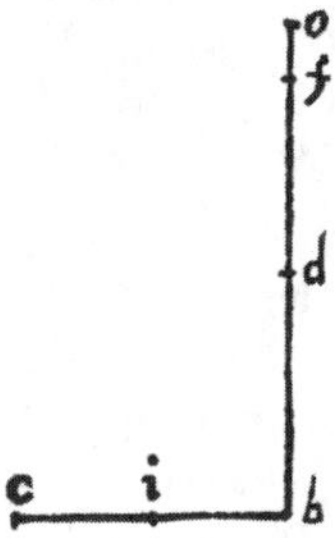

Fig. 125

Example. To find the altitude of a semi-parabola described with an angle of elevation of 55°. From the preceding table the amplitude is seen to be 9396, of which the half is 4698, and the square 22071204. When this is subtracted from the square of the half of *bo*, which is always 25,000,000, the remainder is 2928796, of which the square root is approximately 1710. Adding this to the half of *bo*, namely 5000, we have 6710 for the altitude of *bf.*

[311]

It will be worth while to add a third table giving the altitudes and sublimities for parabolas in which the amplitude is a constant.

Sagr. I shall be very glad to see this; for from it I shall learn the difference of speed and force [*degl' impeti e delle forze*] required to fire projectiles over the same range with what we call mortar shots. This difference will, I believe, vary greatly with the elevation so that if, for example, one wished to employ an elevation of 3° or 4°, or 87° or 88° and yet give the ball the same range which it had with an elevation of 45° (where we have shown the initial speed to be a minimum) the excess of force required will, I think, be very great.

Salv. You are quite right, sir; and you will find that in order to perform this operation completely, at all angles of elevation, you will have to make great strides toward an infinite speed. We pass now to the consideration of the table.

[312]

TABLE GIVING THE ALTITUDES AND SUBLIMITIES OF PARABOLAS OF CONSTANT AMPLITUDE, NAMELY 10000, COMPUTED FOR EACH DEGREE OF ELEVATION.

ANGLE OF ELEVATION	ALTITUDE	SUBLIMITY	ANGLE OF ELEVATION	ALTITUDE	SUBLIMITY
1°	87	286533	46°	5177	4828
2	175	142450	47	5363	4662
3	262	95802	48	5553	4502
4	349	71531	49	5752	4345
5	437	57142	50	5959	4196

6	525	47573	51	6174	4048
7	614	40716	52	6399	3906
8	702	35587	53	6635	3765
9	792	31565	54	6882	3632
10	881	28367	55	7141	3500
11	972	25720	56	7413	3372
12	1063	23518	57	7699	3247
13	1154	21701	58	8002	3123
14	1246	20056	59	8332	3004
15	1339	18663	60	8600	2887
16	1434	17405	61	9020	2771
17	1529	16355	62	9403	2658
18	1624	15389	63	9813	2547
19	1722	14522	64	10251	2438
20	1820	13736	65	10722	2331
21	1919	13024	66	11230	2226
22	2020	12376	67	11779	2122
23	2123	11778	68	12375	2020
24	2226	11230	69	13025	1919
25	2332	10722	70	13237	1819
26	2439	10253	71	14521	1721
27	2547	9814	72	15388	1624
28	2658	9404	73	16354	1528
29	2772	9020	74	17437	1433
30	2887	8659	75	18660	1339
31	3008	8336	76	20054	1246
32	3124	8001	77	21657	1154
33	3247	7699	78	23523	1062
34	3373	7413	79	25723	972
35	3501	7141	80	28356	881
36	3631	6882	81	31569	792
37	3768	6635	82	35577	702
38	3906	6395	83	40222	613
39	4049	6174	84	47572	525
40	4196	5959	85	57150	437
41	4346	5752	86	71503	349
42	4502	5553	87	95405	262
43	4662	5362	88	143181	174
44	4828	5177	89	286499	87
45	5000	5000	90	infinita	

[313]

PROPOSITION XIV

To find for each degree of elevation the altitudes and sublimities of parabolas of constant amplitude.

The problem is easily solved. For if we assume a constant amplitude of 10000, then half the tangent at any angle of elevation will be the altitude. Thus, to illustrate, a parabola having an angle of elevation of 30° and an amplitude of 10000, will have an altitude of 2887, which is approximately one-half the tangent. And now the altitude having been found, the sublimity is derived as follows. Since it has been proved that half the amplitude of a semi-parabola is the mean proportional between the altitude and sublimity, and since the altitude has already been found, and since the semi-amplitude is a constant, namely 5000, it follows that if we divide the square of the semi-amplitude by the altitude we shall obtain the sublimity sought. Thus in our example the altitude was found to be 2887: the square of 5000 is 25,000,000, which divided by 2887 gives the approximate value of the sublimity, namely 8659.

Salv. Here we see, first of all, how very true is the statement made above, that, for different angles of elevation, the greater the deviation from the mean, whether above or below, the greater the initial speed [*impeto e violenza*] required to carry the projectile over the same range. For since the speed is the resultant of two motions, namely, one horizontal and uniform, the other vertical and naturally accelerated; and since the sum of the altitude and sublimity represents this speed, it is seen from the preceding table that this sum is a minimum for an elevation of 45° where the altitude and sublimity are equal, namely, each 5000; and their sum 10000. But if we choose a greater elevation, say 50°, we shall find the altitude 5959, and the sublimity 4196, giving a sum of 10155; in like manner we shall find that this is precisely the value of the speed at 40° elevation, both angles deviating equally from the mean.

Secondly it is to be noted that, while equal speeds are required for each of two elevations that are equidistant from the mean, there is this curious alternation, namely, that the altitude and sublimity at the greater elevation correspond inversely to the sublimity and altitude at the lower elevation. Thus in the preceding example an elevation

[314]

of 50° gives an altitude of 5959 and a sublimity of 4196; while an elevation of 40° corresponds to an altitude of 4196 and a sublimity of 5959. And this holds true in general; but it is to be remembered that, in order to escape tedious calculations, no account has been taken of fractions which are of little moment in comparison with such large numbers.

Sagr. I note also in regard to the two components of the initial speed [*impeto*] that the higher the shot the less is the horizontal and the greater the vertical component; on the other band, at lower elevations where the shot reaches only a small height the horizontal component of the initial speed must be great. In the case of a projectile fired at an elevation of 90°, I quite understand that all the force [*forza*] in the world would

not be sufficient to make it deviate a single finger's breadth from the perpendicular and that it would necessarily fall back into its initial position; but in the case of zero elevation, when the shot is fired horizontally, I am not so certain that some force, less than infinite, would not carry the projectile some distance; thus not even a cannon can fire a shot in a perfectly horizontal direction, or as we say, point blank, that is, with no elevation at all. Here I admit there is some room for doubt. The fact I do not deny outright, because of another phenomenon apparently no less remarkable, but yet one for which I have conclusive evidence. This phenomenon is the impossibility of stretching a rope in such a way that it shall be at once straight and parallel to the horizon; the fact is that the cord always sags and bends and that no force is sufficient to stretch it perfectly straight.

Salv. In this case of the rope then, Sagredo, you cease to wonder at the phenomenon because you have its demonstration; but if we consider it with more care we may possibly discover some correspondence between the case of the gun and that of the string. The curvature of the path of the shot fired horizontally appears to result from two forces, one (that of the weapon) drives it horizontally and the other (its own weight) draws it vertically downward. So in stretching the rope you have the force which pulls it horizontally and its own weight which acts downwards. The circumstances in these two cases are, therefore, very similar. If then you attribute to the weight of the rope a power and energy [*possanza ed energia*] sufficient to oppose and overcome any stretching force, no matter how great, why deny this power to the bullet?

[315]

Besides I must tell you something which will both surprise and please you, namely, that a cord stretched more or less tightly assumes a curve which closely approximates the parabola. This similarity is clearly seen if you draw a parabolic curve on a vertical plane and then invert it so that the apex will lie at the bottom and the base remain horizontal; for, on hanging a chain below the base, one end attached to each extremity of the base, you will observe that, on slackening the chain more or less, it bends and fits itself to the parabola; and the coincidence is more exact in proportion as the parabola is drawn with less curvature or, so to speak, more stretched; so that in parabolas described with elevations less than 45° the chain fits its parabola almost perfectly.

Sagr. Then with a fine chain one would be able to quickly draw many parabolic lines upon a plane surface.

Salv. Certainly and with no small advantage as I shall show you later.

Simp. But before going further, I am anxious to be convinced at least of that proposition of which you say that there is a rigid demonstration; I refer to the statement that it is impossible by any force whatever to stretch a cord so that it will lie perfectly straight and horizontal.

Sagr. I will see if I can recall the demonstration; but in order to understand it, Simplicio, it will be necessary for you to take for granted concerning machines what is evident not alone from experiment but also from theoretical considerations, namely, that the velocity of a moving body [*velocità del movente*], even when its force [*forza*] is small, can overcome a very great resistance exerted by a slowly moving body, whenever the velocity of the moving body bears to that of the resisting body a greater ratio than the resistance [*resistenza*] of the resisting body to the force [*forza*] of the moving body.

[316]

Simp. This I know very well for it has been demonstrated by Aristotle in his *Questions in Mechanics*; it is also clearly seen in the lever and the steelyard where a counterpoise weighing not more than 4 pounds will lift a weight of 400 provided that the distance of the counterpoise from the axis about which the steelyard rotates be more than one hundred times as great as the distance between this axis and the point of support for the large weight. This is true because the counterpoise in its descent traverses a space more than one hundred times as great as that moved over by the large weight in the same time; in other words the small counterpoise moves with a velocity which is more than one hundred times as great as that of the large weight.

Sagr. You are quite right; you do not hesitate to admit that however small the force [*forza*] of the moving body it will overcome any resistance, however great, provided it gains more in velocity than it loses in force and weight [*vigore e gravità*]. Now let us return to the case of the cord. In the accompanying figure *ab* represents a line passing through two fixed points *a* and *b*; at the extremities of this line hang, as you see, two

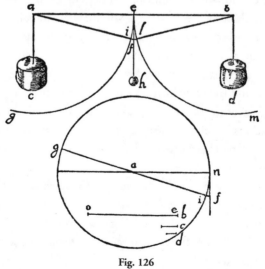

Fig. 126

large weights *c* and *d*, which stretch it with great force and keep it truly straight, seeing that it is merely a line without weight. Now I wish to remark that if from the middle point of this line, which we may call *e*, you suspend any small weight, say *h*, the

[317]

line *ab* will yield toward the point *f* and on account of its elongation will compel the two heavy weights *c* and *d* to rise. This I shall demonstrate as follows: with the points *a* and *b* as centers describe the two quadrants, *eig* and *elm*; now since the two semi-diameters *ai* and *bl* are equal to *ae* and *eb*, the remainders *fi* and *fl* are the excesses of the lines *af* and *fb* over *ae* and *eb*; they therefore determine the rise of the weights *c* and *d*, assuming of course that the weight *h* has taken the position *f*. But the weight *h* will take the position *f*, whenever the line *ef* which represents the descent of *h* bears to the line *fi*—that is, to the rise of the weights *c* and *d*—a ratio which is greater than the ratio of the weight of the two large bodies to that of the body *h*. Even when the weights of *c* and *d* are very great and that of *h* very small this will happen; for the excess of the weights *c* and *d* over the weight of *h* can never be so great but that the excess of the tangent *ef* over the segment *fi* may be proportionally greater. This may be proved as follows: Draw a circle of diameter *gai*; draw the line *bo* such that the ratio of its length to another length *c*, *c>d*, is the same as the ratio of the weights *c* and *d* to the weight *h*. Since *c>d*, the ratio of *bo* to *d* is greater than that of *bo* to *c*. Take *be* a third proportional to *ob* and *d*; prolong the diameter *gi* to a point *f* such that *gi:if=oe:eb*; and from the point *f* draw the tangent *fn*; then since we already have *oe:eb=gi:if*, we shall obtain, by compounding ratios, *ob:eb=gf:if*. But *d* is a mean proportional between *ob* and *be*, while *nf* is a mean proportional between *gf* and *fi*. Hence *nf* bears to *fi* the same ratio as that of *cb* to *d*, which is greater than that of the weights *c* and *d* to the weight *h*. Since then the descent, or velocity, of the weight *h* bears to the rise, or velocity, of the weights *c* and *d* a greater ratio than the weight of the bodies *c* and *d* bears to the weight of *h*, it is clear that the weight *h* will descend and the line *ab* will cease to be straight and horizontal.

And now this which happens in the case of a weightless cord *ab* when any small weight *h* is attached at the point *e*, happens also when the cord is made of ponderable matter but without any attached weight; because in this case the material of which the cord is composed functions as a suspended weight.

Simp. I am fully satisfied. So now Salviati can explain, as he promised, the advantage of such a chain and, afterwards, present the speculations of our Academician on the subject of impulsive forces [*forza della percossa*].

Salv. Let the preceding discussions suffice for to-day; the hour is already late and the time remaining will not permit us to clear up the subjects proposed; we may therefore postpone our meeting until another and more opportune occasion.

[318]

Sagr. I concur in your opinion, because after various conversations with intimate friends of our Academician I have concluded that this question of impulsive forces is very obscure, and I think that, up to the present, none of those who have treated this subject have been able to clear up its dark corners which lie almost beyond the reach of human imagination; among the various views which I have heard expressed one, strangely fantastic, remains in my memory, namely, that impulsive forces are indeterminate, if not infinite. Let us, therefore, await the convenience of Salviati. Meanwhile tell me what is this which follows the discussion of projectiles.

Salv. These are some theorems pertaining to the centers of gravity of solids, discovered by our Academician in his youth, and undertaken by him because he considered the treatment of Federigo Comandino to be somewhat incomplete. The propositions which you have before you would, he thought, meet the deficiencies of Comandino's book. The investigation was undertaken at the instance of the Illustrious Marquis Guid' Ubaldo Dal Monte, a very distinguished mathematician of his day, as is evidenced by his various publications. To this gentleman our Academician gave a copy of this work, hoping to extend the investigation to other solids not treated by Comandino. But a little later there chanced to fall into his hands the book of the great geometrician, Luca Valerio, where he found the subject treated so completely that he left off his own investigations, although the methods which he employed were quite different from those of Valerio.

Sagr. Please be good enough to leave this volume with me until our next meeting so that I may be able to read and study these propositions in the order in which they are written.

Salv. It is a pleasure to comply with your request and I only hope that the propositions will be of deep interest to you.

END OF FOURTH DAY.

APPENDIX

Containing some theorems, and their proofs, dealing with centers of gravity of solid bodies, written by the same Author at an earlier date.[42]

[FINIS]

---

42. Following the example of the National Edition, this *Appendix* which covers 18 pages of the Leyden Edition of 1638 is here omitted as being of minor interest. *[Trans.]*

Johannes Kepler

(1571-1630)

HIS LIFE AND WORK

If an award were ever given to the person in history who was most dedicated to the pursuit of absolute precision, the German astronomer Johannes Kepler might well be the recipient. Kepler was so obsessed with measurements that he even calculated his own gestational period to the minute—224 days, 9 hours, 53 minutes. (He had been born prematurely.) So it is no surprise that he toiled over his astronomical research to such a degree that he ultimately produced the most exact astronomical tables of his time, leading to the eventual acceptance of the sun-centered (heliocentric) theory of the planetary system.

Like Copernicus, whose work inspired him, Kepler was a deeply religious man. He viewed his continual study of universal properties as a fulfillment of his Christian duty to understand the very universe that God created. But unlike Copernicus, Kepler's life was anything but quiet and lacking in contrast. Always short of money, Kepler often resorted to publishing astrological calendars and horoscopes, which, ironically, gained him some local notoriety when their predictions turned out to be quite accurate. Kepler also suffered the early deaths of several of his children, as well as the indignity of having to defend in court his eccentric mother, Katherine, who had a reputation for practicing witchcraft and was nearly burned at the stake.

Kepler entered into a series of complex relationships, most notably with Tycho Brahe, the great naked-eye astronomical observer. Brahe dedicated years of his life to

recording and measuring celestial bodies, but he lacked the mathematical and analytical skills necessary to understand planetary motion. A man of wealth, Brahe hired Kepler to make sense of his observations of the orbit of Mars, which had perplexed astronomers for many years. Kepler painstakingly mapped Brahe's data on the motion of Mars to an ellipse, and this success lent mathematical credibility to the Copernican model of a sun-centered system. His discovery of elliptical orbits helped usher in a new era in astronomy. The motions of planets could now be predicted.

In spite of his achievements, Kepler never gained much wealth or prestige and was often forced to flee the countries where he sojourned because of religious upheaval and civil unrest. By the time he died at the age of fifty-nine in 1630 (while attempting to collect an overdue salary), Kepler had discovered three laws of planetary motion, which are still taught to students in physics classes in the twenty-first century. And it was Kepler's Third Law, not an apple, that led Isaac Newton to discover the law of gravitation.

Johannes Kepler was born on December 27, 1571, in the town of Weil der Stadt, in Württemburg (now part of Germany). His father, Heinrich Kepler, was, according to Johannes, "an immoral, rough, and quarrelsome soldier" who deserted his family on several occasions to join up with mercenaries to battle a Protestant uprising in Holland. Heinrich is believed to have died somewhere in the Netherlands. The young Johannes lived with his mother, Katherine, in his grandfather's inn, where he was put to work at an early age waiting tables, despite his poor health. Kepler had nearsightedness as well as double vision, which was believed to have been caused by a near-fatal bout of smallpox; and he also suffered from abdominal problems and "crippled" fingers that limited his career potential choice, in the view of his family, to a life in the ministry.

"Bad-tempered" and "garrulous" were words Kepler used to describe his mother, Katherine, but he was aware from a young age that his father was the cause. Katherine herself had been raised by an aunt who practiced witchcraft and was burned at the stake. So it was no surprise to Kepler when his own mother faced similar charges later in her life. In 1577, Katherine showed her son the "great comet" that appeared in the sky that year, and Kepler later acknowledged that this shared moment with his mother had a lasting impact on his life. Despite a childhood filled with pain and anxiety, Kepler was obviously gifted, and he managed to procure a scholarship reserved for promising male children of limited means who lived in the German province of Swabia. He attended the German Schreibschule in Leonberg before transferring to a Latin school, which was instrumental in providing him with the Latin writing style he later employed in his work. Being frail and precocious, Kepler was beaten regularly by classmates, who considered him a know-it-all, and he soon turned to religious study as a way of escaping his predicament.

In 1587, Kepler enrolled at Tubingen University, where he studied theology and philosophy. He also established himself there as a serious student of mathematics and astronomy, and became an advocate of the controversial Copernican heliocentric theory. So public was young Kepler in his defense of the Copernican model of the universe that it was not uncommon for him to engage in public debate on the subject. Despite his main interest in theology, he was growing more and more intrigued by the mystical appeal of a heliocentric universe. Although he had intended to graduate from Tubingen in 1591 and join the university's theology faculty, a recommendation to a post in mathematics and astronomy at the Protestant school in Graz, Austria, proved irresistible. So, at the age of twenty-two, Kepler deserted a career in the ministry for the study of science. But he would never abandon his belief in God's role in the creation of the universe.

In the sixteenth century, the distinction between astronomy and astrology was fairly ambiguous. One of Kepler's duties as a mathematician in Graz was to compose an astrological calendar complete with predictions. This was a common practice at the time, and Kepler was clearly motivated by the extra money the job provided, but he could not have anticipated the public's reaction when his first calendar was published. He predicted an extraordinarily cold winter, as well as a Turkish incursion, and when both predictions came true, Kepler was triumphantly hailed as a prophet. Despite the clamor, he would never hold much respect for the work he did on the annual almanacs. He called astrology "the foolish little daughter of astronomy" and was equally dismissive of the public' s interest and the astrologer's intentions. "If ever astrologers are correct," he wrote, "it ought to be credited to luck." Still, Kepler never failed to turn to astrology whenever money became tight, which was a recurring theme in his life, and he did hold out hope of discovering some true science in astrology.

One day, while lecturing on geometry in Graz, Kepler experienced a sudden revelation that set him on a passionate journey and changed the course of his life. It was, he felt, the secret key to understanding the universe. On the blackboard, in front of the class, he drew an equilateral triangle within a circle, and another circle drawn within the triangle. It occurred to him that the ratio of the circles was indicative of the ratio of the orbits of Saturn and Jupiter. Inspired by this revelation, he assumed that all six planets known at the time were arranged around the sun in such a way that the geometric figures would fit perfectly between them. Initially he tested this hypothesis without success, using two-dimensional plane figures such as the pentagon, the square, and the triangle. He then returned to the Pythagorean solids, used by the ancient Greeks, who discovered that only five solids could be constructed from regular geometric figures. To Kepler, this explained why there could only be six planets (Mercury, Venus, Earth, Mars, Jupiter, and Saturn) with five spaces between them, and why these

spaces were not uniform. This geometric theory regarding planetary orbits and distances inspired Kepler to write *Mystery of the Cosmos* (*Mysterium Cosmographicum*), published in 1596. It took him about a year to write, and although the scheme was reasonably accurate, he was clearly very sure that his theories would ultimately bear out:

> *And how intense was my pleasure from this discovery can never be expressed in words. I no longer regretted the time wasted. Day and night I was consumed by the computing, to see whether this idea would agree with the Copernican orbits, or if my joy would be carried away by the wind. Within a few days everything worked, and I watched as one body after another fit precisely into its place among the planets.*

Kepler spent the rest of his life trying to obtain the mathematical proof and scientific observations that would justify his theories. *Mystery of the Cosmos* was the first decidedly Copernican work published since Copernicus' own *On the Revolutions*, and as a theologian and astronomer Kepler was determined to understand how and why God designed the universe. Advocating a heliocentric system had serious religious implications, but Kepler maintained that the sun's centrality was vital to God's design, as it kept the planets aligned and in motion. In this sense, Kepler broke with Copernicus' heliostatic system of a sun "near" the center and placed the sun directly in the center of the system.

Today, Kepler's polyhedra appear impracticable. But although the premise of *Mystery of the Cosmos* was erroneous, Kepler's conclusions were still astonishingly accurate and decisive, and were essential in shaping the course of modern science. When the book was published, Kepler sent a copy to Galileo, urging him to "believe and step forth," but the Italian astronomer rejected the work because of its apparent speculations. Tycho Brahe, on the other hand, was immediately intrigued. He viewed Kepler's work as new and exciting, and he wrote a detailed critique in the book's support. Reaction to *Mystery of the Cosmos*, Kepler would later write, changed the direction of his entire life.

In 1597, another event would change Kepler's life, as he fell in love with Barbara Müller, the first daughter of a wealthy mill owner. They married on April 27 of that year, under an unfavorable constellation, as Kepler would later note in his diary. Once again, his prophetic nature emerged as the relationship and the marriage dissolved. Their first two children died very young, and Kepler became distraught. He immersed himself in his work to distract himself from the pain, but his wife did not understand his pursuits. "Fat, confused, and simpleminded" was how he described her in his diary, though the marriage did last fourteen years, until her death in 1611 from typhus.

In September 1598, Kepler and other Lutherans in Graz were ordered to leave town by the Catholic archduke, who was bent on removing the Lutheran religion from Austria. After a visit to Tycho Brahe's Benatky Castle in Prague, Kepler was invited by the wealthy Danish astronomer to stay there and work on his research. Kepler was somewhat wary of Brahe, even before having met him. "My opinion of Tycho is this: he is superlatively rich, but he knows not how to make proper use of it, as is the case with most rich people," he wrote. "Therefore, one must try to wrest his riches from him."

If his relationship with his wife lacked complexity, Kepler more than made up for it when he entered into a working arrangement with the aristocratic Brahe. At first, Brahe treated the young Kepler as an assistant, carefully doling out assignments without giving him much access to detailed observational data. Kepler badly wanted to be regarded as an equal and given some independence, but the secretive Brahe wanted to use Kepler to establish his own model of the solar system—a non-Copernican model that Kepler did not support.

Kepler was immensely frustrated. Brahe had a wealth of observational data but lacked the mathematical tools to fully comprehend it. Finally, perhaps to pacify his restless assistant, Brahe assigned Kepler to study the orbit of Mars, which had confused the Danish astronomer for some time because it appeared to be the least circular. Kepler initially thought he could solve the problem in eight days, but the project turned out to take him eight years. Difficult as the research proved to be, it was not without its rewards, as the work led Kepler to discover that Mars's orbit precisely described an ellipse, as well as to formulate his first two "planetary laws," which he published in 1609 in *The New Astronomy*.

A year and a half into his working relationship with Brahe, the Danish astronomer became very ill at dinner and died a few days later of a bladder infection. Kepler took over the post of Imperial Mathematician and was now free to explore planetary theory without being constrained by the watchful eye of Tycho Brahe. Realizing an opportunity, Kepler immediately went after the Brahe data that he coveted before Brahe's heirs could take control of them. "I confess that when Tycho died," Kepler wrote later, "I quickly took advantage of the absence, or lack of circumspection, of the heirs, by taking the observations under my care, or perhaps usurping them." The result was Kepler's *Rudolphine Tables*, a compilation of the data from thirty years of Brahe's observations. To be fair, on his deathbed Brahe had urged Kepler to complete the tables; but Kepler did not frame the work according to any Tychonic hypothesis, as Brahe had hoped. Instead, Kepler used the data, which included calculations using logarithms he had developed himself, in predicting planetary positions. He was able to predict transits of the sun by Mercury and Venus, though he did not live long enough to witness them.

Kepler did not publish *Rudolphine Tables* until 1627, however, because the data he discovered constantly led him in new directions.

After Brahe's death, Kepler witnessed a nova, which later became known as "Kepler's nova," and he also experimented in optical theories. Though scientists and scholars view Kepler's optical work as minor in comparison with his accomplishments in astronomy and mathematics, the publication in 1611 of his book *Dioptrices,* changed the course of optics.

In 1605, Kepler announced his first law, the law of ellipses, which held that the planets move in ellipses with the sun at one focus. Earth, Kepler asserted, is closest to the sun in January and farthest from it in July as it travels along its elliptical orbit. His second law, the law of equal areas, maintained that a line drawn from the Sun to a planet sweeps out equal areas in equal times. Kepler demonstrated this by arguing that an imaginary line connecting any planet to the sun must sweep over equal areas in equal intervals of time. He published both laws in 1609 in his book *New Astronomy* (*Astronomia Nova*).

Yet despite his status as Imperial Mathematician and as a distinguished scientist whom Galileo sought out for an opinion on his new telescopic discoveries, Kepler was unable to secure for himself a comfortable existence. Religious upheaval in Prague jeopardized his new homeland, and in 1611 his wife and his favorite son died. Kepler was permitted, under exemption, to return to Linz, and in 1613 he married Susanna Reuttinger, a twenty-four-year-old orphan who would bear him seven children, only two of whom would survive to adulthood. It was at this time that Kepler's mother was accused of witchcraft, and in the midst of his own personal turmoil he was forced to defend her against the charge in order to prevent her being burned at the stake. Katherine was imprisoned and tortured, but her son managed to obtain an acquittal and she was released.

Because of these distractions, Kepler's return to Linz was not a productive time initially. Distraught, he turned his attention away from tables and began working on *Harmonies of the World* (*Harmonice Mundi*), a passionate work which Max Caspar, in his biography of Kepler, described as "a great cosmic vision, woven out of science, poetry, philosophy, theology, mysticism." Kepler finished *Harmonies of the World* on May 27, 1618. In this series of five books, he extended his theory of harmony to music, astrology, geometry, and astronomy. The series included his third law of planetary motion, the law that would inspire Isaac Newton some sixty years later, which maintained that the cubes of mean distances of the planets from the sun are proportional to the squares of their periods of revolution. In short, Kepler discovered how planets orbited, and in so doing paved the way for Newton to discover why.

Kepler believed he had discovered God 's logic in designing the universe, and he was unable to hide his ecstasy. In Book 5 of *Harmonies of the World* he wrote:

I dare frankly to confess that I have stolen the golden vessels of the Egyptians to build a tabernacle for my God far from the bounds of Egypt. If you pardon me, I shall rejoice; if you reproach me, I shall endure. The die is cast, and I am writing the book, to be read either now or by posterity, it matters not. It can wait a century for a reader, as God himself has waited six thousand years for a witness.

The Thirty Years War, which beginning in 1618 decimated the Austrian and German lands, forced Kepler to leave Linz in 1626. He eventually settled in the town of Sagan, in Silesia. There he tried to finish what might best be described as a science fiction novel, which he had dabbled at for years, at some expense to his mother during her trial for witchcraft. *Dream of the Moon* (*Somnium seu astronomia lunari*), which features an interview with a knowing "demon" who explains how the protagonist could travel to the moon, was uncovered and presented as evidence during Katherine's trial. Kepler spent considerable energy defending the work as pure fiction and the demon as a mere literary device. The book was unique in that it was not only ahead of its time in terms of fantasy but also a treatise supporting Copernican theory.

In 1630, at the age of fifty-eight, Kepler once again found himself in financial straits. He set out for Regensburg, where he hoped to collect interest on some bonds in his possession as well as some money he was owed. However, a few days after his arrival he developed a fever, and died on November 15. Though he never achieved the mass renown of Galileo, Kepler produced a body of work that was extraordinarily useful to professional astronomers like Newton who immersed themselves in the details and accuracy of Kepler's science. Johannes Kepler was a man who preferred aesthetic harmony and order, and all that he discovered was inextricably linked with his vision of God. His epitaph, which he himself composed, reads: "I used to measure the heavens; now I shall measure the shadows of the earth. Although my soul was from heaven, the shadow of my body lies here."

HARMONIES

of the

WORLD

BOOK FIVE

Concerning the very perfect harmony of the celestial movements, and the genesis of eccentricities and the semidiameters, and as periodic times from the same.

After the model of the most correct astronomical doctrine of today, and the hypothesis not only of Copernicus but also of Tycho Brahe, whereof either hypotheses are today publicly accepted as most true, and the Ptolemaic as outmoded.

I commence a sacred discourse, a most true hymn to God the Founder, and I judge it to be piety, not to sacrifice many hecatombs of bulls to Him and to burn incense of innumerable perfumes and cassia, but first to learn myself, and afterwards to teach others too, how great He is in wisdom, how great in power, and of what sort in goodness. For to wish to adorn in every way possible the things that should receive adornment and to envy no thing its goods—this I put down as the sign of the greatest goodness, and in this respect I praise Him as good that in the heights of His wisdom He finds everything whereby each

thing may be adorned to the utmost and that He can do by His unconquerable power all that He has decreed.

Galen, *on the Use of Parts*. Book III

PROEM

[268] As regards that which I prophesied two and twenty years ago (especially that the five regular solids are found between the celestial spheres), as regards that of which I was firmly persuaded in my own mind before I had seen Ptolemy's *Harmonies*, as regards that which I promised my friends in the title of this fifth book before I was sure of the thing itself, that which, sixteen years ago, in a published statement, I insisted must be investigated, for the sake of which I spent the best part of my life in astronomical speculations, visited Tycho Brahe, [269] and took up residence at Prague: finally, as God the Best and Greatest, Who had inspired my mind and aroused my great desire, prolonged my life and strength of mind and furnished the other means through the liberality of the two Emperors and the nobles of this province of Austria-on-the-Anisana: after I had discharged my astronomical duties as much as sufficed, finally, I say, I brought it to light and found it to be truer than I had even hoped, and I discovered among the celestial movements the full nature of harmony, in its due measure, together with all its parts unfolded in Book III—not in that mode wherein I had conceived it in my mind (this is not last in my joy) but in a very different mode which is also very excellent and very perfect. There took place in this intervening time, wherein the very laborious reconstruction of the movements held me in suspense, an extraordinary augmentation of my desire and incentive for the job, a reading of the *Harmonies* of Ptolemy, which had been sent to me in manuscript by John George Herward, Chancellor of Bavaria, a very distinguished man and of a nature to advance philosophy and every type of learning. There, beyond my expectations and with the greatest wonder, I found approximately the whole third book given over to the same consideration of celestial harmony, fifteen hundred years ago. But indeed astronomy was far from being of age as yet; and Ptolemy, in an unfortunate attempt, could make others subject to despair, as being one who, like Scipio in Cicero, seemed to have recited a pleasant Pythagorean dream rather than to have aided philosophy. But both the crudeness of the ancient philosophy and this exact agreement in our meditations, down to the last hair, over an interval of fifteen centuries, greatly strengthened me in getting on with the job. For what need is there of many men? The very nature of things, in order to reveal herself to mankind, was at work in the different interpreters of different ages, and was the finger of God—to use the Hebrew expression; and here, in the minds of two men, who had wholly given themselves up to the contemplation of nature, there was the same conception as to the configuration of the world, although neither had

been the other's guide in taking this route. But now since the first light eight months ago, since broad day three months ago, and since the sun of my wonderful speculation has shone fully a very few days ago: nothing holds me back. I am free to give myself up to the sacred madness, I am free to taunt mortals with the frank confession that I am stealing the golden vessels of the Egyptians, in order to build of them a temple for my God, far from the territory of Egypt. If you pardon me, I shall rejoice; if you are enraged, I shall bear up. The die is cast, and I am writing the book—whether to be read by my contemporaries or by posterity matters not. Let it await its reader for a hundred years, if God Himself has been ready for His contemplator for six thousand years.

The chapters of this book are as follows:

1. Concerning the five regular solid figures.
2. On the kinship between them and the harmonic ratios.
3. Summary of astronomical doctrine necessary for speculation into the celestial harmonies.
4. In what things pertaining to the planetary movements the simple consonances have been expressed and that all those consonances which are present in song are found in the heavens.
5. That the clefs of the musical scale, or pitches of the system, and the genera of consonances, the major and the minor, are expressed in certain movements.
6. That the single musical Tones or Modes are somehow expressed by the single planets.
7. That the counterpoints or universal harmonies of all the planets can exist and be different from one another.
8. That four kinds of voice are expressed in the planets: soprano, contralto, tenor, and bass.
9. Demonstration that in order to secure this harmonic arrangement, those very planetary eccentricities which any planet has as its own, and no others, had to be set up.
10. Epilogue concerning the sun, by way of very fertile conjectures.

[270] Before taking up these questions, it is my wish to impress upon my readers the very exhortation of Timaeus, a pagan philosopher, who was going to speak on the same things: it should be learned by Christians with the greatest admiration, and shame too, if they do not imitate him: Ἀλλ' ὦ Σώκρατεσ, τοῦτο γε δὴ πντες, ὅσοι καὶ κατὰ βραχὺ σωφροσυνης μετέουσιν, ἐπὶ πασῇ ὁρμῇ καὶ σμίκρου καὶ μεγάλου πράγματοσ θεὸν ἀει που καλοῦσιν. ἡμᾶς δὲ τοὺς περὶ τοῦ πὰντος λόγους ποιεῖσθαι πη μέλλοντας..., εἰ μὴ πανταπασι παραλλάτομεν, ἀνάγκη θεοὺς τε καί θεὰς ἐπικαλουμενουσ εὔχεσθαι πάντα, κατὰ νοῦν ἐκεῖνοισ μέν μάλιστα, ἑπομένως δέ ἡμῖν εἰπεῖν. *For truly, Socrates, since all who*

*have the least particle of intelligence always invoke God whenever they enter upon any busi-
ness, whether light or arduous; so too, unless we have clearly strayed away from all sound
reason, we who intend to have a discussion concerning the universe must of necessity make
our sacred wishes and pray to the Gods and Goddesses with one mind that we may say such
things as will please and be acceptable to them in especial and, secondly, to you too.*

1. CONCERNING THE FIVE REGULAR SOLID FIGURES

[271] It has been said in the second book how the regular plane figures are fitted
together to form solids; there we spoke of the five regular solids, among others, on
account of the plane figures. Nevertheless their number, five, was there demonstrated;
and it was added why they were designated by the Platonists as the figures of the world,
and to what element any solid was compared on account of what property. But now,
in the anteroom of this book, I must speak again concerning these figures, on their own
account, not on account of the planes, as much as suffices for the celestial harmonies;
the reader will find the rest in the *Epitome of Astronomy*, Volume II, Book IV.

Accordingly, from the *Mysterium Cosmographicum*, let me here briefly inculcate the
order of the five solids in the world, whereof three are primary and two secondary. For
the *cube* (1) is the outmost and the most spacious, because firstborn and having the
nature (*rationem*) of a *whole*, in the very form of its generation. There follows the *tetrahedron* (2), as if made a *part*, by cutting up the cube; nevertheless it is primary too, with
a solid trilinear angle, like the cube. Within the tetrahedron is the *dodecahedron* (3), the
last of primary figures, namely, like a solid composed of parts of a cube and similar
parts of a tetrahedron, *i.e.*, of irregular tetrahedrons, wherewith the cube inside is
roofed over. Next in order is the *icosahedron* (4) on account of its similarity, the last of
the secondary figures and having a plurilinear solid angle. The *octahedron* (5) is inmost,
which is similar to the cube and the first of the secondary figures and to which as
inscriptile the first place is due, just as the first outside place is due to the cube as cir-
cumscriptile.

[272] However, there are as it were two noteworthy weddings of these figures,
made from different classes: the males, the cube and the dodecahedron, among the primary; the females, the octahedron and the icosahedron, among the secondary, to which
is added one as it were bachelor or hermaphrodite, the tetrahedron, because it is
inscribed in itself, just as those female solids are inscribed in the males and are as it were
subject to them, and have the signs of the feminine sex, opposite the masculine, namely, angles opposite planes. Moreover, just as the tetrahedron is the element, bowels, and
as it were rib of the male cube, so the feminine octahedron is the element and part of
the tetrahedron in another way; and thus the tetrahedron mediates in this marriage.

The main difference in these wedlocks or family relationships consists in the

following: the ratio of the cube is *rational*. For the tetrahedron is one third of the body of the cube, and the octahedron half of the tetrahedron, one sixth of the cube; while the ratio of the dodecahedron's wedding is *irrational* (*ineffabilis*) but *divine*.

The union of these two words commands the reader to be careful as to their significance. For the word *ineffabilis* here does not of itself denote any nobility, as elsewhere in theology and divine things, but denotes an inferior condition. For in geometry, as was said in the first book, there are many irrationals, which do not on that account participate in a divine proportion too. But you must look in the first book for what the divine ratio, or rather the divine section, is. For in other proportions there are four terms present; and three, in a continued proportion; but the divine requires a single relation of terms outside of that of the proportion itself, namely in such fashion that the two lesser terms, as parts make up the greater term, as a whole. Therefore, as much as is taken away from this wedding of the dodecahedron on account of its employing an irrational proportion,

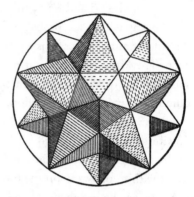

is added to it conversely, because its irrationality approaches the divine. This wedding also comprehends the solid star too, the generation whereof arises from the continuation of five planes of the dodecahedron till they all meet in a single point. See its generation in Book II.

Lastly, we must note the ratio of the spheres circumscribed around them to those inscribed in them: in the case of the tetrahedron it is rational, 100,000 : 33,333 or 3 : 1; in the wedding of the cube it is irrational, but the radius of the inscribed sphere is rational in square, and is itself the square root of one third the square on the radius (of the circumscribed sphere), namely 100,000 : 57,735; in the wedding of the dodecahedron, clearly irrational, 100,000 : 79,465; in the case of the star, 100,000 : 52,573, half the side of the icosahedron or half the distance between two rays.

2. ON THE KINSHIP BETWEEN THE HARMONIC RATIOS AND THE FIVE REGULAR FIGURES

[273] This kinship (*cognatio*) is various and manifold; but there are four degrees of kinship. For either the sign of kinship is taken from the outward form alone which the figures have, or else ratios which are the same as the harmonic arise in the construction of the side, or result from the figures already constructed, taken simply or together; or, lastly, they are either equal to or approximate the ratios of the spheres of the figure.

In the first degree, the ratios, where the character or greater term is 3, have kin-

ship with the triangular plane of the tetrahedron, octahedron, and icosahedron; but where the greater term is 4, with the square plane of the cube; where 5, with the pentagonal plane of the dodecahedron. This similitude on the part of the plane can also be extended to the smaller term of the ratio, so that wherever the number 3 is found as one term of the continued doubles, that ratio is held to be akin to the three figures first named: for example, 1 : 3 and 2 : 3 and 4 : 3 and 8 : 3, et cetera; but where the number is 5, that ratio is absolutely assigned to the wedding of the dodecahedron: for example, 2 : 5 and 4 : 5 and 8 : 5, and thus 3 : 5 and 3 : 10 and 6 : 5 and 12 : 5 and 24:5. The kinship will be less probable if the sum of the terms expresses this similitude, as in 2 : 3 the sum of the terms is equal to 5, as if to say that 2 : 3 is akin to the dodecahedron. The kinship on account of the outward form of the solid angle is similar: the solid angle is trilinear among the primary figures, quadrilinear in the octahedron, and quinquelinear in the icosahedron. And so if one term of the ratio participates in the number 3, the ratio will be connected with the primary bodies; but if in the number 4, with the octahedron; and finally, if in the number 5, with the icosahedron. But in the feminine solids this kinship is more apparent, because the characteristic figure latent within follows upon the form of the angle: the tetragon in the octahedron, the pentagon in the icosahedron; and so 3 : 5 would go to the sectioned icosahedron for both reasons.

The second degree of kinship, which is genetic, is to be conceived as follows: First, some harmonic ratios of numbers are akin to one wedding or family, namely, perfect ratios to the single family of the cube; conversely, there is the ratio which is never fully expressed in numbers and cannot be demonstrated by numbers in any other way, except by a long series of numbers gradually approaching it: this ratio is called *divine*, when it is perfect, and it rules in various ways throughout the dodecahedral wedding. Accordingly, the following consonances begin to shadow forth that ratio: 1:2 and 2: 3 and 2 : 3 and 5 : 8. For it exists most imperfectly in 1 : 2, more perfectly in 5 : 8, and still more perfectly if we add 5 and 8 to make 13 and take 8 as the numerator, if this ratio has not stopped being harmonic.

Further, in constructing the side of the figure, the diameter of the globe must be cut; and the octahedron demands its bisection, the cube and the tetrahedron its trisection, the dodecahedral wedding its quinquesection. Accordingly, the ratios between the figures are distributed according to the numbers which express those ratios. But the square on the diameter is cut too, or the square on the side of the figure is formed from a fixed part of the diameter. And then the squares on the sides are compared with the square on the diameter, and they constitute the following ratios: in the cube 1 : 3, in the tetrahedron 2 : 3, in the octahedron 1 : 2. Wherefore, if the two ratios are put together, the cubic and the tetrahedral will give 1 : 2; the cubic and the octahedral,

2 : 3; the octahedral and the tetrahedral, 3 : 4. The sides in the dodecahedral wedding are irrational.

Thirdly, the harmonic ratios follow in various ways upon the already constructed figures. For either the number of the sides of the plane is compared with the number of lines in the total figure; [274] and the following ratios arise: in the cube, 4:12 or 1:3; in the tetrahedron 3 : 6 or 1 : 2; in the octahedron 3 : 12 or 1 : 4; in the dodecahedron 5 : 30 or 1 : 6; in the icosahedron 3 : 30 or 1 : 10. Or else the number of sides of the plane is compared with the number of planes; then the cube gives 4 : 6 or 2 : 3, the tetrahedron 3 : 4, the octahedron 3 : 8, the dodecahedron 5 : 12, the icosahedron 3 : 20. Or else the number of sides or angles of the plane is compared with the number of solid angles, and the cube gives 4 : 8 or 1 : 2, the tetrahedron 3 : 4, the octahedron 3 : 6 or 1 : 2, the dodecahedron with its consort 5 : 20 or 3 : 12 (*i.e.*, 1 : 4). Or else the number of planes is compared with the number of solid angles, and the cubic wedding gives 6 : 8 or 3 : 4, the tetrahedron the ratio of equality, the dodecahedral wedding 12 : 20 or 3 : 5. Or else the number of all the sides is compared with the number of the solid angles, and the cube gives 8 : 12 or 2 : 3, the tetrahedron 4 : 6 or 2 : 3, and the octahedron 6 : 12 or 1 : 2, the dodecahedron 20 : 30 or 2 : 3, the icosahedron 12:30 or 2:5.

Moreover, the bodies too are compared with one another, if the tetrahedron is stowed away in the cube, the octahedron in the tetrahedron and cube, by geometrical inscription. The tetrahedron is one third of the cube, the octahedron half of the tetrahedron, one sixth of the cube, just as the octahedron, which is inscribed in the globe, is one sixth of the cube which circumscribes the globe. The ratios of the remaining bodies are irrational.

The fourth species or degree of kinship is more proper to this work: the ratio of the spheres inscribed in the figures to the spheres circumscribing them is sought, and what harmonic ratios approximate them is calculated. For only in the tetrahedron is the diameter of the inscribed sphere rational, namely, one third of the circumscribed sphere. But in the cubic wedding the ratio, which is single there, is as lines which are rational only in square. For the diameter of the inscribed sphere is to the diameter of the circumscribed sphere as the square root of the ratio 1 : 3. And if you compare the ratios with one another, the ratio of the tetrahedral spheres is the square of the ratio of the cubic spheres. In the dodecahedral wedding there is again a single ratio, but an irrational one, slightly greater than 4 : 5. Therefore the ratio of the spheres of the cube and octahedron is approximated by the following consonances: 1 : 2, as proximately greater, and 3 : 5, as proximately smaller. But the ratio of the dodecahedral spheres is approximated by the consonances 4 : 5 and 5 : 6, as proximately smaller, and 3 : 4 and 5 : 8, as proximately greater.

But if for certain reasons 1 : 2 and 1 : 3 are arrogated to the cube, the ratio of the spheres of the cube will be to the ratio of the spheres of the tetrahedron as the consonances 1 : 2 and 1 : 3, which have been ascribed to the cube, are to 1 : 4 and 1 : 9, which are to be assigned to the tetrahedron, if this proportion is to be used. For these ratios, too, are as the squares of those consonances. And because 1 : 9 is not harmonic, 1 : 8 the proximate ratio takes its place in the tetrahedron. But by this proportion approximately 4 : 5 and 3 : 4 will go with the dodecahedral wedding. For as the ratio of the spheres of the cube is approximately the cube of the ratio of the dodecahedral, so too the cubic consonances 1 : 2 and 2 : 3 are approximately the cubes of the consonances 4 : 5 and 3 : 4. For 4 : 5 cubed is 64 : 125, and 1 : 2 is 64 : 128. So 3 : 4 cubed is 27 : 64, and 1 : 3 is 27 : 81.

3. A SUMMARY OF ASTRONOMICAL DOCTRINE NECESSARY FOR SPECULATION INTO THE CELESTIAL HARMONIES

First of all, my readers should know that the ancient astronomical hypotheses of Ptolemy, in the fashion in which they have been unfolded in the *Theoricae* of Peurbach and by the other writers of epitomes, are to be completely removed from this discussion and cast out of [275] the mind. For they do not convey the true lay out of the bodies of the world and the polity of the movements.

Although I cannot do otherwise than to put solely Copernicus' opinion concerning the world in the place of those hypotheses and, if that were possible, to persuade everyone of it; but because the thing is still new among the mass of the intelligentsia (*apud vulgus studiosorum*), and the doctrine that the Earth is one of the planets and moves among the stars around a motionless sun sounds very absurd to the ears of most of them: therefore those who are shocked by the unfamiliarity of this opinion should know that these harmonical speculations are possible even with the hypotheses of Tycho Brahe—because that author holds, in common with Copernicus, everything else which pertains to the lay out of the bodies and the tempering of the movements, and transfers solely the Copernican annual movement of the Earth to the whole system of planetary spheres and to the sun, which occupies the centre of that system, in the opinion of both authors. For after this transference of movement it is nevertheless true that in Brahe the Earth occupies at any time the same place that Copernicus gives it, if not in the very vast and measureless region of the fixed stars, at least in the system of the planetary world. And accordingly, just as he who draws a circle on paper makes the writing-foot of the compass revolve, while he who fastens the paper or tablet to a turning lathe draws the same circle on the revolving tablet with the foot of the compass or stylus motionless; so too, in the case of Copernicus the Earth, by the real movement of its body, measures out a circle revolving midway between the circle of Mars on the

outside and that of Venus on the inside; but in the case of Tycho Brahe the whole planetary system (wherein among the rest the circles of Mars and Venus are found) revolves like a tablet on a lathe and applies to the motionless Earth, or to the stylus on the lathe, the midspace between the circles of Mars and Venus; and it comes about from this movement of the system that the Earth within it, although remaining motionless, marks out the same circle around the sun and midway between Mars and Venus, which in Copernicus it marks out by the real movement of its body while the system is at rest. Therefore, since harmonic speculation considers the eccentric movements of the planets, as if seen from the sun, you may easily understand that if any observer were stationed on a sun as much in motion as you please, nevertheless for him the Earth, although at rest (as a concession to Brahe), would seem to describe the annual circle midway between the planets and in an intermediate length of time. Wherefore, if there is any man of such feeble wit that he cannot grasp the movement of the Earth among the stars, nevertheless he can take pleasure in the most excellent spectacle of this most divine construction, if he applies to their image in the sun whatever he hears concerning the daily movements of the Earth in its eccentric—such an image as Tycho Brahe exhibits, with the Earth at rest.

And nevertheless the followers of the true Samian philosophy have no just cause to be jealous of sharing this delightful speculation with such persons, because their joy will be in many ways more perfect, as due to the consummate perfection of speculation, if they have accepted the immobility of the sun and the movement of the Earth.

Firstly [I], therefore, let my readers grasp that today it is absolutely certain among all astronomers that all the planets revolve around the sun, with the exception of the moon, which alone has the Earth as its centre: the magnitude of the moon's sphere or orbit is not great enough for it to be delineated in this diagram in a just ratio to the rest. Therefore, to the other five planets, a sixth, the Earth, is added, which traces a sixth circle around the sun, whether by its own proper movement with the sun at rest, or motionless itself and with the whole planetary system revolving.

Secondly [II]: It is also certain that all the planets are eccentric, *i.e.*, they change their distances from the sun, in such fashion that in one part of their circle they become farthest away from the sun, [276] and in the opposite part they come nearest to the sun. In the accompanying diagram three circles apiece have been drawn for the single planets: none of them indicate the eccentric route of the planet itself; but the mean circle, such as *BE* in the case of Mars, is equal to the eccentric orbit, with respect to its longer diameter. But the orbit itself, such as *AD*, touches *AF*, the upper of the three, in one place *A*, and the lower circle *CD*, in the opposite place *D*. The circle *GH* made with dots and described through the centre of the sun indicates the route of the sun according to Tycho Brahe. And if the sun moves on this route, then absolutely all the

points in this whole planetary system here depicted advance upon an equal route, each upon his own. And with one point of it (namely, the centre of the sun) stationed at one point of its circle, as here at the lowest, absolutely each and every point of the system will be stationed at the lowest part of its circle. However, on account of the smallness of the space the three circles of Venus unite in one, contrary to my intention.

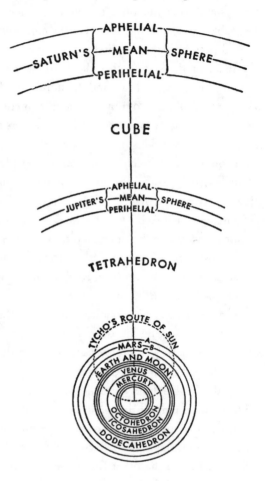

Thirdly [III]: Let the reader recall from my *Mysterium Cosmographicum*, which I published twenty-two years ago, that the number of the planets or circular routes around the sun was taken by the very wise Founder from the five regular solids, concerning which Euclid, so many ages ago, wrote his book which is called the *Elements* in that it is built up out of a series of propositions. But it has been made clear in the second book of this work that there cannot be more regular bodies, *i.e.*, that regular plane figures cannot fit together in a solid more than five times.

Fourthly [IV]: As regards the ratio of the planetary orbits, the ratio between two neighbouring planetary orbits is always of such a magnitude that it is easily apparent that each and every one of them approaches the single ratio of the spheres of one of the five regular solids, namely, that of the sphere circumscribing to the sphere inscribed in the figure. Nevertheless it is not wholly equal, as I once dared to promise concerning the final perfection of astronomy. For, after completing the demonstration of the intervals from Brahe's observations, I discovered the following: if the angles of the cube [277] are applied to the inmost circle of Saturn, the centres of the planes are approximately tangent to the middle circle of Jupiter; and if the angles of the tetrahedron are placed against the inmost circle of Jupiter, the centres of the planes of the tetrahedron

are approximately tangent to the outmost circle of Mars; thus if the angles of the octahedron are placed against any circle of Venus (for the total interval between the three has been very much reduced), the centres of the planes of the octahedron penetrate and descend deeply within the outmost circle of Mercury, but nonetheless do not reach as far as the middle circle of Mercury; and finally, closest of all to the ratios of the dodecahedral and icosahedral spheres—which ratios are equal to one another—are the ratios or intervals between the circles of Mars and the Earth, and the Earth and Venus; and those intervals are similarly equal, if we compute from the inmost circle of Mars to the middle circle of the Earth, but from the middle circle of the Earth to the middle circle of Venus. For the middle distance of the Earth is a mean proportional between the least distance of Mars and the middle distance of Venus. However, these two ratios between the planetary circles are still greater than the ratios of those two pairs of spheres in the figures, in such fashion that the centres of the dodecahedral planes are not tangent to the outmost circle of the Earth, and the centres of the icosahedral planes are not tangent to the outmost circle of Venus; nor, however, can this gap be filled by the semidiameter of the lunar sphere, by adding it, on the upper side, to the greatest distance of the Earth and subtracting it, on the lower, from the least distance of the same. But I find a certain other ratio of figures—namely, if I take the augmented dodecahedron, to which I have given the name of echinus, (as being fashioned from twelve quinquangular stars and thereby very close to the five regular solids), if I take it, I say, and place its twelve points in the inmost circle of Mars, then the sides of the pentagons, which are the bases of the single rays or points, touch the middle circle of Venus. In short: the cube and the octahedron, which are consorts, do not penetrate their planetary spheres at all; the dodecahedron and the icosahedron, which are consorts, do not wholly reach to theirs, the tetrahedron exactly touches both: in the first case there is falling short; in the second, excess; and in the third, equality, with respect to the planetary intervals.

Wherefore it is clear that the very ratios of the planetary intervals from the sun have not been taken from the regular solids alone. For the Creator, who is the very source of geometry and, as Plato wrote, "practices eternal geometry," does not stray from his own archetype. And indeed that very thing could be inferred from the fact that all the planets change their intervals throughout fixed periods of time, in such fashion that each has two marked intervals from the sun, a greatest and a least; and a fourfold comparison of the intervals from the sun is possible between two planets: the comparison can be made between either the greatest, or the least, or the contrary intervals most remote from one another, or the contrary intervals nearest together. In this way the comparisons made two by two between neighbouring planets are twenty in number, although on the contrary there are only five regular solids. But it is consonant that if the Creator had any concern for the ratio of the spheres in general, He would

also have had concern for the ratio which exists between the varying intervals of the single planets specifically and that the concern is the same in both cases and the one is bound up with the other. If we ponder that, we will comprehend that for setting up the diameters and eccentricities conjointly, there is need of more principles, outside of the five regular solids.

Fifthly [V]: To arrive at the movements between which the consonances have been set up, once more I impress upon the reader that in the *Commentaries on Mars* I have demonstrated from the sure observations of Brahe that daily arcs, which are equal in one and the same eccentric circle, are not traversed with equal speed; but that these differing *delays in equal parts of the eccentric observe the ratio of their distances from the sun,* the source of movement; and conversely, that if equal times are assumed, namely, one natural day in both cases, the corresponding *true diurnal arcs* [278] *of one eccentric orbit have to one another the ratio which is the inverse of the ratio of the two distances from the sun.* Moreover, I demonstrated at the same time that *the planetary orbit is elliptical and the sun, the source of movement, is at one of the foci of this ellipse; and so, when the planet has completed a quarter of its total circuit from its aphelion, then it is exactly at its mean distance from the sun, midway between its greatest distance at the aphelion and its least at the perihelion.* But from these two axioms it results *that the diurnal mean movement of the planet in its eccentric is the same as the true diurnal arc of its eccentric at those moments wherein the planet is at the end of the quadrant of the eccentric measured from the aphelion, although that true quadrant appears still smaller than the just quadrant.* Furthermore, it follows *that the sum of any two true diurnal eccentric arcs, one of which is at the same distance from the aphelion that the other is from the perihelion, is equal to the sum of the two mean diurnal arcs.* And as a consequence, *since the ratio of circles is the same as that of the diameters, the ratio of one mean diurnal arc to the sum of all the mean and equal arcs in the total circuit is the same as the ratio of the mean diurnal arc to the sum of all the true eccentric arcs, which are the same in number but unequal to one another.* And those things should first be known concerning the true diurnal arcs of the eccentric and the true movements, so that by means of them we may understand the movements which would be apparent if we were to suppose an eye at the sun.

Sixthly [VI]: But as regards the arcs which are apparent, as it were, from the sun, it is known even from the ancient astronomy that, among true movements which are equal to one another, that movement which is farther distant from the centre of the world (as being at the aphelion) will appear smaller to a beholder at that centre, but the movement which is nearer (as being at the perihelion) will similarly appear greater. Therefore, since moreover the true diurnal arcs at the near distance are still greater, on account of the faster movement, and still smaller at the distant aphelion, on account of the slowness of the movement, I demonstrated in the *Commentaries on Mars* that *the*

ratio of the apparent diurnal arcs of one eccentric circle is fairly exactly the inverse ratio of the squares of their distances from the sun. For example, if the planet one day when it is at a distance from the sun of 10 parts, in any measure whatsoever, but on the opposite day, when it is at the perihelion, of 9 similar parts: it is certain that from the sun its apparent progress at the aphelion will be to its apparent progress at the perihelion, as 81 : 100.

But that is true with these provisos: First, that the eccentric arcs should not be great, lest they partake of distinct distances which are very different—*i.e.*, lest the distances of their termini from the apsides cause a perceptible variation; second, that the eccentricity should not be very great, for the greater its eccentricity (*viz.*, the greater the arc becomes) the more the angle of its apparent movement increases beyond the measure of its approach to the sun, by Theorem 8 of Euclid's *Optics*; none the less in small arcs even a great distance is of no moment, as I have remarked in my *Optics*, Chapter 11. But there is another reason why I make that admonition. For the eccentric arcs around the mean anomalies are viewed obliquely from the centre of the sun. This obliquity subtracts from the magnitude of the apparent movement, since conversely the arcs around the apsides are presented directly to an eye stationed as it were at the sun. Therefore, when the eccentricity is very great, then the eccentricity takes away perceptibly from the ratio of the movements; if without any diminution we apply the mean diurnal movement to the mean distance, as if at the mean distance, it would appear to have the same magnitude which it does have—as will be apparent below in the case of Mercury. All these things are treated at greater length in Book V of the *Epitome of Copernican Astronomy*, but they have been mentioned here too because they have to do with the very terms of the celestial consonances, considered in themselves singly and separately.

Seventhly [VII]: If by chance anyone runs into those diurnal movements which are apparent [279] to those gazing not as it were from the sun but from the Earth, with which movements Book VI of the *Epitome of Copernican Astronomy* deals, he should know that their rationale is plainly not considered in this business. Nor should it be, since the Earth is not the source of the planetary movements, nor can it be, since with respect to deception of sight they degenerate not only into mere quiet or apparent stations but even into retrogradation, in which way a whole infinity of ratios is assigned to all the planets, simultaneously and equally. Therefore, in order that we may hold for certain what sort of ratios of their own are constituted by the single real eccentric orbits (although these too are still apparent, as it were to one looking from the sun, the source of movement), first we must remove from those movements of their own this image of the adventitious annual movement common to all five, whether it arises from the movement of the Earth itself, according to Copernicus, or from the annual movement

of the total system, according to Tycho Brahe, and the winnowed movements proper to each planet are to be presented to sight.

Eighthly [VIII]: So far we have dealt with the different delays or arcs of one and the same planet. Now we must also deal with the comparison of the movements of two planets. Here take note of the definitions of the terms which will be necessary for us. We give the name of *nearest apsides* of two planets to the perihelion of the upper and the aphelion of the lower, notwithstanding that they tend not towards the same region of the world but towards distinct and perhaps contrary regions. By *extreme movements* understand the slowest and the fastest of the whole planetary circuit; by *converging or converse extreme movements*, those which are at the nearest apsides of two planets— namely, at the perihelion of the upper planet and the aphelion of the lower; by *diverging or diverse*, those at the opposite apsides—namely, the aphelion of the upper and the perihelion of the lower. Therefore again, a certain part of my *Mysterium Cosmographicum*, which was suspended twenty-two years ago, because it was not yet clear, is to be completed and herein inserted. For after finding the true intervals of the spheres by the observations of Tycho Brahe and continuous labour and much time, at last, at last the right ratio of the periodic times to the spheres

> though it was late, looked to the unskilled man,
> yet looked to him, and, after much time, came,

and, if you want the exact time, was conceived mentally on the 8th of March in this year One Thousand Six Hundred and Eighteen but unfelicitously submitted to calculation and rejected as false, finally, summoned back on the 15th of May, with a fresh assault undertaken, outfought the darkness of my mind by the great proof afforded by my labor of seventeen years on Brahe's observations and meditation upon it uniting in one concord, in such fashion that I first believed I was dreaming and was presupposing the object of my search among the principles. But it is absolutely certain and exact that *the ratio which exists between the periodic times of any two planets is precisely the ratio of the $3/2$th power of the mean distances,* i.e., *of the spheres themselves,* provided, however, that the arithmetic mean between both diameters of the elliptic orbit be slightly less than the longer diameter. And so if any one take the period, say, of the Earth, which is one year, and the period of Saturn, which is thirty years, and extract the cube roots of this ratio and then square the ensuing ratio by squaring the cube roots, he will have as his numerical products the most just ratio of the distances of the Earth and Saturn from the sun.[1] For the cube root of 1 is 1, and the square of it is 1; and the cube root of 30 is greater than 3, and therefore the square of it is greater than 9. And Saturn, at

---

1. For in the *Commentaries on Mars*, chapter 48, page 232, I have proved that this Arithmetic mean is either the diameter of the circle which is equal in length to the elliptic orbit, or else is very slightly less.

its mean distance from the sun, is slightly higher [280] than nine times the mean distance of the Earth from the sun. Further on, in Chapter 9, the use of this theorem will be necessary for the demonstration of the eccentricities.

Ninthly [IX]: If now you wish to measure with the same yardstick, so to speak, the true daily journeys of each planet through the ether, two ratios are to be compounded—the ratio of the true (not the apparent) diurnal arcs of the eccentric, and the ratio of the mean intervals of each planet from the sun (because that is the same as the ratio of the amplitude of the spheres), *i.e., the true diurnal arc of each planet is to be multiplied by the semidiameter of its sphere:* the products will be numbers fitted for investigating whether or not those journeys are in harmonic ratios.

Tenthly [X]: In order that you may truly know how great any one of these diurnal journeys appears to be to an eye stationed as it were at the sun, although this same thing can be got immediately from the astronomy, nevertheless it will also be manifest if you multiply the ratio of the journeys by the inverse ratio not of the mean, but of the true intervals which exist at any position on the eccentrics: *multiply the journey of the upper by the interval of the lower planet from the sun, and conversely multiply the journey of the lower by the interval of the upper from the sun.*

Eleventhly [XI]: And in the same way, if the apparent movements are given, at the aphelion of the one and at the perihelion of the other, or conversely or alternately, the ratios of the distances of the aphelion of the one to the perihelion of the other may be elicited. But where the mean movements must be known first, *viz.*, the inverse ratio of the periodic times, wherefrom the ratio of the spheres is elicited by Article VIII above: then *if the mean proportional between the apparent movement of either one of its mean movement be taken, this mean proportional is to the semidiameter of its sphere* (which is already known) *as the mean movement is to the distance or interval sought.* Let the periodic times of two planets be 27 and 8. Therefore the ratio of the mean diurnal movement of the one to the other is 8 : 27. Therefore the semidiameters of their spheres will be as 9 to 4. For the cube root of 27 is 3, that of 8 is 2, and the squares of these roots, 3 and 2, are 9 and 4. Now let the apparent aphelial movement of the one be 2 and the perihelial movement of the other $33^{1}/_{3}$. The mean proportionals between the mean movements 8 and 27 and these apparent ones will be 4 and 30. Therefore if the mean proportional 4 gives the mean distance of 9 to the planet, then the mean movement of 8 gives an aphelial distance 18, which corresponds to the apparent movement 2; and if the other mean proportional 30 gives the other planet a mean distance of 4, then its mean movement of 27 will give it a perihelial interval of $3^{3}/_{5}$. I say, therefore, that the aphelial distance of the former is to the perihelial distance of the latter as 18 to $3^{3}/_{5}$. Hence it is clear that if the consonances between the extreme movements of two planets are found and the periodic times are established for both, the extreme and the mean

distances are necessarily given, wherefore also the eccentricities.

Twelfthly [XII]: It is also possible, from the different extreme movements of one and the same planet, to find the *mean movement*. The mean movement is not exactly the arithmetic mean between the extreme movements, nor exactly the geometric mean, but it is as much less than the geometric mean as the geometric mean is less than the (arithmetic) mean between both means. Let the two extreme movements be 8 and 10: the mean movement will be less than 9, and also less than the square root of 80 by half the difference between 9 and the square root of 80. In this way, if the aphelial movement is 20 and the perihelial 24, the mean movement will be less than 22, even less than the square root of 480 by half the difference between that root and 22. There is use for this theorem in what follows.

[281] Thirteenthly [XIII]: From the foregoing the following proposition is demonstrated, which is going to be very necessary for us: Just as the ratio of the mean movements of two planets is the inverse ratio of the $3/2$th powers of the spheres, so the ratio of two apparent converging extreme movements always falls short of the ratio of the $3/2$th powers of the intervals corresponding to those extreme movements; and in what ratio the product of the two ratios of the corresponding intervals to the two mean intervals or to the semidiameters of the two spheres falls short of the ratio of the square roots of the spheres, in that ratio does the ratio of the two extreme converging movements exceed the ratio of the corresponding intervals; but if that compound ratio were to exceed the ratio of the square roots of the spheres, then the ratio of the converging movements would be less than the ratio of their intervals.[1]

Let the ratio of the spheres be *DH : AE*; let the ratio of the mean movements be *HI : EM*, the $3/2$th power of the inverse of the former. Let the least interval of the sphere of the first be *CG*; and the greatest interval of the sphere of the second be *BF*; and first let *DH : CG* comp. *BF : AE* be smaller than the $1/2$th power of *DH : AE*. And let *GH* be the apparent perihelial movement of the upper planet, and *FL* the aphelial of the lower, so that they are converging extreme movements.

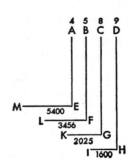

I say that

$$GK : FL = BF : CG$$
$$BF^{3/2} : CG^{3/2}.$$

For

$$HI : GK = CG^2 : DH^2$$

and
$$FL : EM = AE^2 : BF^2.$$
Hence
$$HI : GK \text{ comp. } FL : EM = CG^2 : DH^2 \text{ comp. } AE^2 : BF^2.$$
But
$$CG : DH \text{ comp. } AE : BF < AE^{1/2} : DH^{1/2}$$
by a fixed ratio of defect, as was assumed. Therefore too
$$HI : GK \text{ comp. } FL : EM \ AE^{2/2} : DH^{2/2}$$
$$AE : DH$$
by a ratio of defect which is the square of the former. But by number VIII
$$HI : EM = AE^{3/2} : DH^{3/2}.$$
Therefore let the ratio which is smaller by the total square of the ratio of defect be divided into the ratio of the $^3/_2$th powers; that is,
$$HI : EM \text{ comp. } GK : HI \text{ comp. } EM : FL \ AE^{1/2} : DH^{1/2}$$
by the excess squared. But
$$HI : EM \text{ comp. } GK : HI \text{ comp. } EM : FL = GK : FL.$$
Therefore
$$GK : FL \ AE^{1/2} : DH^{1/2}$$
by the excess squared. But
$$AE : DH = AE : BF \text{ comp. } BF : CG \text{ comp. } CG : DH.$$
And
$$CG : DH \text{ comp. } AE : BF \ AE^{1/2} : DH^{1/2}$$
by the simple defect. Therefore
$$BF : CG \ AE^{1/2} : DH^{1/2}$$
by the simple excess. But
$$GK : FL \ AE^{1/2} : DH^{1/2}$$
but by the excess squared. But the excess squared is greater than the simple excess. Therefore the ratio of the movements GK to FL is greater than the ratio of the corresponding intervals BF to CG.

In fully the same way, it is demonstrated even contrariwise that if the planets approach one another in G and F beyond the mean distances in H and E, in such fashion that the ratio of the mean distances $DH : AE$ becomes less than $DH^{1/2} : AE^{1/2}$, then the ratio of the movements $GK : FL$ becomes less than the ratio of the corresponding intervals $BF : CG$. For you need to do nothing more than to change the words *greater* to *less*, > to <, *excess* to *defect*, and conversely.

In suitable numbers, because the square root of $^4/_9$ is $^2/_3$; and $^5/_8$ is even greater than $^2/_3$ by the ratio of excess $^{15}/_{16}$; and the square of the ratio 8 : 9 [282] is the ratio 1600 : 2025, *i.e.*, 64 : 81; and the square of the ratio 4 : 5 is the ratio 3456 : 5400, *i.e.*,

16 : 25; and finally the $3/_2$th power of the ratio 4 : 9 is the ratio 1600 : 5400, *i.e.*, 8 : 27: therefore too the ratio 2025 : 3456, *i.e.*, 75 : 128, is even greater than 5 : 8, *i.e.*, 75 : 120, by the same ratio of excess (*i.e.*, 120 : 128), 15 : 16; whence 2025 : 3456, the ratio of the converging movements, exceeds 5 : 8, the inverse ratio of the corresponding intervals, by as much as 5 : 8 exceeds 2 : 3, the square root of the ratio of the spheres. Or, what amounts to the same thing, the ratio of the two converging intervals is a mean between the ratio of the square roots of the spheres and the inverse ratio of the corresponding movements.

Moreover, from this you may understand that the ratio of the diverging movements is much greater than the ratio of the $3/_2$th powers of the spheres, since the ratio of the $3/_2$th powers is compounded with the squares of the ratio of the aphelial interval to the mean interval, and that of the mean to the perihelial.

4. IN WHAT THINGS HAVING TO DO WITH THE PLANETARY MOVEMENTS HAVE THE HARMONIC CONSONANCES BEEN EXPRESSED BY THE CREATOR, AND IN WHAT WAY?

Accordingly, if the image of the retrogradation and stations is taken away and the proper movements of the planets in their real eccentric orbits are winnowed out, the following distinct things still remain in the planets: 1) The distances from the sun. 2) The periodic times. 3) The diurnal eccentric arcs. 4) The diurnal delays in those arcs. 5) The angles at the sun, and the diurnal area apparent to those as it were gazing from the sun. And again, all of these things, with the exception of the periodic times, are variable in the total circuit, most variable at the mean longitudes, but least at the extremes, when, turning away from one extreme longitude, they begin to return to the opposite. Hence when the planet is lowest and nearest to the sun and thereby delays the least in one degree of its eccentric, and conversely in one day traverses the greatest diurnal arc of its eccentric and appears fastest from the sun: then its movement remains for some time in this strength without perceptible variation, until, after passing the perihelion, the planet gradually begins to depart farther from the sun in a straight line; at that same time it delays longer in the degrees of its eccentric circle; or, if you consider the movement of one day, on the following day it goes forward less and appears even more slow from the sun until it has drawn close to the highest apsis and made its distance from the sun very great: for then longest of all does it delay in one degree of its eccentric; or on the contrary in one day it traverses its least arc and makes a much smaller apparent movement and the least of its total circuit.

Finally, all these things may be considered either as they exist in any one planet at different times or as they exist in different planets: whence, by the assumption of an infinite amount of time, all the affects of the circuit of one planet can concur in the

same moment of time with all the affects of the circuit of another planet and be compared, and then the total eccentrics, as compared with one another, have the same ratio as their semidiameters or mean intervals; but the arcs of two eccentrics, which are similar or designated by the same number (of degrees), nevertheless have their true lengths unequal in the ratio of their eccentrics. For example, one degree in the sphere of Saturn is approximately twice as long as one degree in the sphere of Jupiter. And conversely, the diurnal arcs of the eccentrics, as expressed in astronomical terms, do not exhibit the ratio of the true journeys which the globes complete in one day [283] through the ether, because the single units in the wider circle of the upper planet denote a quarter part of the journey, but in the narrower circle of the lower planet a smaller part.

Therefore let us take the second of the things which we have posited, namely, the periodic times of the planets, which comprehend the sums made up of all the delays—long, middling, short—in all the degrees of the total circuit. And we found that from antiquity down to us, the planets complete their periodic returns around the sun, as follows in the table:

	Days	Minutes of a day	Therefore the mean diurnal moments		
			Min.	Sec.	Thirds
Saturn	10,759	12	2	0	27
Jupiter	4,332	37	4	59	8
Mars	686	59	31	26	31
Earth with Moon	365	15	59	8	11
Venus	224	42	96	7	39
Mercury	87	58	245	32	25

Accordingly, in these periodic times there are no harmonic ratios, as is easily apparent, if the greater periods are continuously halved, and the smaller are continuously doubled, so that, by neglecting the intervals of an octave, we can investigate the intervals which exist within one octave.

	Saturn	Jupiter	Mars	Earth	Venus	Mercury	
	10,759^{D}12'						
	5,379^{D}36'	4,332^{D}37'				87^{D}58'	
Halves	2,689^{D}48'	2,166^{D}19'			224^{D}42'	175^{D}56'	Doubles
	1,344^{D}54'	1,083^{D}10'	686^{D}59'	365^{D}15'	449^{D}24'	351^{D}52'	
	672^{D}27'	541^{D}35'					

All the last numbers, as you see, are counter to harmonic ratios and seem, as it were, irrational. For let 687, the number of days of Mars, receive as its measure 120, which is the number of the division of the chord: according to this measure Saturn will have 117 for one sixteenth of its period, Jupiter less than 95 for one eighth of its peri-

od, the Earth less than 64, Venus more than 78 for twice its period, Mercury more than 61 for four times its period. These numbers do not make any harmonic ratio with 120, but their neighbouring numbers—60, 75, 80, and 96—do. And so, whereof Saturn has 120, Jupiter has approximately 97, the Earth more than 65, Venus more than 80, and Mercury less than 63. And whereof Jupiter has 120, the Earth has less than 81, Venus less than 100, Mercury less than 78. Likewise, whereof Venus has 120, the Earth has less than 98, Mercury more than 94. Finally, whereof the Earth has 120, Mercury has less than 116. But if the free choice of ratios had been effective here, consonances which are altogether perfect but not augmented or diminished would have been taken. Accordingly we find that God the Creator did not wish to introduce harmonic ratios between the sums of the delays added together to form the periodic times.

[284] And although it is a very probable conjecture (as relying on geometrical demonstrations and the doctrine concerning the causes of the planetary movements given in the *Commentaries on Mars*) that the bulks of the planetary bodies are in the ratio of the periodic times, so that the globe of Saturn is about thirty times greater than the globe of the Earth, Jupiter twelve times, Mars less than two, the Earth one and a half times greater than the globe of Venus and four times greater than the globe of Mercury: not therefore will even these ratios of bodies be harmonic.

But since God has established nothing without geometrical beauty, which was not bound by some other prior law of necessity, we easily infer that the periodic times have got their due lengths, and thereby the mobile bodies too have got their bulks, from something which is prior in the archetype, in order to express which thing these bulks and periods have been fashioned to this measure, as they seem disproportionate. But I have said that the periods are added up from the longest, the middling, and the slowest delays: accordingly geometrical fitnesses must be found either in these delays or in anything which may be prior to them in the mind of the Artisan. But the ratios of the delays are bound up with the ratios of the diurnal arcs, because the arcs have the inverse ratio of the delays. Again, we have said that the ratios of the delays and intervals of any one planet are the same. Then, as regards the single planets, there will be one and the same consideration of the following three: the arcs, the delays in equal arcs, and the distance of the arcs from the sun or the intervals. And because all these things are variable in the planets, there can be no doubt but that, if these things were allotted any geometrical beauty, then, by the sure design of the highest Artisan, they would have been received that at their extremes, at the aphelial and perihelial intervals, not at the mean intervals lying in between. For, given the ratios of the extreme intervals, there is no need of a plan to fit the intermediate ratios to a definite number. For they follow of themselves, by the necessity of planetary movement, from one extreme through all the intermediates to the other extreme.

Therefore the intervals are as follows, according to the very accurate observations of Tycho Brahe, by the method given in the *Commentaries on Mars* and investigated in very persevering study for seventeen years.

INTERVALS COMPARED WITH HARMONIC RATIOS[1]

Of Two Planets *Converging Diverging*		Of Single Planets
$a/_b=2/_1,$ $b/_c=5/_3$	Saturn's aphelion 10,052. a. perihelion 8,968. b.	More than a minor whole tone $^{10,000}/_{9,000}$ Less than a major whole tone $^{10,000}/_{8,935}$
$c/_f=4/_1,$ $d/_e=3/_1$	Jupiter's aphelion 5,451. c. perihelion 4,949. d.	No concordant ratio but approximately 11 : 10, a discordant or diminished 6 : 5.
$e/_h=5/_3,$ $f/_g=17/_{20}$	Mar's aphelion 1,665. e. perihelion 1,382. f.	Here 1662 : 1385 would be the consonance 6 : 5, and 1665 : 1332 would be 5 : 4
$\dfrac{g}{k}=\dfrac{2}{1\frac{1}{2}}\,viz\dfrac{1000}{710},\dfrac{h}{i}=\dfrac{27}{20}$	Earth's aphelion 1,018. g. perihelion 982. h.	Here 1025 : 984 would be the diesis 24 : 25. Therefore it does not have the diesis.
$i/_m=12/_5,$ $k/_i=243/_{160}$	Venus' aphelion 729. i. perihelion 719. k.	Less than a sesquicomma. More than one third of a diesis.
	Mercury's aphelion 470. l. perihelion 307. m.	243 : 160, greater than a perfect fifth but less than a harmonic 8 : 5

[285] Therefore the extreme intervals of no one planet come near consonances except those of Mars and Mercury.

But if you compare the extreme intervals of different planets with one another, some harmonic light begins to shine. For the extreme diverging intervals of Saturn and Jupiter make slightly more than the octave; and the converging, a mean between the major and minor sixths. So the diverging extremes of Jupiter and Mars embrace approximately the double octave; and the converging, approximately the fifth and the

---

1. General Note: Throughout this text Kepler's *concinna* and *inconcinna* are translated as "concordant" and "discordant." *Concinna* is usually used by Kepler of all intervals whose ratios occur within the "natural system" or the just intonation of the scale. *Inconcinna* refers to all ratios that lie outside of this system of tuning. "Consonant" (*consonans*) and "dissonant" (*dissonans*) refer to qualities which can be applied to intervals within the musical system, in other words to "concords." "Harmony" (*harmonia*) is used sometimes in the sense of "concordance" and sometimes in the sense of "consonance."

Genus durum and *genus molle* are translated either as "major mode" and "minor mode," or as "major scale" and "minor scale," or as "major kind" and "minor kind" (of consonances). The use of *modus*, to refer to the ecclesiastical modes, occurs only in Chapter 6.

As our present musical terms do not apply strictly to the music of the sixteenth and seventeenth centuries, a brief explanation of terms here may be useful. This material is taken from Kepler's *Harmonies of the World*, Book III.

An octave system in the minor scale (*Systema octavae in cantu molli*)

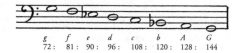

	g	f	e	d	c	b	A	G
Ratios of string lengths:	72:	81:	90:	96:	108:	120:	128:	144

octave. But the diverging extremes of the Earth and Mars embrace somewhat more than the major sixth; the converging, an augmented fourth. In the next couple, the Earth and Venus, there is again the same augmented fourth between the converging extremes; but we lack any harmonic ratio between the diverging extremes: for it is less than the semi-octave (so to speak), *i.e.*, less than the square root of the ratio 2 : 1. Finally, between the diverging extremes of Venus and Mercury there is a ratio slightly less than the octave compounded with the minor third; between the converging there is a slightly augmented fifth.

In the major scale (*In cantu duro*)

g   f   e   d   c   B   A   G

Ratios of string lengths:　　360 :405 :　432 :　480 :　540 :　576 :　640 :　720

As in all music, these scales can be repeated at one or more octaves above. The ratios would then all be halved, *i.e.*,

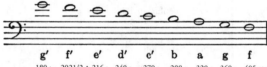

g'　 f'　 e'　 d'　 c'　 b　 a　 g　 f

180 :　2021/2 : 216 :　240 :　270 :　288 :　320 :　360 :　405 etc.

Various intervals which Kepler considers are:

80 : 81	*comma* (of Didymus), difference between major and minor whole tones (8/9 ÷ 9/10)	
24 : 25	*diesis* [difference between e – e flat or B – b flat or between a semitone and a minor whole tone (15/16 ÷ 9/10)]	
128 : 135	*lemma* [difference between a semitone and a major whole tone (15/16 ÷ 8/9)]	
243 : 256	*Plato's lemma* (not found in this system but in the Pythagorean tuning)	
15 : 16	*semitone*	minor mode between e flat – d, b flat – A
		major mode between e – d, B – A
9 : 10	*minor whole tone*	minor mode f – e flat, c – b flat
		major mode e – d, B – A
8 : 9	*major whole tone*	minor mode: g – f, d – c, A – G
		major mode: g – f, d – c, A – G
27 : 32	*sub-minor third*	(major and minor modes: f – d, c – A)
5 : 6	*minor third*	minor mode: e – flat – c, b flat – G
		major mode: g – e, d – B
4 : 5	*major third*	minor mode: g – e – flat, d – b – flat
		major mode: e – c, B – G
64 : 81	*ditone* (Pythagorean third) (major and minor modes: a – f)	
243 : 320	*lesser imperfect fourth* (inversion of "greater imperfect fifth") see below	
3 : 4	*perfect fourth*	minor mode: g – d, f – c, e flat – b flat, d – A, c – G
		major mode: g – d, f – c, e – B,　　, d – A, c – G
20 : 27	*greater imperfect fourth*	minor mode: b' flat – f
		major mode: a – e
32 : 45	*augmented fourth*	minor mode: a – e flat
		major mode: b – f
45 : 64	*diminished fifth*	minor mode: e – flat – A
		major mode: f – B
27 : 40	*lesser imperfect fifth*	minor mode: f – b flat
		major mode: e – A
2 : 3	*perfect fifth*	minor mode: g – c, d – G
		major mode: g – c, d – G
160 : 243	*greater imperfect fifth* (compound of ditone and minor third 64/81 x 5/6)	
81 : 128	*imperfect minor sixth* (minor and major modes: f – A)	
5 : 8	*minor sixth*	minor mode: e flat – G, b^{1b}+ – d
		major mode: g – B, c' – e
3 : 5	*major sixth*	minor mode: g – B flat, c' – e flat
		major mode: e – G, b – d
64 : 27	*greater major sixth*	minor mode: d' – f, a – c
		major mode: d' – f, a – c
1 : 2	*octave* (g – G, a – A, b – B, b flat – b flat)	

All these are simple intervals. When one or more octaves are added to any simple intervals the resultant interval is a "compound" interval.

1 : 3 equals 1/2 x 2/3—an octave and a perfect fifth

3 : 32 equals (1/2)^3 x 3/4—three octaves and a perfect fourth

1 : 20 equals (1/2)^4 x 16/20—four octaves and a major third

Accordingly, although one interval was somewhat removed from harmonic ratios, this success was an invitation to advance further. Now my reasonings were as follows: First, in so far as these intervals are lengths without movement, they are not fittingly examined for harmonic ratios, because movement is more properly the subject of consonances, by reason of speed and slowness. Second, inasmuch as these same intervals are the diameters of the spheres, it is believable that the ratio of the five regular solids applied proportionally is more dominant in them, because the ratio of the geometrical solid bodies to the celestial spheres (which are everywhere either encompassed by celestial matter, as the ancients hold, or to be encompassed successively by the accumulation of many revolutions) is the same as the ratio of the plane figures which may be inscribed in a circle (these figures engender the consonances) to the celestial circles of movements and the other regions wherein the movements take place. Therefore, if we are looking for consonances, we should look for them not in these intervals in so far as they are the semidiameters of spheres but in them in so far as they are the measures of the movements, *i.e.*, in the movements themselves, rather. Absolutely no other than the mean intervals can be taken as the semidiameters of the spheres; but we are here dealing with the extreme intervals. Accordingly, we are not dealing with the intervals in respect to their spheres but in respect to their movements.

Accordingly, although for these reasons I had passed on to the comparison of the extreme movements, at first the ratios of the movements remained the same in magnitude as those which were previously the ratios of the intervals, only inverted. Wherefore too, certain ratios, which are discordant and foreign to harmonies, as before, have been found between the movements. But once again I judged that this happened to me deservedly, because I compared with one another eccentric arcs which

Concords: All intervals from diesis downward on above list.

Consonances: Minor and major thirds and sixths, perfect fourth, fifth, and octave.

"Adulterine" consonances: sub-minor third, ditone, lesser imperfect fourth and fifth, greater imperfect fourth and fifth, imperfect minor sixth, greater major sixth.

Dissonances: All other intervals.

Throughout this work Kepler, after the fashion of the theorists of his time, uses the ratios of string lengths rather than the ratios of vibrations as is usually done today. String lengths are, of course, inversely proportionate to the vibrations. That is, string lengths 4 : 5 are expressed in vibrations as 5 : 4. This accounts for the descending order of the scale, which follows the increasing numerical order. It is an interesting fact that Kepler's minor and major scales are inversions of each other and hence, when expressed in ratios of vibrations, are in the opposite order from those in ratios of string lengths:

Notes resulting from ratios of vibrations

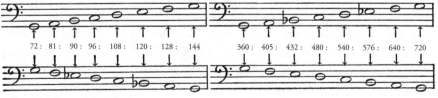

| 72 : | 81 : | 90 : | 96 : | 108 : | 120 : | 128 : | 144 |

| 360 : | 405 : | 432 : | 480 : | 540 : | 576 : | 640 : | 720 |

Notes resulting from ratios of string lengths

An arbitrary pitch G is chosen to situate these ratios. This g or "gamma" was usually the lowest tone of the sixteenth-century musical gamut.

Elliott Carter, Jr.

are not expressed and numbered by a measure of the same magnitude but are numbered in degrees and minutes which are of diverse magnitude in diverse planets, nor do they from our place give the appearance of being as great as the number of each says, except only at the centre of the eccentric of each planet, which centre rests upon no body; and hence it is also unbelievable that there is any sense or natural instinct in that place in the world which is capable of perceiving this; or, rather, it was impossible, if I was comparing the eccentric arcs of different planets with respect to their appearance at their centres, which are different for different planets. But if diverse apparent magnitudes are compared with one another, they ought to be apparent in one place in the world in such a way that that which possesses the faculty of comparing them may be present in that place from which they are all apparent. Accordingly, I judged that the appearance of these eccentric arcs should be removed from the mind or else should be formed differently. But if I removed the appearance and applied my mind to the diurnal journeys of the planets, I saw that I had to employ the rule which I gave in Article IX of the preceding chapter. [286] Accordingly if the diurnal arcs of the eccentric are multiplied by the mean intervals of the spheres, the following journeys are produced:

		Diurnal movements	Mean intervals	Diurnal journeys
Saturn	at aphelion	1'53"	9510	1065
	at perihelion	2'7"		1208
Jupiter	at aphelion	4'44"	5200	1477
	at perihelion	5'15"		1638
Mars	at aphelion	28'44"	1524	2627
	at perihelion	34'34"		3161
Earth	at aphelion	58'60"	1000	3486
	at perihelion	60'13"		3613
Venus	at aphelion	95'29"	724	4149
	at perihelion	96'50"		4207
Mercury	at aphelion	201'0"	388	4680
	at perihelion	307'3"		7148

Thus Saturn traverses barely one seventh of the journey of Mercury; and hence, as Aristotle judged consonant with reason in Book II of *On the Heavens*, the planet which is nearer the sun always traverses a greater space than the planet which is farther away—as cannot hold in the ancient astronomy.

And indeed, if we weigh the thing fairly carefully, it will appear to be not very probable that the most wise Creator should have established harmonies between the

planetary journeys in especial. For if the ratios of the journeys are harmonic, all the other affects which the planets have will be necessitated and bound up with the journeys, so that there is no room elsewhere for establishing harmonies. But whose good will it be to have harmonies between the journeys, or who will perceive these harmonies? For there are two things which disclose to us harmonies in natural things: either light or sound: light apprehended through the eyes or hidden senses proportioned to the eyes, and sound through the ears. The mind seizes upon these forms and, whether by instinct (on which Book IV speaks profusely) or by astronomical or harmonic ratiocination, discerns the concordant from the discordant. Now there are no sounds in the heavens, nor is the movement so turbulent that any noise is made by the rubbing against the ether. Light remains. If light has to teach these things about the planetary journeys, it will teach either the eyes or a sensorium analogous to the eyes and situated in a definite place; and it seems that sense-perception must be present there in order that light of itself may immediately teach. Therefore there will be sense-perception in the total world, namely in order that the movements of all the planets may be presented to sense-perceptions at the same time. For that former route—from observations through the longest detours of geometry and arithmetic, through the ratios of the spheres and the other things which must be learned first, down to the journeys which have been exhibited—is too long for any natural instinct, for the sake of moving which it seems reasonable that the harmonies have been introduced.

Therefore with everything reduced to one view, I concluded rightly [287] that the true journeys of the planets through the ether should be dismissed, and that we should turn our eyes to the apparent diurnal arcs, according as they are all apparent from one definite and marked place in the world—namely, from the solar body itself, the source of movement of all the planets; and we must see, not how far away from the sun any one of the planets is, nor how much space it traverses in one day (for that is something for ratiocination and astronomy, not for instinct), but how great an angle the diurnal movement of each planet subtends in the solar body, or how great an arc it seems to traverse in one common circle described around the sun, such as the ecliptic, in order that these appearances, which were conveyed to the solar body by virtue of light, may be able to flow, together with the light, in a straight line into creatures, which are partakers of this instinct, as in Book IV we said the figure of the heavens flowed into the foetus by virtue of the rays.

Therefore, if you remove from the proper planetary movement the parallaxes of the annual orbit, which gives them the mere appearances of stations and retrogradations, Tycho's astronomy teaches that the diurnal movements of the planets in their orbits (which are apparent as it were to spectator at the sun) are as shown in the table on the opposite page.

Note that the great eccentricity of Mercury makes the ratio of the movements differ somewhat from the ratio of the square of the distances. For if you make the square of the ratio of 100, the mean distance, to 121, the aphelial distance, be the ratio of the aphelial movement to the mean movement of 245'32", then an aphelial movement of 167 will be produced; and if the square of the ratio of 100 to 79, the perihelial distance, be the ratio of the perihelial to the same mean movement, then the perihelial movement will become 393; and both cases are greater than I have here laid down, because the mean movement at the mean anomaly, viewed very obliquely, does not appear as great, *viz.*, not as great as 245'32", but about 5' less. Therefore, too, lesser aphelial and perihelial movements will be elicited. But the aphelial (appears) lesser and the perihelial greater, on account of theorem 8, Euclid's *Optics*, as I remarked in the preceding Chapter, Article VI.

Harmonies Between Two Planets		Apparent Diurnal Movements			Harmonies Between the Movements of Single Planets
Diverging	*Converging*				
		Saturn	at aphelion	1'46" a.	1 : 48": 2'15" = 4 : 5,
			at perihelion	2'15" b.	major third
$^a/_d = ^1/_3$,	$^b/_c = ^1/_2$				
		Jupiter	at aphelion	4'30" c.	4'35": 5'30" = 5 : 6,
			at perihelion	5'30" d.	minor third
$^c/_f = ^1/_8$,	$^d/_e = ^5/_{24}$				
		Mars	at aphelion	26'14" e.	25'21" : 38'1" = 2 : 3,
			at perihelion	38'1" f.	the fifth
$^e/_h = ^5/_{12}$,	$^f/_g = ^2/_3$				
		Earth	at aphelion	57'3" g.	57'28": 61'18" = 15 :
			at perihelion	61'18" h.	16, semitone
$^g/_k = ^3/_5$,	$^h/_i = ^5/_8$				
		Venus	at aphelion	94'50" i.	94'50": 98'47" = 24 :
			at perihelion	97'37" k.	25, diesis
$^i/_m = ^1/_4$,	$^k/_l = ^3/_5$				
		Mercury	at aphelion	164'0" 1.	164'0" : 394'0" = 5 : 12,
			at perihelion	384'0" m.	octave and minor third

Accordingly, I could mentally presume, even from the ratios of the diurnal eccentric arcs given above, that there were harmonies and concordant intervals between these extreme apparent movements of the single planets, since I saw that everywhere there the square roots of harmonic ratios were dominant, but knew that the ratio of the apparent movements was the square of the ratio of the eccentric movements. But it is

possible by experience itself, or without any ratiocination to prove what is affirmed, as you see [288] in the preceding table. The ratios of the apparent movements of the single planets approach very close to harmonies, in such fashion that Saturn and Jupiter embrace slightly more than the major and minor thirds, Saturn with a ratio of excess of 53 : 54, and Jupiter with one of 54 : 55 or less, namely approximately a sesquicomma; the Earth, slightly more (namely 137 : 138, or barely a semicomma) than a semitone; Mars somewhat less (namely 29 : 30, which approaches 34 : 35 or 35 : 36) than a fifth; Mercury exceeds the octave by a minor third rather than a whole tone, *viz.*, it is about 38 : 39 (which is about two commas, *viz.*, 34 : 35 or 35 : 36) less than a whole tone. Venus alone falls short of any of the concords the diesis; for its ratio is between two and three commas, and it exceeds two thirds of a diesis, and is about 34:35 or 35:36, a diesis diminished by a comma.

The moon, too, comes into this consideration. For we find that its hourly apogeal movement in the quadratures, *viz.*, the slowest of all its movements, to be 26'26"; its perigeal movement in the syzygies, *viz.*, the fastest of all, 35'12", in which way the perfect fourth is formed very precisely. For one third of 26'26" is 8'49", the quadruple of which is 35'16". And note that the consonance of the perfect fourth is found nowhere else between the apparent movements; note also the analogy between the fourth in consonances and the quarter in the phases. And so the above things are found in the movements of the single planets.

But in the extreme movements of two planets compared with one another, the radiant sun of celestial harmonies immediately shines at first glance, whether you compare the diverging extreme movements or the converging. For the ratio between the diverging movements of Saturn and Jupiter is exactly the duple or octave; that between the diverging, slightly more than triple or the octave and the fifth. For one third of 5'30" is 1'50", although Saturn has 1'46" instead of that. Accordingly, the planetary movements will differ from a consonance by a diesis more or less, *viz.*, 26 : 27 or 27:28; and with less than one second acceding at Saturn's aphelion, the excess will be 34 : 35, as great as the ratio of the extreme movements of Venus. The diverging and converging movements of Jupiter and Mars are under the sway of the triple octave and the double octave and a third, but not perfectly. For one eighth of 38'1" is 4'45", although Jupiter has 4'30"; and between these numbers there is still a difference of 18 : 19, which is a mean between the semitone of 15 : 16 and the diesis of 24 : 25, namely, approximately a perfect lemma of 128 : 135.[1] Thus one fifth of 26'14" is 5'15", although Jupiter has 5'30"; accordingly in this case the quintuple ratio is diminished in the ratio of 21 : 22, the augment in the case of the other ratio, *viz.*, approximately a diesis of 24 : 25.

1. cf. Footnote to *Intervals Compared with Harmonic Ratios*, p. 186.

The consonance 5 : 24 comes nearer, which compounds a minor instead of a major third with the double octave. For one fifth of 5'30" is 1'6", which if multiplied by 24 makes 26'24", does not differ by more than a semicomma. Mars and the Earth have been allotted the least ratio, exactly the sesquialteral or perfect fifth: for one third of 57'3" is 19'1", the double of which is 38'2", which is Mars' very number, *viz.*, 38'11". They have also been allotted the greater ratio of 5 : 12, the octave and minor third, but more imperfectly. For one twelfth of 61'18" is 5'6½," which if multiplied by 5 gives 25'33", although instead of that Mars has 26'14". Accordingly, there is a deficiency of a diminished diesis approximately, *viz.*, 35 : 36. But the Earth and Venus together have been allotted 3 : 5 as their greatest consonance and 5 : 8 as their least, the major and minor sixths, but again not perfectly. For one fifth of 97'37", which if multiplied by 3 gives 58'33", which is greater than the movement of the Earth in the ratio 34 : 35, which is approximately 35 : 36: by so much do the planetary ratios differ from the harmonic. Thus one eighth of 94'50" is 11'51"+, five times which is 59'16", which is approximately equal to the mean movement of the Earth. Wherefore here the planetary ratio is less than the harmonic [289] in the ratio of 29 : 30 or 30:31, which is again approximately 35 : 36, the diminished diesis; and thereby this least ratio of these planets approaches the consonance of the perfect fifth. For one third of 94'50" is 31'37", the double of which is 63'14", of which the 61'18" of the perihelial movement of the Earth falls short in the ratio of 31 : 32, so that the planetary ratio is exactly a mean between the neighbouring harmonic ratios. Finally, Venus and Mercury have been allotted the double octave as their greatest ratio and the major sixth as their least, but not absolute-perfectly. For one fourth of 384' is 96'0", although Venus has 94'50". Therefore the quadruple adds approximately one comma. Thus one fifth of 164' is 32'48", which if multiplied by 3 gives 98'24", although Venus has 97'37". Therefore the planetary ratio is diminished by about two thirds of a comma, *i.e.*, 126 : 127.

Accordingly the above consonances have been ascribed to the planets; nor is there any ratio from among the principal comparisons (*viz.*, of the converging and diverging extreme movements) which does not approach so nearly to some consonance that, if strings were tuned in that ratio, the ears would not easily discern their imperfection—with the exception of that one excess between Jupiter and Mars.

Moreover, it follows that we shall not stray far away from consonances if we compare the movements of the same field. For if Saturn's 4 : 5 comp. 53 : 54 are compounded with the intermediate 1 : 2, the product is 2 : 5 comp. 53 : 54, which exists between the aphelial movements of Saturn and Jupiter. Compound with that Jupiter's 5:6 comp. 54 : 55, and the product is 5 : 12 comp. 54 : 55, which exist between the perihelial movements of Saturn and Jupiter. Thus compound Jupiter's 5 : 6 comp. 54:55 with the intermediate ensuing ratio of 5 : 24 comp. 158 : 157, the product will be 1:6

comp. 36 : 35 between the aphelial movements. Compound the same 5 : 24 comp. 158 : 157 with Mars' 2 : 3 comp. 30 : 29, and the product will be 5 : 36 comp. 25 : 24 approximately, *i.e.*, 125 : 864 or about 1 : 7, between the perihelial movements. This ratio is still alone discordant. With 2 : 3 the third ratio among the intermediates, compound Mars' 2 : 3 less 29 : 30; the result will be 4 : 9 comp. 30 : 29, *i.e.*, 40 : 87, another discord between the aphelial movements. If instead of Mars' you compound the Earth's 15 : 16 comp. 137 : 138, you will make 5 : 8 comp. 137 : 138 between the perihelial movements. And if with the fourth of the intermediates, 5 : 8 comp. 31 : 30, or 2 : 3 comp. 31 : 32, you compound the Earth's 15 : 16 comp. 137 : 138, the product will be approximately 3 : 5 between the aphelial movements of the Earth and Venus. For one fifth of 94'50" is 18'58", the triple of which is 56'54", although the Earth has 57'3". If you compound Venus' 34 : 35 with the same ratio, the result will be 5 : 8 between the perihelial movements. For one eighth of 97'37" is 12'12"+ which if multiplied by 5 gives 61'1", although the Earth has 61'18". Finally, if with the last of the intermediate ratios, 3 : 5 comp. 126 : 127 you compound Venus' 34 : 35, the result is 3 : 5 comp. 24 : 25, and the interval, compounded of both, between the aphelial movements, is dissonant. But if you compound Mercury's 5 : 12 comp. 38 : 39, the double octave or 1 : 4 will be diminished by approximately a whole diesis, in proportion to the perihelial movements.

Accordingly, perfect consonances are found: between the converging movements of Saturn and Jupiter, the octave; between the converging movements of Jupiter and Mars, the octave and minor third approximately; between the converging movements of Mars and the Earth, the fifth; between their perihelial, the minor sixth; between the extreme converging movements of Venus and Mercury, the major sixth; between the diverging or even between the perihelial, the double octave: whence without any loss to an astronomy which has been built, most subtly of all, upon Brahe's observations, it seems that the residual very slight discrepancy can be discounted, especially in the movements of Venus and Mercury.

But you will note that where there is no perfect major consonance, as between Jupiter and Mars, there alone have I found the placing of the solid figure to be approximately perfect, since the perihelial distance of Jupiter is approximately three times the aphelial distance of Mars, in such fashion that this pair of planets strives after the perfect consonance in the intervals which it does not have in the movements.

[290] You will note, furthermore, that the major planetary ratio of Saturn and Jupiter exceeds the harmonic, *viz.*, the triple, by approximately the same quantity as belongs to Venus; and the common major ratio of the converging and diverging movements of Mars and the Earth are diminished by approximately the same. You will note thirdly that, roughly speaking, in the upper planets the consonances are established

between the converging movements, but in the lower planets, between movements in the same field. And note fourthly that between the aphelial movements of Saturn and the Earth there are approximately five octaves; for one thirty-second of 57'3" is 1'47", although the aphelial movement of Saturn is 1'46".

Furthermore, a great distinction exists between the consonances of the single planets which have been unfolded and the consonances of the planets in pairs. For the former cannot exist at the same moment of time, while the latter absolutely can; because the same planet, moving at its aphelion, cannot be at the same time at the opposite perihelion too, but of two planets one can be at its aphelion and the other at its perihelion at the same moment of time. And so the ratio of plain-song or monody, which we call choral music and which alone was known to the ancients,[1] to polyphony—called "figured song,";[2] the invention of the latest generations—is the same as the ratio of the consonances which the single planets designate to the consonances of the planets taken together. And so, further on, in Chapters 5 and 6, the single planets will be compared to the choral music of the ancients and its properties will be exhibited in the planetary movements. But in the following chapters, the planets taken together and the figured modern music will be shown to do similar things.

5. IN THE RATIOS OF THE PLANETARY MOVEMENTS WHICH ARE APPARENT AS IT WERE TO SPECTATORS AT THE SUN, HAVE BEEN EXPRESSED THE PITCHES OF THE SYSTEM, OR NOTES OF THE MUSICAL SCALE, AND THE MODES OF SONG (GENERA CANTUS), THE MAJOR AND THE MINOR[3]

Therefore by now I have proved by means of numbers gotten on one side from astronomy and on the other side from harmonies that, taken in every which way, harmonic ratios hold between these twelve termini or movements of the six planets revolving around the sun or that they approximate such ratios within an imperceptible part of least concord. But just as in Book III in the first chapter, we first built up the single harmonic consonances separately, and then we joined together all the consonances—as many as there were—in one common system or musical scale, or, rather, in one octave of them which embraces the rest in power, and by means of them we separated the others into their degrees or pitches (loca) and we did this in such a way that there would be a scale; so now also, after the discovery of the consonances (harmoniis) which

---

1. The choral music of the Greeks was monolinear, everyone singing the same melody together—E. C., Jr.

2. In plain-song all the time values of the notes were approximately equal, while in "figured song" time values of different lengths were indicated by the notes, which gave composers an opportunity both to regulate the way different contrapuntal parts joined together and to produce many expressive effects. Practically all melodies since this time are in "figured song" style.—E. C., Jr.

3. See note to *Intervals Compared with Harmonic Ratios*.

God Himself has embodied in the world, we must consequently see whether those single consonances stand so separate that they have no kinship with the rest, or whether all are in concord with one another. Notwithstanding it is easy to conclude, without any further inquiry, that those consonances were fitted together by the highest prudence in such fashion that they move one another about within one frame, so to speak, and do not jolt one another out of it; since indeed we see that in such a manifold comparison of the same terms there is no place where consonances do not occur. For unless in one scale all the consonances were fitted to all, it could easily have come about (and it has come about wherever necessity thus urges it) that many dissonances should exist. For example, if someone had set up a major sixth between the first and the second term, and likewise a major third between the second and the third term, without taking the first into account, then he would admit a dissonance and the discordant interval 12 : 25 between the first and third.

But come now, let us see whether that which we have already inferred by reasoning is really found in this way. [291] But let me premise some cautions, that we may be the less impeded in our progress. First, for the present, we must conceal those augments or diminutions which are less than a semitone; for we shall see later on what causes they have. Second, by continuous doubling or contrary halving of the movements, we shall bring everything within the range of one octave, on account of the sameness of consonance in all the octaves.

Accordingly the numbers wherein all the pitches or clefs (*loca seu claves*) of the octave system are expressed have been set out in a table in Book III, Chapter 7[1], *i.e.*,

1. The table is as follows:

Concordant Intervals	Lengths of Strings	In familiar notes
	1080	High g
Semitone		
	1152	f #
Lemma		
	1215	f
Semitone		
	1296	e
Diesis		
	1350	e ♭
Semitone		
	1440	d
Semitone		
	1536	c #
Lemma		
	1620	c
Semitone		
	1728	b
Diesis		
	1800	b ♭
Semitone		
	1920	A
Semitone		
	2048	G #
Lemma		
	2160	Low G

understand these numbers of the length of two strings. As a consequence, the speeds of the movements will be in the inverse ratios.

Now let the planetary movements be compared in terms of parts continuously halved. Therefore

Movement of Mercury	at perihelion,	7th subduple, or $1/_{128}$,	3'0"
	at aphelion,	6th subduple, or $1/_{64}$,	2'34"
Movement of Venus	at perihelion,	5th subduple, or $1/_{32}$,	3'3"
	at aphelion,	5th subduple, or $1/_{32}$,	2'58"
Movement of Earth	at perihelion,	5th subduple, or $1/_{32}$,	1'55"
	at aphelion,	5th subduple, or $1/_{32}$,	1'47"
Movement of Mars	at perihelion,	4th subduple, or $1/_{16}$,	2'23"
	at aphelion,	3rd subduple, or $1/_8$,	3'17"
Movement of Jupiter	at perihelion,	subduple, or $1/_2$,	2'45"
	at aphelion,	subduple, or $1/_2$	2'15"
Movement of Saturn	at perihelion,		2'15"
	at aphelion,		1'46"

Now the aphelial movement of Saturn at its slowest—i.e., the slowest movement—marks G, the lowest pitch in the system with the number 1'46". Therefore the aphelial movement of the Earth will mark the same pitch, but five octaves higher, because its number is 1'47", and who wants to quarrel about one second in the aphelial movement of Saturn? But let us take it into account, nevertheless; the difference will not be greater than 106 : 107, which is less than a comma. If you add 27", one quarter of this 1'47", the sum will be 2'14", although the perihelial movement of Saturn has 2'15"; similarly the aphelial movement of Jupiter, but one octave higher. Accordingly, these two movements mark the note b, or else are very slightly higher. Take 36", one third of 1'47", and add it to the whole; you will get as a sum 2'23" for the note c; and here's the perihelion of Mars of the same magnitude but four octaves higher. To this same 1'47" add also 54", half of it, and the sum will be 2'41" for the note d; and here the perihelion of Jupiter is at hand, but one octave higher, for it occupies the nearest number, viz., 2'45". If you add two thirds, viz., 1'11", the sum will be 2'58"; and here's the aphelion of Venus at 2'58". Accordingly, it will mark the pitch or the note e, but five octaves higher. And the perihelial movement of Mercury, which is 3'0", does not exceed it by much but is seven octaves higher. Finally, divide the double of 1'47", viz., 3'34", into nine parts and subtract one part of 24" from the whole; 3'10" will be left for the note f, which the 3'17" of the aphelial movement of Mars marks approximately but three octaves higher; and this number is slightly greater than the just number and approaches the note f sharp. For if one sixteenth of 3'34", viz., 13$1/_2$", is subtracted from 3'34", then 3'20$1/_2$" is left, to which 3'17" is very near. And indeed in

music *f* sharp is often employed in place of *f,* as we can see everywhere.

Accordingly all the notes of the major scale (*cantus duri*) (except the note *a* which was not marked by harmonic division, in Book III, Chapter 2) are marked by all the extreme movements of the planets, except the perihelial movements of Venus and the Earth [292] and the aphelial movement of Mercury, whose number, 2'34", approaches the note *c* sharp. For subtract from the 2'41" of *d* one sixteenth or 10", and 2'30" remains for the note *c* sharp. Thus only the perihelial movement of Venus and the Earth are missing from this scale, as you may see in the table.

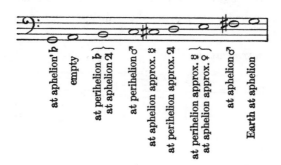

On the other hand, if the beginning of the scale is made at 2'15", the aphelial movement of Saturn, and we must express the note *G* in those degrees: then for the note *A* is 2'32", which closely approaches the aphelial movement of Mercury; for the note *b* flat, 2'42", which is approximately the perihelial movement of Jupiter, by the equipollence of octaves; for the note *c,* 3'0", approximately the perihelial movement of Mercury and Venus; for the note *d,* 3'23" and the aphelial movement of Mars is not much graver, *viz.,* 3'17", so that here the number is about as much less than its note as previously the same number was greater than its note; for the note *e* flat, 3'36", which the aphelial movement of the Earth approximates; for the note *e,* 3'50", and the perihelial movement of the Earth is 3'49"; but the aphelial movement of Jupiter again

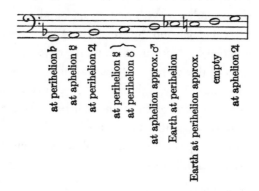

occupies *g*. In this way, all the notes except *f* are expressed within one octave of the minor scale by most of the aphelial and perihelial movements of the planets, especially by those which were previously omitted, as you see in the table.

Previously, however, *f* sharp was marked and *a* omitted; now *a* is marked, *f* sharp is omitted; for the harmonic division in Chapter 2 also omitted the note *f.*

Accordingly, the musical scale or system of one octave with all its pitches, by means of which natural song[1] is transposed in music, has been expressed in the heavens by a twofold way and in two as it were modes of song. There is this sole difference: in our harmonic sectionings both ways start together from one and the same terminus *G*; but here, in the planetary movements, that which was previously *b* now becomes *G* in the minor mode.

In the celestial movements, as follows:

By harmonic sectionings, as follows:

For as in music 2160 : 1800, or 6 : 5, so in that system which the heavens express, 1728 : 1440, namely, also 6 : 5; and so for most of the remaining, 2160 : 1800, 1620, 1440, 1350, 1080 as 1728 : 1440, 1296, 1152, 1080, 864.

Accordingly you won't wonder any more that a very excellent order of sounds or pitches in a musical system or scale has been set up by men, since you see that they are doing nothing else in this business except to play the apes of God the Creator and to act out, as it were, a certain drama of the ordination of the celestial movements.

But there still remains another way whereby we may understand the twofold musical scale in the heavens, where one and the same system but a twofold tuning (*tensio*) is embraced, one at the aphelial movement of Venus, the other at the perihelial, because the variety of movements of this planet is of the least magnitude, as being such as is comprehended within the magnitude of the diesis, the least concord. And the aphelial tuning (*tensio*), as above, has been given to the aphelial movements of Saturn, the Earth, Venus, and (relatively speaking) Jupiter, in *G, e, b,* but to the perihelial movements of Mars and (relatively speaking) Saturn and, as is apparent at first glance, to

---

1. Natural song: music in the basic major or minor system without accidentals. E. C., Jr.

those of Mercury, in *c, e,* and *b.* On the other hand, the perihelial tuning supplies a pitch even for the aphelial movements of Mars, Mercury, and (relatively speaking) Jupiter, but to the perihelial movements of Jupiter, Venus, and (relatively speaking) Saturn, and to a certain extent to that of the Earth and indubitably to that of Mercury too. For let us suppose that now not the aphelial movement of Venus but the 3'3" of the perihelial gets the pitch of *e;* it is approached very closely by the 3'0" of the peri-helial movement of Mercury, through a double octave, at the end of Chapter 4. But if 18" or one tenth of this perihelial movement of Venus is subtracted, 2'45" remains, the perihelion of Jupiter, which occupies the pitch of *d;* and if one fifteenth or 12" is added, the sum will be 3'15", approximately the perihelion of Mars which occupies the pitch of *f;* and thus in *b,* the perihelial movement of Saturn and the aphelial movement of Jupiter have approximately the same tuning. But one eighth, or 23", if multiplied by 5, gives 1'55", which is the perihelial movement of the Earth; and, although it does not square with the foregoing in the same scale, as it does not give the interval 5 : 8 below *e* nor 24 : 25 above *G,* nevertheless if now the perihelial movement of Venus and so too the aphelial movement of Mercury, outside of the order, occupy the pitch *e*-flat instead of *e,* then there the perihelial movement of the Earth will occupy the pitch of *G,* and the aphelial movement of Mercury is in concord, because 1'1", or one third of 3'3", if multiplied by 5, gives 5'5", half of which, or 2'32", approximates the aphelion of Mercury, which in this extraordinary adjustment will occupy the pitch of *c.* Therefore, all these movements are of the same tuning with respect to one another; but the perihelial movement of Venus together with the three (or five) prior movements, *viz.,* in the same harmonic mode, divides the scale differently from the aphelial move-ment of the same in its tuning, *viz.,* in the major mode (*denere duro*). Moreover, the perihelial movement of Venus, together with the two posterior movements, divides the same scale differently, *viz.,* not into concords but merely into a different order of con-cords, namely one which belongs to the minor mode (*generis mollis*).

But it is sufficient to have laid before the eyes in this chapter what is the case casu-ally, but it will be disclosed in Chapter 9 by the most lucid demonstrations why each and every one of these things was made in this fashion and what the causes were not merely of harmony but even of the very least discord.

6. IN THE EXTREME PLANETARY MOVEMENTS THE MUSICAL MODES OR TONES HAVE SOMEHOW BEEN EXPRESSED

[294] This follows from the aforesaid and there is no need of many words; for the single planets somehow mark the pitches of the system with their perihelial movement, in so far as it has been appointed to the single planets to traverse a certain fixed inter-val in the musical scale comprehended by the definite notes of it or the pitches of the

system, and beginning at that note or pitch of each planet which in the preceding chapter fell to the aphelial movement of that planet: *G* to Saturn and the Earth, *b* to Jupiter, which can be transposed higher to *G*, *f*-sharp to Mars, *e* to Venus, *a* to Mercury in the higher octave. See the single movements in the familiar terms of notes. They do not form articulately the intermediate positions, which you here see filled by notes, as they do the extremes, because they struggle from one extreme to the opposite not by leaps and intervals but by a continuum of tunings and actually traverse all the means (which are potentially infinite)—which cannot be expressed by me in any other way than by a continuous series of intermediate notes. Venus remains approximately in unison and does not equal even the least of the concordant intervals in the difference of its tension.

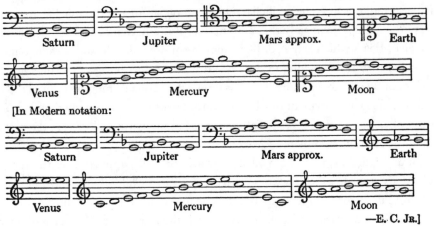

[In Modern notation:

—E. C. Jr.]

But the signature of two accidentals (flats) in a common staff and the formation of the skeletal outline of the octave by the inclusion of a definite concordant interval are a certain first beginning of the distinction of Tones or Modes (*modorum*). Therefore the musical Modes have been distributed among the planets. But I know that for the formation and determination of distinct Modes many things are requisite, which belong to human song, as containing (a) distinct (order of) intervals; and so I have used the word *somehow*.

But the harmonist will be free to choose his opinion as to which Mode each planet expresses as its own, since the extremes have been assigned to it here. From among the familiar Modes, I should give to Saturn the Seventh or Eighth, because if you place its key-note at *G*, the perihelial movement ascends to *b*; to Jupiter, the First or Second Mode, because its aphelial movement has been fitted to *G* and its perihelial movement arrives at *b* flat; to Mars, the Fifth or Sixth Mode, not only because Mars comprehends approximately the perfect fifth, which interval is common to all the Modes, but principally because when it is reduced with the others to a common system, it attains *c* with

its perihelial movement and touches *f* with its aphelial, which is the key-note of the Fifth or Sixth Mode or Tone; I should give the Third or Fourth Mode to the Earth, because its movement revolves within a semitone, while the first interval of those Modes is a semitone; but to Mercury will belong indifferently all the Modes or Tones on account of the greatness of its range; to Venus, clearly none on account of the smallness of its range; but on account of the common system the Third and Fourth Mode, because with reference to the other planets it occupies *e*. (The Earth sings MI, FA, MI so that you may infer even from the syllables that in this our domicile MIsery and FAmine obtain.)[1]

7. The Universal Consonances of All Six Planets, Like Common Four-Part Counterpoint, Can Exist

[295] But now, Urania, there is need for louder sound while I climb along the harmonic scale of the celestial movements to higher things where the true archetype of the fabric of the world is kept hidden. Follow after, ye modern musicians, and judge the thing according to your arts, which were unknown to antiquity. Nature, which is never not lavish of herself, after a lying-in of two thousand years, has finally brought you forth in these last generations, the first true images of the universe. By means of your concords of various voices, and through your ears, she has whispered to the human mind, the favorite daughter of God the Creator, how she exists in the innermost bosom.

(Shall I have committed a crime if I ask the single composers of this generation for some artistic motet instead of this epigraph? The Royal Psalter and the other Holy Books can supply a text suited for this. But alas for you! No more than six are in concord in the heavens. For the moon sings here monody separately, like a dog sitting on the Earth. Compose the melody; I, in order that the book may progress, promise that I will watch carefully over the six parts. To him who more properly expresses the celestial music described in this work, Clio will give a garland, and Urania will betroth Venus his bride.)

It has been unfolded above what harmonic ratios two neighbouring planets would embrace in their extreme movements. But it happens very rarely that two, especially the slowest, arrive at their extreme intervals at the same time; for example, the apsides of Saturn and Jupiter are about 81° apart. Accordingly, while this distance between them measures out the whole zodiac by definite twenty-year leaps,[2] eight hundred years pass by, and nonetheless the leap which concludes the eighth century, does not

---

1. See note on hexachordal system.
2. That is to say, since Saturn and Jupiter have one revolution with respect to one another every twenty years, they are 81° apart once every twenty years, while the end-positions of this 81° interval traverse the ecliptic in leaps, so to speak, and coincide with the apsides approximately once in eight hundred years. C. G. W.

carry precisely to the very apsides; and if it digresses much further, another eight hundred years must be awaited, that a more fortunate leap than that one may be sought; and the whole route must be repeated as many times as the measure of digression is contained in the length of one leap. Moreover, the other single pairs of planets have periods as that, although not so long. But meanwhile there occur also other consonances of two planets, between movements whereof not both are extremes but one or both are intermediate; and those consonances exist as it were in different tunings (*tensionibus*). For, because Saturn tends from *G* to *b*, and slightly further, and Jupiter from *b* to *d* and further; therefore between Jupiter and Saturn there can exist the following consonances, over and above the octave: the major and minor third and the perfect fourth, either one of the thirds through the tuning which maintains the amplitude of the remaining one, but the perfect fourth through the amplitude of a major whole tone. For there will be a perfect fourth not merely from *G* of Saturn to *cc* of Jupiter but also from *A* of Saturn to *dd* of Jupiter and through all the intermediates between the *G* and *A* of Saturn and the *cc* and *dd* of Jupiter. But the octave and the perfect fifth exist solely at the points of the apsides. But Mars, which got a greater interval as its own, received it in order that it should also make an octave with the upper planets through some amplitude of tuning. Mercury received an interval great enough for it to set up almost all the consonances with all the planets within one of its periods, which is not longer than the space of three months. On the other hand, the Earth, and Venus much more so, on account of the smallness of their intervals, limit the consonances, which they form not merely with the others but with one another in especial, to visible fewness. But if three planets are to concord in one harmony, many periodic returns are to be awaited; nevertheless there are many consonances, so that they may so much the more easily take place, while each nearest consonance follows after its neighbour, and very often threefold consonances are seen to exist between Mars, the Earth, and Mercury. But the consonances of four planets now begin to be scattered throughout centuries, and those of five planets throughout thousands of years.

But that all six should be in concord [296] has been fenced about by the longest intervals of time; and I do not know whether it is absolutely impossible for this to occur twice by precise evolving or whether that points to a certain beginning of time, from which every age of the world has flowed.

But if only one sextuple harmony can occur, or only one notable one among many, indubitably that could be taken as a sign of the Creation. Therefore we must ask, in exactly how many forms are the movements of all six planets reduced to one common harmony? The method of inquiry is as follows: let us begin with the Earth and Venus, because these two planets do not make more than two consonances and (wherein the cause of this thing is comprehended) by means of very short intensifications of the movements.

Therefore let us set up two, as it were, skeletal outlines of harmonies, each skeletal outline determined by the two extreme numbers wherewith the limits of the tunings are designated, and let us search out what fits in with them from the variety of movements granted to each planet.

HARMONIES OF ALL THE PLANETS, OR UNIVERSAL HARMONIES
IN THE MAJOR MODE

In order that ♭ may be in concord	At gravest Tuning	At most acute Tuning	[Modern notation
☿ e⁷ b⁶ g⁶	380'20" 285'15" 228'12"	292'48" 234'16"	5 x 8va
♀ e⁶ e⁵	190'10" 95'5"	195'14" 97'37"	4 x 8va
☉ g⁴ b³	57'3" 35'39"	58'34" 36'36"	2 x 8va
♂ g³	28'32"	29'17"	8va
♃ b		4'34"	
♭ B G	2'14" 1'47"	1'49"	

E. C., Jr.]

In order that c may be in concord	At gravest Tuning	At most acute Tuning	[Modern notation
☿ e⁷ c⁷ g⁶	380'20" 204'16" 228'12"	312'21" 234'16"	5 x 8va
♀ e⁶ e⁵	190'10" 95'5"	195'14" 97'37"	4 x 8va
☉ g⁴ c⁴	57'3" 38'2"	58'34" 39'3"	☉ g⁴ b³

♂ g³		28'32"	29'17"
♃ c¹		4'45"	4'53"
♄ G		1'47"	1'49"

E. C., Jr.]

E. C., Jr.]

Saturn joins in this universal consonance with its aphelial movement, the Earth with its aphelial, Venus approximately with its aphelial; at highest tuning, Venus joins with its perihelial; at mean tuning, Saturn joins with its perihelial, Jupiter with its aphelial, Mercury with its perihelial. So Saturn can join in with two movements, Mars with two, Mercury with four. But with the rest remaining, the perihelial movement of Saturn and the aphelial of Jupiter are not allowed. But in their place, Mars joins in with perihelial movement.

The remaining planets join in with single movements, Mars alone with two, and Mercury with four.

[297] Accordingly, the second skeletal outline will be that wherein the other possible consonance, 5 : 8, exists between the Earth and Venus. Here one eighth of the 94'50" of the diurnal aphelial movement of Venus or 11'51"+, if multiplied by 5, equals the 59'16" of the movement of the Earth; and similar parts of the 97'37" of the perihelial movement of Venus are equal to the 61'1" of the movement of the Earth. Accordingly, the other planets are in concord in the following diurnal movements:

HARMONIES OF ALL THE PLANETS, OR UNIVERSAL HARMONIES
IN THE MINOR MODE

In order that ♭ may be in concord	At gravest Tuning	At most acute Tuning	[Modern notation
♃ e♭⁷ b♭⁷ g⁶	379'20" 284'32" 237'4"	295'56" 244'4"	5 x 8va
♀ e♭⁶ e♭⁵	189'40" 94'50"	195'14" 97'37"	4 x 8va
♂ g⁴ b♭⁴	59'16" 35'35"	61'1" 36'37"	2 x 8va

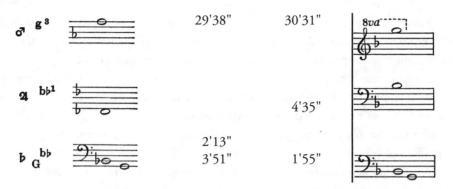

		29'38"	30'31"	
♂ g³				
♃ bb¹			4'35"	
♄ G bb		2'13" 3'51"	1'55"	

E. C., Jr.]

Here again, in the mean tuning Saturn joins in with its perihelial movement, Jupiter with its aphelial, Mercury with its perihelial. But at highest tuning approximately the perihelial movement of the Earth joins in.

In order that c *may be in concord*	At gravest Tuning	At most acute Tuning	[Modern notation
☿ eb⁷ c⁷ g⁶	379'20" 316'5" 237'4"	325'26" 244'4"	5 x 8va
♀ eb⁶ c⁶ eb⁵	189'40" 94'50"	195'14" 162'43" 97'37"	4 x 8va
♁ g⁴	59'16"	61'1"	2 x 8va
♂ g³	29'38"	30'31"	8va
♃ c¹	4'56"	5'5"	
♄ G	3'51"	1'55"	

E. C., Jr.]

And here, with the aphelial movement of Jupiter and the perihelial movement of Saturn removed, the aphelial movement of Mercury is practically admitted besides the perihelial. The rest remain.

Therefore astronomical experience bears witness that the universal consonances of all the movements can take place, and in the two modes (*generum*), the major and minor, and in both genera of form, or (if I may say so) in respect to two pitches and in any one of the four cases, with a certain latitude of tuning and also with a certain variety in the particular consonances of Saturn, Mars, and Mercury, of each with the rest; and that is not afforded by the intermediate movements alone, but by all the extreme movements too, except the aphelial movement of Mars and the perihelial movement of Jupiter; because since the former occupies *f* sharp; and the latter, *d* Venus, which occupies perpetually the intermediate *e* flat or *e*, does not allow those neighbouring dissonances in the universal consonance, as she would do if she had space to go beyond *e* or *e* flat. This difficulty is caused by the wedding of the Earth and Venus, or the male and the female. These two planets divide the kinds (*genera*) of consonances into the major and masculine and the minor and feminine, according as the one spouse has gratified the other—namely, either the Earth is in its aphelion, as if preserving [298] its marital dignity and performing works worthy of a man, with Venus removed and pushed away to her perihelion as to her distaff; or else the Earth has kindly allowed her to ascend into aphelion or the Earth itself has descended into its perihelion towards Venus and as it were, into her embrace, for the sake of pleasure, and has laid aside for a while its shield and arms and all the works befitting a man; for at that time the consonance is minor.

But if we command this contradictory Venus to keep quiet, *i.e.*, if we consider what the consonances not of all but merely of the five remaining planets can be, excluding the movement of Venus, the Earth still wanders around its g string and does not ascend a semitone above it. Accordingly *b*-flat, *b*, *c*, *d*, *e*-flat, and *e* can be in concord with *g*, whereupon, as you see, Jupiter, marking the d string with its perihelial movement, is brought in. Accordingly, the difficulty about Mars' aphelial movement remains. For the aphelial movement of the Earth, which occupies *g*, does not allow it on *f* sharp; but the perihelial movement, as was said above in Chapter V, is in discord with the aphelial movement of Mars by about half a diesis.

HARMONIES OF THE FIVE PLANETS, WITH VENUS LEFT OUT

Major mode (Genus durum)	At gravest Tuning	At most acute Tuning	[Modern notation
d⁷ b⁶ g⁶	342'18" 285'15" 228'12"	351'24" 292'48" 234'16"	5 x 8va
♀ in d⁶ discord e⁵	171'9" 95'5"	175'42" 97'37"	4 x 8va

		At gravest tuning	At most acute tuning	[Modern notation:
♂	g⁴	57'3"	58'34"	2 x 8va
	b³	35'39"	36'36"	
	g³	28'31"	29'17"	8va
♃	d¹	5'21"	5'30"	
	b¹		4'35"	
♭	B	2'13"		
	G	1'47"		

E. C., Jr.]

Here at the most grave tuning, Saturn and the Earth join in with their aphelial movements; at the mean tuning, Saturn with its perihelial and Jupiter with its aphelial; at the most acute, Jupiter with its perihelial.

Minor mode (Genus molle)		*At gravest tuning*	*At most acute tuning*	[*Modern notation:*
♄	d⁷	342'18"	351'24"	5 x 8va
	b⁶	273'50"	280'57"	
	g⁶	228'12"	234'16"	
♀ in discord	d⁶	171'9"	175'42"	4 x 8va
	e⁵	95'5"	97'37"	
♂	g⁴	57'3"	58'34"	2 x 8va
	b³	34'14"	35'8"	
	g³	28'31"	29'17"	8va
♃	d¹			
		5'21"	5'30"	
♭	B	2'8"	2'12"	
	G	1'47"	1'50"	

E. C., Jr.]

677

Here the aphelial movement of Jupiter is not allowed, but at the most acute tuning Saturn practically joins in with its perihelial movement.

But there can also exist the following harmony of the four planets, Saturn, Jupiter, Mars, and Mercury, wherein too the aphelial movement of Mars is present, but it is without latitude of tuning.

In order that b *may be in concord*   *[Modern notation:*

☿ d⁷ b⁶	335'50" 279'52"	5 x 8va
f♯⁶ d⁶	209'52" 167'55"	4 x 8va
♂ b³	34'59"	2 x 8va
f♯³	26'14"	8va
♃ d¹	5'15"	
♭ B	2'11"	

E. C., Jr.]

In order that a *may*

in concord
[Modern notation:

☿ d⁷ a⁶		5 x 8va
f♯⁶ d⁶		4 x 8va
♂ a³		2 x 8va
f♯³		8va

E. C., Jr.]

Accordingly the movements of the heavens are nothing except a certain everlasting polyphony (intelligible, not audible) with dissonant tunings, like certain syncopations or cadences (wherewith men imitate these natural dissonances), which tends towards fixed and prescribed clauses—the single clauses having six terms (like voices)—and which marks out and distinguishes the immensity of time with those notes.[1] Hence it

1. The comparison Kepler draws between the celestial harmonies and the polyphonic music of his time may be clarified by a simple example for four voices from—Palestrina, *O Crux:*

X   *Consonant harmonies*
Y   *Dissonant syncopations*
Z   *Resolutions of dissonances*

As will be observed each of the few voices (as it would also be with the six to which Kepler refers) moves from one consonant chord to another while following a graceful melodic line. Sometimes bits of scales or passing tones are added to give a voice more melodic freedom expressiveness. For the same reason a voice may remain on the same note while the other voices change to a new chord. When this becomes a dissonance (called a syncopation) in the new chord it usually resolves by moving one step downward to a tone that is consonant with the other voices. As in this example each section or "caluse" ends with a cadence.

E. C., Jr.

is no longer a surprise that man, the ape of his Creator, should finally have discovered the art of singing polyphonically (*per concentum*), which was unknown to the ancients, namely in order that he might play the everlastingness of all created time in some short part of an hour by means of an artistic concord of many voices and that he might to some extent taste the satisfaction of God the Workman with His own works, in that very sweet sense of delight elicited from this music which imitates God.

8. In the Celestial Harmonies Which Planet Sings Soprano, Which Alto, Which Tenor, and Which Bass?

Although these words are applied to human voices, while voices or sounds do not exist in the heavens, on account of the very great tranquillity of movements, and not even the subjects in which we find the consonances are comprehended under the true genus of movement, since we were considering the movements solely as apparent from the sun, and finally, although there is no such cause in the heavens, as in human singing, for requiring a definite number of voices in order to make consonance (for first there was the number of the six planets revolving around the sun, from the number of the five intervals taken from the regular figures, and then afterwards—in the order of nature, not of time—the congruence of the movements was settled): I do not know why but nevertheless this wonderful congruence with human song has such a strong effect upon me that I am compelled to pursue this part of the comparison, also, even without any solid natural cause. For those same properties which in Book III, [300] Chapter 16, custom ascribed to the bass and nature gave legal grounds for so doing are somehow possessed by Saturn and Jupiter in the heavens; and we find those of the tenor in Mars, those of the alto are present in the Earth and Venus, and those of the soprano are possessed by Mercury, if not with equality of intervals, at least proportionately. For howsoever in the following chapter the eccentricities of each planet are deduced from their proper causes and through those eccentricities the intervals proper to the movements of each, none the less there comes from that the following wonderful result (I do not know whether it is occasioned by the procurement and mere tempering of necessities): (1) as the bass is opposed to the alto, so there are two planets which have the nature of the alto, two that of the bass, just as in any Mode of song there is one (bass and one alto) on either side, while there are single representatives of the other single voices. (2) As the alto is practically supreme in a very narrow range (*in angustiis*) on account of necessary and natural causes unfolded in Book III, so the almost innermost planets, the Earth and Venus, have the narrowest intervals of movements, the Earth not much more than a semitone, Venus not even a diesis. (3) And as the tenor is free, but none the less progresses with moderation, so Mars alone—with

the single exception of Mercury—can make the greatest interval, namely a perfect fifth. (4) And as the bass makes harmonic leaps, so Saturn and Jupiter have intervals which are harmonic, and in relation to one another pass from the octave to the octave and perfect fifth. (5) And as the soprano is the freest, more than all the rest, and likewise the swiftest, so Mercury can traverse more than an octave in the shortest period. But this is altogether *per accidens*; now let us hear the reasons for the eccentricities.

9. THE GENESIS OF THE ECCENTRICITIES IN THE SINGLE PLANETS FROM THE PROCUREMENT OF THE CONSONANCES BETWEEN THEIR MOVEMENTS

Accordingly, since we see that the universal harmonies of all six planets cannot take place by chance, especially in the case of the extreme movements, all of which we see concur in the universal harmonies—except two, which concur in harmonies closest to the universal—and since much less can it happen by chance that all the pitches of the system of the octave (as set up in Book III) by means of harmonic divisions are designated by the extreme planetary movements, but least of all that the very subtle business of the distinction of the celestial consonances into two modes, the major and minor, should be the outcome of chance, without the special attention of the Artisan: accordingly it follows that the Creator, the source of all wisdom, the everlasting approver of order, the eternal and superexistent geyser of geometry and harmony, it follows, I say, that He, the Artisan of the celestial movements Himself, should have conjoined to the five regular solids the harmonic ratios arising from the regular plane figures, and out of both classes should have formed one most perfect archetype of the heavens: in order that in this archetype, as through the five regular solids the shapes of the spheres shine through on which the six planets are carried, so too through the consonances, which are generated from the plane figures, and deduced from them in Book III, the measures of the eccentricities in the single planets might be determined so as to proportion the movements of the planetary bodies; and in order that there should be one tempering together of the ratios and the consonances, and that the greater ratios of the spheres should yield somewhat to the lesser ratios of the eccentricities necessary for procuring the consonances, and conversely those in especial of the harmonic ratios which had a greater kinship with each solid figure should be adjusted to the planets— in so far as that could be effected by means of consonances. And in order that, finally, in that way both the ratios of the spheres and the eccentricities of the single planets might be born of the archetype simultaneously, while from the amplitude of the spheres and the bulk of the bodies the periodic times of the single planets might result.

[301] While I struggle to bring forth this process into the light of human intellect by means of the elementary form customary with geometers, may the Author of the

heavens be favourable, the Father of intellects, the Bestower of mortal senses, Himself immortal and superblessed, and may He prevent the darkness of our mind from bringing forth in this work anything unworthy of His Majesty, and may He effect that we, the imitators of God by the help of the Holy Ghost, should rival the perfection of His works in sanctity of life, for which He choose His church throughout the Earth and, by the blood of His Son, cleansed it from sins, and that we should keep at a distance all the discords of enmity, all contentions, rivalries, anger, quarrels, dissensions, sects, envy, provocations, and irritations arising through mocking speech and the other works of the flesh; and that along with myself, all who possess the spirit of Christ will not only desire but will also strive by deeds to express and make sure their calling, by spurning all crooked morals of all kinds which have been veiled and painted over with the cloak of zeal or of the love of truth or of singular erudition or modesty over against contentious teachers, or with any other showy garment. Holy Father, keep us safe in the concord of our love for one another, that we may be one, just as Thou art one with Thine Son, Our Lord, and with the Holy Ghost, and just as through the sweetest bonds of harmonies Thou hast made all Thy works one; and that from the bringing of Thy people into concord the body of Thy Church may be rebuilt up in the Earth, as Thou didst erect the heavens themselves out of harmonies.

Prior Reasons

I. Axiom. *It is reasonable that, wherever in general it could have been done, all possible harmonies were due to have been set up between the extreme movements of the planets taken singly and by twos, in order that that variety should adorn the world.*

II. Axiom. *The five intervals between the six spheres to some extent were due to correspond to the ratio of the geometrical spheres which inscribe and circumscribe the five regular solids, and in the same order which is natural to the figures.*

Concerning this, see Chapter 1 and the *Mysterium Cosmographicum* and the *Epitome of Copernican Astronomy*.

III. Proposition. *The intervals between the Earth and Mars, and between the Earth and Venus, were due to be least, in proportion to their spheres, and thereby approximately equal; middling and approximately equal between Saturn and Jupiter, and between Venus and Mercury; but greatest between Jupiter and Mars.*

For by Axiom II, the planets corresponding in position to the figures which make the least ratio of geometrical spheres ought likewise to make the least ratio; but those which correspond to the figures of middling ratio ought to make the greatest; and those which correspond to the figures of greatest ratio, the greatest. But the order holding between the figures of the dodecahedron and the icosahedron is the same as that between the pairs of planets, Mars and the Earth, and the Earth and Venus, and the

order of the cube and octahedron is the same as that of the pair Saturn and Jupiter and that of the pair Venus and Mercury; and, finally, the order of the tetrahedron is the same as that of the pair Jupiter and Mars (see Chapter 3). Therefore, the least ratio will hold between the planetary spheres first mentioned, while that between Saturn and Jupiter is approximately equal to that between Venus and Mercury; and, finally, the greatest between the spheres of Jupiter and Mars.

IV. Axiom. *All the planets ought to have their eccentricities diverse, no less than a movement in latitude, and in proportion to those eccentricities also their distances from the sun, the source of movement, diverse.*

As the essence of movement consists not in *being* but in *becoming*, so too the form or figure of the region which any planet traverses in its movement does not become solid immediately from the start but in the succession of time acquires at last not only length but also breadth and depth (its perfect ternary of dimensions); and, gradually, thus, by the interweaving and piling up of many circuits, the form of a concave sphere comes to be represented—just as out of the silk-worm's thread, by the interweaving and heaping together of many circles, the cocoon is built.

V. Proposition. *Two diverse consonances were to have been attributed to each pair of neighbouring planets.*

For, by Axiom IV, any planet has a longest and a shortest distance from the sun, wherefore, by Chapter 3, it will have both a slowest movement and a fastest. Therefore, there are two primary comparisons of the extreme movements, one of the diverging movements in the two planets, and the other of the converging. Now it is necessary that they be diverse from one another, because the ratio of the diverging movements will be greater, that of the converging, lesser. But, moreover, diverse consonances had to exist by way of diverse pairs of planets, so that this variety should make for the adornment of the world—by Axiom I—and also because the ratios of the intervals between two planets are diverse, by Proposition III. But to each definite ratio of the spheres there correspond harmonic ratios, in quantitative kinship, as has been demonstrated in Chapter 5 of this book.

VI. Proposition. *The two least consonances, 4 : 5 and 5 : 6, do not have a place between two planets.*

For

$$5 : 4 = 1{,}000 : 800$$

and

$$6 : 5 = 1{,}000 : 833.$$

But the spheres circumscribed around the dodecahedron and icosahedron have a greater ratio to the inscribed spheres than $1{,}000 : 795$, etc., and these two ratios indicate the intervals between the nearest planetary spheres, or the least distances. For in

the other regular solids the spheres are farther distant from one another. But now the ratio of the movements is even greater than the ratios of the intervals, unless the ratio of the eccentricities to the spheres is vast—by Article XIII of Chapter 3. Therefore the least ratio of the movements is greater than 4 : 5 and 5 : 6. Accordingly, these consonances, being hindered by the regular solids, receive no place among the planets.

VII. Proposition. *The consonance of the perfect fourth can have no place between the converging movements of two planets, unless the ratios of the extreme movements proper to them are, if compounded, more than a perfect fifth.*

For let 3 : 4 be the ratio between the converging movements. And first, let there be no eccentricity, no ratio of movements proper to the single planets, but both the converging and the mean movements the same; then it follows that the corresponding intervals, which by this hypothesis will be the semidiameters of the spheres, constitute the $2/_3$d power of this ratio, *viz.*, 4480 : 5424 (by Chapter 3). But this ratio is already less than the ratio of the spheres of any regular figure; and so the whole inner sphere would be cut by the regular planes of the figure inscribed in any outer sphere. But this is contrary to Axiom II.

Secondly, let there be some composition of the ratios between the extreme movements, and let the ratio of the converging movements be 3 : 4 or 75 : 100, but let the ratio of the corresponding intervals be 1,000 : 795, since no regular figure has a lesser ratio of spheres. And because the inverse ratio of the movements exceeds this ratio of the intervals by the excess 750 : 795, then if this excess is divided into the ratio 1,000 : 795, according to the doctrine of Chapter 3, the result will be 9434 : 7950, the square root of the ratio of the spheres. Therefore the square of this ratio, *viz.*, 8901 : 6320, *i.e.*, 10,000 : 7,100 is the ratio of the spheres. Divide this by 1000 : 795, the ratio of the converging intervals, the result will be 7100 : 7950, about a major whole tone. The compound of the two ratios which the mean movements have to the converging movements on either side must be at least so great, in order that the perfect fourth may be possible between the converging movements. Accordingly, the compound ratio of the diverging extreme intervals to the converging extreme intervals is about the square root of this ratio, *i.e.*, two tones, and again the converging intervals are the square of this, *i.e.*, more than a perfect fifth. Accordingly, if the compound of the proper movements of two neighbouring planets is less than a perfect fifth, a perfect fourth will not be possible between their converging movements.

VIII. Proposition. *The consonances 1 : 2 and 1 : 3, i.e., the octave and the octave plus a fifth were due to Saturn and Jupiter.*

For they are the first and highest of the planets and have obtained the first figure, the cube, by Chapter 1 of this book; and these consonances are first in the order of nature and are chief in the two families of figures, the bisectorial or tetragonal and the

triangular, by what has been said in Book I. But that which is chief, the octave 1 : 2, is approximately greater than the ratio of the spheres of the cube, [303] which is 1:√3; wherefore it is fitted to become the lesser ratio of the movements of the planets on the cube, by Chapter 3, Article XIII; and, as a consequence, 1 : 3 serves as the greater ratio.

But this is also the same as what follows: for if some consonance is to some ratio of the spheres of the figures, as the ratio of the movements apparent from the sun is to the ratio of the mean intervals, such a consonance will duly be attributed to the movements. But it is natural that the ratio of the diverging movements should be much greater than the ratio of the $3/_2$th powers of the spheres, according to the end of Chapter 3, *i.e.*, it approaches the square of the ratio of the spheres; and moreover 1 : 3 is the square of the ratio of the spheres of the cube, which we call the ratio of 1 : √3. Therefore, the ratio of the diverging movements of Saturn and Jupiter is 1 : 3. (See above, Chapter 2, for many other kinships of these ratios with the cube.)

IX. Proposition. *The private ratios of the extreme movements of Saturn and Jupiter compounded were due to be approximately 2 : 3, a perfect fifth.*

This follows from the preceding; if the perihelial movement of Jupiter is triple the aphelial movement of Saturn, and conversely the aphelial movement of Jupiter is double the perihelial of Saturn, then 1 : 2 and 1 : 3 compounded inversely give 2 : 3.

X. Axiom. *When choice is free in other respects, the private ratio of movements, which is prior in nature or of a more excellent mode or even which is greater, is due to the higher planet.*

XI. Proposition. *The ratio of the aphelial movement of Saturn to the perihelial was due to be 4 : 5, a major third, but that of Jupiter's movements 5 : 6, a minor third.*

For as compounded together they are equivalent to 2 : 3; but 2 : 3 can be divided harmonically no other way than into 4 : 5 and 5 : 6. Accordingly God the composer of harmonies divided harmonically the consonance 2 : 3, (by Axiom I) and the harmonic part of it which is greater and of the more excellent major mode, as masculine, He gave to Saturn the greater and higher planet, and the lesser ratio 5 : 6 to the lower one, Jupiter (by Axiom X).

XII. Proposition. *The great consonance of 1 : 4, the double octave, was due to Venus and Mercury.*

For as the cube is the first of the primary figures, so the octahedron is the first of the secondary figures, by Chapter 1 of this book. And as the cube considered geometrically is outer and the octahedron is inner, *i.e.*, the latter can be inscribed in the former, so also in the world Saturn and Jupiter are the beginning of the upper and outer planets, or from the outside; and Mercury and Venus are the beginning of the inner planets, or from the inside, and the octahedron has been placed between their circuits: (see Chapter 3). Therefore, from among the consonances, one which is primary and

cognate to the octahedron is due to Venus and Mercury. Furthermore, from among the consonances, after 1 : 2 and 1 : 3, there follows in natural order 1 : 4; and that is cognate to 1 : 2, the consonance of the cube, because it has arisen from the same cut of figures, *viz.*, the tetragonal, and is commensurable with it, *viz.*, the double of it; while the octahedron is also akin to, and commensurable with the cube. Moreover, 1 : 4 is cognate to the octahedron for a special reason, on account of the number four being in that ratio, while a quadrangular figure lies concealed in the octahedron and the ratio of its spheres is said to be 1 : $\sqrt{2}$.

Accordingly the consonance 1 : 4 is a continued power of this ratio, in the ratio of the squares, *i.e.*, the 4th power of 1 : $\sqrt{2}$ (see Chapter 2). Therefore, 1 : 4 was due to Venus and Mercury. And because in the cube 1 : 2 has been made the smaller consonance of the two, since the outermost position is over against it, in the octahedron there will be 1 : 4, the greater consonance of the two, as the innermost position is over against it. But too, this is the reason why 1 : 4 has here been given as the greater consonance, not as the smaller.[1] For since the ratio of the spheres of the octahedron is the ratio of 1 : $\sqrt{3}$, then if it is postulated that the inscription of the octahedron among the planets is perfect (although it is not perfect, but penetrates Mercury's sphere to some extent—which is of advantage to us): accordingly, the ratio of the converging movements must be less than the $^{3}/_{2}$th powers of 1 : $\sqrt{3}$; but indeed 1 : 3 is plainly the square of the ratio 1 : $\sqrt{3}$ and is thus greater than the exact ratio; all the more then will 1 : 4 be greater than the exact ratio, as greater than 1 : 3. Therefore, not even the square root of 1 : 4 is allowed between the converging movements. Accordingly, 1 : 4 cannot be less than the octahedric; so it will be greater.

Further: 1 : 4 is akin to the octahedric square, where the ratio of the inscribed and circumscribed circles is 1 : $\sqrt{2}$, just as 1 : 3 is akin to the cube, where the ratio of the spheres is 1 : $\sqrt{3}$. For as 1 : 3 is a power of 1 : $\sqrt{3}$, *viz.*, its square, [304] so too here 1:4 is a power of 1 : $\sqrt{2}$, *viz.*, twice its square, *i.e.*, its quadruple power. Wherefore, if 1:3 was due to have been the greater consonance of the cube (by Proposition VII), accordingly 1 : 4 ought to become the greater consonance of its octahedron.

XIII. Proposition. *The greater consonance of approximately 1 : 8, the triple octave, and the smaller consonance of 5 : 24, the minor third and double octave, were due to the extreme movements of Jupiter and Mars.*

For the cube has obtained 1 : 2 and 1 : 3, while the ratio of the spheres of the tetrahedron, which is situated between Jupiter and Mars, called the triple ratio, is the square of the ratio of the spheres of the cube, which is called the ratio of 1 : $\sqrt{3}$. Therefore, it was proper that ratios of movements which are the squares of the cubic ratios should

---

1. *Smaller* (lesser) and *greater* consonances are equivalent to our modern "more closely spaced" and "more widely spaced" consonances. E. C., Jr.

be applied to the tetrahedron. But of the ratios 1 : 2 and 1 : 3 the following ratios are the squares: 1 : 4 and 1 : 9. But 1 : 9 is not harmonic, and 1 : 4 has already been used up in the octahedron. Accordingly, consonances neighbouring upon these ratios were to have been taken, by Axiom I. But the lesser ratio 1 : 8 and the greater 1 : 10 are the nearest. Choice between these ratios is determined by kinship with the tetrahedron, which has nothing in common with the pentagon, since 1 : 10 is of a pentagonal cut, but the tetrahedron has greater kinship with 1 : 8 for many reasons (see Chapter 2).

Further, the following also makes for 1 : 8: just as 1 : 3 is the greater consonance of the cube and 1 : 4 the greater consonance of the octahedron, because they are powers of the ratios between the spheres of the figures, so too 1 : 8 was due to be the greater consonance of the tetrahedron, because as its body is double that of the octahedron inscribed in it, as has been said in Chapter 1, so too the term 8 in the tetrahedral ratio is double the term 4 in the tetrahedral ratio.

Further, just as 1 : 2 the smaller consonance of the cube, is one octave, and 1 : 4, the greater consonance of the octahedron, is two octaves, so already 1 : 8, the greater consonance of the tetrahedron, was due to be three octaves. Moreover, more octaves were due to the tetrahedron than to the cube and octahedron, because, since the smaller tetrahedral consonance is necessarily greater than all the lesser consonances in the other figures (for the ratio of the tetrahedral spheres is greater than all the spheres of figures): too the greater tetrahedral consonance was due to exceed the greater consonances of the others in number of octaves. Finally, the triple of octave intervals has kinship with the triangular form of the tetrahedron, and has a certain perfection, as follows: every three is perfect; since even the octuple, the term (of the triple octave), is the first cubic number of perfect quantity, namely of three dimensions.

A greater consonance neighbouring upon 1 : 4 or 6 : 24 is 5 : 24, while a lesser is 6 : 20 or 3 : 10. But again 3 : 10 is of the pentagonal cut, which has nothing in common with the tetrahedron. But on account of the numbers 3 and 4 (from which the numbers 12, 24 arise) 5 : 24 has kinship with the tetrahedron. For we are here neglecting the other lesser terms, *viz.*, 5 and 3, because their lightest degree of kinship is with figures, as it is possible to see in Chapter 2. Moreover, the ratio of the spheres of the tetrahedron is triple; but the ratio of the converging intervals too ought to be approximately so great, by Axiom II. By Chapter 3, the ratio of the converging movements approaches the inverse ratio of the $3/_2$th powers of the intervals, but the $3/_2$th power of 3 : 1 is approximately 1000 : 193. Accordingly, whereof the aphelial movement of Mars is 1000, the (perihelial) of Jupiter will be slightly greater than 193 but much less than 333, which is one third of 1,000. Accordingly, not the consonance 10 : 3, *i.e.*, 1,000 : 333, but the consonance 24 : 5, *i.e.*, 1,000 : 208, takes place between the converging movements of Jupiter and Mars.

XIV. Proposition. *The private ratio of the extreme movements of Mars was due to be greater than 3 : 4, the perfect fourth, and approximately 18 : 25.*

For let there be the exact consonances 5 : 24 and 1 : 8 or 3 : 24, which are commonly attributed to Jupiter and Mars (Proposition XIII). Compound inversely 5 : 24, the lesser with 3 : 24, the greater; 3 : 5 results as the compound of both ratios. But the proper ratio of Jupiter alone has been found to be 5 : 6, in Proposition XI, above. Then compound this inversely with the composition 3 : 5, *i.e.*, compound 30 : 25 and 18:30; there results as the proper ratio of Mars 18 : 25, which is greater than 18 : 24 or 3 : 4. But it will become still greater, if, on account of the ensuing reasons, the common greater consonance 1 : 8 is increased.

XV. Proposition. *The consonances 2 : 3, the fifth; 5 : 8, the minor sixth; and 3 : 5, the major sixth were to have been distributed among the converging movements of Mars and the Earth, the Earth and Venus, Venus and Mercury, and in that order.*

For the dodecahedron and the icosahedron, the figures interspaced between Mars, the Earth, and Venus have the least ratio between their circumscribed and inscribed spheres. [305] Therefore from among possible consonances the least are due to them, as being cognate for this reason, and in order that Axiom II may have place. But the least consonances of all, *viz.*, 5 : 6 and 4 : 5, are not possible, by Proposition IV. Therefore, the nearest consonances greater than they, *viz.*, 3 : 4 or 2 : 3 or 5 : 8 or 3:5 are due to the said figures.

Again, the figure placed between Venus and Mercury, *viz.*, the octahedron, has the same ratio of its spheres as the cube. But by Proposition VII, the cube received the octave as the lesser consonance existing between the converging movements. Therefore, by proportionality, so great a consonance, *viz.*, 1 : 2, would be due to the octahedron as the lesser consonance, if no diversity intervened. But the following diversity intervenes: if compounded together, the private ratios of the single movements of the cubic planets, *viz.*, Saturn and Jupiter, did not amount to more than 2 : 3; while, if compounded, the ratios of the single movements of the octahedral planets, *viz.*, Venus and Mercury will amount to more than 2 : 3, as is apparent easily, as follows: For, as the proportion between the cube and octahedron would require if it were alone, let the lesser octahedral ratio be greater than the ratios here given, and thereby clearly as great as was the cubic ratio, *viz.*, 1 : 2; but the greater consonance was 1 : 4, by Proposition XII. Therefore if the lesser consonance 1 : 2 is divided into the one we have just laid down, 1 : 2, still remains as the compound of the proper movements of Venus and Mercury; but 1 : 2 is greater than 2 : 3 the compound of the proper movements of Saturn and Jupiter; and indeed a greater eccentricity follows upon this greater compound, by Chapter 3, but a lesser ratio of the converging movements follows upon the greater eccentricity, by the same Chapter 3. Wherefore by the addition of a greater

eccentricity to the proportion between the cube and the octahedron it comes about that a lesser ratio than 1 : 2 is also required between the converging movements of Venus and Mercury. Moreover, it was in keeping with Axiom I that, with the consonance of the octave given to the planets of the cube, another consonance which is very near (and by the earlier demonstration less than 1 : 2) should be joined to the planets of the octahedron. But 3 : 5 is proximately less than 1 : 2, and as the greatest of the three it was due to the figure having the greatest ratio of its spheres, *viz.*, the octahedron. Accordingly, the lesser ratios, 5 : 8 and 2 : 3 or 3 : 4, were left for the icosahedron and dodecahedron, the figures having a lesser ratio of their spheres.

But these remaining ratios have been distributed between the two remaining planets, as follows. For as, from among the figures, though of equal ratios between their spheres, the cube has received the consonance 1 : 2, while the octahedron the lesser consonance 3 : 5, in that the compound ratio of the private movements of Venus and Mercury exceeded the compound ratio of the private movements of Saturn and Jupiter; so also although the dodecahedron has the same ratio of its spheres as the icosahedron, a lesser ratio was due to it than to the icosahedron, but very close on account of a similar reason, *viz.*, because this figure is between the Earth and Mars, which had a great eccentricity in the foregoing. But Venus and Mercury, as we shall hear in the following, have the least eccentricities. But since the octahedron has 3 : 5, the icosahedron, whose species are in a lesser ratio, has the next slightly lesser, *viz.*, 5 : 8; accordingly, either 2 : 3, which remains, or 3 : 4 was left for the dodecahedron, but more likely 2:3, as being nearer to the icosahedral 5 : 8; since they are similar figures.

But 3 : 4 indeed was not possible. For although, in the foregoing, the private ratio of the extreme movements of Mars was great enough, yet the Earth—as has already been said and will be made clear in what follows—contributed its own ratio, which was too small for the compound ratio of both to exceed the perfect fifth. Accordingly, Proposition VII, 3 : 4 could not have place. And all the more so, because—as will follow in Proposition XVII—the ratio of the converging intervals was due to be greater than 1,000 : 795.

XVI. Proposition. *The private ratios of movements of Venus and Mercury, if compounded together, were due to make approximately 5 : 12.*

For divide the lesser harmonic ratio attributed in Proposition XV to this pair jointly into the greater of them, 1 : 4 or 3 : 12, by Proposition XII; there results 5 : 12, the compound ratio of the private movements of both. And so the private ratio of the extreme movements of Mercury alone is less than 5 : 12, the magnitude of the private movement of Venus. Understand this of these first reasons. For below, by the second reasons, through the addition of some variation to the joint consonances of both, it results that only the private ratio of Mercury is perfectly 5 : 12.

XVII. Proposition. *The consonance between the diverging movements of Venus and the Earth could not be less than 5 : 12.*

For in the private ratio of its movements Mars alone has received more than the perfect fourth and more than 18 : 25, by Proposition XIV. But their lesser consonance is the perfect fifth, [306] by Proposition XV. Accordingly, the ratio compounded of these two parts is 12 : 25. But its own private ratio is due to the Earth, by Axiom IV. Therefore, since the consonance of the diverging movements is made up out of the said three elements, it will be greater than 12 : 25. But the nearest consonance greater than 12 : 25, *i.e.*, 60 : 125, is 5 : 12, *viz.*, 60 : 144. Wherefore, if there is need of a consonance for this greater ratio of the two planets, by Axiom I, it cannot be less than 60:144 or 5 : 12.

Therefore up to now all the remaining pairs of planets have received their two consonances by necessary reasons; the pair of the Earth and Venus alone has as yet been allotted only one consonance, 5 : 8, by the axioms so far employed. Therefore, we must now take a new start and inquire into its remaining consonance, *viz.*, the greater, or the consonance of the diverging movements.

Posterior Reasons

XVIII. Axiom. *The universal consonances of movements were to be constituted by a tempering of the six movements, especially in the case of the extreme movements.*

This is proved by Axiom I.

XIX. Axiom. *The universal consonances had to come out the same within a certain latitude of movements, namely, in order that they should occur the more frequently.*

For if they had been limited to indivisible points of the movements, it could have happened that they would never occur, or very rarely.

XX. Axiom. *As the most natural division of the kinds* (generum) *of consonances is into major and minor, as has been proved in Book 3, so the universal consonances of both kinds had to be procured between the extreme movements of the planets.*

XXI. Axiom. *Diverse species of both kinds of consonances had to be instituted, so that the beauty of the world might well be composed out of all possible forms of variety—and by means of the extreme movements, at least by means of some extreme movements.*

By Axiom I.

XXII. Proposition. *The extreme movements of the planets had to designate pitches or strings* (chordas) *of the octave system, or notes* (claves) *of as musical scale.*

For the genesis and comparison of consonances beginning from one common term has generated the musical scale, or the division of the octave into its pitches or tones (*sonos*), as has been proved in Book 3. Accordingly, since varied consonances between

the extremes of movements are required, by Axioms I, XX, and XXI, wherefore the real division of some celestial system or harmonic scale by the extremes of movements is required.

XXIII. Proposition. *It was necessary for there to be one pair of planets, between the movements of which no consonances could exist except the major sixth 3 : 5 and the minor sixth 5 : 8.*

For since the division into kinds of consonances was necessary, by Axiom XX, and by means of the extreme movements at the apsides, by XXII, because solely the extremes, *viz.*, the slowest and the fastest, need the determination of a manager and orderer, the intermediate tensions come of themselves, without any special care, with the passage of the planet from the slowest movement to the fastest: accordingly, this ordering could not take place otherwise than by having the diesis or 24 : 25 designated by the extremes of the two planetary movements, in that the kinds of consonances are distinguished by the diesis, as was unfolded in Book 3.

But the diesis is the difference either between two thirds, 4 : 5 and 5 : 6, or between two sixths, 3 : 5 and 5 : 8, or between those ratios increased by one or more octave intervals. But the two thirds, 4 : 5 and 5 : 6, did not have place between two planets, by Proposition VI, and neither the thirds nor the sixths increased by the interval of an octave have been found, except 5 : 12 in the pair of Mars and the Earth, and still not otherwise than along with the related 2 : 3, and so the intermediate ratios 5:8 and 3 : 5 and 1 : 2 were alike admitted. Therefore, it remains that the two sixths, 3:5 and 5 : 8, were to be given to one pair of planets. But too the sixths alone were to be granted to the variation of their movements, in such fashion that they would neither expand their term to the proximately greater interval of one octave, 1 : 2, [307] nor contract them to the narrows of the proximately lesser interval of the fifth, 2 : 3. For, although it is true that the same two planets, which make a perfect fifth with their extreme converging movements, can also make sixths and thus traverse the diesis too, still this would not smell of the singular providence of the Orderer of movements. For the diesis, the least interval—which is potentially latent in all the major intervals comprehended by the extreme movements—is itself at that time traversed by the intermediate movements varied by continuous tension, but it is not determined by their extremes, since the part is always less than the whole, *viz.*, the diesis than the greater interval 3 : 4 which exists between 2 : 3 and 1 : 2 and which whole would be here assumed to be determined by the extreme movements.

XXIV. Proposition. *The two planets which shift the kind (genus) of harmony, which is the difference between the private ratios of the extreme movements, ought to make a diesis, and the private ratio of one ought to be greater than a diesis, and they ought to make one of the sixths with their aphelial movements and the other with their perihelial.*

For, since the extremes of the movements make two consonances differing by a single diesis, that can take place in three ways. For either the movement of one planet will remain constant and the movement of the other will vary by a diesis, or both will vary by half a diesis and make 3 : 5, a major sixth, when the upper is at its aphelion and the lower in its perihelion, and when they move out of those intervals and advance towards one another, the upper into its perihelion and the lower into its aphelion, they make 5 : 8, a minor sixth; or, finally, one varies its movement from aphelion to perihelion more than the other does, and there is an excess of one diesis, and thus there is a major sixth between the two aphelia, and a minor sixth between the two perihelia. But the first way is not legitimate, for one of these planets would be without eccentricity, contrary to Axiom IV. The second way was less beautiful and less expedient; less beautiful, because less harmonic, for the private ratios of the movements of the two planets would have been out of tune (*inconcinnae*), for whatever is less than a diesis is out of tune; moreover it occasions one single planet to labour under this ill-concordant small difference—except that indeed it could not take place, because in this way the extreme movements would have wandered from the pitches of the system or the notes (*clavibus*) of the musical scale, contrary to Proposition XXII. Moreover, it would have been less expedient, because the sixths would have occurred only at those moments in which the planets would have been at the contrary apsides; there would have been no latitude within which these sixths and the universal consonances related to them could have occurred; accordingly, these universal consonances would have been very rare, with all the (*harmonic*) positions of the planets reduced to the narrow limits of definite and single points on their orbits, contrary to Axiom XIX. Accordingly, the third way remains: that both of the planets should vary their own private movements, but one more than the other, by one full diesis at the least.

XXV. Proposition. *The higher of the planets which shift the kind of harmony ought to have the ratio of its private movements less than a minor whole tone 9 : 10; while the lower, less than a semitone 15 : 16.*

For they will make 3 : 5 either with their aphelial movements or with their perihelial, by the foregoing proposition. Not with their perihelial, for then the ratio of their aphelial movements would be 5 : 8. Accordingly, the lower planet would have its private ratio one diesis more than the upper would, by the same foregoing proposition. But that is contrary to Axiom X. Accordingly, they make 3 : 5 with their aphelial movements, and with their perihelial 5 : 8, which is 24 : 25 less than the other. But if the aphelial movements make 3 : 5, a major sixth, therefore, the aphelial movement of the upper together with the perihelial of the lower will make more than a major sixth; for the lower planet will compound directly its full private ratio.

In the same way, if the perihelial movements make 5 : 8, a minor sixth, the perihelial

movement of the upper and the aphelial movement of the lower will make less than a minor sixth; for the lower planet will compound inversely its full private ratio. But if the private ratio of the lower equalled the semitone 15 : 16, then too a perfect fifth could occur over and above the sixths, because the minor sixth, diminished by a semitone, because the perfect fifth; but this is contrary to Proposition XXIII. Accordingly, the lower planet has less than a semitone in its own interval. And because the private ratio of the upper is one diesis greater than the private ratio of the lower, but the diesis compounded with the semitone makes 9 : 10 the minor whole tone.

XXVI. Proposition. *On the planets which shift the kind of harmony, the upper was due to have either a diesis squared, 576 : 625, i.e., approximately 12 : 13, as* [308] *the interval made by its extreme movements, or the semitone 15 : 16, or something intermediate differing by the comma 80 : 81 either from the former or the latter; while the lower planet, either the simple diesis 24 : 25, or the difference between a semitone and a diesis, which is 125 : 128, i.e., approximately 42 : 43; or, finally and similarly, something intermediate differing either from the former or from the latter by the comma 80 : 81, viz., the upper planet ought to make the diesis squared diminished by a comma, and the lower, the simple diesis diminished by a comma.*

For, by Proposition XXV, the private ratio of the upper ought to be greater than a diesis, but by the preceding proposition less than the (minor) whole tone 9 : 10. But indeed the upper planet ought to exceed the lower by one diesis, by Proposition XXIV. And harmonic beauty persuades us that, even if the private ratios of these planets cannot be harmonic, on account of their smallness, they should at least be from among the concordant (*ex concinnis*) if that is possible, by Axiom I. But there are only two concords less than 9 : 10, the (minor) whole tone, *viz.*, the semitone and the diesis; but they differ from one another not by the diesis but by some smaller interval, 125 : 128. Accordingly, the upper cannot have the semitone; nor the lower, the diesis; but either the upper will have the semitone 15 : 16, and the lower, 125 : 128, *i.e.*, 42 : 43; or else the lower will have the diesis 24 : 25, but the upper the diesis squared, approximately 12 : 13. But since the laws of both planets are equal, therefore, if the nature of the concordant had to be violated in their private ratios, it had to be violated equally in both, so that the difference between their private intervals could remain an exact diesis, which is necessary for distinguishing the kinds of consonances, by Proposition XXIV. But the nature of the concordant was then violated equally in both, if the interval whereby the private ratio of the upper planet fell short of the diesis squared and exceeded the semitone is the same interval whereby the private ratio of the lower planet fell short of a simple diesis and exceeded the interval 125 : 128.

Furthermore, this excess or defect was due to be the comma 80 : 81, because, once more, no other interval was designated by the harmonic ratios, and in order that the

comma might be expressed among the celestial movements as it is expressed in harmonics, namely, by the mere excess and defect of the intervals in respect to one another. For in harmonies the comma distinguishes between major and minor whole tones and does not appear in any other way.

It remains for us to inquire which ones of the intervals set forth are preferable—whether the diesis, the simple diesis for the lower planet and the diesis squared for the upper, or the semitone for the upper and 125 : 128 for the lower. And the dieses win by the following arguments: For although the semitone has been variously expressed in the musical scale, yet its allied ratio 125 : 128 has not been expressed. On the other hand, the diesis has been expressed variously and the diesis squared somehow, *viz.*, in the resolution of whole tones into dieses, semitones, and lemmas; for then, as has been said in Book III, Chapter 8, two dieses proximately succeed one another in two pitches. The other argument is that in the distinction into kinds, the laws of the diesis are proper but not at all those of the semitone. Accordingly, there had to be greater consideration of the diesis than of the semitone. It is inferred from everything that the private ratio of the upper planet ought to be 2916 : 3125 or approximately 14 : 15, and that of the lower, 243 : 250 or approximately 35 : 36.

It is asked whether the Highest Creative Wisdom has been occupied in making these tenuous little reckonings. I answer that it is possible that many reasons are hidden from me, but if the nature of harmony has not allowed weightier reasons—since we are dealing with ratios which descend below the magnitude of all concords—it is not absurd that God has followed even those reasons, wherever they appear tenuous, since He has ordained nothing without cause. It would be far more absurd to assert that God has taken at random these magnitudes below the limits prescribed for them, the minor whole tone; and it is not sufficient to say: He took them of that magnitude because He chose to do so. For in geometrical things, which are subject to free choice, God chose nothing without a geometrical cause of some sort, as is apparent in the edges of leaves, in the scales of fishes, in the skins of beasts and their spots and the order of the spots, and similar things.

XXVII. Proposition. *The ratio of movements of the Earth and Venus ought to have been greater than a major sixth between the aphelial movements; less than a minor sixth between the perihelial movements.*

By Axiom XX it was necessary to distinguish the kinds of consonances. But by Proposition XXIII that could not be done except through the sixths. Accordingly, since by Proposition XV the Earth and Venus, planets next to one another and icosahedral, had received the minor sixth, 5 : 8, it was necessary for the other sixth, 3 : 5, to be assigned to them, but not between the converging or diverging extremes, but between the extremes of the same field, one sixth [309] between the aphelial, and the other

between the perihelial, by Proposition XXIV. Furthermore, the consonance 3 : 5 is cognate to the icosahedron, since both are of the pentagonal cut. See Chapter 2.

Behold the reason why exact consonances are found between the aphelial and perihelial movements of these two planets, but not between the converging, as in the case of the upper planets.

XXVIII. Proposition. *The private ratio of movements fitting the Earth was approximately 14 : 15, Venus, approximately 35 : 36.*

For these two planets had to distinguish the kinds of consonances, by the preceding proposition; therefore, by Proposition XXVI, the Earth as the higher was due to receive the interval 2916 : 3125, *i.e.*, approximately 14 : 15, but Venus as the lower the interval 243 : 250, *i.e.*, approximately 35 : 36.

Behold the reason why these two planets have such small eccentricities and, in proportion to them, small intervals or private ratios of the extreme movements, although nevertheless the next higher planet, Mars, and the next lower, Mercury, have marked eccentricities and the greatest of all. And astronomy confirms the truth of this; for in Chapter 4 the Earth clearly had 14 : 15, but Venus 34 : 35, which astronomical certitude can barely discern from 35 : 36 in this planet.

XXIX. Proposition. *The greater consonance of the movements of Mars and the Earth, viz., that of the diverging movements, could not be from among the consonances greater than 5 : 12.*

Above, in Proposition XVII, it was not any one of the lesser ratios; but now it is not any one of the greater ratios either. For the other common or lesser consonance of these two planets is 2 : 3, when the private ratio of Mars, which by Proposition XIV exceeds 18 : 25, makes more than 12 : 25, *i.e.*, 60 : 125. Accordingly, compound the private ratio of the Earth 14 : 15, *i.e.*, 50 : 60, by the preceding proposition. The compound ratio is greater than 56 : 125, which is approximately 4 : 9, *viz.*, slightly greater than an octave and a major whole tone. But the next greater consonance than the octave and whole tone is 5 : 12, the octave and minor third.

Note that I do not say that this ratio is neither greater nor smaller than 5 : 12; but I say that if it is necessary for it to be harmonic, no other consonance will belong to it.

XXX. Proposition. *The private ratio of movements of Mercury was due to be greater than all the other private ratios.*

For by Proposition XVI the private movements of Venus and Mercury compounded together were due to make about 5 : 12. But the private ratio of Venus, taken separately, is only 243 : 250, *i.e.*, 1458 : 1500. But if it is compounded inversely with 5 : 12, *i.e.*, 625 : 1500, Mercury singly is left with 625 : 1458, which is greater than an octave and a major whole tone; although the private ratio of Mars, which is the greatest of all these among the remaining planets, is less than 2 : 3, *i.e.*, the perfect fifth.

And thereby the private ratios of Venus and Mercury, the lowest planets, if compounded together, are approximately equal to the compounded private ratios of the four higher planets, because, as will now be apparent immediately, the compounded private ratios of Saturn and Jupiter exceed 2 : 3; those of Mars fall somewhat short of 2 : 3: all compounded, 4 : 9, *i.e.*, 60 : 135. Compound the Earth's 14 : 15, *i.e.*, 56:60, the result will be 56 : 135, which is slightly greater than 5 : 12, which just now was the compound of the private ratios of Venus and Mercury. But this has not been sought for nor taken from any separate and singular archetype of beauty but comes of itself, by the necessity of the causes bound together by the consonances hitherto established.

XXXI. Proposition. *The aphelial movement of the Earth had to harmonize with the aphelial movement of Saturn, through some certain number of octaves.*

For, by Proposition XVIII, it was necessary for there to be universal consonances, wherefore also there had to be a consonance of Saturn with the Earth and Venus. But if one of the extreme movements of Saturn had harmonized with neither of the Earth's and Venus', this would have been less harmonic than if both of its extreme movements had harmonized with these planets, by Axiom I. Therefore both of Saturn's extreme movements had to harmonize, the aphelial with one of these two planets, the perihelial with the other, since nothing would hinder, as was the case with the first planet. Accordingly these consonances will be either identisonant[1] (*identisonae*) or diversisonant (*diversisonae*), *i.e.*, either of continued double proportion or of some other. But both of them cannot be of some other proportion, for between the terms 3 : 5 (which determine the greater consonance between the aphelial movements of the Earth and Venus, by Proposition XXVII) two harmonic means cannot be set up; for the sixth cannot be divided into three intervals (see Book III). Accordingly, Saturn could not, [310] by means of both its movements, make an octave with the harmonic means between 3 and 5; but in order that its movements should harmonize with the 3 of the Earth and the 5 of Venus, it is necessary that one of those terms should harmonize identically, or through a certain number of octaves, with the others, *viz.*, with one of the said planets. But since the identisonant consonances are more excellent, they had to be established between the more excellent extreme movements, *viz.*, between the aphelial, because too they have the position of a principle on account of the altitude of the planets and because the Earth and Venus claim as their private ratio somehow and as a prerogative the consonance 3 : 5, with which as their greater consonance we are now dealing. For although, by Proposition XXII, this consonance belongs to the perihelial movement of Venus and some intermediate movement of the Earth, yet the start is made at the extreme movements and the intermediate movements come after the beginnings.

---

1. "Identisonant consonances" are such as 3 : 5, 3 : 10, 3 : 20, etc.

Now, since on one side we have the aphelial movement of Saturn at its greatest altitude, on the other side the aphelial movement of the Earth rather than Venus is to be joined with it, because of these two planets which distinguish the kinds of harmony, the Earth, again, has the greater altitude. There is also another nearer cause: the posterior reasons—with which we are now dealing—take away from the prior reasons but only with respect to minima, and in harmonics that is with respect to all intervals less than concords. But by the prior reasons the aphelial movement not of Venus but of the Earth, will approximate the consonance of some number of octaves to be established with the aphelial movement of Saturn. For compound together, first, 4 : 5 the private ratio of Saturn's movements, *i.e.*, from the aphelion to the perihelial of Saturn (Proposition XI), secondly, the 1 : 2 of the converging movements of Saturn and Jupiter, *i.e.*, from the perihelion of Saturn to the aphelion of Jupiter (by Proposition VIII), thirdly, the 1 : 8 of the diverging movements of Jupiter and Mars, *i.e.*, from the aphelion of Jupiter to the perihelion of Mars (by Proposition XIV), fourthly, the 2 : 3 of the converging movements of Mars and the Earth, *i.e.*, from the perihelion of Mars to the aphelion of the Earth (by Proposition XV): you will find between the aphelion of Saturn and the perihelion of the Earth the compound ratio 1 : 30, which falls short of 1 : 32, or five octaves, by only 30 : 32, *i.e.*, 15 : 16 or a semitone. And so, if a semitone, divided into particles smaller than the least concord, is compounded with these four elements there will be a perfect consonance of five octaves between the aphelial movements of Saturn and the Earth, which have been set forth. But in order for the same aphelial movement of Saturn to make some number of octaves with the aphelial movement of Venus, it would have been necessary to snatch approximately a whole perfect fourth from the prior reasons; for if you compound 3 : 5, which exists between the aphelial movements of the Earth and Venus, with the ratio 1 : 30 compounded of the four prior elements, then as it were from the prior reasons, 1 : 50 is found between the aphelial movements of Saturn and Venus: This interval differs from 1 : 32, or five octaves, by 32 : 50, *i.e.*, 16 : 25, which is a perfect fifth and a diesis; and from six octaves, or 1 : 64, it differs by 50 : 64, *i.e.*, 25 : 32, or a perfect fourth minus a diesis. Accordingly, an indentisonant consonance was due to be established, not between the aphelial movements of Venus and Saturn but between those of Venus and the Earth, so that Saturn might keep a diversisonant consonance with Venus.

XXXII. Proposition. *In the universal consonances of planets of the minor scale the exact aphelial movement of Saturn could not harmonize precisely with the other planets.*

For the Earth by its aphelial movement does not concur in the universal consonance of the minor scale, because the aphelial movements of the Earth and Venus make the interval 3 : 5, which is of the major scale (by Proposition XVII). But by its aphelial movement Saturn makes an identisonant consonance with the aphelial movement of

the Earth (by Proposition XXXI). Therefore, neither does Saturn concur by its aphelial movement. Nevertheless, in place of the aphelial movement there follows some faster movement of Saturn, very near to the aphelial, and also in the minor scale—as was apparent in Chapter 7.

XXXIII. Proposition. *The major kind of consonances and musical scale is akin to the aphelial movements; the minor to the perihelial.*

For although a major consonance (*dura harmonia*) is set up not only between the aphelial movement of the Earth and the aphelial movement of Venus but also between the lower aphelial movements and the lower movements of Venus as far as its perihelion; and, conversely, there is a minor consonance not merely between the perihelial movement of Venus and the perihelial of the Earth but also between the higher movements of Venus as far as the aphelion and the higher movements of the Earth (by Propositions XX and XXIV). Accordingly, the major scale is designated properly only in the aphelial movements, the minor, only in the perihelial.

XXXIV. Proposition. *The major scale is more akin to the upper of the two planets, the minor, to the lower.*

[311] For, because the major scale is proper to the aphelial movements, the minor, to the perihelial (by the preceding proposition), while the aphelial are slower and graver than the perihelial; accordingly, the major scale is proper to the slower movements, the minor to the faster. But the upper of the two planets is more akin to the slow movements, the lower, to the fast, because slowness of the private movement always follows upon altitude in the world. Therefore, of two planets which adjust themselves to both modes, the upper is more akin to the major mode of the scale, the lower, to the minor. Further, the major scale employs the major intervals 4 : 5 and 3 : 5, and the minor, the minor ones, 5 : 6 and 5 : 8. But, moreover, the upper planet has both a greater sphere and slower, *i.e.*, greater movements and a lengthier circuit; but those things which agree greatly on both sides are rather closely united.

XXXV. Proposition. *Saturn and the Earth embrace the major scale more closely, Jupiter and Venus, the minor.*

For, first, the Earth, as compared with Venus and as designating both scales along with Venus, is the upper. Accordingly, by the preceding proposition, the Earth embraces the major scale chiefly; Venus, the minor. But with its aphelial movement Saturn harmonizes with the Earth's aphelial movement, through an octave (by Proposition XXXI): wherefore too (by Proposition XXXIII) Saturn embraces the major scale. Secondly, by the same proposition, Saturn by means of its aphelial movement nurtures more the major scale and (by Proposition XXXII) spits out the minor scale. Accordingly, it is more closely related to the major scale than to the minor, because the scales are properly designated by the extreme movements.

Now as regards Jupiter, in comparison with Saturn it is lower; therefore as the major scale is due to Saturn, so the minor is due to Jupiter, by the preceding proposition.

XXXVI. Proposition. *The perihelial movement of Jupiter had to concord with the perihelial movement of Venus in one scale but not also in the same consonance; and all the less so, with the perihelial movement of the Earth.*

For, because the minor scale chiefly was due to Jupiter, by the preceding proposition, while the perihelial movements are more akin to the minor scale (by Proposition XXX), accordingly, by its perihelial movement Jupiter had to designate the key of the minor scale, *viz.*, its definite pitch or key-note (*phthongum*). But too the perihelial movements of Venus and the Earth designate the same scale (by Proposition XXVIII); therefore the perihelial movement of Jupiter was to be associated with their perihelial movements in the same tuning, but it could not constitute a consonance with the perihelial movements of Venus. For, because (by Proposition VIII) it had to make about 1 : 3 with the aphelial movement of Saturn, *i.e.*, the note (*clavem*) d of that system, wherein the aphelial movement of Saturn strikes the note G, but the aphelial movement of Venus the note e: accordingly, it approached the note e within an interval of least consonance. For the least consonance is 5 : 6, but the interval between d and e is much smaller, *viz.*, 9 : 10, a whole tone. And although in the perihelial tension (*tensione*) Venus is raised from the d of the aphelial tension yet this elevation is less than a diesis, (by Proposition XXVIII). But the diesis (and hence any smaller interval) if compounded with a minor whole tone does not yet equal 5 : 6 the interval of least consonance. Accordingly, the perihelial movement of Jupiter could not observe 1 : 3 or thereabouts with the aphelial movement of Saturn and at the same time harmonize with Venus. Nor with the Earth. For if the perihelial movement of Jupiter had been adjusted to the key of the perihelial movement of Venus in the same tension in such fashion that below the quantity of least concord it should preserve with the aphelial movement of Saturn the interval 1 : 3, *viz.*, by differing from the perihelial movement of Venus by a minor whole tone, 9 : 10 or 36 : 40 (besides some octaves) towards the low. Now the perihelial movement of the Earth differs from the same perihelial movement of Venus by 5 : 8, *i.e.*, by 25 : 40. And so the perihelial movements of the Earth and Jupiter differ by 25 : 36, over and above some number of octaves. But that is not harmonic, because it is the square of 5 : 6, or a perfect fifth diminished by one diesis.

XXXVII. Proposition. *It was necessary for an interval equal to the interval of Venus to accede to the 2 : 3 of the compounded private consonances of Saturn and Jupiter and to 1 : 3 the great consonance common to them.*

For with its aphelial movement Venus assists in the proper designation of the major scale; with its perihelial, that of the minor scale, by Propositions XXVII and

XXXIII. But by its aphelial movement Saturn had to be in concord also with the major scale and thus with the aphelial movement of Venus, by Proposition XXXV, but Jupiter's perihelial with the perihelial of Venus, by the preceding proposition. Accordingly, as great as Venus makes its interval from aphelial to perihelial to be, so great an interval must also accede to that movement of Jupiter which makes 1 : 3 with the aphelial movement of Saturn—to the very perihelial movement of Jupiter. But the consonance of the converging movements of Jupiter and Saturn is precisely 1 : 2, by Proposition VIII. Accordingly, if the interval 1 : 2 is divided into the interval [312] greater than 1 : 3, there results, as the compound of the private ratios of both, something which is proportionately greater than 2 : 3.

Above, in Proposition XXVI, the private ratio of the movements of Venus was 243 : 250 or approximately 35 : 36; but in Chapter 4, between the aphelial movement of Saturn and the perihelial movement of Jupiter there was found a slightly greater excess beyond 1 : 3, viz., between 26 : 27 and 27 : 28. But the quantity here prescribed is absolutely equalled, by the addition of a single second to the aphelial movement of Saturn, and I do not know whether astronomy can discern that difference.

XXXVIII. Proposition. *The increment 243 : 250 to 2 : 3, the compound of the private ratios of Saturn and Jupiter, which was up to now being established by the prior reasons, was to be distributed among the planets in such fashion that of it the comma 80 : 81 should accede to Saturn and the remainder, 19,683 : 20,000 or approximately 62 : 63, to Jupiter.*

It follows from Axiom XIX that this was to have been distributed between both planets so that each could with some latitude concur in the universal consonances of the scale akin to itself. But the interval 243 : 250 is smaller than all concords: accordingly no harmonic rules remain whereby it may be divided into two concordant parts, with the single exception of those of which there was need in the division of 24 : 25, the diesis, above in Proposition XXVI; namely, in order that it may be divided into the comma 80 : 81 (which is a primary one of those intervals which are subordinate to the concordant) and into the remainder 19,683 : 20,000, which is slightly greater than a comma, viz., approximately 62 : 63. But not two but one comma had to be taken away, lest the parts should become too unequal, since the private ratios of Saturn and Jupiter are approximately equal (according to Axiom X extended even to concords and parts smaller than those) and also because the comma is determined by the intervals of the major whole tone and minor whole tone, not so two commas. Furthermore, to Saturn the higher and mightier planet was due not that part which was greater, although Saturn had the greater private consonance 4 : 5, but that one which is prior and more beautiful, i.e., more harmonic. For in Axiom X the consideration of priority and harmonic perfection comes first, and the consideration of quantity comes last, because

there is no beauty in quantity of itself. Thus the movements of Saturn become 64 : 81, an adulterine[1] major third, as we have called them in Book III, Chapter 12, but those of Jupiter, 6,561 : 8,000.

I do not know whether it should be numbered among the causes of the addition of a comma to Saturn that the extreme intervals of Saturn can constitute the ratio 8:9, the major whole tone, or whether that resulted without further ado from the preceding causes of the movements. Accordingly, you here have, in place of a corollary, the reason why, above in Chapter 4, the intervals of Saturn were found to embrace approximately a major whole tone.

XXXIX. Proposition. *Saturn could not harmonize with its exact perihelial movement in the universal consonances of the planets of the major scale, nor Jupiter with its exact aphelial movement.*

For since the aphelial movement of Saturn had to harmonize exactly with the aphelial movements of the Earth and Venus (by Proposition XXXI), that movement of Saturn which is 4 : 5 or one major third faster than its aphelial will also harmonize with them. For the aphelial movements of the Earth and Venus make a major sixth, which, by the demonstrations of Book III, is divisible into a perfect fourth and a major third, therefore the movement of Saturn, which is still faster than this movement already harmonized but none the less below the magnitude of a concordant interval, will not exactly harmonize. But such a movement is Saturn's perihelial movement itself, because it differs from its aphelial movement by more than the interval 4 : 5, *viz.*, one comma or 80 : 81 more (which is less than the least concord), by Proposition XXXVIII. Accordingly the perihelial movement of Saturn does not exactly harmonize. But neither does the aphelial movement of Jupiter do so precisely. For while it does not harmonize precisely with the perihelial movement of Saturn, it harmonizes at a distance of a perfect octave (by Proposition VIII), wherefore, according to what has been said in Book III, it cannot precisely harmonize.

XL. Proposition. *It was necessary to add the lemma of Plato to 1 : 8, or the triple octave, the joint consonance of the diverging movements of Jupiter and Mars established by the prior reasons.*

For because, by Proposition XXXI, there had to be 1 : 32, *i.e.*, 12 : 384, between the aphelial movements of Saturn and the Earth, but there had to be 3:2, *i.e.*, 384:256, from the aphelion of the Earth to the perihelion of Mars [313] (by Proposition XV), and from the aphelion of Saturn to its perihelion, 4 : 5 or 12 : 15 with its increment (by Proposition XXXVII); finally, from the perihelion of Saturn to the aphelion of Jupiter 1 : 2 or 15 : 30 (by Proposition VIII); accordingly, there remains 30 : 256 from

---

1 See footnote to *Intervals Compared with Harmonic Ratios.*

the aphelion of Jupiter to the perihelion of Mars, by the subtraction of the increment of Saturn. But 30 : 256 exceeds 32 : 256 by the interval 30 : 32, *i.e.*, 15 : 16 or 240 : 256, which is a semitone. Accordingly, if the increment of Saturn, which (by Proposition XXXVIII) had to be 80 : 81, *i.e.*, 240 : 243, is compounded inversely with 240 : 243, the result is 243 : 256; but that is the lemma of Plato,[1] *viz.*, approximately 19 : 20, see Book III. Accordingly, Plato's lemma had to be compounded with the 1 : 8.

And so the great ratio of Jupiter and Mars, *viz.*, of the diverging movements, ought to be 243 : 2,048, which is somehow a mean between 243 : 2,187 and 243 : 1,944, *i.e.*, between 1 : 9 and 1 : 8, whereof proportionality required the first, above; and a nearer harmonic concord, the second.

XLI. Proposition. *The private ratio of the movements of Mars has necessarily been made the square of the harmonic ratio 5 : 6, viz., 25 : 86.*

For, because the ratio of the diverging movements of Jupiter and Mars had to be 243 : 2,048, *i.e.*, 729 : 6,144, by the preceding proposition, but that of the converging movements 5 : 24, *i.e.*, 1,280 : 6,144 (by Proposition XIII), therefore the compound of the private ratios of both was necessarily 729 : 1,280 or 72,900 : 128,000. But the private ratio of Jupiter alone had to be 6,561 : 8,000, *i.e.*, 104,976 : 128,000 (by Proposition XXVIII). Therefore, if the compound ratio of both is divided by this, the private ratio of Mars will be left as 72,900 : 104,976, *i.e.*, 25 : 36, the square root of which is 5 : 6.

In another fashion, as follows: There is 1 : 32 or 120 : 3,840 from the aphelial movement of Saturn to the aphelial movement of the Earth, but from that same movement to the perihelial of Jupiter there is 1 : 3 or 120 : 360, with its increment. But from this to the aphelial movement of Mars is 5 : 24 or 360 : 1,728. Accordingly, from the aphelial movement of Mars to the aphelial movement of the Earth, there remains 1,728 : 3,840 minus the increment of the ratio of the diverging movements of Saturn and Jupiter. But from the same aphelial movement of the Earth to the perihelial of Mars there is 3 : 2, *i.e.*, 3,840 : 2,500. Therefore between the aphelial and perihelial movements of Mars there remains the ratio 1,728 : 2,560, *i.e.*, 27 : 40 or 81 : 120, minus the said increment. But 81 : 120 is a comma less than 80 : 120 or 2 : 3. Therefore, if a comma is taken away from 2 : 3, and the said increment (which by Proposition XXXVIII is equal to the private ratio of Venus) is taken away too, the private ratio of Mars is left. But the private ratio of Venus is the diesis diminished by a comma, by Proposition XXVI. But the comma and the diesis diminished by a comma make a full diesis or 24 : 25. Therefore if you divide 2 : 3, *i.e.*, 24 : 36 by the diesis 24 : 25, Mars' private ratio of 25 : 36 is left, as before, the square root of which, or 5 : 6, goes to the intervals, by Chapter 3.

1. *Timaeus*, 36.

Behold again the reason why—above, in Chapter 4—the extreme intervals of Mars have been found to embrace the harmonic ratio 5 : 6.

XLII. Proposition. *The great ratio of Mars and the Earth, or the common ratio of the diverging movements, has been necessarily made to be 54 : 125, smaller than the consonance 5 : 12 established by the prior reasons.*

For the private ratio of Mars had to be a perfect fifth, from which a diesis has been taken away, by the preceding proposition. But the common or minor ratio of the converging movements of Mars and the Earth had to be a perfect fifth or 2 : 3, by Proposition XV. Finally, the private ratio of the Earth is the diesis squared, from which a comma is taken away, by Propositions XXVI and XXVIII. But out of these elements is compounded the major ratio or that of the diverging movements of Mars and the Earth—and it is two perfect fifths (or 4 : 9, *i.e.*, 108 : 243) plus a diesis diminished by a comma, *i.e.*, plus 243 : 250; namely, it is 108 : 250 or 54 : 125, *i.e.*, 608 : 1,500. But this is smaller than 625 : 1,500, *i.e.*, than 5 : 12, in the ratio 602 : 625, which is approximately 36 : 37, smaller than 625 : 1,5000, *i.e.*, than 5 : 12, in the ratio 602:625, which is approximately 36 : 37, smaller than the least concord.

XLIII. Proposition. *The aphelial movement of Mars could not harmonize in some universal consonance; nevertheless it was necessary for it to be in concord to some extent in the scale of the minor mode.*

For, because the perihelial movement of Jupiter has the pitch *d* of acute tuning in the minor mode, and the consonance 5 : 24 ought to have existed between that and the aphelial movement of Mars, therefore, the aphelial movement of Mars occupies the adulterine pitch of the same acute tuning. I say *adulterine* for, although in Book III, Chapter 12, the adulterine consonances were reviewed and deduced from the composition of systems, certain ones which exist in the simple natural system were omitted. [314] And so, after the line which ends 81 : 120, the reader may add: if you divide into it 4 : 5 or 32 : 40, there remains 27 : 32, the subminor sixth,[1] which exists between *d* and *f* or *c* and *e*[2] or *a* and *c* of even the simple octave. And in the ensuing table, the following should be in the first line; for 5 : 6 there is 27 : 32, which is deficient.

From that it is clear that in the natural system the true note (*clavem*) *f*, as regulated by my principles, constitutes a deficient or adulterine minor sixth with the note *d*. Accordingly since between the perihelial movement of Jupiter set up in the true note *d* and the aphelial movement of Mars there is a perfect minor sixth over and above the double octave, but not the diminished (by Proposition XIII), it follows that with its aphelial movement Mars designates the pitch which is one comma higher than the true note *f*, and so it will concord not absolutely but merely to a certain extent in this scale.

---

1. Here "sixth" (*sexta*) should probably be "third" (*tertia*). E. C., Jr.
2. *C* and *e* do not produce a subminor third in the "natural system." E. C., Jr.

But it does not enter into either the pure or the adulterine universal harmony. For the perihelial movement of Venus occupies the pitch of *e* in this tuning (*tensionem*). But there is dissonance between *e* and *f*, on account of their nearness. Therefore, Mars is in discord with the perihelial movement of one of the planets, *viz.*, Venus. But too it is in discord with the other movements of Venus; they are diminished by a comma less than a diesis: wherefore, since there is a semitone and a comma between the perihelial movement of Venus and the aphelial movement of Mercury, accordingly, between the aphelion of Venus and the aphelion of Mars there will be a semitone and a diesis (neglecting the octaves), *i.e.*, a minor whole tone, which is still a dissonant interval. Now the aphelial movement of Mars concords to that extent in the scale of the minor mode, but not in that of the major. For since the aphelial movement of Venus concords with the *e* of the major mode, while the aphelial movement of Mars (neglecting the octaves) has been made a minor whole tone higher than *e*, then necessarily the aphelial movement of Mars in this tuning would fall midway between *f* and *f* sharp and would make with *g* (which in this tuning would be occupied by the aphelial movement of the Earth) the plainly discordant interval 25 : 27, *viz.*, a major whole tone diminished by a diesis.

In the same way, it will be proved that the aphelial movement of Mars is also in discord with the movements of the Earth. For because it makes a semitone and comma with the perihelial movement of Venus, *i.e.*, 14 : 15 (by what has been said), but the perihelial movements of the Earth and Venus make a minor sixth 5 : 8 or 15 : 24 (by Proposition XXVII). Accordingly, the aphelial movement of Mars together with the perihelial movement of the Earth (the octaves added to it) will make 14 : 24 or 7 : 12, a discordant interval and one not harmonic, like 7 : 6. For any interval between 5 : 6 and 8 : 9 is dissonant and discordant, as 6 : 7 in this case. But no other movement of the Earth can harmonize with the aphelial movement of Mars. For it was said above that it makes the discordant interval 25 : 27 with the Earth (neglecting the octaves); but all from 6 : 7 or 24 : 28 to 25 : 27 are smaller than the least harmonic interval.

XLIV. Corollary. *Accordingly it is clear from the above Proposition XLIII concerning Jupiter and Mars, and from Proposition XXXIX concerning Saturn and Jupiter, and from Proposition XXXVI concerning Jupiter and the Earth, and from Proposition XXXII concerning Saturn, why—in Chapter 5, above—it was found that all the extreme movements of the planets had not been adjusted perfectly to one natural system or musical scale, and that all those which had been adjusted to a system of the same tuning did not distinguish the pitches (loca) of that system in a natural way or effect a purely natural succession of concordant intervals. For the reasons are prior whereby the single planets came into possession of their single consonances; those whereby all the planets, of the universal consonances; and finally, those whereby the universal consonances of the two modes, the major and the minor: when all those have been posited, an omniform adjustment to one natural system is pre-*

vented. But if those causes had not necessarily come first, there is no doubt that either one system and one tuning of it would have embraced the extreme movements of all the planets; or, if there was need of two systems for the two modes of song, the major and minor, the very order of the natural scale would have been expressed not merely in one mode, the major, but also in the remaining minor mode. Accordingly, here in Chapter 5, you have the promised causes of the discords through least intervals and intervals smaller than all concords.

XLV. Proposition. *It was necessary for an interval equal to the interval of Venus to be added to the common major consonance of Venus and Mercury, the double octave, and also the private consonance of Mercury, which were established above in Propositions XII and XIII by the prior reasons,* [315] *in order that the private ratio of Mercury should be a perfect 5 : 12 and that thus Mercury should with both its movements harmonize with the single perihelial movement of Venus.*

For, because the aphelial movement of Saturn, the highest and outmost planet, circumscribed around its regular solid, had to harmonize with the aphelial movement of the Earth, the highest movement of the Earth, which divides the classes of figures; it follows by the laws of opposites that the perihelial movement of Mercury as the innermost planet, inscribed in its figure, the lowest and nearest to the sun, should harmonize with the perihelial movement of the Earth, with the lowest movement of the Earth, the common boundary: the former in order to designate the major mode of consonances, the latter the minor mode, by Propositions XXXIII and XXXIV. But the perihelial movement of Venus had to harmonize with the perihelial movement of the Earth in the consonance 5 : 3, by Proposition XXVII; therefore too the perihelial movement of Mercury had to be tempered with the perihelial of Venus in one scale. But by Proposition XII the consonance of the diverging movements of Venus and Mercury was determined by the prior reasons to be 1 : 4; therefore, now by these posterior reasons it was to be adjusted by the accession of the total interval of Venus. Accordingly, not from further on, from the aphelion, but from the perihelion of Venus to the perihelion of Mercury there is a perfect double octave. But the consonance 3 : 5 of the converging movements is perfect, by Proposition XV. Accordingly if 1 : 4 is divided by 3 : 5, there remains to Mercury singly the private ratio 5 : 12, perfect too, but not further (by Proposition XVI, through the prior reasons) diminished by the private ratio of Venus.

Another reason. Just as only Saturn and Jupiter are touched nowhere on the outside by the dodecahedron and icosahedron wedded together, so only Mercury is untouched on the inside by these same solids, since they touch Mars on the inside, the Earth on both sides, and Venus on the outside. Accordingly, just as something equal to the private ratio of Venus has been added distributively to the private ratios of movements of Saturn and Jupiter, which are supported by the cube and tetrahedron; so now some-

thing as great was due to accede to the private ratio of solitary Mercury, which is comprehended by the associated figures of the cube and tetrahedron; because, as the octahedron, a single figure among the secondary figures, does the job of two among the primary, the cube and tetrahedron (concerning which see Chapter 1), so too among the lower planets there is one Mercury in place of two of the upper planets, *viz.*, Saturn and Jupiter.

Thirdly, just as the aphelial movement of the highest planet Saturn had to harmonize, in some number of octaves, *i.e.*, in the continued double ratio, 1 : 32, with the aphelial movement of the higher and nearer of the two planets which shift the mode of consonance (by Proposition XXXI); so, *vice versa*, the perihelial movement of the lowest planet Mercury, again through some number of octaves, *i.e.*, in the continued double ratio, 1 : 4, had to harmonize with the perihelial movement of the lower and similarly nearer of the two planets which shift the mode of consonance.

Fourthly, of the three upper planets, Saturn, Jupiter, and Mars, the single but extreme movements concord with the universal consonances; accordingly both extreme movements of the single lower planet, *viz.*, Mercury, had to concord with the same; for the middle planets, the Earth and Venus, had to shift the mode of consonances, by Propositions XXXIII and XXXIV.

Finally, in the three pairs of the upper planets perfect consonances have been found between the converging movements, but adjusted (*fermentatae*) consonances between the diverging movements and private ratios of the single planets; accordingly, in the two pairs of the lower planets, conversely, perfect consonances had to be found not between the converging movements chiefly, nor between the diverging, but between the movements of the same field. And because two perfect consonances were due to the Earth and Venus, therefore two perfect consonances were due to Venus and Mercury also. And the Earth and Venus had to receive as perfect a consonance between their aphelial movements as between their perihelial, because they had to shift the mode of their consonance; but Venus and Mercury, as not shifting the mode of their consonance, did not also require perfect consonances between both pairs, the aphelial movements and the perihelial; but there came in place of the perfect consonance of the aphelial movements, as being already adjusted the perfect consonance of the converging movements, so that just as Venus, the higher of the lower planets, has the least private ratio of all the private ratios of movements (by Proposition XXVI), and Mercury, the lower of the lower, has received the greatest ratio of all the private ratios of movements (by Proposition XXX), so too the private ratio of Venus should be the most imperfect of all the private ratios or the farthest removed from consonances, while the private ratio of Mercury should be most perfect of all the private ratios, *i.e.*, an absolute consonance without adjustment, and that finally the relations should be everywhere opposite.

For He Who is before the ages and on into the ages thus adorned the great things of His wisdom: nothing excessive, nothing defective, no room for any censure. How lovely are his works! All things, in twos, one [316] *against one, none lacking its opposite. He has strengthened the goods—adornment and propriety—of each and every one and established them in the best reasons, and who will be satiated seeing their glory?*

XLVI. Axiom. *If the interspacing of the solid figures between the planetary spheres is free and unhindered by the necessities of antecedent causes, then it ought to follow to perfection the proportionality of geometrical inscriptions and circumscriptions, and thereby the conditions of the ratio of the inscribed to the circumscribed spheres.*

For nothing is more reasonable than that physical inscription should exactly represent the geometrical, as the work, its pattern.

XLVII. Proposition. *If the inscription of the regular solids among the planets was free, the tetrahedron was due to touch with its angles precisely the perihelial sphere of Jupiter above it, and with centres of its planes precisely the aphelial sphere of Mars below it. But the cube and the octahedron, each placing its angles in the perihelial sphere of the planet above, were due to penetrate the sphere of the inside planet with the centres of their planes, in such fashion that those centres should turn within the aphelial and perihelial spheres: on the other hand, the dodecahedron and icosahedron, grazing with their angles the perihelial spheres of their planets on the outside, were due not quite to touch with the centres of their planes the aphelial spheres of their inner planets. Finally, the dodecahedral echinus, placing its angles in the perihelial sphere of Mars, was due to come very close to the aphelial sphere of Venus with the midpoints of its converted sides which interdistinguish two solid rays.*

For the tetrahedron is the middle one of the primary figures, both in genesis and in situation in the world; accordingly, it was due to remove equally both regions, that of Jupiter and that of Mars. And because the cube was above it and outside it, and the dodecahedron was below it and within it, therefore it was natural that their inscription should strive for the contrariety wherein the tetrahedron held a mean, and that the one of them should make an excessive inscription, and the other a defective, *viz.*, the one should somewhat penetrate the inner sphere, the other not touch it. And because the octahedron is cognate to the cube and has an equal ratio of spheres, but the icosahedron to the dodecahedron, accordingly, whatever the cube has of perfection of inscription, the same was due to the octahedron also, and whatever the dodecahedron, the same to the icosahedron too. And the situation of the octahedron's similar to the situation of the cube, but that of the icosahedron to the situation of the dodecahedron, because as the cube occupies the one limit to the outside, so the octahedron occupies the remaining limit to the inside of the world, but the dodecahedron and icosahedron are midway: accordingly even a similar inscription was proper, in the case of the dodecahedron, one penetrating the sphere of the inner planet, in that of the icosahedron, one falling short of it.

But the echinus, which represents the icosahedron with the apexes of its angles and the dodecahedron with the bases, was due to fill, embrace, or dispose both regions, that between Mars and the Earth with the dodecahedron as well as that between the Earth and Venus with the icosahedron. But the preceding axiom makes clear which of the opposites was due to which association. For the tetrahedron, which has a rational inscribed sphere, has been allotted the middle position among the primary figures and is surrounded on both sides by figures of incommensurable spheres, whereof the outer is the cube, the inner the dodecahedron, by Chapter 1 of this book. But this geometrical quality, *viz.*, the rationality of the inscribed sphere, represents in nature the perfect inscription of the planetary sphere. Accordingly, the cube and its allied figure have their inscribed spheres rational only in square, *i.e.*, in power alone; accordingly, they ought to represent a semiperfect inscription, where, even if not the extremity of the planetary sphere, yet at least something on the inside and rightfully a mean between the aphelial and perihelial spheres—if that is possible through other reasons—is touched by the centres of the planes of the figures. On the other hand, the dodecahedron and its allied figure have their inscribed spheres clearly irrational both in the length of the radius and in the square; accordingly, they ought to represent a clearly imperfect inscription and one touching absolutely nothing of the planetary sphere, *i.e.*, falling short and not reaching as far as the aphelial sphere of the planet with the centres of its planes.

Although the echinus is cognate to the dodecahedron and its allied figure, nevertheless it has a property similar to the tetrahedron. For the radius of the sphere inscribed in its inverted sides is indeed incommensurable with the radius of the circumscribed sphere, but it is, however, commensurable with the length of the distance between two neighbouring angles. And so the perfection of the commensurability of rays is approximately as great as in the tetrahedron; but elsewhere the imperfection is as great as in the [317] dodecahedron and its allied figure. Accordingly it is reasonable too that the physical inscription belonging to it should be neither absolutely tetrahedral nor absolutely dodecahedral but of an intermediate kind; in order that (because the tetrahedron was due to touch the extremity of the sphere with its planes, and the dodecahedron, to fall short of it by a definite interval) this wedge-shaped figure with the inverted sides should stand between the icosahedral space and the extremity of the inscribed sphere and should nearly touch this extremity—if nevertheless this figure was to be admitted into association with the remaining five, and if its laws could be allowed, with the laws of the others remaining. Nay, why do I say "could be allowed"? For they could not do without them. For if an inscription, which was loose and did not come into contact fitted the dodecahedron, what else could confine that indefinite

looseness within the limits of a fixed magnitude, except this subsidiary figure cognate to the dodecahedron and icosahedron, and which comes almost into contact with its inscribed sphere and does not fall short (if indeed it does fall short) any more than the tetrahedron exceeds and penetrates—with which magnitude we shall deal in the following.

This reason for the association of the echinus with the two cognate figures (*viz.*, in order that the ratio of the spheres of Mars and Venus, which they had left indefinite, should be made determinate) is rendered very probable by the fact that 1,000, the semidiameter of the sphere of the Earth, is found to be practically a mean proportional between the perihelial sphere of Mars and the aphelial sphere of Venus; as if the interval, which the echinus assigns to the cognate figures, has been divided between them as proportionally as possible.

XLVIII. Proposition. *The inscription of the regular solid figures between the planetary spheres was not the work of pure freedom; for with respect to very small magnitudes it was hindered by the consonances established between the extreme movements.*

For, by Axioms I and II, the ratio of the spheres of each figure was not due to be expressed immediately by itself, but by means of it the consonances most akin to the ratios of the spheres were first to be sought and adjusted to the extreme movements.

Then, in order that, by Axioms XVIII and XX, the universal consonances of the two modes could exist, it was necessary for the greater consonances of the single pairs to be readjusted somewhat, by means of the posterior reasons. Accordingly, in order that those things might stand, and be maintained by their own reasons, intervals were required which are somewhat discordant with those which arise from the perfect inscription of figures between the spheres, by the laws of movements unfolded in Chapter 3. In order that it be proved and made manifest how much is taken away from the single planets by the consonances established by their proper reasons; come, let us build up, out of them, the intervals of the planets from the sun, by a new form of calculation not previously tried by anyone.

Now there will be three heads to this inquiry: First, from the two extreme movements of each planet the similar extreme intervals between it and the sun will be investigated, and by means of them the radius of the sphere in those dimensions, of the extreme intervals, which are proper to each planet. Secondly, by means of the same extreme movements, in the same dimensions for all, the mean movements and their ratio will be investigated. Thirdly, by means of the ratio of the mean movements already disclosed, the ratio of the spheres or mean intervals and also one ratio of the

extreme intervals, will be investigated; and the ratio of the mean intervals will be compared with the ratios of the figures.

As regards the first: we must repeat, from Chapter 3, Article VI, that the ratio of the extreme movements is the inverse square of the ratio of the corresponding intervals from the sun. Accordingly, since the ratio of the squares is the square of the ratio of its sides, therefore, the numbers, whereby the extreme movements of the single planets are expressed, will be considered as squares and the extraction of their roots will give the extreme intervals, whereof it is easy to take the arithmetic mean as the semidiameter of the sphere and the eccentricity. Accordingly the consonances so far established have prescribed.

[318] *Planets Props.*	*Ratios of movements*	*The roots either prolonged or of their multiples*	*Therefore the semidiameter of the sphere*	*Eccen- tricity*	*In dimensions whereof the semidiameter of the sphere is 100,000*
Saturn by XXXVIII	64 : 81	80 : 90	85	5	5,882
Jupiter by XXXVIII	6,561 : 8,000	81,000 : 89,444	85,222	4,222	4,954
Mars by XLI	25 : 36	50 : 60	55	5	9,091
Earth by XXVIII	2,916 : 3,125	93,531 : 96,825	95,178	1,647	1,730
Venus by XXVIII	243 : 250	9,859 : 10,000	99,295	705	710
Mercury by XLV	5 : 12	63,250 : 98,000	80,625	17,375	21,551

For the second of the things proposed, we again have need of Chapter 3, Article XII, where it was shown that the number which expresses the movement which is as a mean in the ratio of the extremes is less than their arithmetic mean, also less than the geometric mean by half the difference between the geometric and arithmetic means. And because we are investigating all the mean movements in the same dimensions, therefore let all the ratios hitherto established between different twos and also all the private ratios of the single planets be set out in the measure of the least common divisible. Then let the means be sought: the arithmetic, by taking half the difference between the extreme movements of each planet, the geometric, by the multiplication of one extreme into the other and extracting the square root of the product; then by subtracting half the difference of the means from the geometric mean, let the number of the mean movement be constituted in the private dimensions of each planet, which can easily, by the rule of ratios, be converted into the common dimensions.

[319] Therefore, from the prescribed consonances, the ratio of the mean diurnal movements has been found, *viz.*, the ratio between the numbers of the degrees and minutes of each planet. It is easy to explore how closely that approaches to astronomy.

Harmonic ratios of two	Numbers of the extreme movements	Private ratios of the single planets	Continued means of the single planets		Halves of the differences	Number of the mean movement in dimensions	
			Arithmetic	Geometric		Private	Common
1	♄ 139,968	64					
			72.50	72.00	.25	71.75	156,917
1	♄ 177,147	81					
2	♃ 354,294	6,561					
			7,280.5	7,244.9	17.8	7,227.1	390,263
5	♃ 432,000	8,000					
24	♂ 2,073,600	25					
			30.50	30.00	.25	29.75	2,467,584
2	♂ 2,985,984	36					
32 3	♁ 4,478,976	2,916					
			3,020.500	3,018.692	.904	3,017.788	4,635,322
5	♁ 4,800,000	3,125					
5 8	♀ 7,464,960	243					
			246.500	246.475	.0125	246.4625	7,571,328
1 3	♀ 7,680,000	250					
5	☿ 12,800,000	5					
			8.500	7.746	.377	7.369	18,864,680
4	☿ 30,720,000	12					

The third head of things proposed requires Chapter 3, Article VIII. For when the ratio of the mean diurnal movements of the single planets has been found, it is possible to find the ratio of the spheres too. For the ratio of the mean movements is the $3/2$th power of the inverse ratio of the spheres. But, too, the ratio of the cube numbers is the $3/2$th power of the ratio of the squares of those same square roots, given in the table of Clavius, which he subjoined to his *Practical Geometry*. Wherefore, if the numbers of our mean movements (curtailed, if need be, of an equal number of ciphers) are sought among the cube numbers of that table, they will indicate on the left, under the heading of the squares, the numbers of the ratio of the spheres; then the eccentricities ascribed above to the single planets in the private ratio of the semidiameters of each may easily be converted by the rule of ratios into dimensions common to all, so that, by their addition to the semidiameters of the spheres and subtraction from them, the extreme intervals of the single planets from the sun may be established. Now we shall give to the semidiameter of the terrestrial sphere the round number 100,000, as is the practice in astronomy, and with the following design: because this number or its square

or its cube is always made up of mere ciphers; and so too we shall raise the mean movement of the Earth to the number 10,000,000,000 and by the rule of ratios make the number of the mean movement of any planet be to the number of the mean movement of the Earth, as 10,000,000,000 is to the new measurement. And so the business can be carried on with only five cube roots, by comparing those single cube roots with the one number of the Earth.

Numbers of the mean movements							
In the original dimensions	*In the new dimensions found in inverse order among the cubes*	*Numbers of the ratio of the spheres found among the squares*	*Semi-diameters as above*	*Eccentricities in dimensions Private as above*	*Common*	*Extreme intervals resulting Aphelion*	*Perihelion*
♄ 156,917	29,539,960	9,556	85	5	562	10,118	8,994
♃ 390,263	11,877,400	5,206	85,222	4,222	258	5,464	4,948
♂ 2,467,584	1,878,483	1,523	55	5	138	1,661	1,384
♁ 4,635,322	1,000,000	1,000	95,178	1,647	17	1,017	983
♀ 7,571,328	612,220	721	99,295	705	5	726	716
☿ 18,864,680	245,714	392	80,625	17,375	85	476	308

Accordingly, it is apparent in the last column what the numbers turn out to be whereby the converging intervals of two planets are expressed. All of them approach very near to those intervals, which I found from Brahe's observations. In Mercury alone is there some small difference. For astronomy is seen to give the following intervals to it: 470, 388, 306, all shorter. It seems that the reason for the dissonance may be referred either to the fewness of the observations or to the magnitude of the eccentricity. (See Chapter 3). But I hurry on to the end of the calculation.

For now it is easy to compare the ratio of the spheres of the figures with the ratio of the converging intervals.

[320] For if the semidiameter of the sphere circumscribed around the figure

which is commonly 100,000	*becomes:*	*Then the semidiameter of the sphere or circle inscribed in:*	*instead of:*	*becomes:*	*Although by the consonances the interval is:*	
In the cube	8,994	♄ (Saturn)	57,735	5,194	Mean	♃ 5,206
In the tetrahedron	4,948	♃ (Jupiter)	33,333	1,649	Aphelial	♂ 1,661
In the dodecahedron	1,384	♂ (Mars)	79,465	1,100	Aphelial	♁ 1,018
In the icosahedron	983	♁ (Earth)	79,465	781	Aphelial	♀ 726
In the echinus	1,384	♂ (Mars)	52,573	728	Aphelial	♀ 726
In the octahedron	716	♀ (Venus)	57,735	413	Mean	☿ 392

In the square in

| the octahedron | 716 ♀ (Venus) | 70,711 | 506 | Aphelial | ☿ | 476 |
| | or 476 ☿ (Mercury) | 70,711 | 336 | Perihelial | ☿ | 308 |

That is to say, the planes of the cube extend down slightly below the middle circle of Jupiter; the octahedral planes, not quite to the middle circle of Mercury; the tetrahedral, slightly below the highest circle of Mars; the sides of the echinus, not quite to the highest circle of Venus; but the planes of the dodecahedron fall far short of the aphelial circle of the Earth; the planes of the icosahedron also fall short of the aphelial circle of Venus, and approximately proportionally; finally, the square in the octahedron is quite inept, and not unjustly, for what are plane figures doing among solids? Accordingly, you see that if the planetary intervals are deduced from the harmonic ratios of movements hitherto demonstrated, it is necessary that they turn out as great as these allow, but not as great as the laws of free inscription prescribed in Proposition XLV would require: because this κόσμοσ γεωμέτρικοσ (geometrical adornment) of perfect inscription was not fully in accordance with that other κόδμον ἁρμόνικον ἐν-δεχόμενον (possible harmonic adornment)—to use the words of Galen, taken from the epigraph to this Book V. So much was to be demonstrated by the calculation of numbers, for the elucidation of the prescribed proposition.

I do not hide that if I increase the consonance of the diverging movements of Venus and Mercury by the private ratio of the movements of Venus, and, as a consequence, diminish the private ratio of Mercury by the same, then by this process I produce the following intervals between Mercury and the sun: 469,388,307, which are very precisely represented by astronomy. But, in the first place, I cannot defend that diminishing by harmonic reasons. For the aphelial movement of Mercury will not square with that musical scale, nor in the planets which are opposite in the world is the planetary principle (*ratio*) of opposition of all conditions kept. Finally, the mean diurnal movement of Mercury becomes too great, and thereby the periodic time, which is the most certain fact in all astronomy, is shortened too much. And so I stay within the harmonic polity here employed and confirmed throughout the whole of Chapter 9. But none the less with this example I call you all forth, as many of you as have happened to read this book and are steeped in the mathematical disciplines and the knowledge of highest philosophy: work hard and either pluck up one of the consonances applied everywhere, interchange it with some other, and test whether or not you will come so near to the astronomy posited in Chapter 4, or else try by reasons whether or not you can build with the celestial movements something better and more expedient and destroy in part or in whole the layout applied by me. But let whatever pertains to the glory of Our Lord and Founder be equally permissible to you by way of this book, and up to this very hour I myself have taken the liberty of everywhere changing those

things which I was able to discover on earlier days and which were the conceptions of a sluggish care or hurrying ardour.

[321] XLIX. Envoi. *It was good that in the genesis of the intervals the solid figures should yield to the harmonic ratios, and the major consonances of two planets to the universal consonances of all, in so far as this was necessary.*

With good fortune we have arrived at 49, the square of 7; so that this may come as a kind of Sabbath, since the six solid eights of discourse concerning the construction of the heavens has gone before. Moreover, I have rightly made an *envoi* which could be placed first among the axioms: because God also, enjoying the works of His creation, "saw all things which He had made, and behold! they were very good."

There are two branches to the *envoi*: First, there is a demonstration concerning consonances in general, as follows: For where there is choice among different things which are not of equal weight, there the more excellent are to be put first and the more vile are to be detracted from, in so far as that is necessary, as the very word ὁ κόδμος, which signifies *adornment,* seems to argue. But inasmuch as life is more excellent than the body, the form than the material, by so much does harmonic adornment excel the geometrical.

For as life perfects the bodies of animate things, because they have been born for the exercise of life—as follows from the archetype of the world, which is the divine essence—so movement measures the regions assigned to the planets, each that of its own planet: because that region was assigned to the planet in order that it should move. But the five regular solids, by their very name, pertain to the intervals of the regions and to the number of them and the bodies; but the consonances to the movements. Again, as matter is diffuse and indefinite of itself, the form definite, unified, and determinant of the material, so too there are an infinite number of geometric ratios, but few consonances. For although among the geometrical ratios there are definite degrees of determinations, formation, and restriction, and no more than three can exist from the ascription of spheres to the regular solids; but nevertheless an accident common to all the rest follows upon even these geometrical ratios: an infinite possible section of magnitudes is presupposed, which those ratios whose terms are mutually incommensurable somehow involve in actuality too. But the harmonic ratios are all rational, the terms of all are commensurable and are taken from a definite and finite species of plane figures. But infinity of section represents the material, while commensurability or rationality of terms represents the form. Accordingly, as material desires the form, as the rough-hewn stone, of a just magnitude indeed, the form of a human body, so the geometric ratios of figures desire the consonances—not in order to fashion and form those consonances, but because this material squares better with this form, this quantity of stone with this statue, even this ratio of regular solids with this consonance—therefore in order so that

they are fashioned and formed more fully, the material by its form, the stone by the chisel into the form of an animate being; but the ratio of the spheres of the figure by its own, *i.e.*, the near and fitting, consonance.

The things which have been said up to now will become clearer from the history of my discoveries. Since I had fallen into this speculation twenty-four years ago, I first inquired whether the single planetary spheres are equal distances apart from one another (for the spheres are apart in Copernicus, and do not touch one another), that is to say, I recognized nothing more beautiful than the ratio of equality. But this ratio is without head or tail: for this material equality furnished no definite number of mobile bodies, no definite magnitude for the intervals. Accordingly, I meditated upon the similarity of the intervals to the spheres, *i.e.*, upon the proportionality. But the same complaint followed. For although to be sure, intervals which were altogether unequal were produced between the spheres, yet they were not unequally equal, as Copernicus wishes, and neither the magnitude of the ratio nor the number of the spheres was given. I passed on to the regular plane figures: [322] intervals were formed from them by the ascription of circles. I came to the five regular solids: here both the number of the bodies and approximately the true magnitude of the intervals was disclosed, in such fashion that I summoned to the perfection of astronomy the discrepancies remaining over and above. Astronomy was perfect these twenty years; and behold! there was still a discrepancy between the intervals and the regular solids, and the reasons for the distribution of unequal eccentricities among the planets were not disclosed. That is to say, in this house the world, I was asking not only why stones of a more elegant form but also what form would fit the stones, in my ignorance that the Sculptor had fashioned them in the very articulate image of an animated body. So, gradually, especially during these last three years, I came to the consonances and abandoned the regular solids in respect to minima, both because the consonances stood on the side of the form which the finishing touch would give, and the regular solids, on that of the material—which in the world is the number of bodies and the rough-hewn amplitude of the intervals—and also because the consonances gave the eccentricities, which the regular solids did not even promise—that is to say, the consonances made the nose, eyes, and remaining limbs a part of the statue, for which the regular solids had prescribed merely the outward magnitude of the rough-hewn mass.

Wherefore, just as neither the bodies of animate beings are made nor blocks of stone are usually made after the pure rule of some geometrical figure, but something is taken away from the outward spherical figure, however elegant it may be (although the just magnitude of the bulk remains), so that the body may be able to get the organs necessary for life, and the stone the image of the animate being; so too as the ratio which the regular solids had been going to prescribe for the planetary spheres is inferi-

or and looks only towards the body and material, it has to yield to the consonances, in so far as that was necessary in order for the consonances to be able to stand closely by and adorn the movement of the globes.

The other branch of the *envoi*, which concerns universal consonances, has a proof closely related to the first. (As a matter of fact, it was in part assumed above, in XVIII, among the Axioms.) For the finishing touch of perfection, as it were, is due rather to that which perfects the world more; and conversely that thing which occupies a second position is to be detracted from, if either is to be detracted from. But the universal harmony of all perfects the world more than the single twin consonances of different neighbouring twos. For harmony is a certain ratio of unity; accordingly the planets are more united, if they all are in concord together in one harmony, than if each two concord separately in two consonances. Wherefore, in the conflict of both, either one of the two single consonances of two planets was due to yield, so that the universal harmonies of all could stand. But the greater consonances, those of the diverging movements, were due to yield rather than the lesser, those of the converging movements. For if the divergent movements diverge, then they look not towards the planets of the given pair but towards other neighbouring planets, and if the converging movements converge, then the movements of one planet are converging toward the movement of the other, conversely: for example, in the pair Jupiter and Mars the aphelial movement of Jupiter verges toward Saturn, the perihelial of Mars towards the Earth: but the perihelial movement of Jupiter verges toward Mars, the aphelial of Mars toward Jupiter. Accordingly the consonance of the converging movements is more proper to Jupiter and Mars; the consonance of the diverging movements is somehow more foreign to Jupiter and Mars. But the ratio of union which brings together neighbouring planets by twos and twos is less disturbed if the consonance which is more foreign and more removed from them should be adjusted than if the private ratio should be, *viz.*, the one which exists between the more neighbouring movements of neighbouring planets. None the less this adjustment was not very great. For the proportionality has been found in which may stand the universal consonances of all the planets may exist (and these in two distinct modes), and in which (with a certain latitude of tuning merely equal to a comma) may also be embraced the single consonances of two neighbouring planets; the consonances of the converging movements in four pairs, perfect, of the aphelial movements in one pair, of the perihelial movements in two pairs, likewise perfect; the consonances of the diverging movements in four pairs, these, however, within the difference of one diesis (the very small interval by which the human voice [323] in figured song nearly always errs; the single consonance of Jupiter and Mars, this between the diesis and the semitone. Accordingly it is apparent that this mutual yielding is everywhere very good.)

Accordingly let this do for our *envoi* concerning the work of God the Creator. It now remains that at last, with my eyes and hands removed from the tablet of demonstrations and lifted up towards the heavens, I should pray, devout and supplicating, to the Father of lights: *O Thou Who dost by the light of nature promote in us the desire for the light of grace, that by its means Thou mayest transport us into the light of glory, I give thanks to Thee, O Lord Creator, Who hast delighted me with Thy makings and in the works of Thy hands have I exulted. Behold! now, I have completed the work of my profession, having employed as much power of mind as Thou didst give to me; to the men who are going to read those demonstrations I have made manifest the glory of Thy works, as much of its infinity as the narrows of my intellect could apprehend. My mind has been given over to philosophizing most correctly: if there is anything unworthy of Thy designs brought forth by me—a worm born and nourished in a wallowing place of sins—breathe into me also that which Thou dost wish men to know, that I may make the correction: If I have been allured into rashness by the wonderful beauty of Thy works, or if I have loved my own glory among men, while I am advancing in the work destined for Thy glory, be gentle and merciful and pardon me; and finally deign graciously to effect that these demonstrations give way to Thy glory and the salvation of souls and nowhere be an obstacle to that.*

10. EPILOGUE CONCERNING THE SUN, BY WAY OF CONJECTURE[1]

From the celestial music to the hearer, from the Muses to Apollo the leader of the Dance, from the six planets revolving and making consonances to the Sun at the centre of all the circuits, immovable in place but rotating into itself. For although the harmony is most absolute between the extreme planetary movements, not with respect to the true speeds through the ether but with respect to the angles which are formed by joining with the centre of the sun the termini of the diurnal arcs of the planetary orbits; while the harmony does not adorn the termini, *i.e.*, the single movements, in so far as they are considered in themselves but only in so far as by being taken together and compared with one another, they become the object of some mind; and although no object is ordained in vain, without the existence of some thing which may be moved by it, while those angles seem to presuppose some action similar to our eyesight or at least to that sense-perception whereby, in Book IV, the sublunary nature perceived the angles of rays formed by the planets on the Earth: still it is not easy for dwellers on the Earth to conjecture what sort of sight is present in the sun, what eyes there are, or what other instinct there is for perceiving those angles even without eyes and for evaluating the harmonies of the movements entering into the antechamber of the mind by whatever doorway, and finally what mind there is in the sun. None the less, however those

---

1. See Kepler's commentary on this epilogue in the *Epitome*, pages 10-11.

things may be, this composition of the six primary spheres around the sun, cherishing it with their perpetual revolutions and as it were adoring it (just as, separately, four moons accompany the globe of Jupiter, two Saturn, but a single moon by its circuit encompasses, cherishes, fosters the Earth and us its inhabitants, and ministers to us) and this special business of the harmonies, which is a most clear footprint of the highest providence over solar affairs, now being added to that consideration, [324] wrings from me the following confession: not only does light go out from the sun into the whole world, as from the focus or eye of the world, as life and heat from the heart, as every movement from the King and mover, but conversely also by royal law these returns, so to speak, of every lovely harmony are collected in the sun from every province in the world, nay, the forms of movements by twos flow together and are bound into one harmony by the work of some mind, and are as it were coined money from silver and gold bullion; finally, the curia, palace, and praetorium or throne-room of the whole realm of nature are in the sun, whatsoever chancellors, palatines, prefects the Creator has given to nature: for them, whether created immediately from the beginning or to be transported hither at some time, has He made ready those seats. For even this terrestrial adornment, with respect to its principal part, for quite a long while lacked the contemplators and enjoyers, for whom however it had been appointed; and those seats were empty. Accordingly the reflection struck my mind, what did the ancient Pythagoreans in Aristotle mean, who used to call the centre of the world (which they referred to as the "fire" but understood by that the sun) "the watchtower of Jupiter," Διος φυλακὴν; what, likewise, was the ancient interpreter pondering in his mind when he rendered the verse of the Psalm as: "He has placed His tabernacle in the sun."

But also I have recently fallen upon the hymn of Proclus the Platonic philosopher (of whom there has been much mention in the preceding books), which was composed to the Sun and filled full with venerable mysteries, if you excise that one κλῦθ (hear me) from it; although the ancient interpreter already cited has explained this to some extent, viz., in invoking the sun, he understands Him Who has placed His tabernacle in the sun. For Proclus lived at a time in which it was a crime, for which the rulers of the world and the people itself inflicted all punishments, to profess Jesus of Nazareth, God Our Savior, and to contemn the gods of the pagan poets (under Constantine, Maxentius, and Julian the Apostate). Accordingly Proclus, who from his Platonic philosophy indeed, by the natural light of the mind, had caught a distant glimpse of the Son of God, that true light which lighteth every man coming into this world, and who already knew that divinity must never be sought with a superstitious mob in sensible things, nevertheless preferred to seem to look for God in the sun rather than in Christ a sensible man, in order that at the same time he might both deceive the pagans by

honoring verbally the Titan of the poets and devote himself to his philosophy, by drawing away both the pagans and the Christians from sensible beings, the pagans from the
visible sun, the Christians from the Son of Mary, because, trusting too much to the
natural light of reason, he spit out the mystery of the Incarnation; and finally that at
the same time he might take over from them and adopt into his own philosophy whatever the Christians had which was most divine and especially consonant with Platonic
philosophy.[1] And so the accusation of the teaching of the Gospel concerning Christ is
laid against this hymn of Proclus, in its own matters: let that Titan keep as his private
possessions χρῦσα ἡνία (golden reins) and ταμιεῖυν φαοῦς, μεσσατὶην, αἰθερος
ἔδρην, κοδμοῦ κραδιαῖον ἐριφεγγέᾳ κυκλὸν (a treasury of light, a seat at the mid-
part of the ether, a radiant circle at the heart of the world), which visible aspect
Copernicus too bestows upon him; let him even keep his παλιννοστοὺς διφρείς
(cyclical chariot-drivings), although according to the ancient Pythagoreans he does not
possess them but in their place τὸ κέντρον, Διὸς φυλακήν (the centre, the watchtower of Zeus)—which doctrine, misshapen by the forgetfulness of ages, as by a flood,
was not recognized by their follower Proclus; let him also keep his γενεθλὴν
Βλαστησασαν (offspring born) of himself, and whatever else is of nature; in turn, let
the philosophy of Proclus yield to Christian doctrines, [325] let the sensible sun yield
to the Son of Mary, the Son of God, Whom Proclus addresses under the name of the
Titan ζωαρκεὸς, ὦ ἄνα, πηγῆς αὐτὸς ἔχων κλῆδα (O lord, who dost hold the key
of the life-supporting spring), and that πάντα τεῆς ἐπλήσας ἐλερσινοοῖο
προνόιης (thou didst fulfill all things with thy mind-awakening foresight), and that
immense power over the μοιράων (fates), and things which were read of in no philosophy before the promulgation of the Gospel,[2] the demons dreading him as their threatening scourge, the demons lying in ambush for souls, ὄφρα ὑφιτενοὺς λαθοῖντο
πατρὸς περιφέγγεοσ αὐλῆς (in order that they might escape the notice of the light-
filled hall of the lofty father); and who except the Word of the Father is that εἰκὼν
παγγενεταο, θεοῦ, οὐφάευτος ἀπ᾽ ἀρρήτου γενετῆρος παύσατο στοιχεῖων
ὀρυμάγδος ἐπ ἀλληλοῖσιν ἰόντων (image of the all-begetting father, upon whose
manifestation from an ineffable mother the sin of the elements changing into one
another ceased), according to the following: *The Earth was unwrought and a chaotic
mass, and darkness was upon the face of the abyss, and God divided the light from the darkness, the waters from the waters, the sea from the dry land; and: all things were made by
the very Word.* Who except Jesus of Nazareth the Son of God, ψυχῶν ἀναγωγεύς (the
shepherd of souls), to whom ἱκεσιὴ πολυδάκρυος (the prayer of a tearful suppliant)

1. It was the judgment of the ancients concerning his book *Metroace* that in it he set forth, not without divine rapture, his universal doctrine
concerning God; and by the frequent tears of the author apparent in it all suspicion was removed from the hearers. None the less this same man wrote
against the Christians eighteen epichiremata, to which John Philoponus opposed himself, reproaching Proclus with ignorance of Greek thought, which
none the less he had undertaken to defend. That is to say, Proclus concealed those things which did not make for his own philosophy.
2. Nevertheless in Suidas some similar things are attributed to ancient Orpheus, nearly equal to Moses, as if his pupil; see too the hymns of
Orpheus, on which Proclus wrote commentaries.

is to be offered, in order that He cleanse us from sins and wash us of the filth τῆς γενεθλῆς (of generation)—as if Proclus acknowledged the forms of original sin—and guard us from punishment and evil, πρηυνῶν θόον ὄμμα δικῆς (by making mild the quick eye of justice), namely, the wrath of the Father? And the other things we read of, which are as it were taken from the hymn of Zacharias (or, accordingly, was that hymn a part of the *Metroace*?) Αχλυν ἀποσκεδάσας ὀλεσίμβροτον ἰολοχεύτον (dispersing the poisonous, man-destroying mist), *viz.*, in order that He may give to souls living in darkness and the shadows of death the φάος ἁγνον (holy light) and ὄλβον ἀστυφελικτὸν ἀπ ἐυσεβίνἐρατείης (unshaken happiness from lovely piety); for that is to serve God in holiness and justice all our days.

Accordingly, let us separate out these and similar things and restore them to the doctrine of the Catholic Church to which they belong. But let us see what the principal reason is why there has been mention made of the hymn. For this same sun which ὕψοθεν ἀρμνίης ῥῦμα πλοῦσιον ἐξοτεύει (sluices the rich flow of harmony from on high)—so too Orpheus κόσμου τὸν ἐναρμόνιον δρόμον ἕλκων (making move the harmonious course of the world)—the same, concerning whose stock Phoebus about to rise κιθαρῇ ὑπὸ θέσκελα μέλπων εὐνάξει μεγὰ κῦμα βαρυφλοισβοῖο γενεθλῆς (sings marvellous things on his lyre and lulls to sleep the heavy-sounding surge of generation) and in whose dance Paean is the partner, πλήσας ἁρμονίης παναπήμονος εὔρεα κόσμν (striking the wide sweep of innocent harmony)—him, I say, does Proclus at once salute in the first verse of the hymn as πῦρος νοεροῦ βασιλέα (king of intellectual fire). By that commencement, at the same time, he indicates what the Pythagoreans understood by the word of fire (so that it is surprising that the pupil should disagree with the masters in the position of the centre) and at the same time he transfers his whole hymn from the body of the sun and its quality and light, which are sensibles, to the intelligibles, and he has assigned to that πῦρ νοερὸς (intellectual fire) of his—perhaps the artisan fire of the Stoics—to that created God of Plato, that chief or self-ruling mind, a royal throne in the solar body, confounding into one the creature and Him through Whom all things have been created. But we Christians, who have been taught to make better distinctions, know that this eternal and uncreated "Word," Which was "with God" and Which is contained by no abode, although He is within all things, excluded by none, although He is outside of all things, took up into unity of person flesh out of the womb of the most glorious Virgin Mary, and, when the ministry of His flesh was finished, occupied as His royal abode the heavens, wherein by a certain excellence over and above the other parts of the world, *viz.*, through His glory and majesty, His celestial Father too is recognized to dwell, and has also promised to His faithful, mansions in that house of His Father: as for the remainder concerning that abode, we believe it superfluous to inquire into it too curiously or to forbid the

senses or natural reasons to investigate that which the eye has not seen nor the ear heard and into which the heart of man has not ascended; but we duly subordinate the created mind—of whatsoever excellence it may be—to Its Creator, and we introduce neither God-intelligences with Aristotle and the pagan philosophers nor armies of innumerable planetary spirits with the Magi, nor do we propose that they are either to be adored or summoned to intercourse with us by theurgic superstitions, for we have a careful fear of that; but we freely inquire by natural reasons what sort of thing each mind is, especially if in the heart of the world [326] there is any mind bound rather closely to the nature of things and performing the function of the soul of the world—or if also some intelligent creatures, of a nature different from human perchance do inhabit or will inhabit the globe thus animated (see my book *on the New Star*, Chapter 24, "On the Soul of the World and Some of Its Functions"). But if it is permissible, using the thread of analogy as a guide, to traverse the labyrinths of the mysteries of nature, not ineptly, I think, will someone have argued as follows: The relation of the six spheres to their common centre, thereby the centre of the whole world, is also the same as that of διανοὶα (discussive intellection) to νοῦς (intuitive intellection), according as those faculties are distinguished by Aristotle, Plato, Proclus, and the rest; and the relation of the single planets' revolutions in place around the sun to the ἀμετάθεδον (unvarying) rotation of the sun in the central space of the whole system (concerning which the sun-spots are evidence; this has been demonstrated in the *Commentaries on the Movement of Mars*) is the same as the relation of τὸ διανοητικὸν to τὸ νοερὸν, that of the manifold discourses of ratiocination to the most simple intellection of the mind. For as the sun rotating into itself moves all the planets by means of the form emitted from itself, so too—as the philosophers teach—mind, by understanding itself and in itself all things, stirs up ratiocinations, and by dispersing and unrolling its simplicity into them, makes everything to be understood. And the movements of the planets around the sun at their centre and the discourses of ratiocinations are so interwoven and bound together that, unless the Earth, our domicile, measured out the annual circle, midway between the other spheres—changing from place to place, from station to station—never would human ratiocination have worked its way to the true intervals of the planets and to the other things dependent from them, never would it have constituted astronomy. (See the *Optical Part of Astronomy*, Chapter 9.)

On the other hand, in a beautiful correspondence, simplicity of intellection follows upon the stillness of the sun at the centre of the world, in that hitherto we have always worked under the assumption that those solar harmonies of movements are defined neither by the diversity of regions nor by the amplitude of the expanses of the world. As a matter of fact, if any mind observes from the sun those harmonies, that mind is without the assistance afforded by the movement and diverse stations of his

abode, by means of which it may string together ratiocinations and discourse necessary for measuring out the planetary intervals. Accordingly, it compares the diurnal movements of each planet, not as they are in their own orbits but as they pass through the angles at the centre of the sun. And so if it has knowledge of the magnitude of the spheres, this knowledge must be present in it *a priori*, without any toil of ratiocination: but to what extent that is true of human mind and of sublunary nature has been made clear above, from Plato and Proclus.

Under these circumstances, it will not have been surprising if anyone who has been thoroughly warmed by taking a fairly liberal draft from that bowl of Pythagoras which Proclus gives to drink from in the very first verse of the hymn, and who has been made drowsy by the very sweet harmony of the dance of the planets begins to dream (by telling a story he may imitate Plato's Atlantis and, by dreaming, Cicero's Scipio): throughout the remaining globes, which follow after from place to place, there have been disseminated discursive or ratiocinative faculties, whereof that one ought assuredly to be judged the most excellent and absolute which is in the middle position among those globes, *viz.*, in man's earth, while there dwells in the sun simple intellect, πῦρ νοερὸν, or νοῦς, the source, whatsoever it may be, of every harmony.

For if it was Tycho Brahe's opinion concerning that bare wilderness of globes that it does not exist fruitlessly in the world but is filled with inhabitants: with how much greater probability shall we make a conjecture as to God's works and designs even for the other globes, from that variety which we discern in this globe of the Earth. For He Who created the species which should inhabit the waters, beneath which however there is no room for the air [327] which living things draw in; Who sent birds supported on wings into the wilderness of the air; Who gave white bears and white wolves to the snowy regions of the North, and as food for the bears the whale, and for the wolves, birds' eggs; Who gave lions to the deserts of burning Libya and camels to the widespread plains of Syria, and to the lions an endurance of hunger, and to the camels an endurance of thirst: did He use up every art in the globe of the Earth so that He was unable, every goodness so that he did not wish, to adorn the other globes too with their fitting creatures, as either the long or short revolutions, or the nearness or removal of the sun, or the variety of eccentricities or the shine or darkness of the bodies, or the properties of the figures wherewith any region is supported persuaded?

Behold, as the generations of animals in this terrestrial globe have an image of the male in the dodecahedron, of the female in the icosahedron—whereof the dodecahedron rests on the terrestrial sphere from the outside and the icosahedron from the inside: what will we suppose the remaining globes to have, from the remaining figures? For whose good do four moons encircle Jupiter, two Saturn, as does this our moon this our domicile? But in the same way we shall ratiocinate concerning the globe of the sun

also, and we shall as it were incorporate conjectures drawn from the harmonies, *et cetera*—which are weighty of themselves—with other conjectures which are more on the side of the bodily, more suited for the apprehension of the vulgar. Is that globe empty and the others full, if everything else is in due correspondence? If as the Earth breathes forth clouds, so the sun black smoke? If as the Earth is moistened and grows under showers, so the sun shines with those combusted spots, while clear flamelets sparkle in its all fiery body. For whose use is all this equipment, if the globe is empty? Indeed, do not the senses themselves cry out that fiery bodies dwell here which are receptive of simple intellects, and that truly the sun is, if not the king, at least the queen πῦρος νοεροῦ (of intellectual fire)?

Purposely I break off the dream and the very vast speculation, merely crying out with the royal Psalmist: *Great is our Lord and great His virtue and of His wisdom there is no number: praise Him, ye heavens, praise Him, ye sun, moon, and planets, use every sense for perceiving, every tongue for declaring your Creator. Praise Him, ye celestial harmonies, praise Him, ye judges of the harmonies uncovered* (and you before all, old happy Mastlin, for you used to animate these cares with words of hope): *and thou my soul, praise the Lord thy Creator, as long as I shall be: for out of Him and through Him and in Him are all things,* καὶ τὰ αἰσθητὰ καὶ τὰ νοερὰ (*both the sensible and the intelligible*); *for both whose whereof we are utterly ignorant and those which we know are the least part of them; because there is still more beyond. To Him be praise, honour, and glory, world without end. Amen.*

THE END

This work was completed on the 17th or 27th day of May, 1618; but Book V was reread (while the type was being set) on the 9th or 19th of February, 1619. At Linz, the capital of Austria—above the Enns.

Isaac Newton

(1642-1727)

HIS LIFE AND WORK

On February 5, 1676, Isaac Newton penned a letter to his bitter enemy, Robert Hooke, which contained the sentence, "If I have seen farther, it is by standing on the shoulders of giants." Often described as Newton's nod to the scientific discoveries of Copernicus, Galileo, and Kepler before him, it has become one of the most famous quotes in the history of science. Indeed, Newton did recognize the contributions of those men, some publicly and others in private writings. But in his letter to Hooke, Newton was referring to optical theories, specifically the study of the phenomena of thin plates, to which Hooke and Renè Descartes had made significant contributions.

Some scholars have interpreted the sentence as a thinly veiled insult to Hooke, whose crooked posture and short stature made him anything but a giant, especially in the eyes of the extremely vindictive Newton. Yet despite their feuds, Newton did appear to humbly acknowledge the noteworthy research in optics of both Hooke and Descartes, adopting a more conciliatory tone at the end of the letter.

Isaac Newton is considered the father of the study of infinitesimal calculus, mechanics and planetary motion, and the theory of light and color. But he secured his place in history by formulating gravitational force and defining the laws of motion and attraction in his landmark work, *Mathematical Principles of Natural Philosophy* (*Philosophiae Naturalis Principia Mathematica*) generally known as *Principia*. There

Newton fused the scientific contributions of Copernicus, Galileo, Kepler, and others into a dynamic new symphony. *Principia*, the first book on theoretical physics, is roundly regarded as the most important work in the history of science and the scientific foundation of the modern worldview.

Newton wrote the three books that form *Principia* in just eighteen months and, astonishingly, between severe emotional breakdowns—likely compounded by his competition with Hooke. He even went to such vindictive lengths as to remove from the book all references to Hooke's work, yet his hatred for his fellow scientist may have been the very inspiration for *Principia*.

The slightest criticism of his work, even if cloaked in lavish praise, often sent Newton into dark withdrawal for months or years. This trait revealed itself early in Newton's life and has led some to wonder what other questions Newton might have answered had he not been obsessed with settling personal feuds. Others have speculated that Newton's scientific discoveries and achievements were the result of his vindictive obsessions and might not have been possible had he been less arrogant.

As a young boy, Isaac Newton asked himself the questions that had long mystified humanity, and then went on to answer many of them. It was the beginning of a life full of discovery, despite some anguishing first steps. Isaac Newton was born in the English industrial town of Woolsthorpe, Lincolnshire, on Christmas Day of 1642, the same year in which Galileo died. His mother did not expect him to live long, as he was born very prematurely; he would later describe himself as having been so small at birth he could fit into a quart pot. Newton's yeoman father, also named Isaac, had died three month's earlier, and when Newton reached two years of age, his mother, Hannah Ayscough, remarried, wedding Barnabas Smith, a rich clergyman from North Witham.

Apparently there was no place in the new Smith family for the young Newton, and he was placed in the care of his grandmother, Margery Ayscough. The specter of this abandonment, coupled with the tragedy of never having known his father, haunted Newton for the rest of his life. He despised his stepfather; in journal entries for 1662 Newton, examining his sins, recalled "threatening my father and mother Smith to burne them and the house over them."

Much like his adulthood, Newton's childhood was filled with episodes of harsh, vindictive attacks, not only against perceived enemies but against friends and family as well. He also displayed the kind of curiosity early on that would define his life's achievements, taking an interest in mechanical models and architectural drawing. Newton spent countless hours building clocks, flaming kites, sundials, and miniature mills (powered by mice) as well as drawing elaborate sketches of animals and ships. At the age of five he attended schools at Skillington and Stoke but was considered one of the poorest students, receiving comments in teachers' reports such as "inattentive" and

"idle." Despite his curiosity and demonstrable passion for learning, he was unable to apply himself to schoolwork.

By the time Newton reached the age of ten, Barnabas Smith had passed away and Hannah had come into a considerable sum from Smith's estate. Isaac and his grandmother began living with Hannah, a half-brother, and two half-sisters. Because his work at school was uninspiring, Hannah decided that Isaac would be better off managing the farm and estate, and she pulled him out of the Free Grammar School in Grantham. Unfortunately for her, Newton had even less skill or interest in managing the family estate than he had in schoolwork. Hannah's brother, William, a clergyman, decided that it would be best for the family if the absent-minded Isaac returned to school to finish his education.

This time, Newton lived with the headmaster of the Free Grammar School, John Stokes, and he seemed to turn a corner in his education. One story has it that a blow to the head, administered by a schoolyard bully, somehow enlightened him, enabling the young Newton to reverse the negative course of his educational promise. Now demonstrating intellectual aptitude and curiosity, Newton began preparing for further study at a university. He decided to attend Trinity College, his uncle William's alma mater, at Cambridge University.

At Trinity, Newton became a subsizar, receiving an allowance toward the cost of his education in exchange for performing various chores such as waiting tables and cleaning rooms for the faculty. But by 1664 he was elected scholar, which guaranteed him financial support and freed him from menial duties. When the university closed because of the bubonic plague in 1665, Newton retreated to Lincolnshire. In the eighteen months he spent at home during the plague he devoted himself to mechanics and mathematics, and began to concentrate on optics and gravitation. This "annus mirabilis" (miraculous year), as Newton called it, was one of the most productive and fruitful periods of his life. It is also around this time that an apple, according to legend, fell onto Newton's head, awakening him from a nap under a tree and spurring him on to define the laws of gravity. However far-fetched the tale, Newton himself wrote that a falling apple had "occasioned" his foray into gravitational contemplation, and he is believed to have performed his pendulum experiments then. "I was in the prime of my age for invention," Newton later recalled, "and minded Mathematicks and Philosophy more then at any time since."

When he returned to Cambridge, Newton studied the philosophy of Aristotle and Descartes, as well as the science of Thomas Hobbes and Robert Boyle. He was taken by the mechanics of Copernicus and Galileo's astronomy, in addition to Kepler's optics. Around this time, Newton began his prism experiments in light refraction and dispersion, possibly in his room at Trinity or at home in Woolsthorpe. A development at

the university that clearly had a profound influence on Newton's future—was the arrival of Isaac Barrow, who had been named the Lucasian Professor of Mathematics. Barrow recognized Newton's extraordinary mathematical talents, and when he resigned his professorship in 1669 to pursue theology he recommended the twenty-seven-year-old Newton as his replacement.

Newton's first studies as Lucasian Professor centered in the field of optics. He set out to prove that white light was composed of a mixture of various types of light, each producing a different color of the spectrum when refracted by a prism. His series of elaborate and precise experiments to prove that light was composed of minute particles drew the ire of scientists such as Hooke, who contended that light traveled in waves. Hooke challenged Newton to offer further proof of his eccentric optical theories. Newton's way of responding was one he did not outgrow as he matured. He withdrew, set out to humiliate Hooke at every opportunity, and refused to publish his book, Opticks, until after Hooke's death in 1703.

Early in his tenure as Lucasian Professor, Newton was well along in his study of pure mathematics, but he shared his work with very few of his colleagues. Already by 1666, he had discovered general methods of solving problems of curvature—what he termed "theories of fluxions and inverse fluxions." The discovery set off a dramatic feud with supporters of the German mathematician and philosopher Gottfried Wilhelm Leibniz, who more than a decade later published his findings on differential and integral calculus. Both men arrived at roughly the same mathematical principles, but Leibniz published his work before Newton. Newton's supporters claimed that Leibniz had seen the Lucasian Professor's papers years before, and a heated argument between the two camps, known as the Calculus Priority Dispute, did not end until Leibniz died in 1716. Newton's vicious attacks which often spilled over to touch on views about God and the universe, as well as his accusations of plagiarism, left Leibniz impoverished and disgraced.

Most historians of science believe that the two men in fact arrived at their ideas independently and that the dispute was pointless. Newton's vitriolic aggression toward Leibniz took a physical and emotional toll on Newton as well. He soon found himself involved in another battle, this time over his theory of color, and in 1678 he suffered a severe mental breakdown. The next year, his mother, Hannah passed away, and Newton began to distance himself from others. In secret, he delved into alchemy, a field widely regarded already in Newton's time as fruitless. This episode in the scientist's life has been a source of embarrassment to many Newton scholars. Only long after Newton died did it become apparent that his interest in chemical experiments was related to his later research in celestial mechanics and gravitation.

Newton had already begun forming theories about motion by 1666, but he was as yet unable to adequately explain the mechanics of circular motion. Some fifty years earlier, the German mathematician and astronomer Johannes Kepler had proposed three laws of planetary motion, which accurately described how the planets moved in relation to the sun, but he could not explain why the planets moved as they did. The closest Kepler came to understanding the forces involved was to say that the sun and the planets were "magnetically" related.

Newton set out to discover the cause of the planets' elliptical orbits. By applying his own law of centrifugal force to Kepler's third law of planetary motion (the law of harmonies) he deduced the inverse-square law, which states that the force of gravity between any two objects is inversely proportional to the square of the distance between the object's centers. Newton was thereby coming to recognize that gravitation is universal—that one and the same force causes an apple to fall to the ground and the moon to race around the earth. He then set out to test the inverse-square relation against known data. He accepted Galileo's estimate that the moon is sixty earth radii from the earth, but the inaccuracy of his own estimate of the earth's diameter made it impossible to complete the test to his satisfaction. Ironically, it was an exchange of letters in 1679 with his old adversary Hooke that renewed his interest in the problem. This time, he turned his attention to Kepler's second law, the law of equal areas, which Newton was able to prove held true because of centripetal force. Hooke, too, was attempting to explain the planetary orbits, and some of his letters on that account were of particular interest to Newton.

At an infamous gathering in 1684, three members of the Royal Society—Robert Hooke, Edmond Halley, and Christopher Wren, the noted architect of St. Paul's Cathedral—engaged in a heated discussion about the inverse-square relation governing the motions of the planets. In the early 1670s, the talk in the coffeehouses of London and other intellectual centers was that gravity emanated from the sun in all directions and fell off at a rate inverse to the square of the distance, thus becoming more and more diluted over the surface of the sphere as that surface expands. The 1684 meeting was, in effect, the birth of *Principia*. Hooke declared that he had derived from Kepler's law of ellipses the proof that gravity was an emanating force, but would withhold it from Halley and Wren until he was ready to make it public. Furious, Halley went to Cambridge, told Newton Hooke's claim, and proposed the following problem. "What would be the form of a planet's orbit about the sun if it were drawn towards the sun by a force that varied inversely as the square of the distance?" Newton's response was staggering. "It would be an ellipse," he answered immediately, and then told Halley that he had solved the problem four years earlier but had misplaced the proof in his office.

At Halley's request, Newton spent three months reconstituting and improving the proof. Then, in a burst of energy sustained for eighteen months, during which he was so caught up in his work that he often forgot to eat, he further developed these ideas until their presentation filled three volumes. Newton chose to title the work *Philosophiae Naturalis Principia Mathematica*, in deliberate contrast with Descartes' *Principia Philosophiae*. The three books of Newton's *Principia* provided the link between Kepler's laws and the physical world. Halley reacted with "joy and amazement" to Newton's discoveries. To Halley, it seemed the Lucasian Professor had succeeded where all others had failed, and he personally financed publication of the massive work as a masterpiece and a gift to humanity.

Where Galileo had shown that objects were "pulled" toward the center of the earth, Newton was able to prove that this same force, gravity, affected the orbits of the planets. He was also familiar with Galileo's work on the motion of projectiles, and he asserted that the moon's orbit around the earth adhered to the same principles. Newton demonstrated that gravity explained and predict the moon's motions as well as the rising and falling of the tides on earth. Book 1 of *Principia* encompasses Newton's three laws of motion:

1. Every body perseveres in its state of resting, or uniformly moving in a right line, unless it is compelled to change that state by forces impressed upon it.
2. The change of motion is proportional to the motive force impressed; and is made in the direction of the right line in which that force is impressed.
3. To every action there is always opposed an equal reaction; or, the mutual actions of two bodies upon each other are always equal, and directed to contrary directions.

Book 2 began for Newton as something of an afterthought to Book 1; it was not included in the original outline of the work. It is essentially a treatise on fluid mechanics, and it allowed Newton room to display his mathematical ingenuity. Toward the end of the book, Newton concludes that the vortices invoked by Descartes to explain the motions of planets do not hold up to scrutiny, for the motions could be performed in free space without vortices. How that is so, Newton wrote, "may be understood by the first Book; and I shall now more fully treat of it in the following Book."

In Book 3, subtitled *System of the World*, by applying the laws of motion from book 1 to the physical world Newton concluded that "there is a power of gravity tending to all bodies, proportional to the several quantities of matter which they contain." He thus demonstrated that his law of universal gravitation could explain the motions of the six known planets, as well as moons, comets, equinoxes, and tides. The law states that all matter is mutually attracted with a force directly proportional to the product of their masses and inversely proportional to the square of the distance between them.

Newton, by a single set of laws, had united the earth with all that could be seen in the skies. In the first two "Rules of Reasoning" from Book 3, Newton wrote:

We are to admit no more causes of natural things than such as are both true and sufficient to explain their appearances. Therefore, to the same natural effects we must, as far as possible, assign the same causes.

It is the second rule that actually unifies heaven and earth. An Aristotelian would have asserted that heavenly motions and terrestrial motions are manifestly not the same natural effects and that Newton's second rule could not, therefore, be applied. Newton saw things otherwise.

Principia was moderately praised upon its publication in 1687, but only about five hundred copies of the first edition were printed. However, Newton's nemesis, Robert Hooke, had threatened to spoil any coronation Newton might have enjoyed. After Book 2 appeared, Hooke publicly claimed that the letters he had written in 1679 had provided scientific ideas that were vital to Newton's discoveries. His claims, though not without merit, were abhorrent to Newton, who vowed to delay or even abandon publication of Book 3. Newton ultimately relented and published the final book of *Principia*, but not before painstakingly removing from it every mention of Hooke's name.

Newton's hatred for Hooke consumed him for years afterward. In 1693, he suffered yet another nervous breakdown and retired from research. He withdrew from the Royal Society until Hooke's death in 1703, then was elected its president and reelected each year until his own death in 1727. He also withheld publication of *Opticks*, his important study of light and color that would become his most widely read work, until after Hooke was dead.

Newton began the eighteenth century in a government post as warden of the Royal Mint, where he utilized his work in alchemy to determine methods for reestablishing the integrity of the English currency. As president of the Royal Society, he continued to battle perceived enemies with inexorable determination, in particular carrying on his longstanding feud with Leibniz over their competing claims to have invented calculus. He was knighted by Queen Anne in 1705, and lived to see publication of the second and third editions of *Principia*.

Isaac Newton died in March 1727, after bouts of pulmonary inflammation and gout. As was his wish, Newton had no rival in the field of science. The man who apparently formed no romantic attachments with women (some historians have speculated on possible relationships with men, such as the Swiss natural philosopher Nicolas Fatio de Duillier) cannot, however, be accused of a lack of passion for his work. The poet Alexander Pope, a contemporary of Newton's, most elegantly described the great thinker's gift to humanity:

Nature and Nature's laws lay hid in night:
God said, "Let Newton be! and all was light."

For all the petty arguments and undeniable arrogance that marked his life, toward its end Isaac Newton was remarkably poignant in assessing his accomplishments: "I do not know how I may appear to the world, but to myself I seem to have been only like a boy, playing on the sea-shore, and diverting myself, in now and then finding a smoother pebble or prettier shell than ordinary, whilst the great ocean of truth lay all undiscovered before me."

THE
MATHEMATICAL PRINCIPLES
OF
NATURAL PHILOSOPHY.

DEFINITIONS.

DEFINITION I.

THE QUANTITY OF MATTER IS THE MEASURE OF THE SAME,
ARISING FROM ITS DENSITY AND BULK CONJUNCTLY.

Thus air of a double density, in a double space, is quadruple in quantity; in a triple space, sextuple in quantity. The same thing is to be understood of snow, and fine dust or powders, that are condensed by compression or liquefaction; and of all bodies that are by any causes whatever differently condensed. I have no regard in this place to a medium, if any such there is, that freely pervades the interstices between the parts of bodies. It is this quantity that I mean hereafter everywhere under the name of body or mass, And the same is known by the weight of each body; for it is proportional to the weight, as I have found by experiments on pendulums, very accurately made, which shall be shewn hereafter.

DEFINITION II.

THE QUANTITY OF MOTION IS THE MEASURE OF THE SAME,
ARISING FROM THE VELOCITY AND QUANTITY OF MATTER
CONJUNCTLY.

The motion of the whole is the sum of the motions of all the parts; and therefore in a body double in quantity, with equal velocity, the motion is double; with twice the velocity, it is quadruple.

DEFINITION III.

THE *VIS INSITA*, OR INNATE FORCE OF MATTER, IS A POWER
OF RESISTING, BY WHICH EVERY BODY, AS MUCH AS IN IT
LIES, ENDEAVOURS TO PERSEVERE IN ITS PRESENT STATE,
WHETHER IT BE OF REST, OR OF MOVING UNIFORMLY
FORWARD IN A RIGHT LINE.

This force is ever proportional to the body whose force it is: and differs nothing from the inactivity of the mass, but in our manner of conceiving it. A body, from the inactivity of matter, is not without difficulty put out of its state of rest or motion. Upon which account, this *vis insita*, may, by a most significant name, be called *vis inertiæ*, or force of inactivity. But a body exerts this force only when another force, impressed upon it, endeavours to change its condition; and the exercise of this force may be considered both as resistance and impulse; it is resistance, in so far as the body, for maintaining its present state, withstands the force impressed; it is impulse, in so far as the body, by not easily giving way to the impressed force of another, endeavours to change the state of that other. Resistance is usually ascribed to bodies at rest, and impulse to those in motion; but motion and rest, as commonly conceived, are only relatively distinguished; nor are those bodies always truly at rest, which commonly are taken to be so.

DEFINITION IV.

AN IMPRESSED FORCE IS AN ACTION EXERTED UPON A BODY,
IN ORDER TO CHANGE ITS STATE, EITHER OF REST, OR OF
MOVING UNIFORMLY FORWARD IN A RIGHT LINE.

This force consists in the action only; and remains no longer in the body, when the action is over. For a body maintains every new state it acquires, by its *vis inertiæ* only. Impressed forces are of different origins as from percussion, from pressure, from centripetal force.

DEFINITION V.

A CENTRIPETAL FORCE IS THAT BY WHICH BODIES ARE
DRAWN OR IMPELLED, OR ANY WAY TEND, TOWARDS A POINT
AS TO A CENTRE.

Of this sort is gravity, by which bodies tend to the centre of the earth magnetism, by which iron tends to the loadstone; and that force, whatever it is, by which the planets are

perpetually drawn aside from the rectilinear motions, which otherwise they would pursue, and made to revolve in curvilinear orbits. A stone, whirled about in a sling, endeavours to recede from the hand that turns it; and by that endeavour, distends the sling, and that with so much the greater force, as it is revolved with the greater velocity, and as soon as ever it is let go, flies away. That force which opposes itself to this endeavour, and by which the sling perpetually draws back the stone towards the hand, and retains it in its orbit, because it is directed to the hand as the centre of the orbit, I call the centripetal force. And the same thing is to be understood of all bodies, revolved in any orbits. They all endeavour to recede from the centres of their orbits; and were it not for the opposition of a contrary force which restrains them to, and detains them in their orbits, which I therefore call centripetal, would fly off in right lines, with an uniform motion. A projectile, if it was not for the force of gravity, would not deviate towards the earth, but would go off from it in a right line, and that with an uniform motion, if the resistance of the air was taken away. It is by its gravity that it is drawn aside perpetually from its rectilinear course, and made to deviate towards the earth, more or less, according to the force of its gravity, and the velocity of its motion. The less its gravity is, for the quantity of its matter, or the greater the velocity with which it is projected, the less will it deviate from a rectilinear course, and the farther it will go. If a leaden hall, projected from the top of a mountain by the force of gunpowder with a given velocity, and in a direction parallel to the horizon, is carried in a curve line to the distance of two miles before it falls to the ground; the same, if the resistance of the air were taken away, with a double or decuple velocity, would fly twice or ten times as far. And by increasing the velocity, we may at pleasure increase the distance to which it might be projected, and diminish the curvature of the line, which it might describe, till at last it should fall at the distance of 10, 30, or 90 degrees, or even might go quite round the whole earth before it falls; or lastly, so that it might never fall to the earth, but go forward into the celestial spaces, and proceed in its motion *in infinitum*. And after the same manner that a projectile, by the force of gravity, may be made to revolve in an orbit, and go round the whole earth, the moon also, either by the force of gravity, if it is endued with gravity, or by any other force, that impels it towards the earth, may be perpetually drawn aside towards the earth, out of the rectilinear way, which by its innate force it would pursue; and would be made to revolve in the orbit which it now describes; nor could the moon without some such force, be retained in its orbit. If this force was too small, it would not sufficiently turn the moon out of a rectilinear course: if it was too great, it would turn it too much, and draw down the moon from its orbit towards the earth. It is necessary, that the force be of a just quantity, and it belongs to the mathematicians to find the force, that may serve exactly to retain a body in a given orbit, with a given velocity; and *vice versa*, to determine the curvilinear way,

...to which a body projected from a given place, with a given velocity, may be made to deviate from its natural rectilinear way, by means of a given force.

The quantity of any centripetal force may be considered as of three kinds; absolute, accelerative, and motive.

DEFINITION VI.

THE ABSOLUTE QUANTITY OF A CENTRIPETAL FORCE IS THE MEASURE OF THE SAME PROPORTIONAL TO THE EFFICACY OF THE CAUSE THAT PROPAGATES IT FROM THE CENTRE, THROUGH THE SPACES ROUND ABOUT.

Thus the magnetic force is greater in one load-stone and less in another according to their sizes and strength of intensity.

DEFINITION VII.

THE ACCELERATIVE QUANTITY OF A CENTRIPETAL FORCE IS THE MEASURE OF THE SAME, PROPORTIONAL TO THE VELOCITY WHICH IT GENERATES IN A GIVEN TIME.

Thus the force of the same load-stone is greater at a less distance, and less at a greater: also the force of gravity is greater in valleys, less on tops of exceeding high mountains; and yet less (as shall hereafter be shown), at greater distances from the body of the earth; but at equal distances, it is the same everywhere; because (taking away, or allowing for, the resistance of the air), it equally accelerates all falling bodies, whether heavy or light, great or small.

DEFINITION VIII.

THE MOTIVE QUANTITY OF A CENTRIPETAL FORCE, IS THE MEASURE OF THE SAME, PROPORTIONAL TO THE MOTION WHICH IT GENERATES IN A GIVEN TIME.

Thus the weight is greater in a greater body, less in a less body; and, in the same body, it is greater near to the earth, and less at remoter distances. This sort of quantity is the centripetency, or propension of the whole body towards the centre, or, as I may say, its weight; and it is always known by the quantity of an equal and contrary force just sufficient to hinder the descent of the body.

These quantities of forces, we may, for brevity's sake, call by the names of motive, accelerative, and absolute forces; and, for distinction's sake, consider them, with respect

to the bodies that tend to the centre; to the places of those bodies; and to the centre of force towards which they tend; that is to say, I refer the motive force to the body as an endeavour and propensity of the whole towards a centre, arising from the propensities of the several parts taken together; the accelerative force to the place of the body, as a certain power or energy diffused from the centre to all places around to move the bodies that are in them; and the absolute force to the centre, as endued with some cause, without which those motive forces would not be propagated through the spaces round about; whether that cause be some central body (such as is the load-stone, in the centre of the magnetic force, or the earth in the centre of the gravitating force), or anything else that does not yet appear. For I here design only to give a mathematical notion of those forces, without considering their physical causes and seats.

Wherefore the accelerative force will stand in the same relation to the motive, as celerity does to motion. For the quantity of motion arises from the celerity drawn into the quantity of matter; and the motive force arises from the accelerative force drawn into the same quantity of matter. For the sum of the actions of the accelerative force, upon the several articles of the body, is the motive force of the whole. Hence it is, that near the surface of the earth, where the accelerative gravity, or force productive of gravity, in all bodies is the same, the motive gravity or the weight is as the body: but if we should ascend to higher regions, where the accelerative gravity is less, the weight would be equally diminished, and would always be as the product of the body, by the accelerative gravity. So in those regions, where the accelerative gravity is diminished into one half, the weight of a body two or three times less, will be four or six times less.

I likewise call attractions and impulses, in the same sense, accelerative, and motive; and use the words attraction, impulse or propensity of any sort towards a centre, promiscuously, and indifferently, one for another; considering those forces not physically, but mathematically: wherefore, the reader is not to imagine, that by those words, I anywhere take upon me to define the kind, or the manner of any action, the causes or the physical reason thereof, or that I attribute form, in a true and physical sense, to certain centres (which are only mathematical points); when at any time I happen to speak of centres as attracting, or as endued with attractive powers.

SCHOLIUM.

Hitherto I have laid down the definitions of such words as are less known, and explained the sense in which I would have them to be understood in the following discourse. I do not define time, space, place and motion, as being well known to all. Only I must observe that the vulgar conceive those quantities under no other notions but from the relation they bear to sensible objects. And thence arise certain prejudices, for the removing of which, it will be convenient to distinguish them into absolute and relative, true and apparent, mathematical and common.

I. Absolute, true, and mathematical time, of itself, and from its own nature flows equably without regard to anything external, and by another name is called duration: relative, apparent, and common time, is some sensible and external (whether accurate or unequable) measure of duration by the means of motion, which is commonly used instead of true time; such as an hour, a day, a month, a year.

II. Absolute space, in its own nature, without regard to anything external, remains always similar and immovable. Relative space is some movable dimension or measure of the absolute spaces; which our senses determine by its position to bodies; and which is vulgarly taken for immovable space; such is the dimension of a subterraneous, an æreal, or celestial space, determined by its position in respect of the earth. Absolute and relative space, are the same in figure and magnitude; but they do not remain always numerically the same. For if the earth, for instance, moves, a space of our air, which relatively and in respect of the earth remains always the same, will at one time be one part of the absolute space into which the air panes; at another time it will be another part of the same, and so, absolutely understood, it will be perpetually mutable.

III. Place is a part of space which a body takes up, and is according to the space, either absolute or relative. I say, apart of space; not the situation, nor the external surface of the body. For the places of equal solids are always equal; but their superfices, by reason of their dissimilar figures, are often unequal. Positions properly have no quantity, nor are they so much the places themselves, as the properties of places. The motion of the whole is the same thing with the sum of the motions of the parts; that is, the translation of the whole, out of its place, is the same thing with the sum of the translations of the parts out of their places; and therefore the place of the whole is the same thing with the sum of the places of the parts, and for that reason, it is internal, and in the whole body.

IV. Absolute motion is the translation of a body from one absolute place into another; and relative motion, the translation from one relative place into another. Thus in a ship under sail, the relative place of a body is that part of the ship which the body possesses; or that part of its cavity which the body fills, and which therefore moves together with the ship: and relative rest is the continuance of the body in the same part of the ship, or of its cavity. But real, absolute rest, is the continuance of the body in the same part of that immovable space, in which the ship itself, its cavity, and all that it contains, is moved. Wherefore, if the earth is really at rest, the body, which relatively rests in the ship, will really and absolutely move with the same velocity which the ship has on the earth. But if the earth also moves, the true and absolute motion of the body will arise, partly from the true motion of the earth, in immovable space; partly from the relative motion of the ship on the earth; and if the body moves also relatively in the ship; its true motion will arise, partly from the true motion of the earth, in immovable

space, and partly from the relative motions as well of the ship on the earth, as of the body in the ship; and from these relative motions will arise the relative motion of the body on the earth. As if that part of the earth, where the ship is, was truly moved toward the east, with a velocity of 10010 parts; while the ship itself, with a fresh gale, and full sails, is carried towards the west, with a velocity expressed by 10 of those parts; but a sailor walks in the ship towards the east, with 1 part of the said velocity; then the sailor will be moved truly in immovable space towards the east, with a velocity of 10001 parts and relatively on the earth towards the west, with a velocity of 9 of those parts.

Absolute time, in astronomy, is distinguished from relative, by the equation or correction of the vulgar time. For the natural days are truly unequal, though they are commonly considered as equal, and used for a measure of time; astronomers correct this inequality for their more accurate deducing of the celestial motions. It may be that there is no such thing as an equable motion whereby time may be accurately measured. All motions may be accelerated and retarded, but the true, or equable progress of absolute time is liable to no change. The duration or perseverance of the existence of things remains the same, whether the motions are swift or slow, or none at all: and therefore it ought to be distinguished from what are only sensible measures thereof; and out of which we collect it, by means of the astronomical equation. The necessity of which equation, for determining the times of a phænomenon, is evinced as well from the experiments of the pendulum clock, as by eclipses of the satellites of *Jupiter*.

As the order of the parts of time is immutable, so also is the order of the parts of space. Suppose those parts to be moved out of their places, and they will be moved (if the expression may be allowed) out of themselves. For times and spaces are, as it were, the places as well of themselves as of all other things. All things are placed in time as to order of succession; and in space as to order of situation. It is from their essence or nature that they are places; and that the primary places of things should be moveable, is absurd. These are therefore the absolute places; and translations out of those places, are the only absolute motions.

But because the parts of space cannot be seen, or distinguished from one another by our senses, therefore in their stead we use sensible measures of them. For from the positions and distances of things from any body considered as immovable, we define all places; said then with respect to such places, we estimate all motions, considering bodies as transferred from some of those places into others. And so, instead of absolute places and motions, we use relative ones; and that without any inconvenience in common affairs; but in philosophical disquisitions, we ought to abstract from our senses, and consider things themselves, distinct from what are only sensible measures of them. For it may be that there is no body really at rest, to which the places and motions of others may be referred.

But we may distinguish rest and motion, absolute and relative, one from the other by their properties, causes and effects. It is a property of rest, that bodies really at rest do rest in respect to one another. And therefore as it is possible, that in the remote regions of the fixed stars, or perhaps far beyond them, there may be some body absolutely at rest; but impossible to know, from the position of bodies to one another in our regions whether any of these do keep the same position to that remote body; it follows that absolute rest cannot be determined from the position of bodies in our regions.

It is a property of motion, that the parts, which retain given positions to their wholes, do partake of the motions of those wholes. For all the parts of revolving bodies endeavour to recede from the axis of motion; and the impetus of bodies moving forward, arises from the joint impetus of all the parts. Therefore, if surrounding bodies are moved, those that are relatively at rest within them, will partake of their motion. Upon which account, the true and absolute motion of a body cannot be determined by the translation of it from those which only seem to rest; for the external bodies ought not only to appear at rest, but to be really at rest. For otherwise, all included bodies, beside their translation from near the surrounding ones, partake likewise of their true motions; and though that translation were not made they would not be really at rest, but only seem to be so. For the surrounding bodies stand in the like relation to the surrounded as the exterior part of a whole does to the interior, or as the shell does to the kernel; but, if the shell moves, the kernel will also move, as being part of the whole, without any removal from near the shell.

A property, near akin to the preceding, is this, that if a place is moved, whatever is placed therein moves along with it; and therefore a body, which is moved from a place in motion, partakes also of the motion of its place. Upon which account, all motions, from places in motion, are no other than parts of entire and absolute motions; and every entire motion is composed of the motion of the body out of its first place, and the motion of this place out of its place; and so on, until we come to some immovable place, as in the before-mentioned example of the sailor. Wherefore, entire and absolute motions can be not otherwise determined than by immovable places; and for that reason I did before refer those absolute motions to immovable places, but relative ones to movable places. Now no other places are immovable but those that, from infinity to infinity, do all retain the same given position one to another; and upon this account must ever remain unmoved; and do thereby constitute immovable space.

The causes by which true and relative motions are distinguished, one from the other, are the forces impressed upon bodies to generate motion. True motion is neither generated nor altered, but by some force impressed upon the body moved; but relative motion may be generated or altered without any force impressed upon the body. For it is sufficient only to impress some force on other bodies with which the former is

compared, that by their giving way, that relation may be changed, in which the relative rest or motion of this other body did consist. Again, true motion suffers always some change from any force impressed upon the moving body; but relative motion does not necessarily undergo any change by such forces. For if the same forces are likewise impressed on those other bodies, with which the comparison is made, that the relative position may be preserved, then that condition will be preserved in which the relative motion consists. And therefore any relative motion may be changed when the true motion remains unaltered, and the relative may be preserved when the true suffers some change. Upon which accounts, true motion does by no means consist in such relations.

The effects which distinguish absolute from relative motion are, the forces of receding from the axis of circular motion. For there are no such forces in a circular motion purely relative, but in a true and absolute circular motion, they are greater or less, according to the quantity of the motion. If a vessel, hung by a long cord, is so often turned about that the cord is strongly twisted, then filled with water, and held at rest together with the water; after, by the sudden action of another force, it is whirled about the contrary way, and while the cord is untwisting itself, the vessel continues for some time in this motion; the surface of the water will at first be plain, as before the vessel began to move; but the vessel, by gradually communicating its motion to the water, will make it begin sensibly to revolve, and recede by little and little from the middle, and ascend to the sides of the vessel, forming itself into a concave figure (as I have experienced), and the swifter the motion becomes, the higher will the water rise, till at last, performing its revolutions in the same times with the vessel, it becomes relatively at rest in it. This ascent of the water shows its endeavour to recede from the axis of its motion; and the true and absolute circular motion of the water, which is here directly contrary to the relative, discovers itself, and may be measured by this endeavour. At first, when the relative motion of the water in the vessel was greatest, it produced no endeavour to recede from the axis; the water showed no tendency to the circumference, nor any ascent towards the sides of the vessel, but remained of a plain surface, and therefore its true circular motion had not yet begun. But afterwards, when the relative motion of the water had decreased, the ascent thereof towards the sides of the vessel proved its endeavour to recede from the axis; and this endeavour showed the real circular motion of the water perpetually increasing' till it had acquired, its greatest quantity, when the water rested relatively in the vessel. And therefore this endeavour does not depend upon any translation of the water in respect of the ambient bodies, nor can true circular motion be defined by such translation. There is only one real circular motion of any one revolving body, corresponding to only one power of endeavouring to recede from its axis of motion, as its proper and adequate effect; but relative motions, in one and the same body, are innumerable, according to the various relations it bears to external

bodies, and like other relations, are altogether destitute of any real effect, any otherwise than they may perhaps partake of that one only true motion. And therefore in their system who suppose that our heavens, revolving below the sphere of the fixed stars, carry the planets along with them; the several parts of those heavens, and the planets, which are indeed relatively at rest in their heavens, do yet really move. For they change their position one to another (which never happens to bodies truly at rest), and being carried together with their heavens, partake of their motions, and as parts of revolving wholes, endeavour to recede from the axis of their motions.

Wherefore relative quantities are not the quantities themselves, whose names they bear, but those sensible measures of them (either accurate or inaccurate), which are commonly used instead of the measured quantities themselves. And if the meaning of words is to be determined by their use, then by the names time, space, place and motion, their measures are properly to be understood; and the expression will be unusual, and purely mathematical, if the measured quantities themselves are meant. Upon which account, they do strain the sacred writings, who there interpret those words for the measured quantities. Nor do those less defile the purity of mathematical and philosophical truths, who confound real quantities themselves with their relations and vulgar measures.

It is indeed a matter of great difficulty to discover, and effectually to distinguish, the true motions of particular bodies from the apparent; because the parts of that immovable space, in which those motions are performed, do by no means come under the observation of our senses. Yet the thing is not altogether desperate; for we have some arguments to guide us, partly from the apparent motions, which are the differences of the true motions; partly from the forces, which are the causes and effects of the true motions. For instance, if two globes, kept at a given distance one from the other by means of a cord that connects them, were revolved about their common centre of gravity, we might, from the tension of the cord, discover the endeavour of the globes to recede from the axis of their motion, and from thence we might compute the quantity of their circular motions. And then if any equal forces should be impressed at once on the alternate faces of the globes to augment or diminish their circular motions, from the increase or decrease of the tension of the cord, we might infer the increment or decrement of their motions; and thence would be found on what faces those forces ought to be impressed, that the motions of the globes might be most augmented; that is, we might discover their hindermost faces, or those which, in the circular motion, do follow. But the faces which follow being known, and consequently the opposite ones that precede, we should likewise know the determination of their motions. And thus we might find both the quantity and the determination of this circular motion, even in an immense vacuum, where there was nothing external or sensible with which the

globes could be compared. But now, if in that space some remote bodies were placed that kept always a given position one to another, as the fixed stars do in our regions, we could not indeed determine from the relative translation of the globes among those bodies, whether the motion did belong to the globes or to the bodies. But if we observed the cord, and found that its tension was that very tension which the motions of the globes required, we might conclude the motion to be in the globes, and the bodies to be at rest; and then, lastly, from the translation of the globes among the bodies, we should find the determination of their motions. But how we are to collect the true motions from their causes, effects, and apparent differences; and, *vice versa*, how from the motions, either true or apparent, we may come to the knowledge of their causes and effects, shall be explained more at large in the following tract For to this end it was that I composed it.

AXIOMS, OR LAWS OF MOTION.

LAW I.

EVERY BODY PERSEVERES IN ITS STATE OF REST, OR OF UNIFORM MOTION IN A RIGHT LINE, UNLESS IT IS COMPELLED TO CHANGE THAT STATE BY FORCES IMPRESSED THEREON.

Projectiles persevere in their motions, so far as they are not retarded by the resistance of the air, or impelled downwards by the force of gravity A top, whose parts by their cohesion are perpetually drawn aside from rectilinear motions, does not cease its rotation, otherwise than as it is retarded by the air. The greater bodies of the planets and comets, meeting with less resistance in more free spaces, preserve their motions both progressive and circular for a much longer time.

LAW II.

THE ALTERATION OF MOTION IS EVER PROPORTIONAL TO THE MOTIVE FORCE IMPRESSED; AND IS MADE IN THE DIRECTION OF THE RIGHT LINE IN WHICH THAT FORCE IS IMPRESSED.

If any force generates a motion, a double force will generate double the motion, a triple force triple the motion, whether that force be impressed altogether and at once, or gradually and successively. And this motion (being always directed the same way

with the generating force), if the body moved before, is added to or subducted from the former motion, according as they directly conspire with or are directly contrary to each other; or obliquely joined, when they are oblique, so as to produce a new motion compounded from the determination of both.

LAW III.

TO EVERY ACTION THERE IS ALWAYS OPPOSED AN EQUAL REACTION: OR THE MUTUAL ACTIONS OF TWO BODIES UPON EACH OTHER ARE ALWAYS EQUAL, AND DIRECTED TO CONTRARY PARTS.

Whatever draws or presses another is as much drawn or pressed by that other. If you press a stone with your finger, the finger is also pressed by the stone. If a horse draws a stone tied to a rope, the horse (if I may so say) will be equally drawn back towards the stone: for the distended rope, by the same endeavour to relax or unbend itself, will draw the horse as much towards the stone, as it does the stone towards the horse, and will obstruct the progress of the one as much as it advances that of the other.

If a body impinge upon another, and by its force change the motion of the other, that body also (because of the equality of the mutual pressure) will undergo an equal change, in its own motion, towards the contrary part. The changes made by these actions are equal, not in the velocities but in the motions of bodies; that is to say, if the bodies are not hindered by any other impediments. For, because the motions are equally changed, the changes of the velocities made towards contrary parts are reciprocally proportional to the bodies. This law takes place also in attractions, as will be proved in the next scholium.

COROLLARY I.

A BODY BY TWO FORCES CONJOINED WILL DESCRIBE THE DIAGONAL OF A PARALLELOGRAM, IN THE SAME TIME THAT IT WOULD DESCRIBE THE SIDES, BY THOSE FORCES APART.

If a body in a given time, by the force M impressed apart in the place A, should with an uniform motion be carried from A to B; and by the force N impressed apart in the same place, should be carried from A to C; complete the parallelogram ABCD, and, by both forces acting together, it will in the same time be carried in the diagonal from A to D. For since the force N acts in the direction of the line AC, parallel to BD, this force (by the second law) will not at all alter the

velocity generated by the other force M, by which the body is carried towards the line BD. The body therefore will arrive at the line BD in the same time, whether the force N be impressed or not; and therefore at the end of that time it will be found somewhere in the line BD. By the same argument, at the end of the same time it will be found somewhere in the line CD. Therefore it will be found in the point D, where both lines meet. But it will move in a right line from A to D, by Law I.

COROLLARY II.

AND HENCE IS EXPLAINED THE COMPOSITION OF ANY ONE DIRECT FORCE AD, OUT OF ANY TWO OBLIQUE FORCES AC AND CD; AND, ON THE CONTRARY, THE RESOLUTION OF ANY ONE DIRECT FORCE AD INTO TWO OBLIQUE FORCES AC AND CD: WHICH COMPOSITION AND RESOLUTION ARE ABUNDANTLY CONFIRMED FROM MECHANICS.

As if the unequal radii OM and ON drawn from the centre O of any wheel, should sustain the weights A and P by the cords MA and NP; and the forces of those weights to move the wheel were required. Through the centre O draw the right line KOL, meeting the cords perpendicularly in K and L; and from the centre O, with OL the greater of the distances OK and OL, describe a circle, meeting the cord MA in D: and drawing OD, make AC parallel and DC perpendicular thereto. Now, it being indifferent whether the points K, L, D, of the cords be fixed to the plane of the wheel or not, the weights will have the same effect whether they are suspended from the points K and L, or from D and L. Let the whole force of the weight A be represented by the line AD, and let it be resolved into the forces AC

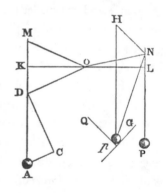

and CD; of which the force AC, drawing the radius OD directly from the centre, will have no effect to move the wheel: but the other force DC, drawing the radius DO perpendicularly, will have the same effect as if it drew perpendicularly the radius OL equal to OD; that is, it will have the same effect as the weight P, if that weight is to the weight A as the force DC is to the force DA; that is (because of the similar triangles ADC, DOK), as OK to OD or OL. Therefore the weights A and P, which are reciprocally as the radii OK and OL that lie in the same right line, will be equipollent, and so remain in equilibrio; which is the well known property of the balance, the lever, and the wheel. If either weight is greater than in this ratio, its force to move the wheel will be so much greater.

If the weight p, equal to the weight P, is partly suspended by the cord Np, partly sustained by the oblique plane pG; draw pH, NH, the former perpendicular to the horizon, the latter to the plane pG; and if the force of the weight p tending downwards is represented by the line pH, it may be resolved into the forces pN, HN. If there was any plane pQ, perpendicular to the cord pN, cutting the other plane pG in a line parallel to the horizon, and the weight p was supported only by those planes pQ, pG, it would press those planes perpendicularly with the forces pN, HN; to wit, the plane pQ with the force pN, and the plane pG with the force HN. And therefore if the plane pQ was taken away, so that the weight might stretch the cord, because the cord, now sustaining the weight, supplies the place of the plane that was removed, it will be strained by the same force N which pressed upon the plane before. Therefore, the tension of this oblique cord pN will be to that of the other perpendicular cord PN as pN to pH. And therefore if the weight p is to the weight A in a ratio compounded of the reciprocal ratio of the least distances of the cords PN, AM, from the centre of the wheel, and of the direct ratio of pH to pN, the weights will have the same effect towards moving the wheel and will therefore sustain each other; as any one may find by experiment.

But the weight p pressing upon those two oblique planes may be considered as a wedge between the two internal surfaces of a body split by it; and hence the forces of the wedge and the mallet may be determined; for because the force with which the weight p presses the plane pQ is to the force with which the same, whether by its own gravity, or by the blow of a mallet, is impelled in the direction of the line pH towards both the planes, as pH to pH; and to the force with which it presses the other plane pG, as pN to NH. And thus the force of the screw may be deduced from a like resolution of forces; it being no other than a wedge impelled with the force of a lever. Therefore the use of this Corollary spreads far and wide, and by that diffusive extent the truth thereof is farther confirmed. For on what has been said depends the whole doctrine of mechanics variously demonstrated by different authors. For from hence are easily deduced the forces of machines, which are compounded of wheels, pullies, levers, cords, and weights, ascending directly or obliquely, and other mechanical powers; as also the force of the tendons to move the bones of animals.

COROLLARY III.

THE QUANTITY OF MOTION, WHICH IS COLLECTED BY TAKING THE SUM OF THE MOTIONS DIRECTED TOWARDS THE SAME PARTS, AND THE DIFFERENCE OF THOSE THAT ARE DIRECTED TO CONTRARY PARTS, SUFFERS NO CHANGE FROM THE ACTION OF BODIES AMONG THEMSELVES.

For action and its opposite re-action are equal, by Law III, and therefore, by Law II, they produce in the motions equal changes towards opposite parts. Therefore if the motions are directed towards the same parts, whatever is added to the motion of the preceding body will be subducted from the motion of that which follows; so that the sum win be the same as before. If the bodies meet, with contrary motions, there will be an equal deduction from the motions of both; and therefore the difference of the motions directed towards opposite parts will remain the same.

Thus if a spherical body A with two parts of velocity is triple of a spherical body B which follows in the same right line with ten parts of velocity, the motion of A will be to that of B as 6 to 10. Suppose, then, their motions to be of 6 parts and of 10 parts, and the sum will be 16 parts. Therefore, upon the meeting of the bodies, if A acquire 3, 4, or 5 parts of motion, B will lose as many; and therefore after reflexion A will proceed with 9, 10, or 11 parts, and B with 7, 6, or 5 parts; the sum remaining always of 16 parts as before. If the body A acquire 9, 10, 11, or 12 parts of motion, and therefore after meeting proceed with 15, 16, 17, or 18 parts, the body B, losing so many parts as A has got, will either proceed with 1 part, having lost 9, or stop and remain at rest, as having lost its whole progressive motion of 10 parts; or it will go back with 1 part, having not only lost its whole motion, but (if I may so say) one part more; or it will go back with 2 parts, because a progressive motion of 12 parts is taken off. And so the sums of the conspiring motions 15+1 or 16+0, and the differences of the contrary motions 17-1 and 18-2, will always be equal to 16 parts, as they were before the meeting and reflexion of the bodies. But, the motions being known with which the bodies proceed after reflexion, the velocity of either will be also known, by taking the velocity after to the velocity before reflexion, as the motion after is to the motion before. As in the last case, where the motion of the body A was of 6 parts before reflexion and of 18 parts after, and the velocity was of 2 parts before reflexion, the velocity thereof after reflexion will be found to be of 6 parts; by saying, as the 6 parts of motion, before to 18 parts after, so are 2 parts of velocity before reflexion to 6 parts after.

But if the bodies are either not spherical, or, moving in different right lines, impinge obliquely one upon the other, and their motions after reflexion are required, in those cases we are first to determine the position of the plane that touches the concurring bodies in the point of concourse; then the motion of each body (by Corol. II) is to be resolved into two, one perpendicular to that plane, and the other parallel to it. This done, because the bodies act upon each other in the direction of a line perpendicular to this plane, the parallel motions are to be retained the same after reflexion as before; and to the perpendicular motions we are to assign equal changes towards the contrary parts; in such manner that the sum of the conspiring and the difference of the contrary motions may remain the same as before. From such kind of reflexions also

sometimes arise the circular motions of bodies about their own centres. But these are cases which I do not consider in what follows; and it would be too tedious to demonstrate every particular that relates to this subject.

COROLLARY IV.

The common centre of gravity of two or more bodies does not alter its state of motion or rest by the actions of the bodies among themselves: and therefore the common centre of gravity of all bodies acting upon each other (excluding outward actions and impediments) is either at rest, or moves uniformly in a right line.

For if two points proceed with an uniform motion in right lines, and their distance be divided in a given ratio, the dividing point will be either at rest, or proceed uniformly in a right line. This is demonstrated hereafter in Lem. XXIII and its Corol., when the points are moved in the same plane; and by a like way of arguing, it may be demonstrated when the points are not moved in the same plane. Therefore if any number of bodies move uniformly in right lines, the common centre of gravity of any two of them is either at rest, or proceeds uniformly in a right line; because the line which connects the centres of those two bodies so moving is divided at that common centre in a given ratio. In like manner the common centre of those two and that of a third body will be either at rest or moving uniformly in a right line because at that centre the distance between the common centre of the two bodies, and the centre of this last, is divided in a given ratio. In like manner the common centre of these three, and of a fourth body, is either at rest, or moves uniformly in a right line; because the distance between the common centre of the three bodies, and the centre of the fourth is there also divided in a given ratio, and so on ad infinitum. Therefore, in a system of bodies where there is neither any mutual action among themselves, nor any foreign force impressed upon them from without, and which consequently move uniformly in right lines, the common centre of gravity of them all is either at rest or moves uniformly forward in a right line.

Moreover, in a system of two bodies mutually acting upon each other, since the distances between their centres and the common centre of gravity of both are reciprocally as the bodies, the relative motions of those bodies, whether of approaching to or of receding from that centre, will be equal among themselves. Therefore since the changes which happen to motions are equal and directed to contrary parts, the common centre of those bodies, by their mutual action between themselves, is neither promoted nor

retarded, nor suffers any change as to its state of motion or rest. But in a system of several bodies, because the common centre of gravity of any two acting mutually upon each other suffers no change in its state by that action; and much less the common centre of gravity of the others with which that action does not intervene: but the distance between those two centres is divided by the common centre of gravity of all the bodies into parts reciprocally proportional to the total sums of those bodies whose centres they are: and therefore while those two centres retain their state of motion or rest, the common centre of all does also retain its state: it is manifest that the common centre of all never suffers any change in the state of its motion or rest from the actions of any two bodies between themselves. But in such a system all the actions of the bodies among themselves either happen between two bodies, or are composed of actions interchanged between some two bodies; and therefore they do never produce any alteration in the common centre of all as to its state of motion or rest. Wherefore since that centre, when the bodies do not act mutually one upon another, either is at rest or moves uniformly forward in some right line, it will, notwithstanding the mutual actions of the bodies among themselves, always persevere in its state, either of rest, or of proceeding uniformly in a right line, unless it is forced out of this state by the action of some power impressed from without upon the whole system. And therefore the same law takes place in a system consisting of many bodies as in one single body, with regard to their persevering in their state of motion or of rest. For the progressive motion, whether of one single body, or of a whole system of bodies, is always to be estimated from the motion of the centre of gravity.

COROLLARY V.

THE MOTIONS OF BODIES INCLUDED IN A GIVEN SPACE ARE THE SAME AMONG THEMSELVES, WHETHER THAT SPACE IS AT REST, OR MOVES UNIFORMLY FORWARDS IN A RIGHT LINE WITHOUT ANY CIRCULAR MOTION.

For the differences of the motions tending towards the same parts, and the sums of those that tend towards contrary parts, are, at first (by supposition), in both cases the same; and it is from those sums and differences that the collisions and impulses do arise with which the bodies mutually impinge one upon another. Wherefore (by Law II), the effects of those collisions will be equal in both cases; and therefore the mutual motions of the bodies among themselves in the one case will remain equal to the mutual motions of the bodies among themselves in the other. A clear proof of which we have from the experiment of a ship; where all motions happen after the same manner, whether the ship is at rest, or is carried uniformly forwards in a right line.

COROLLARY VI.

IF BODIES, ANY HOW MOVED AMONG THEMSELVES, ARE
URGED IN THE DIRECTION OF PARALLEL LINES BY EQUAL
ACCELERATIVE FORCES, THEY WILL ALL CONTINUE TO MOVE
AMONG THEMSELVES, AFTER THE SAME MANNER AS IF THEY
HAD BEEN URGED BY NO SUCH FORCES.

For these forces acting equally (with respect to the quantities of the bodies to be moved), and in the direction of parallel lines, will (by Law II) move all the bodies equally (as to velocity), and therefore will never produce any change in the positions or motions of the bodies among themselves.

SCHOLIUM.

Hitherto I have laid down such principles as have been received by mathematicians, and are confirmed by abundance of experiments. By the first two Laws and the first two Corollaries, Galileo discovered that the descent of bodies observed the duplicate ratio of the time, and that the motion of projectiles was in the curve of a parabola; experience agreeing with both, unless so far as these motions are a little retarded by

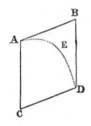

the resistance of the air. When a body is falling, the uniform force of its gravity acting equally, impresses, in equal particles of time, equal forces upon that body, and therefore generates equal velocities; and in the whole time impresses a whole force, and generates a whole velocity proportional to the time. And the spaces described in proportional times are as the velocities and the times conjunctly; that is, in a duplicate ratio of the times. And when a body is thrown upwards, its uniform gravity impresses forces and takes off velocities proportional to the times; and the times of ascending to the greatest heights are as the velocities to be taken off, and those heights are as the velocities and the times conjunctly, or in the duplicate ratio of the velocities. And if a body be projected in any direction, the motion arising from its projection is compounded with the motion arising from its gravity. As if the body A by its motion of projection alone could describe in a given time the right line AB, and with its motion of falling alone could describe in the same time the altitude AC; complete the paralellogram ABDC, and the body by that compounded motion will at the end of the time be found in the place D; and the curve line AED, which that body describes, will be a parabola, to which the right line AB will be a tangent in A; and whose ordinate BD will be as the square of the line AB. On the same Laws and Corollaries depend those things which have been demonstrated concerning the times

of the vibration of pendulums, and are confirmed by the daily experiments of pendulum clocks. By the same, together with the third Law, Sir Christ. Wren, Dr. Wallis, and Mr. Huygens, the greatest geometers of our times, did severally determine the rules of the congress and reflexion of hard bodies, and much about the same time communicated their discoveries to the Royal Society, exactly agreeing among themselves as to those rules. Dr. Wallis, indeed, was something more early in the publication; then followed Sir Christopher Wren, and, lastly, Mr. Huygens. But Sir Christopher Wren confirmed the truth of the thing before the Royal Society by the experiment of pendulums,

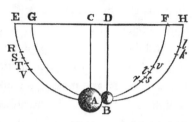

which Mr. Mariotte soon after thought fit to explain in a treatise entirely upon that subject. But to bring this experiment to an accurate agreement with the theory, we are to have a due regard as well to the resistance of the air as to the elastic force of the concurring bodies. Let the spherical bodies A, B be suspended by the parallel and equal strings AC, BD, from the centres C, D. About these centres, with those intervals, describe the semicircles EAF, GBH, bisected by the radii CA, DB. Bring the body A to any point R of the LAP, and (withdrawing the body B) let it go from thence, and after one oscillation suppose it to return to the point V: then RV will be the retardation arising from the resistance of the air. Of this RV let ST be a fourth part, situated in the middle, to wit, so as RS and TV may be equal, and RS may be to ST as 3 to 2 then will ST represent very nearly the retardation during the descent from S to A. Restore the body B to its place: and, supposing the body A to be let fall from the point S, the velocity thereof in the place of reflexion A, without sensible error, will be the same as if it had descended in vacuo from the point T. Upon which account this velocity may be represented by the chord of the arc TA. For it is a proposition well known to geometers, that the velocity of a pendulous body in the lowest point is as the chord of the arc which it has described in its descent. After reflexion, suppose the body A comes to the place s, and the body B to the place k. Withdraw the body B, and find the place v, from which if the body A, being let go, should after one oscillation return to the place r, st may be a fourth part of rv, so placed in the middle thereof as to leave rs equal to tv, and let the chord of the arc tA represent the velocity which the body A had in the place A immediately after reflexion. For t will be the true and correct place to which the body A should have ascended, if the resistance of the air had been taken off. In the same way we are to correct the place k to which the body B ascends, by finding the place l to which it should have ascended in vacuo. And thus everything may be subjected to experiment, in the same manner as if we were really placed in vacuo. These things being done, we are to take the product (if I may so say) of the body A, by the chord of

the arc TA (which represents its velocity), that we may have its motion in the place A immediately before reflexion; and then by the chord of the arc tA, that we may have its motion in the place A immediately after reflexion. And so we are to take the product of the body B by the chord of the arc Bl that we may have the motion of the same immediately after reflexion. And in like manner, when two bodies are let go together from different places, we are to find the motion of each, as well before as after reflexion; and then we may compare the motions between themselves, and collect the effects of the reflexion. Thus trying the thing with pendulums of ten feet, in unequal as well as equal bodies, and making the bodies to concur after a descent through large spaces, as of 8, 12, or 16 feet, I found always, without an error of 3 inches, that when the bodies concurred together directly, equal changes towards the contrary parts were produced in their motions, and, of consequence, that the action and reaction were always equal. As if the body A impinged upon the body B at rest with 9 parts of motion, and losing 7, proceeded after reflexion with 2, the body B was carried backwards with those 7 parts. If the bodies concurred with contrary motions, A with twelve parts of motion, and B with six, then if A receded with 2, B receded with 8; to wit, with a deduction of 14 parts of motion on each side. For from the motion of A subducting twelve parts, nothing will remain; but subducting 2 parts more, a motion will be generated of 2 parts towards the contrary way; and so, from the motion of the body B of 6 parts, subducting 14 parts, a motion is generated of 8 parts towards the contrary way. But if the bodies were made both to move towards the same way, A, the swifter, with 14 parts of motion, B, the slower, with 5, and after reflexion A went on with 5, B likewise went on with 14 parts; 9 parts being transferred from A to B. And so in other cases. By the congress and collision of bodies, the quantity of motion, collected from the sum of the motions directed towards the same way, or from the difference of those that were directed towards contrary ways, was never changed. For the error of an inch or two in measures may be easily ascribed to the difficulty of executing everything with accuracy. It was not easy to let go the two pendulums so exactly together that the bodies should impinge one upon the other in the lowermost place AB; nor to mark the places s, and k, to which the bodies ascended after congress. Nay, and some errors, too, might have happened from the unequal density of the parts of the pendulous bodies themselves, and from the irregularity of the texture proceeding from other causes.

But to prevent an objection that may perhaps be alledged against the rule, for the proof of which this experiment was made, as if this rule did suppose that the bodies were either absolutely hard, or at least perfectly elastic (whereas no such bodies are to be found in nature), I must add, that the experiments we have been describing, by no means depending upon that quality of hardness, do succeed as well in soft as in hard bodies. For if the rule is to be tried in bodies not perfectly hard, we are only to dimin-

ish the reflexion in such a certain proportion as the quantity of the elastic force requires. By the theory of Wren and Huygens, bodies absolutely hard return one from another with the same velocity with which they meet. But this may be affirmed with more certainty of bodies perfectly elastic. In bodies imperfectly elastic the velocity of the return is to be diminished together with the elastic force; because that force (except when the parts of bodies are bruised by their congress, or suffer some such extension as happens under the strokes of a hammer) is (as far as I can perceive) certain and determined, and makes the bodies to return one from the other with a relative velocity, which is in a given ratio to that relative velocity with which they met. This I tried in balls of wool, made up tightly, and strongly compressed. For, first, by letting go the pendulous bodies, and measuring their reflexion, I determined the quantity of their elastic force; and then, according to this force, estimated the reflexions that ought to happen in other cases of congress. And with this computation other experiments made afterwards did accordingly agree; the balls always receding one from the other with a relative velocity, which was to the relative velocity with which they met as about 5 to 9. Balls of steel returned with almost the same velocity: those of cork with a velocity something less; but in balls of glass the proportion was as about 15 to 16. And thus the third Law, so far as it regards percussions and reflexions, is proved by a theory exactly agreeing with experience.

In attractions, I briefly demonstrate the thing after this manner. Suppose an obstacle is interposed to hinder the congress of any two bodies A, B, mutually attracting one the other: then if either body, as A, is more attracted towards the other body B, than that other body B is towards the first body A, the obstacle will be more strongly urged by the pressure of the body A than by the pressure of the body B, and therefore will not remain in equilibrio: but the stronger pressure will prevail, and will make the system of the two bodies, together with the obstacle, to move directly towards the parts on which B lies; and in free spaces, to go forward in infinitum with a motion perpetually accelerated; which is absurd and contrary to the first Law. For, by the first Law, the system ought to persevere in its state of rest, or of moving uniformly forward in a right line; and therefore the bodies must equally press the obstacle, and be equally attracted one by the other. I made the experiment on the loadstone and iron. If these, placed apart in proper vessels, are made to float by one another in standing water, neither of them will propel the other; but, by being equally attracted, they will sustain each other's pressure, and rest at last in an equilibrium.

So the gravitation betwixt the earth and its parts is mutual. Let the earth FI be cut by any plane EG into two parts EGF and EGI, and their weights one towards the other will be mutually equal. For if by another plane HK, parallel to the former EG, the greater part EGI is cut into two parts EGKH and HKI, whereof HKI is equal to the

part EFG, first cut off, it is evident that the middle part EGKH, will have no propen-sion by its proper weight towards either side, but will hang as it were, and rest in an equilibrium betwixt both. But the one extreme part HKI will with its whole weight bear upon and press the middle part towards the other extreme part EGF; and therefore the force with which EGI, the sum of the parts HKI and EGKH, tends towards the third part EGF, is equal to the weight of the part HKI, that is, to the weight of the third part EGF. And therefore the weights of the two parts EGI and EGF, one towards the other, are equal, as I was to prove.

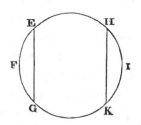

And indeed if those weights were not equal, the whole earth floating in the nonresist-ing æther would give way to the greater weight, and, retiring from it, would be carried off in infinitum.

And as those bodies are equipollent in the congress and reflexion, whose velocities are reciprocally as their innate forces, so in the use of mechanic instruments those agents are equipollent, and mutually sustain each the contrary pressure of the other, whose velocities, estimated according to the determination of the forces, are recipro-cally as the forces.

So those weights are of equal force to move the arms of a balance; which during the play of the balance are reciprocally as their velocities upwards and downwards; that is, if the ascent or descent is direct, those weights are of equal force, which are recipro-cally as the distances of the points at which they are suspended from the axis of the bal-ance; but if they are turned aside by the interposition of oblique planes, or other obsta-cles, and made to ascend or descend obliquely, these bodies will be equipollent, which are reciprocally as the heights of their ascent and descent taken according to the per-pendicular; and that on account of the determination of gravity downwards.

And in like manner in the pulley, or in a combination of pullies, the force of a hand drawing the rope directly, which is to the weight, whether ascending directly or obliquely, as the velocity of the perpendicular ascent of the weight to the velocity of the hand that draws the rope, will sustain the weight.

In clocks and such like instruments, made up from a combination of wheels, the contrary forces that promote and impede the motion of the wheels, if they are recip-rocally as the velocities of the parts of the wheel on which they are impressed, will mutually sustain the one the other.

The force of the screw to press a body is to the force of the hand that turns the handles by which it is moved as the circular velocity of the handle in that part where it is impelled by the hand is to the progressive velocity of the screw towards the pressed body.

The forces by which the wedge presses or drives the two parts of the wood it cleaves are to the force of the mallet upon the wedge as the progress of the wedge in the direction of the force impressed upon it by the mallet is to the velocity with which the parts of the wood yield to the wedge, in the direction of lines perpendicular to the sides of the wedge. And the like account is to be given of all machines.

The power and use of machines consist only in this, that by diminishing the velocity we may augment the force, and the contrary: from whence in all sorts of proper machines, we have the solution of this problem; To move a given weight with a given power, or with a given force to overcome any other given resistance. For if machines are so contrived that the velocities of the agent and resistant are reciprocally as their forces, the agent will just sustain the resistant, but with a greater disparity of velocity will overcome it. So that if the disparity of velocities is so great as to overcome all that resistance which commonly arises either from the attrition of contiguous bodies as they slide by one another, or from the cohesion of continuous bodies that are to be separated, or from the weights of bodies to be raised, the excess of the force remaining, after all those resistances are overcome, will produce an acceleration of motion proportional thereto, as well in the parts of the machine as in the resisting body. But to treat of mechanics is not my present business. I was only willing to show by those examples the great extent and certainty of the third Law of motion. For if we estimate the action of the agent from its force and velocity conjunctly, and likewise the reaction of the impediment conjunctly from the velocities of its several parts, and from the forces of resistance arising from the attrition, cohesion, weight, and acceleration of those parts. the action and reaction in the use of all sorts of machines will be found always equal to one another. And so far as the action is propagated by the intervening instruments, and at last impressed upon the resisting body, the ultimate determination of the action will be always contrary to the determination of the reaction.

BOOK I.

OF THE MOTION OF BODIES.

SECTION I.

Of the method of first and last ratios of quantities, by the help whereof we demonstrate the propositions that follow.

LEMMA I.

QUANTITIES, AND THE RATIOS OF QUANTITIES, WHICH IN
ANY FINITE TIME CONVERGE CONTINUALLY TO EQUALITY,
AND BEFORE THE END OF THAT TIME APPROACH NEARER
THE ONE TO THE OTHER THAN BY ANY GIVEN DIFFERENCE,
BECOME ULTIMATELY EQUAL.

If you deny it, suppose them to be ultimately unequal, and let D be their ultimate difference. Therefore they cannot approach nearer to equality than by that given difference D; which is against the supposition.

LEMMA II.

IF IN ANY FIGURE AacE, TERMINATED BY THE RIGHT LINES
Aa, AE, AND THE CURVE acE, THERE BE INSCRIBED ANY
NUMBER OF PARALLELOGRAMS AB, BC, CD,
&C., COMPREHENDED UNDER EQUAL BASES
AB, BC, CD, &C., AND THE SIDES, BB,
CC, DD, &C., PARALLEL TO ONE SIDE AA
OF THE FIGURE; AND THE PARALLELOGRAMS
AKBL, BLCM, CMDN, &C., ARE COMPLETED.
THEN IF THE BREADTH OF THOSE
PARALLELOGRAMS BE SUPPOSED TO BE
DIMINISHED, AND THEIR NUMBER TO BE
AUGMENTED IN INFINITUM; I SAY, THAT
THE ULTIMATE RATIOS WHICH THE INSCRIBED FIGURE
AKBLCMDD, THE CIRCUMSCRIBED FIGURE AALBMENDOE,
AND CURVILINEAR FIGURE AABCDE, WILL HAVE TO ONE
ANOTHER, ARE RATIOS OF EQUALITY.

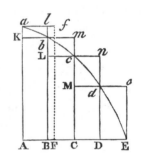

For the difference of the inscribed and circumscribed figures is the sum of the parallelograms Kl, Lm, Mn, Do, that is (from the equality of all their bases), the rectangle under one of their bases Kb and the sum of their altitudes Aa, that is, the rectangle ABla. But this rectangle, because its breadth AB is supposed diminished in infinitum, becomes less than any given space. And therefore (by Lem. I) the figures inscribed and circumscribed become ultimately equal one to the other; and much more will the intermediate curvilinear figure be ultimately equal to either.   Q.E.D.

LEMMA III.

The same ultimate ratios are also ratios of equality, when the breadths, AB, BC, DC, &c., of the parallelograms are unequal, and are all diminished in infinitum.

For suppose AF equal to the greatest breadth, and complete the parallelogram FAaf. This parallelogram will be greater than the difference of the inscribed and circumscribed figures; but, because its breadth AF is diminished in infinitum, it will become less than any given rectangle.   Q.E.D.

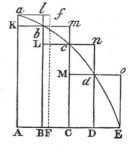

COR. 1. Hence the ultimate sum of those evanescent parallelograms will in all parts coincide with the curvilinear figure.

COR. 2. Much more will the rectilinear figure comprehended under the chords of the evanescent arcs ab, bc, cd, &c., ultimately coincide with the curvilinear figure.

COR. 3. And also the circumscribed rectilinear figure comprehended under the tangents of the same arcs.

COR. 4 And therefore these ultimate figures (as to their perimeters E) are not rectilinear, but curvilinear limits of rectilinear figures.

LEMMA IV.

IN TWO FIGURES AacE, PprT, YOU INSCRIBE (AS BEFORE) TWO RANKS OF PARALLELOGRAMS, AN EQUAL NUMBER IN EACH RANK, AND, WHEN THEIR BREADTHS ARE DIMINISHED IN INFINITRUM, THE ULTIMATE RATIOS OF THE PARALLELOGRAMS IN ONE FIGURE TO THOSE IN THE OTHER, EACH TO EACH RESPECTIVELY, ARE THE SAME; I SAY THAT THOSE TWO FIGURES AacE, PprT, ARE TO ONE ANOTHER IN THAT SAME RATIO.

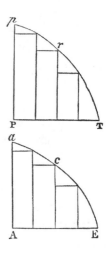

For as the parallelograms in the one are severally to the parallelograms in the other, so (by composition) is the sum of all in the one to the sum of all in the other; and so is the one figure to the other; because (by Lem. III) the former figure to the former sum, and the latter figure to the latter sum, are both in the ratio of equality.   Q.E.D.

COR. Hence if two quantities of any kind are any how divided into an equal number of parts, and those parts, when their number is augmented, and their magnitude diminished in infinitum, have a given ratio one to the other, the first to the first, the second to the second, and so on in order, the whole quantities will be one to the other in that same given ratio. For if, in the figures of this Lemma, the parallelograms are taken one

to the other in the ratio of the parts, the sum of the parts will always be as the sum of the parallelograms; and therefore supposing the number of the parallelograms and parts to be augmented, and their magnitudes diminished in infinitum, those sums will be in the ultimate ratio of the parallelogram in the one figure to the correspondent parallelogram in the other; that is (by the supposition), in the ultimate ratio of any part of the one quantity to the correspondent part of the other.

LEMMA V.

IN SIMILAR FIGURES, ALL SORTS OF HOMOLOGOUS SIDES,
WHETHER CURVILINEAR OR RECTILINEAR, ARE PROPORTIONAL;
AND THE AREAS ARE IN THE DUPLICATE RATIO OF THE
HOMOLOGOUS SIDES.

LEMMA VI.

IF ANY ARC ACB, GIVEN IN POSITION
IS SUBTENDED BY ITS CHORD AB, AND
IN ANY POINT A, IN THE MIDDLE OF
THE CONTINUED
CURVATURE, IS TOUCHED BY A RIGHT
LINE AD, PRODUCED BOTH WAYS;
THEN IF THE POINTS A AND B
APPROACH ONE ANOTHER AND MEET, I
SAY THE ANGLE BAD, CONTAINED BETWEEN THE CHORD
AND THE TANGENT, WILL BE DIMINISHED IN INFINITUM,
AND ULTIMATELY WILL VANISH.

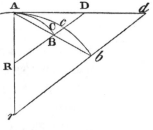

For if that angle does not vanish, the arc ACB will contain with the tangent AD an angle equal to a rectilinear angle; and therefore the curvature at the point A will not be continued, which is against the supposition.

LEMMA VII.

THE SAME THINGS BEING SUPPOSED, I SAY THAT THE ULTIMATE
RATIO OF THE ARC, CHORD, AND TANGENT, ANY ONE TO ANY
OTHER, IS THE RATIO OF EQUALITY.

For while the point B approaches towards the point A, consider always AB and AD as produced to the remote points b and d, and parallel to the secant BD draw bd: and let the arc Acb be always similar to the arc ACB. Then, supposing the points A and B to coincide, the angle dAb will vanish, by the preceding Lemma; and therefore the right

lines Ab, Ad (which are always finite), and the intermediate arc Acb, will coincide, and become equal among themselves. Wherefore, the rightlines AB, AD, and the intermediate arc ACB (which are always proportional to the former), will vanish, and ultimately acquire the ratio of equality. Q.E.D.

COR. 1. Whence if through B we draw BF parallel to the tangent, always cutting any right line AF passing through A in F, this line BF will be ultimately in the ratio of equality with the evanescent arc ACB; because, completing the parallelogram AFBD, it is always in a ratio of equality with AD.

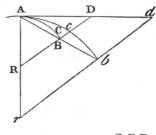

COR. 2. And if through B and A more right lines are drawn, as BE, BD, AF, AG, cutting the tangent AD and its parallel BF; the ultimate ratio of all the abscissas AD, AE, BF, BG, and of the chord and arc AB, any one to any other, will be the ratio of equality.

COR. 3. And therefore in all our reasoning about ultimate ratios, we may freely use any one of those lines for any other.

LEMMA VIII.

IF THE RIGHT LINES AR, BR, WITH THE ARC ACB, THE CHORD AB, AND THE TANGENT AD, CONSTITUTE THREE TRIANGLES RAB, RACB, RAD, AND THE POINTS A AND B APPROACH AND MEET: I SAY, THAT THE ULTIMATE FORM OF THESE EVANESCENT TRIANGLES IS THAT OF SIMILITUDE, AND THEIR ULTIMATE RATIO THAT OF EQUALITY.

For while the point B approaches towards the point A, consider always AB, AD, AR, as produced to the remote points b, d, and r, and rbd as drawn parallel to RD, and let the arc Acb be always similar to the arc ACB. Then supposing the points A and B to coincide, the angle bAd will vanish; and therefore the three triangles rAb, rAci, rAd(which are always finite), will coincide, and on that account become both similar and equal. And therefore the triangles RAB, RACB, RAD which are always similar and proportional to these, will ultimately become both similar and equal among themselves. Q.E.D.

COR. And hence in all reasonings about ultimate ratios, we may indifferently use any one of those triangles for any other.

LEMMA IX.

IF A RIGHT LINE AE. AND A CURVE LINE ABC, BOTH GIVEN
BY POSITION, CUT EACH OTHER IN A GIVEN ANGLE, A; AND
TO THAT RIGHT LINE, IN ANOTHER GIVEN ANGLE, BD, CE
ARE ORDINATELY APPLIED, MEETING THE CURVE IN B, C;
AND THE POINTS B AND C TOGETHER APPROACH TOWARDS
AND MEET IN THE POINT A: I SAY THAT THE AREAS OF THE
TRIANGLES ABD, ACE, WILL ULTIMATELY BE ONE TO THE
OTHER IN THE DUPLICATE RATIO OF THE SIDES.

For while the points B, C, approach towards the point A, suppose always AD to
be produced to the remote points d and e, so as Ad, Ae may be proportional to AD,
AE; and the ordinates db, ec, to be drawn parallel to the ordinates DB and EC, and
meeting AB and AC produced in b and c. Let the curve Abc be similar to the curve
ABC, and draw the right line Ag so as to touch both
curves in A, and cut the ordinates DB, EC, db ec, in
F, G, f, g. Then, supposing the length Ae to remain
the same, let the points B and C meet in the point A;
and the angle cAg vanishing, the curvilinear areas
Abd, Ace will coincide with the rectilinear areas Afd,
A; and therefore (by Lem. V) will be one to the other
in the duplicate ratio of the sides Ad, Ae. But the
areas ABD, ACE are always proportional to these
areas; and so the sides AD, AE are to these sides. And

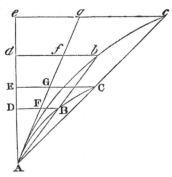

therefore the areas ABD, ACE are ultimately one to the other in the duplicate ratio of
the sides AD, AE.   Q.E.D.

LEMMA X.

THE SPACES WHICH A BODY DESCRIBES BY ANY FINITE FORCE
URGING IT, WHETHER THAT FORCE IS DETERMINED AND
IMMUTABLE, OR IS CONTINUALLY AUGMENTED OR CONTINUALLY
DIMINISHED, ARE IN THE VERY BEGINNING OF THE MOTION ONE
TO THE OTHER IN THE DUPLICATE RATIO OF THE TIMES.

Let the times be represented by the lines AD, AE, and the velocities generated in
those times by the ordinates DB, EC. The spaces described with these velocities will be
as the areas ABD, ACE, described by those ordinates, that is, at the very beginning of
the motion (by Lem. IX), in the duplicate ratio of the times AD, AE.   Q.E.D.

Cor. 1. And hence one may easily infer, that the errors of bodies describing similar parts of similar figures in proportional times, are nearly as the squares of the times in which they are generated; if so be these errors are generated by any equal forces similarly applied to the bodies, and measured by the distances of the bodies from those places of the similar figures, at which, without the action of those form, the bodies would have arrived in those proportional times.

Cor. 2. But the errors that are generated by proportional forces, similarly applied to the bodies at similar parts of the similar figures, are as the forces and the squares of the times conjunctly.

Cor. 3. The same thing is to be understood of any spaces whatsoever described by bodies urged with different forces; all which, in the very beginning of the motion, are as the forces and the squares of the times conjunctly.

Cor. 4. And therefore the forces are as the spaces described in the very beginning of the motion directly, and the squares of the times inversely.

Cor. 5. And the squares of the times are as the spaces described directly, and the forces inversely.

SCHOLIUM.

If in comparing indetermined quantities of different sorts one with another, any one is said to be as any other directly or inversely, the meaning is, that the former is augmented or diminished in the same ratio with the latter, or with its reciprocal. And if any one is said to be as any other two or more directly or inversely, the meaning is, that the first is augmented or diminished in the ratio compounded of the ratios in which the others, or the reciprocals of the others, are augmented or diminished. As if A is said to be as B directly, and C directly, and D inversely, the meaning is, that A is augmented or diminished in the same ratio with $B \times C \times \frac{1}{D}$, that is to say, that A and $\frac{BC}{D}$ are one to the other in a given ratio.

LEMMA XI.

The evanescent subtense of the angle of contact, in all curves which at the point of contact have a finite curvature, is ultimately in the duplicate ratio of the subtense of the conterminate arc.

Case 1. Let AB be that arc, AD its tangent, BD the subtense of the angle of contact perpendicular on the tangent, AB the subtense of the arc. Draw BG perpendicular to the subtense AB, and AG to the tangent AD, meeting in G; then let the points D, B, and G, approach to the points d, b, and g, and suppose J to be the ultimate intersection

of the lines BG, AG, when the points D, B, have come to A. It is evident that the distance GJ may be less than any assignable. But (from the nature of the circles passing through q the points A, B, G, A, *b*, *g*,) AB² = AG × BD, and A² = A*g* × *bd*; and therefore the ratio of AB² to A*b*² is compounded of the ratios of AG to A*g*, and of B*d* to *bd*. But because GJ may be assumed of less length than any assignable, the ratio of AG to A*g* may be such as to differ from the ratio of equality by less than any assignable difference; and therefore the ratio of AB² to A*b*² may be such as to differ from the ratio of BD to bd by less than any assignable difference. Therefore, by Lem. I, the ultimate ratio of AB² to A*b*² is the same with the ultimate ratio of BD to bd. 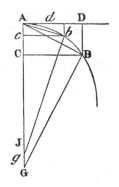 Q.E.D.

CASE 2. Now let BD be inclined to AD in any given angle, and the ultimate ratio of BD to *bd* will always be the same as before and therefore the same with the ratio of AB² to A*b*². Q.E.D.

CASE. 3. And if we suppose the angle D not to be given, but that the right line BD converges to a given point, or is determined by any other condition whatever; nevertheless the angles D, *d*, being determined by the same law, will always draw nearer to equality, and approach nearer to each other than by any assigned difference, and therefore, by Lem. I, will at last be equal; and therefore the lines BD, *bd* are in the same ratio to each other as before. Q.E.D.

COR. 1. Therefore since the tangents AD, A*d*, the arcs AB, A*b*, and their sines, BC, *bc*, become ultimately equal to the chords AB, A*b*, their squares will ultimately become as the subtenses BD, *bd*.

COR. 2. Their squares are also ultimately as the versed sines of the arcs, bisecting the chords, and converging to a given point. For those versed sines are as the subtenses BD, *bd*.

COR. 3. And therefore the versed sine is in the duplicate ratio of the time in which a body will describe the arc with a given velocity.

COR. 4. The rectilinear triangles ADB, A*db* are ultimately in the triplicate ratio of the sides AD, A*d*, and in a sesquiplicate ratio of the sides DB, *db*; as being in the ratio compounded of the sides AD to DB, and of A*d* to *db*. So also the triangles ABC, Abc are ultimately in the triplicate ratio of the sides BC, *bc*. What I call the sesquiplicate ratio is the subduplicate of the triplicate, as being compounded of the simple and subduplicate ratio.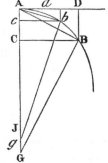

COR. 5. And because DB, *db* are ultimately parallel and in the duplicate ratio of the lines AD, A*d*, the ultimate curvilinear areas ADB, A*db* will be (by the nature of the parabola) two thirds of the rectilinear triangles ADB, A*db*; and the segments AB, A*b* will be one third of the same triangles. And thence those areas and those segments will be in the triplicate ratio as well of the tangents AD, A*d*, as of the chords and arcs AB, AB.

SCHOLIUM.

But we have all along supposed the angle of contact to be neither infinitely greater nor infinitely less than the angles of contact made by circles and their tangents; that is, that the curvature at the point A is neither infinitely small nor infinitely great, or that the interval AJ is of a finite magnitude. For DB may be taken as AD^3: in which case no circle can be drawn through the point A, between the tangent AD and the curve AB, and therefore the angle of contact will be infinitely less than those of circle. And by a like reasoning, if DB be made successfully as AD^4, AD^5 AD^6, AD^7 &c., we shall have a series of angles of contact, proceeding in infinitum, wherein every succeeding term is infinitely less than the preceding. And if DB be made successively as AD^2, $AD^{3/}{}_2$ $AD^{4/}{}_3$ $AD^{5/}{}_4$ $AD^{6/}{}_5$ AD^7, &c., we shall have another infinite series of angles of contact, the first of which is of the same sort with those of circles, the second infinitely greater, and every succeeding one infinitely greater than the preceding. But between any two of these angles another series of intermediate angles of contact may be interposed, proceeding both ways in infinitum, wherein every succeeding angle shall be infinitely greater or infinitely less than the preceding. As if between the terms AD^2 and AD^3 there were interposed the series $AD^{13/}{}_6$, $AD^{11/}{}_5$ $AD^{9/}{}_4$ $AD^{7/}{}_3$ $AD^{5/}{}_2$ $AD^{8/}{}_3$ $AD^{11/}{}_4$ $AD^{14/}{}_5$ $AD^{17/}{}_6$, &c. And again, between any two angles of this series, a new series of intermediate angles may be interposed, differing from one another by infinite intervals. Nor is nature confined to any bounds.

Those things which have been demonstrated of curve lines, and the superfices which they comprehend, may be easily applied to the curve superfices and contents of solids. These Lemmas are premised to avoid the tediousness of deducing perplexed demonstrations ad absurdum, according to the method of the ancient geometers. For demonstrations are more contracted by the method of indivisibles: but because the hypothesis of indivisibles seems somewhat harsh, and therefore that method is reckoned less geometrical, I chose rather to reduce the demonstrations of the following propositions to the first and last sums and ratios of nascent and evanescent quantities, that is, to the limits of those sums and ratios; and so to premise, as short as I could, the demonstrations of those limits. For hereby the same thing is performed as by the method of indivisibles; and now those principles being demonstrated, we may use

them with more safety. Therefore if hereafter I should happen to consider quantities as made up of particles, or should use little curve lines for right ones, I would not be understood to mean indivisibles, but evanescent divisible quantities; not the sums and ratios of determinate parts, but always the limits of sums and ratios; and that the force of such demonstrations always depends on the method laid down in the foregoing Lemmas.

Perhaps it may be objected, that there is no ultimate proportion, of evanescent quantities; because the proportion, before the quantities have vanished, is not the ultimate, and when they are vanished, is none. But by the same argument, it may be alledged, that a body arriving at a certain place, and there stopping, has no ultimate velocity: because the velocity, before the body comes to the place, is not its ultimate velocity; when it has arrived, is none. But the answer is easy; for by the ultimate velocity is meant that with which the body is moved, neither before it arrives at its last place and the motion ceases, nor after, but at the very instant it arrives; that is, that velocity with which the body arrives at its last place, and with which the motion ceases. And in like manner, by the ultimate ratio of evanescent quantities is to be understood the ratio of the quantities not before they vanish, nor afterwards, but with which they vanish. In like manner the first ratio of nascent quantities is that with which they begin to be. And the first or last sum is that with which they begin and cease to be (or to be augmented or diminished). There is a limit which the velocity at the end of the motion may attain, but not exceed. This is the ultimate velocity. And there is the like limit in all quantities and proportions that begin and cease to be. And since such limits are certain and definite, to determine the same is a problem strictly geometrical. But whatever is geometrical we may be allowed to use in determining and demonstrating any other thing that is likewise geometrical.

It may also be objected, that if the ultimate ratios of evanescent quantities are given, their ultimate magnitudes will be also given: and so all quantities will consist of indivisibles, which is contrary to what Euclid has demonstrated concerning incommensurables, in the 10th Book of his Elements. But this objection is founded on a false supposition. For those ultimate ratios with which quantities vanish are not truly the ratios of ultimate quantities, but limits towards which the ratios of quantities decreasing without limit do always converge; and to which they approach nearer than by any given difference, but never go beyond, nor in effect attain to, till the quantities are diminished in infinitum. This thing will appear more evident in quantities infinitely great. If two quantities, whose difference is given, be augmented in infinitum, the ultimate ratio of these quantities will be given, to wit, the ratio of equality; but it does not from thence follow, that the ultimate or greatest quantities themselves, whose ratio that is, will be given. Therefore if in what follows, for the sake of being

more easily understood, I should happen to mention quantities as least, or evanescent, or ultimate, you are not to suppose that quantities of any determinate magnitude are meant, but such as are conceived to be always diminished without end.

SECTION II.

OF THE INVENTION OF CENTRIPETAL FORCES.

PROPOSITION I THEOREM I.

THE AREAS, WHICH REVOLVING BODIES DESCRIBE BY RADII DRAWN TO AN IMMOVABLE CENTRE OF FORCE DO LIE IN THE SAME IMMOVABLE PLANES, AND ARE PROPORTIONAL TO THE TIMES IN WHICH THEY ARE DESCRIBED.

For suppose the time to be divided into equal parts, and in the first part of that time let the body by its innate force describe the right line AB. In the second part of that time, the same would (by Law I.), if not hindered, proceed directly to c, along the line Bc equal to AB; so that by the radii AS, BS, cS, drawn to the centre, the equal areas ASB, BSc, would be described. But when the body is arrived at B, suppose that a centripetal force acts at once with a great impulse, and, turning aside the body from the right line Bc, compels it afterwards to continue its motion along the right line BC. Draw cC parallel to BS meeting BC in C; and at the end of the second part of the time, the body (by Cor. I. of the Laws) will be found in C, in the same plane with the triangle ASB. Join SC, and; because SB and Cc are parallel, the triangle SBC will be equal to the triangle SB, and therefore

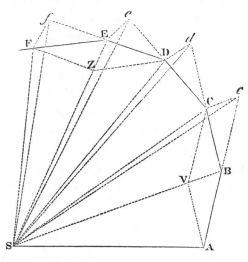

also to the triangle SAB. By the like argument, if the centripetal force acts successively in C, D, E, &c., and makes the body, in each single particle of time, to describe the right lines CD, DE, EF, &c., they will all lie in the same plane; and the triangle SCD will be equal to the triangle SBC, and SDE to SCD, and SEF to SDE. And therefore,

in equal times, equal areas are described in one immovable plane: and, by composition, any sums SADS, SAFS, of those areas, are one to the other as the times in which they are described. Now let the number of those triangles be augmented, and their breadth diminished in infinitum; and (by Cor. 4, Lem. III.) their ultimate perimeter ADF will be a curve line: and therefore the centripetal force, by which the body is perpetually drawn back from the tangent of this curve, will act continually; and any described areas SADS, SAFS, which are always proportional to the times of description, will, in this case also, be proportional to those times. Q.E.D.

Cor. 1. The velocity of a body attracted towards an immovable centre, in spaces void of resistance, is reciprocally as the perpendicular let fall from that centre on the right line that touches the orbit. For the velocities in those places A, B, C, D, E, are as the bases AB, BC, CD, DE, EF, of equal triangles; and these bases are reciprocally as the perpendiculars let fall upon them.

Cor. 2. If the chords AB, BC of two arcs, successively described in equal times by the same body, in spaces void of resistance, are completed into a parallelogram ABCV, and the diagonal BV of this parallelogram, in the position which it ultimately acquires when those arcs are diminished in infinitum, is produced both ways, it will pass through the centre of force

Cor. 3. If the chords AB, BC, and DE, EF, of arcs described in equal times, in spaces void of resistance, are completed into the parallelograms ABCV, DEFZ: the forces in B and E are one to the other in the ultimate ratio of the diagonals BV, EZ, when those arcs are diminished in infinitum. For the motions BC and EF of the body (by Cor. 1 of the Laws) are compounded of the motions Bc, BV, and Ef, EZ: but BV and EZ, which are equal to Cc and Ff, in the demonstration of this Proposition, were generated by the impulses of the centripetal force in B and E, and are therefore proportional to those impulses.

Cor. 4. The forces by which bodies, in spaces void of resistance, are drawn back from rectilinear motions, and turned into curvilinear orbits, are one to another as the versed sines of arcs described in equal times; which versed sines tend to the centre of force, and bisect the chords when those axes are diminished to infinity. For such versed sines are the halves of the diagonals mentioned in Cor. 3.

Cor. 5. And therefore those forces are to the force of gravity as the said versed sines to the versed sines perpendicular to the horizon of those parabolic arcs which projectiles describe in the same time.

Cor. 6. And the same things do all hold good (by Cor. 5 of the Laws), when the planes in which the bodies are moved, together with the centres of force which are placed in those planes, are not at rest, but move uniformly forward in right lines.

PROPOSITION II. THEOREM II.

Every body that moves in any curve line described in a plane, and by a radius, drawn to a point either immovable, or moving forward with an uniform rectilinear motion, describes about that point areas proportional to the times, is urged by a centripetal force directed to that point.

CASE. 1. For every body that moves in a curve line, is (by Law 1) turned aside from its rectilinear course by the action of some force that impels it. And that force by which the body is turned off from its rectilinear course, and is made to describe, in equal times, the equal least triangles SAB, SBC, SCD, &c., about the immovable point S (by Prop. XL. Book 1, Elem. and Law II), acts in the place B, according to the direction of a line parallel to cC, that is, in the direction of the line BS, and in the place C, according to the direction of a line parallel to dD, that is, in the direction of the line CS, &c.; and therefore acts always in the direction of lines tending to the immovable point S.

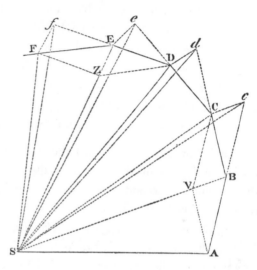

Q.E.D.

CASE 2. And (by Cor. 5 of the Laws) it is indifferent whether the superfices in which a body describes a curvilinear figure be quiescent, or moves together with the body, the figure described, and its point S, uniformly forward in right lines.

COR. 1. In non-resisting spaces or mediums, if the areas are not proportional to the times, the forces are not directed to the point in which the radii meet; but deviate therefrom in consequentia, or towards the parts to which the motion is directed, if the description of the areas is accelerated; but in antecedentia, if retarded.

COR. 2. And even in resisting mediums, if the description of the areas is accelerated, the directions of the forces deviate from the point in which the radii meet, towards the parts to which the motion tends.

SCHOLIUM.

A body may be urged by a centripetal force compounded of several forces; in which case the meaning of the Proposition is that the force which results out of all tends to the point S. But if any force acts perpetually in the direction of lines perpendicular to the described surface, this force will make the body to deviate from the plane of its motion: but will neither augment nor diminish the quantity of the described surface. and is therefore to be neglected in the composition of forces.

PROPOSITION III. THEOREM III.

EVERY BODY, THAT BY A RADIUS DRAWN TO THE CENTRE OF
ANOTHER BODY, HOWSOEVER MOVED, DESCRIBES AREAS
ABOUT THAT CENTRE PROPORTIONAL TO THE TIMES, IS
URGED BY A FORCE COMPOUNDED OUT OF THE CENTRIPETAL
FORCE TENDING TO THAT OTHER BODY, AND OF ALL
THE ACCELERATIVE FORCE BY WHICH THAT OTHER
BODY IS IMPELLED.

Let L represent the one, and T the other body; and (by Cor. 6 of the Laws) if both bodies are urged in the direction of parallel lines, by a new force equal and contrary to that by which the second body T is urged, the first body L will go on to describe about the other body T the same areas as before: but the force by which that other body T was urged will be now destroyed by an equal and contrary force; and therefore (by Law I.) that other body T, now left to itself, will either rest, or move uniformly forward in a right line: and the first body L impelled by the difference of the forces, that is, by the force remaining, will go on to describe about the other body T areas proportional to the times. And therefore (by Theor. II.) the difference of the forces is directed to the other body T as its centre.   Q.E.D

COR. 1. Hence if the one body L, by a radius drawn to the other body T, describes areas proportional to the times; and from the whole force, by which the first body L is urged (whether that force is simple, or, according to Cor. 2 of the Laws, compounded out of several forces), we subduct (by the same Cor.) that whole accelerative force by which the other body is urged; the whole remaining force by which the first body is urged will tend to the other body T, as its centre.

COR. 2. And, if these areas are proportional to the times nearly, the remaining force will tend to the other body T nearly.

COR. 3. And vice versa, if the remaining force tends nearly to the other body T, those areas will be nearly proportional to the times.

COR. 4. If the body L, by a radius drawn to the other body T, describes areas, which, compared with the times, are very unequal; and that other body T be either at rest, or moves uniformly forward in a right line: the action of the centripetal force tending to that other body T is either none at all, or it is mixed and compounded with very powerful actions of other forces: and the whole force compounded of them all, if they are many, is directed to another (immovable or moveable) centre. The same thing obtains, when the other body is moved by any motion whatsoever; provided that centripetal force is taken, which remains after subducting that whole force acting upon that other body T.

SCHOLIUM.

Because the equable description of areas indicates that a centre is respected by that force with which the body is most affected, and by which it is drawn back from its rectilinear motion, and retained in its orbit; why may we not be allowed, in the following discourse, to use the equable description of areas as an indication of a centre, about which all circular motion is performed in free spaces?

PROPOSITION IV. THEOREM IV.

THE CENTRIPETAL FORCES OF BODIES, WHICH BY EQUABLE MOTIONS DESCRIBE DIFFERENT CIRCLES, TEND TO THE CENTRES OF THE SAME CIRCLES; AND ARE ONE TO THE OTHER AS THE SQUARES OF THE ARCS DESCRIBED IN EQUAL TIMES APPLIED TO THE RADII OF THE CIRCLES.

These forces tend to the centres of the circles (by Prop. II, and Cor. 2, Prop. I.), and are one to another as the versed sines of the least arcs described in equal times (by Cor. 4, Prop. I.); that is, as the squares of the same arcs applied to the diameters of the circles (by Lem. VII.); and therefore since those arcs are as arcs described in any equal times, and the diameters are as the radii, the forces will be as the squares of any arcs described in the same time applied to the radii of the circles. Q.E.D.

COR. 1. Therefore, since those arcs are as the velocities of the bodies the centripetal forces are in a ratio compounded of the duplicate ratio of the velocities directly, and of the simple ratio of the radii inversely.

COR. 2. And since the periodic times are in a ratio compounded of the ratio of the radii directly, and the ratio of the velocities inversely, the centripetal forces are in a ratio compounded of the ratio of the radii directly, and the duplicate ratio of the periodic times inversely.

COR. 3. Whence if the periodic times are equal, and the velocities therefore as the radii, the centripetal forces will be also as the radii; and the contrary.

Cor. 4. If the periodic times and the velocities are both in the subduplicate ratio of the radii, the centripetal forces will be equal among themselves; and the contrary.

Cor. 5. If the periodic times are as the radii, and therefore the velocities equal, the centripetal forces will be reciprocally as the radii; and the contrary.

Cor. 6. If the periodic times are in the sesquiplicate ratio of the radii, and therefore the velocities reciprocally in the subduplicate ratio of the radii, the centripetal forces will be in the duplicate ratio of the radii inversely; and the contrary.

Cor. 7. And universally, if the periodic time is as any power R^n of the radius R, and therefore the velocity reciprocally as the power R^{n-1} of the radius, the centripetal force will be reciprocally as the power R^{2n-1} of the radius; and the contrary.

Cor. 8. The same things all hold concerning the times, the velocities, and forces by which bodies describe the similar parts of any similar figures that have their centres in a similar position with those figures; as appears by applying the demonstration of the preceding cases to those. And the application is easy, by only substituting the equable description of areas in the place of equable motion, and using the distances of the bodies from the centres instead of the radii.

Cor. 9. From the same demonstration it likewise follows, that the arc which a body, uniformly revolving in a circle by means of a given centripetal force, describes in any time, is a mean proportional between the diameter of the circle, and the space which the same body falling by the same given force would descend through in the same given time.

SCHOLIUM.

The case of the 6th Corollary obtains in the celestial bodies (as Sir Christopher Wren, Dr. Hooke, and Dr. Halley have severally observed); and therefore in what follows, I intend to treat more at large of those things which relate to centripetal force decreasing in a duplicate ratio of the distances from the centres.

Moreover, by means of the preceding Proposition and its Corollaries, we may discover the proportion of a centripetal force to any other known force, such as that of gravity. For if a body by means of its gravity revolves in a circle concentric to the earth, this gravity is the centripetal force of that body. But from the descent of heavy bodies, the time of one entire revolution, as well as the arc described in any given time, is given (by Cor. 9 of this Prop.). And by such propositions, Mr. Huygens, in his excellent book De Horologio Oscillatorio, has compared the force of gravity with the centrifugal forces of revolving bodies.

The preceding Proposition may be likewise demonstrated after this manner. In any circle suppose a polygon to be inscribed of any number of sides. And if a body, moved with a given velocity along the sides of the polygon, is reflected from the circle at the

several angular points, the force, with which at every reflection it strikes the circle, will be as its velocity: and therefore the sum of the forces, in a given time, will be as that velocity and the number of reflections conjunctly; that is (if the species of the polygon be given), as the length described in that given time, and increased or diminished in the ratio of the same length to the radius of the circle; that is, as the square of that length applied to the radius; and therefore the polygon, by having its sides diminished in infinitum, coincides with the circle, as the square of the arc described in a given time applied to the radius. This is the centrifugal force, with which the body impels the circle; and to which the contrary force, wherewith the circle continually repels the body towards the centre, is equal.

PROPOSITION V. PROBLEM I.

THERE BEING GIVEN, IN ANY PLACES, THE VELOCITY WITH
WHICH A BODY DESCRIBES A GIVEN FIGURE, BY MEANS OF
FORCES DIRECTED TO SOME COMMON CENTRE: TO FIND
THAT CENTRE.

Let the three right lines PT, TQV, VR touch the figure described in as many points, P, Q, R, and meet in T and V. On the tangents erect the perpendiculars PA, QB, RC, reciprocally proportional to the velocities of the body in the points P, Q, R, from which the perpendiculars were raised; that is, so that PA may be to QB as the velocity in Q to the velocity in P, and QB to RC as the velocity in R to the velocity in Q. Through the ends A, B, C, of the perpendiculars draw AD, DBE, EC, at right angles, meeting in D and E: and the right lines TD, VE produced, will meet in S, the centre required.

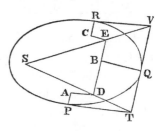

For the perpendiculars let fall from the centre S on the tangents PT, QT, are reciprocally as the velocities of the bodies in the points P and Q (by Cor. 1, Prop. I.), and therefore, by construction, as the perpendiculars AP, BQ directly; that is, as the perpendiculars let fall from the point D on the tangents. Whence it is easy to infer that the points S, D, T, are in one right line. And by the like argument the points S, E, V are also in one right line; and therefore the centre S is in the point where the right lines TD, VE meet.   Q.E.D.

PROPOSITION VI. THEOREM V.

IN A SPACE VOID OF RESISTANCE, IF A BODY REVOLVES IN
ANY ORBIT ABOUT AN IMMOVABLE CENTRE, AND IN THE

LEAST TIME DESCRIBES ANY ARC JUST THEN NASCENT; AND
THE VERSED SINE OF THAT ARC IS SUPPOSED TO BE DRAWN
BISECTING THE CHORD, AND PRODUCED PASSING THROUGH
THE CENTRE OF FORCE: THE CENTRIPETAL FORCE IN THE
MIDDLE OF THE ARC WILL BE AS THE VERSED SINE DIRECTLY
AND THE SQUARE OF THE TIME INVERSELY.

For the versed sine in a given time is as the force (by Cor. 4, Prop. 1); and augmenting the time in any ratio, because the arc will be augmented in the same ratio, the
versed sine will be augmented in the duplicate of that ratio (by Cor. 2 and 3, Lem. XI.),
and therefore is as the force and the square of the time. Subduct on both sides the
duplicate ratio of the time, and the force will be as the versed sine directly, and the
square of the time inversely. Q.E.D.

And the same thing may also be easily demonstrated by Corol. 4, Lem., X.

COR. 1. If a body P revolving about the centre S describes a curve line APQ, which
a right line ZPR touches in any point P; and from any other point Q of the curve, QR
is drawn parallel to the distance SP, meeting the tangent
in R; and QT is drawn perpendicular to the distance SP;
the centripetal force will be reciprocally as the solid
$\frac{SP^2 \times QT^2}{QR}$, if the solid be taken of that magnitude which

it ultimately acquires when the points P and Q coincide.
For QR is equal to the versed sine of double the arc QP,
whose middle is P : and double the triangle SQP, or SP × QT is proportional to the
time in which that double arc is described; and therefore may be used for the exponent
of the time.

COR. 2. By a like reasoning, the centripetal force is reciprocally as the solid $\frac{SY^2 \times QP^2}{QR}$
; if SY is a perpendicular from the centre of force on PR the tangent of the orbit. For
the rectangles SY × QP and SP × QT are equal.

COR. 3. If the orbit is either a circle, or touches or cuts a circle concentrically, that
is, contains with a circle the least angle of contact or section, having the same curvature and the same radius of curvature at the point P; and if PV be a chord of this circle, drawn from the body through the centre of force; the centripetal force will be
reciprocally as the solid SY² × PV– For PV is $\frac{QP^2}{QR}$.

COR. 4. The same things being supposed, the centripetal force is as the square of
the velocity directly, and that chord inversely. For the velocity is reciprocally as the perpendicular SY, by Cor. 1. Prop. I.

COR. 5. Hence if any curvilinear figure APQ is given, and therein a point S is also given, to which a centripetal force is perpetually directed, that law of centripetal force may be found, by which the body P will be continually drawn back from a rectilinear course, and, being detained in the perimeter of that figure, will describe the same by a perpetual revolution. That is, we are to find, by computation, either the solid $\frac{SP^2 \times QT^2}{QR}$ or the solid $SY^2 \times PV$, reciprocally proportional to this force. Examples of this we shall give in the following Problems.

PROPOSITION VII. PROBLEM II.

IF A BODY REVOLVES IN THE CIRCUMFERENCE OF A CIRCLE; IT IS PROPOSED TO FIND THE LAW OF CENTRIPETAL FORCE DIRECTED TO ANY GIVEN POINT.

Let VQPA be the circumference of the circle; S the given point to which as to a centre the force tends; P the body moving in the circumference; Q the next place into which it is to move; and PRZ the tangent of the circle at the preceding L place. Through the point S draw the chord PV, and the diameter VA of the circle: join AP, and draw QT perpendicular to SP, which produced,

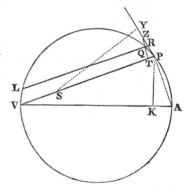

may meet the tangent PR in Z; and lastly, through the point Q, draw LR parallel to SP, meeting the circle in L, and the tangent PZ in R. And, because of the similar triangles ZQR, ZTP, VPA, we shall have RP², that is, QRL to QT² as AY² to PV². And therefore $\frac{QRL \times PV^2}{AV^2}$ is equal to QT². Multiply those equals by $\frac{SP^2 \times PV^3}{AV^2} = \frac{SP^2 \times QT^2}{QR}$, and the points P and Q coinciding, for RL write PV; then we shall have $\frac{SP^2 \times PV^3}{AV^2} = \frac{SP^2 \times QT^2}{QR}$. And therefore (by Cor 1 and 5,

Prop. VI.) the centripetal force is reciprocally as $\frac{SP^2 \times PV^3}{AV^2}$; that is (because AV² is given), reciprocally as the square of the distance or altitude SP, and the cube of the chord PV conjunctly. Q.E.I.

THE SAME OTHERWISE.

On the tangent PR produced let fall the perpendicular SY; and (because of the similar triangles SYP, VPA), we shall have AV to PV as SP to SY, and therefore $\frac{SP \times PV}{AV} = SY$, and $\frac{SP^2 \times PV^3}{AV^2} = SY^2 \times PV$. And therefore (by Corol. 3 and 5, Prop. VI), the

centripetal force is reciprocally as $\dfrac{SP^2 \times PV^3}{AV^2}$ that is (because AV is given), reciprocally as

$SP^2 \times PV^3$. Q.E.I.

COR. 1. Hence if the given point S, to which the centripetal force always tends, is placed in the circumference of the circle, as at V, the centripetal force will be reciprocally as the quadrato-cube (or fifth power) of the altitude SP.

COR. 2. The force by which the body P in the circle APTV revolves about the centre of force S is to the force by which the same body P may revolve in the same circle, and in the same periodic time, about any other centre of force R, as $RP^2 \times SP$ to the cube of the right line SG, which from the first centre of force S is drawn parallel to the distance PR. of the body from the second centre of force R, meeting the tangent PG of the orbit in G. For by the construction of this Proposition, the former force is to the latter as $RP^2 \times PT^3$ to $SP^2 \times PV^3$; that is, as $SP \times RP^2$ to$\dfrac{SP^3 \times PV^3}{PT^3}$; or (because of the similar triangles PSG, TPV) to SG^3.

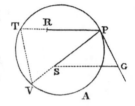

COR. 3. The force by which the body P in any orbit revolves about the centre of force S, is to the force by which the same body may revolve in the same orbit, and the same periodic time, about any other centre of force R, as the solid $SP \times RP^2$, contained under the distance of the body from the first centre of force S, and the square of its distance from the second centre of force R, to the cube of the right line SG, drawn from the first centre of the force S, parallel to the distance RP of the body from the second centre of force R, meeting the tangent PG of the orbit in G. For the force in this orbit at any point P is the same as in a circle of the same curvature.

PROPOSITION VIII. PROBLEM III.

IF A BODY MOVES IN THE SEMI-CIRCUMFERENCE PQA; IT IS
PROPOSED TO FIND THE LAW OF THE CENTRIPETAL FORCE
LENDING TO A POINT S, SO REMOTE, THAT ALL THE LINES
PS, RS DRAWN THERETO, MAY BE TAKEN FOR PARALLELS.

From C, the centre of the semi-circle, let the semi-diameter CA be drawn, cutting the parallels at right angles in M and N, and join CP. Because of the similar triangles CPM, PZT, and RZQ, we shall have CP^2 to PM^2 as PR^2 to QT^2; and, from the nature of the circle, PR^2 is equal to the rectangle $QR \times \overline{RN+QN}$ or, the points P, Q coinciding, to the rectangle $QR \times 2PM$. Therefore CP^2 is

to PM^2 as $QR \times 2PM$ to QT^2; and$\dfrac{QT^2}{QR} = \dfrac{2PM^3}{CP^2}$, and $\dfrac{QT^2 \times SP^2}{QR} = \dfrac{2PM^3 \times SP^2}{CP^2}$. And

therefore (by Corol. 1 and 5, Prop. VI.), the centripetal

force is reciprocally as $\frac{2PM^3 \times SP^2}{CP^2}$; that is (neglecting the

given ratio $\frac{2SP^2}{CP^2}$), reciprocally as PM³.

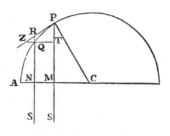

Q.E.I.

And the same thing is likewise easily inferred from the preceding Proposition.

SCHOLIUM

And by a like reasoning, a body will be moved in an ellipsis, or even in an hyperbola, or parabola, by a centripetal force which is reciprocally as the cube of the ordinate directed to an infinitely remote centre of force.

PROPOSITION IX. PROBLEM IV.

IF A BODY REVOLVES IN A SPIRAL PQS, CUTTING ALL THE RADII SP, SQ, &C., IN A GIVEN ANGLE; IT IS PROPOSED TO FIND THE LAW OF THE CENTRIPETAL FORCE TENDING TO THE CENTRE OF THAT SPIRAL.

Suppose the indefinitely small angle PSQ to be given; because, then, all the angles are given, the figure SPRQT will be given in specie. Therefore the ratio $\frac{QT}{QR}$ is also given, $\frac{QT^2}{QR}$ is as QT, that is

(because the figure is given in specie), as SP. But if the angle PSQ is any way changed, the right line QR, subtending the angle of contact QPR (by

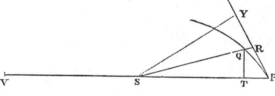

Lemma XI) will be changed in the duplicate ratio of PR or QT Therefore the ratio $\frac{QT^2}{QR}$ remains the same as before, that is, as SP. And $\frac{QT^2 \times SP^2}{QR}$ is as SP³, and therefore (by Corol. 1 and 5, Prop. VI) the centripetal force is reciprocally as the cube of the distance SP.

Q.E.I.

THE SAME OTHERWISE.

The perpendicular SY let fall upon the tangent, and the chord PV of the circle concentrically cutting the spiral, are in given ratios to the height SP; and therefore SP³ is as SY² × PV, that is (by Corel. 3 and 5, Prop. VI) reciprocally as the centripetal force.

LEMMA XII.

All parallelograms circumscribed about any conjugate diameters of a given ellipsis or hyperbola are equal among themselves.

This is demonstrated by the writers on the conic sections.

PROPOSITION X. PROBLEM V.

If a body revolves in an ellipsis; it is proposed to find the law of the centripetal force tending to the centre of the ellipsis.

Suppose CA, CB to be semi-axes of the ellipsis; GP, DK, conjugate diameters; PF, QT perpendiculars to those diameters; Qv an ordinate to the diameter GP; and if the parallelogram

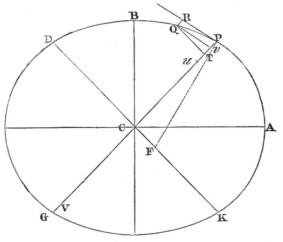

QvPR be completed, then (by the properties of the conic sections) the rectangle PvG will be to Qv^2 as PC^2 to CD^2; and (because of the similar triangles QvT, PCF), Qv^2 to QT^2 as PC^2 to PF^2; and, by composition, the ratio of PvG to QT^2 is compounded of the ratio of PC^2 to CD^2, and of the ratio of PC^2 to PF^2, that is, vG to $\dfrac{QT^2}{Pv}$ as PC^2

to $\dfrac{CD^2 \times PF^2}{PC^2}$. Put QR for Pv, and (by Lem. XII), BC × CA for CD × PF; also (the points P and Q coinciding) 2PC for vG; and multiplying the extremes and means together, we shall have $\dfrac{QT^2 \times PC^2}{QR}$ equal to $\dfrac{2BC^2 \times CA^2}{PC}$. Therefore (by Cor. 5, Prop. VI), the

centripetal force is reciprocally as $\dfrac{2BC^2 \times CA^2}{PC}$; that is (because $2BC^2 \times CA^2$ is given),

reciprocally as $\dfrac{1}{PC}$; that is, directly as the distance PC. QEI.

The same otherwise.

In the right line PG on the other side of the point T, take the point u so that Tu may be equal to Tv; then take uV, such as shall be to vG as DC^2 to PC^2. And because

Qu^2 is to PuG as DC^2 to PC^2 (by the conic sections), we shall have $Qv^2 = Pv \times uV$. Add the rectangle uPv to both sides, and the square of the chord of the arc PQ will be equal to the rectangle VPv; and therefore a circle which touches the conic section in P, and passes through the point Q, will pass also through the point V. Now let the points P and Q meet, and the ratio of uV to vG, which is the same with the ratio of DC^2 to PC^2, will become the ratio of PV to PG, or PV to 2PC; and therefore PV will be equal to $\frac{2DC^2}{PC}$. And therefore the force by which the body P revolves in the ellipsis will be

reciprocally as $\frac{2DC^2}{PC} \times PF2$ (by Cor. 3, Prop. VI); that is (because 2DC2 × PF2 is

given) directly as PC.   Q.E.I.

COR. 1. And therefore the force is as the distance of the body from the centre of the ellipsis; and, vice versa, if the force is as the distance, the body will move in an ellipsis whose centre coincides with the centre of force, or perhaps in a circle into which the ellipsis may degenerate.

COR. 2. And the periodic times of the revolutions made in all ellipses whatsoever about the same centre will be equal. For those times in similar ellipses will be equal (by Corol. 3 and 8, Prop. IV); but in ellipses that have their greater axis common, they are one to another as the whole areas of the ellipses directly, and the parts of the areas described in the same time inversely; that is, as the lesser axes directly, and the velocities of the bodies in their principal vertices inversely; that is, as those lesser axes directly, and the ordinates to the same point of the common axes inversely; and therefore (because of the equality of the direct and inverse ratios) in the ratio of equality.

SCHOLIUM.

If the ellipsis, by having its centre removed to an infinite distance, degenerates into a parabola, the body will move in this parabola; and the force, now tending to a centre infinitely remote, will become equable. Which is Galileo's theorem. And if the parabolic section of the cone (by changing the inclination of the cutting plane to the cone) degenerates into an hyperbola, the body will move in the perimeter of this hyperbola, having its centripetal force changed into a centrifugal force. And in like manner as in the circle, or in the ellipsis, if the forces are directed to the centre of the figure placed in the abscissa, those forces by increasing or diminishing the ordinates in any given ratio, or even by changing the angle of the inclination of the ordinates to the abscissa, are always augmented or diminished in the ratio of the distances from the centre; provided the periodic times remain equal; so also in all figures whatsoever, if the ordinates are augmented or diminished in any given ratio, or their inclination is any way changed, the periodic time remaining the same, the forces directed to any centre

placed in the abscissa are in the several ordinates augmented or diminished in the ratio of the distances from the centre.

SECTION III.

OF THE MOTION OF BODIES IN ECCENTRIC CONIC SECTIONS.

PROPOSITION XL PROBLEM VI.

IF A BODY REVOLVES IN AN ELLIPSIS; IT IS REQUIRED TO FIND THE LAW OF THE CENTRIPETAL FORCE TENDING TO THE FOCUS OF THE ELLIPSIS.

Let S be the focus of the ellipsis. Draw SP cutting the diameter DK of the ellipsis in E, and the ordinate Qv in x; and complete the parallelogram QxPR. It is evident that EP is equal to the greater semi-axis AC: for drawing HI from the other focus H of the ellipsis parallel to EC, because CS, CH are equal, ES, EI will be also equal; so that EP is the half sum of PS, PI, that is (because of the parallels HI, PR, and the equal angles IPR, HPZ), of PS, PH, which taken together are equal to the whole axis 2AC. Draw QT perpendicular to SP, and putting L for the principal latus rectum of the

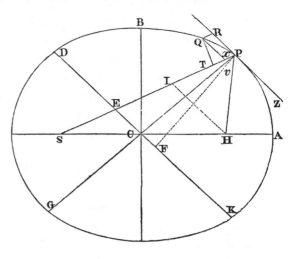

ellipsis $(\frac{2BC^2}{AC})$, we shall have L × QR to L × Pv as QR to Pv, that is, as PE or AC to PC; and L × Pv to GvP as L to Gv; and GvP to Qv² as PC² to CD²; and by (Corol. 2, Lem. VII) the points Q and P coinciding, Qv², is to Qx² in the ratio of equality; and Qx² or Qv² is to QT² as EP² to PF² that is, as CA² to PF², or (by Lem. XII) as CD² to CB². And compounding all those ratios together, we shall have L × QR to QT² as AC × L × PC² × CD², or 2CB² × PC² × CD² to PC × GvX CD² × CB², or as 2PC to Gv. But the points Q and P coinciding, 2PC and Gr are equal. And therefore the quantities L × QR and QT², proportional to these, will be also equal.

Let those equals be drawn into $\frac{SP^2}{QR}$ and $L \times SP^2$ will become equal to $\frac{SP^2 \times QT^2}{QR}$. And therefore (by Corol. 1 and 5, Prop. VI) the centripetal force is reciprocally as $L \times SP^2$, that is, reciprocally in the duplicate ratio of the distance SP.   Q.E.I.

THE SAME OTHERWISE.

Since the force tending to the centre of the ellipsis, by which the body P may revolve in that ellipsis, is (by Corol. 1, Prop. X.) as the distance CP of the body from the centre C of the ellipsis; let CE be drawn parallel to the tangent PR of the ellipsis; and the force by which the same body P may revolve about any other point S of the ellipsis, if CE and PS intersect in E, will be as $\frac{PE^3}{SP^2}$ (by Cor. 3, Prop. VII.); that is, if the point S is the focus of the ellipsis, and therefore PE be given as SP^2 reciprocally. Q.E.I.

With the same brevity with which we reduced the fifth Problem to the parabola, and hyperbola, we might do the like here: but because of the dignity of the Problem and its use in what follows, I shall confirm the other cases by particular demonstrations.

PROPOSITION XII. PROBLEM VII.

SUPPOSE A BODY TO MOVE IN AN HYPERBOLA; IT IS REQUIRED TO FIND THE LAW OF THE CENTRIPETAL FORCE TENDING TO THE FOCUS OF THAT FIGURE.

Let CA, CB be the semi-axes of the hyperbola; PG, KD other conjugate diameters; PF a perpendicular to the diameter KD; and Qv an ordinate to the diameter GP. Draw SP cutting the diameter DK in E, and the ordinate Qv in x, and complete the parallelogram QRPx. It is evident that EP is equal to the semi-transverse axis AC; for drawing HI, from the other focus H of the hyperbola, parallel to EC, because CS, CH are equal, ES, EI will be also equal; so that EP is the half difference of PS, PI; that is (because of the parallels IH, PR, and the equal angles IPR HPZ), of PS, PH, the difference of which is equal to the whole axis 2AC. Draw QT perpendicular to SP; and putting L for the principal latus rectum of the hyperbola (that is, for $\frac{2BC^2}{AC}$), we shall have $L \times QR$ to $L \times Pv$ as QR to Pv, or Px to Pv, that is (because of the similar triangles Pxv, PEC), as PE to PC, or AC to PC. And $L \times Pv$ will be to $Gv \times Pv$ as L to Gv; and (by the properties of the conic sections) the rectangle GvP is to Qv^2 as PC^2 to CD^2; and by (Cor. 2, Lem. VII), Qv^2 to Qx^2, the points Q and P coinciding, becomes a ratio of equality; and Qx^2 or Qv^2 is to QT^2 as EP^2 to PF^2, that is, as CA^2 to PF^2, or (by Lem. XII.) as CD^2 to CB^2: and, compounding all those ratios together, we shall have $L \times QR$ to QT2 as $AC \times L \times PC^2 \times CD^2$, or $2CB^2 \times PC^2 \times CD^2$ to $PC \times Gv$

$\times CD^2 \times CB^2$, or as 2PC to Gv. But the points P and Q coinciding, 2PC and Gv are equal. And therefore the quantities $L \times QR$ and QT^2, proportional to them, will be also equal. Let those equals be drawn into $\frac{SP^2}{QR}$, and we shall have $L \times SP^2$ equal to $\frac{SP^2 \times QT^2}{QR}$.

And therefore (by Cor. 1 and 5, Prop. VI.) the centripetal force is reciprocally as $L \times SP^2$, that is, reciprocally in the duplicate ratio of the distance SP. Q. E. I.

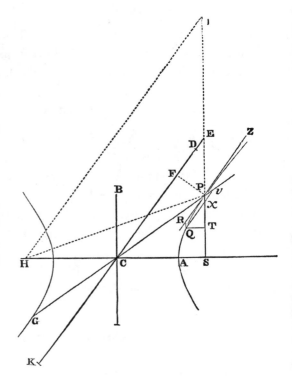

THE SAME OTHERWISE.

Find out the force tending from the centre C of the hyperbola. This will be proportional to the distance CP. But from thence (by Cor. 3, Prop. VII.) the force tending to the focus S will be as $\frac{P}{S}$ that is, because PE is given reciprocally as SP^2. Q.E.I.

And the same way may it be demonstrated, that the body having its centripetal changed into a centrifugal force, will move in the conjugate hyperbola.

LEMMA XIII.

THE LATUS RECTUM OF A PARABOLA BELONGING TO ANY VERTEX IS QUADRUPLE THE DISTANCE OF THAT VERTEX FROM THE FOCUS OF THE FIGURE.

This is demonstrated by the writers on the conic sections.

LEMMA XIV.

THE PERPENDICULAR, LET FALL FROM THE FOCUS OF A PARABOLA ON ITS TANGENT, IS A MEAN PROPORTIONAL

BETWEEN THE DISTANCES OF THE FOCUS FROM THE
POINT OF CONTACT, AND FROM THE PRINCIPAL
VERTEX OF THE FIGURE.

For, let AP be the parabola, S its focus, A its principal vertex, P the point of contact, PO an ordinate to the principal diameter, PM the tangent meeting the principal diameter in M, and SN the perpendicular from 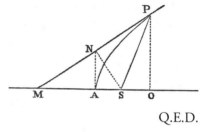 the focus on the tangent: join AN, and because of the equal lines MS and SP, MN and NP, MA and AO, the right lines AN, OP, will be parallel; and thence the triangle SAN will be right-angled at A, and similar to the equal triangles SNM, SNP; therefore PS is to SN as SN to SA.

Q.E.D.

COR. 1. PS^2 is to SN^2 as PS to SA.

COR. 2. And because SA is given, SN^2 will be as PS.

COR. 3. And the concourse of any tangent PM, with the right line SN, drawn from the focus perpendicular on the tangent falls in the right line AN that touches the parabola in the principal vertex.

PROPOSITION XIII. PROBLEM VIII.

IF A BODY MOVES IN THE PERIMETER OF A PARABOLA; IT IS
REQUIRED TO FIND THE LAW OF THE CENTRIPETAL FORCE
TENDING TO THE FOCUS OF THAT FIGURE.

Retaining the construction of the preceding Lemma, let P be the body in the perimeter of the parabola; and from the place Q, into which it is next to succeed, draw QR parallel and QT perpendicular to SP, as also Qv parallel to the tangent, and meet-

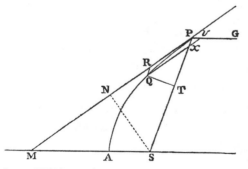

ing the diameter PG in v, and the distance SP in x. Now, because of the similar triangles Pxv, SPM, and of the equal sides SP, SM of the one, the sides Px or QR and Pv of the other will be also equal. But (by the conic sections) the square of the ordinate Qv is equal to the rectangle under the latus rectum and the segment Pv of the diameter; that is (by Lem. XIII.), to the rectangle 4PS × Pv, or 4PS × QR; and the points P and Q coinciding, the ratio of Qv to Qx (by Cor. 2, Lem. VII.,) becomes a ratio of equality. And therefore Qx^2, in this case, becomes equal to the rectangle 4PS × QR. But (because of

the similar triangles QxT, SPN), Q^2 is to QT^2 as PS^2 to SN^2, that is (by Cor. 1, Lem. XIV.), as PS to SA; that is, as 4PS × QR to 4SA × QR, and therefore (by Prop. IX. Lib. Y., Elem.) QT2 and 4SA × QR are equal. Multiply these equals by $\frac{SP^2}{QR}$ and $\frac{SP^2 \times QT^2}{QR}$ will become equal to SP^2 × 4SA: and therefore (by Cor. 1 and 5, Prop. VI.), the centripetal force is reciprocally as SP^2 × 4SA; that is, because 4SA is given, reciprocally in the duplicate ratio of the distance SP.   Q.E.D.

COR. 1. From the three last Propositions it follows, that if any body P goes from the place P with any velocity in the direction of any right line PR, and at the same time is urged by the action of a centripetal force that is reciprocally proportional to the square of the distance of the places from the centre, the body will move in one of the conic sections, having its focus in the centre of force; and the contrary. For the focus, the point of contact, and the position of the tangent, being given, a conic section may be described, which at that point shall have a given curvature. But the curvature is given from the centripetal force and velocity of the body being given; and two orbits, mutually touching one the other, cannot be described by the same centripetal force and the same velocity.

COR. 2. If the velocity with which the body goes from its place P in such, that in any infinitely small moment of time the lineola PR may be thereby described; and the centripetal force such as in the same time to move the same body through the space QR; the body will move in one of the conic sections, whose principal latus rectum is the quantity in its ultimate state, when the lineolæ PR, QR are diminished in infinitum. In these Corollaries I consider the circle as an ellipsis; and I except the case where the body descends to the centre in a right line.

PROPOSITION XIV. THEOREM VI

IF SEVERAL BODIES REVOLVE ABOUT ONE COMMON CENTRE,
AND THE CENTRIPETAL FORCE IS RECIPROCALLY IN THE
DUPLICATE RATIO OF THE DISTANCE OF PLACES FROM THE
CENTRE; I SAY, THAT THE PRINCIPAL LATERA RECTA OF THEIR
ORBITS ARE IN THE DUPLICATE RATIO OF THE AREAS, WHICH
THE BODIES BY RADII DRAWN TO THE CENTRE DESCRIBE IN
THE SAME TIME.

For (by Cor 2, Prop. XIII) the latus rectum L is equal to the quantity $\frac{QT^2}{QR}$ in its ultimate state when the points P and Q coincide. But the lineola QR in a given time is as the generating centripetal force; that is (by supposition), reciprocally as SP^2.

And therefore $\frac{QT^2}{QR}$ is as $QT^2 \times SP^2$; that is the latus

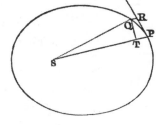

rectum L is in the duplicate ratio of the area QT × SP. Q.E.D.

COR. Hence the whole area of the ellipsis, and the rectangle under the axes, which is proportional to it, is in the ratio compounded of the subduplicate ratio of the latus rectum, and the ratio of the periodic time. For the whole area is as the area QT × SP, described in a given time, multiplied by the periodic time.

PROPOSITION XV. THEOREM VII.

THE SAME THINGS BEING SUPPOSED, I SAY, THAT THE PERIODIC TIMES IN ELLIPSES, ARE IN THE SESQUIPLICATE RATIO OF THEIR GREATER AXES.

For the lesser axis is a mean proportional between the greater axis and the latus rectum; and, therefore, the rectangle under the axes is in the ratio compounded of the subduplicate ratio of the latus rectum and the sesquiplicate ratio of the greater axis. But this rectangle (by Cor. 3, Prop. XIV) is in a ratio compounded of the subduplicate ratio of the latus rectum, and the ratio of the periodic time. Subduct from both sides the subduplicate ratio of the latus rectum, and there will remain the sesquiplicate ratio of the greater axis, equal to the ratio of the periodic time. Q.E.D.

COR. Therefore the periodic times in ellipses are the same as in circles whose diameters are equal to the greater axes of the ellipses.

PROPOSITION XVI. THEOREM VIII

THE SAME THINGS BEING SUPPOSED, AND RIGHT LINES BEING, DRAWN TO THE BODIES THAT SHALL TOUCH THE ORBITS, AND PERPENDICULARS BEING LET FALL ON THOSE TANGENTS FROM THE COMMON FOCUS; I SAY, THAT THE VELOCITIES OF THE BODIES ARE IN A RATIO COMPOUNDED OF THE RATIO OF THE PERPENDICULARS INVERSELY, AND THE SUBDUPLICATE RATIO OF THE PRINCIPAL LATERA RECTA DIRECTLY.

From the focus S draw SY perpendicular to the tangent PR, and the velocity of the body P will be reciprocally in the subduplicate ratio of the quantity $\frac{SY^2}{L}$. For that velocity is as the infinitely small arc PQ described in a given moment of time that is (by

Lem. VII), as the tangent PR; that is (because of the proportionals PR to QT, and SP to SY), as $\frac{SP \times QT}{SY}$; or as SY reciprocally, and SP × QT directly; but SP × QT is as the area described in the given time, that is (by Prop. XIV), in the subduplicate ratio of the latus rectum. Q.E.D.

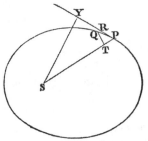

COR. 1. The principal latera recta are in a ratio compounded of the duplicate ratio of the perpendiculars and the duplicate ratio of the velocities.

COR. 2. The velocities of bodies, in their greatest and least distances from the common focus, are in the ratio compounded of the ratio of the distances inversely, and the subduplicate ratio of the principal latera recta directly. For those perpendiculars are now the distances.

COR. 3. And therefore the velocity in a conic section, at its greatest or least distance from the focus, is to the velocity in a circle, at the same distance from the centre, in the subduplicate ratio of the principal latus rectum to the double of that distance.

COR. 4. The velocities of the bodies revolving in ellipses, at their mean distances from the common focus, are the same as those of bodies revolving in circles, at the same distances; that is (by Cor. 6. Prop. IV), reciprocally in the subduplicate ratio of the distances. For the perpendiculars are now the lesser semi-axes, and these are as mean proportionals between the distances and the latera recta. Let this ratio inversely be compounded with the subduplicate ratio of the latera recta directly, and we shall have the subduplicate ratio of the distance inversely.

COR. 5. In the same figure, or even in different figures, whose principal latera recta are equal, the velocity of a body is reciprocally as the perpendicular let fall from the focus on the tangent.

COR. 6. In a, parabola, the velocity is reciprocally in the subduplicate ratio of the distance of the body from the focus of the figure; it is more variable in the ellipsis, and less in the hyperbola, than according to this ratio. For (by Cor. 2, Lem. XIV) the perpendicular let fall from the focus on the tangent of a parabola is in the subduplicate ratio of the distance. In the hyperbola the perpendicular is less variable; in the ellipsis more.

COR. 7. In a parabola, the velocity of a body at any distance from the focus is to the velocity of a body revolving in a circle, at the same distance from the centre, in the subduplicate ratio of the number 2 to 1; in the ellipsis it is less, and in the hyperbola greater, than according to this ratio. For (by Cor. 2 of this Prop.) the velocity at the vertex of a parabola is in this ratio, and (by Cor. 6 of this Prop. and Prop. IV) the same proportion holds in all distances. And hence, also, in a parabola, the velocity is everywhere equal to the velocity of a body revolving in a circle at half the distance; in the ellipsis it is less, and in the hyperbola greater.

COR. 8. The velocity of a body revolving in any conic section is to the velocity of a body revolving in a circle, at the distance of half the principal latus rectum of the section, as that distance to the perpendicular let fall from the focus on the tangent of the section. This appears from Cor. 5.

COR. 9. Wherefore since (by Cor. 6, Prop. IV), the velocity of a body revolving in this circle is to the velocity of another body revolving in any other circle reciprocally in the subduplicate ratio of the distances; therefore, ex æquo, the velocity of a body revolving in a conic section will be to the velocity of a body revolving in a circle at the same distance as a mean proportional between that common distance, and half the principal latus rectum of the section, to the perpendicular let fall from the common focus upon the tangent of the section.

PROPOSITION XVII. PROBLEM IX.

SUPPOSING THE CENTRIPETAL FORM TO BE RECIPROCALLY PROPORTIONAL TO THE SQUARES OF THE DISTANCES OF PLACES FROM THE CENTRE, AND THAT THE ABSOLUTE QUANTITY OF THAT FORCE IS KNOWN; IT IS REQUIRED TO DETERMINE THE LINE WHICH A BODY WILL DESCRIBE THAT IS LET GO FROM A GIVEN PLACE WITH A GIVEN VELOCITY IN THE DIRECTION OF A GIVEN RIGHT LINE.

Let the centripetal force tending to the point S be such as will make the body p revolve in any given orbit pq; and suppose the velocity of this body in the place p is known. Then from the place P suppose the body P to be let go with a given velocity in the direction of the line PR; but by virtue of a centripetal force to be immediately turned aside from that right line into the conic section PQ. This, the right line PR will therefore touch in P. Suppose likewise that the right line pr touches the orbit pq in p;

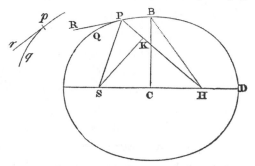

and if from S you suppose perpendiculars let fall on those tangents, the principal latus rectum of the conic section (by Cor. 1, Prop. XVI) will be to the principal latus rectum of that orbit in a ratio compounded of the duplicate ratio of the perpendiculars, and the duplicate ratio of the velocities; and is therefore given. Let this latus rectum be L; the focus S of the conic section is also given. Let the angle RPH be the complement of the angle RPS to two right; and the line PH, in which the other focus H is placed,

is given by position. Let fall SK perpendicular on PH, and erect the conjugate semi-axis BC; this done, we shall have $SP^2 - 2KPH + PH^2 = SH^2 \backsim 4CH^2 = 4BH^2 - 4BC^2 = PH^2 - L \times \overline{SP + PI} = SP^2 + 2SPH + PH^2 - L \times \overline{P + PH}$. Add on both sides $2KPH - SP^2 - PH2 + L \times \overline{P + PH}$, and we shall have $L \times \overline{P + PH} = 2SPH + 2KPH$, or SP + PH to PH, as 2SP + 2KP to L. Whence PH is given both in length and position. That is, if the velocity of the body in P is such that the latus rectum L is less than 2SP + 2KP, PH will lie on the same side of the tangent PR with the line SP; and therefore the figure will be an ellipsis, which from the given foci S, H, and the principal axis SP + PH, is given also. But if the velocity of the body is so great, that the latus rectum L becomes equal to 2SP + 2KP, the length PH will be infinite; and therefore, the figure will be a parabola, which has its axis SH parallel to the line PK, and is thence given. But if the body goes from its place P with a yet greater velocity, the length, PH is to be taken on the other side the tangent; and so the tangent passing between the foci, the figure will be an hyperbola having its principal axis equal to the difference of the lines SP and PH, and thence is given. For if the body, in these cases, revolves in a conic section so found; it is demonstrated in Prop. XI XII, and XIII, that the centripetal force will be reciprocally as the square of the distance of the body from the centre of force S; and therefore we have rightly determined the line PQ, which a body let go from a given place P with a given velocity, and in the direction of the right line PR given by position, would describe with such a force.   Q.E.F.

COR. 1. Hence in every conic section, from the principal vertex D, the latus rectum L, and the focus S given, the other focus H is given, by taking DH to DS as the latus rectum to the difference between the latus rectum and 4DS. For the proportion, SP + PH to PH as 2SP + 2KP to L, becomes, in the case of this Corollary, DS + DH to DH as 4DS to L, and by division DS to DH as 4DS – L to L.

COR. 2. Whence if the velocity of a body in the principal vertex D is given, the orbit may be readily found; to wit, by taking its latus rectum to twice the distance DS, in the duplicate ratio of this given velocity to the velocity of a body revolving in a circle at the distance DS (by Cor. 3, Prop. XVI), and then taking DH to DS as the latus rectum to the difference between the latus rectum and 4DS.

COR. 3. Hence also if a body move in any conic section, and is forced out of its orbit by any impulse, you may discover the orbit in which it will afterwards pursue its course. For by compounding the proper motion of the body with that motion, which the impulse alone would generate, you will have the motion with which the body will go off from a given place of impulse in the direction of a right line given in position.

COR. 4. And if that body is continually disturbed by the action of some foreign force, we may nearly know its course, by collecting the changes which that force introduces in some points, and estimating the continual changes it will undergo in the intermediate places, from the analogy that appears in the progress of the series.

SCHOLIUM.

If a body P, by means of a centripetal force tending to any given point R, move in the perimeter of any given conic section whose centre is C; and the law of the centripetal force is required: draw CG parallel to the radius RP, and meeting the tangent PG of the orbit in G; and the force required (by Cor. 1, and Schol. Prop. X., and Cor. 3, Prop. VII.) will be as $\frac{CG^3}{RP^2}$.

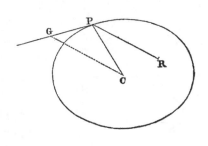

SECTION IV.

Of the finding of elliptic, parabolic, and hyperbolic orbits, from the focus given.

LEMMA XV.

IF FROM THE TWO FOCI S, H, OF ANY ELLIPSIS OR HYBERBOLA, WE DRAW TO ANY THIRD POINT V THE RIGHT LINES SV, HV, WHEREOF ONE HV IS EQUAL TO THE PRINCIPAL AXIS OF THE FIGURE, THAT IS, TO THE AXIS IN WHICH THE FOCI ARE SITUATED, THE OTHER, SV, IS BISECTED IN T BY THE PERPENDICULAR TR LET FALL UPON IT; THAT PERPENDICULAR TR WILL SOMEWHERE TOUCH THE CONIC SECTION : AND, VICE VERSA, IF IT DOES TOUCH IT, HV WILL BE EQUAL TO THE PRINCIPAL AXIS OF THE FIGURE.

For, let the perpendicular TR cut the right line HV, produced, if need be, in R; and join SR. Because TS, TV are equal, therefore the right lines SR, VR, as well as the angles TRS, TRV, will be also equal. Whence the point R will be in the conic section, and the perpendicular TR will touch the same; and the contrary.

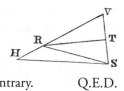

Q.E.D.

PROPOSITION XVIII. PROBLEM X.

FROM A FOCUS AND THE PRINCIPAL AXES GIVEN, TO DESCRIBE ELLIPTIC AND HYPERBOLIC TRAJECTORIES, WHICH SHALL PASS THROUGH GIVEN POINTS, AND TOUCH RIGHT LINES GIVEN BY POSITION.

Let S be the common focus of the figures; AB the length of the principal axis of any trajectory; P a point through which the trajectory should pass; and TR a right line which it should touch. About the centre P, with the interval AB – SP, if the orbit is an ellipse, or AB + SP, if the orbit is an hyperbola, describe the circle HG. On the tan-

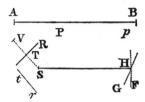

gent TR let fall the perpendicular ST, and produce the same to V, so that TV may be equal to ST; and about V as a centre with the interval. AB describe the circle FH. In this manner, whether two points P, p, are given, or two tangents TR, tr, or a point P and a tangent TR, we are to describe two circles. Let H be their common intersection, and from the foci S, H, with the given axis describe the trajectory: I say, the thing is done. For (because PH + SP in the ellipse, and PH – SP in the hyperbola, is equal to the axis) the described trajectory will pass through the point P, and (by the preceding Lemma) will touch the right line TR. And by the same argument it will either pass through the two points P, p, or touch the two right lines TR, tr. Q.E.F.

PROPOSITION XIX PROBLEM XI.

ABOUT A GIVEN FOCUS, TO &SCRIBE A PARABOLIC TRAJEC-TORY, WHICH SHALL PASS THROUGH GIVEN POINTS, AND TOUCH RIGHT LINES GIVEN BY POSITION.

Let S be the focus, P a point, and TR a tangent of the trajectory to be described. About P as a centre, with the interval PS, describe the circle FG. From the focus let fall ST perpendicular on the tangent, and produce the same to V, so as TV may be equal to ST. After the same manner another circle *fg* is to be described, if another point *p* is given; or another point *v* is to be found, if another tangent *tr* is given; then draw the right line IF, which shall touch the two circles FG, *fg*, if two points P, *p* are given; or pass through the two points V, *v*, if two tangents TR, *tr*, are given: or touch the circle FG, and pass through the point V, if the point P and the tangent TR are given. On FI let fall the perpendicular SI, and bisect the same in K; and with the axis SK and principal vertex K describe a

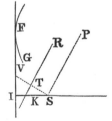

parabola: I say the thing is done. For this parabola (because SK is equal to IK, and SP to FP) will pass through the point P; and (by Cor. 3, Lem. XIV) because ST is equal to TV, and STR a right angle, it will touch the right line TR. Q.E.F.

PROPOSITION XX. PROBLEM XII.

ABOUT A GIVEN FOCUS TO DESCRIBE ANY TRAJECTORY

GIVEN IN SPECIE WHICH SHALL PASS THROUGH GIVEN POINTS, AND TOUCH RIGHT LINES GIVEN BY POSITION.

CASE 1. About the focus S it is required to describe a trajectory ABC, passing through two points B,C. Because the trajectory is given in specie, the ratio of the principal axis to the distance of the foci will be given. In that ratio take KB to BS, and LC to CS. About the centres B, C, with the intervals BK, CL, describe two circles; and on the right line KL, that touches the same in K and L, let fall the perpendicular SG; which out in A and *a*, so that GA may be to AS, and G*a* to *a*S, as KB to BS; and with

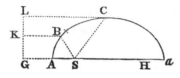

the axis A*a*, and vertices A, *a*, describe a trajectory: I say the thing is done. For let H be the other focus of the described figure, and seeing GA is to AS as G*a* to *a*S, then by division we shall have G*a*-GA, or A*a* to *a*S-AS, or SH in the same ratio, and therefore in the ratio which the principal axis of the figure to be described has to the distance of its foci; and therefore the described figure is of the same species with the figure which was to be described. And since KB to BS, and LC to CS, are in the same ratio, this figure will pass through the points B, C, as is manifest from the conic sections.

CASE 2. About the focus S it is required to describe a trajectory which shall somewhere touch two right lines TR, *tr*. From the focus on those tangents let fall the perpendiculars ST, S*t*, which produce to V, *v*, so that TV, *tv* may be equal to TS, *t*S. Bisect V*v* in O, and erect the indefinite perpendicular OH, and cut the right line VS infinitely produced in K and *k*, so that VK be to KS, and V*k* to *k*S, as the principal axis of the trajectory to be described is to the distance of its foci. On the diameter K*k* describe a circle cutting OH in H; and with the foci S, H, and prin-

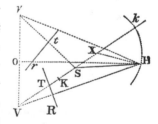

cipal axis equal to VH, describe a trajectory: I say, the thing is done. For bisecting K*k* in X, and joining HX, HS, HV, H*v*, because VK is to KS as V*k* to *k*S; and by composition, as VK + V*k* to KS + *k*S; and by division, as V*k* – VK to *k*S – KS, that is, as 2VX to 2KX, and 2KX to 2SX, and therefore as VX to HX and HX to SX, the triangles VXH, HXS will be similar; therefore VH will be to SH as VX to XH; and therefore as VK to KS. Wherefore VH, the principal axis of the described trajectory, has the same ratio to SH, the distance of the foci, as the principal axis of the trajectory which was to be described has to the distance of its foci; and is therefore of the same species. And seeing VH, *v*H are equal to the principal axis, and VS, *v*S are perpendicularly bisected by the right lines TR, tr, it is evident (by Lem. XV) that those right lines touch the described trajectory. Q.E.F.

CASE. 3. About the focus S it is required to describe a trajectory, which shall touch

a right line TR in a given Point R. On the right line TR let fall the perpendicular ST, which produce to V, so that TV may be equal to ST; join VR, and out the right line VS indefinitely produced in K and *k*, so that VK may be to SK, and V*k* to S*k*, as the principal axis of the ellipsis to be described to the distance of its foci; and on the diameter K*k* describing a circle, cut the right line VR pro-
duced in H; then with the foci S, H, and principal axis equal to VH, describe a trajectory: I say, the thing is done. For VH is to SH as VK to SK, and therefore as the principal axis of the trajectory which was to be

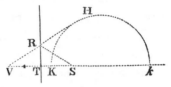

described to the distance of its foci (as appears from what we have demonstrated in Case 2); and therefore the described trajectory is of the same species with that which was to be described; but that the right line TR, by which the angle VRS is bisected, touches the trajectory in the point R, is certain from the properties of the conic sections.   Q.E.F.

CASE 4. About the focus S it is required to describe a trajectory APB that shall touch a right line TR, and pass through any given point P without the tangent, and shall be similar to the figure *apb*, described with the principal axis *ab*, and foci *s*, *h*. On the tangent TR let fall the perpendicular ST, which produce to V, so that TV may be equal to ST; and making the angles *hsq*, *shq*, equal to the angles VSP, SVP, about *q* as

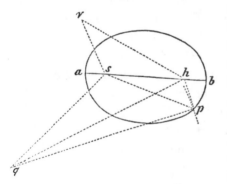

a centre, and with an interval which shall be to *ab* as SP to VS, describe a circle cutting the figure *apb* in *p*: join *sp*, and draw SH such that it may be to *sh* as SP is to *sp*, and may make the angle PSH equal to the angle *psh*, and the angle VSH equal to the angle *psq*. Then with the foci S, H, and principal axis AB, equal to the distance VH, describe a conic section: I say, the thing is done; for if *sv* is drawn so that it shall be to *sp* as *sh* is to *sq*,

and shall make the angle *vsp* equal to the angle *hsq*, and the angle *vsh* equal to the angle *psq*, the triangles *svh*, *spq*, will be similar, and therefore *vh* will be to *pq* as *sh* is to *sq*; that is (because of the similar triangles VSP, *hsq*, as VS is to SP, or as *ab* to *pq*. Wherefore *vh* and *ab* are equal. But, because of the similar triangles VSH, *vsh*, VH is to SH, or as *vh* to *sh*; that is, the axis of the conic section now described is to the distance of its foci as the axis *ab* to the distance of the foci *sh*; and therefore the figure now described is similar to the figure *aph*. But, because the

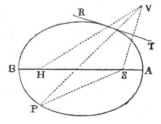

triangle PSH is similar to the triangle *psh*, this figure passes through the point P; and because VH is equal to its axis, and VS is perpendicularly bisected by the right line TR, the said figure touches the right line TR.   Q.E.F.

LEMMA XVI.

From three given points to draw to a fourth point that is not given three right lines whose differences shall be either given., or none at all.

CASE 1. Let the given points be A, B, C, and Z the fourth point which we are to find; because of the given difference of the lines AZ, BZ, the locus of the point Z will be an hyperbola whose foci are A and B, and whose principal axis is the given difference. Let that axis be MN. Taking PM to MA as MN is to AB, erect PR perpendicular to AB, and let fall ZR perpendicular to PR; then from the nature of the hyperbola, ZR will be to AZ as MN is to AB. And by the like argument, the locus of the point Z will be another hyperbola, whose foci are A, C, and whose principal axis is the difference between AZ and CZ; and QS a perpendicular on AC may be drawn, to which (QS) if from any point Z of this hyperbola a perpendicular ZS is let fall (this ZS), shall be to AZ as the difference between AZ and CZ is to AC. Wherefore the ratios of ZR and ZS to AZ are given, and consequently the ratio of ZR to ZS one to the

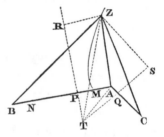

other; and therefore if the right lines RP, SQ, meet in T, and TZ and TA are drawn, the figure TRZS will be given in specie, and the right line TZ, in which the point Z is somewhere placed, will be given in position. There will be given also the right line TA, and the angle ATZ; and because the ratios of AZ and TZ to ZS are given, their ratio to each other is given also; and thence will be given likewise the triangle ATZ, whose vertex is the point Z.   Q.E.I.

CASE 2. If two of the three lines, for example AZ and BZ, are equal, draw the right line TZ so as to bisect the right line AB; then find the triangle ATZ as above. Q.E.I.

CASE 3. If all the three are equal, the point Z will be placed in the centre of a circle that passes through the points A, B, C.   Q.E.I.

This problematic Lemma is likewise solved in Apollonius's Book of Tactions restored by Vieta.

PROPOSITION XXI. PROBLEM XIII.

About a given focus to describe a trajectory that

SHALL PASS THROUGH GIVEN POINTS AND TOUCH RIGHT LINES GIVEN BY POSITION.

Let the focus S, the point P, and the tangent TR be given, and suppose that the other focus H is to be found. On the tangent let fall the perpendicular ST, which produce to Y, so that TY may be equal to ST, and YH will be equal to the principal axis. Join SP, HP, and SP will be the difference between HP and the principal axis. After this

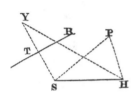

manner, if more tangents TR are given, or more points P, we shall always determine as many lines YH, or PH, drawn from the said points Y or P, to the focus H, which either shall be equal to the axes, or differ from the axes by given lengths SP; and therefore which shall either be equal among themselves, or shall have given differences; from whence (by the preceding Lemma), that other focus H is given. But having the foci and the length of the axis (which is either YH, or, if the trajectory be an ellipse, PH + SP; or PH-SP, if it be an hyperbola), the trajectory is given. Q.E.I.

SCHOLIUM.

When the trajectory is an hyperbola, I do not comprehend its conjugate hyperbola under the name of this trajectory. For a body going on with a continued motion can never pass out of one hyperbola into its conjugate hyperbola.

The case when three points are given is more readily solved thus. Let B, C, D, be the given points. Join BC, CD, and produce them to E, F, so as EB may be to EC as SB to SC; and FC to FD as SC to SD. On EF drawn and produced let fall the perpendiculars SG, BH, and in GS produced indefinitely take GA to AS, and Ga to aS,

as HB is to BS; then A will be the vertex, and Aa the principal axis of the trajectory; which, according as GA is greater than, equal to, or less than AS, will be either an ellipse, a parabola, or an hyperbola; the point a in the first case falling on the same side of the line GF as the point A; in the second, going off to an infinite distance; in the third, falling on the other side of the line GF. For if on GF the perpendiculars CI, DK are

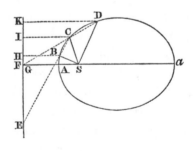

let fall, IC will be to HB as EC to EB; that is, as SC to SB: and by permutation, IC to SC as HB to SB, or as GA to SA. And, by the like argument, we may prove that KD is to SD in the same ratio. Wherefore the points B, C, D lie in a conic section described about the focus S, in such manner that all the right lines drawn from the focus S to the

several points of the section, and the perpendiculars let fall from the same points on the right line GF, are in that given ratio.

That excellent geometer M. De la Hire has solved this Problem much after the same way, in his Conics, Prop. XXV., Lib. VIII.

SECTION V.

How the orbits are to be found when neither focus is given.

LEMMA XVII.

IF FROM ANY POINT P OF A GIVEN CONIC SECTION, TO THE FOUR PRODUCED SIDES AB, CD, AC, DB, OF ANY TRAPEZIUM ABDC INSCRIBED IN THAT SECTION, AS MANY RIGHT LINES PQ, PR, PS, PT ARE DRAWN IN GIVEN ANGLES, EACH LINE TO EACH SIDE, THE RECTANGLE PQ × PR OF THOSE ON THE OPPOSITE SIDES AB, CD, WILL BE TO THE RECTANGLE PS × PT OF THOSE ON THE OTHER TWO OPPOSITE SIDES AC, BD, IN A GIVEN RATIO.

CASE 1. Let us suppose, first, that the lines drawn to one pair of opposite sides are parallel to either of the other sides; as PQ and PR to the side AC and PS and PT to the side AB. And farther, that one pair of the opposite sides, as AC and BD, are parallel betwixt themselves; then the right line which bisects those parallel sides will be one of the diameters of the conic section, and will likewise bisect RQ. Let O be the point in which RQ is bisected, and PO will be an ordinate to that diameter. Produce PO to K, so that OK may be equal to PO, and OK will be an ordinate on the other side of that diameter. Since, therefore, the points A, B, P and K are placed in the conic section, and PK cuts AB in a given angle, the rectangle PQK (by Prop. XVII., XIX, XXI and XXIII, Book III., of Apollonius's Conics) will be to the rectangle AQB in a given ratio. But QK and PR are equal, as being the differences of the equal lines OK, OP, and OQ, OR; whence the rectangles PQK and PQ × PR are equal; and therefore the rectangle PQ × PR is to the rectangle A B, that *s*, to the rectangle PS × PT in a given ratio.   Q.E.D.

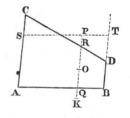

CASE 2. Let us next suppose that the opposite sides AC and BD of the trapezium are not parallel. Draw B*d* parallel to AC, and meeting as well the right line ST in *t*, as the conic section in *d*. Join C*d* cutting PQ in *r*, and draw DM parallel to PQ, cutting C*d* in M, and AB in N. Then (because of the similar triangles BT*t*, DBIN),Bt or PQ

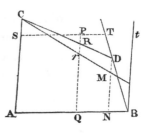

is to Tt as DN to NB. And so Rr is to AQ or PS as DM to AN. Wherefore, by multiplying the antecedents by the antecedents, and the consequents by the consequents, as the rectangle PQ × Rr is to the rectangle PS × Tt, so will the rectangle NDM be to the rectangle ANB; and (by Case 1) so is the rectangle PQ × Pr to the rectangle PS × Pt; and by division, so is the rectangle PQ × PR to the rectangle PS × PT.   Q.E.D.

CASE 3. Let us suppose, lastly, the four lines PQ, PR, PS, PT, not to be parallel to

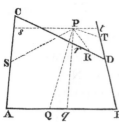

the sides AC, AB, but anyway inclined to them. In their place draw Pq, Pr, parallel to AC. and Ps, Pt parallel to AB; and because the angles of the triangles PQq, PRr, PSs, PTt are given, the ratios of PQ to Pq, PR to Pr, PS to Ps, PT to Pt will be also given; and therefore the compounded ratios PQ × PR to Pqx Pr, and PS × PT to Ps × Pt are given. But from what we have demonstrated before, the ratio of Pq × Pr to Ps × Pt is given; and therefore also the ratio of PQ × PR to PS × PT.   Q.E.D.

LEMMA XVIII.

THE SAME THINGS SUPPOSED, IF THE RECTANGLE
PQ × PR OF THE LINES DRAWN TO THE TWO
OPPOSITE SIDES OF THE TRAPEZIUM IS TO THE
RECTANGLE PS × PT OF THOSE DRAWN TO
THE OTHER TWO SIDES IN A GIVEN RATIO, THE
POINT P, FROM WHENCE THOSE LINES ARE DRAWN,
WILL BE PLACED IN A CONIC SECTION DESCRIBED
ABOUT THE TRAPEZIUM.

Conceive a conic section to be described passing through the points A, B, C, D, and any one of the infinite number of points P, as for example p; I say, the point P will be always placed in this section. If you deny the thing, join AP cutting this conic section somewhere else, if possible, than in P, as in b. Therefore if from those points p and b, in the given angles to the sides of the trapezium, we draw the right lines pq, pr, ps, pt, and bk, bn, bf, bd, we shall have, as bk × bn to bf × bd so (by Lem. XVII) pq × pr to ps × pt; and so (by supposition). PQ × PR to PS × PT. And

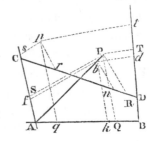

because of the similar trapezia bkAf, PQAS, as *bk* to *bf,* so PQ to PS. Wherefore by dividing the terms of the preceding proportion by the correspondent terms of this, we shall have *bn* to *bd* as PR to PT. And therefore the equiangular trapezia D*nbd,* DRPT, are similar, and consequently their diagonals D*b,* DP do coincide. Wherefore *b* falls in the intersection of the right lines AP, DP, and consequently coincides with the point P. And therefore the point P, wherever it is taken, falls to be in the assigned conic section.

Q.E.D.

COR. Hence if three right lines PQ, PR, PS, are drawn from a common point P, to as many other right lines given in position, AB, CD, AC, each. to each, in as many angles respectively given, and the rectangle PQ × PR under any two of the lines drawn be to the square of the third PS in a given ratio; the point P, from which the right lines are drawn, will be placed in a conic section that touches the lines AB, CD in A and C; and the contrary. For the position of the three right lines AB, CD, AC remaining the same, let the line BD approach to and coincide with the line AC; then let the line PT come likewise to coincide with the line PS; and the rectangle PS × PT will become PS^2 and the right lines AB, CD, which before did cut the curve in the points A and B, C and D, can no longer cut, but only touch, the curve in those coinciding points.

SCHOLIUM.

In this Lemma, the name of conic section is to be understood in a large sense, comprehending as well the rectilinear section through the vertex of the cone, as the circular one parallel to the base. For if the point p happens to be in a right line, by which the points A and D, or C and B are joined, the conic section will be changed into two right lines, one of which is that right line upon which the point p falls, and the other is a right line that joins the other two of the four points. If the two opposite angles of the trapezium taken together are equal to two right angles, and if the four lines PQ, PR, PS, PT, are drawn to the sides thereof at right angles, or any other equal angles, and the rectangle PQ × PR under two of the lines drawn PQ and PR, is equal to the rectangle PS × PT under the other two PS and PT, the conic section will become a circle. And the same thing will happen if the four lines are drawn in any angles, and the rectangle PQ × PR, under one pair of the lines drawn, is to the rectangle PS × PT under the other pair as the rectangle under the sines of the angles S, T, in which the two last lines PS, PT are drawn to the rectangle under the sines of the angles Q, R, in which the first two PQ, PR are drawn. In all other cases the locus of the point P will be one of the three figures which pass commonly by the name of the conic sections. But in room of the trapezium ABCD, we may substi-

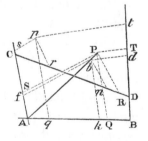

tute a quadrilateral figure whose two opposite sides cross one another like diagonals. And one or two of the four points A, B, C, D may be supposed to be removed to an infinite distance, by which means the sides of the figure which converge to those points, will become parallel; and in this case the conic section will pass through the other points, and will go the same way as the parallels in infinitum.

LEMMA XIX.

TO FIND A POINT P FROM WHICH IF FOUR RIGHT LINES PQ, PR, PS, PT ARE DRAWN TO AS MANY OTHER RIGHT LINES AB, CD, AC, BD, GIVEN BY POSITION, EACH TO EACH, AT GIVEN ANGLES, THE RECTANGLE PQ × PR, UNDER ANY TWO OF THE LINES DRAWN, SHALL BE TO THE RECTANGLE PS × PT, UNDER THE OTHER TWO, IN A GIVEN RATIO.

Suppose the lines AB, CD, to which the two right lines PQ, PR, containing one of the rectangles, are drawn to meet two other lines, given by position, in the points A, B, C, D. From one of those, as A, draw any right line AH, in which you would find the point P. Let this cut the opposite lines BD, CD, in H and I; and, because all the angles of the figure are given, the ratio of PQ to PA, and PA to PS, and therefore of PQ to PS, will be also given. Subducting this ratio from the given ratio of PQ × PR to PS × PT, the ratio of PR to PT will be given; and adding the given ratios of PI to PR, and PT to PH, the ratio of PI to PH, and therefore the point P will be given. Q.E.I.

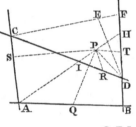

CoR. 1. Hence also a tangent may be drawn to any point D of the locus of all the points P. For the chord PD, where the points P and D meet, that is, where AH is drawn through the point D, becomes a tangent. In which case the ultimate ratio of the evanescent lines IP and PH will be found as above. Therefore draw CF parallel to AD, meeting BD in F, and cut it in E in the same ultimate ratio, then DE will be the tangent; because CF and the evanescent IH are parallel, and similarly cut in E and P.

CoR. 2. Hence also the locus of all the points P may be determined. Through any of the points A, B, C, D, as A, draw AE touching the locus, and through any other point B parallel to the tangent, draw BF meeting the locus in F; and find the point F by this Lemma. Bisect BF in G, and, drawing the indefinite line AG, this will be the position of the diameter to which BG and FG are ordinates. Let this AG meet the locus in H, and AH will be its diameter or latus transversum, to which the latus rectum will be as BG² to AG X, GH. If AG nowhere meets the locus, the line AH being infinite,

the locus will be a parabola; and its latus rectum corresponding to the diameter AG will be $\frac{BG^2}{AG}$. But if it does meet it anywhere, the locus will be an hyperbola, when the points A and H are placed on the same side the point G; and an ellipsis, if the point G falls between the points A and H; unless, perhaps, the angle AGB is a right angle, and at the same time BG² equal to the rectangle AGH, in which case the locus will be a circle.

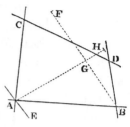

And so we have given in this Corollary a solution of that famous Problem of the ancients concerning four lines, begun by Euclid, and carried on by Apollonius; and this not an analytical calculus, but a geometrical composition, such as the ancients required.

LEMMA XX.

IF THE TWO OPPOSITE ANGULAR POINTS A AND P OF ANY PARALLELOGRAM ASPQ TOUCH ANY CONIC SECTION IN THE POINTS A AND P; AND THE SIDES AQ, AS OF ONE OF THOSE ANGLES, INDEFINITELY PRODUCED, MEET THE SAME CONIC SECTION IN B AND C; AND FROM THE POINTS OF CONCOURSE B AND C TO ANY FIFTH POINT D OF THE CONIC SECTION, TWO RIGHT LINES BD, CD ARE DRAWN MEETING THE TWO OTHER SIDES PS, PQ OF THE PARALLELOGRAM, INDEFINITELY PRODUCED IN T AND R; THE PARTS PR AND PT, CUT OFF FROM THE SIDES, WILL ALWAYS BE ONE TO THE OTHER IN A GIVEN RATIO. AND VICE VERSA, IF THOSE PARTS CUT OFF ARE ONE TO THE OTHER IN A GIVEN RATIO, THE LOCUS OF THE POINT D WILL BE A CONIC SECTION PASSING THROUGH THE FOUR POINTS A, B, C, P

CASE 1. Join BP, CP, and from the point D draw the two right lines DG, DE, of which the first DG shall be parallel to AB and meet PB, PQ, CA in H, I, G; and the other DE shall be parallel to AC, and meet PC, PS, AB, in F, K, E; and (by Lem. XVII)

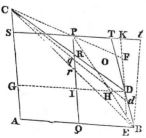

the rectangle DE × DF will be to the rectangle DG × DH in a given ratio. But PQ is to DE (or IQ) as PB to HB, and consequently as PT to DH; and by permutation PQ is to PT as DE to DH. Likewise PR is to DF as RC to DC, and therefore as (IG or) PS to DG; and by permutation PR is to PS as DF to DG; and, by compounding those ratios, the rectangle PQ × PR will

be to the rectangle PS × PT as the rectangle DE × DF is to the rectangle DG × DH and consequently in a given ratio. But PQ and PS are given, and therefore the ratio of PR to PT is given. Q.E.D.

CASE.. 2. But if PR and PT are supposed to be in a given ratio one to the other, then by going back again, by a like reasoning, it will follow that the rectangle DE × DF is to the rectangle DG × DH in a given ratio); and so the point D (by Lem. XVIII) will lie in a conic section passing through the points A, B, C, P, as its locus. Q.E.D.

COR. 1. Hence if we draw BC cutting PQ in r and in PT take Pt to Pr in the same ratio which PT has to PR; then B*t* will touch the conic section in the point B. For suppose the point D to coalesce with the point B, so that the chord BD vanishing, BT shall become a tangent, and CD and BT will coincide with CB and B*t*.

COR. 2. And, vice versa, if B*t* is a tangent, and the lines BD, CD meet in any point D of a conic section, PR will be to PT as Pr to Pt. And, on the contrary, if PR is to PT as Pr to P*t*, then BD and CD will meet in some point D of a conic section.

COR. 3. One conic section cannot cut another conic section in more than four points. For, if it is possible, let two conic sections pass through the five points A, B, C, P, O; and let the right line BD cut them in the points D, d, and the right line Cd cut the right line PQ in *q*. Therefore PR is to PT as Pq to PT: whence PR and P*q* are equal one to the other, against the supposition.

LEMMA XXI.

IF TWO MOVEABLE AND INDEFINITE RIGHT LINES BM, CM DRAWN THROUGH GIVEN POINTS B, C, AS POLES, DO BY THEIR POINT OF CONCOURSE M DESCRIBE A THIRD RIGHT LINE MN GIVEN BY POSITION; AND OTHER TWO INDEFINITE RIGHT LINES BD, CD ARE DRAWN, MAKING WITH THE FORMER TWO AT THOSE GIVEN POINTS B, C, GIVEN ANGLES, MBD, MCD : I SAY, THAT THOSE TWO RIGHT LINES BD, CD WILL BY THEIR POINT OF CONCOURSE D DESCRIBE A CONIC SECTION PASSING THROUGH THE POINTS B, C. AND, VICE VERSA, IF THE RIGHT LINES BD, CD DO BY THEIR POINT OF CONCOURSE D DESCRIBE A CONIC SECTION PASSING THROUGH THE GIVEN POINTS B, C, A, AND THE ANGLE DBM IS ALWAYS EQUAL TO THE GIVEN ANGLE ABC, AS WELL AS THE ANGLE DCM ALWAYS EQUAL TO THE GIVEN ANGLE; ACB, THE POINT M WILL LIE IN A RIGHT LINE GIVEN BY POSITION, AS ITS LOCUS.

For in the right line MN let a point N be given, and when the moveable point M falls on the immoveable point N, let the moveable point D fall on an immovable point P. Join CN, BN, CP BP and from the point P draw the right lines PT, PR meeting BD,

CD in T and R, and making the angle BPT equal to the given angle BNM, and the angle CPR equal to the given angle CNM. Wherefore since (by supposition) the angles MBD, NBP are equal, as also the angles MCD, NCP, take away the angles NBD and NCD that are common, and there will remain the angles NBM and PBT, NCM and PCR equal; and therefore the triangles NBM, PBT are similar, as also the triangles NCM, PCR. Wherefore PT is to NM as PB to NB; and PR to NM as PC to NC. But the points, B, C, N, P are immovable: wherefore PT and PR have a given ratio to NM and consequently a given ratio

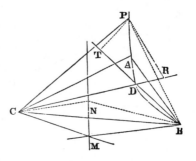

between themselves; and therefore, (by Lemma XX) the point D wherein the moveable right lines BT and CR perpetually concur, will be placed in a conic section passing through the points B, C, P.   Q.E.D.

And, *vice versa*, if the moveable point D lies in a conic section passing through the given points B, C, A; and the angle DBM is always equal to the given angle ABC, and the angle DCM always equal to the given angle ACB, and when the point D falls suc-

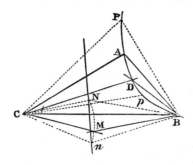

cessively on any two immovable points *p*, P, of the conic section, the moveable point M falls successively on two immovable points *n*, N. Through these points *n*, N, draw the right line *n*N: this line *n*N will be the perpetual locus of that moveable point M. For, if possible, let the point M be placed in any curve line. Therefore the point D will be placed in a conic section passing through the five points B, C, A, *p*, P, when the point M is perpetually placed in a

curve line. But from what was demonstrated before, the point D will be also placed in a conic section passing through the same five points B, C, A, *p*, P, when the point M is perpetually placed in a right line. Wherefore the two conic sections will both pass through the same five points, against Corol. 3, Lem. XX. It is therefore absurd to suppose that the point M is placed in a curve line.   Q.E.D.

PROPOSITION XXII. PROBLEM XIV.

TO DESCRIBE A TRAJECTORY THAT SHALL PASS THROUGH FIVE GIVEN POINTS.

Let the five given points be A, B, C, P, D. From any one of them, as A, to any other two as B, C, which may be called the poles, draw the right lines AB, AC, and parallel to those the lines TPS, PRQ through the fourth point P. Then from the two

poles B, C, draw through the fifth point D two indefinite lines BDT, CRD, meeting with the last drawn lines TPS, PRQ (the former with the former, and the latter with

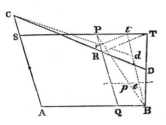

the latter) in T and R. Then drawing, the right line tr parallel to TR, cutting off from the right lines PT, PR, any segments P*t*, P*r*, proportional to PT, PR; and if through their extremities, t, r, and the poles B, C, the right lines B*t*, C*r* are drawn, meeting in *d*, that point *d* will be placed in the trajectory required. For (by Lem. XX) that point d is placed in a conic section passing through the four points A, B, C, P; and the lines R*r*, T*t* vanishing, the point d comes to coincide with the point D. Wherefore the conic section passes through the five points A, B, C, P, D.   Q.E.D.

THE SAME OTHERWISE.

Of the given points join any three, as A, B, C; and about two of them B, C, as poles, making the angles ABC, ACB of a given magnitude to revolve, apply the legs BA, CA, first to the point D, then to the point P, and mark the points M, N, in which the other legs BL, CL intersect each other in both cases.

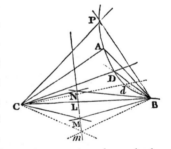

Draw the indefinite right line MN, and let those moveable angles revolve about their poles B, C, in such manner that the intersection, which is now supposed to be m, of the legs BL, CL, or BM, CM, may always fall in that indefinite right line MN; and the intersection, which is now supposed to be d, of the legs BA CA, or BD, CD, will describe the trajectory required, PAD B. For (by Lem. XXI) the point d will be placed in a conic section passing through the points B, C; and when the point m comes to coincide with the points L, M, N, the point d will (by construction) come to coincide with the points A, D, P. Wherefore a conic section will be described that shall pass through the five points A, B, C, P, D.

Q.E.F.

COR. 1. Hence a right line may be readily drawn which shall be a tangent to the trajectory in any given point B. Let the point d come to coincide with the point B, and the right line B*d* will become the tangent required.

COR. 2. Hence also may be found the centres, diameters, and latera recta of the trajectories, as in Cor. 2, Lem. XIX.

SCHOLIUM.

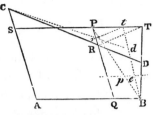

The former of these constructions will become something more simple by joining BP, and in that line, produced, if need be, taking B*p* to BP as PR is to PT; and through *p* draw the indefinite right line *pe* parallel to S PT, and in that line pe taking always *pe* equal to P*r*, and draw the right lines B*e*, C*r* to meet in *d*. For since P*r* to P*t*, PR to PT, *p*B to PB, *pe* to P*t*, are all in the same ratio, *pe* and P*r* will be always be equal. After this manner the points of the trajectory are most readily found, unless you would rather describe the curve mechanically, as in the second construction.

PROPOSITION XXIII. PROBLEM XV.

To describe a trajectory that shall pass through four given points, and touch a right line given by position.

CASE. 1. Suppose that HB is the given tangent, B the point of contact, and C, D, P, the three other given points. Join BC, and draw PS parallel to BH, and PQ parallel to BC; complete the parallelogram BSPQ. Draw BD cutting SP in T, and CD cutting PQ in R. Lastly, draw any line t*r* parallel to TR, cutting off from PQ, PS, the segments P*r*, P*t* proportional to PR, PT respectively; and draw C*r*, B*t* their point of concourse *d* will (by Lem. XX) always fall on the trajectory to be described.

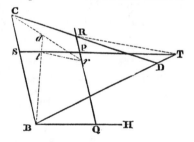

The same otherwise.

Let the angle CBH of a given magnitude revolve about the pole B, as also the rectilinear radius DC, both ways produced, about the pole C. Mark the points M, N, on which the leg BC of the angle cuts that radius when BH, the other leg thereof, meets the same radius in the points P and D. Then drawing the indefinite line MN, let that radius CP or CD and the leg BC of the angle perpetually meet in this line; and the point of concourse of the other leg BH with the radius will delineate the trajectory required.

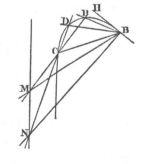

For if in the constructions of the preceding Problem the point A comes to a coincidence with the point B, the lines CA and CB will coincide, and the line AB, in its last situation, will become the tangent BH; and therefore the constructions there set down will become the same with the constructions here described. Wherefore the concourse of the leg BH with the radius will describe a conic section passing through the points C, D, P, and touching the line BH in the point B. Q.E.F.

CASE. 2. Suppose the four points B, C, D, P, given, being situated without the tangent HI. Join each two by the lines BD, CP meeting in G, and cutting the tangents in H and L. Cut the tangent in A in such manner that HA may be to IA as the rectangle under a mean proportional between CG and GP, and a mean proportional between

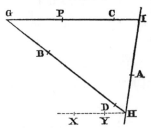

BH and HD is to a rectangle under a mean proportional between GD and GB, and a mean proportional between PI and IC, and A will be the point of contact. For if HX, a parallel to the right line PI, cuts the trajectory in any points X and Y, the point A (by the properties of the conic sections) will come to be so placed, that HA^2 will become to AI^2 in a ratio that is compounded out of the ratio of the rectangle XHY to the rectangle BHD, or of the rectangle CGP to the rectangle DGB; and the ratio of the rectangle BHD to the rectangle PIC. But after the point of contact A is found, the trajectory will be described as in the first Case. Q.E.F. But the point A may be taken either between or without the points H and I, upon which account a twofold trajectory may be described.

PROPOSITION XXIV. PROBLEM XVI.

To describe a trajectory that shall pass through three given points, and touch two right lines given by position.

Suppose HI, KL to be the given tangents, and B, C, D, the given points. Through any two of those points, as B, D, draw the indefinite right line BD meeting the tangents in the points H, K. Then likewise through any other two of these points, as C, D, draw the indefinite right line CD meeting the tangents in the points I, L. Cut the lines drawn in R and S, so that HR may be to KR as the mean proportional between BH and HD is to the mean proportional between BK and KD; and IS to LS as the mean proportional between CI and ID is to the mean proportional between CL and LD. But you may cut, at pleasure, either within or between the

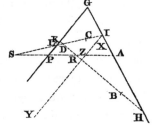

points K and H, I and L, or without them; then draw RS cutting the tangents in A and P, and A and P will be the points of contact. For if A and P are supposed to be the points of contact, situated anywhere else in the tangents, and through any of the points H, I, K, L, as I, situated in either tangent HI, a right line IY is drawn parallel to the other tangent KL, and meeting the curve in X and Y, and in that right line there be taken IZ equal to a mean proportional between IX and IY, the rectangle XIY or IZ², will (by the properties of the conic sections) be to LP² as the rectangle CID is to the rectangle CLD, that is (by the construction), as SI is to SL², and therefore IZ is to LP as SI to SL. Wherefore the points S, P, Z, are in one right line. Moreover, since the tangents meet in G, the rectangle XIY or IZ² will (by the properties of the conic sections) be to IA² as GP² is to GA², and consequently IZ will be to IA as GP to GA. Wherefore the points P, Z, A, lie in one right line, and therefore the points S, P, and A are in one right line. And the same argument will prove that the points R., P, and A are in one right line. Wherefore the points of contact A and P lie in the right line RS. But after these points are found, the trajectory may be described, as in the first Case of the preceding Problem.   Q.E.F.

In this Proposition, and Case 2 of the foregoing, the constructions are the same, whether the right line XY cut the trajectory in X and Y, or not; neither do they depend upon that section. But the constructions being demonstrated where that right line does cut the trajectory, the constructions where it does not are also known; and therefore, for brevity's sake, I omit any farther demonstration of them.

LEMMA XXII.

TO TRANSFORM FIGURES INTO OTHER FIGURES OF THE SAME KIND.

Suppose that any figure HGI is to be transformed. Draw, at pleasure, two parallel lines AO, BL, cutting any third line AB, given by position, in A and B, and from any point G of the figure, draw out any right line GD, parallel to OA, till it meet the right line AB. Then from any given point O in the line OA, draw to the point D the right line OD, meeting BL in d; and from the point of concourse raise the right line dg containing any given angle with the right line BL, and having such ratio to Od as DG has to OD; and g will be the point in the new figure hgi, corresponding to the point G. And in like manner the several points of the first figure will give as many correspondent points of the new figure. If we therefore conceive the point G to be carried

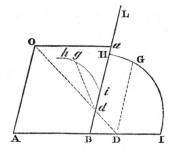

along by a continual motion through all the points of the first figure, the point g will be likewise carried along by a continual motion through all the points of the new figure, and describe the same. For distinction's sake, let us call DG the first ordinate, dg, the new ordinate, AD the first abscissa, ad the new abscissa; O the pole. OD the abscinding radius, OA the first ordinate radius, and Oa (by which the parallelogram OABa is completed) the new ordinate radius.

I say, then, that if the point G is placed in a right line given by position, the point g will be also placed in a right line given by position. If the point G is placed in a conic section, the point g, will be likewise placed in a conic section. And here I understand the circle as one of the conic sections. But farther,. if the point G is placed in a line of the third analytical order, the point g will also be placed in a line of the third order, and so on in curve lines of higher orders. The two lines in which the points G, g, are placed, will be always of the same analytical order. For as ad is to OA, so are Od to OD, dg, to DG, and AB to AD; and therefore AD is equal to $\frac{OA \times AB}{ad}$, and DG equal to $\frac{OA \times dg}{ad}$. Now if the point G is placed in a right line, and therefore, in any equation by which the relation between the abscissa AD and the ordinate GD is expressed, those indetermined lines AD and DG rise no higher than to one dimension, by writing this equation $\frac{OA \times AB}{ad}$ in place of AD, and $\frac{OA \times dg}{ad}$ in place of DG, a new equation will be produced, in which the new abscissa ad and new ordinate dg rise only to one dimension; and which therefore must denote a right line. But if AD and DG (or either of them) had risen to two dimensions in the first equation, ad and dg would likewise have risen to two dimensions in the second equation. And so on in three or more dimensions. The indetermined lines, ad, dg in the second equation, and AD, DG, in the first, will always rise to the same number of dimensions; and therefore the lines in which the points G, g, are placed are of the same analytical order.

I say farther, that if any right line touches the curve line in the first figure, the same right line transferred the same way with the curve into the new figure will touch that curve line in the new figure, and *vice versa*. For if any two points of the curve in the first figure are supposed to approach one the other till they come to coincide, the same points transferred will approach one the other till they come to coincide in the new figure; and therefore the right lines with which those points are joined will become together tangents of the curves in both figures. I might have given demonstrations of these assertions in a more geometrical form; but I study to be brief.

Wherefore if one rectilinear figure is to be transformed into another, we need only transfer the intersections of the right lines of which the first figure consists, and through the transferred intersections to draw right lines in the new figure. But if a curvilinear figure is to be transformed, we must transfer the points, the tangents, and other right lines, by means of which the curve line is defined. This Lemma is of use in

the solution of the more difficult Problems; for thereby we may transform the proposed figures, if they are intricate, into others that are more simple. Thus any right lines converging to a point are transformed into parallels, by taking for the first ordinate radius any right line that passes through the point of concourse of the converging lines, and that because their point of concourse is by this means made to go off *in infinitum*; and parallel lines are such as tend to a point infinitely remote. And after the problem is solved in the new figure, if by the inverse operations we transform the new into the first figure, we shall have the solution required.

This Lemma is also of use in the solution of solid problems. For as often as two conic sections occur, by the intersection of which a problem may be solved, any one of them may be transformed, if it is an hyperbola or a parabola, into an ellipsis, and then this ellipsis may be easily changed into a circle. So also a right line and a conic section, in the construction of plane problems, may be transformed into a right line and a circle.

PROPOSITION XXV. PROBLEM XVII.

To describe a trajectory that shall pass through two given points, and touch three right lines given by position.

Through the concourse of any two of the tangents one with the other, and the concourse of the third tangent with the right line which passes through the two given points, draw an indefinite right line; and, taking this line for the first ordinate radius, transform the figure by the preceding Lemma into a new figure. In this figure those two tangents will become parallel to each other, and the third tangent will be parallel to the right line that passes through the two given points. Suppose *hi*, *kl* to be those two parallel tangents, *ik* the third tangent, and *hl* a right line parallel thereto, passing through those points *a*, *b*, through which the conic section ought to pass in this new figure; and completing the parallelogram *hikl*, let the right lines *hi*, *ik*, *kl* be so cut in *c*, *d*, *e*, that *hc* may be to the square root of the rectangle *ahb*, *ic*, to *id*, and *ke* to *kd*, as the sum of the right lines *hi* and *kl* is to the sum of the three lines, the first whereof is the right line *ik*, and the other two are the square roots of the rectangles *ahb* and *alb*, and *c*, *d*, *e*, will be the points of contact. For by the properties of the conic sections, hc^2 to the rectangle *ahb*, and ic^2 to id^2, and ke^2 to kd^2, and el^2 to the rectangle *alb*, are all in the same ratio; and therefore *hc* to the square root of *ahb*, *ic* to *id*, *ke* to *kd*, and *el* to the square root of *alb*, are in the subduplicate of that ratio; and

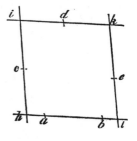

by composition, in the given ratio of the sum of all the antecedents *hi + kl*, to the sum of all the consequents √*ahb* + *ik* +√*alb*. Wherefore from that given ratio we have the points of contact c, d, e, in the new figure. By the inverted operations of the last Lemma, let those points be transferred into the first figure, and the trajectory will be there described by Prob. XIV. Q.E.F. But according as the points *a, b*, fall between the points *k, l*, or without them, the points *c, d, e*, must be taken either between the points, *h, i, k, l*, or without them. If one of the points *a, b*, falls between the points *h, i*, and the other without the points *h, l*, the Problem is impossible.

PROPOSITION XXVI. PROBLEM XVIII.

To describe a trajectory that shall pass through a given point, and touch four right lines given by position.

From the common intersections, of any two of the tangents to the common intersection of the other two, draw an indefinite right line; and taking this line for the first ordinate radius, transform the figure (by Lem. XXII) into a new figure, and the two pairs of tangents, each of which before concurred in the first ordinate radius, will now become parallel. Let *hi* and *kl*, *ik* and *hl*, be those pairs of parallels completing the parallelogram *hikl*. And let *p* be the point in this new figure corresponding to the given point in the first figure. Through O the centre of the figure draw *pq*: and O*q* being equal to O*p*, *q* will be the other point through which the conic section must pass in this new figure. Let this point be transferred, by the inverse operation of Lem. XXII into the first figure, and there we shall have the two points through which the trajectory is to be described. But through those points that trajectory may be described by Prop. XVII.

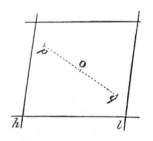

LEMMA XXIII.

If two right lines, as AC, BD given by position, and terminating in given points A, B are in a given ratio one to the other, and the right line CD, by which the indetermined points C, D are joined is cut in K in a given ratio; I say, that the point K will be placed in a right line given by position.

For let the right lines AC, BD meet in E, and in BE take BG to AE as BD is to AC, and let FD be always equal to the given line EG; and, by construction, EC will

be to GD, that is, to EF, as AC to BD, and therefore in a given ratio; and therefore the triangle EFC will be given in kind. Let CF be cut in L so as CL may be to CF in the ratio of CK to CD; and because that is a given ratio, the triangle EFL will be given in kind, and therefore the point L will be placed in the right line EL given by position. Join LK, and the triangles CLK, CFD will be similar; and because FD is a given line, and LK is to FD) in a given ratio, LK will be also given To this let EH be taken equal, and ELKH will be

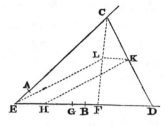

always a parallelogram. And therefore the point K is always placed in the side HK (given by position) of that parallelogram.   Q.E.D.

COR. Because the figure EFLC is given in kind, the three right lines EF, EL, and EC, that is, GD, HK, and EC, will have given ratios to each other.

LEMMA XXIV.

IF THREE RIGHT LINES, TWO WHEREOF ARE PARALLEL, AND
GIVEN BY POSITION, TOUCH ANY CONIC SECTION; I SAY,
THAT THE SEMI-DIAMETER OF THE SECTION WHICH IS
PARALLEL TO THOSE TWO IS A MEAN PROPORTIONAL
BETWEEN THE SEGMENTS OF THOSE TWO THAT ARE
INTERCEPTED BETWEEN THE POINTS OF CONTACT AND
THE THIRD TANGENT.

Let AF, GB be the two parallels touching the conic section ADB in A and B; EF the third right line touching the conic section in I, and meeting the two former tangents in F and G, and let CD be the semi-diameter of the figure parallel to those tangents; I say, that AF, CD, BG are continually proportional.

For if the conjugate diameters AB, DM meet the tangent FG in E and H, and cut one the other in C, and the parallelogram IKCL be completed; from the nature of the conic sections, EC will be to CA, as CA to CL; and so by division, EC − CA to CA − CL, or EA to AL; and by composition, EA to EA + AL or EL, as EC to EC+CA or EB; and therefore (because of

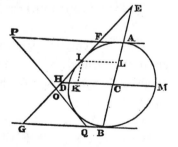

the similitude of the triangles EAF, EI, I, ECH, EBG) AF is to Ll as CH to BG. Likewise, from the nature of the conic sections, LI (or CK) is to CD as CD to CH; and therefore (*ex æquo perturbate*) AF is to CD as CD to BG.   Q.E.D.

Cor. 1. Hence if two tangents FG, PQ meet two parallel tangents AF, BG in F and G, P and Q, and cut one the other in O; AF (*ex æquoperturbate*) will be to BQ as AP to BG, and by division, as FP to GQ, and therefore as FO to OG.

Cor. 2. Whence also the two right lines PG, FQ drawn through the points P and G, F and Q, will meet in the right line ACB passing through the centre of the figure and the points of contact A, B.

LEMMA XXV.

If four sides of a parallelogram indefinitely produced touch any conic section, and are cut by a fifth tangent; I say, that, taking those segments of any two conterminous sides that terminate in opposite angles of the parallelogram, either segment is to the side from which it is cut off as that part of the other conterminous side which is intercepted between the point of contact and the third side is to the other segment.

Let the four sides ML, IK, KL, MI, of the parallelogram MLIK touch the conic section in A, B, C, D; and let the fifth tangent FQ out those sides in F, Q, H, and E;

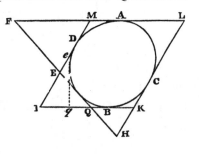

and taking the segments ME, KQ of the sides MI, KI, or the segments KH, MF of the sides KL, ML, I say, that ME is to MI as BK to KQ; and KH to KL as AM to MF. For, by Cor. 1 of the preceding Lemma, ME is to EI as (AM or) BK to BQ; and, by composition, ME is to MI as BK to KQ. Q.E.D. Also KH is to HL as (BK or) AM to AF; and by division, KH to KL as AM to MF. Q.E.D.

Cor. 1. Hence if a parallelogram IKLM described about a given conic section is given, the rectangle KQ × ME, as also the rectangle KH × MF equal thereto, will be given. For, by reason of the similar triangles KQH, MFE, those rectangles are equal.

Cor. 2. And if a sixth tangent *eq* is drawn meeting the tangents KI, MI in *q* and *e*, the rectangle KQ × ME will be equal to the rectangle K*q* × M*e*, and KQ will be to M*e* as K*q* to ME, and by division as Q*q* to E*e*.

Cor. 3. Hence, also, if E*q*, *e*Q, are joined and bisected, and a right line is drawn through the points of bisection, this right line will pass through the centre of the conic

section. For since Q*q* is to E*e* as KQ to M*e*, the same right line will pass through the middle of all the lines E*q*, *e*Q, MK (by Lem, XXIII), and the middle point of the right line MK is the centre of the section.

PROPOSITION XXVII. PROBLEM XIX.

TO DESCRIBE A TRAJECTORY THAT MAY TOUCH FIVE RIGHT LINES GIVEN BY POSITION.

Supposing ABG, BCF, GCD, FDE, EA to be the tangents given by position. Bisect in M and N, AF, BE, the diagonals of the quadrilateral figure ABPE contained under any four of them; and (by Cor. 3, Lem. XXV) the right line MN drawn through the points bisection will pass through the centre of the trajectory. Again, bisect in P and Q the diagonals (if I may so call them) BD, GF of the quadrilateral figure BGDF contained under any other four tangents, and the right line PQ drawn through the points of bisection will pass through the centre of the trajectory; and therefore the centre will be given in the

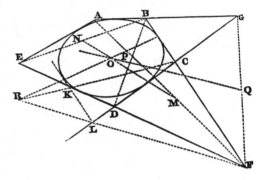

concourse of the bisecting lines. Suppose it to be O. Parallel to any tangent BC draw KL at such distance that the centre O may be placed in the middle between the parallels; this KL will touch the trajectory to be described. Let this cut any other two tangents GCD, FDE, in L and K. Through the points C and K, F and L, where the tangents not parallel, CL, FK meet the parallel tangents CF, KL, draw CK, FL meeting in R; and the right line OR drawn and produced, will cut the parallel tangents CF, KL, in the points of contact. This appears from Cor. 2, Lem. XXIV. And by the same method the other points of contact may be found, and then the trajectory may be described by Prob. XIV.   Q.E.F.

SCHOLIUM.

Under the preceding Propositions are comprehended those Problems wherein either the centres or asymptotes of the trajectories are given. For when points and tangents and the centre are given, as many other points and as many other tangents are given at an equal distance on the other side of the centre. And an asymptote is to be considered as a tangent, and its infinitely remote extremity (if we may say so) is a point of contact. Conceive the point of contact of any tangent removed *in infinitum*, and the

tangent will degenerate into an asymptote, and the constructions of the preceding Problems will be changed into the constructions of those Problems wherein the asymptote is given.

After the trajectory is described, we may find its axes and foci in this manner. In the construction and figure of Lem. XXI, let those legs BP, CP, of the moveable angles PBN, PCN, by the concourse of which the trajectory was described, be made parallel one to the other; and retaining that position, let them revolve about their poles B, C, in that figure. In the mean while let the other legs CN, BN, of those angles, by their concourse K or k, describe the circle BKGC. Let O be the centre of this circle; and from this centre upon the ruler MN, wherein those legs CN, BN did concur while the trajectory was described,

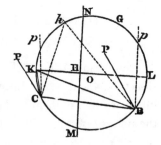

let fall the perpendicular OH meeting the circle in K and L. And when those other legs CK,BK meet in the point K that is nearest to the ruler, the first legs CP, BP will be parallel to the greater axis, and perpendicular on the lesser; and the contrary will happen if those legs meet in the remotest point L. Whence if the centre of the trajectory is given the axes will be given; and those being given, the foci will be readily found.

But the squares of the axes are one to the other as KH to LH, and thence it is easy to describe a trajectory given in kind through four given points. For if two of the given points are made the poles C, B, the third will give the moveable angles PCK, PBK; but those being given, the circle BGKC may be described. Then, because the trajectory is given in kind, the ratio of OH to OK, and therefore OH itself, will be given. About the centre O, with the interval OH, describe another circle, and the right line that touches this circle, and passes through the concourse of the legs CK, BK, when the first legs CP, BP meet in the fourth given point, will be the ruler MN, by means

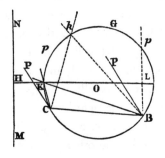

of which the trajectory may be described. Whence also on the other hand a trapezium given in kind (excepting a few cases that are impossible) maybe inscribed in a given conic section.

There are also other Lemmas, by the help of which trajectories given in kind may be described through given points, and touching given lines. Of such a sort is this, that if a right line is drawn through any point given by position, that may cut a given conic section in two points, and the distance of the intersections is bisected, the point of bisection will touch another

conic section of the same kind with the former, and having its axes parallel to the axes of the former. But I hasten to things of greater use.

LEMMA XXVI.

To place the three angles of a triangle, given both in kind and magnitude, in respect of as many right lines given by position, provided they are not all parallel among themselves, in such manner that the several angles may touch the several lines.

Three indefinite right lines AB, AC BC are given by position, and it is required so to place the triangle DEF that its angle D may touch the line AB, its angle E the line AC, and its angle F the line BC. Upon DE, DF, and EF, describe three segments of circles DRE, DGF; EMF, capable of angles equal to the angles BAC, ABC, ACB respectively. But those segments are to be described towards such sides of the lines DE, DF, EF, that the letters DRED may turn round about in the same order with the letters BACB; the letters DGFD in the same order with the letters ABCA; and the letters

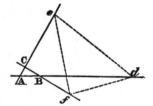

EMFE in the same order with the letters ACBA; then, completing those segments into entire circles let the two former circles cut one the other in G, and suppose P and Q to be their centres. Then joining GP, PQ, take Ga to AB as GP is to PQ; and about the centre G, with the interval Ga, describe a circle that may cut the first circle DGE in a. Join aD cutting the second circle DFG in b, as well as aE cutting the third circle EMF in c. Complete the figure ABCdef similar and equal to the figure abcDEF: I say, the thing is done.

For drawing Fc meeting aD in n, and joining aG, bG, QG, QD, PD, by construction the angle EaD is equal to the angle CAB, and the angle F equal to the angle ACB; and therefore the triangle anc equiangular to the triangle ABC. Wherefore the angle anc or FnD is equal to the angle ABC, and consequently to the angle FbD; and therefore the point n falls on the point b. Moreover the angle GPQ, which is half the angle GPD at the centre, is equal to the angle GaD at the circumference; and the angle GQP, which is half the angle GQD at the centre, is equal to the complement to two right angles of the angle GbD at the circumference, and therefore equal to the angle

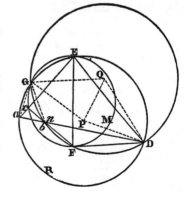

G*ba*. Upon which account the triangles GPQ, G*ab*, are similar, and G*a* is to *ab* as GP to PQ; that is (by, construction), as G*a* to AB. Wherefore *ab* and AB are equal; and consequently the triangles *abc*, ABC, which we have now proved to be similar, are also equal. And therefore since the angles D, E, F, of the triangle DEF do respectively touch the sides *ab*, *ac*, *bc* of the triangle *abc*, the figure ABC*def* may be completed similar and equal to the figure *abc*DEF, and by completing it the Problem will be solved.   Q.E.F.

Cor. Hence a right line may be drawn whose parts given in length may be intercepted between three right lines given by position. Suppose the triangle DEF, by the access of its point D to the side EF, and by having the sides DE, DF placed *in directum* to be changed into a right line whose given part DE is to be interposed between the right lines AB, AC given by position; and its given part DF is to be interposed between the right lines AB, BC, given by position; then, by applying the preceding construction to this case, the Problem will be solved.

PROPOSITION XXVII. PROBLEM XX.

To describe a trajectory given both in kind and
magnitude, given parts of which shall be interposed
between three right lines given by position.

Suppose a trajectory is to be described that may be similar and equal to the curve line DEF, and may be cut by three right lines AB, AC, BC, given by position, into parts DE and EF, similar and equal to the given parts of this curve line.

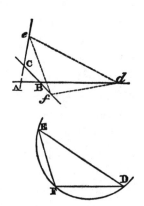

Draw the right lines DE, EF, DF: and place the angles D, E, F, of this triangle DEF, so as to touch those right lines given by position (by Lem. XXVI). Then about the triangle describe the trajectory, similar and equal to the curve DEF.   Q.E.F.

LEMMA XXVII.

To describe a trapezium given in kind, the angles
whereof may be so placed, in respect of four right
lines given by position, that are neither all
parallel among themselves, nor converge to one
common point, that the several angles may touch
the several lines.

Let the four right lines ABC, AD, BD, CE, be given by position; the first cutting the second in A, the third in B, and the fourth in C; and suppose a trapezium *fghi* is to be described that may be similar to the trapezium FGHI, and whose angle *f*, equal to the given angle F, may touch the right line ABC; and the other angles *g, h, i*, equal to the other given angles, G, H, I, may touch the other lines AD, BD, CE, respectively. Join FH, and upon FG, FH, FI describe as many segments of circles FSG, FTH, FVI, the first of which FSG may be capable of an angle equal to the angle BAD; the second FTH capable of an angle equal to the angle CBD; and the third FVI of an angle equal to the angle ACE. But the segments are to be described towards those sides of the lines FG, FH, FI, that the circular order of the letters FSGF may be the same as of the let-

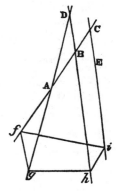

ters BADB, and that the letters FTHF may turn about in the same order as the letters CBDC and the letters FVIF in the same order as the letters ACEA. Complete the segments into entire circles, and let P be the centre of the first circle FSG, Q the centre of the second FTH. Join and produce both ways the line PQ, and in it take QR in the same ratio to PQ as BC has to AB. But QR is to be taken towards that side of the point Q, that the order of the letters P, Q, R may be the same as of the letters A, B, C; and about the centre R with the interval RF describe a fourth circle FN*c* cutting the third circle FVI in *c*. Join F*c* cutting the first circle in *a*, and the second in *b*. Draw *a*G, *b*H, *c*I, and let the figure ABC*fghi* be made similar to the figure *abc*FGHI; and the trapezium *fghi* will be that which was required to be described.

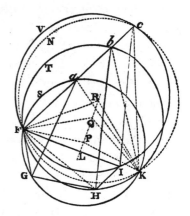

For let the two first circles FSG, FTH cut one the other in K; join PK, QK, RK, *a*K, *b*K, *c*K, and produce QP to L. The angles F*a*K, F*b*K, F*c*K at the circumferences are the halves of the angles FPK, FQK, FRK, at the centres, and therefore equal to LPK, LQK, LRK, the halves of those angles. Wherefore the figure PQRK is equiangular and sim-

ilar to the figure *abc*K, and consequently *ab* is to *bc* as PQ to QR, that is, as AB to BC. But by construction, the angles *f*A*g*, *f*B*h*, *f*C*i*, are equal to the angles F*a*G, F*b*H, F*c*I. And therefore the figure ABC may be completed similar to the figure *abc*FGHI. Which done a trapezium *fghi* will be constructed similar to the trapezium FGHI, and which by its angles *f, g, h, i* will touch the right lines ABC, AD, BD, CE.   Q.E.F.

COR. Hence a right line may be drawn whose parts intercepted in a given order, between four right lines given by position, shall have a given proportion among themselves. Let the angles FGH, GHI, be so far increased that the right lines FG, GH, HI, may lie *in directum*; and by constructing the Problem in this case, a right line *fghi* will be drawn, whose parts *fg*, *gh*, *hi*, intercepted between the four right lines given by position, AB and AD, AD and BD, BD and CE, will be one to another as the lines FG, GH, HI, and will observe the same order among themselves. But the same thing may be more readily done in this manner.

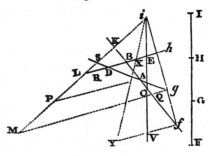

Produce AB to K and BD to L, so as BK may be to AB as HI to GH; and DL to BD as GI to FG; and join KL meeting the right line CE in *i*. Produce *i*L to M, so as LM may be to *i*L as GH to HI; then draw MQ parallel to LB, and meeting the right line AD in *g*, and join *gi* cutting AB, BD in *f*, *h*; I say, the thing, is done.

For let M*g* cut the right line AB in Q, and AD the right line KL in S, and draw AP parallel to BD, and meeting *i*L in P, and *g*M to L*h* (*g*, to *hi*, M*i* to L*i*, GI to HI, AK to BK) and AP to BL, will be in the same ratio. Cut DL in R, so as DL to RL may be in that same ratio; and because *g*S to *g*M, AS to AP, and DS to DL are proportional; therefore (*ex æquo*) as *g*S to L*h*, so will AS be to BL, and DS to RL; and mixtly, BL, – RL to L*h* – BL, as AS – DS to *g*S – AS. That is, BR is to B*h* as AD is to A*g*, and therefore as BD to *g*Q. And alternately BR is to BD as B*h* to *g*Q, or as *fh* to *fg*. But by construction the line BL was cut in D and R in the same ratio as the line FI in G and H; and therefore BR is to BD as FH to FG. Wherefore *fh* is to *fg* as FH to FG. Since, therefore, *gi* to *hi* likewise is as M*i* to L*i*, that is, as GI to HI, it is manifest that the lines FI, *fi*, are similarly out in G and H, *g* and *h*.   Q.E.F.

In the construction of this Corollary, after the line LK is drawn cutting CE in *i*, we may produce *i*E to V, so as EV may be to E*i* as FH to HI, and then draw V parallel to BD. It will come to the same, if about the centre *i* with an interval IH, we describe a circle cutting BD in X, and produce *i*X to Y so as *i*Y may be equal to IF, and then draw Y*f* parallel to BD.

Sir Christopher Wren and Dr. Wallis have long ago given other solutions of this Problem.

PROPOSITION XXIX. PROBLEM XXI

TO DESCRIBE A TRAJECTORY GIVEN IN KIND, THAT MAY BE CUT
BY FOUR RIGHT LINES GIVEN BY POSITION, INTO PARTS GIVEN
IN ORDER, KIND, AND PROPORTION.

Suppose a trajectory is to be described that may be similar to the curve line FGHI, and whose parts, similar and proportional to the parts FG, GH, HI of the other, may be intercepted between the right lines AB and AD, AD, and BD, BD and CE given by position, viz., the first between the first pair of those lines, the second between the second, and the third between the third. Draw the right lines FG, GH, HI, FI; and (by Lem. XXVII) describe a trapezium *fghi* that may be similar to the trapezium FGHI and whose angles *f, g, h, i*, may touch the right lines given by position AB, AD, BD, CE, severally according to their order. And then about this trapezium describe a trajectory, that trajectory will be similar to the curve line FGHI.

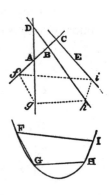

SCHOLIUM.

This problem may be likewise constructed in the following manner. Joining FG, GH, HI, FI, produce GF to V, and join FH, IG, and make the angles CAK, DAL equal to the angles FGH, VFH. Let AK, AL meet the right line BD in K and L, and thence draw KM, LN, of which let KM make the angle AKM equal to the angle GHI, and be itself to AK as HI is to GH; and let LN make the angle ALN equal to the angle FHI, and be itself to AL as HI to FH. But AK, KM, AL, LN are to be drawn towards those sides of the lines AD, AK, AL, that the letters CAKMC, ALKA, DALND may be carried round in the same order as the letters FGHIF; and draw MN meeting the right line CE in *i*. Make the angle *i*EP equal to the angle IGF, and let PE be to E*i* as FG to GI; and through P draw PQ*f* that may with the right line ADE contain an angle PQE equal to the angle FIG, and may meet the right line AB in *f*, and join *fi*.

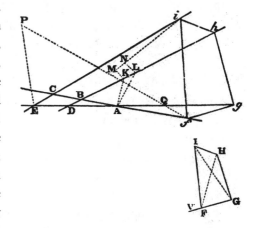

But PE and PQ are to be drawn towards those sides of the lines CE, PE, that the circular order of the letters PF P and PEQP may be the same as of the letters FGHIF; and if upon the line *fi*, in the same order of letters, and similar to the trapezium FGHI, a trapezium *fghi* is constructed, and a trajectory given in kind is circumscribed about it, the Problem will be solved.

So far concerning the finding of the orbits. It remains that we determine the motions of bodies in the orbits so found.

SECTION VI.

How the motions are to be found in given orbits.

PROPOSITION XXX. PROBLEM XXII.

TO FIND AT ANY ASSIGNED TIME THE PLACE OF A BODY
MOVING IN A GIVEN PARABOLIC TRAJECTORY.

Let S be the focus, and A the principal vertex of the parabola; and suppose 4AS 3 M equal to the parabolic area to be out off APS, which either was described by the radius SP, since the body's departure from the vertex, or is to be described thereby before its arrival there. Now the quantity of that area to be cut off is known from the time which is proportional to it. Bisect AS in G, and erect the perpendicular GH equal to 3M, and a circle described about the centre H, with the interval HS, will cut the parabola in the place P required. For

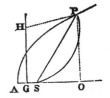

letting fall PO perpendicular on the axis, and drawing PH, there will be AG2 + GH2 $(=HP2= \overline{AO-AG}^2+ \overline{PO-GH}^2$ = AO2 + PO2 − 2GAO − 2GH + PO +AG2+GH2. Whence 2GH 3 PO (=AO2+PO2 − 2GAO) = AO2 + $^3/_4$ PO2. For AO2 write AO 3 $\frac{AO = 3AS}{6}$; then dividing all the terms by 3PO, and multiplying them by 2AS, we shall

have 4/3GH 3 AS (= $^1/_6$AO 3 PO + $^1/_2$AS 3 PO = $\frac{4AO-3SO}{6}$ 3 PO = $\overline{APO-SPO}$ 3 PO = to the area *APO - SPO*)| = to the area APS. But GH was 3M, and therefore $^4/_3$GH 3 AS is 4AS × M Wherefore the area cut off APS is equal to the area that was to be cut off 4AS × M.   Q.E.D.

COR. 1. Hence GH is to AS as the time in which the body described the arc AP to the time in which the body described the arc between the vertex A and the perpendicular erected from the focus S upon the axis.

COR. 2. And supposing a circle ASP perpetually to pass through the moving body P, the velocity of the point H is to the velocity which the body had in the vertex A as 3 to S; and therefore in the same ratio is the line GH to the right line which the body, in the time of its moving from A to P, would describe with that velocity which it had in the vertex A.

COR. 3. Hence, also, on the other hand, the time may be found in which the body has described any assigned arc AP. Join AP, and on its middle point erect a perpendicular meeting the right line GH in H.

LEMMA XXVIII.

There is no oval figure whose area, cut of by right lines at pleasure, can be universally found by means of equations of any number of finite terms and dimensions.

Suppose that within the oval any point is given, about which as a pole a right line is perpetually revolving with an uniform motion, while in that right line a moveable point going out from the pole moves always forward with a velocity proportional to the square of that right line with in the oval. By this motion that point will describe a spiral with infinite circumgyrations. Now if a portion of the area of the oval cut off by that right line could be found by a finite equation, the distance of the point from the pole, which is proportional to this area, might be found by the same equation, and therefore all the points of the spiral might be found by a finite equation also; and therefore the intersection of a right line given in position with the spiral might also be found by a finite equation. But every right line infinitely produced cuts a spiral in an infinite number of points; and the equation by which any one intersection of two lines is found at the same time exhibits all their intersections by as many roots, and therefore rises to as many dimensions as there are intersections. Because two circles mutually cut one another in two points, one of those intersections is not to be found but by an equation of two dimensions, by which the other intersection may be also found. Because there may be four intersections of two conic sections, any one of them is not to be found universally, but by an equation of four dimensions, by which they may be all found together. For if those intersections are severally sought, because the law and condition of all is the same, the calculus will be the same in every case, and therefore the conclusion always the same, which must therefore comprehend all those intersections at once within itself, and exhibit them all indifferently. Hence it is that the intersections of the conic sections with the curves of the third order, because they may amount to six, come out together by equations of six dimensions; and the intersections of two curves of the third order, because they may amount to nine, come out together by equations of nine dimensions. If this did not necessarily happen, we might reduce all solid to plane Problems, and those higher than solid to solid Problems. But here I speak of curves irreducible in power. For if the equation by which the curve is defined may be reduced to a lower power, the curve will not be one single curve, but composed of two, or more, whose intersections may be severally found by different calculusses. After the same manner the two intersections of right lines with the conic sections come out always by equations of two dimensions; the three intersections of right lines with the irreducible curves of the third order by equations of three dimensions; the four intersections of

right lines with the irreducible curves of the fourth order, by equations of four dimensions; and so on *in infinitum*. Wherefore the innumerable intersections of a right line with a spiral, since this is but one simple curve and not reducible to more curves, require equations infinite in number of dimensions and roots, by which they may be all exhibited together. For the law and calculus of all is the same. For if a perpendicular is let fall from the pole upon that intersecting right line, and that perpendicular together with the intersecting line revolves about the pole, the intersections of the spiral will mutually pass the one into the other; and that which was first or nearest, after one revolution, will be the second; after two, the third; and so on: nor will the equation in the mean time be changed but as the magnitudes of those quantities are changed, by which the position of the intersecting line is determined. Wherefore since those quantities after every revolution return to their first magnitudes, the equation will return to its first form; and consequently one and the same equation will exhibit all the intersections, and will therefore have an infinite number of roots, by which they may be all exhibited. And therefore the intersection of a right line with a spiral cannot be universally found by any finite equation; and of consequence there is no oval figure whose area, out off by right lines at pleasure, can be universally exhibited by any such equation.

By the same argument, if the interval of the pole and point by which the spiral is described is taken proportional to that part of the perimeter of the oval which is cut off, it may be proved that the length of the perimeter cannot be universally exhibited by any finite equation. But here I speak of ovals that are not touched by conjugate figures running out *in infinitum*.

COR. Hence the area of an ellipsis, described by a radius drawn from the focus to the moving body, is not to be found from the time given by a finite equation; and therefore cannot be determined by the description of curves geometrically rational. Those curves I call geometrically rational, all the points whereof may be determined by lengths that are definable by equations; that is, by the complicated ratios of lengths. Other curves (such as spirals, quadratrixes, and cycloids) I call geometrically irrational. For the lengths which are or are not as number to number (according to the tenth Book of Elements) are arithmetically rational or irrational. And therefore I cut off an area of an ellipsis proportional to the time in which it is described by a curve geometrically irrational, in the following manner.

PROPOSITION XXXI. PROBLEM XXIII.

TO FIND THE PLACE OF A BODY MOVING IN A GIVEN ELLIPTIC TRAJECTORY AT ANY ASSIGNED TIME.

Suppose A to be the principal vertex, S the focus, and O the centre of the ellipsis APB; and let P be the place of the body to be found. Produce OA to G so as OG may be to OA as OA to OS. Erect the perpendicular GH; and about the centre O, with the interval OG, describe the circle GEF; and on the ruler GH, as a base, suppose the wheel GEF to move forwards, revolving about its axis, and in the mean time by its point A

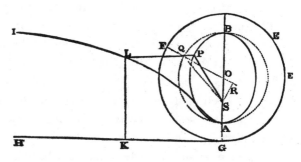

describing the cycloid ALI. Which done, take GK to the perimeter GEFG of the wheel, in the ratio of the time in which the body proceeding from A described the arc AP, to the time of a whole revolution in the ellipsis. Erect the perpendicular KL meeting the cycloid in L; then LP drawn parallel to KG will meet the ellipsis in P, the required place of the body.

For about the centre O with the interval OA describe the semi-circle AQB, and let LP, produced, if need be, meet the arc AQ in Q, and join SQ, OQ. Let OQ meet the arc EFG in F, and upon OQ let fall the perpendicular SR. The area APS is as the area AQS, that is, as the difference between the sector OQA and the triangle OQS, or as the difference of the rectangles $\frac{1}{2}$OQ × AQ, and $\frac{1}{2}$OQ × SR, that is, because $\frac{1}{2}$OQ is given, as the difference between the arc AQ and the right line SR; and therefore (because of the equality of the given ratios SR to the sine of the arc AQ, OS to OA, OA to OG, AQ to GF; and by division, AQ – SR to GF – sine of the arc AQ) as GK, the difference between the arc GF and the sine of the arc AQ. Q.E.D.

SCHOLIUM.

But since the description of this curve is difficult, a solution by approximation will be preferable. First, then, let there be found a certain angle B which may be to an angle of 57,29578 degrees, which an arc equal to the radius subtends, as SH, the distance of the foci, to AB, the diameter of the ellipsis. Secondly, a certain length L, which may be to the radius in the same ratio inversely. And these being found, the Problem may be solved by the following analysis. By any construction (or even by conjecture), suppose we know

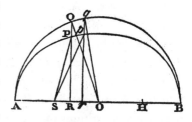

P the place of the body near its true place p. Then letting fall on the axis of the ellipsis the ordinate PR from the proportion of the diameters of the ellipsis, the ordinate

RQ of the circumscribed circle AQB will be given; which ordinate is the sine of the angle AOQ, supposing AO to be the radius, and also cuts the ellipsis in P. It will be sufficient if that angle is found by a rude calculus in numbers near the truth. Suppose we also know the angle proportional to the time, that is, which is to four right angles as the time in which the body described the arc Ap, to the time of one revolution in the ellipsis. Let this angle be N. Then take an angle D, which may be to the angle B as the sine of the angle AOQ to the radius; and an angle E which may be to the angle N – AOQ + D as the length L to the same length L diminished by the cosine of the angle AOQ, when that angle is less than a right angle, or increased thereby when greater. In the next place, take an angle F that may be to the angle B as the sine of the angle AOQ + E to the radius, and an angle G, that may be to the angle N – AOQ – E + F as the length L to the same length L diminished by the cosine of the angle AOQ + E, when that angle is less than a right angle, or increased thereby when greater. For the third time take an angle H, that may be to the angle B as the sine of the angle AOQ + E + G to the radius; and an angle I to the angle N – AOQ – E – G + H, as the length L is to the same length L diminished by the cosine of the angle AOQ + E + G, when that angle is less than a right angle, or increased thereby when greater. And so we may proceed *in infinitum*. Lastly, take the angle AOq equal to the angle AOQ + E + G + I +, &c. and from its cosine Or and the ordinate pr, which is to its sine qr as the lesser axis of the ellipsis to the greater, we shall have p the correct place of the body. When the angle N – AOQ, + D happens to be negative, the sign + of the angle E must be every where changed into –, and the sign – into+. And the same thing is to be understood of the signs of the angles G and I, when the angles N – AOQ – E + F, and N – AOQ – E – G + H come out negative. But the infinite series AOQ + E + G + I +, &c. converges so very fast, that it will be scarcely ever needful to proceed beyond the second term E. And the calculus is founded upon this Theorem, that the area APS is as the difference between the arc AQ and the right line let fall from the focus S perpendicularly upon the radius OQ.

And by a calculus not unlike, the Problem is solved in the hyperbola. Let its centre be O, its vertex A, its focus S, and asymptote OK; and suppose the quantity of the area to be cut off is known, as being proportional to the time. Let that be A, and by conjecture suppose we know the position of a right line SP, that cuts off an area APS near the truth. Join OP, and from A and P to the asymptote draw AI, PK parallel to the other asymptote; and by the table of logarithms the area AIKP will be given, and equal thereto the area OPA, which subducted from the triangle OPS, will leave the area cut off APS. And by

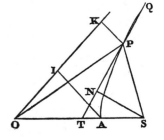

applying 2APS – 2A, or 2A – 2APS, the double difference of the area A that was to be cut off, and the area APS that is cut off, to the line SN that is let fall from the focus S, perpendicular upon the tangent TP, we shall have the length of the chord PQ. Which chord PQ is to be inscribed between A and P, if the area APS that is cut off be greater than the area, A that was to be cut off, but towards the contrary side of the point P, if otherwise: and the point Q will be the place of the body more accurately. And by repeating the computation the place may be found perpetually to greater and greater accuracy.

And by such computations we have a general analytical resolution of the Problem. But the particular calculus that follows is better fitted for astronomical purposes. Supposing AO, OB, OD, to be the semi-axis of the ellipsis, and L its latus rectum, and D the difference betwixt the lesser semi-axis OD, and $\frac{1}{2}$L, the half of the latus rectum: let an angle Y be found, whose sine may be to the radius as the rectangle under that difference D, and AO + OD the half sum of the axes to the square of the greater axis AB. Find also an angle Z, whose sine may be to the radius as the double rectangle under the distance of the foci

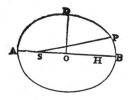

SH and that difference D to triple the square of half the greater semi-axis AO. Those angles being once found, the place of the body may be thus determined. Take the angle T proportional to the time in which the arc BP was described, or equal to what is called the mean motion; and an angle V the first equation of the mean motion to the angle Y, the greatest first equation, as the sine of double the angle T is to the radius; and an angle X, the second equation, to the angle Z, the second greatest equation, as the cube of the sine of the angle T is to the cube of the radius. Then take the angle BHP the mean motion equated equal to T + X + V, the sum of the angles T, V, X, if the angle T is less than a right angle; or equal to T + X – V, the difference of the same, if that angle T is greater than one and less than two right angles; and if HP meets the ellipsis in P, draw SP, and it will cut off the area BSP nearly proportional to the time.

This practice seems to be expeditious enough, because the angles V and X, taken in second minutes, if you please, being very small, it will be sufficient to find two or three of their first figures. But it is likewise sufficiently accurate to answer to the theory of the planet's motions. For even in the orbit of Mars, where the greatest equation of the centre amounts to ten degrees, the error will scarcely exceed one second. But when the angle of the mean motion equated BHP is found, the angle of the true motion BSP, and the distance SP, are readily had by the known methods.

And so far concerning the motion of bodies in curve lines. But it may also come to pass that a moving body shall ascend or descend in a right line; and I shall now go on to explain what belongs to such kind of motions.

SECTION VII.

Concerning the rectilinear ascent and descent of bodies.

PROPOSITION XXXII. PROBLEM XXIV.

SUPPOSING THAT THE CENTRIPETAL FORCE IS RECIPROCALLY
PROPORTIONAL TO THE SQUARE OF THE DISTANCE OF THE
PLACES FROM THE CENTRE; IT IS REQUIRED TO DEFINE
THE SPACES WHICH A BODY, FALLING DIRECTLY,
DESCRIBES IN GIVEN TIMES.

CASE. 1. If the body does not fall perpendicularly, it will (by Cor. I Prop. XIII)
describe some conic section whose focus is placed in the centre of force. Suppose that
conic section to be ARPB and its focus S. And, first, if the figure
be an ellipsis, upon the greater axis thereof AB describe the semicircle ADB, and let the right line DPC pass through the falling
body, making right angles with the axis; and drawing DS, PS, the
area ASD will be proportional to the area ASP, and therefore also
to the time. The axis AB still remaining the same, let the breadth
of the ellipsis be perpetually diminished, and the area ASD will
always remain proportional to the time. Suppose that breadth to
be diminished *in infinitum*; and the orbit APB in that case coinciding with the axis AB, and the focus S with the extreme point of
the axis B, the body will descend. in the right line AC, and the

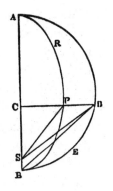

area ABD will become proportional to the time. Wherefore the space AC will be given
which the body describes in a given time by its perpendicular fall from the place A, if
the area ABD is taken proportional to the time, and from the point D the right line
DC is let fall perpendicularly on the right line AB. Q.E.I.

CASE.. 2. If the figure RPB is an hyperbola, on the same principal diameter AB describe the rectangular hyperbola BED; and
because the areas CSP, CB P, SP B, are severally to the several
areas CSD, CBED, SDEB, in the given ratio of the heights CP,
CD, and the area. SP/B is proportional to the time in which the
body P will move through the arc P B, the area SDEB will be
also proportional to that time. Let the latus rectum of the hyperbola RPB be diminished *in infinitum*, the latus transversum
remaining the same; and the arc PB will come to coincide with
the right line CB, and the focus S, with the vertex B, and the

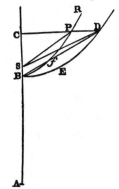

right line SD with the right line BD. And therefore the area BDEB will be proportional to the time in which the body C, by its perpendicular descent, describes the line CB. Q.E.I.

CASE. 3. And by the like argument, if the figure RPB is a parabola, and to the same principal vertex B another parabola BED is described, that may always remain given while the former parabola in whose perimeter the body P moves, by having its latus rectum diminished and reduced to nothing, comes to coincide with the line CB, the parabolic segment BDEB will be proportional to the time in which that body P or C will descend to the centre S or B. Q.E.I.

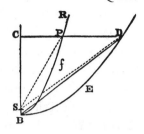

PROPOSITION XXXIII. THEOREM IX.

THE THINGS ABOVE FOUND BEING SUPPOSED, I SAY, THAT THE VELOCITY OF A FALLING BODY IN ANY PLACE C IS TO THE VELOCITY OF A BODY, DESCRIBING A CIRCLE ABOUT THE CENTRE B AT THE DISTANCE BC, IN THE SUBDUPLICATE RATIO OF AC, THE DISTANCE OF THE BODY FROM THE REMOTER VERTEX A OF THE CIRCLE OR RECTANGULAR HYPERBOLA, TO $^1/_2$AB, THE PRINCIPAL SEMI-DIAMETER OF THE FIGURE.

Let AB, the common diameter of both figures RPB, DEB, be bisected in O; and draw the right line PT that may touch the figure RPB in P, and likewise cut that common diameter AB (produced, if need be) in T; and let SY be perpendicular to this line, and BQ to this diameter, and suppose the latus rectum of the figure RPB to be L. From Cor. 9, Prop. XVI, it is manifest that the velocity of a body, moving in the line RPB about the centre S, in any place P, is to the velocity of a body describing a circle about the same centre, at the distance SP, in the subduplicate ratio of the rectangle $^1/_2$L × SP to SY^2 For by the properties of the conic sections ACB is to CP^2 as 2AO to L, and therefore $\frac{2CP^2 \times AO}{ACB}$ is equal to L. Therefore those velocities are to each other in the

subduplicate ratio of $\frac{CP^2 \times AO \times SP}{ACB}$ to SY^2. Moreover, by the properties of the conic sections, CO is to BO as BO to TO and (by composition or division) as CB to BT. Whence (by division or composition) BO – or + CO will be to BO as CT to BT, that is, AC will be to AO as CP to BQ; and therefore $\frac{CP^2 \times AO \times SP}{ACB}$ is equal to $\frac{BQ^2 \times AC \times SP}{AO \times BC}$. Now suppose CP, the breadth of the figure RPB, to be diminished *in infinitum*, so as the point P may come to coincide with the point C, and the point S with the point B,

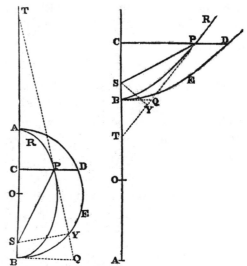

and the line SP with the line BC, and the line SY with the line BQ; and the velocity of the body now descending perpendicularly in the line CB will be to the velocity of a body describing a circle about the centre B, at the distance BC, in the subduplicate ratio of $\frac{BQ^2 \times AC \times SP}{AO \times BC}$ to SY², that is (neglecting the ratios of equality of SP to BC, and BQ² to SY²), in the subduplicate ratio of AC to AO, or $^1/_2$AB.   Q.E.D.

COR. 1. When the points B and S come to coincide, TC will become to TS as AC to AO.

COR. 2. A body revolving in any circle at a given distance from the centre, by its motion converted upwards, will ascend to double its distance from the centre.

PROPOSITION XXXIV. THEOREM X.

IF THE FIGURE BED IS A PARABOLA, I SAY, THAT THE VELOC-
ITY OF A FALLING BODY IN ANY PLACE C IS EQUAL TO THE
VELOCITY BY WHICH A BODY MAY UNIFORMLY DESCRIBE A
CIRCLE ABOUT THE CENTRE B AT HALF THE INTERVAL BC

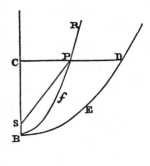

For (by Cor. 7, Prop. XVI) the velocity of a body describing a parabola RPB about the centre S, in any place P, is equal to the velocity of a body uniformly describing a circle about the same centre S at half the interval SP. Let the breadth CP of the parabola be diminished *in infinitum*, so as the parabolic arc P B may come to coincide with the right line CB, the centre S with the vertex B, and the interval SP with the interval BC, and the proposition will be manifest.   Q.E.D.

PROPOSITION XXXV. THEOREM XI

THE SAME THINGS SUPPOSED, I SAY, THAT THE AREA OF THE
FIGURE DES, DESCRIBED BY THE INDEFINITE RADIUS SD, IS

EQUAL TO THE AREA WHICH A BODY WITH A RADIUS
EQUAL TO HALF THE LATUS RECTUM OF THE FIGURE DES,
BY UNIFORMLY REVOLVING ABOUT THE CENTRE S, MAY
DESCRIBE IN THE SAME TIME.

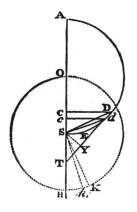 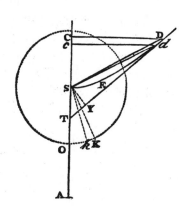

For suppose a body C in the smallest moment of time describes in falling the infinitely little line Cc, while another body K, uniformly revolving about the centre S in the circle OKk, describes the arc Kk. Erect the perpendiculars CD, cd, meeting the figure DES in D, d. Join SD, Sd, SK Sk, and draw Dd meeting the axis AS in T, and thereon let fall the perpendicular SY.

CASE. 1. If the figure DES is a circle, or a rectangular hyperbola, bisect its transverse diameter AS in O, and SO will be half the latus rectum. And because TC is to TD as Cc to Dd, and TD to TS as CD to SY; *ex æquo* TC will be to TS as CD × Cc to SY × Dd. But (by Cor. 1, Prop. XXXIII) TC is to TS as AC to AO; to wit, if in the coalescence of the points D, d, the ultimate ratios of the lines are taken. Wherefore AC is to AO or SK as CD × Cc to SY × Dd. Farther, the velocity of the descending body in C is to the velocity of a body describing a circle about the centre S, at the interval SC, in the subduplicate ratio of AC to AO or SK (by Prop. XXXIII); and this velocity is to the velocity of a body describing the circle OKk in the subduplicate ratio of SK to SC (by Cor. 6, Prop IV); and, *ex æquo*, the first velocity to the last, that is, the little line Cc to the arc Kk, in the subduplicate ratio of AC to SC, that is, in the ratio of AC to CD. Wherefore CD × C is equal to AC × Kk, and consequently AC to SK as AC × Kk to SY × Dd, and thence SK × Kk equal to SY × Dd, and $\frac{1}{2}$SK × Kk equal to $\frac{1}{2}$SY × Dd, that is, the area KSk equal to the area SDd. Therefore in every moment of time two equal particles, KSk and SDd, of areas are generated, which, if their magnitude is diminished, and their number increased *in infinitum*, obtain the ratio of equality, and consequently (by Cor. Lem. IV), the whole areas together generated are always equal.   Q.E.D.

CASE. 2. But if the figure DES is a parabola, we shall find, as above, CD × Cc to SY × Dd as TC to TS, that is, as 2 to 1; and that therefore $\frac{1}{4}$CD × Cc is equal to $\frac{1}{2}$SY × Dd. But the velocity of the falling body in C is equal to the velocity with which a

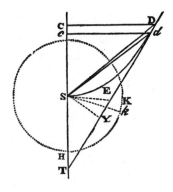

circle may be uniformly described at the interval ½ SC (by Prop. XXXIV). And this velocity to the velocity with which a circle may be described with the radius SK, that is, the little line C*c* to the arc K*k*, is (by Cor. 6, Prop. IV) in the subduplicate ratio of SK to ¹/₂SC; that is, in the ratio of SK to ½ CD. Wherefore ½ SK × K*k* is equal to ¼ CD X. C*c*, and therefore equal to ½ SY × D*d*; that is, the area KS*k* is equal to the area SD*d*, as above. Q.E.D.

PROPOSITION XXXVI. PROBLEM XXV.

TO DETERMINE THE TIMES OF THE DESCENT OF A BODY FALLING FROM A GIVEN PLACE A.

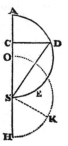

Upon the diameter AS, the distance of the body from the centre at the beginning, describe the semi-circle ADS, as likewise the semi-circle OKH equal thereto, about the centre S. From any place C of the body erect the ordinate CD. Join SD, and make the sector OSK equal to the area ASD. It is evident (by Prop. XXXV) that the body in falling will describe the space AC in the same time in which another body, uniformly revolving about the centre S, may describe the arc OK. Q.E.F.

PROPOSITION XXXVII. PROBLEM XXVI.

TO DEFINE THE TIMES OF THE ASCENT OR DESCENT OF A BODY PROJECTED UPWARDS OR DOWNWARDS FROM A GIVEN PLACE.

Suppose the body to go off from the given place G, in the direction of the line GS, with any velocity. In the duplicate ratio of this velocity to the uniform velocity in a circle, with which the body may revolve about the centre S at the given interval SG, take GA to ¹/₂AS. If that ratio is the same as of the number 2 to 1, the point A is infinitely remote; in which case a parabola is to be described with any latus rectum to the vertex S, and axis SG; as appears by Prop. XXXIV. But if that ratio is less or greater than the ratio of 2 to 1, in the former case a circle, in the latter a rectangular hyperbola, is to be described on the diameter SA; as appears by Prop. XXXIII. Then about the centre S, with an interval equal to half the latus rectum, describe the circle H K; and at the place G of the ascending or descending body, and at any other place C, erect the

perpendiculars GI, CD, meeting the conic section or circle in I and D. Then joining SI, SD, let the sectors HSK, HS*k* be made equal to the segments SEIS, SEDS, and (by Prop. XXXV) the body G will describe the space GC in the same time in which the body K may describe the arc K*k*. Q.E.F.

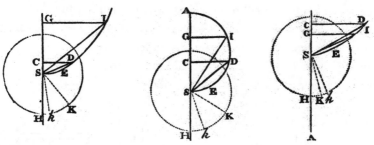

PROPOSITION XXXVIII. THEOREM XII.

Supposing that the centripetal force is proportional to the altitude or distance of places from the centre, I say, that the times and velocities of falling bodies, and the spaces which they describe, are respectively proportional to the arcs, and the right and versed sines of the arcs.

Suppose the body to fall from any place A in the right line AS; and about the centre of force S, with the interval AS, describe the quadrant of a circle AE; and let CD be the right sine of any arc AD; and the body A will in the time AD in falling describe the space AC, and in the place C will acquire the velocity CD.

This is demonstrated the same way from Prop. X, as Prop. XXXII was demonstrated from Prop. XI.

COR. 1. Hence the times are equal in which one body falling from the Place A arrives at the centre S, and another body revolving describes the quadrantal arc ADE.

COR. 2. Wherefore all the times are equal in which bodies falling from whatsoever places arrive at the centre. For all the periodic times of revolving bodies are equal (by Cor. 3, Prop. IV).

PROPOSITION XXXIX. PROBLEM XXVII.

Supposing a centripetal force of any kind, and granting the quadratures of curvilinear figures; it is required to find the velocity of a body, ascending

OR DESCENDING IN A RIGHT LINE, IN THE SEVERAL PLACES
THROUGH WHICH IT PASSES; AS ALSO THE TIME IN WHICH IT
WILL ARRIVE AT ANY PLACE: AND VICE VERSA.

Suppose the body E to fall from any place A in the right line ADEC; and from its place E imagine a perpendicular EG always erected proportional to the centripetal force in that place tending to the centre C; and let BFG be a curve line, the locus of the point G. And in the beginning of the motion suppose EG to coincide with the perpendicular AB; and the velocity of the body in any place E will be as a right line whose square is equal to the curvilinear area ABGE.   Q.E.I.

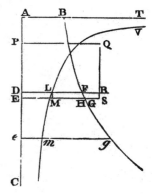

In EG take EM reciprocally proportional to a right line whose square is equal to the area ABGE, and let VLM be a curve line wherein the point M is always placed, and to which the right line AB produced is an asymptote; and the time in which the body in falling describes the line AE, will be as the curvilinear area ABTVME.   Q.E.I.

For in the right line AE let there be taken the very small line DE of a given length, and let DLF be the place of the line EMG, when the body was in D; and if the centripetal force be such, that a right line, whose square is equal to the area ABGE, is as the velocity of the descending body, the area itself will be as the square of that velocity; that is, if for the velocities in D and E we write V and V + I, the area ABFD will be as VV, and the area ABGE as VV + 2VI + II; and by division, the area DFGE as 2VI + II, and therefore $\frac{DFGE}{DE}$ will be as $\frac{2VI+II}{DE}$; that is, if we take the first ratios of those quantities when just nascent, the length DF is as the quantity $\frac{2VI}{DE}$, and therefore also as half that quantity $\frac{I+V}{DE}$. But the time in which the body in falling describes the very small line DE, is as that line directly and the velocity V inversely; and the force will be as the increment I of the velocity directly and the time inversely; and therefore if we take the first ratios when those quantities are just nascent, as $\frac{I+V}{DE}$ that is, as the length DF. Therefore a force proportional to DF or EG will cause the body to descend with a velocity that is as the right line whose square is equal to the area ABGE.   Q.E.D.

Moreover, since the time in which a very small line DE of a given length may be described is as the velocity inversely, and therefore also inversely as a right line whose square is equal to the area ABFD; and since the line DL, and by consequence the nascent area DLME, will be as the same right line inversely, the time will be as the area DLME, and the sum of all the times will be as the sum of all the areas; that is (by

Cor. Lem. IV), the whole time in which the line AE is described will be as the whole area ATVME.   Q.E.D.

Cor.. 1. Let P be the place from whence a body ought to fall, so as that, when urged by any known uniform centripetal force (such as gravity is vulgarly supposed to be), it may acquire in the place D a velocity equal to the velocity which another body, falling by any force whatever, both acquired in that place D. In the perpendicular DF let there be taken DR, which may he a DF as that uni-

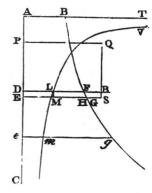

form force to the other force in the place D. Complete the rectangle PDRQ, and cut off the area ABFD equal to that rectangle. Then A will be the place from whence the other body fell. For completing the rectangle DRSE, since the area ABFD is to the area DFGE as VV to 2VI, and therefore as 1/2 V to I, that is, as half the whole veloc- ity to the increment of the velocity of the body falling by the unequable force; and in like manner the area PGRD to the area DRSE as half the whole velocity to the incre- ment of the velocity of the body falling by the uniform force; and since those increments (by reason of the equality of the nascent times) are as the generating forces, that is, as the ordinates DF, DR, and consequently as the nascent areas DFGE, DRSE; therefore, *ex æquo*, the whole areas ABFD, PQRD will be to one another as the halves of the whole velocities; and therefore, because the velocities are equal, they become equal also.

Cor. 2. Whence if any body be projected either upwards or downwards with a given velocity from any place D, and there be given the law of centripetal force acting on it, its velocity will be found in any other place, as *e*, by erecting the ordinate *eg*, and taking that velocity to the velocity in the place D as a right line whose square is equal to the rectangle PQRD, either increased by the curvilinear area DF, if the place *e* is below the place D, or diminished by the same area DF, if it be higher, is to the right line whose square is equal to the rectangle PQRD alone.

Cor. 3. The time is also known by erecting the ordinate *em* reciprocally propor- tional to the square root of PQRD + or - DF, and taking the time in which the body has described the line D to the time in which another body has fallen with an uniform force from P, and in falling arrived at D in the proportion of the curvilinear area DL to the rectangle 2PD X DL. For the time in which a body falling with an uniform force hath described the line PD, is to the time in which the same body has described the line PE in the subduplicate ratio of PD to PE: that is (the very small line DE being just nascent), in the ratio of PD to PD + 1/2 DE, or 2PD to 2PD + DE, and, by division, to the time in which the body hath described the small line DE, as 2PD to DE, and

therefore as the rectangle 2PD × DL to the area DLME; and the time in which both the bodies described the very small line DE is to the time in which the body moving unequably hath described the line D*e* as the area DLME to the area DL*me*; and, *ex aquo*, the first mentioned of these times is to the last as the rectangle 2PD × DL to the area DL*me*.

SECTION VIII.

Of the invention of orbits wherein bodies will revolve, being acted upon by any sort of centripetal force.

PROPOSITION XL. THEOREM XIII.

IF A BODY, ACTED UPON BY ANY CENTRIPETAL FORCE, IS ANY
HOW MOVED, AND ANOTHER BODY ASCENDS OR DESCENDS
IN A RIGHT LINE, AND THEIR VELOCITIES BE EQUAL IN ANY
ONE CASE OF EQUAL ALTITUDES, THEIR VELOCITIES WILL BE
ALSO EQUAL AT ALL EQUAL ALTITUDES.

Let a body descend from A through D and E, to the centre C; and let another body move from V in the curve line VIK*k*. From the centre C, with any distances, describe the concentric circles DI, EK, meeting the right line AC in D and E, and. the curve VIK in I and K. Draw IC meeting KE in N, and on IK let fall the perpendicular NT; and let the interval DE or IN between the circumferences of the circles be very small; and imagine the bodies in D and I to have equal velocities. Then because the distances CD and CI are equal, the centripetal forces in D and I will be also equal. Let those forces be expressed by the equal lineolæ DE and IN; and let the force IN (by Cor. 2 of the Laws of Motion) be resolved into two others, NT and IT. Then the force NT acting in the direction of the line NT perpendicular to the path ITK of the body will not at all affect or change the velocity of the body in that path, but only draw it aside from a rectilinear course, and make it deflect perpetually from the tangent of the orbit, and proceed in the curvilinear path ITK*k*. That whole force, therefore, will be spent in producing this effect; but the other force IT, acting in the direction of the course of the body, will be all employed in accelerating it, and in the least given time will produce an acceleration proportional to itself. Therefore the accelerations of the bodies in D and I, produced in equal times, are as the lines DE, IT (if we take the first ratios of the nascent lines DE, IN, IK, IT, NT); and in unequal times as those lines and the times conjunctly. But the

times in which DE and IK are described, are, by reason of the equal velocities (in D and I) as the spaces described DE and IK, and therefore the accelerations in the course of the bodies through the lines DE and IK are as DE and IT, and DE and IK conjunctly; that is, as the square of DE to the rectangle IT into IK. But the rectangle IT × IK is equal to the square of IN, that is, equal to the square of DE; and therefore the accelerations generated in the passage of the bodies from D and I to E and K are equal. Therefore the velocities of the bodies in E and K are also equal. and by the same reasoning they will always be found equal in any subsequent equal distances.   Q.E.D.

By the same reasoning, bodies of equal velocities and equal distances from the centre will be equally retarded in their ascent to equal distances.   Q.E.D.

COR. 1. Therefore if a body either oscillates by hanging to a string, or by any polished and perfectly smooth impediment is forced to move in a curve line; and another body ascends or descends in a right line, and their velocities be equal at any one equal altitude, their velocities will be also equal at all other equal altitudes. For by the string of the pendulous body, or by the impediment of a vessel perfectly smooth, the same thing will be effected as by the transverse force NT. The body is neither accelerated nor retarded by it, but only is obliged to leave its rectilinear course.

COR. 2. Suppose the quantity P to be the greatest distance from the centre to which a body can ascend, whether it be oscillating, or revolving in a trajectory, and so the same projected upwards from any point of a trajectory with the velocity it has in that point. Let the quantity A be the distance of the body from the centre in any other point of the orbit; and let the centripetal force be always as the power A^{n-1}, of the quantity A, the index of which power $n - 1$ is any number n diminished by unity. Then the velocity in every altitude A will be as $\sqrt{P^n - A^n}$, and therefore will be given. For by Prop. XXXIX, the velocity of a body ascending and descending in a right line is in that very ratio.

PROPOSITION XLI. PROBLEM XXVIII.

SUPPOSING A CENTRIPETAL FORCE OF ANY KIND, AND GRANTING THE QUADRATURES OF CURVILINEAR FIGURES, IT IS REQUIRED TO FIND AS WELL THE TRAJECTORIES IN WHICH BODIES WILL MOVE, AS THE TIMES OF THEIR MOTIONS IN THE TRAJECTORIES FOUND.

Let any centripetal force tend to the centre C, and let it be required to find the trajectory VIK*k*. Let there be given the circle VR, described from the centre C with any interval CV; and from the same centre describe any other circles ID, KE cutting the trajectory in I and K, and the right line CV in D and E. Then draw the right line

CNIX cutting the circles KE, VR in N and X, and the right line CKY meeting the circle VR in Y. Let the points I and K be indefinitely near; and let the body go on from V through I and K to k; and let the point A be the place from whence another body is to fall, so as in the place D to acquire a velocity equal to the velocity of the first body in I. And things remaining as in Prop. XXXIX, the lineola IK, described in the least given time will be as the velocity, and therefore as the right line whose square is equal to the area ABFD, and the triangle ICK proportional to the time will be

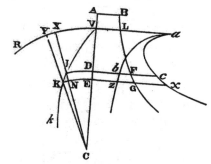

given, and therefore KN will be reciprocally as the altitude IC; that is (if there be given any quantity Q, and the altitude IC be called A), as $\frac{Q}{A}$. This quantity $\frac{Q}{A}$ call Z, and suppose the magnitude of Q to be such that in some case $\sqrt{ABFD}$ may be to Z as IK to KN, and then in all cases $\sqrt{ABPD}$ will be to Z as IK to KN, and ABFD to ZZ as IK^2 to KN^2, and by division ABFD – ZZ to ZZ as IN^2 to KN^2, and therefore $\sqrt{\overline{ABFD-ZZ}}$ to Z, or $\frac{Q}{A}$ as IN to KN; and therefore A × KN will be equal to $\frac{Q \times IN}{ABFD-ZZ}$.

Therefore since YX × XC is to A × KN as CX^2, to AA, the rectangle XY × XC will be equal to $\frac{Q \times IN \times CX^2}{AA\sqrt{ABFD-ZZ}}$. Therefore in the perpendicular DF let there be taken

continually Db, Dc equal to $\frac{Q}{2\sqrt{ABFD-ZZ}}, \frac{Q \times CX^2}{2AA\sqrt{ABFD-ZZ}}$ respectively, and let the curve lines ab, ac, the foci of the points b and c, be described: and from the point V let the perpendicular Va be erected to the line AC, cutting off the curvilinear areas VDba, VDca, and let the ordinates Ez, Ex, be erected also. Then because the rectangle Db × IN or DbzE is equal to half the rectangle A × KN, or to the triangle ICK; and the rectangle Dc × IN or DcxE is equal to half the rectangle YX × XC, or to the triangle XCY; that is, because the nascent particles DbzE, ICK of the areas VDba, VIC are always equal; and the nascent particles DcxE, XCY of the areas VDca, VCX are always equal; therefore the generated area VDca will be equal to the generated area VIC, and therefore proportional to the time; and the generated area VDca is equal to the generated sector VCX. If, therefore, any time be given during which the body has been moving from V, there will be also given the area proportional to it VDba; and thence will be given the altitude of the body CD or CI; and the area VDca, and the sector VCX equal thereto, together with its angle VCI. But the angle VCI, and the altitude CI being given, there is also given the place I, in which the body will be found at the end of that time.

Cor. 1. Hence the greatest and least altitudes of the bodies, that is, the apsides of the trajectories, may be found very readily. For the apsides are those points in which a right line IC drawn through the centre falls perpendicularly upon the trajectory VIK; which comes to pass when the right lines IK and NK become equal; that is, when the area ABFD is equal to ZZ.

COR. 2. So also the angle KIN, in which the trajectory at any place cuts the line IC, may be readily found by the given altitude IC of the body: to wit, by making the sine of that angle to radius as KN to IK that is, as Z to the square root of the area ABFD.

COR. 3. If to the centre C, and the principal vertex V, there be described a conic section VRS; and from any point thereof, as R, there be drawn the tangent RT meeting the axis CV indefinitely produced in the point T; and then joining CR there be drawn the right line CP, equal to the abscissa CT, making an angle VCP proportional to the sector VCR: and if a centripetal force, reciprocally proportional to the cubes of the distances of the places from the centre, tends to the centre C; and from the place V there sets out a body with a just velocity in the direction of a line perpendicular to the right line CV; that body will proceed in a trajectory VPQ, which the point P will always touch; and therefore if the conic section VRS be an hyperbola, the body will descend to the

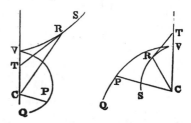

centre; but if it be an ellipsis, it will ascend perpetually, and go farther and farther off *in infinitum.* And, on the contrary, if a body endued with any velocity goes off from the place V, and according, as it begins either to descend obliquely to the centre, or ascends obliquely from it, the figure VRS be either an hyperbola or an ellipsis, the trajectory may be found by increasing or diminishing the angle VCP in a given ratio. And the centripetal force becoming centrifugal, the body will ascend obliquely in the trajectory VPQ, which is found by taking the angle VCP proportional to the elliptic sector VRC, and the length CP equal to the length CT, as before. All these things follow from the foregoing Proposition, by the quadrature of a certain curve, the invention of which, as being easy enough, for brevity's sake I omit.

PROPOSITION XLII. PROBLEM XXIX.

THE LAW OF CENTRIPETAL FORCE BEING GIVEN, IT IS
REQUIRED TO FIND THE MOTION OF A BODY SETTING OUT
FROM A GIVEN PLACE, WITH A GIVEN VELOCITY, IN THE
DIRECTION OF A GIVEN RIGHT LINE.

Suppose the same things as in the three preceding propositions; and let the body go off from the place I in the direction of the little line, IK, with the same velocity as another body, by falling with an uniform centripetal force from the place P, may acquire in D; and let this uniform force be to the force with which the body is at first urged in I, as DR to DF. Let the body go on towards *k*; and about the centre C, with

the interval C*k*, describe the circle *ke*, meeting the right line PD in *e*, and let there be erected the lines *eg*, *ev*, *ew*, ordinately applied to the curves BF*g*, *abv*, *acw*. From the given rectangle PDRQ and the given law of centripetal force, by which the first body

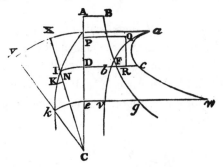

is acted on, the curve line BF*g* is also given, by the construction of Prop. XXVII, and its Cor. 1. Then from the given angle CIK is given the proportion of the nascent lines IK, KN; and thence, by the construction of Prob. XXVIII, there is given the quantity Q, with the curve lines *abv*, *acw*; and therefore, at the end of any time D*gve*, there is given both the altitude of the body C*e* or C*k*, and the area D*cwe*, with the sector equal to it XC*y*, the angle IC*k*, and the place *k*, in which the body will then be found.   Q.E.I.

We suppose in these Propositions the centripetal force to vary in its recess from the centre according to some law, which any one may imagine at pleasure; but at equal distances from the centre to be everywhere the same.

I have hitherto considered the motions of bodies in immovable orbits. It remains now to add something concerning their motions in orbits which revolve round the centres of force.

SECTION IX.

Of the motion of bodies in moveable orbits; and of the motion of the apsides.

PROPOSITION XLIII. PROBLEM XXX.

IT IS REQUIRED TO MAKE A BODY MOVE IN A TRAJECTORY
THAT REVOLVES ABOUT THE CENTRE OF FORCE IN THE
SAME MANNER AS ANOTHER BODY IN THE SAME TRAJECTORY
AT REST.

In the orbit VPK, given by position, let the body P revolve, proceeding from V towards K. From the centre C let there be continually drawn C*p*, equal to CP, making the angle VC*p* proportional to the angle VCP; and the area which the line C*p* describes will be to the area VCP, which the line CP describes at the same time, as the velocity of the describing line C*p* to the velocity of the describing line CP; that is, as the angle VC*p* to the angle VCP, therefore in a given ratio, and therefore proportional to the time. Since, then, the area described by the line C*p* in an immovable plane

is proportional to the time, it is manifest that a body, being acted upon by a just quantity of centripetal force may revolve with the point p in the curve line which the same point p, by the method just now explained, may be made to describe an immovable plane. Make the angle VCu equal to the angle PCp, and the line Cu equal to CV, and the figure uCp equal to the figure VCP, and the body being always in the point p, will move in the perimeter of the revolving figure uCp, and will describe its (revolving) arc up in the same time that the other body P describes the similar and equal are VP in the quiescent

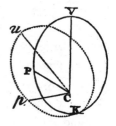

figure VPK. Find, then, by Cor. 5, Prop. VI., the centripetal force by which the body may be made to revolve in the curve line which the point p describes in an immovable plane, and the Problem will be solved.   *Q.E.F.*

PROPOSITION XLIV. THEOREM XIV.

THE DIFFERENCE OF THE FORCES, BY WHICH TWO BODIES
MAY BE MADE TO MOVE EQUALLY, ONE IN A QUIESCENT, THE
OTHER IN THE SAME ORBIT REVOLVING IT IN A TRIPLICATE
RATIO OF THEIR COMMON ALTITUDES INVERSELY.

Let the parts of the quiescent orbit VP, PK be similar and equal to the parts of the revolving orbit up, pk; and let the distance of the points P and K be supposed of the utmost smallness. Let fall a perpendicular kr from the point k to the right line pC, and produce it to m, so that mr may be to kr as the angle VCp to the angle VCP. Because

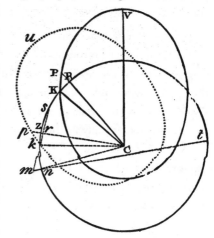

the altitudes of the bodies PC and pC, KC and kC, are always equal, it is manifest that the increments or decrements of the lines PC and pC are always equal; and therefore if each of the several motions of the bodies in the places P and p be resolved into two (by Cor. 2 of the Laws of Motion), one of which is directed towards the centre, or according to the lines PC, pC, and the other, transverse to the former, hath a direction perpendicular to the lines PC and C; the motions towards the centre will be equal, and the transverse motion of the body p will be to the transverse motion of the body P as the angular motion of the line pC to the angular motion of the line PC; that is, as

the angle VCp to the angle VCP. Therefore, at the same time that the body P, by both its motions, comes to the point K, the body p, having an equal motion towards the centre, will be equally moved from p towards C; and therefore that time being expired, it will be found somewhere in the line mkr, which, passing through the point k, is perpendicular to the line pC; and by its transverse motion will acquire a distance from the line pC, that will be to the distance which the other body P acquires from the line PC as the transverse motion of the body p to the transverse motion of the other body P. Therefore since kr is equal to the distance which the body P acquires from the line PC, and mr is to kr as the angle VCp to the angle VCP, that is, as the transverse motion of the body p to the transverse motion of the body P, it is manifest that the body p, at the expiration of that time, will be found in the place m. These things will be so, if the bodies p and P are equally moved in the directions of the lines pC and PC, and are therefore urged with equal forces in those directions. But if we take an angle pCn that is to the angle pCk as the angle VCp to the angle VCP, and nC be equal to kC, in that case the body p at the expiration of the time will really be in n; and is therefore urged with a greater force than the body P, if the angle nCp is greater than the angle kCp, that is, if the orbit upk, move either *in consequentia,* or *in antecedentia,* with a celerity greater than the double of that with which the line CP moves *in consequentia;* and with a less force if the orbit moves slower *in antecedentia.* And the difference of the forces will be as the interval mn of the places through which the body would be carried by the action of that difference in that given space of time. About the centre C with the interval Cn or Ck suppose a circle described cutting the lines mr, mn produced in s and t, and the rectangle $mn \times mt$ will be equal to the rectangle $mk \times ms$, and therefore mn will be equal to $\frac{mk \times ms}{mt}$. But since the triangles pCk, pCn, in a given time, are of a given magnitude, kr, and mr, and their difference mk, and their sum ms, are reciprocally as the altitude pC, and therefore the rectangle $mk \times ms$ is reciprocally as the square of the altitude pC. But, moreover, mt is directly as $\frac{1}{2}mt$, that is, as the altitude pC. These are the first ratios of the nascent lines; and hence $\frac{mk \cdot ms}{mt}$, that is, the nascent lineola mn, and the difference of the forces proportional thereto, are reciprocally as the cube of the altitude pC.   Q.E.D.

COR. 1. Hence the difference of the forces in the places P and p, or K and k, is to the force with which a body may revolve with a circular motion from R to K, in the same time that the body P in an immovable orb describes the arc PK, as the nascent line mn to the versed sine of the nascent arc R, that is, as $\frac{mk \cdot ms}{mt}$ to $\frac{rk^2}{2kC}$ or as $mk \times ms$ to the square of rk; that is, if we take given quantities F and G in the same ratio to one another as the angle VCP bears to the angle VCp, as GG − FF to FF. And, therefore, if from the centre C, with any distance CP or Cp, there be described a circular sector equal to the whole area VPC, which the body revolving, in an immovable orbit has by

a radius drawn to the centre described in any certain time, the difference of the forces, with which the body P revolves in an immovable orbit, and the body p in a movable orbit, will be to the centripetal force, with which another body by a radius drawn to the centre can uniformly describe that sector in the same time as the area VPC is described, as GG − FF to FF. For that sector and the area pCk are to one another as the times in which they are described.

Cor. 2. If the orbit VPK be an ellipsis, having its focus C, and its highest apsis V, and we suppose the ellipsis upk similar and equal to it, so that pC may be always equal to PC, and the angle VCp be to the angle VCP in the given ratio of G, to F; and for the altitude PC or pC we put A, and 2R for the latus rectum of the ellipsis, the force with which a body may be made to revolve in a movable ellipsis will be as $\dfrac{FF}{AA} + \dfrac{RGG-RFF}{A^3}$, and *vice versa*. Let the force with which a body may revolve in an immovable ellipsis be expressed by the quantity $\dfrac{FF}{AA}$,

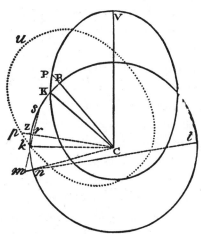

and the force in V will be $\dfrac{FF}{CV^2}$. But the force with which a body may revolve in

a circle at the distance CV, with the same velocity as a body revolving in an ellipsis has in V, is to the force with which a body revolving in an ellipsis is acted upon in the apsis V, as half the latus rectum of the ellipsis to the semi-diameter CV of the circle, and therefore is as $\dfrac{RFF}{CV^3}$; and the force which is to this, as GG − FF to FF, is as $\dfrac{RGG-RFF}{CV^3}$: and this force (by Cor. 1 of this Prop.) is the difference of the forces in V, with which the body P revolves in the immovable ellipsis VPK, and the body p in the movable ellipsis upk. Therefore since by this Prop. that difference at any other altitude A is to itself at the altitude CV as $\dfrac{1}{A^3}$ to $\dfrac{1}{CV^3}$ the same difference in every altitude A will be as

$\dfrac{RGG-RFF}{CV^3}$. Therefore to the force $\dfrac{FF}{AA}$, by which the body may revolve in an

immovable ellipsis VPK add the excess $\dfrac{RGG-RFF}{A^3}$, and the sum will be the whole force

$\dfrac{FF}{AA} + \dfrac{RGG-RFF}{A^3}$ by which a body may revolve in the same time in the movable ellipsis upk.

Cor. 3. In the same manner it will be found, that, if the immovable orbit VPK be an ellipsis having its centre in the centre of the forces C, and there be supposed a movable ellipsis upk, similar, equal, and concentrical to it; and 2R be the principal latus rectum of that ellipsis, and 2T the latus transversum, or greater axis; and

the angle VCp be continually to the angle VCP as G to F; the forces with which bodies may revolve in the immovable and movable ellipsis, in equal times, will be as $\frac{FFA}{T^3}$ and $\frac{FFA}{T^3} + \frac{RGG-RFF}{A^3}$ respectively.

COR. 4. And universally, if the greatest altitude CV of the body be called T, and the radius of the curvature which the orbit VPK has in V, that is, the radius of a circle equally curve, be called R, and the centripetal force with which a body may revolve in any immovable trajectory VPK at the place V be called $\frac{VFF}{TT}$, and in other places P be indefinitely styled X; and the altitude CP be called A, and G – be taken to F in the given ratio of the angle VCp to the angle VCP; the centripetal force with which the same body will perform the same motions in the same time, in the same trajectory *upk* revolving with a circular motion, will be as the sum of the forces $X + \frac{VRGG-VRFF}{A^3}$.

COR. 5. Therefore the motion of a body in an immovable orbit being given, its angular motion round the centre of the forces may be increased or diminished in a given ratio; and thence new immovable orbits may be found in which bodies may revolve with new centripetal forces.

COR. 6. Therefore if there be erected the line VP of an indeterminate length, perpendicular to the line CV given by position, and CP be drawn, and Cp equal to it, making the angle VCp having a given ratio to the angle VCP, the force with which a body may revolve in the curve line V, which the point p is continually describing, will be reciprocally as the cube of the altitude Cp. For the body P, by its *vis inertiæ* alone, no other force impelling it, will proceed uniformly in the right line VP. Add, then, a force tending to the centre C reciprocally as the cube of the altitude CP or Cp, and (by what was just demonstrated)

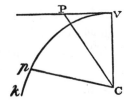

the body will deflect from the rectilinear motion into the curve line V*pk*. But this curve V*pk* is the same with the curve VPQ found in Cor. 3, Prop XLI, in which, I said, bodies attracted with such forces would ascend obliquely.

PROPOSITION XLV. PROBLEM XXXI.

TO FIND THE MOTION OF THE APSIDES IN ORBITS APPROACHING VERY NEAR TO CIRCLES.

This problem is solved arithmetically by reducing the orbit, which a body revolving in a movable ellipsis (as in Cor. 2 and 3 of the above Prop.) describes in an immovable place, to the figure of the orbit whose apsides are required; and then seeking the apsides of the orbit which that body describes in an immovable plane. But orbits acquire the same figure, if the centripetal forces with which they are described, compared between themselves, are made proportional at equal altitudes. Let the point V be the

highest apsis, and write T for the greatest altitude CV, A for any other altitude CP or Cp, and ✕ for the difference of the altitudes CV − CP; and the force with which a body moves in an ellipsis revolving about its focus C (as in Cor. 2), and which in Cor. 2 was as $\dfrac{FF}{AA} + \dfrac{RGG - RFF}{A^3}$,

that is as, $\dfrac{FFA + RGG - RFF}{A^3}$, by substituting T − ✕ for A, will become as $\dfrac{RGG - RFF + TFF - FFX}{A^3}$.

In like manner any other centripetal force is to be reduced to a fraction whose denominator is A^3, and the numerators are to be made analogous by collating together the homologous terms. This will be made plainer by Examples.

Example 1. Let us suppose the centripetal force to be uniform, and therefore as $\dfrac{A^3}{A^3}$ or,

writing T - ✕ for A in the numerator, as $\dfrac{T^3 - 3TTX + 3TXX - X^3}{A^3}$. Then collating together the

correspondent terms of the numerators, that is, those that consist of given quantities, with those of given quantities, and those of quantities not given with those of quantities not given, it will become RGG − RFF + TFF to T^3 as − FFX to 3TTX + 3TXX − X^3, or as − FF to − 3TT + 3TX − XX. Now since the orbit is supposed extremely near to a circle, let it coincide with a circle; and because in that case R and T become equal, and ✕ is infinitely diminished, the last ratios will be, as RGG to T^2, so − FF, to − 3TT, or as GG to TT, so FF to 3TT; and again, as GG to FF, so TT to 3TT, that is, as 1 to 3; and therefore G is to F, that is, the angle VCp to the angle VCP, as I to $\sqrt{3}$. Therefore since the body, in an immovable ellipsis, in descending from the upper to the lower apsis, describes an angle, if I may so speak, of 180 deg., the other body in a movable ellipsis, and therefore in the immovable orbit we are treating of, will in its descent from the upper to the lower apsis, describe an angle VCp of $\dfrac{T^3 - 3TTX + 3TXX - X^3}{A^3}$ deg. And this comes to pass by reason of the likeness of this orbit which a body acted upon by an uniform centripetal force describes, and of that orbit which a body performing its circuits in a revolving ellipsis will describe in a quiescent plane. By this collation of the terms, these orbits are made similar; not universally, indeed, but then only when they approach very near to a circular figure. A body, therefore revolving with an uniform centripetal force in an orbit nearly circular, will always describe an angle of $\dfrac{T^3 - 3TTX + 3TXX - X^3}{A^3}$

deg., or 103 deg., 55 m., 23 sec., at the centre; moving from the upper apsis to the lower apsis when it has once described that angle, and thence returning to the upper apsis when it has described that angle again; and so on *in infinitum*.

Exam. 2. Suppose the centripetal force to be as any power of the altitude A, as, for example, A^{n-3}, or $\dfrac{A^n}{A^3}$; where $n - 3$ and n signify any indices of powers whatever, whether integers or

fractions, rational or surd, affirmative or negative. That numerator A^n or $\overline{T - X\,|}^n$ being reduced

to an indeterminate series by my method of converging series, will become $T^n - nXT^{n-1} + \frac{mn-n}{2}$; XXT^{n-2}, &c. And conferring these terms with the terms of the other numerator RGG – RFF + TFF – FFX, it becomes as RGG – RFF + TFF to T^n) so – FF to – $nT^{n-1} + \frac{nn-n}{2} XT^{n-2}$, &c. And taking the last ratios where the orbits approach to circles, it becomes as RGG to T^n, so – FF to – nT^{n-1}, or as GG to T^{n-1}, so FF to nT^{n-1}; and again, GG to FF, so T^{n-1} to nT^{n-1}, that is, as 1 to n.; and therefore G is to F, that is the angle VCp to the angle VCP, as 1 to $\sqrt{n}$. Therefore since the angle VCP, described in the descent of the body from the upper apsis to the lower apsis in an ellipsis, is of 180 deg., the angle VCp, described in the descent of the body from the upper apsis to the lower apsis in an orbit nearly circular which a body describes with a centripetal force proportional to the power A^{n-3}, will be equal to an angle of $\frac{180}{\sqrt{n}}$ deg., and this angle being repeated, the body will return from the lower to the upper apsis, and so on *in infinitum*. As if the centripetal force be as the distance of the body from the centre, that is, as A, or $\frac{A^4}{A^3}$ n will be equal to 4, and $\sqrt{n}$ equal to 2; and therefore the angle

between the upper and the lower apsis will be equal to $\frac{180}{2}$ deg., or 90 deg. Therefore the body having performed a fourth part of one revolution, will arrive at the lower apsis, and having performed another fourth part, will arrive at the upper apsis, and so on by turns *in infinitum*. This appears also from Prop. X. For a body acted on by this centripetal force will revolve in an immovable ellipsis, whose centre is the centre of force. If the centripetal force is reciprocally as the distance, that is, directly as $\frac{1}{A}$ or $\frac{A^2}{A^3}$,

n will be equal to 2; and therefore the angle between the upper and lower apsis will be $\frac{180}{\sqrt{2}}$ deg., or 127 deg., 16 min., 45 sec.; and therefore a body revolving with such a force, will by a perpetual repetition of this angle, move alternately from the upper to the lower and from the lower to the upper apsis for ever. So, also, if the centripetal force be reciprocally as the biquadrate root of the eleventh power of the altitude, that is, reciprocally as $A^{\frac{11}{4}}$, and, therefore, directly as $A^{\frac{11}{4}}$, or as $\frac{A^{\frac{1}{4}}}{A^3}$ n will be equal to $\frac{1}{4}$, and

$\frac{180}{\sqrt{n}}$ deg. will be equal to 360 deg.; and therefore the body parting from the upper apsis, and from thence perpetually descending, will arrive at the lower apsis when it has completed one entire revolution; and thence ascending perpetually, when it has completed another entire revolution, it will arrive again at the upper apsis; and so alternately forever.

Exam. 3. Taking m and n for any indices of the powers of the altitude, and b and c for any given numbers, suppose the centripetal force to be as

$\frac{bA^m + cA^n}{A^3}$, that is, as $b \text{ into } \overline{T-X}^m + c \text{ into } \overline{T-X}^n$ or (by the method of converging series

above-mentioned) as $\dfrac{bT^m + cT^n - mbXT^{m-l} ncXT^{n-1} + \frac{mm-m}{2} - bXXT^{m-2} + \frac{nn-n}{2} cXXT^{n-2}, \&c.}{A^3}$

and comparing the terms of the numerators, there will arise RGG − RFF + TFF to $bT^m + cT^n$ as − FF to $mbT^{m-1} - ncT^{n-1} + \frac{mm-m}{2} bXT^{m-2} + \frac{nn-n}{2} cXT^{n-2}$, &c. And taking the last ratios that arise when the orbits come to a circular form, there will come forth GG to $bT^{m-1} + cT^{n-1}$ as FF to $mbT^{m-1} + ncT^{n-1}$; and again, GG to FF as $bT^{m-1} + cT^{n-1}$ to $mbT^{n-1} + ncT^{n-1}$. This proportion, by expressing the greatest altitude CV or T arithmetically by unity, becomes, GG to FF as $b + c$ to $mb + nc$, and therefore as 1 to $\frac{mb+nc}{b+c}$. Whence G becomes to F, that is, the angle VCp to the

angle VCP, as 1 to $\sqrt{\frac{mb+nc}{b+c}}$. And therefore since the angle VCP between the upper and the lower apsis, in an immovable ellipsis, is of 180 deg., the angle VCp between the same apsides in an orbit which a body describes with a centripetal force, that is, as $\frac{bA^m + cA^n}{A^3}$, will be equal to an angle of 180 $\sqrt{\frac{b+c}{mb+nc}}$ deg. And by the same reasoning, if

the centripetal force be as $\dfrac{bA^m + cA^n}{A^3}$, the angle between the apaides will be found equal

to 180 $\sqrt{\frac{b-c}{mb-nc}}$ deg. After the same manner the Problem is solved in more difficult cases. The quantity to which the centripetal force is proportional must always be resolved into a converging series whose denominator is A^3. Then the given part of the numerator arising from that operation is to be supposed in the same ratio to that part of it which is not given, as the given part of this numerator RGG − RFF + TFF − FFX is to that part of the same numerator which is not given. And taking away the superfluous quantities, and writing unity for T, the proportion of G to F is obtained.

COR. 1. Hence if the centripetal force be as any power of the altitude, that power may be found from the motion of the apsides; and so contrariwise. That is, if the whole angular motion, with which the body returns to the same apsis, be to the angular motion of one revolution, or 360 deg., as any number as m to another as n, and the altitude called A; the force will be as the power $A^{\frac{nm}{mm}-3}$ of the altitude A; the index of

which power is $\frac{nm}{mm}-3$. This appears by the second example. Hence it is plain that the force in its recess from the centre cannot decrease in a greater then a triplicate ratio of the altitude. A body revolving with such a force, and parting from the apsis, if it once begins to descend, can never arrive at the lower apsis or least altitude, but will descend

to the centre, describing the curve line treated of in Cor. 3, Prop. XLI. But if it should, at its parting from the lower apsis, begin to ascend ever so little, it will ascend *in infinitum*, and never come to the upper apsis; but will describe the curve line spoken of in the same Cor. 3, and Cor. 6, Prop. XLIV. So that where the force in its recess from the centre decreases in a greater than a triplicate ratio of the altitude, the body at its parting from the apsis, will either descend to the centre, or ascend *in infinitum*, according as it descends or ascends at the beginning of its motion. But if the force in its recess from the centre either decreases in a less than a triplicate ratio of the altitude, or increases in any ratio of the altitude whatsoever, the body will never descend to the centre, but will at some time arrive at the lower apsis; and, on the contrary, if the body alternately ascending and descending from one apsis to another never comes to the centre, then either the force increases in the recess from the centre, or it decreases in a less than a triplicate ratio of the altitude; and the sooner the body returns from one apsis to another, the farther is the ratio of the forces from the triplicate ratio. As if the body should return to and from the upper apsis by an alternate descent and ascent in S revolutions, or in 4, or 2, or $1\frac{1}{2}$; that is, if m should be to n as 8, or 4, or 2, or $1\frac{1}{2}$ to 1, and therefore $\frac{nm}{mm} - 3$ be $\frac{1}{64} - 3$ or $\frac{1}{16} - 3$, or $\frac{1}{4} - 3$, or $\frac{4}{9} - 3$; then the force will be as $A^{1/64 - 3}$ 1 or $A^{1/16 - 3}$, or $A^{1/4 - 3}$, or $A^{4/9 - 3}$; that is, it will be reciprocally as $A^{3 - 1/64}$, or $A^{3 - 1/16}$, or $A^{3 - 1/4}$, or $A^{3 - 4/9}$. If the body after each revolution returns to the same apsis, and the apsis remains unmoved, then m will be to n as 1 to 1, and therefore $A^{\frac{nm}{mm} - 3}$ will be equal to A^{-2}, or $\frac{1}{AA}$; and therefore the decrease of the forces will be in a duplicate ratio of the altitude; as was demonstrated above. If the body in three fourth parts, or two thirds, or one third, or one fourth part of an entire revolution, return to the same apsis; m will be to n. as $\frac{3}{4}$ or $\frac{2}{3}$ or $\frac{1}{3}$ or $\frac{1}{4}$ to 1, and therefore $A^{\frac{nm}{mm} - 3}$ is equal to $A^{16/9 - 3}$, or $A^{9/4 - 3}$ or $A^{9 - 3}$, or $A^{16 - 3}$; and therefore the force is either reciprocally as $A^{11/9}$ or $A^{3/4}$, or directly as A^6 or A^{13}. Lastly if the body in its progress from the upper apsis to the same upper apsis again, goes over one entire revolution and three deg. more, and therefore that apsis in each revolution of the body moves three deg. *in consequentia*; then m will be to n as 363 deg. to 360 deg. or as 121 to 120, and therefore $A^{\frac{nm}{mm} - 3}$ will be equal to $A^{-\frac{29523}{14641}}$ and

therefore the centripetal force will be reciprocally as $A^{\frac{29523}{14641}}$ or reciprocally as very nearly. Therefore the centripetal force decreases in a ratio something greater than the duplicate; but approaching $59\frac{3}{4}$ times nearer to the duplicate than the triplicate.

COR. 2. Hence also if a body, urged by a centripetal force which is reciprocally as the square of the altitude, revolves in an ellipsis whose focus is in the centre of the

forces; and a new and foreign force should be added to or subducted from this centripetal force, the motion of the apsides arising from that foreign force may (by the third Example) be known; and so on the contrary. As if the force with which the body revolves in the ellipsis be as $\frac{1}{AA}$ and the foreign force subducted as cA, and therefore

the remaining force as $\frac{A-cA^4}{A^3}$; then (by the third Example) b will be equal to 1, m equal to 1, and n equal to 4; and therefore the angle of revolution between the apsides is equal to $180\sqrt{\frac{1-c}{1-4c}}$ deg. Suppose that foreign force to be 357.45 parts less than the

other force with which the body revolves in the ellipsis; that is, c to be $\frac{A-cA^4}{A^3}$; A or T

being equal to 1; and then $180\sqrt{\frac{1-c}{1-4c}}$ will be $180\sqrt{\frac{35645}{35345}}$ or 180.7623, that is, 180 deg., 45 min., 44 sec. Therefore the body, parting from the upper apsis, will arrive at the lower apsis with an angular motion of 180 deg., 45 min., 44 sec, and this angular motion being repeated, will return to the upper apsis; and therefore the upper apsis in each revolution will go forward 1 deg., 31 min., 28 sec. The apsis of the moon is about twice as swift.

So much for the motion of bodies in orbits whose planes pass through the centre of force. It now remains to determine those motions in eccentrical planes. For those authors who treat of the motion of heavy bodies used to consider the ascent and descent of such bodies, not only in a perpendicular direction, but at all degrees of obliquity upon any given planes; and for the same reason we are to consider in this place the motions of bodies tending to centres by means of any forces whatsoever, when those bodies move in eccentrical planes. These planes are supposed to be perfectly smooth and polished, so as not to retard the motion of the bodies in the least. Moreover, in these demonstrations, instead of the planes upon which those bodies roll or slide, and which are therefore tangent planes to the bodies, I shall use planes parallel to them, in which the centres of the bodies move, and by that motion describe orbits. And by the same method I afterwards determine the motions of bodies performed in curve superficies.

SECTION X.

Of the motion of bodies in given superficies, and of the reciprocal motion of funependulous bodies.

PROPOSITION XLVI. PROBLEM XXXII.

ANY KIND OF CENTRIPETAL FORCE BEING SUPPOSED, AND
THE CENTRE OF FORCE, AND ANY PLANE WHATSOEVER IN
WHICH THE BODY REVOLVES, BEING GIVEN, AND THE
QUADRATURES OF CURVILINEAR FIGURES BEING ALLOWED; IT
IS REQUIRED TO DETERMINE THE MOTION OF A BODY
GOING OFF FROM A GIVEN PLACE, WITH A GIVEN VELOCITY,
IN THE DIRECTION OF A GIVEN RIGHT LINE IN THAT PLANE.

Let S be the centre of force, SC the least distance of that centre from the given plane, P a body issuing from the place P in the direction of the right line PZ, Q the same body revolving in its trajectory, and PQR the trajectory itself which is required to be found, described in that given plane. Join CQ, QS, and if in QS we take SV proportional to the centripetal force with which the body is attracted towards the centre

S, and draw VT parallel to CQ, and meeting SC in T; then will the force SV be resolved into two (by Cor. 2, of the Laws of Motion), the force ST, and the force TV; of which ST attracting the body in the direction of a line perpendicular to that plane, does not at all change its motion in that plane. But the action of the other force TV, coinciding with the position of the plane itself, attracts the body directly towards the given point C in that plane; and therefore causes the body to move in this plane in

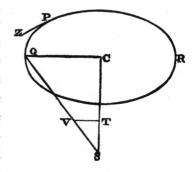

the same manner as if the force ST were taken away, and the body were to revolve in free space about the centre C by means of the force TV alone. But there being given the centripetal force TV with which the body Q revolves in free space about the given centre C, there is given (by Prop. XLII) the trajectory PQR which the body describes; the place Q, in which the body will be found at any given time; and, lastly, the velocity of the body in that place Q. And so è contra.   *Q.E.I.*

PROPOSITION XLVII. THEOREM XV.

SUPPOSING THE CENTRIPETAL FORCE TO BE PROPORTIONAL
TO THE DISTANCE OF THE BODY FROM THE CENTRE; ALL
BODIES REVOLVING IN ANY PLANES WHATSOEVER WILL
DESCRIBE ELLIPSES, AND COMPLETE THEIR REVOLUTIONS IN
EQUAL TIMES; AND THOSE WHICH MOVE IN RIGHT LINES

RUNNING BACKWARDS AND FORWARDS ALTERNATELY, WILL
COMPLETE THEIR SEVERAL PERIODS OF GOING AND
RETURNING IN THE SAME TIMES.

For letting all things stand as in the foregoing Proposition, the force SV, with which the body Q revolving in any plane PQR is attracted towards the centre S, is as the distance SQ; and therefore because SV and SQ, TV and CQ are proportional, the force TV with which the body is attracted towards the given point C in the plane of the orbit is as the distance CQ. Therefore the forces with which bodies found in the plane PQR are attracted towards the point C, are in proportion to the distances equal to the forces with which the same bodies are attracted every way towards the centre S; and therefore the bodies will move in the same times, and in the same figures, in any plane PQR about the point C as they would do in free spaces about the centre S; and therefore (by Cor. 2, Prop. X, and Cor. 2, Prop. XXXVIII.) they will in equal times either describe ellipses in that plane about the centre C, or move to and fro in right line passing through the centre C in that plane; completing the same periods of time in all cases.   *Q.E.D.*

SCHOLIUM.

The ascent and descent of bodies in curve superficies has a near relation to these motions we have been speaking of. Imagine curve lines to be described on any plane, and to revolve about any given axes passing through the centre of force, and by that revolution to describe curve superficies; and that the bodies move in such sort that their centres may be always found in these superficies. If those bodies reciprocate to and fro with an oblique ascent and descent, their motions will be performed in planes passing through the axis, and therefore in the curve lines, by whose revolution those curve superficies were generated. In those cases, therefore, it will be sufficient to consider the motion in those curve lines.

PROPOSITION XLVIII. THEOREM XVI.

IF A WHEEL STANDS UPON THE OUTSIDE OF A GLOBE AT
RIGHT ANGLES THERETO, AND REVOLVING ABOUT ITS OWN
AXIS GOES FORWARD IN A GREAT CIRCLE, THE LENGTH OF
THE CURVILINEAR PATH WHICH ANY POINT, GIVEN IN THE
PERIMETER OF THE WHEEL, HATH DESCRIBED SINCE THE
TIME THAT IT TOUCHED THE GLOBE (WHICH CURVILINEAR
PATH WE MAY CALL THE CYCLOID OR EPICYCLOID), WILL BE
TO DOUBLE THE VERSED SINE OF HALF THE ARC WHICH

SINCE THAT TIME HAS TOUCHED THE GLOBE IN PASSING
OVER IT, AS THE SUM OF THE DIAMETERS OF THE GLOBE
AND THE WHEEL TO THE SEMI-DIAMETER OF THE GLOBE.

PROPOSITION XLIX. THEOREM XVII.

IF A WHEEL STAND UPON THE INSIDE OF A CONCAVE GLOBE
AT RIGHT ANGLES THERETO, AND REVOLVING ABOUT ITS
OWN AXIS GO FORWARD IN ONE OF THE GREAT CIRCLES OF
THE GLOBE, THE LENGTH OF THE CURVILINEAR PATH WHICH
ANY POINT, GIVEN IN THE PERIMETER OF THE WHEEL, HATH
DESCRIBED SINCE IT TOUCHED THE GLOBE, WILL BE TO THE
DOUBLE OF THE VERSED SINE OF HALF THE ARC WHICH IN
ALL THAT TIME HAS TOUCHED THE GLOBE IN PASSING OVER
IT, AS THE DIFFERENCE OF THE DIAMETERS OF THE GLOBE
AND THE WHEEL TO THE SEMI-DIAMETER OF THE GLOBE.

Let ABL be the globe, C its centre, BPV the wheel insisting thereon, E the centre
of the wheel, B the point of contact, and P the given point in the perimeter of the

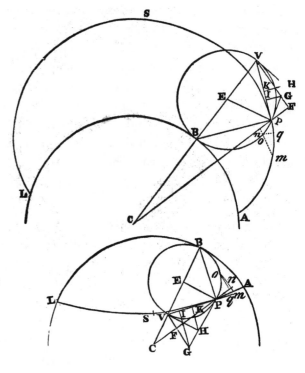

wheel. Imagine this wheel to
proceed in the great circle
ABL from A through B
towards L, and in its progress
to revolve in such a manner
that the arcs AB, PB may be
always equal one to the other,
and the given point P in the
perimeter of the wheel may
describe in the mean time the
curvilinear path AP. Let AP be
the whole curvilinear path
described since the wheel
touched the globe in A, and
the length of this path AP will
be to twice the versed sine of
the are $^1/_2$PB as 2CE to CB.
For let the right line CE (produced if need be) meet the
wheel in V, and join CP, BP,

EP, VP; produce CP, and let fall thereon the perpendicular VF. Let PH, VH, meeting in H, touch the circle in P and V, and let PH cut VF in G, and to VP let fall the perpendiculars GI, HK. From the centre C with any interval let there be described the circle *nom*, cutting the right line CP in *n*, the perimeter of the wheel BP in *o*, and the curvilinear path AP in *m*; and from the centre V with the interval V*o* let there be described a circle cutting VP produced in *q*.

Because the wheel in its progress always revolves about the point of contact B, it is manifest that the right line BP is perpendicular to that curve line AP which the point P of the wheel describes, and therefore that the right line VP will touch this curve in the point P. Let the radius of the circle *nom* be gradually increased or diminished so that at last it become equal to the distance CP; and by reason of the similitude of the evanescent figure P*nomq*, and the figure PFGVI, the ultimate ratio of the evanescent lineolæ P*m*, P*n*, P*o*, P*q*, that is, the ratio of the momentary mutations of the curve AP, the right line CP, the circular arc BP, and the right line VP, will be the same as of the lines PV, PF, PG, PI, respectively. But since VF is perpendicular to CF, and VH to CV, and therefore the angles HVG, VCF equal; and the angle VHG (because the angles of the quadrilateral figure HVEP are right in V and P) is equal to the angle CEP, the triangles V HG, CEP will be similar; and thence it will come to pass that as EP is to CE so is HG to HV or HP, and so KI to KP, and by composition or division as CB to CE so is PI to PK, and doubling the consequents as CB to 2CE so PI to PV, and so is P*q* to P*m*. Therefore the decrement of the line VP, that is, the increment of the line BV-VP to the increment of the curve line AP is in a given ratio of CB to 2CE, and therefore (by Cor. Lem. IV) the lengths BV – VP and AP, generated by those increments, are in the same ratio. But if BV be radius, VP is the cosine of the angle BVP or $^1/_2$BEP, and therefore BV – VP is the versed sine of the same angle, and therefore in this wheel, whose radius is $^1/_2$BV, BV – VP will be double the versed sine of the arc $^1/_2$BP. Therefore AP is to double the versed sine of the arc $^1/_2$BP as 2CE to CB.   *Q.E.D.*

The line AP in the former of these Propositions we shall name the cycloid without the globe, the other in the latter Proposition the cycloid within the globe, for distinction sake.

COR. 1. Hence if there be described the entire cycloid ASL, and the same be bisected in S, the length of the part PS will be to the length PV (which is the double of the sine of the angle VBP, when EB is radius) as 2CE to CB, and therefore in a given ratio.

COR. 2. And the length of the semi-perimeter of the cycloid AS will be equal to a right line which is to the diameter of the wheel BV as 2CE to CB.

PROPOSITION L. PROBLEM XXXIII.

TO CAUSE A PENDULOUS BODY TO OSCILLATE IN A GIVEN CYCLOID.

Let there be given within the globe QVS described with the centre C, the cycloid QRS, bisected in R, and meeting the superficies of the globe with its extreme points Q and S on either hand. Let there be drawn CR bisecting the arc QS in O, and let it be produced to A in such sort that CA may be to CO as CO to CR. About the centre C, with the interval CA, let there be described an exterior globe DAF; and within this globe, by a wheel whose diameter is AO, let there be described two semi-cycloids AQ, AS, touching the interior globe in Q and S, and meeting the exterior globe in A. From that point A, with a thread APT in length equal to the line AR, let the body T depend, and oscillate in such manner between the two semi-cycloids AQ, AS, that, as often as the pendulum parts from the perpendicular AR, the upper part of the thread AP may be applied to that semi-cycloid APS towards which the motion tends, and fold itself round that curve line, as if it were some solid obstacle, the remaining part of the same thread PT which has not yet touched the semi-cycloid continuing straight. Then will the weight T oscillate in the given cycloid QRS. *Q.E.F.*

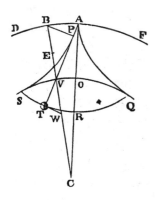

For let the thread PT meet the cycloid QRS in T, and the circle QOS in V, and let CV be drawn; and to the rectilinear part of the thread PT from the extreme points P and T let there be erected the perpendiculars BP, TW, meeting the right line CV in B and W. It is evident, from the construction and generation of the similar figures AS, SR, that those perpendiculars PB, TW, cut off from CV the lengths VB, VW equal the diameters of the wheels OA, OR. Therefore TP is to VP (which is double the sine of the angle VBP when $\frac{1}{2}$BV is radius) as BW to BV, or AO +OR to AO, that is (since CA and CO, CO and CR, and by division AO and OR are proportional), as CA + CO to CA, or, if BV be bisected in E, as 2CE to CB. Therefore (by Cor. 1, Prop. XLIX), the length of the rectilinear part of the thread PT is always equal to the arc of the cycloid PS, and the whole thread APT is always equal to the half of the cycloid APS, that is (by Cor. 2, Prop. XLIX), to the length AR. And therefore contrariwise, if the string remain always equal to the length AR, the point T will always move in the given cycloid QRS. *Q.E.D.*

Cor. The string AR is equal to the semi-cycloid AS, and therefore has the same ratio to AC the semi-diameter of the exterior globe as the like semi-cycloid SR has to CO the semi-diameter of the interior globe.

PROPOSITION LI. THEOREM XVIII.

IF A CENTRIPETAL FORCE TENDING, ON ALL SIDES TO THE
CENTRE C OF A GLOBE, BE IN ALL PLACES AS THE DISTANCE
OF THE PLACE FROM THE CENTRE, AND BY THIS FORCE
ALONE ACTING, UPON IT, THE BODY T OSCILLATE (IN THE
MANNER ABOVE DESCRIBED) IN THE PERIMETER OF THE
CYCLOID QRS; I SAY, THAT ALL THE OSCILLATIONS, HOW
UNEQUAL SOEVER IN THEMSELVES, WILL BE PERFORMED
IN EQUAL TIMES.

For upon the tangent TW infinitely produced let fall the perpendicular CX, and join CT. Because the centripetal force with which the body T is impelled towards C is as the distance CT, let this (by Cor. 2, of the Laws) be resolved into the parts CX, TX, of which CX. impelling the body directly from P stretches the thread PT, and by the resistance the thread makes to it is totally employed, producing no other effect; but the other part TX, impelling the body transversely or towards X, directly accelerates the motion in the cycloid. Then it is plain that the acceleration of the body, proportional to this accelerating force, will be every moment as the length TX, that is (because CV,

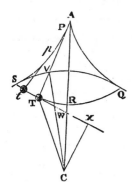

WV, and TX, TW proportional to them are given), as the length TW, that is (by Cor. 1, Prop. XLIX) as the length of the arc of the cycloid TR. If therefore two pendulums APT, A*pt*, be unequally drawn aside from the perpendicular AR, and let fall together, their accelerations will be always as the arcs to be described TR, *t*R. But the parts described at the beginning of the motion are as the accelerations, that is, as the wholes that are to be described at the beginning, and therefore the parts which remain to be described, and the subsequent accelera- tions proportional to those parts, are also as the wholes, and so on. Therefore the accelerations, and consequently the velocities generated, and the parts described with those velocities, and the parts to be described, are always as the wholes; and therefore the parts to be described preserving a given ratio to each other will vanish together, that is, the two bodies oscillating will arrive togeth- er at the perpendicular AR. And since on the other hand the ascent of the pendu- lums from the lowest place R through the same cycloidal arcs with a retrograde motion, is retarded in the several places they pass through by the same forces by which their descent was accelerated; it is plain that the velocities of their ascent and descent through the same arcs are equal, and consequently performed in equal times; and, therefore, since the two parts of the cycloid RS and RQ lying on either

side of the perpendicular are similar and equal, the two pendulums will perform as well the wholes as the halves of their oscillations in the same times.   *Q.E.D.*

COR. The force with which the body T is accelerated or retarded in any place T of the cycloid, is to the whole weight of the same body in the highest place S or Q as the are of the cycloid TR is to the arc SR or QR.

PROPOSITION LII. PROBLEM XXXIV.

TO DEFINE THE VELOCITIES OF THE PENDULUMS IN THE SEVERAL PLACES, AND THE TIMES IN WHICH BOTH THE ENTIRE OSCILLATIONS, AND THE SEVERAL PARTS OF THEM ARE PERFORMED.

About any centre G, with the interval GH equal to the arc of the cycloid RS, describe a semi-circle HKM bisected by the semi-diameter GK. And if a centripetal

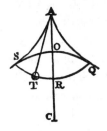

force proportional to the distance of the places from the centre tend to the centre G, and it be in the perimeter HIK equal to the centripetal force in the perimeter of the globe QOS tending towards its centre, and at the same time that the pendulum T is let fall from the highest place S, a body, as L, is let fall from H to G; then because the forces which act upon the bodies are equal at the beginning, and always proportional to the spaces to be described TR, LG, and therefore if TR and LG are equal, are also equal in the places T and L, it is plain that those bodies describe at the beginning equal spaces ST, HL, and therefore are still acted upon equally, and continue to describe equal spaces. Therefore by Prop. XXXVIII, the time in which the body describes the arc ST is to the time of one oscil-

lation, as the arc HI the time in which the body H arrives at L, to the semi-periphery HKM, the time in which the body H will come to M. And the velocity of the pendulous body in the place T is to its velocity in the lowest place R, that is, the velocity of the body H in the place L to its velocity in the place G, or the

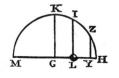

momentary increment of the line HL, to the momentary increment of the line HG (the arcs HI, HK increasing with an equable flux) as the ordinate LI to the radius GK, or as $\sqrt{SR^2 - TR^2}$ to SR. Hence, since in unequal oscillations there are described in equal time arcs proportional to the entire arcs of the oscillations, there are obtained from the times given, both the velocities and the arcs described in all the oscillations universally. Which was first required.

Let now any pendulous bodies oscillate in different cycloids described within different globes, whose absolute forces are also different; and if the absolute force of any

globe QOS be called V, the accelerative force with which the pendulum is acted on in the circumference of this globe, when it begins to move directly towards its centre, will be as the distance of the pendulous body from that centre and the absolute force of the globe conjunctly, that is, as CO × V. Therefore the lineola HY, which is as this accelerated force CO × V, will be described in a given time; and if there be erected the perpendicular YZ meeting the circumference in Z, the nascent arc HZ will denote that given time. But that nascent arc HZ is in the subduplicate ratio of the rectangle GHY, and therefore as $\sqrt{GH \times CO \times V}$. Whence the time of an entire oscillation in the cycloid QRS (it being as the semi-periphery HKM, which denotes that entire oscillation, directly; and as the arc HZ which in like manner denotes a given time inversely) will be as GH directly and $\sqrt{GH \times CO \times V}$ inversely; that is, because GH and SR are equal, as

$\sqrt{\dfrac{SR}{CO \times V}}$ or (by Cor. Prop. L,) as $\sqrt{\dfrac{AR}{AC \times V}}$. Therefore the oscillations in all globes and cycloids, performed with what absolute forces soever, are in a ratio compounded of the subduplicate ratio of the length of the string directly, and the subduplicate ratio of the distance between the point of suspension and the centre of the globe inversely, and the subduplicate ratio of the absolute force of the globe inversely also. Q.E.I.

COR. 1. Hence also the times of oscillating, falling, and revolving bodies may be compared among themselves. For if the diameter of the wheel with which the cycloid is described within the globe is supposed equal to the semi-diameter of the globe, the cycloid will become a right line passing through the centre of the globe, and the oscillation will be changed into a descent and subsequent ascent in that right line. Whence there is given both the time of the descent from any place to the centre, and the time equal to it in which the body revolving uniformly about the centre of the globe at any distance describes an arc of a quadrant. For this time (by Case 2) is to the time of half the oscillation in any cycloid QRS as 1 to $\sqrt{\dfrac{AR}{AC \times V}}$.

COR. 2. Hence also follow what Sir *Christopher Wren* and M. *Huygens*, have discovered concerning the vulgar cycloid. For if the diameter of the globe be infinitely increased, its sphærical superficies will be changed into a plane, and the centripetal force will act uniformly in the direction of lines perpendicular to that plane, and this cycloid of our's will become the same with the common cycloid. But in that case the length of the arc of the cycloid between that plane and the describing point will become equal to four times the versed sine of half the arc of the wheel between the same plane and the describing point, as was discovered by Sir *Christopher Wren*. And a pendulum between two such cycloids will oscillate in a similar and equal cycloid in equal times, as M. *Huygens* demonstrated. The descent of heavy bodies also in the time of one oscillation will be the same as M. *Huygens* exhibited.

The propositions here demonstrated are adapted to the true constitution of the Earth, in so far as wheels moving in any of its great circles will describe, by the motions of nails fixed in their perimeters, cycloids without the globe; and pendulums, in mines and deep caverns of the Earth, must oscillate in cycloids within the globe, that those oscillations may be performed in equal times. For gravity (as will be shewn in the third book) decreases in its progress from the superficies of the Earth; upwards in a duplicate ratio of the distances from the centre of the Earth; downwards in a simple ratio of the same.

PROPOSITION LIII. PROBLEM XXXV.

GRANTING THE QUADRATURES OF CURVILINEAR FIGURES, IT IS REQUIRED TO FIND THE FORCES WITH WHICH BODIES MOVING IN GIVEN CURVE LINES MAY ALWAYS PERFORM THEIR OSCILLATIONS IN EQUAL TIMES.

Let the body T oscillate in any curve line STRQ, whose axis is AR passing through the centre of force C. Draw TX touching that curve in any place of the body T, and in that tangent TX take TY equal to the arc TR. The length of that arc is known from the common methods used for the quadratures of figures. From the point Y draw the right line YZ perpendicular to the tangent. Draw CT meeting that perpendicular in Z, and the centripetal force will be proportional to the right line TZ.   *Q.E.I.*

For if the force with which the body is attracted from T towards C be expressed by the right line TZ taken proportional to it, that force will he resolved into two forces TY, YZ, of which YZ drawing the body in the direction of the length of the thread PT, does not at all change its motion; whereas the other force TY directly accelerates or retards its motion in the curve STRQ. Wherefore since that force is as the space to be described TR, the accelerations or retardations of the body in describing two proportional parts (a greater and a less) of two oscillations, will be always as those parts, and therefore will cause those parts to be described together. But bodies which continually describe together parts proportional to the wholes, will describe the wholes together also.   *Q.E.D.*

COR. 1. Hence if the body T, hanging by a rectilinear thread AT from the centre A, describe the circular arc STRQ, and in the mean time be acted on by any force tending downwards with parallel directions, which is to the uniform force of gravity as the arc TR to its sine TN, the times of the several oscillations will be equal. For because

TZ, AR are parallel, the triangles ATN, ZTY are similar; and therefore TZ will be to AT as TY to TN; that is, if the uniform force of gravity be expressed by the given length AT, the force TZ, by which the oscillations become isochronous, will be to the force of gravity AT, as the arc TR equal to TY is to TN the sine of that arc.

COR. 2. And therefore in clocks, if forces were impressed by some machine upon the pendulum which preserves the motion, and so compounded with the force of gravity that the whole force tending downwards should be always as a line produced by applying the rectangle under the arc TR and the radius AR to the sine TN, all the oscillations will become isochronous.

PROPOSITION LIV. PROBLEM XXXVI.

GRANTING THE QUADRATURES OF CURVILINEAR FIGURES, IT IS REQUIRED TO FIND THE TIMES IN WHICH BODIES BY MEANS OF ANY CENTRIPETAL FORCE WILL DESCEND OR ASCEND IN ANY CURVE LINES DESCRIBED IN A PLANE PASSING THROUGH THE CENTRE OF FORCE.

Let the body descend from any place S, and move in any curve ST R given in a plane passing through the centre of force C. Join CS, and let it be divided into innumerable equal parts, and let D*d* be one of those parts. From the centre C, with the intervals CD, C*d*, let the circles DT, *dt* be described, meeting the curve line ST*t*R in

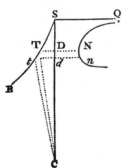

T and *t*. And because the law of centripetal force is given, and also the altitude CS from which the body at first fell, there will be given the velocity of the body in any other altitude CT (by Prop. XXXIX). But the time in which the body describes the lineola T*t* is as the length of that lineola, that is, as the secant of the angle *t*TC directly, and the velocity inversely. Let the ordinate DN, proportional to this time, be made perpendicular to the right line CS at the point D, and because D*d* is given, the rectangle D*d* × DN, that is, the area DN*nd*, will be proportional to the same time. Therefore if PN*n* be a curve line in which the point N is perpetually found, and its asymptote be the right line SQ standing upon the line CS at right angles, the area SQPND will be proportional to the time in which the body in its descent hath described the line ST; and therefore that area being found, the time is also given. *Q.E.I.*

PROPOSITION LV. THEOREM XIX.

IF A BODY MOVE IN ANY CURVE SUPERFICIES, WHOSE AXIS
PASSES THROUGH THE CENTRE OF FORCE, AND FROM THE
BODY A PERPENDICULAR BE LET FALL UPON THE AXIS; AND A
LINE PARALLEL AND EQUAL THERETO BE DRAWN FROM ANY
GIVEN POINT OF THE AXIS; I SAY, THAT THIS PARALLEL LINE
WILL DESCRIBE AN AREA PROPORTIONAL TO THE TIME.

Let BKL be a curve superficies, T a body revolving in it, STR a trajectory which the body describes in the same, S the beginning of the trajectory, OMK the axis of the curve superficies, TN a right line let fall perpendicularly from the body to the axis; OP a line parallel and equal thereto drawn from the given point O in the axis; AP the orthographic projection of the trajectory described by the point P in the plane AOP in which the revolving line OP is found; A the beginning of that projection, answering to

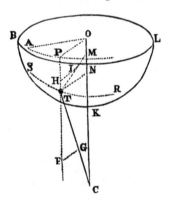

the point S; TC a right line drawn from the body to the centre; TG a part thereof proportional to the centripetal force with which the body tends towards the centre C; TM a right line perpendicular to the curve superficies; T1 a part thereof proportional to the force of pressure with which the body urges the superficies, and therefore with which it is again repelled by the superficies towards M; PTF a right line parallel to the axis and passing through the body, and GF, IH right lines let fall perpendicularly from the points G and I upon that parallel PHTF. I say, now, that the area AOP, described by the radius OP from the beginning of the motion, is proportional to the time. For the force TG (by Cor. 2, of the Laws of Motion) is resolved into the forces TF, FG; and the force TI into the forces TH, HI; but the forces TF, TH, acting in the direction of the line PF perpendicular to the plane AOP, introduce no change in the motion of the body but in a direction perpendicular to that plane. Therefore its motion, so far as it has the same direction with the position of the plane, that is, the motion of the point P, by which the projection AP of the trajectory is described in that plane, is the same as if the forces TF, TH were taken away, and the body were acted on by the forces FG, HI alone; that is, the same as if the body were to describe in the plane AOP the curve AP by means of a centripetal force tending to the centre O, and equal to the sum of the forces FG and HI. But with such a force as that (by Prop. 1) the area AOP will be described proportional to the time.   *Q.E.D.*

Cor. By the same reasoning, if a body, acted on by forces tending to two or more centres in any the same right line CO, should describe in a free space any curve line ST, the area AOP would be always proportional to the time.

PROPOSITION LVI. PROBLEM XXXVII.

GRANTING THE QUADRATURES OF CURVILINEAR FIGURES, AND SUPPOSING THAT THERE ARE GIVEN BOTH THE LAW OF CENTRIPETAL FORCE TENDING TO A GIVEN CENTRE, AND THE CURVE SUPERFICIES WHOSE AXIS PASSES THROUGH THAT CENTRE; IT IS REQUIRED TO FIND THE TRAJECTORY WHICH A BODY WILL DESCRIBE IN THAT SUPERFICIES, WHEN GOING OFF FROM A GIVEN PLACE WITH A GIVEN VELOCITY, AND IN A GIVEN DIRECTION IN THAT SUPERFICIES.

The last construction remaining, let the body T go from the given place S, in the direction of a line given by position, and turn into the trajectory sought STR, whose orthographic projection in the plane BDO is AP. And from the given velocity of the body in the altitude SC, its velocity in any other altitude TC will be also given. With that velocity, in a given moment of time, let the body describe the particle T*t* of its trajectory, and let P*p* be the projection of that particle described in the plane AOP. Join O*p*, and a little circle being described upon the curve superficies about the centre T with the interval T*t* let the projection of that little circle in the plane AOP be the ellipsis *p*Q. And because the magnitude of that little circle T*t*, and TN or PO its distance from the axis CO is also given, the ellipsis *p*Q will be given both in kind and magnitude, as also its position to the right line PO. And since the area PO*p* is proportional to the time, and therefore given because the time is given, the angle PO*p* will be given. And thence will be given *p* the common intersection of the ellipsis and the right line O*p*, together with the angle OP*p*, in which the projection AP*p* of the trajectory cuts the line OP. But from thence (by conferring Prop. XLI, with its 2d Cor.) the manner of determining the curve AP*p* easily appears. Then from the several points P of that projection erecting to the plane AOP, the perpendiculars PT meeting the curve superficies in T, there will be given the several points T of the trajectory.   *Q.E.I.*

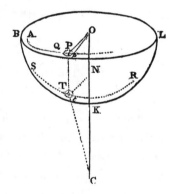

SECTION XI.

Of the motions of bodies tending to each other with centripetal forces.

I have hitherto been treating of the attractions of bodies towards an immovable centre; though very probably there is no such thing existent in nature. For attractions are made towards bodies, and the actions of the bodies attracted and attracting are always reciprocal and equal, by Law III; so that if there are two bodies, neither the attracted nor the attracting body is truly at rest, but both (by Cor. 4, of the Laws of Motion), being as it were mutually attracted, revolve about a common centre of gravity. And if there be more bodies, which are either attracted by one single one which is attracted by them again, or which all of them, attract each other mutually, these bodies will be so moved among themselves, as that their common centre of gravity will either be at rest, or move uniformly forward in a right line. I shall therefore at present go on to treat of the motion of bodies mutually attracting each other; considering the centripetal forces as attractions; though perhaps in a physical strictness they may more truly be called impulses. But these propositions are to be considered as purely mathematical; and therefore, laying aside all physical considerations, I make use of a familiar way of speaking, to make myself the more easily understood by a mathematical reader.

PROPOSITION LVII. THEOREM XX.

Two bodies attracting each other mutually describe similar figures about their common centre of gravity, and about each other mutually.

For the distances of the bodies from their common centre of gravity are reciprocally as the bodies; and therefore in a given ratio to each other; and thence, by composition of ratios, in a given ratio to the whole distance between the bodies. Now these distances revolve about their common term with an equable angular motion, because lying in the same right line they never change their inclination to each other mutually. But right lines that are in a given ratio to each other, and revolve about their terms with an equal angular motion, describe upon planes, which either rest with those terms, or move with any motion not angular, figures entirely similar round those terms. Therefore the figures described by the revolution of these distances are similar. *Q.E.D.*

PROPOSITION LVIII. THEOREM XXI.

If two bodies attract each other mutually with forces of any kind, and in the mean time revolve about the

COMMON CENTRE OF GRAVITY; I SAY, THAT, BY THE SAME
FORCES, THERE MAY BE DESCRIBED ROUND EITHER BODY
UNMOVED A FIGURE SIMILAR AND EQUAL TO THE FIGURES
WHICH THE BODIES SO MOVING DESCRIBE ROUND EACH
OTHER MUTUALLY.

Let the bodies S and P revolve about their common centre of gravity C, proceeding from S to T, and from P to Q. From the given point *s* lot there be continually drawn *sp*, *sq*, equal and parallel to SP, TQ; and the curve *pqv*, which the point *p* describes in its revolution round the immovable point *s*, will be similar and equal to the curves which the bodies S and P describe about each other mutually; and therefore, by Theor. XX, similar

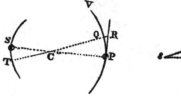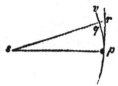

to the curves ST and PQV which the same bodies describe about their common centre of gravity C; and that because the proportions of the lines SC, CP, and SP or *sp*, to each other, are given.

CASE. 1. The common centre of gravity C (by Cor. 4, of the Laws of Motion) is either at rest, or moves uniformly in a right line. Let us first suppose it at rest, and in *s* and *p* let there be placed two bodies, one immovable in *s*, the other movable in *p*, similar and equal to the bodies S and P. Then let the right lines PR and *pr* touch the curves PQ and *pq* in P and *p*, and produce CQ and *sq* to R and *r*. And because the figures CPRQ, *sprq* are similar, RQ will be to *rq* as CP to *sp*, and therefore in a given ratio. Hence if the force with which the body P is attracted towards the body S, and by consequence towards the intermediate point the centre C, were to the force with which the body *p* is attracted towards the centre *s*, in the same given ratio, these forces would in equal times attract the bodies from the tangents PR, *pr* to the arcs PQ, *pq*, through the intervals proportional to them RQ, *rq*; and therefore this last force (tending to *s*) would make the body *p* revolve in the curve *pqv*, which would become similar to the curve PQV, in which the first force obliges the body P to revolve; and their revolutions would be completed in the same times But because those forces are not to each other in the ratio of CP to *sp*, but (by reason of the similarity and equality of the bodies S and *s*, P and *p* and the equality of the distances SP, *sp*) mutually equal, the bodies in equal times will be equally drawn from the tangents; and therefore that the body *p* may be attracted through the greater interval *rq*, there is required a greater time, which will be in the subduplicate ratio of the intervals; because, by Lemma X, the spaces described at the very beginning of the motion are in a duplicate ratio of the times. Suppose, then the velocity of the body *p* to be to the velocity of the body P in a subduplicate ratio of the

distance *sp* to the distance CP, so that the arcs *pq*, PQ, which are in a simple proportion to each other, may be described in times that are in a subduplicate ratio of the distances; and the bodies P, *p*, always attracted by equal forces, will describe round the quiescent centres C and *s* similar figures PQV, *pqv*, the latter of which *pqv* is similar and equal to the figure which the body P describes round the movable body S.   *Q.E.D.*

CASE., 2. Suppose now that the common centre of gravity, together with the space in which the bodies are moved among themselves, proceeds uniformly in a right line; and (by Cor. 6, of the Laws of Motion) all the motions in this space will be performed in the same manner as before; and therefore the bodies will describe mutually about each other the same figures as before, which will be therefore similar and equal to the figure *pqv*.   *Q.E.D.*

COR. 1. Hence two bodies attracting each other with forces proportional to their distance, describe (by Prop. X) both round their common centre of gravity, and round each other mutually concentrical ellipses; and, *vice versa*, if such figures are described, the forces are proportional to the distances.

COR. 2. And two bodies, whose forces are reciprocally proportional to the square of their distance, describe (by Prop. XI, XII, XIII), both round their common centre of gravity, and round each other mutually, conic sections having their focus in the centre about which the figures are described. And, *vice versa*, if such figures are described, the centripetal forces are reciprocally proportional to the squares of the distance.

COR. 3. Any two bodies revolving round their common centre of gravity describe areas proportional to the times, by radii drawn both to that centre and to each other mutually.

PROPOSITION LIX. THEOREM XXII.

THE PERIODIC TIME OF TWO BODIES S AND P REVOLVING
ROUND THEIR COMMON CENTRE OF GRAVITY C, IS TO THE
PERIODIC TIME OF ONE OF THE BODIES P REVOLVING
ROUND THE OTHER S REMAINING UNMOVED, AND
DESCRIBING A FIGURE SIMILAR AND EQUAL TO THOSE
WHICH THE BODIES DESCRIBE ABOUT EACH OTHER
MUTUALLY, IN A SUBDUPLICATE RATIO OF THE OTHER BODY
S TO THE SUM OF THE BODIES S + P.

For, by the demonstration of the last Proposition, the times in which any similar arcs PQ and *pq* are described are in a subduplicate ratio of the distances CP and SP, or *sp*, that is, in a subduplicate ratio of the ody S to the sum of the bodies S + P. And by composition of ratios, the sums of the times in which all the similar arcs PQ and *pq*

are described, that is, the whole times in which the whole similar figures are described are in the same subduplicate ratio. *Q.E.D.*

PROPOSITION LX. THEOREM XXIII.

IF TWO BODIES S AND P, ATTRACTING EACH OTHER WITH FORCES RECIPROCALLY PROPORTIONAL TO THE SQUARES OF THEIR DISTANCE, REVOLVE ABOUT THEIR COMMON CENTRE OF GRAVITY; I SAY, THAT THE PRINCIPAL AXIS OF THE ELLIPSIS WHICH EITHER OF THE BODIES, AS P, DESCRIBES BY THIS MOTION ABOUT THE OTHER S, WILL BE TO THE PRINCIPAL AXIS OF THE ELLIPSIS, WHICH THE SAME BODY P MAY DESCRIBE IN THE SAME PERIODICAL TIME ABOUT THE OTHER BODY S QUIESCENT, AS THE SUM OF THE TWO BODIES S + P TO THE FIRST OF TWO MEAN PROPORTIONALS BETWEEN THAT SUM AND THE OTHER BODY S.

For if the ellipses described were equal to each other, their periodic times by the last Theorem would be in a subduplicate ratio of the body S to the sum of the bodies S + P. Let the periodic time in the latter ellipsis be diminished in that ratio, and the periodic times will become equal; but, by Prop. XV, the principal axis of the ellipsis will be diminished in a ratio sesquiplicate to the former ratio; that is, in a ratio to which the ratio of S to S + P is triplicate; and therefore that axis will be to the principal axis of the other ellipsis as the first of two mean proportionals between S + P and S to S + P. And inversely the principal axis of the ellipsis described about the movable body will be to the principal axis of that described round the immovable as S + P to the first of two mean proportionals between S + P and S. *Q.E.D.*

PROPOSITION LXI. THEOREM XXIV.

IF TWO BODIES ATTRACTING EACH OTHER WITH ANY KIND OF FORCES, AND NOT OTHERWISE AGITATED OR OBSTRUCTED, ARE MOVED IN ANY MANNER WHATSOEVER, THOSE MOTIONS WILL BE THE SAME AS IF THEY DID NOT AT ALL ATTRACT EACH OTHER MUTUALLY, BUT WERE BOTH ATTRACTED WITH THE SAME FORCES BY A THIRD BODY PLACED IN THEIR COMMON CENTRE OF GRAVITY; AND THE LAW OF THE ATTRACTING FORCES WILL BE THE SAME IN RESPECT OF THE DISTANCE OF THE BODIES FROM THE COMMON CENTRE, AS IN RESPECT OF THE DISTANCE BETWEEN THE TWO BODIES.

For those forces with which the bodies attract each other mutually, by tending to the bodies, tend also to the common centre of gravity lying directly between them; and therefore are the same as if they proceeded from in intermediate body. *Q.E.D.*

And because there is given the ratio of the distance of either body from that common centre to the distance between the two bodies, there is given, of course, the ratio of any power of one distance to the same power of the other distance; and also the ratio of any quantity derived in any manner from one of the distances compounded any how with given quantities, to another quantity derived in like manner from the other distance, and as many given quantities having that given ratio of the distances to the first Therefore if the force with which one body is attracted by another be directly or inversely as the distance of the bodies from each other, or as any power of that distance; or, lastly, as any quantity derived after any manner from that distance compounded with given quantities; then will the same force with which the same body is attracted to the common centre of gravity be in like manner directly or inversely as the distance of the attracted body from the common centre, or as any power of that distance; or, lastly, as a quantity derived in like sort from that distance compounded with analogous given quantities. That is, the law of attracting force will be the same with respect to both distances. *Q.E.D.*

PROPOSITION LXII. PROBLEM XXXVIII.

TO DETERMINE THE MOTIONS OF TWO BODIES WHICH
ATTRACT EACH OTHER WITH FORCES RECIPROCALLY
PROPORTIONAL TO THE SQUARES OF THE DISTANCE
BETWEEN THEM, AND ARE LET FULL FROM GIVEN PLACES.

The bodies, by the last Theorem, will be moved in the same manner as if they were attracted by a third placed in the common centre of their gravity : and by the hypothesis that centre will be quiescent at the beginning of their motion, and therefore (by Cor. 4, of the Laws of Motion) will be always quiescent. The motions of the bodies are therefore to be determined (by Prob. XXV) in the same manner as if they were impelled by forces tending to that centre; and then we shall have the motions of the bodies attracting each other mutually. *Q.E.I.*

PROPOSITION LXIII. PROBLEM XXXIX.

TO DETERMINE THE MOTIONS OF TWO BODIES ATTRACTING
EACH OTHER WITH FORCES RECIPROCALLY PROPORTIONAL TO
THE SQUARES OF THEIR DISTANCE, AND GOING OFF FROM
GIVEN PLACES IN GIVEN DIRECTIONS WITH GIVEN VELOCITIES.

The motions of the bodies at the beginning being given, there is given also the uniform motion of the common centre of gravity, and the motion of the space which moves along with this centre uniformly in a right line, and also the very first, or beginning motions of the bodies in respect of this space. Then (by Cor. 5, of the Laws, and the last Theorem) the subsequent motions will be performed in the same manner in that space, as if that space together with the common centre of gravity were at rest, and as if the bodies did not attract each other, but were attracted by a third body placed in that centre. The motion therefore in this movable space of each body going off from a given place, in a given direction, with a given velocity, and acted upon by a centripetal force tending to that centre, is to be determined by Prob. IX and XXVI, and at the same time will be obtained the motion of the other round the same centre. With this motion compound the uniform progressive motion of the entire system of the space and the bodies revolving in it, and there will be obtained the absolute motion of the bodies in immovable space.   Q.E.I.

PROPOSITION LXIV. PROBLEM XL.

SUPPOSING FORCES WITH WHICH BODIES MUTUALLY ATTRACT EACH OTHER TO INCREASE IN A SIMPLE RATIO OF THEIR DISTANCES FROM THE CENTRES; IT IS REQUIRED TO FIND THE MOTIONS OF SEVERAL BODIES AMONG THEMSELVES.

Suppose the first two bodies T and L to have their common centre of gravity in D. These, by Cor. 1, Theor. XXI, will describe ellipses having their centres in D, the magnitudes of which ellipses are known by Prob. V.

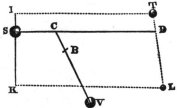

Let now a third body S attract the two former T and L with the accelerative forces ST, SL, and let it be attracted again by them. The force ST (by Cor. 2, of the Laws of Motion) is resolved into the forces SD, DT; and the force SL into the forces SD and DL. Now the forces DT, DL, which are as their sum TL, and therefore as the accelerative forces with which the bodies T and L attract each other mutually, added to the forces of the bodies T and L, the first to the first, and the last to the last, compose forces proportional to the distances DT and DL as before, but only greater than those former forces; and therefore (by Cor. 1, Prop. X, and Cor. 1, and 8, Prop. IV) they will cause those bodies to describe ellipses as before, but with a swifter motion. The remaining accelerative forces SD and DL by the motive forces SD × T and SD × L, which are as the bodies attracting those bodies equally and

in the direction of the lines TI, LK parallel to DS, do not at all change their situations with respect to one another, but cause them equally to approach to the line IK; which must be imagined drawn through the middle of the body S, and perpendicular to the line DS. But that approach to the line IK will be hindered by causing the system of the bodies T and L on one side, and the body S on the other, with proper velocities, to revolve round the common centre of gravity P. With such a motion the body S, because the sum of the motive forces SD × T and SD × L is proportional to the distance CS, tends to the centre C, will describe an ellipsis round the same centre C; and the point D, because the lines CS and CD are proportional, will describe a like ellipsis over against it. But the bodies T and L, attracted by the motive forces SD × T and SD × L, the first by the first, and the last by the last, equally and in the direction of the parallel lines TI and LK, as was said before, will (by Cor. 5 and 6, of the Laws of Motion) continue to describe their ellipses round the movable centre D, as before.   Q.E.I.

Let there be added a fourth body V, and, by the like reasoning, it will be demonstrated that this body and the point C will describe ellipses about the common centre of gravity B; the motions of the bodies T, L, and S round the centres D and C remaining the same as before; but accelerated. And by the same method one may add yet more bodies at pleasure.   Q.E.I.

This would be the case, though the bodies T and L attract each other mutually with accelerative forces either greater or less than those with which they attract the other bodies in proportion to their distance. Let all the mutual accelerative attractions be to each other as the distances multiplied into the attracting bodies; and from what has gone before it will easily be concluded that all the bodies will describe different ellipses with equal periodical times about their common centre of gravity B, in an immovable plane.   Q.E.I.

PROPOSITION LXV. THEOREM XXV.

BODIES, WHOSE FORCES DECREASE IN A DUPLICATE RATIO
OF THEIR DISTANCES FROM THEIR CENTRES, MAY MOVE
AMONG THEMSELVES IN ELLIPSES; AND BY RADII DRAWN TO
THE FOCI MAY DESCRIBE AREAS PROPORTIONAL TO THE
TIMES VERY NEARLY.

In the last Proposition we demonstrated that case in which the motions will be performed exactly in ellipses. The more distant the law of the forces is from the law in that case, the more will the bodies disturb each other's motions; neither is it possible that bodies attracting each other mutually according to the law supposed in this Proposition should move exactly in ellipses, unless by keeping a certain proportion of

distances from each other. However, in the following cases the orbits will not much differ from ellipses.

CASE. 1. Imagine several lesser bodies to revolve about some very great one at different distances from it, and suppose absolute forces tending to every one of the bodies proportional to each. And because (by Cor. 4, of the Laws) the common centre of gravity of them all is either at rest, or moves uniformly forward in a right line, suppose the lesser bodies so small that the great body may be never at a sensible distance from that centre; and then the great body will, without any sensible error, be either at rest, or move uniformly forward in a right line; and the lesser will revolve about that great one in ellipses, and by radii drawn thereto will describe areas proportional to the times; if we except the errors that may be introduced by the receding of the great body from the common centre of gravity, or by the mutual actions of the lesser bodies upon each other. But the lesser bodies may be so far diminished, as that this recess and the mutual actions of the bodies on each other may become less than any assignable; and therefore so as that the orbits way become ellipses, and the areas answer to the times, without any error that is not less than any assignable. Q.E.O.

CASE. 2. Let us imagine a system of lesser bodies revolving about a very great one in the manner just described, or any other system of two bodies revolving about each other to be moving uniformly forward in a right line, and in the mean time to be impelled sideways by the force of another vastly greater body situate at a great distance. And because the equal accelerative forces with which the bodies are impelled in parallel directions do not change the situation of the bodies with respect to each other, but only oblige the whole system to change its place while the parts still retain their motions among themselves, it is manifest that no change in those motions of the attracted bodies can arise from their attractions towards the greater, unless by the inequality of the accelerative attractions, or by the inclinations of the lines towards each other, in whose directions the attractions are made. Suppose, therefore, all the accelerative attractions made towards the great body to be among themselves as the squares of the distances reciprocally; and then, by increasing the distance of the great body till the differences of the right lines drawn from that to the others in respect of their length, and the inclinations of those lines to each other, be less than any given, the motions of the parts of the system will continue without errors that are not less than any given. And because, by the small distance of those parts from each other, the whole system is attracted as if it were but one body, it will therefore be moved by this attraction as if it were one body; that is, its centre of gravity will describe about the great body one of the conic sections (that is, a parabola or hyperbola when the attraction is but languid and an ellipsis when it is more vigorous); and by radii drawn thereto, it will describe areas proportional to the times, without any errors but those which arise from the distances of the parts, which are by the supposition exceedingly small, and may be diminished at pleasure. Q.E.O.

By a like reasoning one may proceed to more compounded cases *in infinitum.*

COR. 1. In the second Case, the nearer the very great body approaches to the system of two or more revolving bodies, the greater will the perturbation be of the motions of the parts of the system among themselves; because the inclinations of the lines drawn from that great body to those parts become greater; and the inequality of the proportion is also greater.

COR. 2. But the perturbation will be greatest of all, if we suppose the accelerative attractions of the parts of the system towards the greatest body of all are not to each other reciprocally as the squares of the distances from that great body; especially if the inequality of this proportion be greater than the inequality of the proportion of the distances from the great body. For if the accelerative force, acting in parallel directions and equally, causes no perturbation in the motions of the parts of the system, it must of course, when it acts unequally, cause a perturbation somewhere, which will be greater or less as the inequality is greater or less. The excess of the greater impulses acting upon some bodies, and not acting upon others, must necessarily change their situation among themselves, And this perturbation, added to the perturbation arising from the inequality and inclination of the lines, makes the whole perturbation greater.

COR. 3. Hence if the parts of this system move in ellipses or circles without any remarkable perturbation, it is manifest that, if they are at all impelled by accelerative forces tending to any other bodies, the impulse is very weak, or else is impressed very near equally and in parallel directions upon all of them.

PROPOSITION LXVI. THEOREM XXVI.

IF THREE BODIES WHOSE FORCES DECREASE IN A DUPLICATE
RATIO OF THE DISTANCES ATTRACT EACH OTHER MUTUALLY;
AND THE ACCELERATIVE ATTRACTIONS OF ANY TWO
TOWARDS THE THIRD BE BETWEEN THEMSELVES RECIPROCALLY
AS THE SQUARES OF THE DISTANCES; AND THE TWO LEAST
REVOLVE ABOUT THE GREATEST; I SAY, THAT THE INTERIOR
OF THE TWO REVOLVING BODIES WILL, BY RADII DRAWN TO
THE INNERMOST AND GREATEST, DESCRIBE ROUND THAT
BODY AREAS MORE PROPORTIONAL TO THE TIMES, AND A
FIGURE MORE APPROACHING TO THAT OF AN ELLIPSIS HAVING
ITS FOCUS IN THE POINT OF CONCOURSE OF THE
RADII, IF THAT GREAT BODY BE AGITATED BY THOSE
ATTRACTIONS, THAN IT WOULD DO IF THAT REAL BODY
WERE NOT ATTRACTED AT ALL BY THE LESSER, BUT
REMAINED AT REST; OR THAN IT WOULD IF THAT GREAT

BODY WERE VERY MUCH MORE OR VERY MUCH LESS ATTRACTED, OR VERY MUCH MORE OR VERY MUCH LESS AGITATED, BY THE ATTRACTIONS.

This appears plainly enough from the demonstration of the second Corollary of the foregoing Proposition; but it may be made out after this manner by a way of reasoning more distinct and more universally convincing.

CASE. 1. Let the lesser bodies P and S revolve in the same plane about the greatest body T, the body P describing the interior orbit PAB, and S the exterior orbit ESE. Let SK, be the mean distance of the bodies P and S; and let the accelerative attraction of the body P towards S, at that mean distance, be expressed by that line SK. Make SL to SK as the square of SK to the square of SP, and SL will be the accelerative attraction of the body P towards S at any distance SP. Join PT, and draw LM parallel to it meeting ST in M; and the attraction SL will be resolved (by Cor. 2, of the Laws of Motion) into the attractions SM, LM. And so the body P will be urged with a threefold accelerative

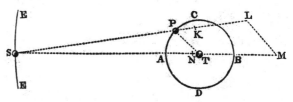

force. One of these forces tends towards T, and arises from the mutual attraction of the bodies T and P. By this force alone the body P would describe round the body T, by the radius PT, areas proportional to the times, and an ellipsis whose focus is in the centre of the body T; and this it would do whether the body T remained unmoved, or whether it were agitated by that attraction. This appears from Prop. XI and Cor. 2 and 3 of Theor. XXI. The other force is that of the attraction LM, which, because it tends from P to T, will be superadded to and coincide with the former force; and cause the areas to be still proportional to the times, by Cor. 3, Theor. XXI. But because it is not reciprocally proportional to the square of the distance PT, it will compose, when added to the former, a force varying from that proportion; which variation will be the greater by how much the proportion of this force to the former is greater, *caeteris paribus.* Therefore, since by Prop. XI, and by Cor. 2, Theor. XXI, the force with which the ellipsis is described about the focus T ought to be directed to that focus, and to be reciprocally proportional to the square of the distance PT, that compounded force varying from that proportion will make the orbit PAB vary from the figure of an ellipsis that has its focus in the point T; and so much the more by how much the variation from that proportion is greater; and by consequence by how much the proportion of the second force LM to the first force is greater, caerteris paribus. But now the third force SM, attracting the body P in a direction parallel to ST, composes with the other force a new force which is no longer directed from P to T; and which varies so much more from

this direction by how much the proportion of this third force to the other forces is greater, *caeteris paribus*; and therefore causes the body P to describe, by the radius TP, areas no longer proportional to the times; and therefore makes the variation from that proportionality so much greater by how much the proportion of this force to the others is greater. But this third force will increase the variation of the orbit PAB from the elliptical figure before-mentioned upon two accounts; first because that force is not directed from P to T; and, secondly, because it is not reciprocally proportional to the square of the distance PT. These things being premised, it is manifest that the areas are then most nearly proportional to the times, when that third force is the least possible, the rest preserving their former quantity; and that the orbit PAB does then approach nearest to the elliptical figure above-mentioned, when both the Second and third, but especially the third force, is the least possible; the first force remaining in its former quantity.

Let the accelerative attraction of the body T towards S be expressed by the line SN; then if the accelerative attractions SM and SN were equal, these, attracting the bodies T and P equally and in parallel directions would not at all change their situation with respect to each other. The motions of the bodies between themselves would be the same in that case as if those attractions did not act at all, by Cor. 6, of the Laws of Motion. And, by a like reasoning, if the attraction SN is less than the attraction SM, it will take away out of the attraction SM the part SN, so that there will remain only the part (of the attraction) MN to disturb the proportionality of the areas and times, and the elliptical figure of the orbit. And in like manner if the attraction SN be greater than the attraction SM, the perturbation of the orbit and proportion will be produced by the difference MN alone. After this manner the attraction SN reduces always the attraction SM to the attraction MN, the first and second attractions remaining perfectly unchanged; and therefore the areas and times come then nearest to proportionality, and the orbit PAB to the above-mentioned elliptical figure, when the attraction MN is either none, or the least that is possible; that is, when the accelerative attractions of the bodies P and T approach as near is possible to equality; that is, when the attraction SN is neither none at all, nor less than the least of all the attractions SM, but is, as it were, a mean between the greatest and least of all those attractions SM, that is, not much greater nor much less than the attraction SK.   *Q.E.D.*

CASE. 2. Let now the lesser bodies P, S, revolve about a greater T in different planes; and the force LM, acting in the direction of the line PT Situate in the plane of the orbit PAB, will have the same effect as before; neither will it draw the body P from the plane of its orbit. But the other force NM acting in the direction of a line parallel to ST (and which, therefore, when the body S is without the line of the nodes is inclined to the plane of the orbit PAB), besides the perturbation of the motion just

now spoken of as to longitude, introduces another perturbation also as to latitude, attracting the body P out of the plane of its orbit. And this perturbation, in any given situation of the bodies P and T to each other, will be as the generating force MN; and therefore becomes least when the force MN is least, that is (as was just now shown), where the attraction SN is not much greater nor much less than the attraction SK.

Q.E.D.

COR. 1. Hence it may be easily collected, that if several less bodies P, S, R, &c., revolve about a very great body T, the motion of the innermost revolving body P will be least disturbed by the attractions of the others, when the great body is as well attracted and agitated by the rest (according to the ratio of the accelerative forces) as the rest are by each other mutually.

COR. 2. In a system of three bodies, T, P, S, if the accelerative attractions of any two of them towards a third be to each other reciprocally as the squares of the distances, the body P, by the radius PT, will describe its area about the body T swifter near the conjunction A and the opposition B than it will near the quadratures C and D. For every force with which the body P is acted on and the body T is not, and which does not act in the direction of the line PT, does either accelerate or retard the description of the area, according as it is directed, whether *in consequentia* or *in antecedentia*. Such is the force NM. This force in the passage of the body P from O to A is directed *in consequentia* to its motion, and therefore accelerates it; then as far as D *in antecedentia*, and retards the motion; then *in consequentia* as far as B; and lastly *in antecedentia* as it moves from B to C.

COR. 3. And from the same reasoning it appears that the body P, *caeteris paribus*, moves more swiftly in the conjunction and opposition than in the quadratures.

COR. 4. The orbit of the body P, *caeteris paribus*, is more curve at the quadratures than at the conjunction and opposition. For the swifter bodies move, the less they deflect from a rectilinear path. And besides the force KL, or NM, at the conjunction and opposition, is contrary to the force with which the body T attracts the body P, and therefore diminishes that force; but the body P will deflect the less from a rectilinear path the less it is impelled towards the body T.

COR. 5. Hence the body P, *caeteris paribus*, goes farther from the body T at the quadratures than at the conjunction and opposition. This is said, however, supposing no regard had to the motion of eccentricity.

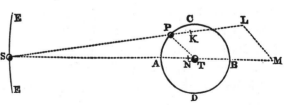

For if the orbit of the body P be eccentrical, its eccentricity (as will be shewn presently by Cor. 9) will be greatest when the apsides are in

the syzygies; and thence it may sometimes come to pass that the body P, in its near approach to the farther apsis, may go farther from the body T at the syzygies than at the quadratures.

COR. 6. Because the centripetal force of the central body T, by which the body P is retained in its orbit, is increased at the quadratures by the addition caused by the force LM, and diminished at the syzygies by the subduction caused by the force KL, and, because the force KL is greater than LM, it is more diminished than increased; and, moreover, since that centripetal force (by Cor. 2, Prop. IV) is in a ratio compounded of the simple ratio of the radius TP directly, and the duplicate ratio of the periodical time inversely; it is plain that this compounded ratio is diminished by the action of the force KL; and therefore that the periodical time, supposing the radius of the orbit PT to remain the same, will be increased, and that in the subduplicate of that ratio in which the centripetal force is diminished; and, therefore, supposing this radius increased or diminished, the periodical time will be increased more or diminished less than in the sesquiplicate ratio of this radius, by Cor. 6, Prop. IV. If that force of the central body should gradually decay, the body P being less and less attracted would go farther and farther from the centre T; and, on the contrary, if it were increased, it would draw nearer to it. Therefore if the action of the distant body S, by which that force is diminished, were to increase and decrease by turns, the radius TP will be also increased and diminshed by turns; and the periodical time will be increased and diminished in a ratio compounded of the sesquiplicate ratio of the radius, and of the subduplicate of that ratio in which the centripetal force of the central body T is diminished or increased, by the increase or decrease of the action of the distant body S.

COR. 7. It also follows, from what was before laid down, that the axis of the ellipsis described by the body P, or the line of the apsides, does as to its angular motion go forwards and backwards by turns, but more forwards than backwards, and by the excess of its direct motion is in the whole carried forwards. For the force with which the body P is urged to the body T at the quadratures, where the force MN vanishes, is compounded of the force LM and the centripetal force with which the body T attracts the body P. The first force LM, if the distance PT be increased, is increased in nearly the same 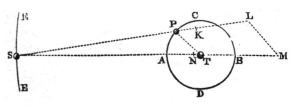 proportion with that distance, and the other force decreases in the duplicate ratio of the distance; and therefore the sum of these two forces decreases in a less than the duplicate ratio of the distance PT; and therefore, by Cor. 1, Prop. XLV, will make the line of the apsides, or, which is the same thing, the upper apsis, to go backward. But at

the conjunction and opposition the force with which the body P is urged towards the body T is the difference of the force KL, and of the force with which the body T attracts the body P; and that difference, because the force KL is very nearly increased in the ratio of the distance PT, decreases in more than the duplicate ratio of the distance PT; and therefore, by Cor. 1, Prop. XLV, causes the line of the apsides to go forwards. In the places between the syzygies and the quadratures, the motion of the line of the apsides depends upon both of these causes conjunctly, so that it either goes forwards or backwards in proportion to the excess of one of these causes above the other. Therefore since the force KL in the syzygies is almost twice as great as the force LM in the quadratures, the excess will be on the side of the force KL, and by consequence the line of the apsides will be carried forwards. The truth of this and the foregoing Corollary will be more easily understood by conceiving the system of the two bodies T and P to be surrounded on every side by several bodies S, S, S, &c., disposed about the orbit ESE. For by the actions of these bodies the action of the body T will be diminished on every side, and decrease in more than a duplicate ratio of the distance.

COR. 8. But since the progress or regress of the apsides depends upon the decrease of the centripetal force, that is, upon its being in a greater or less ratio than the duplicate ratio of the distance TP, in the passage of the body from the lower apsis to the upper; and upon a like increase in its return to the lower apsis again; and therefore becomes greatest where the proportion of the force at the upper apsis to the force at the lower apsis recedes farthest from the duplicate ratio of the distances inversely; it is plain, that, when the apsides are in the syzygies, they will, by reason of the subducting force KL or NM – LM, go forward more swiftly; and in the quadratures by the additional force LM go backward more slowly. Because the velocity of the progress or slowness of the regress is continued for a long time; this inequality becomes exceedingly great.

COR. 9. If a body is obliged, by a force reciprocally proportional to the square of its distance from any centre, to revolve in an ellipsis round that centre and afterwards in its descent from the upper apsis to the lower apsis, that force by a perpetual accession of new force is increased in more than a duplicate ratio of the diminished distance; it is manifest that the body being impelled always towards the centre by the perpetual accession of this new force, will incline more towards that centre than if it were urged by that force alone which decreases in a duplicate ratio of the diminished distance, and therefore will describe an orbit interior to that elliptical orbit, and at the lower apsis approaching nearer to the centre than before. Therefore the orbit by the accession of this new force will become more eccentrical. If now, while the body is returning from the lower to the upper apsis, it should decrease by the same degrees by which it increases before the body would return to its first distance; and therefore if the force decreases in

a yet greater ratio, the body, being now less attracted than before, will ascend to a still greater distance, and so the eccentricity of the orbit will be increased still more. Therefore if the ratio of the increase and decrease of the centripetal force be augmented each revolution, the eccentricity will be augmented also; and, on the contrary, if that ratio decrease, it will be diminished.

Now, therefore, in the system of the bodies T, P, S, when the apsides of the orbit PAB are in the quadratures, the ratio of that increase and decrease is least of all, and becomes greatest when the apsides are in the syzygies. If the apsides are placed in the quadratures, the ratio near the apsides is less, and near the syzygies greater, than the duplicate ratio of the distances; and from that greater ratio arises a direct motion of the line of the apsides, as was just now said. But if we consider the ratio of the whole increase or decrease in the progress between the apsides, this is less than the duplicate ratio of the distances. The force in the lower is to the force in the upper apsis in less than a duplicate ratio of the distance of the upper apsis from the focus of the ellipsis to the distance of the lower apsis from the same focus; and, contrariwise, when the apsides are placed in the syzygies, the force in the lower apsis is to the force in the upper apsis in a greater than a duplicate ratio of the distances. For the forces LM in the quadratures added to the forces of the body T compose forces in a less ratio; and the forces KL in the syzygies subducted from the forces of the body T, leave the forces in a greater ratio. Therefore the ratio of the whole increase and decrease in the passage between the apsides is least at the quadratures and greatest at the syzygies; and therefore in the passage of the apsides from the quadratures to the syzygies it is continually augmented, and increases the eccentricity of the ellipses; and in the passage from the syzygies to the quadratures it is perpetually decreasing, and diminishes the eccentricity.

COR. 10. That we may give an account of the errors as to latitude, let us suppose the plane of the orbit EST to remain immovable; and from the cause of the errors above explained, it is manifest, that, of the two forces NM, ML, which are the only and entire cause of them, the force ML acting always in the plane of the orbit PAB never disturbs the motions as to latitude; and that the force NM, when the nodes are in the syzygies, acting also in the same plane of the orbit, does not at that time affect those motions.

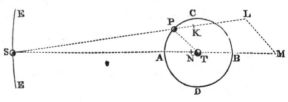

But when the nodes are in the quadratures, it disturbs them very much, and, attracting the body P perpetually out of the plane of its orbit, it diminishes the inclination of the plane in the passage of the body from the quadratures to the syzygies, and again increases the same in the passage from the syzygies to the quadratures. Hence it comes

to pass that when the body is in the syzygies, the inclination is then least of all, and returns to the first magnitude nearly, when the body arrives at the next node. But if the nodes are situate at the octants after the quadratures, that is, between C and A, D and B, it will appear, from what was just now shewn, that in the passage of the body P from either node to the ninetieth degree from thence, the inclination of the plane is perpetually diminished; then, in the passage through the next 45 degrees to the next quadrature, the inclination is increased; and afterwards, again, in its passage through another 45 degrees to the next node, it is diminished. Therefore the inclination is more diminished than increased, and is therefore always less in the subsequent node than in the preceding one, And, by a like reasoning, the inclination is more increased than diminished when the nodes are in the other octants between A and D, B and C. The inclination, therefore, is the greatest of all when the nodes are in the syzygies. In their passage from the syzygies to the quadratures the inclination is diminished at each appulse of the body to the nodes: and becomes least of all when the nodes are in the quadratures, and the body in the syzygies; then it increases by the same degrees by which it decreased before; and, when the nodes come to the next syzygies, returns to its former magnitude.

COR. 11. Because when the nodes are in the quadratures the body P is perpetually attracted from the plane of its orbit; and because this attraction is made towards S in its passage from the node C through the conjunction A to the node D; and to the contrary part in its passage from the node D through the opposition B to the node C; it is manifest that, in its motion from the node C, the body recedes continually from the former plane CD of its orbit till it comes to the next node; and therefore at that node, being now at its greatest distance from the first plane CD, it will pass through the plane of the orbit EST not in D, the other node of that plane, but in a point that lies nearer to the body S, which therefore becomes a new place of the node *in antecedentia* to its former place. And, by a like reasoning the nodes will continue to recede in their passage from this node to the next. The nodes, therefore, when situate in the quadratures, recede perpetually; and at the syzygies, where no perturbation can be produced in the motion as to latitude, are quiescent: in the intermediate places they partake of both conditions, and recede more slowly; and, therefore, being always either retrograde or stationary, they will be carried backwards, or *in antecedentia*, each revolution.

COR. 12. All the errors described in these corrollaries are a little greater at the conjunction of the bodies P, S, than at their opposition; because the generating forces NM and ML are greater.

COR. 13. And since the causes and proportions of the errors and variations mentioned in these Corollaries do not depend upon the magnitude of the body S, it follows that all things before demonstrated will happen, if the magnitude of the body S

be imagined so great as that the system of the two bodies P and T may revolve about it. And from this increase of the body S, and the consequent increase of its centripetal force, from which the errors of the body P arise, it will follow that all these errors, at equal distances, will be greater in this case, than in the other where the body S revolves about the system of the bodies P and T.

COR. 14. But since the forces NM, ML, when the body S is exceedingly distant, are very nearly as the force SK and the ratio PT to ST conjunctly; that is, if both the distance PT and the absolute force of the body S be given, as reciprocally; and since those forces NM, ML are the causes of all the errors and effects treated of in the foregoing Corollaries; it is manifest that all those effects, if the system of bodies T and P continue as before, and only the distance ST and the absolute force of the body S be changed, will be very nearly in a ratio compounded of the direct ratio of the absolute force of the body S, and the triplicate inverse ratio of the distance ST. Hence if the system of bodies T and P revolve about a distant body S, those forces NM, ML, and their effects, will be (by Cor. 2 and 6, Prop IV) reciprocally in a duplicate ratio of the periodical time. And thence, also, if the magnitude of the body S be proportional to its absolute force, those forces, NM, ML, and their effects, will be directly as the cube of the apparent diameter of the distant body S viewed from T, and so *vice versa*. For these ratios are the same as the compounded ratio above mentioned.

COR. 15. And because if the orbits ESE and PAB, retaining their figure, proportions, and inclination to each other, should alter their magnitude; and the forces of the bodies S and T should either remain, or be changed in any given ratio; these forces (that is, the force of the body T, which obliges the body P to deflect from a rectilinear course into the orbit PAB, and the force of the body S, which causes the body P to deviate from that orbit) would act always in the same manner, and in the same proportion; it follows, that all the effects will be similar and proportional, and the times of those effects proportional also; that is, that all the linear errors will be as the diameters of the orbits, the angular errors the same as before; and the times of similar linear errors, or equal angular errors, as the periodical times of the orbits.

COR. 16. Therefore if the figures of the orbits and their inclination to each other be given, and the magnitudes, forces, and distances of the bodies be any how changed, we may, from the errors and times of those errors in one case, collect very nearly the errors and times of the errors in any other case. But this may be done more expeditiously by the following method. The forces NM, ML, other things remaining unaltered, are as the radius TP; and their periodical effects (by Cor. 2, Lem. X) are as the forces and the square of the periodical time of the body P conjunctly. These are the linear errors of the body P; and hence the angular errors as they appear from the centre T (that is, the motion of the apsides and of the nodes, and all the apparent errors as to longitude

and latitude) are in each revolution of the body P as the square of the time of the revolution, very nearly. Let these ratios be compounded with the ratios in Cor. 14, and in any system of bodies T, P, S, where P revolves about T very near to it, and T revolves about S at a great distance, the angular errors of the body P, observed from the centre T, will be in each revolution of the body P as the square of the periodical time of the body P directly, and the square of the periodical time of the body T inversely. And therefore the mean motion of the line of the apsides will be in a given ratio to the mean motion of the nodes; and both those motions will be as the periodical time of the body P directly, and the square of the periodical time of the body T inversely. The increase or diminution of the eccentricity and inclination of the orbit PAB makes no sensible variation in the motions of the apsides and nodes, unless that increase or diminution be very great indeed.

COR. 17. Since the line LM becomes sometimes greater and sometimes less than the radius PT, let the mean quantity of the force LM be expressed by that radius PT; and then that mean force will be to the mean force SK or SN (which may be also expressed by ST) as the length PT to the length ST. But the mean force SN or ST, by which the body T is retained in the orbit it describes about S, is to the force with which the body P is retained in its orbit about T in a ratio compounded of the ratio of the radius ST to the radius PT, and the duplicate ratio of the periodical time of the body P

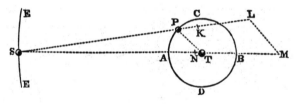

about T to the periodical time of the body T about S. And, *ex aequo*, the mean force LM is to the force by which the body P is retained in its orbit about T (or by which the same body P might revolve at the distance PT in the same periodical time about any immovable point T) in the same duplicate ratio of the periodical times. The periodical times therefore being given, together with the distance PT, the mean force LM is also given; and that force being given, there is given also the force MN, very nearly, by the analogy of the lines PT and MN.

COR. 18. By the same laws by which the body P revolves about the body T, let us suppose many fluid bodies to move round T at equal distances from it; and to be so numerous that they may all become contiguous to each other, so as to form a fluid annulus, or ring, of a round figure, and concentrical to the body T; and the several parts of this annulus, performing their motions by the same law as the body P, will draw nearer to the body T, and move swifter in the conjunction and opposition of themselves and the body S, than in the quadratures. And the nodes of this annulus, or its intersections with the plane of the orbit of the body S or T, will rest at the syzygies but

out of the syzygies they will be carried backward, or *in antecedentia* with the greatest swiftness in the quadratures, and more slowly in other places. The inclination of this annulus also will vary, and its axis will oscillate each revolution, and when the revolution is completed will return to its former situation, except only that it will be carried round a little by the praecession of the nodes.

COR. 19. Suppose now the sphaerical body T, consisting of some matter not fluid, to be enlarged, and to extend itself on every side as far as that annulus, and that a channel were cut all round its circumference containing water; and that this sphere revolves uniformly about its own axis in the same periodical time. This water being accelerated and retarded by turns (as in the last Corollary), will be swifter at the syzygies, and slower at the quadratures, than the surface of the globe, and so will ebb and flow in its channel after the manner of the sea. If the attraction of the body S were taken away, the water would acquire no motion of flux and reflux by revolving round the quiescent centre of the globe. The case is the same of a globe moving uniformly forwards in a right line, and in the mean time revolving about its centre (by Cor. 5 of the Laws of Motion), and of a globe uniformly attracted from its rectilinear course (by Cor. 6, of the same Laws). But let the body S come to act upon it, and by its unequable attraction the water will receive this new motion; for there will be a stronger attraction upon that part of the water that is nearest to the body, and a weaker upon that part which is more remote. And the force LM will attract the water downwards at the quadratures, and depress it as far as the syzygies; and the force KL will attract it upwards in the syzygies, and withhold its descent, and make it rise as far as the quadratures; except only in so far as the motion of flux and reflux may be directed by the channel of the water, and be a little retarded by friction.

COR. 20. If, now, the annulus becomes hard, and the globe is diminished, the motion of flux and reflux will cease; but the oscillating motion of the inclination and the praecession of the nodes will remain. Let the globe have the same axis with the annulus, and perform its revolutions in the same times, and at its surface touch the annulus within, and adhere to it; then the globe partaking of the motion of the annulus, this whole compages will oscillate, and the nodes will go backward, for the globe, as we shall show presently, is perfectly indifferent to the receiving of all impressions. The greatest

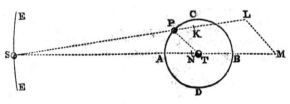

angle of the inclination of the annulus single is when the nodes are in the syzygies. Thence in the progress of the nodes to the quadratures, it endeavours to diminish its inclination, and by that endeavour impresses a motion upon the whole globe.

The globe retains this motion impressed, till the annulus by a contrary endeavour destroys that motion, and impresses a new motion in a contrary direction. And by this means the greatest motion of the decreasing inclination happens when the nodes are in the quadratures, and the least angle of inclination in the octants after the quadratures; and, again, the greatest motion of reclination happens when the nodes are in the syzygies; and the greatest angle of reclination in the octants following. And the case is the same of a globe without this annulus, if it be a little higher or a little denser in the equatorial than in the polar regions; for the excess of that matter in the regions near the equator supplies the place of the annulus. And though we should suppose the centripetal force of this globe to be any how increased, so that all its parts were to tend downwards, as the parts of our earth gravitate to the centre, yet the phaenomena of this and the preceding Corollary would scarce be altered; except that the places of the greatest and least height of the water will be different; for the water is now no longer sustained and kept in its orbit by its centrifugal force, but by the channel in which it flows. And, besides, the force LM attracts the water downwards most in the quadratures, and the force KL or NM – LM attracts it upwards most in the syzygies. And these forces conjoined cease to attract the water downwards, and begin to attract it upwards in the octants before the syzygies; and cease to attract the water upwards, and begin to attract the water downwards in the octants after the syzygies. And thence the greatest height of the water may happen about the octants after the syzygies; and the least height about the octants after the quadratures; excepting only so far as the motion of ascent or descent impressed by these forces may by the *vis insita* of the water continue a little longer, or be stopped a little sooner by impediments in its channel.

COR. 21. For the same reason that redundant matter in the equatorial regions of a globe causes the nodes to go backwards, and therefore by the increase of that matter that retrogradation is increased, by the diminution is diminished, and by the removal quite ceases: it follows, that, if more than that redundant matter be taken away, that is, if the globe be either, more depressed, or of a more rare consistence near the equator than near the poles, there will arise a motion of the nodes *in consequentia.*

COR. 22. And thence from the motion of the nodes is known the constitution of the globe. That is, if the globe retains unalterably the same poles, and the motion (of the nodes) be *in antecedentia*, there is a redundance of the matter near the equator; but if *in consequentia*, a deficiency. Suppose a uniform and exactly sphaerical globe to be first at rest in a free space; then by some impulse made obliquely upon its superficies to be driven from its place, and to receive a motion partly circular and partly right forward. Because this globe is perfectly indifferent to all the axes that pass through its centre, nor has a greater propensity to one axis or to one situation of the axis than to any other, it is manifest that by its own force it will never change its axis, or the inclination

of it. Let now this globe be impelled obliquely by a new impulse in the same part of its superficies as before and since the effect of an impulse is not at all changed by its coming sooner or later, it is manifest that these two impulses, successively impressed, will produce the same motion as if they were impressed at the same time; that is, the same motion as if the globe had been impelled by a simple force compounded of them both (by Cor. 2, of the Laws), that is, a simple motion about an axis of a given inclination. And the ease is the same if the second impulse were made upon any other place of the equator of the first motion; and also if the first impulse were made upon any place in the equator of the motion which would be generated by the second impulse alone; and therefore, also, when both impulses are made in any places whatsoever; for these impulses will generate the same circular motion as if they were impressed together, and at once, in the place of the intersections of the equators of those motions, which would be generated by each of them separately. Therefore, a homogeneous and perfect globe will not retain several distinct motions, but will unite all those that are impressed on it, and reduce them into one; revolving, as far as in it lies, always with a simple and uniform motion about one single given axis, with an inclination perpetually invariable. And the inclination of the axis, or the velocity of the rotation, will not be changed by centripetal force. For if the globe be supposed to be divided into two hemispheres, by any plane whatsoever passing through its own centre, and the centre to which the force is directed, that force will always urge each hemisphere equally; and therefore will not incline the globe any way as to its motion round its own axis. But let there be added any where between the pole and the equator a heap of new matter like a mountain, and this, by its perpetual endeavour to recede from the centre of its motion, will disturb the motion of the globe, and cause its poles to wander about its superficies, describing circles about themselves and their opposite points. Neither can this enormous evagation of the poles be corrected, unless by placing that mountain either in one of the poles; in which case, by Cor. 21, the nodes of the equator will go forwards; or in the equatorial regions, in which case, by Cor. 20, the nodes will go backwards; or, lastly, by adding on the other side of the axis anew quantity of matter, by which the mountain may be balanced in its motion; and then the nodes will either go forwards or backwards, as the mountain and this newly added matter happen to be nearer to the pole or to the equator.

PROPOSITION LXVII. THEOREM XXVII.

THE SAME LAWS OF ATTRACTION BEING SUPPOSED, I SAY,
THAT THE EXTERIOR BODY S DOES, BY RADII DRAWN TO
THE POINT O, THE COMMON CENTRE OF GRAVITY OF THE
INTERIOR BODIES P AND T, DESCRIBE ROUND THAT CENTRE

AREAS MORE PROPORTIONAL TO THE TIMES, AND AN ORBIT
MORE APPROACHING TO THE FORM OF AN ELLIPSIS HAVING
ITS FOCUS IN THAT CENTRE, THAN IT CAN DESCRIBE ROUND
THE INNERMOST AND GREATEST BODY T BY RADII DRAWN
TO THAT BODY.

For the attractions of the body S towards T and P compose its absolute attraction, which is more directed towards O, the common centre of gravity of the bodies T and P, than it is to the greatest body T; and which is more in a reciprocal proportion to the square of the distance SO, than it is to the square of the distance ST; as will easily appear by a little consideration.

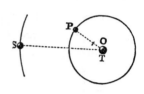

PROPOSITION LXVIII. THEOREM XXVIII.

THE SAME LAWS OF ATTRACTION SUPPOSED, I SAY, THAT
THE EXTERIOR BODY S WILL, BY RADII DRAWN TO O, THE
COMMON CENTRE OF GRAVITY OF THE INTERIOR BODIES P
AND T, DESCRIBE ROUND THAT CENTRE AREAS MORE
PROPORTIONAL TO THE TIMES, AND AN ORBIT MORE
APPROACHING TO THE FORM OF AN ELLIPSIS HAVING ITS
FOCUS IN THAT CENTRE, IF THE INNERMOST AND GREATEST
BODY BE AGITATED BY THESE ATTRACTIONS AS WELL AS THE
REST, THAN IT WOULD DO IF THAT BODY WERE EITHER AT
REST AS NOT ATTRACTED, OR WERE MUCH MORE OR MUCH
LESS ATTRACTED, OR MUCH MORE OR MUCH LESS AGITATED.

This may be demonstrated after the same manner as Prop. LXVI, but by a more prolix reasoning, which I therefore pass over. It will be sufficient to consider it after this manner. From the demonstration of the last Proposition it is plain that the centre, towards which the body S is urged by the two forces conjunctly, is very near to the common centre of gravity of those two other bodies. If this centre were to coincide with that common centre, and moreover the common centre of gravity of all the three bodies were at rest, the body S on one side, and the common centre of gravity of the other two bodies on the other side, would describe true ellipses about that quiescent common centre. This appears from Cor. 2, Prop LVIII, compared with what was demonstrated in Prop. LXIV, and LXV. Now this accurate elliptical motion will be disturbed a little by the distance of

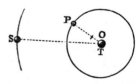

the centre of the two bodies from the centre towards which the third body S is attracted. Let there be added, moreover, a motion to the common centre of the three, and the perturbation will be increased yet more. Therefore the perturbation is least when the common centre of the three bodies is at rest; that is, when the innermost and greatest body T is attracted according to the same law as the rest are; and is always greatest when the common centre of the three, by the diminution of the motion of the body T, begins to be moved, and is more and more agitated.

COR. And hence if more lesser bodies revolve about the great one, it may easily be inferred that the orbits described will approach nearer to ellipses; and the descriptions of areas will be more nearly equable, if all the bodies mutually attract and agitate each other with accelerative forces that are as their absolute forces directly, and the squares of the distances inversely; and if the focus of each orbit be placed in the common centre of gravity of all the interior bodies (that is, if the focus of the first and innermost orbit be placed in the centre of gravity of the greatest and innermost body; the focus of the second orbit in the common centre of gravity of the two innermost bodies; the focus of the third orbit in the common centre of gravity of the three innermost; and so on), than if the innermost body were at rest, and was made the common focus of all the orbits.

PROPOSITION LXIX. THEOREM XXIX.

IN A SYSTEM OF SEVERAL BODIES A, B, C, D, &C., IF ANY ONE OF THOSE BODIES, AS A, ATTRACT ALL THE REST, B, C, D, &C., WITH ACCELERATIVE FORCES THAT ARE RECIPROCALLY AS THE SQUARES OF THE DISTANCES FROM THE ATTRACTING BODY; AND ANOTHER BODY, AS B, ATTRACTS ALSO THE REST, A, C, D, &C., WITH FORCES THAT ARE RECIPROCALLY AS THE SQUARES OF THE DISTANCES FROM THE ATTRACTING BODY; THE ABSOLUTE FORCES OF THE ATTRACTING BODIES A AND B WILL BE TO EACH OTHER AS THOSE VERY BODIES A AND B TO WHICH THOSE FORCES BELONG.

For the accelerative attractions of all the bodies B, C, D, towards A, are by the supposition equal to each other at equal distances; and in like manner the accelerative attractions of all the bodies towards B are also equal to each other at equal distances. But the absolute attractive force of the body A to the absolute attractive force of the body B as the accelerative attraction of all the bodies towards A to the accelerative attraction of all the bodies towards B at equal distances; and so is also the accelerative

attraction of the body B towards A to the accelerative attraction of the body K towards B. But the accelerative attraction of the body B towards A is to the accelerative attraction of the body A towards B as the mass of the body A to the mass of the body B; because the motive force which (by the 2d, 7th, and 8th Definition) are as the accelerative forces and the bodies attracted conjunctly are here equal to one another by the third Law. Therefore the absolute attractive force of the body A is to the absolute attractive force of the body B as the mass of the body A to the mass of the body B. *Q.E.D.*

COR. 1. Therefore if each of the bodies of the system A, 13, C, D, &c. does singly attract all the rest with accelerative forces that are reciprocally as the squares of the distances from the attracting body, the absolute forces of all those bodies will be to each other as the bodies themselves.

COR. 2. By a like reasoning, if each of the bodies of the system A, B, C, D, &c., does singly attract all the rest with accelerative forces, which are either reciprocally or directly in the ratio of any power whatever of the distances from the attracting body; or which are defined by the distances from each of the attracting bodies according to any common law; it is plain that the absolute forces of those bodies are as the bodies themselves.

COR. 3. In a system of bodies whose forces decrease in the duplicate ratio of the distances, if the lesser revolve about one very great one in ellipses, having their common focus in the centre of that great body, and of a figure exceedingly accurate; and moreover by radii drawn to that great body describe areas proportional to the times exactly; the absolute forces of those bodies to each other will be either accurately or very nearly in the ratio of the bodies. And so on the contrary. This appears from Cor. of Prop. XLVIII, compared with the first Corollary of this Prop.

SCHOLIUM.

These Propositions naturally lead us to the analogy there is between centripetal forces, and the central bodies to which those forces used to be directed; for it is reasonable to suppose that forces which are directed to bodies should depend upon the nature and quantity of those bodies, as we see they do in magnetical experiments. And when such cases occur, we are to compute the attractions of the bodies by assigning to each of their particles its proper force, and then collecting the sum of them all. I here use the word attraction in general for any endeavour, of what kind soever, made by bodies to approach to each other; whether that endeavour arise from the action of the bodies themselves, as tending mutually to or agitating each other by spirits emitted; or whether it arises from the action of the aether or of the air, or of any medium whatsoever, whether corporeal or incorporeal, any how impelling bodies placed therein towards each other.

In the same general sense I use the word impulse, not defining in this treatise the species or physical qualities of forces, but investigating the quantities and mathematical proportions of them; as I observed before in the Definitions. In mathematics we are to investigate the quantities of forces with their proportions consequent upon any conditions supposed; then, when we enter upon physics, we compare those proportions with the phenomena of Nature, that we may know what conditions of those forces answer to the several kinds of attractive bodies. And this preparation being made, we argue more safely concerning the physical species, causes, and proportions of the forces. Let us see, then, with what forces sphaerical bodies consisting of particles endued with attractive powers in the manner above spoken of must act mutually upon one another; and what kind of motions will follow from thence.

SECTION XII.

Of the attractive forces of sphaerical bodies.

PROPOSITION LXX. THEOREM XXX.

IF TO EVERY POINT OF A SPHAERICAL SURFACE THERE TEND
EQUAL CENTRIPETAL FORCES DECREASING IN THE DUPLICATE
RATIO OF THE DISTANCES FROM THOSE POINTS, I SAY, THAT
A CORPUSCLE PLACED WITHIN THAT SUPERFICIES WILL NOT
BE ATTRACTED BY THOSE FORCES ANY WAY.

Let HIKL, be that sphaerical superficies, and P a corpuscle placed within. Through P let there be drawn to this superficies to two lines HK, IL, intercepting very small arcs HI, KL; and because (by Cor. 3, Lem. VII) the triangles HPI, LPK are alike,

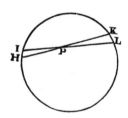

those arcs will be proportional to the distances HP LP; and any particles at HI and KL of the sphaerical superficies, terminated by right lines passing through P, will be in the duplicate ratio of those distances. Therefore the forces of these particles exerted upon the body P are equal between themselves. For the forces are as the particles directly, and the squares of the distances inversely. And these two ratios compose the ratio of equality. The attractions therefore, being made equally towards contrary parts, destroy each other. And by a like reasoning all the attractions through the whole sphaerical superficies are destroyed by contrary attractions. Therefore the body P will not be any way impelled by those attractions. *Q.E.D.*

PROPOSITION LXXI. THEOREM XXXI.

THE SAME THINGS SUPPOSED AS ABOVE, I SAY, THAT A
CORPUSCLE PLACED WITHOUT THE SPHAERICAL SUPERFICIES
IS ATTRACTED TOWARDS THE CENTRE OF THE SPHERE WITH
A FORCE RECIPROCALLY PROPORTIONAL TO THE SQUARE OF
ITS DISTANCE FROM THAT CENTRE.

Let AHKB, *ahkb*, be two equal sphaerical superficies described about the centre S, *s*; their diameters AB, *ab*; and let P and *p* be two corpuscles situate without the spheres in those diameters produced. Let there A be drawn from the corpuscles the lines PHK,

PIL, *phk, pil,* cutting off from the great circles AHB, *ahb*, the equal arcs HK, *hk*, IL, *il*; and to those lines let fall the perpendiculars SD, *sd*, SE, *se*,

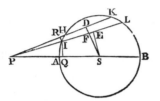 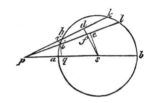

IR, *ir*; of which let SD, *sd*, cut PL, *pl*, in F and *f*. Let fall also to the diameters the perpendiculars IQ, *iq*. Let now the angles DPE, *dpe*, vanish; and because DS and *ds*, ES and *es* are equal, the lines PE, PF, and *pe, pf*, and the lineally DF, *df* may be taken for equal; because their last ratio, when the angles DPE, *dpe* vanish together, is the ratio of equality. These things then supposed, it will be, as PI to PF so is RI to DF, and as *pf* to *pi* so is *df* or DF to *ri*; and, *ex aequo*, as PI × *pf* to PF × *pi* so is RI to *ri*, that is (by Cor. 3, Lem. VII), so is the arc IH to the arc *ih*. Again, PI is to PS as IQ to SE, and ps to pi as se or SE to iq; and, *ex aequo*, PI × *ps* to PS × *pi* as IQ to *iq*. And compounding the ratios $PI^2 \times pf \times ps$ is to $pi^2 \times PF \times PS$, as IH × IQ to *ih* × *iq*; that is, as the circular superficies which is described by the arc IH, as the semi-circle AKB revolves about the diameter AB, is to the circular superficies described by the arc *ih* as the semi-circle *akb* revolves about the diameter *ab*. And the forces with which these superficies attract the corpuscles P and *p* in the direction of lines tending to those superficies are by the hypothesis as the superficies themselves directly, and the squares of the distances of the superficies from those corpuscles inversely; that is, as *pf* × *ps* to PF × PS. And these forces again are to the oblique parts of them which (by the resolution of forces as in Cor. 2, of the Laws) tend to the centres in the directions of the lines PS, *ps*, as PI to PQ, and *pi* to *pq*; that is (because of the like triangles PIQ and PSF, *piq* and *psf*), as PS to PF and *ps* to *pf*. Thence *ex aequo*, the attraction of the corpuscle P towards S is to the attraction of the corpuscle *p* towards *s* as $\frac{PF \times pf \times ps}{PS}$ is to $\frac{pf \times PF \times PS}{ps}$ that is, as

ps^2 to PS^2. And, by a like reasoning the forces with which the superficies described by

the revolution of the arcs KL, *kl* attract those corpuscles, will be as *ps*² to *PS*². And in the same ratio will be the forces of all the circular superficies into which each of the sphaerical superficies may be divided by taking *sd* always equal to SD, and *se* equal to SE. And therefore, by composition, the forces of the entire sphaerical superficies exerted upon those corpuscles will be in the same ratio.   *Q.E.D.*

PROPOSITION LXXII. THEOREM XXXII.

IF TO THE SEVERAL POINTS OF A SPHERE THERE TEND EQUAL
CENTRIPETAL FORCES DECREASING IN A DUPLICATE RATIO OF
THE DISTANCES FROM THOSE POINTS; AND THERE BE GIVEN
BOTH THE DENSITY OF THE SPHERE AND THE RATIO OF
THE DIAMETER OF THE SPHERE TO THE DISTANCE OF THE
CORPUSCLE FROM ITS CENTRE; I SAY, THAT THE FORCE WITH
WHICH THE CORPUSCLE IS ATTRACTED IS PROPORTIONAL TO
THE SEMI-DIAMETER OF THE SPHERE.

For conceive two corpuscles to be severally attracted by two spheres, one by one, the other by the other, and their distances from the centres of the spheres to be proportional to the diameters of the spheres respectively , and the spheres to be resolved into like particles, disposed in a like situation to the corpuscles. Then the attractions of one corpuscle towards the several particles of one sphere will be to the attractions of the other towards as many analogous particles of the other sphere in a ratio compounded of the ratio of the particles, directly, and the duplicate ratio of the distances inversely. But the particles are as the spheres, that is, in a triplicate ratio of the diameters, and the distances are as the diameters; and the first ratio directly with the last ratio taken twice inversely, becomes the ratio of diameter to diameter.   *Q.E.D.*

COR. 1. Hence if corpuscles revolve in circles about spheres composed of matter equally attracting, and the distances from the centres of the spheres be proportional to their diameters, the periodic times will be equal.

COR. 2. And, *vice versa,* if the periodic times are equal, the distances will be proportional to the diameters. These two Corollaries appear from Cor. 3, Prop. IV.

COR. 3. If to the several points of any two solids whatever, of like figure and equal density, there tend equal centripetal forces decreasing in a duplicate ratio of the distances from those points, the forces, with which corpuscles placed in a like situation to those two solids will be attracted by them, will be to each other as the diameters of the solids.

PROPOSITION LXXIII. THEOREM XXXIII.

IF TO THE SEVERAL POINTS OF A GIVEN SPHERE THERE TEND
EQUAL CENTRIPETAL FORCES DECREASING IN A DUPLICATE
RATIO OF THE DISTANCES FROM THE POINTS; I SAY, THAT A
CORPUSCLE PLACED WITHIN THE SPHERE IS ATTRACTED BY A
FORCE PROPORTIONAL TO ITS DISTANCE FROM THE CENTRE.

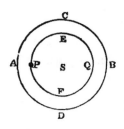

In the sphere ABCD, described about the centre S, let there be placed the corpuscle P; and about the same centre S, with the interval SP, conceive described an interior sphere PEQF. It is plain (by Prop. LXX) that the concentric sphaerical superficies, of which the difference AEBF of the spheres is composed, have no effect at all upon the body P, their attractions being destroyed by contrary attractions. There remains, therefore, only the attraction of the interior sphere PEQF. And (by Prop. LXXII) this is as the distance PS. *Q.E.D.*

SCHOLIUM.

By the superficies of which I here imagine the solids composed, I do not mean superficies purely mathematical, but orbs so extremely thin that their thickness is as nothing; that is, the evanescent orbs of which the sphere will at last consist, when the number of the orbs is increased, and their thickness diminished without end. In like manner, by the points of which lines, surfaces, and solids are said to be composed, are to be understood equal particles, whose magnitude is perfectly inconsiderable.

PROPOSITION LXXIV. THEOREM XXXIV.

THE SAME THINGS SUPPOSED, I SAY, THAT A CORPUSCLE
SITUATE WITHOUT THE SPHERE IS ATTRACTED WITH A
FORCE RECIPROCALLY PROPORTIONAL TO THE SQUARE OF
ITS DISTANCE FROM THE CENTRE.

For suppose the sphere to be divided into innumerable concentric sphaerical superficies, and the attractions of the corpuscle arising from the several superficies will be reciprocally proportional to the square of the distance of the corpuscle from the centre of the sphere (by Prop. LXXI). And, by composition, the sum of those attractions, that is, the attraction of the corpuscle towards the entire sphere, will be in the same ratio. *Q.E.D.*

Cor. 1. Hence the attractions of homogeneous spheres at equal distances from the centres will be as the spheres themselves. For (by Prop. LXXII) if the distances be proportional to the diameters of the spheres, the forces will be as the diameters. Let the greater distance be diminished in that ratio; and the distances now being equal, the attraction will be increased in the duplicate of that ratio; and therefore will be to the other attraction in the triplicate of that ratio; that is, in the ratio of the spheres.

Cor. 2. At any distances whatever the attractions are as the spheres applied to the squares of the distances.

Cor. 3. If a corpuscle placed without an homogeneous sphere is attracted by a force reciprocally proportional to the square of its distance from the centre, and the sphere consists of attractive particles, the force of every particle will decrease in a duplicate ratio of the distance from each particle.

PROPOSITION LXXV. THEOREM XXXV.

If to the several points of a given sphere there tend equal centripetal forces decreasing in a duplicate ratio of the distances from the points; I say, that another similar sphere will be attracted by it with a force reciprocally proportional to the square of the distance of the centres.

For the attraction of every particle is reciprocally as the square of its distance from the centre of the attracting sphere (by Prop. LXXIV), and is therefore the same as if that whole attracting force issued from one single corpuscle placed in the centre of this sphere. But this attraction is as great as on the other hand the attraction of the same corpuscle would be, if that were itself attracted by the several particles of the attracted sphere with the same force with which they are attracted by it. But that attraction of the corpuscle would be (by Prop. LXXIV) reciprocally proportional to the square of its distance from the centre of the sphere; therefore the attraction of the sphere, equal thereto, is also in the same ratio. *Q.E.D.*

Cor. 1. The attractions of spheres towards other homogeneous spheres, are as the attracting spheres applied to the squares of the distances of their centres from the centres of those which they attract.

Cor. 2. The case is the same when the attracted sphere does also attract. For the several points of the one attract the several points of the other with the same force with which they themselves are attracted by the others again; and therefore since in all attractions (by Law III) the attracted and attracting point are both equally acted on, the force will be doubled by their mutual attractions, the proportions remaining.

COR. 3. Those several truths demonstrated above concerning the motion of bodies about the focus of the conic sections will take place when an attracting sphere is placed in the focus, and the bodies move without the sphere.

COR. 4. Those things which were demonstrated before of the motion of bodies about the centre of the conic sections take place when the motions are performed within the sphere.

PROPOSITION LXXVI. THEOREM XXXVI.

IF SPHERES BE HOWEVER DISSIMILAR (AS TO DENSITY OF
MATTER AND ATTRACTIVE FORCE) IN THE SAME RATIO
ONWARD FROM THE CENTRE TO THE CIRCUMFERENCE; BUT
EVERY WHERE SIMILAR, AT EVERY GIVEN DISTANCE FROM
THE CENTRE, ON ALL SIDES ROUND ABOUT; AND THE
ATTRACTIVE FORCE OF EVERY POINT DECREASES IN THE
DUPLICATE RATIO OF THE DISTANCE OF THE BODY ATTRACTED;
I SAY, THAT THE WHOLE FORCE WITH WHICH ONE OF THESE
SPHERES ATTRACTS THE OTHER WILL BE RECIPROCALLY
PROPORTIONAL TO THE SQUARE OF THE DISTANCE OF
THE CENTRES.

Imagine several concentric similar spheres, AB, CD, EF, &c., the innermost of which added to the outermost may compose a matter more dense towards the centre, or subducted from them may leave the same more lax and rare. Then, by Prop. LXXV, these

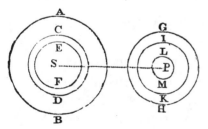

spheres will attract other similar concentric spheres GH, IK, LM, &c., each the other, with forces reciprocally proportional to the square of the distance SP. And, by composition or division, the sum of all those forces, or the excess of any of them above the others; that is, the entire force with which the whole sphere AB (composed of any concentric spheres or of their differences) will attract the whole sphere GH (composed of any concentric spheres or their differences) in the same ratio. Let the number of the concentric spheres be increased *in infinitum*, so that the density of the matter together with the attractive force may, in the progress from the circumference to the centre, increase or decrease according to any given law; and by the addition of matter not attractive, let the deficient density be supplied, that so the spheres may acquire any form desired; and the force with which one of these attracts the other will be still, by the former reasoning, in the same ratio of the square of the distance inversely.   *Q.E.D.*

COR. 1. Hence if many spheres of this kind, similar in all respects, attract each other mutually, the accelerative attractions of each to each, at any equal distances of the centres, will be as the attracting spheres.

COR. 2. And at any unequal distances, as the attracting spheres applied to the squares of the distances between the centres.

COR. 3. The motive attractions, or the weights of the spheres towards one another, will be at equal distances of the centres as the attracting and attracted spheres conjunctly; that is, as the products arising from multiplying the spheres into each other.

COR. 4. And at unequal distances, as those products directly, and the squares of the distances between the centres inversely.

COR. 5. These proportions take place also when the attraction arises from the attractive virtue of both spheres mutually exerted upon each other. For the attraction is only doubled by the conjunction of the forces, the proportions remaining as before.

COR. 6. If spheres of this kind revolve about others at rest, each about each : and the distances between the centres of the quiescent and revolving bodies are proportional to the diameters of the quiescent bodies; the periodic times will be equal.

COR. 7. And, again, if the periodic times are equal, the distances will be proportional to the diameters.

COR. 8. All those truths above demonstrated, relating to the motions of bodies about the foci of conic sections, will take place when an attracting sphere, of any form and condition like that above described, is placed in the focus.

COR. 9. And also when the revolving bodies are also attracting spheres of any condition like that above described.

PROPOSITION LXXVII. THEOREM XXXVII.

IF TO THE SEVERAL POINTS OF SPHERES THERE TEND
CENTRIPETAL FORCES PROPORTIONAL LO THE DISTANCES
OF THE POINTS FROM THE ATTRACTED BODIES; I SAY,
THAT THE COMPOUNDED FORCE WITH WHICH TWO
SPHERES ATTRACT EACH OTHER MUTUALLY IS AS THE
DISTANCE BETWEEN THE CENTRES OF THE SPHERES.

CASE. 1. Let AEBF be a sphere; S its centre, P a corpuscle attracted : PASB the axis of the sphere passing through the centre of the corpuscle; EF, *ef* two planes cutting the sphere, and perpendicular to the axis, and equidistant, one on one side, the other on the other, from the centre of the sphere; G and *g* the intersections of the planes and the axis; and H any point in the plane EF. The centripetal force of the point H upon the corpuscle P, exerted in the direction of the line PH, is as the distance PH; and (by

Cor. 2, of the Laws) the same exerted in the direction of the line PG, or towards the centre S, is as the length PG. Therefore the force of all the points in the plane EF (that is, of that whole plane) by which the corpuscle P is attracted towards the centre S is as

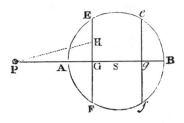

the distance PG multiplied by the number of those points, that is, as the solid contained under that plane EF and the distance PG. And in like manner the force of the plane *ef*, by which the corpuscle P is attracted towards the centre S, is as that plane drawn into its distance Pg, or as the equal plane EF drawn into that distance Pg; and the sum of the forces of both planes as the plane EF drawn into the sum of the distances PG + Pg, that is, as that plane drawn into twice the distance PS of the centre and the corpuscle; that is, as twice the plane EF drawn into the distance PS, or as the sum of the equal planes EF + *ef* drawn into the same distance. And, by a like reasoning, the forces of all the planes in the whole sphere, equi-distant on each side from the centre of the sphere, are as the sum of those planes drawn into the distance PS, that is, as the whole sphere and the distance PS conjunctly. *Q.E.D.*

CASE. 2. Let now the corpuscle P attract the sphere AEBF. And, by the same reasoning, it will appear that the force with which the sphere is attracted is as the distance PS. *Q.E.D.*

CASE. 3. Imagine another sphere composed of innumerable corpuscles P; and because the force with which every corpuscle is attracted is as the distance of the corpuscle from the centre of the first sphere, and as the same sphere conjunctly, and is therefore the same as if it all proceeded from a single corpuscle situate in the centre of the sphere, the entire force with which all the corpuscles in the second sphere are attracted, that is, with which that whole sphere is attracted, will be the same as if that sphere were attracted by a force issuing from a single corpuscle in the centre of the first sphere; and is therefore proportional to the distance between the centres of the spheres. *Q.E.D.*

CASE. 4. Let the spheres attract each other mutually, and the force will be doubled, but the proportion will remain. *Q.E.D.*

CASE. 5. Let the corpuscle *p* be placed within the sphere AEBF; and because the force of the Plane *ef* upon the corpuscle is as the solid contained under that plane and the distance *pg*, and the contrary force of the plane EF as the solid contained under that plane and the distance Pg; the force compounded of both will be as the difference of the solids, that is, as the sum of the equal planes drawn into half the difference

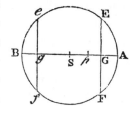

of the distances; that is, as that sum drawn into pS, the distance of the corpuscle from the centre of the sphere. And, by a like reasoning, the attraction of all the planes EF, *ef*, throughout the whole sphere, that is, the attraction of the whole sphere, is conjunctly as the sum of all the planes, or as the whole sphere, and as pS, the distance of the corpuscle from the centre of the sphere. $Q.E.D.$

CASE. 6. And if there be composed a new sphere out of innumerable corpuscles such as p, situate within the first sphere AEBF, it may be proved, as before, that the attraction, whether single of one sphere towards the other, or mutual of both towards each other, will be as the distance pS of the centres. $Q.E.D.$

PROPOSITION LXXVIII. THEOREM XXXVIII.

IF SPHERES IN THE PROGRESS FROM THE CENTRE TO THE CIRCUMFERENCE BE HOWEVER DISSIMILAR AND UNEQUABLE, BUT SIMILAR ON EVERY SIDE ROUND ABOUT AT ALL GIVEN DISTANCES FROM THE CENTRE; AND THE ATTRACTIVE FORCE OF EVERY POINT BE AS THE DISTANCE OF THE ATTRACTED BODY; I SAY, THAT THE ENTIRE FORCE WITH WHICH TWO SPHERES OF THIS KIND ATTRACT EACH OTHER MUTUALLY, IS PROPORTIONAL TO THE DISTANCE BETWEEN THE CENTRES OF THE SPHERES.

This is demonstrated from the foregoing Proposition, in the same manner as Proposition LXXVI was demonstrated from Proposition LXXV.

COR. Those things that were above demonstrated in Prop, X and LXIV, of the motion of bodies round the centres of conic sections, take place when all the attractions are made by the force of sphaerical bodies of the condition above described, and the attracted bodies are spheres of the same kind.

SCHOLIUM.

I have now explained the two principal cases of attractions; to wit, when the centripetal forces decrease in a duplicate ratio of the distances, or increase in a simple ratio of the distances, causing the bodies in both cases to revolve in conic sections, and composing sphaerical bodies whose centripetal forces observe the same law of increase or decrease in the recess from the centre as the forces of the particles themselves do; which is very remarkable. It would be tedious to run over the other cases, whose conclusions are less elegant and important, so particularly as I have done these. I choose rather to comprehend and determine them all by one general method as follows.

LEMMA XXIX.

If about the centre S there be described any circle as
AEB, and about the centre P there be also described
two circles EF, EF, cutting the first in E and e, and
the line PS in F and f; and there be let fall to PS the
perpendiculars ED, ed; I say, that if the distance of
the arcs EF, ef be supposed to be infinitely diminished,
the last ratio of the line Dd to the evanescent line
Ff is the same as that of the line PE to the line PS.

For if the line P*e* cut the arc EF in *q*, and the right line E*e*, which coincides with the evanescent arc E*e*, be produced, and meet the right line PS in T; and there be let fall from S to PE the

perpendicular SG; then, because
of the like triangles DTE, *d*T*e*,
DES, it will be as D*d* to E*e* so DT
to TE, or DE to ES; and because
the triangles, E*eq*, ESG (by Lem.
VIII, and Cor. 3, Lem. VII) are
similar, it will be as E*e* to *eq* or F*f*
so ES to SG; and, *ex aequo*, as D*d*

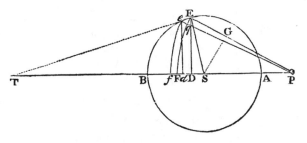

to F*f* so DE to SG; that is (because of the similar triangles PDE, PGS), so is PE to PS.   Q.E.D.

PROPOSITION LXXIX. THEOREM XXXIX.

Suppose a superficies as EF*fe* to have its breadth
infinitely diminished, and to be just vanishing; and
that the same superficies by its revolution round the
axis PS describes a spherical concavo-convex solid, to
the several equal particles of which there tend equal
centripetal forces; I say, that the force with which
that solid attracts a corpuscle situate in P is in a
ratio compounded of the ratio of the solid DE2 × Ff
and the ratio of the force with which the given particle
in the plane Ff would attract the same corpuscle.

For if we consider, first, the force of the sphaerical superficies FE which is generated by the revolution of the arc FE, and is cut any where, as in *r*, by the line *de*, the annular part of the superficies generated by the revolution of the arc *r*E will be as the lineola D*d*, the radius of the sphere PE remainimg the same; as Archimedes has

demonstrated in his Book of the Sphere and Cylinder. And the force of this superficies exerted in the direction of the lines PE or Pr situate all round in the conical superficies, will be as this annular superficies itself; that is as the lineola Dd, or, which is the same, as the rectangle under the given radius PE of the sphere and the lineola Dd; but that force, exerted in the direction of the line PS tending to the centre S, will be less in the ratio PD to PE, and therefore will be as PD × Dd. Suppose now the line DF to be divided into innumerable little equal particles, each of which call Dd, and then the superficies FE will be divided into so many equal annuli, whose forces will be as the

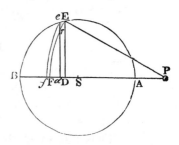

sum of all the rectangles PD × Dd, that is, as $\frac{1}{2}$PF^2 – $\frac{1}{2}$PD^2 and therefore as DE^2 × Ff. Let now the superficies FE be drawn into the altitude Ff, and the force of the solid EFfe exerted upon the corpuscle P will be as DE^2 × Ff, that is, if the force be given which any given particle as Ff exerts upon the corpuscle P at the distance PE. But if that force be not given, the force of the solid EFfe will be as the solid DE^2 × Ff and that force not given, conjunctly. *Q.E.D.*

PROPOSITION LXXX. THEOREM XL.

IF TO THE SEVERAL EQUAL PARTS OF A SPHERE ABE DESCRIBED ABOUT THE CENTRE S THERE TEND EQUAL CENTRIPETAL FORCES; AND FROM THE SEVERAL POINTS D IN THE AXIS OF THE SPHERE AB IN WHICH A CORPUSCLE, AS P, IS PLACED, THERE BE ERECTED THE PERPENDICULARS DE MEETING THE SPHERE IN E, AND IF IN THOSE PERPENDICULARS THE LENGTHS DN BE TAKEN AS THE QUANTITY $\frac{DE^2 \times PS}{PE}$, AND AS THE FORCE WHICH A PARTICLE OF THE SPHERE SITUATE IN THE AXIS EXERTS AT THE DISTANCE PE UPON THE CORPUSCLE P CONJUNCTLY; I SAY, THAT THE WHOLE FORCE WITH WHICH THE CORPUSCLE P IS ATTRACTED TOWARDS THE SPHERE IS AS THE AREA ANB, COMPREHENDED UNDER THE AXIS OF THE SPHERE AB, AND THE CURVE LINE ANB, THE LOCUS OF THE POINT N.

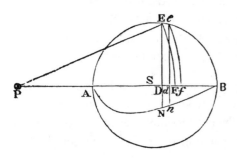

For supposing the construction in the last Lemma and Theorem to stand, conceive the axis of the sphere AB to be divided into innumerable equal particles Dd, and the whole sphere to be divided into so many sphaerical concavo-convex laminae EFfe; and erect the perpendicular dn. By the last

Theorem, the force with which the laminae EFfe attracts the corpuscle P is as DE^2 × Ff and the force of one particle exerted at the distance PE or PF, conjunctly. But (by the last Lemma) Dd is to Ff as PE to PS, and therefore Ff is equal to $\frac{PS \times Dd}{PE}$; and DE^2

x Ff is equal to $Dd \times \frac{DE^2 \times PS}{PE}$; and therefore the force of the laminae EFfe is as

$Dd \times \frac{DE^2 \times PS}{PE}$ and the force of a particle exerted at the distance PF conjunctly; that is, by the supposition, as DN × Dd, or as the evanescent area DNnd. Therefore the forces of all the laminae, exerted upon the corpuscle P are as all the areas DNnd, that is, the whole force of the sphere will be as the whole area ANB.   *Q.E.D.*

Cor. 1. Hence if the centripetal force tending to the several particles remain always the same at all distances, and DN be made as $\frac{DE^2 \times PS}{PE}$, the whole force with which the

corpuscle is attracted by the sphere is as the area ANB.

Cor. 2. If the centripetal force of the particles be reciprocally as the distance of the corpuscle attracted by it, and DN be made as $\frac{DE^2 \times PS}{PE^2}$, the force with which the

corpuscle P is attracted by the whole sphere will be as the area ANB.

Cor. 3. If the centripetal force of the particles be reciprocally as the cube of the distance of the Corpuscle attracted by it, and DN be made as $\frac{DE^2 \times PS}{PE^4}$, the force with

which the corpuscle is attracted by the whole sphere will be as the area ANB.

Cor. 4. And universally if the centripetal force tending to the several particles of the sphere be supposed to be reciprocally as the quantity V; and DN be made as $\frac{DE^2 \times PS}{PE \times V}$; the force with which a corpuscle is attracted by the whole sphere will be as

the area ANB.

PROPOSITION LXXXI. PROBLEM XLI.

The things remaining as above, it is required to measure the area ANB.

From the point P let there be drawn the right line PH touching the sphere in H; and to the axis PAB, letting fall the perpendicular HI, bisect PI in L; and (by Prop. XII, Book II, Elem.) PE^2 is equal to PS^2+SE^2+2PSD. But because the triangles SPH, SHI are alike, SE^2 or SH^2 is equal to the rectangle PSI. Therefore PE^2 is equal to the rectangle contained under PS and PS + SI + 2SD; that is, under PS and 2LS + SD; that is, under PS and 2LD. Moreover DE^2 is equal to SE^2 − SD^2, or SE^2 − LS^2+2SLD − LD^2,

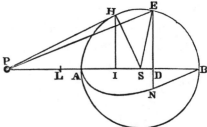

that is, $2SLD - LD^2 - ALB$. For $LS^2 - SE^2$ or $LS^2 - SA^2$ (by Prop. VI, Book II, Elem.) is equal to the rectangle ALB. Therefore if instead of DE^2, we write $2SLD - LD^2 - ALB$, the quantity $\frac{DE^2 \times PS}{PE \times V}$, which (by Cor. 4 of the foregoing,

Prop.) is as the length of the ordinate DN, will now resolve itself into three parts $\frac{2SLD \times PS}{PE \times V} - \frac{LD^2 \times PS}{PE \times V} - \frac{ALB \times PS}{PE \times V}$ where if instead of V we

write the inverse ratio of the centripetal force, and instead of PE the mean proportional between PS and 2LD, those three parts will become ordinates to so many curve lines, whose areas are discovered by the common methods. 　*Q.E.D.*

EXAMPLE 1. If the centripetal force tending to the several particles of the sphere be reciprocally as the distance; instead of V write PE the distance, then $2PS \times LD$ for PE^2; and DN will become as $SL - \frac{1}{2}LD - \frac{ALB}{LD}$. Suppose DN equal to its double

$2SL - LD - \frac{ALB}{LD}$; and 2SL the given part of the ordinate drawn into the length AB will describe the rectangular area 2SL 3 AB; and the indefinite part LD, drawn perpendicularly into the same length with a continued motion, in such sort as in its motion one way or another it may either by increasing or decreasing remain always equal to the length LD, will describe the area $\frac{LB^2 - LA^2}{2}$, that is, the area $SL \times AB$; which taken from the former area $2SL \times AB$, leaves the area $SL \times AB$. But the third part $\frac{ALB}{LD}$ drawn after the same manner with a continued motion perpendicularly into the same length, will describe the area of an hyperbola, which subducted from the area $SL \times AB$ will leave ANB the area sought. Whence arises this construction of the Problem. At the points, L, A, B, erect the perpendiculars L*l*, A*a*, B*b*; making A*a* equal to LB, and B*b* equal to LA. Making L*l* and LB asymptotes, describe through the points *a*, *b*, the hyperbolic

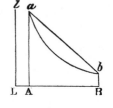

curve *ab*. And the chord *ba* being drawn, will inclose the area aba equal to the area sought ANB.

EXAMPLE 2. If the centripetal force tending to the several particles of the sphere be reciprocally as the cube of the distance, or (which is the same thing) as that cube applied to any given plane; write $\frac{PE^3}{2AS^2}$ for V, and $2PS \times LD$ for PE^2; and DN will

become as $\frac{SL \times AS^2 AS^2 ALB \times AS^2}{PS \times LD 2PS 2PS \times LD^2}$ that is (because PS, AS, SI are continually

proportional), as $\dfrac{LSI}{LD} - \dfrac{1}{2}SI - \dfrac{ALB \times SI}{2LD^2}$. If we draw then these three parts into the length

AB, the first $\dfrac{LSI}{LD}$ will generate the area of an hyperbola; the second $\frac{1}{2}SI$ the area $\frac{1}{2}AB \times SI$; the third $\dfrac{ALB \times SI}{2LD^2}$ the area $\dfrac{ALB \times SI}{2LA} \dfrac{ALB \times SI}{2LB}$, that is,

$\frac{1}{2}AB \times SI$. From the first subduct the sum of the second and third, and there will remain ANB, the area sought. Whence arises this construction of the problem. At the points L, A, S, B, erect the perpendiculars Ll Aa Ss, Bb, of which suppose Ss equal to SI; and through the point s, to the asymptotes Ll, LB, describe the hyperbola asb meeting the perpendiculars Aa, Bb, in a and b; and the rectangle 2ASI, subducted from the hyberbolic area AasbB, will leave ANB the area sought.

EXAMPLE 3. If the centripetal force tending to the several particles of the spheres decrease in a quadruplicate ratio of the distance from the particles; write $\dfrac{PE^4}{2AS^3}$ for V, then $\sqrt{2PS+LD}$ for PE, and DN will become as

$\dfrac{SI^2 \times SL}{\sqrt{2SI}} \times \dfrac{1}{\sqrt{LD^3}} - \dfrac{SI^2}{2\sqrt{2SI}} \times \dfrac{1}{\sqrt{LD}} - \dfrac{SI^2 \times ALB}{2\sqrt{2SI}} \times \dfrac{1}{\sqrt{LD^5}}$. These three parts drawn into the length AB, produce so many areas, viz.

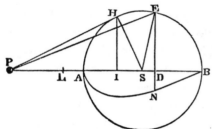

$\dfrac{2SI^2 \times SL}{\sqrt{2SI}}$ into $\dfrac{1}{\sqrt{LA}} - \dfrac{1}{\sqrt{LB}}$; $\dfrac{SI^2}{\sqrt{2SI}}$ into $\sqrt{LB} - \sqrt{LA}$; and $\dfrac{SI^2 \times ALB}{3\sqrt{2SI}}$ into $\dfrac{1}{\sqrt{LA^3}} - \dfrac{1}{\sqrt{LB^3}}$. And these after due reduction come forth $\dfrac{2SI^2 \times SL}{LI}$, SI^2, and $SI^2 + \dfrac{2SI^3}{3LI}$. And these by subducting the last from the first, become $\dfrac{4SI^3}{3LI}$.

Therefore the entire force with which the corpuscle P is attracted towards the centre of the sphere is as s$\dfrac{SI^3}{PI}$, that is, reciprocally as $PS^3 \times PI$ Q.E.I.

By the same method one may determine the attraction of a corpuscle situate within the sphere, but more expeditiously by the following Theorem.

PROPOSITION LXXXII. THEOREM XLI.

IN A SPHERE DESCRIBED ABOUT THE CENTRE S WITH THE INTERVAL SA, IF THERE BE TAKEN SI, SA, SP CONTINUALLY PROPORTIONAL; I SAY, THAT THE ATTRACTION OF A CORPUSCLE WITHIN THE SPHERE

IN ANY PLACE I IS TO ITS ATTRACTION WITHOUT THE SPHERE IN THE
PLACE P IN A RATIO COMPOUNDED OF THE SUBDUPLICATE RATIO OF
IS, PS, THE DISTANCES FROM THE CENTRE, AND THE SUBDUPLICATE
RATIO OF THE CENTRIPETAL FORCES TENDING TO THE CENTRE IN
THOSE PLACES P AND I.

As if the centripetal forces of the particles of the sphere be reciprocally as the distances
of the corpuscle attracted by them; the force with
which the corpuscle situate in I is attracted by the
entire sphere will be to the force with which it is
attracted in P in a ratio compounded of the
subduplicate ratio of the distance SI to the distance SP, and the subduplicate ratio of the centripetal force in the place I arising from any particle in the centre to the centripetal force in the
place P arising from the same particle in the cen-

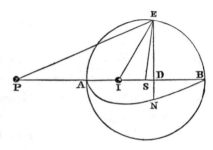

tre; that is, in the subduplicate ratio of the distances SI, SP to each other reciprocally. These
two subduplicate ratios compose the ratio of equality, and therefore the attractions in I and
P produced by the whole sphere are equal. By the like calculation, if the forces of the particles of the sphere are reciprocally in a duplicate ratio of the distances, it will be found that
the attraction in I is to the attraction in P as the distance SP to the semi-diameter SA of
the sphere. If those forces are reciprocally in a triplicate ratio of the distances, the attractions in I and P will be to each other as SP^2 to SA^2; if in a quadruplicate ratio, as SP^3 to
SA^3. Therefore since the attraction in P was found in this last case to be reciprocally as PS^3
$\times$ PI, the attraction in I will be reciprocally as $SA^3 \times$ PI, that is, because SA^3 is given reciprocally as PI. And the progression is the same *in infinitum*. The demonstration of this
Theorem is as follows:

The things remaining as above constructed, and a corpuscle being in any place P,
the ordinate DN was found to be as $\frac{DE^2 \times PS}{PE \times V}$. Therefore if IE be drawn, that ordinate
for any other place of the corpuscle, as I, will become (*mutatis mutandis*) as $\frac{DE^2 \times IS}{IE \times V}$.
Suppose the centripetal forces flowing from any point of the sphere, as E, to be to each
other at the distances IE and PE as PE^n to IE^n (where the number n denotes the index
of the powers of PE and IE), and those ordinates will become as $\frac{DE^2 \times PS}{PE \times PE^n}$ and $\frac{DE^2 \times IS}{IE \times IE^n}$
whose ratio to each other is as $PS \times IE \times IE^N$ to $IS \times PE \times PE^N$.
Because SI, SE, SP are in continued proportion, the triangles SPE, SEI are alike; and
thence IE is to PE as IS to SE or SA. For the ratio of IE to PE write the ratio of IS to
SA; and the ratio of the ordinates becomes that of $PS \times IE^N$ to $SA \times PE^N$. But the
ratio of PS to SA is subduplicate of that of the distances PS, SI; and the ratio of IE^N

to PEⁿ (because IE is to PE as IS to SA) is subduplicate of that of the forces at the distances PS, IS. Therefore the ordinates, and consequently the areas which the ordinates describe, and the attractions proportional to them, are in a ratio compounded of those subduplicate ratios.

Q.E.D.

PROPOSITION LXXXIII. PROBLEM XLII.

TO FIND THE FORCE WITH WHICH A CORPUSCLE PLACED IN
THE CENTRE OF A SPHERE IS ATTRACTED TOWARDS ANY
SEGMENT OF THAT SPHERE WHATSOEVER.

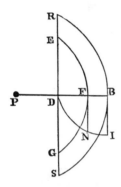

Let P be a body in the centre of that sphere and RBSD a segment thereof contained under the plane RDS, and the sphaerical superficies RBS. Let DB be cut in F by a sphaerical superficies EFG described from the centre P, and let the segment be divided into the parts BREFGS, FEDG. Let us suppose that segment to be not a purely mathematical but a physical superficies, having some, but a perfectly inconsiderable thickness. Let that thickness be called O, and (by what *Archimedes* has demonstrated) that superficies will be as PF × DF x 0. Let us suppose besides the attractive forces of the particles of the sphere to be reciprocally as that power of the distances, of which n is index; and the force with which the superficies EFG attracts the body P will be (by Prop. LXXIX) as $\dfrac{DE^2 \times O}{PF^n}$, that is, as $\dfrac{2DF \times O}{PF^{n-1}} - \dfrac{DF^2 \times O}{PF^n}$. Let the perpendicular FN drawn into O be proportional to this quantity; and the curvilinear area BDI, which the ordinate FN, drawn through the length DB with a continued motion will describe, will be as the whole force with which the whole segment RBSD attracts the body P.

Q.E.I.

PROPOSITION LXXXIV. PROBLEM XLIII.

TO FIND THE FORCE WITH WHICH A CORPUSCLE, PLACED WITH-
OUT THE CENTRE OF A SPHERE IN THE AXIS OF ANY SEGMENT, IS
ATTRACTED BY THAT SEGMENT.

Let the body P placed in the axis ADB of the segment EBK be attracted by that segment. About the centre P, with the interval PE, let the sphaerical superficies EFK be described; and let it divide the segment into two parts EBKFE and EFKDE. Find the force of the first of those parts by Prop. LXXXI, and the force of the latter part by Prop. LXXXIII, and the sum of the forces will be the force of the whole segment EBKDE.

Q.E.I.

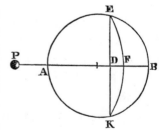

SCHOLIUM.

The attractions of sphaerical bodies being now explained, it comes next in order to treat of the laws of attraction in other bodies consisting in like manner of attractive particles; but to treat of them particularly is not necessary to my design. It will be sufficient to subjoin some general propositions relating to the forces of such bodies, and the motions thence arising, because the knowledge of these will be of some little use in philosophical inquiries.

SECTION XIII.

Of the attractive forces of bodies which are not of a sphaerical figure.

PROPOSITION. LXXXV. THEOREM XLII.

IF A BODY BE ATTRACTED BY ANOTHER, AND ITS ATTRACTION BE VASTLY STRONGER WHEN IT IS CONTIGUOUS TO THE ATTRACTING BODY THAN WHEN THEY ARE SEPARATED FROM ONE ANOTHER BY A VERY SMALL INTERVAL; THE FORCES OF THE PARTICLES OF THE ATTRACTING BODY DECREASE, IN THE RECESS OF THE BODY ATTRACTED, IN MORE THAN A DUPLICATE RATIO OF THE DISTANCE OF THE PARTICLES.

For if the forces decrease in a duplicate ratio of the distances from the particles, the attraction towards a sphaerical body being (by Prop. LXXIV) reciprocally as the square of the distance of the attracted body from the centre of the sphere, will not be sensibly increased by the contact, and it will be still less increased by it, if the attraction, in the recess of the body attracted, decreases in a still less proportion. The proposition, therefore, is evident concerning attractive spheres. And the case is the same of concave sphaerical orbs attracting external bodies. And much more does it appear in orbs that attract bodies placed within them, because there the attractions diffused through the cavities of those orbs are (by Prop. LXX) destroyed by contrary attractions, and therefore have no effect even in the Place of contact. Now if from these spheres and sphaerical orbs we take away any parts remote from the place of contact, and add new parts any where at pleasure, we may change the figures of the attractive bodies at pleasure; but the parts added or taken away, being remote from the place of contact, will cause no remarkable excess of the attraction arising from the contact of the two bodies. Therefore the proposition holds good in bodies of all figures. *Q.E.D.*

PROPOSITION LXXXVI. THEOREM XLIII.

IF THE FORCES OF THE PARTICLES OF WHICH AN
ATTRACTIVE BODY IS COMPOSED DECREASE, IN THE RECESS
OF THE ATTRACTIVE BODY, IN A TRIPLICATE OR MORE THAN
A TRIPLICATE RATIO OF THE DISTANCE FROM THE PARTICLES,
THE ATTRACTION WILL BE VASTLY STRONGER IN THE POINT
OF CONTACT THAN WHEN THE ATTRACTING AND ATTRACTED
BODIES ARE SEPARATED FROM EACH OTHER, THOUGH BY
NEVER SO SMALL AN INTERVAL.

For that the attraction is infinitely increased when the attracted corpuscle comes to touch an attracting sphere of this kind, appears, by the solution of Problem XLI, exhibited in the second and third Examples. The same will also appear (by comparing those Examples and Theorem XLI together) of attractions of bodies made towards concavo-convex orbs, whether the attracted bodies be placed without the orbs, or in the cavities within them. And by adding to or taking from those spheres and orbs any attractive matter any where without the place of contact, so that the attractive bodies may receive any assigned figure, the Proposition will hold good of all bodies universally.   *Q.E.D.*

PROPOSITION LXXXVII. THEOREM XLIV.

IF TWO BODIES SIMILAR TO EACH OTHER, AND CONSISTING
OF MATTER EQUALLY ATTRACTIVE, ATTRACT SEPARATELY
TWO CORPUSCLES PROPORTIONAL TO THOSE BODIES, AND IN
A LIKE SITUATION TO THEM, THE ACCELERATIVE
ATTRACTIONS OF THE CORPUSCLES TOWARDS THE ENTIRE
BODIES WILL BE AS THE ACCELERATIVE ATTRACTIONS OF THE
CORPUSCLES TOWARDS PARTICLES OF THE BODIES PROPORTIONAL
TO THE WHOLES, AND ALIKE SITUATED IN THEM.

For if the bodies are divided into particles proportional to the wholes, and alike situated in there, it will be, as the attraction towards any particle of one of the bodies to the attraction towards the correspondent particle in the other body, so are the attractions towards the several particles of the first body, to the attractions towards the several correspondent particles of the other body; and, by composition, so is the attraction towards the first whole body to the attraction towards the second whole body.   *Q.E.D.*

COR. 1. Therefore if, as the distances of the corpuscles attracted increase, the attractive forces of the particles decrease in the ratio of any power of the distances, the accelerative attractions towards the whole bodies will be as the bodies directly, and those powers of the distances inversely. As if the forces of the particles decrease in a duplicate ratio of the distances from the corpuscles attracted, and the bodies are as A^3 and B^3, and therefore both the cubic sides of the bodies, and the distance of the attracted corpuscles from the bodies, are as A and B; the accelerative attractions towards the bodies will be as $\frac{A^3}{A^2}$ and $\frac{B^3}{B^2}$ that is, as A and B the cubic sides of those bodies. If the forces of the particles decrease in a triplicate ratio of the distances from the attracted corpuscles, the accelerative attractions towards the whole bodies will be as $\frac{A^3}{A^3}$ and $\frac{B^3}{B^3}$ that is, equal.

If the forces decrease in a quadruplicate ratio, the attractions towards the bodies will be as $\frac{A^3}{A^4}$ and $\frac{B^3}{B^4}$, that is, reciprocally as the cubic sides A and B. And so in other cases.

COR. 2. Hence, on the other hand, from the forces with which like bodies attract corpuscles similarly situated, may be collected the ratio of the decrease of the attractive forces of the particles as the attracted corpuscle recedes from them; if so be that decrease is directly or inversely in any ratio of the distances.

PROPOSITION LXXXVIII. THEOREM XLV.

IF THE ATTRACTIVE FORCES OF THE EQUAL PARTICLES OF ANY BODY BE AS THE DISTANCE OF THE PLACES FROM THE PARTICLES, THE FORCE OF THE WHOLE BODY WILL TEND TO ITS CENTRE OF GRAVITY; AND WILL BE THE SAME WITH THE FORCE OF A GLOBE, CONSISTING OF SIMILAR AND EQUAL MATTER, AND HAVING ITS CENTRE IN THE CENTRE OF GRAVITY.

Let the particles A, B, of the body RSTV attract any corpuscle Z with forces which, supposing the particles to be equal between themselves, are as the distances AZ, BZ; but, if they are supposed unequal, are as those particles and their distances AZ, BZ, conjunctly, or (if I may so speak) as those particles drawn into their digtances AZ, BZ respectively. And let those forces be expressed by the contents under A × AZ, and B × BZ. Join AB, and let it be cut in G, so that AG may be to BG as the particle B to the particle A; and G will be the common centre of gravity of the particles A and B. The force A × AZ will (by Cor. 2, of the Laws) be 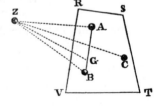 resolved into the forces A × GZ and A × AG; and the force B × RZ into the forces B × GZ and B × BG. Now the forces A × AG and B × BG, because A is proportional

to B, and BG to AG, are equal, and therefore having contrary directions destroy one another. There remain then the forces A × GZ and B × GZ. These tend from Z towards the centre G, and compose the force $\overline{A+B}$ × GZ; that is, the same force as if the attractive particles A and B were placed in their common centre of gravity G, composing there a little globe.

By the same reasoning, if there be added a third particle C, and the force of it be compounded with the force $\overline{A+B}$ × GZ tending to the centre G, the force thence arising will tend to the common centre of gravity of that globe in G and of the particle C; that is, to the common centre of gravity of the three particles A, B, C; and will be the same as if that globe and the particle C were placed in that common centre composing a greater globe there; and so we may go on *in infinitum*. Therefore the whole force of all the particles of any body whatever RSTV is the same as if that body, without removing its centre of gravity, were to put on the form of a globe.   *Q.E.D.*

COR. Hence the motion of the attracted body Z will be the same as if the attracting body RSTV were sphaerical and therefore if that attracting body be either at rest, or proceed uniformly in a right line, the body attracted will move in an ellipsis having its centre in the centre of gravity of the attracting body.

PROPOSITION LXXXIX. THEOREM XLVI.

IF THERE BE SEVERAL BODIES CONSISTING OF EQUAL PARTICLES WHOSE FORCES ARE AS THE DISTANCES OF THE PLACES FROM EACH, THE FORCE COMPOUNDED OF ALL THE FORCES BY WHICH ANY CORPUSCLE IS ATTRACTED WILL TEND TO THE COMMON CENTRE OF GRAVITY OF THE ATTRACTING BODIES; AND WILL BE THE SAME AS IF THOSE ATTRACTING BODIES, PRESERVING THEIR COMMON CENTRE OF GRAVITY, SHOULD UNITE THERE, AND BE FORMED INTO A GLOBE.

This is demonstrated after the same manner as the foregoing Proposition.

COR. Therefore the motion of the attracted body will be the same as if the attracting bodies, preserving their common centre of gravity, should unite there, and be formed into a globe. And, therefore, if the common centre of gravity of the attracting bodies be either at rest, or proceed uniformly in a right line, the attracted body will move in an ellipsis having its centre in the common centre of gravity of the attracting bodies.

PROPOSITION XC. PROBLEM XLIV.

IF TO THE SEVERAL POINTS OF ANY CIRCLE THERE TEND EQUAL CENTRIPETAL FORCES, INCREASING OR DECREASING IN ANY RATIO

OF THE DISTANCES; IT IS REQUIRED TO FIND THE FORCE WITH WHICH A CORPUSCLE IS ATTRACTED, THAT IS, SITUATE ANY WHERE IN A RIGHT LINE WHICH STANDS AT RIGHT ANGLES TO THE PLANE OF THE CIRCLE AT ITS CENTRE.

Suppose a circle to be described about the centre A with any interval AD in a plane to which the right line AP is perpendicular; and let it be required to find the force with which a corpuscle P is attracted towards the same. From any point E of the circle, to the attracted corpuscle P, let there be drawn the right line PE. In the right line PA take PF equal to PE, and make a perpendicular FK, erected at F, to be as the force with which the point E attracts the corpuscle P. And let the curve line IKL be the locus of the point K. Let that curve meet the plane of the circle in L. In PA take PH equal to PD,and erect the perpendicular HI meeting that curve in I; and the attraction of the corpuscle P towards the circle will be as the area AHIL drawn into the altitude AP. *Q.E.I.*

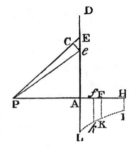

For let there be taken in AE a very small line E*e*. Join P*e*, and in PE, PA take PC, P*f* equal to P*e*. And because the force, with which any point E of the annulus described about the centre A with the interval AP in the aforesaid plane attracts to itself the body P, is supposed to be as FK; and, therefore, the force with which that point attracts the body P towards A is as $\frac{AP \times FK}{PE}$; and the force with which the whole annulus attracts the body P towards A is as the annulus and $\frac{AP \times FK}{PE}$ conjunctly; and that annulus also is as the rectangle under the radius AE and the breadth E*e*, and this rectangle (because PE and AE, E*e* and CE are proportional) is equal to the rectangle PE × CE or PE × F*f*, the force with which that annulus attracts the body P towards A will be as PE × F*f* and $\frac{AP \times FK}{PE}$ conjunctly; that is, as the

content under F*f* × FK × AP, or as the area FK*kf* drawn into AP. And therefore the sum of the forces with which all the annuli, in the circle described about the centre A with the interval AD, attract the body P towards A, is as the whole area AHIKL drawn into AP. *Q.E.D.*

COR. 1. Hence if the forces of the points decrease in the duplicate ratio of the distances, that is, if FK be as $\frac{1}{PF^2}$, and therefore the area AHIKL as $\frac{1}{PA} - \frac{1}{PH}$; the attraction of the corpuscle P towards the circle will be as $1 - \frac{PA}{PH}$; that is, as $\frac{AH}{PH}$.

COR. 2. And universally if the forces of the points at the distances D be reciprocally as any power D^n of the distances; that is, if FK be as $\frac{1}{D^n}$ and therefore the area AHIKL as

$\frac{1}{PA^{n-1}} - \frac{1}{PH^{n-1}}$; the attraction of the corpuscle P towards the circle will be as $\frac{1}{PA^{n-2}} - \frac{PA}{PH^{n-1}}$.

COR. 3. And if the diameter of the circle be increased *in infinitum*, and the number n be greater than unity; the attraction of the corpuscle P towards the whole infinite plane will be reciprocally as PA^{n-2}, because the other term $\frac{PA}{PH^{n-1}}$ vanishes.

PROPOSITION XCI. PROBLEM XLV.

TO FIND THE ATTRACTION OF A CORPUSCLE SITUATE IN THE
AXIS OF A ROUND SOLID, TO WHOSE SEVERAL POINTS THERE
TEND EQUAL CENTRIPETAL FORCES DECREASING IN ANY
RATIO OF THE DISTANCES WHATSOEVER.

Let the corpuscle P, situate in the axis AB of the solid DECG, be attracted towards that solid. Let the solid be cut by any circle as RFS, perpendicular to the axis; and in its semi-diameter FS, in any plane PALKB passing through the axis,

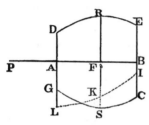

let there be taken (by Prop. XC) the length FK proportional to the force with which the corpuscle P is attracted towards that circle. Let the locus of the point K be the curve line LKI, meeting the planes of the outermost circles AL and BI in L and I; and the attraction of the corpuscle P towards the solid will be as the area LABI.   *Q.E.I.*

COR. 1. Hence if the solid be a cylinder described by the parallelogram ADEB revolved about the axis AB, and the centripetal forces tending to the several points be reciprocally as the squares of the distances from the points; the attraction of the corpuscle P towards this cylinder will be as AB – PE + PD. For the ordinate FK (by Cor. 1, Prop. XC) will be as $1 - \frac{PF}{PR}$. The part 1 of this quantity, drawn into the length AB, describes the area 1 x AB; and the other part $\frac{PF}{PR}$, drawn into the length PB describes the area 1 into $\overline{PE-AD}$ (as may be easily shewn from the quadrature of the curve LKI); and, in like manner, the same part drawn into the length PA describes the area 1 into $\overline{PD-AD}$, and drawn into AB, the difference of PB and PA, describes 1 into $\overline{PE-PD}$, the difference of the areas. From the first content 1 x AB take away the last content 1 into $\overline{PE-PD}$,

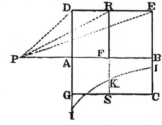

and there will remain the area LABI equal to 1 into $\overline{AB-PE+PD}$. Therefore the force, being proportional to this area, is as AB - PE + PD.

COR. 2. Hence also is known the force by which a spheroid AGBC attracts any body P situate externally in its axis AB. Let NKRM be a conic section whose ordinate ER perpendicular to PE may be always equal to the length of the line PD, continually drawn to the point D in which that ordinate cuts the spheroid From the vertices A, B, of the spheroid, let there be erected to its axis AB the perpendiculars AK, BM,

respectively equal to AP, BP, and therefore meeting the conic section in K and M; and join KM cutting off from it the segment KMRK. Let S be the centre of the spheroid, and SC its greatest semi-diameter; and the force with which the spheroid attracts the body P will be to the force with which a sphere described with the diameter AB attracts the same body as $\frac{AS \times CS^2 - PS \times KMRK}{PS^2 + CS^2 - AS^2}$ is to $\frac{AS^3}{3PS^2}$. And by a calculation

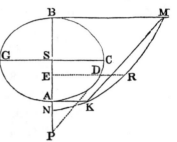

founded on the same principles may be found the forces of the segments of the spheroid.

COR. 3. If the corpuscle be placed within the spheroid and in its axis, the attraction will be as its distance from the centre. This may be easily collected from the following reasoning, whether the particle be in the axis or in any other given diameter. Let AGOF be an attracting spheroid, S its centre, and P the body attracted. Through the body P let there be drawn the semi-diameter SPA, and two right lines DE, FG meeting the spheroid in D and E, F and G; and let PCM, HLN be the superficies of two interior spheroids similar and concentrical to the exterior, the first of which passes through the body P, and cuts the right lines DE, FG in B and C; and the latter cuts the same right lines in H and I, K and L. Let the spheroids have all one common axis, and the parts of the right lines intercepted on both sides DP and BE, FP and CG, DH and IE, FK and LG, will be mutually equal; because the right lines DE, PB, and HI, are bisected in the same point, as are also the right lines FG, PC, and KL. Conceive now DPF, EPG to represent opposite cones described with the infinitely small vertical angles DPF, EPG, and the lines DH, EI to be

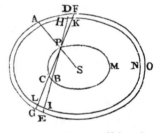

infinitely small also. Then the particles of the cones DHKF, GLIE, cut off by the spheroidical superficies, by reason of the equality of the lines DH and EI, will be to one another as the squares of the distances from the body P, and will therefore attract that corpuscle equally. And by a like reasoning if the spaces DPF, EGCB be divided into particles by the superficies of innumerable similar spheroids concentric to the former and having one common axis, all these particles will equally attract on both aides the body P towards contrary parts. Therefore the forces of the cone DPF, and of the conic segment EGCB, are equal, and by their contrariety destroy each other. And the case is the same of the forces of all the matter that lies without the interior spheroid PCBM. Therefore the body P is attracted by the interior spheroid PCBM alone, and therefore (by Cor. 3, Prop. LXXII) its attraction is to the force with which the body A is attracted by the whole spheroid AGOD as the distance PS to the distance AS. *Q.E.D.*

PROPOSITION XCII. PROBLEM XLVI.

AN ATTRACTING BODY BEING GIVEN, IT IS REQUIRED TO FIND THE RATIO OF THE DECREASE OF THE CENTRIPETAL FORCES TENDING TO ITS SEVERAL POINTS.

The body given must be formed into a sphere, a cylinder, or some regular figure, whose law of attraction answering to any ratio of decrease may be found by Prop. LXXX, LXXXI, and XCI. Then, by experiments, the force of the attractions must be found at several distances, and the law of attraction towards the whole, made known by that means, will give the ratio of the decrease of the forces of the several parts; which was to be found.

PROPOSITION XCIII. THEOREM XLVII.

IF A SOLID BE PLANE ON ONE SIDE, AND INFINITELY EXTENDED ON ALL OTHER SIDES, AND CONSIST OF EQUAL PARTICLES EQUALLY ATTRACTIVE, WHOSE FORCES DECREASE, IN THE RECESS FROM THE SOLID, IN THE RATIO OF ANY POWER GREATER THAN THE SQUARE OF THE DISTANCES, AND A CORPUSCLE PLACED TOWARDS EITHER PART OF THE PLANE IS ATTRACTED BY THE FORCE OF THE WHOLE SOLID; I SAY, THAT THE ATTRACTIVE FORCE OF THE WHOLE SOLID, IN THE RECESS FROM ITS PLACE SUPERFICIES, WILL DECREASE IN THE RATIO OF A POWER WHOSE SIDE IS THE DISTANCE OF THE CORPUSCLE FROM THE PLANE, AND ITS INDEX LESS BY 3 THAN THE INDEX OF THE POWER OF THE DISTANCES.

CASE.: 1. Let LG*l* be the plane by which the solid is terminated. Let the solid lie on that hand of the plane that is towards I, and let it be resolved into innumerable planes *m*HM, *n*IN, *o*KO, &c., parallel to GL. And first let the attracted body C be placed without the solid. Let there be drawn

CGHI perpendicular to those innumerable planes, and let the attractive forces of the points of the solid decrease in the ratio of a power of the distances whose index is the number n not less than 3. Therefore (by Cor. 3, Prop. XC) the force with which any plane *m*HM attracts the point C reciprocally as CH^{n-2}. In the plane *m*HM take the length HM reciprocally proportional to CH^{n-2}, and that force will be as HM. In like manner in the several

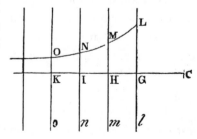

planes *l*GL, *n*IN, *o*KO, &c., take the lengths GL, IN, KO, &c., reciprocally proportional to CG^{n-2}, CI^{n-2}, CK^{n-2}, &c., and the forces of those planes will be as the lengths so taken, and therefore the sum of the forces as the sum of the lengths, that is, the force of the whole solid as the area GLOK

produced infinitely towards OK. But that area (by the known methods of quadratures) is reciprocally as CG^{n-3}, and therefore the force of the whole solid is reciprocally as CG^{n-3}.   *Q.E.D.*

CASE. 2. Let the corpuscle C be now placed on that hand of the plane *I*GL that is within the solid, and take the distance CK equal to the distance CG. And the part of the solid LG*lo*KO terminated by the parallel planes *I*GL, *o*KO, will attract the corpuscle C, situate in the middle, neither one way nor another, the contrary actions of the opposite points destroying one another by reason of their equality. Therefore the corpuscle C is attracted by the force only of the solid situate beyond the plane OK.

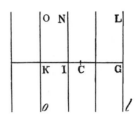

But this force (by Case 1) is reciprocally as CK^{n-3}, that is, (because CG, CK are equal) reciprocally as CK^{n-3}.   *Q.E.D.*

COR. 1. Hence if the solid LGIN be terminated on each side by two infinite parallel planes LG, IN, its attractive force is known, subducting from the attractive force of the whole infinite solid LGKO the attractive force of the more distant part NIKO infinitely produced towards KO.

COR. 2. If the more distant part of this solid be rejected, because its attraction compared with the attraction of the nearer part is inconsiderable, the attraction of that nearer part will, as the distance increases, decrease nearly in the ratio of the power CG^{n-3}.

COR. 3. And hence if any finite body, plane on one side, attract a corpuscle situate over against the middle of that plane, and the distance between the corpuscle and the plane compared with the dimensions of the attracting body be extremely small; and the attracting body consist of homogeneous particles, whose attractive forces decrease in the ratio of any power of the distances greater than the quadruplicate; the attractive force of the whole body will decrease very nearly in the ratio of a power whose side is that very small distance, and the index less by 3 than the index of the former power. This assertion does not hold good, however, of a body consisting of particles whose attractive forces decrease in the ratio of the triplicate power of the distances; because, in that case, the attraction of the remoter part of the infinite body in the second Corollary is always infinitely greater than the attraction of the nearer part.

SCHOLIUM.

If a body is attracted perpendicularly towards a given plane, and from the law of attraction given, the motion of the body be required; the Problem will be solved by seeking (by Prop. XXXIX) the motion of the body descending in a right line towards that plane, and (by Cor. 2, of the Laws) compounding that motion with an uniform motion performed in the direction of lines parallel to that plane. And, on the contrary,

if there be required the law of the attraction tending towards the plane in perpendicular directions, by which the body may be caused to move in any given curve line, the Problem will be solved by working after the manner of the third Problem.

But the operations may be contracted by resolving the ordinates into converging series. As if to a base A the length B be ordinately applied in any given angle, and that length be as any power of the base $A^{\frac{m}{n}}$; and there be sought the force with which a body, either attracted towards the base or driven from it in the direction of that ordinate, may be caused to move in the curve line which that ordinate always describes with its superior extremity; I suppose the base to be increased by a very small part O, and I resolve the ordinate $\overline{A+O}^{\frac{m}{n}}$ into an infinite series

$$A^{\frac{m}{n}}+\frac{m}{n}OA^{\frac{m-n}{n}}+\frac{mm-mn}{2nn}OOA^{\frac{m-2}{n}} \text{ c\&.,}$$ and I suppose the force proportional to the term

of this series in which O is of two dimensions, that is, to the term $\frac{mm-mn}{2nn}OOA^{\frac{m-2n}{n}}$.

Therefore the force sought is as $\frac{mm-mn}{nn}A^{\frac{m-2n}{n}}$, or, which is the same thing, as

$\frac{mm-mn}{nn}B^{\frac{m-2n}{m}}$.

As if the ordinate describe a parabola, m being = 2, and n = 1, the force will be as the given quantity 2B°, and therefore is given. Therefore with a given force the body will move in a parabola, as *Galileo* has demonstrated. If the ordinate describe an hyperbola, m being = 0 − 1, and n = 1, the force will be as 2A^{-3} or 2B^3; and therefore a force which is as the cube of the ordinate will cause the body to move in an hyperbola. But leaving this kind of propositions, I shall go on to some others relating to motion which I have not yet touched upon.

SECTION XIV.

Of the motion of very small bodies when agitated by centripetal forces tending to the several parts of any very great body.

PROPOSITION XCIV. THEOREM XLVIII.

IF TWO SIMILAR MEDIUMS BE SEPARATED FROM EACH OTHER BY A
SPACE TERMINATED ON BOTH SIDES BY PARALLEL PLANES, AND A
BODY IN ITS PASSAGE THROUGH THAT SPACE BE ATTRACTED OR
IMPELLED PERPENDICULARLY TOWARDS EITHER OF THOSE MEDIUMS,
AND NOT AGITATED OR HINDERED BY ANY OTHER FORCE; AND THE
ATTRACTION BE EVERY WHERE THE SAME AT EQUAL DISTANCES

FROM EITHER PLANE, TAKEN TOWARDS THE SAME HAND OF
THE PLANE; I SAY, THAT THE SINE OF INCIDENCE UPON
EITHER PLANE WILL BE TO THE SINE OF EMERGENCE FROM
THE OTHER PLANE IN A GIVEN RATIO.

CASE. 1. Let A*a* and B*b* be two parallel planes and let the body light upon the first, plane A*a* in the direction of the line GH, and in its whole passage through the intermediate space let it be attracted or impelled towards the medium of incidence, and by that action let it be made to describe a curve line HI, and let it emerge in the direction of the line IK. Let there be erected IM perpendicular to B*b* the plane of emergence, and meeting the line of incidence GH prolonged in M, and the plane of incidence A*a* in R; and let the line of emergence KI be produced and meet HM in L. About the centre L, with the interval LI, let a circle be described cutting both HM in P and Q, and MI produced in N; and, first, if the attraction or impulse be supposed uniform, the

curve HI (by what *Galileo* has demonstrated) be a parabola, whose property is that of a rectangle under its given latus rectum and the line IM is equal to the square of HM; and moreover the line HM will be bisected in L. Whence if to MI there be let fall the perpendicular LO, MO, OR will be equal; and adding the equal lines ON, OI, the wholes MN, IR will be equal also. Therefore since IR is given, MN is also given, and the rectangle NMI is to the rectangle under the latus rectum and IM, that is, to HM2 in a given ratio.

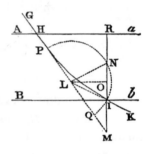

But the rectangle NMI is equal to the rectangle PMQ, that is, to the difference of the squares ML2, and PL2 or LI2; and HM2 hath a given ratio to its fourth part ML2; therefore the ratio of ML2 – LI2 to ML2 is given, and by conversion the ratio of LI2 to ML2, and its subduplicate, the ratio of LI to ML. But in every triangle, as LMI, the sines of the angles are proportional to the opposite sides. Therefore the ratio of the sine of the angle of incidence LMR to the sine of the angle of emergence LIR is given. *Q.E.D..*

CASE. 2. Let now the body pass successively through several spaces terminated with parallel planes A*ab*B, B*bc*C, &c., and let it be acted on by a force which is uniform in each of them separately, but different in the different spaces; and by what was just demonstrated, the sine of the angle of incidence on the first plane A*a* is to the sine of emergence from the second plane B*b* in a

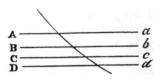

given ratio; and this sine of incidence upon the second plane B*b* will be to the sine of emergence from the third plane C*c* in a given ratio; and this sine to the sine of emergence from the fourth plane D*d* in a given ratio; and so on *in infinitum*; and, by equality, the sine of incidence on the first plane to the sine of emergence from the last plane in a given ratio. Let now the intervals of the planes be diminished, and their number be infinitely increased, so that the action of attraction or impulse,

exerted according to any assigned law, may become continual, and the ratio of the sine of incidence on the first plane to the sine of emergence from the last plane being all along given, will be given then also.   *Q.E.D.*

PROPOSITION XCV. THEOREM XLIX.

THE SAME THINGS BEING SUPPOSED, I SAY, THAT THE VELOCITY OF THE BODY BEFORE ITS INCIDENCE IS TO ITS VELOCITY AFTER EMER-GENCE AS THE SINE OF EMERGENCE TO THE SINE OF INCIDENCE.

Make AH and I*d* equal, and erect the perpendiculars AG, *d*K meeting the lines of incidence and emergence GH, IK, in G and K. In GH take TH equal to IK, and to the plane A*a* let fall a perpendicular T*v*. And (by Cor. 2 of the Laws of Motion) let the motion of the body be resolved into two, one perpendicular to the planes A*a*, B*b*, C*c*, &c., and another parallel to

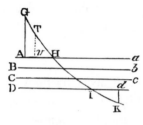

them. The force of attraction or impulse, acting in directions perpendicular to those planes, does not at all alter the motion in parallel directions; and therefore the body proceeding with this motion will in equal times go through those equal parallel intervals that lie between the line AG and the point H, and between the point I and the line *d*K; that is, they will describe the lines GH, IK in equal times. Therefore the velocity before incidence is to the velocity after emergence as GH to IK or TH, that is, as AH or Id to *v*H, that is (supposing TH or IK radius), as the sine of emergence to the sine of incidence.   *Q.E.D.*

PROPOSITION XCVI. THEOREM L.

THE SAME THINGS BEING SUPPOSED, AND THAT THE MOTION BEFORE INCIDENCE IS SWIFTER THAN AFTERWARDS; I SAY, THAT IF THE LINE OF INCIDENCE BE INCLINED CONTINUALLY, THE BODY WILL BE AT LAST REFLECTED, AND THE ANGLE OF REFLEXION WILL BE EQUAL TO THE ANGLE OF INCIDENCE.

For conceive the body passing between the parallel planes A*a*, B*b*, C*c*, &c., to describe parabolic arcs as above; and let those arcs be HP, PQ, QR, &c. And let the obliquity of the line of incidence GH to the first plane A*a* be such that the sine of incidence maybe to the radius of the circle whose sine it is, in the same ratio which the same sine of incidence hath to the sine of emergence from the plane D*d* into the space D*de*E; and because the sine of emergence is now become equal to radius, the angle of emergence will be a right one, and therefore the line of emergence will coincide with the plane D*d*. Let the body come to this plane in the point R; and because the line of

emergence coincides with that plane, it is manifest that the body can proceed no farther towards the plane E*e*. But neither can it proceed in the line of emergence R*d*;
because it is perpetually attracted or impelled towards the medium of incidence. It will
return, therefore, between the planes C*c*, D*d*,
describing an are of a parabola QR*q*, whose principal
vertex (by what *Galileo* has demonstrated) is in R,
cutting the plane C*c* in the same angle at *q*, that it

did before at Q; then going on in the parabolic arcs *qp*, *ph*, &c., similar and equal to
the former arcs QP, PH, &c., it will cut the rest of the planes in the same angles at *p*,
h, &c., as it did before in P, H, &c., and will emerge at last with the same obliquity at
h with which it first impinged on that plane at H. Conceive now the intervals of the
planes A*a*, B*b*, C*c*, D*d*, E*e*, &c., to be infinitely diminished, and the number infinitely increased, so that the action of attraction or impulse, exerted according to any
assigned law, may become continual; and, the angle of emergence remaining all along
equal to the angle of incidence, will be equal to the same also at last.   *Q.E.D.*

SCHOLIUM.

These attractions bear a great resemblance to the reflexions and refractions of
light made in a given ratio of the secants, as was discovered by *Snellius*; and consequently in a given ratio of the sines, as was exhibited by *Des Cartes*. For it is now certain from the phenomena of *Jupiter's* satellites, confirmed by the observations of different astronomers, that light is propagated in succession, and requires about seven
or eight minutes to travel from the sun to the earth. Moreover, the rays of light that
are in our air (as lately was discovered by *Grimaldus*, by the admission of light into
a dark room through a small hole, which I have also tried) in their passage near the
angles of bodies, whether transparent or opaque (such as the circular and rectangular edges of gold, silver and brass coins, or of knives, or broken pieces of stone or
glass), are bent or inflected round those bodies as if they were attracted to them; and
those rays which in
their passage come
nearest to the bodies
are the most inflected,
as if they were most
attracted; which thing
I myself have also care-

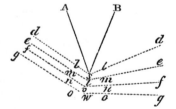

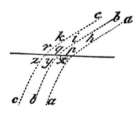

fully observed. And those which pass at greater distances are less inflected; and those
at still greater distances are a little inflected the contrary way, and form three fringes
of colours. In the figure s represents the edge of a knife, or any kind of wedge A*s*B;

and *gowog, fnunf, emtme, dlsld,* are rays inflected towards the knife in the arcs *owo, nvn, mtm, lsl,* which inflection is greater or less according to their distance from the knife. Now since this inflection of the rays is performed in the air without the knife, it follows that the rays which fall upon the knife are first inflected in the air before they touch the knife. And the case is the same of the rays falling upon glass. The refraction, therefore, is made not in the point of incidence, but gradually, by a continual inflection of the rays; which is done partly in the air before they touch the glass, partly (if I mistake not) within the glass, after they have entered it; as is represented in the rays *ckzc, biyb, ahxa,* falling upon *r, q, p,* and inflected between *k* and *z, i* and *y, h* and *x.* Therefore because of the analogy there is between the propagation of the rays of light and the motion of bodies, I thought it not amiss to add the following Propositions for optical uses; not at all considering the nature of the rays of light, or inquiring whether they are bodies or not; but only determining the trajectories of bodies which are extremely like the trajectories of the rays.

PROPOSITION XCVII. PROBLEM XLVII.

SUPPOSING THE SINE OF INCIDENCE UPON ANY SUPERFICIES TO BE IN A GIVEN RATIO TO THE SINE OF EMERGENCE; AND THAT THE INFLECTION OF THE PATHS OF THOSE BODIES NEAR THAT SUPERFICIES IS PERFORMED IN A VERY SHORT SPACE, WHICH MAY BE CONSIDERED AS A POINT; IT IS REQUIRED TO DETERMINE SUCH A SUPERFICIES AS MAY CAUSE ALL THE CORPUSCLES ISSUING FROM ANY ONE GIVEN PLACE TO CONVERGE TO ANOTHER GIVEN PLACE.

Let A be the place from whence the corpuscles diverge; B the place to which they should converge; CDE the curve line which by its revolution round the axis AB describes the superficies sought; D, E, any two points of that curve; and EF, EG, perpendiculars let fall on the paths of the bodies AD, DB. Let the point D approach to and coalesce with the point E; and the ultimate ratio of the line DF by which AD is increased, to the line DG by which DB is diminished, will be the same as that of the sine of incidence to the sine of emergence. Therefore the ratio of the increment of the line AD to the decrement of the line DB is given; and therefore if in the axis AB there be taken any where the point C through which the curve CDE must pass, and CM the increment of AC be taken in that given ratio to CN the decrement

of BC, and from the centres A, B, with the intervals AM, BN, there be described two circles cutting each other in D; that point D will touch the curve sought CDE, and, by touching it any where at pleasure, will determine that curve.   *Q.E.I.*

COR. 1. By causing the point A or B to go off sometimes *in infinitum*, and sometimes to move towards other parts of the point C, will be obtained all those figures which *Cartesius* has exhibited in his Optics and Geometry relating to refractions. The invention of which *Cartesius* having thought fit to conceal, is here laid open in this Proposition.

COR. 2. If a body lighting on any superficies CD in the direction of a right line AD, drawn according to any law, should emerge in the direction of another right line DK; and from the point C there be drawn curve lines CP, CQ, always perpendicular to AD, DK;

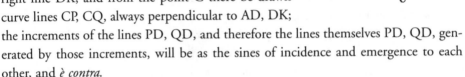

the increments of the lines PD, QD, and therefore the lines themselves PD, QD, generated by those increments, will be as the sines of incidence and emergence to each other, and *è contra*.

PROPOSITION XCVIII. PROBLEM XLVIII.

THE SAME THINGS SUPPOSED; IF ROUND THE AXIS AB ANY ATTRACTIVE SUPERFICIES BE DESCRIBED AS CD, REGULAR OR IRREGULAR, THROUGH WHICH THE BODIES ISSUING FROM THE GIVEN PLACE A MUST PASS; IT IS REQUIRED TO FIND A SECOND ATTRACTIVE SUPERFICIES EF, WHICH MAY MAKE THOSE BODIES CONVERGE TO A GIVEN PLACE B.

Let a line joining AB cut the first superficies in C and the second in E, the point D being taken any how at pleasure. And supposing the sine of incidence on the first superficies to the sine of emergence from the same, and the sine of emergence from the second superficies to the sine of incidence on the same, to be as any given quantity M to another given quantity N; then produce AB to G, so that BG may be to CE as M − N to N; and AD to H, so that AH

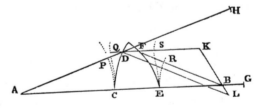

may be equal to AG; and DF to K, so that DK may be to DH as N to M. Join KB, and about the centre D with the interval DH describe a circle meeting KB produced in L, and draw BF parallel to DL; and the point F will touch the line EF, which, being turned round the axis AB, will describe the superficies sought.   *Q.E.F.*

For conceive the lines CP, CQ to be every where perpendicular to AD, DF, and the lines ER, ES to FB, FD respectively, and therefore QS to be always equal to CE; and (by Cor. 2, Prop. XCVII) PD will be to QD as M to N, and therefore as DL, to

DK, or FB to FK; and by division as DL − FB or PH − PD - FB to FD or FQ − QD; and by composition as PH − FB to FQ, that is (because PH and CG, QS and CE, are equal), as CE + BG − FR to CE − FS. But (because BG is to CE as M − N to N) it comes to pass also that CE + BG is to CE as M to N; and therefore, by division, FR is to FS as M to N; and therefore (by Cor. 2, Prop. XCVII) the superficies EF compels a body, falling upon it in the direction DF, to go on in the line FR to the place B.   *Q.E.D.*

SCHOLIUM.

In the same manner one may go on to three or more superficies. But of all figures the sphaerical is the most proper for optical uses. If the object glasses of telescopes were made of two glasses of a sphaerical figure, containing water between them, it is not unlikely that the errors of the refractions made in the extreme parts of the superficies of the glasses may be accurately enough corrected by the refractions of the water. Such object glasses are to be preferred before elliptic and hyperbolic glasses, not only because they may be formed with more ease and accuracy, but because the pencils of rays situate without the axis of the glass would be more accurately refracted by them. But the different refrangibility of different rays is the real obstacle that hinders optics from being made perfect by sphaerical or any other figures. Unless the errors thence arising can be corrected, all the labour spent in correcting the others is quite thrown away.

BOOK II.
OF THE MOTION OF BODIES.

SECTION I.

Of the motion of bodies that are resisted in the ratio of the velocity.

PROPOSITION I. THEOREM I.

IF A BODY IS RESISTED IN THE RATIO OF ITS VELOCITY, THE
MOTION LOST BY RESISTANCE IS AS THE SPACE GONE OVER
IN ITS MOTION.

For since the motion lost in each equal particle of time is as the velocity, that is, as the particle of space gone over, then, by composition, the motion lost in the whole time will be as the whole space gone over. *Q.E.D.*

COR. Therefore if the body, destitute of all gravity, move by its innate force only in free spaces, and there be given both its whole motion at the beginning, and also the motion remaining after some part of the way is gone over, there will be given also the whole space which the body can describe in an infinite time. For that space will be to the space now described as the whole motion at the beginning is to the part lost of that motion.

LEMMA I.

Quantities proportional to their differences are continually proportional.

Let A be to A — B as B to B — C and C to C — D, &c., and, by conversion, A will be to B as B to C and C to D, &c. *Q.E.D.*

PROPOSITION II. THEOREM II.

IF A BODY IS RESISTED IN THE RATIO OF ITS VELOCITY,
AND MOVES, BY ITS VIS INSITA, ONLY, THROUGH A SIMILAR
MEDIUM, AND THE TIMES BE TAKEN EQUAL, THE VELOCITIES
IN THE BEGINNING OF EACH OF THE TIMES ARE IN A
GEOMETRICAL PROGRESSION, AND THE SPACES DESCRIBED
IN EACH OF THE TIMES ARE AS THE VELOCITIES.

912

CASE 1. Let the time be divided into equal particles; and if at the very beginning of each particle we suppose the resistance to act with one single impulse which is as the velocity, the decrement of the velocity in each of the particles of time will be as the same velocity. Therefore the velocities are proportional to their differences, and therefore (by Lem. 1, Book II) continually proportional. Therefore if out of an equal number of particles there be compounded any equal portions of time, the velocities at the beginning of those times will be as terms in a continued progression, which are taken by intervals, omitting every where an equal number of intermediate terms. But the ratios of these terms are compounded of the equal ratios of the intermediate terms equally repeated, and therefore are equal. Therefore the velocities, being proportional to those terms, are in geometrical progression. Let those equal particles of time be diminished, and their number increased *in infinitum*, so that the impulse of resistance may become continual; and the velocities at the beginnings of equal times, always continually proportional, will be also in this case continually proportional. *Q.E.D.*

CASE 2. And, by division, the differences of the velocities, that is, the parts of the velocities lost in each of the times, are as the wholes; but the spaces described in each of the times are as the lost parts of the velocities (by Prop. 1, Book 1), and therefore are also as the wholes. *Q.E.D.*

COROL. Hence if to the rectangular asymptotes AC, CH, the hyperbola BG is described, and AB, DG be drawn perpendicular to the asymptote AC, and both the velocity of the body, and the resistance of the medium, at the very beginning of the motion, be expressed by any given line AC, and, after some time is elapsed, by the indefinite line DC; the time may be expressed by the area ABGD, and the space described in that time by the line AD. For if that area, by the motion of the point D, be uniformly increased in the same manner as the time, the right line DC will decrease in a geometrical ratio in the same manner as the velocity; and the parts of the right line AC, described in equal times, will decrease in the same ratio.

PROPOSITION III. PROBLEM I.

TO DEFINE THE MOTION OF A BODY WHICH, IN A SIMILAR
MEDIUM, ASCENDS OR DESCENDS IN A RIGHT LINE, AND IS
RESISTED IN THE RATIO OF ITS VELOCITY, AND ACTED UPON
BY AN UNIFORM FORCE OF GRAVITY.

The body ascending, let the gravity be expounded by any given rectangle BACH; and the resistance of the medium, at the beginning of the ascent, by the rectangle BADE, taken on the contrary side of the right line AB. Through the point B, with the rectangular asymptotes AC, CH, describe an hyperbola, cutting the perpendiculars

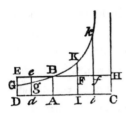

DE, *de*, in G, *g*; and the body ascending will in the time DG*gd* describe the space EG*ge*; in the time DGBA, the space of the whole ascent EGB; in the time ABKI, the space of descent BFK; and in the time IK*ki* the space of descent KF*fk*; and the velocities of the bodies (proportional to the resistance of the medium) in these periods of time will be ABED, AB*ed*, O, ABFI, AB*fi* respectively; and the greatest velocity which the body can acquire by descending will be BACH.

For let the rectangle BACH be resolved into innumerable rectangles A*k*, KI, L*m*, M*n*, &c., which shall be as the increments of the velocities produced in so many equal times; then will O, A*k*, A*l*, A*m*, A*n*, &c., be as the whole velocities, and therefore (by supposition) as the resistances of the medium in the beginning of each of the equal times. Make AC to AK, or ABHC to AB*k*K, as the force of gravity to the resistance in the beginning of the second time; then from the force of grav-

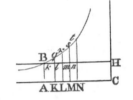

ity subduct the resistances, and ABHC, K*k*HC, L*l*HC, M*m*HC, &c., will be as the absolute forces with which the body is acted upon in the beginning of, each of the times, and therefore (by Law I) as the increments of the velocities, that is, as the rectangles A*k*, K*l*, L*m*, M*n*, &c., and therefore (by Lem. 1, Book II) in a geometrical progression. Therefore, if the right lines K*k*, L*l*, M*m*, N*n*, &c., are produced so as to meet the hyperbola in *q*, *r*, *s*, *t*, &c., the areas AB*q*K, K*qr*L, L*rs*M, M*st*N, &c., will be equal, and therefore analogous to the equal times and equal gravitating forces. But the area AB*q*K (by Corol. 3, Lem. VII and VIII, Book I) is to the area B*kq* as K*q* to ½*kq*, or AC to ½AK, that is, as the force of gravity to the resistance in the middle of the first time. And by the like reasoning, the areas *q*KL*r*, *r*LM*s*, *s*MN*t*, &c., are to the areas *qklr*, *rlms*, *smnt*, &c., as the gravitating forces to the resistances in the middle of the second, third, fourth time, and so on. Therefore since the equal areas BAK*q*, *q*KL*r*, *r*LM*s*, *s*MN*t*, &c., are analogous to the gravitating forces, the areas B*kq*, *qklr*, *rlms*, *smnt*, &c., will be analogous to the resistances in the middle of each of the times, that is (by supposition), to the velocities, and so to the spaces described. Take the sums of the analogous quantities, and the areas B*kq*, B*lr*, B*ms*, B*nt*, &c., will be analogous to the whole spaces described; and also the areas AB*q*K, AB*r*L, AB*s*M, AB*t*N, &c., to the times. Therefore the body, in descending, will in anytime AB*r*L describe the space B*lr*, and in the time L*rt*N the space *rlnt*.   Q.E.D. And the like demonstration holds in ascending motion.

COROL. 1. Therefore the greatest velocity that the body can acquire by filling is to the velocity acquired in any given time as the given force of gravity which perpetually acts upon it to the resisting force which opposes it at the end of that time.

COROL. 2. But the time being augmented in an arithmetical progression, the sum of that greatest velocity and the velocity in the ascent, and also their difference in the descent, decreases in a geometrical progression.

COROL. 3. Also the differences of the spaces, which are described in equal differences of the times, decrease in the same geometrical progression.

COROL. 4. The space described by the body is the difference of two spaces, whereof one is as the time taken from the beginning of the descent, and the other as the velocity; which [spaces] also at the beginning of the descent are equal among themselves.

PROPOSITION IV. PROBLEM II.

SUPPOSING, THE FORCE OF GRAVITY IN ANY SIMILAR MEDIUM TO
BE UNIFORM, AND TO TEND PERPENDICULARLY TO THE PLANE OF
THE HORIZON; TO DEFINE THE MOTION OF A PROJECTILE THERE-
IN, WHICH SUFFERS RESISTANCE PROPORTIONAL TO ITS VELOCITY.

Let the projectile go from any place D in the direction of any right line DP, and let its velocity at the beginning of the motion be expounded by the length DP. From the point P let fall the perpendicular PC on the horizontal line DC, and cut DC in A, so that DA may be to AC as the resistance of the medium arising from the

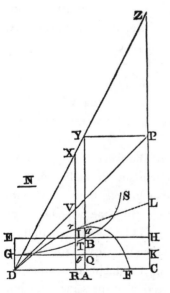

motion upwards at the beginning to the force of gravity; or (which comes to the same) so that the rectangle under DA and DP may be to that under AC and CP as the whole resistance at the beginning of the motion to the force of gravity. With the asymptotes DC, CP describe any hyperbola GTBS cutting the perpendiculars DG, AB in G and B; complete the parallelogram DGKC, and let its side GK out AB in Q. Take a line N in the same ratio to QB as DC is in to CP; and from any point R of the right line DC erect RT perpendicular to it, meeting the hyperbola in T, and the right lines EH, GK, DP in I, t, and V; in that perpendicular take Vr equal to $\frac{tGT}{N}$, or which is the same thing, take Rr equal to $\frac{GTIE}{N}$; and the projectile in the time DRTG will arrive at the point r describing the curve line DraF, the locus of the point r, thence it will come to its greatest height a in the perpendicular

AB; and afterwards ever approach to the asymptote PC. And its velocity in any point r will be as the tangent rL to the curve.   *Q.E.I.*

For N is to QB as DC to CP or DR to RV, and therefore RV is equal to $\dfrac{DR \times QB}{N}$

and Rr (that is, RV — Vr, or $\dfrac{DR \times QB - tGT}{N}$) is equal to $\dfrac{DR \times AB - RDGT}{N}$. Now let the time be expounded by the area RDGT and (by Laws, Cor. 2), distinguish the motion of the body into two others, one of ascent, the other lateral. And since the resistance is as the motion, let that also be distinguished into two parts proportional and contrary to the parts of the motion : and therefore the length described by the lateral motion will be (by Prop. II, Book II) as the line DR, and the height (by Prop. III, Book II) as the area DR x AB — RDGT, that is, as the line Rr. But in the very beginning of the motion the area RDGT is equal to the rectangle DR x AQ, and therefore that line Rr (or $\dfrac{DR \times AB - DR \times AQ}{N}$) will then be to DR as AB — AQ or QB to N, that is, as CP to DC; and therefore as the motion upwards to the motion lengthwise at the beginning. Since, therefore, Rr is always as the height, and DR always as the length, and Rr is to DR at the beginning as the height to the length, it follows, that Rr is always to DR as the height to the length; and therefore that the body will move in the line DraF, which is the locus of the point r.   *Q.E.D.*

COR. 1. Therefore Rr is equal to $\dfrac{DR \times AB}{N} - \dfrac{RDGT}{N}$; and therefore if RT be produced to X so that RX may be equal to $\dfrac{DR \times AB}{N}$, that is, if the parallelogram ACPY be completed, and DY cutting CP in Z be drawn, and RT be produced till it meets DY in X; Xr will be equal to $\frac{RDGT}{N}$, and therefore proportional to the time.

COR. 2. Whence if innumerable lines CR, or, which is the same, innumerable lines ZX, be taken in a geometrical progression, there will be as many lines Xr in an arithmetical progression. And hence the curve DraF is easily delineated by the table of logarithms.

COR. 3. If a parabola be constructed to the vertex D, and the diameter DG produced downwards, and its latus rectum is to 2 DP as the whole resistance at the beginning of

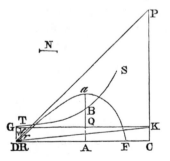

the motion to the gravitating force, the velocity with which the body ought to go from the place D, in the direction of the right line DP, so as in an uniform resisting medium to describe the curve DraF, will be the same as that with which it ought to go from the same place D in the direction of the same right line DP, so as to describe a parabola in a non-resisting medium. For the latus rectum of this parabola, at the

very beginning of the motion, is $\frac{DV^2}{Vr}$; and Vr is $\frac{tGT}{N}$ $_{or}$ $\frac{DR \times Tt}{2N}$ or $\frac{CK \times DR}{DC}$. But a right

line, which, if drawn, would touch the hyperbola GTS in G, is parallel to DK, and

therefore Tt is $\frac{QB \times DC}{CP}$, and N is $\frac{DR^2 \times CK \times CP}{2DC^2 \times QB}$. And therefore Vr is equal to $\frac{DV^2 \times CK \times CP}{2DP \times QB}$, that is (because DR and DC, DV and DP are proportionals), to

$\frac{DV^2}{Vr}$; and the latus rectum $\frac{2DP^2 \times QB}{CK \times CP}$ comes out $\frac{2DP^2 \times DA}{AC \times CP}$, that is (because QB and

CK, DA and AC are proportional), $\frac{2DP^2 \times DA}{AC \times CP}$, and therefore is to 2DP as DP x DA to CP x AC; that is, as the resistance to the gravity. *Q.E.D.*

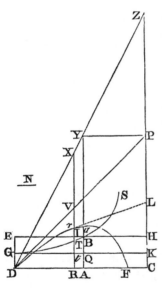

COR. 4. Hence if a body be projected from any place D with a given velocity, in the direction of a right line DP given by position, and the resistance of the medium, at the beginning of the motion, be given, the curve D*ra*F, which that body will describe, may be found. For the velocity being given, the latus rectum of the parabola is given, as is well known. And taking 2DP to that latus rectum, as the force of gravity to the resisting force, DP is also given. Then cutting DC in A, so that CP × AC may be to DP × DA in the same ratio of the gravity to the resistance, the point A will be given. And hence the curve D*ra*F is also given.

COR. 5. And, on the contrary, if the curve D*ra*F be given, there will be given both the velocity of the body and the resistance of the medium in each of the places *r*. For the ratio of CP × AC to DP × DA being given, there is given both the resistance of the medium at the beginning of the motion and the latus rectum of the parabola; and thence the velocity at the beginning of the motion is given also. Then from the length of the tangent L there is given both the velocity proportional to it, and the resistance proportional to the velocity in any place *r*.

COR. 6. But since the length 2DP is to the latus rectum of the parabola as the gravity to the resistance in D; and, from the velocity augmented, the resistance is augmented in the same ratio, but the latus rectum of the parabola is augmented in the duplicate of that ratio, it is plain that the length 2DP is augmented in that simple ratio only; and is therefore always proportional to the velocity; nor will it be augmented or diminished by the change of the angle CDP, unless the velocity be also changed.

COR. 7. Hence appears the method of determining the curve D*ra*F nearly from the phenomena, and thence collecting the resistance and velocity with which the body is projected. Let two similar and equal bodies be projected with the same velocity, from the place D, in different angles CDP, CD*p*; and let the places F, *f*, where they fall upon the horizontal plane DC, be known. Then taking any length for DP or D*p* suppose the resistance in D to be to the gravity in any ratio whatsoever, and let that ratio be expounded by any length SM. Then, by computation, from that assumed length DP, find the lengths DF, D*f*; and from the ratio, found by calculation, subduct the same ratio as found by experiment; and let the difference be expounded by the perpendicular MN. Repeat the same a second and a third time, by assuming always a new ratio SM of the resistance to the gravity, and collecting a new difference MN. Draw the affirmative differences on one side of the right line SM, and the negative on the other side; and through the points N, N, N, draw a regular curve NNN, cutting the right line SMMM in X, and SX will be the true ratio of the resistance to the gravity, which was to be found.

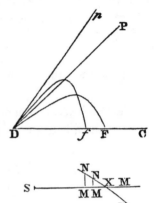

From this ratio the length DF is to be collected by calculation; and a length, which is to the assumed length DP as the length DF known by experiment to the length DF just now found, will be the true length DP. This being known, you will have both the curve line D*ra*F which the body describes, and also the velocity and resistance of the body in each place.

SCHOLIUM.

But, yet, that the resistance of bodies is in the ratio of the velocity, is more a mathematical hypothesis than a physical one. In mediums void of all tenacity, the resistances made to bodies are in the duplicate ratio of the velocities. For by the action of a swifter body, a greater motion in proportion to a greater velocity is communicated to the same quantity of the medium in a less time; and in an equal time, by reason of a greater quantity of the disturbed medium, a motion is communicated in the duplicate ratio greater; and the resistance (by Law II and III) is as the motion communicated. Let us, therefore see what motions arise from this law of resistance.

SECTION II.

Of the motion of bodies that are resisted in the duplicate ratio of their velocities.

PROPOSITION V. THEOREM III.

IF A BODY IS RESISTED IN THE DUPLICATE RATIO OF ITS VELOCITY,
AND MOVES BY ITS INNATE FORCE ONLY THROUGH A SIMILAR
MEDIUM, AND THE TIMES BE TAKEN IN A GEOMETRICAL PROGRES-
SION, PROCEEDING FROM LESS TO GREATER TERMS: I SAY, THAT THE
VELOCITIES AT THE BEGINNING OF EACH OF THE TIMES ARE IN THE
SAME GEOMETRICAL PROGRESSION INVERSELY; AND THAT THE
SPACES ARE EQUAL, WHICH ARE DESCRIBED IN EACH OF THE TIMES.

For since the resistance of the medium is proportional to the square of the velocity, and the decrement of the velocity is proportional to the resistance: if the time be divided into innumerable equal particles, the squares of the velocities at the beginning of each of the times will be proportional to the differences of the same velocities. Let those particles of time be AK, KL, LM, &c., taken in the right line CD; and erect the perpendiculars AB, Kk, Ll, Mm, &c., meeting the hyperbola, BklmG, described with the centre C, and the rectangular asymptotes CD, CH, in B, k, l, m, &c.; then AB will be to Kk as CK to CA, and, by division, AB — Kk to Kk as AK to CA, and alternately, AB — Kk to AK as Kk to CA; and therefore as AB $\times$ Kk to AB $\times$ CA. Therefore since AK and AB $\times$ CA are given, AB — Kk will be as AB $\times$ Kk; and, lastly, when AB and Kk coin-

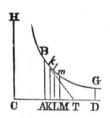

cide, as. And, by the like reasoning, Kk – Ll, Ll – Mm, &c., will be as, Kk^2, Ll^2, &c. Therefore the squares of the lines AB, Kk, Ll, Mm, &c., are as their differences; and, therefore, since the squares of the velocities were shewn above to be as their differences, the progression of both will be alike. This being demonstrated it follows also that the areas described by these lines are in a like progression with the spaces described by these velocities. Therefore if the velocity at the beginning of the first time AK be expounded by the line AB, and the velocity at the beginning of the second time KL by the line Kk, and the length described in the first time by the area AKkB, all the following velocities will be expounded by the following lines Ll, Mm, &c., and the lengths described, by the areas Kl, Lm, &c. And, by composition, if the whole time be expounded by AM, the sum of its parts, the whole length described will be expounded by AMmB the sum of its parts. Now conceive the time AM to be divided into the parts AK, KL, LM, &c so that CA, CK, CL, CM, &c. may be in a geometrical progression; and those parts will be in the same progression, and the velocities AB, Kk, Ll, Mm, &c., will be in the same progression inversely, and the spaces described Ak, Kl, Lm, &c., will be equal.   *Q.E.D.*

COR. 1. Hence it appears, that if the time be expounded by any part AD of the asymptote, and the velocity in the beginning of the time by the ordinate AB, the velocity at the end of the time will be expounded by the ordinate DG; and the whole space described by the adjacent hyperbolic area ABGD; and the space which any body can describe in the same time AD, with the first velocity AB, in a non-resisting medium, by the rectangle AB $\times$ AD.

COR. 2. Hence the space described in a resisting medium is given, by taking it to the space described with the uniform velocity AB in a non-resisting medium, as the hyperbolic area ABGD to the rectangle AB × AD.

COR. 3. The resistance of the medium is also given, by making it equal, in the very beginning of the motion, to an uniform centripetal force, which could generate, in a body falling through a non-resisting medium, the velocity AB in the time AC. For if BT be drawn touching the hyperbola in B, and meeting the asymptote in T, the right line AT will be equal to AC, and will express the time in which the first resistance, uniformly continued, may take away the whole velocity AB.

COR. 4. And thence is also given the proportion of this resistance to the force of gravity, or any other given centripetal force.

COR. 5. And, *vice versa*, if there is given the proportion of the resistance to any given centripetal force, the time AC is also given, in which a centripetal force equal to the resistance may generate any velocity as AB; and thence is given the point B, through which the hyperbola, having CH, CD for its asymptotes, is to be described; as also the space ABGD, which a body, by beginning its motion with that velocity AB, can describe in any time AD, in a similar resisting medium.

PROPOSITION VI. THEOREM IV.

HOMOGENEOUS AND EQUAL SPHERICAL BODIES, OPPOSED BY
RESISTANCES THAT ARE IN THE DUPLICATE RATIO OF THE
VELOCITIES, AND MOVING ON BY THEIR INNATE FORCE ONLY,
WILL, IN TIMES WHICH ARE RECIPROCALLY AS THE VELOCITIES
AT THE BEGINNING, DESCRIBE EQUAL SPACES, AND LOSE
PARTS OF THEIR VELOCITIES PROPORTIONAL TO THE WHOLES.

To the rectangular asymptotes CD, CH describe any hyperbola B*b*E*e*, cutting the perpendiculars AB, *ab*, DE, *de* in B, *b*, E, *e*, let the initial velocities be expounded by the perpendiculars AB, DE, and the times by the lines A*a*, D*d*. Therefore as A*a* is to D*d*, so (by the hypothesis) is DE to AB, and so (from the nature of the hyperbola) is CA

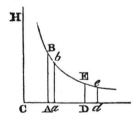

to CD; and, by composition, so is C*a* to C*d*. Therefore the areas AB*ba*, DE*ed*, that is, the spaces described, are equal among themselves, and the first velocities AB, DE are proportional to the last *ab*, *de*, and therefore, by division, proportional to the parts of the velocities lost, AB — *ab*, DE — *de*.   Q.E.D.

PROPOSITION VII. THEOREM V.

IF SPHERICAL BODIES ARE RESISTED IN THE DUPLICATE
RATIO OF THEIR VELOCITIES, IN TIMES WHICH ARE AS THE
FIRST MOTION DIRECTLY, AND THE FIRST RESISTANCES

INVERSELY, THEY WILL LOSE PARTS OF THEIR MOTIONS PROPOR-
TIONAL TO THE WHOLES, AND WILL DESCRIBE SPACES PROPOR-
TIONAL TO THOSE TIMES AND THE FIRST VELOCITIES CONJUNCTLY.

For the parts of the motions lost are as the resistances and times conjunct-ly. Therefore, that those parts may be proportional to the wholes, the resistance and time conjunctly ought to be as the motion. Therefore the time will be as the motion directly and the resistance inversely. Wherefore the particles of the times being taken in that ratio, the bodies will ,always lose parts of their motions proportional to the wholes, and therefore will retain velocities always proportional to their first velocities. And because of the given ratio of the velocities, they will always describe spaces which are as the first velocities and the times conjunctly.   *Q.E.D.*

COR. 1. Therefore if bodies equally swift are resisted in a duplicate ratio of their diameters, homogeneous globes moving with any velocities whatsoever, by describing spaces proportional to their diameters, will lose parts of their motions proportional to the wholes. For the motion of each globe will be as its velocity and mass conjunctly, that is, as the velocity and the cube of its diameter; the resis-tance (by supposition) will be as the square of the diameter and the square of the velocity conjunctly; and the time (by this proposition) is in the former ratio directly, and in the latter inversely, that is, as the diameter directly and the velocity inversely; and therefore the space, which is proportional to the time and velocity is as the diameter.

COR. 2. If bodies equally swift are resisted in a sesquiplicate ratio of their diameters, homogeneous globes, moving with any velocities whatsoever, by describing spaces that are in a sesquiplicate ratio of the diameters, will lose parts of their motions proportional to the wholes.

COR. 3. And universally, if equally swift bodies are resisted in the ratio of any power of the diameters, the spaces, in which homogeneous globes, moving with any velocity whatsoever, will lose parts of their motions proportional to the wholes, will be as the cubes of the diameters applied to that power. Let those diameters be D and E; and if the resistances, where the velocities are supposed equal, are as D^n and E^n; the spaces in which the globes, moving with any velocities whatsoever, will lose parts of their motions proportional to the wholes, will be as D^{3-n} and E^{3-n}. And therefore homogeneous globes, in describing spaces proportional to and, will retain their velocities in the same ratio to one another as at the beginning.

COR. 4. Now if the globes are not homogeneous, the space described by the denser globe must be augmented in the ratio of the density. For the motion, with an equal velocity, is greater in the ratio of the density, and the time (by

this Prop.) is augmented in the ratio of motion directly, and the space described in the ratio of the time.

Cor. 5. And if the globes move in different mediums, the space, in a medium which, *caeteris paribus*, resists the most, must be diminished in the ratio of the greater resistance. For the time (by this Prop.) will be diminished in the ratio of the augmented resistance, and the space in the ratio of the time.

LEMMA II.

The moment of any *genitum* is equal to the moments of each of the generating sides drawn into the indices of the powers of those sides, and into their co-efficients continually.

I call any quantity a *genitum* which is not made by addition or subduction of divers parts, but is generated or produced in arithmetic by the multiplication, division, or extraction of the root of any terms whatsoever; in geometry by the invention of contents and sides, or of the extremes and means of proportionals. Quantities of this kind are products, quotients, roots, rectangles, squares, cubes, square and cubic sides, and the like. These quantities I here consider as variable and indetermined, and increasing or decreasing, as it were, by a perpetual motion or flux; and I understand their momentaneous increments or decrements by the name of moments; so that the increments may be esteemed as added or affirmative moments; and the decrements as subducted or negative ones. But take care not to look upon finite particles as such. Finite particles are not moments, but the very quantities generated by the moments. We are to conceive them as the just nascent principles of finite magnitudes. Nor do we in this Lemma regard the magnitude of the moments, but their first proportion, as nascent. It will be the same thing, if, instead of moments, we use either the velocities of the increments and decrements (which may also be called the motions, mutations, and fluxions of quantities), or any finite quantities proportional to those velocities. The co-efficient of any generating side is the quantity which arises by applying the genitum to that side.

Wherefore the sense of the Lemma is, that if the moments of any quantities A, B, C, &c., increasing or decreasing by a perpetual flux, or the velocities of the mutations which are proportional to them, be called a, b, c, &c., the moment or mutation of the generated rectangle AB will be aB + bA; the moment of the generated content ABC will be aBC + bAC + cAB; and the moments of the generated powers A^2, A^3, A^4, $A^{\frac{1}{2}}$, $A^{\frac{3}{2}}$, $A^{\frac{1}{3}}$, $A^{\frac{2}{3}}$, A^{-1}, A^{-2}, $A^{-\frac{1}{2}}$, will be $2a$A, $3a$A^2, $4a$A^3, $\frac{1}{2}a$A$^{-\frac{1}{2}}$, $\frac{3}{2}a$A$^{\frac{1}{2}}$, $\frac{1}{3}a$A$^{-\frac{2}{3}}$, $\frac{2}{3}a$A$^{-\frac{1}{3}}$,

$-a$A^{-2}, $-2a$A^{-3}, $-\frac{1}{2}a$A$^{-\frac{3}{2}}$ respectively; and, in general, that the moment of any power $A^{\frac{n}{m}}$,

will be $\frac{n}{m}aA^{\frac{n-m}{m}}$. Also, that the moment of the generated quantity A^2B will be $2aAB$ $+bA^2$; the moment of the generated quantity $A^3B^4C^2$ will be $3aA^2B^4C^2 + 4bA^3B^3C^2$ $+ 2cA^3B^4C$; and the moment of the generated quantity $\frac{A^3}{B^2}$ or A^3B^{-2} will be $3aA^2B^{-2}$ $- sbA^3B^{-3}$; and so on. The Lemma is thus demostrated.

CASE 1. Any rectangle, as AB, augmented by a perpetual flux, when, as yet, there wanted of the sides A and B half their moments $\frac{1}{2}a$ and $\frac{1}{2}b$, was $A-\frac{1}{2}a$ into $B-\frac{1}{2}b$, or

$AB-\frac{1}{2}aB-\frac{1}{2}bA+\frac{1}{4}ab$; but as soon as the sides A and B are augmented by the other half

moments, the rectangle becomes $A+\frac{1}{2}a$ into $B+\frac{1}{2}b$, or $AB+\frac{1}{2}aB+\frac{1}{2}bA+\frac{1}{4}ab$. From this rectangle subduct the former rectangle, and there will remain the excess $aB + bA$. Therefore with the whole increments a and b of the sides, the increment $aB + bA$ of the rectangle is generated.   Q.E.D.

CASE 2. Suppose AB always equal to G, and then the moment of the content ABC or GC (by Case 1) will be, $gC + cG$, that is (putting AB and $aB + BA$ for G and g), $aBC + bAC + cAB$. And the reasoning is the same for contents under ever so many sides.   Q.E.D.

CASE 3. Suppose the sides A, B, and C, to be always equal among themselves; and the moment $aB + bA$, of A^2, that is, of the rectangle AB, will be $2aA$; and the moment $aBC + bAC + cAB$ of A^3, that is, of the content ABC, will be $3aA^2$. And by the same reasoning the moment of any power A^n is naA^{n-1}.   Q.E.D.

CASE 4. Therefore since $\frac{1}{A}$ into A is 1, the moment of $\frac{1}{A}$ drawn into A, together with $\frac{1}{A}$ drawn into a, will be the moment of 1, that is, nothing. Therefore the moment of $\frac{1}{A}$, or of A^{-1}, is

$\frac{-a}{A^2}$. And generally since $\frac{1}{A^n}$ into A^n is 1, the moment of $\frac{1}{A^n}$ drawn into A^n together with $\frac{1}{A^n}$ into naA^{n-1} will be nothing. And, therefore, the moment o $\frac{1}{A^n}$ or A^{-n} will $-\frac{na}{A^{n+1}}$.   QE.D.

CASE 5. And since $A^{\frac{1}{2}}$ into $A^{\frac{1}{2}}$ is A, the moment of $A^{\frac{1}{2}}$ drawn into $2A^{\frac{1}{3}}$ will be a (by Case 3);

and, therefore, the moment of $A^{\frac{1}{2}}$ will be $\frac{a}{2A^{\frac{1}{2}}}$ or $\frac{1}{2}aA-\frac{1}{2}$. And, generally, putting $A^{\frac{m}{n}}$ equal to B,

then A^m will be equal to B^n, and therefore maA^{m-1} equal to nbB^{n-1}, and maA^{-1} equal to nbB^{-1}, or

$nbA-\frac{m}{n}$; and therefore $AB-\frac{1}{2}aB-\frac{1}{2}bA+\frac{1}{4}ab$ is equal to b, that is, equal to the moment $A^{\frac{m}{n}}$.   Q.E.D.

CASE 6. Therefore the moment of any generated quantity $A^m B^n$ is the moment of A^m drawn into B^n, together with the moment of B^n drawn into A^m, that is, $maA^{m-1}B^n + nbB^{n-1}$; and that whether the indices m and n of the powers be whole numbers or fractions, affirmative or negative. And the reasoning is the same for contents under more powers. Q.E.D.

COR. 1. Hence in quantities continually proportional, if one term is given, the moments of the rest of the terms will be as the same terms multiplied by the number of intervals between them and the given term. Let A, B, C, D, E, F, be continually proportional; then if the term C is given, the moments of the rest of the terms will be among themselves as — 2A, — B, D, 2E, 3F.

COR. 2. And if in four proportionals the two means are given, the moments of the extremes will be as those extremes. The same is to be understood of the sides of any given rectangle.

COR. 3. And if the sum or difference of two squares is given, the moments of the sides will be reciprocally as the sides.

SCHOLIUM.

In a letter of mine to Mr. J. *Collins*, dated *December* 10, 1672, having described a method of tangents, which I suspected to be the same with *Slusius's* method, which at that time was not made public, I subjoined these words: *This is one particular, or rather a Corollary, of a general method, which extends itself, without any troublesome calculation, not only to the drawing of tangents to any curve lines, whether geometrical or mechanical, or any how respecting right lines or other curves, but also to the resolving other abstruser kinds of problems about the crookedness, areas, lengths, centres of gravity of curves, &c.; nor is it (as* Hudden's *method de Maximis & Minimis) limited to equations which are free from surd quantities. This method I have interwoven with that other of working in equations, by reducing them to infinite series.* So far that letter. And these last words relate to a treatise I composed on that subject in the year 1671. The foundation of that general method is contained in the preceding Lemma.

PROPOSITION VIII. THEOREM VI.

IF A BODY IN AN UNIFORM MEDIUM, BEING UNIFORMLY ACTED UPON BY THE FORCE OF GRAVITY, ASCENDS OR DESCENDS IN A RIGHT LINE; AND THE WHOLE SPACE DESCRIBED BE DISTINGUISHED INTO EQUAL PARTS, AND IN THE BEGINNING, OF EACH OF THE PARTS (BY ADDING OR SUBDUCTING THE RESISTING FORCE OF THE MEDIUM TO

OR FROM THE FORCE OF GRAVITY, WHEN THE BODY
ASCENDS OR DESCENDS) YOU COLLECT THE ABSOLUTE
FORCES; I SAY, THAT THOSE ABSOLUTE FORCES ARE IN A
GEOMETRICAL PROGRESSION.

For let the force of gravity be expounded by the given line AC; the force of resistance by the indefinite line AK; the absolute force in the descent of the body by the
difference KC; the velocity of the body by a line AP, which shall be a mean proportional between AK and AC, and therefore in a subduplicate ratio of the resistance; the
increment of the resistance made in a given particle of time by the lineola KL, and the
contemporaneous increment of the velocity by the lineola PQ; and with the centre C,

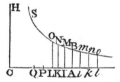

and rectangular asymptotes CA, CH, describe any hyperbola
BNS meeting the erected perpendiculars AB, KN, LO in B, N
and O. Because AK is as AP², the moment KL of the one will
be as the moment 2APQ of the other, that is, as AP × KC; for
the increment PQ of the velocity is (by Law II) proportional to
the generating force KC. Let the ratio of KL be compounded with the ratio KN, and
the rectangle KL × KN will become as AP × KC × KN; that is (because the rectangle KC × KN is given), as AP. But the ultimate ratio of the hyperbolic area KNOL to
the rectangle KL × KN becomes, when the points K and L coincide, the ratio of equality. Therefore that hyperbolic evanescent area is as AP. Therefore the whole hyperbolic
area ABOL is composed of particles KNOL which are always proportional to the velocity AP; and therefore is itself proportional to the space described with that velocity. Let
that area be now divided into equal parts, as ABMI, IMNK, KNOL, &c., and the
absolute forces AC, IC, KC, LC, &c., will be in a geometrical progression. Q.E.D. And
by a like reasoning, in the ascent of the body, taking, on the contrary side of the point
A, the equal areas AB*mi*, *imnk*, *knol*, &c., it will appear that the absolute forces AC,
*i*C, *k*C, *ι*C, &c., are continually proportional. Therefore if all the spaces in the ascent
and descent are taken equal, all the absolute forces *ι*C, *k*C, *i*C, AC, IC, KC, LC, &c.,
will be continually proportional.   Q.E.D.

CoR. 1. Hence if the space described be expounded by the hyperbolic area ABNK,
the force of gravity, the velocity of the body, and the resistance of the medium, may be
expounded by the lines AC, AP, and AK respectively; and *vice versa.*

CoR. 2. And the greatest velocity which the body can ever acquire in an infinite
descent will be expounded by the line A.C.

CoR. 3. Therefore if the resistance of the medium answering to any given velocity be
known, the greatest velocity will be found, by taking it to that given velocity in a ratio subduplicate of the ratio which the force of gravity bears to that known resistance of the medium.

PROPOSITION IX. THEOREM VII.

SUPPOSING WHAT IS ABOVE DEMONSTRATED, I SAY, THAT IF THE
TANGENTS OF ANGLES OF THE SECTOR OF A CIRCLE, AND OF AN
HYPERBOLA, BE TAKEN PROPORTIONAL TO THE VELOCITIES, THE
RADIUS BEING OF A FIT MAGNITUDE, ALL THE TIME OF THE ASCENT
TO THE HIGHEST PLACE WILL BE AS THE SECTOR OF THE CIRCLE,
AND ALL THE TIME OF DESCENDING FROM THE HIGHEST PLACE AS
THE SECTOR OF THE HYPERBOLA.

To the right line AC, which expresses the force of gravity, let AD be drawn perpendicular
and equal. From the centre D with the semi-diameter
AD describe as well the quadrant AÆ of a circle, as the
rectangular hyperbola AVZ, whose axis is AK, principal vertex A, and asymptote DC. Let Dp, DP be
drawn; and the circular sector AtD will be as all the
time of the ascent to the highest place; and the hyperbolic sector ATD as all the time of descent from the
highest place; if so be that the tangents Ap, AP of those
sectors be as the velocities.

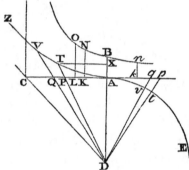

CASE 1. Draw Dtq cutting off the moments or
least particles tDv and qDp, described in the same time, of the sector ADt and of the triangle
ADp. Since those particles (because of the common angle D) are in a duplicate ratio of the sides,
the particle tDv will be as $\frac{qDp \times tD^2}{pD^2}$, that is (because tD is given), as $\frac{qDp}{pD^2}$. But pD^2 is $AD^2 + Ap^2$,

that is $AD^2 + AD \times Ak$, or $AD \times Ck$; and qDp is $\frac{1}{2}AD \times pq$. Therefore tDv, the particle of the

sector, is as $\frac{pq}{Ck}$; that is, as the least decrement pq of the velocity directly, and the force Ck which
diminishes the velocity, inversely; and therefore as the particle of time answering to the
decrement of the velocity. And, by composition, the sum of all the particles tDv in the sector ADt will be as the sum of the particles of time answering to each of the lost particles pq
of the decreasing velocity Ap, till that velocity, being diminished into nothing, vanishes; that
is, the whole sector ADt is as the whole time of ascent to the highest place.   Q.E.D.

CASE 2. Draw DQV cutting off the least particles TDV and PDQ of the sector
DAV, and of the triangle DAQ; and these particles will be to each other as DT^2 to DP^2,
that is (if TX and AP are parallel), as DX^2 to DA^2 or TX^2 to AP^2; and, by division, as
$DX^2 - TX^2$ to $DA^2 - AP^2$. But, from the nature of the hyperbola, $DX^2 - TX^2$ is
AD^2; and, by the supposition, AP^2 is $AD \times AK$. Therefore the particles are to each other as

AD² to AD² — AD × AK; that is, as AD to AD — AK or AC to CK: and therefore the particle TDV of the sector is $\frac{PDQ \times AC}{CK}$; and CK therefore (because AC and AD are given) as $\frac{PQ}{CK}$; that is, as the increment of the velocity directly, and as the force generating the increment inversely; and therefore as the particle of the time answering to the increment. And, by composition, the sum of the particles of time, in which all the particles PQ of the velocity AP are generated, will be as the sum of the particles of the sector ATD; that is, the whole time will be as the whole sector.   Q.E.D.

COR. 1. Hence if AB be equal to a fourth part of AC, the space which a body will describe by falling in any time will be to the space which the body could describe, by moving uniformly on in the same time with its greatest velocity AC, as the area ABNK, which expresses the space described in falling to the area ATD, which expresses the time. For since AC is to AP as AP to AK, then (by Cor. 1, Lem. II, of this Book) LK is to PQ as 2AK to AP, that is, as 2AP to AC, and thence LK is to $\frac{1}{2}$PQ is AP to $\frac{1}{4}$AC

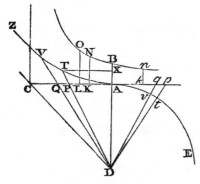

or AB; and KN is to AC or AD as AB to CK; and therefore, *ex aequo*, LKNO to DPQ as AP to CK. But DPQ was to DTV as CK to AC. Therefore, *ex aequo*, LKNO is to DTV as AP to AC; that is, as the velocity of the falling body to the greatest velocity which the body by falling can acquire. Since, therefore, the moments LKNO and DTV of the areas ABNK and ATD are as the velocities, all the parts of those areas generated in the same time will be as the spaces described in the same time; and therefore the whole areas ABNK and ADT, generated from the beginning, will be as the whole spaces described from the beginning of the descent.   Q.E.D.

COR. 2. The same is true also of the space described in the ascent. That is to say, that all that space is to the space described in the same time, with the uniform velocity AC, as the area AB*nk* is to the sector AD*t*.

COR. 3. The velocity of the body, falling in the time ATD, is to the velocity which it would acquire in the same time in a non-resisting space, as the triangle APD to the hyperbolic sector ATD. For the velocity in a non-resisting medium would be as the time ATD, and in a resisting medium is as AP, that is, as the triangle APD. And those velocities, at the beginning of the descent, are equal among themselves, as well as those areas ATD, APD.

COR. 4. By the same argument, the velocity in the ascent is to the velocity with which the body in the same time, in a non-resisting space, would lose

all its motion of ascent, as the triangle A*p*D to the circular sector A*t*D; or as the right line A*p* to the arc A*t*.

COR. 5. Therefore the time in which a body, by falling in a resisting medium, would acquire the velocity AP, is to the time in which it would acquire its greatest velocity AC, by falling in a non-resisting space, as the sector ADT to the triangle ADC: and the time in which it would lose its velocity A*p*, by ascending in a resisting medium, is to the time in which it would lose the same velocity by ascending in a non-resisting space, as the arc A*t* to its tangent A*p*.

COR. 6. Hence from the given time there is given the space described in the ascent or descent. For the greatest velocity of a body descending *in infinitum* is given (by Corol. 2 and 3, Theor. VI, of this Book); and thence the time is given in which a body would acquire that velocity by falling in a non-misting space. And taking the sector ADT or AD*t* to the triangle ADC in the ratio of the given time to the time just now found, there will be given both the velocity AP or A*p*, and the area ABNK or AB*nk*, which is to the sector ADT, or AD*t*, as the space sought to the space which would, in the given time, be uniformly described with that greatest velocity found just before.

COR. 7. And by going backward, from the given space of ascent or descent AB*nk* or ABNK, there will be given the time AD*t* or ADT.

PROPOSITION X. PROBLEM III.

SUPPOSE THE UNIFORM FORCE OF GRAVITY TO TEND DIRECTLY
TO THE PLANE OF THE HORIZON, AND THE RESISTANCE TO BE AS
THE DENSITY OF THE MEDIUM AND THE SQUARE OF THE
VELOCITY CONJUNCTLY: IT IS PROPOSED TO FIND THE DENSITY
OF THE MEDIUM IN EACH PLACE, WHICH SHALL MAKE THE BODY
MOVE IN ANY GIVEN CURVE LINE; THE VELOCITY OF THE BODY
AND THE RESISTANCE OF THE MEDIUM IN EACH PLACE.

Let PQ be a plane perpendicular to the plane of the scheme itself; PFHQ a curve line meeting that plane in the points P and Q; G, H, I, K four places of the body going

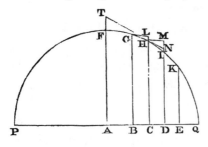

on in this curve from F to Q; and GB, HC, ID, KE four parallel ordinates let fall from these points to the horizon, and standing on the horizontal line PQ at the points B, C, D, E; and let the distances BC, CD, DE, of the ordinates be equal among themselves. From the points G and H let the right lines GL, HN, be drawn touching the curve in G and H, and meeting the ordinates CH, DI, produced upwards, in L and N: and complete the parallelogram

HCDM. And the times in which the body describes the arcs GH, HI, will be in a subduplicate ratio of the altitudes LH, NI, which the bodies would describe in those times, by falling from the tangents; and the velocities will be as the lengths described GH, HI directly, and the times inversely. Let the times be expounded by T and t, and the velocities by $\frac{GH}{T}$ and $\frac{HI}{t}$; and the decrement of the velocity produced in the time

t will be expounded by $\frac{GH}{T} - \frac{HI}{t}$. This decrement arises from the resistance which retards the body, and from the gravity which accelerates it. Gravity, in a falling body, which in its fall describes the space NI, produces a velocity with which it would be able to describe twice that space in the same time, as *Galileo* has demonstrated; that is, the velocity $\frac{2NI}{t}$: but if the body describes the arc HI, it augments that arc only by the

length HI - HN or $\frac{MI \times NI}{HI}$; and therefore generates only the velocity $\frac{2MI \times NI}{t \times HI}$. Let this velocity be added to the before mentioned decrement, and we shall have the decrement of the velocity arising from the resistance alone, that is, $\frac{GH}{T} - \frac{HI}{t} + \frac{2MI \times NI}{t \times HI}$. Therefore

since, in the same time, the action of gravity generates, in a falling body, the velocity

$\frac{2NI}{t}$, the resistance will be to the gravity as $\frac{GH}{T} - \frac{HI}{t} + \frac{2MI \times NI}{t \times HI}$ to $\frac{2NI}{t}$ or as

$\frac{t \times GH}{T} - HI + \frac{2MI \times NI}{HI}$ to 2NI.

Now for the abscissas CB, CD, CE, put — o, o, $2o$. For the ordinate CH put P; and for MI put any series $Qo + Ro^2 + So^3 +$, &c. And all the terms of the series after the first, that is, $Ro^2 + So^3 +$, &c., will be NI; and the ordinates DI, EK, and BG will be P — Qo — Ro^2 — So^3 —, &c., P — $2Qo$ — $4Ro^2$ — $8So^3$ -, &c., and P + Qo — Ro^2 +So^3 —, &c., respectively. And by squaring the differences of the ordinates BG — CH and CH - DI, and to the squares thence produced adding the squares of BC and CD themselves, you will have $oo + QQoo — 2QRo^3$ +,&c., and $oo + QQoo + 2QRo^3$ +,&c., the squares of the arcs GH,HI; whose roots $o\sqrt{1+QQ} - \frac{QRoo}{\sqrt{1+QQ}}$, and $\sqrt{1+QQ} - \frac{QRoo}{\sqrt{1+QQ}}$ are the arcs GH and

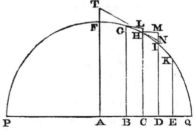

HI. Moreover, if from the ordinate CH there be subducted half the sum of the ordinates BG and DI, and from the ordinate DI there be subducted half the sum of the ordinates CH and EK, there will remain Roo and $Roo + 3So^3$, the versed sines of the arcs GI and

HK. And these are proportional to the lineolae LH and NI, and therefore in the duplicate ratio of the infinitely small times T and t: and thence the ratio $\frac{t}{T}$ is $\sqrt{\frac{R+3So}{R}}$ or

$$\frac{R+\frac{3}{2}So}{R} \quad \text{and} \quad \frac{t \times GH}{T} - HI + \frac{2MI \times NI}{HI}$$, by substituting the values of $\frac{t}{T}$, GH, HI, MI and

NI just found, becomes $\frac{3Soo}{2R}\sqrt{1+QQ}$. And since 2NI is 2Roo, the resistance will be now

to the gravity as $\frac{3Soo}{2R}\sqrt{1+QQ}$ to 2Roo, that is, as $3S\sqrt{1+Q\mathrm{C}}$ to 4RR.

And the velocity will be such, that a body going off therewith from any place H, in the direction of the tangent HN, would describe, *in vacuo*, a parabola whose diameter is HC, and its latus rectum $\frac{HN^2}{NI}$ or $\frac{1+QQ}{R}$.

And the resistance is as the density of the medium and the square of the velocity conjunctly; and therefore the density of the medium is as the resistance directly, and the square of the velocity inversely; that is, as $\frac{3S\sqrt{1+QQ}}{4RR}$ directly and $\frac{1+QQ}{R}$ inversely;

that is, as $\frac{S}{R\sqrt{1+QQ}}$. Q.E.I.

COR. 1. If the tangent HN be produced both ways, so as to meet any ordinate AF in T $\frac{HT}{AC}$ will be equal to $\sqrt{1+QQ}$, and therefore in what has gone before may be put for

$\sqrt{1+QQ}$. By this means the resistance will be to the gravity as 3S x HT to 4RR x AC;

the velocity will be as $\frac{HT}{AC\sqrt{R}}$, and the density of the medium will be as $\frac{S \times AC}{R \times HT}$.

COR. 2. And hence, if the curve line PFHQ be defined by the relation between the base or abscissa AC and the ordinate CH, as is usual, and the value of the ordinate be resolved into a converging series, the Problem will be expeditiously solved by the first terms of the series; as in the following examples.

EXAMPLE 1. Let the line PFHQ be a semi-circle described upon the diameter PQ, to find the density of the medium that shall make a projectile move in that line.

Bisect the diameter PQ in A; and call AQ, n; AC, a; CH, e; and CD, o; then DI^2 or $AQ^2 - AD^2 = nn - aa - 2ao - oo$, or $ee - 2ao - oo$; and the root being extracted by our method, will give $DI = e - \frac{ao}{e} - \frac{oo}{2e} - \frac{aaoo}{2e^3} - \frac{ao^3}{2e^3} - \frac{a^3o^3}{2e^5} -$, &c. Here put nn for $es + aa$, and DI

will become $= e - \frac{ao}{e} - \frac{nnoo}{2e^3} - \frac{anno^3}{2e^5} -$, &c.

Such series I distinguish into successive terms after this manner: I call that the first

term in which the infinitely small quantity o is not found; the second, in which that quantity is of one dimension only; the third, in which it arises to two dimensions; the fourth, in which it is of three; and so *ad infinitum*. And the first term, which here is e, will always denote the length of the ordinate CH, standing at the beginning of the indefinite quantity o. The second term, which here is $\frac{ao}{e}$, will denote the difference between CH and DN; that is, the lineola, MN which is cut off by completing the parallelogram HCDM; and therefore always determines the position of the tangent HN; as, in this case, by taking MN to

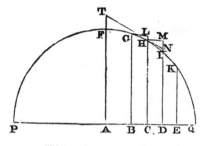

HM as $\frac{ao}{e}$ to o, or a to e. The third term, which here is $\frac{nnoo}{2e^3}$, will represent the lineola IN, which lies between the tangent and the curve; and therefore determines the angle of contact IHN, or the curvature which the curve line has in H. If that lineola IN is of a finite magnitude, it will be expressed by the third term, together with those that follow *in infinitum*. But if that lineola be diminished *in infinitum*, the terms following become infinitely less than the third term, and therefore may be neglected. The fourth term determines the variation of the curvature; the fifth, the variation of the variation; and so on. Whence, by the way, appears no contemptible use of these series in the solution of problems that depend upon tangents, and the curvature of curves.

Now compare the series $e - \frac{ao}{e} - \frac{nnoo}{2e^3} - \frac{anno^3}{2e^5} -$ &c., with the series $P - Qo - Roo - So^3 -$ &c., and for P, Q, R and S, put e, $\frac{a}{e}$, $\frac{nn}{2e^3}$, $\frac{ann}{2e^5}$, and for $\sqrt{1+QQ}$ put $\sqrt{1+\frac{aa}{ee}}$ or $\frac{n}{e}$; and the density of the medium will come out as $\frac{a}{ne}$; that is (because n is given), as $\frac{a}{e}$ or $\frac{AC}{CH}$, that is, as that length of the tangent HT, which is terminated at the semi-diameter AF standing perpendicularly on PQ: and the resistance will be to the gravity as $3a$ to $2n$, that is, as 3AC to the diameter PQ of the circle; and the velocity will be as $\sqrt{CH}$. Therefore if the body goes from the place F, with a due velocity, in the direction of a line parallel to PQ, and the density of the medium in each of the places H is as the length of the tangent HT, and the resistance also in any place H is to the force of gravity as 3AC to PQ, that body will describe the quadrant FHQ of a circle. Q.E.I.

But if the same body should go from the plus P, in the direction of a line perpendicular to PQ, and should begin to move in an arc of the semicircle PFQ, we must take AC or a on the contrary side of the centre A; and therefore its sign must be changed, and we must put $-a$ for $+a$. Then the density of the medium would come out as $-\frac{a}{e}$. But nature does not admit of a negative density, that is, a density which accelerates the motion of bodies; and therefore it cannot naturally come to pass that a body by ascending

from P should describe the quadrant PF of a circle. To produce such an effect, a body ought to be accelerated by an impelling medium, and not impeded by a resisting one.

EXAMPLE 2. Let the line PFQ be a parabola, having its axis AF perpendicular to the horizon PQ, to find the density of the medium, which will make a projectile move in that line.

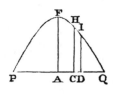

From the nature of the parabola, the rectangle PDQ is equal to the rectangle under the ordinate DI and some given right line; that is, if that right line be called b; PC, a; PQ, c; CH, e; and CD, o; the rectangle $a + o$ into $c - a - o$ or $ac - aa - 2ao + cc - oo$, is equal to the rectangle b into DI, and therefore DI is equal to $\frac{ac - aa}{b} + \frac{c - 2a}{b}o - \frac{oo}{b}$. Now the second term $\frac{c - 2a}{b}o$ of this series is to be put for Qo, and the third term $\frac{oo}{b}$ for Roo. But since there are no more terms, the co-efficient S of the fourth term will vanish; and therefore the quantity $\frac{S}{R\sqrt{1 + QC}}$, to which the density of the medium is proportional, will be nothing. Therefore, where the medium is of no density, the projectile will move in a parabola; as *Galileo* hath heretofore demonstrated. Q.E.I.

EXAMPLE 3. Let the line AGK be an hyperbola, having its asymptote NX perpendicular to the horizontal plane AK, to find the density of the medium that will make a projectile move in that line.

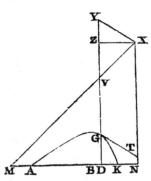

Let MX be the other asymptote, meeting the ordinate DG produced in V; and from the nature of the hyperbola, the rectangle of XV into VG will be given. There is also given the ratio of DN to VX, and therefore the rectangle of DN into VG is given. Let that be bb: and, completing the parallelogram DNXZ, let BN be called a; BD, o, NX, c; and let the given ratio of VZ to ZX or DN be $\frac{m}{n}$. Then DN will be equal to $a - o$, VG equal to $\frac{bb}{a - o}$, VZ equal to $\frac{m}{n} \times \overline{a - o}$

and GD or NX - VZ - VG equal to $c - \frac{m}{n}a + \frac{m}{n}o - \frac{bb}{a - o}$. Let the term $\frac{bb}{a - o}$ be resolved into the converging series $\frac{bb}{a} + \frac{bb}{aa}o + \frac{bb}{a^3}oo + \frac{bb}{a^4}o^3$, &c., and GD will become equal to

$$c - \frac{m}{n}a - \frac{bb}{a} - \frac{m}{n}o + \frac{bb}{aa}o - \frac{bb}{a^3}o^2 - \frac{bb}{a^4}o^3$$ &c. The second term $\frac{m}{n}o - \frac{bb}{aa}o$ of this series is to be used

for Q_o; the third $\frac{bb}{a^3}o^2$, with its sign changed for R_o^2; and the fourth $\frac{bb}{a^4}o^3$, with its sign changed also for S_o^3, and their coefficients $\frac{m}{n} - \frac{bb}{aa}$, $\frac{bb}{a^3}$ and $\frac{bb}{a^4}$ are to be put for Q, R, and S in the former rule. Which being done, the density of the medium will come out as $\frac{bb}{a^3}\sqrt{1 + \frac{mm}{nn} - \frac{2mbb}{naa} + \frac{b^4}{a^4}}$ or $\dfrac{1}{\sqrt{aa + \frac{mm}{nn}aa - \frac{2mbb}{n}aa + \frac{b^4}{aa}}}$, that is, if in VZ you take VY equal to VG, as $\frac{1}{XY}$. For aa and $\frac{XY^2}{VG}$ are the squares of XZ and ZY. But the ratio of the resistance to gravity is found to be that of 3XY to 2YG; and the velocity is that with which the body would describe a parabola, whose vertex is G, diameter DG, latus rectum $\frac{XY^2}{VG}$.

Suppose, therefore, that the densities of the medium in each of the places G are reciprocally as the distances XY, and that the resistance in any place G is to the gravity as 3XY to 2YG; and a body let go from the place A, with a due velocity, will describe that hyperbola AGK. Q.E.I.

EXAMPLE 4. Suppose, indefinitely, the line AGK to be an hyperbola described with the centre X, and the asymptotes MX, NX, so that, having constructed the rectangle XZDN, whose side ZD cuts the hyperbola in G and its asymptote in V, VG may be reciprocally as any power DN^n of the line ZX or DN, whose index is the number n: to find the density of the inedium in whichs projected body will describe this curve.

For BN, BD, NX, put A, O, C, respectively, and let VZ be to XZ or DN as d to e, and VG be equal to $\frac{bb}{DN^n}$;

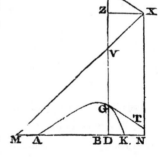

then DN will be equal to A – O, $VG = \dfrac{bb}{\overline{A-O}^n}$,

$VZ = \dfrac{d}{e}\overline{A-O}$, and GD or NX - VZ - VG equal to

$C - \dfrac{d}{e}A + \dfrac{d}{e}O - \dfrac{bb}{\overline{A-O}^n}$. Let the term $\overline{A-O}^n$ be resolved into an infinite series

$$\frac{bb}{A^n} + \frac{nbb}{A^{n+1}} \times O + \frac{nn+n}{2A^{n+2}} \times bbO^2 + \frac{n^3 + 3nn + 2n}{6A^{n+3}} \times bbO^3,$$ &c, and GD will be equal to

$$C - \frac{d}{e}A - \frac{bb}{A^n} + \frac{d}{e}O - \frac{nbb}{A^{n+1}}O - \frac{+nn+n}{2A^{n+2}}bbO^2 - \frac{+n^3 + 3nn + 2n}{6A^{n+3}}bbO,$$ &c. The second term $\dfrac{d}{e}O - \dfrac{nbb}{A^{n+1}}$

of this series is to be used for Q_o, the third $\dfrac{nn+n}{2A^{n+2}}bbO^2$ for R_{oo}, the fourth $\dfrac{n^3 + 3nn + 2n}{6A^{n+3}}bbO^3$ for S_o^3. And thence the density of the medium $\dfrac{S}{R\sqrt{1+QQ}}$ in

any place G, will be $\sqrt[n+2]{3\sqrt{A^2 + \frac{dd}{ee}A^2 - \frac{2dnbb}{eA^n}A + \frac{nnb^4}{A^{2n}}}}$, and therefore if in VZ you take VY

equal to $n \times$ VG, that density is reciprocally as XY. For A^2 and $\frac{dd}{ee}A^2 - \frac{2dnbb}{eA^n}A + \frac{nnb^4}{A^{2n}}$ are the squares of XZ and ZY. But the resistance in the same place G is to the force of gravity as $3S \times \frac{XY}{A}$ to 4RR, that is, as XY to $\frac{2nn+2n}{n+2}$ VG.

And the velocity there is the same wherewith the projected body would move in a parabola, whose vertex is G, diameter GD, and latus rectum $\frac{1+QR}{R}$ or $\frac{2XY^2}{nn+n \times VC}$. Q.E.I.

SCHOLIUM.

In the same manner that the density of the medium comes out to be as $\frac{S \times AC}{R \times HT}$ in Cor. 1, if the resistance is put as any power V^n of the velocity V, the density of the medium will come out to be as $\frac{S}{4-n} \times \overline{\frac{AC}{HT}}^{n-1}$. And therefore if a curve can be found, such that the ratio of $\frac{S}{R^{\frac{4-n}{2}}}$ to $\overline{\frac{HT}{AC}}^{n-1}$, or of $\frac{S^2}{R^{4-n}}$ to $\overline{1+QQ}^{n-1}$ may be given; the body, in an

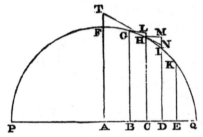

uniform medium, whose resistance is as the

power V^n of the velocity V, will move in this curve. But let us return to more simple curves.

Because there can be no motion in a parabola except in a non-resisting medium, but in the hyperbolas here described it is produced by a perpetual resistance; it is evident that the line which a projectile describes in an uniformly resisting medium approaches nearer to these hyperbolas than to a parabola. That line is certainly of the hyperbolic kind, but about the vertex it is more distant from the asymptotes, and in the parts remote from the vertex draws nearer to them than these hyperbolas here described. The difference, however, is not so great between the one and the other but that these latter may be commodiously enough used in practice instead of the former. And perhaps these may prove more useful than an hyperbola that is more accurate, and at the same time more compounded. They may be made use of, then, in this manner.

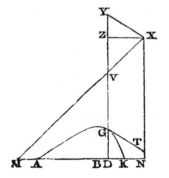

Complete the parallelogram XYGT, and the right line GT will touch the hyperbola in G, and therefore the density of the medium in G is reciprocally as the tangent GT, and the velocity there as $\sqrt{\dfrac{GT^2}{GV}}$ and the resistance

is to the force of gravity as $\dfrac{2nn+2n}{n+2} \times GV$.

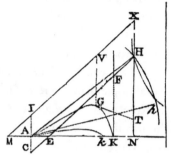

Therefore if a body projected from the place A, in the direction of the right line AH, describes the hyperbola AGK and AH produced meets the asymptote NX in H, and AI drawn parallel to it meets the other asymptote MX in I; the density of the medium in A will be reciprocally as AH, and the velocity of the body as $\sqrt{\dfrac{AH^2}{AI}}$, and the resistance to the force of

gravity as AH to $\dfrac{AH^2}{AI}$. Hence the following rules are deduced.

RULE 1. If the density of the medium at A, and the velocity with which the body is projected remain the same, and the angle NAH be changed; the lengths AH, AI, HX will remain. Therefore if those lengths, in any one case, are found, the hyperbola may afterwards be easily determined from any given angle NAH.

RULE 2. If the angle NAH, and the density of the medium at A, remain the same, and the velocity with which the body is projected be changed, the length AH will continue the same; and AI will be changed in a duplicate ratio of the velocity reciprocally.

RULE 3. If the angle NAH, the velocity of the body at A, and the accelerative gravity remain the same, and the proportion of the resistance at A to the motive gravity be augmented in any ratio; the proportion of AH to AI will be augmented in the same ratio, the latus rectum of the above mentioned parabola remaining the same, and also the length $\dfrac{AH^2}{AI}$ proportional to it; and therefore AH will be diminished in the

same ratio, and AI will be diminished in the duplicate of that ratio. But the proportion of the resistance to the weight is augmented, when either the specific gravity is made less, the magnitude remaining equal, or when the density of the medium is made greater, or when, by diminishing the magnitude, the resistance becomes diminished in a less ratio than the weight.

RULE 4. Because the density of the medium is greater near the vertex of the hyperbola than it is in the place A, that a mean density may be preserved, the ratio of the least of the tangents GT to the tangent AH ought to be found, and the density in A augmented in a ratio a little greater than that of half the sum of those tangents to the least of the tangents GT.

RULE 5. If the lengths AH, AI are given, and the figure AGK is to be described, produce HN to X, so that HX may be to AI as $n + 1$ to 1; and with the centre X, and the asymptotes MX, NX, describe an hyperbola through the point A, such that AI may be to any of the lines VG as XV^n to XI^n.

RULE 6. By how much the greater the number it is, so much the more accurate are these hyperbolas in the ascent of the body from A, and less accurate in its descent to K; and the contrary. The conic hyperbola, keeps a mean ratio between these, and is more simple than the rest. Therefore if the hyperbola be of this kind, and you are to find the point K, where the projected body falls upon any right line AN passing through the point A, let AN produced meet the asymptotes MX, NX in M and N, and take NK equal to AM.

RULE 7. And hence appears an expeditious method of determining this hyperbola from the phenomena. Let two similar and equal bodies be projected with the same velocity, in different angles HAK, hAk, and let them fall upon the plane of the horizon in K and k; and note the proportion of AK to Ak. Let it be as d to e. Then erecting a perpendicular AI of any length, assume any how the length AH or Ah, and thence graphically, or by scale and compass, collect the lengths AK, Ak (by Rule 6). If the ratio of AK to Ak be the same with that of d to e, the length of AH was rightly assumed. If not, take on the indefinite right line SM, the length SM equal to the assumed AH; and

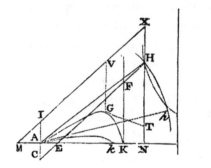
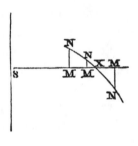

erect a perpendicular MN equal to the difference $\frac{AK}{Ak} - \frac{d}{e}$ of the ratios drawn into any given right line. By the like method, from several assumed lengths AH, you may find several points N; and draw through them all a regular curve NNXN, cutting the right line SMMM in X. Lastly, assume AR equal to the abscissa SX, and thence find again the length AK; and the lengths, which are to the assumed length AI, and this last AH, as the length AK known by experiment, to the length AK last found, will be the true lengths AI and AH, which were to be found. But these being given, there will be given also the resisting force of the medium in the place A, it being to the force of gravity as

AH to $^4/_3$AI. Let the density of the medium be increased by Rule 4, and if the resisting force just found be increased in the same ratio, it will become still more accurate.

RULE 8. The lengths AH, HX being found; let there be now required the position of the line AH, according to which a projectile thrown with that given velocity shall fall upon any point K. At the points A and K, erect the lines AC, KF perpendicular to the horizon; whereof let AC be drawn downwards, and be equal to AI or $^1/_2$HX. With the asymptotes AK, KF, describe an hyperbola, whose conjugate shall pass through the point C; and from the centre A, with the interval AH, describe a circle cutting that

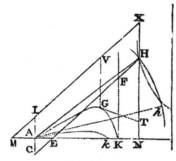

hyperbola in the point H; then the projectile thrown in the direction of the right line AH will fall upon the point K. Q.E.I. For the point H, because of the given length AH, must be somewhere in the circumference of the described circle. Draw CH meeting AK and KF in E and F; and because CH, MX are parallel, and AC, AI equal, AE will be equal to AM, and therefore also equal to KN. But CE is to AE as FH to KN, and therefore CE and FH are equal. Therefore the point H falls upon the hyperbolic curve described with the asymptotes AK, KF whose conjugate passes through the point C; and is therefore found in the common intersection of this hyperbolic curve and the circumference of the described circle. Q.E.D. It is to be observed that this operation is the same, whether the right line AKN be parallel to the horizon, or inclined thereto in any angle; and that from two intersections H, h, there arise two angles NAH, NAh; and that in mechanical practice it is sufficient once to describe a circle, then to apply a ruler CH, of an indeterminate length, so to the point C, that its part FH, intercepted between the circle and the right line FK, may be equal to its part CE placed between the point C and the right line AK.

What has been said of hyperbolas may be easily applied to parabolas. For if a parabola be represented by XAGK, touched by a right line XV in the vertex X, and the

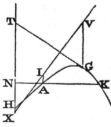

ordinates IA, VG be as any powers XI^n, XV^n, of the abscissas XI, XV; draw XT, GT, AH, whereof let XT be parallel to VG, and let GT, AH touch the parabola in G and A: and a body projected from any place A, in the direction of the right line AH, with a due velocity, will describe this parabola, if the density of the medium in each of the places G be reciprocally as the tangent GT. In that case the velocity in G will be the same as would cause a body, moving in a non-resisting space, to describe a conic parabola, having G for its vertex, VG produced downwards for its diameter, and $\dfrac{2GT^2}{nn - n \times VG}$ for its

latus rectum. And the resisting force in G will be to the force of gravity as GT to

$\frac{2nn-2n}{n-2}$ VG. Therefore if NAK represent an horizontal line, and both the density of the medium at A, and the velocity with which the body is projected, remaining the same, the angle NAH be any how altered, the lengths AH, AI, HX will remain; and thence will be given the vertex X of the parabola, and the position of the right line XI; and by taking VG to IA as XV^n to XI^n, there will be given all the points G of the parabola, through which the projectile will pass.

SECTION III.

Of the motions of bodies which are resisted partly in the ratio of the velocities, and partly in the duplicate of the same ratio.

PROPOSITION XI. THEOREM VIII.

IF A BODY BE RESISTED PARTLY IN THE RATIO AND PARTLY IN
THE DUPLICATE RATIO OF ITS VELOCITY, AND MOVES IN A
SIMILAR MEDIUM BY ITS INNATE FORCE ONLY; AND THE
TIMES BE TAKEN IN ARITHMETICAL PROGRESSION; THEN
QUANTITIES RECIPROCALLY PROPORTIONAL TO THE VELOCITIES,
INCREASED BY A CERTAIN GIVEN QUANTITY,
WILL BE IN GEOMETRICAL PROGRESSION.

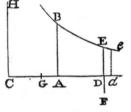

With the centre C, and the rectangular asymptotes CADd and CH, describe an hyperbola BEe, and let AB, DE, de, be parallel to the asymptote CH. In the asymptote CD let A, G be given points; and if the time be expounded by the hyperbolic area ABED uniformly increasing, I say, that the velocity may be expressed by the length DF, whose reciprocal GD, together with the given line CG, compose the length CD increasing in a geometrical progression.

For let the areola DEed be the least given increment of the time, and Dd will be reciprocally as DE, and therefore directly as CD. Therefore the decrement of $\frac{1}{GD}$, which (by Lem. II, Book II) is $\frac{Dd}{GD^2}$, will be also as $\frac{CD}{GD^2}$ or $\frac{CG+GD}{GD^2}$, that is, as $\frac{1}{GD} + \frac{CG}{GD^2}$. Therefore the time ABED uniformly increasing by the addition of the given particles EDde, it follows that $\frac{1}{GD}$ decreases in the same ratio with the velocity. For the decrement of the velocity is as the resistance, that is (by the supposition), as the sum

of two quantities, whereof one is as the velocity, and the other as the square of the velocity; and the decrement of $\frac{1}{GD}$ is as the sum of the quantities $\frac{1}{GD}$ and $\frac{CG}{GD^2}$, whereof the first is $\frac{1}{GD}$ itself, and the last $\frac{CG}{GD^2}$ is as $\frac{1}{GD^2}$: therefore $\frac{1}{GD}$ is as the velocity, the decrements of both being analogous. And if the quantity GD reciprocally proportional to $\frac{1}{GD}$, be augmented by the given quantity CG; the sum CD, the time ABED uniformly increasing, will increase in a geometrical progression.   Q.E.D.

Cor. 1. Therefore, if, having the points A and G given, the time be expounded by the hyperbolic area ABED, the velocity may be expounded by $\frac{1}{GD}$ the reciprocal of GD.

Cor. 2. And by taking GA to GD as the reciprocal of the velocity at the beginning to the reciprocal of the velocity at the end of any time ABED, the point G will be found. And that point being found the velocity may be found from any other time given.

PROPOSITION XII. THEOREM IX.

THE SAME THINGS BEING SUPPOSED, I SAY, THAT IF THE SPACES DESCRIBED ARE TAKEN IN ARITHMETICAL PROGRESSION, THE VELOCITIES AUGMENTED BY A CERTAIN GIVEN QUANTITY WILL BE IN GEOMETRICAL PROGRESSION.

In the asymptote CD let there be given the point R, and, erecting the perpendic-

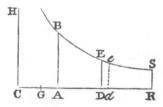

ular RS meeting the hyperbola in S, let the space described be expounded by the hyperbolic area RSED; and the velocity will be as the length GD, which, together with the given line CG, composes a length CD decreasing in a geometrical progression, while the space RSED increases in an arithmetical progression.

For, because the increment ED*de* of the space is given, the lineola D*d*, which is the decrement of GD, will be reciprocally as ED, and therefore directly as CD; that is, as the sum of the same GD and the given length CG. But the decrement of the velocity, in a time reciprocally proportional thereto, in which the given particle of space D*de*E is described, is as the resistance and the time conjunctly, that is, directly as the sum of two quantities, whereof one is as the velocity, the other as the square of the velocity, and inversely as the velocity; and therefore directly as the sum of two quantities, one of which is given, the other is as the velocity. Therefore the decrement both of the velocity and the line GD is as a given quantity and a decreasing quantity conjunctly; and, because the decrements are analogous, the decreasing quantities will always be analogous; viz., the velocity, and the line GD.   Q.E.D.

COR. 1. If the velocity be expounded by the length GD, the space described will be as the hyperbolic area DESR.

COR. 2. And if the point R be assumed any how, the point G will be found, by taking GR to GD as the velocity at the beginning to the velocity after any space RSED is described. The point G being given, the space is given from the given velocity: and the contrary.

COR. 3. Whence since (by Prop. XI) the velocity is given from the given time, and (by this Prop.) the space is given from the given velocity; the space will be given from the given time: and the contrary.

PROPOSITION XIII. THEOREM X.

SUPPOSING THAT A BODY ATTRACTED DOWNWARDS BY AN UNIFORM GRAVITY ASCENDS OR DESCENDS IN A RIGHT LINE; AND THAT THE SAME IS RESISTED PARTLY IN THE RATIO OF ITS VELOCITY, AND PARTLY IN THE DUPLICATE RATIO THEREOF: I SAY, THAT, IF RIGHT LINES PARALLEL TO THE DIAMETERS OF A CIRCLE AND AN HYPERBOLA BE DRAWN THROUGH THE ENDS OF THE CONJUGATE DIAMETERS, AND THE VELOCITIES BE AS SOME SEGMENTS OF THOSE PARALLELS DRAWN FROM A GIVEN POINT, THE TIMES WILL BE AS THE SECTORS OF THE AREAS CUT OF BY RIGHT LINES DRAWN FROM THE CENTRE TO THE ENDS OF THE SEGMENTS; AND THE CONTRARY.

CASE 1. Suppose first that the body is ascending, and from the centre D, with any semi-diameter DB, describe a quadrant BETF of a circle, and through the end B of the semi-diameter DB draw the indefinite line BAP, paral-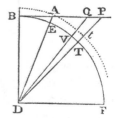lel to the semi-diameter DF. In that line let there be given the point A, and take the segment AP proportional to the velocity. And since one part of the resistance is as the velocity, and another part as the square of the velocity, let the whole resistance be as $AP^2 - 2BAP$. Join DA, DP, cutting the circle in E and T, and let the gravity be expounded by DA^2, so that the gravity shall be to the resistance in P as DA^2 to $AP^2 + 2BAP$; and the time of the whole ascent will be as the sector EDT of the circle.

For draw DVQ, cutting off the moment PQ of the velocity AP, and the moment DTV of the sector DET answering to a given moment of time; and that decrement PQ of the velocity will be as the sum of the forces of gravity DA^2 and of resistance

$AP^2 + 2BAP$, that is (by Prop. XII, Book II, Elem.), as DP^2. Then the area DPQ, which is proportional to PQ, is as DP^2, and the area DTV, which is to the area DPQ as DT^2 to DP^2, is as the given quantity DT^2. Therefore the area EDT decreases uniformly according to the rate of the future time, by subduction of given particles DTV, and is therefore proportional to the time of the whole ascent. Q.E.D.

CASE 2. If the velocity in the ascent of the body be expounded by the length AP as before, and the resistance be made as $AP^2 + 2BAP$, and if the force of gravity be less than can be expressed by DA^2; take BD of such a length, that $AB^2 - BD^2$ may be proportional to the gravity, and let DF be perpendicular and equal to DB, and through the vertex F describe the hyperbola FTVE, whose conjugate semi-diameters are DB and DF, and which cuts DA in E, and DP, DQ in T and V; and the time of the whole ascent will be as the hyperbolic sector TDE.

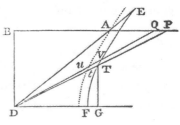

For the decrement PQ of the velocity, produced in a given particle of time, is as the sum of the resistance $AP^2 + 2BAP$ and of the gravity $AB^2 - BD^2$, that is, as $BP^2 - BD^2$. But the area DTV is to the area DPQ as DT^2 to DP^2; and, therefore, if GT be drawn perpendicular to DF, as GT^2 or $GD^2 - GF^2$ to , and as GD^2 to BP^2, and, by division, as DF^2 to $BP^2 - BD^2$. Therefore since the area DPQ is as PQ, that is, as $BP^2 - BD^2$, the area DTV will be as the given quantity DF^2. Therefore the area EDT decreases uniformly in each of the equal particles of time, by the subduction of so many given particles DTV, and therefore is proportional to the time. Q.E.D.

CASE 3. Let AP be the velocity in the descent of the body, and $AP^2 \cdot$ the force of resistance, and $BD^2 - AB^2$ the force of gravity, the angle DBA being a right one. And if with the centre D, and the principal vertex B, there be described a rectangular hyper-

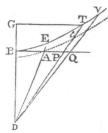

bola BETV cutting DA, DP, and DQ produced in E, T, and V; the sector DET of this hyperbola will be as the whole time of descent.

For the increment PQ of the velocity, and the area DPQ proportional to it, is as the excess of the gravity above the resistance, that is, as $BD^2 - AB^2 - 2BAP - AP^2$ or $BD^2 - BP^2$. And the area DTV is to the area DPQ as DT^2 to DP^2; and therefore as GT^2 or $GD^2 - BD^2$ to BP^2, and as GD^2 to BD^2, and, by division, as BD^2 to $BD^2 - BP^2$. Therefore since the area DPQ is as $BD^2 - BP^2$, the area DTV will be as the given quantity BD^2. Therefore the area EDT increases uniformly in the several equal particles of time by the addition of as many given particles DTV, and therefore is proportional to the time of the descent. Q.E.D.

Cor. If with the centre D and the semi-diameter DA there be drawn through the vertex A an arc At similar to the arc ET, and similarly subtending the angle ADT, the velocity AP will be to the velocity which the body in the time EDT, in a non-resisting space, can lose in its ascent, or acquire in its descent, as the area of the triangle DAP to the area of the sector DAt; and therefore is given from the time given. For the velocity in a non-resisting medium is proportional to the time, and therefore to this sector; in a resisting medium, it is as the triangle; and in both mediums, where it is least, it approaches to the ratio of equality, as the sector and triangle do.

SCHOLIUM.

One may demonstrate also that case in the ascent of the body, where the force of gravity is less than can be expressed by DA^2 or $AB^2 + DB^2$, and greater than can be expressed by $AB^2 - DB^2$, and must be expressed by AB^2. But I hasten to other things.

PROPOSITION XIV. THEOREM XI.

The same things being supposed, I say, that the space described in the ascent or descent is as the difference of the area by which the time is expressed, and of some other area which is augmented or diminished in an arithmetical progression; if the forces compounded of the resistance and the gravity be taken in a geometrical progression.

Take AC (in these three figures) proportional to the gravity, and AK to the resistance; but take them on the same side of the point A, if the body is descending, otherwise on the contrary. Erect Ab, which make to DB as DB^2 to 4BAC: and to the rectangular asymptotes CK, CH, describe the hyperbola bN; and, erecting KN perpendicular to CK, the area AbNK will be augmented or diminished in an arithmetical progression, while the forces CK are taken in a geometrical progression. I say, therefore, that the distance of the body from its greatest altitude is as the excess of the area AbNK above the area DET.

For since AK is as the resistance, that is, as $AP^2 \times 2BAP$; assume any given quantity

Z, and put AK equal to $\dfrac{AP^2 + 2BAP}{Z}$; then (by Lem. II of this Book) the moment KL of

AK will be equal to $\dfrac{2APQ + 2BA \times PQ}{Z}$ or $\dfrac{2BPQ}{Z}$, and the moment KLON of the area

AbNK will be equal to $\dfrac{2BPQ \times LO}{Z}$ or $\dfrac{BPQ \times BD^3}{2Z \times CK \times AB}$.

Case 1. Now if the body ascends, and the gravity be as $AB^2 + BD^2$, BET being a

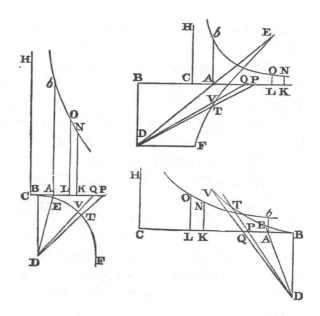

circle, the line AC, which is proportional to the gravity, will be $\frac{AB^2 + BD^2}{Z}$, and DP^2 or $AP^2 + 2BAP + AB^2 + BD^2$ will be $AK \times Z + AC \times Z$ or $CK \times Z$; and therefore the area DTV will be to the area DPQ as DT^2 or DB^2 to $CK \times Z$.

CASE 2. If the body ascends, and the gravity be as $AB^2 - BD^2$, the line AC will be

$\frac{AB^2 - BD^2}{Z}$, and DT^2 will be to DP^2 as DF^2 or DB^2 to $BP^2 - BD^2$ or $AP^2 + 2BAP + AB^2 - BD^2$,

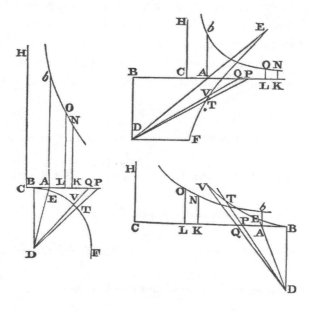

that is, to AK x Z + AC x Z or CK x Z. And therefore the area DTV will be to the area DPQ as DB^2 to CK x Z.

CASE 3. And by the same reasoning, if the body descends, and therefore the gravity is as $BD^2 - AB^2$, and the line AC becomes equal to $\frac{BD^2 - AB^2}{Z}$; the area DTV will be to the area DPQ as DB^2 to CK $\times$ Z: as above.

Since, therefore, these areas are always in this ratio, if for the area DTV, by which the moment of the time, always equal to itself, is expressed, there be put any determinate rectangle, as BD $\times$ m, the area DPQ, that is, $^1/_2$BD $\times$ PQ, will be to BD $\times$ m as CK $\times$ Z to BD^2. And thence $PQ \times BD^3$ becomes equal to 2BD $\times$ m $\times$ CK $\times$ Z, and the moment KLON of the area AbNK, found before, becomes $\frac{BP \times BD \times m}{AB}$. From the area DET subduct its moment DTV or BD x m, and there will remain $\frac{AP \times BD \times m}{AB}$. Therefore the difference of the moments, that is, the moment of the difference of the areas, is equal to $\frac{AP \times BD \times m}{AB}$; and therefore (because of the given quantity $\frac{BD \times m}{AB}$) as the velocity AP; that is, as the moment of the space which the body describes in its ascent or descent. And therefore the difference of the areas, and that space, in creasing or decreasing by proportional moments, and beginning together or vanishing together, are proportional. Q.E.D.

COR. If the length, which arises by applying the area DET to the line BD, be called M; and another length V be taken in that ratio to the length M which the line DA has to the line DE; the space which a body, in a resisting medium, describes in its whole ascent or descent, will be to the space which a body, in a non-resisting medium, falling from rest, can describe in the same time, as the difference of the aforesaid areas to BL; and therefore is given from the time given. For the space in a non-resisting medium is in a duplicate ratio of the time, or as V^2; and, because BD and AB are given, as $\frac{BD \times V^2}{AB}$. This area is equal to the area $\frac{DA^2 \times BD \times M^2}{DE^2 \times AB}$ and the moment of M is m; and therefore the moment of this area is $\frac{DA^2 \times BD \times 2M \times m}{DE^2 \times AB}$. But this moment is to the moment of the difference of the aforesaid areas DET and AbNK, viz., to $\frac{AP \times BD \times m}{AB}$, as $\frac{DA^2 \times BD \times M}{DE^2}$ to $\frac{1}{2}BD \times AP$, or as $\frac{DA^2}{DE^2}$ into DET to DAP; and, therefore, when the areas DET and DAP are least, in the ratio of equality. Therefore the area $\frac{BD \times V^2}{AB}$ and the

difference of the areas DET and AbNK, when all these areas are least, have equal moments; and are therefore equal. Therefore since the velocities, and therefore also the spaces in both mediums described together, in the beginning of the descent, or the end of the ascent, approach to equality, and therefore us then one to another as the area $\frac{BD \times V^2}{AB}$, and the difference of the areas DET and AbNK; and moreover since the space,

in a non-resisting medium, is perpetually as $\frac{BD \times V^2}{AB}$, and the space, in a resisting medium, is perpetually as the difference of the areas DET and AbNK; it necessarily follows, that the spaces, in both mediums, described in any equal times, are one to another as that area $\frac{BD \times V^2}{AB}$ and the difference of the areas DET and AbNK. Q.E.D.

SCHOLIUM.

The resistance of spherical bodies in fluids arises partly from the tenacity, partly from the attrition, and partly from the density of the medium. And that part of the resistance which arises from the density of the fluid as I said, in a duplicate ratio of the velocity; the other part, which arises from the tenacity of the fluid, is uniform, or as the moment of the time; and, therefore, we might now proceed to the motion of bodies, which are resisted partly by an uniform force, or in the ratio of the moments of the time, and partly in the duplicate ratio of the velocity. But it is sufficient to have cleared the way to this speculation in Prop. VIII and IX foregoing, and their Corollaries. For in those Propositions, instead of the uniform resistance made to an ascending body arising from its gravity, one may substitute the uniform resistance which arises from the tenacity of the medium, when the body moves by its *vis insita* alone; and when the body ascends in a right line, add this uniform resistance to the force of gravity, and subduct it when the body descends in a right line. One might also go on to the motion of bodies which are resisted in part uniformly, in part in the ratio of the velocity, and in part in the duplicate ratio of the same velocity. And I have opened a way to this in Prop. XIII and XIV foregoing, in which the uniform resistance arising from the tenacity of the medium may be substituted for the force of gravity, or be compounded with it as before. But I hasten to other things.

SECTION IV.

Of the circular motion of bodies in resisting mediums.

LEMMA III.

LET PQR BE A SPIRAL CUTTING ALL THE RADII SP, SQ, SR, &C., IN EQUAL ANGLES. DRAW THE RIGHT LINE PT TOUCHING THE SPIRAL

IN ANY POINT P, AND CUTTING, THE RADIUS SQ IN T; DRAW PO, QO PERPENDICULAR TO THE SPIRAL, AND MEETING IN O, AND JOIN SO. I SAY, THAT IF THE POINTS P AND Q APPROACH AND COINCIDE, THE ANGLE PSO WILL BECOME A RIGHT ANGLE, AND THE ULTI-MATE RATIO OF THE RECTANGLE $TQ \times 2PS$ TO PQ^2 WILL BE THE RATIO OF EQUALITY.

For from the right angles OPQ, OQR, subduct the equal angles SPQ, SQR, and there will remain the equal angles OPS, OQS. Therefore a circle which passes through the points OSP will pass also through the point Q. Let the points P and Q coincide, and this circle will touch the spiral in the place of coincidence PQ, and will therefore cut the right line OP perpendicularly. Therefore OP will become a diameter of this circle, and the angle OSP, being in a semi-circle, becomes a right one.   Q.E.D.

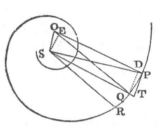

Draw QD, SE perpendicular to OP, and the ultimate ratios of the lines will be as follows: TQ to PD as TS or PS to PE, or 2PO to 2PS; and PD to PQ as PQ to 2PO; and, *ex aequo perturbatè*, to TQ to PQ as PQ to 2PS. Whence PQ^2 becomes equal to TQ x 2PS.   Q.E.D.

PROPOSITION XV. THEOREM XII.

IF THE DENSITY OF A MEDIUM IN EACH PLACE THEREOF BE RECIPRO-CALLY AS THE DISTANCE OF THE PLACES FROM AN IMMOVABLE CEN-TRE AND, THE CENTRIPETAL FORCE BE IN THE DUPLICATE RATIO OF THE DENSITY; I SAY, THAT A BODY MAY REVOLVE IN A SPIRAL WHICH CUTS ALL THE RADII DRAWN FROM THAT CENTRE IN A GIVEN ANGLE.

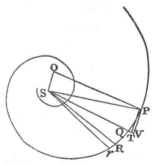

Suppose every thing to be as in the foregoing Lemma, and produce SQ to V so that SV may be equal to SP. In any time let a body, in a resisting medium, describe the least arc PQ, and in double the time the least arc PR; and the decrements of those arcs arising from the resistance, or their differences from the arcs which would be described in a non-resisting medium in the same times, will be to each other as the squares of the times in which they are generated; therefore the decrement of the arc PQ is the fourth part of the decrement of the arc PR. Whence also if the area QSr be taken equal to the area PSQ, the decrement of the arc PQ will be equal

to half the lineola Rr; and therefore the force of resistance and the centripetal force are to each other as the lineola $\frac{1}{2}$Rr and TQ which they generate in the same time. Because

the centripetal force with which the body is urged in P is reciprocally as SP^2, and (by Lem. X, Book I) the lineola TQ, which is generated by that force, is in a ratio compounded of the ratio of this force and the duplicate ratio of the time in which the arc PQ is described (for in this case I neglect the resistance, as being infinitely less than the centripetal force), it follows that TQ$\times$SP^2, that is (by the last Lemma), $\frac{1}{2}$PQ^2 $\times$SP, will be in a duplicate ratio of the time, and therefore the time is as $\sqrt{PQ}$ x SP; and the velocity of the body, with which the arc PQ is described in that time, as $\frac{PQ}{PQ \times \sqrt{SP}}$ or $\frac{1}{\sqrt{SP}}$, that is, in the subduplicate ratio of SP reciprocally.

And, by a like reasoning, the velocity with which the arc QR is described, is in the subduplicate ratio of SQ reciprocally. Now those arcs PQ and QR are as the describing velocities to each other; that is, in the subduplicate ratio of SQ to SP, or as SQ to $\sqrt{SP \times SQ}$; and, because of the equal angles SPQ, SQr, and the equal areas PSQ, QSr, the arc PQ is to the arc Qr as SQ to SP. Take the differences of the proportional consequents, and the arc PQ will be to the arc Rr as SQ to SP$-\overline{\sqrt{SP \times SQ}}$ or $\supset$. For the

points P and Q coinciding, the ultimate ratio of SP$-\overline{\sqrt{SP \times SQ}}$ to $\frac{1}{2}$VQ is the ratio of equality. Because the decrement of the arc PQ arising from the resistance, or its double Rr, is as the resistance and the square of the time conjunctly, the resistance will be as $\frac{Rr}{PQ^2 \times SP}$. But PQ was to R$r$ as SQ to $\frac{1}{2}$VQ, and thence $\frac{Rr}{PQ^2 \times SP}$ becomes as

$$\frac{\frac{1}{2}VQ}{PQ \times SP \times SQ}, \quad \text{or as} \quad \frac{\frac{1}{2}OS}{OP \times SP^2}.$$ For the points P and Q coinciding, SP and SQ coincide also, and the angle PVQ becomes a right one; and, because of the similar triangles PVQ, PSO, PQ becomes to $\frac{1}{2}$VQ   as OP to $\frac{1}{2}$OS. Therefore $\frac{OS}{OP \times SP^2}$ is as the

resistance, that is, in the ratio of the density of the medium in P and the duplicate ratio of the velocity conjunctly. Subduct the duplicate ratio of the velocity, namely, the ratio $\frac{1}{SP}$, and there will remain the density of the medium in P, as $\frac{OS}{OP \times SP}$. Let the spiral be

given, and, because of the given ratio of OS to OP, the density of the medium in P will be as $\frac{1}{SP}$. Therefore in a medium whose density is reciprocally as SP the distance from the centre, a body will revolve in this spiral.   Q.E.D.

CoR. 1. The velocity in any place P, is always the same wherewith a body in a non-resisting medium with the same centripetal force would revolve in a circle, at the same distance SP from the centre.

Cor. 2. The density of the medium, if the distance SP be given, is as $\dfrac{OS}{SP}$, but if that distance is not given, as $\dfrac{OS}{OP \times SP}$. And thence a spiral may be fitted to any density of the medium.

Cor. 3. The force of the resistance in any place P is to the centripetal force in the same place as $\frac{1}{2}$ OS to OP. For those forces are to each other as $\frac{1}{2}$ Rr and TQ, or as

$$\dfrac{\frac{1}{4}VQ \times PC}{SQ} \quad \text{and} \quad \dfrac{\frac{1}{2}PQ^2}{SP},$$

that is, as $\frac{1}{2}$ VQ and PQ, or $\frac{1}{2}$ OS and OP. The spiral therefore being given, there is given the proportion of the resistance to the centripetal force; and, *vice versa*, from that proportion given the spiral is given.

Cor. 4. Therefore the body cannot revolve in this spiral, except where the force of resistance is less than half the centripetal force. Let the resistance be made equal to half the centripetal force, and the spiral will coincide with the right line PS, and in that right line the body will descend to the centre with a velocity that is to the velocity, with which it was proved before, in the case of the parabola (Theor. X, Book I), the descent would be made in a non-resisting medium, in the subduplicate ratio of unity to the number two. And the times of the descent will be here reciprocally as the velocities, and therefore given.

Cor. 5. And because at equal distances from the centre the velocity is the same in the spiral PQR as it is in the right line SP, and the length of the spiral is to the length of the right line PS in a given ratio, namely, in the ratio of OP to OS; the time of the descent in the spiral will be to the time of the descent in the right line SP in the same given ratio, and therefore given.

Cor. 6. If from the centre S, with any two given intervals, two circles are described; and these circles remaining, the angle which the spiral makes with the radius PS be any how changed; the number of revolutions which the body can complete in the space between the circumferences of those circles, going round in the spiral from one circumference

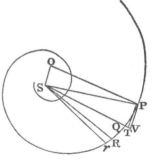

to another, will be as $\dfrac{PS}{OS}$, or as the tangent of the angle which the spiral makes with the radius PS; and the time of the same revolutions will be as $\dfrac{OP}{OS}$, that is, as the secant of the same angle, or reciprocally as the density of the medium.

Cor. 7. If a body, in a medium whose density is reciprocally as the distances of places from the centre, revolves in any curve AEB about that centre, and cuts the first

radius AS in the same angle in B as it did before in A, and that with a velocity that shall be to its first velocity in A reciprocally in a subduplicate ratio of the distances from the

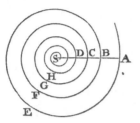

centre (that is, as AS to a mean proportional between AS and BS) that body will continue to describe innumerable similar revolutions BFC, CGD, &c., and by its intersections will distinguish the radius AS into parts AS, BS, CS, DS, &c., that are continually proportional. But the times of the revolutions will be as the perimeters of the orbits AEB, BFC, CGD, &c., directly, and the velocities at the beginnings A, B, C of those orbits inversely; that is as $\frac{3}{AS^2}$, $\frac{3}{BS^2}$, $\frac{3}{CS^2}$. And the whole time in which the body will arrive at the centre, will be to the time of the first revolution as the sum of all the continued proportionals $AS^{\frac{3}{2}}$, $BS^{\frac{3}{2}}$, $CS^{\frac{3}{2}}$, going on *ad infinitum*, to the first term $AS^{\frac{3}{2}}$; that is, as the first term $AS^{\frac{3}{2}}$ to the difference of the two first $AS^{\frac{3}{2}}$ - $BS^{\frac{3}{2}}$

or as $\frac{2}{3}$ AS to AB very nearly. Whence the whole time may be easily found.

COR. 8. From hence also may be deduced, near enough, the motions of bodies in mediums whose density is either uniform, or observes any other assigned law. From the centre S, with intervals SA, SB, SC, &c., continually proportional, describe as many circles; and suppose the time of the revolutions between the perimeters of any two of those circles, in the medium whereof we treated, to be to the time of the revolutions between the same in the medium proposed as the mean density of the proposed medium between those circles to the mean density of the medium whereof we treated, between the same circles, nearly: and that the secant of the angle in which the spiral above determined, in the medium whereof we treated, cuts the radius AS, is in the same ratio to the secant of the angle in which the new spiral, in the proposed medium, cuts the same radius: and also that the number of all the revolutions between the same two circles is nearly as the tangents of those angles. If this be done every where between every two circles, the motion will be continued through all the circles. And by this means one may without difficulty conceive at what rate and in what time bodies ought to revolve in any regular medium.

COR. 9. And although these motions becoming eccentrical should be performed in spirals approaching to an oval figure, yet, conceiving the several revolutions of those spirals to be at the same distances from each other, and to approach to the centre by the same degrees as the spiral above described, we may also understand how the motions of bodies may be performed in spirals of that kind.

PROPOSITION XVI. THEOREM XIII.

IF THE DENSITY OF THE MEDIUM IN EACH OF THE PLACES BE RECIP-
ROCALLY AS THE DISTANCE OF THE PLACES FROM THE IMMOVEABLE
CENTRE, AND THE CENTRIPETAL FORCE BE RECIPROCALLY AS ANY
POWER OF THE SAME DISTANCE, I SAY, THAT THE BODY MAY
REVOLVE IN A SPIRAL INTERSECTING ALL THE RADII DRAWN FROM
THAT CENTRE IN A GIVEN ANGLE.

This is demonstrated in the same manner as the foregoing Proposition. For if the centripetal force in P be reciprocally as any power SP^{n+1} of the distance SP whose index is $n + 1$;
it will be collected, as above, that the time in which the body
describes any arc PQ, will be as $PQ \times PS^{\frac{1}{2}n}$; and the resistance
in P as $\dfrac{Rr}{PQ^2 \times SP^n}$,

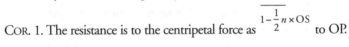

or as $\dfrac{1-\frac{1}{2}n \times VQ}{PQ \times SP^n \times SQ}$, and therefore as $\overline{1-\frac{1}{2}n \times OS} \over OP \times SP^{n+1}$, that is,

(because $\dfrac{\overline{1-\frac{1}{2}n \times OS}}{OP}$ is a given quantity), reciprocally as SP^{n+1}.
And therefore, since the velocity is reciprocally as
$SP^{\frac{1}{2}n}$, the density in P will be reciprocally as SP.

COR. 1. The resistance is to the centripetal force as $\overline{1-\frac{1}{2}n \times OS}$ to OP.

COR. 2. If the centripetal force be reciprocally as SP^3, $1-\frac{1}{2}n$ will be $= 0$; and therefore the
resistance and density of the medium will be nothing, as in Prop. IX, Book I.

COR. 3. If the centripetal force be reciprocally as any power of the radius SP, whose
index is greater than the number 3, the affirmative resistance will be changed into a negative.

SCHOLIUM.

This Proposition and the former, which relate to mediums of unequal density, are to
be understood of the motion of bodies that are so small, that the greater density of the medium on one side of the body above that on the other is not to be considered. I suppose also
the resistance, *caeteris paribus*, to be proportional to its density. Whence, in mediums whose
force of resistance is not as the density, the density must be so much augmented or diminished, that either the excess of the resistance maybe taken away, or the defect supplied.

PROPOSITION XVII. PROBLEM IV.

TO FIND THE CENTRIPETAL FORCE AND THE RESISTING
FORCE OF THE MEDIUM, BY WHICH A BODY, THE LAW OF THE
VELOCITY BEING GIVEN, SHALL REVOLVE IN A GIVEN SPIRAL.

Let that spiral be PQR. From the velocity, with which
the body goes over the very small arc PQ, the time will be
given; and from the altitude TQ, which is as the centripetal
force, and the square of the time, that force will be given.
Then from the difference RS*r* of the areas PSQ and QSR
described in equal particles of time, the retardation of the
body will be given; and from the retardation will be found
the resisting force and density of the medium.

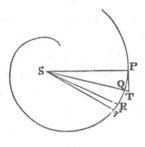

PROPOSITION XVIII. PROBLEM V.

THE LAW OF CENTRIPETAL FORCE BEING GIVEN, TO FIND
THE DENSITY OF THE MEDIUM IN EACH OF THE PLACES
THEREOF, BY WHICH A BODY MAY DESCRIBE A GIVEN SPIRAL.

From the centripetal force the velocity in each place must be found; then
from the retardation of the velocity the density of the medium is found, as in
the foregoing Proposition.

But I have explained the method of managing these Problems in the tenth
Proposition and second Lemma, of this Book; and will no longer detain the reader in
these perplexed disquisitions. I shall now add some things relating to the forces of progressive bodies, and to the density and resistance of those mediums in which the
motions hitherto treated of, and those akin to them, are performed.

SECTION V.

Of the density and compression of fluids; and of hydrostatics.

THE DEFINITION OF A FLUID.

A fluid is any body whose parts yield to any force impressed on it, by
yielding, are easily moved among themselves.

PROPOSITION XIX. THEOREM XIV.

ALL THE PARTS OF A HOMOGENEOUS AND UNMOVED FLUID
INCLUDED IN ANY UNMOVED VESSEL, AND COMPRESSED ON EVERY

SIDE (SETTING ASIDE THE CONSIDERATION OF CONDENSATION,
GRAVITY, AND ALL CENTRIPETAL FORCES), WILL BE EQUALLY PRESSED
ON EVERY SIDE, AND REMAIN IN THEIR PLACES WITHOUT ANY
MOTION ARISING FROM THAT PRESSURE.

CASE 1. Let a fluid be included in the spherical vessel ABC, and uniformly compressed on every side: I say, that no part of it will be moved by that pressure. For if, any part, as D, be moved, all such parts at the same distance from the centre on every side must necessarily be moved at the same time by a like motion; because the pressure of them all is similar and equal; and all other motion is excluded that does not arise from that pressure. But if these parts come all of them nearer to the centre, the fluid must be condensed towards the centre, contrary to the supposition. If they recede from it, the fluid must be condensed towards the circumference; which is also contrary to the supposition. Neither can they move in any one direction retaining their distance from the centre, because for the same reason, they may move in a contrary direction; but the same part cannot be moved contrary ways at the same time. Therefore no part of the fluid will be moved from its place. 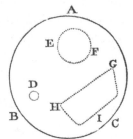 Q.E.D.

CASE 2. I say now, that all the spherical parts of this fluid are equally pressed on every side. For let EF be a spherical part of the fluid; if this be not pressed equally on every side, augment the lesser pressure till it be pressed equally on every side; and its parts (by Case 1) will remain in their places. But before the increase of the pressure, they would remain in their places (by Case 1); and by the addition of a new pressure they will be moved, by the definition of a fluid, from those places. Now these two conclusions contradict each other. Therefore it was false to say that the sphere EF was not pressed equally on every side. Q.E.D.

CASE 3. I say besides, that different spherical parts have equal pressures. For the contiguous spherical parts press each other mutually and equally in the point of contact (by Law III). But (by Case 2) they are pressed on every side with the same force. Therefore any two spherical parts not contiguous, since an intermediate spherical part can touch both, will be pressed with the same force. Q.E.D.

CASE: 4. 1 say now, that all the parts of the fluid are every where pressed equally. For any two parts may be touched by spherical parts in any points whatever; and there they will equally press those spherical parts (by Case 3), and are reciprocally equally pressed by them (by Law III). Q.E.D.

CASE 5. Since, therefore, any part GHI of the fluid is inclosed by the rest of the fluid as in a vessel, and is equally pressed on every side; and also its parts equally press one another, and are at rest among themselves; it is manifest that all the parts of any fluid

as GHI, which is pressed equally on every side, do press each other mutually and equally, and are at rest among themselves. Q.E.D.

CASE 6. Therefore if that fluid be included in a vessel of a yielding substance, or that is not rigid, and be not equally pressed on every side, the same will give way to a stronger pressure, by the Definition of fluidity.

CASE 7. And therefore, in an inflexible or rigid vessel, a fluid will not sustain a stronger pressure on one side than on the other, but will give way to it, and that in a moment of time; because the rigid side of the vessel does not follow the yielding liquor. But the fluid, by thus yielding, will press against the opposite side, and so the pressure will tend on every side to equality. And because the fluid, as soon as it endeavours to recede from the part that is most pressed, is withstood by the resistance of the vessel on the opposite side, the pressure will on every side be reduced to equality, in a moment of time, without any local motion : and from thence the parts of the fluid (by Case 5) will press each other mutually and equally, and be at rest among themselves. Q.E.D.

COR. Whence neither will a motion of the parts of the fluid among themselves be changed by a pressure communicated to the external superficies, except so far as either the figure of the superficies may be somewhere altered, or that all the parts of the fluid, by pressing one another more intensely or remissly, may slide with more or less difficulty among themselves.

PROPOSITION XX. THEOREM XV.

IF ALL THE PARTS OF A SPHERICAL FLUID, HOMOGENEOUS AT EQUAL
DISTANCES FROM THE CENTRE, LYING ON A SPHERICAL CONCENTRIC
BOTTOM, GRAVITATE TOWARDS THE CENTRE OF THE WHOLE, THE
BOTTOM WILL SUSTAIN THE WEIGHT OF A CYLINDER, WHOSE BASE IS
EQUAL TO THE SUPERFICIES OF THE BOTTOM, AND WHOSE ALTI-
TUDE IS THE SAME WITH THAT OF THE INCUMBENT FLUID.

Let DHM be the superficies of the bottom, and AEI the upper superficies of the fluid. Let the fluid be distinguished into concentric orbs of equal thickness, by the innumerable spherical superficies BFK, CGL: and conceive the force of gravity to act only in the upper superficies of every orb, and the actions to be equal on the equal parts of all the superficies. Therefore the upper superficies AE is pressed by the single force of its own gravity, by which all the parts of the upper orb, and the second superficies BFK, will (by Prop. XIX), according to its measure, be equally pressed. The second superficies BFK is pressed likewise by the force of its own gravity, which, added to the former force, makes the pressure double. The third superficies CGL is, according to its measure, acted on by this pressure and the force of its own gravity besides, which makes

its pressure triple. And in like manner the fourth superficies receives a quadruple pressure, the fifth superficies a quintuple, and so on. Therefore the pressure acting on every superficies is not as the solid quantity of the incumbent fluid, but as the number of the orbs reaching to the upper surface of the fluid; and is equal to the gravity of the lowest orb multiplied by the number of orbs: that is, to the gravity of a solid whose ultimate ratio to the cylinder above-mentioned (when the number of the orbs is increased and their thickness diminished, *ad infinitum*, so that the action of gravity from the lowest superficies to the uppermost may become continued) is the ratio of equality. Therefore the lowest superficies sustains the weight of the cylinder above determined. Q.E.D. And

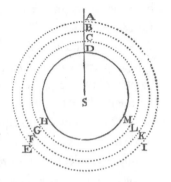

by a like reasoning the Proposition will be evident, where the gravity of the fluid decreases in any assigned ratio of the distance from the centre, and also where the fluid is more rare above and denser below. Q.E.D.

Cor. 1. Therefore the bottom is not pressed by the whole weight of the incumbent fluid, but only sustains that part of it which is described in the Proposition; the rest of the weight being sustained archwise by the spherical figure of the fluid.

Cor. 2. The quantity of the pressure is the same always at equal distances from the centre, whether the superficies pressed be parallel to the horizon, or perpendicular, or oblique; or whether the fluid, continued upwards from the compressed superficies, rises perpendicularly in a rectilinear direction, or creeps obliquely through crooked cavities and canals, whether those passages be regular or irregular, wide or narrow. That the pressure is not altered by any of these circumstances, may be collected by applying the demonstration of this Theorem to the several cases of fluids.

Cor. 3. From the same demonstration it may also be collected (by Prop. XIX), that the parts of a heavy fluid acquire no motion among themselves by the pressure of the incumbent weight, except that motion which arises from condensation.

Cor. 4. And therefore if another body of the same specific gravity, incapable of condensation, be immersed in this fluid, it will acquire no motion by the pressure of the incumbent weight: it will neither descend nor ascend, nor change its figure. If it be spherical, it will remain so, notwithstanding the pressure; if it be square, it will remain square; and that, whether it be soft or fluid; whether it swims freely in the fluid, or lies at the bottom. For any internal part of a fluid is in the same state with the submersed body; and the case of all submersed bodies that have the same magnitude, figure, and specific gravity, is alike. If a submersed body, retaining its weight, should dissolve and put on the form of a fluid, this body, if before it would have ascended, descended, or

from any pressure assume a new figure, would now likewise ascend, descend, or put on a new figure; and that, because its gravity and the other causes of its motion remain. But (by Case 5, Prop. XIX) it would now be at rest, and retain its figure. Therefore also in the former case.

COR. 5. Therefore a body that is specifically heavier than a fluid contiguous to it will sink; and that which is specifically lighter will ascend, and attain so much motion and change of figure as that excess or defect of gravity is able to produce. For that excess or defect is the same thing as an impulse, by which a body, otherwise in equilibrium with the parts of the fluid, is acted on; and may be compared with the excess or defect of a weight in one of the scales of a balance.

COR. 6. Therefore bodies placed in fluids have a twofold gravity the one true and absolute, the other apparent, vulgar, and comparative. Absolute gravity is the whole force with which the body tends downwards; relative and vulgar gravity is the excess of gravity with which the body tends downwards more than the ambient fluid. By the first kind of gravity the parts of all fluids and bodies gravitate in their proper places; and therefore their weights taken together compose the weight of the whole. For the whole taken together is heavy, as may be experienced in vessels full of liquor; and the weight of the whole is equal to the weights of all the parts, and is therefore composed of them. By the other kind of gravity bodies do not gravitate in their places; that is, compared with one another, they do not preponderate, but, hindering one another's endeavours to descend, remain in their proper places, as if they were not heavy. Those things which are in the air, and do not preponderate, are commonly looked on as not heavy. Those which do preponderate are commonly reckoned heavy, in as much as they are not sustained by the weight of the air. The common weights are nothing else but the excess of the true weights above the weight of the air. Hence also, vulgarly, those things are called light which are less heavy, and, by yielding to the preponderating air, mount upwards. But these are only comparatively light and not truly so, because they descend *in vacuo*. Thus, in water, bodies which; by their greater or less gravity, descend or ascend, are comparatively and apparently heavy or light; and their comparative and apparent gravity or levity is the excess or defect by which their true gravity either exceeds the gravity of the water or is exceeded by it. But those things which neither by preponderating descend, nor, by yielding to the preponderating fluid, ascend, although by their true weight they do increase the weight of the whole, yet comparatively, and in the sense of the vulgar, they do not gravitate in the water. For these cases are alike demonstrated.

COR. 7. These things which have been demonstrated concerning gravity take place in any other centripetal forces.

COR. 8. Therefore if the medium in which any body moves be acted on either by its own gravity, or by any other centripetal force, and the body be urged more powerfully by the same force; the difference of the forces is that very motive force, which, in the foregoing Propositions, I have considered as a centripetal force. But if the body be more lightly urged by that force, the difference of the forces becomes a centrifugal force, and is to be considered as such.

COR. 9. But since fluids by pressing the included bodies do not change their external figures, it appears also (by Cor. Prop. XIX) that they will not change the situation of their internal parts in relation to one another; and therefore if animals were immersed therein, and that all sensation did arise from the motion of their parts, the fluid will neither hurt the immersed bodies, nor excite any sensation, unless so far as those bodies may be condensed by the compression. And the case is the same of any system of bodies encompassed with a compressing fluid. All the parts of the system will be agitated with the same motions as if they were placed in a vacuum, and would only retain their comparative gravity; unless so far as the fluid may somewhat resist their motions, or be requisite to conglutinate them by compression.

PROPOSITION XXI. THEOREM XVI.

LET THE DENSITY OF ANY FLUID BE PROPORTIONAL TO THE COMPRESSION, AND ITS PARTS BE ATTRACTED DOWNWARDS BY A CENTRIPETAL FORCE RECIPROCALLY PROPORTIONAL TO THE DISTANCES FROM THE CENTRE: I SAY, THAT, IF THOSE DISTANCES BE TAKEN CONTINUALLY PROPORTIONAL, THE DENSITIES OF THE FLUID AT THE SAME DISTANCES WILL BE ALSO CONTINUALLY PROPORTIONAL.

Let ATV denote the spherical bottom of the fluid, S the centre, SA, SB, SC, SD, SE, SF, &c., distances continually proportional. Erect the perpendiculars AH, BI, CK, DL, EM, FN, &c., which shall be as the densities of the medium in the places A, B, C, D, E, F; and the specific gravities in those places will be as $\frac{AH}{AS}$, $\frac{BI}{BS}$, $\frac{CK}{CS}$, &c., or, which is all one, as $\frac{AH}{AB}$, $\frac{BI}{BC}$, $\frac{CK}{CD}$. Suppose, first, these gravities to be uniformly continued from A to B, from B to C, from C to D, &c., the decrements in the points B, C, D, &c., being taken by steps. And these gravities drawn into the altitudes AB, BC, CD, &c., will give the pressures AH, BI, CK, &c., by which the bottom ATV is acted on (by Theor. XV). Therefore the particle A sustains all the pressures AH, BI, CK, DL, &c., proceeding *in infinitum*; and the particle B sustains the pressures of all but the first AH; and the particle C all but the two first AH, BI; and so on: and therefore the density AH of the first particle A is to the density BI of the second particle B as the

sum of all AH + BI + CK + DL, *in infinitum*, to the sum of all BI + CK + DL, &c. And BI the density of the second particle B is to CK the density of the third C, as the sum of all BI + CK + DL, &c., to the sum of all CK + DL, &c. Therefore these sums

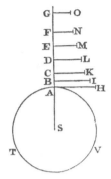

are proportional to their differences AH, BI, CK, &c., and therefore continually proportional (by Lem. I of this Book); and therefore the differences AH, BI, CK, &c., proportional to the sums, are also continually proportional. Wherefore since the densities in the places A, B, C, &c., are as AH, BI, CK, &c., they will also be continually proportional. Proceed intermissively, and, *ex aequo*, at the distances SA, SC, SE, continually proportional, the densities AH, CK, EM will be continually proportional. And by the same reasoning, at any distances SA, SD, SG, continually proportional, the densities AH, DL, GO, will be continually proportional. Let now the points A, B, C, D, E, &c., coincide, so that the progression of the specific gravities from the bottom A to the top of the fluid may be made continual; and at any distances SA, SD, SG, continually proportional, the densities AH, DL, GO, being all along continually proportional, will still remain continually proportional.   Q.E.D.

COR. Hence if the density of the fluid in two places, as A and E, be given, its density in any other place Q may be collected. With the centre S, and the rectangular asymptotes SQ, SX, describe an hyperbola cutting the perpendiculars AH, EM, QT in *a, e,* and *q,* as also the perpendiculars HX, MY, TZ, let fall upon the asypmtote SX, in *h, m,* and *t.* Make the area

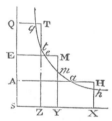

Y*mt*Z to the given area Y*mh*X as the given area E*eq*Q to the given area E*ea*A; and the line Z*t* produced will cut off the line Q*t* proportional to the density. For if the lines SA, SE, SQ are continually proportional, the areas E*eq*Q, E*ea*A will be equal, and thence the areas Y*mt*Z, X*hm*Y, proportional to them, will be also equal: and the lines SX, SY, SZ, that is, AH, EM, QT continually proportional, as they ought to be. And if the lines SA, SE, SQ, obtain any other order in the series of continued proportionals, the lines AH, EM, QT, because of the proportional hyperbolic areas, will obtain the same order in another series of quantities continually proportional.

PROPOSITION XXII. THEOREM XVII.

LET THE DENSITY OF ANY FLUID BE PROPORTIONAL TO THE COM-
PRESSION, AND ITS PARTS BE ATTRACTED DOWNWARDS BY A GRAVI-
TATION RECIPROCALLY PROPORTIONAL TO THE SQUARES OF THE
DISTANCES FROM THE CENTRE : I SAY, THAT IF THE DISTANCES BE
TAKEN IN HARMONIC PROGRESSION, THE DENSITIES OF THE FLUID
AT THOSE DISTANCES WILL BE IN A GEOMETRICAL PROGRESSION.

Let S denote the centre, and SA, SB, SC, SD, SE, the distances in F geometrical progression. Erect the perpendiculars AH, BI, CK, &c., which shall be as the densities of the fluid in the places A, B, C, D, E, &c., and the specific gravities thereof in those places will be as $\frac{AH}{SA^2}$, $\frac{BI}{SB^2}$, $\frac{CK}{SC^2}$, &c. Suppose these gravities to be uniformly

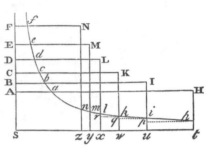

continued, the first from A to B, the second from B to C, the third from C to D, &c. And these drawn into the altitudes AD, BC, CD, DE, &c., or, which is the same thing, into the distances SA, SB, SC, &c., proportional to those altitudes, will give $\frac{AH}{SA}$, $\frac{BI}{SB}$, $\frac{CK}{SC}$, &c., the

exponents of the pressures. Therefore since the densities are as the sums of those pressures, the differences AH - BI, BI - CK, &c., of the densities will be as the differences of those sums $\frac{AH}{SA}$, $\frac{BI}{SB}$, $\frac{CK}{SC}$, &c. With the centre S, and the asymptotes SA, Sx, describe any hyperbola, cutting the perpendiculars AH, BI, CK, &c., in a, b, c, &c., and the perpendiculars Ht, Iu, Kw, let fall upon the asymptote Sx, in h, i, k; and the differences of the densities tu, uw, &c, will be as $\frac{AH}{SA}$,

$\frac{BI}{SB}$, &c. And the rectangles tu x th, uw x ui, &c., or tp, uq, &c., as $\frac{AH \times th}{SA}$, $\frac{BI \times ui}{SB}$ &c., that is, as Aa, Bb, &c. For, by the nature of the hyperbola, SA is to AH or St as th to Aa, and therefore $\frac{AH \times th}{SA}$ is equal to Aa. And, by a like reasoning, $\frac{BI \times ui}{SB}$ is equal to Bb,&c. But Aa, Bb, Cc, &c., are continually proportional, and therefore proportional to their differences Aa − Bb, Bb − Cc, &c., therefore the rectangles tp, ug, &c., are proportional to those differences; as also the sums of the rectangles tp + uq, or tp + uq + wr to the sums of the differences Aa − Cc or Aa − Dd. Suppose several of these terms and the sum of all the differences, as Aa − Ff, will be proportional to the sum of all the rectangles, as zthn. Increase the number of terms, and diminish the distances of the points A, B, C; &c., in infinitum, and those rectangles will become equal to the hyperbolic area zthn, and therefore the difference Aa − Ff is proportional to this area. Take now any distances, as SA, SD, SF, in harmonic progression, and the differences Aa − Dd, Dd − Ff will be equal; and therefore the areas thlx, xlnz, proportional to those differences will be equal among themselves, and the densities St, Sx, Sz, that is, AH, DI, FN, continually proportional. Q.E.D.

CoR. Hence if any two densities of the fluid, as AH and BI, be given, the area thiu, answering to their difference tu, will be given; and thence the density FN will be found at any height SF, by talking the area thnz to that given area thiu as the difference Aa - Ff to the difference Aa - Bb.

SCHOLIUM.

By a like reasoning it may be proved, that if the gravity of the particles of a fluid be diminished in a triplicate ratio of the distances from the centre; and the reciprocals of the squares of the distances SA, SB, SC, &c., (namely, $\frac{SA^3}{SA^2}, \frac{SA^3}{SB^2}, \frac{SA^3}{SC^2}$) be taken in an

arithmetical progression, the densities AH, BI, CK, &c., will be in a geometrical progression. And if the gravity be diminished in a quadruplicate ratio of the distances, and the reciprocals of the cubes of the distances (as $\frac{SA^4}{SA^3}, \frac{SA^4}{SB^3}, \frac{SA^4}{SC^3}$, &c.,) be taken in

arithmetical progression, the densities AH, BI, CK, &c., will be in geometrical progression. And so *in infinitum*. Again; if the gravity of the particles of the fluid be the same at all distances, and the distances be in arithmetical progression, the densities will be in a geometrical progression as Dr. Halley has found. If the gravity be as the distance, and the squares of the distances be in arithmetical progression, the densities will be in geometrical progression. And so *in infinitum*. These things will be so, when the density of the fluid condensed by compression is as the force of compression; or, which is the same thing, when the space possessed by the fluid is reciprocally as this force. Other laws of condensation may be supposed, as that the cube of the compressing force may be as the biquadrate of the density; or the triplicate ratio of the force the same with the quadruplicate ratio of the density : in which case, if the gravity be reciprocally as the square of the distance from the centre, the density will be reciprocally as the cube of the distance. Suppose that the cube of the compressing force be as the quadrato-cube of the density; and if the gravity be reciprocally as the square of the distance, the density will be reciprocally in a sesquiplicate ratio of the distance. Suppose the compressing force to be in a duplicate ratio of the density, and the gravity reciprocally in a duplicate ratio of the distance, and the density will be reciprocally as the distance. To run over all the cases that might be offered would be tedious. But as to our own air, this is certain from experiment, that its density is either accurately, or very nearly at least, as the compressing force; and therefore the density of the air in the atmosphere of the earth is as the weight of the whole incumbent air, that is, as the height of the mercury in the barometer.

PROPOSITION XXIII. THEOREM XVIII.

IF A FLUID BE COMPOSED OF PARTICLES MUTUALLY FLYING
EACH OTHER, AND THE DENSITY BE AS THE COMPRESSION, THE

CENTRIFUGAL FORCES OF THE PARTICLES WILL BE
RECIPROCALLY PROPORTIONAL TO THE DISTANCES OF THEIR
CENTRES. AND, VICE VERSA, PARTICLES FLYING EACH OTHER,
WITH FORCES THAT ARE RECIPROCALLY PROPORTIONAL TO THE
DISTANCES OF THEIR CENTRES, COMPOSE AN ELASTIC FLUID,
WHOSE DENSITY IS AS THE COMPRESSION.

Let the fluid be supposed to be included in a cubic space ACE, and then to be reduced by compression into a lesser cubic space *ace*; and the distances of the particles retaining a like situation with respect to each other in both the spaces, will be as the sides AB, *ab* of the cubes; and the densities of the mediums will be reciprocally as the containing spaces AB^3, ab^3. In the plane side of the greater cube ABCD take the square DP equal to the plane side *db* of the lesser cube : and, by the supposition, the pressure with which the square DP urges the inclosed fluid will be to the pressure with which that square *db* urges the inclosed fluid as the densities of the mediums are to each other, that is, as ab^3 to AB^3. But the pressure with which the square DB urges the included fluid is to the pressure with which the square DP urges the same fluid as the square DB to the square DP, that is, as AB^2 to ab^2. Therefore, *ex aequo*, the pressure

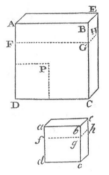

with which the square DB urges the fluid is to the pressure with which the square *db* urges the fluid as *ab* to AB. Let the planes FGH, *fgh*, be drawn through the middles of the two cubes, and divide the fluid into two parts. These parts will press each other mutu-
ally with the same forces with which they are themselves pressed by the planes AC, *ac*, that is, in the proportion of *ab* to AB: and therefore the centrifugal forces by which these pressures are sustained are in the same ratio. The number of the particles being equal, and the situation alike, in both cubes, the forces which all the particles exert, according to the planes FGH, *fgh*, upon all, are as the forces which each exerts on each. Therefore the forces which each exerts on each, according to the plane FGH in the greater cube, are to the forces which each exerts on each, according to the plane *fgh* in the lesser cube, as *ab* to AB, that is, reciprocally as the distances of the particles from each other.   Q.E.D.

And, *vice versa*, if the forces of the single particles are reciprocally as the distances, that is, reciprocally as the sides of the cubes AB, *ab*; the sums of the forces will be in the same ratio, and the pressures of the sides DB, *db* as the sum of the forces; and the pressure of the square DP to the pressure of the side DB as ab^2 to AB^2. And, *ex aequo*, the pressure of the square DP to the pressure of the side *db* as ab^3 to AB^3; that is, the force of compression in the one to the force of compression in the other as the density in the former to the density in the latter.   Q.E.D.

SCHOLIUM.

By a like reasoning, if the centrifugal forces of the particles are reciprocally in the duplicate ratio of the distances between the centres, the cubes of the compressing forces will be as the biquadrates of the densities. If the centrifugal forces be reciprocally in the triplicate or quadruplicate ratio of the distances, the cubes of the compressing forces will be as the quadrato-cubes, or cubo-cubes of the densities. And universally, if D be put for the distance, and E for the density of the compressed fluid, and the centrifugal forces be reciprocally as any power D^n of the distance, whose index is the number n, the compressing forces will be as the cube roots of the power E^{n+2}, whose index is the number $n + 2$; and the contrary. All these things are to be understood of particles whose centrifugal forces terminate in those particles that are next them, or are diffused not much further. We have an example of this in magnetical bodies. Their attractive virtue is terminated nearly in bodies of their own kind that are next them. The virtue of the magnet is contracted by the interposition of an iron plate, and is almost terminated at it: for bodies further off are not attracted by the magnet so much as by the iron plate. If in this manner particles repel others of their own kind that lie next them, but do not exert their virtue on the more remote, particles of this kind will compose such fluids as are treated of in this Proposition. If the virtue of any particle diffuse itself every way *in infinitum*, there will be required a greater force to produce an equal condensation of a greater quantity of the fluid. But whether elastic fluids do really consist of particles so repelling each other, is a physical question. We have here demonstrated mathematically the property of fluids consisting of particles of this kind, that hence philosophers may take occasion to discuss that question.

SECTION VI.

Of the motion and resistance of funependulous bodies.

PROPOSITION XXIV. THEOREM XIX.

THE QUANTITIES OF MATTER IN FUNEPENDULOUS BODIES, WHOSE CENTRES OF OSCILLATION, ARE EQUALLY DISTANT FROM THE CENTRE OF SUSPENSION, ARE IN A RATIO COMPOUNDED OF THE RATIO OF THE WEIGHTS AND THE DUPLICATE RATIO OF THE TIMES OF THE OSCILLATIONS IN VACUO.

For the velocity which a given force can generate in a given matter in a given time is as the force and the time directly, and the matter inversely. The greater the force or the time is, or the less the matter, the greater velocity will be generated. This is manifest from the second Law of Motion. Now if pendulums are of the same length, the

motive forces in places equally distant from the perpendicular are as the weights: and therefore if two bodies by oscillating describe equal arcs, and those arcs are divided into equal parts; since the times in which the bodies describe each of the correspondent parts of the arcs are as the times of the whole oscillations, the velocities in the correspondent parts of the oscillations will be to each other as the motive forces and the whole times of the oscillations directly, and the quantities of matter reciprocally: and therefore the quantities of matter are as the forces and the times of the oscillations directly and the velocities reciprocally. But the velocities reciprocally are as the times, and therefore the times directly and the velocities reciprocally are as the squares of the times; and therefore the quantities of matter are as the motive forces and the squares of the times, that is, as the weights and the squares of the times.   Q.E.D.

COR. 1. Therefore if the times are equal, the quantities of matter in each of the bodies are as the weights.

COR. 2. If the weights are equal, the quantities of matter will be as the squares of the times.

COR. 3. If the quantities of matter are equal, the weights will be reciprocally as the squares of the times.

COR. 4. Whence since the squares of the times, *caeteris paribus*, are as the lengths of the pendulums, therefore if both the times and quantities of matter are equal, the weights will be as the lengths of the pendulums.

COR. 5. And universally, the quantity of matter in the pendulous body is as the weight and the square of the time directly, and the length of the pendulum inversely.

COR. 6. But in a non-resisting medium, the quantity of matter in the pendulous body is as the comparative weight and the square of the time directly, and the length of the pendulum inversely. For the comparative weight is the motive force of the body in any heavy medium, as was shewn above; and therefore does the same thing in such a non-resisting medium as the absolute weight does in a vacuum.

COR. 7. And hence appears a method both of comparing bodies one among another, as to the quantity of matter in each; and of comparing the weights of the same body in different places, to know the variation of its gravity. And by experiments made with the greatest accuracy, I have always found the quantity of matter in bodies to be proportional to their weight.

PROPOSITION XXV. THEOREM XX.

FUNEPENDULOUS BODIES THAT ARE, IN ANY MEDIUM,
RESISTED IN THE RATIO OF THE MOMENTS OF TIME, AND
FUNEPENDULOUS BODIES THAT MOVE IN A NON-RESISTING
MEDIUM OF THE SAME SPECIFIC GRAVITY, PERFORM THEIR
OSCILLATIONS IN A CYCLOID IN THE SAME TIME, AND
DESCRIBE PROPORTIONAL PARTS OF ARCS TOGETHER.

Let AB be an arc of a cycloid, which a body D, by vibrating in a non-resisting medium, shall describe in any time. Bisect that arc in C, so that C may be the lowest point thereof; and the accelerative force with which the body is urged in any place D, or *d* or E will be as the length of the arc CD, or C*d*, or CE. Let that force be expressed by that same arc; and since the resistance is as the moment of the time, and therefore given, let it be expressed by the given part CO of the cycloidal arc, and take the arc O*d*

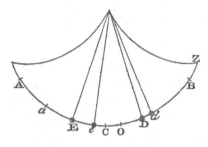

in the same ratio to the arc CD that the arc OB has to the arc CB: and the force with which the body in *d* is urged in a resisting medium, being the excess of the force C*d* above the resistance CO, will be expressed by the arc O*d*, and will therefore be to the force with which the body D is urged in a non-resisting medium in the place D, as the arc O*d* to the arc CD; and therefore also in the place B, as the arc OB to the arc CB. Therefore if two bodies D, *d* go from the place B, and are urged by these forces; since the forces at the beginning are as the arc CB and OB, the first velocities and arcs first described will be in the same ratio. Let those area be BD and B*d*, and the remaining arcs CD, O*d*, will be in the same ratio. Therefore the forces, being proportional to those arcs CD, O*d*, will remain in the same ratio as at the beginning, and therefore the bodies will continue describing together arcs in the same ratio. Therefore the forces and velocities and the remaining arcs CD; O*d*, will be always as the whole arcs CB, OB, and therefore those remaining arcs will be described together. Therefore the two bodies D and *d* will arrive together at the places C and O; that which moves in the non-resisting medium, at the place C, and the other, in the resisting medium, at the place O. Now since the velocities in C and O are as the arcs CB, OB, the arcs which the bodies describe when they go farther will be in the same ratio. Let those arcs be CE and O*e*. The force with which the body D in a non-resisting medium is retarded in E is as CE, and the force with which the body *d* in the resisting medium is retarded in *e*, is as the sum of the force C*e* and the resistance CO, that is, as O*e*; and therefore the forces with which the bodies are retarded are as the arcs CB, OB, proportional to the arcs CE, O*e*; and therefore the velocities, retarded in that given ratio, remain in the same given ratio. Therefore the velocities and the arcs described with those velocities are always to each other in that given ratio of the arcs CB and OB; and therefore if the entire arcs AB, *a*B are taken in the same ratio, the bodies D and *d* will describe those arcs together, and in the places A and *a* will lose all their motion together. Therefore the whole oscillations are isochronal, or are performed in equal times; and any parts of the arcs, as BD, B*d*, or BE, B*e*, that are described together, are proportional to the whole arcs BA, B*a*.   Q.E.D.

Cor. Therefore the swiftest motion in a resisting medium does not fall upon the lowest point C, but is found in that point O, in which the whole arc described B*a* is bisected. And the body, proceeding from thence to *a*, is retarded at the same rate with which it was accelerated before in its descent from B to O.

PROPOSITION XXVI. THEOREM XXI.

FUNEPENDULOUS BODIES, THAT ARE RESISTED IN THE RATIO OF THE VELOCITY, HAVE THEIR OSCILLATIONS IN A CYCLOID ISOCHRONAL.

For if two bodies, equally distant from their centres of suspension, describe, in oscillating, unequal arcs, and the velocities in the correspondent parts of the arcs be to each other as the whole arcs; the resistances, proportional to the velocities, will be also to each other as the same arcs. Therefore if these resistances be subducted from or added to the motive forces arising from gravity which are as the same arcs, the differences or sums will be to each other in the same ratio of the arcs; and since the increments and decrements of the velocities are as these differences or sums, the velocities will be always as the whole arcs; therefore if the velocities are in any one case as the whole arcs, they will remain always in the same ratio. But at the beginning of the motion, when the bodies begin to descend and describe those arcs, the forces, which at that time are proportional to the arcs, will generate velocities proportional to the arcs. Therefore the velocities will be always as the whole arcs to be described, and therefore those arcs will be described in the same time. Q.E.D.

PROPOSITION XXVII. THEOREM XXII.

IF FUNEPENDULOUS BODIES ARE RESISTED IN THE DUPLICATE RATIO OF THEIR VELOCITIES, THE DIFFERENCES BETWEEN THE TIMES OF THE OSCILLATIONS IN A RESISTING MEDIUM, AND THE TIMES OF THE OSCILLATIONS IN A NON-RESISTING MEDIUM OF THE SAME SPECIFIC GRAVITY, WILL BE PROPOR-TIONAL TO THE ARCS DESCRIBED IN OSCILLATING NEARLY.

For let equal pendulums in a resisting medium describe the unequal arcs A, B; and the resistance of the body in the arc A will be to the resistance of the body in the correspondent part of the arc B in the duplicate ratio of the velocities, that is, as AA to BB nearly. If the resistance in the arc B were to the resistance in the arc A as AB to AA, the times in the arcs A and B would be

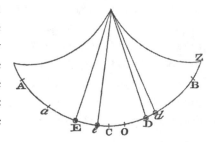

equal (by the last Prop.) Therefore the resistance AA in the arc A, or AB in the arc B, causes the excess of the time in the arc A above the time in a non-resisting medium; and the resistance BB causes the excess of the time in the arc B above the time in a non-resisting medium. But those excesses are as the efficient forces AB and BB nearly, that is, as the arcs A and B.   Q.E.D.

COR. 1. Hence from the times of the oscillations in unequal arcs in a resisting medium, may be known the times of the oscillations in a non-resisting medium of the same specific gravity. For the difference of the times will be to the excess of the time in the lesser arc above the time in a non-resisting medium as the difference of the arcs to the lesser arc.

COR. 2. The shorter oscillations are more isochronal, and very short ones are performed nearly in the same times as in a non-resisting medium. But the times of those which are performed in greater arcs are a little greater, because the resistance in the descent of the body, by which the time is prolonged, is greater, in proportion to the length described in the descent than the resistance in the subsequent ascent, by which the time is contracted. But the time of the oscillations, both short and long, seems to be prolonged in some measure by the motion of the medium. For retarded bodies are resisted somewhat less in proportion to the velocity, and accelerated bodies somewhat more than those that proceed uniformly forwards; because the medium, by the motion it has received from the bodies, going forwards the same way with them, is more agitated in the former case, and less in the latter; and so conspires more or less with the bodies moved. Therefore it resists the pendulums in their descent more, and in their ascent less, than in proportion to the velocity; and these two causes concurring prolong the time.

PROPOSITION XXVIII. THEOREM XXIII.

IF A FUNEPENDULOUS BODY, OSCILLATING IN A CYCLOID, BE
RESISTED IN THE RATIO OF THE MOMENTS OF THE TIME, ITS
RESISTANCE WILL BE TO THE FORCE OF GRAVITY AS THE EXCESS
OF THE ARC DESCRIBED IN THE WHOLE DESCENT ABOVE THE
ARC DESCRIBED IN THE SUBSEQUENT ASCENT TO TWICE THE
LENGTH OF THE PENDULUM.

Let BC represent the arc described in the descent, Ca the arc described in the ascent, and Aa the difference of the axes : and things remaining as they were constructed and demonstrated in Prop. XXV, the force with which the oscillating body is urged in any place D will be to the force of resistance as the arc CD to the arc CO,

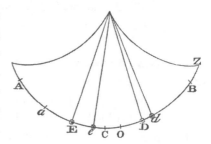

which is half of that difference A*a*. Therefore the force with which the oscillating body is urged at the beginning or the highest point of the cycloid, that is, the force of gravity, will be to the resistance as the arc of the cycloid, between that highest point and lowest point C, is to the arc M; that is (doubling those arcs), as the whole cycloidal arc, or twice the length of the pendulum, to the arc A*a*.   Q.E.D.

PROPOSITION XXIX. PROBLEM VI.

SUPPOSING THAT A BODY OSCILLATING IN A CYCLOID IS RESISTED IN A DUPLICATE RATIO OF THE VELOCITY: TO FIND THE RESISTANCE IN EACH PLACE.

Let B*a* be an arc described in one entire oscillation, C the lowest point of the cycloid, and CZ half the whole cycloidal arc, equal to the length of the pendulum; and

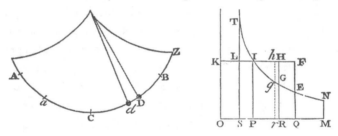

let it be required to find the resistance of the body in any place D. Cut the indefinite right line OQ in the points O, S, P, Q, so that (erecting the perpendiculars OK, ST, PI, QE, and with the centre O, and the aysmptotes OK, OQ, describing the hyperbola TIGE cutting the perpendiculars ST, PI, QE in T, I, and E, and through the point I drawing KF, parallel to the asymptote OQ, meeting the asymptote OK in K, and the perpendiculars ST and QE in L and F) the hyperbolic area PIEQ may be to the hyperbolic area PITS as the arc BC, described in the descent of the body, to the arc C*a* described in the ascent; and that the area IEF may be to the area ILT as OQ to OS. Then with the perpendicular MN cut off the hyperbolic area PINM, and let that area be to the hyperbolic area PIEQ as the arc CZ to the arc BC described in the descent. And if the perpendicular. RG cut off the hyperbolic area PIGR, which shall be to the area PIEQ as any arc CD to the arc BC described in the whole descent, the resistance in any place D will be to the force of gravity as the area $\frac{OR}{OQ}$ IEF – IGH to the area PINM.

For since the forces arising from gravity with which the body is urged in the places Z, B, D, *a*, are as the arcs CZ, CB, CD, C*a* and those arcs are as the areas PINM, PIFQ, PIGR, PITS; let those areas be the exponents both of the arcs and of the forces respectively. Let D*d* be a very small space described by the body in its descent: and let it be expressed by the very small area RG*gr* comprehended between the parallels RG,

rg; and produce rg to h, so that GHhg and RGgr may be the contemporaneous decrements of the areas IGH, PIGR. And the increment $\text{GH}hg - \frac{Rr}{OQ}\text{IEF}$, or $Rr \times \text{HG} - \frac{Rr}{OQ}\text{IEF}$, of the area $\frac{OR}{OQ}\text{IEF} - \text{IGH}$ will be to the decrement RGgr, or $Rr \times$ RG, of the area PIGR, as $\text{HG} - \frac{\text{IEF}}{OQ}$ to RG; and therefore as $\text{OR} \times \text{HG} - \frac{OR}{OQ}\text{IEF}$ to OR x GR or OP x PI, that is (because of the equal quantities OR x HG, OR x HR - OR x GR, ORHK - OPIK, PIHR and PIGR + IGH), as $\text{PIGR} + \text{IGH} - \frac{OR}{OQ}\text{IEF}$ to OPIK. Therefore if the area $\frac{OR}{OQ}\text{IEF} - \text{IGH}$ be called Y, and RGgr the decrement of the area PIGR be given, the increment of the area Y will be as PIGR – Y.

Then if V represent the force arising from the gravity, proportional to the arc CD to be described, by which the body is acted upon in D, and R be put for the resistance, V - R will be the whole force with which the body is urged in D. Therefore the increment of the velocity is as V - R and the particle of time in which it is generated conjunctly. But the velocity itself is as the contemporaneous increment of the space described directly and the same particle of time inversely. Therefore, since the resistance is, by the supposition, as the square of the velocity, the increment of the resistance will (by Lem. II) be as the velocity and the increment of the velocity conjunctly, that is, as the moment of the space and V - R conjunctly; and, therefore, if the moment of the space be given, as V - R; that is, if for the force V we put its exponent PIGR, and the resistance R be expressed by any other area Z, as PIGR – Z.

Therefore the area PIGR uniformly decreasing by the subduction of given moments, the area Y increases in proportion of PIGR - Y, and the area Z in proportion of PIGR – Z. And therefore if the areas Y and Z begin together, and at the beginning are equal, these, by the addition of equal moments, will continue to be equal; and in like manner decreasing by equal moments, will vanish together. And, *vice versa*, if they together begin and vanish, they will have equal moments and be always equal; and that, because if the resistance Z be augmented, the velocity together with the arc Ca, described in the ascent of the body, will be diminished; and the point in which all the motion together with the resistance ceases coming nearer to the point C, the resistance vanishes sooner than the area Y. And the contrary will happen when the resistance is diminished.

Now the area Z begins and ends where the resistance is nothing, that is, at the beginning of the motion where the arc CD is equal to the arc CB, and the right line RG falls upon the right line QE; and at the end of the motion where the arc CD is equal to the arc Ca, and RG falls upon the right line ST. And the area Y or $\frac{OR}{OQ}\text{IEF} - \text{IGH}$

begins and ends also where the resistance is nothing, and therefore where $\frac{OR}{OQ}$ IEF and IGH are equal; that is (by the construction), where the right line RG falls successively

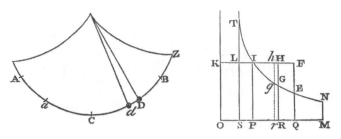

upon the right lines QE and ST. Therefore those areas begin and vanish together, and are therefore always equal. Therefore the area $\frac{OR}{OQ}$ IEF − IGH is equal to the area Z, by

which the resistance is expressed, and therefore is to the area, PINM, by which the gravity is expressed, as the resistance to the gravity.   Q.E.D.

COR. 1. Therefore the resistance in the lowest place C is to the force of gravity as the area $\frac{OP}{OQ}$ IEF to the area PINM.

COR. 2. But it becomes greatest where the area PIHR is to the area IEF as OR to OQ. For in that case its moment (that is, PIGR − Y) becomes nothing.

COR. 3. Hence also may be known the velocity in each place, as being in the subduplicate ratio of the resistance, and at the beginning of the motion equal to the velocity of the body oscillating in the same cycloid without any resistance.

However, by reason of the difficulty of the calculation by which the resistance and the velocity are found by this Proposition, we have thought fit to subjoin the Proposition following.

PROPOSITION XXX. THEOREM XXIV.

IF A RIGHT LINE AB BE EQUAL TO THE ARC OF A CYCLOID
WHICH AN OSCILLATING BODY DESCRIBES, AND AT EACH OF
ITS POINTS D THE PERPENDICULARS DK BE ERECTED,
WHICH SHALL BE TO THE LENGTH OF THE PENDULUM AS
THE RESISTANCE OF THE BODY IN THE CORRESPONDING
POINTS OF THE ARC TO THE FORCE OF GRAVITY; I SAY, THAT
THE DIFFERENCE BETWEEN THE ARC DESCRIBED IN THE
WHOLE DESCENT AND THE ARC DESCRIBED IN THE WHOLE

SUBSEQUENT ASCENT DRAWN INTO HALF THE SUM OF THE SAME ARCS WILL BE EQUAL TO THE AREA BKa WHICH ALL THOSE PERPENDICULARS TAKE UP.

Let the arc of the cycloid, described in one entire oscillation, be expressed by the right line *a*B, equal to it, and the arc which would have been described *in vacuo* by the length AB. Bisect AB in C, and the point C will represent the lowest point of the cycloid, and CD will be as the force arising from gravity, with which the body in D is urged in the direction of the tangent of the cycloid, and will have the same ratio to the length of the pendulum as the force in D has to the force of gravity. Let that force, therefore, be expressed by that length CD, and the force of gravity by the length of the pendulum; and if in DE you take DK in the same ratio to the length of the pendulum as the resistance has to the gravity, DK will lie the exponent of the resistance. From the centre C with the interval CA or CB describe a semi-circle BE*e*A. Let the body describe, in the least time, the space D*d*; and, erecting the perpendiculars DE, *de*, meeting the circumference in E and *e*, they will be as the velocities which the body descending *in vacuo* from the point B would acquire in the places D and *d*. This appears by Prop. LII, Book I. Let therefore, these velocities be expressed by those perpendiculars DE, *de*; and let DF be the velocity which it acquires in D by falling from B in the resisting medium. And if from the centre C with the interval CF we describe the circle F*f*M meeting the right lines *de* and AB in *f* and M, then M will be the place to which it would thenceforward, without farther resistance, ascend, and *df* the velocity it would acquire in *d*. Whence, also, if F*g* represents the moment of the velocity which the body D, in describing the least space D*d*, loses by the resistance of the medium; and CN be taken equal to C*g*, then will N be the place to which the body, if it met no farther resistance, would thenceforward ascend, and MN will be the decrement of the ascent arising from the loss of that velocity. Draw F*m* perpendicular to *df*, and the decrement F*g* of the velocity DF generated by the resistance DK will be to the increment *fm* of the same velocity, generated by the force CD, as the generating force DK to the generating force CD. But because of the similar triangles F*mf*, F*hg*, FDC, *fm* is to F*m* or D*d* as CD to DF; and, *ex aequo*, F*g* to D*d* as DK to DF. Also F*h* is to F*g*, as DF to CF; and, *ex aequo perturbate*, F*h* or MN to D*d* as DK to CF or CM; and therefore the sum of all the MN × CM will be equal to the sum of all the D*d* × DK. At the moveable point M suppose always a rectangular ordinate erected equal to the indeterminate CM, which by a continual motion is drawn into the whole length A*a*; and the trapezium described by that motion, or its equal, the rectangle A*a* × $\frac{1}{2}$*a*B, will be equal to the sum of all the MN x CM, and therefore to the sum of all the D*d* x DK, that is, to the area BKVT*a*. Q.E.D.

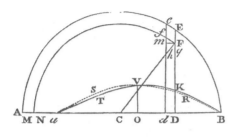

COR. Hence from the law of resistance, and the difference Aa of the arcs Ca, CB, may be collected the proportion of the resistance to the gravity nearly.

For if the resistance DK be uniform, the figure BKTa will be a rectangle under Ba and DK; and thence the rectangle under $\frac{1}{2}$ Ba and Aa will be equal to the rectangle

under Ba and DK, and DK will be equal to $\frac{1}{2}$ Aa. Wherefore since DK is the exponent of the resistance, and the length of the pendulum the exponent of the gravity, the resistance will be to the gravity as $\frac{1}{2}$ Aa to the length of the pendulum; altogether as in Prop. XXVIII is demonstrated.

If the resistance be as the velocity, the figure BKTa will be nearly an ellipsis. For if a body, in a non-resisting medium, by one entire oscillation, should describe the length BA, the velocity in any place D would be as the ordinate DE of the circle described on the diameter AB. Therefore since Ba in the resisting medium, and BA in the non-resisting one, are described nearly in the same times; and therefore the velocities in each of the points of Ba are to the velocities in the correspondent points of the length BA nearly as Ba is to BA, the velocity in the point D in the resisting medium will be as the ordinate of the circle or ellipsis described upon the diameter Ba; and therefore the figure BKVTa will be nearly an ellipsis. Since the resistance is supposed proportional to the velocity, let OV be the exponent of the resistance in the middle point O; and an ellipsis BRVSa described with the centre O, and the semiaxes OB, OV, will be nearly equal to the figure BKVTa, and to its equal the rectangle Aa x BO. Therefore Aa x BO is to OV x BO as the area of this ellipsis to OV x BO; that is, Aa is to OV as the area of the semi-circle to the square of the radius, or as 11 to 7 nearly; and, therefore, $\frac{7}{11}$ Aa is to the length of the pendulum as the resistance of the oscillating body in O to its gravity.

Now if the resistance DK be in the duplicate ratio of the velocity, the figure BKVTa will be almost a parabola having V for its vertex and OV for its axis, and therefore will be nearly equal to the rectangle under $\frac{2}{3}$ Ba and OV. Therefore the rectangle

under $\frac{1}{2}$ Ba and Aa is equal to the rectangle $\frac{2}{3}$ Ba x OV, and therefore OV is equal to

$\frac{3}{4}$ Aa; and therefore the resistance in O made to the oscillating body is to its gravity as

$\frac{3}{4}$ Aa to the length of the pendulum.

And I take these conclusions to be accurate enough for practical uses. For since an ellipsis or parabola BRVSa falls in with the figure BKVTa in the middle point V, that figure, if greater towards the part BRV or VSa than the other, is less towards the contrary part, and is therefore nearly equal to it.

PROPOSITION XXXI. THEOREM XXV.

If the resistance made to an oscillating body in each of the proportional parts of the arcs described be augmented or diminished in a given ratio, the difference between the are described in the descent and the arc described in the subsequent ascent will be augmented or diminished in the same ratio.

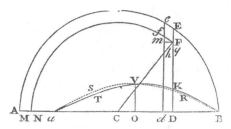

For that difference arises from the retardation of the pendulum by the resistance of the medium, and therefore is as the whole retardation and the retarding resistance proportional thereto. In the foregoing Proposition the rectangle under the right line $\frac{1}{2}$ aB and the difference Aa of the arcs CB, Ca, was equal to the area BKTa. And that area, if the length aB remains, is augmented or diminished in the ratio of the ordinates DK; that is, in the ratio of the resistance and is therefore as the length aB and the resistance conjunctly. And therefore the rectangle under Aa and $\frac{1}{2}$ aB is as aB and the resistance conjunctly, and therefore Aa is as the resistance.　　Q.E.D.

Cor. 1. Hence if the resistance be as the velocity, the difference of the arcs in the same medium will be as the whole arc described: and the contrary.

Cor. 2. If the resistance be in the duplicate ratio of the velocity, that difference will be in the duplicate ratio of the whole arc: and the contrary.

Cor. 3. And universally, if the resistance be in the triplicate or any other ratio of the velocity, the difference will be in the same ratio of the whole arc: and the contrary.

Cor. 4. If the resistance be partly in the simple ratio of the velocity, and partly in the duplicate ratio of the same, the difference will be partly in the ratio of the whole arc, and partly in the duplicate ratio of it: and the contrary. So that the law and ratio of the resistance will be the same for the velocity as the law and ratio,of that difference for the length of the arc.

Cor. 5. And therefore if a pendulum describe successively unequal arcs, and we can find the ratio of the increment or decrement of this difference for the length of the arc described, there will be had also the ratio of the increment or decrement of the resistance for a greater or less velocity.

GENERAL SCHOLIUM.

From these propositions we may find the resistance of mediums by pendulums oscillating therein. I found the resistance of the air by the following experiments. I suspended

a wooden globe or ball weighing $57^7/_{22}$ ounces troy, its diameter $6^7/_8$ *London* inches, by a fine thread on a firm hook, so that the distance between the hook and the centre of oscillation of the globe was $10^1/_2$ feet. I marked on the thread a point 10 feet and 1 inch distant from the centre of suspension; and even with that point I placed a ruler divided into inches, by the help whereof I observed the lengths of the arcs described by the pendulum. Then I numbered the oscillations in which the globe would lose $^1/_8$ part of its motion. If the pendulum was drawn aside from the perpendicular to the distance of 2 inches, and thence let go, so that in its whole descent it described an arc of 2 inches, and in the first whole oscillation, compounded of the descent and subsequent ascent, an arc of almost 4 inches, the same in 164 oscillations lost $^1/_8$ part of its motion, so as in its last ascent to describe an arc of $1^3/_4$ inches. If in the first descent it described an arc of 4 inches, it lost $^1/_8$ part of its motion in 121 oscillations, so as in its last ascent to describe an arc of $3^1/_2$ inches. If in the first descent it described an arc of 8, 16, 32, or 64 inches, it lost $^1/_8$ part of its motion in 69, $35^1/_2$, $18^1/_2$, $9^2/_3$ oscillations, respectively. Therefore the difference between the arcs described in the first descent and the last ascent was in the 1st, 2d, 3d, 4th, 5th, 6th cases, $^1/_4$, $^1/_2$, 1, 2, 4, 8 inches respectively. Divide those differences by the number of oscillations in each case, and in one mean oscillation, wherein an arc of $3^3/_4$, $7^1/_2$, 15, 30, 60, 120 inches was described, the difference of the arcs described in the descent and subsequent ascent will be $^1/_{656}$, $^1/_{242}$, $^1/_{69}$, $^4/_{71}$, $^8/_{37}$, $^{24}/_{29}$ parts of an inch, respectively. But these differences in the greater oscillations are in the duplicate ratio of the arcs described nearly, but in lesser oscillations something greater than in that ratio; and therefore (by Cor. 2, Prop. XXXI of this Book) the resistance of the globe, when it moves very swift, is in the duplicate ratio of the velocity, nearly; and when it moves slowly, somewhat greater than in that ratio.

Now let V represent the greatest velocity in any oscillation, and let A, B, and C be given quantities, and let us suppose the difference of the arcs to be $\text{AV} + \text{BV}^2 + \text{CV}^2$. Since the greatest velocities are in the cycloid as $^1/_2$ the arcs described in oscillating, and in the circle as $^1/_2$ the chords of those arcs; and therefore in equal arcs are greater in the cycloid than in the circle in the ratio of $^1/_2$ the arcs to their chords; but the times in the circle are greater than in the cycloid, in a reciprocal ratio of the velocity; it is plain that the differences of the arcs (which are as the resistance and the square of the time conjunctly) are nearly the same in both curves: for in the cycloid those differences must be on the one hand augmented, with the resistance, in about the duplicate ratio of the arc to the chord, because of the velocity augmented in the simple ratio of the same; and on the other hand diminished, with the square of the time in the same duplicate ratio. Therefore to reduce these observations to the cycloid, we must take the same differences of the arcs as were observed in the circle, and suppose the greatest velocities analogous

to the half, or the whole arcs, that is, to the numbers $^1/_2$, 1, 2, 4, 8, 16. Therefore in the 2d, 4th, and 6th cases, put 1, 4, and 16 for V; and the difference of the arcs in the 2d case will become $\dfrac{\frac{1}{2}}{121} = A + B + C$; in the 4th case, $\dfrac{\frac{2}{1}}{352} = 4A + 8B + 16C$;

in the 6th case, $\dfrac{\frac{8}{2}}{9^3} = 16A + 64B + 256C$. These equations reduced give A =

0,0000916, B = 0,0010847, and C = 0,0029558. Therefore the difference of the arcs is as $0,\,0000916,\ V\ =\ 0,\,0010847V^{\frac{3}{2}}\ +\ 0,\,0029558V^2$: and therefore since (by Cor. Prop.

XXX, applied to this case) the resistance of the globe in the middle of the arc described in oscillating, where the velocity is V, is to its weight as $\dfrac{7}{11}AV + \dfrac{7}{10}BV^{\frac{3}{2}} + \dfrac{3}{4}CV^2$ to

the length of the pendulum, if for A, B, and C you put the numbers found, the resistance of the globe will be to its weight as $0,0000583V + 0,0007593V^{\frac{3}{2}} + 0,0022169V^2$ to

the length of the pendulum between the centre of suspension and the ruler, that is, to 121 inches. Therefore since V in the second case represents 1, in the 4th case 4, and in the 6th case 16, the resistance will be to the weight of the globe, in the 2d case, as 0,0030345 to 121; in the 4th, as 0,041748 to 121; in the 6th, as 0,61705 to 121.

The arc, which the point marked in the thread described in the 6th case, was of $121 - \dfrac{8}{9\frac{2}{3}}$, or 119 $^5/_{29}$ inches. And therefore since the radius was 121 inches, and the

length of the pendulum between the point of suspension and the centre of the globe was 126 inches, the arc which the centre of the globe described was 124 $^3/_{31}$ inches. Because the greatest velocity of the oscillating body, by reason of the resistance of the air, does not fall on the lowest point of the arc described, but near the middle place of the whole arc, this velocity will be nearly the same as if the globe in its whole descent in a non-resisting medium should describe 62 $^3/_{62}$ inches, the half of that arc, and that in a cycloid, to which we have above reduced the motion of the pendulum; and therefore that velocity will be equal to that which the globe would acquire by falling perpendicularly from a height equal to the versed sine of that arc. But that versed sine in the cycloid is to that are 62 $^3/_{62}$ as the same arc to twice the length of the pendulum 252, and therefore equal to 15,278 inches. Therefore the velocity of the pendulum is the same which a body would acquire by falling, and in its fall describing a space of 15,278 inches. Therefore with such a velocity the globe meets with a resistance which is to its weight as 0,61705 to 121, or (if we take that part only of the resistance which is in the duplicate ratio of the velocity) as 0,56752 to 121.

I found, by an hydrostatical experiment, that the weight of this wooden globe was to the weight of a globe of water of the same magnitude as 55 to 97: and therefore since 121 is to 213,4 in the same ratio, the resistance made to this globe of water, moving forwards with the above-mentioned velocity, will be to its weight as 0,56752 to 213,4, that is, as 1 to 376 $^1/_{50}$. Whence since the weight of a globe of water, in the time in which the globe with a velocity uniformly continued describes a length of 30,556 inches, will generate all that velocity in the falling globe, it is manifest that the force of resistance uniformly continued in the same time will take away a velocity, which will be less than the other in the ratio of 1 to 376$^1/_{50}$, that is, the $\dfrac{1}{376\frac{1}{50}}$ part of the whole velocity.

And therefore in the time that the globe, with the same velocity uniformly continued, would describe the length of its semi-diameter, or 3$^7/_{16}$ inches, it would lose the $^1/_{3342}$ part of its motion.

I also counted the oscillations in which the pendulum lost $^1/_4$ part of its motion. In the following table the upper numbers denote the length of the arc described in the first descent, expressed in inches and parts of an inch; the middle numbers denote the length of the arc described in the last ascent; and in the lowest place are the numbers of the oscillations. I give an account of this experiment, as being more accurate than that in which only $^1/_8$ part of the motion was lost. I leave the calculation to such as are disposed to make it.

First descent	2	4	8	16	32	64
Last ascent	1 $^1/_2$	3	6	12	24	48
Numb. of oscill.	374	272	162 $^1/_2$	83 $^1/_3$	41 $^2/_3$	22 $^2/_3$

I afterward suspended a leaden globe of 2 inches in diameter, weighing 26 $^1/_4$ ounces troy by the same thread, so that between the centre of the globe and the point of suspension there was an interval of 10 $^1/_2$ feet, and I counted the oscillations in which a given part of the motion was lost. The first of the following tables exhibits the number of oscillations in which $^1/_8$ part of the whole motion was lost; the second the number of oscillations in which there was lost $^1/_4$ part of the same.

First descent	1	2	4	8	16	32	64
Last ascent	$^7/_8$	$^7/_4$	3 $^1/_2$	7	14	28	56
Numb. of oscill.	226	228	193	140	90 $^1/_2$	53	30
First descent	1	2	4	8	16	32	64
Last ascent	$^3/_4$	1 $^1/_2$	3	6	12	24	48
Numb. of oscill.	510	518	420	318	204	121	70

Selecting in the first table the 3d, 5th, and 7th observations, and expressing the greatest velocities in these observations particularly by the numbers 1, 4, 16 respectively,

and generally by the quantity V as above there will come out in the 3d observation $\frac{1}{2}$ =A + B + C, in the 5th observation $\frac{2}{90\frac{1}{2}}$ =4A + 8B + 16C, in the 7th

observation 8/30 = 16A + 64B + 256C. These equations reduced give A = 0,001414, B = 0,000297, C = 0,000879. And thence the resistance of the globe moving with the velocity V will be to its weight 261, ounces in the same ratio as 0, 0009V + 0, 000208V $\frac{2}{3}$ + 0, 000659V^2 to 121 inches, the length of the pendulum. And if we regard that part only of the resistance which is in the duplicate ratio of the velocity, it will be to the weight of the globe as 0,000659V^2 to 121 inches. But this part of the resistance in the first experiment was to the weight of the wooden globe of 57$^7/_{22}$ ounces as 0,002217V^2 to 121; and thence the resistance of the wooden globe is to the resistance of the leaden one (their velocities being equal) as 57$^7/_{22}$ into 0,002217 to 26$^1/_4$ into 0,000659, that is, as 7$^1/_3$ to 1. The diameters of the two globes were 6$^7/_8$ and 2 inches, and the squares of these are to each other as 47$^1/_4$, and 4, or 11$^{13}/_{16}$ and 1, nearly. Therefore the resistances of these equally swift globes were in less than a duplicate ratio of the diameters. But we have not yet considered the resistance of the thread, which was certainly very considerable, and ought to be subducted from the resistance of the pendulums here found. I could not determine this accurately, but I found it greater than a third part of the whole resistance of the lesser pendulum; and thence I gathered that the resistances of the globes, when the resistance of the thread is subducted, are nearly in the duplicate ratio of their diameters. For the ratio of 7$^1/_3$ - $^1/_3$ to 1 - $^1/_3$, or 10$^1/_2$ to 1 is not very different from the duplicate ratio of the diameters 11$^{13}/_{16}$ to 1.

Since the resistance of the thread is of less moment in greater globes, I tried the experiment also with a globe whose diameter was, 18$^3/_4$ inches. The length of the pendulum between the point of suspension and the centre of oscillation was 122$^1/_2$ inches, and between the point of suspension and the knot in the thread 109$^1/_2$ inches. The arc described by the knot at the first descent of the pendulum was 32 inches. The arc described by the same knot in the last ascent after five oscillations was 28 inches. The sum of the arcs, or the whole arc described in one mean oscillation, was 60 inches. The difference of the arcs 4 inches. The $^1/_{10}$ part of this, or the difference between the descent and ascent in one mean oscillation, is $^2/_5$ of an inch. Then as the radius 109 $^1/_2$ to the radius 122$^1/_2$, so is the whole arc of 60 inches described by the knot in one mean oscillation to the whole arc of 67$^1/_8$ inches described by the centre of the globe in one mean oscillation; and so is the difference $^2/_5$ to a new difference 0,4475. If the length of the arc described were to remain, and the length of the pendulum should be augmented in the ratio of 126 to 122$^1/_2$, the time of the oscillation would be augmented, and the velocity of the pendulum would be diminished in the subduplicate of

that ratio; so that the difference 0,4475 of the arcs described in the descent and subsequent ascent would remain. Then if the arc described be augmented in the ratio of $124^3/_{31}$ to $67^1/_8$, that difference 0,4475 would be augmented in the duplicate of that ratio, and so would become 1,5295. These things would be so upon the supposition that the resistance of the pendulum were in the duplicate ratio of the velocity. Therefore if the pendulum describe the whole arc of $124^3/_{31}$ inches, and its length between the point of suspension and the centre of oscillation be 126 inches, the difference of the arcs described in the descent and subsequent ascent would be 1,5295 inches. And this difference multiplied into the weight of the pendulous globe, which was 208 ounces, produces 318,136. Again; in the pendulum above-mentioned, made of a wooden globe, when its centre of oscillation, being 126 inches from the point of suspension, described the whole arc of $124^3/_{31}$ inches, the difference of the arcs described in the descent and ascent was $^{126}/_{121}$ into $\dfrac{8}{9\frac{2}{3}}$. This multiplied into the weight of the globe, which was

$5^7/_{22}$ ounces, produces 49,396. But I multiply these differences into the weights of the globes, in order to find their resistances. For the differences arise from the resistances, and are as the resistances directly and the weights inversely. Therefore the resistances are as the numbers 318,136 and 49,396. But that part of the resistance of the lesser globe which is in the duplicate ratio of the velocity, was to the whole resistance as 0,56752 to 0,61675, that is, as 45,453 to 49,396; whereas that part of the resistance of the greater globe is almost equal to its whole resistance; and so those parts are nearly as 318,136 and 45,453, that is, as 7 and 1. But the diameters of the globes are $18^3/_4$ and $6\,^7/_8$; and their squares $351^9/_{16}$ and $47^{17}/_{64}$ are as 7,438 and 1, that is, as the resistances of the globes 7 and 1, nearly. The difference of these ratios is scarce greater than may arise from the resistance of the thread. Therefore those parts of the resistances which are, when the globes are equal, as the squares of the velocities, are also, when the velocities are equal, as the squares of the diameters of the globes.

But the greatest of the globes I used in these experiments was not perfectly spherical, and therefore in this calculation I have, for brevity's sake, neglected some little niceties; being not very solicitous for an accurate calculus in an experiment that was not very accurate. So that I could wish that these experiments were tried again with other globes, of a larger size, more in number, and more accurately formed; since the demonstration of a vacuum depends thereon. If the globes be taken in a geometrical proportion, as suppose whose diameters are 4, 8, 16, 32 inches; one may collect from the progression observed in the experiments what would happen if the globes were still larger.

In order to compare the resistances of different fluids with each other, I made the following trials. I procured a wooden vessel 4 feet long, 1 foot broad, and 1 foot high.

This vessel, being uncovered, I filled with spring water, and, having immersed pendulums therein, I made them oscillate in the water. And I found that a leaden globe weighing 166 $\frac{1}{6}$, ounces, and in diameter 3 $\frac{5}{8}$ inches, moved therein as it is set down in the following table; the length of the pendulum from the point of suspension to a certain point marked in the thread being 126 inches, and to the centre of oscillation 134 $\frac{3}{8}$ inches.

The arc described in the first descent, by a point marked in the thread was inches.	64	32	16	8	4	2	1	$\frac{1}{2}$	$\frac{1}{4}$
The arc described in the last ascent was inches.	48	24	12	6	3	$1\frac{1}{2}$	$\frac{3}{4}$	$\frac{3}{8}$	$\frac{3}{16}$
The difference of the arcs, proportional to the motion lost, was inches.	16	8	4	2	1	$\frac{1}{2}$	$\frac{1}{4}$	$\frac{1}{8}$	$\frac{1}{16}$
The number of the oscillations in water.			$\frac{29}{60}$	$1\frac{1}{3}$	3	7	$11\frac{1}{4}$	$12\frac{2}{3}$	$13\frac{1}{3}$
The number of the oscillations in air.	$85\frac{1}{2}$	287	535						

In the experiments of the 4th column there were equal motions lost in 535 oscillations made in the air, and $1\frac{1}{5}$ in water. The oscillations in the air were indeed a little swifter than those in the water. But if the oscillations in the water were accelerated in such a ratio that the motions of the pendulums might be equally swift in both mediums, there would be still the same number $1\frac{1}{5}$ is of oscillations in the water, and by these the same quantity of motion would be lost as before; because the resistance if increased, and the square of the time diminished in the same duplicate ratio. The pendulums, therefore, being of equal velocities, there were equal motions lost in 535 oscillations in the air, and $1\frac{1}{5}$ in the water; and therefore the resistance of the pendulum in the water is to its resistance in the air as 535 to $1\frac{1}{5}$. This is the proportion of the whole resistances in the case of the 4th column.

Now let $AV + CV^2$ represent the difference of the arcs described in the descent and subsequent ascent by the globe moving in air with the greatest velocity V; and since the greatest velocity is in the case of the 4th column to the greatest velocity in the case of the 1st column as 1 to 8; and that difference of the arcs in the case of the 4th column to the difference in the case of the 1st column as $\frac{2}{535}$ to $\frac{16}{85\frac{1}{2}}$, or as $85\frac{1}{2}$ to 4280; put in these cases 1 and 8 for the velocities, and $85\frac{1}{2}$ and 4280 for the differences of the arcs, and $A + C$ will be $= 85\frac{1}{2}$ and $8A + 64C = 4280$ or $A + 8C = 535$; and then by reducing these equations, there will come out $7C = 449\frac{1}{2}$ and $C = 64\frac{3}{14}$ and $A = 21\frac{2}{7}$; and therefore the resistance, which is as $\frac{7}{11}AV + \frac{3}{4}CV^2$, will become as $13\frac{6}{11} V + 48\frac{9}{56} V^2$. Therefore in the case of the 4th column, where the velocity was 1, the

whole resistance is to its part proportional to the square of the velocity as $13\ ^6/_{11}V + 48\ ^9/_{56}\ V^2$ or $61\ ^{13}/_{17}$ to $48\ ^9/_{56}$; and therefore the resistance of the pendulum in water is to that part of the resistance in air, which is proportional to the square of the velocity, and which in swift motions is the only part that deserves consideration, as $61^{13}/_{17}$ to $48^9/_{56}$ and 535 to $1^1/_5$ conjunctly, that is, as 571 to 1. If the whole thread of the pendulum oscillating in the water had been immersed, its resistance would have been still greater; so that the resistance of the pendulum oscillating in the water, that is, that part which is proportional to the square of the velocity, and which only needs to be considered in swift bodies, is to the resistance of the same whole pendulum, oscillating in air with the same velocity, as about 950 to 1, that is as, the density of water to the density of air, nearly.

In this calculation we ought also to have taken in that part of the resistance of the pendulum in the water which was as the square of the velocity; but I found (which will perhaps seem strange) that the resistance in the water was augmented in more than a duplicate ratio of the velocity. In searching after the cause, I thought upon this, that the vessel was too narrow for the magnitude of, the pendulous globe, and by its narrowness obstructed the motion of the water as it yielded to the oscillating globe. For when, I immersed a pendulous globe, whose diameter was one inch only, the resistance was augmented nearly in a duplicate ratio of the velocity. I tried this by making a pendulum of two globes, of which the lesser and lower oscillated in the water, and the greater and higher was fastened to the thread just above the water, and, by oscillating in the air, assisted the motion of the pendulum, and continued it longer. The experiments made by this contrivance proved according to the following table.

Arc descr. in first descent	16	8	4	2	1	$^1/_2$	$^1/_4$
Arc descr. in last ascent	12	6	3	$1^1/_2$	$^3/_4$	$^3/_8$	$^3/_{16}$
Diff. of arcs, proport. to motion lost	4	2	1	$^1/_2$	$^1/_4$	$^1/_8$	$^1/_{16}$
Number of oscillations	$3\,^3/_8$	$6\,^1/_2$	$12^1/_{12}$	$21^1/_5$	34	53	$62^1/_5$

In comparing the resistances of the mediums with each other, I also caused iron pendulums to oscillate in quicksilver. The length of the iron wire was about 3 feet, and the diameter of the pendulous globe about $^1/_3$ of an inch. To the wire, just above the quicksilver, there was fixed another leaden globe of a bigness sufficient to continue the motion of the pendulum for some time. Then a vessel, that would hold about 3 pounds of quicksilver, was filled by turns with quicksilver and common water, that, by making the pendulum oscillate successively in these two different fluids, I might find the proportion of their resistances; and the resistance of the quicksilver proved to be to the resistance of water as about 13 or 14 to 1; that is, as the density of quicksilver to the density of water. When I made use of a pendulous globe something bigger, as of one

whose diameter was about $1/2$ or $2/3$ of an inch, the resistance of the quicksilver proved to be to the resistance of the water as about 12 or 10 to 1. But the former experiment is more to be relied on, because in the latter the vessel was too narrow in proportion to the magnitude of the immersed globe; for the vessel ought to have been enlarged together with the globe. I intended to have repeated these experiments with larger vessels, and in melted metals, and other liquors both cold and hot; but I had not leisure to try all: and besides, from what is already described, it appears sufficiently that the resistance of bodies moving swiftly is nearly proportional to the densities of the fluids in which they move. I do not say accurately; for more tensious fluids, of equal density, will undoubtedly resist more than those that are more liquid; as cold oil more than warm, warm oil more than rainwater, and water more than spirit of wine. But in liquors, which are sensibly fluid enough, as in air, in salt and fresh water, in spirit of wine, of turpentine, and salts, in oil cleared of its faeces by distillation and warmed, in oil of vitriol, and in mercury, and melted metals, and any other suchlike, that are fluid enough to retain for some time the motion impressed upon them by the agitation of the vessel, and which being poured out are easily resolved into drops, I doubt not but the rule already laid down may be accurate enough, especially if the experiments be made with larger pendulous bodies and more swiftly moved.

Lastly, since it is the opinion of some that there is a certain ethereal medium extremely rare and subtile, which freely pervades the pores of all bodies; and from such a medium, so pervading the pores of bodies, some resistance must needs arise; in order to try whether the resistance, which we experience in bodies in motion, be made upon their outward superficies only, or whether their internal parts meet with any considerable resistance upon their superficies, I thought of the following experiment. I suspended a round deal box by a thread 11 feet long on a steel hook, by means of a ring of the same metal, so as to make a pendulum of the aforesaid length. The hook had a sharp hollow edge on its upper part, so that the upper arc of the ring pressing on the edge might move the more freely; and the thread was fastened to the lower arc of the ring. The pendulum being thus prepared, I drew it aside from the perpendicular to the distance of about 6 feet, and that in a plane perpendicular to the edge of the hook, lest the ring, while the pendulum oscillated, should slide to and fro on the edge of the hook: for the point of suspension, in which the ring touches the hook, ought to remain immovable. I therefore accurately noted the place to which the pendulum was brought, and letting it go, I marked three other places, to which it returned at the end of the 1st, 2d, and 3d oscillation. This I often repeated, that I might find those places as accurately as possible. Then I filled the box with lead and other heavy metals that were near at hand. But, first, I weighed the box when empty, and that part of the thread that went round it, and half the remaining part, extended between the hook and the suspended

box; for the thread so extended always acts upon the pendulum, when drawn aside from the perpendicular, with half its weight. To this weight I added the weight of the air contained in the box. And this whole weight was about $^1/_{78}$ of the weight of the box when filled with the metals. Then because the box when full of the metals, by extending the thread with its weight, increased the length of the pendulum, I shortened the thread so as to make the length of the pendulum, when oscillating, the same as before. Then drawing aside the pendulum to the place first marked, and letting it go, I reckoned about 77 oscillations before the box returned to the second mark, and as many afterwards before it came to the third mark, and as many after that before it came to the fourth mark. From whence I conclude that the whole resistance of the box, when full, had not a greater proportion to the resistance of the box, when empty, than 78 to 77. For if their resistances were equal, the box, when full, by reason of its *vis insita*, which was 78 times greater than the *vis insita* of the same when empty, ought to have continued its oscillating motion so much the longer, and therefore to have returned to those marks at the end of 78 oscillations. But it returned to them at the end of 77 oscillations.

Let, therefore, A represent the resistance of the box upon its external superficies, and B the resistance of the empty box on its internal superficies; and if the resistances to the internal parts of bodies equally swift be as the matter, or the number of particles that are resisted, then 78B will be the resistance made to the internal parts of the box, when full; and therefore the whole resistance A + B of the empty box will be to the whole resistance A + 78B of the full box as 77 to 78, and, by division, A + B to 77B as 77 to 1; and thence A + B to B as 77 x 77 to 1, and, by division again, A to B as 5928 to 1. Therefore the resistance of the empty box in its internal parts will be above 5000 times less than the resistance on its external superficies. This reasoning depends upon the supposition that the greater resistance of the full box arises not from any other latent cause, but only from the action of some subtile fluid upon the included metal.

This experiment is related by memory, the paper being lost in which I had described it; so that I have been obliged to omit some fractional parts, which are slipt out of my memory; and I have no leisure to try it again. The first time I made it, the hook being weak, the full box was retarded sooner. The cause I found to be, that the hook was not strong enough to bear the weight of the box; so that, as it oscillated to and fro, the hook was bent sometimes this and sometimes that way. I therefore procured a hook of sufficient strength, so that the point of suspension might remain unmoved, and then all things happened as is above described.

SECTION VII.

Of the motion of fluids, and the resistance made to projected bodies.

PROPOSITION XXXII. THEOREM XXVI.

SUPPOSE TWO SIMILAR SYSTEMS OF BODIES CONSISTING
OF AN EQUAL NUMBER OF PARTICLES, AND LET THE
CORRESPONDENT PARTICLES BE SIMILAR AND PROPORTIONAL,
EACH IN ONE SYSTEM TO EACH IN THE OTHER, AND HAVE A
LIKE SITUATION AMONG THEMSELVES, AND THE SAME GIVEN
RATIO OF DENSITY TO EACH OTHER; AND LET THEM BEGIN
TO MOVE AMONG THEMSELVES IN PROPORTIONAL TIMES,
AND WITH LIKE MOTIONS (THAT IS, THOSE IN ONE SYSTEM
AMONG ONE ANOTHER, AND THOSE IN THE OTHER AMONG
ONE ANOTHER). AND IF THE PARTICLES THAT ARE IN THE
SAME SYSTEM DO NOT TOUCH ONE ANOTHER, EXCEPT IN
THE MOMENTS OF REFLEXION; NOR ATTRACT, NOR REPEL
EACH OTHER, EXCEPT WITH ACCELERATIVE FORCES THAT
ARE AS THE DIAMETERS OF THE CORRESPONDENT PARTICLES
INVERSELY, AND THE SQUARES OF THE VELOCITIES DIRECTLY;
I SAY, THAT THE PARTICLES OF THOSE SYSTEMS WILL
CONTINUE TO MOVE AMONG THEMSELVES WITH LIKE
MOTIONS AND IN PROPORTIONAL TIMES.

Like bodies in like situations are said to be moved among themselves with like motions and in proportional times, when their situations at the end of those times are always found alike in respect of each other; as suppose we compare the particles in one system with the correspondent particles in the other. Hence the times will be proportional, in which similar and proportional parts of similar figures will be described by correspondent particles. Therefore if we suppose two systems of this kind, the correspondent particles, by reason of the similitude of the motions at their beginning, will continue to be moved with like motions, so long as they move without meeting one another; for if, they are acted on by no forces, they will go on uniformly in right lines, by the 1st Law. But if they do agitate one another with some certain forces, and those forces are as the diameters of the correspondent particles inversely and the squares of the velocities directly, then, because the particles are in like situations, and their forces are proportional, the whole forces with which correspondent particles are agitated, and which are compounded of each of the agitating forces (by Corol. 2 of the Laws), will

have like directions, and have the same effect as if they respected centres placed alike among the particles; and those whole forces will be to each other as the several forces which compose them, that is, as the diameters of the correspondent particles inversely, and the squares of the velocities directly: and therefore will came, correspondent particles to continue to describe like figures. These things will be so (by Cor. 1 and 8, Prop. IV., Book I), if those centres are at rest; but if they are moved, yet, by reason of the similitude of the translations, their situations among the particles of the system will remain similar, so that the changes introduced into the figures described by the particles will still be similar. So that the motions of correspondent and similar particles will continue similar till their first meeting with each other; and thence will arise similar collisions, and similar reflexions: which will again beget similar motions of the particles among themselves (by what was just now shewn), till they mutually fall upon one another again, and so on *ad infinitum.*

COR. 1. Hence if any two bodies, which are similar and in like situations to the correspondent particles of the systems, begin to move amongst them in like manner and in proportional times, and their magnitudes and densities be to each other as the magnitudes and densities of the corresponding particles, these bodies will continue to be moved in like manner and in proportional times; for the case of the greater parts of both systems and of the particles is the very same.

COR. 2. And if all the similar and similarly situated parts of both systems be at rest among themselves; and two of them, which are greater than the rest, and mutually correspondent in both systems, begin to move in lines alike posited, with any similar motion whatsoever, they will excite similar motions in the rest of the parts of the systems, and will continue to move among those parts in like manner and in proportional times; and will therefore describe spaces proportional to their diameters.

PROPOSITION XXXIII. THEOREM XXVII.

THE SAME THINGS BEING SUPPOSED, I SAY, THAT THE GREATER PARTS OF THE SYSTEMS ARE RESISTED IN A RATIO COMPOUNDED OF THE DUPLICATE RATIO OF THEIR VELOCITIES, AND THE DUPLICATE RATIO OF THEIR DIAMETERS, AND THE SIMPLE RATIO OF THE DENSITY OF THE PARTS OF THE SYSTEMS.

For the resistance arises partly from the centripetal or centrifugal forces with which the particles of the system mutually act on each other, partly from the collisions and reflexions of the particles and the greater parts. The resistances of the first kind are to each other as the whole motive forces from which they arise, that is, as the whole accelerative forces and the quantities of matter in corresponding parts; that is (by the sup-

position), as the squares of the velocities directly, and the distances of the corresponding particles inversely, and the quantities of matter in the correspondent parts directly:
and therefore since the distances of the particles in one system are to the correspondent
distances of the particles of the others as the diameter of one particle or part in the former system to the diameter of the correspondent particle or part in the other, and since
the quantities of matter are as the densities of the parts and the cubes of the diameters;
the resistances are to each other as the squares of the velocities and the squares of the
diameters and the densities of the parts of the systems. Q.E.D. The resistances of the
latter sort are as the number of correspondent reflexions and the forces of those reflexions conjunctly; but the number of the reflexions are to each other as the velocities of
the corresponding parts directly and the spaces between their reflexions inversely. And
the forces of the reflexions are as the velocities and the magnitudes and the densities of
the corresponding parts conjunctly; that is, as the velocities and the cubes of the diameters and the densities of the parts. And, joining all these ratios, the resistances of the
corresponding parts are to each other as the squares of the velocities and the squares of
the diameters and the densities of the parts conjunctly.   Q.E.D.

COR. 1. Therefore if those systems are two elastic fluids, like our air, and their parts
are at rest among themselves; and two similar bodies proportional in magnitude and
density to the parts of the fluids, and similarly situated among those parts, be any how
projected in the direction of lines similarly posited; and the accelerative forces with,
which the particles of the fluids mutually act upon each other are as the diameters of
the bodies projected inversely and the squares of their velocities directly; those bodies
will excite similar motions in the fluids in proportional times, and will describe similar spaces and proportional to their diameters.

COR. 2. Therefore in the same fluid a projected body that moves swiftly meets with
a resistance that is, in the duplicate ratio of its velocity, nearly. For if the forces with
which distant particles act mutually upon one another should be augmented in the
duplicate ratio of the velocity, the projected body would be resisted in the same duplicate ratio accurately; and therefore in a medium, whose parts when at a distance do not
act mutually with any force on one another, the resistance is in the duplicate ratio of
the velocity accurately. Let there be, therefore, three mediums A, B, C, consisting of
similar and equal parts regularly disposed at equal distances. Let the parts of the mediums A and B recede from each other with forces that are among themselves as T and
V; and let the parts of the medium C be entirely destitute of any such forces. And if
four equal bodies D, E, F, G, move in these mediums, the two first D and E in the two
first A and B, and the other two F and G in the third C; and if the velocity of the body
D be to the velocity of the body E, and the velocity of the body F to the velocity of the
body G, in the subduplicate ratio of the force T to the force V: the resistance of the

body D to the resistance of the body E, and the resistance of the body F to the resistance of the body G, will be in the duplicate ratio of the velocities; and therefore the resistance of the body D will be to the resistance of the body F as the resistance of the body E to the resistance of the body G. Let the bodies D and F be equally swift, as also the bodies E and G; and, augmenting the velocities of the bodies D and F in any ratio, and diminishing the forces of the particles of the medium B in the duplicate of the same ratio, the medium B will approach to the form and condition of the medium C at pleasure; and therefore the resistances of the equal and equally swift bodies E and G in these mediums will perpetually approach to equality so that their difference will at last become less than any given. Therefore since the resistances of the bodies D and F are to each other as the resistances of the bodies E and G, those will also in like manner approach to the ratio of equality. Therefore the bodies D and F, when they move with very great swiftness, meet with resistances very nearly equal; and therefore since the resistance of the body F is in a duplicate ratio of the velocity, the resistance of the body D will be nearly in the same ratio.

COR. 3. The resistance of a body moving very swift in an elastic fluid is almost the same as if the parts of the fluid were destitute of their centrifugal forces, and did not fly from each other; if so be that the elasticity of the fluid arise from the centrifugal forces of the particles, and the velocity be so great as not to allow the particles time enough to act.

COR. 4. Therefore, since the resistances of similar and equally swift bodies, in a medium whose distant parts do not fly from each other, are as the squares of the diameters, the resistances made to bodies moving with very great and equal velocities in an elastic fluid will be as the squares of the diameters, nearly.

COR. 5. And since similar, equal, and equally swift bodies, moving through mediums of the same density, whose particles do not fly from each other mutually, will strike against an equal quantity of matter in equal times, whether the particles of which the medium consists be more and smaller, or fewer and greater, and therefore impress on that matter an equal quantity of motion, and in return (by the 3d Law of Motion) suffer an equal re-action from the same, that is, are equally resisted; it is manifest, also, that in elastic fluids of the same density, when the bodies move with extreme swiftness, their resistances are nearly equal, whether the fluids consist of gross parts, or of parts ever so subtile. For the resistance of projectiles moving with exceedingly great celerities is not much diminished by the subtilty of the medium.

COR. 6. All these things are so in fluids whose elastic force takes its rise from the centrifugal forces of the particles. But if that force arise from some other cause, as from the expansion of the particles after the manner of wool, or the boughs of trees, or any other cause, by which the particles are hindered from moving freely among

themselves, the resistance, by reason of the lesser fluidity of the medium, will be greater than in the Corollaries above.

PROPOSITION XXXIV THEOREM XXVIII.

IF IN A RARE MEDIUM, CONSISTING OF EQUAL PARTICLES
FREELY DISPOSED AT EQUAL DISTANCES FROM EACH OTHER,
A GLOBE AND A CYLINDER DESCRIBED ON EQUAL DIAMETERS
MOVE WITH EQUAL VELOCITIES IN THE DIRECTION OF THE
AXIS OF THE CYLINDER, THE RESISTANCE OF THE GLOBE
WILL BE BUT HALF SO GREAT AS THAT OF THE CYLINDER.

For since the action of the medium upon the body is the same (by Cor. 5 of the Laws) whether the body move in a quiescent medium, or whether the particles of the medium impinge with the same velocity upon the quiescent body, let us consider the body as if it were quiescent, and see with what force it would be impelled by the moving medium. Let, therefore, ABKI represent a spherical body described from the centre C with the semi-diameter CA, and let the particles of the medium impinge with a given velocity upon that spherical body in the directions of right lines parallel to AC; and let FB be one of those right lines. In FB take LB equal to the semi-diameter CB, and draw BD touching the sphere in B. Upon KC and BD let fall the perpendiculars BE, LD; and

the force with which a particle of the medium, impinging on the globe obliquely in the direction FB, would strike the globe in B, will be to the force with which the same particle, meeting the cylinder ONGQ described about the globe with the axis ACI, would strike it perpendicularly in b, as LD to LB, or BE to BC. Again; the efficacy of this force to move the globe, according to the direction of its incidence FB or AC, is to the effi-

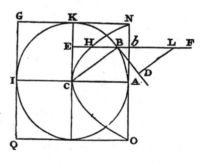

cacy of the same to move the globe, according to the direction of its determination, that is, in the direction of the right line BC in which it impels the globe directly, as BE to BC. And, joining these ratios, the efficacy of a particle, falling upon the globe obliquely in the direction of the right line FB, to move the globe in the direction of its incidence, is to the efficacy of the same particle falling in the same line perpendicularly on the cylinder, to move it in the same direction, as BE2 to BC2. Therefore if in bE, which is perpendicular to the circular base of the cylinder NAO, and equal to the radius AC, we take bH equal to BE2/CB; then bH will be to bE as the effect of the particle upon the globe to the effect of the particle upon the cylinder. And therefore

the solid which is formed by all the right lines bH will be to the solid formed by all the right lines bE as the effect of all the particles upon the globe to the effect of all the particles upon the cylinder. But the former of these solids is a paraboloid whose vertex is C, its axis CA, and *latus rectum* CA, and the latter solid is a cylinder circumscribing the paraboloid; and it is known that a paraboloid is half its circumscribed cylinder. Therefore the whole force of the medium upon the globe is half of the entire force of the same upon the cylinder. And therefore if the particles of the medium are at rest, and the cylinder and globe move with equal velocities, the resistance of the globe will be half the resistance of the cylinder.

Q.E.D.

SCHOLIUM.

By the same method other figures may be compared together as to their resistance; and those may be found which are most apt to continue their motions in resisting mediums. As if upon the circular base CEBH from the centre O, with the radius OC, and the altitude OD, one would construct a frustum CBGF of a cone, which should meet with less resistance than any other frustum constructed with the same base and altitude, and forwards towards D in the direction of its axis: bisect the altitude OD in Q, and produce OQ to S, so that QS may be equal to QC, and S will be the vertex of the cone whose frustum is sought.

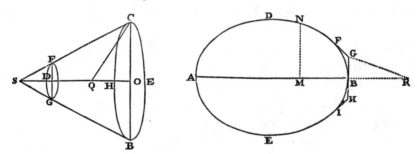

Whence, by the bye, since the angle CSB is always acute, it follows, that, if the solid ADBE be generated by the convolution of an elliptical or oval figure ADBE about its axis AB, and the generating figure be touched by three right lines FG, GH, HI, in the points F, B, and I, so that GH shall be perpendicular to the axis in the point of contact B, and FG, HI maybe inclined to GH in the angles FGB, BHI of 135 degrees: the solid arising from the convolution of the figure ADFGHIE about the same axis AB will be less resisted than the former solid; if so be that both move forward in the direction of their axis AB, and that the extremity B of each go foremost. Which Proposition I conceive may be of use in the building of ships.

If the figure DNFG be such a curve, that if, from any point thereof, as N, the perpendicular NM be let fall on the axis AB, and from the given point G there be drawn

the right line GR parallel to a right line touching the figure in N, and cutting the axis produced in R, MN becomes to GR as GR^3 to $4BR \times GB^2$, the solid described by the revolution of this figure about its axis AB, moving in the before-mentioned rare medium from A towards B, will be less resisted than any other circular solid whatsoever, described of the same length and breadth.

PROPOSITION XXXV. PROBLEM VII.

IF A RARE MEDIUM CONSIST OF VERY SMALL QUIESCENT PARTICLES OF EQUAL MAGNITUDES, AND FREELY DISPOSED AT EQUAL DISTANCES FRONT ONE ANOTHER: TO FIND THE RESISTANCE OF A GLOBE MOVING UNIFORMLY FORWARD IN THIS MEDIUM.

CASE 1. Let a cylinder described with the same diameter and altitude be conceived to go forward with the same velocity in the direction of its axis through the same medium; and let us suppose that the particles of the medium, on which the globe or cylinder falls, fly back with as great a force of reflexion as possible. Then since the resistance of the globe (by the last Proposition) is but half the resistance of the cylinder, and since the globe is to the cylinder as 2 to 3, and since the cylinder by falling perpendicularly on the particles, and reflecting them with the utmost force, communicates to them a velocity double to its own; it follows that the cylinder, in moving forward uniformly half the length of its axis, will communicate a motion to the particles which is to the whole motion of the cylinder as the density of the medium to the density of the cylinder; and that the globe, in the time it describes one length of its diameter in moving uniformly forward, will communicate the same motion to the particles; and in the time that it describes two thirds of its diameter, will communicate a motion to the particles which is to the whole motion of the globe as the density of the medium to; the density of the globe. And therefore the globe meets with a resistance, which is to the force by which its whole motion may be either taken away or generated in the time in which it describes two thirds of its diameter moving uniformly forward, as the density of the medium to the density of the globe.

CASE 2. Let us suppose that the particles of the medium incident on the globe or cylinder are not reflected; and then the cylinder falling perpendicularly on the particles will communicate its own simple velocity to them, and therefore meets a resistance but half so great as in the former case, and the globe also meets with a resistance but half so great.

CASE 3. Let us suppose the particles of the medium to fly back from the globe with a force which is neither the greatest, nor yet none at all, but with a certain mean force;

then the resistance of the globe will be in the same mean ratio between the resistance in the first case and the resistance in the second. Q.E.I.

Cor. 1. Hence if the globe and the particles are infinitely bard, and destitute, of all elastic force, and therefore of all force of reflexion; the resistance of the globe will be to the force by which its whole motion may be destroyed or generated, in the time that the globe describes four third parts of its diameter, as the density of the medium to the density of the globe.

Cor. 2. The resistance of the globe, *caeteris paribus*, is in the duplicate ratio of the velocity.

Cor. 3. The resistance of the globe, *caeteris paribus*, is in the duplicate ratio of the diameter.

Cor. 4. The resistance of the globe is, *caeteris paribus*, as the density of the medium.

Cor. 5. The resistance of the globe is in a ratio compounded of the duplicate ratio of the velocity, and the duplicate ratio of the diameter, and the ratio of the density of the medium.

Cor. 6. The motion of the globe and its resistance maybe thus expounded. Let AB be the time in which the globe may, by its resistance uniformly continued, lose its whole motion. Erect AD, BC perpendicular to AB. Let BC be that whole motion, and through the point C, the asymptotes being AD, AB, describe the hyperbola CF. Produce AB to any point E. Erect the perpendicular EF meeting the hyperbola in F. Complete the parallelogram CBEG, and draw AF meeting BC in H. Then if the globe in any time BE, with its first motion BC uniformly continued, describes in a non-resisting medium the space CBEG expounded by the area of the parallelogram, the same in a resisting medium will describe the space CBEF expounded by the area of the

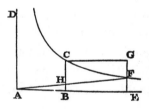

hyperbola; and its motion at the end of that time, will be expounded by EF, the ordinate of the hyperbola, there being lost of its motion the part FG. And its resistance at the end of the same time will be expounded by the length BH, there being lost of its resistance the part CH. All these things appear by Cor. 1 and 3, Prop. V., Book II.

Cor. 7. Hence if the globe in the time T by the resistance R uniformly continued lose its whole motion M, the same globe in the time *t* in a resisting medium, wherein the resistance R decreases in a duplicate ratio of the velocity, will lose out of its motion M the part $\frac{tM}{T+t}$, the part $\frac{TM}{T+t}$ remaining; and will describe a space

which is to the space described in the same time *t*, with the uniform motion M, as the

logarithm of the number $\frac{T+t}{T}$ multiplied by the number 2,302585092994 is to

the number t because the hyperbolic area BCFE is to the rectangle BCGH in that proportion.

SCHOLIUM.

I have exhibited in this Proposition the resistance and retardation of spherical projectiles in mediums that are not continued, and shewn that this resistance is to the force by which the whole motion of the globe may be destroyed or produced in the time in which the globe can describe two thirds of its diameter, with a velocity uniformly continued, as the density of the medium to the density of the globe, if so be the globe and the particles of the medium be perfectly elastic, and are endued with the utmost force of reflexion; and that this force, where the globe and particles of the medium are infinitely hard and void of any reflecting force, is diminished one half. But in continued mediums, as water, hot oil, and quicksilver, the globe as it passes through them does not immediately strike against all the particles of the fluid that generate the resistance made to it, but presses only the particles that lie next to it, which press the particles beyond, which press other particles, and so on; and in these mediums the resistance is diminished one other half. A globe in these extremely fluid mediums meets with a resistance that is to the force by which its whole motion may be destroyed or generated in the time wherein it can describe, with that motion uniformly continued, eight third parts of its diameter, as the density of the medium to the density of the globe. This I shall endeavour to shew in what follows.

PROPOSITION XXXVI. PROBLEM VIII.

TO DEFINE THE MOTION OF WATER RUNNING OUT OF A CYLINDRICAL VESSEL THROUGH A HOLE MADE AT THE BOTTOM.

Let ACDB be a cylindrical vessel, AB the mouth of it, CD the bottom parallel to the horizon, EF a circular hole in the middle of the bottom, G the centre of the hole, and GH the axis of the cylinder perpendicular to the horizon. And suppose a cylinder of ice APQB to be of the same breadth with the cavity of the vessel, and to have the same axis, and to descend perpetually with an uniform motion, and that its parts, as soon as they touch the superficies AB, dissolve into water, and flow down by their weight into the vessel, and in their fall compose the cataract or column of water ABNFEM, passing through the hole EF, and filling up the same exactly. Let the uniform velocity of the descending ice and of the contiguous water in the circle AB be that which the water would acquire by falling through the space IH; and let IH and HG lie in the same right

line; and through the point I let there be drawn the right line KL parallel to the horizon, and meeting the ice on both the sides thereof in K and L. Then the velocity of the water running out at the hole EF will be the same that it would acquire by falling from I through the space IG. Therefore, by *Galileo's* Theorems, IG will be to IH in the duplicate ratio of the velocity of the water that runs out at the hole to the velocity of the water in the circle AB, that is, in the duplicate ratio of the circle AB to the circle EF: those circles being reciprocally as the velocities of the water which in the same time and in equal quantities passes severally through each of them, and completely fills them both. We are now considering the velocity with which the water tends to the plane of the horizon. But the motion parallel to the same, by which the parts of the falling water approach to each other, is not here taken notice of; since it is neither produced by gravity, nor at all changes the motion perpendicular to the horizon which the gravity produces. We suppose, indeed, that the parts of the water cohere a little, that by their cohesion they may in falling approach to each other with motions parallel to the horizon in order to form one single cataract, and to prevent their being divided into several: but the motion parallel to the horizon arising from this cohesion does not come under our present consideration.

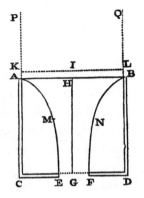

CASE 1. Conceive now the whole cavity in the vessel, which encompasses the falling water ABNPEM, to be full of ice, so that the water may pass through the ice as through a funnel. Then if the water pass very near to the ice only, without touching it; or, which is the same thing, if by reason of the perfect smoothness of the surface of the ice, the water, though touching it, glides over it with the utmost freedom, and without the least resistance; the water will run through the hole EF with the same velocity as before, and the whole weight of the column of water ABNFEM will be all taken up as before in forcing out the water, and the bottom of the vessel will sustain the weight of the ice encompassing that column.

Let now the ice in the vessel dissolve into water; yet will the efflux of the water remain, as to its velocity, the same as before. It will not be less, because the ice now dissolved will endeavour to descend; it will not be greater, because the ice, now become water, cannot descend without hindering the descent of other water equal to its own descent. The same force ought always to generate the same velocity in the effluent water.

But the hole at the bottom of the vessel, by reason of the oblique motions of the particles of the effluent water, must be a little greater than before. For now the particles

of the water do not all of them pass through the hole perpendicularly, but, flowing down on all parts from the sides of the vessel, and converging towards the hole, pass through it with oblique motions; and in tending downwards meet in a stream whose diameter is a little smaller below the hole than at the hole itself; its diameter being to the diameter of the hole as 5 to 6, or as $5^1/_2$ to $6^1/_2$ very nearly, if I took the measures of those diameters right. I procured a very thin flat plate, having a hole pierced in the middle, the diameter of the circular hole being $^5/_8$ parts of an inch. And that the stream of running waters might not be accelerated in falling, and by that acceleration become narrower, I fixed this plate not to the bottom, but to the side of the vessel, so as to make the water go out in the direction of a line parallel to the horizon. Then, when the vessel was full of water, I opened the hole to let it run out; and the diameter of the stream, measured with great accuracy at the distance of about half an inch from the hole, was $^{21}/_{46}$ of an inch. Therefore the diameter of this circular hole was to the diameter of the stream very nearly as 25 to 21. So that the water in passing through the hole converges on all sides, and, after it has run out of the vessel, becomes smaller by converging in that manner, and by becoming smaller is accelerated till it comes to the distance of half an inch from the hole, and at that distance flows in a smaller stream and with greater celerity than in the hole itself, and this in the ratio of 25×25 to 21×21, or 17 to 12, very nearly; that is, in about the subduplicate ratio of 2 to 1. Now it is certain from experiments, that the quantity of water running out in a given time through a circular hole made in the bottom of a vessel is equal to the quantity, which, flowing with the aforesaid velocity, would run out in the same time through another circular hole, whose diameter is to the diameter of the former as 21 to 25. And therefore that running water in passing through the hole itself has a velocity downwards equal to that which a heavy body would acquire in falling through half the height of the stagnant water in the vessel, nearly. But, then, after it has run out, it is still accelerated by converging, till it arrives at a distance from the hole that is nearly equal to its diameter, and acquires a velocity greater than the other in about the subduplicate ratio of 2 to 1; which velocity a heavy body would nearly acquire by falling through the whole height of the stagnant water in the vessel.

Therefore in what follows let the diameter of the stream be represented by that lesser hole which we called EF. And imagine another plane VW above the hole EF, and parallel to the plane thereof, to be placed at a distance equal to the diameter of the same hole, and to be pierced through with a greater hole ST, of such a magnitude that a stream which will exactly fill the lower hole EF way pass through it; the diameter of which hole will therefore be to the diameter of the lower hole as 25 to 21, nearly. By this means the water will run perpendicularly out at the lower hole; and the quantity of the water running out will be, according to the magnitude of this last hole, the same,

very nearly, which the solution of the Problem requires. The space included between the two planes and the falling stream may be considered as the bottom of the vessel. But, to make the solution more simple and mathematical, it is better to take the lower plane alone for the bottom of the vessel, and to suppose that the water which flowed through the ice as through a funnel, and ran out of the vessel through the hole EF made in the lower plane, preserves its motion continually, and that the ice continues at

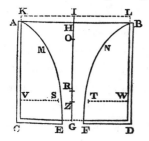

rest. Therefore in what follows let ST be the diameter of a circular hole described from the centre Z, and let the stream run out of the vessel through that hole, when the water in the vessel is all fluid. And let EF be the diameter of the hole, which the stream, in falling through, exactly fills up, whether the water runs out of the vessel by that upper hole ST, or flows through the middle of the ice in the vessel, as through a funnel. And let the diameter of the upper hole ST be to the diameter of the lower EF as about 25 to 21, and let the perpendicular distance between the planes of the holes be equal to the diameter of the lesser hole EF. Then the velocity of the water downwards, in running out of the vessel through the hole ST, will be in that hole the same that a body may acquire by falling from half the height IZ; and the velocity of both the falling streams will be in the hole EF, the same which a body would acquire by falling from the whole height IG.

CASE 2. If the hole EF be not in the middle of the bottom of the vessel, but in some other part thereof, the water will still run out with the same velocity as before, if the magnitude of the hole be the same. For though an heavy body takes a longer time in descending to the same depth, by an oblique line, than by a perpendicular line, yet in both cases it acquires in its descent the same velocity; as *Galileo* has demonstrated.

CASE 3. The velocity of the water is the same when it runs out through a hole in the side of the vessel. For if the hole be small, so that the interval between the superficies AB and KL may vanish as to sense, and the stream of water horizontally issuing out may form a parabolic figure; from the *latus rectum* of this parabola may be collected, that the velocity of the effluent water is that which a body may acquire by falling the height IG or HG of the stagnant water in the vessel. For, by making an experiment, I found that if the height of the stagnant water above the hole were 20 inches, and the height of the hole above a plane parallel to the horizon were also 20 inches, a stream of water springing out from thence would fall upon the plane, at the distance of 37 inches, very nearly, from a perpendicular let fall upon that plane from the hole. For without resistance the stream would have fallen upon the plane at the distance of 40 inches, the *latus rectum* of the parabolic stream being 80 inches.

CASE 4. If the effluent water tend upward, it will still issue forth with the same velocity. For the small stream of water springing upward, ascends with a perpendicular motion to GH or GI, the height of the stagnant water in the vessel; excepting in so far as its ascent is hindered a little by the resistance of the air; and therefore it springs out with the same velocity that it would acquire in falling from that height. Every particle of the stagnant water is equally pressed on all sides (by Prop. XIX., Book II), and, yielding to the pressure, tends always with an equal force, whether it descends through the hole in the bottom of the vessel, or gushes out in an horizontal direction through a hole in the side, or passes into a canal, and springs up from thence through a little hole made in the upper part of the canal. And it may not only be collected from reasoning, but is manifest also from the well-known experiments just mentioned, that the velocity with which the water runs out is the very same that is assigned in this Proposition.

CASE 5. The velocity of the effluent water is the same, whether the figure of the hole be circular, or square, or triangular, or any other figure equal to the circular; for the velocity of the effluent water does not depend upon the figure of the hole, but arises from its depth below the plane KL.

CASE 6. If the lower part of the vessel ABDC be immersed into stagnant water, and

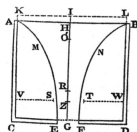

the height of the stagnant water above the bottom of the vessel be GR, the velocity with which the water that is in the vessel will run out at the hole EF into the stagnant water will be the same which the water would acquire by falling, from the height IR; for the weight of all the water in the vessel that is below the superficies of the stagnant water will be sustained in equilibrio by the weight of the stagnant water, and therefore does not at all accelerate the motion of the descending water in the vessel. This case will also appear by experiments, measuring the times in which the water will run out.

COR. 1. Hence if CA the depth of the water be produced to K, so that AK may be to CK in the duplicate ratio of the area of a hole made in any part of the bottom to the area of the circle AB, the velocity of the effluent water will be equal to the velocity which the water would acquire by falling from the height KC.

COR. 2. And the force with which the whole motion of the effluent water may be generated is equal to the weight of a cylindric column of water, whose base is the hole EF, and its altitude 2GI or 2CK. For the effluent water, in the time it becomes equal to this column, may acquire, by falling by its own weight from the height GI, a velocity equal to that with which it runs out.

COR. 3. The weight of all the water in the vessel ABDC is to that part of the weight which is employed in forcing out the water as the sum of the circles AB and EF

to twice the circle EF. For let IO be a mean proportional between IH and IG, and the water running out at the hole EF will, in the time that a drop falling from I would describe the altitude IG, become equal to a cylinder whose base is the circle EF and its altitude 2IG, that is, to a cylinder whose base is the circle AB, and whose altitude is 2IO. For the circle EF is to the circle AB in the subduplicate ratio of the altitude IH to the altitude IG; that is, in the simple ratio of the mean proportional IO to the altitude IG. Moreover, in the time that a drop falling from I can describe the altitude IH, the water that runs out will have become equal to a cylinder whose base is the circle AB, and its altitude 2IH; and in the time that a drop falling from I through H to G describes HG, the difference of the altitudes, the effluent water, that is, the water contained within the solid ABNFEM, will be equal to the difference of the cylinders, that is, to a cylinder whose base is AB, and its altitude 2HO. And therefore all the water contained in the vessel ABDC is to the whole falling water contained in the said solid ABNFEM as HG to 2HO, that is, as HO + OG to 2HO, or IH + IO to 2IH. But the weight of all the water in the solid ABNFEM is employed in forcing out the water; and therefore the weight of all the water in the vessel is to that part of the weight that is employed in forcing out the water as IH + IO to 21H, and therefore as the sum of the circles EF and AB to twice the circle EF.

COR. 4. And hence the weight of all the water in the vessel ABDC is to the other part of the weight which is sustained by the bottom of the vessel as the sum of the circles AB and EF to the difference of the same circles.

COR. 5. And that part of the weight which the bottom of the vessel sustains is to the other part of the weight employed in forcing out the water as the difference of the circles AB and EF to twice the lesser circle EP, or as the area of the bottom to twice the hole.

COR. 6. That part of the weight which presses upon the bottom is to the whole weight of the water perpendicularly incumbent thereon as the circle AB to the sum of the circles AB and EF, or as the Circle AB to the excess of twice the circle AB above the area of the bottom. For that part of the weight which presses upon the bottom is to the weight of the whole water in the vessel as the difference of the circles AB and EF to the sum of the same circles (by Cor. 4); and the weight of the whole water in the vessel is to the weight of the whole water perpendicularly incumbent on the bottom as the circle AB to the difference of the circles AB and EF. Therefore, *ex aequo perturbatè;*, that part of the weight which presses upon the bottom is to the weight of the whole water perpendicularly incumbent thereon as the circle AB to the sum of the circles AB and EF, or the excess of twice the circle AB above the bottom.

COR. 7. If in the middle of the hole EF there be placed the little circle PQ described about the centre G, and parallel to the horizon, the weight of water which

that little circle sustains is greater than the weight of a third part of a cylinder of water whose base is that little circle and its height GH. For let ABNFEM be the cataract or column of falling water whose axis is GH, as above, and let all the water, whose fluidity is not requisite for the ready and quick descent of the water, be supposed to be congealed, as well round about the cataract, as above the little circle. And let PHQ be the column of water congealed above the little circle, whose vertex is H, and its altitude GH. And suppose this cataract to fall with its whole weight downwards, and not in the least to lie against or to press PHQ, but to glide freely by it without any friction, unless, perhaps, just at the very vertex of the ice, where the cataract at the beginning of its fill may tend to a concave figure. And as the congealed water AMEC, BNFD, lying round the cataract, is convex in its internal superficies AME, BNF, towards the falling cataract, so this column PHQ will be convex towards the cataract also, and will therefore be greater

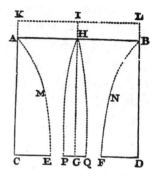

than a cone whose base is that little circle PQ and its altitude GH; that is, greater than a third part of a cylinder described with the same base and altitude. Now that little circle sustains the weight of this column, that is, a weight greater than the weight of the cone, or a third part of the cylinder.

COR. 8. The weight of water which the circle PQ, when very small, sustains, seems to be less than the weight of two thirds of a cylinder of water whose base is that little circle, and its altitude HG. For, things standing as above supposed, imagine the half of a spheroid described whose base is that little circle, and its semi-axis or altitude HG. This figure will be equal to two thirds of that cylinder, and will comprehend within it the column of congealed water PHQ, the weight of which is sustained by that little circle. For though the motion of the water tends directly downwards, the external superficies of that column must yet meet the base PQ in an angle somewhat acute, because the water in its fall is perpetually accelerated, and by reason of that acceleration become narrower. Therefore, since that angle is less than a right one, this column in the lower parts thereof will lie within the hemi-spheroid. In the upper parts also it will be acute or pointed; because to make it otherwise, the horizontal motion of the water must be at the vertex infinitely more swift than its motion towards the horizon. And the less this circle PQ is, the more acute will the vertex of this column be; and the circle being diminished *in infinitum*, the angle PHQ will be diminished *in infinitum*, and therefore the column will lie within the hemi-spheroid. Therefore that column is less than that hemi-spheroid, or than two-third parts of the cylinder whose base is that little circle, and its altitude GH. Now the little circle sustains a force of water equal to the weight

of this column, the weight of the ambient water being employed in causing its efflux out at the hole.

COR. 9. The weight of water which the little circle PQ sustains, when it is very small, is very nearly equal to the weight of a cylinder of water whose base is that little circle, and its altitude $^1/_2$GH; for this weight is an arithmetical mean between the weights of the cone and the hemi-spheroid above mentioned. But if that little circle be not very small, but on the contrary increased till it be equal to the hole EF, it will sustain the weight of all the water lying perpendicularly above it, that is, the weight of a cylinder of water whose base is that little circle, and its altitude GH.

COR. 10. And (as far as I can judge) the weight which this little circle sustains is always to the weight of a cylinder of water whose base is that little circle, and its altitude $^1/_2$GH, as EF^2 to $EF^2 - ^1/_2PQ^2$, or as the circle EF to the excess of this circle above half the little circle PQ, very nearly.

LEMMA IV.

IF A CYLINDER MOVE UNIFORMLY FORWARD IN THE DIRECTION
OF ITS LENGTH, THE RESISTANCE MADE THERETO IS NOT AT
ALL CHANGED BY AUGMENTING OR DIMINISHING THAT
LENGTH; AND, IS THEREFORE THE SAME WITH THE RESISTANCE
OF A CIRCLE, DESCRIBED WITH THE SAME DIAMETER, AND
MOVING, FORWARD WITH THE SAME VELOCITY IN THE DIRECTION
OF A RIGHT LINE PERPENDICULAR TO ITS PLANE.

For the sides are not at all opposed to the motion; and a cylinder becomes a circle when its length is diminished *in infinitum.*

PROPOSITION XXXVII. THEOREM XXIX.

IF A CYLINDER MOVE UNIFORMLY FORWARD IN A COMPRESSED,
INFINITE, AND NON-ELASTIC FLUID, IN THE DIRECTION OF ITS
LENGTH, THE RESISTANCE ARISING FROM THE MAGNITUDE OF ITS
TRANSVERSE SECTION IS TO THE FORCE BY WHICH ITS
WHOLE MOTION MAY BE DESTROYED OR GENERATED, IN THE
TIME THAT IT MOVES FOUR TIMES ITS LENGTH, AS THE
DENSITY OF THE MEDIUM TO THE DENSITY OF THE
CYLINDER, NEARLY.

For let the vessel ABDC touch the surface of stagnant water with its bottom CD, and let the water run out of this vessel into the stagnant water through the cylindric canal EFTS perpendicular to the horizon; and let the little circle PQ be placed parallel

to the horizon any where in the middle of the canal; and produce CA to K, so that AK may be to CK in the duplicate of the ratio, which the excess of the orifice of the canal EF above the little circle PQ bears to the circle AB. Then it is manifest (by Case 5, Case 6, and Cor. 1, Prop. XXXVI) that the velocity of the water passing through the annular space between the little circle and the sides of the vessel will be the very same which the water would acquire by falling, and in its fall describing the altitude KC or IG.

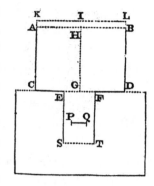

And (by Cor. 10, Prop. XXXVI) if the breadth of the vessel be infinite, so that the lineola HI may vanish, and the altitudes IG, HG become equal; the force of the water that flows down and presses upon the circle will be to the weight of a cylinder whose base is that little circle, and the altitude $^{1}/_{2}$IG, as EF^2 to $EF^2 - {}^{1}/_{2}PQ^2$, very nearly. For the force of the water flowing downward uniformly through the whole canal will be the same upon the little circle PQ in whatsoever part of the canal it be placed.

Let now the orifices of the canal EF, ST be closed, and let the little circle ascend in the fluid compressed on every side, and by its ascent let it oblige the water that lies above it to descend through the annular space between the little circle and the sides of the canal. Then will the velocity of the ascending little circle be to the velocity of the descending water as the difference of the circles EF and PQ is to the circle PQ; and the velocity of the ascending little circle will lie to the sum of the velocities, that is, to the relative velocity of the descending water with which it passes by the little circle in its ascent, as the difference of the circles EF and PQ to the circle EF, or as $EF^2 - PQ^2$ to EF^2. Let that relative velocity be equal to the velocity with which it was shewn above that the water would pass through the annular space, if the circle were to remain unmoved, that is, to the velocity which the water would acquire by falling, and in its fall describing the altitude IG; and the force of the water upon the ascending circle will be the same as before (by Cor. 5, of the Laws of Motion); that is, the resistance of the ascending little circle will be to the weight of a cylinder of water whose base is that little circle, and its altitude $^{1}/_{2}$IG, as EF^2 to $EF^2 - {}^{1}/_{2}PQ^2$, nearly. But the velocity of the little circle will be to the velocity which the water acquires by falling, and in its fall describing the altitude IG, as $EF^2 - PQ^2$ to EF^2.

Let the breadth of the canal be increased *in infinitum*; and the ratios between $EF^2 - PQ^2$ and $EF^2 - {}^{1}/_{2}PQ^2$, will become at last ratios of equality. And therefore the velocity of the little circle will now be the same which the water would acquire in falling, and in its fall describing the altitude IG; and the resistance will become equal to the

weight of a cylinder whose base is that little circle, and its altitude half the altitude IG, from which the cylinder must fall to acquire the velocity of the ascending circle; and with this velocity the cylinder in the time of its fall will describe four times its length. But the resistance of the cylinder moving forward with this velocity in the direction of its length is the same with the resistance of the little circle (by Lem. IV), and is therefore nearly equal to the force by which its motion may be generated while it describes four times its length.

If the length of the cylinder be augmented or diminished, its motion, and the time in which it describes four times its length, will be augmented or diminished in the same ratio, and therefore the force by which the motion so increased or diminished, may be destroyed or generated, will continue the same; because the time is increased or diminished in the same proportion; and therefore that force remains still equal to the resistance of the cylinder, because (by Lem. IV) that resistance will also remain the same.

If the density of the cylinder be augmented or diminished, its motion, and the force by which its motion may be generated or destroyed in the same time, will be augmented or diminished in the same ratio. Therefore the resistance of any cylinder whatsoever will be to the force by which its whole motion may be generated or destroyed, in the time during which it moves four times its length, as the density of the medium to the density of the cylinder, nearly.   Q.E.D.

A fluid must be compressed to become continued; it must be continued and nonelastic, that all the pressure arising from its compression may be propagated in an instant; and so, acting equally upon all parts of the body moved, may produce no change of the resistance. The pressure arising from the motion of the body is spent in generating a motion in the parts of the fluid, and this creates the resistance. But the pressure arising from the compression of the fluid, be it ever so forcible, if it be propagated in an instant, generates no motion in the parts of a continued fluid, produces no change at all of motion therein; and therefore neither augments nor lessens the resistance. This is certain, that the action of the fluid arising from the compression cannot be stronger on the hinder parts of the body moved than on its fore parts, and therefore cannot lessen the resistance described in this proposition. And if its propagation be infinitely swifter than the motion of the body pressed, it will not be stronger on the fore parts than on the hinder parts. But that action will be infinitely swifter, and propagated in an instant, if the fluid be continued and nonelastic.

Cor. 1. The resistances, made to cylinders going uniformly forward in the direction of their lengths through continued infinite mediums are in a ratio compounded of the duplicate ratio of the velocities and the duplicate ratio of the diameters, and the ratio of the density of the mediums.

Cor. 2. If the breadth of the canal be not infinitely increased but the cylinder go forward in the direction of its length through an included quiescent medium, its axis all the while coinciding with the axis of the canal, its resistance will be to the force by which its whole motion, in the time in which it describes four times its length, may be generated or destroyed, in a ratio compounded of the ratio of EF^2 to $EF^2 - \frac{1}{2}PQ^2$ once, and the ratio of EF^2 to $EF^2 - PQ^2$ twice, and the ratio of the density of the medium to the density of the cylinder.

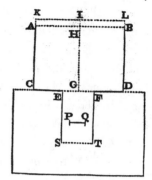

Cor. 3. The same thing supposed, and that a length L is to the quadruple of the length of the cylinder in a ratio compounded of the ratio $EF^2 - \frac{1}{2}PQ^2$ to EF^2 once, and the ratio of $EF^2 - PQ^2$ to EF^2 twice; the resistance of the cylinder will be to the force by which its whole motion, in the time during which it describes the length L, may be destroyed or generated, as the density of the medium to the density of the cylinder.

SCHOLIUM.

In this proposition we have investigated that resistance alone which arises from the magnitude of the transverse section of the cylinder, neglecting that part of the same which may arise from the obliquity of the motions. For as, in Case 1, of Prop. XXXVI., the obliquity of the motions with which the parts of the water in the vessel converged on every side to the hole EF hindered the efflux of the water through the hole, so, in this Proposition, the obliquity of the motions, with which the parts of the water, pressed by the antecedent extremity of the cylinder, yield to the pressure, and diverge on all sides, retards their passage through the places that lie round that antecedent extremity, toward the hinder parts of the cylinder, and causes the fluid to be moved to a greater distance; which increases the resistance, and that in the same ratio almost in which it diminished the efflux of the water out of the vessel, that is, in the duplicate ratio of 25 to 21, nearly. And as, in Case 1, of that Proposition, we made the parts of the water pass through the hole EF perpendicularly and in the greatest plenty, by supposing all the water in the vessel lying round the cataract to be frozen, and that part of the water whose motion was oblique and useless to remain without motion, so in this Proposition, that the obliquity of the motions may be taken away, and the parts of the water may give the freest passage to the cylinder, by yielding to it with the most direct and quick motion possible, so that only so much resistance may remain as arises from the magnitude of the transverse section, and which is incapable of diminution, unless by diminishing the diameter of the cylinder; we must conceive those parts of the fluid

whose motions are oblique and useless, and produce resistance, to be at rest among themselves at both extremities of the cylinder, and there to cohere and be joined to the cylinder.

Let ABCD be a rectangle, and let AE and BE be two parabolic arcs, described with the axis AB, and with a *latus rectum* that is to the space HG, which must be described by the cylinder in falling, in order to acquire the velocity with which it moves, as HG to $\frac{1}{2}$ AB. Let CF and DF be two other parabolic arcs described with the axis CD, and a *latus rectum* quadruple of the former; and by the convolution of the figure about the axis EF let there be generated a solid, whose middle part ABDO is the cylinder we are here speaking of, and whose extreme parts ABE and CDF contain the parts of the fluid at

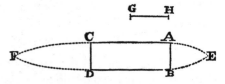

rest among themselves, and concreted into two hard bodies, adhering to the cylinder at each end like a head and tail. Then if this solid EACFDB move in the direction of the length of its axis FE toward the parts beyond E, the resistance will be the same which we have here determined in this Proposition, nearly; that is, it will have the same ratio to the force with which the whole motion of the cylinder may be destroyed or generated, in the time that it is describing the length 4AC with that motion uniformly continued, as the density of the fluid has to the density of the cylinder, nearly. And (by Cor. 7, Prop. XXXVI) the resistance must be to this force in the ratio of 2 to 3, at the least.

LEMMA V.

IF A CYLINDER, A SPHERE, AND A SPHEROID, OF EQUAL BREADTHS
BE PLACED SUCCESSIVELY IN THE MIDDLE OF A CYLINDRIC CANAL,
SO THAT THEIR AXES MAY COINCIDE WITH THE AXIS OF THE
CANAL, THESE BODIES WILL EQUALLY HINDER THE PASSAGE OF
THE WATER THROUGH THE CANAL.

For the spaces lying between the sides of the canal, and the cylinder, sphere, and spheroid, through which the water passes, are equal; and the water will pass equally through equal spaces.

This is true, upon the supposition that all the water above the cylinder, sphere, or spheroid, whose fluidity is not necessary to make the passage of the water the quickest possible, is congealed, as was explained above in Cor. 7, Prop. XXXVI.

LEMMA VI.

THE SAME SUPPOSITION REMAINING, THE FORE-MENTIONED
BODIES ARE EQUALLY ACTED ON BY THE WATER FLOWING
THROUGH THE CANAL.

This appears by Lem. V and the third Law. For the water and the bodies act upon each other mutually and equally.

LEMMA VII.

IF THE WATER BE AT REST IN THE CANAL, AND THESE BODIES MOVE WITH EQUAL VELOCITY AND THE CONTRARY WAY THROUGH THE CANAL, THEIR RESISTANCES WILL BE EQUAL AMONG THEMSELVES.

This appears from the last Lemma, for the relative motions remain the same among themselves.

SCHOLIUM.

The case is the same of all convex and round bodies, whose axes coincide with the axis of the canal. Some difference may arise from a greater or less friction; but in these *Lemmata* we suppose the bodies to be perfectly smooth, and the medium to be void of all tenacity and friction; and that those parts of the fluid which by their oblique and superfluous motions may disturb, hinder, and retard the flux of the water through the canal, are at rest among themselves; being fixed like water by frost, and adhering to the fore and hinder parts of the bodies in the manner explained in the Scholium of the last Proposition; for in what follows we consider the very least resistance that round bodies described with the greatest given transverse sections can possibly meet with.

Bodies swimming upon fluids, when they move straight forward, cause the fluid to ascend at their fore parts and subside at their hinder parts, especially if they are of an obtuse figure; and thence they meet with a little more resistance than if they were acute at the head and tail. And bodies moving in elastic fluids, if they are obtuse behind and before, condense the fluid a little more at their fore parts, and relax the same at their hinder parts; and therefore meet also with a little more resistance than if they were acute at the head and tail. But in these Lemmas and Propositions we are not treating of elastic, but non-elastic fluids; net of bodies floating on the surface of the fluid, but deeply immersed therein. And when the resistance of bodies in non-elastic fluids is once known, we may then augment this resistance a little in elastic fluids, as our air; and in the surfaces of stagnating fluids, as lakes and seas.

PROPOSITION XXXVIII. THEOREM XXX.

IF A GLOBE MOVE UNIFORMLY FORWARD IN A COMPRESSED, INFINITE, AND NONELASTIC FLUID, ITS RESISTANCE IS TO THE FORCE BY WHICH ITS WHOLE MOTION MAY BE

DESTROYED OR GENERATED, IN THE TIME THAT IT
DESCRIBES EIGHT THIRD PARTS OF ITS DIAMETER, AS THE
DENSITY OF THE FLUID TO THE DENSITY OF THE GLOBE,
VERY NEARLY.

For the globe is to its circumscribed cylinder as two to three; and therefore the force which can destroy all the motion of the cylinder, while the same cylinder is describing the length of four of its diameters, will destroy all the motion of the globe, while the globe is describing two thirds of this length, that is, eight third parts of its own diameter. Now the resistance of the cylinder is to this force very nearly as the density of the fluid to the density of the cylinder or globe (by Prop. XXXVII), and the resistance of the globe is equal to the resistance of the cylinder (by Lem. V, VI, and VII). Q.E.D.

COR. 1. The resistances of globes in infinite compressed mediums are in a ratio compounded of the duplicate ratio of the velocity, and the duplicate ratio of the diameter, and the ratio of the density of the mediums.

COR. 2. The greatest velocity, with which a globe can descend by its comparative weight through a resisting fluid, is the same which it may acquire by falling with the same weight, and without any resistance, and in its fall describing a space that is, to four third parts of its diameter as the density of the globe to the density of the fluid. For the globe in the time of its fall, moving with the velocity acquired in falling, will describe a space that will be to eight third parts of its diameter as the density of the globe to the density of the fluid; and the force of its weight which generates this motion will be to the force that can generate the same motion, in the time that the globe describes eight third parts of its diameter, with the same velocity as the density of the fluid to the density of the globe; and therefore (by this Proposition) the force of weight will be equal to the force of resistance, and therefore cannot accelerate the globe.

COR. 3. If there be given both the density of the globe and its velocity at the beginning of the motion, and the density of the compressed quiescent fluid in which the globe moves, there is given at any time both the velocity of the globe and its resistance, and the space described by it (by Cor. 7, Prop. XXXV).

COR. 4. A globe moving in a compressed quiescent fluid of the same density with itself will lose half its motion before it can describe the length of two of its diameters (by the same Cor. 7).

PROPOSITION XXXIX. THEOREM XXXI.

IF A GLOBE MOVE UNIFORMLY FORWARD THROUGH A FLUID
INCLOSED AND COMPRESSED IN A CYLINDRIC CANAL, ITS

RESISTANCE IS TO THE FORCE BY WHICH ITS WHOLE MOTION
MAY BE GENERATED OR DESTROYED, IN THE TIME IN WHICH
IT DESCRIBES EIGHT THIRD PARTS OF ITS DIAMETER, IN A
RATIO COMPOUNDED OF THE RATIO OF LIKE ORIFICE OF
THE CANAL TO THE EXCESS OF THAT ORIFICE ABOVE HALF
THE GREATEST CIRCLE OF THE GLOBE; AND THE DUPLICATE
RATIO OF THE ORIFICE OF THE CANAL TO THE EXCESS OF
THAT ORIFICE ABOVE THE GREATEST CIRCLE OF THE GLOBE;
AND THE RATIO OF THE DENSITY OF THE FLUID TO THE
DENSITY OF THE GLOBE, NEARLY.

This appears by Cor. 2, Prop. XXXVII, and the demonstration proceeds in the same manner as in the foregoing Proposition.

SCHOLIUM.

In the last two Propositions we suppose (as was done before in Lem. V) that all the water which precedes the globe, and whose fluidity increases the resistance of the same, is congealed. Now if that water becomes fluid, it will somewhat increase the resistance. But in these Propositions that increase is so small, that it may be neglected, because the convex superficies of the globe produces the very same effect almost as the congelation of the water.

PROPOSITION XL. PROBLEM IX.

To find by phenomena the resistance of a globe moving through a perfectly fluid compressed medium.

Let A be the weight of the globe *in vacuo,* B its weight in the resisting medium, D the diameter of the globe, F a space which is to $^4/_3$D as the density of the globe to the density of the medium, that is, as A to A − B, G the time in which the globe falling with the weight B without resistance describes the space F, and H the velocity which the body acquires by that fall. Then H will be the greatest velocity with which the globe can possibly descend with the weight B in the resisting medium, by Cor. 2, Prop XXXVIII; and the resistance which the globe meets with, when descending with that velocity, will be equal to its weight B; and the resistance it meets with in any other velocity will be to the weight B in the duplicate ratio of that velocity to the greatest velocity H, by Cor. 1, Prop. XXXVIII.

This is the resistance that arises from the inactivity of the matter of the fluid. That resistance which arises from the elasticity, tenacity, and friction of its parts, may be thus investigated.

Let the globe be let fall so that it may descend in the fluid by the weight B; and let P be the time of falling, and let that time be expressed in seconds, if the time G be given in seconds. Find the absolute number N agreeing to the logarithm $0,4342944819$ $^{2P}/_G$ and let L be the logarithm of the number $\frac{N+1}{N}$: and the velocity acquired in falling will be $\frac{N-1}{N+1}$ H, and the height described will be $\frac{2PF}{G}$ — $1,3862943611F + 4,605170186LF$. If the fluid be of a sufficient depth, we may neglect the term $4,605170186LF$; and $\frac{2PF}{G}$ - $1,3862943611F$ will be the altitude described, nearly. These things appear by Prop. IX, Book II, and its Corollaries, and are true upon this supposition, that the globe meets with no other resistance but that which arises from the inactivity of matter. Now if it really meet with any resistance of another kind, the descent will be slower, and from the quantity of that retardation will be known the quantity of this new resistance.

That the velocity and descent of a body falling in a fluid might more easily be known, I have composed the following table; the first column of which denotes the times of descent; the second shews the velocities acquired in falling, the greatest velocity being 100000000; the third exhibits the spaces described by falling in those times, 2F being the space which the body describes in the time G with the greatest velocity; and the fourth gives the spaces described with the greatest velocity in the same times.

The numbers in the fourth column are $^{2P}/_G$, and by subducting the number $1,3862944 - 4,6051702L$, are found the numbers in the third column; and these numbers must be multiplied by the space F to obtain the spaces described in falling. A fifth column is added to all these, containing the spaces described in the same times by a body falling *in vacuo* with the force of B its comparative weight.

The Times P.	Velocities of the body falling in the fluid.	The space described in falling in the fluid.	The spaces described with the greatest motion.	The spaces described by falling *in vacuo*.
0,001G	$99999^{29}/_{30}$	0,000001F	0,002F	0,00001F
0,01G	999967	0,0001F	0,02F	0,0001F
0,1G	9966799	0,0099834F	0,2F	0,01F
0,2G	19737532	0,0397361F	0,4F	0,04F
0,3G	29131261	0,0886815F	0,6F	0,09F
0,4G	37994896	0,1559070F	0,8F	0,16F
0,5G	46211716	0,2402290F	1,0F	0,25F
0,6G	53704957	0,3402706F	1,2F	0,36F
0,7G	60436778	0,4545405F	1,4F	0,19F
0,8G	66403677	0,5815071F	1,6F	0,64F
0,9G	71629787	0,7196609F	1,8F	0,81F
1G	76159416	0,8675617F	2F	1F
2G	96402758	2,6500055F	4F	4F
3G	99505475	4,6186570F	6F	9F
4G	99932930	6,6143765F	8F	16F
5G	99990920	8,6137964F	10F	25F
6G	99998771	10,6137179F	12F	36F
7G	99999834	12,6137073F	14F	49F
8G	99999980	14,6137059F	16F	64F
9G	39999997	16,6137057F	18F	81F
10G	$99999999^{3}/_{5}$	18,6137056F	20F	100F

SCHOLIUM.

In order to investigate the resistances of fluids from experiments, I procured a square wooden vessel, whose length and breadth on the inside was 9 inches *English* measure, and its depth 9 feet $^1/_2$; this I filled with rain-water: and having provided globes made up of wax, and lead included therein, I noted the times of the descents of these globes, the height through which they descended being 112 inches. A solid cubic foot of *English* measure contains 76 pounds *troy* weight of rain water; and a solid inch contains $^{19}/_{36}$ ounces *troy* weight, or $253^1/_3$ grains; and a globe of water of one inch in diameter contains 132,645 grains in air, or 132,8 grains *in vacuo*; and any other globe will be as the excess of its weight *in vacuo* above its weight in water.

Exper. 1. A globe whose weight was $156^1/_4$ grains in air, and 77 grains in water, described the whole height of 112 inches in 4 seconds. And, upon repeating the experiment, the globe spent again the very same time of 4 seconds in falling.

The weight of this globe *in vacuo* is $156^{13}/_{38}$ grains; and the excess of this weight above the weight of the globe in water is $79^{13}/_{38}$ grains. Hence the diameter of the globe appears to be 0,84224 parts of an inch. Then it will be, as that excess to the weight of the globe *in vacuo*, so is the density of the water to the density of the globe; and so is $^8/_3$ parts of the diameter of the globe (viz. 2,24597 inches) to the space 2F, which will be therefore 4,4256 inches. Now a globe falling *in vacuo* with its whole weight of $156^{13}/_{38}$ grains in one second of time will describe $193^1/_3$ inches; and falling in water in the same time with the weight of 77 grains without resistance, will describe 95,219 inches; and in the time G, which is to one second of time in the subduplicate ratio of the space F, or of 2,2128 inches to 95,219 inches, will describe 2,2128 inches, and will acquire the greatest velocity H with which it is capable of descending in water. Therefore the time G is 0",15244. And in this time G, with that greatest velocity H, the globe will describe the space 2F, which is 4,4256 inches; and therefore in 4 seconds will describe a space of 116,1245 inches. Subduct the space 1,3862944F, or 3,0676 inches, and there will remain a space of 113,0569 inches, which the globe falling through water in a very wide vessel will describe in 4 seconds. But this space, by reason of the narrowness of the wooden vessel before mentioned, ought to be diminished in a ratio compounded of the subduplicate ratio of the orifice of the vessel to the excess of this orifice above half a great circle of the globe, and of the simple ratio of the same orifice to its excess above a great circle of the globe, that is, in a ratio of 1 to 0,9914. This done, we have a space of 112,08 inches, which a globe falling through the water in this wooden vessel in 4 seconds of time ought nearly to describe by this theory; but it described 112 inches by the experiment.

EXPER. 2. Three equal globes, whose weights were severally $76^{1}/_{3}$ grains in air, and $5^{1}/_{16}$ grains in water, were let fall successively; and every one fell through the water in 15 seconds of time, describing in its fall a height of 112 inches.

By computation, the weight of each globe *in vacuo* is $76^{5}/_{12}$ grains; the excess of this weight above the weight in water is 71 grains $^{17}/_{48}$; the diameter of the globe 0,81296 of an inch; $^{8}/_{3}$ parts of this diameter 2,16789 inches; the space 2F is 2,3217 inches; the space which a globe of $5^{1}/_{16}$ grains in weight would describe in one second without resistance, 12,808 inches, and the time G0",301056. Therefore the globe, with the greatest velocity it is capable of receiving from a weight of $5^{1}/_{16}$ grains in its descent through water, will describe in the time 0",301056 the space of 2,3217 inches; and in 15 seconds the space 115,678 inches. Subduct the space 1,3862944F, or 1,609 inches, and there remains the space 114,069 inches; which therefore the falling globe ought to describe in the same time, if the vessel were very wide. But because our vessel was narrow, the space ought to be diminished by about 0,895 of an inch. And so the space will remain 113,174 inches, which a globe falling in this vessel ought nearly to describe in 15 seconds, by the theory. But by the experiment it described 112 inches. The difference is not sensible.

EXPER. 3. Three equal globes, whose weights were severally 121 grains in air, and 1 grain in water, were successively let fall; and they fell through the water in the times 46", 47", and 50", describing a height of 112 inches.

By the theory, these globes ought to have fallen in about 40". Now whether their falling more slowly were occasioned from hence, that in slow motions the resistance arising from the force of inactivity does really bear a less proportion to the resistance arising from other causes; or whether it is to be attributed to little bubbles that might chance to stick to the globes, or to the rarefaction of the wax by the warmth of the weather, or of the hand that let them fall; or, lastly, whether it proceeded from some insensible errors in weighing the globes in the water, I am not certain. Therefore the weight of the globe in water should be of several grains, that the experiment may be certain, and to be depended on.

EXPER. 4. I began the foregoing experiments to investigate the resistances of fluids, before I was acquainted with the theory laid down in the Propositions immediately preceding. Afterward, in order to examine the theory after it was discovered, I procured a wooden vessel, whose breadth on the inside was 82 inches, and its depth 15 feet and $^{1}/_{3}$. Then I made four globes of wax, with lead included, each of which weighed $139^{1}/_{4}$ grains in air, and $7^{1}/_{8}$ grains in water. These I let fall, measuring the times of their falling in the water with a pendulum oscillating to half seconds. The globes were cold, and had remained so some time, both when they were weighed and when they were let fall; because warmth rarefies the wax, and by rarefying it diminishes the weight of the globe

in the water; and wax, when rarefied, is not instantly reduced by cold to its former density. Before they were let fall, they were totally immersed under water, lest, by the weight of any part of them that might chance to be above the water, their descent should be accelerated in its beginning. Then, when after their immersion they were perfectly at rest, they were let go with the greatest care, that they might not receive any impulse from the hand that let them down. And they fell successively in the times of $47^1/_2$, $48^1/_2$, 50, and 51 oscillations, describing a height of 15 feet and 2 inches. But the weather was now a little colder than when the globes were weighed, and therefore I repeated the experiment another day; and then the globes fell in the times of 49, $49^1/_2$, 50, and 53; and at a third trial in the times of $49^1/_2$, 50, 51, and 53 oscillations. And by making the experiment several times over, I found that the globes fell mostly in the times of $49^1/_2$ and 50 oscillations. When they fell slower, I suspect them to have been retarded by striking against the sides of the vessel.

Now, computing from the theory, the weight of the globe *in vacuo* is $139^2/_5$ grains; the excess of this weight above the weight of the globe in water $132^{11}/_{46}$ grains; the diameter of the globe 0,99868 of an inch; $^8/_3$ parts of the diameter 2,66315 inches; the space 2F 2,8066 inches; the space which a globe weighing $7^1/_8$ grains falling without resistance describes in a second of time 9,88164 inches; and the time G0",376843. Therefore the, globe with the greatest velocity with which it is capable of descending through the water by the force of a weight of $7^1/_8$ grains, will in the time 0",376843 describe a space of 2,8066 inches, and in one second of time a space of 7,44766 inches, and in the time 25", or in 50 oscillations, the space 186,1915 inches. Subduct the space 1,366294F, or 1,9454 inches, and there will remain the space 184,2461 inches which the globe will describe in that time in a very wide vessel. Because our vessel was narrow, let this space be diminished in a ratio compounded of the subduplicate ratio of the orifice of the vessel to the excess of this orifice above half a great circle of the globe, and of the simple ratio of the same orifice to its excess above a great circle of the globe; and we shall have the space of 181,86 inches, which the globe ought by the theory to describe in this vessel in the time of 50 oscillations, nearly. But it described the space of 182 inches, by experiment, in $49^1/_2$ or 50 oscillations.

EXPER. 5. Four globes weighing $154^3/_8$ grains in air, and $21^1/_2$ grains in water, being let fall several times, fell in the times of $28^1/_2$, 29, $29^1/_2$, and 30, and sometimes of 31, 32, and 33 oscillations, describing a height of 15 feet and 2 inches.

They ought by the theory to have fallen in the time of 29 oscillations, nearly.

EXPER. 6. Five globes, weighing $212^3/_8$ grains in air, and $79^1/_2$ in water, being several times let fall, fell in the times of 15, $15^1/_2$, 16, 17, and 18 oscillations, describing a height of 15 feet and 2 inches.

By the theory they ought to have fallen in the time of 15 oscillations, nearly.

EXPER. 7. Four globes, weighing $293^3/_8$ grains in air, and $357/_8$ grains in water, being let fall several times, fell in the times of $29^1/_2$, 30, $30^1/_2$, 31, 32, and 33 oscillations, describing a height of 15 feet and 1 inch and $^1/_2$.

By the theory they ought to have fallen in the time of 28 oscillations, nearly.

In searching for the cause that occasioned these globes of the same weight and magnitude to fall, some swifter and some slower, I hit upon this; that the globes, when they were first let go and began to fall, oscillated about their centres; that side which chanced to be the heavier descending first, and producing an oscillating motion. Now by oscillating thus, the globe communicates a greater motion to the water than if it descended without any oscillations; and by this communication loses part of its own motion with which it should descend; and therefore as this oscillation is greater or lesser it will be more or less retarded. Besides, the globe always recedes from that side of itself which is descending in the oscillation, and by so receding comes nearer to the sides of the vessel, so as even to strike against them sometimes. And the heavier the globes are, the stronger this oscillation is; and the greater they are, the more is the water agitated by it. Therefore to diminish this oscillation of the globes, I made new ones of lead and wax, sticking the lead in one side of the globe very near its surface; and I let fall the globe in such a manner, that, as near as possible, the heavier side might be lowest at the beginning of the descent. By this means the oscillations became much less than before, and the times in which the globes fell were not so unequal: as in the following experiments.

EXPER. 8. Four globes weighing 139 grains in air, and $6^1/_2$ in water, were let fall several times, and fell mostly in the time of 51 oscillations, never in more than 52, or in fewer than 50, describing a height of 182 inches.

By the theory they ought to fall in about the time of 52 oscillations.

EXPER. 9. Four globes weighing $273^1/_4$ grains in air, and $140\ ^3/_4$ in water, being several times let fall, fell in never fewer than 12, and never more than 13 oscillations, describing a height of 182 inches.

These globes by the theory ought to have fallen in the time of $11^1/_3$ oscillations, nearly.

EXPER. 10. Four globes, weighing 384 grains in air, and $119^1/_2$ in water, being let fall several times, fell in the times of $17^3/_4$, 18, $18^1/_2$, and 19 oscillations describing a height of $181^1/_2$ inches. And when they fell in the time of 19 oscillations, I sometimes heard them hit against the sides of the vessel before they reached the bottom.

By the theory they ought to have fallen in the time of $15^5/_9$ oscillations, nearly.

EXPER. 11. Three equal globes, weighing 48 grains in the air, and $3^{29}/_{32}$ in water, being several times let fall, fell in the times of $43^1/_2$, 44, $44^1/_2$, 45, and

46 oscillations, and mostly in 44 and 45, describing a height of $182^1/_2$ inches, nearly.

By the theory they ought to have fallen in the time of 46 oscillations and $^5/_9$, nearly.

EXPER. 12. Three equal globes, weighing 141 grains in air, and $4\,^3/_8$ in water, being let fall several times, fell in the times of 61, 62, 63, 64, and 65 oscillations, describing a space of 162 inches.

And by the theory they ought to have fallen in $64^1/_2$ oscillations, nearly.

From these experiments it is manifest, that when the globes fell slowly, as in the second, fourth, fifth, eighth, eleventh, and twelfth experiments, the times of falling are rightly exhibited by the theory; but when the globes fell more swiftly, as in the sixth, ninth, and tenth experiments, the resistance was somewhat greater than in the duplicate ratio of the velocity. For the globes in falling oscillate a little; and this oscillation, in those globes that are light and fall slowly, soon ceases by the weakness of the motion; but in greater and heavier globes, the motion being strong, it continues longer, and is not to be checked by the ambient water till after several oscillations. Besides, the more swiftly the globes move, the less are they pressed by the fluid at their hinder parts; and if the velocity be perpetually increased, they will at last leave an empty space behind them, unless the compression of the fluid be increased at the same time. For the compression of the fluid ought to be increased (by Prop. XXXII and XXXIII) in the duplicate ratio of the velocity, in order to preserve the resistance in the same duplicate ratio. But because this is not done, the globes that move swiftly are not so much pressed at their hinder parts as the others; and by the defect of this pressure it comes to pass that their resistance is a little greater than in a duplicate ratio of their velocity.

So that the theory agrees with the phaenomena of bodies falling in water It remains that we examine the phaenomena of bodies falling in air.

EXPER. 13. From the top of St. *Paul's* Church in *London*, in *June* 1710, there were let fall together two glass globes, one full of quicksilver, the other of air; and in their fall they described a height of 220 *English* feet. A wooden table was suspended upon iron hinges on one side, and the other side of the same was supported by a wooden pin. The two globes lying upon this table were let fall together by pulling out the pin by means of an iron wire reaching from thence quite down to the ground; so that, the pin being removed, the table, which had then no support but the iron hinges, fell downward, and turning round upon the hinges, gave leave to the globes to drop off from it. At the same instant, with the same pull of the iron wire that took out the pin, a pendulum oscillating to seconds was let go, and began to oscillate. The diameters and weights of the globes, and their times of falling, are exhibited in the following table.

The globes filled with mercury.			The globes full of air.		
Weights.	Diameters.	Times in falling.	Weights.	Diameters.	Times in falling.
908 grains	0,8 of an inch	4"	510 grains	5,1 inches	8" 1/2
983	0,8	4 -	642	5,2	8
866	0,8	4	599	5,1	8
747	0,75	4 +	515	5,0	8 1/4
808	0,75	4	483	5,0	8 1/2
784	0,75	4 +	641	5,2	8

But the times observed must be corrected; for the globes of mercury (by *Galileo's* theory), in 4 seconds of time, will describe 257 *English* feet, and 220 feet in only 3"42"'. So that the wooden table, when the pin was taken out, did not turn upon its hinges so quickly as it ought to have done; and the slowness of that revolution hindered the descent of the globes at the beginning. For the globes lay about the middle of the table, and indeed were rather nearer to the axis upon which it turned than to the pin. And hence the times of falling were prolonged about 18"'; and therefore ought to be corrected by subducting that excess, especially in the larger globes, which, by reason of the largeness of their diameters, lay longer upon the revolving table than the others. This being done, the times in which the six larger globes fell will come forth 8" 12"', 7" 42"', 7" 42"', 7" 57"', 8" 12"' and 7" 42"'.

Therefore the fifth in order among the globes that were full of air being 5 inches in diameter, and 483 grains in weight, fell in 8" 12"', describing a space of 220 feet. The weight of a bulk of water equal to this globe is 16600 grains; and the weight of an equal bulk of air is 16600/860 grains, or $19^3/_{10}$ grains; and therefore the weight of the globe *in vacuo* is $502^3/_{10}$ grains; and this weight is to the weight of a bulk of air equal to the globe as $502^3/_{10}$ to $19^3/_{10}$; and so is 2F to $^8/_3$ of the diameter of the globe, that is, to $13^1/_3$ inches. Whence 2F becomes 28 feet 11 inches. A globe, falling *in vacuo* with its whole weight of $502^3/_{10}$ grains, will in one second of time describe $193^1/_3$ inches as above; and with the weight of 483 grains will describe 185,905 inches; and with that weight 483 grains *in vacuo* will describe the space F, or 14 feet $5^1/_2$ inches, in the time of 57"' 58"', and acquire the greatest velocity it is capable of descending with in the air. With this velocity the globe in 8" 12"' of time will describe 245 feet and $5^1/_3$ inches. Subduct 1,3863F, or 20 feet and $^1/_2$ an inch, and there remain 225 feet 5 inches. This space, therefore, the falling globe ought by this theory to describe in 8" 12"'. But by the experiment it described a space of 220 feet The difference is insensible.

By like calculations applied to the other globes full of air, I composed the following table.

The weight of the globes.	The diameters.	The times of falling from a height of 220 feet.		The space which they would describe by the theory.		The excesses.	
510 grains	5,1 inches	8"	12'''	226 feet	11 inch.	6 feet	11 inch.
642	5,2	7	42	230	9	10	9
599	5,1	7	42	227	10	7	0
515	5	7	57	224	5	4	5
483	5	8	12	225	5	5	5
641	5,2	7	42	230	7	10	7

EXPER. 14. *Anno* 1719, in the month of *July,* Dr. *Desaguliers* made some experiments of this kind again, by forming hogs' bladders into spherical orbs; which was done by means of a concave wooden sphere, which the bladders, being wetted well first, were put into. After that being blown full of air, they were obliged to fill up the spherical cavity that contained them; and then, when dry, were taken out. These were let fall from the lantern on the top of the cupola of the same church, namely, from a height of 272 feet; and at the same moment of time there was let fall a leaden globe, whose weight was about 2 pounds *troy* weight. And in the mean time some persons standing in the upper part of the church where the globes were let fall observed the whole times of falling; and others standing on the ground observed the differences of the times between the fall of the leaden weight and the fall of the bladder. The times were measured by pendulums oscillating to half seconds. And one of those that stood upon the ground had a machine vibrating four times in one second; and another had another machine accurately made with a pendulum vibrating four times in a second also. One of those also who stood at the top of the church had a like machine; and these instruments were so contrived, that their motions could be stopped or renewed at pleasure. Now the leaden globe fell in about four seconds and $1/4$ of time; and from the addition of this time to the difference of time above spoken of, was collected the whole time in which the bladder was falling. The times which the five bladders spent in falling, after the leaden globe had reached the ground, were, the first time, $14^3/_4$", $12^3/_4$", $14^5/_8$", $17^3/_4$", and $16^7/_8$"; and the second time, $14^1/_2$", $14^1/_4$", 14", 19", and $16^3/_4$". Add to these 4", the time in which the leaden globe was falling, and the whole times in which the five bladders fell were, the first time, 19", 17", $18^7/_8$", 22", and $21^1/_8$"; and the second time, $18^3/_4$", $18^1/_2$", $18^1/_4$", $23^1/_4$", and 21". The times observed at the top of the church were, the first time, $19^3/_8$", $17^1/_4$", $18^3/_4$", $22^1/_8$", and 21 $5/_8$"; and the second time, 19", $18^5/_8$", $18^3/_8$", 24", and $21^1/_4$". But the bladders did not always fall directly down, but sometimes fluttered a little in the air, and waved to and fro, as they were descending. And by these motions the times of their falling were prolonged, and increased by half a second sometimes, and sometimes by a whole second. The second and fourth bladder fell most directly the first time, and the

first and third the second time. The fifth bladder was wrinkled, and by its wrinkles was a little retarded. I found their diameters by their circumferences measured with a very fine thread wound about them twice. In the following table I have compared the experiments with the theory; making the density of air to be to the density of rain-water as 1 to 860, and computing the spaces which by the theory the globes ought to describe in falling.

The weights of the bladders.	The diameters	The times of falling from a height of 272 feet	The spaces which by the theory ought to have been described in those times.		The difference between the theory and the experiments.	
128 grains	5,28 inches	19"	271 feet	11 inches	- 0 ft.	1 in.
156	5,19	17	272	0 1/2	+ 0	0 1/2
137 1/2	5,3	18	272	7	+ 0	7
97 1/2	5,26	22	277	4	+ 5	4
99 1/8	5	21 1/8	282	0	+ 10	0

Our theory, therefore, exhibits rightly, within a very little, all the resistance that globes moving either in air or in water meet with; which appears to be proportional to the densities of the fluids in globes of equal velocities and magnitudes.

In the Scholium subjoined to the sixth Section, we shewed, by experiments of pendulums, that the resistances of equal and equally swift globes moving in air, water, and quicksilver, are as the densities of the fluids. We here prove the same more accurately by experiments of bodies falling in air and water. For pendulums at each oscillation excite a motion in the fluid always contrary to the motion of the pendulum in its return; and the resistance arising from this motion, as also the resistance of the thread by which the pendulum is suspended, makes the whole resistance of a pendulum greater than the resistance deduced from the experiments of falling bodies. For by the experiments of pendulums described in that Scholium, a globe of the same density as water in describing the length of its semi-diameter in air would lose the $1/3342$ part of its motion. But by the theory delivered in this seventh Section, and confirmed by experiments of falling bodies, the same globe in describing the same length would lose only a part of its motion equal to $1/4586$, supposing the density of water to be to the density of air as 860 to 1. Therefore the resistances were found greater by the experiments of pendulums (for the reasons just mentioned) than by the experiments of falling globes; and that in the ratio of about 4 to 3. But yet since the resistances of pendulums oscillating, in air, water, and quicksilver, are alike increased by like causes, the proportion of the resistances in these mediums will be rightly enough exhibited by the experiments of pendulums, as well as by the experiments of falling bodies. And from all this it may be concluded, that the resistances of bodies, moving in any fluids whatsoever, though of the most extreme fluidity, are, *caeteris paribus*, as the densities of the fluids.

These things being thus established, we may now determine what part of its motion any globe projected in any fluid whatsoever would nearly lose in a given time. Let D be the diameter of the globe, and V its velocity at the beginning of its motion, and T the time in which a globe with the velocity V can describe *in vacuo* a space that is, to the space $^8/_3$D as the density of the globe to the density of the fluid; and the globe projected in that fluid will, in any other time t lose the part $\frac{tV}{T+t}$, the part $\frac{TV}{T+t}$ remaining; and will describe a space, which will be to that described in the same time *in vacuo* with the uniform velocity V, as the logarithm of the number $\frac{T+t}{T}$ multiplied by the number 2,302585093 is the number $^t/_T$ by Cor. 7, Prop. XXXV. In slow motions the resistance may be a little less, because the figure of a globe is more adapted to motion than the figure of a cylinder described with the same diameter. In swift motions the resistance may be a little greater, because the elasticity and compression of the fluid do not increase in the duplicate ratio of the velocity. But these little niceties I take no notice of.

And though air, water, quicksilver, and the like fluids, by the division of their parts *in infinitum*, should be subtilized, and become mediums infinitely fluid, nevertheless, the resistance they would make to projected globes would be the same. For the resistance considered in the preceding Propositions arises from the inactivity of the matter; and the inactivity of matter is essential to bodies, and always proportional to the quantity of matter. By the division of the parts of the fluid the resistance arising from the tenacity and friction of the parts may be indeed diminished; but the quantity of matter will not be at all diminished by this division; and if the quantity of matter be the same, its force of inactivity will be the same; and therefore the resistance here spoken of will be the same, as being always proportional to that force. To diminish this resistance, the quantity of matter in the spaces through which the bodies move must be diminished; and therefore the celestial spaces, through which the globes of the planets and comets are perpetually passing towards all parts, with the utmost freedom, and without the least sensible diminution of their motion, must be utterly void of any corporeal fluid, excepting, perhaps, some extremely rare vapours and the rays of light.

Projectiles excite a motion in fluids as they pass through them, and this motion arises from the excess of the pressure of the fluid at the fore parts of the projectile above the pressure of the same at the hinder parts; and cannot be less in mediums infinitely fluid than it is in air, water, and quicksilver, in proportion to the density of matter in each. Now this excess of pressure does, in proportion to its quantity, not only excite a motion in the fluid, but also acts upon the projectile so as to retard its motion; and therefore the resistance in every fluid is as the motion excited by the projectile in the fluid; and cannot be less in the most subtile rather in proportion to the density of that

aether, than it is in air, water, and quicksilver, in proportion to the densities of those fluids.

SECTION VIII.

Of motion propagated through fluids.

PROPOSITION XLI. THEOREM XXXII.

A PRESSURE IS NOT PROPAGATED THROUGH A FLUID IN
RECTILINEAR DIRECTIONS UNLESS WHERE THE PARTICLES
OF THE FLUID LIE IN A RIGHT LINE.

If the particles *a, b, c, d, e*, lie in a right line, the pressure may be indeed directly propagated from *a* to *e*; but then the particle *e* will urge the obliquely posited particles *f* and *g* obliquely, and those particles *f* and *g* will not sustain this pressure, unless they be supported by the particles *h* and *k* lying beyond them; but the particles that support

them are also pressed by them; and those particles cannot sustain that pressure, without being supported by, and pressing upon, those particles that lie still farther, as *l* and *m*, and so on *in infinitum*. Therefore the pressure, as soon as it is propagated to particles that lie out of right lines, begins to deflect towards one hand and the other, and will be propagated obliquely *in infinitum*; and after it has begun to be propagated obliquely, if it reaches more distant particles lying out of the light line, it will deflect again on each hand and this it will do as often as it lights on particles that do not lie exactly in a right line.   Q.E.D.

Cor. If any part of a pressure, propagated through a fluid from a given point, be intercepted by any obstacle, the remaining part, which is not intercepted, will deflect into the spaces behind the obstacle. This may be demonstrated also after the following manner. Let a pressure be propagated from the point A towards any part, and, if it be possible, in rectilinear directions; and the obstacle NBCK being perforated in BC, let all the pressure be intercepted but the coniform part APQ passing through the circular hole BC. Let the cone APQ be divided into frustums by the transverse planes, *de*, *fg*, *hi*. Then while the cone ABC, propagating the pressure, urges the conic frustum *degf* beyond it on the superficies *de*, and this frustum urges the next frustum *fgih* on the superficies *fg*, and that frustum urges a third frustum, and so *in infinitum*; it is manifest (by the third Law) that the first frustum *defg* is, by the re-action of the second frustum *fghi*, as much urged and pressed on the superficies *fg*, as it urges and presses that second frustum. Therefore the frustum *degf* is compressed on both sides, that is,

between the cone A*de* and the frustum *fhig*, and therefore (by Case 6, Prop. XIX) cannot preserve its figure, unless it be compressed with the same force on all sides.

Therefore with the same force with which it is pressed on the superficies *de*, *fg*, it will endeavour to break forth at the sides *df*, *eg*; and there (being not in the least tenacious or hard, but perfectly fluid) it will run out, expanding itself, unless there be an ambient fluid opposing that endeavour. Therefore, by the effort it makes to run out, it will press the ambient fluid, at its sides *df*, *eg*, with the same force that it

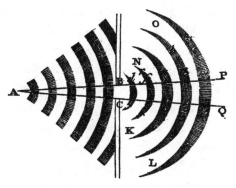

does the frustum *fghi*; and therefore, the pressure will be propagated as much from the sides *df*, *eg*, into the spaces NO, KL this way and that way, as it is propagated from the superficies *fg*, towards PQ.   Q.E.D.

PROPOSITION XLII. THEOREM XXXIII.

ALL MOTION PROPAGATED THROUGH A FLUID DIVERGES FROM A RECTILINEAR PROGRESS INTO THE UNMOVED SPACES.

CASE 1. Let a motion be propagated from the point A through the hole BC, and, if it be possible, let it proceed in the conic space BCQP according to right lines diverging from the point A. And let us first suppose this motion to be that of waves in the surface of standing water; and let *de*, *fg*, *hi*, *kl*, &c., be the tops of the several waves, divided from each other by as any intermediate valleys or hollows. Then, because the water in the ridges of the waves is higher than in the unmoved parts of the fluid KL, NO, it will run down from off the tops of those ridges, *e*, *g*, *i*, *l*, &c., *d*, *f*, *h*, *k*, &c., this way and that way towards KL and NO; and because the water is more depressed in the hollows of the waves than in the unmoved parts of the fluid KL, NO, it will run

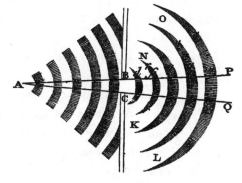

down into those hollows out of those unmoved parts. By the first deflux the ridges of the waves will dilate themselves this way and that way, and be propagated towards KL and NO. And because the motion of the waves from A towards PQ is carried on by a

continual deflux from the ridges of the waves into the hollows next to them, and therefore cannot be swifter than in proportion to the celerity of the descent; and the descent of the water on each side towards KL and NO must be performed with the same velocity; it follows that the dilatation of the waves on each side towards KL and NO will be propagated with the game velocity as the waves themselves go forward with directly from A to PQ, And therefore the whole space this way and that way towards KL and NO will be filled by the dilated waves *rfgr, shis, tkit, vmnv,* &c. Q.E.D. That these things are so, anyone may find by making the experiment in still water.

CASE 2. Let us suppose that *de, fg, hi, kl, mn,* represent pulses successively propagated from the point A through an elastic medium. Conceive the pulses to be propagated by successive condensations and rarefactions of the medium, so that the densest part of every pulse may occupy a spherical superficies described about the centre A, and that equal intervals intervene between the successive pulses. Let the lines *de, fg, hi, kl,* &c., represent the densest parts of the pulses, propagated through the hole BC; and because the medium is denser there than in the spaces on either side towards KL and NO, it will dilate itself as well towards those spaces KL, NO, on each hand, as towards the rare intervals between the pulses; and thence the medium, becoming always more rare next the intervals, and more dense next the pulses, will partake of their motion. And because the progressive motion of the pulses arises from the perpetual relaxation of the denser parts towards the antecedent rare intervals; and since the pulses will relax themselves on each hand towards the quiescent parts of the medium KL, NO, with very near the same celerity; therefore the pulses will dilate themselves on all sides into the unmoved parts KL, NO, with almost the same celerity with which they are propagated directly from the centre A; and therefore will fill up the whole space KLON. Q.E.D. And we find the same by experience also in sounds which are heard through a mountain interposed; and, if they come into F, chamber through the window, dilate themselves into all the parts of the room, and are heard in every corner; and not as reflected from the opposite walls, but directly propagated from the window, as far as our sense can judge.

CASE 3. Let us suppose, lastly, that a motion of any kind is propagated from A through the hole BC. Then since the cause of this propagation is that the parts of the medium that are near the centre A disturb and agitate those which lie farther from it; and since the parts which are urged are fluid, and therefore recede every way towards those spaces where they are less pressed, they will by consequence recede towards all the parts of the quiescent medium; as well to the parts on each band, as KL and NO, as to those right before, as PQ; and by this means all the motion, as soon as it has passed through the hole BC, will begin to dilate itself, and from thence, as from its principle and centre, will be propagated directly every way. Q.E.D.

PROPOSITION XLIII. THEOREM XXXIV.

Every tremulous body in an elastic medium propagates the motion of the pulses on every side right forward, but in a non-elastic medium excites a circular motion.

Case 1. The parts of the tremulous body, alternately going and returning, do in going urge and drive before them those parts of the medium that lie nearest, and by that impulse compress and condense them; and in returning suffer those compressed parts to recede again, and expand themselves. Therefore the parts of the medium that lie nearest to the tremulous body move to and fro by turns, in like manner as the parts of the tremulous body itself do; and for the same cause that the parts of this body agitate these parts of the medium, these parts, being agitated by like tremors, will in their turn agitate others next to themselves; and these others, agitated in like manner, will agitate those that lie beyond them, and so on *in infinitum*. And in the same manner as the first parts of the medium were condensed in going, and relaxed in returning, so will the other parts be condensed every time they go, and expand themselves every time they return. And therefore they will not be all going and all returning at the same instant (for in that case they would always preserve determined distances from each other, and there could be no alternate condensation and rarefaction); but since, in the places where they are condensed, they approach to, and, in the places where they are rarefied, recede from each other, therefore some of them will be going while others are returning; and so on *in infinitum*. The parts so going, and in their going condensed, are pulses, by reason of the progressive motion with which they strike obstacles in their way; and therefore the successive pulses produced by a tremulous body will be propagated in rectilinear directions; and that at nearly equal distances from each other, because of the equal intervals of time in which the body, by its several tremors produces the several pulses. And though the parts of the tremulous body go and return in some certain and determinate direction, yet the pulses propagated from thence through the medium will dilate themselves towards the sides, by the foregoing Proposition; and will be propagated on all sides from that tremulous body, as from a common centre, in superficies nearly spherical and concentrical. An example of this we have in waves excited by shaking a finger in water, which proceed not only forward and backward agreeably to the motion of the finger, but spread themselves in the manner of concentrical circles all round the finger, and are propagated on every side. For the gravity of the water supplies the place of elastic force.

Case 2. If the medium be not elastic, then, because its parts cannot be condensed by the pressure arising from the vibrating parts of the tremulous body, the motion will

be propagated in an instant towards the parts where the medium yields most easily, that is, to the parts which the tremulous body would otherwise leave vacuous behind it. The case is the same with that of a body projected in any medium whatever. A medium yielding to projectiles does not recede *in infinitum*, but with a circular motion comes round to the spaces which the body leaves behind it. Therefore as often as a tremulous body tends to any part, the medium yielding to it comes round in a circle to the parts which the body leaves; and as often as the body returns to the first place, the medium will be driven from the place it came round to, and return to its original place. And though the tremulous body be not firm and hard, but every way flexible, yet if it continue of a given magnitude, since it cannot impel the medium by its tremors any where without yielding to it somewhere else, the medium receding from the parts of the body where it is pressed will always come round in a circle to the parts that yield to it. Q.E.D.

COR. It is a mistake, therefore, to think, as some have done, that the agitation of the parts of flame conduces to the propagation of a pressure in rectilinear directions through an ambient medium. A pressure of that kind must be derived not from the agitation only of the parts of flame, but from the dilatation of the whole.

PROPOSITION XLIV. THEOREM XXXV.

IF WATER ASCEND AND DESCEND ALTERNATELY IN THE
ERECTED LEGS KL, MN, OF A CANAL OR PIPE; AND A
PENDULUM BE CONSTRUCTED WHOSE LENGTH BETWEEN
THE POINT OF SUSPENSION AND THE CENTRE OF OSCILLATION
IS EQUAL TO HALT THE LENGTH OF THE WATER IN THE
CANAL; I SAY, THAT THE WATER WILL ASCEND AND DESCEND
IN THE SAME TIMES IN WHICH THE PENDULUM OSCILLATES.

I measure the length of the water along the axes of the canal and its legs, and make it equal to the sum of those axes; and take no notice of the resistance of the water arising from its attrition by the sides of the canal. Let, therefore, AB, CD, represent the mean height of the water in both legs; and when the water in the leg KL ascends to the height EF, the water will descend in the leg MN to the height GH. Let P be a pendulous body, VP the thread, V the point of suspension, RPQS the cycloid which the pendulum describes, P its lowest point, PQ an arc equal to the height AE. The force with which the motion of the water is accelerated and retarded alternately is the excess of the weight of the water in one leg above the weight in the other; and, therefore, when the water in the leg KL ascends to EF, and in the other leg descends to GH, that force is double the weight of the water EABF, and therefore is to the weight of the whole

water as AE or PQ to VP or PR. The force also with which the body P is accelerated or retarded in any place, as Q, of a cycloid, is (by Cor. Prop. LI) to its whole weight as its distance PQ from the lowest place P to the length PR of the cycloid. Therefore the

motive forces of the water and pendulum, describing the equal spaces AE, PQ, are as the weights to be moved; and therefore if the water and pendulum are quiescent at first, those forces will move them in equal times, and will cause them to go and return together with a reciprocal motion. Q.E.D.

Cor. 1. Therefore the reciprocations of the water in ascending and descending are all performed in equal times, whether the motion be more or less intense or remiss.

Cor. 2. If the length of the whole water in the canal be of $6^1/_9$ feet of *French* measure, the water will descend in one second of time, and will ascend in another second, and so on by turns *in infinitum*, for a pendulum of $3^1/_{18}$ such feet in length will oscillate in one second of time.

Cor. 3. But if the length of the water be increased or diminished, the time of the reciprocation will be increased or diminished in the subduplicate ratio of the length.

PROPOSITION XLV. THEOREM XXXVI.

THE VELOCITY OF WAVES IS IN THE SUBDUPLICATE RATIO OF THE BREADTHS.

This follows from the construction of the following Proposition.

PROPOSITION XLVI. PROBLEM X.

TO FIND THE VELOCITY OF WAVES.

Let a pendulum be constructed, whose length between the point of suspension and the centre of oscillation is equal to the breadth of the waves and in the time that the pendulum will perform one single oscillation the waves will advance forward nearly a space equal to their breadth.

That which I call the breadth of the waves is the transverse measure lying between the deepest part of the hollows, or the tops of the ridges. Let ABCDEF represent the

surface of stagnant water ascending and descending in successive waves; and let A, C, E, &c., be the tops of the waves; and let B, D, F, &c., be the intermediate hollows. Because the motion of the waves is carried on by the successive ascent and descent of the water, so that the parts thereof, as A, C, E, &c., which are highest at one time become lowest immediately after; and because the motive force, by which the highest parts descend and the lowest ascend, is the weight of the elevated water, that alternate ascent and descent will be analogous to the reciprocal motion of the water in the canal, and observe the same laws as to the times of its ascent and descent; and therefore (by Prop. XLIV) if the distances between the highest places of the waves A, C, E, and the lowest B, D, F, be equal to twice the length of any pendulum, the highest parts A, C, E, will become the lowest in the time of one oscillation, and in the time of another oscillation will ascend again. Therefore between the passage of each wave, the time of two oscillations will intervene; that is, the wave will describe its breadth in the time that pendulum will oscillate twice; but a pendulum of four times that length, and which therefore is equal to the breadth of the waves, will just oscillate once in that time.　　　　　Q.E.D.

Cor. 1. Therefore waves, whose breadth is equal to $3^1/_{18}$ *French* feet, will advance through a space equal to their breadth in one second of time; and therefore in one minute will go over a space of $183^1/_3$ feet; and in an hour a space of 11000 feet, nearly.

Cor. 2. And the velocity of greater or less waves will be augmented or diminished in the subduplicate ratio of their breadth.

These things are true upon the supposition that the parts of water ascend or descend in a right line; but, in truth, that ascent and descent is rather performed in a circle; and therefore I propose the time defined by this Proposition as only near the truth.

PROPOSITION XLVII. THEOREM XXXVII.

IF PULSES ARE PROPAGATED THROUGH A FLUID, THE
SEVERAL PARTICLES OF THE FLUID, GOING AND
RETURNING WITH THE SHORTEST RECIPROCAL MOTION,
ARE ALWAYS ACCELERATED OR RETARDED ACCORDING
TO THE LAW OF THE OSCILLATING PENDULUM.

Let AB, BC, CD, &c., represent equal distances of successive pulses; ABC the line of direction of the motion of the successive pulses propagated from A to B; E, F, G

three physical points of the quiescent medium situate in the right line AC at equal distances from each other; E*e*, F*f*, G*g* equal spaces of extreme shortness, through which those points go and return with a reciprocal motion in each vibration; ϵ, ϕ, γ any intermediate places of the same points; EF, FG physical lineolae, or linear parts of the medium lying between those points, and successively transferred into the places $\epsilon\phi$, $\phi\gamma$, and *ef*, *fg*. Let there be drawn the right line PS equal to the right line E*e*. Bisect the same in O, and from the centre O, with the interval OP, describe the circle SIP*i*. Let the whole time of one vibration; with its proportional parts, be expounded by the whole circumference of this circle and its parts, in such sort, that, when any time PH or PHS*h* is completed, if there be let fall to PS the perpendicular HL or *hl*, and there be taken E*e* equal to PL or P*l*, the physical point E may be found in ϵ. A point, as E, moving according to this law with a reciprocal motion, in its going from E through ϵ to *e*, and returning again through ϵ to E, will perform its several vibrations with the degrees of acceleration and retardation with those of an oscillating pendulum. We are now to prove that the several physical points of the medium will be agitated with such a kind of motion. Let us suppose, then, that a medium hath such a motion excited in it from any cause whatsoever, and consider what will follow from thence.

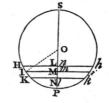

In the circumference PHS*h* let there be taken the equal arcs, HI, IK, or *hi*, *ik*, having the same ratio to the whole circumference as the equal right lines EF, FG have to BC, the whole interval of the pulses. Let fell the perpendiculars IM, KN, or *im*, *kn*; then because the points E, F, G are successively agitated with like motions, and perform their entire vibrations composed of their going and return, while the pulse is transferred from B to C; if PH or PHS*h* be the time elapsed since the beginning of the motion of the point E, then will PI or PHS*i* be the time elapsed since the beginning of the motion of the point F, and PK or PHS*k* the time elapsed since the beginning of the motion of the point G; and therefore Eϵ, Fϕ, Gγ, will be respectively equal to PL, PM, PN, while the points are going, and to P*l*, P*m*, P*n*, when the points are returning. Therefore $\epsilon\gamma$ or EG + Gγ - Eϵ will, when the points are going, be equal to EG - LN and in their return equal to EG + *ln*. But $\epsilon\gamma$ is the breadth or expansion of the part EG of the medium in the place $\epsilon\gamma$; and therefore the expansion of that part in its going is to its mean expansion as EG − LN to EG; and in its return, as EG + *ln* or EG + LN to EG.

Therefore since LN is to KH as IN to the radius OP, and KH to EG as the circumference PHS*h*P to BC; that is, if we put V for the radius of a circle whose circumference is equal to BC the interval of the pulses, as OP to V; and, *ex aequo*, LN to EG as IM to V; the expansion of the part EG, or of the physical point F in the place $\epsilon\gamma$, to the mean expansion of the same part in its first place EG, will be as V - IM to V in going, and as V + *im* to V in its return. Hence the elastic force of the point F in the place $\epsilon\gamma$ to its mean elastic force in the place EG is as $\frac{1}{V-IM}$ to $^1/_V$ in its going, and

as $\frac{1}{V+im}$ to $^1/_V$ in its return. And by the same reasoning the elastic forces of the physical points E and G in going are as $\frac{1}{V-HL}$ and $\frac{1}{V-KN}$ to $^1/_V$; and the difference of the forces to the mean elastic force of the medium as $\frac{HL-KN}{VV-V\times HL-V\times KN+HI\times KN}$ to $^1/_V$; that is, as $\frac{HL-KN}{VV}$ to $^1/_V$, or as HL

- KN to V; if we suppose (by reason of the very short extent of the vibrations) HL and KN to be indefinitely less than the quantity V. Therefore since the quantity V is given, the difference of the form is as HL - KN; that is (because HL - KN is proportional to HK, and OM to OI or OP; and because HK and OP are given) as OM; that is, if F*f* be bisected in Ω, as $\Omega\phi$. And for the same reason the difference of the elastic forces of the physical points ϵ and γ, in the return of the physical lineola $\epsilon\gamma$, is as $\Omega\phi$. But that difference (that is, the excess of the elastic force of the point ϵ above the elastic force of the point γ) is the very force by which the intervening physical lineola $\epsilon\gamma$ of the medium is accelerated in going, and retarded in returning; and therefore the accelerative force of the physical lineola $\epsilon\gamma$ is as its distance from Ω, the middle place of the vibration, Therefore (by Prop. XXXVIII, Book I) the time is rightly expounded by the arc PI; and the linear part of the medium $\epsilon\gamma$ is moved according to the law above-mentioned, that is, according to the law of a pendulum oscillating; and the case is the same of all the linear parts of which the whole medium is compounded. Q.E.D.

COR. Hence it appears that the number of the pulses propagated is the same with the number of the vibrations of the tremulous body, and is not multiplied in their progress. For the physical lineola $\epsilon\gamma$ as soon as it returns to its first place is at rest; neither will it move again, unless it receives a new motion either from the impulse of the tremulous body, or of the pulses propagated from that body. As soon, therefore, as the pulses cease to be propagated from the tremulous body, it will return to a state of rest, and move no more.

PROPOSITION XLVIII. THEOREM XXXVIII.

THE VELOCITIES OF PULSES PROPAGATED IN AN ELASTIC FLUID
ARE IN A RATIO COMPOUNDED OF THE SUBDUPLICATE RATIO OF

THE ELASTIC FORCE DIRECTLY, AND THE SUBDUPLICATE RATIO
OF THE DENSITY INVERSELY; SUPPOSING THE ELASTIC FORCE OF
THE FLUID TO BE PROPORTIONAL TO ITS CONDENSATION.

CASE 1. If the mediums be homogeneous, and the distances of the pulses in those mediums be equal amongst themselves, but the motion in one medium is more intense than in the other, the contractions and dilatations of the correspondent parts will be as those motions; not that this proportion is perfectly accurate. However, if the contractions and dilatations are not exceedingly intense, the error will not be sensible; and therefore this proportion may be considered as physically exact. Now the motive elastic forces are as the contractions and dilatations; and the velocities generated in the same time in equal parts are as the forces. Therefore equal and corresponding parts of corresponding pulses will go and return together, through spaces proportional to their contractions and dilatations, with velocities that are as those spaces; and therefore the pulses, which in the time of one going and returning advance forward a space equal to their breadth, and are always succeeding into the places of the pulses that immediately go before them, will, by reason of the equality of the distances, go forward in both mediums with equal velocity.

CASE 2. If the distances of the pulses or their lengths are greater in one medium than in another, let us suppose that the correspondent parts describe spaces, in going and returning, each time proportional to the breadths of the pulses; then will their contractions and dilatations be equal; and therefore if the mediums are homogeneous, the motive elastic form, which agitate them with a reciprocal motion, will be equal also. Now the matter to be moved by these forces is as the breadth of the pulses; and the space through which they move every time they go and return is in the same ratio. And, moreover, the time of one going and returning is in a ratio compounded of the subduplicate ratio of the matter, and the subduplicate ratio of the space; and therefore is as the space. But the pulses advance a space equal to their breadths in the times of going once and returning once; that is, they go over spaces proportional to the times, and therefore are equally swift.

CASE 3. And, therefore in mediums of equal density and elastic force all the pulses are equally swift. Now if the density or the elastic force of the medium were augmented, then, because the motive force is increased in the ratio of the elastic force, and the matter to be moved is increased in the ratio of the density, the time which is necessary for producing the same motion as before will be increased in the subduplicate ratio of the density, and will be diminished in the subduplicate ratio of the elastic force. And therefore the velocity of the pulses will be in a ratio compounded of the subduplicate ratio of the density of the medium inversely, and the subduplicate ratio of the elastic force directly. Q.E.D.

This Proposition will be made more clear from the construction of the following Problem.

PROPOSITION XLIX. PROBLEM XI.

THE DENSITY AND ELASTIC FORCE OF A MEDIUM BEING GIVEN, TO FIND THE VELOCITY OF THE PULSES.

Suppose the medium to be pressed by an incumbent weight after the manner of our air; and let A be the height of a homogeneous medium, whose weight is equal to the incumbent weight, and whose density is the same with the density of the compressed medium in which the pulses are propagated. Suppose a pendulum to be constructed whose length between the point of suspension and the centre of oscillation is A: and in the time in which that pendulum will perform one entire oscillation composed of its going and returning, the pulse will be propagated right onwards through a space equal to the circumference of a circle described with the radius A.

For, letting those things stand which were constructed in Prop. XLVII, if any physical line, as EF, describing the space PS in each vibration, be acted on in the extremities P and S of every going and return that it makes by an elastic force that is equal to its weight, it will perform its several vibrations in the time in which the same might oscillate in a cycloid whose whole perimeter is equal to the length PS; and that because equal forces will impel equal corpuscles through equal spares in the same or equal times. Therefore since the times of the oscillations are in the subduplicate ratio of the lengths of the pendulums, and the length of the pendulum is equal to half the arc of the whole cycloid, the time of one vibration would be to the time of the oscillation of a pendulum whose length is A in the subduplicate ratio of the length $\frac{1}{2}$PS or PO to the length A. But the elastic force with which the physical lineola EG is urged, when it is found in its extreme places P, S, was (in the demonstration of Prop. XLVII) to its whole elastic force as HL − KN to V, that is (since the point K now falls upon P), as HK to V: and all that force, or which is the same thing, the incumbent weight by which the lineola EG is compressed, is to the weight of the lineola as the altitude A of the incumbent weight to EG the length of the lineola; and therefore, *ex aequo*, the force with which the lineola EG is urged in the places P and S is to the weight of that lineola as HK × A to V × EG; or as PO x A to VV; because HK was to EG as PO to V. Therefore since the times in which equal bodies are impelled through equal spaces are reciprocally in the subduplicate ratio of the forces, the time of one vibration, produced by the action of that elastic force, will be to the time of a vibration, produced by the impulse of the weight in a subduplicate ratio of VV to PO × A, and therefore to the time of the oscillation of a pendulum whose length is A in the subduplicate ratio of VV to PO × A, and

the subduplicate ratio of PO to A conjunctly; that is, in the entire ratio of V to A. But in the time of one vibration composed of the going and returning of the pendulum, the pulse will be propagated right onward through a space equal to its breadth BC. Therefore the time in which a, pulse runs over the space BC is to the time of one oscillation composed of the going and returning of the pendulum as V to A, that is, as BC too the circumference of a circle whose radius is A. But the time in which the pulse will run over the space BC is to the time in which it will run over a length equal to that circumference in the same ratio; and therefore in the time of such an oscillation the pulse will run over a length equal to that circumference. Q.E.D.

Cor. 1. The velocity of the pulses is equal to that which heavy bodies acquire by falling with an equally accelerated motion, and in their fall describing half the altitude A. For the pulse will, in the time of this fall, supposing it to move with the velocity acquired by that fall, run over a space that will be equal to the whole altitude A; and therefore in the time of one oscillation composed of one going and return, will go over a space equal to the circumference of a circle described with the radius A; for the time of the fall is to the time of oscillation as the radius of a circle to its circumference.

Cor. 2. Therefore since that altitude A is as the elastic force of the fluid directly, and the density of the same inversely, the velocity of the pulses will be in a ratio compounded of the subduplicate ratio of the density inversely, and the subduplicate ratio of the elastic force directly.

PROPOSITION L. PROBLEM XII.

To find the distances of the pulses.

Let the number of the vibrations of the body, by whose tremor the pulses are produced, be found to any given time. By that number divide the space which a pulse can go over in the same time, and the part found will be the breadth of one pulse. Q.E.I.

SCHOLIUM.

The last Propositions respect the motions of light and sounds; for since light is propagated in right lines, it is certain that it cannot consist in action alone (by Prop. XLI and XLII). As to sounds, since they arise from tremulous bodies, they can be nothing else but pulses of the air propagated through it (by Prop. XLIII); and this is confirmed by the tremors which sounds, if they be loud and deep, excite in the bodies near them, as we experience in the sound of drums; for quick and short tremors are less easily excited. But it is well known that any sounds, falling upon strings in unison with the sonorous bodies, excite tremors in those strings. This is also confirmed from the velocity of sounds; for since the specific gravities of rain-water and quicksilver are to one another as about 1 to $13^2/_3$, and when the mercury in the barometer is at the height of 30 inches of our measure, the specific gravities of the air and of rain-water are to one another as about 1 to 870, therefore the specific gravity of air and quicksilver are to each other as 1 to 11890. Therefore when the height of the quicksilver is at 30 inches, a height of uniform air, whose weight would be sufficient to compress our air to the density we find it to be of, must be equal to 356700 inches, or 29725 feet of our measure; and this is that very height of the medium, which I have called A in the construction of the foregoing Proposition. A circle whose radius is 29725 feet is 186768 feet in circumference. And since a pendulum $39^1/_5$ inches in length completes one oscillation, composed of its going and return, in two seconds of time, as is commonly known, it follows that a pendulum 29725 feet, or 356700 inches in length will perform a like oscillation in $190^3/_4$ seconds. Therefore in that time a sound will go right onwards 186768 feet, and therefore in one second 979 feet.

But in this computation we have made no allowance for the crassitude of the solid particles of the air, by which the sound is propagated instantaneously. Because the weight of air is to the weight of water as 1 to 870, and because salts are almost twice as dense as water; if the particles of air are supposed to be of near the same density as those of water or salt, and the rarity of the air arises from the intervals of the particles; the diameter of one particle of air will be to the interval between the centres of the particles as 1 to about 9 or 10, and to the interval between the particles themselves as 1 to 8 or 9. Therefore to 979 feet, which, according to the above calculation, a sound will advance forward in one second of time, we may add $979/_9$, or about 109 feet, to compensate for the crassitude of the particles of the air: and then a sound will go forward about 1088 feet in one second of time.

Moreover, the vapours floating in the air being of another spring, and a different tone, will hardly, if at all, partake of the motion of the true air in which the sounds are propagated. Now if these vapours remain unmoved that motion will be propagated the

swifter through the true air alone, and that in the subduplicate ratio of the defect of the matter. So if the atmosphere consist of ten parts of true air and one part of vapours, the motion of sounds will be swifter in the subduplicate ratio of 11 to 10, or very nearly in the entire ratio of 21 to 20, than if it were propagated through eleven parts of true air: and therefore the motion of sounds above discovered must be increased in that ratio. By this means the sound will pass through 1142 feet in one second of time.

These things will be found true in spring and autumn, when the air is rarefied by the gentle warmth of those seasons, and by that means its elastic force becomes somewhat more intense. But in winter, when the air is condensed by the cold, and its elastic force is somewhat remitted, the motion of sounds will be slower in a subduplicate ratio of the density; and, on the other hand, swifter in the summer.

Now by experiments it actually appears that sounds do really advance in one second of time about 1142 feet of *English* measure, or 1070 feet of *French* measure.

The velocity of sounds being known, the intervals of the pulses are known also. For M. *Sauveur*, by some experiments that he made, found that an open pipe about five *Paris* feet in length gives a sound of the same tone with a viol-string that vibrates a hundred times in one second. Therefore there are near 100 pulses in a space of 1070 *Paris* feet, which a sound runs over in a second of time; and therefore one pulse fills up a space of about $10^7/_{10}$ *Paris* feet, that is, about twice the length of the pipe. From whence it is probable that the breadths of the pulses, in all sounds made in open pipes, are equal to twice the length of the pipes.

Moreover, from the Corollary of Prop. XLVII appears the reason why the sounds immediately cease with the motion of the sonorous body, and why they are heard no longer when we are at a great distance from the sonorous bodies than when we are very near them. And besides, from the foregoing principles, it plainly appears how it comes to pass that sounds are so mightily increased in speaking-trumpets; for all reciprocal motion uses to be increased by the generating cause at each return. And in tubes hindering the dilatation of the sounds, the motion decays more slowly, and recurs more forcibly; and therefore is the more increased by the new motion impressed at each return. And these are the principal phaenomena of sounds.

SECTION IX.

Of the circular motion of fluids.

HYPOTHESIS.

THE RESISTANCE ARISING FROM THE WANT OF LUBRICITY IN THE PARTS OF A FLUID, IS, CÆTERIS PARIBUS, PROPORTIONAL TO

THE VELOCITY WITH WHICH THE PARTS OF THE FLUID ARE
SEPARATED FROM EACH OTHER.

PROPOSITION LI. THEOREM XXXIX.

IF A SOLID CYLINDER INFINITELY LONG, IN AN UNIFORM
AND INFINITE FLUID, REVOLVE WITH AN UNIFORM MOTION
ABOUT AN AXIS GIVEN IN POSITION, AND THE FLUID BE
FORCED ROUND BY ONLY THIS IMPULSE OF THE CYLINDER,
AND EVERY PART OF THE FLUID PERSEVERE UNIFORMLY IN
ITS MOTION; I SAY, THAT THE PERIODIC TIMES OF THE
PARTS OF THE FLUID ARE AS THEIR DISTANCES FROM THE
AXIS OF THE CYLINDER.

Let AFL be a cylinder turning uniformly about the axis S, and let the concentric circles BGM, CHN, DIO, EKP, &c., divide the fluid into innumerable concentric cylindric solid orbs of the same thickness. Then, because the fluid is homogeneous, the impressions which the contiguous orbs make upon each other mutually will be (by the Hypothesis) as their translations from each other, and as the contiguous superficies

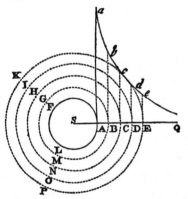

upon which the impressions are made. If the impression made upon any orb be greater or less on its concave than on its convex side, the stronger impression will prevail, and will either accelerate or retard the motion of the orb, according as it agrees with, or is contrary to, the motion of the same. Therefore, that every orb may persevere uniformly in its motion, the impressions made on both sides must be equal and their directions contrary. Therefore since the impressions are as the contiguous superficies, and as their translations from one

another, the translations will be inversely as the superficies, that is, inversely as the distances of the superficies from the axis. But the differences of the angular motions about the axis are as those translations applied to the distances, or as the translations directly and the distances inversely; that is, joining these ratios together, as the squares of the distances inversely. Therefore if there be erected the lines Aa, Bb, Cc, Dd, Ee, &c., perpendicular to the several parts of the infinite right line SABCDEQ, and reciprocally proportional to the squares of SA, SB, SC, SD, SE, &c., and through the extremities of those perpendiculars there be supposed to pass an hyperbolic curve, the sums of the differences, that is, the whole angular motions, will be as the correspondent sums of

the lines A*a*, B*b*, C*c*, D*d*, E*e*, that is (if to constitute a medium uniformly fluid the number of the orbs be increased and their breadth diminished in, infinitum), as the hyperbolic areas A*a*Q, B*b*Q, C*c*Q, D*d*Q, E*e*Q, &c., analogous to the sums; and the times, reciprocally proportional to the angular motions, will be also reciprocally proportional to those areas. Therefore the periodic time of any particle as D, is reciprocally as the area D*d*Q, that is (as appears from the known methods of quadratures of curves), directly as the distance SD. Q.E.D.

COR. 1. Hence the angular motions of the particles of the fluid are reciprocally as their distances from the axis of the cylinder, and the absolute velocities are equal.

COR. 2. If a fluid be contained in a cylindric vessel of an infinite length, and contain another cylinder within, and both the cylinders revolve about one common axis, and the times of their revolutions be as their semi-diameters, and every part of the fluid perseveres in its motion, the periodic times of the several parts will be as the distances from the axis of the cylinders.

COR. 3. If there be added or taken away any common quantity of angular motion from the cylinder and fluid moving in this manner; yet because this new motion will not alter the mutual attrition of the parts of the fluid, the motion of the parts among themselves will not be changed; for the translations of the parts from one another depend upon the attrition. Any part will persevere in that motion, which, by the attrition made on both sides with contrary directions, is no more accelerated than it is retarded.

COR. 4. Therefore if there be taken away from this whole system of the cylinders and the fluid all the angular motion of the outward cylinder, we shall have the motion of the fluid in a quiescent cylinder.

COR. 5. Therefore if the fluid and outward cylinder are at rest, and the inward cylinder revolve uniformly, there will be communicated a circular motion to the fluid, which will be propagated by degrees through the whole fluid; and will go on continually increasing, till such time as the several parts of the fluid acquire the motion determined in Cor. 4.

COR. 6. And because the fluid endeavours to propagate its motion still farther, its impulse will carry the outmost cylinder also about with it, unless the cylinder be violently detained; and accelerate its motion till the periodic times of both cylinders become equal among themselves. But if the outward cylinder be violently detained, it will make an effort to retard the motion of the fluid; and unless the inward cylinder preserve that motion by means of some external force impressed thereon, it will make it cease by degrees.

All these things will be found true by making the experiment in deep standing water.

PROPOSITION LII. THEOREM XL.

IF A SOLID SPHERE, IN AN UNIFORM AND INFINITE FLUID,
REVOLVES ABOUT AN AXIS GIVEN IN POSITION WITH AN
UNIFORM MOTION, AND THE FLUID BE FORCED ROUND BY
ONLY THIS IMPULSE OF THE SPHERE; AND EVERY PART OF
THE FLUID PERSEVERES UNIFORMLY IN ITS MOTION; I SAY,
THAT THE PERIODIC TIMES OF THE PARTS OF THE FLUID
ARE AS THE SQUARES OF THEIR DISTANCES FROM THE
CENTRE OF THE SPHERE.

CASE 1. Let AFL be a sphere turning uniformly about the axis S, and let the concentric circles BGM, CHN, DIO, EKP, &c., divide the fluid into innumerable concentric orbs of the same thickness. Suppose those orbs to be solid; and, because the fluid is homogeneous, the impressions which the contiguous orbs make one upon another will be (by the supposition) as their translations from one another, and the contiguous superficies upon which the impressions are made.

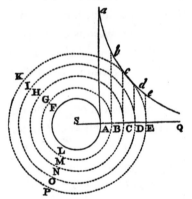

If the impression upon any orb be greater or less upon its concave than upon its convex side, the more forcible impression will prevail, and will either accelerate or retard the velocity of the orb, according as it is directed with a conspiring or contrary motion to that of the orb. Therefore that every orb may persevere uniformly in its motion, it is necessary that the impressions made upon both sides of the orb should be equal, and have contrary directions. Therefore since the impressions are as the contiguous superficies, and as their translations from one another, the translations will be inversely as the superficies, that is, inversely as the squares of the distances of the superficies from the centre. But the differences of the angular motions about the axis are as those translations applied to the distances, or as the translations directly and the distances inversely; that is: by compounding those ratios, as the cubes of the distances inversely, Therefore if upon the several parts of the infinite right line SABCDEQ there be erected the perpendiculars Aa, Bb, Cc, Dd, Ee, &c., reciprocally proportional to the cubes of SA, SB, SC, SD, SE, &c., the sums of the differences, that is, the whole angular motions will be as the corresponding sums of the lines Aa, Bb, Cc, Dd, Ee, &c., that is (if to constitute an uniformly fluid medium the number of the orbs be increased and their thickness diminished *in infinitum*), as the hyperbolic areas AaQ, BbQ, CcQ,

DdQ, EeQ, &c., analogous to the sums; and the periodic times being reciprocally proportional to the angular motions, will be also reciprocally proportional to those areas. Therefore the periodic time of any orb DIO is reciprocally as the area DdQ, that is (by the known methods of quadratures), directly as the square of the distance SD. Which was first to be demonstrated.

CASE 2. From the centre of the sphere let there be drawn a great number of indefinite right lines, making given angles with the axis, exceeding one another by equal differences; and, by these lines revolving about the axis, conceive the orbs to be cut into innumerable annuli; then will every annulus have four annuli contiguous to it, that is, one on its inside, one on its outside, and two on each hand. Now each of these annuli cannot be impelled equally and with contrary directions by the attrition of the interior and exterior annuli, unless the motion be communicated according to the law which we demonstrated in Case 1. This appears from that demonstration. And therefore any series of annuli, taken in any right line extending itself *in infinitum* from the globe, will move according to the law of Case 1, except we should imagine it hindered by the attrition of the annuli on each side of it. But now in a motion, according to this law, no such is, and therefore cannot be, any obstacle to the motions persevering according to that law. If annuli at equal distances from the centre revolve either more swiftly or more slowly near the poles than near the ecliptic, they will be accelerated if slow, and retarded if swift, by their mutual attrition; and so the periodic times will continually approach to equality, according to the law of Case 1. Therefore this attrition will not at all hinder the motion from going on according to the law of Case 1, and therefore that law will take place; that is, the periodic times of the several annuli will be as the squares of their distances from the centre of the globe. Which was to be demonstrated in the second place.

CASE 3. Let now every annulus be divided by transverse sections into innumerable particles constituting a substance absolutely and uniformly fluid; and because these sections do not at all respect the law of circular motion, but only serve to produce a fluid substance, the law of circular motion will continue the same as before. All the very small annuli will either not at all change their asperity and force of mutual attrition upon account of these sections, or else they will change the same equally. Therefore the proportion of the causes remaining the same, the proportion of the effects will remain the same also; that is, the proportion of the motions and the periodic times. Q.E.D. But now as the circular motion, and the centrifugal force thence arising, is greater at the ecliptic than at the poles. There must be some cause operating to retain the several particles in their circles; otherwise the matter that is at the ecliptic will always recede from the centre, and come round about to the poles by the outside of the vortex, and from thence return by the axis to the ecliptic with a perpetual circulation.

COR. 1. Hence the angular motions of the parts of the fluid about the axis of the globe are reciprocally as the squares of the distances from the centre of the globe, and the absolute velocities are reciprocally as the same squares applied to the distances from the axis.

COR. 2. If a globe revolve with a uniform motion about an axis of a given position in a similar and infinite quiescent fluid with an uniform motion, it will communicate a whirling motion to the fluid like that of a vortex, and that motion will by degrees be propagated onward *in infinitum*; and this motion will be increased continually in every part of the fluid, till the periodical times of the several parts become as the squares of the distances from the centre of the globe.

COR. 3. Because the inward parts of the vortex are by reason of their greater velocity continually pressing upon and driving forward the external parts, and by that action are perpetually communicating motion to them, and at the same time those exterior parts communicate the same quantity of motion to those that lie still beyond them, and by this action preserve the quantity of their motion continually unchanged, it is plain that the motion is perpetually transferred from the centre to the circumference of the vortex, till it is quite swallowed up and lost in the boundless extent of that circumference. The matter between any two spherical superficies concentrical to the vortex will never be accelerated; because that matter will be always transferring the motion it receives from the matter nearer the centre to that matter which lies nearer the circumference.

COR. 4. Therefore, in order to continue a vortex in the same state of motion, some active principle is required from which the globe may receive continually the same quantity of motion which it is always communicating to the matter of the vortex. Without such a principle it will undoubtedly come to pass that the globe and the inward parts of the vortex, being always propagating their motion to the outward parts, and not receiving any new motion, will gradually move slower and slower, and at last be carried round no longer.

COR. 5. If another globe should be swimming in the same vortex at a certain distance from its centre, and in the mean time by some force revolve constantly about an axis of a given inclination, the motion of this globe will drive the fluid round after the manner of a vortex; and at first this new and small vortex will revolve with its globe about the centre of the other; and in the mean time its motion will creep on farther and farther, and by degrees be propagated *in infinitum*, after the manner of the first vortex. And for the same reason that the globe of the new vortex was carried about before by the motion of the other vortex, the globe of this other will be carried about by the motion of this new vortex, so that the two globes will revolve about some intermediate point, and by reason of that circular motion mutually fly from each other,

unless some force restrains them. Afterward, if the constantly impressed forces, by which the globes persevere in their motions, should cease, and every thing be left to act according to the laws of mechanics, the motion of the globes will languish by degrees (for the reason assigned in Cor. 3 and 4) and the vortices at last will quite stand still.

COR. 6. If several, globes in given places should constantly revolve with determined velocities about axes given in position, there would arise front them as many vortices going on *in infinitum*. For upon the same account that any one globe propagates its motion *in infinitum*, each globe apart will propagate its own motion *in infinitum* also; so that every part of the infinite fluid will be agitated with a motion resulting from the actions of all the globes. Therefore the vortices will not be confined by any certain limits, but by degrees run mutually into each other; and by the mutual actions of the vortices on each other, the globes will be perpetually moved from their places, as was shewn in the last Corollary; neither can they possibly keep any certain position among themselves, unless some force restrains them. But if those forces, which are constantly impressed upon the globes to continue these motions, should cease, the matter (for the reason assigned in Cor. 3 and 4) will gradually stop, and cease to move in vortices.

COR. 7. If a similar fluid be inclosed in a spherical vessel, and, by the uniform rotation of a globe in its centre, is driven round in a vortex; and the globe and vessel revolve the same way about the same axis, and their periodical times be as the squares of the semi-diameters; the parts of the fluid will not go on in their motions without acceleration or retardation, till their periodical times are as the squares of their distances from the centre of the vortex. No constitution of a vortex can be permanent but this.

COR. 8. If the vessel, the inclosed fluid, and the globe, retain this motion, and revolve besides with a common angular motion about any given axis, because the mutual attrition of the parts of the fluid is not changed by this motion, the motions of the parts among each other will not be changed; for the translations of the parts among themselves depend upon this attrition. Any part will persevere in that motion in which its attrition on one side retards it just as much an its attrition on the other side accelerates it.

COR. 9. Therefore if the vessel be quiescent, and the motion of the globe be given, the motion of the fluid will be given. For conceive a plane to pass through the axis of the globe, and to revolve with a contrary motion; and suppose the sum of the time of this revolution and of the revolution of the globe to be to the time of the revolution of the globe as the square of the semi-diameter of the vessel to the square of the semi-diameter of the globe; and the periodic times of the parts of the fluid in respect of this plane will be as the squares of their distances from the centre of the globe.

COR. 10. Therefore if the vessel move about the same axis with the globe, or with a given velocity about a different one, the motion of the fluid will be given. For if from the whole system we take away the angular motion of the vessel, all the motions will remain the same among themselves as before, by Cor. 8, and those motions will be given by Cor. 9.

COR. 11. If the vessel and the fluid are quiescent, and the globe revolves with an uniform motion, that motion will be propagated by degrees through the whole fluid to the vessel, and the vessel will be carried round by it, unless violently detained; and the fluid and the vessel will be continually accelerated till their periodic times become equal to the periodic times of the globe. If the vessel be either withheld by some force, or revolve with any constant and uniform motion, the medium will come by little and little to the state of motion defined in Cor. 8, 9, 10, nor will it ever persevere in any other state. But if then the forces, by which the globe and vessel revolve with certain motions, should cease, and the whole system be left to act according to the mechanical laws, the vessel and globe, by means of the intervening fluid, will act upon each other, and will continue to propagate their motions through the fluid to each other, till their periodic times become equal among themselves, and the whole system revolves together like one solid body.

SCHOLIUM.

In all these reasonings I suppose the fluid to consist of matter of uniform density and fluidity; I mean, that the fluid is such, that a globe placed any where therein may propagate with the same motion of its own, at distances from itself continually equal, similar and equal motions in the fluid in the same interval of time. The matter by its circular motion endeavours to recede from the axis of the vortex, and therefore presses all the matter that lies beyond. This pressure makes the attrition greater, and the separation of the parts more difficult; and by consequence diminishes the fluidity of the matter. Again; if the parts of the fluid are in any one place denser or larger than in the others, the fluidity will be less in that place, because there are fewer superficies where the parts can be separated from each other. In these cases I suppose the defeat of the fluidity to be supplied by the smoothness or softness of the parts, or some other condition; otherwise the matter where it is less fluid will cohere more, and be more sluggish, and therefore will receive the motion more slowly, and propagate it farther than agrees with the ratio above assigned. If the vessel be not spherical, the particles will move in lines not circular, but answering to the figure of the vessel; and the periodic times will be nearly as the squares of the mean distances from the centre. In the parts between the centre and the circumference the motions will be slower where the spaces are wide, and swifter where narrow; but yet the particles win not tend to the circumference at all the

more for their greater swiftness; for they then describe arcs of less curvity, and the conatus of receding from the centre is as much diminished by the diminution of this curvature as it is augmented by the increase of the velocity. As they go out of narrow into wide spaces, they recede a little farther from the centre, but in doing so are retarded; and when they come out of wide into narrow spaces, they are again accelerated; and so each particle is retarded and accelerated by turns for ever. These things win come to pass in a rigid vessel; for the state of vortices in an infinite fluid is known by Cor. 6 of this Proposition.

I have endeavoured in this Proposition to investigate the properties of vortices, that I might find whether the celestial phaenomena can be explained by them; for the phaenomenon is this, that the periodic times of the planets revolving about Jupiter are in the sesquiplicate ratio of their distances from Jupiter's centre; and the same rule obtains also among the planets that revolve about the sun. And these rules obtain also with the greatest accuracy, as far as has been yet discovered by astronomical observation. Therefore if those planets are carried round in vortices revolving about Jupiter and the sun, the vortices must revolve according to that law. But here we found the periodic times of the parts of the vortex to be in the duplicate ratio of the distances from the centre of motion; and this ratio cannot be diminished and reduced to the sesquiplicate, unless either the matter of the vortex be more fluid the farther it is from the centre, or the resistance arising from the want of lubricity in the parts of the fluid should, as the velocity with which the parts of the fluid are separated goes on increasing, be augmented with it in a greater ratio than that in which the velocity increases. But neither of these suppositions seem reasonable. The more gross and less fluid parts will tend to the circumference, unless they are heavy towards the centre. And though, for the sake of demonstration, I proposed, at the beginning of this Section, an Hypothesis that the resistance is proportional to the velocity, nevertheless, it is in truth probable that the resistance is in a less ratio than that of the velocity; which granted, the periodic times of the parts of the vortex will be in a greater than the duplicate ratio of the distances from its centre. If, as some think, the vortices move more swiftly near the centre, then slower to a certain limit, then again swifter near the circumference, certainly neither the sesquiplicate, nor any other certain and determinate ratio, can obtain in them. Let philosophers then see how that phaenomenon of the sesquiplicate ratio can be accounted for by vortices.

PROPOSITION LIII. THEOREM XLI.

BODIES CARRIED ABOUT IN A VORTEX, AND RETURNING IN
THE SAME ORB, ARE OF THE SAME DENSITY WITH THE
VORTEX, AND ARE MOVED ACCORDING TO THE SAME LAW

WITH THE PARTS OF THE VORTEX, AS TO VELOCITY AND DIRECTION OF MOTION.

For if any small part of the vortex, whose particles or physical points preserve a given situation among each other, be supposed to be congealed, this particle will move according to the same law as before, since no change is made either in its density, *vis insita*, or figure. And again; if a congealed or solid part of the vortex be of the same density with the rest of the vortex, and be resolved into a fluid, this will move according to the same law as before, except in so far as its particles, now become fluid, may be moved among themselves. Neglect, therefore, the motion of the particles among themselves as not at all concerning the progressive motion of the whole, and the motion of the whole will be the same as before. But this motion will be the same with the motion of other parts of the vortex at equal distances from the centre; because the solid, now resolved into a fluid, is become perfectly like to the other parts of the vortex. Therefore a solid, if it be of the same density with the matter of the vortex, will move with the same motion as the parts thereof, being relatively at rest in the matter that surrounds it. If it be more dense, it will endeavour more than before to recede from the centre; and therefore overcoming that force of the vortex, by which, being, as it were, kept in equilibrio, it was retained in its orbit, it will recede from the centre, and in its revolution describe a spiral, returning no longer into the same orbit. And, by the same argument, if it be more rare, it will approach to the centre. Therefore it can never continually go round in the same orbit, unless it be of the same density with the fluid. But we have shewn in that case that it would revolve according to the same law with those parts of the fluid that are at the same or equal distances from the centre of the vortex.

COR. 1. Therefore a solid revolving in a vortex, and continually going round in the same orbit, is relatively quiescent in the fluid that carries it.

COR. 2. And if the vortex be of an uniform density, the same body may revolve at any distance from the centre of the vortex.

SCHOLIUM.

Hence it is manifest that the planets are not carried round in corporeal vortices; for, according to the *Copernican* hypothesis, the planets going round the sun revolve in ellipses, having the sun in their common focus and by radii drawn to the sun describe areas proportional to the times. But now the parts of a vortex can never revolve with such a motion. Let AD, BE, CF, represent three orbits described about the sun S, of which let the utmost circle CF be concentric to the sun; and let the aphelia of the two innermost be A, B; and their perihelia D, E. Therefore a body revolving in the orb CF,

describing, by a radius drawn to the sun, areas proportional to the times, will move with an uniform motion. And, according to the laws of astronomy, the body revolving in the orb BE will move slower in its aphelion B, and swifter in its perihelion E; whereas, according to the laws of mechanics, the matter of the vortex ought to move more swiftly in the narrow space between A and C than in the wide space between D and F; that is, more swiftly in the aphelion than in the perihelion. Now these two conclusions contradict each other. So at the beginning of the sign of Virgo, where the aphelion, of Mars is at present, the distance between the orbits of Mars and Venus is to the distance between the same orbits, at the beginning of the sign of Pisces, as about 3 to 2; and therefore the matter of the vortex between those orbits ought to be swifter at the beginning of Pisces than at the beginning of

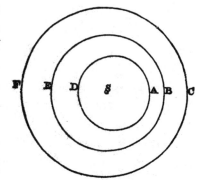

Virgo in the ratio of 3 to 2; for the narrower the space is through which the same quantity of matter passes in the same time of one revolution, the greater will be the velocity with which it passes through it. Therefore if the earth being relatively at rest in this celestial matter should be carried round by it, and revolve together with it about the sun, the velocity of the earth at the beginning of Pisces would be to its velocity at the beginning of Virgo in a sesquialteral ratio. Therefore the sun's apparent diurnal motion at the beginning of Virgo ought to be above 70 minutes, and at the beginning of Pisces less than 48 minutes; whereas, on the contrary, that apparent motion of the sun is really greater at the beginning of Pisces than at the beginning of Virgo, as experience testifies; and therefore the earth is swifter at the beginning of Virgo than at the beginning of Pisces; so that the hypothesis of vortices is utterly irreconcileable with astronomical phaenomena, and rather serves to perplex than explain the heavenly motions. How these motions are performed in free spaces without vortices, may be understood by the first Book; and I shall now more fully treat of it in the following Book.

BOOK III.

In the preceding Books I have laid down the principles of philosophy, principles not philosophical, but mathematical; such, to wit, as we may build our reasonings upon in philosophical inquiries. These principles are the laws and conditions of certain motions, and powers or forces, which chiefly have respect to philosophy; but, lest they should have appeared of themselves dry and barren, I have illustrated them here and

there with some philosophical scholiums, giving an account of such things as are of more general nature, and which philosophy seems chiefly to be founded on; such as the density and the resistance of bodies, spaces void of all bodies, and the motion of light and sounds. It remains that, from the same principles, I now demonstrate the frame of the System of the World. Upon this subject I had, indeed, composed the third Book in a popular method, that it might be read by many; but afterward, considering that such as had not sufficiently entered into the principles could not easily discern the strength of the consequences, nor lay aside the prejudices to which they had been many years accustomed, therefore, to prevent the disputes which might be raised upon such accounts, I chose to reduce the substance of this Book into the form of Propositions (in the mathematical way), which should be read by those only who had first made themselves masters of the principles established in the preceding Books: not that I would advise any one to the previous study of every Proposition of those Books; for they abound with such as might cost too much time, even to readers of good mathematical learning. It is enough if one carefully reads the Definitions, the Laws of Motion, and the first three Sections of the first Book, he may then pass on to this Book, and consult such of the remaining Propositions of the first two Books, as the references in this, and his occasions, shall require.

RULES OF REASONING IN PHILOSOPHY.

RULE I.

WE ARE TO ADMIT NO MORE CAUSES OF NATURAL THINGS THAN SUCH AS ARE BOTH TRUE AND SUFFICIENT TO EXPLAIN THEIR APPEARANCES.

To this purpose the philosophers say that Nature does nothing in vain, and more is in vain when less will serve; for Nature is pleased with simplicity, and affects not the pomp of superfluous causes.

RULE II.

THEREFORE TO THE SAME NATURAL EFFECTS WE MUST, AS FAR AS POSSIBLE, ASSIGN THE SAME CAUSES.

As to respiration in a man and in a beast; the descent of stones in Europe and in *America*; the light of our culinary fire and of the sun; the reflection of light in the earth, and in the planets.

RULE III.

The qualities of bodies, which admit neither intension nor remission of degrees, and which are found to belong to all bodies within the reach of our experiments, are to be esteemed the universal qualities of all bodies whatsoever.

For since the qualities of bodies are only known to us by experiments, we are to hold for universal all such as universally agree with experiments; and such as are not liable to diminution can never be quite taken away. We are certainly not to relinquish the evidence of experiments for the sake of dreams and vain fictions of our own devising; nor are we to recede from the analogy of Nature, which uses to be simple, and always consonant to itself. We no other way know the extension of bodies than by our senses, nor do these reach it in all bodies; but because we perceive extension in all that are sensible, therefore we ascribe it universally to all others also. That abundance of bodies are hard, we learn by experience; and because the hardness of the whole arises from the hardness of the parts, we therefore justly infer the hardness of the undivided particles not only of the bodies we feel but of all others. That all bodies are impenetrable, we gather not from reason, but from sensation. The bodies which we handle we find impenetrable, and thence conclude impenetrability to be an universal property of all bodies whatsoever. That all bodies are moveable, and endowed with certain powers (which we call the *vires inertiae*) of persevering in their motion, or in their rest, we only infer from the like properties observed in the bodies which we have seen. The extension, hardness, impenetrability, mobility, and *vis inertia* of the whole, result from the extension, hardness, impenetrability, mobility, and *vires inertia* of the parts; and thence we conclude the least particles of all bodies to be also all extended, and hard and impenetrable, and moveable, and endowed with their proper *vires inertiae*. And this is the foundation of all philosophy. Moreover, that the divided but contiguous particles of bodies may be separated from one another, is matter of observation; and, in the particles that remain undivided, our minds are able to distinguish yet lesser parts, as is mathematically demonstrated. But whether the parts so distinguished, and not yet divided, may, by the powers of Nature, be actually divided and separated from one another, we cannot certainly determine. Yet, had we the proof of but one experiment that any undivided particle, in breaking a hard and solid body, suffered a division, we might by virtue of this rule conclude that the undivided as well as the divided particles may be divided and actually separated to infinity.

Lastly, if it universally appears, by experiments and astronomical observations, that all bodies about the earth gravitate towards the earth, and that in proportion to the

quantity of matter which they severally contain, that the moon likewise, according to the quantity of its matter, gravitates towards the earth; that, on the other hand, our sea gravitates towards the moon; and all the planets mutually one towards another; and the comets in like manner towards the sun; we must in consequence of this rule, universally allow that all bodies whatsoever are endowed with a principle of mutual gravitation. For the argument from the appearances concludes with more force for the universal gravitation of all bodies than for their impenetrability; of which, among those in the celestial regions, we have no experiments, nor any manner of observation. Not that I affirm gravity to be essential to bodies: by their *vis insita* I mean nothing but their *vis inertiae*. This is immutable. Their gravity is diminished as they recede from the earth.

RULE IV.

IN EXPERIMENTAL PHILOSOPHY WE ARE TO LOOK UPON PROPOSITIONS COLLECTED BY GENERAL INDUCTION FROM PHAENOMENA AS ACCURATELY OR VERY NEARLY TRUE, NOTWITHSTANDING ANY CONTRARY HYPOTHESES THAT MAY BE IMAGINED, TILL SUCH TIME AS OTHER PHAENOMENA OCCUR, BY WHICH THEY MAY EITHER BE MADE MORE ACCURATE, OR LIABLE TO EXCEPTIONS.

This rule we must follow, that the argument of induction may not be evaded by hypotheses.

PHAENOMENA, OR APPEARANCES.

PHAENOMENON I.

THAT THE CIRCUMJOVIAL PLANETS, BY RADII DRAWN TO JUPITER'S CENTRE, DESCRIBE AREAS PROPORTIONAL TO THE TIMES OF DESCRIPTION; AND THAT THEIR PERIODIC TIMES, THE FIXED STARS BEING AT REST, ARE IN THE SESQUIPLICATE PROPORTION OF THEIR DISTANCES FROM ITS CENTRE.

This we know from astronomical observations. For the orbits of these planets differ but insensibly from circles concentric to Jupiter; and their motions in those circles are found to be uniform. And all astronomers agree that their periodic times are in the sesquiplicate proportion of the semi-diameters of their orbits; and so it manifestly appears from the following table.

The periodic times of the satellites of Jupiter.
$1^d.\ 18^h.\ 27'.\ 34''.\ 3^d.\ 13^h.\ 13'\ 42''.\ 7^d.\ 42'\ 36''.\qquad 16^d.\ 16^b.\ 32'\ 9''.$
The distances of the satellites from Jupiter's centre.

From the observations of	1	2	3	4	
Borelli	$5^2/_3$	$8^2/_3$	14	$24^2/_3$	⎫ *semi-diameter of*
Townly *by the Microm*	5,52	8,78	13,47	24,72	⎬ *Jupiter.*
Cassini *by the Telescope.*	5	8	13	23	
Cassini *by the eclip. of the satel*	$5^2/3$	9	$14^{23}/_{60}$	$25^3/_{10}$	⎭
From the periodic times	5,667	9,017	14,384	25,299	

Mr. *Pound* has determined, by the help of excellent micrometers, the diameters of Jupiter and the elongation of its satellites after the following manner. The greatest heliocentric elongation of the fourth satellite from Jupiter's centre was taken with a micrometer in a 15 feet telescope, and at the mean distance of Jupiter from the earth was found about 8' 16". The elongation of the third satellite was taken with a micrometer in a telescope of 123 feet, and at the same distance of Jupiter from the earth was found 4' 42". The greatest elongations of the other satellites, at the same distance of Jupiter from the earth, are found from the periodic times to be 2' 56" 47''', and 1' 51" 6'''.

The diameter of Jupiter taken with the micrometer in a 123 feet telescope several times, and reduced to Jupiter's mean distance from the earth, proved always less than 40", never less than 38", generally 39". This diameter in shorter telescopes is 40", or 41"; for Jupiter's light is a little dilated by the unequal refrangibility of the rays, and this dilatation bears a less ratio to the diameter of Jupiter in the longer and more perfect telescopes than in those which are shorter and less perfect. The times in which two satellites, the first and the third, passed over Jupiter's body, were observed, from the beginning of the ingress to the beginning of the egress, and from the complete ingress to the complete egress, with the long telescope. And from the transit of the first satellite, the diameter of Jupiter at its mean distance from the earth came forth $37^1/_8$", and from the transit of the third $37^3/_8$". There was observed also the time in which the shadow of the first satellite passed over Jupiter's body, and thence the diameter of Jupiter at its mean distance from the earth came out about 37". Let us suppose its diameter to be $37^1/_4$" very nearly, and then the greatest elongations of the first, second, third, and fourth satellite will be respectively equal to 5,965, 9,494, 15,141, and 26,63 semi-diameters of Jupiter.

PHAENOMENON II.

That the circumsatural planets, by radii drawn to Saturn's centre, describe areas proportional to the times of description; and that their periodic times, the fixed stars being at rest, are in the sesquiplicate proportion of their distances from its centre.

For, as *Cassini* from his own observations has determined, their distances from Saturn's centre and their periodic times are as follow.

The periodic times of the satellites of Saturn.
$1^d. 21^h. 18' 27''. 2^d. 17^h. 41' 22''. 4^d. 12^h. 25' 12''. 15^d. 22^h. 41' 14''. 79^d. 7^h. 48' 00''.$

The distances of the satellites from Saturn's centre, in semi-diameters of its ring.

From observations	$1^{19}/_{20}$	$2^1/_2$	$3^1/_2$	8	24
From the periodic times	1,93	2,47	3,45	8	23,35

The greatest elongation of the fourth satellite from Saturn's centre is commonly determined from the observations to be eight of these semi-diameters very nearly. But the greatest elongation of this satellite from Saturn's centre, when taken with an excellent micrometer in Mr. *Huygens'* telescope of 123 feet, appeared to be eight semi-diameters and $^7/_{19}$ of a semi-diameter. And from this observation and the periodic times the distances of the satellites from Saturn's centre in semi-diameters of the ring are 2,1, 2,69, 3,75, 8,7, and 25,35. The diameter of Saturn observed in the same telescope was found to be to the diameter of the ring as 3 to 7; and the diameter of the ring, *May* 29-29, 1719, was found to be 43''; and thence the diameter of the ring when Saturn is at its mean distance from the earth is 42'', and the diameter of Saturn 18''. These things appear so in very long and excellent telescopes, because in such telescopes the apparent magnitudes of the heavenly bodies bear a greater proportion to the dilatation of light in the extremities of those bodies than in shorter telescopes.

If we, then, reject all the spurious light, the diameter of Saturn will not amount to more than 16''.

PHAENOMENON III.

That the five primary planets, Mercury, Venus, Mars, Jupiter, and Saturn, with their several orbits, encompass the sun.

That Mercury and Venus revolve about the sun, is evident from their moon-like appearances. When they shine out with a full face, they are, in respect of us, beyond or above the sun; when they appear half full, they are about the same height on one side or other of the sun; when horned, they are below or between us and the sun; and they are sometimes, when directly under, seen like spots traversing the sun's disk. That Mars surrounds the sun, is as plain from its full face when near its conjunction with the sun, and from the gibbous figure which it shews in its quadratures. And the same thing is demonstrable of Jupiter and Saturn, from their appearing full in all situations; for the shadows of their satellites that appear sometimes upon their disks make it plain that the light they shine with is not their own, but borrowed from the sun.

PHAENOMENON IV.

THAT THE FIXED STARS BEING AT REST, THE PERIODIC TIMES OF THE FIVE PRIMARY PLANETS, AND (WHETHER OF THE SUN ABOUT THE EARTH, OR) OF THE EARTH ABOUT THE SUN, ARE IN THE SESQUIPLICATE PROPORTION OF THEIR MEAN DISTANCES FROM THE SUN.

This proportion, first observed by *Kepler*, is now received by all astronomers; for the periodic times are the same, and the dimensions of the orbits are the same, whether the sun revolves about the earth, or the earth about the sun. And as to the measures of the periodic times, all astronomers are agreed about them. But for the dimensions of the orbits, *Kepler* and *Bullialdus*, above all others, have determined them from observations with the greatest accuracy; and the mean distances corresponding to the periodic times differ but insensibly from those which they have assigned, and for the most part fall in between them; as we may see from the following table.

The periodic times with respect to the fixed stars, of the planets and earth revolving about the sun, in days and decimal parts of a day.

♄	♃	♂	♁	♀	☿
10759,275	4332,514	686,9785	365,2565	224,6176	87,9692

The mean distances of the planets and of the earth from the sun.

	♄	♃	♂
According to Kepler	951000.	519650.	152350.
" to Bullialdus	954198.	522520.	152350.
" to the periodic times	954006.	520096.	152369

	♂	♀	☿
According to Kepler	100000.	72400.	38806
" to Bullialdus	100000.	72398.	38585
" to the periodic times	100000.	72333.	38710.

As to Mercury and Venus, there can be no doubt about their distances from the sun; for they are determined by the elongations of those planet's from the sun; and for the distances of the superior planets, all dispute is cut off by the eclipses of the satellites of Jupiter. For by those eclipses the position of the shadow which Jupiter projects is determined; whence we have the heliocentric longitude of Jupiter. And from its heliocentric and geocentric longitudes compared together, we determine its distance.

PHAENOMENON V.

THEN THE PRIMARY PLANETS, BY RADII DRAWN TO THE EARTH, DESCRIBE AREAS NO WISE PROPORTIONAL TO THE TIMES; BUT THAT THE AREAS WHICH THEY DESCRIBE BY RADII DRAWN TO THE SUN ARE PROPORTIONAL TO THE TIMES OF DESCRIPTION.

For to the earth they appear sometimes direct, sometimes stationary, nay, and sometimes retrograde. But from the sun they are always seen direct, and to proceed with a motion nearly uniform, that is to say, a little swifter in the perihelion and a little slower in the aphelion distances, so as to maintain an equality in the description of the areas. This a noted proposition among astronomers, and particularly demonstrable in Jupiter, from the eclipses of his satellites; by the help of which eclipses, as we have said, the heliocentric longitudes of that planet, and its distances from the sun, are determined.

PHAENOMENON VI.

THAT THE MOON, BY A RADIUS DRAWN TO THE EARTH'S CENTRE, DESCRIBES AN AREA PROPORTIONAL TO THE TIME OF DESCRIPTION.

This we gather from the apparent motion of the moon, compared with its apparent diameter, it is true that the motion of the moon is a little disturbed by the action of the sun: but in laying down these Phaenomena, I neglect those small and inconsiderable errors.

PROPOSITIONS.

PROPOSITION I. THEOREM I.

THAT THE FORCES, BY WHICH THE CIRCUMJOVIAL PLANETS ARE
CONTINUALLY DRAWN OF FROM RECTILINEAR MOTIONS, AND
RETAINED IN THEIR PROPER ORBITS, TEND TO JUPITER'S CENTRE;
AND ARE RECIPROCALLY AS THE SQUARES OF THE DISTANCES OF
THE PLACES OF THOSE PLANETS FROM THAT CENTRE.

The former part of this Proposition appears from Phaen. I, and Prop. II or III,
Book I; the latter from Phaen. I, and Cor. 6, Prop. IV, of the same Book.

The same thing we are to understand of the planets which encompass
Saturn, by Phaen. II.

PROPOSITION II. THEOREM II.

THAT THE FORCES, BY WHICH THE PRIMARY PLANETS ARE
CONTINUALLY DRAWN OFF FROM RECTILINEAR MOTIONS, AND
RETAINED IN THEIR PROPER ORBITS, TEND TO THE SUN; AND
ARE RECIPROCALLY AS THE SQUARES OF THE DISTANCES OF
THE PLACES OF THOSE PLANETS FROM THE SUN'S CENTRE.

The former part of the Proposition is manifest from Phaen. V, and Prop. II, Book
I; the latter from Phaen. IV, and Cor. 6, Prop. IV, of the same Book. But this part of
the Proposition is, with great accuracy, demonstrable from the quiescence of the aphelion points; for a very small aberration from the reciprocal duplicate proportion would
(by Cor. 1, Prop. XLV, Book I) produce a motion of the apsides sensible enough in
every single revolution, and in many of them enormously great.

PROPOSITION III. THEOREM III.

THAT THE FORCE BY WHICH THE MOON IS RETAINED IN ITS ORBIT
LEADS TO THE EARTH; AND IS RECIPROCALLY AS THE SQUARE OF
THE DISTANCE OF ITS PLACE FROM THE EARTH'S CENTRE.

The former part of the Proposition is evident from Phaen. VI, and Prop. II or III,
Book I; the latter from the very slow motion of the moon's apogee; which in every sin-
gle revolution amounting but to 30° 31' *in consequentia*, may be neglected. For (by
Cor. 1, Prop. XLV, Book I) it appears, that, if the distance of the moon from the earth's

centre is to the semi-diameter of the earth as D to 1, the force from which such a motion will result, is reciprocally as $D^2 \, ^4/_{243}$, i.e., reciprocally as the power of D, whose exponent is $2^4/_{243}$ that is to say, in the proportion of the distance something greater than reciprocally duplicate, but which comes $59^3/_4$ times nearer to the duplicate than to the triplicate proportion. But in regard that this motion is owing to the action of the sun (as we shall afterwards shew), it is here to be neglected. The action of the sun, attracting the moon from the earth, is nearly as the moon's distance from the earth; and therefore (by what we have shewed in Cor. 2, Prop. XLV, Book I) is to the centripetal force of the moon as 2 to 357,45, or nearly so; that is, as 1 to $178^{29}/_{40}$. And if we neglect so inconsiderable a force of the sun, the remaining force, by which the moon is retained in its orb, will be reciprocally as D^2. This will yet more fully appear from comparing this force with the force of gravity, as is done in the next Proposition.

COR. If we augment the mean centripetal force by which the moon is retained in its orb, first in the proportion of $177^{29}/_{40}$ to $178^{29}/_{40}$, and then in the duplicate proportion of the semi-diameter of the earth to the mean distance of the centres of the moon and earth, we shall have the centripetal force of the moon at the surface of the earth; supposing this force, in descending to the earth's surface, continually to increase in the reciprocal duplicate proportion of the height.

PROPOSITION IV. THEOREM IV.

THAT THE MOON GRAVITATES TOWARDS THE EARTH, AND BY
THE FORCE OF GRAVITY IS CONTINUALLY DRAWN OF FROM A
RECTILINEAR MOTION, AND RETAINED IN ITS ORBIT.

The mean distance of the moon from the earth in the syzygies in semi-diameters of the earth, is, according to *Ptolemy* and most astronomers, 59; according to *Vendelin* and *Huygens*, 60; to *Copernicus*, $60^1/_3$; to *Street*, $60^2/_5$; and to *Tycho*, $56^1/_2$. But *Tycho*, and all that follow his tables of refraction, making the refractions of the sun and moon (altogether against the nature of light) to exceed the refractions of the fixed stars, and that by four or five minutes *near the horizon*, did thereby increase the moon's *horizontal* parallax by a like number of minutes, that is, by a twelfth or fifteenth part of the whole parallax. Correct this error, and the distance will become about $60^1/_2$ semi-diameters of the earth, near to what others have assigned. Let us assume the mean distance of 60 diameters in the syzygies; and suppose one revolution of the moon, in respect of the fixed stars, to be completed in $27^d. \, 7^h. \, 43'$, as astronomers have determined; and the circumference of the earth to amount to 123249600 *Paris* feet, as the French have found by mensuration. And now if we imagine the moon, deprived of all motion, to be let go, so as to descend towards the earth with the impulse of all that

force by which (by Cor. Prop. III) it is retained in its orb, it will in the space of one minute of time, describe in its fall $15^1/_{12}$ *Paris* feet. This we gather by a calculus, founded either upon Prop. XXXVI, Book I, or (which comes to the same thing) upon Cor. 9, Prop. IV, of the same Book. For the versed sine of that arc, which the moon, in the space of one minute of time, would by its mean motion describe at the distance of 60 semi-diameters of the earth, is nearly $15^1/_{12}$ *Paris* feet, or more accurately 15 feet, 1 inch, and 1 line $^4/_9$. Wherefore, since that force, in approaching to the earth, increases in the reciprocal duplicate proportion of the distance, and, upon that account, at the surface of the earth, is 60×60 times greater than at the moon, a body in our regions, falling with that force, ought in the space of one minute of time, to describe $60 \times 60 \times 15^1/_{12}$ *Paris* feet; and, in the space of one second of time, to describe $15^1/_{12}$ of those feet; or more accurately 15 feet, 1 inch, and 1 line $^4/_9$. And with this very force we actually find that bodies here upon earth do really descend; for a pendulum oscillating seconds in the latitude of *Paris* will be 3 *Paris* feet, and 8 lines 12 in length, as Mr. *Huygens* has observed. And the space which a heavy body describes by falling in one second of time is to half the length of this pendulum in the duplicate ratio of the circumference of a circle to its diameter (as Mr. *Huygens* has also shewn), and is therefore 15 *Paris* feet, 1 inch, 1 line $^7/_9$. And therefore the force by which the moon is retained in its orbit becomes, at the very surface of the earth, equal to the force of gravity which we observe in heavy bodies there. And therefore (by Rule I and II) the force by which the moon is retained in its orbit is that very same force which we commonly call gravity; for, were gravity another force different from that, then bodies descending to the earth with the joint impulse of both forces would fall with a double velocity, and in the space of one second of time would describe $30^1/_6$ *Paris* feet; altogether against experience.

This calculus is founded on the hypothesis of the earth's standing still for if both earth and moon move about the sun, and at the same time about their common centre of gravity, the distance of the centres of the moon and earth from one another will be $60^1/_2$ semi-diameters of the earth; as may be found by a computation from Prop. LX, Book I.

SCHOLIUM.

The demonstration of this Proposition may be more diffusely explained after the following manner. Suppose several moons to revolve about the earth, as in the system of Jupiter or Saturn; the periodic times of these moons (by the argument of induction) would observe the same law which *Kepler* found to obtain among the planets; and therefore their centripetal forces would be reciprocally as the squares of the distances from the centre of the earth, by Prop. I, of this Book. Now if the lowest of these were very small, and were so near the earth as almost to touch the tops of the highest mountains, the

centripetal force thereof, retaining it in its orb, would be very nearly equal to the weights of any *terrestrial* bodies that should be found upon the tops of those mountains, as may be known by the foregoing computation. Therefore if the same little moon should be deserted by its centrifugal force that carries it through its orb, and so be disabled from going onward therein, it would descend to the earth; and that with the same velocity as heavy bodies do actually fall with upon the tops of those very mountains; because of the equality of the forces that oblige them both to descend. And if the force by which that lowest moon would descend were different from gravity, and if that moon were to gravitate towards the earth, as we find terrestrial bodies do upon the tops of mountains, it would then descend with twice the velocity, as being impelled by both these form conspiring together. Therefore since both these forces, that is, the gravity of heavy bodies, and the centripetal forces of the moons, respect the centre of the earth, and are similar and equal between themselves, they will (by Rule I and II) have one and the same cause. And therefore the force which retains the moon in its orbit is that very force which we commonly call gravity; because otherwise this little moon at the top of a mountain must either be without gravity, or fall twice as swiftly as heavy bodies are wont to do.

PROPOSITION V. THEOREM V.

THAT THE CIRCUMJOVIAL PLANETS GRAVITATE TOWARDS JUPITER; THE CIRCUMSATURNAL TOWARDS SATURN; THE CIRCUMSOLAR TOWARDS THE SUN; AND BY THE FORCES OF THEIR GRAVITY ARE DRAWN OFF FROM RECTILINEAR MOTIONS, AND RETAINED IN CURVILINEAR ORBITS.

For the revolutions of the circumjovial planets about Jupiter, of the circumsaturnal about Saturn, and of Mercury and Venus, and the other circumsolar planets, about the sun, are appearances of the same sort with the revolution of the moon about the earth; and therefore, by Rule II, must be owing to the same sort of causes; especially since it has been demonstrated, that the forces upon which those revolutions depend tend to the centres of Jupiter, of Saturn, and of the sun; and that those forces, in receding from Jupiter, from Saturn, and from the sun, decrease in the same proportion, and according to the same low, as the force of gravity does in receding from the earth.

COR. 1. There is, therefore, a power of gravity tending to all the planets; for, doubtless, Venus, Mercury, and the rest, are bodies of the same sort with Jupiter and Saturn. And since all attraction (by Law III) is mutual, Jupiter will therefore gravitate towards all his own satellites, Saturn towards his, the earth towards the moon, and the sun towards all the primary planets.

COR. 2. The force of gravity which tends to any one planet is reciprocally as the square of the distance of places from that planet's centre.

COR. 3. All the planets do mutually gravitate towards one another, by Cor. 1 and 2. And hence it is that Jupiter and Saturn, when near their conjunction, by their mutual attractions sensibly disturb each other's motions. So the sun disturbs the motions of the moon; and both sun and moon disturb our sea, as we shall hereafter explain.

SCHOLIUM.

The force which retains the celestial bodies in their orbits has been hitherto called centripetal force; but it being now made plain that it can be no other than a gravitating force, we shall hereafter call it gravity. For the cause of that centripetal force which retains the moon in its orbit will extend itself to all the planets, by Rule I, II, and IV.

PROPOSITION VI. THEOREM VI.

THAT ALL BODIES GRAVITATE TOWARDS EVERY PLANET; AND THAT THE WEIGHTS OF BODIES TOWARDS ANY THE *SAME* PLANET, AT EQUAL DISTANCES FROM THE CENTRE OF THE PLANET, ARE PROPORTIONAL TO THE QUANTITIES OF MATTER WHICH THEY SEVERALLY CONTAIN.

It has been, now of a long time, observed by others, that all sorts of heavy bodies (allowance being made for the inequality of retardation which they suffer from a small power of resistance in the air) descend to the earth *from equal heights* in equal times; and that equality of times we may distinguish to a great accuracy, by the help of pendulums. I tried the thing in gold, silver, lead, glass, sand, common salt, wood, water, and wheat. I provided two wooden boxes, round and equal: I filled the one with wood, and suspended an equal weight of gold (as exactly as I could) in the centre of oscillation of the other. The boxes hanging by equal threads of 11 feet made a couple of pendulum perfectly equal in weight and figure, and equally receiving the resistance of the air. And, placing the one by the other, I observed them to play together forward and backward, for a long time, with equal vibrations. And therefore the quantity of matter in the gold (by Cor. 1 and 6, Prop. XXIV, Book II) was to the quantity of matter in the wood as the action of the motive force (or *vis motrix*) upon all the gold to the action of the same upon all the wood; that is, as the weight of the one to the weight of the other: and the like happened in the other bodies. By these experiments, in bodies of the same weight, I could manifestly have discovered a difference of matter less than the thousandth part of the whole, had any such been. But, without all doubt, the nature of gravity towards the planets is the same as towards the earth. For, should we imagine

our terrestrial bodies removed to the orb of the moon, and there, together with the moon, deprived of all motion, to be let go, so as to fall together towards the earth, it is certain, from what we have demonstrated before, that, in equal times, they would describe equal spaces with the moon, and of consequence are to the moon, in quantity of matter, as their weights to its weight. Moreover, since the satellites of Jupiter perform their revolutions in times which observe the sesquiplicate proportion of their distances from Jupiter's centre, their accelerative gravities towards Jupiter will be reciprocally as the squares of their distances from Jupiter's centre; that is, equal, at equal distances. And, therefore, these satellites, if supposed to fall *towards Jupiter* from equal heights, would describe equal spaces in equal times, in like manner as heavy bodies do on our earth. And, by the same argument, if the circumsolar planets were supposed to be let fall at equal distances from the sun, they would, in their descent towards the sun, describe equal spaces in equal times. But forces which equally accelerate unequal bodies must be as those bodies: that is to say, the weights of the planets *towards the sun* must be as their quantities of matter. Further, that the weights of Jupiter and of his satellites towards the sun are proportional to the several quantities of their matter, appears from the exceedingly regular motions of the satellites (by Cor. 3, Prop. LXV, Book I). For if some of those bodies were more strongly attracted to the sun in proportion to their quantity of matter than others, the motions of the satellites would be disturbed by that inequality of attraction (by Cor. 2, Prop. LXV, Book I). If, at equal distances from the sun, any satellite, in proportion to the quantity of its matter, did gravitate towards the sun with a force greater than Jupiter in proportion to his, according to any given proportion, suppose of d to e; then the distance between the centres of the sun and of the satellite's orbit would be always greater than the distance between the centres of the sun and of Jupiter nearly in the subduplicate of that proportion: as by some computations I have found. And if the satellite did gravitate towards the sun with a force, lesser in the proportion of e to d, the distance of the centre of the satellite's orb from the sun would be less than the distance of the centre of Jupiter from the sun in the subduplicate of the same proportion. Therefore if, at equal distances from the sun, the accelerative gravity of any satellite towards the sun were greater or less than the accelerative gravity of Jupiter towards the sun but by one $1/1000$ part of the whole gravity, the distance of the centre of the satellite's orbit from the sun would be greater or less than the distance of Jupiter from the sun by one $1/2000$ part of the whole distance; that is, by a fifth part of the distance of the utmost satellite from the centre of Jupiter; an eccentricity of the orbit which would be very sensible. But the orbits of the satellites are concentric to Jupiter, and therefore the accelerative gravities of Jupiter, and of all its satellites towards the sun, are equal among themselves. And by the same argument, the weights of Saturn and of his satellites towards the sun, at equal distances

from the sun, are as their several quantities of matter; and the weights of the moon and of the earth towards the sun are either none, or accurately proportional to the masses of matter which they contain. But some they are, by Cor. 1 and 3, Prop. V.

But further; the weights of all the parts of every planet towards any other planet are one to another as the matter in the several parts; for if some parts did gravitate more, others less, than for the quantity of their matter, then the whole planet, according to the sort of parts with which it most abounds, would gravitate more or less than in proportion to the quantity of matter in the whole. Nor is it of any moment whether these parts are external or internal; for if, for example, we should imagine the terrestrial bodies with us to be raised up to the orb of the moon, to be there compared with its body: if the weights of such bodies were to the weights of the external parts of the moon as the quantities of matter in the one and in the other respectively; but to the weights of the internal parts in a greater or less proportion, then likewise the weights of those bodies would be to the weight of the whole moon in a greater or less proportion; against what we have shewed above.

COR. 1. Hence the weights of bodies do not depend upon their forms and textures; for if the weights could be altered with the forms, they would be greater or less, according to the variety of forms, in equal matter; altogether against experience,

COR. 2. Universally, all bodies about the earth gravitate towards the earth; and the weights of all, at equal distances from the earth's centre, are as the quantities of matter which they severally contain. This is the quality of all bodies within the reach of our experiments; and therefore (by Rule III) to be affirmed of all bodies whatsoever. If the *aether*, or any other body, were either altogether void of gravity, or were to gravitate lest in proportion to its quantity of matter, then, because (according to *Aristotle, Des Cartes*, and others) there is no difference betwixt that and other bodies but in *mere* form of matter, by a successive change from form to form, it might be changed at last into a body of the same condition with those which gravitate most in proportion to their quantity of matter; and, on the other hand, the heaviest bodies, acquiring the first form of that body, might by degrees quite lose their gravity. And therefore the weights would depend upon the forms of bodies, and with those forms might be changed: contrary to what was proved in the preceding Corollary.

COR. 3. All spaces are not equally full; for if all spaces were equally full, then the specific gravity of the fluid which fills the region of the air, on account of the extreme density of the matter, would fall nothing short of the specific gravity of quicksilver, or gold, or any other the most dense body; and, therefore, neither gold, nor any other body, could descend in air; for bodies do not descend in fluids, unless they are specifically heavier than the fluids. And if the quantity of matter in a given space can, by any rarefaction, be diminished, what should hinder a diminution to infinity?

Cor. 4. If all the solid particles of all bodies are of the same density, nor can be rarefied without pores, a void, space, or vacuum must be granted.

By bodies of the same density, I mean those whose *vires inertiae* are in the proportion of their bulks.

Cor. 5. The power of gravity is of a different nature from the power of magnetism; for the magnetic attraction is not as the matter attracted. Some bodies are attracted more by the magnet; others less; most bodies not at all. The power of magnetism in one and the same body may be increased and diminished; and is sometimes far stronger, for the quantity of matter, than the power of gravity; and in receding from the magnet decreases not in the duplicate but almost in the triplicate proportion of the distance, as nearly as I could judge from some rude observations.

PROPOSITION VII. THEOREM VII.

THAT THERE IS A POWER OF GRAVITY TENDING TO ALL BODIES, PROPORTIONAL TO THE SEVERAL QUANTITIES OF MATTER WHICH THEY CONTAIN.

That all the planets mutually gravitate one towards another, we have proved before; as well as that the force of gravity towards every one of them, considered apart, is reciprocally as the square of the distance of places from the centre of the planet. And thence (by Prop. LXIX, Book I, and its Corollaries) it follows, that the gravity tending towards all the planets is proportional to the matter which they contain.

Moreover, since all the parts of any planet A gravitate towards any other planet B; and the gravity of every part is to the gravity of the whole as the matter of the part to the matter of the whole; and (by Law III) to every action corresponds an equal re-action; therefore the planet B will, on the other hand, gravitate towards all the parts of the planet A; and its gravity towards any one part will be to the gravity towards the whole as the matter of the part to the matter of the whole. Q.E.D.

Cor. 1. Therefore the force of gravity towards any whole planet arises from, and is compounded of, the forces of gravity towards all its parts. Magnetic and electric attractions afford us examples of this; for all attraction towards the whole arises from the attractions towards the several parts. The thing may be easily understood in gravity, if we consider a greater planet, as formed of a number of lesser planets, meeting together in one globe; for *hence it would appear that* the force of the whole must arise from the forces of the component parts. If it is objected, that, according to this law, all bodies with us must mutually gravitate one towards another, whereas no such gravitation any where appears, I answer, that since the gravitation towards these bodies is to the gravitation towards the whole earth as these bodies are to the whole earth, the gravitation towards them must be far less than to fall under the observation of our senses.

Cor. 2. The force of gravity towards the several equal particles of any body is reciprocally as the square of the distance of places from the particles; as appears from Cor. 3, Prop. LXXIV, Book I.

PROPOSITION VIII. THEOREM VIII.

In two spheres mutually gravitating, each towards the other, if the matter in planes on all sides round about and equi-distant from the centres is similar, the weight of either sphere towards the other will be reciprocally as the square of the distance between their centres.

After I had found that the force of gravity towards a whole planet did arise from and was compounded of the forces of gravity towards all its parts, and towards every one part was in the reciprocal proportion of the squares of the distances from the part, I was yet in doubt whether that reciprocal duplicate proportion did accurately hold, or but nearly so, in the total force compounded of so many partial ones; for it might be that the proportion which accurately enough took place in greater distances should be wide of the truth near the surface of the planet, where the distances of the particles are unequal, and their situation dissimilar. But by the help of Prop. LXXV and LXXVI, Book I, and their Corollaries, I was at last satisfied of the truth of the Proposition, as it now lies before us.

Cor. 1. Hence we may find and compare together the weights of bodies towards different planets; for the weights of bodies revolving in circles about planets are (by Cor. 2, Prop. IV, Book I) as the diameters of the circles directly, and the squares of their periodic times reciprocally; and their weights at the surfaces of the planets, or at any other distances from their centres, are (by this Prop.) greater or less in the reciprocal duplicate proportion of the distances. Thus from the periodic times of Venus, revolving about the sun, in $224^d.$ $16\,^3/_4{}^h$, of the utmost circumjovial satellite revolving about Jupiter, in $16^d.$ $16\,^8/_{15}{}^h$.; of the Huygenian satellite about Saturn in $15^d.$ $22\,^2/_3{}^h$. and of the moon about the earth in $27^d.$ $7^h.$ $43'$; compared with the mean distance of Venus from the sun, and with the greatest heliocentric elongations of the outmost circumjovial satellite from Jupiter's centre, $8'\ 16''$; of the Huygenian satellite from the centre of Saturn, $3'\ 4''$; and of the moon from the earth, $10'\ 33''$: by computation I found that the weight of equal bodies, at equal distances from the centres of the sun, of Jupiter, of Saturn, and of the earth, towards the sun, Jupiter, Saturn, and the earth, were one to another, as 1, $^1/_{1067}$, and $^1/_{169282}$, respectively. Then because as the distances are increased or diminished, the weights are diminished or increased in a duplicate ratio,

the weights of equal bodies towards the sun, Jupiter, Saturn, and the earth, at the distances 10000, 997, 791, and 109 from their centres, that is, at their very superficies, will be as 10000, 943, 529, and 435 respectively. How much the weights of bodies are at the superficies of the moon, will be shewn hereafter.

COR. 2. Hence likewise we discover the quantity of matter in the several planets; for their quantities of matter are as the forces of gravity at equal distances from their centres; that is, in the sun, Jupiter, Saturn, and the earth, as 1, $1/1067$, and $1/169282$ respectively. If the parallax of the sun be taken greater or less than 10" 30", the quantity of matter in the earth must be augmented or diminished in the triplicate of that proportion.

COR. 3. Hence also we find the densities of the planets; for (by Prop. LXXII, Book I) the weights of equal and similar bodies towards similar spheres are, at the surfaces of those spheres, as the diameters of the spheres; and therefore the densities of dissimilar spheres are as those weights applied to the diameters of the spheres. But the true diameters of the Sun, Jupiter, Saturn, and the earth, were one to another as 10000, 997, 791, and 109; and the weights towards the same as 10000, 943, 529, and 435 respectively; and therefore their densities are as 100, 94,1, 67, and 400. The density of the earth, which comes out by this computation, does not depend upon the parallax of the sun, but is determined by the parallax of the moon, and therefore is here truly defined. The sun, therefore, is a little denser than Jupiter, and Jupiter than Saturn, and the earth four times denser than the sun; for the sun, by its great heat, is kept in a sort of a rarefied state. The moon is denser than the earth, as shall appear afterward.

COR. 4. The smaller the planets are, they are, *caeteris paribus*, of so much the greater density; for so the powers of gravity on their several surfaces come nearer to equality. They are likewise, *caeteris paribus*, of the greater density, as they are nearer to the sun. So Jupiter is more dense than Saturn, and the earth than Jupiter; for the planets were to be placed at different distances from the sun, that, according to their degrees of density, they might enjoy a greater or less proportion to the sun's heat. Our water, if it were removed as far as the orb of Saturn, would be converted into ice, and in the orb of Mercury would quickly fly away in vapour; for the light of the sun, to which its heat is proportional, is seven times denser in the orb of Mercury than with us: and by the thermometer I have found that a sevenfold heat of our summer sun will make water boil. Nor are we to doubt that the matter of Mercury is adapted to its heat, and is therefore more dense than the matter of our earth; since, in a denser matter, the operations of Nature require a stronger heat.

PROPOSITION IX THEOREM IX.

THAT THE FORCE OF GRAVITY, CONSIDERED DOWNWARD
FROM THE SURFACE OF THE PLANETS, DECREASES NEARLY IN
THE PROPORTION OF THE DISTANCES FROM THEIR CENTRES.

If the matter of the planet were of an uniform density, this Proposition would be accurately true (by Prop. LXXIII. Book I). The error, therefore, can be no greater than what may arise from the inequality of the density.

PROPOSITION X. THEOREM X.

THAT THE MOTIONS OF THE PLANETS IN THE HEAVENS MAY SUBSIST AN EXCEEDINGLY LONG TIME.

In the Scholium of Prop. XL, Book II, I have shewed that a globe of water frozen into ice, and moving freely in our air, in the time that it would describe the length of its semi-diameter, would lose by the resistance of the air $1/4386$ part of its motion; and the same proportion holds nearly in all globes, how great soever, and moved with whatever velocity. But that our globe of earth is of greater density than it would be if the whole consisted of water only, I thus make out. If the whole consisted of water only, whatever was of less density than water, because of its less specific gravity, would emerge and float above. And upon this account, if a globe of terrestrial matter, covered on all sides with water, was less dense than water, it would emerge somewhere; and, the subsiding water falling back, would be gathered to the opposite side. And such is the condition of our earth, which in a great measure is covered with seas. The earth, if it was not for its greater density, would emerge from the seas, and, according to its degree of levity, would be raised more or less above their surface, the water of the seas flowing backward to the opposite side. By the same argument, the spots of the sun, which float upon the lucid matter thereof, are lighter than that matter; and, however the planets have been formed while they were yet in fluid masses, all the heavier matter subsided to the centre. Since, therefore, the common matter of our earth on the surface thereof is about twice as heavy as water, and a little lower, in mines, is found about three, or four, or even five times more heavy, it is probable that the quantity of the whole matter of the earth may be five or six times greater than if it consisted all of water; especially since I have before shewed that the earth is about four times more dense than Jupiter. If, therefore, Jupiter is a little more dense than water, in the space of thirty days, in which that planet describes the length of 459 of its semi-diameters, it would, in a medium of the same density with our air, lose almost a tenth part of its motion. But since the resistance of mediums decreases in proportion to their weight or density, so that water, which is $13^3/_5$ times lighter than quicksilver, resists less in that proportion; and air, which is 860 times lighter than water, resists less in the same proportion; therefore in the heavens, where the weight of the medium in which the planets move is immensely diminished, the resistance will almost vanish.

It is shewn in the Scholium of Prop. XXII, Book II, that at the height of 200 miles above the earth the air is more rare than it is at the superficies of the earth in the ratio of 30 to 0,0000000000003998, or as 75000000000000 to 1 nearly. And hence the planet Jupiter, revolving in a medium of the same density with that superior air, would not lose by the resistance of the medium the 1000000th part of its motion in 1000000 years. In the spaces near the earth the resistance is produced only by the air, exhalations, and vapours. When these are carefully exhausted by the air-pump from under the receiver, heavy bodies fall within the receiver with perfect freedom, and without the least sensible resistance; gold itself, and the lightest down, let fall together, will descend with equal velocity; and though they fall through a space of four, six, and eight feet, they will come to the bottom at the same time; as appears from experiments. And therefore the celestial regions being perfectly void of air and exhalations, the planets and comets meeting no sensible resistance in those spaces will continue their motions through them for an immense tract of time.

HYPOTHESIS I.

That the centre of the system of the world is immovable.

This is acknowledged by all, while some contend that the earth, others that the sun, is fixed in that centre. Let us see what may from hence follow.

PROPOSITION XI. THEOREM XI.

That the common centre of gravity of the earth, the sun, and all the planets, is immovable.

For (by Cor. 4 of the Laws) that centre either is at rest, or moves uniformly forward in a right line; but if that centre moved, the centre of the worb:1 would move also, against the Hypothesis.

PROPOSITION XII. THEOREM XII.

That the sun is agitated by a perpetual motion, but never recedes far from the common centre of gravity of all the planets.

For since (by Cor. 2, Prop. VIII) the quantity of matter in the sun is to the quantity of matter in Jupiter as 1067 to 1; and the distance of Jupiter from the sun is to the semi-diameter of the sun in a proportion but a small matter greater, the common centre of gravity of Jupiter and the sun will fall upon a point a little without the surface of

the sun. By the same argument, since the quantity of matter in the sun is to the quantity of matter in Saturn as 3021 to 1, and the distance of Saturn from the sun is to the semi-diameter of the sun in a proportion but a small matter less, the common centre of gravity of Saturn and the sun will fall upon a point a little within the surface of the sun. And, pursuing the principles of this computation, we should find that though the earth and all the planets were placed on one side of the sun, the distance of the common centre of gravity of all from the centre of the sun would scarcely amount to one diameter of the sun. In other cases, the distances of those centres are always less; and therefore, since that centre of gravity is in perpetual rest, the sun, according to the various positions of the planets must perpetually be moved every way, but will never recede far from that centre.

COR. Hence the common centre of gravity of the earth, the sun, and all the planets, is to be esteemed the centre of the world; for since the earth, the sun, and all the planets, mutually gravitate one towards another, and are therefore, according to their powers of gravity, in perpetual agitation, as the Laws of Motion require, it is plain that their moveable centres cannot be taken for the immovable centre of the world. If that body were to be placed in the centre, towards which other bodies gravitate most (according to common opinion), that privilege ought to be allowed to the sun; but since the sun itself is moved, a fixed point is to be chosen from which the centre of the sun recedes least, and from which it would recede yet less if the body of the sun were denser and greater, and therefore less apt to be moved.

PROPOSITION XIII. THEOREM XIII.

THE PLANETS MOVE IN ELLIPSES WHICH HAVE THEIR COMMON FOCUS IN THE CENTRE OF THE SUN; AND, BY RADII DRAWN TO THAT CENTRE, THEY DESCRIBE AREAS PROPORTIONAL TO THE TIMES OF DESCRIPTION.

We have discoursed above of these motions from the Phaenomena. Now that we know the principles on which they depend, from those principles we deduce the motions of the heavens *à priori*. Because the weights of the planets towards the sun are reciprocally as the squares of their distances from the sun's centre, if the sun was at rest, and the other planets did not mutually act one upon another, their orbits would be ellipses, having the sun in their common focus; and they would describe areas proportional to the times *of description*, by Prop. I and XI, and Cor. 1, Prop. XIII, Book I. But the mutual actions of the planets one upon another are so very small, that they may be neglected; and by Prop. LXVI, Book I, they less disturb the motions of the planets around the sun in motion than if those motions were performed about the sun at rest.

It is true, that the action of Jupiter upon Saturn is not to be neglected; for the force of gravity towards Jupiter is to the force of gravity towards the sun (at equal distances, Cor. 2, Prop. VIII) as 1 to 1067; and therefore in the conjunction of Jupiter and Saturn, because the distance of Saturn from Jupiter is to the distance of Saturn from the sun almost as 4 to 9, the gravity of Saturn towards Jupiter will be to the gravity of Saturn towards the sun as 81 to 16 x 1067; or, as 1 to about 211. And hence arises a perturbation of the orb of Saturn in every conjunction of this planet with Jupiter, so sensible, that astronomers are puzzled with it. As the planet is differently situated in these conjunctions, its eccentricity is sometimes augmented, sometimes diminished; its aphelion is sometimes carried forward, sometimes backward, and its mean motion is by turns accelerated and retarded; yet the whole error in its motion about the sun, though arising from so great a force, may be almost avoided (except in the mean motion) by placing the lower focus of its orbit in the common centre of gravity of Jupiter and the sun (according to Prop. LXVII, Book I), and therefore that error, when it is greatest, scarcely exceeds two minutes; and the greatest error in the mean motion scarcely exceeds two minutes yearly. But in the conjunction of Jupiter and Saturn, the accelerative forces of gravity of the sun towards Saturn, of Jupiter towards Saturn, and of Jupiter towards the sun, are almost as 16, 81, and $\frac{16 \times 81 \times 3021}{25}$ or 156609; and

therefore the difference of the form of gravity of the sun towards Saturn, and of Jupiter towards Saturn, is to the force of gravity of Jupiter towards the sun as 65 to 156609, or as 1 to 2409. But the greatest power of Saturn to disturb the motion of Jupiter is proportional to this difference; and therefore the perturbation of the orbit of Jupiter is much less than that of Saturn's. The perturbations of the other orbits are yet far less, except that the orbit of the earth is sensibly disturbed by the moon. The common centre of gravity of the earth and moon moves in an ellipsis about the sun in the focus thereof, and, by a radius drawn to the sun, describes areas proportional to the times of description. But the earth in the mean time by a menstrual motion is revolved about this common centre.

PROPOSITION XIV. THEOREM XIV.

THE APHELIONS AND NODES OF THE ORBITS OF THE PLANETS ARE FIXED.

The aphelions are immovable by Prop. XI, Book I; and so are the planes of the orbits, by Prop. I of the same Book. And if the planes are fixed, the nodes must be so too. It is true, that some inequalities may arise from the mutual actions of the planets and comets in their revolutions; but these will be so small, that they may be here passed by.

COR. 1. The fixed stars are immovable, seeing they keep the same position to the aphelions and nodes of the planets.

COR. 2. And since these stars are liable to no sensible parallax from the annual motion of the earth, they can have no force, because of their immense distance, to produce any sensible effect in our system. Not to mention that the fixed stars, every where promiscuously dispersed in the heavens, by their contrary attractions destroy their mutual actions, by Prop. LXX, Book I.

SCHOLIUM.

Since the planets near the sun (viz. Mercury, Venus, the, Earth, and Mars) are so small that they can act with but little force upon each other, therefore their aphelions and nodes must be fixed, excepting in so far as they are disturbed by the actions of Jupiter and Saturn, and other higher bodies. And hence we may find, by the theory of gravity, that their aphelions move a little *in consequentia,* in respect of the fixed stars, and that in the sesquiplicate proportion of their several distances from the sun. So that if the aphelion of Mars, in the space of a hundred years, is carried 33' 20" *in consequentia,* in respect of the fixed stars, the aphelions of the Earth, of Venus, and of Mercury, will in a hundred years be carried forwards 17' 40", 10' 53", and 4' 16", respectively. But these motions are so inconsiderable, that we have neglected them in this Proposition.

PROPOSITION XV. PROBLEM I.

TO FIND THE PRINCIPAL DIAMETERS OF THE ORBITS OF THE PLANETS.

They are to be taken in the sub-sesquiplicate proportion of the periodic times, by Prop. XV, Book I, and then to be severally augmented in the proportion of the sum of the masses of matter in the sun and each planet to the first of two mean proportionals betwixt that sum and the quantity of matter in the sun, by Prop. LX, Book I.

PROPOSITION XVI. PROBLEM II.

TO FIND THE ECCENTRICITIES AND APHELIONS OF THE PLANETS.

This Problem is resolved by Prop. XVIII, Book I.

PROPOSITION XVII. THEOREM XV.

THAT THE DIURNAL MOTIONS OF THE PLANETS ARE UNIFORM, AND THAT THE LIBRATION OF THE MOON ARISES FROM ITS DIURNAL MOTION.

The Proposition is proved from the first Law of Motion, and Cor. 22, Prop. LXVI, Book I. Jupiter, with respect to the fixed stars, revolves in 91^h. 56'; Mars in 24^h. 39'; Venus in about 23^h.; the Earth in 23^h. 56'; the Sun in 25$^1/_2$, days, and the moon in 27 days, 7 hours, 43'. These things appear by the Phænomena. The spots in the sun's body return to the same situation on the sun's disk, with respect to the earth, in 27$^1/_2$ days; and therefore with respect to the fixed stars the sun revolves in about 25$^1/_2$ days. But because the lunar day, arising from its uniform revolution about its axis, is menstrual, *that is, equal to the time of its periodic revolution in its orb*, therefore the same face of the moon will be always nearly turned to the upper focus of its orb; but, as the situation of that focus requires, will deviate a little to one side and to the other from the earth in the lower focus; and this is the libration in longitude; for the libration in latitude arises from the moon's latitude, and the inclination of its axis to the plant of the ecliptic. This theory of the libration of the moon, Mr. *N. Mercator*, in his Astronomy, published at the beginning of the year 1676, explained more fully out of the letters I sent him. The utmost satellite of Saturn seems to revolve about its axis with a motion like this of the moon, respecting Saturn continually with the same face; for in its revolution round Saturn, as often as it comes to the eastern part of its orbit, it is scarcely visible, and generally quite disappears; which is like to be occasioned by some spots in that part of its body, which is then turned towards the earth, as M. *Cassini* has observed. So also the utmost satellite of Jupiter seems to revolve about its axis with a like motion, because in that part of its body which is turned from Jupiter it has a spot, which always appears as if it were in Jupiter's own body, whenever the satellite passes between Jupiter and our eye.

PROPOSITION XVIII. THEOREM XVI.

THAT THE AXES OF THE PLANETS ARE LESS THAN THE DIAMETERS DRAWN PERPENDICULAR TO THE AXES.

The equal gravitation of the parts on all sides would give a spherical figure to the planets, if it was not for their diurnal revolution in a circle. By that circular motion it comes to pass that the parts receding from the axis endeavour to ascend about the equator; and therefore if the matter is in a fluid state, by its ascent towards the equator it will enlarge the diameters there, and by its descent towards the poles it will shorten the axis. So the diameter of Jupiter (by the concurring observations of astronomers) is found shorter betwixt pole and pole than from east to west. And, by the same argument, if our earth was not higher about the equator than at the poles, the seas would subside about the poles, and, rising towards the equator, would lay all things there under water.

PROPOSITION XIX. PROBLEM III.

TO FIND THE PROPORTION OF THE AXIS OF A PLANET TO THE DIAMETER, PERPENDICULAR THERETO.

Our countryman, Mr. *Norwood*, measuring a distance of 905751 feet of *London* measure between *London* and *York*, in 1635, and observing the difference of latitudes to be 2° 28', determined the measure of one degree to be 367196 feet of *London* measure, that is 57300 *Paris* toises. M. *Picart*, measuring an arc of one degree, and 22' 55" of the meridian between *Amiens* and *Malvoisine*, found an arc of one degree to be 57060 *Paris* toises. M. *Cassini*, the father, measured the distance upon the meridian from the town of *Collioure* in *Roussillon* to the Observatory of *Paris*; and his son added the distance from the Observatory to the Citadel of *Dunkirk*. The whole distance was 486156$^1/_2$ toises and the difference of the latitudes of *Callioure* and *Dunkirk* was 8 degrees, and 31' 11$^5/_6$". Hence an arc of one degree appears to be 57061 *Paris* toises. And from these measures we conclude that the circumference of the earth is 123249600, and its semi-diameter 19615800 *Paris* feet, upon the supposition that the earth is of a spherical figure.

In the latitude of *Paris* a heavy body falling in a second of time describes 15 *Paris* feet, 1 inch, 1$^7/_8$ line, as above, that is, 2173 lines$^7/_9$. The weight of the body is diminished by the weight of the ambient air. Let us suppose the weight lost thereby to be $^1/_{11000}$ part of the whole weight; then that heavy body falling *in vacuo* will describe a height of 2174 lines in one second of time.

A body in every sidereal day of 23^h. 56' 4" uniformly revolving in a circle at the distance of 19615800 feet from the centre, in one second of time describes an arc of 1433,46 feet; the versed sine of which is 0,05236561 feet, or 7,54064 lines. And therefore the force with which bodies descend in the latitude of *Paris* is to the centrifugal force of bodies in the equator arising from the diurnal motion of the earth as 2174 to 7,54064.

The centrifugal force of bodies in the equator is to the centrifugal force with which bodies recede directly from the earth in the latitude of *Paris* 48° 50' 10" in the duplicate proportion of the radius to the cosine of the latitude, that is, as 7,54064 to 3,267. Add this force to the force with which bodies descend by their weight in the latitude of *Paris*, and a body, in the latitude of *Paris*, falling by its whole undiminished force of gravity, in the time of one second, will describe 2177,267 lines, or 15 *Paris* feet, 1 inch, and 5,267 lines. And the total force of gravity in that latitude will be to the centrifugal force of bodies in the equator of the earth as 2177,267 to 7,54064, or as 289 to 1.

Wherefore if APBQ represent the figure of the earth, now no longer spherical, but generated by the rotation of an ellipsis about its lesser axis PQ; and ACQ*qca* a canal

full of water, reaching from the pole Qq to the centre Cc, and thence rising to the equator Aa; the weight of the water in the leg of the canal ACca will be to the weight of water in the other leg QCcq as 299 to 288, because the centrifugal force arising from the circular motion sustains and takes off one of the 289 parts of the weight (in the one leg), and the weight of 288 in the other sustains the rest. But by computation (from

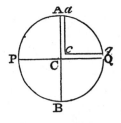

Cor. 2, Prop. XCI, Book I) I find, that, if the matter of the earth was all uniform, and without any motion, and its axis PQ were to the diameter AB as 100 to 101, the force of gravity in the place Q towards the earth would be to the force of gravity in the same place Q towards a sphere described about the centre C with the radius PC, or QC, as 126 to 125. And, by the same argument, the force of gravity in the place A towards the spheroid generated by the rotation of the ellipsis APBQ about the axis AB is to the force of gravity in the same place A, towards the sphere described about the centre C with the radius AC, as 125 to 126. But the force of gravity in the place A towards the earth is a mean proportional betwixt the forces of gravity towards the spheroid and this sphere; because the sphere, by having its diameter PQ diminished in the proportion of 101 to 100, is transformed into the figure of the earth; and this figure, by having a third diameter perpendicular to the two diameters AB and PQ diminished in the same proportion, is converted into the said spheroid; and the force of gravity in A, in either case, is diminished nearly in the same proportion. Therefore the force of gravity in A towards the sphere described about the centre C with the radius AC, is to the force of gravity in A towards the earth as 126 to 125 $^1/_2$. And the force of gravity in the place Q towards the sphere described about the centre C with the radius QC, is to the force of gravity in the place A towards the sphere described about the centre C, with the radius AC, in the proportion of the diameters (by Prop. LXXII, Book I), that is, as 100 to 101. If, therefore, we compound those three proportions 126 to 125, 126 to 125$^1/_2$, and 100 to 101, into one, the force of gravity in the place Q towards the earth will be to the force of gravity in the place A towards the earth as 126 × 126 × 100 to 125 × 125$^1/_2$ × 101; or as 501 to 500.

Now since (by Cor. 3, Prop. XCI, Book I) the force of gravity in either leg of the canal ACca, or QCcq, is as the distance of the places from the centre of the earth, if those legs are conceived to be divided by transverse, parallel, and equidistant surfaces, into parts proportional to the wholes, the weights of any number of parts in the one leg ACca will be to the weights of the same number of parts in the other leg as their magnitudes and the accelerative forces of their gravity conjunctly, that is, as 101 to 100. and 500 to 501, or as 505 to 501. And therefore if the centrifugal force of every part in the leg ACca, arising from the diurnal motion, was to the weight of the same

part as 4 to 505, so that from the weight of every part, conceived to be divided into 505 parts, the centrifugal force might take off four of those parts, the weights would remain equal in each leg, and therefore the fluid would rest in an equilibrium. But the centrifugal force of every part is to the weight of the same part as 1 to 289; that is, the centrifugal force, which should be $^4/_{505}$ parts of the weight, is only $^1/_{289}$ part thereof. And, therefore, I say, by the rule of proportion, that if the centrifugal force $^4/_{505}$ make the height of the water in the leg AC*ca* to exceed the height of the water in the leg QC*cq* by one $^1/_{100}$ part of its whole height, the centrifugal force $^1/_{289}$ will make the excess of the height in the leg AC*ca* only $^1/_{289}$ part of the height of the water in the other leg QC*cq*; and therefore the diameter of the earth at the equator, is to its diameter from pole to pole as 230 to 229. And since the mean semi-diameter of the earth, according to *Picart's* mensuration, is 19615800 *Paris* feet, or 3923,16 miles. (reckoning 5000 feet to a mile), the earth will be higher at the equator than at the poles by 85472 feet, or $17^1/_{16}$ miles. And its height at the equator will be about 19658600 feet, and at the poles 19573000 feet.

If, the density and periodic time of the diurnal revolution remaining the same, the planet was greater or less than the earth, the proportion of the centrifugal force to that of gravity, and therefore also of the diameter betwixt the poles to the diameter at the equator, would likewise remain the same. But if the diurnal motion was accelerated or retarded in any proportion, the centrifugal force would be augmented or diminished nearly in the same duplicate proportion; and therefore the difference of the diameters will be increased or diminished in the same duplicate ratio very nearly. And if the density of the planet was augmented or diminished in any proportion, the force of gravity tending towards it would also be augmented or diminished in the same proportion: and the difference of the diameters contrariwise would be diminished in proportion as the force of gravity is augmented, and augmented in proportion as the force of gravity is diminished. Wherefore, since the earth, in respect of the fixed stars, revolves in 23^h. 56', but Jupiter in 9^h. 56', and the squares of their periodic times are as 29 to 5, and their densities as 400 to $94^1/_2$, the difference of the diameters of Jupiter will be to its lesser diameter as $\frac{29}{5} \times \frac{400}{94\frac{1}{2}} \times \frac{1}{229}$ to 1, or as 1 to $9^1/_2$, nearly. Therefore the diameter

of Jupiter from east to west is to its diameter from pole to pole nearly as $10^1/_3$ to $9^1/_3$. Therefore since its greatest diameter is 37", its lesser diameter lying between the poles will be 33" 25'''. Add thereto about 3" for the irregular refraction of light, and the apparent diameters of this planet will become 40" and 36" 25'''; which are to each other as $11^1/_6$ to $10^1/_6$, very nearly. These things are so upon the supposition that the body of Jupiter is uniformly dense. But now if its body be denser towards the plane of the equator than towards the poles, its diameters may be to each other as 12 to 11, or 13 to 12, or perhaps as 14 to 13.

And *Cassini* observed in the year 1691, that the diameter of Jupiter reaching from east to west is greater by about a fifteenth part than the other diameter. Mr. *Pound* with his 123 feet telescope, and an excellent micrometer, measured the diameters of Jupiter in the year 1719, and found them as follow.

The Times.			Greatest diam.	Lesser diam.	The diam. to each other.
	Day.	Hours.	Parts	Parts	
January	28	6	13,40	12,28	As 12 to 11
March	6	7	13,12	12,20	$13^3/_4$ to $12^3/_4$
March	9	7	13,12	12,08	$12^2/_3$ to $11^2/_3$
April	9	9	12,32	11,48	14 1/2 to 13 1/2

So that the theory agrees with the phaenomena; for the planets are more heated by the sun's rays towards their equators, and therefore are a little more condensed by that heat than towards their poles.

Moreover, that there is a diminution of gravity occasioned by the diurnal rotation of the earth, and therefore the earth rises higher there than it does at the poles (supposing that its matter is uniformly dense), will appear by the experiments of pendulums related under the following Proposition.

PROPOSITION XX. PROBLEM IV.

To find and compare together the weights of bodies in the different regions of our earth.

Because the weights of the unequal legs of the canal of water ACQ*qca* are equal; and the weights of the parts proportional to the whole legs, and alike situated in them, are one to another as the weights of the wholes, and therefore equal betwixt themselves;

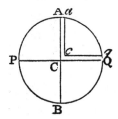

the weights of equal parts, and alike situated in the legs, will be reciprocally as the legs, that is, reciprocally as 230 to 229. And the case is the same in all homogeneous equal bodies alike situated in the legs of the canal. Their weights are reciprocally as the legs, that is, reciprocally as the distances of the bodies from the centre of the earth. Therefore if the bodies are situated in the uppermost parts of the canals, or on the surface of the earth, their weights will be one to another reciprocally as their distances from the centre. And, by the same argument, the weights in all other places round the whole surface of the earth are reciprocally as the distances of the places from the centre; and, therefore, in the hypothesis of the earth's being a spheroid are given in proportion.

Whence arises this Theorem, that the increase of weight in passing from the equator to the poles is nearly as the versed sine of double the latitude; or, which comes to the same thing, as the square of the right sine of the latitude; and the area of the degrees of latitude in the meridian increase nearly in the same proportion. And, therefore, since the latitude of *Paris* is 48° 50', that of places under the equator 00° 00', and that of places under the poles 90°; and the versed sines of double those arcs are 11334,00000 and 20000, the radius being 10000; and the force of gravity at the pole is to the force of gravity at the equator as 230 to 229; and the excess of the force of gravity at the pole to the force of gravity at the equator as 1 to 229; the excess of the force of gravity in the latitude of *Paris* will be to the force of gravity at the equator as $1 \times {}^{11334}/_{20000}$ to 229, or as 5667 to 2290000, And therefore the whole forces of gravity in those places will be one to the other as 2295667 to 2290000. Wherefore since the lengths of pendulums vibrating in equal times are as the forces of gravity, and in the latitude of *Paris*, the length of a pendulum vibrating seconds is 3 *Paris* feet, and $8^1/_2$ lines, or rather because of the weight of the air, 63 lines, the length of a pendulum vibrating in the same time under the equator will be shorter by 1,087 lines. And by a like calculus the following table is made.

Latitude of the place.	Length of the pendulum		Measure of one degree in the meridian.
Deg.	Feet.	Lines.	Toises.
0	3	7,468	56637
5	3	7,482	56642
10	3	7,526	56659
15	3	7,596	56687
20	3	7,692	66724
25	3	7,812	56769
30	3	7,948	56823
35	3	8,099	56882
40	3	8,261	56945
1	3	8,294	56958
2	3	8,327	56971
3	3	8,361	56984
4	3	8,394	56997
45	3	8,428	57010
6	3	8,461	57022
7	3	8,494	57035
8	3	8,528	57048
9	3	8,561	57061
50	3	8,594	57074
55	3	8,756	57137
60	3	8,907	57196
65	3	9,044	57250
70	3	9,162	57295
75	3	9,258	57332
80	3	9,329	57360
85	3	9,372	57377
90	3	9,387	57382

By this table, therefore, it appears that the inequality of degrees is so small, that the figure of the earth, in geographical matters, may be considered as spherical; especially if the earth be a little denser towards the plane of the equator than towards the poles.

Now several astronomers, sent into remote countries to make astronomical observations, have found that pendulum clocks do accordingly move slower near the equator than in our climates. And, first of all, in the year 1672, M. *Richer* took notice of it in the island of *Cayenne*; for when, in the month of *August*, he was observing the transits of the fixed stars over the meridian, he found his clock to go slower than it ought in respect of the mean motion of the sun at the rate of 2' 28" a day. Therefore, fitting up a simple pendulum to vibrate in seconds, which were measured by an excellent clock, he observed the length of that simple pendulum; and this he did over and over every week for ten months together. And upon his return to *France*, comparing the length of that pendulum with the length of the pendulum at *Paris* (which was 3 *Paris* feet and $8^3/_5$ lines), he found it shorter by $1^1/_4$ line.

Afterwards, our friend Dr. *Halley*, about the year 1677, arriving at the island of St. *Helena*, found his pendulum clock to go slower there than at *London* without marking the difference. But he shortened the rod of his clock by more than the $^1/_8$ of an inch, or $1^1/_2$ line; and to effect this, because the length of the screw at the lower end of the rod was not sufficient, he interposed a wooden ring betwixt the nut and the ball.

Then, in the year 1682, M. *Varin* and M. *des Hayes* found the length of a simple pendulum vibrating in seconds at the Royal Observatory of *Paris* to be 3 feet and $8^5/_9$ lines. And by the same method in the island of *Goree*, they found the length of an isochronal pendulum to be 3 feet and $6^5/_9$ lines, differing from the former by two lines. And in the same year, going to the islands of *Guadaloupe* and *Martinico*, they found that the length of an isochronal pendulum in those islands was 3 feet and $6^1/_2$ lines.

After this, M. *Couplet*, the son, in the month of *July* 1697, at the Royal Observatory of *Paris*, so fitted his pendulum clock to the mean motion of the sun, that for a considerable time together the clock agreed with the motion of the sun. In *November* following, upon his arrival at *Lisbon*, he found his clock to go slower than before at the rate of 2' 13", in 24 hours. And next *March* coming to *Paraiba*, he found his clock to go slower than at *Paris*, and at the rate 4' 12" in 24 hours; and he affirms, that the pendulum vibrating in seconds was shorter at *Lisbon* by 21 lines, and at *Paraiba* by 32 lines, than at *Paris*. He had done better to have reckoned those differences $1^1/_3$ and $2^5/_9$ for these differences correspond to the differences of the times 2' 13" and 4' 12". But this gentleman's observations are so gross, that we cannot confide in them.

In the following years, 1699, and 1700, M. *des Hayes*, making another voyage to *America*, determined that in the island of *Cayenne* and *Granada* the length of the pendulum vibrating in seconds was a small matter less than 3 feet and $6^1/_2$ lines; that in the island of St. *Christophers* it was 3 feet and $6^3/_4$, lines; and in the island of St. *Domingo* 3 feet and 7 lines.

And in the year 1704, P. Feuillé, at *Puerto Bello* in *America*, found that the length of the pendulum vibrating in seconds was 3 *Paris* feet, and only 5 $^7/_{12}$ lines, that is, almost 3 lines shorter than at *Paris*, but the observation was faulty. For afterward, going to the island of *Martinico*, he found the length of the isochronal pendulum there 3 *Paris* feet and $5^{10}/_{12}$ lines.

Now the latitude of *Paraiba* is 6° 38' south; that of *Puerto Bello* 9° 33' north; and the latitudes of the islands *Cayenne, Goree, Gaudaloupe, Martinico, Granada,* St. *Christophers,* and St. *Domingo,* are respectively 4° 55', 14° 40", 15° 00', 14° 44', 12° 06', 17° 191, and 19° 48', north. And the excesses of the length of the pendulum at *Paris* above the lengths of the isochronal pendulums observed in those latitudes are a little greater than by the table of the lengths of the pendulum before computed. And therefore the earth is a little higher under the equator than by the preceding calculus, and a little denser at the centre than in mines near the surface, unless, perhaps, the heats of the torrid zone have a little extended the length of the pendulums.

For M. *Picart* has observed, that a rod of iron, which in frosty weather in the winter season was one foot long, when heated by fire, was lengthened into one foot and $^1/_4$ line. Afterward M. *de la Hire* found that a rod of iron, which in the like winter season was 6 feet long, when exposed to the heat of the summer sun, was extended into 6 feet and $^2/_3$ line. In the former case the heat was greater than in the latter; but in the latter it was greater than the heat of the external parts of a human body; for metals exposed to the summer sun acquire a very considerable degree of heat. But the rod of a pendulum clock is never exposed to the heat of the summer sun, nor ever acquires a heat equal to that of the external parts of a human body; and, therefore, though the 3 feet rod of a pendulum clock will indeed be a little longer in the summer than in the winter season, yet the difference will scarcely amount to $^1/_4$ line. Therefore the total difference of the lengths of isochronal pendulums in different climates cannot be ascribed to the difference of heat; nor indeed to the mistakes of the French astronomers. For although there is not a perfect agreement betwixt their observations, yet the errors are so small that they may be neglected; and in this they all agree, that isochronal pendulums are shorter under the equator than at the Royal Observatory of *Paris*, by a difference not less than $1^1/_4$ line, nor greater than $2^2/_3$ lines. By the observations of M. *Richer*, in the island of Cayenne, the difference was $1^1/_4$ line. That difference being corrected by those of M. *des Hayes*, becomes $1^1/_2$ line or $1^3/_4$ line. By the

less accurate observations of others, the same was made about two lines. And this disagreement might arise partly from the errors of the observations, partly from the dissimilitude of the internal parts of the earth, and the height of mountains; partly from the different heats of the air.

I take an iron rod of 3 feet long to be shorter by a sixth part of one line in winter time with us here in *England* than in the summer. Because of the great heats under the equator, subduct this quantity from the difference of one line and a quarter observed by M. *Richer*, and there will remain one line $^1/_{12}$, which agrees very well with $1^{87}/_{1000}$ line collected, by the theory a little before. M. *Richer* repeated his observations, made in the island of *Cayenne*, every week for ten months together, and compared the lengths of the pendulum which he had there noted in the iron rods with the lengths thereof which he observed in *France*. This diligence and care seems to have been wanting to the other observers. If this gentleman's observations are to be depended on, the earth is higher under the equator than at the poles, and that by an excess of about 17 miles; as appeared above by the theory.

PROPOSITION XXI. THEOREM XVII.

THAT THE EQUINOCTIAL POINTS GO BACKWARD, AND THAT THE AXIS OF THE EARTH, BY A NUTATION IN EVERY ANNUAL REVOLUTION, TWICE VIBRATES TOWARDS THE ECLIPTIC, AND AS OFTEN RETURNS TO ITS FORMER POSITION.

The proposition appears from Cor. 20, Prop. LXVI, Book I; but that motion of nutation must be very small, and, indeed, scarcely perceptible.

PROPOSITION XXII. THEOREM XVIII.

THAT ALL THE MOTIONS OF THE MOON, AND ALL THE INEQUALITIES OF THOSE MOTIONS, FOLLOW FROM THE PRINCIPLES WHICH WE HAVE LAID DOWN.

That the greater planets, while they are carried about the sun, may in the mean time carry other lesser planets, revolving about them; and that those lesser planets must move in ellipses which have their foci in the centres of the greater, appears from Prop. LXV, Book I. But then their motions will be several ways disturbed by the action of the sun, and they will suffer such inequalities as are observed in our moon. Thus our moon (by Cor. 2, 3, 4, and 5, Prop. LXVI, Book I) moves faster, and, by a radius drawn to the earth, describes an area greater for the time, and has its orbit less curved, and therefore approaches nearer to the earth in the syzygies than in the quadratures, excepting

in so far as these effects are hindered by the motion of eccentricity; for (by Cor. 9, Prop. LXVI, Book I) the eccentricity is greatest when the apogeon of the moon is in the syzygies, and least when the same is in the quadratures; and upon this account the perigeon moon is swifter, and nearer to us, but the apogeon moon slower, and farther from us, in the syzygies than in the quadratures. Moreover, the apogee goes forward, and the nodes backward; and this is done not with a regular but an unequal motion. For (by Cor. 7 and 8, Prop. LXVI, Book I) the apogee goes more swiftly forward in its syzygies, more slowly backward in its quadratures; and, by the excess of its progress above its regress, advances yearly *in consequentia*. But, contrariwise, the nodes (by Cor. 11, Prop. LXVI, Book I) are quiescent in their syzygies, and go fastest back in their quadratures. Farther, the greatest latitude of the moon (by Cor. 10, Prop. LXVI, Book I) is greater in the quadratures of the moon than in its syzygies. And (by Cor. 6, Prop. LXVI, Book I) the mean motion of the moon is slower in the perihelion of the earth than in its aphelion. And these are the principal inequalities (of the moon) taken notice of by astronomers.

But there are yet other inequalities not observed by former astronomers, by which the motions of the moon are so disturbed, that to this day we have not been able to bring them under any certain rule. For the velocities or horary motions of the apogee and nodes of the moon, and their equations, as well as the difference betwixt the greatest eccentricity in the syzygies, and the least eccentricity in the quadratures, and that inequality which we call the variation, are (by Cor. 14, Prop. LXVI, Book I) in the course of the year augmented and diminished in the triplicate proportion of the sun's apparent diameter. And besides (by Cor. 1 and 2, Lem. 10, and Cor. 16, Prop. LXVI, Book I) the variation is augmented and diminished nearly in the duplicate proportion of the time between the quadratures. But in astronomical calculations, this inequality is commonly thrown into and confounded with the equation of the moon's centre.

PROPOSITION XXIII. PROBLEM V.

To derive the unequal motions of the satellites of Jupiter and Saturn from the motions of our moon.

From the motions of our moon we deduce the corresponding motions of the moons or satellites of Jupiter in this manner, by Cor. 16, Prop. LXVI, Book I. The mean motion of the nodes of the outmost satellite of Jupiter is to the mean motion of the nodes of our moon in a proportion compounded of the duplicate proportion of the periodic times of the earth about the sun to the periodic times of Jupiter about the sun, and the simple proportion of the periodic time of the satellite about Jupiter to the periodic time of our moon about the earth; and, therefore, those nodes, in the space of a

hundred years, are carried 8° 24' backward, or *in antecedentia*. The mean motions of the nodes of the inner satellites are to the mean motion of the nodes of the outmost as their periodic times to the periodic time of the former, by the same Corollary, and are thence given. And the motion of the apsis of every satellite *in consequentia* is to the motion of its nodes *in antecedentia* as the motion of the apogee of our moon to the motion of its nodes (by the same Corollary), and is thence given. But the motions of the apsides thus found must be diminished in the proportion of 5 to 9, or of about 1 to 2, on account of a cause which I cannot here descend to explain. The greatest equations of the nodes, and of the apsis of every satellite, are to the greatest equations of the nodes, and apogee of our moon respectively, as the motions of the nodes and apsides of the satellites, in the time of one revolution of the former equations, to the motions of the nodes and apogee of our moon, in the time of one revolution of the latter equations. The variation of a satellite seen from Jupiter is to the variation of our moon in the same proportion as the whole motions of their nodes respectively during the times in which the satellite and our moon (after parting from) are revolved (again) to the sun, by the same Corollary; and therefore in the outmost satellite the variation does not exceed 5" 12'''.

PROPOSITION XXIV. THEOREM XIX.

THAT THE FLUX AND REFLUX OF THE SEA ARISE FROM THE ACTIONS OF THE SUN AND MOON.

By Cor. 19 and 20, Prop. LXVI, Book I, it appears that the waters of the sea ought twice to rise and twice to fall every day, as well lunar as solar; and that the greatest height of the waters in the open and deep seas ought to follow the appulse of the luminaries to the meridian of the place by a less interval than 6 hours; as happens in all that eastern tract of the *Atlantic* and *AEthiopic* seas between *France* and the *Cape of Good Hope*; and on the coasts of *Chili* and *Peru* in the South Sea; in all which shores the flood falls out about the second, third, or fourth hour, unless where the motion propagated from the deep ocean is by the shallowness of the channels, through which it passes to some particular places, retarded to the fifth, sixth, or seventh hour, and even later. The hours I reckon from the appulse of each luminary to the meridian of the place, as well under as above the horizon; and by the hours of the lunar day I understand the 24th parts of that time which the moon, by its apparent diurnal motion, employs to come about again to the meridian of the place which it left the day before. The force of the sun or moon in raising the sea is greatest in the appulse of the luminary to the meridian of the place; but the force impressed upon the sea at that time continues a little while after the impression, and is afterwards increased by a new though less force still

acting upon it. This makes the sea rise higher and higher, till this new force becoming too weak to raise it any more, the sea rises to its greatest height. And this will come to pass, perhaps, in one or two hours, but more frequently near the shores in about three hours, or even more, where the sea is shallow.

The two luminaries excite two motions, which will not appear distinctly, but between them will arise one mixed motion compounded out of both. In the conjunction or opposition of the luminaries their forces will be conjoined, and bring on the greatest flood and ebb. In the quadratures the sun will raise the waters which the moon depresses, and depress the waters which the moon raises, and from the difference of their forces the smallest of all tides will follow. And because (as experience tells us) the force of the moon is greater than that of the sun, the greatest height of the waters will happen about the third lunar hour. Out of the syzygies and quadratures, the greatest tide, which by the single force of the moon ought to fall out at the third lunar hour, and by the single force of the sun at the third solar hour, by the compounded forces of both must fall out in an intermediate time that approaches nearer to the third hour of the moon than to that of the sun. And, therefore, while the moon is passing from the syzygies to the quadratures, during which time the 3d hour of the sun precedes the 3d hour of the moon, the greatest height of the waters will also precede the 2d hour of the moon, and that, by the greatest interval, a little after the octants of the moon; and, by like intervals, the greatest tide will follow the 3d lunar hour, while the moon is passing from the quadratures to the syzygies. Thus, it happens in the open sea; for in the mouths of rivers the greater tides come later to their height.

But the effects of the luminaries depend upon their distances from the earth; for when they are less distant, their effects are greater, and when more distant, their effects are less, and that in the triplicate proportion of their apparent diameter. Therefore it is that the sun, in the winter time, being then in its perigee, has a greater effect, and makes the tides in the syzygies something greater, and those in the quadratures something less than in the summer season; and every month the moon, while in the perigee, raises greater tides than at the distance of 15 days before or after, when it is in its apogee. Whence it comes to pass that two highest tides do not follow one the other in two immediately succeeding syzygies.

The effect of either luminary doth likewise depend upon its declination or distance from the equator; for if the luminary was placed at the pole, it would constantly attract all the parts of the waters without any intension or remission of its action, and could cause no reciprocation of motion. And, therefore, as the luminaries decline from the equator towards either pole, they will, by degrees, lose their force, and on this account will excite lesser tides in the solstitial than in the equinoctial syzygies. But in the solstitial quadratures they will raise greater tides than in the quadratures about the

equinoxes; because the force of the moon, then situated in the equator, most exceeds the force of the sun. Therefore the greatest tides fall out in those syzygies, and the least in those quadratures, which happen about the time of both equinoxes: and the greatest tide in the syzygies is always succeeded by the least tide in the quadratures, as we find by experience. But, because the sun is less distant from the earth in winter than in summer, it comes to pass that the greatest and least tides more frequently appear before than after the vernal equinox, and more frequently after than before the autumnal.

Moreover, the effects of the luminaries depend upon the latitudes of places. Let A*p*EP represent the earth covered with deep waters; C its centre; P, *p* its poles; AE the equator; P any place without the equator; F*f* the parallel of the place; D*d* the correspondent parallel on the other side of the equator; L the place of the moon three hours before; H the place of the earth directly under it; *h* the opposite place; K, *k* the places

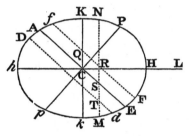

at 90 degrees distance; CH, C*h*, the greatest heights of the sea from the centre of the earth; and CK, C*k*, its least heights: and if with the axes H*h*, K*k*, an ellipsis is described, and by the revolution of that ellipsis about its longer axis H*h* a spheroid HPK*hpk* is formed, this spheroid will nearly represent the figure of the sea; and CF, C*f*, CD, C*d*, will represent the heights of the sea in the places F*f*, D*d*. But farther; in the said revolution of the ellipsis any point N describes the circle NM cutting the parallels F*f*, D*d*, in any places RT, and the equator AE in S; CN will represent the height of the sea in all those places R, S, T, situated in this circle. Wherefore, in the diurnal revolution of any place F, the greatest flood will be in F, at the third hour after the appulse of the moon to the meridian above the horizon; and afterwards the greatest ebb in Q, at the third hour after the setting of the moon; and then the greatest flooding, at the third hour after the appulse of the moon to the meridian under the horizon; and, lastly, the greatest ebb in Q, at the third hour after the rising of the moon; and the latter flood in *f* will be less than the preceding flood in F. For the whole sea is divided into two hemispherical floods, one in the hemisphere KH*h*k on the north side, the other in the opposite hemisphere K*hpk*; which we may therefore call the northern and the southern floods. These floods, being always opposite the one to the other, come by turns to the meridians of all places, after an interval of 12 lunar hours. And seeing the northern countries partake more of the northern flood, and the southern countries more of the southern flood, thence arise tides, alternately greater and less in all places without the equator, in which the luminaries rise and set. But the greatest tide will happen when the moon declines towards the vertex of the place, about the third hour after the appulse of the moon to the meridian above the horizon; and when the

moon changes its declination to the other side of the equator, that which was the greater tide will be changed into a lesser. And the greatest difference of the floods will fall out about the times of the solstices; especially if the ascending node of the moon is about the first of Aries. So it is found by experience that the morning tides in winter exceed those of the evening, and the evening tides in summer exceed those of the morning; at *Plymouth* by the height of one foot, but at *Bristol* by the height of 15 inches, according to the observations of *Collepress* and *Sturmy*.

But the motions which we have been describing suffer some alteration from that force of reciprocation, which the waters, being once moved, retain a little while *by their vis insita*. Whence it comes to pass that the tides may continue for some time, though the actions of the luminaries should cease. This power of retaining the impressed motion lessens the difference of the alternate tides, and makes those tides which immediately succeed after the syzygies greater, and those which follow next after the quadratures less. And hence it is that the alternate tides at *Plymouth* and *Bristol* do not differ much more one from the other than by the height of a foot or 15 inches, and that the greatest tides of all at those ports are not the first but the third after the syzygies. And, besides, all the motions are retarded in their passage through shallow channels, so that the greatest tides of all, in some straits and mouths of rivers, are the fourth or even the fifth after the syzygies.

Farther, it may happen that the tide may be propagated from the ocean through different channels towards the same port, and may pass quicker through some channels than through others; in which case the same tide, divided into two or more succeeding one another, may compound new motions of different kinds. Let us suppose two equal tides flowing towards the same port from different places, the one preceding the other by 6 hours; and suppose the first tide to happen at the third hour of the appulse of the moon to the meridian of the port. If the moon at the time of the appulse to the meridian was in the equator, every 6 hours alternately there would arise equal floods, which, meeting with as many equal ebbs, would so balance one the other, that for that day, the water would stagnate and remain quiet. If the moon then declined from the equator, the tides in the ocean would be alternately greater and less, as was said; and from thence two greater and two lesser tides would be alternately propagated towards that port. But the two greater floods would make the greatest height of the waters to fall out in the middle time betwixt both; and the greater and lesser floods would make the waters to rise to a mean height in the middle time between them, and in the middle time between the two lesser floods the waters would rise to their least height. Thus in the space of 24 hours the waters would come, not twice, as commonly, but once only to their greatest, and once only to their least height; and their greatest height, if the moon declined towards the elevated pole, would happen at the 6th or

30th hour after the appulse of the moon to the meridian; and when the moon changed its declination, this flood would be changed into an ebb. An example of all which Dr. *Halley* has given us, from the observations of seamen in the port of *Batsham*, in the kingdom of *Tounquin*, in the latitude of 20° 50' north. In that port, on the day which follows after the passage of the moon over the equator, the waters stagnate: when the moon declines to the north, they begin to flow and ebb, not twice, as in other ports, but once only every day; and the flood happens at the setting, and the greatest ebb at the rising of the moon. This tide increases with the declination of the moon till the 7th or 8th day; then for the 7 or 8 days following it decreases at the same rate as it had increased before, and ceases when the moon changes its declination, crossing over the equator to the south. After which the flood is immediately changed into an ebb; and thenceforth the ebb happens at the setting and the flood at the rising of the moon; till the moon, again passing the equator, changes its declination. There are two inlets to this port and the neighboring channels, one from the seas of *China*, between the continent and the island of *Leuconia*; the other from the *Indian* sea, between the continent and the island of *Borneo*. But whether there be really two tides propagated through the said channels, one from the *Indian* sea in the space of 12 hours, and one from the sea of *China* in the space of 6 hours, which therefore happening at the 3d and 9th lunar hours, by being compounded together, produce those motions; or whether there be any other circumstances in the state of those seas, I leave to be determined by observations on the neighbouring shores.

Thus I have explained the causes of the motions of the moon and of the sea. Now it is fit to subjoin something concerning the quantity of those motions.

PROPOSITION XXV PROBLEM VI.

TO FIND THE FORCES WITH WHICH THE SUN DISTURBS THE MOTIONS OF THE MOON.

Let S represent the sun, T the earth, P the moon, CADB the moon's orbit. In SP take SK equal to ST; and let SL be to SK in the duplicate proportion of SK to SP: draw LM parallel to PT; and if ST or SK is supposed to represent the accelerated force of gravity of the earth towards the sun, SL will represent the accelerative force of gravity of the moon towards the sun. But that force is compounded of the parts SM and LM, of 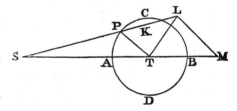 which the force LM, and that part of SM which is represented by TM, disturb the motion of the moon, as we have shewn in Prop. LXVI, Book I, and its Corollaries.

Forasmuch as the earth and moon are revolved about their common centre of gravity, the motion of the earth about that centre will be also disturbed by the like forces; but we may consider the sums both of the forces and of the motions as in the moon, and represent the sum of the forces by the lines TM and ML, which are analogous to them both. The force ML (in its mean quantity) is to the centripetal force by which the moon may be retained in its orbit revolving about the earth at rest, at the distance PT, in the duplicate proportion of the periodic time of the moon about the earth to the periodic time of the earth about the sun (by Cor. 17, Prop. LXVI, Book I); that is, in the duplicate proportion of $27^d.7^h.43'$ to $365^d. 6^h. 9'$; or as 1000 to 178725; or as 1 to $178^{29}/_{40}$. But in the 4th Prop. of this Book we found, that, if both earth and moon were revolved about their common centre of gravity, the mean distance of the one from the other would be nearly $60^1/_2$ mean semi-diameters of the earth; and the force by which the moon maybe kept revolving in its orbit about the earth in rest at the distance PT of $60^1/_2$ semi-diameters of the earth, is to the force by which it may be revolved in the same time, at the distance of 60 semi-diameters, as $60^1/_2$ to 60: and this force is to the force of gravity with us very nearly as 1 to 60 x 60. Therefore the mean force ML is to the force of gravity on the surface of our earth as 1 x $60^1/_2$ to 60 $\times$ 60 $\times$ 60 $\times$ $178^1/_2$, or as 1 to 638092,6; whence by the proportion of the lines TM, ML, the force TM is also given; and these are the forces with which the sun disturbs the motions of the moon.   Q.E.I.

PROPOSITION XXVI. PROBLEM VII.

TO FIND THE HORARY INCREMENT OF THE AREA WHICH THE MOON, BY A RADIUS DRAWN TO THE EARTH, DESCRIBES IN A CIRCULAR ORBIT.

We have above shewn that the area which the moon describes by a radius drawn to the earth is proportional to the time of description, excepting in so far as the moon's motion is disturbed by the action of the sun; and here we propose to investigate the inequality of the moment, or horary increment *of that area or motion so disturbed*. To render the calculus more easy, we shall suppose the orbit of the moon to be circular, and neglect all inequalities but that only which is now under consideration; and, because of the immense distance of the sun, we shall farther suppose that the lines SP and ST are parallel. By this means, the force LM will be always reduced to its mean quantity TP, as well as the force TM to its mean quantity 3PK. These forces (by Cor. 2 of the Laws of Motion) compose the force TL; and this force, by letting fall the perpendicular LE upon the radius TP, if resolved into the forces TE, EL; of which the force TE, acting constantly in the direction of the radius TP, neither accelerates nor retards

the description of the area TPC made by that radius TP; but EL, *acting on the radius* TP in a perpendicular direction, accelerates or retards *the description of the area* in proportion as it accelerates or retards the moon. That acceleration of the moon, in its passage from the quadrature C to the conjunction A, is in every moment of time as the *generating* accelerative force EL, that is, as $\frac{3PK \times TK}{TP}$. Let the time be represented by the TP mean motion of the moon, or (which comes to the same thing) by the angle CTP, or even by the arc CP. At right angles upon CT erect CG equal to CT; and, supposing the quadrantal arc AC to be divided into an infinite number of equal parts P*p*, &c., these *parts* may represent the like *infinite* number of the equal parts of time. Let fall *pk* perpendicular on CT, and draw TG meeting with KP, *kp* produced in F and *f,*

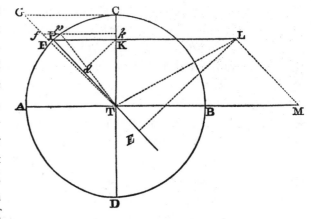

then will FK be equal to TK, and K*k* be to PK as P*p* to T*p*, that is, in a given proportion; and therefore FK x K*k*, or the area FK*kf,* will be as $\frac{3PK \times TK}{TP}$, that is, as

EL; and compounding, the whole area GCKF will be as the sum of all the forces EL impressed upon the moon in the whole time CP; and therefore also as the velocity generated by that sum, that is, as the acceleration of the description of the area CTP, or as the increment of the moment *thereof.* The force by which the moon may in its periodic time CADB of 27^{d}. 7^{h}. 43' be retained revolving about the earth in rest at the distance TP, would cause a body falling in the time CT to describe the length CT, and at the same time to acquire a velocity equal to that with which the moon is moved in its orbit. This appears from Cor. 9, Prop. IV., Book I. But since K*d*, drawn perpendicular on TP, is *but* a third part of EL, and *equal* to the half of TP, or ML, in the octants, the force EL in the octants, where it is greatest, will exceed the force ML in the proportion of 3 to 2; and therefore will be to that force by which the moon in its periodic time may be retained revolving about the earth at rest as 100 to $^2/_3$ x 17872$^1/_2$, or 11915; and in the time CT will generate a velocity equal to 100/11915 parts of the velocity of the moon; but in the time CPA will generate a greater velocity in the proportion of CA to CT or TP. Let the greatest force EL in the octants be represented by the area FK x K*k*, or by the rectangle $^1/_2$ TP × P*p*, which is equal thereto; and the velocity which that greatest force can generate in any time CP will be to the velocity which any other

lesser force EL can generate in the same time as the rectangle $1/_2$TP x CP to the area KCGF; but the velocities generated in the whole time CPA will be one to the other as the rectangle $1/_2$TP x CA to the triangle TCG, or as the quadrantal arc CA to the radius TP; and therefore the latter velocity generated in the whole time will be $100/_{11915}$ parts of the velocity of the moon. To this velocity of the moon, which is proportional to the mean moment of the area (supposing this mean moment to be represented by the number 11915), we add and subtract the half of the other velocity; the sum 11915 + 50, or 11965, will represent the greatest moment of the area in the syzygy A; and the difference 11915 − 50, or 11865, the least moment thereof in the quadratures. Therefore the areas which in equal times are described in the syzygies and quadratures are one to the other as 11965 to 11865. And if to the least moment 11865 we add a moment which shall be to 100, the difference of the two former moments, as the trapezium FKCG to the triangle TCG, or, which comes to the same thing, as the square of the sine PK to the square of the radius TP (that is, as Pd to TP), the sum will represent the moment of the area when the moon is in any intermediate place P.

But these things take place only in the hypothesis that the sun and the earth are at rest, and that the synodical revolution of the moon is finished in 27^d. 7^h. 43'. But since the moon's synodical period is really 29^d. 12^h. 44', the increments of the moments must be enlarged in the same proportion as the time is, that is, in the proportion of 1080853 to 1000000. Upon which account, the whole increment, which was $100/_{11915}$ parts of the mean moment, will now become $100/_{11023}$ parts thereof; and therefore the moment of the area in the quadrature of the moon will be to the moment thereof in the syzygy as 11023 − 50 to 11023 + 50; or as 10973 to 11073; and to the moment thereof, when the moon is in any intermediate place P, as 10973 to 10973 + Pd; that is, supposing TP = 100.

The area, therefore, which the moon, by a radius drawn to the earth, describes in the several little equal parts of time, is nearly as the sum A the number 219,46, and the versed sine of the double distance of the moon from the nearest quadrature, considered in a circle which hath unity for its radius. Thus it is when the variation in the octants is in its mean quantity. But if the variation there is greater or less, that versed sine must be augmented or diminished in the same proportion.

PROPOSITION XXVII. PROBLEM VIII.

FROM THE HORARY MOTION OF THE MOON TO FIND ITS DISTANCE FROM THE EARTH.

The area which the moon, by a radius drawn to the earth, describes in every moment of time, is as the horary motion of the moon and the square of the distance

of the moon from the earth conjunctly. And therefore the distance of the moon from the earth is in a proportion compounded of the subduplicate proportion of the area directly, and the subduplicate proportion of the horary motion inversely.   Q.E.I.

Cor. 1. Hence the apparent diameter of the moon is given; for it is reciprocally as the distance of the moon from the earth. Let astronomers try how accurately this rule agrees with the phænomena.

Cor. 2. Hence also the orbit of the moon may be more exactly defined from the phænomena than hitherto could be done.

PROPOSITION XXVIII. PROBLEM IX.

To find the diameters of the orbit, in which, without eccentricity, the moon would move.

The curvature of the orbit which a body describes, if attracted in lines perpendicular to the orbit, is as the force of attraction directly, and the square of the velocity inversely. I estimate the curvatures of lines compared one with another according to the evanescent proportion of the sines or tangents of their angles of contact to equal radii, supposing those radii to be infinitely diminished. But the attraction of the moon towards the earth in the syzygies is the excess of its gravity towards the earth above the force of the sun 2PK (see Fig. Prop. XXV), by which force the accelerative gravity of the moon towards the sun exceeds the accelerative gravity of the earth towards the sun, or is exceeded by it. But in the quadratures that attraction is the sum of the gravity of the moon towards the earth, and the sun's force KT, by which the moon is attracted towards the earth. And these attractions, putting N for $\frac{AT + CT}{2}$ are nearly as

$$\frac{178725}{AT^2} - \frac{2000}{CT \times N} \quad \text{and} \quad \frac{178725}{CT^2} + \frac{1000}{AT \times N}$$

, or as $178725N \times CT^2 - 2000AT^2 \times CT$, and $178725N \times AT^2 + 1000CT^2 \times AT$. For if the accelerative gravity of the moon towards the earth be represented by the number 178725, the mean force ML, which in the quadratures is PT or TK, and draws the moon towards the earth, will be 1000, and the mean force TM in the syzygies will be 3000; from which, if we subtract the mean force ML, there will remain 2000, the force by which the moon in the syzygies is drawn from the earth, and which we above called 2PK. But the velocity of the moon in the syzygies A and B is to its velocity in the quadratures C and D as CT to AT, and the moment of the area, which the moon by a radius drawn to the earth describes in the syzygies, to the moment of that area *described* in the quadratures conjunctly; that is, as 11073CT to 10973AT. Take this ratio twice inversely, and the former ratio once directly, and the curvature of the orb of the moon in the syzygies will be to the curvature thereof in the quadratures as $120406729 \times 178725AT^2 \times CT^2 \times$

N – 120406729 × 2000AT⁴ × CT to 122611329 × 178725AT² × CT² × N + 122611329 x 1000CT⁴ × AT, that is, as 2151969AT × CT × N – 24081AT³ to 2191371AT × CT × N + 12261CT³.

Because the figure of the moon's orbit is unknown, let us, in its stead, assume the ellipsis DBCA, in the centre of which we suppose the earth to be situated, and the greater axis DC to lie between the quadratures as the lesser AB between the syzygies. But since the plane of this ellipsis is revolved about the earth by an angular motion, and the orbit, whose curvature we now examine, should be described in a plane void of such motion, we are to consider the figure which the moon, while it is revolved in

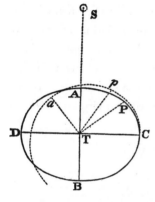

that ellipsis, describes in this plane, that is to say, the figure Cpa, the several points p of which are found by assuming any point P in the ellipsis, which may represent the place of the moon, and drawing Tp equal to TP in such manner that the angle PTp may be equal to the apparent motion of the sun from the time of the last quadrature in C; or (which comes to the same thing) that the angle CTp may be to the angle CTP as the time of the synodic revolution of the moon to the time of the periodic revolution thereof, or as 29ᵈ. 12ʰ. 44' to 27ᵈ. 7ʰ. 43'.

If, therefore, in this proportion we take the angle CTa to the right angle CTA, and make Ta of equal length with TA, we shall have a the lower and C the upper apsis of this orbit Cpa. But, by computation, I find that the difference betwixt the curvature of this orbit Cpa at the vertex a, and the curvature of a circle described about the centre T with the interval TA, is to the difference between the curvature of the ellipsis at the vertex A, and the curvature of the same circle, in the duplicate proportion of the angle CTP to the angle CTp; and that the curvature of the ellipsis in A is to the curvature of that circle in the duplicate proportion of TA to TC; and the curvature of that circle to the curvature of a circle described about the centre T with the interval TC as TC to TA; but that the curvature of this last arch is to the curvature of the ellipsis in C in the duplicate proportion of TA to TC; and that the difference betwixt the curvature of the ellipsis in the vertex C, and the curvature of this last circle, is to the difference betwixt the curvature of the figure Cpa, at the vertex C, and the curvature of this same last circle, in the duplicate proportion of the angle CTp to the angle CTP; all which proportions are easily drawn from the sines of the angles of contact, and of the differences of those angles. But, by comparing those proportions together, we find the curvature of the figure Cpa at a to be to its curvature at C as AT³ – ¹⁶⁸²⁴/₁₀₀₀₀ CT²AT to CT³ + ¹⁶⁸²⁴/₁₀₀₀₀ AT² x CT; where the number ¹⁶⁸²⁴/₁₀₀₀₀ represents the difference of the squares of the angles CTP and CTp, applied to the

square of the lesser angle CTP; or (which is all one) the difference of the squares of the times 27^d. 7^h. 43', and 29^d. 12^h. 44', applied to the square of the time 27^d. 7^h. 43'.

Since, therefore, a represents the syzygy of the moon, and C its quadrature, the proportion now found must be the same with that proportion of the curvature of the moon's orb in the syzygies to the curvature thereof in the quadratures, which we found above. Therefore, in order to find the proportion of CT to AT, let us multiply the extremes and the means, and the terms which come out, applied to AT x CT, become $2062{,}79CT^4 - 2151969N \times CT^3 + 368676N \times AT \times CT^2 + 36342 AT^2 \times CT^2 - 362047N \times AT^2 \times CT + 2191371N \times AT^3 + 4051{,}4AT^4 = 0$. Now if for the half sum N of the terms AT and CT we put 1, and x for their half difference, then CT will be $= 1 + x$, and AT $= 1 - x$. And substituting those values in the equation, after resolving thereof, we shall find x = 0,00719; and from thence, the semi-diameter CT = 1,00719, and the semi-diameter AT = 0,99281, which numbers are nearly as $70^1/_{24}$, and $69^1/_{24}$. Therefore the moon's distance from the earth in the syzygies is to its distance in the quadratures (setting aside the consideration of eccentricity) as $69^1/_{24}$ to $70^1/_{24}$; or, in round numbers, as 69 to 70.

PROPOSITION XXIX. PROBLEM X.

TO FIND THE VARIATION OF THE MOON.

This inequality is owing partly to the elliptic figure of the moon's orbit, partly to the inequality of the moments of the area which the moon by a radius drawn to the earth describes. If the moon P revolved in the ellipsis DBCA about the earth quiescent in the centre of the ellipsis, and by the radius TP, drawn to the earth, described the area CTP, proportional to the time *of description*; and the greatest semi-diameter CT of the ellipsis was to the least TA as 70 to 69; the tangent of the angle CTP would be to the tangent of the angle of the mean motion, computed from the quadrature C, as the semi-diameter TA of the ellipsis to its semi-diameter TC, or as 69 to 70. But the description of the area CTP, as the moon advances from the quadrature to the syzygy, ought to be in such manner accelerated, that the moment of the area in the moon's syzygy may be to the moment thereof in its quadrature as 11073 to 10973; and that the excess of the moment in any intermediate place P above the moment in the quadrature may be as the square of the sine of the angle CTP; which we may effect with accuracy enough, if we diminish the tangent of the angle CTP in the subduplicate proportion of the number 10973 to the number 11073, that is, in proportion of the number 68,6877 to the number 69. Upon which account the tangent of the angle CTP will now be to the tangent of the mean motion as 68,6877 to 70; and the angle CTP in the octants, where the mean motion is 45°, will be found 44° 27' 28", which subtracted from 45°, the

angle of the mean motion, leaves the greatest variation 32' 32". Thus it would be, if the moon, in passing from the quadrature to the syzygy, described an angle CTA of 90 degrees only. But because of the motion of the earth, by which the sun is apparently transferred *in consequentia*, the moon, before it overtakes the sun, describes an angle CTa, greater than a right angle, in the proportion of the time of the synodic revolution of the moon to the time of its periodic revolution, that is, in the proportion of 29^d. 12^h. 44', to 27^d. 7^h. 43'. Whence it comes to pass that all the angles about the centre T are dilated in the same proportion; and the greatest variation, which otherwise would be *but* 32' 32", now augmented in the said proportion, becomes 35' 10".

And this is its magnitude in the mean distance of the sun from the earth, neglecting the differences which may arise from the curvature of the *orbis magnus*, and the stronger action of the sun upon the moon when horned and new, than when gibbous and full. In other distances of the sun from the earth, the greatest variation is in a proportion compounded of the duplicate proportion of the time of the synodic revolution of the moon (the time of the year being given) directly, and the triplicate proportion of the distance of the sun from the earth inversely. And, therefore, in the apogee of the sun, the greatest variation is 33' 14", and in its perigee 37' 11", if the eccentricity of the sun is to the transverse semi-diameter of the *orbis magnus* as 16^{15}/$_{16}$ to 1000.

Hitherto we have investigated the variation in an orb not eccentric, in which, to wit, the moon in its octants is always in its mean distance from the earth. If the moon, on account of its eccentricity, is more or less removed from the earth than if placed in this orb, the variation may be something greater, or something less, than according to this rule. But I leave the excess or defect to the determination of astronomers from the phaenomena.

PROPOSITION XXX. PROBLEM XI.

TO FIND THE HORARY MOTION OF THE NODES OF THE MOON IN A CIRCULAR ORBIT.

Let S represent the sun, T the earth, P the moon, NPn the orbit of the moon, Npn the orthographic projection of the orbit upon the plane of the ecliptic; N, n the nodes, nTNm the line of the nodes produced indefinitely; PI, PK perpendiculars upon the lines ST, Qq; Pp a perpendicular upon the plane of the ecliptic; A, B the moon's syzygies in the plane of the ecliptic; AZ a perpendicular let fall upon Nn, the line of the nodes; Q, q the quadratures of the moon in the plane of the ecliptic, and pK a perpendicular on the line Qq lying between the quadratures. The force of the sun to disturb the motion of the moon (by Prop. XXV) is twofold, one proportional to the line LA the other to the line MT, in the scheme of that Proposition; and the moon by the

former force is drawn towards the earth, by the latter towards the sun, in a direction parallel to the right line ST joining the earth and the sun. The former force LM acts in the direction of the plane of the moon's orbit, and therefore makes no change upon the situation thereof, and is upon that account to be neglected: the latter force MT, by which the plane of the moon's orbit is disturbed, is the same with the force 3PK or 3IT. And this force (by Prop. XXV) is to the force by which the moon may, in its periodic

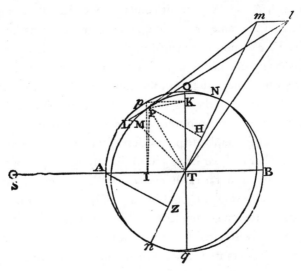

time, be uniformly revolved in a circle about the earth at rest, as 3IT to the radius of the circle multiplied by the number 178,725, or as IT to the radius thereof multiplied by 59,575. But in this calculus, and all that follows, I consider all the lines drawn from the moon to the sun as parallel to the line which joins the earth and the sun; because what inclination there is almost as much diminishes all effects in some cases as it augments them in others; and we are now inquiring after the mean motions of the nodes, neglecting such niceties as are of no moment, and would only serve to render the calculus more perplexed.

Now suppose PM to represent an arc which the moon describes in the least moment of time, and ML a little line, the half of which the moon, by the impulse of the said force 3IT, would describe in the same time; and joining PL, MP, let them be produced to *m* and *l,* where they cut the plane of the ecliptic, and upon T*m* let fall the perpendicular PH. Now, since the right line ML is parallel to the plane of the ecliptic, and therefore can never meet with the right line *ml* which lies in that plane, and yet both those right lines lie in one common plane LMP*ml,* they will be parallel, and upon that account the triangles LMP, *lm*P will be similar. And seeing MP*m* lies in the plane of the orbit, in which the moon did move while in the place P, the point *m* will fall

upon the line Nn, which passes through the nodes N, n, of that orbit. And because the force by which the half of the little line LM is generated, if the whole had been together, and at once impressed in the point P, would have generated that whole line, and caused the moon to move in the arc whose chord is LP; that is to say, would have transferred the moon from the plane MPmT into the plane LPlT; therefore the angular motion of the nodes generated by that force will be equal to the angle mTl. But ml is to mP as ML to MP; and since MP, because of the time given, is also given, ml will be as the rectangle ML x mP, that is, as the rectangle IT x mP. And if Tml is a right angle, the angle mTl will be as $\frac{ml}{Tm}$ and therefore as $\frac{IT \times Pm}{Tm}$, that is (because Tm and mP,

TP and PH are proportional), as $\frac{IT \times PH}{TP}$; and, therefore, because TP is given, as IT x PH. But if the angle Tml or STN is oblique, the angle mTl will be yet less, in proportion of the sine of the angle STN to the radius, or AZ to AT. And therefore the velocity of the nodes is as IT x PH x AZ, or as the solid content of the sines of the three angles TPI, PTN, and STN.

If these are right angles, as happens when the nodes are in the quadratures, and the moon in the syzygy, the little line ml will be removed to an infinite distance, and the angle mTl will become equal to the angle mPl. But in this case the angle mPl is to the angle PTM, which the moon in the same time by its apparent motion describes about the earth, as I to 59,575. For the angle mPl is equal to the angle LPM, that is, to the angle of the moon's deflexion from a rectilinear path; which angle, if the gravity of the moon should have then ceased, the said force of the sun 3IT would by itself have generated in that given time; and the angle PTM is equal to the angle of the moon's deflexion from a rectilinear path; which angle, if the force of the sun 3IT should have then ceased, the force alone by which the moon is retained in its orbit would have generated in the same time. And these forces (as we have above shewn) are the one to the other as 1 to 59,575. Since, therefore, the mean horary motion of the moon (in respect of the fixed stars) is 32' 56" 27''' 12$\frac{1}{2}$ ^{iv}, the horary motion of the node in this case will be 33" 10''' 33^{iv} 12^v. But in other cases the horary motion will be to 33" 10''' 33^{iv} 12^v as the solid content of the sines of the three angles TPI, PTN, and. STN (or of the distances of the moon from the quadrature, of the moon from the node, and of the node from the sun) to the cube of the radius. And as often as the sine of any angle is changed from positive to negative, and from negative to positive, so often must the regressive be changed into a progressive, and the progressive into a regressive motion. Whence it comes to pass that the nodes are progressive as often as the moon happens to be placed between either quadrature, and the node nearest to that quadrature. In other cases they are regressive, and by the excess of the regress above the progress, they are monthly transferred *in antecedentia*.

COR. 1. Hence if from P and M, the extreme points of a least arc PM, on the line Q*q* joining the quadratures we let fall the perpendiculars PK M*k*, and produce the same till they out the line of the nodes N*n* in D and *d*, the horary motion of the nodes will be as the area MPD*d*, and the square of the line AZ conjunctly. For let PK, PH, and AZ, be the three said sines, viz. PK the sine of the distance of the moon from the quadrature, PH the sine of the distance of the moon from the node, and AZ the sine

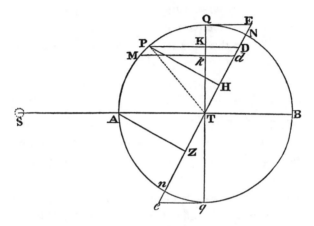

of the distance of the node from the sun; and the velocity of the node will be as the solid content of PK x PH x AZ. But PT is to PK as PM to K*k*; and, therefore, because PT and PTA are given, K*k* will be as PK. Likewise AT is to PD as AZ to PH, and therefore PH is as the rectangle PD x AZ; and, by compounding those proportions, PK x PH is as the solid content K*k* x PD x AZ, and PK x PH x AZ as K*k* x PD x AZ^2; that is, as the area PD*d*M and AZ^2 conjunctly. Q.E.D.

COR. 2. In any given position of the nodes their mean horary motion is half their horary motion in the moon's syzygies; and therefore is to 16" 35''' 16^{iv}. 36^v. as the square of the sine of the distance of the nodes from the syzygies to the square of the radius, or as AZ^2 to AT^2. For if the moon, by an uniform motion, describes the semi-circle QA*q*, the sum of all the areas PD*d*M, during the time of the moon's passage from Q to M, will make up the area QMd*E*, terminating at the tangent QE of the circle; and by the time that the moon has arrived at the point *n*, that sum will make up the whole area EQA*n* described by the line PD: but when the moon proceeds from *n* to *q*, the line PD will fall without the circle, and describe the area *nqe*, terminating at the tangent *qe* of the circle, which area, because the nodes were before regressive, but are now progressive, must be subducted from the former area, and, being itself equal to the area QEN, will leave the semi-circle NQA*n*. While, therefore, the moon describes a semi-circle, the sum of all the areas PD*d*M will be the area of that semi-circle; and while the moon describes a complete circle, the sum of those areas will be the area of

the whole circle. But the area PDdM, when the moon is in the syzygies, is the rectangle of the arc PM into the radius PT; and the sum of all the areas, *every one* equal to this area, in the time that the moon describes a complete circle, is the rectangle of the whole circumference into the radius of the circle; and this rectangle, being double the area of the circle, will be double the quantity of the former sum

If, therefore, the nodes went on with that velocity uniformly continued which they acquire in the moon's syzygies, they would describe a space double of that which they describe in fact; and, therefore, the mean motion, by which, if uniformly continued, they would describe the same space with that which they do in fact describe by an unequal motion, is *but* one-half of that motion which they are possessed of in the moon's syzygies. Wherefore since their greatest horary motion, if the nodes are in the quadratures, is 33" 10"' 33^{iv}. 12^{v}. their mean horary motion in this case will be 16" 35"' 16^{iv}. 36^{v}. And seeing the horary motion of the nodes is every where as AZ^2 and the area PDdM conjunctly, and, therefore, in the moon's syzygies, the horary motion of the nodes is as AZ^3 and the area PDdM conjunctly, that is (because the area PDdM described in the syzygies is given), as AZ^2, therefore the mean motion also will be as AZ^2; and, therefore, when the nodes are without the quadratures, this motion will be to 16" 35"' 16^{iv}. 36^{v}. as AZ^2 to AT^2.   Q.E.D.

PROPOSITION XXXI. PROBLEM XII.

TO FIND THE HORARY MOTION OF THE NODES OF THE MOON IN AN ELLIPTIC ORBIT.

Let Q$pmaq$ represent an ellipsis described with the greater axis Qq, and the lesser axis ab; QAqB a circle circumscribed; T the earth in the common centre of both; S the sun; p the moon moving in this ellipsis; and pm an arc which it describes in the least moment of time; N and n the nodes joined by the line Nn; pK and mk perpendiculars upon the axis Qq, produced both ways till they meet the circle in P and M, and the line of the nodes in D and d. And if the moon, by a radius drawn to the earth, describes an area proportional to the time *of description*, the horary motion of the node in the ellipsis will be as the area pDdm and AZ^2 conjunctly.

For let PF touch the circle in P, and produced meet TN in F; and pf touch the ellipsis in p, and produced meet the same TN in f, and both tangents concur in the axis TQ at Y. And let ML represent the space which the moon, by the impulse of the above-mentioned force 3IT or 3PK, would describe with a transverse motion, in the meantime while revolving in the circle it describes the arc PM; and ml denote the space which the moon revolving in the ellipsis would describe in the same time by the impulse of the same force 3IT or 3PK; and let LP and lp be produced till they meet

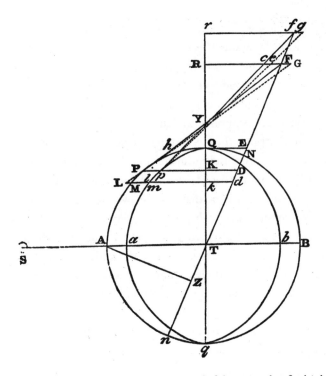

the plane of the ecliptic in G and *g*, and FG and *fg* be joined, of which FG produced may cut *pf*, *pg*, and TGL, in *c*, *e*, and R respectively; and *fg* produced may cut TQ in *r*. Because the force 3IT or 3PK in the circle is to the force 3IT or 3*p*K in the ellipsis as PK to *p*K, or as AT to *a*T, the space ML generated by the former force will be to the space *ml* generated by the latter as PK to *p*K; that is, because of the similar figures PYK*p* and FYR*c*, as FR to *c*R. But (because of the similar triangles PLM, PGF) ML is to FG as PL to PG, that is (on account of the parallels L*k*, PK, GR), as *pl* to *pe*, that is (because of the similar triangles *plm*, *cpe*), as *lm* to *ce*; and inversely as LM is to *lm*, or as PR is to *c*R, so is FG to *ce*. And therefore if *fg* was to *ce* as *fy* to *c*Y, that is, as *fr* to *c*R (that is, as *fr* to FR and FR to *c*R conjunctly, that is, as *f*T to FT, and FG to *ce* conjunctly), because the ratio of FG to *ce*, expunged on both sides, leaves the ratios *fg* to FG and *f*T to FT, *fg* would be to FG as *f*T to FT; and, therefore, the angles which FG and *fg*, would subtend at the earth T would be equal to each other. But these angles (by what we have shewn in the preceding Proposition) are the motions of the nodes, while the moon describes in the circle the arc PM, in the ellipsis the arc *pm*; and therefore the motions of the nodes in the circle and in the ellipsis would be equal to each other. Thus, I say, it would be, if *fg* was to *ce* as *fy* to *c*Y, that is, if *fg* was equal to $\frac{ce \times fY}{cY}$. But because of the similar triangles *fgp*, *cep*, *fg* is to *ce* as *fp* to *cp*; and therefore

fg is equal to $\dfrac{ce \times fp}{cp}$; and therefore the angle which fg subtends in fact is to the former angle which FG subtends, that is to say, the motion of the nodes in the ellipsis is to the motion of the same in the circle as this fg or $\dfrac{ce \times fp}{cp}$ to the force fg

or $\dfrac{ce \times fY}{cY}$, that is, as $fp \times cY$ to $fY \times cp$, or as fp to fY, and cY to cp; that is, if ph parallel to TN meet FP in h, as Fh to FY and FY to FP; that is, as Fh to FP or Dp to DP, and therefore as the area Dpmd to the area DPMd. And, therefore, seeing (by Corol. 1, Prop. XXX) the latter area and AZ^2 conjunctly are proportional to the horary motion of the nodes in the circle, the former area and AZ^2 conjunctly will be proportional to the horary motion of the nodes in the ellipsis.   Q.E.D.

COR. Since, therefore, in any given position of the nodes, the sum of all the areas $pDdm$, in the time while the moon is carried from the quadrature to any place m, is the area mpQEd terminated at the tangent of the ellipsis QE; and the sum of all those areas, in one entire revolution, is the area of the whole ellipsis; the mean motion of the nodes in the ellipsis will be to the mean motion of the nodes in the circle as the ellipsis to the circle; that is, as Ta to TA, or 69 to 70. And, therefore, since (by Corol 2, Prop. XXX) the mean horary motion of the nodes in the circle is to 16" 35"' 16^{iv}. 36^{v}. as AZ^2 to AT^2, if we take the angle 16" 2"' 3^{iv}. 30^{v}. to the angle 16" 35"' 16^{iv}. 36^{v}. as 69 to 70, the mean horary motion of the nodes in the ellipsis will be to 16" 21"' 31^{iv}. 30^{v}. as AZ^2 to AT^2; that is, as the square of the sine of the distance of the node from the sun to the square of the radius.

But the moon, by a radius drawn to the earth, describes the area in the syzygies with a greater velocity than it does that in the quadratures, and upon that account the time is contracted in the syzygies, and prolonged in the quadratures; and together with the time the motion of the nodes is likewise augmented or diminished. But the moment of the area in the quadrature of the moon was to the moment thereof in the syzygies as 10973 to 11073; and therefore the mean moment in the octants is to the excess in the syzygies, and to the defect in the quadratures, as 11023, the half sum of those numbers, to their half difference 50. Wherefore since the time of the moon in the several little equal parts of its orbit is reciprocally as its velocity, the mean time in the octants will be to the excess of the time in the quadratures, and to the defect of the time in the syzygies arising from this cause, nearly as 11023 to 50. But, reckoning from the quadratures to the syzygies, I find that the excess of the moments of the area, in the several places above the least moment in the quadratures, is nearly as the square of the sine of the moon's distance from the quadratures; and therefore the difference betwixt the moment in any place, and the mean moment in the octants, is as the difference betwixt the square of the sine of the moon's distance from the quadratures, and the

square of the sine of 45 degrees, or half the square of the radius; and the increment of the time in the several places between the octants and quadratures, and the decrement thereof between the octants and syzygies, is in the same proportion. But the motion of the nodes, while the moon describes the several little equal parts of its orbit, is accelerated or retarded in the duplicate proportion of the time; for that motion, while the moon describes PM, is (*caeteris paribus*) as ML, and ML is in the duplicate proportion of the time. Wherefore the motion of the nodes in the syzygies, in the time while the moon describes given little parts of its orbit, is diminished in the duplicate proportion of the number 11073 to the number 11023; and the decrement is to the remaining motion as 100 to 10973; but to the whole motion as 100 to 11073 nearly. But the decrement in the places between the octants and syzygies, and the increment in the places between the octants and quadratures, is to this decrement nearly as the whole motion in these places to the whole motion in the syzygies, and the difference betwixt the square of the sine of the moon's distance from the quadrature, and the half square of the radius, to the half square of the radius conjunctly. Wherefore, if the nodes are in the quadratures, and we take two places, one on one side, one on the other, equally distant from the octant and other two distant by the same interval, one from the syzygy, the other from the quadrature, and from the decrements of the motions in the two places between the syzygy and octant we subtract the increments of the motions in the two other places between the octant and the quadrature, the remaining decrement will be equal to the decrement in the syzygy, as will easily appear by computation; and therefore the mean decrement, which ought to be subducted from the mean motion of the nodes, is the fourth part of the decrement in the syzygy. The whole horary motion of the nodes in the syzygies (when the moon by a radius drawn to the earth was supposed to describe an area proportional to the time) was 32" 42"' 7^{iv}. And we have shewn that the decrement of the motion of the nodes, in the time while the moon, now moving with greater velocity, describes the same space, was to this motion as 100 to 11073; and therefore this decrement is 17"' 43^{iv}. 11^{v}. The fourth part of which 4"' 25^{iv}. 48^{v}. subtracted from the mean horary motion above found, 16" 21"' 3^{iv}. 30^{v}. leaves 16" 16"' 37^{iv}. 42^{v}. their correct mean horary motion.

If the nodes are without the quadratures, and two places are considered, one on one side, one on the other, equally distant from the syzygies, the sum of the motions of the nodes, when the moon is in those places, will be to the sum of their motions, when the moon is in the same places and the nodes in the quadratures, as AZ^2 to AT^2. And the decrements of the motions arising from the causes but now explained will be mutually as the motions themselves, and therefore the remaining motions will be mutually betwixt themselves as AZ^2 to AT^2; and the mean motions will be as the remaining motions. And, therefore, in any given position of the nodes, their correct

mean horary motion is to 16" 16"' 37^{iv}. 42^v. as AZ^2 to AT^2; that is, as the square of the sine of the distance of the nodes from the syzygies to the square of the radius.

PROPOSITION XXXII. PROBLEM XIII.

To find the mean motion of the nodes of the moon.

The yearly mean motion is the sum of all the mean horary motions throughout the course of the year. Suppose that the node is in N, and that, after every hour is elapsed, it is drawn back again to its former place; so that, notwithstanding its proper motion, it may constantly remain in the same situation with respect to the fixed stars; while in the mean time the sun S, by the motion of the earth, is seen to leave the node, and to proceed till it completes its apparent annual course by an uniform motion. Let Aa rep-

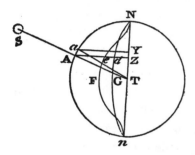

resent a given least arc, which the right line TS always drawn to the sun, by its intersection with the circle NAn, describes in the least given moment of time; and the mean horary motion (from what we have above shewn) will be as AZ^2, that is (because AZ and ZY are proportional), as the rectangle of AZ into ZY, that is, as the area AZYa; and the sum of all the mean horary motions from the beginning will be as the sum of all the areas aYZA, that is, as the area NAZ. But the greatest AZYa is equal to the rectangle of the arc Aa, into the radius of the circle; and therefore the sum of all these rectangles in the whole circle will be to the like sum of all the greatest rectangles as the area of the whole circle to the rectangle of the whole circumference into the radius, that is, as 1 to 2. But the horary motion corresponding to that greatest rectangle was 16" 16"' 37^{iv}. 42^v. and this motion in the complete course of the sidereal year, 365^d. 6^h. 9', amounts to 39° 38' 7" 50"', and therefore the half thereof, 19° 49' 3" 55"', is the mean motion of the nodes corresponding to the whole circle. And the motion of the nodes, in the time while the sun is carried from N to A, is to 19° 49' 3" 55"' as the area NAZ to the whole circle.

Thus it would be if the node was after every hour drawn back again to its former place, that so, after a complete revolution, the sun at the year's end would be found again in the same node which it had left when the year begun. But, because of the motion of the node in the mean time, the sun most needs meet the node sooner; and now it remains that we compute the abbreviation of the time. Since, then, the sun, in the coarse of the year, travels 360 degrees, and the node in the same time by its greatest motion would be carried 39° 39' 7" 50"', or 39,6355 degrees; and the mean motion

of the node in any place N is to its mean motion in its quadratures as AZ^2 to AT^2; the motion of the sun will be to the motion of the node in N as $360AT^2$ to $39,6355AZ^2$; that is, as $9,0927646AT^2$ to AZ^2. Wherefore if we suppose the circumference NAn of the whole circle to be divided into little equal parts, such as Aa, the time in which the sun would describe the little arc Aa, if the circle was quiescent, will be to the time of which it would describe the same arc, supposing the circle together with the nodes to be revolved about the centre T, reciprocally as $9,0827646AT^2$ to $9,0827646AT^2 + AZ^3$; for the time is reciprocally as the velocity with which the little arc is described, and this velocity is the sum of the velocities of both sun and node. If, therefore, the sector NTA represent the time in which the sun by itself, without the motion of the node, would describe the arc NA, and the indefinitely small part ATa of the sector represent the little moment of the time in which it would describe the least arc An; and (letting fall aY perpendicular upon Nn) if in AZ we take dZ of such length that the rectangle of dZ into ZY may be to the least part ATa of the sector as AZ^2 to $9,0827646AT^2 + AZ^2$, that is to say, that dZ may be to $^1/_2$ AZ as AT^2 to $9,0827646AT^2 + AZ^2$; the rectangle of dZ into ZY will represent the decrement of the time arising from the motion of the node, while the arc Aa is described; and if the curve NdGn is the locus where the point d is always found, the curvilinear area NdZ will be as the whole decrement *of time* while the whole arc NA is described; and, therefore, the excess of the sector NAT above the area NdZ will be as the whole time. But because the motion of the node in a less time is less in proportion of the time, the area AaYZ must also be diminished in the same proportion; which may be done by taking in AZ the line eZ of such length, that it may be to the length of AZ as AZ^2 to $9,0827646AT^2 + AZ^2$; for so the rectangle of eZ into ZY will be to the area AZYa as the decrement of the time in which the arc Aa is described to the whole time in which it would have been described, if the node had been quiescent; and, therefore, that rectangle will be as the decrement of the motion of the node. And if the curve NeFn is the locus of the point e, the whole area NaZ, which is the sum of all the decrements *of that motion*, will be as the whole decrement *thereof* during the time in which the arc AN is described; and the remaining area NAe will be as the remaining motion, which is the true motion of the node, during the time in which the whole arc NA is described by the joint motions of both sun and node. Now the area of the semi-circle is to the area of the figure NeFn found by the method of infinite series nearly as 793 to 60. But the motion corresponding *or proportional* to the whole circle was 19° 49' 3" 55'''; and therefore the motion corresponding to double the figure NeFn is 1° 29' 58" 2''', which taken from the former motion leaves 18° 19' 5" 53''', the whole motion of the node with respect to the fixed stars in the interval between two of its conjunctions with the sun; and this motion subducted from the annual motion of the sun 360°, leaves 341° 40' 54" 7''', the motion of the sun in the

interval between the same conjunctions. But as this motion is to the annual motion 360°, so is the motion of the node but just now found 18° 19' 5" 53"' to its annual motion, which will therefore be 19° 18' 1" 23"'; and this is the mean motion of the nodes in the sidereal year. By astronomical tables, it is 19° 21' 21" 50"'. The difference is less than $1/300$ part of the whole motion, and seems to arise from the eccentricity of the moon's orbit, and its inclination to the plane of the ecliptic. By the eccentricity of this orbit the motion of the nodes is too much accelerated; and, on the other hand, by the inclination of the orbit, the motion of the nodes is something retarded, and reduced to its just velocity.

PROPOSITION XXXIII. PROBLEM XIV.

TO FIND THE TRUE MOTION OF THE NODES OF THE MOON.

In the time which is as the area NTA–NdZ (in the preceding Fig.) that motion is as the area NAe, and is thence given; but because the calculus is too difficult, it will be better to use the following construction of the Problem. About the centre C, with any interval CD, describe the circle BEFD; produce DC to A so as AB may be to AC as the mean motion to half the mean true motion when the nodes are in their quadratures (that is, as 19° 18' 1" 23"' to 19° 49' 3" 55"'; and therefore BC to AC as the difference of those motions 0° 31' 2" 32"' to the latter motion 19° 49' 3" 55"', that is, as 1 to 38 $3/10$). Then through the point D draw the indefinite line Gg, touching the cir-

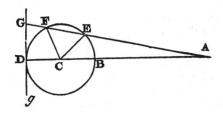

cle in D; and if we take the angle BCE, or BCF, equal to the double distance of the sun from the place of the node, as found by the mean motion, and drawing AE or AF cutting the perpendicular DG in G, we take another angle which shall be to the whole motion of the node in the interval between its syzygies (that is, to 9° 11' 3") as the tangent DG to the whole circumference of the circle BED, and add this last angle (for which the angle DAG may be used) to the mean motion of the nodes, while they are passing from the quadratures to the syzygies, and subtract it from their mean motion while they are passing from the syzygies to the quadratures, we shall have their true motion; for the true motion so found will nearly agree with the true motion which comes out from assuming the times as the area NTA – NdZ, and the motion of the node as the area NAe; as whoever will please to examine and make the computations will find: and this is the semi-menstrual equation of the motion of the nodes. But there is also a menstrual equation, but which is by no means necessary for finding of the moon's latitude; for since the variation of the inclination of the

moon's orbit to the plane of the ecliptic is liable to a twofold inequality, the one semi-menstrual, the other menstrual, the menstrual inequality *of this variation*, and the menstrual equation of the nodes, so moderate and correct each other, that in computing the latitude of the moon both may be neglected.

Cor. From this and the preceding Prop. it appears that the nodes are quiescent in their syzygies, but regressive in their quadratures, by an hourly motion of 16" 19"' 26^{iv}.; and that the equation of the motion of the nodes in the octants is 1° 30'; all which exactly agree with the phaenomena of the heavens.

SCHOLIUM.

Mr. *Machin*, Astron., Prof. Gresh., and Dr. *Henry Pemberton*, separately found out the motion of the nodes by a different method. Mention has been made of this method in another place. Their several papers, both of which I have seen, contained two Propositions, and exactly agreed with each other in both of them. Mr. *Machin's* paper coming first to my hands, I shall here insert it.

OF THE MOTION OF THE MOON'S NODES.

"PROPOSITION I.

The mean motion of the sun from the node is defined by a geometric mean proportional between the mean motion of the sun and that mean motion with which the sun recedes with the greatest swiftness from the node in the quadratures.

"Let T be the earth's place, N*n* the line of the moon's nodes at any given time, KTM a perpendicular thereto, TA a right line revolving about the centre with the same angular velocity with which the sun and the node recede from one another, in such sort that the angle between the quiescent right line N*n* and the revolving line TA may be always equal to the distance of the places of the sun and node. Now if any right line TK be divided into parts TS and SK, and those parts be taken as the mean horary motion of the sun to the mean horary motion of the node in the quadratures, and there be taken the right line TH, a mean proportional between the part TS and the whole TK, this right line will be proportional to the sun's mean motion from the node.

"For let there be described the circle NK*n*M from the centre T and with the radius TK, and about the same centre, with the semi-axis TH and TN, let there be described an ellipsis NH*n*L; and in the time in which the sun recedes from the node through the

arc N*a*, if there be drawn the right line T*ba*, the area of the sector NT*a* will be the exponent of the sum of the motions of the sun and node in the same time. Let, therefore, the extremely small arc *a*A be that which the right line T*ba*, revolving according to the aforesaid law, will uniformly describe in a given particle of time, and the extremely small sector TA*a* will be as the sum of the velocities with which the sun and node are carried two different ways in that time. Now the sun's velocity is almost uniform, its inequality being so small as scarcely to produce the least inequality in the mean motion of the nodes. The other part of this sum, namely, the mean quantity of the velocity of the node, is increased in the recess from the syzygies in a duplicate ratio of the sine of its distance from the sun (by Cor. Prop. XXXI, of this Book), and, being greatest in its quadratures with the sun in K, is in the same ratio to the sun's velocity as SK to TS, that is, as (the difference of the squares of TK and TH, or) the rectangle KHM to TH². But the ellipsis NBH divides the sector AT*a*, the exponent of the sum of these two velocities, into two parts AB*ba* and BT*b*, proportional to the velocities. For produce BT to the circle in β, and from the point B let fall upon the greater axis

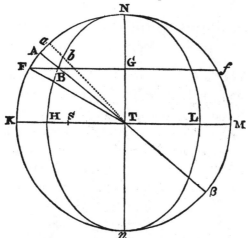

the perpendicular BG, which being produced both ways may meet the circle in the points F and *f*; and because the space AB*ba* is to the sector TB*b* as the rectangle ABβ to BT² (that rectangle being equal to the difference of the squares of TA and TB, because the right line Aβ is equally cut in T, and unequally in B), therefore when the space AB*ba* is the greatest of all in K, this ratio will be the same as the ratio of the rectangle KHM to HT². But the greatest mean velocity of the node was shewn above to be in that very ratio to the velocity of the sun; and therefore in the quadratures the sector AT*a* is divided into parts proportional to the velocities. And because the rectangle KHM is to HT² as FB*f* to BG², and the rectangle ABβ is equal to the rectangle FB*f*, therefore the little area AB*ba*, where it is greatest, is to the remaining sector TB*b* as the

rectangle ABβ to BG². But the ratio of these little areas always was as the rectangle AB(
to BT²; and therefore the little area AB*ba* in the place A is less than its correspondent
little area in the quadratures in the duplicate ratio of BG to BT, that is, in the duplicate ratio of the sine of the sun's distance from the node. And therefore the sum of all
the little areas AB*ba*, to wit, the space ABN, will be as the motion of the node in the
time in which the sun hath been going over the arc NA since he left the node; and the
remaining space, namely, the elliptic sector NTB, will be as the sun's mean motion in
the same time. And because the mean annual motion of the node is that motion which
it performs in the time that the sun completes one period of its course, the mean
motion of the mode from the sun will be to the mean motion of the sun itself as the
area of the circle to the area of the ellipse; that is, as the right line TK to the right line
TH, which is a mean proportional between TK and TS; or, which comes to the same
as the mean proportional TH to the right line TS.

"PROPOSITION II.

THE MEAN MOTION OF THE MOONS NODES BEING GIVEN,
TO FIND THEIR TRUE MOTION.

"Let the angle A be the distance of the sun from the mean place of the node, or
the sun's mean motion from the node. Then if we take the angle B, whose tangent is
to the tangent of the angle A as TH to TK, that is, in the sub-duplicate ratio of the
mean horary motion of the sun to the mean horary motion of the sun from the node,
when the node is in the quadrature, that angle B will be the distance of the sun from
the node's true place. For join FT, and, by the demonstration of the last Proportion,
the angle FTN will be the distance of the sun from the mean place of the node, and

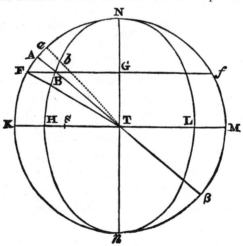

the angle ATN the distance from the true place, and the tangents of these angles are between themselves as TK to TH.

"COR. Hence the angle FTA is the equation of the moon's nodes; and the sine of this angle, where it is greatest in the octants, is to the radius as KH to TK + TH. But the sine of this equation in any other place A is to the greatest sine as the sine of the sums of the angles FTN + ATN to the radius; that is, nearly as the sine of double the distance of the sun from the mean place of the node (namely, 2FTN) to the radius.

"SCHOLIUM.

"If the mean horary motion of the nodes in the quadratures be 16" 16''' 37^{iv}. 42^{v}. that is, in a whole sidereal year, 39° 38' 7" 50''', TH will be to TK in the subduplicate ratio of the number 9,0827646 to the number 10,0827646, that is, as 18,6524761 to 19,6524761. And, therefore, TH is to HK as 18,6524761 to 1; that is, as the motion of the sun in a sidereal year to the mean motion of the node 19° 18' 1" 23$^{2}/_{3}$'''.

"But if the mean motion of the moon's nodes in 20 Julian years is 386° 50' 15", as is collected from the observations made use of in the theory of the moon, the mean motion of the nodes in one sidereal year will be 19° 20' 31" 58'''. and TH will be to HK as 360° to 19° 20' 31" 69'''; that is, as 18,61214 to 1: and from hence the mean horary motion of the nodes in the quadratures will come out 16" 18''' 48^{iv}. And the greatest equation of the nodes in the octants will be 1° 29' 57"."

PROPOSITION XXXIV. PROBLEM XV.

TO FIND THE HORARY VARIATION OF THE INCLINATION OF THE MOON'S ORBIT TO THE PLANE OF THE ECLIPTIC.

Let A and a represent the syzygies; Q and q the quadratures; N and n the nodes; P the place of the moon in its orbit; p the orthographic projection of that place upon the plane of the ecliptic; and mTl the momentaneous motion of the nodes as above. If upon Tm we let fall the perpendicular PG, and joining pG we produce it till it meet Tl in g, and join also Pg, the angle PGp will be the inclination of the moon's orbit to the plane of the ecliptic when the moon is in P; and the angle Pgp will be the inclination of the same after a small moment of time is elapsed; and therefore the angle GPg will be the momentaneous variation of the inclination. But this angle GPg is to the angle GTg as TG to PG and Pp to PG conjunctly. And, therefore, if for the moment of time we assume an hour, since the angle GTg (by Prop. XXX) is to the angle 33" 10''' 33^{iv}. as IT x PG x AZ to AT^3, the angle GPg, (or the horary variation of the inclination) will be to the angle 33" 10''' 33^{iv}. as IT × AZ × TG ×$\frac{Pp}{PG}$ to AT^3. Q.E.I.

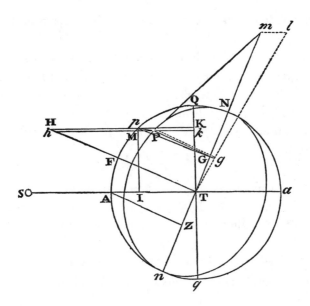

And thus it would be if the moon was uniformly revolved in a circular orbit. But if the orbit is elliptical, the mean motion of the nodes will he diminished in proportion of the lesser axis to the greater, as we have shewn above; and the variation of the inclination will be also diminished in the same proportion.

COR. 1. Upon Nn erect the perpendicular TF, and let pM be the horary motion of the moon in the plane of the ecliptic; upon QT let fall the perpendiculars pK, Mk, and produce them till they meet TF in H and h; then IT will be to AT as Kk to Mp; and TG to Hp as TZ to AT; and, therefore, IT x TG will be equal to $\dfrac{Kk \times Hp \times TZ}{Mp}$, that is, equal to the area HpMh multiplied into the ratio $\dfrac{TZ}{Mp}$: and therefore the horary variation of the inclination will be to 33" 10''' 33^{iv}. as the area HpMh multiplied into AZ x $\dfrac{TZ}{Mp}$ x $\dfrac{Pp}{PG}$ to AT^3.

COR. 2. And, therefore, if the earth and nodes were after every hour drawn back from their new and instantly restored to their old places, so as their situation might continue given for a whole periodic month together, the whole variation of the inclination during that mouth would be to 33" 10''' 33^{iv}. as the aggregate of all the areas HpMh, generated in the time of one revolution of the point p (with due regard in summing to their proper signs + −), multiplied into AZ x TZ x $\dfrac{Pp}{PG}$ to Mp x AT^3;

that is, as the whole circle QAqa multiplied into AZ x TZ x $\dfrac{Pp}{PG}$ to Mp x AT^3, that is,

as the circumference QAqa multiplied into AZ x TZ x $\dfrac{Pp}{PG}$ to 2Mp x AT^2.

COR. 3. And, therefore, in a given position of the nodes, the mean horary variation, from which, if uniformly continued through the whole month, that menstrual variation might be generated, is to 33" 10"' 33^{iv}. as AZ x TZ x $\frac{Pp}{PG}$ to 2AT^2, or as Pp $\times$ $\frac{AZ \times TZ}{\frac{1}{2}AT}$ to PG x 4AT; that is (because Pp is to PG as the sine of the aforesaid inclination to the radius, and $\frac{AZ \times TZ}{\frac{1}{4}AT}$ to 4AT as the sine of double the angle ATn to four times the radius), as the sine of the same inclination multiplied into the sine of double the distance of the nodes from the sun to four times the square of the radius.

COR. 4. Seeing the horary variation of the inclination, when the nodes are in the quadratures, is (by this Prop.) to the angle 33" 10"' 33^{iv}. as IT $\times$ AZ $\times$ TG $\times \frac{Pp}{PG}$ to AT^3, that is, as $\frac{IT \times TG}{\frac{1}{2}AT}$ x $\frac{Pp}{PG}$ to 2AT, that is, as the sine of double the distance of the moon from the quadratures multiplied into $\frac{Pp}{PG}$ to twice the radius, the sum of all the horary variations during the time that the moon, in this situation of the nodes, passes from the quadrature to the syzygy (that is, in the space of 177 $^1/_6$ hours) will be to the sum of as many angles 33" 10"' 33^{iv}. or 5878", as the sum of all the sines of double the distance of the moon from the quadratures multiplied into $\frac{Pp}{PG}$ to the sum of as many diameters; that is, as the diameter multiplied $\frac{Pp}{PG}$ to the circumference; that is, if the inclination be 5° 1', as 7 x $^{874}/_{10000}$ to 22, or as 278 to 10000. And, therefore, the whole variation, composed out of the sum of all the horary variations in the aforesaid time, is 163", or 2' 43".

PROPOSITION XXXV. PROBLEM XVI.

TO A GIVEN TIME TO FIND THE INCLINATION OF THE MOON'S ORBIT TO THE PLANE OF THE ECLIPTIC.

Let AD be the sine of the greatest inclination, and AB the sine of the least. Bisect BD in C; and round the centre 0, with the interval BC, describe the circle BGD. In AC take CE in the same proportion to EB as EB to twice BA. And if to the time given we set off the angle AEG equal to double the distance of the nodes from the

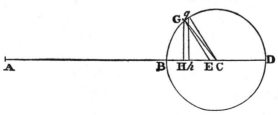

quadratures, and upon AD let fall the perpendicular GH, AH will be the sine of the inclination required.

For GE^2 is equal to GH^2 + HE^2 = BHD + HE^2 = HBD + HE^2 − BH^2 = HBD + BE^2 − 2BH x BE = BE^2 + 2EC x BH = 2EC x AB + 2EC x BH = 2EC x AH; wherefore since 2EC is given, GE^2 will be as AH. Now let AEg represent double the distance of the nodes from the quadratures, in a given moment of time after, and the arc Gg, on account of the given angle GEg, will be as the distance GE. But Hh is to Gg as GH to GC, and, therefore, Hh is as the rectangle GH x Gg, or GH x GE, that is, as $\frac{GH}{GE}$ x

GE^2, or $\frac{GH}{GE}$ x AH; that is, as AH and the sine of the angle AEG conjunctly. If, therefore, in any one case, AH be the sine of inclination, it will increase by the same increments as the sine of inclination doth, by Cor. 3 of the preceding Prop. and therefore win always continue equal to that sine. But when the point G falls upon either point B or D, AH is equal to this sine, and therefore remains always equal thereto.   Q.E.D.

In this demonstration I have supposed that the angle BEG, representing double the distance of the nodes from the quadratures, increaseth uniformly; for I cannot descend to every minute circumstance of inequality. Now suppose that BEG is a right angle, and that Gg is in this case the horary increment of double the distance of the nodes from the sun; then, by Cor. 3 of the last Prop. the horary variation of the inclination in the same case will be to 33" 10''' 33^{iv}. as the rectangle of AH, the sine of the inclination, into the sine of the right angle BEG, double the distance of the nodes from the sun, to four times the square of the radius; that is, as AH, the sine of the mean inclination, to four times the radius; that is, seeing the mean inclination is about 5° 8$^1/_2$, as its sine 896 to 40000, the quadruple of the radius, or as 224 to 10000. But the whole variation corresponding to BD, the difference of the sines, is to this horary variation as the diameter BD to the arc Gg, that is, conjunctly as the diameter BD to the semi-circumference BGD, and as the time of 2079 $^7/_{10}$ hours, in which the node proceeds from the quadratures to the syzygies, to one hour, that is, as 7 to 11, and 2079$^7/_{10}$ to 1. Wherefore, compounding all these proportions, we shall have the whole variation BD to 33" 10''' 33^{iv}. as 224 x 7 x 2079$^7/_{10}$ to 110000, that is, as 29645 to 1000; and from thence that variation BD will come out 16' 23$^1/_2$".

And this is the greatest variation of the inclination, abstracting from the situation of the moon in its orbit; for if the nodes are in the syzygies, the inclination suffers no change from the various positions of the moon. But if the nodes are in the quadratures, the inclination is less when the moon is in the syzygies than when it is in the quadratures by a difference of 2' 43", as we shewed in Cor. 4 of the preceding Prop.; and the whole mean variation BD, diminished by 1' 21$^1/_2$", the half of this excess, becomes 15' 2",

when the moon is in the quadratures; and increased by the same, becomes 17' 45" when the moon is in the syzygies. If, therefore, the moon be in the syzygies, the whole variation in the passage of the nodes from the quadratures to the syzygies will be 17'45"; and, therefore, if the inclination be 5° 17' 20", when the nodes are in the syzygies, it will be 4° 59' 35" when the nodes are in the quadratures and the moon in the syzygies. The truth of all which is confirmed by observations.

Now if the inclination of the orbit should be required when the moon is in the syzygies, and the nodes any where between them and the quadratures, let AB be to AD as the sine of 4° 59' 35" to the sine of 5° 17' 20", and take the angle AEG equal to double the distance of the nodes from the quadratures; and AH will be the sine of the inclination desired, To this inclination of the orbit the inclination of the same is equal, when the moon is 900 distant from the nodes. In other situations of the moon, this menstrual inequality, to which the variation of the inclination is obnoxious in the calculus of the moon's latitude, is balanced, and in a manner took off, by the menstrual inequality of the motion of the nodes (as we said before), and therefore may be neglected in the computation of the said latitude.

SCHOLIUM.

By these computations of the lunar motions I was willing to shew that by the theory of gravity the motions of the moon could be calculated from their physical causes. By the same theory I moreover found that the annual equation of the mean motion of the moon arises from the various dilatation which the orbit of the moon suffers from the action of the sun according to Cor. 6, Prop. LXVI, Book I. The force of this action is greater in the perigeon sun, and dilates the moon's orbit; in the apogeon sun it is less, and permits the orbit to be again contracted. The moon moves slower in the dilated and faster in the contracted orbit; and the annual equation, by which this inequality is regulated, vanishes in the apogee and perigee of the sun. In the mean distance of the sun from the earth it arises to about 11' 50"; in other distances of the sun it is proportional to the equation of the sun's centre, and is added to the mean motion of the moon, while the earth is passing from its aphelion to its perihelion, and subducted while the earth is in the opposite semi-circle. Taking for the radius of the *orbis magnus* 1000, and $16^7/_8$ for the earth's eccentricity, this equation, when of the greatest magnitude, by the theory of gravity comes out 11' 49". But the eccentricity of the earth seems to be something greater, and with the eccentricity this equation will be augmented in the same proportion. Suppose the eccentricity $16^{11}/_{12}$, and the greatest equation will be 11' 51".

Farther; I found that the apogee and nodes of the moon move faster in the perihelion of the earth, where the force of the sun's action is greater, than in the aphelion

thereof, and that in the reciprocal triplicate proportion of the earth's distance from the sun; and hence arise annual equations of those motions proportional to the equation of the sun's centre. Now the motion of the sun is in the reciprocal duplicate proportion of the earth's distance from the sun; and the greatest equation of the centre which this inequality generates is 1° 56' 20", corresponding to the above mentioned eccentricity of the sun, $16^{11}/_{12}$. But if the motion of the sun had been in the reciprocal triplicate proportion of the distance, this inequality would have generated the greatest equation 2° 54' 30"; and therefore the greatest equations which the inequalities of the motions of the moon's apogee and nodes do generate are to 2° 54' 30" as the mean diurnal motion of the moon's apogee and the mean diurnal motion of its nodes are to the mean diurnal motion of the sun. Whence the greatest equation of the mean motion of the apogee comes out 19' 43", and the greatest equation of the mean motion of the nodes 9' 24". The former equation is added, and the latter subducted, while the earth is passing from its perihelion to its aphelion, and contrariwise when the earth is in the opposite semi-circle.

By the theory of gravity I likewise found that the action of the sun upon the moon is something greater when the transverse diameter of the moon's orbit passeth through the sun than when the same is perpendicular upon the line which joins the earth and the sun; and therefore the moon's orbit is something larger in the former than in the latter case. And hence arises another equation of the moon's mean motion, depending upon the situation of the moon's apogee in respect of the sun, which is in its greatest quantity when the moon's apogee is in the octants of the sun, and vanishes when the apogee arrives at the quadratures or syzygies; and it, is added to the mean motion while the moon's apogee is passing from the quadrature of the sun to the syzygy, and subducted while the apogee is passing from the syzygy to the quadrature. This equation, which I shall call the semiannual, when greatest in the octants of the apogee, arises to about 3' 45", so far as I could collect from the phaenomena: and this is its quantity in the mean distance of the sun from the earth, But it is increased and diminished in the reciprocal triplicate proportion of the sun's distance, and therefore is nearly 3' 34" when that distance is greatest, and 3' 56" when least. But when the moon's apogee is without the octants, it becomes less, and is to its greatest quantity as the sine of double the distance of the moon's apogee from the nearest syzygy or quadrature to the radius.

By the same theory of gravity, the action of the sun upon the moon is something greater when the line of the moon's nodes passes through the sun than when it is at right angles with the line which joins the sun and the earth; and hence arises another equation of the moon's mean motion, which I shall call the second semi-annual; and this is greatest when the nodes are in the octants of the sun, and vanishes when they

are in the syzygies or quadratures; and in other positions of the nodes is proportional to the sine of double the distance of either node from the nearest syzygy or quadrature. And it is added to the mean motion of the moon, if the run is *in antecedentia*, to the node which is nearest to him, and subducted if *in consequentia*, and in the octants, where it is of the greatest magnitude, it arises to 47" in the mean distance of the sun from the earth, as I find from the theory of gravity. In other distances of the sun, this equation, greatest in the octants of the nodes, is reciprocally as the cube of the sun's distance from the earth; and therefore in the sun's perigee it comes to about 49", and in its apogee to about 45".

By the same theory of gravity, the moon's apogee goes forward at the greatest rate when it is either in conjunction with or in opposition to the sun, but in its quadratures with the sun it goes backward; and the eccentricity comes, in the former case, to its greatest quantity; in the latter to its least, by Cor. 7, 8, and 9, Prop. LXVI, Book I. And those inequalities, by the Corollaries we have named, are very great, and generate the principal which I call the semiannual equation of the apogee; and this semi-annual equation in its greatest quantity comes to about 12° 18', as nearly as I could collect from the phenomena. Our countryman, *Horrox*, was the first who advanced the theory of the moon's moving in an ellipse about the earth placed in its lower focus. Dr. *Halley* improved the notion, by putting the centre of the ellipsis in an epicycle whose centre is uniformly revolved about the earth; and from the motion in this epicycle the mentioned inequalities in the progress and regress of the apogee, and in the quantity of eccentricity, do arise. Suppose the mean distance of the moon from the earth to

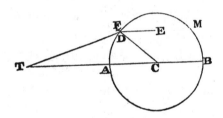

be divided into 100000 parts, and let T represent the earth, and TC the moon's mean eccentricity of 5505 such parts. Produce TC to B, so as CB may be the sine of the greatest semi-annual equation 12° 18' to the radius TC; and the circle BDA described about the centre C, with the interval CB, will be the epicycle spoken of, in which the centre of the moon's orbit is placed, and revolved according to the order of the letters BDA. Set off the angle BCD equal to twice the annual argument, or twice the distance of the sun's true place from the place of the moon's apogee once equated, and CTD will be the semi-annual equation of the moon's apogee, and TD the eccentricity of its orbit, tending to the place of the apogee now twice equated. But, having the moon's mean motion, the place of its apogee, and its eccentricity, as well as the longer axis of its orbit 200000, from these *data* the true place of the moon in its orbit, together with its distance from the earth, may be determined by the methods commonly known.

In the perihelion of the earth, where the force of the sun is greatest, the centre of the moon's orbit moves faster about the centre C than in the aphelion, and that in the reciprocal triplicate proportion of the sun's distance from the earth. But, because the equation of the sun's centre is included in the annual argument, the centre of the moon's orbit moves faster in its epicycle BDA, in the reciprocal duplicate proportion of the sun's distance from the earth. Therefore, that it may move yet faster in the reciprocal simple proportion of the distance, suppose that from D, the centre of the orbit, a right line DE is drawn, tending towards the moon's apogee once equated, that is, parallel to TC; and set off the angle EDF equal to the excess of the aforesaid annual argument above the distance of the moon's apogee from the sun's perigee *in consequentia*, or, which comes to the same thing, take the angle CDF equal to the complement of the sun's true anomaly to 360°; and let DF be to DC as twice the eccentricity of the *orbis magnus* to the sun's mean distance from the earth, and the sun's mean diurnal motion from the moon's apogee to the sun's mean diurnal motion from its own apogee conjunctly, that is, as $33^7/_8$ to 1000, and 52' 27" 16''' to 59' 8" 10''' conjunctly, or as 3 to 100; and imagine the centre of the moon's orbit placed in the point F to be revolved in an epicycle whose centre is D, and radius DF, while the point D moves in the circumference of the circle DABD: for by this means the centre of the moon's orbit comes to describe a certain curve line about the centre Q with a velocity which will be almost reciprocally as the cube of the sun's distance from the earth, as it ought to be.

The calculus of this motion is difficult, but may be rendered more easy by the following approximation. Assuming, as above, the moon's mean distance from the earth of 100000 parts, and the eccentricity TC of 5505 such parts, the line CB or CD will be found $1172^3/_4$ and DF $35^1/_5$, of those parts; and this line DF at the distance TC subtends the angle at the earth, which the removal of the centre of the orbit from the place D to the place F generates in the motion of this centre; and double this line DF in a parallel position, at the distance of the upper focus of the moon's orbit from the earth, subtends at the earth the same angle as DF did before, which that removal generates in the motion of this upper focus; but at the distance of the moon from the earth this double line 2DF at the upper focus, in a parallel position to the first line DF, subtends an angle at the moon, which the said removal generates in the motion of the moon, which angle may be therefore called the second equation of the moon's centre; and this equation, in the mean distance of the moon from the earth, is nearly as the sine of the angle which that line DP contains with the line drawn from the point F to the moon, and when in its greatest quantity amounts to 2' 25". But the angle which the line DF contains with the line drawn from the point F to the moon is found either by subtracting the angle EDP from the mean anomaly of the moon, or by adding the distance of the moon from the sun to the distance of the moons apogee from the

apogee of the sun; and as the radius to the sine of the angle thus found, so is 2' 25" to the second equation of the centre: to be added, if the forementioned sum be less than a semi-circle; to be subducted, if greater. And from the moon's place in its orbit thus corrected, its longitude may be found in the syzygies of the luminaries.

The atmosphere of the earth to the height of 35 or 40 miles refracts the sun's light. This refraction scatters and spreads the light over the earth's shadow; and the dissipated light near the limits of the shadow dilates the shadow. Upon which account, to the diameter of the shadow, as it comes out by the parallax, I add 1 or $1^1/_3$ minute in lunar eclipses.

But the theory of the moon ought to be examined and proved from the phaenomena, first in the syzygies, then in the quadratures, and last of all in the octants: and whoever pleases to undertake the work will find it not amiss to assume the following mean motions of the sun and moon at the Royal Observatory of *Greenwich*, to the last day of *December* at noon, *anno* 1700, O.S. viz. The mean motion of the sun ♉ 20° 43' 40", and of its apogee ♋ 7° 44' 30"; the mean motion of the moon ♒ 15° 21' 00"; of its apogee, ♓ 8° 20' 00"; and of its ascending node ♌ 27° 24' 20"; and the difference of meridians betwixt the Observatory at *Greenwich* and the Royal Observatory at *Paris*, 0^h. 9' 20": but the mean motion of the moon and of its apogee are not yet obtained with sufficient accuracy.

PROPOSITION XXXVI. PROBLEM XVII.

TO FIND THE FORCE OF THE SUN TO MOVE THE SEA.

The sun's force ML or PT to disturb the motions of the moon, was (by Prop. XXV.) in the moon's quadratures, to the force of gravity with us, as 1 to 638092,6; and the force TM − LM or 2PK in the moon's syzygies is double that quantity. But, descending to the surface of the earth, these forces are diminished in proportion of the distances from the Centre of the earth, that is, in the proportion of $60^1/_2$ to 1; and therefore the former force on the earth's surface is to the force of gravity as 1 to 38604600; and by this force the sea is depressed in such places as are 90 degrees distant from the sun, But by the other force, which is twice as great, the sea is raised not only in the places directly under the sun, but in those also which are directly opposed to it; and the sum of these forces is to the force of gravity as 1 to 12868200. And because the same force excites the same motion, whether it depresses the waters in those places which are 90 degrees distant from the sun, or raises them in the places which are directly under and directly opposed to the sun, the aforesaid sum will be the total force of the sun to disturb the sea, and will have the same effect as if the whole was employed in raising the sea in the places directly under and directly opposed to the sun, and did not act at all in the places which are 90 degrees removed from the sun.

And this is the force of the sun to disturb the sea in any given place, where the sun is at the same time both vertical, and in its mean distance from the earth. In other positions of the sun, its force to raise the sea is as the versed sine of double its altitude above the horizon of the place directly, and the cube of the distance from the earth reciprocally.

Cor. Since the centrifugal force of the parts of the earth, arising from the earth's diurnal motion, which is to the force of gravity as 1 to 289, raises the waters under the equator to a height exceeding that under the poles by 85472 *Paris* feet, as above, in Prop. XIX., the force of the sun, which we have now shewed to be to the force of gravity as 1 to 12868200, and therefore is to that centrifugal force as 289 to 12868200, or as 1 to 44527, will be able to raise the waters in the places directly under and directly opposed to the sun to a height exceeding that in the places which are 90 degrees removed from the sun only by one *Paris* foot and $113^1/_{30}$ inches; for this measure is to the measure of 85472 feet as 1 to 44527.

PROPOSITION XXXVII. PROBLEM XVIII.

To find the force of the moon to move the sea.

The force of the moon to move the sea is to be deduced from its proportion to the force of the sun, and this proportion is to be collected from the proportion of the motions of the sea, which are the effects of those forces. Before the mouth of the river *Avon*, three miles below *Bristol*, the height of the ascent of the water in the vernal and autumnal syzygies of the luminaries (by the observations of *Samuel Sturmy*) amounts to about 45 feet, but in the quadratures to 25 only. The former of those heights arises from the sum of the aforesaid forces, the latter from their difference. If, therefore, S and L are supposed to represent respectively the forces of the sun and moon while they are in the equator, as well as in their mean distances from the earth, we shall have L + S to L − S as 45 to 25, or as 9 to 5.

At *Plymouth* (by the observations of *Samuel Colepress*) the tide in its mean height rises to about 16 feet, and in the spring and autumn the height thereof in the syzygies may exceed that in the quadratures by more than 7 or 8 feet. Suppose the greatest difference of those heights to be 9 feet, and L + S will be to L − S as $20^1/_2$ to $11^1/_2$, or as 41 to 23; a proportion that agrees well enough with the former. But because of the great tide at *Bristol*, we are rather to depend upon the observations of *Sturmy*; and, therefore, till we procure something that is more certain, we shall use the proportion of 9 to 5.

But because of the reciprocal motions of the waters, the greatest tides do not happen at the times of the syzygies of the luminaries, but, as we have said before, are the

third in order after the syzygies; or (reckoning from the syzygies) follow next after the third appulse of the moon to the meridian of the place after the syzygies; or rather (as *Sturmy* observes) are the third after the day of the new or full moon, or rather nearly after the twelfth hour from the new or full moon, and therefore fall nearly upon the forty-third hour after the new or full of the moon. But in this port they fall out about the seventh hour after the appulse of the moon to the meridian of the place; and therefore follow next after the appulse of the moon to the meridian, when the moon is distant from the sun, or from opposition with the sun by about 18 or 19 degrees *in consequentia.* So the summer and winter seasons come not to their height in the solstices themselves, but when the sun is advanced beyond the solstices by about a tenth part of its whole course, that is, by about 36 or 37 degrees. In like manner, the greatest tide is raised after the appulse of the moon to the meridian of the place, when the moon has passed by the sun, *or the opposition thereof,* by about a tenth part of the whole motion from *one greatest* tide to *the next following greatest* tide. Suppose that distance about $18^1/_2$ degrees; and the sun's force in this distance of the moon from the syzygies and quadratures will be of less moment to augment and diminish that part of the motion of the sea which proceeds from the motion of the moon than in the syzygies and quadratures themselves in the proportion of the radius to the co-sine of double this distance, or of an angle of 37 degrees; that is, in proportion of 10000000 to 7986355; and, therefore, in the preceding analogy, in place of S we must put 0,7986355S.

But farther; the force of the moon in the quadratures must be diminished, on account of its declination from the equator; for the moon in those quadratures, or rather in $18^1/_2$ degrees past the quadratures, declines from the equator by about 23° 13'; and the force of either luminary to move the sea is diminished as it declines from the equator nearly in the duplicate proportion of the co-sine of the declination; and therefore the force of the moon in those quadratures is only 0,8570327L; whence we have L + 0,7986355S to 0,8570327L – 0,7986355S as 9 to 5.

Farther yet; the diameters of the orbit in which the moon should move, setting aside the consideration of eccentricity, are one to the other as 66 to 70; and therefore the moon's distance from the earth in the syzygies is to its distance in the quadratures, *caeteris paribus,* as 69 to 70; and its distances, when $18^1/_2$, degrees advanced beyond the syzygies, where the greatest tide was excited, and when $18^1/_2$ degrees passed by the quadratures, where the least tide was produced, are to its mean distance as 69,098747 and 69,897345 to $69^1/_2$. But the force of the moon to move the sea is in the reciprocal triplicate proportion of its distance; and therefore its forces, in the greatest and least of those distances, are to its force in its mean distance as 0,9830427 and 1,017522 to 1. From whence we have 1,017522L x 0,7986355S to 0,9830427 x 0,8570327L – 0,7986355S as 9 to 5; and S to L as 1 to 4,4815. Wherefore since the force of the sun is to the force of gravity as 1 to 12868200, the moon's force will be to the force of gravity as 1 to 2671400.

COR. 1. Since the waters excited by the sun's force rise to the height of a foot and $11^1/_{30}$ inches, the moon's force will raise the same to the height of 8 feet and $7^5/_{22}$ inches; and the joint forces of both will raise the same to the height of $10^1/_2$ feet; and when the moon is in its perigee to the height of $12^1/_2$ feet, and more, especially when the wind sets the same way as the tide. And a force of that quantity is abundantly sufficient to excite all the motions of the sea, and agrees well with the proportion of those motions; for in such seas as lie free and open from east to west, as in the *Pacific* sea, and in those tracts of the *Atlantic* and *AEthiopic* seas which lie without the tropics, the waters commonly rise to 6, 9, 12, or 15 feet; but in the *Pacific* sea, which is of a greater depth, as well as of a larger extent, the tides are said to be greater than in the *Atlantic* and *AEthiopic* seas; for to have a full tide raised, an extent of sea from east to west is required of no less than 90 degrees. In the *AEthiopic* sea, the waters rise to a less height within the tropics than in the temperate zones, because of the narrowness of the sea between *Africa* and the southern parts of *America*. In the middle of the open sea the waters cannot rise without falling together, and at the same time, upon both the eastern and western shores, when, notwithstanding, in our narrow seas, they ought to fall on those shores by alternate turns; upon which account there is commonly but a small flood and ebb in such islands as lie far distant from the continent. On the contrary, in some ports, where to fill and empty the bays alternately the waters are with great violence forced in and out through shallow channels, the flood and ebb must be greater than ordinary; as at *Plymouth* and *Chepstow Bridge* in *England*, at the mountains of St. *Michael*, and the town of *Auranches*, in *Normandy*, and at *Cambaia* and *Pegu* in the *East Indies*. In these places the sea is hurried in and out with such violence, as sometimes to lay the shores under water, sometimes to leave them dry for many miles. Nor is this force of the influx and efflux to be broke till it has raised and depressed the waters to 30, 40, or 50 feet and above. And a like account is to be given of long and shallow channels or straits, such as the *Magellanic* straits, and those channels which environ *England*. The tide in such ports and straits, by the violence of the influx and efflux, is augmented above measure. But on such shores as lie towards the deep and open sea with a steep descent, where the waters may freely rise and fall without that precipitation of influx and efflux, the proportion of the tides agrees with the forces of the sun and moon.

COR. 2. Since the moon's force to move the sea is to the force of gravity as 1 to 2871400, it is evident that this force is far less than to appear sensibly in statical or hydrostatical experiments, or even in those of pendulums. It is in the tides only that this force shews itself by any sensible effect.

COR. 3. Because the force of the moon to move the sea is to the like force of the sun as 4,4815 to 1, and the forces (by Cor. 14, Prop. LXVI, Book I) are as the densities

of the bodies of the sun and moon and the cubes of their apparent diameters conjunctly, the density of the moon will be to the density of the *sun* as 4,4815 to 1 directly, and the cube of the moon's diameter to the cube of the sun's diameter inversely; that is (seeing the mean apparent diameters of the moon and sun are 31' 16 $^1/_2$", and 32' 12"), as 4891 to 1000. But the density of the sun was to the density of the earth as 1000 to 4000; and therefore the density of the moon is to the density of the earth as 4891 to 4000, or as 11 to 9. Therefore the body of the moon is more dense and more earthly than the earth itself.

COR. 4. And since the true diameter of the moon (from the observations of astronomers) is to the true diameter of the earth as 100 to 365, the mass of matter in the moon will be to the mass of matter in the earth as I to 39,788.

COR. 5. And the accelerative gravity on the surface of the moon will be about three times less than the accelerative gravity on the surface of the earth.

COR. 6. And the distance of the moon's centre from the centre of the earth will be to the distance of the moon's centre from the common centre, of gravity of the earth and moon as 40,788 to 39,788.

COR. 7. And the mean distance of the centre of the moon from the centre of the earth will be (in the moon's octants) nearly 602, of the greatest semi-diameters of the earth; for the greatest semi-diameter of the earth was 19658600 *Paris* feet, and the mean distance of the centres of the earth and moon, consisting of $60^1/_2$ such semi-diameters, is equal to 1187379440 feet. And this distance (by the preceding Cor.) is to the distance of the moon's centre, from the common centre of gravity of the earth and moon as 40,788 to 39,788; which latter distance, therefore, is 1158268534 feet. And since the moon, in respect of the fixed stars, performs its revolution in 27^d. 7^h. 43$^4/_9$', the versed sine of that angle which the moon in a minute of time describes is 12752341 to the radius 1000,000000,000000; and as the radius is to this versed sine, so are 1158268534 feet to 14,7706353 feet. The moon, therefore, falling towards the earth by that force which retains it in its orbit, would in one minute of time describe 14,7706353 feet; and if we augment this force in the proportion of 178$^{29}/_{40}$ to 177$^{29}/_{40}$, we shall have the total force of gravity at the orbit of the moon, by Cor. Prop. III; and the moon falling by this force, in one minute of time would describe 14,8538067 feet. And at the 60th part of the distance of the moon from the earth's centre, that is, at the distance of 197896573 feet from the centre of the earth, a body falling by its weight, would, in one second of time, likewise describe 14,8538067 feet. And, therefore, at the distance of 19615800, which compose one mean semi-diameter of the earth, a heavy body would describe in falling 15,11175, or 15 feet, 1 inch, and $4^1/_{11}$ lines, in the same time. This will be the descent of bodies in the latitude of 45 degrees. And by the foregoing table, to be found under Prop.

XX, the descent in the latitude of *Paris* will be a little greater by an excess of about $^2/_3$ parts of a line. Therefore, by this computation, heavy bodies in the latitude of *Paris* falling *in vacuo* will describe 15 *Paris* feet, 1 inch, $4^{25}/_{33}$ lines, very nearly, in one second of time. And if the gravity be, diminished by taking away a quantity equal to the centrifugal force arising in that latitude from the earth's diurnal motion, heavy bodies falling there will describe in one second of time 15 feet, 1 inch, and $1^1/_2$ line. And with this velocity heavy bodies do really fall in the latitude of *Paris*, as we have shewn above in Prop. IV and XIX.

COR. 8. The mean distance of the centres of the earth and moon in the syzygies of the moon is equal to 60 of the greatest semi-diameters of the earth, subducting only about one 30th part of a semi-diameter: and in the moon's quadratures the mean distance of the same centres is $60^5/_6$ such semi-diameters of the earth; for these two distances are to the mean distance of the moon in the octants as 69 and 70 to $69^1/_2$, by Prop. XXVIII.

COR. 9. The mean distance of the centres of the earth and moon in the syzygies of the moon is 60 mean semi-diameters of the earth, and a 10th part of one semi-diameter; and in the moon's quadratures the mean distance of the same centres is 61 mean semi-diameters of the earth, subducting one 30th part of one semi-diameter.

COR. 10. In the moon's syzygies its mean horizontal parallax in the latitudes of 0, 30, 38, 45, 52, 60, 90 degrees is 57' 20", 57' 16", 57' 14", 57' 12", 57' 10", 57' 8", 57' 4", respectively.

In these computations I do not consider the magnetic attraction of the earth, whose quantity is very small and unknown: if this quantity should ever be found out, and the measures of degrees upon the meridian, the lengths of isochronous pendulums in different parallels, the laws of the motions of the sea, and the moon's parallax, with the apparent diameters of the sun and moon, should be more exactly determined from phaenomena: we should then be enabled to bring this calculation to a greater accuracy.

PROPOSITION XXXVIII. PROBLEM XIX.

TO FIND THE FIGURE OF THE MOON'S BODY.

If the moon's body were fluid like our sea, the force of the earth to raise that fluid in the nearest and remotest parts would be to the force of the moon by which our sea is raised in the places under and opposite to the moon as the accelerative gravity of the moon towards the earth to the accelerative gravity of the earth towards the moon, and the diameter of the moon to the diameter of the earth conjunctly; that is, as 39,788 to 1, and 100 to 365 conjunctly, or as 1081 to 100. Wherefore, since our sea, by the force of the moon, is raised to $8^3/_5$ feet, the lunar fluid would be raised by the force of the

earth to 93 feet; and upon this account the figure of the moon would be a spheroid, whose greatest diameter produced would pass through the centre of the earth, and exceed the diameters perpendicular thereto by 186 feet. Such a figure, therefore, the moon affects, and must have put on from the beginning. Q.E.I.

COR. Hence it is that the same face of the moon always respects the earth; nor can the body of the moon possibly rest in any other position, but would return always by a libratory motion to this situation; but those librations, however, must be exceedingly slow, because of the weakness of the forces which excite them; so that the face of the moon, which should be always obverted to the earth, may, for the reason assigned in Prop. XVII. be turned towards the other focus of the moon's orbit, without being immediately drawn back, and converted again towards the earth.

LEMMA I.

If APEp represent the earth uniformly dense, marked with the centre C, the poles P, p, and the equator AE; and if about the centre C, with the radius CP, we suppose the sphere Pape to be described, and QR to denote the plane an which a right line, drawn from the centre of the sun to the centre of the earth, insists at right angles; and further suppose that the several particles of the whole exterior earth PapAPepE, without the height of the said sphere, endeavour to recede towards this side and that side from the plane QR, every particle by a force proportional to its distance from that plane; I say, in the first place, that the whole force and efficacy of all the particles that are situate in AE, the circle of the equator, and disposed uniformly without the globe, encompassing, the same after the manner of a ring, to wheel the earth about its centre, is to the whole force and efficacy of as many particles in that point A of the equator which is at the greatest distance from the plane QR, to wheel the earth about its centre with a like circular motion, as 1 to 2. And that circular motion will be performed about an axis lying in the common section of the equator and the plane QR.

For let there be described from the centre K, with the diameter IL, the semi-circle INL. Suppose the semi-circumference INL to be divided into innumerable equal parts,

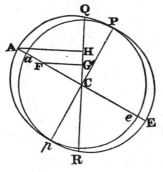
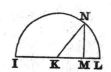

and from the several parts N to the diameter IL let fall the sines NM. Then the sum of the squares of all the sines NM will be equal to the sums of the squares of the sines KM, and both sums together will be equal to the sums of the squares of as many semi-diameters KN; and therefore the sum of the squares of all the sines NM will be but half so great as the sum of the squares of as many semi-diameters KN.

Suppose now the circumference of the circle AE to be divided into the like number of little equal parts, and from every such part P a perpendicular FG to be let fall upon the plane QR, as well as the perpendicular AH from the point A. Then the force by which the particle F recedes from the plane QR will (by supposition) be as that perpendicular PG; and this force multiplied by the distance CG will represent the power of the particle F to turn the earth round its centre. And, therefore, the power of a particle in the place F will be to the power of a particle in the place A as FG x GC to AH x HC; that is, as FC^2 to AC^2: and therefore the whole power of all the particles F, in their proper places F, will be to the power of the like number of particles in the place A as the sum of all the FC^2 to the sum of all the AC^2, that is (by what we have demonstrated before), as 1 to 2.   Q.E.D.

And because the action of those particles is exerted in the direction of lines perpendicularly receding from the plane QR, and that equally from each side of this plane, they will wheel about the circumference of the circle of the equator, together with the adherent body of the earth, round an axis which lies as well in the plane QR as in that of the equator.

LEMMA II.

THE SAME THINGS STILL SUPPOSED, I SAY, IN THE SECOND
PLACE, THAT THE TOTAL FORCE OR POWER OF ALL THE
PARTICLES SITUATED EVERY WHERE ABOUT THE SPHERE TO
TURN THE EARTH ABOUT THE SAID AXIS IS TO THE WHOLE
FORCE OF THE LIKE NUMBER OF PARTICLES, UNIFORMLY
DISPOSED ROUND THE WHOLE CIRCUMFERENCE OF THE
EQUATOR AE IN THE FASHION OF A RING, TO TURN THE WHOLE
EARTH ABOUT WITH THE LIKE CIRCULAR MOTION, AS 2 TO 5.

For let IK be any lesser circle parallel to the equator AE, and let L*l* be any two equal particles in this circle, situated without the sphere P*ape*; and if upon the plane QR, which, is at right angles with a radius drawn to the sun, we let fall the perpendiculars LM, *lm*, the total forces by which these particles recede from the plane QR will be proportional to the perpendiculars LM, *lm*. Let the right line L*l* be drawn parallel to the plane P*ape*, and bisect the same in X; and through the point X draw N*n* parallel to the

plane QR, and meeting the perpendiculars LM, *lm*, in N and *n*; and upon the plane QR let fall the perpendicular XY. And the contrary forces of the particles L and *l* to wheel about the earth contrariwise are as LM x MC, and *lm* x *m*C; that is, as LN x MC

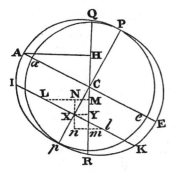

+ NM x MC, and *ln* x *m*C – *nm* x *m*C; or LN x MC + NM x MC, and LN x *m*C – NM x *m*C, and LN x M*m* – NM x $\overline{\text{MC} + n}$, the difference of the two, is the force of both taken together to turn the earth round. The affirmative part of this difference LN x M*m*, or 2LN x NX, is to 2AH x HC, the force of two particles of the same size situated in A, as LX^2 to AC^2; and the negative part $\overline{\text{MC} + m}$, or 2XY x CY, is to 2AH x HC, the force of the same two particles situated in A, as CX^2 to AC^2. And therefore the difference of the parts, that is, the force of the two particles L and *l*, taken together, to wheel the earth about, is to the force of two particles, equal to the former and situated in the place A, to turn in like manner the earth round, as $LX^2 - CX^2$ to AC^2. But if the circumference IK of the circle IK is supposed to be divided into an infinite number of little equal parts L, all the LX^2 will be to the like number of IX^2 as 1 to 2 (by Lem. 1); and to the same number of AC^2 as IX^2 to $2AC^2$; and the same number of CX^2 to as many AC^2 as $2CX^2$ to $2AC^2$. Wherefore the united forces of all the particles in the circumference of the circle IK are to the joint forces of as many particles in the place A as $IX^2 - 2CX^2$ to $2AC^2$; and therefore (by Lem. 1) to the united form of as many particles in the circumference of the circle AE as $IX^2 - 2CX^2$ to AC^2.

Now if P*p*, the diameter of the sphere, is conceived to be divided into an infinite number of equal parts, upon which a like number of circles IK are supposed to insist, the matter in the circumference of every circle IK will be as IX^2; and therefore the force of that matter to turn the earth about will be as IX^2 into $IX^2 - 2CX^2$: and the force of the same matter, if it was situated in the circumference of the circle AE, would be as IX^2 into AC^2. And therefore the force of all the particles of the whole matter situated without the sphere in the circumferences of all the circles is to the force of the like number of particles situated in the circumference of the greatest circle AE as all the IX^2 into $IX^2 - 2CX^2$ to as many IX^2 into AC^2; that is, as all the $AC^2 - CX^2$ into $AC^2 - 3CX^2$ to as many $AC^2 - CX^2$ into AC^2; that is, as all the $AC^4 - 4AC^2$ x $CX^2 + 3CX^4$ to as many $AC^4 - AC^2$ x CX^2; that is, as the whole fluent quantity, whose fluxion is $AC^4 - 4AC^2$ x $CX^2 + 3CX^4$, to the whole fluent quantity, whose fluxion is $AC^4 - AC^2$ x CX^2; and, therefore, by the method of fluxions, as AC^4 x $CX - {}^4/_3AC^2$ x $CX^3 + {}^3/_5CX^5$ to AC^4 x $CX - {}^1/_3 AC^2$ x CX^3; that is, if for CX we write the whole C*p*, or AC, as ${}^4/_{15}AC^5$ to ${}^2/_3AC^5$; that is, as 2 to 5. Q.E.D.

LEMMA III.

The same things still supposed, I say, in the third place, that the motion of the whole earth about the axis above-named arising from the motions of all the particles, will be to the motion of the aforesaid ring about the same axis in a proportion compounded of the proportion of the matter in the earth to the matter in the ring; and the proportion of three squares of the quadrantal arc of any circle to two squares of its diameter, that is, in the proportion of the matter to the matter, and of the number 925275 to the number 1000000.

For the motion of a cylinder revolved about its quiescent axis is to the motion of the inscribed sphere revolved together with it as any four equal squares to three circles inscribed in three of those squares; and the motion of this cylinder is to the motion of an exceedingly thin ring surrounding both sphere and cylinder in their common contact as double the matter in the cylinder to triple the matter in the ring; and this motion of the ring, uniformly continued about the axis of the cylinder, is to the uniform motion of the same about its own diameter performed in the same periodic time as the circumference of a circle to double its diameter.

HYPOTHESIS II.

If the other parts of the earth were taken away, and the remaining ring was carried alone about the sun in the orbit of the earth by the annual motion, while by the diurnal motion it was in the mean time revolved about its own axis inclined to the plane of the ecliptic by an angle of $23^{1}/_{2}$, degrees, the motion of the equinoctial points would be the same, whether the ring were fluid, or whether it consisted of a hard and rigid matter.

PROPOSITION XXXIX. PROBLEM XX.

To find the precession of the equinoxes.

The middle horary motion of the moon's nodes in a circular orbit, when the nodes are in the quadratures, was 16" 35''' 16^{iv}. 36^{v}.; the half of which, 8" 17''' 38^{iv}. 18^{v}. (for

the reasons above explained) is the mean horary motion of the nodes in such an orbit, which motion in a whole sidereal year becomes 20° 11' 46". Because, therefore, the nodes of the moon in such an orbit would be yearly transferred 20° 11' 46" *in antecedentia*; and, if there were more moons, the motion of the nodes of every one (by Cor. 16, Prop. LXVI, Book I) would be as its periodic time; if upon the surface of the earth a moon was revolved in the time of a sidereal day, the annual motion of the nodes of this moon would be to 20° 11' 46" as 23^h. 56', the sidereal day, to 27^d. 7^h. 43', the periodic time of our moon, that is, as 1436 to 39343. And the same thing would happen to the nodes of a ring of moons encompassing the earth, whether these moons did not mutually touch each the other, or whether they were molten, said formed into a continued ring, or whether that ring should become rigid and inflexible.

Let us, then, suppose that this ring is in quantity of matter equal to the whole exterior earth P*ap*AP*ep*E, which lies without the sphere P*ape* (see fig. Lem. II); and because this sphere is to that exterior earth as aC^2 to $AC^2 - aC^2$, that is (seeing PC or aC the least semi-diameter of the earth is to AC the greatest semi-diameter of the same as 229 to 230), as 52441 to 459; if this ring encompassed the earth round the equator, and both together were revolved about the diameter of the ring, the motion of the ring (by Lem. III) would be to the motion of the inner sphere as 459 to 52441 and 1000000 to 925275 conjunctly, that is, as 4590 to 485223; and therefore the motion of the ring would be to the sum of the motions of both ring and sphere as 4590 to 489813. Wherefore if the ring adheres to the sphere, and communicates its motion to the sphere, by which its nodes or equinoctial points recede, the motion remaining in the ring will be to its former motion as 4590 to 489813; upon which account the motion of the equinoctial points will be diminished in the same proportion. Wherefore the annual motion of the equinoctial points of the body, composed of both ring and sphere, will be to the motion 20° 11' 46" as 1436 to 39343 and 4590 to 489813 conjunctly, that is, as 100 to 292369. But the forces by which the nodes of a number of moons (as we explained above), and therefore by which the equinoctial points of the ring recede (that is, the forces 3IT, in fig. Prop. XXX), are in the several particles as the distances of those particles from the plane QR; and by these forces the particles recede from that plane: and therefore (by Lem. II) if the matter of the ring was spread all over the surface of the sphere, after the fashion of the figure P*ap*AP*ep*E, in order to make up that exterior part of the earth, the total force or power of all the particles to wheel about the earth round any diameter of the equator, and therefore to move the equinoctial points, would become less than before in the proportion of 2 to 5. Wherefore the annual regress of the equinoxes now would be to 20° 11' 46" as 10 to 73092; that is, would be 9" 56"' 50^{iv}.

But because the plane of the equator is inclined to that of the ecliptic, this motion is to be diminished in the proportion of the sine 91706 (which is the co-sine of $23^1/_2$ deg.) to the radius 100000; and the remaining motion will now be 9" 7'" 20^{iv}. which is the annual precession of the equinoxes arising from the force of the sun.

But the force of the moon to move the sea, was to the force of the sun nearly as 4,4815 to 1; and the force of the moon to move the equinoxes is to that of the sun in the same proportion. Where the annual precession of the equinoxes proceeding from the force of the moon comes out 40" 52'" 52^{iv}. and the total annual precession arising from the united forces of both will be 50" 00'" 12^{iv}. the quantity of which motion agrees with the phænomena; for the precession of the equinoxes, by astronomical observations, is about 50" yearly.

If the height of the earth at the equator exceeds its height at the poles by more than $17^1/_6$ miles, the matter thereof will be more rare near the surface than at the centre; and the precession of the equinoxes will be augmented by the excess of height, and diminished by the greater rarity.

And now we have described the system of the sun, the earth, moon, and planets, it remains that we add something about the comets.

LEMMA IV.

THAT THE COMETS ARE HIGHER THAN THE MOON, AND IN THE REGIONS OF THE PLANETS.

As the comets were placed by astronomers above the moon, because they were found to have no diurnal parallax, so their annual parallax is a convincing proof of their descending into the regions of the planets; for all the comets which move in a direct course according to the order of the signs, about the end of their appearance become

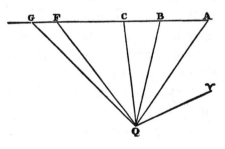

more than ordinarily slow or retrograde, if the earth is between them and the sun; and more than ordinarily swift, if the earth is approaching to a heliocentric opposition with them; where, on the other hand, those which move against the order of the signs, towards the end of their appearance appear swifter than they ought to be, if the earth is between them and the sun; and slower, and perhaps retrograde, if the earth is in the other side of its orbit. And these appearances proceed chiefly from the diverse situations which the earth acquires in the course of its motion, after the same manner as it happens to the planets, which appear sometimes retrograde, sometimes more slowly,

and sometimes more swiftly, progressive according as the motion of the earth falls in with that of the planet, or is directed the contrary way. If the earth move the same way with the comet, but, by an angular motion about the sun, so much swifter that right lines drawn from the earth to the comet converge towards the parts beyond the comet, the comet seen from the earth, because of its slower motion, will appear retrograde; and even if the earth is slower than the comet, the motion of the earth being subducted, the motion of the comet will at least appear retarded; but if the earth tends the contrary way to that of the comet, the motion of the comet will from thence appear accelerated; and from this apparent acceleration, or retardation, or regressive motion, the distance of the comet may be inferred in this manner. Let ΥQA, ΥQB, ΥQC, be three observed longitudes of the comet about the time of its first appearing, and ΥQF its last observed longitude before its disappearing. Draw the right line ABC, whose parts AB, BC, intercepted between the right lines QA and QB, QB and QC, may be one to the other as the two times between the three first observations. Produce AC to G, so as AG may be to AB as the time between the first and last observation to the time between the first and second; and join QG. Now if the comet

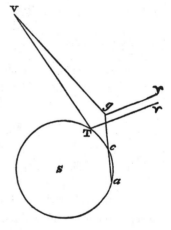

did move uniformly in a right line, and the earth either stood still, or was likewise carried forwards in a right line by an uniform motion, the angle ΥQG would be the longitude of the comet at the time of the last observation. The angle, therefore, FQG, which is the difference of the longitude, proceeds from the inequality of the motions of the comet and the earth; and this angle, if the earth and comet move contrary ways, is added to the angle ΥQG, and accelerates the apparent motion of the comet; but if the comet move the same way with the earth, it is subtracted, and either retards the motion of the comet, or perhaps renders it retrograde, as we have but now explained. This angle, therefore, proceeding chiefly from the motion of the earth, is justly to be esteemed the parallax of the comet; neglecting, to wit, some little increment or decrement that may arise from the unequal motion of the comet in its orbit; and from this parallax we thus deduce the distance of the comet. Let S represent the sun, acT the *orbis magnus*, a the earth's place in the first observation, c the place of the earth in the third observation, T the place of the earth in the last observation, and TΥ a right line drawn to the beginning of Aries. Set off the angle ΥTV equal to the angle ΥQF, that is, equal to the longitude of the comet at the time when the earth is in T; join ac, and produce it to g, so as ag may be to ac as AG to AC; and g will be the place at which the earth would have arrived in the time of the last observation, if

it had continued to move uniformly in the right line ac. Wherefore, if we draw gϒ parallel to Tϒ, and make the angle ϒgV equal to the angle ϒQG, this angle ϒgV will be equal to the longitude of the comet seen from the place g, and the angle TVg will be the parallax which arises from the earth's being transferred from the place g into the place T; and therefore V will be the place of the comet in the plane of the ecliptic. And this place V is commonly lower than the orb of Jupiter.

The same thing may be deduced from the incurvation of the way of the comets; for these bodies move almost in great circles, while their velocity is great; but about the end of their course, when that part of their apparent motion which arises from the parallax bears a greater proportion to their whole apparent motion, they commonly deviate from those circles, and when the earth goes to one side, they deviate to the other; and this deflexion, because of its corresponding with the motion of the earth, must arise chiefly from the parallax; and the quantity thereof is so considerable, as, by my computation, to place the disappearing comets a good deal lower than Jupiter. Whence it follows that when they approach nearer to us in their perigees and perihelions they often descend below the orbs of Mars and the inferior planets.

The near approach of the comets is farther confirmed from the light of their heads; for the light of a celestial body, illuminated by the sun, and receding to remote parts, is diminished in the quadruplicate proportion of the distance; to wit, in one duplicate proportion, on account of the increase of the distance from the sun, and in another duplicate proportion, on account of the decrease of the apparent diameter. Wherefore if both the quantity of light and the apparent diameter of a comet are given, its distance will be also given, by taking the distance of the comet to the distance of a planet in the direct proportion of their diameters and the reciprocal subduplicate proportion of their lights. Thus, in the comet of the year 1682, Mr. *Flamsted* observed with a telescope of 16 feet, and measured with a micrometer, the least diameter of its head, 2' 00"; but the nucleus or star in the middle of the head scarcely amounted to the tenth part of this measure; and therefore its diameter was only 11" or 12"; but in the light and splendor of its head it surpassed that of the comet in the year 1680, and might be compared with the stars of the first or second magnitude. Let us suppose that Saturn with its ring was about four times more lucid; and because the light of the ring was almost equal to the light of the globe within, and the apparent diameter of the globe is about 21", and therefore the united light of both globe and ring would be equal to the light of a globe whose diameter is 30", it follows that the distance of the comet was to the distance of Saturn as 1 to $\sqrt{4}$ inversely, and 12" to 30 directly; that is, as 24 to 30, or 4 to 5. Again; the comet in the month of *April* 1665, as *Hevelius* informs us, excelled almost all the fixed stars in splendor, and even Saturn itself, as being of a much more vivid colour; for this comet was more lucid than that other which had appeared about the end of the

preceding year, and had been compared to the stars of the first magnitude. The diameter of its head was about 6'; but the nucleus, compared with the planets by means of a telescope, was plainly less than Jupiter; and sometimes judged less, sometimes judged equal, to the globe of Saturn within the ring. Since, then, the diameters of the heads of the comets seldom exceed 8' or 12', and the diameter of the nucleus or central star is but about a tenth or perhaps fifteenth part of the diameter of the head, it appears that these stars are generally of about the same apparent magnitude with the planets. But in regard that their light may be often compared with the light of Saturn, yea, and sometimes exceeds it, it is evident that all comets in their perihelions must either be placed below or not far above Saturn; and they are much mistaken who remove them almost as far as the fixed stars; for if it was so, the comets could receive no more light from our sun than our planets do from the fixed stars.

So far we have gone, without considering the obscuration which comets suffer from that plenty of thick smoke which encompasseth their heads, and through which the heads always shew dull, as through a cloud; for by how much the more a body is obscured by this smoke, by so much the more near it must be allowed to come to the sun, that it may vie with the planets in the quantity of light which it reflects. Whence it is probable that the comets descend far below the orb of Saturn, as we proved before from their parallax. But, above all, the thing is evinced from their tails, which must be owing either to the sun's light reflected by a smoke arising from them, and dispersing itself through the aether, or to the light of their own heads. In the former case, we must shorten the distance of the comets, lest we be obliged to allow that the smoke arising from their heads is propagated through such a vast extent of space, and with such a velocity and expansion as will seem altogether incredible; in the latter ease, the whole light of both head and tail is to be ascribed to the central nucleus. But, then, if we suppose all this light to be united and condensed within the disk of the nucleus, certainly the nucleus will by far exceed Jupiter itself in splendor, especially when it emits a very large and lucid tail. If, therefore, under a less apparent diameter, it reflects more light, it must be much more illuminated by the sun, and therefore much nearer to it; and the same argument will bring down the heads of comets sometimes within the orb of Venus, viz., when, being hid under the sun's rays, they emit such huge and splendid tails, like beams of fire, as sometimes they do; for if all that light was supposed to be gathered together into one star, it would sometimes exceed not one Venus only, but a great many such united into one.

Lastly; the same thing is inferred from the light of the heads, which increases in the recess of the comets from the earth towards the sun, and decreases in their return from the sun towards the earth; for so the comet of the year 1665 (by the observations of *Hevelius*), from the time that it was first seen, was always losing of its apparent

motion, and therefore had already passed its perigee; but yet the splendor of its head was daily increasing, till, being hid under the sun's rays, the comet ceased to appear. The comet of the year 1683 (by the observations of the same *Hevelius*), about the end of *July*, when it first appeared, moved at a very slow rate, advancing only about 40 or 45 minutes in its orb in a day's time; but from that time its diurnal motion was continually upon the increase, till *September* 4, when it arose to about 5 degrees; and therefore, in all this interval of time, the comet was approaching to the earth. Which is likewise proved from the diameter of its head, measured with a micrometer: for, *August* 6, *Hevelius* found it only 6' 05", including the coma, which, *September* 2, he observed to be 9' 07", and therefore its head appeared far less about the beginning than towards the end of the motion; though about the beginning, because nearer to the sun, it appeared far more lucid than towards the end, as the same *Hevelius* declares. Wherefore in all this interval of time, on account of its recess from the sun, it decreases in splendor, notwithstanding its access towards the earth. The comet of the year 1618, about the middle of *December*, and that of the year 1680, about the end of the same month, did both move with their greatest velocity, and were therefore then in their perigees; but the greatest splendor of their heads was seen two weeks before, when they had just got clear of the sun's rays; and the greatest splendor of their tails a little more early, when yet nearer to the sun. The head of the former comet (according to the observations of *Cysatus*), *December* 1, appeared greater than the stars of the first magnitude; and, *December* 16 (then in the perigee), it was but little diminished in magnitude, but in the splendor and brightness of its light a great deal. *January* 7, *Kepler*, being uncertain about the head, left off observing. *December* 12, the head of the latter comet was seen and observed by Mr. *Flamsted*, when but 9 degrees distant from the sun; which is scarcely to be done in a star of the third magnitude. *December* 15 and 17, it appeared as a star of the third magnitude, its lustre being diminished by the brightness of the clouds near the setting sun. *December* 26, when it moved with the greatest velocity, being almost in its perigee, it was less than the month of *Pegasus*, a star of the third magnitude. *January* 3, it appeared as a star of the fourth. *January* 9, as one of the fifth. *January* 13, it was hid by the splendor of the moon, then in her increase. *January* 25, it was scarcely equal to the stars of the seventh magnitude. If we compare equal intervals of time on one side and on the other from the perigee, we shall find that the head of the comet, which at both intervals of time was far, but yet equally, removed from the earth, and should have therefore shone with equal splendor, appeared brightest on the side of the perigee towards the sun, and disappeared on the other. Therefore, from the great difference of light in the one situation and in the other, we conclude the great vicinity of the sun and cornet in the former; for the light of comets uses to be regular, and to appear greatest when the heads move fastest, and are therefore in their perigees; excepting in so far as it is increased by their nearness to the sun.

Cor. 1. Therefore the comets shine by the sun's light, which they reflect.

Cor. 2. From what has been said, we may likewise understand why comets are so frequently seen in that hemisphere in which the sun is, and so seldom in the other. If they were visible in the regions far above Saturn, they would appear more frequently in the parts opposite to the sun; for such as were in those parts would be nearer to the earth, whereas the presence of the sun must obscure and hide those that appear in the hemisphere in which he is. Yet, looking over the history of comets, I find that four or five times more have been seen in the hemisphere towards the sun than in the opposite hemisphere; besides, without doubt, not a few, which have been hid by the light of the sun: for comets descending into our parts neither emit tails nor are so well illuminated by the sun, as to discover themselves to our naked eyes, until they are come nearer to us than Jupiter. But the far greater part of that spherical space, which is described about the sun with so small an interval, lies on that side of the earth which regards the sun; and the comets in that greater part are commonly more strongly illuminated, as being for the most part nearer to the sun.

Cor. 3. Hence also it is evident that the celestial spaces are void of resistance; for though the comets are carried in oblique paths, and sometimes contrary to the course of the planets, yet they move every way with the greatest freedom, and preserve their motions for an exceeding long time, even where contrary to the course of the planets. I am out in my judgment if they are not a sort of planets revolving in orbits returning into themselves with a perpetual motion; for, as to what some writers contend, that they are no other than meteors, led into this opinion by the perpetual changes that happen to their heads, it seems to have no foundation; for the heads of comets are encompassed with huge atmospheres, and the lowermost parts of these atmospheres must be the densest; and therefore it is in the clouds only, not in the bodies of the comets themselves, that these changes are seen. Thus the earth, if it was viewed from the planets, would, without all doubt, shine by the light of its cloud and the solid body would scarcely appear through the surrounding clouds. Thus also the belts of Jupiter are formed in the clouds of that planet, for they change their position one to another, and the solid body of Jupiter is hardly to be seen through them; and much more must the bodies of comets be hid under their atmospheres, which are both deeper and thicker.

PROPOSITION XL. THEOREM XX.

That the comets move in some of the conic sections, having their foci in the centre of the sun; and by radii drawn to the sun describe areas proportional to the times.

This proposition appears from Cor. 1, Prop. XIII, Book I, compared with Prop. VIII, XII, and XIII, Book III.

COR. 1. Hence if comets are revolved in orbits returning into themselves, those orbits will be ellipses; and their periodic times be to the periodic times of the planets in the sesquiplicate proportion of their principal axes. And therefore the comets, which for the most part of their course are higher than the planets, and upon that account describe orbits with greater axes, will require a longer time to finish their revolutions. Thus if the axis of a comet's orbit was four times greater than the axis of the orbit of Saturn, the time of the revolution of the comet would be to the time of the revolution of Saturn, that is, to 30 years, as $4 \sqrt{4}$ (or 8) to 1, and would therefore be 240 years.

COR. 2. But their orbits will be so near to parabolas, that parabolas may be used for them without sensible error.

COR. 3. And, therefore, by Cor. 7, Prop. XVI, Book I, the velocity of every comet will always be to the velocity of any planet, supposed to be revolved at the same distance in a circle about the sun, nearly in the subduplicate proportion of double the distance of the planet from the centre of the sun to the distance of the comet from the sun's centre, very nearly. Let us suppose the radius of the *orbis magnus*, or the greatest semi-diameter of the ellipsis which the earth describes, to consist of 100000000 parts; and then the earth by its mean diurnal motion will describe 1720212 of those parts, and $71675^{1}/_{2}$, by its horary motion. And therefore the comet, at the same mean distance of the earth from the sun, with a velocity which is to the velocity of the earth as $\sqrt{2}$ to 1, would by its diurnal motion describe 2432747 parts, and $101364^{1}/_{2}$ parts by its horary motion. But at greater or less distances both the diurnal and horary motion will be to this diurnal and horary motion in the reciprocal subduplicate proportion of the distances, and is therefore given.

COR. 4. Wherefore if the *latus rectum* of the parabola is quadruple of the radius of the *orbis magnus*, and the square of that radius is supposed to consist of 100000000 parts, the area which the comet will daily describe by a radius drawn to the sun will be $1216373^{1}/_{2}$ parts, and the horary area will be $50682^{1}/_{4}$ parts. But, if the *latus rectum* is greater or less in any proportion, the diurnal and horary area will be less or greater in the subduplicate of the same proportion reciprocally.

LEMMA V.

TO FIND A CURVE LINE OF THE PARABOLIC KIND WHICH SHALL PASS THROUGH ANY GIVEN NUMBER OF POINTS.

Let those points be A, B, C, D, E, F, &c., and from the same to any right line HN, given in position, let fall as many perpendiculars AH, BI, CK, DL, EM, FN, &c.

$$b \qquad 2\,b \qquad 3\,b \qquad 4b \qquad 5b$$
$$c \qquad 2\,c \qquad 3c \qquad 4c$$
$$d \qquad 2\,d \qquad 3\,d$$
$$e \qquad 2\,e$$
$$f$$

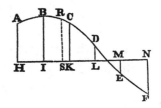

CASE 1. If HI, IK, KL, &c., the intervals of the points H, I, K, L, M &c., are equal, take b, $2b$, $3b$, $4b$, $5b$, &c., the first differences of the perpendiculars AH, BI, CK, &c.; their second differences c, $2c$, $3c$, $4c$, &c.; their third, d, $2d$, $3d$, &c, that is to say, so as AH − BI may be = b, BI − CK = $2b$, CK − DL = $3b$, DL + EM = $4b$, − EM + FN = $5b$, &c.; then $b − 2b = c$, &c., and so on to the last difference, which is here f. Then, erecting any perpendicular RS, which may be considered as an ordinate of the curve required, in order to find the length of this ordinate, suppose the intervals HI, IK, KL, LK &c, to be units, and let AH = a, − HS = p, $^{1}/_{2}\,p$ into − IS = q, $^{1}/_{3}\,q$ into + SK = r, $^{1}/_{4}\,r$ into + SL = s, $^{1}/_{5}\,s$ into + SM = t; proceeding, to wit, to ME, the last perpendicular but one, and prefixing negative signs before the terms HS, IS, &c., which lie from S towards A; and affirmative signs before the terms SK, SL, &c., which lie on the other side of the point S; and, observing well the signs, RS will be = $a + bp + rq + dr + es + ft$, + &c.

CASE 2. But if HI, IK, &c., the intervals of the points H, I, K, L, &c., are unequal, take b, $2b$, $3b$, $4b$, $5b$, &c., the first differences of the perpendiculars AH, BI, CK, &c., divided by the intervals between those perpendiculars; c, $2c$, $3c$, $4c$, &c., their second differences, divided by the intervals between every two; d, $2d$, $3d$, &c., their third differences, divided by the intervals between every three; e, $2e$, &c., their fourth differences, divided by the intervals between every four; and so forth; that is, in such manner, that b may be $\frac{AH-BI}{HI}$, $2b = \frac{BI-CK}{IK}$, $3b = \frac{CK-DL}{KL}$, &c., then $c = \frac{b-2b}{HK}$, $2c = \frac{2b-3b}{IL}$, $3c = \frac{3b-4b}{KM}$, &c., then $d = \frac{c-2c}{HL}$, $2d = \frac{2c-3c}{IM}$, &c. And those differences being found, let AH = a, − HS = p, p into − IS = q, q into + SK = r, r into + SL = s, s into + SM = t; proceeding, to wit, to ME, the last perpendicular but one; and the ordinate RS will be = $a + bp + cq + dr + es + ft$, + &c.

COR. Hence the areas of all curves may be nearly found; for if some number of points of the curve to be squared are found, and a parabola be supposed to be drawn through those points, the area of this parabola will be nearly the same with the area of the curvilinear figure proposed to be squared: but the parabola can be always squared geometrically by methods vulgarly known.

LEMMA VI.

CERTAIN OBSERVED PLACES OF A COMET BEING GIVEN, TO FIND THE PLACE OF THE SAME TO ANY INTERMEDIATE GIVEN TIME.

Let HI, IK, KL, LM (in the preceding Fig.), represent the times between the observations; HA, IB, KC, LD, ME, five observed longitudes of the comet; and HS the given time between the first observation and the longitude required. Then if a regular curve ABCDE is supposed to be drawn through the points A, B, C, D, E, and the ordinate RS is found out by the preceding lemma, RS will be the longitude required.

After the same method, from five observed latitudes, we may find the latitude to a given time.

If the differences of the observed longitudes are small, suppose of 4 or 5 degrees, three or four observations will be sufficient to find a new longitude and latitude; but if the differences are greater, as of 10 or 20 degrees, five observations ought to be used.

LEMMA VII.

THROUGH A GIVEN POINT P TO DRAW A RIGHT LINE BC, WHOSE PARTS PB, PC, CUT OFF BY TWO RIGHT LINES AB, AC, GIVEN IN POSITION, MAY BE ONE TO THE OTHER IN A GIVEN PROPORTION.

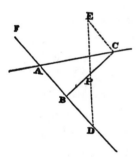

From the given point P suppose any right line PD to be drawn to either of the right lines given, as AB; and produce the same towards AC, the other given right line, as far as *r*, so as PE may be to PD in the given proportion. Let EC be parallel to AD. Draw CPB, and PC will be to PB as PE to PD.   Q.E.F.

LEMMA VIII.

LET ABC BE A PARABOLA, HAVING ITS FOCUS IN S. BY THE CHORD AC BISECTED IN I CUT OFF THE SEGMENT ABCI, WHOSE DIAMETER IS Iμ AND VERTEX μ. IN Iμ PRODUCED TAKE μO EQUAL TO ONE HALF OF Iμ. JOIN OS, AND PRODUCE IT TO ξ, SO AS Sξ MAY BE EQUAL TO 2SO. NOW,

SUPPOSING A COMET TO REVOLVE IN THE ARC CBA, DRAW
ξB, CUTTING AC IN E; I SAY, THE POINT E WILL CUT OFF
FROM THE CHORD AC THE SEGMENT AE, NEARLY PROPOR-
TIONAL TO THE TIME.

For, if we join EO, cutting the parabolic arc ABC in Y, and draw μX touching the
same arc in the vertex μ, and meeting EO in X, the curvilinear area AEXμA will be to
the curvilinear area ACYμA as AE to AC; and, therefore, since the triangle ASE is to
the triangle ASC in the same proportion, the whole area ASEXμA will be to the whole

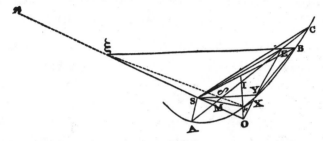

area ASCYμA as AE to AC. But, because ξO is to SO as 3 to 1, and EO to XO in the
same proportion, SK will be parallel to EB; and, therefore, joining BX, the triangle
SEB will be equal to the triangle XEB. Wherefore if to the area ASEXμA we add the
triangle EXB, and from the sum subduct the triangle SEB, there will remain the area
ASBXμA, equal to the area ASEXμA, and therefore in proportion to the area ASCYμA
as AE to AC. But the area ASBYμA is nearly equal to the area ASBXμA; and this area
ASBYμA is to the area ASCYμA as the time of description of the arc AB to the time
of description of the whole arc AC; and, therefore, AE is to AC nearly in the proportion of the times.   Q.E.D.

Cor. When the point B falls upon the vertex μ of the parabola, AE is to AC accurately in the proportion of the times.

SCHOLIUM.

If we join με cutting AC in δ, and in it take ξn in proportion to μB as 27MI to
16Mμ, and draw Bn, this Bn will cut the chord AC, in the proportion of the times,
more accurately than before; but the point n is to be taken beyond or on this side the
point ξ, according as the point B is more or less distant from the principal vertex of
the parabola than the point μ.

LEMMA IX.

THE RIGHT LINES Iμ AND μM, AND THE LENGTH $\frac{AI^2}{4S\mu}$ ARE
EQUAL AMONG THEMSELVES.

For 4Sμ is the *latus rectum* of the parabola belonging to the vertex μ.

LEMMA X.

PRODUCE Sμ TO N AND P, SO AS μN MAY BE ONE THIRD OF
μI, AND SP MAY BE TO SN AS SN TO Sμ; AND IN THE TIME
THAT A COMET WOULD DESCRIBE THE ARC AμC, IF IT WAS
SUPPOSED TO MOVE ALWAYS FORWARDS WITH THE VELOCITY
WHICH IT HATH IN A HEIGHT EQUAL TO SP, IT WOULD
DESCRIBE A LENGTH EQUAL TO THE CHORD AC.

For if the comet with the velocity which it hath in it was in the said time supposed to move uniformly forward in the right line which touches the parabola in μ, the area which it

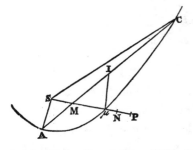

would describe by a radius drawn to the point S would be equal to the parabolic area ASCμA; and therefore the space contained under the length described in the tangent and the length Sμ would be to the space contained under the lengths AC and SM as the area ASCμA to the triangle ASC, that is, as SN to SM. Wherefore AC is to the length described in the tangent as Sμ to SN. But since the velocity of the comet in the height SP (by Cor. 6, Prop. XVI., Book I) is to the velocity of the same in the height Sμ in the reciprocal subduplicate proportion of SP to Sμ, that is, in the proportion of Sμ to SN, the length described with this velocity will be to the length in the same time described in the tangent as Sμ to SN, Wherefore since AC, and the length described with this new velocity, are in the same proportion to the length described in the tangent, they must be equal betwixt themselves.   Q.E.D.

COR. Therefore a comet, with that velocity which it both in the height Sμ + $^2/_3$Iμ, would in the same time describe the chord AC nearly.

LEMMA XI.

IF A COMET VOID OF ALL MOTION WAS LET FALL FROM THE
HEIGHT SN, OR Sμ+ $^1/_3$ Iμ, TOWARDS THE SUN, AND WAS
STILL IMPELLED TO THE SUN BY THE SAME FORCE UNIFORM-
LY CONTINUED BY WHICH IT WAS IMPELLED AT FIRST, THE
SAME, IN ONE HALF OF THAT TIME IN WHICH IT MIGHT
DESCRIBE THE ARC AC IN ITS OWN ORBIT, WOULD IN
DESCENDING DESCRIBE A SPACE EQUAL TO THE LENGTH Iμ.

For in the same time that the comet would require to describe the parabolic arc AC, it would (by the last Lemma), with that velocity which it hath in the height SP, describe the chord AC: and, therefore (by Cor. 7, Prop. XVI, Book I), if it was in the

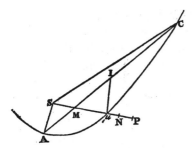

same time supposed to revolve by the force of its own gravity in a circle whose semi-diameter was SP, it would describe an arc of that circle, the length of which would be to the chord of the parabolic arc AC in the subduplicate proportion of 1 to 2. Wherefore if with that weight, which in the height SP it hath towards the sun, it should fall from that height towards the sun, it would

(by Cor. 9, Prop. XVI, Book I) in half the said time describe a space equal to the square of half the said chord applied to quadruple the height SP, that it would describe the space $\frac{AI^2}{4SP}$. But since the weight of the comet towards the sun in the height SN is

to the weight of the same towards the sun in the height SP as SP to Sμ, the comet, by the weight which it both in the height SN, in falling from that height towards the sun, would in the same time describe the space $\frac{AI^2}{4S\mu}$; that is, a space equal to the

length Iμ or μM.   Q.E.D.

PROPOSITION XLI. PROBLEM XXI.

FROM THREE OBSERVATIONS GIVEN TO DETERMINE THE ORBIT OF A COMET MOVING IN A PARABOLA.

This being a Problem of very great difficulty, I tried many methods of resolving it; and several of those Problems, the composition whereof I have given in the first Book, tended to this purpose. But afterwards I contrived the following solution, which is something more simple.

Select three observations distant one from another by intervals of time nearly equal; but let that interval of time in which the comet moves more slowly be somewhat

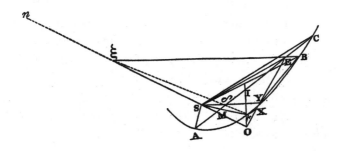

greater than the other; so, to wit, that the difference of the times may be to the sum of the times as the sum of the times to about 600 days; or that the point E may fall upon M nearly, and may err therefrom rather towards I than towards A. If such direct observations are not at hand, a new place of the comet must be found, by Lem. VI.

Let S represent the sun; T, t, τ, three places of the earth in the *orbis magnus*; TA, tB, τC, three observed longitudes of the comet; V the time between the first observation and the second; W the time between the second and the third, X the length which

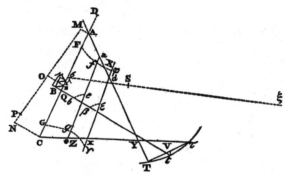

in the whole time V + W the comet might describe with that velocity which it hath in the mean distance of the earth from the sun, which length is to be found by Cor. 3, Prop. XL, Book III; and tV a perpendicular upon the chord Tτ. In the mean observed longitude tB take at pleasure the point B, for the place of the comet in the plane of the ecliptic; and from thence, towards the sun S, draw the line BE, which may be to the perpendicular tV as the content under SB and St^2 to the cube of the hypothenuse of the right angled triangle, whose sides are SB, and the tangent of the latitude of the comet in the second observation to the radius tB. And through the point F, (by Lemma VII) draw the right line AEC, whose parts AE and EC, terminating in the right lines TA and τC, may be one to the other as the times V and W: then A and C will be nearly the places of the comet in the place of the ecliptic in the first and third observations, if B was its place rightly assumed in the second.

Upon AC, bisected in I, erect the perpendicular Ii. Through B draw the obscure line Bi parallel to AC. Join the obscure line Si, cutting AC in λ, and complete the parallelogram iI $\lambda\mu$. Take Iσ equal to 3Iλ; and through the sun S draw the obscure line $\sigma\xi$ equal to 3Sσ + 3$i\lambda$. Then, cancelling the letters A, E, C, I, from the point B towards the point ξ, draw the new obscure line BE, which may be to the former BE in the duplicate proportion of the distance BS to the quantity Sμ + $^1/_3$ $i\lambda$. And through the point E draw again the right line AEC by the same rule as before; that is, so as its parts AE and EC may be one to the other as the times V and W between the observations. Thus A and C will be the places of the comet more accurately.

Upon AC, bisected in I, erect the perpendiculars AM, CN, IO, of which AM and CN may be the tangents of the latitudes in the first and third observations, to the radii TA and τC. Join MN, cutting IO in O. Draw the rectangular parallelogram $i\Lambda\mu$, as before. In IA produced take ID equal to $S\mu + {}^2/_3\lambda$. Then in MN, towards N, take MP, which may be to the above found length X in the subduplicate proportion of the mean distance of the earth from the sun (or of the semi-diameter of the *orbis magnus*) to the distance OD. If the point P fall upon the point N; A, B, and C, will be three places of the comet, through which its orbit is to be described in the plane of the ecliptic. But if the point P falls not upon the point N, in the right line AC take CG equal to NP, so as the points G and P may lie on the same side of the line NC.

By the same method as the points E, A, C, G, were found from the assumed point B, from other points b and (ß assumed at pleasure, find out the new points e, a, c, g, and ϵ, a, κ, γ. Then through G, g, and γ, draw the circumference of a circle G$g\gamma$, cutting the right line τC in Z: and Z will be one place of the comet in the plane of the ecliptic. And in AC, ac, $a\kappa$, taking AF, af, $a\phi$, equal respectively to CG, cg, $\kappa\gamma$; through the points F, f, and ϕ, draw the circumference of a circle F$f\phi$, cutting the right line AT in X; and the point X will be another place of the comet in the plane of the ecliptic. And at the points X and Z, erecting the tangents of the latitudes of the comet to the radii TX and τZ, two places of the comet in its own orbit will be determined. Lastly, if (by Prop. XIX, Book I) to the focus S a parabola is described passing through those two places, this parabola will be the orbit of the comet.   Q.E.I.

The demonstration of this construction follows from the preceding Lemmas, because the right line AC is cut in E in the proportion of the times, by Lem. VII., as it ought to be, by Lem. VIII.; and BE, by Lem. XI., is a portion of the right line BS or Bξ in the plane of the ecliptic, intercepted between the arc ABC and the chord AEC; and MP (by Cor. Lem. X.) is the length of the chord of that arc, which the comet should describe in its proper orbit between the first and third observation, and therefore is equal to MN, providing B is a true place of the comet in the plane of the ecliptic.

But it will be convenient to assume the points B, b, β, not at random, but nearly true. If the angle AQt, at which the projection of the orbit in the plane of the ecliptic cuts the right line tB, is rudely known, at that angle with Bt draw the obscure line AC, which may be to $^4/_3$Tτ in the subduplicate proportion of SQ to St; and, drawing the right line SEB so as its part EB may be equal to the length Vt, the point B will be determined, which we are to use for the first time. Then, cancelling the right line AC, and drawing anew AC according to the preceding construction, and, moreover, finding the length MP, in tB take the point b, by this rule, that, if TA and τC intersect each other in Y, the distance Yb may be to the distance YB in a proportion compounded of the

proportion of MP to MN, and the subduplicate proportion of SB to S*b*. And by the same method you may find the third point β, if you please to repeat the operation the third time; but if this method is followed, two operations generally will be sufficient; for if the distance B*b* happens to be very small, after the points F, *f*, and G, *g*, are found, draw the right lines F*f* and G*g*, and they will out TA and τC in the points required, X and Z.

EXAMPLE.

Let the comet of the year 1680 be proposed. The following table shews the motion thereof, as observed by *Flamsted*, and calculated afterwards by him from his observations, and corrected by Dr. *Halley* from the same observations.

	Time.		Sun's Longitude.	Comet's	
	Appar.	True		Longitude.	Lat. N.
	h. "	h. ' "	o ' "	o ' "	o ' "
1680, *Dec.* 12	4.46	4.46. 0	♉ 1.51.23	♉ 6.32.30	8.28. 0
21	6.32 1/2	6.36.59	11.06.44	♒ 5.08.12	21.42.13
24	6.12	6.17.52	14.09.26	18.49.23	25.23. 5
26	5.14	5.20.44	16.09.22	28.24.13	27.00.52
29	7.55	8.03.02	19.19.42	♓ 13.10.41	28.09.58
30	8.02	8.10.26	20.21.09	17.38.20	28.11.53
1681, *Jan.* 5	5.51	6.01.38	26.22.18	♈ 8.48.53	26.15. 7
9	6.49	7.00.53	♒ 0.29.02	18.44.04	24.11.56
10	5.54	6.06.10	1.27.43	20.40.50	23.43.52
13	6.56	7.08.55	4.33.20	25.59.48	22.17.28
25	7.44	7.58.42	16.45.36	♉ 9.35. 0	17.51.11
30	8.07	8.21.53	21.49.58	13.19.51	16.42.18
Feb. 2	6.20	6.34.51	24.46.59	15.13.53	16.04. 1
5	6.50	7.04.41	27.49.51	16.59.06	15.27. 3

To these you may add some observations of mine.

	Ap.	Comet's	
	Time	Longitude	Lat. N.
	h. '	o ' "	o ' "
1681, *Feb.* 25	8.30	♉ 26.18.35	12.46.46
27	8.15	27.04.30	12.36.12
Mar. 1	11.0	27.52.42	12.23.40
2	8.0	28.12.48	12.19.38
5	11.30	29.18. 0	12.03.16
7	9.30	♊ 0. 4. 0	11.57. 0
9	8.30	0.43. 4	11.45.52

These observations were made by a telescope of 7 feet, with a micrometer and threads placed in the focus of the telescope; by which instruments we determined the positions both of the fixed stars among themselves, and of the comet in respect of the fixed stars. Let A represent the star of the fourth magnitude in the left heel of *Perseus* (*Bayer's o*), B the following star of the third magnitude in the left foot (*Bayer's ζ*), C a star of the sixth magnitude (*Bayer's n*) in the heel of the same foot, and D, E, F, G, H, I, K, L, M, N, O, Z, α, β, γ, δ, other smaller stars in the same foot; and let p, P, Q, R, S, T, V, X, represent the places of the comet in the observations above set down; and, reckoning the distance AB of $80^{7}/_{12}$ parts, AC was $52^{1}/_{4}$ of those parts; BC, $58^{5}/_{6}$; AD, $57^{5}/_{12}$; BD, $82^{6}/_{11}$; CD, $23\ ^{2}/_{3}$; AE, $29^{4}/_{7}$; CE, $57^{1}/_{2}$; DE, $49^{11}/_{12}$; AI, $27^{7}/_{12}$; BI, $52^{1}/_{6}$; CI, $36^{7}/_{12}$; DI, $53^{5}/_{11}$; AK, $38^{2}/_{3}$; BK, 43; CK, $31^{5}/_{9}$; FK, 29; FB, 23; FC, $36^{1}/_{4}$; AH, $18^{6}/_{7}$; DH, $50^{7}/_{8}$; BN, $46^{5}/_{12}$; CN, $31^{1}/_{3}$; BL, $45^{5}/_{12}$; NL, $31^{5}/_{7}$. HO was to HI as 7 to 6, and, produced, did pass between the stars D and E, so as the distance of the star D from this right line was $^{1}/_{6}$CD. LM was to LN as 2 to 9, and, produced, did pass through the star H. Thus were the positions of the fixed stars determined in respect of one another.

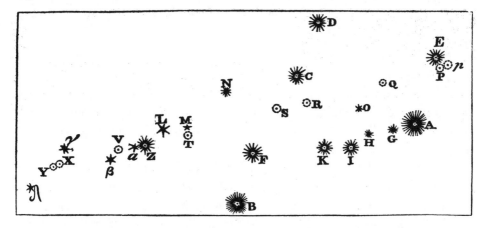

Mr. *Pound* has since observed a second time the positions of these fixed stars amongst themselves, and collected their longitudes and latitudes according to the following table.

The fixed stars.		Their Longitudes	Latitude North.	The fixed stars.		Their Longitudes	Latitude North.
		° ′ ″				° ′ ″	
A	♉	26.41.50	12. 8.36	L	♉	29.33.34	12. 7.48
B		28.40.23	11.17.54	M		29.18.51	12. 7.20
C		27.58.30	12.40.25	N		28.48.29	12.31. 9
E		26.27.17	12.52. 7	Z		29.44.48	11.57.13
F		28,28.37	11.52.22	a		29.52. 3	11.55.48
G		26.56. 8	12. 4.58	ß	♊	0. 8.23	11.48.56
H		27.11.45	12. 2. 1	?		0.40.10	11.55.18
I		27.25. 2	11.53.11	d		1. 3.20	11.30.42
K		27.42. 7	11.53.26				

The positions of the comet to these fixed stars were observed to be as follow:

Friday, *February* 25, O.S. at $8^1/_2{}^h$. P.M. the distance of the comet in p from the star E was less than $3/_{13}$AE, and greater than $1/_5$AE, and therefore nearly equal to $3/_{14}$AE; and the angle ApE was a little obtuse, but almost right. For from A, letting fall a perpendicular on pE, the distance of the comet from that perpendicular was $1/_5p$E.

The same night, at $9^1/_2{}^h$., the distance of the comet in P from the star E was greater than $\frac{1}{4\frac{1}{2}}$AE, and less than $\frac{1}{5\frac{1}{4}}$AE, and therefore nearly equal to $\frac{1}{4\frac{7}{8}}$ of AE, or

$8/_{39}$AE. But the distance of the comet from the perpendicular let fall from the star A upon the right line PE was $4/_5$PE.

Sunday, *February* 27, $8^1/_4{}^h$. P.M. the distance of the comet in Q from the star O was equal to the distance of the stars O and H; and the right line QO produced passed between the stars K and B. I could not, by reason of intervening clouds, determine the position of the star to greater accuracy.

Tuesday, *March* 1, 11^h. P.M. the comet in R lay exactly in a line between the stars K and C, so as the part CR of the right line CRK was a little greater than $1/_3$CK, and a little less than $1/_3$CK + $1/_8$CR, and therefore = $1/_3$CK + $1/_{16}$CR, or $16/_{45}$CK.

Wednesday, *March* 2, 8^h. P.M. the distance of the comet in S from the star C was nearly $4/_9$FC; the distance of the star F from the right line CS produced was $1/_{24}$FC; and the distance of the star B from the same right line was five times greater than the distance of the star F; and the right line NS produced passed between the stars H and I five or six times nearer to the star H than to the star I.

Saturday, *March* 5, $11^1/_2$h. P.M. when the comet was in T, the right line MT was equal to $1/_2$ML, and the right line LT produced passed between B and F four or five times nearer to F than to B, cutting off from BF a fifth or sixth part thereof towards F: and MT produced passed on the outside of the space BF towards the star B four times nearer to the star B than to the star F. M was a very small

star, scarcely to be seen by the telescope; but the star L was greater, and of about the eighth magnitude.

Monday, March 7, $9^1/_2$h. P.M. the comet being in V, the right line Vα produced did pass between B and F, cutting off, from BF towards F, $1/_{10}$ of BF, and was to the right line Vβ as 5 to 4. And the distance of the comet from the right line $\alpha\beta$ was $1/_2$ Vβ.

Wednesday, March 9, $8^1/_2$h. P.M. the comet being in X, the right line γX was equal to $1/_4\gamma\delta$; and the perpendicular let fall from the star δ upon the right γX was $2/_3$ of $\gamma\delta$.

The same night, at 12^h. the comet being in Y, the right line γY was equal to $1/_3$ of $\gamma\delta$, or a little less, as perhaps $5/_{16}$ of $\gamma\delta$; and a perpendicular let fall from the star δ on the right line γY was equal to about $1/_6$ or $1/_7\gamma\delta$. But the comet being then extremely near the horizon, was scarcely discernible, and therefore its place could not be determined with that certainty as in the foregoing observations.

From these observations, by constructions of figures and calculations, I deduced the longitudes and latitudes of the comet; and Mr. Pound, by correcting the places of the fixed stars, hath determined more correctly the places of the comet, which correct places are set down above. Though my micrometer was none of the best, yet the errors in longitude and latitude (as derived from my observations) scarcely exceed one minute. The comet (according to my observations), about the end of its motion, began to decline sensibly towards the north, from the parallel which it described about the end of *February*.

Now, in order to determine the orbit of the comet out of the observations above described, I selected those three which *Flamsted* made, *Dec.* 21, *Jan.* 5, and *Jan.* 25; from which I found St of 9842,1 parts, and Vt of 455, such as the semi-diameter of the *orbis magnus* contains 10000. Then for the first observation, assuming tB of 5657 of those parts, I found SB 9747, BE for the first time 412, Sμ 9503, $i\lambda$ 413, BE for the second time 421, OD 10186, X 8528,4, PM 8450, MN 8475, NP 25; from whence, by the second operation, I collected the distance tb 5640; and by this operation I at last deduced the distances TX 4775 and τZ 11322. From which, limiting the orbit, I found its descending node in ♋, and ascending node in ♑ 1° 53'; the inclination of its plane to the plane of the ecliptic 61° 20 $1/_3$, the vertex thereof (or the perihelion of the comet) distant from the node 8° 39', and in ♐ 27° 43', with latitude 7° 34' south; its *latus rectum* 236,8; and the diurnal area described by a radius drawn to the sun 93585, supposing the square of the semi-diameter of the *orbis magnus* 100000000; that the comet in this orbit moved directly according to the order of the signs, and on *Dec.* 8^d. 00^h. 04' P.M. was in the vertex or perihelion of its orbit. All which I determined by scale and compass, and the chords of angles, taken from the table of natural sines, in a pretty large figure, in which, to wit, the radius of the *orbis magnus* (consisting of 10000 parts) was equal to $16^1/_3$ inches of an English foot.

Lastly, in order to discover whether the comet did truly move in the orbit so determined, I investigated its places in this orbit partly by arithmetical operations, and partly by scale and compass, to the times of some of the observations, as may be seen in the following table:—

The Comet's							
	Dist. from sun.	Longitude computed.	Latitude computed.	Longitude observed.	Latitude observed.	Dif. Lo.	Dif. Lat.
Dec. 12	2792	♉ 6°.32'	8°18½	♉ 6°.31½	8°.26	+ 1	− 7½
29	8403	♓ 13.13⅖	28.00	♓ 13.11¾	28.10 1/12	+ 2	− 10 1/12
Feb. 5	16669	♉ 17.00	15.29⅔	♉ 16.59⅞	15.27⅖	+ 0	+ 2¼
Mar. 5	21737	29.19¾	12. 4	29.20 6/7	12.3 ½	− 1	+ ½

But afterwards Dr. *Halley* did determine the orbit to a greater accuracy by an arithmetical calculus than could be done by linear descriptions; and, retaining the place of the nodes in ♋ and ♑ 1° 53', and the inclination of the plane of the orbit to the ecliptic 61° 20⅓', as well as the time of the comet's being *in perihelio, Dec.* 8^d. 00^h. 04', he found the distance of the perihelion from the ascending node measured in the comet's orbit 9° 20', and the *latus rectum* of the parabola 2430 parts, supposing the mean distance of the sun from the earth to be 100000 parts; and from these data, by an accurate arithmetical calculus, he computed the places of the comet to the times of the observations as follows:—

The Comet's						
True Time.		Dist. from the sun.	Longitude computed	Latitude computed	Errors in	
					Long.	Lat.
	d. h. ' "		° ' "	° ' "	' "	' "
Dec.	12. 4. 46.	28028	♉ 6.29.25	8.26. 0 bor.	− 3. 5	− 2. 0
	21. 6. 37.	61076	♒ 5. 6.30	21.43.20	− 1.42	+ 1. 7
	24. 6. 18.	70008	18.48.20	25.22.40	− 1.3	− 0.25
	26. 5. 20.	75576	28.22.45	27. 1.36	− 1.28	+ 0.44
	29. 8. 3.	84021	♓ 13.12.40	28.10.10	+ 1.59	+ 0.12
	30. 8. 10.	86661	17.40. 5	28.11.20	+ 1.45	− 0.33
Jan.	5. 6. 1.½	101440	♈ 8.49.49	26.15.15	+ 0.56	+ 0. 8
	9. 7. 0.	110959	18.44.36	24.12.54	+ 0.32	+ 0.58
	10. 6. 6.	113162	20.41. 0	23.44.10	+ 0.10	+ 0.18
	13. 7. 9.	120000	26. 0.21	22.17.30	+ 0.33	+ 0. 2
	25. 7. 59.	145370	♉ 9.33.40	17.57.55	− 1.10	+ 1.25
	30. 8. 22.	155303	13.17.41	16.42. 7	− 2.10	− 0.11
Feb.	2. 6. 35	160951	15.11.11	16. 4.15	− 2.42	+ 0.14
	5. 7. 4.½	166686	16.58.55	15.29.13	− 0.41	+ 2. 0
	25. 8. 4	202570	26.15.46	12.48. 0	− 2.49	+ 1.10
Mar.	5. 11. 3	216205	29.18.35	12. 5.40	+ 0.35	+ 2.14

This comet also appeared in the *November* before, and at *Coburg*, in Saxony, was observed by Mr. *Gottfried Kirch*, on the 4th of that month, on the 6th and 11th O.S.; from its positions to the nearest fixed stars observed with sufficient accuracy, sometimes with a two feet, and sometimes with a ten feet telescope; from the difference of longitudes of *Coburg* and *London*, 11°; and from the plates of the fixed stairs observed by Mr. *Pound*, Dr. *Halley* has determined the places of the comet as follows:—

Nov. 3, 17^h. 2', apparent time at *London*, the comet was in a ♌ deg. 51', with 1 deg. 17' 45" latitude north.

November 5, 15^h. 58' the comet was in ♍ 3° 23', with 1° 6' north lat.

November 10, 16^h. 31', the comet was equally distant from two stars in ♌, which are σ and τ in *Bayer*; but it had not quite touched the right line that joins them, but was very little distant from it. In *Flamsted's* catalogue this star σ was then in ♍ 14° 15', with 1 deg. 41' lat. north nearly, and τ in ♍ 17° 3$^1/_2$' with 0 deg. 34' lat. south; and the middle point between those stars was ♍ 15° 39$^1/_2$', with 0° 33$^1/_2$' lat. north. Let the distance of the comet from that right line be about 10' or 12'; and the difference of the longitude of the comet and that middle point will be 7'; and the difference of the latitude nearly 7$^1/_2$'; and thence it follows that the comet was in ♍ 15° 32', with about 26' lat. north.

The first observation from the position of the comet with respect to certain small fixed stars had all the exactness that could be desired; the second also was accurate enough. In the third observation, which was the least accurate, there might be an error of 6 or 7 minutes, but hardly greater. The longitude of the comet, as found in the first and most accurate observation, being computed in the aforesaid parabolic orbit, comes out ♌ 29° 30' 22", its latitude north 1° 25' 7", and its distance from the sun 115546.

Moreover, Dr. *Halley*, observing that a remarkable comet had appeared four times at equal intervals of 575 years (that is, in the mouth of *September* after *Julius Caesar* was killed; *An. Chr.* 531, in the consulate of *Lampadius* and *Orestes*; *An. Chr.* 1106, in the month of *February*; and at the end of the year 1680; and that with a long and remarkable tail, except when it was seen after *Caesar's* death, at which time, by reason of the inconvenient situation of the earth, the tail was not so conspicuous), set himself to find out an elliptic orbit whose greater axis should be 1382957 parts, the mean distance of the earth from the sun containing 10000 such; in which orbit a comet might revolve in 575 years; and, placing the ascending node in ♋ 2° 2', the inclination of the plane of the orbit to the plane of the ecliptic in an angle of 61° 6' 48", the perihelion of the comet in this plane in ♐ 22° 44' 25", the equal time of the perihelion *December* 7^d. 23^h. 9', the distance of the perihelion from the ascending node in the plane of the ecliptic 9° 17' 35", and its conjugate axis 18481,2, he computed the motions of the

comet in this elliptic orbit. The places of the comet, as deduced from the observations, and as arising from computation made in this orbit, may be seen in the following table.

True time.		Longitude observed	Latitude North obs.	Longitude comp.	Latitude computed	Errors in Long.	Lat.
	d. h. '	° ' "	° ' "	° ' "	° ' "	' "	' '
Nov.	3.16.47	♌ 29.51. 0	1.17.45	♌ 29.51.22	1.17.32 N	+ 0.22	– 0.13
	5.15.37	♍ 3.23. 0	1. 6. 0	♍ 3.24.32	1. 6. 9	+ 1.32	+ 0. 9
	10.16.18	15.32. 0	0.27. 0	15.33. 2	0.25. 7	+ 1. 2	–1.53
	16.17.00			≎ 8.16.45	0.53. 7 S		
	18.21.34			18.52.15	1.26.54		
	20.17. 0			28.10.36	1.53.35		
	23.17. 5			♏ 13.22.42	2.29. 0		
Dec.	12. 4.46	♑ 6.32.30	8.28. 0	♑ 6.31.20	8.29. 6 N	– 1.10	+ 1. 6
	21. 6.37	♒ 5. 8.12	21.42.13	♒ 5. 6.14	91.44.42	– 1.58	+ 2.29
	24. 6.18	18.49.23	25.23. 5	18.47.30	25.23.35	– 1.53	+ 0.30
	26. 5.21	28.24.13	27. 0.52	28.21.42	27. 2. 1	– 2.31	+ 1. 9
	29. 8. 3	♓ 13.10.41	28. 9.58	♓ 13.11.14	28.10.38	+ 0.33	+ 0.40
	30. 8.10	17.38. 0	28.11.53	17.38.27	28.11.37	+ 0. 7	– 0.16
Jan.	5. 6. 1 ½	♈ 8.48.53	26.15. 7	♈ 8.48.51	26.14.57	– 0. 2	– 0.10
	9. 7. 1	18.44. 4	24.11.56	18.43.51	24.12.17	– 0.13	+ 0.21
	10. 6. 6	20.40. 5	23.43.32	20.40.23	23.43.25	– 0.27	– 0. 7
	13. 7. 9	25.59.48	22.17.28	26. 0. 8	22.16.32	+ 0.20	– 0.56
	25. 7.59	♉ 9.35. 0	17.56.30	♉ 9.34.11	17.56. 6	– 0.49	– 0.24
	30. 8.22	13.19.51	16.42.18	13.18.28	16.40. 5	– 1.23	– 2.13
Feb.	2. 6.35	15.13.53	16. 4. 1	15.11.59	16. 2.17	– 1.54	– 1.54
	5. 7.4 ½	16.59. 6	15.27. 3	16.59.17	15.27. 0	+ 0.11	– 0. 3
	25. 8.41	26.18.35	12.46.46	26.16.59	12.45.22	– 1.36	– 1.24
Mar.	1.11.10	27.52.42	12.23.40	27.51.47	12.22.28	– 0.55	– 1.12
	5.11.39	29.18. 0	12. 3.16	29.20.11	12. 2.50	+ 2.11	– 0.26
	9. 8.38	♊ 0.43. 4	11.45.52	♊ 0.42.43	11.45.35	– 0.21	–0.17

The observations of this comet from the beginning to the end agree as perfectly with the motion of the comet in the orbit just now described as the motions of the planets do with the theories from whence they are calculated; and by this agreement plainly evince that it was one and the same comet that appeared all that time, and also that the orbit of that comet is here rightly defined.

In the foregoing table we have emitted the observations of *Nov.* 16, 18, 20, and 23, as not sufficiently accurate, for at those times several persons had observed the comet. *Nov.* 17, O.S. *Ponthaeus* and his companions, at 6ʰ. in the morning at *Rome* (that is, 5ʰ. 10' at *London*), by threads directed to the fixed stars, observed the comet in ≎ 8° 30', with latitude 0° 40' south. Their observations may be seen in a treatise which *Ponthaeus* published concerning this comet. *Cellius*, who was present, and communicated his observations in a letter to *Cassini* saw the comet at the same hour in ≎ 8° 30', with latitude 0° 30' south. It was likewise seen by *Galletius* at the

same hour at *Avignon* (that is, at 5^h. 42' morning at *London*) in ♎ 8° 30' 8° without latitude. But by the theory the comet was at that time in ♎ 8° 16' 45", and its latitude was 0° 53' 7" south.

Nov. 18, at 6^h. 30' in the morning at *Rome* (that is, at 5^h. 40' at *London*), *Ponthæus* observed the comet in ♎ 13° 30', with latitude 1° 20' south; and *Cellius* in ♎ 13° 60' with latitude 1° 00' south. But at 5^h. 30' in the morning at *Avignon*, *Galletius* saw it in ♎ 13° 00', with latitude 1° 00' south. In the University of *La Fleche*, in *France*, at 5^h. in the morning (that is, at 5^h. 9' at *London*), it was seen by *P. Ango*, in the middle between two small stars, one of which is the middle of the three which lie in a right line in the southern hand of Virgo, *Bayer's* ψ; and the other is the outmost of the wing, *Bayer's* θ. Whence the comet was then in ♎ 12° 46' with latitude 50' south. And I was informed by Dr. *Halley*, that on the same day at *Boston* in *New England*, in the latitude of $42^1/_2$ deg. at 5^h. in the morning (that is, at 9^h. 44' in the morning at *London*), the comet was seen near ♎ 14°, with latitude 1° 30' south.

Nov. 19, at $4^1/_2{}^h$. at *Cambridge*, the comet (by the observation of a young man) was distant from *Spica* ♍ about 2° towards the north west. Now the spike was at that time in ♎ 19° 23' 47", with latitude 2° 1' 59" south. The same day, at 5^h. in the morning at *Boston* in *New England*, the comet was distant from *Spica* ♍ 1°, with the difference of 40' in latitude. The same day, in the island of *Jamaica*, it was about 1° distant from *Spica* ♍. The same day, Mr. *Arthur Storer*, at the river *Patuxent*, near *Hunting Creek*, in *Maryland*, in the confines of *Virginia*, in lat. $38^1/_2$ ° at 5 in the morning (that is, at 10^h. at *London*), saw the comet above *Spica* ♍, and very nearly joined with it, the distance between them being about $3/_4$ of one deg. And from these observations compared, I conclude, that at 9^h. 44' at *London* the comet was in ♎ 18° 50', with about 1° 25' latitude south. Now by the theory the comet was at that time in ♎ 18° 52' 15", with 1° 26' 54" lat. south.

Nov. 20, *Montenari*, professor of astronomy at *Padua*, at 6^h. in the morning at *Venice* (that is, 5^h. 10' at *London*), saw the comet in ♎ 23°, with latitude 1° 30' south. The same day, at *Boston*, it was distant from *Spica* ♍ by about 4° of longitude east, and therefore was in ♎ 23° 24' nearly.

Nov. 21, *Ponthæus* and his companions, at $7^1/_4{}^h$. in the morning, observed the comet in ♎ 27° 50', with latitude 1° 16' south; *Cellius*, in ♎ 28°; *P. Ango* at 5^h. in the morning, in ♎ 27° 45'; *Montenari* in ♎ 27° 51'. The same day, in the island of *Jamaica*, it was seen near the beginning of ♏, and of about the same latitude with *Spica* ♍, that is, 2° 2'. The same day, at 5^h. morning, at *Ballasore*, in the *East Indies* (that is, at 11^h. 20' of the night preceding at *London*), the distance of the comet from ♍ was taken 7° 35' to the east. It was in a right line between the spike and the balance, and therefore was then in ♎ 26° 58', with about 1° 11' lat. south; and after 5^h. 40' (that is,

at 5^h. morning at *London*), it was in ♎ 28° 12'. with 1° 16' lat. south. Now by the theory the comet was then in ♎ 28° 10' 36", with 1° 53' 35" lat. south.

Nov. 22, the comet was seen by *Montenari* in ♍ 2° 33'; but at *Boston* in *New England*, it was found in about ♍ 3°, and with almost the same latitude as before, that is, 1° 30'. The same day, at 5^h. morning at *Ballasore*, the comet was observed in ♍ 1° 50'; and therefore at 5^h. morning at *London*, the comet was in ♍ 3° 5' nearly. The same day, at $6^1/_2{}^h$. in the morning at *London*, Dr. *Hook* observed it in about ♍ 3° 30', and that in the right line which passeth through *Spica* ♍ and *Cor Leonis*; not, indeed, exactly, but deviating a little from that line towards the north. *Montenari* likewise observed, that this day, and some days after, a right line drawn from the comet through *Spica* passed by the south side of *Cor Leonis* at a very small distance therefrom. The right line through *Cor Leonis* and *Spica* ♍ did cut the ecliptic in ♍ 3° 46' at an angle of 2° 51'; and if the comet had been in this line and in ♍ 3°, its latitude would have been 2° 26'; but since *Hook* and *Montenari* agree that the comet was at some small distance from this line towards the north, its latitude must have been something less. On the 20th, by the observation of *Montenari*, its latitude was almost the same with that of *Spica* ♍, that is, about 1° 30'. But by the agreement of *Hook, Montenari*, and *Ango*, the latitude was continually increasing, and therefore must now, on the 22d, be sensibly greater than 1° 30'; and, taking a mean between the extreme limits but now stated, 2° 26' and 1° 30', the latitude will be about 1° 58'. *Hook* and *Montenari* agree that the tail of the comet was directed towards *Spica* ♍, declining a little from that star towards the south according to *Hook*; but towards the north according to *Montenari*; and, therefore, that declination was scarcely sensible; and the tail, lying nearly parallel to the equator, deviated a little from the opposition of the sun towards the north.

Nov. 23, O.S. at 5^h. morning, at Nuremberg (that is, at $4^1/_2{}^h$. at *London*.), Mr. *Zimmerman*, saw the comet in ♍ 8° 8', with 2° 31' south lat. its place being collected by taking its distances from fixed stars.

Nov. 24, before sun-rising, the comet was seen by *Montenari* in ♍ 12° 52' on the north side of the right line through *Cor Leonis* and *Spica* ♍, and therefore its latitude was something less than 2° 38'; and since the latitude, as we said, by the concurring observations of *Montenari, Ango*, and *Hook*, was continually increasing; therefore, it was now, on the 24th, something greater than 1° 58'; and, taking the mean quantity, may be reckoned 2° 18', without any considerable error. *Ponthaeus* and *Galletius* will have it that the latitude was now decreasing; and *Cellius*, and the observer in *New England*, that it continued the same, viz., of about 1°, or $1^1/_2{}°$. The observations of *Ponthæus* and *Cellius* are more rude, especially those which were made by taking the azimuths and altitudes; as are also the observations of *Galletius*. Those are better which were made by taking the position of the comet to the fixed stars by *Montenari, Hook*,

Ango, and the observer in *New England*, and sometimes by *Ponthaeus* and *Cellius*. The same day, at 5ʰ. morning, at *Ballasore*, the comet was observed in ♍ 11° 45'; and, therefore, at 5ʰ. morning, at *London*, was in ♍ 13° nearly. And, by the theory, the comet was at that time in ♍ 13° 22' 42".

Nov. 25, before sunrise, *Montenari* observed the comet in ♍ 17³/₄ nearly; and *Cellius* observed at the same time that the comet was in a right line between the bright star in the right thigh of Virgo and the southern scale of Libra; and this right line cuts the comet's way in ♍ 18° 36'. And, by the theory, the comet was in ♍ 18¹/₃° nearly.

From all this it is plain that these observations agree with the theory, so far as they agree with one another; and by this agreement it is made clear that it was one and the same comet that appeared all the time from *Nov.* 4 to *Mar.* 9. The path of this comet did twice cut the plane of the ecliptic, and therefore was not a right line. It did cut the ecliptic not in opposite parts of the heavens, but in the end of Virgo and beginning of Capricorn, including an arc of about 98°; and therefore the way of the comet did very much deviate from the path of a great circle; for in the month of *Nov.* it declined at least 3° from the ecliptic towards the south; and in the month of *Dec.* following it declined 29° from the ecliptic towards the north; the two parts of the orbit in which the comet descended towards the sun, and ascended again from the sun, declining one from the other by an apparent angle of above 30°, as observed by *Montenari*. This comet travelled over 9 signs, to wit, from the last deg. of ♌ to the beginning of ♐, beside the sign of ♌, through which it passed before it began to be seen; and there is no other theory by which a comet can go over so great a part of the heavens with a regular motion. The motion of this comet was very unequable; for about the 20th of *Nov.* it described about 5° a day. Then its motion being retarded between *Nov.* 26 and *Dec.* 12, to wit, in the space of 15¹/₂ days, it described only 40°. But the motion thereof being afterwards accelerated, it described near 5° a day, till its motion began to be again retarded. And the theory which justly corresponds with a motion so unequable, and through so great a part of the heavens, which observes the same laws with the theory of the planets, and which accurately agrees with accurate astronomical observations, cannot be otherwise than true.

And, thinking it would not be improper, I have given a true representation of the orbit which this comet described, and of the tail which it emitted in several places, in the annexed figure; protracted in the plane of the trajectory. In this scheme ABC represents the trajectory of the comet, D the sun DE the axis of the trajectory, DF the line of the nodes, GH the intersection of the sphere of the *orbis magnus* with the plane of the trajectory, I the place of the comet *Nov.* 4, *Ann.* 1680; K the place of the same *Nov.* 11; L the place of the same *Nov.* 19; M its place *Dec.* 12; N its place *Dec.* 21; O its

place *Dec.* 29; P its place *Jan.* 5 following; Q its place *Jan.* 25; R its place *Feb.* 5; S its place *Feb.* 25; T its place *March* 5; and V its place *March* 9. In determining the length of the tail, I made the following observations.

Nov. 4 and 6, the tail did not appear; *Nov.* 11, the tail just begun to shew itself, but did not appear above $1/2$ deg. long through a 10 feet telescope; *Nov.* 17, the tail was seen by *Ponthaeus* more than 15° long; *Nov.* 18, in *New-England*, the tail appeared 30° long, and directly opposite to the sun, extending itself to the planet Mars, which was then in ♍, 9° 54'; *Nov.* 19. in *Maryland*, the tail was found 15° or 20° long; *Dec.* 10 (by the observation of Mr. *Flamsted*), the tail passed through the middle of the distance intercepted between the tail of the Serpent of *Ophiuchus* and the star δ in the south wing of *Aquila*, and did terminate near the stars A, ω, *b*, in *Bayer*'s tables. Therefore the end of the tail was in ♉ $19^1/_2$°, with latitude about $34^1/_4$° north; *Dec.* 11, it ascended to the head of *Sagitta* (*Bayer*'s α, β), terminating in ♉ 26° 43', with latitude 38° 34' north; *Dec,* 12, it passed through the middle of *Sagitta*, nor did it reach much farther; terminating in ♒ 4°, with latitude $42^1/_2$° north nearly. But these things are to be understood of the length of the brighter part of the tail; for with a more faint light, observed, too, perhaps, in a serener sky, at *Rome, Dec.* 12, 5^h. 40', by the observation of *Ponthaeus*, the tail arose to 10° above the rump of the Swan, and the side thereof towards the west and towards, the north was 45' distant from this star. But about that time the tail was 3° broad towards the upper end; and therefore the middle thereof was 2° 15' distant from that star towards the south, and the upper end was ♓ in 22°, with latitude 61° north; and thence the tail was about 70° long; *Dec.* 21, it extended almost to *Cassiopeia*'s chair, equally distant from β and from *Schedir*, so as its distance from either of the two was equal to the distance of the one from the other, and therefore did terminate in ♈ 24°, with latitude $47^1/_2$°; *Dec.* 29, it reached to a contact with *Scheat* on its left, and exactly filled up the space between the two stars in the northern foot of *Andromeda*, being 54° in length; and therefore terminated in ♉ 19°, with 35° of latitude; *Jan.* 5, it touched the star p in the breast of *Andromeda* on its right side, and the star (of the girdle on its left; and, according to our observations, was 40° long; but it was curved, and the convex side thereof lay to the south; and near the head of the comet it made an angle of 4° with the circle which passed through the sun and the comet's head; but towards the other end it was inclined to that circle in an angle of about 10° or 11°; and the chord of the tail contained with that circle an angle of 8°. *Jan.* 13, the tail terminated between *Alamech* and *Algol*, with a light that was sensible enough; but with a faint light it ended over against the star κ in *Perseus*'s side. The distance of the end of the tail from the circle passing through the sun and the comet was 3° 50'; and the inclination of the chord of the tail to that circle was $8^1/_2$°. *Jan.* 25 and 26, it shone with a faint light to the length, of 6° or 7°; and for a night or two after,

when there was a very clear sky, it extended to the length of 12°, or something more, with a light that was very faint and very hardly to be seen; but the axis thereof was exactly directed to the bright star in the eastern shoulder of Auriga, and therefore deviated from the opposition of the sun towards the north by an angle of 10°. Lastly, *Feb.* 10, with a telescope I observed the tail 2° long; for that fainter light which I spoke of did not appear through the glasses. But *Ponthæus* writes, that, on *Feb.* 7, he saw the tail 12° long. *Feb.* 25, the comet was without a tail, and so continued till it disappeared.

Now if one reflects upon the orbit described, and duly considers the other appearances of this comet, he will be easily satisfied that the bodies of comets are solid, compact, fixed, and durable, like the bodies of the planets; for if they were nothing else but the vapours or exhalations of the earth, of the sun, and other planets, this comet, in its passage by the neighbourhood of the sun, would have been immediately dissipated; for the heat of the sun is as the density of its rays, that is, reciprocally as the square of the distance of the places from the sun. Therefore, since on *Dec.* 8, when the comet was in its perihelion, the distance thereof from the centre of the sun was to the distance of the earth from the same as about 6 to 1000, the sun's heat on the comet was at that time to the heat of the summer sun with us as 1000000 to 36, or as 28000 to 1. But the heat of boiling water is about 3 times greater than the heat which dry earth acquires from the summer-sun, as I have tried; and the heat of red-hot iron (if my conjecture is right) is about three or four times greater than the heat of boiling water. And therefore the heat which dry earth on the comet, while in its perihelion, might have conceived from the rays of the sun, was about 2000 times greater than the heat of red-hot iron. But by so fierce a heat, vapours and exhalations, and every volatile matter, must have been immediately consumed and dissipated.

This comet, therefore, must have conceived an immense heat from the sun, and retained that heat for an exceeding long time; for a globe of iron of an inch in diameter, exposed red-hot to the open air, will scarcely lose all its heat in an hour's time; but a greater globe would retain its heat longer in the proportion of its diameter, because the surface (in proportion to which it is cooled by the contact of the ambient air) is in that proportion less in respect of the quantity of the included hot matter; and therefore a globe of red hot iron equal to our earth, that is, about 40000000 feet in diameter, would scarcely cool in an equal number of days, or in above 50000 years. But I suspect that the duration of heat may, on account of some latent causes, increase in a yet less proportion than that of the diameter; and I should be glad that the true proportion was investigated by experiments.

It is farther to be observed, that the comet in the month of *December*, just after it had been heated by the sun, did emit a much longer tail, and much more splendid, than in the month of *November* before, when it had not yet arrived at its perihelion;

and, universally, the greatest and most fulgent tails always arise from comets immediately after their passing by the neighbourhood of the sun. Therefore the heat received by the comet conduces to the greatness of the tail: from whence, I think I may infer, that the tail is nothing else but a very fine vapour, which the head or nucleus of the comet emits by its heat.

But we have had three several opinions about the tails of comets; for some will have it that they are nothing else but the beams of the sun's light transmitted through the comets' heads, which they suppose to be transparent; others, that they proceed from the refraction which light suffers in passing from the comet's head to the earth: and, lastly, others, that they are a sort of clouds or vapour constantly rising from the comets' heads, and tending towards the parts opposite to the sun. The first is the opinion of such as are yet unacquainted with optics; for the beams of the sun are seen in a darkened room only in consequence of the light that is reflected, from them by the little particles of dust and smoke which are always flying about in the air; and, for that reason, in air impregnated with thick smoke, those beams appear with great brightness, and move the sense vigorously; in a yet finer air they appear more faint, and are less easily discerned; but in the heavens, where there is no matter to reflect the light, they can never be seen at all. Light is not seen as it is in the beam, but as it is thence reflected to our eyes; for vision can be no otherwise produced than by rays falling upon the eyes; and, therefore, there must be some reflecting matter in those parts where the tails of the comets are seen: for otherwise, since all the celestial spaces are equally illuminated by the sun's light, no part of the heavens could appear with more splendor than another. The second opinion is liable to many difficulties. The tails of comets are never seen variegated with those colours which commonly are inseparable from refraction; and the distinct transmission of the light of the fixed stars and planets to us is a demonstration that the aether or celestial medium is not endowed with any refractive power: for as to what is alleged, that the fixed stars have been sometimes seen by the Egyptians environed with a *Coma* or *Capitlitium*, because that has but rarely happened, it is rather to be ascribed to a casual refraction of clouds; and so the radiation and scintillation of the fixed stars to the refractions both of the eyes and air; for upon laying a telescope to the eye, those radiations and scintillations immediately disappear. By the tremulous agitation of the air and ascending vapours, it happens that the rays of light are alternately turned aside from the narrow space of the pupil of the eye; but no such thing can have place in the much wider aperture of the object-glass of a telescope; and hence it is that a scintillation is occasioned in the former case, which ceases in the latter; and this cessation in the latter case is a demonstration of the regular transmission of light through the heavens, without any sensible refraction. But, to obviate an objection that may be made from the appearing of no tail in such comets as shine but with a faint light, as if

the secondary rays were then too weak to affect the eyes, and for that reason it is that the tails of the fixed stars do not appear, we are to consider, that by the means of telescopes the light of the fixed stars may be augmented above an hundred fold, and yet no tails are seen; that the light of the planets is yet more copious without any tail; but that comets are seen sometimes with huge tails, when the light of their heads is but faint and dull. For so it happened in the comet of the year 1680, when in the month of *December* it was scarcely equal in light to the stars of the second magnitude, and yet emitted a notable tail, extending to the length of 40°, 50°, 60°, or 70°, and upwards; and afterwards, on the 27th and 28th of *January*, when the head appeared but as a star of the 7th magnitude, yet the tail (as we said above), with a light that was sensible enough, though faint, was stretched out to 6 or 7 degrees in length, and with a languishing light that was more difficultly Been, even to 12°, and upwards. But on the 9th and 10th of *February*, when to the naked eye the head appeared no more, through a telescope I viewed the tail of 2° in length. But farther; if the tail was owing to the refraction of the celestial matter, and did deviate from the opposition of the sun, according to the figure of the heavens, that deviation in the same places of the heavens should be always directed towards the same parts. But the comet of the year 1680, *December* 28^d. $8^1/_2{}^h$. P.M. at *London*, was seen in ♓ 8° 41', with latitude north 28° 6'; while the sun was in ♉ 18° 26'. And the comet of the year 1577, *December* 29^d. was in ♓ 8° 41', with latitude north 28° 40', and the sun, as before, in about ♉ 18° 26'. In both cases the situation of the earth was the same, and the comet appeared in the same place of the heavens; yet in the former case the tail of the comet (as well by my observations as by the observations of others) deviated from the opposition of the sun towards the north by an angle of $4^1/_2$ degrees; whereas in the latter there was (according to the observations of *Tycho*) a deviation of 21 degrees towards the south. The refraction, therefore, of the heavens being thus disproved, it remains that the *phaenomena* of the tails of comets must be derived from some reflecting matter.

And that the tails of comets do arise from their heads, and tend towards the parts opposite to the sun, is farther confirmed from the laws which the tails observe. As that, lying in the planes of the comets' orbits which pass through the sun, they constantly deviate from the opposition of the sun towards the parts which the comets' heads in their progress along these orbits have left. That to a spectator, placed in those planes, they appear in the parts directly opposite to the sun; but, as the spectator recedes from those planes, their deviation begins to appear, and daily becomes greater. That the deviation, *caeteris paribus*, appears less when the tail is more oblique to the orbit of the comet, as well as when the head of the comet approaches nearer to the sun, especially if the angle of deviation is estimated near the head of the comet. That the tails which have no deviation appear straight, but the tails which deviate are likewise bended into

a certain curvature. That this curvature is greater when the deviation is greater; and is more sensible when the tail, *caeteris paribus*, is longer; for in the shorter tails the curvature is hardly to be perceived. That the angle of deviation is less near the comet's head, but greater towards the other end of the tail; and that because the convex side of the tail regards the parts from which the deviation is made, and which lie in a right line drawn out infinitely from the sun through the comet's head. And that the tails that are long and broad, and shine with a stronger light, appear more resplendent and more exactly defined on the convex than on the concave side. Upon which accounts it is plain that the *phaenomena* of the tails of comets depend upon the motions of their head

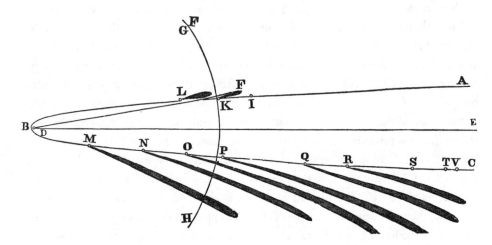

and by no means upon the places of the heavens in which their heads are seen; and that, therefore, the tails of comets do not proceed from the refraction of the heavens, but from their own heads, which furnish the matter that forms the tail. For, as in our air, the smoke of a heated body ascends either perpendicularly if the body is at rest, or obliquely if the body is moved obliquely, so in the heavens, where all bodies gravitate towards the sun, smoke and vapour must (as we have already said) ascend from the sun, and either rise perpendicularly if the smoking body is at rest, or obliquely if the body, in all the progress of its motion, is always leaving those places from which the upper or higher parts of the vapour had risen before; and that obliquity will be least where the vapour ascends with most velocity, to wit, near the smoking body, when that is near the sun. But, because the obliquity varies, the column of vapour will be incurvated; and because the vapour in the preceding sides is something more recent, that is, has ascended something more late; from the body, it will therefore be something more dense on that aide, and must on that account reflect more light, as well as be better defined. I add nothing concerning the sudden uncertain agitation of the tails of comets, and their

irregular figures, which authors sometimes describe, because they may arise from the mutations of our air, and the motions of our clouds, in part obscuring those tails; or, perhaps, from parts of the *Via Lactea*, which might have been confounded with and mistaken for parts of the tails of the comets as they passed by.

But that the atmospheres of comets may furnish a supply of vapours great enough to fill so immense spaces, we may easily understand from the rarity of our own air; for the air near the surface of our earth possesses a space 850 times greater than water of the same weight; and therefore a cylinder of air 850 feet high is of equal weight with a cylinder of water of the same breadth, and but one foot high. But a cylinder of air reaching to the top of the atmosphere is of equal weight with a cylinder of water about 33 feet high: and, therefore, if from the whole cylinder of air the lower part of 850 feet high is taken away, the remaining upper part will be of equal weight with a cylinder of water 32 feet high: and from thence (and by the hypothesis, confirmed by many experiments, that the compression of air is as the weight of the incumbent atmosphere, and that the force of gravity is reciprocally as the square of the distance from the centre of the earth) raising a calculus, by Cor. Prop. XXII, Book II, I found, that, at the height of one semi-diameter of the earth, reckoned from the earth's surface, the air is more rare than with us in a far greater proportion than of the whole space within the orb of Saturn to a spherical space of one inch in diameter; and therefore if a sphere of our air of but one inch in thickness was equally rarefied with the air at the height of one semi-diameter of the earth from the earth's surface, it would fill all the regions of the planets to the orb of Saturn, and far beyond it. Wherefore since the air at greater distances is immensely rarefied, and the *coma* or atmosphere of comets is ordinarily about ten times higher, reckoning from their centres, than the surface of the nucleus, and the tails rise yet higher, they must therefore be exceedingly rare; and though, on account of the much thicker atmospheres of comets, and the great gravitation of their bodies towards the sun, as well as of the particles of their air and vapours mutually one towards another, it may happen that the air in the celestial spaces and in the tails of comets is not so vastly rarefied, yet from this computation it is plain that a very small quantity of air and vapour is abundantly sufficient to produce all the appearances of the tails of comets; for that they are, indeed, of a very notable rarity appears from the shining of the stars through them. The atmosphere of the earth, illuminated by the sun's light, though but of a few miles in thickness, quite obscures and extinguishes the light not only of all the stars, but even of the moon itself; whereas the smallest stars are seen to shine through the immense thickness of the tails of comets, likewise illuminated by the sun, without the least diminution of their splendor. Nor is the brightness of the tails of most comets ordinarily greater than that of our air, an inch or two in thickness, reflecting in a darkened room the light of the sun-beams let in by a hole of the window-shutter.

And we may pretty nearly determine the time spent during the ascent of the vapour from the comet's head to the extremity of the tail, by drawing a right line from the extremity of the tail to the sun, and marking the place where that right line intersects the comet's orbit; for the vapour that is now in the extremity of the tail, if it has ascended in a right line from the sun, must have begun to rise from the head at the time when the head was in the point of intersection. It is trite, the vapour does not rise in a right line from the sun, but, retaining the motion which it had from the comet before its ascent, and compounding that motion with its motion of ascent, arises obliquely; and, therefore, the solution of the Problem will be more exact, if we draw the line which intersects the orbit parallel to the length of the tail; or rather (because of the curvilinear motion of the comet) diverging a little from the line or length of the tail. And by means of this principle I found that the vapour which, *January* 25, was in the extremity of the tail, had begun to rise from the head before *December* 11, and therefore had spent in its whole ascent 45 days; but that the whole tail which appeared on *December* 10 had finished its ascent in the space of the two days then elapsed from the time of the comet's being in its perihelion. The vapour, therefore, about the beginning and in the neighbourhood of the sun rose with the greatest velocity, and afterwards continued to ascend with a motion constantly retarded by its own gravity; and the higher it ascended, the more it added to the length of the tail; and while the tail continued to be seen, it was made up of almost all that vapour which had risen since the time of the comet's being in its perihelion; nor did that part of the vapour which had risen first, and which formed the extremity of the tail, cease to appear, till its too great distance, as well from the sun, from which it received its light, as from our eyes, rendered it invisible. Whence also it is that the tails of other comets which are short do not rise from their heads with a swift and continued motion, and soon after disappear, but are permanent and lasting columns of vapours and exhalations, which, ascending from the heads with a slow motion of many days, and partaking of the motion of the heads which they had from the beginning, continue to go along together with them through the heavens. From whence again we have another argument proving the celestial spaces to be free, and without resistance, since in them not only the solid bodies of the planets and comets, but also the extremely rare vapours of comets' tails, maintain their rapid motions with great freedom, and for an exceeding long time.

Kepler ascribes the ascent of the tails of the comets to the atmospheres of their heads; and their direction towards the parts opposite to the sun to the action of the rays of light carrying along with them the matter of the comets' tails; and without any great incongruity we may suppose, that, in so free spaces, so fine a matter as that of the aether may yield to the action of the rays of the sun's light, though those rays are not able sensibly to move the gross substances in our parts, which are clogged with so palpable a

resistance. Another author thinks that there may be a sort of particles of matter endowed with a principle of levity, as well as others are with a power of gravity; that the matter of the tails of comets may be of the former sort, and that its ascent from the sun may be owing to its levity; but, considering that the gravity of terrestrial bodies is as the matter of the bodies, and therefore can be neither more nor less in the same quantity of matter, I am inclined to believe that this ascent may rather proceed from the rarefaction of the matter of the comets' tails. The ascent of smoke in a chimney is owing to the impulse of the air with which it is entangled. The air rarefied by heat ascends, because its specific gravity is diminished, and in its ascent carries along with it the smoke with which it is engaged; and why may not the tail of a comet rise from the sun after the same manner? For the sun's rays do not act upon the mediums which they pervade otherwise than by reflection and refraction; and those reflecting particles heated by this action, heat the matter of the æther which is involved with them. That matter is rarefied by the heat which it acquires, and because, by this rarefaction, the specific gravity with which it tended towards the sun before is diminished, it will ascend therefrom, and carry along with it the reflecting particles of which the tail of the comet is composed. But the ascent of the vapours is further promoted by their circumgyration about the sun, in consequence whereof they endeavour to recede from the sun, while the sun's atmosphere and the other matter of the heavens are either altogether quiescent, or are only moved with a slower circumgyration derived from the rotation of the sun. And these are the causes of the ascent of the tails of the comets in the neighbourhood of the sun, where their orbits are bent into a greater curvature, and the comets themselves are plunged into the danger and therefore heavier parts of the sun's atmosphere: upon which account they do then emit tails of an huge length; for the tails which then arise, retaining their own proper motion, and in the mean time gravitating towards the sun, must be revolved in ellipses about the sun in like manner as the heads are and by that motion must always accompany the heads, and freely adhere to them. For the gravitation of the vapours towards the sun can no more force the tails to abandon the heads, and descend to the sun, than the gravitation of the heads can oblige them to fall from the tails. They must by their common gravity either fall together towards the sun, or be retarded together in their common ascent therefrom; and, therefore (whether from the causes already described, or from any others), the tails and heads of comets may easily acquire and freely retain any position one to the other, without disturbance or impediment from that common gravitation.

The tails, therefore, that rise in the perihelion positions of the comets will go along with their heads into far remote parts, and together with the heads will either return again from thence to us, after a long course of years, or rather will be there rarefied, and by degrees quite vanish away; for afterwards, in the descent of the heads towards the sun,

new short tails will be emitted from the heads with a slow motion; and those tails by degrees will be augmented immensely, especially in such comets as in their perihelion distances descend as low as the sun's atmosphere; for all vapour in those free spaces is in a perpetual state of rarefaction and dilatation; and from hence it is that the tails of all comets are broader at their upper extremity than near their heads. And it is not unlikely but that the vapour, thus perpetually rarefied and dilated, may be at last dissipated and scattered through the whole heavens, and by little and little be attracted towards the planets by its gravity, and mixed with their atmosphere; for as the seas are absolutely necessary to the constitution of our earth, that from them, the sun, by its heat, may exhale a sufficient quantity of vapours, which, being gathered together into clouds, may drop down in rain, for watering of the earth, and for the production and nourishment of vegetables; or, being condensed with cold on the tops of mountains (as some philosophers with reason judge), may run down in springs and rivers; so for the conservation of the seas, and fluids of the planets, comets seem to be required that, from their exhalations and vapours condensed, the wastes of the planetary fluids spent upon vegetation and putrefaction, and converted into dry earth, may be continually supplied and made up; for all vegetables entirely derive their growths from fluids, and afterwards, in great measure, are turned into dry earth by putrefaction; and a sort of slime is always found to settle at the bottom of putrefied fluids; and hence it is that the bulk of the solid earth is continually increased; and the fluids, if they are not supplied from without, must be in a continual decrease, and quite fail at last. I suspect, moreover, that it is chiefly from the comets that spirit comes, which is indeed the smallest, but the most subtle and useful part of our air, and so much required to sustain the life of all things with us.

The atmospheres of comets, in their descent towards the sun, by running out into the tails, are spent and diminished, and become narrower, at least on that side which regards the sun; and in receding from the sun, when they less run out into the tails, they are again enlarged, if *Hevelius* has justly marked their appearances. But they are seen least of all just after they have been most heated by the sun, and on that account then emit the longest and most resplendent tails; and, perhaps, at the same time, the nuclei are environed with a denser and blacker smoke in the lowermost parts of their atmosphere; for smoke that is raised by a great and intense heat is commonly the denser and blacker. This the head of that comet which we have been describing, at equal distances both from the sun and from the earth, appeared darker after it had passed by its perihelion than it did before; for in the month of *December* it was commonly compared with the stars of the third magnitude, but in *November* with those of the first or second; and such as saw both appearances have described the first as of another and greater comet than the second. For, *November* 19, this comet appeared to a young man at *Cambridge*, though with a pale and dull light, yet equal to *Spica Virginis*; and at that

time it shone with greater brightness than it did afterwards. And *Montenari, November* 20, st. vet. observed it larger than the stars of the first magnitude, its tail being then 2 degrees long. And Mr. *Storer* (by letters which have come into my hands) writes that in the month of *December*, when the tail appeared of the greatest bulk and splendor, the head was but small, and far less than that which was seen in the month of *November* before sun-rising; and, conjecturing at the cause of the appearance, he judged it to proceed from there being a greater quantity of matter in the head at first, which was afterwards gradually spent.

And, which farther makes for the same purpose, I find, that the heads of other comets, which did put forth tails of the greatest bulk and splendour, have appeared but obscure and small. For in *Brazil, March* 5,1668, 7[h]. P.M., St. N. P. *Valentinus Estancius* saw a comet near the horizon, and towards the south west, with a head so small as scarcely to be discerned, but with a tail above measure splendid, so that the reflection thereof from the sea was easily seen by those who stood upon the shore; and it looked like a fiery beam extended 23° in length from the west to south, almost parallel to the horizon. But this excessive splendor continued only three days, decreasing apace afterwards; and while the splendor was decreasing, the bulk of the tail increased: whence in *Portugal* it is said to have taken up one quarter of the heavens, that is, 45 degrees, extending from west to east with a very notable splendor, though the whole tail was not seen in those parts, because the head was always hid under the horizon: and from the increase of the bulk and decrease of the splendor of the tail, it appear that the head was then in its recess from the sun, and had been very near to it in its perihelion, as the comet of 1680 was. And we read, in the *Saxon* Chronicle, of a like comet appearing in the year 1106, *the star whereof was small and obscure* (as that of 1690), *but the splendour of its tail was very bright, and like a huge fiery beam stretched out in a direction between the east and north*, as *Hevelius* has it also from *Simeon*, the monk of *Durham*. This comet appeared in the beginning of *February*, about the evening, and towards the south west part of heaven; from whence, and from the position of the tail, we infer that the head was near the sun. *Matthew Paris* says, *It was distant from the sun by about a cubit, from three of the clock* (rather six) *till nine, putting forth a long tail.* Such also was that most resplendent comet described by *Aristotle*, lib. 1, *Meteor.* 6. *The head whereof could not be seen, because it had set before the sun, or at least was hid under the sun's rays; but next day it was seen as well as might be; for, having left the sun but a very little way, it set immediately after it. And the scattered light of the head, obscured by the too great splendour* (of the tail) *did not yet appear. But afterwards* (as *Aristotle* says) *when the splendour* (of the tail) *was now diminished* (the head of), *the comet recovered its native brightness; and the splendour* (of its tail) *reached now to a third part of the heavens* (that is, to 60°). *This appearance was in the winter season* (an. 4, Olymp. 101), *and, rising to* Orion's

girdle, it there vanished away. It is true that the comet of 1618, which came out directly from under the sun's rays with a very large tail, seemed to equal, if not to exceed, the stars of the first magnitude; but, then, abundance of other comets have appeared yet greater than this, that put forth shorter tails; some of which are said to have appeared as big as Jupiter, others as big as Venus, or even as the moon.

We have said, that comets are a sort of planets revolved in very eccentric orbits about the sun; and as, in the planets which are without tails, those are commonly less which are revolved in lesser orbits, and nearer to the sun, so in comets it is probable that those which in their perihelion approach nearer to the sun are generally of less magnitude, that they may not agitate the sun too much by their attractions. But as to the transverse diameters of their orbits, and the periodic times of their revolutions, I leave them to be determined by comparing comets together which after long intervals of time return again in the same orbit. In the mean time, the following Proposition may give some light in that inquiry.

PROPOSITION XLII. PROBLEM XXII.

TO CORRECT A COMET'S TRAJECTORY FOUND AS ABOVE.

OPERATION 1. Assume that position of the plane of the trajectory which was determined according to the preceding proposition; and select three places of the comet, deduced from very accurate observations, and at great distances one from the other. Then suppose A to represent the time between the first observation and the second, and B the time between the second and the third; but it will be convenient that in one of those times the comet be in its perigeon, or at least not far from it. From those apparent places find, by trigonometric operations; the three true places of the comet in that assumed plane of the trajectory; then through the places found, and about the centre of the sun as the focus, describe a conic section by arithmetical operations, according to Prop. XXI., Book I. Let the areas of this figure which are terminated by radii drawn from the sun to the places found be D and E; to wit, D the area between the first observation and the second, and E the area between the second and third; and let T represent the whole time in which the whole area D + E should be described with the velocity of the comet found by Prop. XVI., Book I.

OPER. 2. Retaining the inclination of the plane of the trajectory to the plane of the ecliptic, let the longitude of the nodes of the plane of the trajectory be increased by the addition of 20 or 30 minutes, which call P. Then from the aforesaid three observed places of the comet let the three true places be found (as before) in this new plane; as also the orbit passing through those places, and the two areas of the same described between the two observations, which call *d* and *e*; and let *t* be the whole time in which the whole area *d* + *e* should be described.

OPER. 3. Retaining the longitude of the nodes in the first operation, let the inclination of the plane of the trajectory to the plane of the ecliptic decreased by adding thereto 20' or 30', which call Q. Then from the aforesaid three observed apparent places of the comet let the three true places be found in this new plane, as well as the orbit passing through them, and the two areas of the same described between the observation, which call δ and ε; and let τ be the whole time in which the whole area δ + δ should be described.

Then taking C to 1 as A to B; and G to 1 as D to E; and *g* to 1 as *d* to *e*; and γ to 1 as δ to ε; let S be the true time between the first observation and the third; and, observing well the signs + and -, let such numbers *m* and *n* be found out as will make 2G – 2C, = *m*G – *mg* + *n*G – *n*τ; and 2T – 2S = *m*T – *mt* + *n*T – *n*τ. And if, in the first operation, I represents the inclination of the plane of the trajectory to the plane of the ecliptic, and K the longitude of either node, then I + *n*Q will be the true inclination of the plane of the trajectory to the plane of the ecliptic, and K + *m*P the true longitude of the node. And, lastly, if in the first, second, and third operations, the quantities R, *r*, and (, represent the parameters of the trajectory, and the quantities $\frac{1}{L}$, $\frac{1}{l}$, $\frac{1}{\lambda}$, the

transverse diameters of the same, then R + *mr* – *m*R + *n*ρ - *n*R will be the true parameter, and $\frac{1}{L + ml - mL + n\lambda - nL}$ will be the true transverse diameter of the trajectory which the comet describes; and from the transverse diameter given the periodic time of the comet is also given. Q.E.I. But the periodic times of the revolutions of comets, and the transverse diameters of their orbits, cannot be accurately enough determined but by comparing comets together which appear at different times. If, after equal intervals of time, several comets are found to have described the same orbit, we may thence conclude that they are all but one and the same comet revolved in the same orbit; and then from the times of their revolutions the transverse diameters of their orbits will be given, and from those diameters the elliptic orbits themselves will be determined.

To this purpose the trajectories of many comets ought to be computed, supposing those trajectories to be parabolic; for such trajectories will always nearly agree with the *phaenomena*, as appears not only from the parabolic trajectory of the comet of the year 1680, which I compared above with the observations, but likewise from that of the notable comet which appeared in the year 1664 and 1665, and was observed by *Hevelius*, who, from his own observations, calculated the longitudes and latitudes thereof, though with little accuracy. But from the same observations Dr. *Halley* did again compute its places; and from those new places determined its trajectory, finding its ascending node in ♓ 21° 13' 55"; the inclination of the orbit to the plane of the ecliptic 21° 18' 40"; the distance of its perihelion from the node, estimated in the comet's orbit, 49° 27' 30", its perihelion in ♌ 8° 40' 30", with heliocentric latitude

south 16° 01' 45"; the comet to have been in its perihelion *November* 21^d. 11^h. 52' P.M. equal time at *London*, or 13^h. 8' at *Dantzick*, O.S.; and that the *latus rectum* of the parabola was 410286 such parts as the sun's mean distance from the earth is supposed to contain 100000. And how nearly the places of the comet computed in this orbit agree with the observations, will appear from the annexed table, calculated by Dr. *Halley*.

Appar. Time at Dantzick.	The observed Distances of the Comet from		The observed Places.			The Places computed in the Orb.	
d.　h.　'		° ' "			° ' "		° ' "
December 3 18.29 ¹/₂	The Lion's heart	46.24.20	Long.	♎	7.01.00	♎	7. 1.29
	The Virgin's spike	22.52.10	Lat. S.		21.39. 0		21.38.50
4.18. 1¹/₂	The Lion's heart	46. 2.45	Long.	♎	6.15. 0	♎	6.16. 5
	The Virgin's spike	23.52.40	Lat. S.		22.24. 0		22.24. 0
7.17.48	The Lion's heart	44.48. 0	Long.	♎	3. 6. 0	♍	3. 7.33
	The Virgin's spike	27.56.40	Lat. S.		25.22. 0		25.21.40
17.14.43	The Lion's heart	63.15.15	Long.	♌	2.56. 0	♌	2.56. 0
	Orion's right shoulder	45.43.30	Lat. S.		49.25. 0		49.25. 0
19.9.25	Procyon	35.13.50	Long.	♊	28.40.30	♊	28.43. 0
	Bright star of Whale's jaw	52.56. 0	Lat. S.		45.48. 0		45.46. 0
20.9. 53¹/₂	Procyon	40.49. 0	Long.	♊	13.03. 0	♊	13. 5. 0
	Bright star of Whale's jaw	40.04. 0	Lat. S		39.54. 0		39.53.40
21.9. 9¹/₂	Orion's right shoulder	26.21.25	Long.	♊	2.16. 0	♊	2.18.30
	Bright star of Whale's jaw	29.28. 0	Lat. S.		33.41. 0		33.39.40
22.9. 0	Orion's right shoulder	29.47. 0	Long.	♉	24.24. 0	♉	24.27. 0
	Bright star of Whale's jaw	20.29.30	Lat. S.		27.45. 0		27.46. 0
26.7.58	The bright star of Aries	23.20. 0	Long.	♉	9. 0. 0	♉	9. 2.28
	Aldebaran	26.44. 0	Lat. S.		12.36. 0		12.34.13
27.6.45	The bright star of Aries	20.45. 0	Long.	♉	7. 5.40	♉	7. 8.45
	Aldebaran	28.10. 0	Lat. S.		10.23. 0		10.23.13
28.7.39	The bright star of Aries	18.29. 0	Long.	♉	5.24.45	♉	5.27.52
	Palilicium	29.37. 0	Lat. S.		8.22.50		8.23.37
31.6.45	Andromeda's girdle	30.48.10	Long.	♉	2. 7.40	♉	2. 8.20
	Palilicium	32.53.30	Lat. S.		4.13. 0		4.16.25
Jan. 1665 7. 7.37¹/₂	Andromeda's girdle	25.11. 0	Long.	♈	28.24.47	♈	28.24. 0
	Palilicium	37.12.25	Lat. N.		0.54. 0		0.53. 0
13.7. 0	Andromeda's head	28. 7.10	Long.	♈	27. 6.54	♈	27. 6.39
	Palilicium.	38.55.20	Lat. N.		3. 6.50		3. 7.40
24.7.29	Andromeda's girdle	20.32.15	Long.	♈	26.29.15	♈	26.28.50
	Palilicium	40. 5. 0	Lat. N.		5.25.50		5.26. 0
Feb. 7. 8.37			Long.	♈	27. 4.46	♈	27.24.55
			Lat. N.		7. 3.29		7. 3.15
22. 8.46			Long.	♈	28.29.46	♈	28.29.58
			Lat. N.		8.12.36		8.10.25
March. 1. 8.16			Long.	♈	29.18 15	♈	29.18.20
			Lat. N.		8.36.26		8.36.12
7. 8.37			Long.	♉	0. 2.48	♉	0. 2.42
			Lat. N.		8.56.30		8.56.56

In *February*, the beginning of the year 1665, the first star of Aries, which I shall hereafter call γ, was in ♈ 28° 30' 15", with 7° 8' 58" north lat.; the second star of Aries was in ♈ 29° 17' 18", with 8° 28' 16" north lat.; and another star of the seventh magnitude, which I call, was in ♈ 28° 24' 45", with 8° 28' 13" north lat. The comet *Feb.* 7ᵈ. 7ʰ. 30' at *Paris* (that is, *Feb.* 7ᵈ. 8ʰ. 37' at *Dantzick*) O.S. made a triangle with those stars γ and A, which was right-angled in γ; and the distance of the comet from the star γ was equal to the distance of the stars γ and A, that is, 1° 19' 46" of a great circle; and therefore in the parallel of the latitude of the star γ it was 1° 20' 26". Therefore if from the longitude of the star γ there be subducted the longitude 1° 20' 26", there will remain the longitude of the comet ♈ 27° 9' 49". M. *Auzout*, from this observation of his, placed the comet in ♈ 27° 0', nearly; and, by the scheme in which Dr. *Hooke* delineated its motion, it was then in ♈ 26° 59' 24". I place it in ♈ 27° 4' 46", taking the middle between the two extremes.

From the same observations, M. *Auzout* made the latitude of the comet at that time 7° and 4' or 5' to the north; but he had done better to have made it 7° 3' 29", the difference of the latitudes of the comet and the star γ being equal to the difference of the longitude of the stars γ and A.

February 22ᵈ. 7ʰ. 30' at *London*, that is, *February* 22ᵈ. 8ʰ. 46' at *Dantzick*, the distance of the comet from the star A, according to Dr. *Hooke's* observation, as was delineated by himself in a scheme, and also by the observations of M. *Auzout*, delineated in like manner by M. *Petit*, was a fifth part of the distance between the star A and the first star of Aries, or 15° 57'; and the distance of the comet from a right line joining the star A and the first of Aries was a fourth part of the same fifth part, that is, 4'; and therefore the comet was in ♈ 28° 29' 46", with 8° 12' 36" north lat.

March 1, 7ʰ. 0' at *London*, that is, *March* 1, 8ʰ. 16' at *Dantzick*, the comet was observed near the second star in Aries, the distance between them being to the distance between the first and second stars in Aries, that is, to 1° 33', as 4 to 45 according to Dr. *Hooke*, or as 2 to 23 according to M. *Gottignies*. And, therefore, the distance of the comet from the second star in Aries was 8' 16" according to Dr. *Hooke*, or 8' 5" according to M. *Gottignies*; or, taking a mean between both, 8' 10". But, according to M. *Gottignies*, the comet had gone beyond the second star of Aries about a fourth or a fifth part of the space that it commonly went over in a day, to wit, about 1' 35" (in which he agrees very well with M. *Auzout*); or, according to Dr. *Hooke*, not quite so much, as perhaps only 1'. Wherefore if to the longitude of the first star in Aries we add 1', and 8' 10" to its latitude, we shall have the longitude of the comet ♈ 29° 18', with 8° 36' 26" north lat.

March 7, 7ʰ. 30' at *Paris* (that is, *March* 7, 8ʰ. 37' at *Dantzick*), from the observations of M. *Auzout*, the distance of the comet from the second star in Aries was equal

to the distance of that star from the star A, that is, 52' 29"; and the difference of the longitude of the comet and the second star in Aries was 45' or 46', or, taking a mean quantity, 45' 30"; and therefore the comet was in ♈ 0° 2' 48". From the scheme of the observations of M. *Auzout*, constructed by M. *Petit*, *Hevelius* collected the latitude of the comet 8° 54'. But the engraver did not rightly trace the curvature of the comet's way towards the end of the motion; and *Hevelius*, in the scheme of M. *Auzout's* observations which he constructed himself, corrected this irregular curvature, and so made the latitude of the comet 8° 55' 30". And, by farther correcting this irregularity, the latitude may become 8° 56', or 8° 57'.

This comet was also seen *March* 9, and at that time its place must have been in ♉ 0° 18', with 9° 3$\frac{1}{2}$' north lat. nearly.

This comet appeared three months together, in which space of time it travelled over almost six signs, and in one of the days thereof described almost 20 deg. Its course did very much deviate from a great circle, bending towards the north, and its motion towards the end from retrograde became direct; and, notwithstanding, its course was so uncommon, yet by the table it appears that the theory, from beginning to end, agrees with the observations no less accurately than the theories of the planets usually do with the observations of them; but we are to subduct about 2' when the comet was swiftest, which we may effect by taking off 12', from the angle between the ascending node and the perihelion, or by making that angle 49° 27, 18". The annual parallax of both these comets (this and the preceding) was very conspicuous, and by its quantity demonstrates the annual motion of the earth in the *orbis magnus*.

This theory is likewise confirmed by the motion of that comet, which in the year 1683 appeared retrograde, in an orbit whose plane contained almost a right angle with the plane of the ecliptic, and whose ascending node (by the computation of Dr. *Halley*) was in ♍ 23° 23'; the inclination of its orbit to the ecliptic 83° 11'; its perihelion in ♊ 25° 29' 30", its perihelion distance from the sun 56020 of such parts as the radius of the *orbis magnus* contains 100000; and the time of its perihelion *July* 2^d. 3^h. 50'. And the places thereof, computed by Dr. *Halley* in this orbit, are compared with the places of the same observed by Mr. *Flamsted*, in the following table:—

1683 Eq. time.	Sun's place	Comet's Long. com.	Lat. Nor. comput.	Comet's Long. obs'd	Lat. Nor. observed	Diff. Long.	Diff. Lat.
d. h. '	o ' "	o ' "	o ' "	o ' "	o ' "	' "	' "
July 13.12.55	♌ 1.02.30	♋ 13.05.42	29.29.13	♋ 13. 6.42	29.29.20	+ 1.00	+ 0.07
15.11.15	2.53.12	11.37.48	29.34. 0	11.39.43	29.34.50	+ 1.55	+ 0.50
17.10.20	4.45.45	10. 7. 6	29.33.30	10. 8.40	29.34. 0	+ 1.34	+ 0.30
23.13.40	10.38.21	5.10.27	28.51.42	5.11.30	28.50.28	+ 1.03	– 1.14
25.14. 5	12.35.28	3.27.53	24.24.47	3.27. 0	28.23.40	– 0.53	– 1. 7
31. 9.42	18.09.22	♊ 27.55. 3	26.22.52	♊ 27.54.24	26.22.25	– 0.39	– 0.27
31.14.55	18.21.53	27.41. 7	26.16.57	27.41. 8	26.14.50	+ 0. 1	– 2. 7
Aug. 2.14 56	20.17.16	25.29.32	25.16.19	25.28.46	25.17.28	– 0.46	+ 1. 9
4.10.49	22.02.50	23.18.20	24.10.49	23.16.55	24.12.19	– 1.25	+ 1.30
6.10. 9	21.16.45	20.42.21	22.47. 5	20.40.32	22.49. 5	– 1.51	+ 2. 0
9.10.26	26.50.52	16. 7.57	20. 6.37	16. 5.55	20. 6.10	– 2. 2	– 0.27
15.14. 1	♍ 2.47.13	3.30.48	11.37.33	3.26.18	11.32. 1	– 4.30	– 5.32
16.15.10	3.48. 2	0.43. 7	9.34.16	0.41.55	9.34.13	– 1.12	– 0. 3
18.16.44	6.45.33	♉ 24.52.53	5.11.15 South.	♉ 24.49. 5	5. 9.11 South	–3.48	– 2. 4
22.14.44	9.35.49	11. 7.14	5.16.58	11.07.12	5.16.58	– 0. 2	– 0. 3
23.15.52	10.36 48	7. 2.18	8.17. 9	7. 1.17	8.16.41	– 1. 1	– 0.28
26.16. 2	13.31.20	♈ 24.45.31	16.38. 0	♈ 24.44.00	16.38.20	– 1.31	+ 0.20

This theory is yet farther confirmed by the motion of that retrograde comet which appeared in the year 1682. The ascending node of this (by Dr. *Halley's* computation) was in ♉ 21° 16' 30"; the inclination of its orbit to the plane of the ecliptic 17° 56' 00"; its perihelion in ♒ 2° 52' 50"; its perihelion distance from the sun 58328 parts, of which the radius of the *orbis magnus* contains 100000; the equal time of the comet's being in its perihelion *Sept.* 4ᵈ. 7ʰ. 39'. And its places, collected from Mr. *Flamsted's* observations, are compared with its places computed from our theory in the following table:

1682 App. time.	Sun's place	Comet's Lon. comp.	Lat. Nor comp.	Com. Long. observed.	Lat. Nor observ.	Diff. Long.	Diff. Lat.
d. h. '	o ' "	o ' "	o ' "	o ' "	o ' "	' "	' "
Aug 19.16.38	♍ 7. 0. 7	♌ 18.14.28	25.50. 7	♌ 18.14.40	25.49.55.	– 0.12	+ 0.12
20.15.38	7.55.52	24.46.23	26.14.42	24.46.22	26.12.52	+ 0. 1	+ 1.50
21. 8.21	8.36.14	29.37.15	26.20. 3	29.38.02	26.17.37	– 0.47	+ 2,26
22. 8. 8	9.33.55	♍ 6.29.53	26. 8.42	♍ 6.30. 3	26. 7.12	– 0.10	+ 1.30
29.08.20	16.22.40	♎ 12.37.54	18.37.47	♎ 12.37.49	18.34. 5	+ 0. 5	+ 3.42
30. 7.46	17.19.41	15.36. 1	17.26.43	15.35.18	17.27.17	+ 0.43	– 0.34
Sept. 1. 7.33	19.16. 9	20.30.53	15.13. 0	20.27. 4	15. 9.49	+ 3.49	+ 3.11
4. 7.22	22.11.28	25.42. 0	12.23.48	25.40.58	12.22. 0	+ 1. 2	+ 1.48
5. 7.32	23.10.29	27. 0.46	11.33.08	26.59.24	11.33.51	+ 1.22	– 0.43
8. 7.16	26. 5.58	29.58.44	9.26.46	29.58.45	9.26.43	– 0. 1	+ 0. 3
9. 7.26	27. 5. 9	♍ 0.44.10	8.49.10	♍ 0.44. 4	8.48.25	+ 0. 6	+ 0.45

This theory is also confirmed by the retrograde motion of the comet that appeared in the year 1723. The ascending node of this comet (according to the computation of Mr. *Bradley*, Savilian Professor of Astronomy at *Oxford*) was in ♈ 14° 16'. The inclination of the orbit to the plane of the ecliptic 49° 59'. Its perihelion was in ♉ 12° 15' 20". Its perihelion distance from the sun 998651 parts, of which the radius of the *orbis*

magnus contains 1000000, and the equal time of its perihelion *September* 16^d. 16^h. 10'. The places of this comet computed in this orbit by Mr. *Bradley*, and compared with the places observed by himself, his uncle Mr. *Pound*, and Dr. *Halley*, may be seen in the following table.

1723 Eq. time.		Comet's Long. obs.	Lat. Nor obs.	Comet's Lon. com.	Lat. Nor comp.	Diff. Lon.	Diff. Lat.
	d. h. '	o ' "	o ' "		o ' "	o ' "	' "	' "
Oct.	9. 8. 5	♒ 7.22.15	5. 2. 0	♒ 7.21.26	5. 2.47	+ 49	− 47
	10. 6.21	6.41.12	7.44.13		6.41.42	7.43.18	− 50	+ 55
	12. 7.22	5.39.58	11.55. 0		5.40.19	11.54.55	− 21	+ 5
	14. 8.57	4.59.49	14.43.50		5. 0.37	14.44. 1	− 48	− 11
	15. 6.35	4.47.41	15.40.51		4.47.45	15.40.55	− 4	− 4
	21. 6.22	4. 2.32	19.41.49		4. 2.21	19.42. 3	+ 11	− 14
	22. 6.24	3.59. 2	20. 8.12		3.59.10	20. 8.17	− 8	− 5
	24. 8. 2	3.55.29	20.55 18		3.55.11	20.55. 9	+ 18	+ 9
	29. 8.56	3.56.17	22.20.27		3.56.42	22.20.10	− 26	+ 17
	30. 6.20	3.58. 9	22.32.28		3.58.17	22.32.12	− 8	+ 16
Nov.	5. 5.53	4.16.30	23.38.33		4.16.23	23.38. 7	+ 7	+ 26
	8. 7. 6	4.29.36	24. 4.30		4.29.54	24. 4.40	− 18	− 10
	14. 6.20	5. 2.16	24.48.46		5. 2.51	24.48.16	− 35	+ 30
	20. 7.45	5.42.20	25.24.45		5.43.13	25.25.17	− 53	− 32
Dec.	7. 6.45	8. 4.13	26.54.18		8. 3.55	26.53.42	+ 18	+ 36

From these examples it is abundantly evident that the motions of comets are no less accurately represented by our theory than the motions of the planets commonly are by the theories of them; and, therefore, by means of this theory, we may enumerate the orbits of comets, and so discover the periodic time of a comet's revolution in any orbit; whence, at last, we shall have the transverse diameters of their elliptic orbits and their aphelion distances.

That retrograde comet which appeared in the year 1607 described an orbit whose ascending node (according to Dr. *Halley*'s computation) was in ♉ 20° 21'; and the inclination of the plane of the orbit to the plane of the ecliptic 17° 2'; whose perihelion was in ♒ 2° 16'; and its perihelion distance from the sun 58680 of such parts as the radius of the *orbis magnus* contains 100000; and the comet was in its perihelion *October* 16^d. 3^h. 50'; which orbit agrees very nearly with the orbit of the comet which was seen in 1682. If these were not two different comets, but one and the same, that comet will finish one revolution in the space of 75 years; and the greater axis of its orbit will be to the greater axis of the *orbis magnus* as $\sqrt[3]{75 \times 75}$ to 1, or as 1778 to 100, nearly. And the aphelion distance of this comet from the sun will be to the mean distance of the earth from the sun as about 35 to 1; from which data it will be no hard matter to determine the elliptic orbit of this comet. But these things are to be supposed on condition, that, after the space of 75 years, the same comet shall return again in the same orbit. The other comets seem to ascend to greater heights, and to require a longer time to perform their revolutions.

But, because of the great number of comets, of the great distance of their aphelions from the sun, and of the slowness of their motions in the aphelions, they will, by their mutual gravitations, disturb each other; so that their eccentricities and the times of their revolutions will be sometimes a little increased, and sometimes diminished. Therefore we are not to expect that the same comet will return exactly in the same orbit, and in the same periodic times: it will be sufficient if we find the changes no greater than may arise from the causes just spoken of.

And hence a reason may be assigned why comets are not comprehended within the limits of a zodiac, as the planets are; but, being confined to no bounds, are with various motions dispersed all over the heavens; namely, to this purpose, that in their aphelions, where their motions are exceedingly slow, receding to greater distances one from another, they may suffer less disturbance from their mutual gravitations: and hence it is that the comets which descend the lowest, and therefore move the slowest in their aphelions, ought also to ascend the highest.

The comet which appeared in the year 1680 was in its perihelion less distant from the sun than by a sixth part of the sun's diameter; and because of its extreme velocity in that proximity to the sun, and some density of the sun's atmosphere, it must have suffered some resistance and retardation; and therefore, being attracted something nearer to the sun in every revolution, will at last fall down upon the body of the sun. Nay, in its aphelion, where it moves the slowest, it may sometimes happen to be yet farther retarded by the attractions of other comets, and in consequence of this retardation descend to the sun. So fixed stars, that have been gradually wasted by the light and vapours emitted from them for a long time, may be recruited by comets that fall upon them; and from this fresh supply of new fuel those old stars, acquiring new splendor, may pass for new stars. Of this kind are such fixed stars as appear on a sudden, and shine with a wonderful brightness at first, and afterwards vanish by little and little. Such was that star which appeared in *Cassiopeia's* chair; which *Cornelius Gemma* did not see upon the 8th of *November*, 1572, though he was observing that part of the heavens upon that very night, and the sky was perfectly serene; but the next night (*November* 9) be saw it shining much brighter than any of the fixed stars, and scarcely inferior to veil us in splendor. *Tycho Brahe* saw it upon the 11th of the same month, when it shone with the greatest lustre; and from that time he observed it to decay by little and little; and in 16 months' time it entirely disappeared. In the month of *November*, when it first appeared, its light was equal to that of *Venus*. In the month of *December* its light was a little diminished, and was now become equal to that of *Jupiter*. In *January* 1573 it was less than *Jupiter*, and greater than *Sirius*; and about the end of *February* and the beginning of *March* became equal to that star. In the months of *April* and *May* it was equal to a star of the second magnitude; in *June, July,* and *August,* to a

star of the third magnitude; in *September, October,* and *November,* to those of the fourth magnitude; in *December* and *January* 1574 to those of the fifth; in *February* to those of the sixth magnitude; and in *March* it entirely vanished. Its colour at the beginning was clear, bright, and inclining to white; afterwards it, turned a little yellow; and in *March* 1573 it became ruddy like *Mars* or *Aldebaran:* in *May* it turned to a kind of dusky whiteness, like that we observe in *Saturn;* and that colour it retained ever after, but growing always more and more obscure. Such also was the star in the right foot of *Serpentarius,* which *Kepler's* scholars first observed *September* 30, O.S. 1604, with a light exceeding that of *Jupiter,* though the night before it was not to be seen; and from that time it decreased by little and little, and in 15 or 16 months entirely disappeared. Such a new star appearing with an unusual splendor is said to have moved *Hipparchus* to observe, and make a catalogue of, the fixed stars. As to those fixed stars that appear and disappear by turns and increase slowly and by degrees, and, scarcely ever exceed the stars of the third magnitude, they seem to be of another kind, which revolve about their axes, and, having a light and a dark side, shew those two different sides by turns. The vapours which arise from the sun, the fixed stars, and the tails of the comets, may meet at last with, and fall into, the atmospheres of the planets by their gravity, and there be condensed and turned into water and humid spirits; and from thence, by a slow heat, pass gradually into the form of salts, and sulphurs, and tinctures, and mud, and clay, and sand, and stones, and coral, and other terrestrial substances.

GENERAL SCHOLIUM.

The hypothesis of vortices is pressed with many difficulties. That every planet by a radius drawn to the sun may describe areas proportional to the times of description, the periodic times of the several parts of the vortices should observe the duplicate proportion of their distances from the sun; but that the periodic times of the planets may obtain the sesquiplicate proportion of their distances from the sun, the periodic times of the parts of the vortex ought to be in the: sesquiplicate proportion of their distances. That the smaller vortices may maintain their lesser revolutions about *Saturn, Jupiter,* and other planets, and swim quietly and undisturbed in the greater vortex of the sun, the periodic times of the parts of the sun's vortex should be equal; but the rotation of the sun and planets about their axes, which ought to correspond with the motions of their vortices, recede far from all these proportions. The motions of the comets are exceedingly regular, are governed by the same laws with the motions of the planets, and can by no means be accounted for by the hypothesis of vortices, for comets are carried with very eccentric motions through all parts of the heavens indifferently, with a freedom that is incompatible with the notion of a vortex.

Bodies projected in our air suffer no resistance but from the air. Withdraw the air, as is done in Mr. *Boyle's* vacuum, and the resistance ceases; for in this void a bit of fine down and a piece of solid gold descend with equal velocity. And the parity of reason must take place in the celestial spaces above the earth's atmosphere; in which spaces, where there is no air to resist their motions, all bodies will move with the greatest freedom; and the planets and comets will constantly pursue their revolutions in orbits given in kind and position, according to the laws above explained; but though these bodies may, indeed, persevere in their orbits by the mere laws of gravity, yet they could by no means have at first derived the regular position of the orbits themselves from those laws.

The six primary planets are revolved about the sun in circles concentric with the sun, and with motions directed towards the same parts, and almost in the same plane. Ten moons are revolved about the earth, Jupiter and Saturn, in circles concentric with them, with the same direction of motion, and nearly in the planes of the orbits of those planets; but it is not to be conceived that mere mechanical causes could give birth to so many regular motions, since the comets range over all parts of the heavens in very eccentric orbits; for by that kind of motion they pass easily through the orbs of the planets, and with great rapidity; and in their aphelions, where they move the slowest, and we detained the longest, they recede to the greatest distances from each other, and thence suffer the least disturbance from their mutual attractions. This most beautiful system of the sun, planets, and comets, could only proceed from the counsel and dominion of an intelligent and powerful Being. And if the fixed stars are the centres of other like systems, these being formed by the like wise counsel, must be all subject to the dominion of One; especially since the light of the fixed stars is of the same nature with the light of the sun, and from every system light passes into all the other systems: and lest the systems of the fixed stars should, by their gravity, fall on each other mutually, he hath placed thou systems at immense distances one from another.

This Being governs all things, not as the soul of the world, but as Lord over all; and on account of his dominion he is wont to be called *Lord God* παιτοκράτωρ, or *Universal Ruler;* for *God* is a relative word, and has a respect to servants; and *Deity* is the dominion of God not over his own body, as those imagine who fancy God to be the soul of the world, but over servants. The Supreme God is a Being eternal, infinite, absolutely perfect; but a being, however perfect, without dominion, cannot be said to be Lord God; for we say, my God, your God, the God of *Israel,* the God of Gods, and Lord of Lords; but we do not say, my Eternal, year Eternal the Eternal of *Israel,* the Eternal of Gods; we do not say,

my Infinite, or my Perfect: these are titles which have no respect to servants. The word *God*[1] usually signifies *Lord*; but every lord is not a God. It is the dominion of a spiritual being which constitutes a God: a true, supreme, or imaginary dominion makes a true, supreme, or imaginary God. And from his true dominion it follows that the true God is a living, intelligent, and powerful Being; and, from his other perfections, that he is supreme, or most perfect. He is eternal and infinite, omnipotent and omniscient; that is, his duration reaches from eternity to eternity; his presence from infinity to infinity; he governs all things and knows all things that are or can be done. He is not eternity or infinity, but eternal and infinite; he is not duration or space, but he endures and is present. He endures for ever, and is every where present; and by existing always and every where, he constitutes duration and space. Since every particle of space is *always*, and every indivisible moment of duration is *every where*, certainly the Maker and Lord of all things cannot be *never* and *no where*. Every soul that has perception is, though in different times and in different organs of sense and motion, still the same indivisible person. There are given successive parts in duration, coexistent parts in space, but neither the one nor the other in the person of a man, or his thinking principle; and much less can they be found in the thinking substance of God. Every man, so far as he is a thing that has perception, is one and the same man during his whole life, in all and each of his organs of sense. God is the same God, always and every where. He is omnipresent not *virtually* only, but also *substantially*; for virtue cannot subsist without substance. In him[2] are all things contained and moved; yet neither affects the other: God suffers nothing from the motion of bodies; bodies find no resistance from the omnipresence of God. It is allowed by all that the Supreme God exists necessarily; and by the same necessity he exists *always* and *every where*. Whence also he is all similar, all eye, all ear, all brain, all arm, all power to perceive, to understand, and to act; but in a manner not at all human, in a manner not at all corporeal, in a manner utterly unknown to us. As a blind man has no idea of colours, so have we no idea of the manner by which the all-wise God perceives and understands all things; He is utterly void of all body and bodily figures and can therefore neither be seen, nor heard, nor touched; nor ought he to be worshipped under the representation of any corporeal thing. We have ideas of his attributes; but what the real substance of any thing is we know not. In bodies, we see only their figures and colours, we hear only the sounds, we touch only their outward surfaces, we smell only the smells, and taste the savours;

---

[1] Dr. Pocock derives the Latin word *Deus* from the Arabic *du* (in the oblique case *di*), which signifies *Lord*. And in this same princes are called *gods, Psal.* lxxxii. ver. 6; and *John* x. ver. 35. And *Moses* is called a *god* to his brother *Aaron*, and a god to *Pharaoh* (*Exod.* iv. ver. 16; and vii. ver. 1). And in the same sense the souls of dead princes were formerly, by the Heathens, called *gods*, but falsely, became of their want of dominion.

[2] This was the opinion of the Ancients. So *Pythagoras*, in *Cicer. de Nat. Deor.* lib. i. *Thales, Anaxagoras, Virgil, Georg.* lib. iv. ver. 220; and *AEneid*, lib. vi. ver. 721. *Philo Allegor.* at the beginning of lib. i. *Aratus*, in his *Phaenom.* at the beginning. So also the sacred writers; as *St. Paul, Acts,* xvii. ver. 27, 28. *St. John's* Gosp. chap. xiv. ver. 2. *Moses*, in *Deut.* iv. ver. 39; and x. ver. 14. *David, Psal.* cxxxix. ver. 7, 8, 9. *Solomon,* 1 *Kings,* viii. ver. 27. *Job*, xxii. ver. 12, 13, 14. *Jeremiah*, xxiii. ver. 23, 24. The Idolaters supposed the sun, moon, and stars, the souls of man, and other parts of the world, to be parts of the Supreme God, and therefore, to be worshipped; but erroneously.

but their inward substances are not to be known either by our, senses, or by any reflex act of our minds: much less, then, have we any idea of the substance of God. We know him only by his most wise and excellent contrivances of things, and final causes; we admire him for his perfections; but we reverence and adore him on account of his dominion: for we adore him as his servants; and a god without dominion, providence, and final causes, is nothing else but Fate and Nature. Blind metaphysical necessity, which is certainly the same always and every where, could produce no variety of things. All that diversity of natural things which we find suited to different times and places could arise from nothing but the ideas and will of a Being necessarily existing. But, by way of allegory, God is said to see, to speak, to laugh, to love, to hate, to desire, to give, to receive, to rejoice, to be angry, to fight, to frame, to work, to build; for our notions of God are taken from the ways of mankind by a certain similitude, which, though not perfect, has some likeness, however. And thus much concerning God; to discourse of whom from the appearances of things, does certainly belong to Natural Philosophy.

Hitherto we have explained the phaenomena of the heavens and of our sea by the power of gravity, but have not yet assigned the cause of this power. This is certain, that it must proceed from a cause that penetrates to the very centres of the sun and planets, without suffering the least diminution of its force; that operates not according to the quantity of the surfaces of the particles upon which it acts (as mechanical causes use to do), but according to the quantity of the solid matter which they contain, and propagates its virtue on all sides to immense distances, decreasing always in the duplicate proportion of the distances. Gravitation towards the sun is made up out of the gravitations towards the several particles of which the body of the sun is composed; and in receding from the sun decreases accurately in the duplicate proportion of the distances as far as the orb of Saturn, as evidently appears from the quiescence of the aphelions of the planets; nay, and even to the remotest aphelions of the comets, if those aphelions are also quiescent, But hitherto I have not been able to discover the cause of those properties of gravity from phaenomena, and I frame no hypotheses; for whatever is not deduced from the phaenomena, is to be called an hypothesis; and hypotheses, whether metaphysical or physical, whether of occult qualities or mechanical, have no place in experimental philosophy. In this philosophy particular propositions are inferred from the phaenomena, and afterwards rendered general by induction. Thus it was that the impenetrability, the mobility, and the impulsive force of bodies, and the laws of motion and of gravitation, were discovered, And to us it is enough that gravity does really exist, and act according to the laws which we have explained, and abundantly serves to account for all the motions of the celestial bodies, and of our sun.

And now we might add something concerning a certain most subtle Spirit which pervades and lies hid in all gross bodies; by the force and action of which Spirit the particles of bodies mutually attract one another at near distances, and cohere, if contiguous; and electric bodies operate to greater distance, as well repelling as attracting the neighbouring corpuscles; and light is emitted, reflected, refracted, inflected, and heats bodies; and all sensation is excited, and the members of animal bodies move at the command of the will, namely, by the vibrations of this Spirit, mutually propagated along the solid filaments of the nerves, from the outward organs of sense to the brain, and from the brain into the muscles. But these are things that cannot be explained in few words, nor are we furnished with that sufficiency of experiments which is required to an accurate determination and demonstration of the laws by which this electric and elastic Spirit operates.

END OF THE MATHEMATICAL PRINCIPLES.

Albert Einstein

(1879-1955)

HIS LIFE AND WORK

Genius isn't always immediately recognized. Although Albert Einstein would become the greatest theoretical physicist who ever lived, when he was in grade school in Germany his headmaster told his father, "He'll never make a success of anything." When Einstein was in his mid-twenties, he couldn't find a decent teaching job even though he had graduated from the Federal Polytechnic School in Zurich as a teacher of mathematics and physics. So he gave up hope of obtaining a university position and applied for temporary work in Bern. With the help of a classmate's father, Einstein managed to secure a civil-service post as an examiner in the Swiss patent office. He worked six days a week, earning $600 a year. That's how he supported himself while working toward his doctorate in physics at the University of Zurich.

In 1903, Einstein married his Serbian sweetheart, Mileva Maric, and the couple moved into a one-bedroom flat in Bern. Two years later, she bore him a son, Hans Albert. The period surrounding Hans's birth was probably the happiest time in Einstein's life. Neighbors later recalled seeing the young father absentmindedly pushing a baby carriage down the city streets. From time to time, Einstein would reach into the carriage and remove a pad of paper on which to jot down notes to himself. It seems likely that the notepad in the baby's stroller contained some of the formulas and equations that led to the theory of relativity and the development of the atomic bomb.

During these early years at the patent office, Einstein spent most of his spare time studying theoretical physics. He composed a series of four seminal scientific papers,

which set forth some of the most momentous ideas in the long history of the quest to comprehend the universe. Space and time would never be looked at the same way again. Einstein's work won him the Nobel Prize in Physics in 1921, as well as much popular acclaim.

As Einstein pondered the workings of the universe, he received flashes of understanding that were too deep for words. "These thoughts did not come in any verbal formulation," Einstein was once quoted as saying. "I rarely think in words at all. A thought comes, and I may try to express it in words afterward."

Einstein eventually settled in the United States, where he publicly championed such causes as Zionism and nuclear disarmament. But he maintained his passion for physics. Right up until his death in 1955, Einstein kept seeking a unified field theory that would link the phenomena of gravitation and electromagnetism in one set of equations. It is a tribute to Einstein's vision that physicists today continue to seek a grand unification of physical theory. Einstein revolutionized scientific thinking in the twentieth century and beyond.

Albert Einstein was born at Ulm, in the former German state of Wüettemberg, on March 14, 1879, and grew up in Munich. He was the only son of Hermann Einstein and Pauline Koch. His father and uncle owned an electrotechnical plant. The family considered Albert a slow learner because he had difficulty with language. (It is now thought that he may have been dyslexic.) Legend has it that when Hermann asked the headmaster of his son's school about the best profession for Albert, the man replied, "It doesn't matter. He'll never make a success of anything."

Einstein did not do well in school. He didn't like the regimentation, and he suffered from being one of the few Jewish children in a Catholic school. This experience as an outsider was one that would repeat itself many times in his life.

One of Einstein's early loves was science. He remembered his father's showing him a pocket compass when he was around five years old, and marveling that the needle always pointed north, even if the case was spun. In that moment, Einstein recalled, he "felt something deeply hidden had to be behind things."

Another of his early loves was music. Around the age of six, Einstein began studying the violin. It did not come naturally to him; but when after several years he recognized the mathematical structure of music, the violin became a lifelong passion—although his talent was never a match for his enthusiasm.

When Einstein was ten, his family enrolled him in the Luitpold Gymnasium, which is where, according to scholars, he developed a suspicion of authority. This trait served Einstein well later in life as a scientist. His habit of skepticism made it easy for him to question many long-standing scientific assumptions.

In 1895, Einstein attempted to skip high school by passing an entrance examination to the Federal Polytechnic School in Zurich, where he hoped to pursue a degree in electrical engineering. This is what he wrote about his ambitions at the time:

> *If I were to have the good fortune to pass my examinations, I would go to Zurich. I would stay there for four years in order to study mathematics and physics. I imagine myself becoming a teacher in those branches of the natural sciences, choosing the theoretical part of them. Here are the reasons which lead me to this plan. Above all, it is my disposition for abstract and mathematical thought, and my lack of imagination and practical ability.*

Einstein failed the arts portion of the exam and so was denied admission to the polytechnic. His family instead sent him to secondary school at Aarau, in Switzerland, hoping that it would earn him a second chance to enter the Zurich school. It did, and Einstein graduated from the polytechnic in 1900. At about that time he fell in love with Mileva Maric, and in 1901, she gave birth out of wedlock to their first child, a daughter named Lieserl. Very little is known for certain about Lieserl, but it appears that she either was born with a crippling condition or fell very ill as an infant, then was put up for adoption, and died at about two years of age. Einstein and Maric married in 1903.

The year Hans was born, 1905, was a miracle year for Einstein. Somehow he managed to handle the demands of fatherhood and a full-time job and still publish four epochal scientific papers, all without benefit of the resources that an academic appointment might have provided.

In the spring of that year, Einstein submitted three papers to the German periodical *Annals of Physics (Annalen der Physik)*. The three appeared together in the journal's volume 17. Einstein characterized the first paper, on the light quantum, as "very revolutionary." In it, he examined the phenomenon of the quantum (the fundamental unit of energy) discovered by the German physicist Max Planck. Einstein explained the photoelectric effect, which holds that for each electron emitted, a specific amount of energy is released. This is the quantum effect that states that energy is emitted in fixed amounts that can be expressed only as whole integers. This theory formed the basis for a great deal of quantum mechanics. Einstein suggested that light be considered a collection of independent particles of energy, but remarkably, he offered no experimental data. He simply argued hypothetically for the existence of these "light quantum" for aesthetic reasons.

Initially, physicists were hesitant to endorse Einstein's theory. It was too great a departure from scientifically accepted ideas of the time, and far beyond anything

Planck had discovered. It was this first paper, titled "On a Heuristic View concerning the Production and Transformation of Light"—not his work on relativity—that won Einstein the Nobel Prize in Physics in 1921.

In his second paper, "On a New Determination of Molecular Dimensions"— which Einstein wrote as his doctoral dissertation—and his third, "On the Movement of Small Particles Suspended in Stationary Liquids Required by the Molecular-Kinetic Theory of Heat," Einstein proposed a method to determine the size and motion of atoms. He also explained Brownian motion, a phenomenon described by the British botanist Robert Brown after studying the erratic movement of pollen suspended in fluid. Einstein asserted that this movement was caused by impacts between atoms and molecules. At the time, the very existence of atoms was still a subject of scientific debate, so there could be no underestimating the importance of these two papers. Einstein had confirmed the atomic theory of matter.

In the last of his 1905 papers, entitled "On the Electrodynamics of Moving Bodies," Einstein presented what became known as the special theory of relativity. The paper reads more like an essay than a scientific communication. Entirely theoretical, it contains no notes or bibliographic citations. Einstein wrote this 9,000-word treatise in just five weeks, yet historians of science consider it every bit as comprehensive and revolutionary as Isaac Newton's *Principia*.

What Newton had done for our understanding of gravity, Einstein had done for our view of time and space, managing in the process to overthrow the Newtonian conception of time. Newton had declared that "absolute, true, and mathematical time, of itself and from its own nature, flows equably without relation to anything external." Einstein held that all observers should measure the same speed for light, regardless of how fast they themselves are moving. Einstein also asserted that the mass of an object is not unchangeable but rather increases with the object's velocity. Experiments later proved that a small particle of matter, when accelerated to 86 percent of the speed of light, has twice as much mass as it does at rest.

Another consequence of relativity is that the relation between energy and mass may be expressed mathematically, which Einstein did in the famous equation $E=mc^2$. This expression—that energy is equivalent to mass times the square of the speed of light—led physicists to understand that even miniscule amounts of matter have the potential to yield enormous amounts of energy. Completely converting to energy just a part of the mass of a few atoms would, then, result in a colossal explosion. Thus did Einstein's modest-looking equation lead scientists to consider the consequences of splitting the atom (nuclear fission) and, at the urging of governments, to develop the atomic bomb. In 1909, Einstein was appointed professor of theoretical physics at the University of Zurich, and three years later he fulfilled his ambition to return to the

Federal Polytechnic School as a full professor. Other prestigious academic appointments and directorships followed. Throughout, he continued to work on his theory of gravity as well as his general theory of relativity. But as his professional status continued to rise, his marriage and health began to deteriorate. He and Mileva began divorce proceedings in 1914, the same year he accepted a professorship at the University of Berlin. When he later fell ill, his cousin Elsa nursed him back to health, and around 1919 they were married.

Where the special theory of relativity radically altered concepts of time and mass, the general theory of relativity changed our concept of space. Newton had written that "absolute space, in its own nature, without relation to anything external, remains always similar and immovable." Newtonian space is Euclidean, infinite, and unbounded. Its geometric structure is completely independent of the physical matter occupying it. In it, all bodies gravitate toward one another without having any effect on the structure of space. In stark contrast, Einstein's general theory of relativity asserts that not only does a body's gravitational mass act on other bodies, it also influences the structure of space. If a body is massive enough, it induces space to curve around it. In such a region, light appears to bend.

In 1919, Sir Arthur Eddington sought evidence to test the general theory. Eddington organized two expeditions, one to Brazil and the other to West Africa, to observe the light from stars as it passed near a massive body—the sun—during a total solar eclipse on May 29. Under normal circumstances such observations would be impossible, as the weak light from distant stars would be blotted out by daylight, but during the eclipse such light would briefly be visible.

In September, Einstein received a telegram from Hendrik Lorentz, a fellow physicist and close friend. It read: "Eddington found star displacement at rim of Sun, preliminary measurements between nine-tenths of a second and twice that value." Eddington's data were in keeping with the displacement predicted by the special relativity theory. His photographs from Brazil seemed to show the light from known stars in a different position in the sky during the eclipse than they were at nighttime, when their light did not pass near the sun. The theory of general relativity had been confirmed, forever changing the course of physics. Years later, when a student of Einstein's asked how he would have reacted had the theory been disproved, Einstein replied, "Then I would have felt sorry for the dear Lord. The theory is correct."

Confirmation of general relativity made Einstein world-famous. In 1921, he was elected a member of the British Royal Society. Honorary degrees and awards greeted him at every city he visited. In 1927, he began developing the foundation of quantum mechanics with the Danish physicist Niels Bohr, even as he continued to pursue his dream of a unified field theory. His travels in the United States led to his appointment

in 1932 as a professor of mathematics and theoretical physics at the Institute for Advanced Study in Princeton, New Jersey.

A year later, he settled permanently in Princeton after the ruling Nazi party in Germany began a campaign against "Jewish science." Einstein's property was confiscated, and he was deprived of German citizenship and positions in German universities. Until then, Einstein had considered himself a pacifist. But when Hitler turned Germany into a military power in Europe, Einstein came to believe that the use of force against Germany was justified. In 1939, at the dawn of World War II, Einstein became concerned that the Germans might be developing the capability to build an atomic bomb—a weapon made possible by his own research and for which he therefore felt a responsibility. He sent a letter to President Franklin D. Roosevelt warning of such a possibility and urging that the United States undertake nuclear research. The letter, composed by his friend and fellow scientist Leo Szilard, became the impetus for the formation of the Manhattan Project, which produced the world's first atomic weapons. In 1944, Einstein put a handwritten copy of his 1905 paper on special relativity up for auction and donated the proceeds—six million dollars—to the Allied war effort.

After the war, Einstein continued to involve himself with causes and issues that concerned him. In November 1952, having shown strong support for Zionism for many years, he was asked to accept the presidency of Israel. He respectfully declined, saying that he was not suited for the position. In April 1955, only one week before his death, Einstein composed a letter to the philosopher Bertrand Russell in which he agreed to sign his name to a manifesto urging all nations to abandon nuclear weapons.

Einstein died of heart failure on April 18, 1955. Throughout his life, he had sought to understand the mysteries of the cosmos by probing it with his thought rather than relying on his senses. "The truth of a theory is in your mind," he once said, "not in your eyes."

THE PRINCIPLE OF RELATIVITY

Translated by W. Perrett and G. B. Jeffery

ON THE ELECTRODYNAMICS OF MOVING BODIES

It is known that Maxwell's electrodynamics—as usually understood at the present time—when applied to moving bodies, leads to asymmetries which do not appear to be inherent in the phenomena. Take, for example, the reciprocal electrodynamic action of a magnet and a conductor. The observable phenomenon here depends only on the relative motion of the conductor and the magnet, whereas the customary view draws a sharp distinction between the two cases in which either the one or the other of these bodies is in motion. For if the magnet is in motion and the conductor at rest, there arises in the neighbourhood of the magnet an electric field with a certain definite energy, producing a current at the places where parts of the conductor are situated. But if the magnet is stationary and the conductor in motion, no electric field arises in the neighbourhood of the magnet. In the conductor, however, we find an electromotive force, to which in itself there is no corresponding energy, but which gives rise—assuming equality of relative motion in the two cases discussed—to electric currents of the same path and intensity as those produced by the electric form in the former case.

Examples of this sort, together with the unsuccessful attempts to discover any motion of the earth relatively to the "light medium," suggest that the phenomena of electrodynamics as well as of mechanics possess no properties corresponding to the idea of absolute rest. They suggest rather that, as has already been shown to the first order of small quantities, the same laws of electrodynamics and optics will be valid for all frames of reference for which the equations of mechanics hold good.[1] We will raise this conjecture (the purport of which will hereafter be called the "Principle of Relativity") to the status of a postulate, and also introduce another postulate, which is only apparently

---

1. The preceding memoir by Lorentz was not at this time known to the author.

irreconcilable with the former, namely, that light is always propagated in empty space with a definite velocity c which is independent of the state of motion of the emitting body. These two postulates suffice for the attainment of a simple and consistent theory of the electrodynamics of moving bodies based on Maxwell's theory for stationary bodies. The introduction of a "luminiferous ether" will prove to be superfluous inasmuch as the view here to be developed will not require an "absolutely stationary space" provided with special properties, nor assign a velocity-vector to a point of the empty space in which electromagnetic processes take place.

The theory to be developed is based—like all electrodynamics—on the kinematics of the rigid body, since the assertions of any such theory have to do with the relationships between rigid bodies (systems of co-ordinates), clocks, and electromagnetic processes. Insufficient consideration of this circumstance lies at the root of the difficulties which the electrodynamics of moving bodies at present encounters.

I. KINEMATICAL PART

§ 1. Definition of Simultaneity

Let us take a system of co-ordinates in which the equations of Newtonian mechanics hold good.[1] In order to render our presentation more precise and to distinguish this system of co-ordinates verbally from others which will be introduced hereafter, we call it the "stationary system."

If a material point is at rest relatively to this system of co-ordinates, its position can be defined relatively thereto by the employment of rigid standards of measurement and the methods of Euclidean geometry, and can be expressed in Cartesian co-ordinates.

If we wish to describe the *motion* of a material point, we give the values of its co-ordinates as functions of the time. Now we must bear carefully in mind that a mathematical description of this kind has no physical meaning unless we are quite clear as to what we understand by "time." We have to take into account that all our judgments in which time plays a part are always judgments of *simultaneous events*. If, for instance, I say, "That train arrives here at 7 o'clock," I mean something like this: "The pointing of the small hand of my watch to 7 and the arrival of the train are simultaneous events."[2]

It might appear possible to overcome all the difficulties attending the definition of "time" by substituting "the position of the small hand of my watch" for "time." And in fact such a definition is satisfactory when we are concerned with defining a time

---

1. I.e. to the first approximation.
2. We shall not here discuss the inexactitude which lurks in the concept of simultaneity of two events at approximately the same place, which can only be removed by an abstraction.

exclusively for the place where the watch is located; but it is no longer satisfactory when we have to connect in time series of events occurring at different places, or—what comes to the same thing—to evaluate the times of events occurring at places remote from the watch.

We might, of course, content ourselves with time values determined by an observer stationed together with the watch at the origin of the co-ordinates, and co-ordinating the corresponding positions of the hands with light signals, given out by every event to be timed, and reaching him through empty space. But this co-ordination has the disadvantage that it is not independent of the standpoint of the observer with the watch or clock, as we know from experience. We arrive at a much more practical determination along the following line of thought.

If at the point A of space there is a clock, an observer at A can determine the time values of events in the immediate proximity of A by finding the positions of the hands which are simultaneous with these events. If there is at the point B of space another clock in all respects resembling the one at A, it is possible for an observer at B to determine the time values of events in the immediate neighbourhood of B. But it is not possible without further assumption to compare, in respect of time, an event at A with an event at B. We have so far defined only an "A time" and a "B time." We have not defined a common "time" for A and B, for the latter cannot be defined at all unless we establish *by definition* that the "time" required by light to travel from A to B equals the "time" it requires to travel from B to A. Let a ray of light start at the "A time" t_A from A towards B, let it at the "B time" t_B be reflected at B in the direction of A, and arrive again at A at the "A time" t'_A.

In accordance with definition the two clocks synchronize if

$$t_B - t_A = t'_A - t_B.$$

We assume that this definition of synchronism is free from contradictions, and possible for any number of points; and that the following relations are universally valid:

1. If the clock at B synchronizes with the clock at A, the clock at A synchronizes with the clock at B.

2. If the clock at A synchronizes with the clock at B and also with the clock at C, the clocks at B and C also synchronize with each other.

Thus with the help of certain imaginary physical experiments we have settled what is to be understood by synchronous stationary clocks located at different places, and have evidently obtained a definition of "simultaneous" or "synchronous," and of "time." The "time" of an event is that which is given simultaneously with the event by a stationary clock located at the place of the event, this clock being synchronous, and

indeed synchronous for all time determinations, with a specified stationary clock.

In agreement with experience we further assume the quantity

$$\frac{2\,\mathrm{AB}}{t'_{\mathrm{A}}-t_{\mathrm{A}}}=c$$

to be a universal constant—the velocity of light in empty space.

It is essential to have time defined by means of stationary clocks in the stationary system, and the time now defined being appropriate to the stationary system we call it "the time of the stationary system."

§ 2. On the Relativity of Lengths and Times

The following reflexions are based on the principle of relativity and on the principle of the constancy of the velocity of light. These two principles we define as follows:—

1. The laws by which the states of physical systems undergo change are not affected, whether these changes of state be referred to the one or the other of two systems of co-ordinates in uniform translatory motion.

2. Any ray of light moves in the "stationary" system of co-ordinates with the determined velocity c, whether the ray be emitted by a stationary or by a moving body. Hence

$$\text{velocity} = \frac{\text{light path}}{\text{time interval}}$$

where time interval is to be taken in the sense of the definition in § 1.

Let there be given a stationary rigid rod; and let its length be l as measured by a measuring-rod which is also stationary. We now imagine the axis of the rod lying along the axis of x of the stationary system of co-ordinates, and that a uniform motion of parallel translation with velocity v along the axis of x in the direction of increasing x is then imparted to the rod. We now inquire as to the length of the moving rod, and imagine its length to be ascertained by the following two operations:—

(*a*) The observer moves together with the given measuring-rod and the rod to be measured, and measures the length of the rod directly by superposing the measuring-rod, in just the same way as if all three were at rest.

(*b*) By means of stationary clocks set up in the stationary system and synchronizing in accordance with § 1, the observer ascertains at what points of the stationary system the two ends of the rod to be measured are located at a definite time. The distance between these two points, measured by the measuring-rod already employed, which in this case is at rest, is also a length which may be designated "the length of the rod."

In accordance with the principle of relativity the length to be discovered by the operation (*a*)—we will call it "the length of the rod in the moving system"—must be

equal to the length l of the stationary rod.

The length to be discovered by the operation (b) we will call "the length of the (moving) rod in the stationary system." This we shall determine on the basis of our two principles, and we shall find that it differs from l.

Current kinematics tacitly assumes that the lengths determined by these two operations are precisely equal, or in other words, that a moving rigid body at the epoch t may in geometrical respects be perfectly represented by *the same* body *at rest* in a definite position.

We imagine further that at the two ends A and B of the rod, clocks are placed which synchronize with the clocks of the stationary system, that is to say that their indications correspond at any instant to the "time of the stationary system" at the places where they happen to be. These clocks are therefore "synchronous in the stationary system."

We imagine further that with each clock there is a moving observer, and that these observers apply to both clocks the criterion established in § 1 for the synchronization of two clocks. Let a ray of light depart from A at the time[1] t_A, let it be reflected at B at the time t_B, and reach A again at the time t'_A. Taking into consideration the principle of the constancy of the velocity of light we find that

$$t_B - t_A = \frac{r_{AB}}{c - v} \quad \text{and} \quad t'_A - t_B = \frac{r_{AB}}{c + v}$$

where r_{AB} denotes the length of the moving rod—measured in the stationary system. Observers moving with the moving rod would thus find that the two clocks were not synchronous, while observers in the stationary system would declare the clocks to be synchronous.

So we see that we cannot attach any *absolute* signification to the concept of simultaneity, but that two events which, viewed from a system of co-ordinates, are simultaneous, can no longer be looked upon as simultaneous events when envisaged from a system which is in motion relatively to that system.

§ 3. THEORY OF THE TRANSFORMATION OF CO-ORDINATES AND TIMES FROM A STATIONARY SYSTEM TO ANOTHER SYSTEM IN UNIFORM MOTION OF TRANSLATION RELATIVELY TO THE FORMER

Let us in "stationary" space take two systems of co-ordinates, i.e. two systems, each of three rigid material lines, perpendicular to one another, and issuing from a point. Let the axes of X of the two systems coincide, and their axes of Y and Z respectively be parallel. Let each system be provided with a rigid measuring-rod and a number of

---

1. "Time" here denotes "time of the stationary" and also "position of hands of the moving clock situated at the place, under discussion."

clocks, and let the two measuring-rods, and likewise all the clocks of the two systems, be in all respects alike.

Now to the origin of one of the two systems (k) let a constant velocity v be imparted in the direction of the increasing x of the other stationary system (K), and let this velocity be communicated to the axes of the co-ordinates, the relevant measuring-rod, and the clocks. To any time of the stationary system K there then will correspond a definite position of the axes of the moving system, and from reasons of symmetry we are entitled to assume that the motion of k may be such that the axes of the moving system are at the time t (this "t" always denotes a time of the stationary system) parallel to the axes of the stationary system.

We now imagine space to be measured from the stationary system K by means of the stationary measuring-rod, and also from the moving system k by means of the measuring-rod moving with it; and that we thus obtain the co-ordinates x, y, z, and ξ, η, ζ respectively. Further, let the time t of the stationary system be determined for all points thereof at which there are clocks by means of light signals in the manner indicated in § 1; similarly let the time τ of the moving system be determined for all points of the moving system at which there are clocks at rest relatively to that system by applying the method, given in § 1, of light signals between the points at which the latter clocks are located.

To any system of values x, y, z, t, which completely defines the place and time of an event in the stationary system, there belongs a system of values ξ, η, ζ, τ, determining that event relatively to the system k, and our task is now to find the system of equations connecting these quantities.

In the first place it is clear that the equations must be *linear* on account of the properties of homogeneity which we attribute to space and time.

If we place $x' = x - vt$, it is clear that a point at rest in the system k must have a system of values x', y, z, independent of time. We first define τ as a function of x', y, z, and t. To do this we have to express in equations that τ is nothing else than the summary of the data of clocks at rest in system k, which have been synchronized according to the rule given in § 1.

From the origin of system k let a ray be emitted at the time τ_0 along the X-axis to x', and at the time τ_1 be reflected thence to the origin of the co-ordinates, arriving there at the time τ_2; we then must have $\frac{1}{2}(\tau_0 + \tau_2) = \tau_1$, or, by inserting the arguments of the function τ and applying the principle of the constancy of the velocity of light in the stationary system:

$$\frac{1}{2}\left[\tau(0,0,0,t) + \tau\left(0,0,0,t + \frac{x'}{c-v} + \frac{x'}{c+v}\right) \right] = \tau\left(x',0,0,t + \frac{x'}{c-v}\right)$$

Hence, if x' be chosen infinitesimally small,

$$\frac{1}{2}\left(\frac{1}{c-v}+\frac{1}{c+v}\right)\frac{\partial\tau}{\partial t}=\frac{\partial\tau}{\partial x'}+\frac{1}{c-v}\frac{\partial\tau}{\partial t}$$

or

$$\frac{\partial\tau}{\partial x'}+\frac{v}{c^2-v^2}\frac{\partial\tau}{\partial t}=0$$

It is to be noted that instead of the origin of the co-ordinates we might have chosen any other point for the point of origin of the ray, and the equation just obtained is therefore valid for all values of x', y, z.

An analogous consideration—applied to the axes of Y and Z—it being borne in mind that light is always propagated along these axes, when viewed from the stationary system, with the velocity $\sqrt{(c^2 - v^2)}$, gives us

$$\frac{\partial\tau}{\partial y}=0, \frac{\partial\tau}{\partial z}=0.$$

Since τ is a linear function, it follows from these equations that

$$\tau = a\left(t - \frac{v}{c^2-v^2}x'\right)$$

where a is a function $\phi(v)$ at present unknown, and where for brevity it is assumed that at the origin of k, $\tau = 0$, when $t = 0$.

With the help of this result we easily determine the quantities ξ, η, ζ by expressing in equations that light (as required by the principle of the constancy of the velocity of light, in combination with the principle of relativity) is also propagated with velocity c when measured in the moving system. For a ray of light emitted at the time $\tau = 0$ in the direction of the increasing ξ

$$\xi = c\tau \quad \text{or} \quad \xi = ac\left(t - \frac{v}{c^2-v^2}x'\right).$$

But the ray moves relatively to the initial point of k, when measured in the stationary system, with the velocity $c - v$, so that

$$\frac{x'}{c-v}=t$$

If we insert this value of t in the equation for ξ, we obtain

$$\xi = a\frac{c^2}{c^2-v^2}x'.$$

In an analogous manner we find, by considering rays moving along the two other axes, that

$$\eta = c\tau = ac\left(t - \frac{v}{c^2-v^2}x'\right)$$

when

$$\frac{y}{\sqrt{\left(c^2 - v^2\right)}} = t, x' = 0$$

Thus

$$\eta = a\frac{c}{\sqrt{\left(c^2 - v^2\right)}} y \quad \text{and} \quad \zeta = a\frac{c}{\sqrt{\left(c^2 - v^2\right)}} z$$

Substituting for x' its value, we obtain

$$\tau = \phi(v)\beta\left(t - vx/c^2\right),$$
$$\xi = \phi(v)\beta(x - vt),$$
$$\eta = \phi(v)y,$$
$$\zeta = \phi(v)z$$

where

$$\beta = \frac{1}{\sqrt{\left(1 - v^2/c^2\right)}},$$

and ϕ is an as yet unknown function of v. If no assumption whatever be made as to the initial position of the moving system and as to the zero point of τ, an additive constant is to be placed on the right side of each of these equations.

We now have to prove that any ray of light, measured in the moving system, is propagated with the velocity c, if, as we have assumed, this is the case in the stationary system; for we have not as yet furnished the proof that the principle of the constancy of the velocity of light is compatible with the principle of relativity.

At the time $t = \tau = 0$, when the origin of the co-ordinates is common to the two systems, let a spherical wave be emitted therefrom, and be propagated with the velocity c in system K. If (x, y, z) be a point just attained by this wave, then

$$x^2 + y^2 + z^2 = c^2 t^2.$$

Transforming this equation with the aid of our equations of transformation we obtain after a simple calculation

$$\xi^2 + \eta^2 + \zeta^2 = c^2\tau^2.$$

The wave under consideration is therefore no less a spherical wave with velocity of propagation c when viewed in the moving system. This shows that our two fundamental principles are compatible.[1]

In the equations of transformation which have been developed there enters an unknown function ϕ of v, which we will now determine.

1. The equations of the Lorentz transformation may be more simply deduced directly from the condition that in virtue of these equations the relation $x^2 + y^2 + z^2 = c^2 t^2$ shall have as its consequence the second relation $\xi^2 + \eta^2 + \zeta^2 = c^2\tau^2$.

For this purpose we introduce a third system of co-ordinates K', which relatively to the system k is in a state of parallel translatory motion parallel to the axis of X, such that the origin of co-ordinates of system k moves with velocity $-v$ on the axis of X. At the time $t = 0$ let all three origins coincide, and when $t = x = y = z = 0$ let the time t' of the system K be zero. We call the co-ordinates, measured in the system K', x', y', z', and by a twofold application of our equations of transformation we obtain

$$t' = \phi(-v)\beta(-v)(\tau + v\xi/c^2) \quad = \phi(v)\phi(-v)t,$$
$$x' = \phi(-v)\beta(-v)(\xi + v\tau) \quad = \phi(v)\phi(-v)x,$$
$$y' = \phi(-v)\eta \quad = \phi(v)\phi(-v)y,$$
$$z' = \phi(-v)\zeta \quad = \phi(v)\phi(-v)z,$$

Since the relations between x', y', z' and x, y, z do not contain the time t, the systems K and K' are at rest with respect to one another, and it is clear that the transformation from K to K' must be the identical transformation. Thus

$$\phi(v)\phi(-v) = 1$$

We now inquire into the signification of $\phi(v)$. We give our attention to that part of the axis of Y of system k which lies between $\xi = 0, \eta = 0, \zeta = 0$ and $\xi = 0, \eta = l, \zeta = 0$. This part of the axis of Y is a rod moving perpendicularly to its axis with velocity v relatively to system K. Its ends possess in K the co-ordinates

$$x_1 = vt, y_1 = \frac{l}{\phi(v)}, z_1 = 0$$

and

$$x_2 = vt, y_2 = z_2 = 0$$

The length of the rod measured in K is therefore $l/\phi(v)$; and this gives us the meaning of the function $\phi(v)$. From reasons of symmetry it is now evident that the length of a given rod moving perpendicularly to its axis, measured in the stationary system, must depend only on the velocity and not on the direction and the sense of the motion. The length of the moving rod measured in the stationary system does not change, therefore, if v and $-v$ are interchanged. Hence follows that $l/\phi(v) = l/\phi(-v)$, or

$$\phi(v) = \phi(-v)$$

It follows from this relation and the one previously found that $\phi(v) = 1$, so that the transformation equations which have been found become

$$\tau = \beta(t - vx/c^2),$$
$$\xi = \beta(x - vt),$$
$$\eta = y,$$
$$\zeta = z$$

where

$$\beta = 1/\sqrt{(1-v^2/c^2)}$$

§ 4. Physical Meaning of the Equations Obtained In Respect to Moving Rigid Bodies and Moving Clocks

We envisage a rigid sphere[1] of radius R, at rest relatively to the moving system k, and with its centre at the origin of co-ordinates of k. The equation of the surface of this sphere moving relatively to the system K with velocity v is

$$\xi^2 + \eta^2 + \zeta^2 = R^2$$

The equation of this surface expressed in x, y, z at the time $t = 0$ is

$$\frac{x^2}{\left(\sqrt{(1-v^2/c^2)}\right)^2} + y^2 + z^2 = R^2$$

A rigid body which, measured in a state of rest, has the form of a sphere, therefore has in a state of motion—viewed from the stationary system—the form of an ellipsoid of revolution with the axes

$$R\sqrt{(1 - v^2/c^2)}, R, R$$

Thus, whereas the Y and Z dimensions of the sphere (and therefore of every rigid body of no matter what form) do not appear modified by the motion, the X dimension appears shortened in the ratio $1:\sqrt{(1 - v^2/c^2)}$, i.e. the greater the value of v, the greater the shortening. For $v = c$ all moving objects—viewed from the "stationary" system—shrivel up into plain figures. For velocities greater than that of light our deliberations become meaningless; we shall, however, find in what follows, that the velocity of light in our theory plays the part, physically, of an infinitely great velocity.

It is clear that the same results hold good of bodies at rest in the "stationary" system, viewed from a system in uniform motion.

Further, we imagine one of the clocks which are qualified to mark the time t when at rest relatively to the stationary system, and the time τ when at rest relatively to the moving system, to be located at the origin of the co-ordinates of k, and so adjusted that it marks the time τ. What is the rate of this clock, when viewed from the stationary system?

Between the quantities x, t, and τ, which refer to the position of the clock, we have, evidently, $x = vt$ and

---

1. That is, a body possessing spherical form when examined at rest.

$$\tau = \frac{1}{\sqrt{\left(1 - v^2 / c^2\right)}}\left(t - vx / c^2\right)$$

Therefore,

$$\tau = t\sqrt{(1 - v^2 / c^2)} = t - (1 - \sqrt{(1 - v^2 / c^2)})t$$

whence it follows that the time marked by the clock (viewed in the stationary system) is slow by $1 - \sqrt{(1 - v^2/c^2)}$ seconds per second, or—neglecting magnitudes of fourth and higher order—by $\frac{1}{2}v^2 c^2$.

From this there ensues the following peculiar consequence. If at the points A and B of K there are stationary clocks which, viewed in the stationary system, are synchronous; and if the clock at A is moved with the velocity v along the line AB to B, then on its arrival at B the two clocks no longer synchronize, but the clock moved from A to B lags behind the other which has remained at B by $\frac{1}{2}tv^2 c^2$ (up to magnitudes of fourth and higher order), t being the time occupied in the journey from A to B.

It is at once apparent that this result still holds good if the clock moves from A to B in any polygonal line, and also when the points A and B coincide.

If we assume that the result proved for a polygonal line is also valid for a continuously curved line, we arrive at this result: If one of two synchronous clocks at A is moved in a closed curve with constant velocity until it returns to A, the journey lasting t seconds, then by the clock which has remained at rest the travelled clock on its arrival at A will be $\frac{1}{2}tv^2 c^2$ second slow. Thence we conclude that a balance-clock[1] at the equator must go more slowly, by a very small amount, than a precisely similar clock situated at one of the poles under otherwise identical conditions.

§ 5. The Composition of Velocities

In the system k moving along the axis of X of the system K with velocity v, let a point move in accordance with the equations

$$\xi = w_\xi\tau, \eta = w_\eta\tau, \zeta = 0$$

where w_ξ and w_η denote constants.

Required: the motion of the point relatively to the system K. If with the help of the equations of transformation developed in § 3 we introduce the quantities x, y, z, t into the equations of motion of the point, we obtain

---

1. Not a pendulum-clock, which is physically a system to which the Earth belongs. This case had to be excluded.

$$x = \frac{w_\xi + v}{1 + vw_\xi / c^2} w,$$

$$y = \frac{\sqrt{\left(1 - v^2 / c^2\right)}}{1 + vw_\xi / c^2} w_{\eta} t,$$

$$z = 0$$

Thus the law of the parallelogram of velocities is valid according to our theory only to a first approximation. We set

$$V^2 = \left(\frac{dx}{dt}\right)^2 + \left(\frac{dy}{dt}\right)^2,$$

$$w^2 = w_\xi^2 + w_\eta^2,$$

$$a = \tan^{-1} w_y / w_x,$$

a is then to be looked upon as the angle between the velocities v and w. After a simple calculation we obtain

$$V = \frac{\sqrt{\left[\left(v^2 + w^2 + 2vw \cos a\right) - \left(vw \sin a / c^2\right)^2\right]}}{1 + vw \cos a / c^2}$$

It is worthy of remark that v and w enter into the expression for the resultant velocity in a symmetrical manner. If w also has the direction of the axis of X, we get

$$V = \frac{v + w}{1 + vw / c^2}.$$

It follows from this equation that from a composition of two velocities which are less than c, there always results a velocity less than c. For if we set $v = c - \kappa$, $w = c - \lambda$, κ and λ being positive and less than c, then

$$V = c \frac{2c - \kappa - \lambda}{2c - \kappa - \lambda + \kappa\lambda/c} < c$$

It follows, further, that the velocity of light c cannot be altered by composition with a velocity less than that of light. For this case we obtain

$$V = \frac{c + w}{1 + w / c} = c$$

We might also have obtained the formula for V, for the case when v and w have the same direction, by compounding two transformations in accordance with § 3. If in addition to the systems K and k figuring in § 3 we introduce still another system of co-ordinates k' moving parallel to k, its initial point moving on the axis of X with the velocity w, we obtain equations between the quantities x, y, z, t and the corresponding

quantities of k', which differ from the equations found in § 3 only in that the place of "v" is taken by the quantity

$$\frac{v + w}{1 + vw/c^2}$$

from which we see that such parallel transformations—necessarily—form a group.

We have now deduced the requisite laws of the theory of kinematics corresponding to our two principles, and we proceed to show their application to electrodynamics.

II. ELECTRODYNAMICAL PART

§ 6. Transformation of the Maxwell-Hertz Equations for Empty Space. On the Nature of the Electromotive Forces Occurring in a Magnetic Field During Motion

Let the Maxwell-Hertz equations for empty space hold good for the stationary system K, so that we have

$$\frac{1}{c}\frac{\partial X}{\partial x} = \frac{\partial N}{\partial y} - \frac{\partial M}{\partial z}, \quad \frac{1}{c}\frac{\partial L}{\partial t} = \frac{\partial Y}{\partial z} - \frac{\partial Z}{\partial y},$$

$$\frac{1}{c}\frac{\partial Y}{\partial t} = \frac{\partial L}{\partial z} - \frac{\partial N}{\partial x}, \quad \frac{1}{c}\frac{\partial M}{\partial t} = \frac{\partial Z}{\partial x} - \frac{\partial X}{\partial z},$$

$$\frac{1}{c}\frac{\partial Z}{\partial t} = \frac{\partial M}{\partial x} - \frac{\partial L}{\partial y}, \quad \frac{1}{c}\frac{\partial N}{\partial t} = \frac{\partial X}{\partial y} - \frac{\partial Y}{\partial x}$$

where (X, Y, Z) denotes the vector of the electric force, and (L, M, N) that of the magnetic force.

If we apply to these equations the transformation developed in § 3, by referring the electromagnetic processes to the system of co-ordinates there introduced, moving with the velocity v, we obtain the equations

$$\frac{1}{c}\frac{\partial X}{\partial \tau} = \frac{\partial}{\partial \tau}\left\{\beta\left(N - \frac{v}{c}Y\right)\right\} - \frac{\partial}{\partial \zeta}\left\{\beta\left(M + \frac{v}{c}Z\right)\right\},$$

$$\frac{1}{c}\frac{\partial}{\partial \tau}\left\{\beta\left(Y - \frac{v}{c}N\right)\right\} = \frac{\partial L}{\partial \xi} \qquad\qquad - \frac{\partial}{\partial \zeta}\left\{\beta\left(N - \frac{v}{c}Y\right)\right\},$$

$$\frac{1}{c}\frac{\partial}{\partial \tau}\left\{\beta\left(Z + \frac{v}{c}M\right)\right\} = \frac{\partial}{\partial \xi}\left\{\beta\left(M + \frac{v}{c}Z\right)\right\} - \frac{\partial L}{\partial \eta},$$

$$\frac{1}{c}\frac{\partial L}{\partial \tau} = \frac{\partial}{\partial \zeta}\left\{\beta\left(Y - \frac{v}{c}N\right)\right\} - \frac{\partial}{\partial \eta}\left\{\beta\left(Z + \frac{v}{c}M\right)\right\},$$

$$\frac{1}{c}\frac{\partial}{\partial \tau}\left\{\beta\left(M + \frac{v}{c}Z\right)\right\} = \frac{\partial}{\partial \xi}\left\{\beta\left(Z + \frac{v}{c}M\right)\right\} - \frac{\partial X}{\partial \xi},$$

$$\frac{1}{c}\frac{\partial}{\partial \tau}\left\{\beta\left(N + \frac{v}{c}Y\right)\right\} = \frac{\partial X}{\partial \eta} \qquad\qquad - \frac{\partial}{\partial \xi}\left\{\beta\left(Y + \frac{v}{c}N\right)\right\},$$

where

$$b = 1/\sqrt{(1 - v^2/c^2)}$$

Now the principle of relativity requires that if the Maxwell-Hertz equations for empty space hold good in system K, they also hold good in system *k*; that is to say that the vectors of the electric and the magnetic force—(x', Y', Z') and (L', M', N')—of the moving system *k*, which are defined by their ponderomotive effects on electric or magnetic masses respectively, satisfy the following equations:—

$$\frac{1}{c}\frac{\partial X'}{\partial \tau} = \frac{\partial N'}{\partial \eta} - \frac{\partial M'}{\partial \zeta}, \qquad \frac{1}{c}\frac{\partial L'}{\partial \tau} = \frac{\partial Y'}{\partial \zeta} - \frac{\partial Z'}{\partial \eta},$$

$$\frac{1}{c}\frac{\partial Y'}{\partial \tau} = \frac{\partial L'}{\partial \zeta} - \frac{\partial N'}{\partial \xi}, \qquad \frac{1}{c}\frac{\partial M'}{\partial \tau} = \frac{\partial Z'}{\partial \xi} - \frac{\partial X'}{\partial \zeta},$$

$$\frac{1}{c}\frac{\partial Z'}{\partial \tau} = \frac{\partial M'}{\partial \xi} - \frac{\partial L'}{\partial \eta}, \qquad \frac{1}{c}\frac{\partial N'}{\partial \tau} = \frac{\partial X'}{\partial \eta} - \frac{\partial Y'}{\partial \xi}.$$

Evidently the two systems of equations found for system *k* must express exactly the same thing, since both systems of equations are equivalent to the Maxwell-Hertz equations for system K. Since, further, the equations of the two systems agree, with the exception of the symbols for the vectors, it follows that the functions occurring in the systems of equations at corresponding places must agree, with the exception of a factor $\psi(v)$, which is common for all functions of the one system of equations, and is independent of ξ, η, ζ and τ but depends upon v. Thus we have the relations

$$X' = \psi(v)X, \qquad\qquad L' = \psi(v)L,$$

$$Y' = \psi(v)\beta\left(Y - \frac{v}{c}N\right), \quad M' = \psi(v)\beta\left(M + \frac{v}{c}Z\right),$$

$$Z' = \psi(v)\beta\left(Z - \frac{v}{c}M\right), \quad N' = \psi(v)\beta\left(N + \frac{v}{c}Y\right).$$

If we now form the reciprocal of this system of equations, firstly by solving the equations just obtained, and secondly by applying the equations to the inverse transformation (from k to K), which is characterized by the velocity $-v$, it follows, when we consider that the two systems of equations thus obtained must be identical, that $\psi(v)\,\psi(-v) = 1$. Further, from reasons of symmetry[1] $\psi(v) = \psi(-v)$, and therefore

$$\psi(v) = 1,$$

and our equations assume the form

$$X' = X, \qquad\qquad L' = L,$$

$$Y' = \beta\left(Y - \frac{v}{c}N\right), \quad M' = \beta\left(M + \frac{v}{c}Z\right),$$

$$Z' = \beta\left(Z - \frac{v}{c}M\right), \quad N' = \beta\left(N - \frac{v}{c}Y\right).$$

As to the interpretation of these equations we make the following remarks: Let a point charge of electricity have the magnitude "one" when measured in the stationary system K, i.e. let it when at rest in the stationary system exert a force of one dyne upon an equal quantity of electricity at a distance of one cm. By the principle of relativity this electric charge is also of the magnitude "one" when measured in the moving system. If this quantity of electricity is at rest relatively to the stationary system, then by definition the vector (X, Y, Z) is equal to the force acting upon it. If the quantity of electricity is at rest relatively to the moving system (at least at the relevant instant), then the force acting upon it, measured in the moving system, is equal to the vector (x', Y', Z'). Consequently the first three equations above allow themselves to be clothed in words in the two following ways:

1. If a unit electric point charge is in motion in an electromagnetic field, there acts upon it, in addition to the electric force, an "electromotive force" which, if we neglect the terms multiplied by the second and higher powers of v/c, is equal to the vector-product of the velocity of the charge and the magnetic force, divided by the velocity of light. (Old manner of expression.)

2. If a unit electric point charge is in motion in an electromagnetic field, the force acting upon it is equal to the electric force which is present at the locality of the charge, and which we ascertain by transformation of the field to a system of co-ordinates at rest relatively to the electrical charge. (New manner of expression.)

The analogy holds with "magnetomotive forces." We see that electromotive force plays in the developed theory merely the part of an auxiliary concept, which owes its introduction to the circumstance that electric and magnetic forces do not exist independently of the state of motion of the system of co-ordinates.

1. If, for example, X = Y = Z = L = M = O, and N ≠ O, then from reasons of symmetry it is clear that when v changes sign without changing its numerical value, Y' must also change sign without changing its numerical value.

Furthermore it is clear that the asymmetry mentioned in the introduction as aris-ing when we consider the currents produced by the relative motion of a magnet and a conductor, now disappears. Moreover, questions as to the "seat" of electrodynamic elec-tromotive forces (unipolar machines) now have no point.

§ 7. THEORY OF DOPPLER'S PRINCIPLE AND OF ABERRATION

In the system K, very far from the origin of co-ordinates, let there be a source of electrodynamic waves, which in a part of space containing the origin of co-ordinates may be represented to a sufficient degree of approximation by the equations

$$X = X_0 \sin\Phi, \quad L = L_0 \sin\Phi,$$
$$Y = Y_0 \sin\Phi, \quad M = M_0 \sin\Phi,$$
$$Z = Z_0 \sin\Phi, \quad N = N_0 \sin\Phi,$$

where

$$\Phi = \omega\left\{t - \frac{1}{c}\left(lx + my + nz\right)\right\}.$$

Here (X_0, Y_0, Z_0) and (L_0, M_0, N_0) are the vectors defining the amplitude of the wave-train, and l, m, n the direction-cosines of the wave-normals. We wish to know the con-stitution of these waves, when they are examined by an observer at rest in the moving system k.

Applying the equations of transformation found in § 6 for electric and magnetic forces, and those found in § 3 for the co-ordinates and the time, we obtain directly

$$X' = X_0 \sin\Phi', \qquad\qquad L' = L_0 \sin\Phi',$$
$$Y' = \beta\left(Y_0 - vN_0/c\right)\sin\Phi', \quad M' = \beta\left(M_0 + vZ_0/c\right)\sin\Phi',$$
$$Z' = \beta\left(Z_0 + vM_0/c\right)\sin\Phi', \quad N = \beta\left(N_0 - vY_0/c\right)\sin\Phi',$$

$$\Phi' = \omega'\left\{\tau - \frac{1}{c}\left(l'\xi + m'\eta + n'\zeta\right)\right\}$$

where

$$\omega' = \omega\beta\left(1 - lv/c\right),$$
$$l' = \frac{l - v/c}{1 - lv/c},$$
$$m' = \frac{m}{\beta\left(1 - lv/c\right)},$$
$$n' = \frac{n}{\beta\left(1 - lv/c\right)}.$$

From the equation for ω' it follows that if an observer is moving with velocity v relatively to an infinitely distant source of light of frequency ν, in such a way that the connecting line "source—observer" makes the angle ϕ with the velocity of the observer

referred to a system of co-ordinates, which is at rest relatively to the source of light, the frequency ν' of the light perceived by the observer is given by the equation

$$\nu' = \nu \frac{1 - \cos\phi \cdot \nu/c}{\sqrt{\left(1 - \nu^2/c^2\right)}}.$$

This is Doppler's principle for any velocities whatever. When $\phi = 0$ the equation assumes the perspicuous form

$$\nu' = \nu \sqrt{\frac{1 - \nu/c}{1 + \nu/c}}.$$

We see that, in contrast with the customary view, when $\nu = -c, \nu' = \infty$.

If we call the angle between the wave-normal (direction of the ray) in the moving system and the connecting line "source—observer" ϕ', the equation for l assumes the form

$$\cos\phi' = \frac{\cos\phi - \nu/c}{1 - \cos\phi \cdot \nu/c}.$$

This equation expresses the law of aberration in its most general form. If $\phi = \frac{1}{2}\pi$, the equation becomes simply

$$\cos\phi' = -\nu/c.$$

We still have to find the amplitude of the waves, as it appears in the moving system. If we call the amplitude of the electric or magnetic force A or A' respectively, accordingly as it is measured in the stationary system or in the moving system, we obtain

$$A'^2 = A^2 \frac{\left(1 - \cos\phi \cdot \nu/c\right)^2}{1 + \nu^2/c^2}.$$

which equation, if $\phi = 0$, simplifies into

$$A'^2 = A^2 \frac{1 - \nu/c}{1 + \nu/c}.$$

It follows from these results that to an observer approaching a source of light with the velocity c, this source of light must appear of infinite intensity.

§ 8. TRANSFORMATION OF THE ENERGY OF LIGHT RAYS. THEORY OF THE PRESSURE OF RADIATION EXERTED ON PERFECT REFLECTORS

Since $A^2/8\pi$ equals the energy of light per unit of volume, we have to regard $A'^2/8\pi$, by the principle of relativity, as the energy of light in the moving system. Thus A'^2/A^2 would be the ratio of the "measured in motion" to the "measured at rest" energy

of a given light complex, if the volume of a light complex were the same, whether measured in K or in k. But this is not the case. If l, m, n are the direction-cosines of the wave-normals of the light in the stationary system, no energy passes through the surface elements of a spherical surface moving with the velocity of light:

$$(x - lct)^2 + (y - mct)^2 + (z - nct)^2 = R^2.$$

We may therefore say that this surface permanently encloses the same light complex. We inquire as to the quantity of energy enclosed by this surface, viewed in system k, that is, as to the energy of the light complex relatively to the system k.

The spherical surface—viewed in the moving system—is an ellipsoidal surface, the equation for which, at the time $\tau = 0$, is

$$(\beta\xi - l\beta\xi v/c)^2 + (\eta - m\beta\xi v/c)^2 + (\zeta - n\beta\xi v/c)^2 = R^2$$

If S is the volume of the sphere, and S' that of this ellipsoid, then by a simple calculation

$$\frac{S'}{S} = \frac{\sqrt{1 - v^2/c^2}}{1 - \cos\phi \cdot v/c}.$$

Thus, if we call the light-energy enclosed by this surface E when it is measured in the stationary system, and E' when measured in the moving system, we obtain

$$\frac{E'}{E} = \frac{A^2 S'}{A^2 S} = \frac{1 - \cos\phi \cdot v/c}{\sqrt{\left(1 - v^2/c^2\right)}},$$

and this formula, when $\phi = 0$, simplifies into

$$\frac{E'}{E} = \sqrt{\frac{1 - v/c}{1 + v/c}}.$$

It is remarkable that the energy and the frequency of a light complex vary with the state of motion of the observer in accordance with the same law.

Now let the co-ordinate plane $\xi = 0$ be a perfectly reflecting surface, at which the plane waves considered in § 7 are reflected. We seek for the pressure of light exerted on the reflecting surface, and for the direction, frequency, and intensity of the light after reflexion.

Let the incidental light be defined by the quantities A, $\cos\phi$, ν (referred to system K). Viewed from k the corresponding quantities are

$$A' = A \frac{1 - \cos\phi \cdot v/c}{\sqrt{\left(1 - v^2/c^2\right)}},$$

$$\cos\phi' = \frac{\cos\phi - v/c}{1 - \cos\phi \cdot v/c},$$

$$v' = v \frac{1 - \cos\phi \cdot v/c}{\sqrt{\left(1 - v^2/c^2\right)}}.$$

For the reflected light, referring the process to system k, we obtain

$$A'' = A'$$
$$\cos\phi'' = -\cos\phi'$$
$$v'' = v'$$

Finally, by transforming back to the stationary system K, we obtain for the reflected light

$$A''' = A'' \frac{1 + \cos\phi'' \cdot v/c}{\sqrt{\left(1 - v^2/c^2\right)}} = A \frac{1 - 2\cos\phi \cdot v/c + v^2/c^2}{1 - v^2/c^2},$$

$$\cos\phi''' = \frac{\cos\phi'' + v/c}{1 + \cos\phi'' \cdot v/c} = -\frac{\left(1 + v^2/c^2\right)\cos\phi - 2v/c}{1 - 2\cos\phi \cdot v/c + v^2/c^2}$$

$$v''' = v'' \frac{1 + \cos\phi'' v/c}{\sqrt{\left(1 - v^2/c^2\right)}} = v \frac{1 - 2\cos\phi \cdot v/c + v^2/c^2}{1 - v^2/c^2}.$$

The energy (measured in the stationary system) which is incident upon unit area of the mirror in unit time is evidently $A^2(c\cos\phi - v)/8\pi$. The energy leaving the unit of surface of the mirror in the unit of time is $A'''^2(-c\cos\phi''' + v)/8\pi$. The difference of these two expressions is, by the principle of energy, the work done by the pressure of light in the unit of time. If we set down this work as equal to the product Pv, where P is the pressure of light, we obtain

$$P = 2 \cdot \frac{A^2}{8\pi} \frac{\left(\cos\phi - v/c\right)^2}{1 - v^2/c^2}.$$

In agreement with experiment and with other theories, we obtain to a first approximation

$$P = 2 \cdot \frac{A^2}{8\pi} \cos^2 \phi.$$

All problems in the optics of moving bodies can be solved by the method here employed. What is essential is that the electric and magnetic force of the light which is influenced by a moving body be transformed into a system of co-ordinates; at rest relatively to the body. By this means all problems in the optics of moving bodies will be reduced to a series of problems in the optics of stationary bodies.

§ 9. TRANSFORMATION OF THE MAXWELL-HERTZ EQUATIONS WHEN CONVECTION-CURRENTS ARE TAKEN INTO ACCOUNT

We start from the equations

$$\frac{1}{c}\left\{\frac{\partial X}{\partial t}+u_x\rho\right\}=\frac{\partial N}{\partial y}-\frac{\partial M}{\partial z}, \quad \frac{1}{c}\frac{\partial L}{\partial t}=\frac{\partial Y}{\partial z}-\frac{\partial Z}{\partial y},$$

$$\frac{1}{c}\left\{\frac{\partial Y}{\partial t}+u_y\rho\right\}=\frac{\partial L}{\partial z}-\frac{\partial N}{\partial x}, \quad \frac{1}{c}\frac{\partial M}{\partial t}=\frac{\partial Z}{\partial x}-\frac{\partial X}{\partial z},$$

$$\frac{1}{c}\left\{\frac{\partial Z}{\partial t}+u_z\rho\right\}=\frac{\partial M}{\partial x}-\frac{\partial L}{\partial y}, \quad \frac{1}{c}\frac{\partial N}{\partial t}=\frac{\partial X}{\partial y}-\frac{\partial Y}{\partial x},$$

where

$$\rho=\frac{\partial X}{\partial x}+\frac{\partial Y}{\partial y}+\frac{\partial Z}{\partial z}$$

denotes 4π times the density of electricity, and (u_x, u_y, u_z) the velocity-vector of the charge. If we imagine the electric charges to be invariably coupled to small rigid bodies (ions, electrons), these equations are the electromagnetic basis of the Lorentzian electrodynamics and optics of moving bodies.

Let these equations be valid in the system K, and transform them, with the assistance of the equations of transformation given in §§ 3 and 6, to the system k. We then obtain the equations

$$\frac{1}{c}\left\{\frac{\partial X'}{\partial \tau}+u_\xi\rho'\right\}=\frac{\partial N'}{\partial \eta}-\frac{\partial M'}{\partial \zeta}, \quad \frac{1}{c}\frac{\partial L'}{\partial \tau}=\frac{\partial Y'}{\partial \zeta}-\frac{\partial Z'}{\partial \eta},$$

$$\frac{1}{c}\left\{\frac{\partial Y'}{\partial \tau}+u_\eta\rho'\right\}=\frac{\partial L'}{\partial \zeta}-\frac{\partial N'}{\partial \xi}, \quad \frac{1}{c}\frac{\partial M'}{\partial \tau}=\frac{\partial Z'}{\partial \xi}-\frac{\partial X'}{\partial \zeta},$$

$$\frac{1}{c}\left\{\frac{\partial Z'}{\partial \tau}+u_\zeta\rho'\right\}=\frac{\partial M'}{\partial \xi}-\frac{\partial L'}{\partial \eta}, \quad \frac{1}{c}\frac{\partial N'}{\partial \tau}=\frac{\partial X'}{\partial \eta}-\frac{\partial Y'}{\partial \xi},$$

where

$$u_\xi=\frac{u_x-v}{1-u_xv/c^2}$$

$$u_\eta=\frac{u_y}{\beta\left(1-u_xv/c^2\right)}$$

$$u_\zeta=\frac{u_z}{\beta\left(1-u_xv/c^2\right)},$$

and

$$\rho' = \frac{\partial X'}{\partial \xi} + \frac{\partial Y'}{\partial \eta} + \frac{\partial Z'}{\partial \zeta}$$

$$= \beta\left(1 - u_x v / c^2\right)\rho.$$

Since—as follows from the theorem of addition of velocities (§ 5)—the vector (u_ξ, u_η, u_ζ) is nothing else than the velocity of the electric charge, measured in the system k, we have the proof that, on the basis of our kinematical principles, the electrodynamic foundation of Lorentz's theory of the electrodynamics of moving bodies is in agreement with the principle of relativity.

In addition I may briefly remark that the following important law may easily be deduced from the developed equations: If an electrically charged body is in motion anywhere in space without altering its charge when regarded from a system of co-ordinates moving with the body, its charge also remains—when regarded from the "stationary" system K—constant.

§ 10. DYNAMICS OF THE SLOWLY ACCELERATED ELECTRON

Let there be in motion in an electromagnetic field an electrically charged particle (in the sequel called an "electron"), for the law of motion of which we assume as follows:

If the electron is at rest at a given epoch, the motion of the electron ensues in the next instant of time according to the equations

$$m\frac{d^2x}{dt^2} = \varepsilon X$$

$$m\frac{d^2y}{dt^2} = \varepsilon Y$$

$$m\frac{d^2z}{dt^2} = \varepsilon Z$$

where x, y, z denote the co-ordinates of the electron, and m the mass of the electron, as long as its motion is slow.

Now, secondly, let the velocity of the electron at a given epoch be v. We seek the law of motion of the electron in the immediately ensuing instants of time.

Without affecting the general character of our considerations, we may and will assume that the electron, at the moment when we give it our attention, is at the origin of the co-ordinates, and moves with the velocity v along the axis of X of the system K. It is then clear that at the given moment ($t = 0$) the electron is at rest relatively to a system of co-ordinates which is in parallel motion with velocity v along the axis of X.

From the above assumption, in combination with the principle of relativity, it is clear that in the immediately ensuing time (for small values of t) the electron, viewed from the system k, moves in accordance with the equations

$$m\frac{d^2\xi}{d\tau^2} = \varepsilon X',$$

$$m\frac{d^2\eta}{d\tau^2} = \varepsilon Y',$$

$$m\frac{d^2\zeta}{d\tau^2} = \varepsilon Z',$$

in which the symbols ξ, η, ζ, τ, x', Y', Z' refer to the system k. If, further, we decide that when $t = x = y = z = 0$ then $\tau = \xi = \eta = \zeta = 0$, the transformation equations of §§ 3 and 6 hold good, so that we have

$$\xi = \beta(x - vt), \eta = y, \zeta = z, \tau = \beta(t - vx/c^2)$$

$$x' = X, Y' = \beta(Y - vN/c), Z' = \beta(Z + vM/c).$$

With the help of these equations we transform the above equations of motion from system k to system K, and obtain

$$\left.\begin{aligned}
\frac{d^2x}{dt^2} &= \frac{\varepsilon}{m\beta^3}X \\
\frac{d^2y}{dt^2} &= \frac{\varepsilon}{m\beta}\left(Y - \frac{v}{c}N\right) \\
\frac{d^2z}{dt^2} &= \frac{\varepsilon}{m\beta}\left(Z + \frac{v}{c}M\right)
\end{aligned}\right\} \dots (A)$$

Taking the ordinary point of view we now inquire as to the "longitudinal" and the "transverse" mass of the moving electron. We write the equations (A) in the form

$$m\beta^3\frac{d^2x}{dt^2} = \varepsilon X = \varepsilon X',$$

$$m\beta^2\frac{d^2y}{dt^2} = \varepsilon\beta\left(Y - \frac{v}{c}N\right) = \varepsilon Y',$$

$$m\beta^2\frac{d^2z}{dt^2} = \varepsilon\beta\left(Z + \frac{v}{c}M\right) = \varepsilon Z',$$

and remark firstly that ϵx', ϵY', ϵZ' are the components of the ponderomotive force acting upon the electron, and are so indeed as viewed in a system moving at the moment with the electron, with the same velocity as the electron. (This force might be measured, for example, by a spring balance at rest in the last-mentioned system.) Now if we call this force simply "the force acting upon the electron,"[1] and maintain the equation—mass x acceleration = force—and if we also decide that the accelerations are to be measured in the stationary system K, we derive from the above equations

1. The definition of force here given is not advantageous, as was first shown by M. Planck. It is more to the point to define force in such a way that the laws of momentum and energy assume the simplest form.

$$\text{Longitudinal mass} = \frac{m}{\left(\sqrt{1 - v^2/c^2}\right)^3}.$$

$$\text{Transverse mass} = \frac{m}{1 - v^2/c^2}.$$

With a different definition of force and acceleration we should naturally obtain other values for the masses. This shows us that in comparing different theories of the motion of the electron we must proceed very cautiously.

We remark that these results as to the mass are also valid for ponderable material points, because a ponderable material point can be made into an electron (in our sense of the word) by the addition of an electric charge, *no matter how small.*

We will now determine the kinetic energy of the electron. If an electron moves from rest at the origin of co-ordinates of the system K along the axis of X under the action of an electrostatic force X, it is clear that the energy withdrawn from the electrostatic field has the value $\int \varepsilon X dx$. As the electron is to be slowly accelerated, and consequently may not give off any energy in the form of radiation, the energy withdrawn from the electrostatic field must be put down as equal to the energy of motion W of the electron. Bearing in mind that during the whole process of motion which we are considering, the first of the equations (A) applies, we therefore obtain

$$W = \int \varepsilon X dx = m \int_0^v \beta^3 v dv$$

$$= mc^2 \left\{ \frac{1}{\sqrt{1 - v^2/c^2}} - 1 \right\}$$

Thus, when $v = c$, W becomes infinite. Velocities greater than that of light have—as in our previous results—no possibility of existence.

This expression for the kinetic energy must also, by virtue of the argument stated above, apply to ponderable masses as well.

We will now enumerate the properties of the motion of the electron which result from the system of equations (A), and are accessible to experiment.

1.   From the second equation of the system (A) it follows that an electric force Y and a magnetic force N have an equally strong deflective action on an electron moving with the velocity v, when $Y = Nv/c$. Thus we see that it is possible by our theory to determine the velocity of the electron from the ratio of the magnetic power of deflexion A_m to the electric power of deflexion A_e, for any velocity, by applying the law

$$\frac{A_m}{A_e} = \frac{v}{c}.$$

This relationship may be tested experimentally, since the velocity of the electron can be directly measured, e.g. by means of rapidly oscillating electric and magnetic fields.

2. From the deduction for the kinetic energy of the electron it follows that between the potential difference, P, traversed and the acquired velocity v of the electron there must be the relationship

$$P = \int X dx = \frac{m}{\varepsilon} c^2 \left\{ \frac{1}{\sqrt{1 - v^2 / c^2}} - \right.$$

3. We calculate the radius of curvature of the path of the electron when a magnetic force N is present (as the only deflective force), acting perpendicularly to the velocity of the electron. From the second of the equations (A) we obtain

$$-\frac{d^2 y}{dt^2} = \frac{v^2}{R} = \frac{\varepsilon}{m} \frac{v}{c} N \sqrt{1 - \frac{v^2}{c^2}}$$

or

$$R = \frac{mc^2}{\varepsilon} \cdot \frac{v/c}{\sqrt{\left(1 - v^2 / c^2\right)}} \cdot \frac{1}{N}$$

These three relationships are a complete expression for the laws according to which, by the theory here advanced, the electron must move.

In conclusion I wish to say that in working at the problem here dealt with I have had the loyal assistance of my friend and colleague M. Besso, and that I am indebted to him for several valuable suggestions.

DOES THE INERTIA OF A BODY DEPEND UPON ITS ENERGY-CONTENT?

Translated from "Ist die Trägheit eins Körpers von seinem Energiegehalt abhängig?" Annalen der Physik, 17, 1905.

The results of the previous investigation lead to a very interesting conclusion, which is here to be deduced.

I based that investigation on the Maxwell-Hertz equations for empty space, together with the Maxwellian expression for the electromagnetic energy of space, and in addition the principle that:

The laws by which the states of physical system alter are independent of the alternative, to which of two systems of co-ordinates, in uniform motion of parallel translation relatively to each other, these alterations of state are referred (principle of relativity).

With these principles[1] as my basis I deduced *inter alia* the following result (§ 8):

Let a system of plane waves of light, referred to the system of co-ordinates (x, y, z), possess the energy l; let the direction of the ray (the wave-normal) make an angle ϕ with the axis of x of the system. If we introduce a new system of co-ordinates (ξ, η, ζ) moving in uniform parallel translation with respect to the system (x, y, z), and having its origin of co-ordinates in motion along the axis of x with the velocity v, then this quantity of light—measured in the system (ξ, η, ζ)—possesses the energy

$$l^* = l \frac{1 - \frac{v}{c}\cos\phi}{\sqrt{1 - v^2/c^2}}$$

where c denotes the velocity of light. We shall make use of this result in what follows.

Let there be a stationary body in the system (x, y, z), and let its energy—referred to the system (x, y, z)—be E_0. Let the energy of the body relative to the system (ξ, η, ζ) moving as above with the velocity v, be H_0.

Let this body send out, in a direction making an angle ϕ with the axis of x, plane waves of light, of energy $1/2 L$ measured relatively to (x, y, z), and simultaneously an equal quantity of light in the opposite direction. Meanwhile the body remains at rest with respect to the system (x, y, z). The principle of energy must apply to this process, and in fact (by the principle of relativity) with respect to both systems of co-ordinates. If we call the energy of the body after the emission of light E_1 or H_1 respectively, measured relatively to the system (x, y, z) or (ξ, η, ζ) respectively, then by employing the relation given above we obtain

$$E_0 = E_1 + \frac{1}{2}L + \frac{1}{2}L,$$

$$H_0 = H_1 + \frac{1}{2}L\frac{1 - \frac{v}{c}\cos\phi}{\sqrt{1 - v^2/c^2}} + \frac{1}{2}L\frac{1 + \frac{v}{c}\cos\phi}{\sqrt{1 - v^2/c^2}}$$

$$= H_1 + \frac{L}{\sqrt{1 - v^2/c^2}}$$

By subtraction we obtain from these equations

---

1. The principle of the constancy of the velocity of light is of course contained in Maxwell's equations.

$$H_0 - E_0 - \left(H_1 - E_1\right) = L\left\{\frac{1}{\sqrt{1 - v^2/c^2}} - 1\right\}.$$

The two differences of the form H − E occurring in this expression have simple physical significations. H and E are energy values of the same body referred to two systems of co-ordinates which are in motion relatively to each other, the body being at rest in one of the two systems (system (x, y, z)). Thus it is clear that the difference H − E can differ from the kinetic energy K of the body, with respect to the other system (ξ, η, ζ), only by an additive constant C, which depends on the choice of the arbitrary additive constants of the energies H and E. Thus we may place

$$H_0 - E_0 = K_0 + C,$$

$$H_1 - E_1 = K_1 + C,$$

since C does not change during the emission of light. So we have

$$K_0 - K_1 = L\left\{\frac{1}{\sqrt{1 - v^2/c^2}} - 1\right\}.$$

The kinetic energy of the body with respect to (ξ, η, ζ) diminishes as a result of the emission of light, and the amount of diminution is independent of the properties of the body. Moreover, the difference $K_0 - K_1$, like the kinetic energy of the electron (§ 10), depends on the velocity.

Neglecting magnitudes of fourth and higher orders we may place

$$K_0 - K_1 = \frac{1}{2}\frac{L}{c^2}v^2.$$

From this equation it directly follows that:

If a body gives off the energy L in the form of radiation, its mass diminishes by L/c^2. The fact that the energy withdrawn from the body becomes energy of radiation evidently makes no difference, so that we are led to the more general conclusion that:

The mass of a body is a measure of its energy-content; if the energy changes by L, the mass changes in the same sense by $L/9 \times 10^{20}$, the energy being measured in ergs, and the mass in grammes.

It is not impossible that with bodies whose energy-content is variable to a high degree (e.g. with radium salts) the theory may be successfully put to the test.

If the theory corresponds to the facts, radiation conveys inertia between the emitting and absorbing bodies.

ALBERT EINSTEIN

ON THE INFLUENCE OF GRAVITATION ON THE PROPAGATION OF LIGHT

Translated from "Über den Einfluss der Schwerkraft auf die Ausbreitung des Lichtes," Annalen der Physik, 35, 1911.

In a memoir published four years ago[1] I tried to answer the question whether the propagation of light is influenced by gravitation. I return to this theme, because my previous presentation of the subject does not satisfy me, and for a stronger reason, because I now see that one of the most important consequences of my former treatment is capable of being tested experimentally. For it follows from the theory here to be brought forward, that rays of light, passing close to the sun, are deflected by its gravitational field, so that the angular distance between the sun and a fixed star appearing near to it is apparently increased by nearly a second of arc.

In the course of these reflexions further results are yielded which relate to gravitation. But as the exposition of the entire group of considerations would be rather difficult to follow, only a few quite elementary reflexions will be given in the following pages, from which the reader will readily be able to inform himself as to the suppositions of the theory and its line of thought. The relations here deduced, even if the theoretical foundation is sound, are valid only to a first approximation.

§ 1. A HYPOTHESIS AS TO THE PHYSICAL NATURE OF THE GRAVITATIONAL FIELD

In a homogeneous gravitational field (acceleration of gravity γ) let there be a stationary system of co-ordinates K, orientated so that the lines of force of the gravitational field run in the negative direction of the axis of z. In a space free of gravitational fields let there be a second system of co-ordinates K', moving with uniform acceleration (γ) in the positive direction of its axis of z. To avoid unnecessary complications, let us for the present disregard the theory of relativity, and regard both systems from the customary point of view of kinematics, and the movements occurring in them from that of ordinary mechanics.

Relatively to K, as well as relatively to K', material points which are not subjected to the action of other material points, move in keeping with the equations

---

1. A. Einstein, Jahrbuch für Radioakt. und Elektronik, 4, 1907

$$\frac{d^2 x}{dt^2} = 0, \frac{d^2 y}{dt^2} = 0, \frac{d^2 z}{dt^2} = -\gamma.$$

For the accelerated system K' this follows directly from Galileo's principle, but for the system K, at rest in a homogeneous gravitational field, from the experience that all bodies in such a field are equally and uniformly accelerated. This experience, of the equal falling of all bodies in the gravitational field, is one of the most universal which the observation of nature has yielded; but in spite of that the law has not found any place in the foundations of our edifice of the physical universe.

But we arrive at a very satisfactory interpretation of this law of experience, if we assume that the systems K and K' are physically exactly equivalent, that is, if we assume that we may just as well regard the system K as being in a space free from gravitational fields, if we then regard K as uniformly accelerated. This assumption of exact physical equivalence makes it impossible for us to speak of the absolute acceleration of the system of reference, just as the usual theory of relativity forbids us to talk of the absolute velocity of a system;[1] and it makes the equal falling of all bodies in a gravitational field seem a matter of course.

As long as we restrict ourselves to purely mechanical processes in the realm where Newton's mechanics holds sway, we are certain of the equivalence of the systems K and K'. But this view of ours will not have any deeper significance unless the systems K and K' are equivalent with respect to all physical processes, that is, unless the laws of nature with respect to K are in entire agreement with those with respect to K'. By assuming this to be so, we arrive at a principle which, if it is really true, has great heuristic importance. For by theoretical consideration of processes which take place relatively to a system of reference with uniform acceleration, we obtain information as to the career of processes in a homogeneous gravitational field. We shall now show, first of all, from the standpoint of the ordinary theory of relativity, what degree of probability is inherent in our hypothesis.

§ 2. ON THE GRAVITATION OF ENERGY

One result yielded by the theory of relativity is that the inertia mass of a body increases with the energy it contains; if the increase of energy amounts to E, the increase in inertia mass is equal to E/c^2, when c denotes the velocity of light. Now is there an increase of gravitating mass corresponding to this increase of inertia mass? If not, then a body would fall in the same gravitational field with varying acceleration according to the energy it contained. That highly satisfactory result of the theory of

---

1. Of course we cannot replace any arbitrary gravitational field by a state of motion of the system without a gravitational field, any more than, by a transformation of relativity, we can transform all points of a medium in any kind of motion to rest.

relativity by which the law of the conservation of mass is merged in the law of conservation of energy could not be maintained, because it would compel us to abandon the law of the conservation of mass in its old form for inertia mass, and maintain it for gravitating mass.

But this must be regarded as very improbable. On the other hand, the usual theory of relativity does not provide us with any argument from which to infer that the weight of a body depends on the energy contained in it. But we shall show that our hypothesis of the equivalence of the systems K and K' gives us gravitation of energy as a necessary consequence.

Let the two material systems S_1 and S_2, provided with instruments of measurement, be situated on the z-axis of K at the distance h from each other,[1] so that the gravitation potential in S_2 is greater than that in S_1 by γh. Let a definite quantity of energy E be emitted from S_2 towards S_1. Let the quantities of energy in S_1 and S_2 be measured by contrivances which—brought to one place in the system z and there compared—shall be perfectly alike. As to the process of this conveyance of energy by radiation we can make no *a priori* assertion, because we do not know the influence of the gravitational field on the radiation and the measuring instruments in S_1 and S_2.

But by our postulate of the equivalence of K and K' we are able, in place of the system K in a homogeneous gravitational field, to set the gravitation-free system K', which moves with uniform acceleration in the direction of positive z, and with the z-axis of which the material systems S_1 and S_2 are rigidly connected.

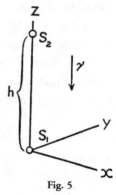

Fig. 5

We judge of the process of the transference of energy by radiation from S_2 to S_1 from a system K_0, which is to be free from acceleration. At the moment when the radiation energy E_2 is emitted from S_2 toward S_1, let the velocity of K' relatively to K_0 be zero. The radiation will arrive at S_1 when the time h/c has elapsed (to a first approximation). But at this moment the velocity of S_1 relatively to K_0 is $\gamma h/c = v$. Therefore by the ordinary theory of relativity the radiation arriving at S_1 does not possess the energy E_2, but a greater energy E_1, which is related to E_2, to a first approximation by the equation[2]

$$E_1 = E_2\left(1 + \frac{v}{c}\right) = E_2\left(1 + \gamma\frac{h}{c^2}\right) \qquad (1)$$

By our assumption exactly the same relation holds if the same process takes place in the system K, which is not accelerated, but is provided with a gravitational field. In this case we may replace γh by the potential Φ of the gravitation vector in S_2, if the arbitrary constant of Φ in S_1 is equated to zero. We then have the equation

1. The dimensions of S1 and S2, are regarded as infinitely small in comparison with h.
2. See above.

$$E_1 = E_2 + \frac{E_2}{c^2}\Phi \qquad\qquad (1a)$$

This equation expresses the law of energy for the process under observation. The energy E_1 arriving at S_1 is greater than the energy E_2, measured by the same means, which was emitted in S_2, the excess being the potential energy of the mass E_2/c^2 in the gravitational field. It thus proves that for the fulfilment of the principle of energy we have to ascribe to the energy E, before its emission in S_2, a potential energy due to gravity, which corresponds to the gravitational mass E/c^2. Our assumption of the equivalence of K and K' thus removes the difficulty mentioned at the beginning of this paragraph which is left unsolved by the ordinary theory of relativity.

The meaning of this result is shown particularly clearly if we consider the following cycle of operations:

1. The energy E, as measured in S_2, is emitted in the form of radiation in S_2 towards S_1, where, by the result just obtained, the energy $E(1 + \gamma h/c^2)$, as measured in S_1, is absorbed.

2. A body W of mass M is lowered from S_2 to S_1, work $M\gamma h$ being done in the process.

3. The energy E is transferred from S_1 to the body W while W is in S_1. Let the gravitational mass M be thereby changed so that it acquires the value M'.

4. Let W be again raised to S_2, work $M'\gamma h$ being done in the process.

5. Let E be transferred from W back to S_2.

The effect of this cycle is simply that S_1 has undergone the increase of energy $E\gamma h/c^2$, and that the quantity of energy $M'\gamma k - M\gamma h$ has been conveyed to the system in the form of mechanical work. By the principle of energy, we must therefore have

$$E\gamma \frac{h}{c^2} = M'\gamma h - M\gamma h,$$

or

$$M' - M = E/c^2 \ldots (1b)$$

The increase in gravitational mass is thus equal to E/c^2, and therefore equal to the increase in inertia mass as given by the theory of relativity.

The result emerges still more directly from the equivalence of the systems K and K', according to which the gravitational mass in respect of K is exactly equal to the inertia mass in respect of K'; energy must therefore possess a gravitational mass which is equal to its inertia mass. If a mass M_0 be suspended on a spring balance in the system K', the balance will indicate the apparent weight $M_0\gamma$ on account of the inertia of M_0. If the quantity of energy E be transferred to M_0, the spring balance, by the law of the inertia of energy, will indicate $(M_0 + E/c^2)\gamma$. By reason of our fundamental assumption

exactly the same thing must occur when the experiment is repeated in the system K, that is, in the gravitational field.

3. TIME AND THE VELOCITY OF LIGHT IN THE GRAVITATIONAL FIELD

If the radiation emitted in the uniformly accelerated system K' in S_2 toward S_1 had the frequency v_2 relatively to the clock in S_2, then, relatively to S_1, at its arrival in S_1 it no longer has the frequency v_2, relatively to an identical clock in S_1, but a greater frequency v_1, such that to a first approximation

$$v_1 = v_2\left(1 + \gamma\frac{h}{c^2}\right). \tag{2}$$

For if we again introduce the unaccelerated system of reference K_0, relatively to which, at the time of the emission of light, K' has no velocity, then S_1, at the time of arrival of the radiation at S_1, has, relatively to K_0, the velocity $\gamma\, h/c$, from which, by Doppler's principle, the relation as given results immediately.

In agreement with our assumption of the equivalence of the systems K' and K, this equation also holds for the stationary system of co-ordinates K, provided with a uniform gravitational field, if in it the transference by radiation takes place as described. It follows, then, that a ray of light emitted in S_2 with a definite gravitational potential, and possessing at its emission the frequency v_2—compared with a clock in S_2—will, at its arrival in S_1, possess a different frequency v_1—measured by an identical clock in S_1. For γh we substitute the gravitational potential Φ of S_2—that of S_1 being taken as zero—and assume that the relation which we have deduced for the homogeneous gravitational field also holds for other forms of field. Then

$$v_1 = v_2\left(1 + \frac{\Phi}{c^2}\right) \tag{2a}$$

This result (which by our deduction is valid to a first approximation) permits, in the first place, of the following application. Let v_0 be the vibration-number of an elementary light-generator, measured by a delicate clock at the same place. Let us imagine them both at a place on the surface of the Sun (where our S_2 is located). Of the light there emitted, a portion reaches the Earth (S_1), where we measure the frequency of the arriving light with a clock U in all respects resembling the one just mentioned. Then by (2a),

$$v = v_0\left(1 + \frac{\Phi}{c^2}\right)$$

where Φ is the (negative) difference of gravitational potential between the surface of the Sun and the Earth. Thus according to our view the spectral lines of sunlight, as compared with the corresponding spectral lines of terrestrial sources of light, must be

somewhat displaced toward the red, in fact by the relative amount

$$\frac{v_0 - v}{v_0} = -\frac{\Phi}{c^2} = 2.10^{-6}$$

If the conditions under which the solar bands arise were exactly known, this shifting would be susceptible of measurement. But as other influences (pressure, temperature) affect the position of the centres of the spectral lines, it is difficult to discover whether the inferred influence of the gravitational potential really exists.[1]

On a superficial consideration equation (2), or (2a), respectively, seems to assert an absurdity. If there is constant transmission of light from S_2 to S_1, how can any other number of periods per second arrive in S_1 than is emitted in S_2? But the answer is simple. We cannot regard v_2 or respectively v_1 simply as frequencies (as the number of periods per second) since we have not yet determined the time in system K. What v_2 denotes is the number of periods with reference to the time-unit of the clock U in S_2, while v_1 denotes the number of periods per second with reference to the identical clock in S_1. Nothing compels us to assume that the clocks U in different gravitation potentials must be regarded as going at the same rate. On the contrary, we must certainly define the time in K in such a way that the number of wave crests and troughs between S_2 and S_1 is independent of the absolute value of time; for the process under observation is by nature a stationary one. If we did not satisfy this condition, we should arrive at a definition of time by the application of which time would merge explicitly into the laws of nature, and this would certainly be unnatural and unpractical. Therefore the two clocks in S_1 and S_2 do not both give the "time" correctly. If we measure time in S_1 with the clock U, then we must measure time in S_2 with a clock which goes $1 + \Phi/c^2$ times more slowly than the clock U when compared with U at one and the same place. For when measured by such a clock the frequency of the ray of light which is considered above is at its emission in S_2

$$v_2\left(1 + \frac{\Phi}{c^2}\right)$$

and is therefore, by (2a), equal to the frequency v_1 of the same ray of light on its arrival in S_1.

This has a consequence which is of fundamental importance for our theory. For if we measure the velocity of light at different places in the accelerated, gravitation-free system K', employing clocks U of identical constitution, we obtain the same magnitude at all these places. The same holds good, by our fundamental assumption, for the system K as well. But from what has just been said we must use clocks of unlike

---

1. L. F. Jewell (Journ. de Phys., 6, 1897, p. 84) and particularly Ch. Fabry and H. Boisson (Comptes rendus, 148, 1909, pp. 688-690) have actually found such displacements of fine spectral lines toward the red end of the spectrum, of the order of magnitude here calculated, but have ascribed them to an effect of pressure in the absorbing layer.

constitution, for measuring time at places with differing gravitation potential. For measuring time at a place which, relatively to the origin of the co-ordinates, has the gravitation potential Φ, we must employ a clock which—when removed to the origin of co-ordinates—goes $(1 + \Phi/c^2)$ times more slowly than the clock used for measuring time at the origin of co-ordinates. If we call the velocity of light at the origin of co-ordinates c_0, then the velocity of light c at a place with the gravitation potential Φ will be given by the relation

$$c = c_0\left(1 + \frac{\Phi}{c^2}\right)$$

(3)

The principle of the constancy of the velocity of light holds good according to this theory in a different form from that which usually underlies the ordinary theory of relativity.

4. BENDING OF LIGHT-RAYS IN THE GRAVITATIONAL FIELD

From the proposition which has just been proved, that the velocity of light in the gravitational field is a function of the place, we may easily infer, by means of Huyghens's principle, that light-rays propagated across a gravitational field undergo deflexion. For let E be a wave front of a plane light-wave at the time t, and let P_1 and P_2 be two points in that plane at

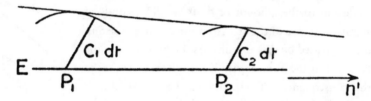

unit distance from each other. P_1 and P_2 lie in the plane of the paper, which is chosen so that the differential coefficient of Φ, taken in the direction of the normal to the plane, vanishes, and therefore also that of c. We obtain the corresponding wave front at time $t + dt$, or, rather, its line of section with the plane of the paper, by describing circles round the points P_1 and P_2 with radii c_1dt and c_2dt respectively, where c_1 and c_2 denote the velocity of light at the points P_1 and P_2 respectively, and by drawing the tangent to these circles. The angle through which the light-ray is deflected in the path cdt is therefore

$$\left(c_1 - c_2\right)dt = -\frac{\partial c}{\partial n'}dt,$$

if we calculate the angle positively when the ray is bent toward the side of increasing n'. The angle of deflexion per unit of path of the light-ray is thus

$$-\frac{1}{c}\frac{\partial c}{\partial n'} \text{ or by (3) } -\frac{1}{c^2}\frac{\partial \Phi}{\partial n'}$$

Finally, we obtain for the deflexion which a light-ray experiences toward the side n' on any path (s) the expression

$$a = -\frac{1}{c^2}\int\frac{\partial \Phi}{\partial n'}ds \qquad (4)$$

We might have obtained the same result by directly considering the propagation of a ray of light in the uniformly accelerated system K', and transferring the result to the system K, and thence to the case of a gravitational field of any form.

By equation (4) a ray of light passing along by a heavenly body suffers a deflexion to the side of the diminishing gravitational potential, that is, on the side directed toward the heavenly body, of the magnitude

$$a = -\frac{1}{c^2}\int_{\theta=-\frac{1}{2}\pi}^{\theta=\frac{1}{2}\pi}\frac{kM}{r^2}\cos\theta\, ds = 2\frac{kM}{r^2\Delta}$$

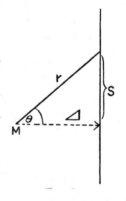

where k denotes the constant of gravitation, M the mass of the heavenly body, Δ the distance of the ray from the centre of the body. A ray of light going past the Sun would accordingly undergo deflexion to the amount of $4\cdot10^{-6}$ = .83 seconds of arc. The angular distance of the star from the centre of the Sun appears to be increased by this amount. As the fixed stars in the parts of the sky near the Sun are visible during total eclipses of the Sun, this consequence of the theory may be compared with experience. With the planet Jupiter the displacement to be expected reaches to about $1/100$ of the amount given. It would be a most desirable thing if astronomers would take up the question here raised. For apart from any theory there is the question whether it is possible with the equipment at present available to detect an influence of gravitational fields on the propagation of light.

THE FOUNDATION OF THE GENERAL THEORY OF RELATIVITY

Translated from "Die Grundlage der allgemeinen Relativitätstheorie," Annalen der Physik, 49, 1916.

A. FUNDAMENTAL CONSIDERATIONS ON THE POSTULATE OF RELATIVITY

§ 1. OBSERVATIONS ON THE SPECIAL THEORY OF RELATIVITY

The special theory of relativity is based on the following postulate, which is also satisfied by the mechanics of Galileo and Newton.

If a system of co-ordinates K is chosen so that, in relation to it, physical laws hold good in their simplest form, the *same* laws also hold good in relation to any other system of co-ordinates K' moving in uniform translation relatively to K. This postulate we call the "special principle of relativity." The word "special" is meant to intimate that the principle is restricted to the case when K' has a motion of uniform translation relatively to K, but that the equivalence of K' and K does not extend to the case of non-uniform motion of K' relatively to K.

Thus the special theory of relativity does not depart from classical mechanics through the postulate of relativity, but through the postulate of the constancy of the velocity of light *in vacuo*, from which, in combination with the special principle of relativity, there follow, in the well-known way, the relativity of simultaneity, the Lorentzian transformation, and the related laws for the behaviour of moving bodies and clocks.

The modification to which the special theory of relativity has subjected the theory of space and time is indeed far-reaching, but one important point has remained unaffected. For the laws of geometry, even according to the special theory of relativity, are to be interpreted directly as laws relating to the possible relative positions of solid bodies at rest; and, in a more general way, the laws of kinematics are to be interpreted as laws which describe the relations of measuring bodies and clocks. To two selected material points of a stationary rigid body there always corresponds a distance of quite definite length, which is independent of the locality and orientation of the body, and is also independent of the time. To two selected positions of the hands of a clock at rest relatively to the privileged system of reference there always corresponds an interval of time of a definite length, which is independent of place and time. We shall soon see that the general theory of relativity cannot adhere to this simple physical interpretation of space and time.

§ 2. THE NEED FOR AN EXTENSION OF THE POSTULATE OF RELATIVITY

In classical mechanics, and no less in the special theory of relativity, there is an inherent epistemological defect which was, perhaps for the first time, clearly pointed

out by Ernst Mach. We will elucidate it by the following example: Two fluid bodies of the same size and nature hover freely in space at so great a distance from each other and from all other masses that only those gravitational forces need be taken into account which arise from the interaction of different parts of the same body. Let the distance between the two bodies be invariable, and in neither of the bodies let there be any relative movements of the parts with respect to one another. But let either mass, as judged by an observer at rest relatively to the other mass, rotate with constant angular velocity about the line joining the masses. This is a verifiable relative motion of the two bodies. Now let us imagine that each of the bodies has been surveyed by means of measuring instruments at rest relatively to itself, and let the surface of S_1 prove to be a sphere, and that of S_2 an ellipsoid of revolution. Thereupon we put the question— What is the reason for this difference in the two bodies? No answer can be admitted as epistemologically satisfactory,[1] unless the reason given is an *observable fact of experience*. The law of causality has not the significance of a statement as to the world of experience, except when *observable facts* ultimately appear as causes and effects.

Newtonian mechanics does not give a satisfactory answer to this question. It pronounces as follows: The laws of mechanics apply to the space R_1, in respect to which the body S_1 is at rest, but not to the space R_2 in respect to which the body S_2 is at rest. But the privileged space R_1 of Galileo, thus introduced, is a merely *factitious* cause, and not a thing that can be observed. It is therefore clear that Newton's mechanics does not really satisfy the requirement of causality in the case under consideration, but only apparently does so, since it makes the factitious cause R_1 responsible for the observable difference in the bodies S_1 and S_2.

The only satisfactory answer must be that the physical system consisting of S_1 and S_2 reveals within itself no imaginable cause to which the differing behaviour of S_1 and S_2 can be referred. The cause must therefore lie *outside* this system. We have to take it that the general laws of motion, which in particular determine the shapes of S_1 and S_2, must be such that the mechanical behaviour of S_1 and S_2 is partly conditioned, in quite essential respects, by distant masses which we have not included in the system under consideration. These distant masses and their motions relative to S_1 and S_2 must then be regarded as the seat of the causes (which must be susceptible to observation) of the different behaviour of our two bodies S_1 and S_2. They take over the rôle of the factitious cause R_1. Of all imaginable spaces R_1, R_2, etc., in any kind of motion relatively to one another, there is none which we may look upon as privileged *a priori* without reviving the above-mentioned epistemological objection. *The laws of physics must be of such a nature that they apply to systems of reference in any kind of motion.* Along this road we arrive at an extension of the postulate of relativity.

1. Of course an answer may be satisfactory from the point of view of epistemology, and yet be unsound physically, if it is in conflict with other experiences.

In addition to this weighty argument from the theory of knowledge, there is a well-known physical fact which favours an extension of the theory of relativity. Let K be a Galilean system of reference, i.e. a system relatively to which (at least in the four-dimensional region under consideration) a mass, sufficiently distant from other masses, is moving with uniform motion in a straight line. Let K' be a second system of reference which is moving relatively to K in *uniformly accelerated* translation. Then, relatively to K', a mass sufficiently distant from other masses would have an accelerated motion such that its acceleration and direction of acceleration are independent of the material composition and physical state of the mass.

Does this permit an observer at rest relatively to K' to infer that he is on a "really" accelerated system of reference? The answer is in the negative; for the above-mentioned relation of freely movable masses to K' may be interpreted equally well in the following way. The system of reference K' is unaccelerated, but the space-time territory in question is under the sway of a gravitational field, which generates the accelerated motion of the bodies relatively to K'.

This view is made possible for us by the teaching of experience as to the existence of a field of force, namely, the gravitational field, which possesses the remarkable property of imparting the same acceleration to all bodies.[1] The mechanical behaviour of bodies relatively to K' is the same as presents itself to experience in the case of systems which we are wont to regard as "stationary" or as "privileged." Therefore, from the physical standpoint, the assumption readily suggests itself that the systems K and K' may both with equal right be looked upon as "stationary," that is to say, they have an equal title as systems of reference for the physical description of phenomena.

It will be seen from these reflexions that in pursuing the general theory of relativity we shall be led to a theory of gravitation, since we are able to "produce" a gravitational field merely by changing the system of co-ordinates. It will also be obvious that the principle of the constancy of the velocity of light *in vacuo* must be modified, since we easily recognize that the path of a ray of light with respect to K' must in general be curvilinear, if with respect to K light is propagated in a straight line with a definite constant velocity.

§ 3. The Space-Time Continuum. Requirement of General Co-Variance for the Equations Expressing General Laws of Nature

In classical mechanics, as well as in the special theory of relativity, the co-ordinates of space and time have a direct physical meaning. To say that a point-event has the X_1 co-ordinate x_1 means that the projection of the point-event on the axis of X_1, determined by rigid rods and in accordance with the rules of Euclidean geometry, is obtained by measuring off a given rod (the unit of length) x_1 times from the origin of

1. Eötvös has proved experimentally that the gravitational field has this property in great accuracy.

co-ordinates along the axis of X_1. To say that a point-event has the X_4 co-ordinates x_4 = t, means that a standard clock, made to measure time in a definite unit period, and which is stationary relatively to the system of co-ordinates and practically coincident in space with the point-event,[1] will have measured off x_4 = t periods at the occurrence of the event.

This view of space and time has always been in the minds of physicists, even if, as a rule, they have been unconscious of it. This is clear from the part which these concepts play in physical measurements; it must also have underlain the reader's reflexions on the preceding paragraph (§ 2) for him to connect any meaning with what he there read. But we shall now show that we must put it aside and replace it by a more general view, in order to be able to carry through the postulate of general relativity, if the special theory of relativity applies to the special case of the absence of a gravitational field.

In a space which is free of gravitational fields we introduce a Galilean system of reference K (x, y, z, t), and also a system of co-ordinates K' (x', y', z', t') in uniform rotation relatively to K. Let the origins of both systems, as well as their axes of Z, permanently coincide. We shall show that for a space-time measurement in the system K' the above definition of the physical meaning of lengths and times cannot be maintained. For reasons of symmetry it is clear that a circle around the origin in the X, Y plane of K may at the same time be regarded as a circle in the X', Y' plane of K'. We suppose that the circumference and diameter of this circle have been measured with a unit measure infinitely small compared with the radius, and that we have the quotient of the two results. If this experiment were performed with a measuring-rod at rest relatively to the Galilean system K, the quotient would be π. With a measuring-rod at rest relatively to K', the quotient would be greater than π. This is readily understood if we envisage the whole process of measuring from the "stationary" system K, and take into consideration that the measuring-rod applied to the periphery undergoes a Lorentzian contraction, while the one applied along the radius does not. Hence Euclidean geometry does not apply to K'. The notion of co-ordinates defined above, which presupposes the validity of Euclidean geometry, therefore breaks down in relation to the system K'. So, too, we are unable to introduce a time corresponding to physical requirements in K', indicated by clocks at rest, relatively to K'. To convince ourselves of this impossibility, let us imagine two clocks of identical constitution placed, one at the origin of co-ordinates, and the other at the circumference of the circle, and both envisaged from the "stationary" system K. By a familiar result of the special theory of relativity, the clock at the circumference—judged from K—goes more slowly than the other, because the former is in motion and the latter at rest. An observer at the common origin of co-ordinates, capable of observing the clock at the circumference by means of light, would therefore

---

1. We assume the possibility of verifying "simultaneity" for events immediately proximate in space, or—to speak more precisely—for immediate proximity or coincidence in space-time, without giving a definition of this fundamental concept.

see it lagging behind the clock beside him. As he will not make up his mind to let the velocity of light along the path in question depend explicitly on the time, he will interpret his observations as showing that the clock at the circumference "really" goes more slowly than the clock at the origin. So he will be obliged to define time in such a way that the rate of a clock depends upon where the clock may be.

We therefore reach this result:—In the general theory of relativity, space and time cannot be defined in such a way that differences of the spatial co-ordinates can be directly measured by the unit measuring-rod, or differences in the time co-ordinate by a standard clock.

The method hitherto employed for laying co-ordinates into the space-time continuum in a definite manner thus breaks down, and there seems to be no other way which would allow us to adapt systems of co-ordinates to the four-dimensional universe so that we might expect from their application a particularly simple formulation of the laws of nature. So there is nothing for it but to regard all imaginable systems of co-ordinates, on principle, as equally suitable for the description of nature. This comes to requiring that:—

The general laws of nature are to be expressed by equations which hold good for all systems of co-ordinates, that is, are co-variant with respect to any substitutions whatever (generally co-variant).

It is clear that a physical theory which satisfies this postulate will also be suitable for the general postulate of relativity. For the sum of *all* substitutions in any case includes those which correspond to all relative motions of three-dimensional systems of co-ordinates. That this requirement of general co-variance, which takes away from space and time the last remnant of physical objectivity, is a natural one, will be seen from the following reflexion. All our space-time verifications invariably amount to a determination of space-time coincidences. If, for example, events consisted merely in the motion of material points, then ultimately nothing would be observable but the meetings of two or more of these points. Moreover, the results of our measurings are nothing but verifications of such meetings of the material points of our measuring instruments with other material points, coincidences between the hands of a clock and points on the clock dial, and observed point-events happening at the same place at the same time.

The introduction of a system of reference serves no other purpose than to facilitate the description of the totality of such coincidences. We allot to the universe four space-time variables x_1, x_2, x_3, x_4 in such a way that for every point-event there is a corresponding system of values of the variables $x_1 \ldots x_4$. To two coincident point-events there corresponds one system of values of the variables $x_1 \ldots x_4$, i.e. coincidence is characterized by the identity of the co-ordinates. If, in place of the variables $x_1 \ldots x_4$, we

introduce functions of them, x'_1, x'_2, x'_3, x'_4, as a new system of co-ordinates, so that the systems of values are made to correspond to one another without ambiguity, the equality of all four co-ordinates in the new system will also serve as an expression for the space-time coincidence of the two point-events. As all our physical experience can be ultimately reduced to such coincidences, there is no immediate reason for preferring certain systems of co-ordinates to others, that is to say, we arrive at the requirement of general co-variance.

§ 4. The Relation of the Four Co-ordinates to Measurement in Space and Time

It is not my purpose in this discussion to represent the general theory of relativity as a system that is as simple and logical as possible, and with the minimum number of axioms; but my main object is to develop this theory in such a way that the reader will feel that the path we have entered upon is psychologically the natural one, and that the underlying assumptions will seem to have the highest possible degree of security. With this aim in view let it now be granted that:

For infinitely small four-dimensional regions the theory of relativity in the restricted sense is appropriate, if the co-ordinates are suitably chosen.

For this purpose we must choose the acceleration of the infinitely small ("local") system of co-ordinates so that no gravitational field occurs; this is possible for an infinitely small region. Let X_1, X_2, X_3, be the co-ordinates of space, and X_4 the appertaining co-ordinate of time measured in the appropriate unit.[1] If a rigid rod is imagined to be given as the unit measure, the co-ordinates, with a given orientation of the system of co-ordinates, have a direct physical meaning in the sense of the special theory of relativity. By the special theory of relativity the expression

$$ds^2 = -dX_1^2 - dX_2^2 - dX_3^2 + dX_4^2 \qquad (1)$$

then has a value which is independent of the orientation of the local system of co-ordinates, and is ascertainable by measurements of space and time. The magnitude of the linear element pertaining to points of the four-dimensional continuum in infinite proximity, we call ds. If the ds belonging to the element $dX_1 \ldots dX_4$ is positive, we follow Minkowski in calling it time-like; if it is negative, we call it space-like.

To the "linear element" in question, or to the two infinitely proximate point-events, there will also correspond definite differentials $dx_1 \ldots dx_4$ of the four-dimensional co-ordinates of any chosen system of reference. If this system, as well as the "local" system, is given for the region under consideration, the $dX\nu$ will allow themselves to be represented here by definite linear homogeneous expressions of the $dx\sigma$:—

1. The unit of time is to be chosen so that the velocity of light *in vacuo* as measured in the "local" system of co-ordinates is to be equal to unity.

$$dX_v = \sum_\sigma a_{v\sigma} dx_\sigma \qquad (2)$$

Inserting these expressions in (1), we obtain

$$ds^2 = \sum_{\tau\sigma} g_{\sigma\tau} dx_\sigma dx_\tau \qquad (3)$$

where the $g_{\sigma\tau}$ will be functions of the x_σ. These can no longer be dependent on the orientation and the state of motion of the "local" system of co-ordinates, for ds^2 is a quantity ascertainable by rod-clock measurement of point-events infinitely proximate in space-time, and defined independently of any particular choice of co-ordinates. The $g_{\sigma\tau}$ are to be chosen here so that $g_{\sigma\tau} = g_{\tau\sigma}$; the summation is to extend over all values of σ and τ, so that the sum consists of 4 x 4 terms, of which twelve are equal in pairs.

The case of the ordinary theory of relativity arises out of the case here considered, if it is possible, by reason of the particular relations of the $g_{\sigma\tau}$ in a finite region, to choose the system of reference in the finite region in such a way that the $g_{\sigma\tau}$ assume the constant values

$$\begin{bmatrix} -1 & 0 & 0 & 0 \\ 0 & -1 & 0 & 0 \\ 0 & 0 & -1 & 0 \\ 0 & 0 & 0 & +1 \end{bmatrix} \qquad (4)$$

We shall find hereafter that the choice of such co-ordinates is, in general, not possible for a finite region.

From the considerations of § 2 and § 3 it follows that the quantities $g\tau\sigma$ are to be regarded from the physical standpoint as the quantities which describe the gravitational field in relation to the chosen system of reference. For, if we now assume the special theory of relativity to apply to a certain four-dimensional region with the co-ordinates properly chosen, then the $g_{\sigma\tau}$ have the values given in (4). A free material point then moves, relatively to this system, with uniform motion in a straight line. Then if we introduce new space-time co-ordinates x_1, x_2, x_3, x_4, by means of any substitution we choose, the $g^{\sigma\tau}$ in this new system will no longer be constants, but functions of space and time. At the same time the motion of the free material point will present itself in the new co-ordinates as a curvilinear non-uniform motion, and the law of this motion will be independent of the nature of the moving particle. We shall therefore interpret this motion as a motion under the influence of a gravitational field. We thus find the occurrence of a gravitational field connected with a space-time variability of the g_σ. So, too, in the general case, when we are no longer able by a suitable choice of co-ordinates to apply the special theory of relativity to a finite region, we shall hold fast to the view

that the $g_{\sigma\tau}$ describe the gravitational field.

Thus, according to the general theory of relativity, gravitation occupies an exceptional position with regard to other forces, particularly the electromagnetic forces, since the ten functions representing the gravitational field at the same time define the metrical properties of the space measured.

B. MATHEMATICAL AIDS TO THE FORMULATION OF GENERALLY COVARIANT EQUATIONS

Having seen in the foregoing that the general postulate of relativity leads to the requirement that the equations of physics shall be covariant in the face of any substitution of the co-ordinates $x_1 \ldots x_4$, we have to consider how such generally covariant equations can be found. We now turn to this purely mathematical task, and we shall find that in its solution a fundamental rôle is played by the invariant ds given in equation (3), which, borrowing from Gauss's theory of surfaces, we have called the "linear element."

The fundamental idea of this general theory of covariants is the following:—Let certain things ("tensors") be defined with respect to any system of co-ordinates by a number of functions of the co-ordinates, called the "components" of the tensor. There are then certain rules by which these components can be calculated for a new system of co-ordinates, if they are known for the original system of co-ordinates, and if the transformation connecting the two systems is known. The things hereafter called tensors are further characterized by the fact that the equations of transformation for their components are linear and homogeneous. Accordingly, all the components in the new system vanish, if they all vanish in the original system. If, therefore, a law of nature is expressed by equating all the components of a tensor to zero, it is generally covariant. By examining the laws of the formation of tensors, we acquire the means of formulating generally covariant laws.

§ 5. CONTRAVARIANT AND COVARIANT FOUR-VECTORS

Contravariant Four-vectors.—The linear element is defined by the four "components" dx_ν, for which the law of transformation is expressed by the equation

$$dx'_\sigma = \sum_\nu \frac{\partial x'_\sigma}{\partial x_\nu} dx_\nu$$

(5)

The dx'_σ are expressed as linear and homogeneous functions of the dx_ν. Hence we may look upon these co-ordinate differentials as the components of a "tensor" of the particular kind which we call a contravariant four-vector. Any thing which is defined relatively to the system of co-ordinates by four quantities A^ν, and which is transformed by the same law

$$A'^\sigma = \sum_\nu \frac{\partial x'_\sigma}{\partial x_\nu} A^\nu,$$

(5a)

we also call a contravariant four-vector. From (5a) it follows at once that the sums $A^\sigma \pm B^\sigma$ are also components of a four-vector, if A^σ and B^σ are such. Corresponding relations hold for all "tensors" subsequently to be introduced. (Rule for the addition and subtraction of tensors.)

Covariant Four-vectors.—We call four quantities $A\nu$ the components of a covariant four-vector, if for any arbitrary choice of the contravariant four-vector B^ν

$$\sum_\nu A_\nu B^\nu = \text{Invariant}$$

(6)

The law of transformation of a covariant four-vector follows from this definition. For if we replace B^ν on the right-hand side of the equation

$$\sum_\sigma A'_\sigma B'^\sigma = \sum_\nu A_\nu B^\nu$$

by the expression resulting from the inversion of (5a),

$$\sum_\sigma \frac{\partial x_\nu}{\partial x'_\sigma} B'^\sigma,$$

we obtain

$$\sum_\sigma B'^\sigma \sum_\nu \frac{\partial x_\nu}{\partial x'_\sigma} A_\nu = \sum_\sigma B'^\sigma A'_\sigma.$$

Since this equation is true for arbitrary values of the B'^σ, it follows that the law of transformation is

$$A'_\sigma = \sum_\nu \frac{\partial x_\nu}{\partial x'_\sigma} A_\nu.$$

(7)

Note on a Simplified Way of Writing the Expressions.—A glance at the equations of this paragraph shows that there is always a summation with respect to the indices which occur twice under a sign of summation (e.g. the index ν in (5)), and only with respect to indices which occur twice. It is therefore possible, without loss of clearness, to omit the sign of summation. In its place we introduce the convention:—If an index occurs twice in one term of an expression, it is always to be summed unless the contrary is expressly stated.

The difference between covariant and contravariant four-vectors lies in the law of transformation ((7) or (5) respectively). Both forms are tensors in the sense of the general remark above. Therein lies their importance. Following Ricci and Levi-Civita, we

denote the contravariant character by placing the index above, the covariant by placing it below.

§ 6. Tensors of the Second and Higher Ranks

Contravariant Tensors.—If we form all the sixteen products of the components $A^{\mu\nu}$ and B^{ν} of two contravariant four-vectors

$$A^{\mu\nu} = A^{\mu}B^{\nu} \tag{8}$$

then by (8) and (5a) $A^{\mu\nu}$ satisfies the law of transformation

$$A'^{\sigma\tau} = \frac{\partial x'_{\sigma}}{\partial x_{\mu}} \frac{\partial x'_{\tau}}{\partial x_{\nu}} A^{\mu\nu} \tag{9}$$

We call a thing which is described relatively to any system of reference by sixteen quantities, satisfying the law of transformation (9), a contravariant tensor of the second rank. Not every such tensor allows itself to be formed in accordance with (8) from two four-vectors, but it is easily shown that any given sixteen $A^{\mu\nu}$ can be represented as the sums of the $A^{\mu}B^{\nu}$ of four appropriately selected pairs of four-vectors. Hence we can prove nearly all the laws which apply to the tensor of the second rank defined by (9) in the simplest manner by demonstrating them for the special tensors of the type (8).

Contravariant Tensors of Any Rank.—It is clear that, on the lines of (8) and (9), contravariant tensors of the third and higher ranks may also be defined with 4^3 components, and so on. In the same way it follows from (8) and (9) that the contravariant four-vector may be taken in this sense as a contravariant tensor of the first rank.

Covariant Tensors.—On the other hand, if we take the sixteen products $A_{\mu\nu}$, of two covariant four-vectors A_{μ} and B_{ν},

$$A_{\mu\nu} = A_{\mu}B_{\nu}, \tag{10}$$

the law of transformation for these is

$$A'_{\sigma\tau} = \frac{\partial x_{\mu}}{\partial x'_{\sigma}} \frac{\partial x_{\nu}}{\partial x'_{\tau}} A_{\mu\nu} \tag{11}$$

This law of transformation defines the covariant tensor of the second rank. All our previous remarks on contravariant tensors apply equally to covariant tensors.

NOTE.—It is convenient to treat the scalar (or invariant) both as a contravariant and a covariant tensor of zero rank.

Mixed Tensors.—We may also define a tensor of the second rank of the type

$$A^{\nu}_{\mu} = A_{\mu}B^{\nu}$$

which is covariant with respect to the index μ, and contravariant with respect to the

index ν. Its law of transformation is

$$A^{\pi}_{\sigma} = \frac{\partial x'_{\tau}}{\partial x_{\nu}} \frac{\partial x_{\mu}}{\partial x'_{\sigma}} A^{\nu}_{\mu} \tag{13}$$

Naturally there are mixed tensors with any number of indices of covariant character, and any number of indices of contravariant character. Covariant and contravariant tensors may be looked upon as special cases of mixed tensors.

Symmetrical Tensors.—A contravariant, or a covariant tensor, of the second or higher rank is said to be symmetrical if two components, which are obtained the one from the other by the interchange of two indices, are equal. The tensor $A^{\mu\nu}$, or the tensor $A_{\mu\nu}$, is thus symmetrical if for any combination of the indices μ, ν,

$$A^{\mu\nu} = A^{\nu\mu}, \tag{14}$$

or respectively,

$$A_{\mu\nu} = A_{\nu\mu} \tag{14a}$$

It has to be proved that the symmetry thus defined is a property which is independent of the system of reference. It follows in fact from (9), when (14) is taken into consideration, that

$$A'^{\sigma\tau} = \frac{\partial x'_{\sigma}}{\partial x_{\mu}} \frac{\partial x'_{\tau}}{\partial x_{\nu}} A^{\mu\nu} = \frac{\partial x'_{\sigma}}{\partial x_{\mu}} \frac{\partial x'_{\tau}}{\partial x_{\nu}} A^{\nu\mu} = \frac{\partial x'_{\sigma}}{\partial x_{\nu}} \frac{\partial x'_{\tau}}{\partial x_{\mu}} A^{\mu\nu} = A'^{\tau\sigma}$$

The last equation but one depends upon the interchange of the summation indices μ and ν, i.e. merely on a change of notation.

Antisymmetrical Tensors.—A contravariant or a covariant tensor of the second, third, or fourth rank is said to be antisymmetrical if two components, which are obtained the one from the other by the interchange of two indices, are equal and of opposite sign. The tensor $A^{\mu\nu}$, or the tensor $A_{\mu\nu}$, is therefore antisymmetrical, if always

$$A^{\mu\nu} = -A^{\nu\mu}, \tag{15}$$

or respectively,

$$A_{\mu\nu} = -A_{\nu\mu} \tag{15a}$$

Of the sixteen components $A^{\mu\nu}$, the four components $A^{\mu\mu}$ vanish; the rest are equal and of opposite sign in pairs, so that there are only six components numerically different (a six-vector). Similarly we see that the antisymmetrical tensor of the third rank $A^{\mu\nu\sigma}$ has only four numerically different components, while the antisymmetrical tensor $A^{\mu\nu\sigma\tau}$ has only one. There are no antisymmetrical tensors of higher rank than the fourth in a continuum of four dimensions.

§ 7. MULTIPLICATION OF TENSORS

Outer Multiplication of Tensors.—We obtain from the components of a tensor of rank n and of a tensor of rank m the components of a tensor of rank $n + m$ by multiplying each component of the one tensor by each component of the other. Thus, for example, the tensors T arise out of the tensors A and B of different kinds,

$$T_{\mu\nu\sigma} = A_{\mu\nu}B_{\sigma},$$
$$T^{\mu\nu\sigma\tau} = A^{\mu\nu}B^{\sigma\tau},$$
$$T^{\sigma\tau}_{\mu\nu} = A_{\mu\nu}B^{\sigma\nu}.$$

The proof of the tensor character of T is given directly by the representations (8), (10), (12), or by the laws of transformation (9), (11), (13). The equations (8), (10), (12) are themselves examples of outer multiplication of tensors of the first rank.

"Contraction" of a Mixed Tensor.—From any mixed tensor we may form a tensor whose rank is less by two, by equating an index of covariant with one of contravariant character, and summing with respect to this index ("contraction"). Thus, for example, from the mixed tensor of the fourth rank $A^{\sigma\tau}_{\mu\nu}$, we obtain the mixed tensor of the second rank,

$$A^{\tau}_{\nu} = A^{\mu\tau}_{\mu\nu} \left(= \sum_{\mu} A^{\mu\tau}_{\mu\nu} \right),$$

and from this, by a second contraction, the tensor of zero rank,

$$A = A^{\nu}_{\nu} = A^{\mu\nu}_{\mu\nu}.$$

The proof that the result of contraction really possesses the tensor character is given either by the representation of a tensor according to the generalization of (12) in combination with (6), or by the generalization of (13).

Inner and Mixed Multiplication of Tensors.—These consist in a combination of outer multiplication with contraction.

Examples.—From the covariant tensor of the second rank $A_{\mu\nu}$ and the contravariant tensor of the first rank B^{σ} we form by outer multiplication the mixed tensor

$$D^{\sigma}_{\mu\nu} = A_{\mu\nu}B^{\sigma}.$$

On contraction with respect to the indices ν and σ, we obtain the covariant four-vector

$$D_{\mu} = D^{\nu}_{\mu\nu} = A_{\mu\nu}B^{\nu}.$$

This we call the inner product of the tensors $A_{\mu\nu}$ and B^{σ}. Analogously we form from the tensors $A_{\mu\nu}$, and $B^{\sigma\tau}$, by outer multiplication and double contraction, the inner

product $A_{\mu\nu}B^{\mu\nu}$. By outer multiplication and one contraction, we obtain from $A\mu\nu$ and $B^{\sigma\tau}$ the mixed tensor of the second rank $D^{\tau}_{\mu} = A_{\mu\nu}B^{\nu\tau}$. This operation may be aptly characterized as a mixed one, being "outer" with respect to the indices μ and τ, and "inner" with respect to the indices ν and σ.

We now prove a proposition which is often useful as evidence of tensor character. From what has just been explained, $A_{\mu\nu}B^{\mu\nu}$ is a scalar if $A_{\mu\nu}$, and $B^{\sigma\tau}$ are tensors. But we may also make the following assertion: If $A_{\mu\nu}B^{\mu\nu}$ is a scalar *for any choice of the tensor* $B^{\mu\nu}$, then $A_{\mu\nu}$ has tensor character. For, by hypothesis, for any substitution,

$$A'_{\sigma\tau} B'^{\sigma\tau} = A'_{\mu\nu} B^{\mu\nu}.$$

But by an inversion of (9)

$$B^{\mu\nu} = \frac{\partial x_{\mu}}{\partial x'_{\sigma}} \frac{\partial x_{\nu}}{\partial x'_{\tau}} B'^{\sigma\tau}.$$

This, inserted in the above equation, gives

$$\left(A'_{\sigma\tau} - \frac{\partial x_{\mu}}{\partial x'_{\sigma}} \frac{\partial x_{\nu}}{\partial x'_{\tau}} A_{\mu\nu} \right) B'^{\sigma\tau} = 0.$$

This can only be satisfied for arbitrary values of $B'^{\sigma\tau}$ if the bracket vanishes. The result then follows by equation (11). This rule applies correspondingly to tensors of any rank and character, and the proof is analogous in all cases.

The rule may also be demonstrated in this form: If B^{μ} and C^{ν} are any vectors, and if, for all values of these, the inner product $A_{\mu\nu}B^{\mu}C^{\nu}$ is a scalar, then $A_{\mu\nu}$ is a covariant tensor. This latter proposition also holds good even if only the more special assertion is correct, that with any choice of the four-vector B^{μ} the inner product $A_{\mu\nu}B^{\mu}B^{\nu}$ is a scalar, if in addition it is known that $A_{\mu\nu}$ satisfies the condition of symmetry $A_{\mu\nu} = A_{\nu\mu}$. For by the method given above we prove the tensor character of $(A_{\mu\nu} + A_{\nu\mu})$, and from this the tensor character of $A_{\mu\nu}$ follows on account of symmetry. This also can be easily generalized to the case of covariant and contravariant tensors of any rank.

Finally, there follows from what has been proved, this law, which may also be generalized for any tensors: If for any choice of the four-vector B^{ν} the quantities $A_{\mu\nu}B^{\nu}$ form a tensor of the first rank, then $A_{\mu\nu}$ is a tensor of the second rank. For, if C^{μ} is any four-vector, then on account of the tensor character of $A_{\mu\nu}B^{\nu}$, the inner product $A_{\mu\nu}B^{\nu}C^{\mu}$ is a scalar for any choice of the two four-vectors B^{ν} and C^{μ}. From which the proposition follows.

§ 8. SOME ASPECTS OF THE FUNDAMENTAL TENSOR $g_{\mu\nu}$

The Covariant Fundamental Tensor.—In the invariant expression for the square of the linear element,

$$ds^2 = g_{\mu\nu}dx_\mu dx_\nu,$$

the part played by the dx_μ is that of a contravariant vector which may be chosen at will. Since further, $g_{\mu\nu} = g_{\nu\mu}$, it follows from the considerations of the preceding paragraph that $g_{\mu\nu}$ is a covariant tensor of the second rank. We call it the "fundamental tensor." In what follows we deduce some properties of this tensor which, it is true, apply to any tensor of the second rank. But as the fundamental tensor plays a special part in our theory, which has its physical basis in the peculiar effects of gravitation, it so happens that the relations to be developed are of importance to us only in the case of the fundamental tensor.

The Contravariant Fundamental Tensor.—If in the determinant formed by the elements $g_{\mu\nu}$, we take the co-factor of each of the $g_{\mu\nu}$ and divide it by the determinant $g = |g_{\mu\nu}|$, we obtain certain quantities $g^{\mu\nu}(= g^{\nu\mu})$ which, as we shall demonstrate, form a contravariant tensor.

By a known property of determinants

$$g_{\mu\sigma}g^{\nu\sigma} = \delta_\mu^\nu \tag{16}$$

where the symbol δ_μ^ν denotes 1 or 0, according as $\mu = \nu$ or $\mu \neq \nu$.

Instead of the above expression for ds^2 we may thus write

$$g_{\mu\sigma}\delta_\nu^\sigma dx_\mu dx_\nu$$

or, by (16)

$$g_{\mu\sigma}g_{\nu\tau}g^{\sigma\tau}dx_\mu dx_\nu$$

But, by the multiplication rules of the preceding paragraphs, the quantities

$$d\xi_\sigma = g_{\mu\sigma}dx_\mu$$

form a covariant four-vector, and in fact an arbitrary vector, since the dx_μ are arbitrary. By introducing this into our expression we obtain

$$ds^2 = g^{\sigma\tau}d\xi_\sigma d\xi_\tau$$

Since this, with the arbitrary choice of the vector $d\xi\sigma$, is a scalar, and $g^{\sigma\tau}$ by its definition is symmetrical in the indices σ and τ, it follows from the results of the preceding paragraph that $g^{\sigma\tau}$ is a contravariant tensor.

It further follows from (16) that δ_μ is also a tensor, which we may call the mixed fundamental tensor.

The Determinant of the Fundamental Tensor.—By the rule for the multiplication of determinants

$$\left|g_{\mu\alpha}g^{\alpha\nu}\right| = \left|g_{\mu\alpha}\right| \times \left|g^{\alpha\nu}\right|$$

On the other hand

$$\left|g_{\mu\alpha}g^{\alpha\nu}\right| = \left|\delta_{\mu}^{\nu}\right| = 1.$$

It therefore follows that

$$\left|g_{\mu\nu}\right| \times \left|g^{\mu\nu}\right| = 1 \qquad (17)$$

The Volume Scalar.—We seek first the law of transformation of the determinant $g = \left|g_{\mu\nu}\right|$. In accordance with (11)

$$g' = \left|\frac{\partial x_{\mu}}{\partial x'_{\sigma}}\frac{\partial x}{\partial x'_{\tau}}g_{\mu\nu}\right|.$$

Hence, by a double application of the rule for the multiplication of determinants, it follows that

$$g' = \left|\frac{\partial x_{\mu}}{\partial x'_{\sigma}}\right| \cdot \left|\frac{\partial x_{\nu}}{\partial x'_{\tau}}\right| \cdot \left|g_{\mu\nu}\right| = \left|\frac{\partial x_{\mu}}{\partial x'_{\sigma}}\right|^2 g,$$

or

$$\sqrt{g'} = \left|\frac{\partial x_{\mu}}{\partial x'_{\sigma}}\right| \cdot \sqrt{g}.$$

On the other hand, the law of transformation of the element of volume

$$d\tau = \int dx_1\,dx_2\,dx_3\,dx_4$$

is, in accordance with the theorem of Jacobi,

$$d\tau' = \left|\frac{\partial x'_{\sigma}}{\partial x_{\mu}}\right| d\tau.$$

By multiplication of the last two equations, we obtain

$$\sqrt{g'}\,d\tau' = \sqrt{g}\,d\tau \qquad (18).$$

Instead of $\sqrt{g}$, we introduce in what follows the quantity $\sqrt{-g}$, which is always real on account of the hyperbolic character of the space-time continuum. The invariant $\sqrt{-g}\,d\tau$ is equal to the magnitude of the four-dimensional element of volume in the "local" system of reference, as measured with rigid rods and clocks in the sense of the special theory of relativity.

Note on the Character of the Space-time Continuum.—Our assumption that the special theory of relativity can always be applied to an infinitely small region, implies that ds^2 can always be expressed in accordance with (1) by means of real quantities $dX_1 \ldots dX_4$. If we denote by $d\tau_0$ the "natural" element of volume dX_1, dX_2, dX_3, dX_4, then

$$d\tau_0 = \sqrt{-g}\, d\tau \qquad\qquad\qquad (18a)$$

If $\sqrt{-g}$ were to vanish at a point of the four-dimensional continuum, it would mean that at this point an infinitely small "natural" volume would correspond to a finite volume in the co-ordinates. Let us assume that this is never the case. Then g cannot change sign. We will assume that, in the sense of the special theory of relativity, g always has a finite negative value. This is a hypothesis as to the physical nature of the continuum under consideration, and at the same time a convention as to the choice of co-ordinates.

But if $-g$ is always finite and positive, it is natural to settle the choice of co-ordinates *a posteriori* in such a way that this quantity is always equal to unity. We shall see later that by such a restriction of the choice of co-ordinates it is possible to achieve an important simplification of the laws of nature.

In place of (18), we then have simply $d\tau' = d\tau$, from which, in view of Jacobi's theorem, it follows that

$$\left| \frac{\partial x'_\sigma}{\partial x_\mu} \right| = 1 \qquad\qquad\qquad (19)$$

Thus, with this choice of co-ordinates, only substitutions for which the determinant is unity are permissible.

But it would be erroneous to believe that this step indicates a partial abandonment of the general postulate of relativity. We do not ask "What are the laws of nature which are covariant in face of all substitutions for which the determinant is unity?" but our question is "What are the generally covariant laws of nature?" It is not until we have formulated these that we simplify their expression by a particular choice of the system of reference.

The Formation of New Tensors by Means of the Fundamental Tensor.—Inner, outer, and mixed multiplication of a tensor by the fundamental tensor give tensors of different character and rank. For example,

$$A^\mu = g^{\mu\sigma} A_\sigma,$$

$$A = g_{\mu\nu} A^{\mu\nu}.$$

The following forms may be specially noted:—

$$A^{\mu\nu} = g^{\mu\alpha} g^{\nu\beta} A_{\alpha\beta},$$

$$A_{\mu\nu} = g_{\mu\alpha} g_{\nu\beta} A^{\alpha\beta}$$

(the "complements" of covariant and contravariant tensors respectively), and

$$B_{\mu\nu} = g_{\mu\nu} g^{\alpha\beta} A_{\alpha\beta}$$

We call $B_{\mu\nu}$ the reduced tensor associated with $A_{\mu\nu}$. Similarly,

$$B^{\mu\nu} = g^{\mu\nu} g_{\alpha\beta} A^{\alpha\beta}.$$

It may be noted that $g^{\mu\nu}$ is nothing more then the complement of $g_{\mu\nu}$, since

$$g^{\mu\alpha} g^{\nu\beta} g_{\alpha\beta} = g^{\mu\alpha} \delta_\alpha^\nu = g^{\mu\nu}.$$

§ 9. The Equation of the Geodetic Line. The Motion of a Particle

As the linear element ds is defined independently of the system of co-ordinates, the line drawn between two points P and P' of the four-dimensional continuum in such a way that $\int ds$ is stationary—a geodetic line—has a meaning which also is independent of the choice of co-ordinates. Its equation is

$$\delta \int_P^{P'} ds = 0 \qquad (20)$$

Carrying out the variation in the usual way, we obtain from this equation four differential equations which define the geodetic line; this operation will be inserted here for the sake of completeness. Let λ be a function of the co-ordinates x_ν, and let this define a family of surfaces which intersect the required geodetic line as well as all the lines in immediate proximity to it which are drawn through the points P and P'. Any such line may then be supposed to be given by expressing its co-ordinates x_ν as functions of λ. Let the symbol δ indicate the transition from a point of the required geodetic to the point corresponding to the same λ on a neighbouring line. Then for (20) we may substitute

$$\left. \begin{array}{c} \int_{\lambda_1}^{\lambda_2} \delta w \, d\lambda = 0 \\[2mm] w^2 = g_{\mu\nu} \dfrac{dx_\mu}{d\lambda} \dfrac{dx_\nu}{d\lambda} \end{array} \right\} \qquad (20a)$$

But since

$$\delta w = \frac{1}{w} \left\{ \frac{1}{2} \frac{\partial g_{\mu\nu}}{\partial x_\sigma} \frac{dx_\mu}{d\lambda} \frac{dx_\nu}{d\lambda} \delta x_\sigma + g_{\mu\nu} \frac{dx_\mu}{d\lambda} \delta \left(\frac{dx_\nu}{d\lambda} \right) \right\},$$

and

$$\delta \left(\frac{dx_\nu}{d\lambda} \right) = \frac{d}{d\lambda} (\delta x_\nu),$$

we obtain from (20a), after a partial integration,

$$\int_{\lambda_1}^{\lambda_2} \kappa_\sigma \delta x_\sigma \, d\lambda = 0,$$

where

$$\kappa_\sigma = \frac{d}{d\lambda}\left\{\frac{g_{\mu\nu}}{w}\frac{dx_\mu}{d\lambda}\right\} - \frac{1}{2w}\frac{\partial g_{\mu\nu}}{\partial x_\sigma}\frac{dx_\mu}{d\lambda}\frac{dx_\nu}{d\lambda} \tag{20b}$$

Since the values of δx_σ are arbitrary, it follows from this that

$$\kappa_\sigma = 0 \tag{20c}$$

are the equations of the geodetic line.

If ds does not vanish along the geodetic line we may choose the "length of the arc" s, measured along the geodetic line, for the parameter λ. Then $w = 1$, and in place of (20c) we obtain

$$g_{\mu\nu}\frac{d^2x_\mu}{ds^2} + \frac{\partial g_{\mu\nu}}{\partial x_\sigma}\frac{dx_\sigma}{ds}\frac{dx_\mu}{ds} - \frac{1}{2}\frac{\partial g_{\mu\nu}}{\partial x_\sigma}\frac{dx_\mu}{ds}\frac{dx_\nu}{ds} = 0$$

or, by a mere change of notation,

$$g_{a\sigma}\frac{d^2x_a}{ds^2} + [\mu\nu, \sigma]\frac{\partial x_\mu}{\partial s}\frac{dx_\nu}{ds} = 0 \tag{20d}$$

where, following Christoffel, we have written

$$[\mu\nu, \sigma] = \frac{1}{2}\left(\frac{\partial g_{\mu\sigma}}{\partial x_\nu} + \frac{\partial g_{\nu\sigma}}{\partial x_\mu} - \frac{\partial g_{\mu\nu}}{\partial x_\sigma}\right) \tag{21}$$

Finally, if we multiply (20d) by $g^{\sigma\tau}$ (outer multiplication with respect to τ, inner with respect to σ), we obtain the equations of the geodetic line in the form

$$\frac{d^2x_\tau}{ds^2} + \{\mu\nu, \tau\}\frac{dx_\mu}{ds}\frac{dx_\nu}{ds} = 0 \tag{22}$$

where, following Christoffel, we have set

$$\{\mu\nu, \tau\} = g^{\tau a}[\mu\nu, a] \tag{23}$$

§ 10. The Formation of Tensors by Differentiation

With the help of the equation of the geodetic line we can now easily deduce the laws by which new tensors can be formed from old by differentiation. By this means we are able for the first time to formulate generally covariant differential equations. We reach this goal by repeated application of the following simple law:

If in our continuum a curve is given, the points of which are specified by the arcual distance s measured from a fixed point on the curve, and if, further, ϕ is an invariant function of space, then $d\phi/ds$ is also an invariant. The proof lies in this, that ds is an invariant as well as $d\phi$.

As

$$\frac{d\phi}{ds} = \frac{\partial\phi}{\partial x_\mu}\frac{dx_\mu}{ds}$$

therefore

$$\psi = \frac{\partial \phi}{\partial x_\mu} \frac{dx_\mu}{ds}$$

is also an invariant, and an invariant for all curves starting from a point of the continuum, that is, for any choice of the vector dx_μ. Hence it immediately follows that

$$A_\mu = \frac{\partial \phi}{\partial x_\mu} \qquad (24)$$

is a covariant four-vector—the "gradient" of ϕ.

According to our rule, the differential quotient

$$\chi = \frac{\partial \psi}{\partial s}$$

taken on a curve, is similarly an invariant. Inserting the value of ψ, we obtain in the first place

$$\chi = \frac{\partial^2 \phi}{\partial x_\mu \partial x_\nu} \frac{dx_\mu}{ds} \frac{dx_\nu}{ds} + \frac{\partial \phi}{\partial x_\mu} \frac{d^2 x_\mu}{ds^2}$$

The existence of a tensor cannot be deduced from this forthwith. But if we may take the curve along which we have differentiated to be a geodetic, we obtain on substitution for d^2x_ν/ds^2 from (22),

$$\chi = \left(\frac{\partial^2 \phi}{\partial x_\mu \partial x_\nu} - \{\mu\nu, \tau\} \frac{\partial \phi}{\partial x_\tau} \right) \frac{dx_\mu}{ds} \frac{dx_\nu}{ds}.$$

Since we may interchange the order of the differentiations, and since by (23) and (21) $\{\mu\nu, \tau\}$ is symmetrical in μ and ν, it follows that the expression in brackets is symmetrical in μ and ν. Since a geodetic line can be drawn in any direction from a point of the continuum, and therefore dx_μ/ds is a four-vector with the ratio of its components arbitrary, it follows from the results of § 7 that

$$A_{\mu\nu} = \frac{\partial^2 \phi}{\partial x_\mu \partial x_\nu} - \{\mu\nu, \tau\} \frac{\partial \phi}{\partial x_\tau} \qquad (25)$$

is a covariant tensor of the second rank. We have therefore come to this result: from the covariant tensor of the first rank

$$A_\mu = \frac{\partial \phi}{\partial x_\mu}$$

we can, by differentiation, form a covariant tensor of the second rank

$$A_{\mu\nu} = \frac{\partial A_\mu}{\partial x_\nu} - \{\mu\nu, \tau\} A_\tau \qquad (26)$$

We call the tensor $A_{\mu\nu}$ the "extension" (covariant derivative) of the tensor A_μ. In the first place we can readily show that the operation leads to a tensor, even if the vector A_μ cannot be represented as a gradient. To see this, we first observe that

$$\psi \frac{\partial \phi}{\partial x_\mu}$$

is a covariant vector, if ψ and ϕ are scalars. The sum of four such terms

$$S_\mu = \psi^{(1)} \frac{\phi \partial^{(1)}}{\partial x_\mu} + . + . + \psi^{(4)} \frac{\partial \phi^{(4)}}{\partial x_\mu},$$

is also a covariant vector, if $\psi^{(1)}$, $\phi^{(1)}$...$\psi^{(4)}$, $\phi^{(4)}$ are scalars. But it is clear that any covariant vector can be represented in the form S_μ. For, if A_μ is a vector whose components are any given functions of the x_ν, we have only to put (in terms of the selected system of co-ordinates)

$$\psi^{(1)} = A_1, \quad \phi^{(1)} = x_1,$$
$$\psi^{(2)} = A_2, \quad \phi^{(2)} = x_2,$$
$$\psi^{(3)} = A_3, \quad \phi^{(3)} = x_3,$$
$$\psi^{(4)} = A_4, \quad \phi^{(4)} = x_4,$$

in order to ensure that S_μ shall be equal to A_μ.

Therefore, in order to demonstrate that $A_{\mu\nu}$ is a tensor if *any* covariant vector is inserted on the right-hand side for A_μ, we only need show that this is so for the vector S_μ. But for this latter purpose it is sufficient, as a glance at the right-hand side of (26) teaches us, to furnish the proof for the case

$$A_\mu = \psi \frac{\partial \phi}{\partial x_\mu}.$$

Now the right-hand side of (25) multiplied by ψ,

$$\psi \frac{\partial^2 \phi}{\partial x_\mu \partial x_\nu} - \{\mu\nu, \tau\} \psi \frac{\partial \phi}{\partial x_\tau}$$

is a tensor. Similarly

$$\frac{\partial \psi}{\partial x_\mu} \frac{\partial \phi}{\partial x_\nu}$$

being the outer product of two vectors, is a tensor. By addition, there follows the tensor character of

$$\frac{\partial}{\partial x_\nu} \left(\psi \frac{\partial \phi}{\partial x_\mu} \right) - \{\mu\nu, \tau\} \left(\psi \frac{\partial \phi}{\partial x_\tau} \right).$$

As a glance at (26) will show, this completes the demonstration for the vector

$$\psi \frac{\partial \phi}{\partial x_\mu}$$

and consequently, from what has already been proved, for any vector A_μ.

By means of the extension of the vector, we may easily define the "extension" of a covariant tensor of any rank. This operation is a generalization of the extension of a vector. We restrict ourselves to the case of a tensor of the second rank, since this suffices to give a clear idea of the law of formation.

As has already been observed, any covariant tensor of the second rank can be represented[1] as the sum of tensors of the type $A_\mu B_\nu$. It will therefore be sufficient to deduce the expression for the extension of a tensor of this special type. By (26) the expressions

$$\frac{\partial A_\mu}{\partial x_\sigma} - \{\sigma\mu, \tau\} A_\tau,$$

$$\frac{\partial B_\nu}{\partial x_\sigma} - \{\sigma\nu, \tau\} B_\tau,$$

are tensors. On outer multiplication of the first by B_ν, and of the second by A_μ, we obtain in each case a tensor of the third rank. By adding these, we have the tensor of the third rank

$$A_{\mu\nu\sigma} = \frac{\partial A_{\mu\nu}}{\partial x_\sigma} - \{\sigma\mu, \tau\} A_{\tau\nu} - \{\sigma\nu, \tau\} A_{\mu\tau} \tag{27}$$

where we have put $A_{\mu\nu} = A_\mu B_\nu$. As the right-hand side of (27) is linear and homogeneous in the $A_{\mu\nu}$, and their first derivatives, this law of formation leads to a tensor, not only in the case of a tensor of the type $A_\mu B_\nu$, but also in the case of a sum of such tensors, i.e. in the case of any covariant tensor of the second rank. We call $A_{\mu\nu\sigma}$ the extension of the tensor $A_{\mu\nu}$.

It is clear that (26) and (24) concern only special cases of extension (the extension of the tensors of rank one and zero respectively).

In general, all special laws of formation of tensors are included in (27) in combination with the multiplication of tensors.

§ 11. SOME CASES OF SPECIAL IMPORTANCE

The Fundamental Tensor.—We will first prove some lemmas which will be useful hereafter. By the rule for the differentiation of determinants

$$dg = g^{\mu\nu} g \, dg_{\mu\nu} = g_{\mu\nu} g \, dg^{\mu\nu} \tag{28}$$

The last member is obtained from the last but one, if we bear in mind that $g_{\mu\nu} dg^{\mu'\nu} = \delta_\mu^{\mu'}$, so that $g_{\mu\nu} g^{\mu\nu} = 4$, and consequently

$$g_{\mu\nu} dg^{\mu\nu} + g^{\mu\nu} dg_{\mu\nu} = 0.$$

From (28), it follows that

---

1. By outer multiplication of the vector with arbitrary components $A_{11}, A_{12}, A_{13}, A_{14}$ by the vector with components 1, 0, 0, 0, we produce a tensor with components

$$\begin{matrix} A_{11} & A_{12} & A_{13} & A_{14} \\ 0 & 0 & 0 & 0 \\ 0 & 0 & 0 & 0 \\ 0 & 0 & 0 & 0 \end{matrix}$$

By the addition of four tensors of this type, we obtain the tensor $A_{\mu\nu}$ with any assigned components.

$$\frac{1}{\sqrt{-g}}\frac{\partial\sqrt{-g}}{\partial x_{\sigma}} = \frac{1}{2}\frac{\partial\log(-g)}{\partial x_{\sigma}} = \frac{1}{2}g^{\mu\nu}\frac{\partial g_{\mu\nu}}{\partial x_{\sigma}} = -\frac{1}{2}g_{\mu\nu}\frac{\partial g^{\mu\nu}}{\partial x_{\sigma}}.\tag{29}$$

Further, from $g_{\mu\sigma}g^{\nu\sigma} = \delta_{\mu}^{\nu}$, it follows on differentiation that

$$\left.\begin{array}{l} g_{\mu\sigma}dg^{\nu\sigma} = -g^{\nu\sigma}dg_{\mu\sigma} \\[2mm] g_{\mu\sigma}\dfrac{\partial g^{\nu\sigma}}{\partial x_{\lambda}} = -g^{\nu\sigma}d\dfrac{\partial g_{\mu\sigma}}{\partial x_{\lambda}} \end{array}\right\}\tag{30}$$

From these, by mixed multiplication by $g^{\sigma\tau}$ and $g_{\nu\lambda}$ respectively, and a change of notation for the indices, we have

$$\left.\begin{array}{l} dg^{\mu\nu} = -g^{\mu\alpha}g^{\nu\beta}dg_{\alpha\beta} \\[2mm] \dfrac{\partial g^{\mu\nu}}{\partial x_{\sigma}} = -g^{\mu\alpha}g^{\nu\beta}\dfrac{\partial g_{\alpha\beta}}{\partial x_{\sigma}} \end{array}\right\}\tag{31}$$

and

$$\left.\begin{array}{l} dg_{\mu\nu} = -g_{\mu\alpha}g_{\nu\beta}dg^{\alpha\beta} \\[2mm] \dfrac{\partial g_{\mu\nu}}{\partial x_{\sigma}} = -g_{\mu\alpha}g_{\nu\beta}\dfrac{\partial g^{\alpha\beta}}{\partial x_{\sigma}} \end{array}\right\}\tag{32}$$

The relation (31) admits of a transformation, of which we also have frequently to make use. From (21)

$$\frac{\partial g_{\alpha\beta}}{\partial x_{\sigma}} = [\alpha\sigma,\ \beta] + [\beta\sigma,\ \alpha]\tag{33}$$

Inserting this in the second formula of (31), we obtain, in view of (23)

$$\frac{\partial g^{\mu\nu}}{\partial x_{\sigma}} = -g^{\mu\tau}\{\tau\sigma,\ \nu\} - g^{\nu\tau}\{\tau\sigma,\ \mu\}\tag{34}$$

Substituting the right-hand side of (34) in (29), we have

$$\frac{1}{\sqrt{-g}}\frac{\partial\sqrt{-g}}{\partial x_{\sigma}} = \{\mu\sigma,\ \mu\}\tag{29a}$$

The "Divergence" of a Contravariant Vector.—If we take the inner product of (26) by the contravariant fundamental tensor $g^{\mu\nu}$, the right-hand side, after a transformation of the first term, assumes the form

$$\frac{\partial}{\partial x_{\nu}}\left(g^{\mu\nu}A_{\mu}\right) - A_{\mu}\frac{\partial g^{\mu\nu}}{\partial x_{\nu}} - \frac{1}{2}\left(\frac{\partial g_{\mu\alpha}}{\partial x_{\nu}} + \frac{\partial g_{\nu\alpha}}{\partial x_{\mu}} - \frac{\partial g_{\mu\nu}}{\partial x_{\alpha}}\right)g^{\mu\nu}A_{\tau}.$$

In accordance with (31) and (29), the last term of this expression may be written

$$\frac{1}{2}\frac{\partial g^{\tau\nu}}{\partial x_{\nu}}A_{\tau} + \frac{1}{2}\frac{\partial g^{\tau\mu}}{\partial x_{\mu}}A_{\tau} + \frac{1}{\sqrt{-g}}\frac{\partial\sqrt{-g}}{\partial x_{\alpha}}g^{\mu\nu}A_{\tau}.$$

As the symbols of the indices of summation are immaterial, the first two terms of this expression cancel the second of the one above. If we then write $g^{\mu\nu}A_{\mu} = A^{\nu}$, so that A^{ν} like A_{μ} is an arbitrary vector, we finally obtain

$$\Phi = \frac{1}{\sqrt{-g}} \frac{\partial}{\partial x_\nu} \left(\sqrt{-g} \, A^\nu \right) \tag{35}$$

This scalar is the *divergence* of the contravariant vector A^ν.

The "Curl" of a Covariant Vector.—The second term in (26) is symmetrical in the indices μ and ν. Therefore $A_{\mu\nu} - A_{\nu\mu}$ is a particularly simply constructed antisymmetrical tensor. We obtain

$$B_{\mu\nu} = \frac{\partial A_\mu}{\partial x_\nu} - \frac{\partial A_\nu}{\partial x_\mu} \tag{36}$$

Antisymmetrical Extension of a Six-vector.—Applying (27) to an antisymmetrical tensor of the second rank $A_{\mu\nu}$, forming in addition the two equations which arise through cyclic permutations of the indices, and adding these three equations, we obtain the tensor of the third rank

$$B_{\mu\nu\sigma} = A_{\mu\nu\sigma} + A_{\nu\sigma\mu} + A_{\sigma\mu\nu} = \frac{\partial A_{\mu\nu}}{\partial x_\sigma} + \frac{\partial A_{\nu\sigma}}{\partial x_\mu} + \frac{\partial A_{\sigma\mu}}{\partial x_\nu} \tag{37}$$

which it is easy to prove is antisymmetrical.

The Divergence of a Six-vector.—Taking the mixed product of (27) by $g^{\mu\alpha}g^{\nu\beta}$, we also obtain a tensor. The first term on the right-hand side of (27) may be written in the form

$$\frac{\partial}{\partial x_\sigma} \left(g^{\mu\alpha} g^{\nu\beta} A_{\mu\nu} \right) - g^{\mu\alpha} \frac{\partial g^{\nu\beta}}{\partial x_\sigma} A_{\mu\nu} - g^{\nu\beta} \frac{\partial g^{\mu\alpha}}{\partial x_\sigma} A_{\mu\nu}.$$

If we write $A_\sigma^{\alpha\beta}$ for $g^{\mu\alpha}g^{\nu\beta}A_{\mu\nu\sigma}$ and $A^{\alpha\beta}$ for $g^{\mu\alpha}g^{\nu\beta}A_{\mu\nu}$, and in the transformed first term replace

$$\frac{\partial g^{\nu\beta}}{\partial x_\sigma} \quad \text{and} \quad \frac{\partial g^{\mu\alpha}}{\partial x_\sigma}$$

by their values as given by (34), there results from the right-hand side of (27) an expression consisting of seven terms, of which four cancel, and there remains

$$A_\sigma^{\alpha\beta} = \frac{\partial A^{\alpha\beta}}{\partial x_\sigma} + \{\sigma\gamma, \alpha\} A^{\gamma\beta} + \{\sigma\gamma, \beta\} A^{\alpha\gamma} \tag{38}$$

This is the expression for the extension of a contravariant tensor of the second rank, and corresponding expressions for the extension of contravariant tensors of higher and lower rank may also be formed.

We note that in an analogous way we may also form the extension of a mixed tensor:—

$$A_{\mu\sigma}^{\alpha} = \frac{\partial A_\mu^\alpha}{\partial x_\sigma} + \{\sigma\mu, \tau\} A_\tau^\alpha + \{\sigma\tau, \alpha\} A_\mu^\tau \tag{39}$$

On contracting (38) with respect to the indices β and σ (inner multiplication by δ_β^σ), we obtain the vector

$$A^\alpha = \frac{\partial A^{\alpha\beta}}{\partial x_\beta} + \{\beta\gamma,\, \beta\} A^{\alpha\gamma} + \{\beta\gamma,\, \alpha\} A^{\gamma\beta}.$$

On account of the symmetry of $\{\beta\gamma,\, \alpha\}$ with respect to the indices β and γ, the third term on the right-hand side vanishes, if $A^{\alpha\beta}$ is, as we will assume, an antisymmetrical tensor. The second term allows itself to be transformed in accordance with (29a). Thus we obtain

$$A^\alpha = \frac{1}{\sqrt{-g}} \frac{\partial\left(\sqrt{-g}\, A^{\alpha\beta}\right)}{\partial x_\beta} \tag{40}$$

This is the expression for the divergence of a contravariant six-vector.

The Divergence of a Mixed Tensor of the Second Rank.—Contracting (39) with respect to the indices α and σ, and taking (29a) into consideration, we obtain

$$\sqrt{-g}\, A_\mu = \frac{\partial\left(\sqrt{-g}\, A_\mu^\sigma\right)}{\partial x_\sigma} - \{\sigma\mu,\, \tau\}\sqrt{-g}\, A_\tau^\sigma \tag{41}$$

If we introduce the contravariant tensor $A^{\rho\sigma} = g^{\rho\tau} A_\tau^\sigma$ in the last term, it assumes the form

$$-[\sigma\mu,\, \rho]\sqrt{-g}\, A^{\rho\sigma}.$$

If, further, the tensor $A^{\rho\sigma}$ is symmetrical, this reduces to

$$-\frac{1}{2}\sqrt{-g}\, \frac{\partial g_{\rho\sigma}}{\partial x_\mu} A^{\rho\sigma}.$$

Had we introduced, instead of $A^{\rho\sigma}$, the covariant tensor $A_{\rho\sigma} = g_{\rho\alpha} g_{\sigma\beta} A^{\alpha\beta}$, which is also symmetrical, the last term, by virtue of (31), would assume the form

$$\frac{1}{2}\sqrt{-g}\, \frac{\partial g^{\rho\sigma}}{\partial x_\mu} A_{\rho\sigma}.$$

In the case of symmetry in question, (41) may therefore be replaced by the two forms

$$\sqrt{-g}\, A_\mu = \frac{\partial\left(\sqrt{-g}\, A_\mu^\sigma\right)}{\partial x_\sigma} - \frac{1}{2}\frac{\partial g^{\rho\sigma}}{\partial x_\mu}\sqrt{-g}\, A^{\rho\sigma} \tag{41a}$$

$$\sqrt{-g}\, A_\mu = \frac{\partial\left(\sqrt{-g}\, A_\mu^\sigma\right)}{\partial x_\sigma} + \frac{1}{2}\frac{\partial g^{\rho\sigma}}{\partial x_\mu}\sqrt{-g}\, A_{\rho\sigma} \tag{41b}$$

which we have to employ later on.

§ 12. The Riemann-Christoffel Tensor

We now seek the tensor which can be obtained from the fundamental tensor *alone*, by differentiation. At first sight the solution seems obvious. We place the fundamental

tensor of the $g_{\mu\nu}$ in (27) instead of any given tensor $A_{\mu\nu}$, and thus have a new tensor, namely, the extension of the fundamental tensor. But we easily convince ourselves that this extension vanishes identically. We reach our goal, however, in the following way. In (27) place

$$A_{\mu\nu} = \frac{\partial A_\mu}{\partial x_\nu} - \{\mu\nu, \rho\} A_\rho,$$

i.e. the extension of the four-vector A_μ. Then (with a somewhat different naming of the indices) we get the tensor of the third rank

$$A_{\mu\sigma\tau} = \frac{\partial^2 A_\mu}{\partial x_\sigma \partial x_\tau} - \{\mu\sigma, \rho\}\frac{\partial A_\rho}{\partial x_\tau} - \{\mu\tau, \rho\}\frac{\partial A_\rho}{\partial x_\sigma} - \{\sigma\tau, \rho\}\frac{\partial A_\mu}{\partial x_\rho}$$
$$+ \left[-\frac{\partial}{\partial x_\tau}\{\mu\sigma, \rho\} + \{\mu\tau, \alpha\}\{\alpha\sigma, \rho\} + \{\sigma\tau, \alpha\}\{\alpha\mu, \rho\} \right] A_\rho.$$

This expression suggests forming the tensor $A_{\mu\sigma\tau} - A_{\mu\tau\sigma}$. For, if we do so, the following terms of the expression for $A_{\mu\sigma\tau}$ cancel those of $A_{\mu\tau\sigma}$, the first, the fourth, and the member corresponding to the last term in square brackets; because all these are symmetrical in σ and τ. The same holds good for the sum of the second and third terms. Thus we obtain

$$A_{\mu\sigma\tau} - A_{\mu\tau\sigma} = B_{\mu\sigma\tau}^\rho A_\rho \qquad (42)$$

where

$$B_{\mu\sigma\tau}^\rho = -\frac{\partial}{\partial x_\tau}\{\mu\sigma, \rho\} + \frac{\partial}{\partial x_\sigma}\{\mu\tau, \rho\} - \{\mu\sigma, \alpha\}\{\alpha\tau, \rho\} + \{\mu\tau, \alpha\}\{\alpha\sigma, \rho\} \qquad (43)$$

The essential feature of the result is that on the right side of (42) the A_ρ occur alone, without their derivatives. From the tensor character of $A_{\mu\sigma\tau} - A_{\mu\tau\sigma}$ in conjunction with the fact that A_ρ is an arbitrary vector, it follows, by reason of § 7, that $B_{\mu\sigma\tau}^\rho$ is a tensor (the Riemann-Christoffel tensor).

The mathematical importance of this tensor is as follows: If the continuum is of such a nature that there is a co-ordinate system with reference to which the $g_{\mu\nu}$ are constants, then all the $B_{\mu\sigma\tau}^\rho$ vanish. If we choose any new system of co-ordinates in place of the original ones, the $g_{\mu\nu}$ referred thereto will not be constants, but in consequence of its tensor nature, the transformed components of $B_{\mu\sigma\tau}^\rho$ will still vanish in the new system. Thus the vanishing of the Riemann tensor is a necessary condition that, by an appropriate choice of the system of reference, the $g_{\mu\nu}$ may be constants. In our problem this corresponds to the case in which,[1] with a suitable choice of the system of reference, the special theory of relativity holds good for a *finite* region of the continuum.

Contracting (43) with respect to the indices τ and ρ we obtain the covariant tensor of second rank

---

1. The mathematicians have proved that this is also a *sufficient* condition.

where $\qquad$ (44)

$$G_{\mu\nu} = B^{\rho}_{\mu\nu\rho} = R_{\mu\nu} + S_{\mu\nu}$$

$$R_{\mu\nu} = -\frac{\partial}{\partial x_{\alpha}}\{\mu\nu, \alpha\} + \{\mu\alpha, \beta\}\{\nu\beta, \alpha\}$$

$$S_{\mu\nu} = \frac{\partial^2 \log\sqrt{-g}}{\partial x_{\mu}\partial x_{\nu}} - \{\mu\nu, \alpha\}\frac{\partial \log\sqrt{-g}}{\partial x_{\alpha}}$$

Note on the Choice of Co-ordinates.—It has already been observed in § 8, in connexion with equation (18a), that the choice of co-ordinates may with advantage be made so that $\sqrt{-g} = 1$. A glance at the equations obtained in the last two sections shows that by such a choice the laws of formation of tensors undergo an important simplification. This applies particularly to $G_{\mu\nu}$, the tensor just developed, which plays a fundamental part in the theory to be set forth. For this specialization of the choice of co-ordinates brings about the vanishing of $S_{\mu\nu}$, so that the tensor $G_{\mu\nu}$ reduces to $R_{\mu\nu}$.

On this account I shall hereafter give all relations in the simplified form which this specialization of the choice of co-ordinates brings with it. It will then be an easy matter to revert to the *generally* covariant equations, if this seems desirable in a special case.

C. THEORY OF THE GRAVITATIONAL FIELD

§ 13. Equations of Motion of a Material Point in the Gravitational Field. Expression for the Field-Components of Gravitation

A freely movable body not subjected to external forces moves, according to the special theory of relativity, in a straight line and uniformly. This is also the case, according to the general theory of relativity, for a part of four-dimensional space in which the system of co-ordinates K_0, may be, and is, so chosen that they have the special constant values given in (4).

If we consider precisely this movement from any chosen system of co-ordinates K_1, the body, observed from K_1, moves, according to the considerations in § 2, in a gravitational field. The law of motion with respect to K_1 results without difficulty from the following consideration. With respect to K_0 the law of motion corresponds to a four-dimensional straight line, i.e. to a geodetic line. Now since the geodetic line is defined independently of the system of reference, its equations will also be the equation of motion of the material point with respect to K_1. If we set

$$\Gamma^{\tau}_{\mu\nu} = -\{\mu\nu, \tau\} \qquad (45)$$

the equation of the motion of the point with respect to K_1, becomes

$$\frac{d^2 x_\tau}{ds^2} = \Gamma_{\mu\nu}^\tau \frac{dx_\mu}{ds} \frac{dx_\nu}{ds} \qquad (46)$$

We now make the assumption, which readily suggests itself, that this covariant system of equations also defines the motion of the point in the gravitational field in the case when there is no system of reference K_0, with respect to which the special theory of relativity holds good in a finite region. We have all the more justification for this assumption as (46) contains only *first* derivatives of the $g_{\mu\nu}$, between which even in the special case of the existence of K_0, no relations subsist.[1]

If the $\Gamma_{\mu\nu}^\tau$ vanish, then the point moves uniformly in a straight line. These quantities therefore condition the deviation of the motion from uniformity. They are the components of the gravitational field.

§ 14. THE FIELD EQUATIONS OF GRAVITATION IN THE ABSENCE OF MATTER

We make a distinction hereafter between "gravitational field" and "matter" in this way, that we denote everything but the gravitational field as "matter." Our use of the word therefore includes not only matter in the ordinary sense, but the electromagnetic field as well.

Our next task is to find the field equations of gravitation in the absence of matter. Here we again apply the method employed in the preceding paragraph in formulating the equations of motion of the material point. A special case in which the required equations must in any case be satisfied is that of the special theory of relativity, in which the $g_{\mu\nu}$, have certain constant values. Let this be the case in a certain finite space in relation to a definite system of co-ordinates K_0. Relatively to this system all the components of the Riemann tensor $B_{\mu\nu\tau}^\rho$, defined in (43), vanish. For the space under consideration they then vanish, also in any other system of co-ordinates.

Thus the required equations of the matter-free gravitational field must in any case be satisfied if all $B_{\mu\sigma\tau}^\rho$ vanish. But this condition goes too far. For it is clear that, e.g., the gravitational field generated by a material point in its environment certainly cannot be "transformed away" by any choice of the system of co-ordinates, i.e. it cannot be transformed to the case of constant $g_{\mu\nu}$.

This prompts us to require for the matter-free gravitational field that the symmetrical tensor $G_{\mu\nu}$, derived from the tensor $B_{\mu\nu\tau}^\rho$, shall vanish. Thus we obtain ten equations for the ten quantities $g_{\mu\nu}$, which are satisfied in the special case of the vanishing of all $B_{\mu\nu\tau}^\rho$. With the choice which we have made of a system of co-ordinates, and taking (44) into consideration, the equations for the matter-free field are

---

1. It is only between the second (and first) derivatives that, by § 12, the relations $B_{\mu\sigma\tau}^\rho = 0$ subsist.

$$\left.\begin{array}{l} \dfrac{\partial \Gamma^{\alpha}_{\mu\nu}}{\partial x_{\alpha}} + \Gamma^{\alpha}_{\mu\beta}\Gamma^{\beta}_{\nu\alpha} = 0 \\[2mm] \sqrt{-g} = 1 \end{array}\right\} \tag{47}$$

It must be pointed out that there is only a minimum of arbitrariness in the choice of these equations. For besides $G_{\mu\nu}$ there is no tensor of second rank which is formed from the $g_{\mu\nu}$ and its derivatives, contains no derivations higher than second, and is linear in these derivatives.[1]

These equations, which proceed, by the method of pure mathematics, from the requirement of the general theory of relativity, give us, in combination with the equations of motion (46), to a first approximation Newton's law of attraction, and to a second approximation the explanation of the motion of the perihelion of the planet Mercury discovered by Leverrier (as it remains after corrections for perturbation have been made). These facts must, in my opinion, be taken as a convincing proof of the correctness of the theory.

§ 15. THE HAMILTONIAN FUNCTION FOR THE GRAVITATIONAL FIELD. LAWS OF MOMENTUM AND ENERGY

To show that the field equations correspond to the laws of momentum and energy, it is most convenient to write them in the following Hamiltonian form:

$$\left.\begin{array}{l} \delta \int H \, d\tau = 0 \\[2mm] H = g^{\mu\nu}\Gamma^{\alpha}_{\mu\beta}\Gamma^{\beta}_{\nu\alpha} \\[2mm] \sqrt{-g} = 1 \end{array}\right\} \tag{47a}$$

where, on the boundary of the finite four-dimensional region of integration which we have in view, the variations vanish.

We first have to show that the form (47a) is equivalent to the equations (47). For this purpose we regard H as a function of the $g^{\mu\nu}$ and the $g^{\mu\nu}_{\sigma}\left(= \partial g^{\mu\nu} / \partial x_{\sigma}\right)$. Then in the first place

$$\delta H = \Gamma^{\alpha}_{\mu\beta}\Gamma^{\beta}_{\nu\alpha}\delta g^{\mu\nu} + 2g^{\mu\nu}\Gamma^{\alpha}_{\mu\beta}\delta\Gamma^{\beta}_{\nu\alpha}$$

$$= -\Gamma^{\alpha}_{\mu\beta}\Gamma^{\beta}_{\nu\alpha}\delta g^{\mu\nu} + 2\Gamma^{\alpha}_{\mu\beta}\delta\left(g^{\mu\nu}\Gamma^{\beta}_{\nu\alpha}\right).$$

But

$$\delta\left(g^{\mu\nu}\Gamma^{\beta}_{\nu\alpha}\right) = -\frac{1}{2}\delta\left[g^{\mu\nu}g^{\beta\nu}\left(\frac{\partial g_{\nu\lambda}}{\partial x_{\alpha}} + \frac{\partial g_{\alpha\lambda}}{\partial x_{\nu}} - \frac{\partial g_{\alpha\nu}}{\partial x_{\lambda}}\right)\right].$$

The terms arising from the last two terms in round brackets are of different sign, and result from each other (since the denomination of the summation indices is immaterial)

---

1. Properly speaking, this can be affirmed only of the tensor

$$G_{\mu\nu} + \lambda g_{\mu\nu}g^{\alpha\beta}G_{\alpha\beta}$$

where λ is a constant. If, however, we set this tensor = 0, we come back again to the equations $G_{\mu\nu} = 0$.

through interchange of the indices μ and β. They cancel each other in the expression for δH, because they are multiplied by the quantity $\Gamma_{\mu\beta}^{\alpha}$, which is symmetrical with respect to the indices μ and β. Thus there remains only the first term in round brackets to be considered, so that, taking (31) into account, we obtain

$$\delta H = \Gamma_{\mu\beta}^{\alpha}\Gamma_{v\alpha}^{\beta}\delta g^{\mu v} + \Gamma_{\mu\beta}^{\alpha}\delta g_{\alpha}^{\mu\beta}$$

Thus

$$\left.\begin{array}{l} \dfrac{\partial H}{\partial g^{\mu v}} = -\Gamma_{\mu\beta}^{\alpha}\Gamma_{v\alpha}^{\beta} \\[3mm] \dfrac{\partial H}{\partial g_{\sigma}^{\mu v}} = \Gamma_{\mu v}^{\sigma} \end{array}\right\} \tag{48}$$

Carrying out the variation in (47a), we get in the first place

$$\frac{\partial}{\partial x_{\alpha}}\left(\frac{\partial H}{\partial g_{\alpha}^{\mu v}}\right) - \frac{\partial H}{\partial g^{\mu v}} = 0, \tag{47b}$$

which, on account of (48), agrees with (47), as was to be proved.

If we multiply (47b) by $g_{\sigma}^{\mu v}$, then because

$$\frac{\partial g_{\sigma}^{\mu v}}{\partial x_{\alpha}} = \frac{\partial g_{\alpha}^{\mu v}}{\partial x_{\sigma}}$$

and, consequently,

$$g_{\sigma}^{\mu v}\frac{\partial}{\partial x_{\alpha}}\left(\frac{\partial H}{\partial g_{\alpha}^{\mu v}}\right) = \frac{\partial}{\partial x_{\alpha}}\left(g_{\sigma}^{\mu v}\frac{\partial H}{\partial g_{\alpha}^{\mu v}}\right) - \frac{\partial H}{\partial g_{\alpha}^{\mu v}}$$

we obtain the equation

$$\frac{\partial}{\partial x_{\alpha}}\left(g_{\sigma}^{\mu v}\frac{\partial H}{\partial g_{\alpha}^{\mu v}}\right) - \frac{\partial H}{\partial x_{\sigma}} = 0$$

or[1]

$$\left.\begin{array}{l} \dfrac{\partial t_{\sigma}^{\alpha}}{\partial x_{\alpha}} = 0 \\[3mm] -d\kappa t_{\sigma}^{\alpha} = g_{\sigma}^{\mu v}\dfrac{\partial H}{\partial g_{\alpha}^{\mu v}} - \delta_{\sigma}^{\alpha}H \end{array}\right\} \tag{49}$$

where, on account of (48), the second equation of (47), and (34)

$$\kappa t_{\sigma}^{\alpha} = \frac{1}{2}\delta_{\sigma}^{\alpha}g^{\mu v}\Gamma_{\mu\beta}^{\lambda}\Gamma_{v\lambda}^{\beta} - g^{\mu v}\Gamma_{\mu\beta}^{\alpha}\Gamma_{v\sigma}^{\beta} \tag{50}$$

It is to be noticed that t_{σ}^{α} is not a tensor; on the other hand (49) applies to all systems of co-ordinates for which $\sqrt{-g} = 1$. This equation expresses the law of conservation of momentum and of energy for the gravitational field. Actually the integration of this equation over a three-dimensional volume V yields the four equations

1. The reason for the introduction of the factor - 2κ will be apparent later.

$$\frac{d}{dx_4}\int t_\sigma^4 \, dV = \int \left(lt_\sigma^1 + mt_\sigma^2 + nt_\sigma^3\right) dS \tag{49a}$$

where l, m, n denote the direction-cosines of direction of the inward drawn normal at the element dS of the bounding surface (in the sense of Euclidean geometry). We recognize in this the expression of the laws of conservation in their usual form. The quantities t_σ^α we call the "energy components" of the gravitational field.

I will now give equations (47) in a third form, which is particularly useful for a vivid grasp of our subject. By multiplication of the field equations (47) by $g^{\nu\sigma}$ these are obtained in the "mixed" form. Note that

$$g^{\nu\sigma}\frac{\partial \Gamma_{\mu\nu}^\alpha}{\partial x_\alpha}\left(g^{\nu\sigma}\Gamma_{\mu\nu}^\alpha\right) - \frac{\partial g^{\nu\sigma}}{\partial x_\alpha}\Gamma_{\mu\nu}^\alpha$$

which quantity, by reason of (34), is equal to

$$\frac{\partial}{\partial x_\alpha}\left(g^{\nu\sigma}\Gamma_{\mu\nu}^\alpha\right) - g^{\nu\beta}\Gamma_{\alpha\beta}^\sigma\Gamma_{\mu\nu}^\alpha - g^{\sigma\beta}\Gamma_{\alpha\beta}^\nu\Gamma_{\mu\nu}^\alpha,$$

or (with different symbols for the summation indices)

$$\frac{\partial}{\partial x_\alpha}\left(g^{\sigma\beta}\Gamma_{\mu\beta}^\alpha\right) - g^{\gamma\delta}\Gamma_{\gamma\beta}^\sigma\Gamma_{\delta\mu}^\beta - g^{\nu\sigma}\Gamma_{\mu\beta}^\alpha\Gamma_{\nu\alpha}^\beta.$$

The third term of this expression cancels with the one arising from the second term of the field equations (47); using relation (50), the second term may be written

$$\kappa\left(t_\mu^\sigma - \frac{1}{2}\delta_\mu^\sigma t\right)$$

where $t = t_\alpha^\alpha$. Thus instead of equations (47) we obtain

$$\left.\begin{array}{c}\dfrac{\partial}{\partial x_\alpha}\left(g^{\sigma\beta}\Gamma_{\mu\beta}^\alpha\right) = -\kappa\left(t_\mu^\sigma - \delta_\mu^\sigma t\right)\\[1.5ex]\sqrt{-g} = 1\end{array}\right\} \tag{51}$$

§ 16. THE GENERAL FORM OF THE FIELD EQUATIONS OF GRAVITATION

The field equations for matter-free space formulated in § 15 are to be compared with the field equation

$$\nabla^2\phi = 0$$

of Newton's theory. We require the equation corresponding to Poisson's equation

$$\nabla^2\phi = 4\pi\lambda\rho,$$

where ρ denotes the density of matter.

The special theory of relativity has led to the conclusion that inert mass is nothing

more or less than energy, which finds its complete mathematical expression in a symmetrical tensor of second rank, the energy-tensor. Thus in the general theory of relativity we must introduce a corresponding energy-tensor of matter T^α_σ, which, like the energy-components t_σ [equations (49) and (50)] of the gravitational field, will have mixed character, but will pertain to a symmetrical covariant tensor.[1]

The system of equation (51) shows how this energy-tensor (corresponding to the density ρ in Poisson's equation) is to be introduced into the field equations of gravitation. For if we consider a complete system (e.g. the solar system), the total mass of the system, and therefore its total gravitating action as well, will depend on the total energy of the system, and therefore on the ponderable energy together with the gravitational energy. This will allow itself to be expressed by introducing into (51), in place of the energy-components of the gravitational field alone, the sums $t^\sigma_\mu + T^\sigma_\mu$ of the energy-components of matter and of gravitational field. Thus instead of (51) we obtain the tensor equation

$$\left. \begin{array}{l} \dfrac{\partial}{\partial x_\alpha}\left(g^{\sigma\beta}T^\alpha_{\mu\beta}\right) = -\kappa\left[\left(t^\sigma_\mu + T^\sigma_\mu\right) - \dfrac{1}{2}\delta^\sigma_\mu\left(t + T\right)\right] \\[2mm] \sqrt{-g} = 1 \end{array} \right\} \tag{52}$$

where we have set $T = T^\mu_\mu$ (Laue's scalar). These are the required general field equations of gravitation in mixed form. Working back from these, we have in place of (47)

$$\left. \begin{array}{l} \dfrac{\partial}{\partial x_\alpha}\Gamma^\alpha_{\mu\nu} + \Gamma^\alpha_{\mu\beta}\Gamma^\beta_{\mu\alpha} = -\kappa\left(T_{\mu\nu} - \dfrac{1}{2}g_{\mu\nu}T\right), \\[2mm] \sqrt{-g} = 1 \end{array} \right\} \tag{53}$$

It must be admitted that this introduction of the energy-tensor of matter is not justified by the relativity postulate alone. For this reason we have here deduced it from the requirement that the energy of the gravitational field shall act gravitatively in the same way as any other kind of energy. But the strongest reason for the choice of these equations lies in their consequence, that the equations of conservation of momentum and energy, corresponding exactly to equations (49) and (49a), hold good for the components of the total energy. This will be shown in § 17.

§ 17. The Laws of Conservation in the General Case

Equation (52) may readily be transformed so that the second term on the right-hand side vanishes. Contract (52) with respect to the indices μ and σ, and after multiplying the resulting equation by $\frac{1}{2}\delta^\sigma_\mu$, subtract it from equation (52). This gives

1. $g_{\alpha\tau}T^\sigma_\mu = T_{\sigma\tau}$ and $g_{\sigma\beta}T^\alpha_\sigma = T^{\sigma\beta}$ are to be symmetrical tensors.

$$\frac{\partial}{\partial x_\alpha}\left(g^{\sigma\beta}\Gamma^\alpha_{\mu\beta} - \frac{1}{2}\delta^\sigma_\mu g^{\lambda\beta}\Gamma^\alpha_{\lambda\beta}\right) = -\kappa\left(t^\sigma_\mu + T^\sigma_\mu\right) \tag{52a}$$

On this equation we perform the operation $\partial/\partial x_\sigma$. We have

$$\frac{\partial^2}{\partial x_\alpha \partial x_\sigma}\left(g^{\sigma}\Gamma^\alpha_{\beta\mu}\right) = -\frac{1}{2}\frac{\partial^2}{\partial x_\alpha \partial x_\sigma}\left[g^{\sigma\beta}g^{\alpha\lambda}\left(\frac{\partial g_{\mu\lambda}}{\partial x_\beta} + \frac{\partial g_{\beta\lambda}}{\partial x_\mu} - \frac{\partial g_{\mu\beta}}{\partial x_\lambda}\right)\right].$$

The first and third terms of the round brackets yield contributions which cancel one another, as may be seen by interchanging, in the contribution of the third term, the summation indices α and σ on the one hand, and β and λ on the other. The second term may be re-modelled by (31), so that we have

$$\frac{\partial^2}{\partial x_\alpha \partial x_\sigma}\left(g^{\sigma\beta}\Gamma^\alpha_{\mu\beta}\right) = \frac{1}{2}\frac{\partial^3 g^{\alpha\beta}}{\partial x_\alpha\, \partial x_\beta \partial x_\mu} \tag{54}$$

The second term on the left-hand side of (52a) yields in the first place

$$-\frac{1}{2}\frac{\partial^2}{\partial x_\alpha \partial x_\mu}\left(g^{\lambda\beta}\Gamma^\alpha_{\lambda\beta}\right)$$

or

$$\frac{1}{4}\frac{\partial^2}{\partial x_\alpha \partial x_\mu}\left[g^{\lambda\beta}g^{\alpha\delta}\left(\frac{\partial g_{\delta\lambda}}{\partial x_\beta} + \frac{\partial g_{\delta\beta}}{\partial x_\lambda} - \frac{\partial g_{\lambda\beta}}{\partial x_\delta}\right)\right].$$

With the choice of co-ordinates which we have made, the term deriving from the last term in round brackets disappears by reason of (29). The other two may be combined, and together, by (31), they give

$$-\frac{1}{2}\frac{\partial^3 g^{\alpha\beta}}{\partial x_\alpha \partial x_\beta \partial x_\mu},$$

so that in consideration of (54), we have the identity

$$\frac{\partial^2}{\partial x_\alpha \partial x_\sigma}\left(g^{\rho\beta}\Gamma_{\mu\beta} - \frac{1}{2}\delta^\delta_\mu g^{\lambda\beta}\Gamma^\alpha_{\lambda\beta}\right) \equiv 0 \tag{55}$$

From (55) and (52a), it follows that

$$\frac{\partial\left(t^\sigma_\mu + T^\sigma_\mu\right)}{\partial x_\sigma} = 0 \tag{56}$$

Thus it results from our field equations of gravitation that the laws of conservation of momentum and energy are satisfied. This may be seen most easily from the consideration which leads to equation (49a); except that here, instead of the energy components t^σ of the gravitational field, we have to introduce the totality of the energy components of matter and gravitational field.

§ 18. THE LAWS OF MOMENTUM AND ENERGY FOR MATTER, AS A CONSEQUENCE OF THE FIELD EQUATIONS

Multiplying (53) by $\partial g^{\mu\nu}/\partial x_\sigma$, we obtain, by the method adopted in § 15, in view of the vanishing of

$$g_{\mu\nu} \frac{\partial g^{\mu\nu}}{\partial x_\sigma},$$

the equation

$$\frac{\partial t_\sigma^\alpha}{\partial x_\alpha} + \frac{1}{2} \frac{\partial g^{\mu\nu}}{\partial x_\sigma} T_{\mu\nu} = 0,$$

or, in view of (56),

$$\frac{\partial T_\sigma^\alpha}{\partial x_\alpha} + \frac{1}{2} \frac{\partial g^{\mu\nu}}{\partial x_\sigma} T_{\mu\nu} = 0 \tag{57}$$

Comparison with (41b) shows that with the choice of system of co-ordinates which we have made, this equation predicates nothing more or less than the vanishing of divergence of the material energy-tensor. Physically, the occurrence of the second term on the left-hand side shows that laws of conservation of momentum and energy do not apply in the strict sense for matter alone, or else that they apply only when the $g^{\mu\nu}$ are constant, i.e. when the field intensities of gravitation vanish. This second term is an expression for momentum, and for energy, as transferred per unit of volume and time from the gravitational field to matter. This is brought out still more clearly by re-writing (57) in the sense of (41) as

$$\frac{\partial T_\sigma^\alpha}{\partial x_\alpha} = \Gamma_{\alpha\sigma}^\beta T_\beta^\alpha \tag{57a}$$

The right side expresses the energetic effect of the gravitational field on matter.

Thus the field equations of gravitation contain four conditions which govern the course of material phenomena. They give the equations of material phenomena completely, if the latter is capable of being characterized by four differential equations independent of one another.[1]

D. MATERIAL PHENOMENA

The mathematical aids developed in part B enable us forthwith to generalize the physical laws of matter (hydrodynamics, Maxwell's electrodynamics), as they are formulated in the special theory of relativity, so that they will fit in with the general theory of relativity. When this is done, the general principle of relativity does not indeed afford us a further limitation of possibilities; but it makes us acquainted with the influence of the gravitational field on all processes, without our having to introduce any new hypothesis whatever.

1. On this question cf. H. Hilbert, Nachr. d. K. Gesellsch. d. Wiss. zu Göttingen, Math.-phys. Klasse, 1915, p. 3.

Hence it comes about that it is not necessary to introduce definite assumptions as to the physical nature of matter (in the narrower sense). In particular it may remain an open question whether the theory of the electromagnetic field in conjunction with that of the gravitational field furnishes a sufficient basis for the theory of matter or not. The general postulate of relativity is unable on principle to tell us anything about this. It must remain to be seen, during the working out of the theory, whether electromagnetics and the doctrine of gravitation are able in collaboration to perform what the former by itself is unable to do.

§ 19. EULER'S EQUATIONS FOR A FRICTIONLESS ADIABATIC FLUID

Let p and ρ be two scalars, the former of which we call the "pressure," the latter the "density" of a fluid; and let an equation subsist between them. Let the contravariant symmetrical tensor

$$T^{\alpha\beta} = -g^{\alpha\beta}p + \rho\frac{dx_\alpha}{ds}\frac{dx_\beta}{ds} \tag{58}$$

be the contravariant energy-tensor of the fluid. To it belongs the covariant tensor

$$T_{\mu\nu} = -g_{\mu\nu}p + g_{\mu\alpha}g_{\mu\beta}\frac{dx_\alpha}{ds}\frac{dx_\beta}{ds}\rho, \tag{58a}$$

as well as the mixed tensor[1]

$$T_\sigma^\alpha = -\delta_\sigma^\alpha p + g_{\sigma\beta}\frac{dx_\alpha}{ds}\frac{dx_\beta}{ds}\rho \tag{58b}$$

Inserting the right-hand side of (58b) in (57a), we obtain the Eulerian hydrodynamical equations of the general theory of relativity. They give, in theory, a complete solution of the problem of motion, since the four equations (57a), together with the given equation between p and ρ, and the equation

$$g_{\alpha\beta}\frac{dx_\alpha}{ds}\frac{dx_\beta}{ds} = 1,$$

are sufficient, $g_{\alpha\beta}$ being given, to define the six unknowns

$$p, \rho, \frac{dx_a}{ds}, \frac{dx_2}{ds}, \frac{dx_3}{ds}, \frac{dx_4}{ds}.$$

If the $g_{\mu\nu}$ are also unknown, the equations (53) are brought in. These are eleven equations for defining the ten functions $g_{\mu\nu}$, so that these functions appear over-defined. We must remember, however, that the equations (57a) are already contained in the equations (53), so that the latter represent only seven independent equations. There is good reason for this lack of definition, in that the wide freedom of the choice of coordinates

---

1. For an observer using a system of reference in the sense of the special theory of relativity for an infinitely small region, and moving with it, the density of energy T_4^4 equals $\rho - p$. This gives the definition of ρ. Thus ρ is not constant for an incompressible fluid.

causes the problem to remain mathematically undefined to such a degree that three of the functions of space may be chosen at will.[1]

§ 20. MAXWELL'S ELECTROMAGNETIC FIELD EQUATIONS FOR FREE SPACE

Let ϕ_ν be the components of a covariant vector—the electromagnetic potential vector. From them we form, in accordance with (36), the components $F_{\rho\sigma}$ of the covariant six-vector of the electromagnetic field, in accordance with the system of equations

$$F_{\rho\sigma} - \frac{\partial \phi_\rho}{\partial x_\sigma} - \frac{\partial \phi_\sigma}{\partial x_\rho} \tag{59}$$

It follows from (59) that the system of equations

$$\frac{\partial F_{\rho\sigma}}{\partial x_\tau} + \frac{\partial F_{\sigma\tau}}{\partial x_\rho} + \frac{\partial F_{\tau\rho}}{\partial x_\sigma} = 0 \tag{60}$$

is satisfied, its left side being, by (37), an antisymmetrical tensor of the third rank. System (60) thus contains essentially four equations which are written out as follows:—

$$\begin{aligned}
\frac{\partial F_{23}}{\partial x_4} + \frac{\partial F_{34}}{\partial x_2} + \frac{\partial F_{42}}{\partial x_3} &= 0 \\
\frac{\partial F_{34}}{\partial x_1} + \frac{\partial F_{41}}{\partial x_3} + \frac{\partial F_{13}}{\partial x_4} &= 0 \\
\frac{\partial F_{41}}{\partial x_2} + \frac{\partial F_{12}}{\partial x_4} + \frac{\partial F_{24}}{\partial x_1} &= 0 \\
\frac{\partial F_{12}}{\partial x_3} + \frac{\partial F_{23}}{\partial x_1} + \frac{\partial F_{31}}{\partial x_2} &= 0
\end{aligned} \tag{60a}$$

This system corresponds to the second of Maxwell's systems of equations. We recognize this at once by setting

$$\begin{aligned}
F_{23} &= H_x, & F_{14} &= E_x \\
F_{31} &= H_y, & F_{24} &= E_y \\
F_{12} &= H_z, & F_{34} &= E_z
\end{aligned} \tag{61}$$

Then in place of (60a) we may set, in the usual notation of three-dimensional vector analysis,

$$\begin{aligned}
-\frac{\partial H}{\partial t} &= \operatorname{curl} E \\
\operatorname{div} H &= 0
\end{aligned} \tag{60b}$$

We obtain Maxwell's first system by generalizing the form given by Minkowski. We introduce the contravariant six-vector associated with $F^{\alpha\beta}$

1. On the abandonment of the choice of co-ordinates with g = - 1, there remain four functions of space with liberty of choice, corresponding to the four arbitrary functions at our disposal in the choice of co-ordinates.

$$F^{\mu\nu} = g^{\mu\alpha}g^{\nu\beta}F_{\alpha\beta} \qquad (62)$$

and also the contravariant vector J^μ of the density of the electric current. Then, taking (40) into consideration, the following equations will be invariant for any substitution whose invariant is unity (in agreement with the chosen co-ordinates):—

$$\frac{\partial}{\partial x_\nu}F^{\mu\nu} = J^\mu \qquad (63)$$

Let

$$\begin{aligned}
F^{23} &= H'_x, & F^{14} &= -E'_x \\
F^{31} &= H'_y, & F^{24} &= -E'_y \\
F^{12} &= H'_z, & F^{34} &= -E'_z
\end{aligned} \right\} \qquad (64)$$

which quantities are equal to the quantities $H_x \ldots E^z$ in the special case of the restricted theory of relativity; and in addition

$$J^1 - j_x, \; J^2 = j_y, \; J^3 = j_z, \; J^4 = \rho,$$

we obtain in place of (63)

$$\left. \begin{aligned}
\frac{\partial E'}{\partial t} + j &= \text{curl } H' \\
\text{div } E' &= \rho
\end{aligned} \right\} \qquad (63a)$$

The equations (60), (62), and (63) thus form the generalization of Maxwell's field equations for free space, with the convention which we have established with respect to the choice of co-ordinates.

The Energy-components of the Electromagnetic Field.—We form the inner product

$$\kappa_\sigma = F_{\sigma\mu}J^\mu \qquad (65)$$

By (61) its components, written in the three-dimensional manner, are

$$\left. \begin{aligned}
\kappa_1 &= \rho E_x + \left[j \cdot H \right]^x \\
\vdots \quad &\vdots \quad \vdots \quad \vdots \\
\kappa_4 &= -\left(jE \right)
\end{aligned} \right\} \qquad (65a)$$

κ_σ is a covariant vector the components of which are equal to the negative momentum, or, respectively, the energy, which is transferred from the electric masses to the electromagnetic field per unit of time and volume. If the electric masses are free, that is, under the sole influence of the electromagnetic field, the covariant vector κ_σ will vanish.

To obtain the energy-components T_σ^ν of the electromagnetic field, we need only give to equation $\kappa_\sigma = 0$ the form of equation (57). From (63) and (65) we have in the first place

$$\kappa_\sigma = F_{\sigma\mu} \frac{\partial F^{\mu\nu}}{\partial x_\nu} = \frac{\partial}{\partial x_\nu}\left(F_{\sigma\mu}F^{\mu\nu}\right) - F^{\mu\rho}\frac{\partial F_{\sigma\mu}}{\partial x_\nu}.$$

The second term of the right-hand side, by reason of (60), permits the transformation

$$F^{\mu\nu}\frac{\partial F_{\sigma\mu}}{\partial x_\nu} = \frac{1}{2}F^{\mu\nu}\frac{\partial F_{\mu\nu}}{\partial x_\sigma} = -\frac{1}{2}g^{\mu\alpha}g^{\nu\beta}F_{\alpha\beta}\frac{\partial F_{\mu\nu}}{\partial x_\sigma},$$

which latter expression may, for reasons of symmetry, also be written in the form

$$-\frac{1}{4}\left[g^{\mu\alpha}g^{\nu\beta}F_{\alpha\beta}\frac{\partial F_{\mu\nu}}{\partial x_\sigma} + g^{\mu\alpha}g^{\nu\beta}\frac{\partial F_{\mu\beta}}{\partial x_\sigma}F_{\mu\nu}\right].$$

But for this we may set

$$-\frac{1}{4}\frac{\partial}{\partial x_\sigma}\left(g^{\mu\alpha}g^{\nu\beta}F_{\alpha\beta}F_{\mu\nu}\right) + -\frac{1}{4}F_{\alpha\beta}F_{\mu\nu}\frac{\partial}{\partial x_\sigma}\left(g^{\mu\alpha}g^{\nu\beta}\right).$$

The first of these terms is written more briefly

$$-\frac{1}{4}\frac{\partial}{\partial x_\sigma}\left(F^{\mu\nu}F_{\mu\nu}\right);$$

the second, after the differentiation is carried out, and after some reduction, results in

$$-\frac{1}{2}F^{\mu\tau}F_{\mu\nu}g^{\nu\rho}\frac{\partial g_{\sigma\tau}}{\partial x_\sigma}.$$

Taking all three terms together we obtain the relation

$$\kappa_\sigma = \frac{\partial T_\sigma^\nu}{\partial x_\nu} - \frac{1}{2}g^{\tau\mu}\frac{\partial g_{\mu\nu}}{\partial x_\sigma}T_\tau^\nu \tag{66}$$

where

$$T_\sigma^\nu = -F_{\sigma\alpha}F^{\nu\alpha} + \frac{1}{4}\delta_\sigma^\nu F_{\alpha\beta}F^{\alpha\beta}.$$

Equation (66), if κ_σ vanishes, is, on account of (30), equivalent to (57) or (57a) respectively. Therefore the T_σ^ν are the energy-components of the electromagnetic field. With the help of (61) and (64), it is easy to show that these energy-components of the electromagnetic field in the case of the special theory of relativity give the well-known Maxwell-Poynting expressions.

We have now deduced the general laws which are satisfied by the gravitational field and matter, by consistently using a system of co-ordinates for which $\sqrt{-g} = 1$. We have thereby achieved a considerable simplification of formulæ and calculations, without failing to comply with the requirement of general covariance; for we have drawn our equations from generally covariant equations by specializing the system of co-ordinates.

Still the question is not without a formal interest, whether with a correspondingly generalized definition of the energy-components of gravitational field and matter, even

without specializing the system of co-ordinates, it is possible to formulate laws of con-servation in the form of equation (56), and field equations of gravitation of the same nature as (52) or (52a), in such a manner that on the left we have a divergence (in the ordinary sense), and on the right the sum of the energy-components of matter and gravitation. I have found that in both cases this is actually so. But I do not think that the communication of my somewhat extensive reflexions on this subject would be worth while, because after all they do not give us anything that is materially new.

E

§ 21. NEWTON'S THEORY AS A FIRST APPROXIMATION

As has already been mentioned more than once, the special theory of relativity as a special case of the general theory is characterized by the $g_{\mu\nu}$ having the constant val-ues (4). From what has already been said, this means complete neglect of the effects of gravitation. We arrive at a closer approximation to reality by considering the case where the $g_{\mu\nu}$ differ from the values of (4) by quantities which are small compared with 1, and neglecting small quantities of second and higher order. (First point of view of approximation.)

It is further to be assumed that in the space-time territory under consideration the $g_{\mu\nu}$ at spatial infinity, with a suitable choice of co-ordinates, tend toward the values (4); i.e. we are considering gravitational fields which may be regarded as generated exclu-sively by matter in the finite region.

It might be thought that these approximations must lead us to Newton's theory. But to that end we still need to approximate the fundamental equations from a second point of view. We give our attention to the motion of a material point in accordance with the equations (16). In the case of the special theory of relativity the components

$$\frac{dx_1}{ds}, \frac{dx_2}{ds}, \frac{dx_3}{ds}$$

may take on any values. This signifies that any velocity

$$v = \sqrt{\left(\frac{dx_1}{dx_4}\right)^2 + \left(\frac{dx_2}{dx_4}\right)^2 + \left(\frac{dx_3}{dx_4}\right)^2}$$

may occur, which is less than the velocity of light *in vacuo*. If we restrict ourselves to the case which almost exclusively offers itself to our experience, of v being small as compared with the velocity of light, this denotes that the components

$$\frac{dx_1}{ds}, \frac{dx_2}{ds}, \frac{dx_3}{ds}$$

are to be treated as small quantities, while dx_4/ds, to the second order of small quantities, is equal to one. (Second point of view of approximation.)

Now we remark that from the first point of view of approximation the magnitudes $\Gamma^{\tau}_{\mu\nu}$ are all small magnitudes of at least the first order. A glance at (46) thus shows that in this equation, from the second point of view of approximation, we have to consider only terms for which $\mu = \nu = 4$. Restricting ourselves to terms of lowest order we first obtain in place of (46) the equations

$$\frac{d^2 x_{\tau}}{dt^2} = \Gamma^{\tau}_{44}$$

where we have set $ds = dz_4 = dt$; or with restriction to terms which from the first point of view of approximation are of first order:—

$$\frac{d^2 x_{\tau}}{dt^2} = [44, \tau] \quad (\tau = 1, 2, 3)$$

$$\frac{d^2 x_4}{dt^2} = -[44. 4]$$

If in addition we suppose the gravitational field to be a quasi-static field, by confining ourselves to the case where the motion of the matter generating the gravitational field is but slow (in comparison with the velocity of the propagation of light), we may neglect on the right-hand side differentiations with respect to the time in comparison with those with respect to the space co-ordinates, so that we have

$$\frac{d^2 x_{\tau}}{dt^2} = -\frac{1}{2}\frac{\partial g_{44}}{\partial x_{\tau}} \quad (\tau = 1, 2, 3) \tag{67}$$

This is the equation of motion of the material point according to Newton's theory, in which $\frac{1}{2} g_{44}$ plays the part of the gravitational potential. What is remarkable in this result is that the component g_{44} of the fundamental tensor alone defines, to a first approximation, the motion of the material point.

We now turn to the field equations (53). Here we have to take into consideration that the energy-tensor of "matter" is almost exclusively defined by the density of matter in the narrower sense, i.e. by the second term of the right-hand side of (58) [or, respectively, (58a) or (58b)]. If we form the approximation in question, all the components vanish with the one exception of $T_{44} = \rho = T$. On the left-hand side of (53) the second term is a small quantity of second order; the first yields, to the approximation in question,

$$\frac{\partial}{\partial x_1}[\mu\nu, 1] + \frac{\partial}{\partial x_2}[\mu\nu, 2] + \frac{\partial}{\partial x_3}[\mu\nu, 3] - \frac{\partial}{\partial x_4}[\mu\nu, 4].$$

For $\mu = \nu = 4$, this gives, with the omission of terms differentiated with respect to time,

$$-\frac{1}{2}\left(\frac{\partial^2 g_{44}}{\partial x_1^2} + \frac{\partial^2 g_{44}}{\partial x_2^2} + \frac{\partial^2 g_{44}}{\partial x_3^2}\right) = -\frac{1}{2}\nabla^2 g_{44}.$$

The last of equations (53) thus yields

$$\nabla^2 g_{44} = \kappa\rho \tag{68}$$

The equations (67) and (68) together are equivalent to Newton's law of gravitation.

By (67) and (68) the expression for the gravitational potential becomes

$$-\frac{\kappa}{8\pi}\int\frac{\rho d\tau}{r} \tag{68a}$$

while Newton's theory, with the unit of time which we have chosen, gives

$$-\frac{K}{c^2}\int\frac{\rho d\tau}{r}$$

in which K denotes the constant $6 \cdot 7 \times 10^{-8}$, usually called the constant of gravitation. By comparison we obtain

$$\kappa = \frac{8\pi K}{c^2} = 1\cdot 87 \times 10^{-27} \tag{69}$$

§ 22. BEHAVIOUR OF RODS AND CLOCKS IN THE STATIC GRAVITATIONAL FIELD. BENDING OF LIGHT-RAYS. MOTION OF THE PERIHELION OF A PLANETARY ORBIT

To arrive at Newton's theory as a first approximation we had to calculate only one component, g_{44}, of the ten $g_{\mu\nu}$ of the gravitational field, since this component alone enters into the first approximation, (67), of the equation for the motion of the material point in the gravitational field. From this, however, it is already apparent that other components of the $g_{\mu\nu}$ must differ from the values given in (4) by small quantities of the first order. This is required by the condition $g = -1$.

For a field-producing point mass at the origin of co-ordinates, we obtain, to the first approximation, the radially symmetrical solution

$$\begin{aligned} g_{\rho\sigma} &= -\delta_{\rho\sigma} - \alpha\frac{x_\rho x_\sigma}{r^3} && (\rho, \sigma = 1, 2, 3) \\ g_{\rho 4} &= -\delta_{4\rho} = 0 && (\rho = 1, 2, 3) \\ g_{44} &= 1 - \frac{\alpha}{r} \end{aligned} \tag{70}$$

where $\delta_{\rho\sigma}$ is 1 or 0, respectively, accordingly as $\rho = \sigma$ or $\rho \neq \sigma$, and r is the quantity $+\sqrt{x_1^2 + x_2^2 + x_3^2}$ on account of (68a)

$$\alpha = \frac{\kappa M}{4\pi}, \tag{70a}$$

if M denotes the field-producing mass. It is easy to verify that the field equations (outside the mass) are satisfied to the first order of small quantities.

We now examine the influence exerted by the field of the mass M upon the metrical properties of space. The relation

$$ds^2 = g_{\mu\nu}dx_\mu dx_\nu.$$

always holds between the "locally" (§ 4) measured lengths and times ds on the one hand, and the differences of co-ordinates dx_ν, on the other hand.

For a unit-measure of length laid "parallel" to the axis of x, for example, we should have to set $ds^2 = -1$; $dx_2 = dx_3 = dx_4 = 0$. Therefore $-1 = g_{11}dx_1^2$. If, in addition, the unit-measure lies on the axis of x, the first of equations (70) gives

$$g_{11} = -\left(1 + \frac{\alpha}{r}\right).$$

From these two relations it follows that, correct to a first order of small quantities,

$$dx = 1 - \frac{\alpha}{2r} \tag{71}$$

The unit measuring-rod thus appears a little shortened in relation to the system of co-ordinates by the presence of the gravitational field, if the rod is laid along a radius.

In an analogous manner we obtain the length of co-ordinates in tangential direction if, for example, we set

$$ds^2 = -1; \quad dx_1 = dx_3 = dx_4 = 0; \quad x_1 = r, \, x_2 = x_3 = 0.$$

The result is

$$-1 = g_{22}dx_2^2 = -dx_2^2 \tag{71a}$$

With the tangential position, therefore, the gravitational field of the point of mass has no influence on the length of rod.

Thus Euclidean geometry does not hold even to a first approximation in the gravitational field, if we wish to take one and the same rod, independently of its place and orientation, as a realization of the same interval; although, to be sure, a glance at (70a) and (69) shows that the deviations to be expected are much too slight to be noticeable in measurements of the earth's surface.

Further, let us examine the rate of a unit clock, which is arranged to be at rest in a static gravitational field. Here we have for a clock period $ds = 1$; $dx_1 = dx_2 = dx_3 = 0$ Therefore

$$1 = g_{44}dx_4^2;$$

$$dx_4 = \frac{1}{\sqrt{g_{44}}} = \frac{1}{\sqrt{\left(1 + \left(g_{44} - 1\right)\right)}} = 1 - \frac{1}{2}\left(g_{44} - 1\right)$$

or

$$dx_4 = 1 + \frac{\kappa}{8\pi}\int\rho\frac{d\tau}{r} \tag{72}$$

Thus the clock goes more slowly if set up in the neighbourhood of ponderable masses.

From this it follows that the spectral lines of light reaching us from the surface of large stars must appear displaced towards the red and of the spectrum.[1]

We now examine the course of light-rays in the static gravitational field. By the special theory of relativity the velocity of light is given by the equation

$$-dx_1^2 - dx_2 - dx_3^2 + dx_4^2 = 0$$

and therefore by the general theory of relativity by the equation

$$ds^2 = g_{\mu\nu}dx_\mu dx_\nu = 0 \qquad (73)$$

If the direction, i.e. the ratio $dx_1 : dx_2 : dx_3$ is given, equation (73) gives the quantities

$$\frac{dx_1}{dx_4}, \frac{dx_2}{dx_4}, \frac{dx_3}{dx_4}$$

and accordingly the velocity

$$\sqrt{\left(\frac{dx_1}{dx_4}\right)^2 + \left(\frac{dx_2}{dx_4}\right)^2 + \left(\frac{dx_3}{dx_4}\right)^2} = \gamma$$

defined in the sense of Euclidean geometry. We easily recognize that the course of the light-rays must be bent with regard to the system of co-ordinates, if the $g_{\mu\nu}$ are not constant. If n is a direction perpendicular to the propagation of light, the Huyghens principle shows that the light-ray, envisaged in the plane (γ, n), has the curvature $-\partial\gamma/\partial n$.

We examine the curvature undergone by a ray of light passing by a mass M at the distance Δ. If we choose the system of co-ordinates in agreement with the accompanying diagram, the total bending of the ray (calculated positively if concave towards the origin) is given in sufficient approximation by

$$\int_{-\infty}^{+\infty} \frac{\partial\gamma}{\partial x_1} dx_2,$$

while (73) and (70) give

$$\gamma = \sqrt{\left(-\frac{g_{44}}{g_{22}}\right)} = 1 - \frac{a}{2r}\left(1 + \frac{x_2^2}{r^2}\right)$$

Carrying out the calculation, this gives

$$B = \frac{2\alpha}{\Delta} = \frac{\kappa M}{2\pi\Delta} \qquad (74)$$

According to this, a ray of light going past the sun undergoes a deflexion of 1.7"; and a ray going past the planet Jupiter a deflexion of about .02".

If we calculate the gravitational field to a higher degree of approximation, and likewise with corresponding accuracy the orbital motion of a material point of relatively

---

1. According to E. Freundlich, spectroscopical observations on fixed stars of certain types indicate the existence of an effect of this kind, but a crucial test of this consequence his not yet been made.

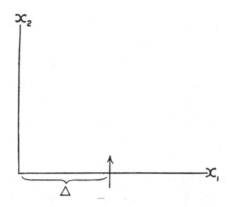

infinitely small mass, we find a deviation of the following kind from the Kepler-Newton laws of planetary motion. The orbital ellipse of a planet undergoes a slow rotation, in the direction of motion, of amount

$$\varepsilon = 24\pi^3 \frac{\alpha^2}{T^2 c^2 \left(1 - e^2\right)} \tag{75}$$

per revolution. In this formula a denotes the major semi-axis, c the velocity of light in the usual measurement, e the eccentricity, T the time of revolution in seconds.[1]

Calculation gives for the planet Mercury a rotation of the orbit of 43" per century, corresponding exactly to astronomical observation (Leverrier); for the astronomers have discovered in the motion of the perihelion of this planet, after allowing for disturbances by other planets, an inexplicable remainder of this magnitude.

HAMILTON'S PRINCIPLE AND THE GENERAL THEORY OF RELATIVITY

Translated from "Hamiltonsches Princip und allgemeine Relativitätstheorie," Sitzungsberichte der Preussischen Akad. Wissenschaften, 1916.

The general theory of relativity has recently been given in a particularly clear form by H. A. Lorentz and D. Hilbert,[2] who have deduced its equations from one single

---

1. For the calculation I refer to the original papers: A. Einstein, Sitzungsber. d. Preuss. Akad. d. Wiss., 1915, p. 831; K. Schwarzschild, *ibid.*, 1916, p. 189.
2. Four papers by Lorentz in the Publications of the Koninkl. Akad. van Wetensch. te Amsterdam, 1915 end 1916; D. Hilbert, Göttinger Nachr., 1915, Part 3.

principle of variation. The same thing will be done in the present paper. But my purpose here is to present the fundamental connexions in as perspicuous a manner as possible, and in as general terms as is permissible from the point of view of the general theory of relativity. In particular we shall make as few specializing assumptions as possible, in marked contrast to Hilbert's treatment of the subject. On the other hand, in
antithesis to my own most recent treatment of the subject, there is to be complete liberty in the choice of the system of co-ordinates.

§ 1. THE PRINCIPLE OF VARIATION AND THE FIELD-
EQUATIONS OF GRAVITATION AND MATTER

Let the gravitational field be described as usual by the tensor[1] of the $g_{\mu\nu}$ (or the
$g^{\mu\nu}$); and matter, including the electromagnetic field, by any number of space-time
functions $q_{(\rho)}$. How these functions may be characterized in the theory of invariants
does not concern us. Further, let $\mathfrak{H}$ be a function of the

$$g^{\mu\nu}, g_\sigma^{\mu\nu}\left(=\frac{\partial g^{\mu\nu}}{\partial x_\sigma}\right) \text{ and } g_{\sigma\tau}^{\mu\nu}\left(=\frac{\partial^2 g^{\mu\nu}}{\partial x_\sigma \partial x_\tau}\right), \text{ the } q_{(\rho)} \text{ and } q_{(\rho)\alpha}\left(=\frac{\partial q_{(\rho)}}{\partial x_\alpha}\right).$$

The principle of variation

$$\delta\int\mathfrak{H}d\tau = 0 \tag{1}$$

then gives us as many differential equations as there are functions $g_{\mu\nu}$, and $q_{(\rho)}$ to be
defined, if the $g^{\mu\nu}$ and $q_{(\rho)}$ are varied independently of one another, and in such a way
that at the limits of integration the $\delta q_{(\rho)}$, $\delta g^{\mu\nu}$, and $\frac{\partial}{\partial x_\sigma}\left(\delta g^{\mu\nu}\right)$ all vanish.

We will now assume that $\mathfrak{H}$ is linear in the $g_{\sigma\tau}^{\mu\nu}$, and that the coefficients of the $g_{\sigma\tau}^{\mu\nu}$
depend only on the $g^{\mu\nu}$. We may then replace the principle of variation (1) by one
which is more convenient for us. For by appropriate partial integration we obtain

$$\int\mathfrak{H}d\tau = \int\overset{*}{\mathfrak{H}}d\tau + F \tag{2}$$

where F denotes an integral over the boundary of the domain in question, and $\overset{*}{\mathfrak{H}}$
depends only on the $g^{\mu\nu}$, $g_\sigma^{\mu\nu}$, $q_{(\rho)}$, $q_{(\rho)a}$, and no longer on the $g_{\sigma\tau}^{\mu\nu}$. From (2) we
obtain, for such variations as are of interest to us,

$$\delta\int\mathfrak{H}d\tau = \delta\int\overset{*}{\mathfrak{H}}d\tau, \tag{3}$$

so that we may replace our principle of variation (1) by the more convenient form

$$\delta\int\overset{*}{\mathfrak{H}}d\tau = 0. \tag{1a}$$

---

1. No use is made for the present of the tensor character of the $g_{\mu\nu}$.

By carrying out the variation of the $g^{\mu\nu}$ and the $q_{(\rho)}$, we obtain, as field-equations of gravitation and matter, the equations[1]

$$\frac{\partial}{\partial x_\alpha}\left(\frac{\partial \mathfrak{H}^*}{\partial g_\alpha^{\mu\nu}}\right) - \frac{\partial \mathfrak{H}^*}{\partial g^{\mu\nu}} = 0 \qquad (4)$$

$$\frac{\partial}{\partial x_\alpha}\left(\frac{\partial \mathfrak{H}^*}{\partial q_{(\rho)\alpha}}\right) - \frac{\partial \mathfrak{H}^*}{\partial q_{(\rho)}} = 0 \qquad (5)$$

§ 2. SEPARATE EXISTENCE OF THE GRAVITATIONAL FIELD

If we make no restrictive assumption as to the manner in which $\mathfrak{H}$ depends on the $g_{\mu\nu}$, $g_\sigma^{\mu\nu}$, $g_\sigma^{\mu\nu}$, $q_{(\rho)}$, $q_{(\rho)\alpha}$, the energy-components cannot be divided into two parts, one belonging to the gravitational field, the other to matter. To ensure this feature of the theory, we make the following assumption

$$\mathfrak{H} = \mathfrak{G} + \mathfrak{M} \qquad (6)$$

where $\mathfrak{G}$ is to depend only on the $g^{\mu\nu}$, $g_\sigma^{\mu\nu}$, $g_\sigma^{\mu\nu}$, and $\mathfrak{M}$ only on $g^{\mu\nu}$, $q_{(\rho)}$, $q_{(\rho)\alpha}$. Equations (4), (4a) then assume the form

$$\frac{\partial}{\partial x_\alpha}\left(\frac{\partial \mathfrak{G}^*}{\partial g_\alpha^{\mu\nu}}\right) - \frac{\partial \mathfrak{G}^*}{\partial g^{\mu\nu}} = \frac{\partial \mathfrak{M}}{\partial g^{\mu\nu}} \qquad (7)$$

$$\frac{\partial}{\partial x_\alpha}\left(\frac{\partial \mathfrak{M}}{\partial q_{(\rho)\alpha}}\right) - \frac{\partial \mathfrak{M}}{\partial q_{(\rho)}} = 0 \qquad (8)$$

Here $\mathfrak{G}^*$ stands in the same relation to $\mathfrak{G}$ as $\mathfrak{H}^*$ to $\mathfrak{H}$.

It is to be noted carefully that equations (8) or (5) would have to give way to others, if we were to assume $\mathfrak{M}$ or $\mathfrak{H}$ to be also dependent on derivatives of the $q_{(\rho)}$ of order higher than the first. Likewise it might be imaginable that the $q_{(\rho)}$ would have to be taken, not as independent of one another, but as connected by conditional equations. All this is of no importance for the following developments, as these are based solely on the equations (7), which have been found by varying our integral with respect to the $g^{\mu\nu}$.

§ 3. PROPERTIES OF THE FIELD EQUATIONS OF GRAVITATION CONDITIONED BY THE THEORY OF INVARIANTS

We now introduce the assumption that

$$ds^2 = g_{\mu\nu}dx_\mu dx_\nu \qquad (9)$$

[1]. For brevity the summation symbols are omitted in the formulæ. Indices occurring twice in a term are always to be taken as summed. Thus in (4), for example, $\frac{\partial}{\partial x_\alpha}\left(\frac{\partial \mathfrak{i}^*}{\partial g_\alpha^{\mu\nu}}\right)$ denotes the term $\sum_\alpha \frac{\partial}{\partial x_\alpha}\left(\frac{\partial \mathfrak{H}^*}{\partial g_\alpha^{\mu\nu}}\right)$

is an invariant. This determines the transformational character of the $g_{\mu\nu}$. As to the transformational character of the $q_{(\rho)}$, which describe matter, we make no supposition. On the other hand, let the functions $H = \dfrac{\mathfrak{H}}{\sqrt{-g}}$, as well as $G = \dfrac{\mathfrak{G}}{\sqrt{-g}}$, and $M = \dfrac{\mathfrak{M}}{\sqrt{-g}}$, be invariants in relation to any substitutions and space-time co-ordinates. From these assumptions follows the general covariance of the equations (7) and (8), deduced from (1). It further follows that G (apart from a constant factor) must be equal to the scalar of Riemann's tensor of curvature; because there is no other invariant with the properties required for G.[1] Thereby $\mathfrak{G}^*$ is also perfectly determined, and consequently the left-hand side of field equation (7) as well.[2]

From the general postulate of relativity there follow certain properties of the function $\mathfrak{G}^*$ which we shall now deduce. For this purpose we carry through an infinitesimal transformation of the co-ordinates, by setting

$$x'_\nu = x_\nu + \Delta x_\nu \tag{10}$$

where the Δx_ν are arbitrary, infinitely small functions of the co-ordinates, and x'_ν are the co-ordinates, in the new system, of the world-point having the co-ordinates x_ν in the original system. As for the co-ordinates, so too for any other magnitude ψ, a law of transformation holds good, of the type

$$\psi' = \psi + \Delta\psi,$$

where $\Delta\psi$ must always be expressible by the Δx_ν. From the covariant property of the $g^{\mu\nu}$ we easily deduce for the $g^{\mu\nu}$ and $g_\sigma^{\mu\nu}$ the laws of transformation

$$\Delta g^{\mu\nu} = g^{\mu\alpha}\frac{\partial\left(\Delta x_\nu\right)}{\partial x_\alpha} + g^{\nu\alpha}\frac{\partial\left(\Delta x_\mu\right)}{\partial x_\alpha} \tag{11}$$

$$\Delta g_\sigma^{\mu\nu} = \frac{\partial\left(\Delta g^{\mu\nu}\right)}{\partial x_\sigma} + g_\alpha^{\mu\nu}\frac{\partial\left(\Delta x_\alpha\right)}{\partial x_\sigma} \tag{12}$$

Since $\mathfrak{G}^*$ depends only on the $g^{\mu\nu}$ and $g_\sigma^{\mu\nu}$, it is possible, with the help of (11) and (12), to calculate $\Delta\mathfrak{G}^*$. We thus obtain the equation

$$\sqrt{-g}\,\Delta\left(\frac{\mathfrak{G}^*}{\sqrt{-g}}\right) = S_\sigma^\nu\frac{\partial(\Delta x_\sigma)}{\partial x_\nu} + 2\frac{\partial\mathfrak{G}^*}{\partial g_\alpha^{\mu\sigma}}g^{\mu\nu}\frac{\partial^2\Delta x_\sigma}{\partial x_\nu\partial x_\alpha}, \tag{13}$$

where for brevity we have set

$$S_\sigma^\nu = 2\frac{\partial\mathfrak{G}^*}{\partial g^{\mu\sigma}}g^{\mu\nu} + 2\frac{\partial\mathfrak{G}^*}{\partial g_\alpha^{\mu\sigma}}g_\alpha^{\mu\nu} + \mathfrak{G}^*\delta_\sigma^\nu - \frac{\partial\mathfrak{G}^*}{\partial g_\nu^{\mu\alpha}}g_\sigma^{\mu\alpha}. \tag{14}$$

1. Herein is to be found the reason why the general postulate of relativity leads to a very definite theory of gravitation.
2. By performing partial integration we obtain
$$\mathfrak{G}^* = \sqrt{-g}\,g^{\mu\nu}[\{\mu\alpha,\,\beta\}\,\{\nu\beta,\,\alpha\} - \{\mu\nu,\,\alpha\}\,\{\alpha\beta,\,\beta\}].$$

From these two equations we draw two inferences which are important for what follows. We know that $\frac{\mathfrak{G}}{\sqrt{-g}}$ is an invariant with respect to any substitution, but we do not know this of $\frac{\mathfrak{G}^*}{\sqrt{-g}}$. It is easy to demonstrate, however, that the latter quantity is an invariant with respect to any *linear* substitutions of the co-ordinates. Hence it follows that the right side of (13) must always vanish if all $\frac{\partial^2 \Delta x_\sigma}{\partial x_\nu \partial x_\alpha}$ vanish. Consequently $\mathfrak{G}^*$ must satisfy the identity

$$S_\sigma^\nu \equiv 0 \tag{15}$$

If, further, we choose the Δx_ν so that they differ from zero only in the interior of a given domain, but in infinitesimal proximity to the boundary they vanish, then, with the transformation in question, the value of the boundary integral occurring in equation (2) does not change. Therefore $\Delta F = 0$, and, in consequence,[1]

$$\Delta \int \mathfrak{G} d\tau = \Delta \int \mathfrak{G}^* d\tau$$

But the left-hand side of the equation must vanish, since both $\frac{\mathfrak{G}}{\sqrt{-g}}$ and $\sqrt{-g}\, dt$ are invariants. Consequently the right-hand side also vanishes. Thus, taking (14), (15), and (16) into consideration, we obtain, in the first place, the equation

$$\int \frac{\partial \mathfrak{G}^*}{\partial g_\alpha^{\mu\sigma}} g^{\mu\nu} \frac{\partial^2 (\Delta x_\sigma)}{\partial x_\nu \partial x_\alpha} d\tau = 0 \tag{16}$$

Transforming this equation by two partial integrations, and having regard to the liberty of choice of the Δx_σ, we obtain the identity

$$\frac{\partial^2}{\partial x_\nu \partial x_\alpha} \left(g^{\mu\nu} \frac{\partial \mathfrak{G}^*}{\partial g_\alpha^{\mu\sigma}} \right) \equiv 0 \tag{17}$$

From the two identities (16) and (17), which result from the invariance of $\frac{\mathfrak{G}}{\sqrt{-g}}$, and therefore from the postulate of general relativity, we now have to draw conclusions.

We first transform the field equations (7) of gravitation by mixed multiplication by $g^{\mu\sigma}$. We then obtain (by interchanging the indices σ and ν), as equivalents of the field equations (7) the equations

$$\frac{\partial}{\partial x_\alpha} \left(g^{\mu\nu} \frac{\partial \mathfrak{G}^*}{\partial g_\alpha^{\mu\sigma}} \right) = - (\mathfrak{T}_\sigma^\nu + t_\sigma^\nu) \tag{18}$$

where we have set

$$\mathfrak{T}_\sigma^\nu = - \frac{\partial \mathfrak{M}}{\partial g^{\mu\sigma}} g^{\mu\nu} \tag{19}$$

---

1. By the introduction of the quantities $\mathfrak{G}$ and $\mathfrak{G}^*$ instead of $\mathfrak{H}$ and $\mathfrak{H}^*$.

$$t_\sigma^\nu = -\left(\frac{\partial \mathfrak{G}^*}{\partial g_\alpha^{\mu\sigma}}g_\alpha^{\mu\nu} + \frac{\partial \mathfrak{G}^*}{\partial g^{\mu\sigma}}g^{\mu\nu}\right) = \tfrac{1}{2}\left(\mathfrak{G}^*\delta_\sigma^\nu - \frac{\partial \mathfrak{G}^*}{\partial g_\nu^{\mu\alpha}}g_\sigma^{\mu\alpha}\right) \quad (20)$$

The last expression for t_μ^ν is vindicated by (14) and (15). By differentiation of (18) with respect to x_ν, and summation for ν, there follows, in view of (17),

$$\frac{\partial}{\partial x_\nu}(\mathfrak{T}_\sigma^\nu + t_\sigma^\nu) = 0 \quad (21)$$

Equation (21) expresses the conservation of momentum and energy. We call $\mathfrak{T}_\sigma^\nu$ the components of the energy of matter, t_σ^ν the components of the energy of the gravitational field.

Having regard to (20), there follows from the field equations (7) of gravitation, by multiplication by $g_\sigma^{\mu\nu}$, and summation with respect to μ and ν,

$$\frac{\partial t_\sigma^\nu}{\partial x_\nu} + \tfrac{1}{2}g_\sigma^{\mu\nu}\frac{\partial \mathfrak{M}}{\partial g^{\mu\nu}} = 0,$$

or, in view of (19) and (21),

$$\frac{\partial \mathfrak{T}_\sigma^\nu}{\partial x_\nu} + \tfrac{1}{2}g_\sigma^{\mu\nu}\mathfrak{T}_{\mu\nu} = 0 \quad (22)$$

where $\mathfrak{T}_{\mu\nu}$ denotes the quantities $g_{\nu\sigma}\mathfrak{T}_{\mu\nu}$. These are four equations which the energy-components of matter have to satisfy.

It is to be emphasized that the (generally covariant) laws of conservation (21) and (22) are deduced from the field equations (7) of gravitation, in combination with the postulate of general covariance (relativity) *alone*, without using the field equations (8) for material phenomena.

COSMOLOGICAL CONSIDERATIONS ON THE GENERAL THEORY OF RELATIVITY

Translated from "Kosmologische Betrachtungen zur allgemeinen Relativitätstheorie," Sitzungsberichte der Preussischen Akad. d. Wissenschaften, 1917.

It is well known that Poisson's equation

$$\nabla^2\phi = 4\pi K\rho \quad (1).$$

in combination with the equations of motion of a material point is not as yet a perfect substitute for Newton's theory of action at a distance. There is still to be taken into account the condition that at spatial infinity the potential ϕ tends toward a fixed limiting value. There is an analogous state of things in the theory of gravitation in general relativity. Here, too, we must supplement the differential equations by limiting conditions at spatial infinity, if we really have to regard the universe as being of infinite spatial extent.

In my treatment of the planetary problem I chose these limiting conditions in the form of the following assumption: it is possible to select a system of reference so that at spatial infinity all the gravitational potentials $g_{\mu\nu}$ become constant. But it is by no means evident *a priori* that we may lay down the same limiting conditions when we wish to take larger portions of the physical universe into consideration. In the following pages the reflexions will be given which, up to the present, I have made on this fundamentally important question.

§ 1. THE NEWTONIAN THEORY

It is well known that Newton's limiting condition of the constant limit for ϕ at spatial infinity leads to the view that the density of matter becomes zero at infinity. For we imagine that there may be a place in universal space round about which the gravitational field of matter, viewed on a large scale, possesses spherical symmetry. It then follows from Poisson's equation that, in order that ϕ may tend to a limit at infinity, the mean density ρ must decrease toward zero more rapidly than $1/r^2$ as the distance r from the centre increases.[1] In this sense, therefore, the universe according to Newton is finite, although it may possess an infinitely great total mass.

From this it follows in the first place that the radiation emitted by the heavenly bodies will, in part, leave the Newtonian system of the universe, passing radially outwards, to become ineffective and lost in the infinite. May not entire heavenly bodies fare likewise? It is hardly possible to give a negative answer to this question. For it follows from the assumption of a finite limit for ϕ at spatial infinity that a heavenly body with finite kinetic energy is able to reach spatial infinity by overcoming the Newtonian forces of attraction. By statistical mechanics this case must occur from time to time, as long as the total energy of the stellar system—transferred to one single star—is great enough to send that star on its journey to infinity, whence it never can return.

We might try to avoid this peculiar difficulty by assuming a very high value for the limiting potential at infinity. That would be a possible way, if the value of the gravitational potential were not itself necessarily conditioned by the heavenly bodies. The

1. ρ is the mean density of matter, calculated for a region which is large as compared with the distance between neighbouring fixed stars, but small in comparison with the dimensions of the whole stellar system.

truth is that we are compelled to regard the occurrence of any great differences of potential of the gravitational field as contradicting the facts. These differences must really be of so low an order of magnitude that the stellar velocities generated by them do not exceed the velocities actually observed.

If we apply Boltzmann's law of distribution for gas molecules to the stars, by comparing the stellar system with a gas in thermal equilibrium, we find that the Newtonian stellar system cannot exist at all. For there is a finite ratio of densities corresponding to the finite difference of potential between the centre and spatial infinity. A vanishing of the density at infinity thus implies a vanishing of the density at the centre.

It seems hardly possible to surmount these difficulties on the basis of the Newtonian theory. We may ask ourselves the question whether they can be removed by a modification of the Newtonian theory. First of all we will indicate a method which does not in itself claim to be taken seriously; it merely serves as a foil for what is to follow. In place of Poisson's equation we write

$$\nabla^2 \phi - \lambda \phi = 4\pi\kappa\rho \tag{2}$$

where λ denotes a universal constant. If ρ_0 be the uniform density of distribution of mass, then

$$\phi = -\frac{4\pi\kappa}{\lambda}\rho_0 \tag{3}$$

is a solution of equation (2). This solution would correspond to the case in which the matter of the fixed stars was distributed uniformly through space, if the density ρ_0 is equal to the actual mean density of the matter in the universe. The solution then corresponds to an infinite extension of the central space, filled uniformly with matter. If, without making any change in the mean density, we imagine matter to be non-uniformly distributed locally, there will be, over and above the ϕ with the constant value of equation (3), an additional ϕ, which in the neighbourhood of denser masses will so much the more resemble the Newtonian field as $\lambda\phi$ is smaller in comparison with $4\pi\kappa\rho$.

A universe so constituted would have, with respect to its gravitational field, no centre. A decrease of density in spatial infinity would not have to be assumed, but both the mean potential and mean density would remain constant to infinity. The conflict with statistical mechanics which we found in the case of the Newtonian theory is not repeated. With a definite but extremely small density, matter is in equilibrium, without any internal material form (pressures) being required to maintain equilibrium.

§ 2. THE BOUNDARY CONDITIONS ACCORDING TO THE GENERAL THEORY OF RELATIVITY

In the present paragraph I shall conduct the reader over the road that I have myself travelled, rather a rough and winding road, because otherwise I cannot hope that he will take much interest in the result at the end of the journey. The conclusion I shall arrive at is that the field equations of gravitation which I have championed hitherto still need a slight modification, so that on the basis of the general theory of relativity those fundamental difficulties may be avoided which have been set forth in § 1 as confronting the Newtonian theory. This modification corresponds perfectly to the transition from Poisson's equation (1) to equation (2) of § 1. We finally infer that boundary conditions in spatial infinity fall away altogether, because the universal continuum in respect of its spatial dimensions is to be viewed as a self-contained continuum of finite spatial (three-dimensional) volume.

The opinion which I entertained until recently, as to the limiting conditions to be laid down in spatial infinity, took its stand on the following considerations. In a consistent theory of relativity there can be no inertia *relatively to "space,"* but only an inertia of masses *relatively to one another.* If, therefore, I have a mass at a sufficient distance from all other masses in the universe, its inertia must fall to zero. We will try to formulate this condition mathematically.

According to the general theory of relativity the negative momentum is given by the first three components, the energy by the last component of the covariant tensor multiplied by $\sqrt{-g}$

$$m\sqrt{-g}\, g_{\mu\alpha} \frac{dx_\alpha}{ds} \tag{4}$$

where, as always, we set

$$ds^2 = -g_{\mu\nu}\, dx_\mu\, dx_\nu \tag{5}$$

In the particularly perspicuous case of the possibility of choosing the system of co-ordinates so that the gravitational field at every point is spatially isotropic, we have more simply

$$ds^2 = -A\left(dx_1^2 + dx_2^2 + dx_3^2\right) + B dx_4^2$$

If, moreover, at the same time

$$\sqrt{-g} = 1 = \sqrt{A^3 B}$$

we obtain from (4), to a first approximation for small velocities,

$$m\frac{A}{\sqrt{B}}\frac{dx_1}{dx_4}, m\frac{A}{\sqrt{B}}\frac{dx_2}{dx_4}, m\frac{A}{\sqrt{B}}\frac{dx_3}{dx_4}$$

for the components of momentum, and for the energy (in the static case)

$$m\sqrt{B}.$$

From the expressions for the momentum, it follows that $m\dfrac{A}{\sqrt{B}}$ plays the part of the rest mass. As m is a constant peculiar to the point of mass, independently of its position, this expression, if we retain the condition $\sqrt{g} - = 1$ at spatial infinity, can vanish only when A diminishes to zero, while B increases to infinity. It seems, therefore, that such a degeneration of the co-efficients $g_{\mu\nu}$ is required by the postulate of relativity of all inertia. This requirement implies that the potential energy $m\sqrt{B}$ becomes infinitely great at infinity. Thus a point of mass can never leave the system; and a more detailed investigation shows that the same thing applies to light-rays. A system of the universe with such behaviour of the gravitational potentials at infinity would not therefore run the risk of wasting away which was mooted just now in connexion with the Newtonian theory.

I wish to point out that the simplifying assumptions as to the gravitational potentials on which this reasoning is based, have been introduced merely for the sake of lucidity. It is possible to find general formulations for the behaviour of the $g_{\mu\nu}$ at infinity which express the essentials of the question without further restrictive assumptions.

At this stage, with the kind assistance of the mathematician J. Grommer, I investigated centrally symmetrical, static gravitational fields, degenerating at infinity in the way mentioned. The gravitational potentials $g_{\mu\nu}$ were applied, and from them the energy-tensor $T_{\mu\nu}$ of matter was calculated on the basis of the field equations of gravitation. But here it proved that for the system of the fixed stars no boundary conditions of the kind can come into question at all, as was also rightly emphasized by the astronomer de Sitter recently.

For the contravariant energy-tensor $T^{\mu\nu}$ of ponderable matter is given by

$$T^{\mu\nu} = \rho\frac{dx_\mu}{ds}\frac{dx_\nu}{ds},$$

where ρ is the density of matter in natural measure. With an appropriate choice of the system of co-ordinates the stellar velocities are very small in comparison with that of light. We may, therefore, substitute $\sqrt{g_{44}}\,dx_4$ for ds. This shows us that all components of $T^{\mu\nu}$ must be very small in comparison with the last component T^{44}. But it was quite impossible to reconcile this condition with the chosen boundary conditions. In the retrospect this result does not appear astonishing. The fact of the small velocities of the stars allows the conclusion that wherever there are fixed stars, the gravitational potential (in our case $\sqrt{B}$) can never be much greater than here on earth. This follows from

statistical reasoning, exactly as in the case of the Newtonian theory. At any rate, our calculations have convinced me that such conditions of degeneration for the $g_{\mu\nu}$ in spatial infinity may not be postulated.

After the failure of this attempt, two possibilities next present themselves.

(*a*) We may require, as in the problem of the planets, that, with a suitable choice of the system of reference, the $g_{\mu\nu}$ in spatial infinity approximate to the values

$$
\begin{array}{cccc}
-1 & 0 & 0 & 0 \\
0 & -1 & 0 & 0 \\
0 & 0 & -1 & 0 \\
0 & 0 & 0 & 1
\end{array}
$$

(*b*) We may refrain entirely from laying down boundary conditions for spatial infinity claiming general validity; but at the spatial limit of the domain under consideration we have to give the $g_{\mu\nu}$ separately in each individual case, as hitherto we were accustomed to give the initial conditions for time separately.

The possibility (*b*) holds out no hope of solving the problem, but amounts to giving it up. This is an incontestable position, which is taken up at the present time by de Sitter.[1] But I must confess that such a complete resignation in this fundamental question is for me a difficult thing. I should not make up my mind to it until every effort to make headway toward a satisfactory view had proved to be vain.

Possibility (*a*) is unsatisfactory in more respects than one. In the first place those boundary conditions pre-suppose a definite choice of the system of reference, which is contrary to the spirit of the relativity principle. Secondly, if we adopt this view, we fail to comply with the requirement of the relativity of inertia. For the inertia of a material point of mass m (in natural measure) depends upon the $g_{\mu\nu}$; but these differ but little from their postulated values, as given above, for spatial infinity. Thus inertia would indeed be *influenced*, but would not be *conditioned* by matter (present in finite space). If only one single point of mass were present, according to this view, it would possess inertia, and in fact an inertia almost as great as when it is surrounded by the other masses of the actual universe. Finally, those statistical objections must be raised against this view which were mentioned in respect of the Newtonian theory.

From what has now been said it will be seen that I have not succeeded in formulating boundary conditions for spatial infinity. Nevertheless, there is still a possible way out, without resigning as suggested under (*b*). For if it were possible to regard the universe as a continuum which is *finite (closed) with respect to its spatial dimensions*, we should have no need at all of any such boundary conditions. We shall proceed to show that both the general postulate of relativity and the fact of the small stellar velocities

1. de Sitter, Akad. van Wetensch. te Amsterdam, 8 Nov., 1916.

are compatible with the hypothesis of a spatially finite universe; though certainly, in order to carry through this idea, we need a generalizing modification of the field equations of gravitation.

§ 3. The Spatially Finite Universe with a Uniform Distribution of Matter

According to the general theory of relativity the metrical character (curvature) of the four-dimensional space-time continuum is defined at every point by the matter at that point and the state of that matter. Therefore, on account of the lack of uniformity in the distribution of matter, the metrical structure of this continuum must necessarily be extremely complicated. But if we are concerned with the structure only on a large scale, we may represent matter to ourselves as being uniformly distributed over enormous spaces, so that its density of distribution is a variable function which varies extremely slowly. Thus our procedure will somewhat resemble that of the geodesists who, by means of an ellipsoid, approximate to the shape of the earth's surface, which on a small scale is extremely complicated.

The most important fact that we draw from experience as to the distribution of matter is that the relative velocities of the stars are very small as compared with the velocity of light. So I think that for the present we may base our reasoning upon the following approximative assumption. There is a system of reference relatively to which matter may be looked upon as being permanently at rest. With respect to this system, therefore, the contravariant energy-tensor $T^{\mu\nu}$ of matter is, by reason of (5), of the simple form

$$\begin{vmatrix} 0 & 0 & 0 & 0 \\ 0 & 0 & 0 & 0 \\ 0 & 0 & 0 & 0 \\ 0 & 0 & 0 & \rho \end{vmatrix} \tag{6}$$

The scalar ρ of the (mean) density of distribution may be *a priori* a function of the space co-ordinates. But if we assume the universe to be spatially finite, we are prompted to the hypothesis that ρ is to be independent of locality. On this hypothesis we base the following considerations.

As concerns the gravitational field, it follows from the equation of motion of the material point

$$\frac{d^2 x_\nu}{ds^2} + \{\alpha\beta, \nu\} \frac{dx_\alpha}{ds} \frac{dx_\beta}{ds} = 0$$

that a material point in a static gravitational field can remain at rest only when g_{44} is independent of locality. Since, further, we presuppose independence of the time co-ordinate x_4 for all magnitudes, we may demand for the required solution that, for all x_ν,

$$g_{44} = 1 \tag{7}$$

Further, as always with static problems, we shall have to set

$$g_{14} = g_{24} = g_{34} = 0 \tag{8}$$

It remains now to determine those components of the gravitational potential which define the purely spatial-geometrical relations of our continuum (g_{11}, g_{12}, $\cdots$ g_{33}). From our assumption as to the uniformity of distribution of the masses generating the field, it follows that the curvature of the required space must be constant. With this distribution of mass, therefore, the required finite continuum of the x_1, x_2, x_3, with constant x_4, will be a spherical space.

We arrive at such a space, for example, in the following way. We start from a Euclidean space of four dimensions, $\xi_1, \xi_2, \xi_3, \xi_4$, with a linear element $d\sigma$; let, therefore,

$$d\sigma^2 = d\xi_1^2 + d\xi_2^2 + d\xi_3^2 + d\xi_4^2 \tag{9}$$

In this space we consider the hyper-surface

$$R^2 = \xi_1^2 + \xi_2^2 + \xi_3^2 + \xi_4^2, \tag{10}$$

where R denotes a constant. The points of this hyper-surface form a three-dimensional continuum, a spherical space of radius of curvature R.

The four-dimensional Euclidean space with which we started serves only for a convenient definition of our hyper-surface. Only those points of the hyper-surface are of interest to us which have metrical properties in agreement with those of physical space with a uniform distribution of matter. For the description of this three-dimensional continuum we may employ the co-ordinates ξ_1, ξ_2, ξ_3 (the projection upon the hyperplane $\xi_4 = 0$) since, by reason of (10), ξ_4 can be expressed in terms of ξ_1, ξ_2, ξ_3. Eliminating ξ_4 from (9), we obtain for the linear element of the spherical space the expression

$$\left. \begin{aligned} d\sigma^2 &= \gamma_{\mu\nu} d\xi_\mu d\xi_\nu \\ \gamma_{\mu\nu} &= \delta_{\mu\nu} + \frac{\xi_\mu \xi_\nu}{R^2 - \rho^2} \end{aligned} \right\} \tag{11}$$

where $\delta_{\mu\nu} = 1$, if $\mu = \nu$; $\delta_{\mu\nu} = 0$, if $\mu \neq \nu$, and $\rho^2 = \xi_1^2 + \xi_2^2 + \xi_3^2$. The co-ordinates chosen are convenient when it is a question of examining the environment of one of the two points $\xi_1 = \xi_2 = \xi_3 = 0$.

Now the linear element of the required four-dimensional space-time universe is also given us. For the potential $g_{\mu\nu}$, both indices of which differ from 4, we have to set

$$g_{\mu\nu} = - \left(\delta_{\mu\nu} + \frac{x_\mu x_\nu}{R^2 - (x_1^2 + x_2^2 + x_3^2)} \right) \tag{12}$$

which equation, in combination with (7) and (8), perfectly defines the behaviour of measuring-rods, clocks, and light-rays.

§ 4. ON AN ADDITIONAL TERM FOR THE FIELD EQUATIONS OF GRAVITATION

My proposed field equations of gravitation for any chosen system of co-ordinates run as follows:—

$$
\left.
\begin{aligned}
G_{\mu\nu} &= -\kappa\left(T_{\mu\nu} - \tfrac{1}{2}g_{\mu\nu}T\right), \\[1mm]
G_{\mu\nu} &= -\frac{\partial}{\partial x_\alpha}\{\mu\nu,\alpha\} + \{\mu\nu,\beta\}\{\nu\beta,\alpha\} \\[1mm]
&\quad + \frac{\partial^2 \log\sqrt{-g}}{\partial x_\mu \partial x_\nu} - \{\mu\nu,\alpha\}\frac{\partial \log\sqrt{-g}}{\partial x_\alpha}
\end{aligned}
\right\}
\tag{13}
$$

The system of equations (13) is by no means satisfied when we insert for the $g_{\mu\nu}$ the values given in (7), (8), and (12), and for the (contravariant) energy-tensor of matter the values indicated in (6). It will be shown in the next paragraph how this calculation may conveniently be made. So that, if it were certain that the field equations (13) which I have hitherto employed were the only ones compatible with the postulate of general relativity, we should probably have to conclude that the theory of relativity does not admit the hypothesis of a spatially finite universe.

However, the system of equations (14) allows a readily suggested extension which is compatible with the relativity postulate, and is perfectly analogous to the extension of Poisson's equation given by equation (2). For on the left-hand side of field equation (13) we may add the fundamental tensor $g_{\mu\nu}$, multiplied by a universal constant, $-\lambda$, at present unknown, without destroying the general covariance. In place of field equation (13) we write

$$
G_{\mu\nu} - \lambda g_{\mu\nu} = -\kappa\left(T_{\mu\nu} - \tfrac{1}{2}g_{\mu\nu}T\right)
\tag{13a}
$$

This field equation, with λ sufficiently small, is in any case also compatible with the facts of experience derived from the solar system. It also satisfies laws of conservation of momentum and energy, because we arrive at (13a) in place of (13) by introducing into Hamilton's principle, instead of the scalar of Riemann's tensor, this scalar increased by a universal constant; and Hamilton's principle, of course, guarantees the validity of laws of conservation. It will be shown in § 5 that field equation (13a) is compatible with our conjectures on field and matter.

§ 5. CALCULATION AND RESULT

Since all points of our continuum are on an equal footing, it is sufficient to carry through the calculation for *one* point, e.g. for one of the two points with the co-ordinates

$$x_1 = x_2 = x_3 = x_4 = 0.$$

Then for the $g_{\mu\nu}$ in (13a) we have to insert the values

$$\begin{matrix} -1 & 0 & 0 & 0 \\ 0 & -1 & 0 & 0 \\ 0 & 0 & -1 & 0 \\ 0 & 0 & 0 & -1 \end{matrix}$$

wherever they appear differentiated only once or not at all. We thus obtain in the first place

$$G_{\mu\nu} = \frac{\partial}{\partial x_1}[\mu\nu, 1] + \frac{\partial}{\partial x_2}[\mu\nu, 2] + \frac{\partial}{\partial x_3}[\mu\nu, 3] + \frac{\partial^2 \log\sqrt{-g}}{\partial x_\mu \partial x_\nu}.$$

From this we readily discover, taking (7), (8), and (13) into account, that all equations (13*a*) are satisfied if the two relations

$$-\frac{2}{R^2} + \lambda = -\frac{\kappa\rho}{2}, \quad -\lambda = -\frac{\kappa\rho}{2},$$

or

$$\lambda = \frac{\kappa\rho}{2} = \frac{1}{R^2} \tag{14}$$

are fulfilled.

Thus the newly introduced universal constant λ defines both the mean density of distribution ρ which can remain in equilibrium and also the radius R and the volume $2\pi^2R^3$ of spherical space. The total mass M of the universe, according to our view, is finite, and is in fact

$$M = \rho \cdot 2\pi^2 R^3 = 4\pi^2 \frac{R}{\kappa} = \pi^2 \sqrt{\frac{32}{\kappa^3\rho}} \tag{15}$$

Thus the theoretical view of the actual universe, if it is in correspondence with our reasoning, is the following. The curvature of space is variable in time and place, according to the distribution of matter, but we may roughly approximate to it by means of a spherical space. At any rate, this view is logically consistent, and from the standpoint of the general theory of relativity lies nearest at hand; whether, from the standpoint of present astronomical knowledge, it is tenable, will not here be discussed. In order to arrive at this consistent view, we admittedly had to introduce an extension of the field equations of gravitation which is not justified by our actual knowledge of gravitation.

It is to be emphasized, however, that a positive curvature of space is given by our results, even if the supplementary term is not introduced. That term is necessary only for the purpose of making possible a quasi-static distribution of matter, as required by the fact of the small velocities of the stars.

DO GRAVITATIONAL FIELDS PLAY AN ESSENTIAL PART IN THE STRUCTURE OF THE ELEMENTARY PARTICLES OF MATTER?

Translated from "Spielen Gravitationsfelder im Aufber der materiellen Elementarteilchen eine wesentliche Rolle?" Sitzungsberichte der Preussischen Akad. d. Wissenschaften, 1919.

Neither the Newtonian nor the relativistic theory of gravitation has so far led to any advance in the theory of the constitution of matter. In view of this fact it will be shown in the following pages that there are reasons for thinking that the elementary formations which go to make up the atom are held together by gravitational forces.

§ 1. DEFECTS OF THE PRESENT VIEW

Great pains have been taken to elaborate a theory which will account for the equilibrium of the electricity constituting the electron. G. Mie, in particular, has devoted deep researches to this question. His theory, which has found considerable support among theoretical physicists, is based mainly on the introduction into the energy-tensor of supplementary terms depending on the components of the electro-dynamic potential, in addition to the energy terms of the Maxwell-Lorentz theory. These new terms, which in outside space are unimportant, are nevertheless effective in the interior of the electrons in maintaining equilibrium against the electric form of repulsion. In spite of the beauty of the formal structure of this theory, as erected by Mie, Hilbert, and Weyl, its physical results have hitherto been unsatisfactory. On the one hand the multiplicity of possibilities is discouraging, and on the other hand those additional terms have not as yet allowed themselves to be framed in such a simple form that the

solution could be satisfactory.

So far the general theory of relativity has made no change in this state of the question. If we for the moment disregard the additional cosmological term, the field equations take the form

$$G_{\mu\nu} = \frac{1}{2} g_{\mu\nu} G = -\kappa T_{\mu\nu}$$

(1)

where $G_{\mu\nu}$ denotes the contracted Riemann tensor of curvature, G the scalar of curvature formed by repeated contraction, and $T_{\mu\nu}$ the energy-tensor of "matter." The assumption that the $T_{\mu\nu}$ do *not* depend on the derivatives of the $g_{\mu\nu}$ is in keeping with the historical development of these equations. For these quantities are, of course, the energy-components in the sense of the special theory of relativity, in which variable $g_{\mu\nu}$ do not occur. The second term on the left-hand side of the equation is so chosen that the divergence of the left-hand side of (1) vanishes identically, so that taking the divergence of (1), we obtain the equation

$$\frac{\partial \mathfrak{T}_{\mu}^{\sigma}}{\partial x_{\sigma}} + \tfrac{1}{2} g_{\mu}^{\sigma\tau} \mathfrak{T}_{\sigma\tau} = 0$$

(2)

which in the limiting case of the special theory of relativity gives the complete equations of conservation

$$\frac{\partial T_{\mu\nu}}{\partial x_{\nu}} = 0.$$

Therein lies the physical foundation for the second term of the left-hand side of (1). It is by no means settled *a priori* that a limiting transition of this kind has any possible meaning. For if gravitational fields do play an essential part in the structure of the particles of matter, the transition to the limiting case of constant $g_{\mu\nu}$ would, for them, lose its justification, for indeed, with constant $g_{\mu\nu}$ there could not be any particles of matter. So if we wish to contemplate the possibility that gravitation may take part in the structure of the fields which constitute the corpuscles, we cannot regard equation (1) as confirmed.

Placing in (1) the Maxwell-Lorentz energy-components of the electromagnetic field $\phi_{\mu\nu}$,

$$T_{\mu\nu} = \frac{1}{4} g_{\mu\nu} \phi_{\sigma\tau} \phi^{\sigma\tau} - \phi_{\mu\sigma} \phi_{\nu\tau} g^{\sigma\tau},$$

(3)

we obtain for (2), by taking the divergence, and after some reduction,[1]

$$\phi_{\mu\sigma} \, \mathfrak{J}^{\sigma} = 0$$

(4)

where, for brevity, we have set

$$\frac{\partial}{\partial x_{\tau}} \left(\sqrt{-g} \phi_{\mu\nu} g^{\mu\sigma} g^{\nu\tau} \right) = \frac{\partial \mathfrak{f}^{\sigma\tau}}{\partial x_{\tau}} = \mathfrak{J}^{\sigma}$$

(5)

1. Cf. e.g. A. Einstein, Sitzungsber. d. Preuss. Akad. d. Wiss., 1916, pp. 187, 188.

In the calculation we have employed the second of Maxwell's systems of equations

$$\frac{\partial \phi_{\mu\nu}}{\partial x_\rho} + \frac{\partial \phi_{\nu\rho}}{\partial x_\mu} + \frac{\partial \phi_{\rho\mu}}{\partial x_\nu} = 0 \tag{6}$$

We see from (4) that the current-density $\mathfrak{J}^\sigma$ must everywhere vanish. Therefore, by equation (1), we cannot arrive at a theory of the electron by restricting ourselves to the electromagnetic components of the Maxwell-Lorentz theory, as has long been known. Thus if we hold to (1) we are driven on to the path of Mie's theory.[1]

Not only the problem of matter, but the cosmological problem as well, leads to doubt as to equation (1). As I have shown in the previous paper, the general theory of relativity requires that the universe be spatially finite. But this view of the universe necessitated an extension of equations (1), with the introduction of a new universal constant λ, standing in a fixed relation to the total mass of the universe (or, respectively, to the equilibrium density of matter). This is gravely detrimental to the formal beauty of the theory.

§ 2. THE FIELD EQUATIONS FREED OF SCALARS

The difficulties set forth above are removed by setting in place of field equations (1) the field equations

$$G_{\mu\nu} - \frac{1}{4} g_{\mu\nu} G = -\kappa T_{\mu\nu} \tag{1a}$$

where $T_{\mu\nu}$ denotes the energy-tensor of the electromagnetic field given by (3).

The formal justification for the factor $-1/4$ in the second term of this equation lies in its causing the scalar of the left-hand side,

$$g^{\mu\nu} \left(G_{\mu\nu} - \frac{1}{4} g_{\mu\nu} G \right),$$

to vanish identically, as the scalar $g^{\nu\mu} T_{\mu\nu}$ of the right-hand side does by reason of (3). If we had reasoned on the basis of equations (1) instead of (1a), we should, on the contrary, have obtained the condition $G = 0$, which would have to hold good everywhere for the $g_{\mu\nu}$, independently of the electric field. It is clear that the system of equations [(1a), (3)] is a consequence of the system [(1), (3)], but not conversely.

We might at first sight feel doubtful whether (1a) together with (6) sufficiently define the entire field. In a generally relativistic theory we need n - 4 differential equations, independent of one another, for the definition of n independent variables, since in the solution, on account of the liberty of choice of the co-ordinates, four quite arbitrary functions of all co-ordinates must naturally occur. Thus to define the sixteen independent quantities $g_{\mu\nu}$ and $\phi_{\mu\nu}$, we require twelve equations, all independent of one another. But as it happens, nine of the equations (1a), and three of the equations (6) are independent of one another.

---

1. Cf. D. Hilbert, Göttinger Nachr., 20 Nov., 1915.

Forming the divergence of (1a), and taking into account that the divergence of $G_{\mu\nu} - \frac{1}{2} g_{\mu\nu} G$ vanishes, we obtain

$$\phi_{\mu\alpha} J^{\alpha} + \frac{1}{4\kappa} \frac{\partial G}{\partial x_{\sigma}} = 0 \qquad (4a)$$

From this we recognize first of all that the scalar of curvature G in the four-dimensional domains in which the density of electricity vanishes, is constant. If we assume that all these parts of space are connected, and therefore that the density of electricity differs from zero only in separate "world-threads," then the scalar of curvature, everywhere outside these world-threads, possesses a constant value G_0. But equation (4a) also allows an important conclusion as to the behaviour of G within the domains having a density of electricity other than zero. If, as is customary, we regard electricity as a moving density of charge, by setting

$$J^{\sigma} = \frac{\mathfrak{J}^{\sigma}}{\sqrt{-g}} = \rho \frac{dx_{\sigma}}{ds}, \qquad (7)$$

we obtain from (4a) by inner multiplication by J^{σ}, on account of the antisymmetry of $\phi_{\mu\nu}$, the relation

$$\frac{\partial G}{\partial x_{\sigma}} \frac{dx_{\sigma}}{ds} = 0 \qquad (8)$$

Thus the scalar of curvature is constant on every world-line of the motion of electricity. Equation (4a) can be interpreted in a graphic manner by the statement: The scalar of curvature plays the part of a negative pressure which, outside of the electric corpuscles, has a constant value G_0. In the interior of every corpuscle there subsists a negative pressure (positive $G - G_0$) the fall of which maintains the electrodynamic force in equilibrium. The minimum of pressure, or, respectively, the maximum of the scalar of curvature, does not change with time in the interior of the corpuscle.

We now write the field equations (1a) in the form

$$\left(G_{\mu\nu} - \frac{1}{2} g_{\mu\nu} G \right) + \frac{1}{4} g_{\mu\nu} G_0 = -\kappa \left(T_{\mu\nu} + \frac{1}{4\kappa} g_{\mu\nu} (G - G_0) \right) \qquad (9)$$

On the other hand, we transform the equations supplied with the cosmological term as already given

$$G_{\mu\nu} - \lambda g_{\mu\nu} = -\kappa \left(T_{\mu\nu} - \frac{1}{2} g_{\mu\nu} T \right)$$

Subtracting the scalar equation multiplied by $1/2$, we next obtain

$$\left(G_{\mu\nu} - \frac{1}{2} g_{\mu\nu} G \right) + g_{\mu\nu} \lambda = -\kappa T.$$

Now in regions where only electrical and gravitational fields are present, the right-hand side of this equation vanishes. For such regions we obtain, by forming the scalar,

$$G + 4\lambda = 0.$$

In such regions, therefore, the scalar of curvature is constant, so that λ may be replaced by $\frac{1}{4}G_0$. Thus we may write the earlier field equation (1) in the form

$$G_{\mu\nu} - \frac{1}{2}g_{\mu\nu}G + \frac{1}{4\kappa}g_{\mu\nu}G_0 = -\kappa T_{\mu\nu} \qquad (10)$$

Comparing (9) with (10), we see that there is no difference between the new field equations and the earlier ones, except that instead of $T_{\mu\nu}$ as tensor of "gravitating mass" there now occurs $T_{\mu\nu} + \frac{1}{4\kappa}g_{\mu\nu}(G - G_0)$ which is independent of the scalar of curvature. But the new formulation has this great advantage, that the quantity λ appears in the fundamental equations as a constant of integration, and no longer as a universal constant peculiar to the fundamental law.

§ 3. ON THE COSMOLOGICAL QUESTION

The last result already permits the surmise that with our new formulation the universe may be regarded as spatially finite, without any necessity for an additional hypothesis. As in the preceding paper I shall again show that with a uniform distribution of matter, a spherical world is compatible with the equations.

In the first place we set

$$ds^2 = -\gamma_{ik}dx_i dx_k + dx_4^2 \left(i, k = 1, 2, 3 \right) \qquad (11)$$

Then if P_{ik} and P are, respectively, the curvature tensor of the second rank and the curvature scalar in three-dimensional space, we have

$$G_{ik} = P_{ik} \left(i, k = 1, 2, 3 \right)$$
$$G_4^i = G_{4i} = G_{44} = 0$$
$$G = -P$$
$$-g = \gamma.$$

It therefore follows for our case that

$$G_{ik} - \frac{1}{2}g_{ik}G = P_{ik} - \frac{1}{2}\gamma_{ik}P \left(i, k = 1, 2, 3 \right)$$
$$G_{44} - \frac{1}{2}g_{44}G = \frac{1}{2}P.$$

We pursue our reflexions, from this point on, in two ways. Firstly, with the support of equation (1a). Here $T_{\mu\nu}$ denotes the energy-tensor of the electro-magnetic field, arising from the electrical particles constituting matter. For this field we have everywhere

$$\mathfrak{T}_1^1 + \mathfrak{T}_2^2 + \mathfrak{T}_3^3 + \mathfrak{T}_4^4 = 0.$$

The individual $\mathfrak{T}_\mu^\nu$ are quantities which vary rapidly with position; but for our purpose we no doubt may replace them by their mean values. We therefore have to choose

$$\mathfrak{T}_1^1 = \mathfrak{T}_2^2 = \mathfrak{T}_3^3 = -\tfrac{1}{3}\mathfrak{T}_4^4 = \text{const.}\ \Bigg\} \\ \mathfrak{T}_\mu^\nu = 0 \ (\text{for } \mu \neq \nu), \tag{12}$$

and therefore

$$T_{ik} = \tfrac{1}{3}\frac{\mathfrak{T}_4^4}{\sqrt{\gamma}}\gamma_{ik}, \ T_{44} = \frac{\mathfrak{T}_4^4}{\sqrt{\gamma}}.$$

In consideration of what has been shown hitherto, we obtain in place of (1a)

$$P_{ik} - \tfrac{1}{2}\gamma_{ik}P = -\tfrac{1}{3}\gamma_{ik}\frac{\kappa\mathfrak{T}_4^4}{\sqrt{\gamma}} \tag{13}$$

$$\tfrac{1}{2}P = -\frac{\kappa\mathfrak{T}_4^4}{\sqrt{\gamma}} \tag{14}$$

The scalar of equation (13) agrees with (14). It is on this account that our fundamental equations permit the idea of a spherical universe. For from (13) and (14) follows

$$P_{ik} + \frac{4}{3}\frac{\kappa\mathfrak{T}_4^4}{\sqrt{\gamma}}\gamma_{ik} = 0 \tag{15}$$

and it is known[1] that this system is satisfied by a (three-dimensional) spherical universe.

But we may also base our reflexions on the equations (9). On the right-hand side of (9) stand those terms which, from the phenomenological point of view, are to be replaced by the energy-tensor of matter; that is, they are to be replaced by

$$\begin{matrix} 0 & 0 & 0 & 0 \\ 0 & 0 & 0 & 0 \\ 0 & 0 & 0 & 0 \\ 0 & 0 & 0 & \rho \end{matrix}$$

where ρ denotes the mean density of matter assumed to be at rest. We thus obtain the equations

$$P_{ik} - \tfrac{1}{2}\gamma_{ik}P - \tfrac{1}{2}\gamma_{ik}G_0 = 0 \tag{16}$$

$$\frac{1}{2}P + \frac{1}{4}G_0 = -\kappa\rho \tag{17}$$

From the scalar of equation (16) and from (17) we obtain

$$G_0 = -\frac{2}{3}P = 2\kappa\rho \tag{18}$$

and consequently from (16)

$$P_{ik} - \kappa\rho\gamma_{ik} = 0 \tag{19}$$

1. Cf. H. Weyl, "Raum, Zeit, Materie," § 33.

which equation, with the exception of the expression for the co-efficient, agrees with (15). By comparison we obtain

$$\mathfrak{T}_4^4 = \tfrac{3}{4}\rho\sqrt{\gamma} \tag{20}$$

This equation signifies that of the energy constituting matter three-quarters is to be ascribed to the electromagnetic field, and one-quarter to the gravitational field.

§ 4. CONCLUDING REMARKS

The above reflexions show the possibility of a theoretical construction of matter out of gravitational field and electromagnetic field alone, without the introduction of hypothetical supplementary terms on the lines of Mie's theory. This possibility appears particularly promising in that it frees us from the necessity of introducing a special constant λ for the solution of the cosmological problem. On the other hand, there is a peculiar difficulty. For, if we specialize (1) for the spherically symmetrical static case we obtain one equation too few for defining the $g_{\mu\nu}$ and $\phi_{\mu\nu}$, with the result that any *spherically symmetrical distribution* of electricity appears capable of remaining in equilibrium. Thus the problem of the constitution of the elementary quanta cannot yet be solved on the immediate basis of the given field equations.

Acknowledgements

T his book would not have been possible without the help of a number of talented people who made different contributions at various stages of the book's development. Among those deserving special thanks are Michael Rosin, a consultant to Running Press, Gil King, and Mrs. Karen Sime, assistant to Professor Stephen Hawking.

Thanks are also due to several past and present members of the staff of Running Press: Carlo DeVito, Kathleen Greczylo, Kelly Pennick, Bill Jones, and Deborah Grandinetti.

Stephen Hawking

Stephen Hawking is considered the most brilliant theoretical physicist since Einstein. He has also done much to popularize science. His book, *A Brief History of Time*, sold more than 10 million copies in 40 languages, achieving the kind of success almost unheard of in the history of science writing. His subsequent books, *The Universe in A Nutshell*, and *The Future of Spacetime*, with Kip S. Thorne and others, have also been well-received.

He was born in Oxford, England on January 8, 1942 (300 years after the death of Galileo). He studied physics at University College, Oxford, received his Ph.D. in Cosmology at Cambridge and since 1979, has held the post of Lucasian Professor of Mathematics. The chair was founded in 1663 with money left in the will of the Reverend Henry Lucas, who had been the Member of Parliament for the University. It was first held by Isaac Barrow, and then in 1669 by Isaac Newton. It is reserved for those individuals considered the most brilliant thinkers of their time.

Professor Hawking has worked on the basic laws that govern the universe. With Roger Penrose, he showed that Einstein's General Theory of Relativity implied space and time would have a beginning in the Big Bang and an end in black holes. The results indicated it was necessary to unify General Relativity with Quantum Theory, the other great scientific development of the first half of the twentieth century. One consequence of such a unification that he discovered was that black holes should not be completely black but should emit radiation and eventually disappear. Another conjecture is that the universe has no edge or boundary in imaginary time.

Stephen Hawking has twelve honorary degrees, and is the recipient of many awards, medals and prizes. He is a Fellow of the Royal Society and a Member of the US National Academy of Sciences. He continues to combine family life (he has three children and one grandchild) and his research into theoretical physics together with an extensive program of travel and public lectures.